Bill James presents. . .

STATS
Minor League Handbook
2000

STATS, Inc.
and
Howe Sportsdata

STATS
PUBLISHING

HOWE SPORTSDATA
A SERVICE OF SPORTSTICKER

Published by STATS Publishing
A division of Sports Team Analysis & Tracking Systems, Inc.

Cover by Marc Elman, Ben Frobig and Chuck Miller

Cover photo by David M. Schofield

First Edition: November, 1999

Printed in the United States of America

ISBN 1-884064-72-8

Acknowledgments

Numerous people contributed to the 2000 versions of the STATS *Major League Handbook*, *Minor League Handbook* and *Player Profiles*. We'd like to thank everyone who had a hand in bringing you the best trio of statistical annuals in the business:

John Dewan, STATS' Chief Executive Officer, continues to make us the No. 1 source for sports statistics. Our President, Alan Leib, will help us grow in the years to come. John and Alan are assisted by Jennifer Manicki. Sue Dewan and Bob Meyerhoff are vice-presidents involved in Research & Development/Special Projects. Sue's team includes Jim Osborne and Andy Tumpowsky. Bob's team includes Joe Sclafani.

Vice President of Publishing Products Don Zminda oversees the department that produces this and all of our other sports titles. Don's department includes Jim Callis, Thom Henninger, Jim Henzler, Chuck Miller and yours truly. Jim Henzler handled all of the programming assignments for this book, while Chuck was responsible for design and layout. Jim Callis' vast minor league knowledge was needed to fill in gaps in this book, while Don and Thom also pored over everything.

Spreading the word about this book and everything else in the world of STATS Publishing falls to Marc Elman and his team. Marc works with Ben Frobig (who created the cover), Mike Janosi, Antoinette Kelly and Mike Sarkis.

Allan Spear heads the Data Collection Department. His staff consists of Jeremy Alpert, Michelle Blanco, Jeff Chernow, Ryan Ellis, Mike Hammer, Derek Kenar, Tony Largo, Jon Passman, Jeff Schinski, Matt Senter, Bill Stephens and Joe Stillwell. Together, they oversee a vast reporter network.

The efforts of the Commercial Products, Fantasy, Interactive Products and Sales departments help pay most of our bills at STATS. Alan Leib oversees our Commercial Products division, which includes Ethan D. Cooperson, Dan Matern and David Pinto. Steve Byrd is in charge of the Fantasy department, which consists of Bill Burke, Jim Corelis, Dan Ford, Stefan Kretschmann, Walter Lis, Marc Moeller, Mike Mooney, Oscar Palacios, Corey Roberts, Eric Robin, Jeff Smith, Yingmin Wang and Rick Wilton. Mike Canter heads the Interactive group and is assisted by Dave Carlson, Jake Costello, Will McCleskey, Tim Moriarty, Dean Peterson, Pat Quinn, John Sasman, Meghan Sheehan, Morris Srinivasan and Nick Stamm. Jim Capuano leads a Sales team comprised of Greg Kirkorsky and Jake Stein.

Our Financial/Administrative/Human Resources/Legal Department ensures that everything runs smoothly at our Morton Grove, Ill., headquarters. Howard Lanin overseas the financial details and is assisted by Kim Bartlett and Betty Moy. Susan Zamechek assists in finance and oversees the administrative aspects of the company with the help of Sherlinda Johnson, while Tracy Lickton is in charge of human resources. Carol Savier aids with legal matters. Art Ashley provides programming support to all four groups.

A curtain call for everyone.

—Tony Nistler

This book is dedicated to
STATS' 1999 Co-Rookies of the Year:

Maya Isabelle Lanin (3/18/99)
Elizabeth Ann Callis (5/10/99)
Scarlett Katherine Costello (6/30/99)
Ivey Grace Topel (8/3/99)

Table of Contents

Introduction

A minor league player's development is loaded with twists and turns. Injuries may slow his progress or limit his potential. Realizing he can't hit a breaking ball or hold his own against righthanded pitching means making adjustments or never nailing down a major league job.

By the time he has played a few professional seasons, he has shown strengths, weaknesses and tendencies. He may display a knack for the longball, an ability to draw walks or a propensity to strike out. A player's profile begins to develop, and the numbers tell us a lot about what kind of ballplayer he has become.

This ninth edition of the *STATS Minor League Handbook* contains the code that gives us a glimpse into a player's development. It houses the complete career stats for every player who appeared in Double-A and Triple-A ball in 1999. The exceptions are players who reached the major leagues in '99. Those players can be found in our companion book, the *STATS Major League Handbook*.

For players in Class-A and Rookie leagues, we supply complete 1999 statistical lines in the section that follows the career register of Double-A and Triple-A players. Beginning with this edition, handedness and positions are provided for players listed in the Class-A and Rookie leagues section.

There's more to help you assess a player's development. The *Minor League Handbook* includes lefty/righty and home/road breakdowns for all Double-A and Triple-A regulars, as well as leader boards for all minor league levels, from short-season leagues to Triple-A.

You also will find totals for each minor league team and league. That information provides insight into the impact a player's surroundings has on his performance. A 20-homer season, for instance, is more significant in the Florida State League than in the California League, even though both are high Class-A circuits. The same is true at the Triple-A level, where a 20-homer campaign is more noteworthy in the International League than in the Pacific Coast League.

Finally, look for major league equivalencies for the top Double-A and Triple-A hitters in each organization. The MLEs, developed by Bill James, translate a hitter's minor league numbers into what they would have looked like in the majors. Adjustments are made for home park (both major and minor league), league and level of competition.

The numbers tell us a lot, and a plethora of information on player development in 1999 can be found in this book. Enjoy the ninth edition of the *Minor League Handbook*.

—Thom Henninger

Career Register

Any player who appeared in Double-A or Triple-A in 1999 gets a profile in this section. The exception is if he also played in the major leagues, in which case his statistics are in our companion book, the *STATS Major League Handbook*.

The profiles have complete major and minor league records for all qualifying players. Most of the statistical abbreviations are common and will be used throughout the book. Here's a quick review:

For all players, **Ht** = Height; **Wt** = Weight; **Age** = age as of June 30, 2000.

For hitters, **G** = games; **AB** = at-bats; **H** = hits; **2B** = doubles; **3B** = triples; **HR** = home runs; **TB** = total bases; **R** = runs; **RBI** = runs batted in; **TBB** = total bases on balls; **IBB** = intentional bases on balls; **SO** = strikeouts; **HBP** = times hit by pitches; **SH** = sacrifice hits; **SF** = sacrifice flies; **SB** = stolen bases; **CS** = times caught stealing; **SB%** = stolen base percentage; **GDP** = times grounded into double plays; **Avg** = batting average; **OBP** = on-base percentage; **SLG** = slugging percentage.

For pitchers, **G** = games pitched; **GS** = games started; **CG** = complete games; **GF** = games finished; **IP** = innings pitched; **BFP** = batters facing pitcher; **H** = hits allowed; **R** = runs allowed; **ER** = earned runs allowed; **HR** = home runs allowed; **SH** = sacrifice hits allowed; **SF** = sacrifice flies allowed; **HB** = hits batsmen; **TBB** = total bases on balls; **IBB** = intentional bases on balls; **SO** = strikeouts; **WP** = wild pitches; **Bk** = balks; **W** = wins; **L** = losses; **Pct.** = winning percentage; **ShO** = shutouts; **Sv** = saves; **ERA** = earned run average.

Class-A (A+, A, A-) and Rookie (R+, R) have separate classifications to distinguish the level of competition.

Andy Abad

Bats: Left **Throws:** Left **Pos:** OF   **Ht:** 6'1" **Wt:** 184 **Born:** 8/25/72 **Age:** 27

Year Team	Lg Org	G	AB	H	2B	3B	HR	TB	R	RBI	TBB	IBB	SO	HBP	SH	SF	SB	CS	SB%	GDP	Avg	OBP	SLG
1993 Red Sox	R Bos	59	230	57	9	2	1	73	24	28	25	0	27	2	2	4	2	2	.50	2	.248	.322	.317
1994 Sarasota	A+ Bos	111	354	102	20	0	2	128	39	35	42	4	58	5	5	5	2	12	.14	9	.288	.367	.362
1995 Trenton	AA Bos	89	287	69	14	3	4	101	29	32	36	2	58	3	6	3	5	7	.42	6	.240	.328	.352
Sarasota	A+ Bos	18	59	17	3	0	0	20	5	10	6	0	13	0	0	0	4	3	.57	0	.288	.354	.339
1996 Sarasota	A+ Bos	58	202	58	15	1	2	81	28	41	37	1	28	3	2	2	10	3	.77	6	.287	.402	.401
Trenton	AA Bos	65	213	59	22	1	4	95	33	39	33	2	41	0	0	3	5	3	.63	4	.277	.369	.446
1997 Trenton	AA Bos	45	165	50	13	0	8	87	37	24	33	3	27	2	0	1	2	4	.33	2	.303	.423	.527
Pawtucket	AAA Bos	68	227	62	7	0	9	96	28	32	36	1	47	2	1	1	3	2	.60	4	.273	.376	.423
1998 Pawtucket	AAA Bos	111	365	112	18	1	16	180	71	66	68	2	70	3	4	5	10	6	.63	7	.307	.415	.493
1999 Pawtucket	AAA Bos	102	377	112	21	4	15	186	61	65	51	5	50	2	2	3	7	2	.78	9	.297	.381	.493
7 Min. YEARS		726	2479	698	142	12	61	1047	355	372	367	20	419	22	22	27	50	44	.53	49	.282	.375	.422

Chuck Abbott

Bats: Right **Throws:** Right **Pos:** SS   **Ht:** 6'1" **Wt:** 180 **Born:** 1/26/75 **Age:** 25

Year Team	Lg Org	G	AB	H	2B	3B	HR	TB	R	RBI	TBB	IBB	SO	HBP	SH	SF	SB	CS	SB%	GDP	Avg	OBP	SLG
1996 Boise	A- Ana	70	268	53	9	2	0	66	41	20	24	0	59	5	4	4	11	5	.69	8	.198	.272	.246
1997 Cedar Rapds	A Ana	133	520	120	21	5	7	172	86	54	62	0	170	3	6	2	31	12	.72	7	.231	.315	.331
1998 Midland	AA Ana	132	525	138	21	9	2	183	74	62	38	0	135	4	8	4	16	9	.64	18	.263	.315	.349
1999 Erie	AA Ana	125	444	106	13	1	6	139	70	46	47	1	138	2	6	2	9	10	.47	10	.239	.313	.313
4 Min. YEARS		460	1757	417	64	17	15	560	271	182	171	1	502	14	24	12	67	36	.65	43	.237	.308	.319

Brent Abernathy

Bats: Right **Throws:** Right **Pos:** 2B   **Ht:** 6'1" **Wt:** 185 **Born:** 9/23/77 **Age:** 22

Year Team	Lg Org	G	AB	H	2B	3B	HR	TB	R	RBI	TBB	IBB	SO	HBP	SH	SF	SB	CS	SB%	GDP	Avg	OBP	SLG
1997 Hagerstown	A Tor	99	379	117	27	2	1	151	69	26	30	0	32	6	6	2	22	13	.63	6	.309	.367	.398
1998 Dunedin	A+ Tor	124	485	159	36	1	3	206	85	65	44	0	38	1	12	6	35	13	.73	11	.328	.381	.425
1999 Knoxville	AA Tor	136	577	168	42	1	13	251	108	62	55	1	47	6	5	7	34	15	.69	11	.291	.355	.435
3 Min. YEARS		359	1441	444	105	4	17	608	262	153	129	1	117	13	23	15	91	41	.69	28	.308	.367	.422

Willie Adams

Pitches: Right **Bats:** Right **Pos:** P   **Ht:** 6'7" **Wt:** 215 **Born:** 10/8/72 **Age:** 27

Year Team	Lg Org	G	GS	CG	GF	IP	BFP	H	R	ER	HR	SH	SF	HB	TBB	IBB	SO	WP	Bk	W	L	Pct.	ShO	Sv	ERA
1993 Madison	A Oak	5	5	0	0	18.2	84	21	10	7	2	1	1	0	8	0	22	1	1	0	2	.000	0	0	3.38
1994 Modesto	A+ Oak	11	5	0	0	45.1	181	41	17	17	7	2	0	0	10	0	42	2	3	7	1	.875	0	2	3.38
Huntsville	AA Oak	10	10	0	0	60.2	256	58	32	29	3	2	3	5	23	2	33	1	1	4	3	.571	0	0	4.30
1995 Huntsville	AA Oak	13	13	0	0	80.2	330	75	33	27	8	2	1	2	17	0	72	1	0	6	5	.545	0	0	3.01
Edmonton	AAA Oak	11	10	1	1	68	288	73	35	33	2	2	2	6	15	5	40	3	0	2	5	.286	0	0	4.37
1996 Edmonton	AAA Oak	19	19	3	0	112	466	95	49	47	12	1	1	6	39	2	80	4	0	10	4	.714	1	0	3.78
1997 Edmonton	AAA Oak	13	12	0	0	75.1	345	105	57	54	13	2	4	2	19	3	58	3	1	5	4	.556	0	0	6.45
1998 Athletics	R Oak	2	2	0	0	3.2	17	3	2	1	0	0	0	1	1	0	3	0	0	0	1	.000	0	0	2.45
Edmonton	AAA Oak	2	2	0	0	3.2	20	8	5	5	2	0	0	0	1	0	1	0	0	1	1	.500	0	0	12.27
1999 Sarasota	A+ Bos	2	2	0	0	13.2	58	14	5	3	1	0	0	1	1	0	6	0	0	1	1	.500	0	0	1.98
Trenton	AA Bos	2	2	0	0	11.2	53	17	6	6	2	0	0	0	2	0	6	2	0	1	1	.500	0	0	4.63
Pawtucket	AAA Bos	11	11	1	0	64.2	290	82	46	37	7	2	3	3	10	0	37	2	3	4	5	.444	1	0	5.15
1996 Oakland	AL	12	12	1	0	76.1	329	76	39	34	11	3	2	5	23	3	68	2	0	3	4	.429	1	0	4.01
1997 Oakland	AL	13	12	0	0	58.1	282	73	53	53	9	3	5	4	32	2	37	2	0	3	5	.375	0	0	8.18
7 Min. YEARS		101	93	5	7	558	2388	592	297	266	59	14	15	26	146	12	400	19	9	40	32	.556	2	2	4.29
2 Maj. YEARS		25	24	1	0	134.2	611	149	92	87	20	6	7	9	55	5	105	4	0	6	9	.400	1	0	5.81

Joel Adamson

Pitches: Left **Bats:** Left **Pos:** P   **Ht:** 6'4" **Wt:** 185 **Born:** 7/2/71 **Age:** 28

Year Team	Lg Org	G	GS	CG	GF	IP	BFP	H	R	ER	HR	SH	SF	HB	TBB	IBB	SO	WP	Bk	W	L	Pct.	ShO	Sv	ERA
1990 Princeton	R+ Phi	12	8	1	3	48	204	55	27	21	2	1	0	3	12	1	39	6	7	2	5	.286	0	1	3.94
1991 Spartanburg	A Phi	14	14	1	0	81	333	72	29	23	5	2	4	3	22	0	84	3	2	4	4	.500	1	0	2.56
Clearwater	A+ Phi	5	5	0	0	29.2	125	28	12	10	1	2	1	1	7	0	20	2	1	2	1	.667	0	0	3.03
1992 Clearwater	A+ Phi	15	15	1	0	89.2	378	90	35	34	4	2	3	7	19	0	52	0	1	5	6	.455	1	0	3.41
Reading	AA Phi	10	10	2	0	59	255	68	36	28	10	3	1	0	13	1	35	3	0	3	6	.333	0	0	4.27
1993 Edmonton	AAA Fla	5	5	0	0	26	125	39	21	20	5	1	1	0	13	0	7	0	1	1	2	.333	0	0	6.92
High Desert	A+ Fla	22	20	6	1	129.2	571	160	83	66	13	3	4	4	30	0	72	5	7	5	5	.500	3	0	4.58
1994 Portland	AA Fla	33	11	2	16	91.1	402	95	51	44	9	5	2	5	32	5	59	0	0	5	6	.455	2	7	4.34
1995 Charlotte	AAA Fla	19	18	2	0	115	471	113	51	42	12	0	3	6	20	0	80	4	2	8	4	.667	0	0	3.29
1996 Charlotte	AAA Fla	44	8	0	14	97.2	424	108	48	41	15	3	3	3	28	2	84	1	0	6	6	.500	0	3	3.78
1997 Tucson	AAA Mil	6	6	0	0	33	138	38	16	16	4	1	1	2	8	0	24	3	1	2	1	.667	0	0	4.36
1999 Pawtucket	AAA Bos	25	3	0	12	43.1	193	60	35	29	5	2	0	6	8	2	14	2	0	2	4	.333	0	2	6.02
Tacoma	AAA Sea	14	6	0	3	36.2	174	48	25	21	4	1	3	6	15	1	15	1	1	2	2	.500	0	0	5.15
1996 Florida	NL	9	0	0	1	11	56	18	9	9	1	2	1	1	7	0	7	0	0	0	0	.000	0	0	7.36
1997 Milwaukee	AL	30	6	0	3	76.1	324	78	36	30	13	4	2	5	19	0	56	0	1	5	3	.625	0	0	3.54
1998 Arizona	NL	5	5	0	0	23	104	25	21	21	5	1	1	3	11	0	14	0	0	0	3	.000	0	0	8.22
9 Min. YEARS		224	129	15	49	880	3793	974	469	395	89	26	26	46	227	12	585	30	23	47	52	.475	7	13	4.04
3 Maj. YEARS		44	11	0	4	110.1	484	121	66	60	19	7	4	9	37	0	77	0	1	5	6	.455	0	0	4.89

3

Carlos Adolfo

Bats: Right **Throws:** Right **Pos:** OF   **Ht:** 5'11" **Wt:** 160 **Born:** 4/20/76 **Age:** 24

				BATTING														BASERUNNING				PERCENTAGES		
Year Team	Lg Org	G	AB	H	2B	3B	HR	TB	R	RBI	TBB	IBB	SO	HBP	SH	SF	SB	CS	SB%	GDP	Avg	OBP	SLG
1994 Vermont	A- Mon	67	252	67	10	3	6	101	41	33	28	0	60	0	0	4	11	7	.61	5	.266	.335	.401
1995 Wst Plm Bch	A+ Mon	28	81	15	1	0	1	19	6	7	5	0	22	0	0	0	1	0	1.00	1	.185	.233	.235
Albany	A Mon	57	214	52	13	5	4	87	31	33	17	0	65	2	1	0	5	6	.45	4	.243	.305	.407
1996 Delmarva	A Mon	132	492	134	20	8	10	200	82	71	47	3	106	1	2	6	18	6	.75	11	.272	.333	.407
1997 Wst Plm Bch	A+ Mon	120	448	101	15	2	11	153	62	50	38	1	91	2	3	0	9	18	.33	8	.225	.289	.342
1998 Jupiter	A+ Mon	88	334	90	16	2	13	149	51	44	37	0	80	4	3	1	10	8	.56	5	.269	.348	.446
Harrisburg	AA Mon	40	130	25	5	0	2	36	10	16	9	1	33	1	1	3	3	0	1.00	4	.192	.245	.277
1999 Ottawa	AAA Mon	16	53	10	2	1	2	20	5	9	3	0	11	1	0	2	0	0	.00	2	.189	.237	.377
Harrisburg	AA Mon	76	221	60	16	0	10	106	37	41	25	2	51	4	1	1	3	2	.60	8	.271	.355	.480
6 Min. YEARS		624	2225	554	98	21	59	871	325	304	209	7	519	15	11	17	60	47	.56	48	.249	.315	.391

Brandon Agamennone

Pitches: Right **Bats:** Right **Pos:** P   **Ht:** 6'2" **Wt:** 190 **Born:** 11/6/75 **Age:** 24

			HOW MUCH HE PITCHED						WHAT HE GAVE UP										THE RESULTS				
Year Team	Lg Org	G	GS	CG	GF	IP	BFP	H	R	ER	HR	SH	SF	HB	TBB	IBB	SO	WP	Bk	W	L	Pct.	ShO	Sv	ERA
1998 Vermont	A- Mon	9	3	0	0	31.2	124	19	6	5	1	0	1	1	11	0	30	0	0	3	1	.750	0	0	1.42
Cape Fear	A Mon	6	6	1	0	35.1	134	24	15	12	2	0	1	2	6	0	29	0	0	2	0	1.000	1	0	3.06
1999 Jupiter	A+ Mon	16	9	0	0	65.2	268	51	31	23	4	2	4	3	15	0	41	1	2	4	2	.667	0	0	3.15
Harrisburg	AA Mon	22	4	0	11	52.1	210	44	19	18	5	3	0	2	14	0	41	2	0	5	2	.714	0	5	3.10
2 Min. YEARS		53	22	1	11	185	736	138	71	58	12	5	6	8	46	0	141	3	2	14	5	.737	1	5	2.82

Stevenson Agosto

Pitches: Left **Bats:** Left **Pos:** P   **Ht:** 5'10" **Wt:** 175 **Born:** 9/2/75 **Age:** 24

			HOW MUCH HE PITCHED						WHAT HE GAVE UP										THE RESULTS				
Year Team	Lg Org	G	GS	CG	GF	IP	BFP	H	R	ER	HR	SH	SF	HB	TBB	IBB	SO	WP	Bk	W	L	Pct.	ShO	Sv	ERA
1994 Angels	R Ana	13	1	0	7	26.1		27	18	13	1	3	1	3	14	0	26	6	1	0	2	.000	0	1	4.44
1995 Angels	R Ana	1	1	0	0	5	22	3	5	3	0	2	1	1	2	0	2	3	0	0	1	.000	0	0	5.40
Boise	A- Ana	13	11	0	1	52.1	224	39	20	17	1	0	3	5	30	2	34	12	0	6	2	.750	0	0	2.92
1996 Cedar Rapids	A Ana	28	28	1	0	156.2	680	143	91	77	12	7	6	7	86	2	121	8	7	8	10	.444	0	0	4.42
1997 Lk Elsinore	A+ Ana	24	21	1	0	137	603	155	91	81	23	2	2	3	50	0	91	11	3	5	8	.385	1	0	5.32
Rancho Cuca	A+ SD	3	3	1	0	22	89	18	7	7	2	3	0	0	6	0	18	1	0	2	0	1.000	1	0	2.86
1990 Rancho Cuca	A+ CD	23	20	0	0	108	505	132	83	73	14	4	6	3	68	0	16	4	5	5	8	.385	0	0	6.08
1999 Mobile	AA SD	40	1	0	5	81	371	81	61	53	13	2	7	1	59	1	59	10	1	3	3	.500	0	0	5.89
6 Min. YEARS		145	89	3	13	588.1	2619	598	376	324	66	23	26	23	315	5	442	66	16	29	34	.460	2	1	4.96

Pat Ahearne

Pitches: Right **Bats:** Right **Pos:** P   **Ht:** 6'3" **Wt:** 195 **Born:** 12/10/69 **Age:** 30

			HOW MUCH HE PITCHED						WHAT HE GAVE UP										THE RESULTS				
Year Team	Lg Org	G	GS	CG	GF	IP	BFP	H	R	ER	HR	SH	SF	HB	TBB	IBB	SO	WP	Bk	W	L	Pct.	ShO	Sv	ERA
1992 Lakeland	A+ Det	1	1	0	0	4.2	17	4	2	1	0	0	0	0	0	0	4	0	0	0	0	.000	0	0	1.93
1993 Lakeland	A+ Det	25	24	2	0	147.1	650	160	87	73	8	7	4	6	48	0	51	3	1	6	15	.286	0	0	4.46
1994 Trenton	AA Det	30	13	2	3	108.2	467	126	55	48	8	1	6	5	25	1	57	5	0	7	5	.583	0	0	3.98
1995 Toledo	AAA Det	25	23	1	0	139.2	599	165	83	73	11	2	5	5	37	3	54	2	0	7	9	.438	1	0	4.70
1996 Norfolk	AAA NYM	5	4	0	0	25.1	108	26	14	13	1	3	0	1	9	1	14	0	1	1	2	.333	0	0	4.62
Duluth-Sup	IND —	1	1	0	0	4.1	24	10	6	6	3	0	0	0	1	0	1	1	0	0	0	.000	0	0	12.46
San Antonio	AA LA	8	8	0	0	45.1	208	59	34	29	3	2	2	1	18	0	21	4	0	2	4	.333	0	0	5.76
Vero Beach	A+ LA	6	6	1	0	47	179	38	16	11	1	2	1	1	5	0	26	2	0	3	2	.600	1	0	2.11
1997 Albuquerque	AAA LA	20	8	0	3	60.2	280	82	43	33	9	4	2	1	20	1	44	2	0	2	4	.333	0	0	4.90
San Antonio	AA LA	14	14	3	0	84	364	109	48	42	1	6	2	2	13	0	45	4	0	4	5	.444	0	0	4.50
1998 Bridgeport	IND —	5	5	0	0	28	123	29	12	8	1	1	1	1	5	0	16	1	0	2	2	.500	0	0	2.57
1999 Bridgeport	IND —	7	7	1	0	46.1	188	35	17	13	4	1	1	0	14	0	43	4	0	6	0	1.000	1	0	2.53
New Haven	AA Sea	17	17	4	0	124	493	114	41	36	6	3	1	3	27	0	80	2	0	8	3	.727	2	0	2.61
1995 Detroit	AL	4	3	0	0	10	55	20	13	13	2	0	0	0	5	1	4	1	0	0	2	.000	0	0	11.70
8 Min. YEARS		164	131	14	6	865.1	3700	957	458	386	58	32	25	26	222	6	456	30	2	48	51	.485	5	0	4.01

Jay Ahrendt

Bats: Left **Throws:** Right **Pos:** C-DH   **Ht:** 6'2" **Wt:** 210 **Born:** 1/23/74 **Age:** 26

				BATTING														BASERUNNING				PERCENTAGES		
Year Team	Lg Org	G	AB	H	2B	3B	HR	TB	R	RBI	TBB	IBB	SO	HBP	SH	SF	SB	CS	SB%	GDP	Avg	OBP	SLG
1996 Will County	IND —	10	33	12	2	0	1	17	6	10	9	2	6	0	0	0	2	2	.50	0	.364	.500	.515
Orioles	R Bal	25	66	21	4	0	1	28	9	11	14	0	15	2	0	0	0	2	.00	0	.318	.430	.424
Bluefield	R+ Bal	3	4	2	0	0	0	2	1	2	1	0	1	0	0	0	0	0	.00	0	.500	.600	.500
1997 Sioux City	IND —	8	10	1	0	0	0	1	1	1	4	0	2	0	0	0	0	0	.00	0	.100	.357	.100
Will County	IND —	39	151	49	4	0	6	71	29	20	14	1	22	2	0	1	1	0	1.00	3	.325	.387	.470
1998 Atlantic Ct	IND —	11	111	30	8	0	1	51	20	11	11	0	13	1	0	1	1	0	1.00	2	.270	.327	.393
Nashua	IND —	22	43	10	4	0	1	17	9	11	8	0	18	1	0	1	1	0	1.00	2	.233	.358	.395
1999 Rancho Cuca	A+ SD	40	121	31	5	1	1	41	14	14	16	0	44	0	0	0	0	1	.00	1	.256	.343	.339
Mobile	AA SD	8	15	3	1	0	0	4	2	2	4	2	8	0	0	0	0	0	.00	0	.200	.368	.267
4 Min. YEARS		199	584	167	26	3	12	235	97	82	81	5	159	6	2	6	5	5	.50	8	.286	.375	.402

4

Paul Ah Yat

Pitches: Left **Bats:** Right **Pos:** P **Ht:** 6'1" **Wt:** 186 **Born:** 10/13/74 **Age:** 25

		HOW MUCH HE PITCHED						WHAT HE GAVE UP									THE RESULTS					
Year Team	Lg Org	G	GS	CG	GF	IP	BFP	H	R	ER	HR	SH	SF	HB	TBB	IBB	SO	WP	Bk	W	L	Pct.	ShO	Sv	ERA
1996 Erie	A- Pit	26	0	0	4	27.2	114	24	15	10	1	1	0	0	6	0	34	0	0	1	1	.500	0	1	3.25
1997 Augusta	A Pit	29	9	0	5	90	366	82	34	29	7	3	0	3	16	1	119	4	0	5	1	.833	0	0	2.90
Lynchburg	A+ Pit	6	6	3	0	48	182	37	8	7	2	2	0	1	4	0	38	1	0	5	1	.833	1	0	1.31
1998 Lynchburg	A+ Pit	14	14	4	0	102.1	410	95	40	31	9	1	3	4	13	2	77	2	0	6	3	.667	3	0	2.73
Carolina	AA Pit	13	13	1	0	84.1	362	84	43	34	10	1	2	3	21	0	60	6	0	5	5	.500	0	0	3.63
1999 Altoona	AA Pit	16	15	0	0	95.1	398	86	41	32	6	4	4	3	30	0	90	4	1	8	4	.667	0	0	3.02
Nashville	AAA Pit	13	11	1	1	64.2	291	75	45	41	10	3	2	4	24	1	41	1	1	4	3	.571	0	0	5.71
4 Min. YEARS		117	68	9	10	512.1	2123	483	226	184	45	15	12	17	114	4	459	18	2	34	18	.654	4	1	3.23

Kurt Airoso

Bats: Right **Throws:** Right **Pos:** OF **Ht:** 6'2" **Wt:** 190 **Born:** 2/12/75 **Age:** 25

		BATTING															BASERUNNING				PERCENTAGES		
Year Team	Lg Org	G	AB	H	2B	3B	HR	TB	R	RBI	TBB	IBB	SO	HBP	SH	SF	SB	CS	SB%	GDP	Avg	OBP	SLG
1996 Jamestown	A- Det	27	78	22	5	2	2	37	12	12	10	0	31	1	2	0	3	1	.75	1	.282	.370	.474
1997 Lakeland	A+ Det	22	62	12	1	2	0	17	12	7	11	0	23	1	1	0	0	0	.00	2	.194	.324	.274
Tigers	R Det	4	10	0	0	0	0	0	1	0	3	0	3	1	0	0	0	0	.00	0	.000	.286	.000
W Michigan	A Det	14	37	11	5	0	0	16	6	2	6	0	15	0	0	1	0	0	.00	0	.297	.386	.432
1998 Lakeland	A+ Det	109	386	112	24	0	15	181	69	61	67	0	106	5	1	1	7	3	.70	7	.290	.401	.469
1999 Jacksnville	AA Det	134	536	146	28	6	10	216	95	72	89	1	113	5	0	6	10	3	.77	8	.272	.377	.403
4 Min. YEARS		310	1109	303	63	10	27	467	195	154	186	1	291	14	2	10	20	7	.74	18	.273	.381	.421

Chad Akers

Bats: Right **Throws:** Right **Pos:** SS **Ht:** 5'8" **Wt:** 160 **Born:** 5/30/72 **Age:** 28

		BATTING															BASERUNNING				PERCENTAGES		
Year Team	Lg Org	G	AB	H	2B	3B	HR	TB	R	RBI	TBB	IBB	SO	HBP	SH	SF	SB	CS	SB%	GDP	Avg	OBP	SLG
1993 Billings	R+ Cin	65	247	66	14	3	2	92	54	35	24	0	26	8	1	3	14	7	.67	4	.267	.348	.372
1994 Chstn-WV	A Cin	133	490	135	23	1	4	172	65	35	52	1	49	2	2	3	41	16	.72	14	.276	.346	.351
1995 Winston-Sal	A+ Cin	103	361	94	14	1	2	116	41	29	27	1	49	1	7	3	25	8	.76	7	.260	.311	.321
1996 Fargo-Mh	IND —	83	330	90	11	0	5	116	84	41	57	2	32	10	2	4	13	12	.52	8	.273	.392	.352
1997 Fargo-Mh	IND —	84	368	117	14	6	4	155	75	43	25	0	41	4	2	5	27	4	.87	6	.318	.363	.421
1998 Fargo-Mh	IND —	83	358	111	30	5	8	175	79	44	29	0	39	2	0	1	12	5	.71	8	.310	.364	.489
1999 Atlantic Ct	IND —	59	243	66	18	3	5	105	42	32	22	1	30	4	3	3	16	4	.80	2	.272	.338	.432
New Haven	AA Sea	1	0	0	0	0	0	0	1	0	0	0	0	0	0	0	0	0	.00	0	.000	.000	.000
Tacoma	AAA Sea	48	192	60	9	3	1	78	31	14	18	1	25	1	1	2	7	3	.70	3	.313	.371	.406
7 Min. YEARS		659	2589	739	133	22	31	1009	472	273	254	6	291	32	18	24	155	59	.72	52	.285	.354	.390

Jay Akin

Pitches: Left **Bats:** Left **Pos:** P **Ht:** 6'2" **Wt:** 200 **Born:** 7/9/74 **Age:** 25

		HOW MUCH HE PITCHED						WHAT HE GAVE UP									THE RESULTS					
Year Team	Lg Org	G	GS	CG	GF	IP	BFP	H	R	ER	HR	SH	SF	HB	TBB	IBB	SO	WP	Bk	W	L	Pct.	ShO	Sv	ERA
1997 Helena	R+ Mil	5	5	1	0	27	99	16	5	3	1	0	0	0	5	0	19	1	0	2	0	1.000	0	0	1.00
Beloit	A Mil	9	9	0	0	48.1	211	52	32	17	3	4	2	3	11	0	25	0	1	1	5	.167	0	0	3.17
1998 Stockton	A+ Mil	44	0	0	15	85	371	95	33	28	6	5	2	2	34	2	75	3	0	2	3	.400	0	2	2.96
1999 Huntsville	AA Mil	46	1	0	12	84	374	93	51	39	9	3	2	4	31	3	62	1	2	2	5	.286	0	0	4.18
3 Min. YEARS		104	15	1	27	244.1	1055	256	121	87	19	12	6	9	81	5	181	5	3	7	13	.350	0	2	3.20

Jose Alberro

Pitches: Right **Bats:** Right **Pos:** P **Ht:** 6'2" **Wt:** 190 **Born:** 6/29/69 **Age:** 31

		HOW MUCH HE PITCHED						WHAT HE GAVE UP									THE RESULTS					
Year Team	Lg Org	G	GS	CG	GF	IP	BFP	H	R	ER	HR	SH	SF	HB	TBB	IBB	SO	WP	Bk	W	L	Pct.	ShO	Sv	ERA
1991 Rangers	R Tex	19	0	0	16	30.1	121	17	6	5	1	1	0	4	9	0	40	1	2	2	0	1.000	0	6	1.48
Charlotte	A+ Tex	5	0	0	0	5.2	33	8	9	6	0	1	0	1	7	2	3	3	0	0	1	.000	0	0	9.53
1992 Gastonia	A Tex	17	0	0	6	20.2	84	18	8	8	2	0	1	1	4	0	26	1	0	1	0	1.000	0	1	3.48
Charlotte	A+ Tex	28	0	0	20	45	175	37	10	6	0	2	0	3	9	0	29	1	1	1	1	.500	0	15	1.20
1993 Tulsa	AA Tex	17	0	0	16	19	78	11	2	2	2	1	0	0	8	1	24	2	1	0	0	.000	0	5	0.95
Okla City	AAA Tex	12	0	0	7	17	85	25	15	13	2	1	2	0	11	0	14	4	0	0	0	.000	0	0	6.88
1994 Okla City	AAA Tex	52	0	0	35	69.2	314	79	40	35	6	6	4	5	36	8	50	3	0	4	3	.571	0	11	4.52
1995 Okla City	AAA Tex	20	10	0	7	77.2	331	73	34	29	4	2	3	4	27	2	55	6	0	4	2	.667	0	0	3.36
1996 Okla City	AAA Tex	29	27	4	0	171	720	154	73	66	12	6	0	8	57	1	140	9	2	9	9	.500	2	0	3.47
1997 Okla City	AAA Tex	16	16	1	0	91.2	387	90	48	43	6	1	1	5	29	1	59	3	1	5	6	.455	1	0	4.22
Columbus	AAA NYY	1	1	1	0	8	32	5	4	3	1	0	1	1	1	0	6	0	0	0	1	.000	0	0	3.38
1998 Columbus	AAA NYY	46	13	1	20	127.1	570	123	76	64	14	3	4	7	69	0	91	10	1	8	10	.444	0	5	4.52
1999 Toledo	AAA Det	14	0	0	5	24	111	28	16	14	4	0	2	1	11	1	21	4	0	2	2	.500	0	0	5.25
Jacksonville	AA Det	1	0	0	0	2.2	13	4	2	1	0	0	0	0	1	0	1	0	0	0	0	.000	0	0	3.38
Calgary	AAA Fla	24	8	0	4	59.2	267	74	46	44	9	1	1	2	16	0	43	5	0	3	2	.600	0	0	6.64
1995 Texas	AL	12	0	0	7	20.2	101	26	18	17	2	0	1	1	12	1	10	2	0	0	0	.000	0	0	7.40
1996 Texas	AL	5	1	0	1	9.1	46	14	6	6	1	0	1	0	7	1	2	0	0	0	1	.000	0	0	5.79
1997 Texas	AL	10	4	0	2	28.1	143	37	33	25	4	2	1	1	17	1	11	3	0	0	3	.000	0	0	7.94
9 Min. YEARS		301	75	7	136	769.1	3321	751	389	339	63	25	19	43	295	16	602	52	9	39	37	.513	3	43	3.97
3 Maj. YEARS		27	5	0	10	58.1	290	77	57	48	7	2	3	2	36	3	23	5	0	0	4	.000	0	0	7.41

5

Juan Alcala

Bats: Right **Throws:** Right **Pos:** C   **Ht:** 6'2" **Wt:** 185 **Born:** 4/15/78 **Age:** 22

Year Team	Lg Org	G	AB	H	2B	3B	HR	TB	R	RBI	TBB	IBB	SO	HBP	SH	SF	SB	CS	SB%	GDP	Avg	OBP	SLG
1997 Mariners	R Sea	29	92	21	5	0	1	29	15	7	7	0	26	0	2	0	0	0	.00	2	.228	.283	.315
Everett	A- Sea	9	33	5	1	0	0	6	3	1	1	0	15	0	0	0	1	0	1.00	1	.152	.176	.182
1998 Everett	A- Sea	29	104	17	2	1	1	24	6	7	5	0	25	0	0	0	1	1	.50	2	.163	.202	.231
1999 Tacoma	AAA Sea	1	1	0	0	0	0	0	0	0	0	0	0	0	0	0	0	0	.00	0	.000	.000	.000
Everett	A- Sea	17	58	12	4	0	1	19	4	8	0	0	17	0	1	0	1	0	1.00	0	.207	.207	.328
Lancaster	A+ Sea	8	14	1	1	0	0	2	0	2	1	0	7	0	0	0	0	0	.00	0	.071	.133	.143
3 Min. YEARS		93	302	56	13	1	3	80	28	25	14	0	90	0	3	0	3	1	.75	5	.185	.222	.265

Israel Alcantara

Bats: Right **Throws:** Right **Pos:** OF   **Ht:** 6'2" **Wt:** 165 **Born:** 5/6/73 **Age:** 27

Year Team	Lg Org	G	AB	H	2B	3B	HR	TB	R	RBI	TBB	IBB	SO	HBP	SH	SF	SB	CS	SB%	GDP	Avg	OBP	SLG
1992 Expos	R Mon	59	224	62	14	2	3	89	29	37	17	4	35	1	0	2	6	5	.55	8	.277	.328	.397
1993 Burlington	A Mon	126	470	115	26	3	18	201	65	73	20	2	125	7	1	5	6	7	.46	5	.245	.283	.428
1994 Wst Plm Bch	A+ Mon	125	471	134	26	4	15	213	65	69	26	0	130	3	1	3	9	3	.75	6	.285	.324	.452
1995 Harrisburg	AA Mon	71	237	50	12	2	10	96	25	29	21	1	81	2	1	1	1	1	.50	5	.211	.280	.405
Wst Plm Bch	A+ Mon	39	134	37	7	2	3	57	16	22	9	0	35	2	2	1	3	0	1.00	0	.276	.329	.425
1996 Harrisburg	AA Mon	62	218	46	5	0	8	75	26	19	14	0	62	1	0	1	1	1	.50	5	.211	.261	.344
Expos	R Mon	7	30	9	2	0	2	17	4	10	3	2	6	0	0	0	0	1	.00	1	.300	.364	.567
Wst Plm Bch	A+ Mon	15	61	19	2	0	4	33	11	14	3	0	13	1	0	1	0	0	.00	1	.311	.348	.541
1997 Harrisburg	AA Mon	89	301	85	9	2	27	179	48	68	29	1	84	3	0	3	4	5	.44	5	.282	.348	.595
1998 St. Pete	A+ TB	38	141	47	5	0	10	82	21	26	21	2	29	2	0	1	1	0	1.00	6	.333	.427	.582
Reading	AA TB	53	203	63	12	2	15	124	36	44	17	2	37	2	0	1	1	0	.00	9	.310	.368	.611
Orlando	AA TB	15	55	13	4	0	3	26	8	18	7	0	15	0	0	3	0	1	.00	0	.236	.308	.473
1999 Trenton	AA Bos	77	293	86	26	0	20	172	48	60	27	0	78	4	0	0	4	2	.67	0	.294	.361	.587
Pawtucket	AAA Bos	24	81	22	3	0	9	52	13	23	9	0	29	3	0	0	0	0	.00	0	.272	.366	.642
8 Min. YEARS		800	2919	788	153	17	147	1416	415	512	223	14	759	31	5	21	35	27	.56	51	.270	.326	.485

Chad Alexander

Bats: Right **Throws:** Right **Pos:** OF   **Ht:** 6'1" **Wt:** 190 **Born:** 5/22/74 **Age:** 26

Year Team	Lg Org	G	AB	H	2B	3B	HR	TB	R	RBI	TBB	IBB	SO	HBP	SH	SF	SB	CS	SB%	GDP	Avg	OBP	SLG
1995 Auburn	A- Hou	71	278	81	15	5	5	121	45	43	25	1	37	7	1	5	7	1	.88	11	.291	.359	.435
Quad City	A Hou	2	7	2	0	0	0	2	2	1	0	0	0	0	0	0	0	0	.00	0	.286	.286	.286
1996 Quad City	A Hou	118	435	115	25	4	13	187	68	69	57	4	108	2	0	3	16	11	.59	11	.264	.350	.430
1997 Kissimmee	A+ Hou	129	469	127	31	6	4	182	67	46	56	1	91	4	2	3	11	8	.58	15	.271	.352	.388
1998 Jackson	AA Hou	128	416	119	33	2	13	195	77	45	71	0	80	5	3	3	6	7	.46	8	.286	.394	.469
New Orleans	AAA Hou	2	5	2	0	0	0	2	1	2	0	0	2	0	0	0	0	0	.00	0	.400	.400	.400
1999 New Orleans	AAA Hou	28	96	23	5	0	2	34	7	8	6	0	22	0	0	0	1	0	.00	3	.240	.279	.354
Jackson	AA Hou	84	317	98	27	3	9	158	42	44	34	1	58	3	0	3	9	5	.64	4	.309	.378	.498
5 Min. YEARS		562	2023	567	136	20	46	881	309	258	249	7	398	21	6	19	49	33	.60	52	.280	.362	.435

Jeff Alfano

Bats: Right **Throws:** Right **Pos:** C   **Ht:** 6'3" **Wt:** 210 **Born:** 8/16/76 **Age:** 23

Year Team	Lg Org	G	AB	H	2B	3B	HR	TB	R	RBI	TBB	IBB	SO	HBP	SH	SF	SB	CS	SB%	GDP	Avg	OBP	SLG
1996 Ogden	R+ Mil	45	159	45	9	0	4	66	29	29	12	0	30	4	2	2	2	2	.50	2	.283	.345	.415
1997 Beloit	A Mil	37	121	28	3	2	2	41	14	16	9	0	32	7	1	1	3	1	.75	4	.231	.319	.339
Ogden	R+ Mil	46	175	63	12	4	7	104	39	29	17	1	31	4	0	0	9	4	.69	4	.360	.426	.594
1998 Stockton	A+ Mil	113	389	94	21	1	4	129	39	40	37	1	93	6	0	1	7	4	.64	14	.242	.316	.332
1999 Huntsville	AA Mil	83	247	61	15	0	5	91	20	31	35	2	65	6	0	0	4	1	.80	10	.247	.354	.368
4 Min. YEARS		324	1091	291	60	7	22	431	141	145	110	4	251	27	3	5	25	12	.68	34	.267	.347	.395

Dusty Allen

Bats: Right **Throws:** Right **Pos:** 1B-OF   **Ht:** 6'4" **Wt:** 215 **Born:** 8/9/72 **Age:** 27

Year Team	Lg Org	G	AB	H	2B	3B	HR	TB	R	RBI	TBB	IBB	SO	HBP	SH	SF	SB	CS	SB%	GDP	Avg	OBP	SLG
1995 Idaho Falls	R+ SD	29	104	34	7	0	4	53	21	24	21	0	19	0	0	2	1	2	.33	2	.327	.433	.510
Clinton	A SD	36	139	37	12	1	5	66	25	31	12	1	29	1	0	0	1	0	1.00	3	.266	.329	.475
1996 Clinton	A SD	77	243	65	10	3	10	111	46	46	67	1	59	4	0	3	4	7	.36	7	.267	.429	.457
Rancho Cuca	A+ SD	55	208	62	15	1	10	109	41	45	38	1	65	2	0	3	3	2	.60	3	.298	.406	.524
1997 Mobile	AA SD	131	475	120	28	4	17	207	85	75	81	0	116	0	0	3	1	4	.20	12	.253	.360	.436
1998 Mobile	AA SD	42	154	39	10	4	6	75	30	42	32	1	26	1	0	2	1	0	1.00	3	.253	.381	.487
Las Vegas	AAA SD	87	292	78	21	1	16	149	42	45	31	0	80	4	0	4	0	2	.00	5	.267	.341	.510
1999 Las Vegas	AAA SD	128	454	124	30	3	18	214	68	89	79	0	143	3	0	2	3	5	.38	5	.273	.381	.471
5 Min. YEARS		585	2069	559	133	17	86	984	358	397	361	4	537	13	0	19	14	22	.39	40	.270	.379	.476

Luke Allen

Bats: Left **Throws:** Right **Pos:** 3B   **Ht:** 6'2" **Wt:** 208 **Born:** 8/4/78 **Age:** 21

Year Team	Lg Org	G	AB	H	2B	3B	HR	TB	R	RBI	TBB	IBB	SO	HBP	SH	SF	SB	CS	SB%	GDP	Avg	OBP	SLG
1997 Great Falls	R+ LA	67	258	89	12	6	7	134	50	40	19	1	53	0	1	0	12	11	.52	3	.345	.390	.519
1998 San Berndno	A+ LA	105	399	119	25	6	4	168	51	46	30	0	93	3	7	4	18	11	.62	9	.298	.349	.421
San Antonio	AA LA	23	78	26	3	1	3	40	9	10	6	1	16	0	1	0	1	2	.33	0	.333	.381	.513

Year Team	Lg Org	G	AB	H	2B	3B	HR	TB	R	RBI	TBB	IBB	SO	HBP	SH	SF	SB	CS	SB%	GDP	Avg	OBP	SLG
1999 San Antonio	AA LA	137	533	150	16	12	14	232	90	82	44	0	102	1	2	2	14	8	.64	8	.281	.336	.435
3 Min. YEARS		332	1268	384	56	25	28	574	200	178	99	2	264	4	11	6	45	32	.58	15	.303	.354	.453

Chip Alley

Bats: Both **Throws:** Right **Pos:** C **Ht:** 6'3" **Wt:** 190 **Born:** 12/20/76 **Age:** 23

Year Team	Lg Org	G	AB	H	2B	3B	HR	TB	R	RBI	TBB	IBB	SO	HBP	SH	SF	SB	CS	SB%	GDP	Avg	OBP	SLG
1995 Orioles	R Bal	12	30	9	4	0	0	13	10	3	11	0	4	1	0	2	0	0	.00	1	.300	.477	.433
1996 Bluefield	R+ Bal	24	67	13	4	0	0	17	7	4	15	0	16	1	0	1	0	2	.00	2	.194	.345	.254
1997 Delmarva	A Bal	82	250	59	17	1	3	87	19	32	34	3	45	8	1	2	7	2	.78	5	.236	.344	.348
1998 Frederick	A+ Bal	112	340	89	23	1	9	141	42	47	60	2	60	4	5	1	0	2	.00	5	.262	.378	.415
1999 Bowie	AA Bal	5	9	1	1	0	0	2	4	0	1	0	3	0	0	0	0	0	.00	0	.111	.200	.222
Orioles	R Bal	2	3	0	0	0	0	0	2	0	2	0	0	0	0	0	0	0	.00	0	.000	.400	.000
Frederick	A+ Bal	41	132	30	6	0	1	39	21	12	23	1	27	1	1	0	0	1	.00	1	.227	.346	.295
5 Min. YEARS		278	831	201	55	2	13	299	105	98	146	6	155	15	7	6	7	7	.50	14	.242	.363	.360

Richard Almanzar

Bats: Right **Throws:** Right **Pos:** 2B **Ht:** 5'10" **Wt:** 165 **Born:** 4/3/76 **Age:** 24

Year Team	Lg Org	G	AB	H	2B	3B	HR	TB	R	RBI	TBB	IBB	SO	HBP	SH	SF	SB	CS	SB%	GDP	Avg	OBP	SLG
1995 Lakeland	A+ Det	42	140	43	9	0	1	55	29	14	18	0	20	4	5	0	11	9	.55	5	.307	.401	.393
Fayetteville	A Det	80	308	76	12	1	0	90	47	16	29	0	32	7	9	0	39	15	.72	5	.247	.326	.292
1996 Lakeland	A+ Det	124	471	144	22	2	1	173	81	36	49	0	49	8	12	3	53	19	.74	5	.306	.379	.367
1997 Jacksonville	AA Det	103	387	94	20	2	5	133	55	35	37	0	43	3	11	0	20	6	.77	11	.243	.314	.344
1998 Toledo	AAA Det	104	306	64	16	1	1	85	36	16	28	0	30	3	4	2	11	7	.61	8	.209	.280	.278
1999 Iowa	AAA ChC	33	93	20	2	3	1	31	13	4	6	0	7	0	2	0	6	1	.86	4	.215	.263	.333
West Tenn	AA ChC	42	151	46	7	0	2	59	27	16	18	0	19	1	2	0	13	7	.65	0	.305	.382	.391
5 Min. YEARS		528	1856	487	88	9	11	626	288	137	185	0	200	26	45	5	153	64	.71	38	.262	.337	.337

Wady Almonte

Bats: Right **Throws:** Right **Pos:** OF **Ht:** 6'0" **Wt:** 195 **Born:** 4/20/75 **Age:** 25

Year Team	Lg Org	G	AB	H	2B	3B	HR	TB	R	RBI	TBB	IBB	SO	HBP	SH	SF	SB	CS	SB%	GDP	Avg	OBP	SLG
1994 Orioles	R Bal	42	120	24	2	0	2	32	11	9	8	0	22	1	1	0	1	2	.33	0	.200	.256	.267
1995 Bluefield	R+ Bal	51	189	58	12	1	6	90	37	30	9	2	49	1	0	2	6	5	.55	4	.307	.338	.476
1996 Orioles	R Bal	1	3	1	0	0	0	1	2	1	1	0	0	0	0	0	1	0	1.00	0	.333	.500	.333
Frederick	A+ Bal	85	287	82	12	2	12	134	45	44	21	2	59	6	4	1	1	5	.17	12	.286	.346	.467
1997 Bowie	AA Bal	69	222	46	7	2	6	75	25	25	27	0	64	5	0	1	2	4	.33	6	.207	.306	.338
Frederick	A+ Bal	57	202	52	13	2	10	99	34	36	16	4	59	4	1	3	4	1	.80	8	.257	.320	.490
1998 Bowie	AA Bal	7	21	1	0	0	1	4	2	2	4	0	9	1	0	0	0	0	.00	2	.048	.231	.190
1999 Bowie	AA Bal	124	482	141	27	4	17	227	68	83	31	1	72	7	0	5	10	10	.50	12	.293	.341	.471
6 Min. YEARS		436	1526	405	73	11	54	662	224	230	117	9	334	25	6	12	25	27	.48	44	.265	.326	.434

Garvin Alston

Pitches: Right **Bats:** Right **Pos:** P **Ht:** 6'1" **Wt:** 185 **Born:** 12/8/71 **Age:** 28

Year Team	Lg Org	G	GS	CG	GF	IP	BFP	H	R	ER	HR	SH	SF	HB	TBB	IBB	SO	WP	Bk	W	L	Pct.	ShO	Sv	ERA
1992 Bend	A- Col	14	12	0	0	73	320	71	40	32	1	5	5	9	29	0	73	7	8	5	4	.556	0	0	3.95
1993 Central Val	A+ Col	25	24	1	0	117	538	124	81	71	11	6	6	8	70	0	90	10	2	5	9	.357	0	0	5.46
1994 Central Val	A+ Col	37	13	0	20	87	382	91	51	35	9	5	0	6	42	1	83	5	2	5	9	.357	0	8	3.62
New Haven	AA Col	4	0	0	1	4.1	22	5	6	6	1	0	0	0	3	0	8	0	0	0	0	.000	0	1	12.46
1995 New Haven	AA Col	47	0	0	20	66.2	271	47	24	21	1	4	2	3	26	3	73	4	0	4	4	.500	0	6	2.84
1996 Colo Sprngs	AAA Col	35	0	0	26	34.1	171	47	23	22	3	1	0	1	27	0	36	2	0	1	4	.200	0	14	5.77
1998 Colo Sprngs	AAA Col	44	0	0	17	67	313	85	53	48	12	1	2	1	32	3	69	2	2	2	4	.333	0	5	6.45
1999 Albuquerque	AAA LA	5	0	0	2	10.2	46	12	6	6	1	1	0	1	4	0	5	1	0	1	2	.333	0	0	5.06
1996 Colorado	NL	6	0	0	4	6	30	9	6	6	1	0	2	1	3	0	5	1	0	1	0	1.000	0	0	9.00
7 Min. YEARS		211	49	1	86	460	2063	482	284	241	39	23	15	29	233	7	437	31	14	23	36	.390	0	34	4.72

Clemente Alvarez

Bats: Right **Throws:** Right **Pos:** C **Ht:** 5'11" **Wt:** 180 **Born:** 5/18/68 **Age:** 32

Year Team	Lg Org	G	AB	H	2B	3B	HR	TB	R	RBI	TBB	IBB	SO	HBP	SH	SF	SB	CS	SB%	GDP	Avg	OBP	SLG
1987 White Sox	R CWS	25	55	10	1	0	1	14	8	4	7	0	8	0	0	0	1	1	.50	1	.182	.274	.255
1988 South Bend	A CWS	15	41	3	0	0	0	3	0	1	3	0	19	0	0	0	0	0	.00	2	.073	.136	.073
Utica	A- CWS	53	132	31	5	1	0	38	15	14	11	0	36	2	4	1	5	2	.71	2	.235	.301	.288
1989 South Bend	A CWS	86	230	51	15	0	0	66	22	22	16	0	59	0	9	1	4	1	.80	6	.222	.271	.287
1990 Sarasota	A+ CWS	37	119	19	4	1	1	28	9	9	8	0	24	0	2	0	0	0	.00	5	.160	.213	.235
South Bend	A CWS	48	127	30	5	0	2	41	14	12	20	0	38	1	5	2	2	1	.67	1	.236	.340	.323
1991 Sarasota	A+ CWS	71	194	40	10	2	1	57	14	22	20	0	41	4	7	1	3	2	.60	6	.206	.292	.294
1992 Birmingham	AA CWS	57	169	24	8	0	1	35	7	10	10	0	52	2	3	0	1	1	.50	5	.142	.199	.207
1993 White Sox	R CWS	2	5	0	0	0	0	0	0	1	0	0	2	0	0	0	0	1	.00	0	.000	.167	.000
Nashville	AAA CWS	11	29	6	0	0	0	6	1	2	1	0	4	0	2	0	0	0	.00	0	.207	.233	.207
Birmingham	AA CWS	35	111	25	4	0	1	32	8	11	8	0	28	1	1	1	0	4	.00	3	.225	.298	.288
1994 Nashville	AAA CWS	87	223	48	8	1	3	67	18	14	17	2	48	2	12	2	0	2	.00	2	.215	.275	.300
1995 Ottawa	AAA Mon	50	143	33	7	0	4	52	15	20	10	1	34	2	3	0	0	0	.00	2	.231	.290	.364
1997 Winston-Sal	A+ CWS	2	4	1	0	0	0	1	0	0	1	0	2	0	0	0	0	0	.00	0	.250	.400	.250

Year Team	Lg Org	G	AB	H	2B	3B	HR	TB	R	RBI	TBB	IBB	SO	HBP	SH	SF	SB	CS	SB%	GDP	Avg	OBP	SLG
																BATTING → BASERUNNING → PERCENTAGES							
Birmingham	AA CWS	79	242	49	10	1	3	70	29	23	27	0	49	5	3	1	0	0	.00	17	.202	.295	.289
1999 Scranton-WB	AAA Phi	9	28	7	4	0	0	11	4	6	3	0	9	0	0	0	0	0	.00	1	.250	.323	.393
Reading	AA Phi	48	142	25	5	1	2	38	12	12	11	0	38	0	5	1	1	1	.50	3	.176	.234	.268
11 Min. YEARS		715	1994	402	86	7	19	559	176	180	176	1	491	20	56	10	17	16	.52	56	.202	.272	.280

Rafael Alvarez

Bats: Both **Throws:** Left **Pos:** OF **Ht:** 5'11" **Wt:** 192 **Born:** 1/22/77 **Age:** 23

BATTING / BASERUNNING / PERCENTAGES

Year Team	Lg Org	G	AB	H	2B	3B	HR	TB	R	RBI	TBB	IBB	SO	HBP	SH	SF	SB	CS	SB%	GDP	Avg	OBP	SLG
1994 Twins	R Min	32	101	32	5	0	2	43	15	10	18	0	14	1	2	0	4	2	.67	4	.317	.425	.426
1995 Fort Wayne	A Min	99	374	106	17	5	5	148	62	36	34	1	53	2	2	4	15	11	.58	5	.283	.343	.396
1996 Fort Myers	A+ Min	6	22	3	0	0	0	3	1	1	1	0	7	0	0	1	0	1	.00	0	.136	.167	.136
Fort Wayne	A Min	119	473	143	30	7	4	199	61	58	43	5	55	3	2	1	11	9	.55	5	.302	.363	.421
1997 Salt Lake	AAA Min	17	48	13	1	1	0	16	10	5	6	0	9	0	1	0	5	0	1.00	1	.271	.352	.333
New Britain	AA Min	16	47	12	0	0	2	18	5	7	5	0	9	1	1	0	1	4	.20	0	.255	.340	.383
Fort Myers	A+ Min	47	122	33	9	1	1	47	13	15	17	0	27	0	3	1	6	2	.75	1	.270	.357	.385
1998 Fort Myers	A+ Min	110	391	114	20	2	4	150	54	38	45	8	51	1	5	3	19	8	.70	5	.292	.364	.384
1999 Salt Lake	AAA Min	6	16	6	1	0	0	7	3	2	0	0	1	0	0	0	0	0	.00	1	.375	.375	.438
Fort Myers	A+ Min	83	304	89	22	4	10	149	47	58	38	4	48	4	1	3	8	4	.67	5	.293	.375	.490
6 Min. YEARS		535	1898	551	105	20	28	780	271	230	207	18	274	12	17	13	69	41	.63	30	.290	.362	.411

Victor Alvarez

Pitches: Left **Bats:** Left **Pos:** P **Ht:** 5'10" **Wt:** 150 **Born:** 11/8/76 **Age:** 23

HOW MUCH HE PITCHED / WHAT HE GAVE UP / THE RESULTS

Year Team	Lg Org	G	GS	CG	GF	IP	BFP	H	R	ER	HR	SH	SF	HB	TBB	IBB	SO	WP	Bk	W	L	Pct.	ShO	Sv	ERA
1997 Great Falls	R+ LA	12	8	0	3	48.1	212	49	30	18	0	0	4	3	17	0	50	2	3	4	1	.800	0	0	3.35
1999 Vero Beach	A+ LA	12	12	1	0	73	280	56	21	16	4	1	1	2	16	0	57	1	1	4	4	.500	0	0	1.97
San Antonio	AA LA	9	9	0	0	56.1	234	58	27	23	5	3	1	2	10	0	43	1	0	4	3	.571	0	0	3.67
2 Min. YEARS		33	29	1	3	177.2	726	163	78	57	9	4	6	7	43	0	150	4	4	12	8	.600	0	0	2.89

Jose Amado

Bats: Right **Throws:** Right **Pos:** 1B **Ht:** 6'1" **Wt:** 180 **Born:** 2/7/75 **Age:** 25

BATTING / BASERUNNING / PERCENTAGES

Year Team	Lg Org	G	AB	H	2B	3B	HR	TB	R	RBI	TBB	IBB	SO	HBP	SH	SF	SB	CS	SB%	GDP	Avg	OBP	SLG
1995 Everett	A- Sea	57	215	57	15	1	8	98	33	33	24	6	19	6	0	5	5	5	.75	4	.265	.348	.456
1996 Wisconsin	A Sea	61	232	67	13	0	5	95	43	36	20	1	20	8	2	3	6	5	.55	5	.289	.361	.409
Lansing	A KC	57	212	74	18	1	5	109	39	47	17	2	17	8	1	2	8	4	.67	6	.349	.414	.514
1997 Lansing	A KC	61	234	80	25	1	4	119	49	45	24	1	18	4	0	6	10	2	.83	8	.342	.403	.509
1998 Wilmington	A+ KC	70	236	62	17	1	4	93	34	28	24	2	28	10	1	2	6	5	.55	11	.263	.353	.394
1999 Wichita	AA KC	121	459	133	29	2	13	205	71	93	54	4	37	3	0	6	13	8	.63	15	.290	.364	.447
5 Min. YEARS		427	1588	473	117	6	39	719	269	282	163	16	139	39	4	24	50	24	.68	49	.298	.372	.453

John Ambrose

Pitches: Right **Bats:** Right **Pos:** P **Ht:** 6'5" **Wt:** 180 **Born:** 11/1/74 **Age:** 25

HOW MUCH HE PITCHED / WHAT HE GAVE UP / THE RESULTS

Year Team	Lg Org	G	GS	CG	GF	IP	BFP	H	R	ER	HR	SH	SF	HB	TBB	IBB	SO	WP	Bk	W	L	Pct.	ShO	Sv	ERA
1994 White Sox	R CWS	11	10	1	0	46.2	195	34	21	19	4	1	2	6	24	0	43	4	3	1	2	.333	0	0	3.66
Hickory	A CWS	3	1	0	1	12.2	58	16	11	10	1	0	0	0	6	0	7	0	0	1	1	.500	0	1	7.11
1995 Hickory	A CWS	14	14	0	0	73	314	65	41	32	6	2	3	3	35	0	49	9	2	4	8	.333	0	0	3.95
South Bend	A CWS	3	3	1	0	16.2	77	18	13	10	2	1	0	0	10	0	15	2	0	1	1	.500	0	0	5.40
1997 Winston-Sal	A+ CWS	27	27	1	0	149.2	688	136	102	91	17	5	9	8	117	2	137	16	5	8	13	.381	1	0	5.47
1998 Birmingham	AA CWS	31	22	0	3	140.2	641	156	90	81	18	2	4	13	69	2	103	14	2	9	12	.429	0	0	5.18
1999 Arkansas	AA StL	34	16	0	17	106.2	483	108	65	56	11	6	6	5	68	0	78	10	0	4	12	.250	0	9	4.73
5 Min. YEARS		123	93	3	21	546	2456	533	343	299	59	17	24	35	329	4	432	55	12	28	49	.364	1	10	4.93

Jesus Ametller

Bats: Left **Throws:** Right **Pos:** 2B **Ht:** 5'8" **Wt:** 175 **Born:** 7/25/74 **Age:** 25

BATTING / BASERUNNING / PERCENTAGES

Year Team	Lg Org	G	AB	H	2B	3B	HR	TB	R	RBI	TBB	IBB	SO	HBP	SH	SF	SB	CS	SB%	GDP	Avg	OBP	SLG
1997 Pr William	A+ StL	60	215	58	10	2	3	81	26	26	15	1	12	0	4	0	3	1	.75	5	.270	.317	.377
1998 Pr William	A+ StL	101	358	112	29	0	1	144	52	38	2	0	29	3	6	5	4	6	.40	8	.313	.318	.402
1999 Arkansas	AA StL	116	397	122	26	2	10	182	53	53	5	0	21	4	1	5	2	1	.67	13	.307	.319	.458
Memphis	AAA StL	2	4	1	0	0	0	1	0	0	0	0	0	0	0	0	0	0	.00	0	.250	.250	.250
3 Min. YEARS		279	974	293	65	4	14	408	131	117	22	1	62	7	11	10	9	8	.53	26	.301	.318	.419

Bill Anderson

Pitches: Right **Bats:** Right **Pos:** P **Ht:** 6'0" **Wt:** 190 **Born:** 9/23/71 **Age:** 28

HOW MUCH HE PITCHED / WHAT HE GAVE UP / THE RESULTS

Year Team	Lg Org	G	GS	CG	GF	IP	BFP	H	R	ER	HR	SH	SF	HB	TBB	IBB	SO	WP	Bk	W	L	Pct.	ShO	Sv	ERA
1994 Rancho Cuca	A+ SD	22	2	0	5	62.1	265	64	36	31	2	2	0	3	24	0	70	2	4	7	0	1.000	0	1	4.48
1997 Mobile	AA SD	7	0	0	3	9.2	43	8	3	2	0	0	0	0	6	0	6	1	0	0	0	.000	0	0	1.86
Rancho Cuca	A+ SD	29	14	0	6	101	429	78	53	45	9	2	2	6	51	0	118	6	2	8	4	.667	0	1	4.01
1998 Mobile	AA SD	13	6	0	0	43	177	32	12	11	3	1	0	0	23	0	39	2	1	3	0	1.000	0	0	2.30
1999 Mobile	AA SD	4	4	0	0	18	83	20	14	14	2	1	1	1	13	0	19	1	0	0	0	.000	0	0	7.00
Nashua	IND —	10	5	1	2	39	151	32	12	9	2	1	0	1	7	0	32	2	0	5	1	.833	0	1	2.08

Year Team	Lg Org	G	GS	CG	GF	IP	BFP	H	R	ER	HR	SH	SF	HB	TBB	IBB	SO	WP	Bk	W	L	Pct.	ShO	Sv	ERA
Erie	AA Ana	5	5	0	0	18.1	83	20	12	11	2	0	0	0	8	0	12	2	0	1	1	.500	0	0	5.40
4 Min. YEARS		90	36	1	16	291.1	1231	254	142	123	20	7	4	12	132	0	296	16	7	24	6	.800	0	3	3.80

Jason Anderson

Pitches: Left **Bats:** Left **Pos:** P **Ht:** 6'2" **Wt:** 195 **Born:** 4/6/76 **Age:** 24

Year Team	Lg Org	G	GS	CG	GF	IP	BFP	H	R	ER	HR	SH	SF	HB	TBB	IBB	SO	WP	Bk	W	L	Pct.	ShO	Sv	ERA
1997 Sou Oregon	A- Oak	14	9	0	1	52.1	238	63	38	29	4	3	0	5	19	0	38	8	2	3	3	.500	0	0	4.99
1998 Modesto	A+ Oak	28	24	1	2	145.2	612	147	67	56	5	5	4	2	53	0	110	5	1	9	4	.692	1	0	3.46
Huntsville	AA Oak	3	3	1	0	17	80	16	15	10	2	1	0	2	11	1	14	1	1	1	1	.500	1	0	5.29
1999 Visalia	A+ Oak	4	4	0	0	25	110	32	9	7	1	0	0	2	7	0	17	1	0	2	1	.667	0	0	2.52
Midland	AA Oak	23	23	0	0	111	531	148	103	85	15	6	7	10	47	0	74	5	3	4	9	.308	0	0	6.89
3 Min. YEARS		72	63	2	3	351	1571	406	232	187	27	15	11	21	137	1	253	20	7	19	18	.514	2	0	4.79

Ryan Anderson

Pitches: Left **Bats:** Left **Pos:** P **Ht:** 6'10" **Wt:** 215 **Born:** 7/12/79 **Age:** 20

Year Team	Lg Org	G	GS	CG	GF	IP	BFP	H	R	ER	HR	SH	SF	HB	TBB	IBB	SO	WP	Bk	W	L	Pct.	ShO	Sv	ERA
1998 Wisconsin	A Sea	22	22	0	0	111.1	474	86	47	40	4	3	3	10	67	0	152	4	3	6	5	.545	0	0	3.23
1999 New Haven	AA Sea	24	24	0	0	134	606	131	77	67	9	2	5	8	86	1	162	9	3	9	13	.409	0	0	4.50
2 Min. YEARS		46	46	0	0	245.1	1080	217	124	107	13	5	8	18	153	1	314	13	6	15	18	.455	0	0	3.93

Alex Andreopoulos

Bats: Left **Throws:** Right **Pos:** C **Ht:** 5'10" **Wt:** 190 **Born:** 8/19/72 **Age:** 27

							BATTING										BASERUNNING				PERCENTAGES		
Year Team	Lg Org	G	AB	H	2B	3B	HR	TB	R	RBI	TBB	IBB	SO	HBP	SH	SF	SB	CS	SB%	GDP	Avg	OBP	SLG
1995 Helena	R+ Mil	3	9	5	0	0	2	11	3	7	4	0	0	0	0	0	0	0	.00	0	.556	.692	1.222
Beloit	A Mil	60	163	49	9	0	1	61	32	20	35	1	16	3	3	1	5	3	.63	2	.301	.431	.374
1996 Stockton	A+ Mil	87	291	88	17	2	5	124	52	41	40	2	33	5	2	4	10	3	.77	5	.302	.391	.426
1997 El Paso	AA Mil	7	26	4	1	0	0	5	1	3	1	0	2	0	0	0	0	0	.00	1	.154	.185	.192
Tucson	AAA Mil	10	15	6	1	0	0	7	3	1	0	0	1	0	0	0	0	0	.00	0	.400	.400	.467
1998 El Paso	AA Mil	113	377	131	35	1	10	188	72	93	54	4	31	9	2	5	2	3	.40	9	.321	.413	.499
1999 Louisville	AAA Mil	71	201	53	8	0	5	76	19	31	25	4	21	2	3	1	1	0	1.00	5	.264	.349	.378
5 Min. YEARS		351	1082	326	71	3	23	472	182	196	159	11	104	19	10	11	18	9	.67	22	.301	.397	.436

Clayton Andrews

Pitches: Left **Bats:** Right **Pos:** P **Ht:** 6'0" **Wt:** 175 **Born:** 5/15/78 **Age:** 22

Year Team	Lg Org	G	GS	CG	GF	IP	BFP	H	R	ER	HR	SH	SF	HB	TBB	IBB	SO	WP	Bk	W	L	Pct.	ShO	Sv	ERA
1996 Medcine Hat	R+ Tor	8	4	0	1	25.2	120	37	23	21	4	0	3	1	10	0	14	1	0	2	4	.333	0	0	7.36
1997 Hagerstown	A Tor	28	15	0	7	114.2	512	120	70	58	8	4	4	5	47	1	112	4	2	7	7	.500	0	0	4.55
1998 Hagerstown	A Tor	27	26	2	0	162	635	112	59	41	7	4	5	6	46	0	193	7	2	10	7	.588	1	0	2.28
1999 Knoxville	AA Tor	25	25	0	0	132.2	593	143	85	58	13	8	3	4	69	0	93	4	2	10	8	.556	0	0	3.93
Syracuse	AAA Tor	3	3	0	0	15	65	10	14	13	5	0	1	0	13	0	9	1	0	0	1	.000	0	0	7.80
4 Min. YEARS		91	73	2	8	450	1925	422	251	191	37	16	16	16	185	1	421	17	6	29	27	.518	1	0	3.82

Jeff Andrews

Pitches: Right **Bats:** Right **Pos:** P **Ht:** 6'3" **Wt:** 190 **Born:** 9/1/74 **Age:** 25

Year Team	Lg Org	G	GS	CG	GF	IP	BFP	H	R	ER	HR	SH	SF	HB	TBB	IBB	SO	WP	Bk	W	L	Pct.	ShO	Sv	ERA
1997 South Bend	A Ari	23	4	0	7	55	237	52	37	32	4	2	1	2	27	1	32	3	0	1	5	.167	0	0	5.24
Lethbridge	R+ Ari	9	9	1	0	49.2	219	55	27	18	3	1	0	3	10	0	50	3	0	3	3	.500	0	0	3.26
1998 South Bend	A Ari	20	17	0	2	123	524	130	62	39	4	4	3	2	28	2	68	7	1	3	8	.273	0	0	2.85
High Desert	A+ Ari	6	3	0	2	25	119	36	19	12	1	0	2	0	7	0	8	0	0	1	1	.500	0	0	4.32
1999 High Desert	A+ Ari	6	6	0	0	29.2	143	41	27	21	5	0	1	2	13	0	25	1	0	0	3	.000	0	0	6.37
El Paso	AA Ari	35	8	0	21	73	323	87	47	43	6	3	5	3	24	3	40	1	1	3	8	.273	0	7	5.30
3 Min. YEARS		99	47	1	32	355.1	1565	401	219	165	23	10	12	12	109	6	223	15	2	11	28	.282	0	7	4.18

Luis Andujar

Pitches: Right **Bats:** Right **Pos:** P **Ht:** 6'2" **Wt:** 215 **Born:** 11/22/72 **Age:** 27

Year Team	Lg Org	G	GS	CG	GF	IP	BFP	H	R	ER	HR	SH	SF	HB	TBB	IBB	SO	WP	Bk	W	L	Pct.	ShO	Sv	ERA
1991 White Sox	R CWS	10	10	0	0	62.1	255	60	27	17	0	1	2	4	10	0	52	3	1	4	4	.500	1	0	2.45
1992 South Bend	A CWS	32	15	1	11	120.1	516	109	49	39	5	2	0	6	47	0	91	5	1	6	5	.545	1	3	2.92
1993 Sarasota	A+ CWS	18	11	2	4	86	345	67	26	19	2	7	0	3	28	0	72	1	0	6	6	.500	0	1	1.99
Birmingham	AA CWS	6	6	0	0	39.2	169	31	9	8	3	3	1	5	18	0	48	1	0	5	0	1.000	0	0	1.82
1994 White Sox	R CWS	2	0	0	0	6	22	3	1	0	0	0	0	1	0	0	6	0	0	1	0	1.000	0	0	0.00
Birmingham	AA CWS	15	15	0	0	76.2	344	90	50	43	5	1	2	8	25	0	64	5	0	3	7	.300	0	0	5.05
1995 Birmingham	AA CWS	27	27	2	0	167.1	689	147	64	53	10	1	5	7	44	0	146	3	1	14	8	.636	1	0	2.85
1996 White Sox	R CWS	1	1	0	0	6	22	3	0	0	0	0	0	1	0	0	3	0	0	1	0	1.000	0	0	0.00
Nashville	AAA CWS	8	7	1	0	38	171	50	26	25	4	0	2	2	8	0	24	1	1	1	4	.200	0	0	5.92
Syracuse	AAA Tor	2	2	0	0	12	55	17	7	3	1	0	2	0	2	0	10	0	0	0	0	.000	0	0	2.25
1997 Syracuse	AAA Tor	13	5	1	7	39	169	47	26	24	6	2	2	3	14	1	29	1	1	1	6	.143	0	1	5.54
1998 Syracuse	AAA Tor	20	0	0	14	34	130	23	9	8	5	2	0	4	6	0	24	2	1	3	2	.600	0	8	2.12
Calgary	AAA CWS	13	9	0	0	50.1	226	62	38	35	8	4	0	4	15	1	46	0	0	3	3	.500	0	0	6.26

Year Team	Lg Org	G	GS	CG	GF	IP	BFP	H	R	ER	HR	SH	SF	HB	TBB	IBB	SO	WP	Bk	W	L	Pct.	ShO	Sv	ERA
1999 Charlotte AAA CWS		52	0	0	35	60	252	62	21	20	3	4	4	3	13	0	59	3	0	4	5	.444	0	16	3.00
1995 Chicago	AL	5	5	0	0	30.1	128	26	12	11	4	0	0	1	14	2	9	0	0	2	1	.667	0	0	3.26
1996 Chicago	AL	5	5	0	0	23	113	32	22	21	4	1	2	0	15	0	6	0	0	0	2	.000	0	0	8.22
Toronto	AL	3	2	0	0	14.1	57	14	8	8	4	0	2	1	1	0	5	1	0	1	1	.500	0	0	5.02
1997 Toronto	AL	17	8	0	5	50	244	76	45	36	9	3	4	0	21	1	28	2	0	0	6	.000	0	0	6.48
1998 Toronto	AL	5	0	0	3	5.2	30	12	6	6	0	0	0	0	2	0	1	0	0	0	0	.000	0	0	9.53
9 Min. YEARS		219	108	8	71	797.2	3365	761	352	294	52	23	21	52	231	2	674	25	6	52	50	.510	3	29	3.32
4 Maj. YEARS		35	20	0	8	123.1	572	160	93	82	21	4	8	2	53	3	49	4	0	3	10	.231	0	0	5.98

Chuck Antczak

Bats: Right **Throws:** Right **Pos:** C   **Ht:** 6'0" **Wt:** 185 **Born:** 10/8/73 **Age:** 26

Year Team	Lg Org	G	AB	H	2B	3B	HR	TB	R	RBI	TBB	IBB	SO	HBP	SH	SF	SB	CS	SB%	GDP	Avg	OBP	SLG
1995 Hickory A CWS		6	5	1	0	0	0	1	0	1	0	0	2	0	0	0	0	0	.00	0	.200	.200	.200
Bristol R+ CWS		24	59	18	4	0	1	25	11	10	6	0	16	7	0	1	2	0	1.00	1	.305	.425	.424
1996 Hickory A CWS		9	13	2	0	0	0	2	0	1	3	0	2	0	1	0	0	0	.00	0	.154	.313	.154
South Bend A CWS		16	31	3	2	0	0	5	3	1	1	0	9	2	1	0	0	0	.00	0	.097	.176	.161
Bristol R+ CWS		7	23	7	0	0	0	7	2	0	2	0	5	0	0	0	0	0	.00	0	.304	.360	.304
Pr William A+ CWS		5	11	1	0	0	0	1	2	0	1	0	2	1	0	0	0	0	.00	0	.091	.231	.091
1997 Hickory A CWS		1	1	1	0	0	0	1	0	1	0	0	0	0	0	1	0	0	.00	0	1.000	.500	1.000
Winston-Sal A+ CWS		5	14	2	0	0	0	2	0	0	0	0	3	0	0	0	0	0	.00	0	.143	.143	.143
1998 Greenville IND —		11	35	4	1	0	0	5	0	3	6	0	7	2	0	1	1	0	1.00	0	.114	.279	.143
1999 Reading AA Phi		8	19	0	0	0	0	0	0	0	0	0	6	0	0	1	0	0	.00	1	.000	.000	.000
Clearwater A+ Phi		15	31	8	2	0	0	10	3	4	2	0	6	2	0	0	0	0	.00	0	.258	.343	.323
5 Min. YEARS		107	242	47	9	0	1	59	21	21	21	0	58	14	2	2	3	0	1.00	5	.194	.294	.244

Brian Anthony

Bats: Left **Throws:** Right **Pos:** 3B   **Ht:** 6'2" **Wt:** 218 **Born:** 10/22/73 **Age:** 26

Year Team	Lg Org	G	AB	H	2B	3B	HR	TB	R	RBI	TBB	IBB	SO	HBP	SH	SF	SB	CS	SB%	GDP	Avg	OBP	SLG
1996 Portland A- Col		30	107	15	5	0	1	23	6	5	10	0	30	0	0	0	1	0	1.00	3	.140	.214	.215
1997 Asheville A Col		83	296	76	17	1	12	131	41	49	23	0	75	2	1	0	4	4	.50	6	.257	.315	.443
1998 Salem A+ Col		123	442	122	19	0	15	186	53	65	29	4	85	5	3	4	7	9	.44	10	.276	.325	.421
1999 Carolina AA Col		64	171	38	9	1	7	70	20	20	11	0	39	1	0	2	1	2	.33	5	.222	.270	.409
Salem A+ Col		36	128	31	7	0	3	47	13	13	8	0	28	0	1	1	0	2	.00	4	.242	.285	.367
4 Min. YEARS		336	1144	282	57	2	38	457	133	152	81	4	257	8	5	7	13	17	.43	28	.247	.299	.399

Eric Anthony

Bats: Left **Throws:** Left **Pos:** OF   **Ht:** 6'2" **Wt:** 210 **Born:** 11/8/67 **Age:** 32

Year Team	Lg Org	G	AB	H	2B	3B	HR	TB	R	RBI	TBB	IBB	SO	HBP	SH	SF	SB	CS	SB%	GDP	Avg	OBP	SLG
1986 Astros R Hou		13	12	3	0	0	0	3	2	0	5	0	5	1	0	0	1	0	1.00	1	.250	.500	.250
1987 Astros R Hou		60	216	57	11	6	10	110	38	46	26	3	58	2	0	1	2	2	.50	4	.264	.347	.509
1988 Asheville A Hou		115	439	120	36	1	29	245	73	89	40	5	101	3	0	3	10	4	.71	10	.273	.336	.558
1989 Columbus AA Hou		107	403	121	16	2	28	225	67	79	35	5	127	3	0	3	14	9	.61	3	.300	.358	.558
Tucson AAA Hou		12	46	10	3	0	3	22	10	11	6	0	11	0	0	0	0	0	.00	0	.217	.308	.478
1990 Columbus AA Hou		4	12	2	0	0	1	5	2	3	3	0	4	0	0	0	0	0	.00	0	.167	.333	.417
Tucson AAA Hou		40	161	46	10	2	6	78	28	26	17	0	41	1	0	3	8	3	.73	4	.286	.352	.484
1991 Tucson AAA Hou		79	318	107	22	2	9	160	57	63	25	6	58	3	0	3	11	5	.69	13	.336	.387	.503
1995 Indianapols AAA Cin		7	24	7	0	0	4	19	7	8	6	3	4	0	0	0	2	0	1.00	2	.292	.433	.792
1996 Indianapols AAA Cin		7	21	5	1	0	2	12	4	7	7	0	8	0	0	0	1	0	.00	0	.238	.429	.571
1997 Okla City AAA Tex		9	36	16	2	0	2	24	3	9	2	0	7	0	0	0	0	0	.00	0	.444	.462	.667
Albuquerque AAA LA		27	105	36	6	1	7	65	18	27	11	1	28	0	0	1	2	3	.40	0	.343	.402	.619
1998 Albuquerque AAA LA		59	188	57	9	2	10	100	34	26	36	3	43	1	0	1	3	3	.50	2	.303	.416	.532
1999 Albuquerque AAA LA		7	20	6	2	0	1	11	4	3	3	1	5	0	0	0	0	0	.00	0	.300	.391	.550
1989 Houston NL		25	61	11	2	0	4	25	7	7	9	2	16	0	0	1	0	0	.00	1	.180	.286	.410
1990 Houston NL		84	239	46	8	0	10	84	26	29	29	3	78	2	1	6	5	0	1.00	4	.192	.279	.351
1991 Houston NL		39	118	18	6	0	1	27	11	7	12	1	41	0	0	2	1	0	1.00	1	.153	.227	.229
1992 Houston NL		137	440	105	15	1	19	179	45	80	38	5	98	1	0	4	5	4	.56	7	.239	.298	.407
1993 Houston NL		145	486	121	19	4	15	193	70	66	49	2	88	2	0	2	3	5	.38	9	.249	.319	.397
1994 Seattle AL		79	262	62	14	1	10	108	31	30	23	4	66	0	0	2	6	2	.75	7	.237	.297	.412
1995 Cincinnati NL		47	134	36	6	0	5	57	19	23	13	2	30	0	0	3	2	1	.67	1	.269	.327	.425
1996 Cincinnati NL		47	123	30	6	0	8	60	22	13	22	2	36	0	0	0	1	0	.00	2	.244	.359	.488
Colorado NL		32	62	15	2	0	4	29	10	9	10	0	20	0	0	1	0	0	.00	1	.242	.342	.468
1997 Los Angeles NL		47	74	18	2	2	2	31	8	5	12	1	18	0	0	0	1	0	1.00	0	.243	.349	.419
11 Min. YEARS		546	2001	593	118	16	112	1079	347	397	222	27	500	14	0	16	53	30	.64	41	.296	.368	.539
9 Maj. YEARS		682	1999	462	81	8	78	793	249	269	217	22	491	5	3	19	24	14	.63	34	.231	.305	.397

Julio Aquino

Pitches: Right **Bats:** Right **Pos:** P   **Ht:** 6'1" **Wt:** 173 **Born:** 12/12/72 **Age:** 27

Year Team	Lg Org	G	GS	CG	GF	IP	BFP	H	R	ER	HR	SH	SF	HB	TBB	IBB	SO	WP	Bk	W	L	Pct.	ShO	Sv	ERA
1994 Great Falls R+ LA		16	12	0	2	81.1	346	105	46	41	3	0	1	2	9	0	55	6	1	3	4	.429	0	1	4.54
1995 San Berndno A+ LA		25	3	0	6	59.2	293	96	59	52	5	2	2	1	23	0	42	5	1	2	2	.500	0	0	7.84
Vero Beach A+ LA		3	0	0	2	3	14	1	0	0	0	0	0	0	3	0	0	0	0	0	0	.000	0	1	0.00
1996 Hudson Val A- TB		22	0	0	10	45	183	36	16	13	2	2	1	2	7	0	46	5	0	3	1	.750	0	3	2.60
1997 St. Pete A+ TB		50	0	0	8	60	240	53	21	19	3	2	2	3	8	0	39	3	1	3	5	.375	0	1	2.85

10

Year Team	Lg Org	HOW MUCH HE PITCHED						WHAT HE GAVE UP								THE RESULTS					
		G	GS	CG	GF	IP	BFP	H	R	ER	HR	SH	SF	HB	TBB	IBB	SO	WP	Bk	W	L	Pct.	ShO	Sv	ERA
1998 St. Pete	A+ TB	34	0	0	23	41	177	45	18	16	1	1	3	3	8	0	38	3	1	1	3	.250	0	9	3.51
1999 Orlando	AA TB	5	0	0	2	6.1	38	18	15	13	3	0	1	2	0	0	4	3	0	0	0	.000	0	0	18.47
6 Min. YEARS		155	15	0	53	296.1	1291	354	175	154	17	7	10	13	58	0	224	25	4	12	15	.444	0	15	4.68

Danny Ardoin

Bats: Right Throws: Right Pos: C   Ht: 6'0" Wt: 205 Born: 7/8/74 Age: 25

Year Team	Lg Org	BATTING															BASERUNNING				PERCENTAGES		
		G	AB	H	2B	3B	HR	TB	R	RBI	TBB	IBB	SO	HBP	SH	SF	SB	CS	SB%	GDP	Avg	OBP	SLG
1995 Sou Oregon	A- Oak	58	175	41	9	1	2	58	28	23	31	0	50	9	5	4	2	1	.67	2	.234	.370	.331
1996 Modesto	A+ Oak	91	317	83	13	3	6	120	55	34	47	0	81	9	3	2	5	7	.42	9	.262	.371	.379
1997 Huntsville	AA Oak	57	208	48	10	1	4	72	26	23	17	0	38	3	0	2	2	3	.40	7	.231	.296	.346
Visalia	A+ Oak	43	145	34	7	1	3	52	16	19	21	0	39	4	1	0	0	1	.00	3	.234	.347	.359
1998 Huntsville	AA Oak	109	363	90	21	0	16	159	67	62	62	0	87	7	6	1	8	4	.67	10	.248	.367	.438
1999 Vancouver	AAA Oak	109	336	85	13	2	8	126	53	46	50	0	78	9	9	1	3	3	.50	12	.253	.364	.375
5 Min. YEARS		467	1544	381	73	8	39	587	245	207	228	0	373	41	24	10	20	19	.51	43	.247	.357	.380

Bronson Arroyo

Pitches: Right Bats: Right Pos: P   Ht: 6'5" Wt: 180 Born: 2/24/77 Age: 23

Year Team	Lg Org	HOW MUCH HE PITCHED						WHAT HE GAVE UP								THE RESULTS					
		G	GS	CG	GF	IP	BFP	H	R	ER	HR	SH	SF	HB	TBB	IBB	SO	WP	Bk	W	L	Pct.	ShO	Sv	ERA
1995 Pirates	R Pit	13	9	0	3	61.1	275	72	39	29	4	2	0	4	9	0	48	5	0	5	4	.556	0	1	4.26
1996 Augusta	A Pit	26	26	0	0	135.2	562	123	64	53	11	9	1	7	36	0	107	10	0	8	6	.571	0	0	3.52
1997 Lynchburg	A+ Pit	24	24	3	0	160.1	658	154	69	59	17	7	0	3	33	0	121	0	0	12	4	.750	1	0	3.31
1998 Carolina	AA Pit	23	22	1	0	127	573	158	91	77	18	4	6	3	51	0	90	7	0	9	8	.529	0	0	5.46
1999 Altoona	AA Pit	25	25	2	0	153	668	167	73	62	15	5	2	7	58	1	100	6	0	15	4	.789	1	0	3.65
Nashville	AAA Pit	3	3	0	0	13	71	22	15	15	1	0	0	1	10	0	11	0	0	0	2	.000	0	0	10.38
5 Min. YEARS		114	109	6	3	650.1	2807	696	351	295	66	27	9	25	197	1	477	37	0	49	28	.636	2	1	4.08

Luis Arroyo

Pitches: Left Bats: Left Pos: P   Ht: 6'0" Wt: 174 Born: 9/29/73 Age: 26

Year Team	Lg Org	HOW MUCH HE PITCHED						WHAT HE GAVE UP								THE RESULTS					
		G	GS	CG	GF	IP	BFP	H	R	ER	HR	SH	SF	HB	TBB	IBB	SO	WP	Bk	W	L	Pct.	ShO	Sv	ERA
1992 Padres	R SD	17	9	0	3	57.2	259	65	45	27	0	1	6	2	21	0	55	4	12	4	4	.500	0	0	4.21
1993 Waterloo	A SD	17	16	1	1	95.2	424	99	59	48	11	7	6	6	46	1	59	5	3	5	7	.417	0	0	4.52
1994 Springfield	A SD	16	16	1	0	99.2	434	86	50	38	8	5	2	1	47	4	76	4	4	8	2	.800	0	0	3.43
Rancho Cuca	A+ SD	10	10	0	0	54.1	243	62	33	29	6	1	1	3	30	0	34	2	0	3	4	.429	0	0	4.80
1995 Rancho Cuca	A+ SD	26	24	0	0	128.2	599	158	97	75	9	8	6	12	62	6	102	7	3	7	10	.412	0	0	5.25
1996 St. Lucie	A+ NYM	22	0	0	4	42	170	36	17	14	1	0	3	1	15	1	28	3	0	1	0	1.000	0	2	3.00
1997 Binghamton	AA NYM	7	0	0	1	14.2	60	14	6	5	2	2	1	0	6	0	9	0	1	0	0	.000	0	0	3.07
St. Lucie	A+ NYM	36	2	0	11	56	231	37	21	13	2	3	1	3	23	2	57	1	3	3	3	.500	0	0	2.09
1998 Norfolk	AAA NYM	8	0	0	5	8	41	11	7	6	1	0	1	1	7	0	7	0	0	0	1	.000	0	0	6.75
Binghamton	AA NYM	57	0	0	16	66.1	280	59	30	19	1	5	2	1	26	3	78	4	1	1	5	.167	0	3	2.58
1999 Knoxville	AA Tor	5	0	0	2	6.2	22	2	1	1	0	0	0	1	0	0	7	0	0	0	0	.000	0	0	1.35
Syracuse	AAA Tor	9	0	0	3	12.2	65	18	13	12	1	1	1	0	9	1	10	1	1	0	1	.000	0	0	8.53
Portland	AA Fla	9	0	0	1	13.2	61	14	11	5	2	2	0	0	8	4	10	0	0	0	1	.000	0	0	3.29
Calgary	AAA Fla	22	0	0	8	33.1	157	42	33	24	6	2	2	3	17	0	26	0	1	2	1	.667	0	0	6.48
8 Min. YEARS		261	77	2	55	689.1	3046	703	423	316	50	37	32	34	317	22	558	31	29	34	39	.466	0	7	4.13

J.D. Arteaga

Pitches: Left Bats: Left Pos: P   Ht: 6'3" Wt: 220 Born: 8/2/74 Age: 25

Year Team	Lg Org	HOW MUCH HE PITCHED						WHAT HE GAVE UP								THE RESULTS					
		G	GS	CG	GF	IP	BFP	H	R	ER	HR	SH	SF	HB	TBB	IBB	SO	WP	Bk	W	L	Pct.	ShO	Sv	ERA
1997 Pittsfield	A- NYM	12	3	0	2	30.1	129	32	15	9	0	1	0	1	4	0	29	1	0	4	2	.667	0	0	2.67
Capital Cty	A NYM	1	1	0	0	6	20	3	0	0	0	0	0	0	0	0	4	0	0	1	0	1.000	0	0	0.00
1998 St. Lucie	A+ NYM	15	2	0	1	37.1	154	37	15	12	1	4	0	0	7	0	28	1	1	2	0	1.000	0	0	2.89
Binghamton	AA NYM	21	18	0	0	119	495	122	48	37	8	6	5	5	25	1	97	2	0	8	7	.533	0	0	2.80
1999 St. Lucie	A+ NYM	1	1	0	0	5	19	3	2	2	1	0	1	0	2	0	0	0	0	0	1	.000	0	0	3.60
Mets	R NYM	2	1	0	0	4	15	4	3	3	1	0	0	0	0	0	3	0	0	0	0	.000	0	0	6.75
Binghamton	AA NYM	11	3	0	1	28.1	133	32	21	18	3	0	2	2	14	0	24	0	0	3	1	.750	0	0	5.72
3 Min. YEARS		63	29	0	4	230	965	233	104	81	14	11	8	8	52	1	185	4	1	18	11	.621	0	0	3.17

Mike Asche

Bats: Right Throws: Right Pos: OF   Ht: 6'2" Wt: 189 Born: 2/13/72 Age: 28

Year Team	Lg Org	BATTING															BASERUNNING				PERCENTAGES		
		G	AB	H	2B	3B	HR	TB	R	RBI	TBB	IBB	SO	HBP	SH	SF	SB	CS	SB%	GDP	Avg	OBP	SLG
1994 Welland	A- Pit	55	204	49	5	1	4	68	22	25	13	0	30	1	3	0	6	3	.67	2	.240	.289	.333
1995 Augusta	A Pit	106	376	100	17	6	6	147	62	59	35	1	60	5	3	3	21	5	.81	6	.266	.334	.391
1996 Lynchburg	A+ Pit	129	498	147	25	6	7	205	79	54	38	1	92	2	8	7	26	5	.84	11	.295	.343	.412
1997 Carolina	AA Pit	15	42	9	1	1	0	12	2	2	4	0	6	0	1	0	0	0	.00	0	.214	.283	.286
Lynchburg	A+ Pit	107	409	125	34	4	11	200	70	70	41	0	77	4	1	8	33	3	.92	5	.306	.368	.489
1998 Lynchburg	A+ Pit	29	103	33	8	0	5	56	24	13	10	0	17	0	0	1	9	0	1.00	1	.320	.377	.544
Carolina	AA Pit	65	212	55	14	4	3	86	44	26	37	0	45	3	1	1	15	6	.71	2	.259	.375	.406
1999 Altoona	AA Pit	7	17	7	2	0	0	9	3	3	1	0	3	0	0	0	1	1	.50	0	.412	.444	.529
6 Min. YEARS		513	1861	525	106	22	36	783	306	252	179	2	330	15	17	20	111	23	.83	27	.282	.347	.421

Chris Ashby

Bats: Right Throws: Right Pos: OF Ht: 6'3" Wt: 196 Born: 12/15/74 Age: 25

					BATTING											BASERUNNING				PERCENTAGES		
Year Team	Lg Org	G	AB	H	2B	3B	HR	TB	R	RBI	TBB	IBB	SO	HBP	SH	SF	SB	CS	SB%	GDP	Avg	OBP	SLG
1993 Yankees	R NYY	49	175	37	12	0	0	49	24	23	32	0	45	6	0	2	5	3	.63	6	.211	.349	.280
Greensboro	A NYY	1	4	3	0	0	0	3	2	0	0	0	0	0	0	0	0	0	.00	0	.750	.800	.750
1994 Yankees	R NYY	45	163	55	8	1	5	80	28	38	21	0	20	1	1	3	2	0	1.00	4	.337	.410	.491
Greensboro	A NYY	6	16	2	1	0	0	3	0	2	2	0	6	0	0	0	0	0	.00	1	.125	.222	.188
1995 Greensboro	A NYY	88	288	79	23	1	9	131	45	45	61	2	68	6	2	2	3	3	.50	9	.274	.409	.455
1996 Tampa	A+ NYY	100	325	80	28	0	6	126	55	46	71	1	78	5	1	1	16	4	.80	5	.246	.388	.388
1997 Norwich	AA NYY	136	457	114	20	1	24	208	92	82	80	2	95	6	0	3	10	7	.59	14	.249	.366	.455
1998 Columbus	AAA NYY	5	11	1	0	0	0	1	0	1	3	0	6	0	0	0	0	0	.00	0	.091	.286	.091
Norwich	AA NYY	126	438	125	24	0	11	182	65	53	65	3	99	7	0	4	17	3	.85	12	.285	.383	.416
1999 Norwich	AA NYY	29	108	27	5	1	3	43	11	16	11	0	20	3	0	2	3	4	.43	3	.250	.331	.398
Columbus	AAA NYY	70	206	55	13	1	9	97	46	32	21	0	39	2	1	0	6	3	.67	5	.267	.341	.471
7 Min. YEARS		655	2191	578	134	5	67	923	368	338	367	8	476	37	5	17	62	27	.70	59	.264	.376	.421

Billy Ashley

Bats: Right Throws: Right Pos: DH-OF Ht: 6' 6" Wt: 245 Born: 7/11/70 Age: 29

					BATTING											BASERUNNING				PERCENTAGES		
Year Team	Lg Org	G	AB	H	2B	3B	HR	TB	R	RBI	TBB	IBB	SO	HBP	SH	SF	SB	CS	SB%	GDP	Avg	OBP	SLG
1988 Dodgers	R LA	9	26	4	0	0	0	4	3	0	1	0	9	0	0	0	1	0	1.00	0	.154	.185	.154
1989 Dodgers	R LA	48	160	38	6	2	1	51	23	19	19	1	42	2	0	3	9	1	.90	4	.238	.321	.319
1990 Bakersfield	A+ LA	99	331	72	13	1	9	114	48	40	25	1	135	3	3	1	17	3	.85	4	.218	.278	.344
1991 Vero Beach	A+ LA	60	206	52	11	2	7	88	18	42	7	0	69	0	0	1	9	2	.82	4	.252	.276	.427
1992 Albuquerque	AAA LA	25	95	20	7	0	2	33	11	10	6	0	42	0	0	0	1	0	1.00	2	.211	.257	.347
San Antonio	AA LA	101	380	106	23	1	24	203	60	66	16	3	111	6	0	2	13	7	.65	9	.279	.317	.534
1993 Albuquerque	AAA LA	125	482	143	31	4	26	260	88	100	35	1	143	2	0	5	6	4	.60	16	.297	.344	.539
1994 Albuquerque	AAA LA	107	388	134	19	4	37	272	93	105	53	7	116	7	0	5	6	4	.60	13	.345	.428	.701
1996 Albuquerque	AAA LA	7	23	8	1	0	1	12	6	9	7	0	9	0	0	0	2	0	1.00	0	.348	.500	.522
1998 Pawtucket	AAA Bos	63	218	59	12	0	14	113	40	51	35	0	72	1	0	2	1	0	1.00	5	.271	.371	.518
1999 St. Paul	IND —	48	194	66	14	0	14	122	40	41	24	0	56	1	0	1	1	0	1.00	5	.340	.414	.629
Toledo	AAA Det	29	112	32	9	0	9	68	19	25	9	0	32	0	0	0	0	0	.00	5	.286	.339	.607
1992 Los Angeles	NL	29	95	21	5	0	2	32	6	6	5	0	34	0	0	0	0	0	.00	2	.221	.260	.337
1993 Los Angeles	NL	14	37	9	0	0	0	9	0	0	2	0	11	0	0	0	0	0	.00	0	.243	.282	.243
1994 Los Angeles	NL	2	6	2	1	0	0	3	0	0	0	0	2	0	0	0	0	0	.00	0	.333	.333	.500
1995 Los Angeles	NL	81	215	51	5	0	8	80	17	27	26	4	88	2	0	2	0	0	.00	8	.237	.320	.372
1996 Los Angeles	NL	71	110	22	2	1	9	53	18	25	21	1	44	1	0	1	0	0	.00	3	.200	.331	.482
1997 Los Angeles	NL	71	131	32	7	0	6	57	12	19	8	0	46	1	0	0	0	0	.00	2	.244	.293	.435
1998 Boston	AL	13	24	7	3	0	3	19	3	7	2	0	11	0	0	0	0	0	.00	0	.292	.346	.792
10 Min. YEARS		721	2615	734	146	14	144	1340	449	508	237	13	836	22	3	20	66	21	.76	67	.281	.343	.512
7 Maj. YEARS		281	618	144	23	1	28	253	56	84	63	5	236	4	0	3	0	0	.00	15	.233	.307	.409

Justin Atchley

Pitches: Left Bats: Left Pos: P Ht: 6'3" Wt: 215 Born: 9/5/73 Age: 26

		HOW MUCH HE PITCHED						WHAT HE GAVE UP										THE RESULTS					
Year Team	Lg Org	G	GS	CG	GF	IP	BFP	H	R	ER	HR	SH	SF	HB	TBB	IBB	SO	WP	Bk	W	L	Pct.	ShO	Sv	ERA
1995 Billings	R+ Cin	13	13	0	0	77	327	91	33	30	4	2	1	2	20	2	65	2	1	10	0	1.000	0	0	3.51
1996 Chstn-WV	A Cin	17	16	0	1	91	392	98	42	35	7	4	2	1	23	0	78	0	1	3	3	.500	0	1	3.46
Winston-Sal	A+ Cin	12	12	0	0	69	290	74	48	39	13	3	3	2	16	0	50	2	0	3	3	.500	0	0	5.09
1997 Chattanooga	AA Cin	13	13	1	0	67	289	75	45	35	8	2	5	1	14	0	48	5	0	4	2	.667	0	0	4.70
1999 Chattanooga	AA Cin	17	17	0	0	97.1	416	114	48	37	9	1	6	1	22	1	70	1	1	4	9	.308	0	0	3.42
Indianapols	AAA Cin	5	4	0	1	23.1	106	39	14	14	5	0	0	0	2	0	6	0	0	2	1	.667	0	1	5.40
4 Min. YEARS		77	75	1	2	424.2	1820	491	230	190	46	12	17	7	97	3	317	10	3	26	18	.591	0	2	4.03

Ross Atkins

Pitches: Right Bats: Right Pos: P Ht: 6'2" Wt: 195 Born: 8/7/73 Age: 26

		HOW MUCH HE PITCHED						WHAT HE GAVE UP										THE RESULTS					
Year Team	Lg Org	G	GS	CG	GF	IP	BFP	H	R	ER	HR	SH	SF	HB	TBB	IBB	SO	WP	Bk	W	L	Pct.	ShO	Sv	ERA
1995 Watertown	A- Cle	13	10	0	1	77	333	52	28	22	2	1	2	2	26	0	46	5	2	5	2	.714	0	1	3.26
1996 Columbus	A Cle	28	28	2	0	169.2	712	156	85	74	19	5	3	6	64	0	129	10	1	11	10	.524	2	0	3.93
1997 Kinston	A+ Cle	27	16	0	3	117	501	98	53	47	10	2	3	2	62	2	84	11	2	8	4	.667	0	0	3.62
1998 Akron	AA Cle	40	5	0	23	77.1	332	73	39	36	9	2	3	5	31	1	38	4	2	7	8	.467	0	10	4.19
1999 Akron	AA Cle	33	7	0	5	87.1	398	90	60	56	10	0	5	6	47	0	43	5	1	6	8	.429	0	3	5.77
5 Min. YEARS		141	66	2	32	512	2198	469	265	235	50	10	16	21	230	3	340	35	8	37	32	.536	2	14	4.13

Rich Aude

Bats: Right Throws: Right Pos: 1B Ht: 6' 5" Wt: 215 Born: 7/13/71 Age: 28

					BATTING											BASERUNNING				PERCENTAGES		
Year Team	Lg Org	G	AB	H	2B	3B	HR	TB	R	RBI	TBB	IBB	SO	HBP	SH	SF	SB	CS	SB%	GDP	Avg	OBP	SLG
1989 Pirates	R Pit	24	88	19	3	0	0	22	13	7	5	0	17	3	0	1	2	0	1.00	1	.216	.278	.250
1990 Augusta	A Pit	128	475	111	23	1	6	154	48	61	41	1	133	7	0	4	3	1	.75	11	.234	.302	.324
1991 Salem	A+ Pit	103	366	97	12	2	3	122	45	43	27	5	72	9	0	4	3	0	1.00	7	.265	.331	.333
1992 Salem	A+ Pit	122	447	128	26	4	9	189	63	60	50	2	79	8	0	1	11	2	.85	10	.286	.368	.423
Carolina	AA Pit	6	20	4	1	0	2	11	4	3	1	0	3	0	0	0	0	0	.00	0	.200	.238	.550
1993 Buffalo	AAA Pit	21	64	24	9	0	4	45	17	16	10	0	15	1	0	1	0	0	.00	1	.375	.461	.703
Carolina	AA Pit	120	422	122	25	3	18	207	66	73	50	7	79	12	1	6	8	4	.67	6	.289	.376	.491
1994 Buffalo	AAA Pit	138	520	146	38	4	15	237	66	79	41	3	83	11	0	2	9	5	.64	14	.281	.345	.456
1995 Calgary	AAA Pit	50	195	65	14	2	9	110	34	42	12	1	30	4	0	5	3	2	.60	11	.333	.375	.564

Year Team	Lg Org	BATTING															BASERUNNING				PERCENTAGES		
		G	AB	H	2B	3B	HR	TB	R	RBI	TBB	IBB	SO	HBP	SH	SF	SB	CS	SB%	GDP	Avg	OBP	SLG
1996 Calgary	AAA Pit	103	394	115	29	0	17	195	69	81	26	2	69	4	0	5	4	4	.50	10	.292	.338	.495
1997 Syracuse	AAA Tor	100	350	99	23	2	15	171	48	59	26	2	88	11	0	3	0	0	1.00	9	.283	.349	.489
1998 Expos	R Mon	2	6	2	1	0	0	3	1	0	1	0	3	1	0	0	0	0	.00	0	.333	.500	.500
Atlantic Ct	IND —	44	163	52	15	1	12	105	35	37	17	0	24	5	0	0	0	1	.00	1	.319	.400	.644
1999 Birmingham	AA CWS	129	486	141	33	2	12	214	63	85	34	5	90	9	0	4	15	3	.83	15	.290	.345	.440
1993 Pittsburgh	NL	13	26	3	1	0	0	4	1	4	1	0	7	0	0	0	0	0	.00	0	.115	.148	.154
1995 Pittsburgh	NL	42	109	27	8	0	2	41	10	19	6	0	20	0	0	0	1	2	.33	4	.248	.287	.376
1996 Pittsburgh	NL	7	16	4	0	0	0	4	0	1	0	0	8	0	0	0	0	0	.00	0	.250	.250	.250
11 Min. YEARS		1090	3996	1125	252	21	122	1785	572	646	341	28	785	85	1	32	61	22	.73	96	.282	.348	.447
3 Maj. YEARS		62	151	34	9	0	2	49	11	24	7	0	35	0	0	0	1	2	.33	4	.225	.259	.325

Jeff Austin

Pitches: Right **Bats:** Right **Pos:** P   **Ht:** 6'0" **Wt:** 185 **Born:** 10/19/76 **Age:** 23

Year Team	Lg Org	HOW MUCH HE PITCHED						WHAT HE GAVE UP										THE RESULTS						
		G	GS	CG	GF	IP	BFP	H	R	ER	HR	SH	SF	HB	TBB	IBB	SO	WP	Bk	W	L	Pct.	ShO	Sv	ERA
1999 Wilmington	A+ KC	18	18	0	0	112.1	473	108	52	47	10	5	3	2	39	0	97	5	0	7	2	.778	0	0	3.77
Wichita	AA KC	6	6	0	0	34.1	155	40	19	17	1	0	1	2	11	1	21	4	0	3	1	.750	0	0	4.46
1 Min. YEARS		24	24	0	0	146.2	628	148	71	64	11	5	4	4	50	1	118	9	0	10	3	.769	0	0	3.93

Robert Averette

Pitches: Right **Bats:** Right **Pos:** P   **Ht:** 6'2" **Wt:** 185 **Born:** 9/30/76 **Age:** 23

Year Team	Lg Org	HOW MUCH HE PITCHED						WHAT HE GAVE UP										THE RESULTS						
		G	GS	CG	GF	IP	BFP	H	R	ER	HR	SH	SF	HB	TBB	IDD	SO	WP	Dk	W	L	Pct.	ShO	Sv	ERA
1997 Billings	R+ Cin	2	1	0	1	2.2	11	3	0	0	0	0	0	0	1	1	3	0	0	0	0	.000	0	0	0.00
Chstn-WV	A Cin	11	3	0	2	26.1	131	42	28	23	3	3	1	0	12	0	20	2	0	2	2	.500	0	1	7.86
1998 Chstn-WV	A Cin	14	14	3	0	84	355	84	38	26	2	6	3	2	26	0	68	4	1	5	4	.556	0	0	2.79
Chattanooga	AA Cin	14	14	0	0	81	355	97	51	46	6	2	3	3	36	2	32	2	0	5	8	.385	0	0	5.11
1999 Rockford	A Cin	19	19	2	0	125.2	521	117	54	36	2	4	3	4	40	3	98	9	0	9	5	.643	2	0	2.58
Chattanooga	AA Cin	6	6	1	0	36.1	164	42	22	21	1	0	1	0	19	0	15	0	0	2	1	.667	0	0	5.20
3 Min. YEARS		66	57	6	3	356	1537	385	193	152	14	15	11	11	134	6	236	17	1	23	20	.535	2	1	3.84

Corey Avrard

Pitches: Right **Bats:** Right **Pos:** P   **Ht:** 6'4" **Wt:** 190 **Born:** 12/6/76 **Age:** 23

Year Team	Lg Org	HOW MUCH HE PITCHED						WHAT HE GAVE UP										THE RESULTS						
		G	GS	CG	GF	IP	BFP	H	R	ER	HR	SH	SF	HB	TBB	IBB	SO	WP	Bk	W	L	Pct.	ShO	Sv	ERA
1995 Savannah	A StL	13	13	0	0	54.1	228	38	25	24	4	1	4	0	33	2	51	6	0	1	6	.143	0	0	3.98
1996 Peoria	A StL	21	21	2	0	110.1	489	105	73	52	6	6	2	8	58	0	103	5	0	5	9	.357	0	0	4.24
1997 Peoria	A StL	20	20	0	0	93.1	437	97	76	66	5	4	4	4	69	1	94	9	0	4	5	.444	0	0	6.36
Pr William	A+ StL	8	8	0	0	40.1	190	30	28	24	1	0	0	2	44	0	50	4	1	0	3	.000	0	0	5.36
1998 Pr William	A+ StL	31	11	0	6	80	345	67	57	45	9	2	6	3	50	0	52	5	0	4	5	.444	0	0	5.06
1999 Potomac	A+ StL	28	0	0	11	32.2	157	32	19	16	2	1	1	4	26	1	40	7	0	2	2	.500	0	0	4.41
Arkansas	AA StL	25	0	0	13	26	109	15	12	9	2	1	2	0	14	1	31	5	0	1	1	.500	0	6	3.12
5 Min. YEARS		146	73	2	30	437	1955	384	290	236	29	15	19	21	294	5	421	41	1	17	31	.354	0	6	4.86

Mike Ayers

Pitches: Left **Bats:** Left **Pos:** P   **Ht:** 5'10" **Wt:** 188 **Born:** 12/23/73 **Age:** 26

Year Team	Lg Org	HOW MUCH HE PITCHED						WHAT HE GAVE UP										THE RESULTS						
		G	GS	CG	GF	IP	BFP	H	R	ER	HR	SH	SF	HB	TBB	IBB	SO	WP	Bk	W	L	Pct.	ShO	Sv	ERA
1996 Augusta	A Pit	27	0	0	7	30.1	134	33	21	14	1	2	2	0	8	0	31	4	0	3	0	1.000	0	0	4.15
1997 Lynchburg	A+ Pit	39	0	0	13	63	288	54	38	35	8	4	2	6	44	6	62	4	0	5	4	.556	0	0	5.00
1998 Augusta	A Pit	4	0	0	1	5.2	37	11	13	11	0	0	1	0	6	1	6	3	0	0	1	.000	0	0	17.47
Lynchburg	A+ Pit	34	0	0	15	40.1	188	53	36	34	5	1	2	5	17	0	31	2	1	3	3	.500	0	0	7.59
1999 Lynchburg	A+ Pit	27	0	0	14	36.2	153	34	13	11	1	2	2	1	16	0	28	4	0	1	2	.333	0	2	2.70
Altoona	AA Pit	11	0	0	3	17	70	10	4	3	1	1	1	0	11	0	16	5	0	0	0	.000	0	0	1.59
4 Min. YEARS		142	0	0	53	193	870	195	125	108	16	10	10	12	102	7	174	22	1	12	10	.545	0	6	5.04

Jesus Azuaje

Bats: Right **Throws:** Right **Pos:** SS   **Ht:** 5'10" **Wt:** 170 **Born:** 1/16/73 **Age:** 27

Year Team	Lg Org	BATTING															BASERUNNING				PERCENTAGES		
		G	AB	H	2B	3B	HR	TB	R	RBI	TBB	IBB	SO	HBP	SH	SF	SB	CS	SB%	GDP	Avg	OBP	SLG
1993 Burlington	R+ Cle	62	254	71	10	1	7	104	46	41	22	0	53	0	1	3	19	2	.90	4	.280	.333	.409
Kinston	A+ Cle	3	11	5	2	0	0	7	1	0	2	0	1	0	0	0	0	2	.00	0	.455	.538	.636
1994 Columbus	A Cle	118	450	127	20	1	7	170	77	57	69	0	72	5	6	0	21	7	.75	6	.282	.384	.378
1995 Norfolk	AAA NYM	5	14	6	1	0	0	7	1	0	2	0	2	0	0	0	1	1	.50	0	.429	.500	.500
Binghamton	AA NYM	24	86	17	5	0	0	22	10	8	11	0	25	2	3	0	1	1	.50	1	.198	.303	.256
St. Lucie	A+ NYM	91	306	73	5	1	2	86	35	20	36	1	55	7	11	0	14	9	.61	5	.239	.332	.281
1996 Capital Cty	A NYM	1	3	2	1	0	0	3	1	1	0	0	0	0	1	1	0	0	.00	0	.667	.500	1.000
Binghamton	AA NYM	86	249	59	16	0	2	81	36	26	45	1	33	1	3	1	5	6	.45	5	.237	.355	.325
1997 Binghamton	AA NYM	100	331	92	15	1	6	127	50	37	45	1	42	8	8	4	11	9	.55	13	.278	.374	.384
Norfolk	AAA NYM	22	49	15	3	0	1	21	11	6	7	1	8	2	0	0	1	0	1.00	3	.306	.414	.429
1998 Norfolk	AAA NYM	10	33	7	3	0	0	10	1	1	2	0	6	0	1	0	0	0	.00	3	.212	.257	.303
Binghamton	AA NYM	110	384	106	22	1	9	151	66	52	52	0	48	4	7	5	15	1	.94	5	.276	.364	.393
1999 Huntsville	AA Mil	119	391	110	21	0	10	161	63	60	70	4	26	11	0	7	34	8	.81	12	.281	.390	.412
7 Min. YEARS		751	2561	690	124	5	42	950	398	309	363	8	371	40	41	21	122	46	.73	60	.269	.366	.371

Darrin Babineaux

Pitches: Right **Bats:** Right **Pos:** P **Ht:** 6'4" **Wt:** 210 **Born:** 7/10/74 **Age:** 25

			HOW MUCH HE PITCHED						WHAT HE GAVE UP										THE RESULTS				
Year Team	Lg Org	G	GS	CG	GF	IP	BFP	H	R	ER	HR	SH	SF	HB	TBB	IBB	SO	WP	Bk	W	L	Pct.	ShO	Sv	ERA
1995 Yakima	A- LA	12	10	0	2	59.1	251	53	33	24	3	1	3	4	18	1	36	0	1	1	6	.143	0	0	3.64
1996 San Berndno	A+ LA	5	5	0	0	17	97	34	27	27	3	0	0	0	14	0	16	3	0	1	3	.250	0	0	14.29
Savannah	A LA	13	12	1	0	71	307	70	45	38	6	1	3	1	30	1	48	6	2	5	5	.500	0	0	4.82
Vero Beach	A+ LA	10	10	1	0	63	267	56	30	23	6	2	0	2	23	0	41	8	2	1	7	.125	0	0	3.29
1997 Vero Beach	A+ LA	18	12	0	0	81.2	350	82	46	40	7	1	3	3	32	0	63	6	1	7	3	.700	0	0	4.41
1998 San Antonio	AA LA	39	4	0	13	77.1	329	66	34	29	8	0	5	1	33	0	56	6	0	5	4	.556	0	3	3.38
Albuquerque	AAA LA	3	0	0	1	4	16	4	2	2	2	0	0	0	0	0	4	0	0	0	0	.000	0	0	4.50
1999 New Britain	AA Min	5	0	0	1	9.2	52	14	10	7	1	0	1	1	4	0	7	2	0	0	0	.000	0	0	6.52
Newark	IND —	35	15	3	6	125.1	529	118	68	50	15	1	3	3	48	1	104	7	0	10	5	.667	2	1	3.59
5 Min. YEARS		140	68	5	23	508.1	2198	497	295	240	51	6	18	15	202	3	375	38	6	30	33	.476	2	4	4.25

Mike Bacsik

Pitches: Left **Bats:** Left **Pos:** P **Ht:** 6'3" **Wt:** 190 **Born:** 11/11/77 **Age:** 22

			HOW MUCH HE PITCHED						WHAT HE GAVE UP										THE RESULTS				
Year Team	Lg Org	G	GS	CG	GF	IP	BFP	H	R	ER	HR	SH	SF	HB	TBB	IBB	SO	WP	Bk	W	L	Pct.	ShO	Sv	ERA
1996 Burlington	R+ Cle	13	13	1	0	69.2	276	49	23	17	3	0	2	1	14	0	61	3	1	4	2	.667	0	0	2.20
1997 Columbus	A Cle	28	28	0	0	139	622	163	94	84	16	7	3	9	47	1	100	12	2	4	14	.222	0	0	5.44
1998 Kinston	A+ Cle	27	27	1	0	165.2	667	147	64	53	17	5	4	4	37	3	128	4	0	10	9	.526	0	0	2.88
1999 Akron	AA Cle	26	26	1	0	149.1	647	164	84	77	24	5	5	7	47	0	84	4	0	11	11	.500	0	0	4.64
4 Min. YEARS		94	94	3	0	523.2	2212	523	265	231	60	17	14	21	145	4	373	23	3	29	36	.446	0	0	3.97

Brooks Badeaux

Bats: Both **Throws:** Right **Pos:** 2B **Ht:** 5'10" **Wt:** 175 **Born:** 10/20/76 **Age:** 23

			BATTING													BASERUNNING				PERCENTAGES		
Year Team	Lg Org	G	AB	H	2B	3B	HR	TB	R	RBI	TBB	IBB	SO	HBP	SH	SF	SB	CS	SB%	GDP	Avg	OBP	SLG
1998 Hudson Val	A- TB	68	267	80	9	4	1	100	48	36	29	0	47	3	7	2	11	4	.73	4	.300	.372	.375
1999 St. Pete	A+ TB	96	342	97	6	1	0	105	68	19	57	1	44	2	5	0	2	7	.22	4	.284	.389	.307
Orlando	AA TB	3	2	1	0	0	1	4	1	1	0	0	0	0	0	0	0	0	.00	0	.500	.500	2.000
2 Min. YEARS		167	611	178	15	5	2	209	117	56	86	1	91	5	12	2	13	11	.54	8	.291	.382	.342

Ed Bady

Bats: Both **Throws:** Right **Pos:** OF **Ht:** 5'11" **Wt:** 170 **Born:** 2/5/73 **Age:** 27

			BATTING													BASERUNNING				PERCENTAGES		
Year Team	Lg Org	G	AB	H	2B	3B	HR	TB	R	RBI	TBB	IBB	SO	HBP	SH	SF	SB	CS	SB%	GDP	Avg	OBP	SLG
1994 Vermont	A- Mon	44	141	35	5	5	2	56	19	21	12	0	51	2	5	0	11	6	.65	3	.248	.316	.397
1995 Vermont	A- Mon	72	295	97	15	3	2	124	51	25	24	3	52	5	2	0	34	19	.64	3	.329	.389	.420
1996 Wst Plm Bch	A+ Mon	128	484	136	9	3	1	154	62	34	42	0	93	10	12	3	42	17	.71	2	.281	.349	.318
1997 Harrisburg	AA Mon	97	267	56	8	4	1	75	36	22	21	3	62	1	10	0	15	5	.75	3	.210	.270	.281
1998 Jupiter	A+ Mon	1	4	1	1	0	0	2	1	0	0	0	0	0	0	0	1	1	.50	0	.250	.250	.500
Harrisburg	AA Mon	58	123	31	4	1	0	37	19	2	15	0	30	0	3	0	10	2	.83	1	.252	.333	.301
Ottawa	AAA Mon	5	13	2	0	0	0	2	0	0	3	0	5	0	0	0	0	0	.00	0	.154	.313	.154
1999 Akron	AA Cle	69	230	56	13	3	2	81	42	33	32	0	68	1	4	2	19	5	.79	3	.243	.336	.352
6 Min. YEARS		474	1557	414	55	19	8	531	230	137	149	6	361	19	36	5	132	55	.71	15	.266	.336	.341

Benito Baez

Pitches: Left **Bats:** Left **Pos:** P **Ht:** 6'0" **Wt:** 160 **Born:** 5/6/77 **Age:** 23

			HOW MUCH HE PITCHED						WHAT HE GAVE UP										THE RESULTS				
Year Team	Lg Org	G	GS	CG	GF	IP	BFP	H	R	ER	HR	SH	SF	HB	TBB	IBB	SO	WP	Bk	W	L	Pct.	ShO	Sv	ERA
1995 Athletics	R Oak	14	11	1	0	70	303	64	35	26	2	2	2	4	28	0	83	2	0	5	1	.833	0	0	3.34
1996 W Michigan	A Oak	32	20	0	4	129.2	557	123	60	50	6	5	6	2	52	1	92	4	1	8	4	.667	0	4	3.47
1997 Visalia	A+ Oak	16	15	1	0	96.2	393	83	40	38	8	1	2	3	28	0	87	0	1	5	5	.500	0	0	3.54
Huntsville	AA Oak	15	7	0	2	42.1	206	64	47	43	8	2	4	1	22	1	27	3	2	2	4	.333	0	0	9.14
1998 Huntsville	AA Oak	34	17	0	11	122.2	579	161	92	79	12	3	5	1	64	0	83	7	1	3	8	.273	0	0	5.80
1999 Midland	AA Oak	37	0	0	9	54.1	243	68	35	33	5	3	7	0	15	2	51	2	2	5	1	.833	0	3	5.47
Vancouver	AAA Oak	11	0	0	4	18	76	18	7	7	2	0	0	0	7	0	19	1	1	0	2	.000	0	1	3.50
5 Min. YEARS		159	70	2	30	533.2	2357	581	316	276	43	16	26	14	216	4	442	19	8	28	25	.528	0	8	4.65

Kevin Baez

Bats: Right **Throws:** Right **Pos:** 2B-SS **Ht:** 5'11" **Wt:** 175 **Born:** 1/10/67 **Age:** 33

			BATTING													BASERUNNING				PERCENTAGES		
Year Team	Lg Org	G	AB	H	2B	3B	HR	TB	R	RBI	TBB	IBB	SO	HBP	SH	SF	SB	CS	SB%	GDP	Avg	OBP	SLG
1988 Little Fall	A- NYM	70	218	58	7	1	1	70	23	19	32	1	30	2	2	3	7	3	.70	3	.266	.361	.321
1989 Columbia	A NYM	123	426	108	25	1	5	150	59	44	58	3	53	6	9	3	11	9	.55	5	.254	.349	.352
1990 Jackson	AA NYM	100	327	70	11	0	2	55	26	28	67	1	11	0	11	0	0	1	.10	7	.020	.012	.024
1991 Tidewater	AAA NYM	65	210	36	8	0	0	44	18	13	12	1	32	4	5	4	0	1	.00	5	.171	.226	.210
1992 Tidewater	AAA NYM	109	352	83	16	1	2	107	30	33	13	1	57	4	5	5	1	1	.50	9	.236	.267	.304
1993 Norfolk	AAA NYM	63	209	54	11	1	2	73	23	21	20	1	29	1	2	1	0	2	.00	3	.258	.325	.349
1994 Rochester	AAA Bal	110	359	85	17	1	2	110	50	42	40	0	52	2	5	5	2	7	.22	13	.237	.313	.306
1995 Toledo	AAA Det	116	376	87	13	2	4	116	30	37	22	1	57	1	10	2	1	6	.14	13	.231	.274	.309
1996 Toledo	AAA Det	98	302	74	12	3	11	125	34	44	24	0	53	2	5	3	0	1	.00	6	.245	.301	.414
1997 Salt Lake	AAA Min	112	383	105	25	3	5	151	38	54	29	0	74	4	3	6	3	4	.43	7	.274	.327	.394
1998 Chattanooga	AA Cin	49	180	46	10	0	0	56	30	22	26	1	27	1	1	2	0	1	.00	6	.256	.349	.311
Indianaplis	AAA Cin	49	137	36	5	0	1	44	21	12	19	0	26	0	2	1	0	1	.00	6	.263	.350	.321
1999 Indianapolis	AAA Cin	20	40	12	3	0	0	15	4	7	11	0	4	0	1	1	0	1	1.00	5	.300	.451	.375

	BATTING																BASERUNNING				PERCENTAGES		
Year Team	Lg Org	G	AB	H	2B	3B	HR	TB	R	RBI	TBB	IBB	SO	HBP	SH	SF	SB	CS	SB%	GDP	Avg	OBP	SLG
Norfolk	AAA NYM	60	175	46	5	0	1	54	15	26	17	1	21	2	0	3	2	0	1.00	2	.263	.330	.309
1990 New York	NL	5	12	2	1	0	0	3	0	0	0	0	0	0	0	2	0	0	.00	2	.167	.167	.250
1992 New York	NL	6	13	2	0	0	0	2	0	0	0	0	0	0	0	0	0	0	.00	1	.154	.154	.154
1993 New York	NL	52	126	23	9	0	0	32	10	7	13	1	17	0	4	0	0	0	.00	1	.183	.259	.254
12 Min. YEARS		1150	3694	906	168	13	36	1208	404	403	360	14	559	31	61	41	34	39	.47	87	.245	.314	.327
3 Maj. YEARS		63	151	27	10	0	0	37	10	7	13	1	17	0	4	0	0	0	.00	4	.179	.244	.245

Cory Bailey

Pitches: Right **Bats:** Right **Pos:** P   **Ht:** 6' 1" **Wt:** 200 **Born:** 1/24/71 **Age:** 29

	HOW MUCH HE PITCHED						WHAT HE GAVE UP										WP	Bk	THE RESULTS					
Year Team	Lg Org	G	GS	CG	GF	IP	BFP	H	R	ER	HR	SH	SF	HB	TBB	IBB	SO	WP	Bk	W	L	Pct.	ShO	Sv	ERA
1991 Red Sox	R Bos	1	0	0	1	2	9	2	1	0	0	0	0	0	1	0	1	0	0	0	0	.000	0	1	0.00
Elmira	A- Bos	28	0	0	25	39	151	19	10	8	2	1	0	3	12	0	54	2	0	2	4	.333	0	15	1.85
1992 Lynchburg	A+ Bos	49	0	0	43	66.1	272	43	20	18	3	6	2	2	30	2	87	5	0	5	7	.417	0	23	2.44
1993 Pawtucket	AAA Bos	52	0	0	40	65.2	264	48	21	21	1	2	2	1	31	3	59	5	1	4	5	.444	0	20	2.88
1994 Pawtucket	AAA Bos	53	0	0	43	61.1	264	44	25	22	4	4	0	1	38	2	52	7	0	4	3	.571	0	19	3.23
1995 Louisville	AAA StL	55	0	0	40	59.1	258	51	30	30	6	6	2	0	30	4	49	7	0	5	3	.625	0	25	4.55
1996 Louisville	AAA StL	22	0	0	8	34	151	29	22	22	1	3	1	0	20	5	27	4	1	2	4	.333	0	1	5.82
1997 Okla City	AAA Tex	42	0	0	33	50.1	219	49	20	19	1	3	1	0	23	7	38	4	0	3	4	.429	0	15	3.40
Phoenix	AAA SF	13	0	0	11	17.1	70	16	4	3	0	1	1	0	6	1	14	1	0	4	0	1.000	0	3	1.56
1998 Fresno	AAA SF	57	0	0	25	94.2	375	79	31	26	4	1	2	3	18	4	76	4	2	7	2	.778	0	10	2.47
1999 Fresno	AAA SF	43	0	0	39	46.1	200	47	24	17	7	2	0	0	17	0	52	3	1	2	1	.667	0	18	3.30
1993 Boston	AL	11	0	0	5	15.2	66	12	7	6	0	1	1	0	12	3	11	2	1	0	1	.000	0	0	3.45
1994 Boston	AL	5	0	0	2	4.1	24	10	6	6	2	0	0	0	3	1	4	0	0	0	1	.000	0	0	12.46
1995 St. Louis	NL	3	0	0	0	3.2	15	2	3	3	0	0	0	0	2	1	5	1	0	0	0	.000	0	0	7.36
1996 St. Louis	NL	51	0	0	12	57	251	57	21	19	1	2	1	1	30	3	38	3	0	5	2	.714	0	0	3.00
1997 San Francisco	NL	7	0	0	4	9.2	45	15	9	9	1	0	1	0	4	0	5	0	0	0	1	.000	0	0	8.38
1998 San Francisco	NL	5	0	0	1	3.1	13	2	1	1	0	0	0	0	1	0	2	0	0	0	0	.000	0	0	2.70
9 Min. YEARS		415	0	0	308	536.1	2233	427	208	186	29	29	11	10	226	28	509	42	5	38	33	.535	0	150	3.12
6 Maj. YEARS		82	0	0	24	93.2	414	98	47	44	5	3	3	1	52	8	65	6	1	5	5	.500	0	0	4.23

Roger Bailey

Pitches: Right **Bats:** Right **Pos:** P   **Ht:** 6' 1" **Wt:** 180 **Born:** 10/3/70 **Age:** 29

	HOW MUCH HE PITCHED						WHAT HE GAVE UP										WP	Bk	THE RESULTS					
Year Team	Lg Org	G	GS	CG	GF	IP	BFP	H	R	ER	HR	SH	SF	HB	TBB	IBB	SO	WP	Bk	W	L	Pct.	ShO	Sv	ERA
1992 Bend	A- Col	11	11	1	0	65.1	271	48	19	16	4	2	1	4	30	0	81	2	1	5	2	.714	0	0	2.20
1993 Central Val	A+ Col	22	22	1	0	111.2	515	139	78	60	9	1	3	6	56	1	84	7	1	4	7	.364	1	0	4.84
1994 New Haven	AA Col	25	24	1	1	159	675	157	70	57	8	5	7	5	56	1	112	6	0	9	9	.500	1	0	3.23
1995 Colo Sprngs	AAA Col	3	3	0	0	16.2	71	15	9	5	0	0	0	0	8	0	7	0	0	0	0	.000	0	0	2.70
1996 Colo Sprngs	AAA Col	9	9	0	0	48.2	214	60	34	34	5	0	3	2	20	0	27	2	0	4	4	.500	0	0	6.29
1998 Asheville	A Col	1	1	0	0	4.2	22	5	2	2	1	0	0	1	5	0	1	1	0	0	0	.000	0	0	3.86
Salem	A+ Col	3	3	0	0	10.1	56	13	11	10	0	1	2	1	11	0	5	2	0	0	2	.000	0	0	8.71
1999 Durham	AAA TB	7	4	0	0	27	123	28	21	17	3	0	1	2	13	0	17	1	0	1	0	1.000	0	0	5.67
Carolina	AA Col	4	4	0	0	18	86	21	16	14	2	2	1	2	10	0	14	2	0	0	3	.000	0	0	7.00
Colo Sprngs	AAA Col	4	4	0	0	21.2	105	31	19	17	1	1	1	0	14	0	15	1	0	0	0	.000	0	0	7.06
1995 Colorado	NL	39	6	0	9	81.1	360	88	49	45	9	7	2	1	39	3	33	7	1	7	6	.538	0	0	4.98
1996 Colorado	NL	24	11	0	4	83.2	385	94	64	58	7	2	4	1	52	0	45	3	0	2	3	.400	0	1	6.24
1997 Colorado	NL	29	29	5	0	191	835	210	103	91	27	7	4	13	70	2	84	4	0	9	10	.474	2	0	4.29
7 Min. YEARS		89	85	3	1	483	2138	517	279	232	33	12	19	23	223	2	363	24	2	23	27	.460	2	0	4.32
3 Maj. YEARS		92	46	5	13	356	1580	392	216	194	43	16	10	15	161	5	162	14	1	18	19	.486	2	1	4.90

Matt Bailie

Pitches: Right **Bats:** Right **Pos:** P   **Ht:** 5'10" **Wt:** 195 **Born:** 10/1/75 **Age:** 24

	HOW MUCH HE PITCHED						WHAT HE GAVE UP										WP	Bk	THE RESULTS					
Year Team	Lg Org	G	GS	CG	GF	IP	BFP	H	R	ER	HR	SH	SF	HB	TBB	IBB	SO	WP	Bk	W	L	Pct.	ShO	Sv	ERA
1998 Martinsvlle	R+ Phi	24	0	0	22	31.2	136	33	13	10	2	2	1	2	6	2	36	1	2	4	2	.667	0	9	2.84
Piedmont	A Phi	2	0	0	0	2.1	13	3	0	0	0	0	0	0	3	0	2	0	0	0	0	.000	0	0	0.00
1999 Clearwater	A+ Phi	2	0	0	2	3	14	2	1	1	0	0	0	0	3	0	5	0	0	0	0	.000	0	0	3.00
Batavia	A- Phi	10	0	0	8	17.1	72	15	8	8	1	1	0	2	4	1	23	4	0	2	2	.500	0	3	4.15
Piedmont	A Phi	6	1	0	4	18	75	13	5	3	0	0	0	0	7	0	24	1	0	0	1	.000	0	1	1.47
Reading	AA Phi	1	1	0	0	6	20	3	0	0	0	0	0	0	1	0	6	0	0	1	0	1.000	0	0	0.00
2 Min. YEARS		45	2	0	36	78.2	330	69	27	22	3	3	1	4	24	3	96	6	2	7	4	.636	0	13	2.52

Rod Bair

Bats: Right **Throws:** Right **Pos:** OF   **Ht:** 5'11" **Wt:** 190 **Born:** 10/29/74 **Age:** 25

	BATTING																BASERUNNING				PERCENTAGES		
Year Team	Lg Org	G	AB	H	2B	3B	HR	TB	R	RBI	TBB	IBB	SO	HBP	SH	SF	SB	CS	SB%	GDP	Avg	OBP	SLG
1996 Portland	A- Col	56	221	48	11	2	4	75	34	33	17	2	29	7	5	4	9	4	.69	2	.217	.289	.339
1997 Salem	A+ Col	16	44	12	3	0	0	15	5	6	0	0	6	2	3	1	2	0	1.00	1	.273	.298	.341
Asheville	A Col	91	356	100	20	1	8	146	50	51	13	1	51	11	3	1	9	6	.60	11	.281	.325	.410
1998 Salem	A+ Col	114	425	127	42	5	8	203	62	60	24	3	64	13	0	5	12	6	.67	11	.299	.351	.478
1999 Carolina	AA Col	125	472	143	34	6	13	228	70	81	28	0	78	16	0	6	14	12	.54	11	.303	.358	.483
4 Min. YEARS		402	1518	430	110	14	33	667	221	231	82	6	228	49	11	17	46	28	.62	36	.283	.337	.439

Jason Baker

Pitches: Right Bats: Right Pos: P   Ht: 6'4" Wt: 195 Born: 11/21/74 Age: 25

		HOW MUCH HE PITCHED						WHAT HE GAVE UP									THE RESULTS					
Year Team	Lg Org	G	GS	CG	GF	IP	BFP	H	R	ER	HR	SH	SF	HB	TBB	IBB	SO	WP	Bk	W	L	Pct.	ShO	Sv	ERA
1993 Expos	R Mon	7	7	0	0	32	132	26	14	8	0	1	3	1	11	0	24	6	0	1	1	.500	0	0	2.25
1994 Vermont	A- Mon	13	13	0	0	61.2	279	55	44	33	4	0	2	5	40	0	21	20	1	6	5	.545	0	0	4.82
1995 Vermont	A- Mon	14	14	0	0	72	317	59	40	33	2	1	0	5	47	1	57	11	0	6	5	.545	0	0	4.13
1996 Delmarva	A Mon	27	27	2	0	160.1	688	127	70	50	6	3	3	16	77	0	147	22	0	9	7	.563	0	0	2.81
1997 Expos	R Mon	2	2	0	0	7	28	4	0	0	0	0	0	1	3	0	8	0	0	0	0	.000	0	0	0.00
Wst Plm Bch	A+ Mon	15	14	1	0	72	326	90	55	48	10	4	3	2	31	0	47	11	2	3	4	.429	1	0	6.00
1998 Harrisburg	AA Mon	25	20	0	2	103.2	476	95	69	65	18	1	3	8	71	1	88	11	1	4	10	.286	0	0	5.64
1999 Ottawa	AAA Mon	11	0	0	7	12.2	69	18	12	12	1	1	0	0	14	0	9	4	0	1	0	1.000	0	0	8.53
Harrisburg	AA Mon	23	1	0	7	31.1	150	29	22	21	4	2	2	1	28	0	24	1	0	1	3	.250	0	2	6.03
7 Min. YEARS		137	98	3	16	552.2	2465	503	326	270	45	13	16	39	322	2	425	86	4	31	35	.470	1	2	4.40

Ryan Balfe

Bats: Both Throws: Right Pos: 3B   Ht: 6'1" Wt: 180 Born: 11/11/75 Age: 24

		BATTING															BASERUNNING				PERCENTAGES		
Year Team	Lg Org	G	AB	H	2B	3B	HR	TB	R	RBI	TBB	IBB	SO	HBP	SH	SF	SB	CS	SB%	GDP	Avg	OBP	SLG
1994 Bristol	R+ Det	43	121	26	3	0	1	32	12	11	23	0	38	1	1	1	2	4	.33	1	.215	.342	.264
1995 Fayetteville	A Det	113	398	104	20	2	10	150	53	40	48	0	85	9	0	1	1	1	.50	11	.261	.353	.397
1996 Lakeland	A+ Det	92	347	97	21	1	11	153	48	66	24	2	66	5	0	3	3	0	1.00	13	.280	.332	.441
1997 Tigers	R Det	2	7	4	0	0	1	7	2	1	1	0	1	0	0	0	0	0	.00	0	.571	.625	1.000
Lakeland	A+ Det	86	312	84	13	2	13	140	40	48	24	3	75	3	1	6	1	1	.50	7	.269	.322	.449
1998 Mobile	AA SD	23	69	16	5	1	2	29	9	11	8	0	10	0	0	0	1	0	1.00	3	.232	.312	.420
1999 Mobile	AA SD	111	400	112	31	3	11	182	69	70	50	4	95	4	0	3	0	1	.00	18	.280	.363	.455
6 Min. YEARS		470	1654	443	93	9	49	701	233	256	178	9	370	22	2	14	8	7	.53	53	.268	.344	.424

Jeff Ball

Bats: Right Throws: Right Pos: 3B   Ht: 5'10" Wt: 185 Born: 4/17/69 Age: 31

		BATTING															BASERUNNING				PERCENTAGES		
Year Team	Lg Org	G	AB	H	2B	3B	HR	TB	R	RBI	TBB	IBB	SO	HBP	SH	SF	SB	CS	SB%	GDP	Avg	OBP	SLG
1990 Auburn	A- Hou	70	263	76	18	1	5	111	40	38	22	1	35	4	3	5	20	5	.80	4	.289	.347	.422
1991 Osceola	A+ Hou	118	392	96	15	3	5	132	53	51	49	4	74	10	3	4	20	8	.71	9	.245	.341	.337
1992 Jackson	AA Hou	93	278	53	14	1	5	84	27	24	20	1	58	10	2	1	5	3	.63	9	.191	.269	.302
1993 Quad City	A Hou	112	389	114	28	2	14	188	68	76	58	3	63	7	1	5	40	19	.68	11	.293	.390	.483
1994 Jackson	AA Hou	111	358	113	30	3	13	188	65	57	34	3	74	5	5	3	9	8	.53	9	.316	.380	.525
1995 Tucson	AAA Hou	110	362	106	25	2	4	147	58	66	25	3	66	7	4	5	11	5	.69	13	.293	.346	.406
1996 Tucson	AAA Hou	116	429	139	31	2	19	231	64	73	34	1	83	1	0	1	10	8	.56	12	.324	.374	.538
1997 Phoenix	AAA SF	126	470	151	38	3	18	249	90	103	58	5	84	5	1	7	10	4	.71	12	.321	.396	.530
1998 Fresno	AAA SF	124	456	135	29	0	21	227	81	80	55	6	86	8	0	1	5	2	.71	18	.296	.381	.498
1999 Vancouver	AAA Oak	96	346	107	22	2	8	157	50	51	37	0	57	3	7	4	7	2	.78	19	.309	.377	.454
1998 San Francisco	NL	2	4	1	0	0	0	1	0	0	0	0	0	0	0	0	0	0	.00	0	.250	.250	.250
10 Min. YEARS		1076	3743	1090	250	19	112	1714	596	609	392	27	680	60	26	36	137	64	.68	116	.291	.364	.458

Travis Baptist

Pitches: Left Bats: Left Pos: P   Ht: 6' 0" Wt: 195 Born: 12/30/71 Age: 28

		HOW MUCH HE PITCHED						WHAT HE GAVE UP									THE RESULTS					
Year Team	Lg Org	G	GS	CG	GF	IP	BFP	H	R	ER	HR	SH	SF	HB	TBB	IBB	SO	WP	Bk	W	L	Pct.	ShO	Sv	ERA
1991 Medcine Hat	R+ Tor	14	14	1	0	85.1	379	100	54	39	5	2	2	1	21	0	48	4	1	4	4	.500	1	0	4.11
1992 Myrtle Bch	A Tor	19	19	2	0	118	455	81	24	19	2	6	2	4	22	0	97	5	4	11	2	.846	1	0	1.45
1993 Knoxville	AA Tor	7	7	0	0	33	139	37	17	15	2	2	3	2	7	0	24	3	0	1	3	.250	0	0	4.09
1994 Syracuse	AAA Tor	24	22	1	0	122.2	539	145	80	62	20	3	4	0	33	2	42	6	2	8	8	.500	0	0	4.55
1995 Syracuse	AAA Tor	15	13	0	0	79	356	83	56	38	12	2	3	2	32	2	52	4	1	3	4	.429	0	0	4.33
1996 Syracuse	AAA Tor	30	21	2	1	141	633	187	91	85	15	5	10	2	48	2	77	7	2	7	6	.538	0	0	5.43
1997 New Britain	AA Min	36	3	0	17	60.2	247	49	27	23	6	8	1	2	26	2	50	4	0	5	6	.455	0	0	3.41
Salt Lake	AAA Min	7	6	1	0	47.2	194	47	16	11	3	0	1	1	9	0	28	2	1	4	1	.800	1	0	2.08
1998 Salt Lake	AAA Min	21	21	1	0	135.2	559	128	53	47	12	3	0	4	41	1	98	7	1	8	5	.615	0	0	3.12
1999 Salt Lake	AAA Min	17	6	0	5	38.2	174	46	24	23	6	0	0	1	17	0	23	3	0	1	3	.250	0	1	5.35
Pawtucket	AAA Bos	17	3	0	2	42.1	195	49	27	25	5	1	0	1	19	0	30	2	0	4	2	.667	0	0	5.31
1998 Minnesota	AL	13	0	0	4	27	123	34	18	17	5	0	6	0	11	1	11	0	0	0	1	.000	0	0	5.67
9 Min. YEARS		207	135	8	15	904	3870	952	467	387	88	32	26	20	275	9	569	47	12	56	44	.560	3	1	3.85

Lorenzo Barcelo

Pitches: Right Bats: Right Pos: P   Ht: 6' 4" Wt: 220 Born: 8/10/77 Age: 22

		HOW MUCH HE PITCHED						WHAT HE GAVE UP									THE RESULTS					
Year Team	Lg Org	G	GS	CG	GF	IP	BFP	H	R	ER	HR	SH	SF	HB	TBB	IBB	SO	WP	Bk	W	L	Pct.	ShO	Sv	ERA
1995 Bellingham	A- SF	12	11	0	0	47	198	43	23	18	3	0	1	2	19	0	34	1	1	3	2	.600	0	0	3.45
1996 Burlington	A SF	26	26	1	0	152.2	633	138	70	60	19	9	5	3	40	0	103	5	0	10	10	.516	0	0	3.54
1997 San Jose	A+ SF	16	16	1	0	89	378	91	45	39	13	1	3	1	30	2	89	1	2	5	4	.556	1	0	3.94
Shreveport	AA SF	5	5	0	0	31.1	132	30	19	14	4	1	0	0	8	0	20	0	2	2	0	1.000	0	0	4.02
Birmingham	AA CWS	6	6	0	0	33.1	147	36	20	18	2	0	1	4	9	0	29	1	0	2	1	.667	0	0	4.86
1998 White Sox	R CWS	3	3	0	0	6	24	6	1	1	0	1	0	1	0	0	9	0	0	0	1	.000	0	0	1.50
1999 White Sox	R CWS	9	9	0	0	42.2	171	36	14	8	0	1	0	1	6	0	57	3	2	2	1	.667	0	0	1.69
Burlington	A CWS	1	1	0	0	5	18	3	2	2	1	0	1	0	6	0	10	0	0	1	0	1.000	0	0	3.60
Birmingham	AA CWS	4	4	0	0	20	79	14	8	8	0	1	2	1	6	0	14	0	0	1	0	.000	0	0	3.60
5 Min. YEARS		82	81	2	0	427	1780	397	202	168	42	11	12	14	124	2	397	11	12	27	20	.574	1	0	3.54

16

Andy Barkett

Bats: Left **Throws:** Left **Pos:** 1B   **Ht:** 6'1" **Wt:** 205 **Born:** 9/5/74 **Age:** 25

Year Team	Lg Org	G	AB	H	2B	3B	HR	TB	R	RBI	TBB	IBB	SO	HBP	SH	SF	SB	CS	SB%	GDP	Avg	OBP	SLG
																	BASERUNNING				PERCENTAGES		
1995 Butte	R+ Tex	45	162	54	11	5	5	90	33	51	33	2	39	3	0	4	1	0	1.00	1	.333	.446	.556
Chston-SC	A Tex	21	78	17	6	0	0	23	7	12	10	0	27	0	0	3	0	3	.00	3	.218	.297	.295
1996 Charlotte	A+ Tex	115	392	112	22	3	6	158	57	54	57	2	59	5	0	4	3	1	.75	6	.286	.380	.403
1997 Tulsa	AA Tex	130	471	141	34	8	8	215	82	65	63	2	86	5	1	2	1	3	.25	15	.299	.386	.456
1998 Tulsa	AA Tex	43	157	42	11	1	2	61	23	31	27	0	22	1	0	1	0	0	.00	2	.268	.376	.389
Oklahoma	AAA Tex	80	255	80	17	5	4	119	38	36	35	2	43	0	0	3	3	4	.43	6	.314	.392	.467
1999 Oklahoma	AAA Tex	132	486	149	32	5	10	221	70	76	44	4	71	6	0	5	7	7	.50	18	.307	.368	.455
5 Min. YEARS		566	2001	595	133	27	35	887	310	325	269	12	347	20	1	22	15	18	.45	51	.297	.382	.443

Brian Barkley

Pitches: Left **Bats:** Left **Pos:** P   **Ht:** 6'2" **Wt:** 185 **Born:** 12/8/75 **Age:** 24

Year Team	Lg Org	G	GS	CG	GF	IP	BFP	H	R	ER	HR	SH	SF	HB	TBB	IBB	SO	WP	Bk	W	L	Pct.	ShO	Sv	ERA
		HOW MUCH HE PITCHED						WHAT HE GAVE UP												THE RESULTS					
1994 Red Sox	R Bos	4	3	0	0	18.2	71	11	7	2	1	1	0	0	4	0	14	2	1	0	1	.000	0	0	0.96
1995 Sarasota	A+ Bos	24	24	2	0	146.2	611	147	66	53	5	2	3	5	37	3	70	4	1	8	10	.444	2	0	3.25
1996 Trenton	AA Bos	22	21	0	0	119.2	535	126	79	76	17	6	5	5	56	4	89	7	2	8	8	.500	0	0	5.72
1997 Trenton	AA Bos	29	29	4	0	178.2	797	208	113	98	18	3	6	3	79	0	121	3	2	12	9	.571	0	0	4.94
1998 Pawtucket	AAA Bos	23	23	1	0	139.1	609	161	81	76	22	3	10	7	50	4	88	5	2	7	9	.438	0	0	4.91
1999 Sarasota	A+ Bos	1	0	0	0	3	12	2	0	0	0	0	0	0	1	0	2	0	0	1	0	1.000	0	0	0.00
Trenton	AA Bos	7	7	0	0	35.1	135	32	10	10	2	0	0	2	6	0	18	0	0	5	0	1.000	0	0	2.55
Pawtucket	AAA Bos	3	3	0	0	14	63	11	9	8	2	1	1	1	7	0	5	1	0	0	1	.000	0	0	5.14
1998 Boston	AL	6	0	0	1	11	59	16	13	12	2	0	2	1	9	1	2	1	0	0	0	.000	0	0	9.82
6 Min. YEARS		113	110	7	0	655.1	2833	698	365	323	67	16	25	23	240	11	407	22	8	41	38	.519	2	0	4.44

Brian Barnes

Pitches: Left **Bats:** Left **Pos:** P   **Ht:** 5'9" **Wt:** 170 **Born:** 3/25/67 **Age:** 33

Year Team	Lg Org	G	GS	CG	GF	IP	BFP	H	R	ER	HR	SH	SF	HB	TBB	IBB	SO	WP	Bk	W	L	Pct.	ShO	Sv	ERA
		HOW MUCH HE PITCHED						WHAT HE GAVE UP												THE RESULTS					
1989 Jamestown	A- Mon	2	2	0	0	9	33	4	1	1	0	0	0	0	3	0	15	1	1	1	0	1.000	0	0	1.00
Wst Plm Bch	A+ Mon	7	7	4	0	50	187	25	9	4	0	3	1	0	16	0	67	4	0	4	3	.571	3	0	0.72
Indianapolis	AAA Mon	1	1	0	0	6	24	5	1	1	0	0	0	0	2	0	5	0	0	1	0	1.000	0	0	1.50
1990 Jacksnville	AA Mon	29	28	3	0	201.1	828	144	78	62	12	7	5	9	87	2	213	8	1	13	7	.650	1	0	2.77
1991 Wst Plm Bch	A+ Mon	2	2	0	0	7	27	3	0	0	0	0	0	0	4	0	6	3	0	0	0	.000	0	0	0.00
Indianapolis	AAA Mon	2	2	0	0	11	44	6	2	2	0	0	1	1	8	0	10	0	0	2	0	1.000	0	0	1.64
1992 Indianapolis	AAA Mon	13	13	2	0	83	338	69	35	34	8	1	2	1	30	1	77	2	2	4	4	.500	1	0	3.69
1994 Charlotte	AAA Cle	13	0	0	2	18.1	80	17	10	8	2	0	0	1	8	2	23	1	0	0	1	.000	0	1	3.93
Albuquerque	AAA LA	9	9	0	0	47	221	57	38	33	9	0	1	1	23	2	44	1	0	5	1	.833	0	0	6.32
1995 Pawtucket	AAA Bos	21	18	2	0	106.1	454	107	62	50	12	0	2	4	30	0	90	5	1	7	5	.583	2	0	4.23
1996 Jacksnville	AA Det	13	12	1	0	74.2	320	74	37	31	8	6	1	4	25	1	74	3	0	4	6	.400	1	0	3.74
Toledo	AAA Det	14	13	2	0	88	373	85	49	39	8	0	1	4	29	0	70	6	1	6	6	.500	0	0	3.99
1997 Toledo	AAA Det	32	18	0	4	115.1	540	143	100	86	16	2	8	7	57	6	86	9	0	7	10	.412	0	0	6.71
1998 Memphis	AAA StL	35	21	0	6	140.2	598	138	66	56	15	3	4	7	39	1	154	5	0	7	5	.583	0	0	3.58
1999 Memphis	AAA StL	36	10	0	7	90	393	104	55	55	16	4	3	3	33	1	88	5	0	4	3	.571	0	0	5.50
1990 Montreal	NL	4	4	1	0	28	115	25	10	9	2	2	0	0	7	0	23	2	0	1	1	.500	0	0	2.89
1991 Montreal	NL	28	27	1	0	160	684	135	82	75	16	9	5	6	84	2	117	5	1	5	8	.385	0	0	4.22
1992 Montreal	NL	21	17	0	2	100	417	77	34	33	9	5	1	3	46	1	65	1	2	6	6	.500	0	0	2.97
1993 Montreal	NL	52	8	0	8	100	442	105	53	49	9	8	3	0	48	2	60	5	1	2	6	.250	0	3	4.41
1994 Cleveland	AL	6	0	0	2	13.1	67	12	10	8	2	0	1	0	15	2	5	0	0	0	1	.000	0	0	5.40
Los Angeles	NL	5	0	0	1	5	29	10	4	4	1	0	0	0	4	1	5	2	0	0	0	.000	0	0	7.20
10 Min. YEARS		229	156	14	19	1047.2	4455	981	543	462	106	27	28	42	394	16	1022	53	6	65	51	.560	6	1	3.97
5 Maj. YEARS		116	56	2	13	406.1	1754	364	193	178	39	24	10	9	204	8	275	15	4	14	22	.389	0	3	3.94

John Barnes

Bats: Right **Throws:** Right **Pos:** OF   **Ht:** 6'2" **Wt:** 205 **Born:** 4/24/76 **Age:** 24

Year Team	Lg Org	G	AB	H	2B	3B	HR	TB	R	RBI	TBB	IBB	SO	HBP	SH	SF	SB	CS	SB%	GDP	Avg	OBP	SLG
																	BASERUNNING				PERCENTAGES		
1996 Red Sox	R Bos	30	101	28	4	0	1	35	9	17	5	0	17	6	0	5	4	0	1.00	3	.277	.333	.347
1997 Michigan	A Bos	130	490	149	19	5	6	196	80	73	65	3	42	5	0	6	19	5	.79	7	.304	.387	.400
1998 Trenton	AA Bos	100	380	104	18	0	14	164	53	36	40	3	47	3	2	4	3	8	.27	11	.274	.344	.432
New Britain	AA Min	20	71	19	4	1	0	25	9	8	9	0	9	1	0	1	1	1	.50	2	.268	.354	.352
1999 New Britain	AA Min	129	452	119	21	1	13	181	62	58	49	3	40	5	1	4	10	2	.83	15	.263	.339	.400
4 Min. YEARS		409	1494	419	66	7	34	601	213	192	168	9	155	20	3	20	37	16	.70	38	.280	.357	.402

Larry Barnes

Bats: Left **Throws:** Left **Pos:** 1B   **Ht:** 6'1" **Wt:** 195 **Born:** 7/23/74 **Age:** 25

Year Team	Lg Org	G	AB	H	2B	3B	HR	TB	R	RBI	TBB	IBB	SO	HBP	SH	SF	SB	CS	SB%	GDP	Avg	OBP	SLG
																	BASERUNNING				PERCENTAGES		
1995 Angels	R Ana	56	197	61	8	3	8	84	42	37	27	0	40	5	1	2	12	5	.71	1	.310	.403	.426
1996 Cedar Rapds	A Ana	131	489	155	36	5	27	282	84	112	58	5	101	6	1	6	9	6	.60	8	.317	.392	.577
1997 Lk Elsinore	A+ Ana	115	446	128	32	2	13	203	68	71	43	4	84	5	1	5	3	4	.43	6	.287	.353	.455
1998 Lk Elsinore	A+ Ana	51	183	45	11	2	7	81	32	33	22	2	49	1	0	0	2	0	1.00	3	.246	.330	.443
Midland	AA Ana	69	245	67	16	4	6	109	30	30	20	0	54	1	2	2	4	2	.67	5	.273	.348	.445
1999 Erie	AA Ana	130	497	142	25	9	20	245	73	100	49	7	99	5	0	16	14	3	.82	7	.286	.346	.493
5 Min. YEARS		552	2057	598	128	25	76	1004	328	388	227	21	427	23	5	31	44	20	.69	30	.291	.363	.488

17

Marty Barnett

Pitches: Right **Bats:** Right **Pos:** P   **Ht:** 6'3" **Wt:** 210 **Born:** 3/10/74 **Age:** 26

Year Team	Lg Org	G	GS	CG	GF	IP	BFP	H	R	ER	HR	SH	SF	HB	TBB	IBB	SO	WP	Bk	W	L	Pct.	ShO	Sv	ERA
1995 Batavia	A- Phi	10	10	0	0	49.1	228	67	45	34	3	2	4	5	10	1	32	9	3	1	6	.143	0	0	6.20
1997 Piedmont	A Phi	6	6	0	0	37	154	34	16	13	1	1	2	2	11	0	28	1	0	2	1	.667	0	0	3.16
Clearwater	A+ Phi	17	15	1	0	97.2	411	102	50	40	10	1	1	0	29	0	62	6	2	5	6	.455	0	0	3.69
1998 Reading	AA Phi	5	5	0	0	24.2	116	31	17	17	5	0	1	2	13	0	21	0	1	0	3	.000	0	0	6.20
Clearwater	A+ Phi	7	6	0	0	27.1	128	34	23	19	4	0	0	1	14	0	13	2	1	0	1	.000	0	0	6.26
1999 Reading	AA Phi	35	0	0	19	53.1	226	43	19	15	2	2	0	0	24	2	33	1	1	2	3	.400	0	7	2.53
Durham	AAA TB	16	0	0	6	28	124	30	17	17	2	1	3	1	14	1	19	4	0	1	0	1.000	0	0	5.46
4 Min. YEARS		96	42	1	25	317.1	1387	341	187	155	27	7	11	11	115	4	208	23	8	11	20	.355	0	7	4.40

Jim Baron

Pitches: Left **Bats:** Left **Pos:** P   **Ht:** 6'3" **Wt:** 210 **Born:** 2/22/74 **Age:** 26

Year Team	Lg Org	G	GS	CG	GF	IP	BFP	H	R	ER	HR	SH	SF	HB	TBB	IBB	SO	WP	Bk	W	L	Pct.	ShO	Sv	ERA
1992 Padres	R SD	14	0	0	3	25	117	24	28	23	0	1	4	1	25	0	18	10	6	2	0	1.000	0	0	8.28
1993 Padres	R SD	13	8	1	2	48.2	220	38	33	24	0	1	3	6	38	0	36	5	1	1	3	.250	0	0	4.44
1994 Springfield	A SD	25	23	0	0	105.2	515	121	83	75	14	2	3	7	76	2	73	14	3	6	6	.500	0	0	6.39
1995 Rancho Cuca	A+ SD	3	0	0	1	2.2	22	7	8	5	1	1	0	0	6	0	3	2	0	0	0	.000	0	0	16.88
Clinton	A SD	11	9	1	1	50.2	232	65	42	35	4	3	2	1	16	2	31	4	0	0	8	.000	0	0	6.22
Idaho Falls	R+ SD	27	1	0	5	43	201	51	31	27	2	0	2	1	19	1	43	8	0	2	3	.400	0	0	5.65
1996 Rancho Cuca	A+ SD	54	0	0	17	87	383	87	44	29	9	2	3	1	35	0	85	7	2	6	3	.667	0	1	3.00
1997 Las Vegas	AAA SD	4	0	0	2	4	21	8	5	5	2	0	0	0	3	0	3	0	0	0	0	.000	0	0	11.25
Mobile	AA SD	19	1	0	4	33.2	152	35	21	17	3	2	0	3	13	1	30	3	0	2	4	.333	0	0	4.54
Rancho Cuca	A+ SD	14	14	0	0	85.1	371	89	50	32	2	4	7	2	28	1	64	4	1	1	7	.125	0	0	3.38
1998 Norwich	AA NYY	23	12	4	6	96.2	403	99	35	25	2	2	2	0	20	0	69	4	0	6	4	.600	0	0	2.33
Columbus	AAA NYY	8	7	1	1	44.1	196	54	32	30	7	0	2	1	19	0	28	3	0	1	5	.167	0	0	6.09
1999 Altoona	AA Pit	29	20	0	3	145	618	141	73	64	13	6	8	4	44	2	75	6	5	9	9	.500	0	0	3.97
8 Min. YEARS		244	95	7	45	771.2	3451	819	485	391	59	24	36	27	342	9	558	70	18	36	52	.409	1	2	4.56

Tucker Barr

Bats: Right **Throws:** Right **Pos:** C   **Ht:** 6'1" **Wt:** 205 **Born:** 5/26/75 **Age:** 25

Year Team	Lg Org	G	AB	H	2B	3B	HR	TB	R	RBI	TBB	IBB	SO	HBP	SH	SF	SB	CS	SB%	GDP	Avg	OBP	SLG
1996 Auburn	A- Hou	44	165	36	12	0	4	60	16	22	5	0	39	1	0	2	1	1	.50	2	.218	.243	.364
1997 Quad City	A Hou	93	309	64	10	1	10	106	42	36	39	0	91	4	0	1	0	2	.00	4	.207	.303	.343
1998 Kissimmee	A+ Hou	57	182	46	10	0	8	80	25	31	23	0	39	2	0	1	0	2	.00	2	.253	.341	.440
1999 Jackson	AA Hou	41	107	27	0	0	5	42	8	15	12	0	20	5	0	0	0	0	.00	3	.252	.355	.393
4 Min. YEARS		235	763	173	32	1	27	288	91	104	79	0	189	12	0	4	1	5	.17	11	.227	.308	.377

Manuel Barrios

Pitches: Right **Bats:** Right **Pos:** P   **Ht:** 6'0" **Wt:** 185 **Born:** 9/21/74 **Age:** 25

Year Team	Lg Org	G	GS	CG	GF	IP	BFP	H	R	ER	HR	SH	SF	HB	TBB	IBB	SO	WP	Bk	W	L	Pct.	ShO	Sv	ERA
1994 Quad City	A Hou	43	0	0	11	65	295	73	44	43	4	5	2	7	23	4	63	8	2	0	6	.000	0	4	5.95
1995 Quad City	A Hou	50	0	0	48	52	219	44	16	13	1	2	1	4	17	1	55	1	0	1	5	.167	0	23	2.25
1996 Jackson	AA Hou	60	0	0	53	68.1	298	60	29	18	4	4	2	3	29	5	69	3	0	6	4	.600	0	23	2.37
1997 New Orleans	AAA Hou	57	0	0	17	82.2	350	70	32	30	5	10	4	1	34	9	77	2	0	4	8	.333	0	0	3.27
1998 Albuquerque	AAA LA	20	2	0	7	36	170	47	25	24	7	1	1	2	15	0	33	4	0	1	3	.250	0	0	6.00
Charlotte	AAA Fla	18	1	0	6	24.1	98	10	10	10	3	0	0	1	9	2	22	0	0	2	0	1.000	0	0	3.70
1999 Indianapols	AAA Cin	49	8	0	9	90.1	399	94	60	53	8	3	2	7	35	0	73	9	2	2	7	.222	0	0	5.28
1997 Houston	NL	2	0	0	0	3	18	6	4	4	0	0	0	0	3	0	3	0	0	0	0	.000	0	0	12.00
1998 Florida	NL	2	0	0	0	2.2	13	4	1	1	1	0	0	0	2	0	1	0	0	0	0	.000	0	0	3.38
Los Angeles	NL	1	0	0	1	1	4	0	0	0	0	0	0	0	2	0	0	0	0	0	0	.000	0	0	0.00
6 Min. YEARS		297	11	0	151	418.2	1829	407	216	191	32	25	12	25	162	21	392	27	4	16	33	.327	0	50	4.11
2 Maj. YEARS		5	0	0	1	6.2	35	10	5	5	1	0	0	0	7	0	4	0	0	0	0	.000	0	0	6.75

Blake Barthol

Bats: Right **Throws:** Right **Pos:** C   **Ht:** 6'0" **Wt:** 200 **Born:** 4/7/73 **Age:** 27

Year Team	Lg Org	G	AB	H	2B	3B	HR	TB	R	RBI	TBB	IBB	SO	HBP	SH	SF	SB	CS	SB%	GDP	Avg	OBP	SLG
1995 Portland	A- Col	56	191	45	10	2	1	62	20	25	22	0	32	4	1	3	5	2	.71	5	.236	.323	.325
1996 Salem	A+ Col	109	375	107	17	2	13	167	58	67	36	0	48	12	6	1	12	5	.71	5	.285	.366	.445
1997 New Haven	AA Col	109	325	79	12	2	6	113	42	39	31	0	76	10	11	2	5	3	.63	6	.243	.326	.348
1998 Salem	A+ Col	122	441	128	37	2	11	202	56	68	46	5	94	7	4	5	5	3	.63	2	.290	.363	.458
1999 Carolina	AA Col	96	322	90	18	3	8	138	41	27	32	2	62	7	5	1	0	1	.00	8	.280	.356	.429
5 Min. YEARS		492	1654	449	94	11	39	682	217	226	167	7	312	40	27	12	27	14	.00	00	.271	.350	.412

Jayson Bass

Bats: Left **Throws:** Left **Pos:** OF   **Ht:** 6'3" **Wt:** 205 **Born:** 6/22/74 **Age:** 26

Year Team	Lg Org	G	AB	H	2B	3B	HR	TB	R	RBI	TBB	IBB	SO	HBP	SH	SF	SB	CS	SB%	GDP	Avg	OBP	SLG
1993 Bristol	R+ Det	35	119	25	6	2	4	47	21	13	14	0	42	2	0	0	2	2	.50	0	.210	.304	.395
1994 Jamestown	A- Det	48	162	44	9	4	5	76	23	18	22	1	52	2	0	0	4	3	.57	2	.272	.366	.469
1995 Fayetteville	A Det	108	368	79	15	6	10	136	47	48	37	1	111	3	1	1	14	3	.82	5	.215	.291	.370
1996 Fayetteville	A Det	104	295	68	12	3	11	119	44	43	54	3	118	2	3	2	19	10	.66	2	.231	.351	.403

Year Team	Lg Org	G	AB	H	2B	3B	HR	TB	R	RBI	TBB	IBB	SO	HBP	SH	SF	SB	CS	SB%	GDP	Avg	OBP	SLG
1997 Lakeland	A+ Det	108	376	97	18	4	13	162	58	53	41	5	130	2	0	4	17	7	.71	4	.258	.331	.431
1998 Lancaster	A+ Sea	110	392	113	26	6	21	214	80	84	40	2	102	4	0	2	31	12	.72	3	.288	.358	.546
1999 New Haven	AA Sea	123	431	114	23	5	21	210	79	67	72	1	160	3	0	5	34	14	.71	3	.265	.370	.487
7 Min. YEARS		636	2143	540	109	30	85	964	352	326	280	13	715	18	4	14	121	51	.70	17	.252	.341	.450

Jayson Bass

Bats: Both Throws: Right Pos: OF   Ht: 6'0" Wt: 180 Born: 6/2/76 Age: 24

Year Team	Lg Org	G	AB	H	2B	3B	HR	TB	R	RBI	TBB	IBB	SO	HBP	SH	SF	SB	CS	SB%	GDP	Avg	OBP	SLG
1994 Braves	R Atl	49	173	25	8	0	0	33	14	4	15	0	33	2	0	1	5	8	.38	2	.145	.220	.191
1995 Danville	R+ Atl	64	268	60	17	4	0	85	38	17	28	2	61	4	0	2	24	8	.75	2	.224	.305	.317
1996 Danville	R+ Atl	57	207	50	11	6	2	79	41	23	34	0	32	6	1	5	22	5	.81	1	.242	.357	.382
Macon	A Atl	5	22	8	0	0	1	11	2	1	0	0	5	1	0	0	3	1	.75	0	.364	.391	.500
1997 Durham	A+ Atl	75	277	71	20	4	4	111	48	34	29	1	57	2	2	0	8	4	.67	6	.256	.331	.401
1998 Danville	A+ Atl	10	38	6	1	1	0	9	3	1	0	0	12	1	0	0	2	1	.67	0	.158	.179	.237
Greenville	AA Atl	86	233	53	10	1	5	80	27	18	37	1	60	1	6	2	11	6	.65	2	.227	.333	.343
1999 Myrtle Bch	A+ Atl	44	164	36	7	3	2	55	20	19	15	1	45	2	1	1	8	3	.73	1	.220	.291	.335
Richmond	AAA Atl	59	153	32	4	1	1	41	20	10	19	0	46	2	2	2	9	2	.82	5	.209	.301	.268
6 Min. YEARS		449	1535	341	78	20	15	504	213	127	177	5	351	21	12	13	92	38	.71	19	.222	.309	.328

Richard Batchelor

Pitches: Right Bats: Right Pos: P   Ht: 6' 1" Wt: 195 Born: 4/8/67 Age: 33

		HOW MUCH HE PITCHED						WHAT HE GAVE UP												THE RESULTS				
Year Team	Lg Org	G	GS	CG	GF	IP	BFP	H	R	ER	HR	SH	SF	HB	TBB	IBB	SO	WP	Bk	W	L	Pct.	ShO	Sv	ERA
1990 Greensboro	A NYY	27	0	0	18	51.1	200	39	15	9	1	0	2	0	14	1	38	2	0	2	2	.500	0	8	1.58
1991 Ft. Laud	A+ NYY	50	0	0	41	62	269	55	28	19	1	6	1	1	22	5	58	4	0	4	7	.364	0	25	2.76
Albany-Colo	AA NYY	1	0	0	1	1	9	5	5	5	0	1	0	0	1	0	0	0	0	0	0	.000	0	0	45.00
1992 Albany-Colo	AA NYY	58	0	0	34	70.2	320	79	40	33	5	1	2	6	34	3	45	4	0	4	5	.444	0	7	4.20
1993 Albany-Colo	AA NYY	36	0	0	32	40.1	162	27	9	4	1	1	0	1	12	0	40	3	0	1	3	.250	0	19	0.89
Columbus	AAA NYY	15	0	0	14	16.1	74	14	5	5	0	0	0	1	8	1	17	3	0	1	1	.500	0	6	2.76
1994 Louisville	AAA StL	53	0	0	13	81.1	347	85	40	32	7	5	3	3	32	6	50	7	0	1	2	.333	0	1	3.54
1995 Louisville	AAA StL	50	6	0	7	85	352	85	39	31	5	4	3	7	16	2	61	0	0	5	4	.556	0	2	3.28
1996 Louisville	AAA StL	51	0	0	44	54.2	242	59	29	25	5	4	2	2	19	5	57	5	0	5	2	.714	0	28	4.12
1997 Louisville	AAA StL	12	0	0	10	14	66	18	9	7	1	0	2	1	6	2	10	2	0	0	2	.000	0	5	4.50
Las Vegas	AAA SD	15	0	0	4	21	93	23	15	15	2	1	1	1	8	2	19	5	0	3	0	1.000	0	6	6.43
1998 Buffalo	AAA Cle	57	0	0	45	58.1	263	58	26	22	3	2	0	4	25	1	64	7	1	4	4	.500	0	22	3.39
1999 Tucson	AAA Ari	30	0	0	28	28	125	29	19	14	2	1	1	2	12	1	23	2	0	0	4	.000	0	12	4.50
1993 St. Louis	NL	9	0	0	2	10	45	14	12	9	1	1	2	0	3	1	4	0	0	0	0	.000	0	0	8.10
1996 St. Louis	NL	11	0	0	7	15	54	9	2	2	0	1	0	0	1	0	11	0	0	2	0	1.000	0	1	1.20
1997 St. Louis	NL	10	0	0	3	16	76	21	12	8	0	2	0	2	7	1	8	0	1	1	1	.500	0	0	4.50
San Diego	NL	13	0	0	5	12.2	62	19	11	11	2	1	0	1	7	1	10	1	0	2	0	1.000	0	0	7.82
10 Min. YEARS		455	6	0	291	584	2526	576	279	221	33	26	17	29	209	29	482	44	1	30	36	.455	0	132	3.41
3 Maj. YEARS		43	0	0	17	53.2	237	63	37	30	3	5	2	3	18	3	33	1	1	5	1	.833	0	0	5.03

Fletcher Bates

Bats: Both Throws: Right Pos: OF   Ht: 6'1" Wt: 193 Born: 3/24/74 Age: 26

Year Team	Lg Org	G	AB	H	2B	3B	HR	TB	R	RBI	TBB	IBB	SO	HBP	SH	SF	SB	CS	SB%	GDP	Avg	OBP	SLG
1994 Mets	R NYM	52	183	39	5	3	5	65	23	29	33	0	49	0	1	4	4	3	.57	1	.213	.327	.355
St. Lucie	A+ NYM	7	24	6	1	1	1	12	2	4	1	0	5	0	0	0	0	0	.00	0	.250	.280	.500
1995 Pittsfield	A- NYM	75	276	90	14	9	6	140	52	37	41	0	72	4	1	3	17	9	.65	1	.326	.417	.507
Binghamton	AA NYM	2	8	0	0	0	0	0	1	0	1	0	6	0	0	0	0	0	.00	0	.000	.111	.000
1996 Capital Cty	A NYM	132	491	127	21	13	15	219	84	72	64	4	162	3	4	3	16	6	.73	3	.259	.346	.446
1997 St. Lucie	A+ NYM	70	253	76	19	11	11	150	49	38	33	6	66	4	0	2	7	6	.54	4	.300	.387	.593
Binghamton	AA NYM	68	245	63	14	2	12	117	44	34	26	0	71	1	1	2	9	3	.75	2	.257	.328	.478
1998 Portland	AA Fla	140	537	147	23	5	11	213	67	60	46	2	118	2	1	1	19	6	.76	4	.274	.333	.397
1999 Portland	AA Fla	139	537	136	28	9	9	209	72	55	39	1	109	2	4	8	18	6	.75	10	.253	.302	.389
6 Min. YEARS		685	2554	684	125	53	70	1125	394	329	284	13	658	16	12	23	90	39	.70	25	.268	.342	.440

Allen Battle

Bats: Right Throws: Right Pos: DH   Ht: 6' 0" Wt: 170 Born: 11/29/68 Age: 31

Year Team	Lg Org	G	AB	H	2B	3B	HR	TB	R	RBI	TBB	IBB	SO	HBP	SH	SF	SB	CS	SB%	GDP	Avg	OBP	SLG
1991 Johnson Cy	R+ StL	17	62	24	6	1	0	32	26	7	14	0	6	1	1	0	7	1	.88	2	.387	.506	.516
Savannah	A StL	48	169	42	7	1	0	51	27	20	27	0	34	1	0	2	12	3	.80	0	.249	.352	.302
1992 Springfield	A StL	67	235	71	10	4	4	101	49	24	41	0	34	10	1	2	22	12	.65	1	.302	.424	.430
St. Pete	A+ StL	60	222	71	9	2	1	87	34	15	35	2	38	4	4	2	21	11	.66	2	.320	.418	.392
1993 Arkansas	AA StL	108	390	107	24	12	3	164	71	40	45	0	75	6	2	3	20	12	.63	4	.274	.356	.421
1994 Louisville	AAA StL	132	520	163	44	7	6	239	104	69	59	2	82	6	1	7	23	8	.74	14	.313	.385	.460
1995 Louisville	AAA StL	47	164	46	12	1	3	69	28	18	28	0	32	1	5	0	7	1	.88	3	.280	.389	.421
1996 Edmonton	AAA Oak	62	224	68	12	4	3	97	53	33	37	0	37	3	6	0	9	3	.75	5	.304	.406	.433
1997 Nashville	AAA CWS	11	27	6	1	0	2	13	6	5	5	0	7	0	0	0	0	0	.00	0	.222	.344	.481
1998 Ottawa	AAA Mon	132	454	138	31	2	11	206	72	68	71	3	81	8	2	6	34	5	.87	13	.304	.403	.454
1000 Iowa	AAA ChC	35	110	27	7	0	3	43	16	14	14	1	30	0	1	1	2	1	.67	1	.245	.328	.391
Cubs	R ChC	3	13	4	0	1	0	6	2	0	1	0	4	1	0	0	1	0	1.00	1	.308	.400	.462
1995 St. Louis	NL	61	118	32	5	0	0	37	13	2	15	0	26	1	3	0	3	3	.50	1	.271	.358	.314

	BATTING																BASERUNNING				PERCENTAGES		
Year Team	Lg Org	G	AB	H	2B	3B	HR	TB	R	RBI	TBB	IBB	SO	HBP	SH	SF	SB	CS	SB%	GDP	Avg	OBP	SLG
1996 Oakland	AL	47	130	25	3	0	1	31	20	5	17	1	26	2	1	1	10	2	.83	3	.192	.293	.238
9 Min. YEARS		722	2590	767	163	35	36	1108	488	313	377	8	460	41	23	25	158	57	.73	46	.296	.391	.428
2 Maj. YEARS		108	248	57	8	0	1	68	33	7	32	1	52	3	4	1	13	5	.72	3	.230	.324	.274

Jose Bautista

Pitches: Right   Bats: Right   Pos: P   Ht: 6' 2"   Wt: 205   Born: 7/25/64   Age: 35

	HOW MUCH HE PITCHED						WHAT HE GAVE UP												THE RESULTS					
Year Team	Lg Org	G	GS	CG	GF	IP	BFP	H	R	ER	HR	SH	SF	HB	TBB	IBB	SO	WP	Bk	W	L	Pct.	ShO	Sv	ERA
1981 Kingsport	R+ NYM	13	11	3	1	66	—	84	54	34	10	—	—	2	17	1	34	1	3	3	6	.333	2	0	4.64
1982 Kingsport	R+ NYM	14	4	0	5	38.1	—	61	44	38	3	—	—	0	19	0	13	3	1	0	4	.000	0	0	8.92
1983 Mets	R NYM	13	13	2	0	81.2	—	66	31	21	2	—	—	0	32	1	44	5	1	4	3	.571	0	0	2.31
1984 Columbia	A NYM	19	18	5	0	135	544	121	52	47	10	7	2	0	35	3	96	3	1	13	4	.765	3	0	3.13
1985 Lynchburg	A+ NYM	27	25	7	1	169	674	145	49	44	8	2	3	3	33	0	109	3	1	15	8	.652	3	1	2.34
1986 Jackson	AA NYM	7	4	0	0	21.2	109	36	22	20	3	0	0	1	8	0	13	3	0	0	1	.000	0	0	8.31
Lynchburg	A+ NYM	18	18	5	0	118.2	486	120	58	52	12	6	4	3	24	1	62	3	3	8	8	.500	1	0	3.94
1987 Jackson	AA NYM	28	25	2	2	169.1	712	174	76	61	9	6	3	4	43	3	95	6	3	10	5	.667	1	0	3.24
1989 Rochester	AAA Bal	15	13	3	1	98.2	398	84	41	31	10	3	4	3	26	1	47	4	2	4	4	.500	1	0	2.83
1990 Rochester	AAA Bal	27	13	3	4	108.2	442	115	51	49	10	3	5	4	15	0	50	3	5	7	8	.467	0	2	4.06
1991 Okla City	AAA Tex	11	3	0	4	32.1	139	38	19	19	4	1	0	1	6	0	22	0	0	0	3	.000	0	0	5.29
Miami	A+ Bal	11	11	4	0	76.1	293	63	23	23	5	1	0	1	11	0	69	1	1	8	2	.800	3	0	2.71
Rochester	AAA Bal	6	0	0	5	15.1	56	8	1	1	1	2	0	0	3	2	7	0	0	1	0	1.000	0	1	0.59
1992 Omaha	AAA KC	40	7	1	16	108.1	476	125	66	59	7	2	4	2	28	0	60	1	1	2	10	.167	0	2	4.90
Memphis	AA KC	1	1	0	0	6	25	6	3	3	1	0	0	0	2	0	7	1	0	1	0	1.000	0	0	4.50
1996 Phoenix	AAA SF	6	6	0	0	39.1	159	41	19	19	1	0	1	4	5	0	18	0	0	2	2	.500	0	0	4.35
1997 Louisville	AAA StL	11	0	0	2	17.1	56	3	0	0	0	0	0	3	2	1	11	0	0	2	0	1.000	0	0	0.00
1998 Norwich	AA NYY	3	3	0	0	8.1	49	17	16	14	5	0	1	1	4	0	4	0	0	0	2	.000	0	0	15.12
Calgary	AAA CWS	35	0	0	26	41.1	181	52	24	18	7	1	2	2	4	0	23	0	0	3	3	.500	0	15	3.92
1999 Ottawa	AAA Mon	16	0	0	5	28.1	126	33	19	18	6	2	2	1	5	1	24	0	0	0	1	.000	0	4	5.72
Norfolk	AAA NYM	20	12	0	0	82.2	374	111	53	49	14	1	1	5	21	1	41	4	0	7	4	.636	0	0	5.33
1988 Baltimore	AL	33	25	3	5	171.2	721	171	86	82	21	2	3	7	45	3	76	4	5	6	15	.286	0	0	4.30
1989 Baltimore	AL	15	10	0	4	78	325	84	46	46	17	1	1	1	15	0	30	0	0	3	4	.429	0	0	5.31
1990 Baltimore	AL	22	0	0	9	26.2	112	28	15	12	4	1	1	0	7	3	15	2	0	1	0	1.000	0	0	4.05
1991 Baltimore	AL	5	0	0	3	5.1	34	13	10	10	1	0	0	1	5	0	3	1	0	0	1	.000	0	0	16.88
1993 Chicago	NL	58	7	1	14	111.2	459	105	38	35	11	4	3	5	27	3	63	4	1	10	3	.769	0	2	2.82
1994 Chicago	NL	58	0	0	24	69.1	293	75	30	30	10	5	4	3	17	7	45	2	1	4	5	.444	0	1	3.89
1995 San Francisco	NL	52	6	0	19	100.2	451	120	77	72	24	8	5	5	26	3	45	1	2	3	8	.273	0	0	6.44
1996 San Francisco	NL	37	1	0	12	69.2	280	66	32	26	10	4	3	2	15	5	28	0	0	3	4	.429	0	0	3.36
1997 Detroit	AL	21	0	0	4	40.1	185	55	32	30	6	1	0	2	12	3	19	1	1	2	2	.500	0	0	6.69
St. Louis	NL	11	0	0	3	12.1	56	15	10	9	2	3	0	1	2	1	4	0	0	0	0	.000	0	0	6.57
15 Min. YEARS		341	187	35	73	1462.2	—	1503	721	620	128	—	—	37	343	15	849	41	22	90	78	.536	14	25	3.81
9 Maj. YEARS		312	49	4	97	685.2	2925	732	376	352	106	29	20	27	171	28	328	16	10	32	42	.432	0	3	4.62

Juan Bautista

Bats: Right   Throws: Right   Pos: SS   Ht: 6'0"   Wt: 170   Born: 6/24/75   Age: 25

	BATTING																BASERUNNING				PERCENTAGES		
Year Team	Lg Org	G	AB	H	2B	3B	HR	TB	R	RBI	TBB	IBB	SO	HBP	SH	SF	SB	CS	SB%	GDP	Avg	OBP	SLG
1993 Albany	A Bal	98	295	70	17	2	0	91	24	28	14	0	72	7	3	4	11	3	.79	11	.237	.284	.308
1994 Orioles	R Bal	21	65	10	2	2	0	16	4	3	2	0	19	1	1	0	3	1	.75	3	.154	.191	.246
1995 Bowie	AA Bal	13	38	4	2	0	0	6	3	0	3	0	5	2	1	0	1	0	1.00	1	.105	.209	.158
High Desert	A+ Bal	99	374	98	13	4	11	152	54	51	18	0	74	7	6	3	22	9	.71	8	.262	.306	.406
1996 Bowie	AA Bal	129	441	103	18	3	3	136	35	33	21	1	102	5	8	2	15	12	.56	6	.234	.275	.308
1997 Orioles	R Bal	3	9	1	0	0	0	1	3	0	1	0	2	2	0	1	1	1	.50	0	.111	.333	.111
Bowie	AA Bal	21	68	17	1	0	0	18	9	3	5	0	17	0	1	1	1	2	.33	2	.250	.297	.265
Birmingham	AA CWS	12	46	11	3	0	0	14	6	4	3	0	15	0	1	0	0	1	.00	2	.239	.286	.304
1998 Birmingham	AA CWS	120	420	107	13	1	5	137	46	34	18	1	98	4	6	3	6	12	.33	18	.255	.290	.326
1999 Tulsa	AA Tex	127	471	116	14	3	8	160	60	45	25	0	114	7	6	0	18	9	.67	12	.246	.294	.340
7 Min. YEARS		643	2227	537	83	15	27	731	244	201	110	2	518	35	33	13	78	50	.61	65	.241	.286	.328

Juan Bautista

Bats: Right   Throws: Right   Pos: 2B   Ht: 6'1"   Wt: 165   Born: 7/20/78   Age: 21

	BATTING																BASERUNNING				PERCENTAGES		
Year Team	Lg Org	G	AB	H	2B	3B	HR	TB	R	RBI	TBB	IBB	SO	HBP	SH	SF	SB	CS	SB%	GDP	Avg	OBP	SLG
1996 Diamondbcks	R Ari	49	140	28	3	1	0	33	14	14	11	0	51	3	0	2	5	2	.71	2	.200	.269	.236
1997 South Bend	A Ari	31	92	12	1	1	0	15	12	4	6	0	32	3	1	0	1	0	1.00	1	.130	.208	.163
Lethbridge	R+ Ari	43	136	28	3	1	1	36	23	14	12	0	35	4	2	2	4	1	.80	4	.206	.286	.265
1998 South Bend	A Ari	71	235	50	13	0	1	66	22	11	19	0	60	5	0	1	7	5	.58	5	.213	.285	.281
Tucson	AAA Ari	9	20	3	0	0	0	3	1	1	2	0	5	1	0	1	0	0	.00	2	.150	.250	.150
High Desert	A+ Ari	6	18	2	0	0	0	5	1	1	1	0	5	1	0	0	0	0	.00	0	.111	.200	.278
1999 El Paso	AA Ari	2	3	0	0	0	0	0	0	0	0	0	2	0	0	0	0	0	.00	0	.000	.000	.000
4 Min. YEARS		211	644	123	20	3	3	158	73	45	51	0	190	17	3	6	17	8	.68	14	.191	.266	.245

Chuck Beale

Pitches: Right   Bats: Right   Pos: P   Ht: 6'0"   Wt: 210   Born: 3/19/74   Age: 26

	HOW MUCH HE PITCHED						WHAT HE GAVE UP												THE RESULTS					
Year Team	Lg Org	G	GS	CG	GF	IP	BFP	H	R	ER	HR	SH	SF	HB	TBB	IBB	SO	WP	Bk	W	L	Pct.	ShO	Sv	ERA
1996 Lowell	A- Bos	28	0	0	26	29	112	16	7	4	1	2	0	1	7	0	33	2	1	0	0	.000	0	16	1.24
1997 Michigan	A Bos	39	9	1	28	89.1	405	111	58	37	5	3	2	2	17	2	86	9	2	2	7	.222	0	12	3.73

Year Team	Lg Org	G	GS	CG	GF	IP	BFP	H	R	ER	HR	SH	SF	HB	TBB	IBB	SO	WP	Bk	W	L	Pct.	ShO	Sv	ERA
		HOW MUCH HE PITCHED						WHAT HE GAVE UP												THE RESULTS					
1998 Trenton	AA Bos	43	0	0	14	69	284	54	31	25	9	3	3	3	31	7	39	4	0	5	3	.625	0	1	3.26
1999 Trenton	AA Bos	29	1	0	6	59	276	71	45	39	6	4	2	1	36	4	41	8	0	2	5	.286	0	1	5.95
4 Min. YEARS		139	10	1	74	246.1	1077	252	141	105	21	12	7	7	91	13	199	23	3	9	15	.375	0	30	3.84

Trey Beamon

Bats: Left **Throws:** Right **Pos:** OF **Ht:** 6' 0" **Wt:** 192 **Born:** 2/11/74 **Age:** 26

Year Team	Lg Org	G	AB	H	2B	3B	HR	TB	R	RBI	TBB	IBB	SO	HBP	SH	SF	SB	CS	SB%	GDP	Avg	OBP	SLG
		BATTING															BASERUNNING				PERCENTAGES		
1992 Pirates	R Pit	13	39	12	1	0	1	16	9	6	4	1	0	0	0	0	0	1	.00	0	.308	.372	.410
Welland	A- Pit	19	69	20	5	0	3	34	15	9	8	0	9	0	0	0	4	3	.57	6	.290	.364	.493
1993 Augusta	A Pit	104	373	101	18	6	0	131	64	45	48	2	60	6	0	4	19	6	.76	12	.271	.360	.351
1994 Carolina	AA Pit	112	434	140	18	9	5	191	69	47	33	4	53	5	4	3	24	9	.73	8	.323	.375	.440
1995 Calgary	AAA Pit	118	452	151	29	5	5	205	74	62	39	4	55	2	2	3	18	8	.69	7	.334	.387	.454
1996 Calgary	AAA Pit	111	378	109	15	3	5	145	62	52	55	6	63	6	3	5	16	3	.84	12	.288	.383	.384
1997 Las Vegas	AAA Pit	90	329	108	19	4	5	150	64	49	48	1	58	9	2	2	14	6	.70	11	.328	.425	.456
1998 Lakeland	A+ Det	2	6	3	0	0	0	3	2	0	3	0	0	0	0	0	0	0	.00	0	.500	.667	.500
Toledo	AAA Det	56	207	49	6	0	3	64	31	18	28	0	38	2	0	3	16	2	.89	2	.237	.329	.309
1999 Charlotte	AAA CWS	18	54	14	5	0	1	22	11	6	3	0	10	0	0	0	4	0	1.00	2	.259	.298	.407
Binghamton	AA NYM	71	246	59	13	0	2	78	32	20	29	0	41	2	1	1	13	10	.57	12	.240	.324	.317
1996 Pittsburgh	NL	24	51	11	2	0	0	13	7	6	4	0	6	0	1	0	1	1	.50	0	.216	.273	.255
1997 San Diego	NL	43	65	18	3	0	0	21	5	7	2	0	17	1	0	0	1	2	.33	1	.277	.309	.323
1998 Detroit	AL	28	42	11	4	0	0	15	4	2	5	0	13	0	1	0	0	1	.00	3	.262	.340	.357
8 Min. YEARS		714	2587	766	129	27	30	1039	433	314	298	18	387	32	12	21	128	48	.73	72	.296	.373	.402
3 Maj. YEARS		95	158	40	9	0	0	49	16	15	11	0	36	1	2	0	3	3	.50	4	.253	.306	.310

Doug Bearden

Bats: Right **Throws:** Right **Pos:** SS **Ht:** 6'2" **Wt:** 180 **Born:** 9/11/75 **Age:** 24

Year Team	Lg Org	G	AB	H	2B	3B	HR	TB	R	RBI	TBB	IBB	SO	HBP	SH	SF	SB	CS	SB%	GDP	Avg	OBP	SLG
		BATTING															BASERUNNING				PERCENTAGES		
1994 White Sox	R CWS	46	165	36	4	1	1	45	15	12	4	0	30	1	1	2	1	1	.50	4	.218	.238	.273
1995 Hickory	A CWS	44	141	22	5	1	2	35	9	12	5	1	44	1	2	0	1	1	.50	6	.156	.190	.248
Bristol	R+ CWS	46	167	39	10	1	3	60	26	22	6	0	40	3	3	2	5	0	1.00	1	.234	.270	.359
1996 Hickory	A CWS	49	169	37	7	0	1	47	12	11	3	0	35	0	2	0	3	0	.00	2	.219	.233	.278
Bristol	R+ CWS	40	127	20	1	0	1	24	6	6	7	0	29	0	3	0	2	1	.67	5	.157	.201	.189
1997 Beloit	A Mil	56	163	36	3	1	0	41	15	14	2	0	37	3	4	0	1	1	.50	4	.221	.244	.252
1998 Stockton	A+ Mil	115	359	83	15	0	1	101	43	26	28	0	80	2	8	2	6	6	.50	1	.231	.289	.281
1999 Jackson	AA Hou	25	83	15	3	0	0	18	7	3	2	0	24	1	0	0	0	0	.00	2	.181	.209	.217
Kissimmee	A+ Hou	45	149	40	7	1	2	55	19	16	8	0	35	2	4	1	1	4	.20	3	.268	.313	.369
6 Min. YEARS		466	1523	328	55	5	11	426	152	122	65	1	354	13	27	7	17	17	.50	28	.215	.252	.280

Ray Beasley

Pitches: Left **Bats:** Right **Pos:** P **Ht:** 5'11" **Wt:** 168 **Born:** 10/26/76 **Age:** 23

Year Team	Lg Org	G	GS	CG	GF	IP	BFP	H	R	ER	HR	SH	SF	HB	TBB	IBB	SO	WP	Bk	W	L	Pct.	ShO	Sv	ERA
		HOW MUCH HE PITCHED						WHAT HE GAVE UP												THE RESULTS					
1996 Danville	R+ Atl	27	0	0	21	36.2	145	28	8	7	0	1	1	1	10	0	47	1	1	1	2	.333	0	12	1.72
Eugene	A- Atl	3	0	0	4	4	19	4	2	0	0	0	0	0	2	0	7	0	0	0	0	.000	0	0	0.00
1997 Macon	A Atl	49	0	0	30	71.1	294	52	28	21	4	4	3	5	26	2	102	2	0	3	4	.429	0	8	2.65
1998 Danville	A+ Atl	54	0	0	20	55.2	241	54	26	22	3	3	2	3	24	4	55	2	1	6	8	.429	0	1	3.56
Richmond	AAA Atl	2	0	0	1	6	28	8	3	3	0	2	0	0	2	0	8	0	0	0	0	.000	0	0	4.50
1999 Greenville	AA Atl	50	0	0	22	81.2	349	84	45	42	8	2	4	3	26	5	71	3	1	7	4	.636	0	3	4.63
4 Min. YEARS		185	0	0	94	255.1	1076	230	112	95	15	12	10	12	90	11	290	8	3	17	18	.486	0	31	3.35

Matt Beaumont

Pitches: Left **Bats:** Left **Pos:** P **Ht:** 6'3" **Wt:** 210 **Born:** 4/22/73 **Age:** 27

Year Team	Lg Org	G	GS	CG	GF	IP	BFP	H	R	ER	HR	SH	SF	HB	TBB	IBB	SO	WP	Bk	W	L	Pct.	ShO	Sv	ERA
		HOW MUCH HE PITCHED						WHAT HE GAVE UP												THE RESULTS					
1994 Boise	A- Ana	12	10	0	0	64	268	52	27	25	2	4	2	7	22	1	77	3	0	3	3	.500	0	0	3.52
1995 Lk Elsinore	A+ Ana	27	26	0	0	175.1	724	162	80	64	15	1	6	7	57	1	149	1	1	16	9	.640	0	0	3.29
1996 Midland	AA Ana	28	28	2	0	161.2	746	198	124	105	20	4	6	12	71	0	132	5	0	7	16	.304	0	0	5.85
1997 Midland	AA Ana	4	3	0	0	9.2	62	24	27	27	5	0	0	0	10	0	11	1	0	0	2	.000	0	0	25.14
Lk Elsinore	A+ Ana	1	1	0	0	1.1	7	2	1	1	0	0	0	0	1	0	1	0	1	0	0	.000	0	0	6.75
1998 Midland	AA Ana	34	18	1	6	128.2	583	124	81	60	10	5	4	10	67	1	107	3	1	9	12	.429	0	1	4.20
1999 Erie	AA Ana	32	12	0	6	106.2	474	97	64	56	13	5	3	7	59	0	76	3	3	5	6	.455	0	1	4.73
6 Min. YEARS		138	98	3	12	647.1	2864	659	404	338	65	19	21	43	287	3	553	16	8	40	48	.455	0	2	4.70

Greg Beck

Pitches: Right **Bats:** Right **Pos:** P **Ht:** 6'3" **Wt:** 215 **Born:** 10/21/72 **Age:** 27

Year Team	Lg Org	G	GS	CG	GF	IP	BFP	H	R	ER	HR	SH	SF	HB	TBB	IBB	SO	WP	Bk	W	L	Pct.	ShO	Sv	ERA
		HOW MUCH HE PITCHED						WHAT HE GAVE UP												THE RESULTS					
1994 Helena	R+ Mil	18	2	0	11	43.2	191	42	26	21	4	3	2	2	20	1	41	3	0	4	3	.571	0	4	4.33
1995 Beloit	A Mil	35	5	0	12	74.1	331	73	46	39	2	1	6	2	35	2	91	7	2	5	2	.714	0	2	4.72
1996 Stockton	A+ Mil	28	28	0	0	152.1	695	197	119	104	18	8	7	12	53	1	96	7	0	9	11	.450	0	0	6.14
1997 Stockton	A+ Mil	27	1	0	11	55	222	33	16	15	4	2	1	3	23	2	46	2	0	4	4	.500	0	0	2.45
El Paso	AA Mil	10	0	0	3	48.1	232	75	46	35	8	2	3	5	15	2	37	5	1	1	5	.167	0	0	6.52
1998 El Paso	AA Mil	30	15	0	6	98	452	135	80	73	14	2	3	8	24	2	76	7	1	9	7	.563	0	0	6.70
Louisville	AAA Mil	10	8	1	0	46	204	49	31	29	8	3	2	0	16	0	37	2	0	4	3	.571	0	0	5.67

21

		HOW MUCH HE PITCHED				WHAT HE GAVE UP								THE RESULTS					
Year Team	Lg Org	G	GS	CG	GF	IP	BFP	H	R	ER	HR	SH	SF	HB	TBB	IBB	SO	WP	Bk	W	L	Pct.	ShO	Sv	ERA
1999 Louisville	AAA Mil	1	0	0	0	0.1	4	3	3	3	1	0	0	0	0	0	0	0	0	0	0	.000	0	0	81.00
Huntsville	AA Mil	26	25	0	1	151.2	648	157	79	75	24	5	7	8	48	1	93	12	0	10	9	.526	0	0	4.45
6 Min. YEARS		193	90	1	42	669.2	2979	764	446	394	83	26	31	42	234	11	517	45	3	46	44	.511	0	6	5.30

Brian Becker

Bats: Right **Throws:** Right **Pos:** 1B   **Ht:** 6'7" **Wt:** 220 **Born:** 5/26/75 **Age:** 25

		BATTING														BASERUNNING				PERCENTAGES		
Year Team	Lg Org	G	AB	H	2B	3B	HR	TB	R	RBI	TBB	IBB	SO	HBP	SH	SF	SB	CS	SB%	GDP	Avg	OBP	SLG
1996 Devil Rays	R TB	52	199	54	12	0	2	72	31	27	13	0	28	3	0	4	3	1	.75	3	.271	.320	.362
1997 Chston-SC	A TB	135	494	116	31	2	11	184	55	70	53	3	120	4	0	9	12	1	.92	12	.235	.309	.372
1998 St. Pete	A+ TB	129	492	139	27	4	8	198	64	63	43	1	116	4	0	8	1	1	.50	14	.283	.340	.402
1999 Orlando	AA TB	129	480	121	24	1	18	201	67	74	42	2	89	4	0	3	0	0	.00	16	.252	.316	.419
4 Min. YEARS		445	1665	430	94	7	39	655	217	234	151	6	353	15	0	24	16	3	.84	45	.258	.321	.393

Robbie Beckett

Pitches: Left **Bats:** Right **Pos:** P   **Ht:** 6'5" **Wt:** 238 **Born:** 7/16/72 **Age:** 27

		HOW MUCH HE PITCHED						WHAT HE GAVE UP												THE RESULTS					
Year Team	Lg Org	G	GS	CG	GF	IP	BFP	H	R	ER	HR	SH	SF	HB	TBB	IBB	SO	WP	Bk	W	L	Pct.	ShO	Sv	ERA
1990 Padres	R SD	10	10	0	0	49.1	236	40	28	24	1	3	1	2	45	0	54	8	3	2	5	.286	0	0	4.38
Riverside	A+ SD	3	3	0	0	16.2	76	13	13	13	0	1	0	0	11	0	11	1	1	2	1	.667	0	0	7.02
1991 Chston-SC	A SD	28	26	1	0	109.1	545	115	111	100	5	1	8	3	117	0	96	20	2	2	14	.125	0	0	8.23
1992 Waterloo	A SD	24	24	1	0	120.2	578	77	88	64	4	1	1	6	140	0	147	20	4	4	10	.286	1	0	4.77
1993 Rancho Cuca	A+ SD	37	10	0	14	83.2	413	75	62	56	7	1	7	2	93	1	88	25	3	2	4	.333	0	4	6.02
1994 Wichita	AA SD	33	0	0	14	40	188	30	28	26	2	4	2	1	40	0	59	10	0	1	3	.250	0	2	5.85
Las Vegas	AAA SD	23	0	0	11	23.2	134	27	36	31	4	0	3	0	39	0	30	7	0	1	0	1.000	0	0	11.79
1995 Memphis	AA SD	36	8	2	11	86.1	400	65	57	46	3	2	3	10	73	4	98	19	0	3	4	.429	1	0	4.80
1996 Portland	AA Fla	3	3	0	0	13	66	17	9	9	1	1	2	0	13	0	7	1	0	1	0	1.000	0	0	6.23
New Haven	AA Col	30	4	0	11	48.2	219	38	30	26	7	4	3	1	46	5	55	3	0	6	3	.667	0	0	4.81
Colo Sprngs	AAA Col	12	0	0	4	12.1	55	6	6	3	0	1	0	1	11	0	15	2	0	0	2	.000	0	1	2.19
1997 Colo Sprngs	AAA Col	45	1	0	17	54.1	267	61	49	41	12	1	3	2	47	2	67	13	0	1	3	.250	0	1	6.79
1998 Colo Sprngs	AAA Col	21	0	0	10	26	137	35	27	26	4	0	3	1	28	0	28	3	0	0	0	.000	0	0	9.00
New Haven	AA Col	22	0	0	8	24.2	121	20	14	14	3	1	0	3	23	0	36	5	0	2	1	.667	0	0	5.11
1999 San Antonio	AA LA	18	16	1	2	97.1	451	82	63	56	7	5	6	13	68	1	92	7	0	7	7	.500	1	1	5.18
Albuquerque	AAA LA	15	5	0	1	44	214	50	42	39	8	0	4	3	38	0	54	2	0	1	3	.250	0	0	7.98
1996 Colorado	NL	5	0	0	2	5.1	31	6	8	8	3	0	1	0	9	0	6	1	0	0	0	.000	0	0	13.50
1997 Colorado	NL	2	0	0	2	1.2	7	1	1	1	0	0	0	0	1	1	2	0	0	0	0	.000	0	0	5.40
10 Min. YEARS		360	110	5	106	850	4100	756	663	574	68	26	46	48	832	13	937	146	14	34	61	.358	3	9	6.08
2 Maj. YEARS		7	0	0	4	7	38	7	9	9	3	0	1	0	10	1	8	1	0	0	0	.000	0	0	11.57

Kevin Beirne

Pitches: Right **Bats:** Left **Pos:** P   **Ht:** 6'4" **Wt:** 210 **Born:** 1/1/74 **Age:** 26

		HOW MUCH HE PITCHED						WHAT HE GAVE UP												THE RESULTS					
Year Team	Lg Org	G	GS	CG	GF	IP	BFP	H	R	ER	HR	SH	SF	HB	TBB	IBB	SO	WP	Bk	W	L	Pct.	ShO	Sv	ERA
1995 White Sox	R CWS	2	0	0	2	3.2	15	2	2	1	0	0	0	1	1	0	3	0	0	0	0	.000	0	2	2.45
Bristol	R+ CWS	9	0	0	7	9	35	4	0	0	0	0	0	0	4	0	12	0	0	1	0	1.000	0	2	0.00
Hickory	A CWS	3	0	0	1	4	16	7	2	2	0	0	0	0	0	0	4	0	0	0	0	.000	0	0	4.50
1996 South Bend	A CWS	26	25	1	0	145.1	627	153	85	67	5	5	5	9	60	0	110	12	3	4	11	.267	0	0	4.15
1997 Winston-Sal	A+ CWS	13	13	1	0	82.2	338	66	38	28	7	1	2	7	28	1	75	5	0	4	4	.500	0	0	3.05
Birmingham	AA CWS	13	12	0	1	75	336	76	51	41	4	2	3	4	41	0	49	2	1	6	4	.600	0	0	4.92
1998 Birmingham	AA CWS	26	26	2	0	167.1	702	142	77	64	12	6	6	6	87	2	153	4	2	13	9	.591	1	0	3.44
Calgary	AAA CWS	2	2	0	0	8	38	12	5	4	1	1	1	1	4	0	6	0	0	0	0	.000	0	0	4.50
1999 Charlotte	AAA CWS	20	20	0	0	113	495	134	75	68	14	1	4	2	36	0	63	12	0	5	5	.500	0	0	5.42
5 Min. YEARS		114	98	4	11	608	2602	596	335	275	43	16	21	30	261	3	475	35	6	33	33	.500	1	4	4.07

Todd Belitz

Pitches: Left **Bats:** Left **Pos:** P   **Ht:** 6'1" **Wt:** 218 **Born:** 10/23/75 **Age:** 24

		HOW MUCH HE PITCHED						WHAT HE GAVE UP												THE RESULTS					
Year Team	Lg Org	G	GS	CG	GF	IP	BFP	H	R	ER	HR	SH	SF	HB	TBB	IBB	SO	WP	Bk	W	L	Pct.	ShO	Sv	ERA
1997 Hudson Val	A- TB	15	15	0	0	74	315	65	41	29	4	1	2	5	18	0	78	0	0	4	5	.444	0	0	3.53
1998 Chston-SC	A TB	21	21	0	0	130	530	99	44	35	8	6	1	8	48	0	123	11	1	6	4	.600	0	0	2.42
St. Pete	A+ TB	7	7	0	0	44.2	188	39	28	25	3	2	3	2	14	0	40	2	0	2	2	.500	0	0	5.04
1999 Orlando	AA TB	28	28	0	0	160.2	712	169	114	103	23	3	6	11	65	1	118	2	4	9	9	.500	0	0	5.77
3 Min. YEARS		71	71	0	0	409.1	1745	372	227	192	38	12	12	26	145	1	359	15	5	21	20	.512	0	0	4.22

Tim Belk

Bats: Right **Throws:** Right **Pos:** 1B   **Ht:** 6'3" **Wt:** 200 **Born:** 4/6/70 **Age:** 30

		BATTING														BASERUNNING				PERCENTAGES		
Year Team	Lg Org	G	AB	H	2B	3B	HR	TB	R	RBI	TBB	IBB	SO	HBP	SH	SF	SB	CS	SB%	GDP	Avg	OBP	SLG
1992 Billings	R+ Cin	73	273	78	13	0	12	127	60	56	35	0	33	4	0	6	15	2	.88	6	.286	.368	.465
1993 Winston-Sal	A+ Cin	134	509	156	23	3	14	227	89	65	48	3	76	6	2	2	9	7	.56	8	.306	.372	.446
1994 Indianapols	AAA Cin	6	18	2	1	0	0	3	1	0	1	0	5	0	1	0	0	1	.00	1	.111	.158	.167
Chattanooga	AA Cin	118	411	127	35	4	10	198	64	86	60	5	41	3	0	11	13	8	.62	7	.309	.392	.482
1995 Indianapols	AAA Cin	57	193	58	11	0	4	81	30	18	16	0	30	2	1	0	2	5	.29	9	.301	.360	.420
1996 Indianapols	AAA Cin	120	436	125	27	3	15	203	63	63	27	1	72	2	1	6	5	2	.71	7	.287	.327	.466
1997 Indianapols	AAA Cin	90	255	74	18	1	8	118	37	38	26	1	45	1	3	4	5	3	.63	7	.290	.353	.463
1998 Toledo	AAA Det	84	292	78	19	1	9	126	40	34	18	1	55	0	0	1	5	0	1.00	6	.267	.315	.432

Year Team	Lg Org	G	AB	H	2B	3B	HR	TB	R	RBI	TBB	IBB	SO	HBP	SH	SF	SB	CS	SB%	GDP	Avg	OBP	SLG
1999 Memphis	AAA StL	21	55	11	4	0	3	24	10	8	9	0	9	0	0	0	1	0	1.00	4	.200	.313	.436
Zion	IND —	31	131	45	11	0	10	86	29	30	12	2	28	0	0	1	3	0	1.00	0	.344	.396	.656
1996 Cincinnati	NL	7	15	3	0	0	0	3	2	0	1	0	2	0	0	0	0	0	.00	0	.200	.250	.200
8 Min. YEARS		734	2573	754	162	11	85	1193	423	398	252	13	394	21	8	31	58	28	.67	49	.293	.357	.464

Jason Bell

Pitches: Right **Bats:** Right **Pos:** P   **Ht:** 6'3" **Wt:** 214 **Born:** 9/30/74 **Age:** 25

Year Team	Lg Org	G	GS	CG	GF	IP	BFP	H	R	ER	HR	SH	SF	HB	TBB	IBB	SO	WP	Bk	W	L	Pct.	ShO	Sv	ERA
1995 Fort Wayne	A Min	9	6	0	2	34.1	139	26	11	5	0	3	0	1	6	0	40	6	2	3	1	.750	0	0	1.31
1996 Fort Myers	A+ Min	13	13	0	0	90.1	350	61	20	17	1	4	2	6	22	0	83	3	0	6	3	.667	0	0	1.69
Hardware Cy	AA Min	16	16	2	0	94	410	93	54	46	13	5	2	5	38	1	94	6	1	2	6	.250	1	0	4.40
1997 New Britain	AA Min	28	28	3	0	164.2	700	163	71	62	19	3	2	5	64	0	142	13	2	11	9	.550	1	0	3.39
1998 New Britain	AA Min	29	29	2	0	169.2	694	148	90	88	21	3	2	5	61	1	166	4	1	8	11	.421	0	0	4.67
1999 Salt Lake	AAA Min	18	15	0	0	76.1	364	96	58	54	12	3	4	3	35	0	72	4	1	5	5	.500	0	0	6.37
New Britain	AA Min	7	7	0	0	47.1	198	46	21	18	4	2	1	2	11	0	34	0	1	3	3	.500	0	0	3.42
5 Min. YEARS		120	114	7	2	676.2	2855	633	325	290	70	23	13	27	237	2	631	36	9	38	38	.500	2	0	3.86

Mike Bell

Bats: Right **Throws:** Right **Pos:** 2B-1B   **Ht:** 6'2" **Wt:** 195 **Born:** 12/7/74 **Age:** 25

Year Team	Lg Org	G	AB	H	2B	3B	HR	TB	R	RBI	TBB	IBB	SO	HBP	SH	SF	SB	CS	SB%	GDP	Avg	OBP	SLG
1993 Rangers	R Tex	60	230	73	13	6	3	107	48	34	27	0	23	4	1	2	9	2	.82	2	.317	.395	.465
1994 Chston-SC	A Tex	120	475	125	22	6	6	177	58	58	47	1	76	3	1	6	16	12	.57	14	.263	.330	.373
1995 Charlotte	A+ Tex	129	470	122	20	1	5	159	49	52	48	0	72	0	3	2	9	8	.53	11	.260	.327	.338
1996 Tulsa	AA Tex	128	484	129	31	3	16	214	62	59	42	1	75	3	4	0	3	1	.75	13	.267	.329	.442
1997 Okla City	AAA Tex	93	328	77	18	2	5	114	35	38	29	0	78	4	0	3	4	2	.67	10	.235	.302	.348
Tulsa	AA Tex	33	123	35	11	0	8	70	17	23	15	0	28	4	2	2	0	1	.00	2	.285	.375	.569
1998 Norfolk	AAA NYM	17	44	8	1	0	2	15	6	8	8	1	7	0	0	1	0	0	.00	0	.182	.302	.341
St. Lucie	A+ NYM	18	63	22	5	2	1	34	11	14	8	2	10	2	2	5	2	1	.67	1	.349	.410	.540
Binghamton	AA NYM	78	275	73	14	1	14	131	47	56	35	1	50	2	0	6	3	5	.38	5	.265	.346	.476
1999 Norfolk	AAA NYM	39	135	37	11	1	1	53	11	25	9	1	23	2	0	2	4	2	.67	5	.274	.324	.393
7 Min. YEARS		715	2627	701	146	22	61	1074	344	367	268	7	442	24	13	29	50	34	.60	63	.267	.337	.409

Mike Bell

Pitches: Left **Bats:** Left **Pos:** P   **Ht:** 6'2" **Wt:** 195 **Born:** 10/14/72 **Age:** 27

Year Team	Lg Org	G	GS	CG	GF	IP	BFP	H	R	ER	HR	SH	SF	HB	TBB	IBB	SO	WP	Bk	W	L	Pct.	ShO	Sv	ERA
1995 Vermont	A- Mon	7	0	0	4	16.2	59	7	5	1	0	1	0	1	5	2	12	0	0	0	0	.000	0	1	0.54
Albany	A Mon	12	0	0	4	20.2	81	13	8	6	0	2	0	1	8	0	14	0	0	3	3	.500	0	2	2.61
1996 Wst Plm Bch	A+ Mon	13	0	0	5	15.1	82	27	19	15	1	2	0	1	11	1	11	1	0	0	1	.000	0	0	8.80
Delmarva	A Mon	40	0	0	15	59.2	232	39	13	9	1	6	0	3	18	0	59	1	1	6	1	.857	0	5	1.36
1997 Wst Plm Bch	A+ Mon	41	3	0	15	81.1	328	60	30	28	2	4	2	5	27	0	56	2	0	5	4	.556	0	4	3.10
1998 Jupiter	A+ Mon	5	0	0	2	7	37	16	8	4	1	0	1	0	2	0	5	2	0	1	0	.000	0	0	5.14
Frederick	A+ Bal	38	0	0	20	60.1	236	53	22	18	3	6	3	2	13	2	38	3	0	7	4	.636	0	7	2.69
1999 Bowie	AA Bal	41	13	0	5	131.1	575	134	80	67	13	4	3	12	49	1	79	3	1	7	7	.500	0	0	4.59
5 Min. YEARS		197	16	0	70	392.1	1630	349	185	148	21	25	9	25	133	6	274	12	2	28	21	.571	0	18	3.40

Rob Bell

Pitches: Right **Bats:** Right **Pos:** P   **Ht:** 6'5" **Wt:** 225 **Born:** 1/17/77 **Age:** 23

Year Team	Lg Org	G	GS	CG	GF	IP	BFP	H	R	ER	HR	SH	SF	HB	TBB	IBB	SO	WP	Bk	W	L	Pct.	ShO	Sv	ERA
1995 Braves	R Atl	10	8	0	0	34	154	38	29	26	2	0	2	2	14	0	33	7	0	1	6	.143	0	0	6.88
1996 Eugene	A- Atl	16	16	0	0	81	356	89	49	46	5	5	3	3	29	1	74	2	0	5	6	.455	0	0	5.11
1997 Macon	A Atl	27	27	1	0	146.2	614	144	72	60	15	5	5	3	41	1	140	7	0	14	7	.667	0	0	3.68
1998 Danville	A+ Atl	28	28	2	0	178.1	736	169	79	65	8	6	6	7	46	0	197	8	0	7	9	.438	0	0	3.28
1999 Reds	R Cin	2	2	0	0	8	36	3	1	1	0	1	0	0	0	0	11	1	0	0	0	.000	0	0	1.13
Chattanooga	AA Cin	12	12	2	0	72	293	75	30	25	7	2	2	0	17	0	68	1	0	3	6	.333	1	0	3.13
5 Min. YEARS		95	93	5	0	520	2179	518	260	223	37	19	18	15	147	2	523	26	0	30	34	.469	1	0	3.86

Mark Bellhorn

Bats: Both **Throws:** Right **Pos:** 2B   **Ht:** 6'1" **Wt:** 214 **Born:** 8/23/74 **Age:** 25

Year Team	Lg Org	G	AB	H	2B	3B	HR	TB	R	RBI	TBB	IBB	SO	HBP	SH	SF	SB	CS	SB%	GDP	Avg	OBP	SLG
1995 Modesto	A+ Oak	56	229	59	12	0	6	89	35	31	27	0	52	4	2	0	5	2	.71	9	.258	.346	.389
1996 Huntsville	AA Oak	131	468	117	24	5	10	181	84	71	73	7	124	4	7	4	19	2	.90	7	.250	.353	.387
1997 Edmonton	AAA Oak	70	241	79	18	3	11	136	54	46	64	2	59	2	3	0	6	6	.50	4	.328	.472	.564
1998 Edmonton	AAA Oak	87	309	77	20	4	10	135	57	44	62	0	90	6	0	1	6	2	.75	8	.249	.384	.437
1999 Athletics	R Oak	12	43	10	3	0	0	13	11	5	11	2	9	0	0	0	0	0	.00	1	.233	.389	.302
Midland	AA Oak	17	57	17	3	0	2	26	12	8	11	0	13	0	0	0	1	0	1.00	2	.298	.412	.456
1997 Oakland	AL	68	224	51	9	1	6	80	33	19	32	0	70	0	5	0	7	1	.88	1	.228	.324	.357
1998 Oakland	AL	11	12	1	1	0	0	2	1	1	3	0	4	1	0	0	2	0	1.00	0	.083	.313	.167
5 Min. YEARS		373	1347	359	80	12	39	580	253	205	248	11	347	16	12	5	37	12	.76	31	.267	.386	.431
2 Maj. YEARS		79	236	52	10	1	6	82	34	20	35	0	74	1	5	0	9	1	.90	1	.220	.324	.347

Francisco Belliard

Bats: Both **Throws:** Right **Pos:** 2B **Ht:** 5'11" **Wt:** 165 **Born:** 11/27/79 **Age:** 20

		BATTING														BASERUNNING				PERCENTAGES		
Year Team	Lg Org	G	AB	H	2B	3B	HR	TB	R	RBI	TBB	IBB	SO	HBP	SH	SF	SB	CS	SB%	GDP	Avg	OBP	SLG
1999 High Desert	A+ Ari	16	47	12	1	1	0	15	4	1	4	0	16	1	2	0	1	1	.50	0	.255	.327	.319
Tucson	AAA Ari	3	7	1	0	0	0	1	0	2	1	0	3	0	0	0	0	0	.00	0	.143	.250	.143
South Bend	A Ari	70	265	66	11	1	0	79	28	15	20	0	64	2	2	0	3	2	.60	7	.249	.307	.298
1 Min. YEARS		89	319	79	12	2	0	95	32	18	25	0	83	3	4	0	4	3	.57	7	.248	.308	.298

Josh Belovsky

Pitches: Right **Bats:** Right **Pos:** P **Ht:** 6'2" **Wt:** 225 **Born:** 4/8/74 **Age:** 26

		HOW MUCH HE PITCHED						WHAT HE GAVE UP										THE RESULTS					
Year Team	Lg Org	G	GS	CG	GF	IP	BFP	H	R	ER	HR	SH	SF	HB	TBB	IBB	SO	WP	Bk	W	L	Pct.	ShO	Sv	ERA
1998 Missn Viejo	IND —	45	0	0	37	56	208	27	11	10	3	4	1	0	15	0	64	5	1	5	1	.833	0	13	1.61
1999 Trenton	AA Bos	1	0	0	0	1.1	10	4	5	5	0	0	0	0	2	0	2	0	0	0	0	.000	0	0	33.75
Sarasota	A+ Bos	48	0	0	43	53.1	223	42	15	14	1	7	0	4	23	5	53	5	0	6	2	.750	0	20	2.36
2 Min. YEARS		94	0	0	80	110.2	441	73	31	29	4	11	1	4	40	5	119	10	1	11	3	.786	0	33	2.36

Alonso Beltran

Pitches: Right **Bats:** Right **Pos:** P **Ht:** 6'3" **Wt:** 180 **Born:** 3/4/72 **Age:** 28

		HOW MUCH HE PITCHED						WHAT HE GAVE UP										THE RESULTS					
Year Team	Lg Org	G	GS	CG	GF	IP	BFP	H	R	ER	HR	SH	SF	HB	TBB	IBB	SO	WP	Bk	W	L	Pct.	ShO	Sv	ERA
1991 Blue Jays	R Tor	14	3	0	7	33	126	26	9	7	0	1	3	1	7	0	30	1	1	2	0	1.000	0	3	1.91
1992 Medcine Hat	R+ Tor	15	15	1	0	91.2	378	78	46	32	7	4	3	7	25	0	66	4	2	4	5	.444	0	0	3.14
1993 St.Cathrnes	A- Tor	15	15	1	0	99	392	63	36	26	4	1	3	6	28	0	101	2	0	11	2	.846	1	0	2.36
1994 Dunedin	A+ Tor	7	5	0	0	25.1	109	22	13	13	4	0	2	1	10	0	10	1	0	2	1	.667	0	0	4.62
1995 Knoxville	AA Tor	28	6	0	7	87	399	111	60	55	8	3	4	5	32	0	54	6	2	3	6	.333	0	1	5.69
1996 Winston-Sal	A+ Cin	14	1	0	4	38.1	148	26	9	8	2	2	0	1	10	1	26	1	2	2	1	.667	0	0	1.88
Chattanooga	AA Cin	3	3	0	0	13.1	62	18	13	12	2	0	0	1	6	0	10	0	0	0	1	.000	0	0	8.10
1997 Lubbock	IND —	18	18	1	0	100.2	452	115	61	58	14	1	2	4	45	0	66	5	1	4	4	.500	1	0	5.19
1999 Altoona	AA Pit	13	0	0	1	18	86	27	18	18	2	0	1	0	9	0	18	1	0	0	2	.000	0	1	9.00
8 Min. YEARS		127	66	3	19	506.1	2152	486	265	229	43	12	18	26	172	1	381	21	8	28	22	.560	2	5	4.07

Esteban Beltre

Bats: Right **Throws:** Right **Pos:** SS **Ht:** 5'10" **Wt:** 180 **Born:** 12/26/67 **Age:** 32

		BATTING														BASERUNNING				PERCENTAGES		
Year Team	Lg Org	G	AB	H	2B	3B	HR	TB	R	RBI	TBB	IBB	SO	HBP	SH	SF	SB	CS	SB%	GDP	Avg	OBP	SLG
1984 Calgary	R+ Mon	18	20	4	0	0	0	4	1	2	2	0	8	0	0	0	1	0	1.00	1	.200	.273	.200
1985 Utica	A- Mon	72	241	48	6	2	0	58	19	22	18	0	58	3	8	1	8	7	.53	4	.199	.262	.241
1986 Wst Plm Bch	A+ Mon	97	285	69	11	1	1	85	24	20	16	2	59	0	4	1	4	2	.67	9	.242	.281	.298
1987 Jacksnville	AA Mon	142	491	104	15	4	4	139	55	34	40	0	98	3	10	0	9	8	.53	7	.212	.275	.283
1988 Jacksnville	AA Mon	35	113	17	2	0	0	19	5	6	3	0	28	0	0	0	1	0	1.00	1	.150	.172	.168
Wst Plm Bch	A+ Mon	69	226	63	5	6	0	80	23	15	11	0	38	1	11	1	4	0	1.00	4	.279	.314	.354
1989 Rockford	A Mon	104	375	80	15	3	2	107	42	33	33	1	83	0	5	1	9	3	.75	8	.213	.276	.285
1990 Indianapols	AAA Mon	133	407	92	11	2	1	110	33	37	32	1	77	2	5	4	8	2	.80	9	.226	.283	.270
1991 Denver	AAA Mil	27	78	14	1	3	0	21	11	9	9	0	16	0	0	0	3	2	.60	5	.179	.264	.269
Vancouver	AAA CWS	88	347	94	11	3	0	111	48	30	23	0	61	0	7	1	8	7	.53	4	.271	.315	.320
1992 Vancouver	AAA CWS	40	161	43	5	2	0	52	17	16	8	1	27	1	5	1	4	4	.50	3	.267	.304	.323
1993 Nashville	AAA CWS	134	489	143	24	4	8	199	67	52	33	1	102	0	5	0	18	6	.75	13	.292	.337	.407
1996 Scranton-WB	AAA Phi	4	15	2	0	0	0	2	1	1	0	0	1	0	0	0	0	0	.00	0	.133	.133	.133
Richmond	AAA Atl	10	28	7	3	0	0	10	3	0	1	0	2	0	0	0	0	0	.00	0	.250	.276	.357
1997 St. Paul	IND —	0	0	0	0	0	0	0	0	0	0	0	0	0	0	0	0	0	.00	0	.000	.000	.000
1998 Salt Lake	AAA Min	133	510	142	24	4	2	180	84	49	39	0	109	0	5	4	26	11	.70	7	.278	.327	.353
1999 Rochester	AAA Bal	92	314	83	19	3	1	111	45	23	23	1	64	1	4	1	5	3	.63	11	.264	.316	.354
Charlotte	AAA CWS	38	121	31	8	0	2	45	27	17	7	0	16	0	3	2	4	0	1.00	6	.256	.292	.372
1991 Chicago	AL	8	6	1	0	0	0	1	0	0	1	0	1	0	0	0	1	0	1.00	1	.167	.286	.167
1992 Chicago	AL	49	110	21	2	0	1	26	21	10	3	0	18	0	2	1	1	0	1.00	3	.191	.211	.236
1994 Texas	AL	48	131	37	5	0	0	42	12	12	16	0	25	0	5	1	2	5	.29	3	.282	.358	.321
1995 Texas	AL	54	92	20	8	0	0	28	7	7	4	0	15	0	3	0	0	0	.00	1	.217	.250	.304
1996 Boston	AL	27	62	16	2	0	0	18	6	6	4	0	14	0	1	1	1	0	1.00	1	.258	.299	.290
14 Min. YEARS		1237	4221	1036	160	37	21	1333	505	366	298	7	847	11	72	17	112	55	.67	94	.245	.296	.316
5 Maj. YEARS		186	401	95	17	0	1	115	46	35	28	0	73	0	11	3	5	5	.50	8	.237	.285	.287

Brian Benefield

Bats: Right **Throws:** Right **Pos:** 2B **Ht:** 6'0" **Wt:** 181 **Born:** 8/12/76 **Age:** 23

		BATTING														BASERUNNING				PERCENTAGES		
Year Team	Lg Org	G	AB	H	2B	3B	HR	TB	R	RBI	TBB	IBB	SO	HBP	SH	SF	SB	CS	SB%	GDP	Avg	OBP	SLG
1997 Watertown	A- Cle	69	265	76	9	1	4	99	47	19	49	3	40	1	2	1	23	7	.77	3	.287	.399	.374
1998 Kinston	A+ Cle	71	260	57	9	2	5	85	44	34	31	1	50	4	4	2	8	4	.67	1	.220	.311	.328
1999 Columbus	A Cle	81	303	83	14	1	15	144	60	51	43	1	67	8	2	5	18	12	.60	4	.274	.373	.475
Akron	AA Cle	44	145	28	3	2	3	44	14	14	16	0	32	0	0	0	3	3	.50	1	.193	.273	.303
3 Min. YEARS		265	972	244	35	6	27	372	165	118	139	5	189	13	8	8	52	26	.67	9	.251	.350	.383

Adam Benes

Pitches: Right **Bats:** Left **Pos:** P **Ht:** 6'2" **Wt:** 195 **Born:** 3/12/73 **Age:** 27

		HOW MUCH HE PITCHED						WHAT HE GAVE UP										THE RESULTS					
Year Team	Lg Org	G	GS	CG	GF	IP	BFP	H	R	ER	HR	SH	SF	HB	TBB	IBB	SO	WP	Bk	W	L	Pct.	ShO	Sv	ERA
1995 New Jersey	A- StL	19	10	0	3	75	311	71	30	28	3	0	4	3	23	0	47	5	2	5	3	.625	0	0	3.36

24

Year Team	Lg Org	G	GS	CG	GF	IP	BFP	H	R	ER	HR	SH	SF	HB	TBB	IBB	SO	WP	Bk	W	L	Pct.	ShO	Sv	ERA
		HOW MUCH HE PITCHED						WHAT HE GAVE UP												THE RESULTS					
1996 Peoria	A StL	43	0	0	15	65	278	58	31	27	4	2	0	2	28	0	64	2	1	2	2	.500	0	0	3.74
1997 Pr William	A+ StL	33	5	0	9	70.1	326	92	54	49	15	3	2	2	29	0	44	4	0	3	3	.500	0	0	6.27
1998 Pr William	A+ StL	10	0	0	1	13.1	58	12	6	2	1	0	0	0	4	0	9	0	0	1	0	1.000	0	0	1.35
Arkansas	AA StL	12	0	0	6	16.1	73	21	12	11	2	1	2	1	2	1	8	2	0	0	0	.000	0	0	6.06
1999 Arkansas	AA StL	28	0	0	10	40.1	182	51	30	24	9	0	2	1	15	1	19	0	1	1	1	.500	0	0	5.36
5 Min. YEARS		145	15	0	44	280.1	1228	305	163	141	34	6	10	9	101	2	191	13	4	12	9	.571	0	0	4.53

Yamil Benitez

Bats: Right **Throws:** Right **Pos:** OF **Ht:** 6' 2" **Wt:** 207 **Born:** 5/10/72 **Age:** 28

Year Team	Lg Org	G	AB	H	2B	3B	HR	TB	R	RBI	TBB	IBB	SO	HBP	SH	SF	SB	CS	SB%	GDP	Avg	OBP	SLG
		BATTING															BASERUNNING				PERCENTAGES		
1990 Expos	R Mon	22	83	19	1	0	1	23	6	5	8	0	18	0	0	0	0	0	.00	1	.229	.297	.277
1991 Expos	R Mon	54	197	47	9	5	5	81	20	38	12	1	55	1	1	5	10	5	.67	3	.239	.279	.411
1992 Albany	A Mon	23	79	13	3	2	1	23	6	6	5	1	49	0	0	0	0	2	.00	1	.165	.214	.291
Jamestown	A- Mon	44	162	44	6	6	3	71	24	23	14	0	52	2	1	0	19	1	.95	5	.272	.337	.438
1993 Burlington	A Mon	111	411	112	21	5	15	188	70	61	29	1	99	3	6	3	18	7	.72	8	.273	.323	.457
1994 Harrisburg	AA Mon	126	475	123	18	4	17	200	58	91	36	2	134	2	1	4	18	15	.55	12	.259	.311	.421
1995 Ottawa	AAA Mon	127	474	123	24	6	18	213	66	69	44	3	128	2	2	2	14	6	.70	10	.259	.324	.449
1996 Ottawa	AAA Mon	114	439	122	20	2	23	215	56	81	28	5	120	1	0	6	11	4	.73	5	.278	.319	.490
1997 Omaha	AAA KC	92	329	97	14	1	21	176	61	71	24	1	82	1	0	4	12	3	.80	8	.295	.341	.535
1999 Louisville	AAA Mil	99	341	73	24	2	12	137	47	49	29	0	103	2	1	1	13	4	.76	7	.214	.279	.402
1995 Montreal	NL	14	39	15	2	1	2	25	8	7	1	0	7	0	0	0	0	2	.00	1	.385	.400	.641
1996 Montreal	NL	11	12	2	0	0	0	2	0	2	0	0	4	0	0	0	0	0	.00	0	.167	.167	.167
1997 Kansas City	AL	53	191	51	7	1	8	84	22	21	10	0	49	1	2	0	2	2	.50	2	.267	.307	.440
1998 Arizona	NL	91	206	41	7	1	9	77	17	30	14	1	46	4	0	1	2	2	.50	6	.199	.262	.374
9 Min. YEARS		812	2990	773	140	33	116	1327	414	494	229	14	840	14	12	25	115	47	.71	60	.259	.312	.444
4 Maj. YEARS		169	448	109	16	3	19	188	47	60	25	1	106	5	2	1	4	6	.40	9	.243	.290	.420

Erik Bennett

Pitches: Right **Bats:** Right **Pos:** P **Ht:** 6' 2" **Wt:** 205 **Born:** 9/13/68 **Age:** 31

Year Team	Lg Org	G	GS	CG	GF	IP	BFP	H	R	ER	HR	SH	SF	HB	TBB	IBB	SO	WP	Bk	W	L	Pct.	ShO	Sv	ERA
		HOW MUCH HE PITCHED						WHAT HE GAVE UP												THE RESULTS					
1989 Bend	A- Ana	15	15	2	0	96	422	96	58	37	4	3	2	3	36	0	96	8	6	6	8	.429	0	0	3.47
1990 Quad City	A Ana	18	18	3	0	108.1	453	91	48	36	9	5	6	4	37	0	100	2	4	7	7	.500	1	0	2.99
1991 Palm Spring	A+ Ana	8	8	1	0	43	192	41	15	12	2	3	0	3	27	0	31	0	0	2	3	.400	0	0	2.51
1992 Quad City	A Ana	8	8	1	0	57.1	238	46	20	17	0	3	5	4	22	0	59	3	1	3	3	.500	1	0	2.67
Palm Spring	A+ Ana	6	6	1	0	42	171	27	19	17	0	2	1	4	15	0	33	2	1	4	2	.667	0	0	3.64
Midland	AA Ana	7	7	0	0	46	195	47	22	20	3	3	2	7	16	0	36	1	0	1	3	.250	0	0	3.91
1993 Midland	AA Ana	11	11	0	0	69.1	308	87	57	50	12	2	6	6	17	1	33	1	0	5	4	.556	0	0	6.49
Vancouver	AAA Ana	18	12	0	1	80.1	353	101	57	54	10	1	0	4	21	0	51	3	0	6	6	.500	0	1	6.05
1994 Vancouver	AAA Ana	45	1	0	14	89.2	375	71	32	28	9	2	4	10	28	2	83	8	2	1	4	.200	0	3	2.81
1995 Vancouver	AAA Ana	28	0	0	12	50.2	206	44	24	24	5	0	2	3	18	2	39	4	1	6	0	1.000	0	2	4.26
Tucson	AAA Hou	14	1	0	4	22.2	110	27	17	12	1	0	3	2	14	2	24	0	0	3	1	.750	0	1	4.76
1996 Salt Lake	AAA Min	17	0	0	4	24	114	27	17	17	4	0	2	2	14	1	10	0	0	3	1	.750	0	0	6.38
1997 Akron	AA Cle	11	1	0	5	24.1	107	26	13	13	1	0	0	1	9	1	20	1	1	2	3	.400	0	0	4.81
1998 Bend	IND —	32	1	0	20	60.1	266	49	45	40	5	5	4	6	26	4	57	1	0	4	4	.500	0	5	5.97
1999 Tri-City	IND —	22	0	0	9	36.2	134	16	4	2	0	2	1	3	11	0	40	1	0	2	1	.667	0	2	0.49
Jackson	AA Hou	20	0	0	8	28.1	122	23	14	13	1	0	1	4	12	3	32	0	0	3	0	.000	0	1	4.13
1995 California	AL	1	0	0	1	0.1	1	0	0	0	0	0	0	0	0	0	0	0	0	0	0	.000	0	0	0.00
1996 Minnesota	AL	24	0	0	10	27.1	130	33	24	24	7	3	1	2	16	1	13	1	0	2	0	1.000	0	1	7.90
11 Min. YEARS		280	89	8	77	879	3766	819	462	392	70	34	39	66	323	16	744	35	16	55	53	.509	2	15	4.01
2 Maj. YEARS		25	0	0	11	27.2	131	33	24	24	7	3	1	2	16	1	13	1	0	2	0	1.000	0	1	7.81

Ryan Bennett

Bats: Right **Throws:** Right **Pos:** C **Ht:** 6'0" **Wt:** 195 **Born:** 7/26/74 **Age:** 25

Year Team	Lg Org	G	AB	H	2B	3B	HR	TB	R	RBI	TBB	IBB	SO	HBP	SH	SF	SB	CS	SB%	GDP	Avg	OBP	SLG
		BATTING															BASERUNNING				PERCENTAGES		
1996 Pittsfield	A- NYM	27	79	19	2	1	0	23	11	14	13	1	21	0	0	2	0	0	.00	1	.241	.340	.291
1997 St. Lucie	A+ NYM	2	2	0	0	0	0	0	0	0	0	0	2	0	0	0	0	0	.00	0	.000	.000	.000
Capital Cty	A NYM	19	42	8	1	0	0	9	6	3	5	0	15	0	0	0	0	0	.00	1	.190	.277	.214
1998 Capital Cty	A NYM	57	175	50	6	1	2	64	20	20	18	0	49	1	3	1	2	0	1.00	3	.286	.354	.366
1999 Binghamton	AA NYM	1	4	0	0	0	0	0	1	0	0	0	2	0	0	0	0	0	.00	0	.000	.000	.000
St. Lucie	A+ NYM	56	165	37	4	0	0	41	19	12	19	0	32	1	3	3	2	1	.67	5	.224	.303	.248
4 Min. YEARS		162	467	114	13	2	2	137	57	49	55	1	121	2	6	6	4	1	.80	10	.244	.323	.293

Jake Benz

Pitches: Left **Bats:** Left **Pos:** P **Ht:** 5'9" **Wt:** 162 **Born:** 2/27/72 **Age:** 28

Year Team	Lg Org	G	GS	CG	GF	IP	BFP	H	R	ER	HR	SH	SF	HB	TBB	IBB	SO	WP	Bk	W	L	Pct.	ShO	Sv	ERA
		HOW MUCH HE PITCHED						WHAT HE GAVE UP												THE RESULTS					
1994 Vermont	A- Mon	28	0	0	12	46	188	24	11	8	1	1	2	4	19	3	36	1	0	4	1	.800	0	3	1.57
1995 Wst Plm Bch	A+ Mon	44	0	0	38	54	220	44	13	7	0	3	2	3	18	3	48	4	1	0	2	.000	0	22	1.17
1996 Harrisburg	AA Mon	34	0	0	20	37.2	181	42	30	25	7	3	2	2	27	3	25	4	0	1	4	.200	0	4	5.97
Wst Plm Bch	A+ Mon	17	0	0	9	20.1	93	19	10	5	0	4	0	0	11	1	14	7	0	2	4	.333	0	2	2.21
1997 Wst Plm Bch	A+ Mon	14	0	0	3	24	94	18	9	7	1	1	1	2	6	0	28	3	0	0	0	.000	0	2	2.63
Harrisburg	AA Mon	23	0	0	9	38.2	169	39	13	10	0	0	1	1	20	0	30	4	0	4	1	.800	0	2	2.33
1998 Harrisburg	AA Mon	16	0	0	7	33.1	133	19	5	4	2	1	1	1	11	3	31	0	0	3	1	.750	0	4	1.08
Ottawa	AAA Mon	25	3	0	8	49.1	230	63	34	32	8	3	1	2	24	2	40	3	0	1	5	.167	0	1	5.84

Year Team	Lg Org	G	GS	CG	GF	IP	BFP	H	R	ER	HR	SH	SF	HB	TBB	IBB	SO	WP	Bk	W	L	Pct.	ShO	Sv	ERA
		HOW MUCH HE PITCHED						WHAT HE GAVE UP												THE RESULTS					
1999 Ottawa	AAA Mon	18	0	0	9	30.1	152	42	27	20	2	1	4	1	20	3	34	2	0	2	3	.400	0	1	5.93
Calgary	AAA Fla	2	0	0	0	4	18	3	1	0	0	0	0	0	3	0	4	0	0	1	0	1.000	0	0	0.00
Portland	AA Fla	23	0	0	11	33.1	152	33	19	16	6	0	2	0	23	0	24	3	1	1	0	1.000	0	0	4.32
6 Min. YEARS		244	3	0	126	371	1629	346	171	134	28	20	16	16	182	18	320	31	2	19	23	.452	0	39	3.25

Angel Berroa

Bats: Right **Throws:** Right **Pos:** SS   **Ht:** 6'0" **Wt:** 175 **Born:** 1/27/80 **Age:** 20

Year Team	Lg Org	G	AB	H	2B	3B	HR	TB	R	RBI	TBB	IBB	SO	HBP	SH	SF	SB	CS	SB%	GDP	Avg	OBP	SLG
		BATTING															BASERUNNING				PERCENTAGES		
1999 Athletics	R Oak	46	169	49	11	4	2	74	42	24	16	0	26	7	0	2	11	4	.73	1	.290	.371	.438
Midland	AA Oak	4	17	1	1	0	0	2	3	0	0	0	2	0	0	0	0	0	.00	0	.059	.059	.118
1 Min. YEARS		50	186	50	12	4	2	76	45	24	16	0	28	7	0	2	11	4	.73	1	.269	.346	.409

Mike Berry

Bats: Right **Throws:** Right **Pos:** 3B   **Ht:** 5'10" **Wt:** 185 **Born:** 8/12/70 **Age:** 29

Year Team	Lg Org	G	AB	H	2B	3B	HR	TB	R	RBI	TBB	IBB	SO	HBP	SH	SF	SB	CS	SB%	GDP	Avg	OBP	SLG
		BATTING															BASERUNNING				PERCENTAGES		
1993 Burlington	A Mon	31	92	22	2	0	1	27	15	6	20	0	22	0	3	0	0	1	.00	4	.239	.375	.293
1994 Burlington	A Mon	94	334	105	18	1	10	155	67	45	53	0	59	1	1	1	7	3	.70	1	.314	.409	.464
1995 Wst Plm Bch	A+ Mon	24	79	13	3	1	1	21	16	2	13	0	16	0	0	0	0	1	.00	1	.165	.283	.266
Visalia	A+ Mon	98	368	113	28	4	9	176	69	61	57	1	70	5	1	3	12	6	.67	9	.307	.404	.478
1996 Frederick	A+ Bal	3	8	1	0	0	0	4	2	1	4	0	2	0	0	0	0	0	.00	1	.125	.417	.500
Bowie	AA Bal	2	7	1	0	0	0	1	1	2	0	0	4	0	0	1	0	0	.00	0	.143	.125	.143
High Desert	A+ Bal	121	463	167	44	5	13	260	109	113	99	3	67	7	0	3	7	4	.64	9	.361	.477	.562
1997 Bowie	AA Bal	53	204	47	10	0	8	81	34	30	24	0	53	3	1	2	1	1	.50	6	.230	.318	.397
Rochester	AAA Bal	54	177	53	11	3	1	73	23	19	13	0	31	1	0	1	1	1	.50	4	.299	.349	.412
1998 Columbus	AAA NYY	25	87	25	6	0	1	34	7	9	10	0	14	0	0	4	0	0	.00	2	.287	.347	.391
Norwich	AA NYY	107	399	117	35	2	14	198	50	63	53	1	58	3	0	5	8	2	.80	5	.293	.376	.496
1999 Carolina	AA Col	90	306	74	15	2	9	120	36	38	26	0	61	2	0	3	0	2	.00	11	.242	.303	.392
7 Min. YEARS		702	2524	738	172	18	68	1150	429	389	372	5	457	22	6	23	36	21	.63	62	.292	.385	.456

Mike Bertotti

Pitches: Left **Bats:** Left **Pos:** P   **Ht:** 6'1" **Wt:** 185 **Born:** 1/18/70 **Age:** 30

Year Team	Lg Org	G	GS	CG	GF	IP	BFP	H	R	ER	HR	SH	SF	HB	TBB	IBB	SO	WP	Bk	W	L	Pct.	ShO	Sv	ERA
		HOW MUCH HE PITCHED						WHAT HE GAVE UP												THE RESULTS					
1991 Utica	A- CWS	14	5	0	3	37.1	186	38	33	24	2	1	3	2	36	0	33	9	0	3	4	.429	0	0	5.79
1992 South Bend	A CWS	11	0	0	5	19.1	86	12	8	8	1	1	1	1	22	0	17	1	1	3	0	.000	0	1	3.72
Utica	A- CWS	17	1	0	5	33.1	164	36	28	23	2	0	1	2	31	0	23	7	1	2	2	.500	0	1	6.21
1993 Hickory	A CWS	9	9	2	0	59.2	248	42	19	14	2	4	0	1	29	1	77	2	3	3	3	.500	0	0	2.11
South Bend	A CWS	17	16	2	0	111	466	93	51	43	5	6	6	6	44	2	108	7	1	5	7	.417	2	0	3.49
1994 Pr William	A+ CWS	16	15	2	0	104.2	435	90	48	41	13	2	1	3	43	0	103	8	1	7	6	.538	1	0	3.53
Birmingham	AA CWS	10	10	1	0	68.1	273	55	25	22	1	2	3	0	21	1	44	5	0	4	3	.571	1	0	2.90
1995 Birmingham	AA CWS	12	12	1	0	63	279	60	38	35	4	0	4	2	36	0	53	8	0	2	7	.222	0	0	5.00
Nashville	AAA CWS	7	6	0	1	32	154	41	34	31	8	0	1	3	17	0	35	0	0	2	3	.400	0	0	8.72
1996 Nashville	AAA CWS	28	9	1	5	82.1	365	80	43	40	10	5	4	2	42	3	73	3	0	5	3	.625	0	1	4.37
1997 Nashville	AAA CWS	21	20	1	0	107.2	505	91	70	64	17	1	7	2	105	0	87	15	0	5	9	.357	0	0	5.35
1998 Calgary	AAA CWS	43	6	0	16	80.1	383	90	56	53	10	3	6	4	50	0	64	8	0	3	2	.600	0	3	5.94
1999 Tacoma	AAA Sea	3	3	0	0	7	43	6	8	8	0	1	0	1	17	0	6	1	0	0	2	.000	0	0	10.29
Midland	AA Oak	20	0	0	6	25.2	141	30	26	24	0	0	1	1	37	0	25	7	0	2	3	.400	0	1	8.42
Waterbury	IND —	7	7	0	0	35.2	159	39	25	24	5	0	3	1	17	0	40	3	0	1	0	.000	0	0	6.06
1995 Chicago	AL	4	4	0	0	14.1	80	23	20	20	6	0	3	3	11	0	15	2	1	1	1	.500	0	0	12.56
1996 Chicago	AL	15	2	0	4	28	130	28	18	16	5	0	1	0	20	3	19	4	0	2	0	1.000	0	0	5.14
1997 Chicago	AL	9	0	0	2	3.2	23	9	3	3	0	0	1	0	2	0	4	0	1	0	0	.000	0	0	7.36
9 Min. YEARS		235	119	10	41	867.1	3887	803	512	454	80	26	41	30	547	7	788	84	7	43	58	.426	4	7	4.71
3 Maj. YEARS		28	6	0	6	46	233	60	41	39	11	0	5	3	33	3	38	6	2	3	1	.750	0	0	7.63

Junior Betances

Bats: Right **Throws:** Right **Pos:** 2B   **Ht:** 5'11" **Wt:** 165 **Born:** 5/26/73 **Age:** 27

Year Team	Lg Org	G	AB	H	2B	3B	HR	TB	R	RBI	TBB	IBB	SO	HBP	SH	SF	SB	CS	SB%	GDP	Avg	OBP	SLG
		BATTING															BASERUNNING				PERCENTAGES		
1994 Helena	R+ Mil	66	212	56	8	3	2	76	37	21	34	1	38	1	6	2	12	6	.67	1	.264	.365	.358
1995 Beloit	A Mil	122	427	125	21	8	1	165	66	52	61	1	67	2	7	7	21	9	.70	9	.293	.378	.386
1996 Stockton	A+ Mil	125	458	116	9	7	1	142	69	41	51	0	61	6	4	6	14	11	.56	9	.253	.332	.310
1997 Kinston	A+ Cle	74	230	64	10	2	4	90	34	26	24	0	34	3	3	3	8	4	.67	5	.278	.350	.391
1998 Akron	AA Cle	76	269	76	10	5	6	114	41	31	25	1	54	2	2	0	11	2	.85	4	.283	.348	.424
1999 Akron	AA Cle	89	306	90	14	5	2	120	41	28	31	1	53	6	1	1	9	6	.60	7	.294	.369	.392
6 Min. YEARS		552	1902	527	72	30	16	707	288	199	226	4	307	20	23	19	75	38	.66	35	.277	.357	.372

Rafael Betancourt

Pitches: Right **Bats:** Right **Pos:** P   **Ht:** 6'2" **Wt:** 176 **Born:** 4/29/75 **Age:** 25

Year Team	Lg Org	G	GS	CG	GF	IP	BFP	H	R	ER	HR	SH	SF	HB	TBB	IBB	SO	WP	Bk	W	L	Pct.	ShO	Sv	ERA
		HOW MUCH HE PITCHED						WHAT HE GAVE UP												THE RESULTS					
1997 Michigan	A Bos	27	0	0	22	32.1	125	26	9	7	2	1	0	0	2	0	52	3	1	0	3	.000	0	11	1.95
1998 Red Sox	R Bos	4	3	0	0	5	22	6	5	4	1	0	1	0	1	0	4	1	1	0	2	.000	0	0	7.20
Sarasota	A+ Bos	20	0	0	4	28	111	22	12	11	2	1	0	0	6	0	33	0	0	3	1	.750	0	2	3.54
Trenton	AA Bos	7	0	0	3	9.1	42	9	7	7	1	0	0	0	3	0	9	0	0	0	0	.000	0	0	6.75

Year Team	Lg Org	G	GS	CG	GF	IP	BFP	H	R	ER	HR	SH	SF	HB	TBB	IBB	SO	WP	Bk	W	L	Pct.	ShO	Sv	ERA
1999 Sarasota	A+ Bos	6	0	0	5	7	25	5	0	0	0	0	0	0	1	0	6	0	0	0	0	.000	0	4	0.00
Trenton	AA Bos	39	0	0	30	54.2	218	50	24	22	7	4	2	0	10	0	57	0	1	6	2	.750	0	13	3.62
3 Min. YEARS		103	3	0	64	136.1	543	118	57	51	12	7	3	0	23	0	161	4	3	9	8	.529	0	30	3.37

Randy Betten

Bats: Right **Throws:** Right **Pos:** 2B-3B   **Ht:** 5'11" **Wt:** 170 **Born:** 7/28/71 **Age:** 28

Year Team	Lg Org	G	AB	H	2B	3B	HR	TB	R	RBI	TBB	IBB	SO	HBP	SH	SF	SB	CS	SB%	GDP	Avg	OBP	SLG
1995 Boise	A- Ana	2	8	3	0	0	0	3	2	2	1	0	2	0	0	0	0	0	.00	0	.375	.444	.375
Cedar Rapds	A Ana	36	60	14	2	0	0	16	8	4	13	0	8	0	0	1	6	2	.75	0	.233	.365	.267
1996 Lk Elsinore	A+ Ana	74	274	71	15	3	3	101	32	34	22	1	49	3	3	1	11	3	.79	6	.259	.320	.369
Midland	AA Ana	28	82	14	2	0	0	16	5	5	5	0	19	0	1	0	3	1	.75	2	.171	.218	.195
1997 Lk Elsinore	A+ Ana	35	116	40	5	2	2	55	18	27	16	1	29	3	4	0	7	5	.58	1	.345	.437	.474
Midland	AA Ana	57	220	64	13	3	3	92	39	24	22	0	45	1	4	1	7	3	.70	5	.291	.357	.418
Vancouver	AAA Ana	23	61	17	4	0	1	24	9	12	7	0	21	0	3	0	1	1	.50	1	.279	.353	.393
1998 Vancouver	AAA Ana	10	10	1	1	0	0	2	1	2	2	0	2	0	0	1	1	1	.50	1	.100	.231	.200
Midland	AA Ana	76	209	48	16	2	2	74	30	19	18	0	50	4	8	2	3	2	.60	6	.230	.300	.354
1999 Edmonton	AAA Ana	12	29	11	1	0	0	12	5	3	0	0	5	0	2	0	0	0	.00	0	.379	.379	.414
Erie	AA Ana	7	20	3	0	1	0	5	3	1	0	0	7	0	1	0	3	0	1.00	0	.150	.150	.250
Lk Elsinore	A+ Ana	15	52	17	2	0	1	22	11	7	3	0	10	1	0	0	3	0	1.00	2	.327	.375	.423
5 Min. YEARS		375	1141	303	61	11	12	422	163	140	109	2	247	12	26	6	45	18	.71	24	.266	.334	.370

Todd Betts

Bats: Left **Throws:** Right **Pos:** 3B   **Ht:** 6'0" **Wt:** 185 **Born:** 6/24/73 **Age:** 27

Year Team	Lg Org	G	AB	H	2B	3B	HR	TB	R	RBI	TBB	IBB	SO	HBP	SH	SF	SB	CS	SB%	GDP	Avg	OBP	SLG
1993 Burlington	R+ Cle	56	168	39	9	0	7	69	40	27	32	2	26	3	0	1	6	1	.86	4	.232	.363	.411
1994 Watertown	A- Cle	65	227	74	18	2	10	126	49	53	54	2	29	4	1	2	3	2	.60	1	.326	.460	.555
1995 Kinston	A+ Cle	109	331	90	15	3	9	138	52	44	88	2	56	6	1	4	2	3	.40	5	.272	.429	.417
1996 Canton-Akrn	AA Cle	77	238	60	13	0	1	76	35	26	38	2	51	5	0	4	0	1	.00	6	.252	.361	.319
1997 Akron	AA Cle	128	439	108	25	1	20	195	65	69	73	6	97	4	1	5	1	3	.25	6	.246	.355	.444
1998 Akron	AA Cle	91	318	86	18	3	17	161	55	46	64	5	71	4	0	2	1	0	1.00	3	.270	.397	.506
Buffalo	AAA Cle	14	35	8	3	0	2	17	5	6	8	0	7	0	0	1	0	0	.00	0	.229	.364	.486
1999 Akron	AA Cle	104	375	105	24	1	19	188	60	67	61	2	65	7	0	3	2	1	.67	3	.280	.388	.501
7 Min. YEARS		644	2131	570	125	10	85	970	361	338	418	23	402	33	3	22	15	11	.58	32	.267	.392	.455

Jim Betzsold

Bats: Right **Throws:** Right **Pos:** OF   **Ht:** 6'3" **Wt:** 210 **Born:** 8/7/72 **Age:** 27

Year Team	Lg Org	G	AB	H	2B	3B	HR	TB	R	RBI	TBB	IBB	SO	HBP	SH	SF	SB	CS	SB%	GDP	Avg	OBP	SLG
1994 Watertown	A- Cle	66	212	61	18	0	12	115	48	46	53	1	68	15	1	2	3	3	.50	2	.288	.457	.542
1995 Kinston	A+ Cle	126	455	122	22	2	25	223	77	71	55	3	137	10	0	4	3	5	.38	4	.268	.357	.490
1996 Canton-Akrn	AA Cle	84	268	64	11	5	3	94	35	35	30	1	74	6	1	1	4	1	.80	3	.239	.328	.351
1997 Akron	AA Cle	118	434	115	21	5	19	203	76	79	60	2	119	10	0	2	4	5	.44	12	.265	.366	.468
1998 Buffalo	AAA Cle	74	209	51	10	1	10	93	36	27	27	0	72	6	0	0	4	4	.50	3	.244	.347	.445
1999 Jackson	AA Hou	38	126	30	6	1	6	56	30	17	22	0	35	5	1	0	4	3	.57	2	.238	.373	.444
New Orleans	AAA Hou	63	198	43	15	0	7	79	29	27	14	0	64	3	0	2	3	2	.60	1	.217	.276	.399
6 Min. YEARS		569	1902	486	103	14	82	863	331	302	261	7	569	55	3	11	25	23	.52	27	.256	.360	.454

Bobby Bevel

Pitches: Left **Bats:** Left **Pos:** P   **Ht:** 5'10" **Wt:** 180 **Born:** 10/10/73 **Age:** 26

Year Team	Lg Org	G	GS	CG	GF	IP	BFP	H	R	ER	HR	SH	SF	HB	TBB	IBB	SO	WP	Bk	W	L	Pct.	ShO	Sv	ERA
1995 Portland	A- Col	25	0	0	8	28	128	24	13	11	0	3	2	1	18	4	25	5	0	2	3	.400	0	1	3.54
1996 Salem	A Col	41	0	0	10	68	286	61	25	24	4	3	1	2	30	2	60	6	0	4	2	.667	0	3	3.18
1997 Salem	A+ Col	50	0	0	18	66	290	69	37	34	5	2	7	9	17	0	57	3	0	4	7	.364	0	3	4.64
1998 Salem	A+ Col	51	0	0	26	91.2	373	72	26	23	4	2	3	4	24	0	92	5	1	6	4	.600	0	3	2.26
1999 Carolina	AA Col	48	0	0	22	67	294	70	37	33	7	4	1	2	27	2	58	9	0	3	7	.300	0	7	4.43
5 Min. YEARS		215	0	0	84	320.2	1371	296	138	125	20	14	14	18	116	8	292	28	1	19	23	.452	0	14	3.51

Jason Beverlin

Pitches: Right **Bats:** Left **Pos:** P   **Ht:** 6'5" **Wt:** 220 **Born:** 11/27/73 **Age:** 26

Year Team	Lg Org	G	GS	CG	GF	IP	BFP	H	R	ER	HR	SH	SF	HB	TBB	IBB	SO	WP	Bk	W	L	Pct.	ShO	Sv	ERA
1994 W Michigan	A Oak	17	1	0	5	41	168	32	12	8	0	1	0	2	14	0	48	3	4	3	2	.600	0	1	1.76
1995 W Michigan	A Oak	22	14	0	1	89	392	76	51	40	4	3	3	8	40	0	84	5	5	3	9	.250	0	0	4.04
Greensboro	A NYY	7	7	1	0	51	198	49	15	15	1	0	0	0	6	0	31	4	0	2	4	.333	1	0	2.65
1996 Norwich	AA NYY	8	4	0	1	16	81	25	21	15	2	0	2	0	6	1	17	0	0	0	3	.000	0	0	8.44
Tampa	A+ NYY	25	1	0	6	46.1	194	43	22	18	5	1	1	1	17	2	38	4	1	2	0	1.000	0	1	3.50
1997 Norwich	AA NYY	25	0	0	8	41.2	203	50	38	36	10	0	0	6	24	0	42	3	0	1	0	1.000	0	0	7.78
Tampa	A+ NYY	7	6	0	0	41.1	167	37	26	22	4	2	2	4	13	1	24	6	0	1	3	.250	0	0	4.79
1998 Norwich	AA NYY	25	9	0	8	81	343	68	34	33	5	2	4	3	38	0	86	6	1	3	5	.375	0	1	3.67
Tampa	A+ NYY	7	5	0	0	32	142	37	23	20	2	0	4	1	16	2	15	2	1	1	3	.250	0	0	5.63
1999 Norwich	AA NYY	28	27	1	0	173.1	743	153	91	71	16	6	7	6	81	0	147	10	1	15	9	.625	0	0	3.69
6 Min. YEARS		171	74	2	29	612.2	2631	570	333	278	49	15	23	31	255	6	532	43	13	31	38	.449	1	3	4.08

Nick Bierbrodt

Pitches: Left **Bats:** Left **Pos:** P **Ht:** 6' 5" **Wt:** 175 **Born:** 5/16/78 **Age:** 22

Year Team	Lg Org	G	GS	CG	GF	IP	BFP	H	R	ER	HR	SH	SF	HB	TBB	IBB	SO	WP	Bk	W	L	Pct.	ShO	Sv	ERA
1996 Diamondbcks	R Ari	8	8	0	0	38	147	25	9	7	1	0	0	0	13	0	46	2	0	1	1	.500	0	0	1.66
Lethbridge	R+ Ari	3	3	0	0	18	72	12	4	1	0	0	1	1	5	0	23	1	0	2	0	1.000	0	0	0.50
1997 South Bend	A Ari	15	15	0	0	75.2	340	77	43	34	4	3	1	9	37	0	64	6	1	2	4	.333	0	0	4.04
1998 High Desert	A+ Ari	24	23	1	0	129.2	560	122	66	49	7	3	6	7	64	0	88	9	0	8	7	.533	0	0	3.40
1999 El Paso	AA Ari	14	14	2	0	76	341	78	45	39	3	2	1	8	37	0	55	5	0	5	6	.455	1	0	4.62
Tucson	AAA Ari	11	11	0	0	43.1	213	57	42	35	9	4	0	3	30	0	43	3	0	1	4	.200	0	0	7.27
4 Min. YEARS		75	74	3	0	380.2	1673	371	209	165	24	12	9	28	186	0	319	26	1	19	22	.463	1	0	3.90

Kurt Bierek

Bats: Left **Throws:** Right **Pos:** 1B **Ht:** 6'4" **Wt:** 220 **Born:** 9/13/72 **Age:** 27

Year Team	Lg Org	G	AB	H	2B	3B	HR	TB	R	RBI	TBB	IBB	SO	HBP	SH	SF	SB	CS	SB%	GDP	Avg	OBP	SLG
1993 Oneonta	A- NYY	70	274	64	6	6	5	97	36	37	19	2	49	3	1	1	4	4	.50	4	.234	.290	.354
1994 Greensboro	A NYY	133	467	118	24	6	14	196	78	73	69	2	101	8	2	3	8	1	.89	10	.253	.356	.420
1995 Tampa	A+ NYY	126	447	111	16	2	4	143	60	53	61	3	73	4	2	2	3	4	.43	11	.248	.342	.320
1996 Tampa	A+ NYY	88	320	97	14	2	11	148	48	55	41	3	40	6	0	3	6	3	.67	5	.303	.389	.463
1997 Norwich	AA NYY	133	473	128	32	2	18	218	77	78	56	2	89	7	0	2	4	4	.50	8	.271	.355	.461
1008 Columbus	AAA NYY	14	50	15	5	1	1	25	8	8	5	0	8	0	0	0	0	0	.00	2	.300	.364	.500
Norwich	AA NYY	95	344	81	13	2	13	137	44	61	50	1	61	3	0	2	0	1	.00	8	.235	.336	.398
1999 Columbus	AAA NYY	135	532	149	42	4	23	268	84	95	48	1	99	6	1	7	5	3	.63	14	.280	.342	.504
7 Min. YEARS		794	2907	763	152	25	89	1232	435	460	349	14	520	37	6	20	30	20	.60	62	.262	.347	.424

Steve Bieser

Bats: Left **Throws:** Right **Pos:** OF **Ht:** 5'10" **Wt:** 180 **Born:** 8/4/67 **Age:** 32

Year Team	Lg Org	G	AB	H	2B	3B	HR	TB	R	RBI	TBB	IBB	SO	HBP	SH	SF	SB	CS	SB%	GDP	Avg	OBP	SLG
1989 Batavia	A- Phi	25	75	18	3	1	1	26	13	13	12	0	20	2	2	2	2	1	.67	1	.240	.352	.347
1990 Batavia	A- Phi	54	160	37	11	1	0	50	36	12	26	1	27	1	2	2	13	2	.87	3	.231	.339	.313
1991 Spartanburg	A Phi	60	168	41	6	0	0	47	25	13	31	0	35	3	4	3	17	4	.81	4	.244	.366	.280
1992 Clearwater	A+ Phi	73	203	58	6	5	0	74	33	10	39	3	28	9	8	0	8	8	.50	2	.286	.422	.365
Reading	AA Phi	33	139	38	5	4	0	51	20	8	6	0	25	4	4	0	8	3	.73	3	.273	.322	.367
1993 Reading	AA Phi	53	170	53	6	3	1	68	21	19	15	1	24	2	1	0	9	5	.64	2	.312	.374	.400
Scranton-WB	AAA Phi	20	83	21	4	0	0	26	3	4	2	0	14	1	1	0	3	0	1.00	0	.253	.279	.301
1994 Scranton-WB	AAA Phi	93	228	61	13	1	0	76	42	15	17	1	40	5	4	2	12	8	.60	2	.268	.329	.333
1995 Scranton-WB	AAA Phi	95	245	66	12	6	1	93	37	33	22	1	56	10	6	2	14	5	.74	5	.269	.351	.380
1996 Ottawa	AAA Mon	123	382	123	24	4	1	158	63	32	35	4	55	6	23	2	27	7	.79	6	.322	.386	.414
1997 Norfolk	AAA NYM	41	122	20	5	0	0	25	6	4	9	0	20	5	2	0	4	3	.57	1	.164	.250	.205
1998 Nashville	AAA Pit	82	206	53	11	4	1	75	30	24	33	1	30	10	4	6	13	2	.87	4	.257	.376	.364
1999 Nashville	AAA Pit	6	13	3	1	0	0	4	3	3	2	0	4	1	0	0	0	0	.00	0	.231	.375	.308
Altoona	AA Pit	40	148	31	5	2	4	52	24	23	21	0	32	4	0	1	3	4	.43	2	.209	.322	.351
Memphis	AAA StL	58	180	56	13	2	4	85	25	16	16	0	30	3	5	0	8	0	1.00	2	.311	.377	.472
1997 New York	NL	47	69	17	3	0	0	20	16	4	7	1	20	4	0	1	2	3	.40	0	.246	.346	.290
1998 Pittsburgh	NL	13	11	3	1	0	0	4	2	1	2	0	2	0	0	0	0	0	.00	1	.273	.385	.364
11 Min. YEARS		862	2522	679	125	33	13	909	381	229	286	12	440	66	66	20	141	52	.73	37	.269	.356	.360
2 Maj. YEARS		60	80	20	4	0	0	24	18	5	9	1	22	4	0	1	2	3	.40	1	.250	.351	.300

Alberto Blanco

Pitches: Left **Bats:** Left **Pos:** P **Ht:** 6'1" **Wt:** 200 **Born:** 6/27/76 **Age:** 24

Year Team	Lg Org	G	GS	CG	GF	IP	BFP	H	R	ER	HR	SH	SF	HB	TBB	IBB	SO	WP	Bk	W	L	Pct.	ShO	Sv	ERA
1993 Astros	R Hou	9	1	0	1	18	80	15	4	4	0	0	1	1	11	0	32	2	0	0	1	.000	0	1	2.00
1994 Quad City	A Hou	27	19	0	3	117	520	118	70	61	13	4	4	5	66	0	101	11	3	7	9	.438	0	0	4.69
1995 Quad City	A Hou	11	11	1	0	54.2	231	47	22	19	2	0	3	1	19	0	58	3	0	3	3	.500	1	0	3.13
1996 Quad City	A Hou	11	11	0	0	46.2	198	42	25	18	3	0	2	3	15	0	58	3	0	2	2	.500	0	0	3.47
1997 Jackson	AA Hou	1	1	0	0	7	30	5	2	2	1	0	0	1	3	0	4	0	0	1	0	1.000	0	0	2.57
Astros	R Hou	2	2	0	0	5	19	1	0	0	0	0	0	0	1	0	11	0	0	0	0	.000	0	0	0.00
Kissimmee	A+ Hou	19	19	1	0	114.1	467	83	45	36	4	5	4	11	45	0	95	6	2	7	4	.636	1	0	2.83
1998 Kissimmee	A+ Hou	2	2	0	0	11.1	50	12	9	8	1	1	1	0	3	0	13	1	0	0	0	.000	0	0	6.35
Jackson	AA Hou	12	12	0	0	59.1	261	65	43	38	10	4	3	1	24	0	60	4	2	4	4	.500	0	0	5.76
1999 Jacksnville	AA Det	37	4	0	11	72	307	58	37	30	10	2	3	3	37	1	62	1	4	3	2	.600	0	1	3.75
7 Min. YEARS		131	82	2	15	505.1	2163	446	257	216	44	16	21	27	224	1	494	31	11	27	25	.519	2	2	3.85

Matt Blank

Pitches: Left **Bats:** Left **Pos:** P **Ht:** 6'2" **Wt:** 200 **Born:** 4/5/76 **Age:** 24

Year Team	Lg Org	G	GS	CG	GF	IP	BFP	H	R	ER	HR	SH	SF	HB	TBB	IBB	SO	WP	Bk	W	L	Pct	ShO	Sv	ERA
1997 Vermont	A- Mon	16	15	2	0	95.2	375	74	26	18	2	1	3	2	14	0	84	0	0	6	4	.600	1	0	1.69
1998 Cape Fear	A Mon	21	21	2	0	134.2	539	121	45	39	6	4	2	9	24	0	114	1	1	9	2	.818	2	0	2.61
Jupiter	A+ Mon	8	6	0	1	42.1	170	33	14	11	2	0	1	4	10	0	26	0	1	5	1	.833	0	0	2.34
1999 Jupiter	A+ Mon	14	14	3	0	90	348	64	26	24	5	3	3	2	19	1	66	1	2	9	5	.643	1	0	2.40
Harrisburg	AA Mon	15	14	0	0	85	363	94	41	37	14	5	2	0	26	0	42	3	0	6	3	.667	0	0	3.92
3 Min. YEARS		74	70	7	1	447.2	1795	386	152	129	29	13	11	17	93	1	332	5	4	35	15	.700	3	0	2.59

Ron Blazier

Pitches: Right Bats: Right Pos: P   Ht: 6'5" Wt: 249 Born: 7/30/71 Age: 28

Year Team	Lg Org	G	GS	CG	GF	IP	BFP	H	R	ER	HR	SH	SF	HB	TBB	IBB	SO	WP	Bk	W	L	Pct.	ShO	Sv	ERA
1990 Princeton	R+ Phi	14	13	1	1	78.2	331	79	46	39	10	1	3	1	29	1	45	3	1	3	5	.375	0	0	4.46
1991 Batavia	A- Phi	24	8	0	8	72.1	312	81	40	37	11	2	1	3	17	3	77	2	1	7	5	.583	0	2	4.60
1992 Spartanburg	A Phi	30	21	2	6	159.2	640	141	55	47	10	2	5	5	32	0	149	4	0	14	7	.667	0	0	2.65
1993 Clearwater	A+ Phi	27	23	1	1	155.1	663	171	80	68	8	4	4	6	40	5	86	1	1	9	8	.529	0	0	3.94
1994 Clearwater	A+ Phi	29	29	0	0	173.1	715	177	73	65	15	4	6	9	36	1	120	2	2	13	5	.722	0	0	3.38
1995 Reading	AA Phi	56	3	0	17	106.2	431	93	44	39	11	5	2	0	31	7	102	2	1	4	5	.444	0	1	3.29
1996 Scranton-WB	AAA Phi	33	0	0	23	42	168	33	15	12	1	1	2	2	9	2	38	1	0	4	0	1.000	0	12	2.57
1997 Clearwater	A+ Phi	15	0	0	9	30.2	123	24	11	10	0	1	1	0	8	1	45	7	1	2	3	.400	0	3	2.93
Scranton-WB	AAA Phi	11	0	0	8	14.2	68	17	9	6	4	1	1	0	3	0	10	0	0	0	3	.000	0	1	3.68
1999 Delmarva	A Bal	2	0	0	2	5	20	4	2	2	1	0	0	1	0	0	7	0	0	1	0	1.000	0	1	3.60
Bowie	AA Bal	19	0	0	6	31.2	145	40	27	26	6	2	0	2	12	0	28	1	0	1	1	.500	0	0	7.39
1996 Philadelphia	NL	27	0	0	9	38.1	173	49	30	25	6	3	2	0	10	3	25	3	0	3	1	.750	0	0	5.87
1997 Philadelphia	NL	36	0	0	7	53.2	240	62	31	30	8	1	4	0	21	3	42	2	0	1	1	.500	0	0	5.03
9 Min. YEARS		260	97	4	81	870	3616	860	402	351	77	23	25	29	217	20	707	23	7	58	42	.580	0	20	3.63
2 Maj. YEARS		63	0	0	16	92	413	111	61	55	14	4	6	0	31	6	67	5	0	4	2	.667	0	0	5.38

David Bleazard

Pitches: Right Bats: Right Pos: P   Ht: 6'0" Wt: 175 Born: 3/7/74 Age: 26

Year Team	Lg Org	G	GS	CG	GF	IP	BFP	H	R	ER	HR	SH	SF	HB	TBB	IBB	SO	WP	Bk	W	L	Pct.	ShO	Sv	ERA
1996 Medcine Hat	R+ Tor	20	0	0	19	23.2	115	29	16	12	0	0	1	2	14	0	31	1	0	0	0	.000	0	10	4.56
1997 Hagerstown	A Tor	10	10	0	0	59.2	250	52	25	22	1	1	2	5	20	0	58	5	4	5	0	1.000	0	0	3.32
1998 Dunedin	A+ Tor	14	0	0	4	19	88	20	14	9	1	1	0	2	11	0	20	4	1	1	0	1.000	0	0	4.26
1999 Dunedin	A+ Tor	14	13	1	1	90.2	374	73	36	23	1	2	1	2	30	1	58	5	1	6	6	.500	0	0	2.28
Knoxville	AA Tor	15	15	1	0	86.2	358	81	36	31	4	1	4	4	34	0	49	7	2	5	3	.625	1	0	3.22
4 Min. YEARS		73	38	2	24	279.2	1185	255	127	97	7	5	8	15	109	1	216	22	8	17	9	.654	1	10	3.12

Darin Blood

Pitches: Right Bats: Both Pos: P   Ht: 6'2" Wt: 200 Born: 8/31/74 Age: 25

Year Team	Lg Org	G	GS	CG	GF	IP	BFP	H	R	ER	HR	SH	SF	HB	TBB	IBB	SO	WP	Bk	W	L	Pct.	ShO	Sv	ERA
1995 Bellingham	A- SF	14	13	0	0	74.1	315	63	26	21	2	4	0	3	32	0	78	6	1	6	3	.667	0	0	2.54
1996 San Jose	A+ SF	27	25	2	0	170	717	140	59	50	4	5	2	10	71	0	193	26	2	17	6	.739	2	0	2.65
1997 Shreveport	AA SF	27	27	0	0	156	698	152	89	75	12	7	8	8	83	0	90	14	2	8	10	.444	0	0	4.33
1998 Fresno	AAA SF	19	19	1	0	114	496	138	63	59	9	6	2	7	37	0	63	3	0	4	5	.444	1	0	4.66
Rochester	AAA Bal	6	6	1	0	32.2	131	24	11	9	2	0	0	5	13	0	14	1	0	3	2	.600	0	0	2.48
1999 Rochester	AAA Bal	12	10	0	0	43.2	211	53	43	42	3	1	4	2	38	0	21	5	1	0	4	.000	0	0	8.66
5 Min. YEARS		105	100	4	0	590.2	2568	570	291	256	32	23	16	35	274	0	459	55	6	38	30	.559	4	0	3.90

Jaime Bluma

Pitches: Right Bats: Right Pos: P   Ht: 5'11" Wt: 195 Born: 5/18/72 Age: 28

Year Team	Lg Org	G	GS	CG	GF	IP	BFP	H	R	ER	HR	SH	SF	HB	TBB	IBB	SO	WP	Bk	W	L	Pct.	ShO	Sv	ERA
1994 Eugene	A- KC	26	0	0	23	36.1	133	19	5	4	0	1	1	0	6	0	35	0	0	2	1	.667	0	12	0.99
Wilmington	A+ KC	7	0	0	7	9.2	34	7	2	1	0	0	0	0	0	0	5	0	0	4	0	1.000	0	2	0.93
1995 Wichita	AA KC	42	0	0	40	55.1	214	38	19	19	9	3	1	1	9	2	31	1	0	4	3	.571	0	22	3.09
Omaha	AAA KC	18	0	0	10	23.2	101	21	13	8	1	3	3	0	14	4	12	3	0	0	0	.000	0	4	3.04
1996 Omaha	AAA KC	52	0	0	47	57.2	251	57	22	20	7	0	2	1	20	3	40	5	2	1	2	.333	0	25	3.12
Wichita	AA KC	14	0	0	9	14.1	67	19	13	10	4	0	1	0	7	2	8	0	0	0	1	.000	0	2	6.28
1998 Omaha	AAA KC	39	0	0	18	62	291	67	44	37	10	1	0	4	35	6	38	5	0	1	2	.333	0	0	5.37
1999 Wichita	AA KC	30	0	0	22	38.1	169	40	25	23	9	0	1	0	16	3	21	0	1	2	6	.250	0	6	5.40
Omaha	AAA KC	17	0	0	10	22.1	92	21	10	8	5	1	0	0	4	1	19	0	0	0	0	.000	0	3	3.22
1996 Kansas City	AL	17	0	0	10	20	82	18	9	8	2	1	2	1	4	1	14	1	0	0	0	.000	0	5	3.60
5 Min. YEARS		245	0	0	186	319.2	1352	289	158	130	45	9	9	6	111	21	209	14	3	14	15	.483	0	75	3.66

Hiram Bocachica

Bats: Right Throws: Right Pos: 2B   Ht: 5'11" Wt: 165 Born: 3/4/76 Age: 24

Year Team	Lg Org	G	AB	H	2B	3B	HR	TB	R	RBI	TBB	IBB	SO	HBP	SH	SF	SB	CS	SB%	GDP	Avg	OBP	SLG
1994 Expos	R Mon	43	168	47	9	0	5	71	31	16	15	0	42	2	2	0	11	4	.73	1	.280	.346	.423
1995 Albany	A Mon	96	380	108	20	10	2	154	65	30	52	3	78	8	3	1	47	17	.73	4	.284	.381	.405
1996 Expos	R Mon	9	32	8	3	0	0	11	11	2	5	1	3	1	0	0	2	1	.67	0	.250	.368	.344
Wst Plm Bch	A+ Mon	71	267	90	17	5	2	123	50	26	34	0	47	6	3	3	21	3	.88	6	.337	.419	.461
1997 Harrisburg	AA Mon	119	443	123	19	3	11	181	82	35	41	1	98	13	1	3	29	12	.71	3	.278	.354	.409
1998 Harrisburg	AA Mon	80	296	78	18	4	4	116	39	27	21	2	61	11	2	1	20	8	.71	1	.264	.334	.392
Ottawa	AAA Mon	12	41	8	3	1	0	13	5	5	6	0	14	1	0	0	2	0	1.00	1	.195	.313	.317
Albuquerque	AAA LA	26	101	24	7	1	4	45	16	16	13	1	24	6	1	0	5	3	.63	1	.238	.358	.446
1999 San Antonio	AA LA	123	477	139	22	10	11	214	84	60	60	0	71	13	4	5	30	15	.67	5	.291	.382	.449
6 Min. YEARS		579	2205	625	118	34	39	928	383	217	247	8	438	61	16	13	167	63	.73	22	.283	.369	.421

Kurt Bogott

Pitches: Left Bats: Left Pos: P Ht: 6'4" Wt: 195 Born: 9/30/72 Age: 27

Year Team	Lg Org	G	GS	CG	GF	IP	BFP	H	R	ER	HR	SH	SF	HB	TBB	IBB	SO	WP	Bk	W	L	Pct.	ShO	Sv	ERA
1993 Red Sox	R Bos	3	2	0	0	15	57	10	3	3	1	0	0	2	4	0	20	3	0	0	1	.000	0	0	1.80
Utica	A- Bos	13	10	0	0	56.2	260	64	37	28	4	2	1	3	23	0	53	8	3	1	7	.125	0	0	4.45
1994 Red Sox	R Bos	3	2	0	0	13.2	49	7	1	1	0	0	0	1	3	0	12	2	0	1	0	1.000	0	0	0.66
Lynchburg	A+ Bos	6	6	0	0	26.1	127	32	23	18	1	1	1	1	14	0	14	2	0	2	3	.400	0	0	6.15
1995 Sarasota	A+ Bos	41	9	0	15	88.2	388	89	44	30	3	4	1	4	41	0	62	8	3	6	4	.600	0	0	3.05
Trenton	AA Bos	2	0	0	2	3.1	13	3	1	1	1	0	0	0	1	0	2	0	0	0	1	.000	0	0	2.70
1996 Knoxville	AA Tor	33	0	0	9	54	256	64	34	32	2	0	2	5	29	2	56	12	1	2	2	.500	0	3	5.33
Dunedin	A+ Tor	19	0	0	8	30.1	133	22	16	6	2	0	0	3	20	1	41	8	0	1	1	.500	0	4	1.78
1997 Syracuse	AAA Tor	16	0	0	6	21.2	106	23	20	19	2	2	2	3	15	1	16	1	0	1	3	.250	0	0	7.89
Knoxville	AA Tor	35	1	0	14	64.2	284	66	32	28	10	1	3	6	25	2	77	6	1	2	1	.667	0	2	3.90
1998 Dunedin	A+ Tor	3	0	0	0	6.1	21	2	0	0	0	0	0	0	1	0	8	0	0	0	0	.000	0	0	0.00
1999 Syracuse	AAA Tor	46	4	0	10	85.2	392	80	52	44	11	3	3	8	44	4	76	9	0	8	6	.571	0	1	4.62
7 Min. YEARS		220	34	0	64	466.1	2086	462	263	210	37	13	13	36	220	10	437	59	8	24	29	.453	0	10	4.05

Gary Bohannon

Pitches: Right Bats: Right Pos: P Ht: 6'4" Wt: 175 Born: 2/19/76 Age: 24

Year Team	Lg Org	G	GS	CG	GF	IP	BFP	H	R	ER	HR	SH	SF	HB	TBB	IBB	SO	WP	Bk	W	L	Pct.	ShO	Sv	ERA
1998 Kingsport	R+ NYM	10	10	1	0	59.2	238	56	19	17	1	1	0	0	5	0	49	2	1	6	3	.667	1	0	2.56
1999 Binghamton	AA NYM	2	0	0	0	2	23	12	13	11	0	1	1	1	3	0	0	0	0	0	0	.000	0	0	49.50
St. Lucie	A+ NYM	32	12	1	8	108	480	131	66	53	4	7	5	8	30	2	58	5	1	6	6	.500	0	2	4.42
2 Min. YEARS		44	22	2	8	169.2	741	199	98	81	5	9	6	9	38	2	107	7	2	12	9	.571	1	2	4.30

Rod Bolton

Pitches: Right Bats: Right Pos: P Ht: 6'2" Wt: 190 Born: 9/23/68 Age: 31

Year Team	Lg Org	G	GS	CG	GF	IP	BFP	H	R	ER	HR	SH	SF	HB	TBB	IBB	SO	WP	Bk	W	L	Pct.	ShO	Sv	ERA
1990 Utica	A- CWS	6	6	1	0	44	168	27	4	2	0	1	0	3	11	0	45	0	0	5	1	.833	1	0	0.41
South Bend	A CWS	7	7	3	0	51	196	34	14	11	0	1	1	1	12	1	50	1	1	5	1	.833	1	0	1.94
1991 Sarasota	A+ CWS	15	15	5	0	103.2	412	81	29	22	2	5	1	2	23	0	77	3	1	7	6	.538	2	0	1.91
Birmingham	AA CWS	12	12	3	0	89	360	73	26	16	3	0	2	8	21	1	57	3	0	8	4	.667	2	0	1.62
1992 Vancouver	AAA CWS	27	27	3	0	187.1	781	174	72	61	9	9	4	1	59	2	111	9	2	11	9	.550	2	0	2.93
1993 Nashville	AAA CWS	18	16	1	1	115.2	480	108	40	37	10	2	3	3	37	2	75	11	0	10	1	.909	0	1	2.88
1994 Nashville	AAA CWS	17	17	1	0	116	480	108	43	33	4	6	1	4	35	2	63	2	0	7	5	.583	0	0	2.56
1995 Nashville	AAA CWS	20	20	3	0	131.1	534	127	44	42	13	2	2	7	23	1	76	2	0	14	3	.824	1	0	2.88
1997 Indianapols	AAA Cin	28	27	1	0	169.2	730	185	96	81	21	6	4	3	47	0	108	16	2	9	8	.529	1	0	4.30
1998 Indianapols	AAA Cin	29	29	1	0	177	746	166	82	75	15	3	2	5	64	1	117	6	1	12	11	.522	1	0	3.81
1999 Scranton-WB	AAA Phi	24	24	4	0	153	655	161	76	65	10	5	1	1	52	3	85	6	0	11	10	.524	2	0	3.82
1993 Chicago	AL	9	8	0	0	42.1	197	55	40	35	4	1	4	1	16	0	17	4	0	2	6	.250	0	0	7.44
1995 Chicago	AL	8	3	0	2	22	109	33	23	20	4	0	1	0	14	1	10	1	0	0	2	.000	0	0	8.18
9 Min. YEARS		203	200	26	1	1337.2	5548	1244	526	445	87	40	21	38	384	13	864	59	7	99	59	.627	13	1	2.99
2 Maj. YEARS		17	11	0	2	64.1	306	88	63	55	8	1	5	1	30	1	27	5	0	2	8	.200	0	0	7.69

Jim Bonnici

Bats: Right Throws: Right Pos: DH Ht: 6'4" Wt: 230 Born: 1/21/72 Age: 28

Year Team	Lg Org	G	AB	H	2B	3B	HR	TB	R	RBI	TBB	IBB	SO	HBP	SH	SF	SB	CS	SB%	GDP	Avg	OBP	SLG
1991 Mariners	R Sea	51	178	59	2	4	0	69	36	38	44	0	31	6	0	5	8	2	.80	1	.331	.468	.388
1992 Bellingham	A- Sea	53	168	44	6	1	4	64	13	20	22	2	54	2	1	0	5	2	.71	3	.262	.354	.381
1993 Riverside	A+ Sea	104	375	115	21	1	9	165	69	58	58	2	72	9	3	1	0	0	.00	7	.307	.411	.440
1994 Riverside	A+ Sea	113	397	111	23	3	10	170	71	71	58	0	81	18	0	3	1	2	.33	14	.280	.393	.428
1995 Port City	AA Sea	138	508	144	36	3	20	246	75	91	76	15	97	9	0	3	2	2	.50	14	.283	.384	.484
1996 Tacoma	AAA Sea	139	497	145	25	0	26	248	76	74	59	4	100	2	1	3	1	3	.25	13	.292	.367	.499
1997 Tacoma	AAA Sea	1	4	1	0	0	0	1	0	1	1	0	1	0	0	0	0	0	.00	0	.250	.400	.250
1999 Toledo	AAA Det	22	58	13	3	0	2	22	10	4	6	0	25	1	0	1	0	0	.00	0	.224	.303	.379
8 Min. YEARS		621	2185	632	116	12	71	985	350	357	324	23	461	47	5	16	17	11	.61	52	.289	.390	.451

Toby Borland

Pitches: Right Bats: Right Pos: P Ht: 6'6" Wt: 193 Born: 5/29/69 Age: 31

Year Team	Lg Org	G	GS	CG	GF	IP	BFP	H	R	ER	HR	SH	SF	HB	TBB	IBB	SO	WP	Bk	W	L	Pct.	ShO	Sv	ERA
1988 Martinsvlle	R+ Phi	34	0	0	23	49	215	42	26	22	1	2	1	2	29	1	43	2	1	2	3	.400	0	12	4.04
1989 Spartanburg	A Phi	47	0	0	46	66.2	296	62	29	22	3	2	2	7	35	1	48	15	1	4	5	.444	0	9	2.97
1990 Clearwater	A+ Phi	44	0	0	23	59.2	257	44	21	15	1	7	1	3	35	4	44	6	1	1	2	.333	0	5	2.26
Reading	AA Phi	11	0	0	6	25	100	16	6	4	1	0	2	1	11	1	26	2	0	4	1	.800	0	1	1.44
1991 Reading	AA Phi	59	0	0	50	76.2	358	68	31	23	2	2	5	2	56	5	72	5	3	8	3	.727	0	24	2.70
1992 Scranton-WB	AAA Phi	27	0	0	6	27.1	131	25	23	22	2	3	1	2	26	3	25	4	0	0	1	.000	0	1	7.24
Reading	AA Phi	32	0	0	18	42	196	39	23	16	2	2	1	1	32	3	45	3	0	2	4	.333	0	5	3.43
1993 Scranton-WB	AAA Phi	26	0	0	15	29.2	136	31	20	19	4	4	0	1	20	3	26	2	1	2	4	.333	0	1	5.76
Reading	AA Phi	44	0	0	37	53.2	259	38	17	15	2	1	2	2	20	1	74	1	0	2	2	.500	0	13	2.52
1994 Scranton-WB	AAA Phi	27	1	0	15	53.2	214	36	12	10	2	1	3	1	21	7	61	2	1	4	1	.800	0	4	1.68
1995 Scranton-WB	AAA Phi	8	0	0	3	11.1	45	5	0	0	0	0	0	0	6	1	15	2	0	0	0	.000	0	1	0.00
1997 Pawtucket	AAA Bos	28	2	0	13	47.1	213	50	22	21	5	0	0	2	25	3	46	5	0	2	0	1.000	0	3	3.99
1998 Reading	AA Phi	8	0	0	8	9.1	51	18	12	10	4	1	0	0	5	0	13	1	0	1	3	.250	0	3	9.64
Scranton-WB	AAA Phi	13	0	0	8	12.2	52	14	8	8	1	1	0	1	8	0	15	1	0	0	2	.000	0	5	5.68

Year Team	Lg Org	G	GS	CG	GF	IP	BFP	H	R	ER	HR	SH	SF	HB	TBB	IBB	SO	WP	Bk	W	L	Pct.	ShO	Sv	ERA
Charlotte	AAA Fla	19	0	0	6	36.2	158	33	12	11	3	0	1	1	21	1	26	4	1	3	0	1.000	0	1	2.70
1999 Edmonton	AAA Ana	21	0	0	10	27	136	31	24	21	5	1	3	3	23	2	34	2	0	2	1	.667	0	0	7.00
1994 Philadelphia	NL	24	0	0	7	34.1	144	31	10	9	1	1	0	4	14	3	26	4	0	1	0	1.000	0	1	2.36
1995 Philadelphia	NL	50	0	0	18	74	339	81	37	31	3	3	2	5	37	7	59	12	0	1	3	.250	0	6	3.77
1996 Philadelphia	NL	69	0	0	11	90.2	399	83	51	41	9	4	1	3	43	3	76	10	0	7	3	.700	0	0	4.07
1997 New York	NL	13	0	0	5	13.1	65	11	9	9	1	0	0	1	14	0	7	3	0	0	1	.000	0	1	6.08
Boston	AL	3	0	0	0	3.1	24	6	5	5	1	0	0	2	7	0	1	0	0	0	0	.000	0	0	13.50
1998 Philadelphia	NL	6	0	0	3	9	39	8	5	5	1	1	0	0	5	0	9	2	0	0	0	.000	0	0	5.00
11 Min. YEARS		451	3	0	286	627.2	2777	552	286	239	38	26	23	27	368	36	613	57	9	37	32	.536	0	86	3.43
5 Maj. YEARS		165	0	0	44	224.2	1010	220	117	100	16	9	3	15	120	13	178	31	0	9	7	.563	0	8	4.01

Joe Borowski

Pitches: Right **Bats:** Right **Pos:** P   **Ht:** 6' 2" **Wt:** 225 **Born:** 5/4/71 **Age:** 29

Year Team	Lg Org	G	GS	CG	GF	IP	BFP	H	R	ER	HR	SH	SF	HB	TBB	IBB	SO	WP	Bk	W	L	Pct.	ShO	Sv	ERA
1990 White Sox	R CWS	12	11	0	0	61.1	286	74	47	38	3	1	2	2	25	0	67	2	2	2	8	.200	0	0	5.58
1991 Kane County	A Bal	49	0	0	28	81	344	60	26	23	2	4	4	3	43	2	76	4	0	7	2	.778	0	13	2.56
1992 Frederick	A+ Bal	48	0	0	36	80.1	362	71	40	33	3	5	6	3	50	3	85	2	0	5	6	.455	0	10	3.70
1993 Frederick	A+ Bal	42	2	0	27	62.1	280	61	30	25	5	2	2	3	37	0	70	8	0	1	1	.500	0	11	3.61
Bowie	AA Bal	9	0	0	5	17.2	75	11	0	0	0	3	0	0	11	3	17	0	1	3	0	1.000	0	0	0.00
1994 Bowie	AA Bal	49	0	0	37	66	277	52	14	14	3	4	1	0	28	3	73	4	0	3	4	.429	0	14	1.91
1995 Bowie	AA Bal	16	0	0	14	20.2	83	16	9	9	2	0	0	0	7	1	32	1	0	2	2	.500	0	7	3.92
Rochester	AAA Bal	28	0	0	22	35.2	149	32	16	16	3	5	1	0	18	2	32	1	0	1	3	.250	0	6	4.04
1996 Richmond	AAA Atl	34	0	0	19	53.1	224	42	25	22	4	4	4	0	30	1	40	1	0	1	5	.167	0	3	3.71
1997 Richmond	AAA Atl	21	0	0	4	37.2	159	32	16	15	3	2	0	1	19	2	34	4	0	1	2	.333	0	2	3.58
1998 Columbus	AAA NYY	45	0	0	10	73.2	320	66	25	24	6	3	4	2	39	1	67	3	0	3	3	.500	0	4	2.93
1999 Louisville	AAA Mil	58	0	0	28	89	399	94	59	54	7	4	6	3	44	3	70	1	0	6	2	.750	0	5	5.46
1995 Baltimore	AL	6	0	0	3	7.1	30	5	1	1	0	0	0	0	4	0	3	0	0	0	0	.000	0	0	1.23
1996 Atlanta	NL	22	0	0	8	26	121	33	15	14	4	5	0	1	13	4	15	1	0	2	4	.333	0	0	4.85
1997 Atlanta	NL	20	0	0	8	24	111	27	11	10	2	1	0	0	16	4	6	0	0	2	2	.500	0	0	3.75
New York	AL	1	0	0	1	2	12	2	2	2	0	0	0	0	4	1	2	0	0	0	1	.000	0	0	9.00
1998 New York	AL	8	0	0	6	9.2	42	11	7	7	0	0	0	0	4	0	7	0	0	1	0	1.000	0	0	6.52
10 Min. YEARS		411	13	0	230	678.2	2958	611	307	273	41	37	30	17	351	21	663	33	4	35	38	.479	0	78	3.62
4 Maj. YEARS		57	0	0	26	69	316	78	36	34	6	6	0	1	41	9	33	1	0	5	7	.417	0	0	4.43

Shawn Boskie

Pitches: Right **Bats:** Right **Pos:** P   **Ht:** 6' 3" **Wt:** 210 **Born:** 3/28/67 **Age:** 33

Year Team	Lg Org	G	GS	CG	GF	IP	BFP	H	R	ER	HR	SH	SF	HB	TBB	IBB	SO	WP	Bk	W	L	Pct.	ShO	Sv	ERA
1986 Wytheville	R+ ChC	14	12	1	0	54	268	42	41	32	4	0	1	7	57	1	40	15	0	4	4	.500	0	0	5.33
1987 Peoria	A ChC	26	25	1	0	149	657	149	91	72	12	4	5	17	56	2	100	7	5	9	11	.450	0	0	4.35
1988 Winston-Sal	A+ ChC	27	27	4	0	186	825	176	83	70	9	4	7	17	89	1	164	14	4	12	7	.632	2	0	3.39
1989 Charlotte	AA ChC	28	28	5	0	181	813	196	105	88	10	3	8	19	84	3	164	11	1	11	8	.579	0	0	4.38
1990 Iowa	AAA ChC	8	8	1	0	51	217	46	22	18	1	2	1	2	21	1	51	1	0	4	2	.667	0	0	3.18
1991 Iowa	AAA ChC	7	6	2	0	45.1	186	43	19	18	1	5	1	2	11	0	29	1	1	2	2	.500	0	0	3.57
1992 Iowa	AAA ChC	2	2	0	0	7.1	32	8	4	3	0	0	0	0	3	0	3	0	0	0	0	.000	0	0	3.68
1993 Iowa	AAA ChC	11	11	1	0	71.2	300	70	35	34	4	2	1	7	21	0	35	1	0	6	1	.857	0	0	4.27
1995 Lk Elsinore	A+ Ana	3	3	0	0	11	53	15	7	5	1	0	0	0	4	0	8	0	0	0	0	.000	0	0	4.09
Vancouver	AAA Ana	1	1	0	0	6	25	4	2	2	1	0	0	0	4	0	1	0	0	1	0	1.000	0	0	3.00
1998 Ottawa	AAA Mon	13	13	0	0	87	375	100	48	44	7	0	2	5	21	1	51	5	0	5	7	.417	0	0	4.55
1999 Albuquerque	AAA LA	15	15	0	0	86.1	401	111	66	56	14	3	4	4	37	2	62	5	0	4	8	.333	0	0	5.84
1990 Chicago	NL	15	15	1	0	97.2	415	99	42	40	8	8	2	1	31	3	49	3	2	5	6	.455	0	0	3.69
1991 Chicago	NL	28	20	0	2	129	582	150	78	75	14	8	6	5	52	4	62	1	1	4	9	.308	0	0	5.23
1992 Chicago	NL	23	18	0	2	91.2	393	96	55	51	14	9	6	4	36	3	39	5	1	5	11	.313	0	0	5.01
1993 Chicago	NL	39	2	0	10	65.2	277	63	30	25	7	4	1	7	21	2	39	5	0	5	3	.625	0	0	3.43
1994 Chicago	NL	2	0	0	0	3.2	14	3	0	0	0	0	0	0	0	0	2	1	0	0	0	.000	0	0	0.00
Philadelphia	NL	18	14	1	1	84.1	367	85	56	49	14	2	3	3	29	2	59	6	0	4	6	.400	0	0	5.23
Seattle	AL	2	1	0	0	2.2	13	4	2	2	1	0	0	0	1	1	0	0	0	0	1	.000	0	0	6.75
1995 California	AL	20	20	1	0	111.2	494	127	73	70	16	4	6	7	25	0	51	4	0	7	7	.500	0	0	5.64
1996 California	AL	37	28	1	1	189.1	860	226	126	112	40	6	4	13	67	7	133	10	0	12	11	.522	0	0	5.32
1997 Baltimore	AL	28	9	0	8	77	349	95	57	55	14	2	7	2	26	1	50	1	0	6	6	.500	0	1	6.43
1998 Montreal	NL	5	5	0	0	11.2	90	34	21	18	5	1	1	2	4	1	10	0	0	1	3	.250	0	0	9.17
11 Min. YEARS		155	151	15	0	935.2	4152	960	523	442	64	23	30	80	408	11	708	60	11	58	50	.537	2	0	4.25
9 Maj. YEARS		217	132	4	24	870.1	3854	982	540	497	133	44	36	44	292	24	494	36	4	49	63	.438	0	1	5.14

Heath Bost

Pitches: Right **Bats:** Right **Pos:** P   **Ht:** 6'4" **Wt:** 200 **Born:** 10/13/74 **Age:** 25

Year Team	Lg Org	G	GS	CG	GF	IP	BFP	H	R	ER	HR	SH	SF	HB	TBB	IBB	SO	WP	Bk	W	L	Pct.	ShO	Sv	ERA
1995 Portland	A- Col	10	0	0	1	16	63	15	6	6	1	0	0	0	0	0	25	1	0	1	0	1.000	0	0	3.38
Asheville	A Col	9	2	0	4	23.2	90	20	6	4	1	0	0	1	3	0	17	1	2	4	1	.800	0	0	1.52
1996 New Haven	AA Col	4	0	0	2	6	24	5	1	1	0	0	0	0	2	0	7	0	0	1	0	1.000	0	0	1.50
Asheville	A Col	41	0	0	29	76	293	45	13	11	3	6	0	1	19	5	102	2	0	5	2	.714	0	15	1.30
1997 Salem	A+ Col	13	0	0	10	15	57	9	4	4	1	1	0	0	2	0	9	0	0	1	0	1.000	0	3	2.40
Colo Sprngs	AAA Col	2	0	0	0	3	21	10	8	7	1	0	1	0	1	0	3	0	0	0	0	.000	0	0	21.00
New Haven	AA Col	38	0	0	32	43	180	44	18	17	3	0	0	0	10	1	45	5	0	2	2	.500	0	20	3.56
1998 New Haven	AA Col	41	0	0	14	46.1	193	43	20	17	2	5	0	4	11	0	48	3	1	4	2	.667	0	3	3.30
1999 Colo Sprngs	AAA Col	38	6	0	8	86.1	378	120	59	53	10	2	1	4	12	2	67	0	0	5	4	.556	0	0	5.53
5 Min. YEARS		196	8	0	100	315.1	1299	311	135	120	22	14	2	10	60	8	323	12	3	23	12	.657	0	40	3.42

Mike Bovee

Pitches: Right Bats: Right Pos: P   Ht: 5'10" Wt: 219 Born: 8/21/73 Age: 26

Year Team	Lg Org	G	GS	CG	GF	IP	BFP	H	R	ER	HR	SH	SF	HB	TBB	IBB	SO	WP	Bk	W	L	Pct.	ShO	Sv	ERA
1991 Royals	R KC	11	11	0	0	61.2	251	52	19	14	1	0	1	1	12	0	76	4	0	3	1	.750	0	0	2.04
1992 Appleton	A KC	28	24	1	0	149.1	618	143	85	59	8	4	9	3	41	1	120	13	3	9	10	.474	0	0	3.56
1993 Rockford	A KC	20	20	2	0	109	469	118	58	51	1	4	4	6	30	0	111	15	0	5	9	.357	0	0	4.21
1994 Wilmington	A+ KC	28	26	0	1	169.2	675	149	58	50	10	4	3	4	32	0	154	8	1	13	4	.765	0	0	2.65
1995 Wichita	AA KC	20	20	1	0	114	486	118	60	53	12	2	4	2	43	0	72	4	0	8	6	.571	0	0	4.18
1996 Wichita	AA KC	27	27	3	0	176.2	783	223	113	95	21	9	8	6	40	1	102	10	0	10	11	.476	2	0	4.84
1997 Midland	AA Ana	20	13	3	1	102	424	117	53	48	7	3	5	4	23	0	61	7	0	8	2	.800	0	0	4.24
Vancouver	AAA Ana	12	12	1	0	89	377	92	38	34	7	4	2	7	25	0	71	4	0	4	3	.571	0	0	3.44
1998 Vancouver	AAA Ana	48	8	1	13	95	436	109	61	59	6	7	3	6	50	4	76	4	0	3	12	.200	1	1	5.59
1999 Syracuse	AAA Tor	19	3	0	6	35.2	175	49	29	29	6	2	2	2	20	1	32	1	0	2	0	.000	0	1	7.32
Erie	AA Ana	26	0	0	23	34	132	26	6	5	2	0	1	2	5	0	33	0	0	1	1	.500	0	12	1.32
1997 Anaheim	AL	3	0	0	3	3.1	14	3	2	2	1	0	0	0	1	0	5	0	0	0	0	.000	0	0	5.40
9 Min. YEARS		259	164	12	44	1136	4826	1196	580	497	81	39	42	43	321	7	908	70	4	64	61	.512	3	14	3.94

Brent Bowers

Bats: Right Throws: Left Pos: OF   Ht: 6'4" Wt: 215 Born: 5/2/71 Age: 29

Year Team	Lg Org	G	AB	H	2B	3B	HR	TB	R	RBI	TBB	IBB	SO	HBP	SH	SF	SB	CS	SB%	GDP	Avg	OBP	SLG
1989 Medcine Hat	R+ Tor	54	207	46	2	2	0	52	16	13	19	0	55	0	0	1	6	2	.75	5	.222	.286	.251
1990 Medcine Hat	R+ Tor	60	212	58	7	3	3	80	30	27	31	0	35	1	1	0	19	8	.70	2	.274	.369	.377
1991 Myrtle Bch	A Tor	120	402	101	8	4	2	123	53	44	31	1	76	2	9	4	35	12	.74	11	.251	.305	.306
1992 Dunedin	A+ Tor	128	524	133	10	3	3	158	74	46	34	0	99	3	8	1	31	15	.67	4	.254	.302	.302
1993 Knoxville	AA Tor	141	577	143	23	4	5	189	63	43	21	1	121	3	13	0	36	19	.65	5	.248	.278	.328
1994 Knoxville	AA Tor	127	472	129	18	11	4	181	52	49	20	4	75	1	7	2	15	8	.65	8	.273	.303	.383
1995 Syracuse	AAA Tor	111	305	77	16	5	5	118	38	26	10	0	57	1	1	1	5	1	.83	3	.252	.278	.387
1996 Bowie	AA Bal	58	228	71	11	1	9	111	37	25	17	2	40	2	3	0	10	4	.71	1	.311	.364	.487
Rochester	AAA Bal	49	206	67	8	4	4	95	40	19	14	0	41	0	3	0	9	3	.75	1	.325	.368	.461
1997 Scranton-WB	AAA Phi	39	110	28	2	0	3	39	15	7	8	0	28	1	0	1	1	1	.50	1	.255	.308	.355
1998 Norfolk	AAA NYM	82	275	67	8	3	5	96	36	31	21	0	59	0	3	5	17	6	.74	6	.244	.292	.349
Knoxville	AA Tor	27	107	30	5	1	2	43	19	12	16	1	18	0	1	0	9	1	.90	3	.280	.374	.402
1999 West Tenn	AA ChC	35	100	16	4	0	2	26	10	9	11	1	16	1	1	1	4	0	1.00	2	.160	.248	.260
1996 Baltimore	AL	21	39	12	2	0	0	14	6	3	0	0	7	0	0	0	1	0	.00	1	.308	.308	.359
11 Min. YEARS		1031	3725	966	122	41	47	1311	483	351	253	10	720	15	50	16	197	80	.71	52	.259	.308	.352

Cedrick Bowers

Pitches: Left Bats: Right Pos: P   Ht: 6'2" Wt: 210 Born: 2/10/78 Age: 22

Year Team	Lg Org	G	GS	CG	GF	IP	BFP	H	R	ER	HR	SH	SF	HB	TBB	IBB	SO	WP	Bk	W	L	Pct.	ShO	Sv	ERA
1996 Devil Rays	R TB	13	13	0	0	60.1	268	50	39	36	2	0	2	3	39	0	85	5	5	3	5	.375	0	0	5.37
1997 Chston-SC	A TB	28	28	0	0	157	657	119	74	56	11	4	3	3	78	0	164	15	1	8	10	.444	0	0	3.21
1998 St. Pete	A+ TB	28	26	0	1	150	655	144	89	73	14	6	4	1	80	1	156	6	2	5	9	.357	0	0	4.38
1999 Orlando	AA TB	27	27	1	0	125	567	125	94	83	18	3	5	4	76	0	138	12	1	6	9	.400	0	0	5.98
4 Min. YEARS		96	94	1	1	492.1	2147	438	296	248	45	13	14	11	273	1	543	38	9	22	33	.400	0	0	4.53

Shane Bowers

Pitches: Right Bats: Right Pos: P   Ht: 6'5" Wt: 220 Born: 7/27/71 Age: 28

Year Team	Lg Org	G	GS	CG	GF	IP	BFP	H	R	ER	HR	SH	SF	HB	TBB	IBB	SO	WP	Bk	W	L	Pct.	ShO	Sv	ERA
1993 Elizabethtn	R+ Min	7	1	0	4	11.1	48	13	7	6	0	1	1	0	1	0	13	3	0	2	0	1.000	0	0	4.76
1994 Fort Wayne	A Min	27	11	1	9	81.2	333	76	32	30	3	5	1	6	18	1	72	8	0	6	4	.600	0	5	3.31
Fort Myers	A+ Min	13	0	0	5	17.2	85	28	7	7	1	0	0	4	4	0	19	2	0	0	0	.000	0	0	3.57
1995 Fort Myers	A+ Min	23	23	1	0	145.2	580	119	43	35	6	2	4	12	32	1	103	6	1	13	5	.722	0	0	2.16
1996 Hardware Cy	AA Min	27	22	1	1	131	569	134	71	61	15	2	3	6	42	1	96	11	0	6	8	.429	0	0	4.19
1997 New Britain	AA Min	14	13	1	0	71.1	299	65	29	27	6	2	3	4	22	0	59	2	0	7	2	.778	1	0	3.41
Salt Lake	AAA Min	9	9	1	0	56.1	247	64	35	30	12	1	4	3	14	0	46	2	0	6	2	.750	0	0	4.79
1998 Salt Lake	AAA Min	33	16	2	2	110	498	137	76	72	18	1	1	1	40	0	101	6	0	9	7	.563	0	0	5.89
1999 Salt Lake	AAA Min	31	18	0	1	122	560	149	86	77	25	2	5	1	54	0	103	11	0	7	4	.636	0	0	5.68
1997 Minnesota	AL	5	5	0	0	19	92	27	20	17	2	0	1	1	8	0	7	1	0	0	3	.000	0	0	8.05
7 Min. YEARS		184	113	7	22	747	3219	785	386	345	86	16	22	33	227	3	612	51	1	56	32	.636	1	5	4.16

Justin Bowles

Bats: Left Throws: Left Pos: OF   Ht: 6'0" Wt: 185 Born: 8/20/73 Age: 26

Year Team	Lg Org	G	AB	H	2B	3B	HR	TB	R	RBI	TBB	IBB	SO	HBP	SH	SF	SB	CS	SB%	GDP	Avg	OBP	SLG
1996 Sou Oregon	A Oak	56	214	61	20	1	11	116	41	45	31	2	53	1	0	0	8	3	.73	1	.285	.378	.542
Huntsville	AA Oak	3	12	4	0	0	0	4	1	2	0	0	5	1	0	0	0	0	.00	0	.333	.385	.333
1997 Modesto	A+ Oak	107	394	129	39	9	7	207	66	51	56	2	85	5	5	5	6	3	.67	3	.327	.413	.525
1998 Huntsville	AA Oak	74	274	76	21	1	10	129	50	48	37	0	60	1	4	3	2	1	.67	11	.277	.362	.471
1999 Midland	AA Oak	131	489	140	27	8	20	243	73	73	44	1	122	2	3	4	10	7	.59	13	.286	.345	.497
4 Min. YEARS		371	1383	410	107	19	48	699	231	219	168	5	325	10	12	12	26	14	.65	28	.296	.374	.505

Josh Bradford

Pitches: Right Bats: Right Pos: P Ht: 6'5" Wt: 185 Born: 4/19/74 Age: 26

		HOW MUCH HE PITCHED						WHAT HE GAVE UP												THE RESULTS					
Year Team	Lg Org	G	GS	CG	GF	IP	BFP	H	R	ER	HR	SH	SF	HB	TBB	IBB	SO	WP	Bk	W	L	Pct.	ShO	Sv	ERA
1996 St.Cathrnes	A- Tor	18	7	0	3	53.2	232	49	27	20	1	1	3	4	17	0	63	8	2	5	4	.556	0	1	3.35
1997 Dunedin	A+ Tor	28	23	2	3	158.2	701	173	104	88	11	0	5	11	65	3	92	18	5	8	8	.500	1	0	4.99
1998 Dunedin	A+ Tor	17	12	1	3	70.2	316	75	43	39	4	4	1	7	30	0	46	5	0	4	4	.500	0	1	4.97
1999 Syracuse	AAA Tor	1	1	0	0	4	24	9	8	8	2	0	0	0	3	0	2	1	0	0	1	.000	0	0	18.00
Knoxville	AA Tor	34	12	0	6	105	465	109	65	62	9	1	4	5	53	1	83	11	0	5	4	.556	0	2	5.31
4 Min. YEARS		98	55	3	15	392	1738	415	247	217	27	6	13	27	168	4	286	43	7	22	21	.512	1	4	4.98

Milton Bradley

Bats: Both Throws: Right Pos: OF Ht: 6'0" Wt: 170 Born: 4/15/78 Age: 22

		BATTING															BASERUNNING				PERCENTAGES		
Year Team	Lg Org	G	AB	H	2B	3B	HR	TB	R	RBI	TBB	IBB	SO	HBP	SH	SF	SB	CS	SB%	GDP	Avg	OBP	SLG
1996 Expos	R Mon	31	109	27	7	1	1	39	18	12	13	0	14	1	1	2	7	4	.64	2	.248	.328	.358
1997 Vermont	A- Mon	50	200	60	7	5	3	86	29	30	17	1	34	0	1	2	7	7	.50	6	.300	.352	.430
Expos	R Mon	9	25	5	2	0	1	10	6	2	4	0	4	1	0	0	2	2	.50	0	.200	.333	.400
1998 Cape Fear	A Mon	75	281	85	21	4	6	132	54	50	23	1	57	4	3	3	13	8	.62	7	.302	.360	.470
Jupiter	A+ Mon	67	261	75	14	1	5	106	55	34	30	2	42	5	1	2	17	9	.65	3	.287	.369	.406
1999 Harrisburg	AA Mon	87	346	114	22	5	12	182	62	50	33	0	61	3	1	2	14	10	.58	5	.329	.391	.526
4 Min. YEARS		319	1222	366	73	16	28	555	224	178	120	4	212	14	7	11	60	40	.60	23	.300	.366	.454

Ryan Bradley

Pitches: Right Bats: Right Pos: P Ht: 6'4" Wt: 226 Born: 10/26/75 Age: 24

		HOW MUCH HE PITCHED						WHAT HE GAVE UP												THE RESULTS					
Year Team	Lg Org	G	GS	CG	GF	IP	BFP	H	R	ER	HR	SH	SF	HB	TBB	IBB	SO	WP	Bk	W	L	Pct.	ShO	Sv	ERA
1997 Oneonta	A- NYY	14	0	0	9	26.2	103	22	5	4	1	0	0	0	5	1	22	0	1	3	1	.750	0	1	1.35
1998 Tampa	A+ NYY	32	11	1	18	94.2	383	59	29	25	1	5	1	6	30	4	112	16	2	7	4	.636	1	7	2.38
Norwich	AA NYY	3	3	1	0	25	89	8	4	4	1	0	0	0	8	0	25	2	0	2	0	1.000	1	0	1.44
Columbus	AAA NYY	3	3	0	0	16	72	15	13	11	4	0	0	0	13	0	12	1	0	0	1	.000	0	0	6.19
1999 Columbus	AAA NYY	29	24	1	1	145	664	163	112	100	28	5	9	10	73	0	118	23	1	5	12	.294	0	0	6.21
1998 New York	AL	5	1	0	1	12.2	59	12	9	8	2	0	1	1	9	0	13	0	0	2	1	.667	0	0	5.68
3 Min. YEARS		81	41	3	28	307.1	1311	267	163	144	39	6	10	16	129	5	289	40	4	17	18	.486	2	8	4.22

Terry Bradshaw

Bats: Left Throws: Right Pos: OF Ht: 6'0" Wt: 195 Born: 2/3/69 Age: 31

		BATTING															BASERUNNING				PERCENTAGES		
Year Team	Lg Org	G	AB	H	2B	3B	HR	TB	R	RBI	TBB	IBB	SO	HBP	SH	SF	SB	CS	SB%	GDP	Avg	OBP	SLG
1990 Hamilton	A- StL	68	236	55	5	1	3	71	37	13	24	1	60	1	2	1	15	3	.83	4	.233	.305	.301
1991 Savannah	A StL	132	443	105	17	1	7	145	90	42	99	1	117	10	4	5	64	15	.81	6	.237	.384	.327
1993 St. Pete	A+ StL	125	461	134	25	6	5	186	84	51	82	1	60	7	7	5	43	17	.72	8	.291	.402	.403
1994 Arkansas	AA StL	114	425	119	25	8	10	190	65	52	50	4	69	7	2	4	13	10	.57	5	.280	.362	.447
Louisville	AAA StL	22	80	20	4	0	4	36	16	8	6	0	10	2	1	0	5	1	.83	2	.250	.318	.450
1995 Louisville	AAA StL	111	389	110	24	8	8	174	65	42	53	0	60	3	7	1	20	7	.74	6	.283	.372	.447
1996 Louisville	AAA StL	102	389	118	23	1	12	179	56	44	42	1	64	2	0	2	21	9	.70	6	.303	.372	.460
1997 Louisville	AAA StL	130	453	113	17	6	8	166	79	43	61	1	79	9	1	0	26	10	.72	12	.249	.350	.366
1998 Omaha	AAA KC	105	295	78	12	0	13	129	61	35	51	2	52	4	1	1	12	6	.67	2	.264	.379	.437
1999 Ottawa	AAA Mon	56	127	25	5	3	0	36	13	10	16	1	31	3	1	1	4	2	.67	1	.197	.299	.283
1995 St. Louis	NL	19	44	10	1	1	0	13	6	2	2	0	10	0	0	0	1	2	.33	0	.227	.261	.295
1996 St. Louis	NL	15	21	7	1	0	0	8	4	3	3	0	2	0	0	0	0	1	.00	0	.333	.417	.381
9 Min. YEARS		965	3298	877	157	34	70	1312	566	340	484	12	602	48	26	20	223	80	.74	50	.266	.366	.398
2 Maj. YEARS		34	65	17	2	1	0	21	10	5	5	0	12	0	0	0	1	3	.25	0	.262	.314	.323

J.D. Brammer

Pitches: Right Bats: Right Pos: P Ht: 6'4" Wt: 235 Born: 1/30/75 Age: 25

		HOW MUCH HE PITCHED						WHAT HE GAVE UP												THE RESULTS					
Year Team	Lg Org	G	GS	CG	GF	IP	BFP	H	R	ER	HR	SH	SF	HB	TBB	IBB	SO	WP	Bk	W	L	Pct.	ShO	Sv	ERA
1996 Watertown	A- Cle	17	0	0	5	38	173	27	22	15	0	0	3	3	28	1	49	8	5	5	0	1.000	0	1	3.55
1997 Columbus	A Cle	28	23	0	1	116.2	542	132	102	91	11	2	7	18	50	0	105	9	4	6	10	.375	0	1	7.02
1998 Kinston	A+ Cle	15	0	0	8	27	106	15	6	4	1	0	0	1	8	0	33	1	1	3	2	.600	0	2	1.33
Akron	AA Cle	11	0	0	4	20.2	95	21	12	12	3	0	1	1	10	1	23	4	2	1	0	1.000	0	3	5.23
1999 Akron	AA Cle	47	0	0	24	75.2	349	53	44	40	6	4	3	9	60	0	69	11	3	3	2	.600	0	8	4.76
4 Min. YEARS		118	23	0	42	278	1265	248	186	162	21	6	14	32	156	2	279	33	15	18	14	.563	0	15	5.24

Ryan Brannan

Pitches: Right Bats: Right Pos: P Ht: 6'3" Wt: 225 Born: 4/27/75 Age: 25

		HOW MUCH HE PITCHED						WHAT HE GAVE UP												THE RESULTS					
Year Team	Lg Org	G	GS	CG	GF	IP	BFP	H	R	ER	HR	SH	SF	HB	TBB	IBB	SO	WP	Bk	W	L	Pct.	ShO	Sv	ERA
1997 Clearwater	A+ Phi	21	0	0	18	27.1	108	20	2	1	0	5	0	0	8	0	25	2	2	0	0	.000	0	10	0.33
Reading	AA Phi	45	0	0	41	52.1	223	52	18	18	2	7	1	5	20	2	39	3	2	4	2	.667	0	20	3.10
1998 Scranton-WB	AAA Phi	16	0	0	12	16.2	88	21	18	14	0	1	1	3	13	2	12	3	0	1	1	.500	0	2	7.56
Reading	AA Phi	41	0	0	26	55.2	254	55	31	22	5	5	2	4	29	3	42	4	1	4	4	.556	0	6	3.56
1999 Clearwater	A+ Phi	28	13	0	11	77.1	370	86	63	42	8	1	4	13	40	0	39	10	1	4	4	.500	0	0	4.89
Reading	AA Phi	5	0	0	1	4.1	28	9	8	8	0	1	1	1	4	1	1	1	0	0	0	.000	0	0	16.62
3 Min. YEARS		156	13	0	109	233.2	1071	243	140	105	15	20	9	26	114	8	158	23	6	14	11	.560	0	38	4.04

Jeff Branson

Bats: Left **Throws:** Right **Pos:** SS **Ht:** 6' 0" **Wt:** 180 **Born:** 1/26/67 **Age:** 33

Year Team	Lg Org	G	AB	H	2B	3B	HR	TB	R	RBI	TBB	IBB	SO	HBP	SH	SF	SB	CS	SB%	GDP	Avg	OBP	SLG
1989 Cedar Rapds	A Cin	127	469	132	28	1	10	192	70	68	41	3	90	2	4	4	5	6	.45	10	.281	.339	.409
1990 Chattanooga	AA Cin	63	233	49	9	1	2	66	19	29	13	2	48	0	1	2	3	1	.75	4	.210	.250	.283
Cedar Rapds	A Cin	62	239	60	13	4	6	99	37	24	24	3	45	0	0	2	11	3	.79	6	.251	.317	.414
1991 Chattanooga	AA Cin	88	304	80	13	3	2	105	35	28	31	2	51	1	2	5	3	7	.30	4	.263	.328	.345
Nashville	AAA Cin	43	145	35	4	1	0	41	10	11	8	2	31	0	1	0	5	4	.56	1	.241	.281	.283
1992 Nashville	AAA Cin	36	123	40	6	3	4	64	18	12	9	1	19	0	1	0	0	3	.00	1	.325	.371	.520
1997 Indianapols	AAA Cin	15	57	12	3	0	1	18	7	4	6	0	10	0	1	0	0	0	.00	1	.211	.286	.316
1998 Buffalo	AAA Cle	12	46	12	4	1	0	18	5	2	5	1	9	0	0	0	0	0	.00	0	.261	.333	.391
1999 Indianapols	AAA Cin	124	430	109	18	2	7	152	57	56	46	3	86	1	1	2	2	2	.50	3	.253	.326	.353
1992 Cincinnati	NL	72	115	34	7	1	0	43	12	15	5	2	16	0	2	1	0	1	.00	4	.296	.322	.374
1993 Cincinnati	NL	125	381	92	15	1	3	118	40	22	19	2	73	0	8	4	4	1	.80	4	.241	.275	.310
1994 Cincinnati	NL	58	109	31	4	1	6	55	18	16	5	2	16	0	2	0	0	0	.00	4	.284	.316	.505
1995 Cincinnati	NL	122	331	86	18	2	12	144	43	45	44	14	69	2	1	6	2	1	.67	9	.260	.345	.435
1996 Cincinnati	NL	129	311	76	16	4	9	127	34	37	31	4	67	1	7	3	2	0	1.00	9	.244	.312	.408
1997 Cincinnati	NL	65	98	15	3	1	1	23	9	5	7	1	23	0	1	0	1	0	1.00	3	.153	.210	.235
Cleveland	AL	29	72	19	4	0	2	29	5	7	7	0	17	1	0	2	0	2	.00	1	.264	.329	.403
1998 Cleveland	AL	63	100	20	4	1	1	29	6	9	3	0	21	0	1	1	0	0	.00	1	.200	.221	.290
7 Min. YEARS		570	2046	529	98	16	32	755	258	234	183	17	389	4	11	15	29	26	.53	30	.259	.319	.369
7 Maj. YEARS		660	1517	373	71	11	34	568	167	156	121	25	302	4	22	17	9	5	.64	35	.246	.300	.374

Bryan Braswell

Pitches: Left **Bats:** Left **Pos:** P **Ht:** 6'1" **Wt:** 200 **Born:** 6/30/75 **Age:** 25

Year Team	Lg Org	G	GS	CG	GF	IP	BFP	H	R	ER	HR	SH	SF	HB	TBB	IBB	SO	WP	Bk	W	L	Pct.	ShO	Sv	ERA
1996 Auburn	A- Hou	15	14	0	1	73	325	70	40	35	2	1	2	11	29	2	77	9	1	4	8	.333	0	0	4.32
1997 Quad City	A Hou	19	19	1	0	116.1	495	107	70	49	10	0	4	2	32	0	118	2	5	6	6	.500	0	0	3.79
1998 Kissimmee	A+ Hou	27	26	2	0	159.2	698	176	92	70	22	3	3	4	48	0	118	7	2	11	9	.550	1	0	3.95
1999 Jackson	AA Hou	28	28	1	0	171.1	741	180	104	86	27	4	6	4	54	0	131	10	0	9	10	.474	0	0	4.52
4 Min. YEARS		89	87	4	1	520.1	2259	533	306	240	61	8	15	21	163	2	444	28	8	30	33	.476	1	0	4.15

Danny Bravo

Bats: Both **Throws:** Right **Pos:** 3B-2B **Ht:** 5'11" **Wt:** 175 **Born:** 5/27/77 **Age:** 23

Year Team	Lg Org	G	AB	H	2B	3B	HR	TB	R	RBI	TBB	IBB	SO	HBP	SH	SF	SB	CS	SB%	GDP	Avg	OBP	SLG
1996 Wst Plm Bch	A+ Mon	48	137	27	2	2	0	33	15	12	14	0	30	1	3	0	3	4	.43	0	.197	.276	.241
Delmarva	A Mon	18	61	14	6	1	0	22	10	7	2	0	14	1	2	1	1	0	1.00	1	.230	.262	.361
1997 Wst Plm Bch	A+ Mon	15	37	6	1	1	0	9	3	0	2	0	5	0	0	0	0	0	.00	0	.162	.205	.243
Cape Fear	A Mon	73	253	68	9	1	3	88	28	34	9	0	31	4	3	3	3	4	.43	4	.269	.301	.348
1998 Cape Fear	A Mon	101	343	95	12	4	4	127	48	44	32	2	65	8	14	1	7	10	.41	11	.277	.352	.370
Jupiter	A+ Mon	24	71	11	1	0	0	12	5	3	8	0	14	2	0	2	1	1	.50	0	.155	.253	.169
1999 Jupiter	A+ Mon	7	20	6	3	0	1	12	5	3	1	0	5	1	2	0	0	0	.00	1	.300	.364	.600
Harrisburg	AA Mon	12	28	4	1	0	0	5	0	2	1	0	6	0	1	0	0	0	.00	0	.143	.172	.179
Birmingham	AA CWS	76	270	76	12	1	2	96	49	38	41	2	39	2	3	3	6	5	.55	9	.281	.377	.356
4 Min. YEARS		374	1220	307	47	10	10	404	163	143	110	3	209	19	28	10	21	24	.47	26	.252	.321	.331

Jason Brester

Pitches: Left **Bats:** Left **Pos:** P **Ht:** 6'3" **Wt:** 190 **Born:** 12/7/76 **Age:** 23

Year Team	Lg Org	G	GS	CG	GF	IP	BFP	H	R	ER	HR	SH	SF	HB	TBB	IBB	SO	WP	Bk	W	L	Pct.	ShO	Sv	ERA
1995 Bellingham	A- SF	8	6	0	0	24	104	23	11	11	3	0	1	3	12	0	17	0	0	1	0	1.000	0	0	4.13
1996 Burlington	A SF	27	27	0	0	157	659	139	78	69	14	4	7	3	64	0	143	13	1	10	9	.526	0	0	3.96
1997 San Jose	A+ SF	26	26	0	0	142.1	625	164	80	67	14	4	3	3	52	0	172	10	7	9	9	.500	0	0	4.24
1998 Shreveport	AA SF	19	19	0	0	113	490	117	58	48	11	7	4	0	44	3	79	4	2	2	8	.200	0	0	3.82
New Haven	AA Col	5	4	0	0	22.2	97	22	7	4	0	1	0	1	7	0	15	3	1	2	0	1.000	0	0	1.59
1999 Carolina	AA Col	11	11	0	0	59.1	268	71	45	38	8	1	1	2	26	0	44	3	3	2	6	.250	0	0	5.76
Reading	AA Phi	16	16	3	0	105.1	436	105	48	44	8	4	6	2	26	1	87	6	2	7	5	.583	1	0	3.76
5 Min. YEARS		112	109	3	0	623.2	2679	641	327	281	48	21	21	12	231	4	557	39	16	33	37	.471	1	0	4.06

Ryan Brewer

Pitches: Right **Bats:** Left **Pos:** P **Ht:** 6'2" **Wt:** 185 **Born:** 10/31/73 **Age:** 26

Year Team	Lg Org	G	GS	CG	GF	IP	BFP	H	R	ER	HR	SH	SF	HB	TBB	IBB	SO	WP	Bk	W	L	Pct.	ShO	Sv	ERA
1996 Lubbock	IND —	8	8	4	0	61.1	247	49	20	14	3	5	0	2	17	3	39	3	1	5	3	.625	1	0	2.05
Spokane	A- KC	17	2	0	11	43	182	41	20	16	4	4	2	1	16	0	39	3	0	3	2	.600	0	5	3.35
1997 Wilmington	A+ KC	47	0	0	19	105	439	100	41	39	5	6	0	3	29	4	93	4	0	5	4	.556	0	7	3.34
1998 Wilmington	A+ KC	26	0	0	13	41	189	36	12	7	2	3	1	0	11	0	00	1	0	0	1	.769	0	0	1.51
Omaha	AAA KC	1	0	0	1	2	7	0	0	0	0	0	0	0	0	0	0	0	0	0	0	.000	0	0	0.00
Wichita	AA KC	20	0	0	6	36	161	47	16	16	3	2	1	0	12	3	30	3	0	3	0	1.000	0	1	4.00
1999 Wichita	AA KC	42	1	0	20	66.2	291	85	45	41	9	6	3	3	17	3	34	5	1	5	2	.714	0	3	5.54
4 Min. YEARS		161	11	4	70	355	1496	358	154	133	26	28	7	9	102	16	271	22	2	24	12	.667	1	25	3.37

Kary Bridges

Bats: Left **Throws:** Right **Pos:** 2B **Ht:** 5'10" **Wt:** 170 **Born:** 10/27/72 **Age:** 27

							BATTING											BASERUNNING				PERCENTAGES		
Year Team	Lg Org	G	AB	H	2B	3B	HR	TB	R	RBI	TBB	IBB	SO	HBP	SH	SF	SB	CS	SB%	GDP	Avg	OBP	SLG
1993 Quad City	A Hou	65	263	74	9	0	3	92	37	24	31	1	18	2	1	3	15	10	.60	7	.281	.358	.350
1994 Quad City	A Hou	117	447	135	20	4	1	166	66	53	38	3	29	3	8	4	14	11	.56	9	.302	.358	.371
1995 Jackson	AA Hou	118	418	126	22	4	3	165	56	43	49	3	17	0	6	4	10	12	.45	12	.301	.372	.395
1996 Jackson	AA Hou	87	338	110	12	2	4	138	51	33	32	1	14	1	7	3	4	5	.44	11	.325	.382	.408
Tucson	AAA Hou	42	140	44	9	1	1	58	24	21	9	1	8	1	0	2	1	3	.25	3	.314	.355	.414
1997 New Orleans	AAA Hou	23	64	11	1	2	0	16	6	3	5	0	9	1	0	1	1	0	1.00	0	.172	.239	.250
Carolina	AA Pit	66	283	95	17	1	3	123	43	29	9	0	10	0	3	2	9	5	.64	7	.336	.354	.435
Calgary	AAA Pit	33	95	25	4	0	0	29	9	6	7	1	6	0	1	0	1	0	1.00	3	.263	.314	.305
1998 West Tenn	AA ChC	48	196	60	7	1	0	69	30	21	18	1	9	0	1	0	6	4	.60	4	.306	.363	.352
Iowa	AAA ChC	64	181	39	10	1	0	51	25	14	11	0	12	1	0	2	0	2	.00	4	.215	.262	.282
1999 Iowa	AAA ChC	10	25	3	0	0	0	3	1	0	1	0	5	0	0	0	0	0	.00	0	.120	.154	.120
Oklahoma	AAA Tex	75	239	82	14	0	7	117	38	39	21	2	14	1	4	3	6	3	.67	6	.343	.394	.490
7 Min. YEARS		748	2689	804	125	16	22	1027	386	286	231	13	151	10	31	25	67	55	.55	68	.299	.354	.382

Anthony Briggs

Pitches: Right **Bats:** Right **Pos:** P **Ht:** 6'1" **Wt:** 155 **Born:** 9/14/73 **Age:** 26

		HOW MUCH HE PITCHED						WHAT HE GAVE UP										THE RESULTS						
Year Team	Lg Org	G	GS	CG	GF	IP	BFP	H	R	ER	HR	SH	SF	HB	TBB	IBB	SO	WP	Bk	W	L	Pct.	ShO	Sv	ERA
1994 Braves	R Atl	1	0	0	1	4	14	1	0	0	0	0	0	0	1	0	1	0	0	0	0	.000	0	0	0.00
Idaho Falls	R+ Atl	20	0	0	5	49.2	227	58	30	22	1	2	2	2	21	2	45	6	0	2	3	.400	0	1	3.99
1995 Macon	A Atl	29	24	1	1	147.1	635	145	76	49	12	2	1	4	56	1	114	9	0	5	8	.615	1	0	2.99
1996 Durham	A+ Atl	31	18	1	3	124.2	548	131	84	61	10	7	9	3	60	1	76	9	1	9	10	.474	0	0	4.40
1997 Durham	A+ Atl	17	0	0	10	30	129	27	16	15	2	1	1	0	13	2	25	3	0	1	2	.333	0	3	4.50
Greenville	AA Atl	19	13	0	0	94.1	413	91	64	57	11	4	2	0	43	0	59	4	2	6	3	.667	0	0	5.44
1998 Greenville	AA Atl	6	0	0	3	12.2	55	12	9	8	0	1	1	0	8	0	10	6	0	1	0	1.000	0	0	5.68
Richmond	AAA Atl	28	21	0	5	121.2	536	125	82	72	16	1	4	1	57	0	91	9	1	7	10	.412	0	0	5.33
1999 Colo Sprngs	AAA Col	10	1	0	2	17.2	95	30	25	15	2	3	5	1	10	1	5	0	0	1	1	.500	0	0	7.64
Rockies	R Col	3	3	0	0	7.1	33	11	3	2	0	0	0	0	1	0	5	0	0	0	0	.000	0	0	2.45
Carolina	AA Col	4	0	0	1	4	22	7	5	5	0	1	1	0	4	0	4	0	0	0	1	.000	0	0	11.25
6 Min. YEARS		168	80	2	31	613.1	2707	638	394	306	54	22	26	11	274	7	435	46	4	35	35	.500	1	4	4.49

Jim Brink

Pitches: Right **Bats:** Right **Pos:** P **Ht:** 6'0" **Wt:** 185 **Born:** 9/11/76 **Age:** 23

		HOW MUCH HE PITCHED						WHAT HE GAVE UP										THE RESULTS						
Year Team	Lg Org	G	GS	CG	GF	IP	BFP	H	R	ER	HR	SH	SF	HB	TBB	IBB	SO	WP	Bk	W	L	Pct.	ShO	Sv	ERA
1998 Sou Oregon	A- Oak	24	1	0	17	56.1	241	63	32	27	4	1	2	1	16	2	43	2	2	5	0	1.000	0	11	4.31
1999 Midland	AA Oak	5	0	0	2	8	35	10	7	7	4	0	0	1	1	0	4	0	0	1	1	.500	0	0	7.88
Modesto	A+ Oak	47	0	0	41	45.1	204	53	24	23	2	5	4	0	18	3	38	0	0	1	0	1.000	0	29	4.57
2 Min. YEARS		76	1	0	60	109.2	480	126	63	57	10	6	6	2	35	5	85	2	2	7	1	.875	0	40	4.68

Darryl Brinkley

Bats: Right **Throws:** Right **Pos:** OF **Ht:** 5'11" **Wt:** 205 **Born:** 12/23/68 **Age:** 31

							BATTING											BASERUNNING				PERCENTAGES		
Year Team	Lg Org	G	AB	H	2B	3B	HR	TB	R	RBI	TBB	IBB	SO	HBP	SH	SF	SB	CS	SB%	GDP	Avg	OBP	SLG
1994 Winnipeg	IND —	72	294	86	18	3	8	134	48	44	21	0	31	6	3	1	32	13	.71	5	.293	.351	.456
1995 Winnipeg	IND —	30	131	44	2	1	4	60	22	19	8	1	13	3	1	2	6	4	.60	4	.336	.382	.458
1996 Rancho Cuca	A+ SD	65	259	94	28	2	9	153	52	59	23	2	37	2	0	6	18	10	.64	13	.363	.410	.591
Memphis	AA SD	60	203	60	9	0	9	96	36	29	22	2	33	3	1	1	13	5	.72	2	.296	.371	.473
1997 Mobile	AA SD	55	215	66	14	1	5	97	41	33	26	1	30	5	0	0	10	9	.53	6	.307	.394	.451
1998 Nashville	AAA Pit	114	372	132	23	3	9	188	57	51	27	2	53	13	0	1	10	8	.56	9	.355	.416	.505
1999 Nashville	AAA Pit	111	372	120	35	2	14	201	68	75	31	0	58	1	0	3	5	5	.50	11	.323	.373	.540
6 Min. YEARS		507	1846	602	129	12	58	929	324	310	158	8	255	33	5	14	94	54	.64	50	.326	.387	.503

Jorge Brito

Bats: Right **Throws:** Right **Pos:** C **Ht:** 6'1" **Wt:** 190 **Born:** 6/22/66 **Age:** 34

							BATTING											BASERUNNING				PERCENTAGES		
Year Team	Lg Org	G	AB	H	2B	3B	HR	TB	R	RBI	TBB	IBB	SO	HBP	SH	SF	SB	CS	SB%	GDP	Avg	OBP	SLG
1986 Medford	A- Oak	21	59	9	2	0	0	11	4	5	4	0	17	2	0	1	0	2	.00	3	.153	.227	.186
1987 Medford	A- Oak	40	110	20	1	0	1	24	7	15	12	0	54	1	1	2	0	0	.00	3	.182	.264	.218
1988 Modesto	A+ Oak	96	300	65	15	0	5	95	38	27	47	0	104	8	3	3	0	0	.00	6	.217	.335	.317
1989 Modesto	A+ Oak	16	54	13	2	0	1	18	8	6	5	0	14	1	1	0	0	0	.00	2	.241	.317	.333
Tacoma	AAA Oak	5	15	3	1	0	0	4	2	0	2	0	6	0	0	0	0	1	.00	2	.200	.294	.267
Huntsville	AA Oak	24	73	16	2	2	0	22	13	8	20	0	23	0	0	2	1	1	.50	2	.219	.387	.301
Madison	A Oak	43	143	30	4	1	3	45	20	14	22	1	46	2	1	0	1	0	1.00	9	.210	.323	.315
1990 Huntsville	AA Oak	57	164	44	6	1	2	58	17	20	30	1	49	3	3	1	0	1	.00	6	.268	.389	.354
1991 Tacoma	AAA Oak	22	73	17	2	0	1	22	6	3	4	0	20	0	0	0	0	1	.00	6	.233	.273	.301
Huntsville	AA Oak	65	203	41	11	0	1	55	26	23	28	0	50	4	2	1	0	1	.00	2	.202	.309	.271
1992 Tacoma	AAA Oak	18	35	5	2	0	0	7	4	1	2	0	17	0	0	0	0	0	.00	0	.143	.189	.200
Huntsville	AA Oak	33	72	15	2	0	2	23	10	6	13	0	21	1	3	0	2	0	1.00	3	.208	.337	.319
1993 Huntsville	AA Oak	18	36	10	3	0	4	25	6	11	10	1	10	0	2	1	0	0	.00	1	.278	.449	.694
1994 New Haven	AA Col	63	200	46	11	1	5	74	18	25	18	3	59	2	1	2	2	0	1.00	6	.230	.297	.370
Colo Sprngs	AAA Col	21	64	24	5	0	3	38	13	19	7	1	14	0	1	0	0	0	.00	3	.375	.437	.594
1995 Colo Sprngs	AAA Col	32	96	22	4	1	2	34	9	15	2	0	20	1	1	2	0	0	.00	3	.229	.248	.354
1996 Colo Sprngs	AAA Col	53	159	54	17	0	7	92	32	31	24	1	37	4	0	1	1	0	1.00	6	.340	.436	.579
1997 Syracuse	AAA Tor	8	30	7	3	0	2	16	3	4	3	0	10	2	0	1	0	0	1.00	2	.233	.343	.533

Year Team	Lg Org	G	AB	H	2B	3B	HR	TB	R	RBI	TBB	IBB	SO	HBP	SH	SF	SB	CS	SB%	GDP	Avg	OBP	SLG
1998 Louisville	AAA Mil	77	232	66	17	0	9	110	34	36	22	0	61	8	4	3	3	1	.75	4	.284	.362	.474
1999 Huntsville	AA Mil	26	67	20	2	1	3	33	11	7	4	0	15	2	0	0	0	0	.00	1	.299	.356	.493
Louisville	AAA Mil	4	18	1	0	0	0	1	0	0	0	0	9	0	0	0	0	0	.00	0	.056	.056	.056
1995 Colorado	NL	18	51	11	3	0	0	14	5	7	2	0	17	1	1	0	1	0	1.00	0	.216	.259	.275
1996 Colorado	NL	8	14	1	0	0	0	1	1	0	1	0	8	2	1	0	0	0	.00	0	.071	.235	.071
14 Min. YEARS		742	2203	528	112	7	51	807	281	276	279	8	656	43	25	17	10	8	.56	67	.240	.334	.366
2 Maj. YEARS		26	65	12	3	0	0	15	6	7	3	0	25	3	2	0	1	0	1.00	1	.185	.254	.231

Bats: Right **Throws:** Right **Pos:** C

Juan Brito

Ht: 5'11" **Wt:** 185 **Born:** 11/7/79 **Age:** 20

Year Team	Lg Org	G	AB	H	2B	3B	HR	TB	R	RBI	TBB	IBB	SO	HBP	SH	SF	SB	CS	SB%	GDP	Avg	OBP	SLG
1997 Royals	R KC	25	70	22	4	0	3	35	14	15	5	1	5	1	1	0	0	0	.00	1	.314	.368	.500
1998 Lansing	A KC	63	212	52	7	0	0	59	16	22	17	0	41	2	1	2	2	2	.50	6	.245	.305	.278
1999 Wilmington	A+ KC	14	46	13	1	0	0	14	3	1	1	0	11	0	0	0	0	0	.00	1	.283	.298	.304
Wichita	AA KC	4	11	1	0	0	0	1	0	0	2	0	3	0	0	0	0	0	.00	2	.091	.231	.091
Chstn-WV	A KC	61	208	50	6	0	0	56	14	19	11	0	37	1	3	0	1	2	.33	8	.240	.282	.269
Omaha	AAA KC	2	7	2	2	0	0	4	1	0	0	0	2	0	0	0	0	0	.00	0	.286	.286	.571
3 Min. YEARS		169	554	140	20	0	3	169	48	57	36	1	99	4	5	2	3	4	.43	18	.253	.302	.305

Bats: Right **Throws:** Right **Pos:** 2B

Tilson Brito

Ht: 6' 0" **Wt:** 180 **Born:** 5/28/72 **Age:** 28

Year Team	Lg Org	G	AB	H	2B	3B	HR	TB	R	RBI	TBB	IBB	SO	HBP	SH	SF	SB	CS	SB%	GDP	Avg	OBP	SLG
1992 Blue Jays	R Tor	54	189	58	10	4	3	85	36	36	22	1	22	6	0	5	16	8	.67	5	.307	.387	.450
Knoxville	AA Tor	7	24	5	1	2	0	10	2	2	0	0	9	0	0	0	0	0	.00	0	.208	.208	.417
1993 Dunedin	A+ Tor	126	465	125	21	3	6	170	80	44	59	0	60	10	10	3	27	16	.63	8	.269	.361	.366
1994 Knoxville	AA Tor	139	476	127	17	7	5	173	61	57	35	2	68	8	9	7	33	12	.73	7	.267	.323	.363
1995 Syracuse	AAA Tor	90	327	79	16	3	7	122	49	32	29	0	69	4	2	1	17	8	.68	6	.242	.310	.373
1996 Syracuse	AAA Tor	108	400	111	22	8	10	179	63	54	38	1	65	5	3	4	11	10	.52	8	.278	.345	.448
1997 Modesto	A+ Oak	4	9	3	1	0	1	7	3	3	2	0	1	2	0	0	0	0	.00	0	.333	.538	.778
1998 Tacoma	AAA Sea	42	143	37	12	1	2	57	20	12	8	0	29	2	3	1	0	1	.00	4	.259	.305	.399
1999 Charlotte	AAA CWS	111	406	129	30	5	11	202	60	58	34	3	66	12	3	3	6	4	.60	5	.318	.385	.498
1996 Toronto	AL	26	80	19	7	0	1	29	10	7	10	0	18	3	2	0	1	1	.50	0	.238	.344	.363
1997 Toronto	AL	49	126	28	3	0	0	31	9	8	9	0	28	2	0	2	1	0	1.00	2	.222	.281	.246
Oakland	AL	17	46	13	2	1	2	23	8	6	1	0	10	0	2	0	0	0	.00	0	.283	.298	.500
8 Min. YEARS		681	2439	674	130	33	45	1005	374	298	227	7	389	49	30	24	110	59	.65	43	.276	.347	.412
2 Maj. YEARS		92	252	60	12	1	3	83	27	21	20	0	56	5	4	2	2	1	.67	2	.238	.329	.329

Pitches: Right **Bats:** Right **Pos:** P

Corey Brittan

Ht: 6'6" **Wt:** 196 **Born:** 2/23/75 **Age:** 25

Year Team	Lg Org	G	GS	CG	GF	IP	BFP	H	R	ER	HR	SH	SF	HB	TBB	IBB	SO	WP	Bk	W	L	Pct.	ShO	Sv	ERA
1996 Pittsfield	A- NYM	14	14	2	0	98	390	74	30	25	2	4	0	2	20	0	84	5	2	8	3	.727	0	0	2.30
1997 St. Lucie	A+ NYM	51	1	0	18	78	338	91	35	31	5	4	0	1	21	4	57	2	0	3	5	.375	0	3	3.58
1998 Binghamton	AA NYM	9	0	0	3	9.1	40	9	4	4	0	0	1	0	4	0	5	3	0	1	1	.500	0	0	3.86
St. Lucie	A+ NYM	34	0	0	17	67	290	74	35	29	1	2	2	2	14	0	40	5	1	4	2	.667	0	2	3.90
1999 Binghamton	AA NYM	54	0	0	27	90.2	375	84	36	28	6	3	2	1	23	0	60	3	2	2	4	.333	0	7	2.78
4 Min. YEARS		162	15	2	65	343	1433	332	140	117	14	14	6	8	82	4	246	18	5	18	15	.545	0	12	3.07

Bats: Right **Throws:** Right **Pos:** 2B

J.J. Brock

Ht: 5'11" **Wt:** 175 **Born:** 12/4/74 **Age:** 25

Year Team	Lg Org	G	AB	H	2B	3B	HR	TB	R	RBI	TBB	IBB	SO	HBP	SH	SF	SB	CS	SB%	GDP	Avg	OBP	SLG
1998 South Bend	A Ari	91	354	92	19	3	2	123	45	21	26	1	75	3	6	2	4	8	.33	10	.260	.314	.347
1999 South Bend	A Ari	48	172	38	8	3	1	55	19	13	12	0	27	1	2	2	2	2	.50	6	.221	.273	.320
El Paso	AA Ari	43	136	26	4	2	0	34	13	8	4	1	26	2	1	0	0	1	.00	5	.191	.225	.250
2 Min. YEARS		182	662	156	31	8	3	212	77	42	42	2	128	6	9	4	6	11	.35	21	.236	.286	.320

Bats: Left **Throws:** Left **Pos:** OF

Tarrik Brock

Ht: 6'3" **Wt:** 170 **Born:** 12/25/73 **Age:** 26

Year Team	Lg Org	G	AB	H	2B	3B	HR	TB	R	RBI	TBB	IBB	SO	HBP	SH	SF	SB	CS	SB%	GDP	Avg	OBP	SLG
1991 Bristol	R+ Det	55	177	47	7	3	1	63	26	13	22	0	42	3	1	1	14	6	.70	3	.266	.355	.356
1992 Fayetteville	A Det	100	271	59	5	4	0	72	35	17	31	1	69	4	5	1	15	10	.60	2	.218	.306	.266
1993 Fayetteville	A Det	116	427	92	8	4	3	117	60	47	54	2	108	5	5	4	25	16	.61	5	.215	.308	.274
1994 Lakeland	A+ Det	86	331	77	17	14	2	128	43	32	38	2	89	2	2	2	15	6	.71	5	.233	.314	.387
Trenton	AA Det	34	115	16	1	4	2	31	12	11	13	0	43	2	1	0	3	3	.50	2	.139	.238	.270
1995 Toledo	AAA Det	9	31	6	1	0	0	7	4	0	2	0	17	0	0	0	2	0	1.00	0	.194	.242	.226
Jacksnville	AA Det	9	26	3	0	0	0	3	4	2	3	0	14	1	1	0	2	0	1.00	0	.115	.233	.115
Lakeland	A+ Det	28	91	19	3	0	0	22	12	5	12	0	32	0	1	0	5	3	.63	2	.209	.301	.242
Visalia	A+ Det	45	138	31	5	2	1	43	21	15	17	0	52	4	2	1	11	1	.92	2	.225	.327	.312
1996 Lakeland	A+ Det	53	212	59	11	4	5	93	42	27	17	0	61	5	0	3	8	2	.82	4	.278	.342	.439
Jacksnville	AA Det	37	102	13	2	0	0	15	14	6	10	0	36	1	0	0	3	3	.50	0	.127	.212	.147
Fayettevlle	A Det	32	119	35	5	2	1	47	21	11	14	1	31	4	0	1	11	6	.65	3	.294	.384	.395
1997 Lancaster	A+ Sea	132	402	108	21	12	7	174	88	47	78	1	106	6	6	6	40	8	.83	3	.269	.395	.433

36

Year Team	Lg Org	G	AB	H	2B	3B	HR	TB	R	RBI	TBB	IBB	SO	HBP	SH	SF	SB	CS	SB%	GDP	Avg	OBP	SLG
1998 Orlando	AA Sea	111	372	103	28	7	15	190	76	65	59	4	110	6	1	5	17	9	.65	2	.277	.380	.511
Tacoma	AAA Sea	24	94	23	2	3	1	34	14	14	9	0	28	0	1	1	5	0	1.00	1	.245	.308	.362
1999 Carolina	AA Col	66	218	54	10	1	7	87	40	23	39	0	67	1	1	1	7	4	.64	2	.248	.363	.399
West Tenn	AA ChC	54	189	41	10	4	1	62	29	9	33	1	60	0	1	1	9	4	.69	0	.217	.332	.328
9 Min. YEARS		991	3315	786	136	64	46	1188	541	344	451	12	965	44	28	20	186	82	.69	39	.237	.334	.358

Troy Brohawn

Pitches: Left Bats: Left Pos: P   Ht: 6'1" Wt: 190 Born: 1/14/73 Age: 27

Year Team	Lg Org	G	GS	CG	GF	IP	BFP	H	R	ER	HR	SH	SF	HB	TBB	IBB	SO	WP	Bk	W	L	Pct.	ShO	Sv	ERA
1994 San Jose	A+ SF	4	4	0	0	16.2	80	27	15	13	2	1	0	2	5	0	13	1	0	0	2	.000	0	0	7.02
1995 San Jose	A+ SF	11	10	0	1	65.1	246	45	14	12	4	1	1	1	20	0	57	5	1	7	3	.700	0	0	1.65
1996 Shreveport	AA SF	28	28	0	0	156.2	668	163	99	80	30	7	3	6	49	0	82	8	3	9	10	.474	0	0	4.60
1997 Shreveport	AA SF	26	26	1	0	169	695	148	57	48	10	3	1	2	64	0	98	4	3	13	5	.722	1	0	2.56
1998 Fresno	AAA SF	30	19	0	4	121.2	528	144	75	71	18	11	5	3	36	1	87	8	0	10	8	.556	0	0	5.25
1999 Tucson	AAA Ari	3	2	0	0	13.2	67	22	8	5	1	3	0	0	3	0	12	0	0	1	0	1.000	0	0	3.29
6 Min. YEARS		102	89	1	5	543	2284	549	268	229	65	26	10	14	177	1	349	26	7	40	28	.588	1	0	3.80

Antone Brooks

Pitches: Left Bats: Left Pos: P   Ht: 6'0" Wt: 170 Born: 12/20/73 Age: 26

Year Team	Lg Org	G	GS	CG	GF	IP	BFP	H	R	ER	HR	SH	SF	HB	TBB	IBB	SO	WP	Bk	W	L	Pct.	ShO	Sv	ERA
1995 Eugene	A- Atl	15	0	0	5	17	67	9	5	1	0	0	0	0	8	1	26	0	0	2	0	1.000	0	0	0.53
1996 Macon	A Atl	43	0	0	26	80.1	334	57	24	20	5	2	2	5	36	4	101	8	0	9	4	.692	0	10	2.24
Durham	A+ Atl	2	0	0	1	3	10	1	0	0	0	0	0	0	0	0	6	0	0	0	0	.000	0	0	0.00
1997 Greenville	AA Atl	14	0	0	3	20.2	93	21	14	11	3	0	2	2	8	1	10	1	0	1	0	1.000	0	0	4.79
1998 Greenville	AA Atl	26	0	0	7	38	168	42	16	15	1	3	4	1	19	0	37	2	0	6	3	.667	0	1	3.55
1999 Richmond	AAA Atl	43	0	0	18	56	241	57	28	24	2	5	5	0	21	0	39	3	0	3	5	.375	0	1	3.86
5 Min. YEARS		143	0	0	60	215	913	187	87	71	12	10	13	8	92	6	219	14	0	21	12	.636	0	12	2.97

Jerry Brooks

Bats: Right Throws: Right Pos: 1B   Ht: 6'0" Wt: 195 Born: 3/23/67 Age: 33

Year Team	Lg Org	G	AB	H	2B	3B	HR	TB	R	RBI	TBB	IBB	SO	HBP	SH	SF	SB	CS	SB%	GDP	Avg	OBP	SLG
1988 Great Falls	R+ LA	68	284	99	21	3	8	150	63	60	24	0	25	4	0	9	7	4	.64	9	.347	.394	.526
1989 Bakersfield	A+ LA	141	565	164	39	1	16	253	70	87	25	0	79	6	0	8	9	6	.60	10	.290	.323	.448
1990 San Antonio	AA LA	106	391	118	19	0	9	164	52	58	26	4	39	4	1	5	5	8	.38	7	.302	.347	.419
1991 Albuquerque	AAA LA	125	429	126	20	7	13	199	64	82	29	5	49	6	1	4	3	5	.57	14	.294	.344	.464
1992 Albuquerque	AAA LA	129	467	124	36	1	14	204	77	78	39	1	68	4	0	7	3	2	.60	9	.266	.323	.437
1993 Albuquerque	AAA LA	116	421	145	28	4	11	214	67	71	21	2	44	2	3	7	3	4	.43	11	.344	.373	.508
1994 Albuquerque	AAA LA	115	390	125	23	1	16	198	76	79	31	3	34	5	0	3	4	1	.80	13	.321	.375	.508
1995 Indianapolis	AAA Cin	90	325	92	19	2	14	157	41	52	22	0	38	5	0	2	3	1	.75	16	.283	.335	.483
1996 Charlotte	AAA Fla	136	466	134	29	2	34	269	72	107	32	3	78	2	0	2	5	5	.50	17	.288	.335	.577
1999 Norfolk	AAA NYM	79	241	57	13	1	9	99	32	27	34	2	50	2	0	1	0	2	.00	3	.237	.335	.411
1993 Los Angeles	NL	9	9	2	1	0	1	6	2	1	0	0	2	0	0	0	0	0	.00	0	.222	.222	.667
1996 Florida	NL	8	5	2	0	1	0	4	2	3	1	0	1	1	0	0	0	0	.00	0	.400	.571	.800
10 Min. YEARS		1105	3980	1184	247	22	144	1907	614	701	283	20	504	40	5	49	43	36	.54	109	.297	.346	.479
2 Maj. YEARS		17	14	4	1	1	1	10	4	4	1	0	3	1	0	0	0	0	.00	0	.286	.375	.714

Jason Brosnan

Pitches: Left Bats: Left Pos: P   Ht: 6'1" Wt: 190 Born: 1/26/68 Age: 32

Year Team	Lg Org	G	GS	CG	GF	IP	BFP	H	R	ER	HR	SH	SF	HB	TBB	IBB	SO	WP	Bk	W	L	Pct.	ShO	Sv	ERA
1989 Great Falls	R+ LA	13	13	0	0	67	294	41	24	19	1	1	1	3	55	0	89	10	4	6	2	.750	0	0	2.55
1990 Bakersfield	A+ LA	26	25	0	0	136	607	113	63	47	4	3	4	7	91	1	157	7	2	12	4	.750	0	0	3.11
1991 San Antonio	AA LA	2	2	0	0	7.2	49	15	15	15	2	0	0	0	11	0	8	0	0	0	1	.000	0	0	17.61
Vero Beach	A+ LA	11	9	0	0	36.1	164	34	27	23	2	1	2	2	21	0	25	5	0	1	2	.333	0	0	5.70
1992 Albuquerque	AAA LA	8	0	0	3	8.2	44	13	9	8	2	1	0		4	0	12	2	0	0	0	.000	0	1	8.31
San Antonio	AA LA	8	8	0	0	32.1	163	44	33	28	9	2	2	1	21	1	27	4	0	1	7	.125	0	0	7.79
Vero Beach	A+ LA	18	8	2	3	58	255	69	32	30	2	2	2	1	26	2	51	11	1	3	4	.429	0	0	4.66
1993 Vero Beach	A+ LA	23	0	0	9	25.2	127	30	22	13	1	1	1	1	19	2	32	4	0	0	2	.000	0	1	4.56
Bakersfield	A+ LA	9	6	0	1	36.1	161	36	20	14	2	1	1	2	15	0	34	4	0	4	1	.800	0	0	3.47
San Antonio	AA LA	3	3	0	0	20.1	83	21	11	10	1	0	0	0	7	0	10	1	0	2	0	.000	0	0	4.43
1994 San Antonio	AA LA	17	1	0	8	30.2	141	34	16	12	3	0	1	2	12	1	29	3	0	2	3	.400	0	1	3.52
Albuquerque	AAA LA	24	7	0	5	61.2	275	75	36	36	4	2	1	0	30	0	43	3	2	4	4	.333	0	1	5.25
1995 Albuquerque	AAA LA	23	1	0	11	31	128	30	16	15	3	0	2	0	9	1	18	0	1	2	0	1.000	0	2	4.35
San Antonio	AA LA	19	0	0	7	22.2	94	24	9	9	1	1	2	1	4	0	21	1	0	1	0	1.000	0	2	3.57
1996 Tacoma	AAA Sea	12	2	0	3	31.2	125	19	14	10	2	1	1	3	15	1	26	2	0	3	1	.750	0	0	2.84
Port City	AA Sea	30	9	1	7	77	327	71	33	31	8	2	2	1	32	1	76	2	1	5	6	.455	1	1	3.62
1997 Memphis	AA Sea	40	0	0	21	53.1	233	44	16	15	7	2	1	4	11	1	62	2	1	2	3	.400	0	5	2.53
1998 Vancouver	AAA Ana	10	0	0	4	13	55	13	6	5	2	0	0	2	5	0	11	3	0	0	0	.000	0	0	3.46
Midland	AA Ana	16	0	0	6	24.2	102	32	20	17	0	2	1	1	13	1	24	1	0	3	0	1.000	0	6	6.20
1999 New Haven	AA Sea	28	1	0	15	50	193	32	14	13	4	3	1	2	15	2	44	4	0	3	0	1.000	0	6	2.34
11 Min. YEARS		340	95	3	103	824	3618	790	436	370	67	23	23	33	416	14	799	69	11	50	42	.543	1	21	4.04

Terry Bross

Pitches: Right **Bats:** Right **Pos:** P **Ht:** 6' 9" **Wt:** 240 **Born:** 3/30/66 **Age:** 34

Year Team	Lg Org	G	GS	CG	GF	IP	BFP	H	R	ER	HR	SH	SF	HB	TBB	IBB	SO	WP	Bk	W	L	Pct.	ShO	Sv	ERA
1987 Little Fall	A- NYM	10	3	0	1	28	129	22	23	12	3	2	1	0	20	0	21	1	1	2	0	1.000	0	0	3.86
1988 Little Fall	A- NYM	20	6	0	8	55.1	248	43	25	19	2	1	2	1	38	0	59	2	2	2	1	.667	0	1	3.09
1989 St. Lucie	A+ NYM	35	0	0	26	58	234	39	21	18	1	0	4	1	26	3	47	3	1	8	2	.800	0	11	2.79
1990 Jackson	AA NYM	58	0	0	48	71.2	289	46	21	21	4	5	3	2	40	5	51	4	4	3	4	.429	0	28	2.64
1991 Tidewater	AAA NYM	27	0	0	10	33	159	31	21	16	0	1	1	1	32	2	23	3	2	2	0	1.000	0	2	4.36
Williamsprt	AA NYM	20	0	0	16	25.1	98	13	12	7	1	2	1	0	11	0	28	1	1	2	0	1.000	0	5	2.49
1992 Las Vegas	AAA SD	49	0	0	12	85.2	356	83	36	31	4	5	6	0	30	3	42	5	1	7	3	.700	0	3	3.26
1993 Phoenix	AAA SF	54	0	0	8	79.1	343	76	37	35	5	1	5	1	37	1	69	3	2	4	4	.500	0	5	3.97
1994 Indianaplos	AAA Cin	38	14	0	1	110.1	449	86	42	37	8	4	2	1	43	3	82	4	0	6	2	.750	0	0	3.02
1999 Tucson	AAA Ari	2	0	0	1	2.1	13	6	3	3	1	0	0	0	1	0	0	0	0	0	0	.000	0	0	11.57
1991 New York	NL	8	0	0	4	10	39	7	2	2	1	1	0	0	3	0	5	0	0	0	0	.000	0	0	1.80
1993 San Francisco	NL	2	0	0	1	2	10	3	2	2	1	0	0	0	1	0	1	0	0	0	0	.000	0	0	9.00
9 Min. YEARS		313	23	0	151	549	2318	445	241	199	29	21	25	7	278	17	422	26	14	36	16	.692	0	52	3.26
2 Maj. YEARS		10	0	0	5	12	49	10	4	4	2	1	0	0	4	0	6	0	0	0	0	.000	0	0	3.00

Ben Broussard

Bats: Left **Throws:** Left **Pos:** OF **Ht:** 6'2" **Wt:** 220 **Born:** 9/24/76 **Age:** 23

Year Team	Lg Org	G	AB	H	2B	3B	HR	TB	R	RBI	TBB	IBB	SO	HBP	SH	SF	SB	CS	SB%	GDP	Avg	OBP	SLG
1999 Billings	R+ Cin	38	145	59	11	2	14	116	39	48	34	2	30	4	0	1	1	0	1.00	1	.407	.527	.800
Clinton	A Cin	5	20	11	4	1	2	23	8	6	3	0	4	0	0	0	0	0	.00	1	.550	.609	1.150
Chattanooga	AA Cin	35	127	27	5	0	8	56	26	21	11	1	41	3	0	0	1	0	1.00	0	.213	.291	.441
1 Min. YEARS		78	292	97	20	3	24	195	73	75	48	3	75	7	0	1	2	0	1.00	1	.332	.437	.668

Scott Brow

Pitches: Right **Bats:** Right **Pos:** P **Ht:** 6' 3" **Wt:** 200 **Born:** 3/17/69 **Age:** 31

Year Team	Lg Org	G	GS	CG	GF	IP	BFP	H	R	ER	HR	SH	SF	HB	TBB	IBB	SO	WP	Bk	W	L	Pct.	ShO	Sv	ERA
1990 St.Cathrnes	A- Tor	9	7	0	1	39.2	165	34	18	10	2	2	0	2	11	0	39	4	0	3	1	.750	0	0	2.27
1991 Dunedin	A+ Tor	15	12	0	1	69.2	306	73	50	37	5	3	3	2	28	1	31	2	5	3	7	.300	0	0	4.78
1992 Dunedin	A+ Tor	25	25	3	0	170.2	690	143	53	46	8	4	5	7	44	2	107	3	3	14	2	.875	1	0	2.43
1993 Knoxvllle	AA Tor	3	3	1	0	19	74	13	0	7	3	1	1	0	0	0	12	0	0	1	2	.333	0	0	3.32
Syracuse	AAA Tor	20	19	2	0	121.1	510	119	63	59	8	3	8	6	37	1	64	4	2	6	8	.429	0	0	4.38
1994 Syracuse	AAA Tor	14	13	1	0	79.1	346	77	45	38	9	1	2	3	38	0	30	2	0	5	3	.625	1	0	4.31
1995 Syracuse	AAA Tor	11	5	0	1	31	164	52	39	31	7	2	3	1	18	1	14	1	0	1	5	.167	0	0	9.00
1996 Syracuse	AAA Tor	18	11	0	2	76.2	331	84	49	42	6	0	3	0	26	1	52	1	0	5	4	.556	0	0	4.93
1997 Richmond	AAA Atl	61	1	0	50	83	369	89	44	41	12	1	1	2	35	2	62	6	1	5	9	.357	0	18	4.45
1998 Columbus	AAA NYY	30	3	0	8	59.1	273	74	42	36	8	2	3	1	26	0	35	3	0	3	2	.600	0	0	5.46
1999 Edmonton	AAA Ana	64	0	0	32	79	352	94	53	50	7	3	5	1	31	2	48	6	0	1	6	.143	0	15	5.70
1993 Toronto	AL	6	3	0	1	18	83	19	15	12	2	1	2	1	10	1	7	0	0	1	1	.500	0	0	6.00
1994 Toronto	AL	18	0	0	9	29	141	34	27	19	4	1	2	1	19	2	15	6	0	0	3	.000	0	2	5.90
1996 Toronto	AL	18	1	0	9	38.2	180	45	25	24	5	1	1	0	25	1	23	2	1	1	0	1.000	0	0	5.59
1998 Arizona	NL	17	0	0	5	21.1	98	22	17	17	2	2	1	0	14	2	13	0	0	1	0	1.000	0	0	7.17
10 Min. YEARS		270	99	7	94	828.2	3580	852	468	397	75	22	34	25	303	10	494	34	11	47	49	.490	2	33	4.31
4 Maj. YEARS		59	4	0	24	107	502	120	84	72	13	5	6	2	68	6	58	8	1	3	4	.429	0	2	6.06

Alvin Brown

Pitches: Right **Bats:** Right **Pos:** P **Ht:** 6'1" **Wt:** 200 **Born:** 9/2/70 **Age:** 29

Year Team	Lg Org	G	GS	CG	GF	IP	BFP	H	R	ER	HR	SH	SF	HB	TBB	IBB	SO	WP	Bk	W	L	Pct.	ShO	Sv	ERA
1993 Bristol	R+ Det	15	6	0	4	39	182	27	30	27	2	0	1	4	47	0	30	14	0	2	2	.500	0	1	6.23
1994 Lakeland	A+ Det	4	0	0	3	7	40	11	8	7	0	0	2	0	7	0	9	1	0	0	0	.000	0	0	9.00
Fayettevlle	A Det	33	12	1	11	97.2	441	61	60	47	3	4	0	7	83	0	109	27	2	6	7	.462	1	0	4.33
1995 Lakeland	A+ Det	9	9	0	0	46.2	202	35	23	22	1	1	1	4	33	0	35	9	1	2	3	.400	0	0	4.24
1996 San Berndno	A+ LA	42	2	0	16	68.2	306	43	40	29	2	5	2	2	62	0	84	17	1	2	4	.333	0	2	3.80
1997 San Antonio	AA LA	16	16	2	0	96.1	406	83	48	40	9	2	2	5	33	0	67	9	2	6	5	.545	1	0	3.74
Albuquerque	AAA LA	12	11	1	0	61.2	291	74	50	42	9	4	2	1	35	0	43	6	1	4	6	.400	1	0	6.13
1999 Altoona	AA Pit	7	6	0	0	26.1	124	29	22	19	0	3	3	1	17	0	15	6	1	4	1	.800	0	0	6.49
Lafayette	IND —	1	0	0	1	6	23	3	2	2	0	0	1	2	1	0	5	1	0	0	0	.000	0	0	3.00
Erie	AA Ana	6	0	0	4	6.2	39	9	6	5	0	0	0	2	7	0	6	3	0	0	1	.000	0	2	6.75
6 Min. YEARS		145	62	4	39	456	2054	375	289	240	26	19	12	28	325	0	403	93	8	26	29	.473	3	5	4.74

Elliot Brown

Pitches: Right **Bats:** Both **Pos:** P **Ht:** 6'3" **Wt:** 185 **Born:** 6/7/75 **Age:** 25

Year Team	Lg Org	G	GS	CG	GF	IP	BFP	H	R	ER	HR	SH	SF	HB	TBB	IBB	SO	WP	Bk	W	L	Pct.	ShO	Sv	ERA
1997 Chston-SC	A TB	33	16	0	6	118.2	525	117	73	57	11	4	2	8	45	0	86	12	0	5	8	.385	0	3	4.32
1998 Chston-SC	A TB	40	15	0	2	107	475	123	72	59	10	1	5	10	40	0	59	8	1	2	7	.222	0	0	4.96
1999 Orlando	AA TB	10	1	0	5	18.2	89	25	18	16	2	0	1	0	12	0	12	3	0	0	0	.000	0	0	7.71
St. Pete	A+ TB	38	0	0	15	57.1	230	44	20	17	1	2	1	3	14	1	42	5	0	5	3	.625	0	3	2.67
3 Min. YEARS		121	32	0	31	301.2	1319	309	183	149	24	7	9	21	111	1	199	28	1	12	20	.375	0	6	4.45

Jamie Brown

Pitches: Right **Bats:** Right **Pos:** P **Ht:** 6'2" **Wt:** 205 **Born:** 3/31/77 **Age:** 23

		HOW MUCH HE PITCHED						WHAT HE GAVE UP												THE RESULTS					
Year Team	Lg Org	G	GS	CG	GF	IP	BFP	H	R	ER	HR	SH	SF	HB	TBB	IBB	SO	WP	Bk	W	L	Pct.	ShO	Sv	ERA
1997 Watertown	A- Cle	13	13	1	0	73	303	66	35	25	6	1	2	4	15	0	57	1	1	10	2	.833	0	0	3.08
1998 Kinston	A+ Cle	27	27	2	0	172.2	717	162	91	73	12	10	3	11	44	1	148	4	2	11	9	.550	0	0	3.81
Akron	AA Cle	1	1	0	0	7	28	5	2	2	1	0	0	1	1	0	5	0	0	1	0	1.000	0	0	2.57
1999 Akron	AA Cle	23	23	1	0	138	586	140	72	70	11	7	10	13	39	1	98	2	3	5	9	.357	0	0	4.57
Buffalo	AAA Cle	1	0	0	0	5	23	8	4	3	0	1	1	0	1	0	2	0	0	1	0	1.000	0	0	5.40
3 Min. YEARS		65	64	4	0	395.2	1657	381	204	173	30	19	16	29	100	2	310	7	6	28	20	.583	0	0	3.94

Randy Brown

Bats: Right **Throws:** Right **Pos:** 2B **Ht:** 5'11" **Wt:** 160 **Born:** 5/1/70 **Age:** 30

		BATTING														BASERUNNING				PERCENTAGES		
Year Team	Lg Org	G	AB	H	2B	3B	HR	TB	R	RBI	TBB	IBB	SO	HBP	SH	SF	SB	CS	SB%	GDP	Avg	OBP	SLG
1990 Elmira	A- Bos	74	212	50	4	0	1	57	27	8	17	0	47	4	9	0	17	4	.81	1	.236	.305	.269
1991 Red Sox	R Bos	44	143	27	7	0	0	34	25	10	23	0	31	2	3	1	19	0	1.00	4	.189	.308	.238
Winter Havn	A+ Bos	63	135	21	3	0	0	24	14	5	16	0	42	1	4	0	10	3	.77	2	.156	.250	.178
1992 Winter Havn	A+ Bos	121	430	101	18	2	2	129	39	24	28	0	115	6	8	4	8	9	.47	1	.235	.288	.300
1993 Lynchburg	A+ Bos	128	483	114	25	7	2	159	57	45	25	0	127	13	2	4	10	8	.56	6	.236	.290	.329
1994 New Britain	AA Bos	114	389	87	14	2	8	129	51	30	30	0	102	5	7	4	9	5	.64	1	.224	.285	.332
1995 Pawtucket	AAA Bos	74	212	53	6	1	2	67	27	12	10	0	53	4	4	2	5	1	.83	4	.250	.294	.316
1996 Pawtucket	AAA Bos	3	6	1	0	0	0	1	0	1	1	0	1	0	0	0	0	0	.00	1	.167	.286	.167
Trenton	AA Bos	72	245	73	15	2	11	125	46	38	27	2	56	5	1	0	9	4	.69	3	.298	.379	.510
1997 Trenton	AA Bos	97	336	86	11	4	8	129	51	49	38	3	102	4	3	4	9	7	.56	6	.256	.335	.384
Norwich	AA NYY	19	60	13	2	0	3	24	10	8	9	0	22	2	0	0	2	1	.67	1	.217	.338	.400
1998 Nashville	AAA Pit	14	49	9	1	0	1	13	8	6	4	0	15	0	0	1	1	1	.50	1	.184	.241	.265
Carolina	AA Pit	80	257	75	18	6	7	126	39	35	22	1	77	5	3	2	9	5	.64	4	.292	.357	.490
1999 New Haven	AA Sea	46	167	43	7	5	6	78	30	22	19	1	37	1	2	0	0	4	.00	3	.257	.337	.467
Tacoma	AAA Sea	44	156	40	7	1	6	67	15	27	9	1	48	1	6	0	4	2	.67	6	.256	.301	.429
10 Min. YEARS		993	3280	793	138	30	57	1162	439	320	278	8	875	53	52	22	112	54	.67	43	.242	.309	.354

Ray Brown

Bats: Left **Throws:** Right **Pos:** 1B-DH **Ht:** 6'2" **Wt:** 205 **Born:** 7/30/72 **Age:** 27

		BATTING														BASERUNNING				PERCENTAGES		
Year Team	Lg Org	G	AB	H	2B	3B	HR	TB	R	RBI	TBB	IBB	SO	HBP	SH	SF	SB	CS	SB%	GDP	Avg	OBP	SLG
1994 Billings	R+ Cin	60	218	80	19	3	9	132	50	49	27	1	32	10	0	5	3	5	.38	5	.367	.450	.606
1995 Winston-Sal	A+ Cin	122	445	118	26	0	19	201	63	77	52	12	85	11	0	4	3	2	.60	8	.265	.354	.452
Chstn-WV	A Cin	6	17	2	1	0	0	3	3	0	4	0	3	0	0	0	0	0	.00	0	.118	.286	.176
1996 Chattanooga	AA Cin	115	364	119	26	5	13	194	68	52	52	7	62	3	0	3	2	1	.67	11	.327	.412	.533
1997 Las Vegas	AAA SD	41	140	36	13	0	2	55	12	15	11	1	28	1	0	1	1	0	1.00	11	.257	.316	.393
Mobile	AA SD	57	179	63	16	0	4	91	28	30	33	1	33	1	0	1	1	0	1.00	8	.352	.453	.508
1998 Wichita	AA KC	114	402	128	31	1	21	224	79	96	57	5	57	3	1	6	4	2	.67	16	.318	.402	.557
1999 Wichita	AA KC	13	44	14	4	0	1	21	8	11	8	0	5	0	0	0	0	0	.00	2	.318	.423	.477
6 Min. YEARS		528	1809	560	136	9	69	921	311	330	244	27	305	29	2	19	14	10	.58	59	.310	.396	.509

Richard Brown

Bats: Left **Throws:** Left **Pos:** OF **Ht:** 6'1" **Wt:** 196 **Born:** 4/28/77 **Age:** 23

		BATTING														BASERUNNING				PERCENTAGES		
Year Team	Lg Org	G	AB	H	2B	3B	HR	TB	R	RBI	TBB	IBB	SO	HBP	SH	SF	SB	CS	SB%	GDP	Avg	OBP	SLG
1996 Yankees	R NYY	47	164	47	8	3	0	61	33	23	23	1	32	1	1	3	2	1	.67	2	.287	.372	.372
1997 Yankees	R NYY	10	30	11	3	0	0	14	7	3	5	0	6	0	0	1	0	0	.00	2	.367	.444	.467
1998 Yankees	R NYY	6	14	6	0	0	2	12	6	2	1	0	3	1	0	0	2	0	1.00	0	.429	.500	.857
Tampa	A+ NYY	80	282	84	13	3	11	136	46	38	45	1	54	5	2	0	8	6	.57	3	.298	.404	.482
1999 Norwich	AA NYY	104	383	100	18	8	6	152	46	54	34	0	81	3	0	4	5	8	.38	6	.261	.323	.397
4 Min. YEARS		247	873	248	42	14	19	375	138	120	108	2	176	10	3	8	17	15	.53	13	.284	.366	.430

Vick Brown

Bats: Right **Throws:** Right **Pos:** 2B **Ht:** 6'1" **Wt:** 170 **Born:** 11/14/72 **Age:** 27

		BATTING														BASERUNNING				PERCENTAGES		
Year Team	Lg Org	G	AB	H	2B	3B	HR	TB	R	RBI	TBB	IBB	SO	HBP	SH	SF	SB	CS	SB%	GDP	Avg	OBP	SLG
1993 Yankees	R NYY	52	212	52	7	1	0	61	31	15	19	1	44	7	1	3	18	2	.90	1	.245	.324	.288
1994 Greensboro	A NYY	117	382	88	8	1	0	98	69	20	73	0	79	4	4	1	27	10	.73	4	.230	.359	.257
1995 Greensboro	A NYY	118	432	98	10	1	2	116	66	36	44	0	93	6	8	1	24	9	.73	11	.227	.306	.269
1996 Tampa	A+ NYY	35	89	18	3	0	0	21	17	7	14	0	22	2	2	0	2	0	1.00	3	.202	.324	.236
Greensboro	A NYY	25	91	29	6	0	1	38	8	9	11	0	23	1	0	0	9	2	.82	0	.319	.398	.418
1997 Tampa	A+ NYY	123	463	135	19	4	2	168	77	42	38	0	78	11	6	5	55	13	.81	6	.292	.356	.363
1998 Norwich	AA NYY	102	352	105	14	3	6	143	62	34	40	0	75	6	1	0	35	10	.78	7	.298	.379	.406
1999 Norwich	AA NYY	132	482	121	19	1	5	157	86	48	83	0	101	7	5	5	50	14	.78	15	.251	.366	.326
7 Min. YEARS		704	2503	646	86	11	16	802	416	211	322	1	515	44	27	15	220	60	.79	47	.258	.351	.320

Mo Bruce

Bats: Right **Throws:** Right **Pos:** 2B **Ht:** 5'10" **Wt:** 190 **Born:** 5/1/75 **Age:** 25

		BATTING														BASERUNNING				PERCENTAGES		
Year Team	Lg Org	G	AB	H	2B	3B	HR	TB	R	RBI	TBB	IBB	SO	HBP	SH	SF	SB	CS	SB%	GDP	Avg	OBP	SLG
1996 Kingsport	R+ NYM	11	38	7	0	1	0	9	5	4	0	0	7	1	0	1	2	1	.67	1	.184	.200	.237
Mets	R NYM	30	120	33	5	3	0	44	16	7	3	0	15	0	3	1	6	1	.86	1	.275	.290	.367
1997 Kingsport	R+ NYM	34	128	47	8	3	3	70	35	21	16	0	20	2	0	0	14	4	.78	1	.367	.445	.547

Year Team	Lg Org	G	AB	H	2B	3B	HR	TB	R	RBI	TBB	IBB	SO	HBP	SH	SF	SB	CS	SB%	GDP	Avg	OBP	SLG
Pittsfield	A- NYM	29	115	40	7	3	4	65	26	14	11	0	23	2	0	2	12	2	.86	4	.348	.408	.565
1998 Capital Cty	A NYM	126	516	176	24	4	15	253	81	74	41	4	107	1	1	1	45	15	.75	5	.341	.390	.490
1999 Binghamton	AA NYM	133	500	135	25	4	9	195	80	76	61	2	134	4	5	5	33	11	.75	9	.270	.351	.390
4 Min. YEARS		363	1417	438	69	18	31	636	243	196	132	6	306	10	9	10	112	34	.77	21	.309	.370	.449

Cliff Brumbaugh

Bats: Right **Throws:** Right **Pos:** OF   **Ht:** 6'2" **Wt:** 205 **Born:** 4/21/74 **Age:** 26

Year Team	Lg Org	G	AB	H	2B	3B	HR	TB	R	RBI	TBB	IBB	SO	HBP	SH	SF	SB	CS	SB%	GDP	Avg	OBP	SLG
1995 Hudson Val	A- Tex	74	282	101	19	4	2	134	44	45	39	4	51	2	0	2	15	3	.83	11	.358	.437	.475
1996 Chston-SC	A Tex	132	458	111	23	7	6	166	70	45	72	2	103	1	1	2	20	7	.74	5	.242	.345	.362
1997 Charlotte	A+ Tex	139	522	136	27	4	15	216	78	70	47	2	99	6	0	4	13	11	.54	7	.261	.326	.414
1998 Tulsa	AA Tex	132	483	125	34	1	15	206	65	76	54	5	77	4	3	5	1	3	.25	12	.259	.335	.427
1999 Tulsa	AA Tex	135	513	144	35	3	25	260	94	89	71	1	88	2	0	4	18	4	.82	5	.281	.368	.507
Oklahoma	AAA Tex	4	12	3	0	0	0	3	1	1	0	0	2	0	0	0	0	0	.00	0	.250	.250	.250
5 Min. YEARS		616	2270	620	138	19	63	985	352	326	283	14	420	15	4	17	67	28	.71	40	.273	.355	.434

Clay Bruner

Pitches: Right **Bats:** Right **Pos:** P   **Ht:** 6'3" **Wt:** 180 **Born:** 10/16/76 **Age:** 23

Year Team	Lg Org	G	GS	CG	GF	IP	BFP	H	R	ER	HR	SH	SF	HB	TBB	IBB	SO	WP	Bk	W	L	Pct.	ShO	Sv	ERA
1995 Det	R Det	5	4	0	0	16	77	15	12	7	1	3	0	3	10	0	15	1	0	0	1	.000	0	0	3.94
1996 Fayettevlle	A Det	27	26	0	1	156.2	669	124	64	45	6	3	2	4	77	0	152	13	0	14	5	.737	0	0	2.59
1997 W Michigan	A Det	24	24	3	0	166.1	664	134	52	44	11	2	7	4	48	1	135	9	1	15	3	.833	2	0	2.38
1998 Jacksnville	AA Det	28	28	1	0	171	739	173	90	72	15	4	6	6	66	0	91	8	2	10	6	.625	0	0	3.79
1999 Jacksnville	AA Det	7	5	0	1	25.1	129	47	32	25	0	0	3	1	10	0	9	2	0	1	3	.250	0	1	8.88
5 Min. YEARS		91	87	4	2	535.1	2278	493	250	193	33	12	18	18	211	1	402	33	3	40	18	.690	2	1	3.24

Justin Brunette

Pitches: Left **Bats:** Left **Pos:** P   **Ht:** 6'1" **Wt:** 200 **Born:** 10/7/75 **Age:** 24

Year Team	Lg Org	G	GS	CG	GF	IP	BFP	H	R	ER	HR	SH	SF	HB	TBB	IBB	SO	WP	Bk	W	L	Pct.	ShO	Sv	ERA
1997 New Jersey	A- StL	8	0	0	2	5.2	29	10	6	5	0	0	0	0	0	0	6	1	1	1	0	1.000	0	0	7.94
1999 Peoria	A StL	38	0	0	12	44.2	181	34	9	9	2	2	1	1	16	1	44	2	1	3	1	.750	0	2	1.81
Arkansas	AA StL	18	0	0	3	18.1	82	21	12	4	3	0	0	0	7	0	23	1	0	1	2	.333	0	0	1.96
2 Min. YEARS		62	0	0	17	68.2	292	68	27	18	5	2	1	1	23	1	73	4	2	5	3	.625	0	2	2.36

Matt Bryant

Bats: Right **Throws:** Right **Pos:** SS   **Ht:** 6'0" **Wt:** 180 **Born:** 4/28/75 **Age:** 25

Year Team	Lg Org	G	AB	H	2B	3B	HR	TB	R	RBI	TBB	IBB	SO	HBP	SH	SF	SB	CS	SB%	GDP	Avg	OBP	SLG
1997 Canton	IND —	64	224	73	15	1	5	105	40	53	22	3	36	0	5	4	5	0	1.00	2	.326	.380	.469
1998 Augusta	A Pit	59	177	53	4	1	2	65	24	18	26	0	29	2	2	4	1	5	.17	3	.299	.388	.367
Lynchburg	A+ Pit	51	177	49	7	1	2	64	20	13	17	0	38	0	0	0	1	1	.50	5	.277	.340	.362
1999 Altoona	AA Pit	12	24	6	0	0	0	6	1	1	2	0	7	0	0	0	0	0	.00	0	.250	.308	.250
Lynchburg	A+ Pit	26	102	29	4	0	0	33	9	11	11	0	12	0	1	0	4	1	.80	3	.284	.354	.324
3 Min. YEARS		212	704	210	30	3	9	273	94	96	78	3	122	2	8	8	11	7	.61	13	.298	.366	.388

Jim Buccheri

Bats: Right **Throws:** Right **Pos:** OF   **Ht:** 5'11" **Wt:** 165 **Born:** 11/12/68 **Age:** 31

Year Team	Lg Org	G	AB	H	2B	3B	HR	TB	R	RBI	TBB	IBB	SO	HBP	SH	SF	SB	CS	SB%	GDP	Avg	OBP	SLG
1988 Sou Oregon	A- Oak	58	232	67	8	1	0	77	42	17	20	0	35	4	0	3	25	7	.78	7	.289	.351	.332
1989 Madison	A Oak	115	433	101	9	0	2	116	56	28	26	1	61	5	3	3	43	12	.78	5	.233	.283	.268
1990 Modesto	A+ Oak	36	125	35	4	1	0	41	27	7	25	0	16	2	2	0	15	9	.63	2	.280	.408	.328
Huntsville	AA Oak	84	278	58	2	1	0	62	39	22	40	0	38	3	7	1	14	6	.70	5	.209	.314	.223
1991 Huntsville	AA Oak	100	340	72	15	0	0	87	48	22	71	0	60	7	5	4	35	7	.83	5	.212	.355	.256
1992 Huntsville	AA Oak	20	60	9	2	1	1	16	8	5	9	0	18	0	1	1	5	3	.63	2	.150	.257	.267
Reno	A+ Oak	63	259	95	14	2	4	125	65	38	56	3	40	2	2	2	33	13	.72	5	.367	.480	.483
Tacoma	AAA Oak	46	127	38	6	3	0	50	24	13	27	1	25	2	0	0	10	5	.67	2	.299	.429	.394
1993 Modesto	A+ Oak	2	7	2	0	0	0	2	3	1	2	0	2	1	0	0	0	0	.00	1	.286	.500	.286
Tacoma	AAA Oak	90	293	81	9	3	2	102	45	40	39	1	46	2	10	1	12	9	.57	6	.276	.364	.348
1994 Tacoma	AAA Oak	121	448	136	8	3	3	159	59	39	42	1	45	4	7	2	32	14	.70	8	.304	.367	.355
1995 Ottawa	AAA Mon	133	470	126	16	4	0	150	64	30	49	5	58	3	11	2	44	11	.80	7	.268	.340	.319
1996 Ottawa	AAA Mon	65	206	53	3	4	1	67	40	12	33	0	28	2	1	2	33	6	.85	1	.257	.362	.325
1997 St. Pete	A+ TB	30	104	30	3	0	0	33	20	11	27	0	20	1	3	2	25	7	.79	2	.245	.333	.289
1998 Durham	AAA TB	106	351	107	14	3	6	145	51	34	25	1	28	5	6	0	37	13	.74	11	.305	.360	.413
1999 Durham	AAA TB	6	8	1	1	0	0	2	2	2	0	0	1	0	1	0	2	0	1.00	1	.125	.273	.250
Orlando	AA TB	45	161	50	8	1	1	63	18	16	15	0	24	3	3	0	5	4	.56	2	.311	.380	.391
Binghamton	AA NYM	4	17	5	1	1	0	8	1	1	0	0	4	0	1	0	0	0	.00	0	.294	.294	.471
Norfolk	AAA NYM	32	92	21	3	0	0	24	9	5	4	0	15	0	1	0	4	1	.80	4	.228	.260	.261
12 Min. YEARS		1184	4111	1107	132	28	20	1355	630	345	512	13	563	46	64	25	374	127	.75	77	.269	.355	.330

40

Brian Buchanan

Bats: Right **Throws:** Right **Pos:** OF **Ht:** 6' 4" **Wt:** 230 **Born:** 7/21/73 **Age:** 26

						BATTING										BASERUNNING				PERCENTAGES		
Year Team	Lg Org	G	AB	H	2B	3B	HR	TB	R	RBI	TBB	IBB	SO	HBP	SH	SF	SB	CS	SB%	GDP	Avg	OBP	SLG
1994 Oneonta	A- NYY	50	177	40	9	2	4	65	28	26	24	2	53	6	0	2	5	3	.63	2	.226	.335	.367
1995 Greensboro	A NYY	23	96	29	3	0	3	41	19	12	9	1	17	1	0	0	7	1	.88	1	.302	.368	.427
1996 Tampa	A+ NYY	131	526	137	22	4	10	197	65	58	37	6	108	10	1	1	23	8	.74	14	.260	.321	.375
1997 Columbus	AAA NYY	18	61	17	1	0	4	30	8	7	4	0	11	3	1	1	2	1	.67	3	.279	.348	.492
Norwich	AA NYY	116	470	145	25	2	10	204	75	69	32	0	85	11	0	6	11	9	.55	11	.309	.362	.434
1998 Salt Lake	AAA Min	133	500	139	29	3	17	225	74	82	36	1	90	9	1	1	14	2	.88	7	.278	.337	.450
1999 Salt Lake	AAA Min	107	391	116	24	1	10	172	67	60	28	0	85	9	0	3	11	2	.85	14	.297	.355	.440
6 Min. YEARS		578	2221	623	113	12	58	934	336	314	170	10	449	49	3	14	73	26	.74	52	.281	.343	.421

Bucky Buckles

Pitches: Right **Bats:** Right **Pos:** P **Ht:** 6'1" **Wt:** 190 **Born:** 6/19/73 **Age:** 27

		HOW MUCH HE PITCHED						WHAT HE GAVE UP										THE RESULTS					
Year Team	Lg Org	G	GS	CG	GF	IP	BFP	H	R	ER	HR	SH	SF	HB	TBB	IBB	SO	WP	Bk	W	L	Pct.	ShO	Sv	ERA
1994 Hudson Val	A- Tex	27	0	0	24	45.2	173	31	10	7	0	0	2	2	8	0	51	1	0	3	1	.750	0	18	1.38
1995 Charlotte	A+ Tex	48	0	0	43	69	293	70	29	24	5	5	2	0	21	3	43	4	2	2	9	.182	0	16	3.13
1996 Charlotte	A+ Tex	21	3	0	5	55	228	55	25	22	3	5	1	2	13	1	43	2	1	1	4	.200	0	0	3.60
1997 Tulsa	AA Tex	34	0	0	19	45	204	59	38	35	5	0	2	1	20	0	29	2	0	2	2	.500	0	1	7.00
Okla City	AAA Tex	5	0	0	1	11.2	50	12	3	1	0	2	1	0	4	0	5	0	0	0	0	.000	0	0	0.77
1998 Rangers	R Tex	2	2	0	0	3	9	0	0	0	0	0	0	0	0	0	2	0	0	0	0	.000	0	0	0.00
Charlotte	A+ Tex	18	0	0	9	31.1	122	21	4	2	1	1	1	0	15	1	18	0	0	4	0	1.000	0	1	0.57
1999 Rangers	R Tex	1	1	0	0	2	10	4	2	1	0	0	0	0	0	0	1	0	0	0	1	.000	0	0	4.50
Tulsa	AA Tex	36	5	0	10	72.1	319	71	40	30	10	4	3	6	34	3	39	4	0	10	4	.714	0	1	3.73
6 Min. YEARS		192	11	0	111	335	1408	323	151	122	24	17	12	11	115	8	231	13	3	22	21	.512	0	37	3.28

Mark Budzinski

Bats: Left **Throws:** Left **Pos:** OF **Ht:** 6'2" **Wt:** 175 **Born:** 8/26/73 **Age:** 26

						BATTING										BASERUNNING				PERCENTAGES		
Year Team	Lg Org	G	AB	H	2B	3B	HR	TB	R	RBI	TBB	IBB	SO	HBP	SH	SF	SB	CS	SB%	GDP	Avg	OBP	SLG
1995 Watertown	A- Cle	70	253	64	12	8	3	101	50	25	52	1	49	8	3	2	15	5	.75	3	.253	.394	.399
1996 Columbus	A Cle	74	260	68	12	4	3	97	42	38	59	4	68	4	2	1	12	3	.80	5	.262	.404	.373
1997 Kinston	A+ Cle	68	241	69	13	3	7	109	43	39	48	1	61	1	2	0	6	4	.60	3	.286	.407	.452
1998 Akron	AA Cle	127	478	125	21	5	10	186	68	62	50	2	125	1	4	2	12	8	.60	9	.262	.331	.389
1999 Akron	AA Cle	86	297	84	17	6	6	131	58	46	48	0	63	5	2	0	9	4	.69	3	.283	.391	.441
Buffalo	AAA Cle	47	133	38	7	3	2	57	24	17	22	2	36	0	2	0	4	2	.67	3	.286	.387	.429
5 Min. YEARS		472	1662	448	82	29	31	681	285	227	279	10	402	19	15	5	58	26	.69	26	.270	.380	.410

Shawn Buhner

Bats: Right **Throws:** Right **Pos:** 1B **Ht:** 6'2" **Wt:** 200 **Born:** 8/29/72 **Age:** 27

						BATTING										BASERUNNING				PERCENTAGES		
Year Team	Lg Org	G	AB	H	2B	3B	HR	TB	R	RBI	TBB	IBB	SO	HBP	SH	SF	SB	CS	SB%	GDP	Avg	OBP	SLG
1994 Bellingham	A- Sea	53	153	44	12	0	4	68	19	19	16	1	39	0	0	4	4	2	.67	2	.288	.347	.444
1995 Wisconsin	A Sea	87	292	70	14	3	2	96	24	36	16	2	65	6	0	4	0	2	.00	9	.240	.289	.329
1996 Lancaster	A+ Sea	69	239	50	19	1	3	80	28	25	20	0	55	9	1	1	0	0	.00	10	.209	.294	.335
1997 Lancaster	A+ Sea	111	397	102	22	1	11	159	66	53	49	3	126	7	0	3	4	1	.80	5	.257	.346	.401
1998 Orlando	AA Sea	99	348	84	14	2	10	132	48	49	47	0	98	3	4	0	1	3	.25	15	.241	.337	.379
1999 Tacoma	AAA Sea	43	146	35	8	0	1	46	17	12	10	0	43	3	0	2	0	1	.00	9	.240	.298	.315
6 Min. YEARS		462	1575	385	89	7	31	581	202	194	158	6	426	28	5	14	9	9	.50	50	.244	.322	.369

Jason Bullard

Pitches: Right **Bats:** Right **Pos:** P **Ht:** 6'2" **Wt:** 185 **Born:** 10/23/68 **Age:** 31

		HOW MUCH HE PITCHED						WHAT HE GAVE UP										THE RESULTS					
Year Team	Lg Org	G	GS	CG	GF	IP	BFP	H	R	ER	HR	SH	SF	HB	TBB	IBB	SO	WP	Bk	W	L	Pct.	ShO	Sv	ERA
1991 Welland	A- Pit	6	0	0	6	7	28	4	0	0	0	0	0	0	4	0	8	0	0	0	0	.000	0	4	0.00
Augusta	A Pit	21	0	0	17	25.2	116	21	13	10	1	1	0	1	15	1	29	2	1	2	2	.500	0	7	3.51
1992 Carolina	AA Pit	19	0	0	10	24.1	121	37	25	20	3	2	2	2	11	1	23	3	0	0	0	.000	0	3	7.40
1993 Pirates	R Pit	4	0	0	1	7	33	11	3	3	0	1	0	1	2	0	8	1	0	0	1	.000	0	0	3.86
1994 St. Paul	IND —	33	4	0	23	59.1	248	53	31	25	2	5	2	4	25	1	47	10	0	6	5	.545	0	10	3.79
1995 Colo Sprngs	AAA Col	4	0	0	1	8.2	48	18	13	7	1	0	0	1	5	1	5	0	1	0	0	.000	0	0	7.27
St. Paul	IND —	17	17	0	0	88.1	406	113	58	51	9	0	5	7	33	1	47	8	0	3	3	.500	0	0	5.20
1996 Norfolk	AAA NYM	24	0	0	7	38.2	178	45	23	21	2	2	2	6	16	1	24	6	0	0	3	.000	0	0	4.89
Binghamton	AA NYM	8	0	0	3	10	46	11	4	3	0	1	0	0	5	2	10	0	0	0	0	.000	0	0	2.70
Canton-Akrn	AA Cle	9	0	0	5	11	45	7	3	3	1	2	0	1	6	1	12	0	0	1	1	.500	0	0	2.45
1997 Bowie	AA Bal	61	0	0	15	92.2	391	84	39	27	6	3	4	10	38	9	77	10	0	7	2	.778	0	3	2.62
1998 Richmond	AAA Atl	36	0	0	13	55	235	56	36	30	3	1	2	3	22	0	48	14	0	1	2	.333	0	0	4.91
Greenville	AA Atl	17	0	0	15	17	66	9	3	2	0	1	1	0	8	1	13	0	0	1	1	.500	0	10	1.06
1999 Greenville	AA Atl	5	0	0	1	7.2	53	16	18	16	2	0	1	1	12	2	5	1	0	0	1	.000	0	0	18.78
Somerset	IND —	46	0	0	22	50	227	55	32	22	5	3	1	3	23	3	43	8	0	3	3	.500	0	6	3.96
9 Min. YEARS		310	21	0	139	502.1	2241	540	301	240	35	22	20	40	225	24	399	63	2	24	26	.480	0	43	4.30

Nate Bump

Pitches: Right **Bats:** Right **Pos:** P **Ht:** 6'2" **Wt:** 185 **Born:** 7/24/76 **Age:** 23

		HOW MUCH HE PITCHED						WHAT HE GAVE UP										THE RESULTS					
Year Team	Lg Org	G	GS	CG	GF	IP	BFP	H	R	ER	HR	SH	SF	HB	TBB	IBB	SO	WP	Bk	W	L	Pct.	ShO	Sv	ERA
1998 Salem-Keizr	A- SF	2	2	0	0	8	31	5	0	0	0	0	0	2	3	0	8	1	0	0	0	.000	0	0	0.00

41

Year Team	Lg Org	G	GS	CG	GF	IP	BFP	H	R	ER	HR	SH	SF	HB	TBB	IBB	SO	WP	Bk	W	L	Pct.	ShO	Sv	ERA
San Jose	A+ SF	11	11	0	0	61.2	240	37	13	12	2	1	1	2	24	0	61	2	0	6	1	.857	0	0	1.75
1999 Shreveport	AA SF	17	17	1	0	92.1	394	85	40	34	9	6	0	5	32	0	59	2	0	4	10	.286	1	0	3.31
Portland	AA Fla	8	8	0	0	43	203	57	38	29	3	1	2	5	12	0	33	1	0	2	6	.250	0	0	6.07
2 Min. YEARS		38	38	1	0	205	868	184	91	75	14	8	3	14	71	0	161	6	0	12	17	.414	1	0	3.29

Pitches: Right **Bats:** Right **Pos:** P

Rob Burger

Ht: 6'1" **Wt:** 175 **Born:** 3/25/76 **Age:** 24

Year Team	Lg Org	G	GS	CG	GF	IP	BFP	H	R	ER	HR	SH	SF	HB	TBB	IBB	SO	WP	Bk	W	L	Pct.	ShO	Sv	ERA
1994 Martinsvlle	R+ Phi	7	5	0	0	19	83	20	13	12	3	0	0	0	8	0	30	1	1	1	1	.500	0	0	5.68
1995 Martinsvlle	R+ Phi	9	9	0	0	40.2	188	47	25	21	1	0	2	3	23	0	54	5	0	2	4	.333	0	0	4.65
1996 Piedmont	A Phi	27	26	2	1	160	673	129	74	60	9	5	8	9	61	0	171	7	6	10	12	.455	2	0	3.38
1997 Clearwater	A+ Phi	28	27	1	0	160.2	682	131	79	64	8	2	3	13	93	0	154	17	3	11	9	.550	1	0	3.59
1998 Reading	AA Phi	33	19	1	10	115	529	119	88	77	21	3	3	8	69	1	102	10	0	3	11	.214	0	0	6.03
1999 Reading	AA Phi	9	9	0	0	27.1	156	29	43	41	5	2	2	5	45	0	23	7	0	0	6	.000	0	0	13.50
Phillies	R Phi	9	2	0	4	22.2	102	19	8	7	0	1	0	3	15	0	31	7	0	1	1	.500	0	0	2.78
Clearwater	A+ Phi	6	5	0	0	24	114	15	10	8	1	1	0	2	24	0	23	5	0	1	2	.333	0	0	3.00
6 Min. YEARS		128	102	4	15	569.1	2527	509	340	290	48	14	18	43	338	1	588	59	10	29	46	.387	3	0	4.58

Pitches: Left **Bats:** Left **Pos:** P

Enrique Burgos

Ht: 6'4" **Wt:** 230 **Born:** 10/7/65 **Age:** 34

Year Team	Lg Org	G	GS	CG	GF	IP	BFP	H	R	ER	HR	SH	SF	HB	TBB	IBB	SO	WP	Bk	W	L	Pct.	ShO	Sv	ERA
1983 Blue Jays	R Tor	13	8	1	1	49		52	37	26	1	—	—	2	32	2	19	4	2	0	9	.000	0	0	4.78
1984 Florence	A Tor	2	0	0	0	1	7	2	2	2	0	0	0	0	1	0	1	0	0	0	0	.000	0	0	18.00
Blue Jays	R Tor	12	10	1	0	71.2	319	74	37	19	1	6	2	1	22	0	38	9	1	4	5	.444	0	0	2.39
1985 Florence	A Tor	26	0	0	12	47.2	240	55	39	35	2	5	2	1	44	2	32	7	1	3	1	.750	0	1	6.61
Kinston	A+ Tor	7	1	0	1	8.1	47	12	11	11	1	0	2	0	10	0	5	1	0	0	2	.000	0	0	11.88
1986 Florence	A Tor	28	10	0	6	85	418	92	76	61	5	5	5	2	70	0	71	15	0	3	8	.273	0	2	6.46
Ventura	A+ Tor	9	9	0	0	45.2	205	46	27	20	1	1	4	0	31	0	37	5	1	1	3	.250	0	0	3.94
1987 Knoxville	AA Tor	17	5	0	6	45.1	222	33	27	22	4	2	1	1	55	0	45	3	1	2	3	.400	0	1	4.37
Myrtle Bch	A Tor	23	0	0	13	38.1	159	22	15	9	2	2	1	0	24	1	36	8	0	5	2	.714	0	7	2.11
1988 Syracuse	AAA Tor	2	0	0	0	2.1	13	4	2	2	0	0	0	0	2	0	2	2	0	0	0	.000	0	0	7.71
Dunedin	A+ Tor	33	4	0	13	49.2	239	61	28	26	0	3	1	0	37	2	55	9	3	1	5	.167	0	1	4.71
1989 Dunedin	A+ Tor	8	0	0	3	12.2	59	8	7	3	0	1	2	0	7	0	15	1	0	2	0	1.000	0	0	2.13
Miami	A+ Tor	15	1	0	11	20.2	92	20	14	9	0	1	1	0	13	0	18	4	0	1	1	.500	0	0	3.92
Myrtle Bch	A Tor	16	1	0	10	16.2	82	16	11	5	0	2	0	2	20	2	15	3	0	0	2	.000	0	1	2.70
1993 Omaha	AAA KC	48	0	0	26	62.2	263	36	26	22	4	2	3	1	37	0	91	9	0	2	4	.333	0	3	3.16
1994 Omaha	AAA KC	57	0	0	45	56.1	248	44	24	18	5	2	1	1	33	3	68	8	1	1	4	.200	0	19	2.88
1995 Phoenix	AAA SF	41	2	0	13	58.2	273	63	44	40	7	5	3	0	40	5	77	4	1	2	6	.250	0	2	6.14
1999 Altoona	AA Pit	5	0	0	2	4	14	1	1	1	0	1	0	0	3	0	3	0	0	0	1	.000	0	0	2.25
1993 Kansas City	AL	5	0	0	3	5	28	5	5	5	0	0	0	1	6	1	6	3	0	0	1	.000	0	0	9.00
1995 San Francisco	NL	5	0	0	2	8.1	44	14	8	8	1	0	0	1	6	0	12	2	0	0	0	.000	0	0	8.64
11 Min. YEARS		362	51	2	162	675.2	—	641	428	331	33	—	—	11	481	17	627	92	11	27	56	.325	0	43	4.41
2 Maj. YEARS		10	0	0	5	13.1	72	19	13	13	1	0	0	2	12	1	18	5	0	0	1	.000	0	0	8.78

Pitches: Left **Bats:** Left **Pos:** P

Travis Burgus

Ht: 6'2" **Wt:** 190 **Born:** 11/6/72 **Age:** 27

Year Team	Lg Org	G	GS	CG	GF	IP	BFP	H	R	ER	HR	SH	SF	HB	TBB	IBB	SO	WP	Bk	W	L	Pct.	ShO	Sv	ERA
1995 Elmira	A- Fla	15	15	0	0	88	369	84	45	34	7	3	3	4	29	0	68	4	1	7	5	.583	0	0	3.48
1996 Kane County	A Fla	30	7	1	11	96.1	404	80	29	19	1	4	3	5	39	1	111	9	1	5	4	.556	0	4	1.78
1997 Portland	AA Fla	16	9	0	1	52	244	63	47	39	12	0	1	4	26	1	29	0	0	4	3	.571	0	0	6.75
1998 Portland	AA Fla	38	0	0	14	57	242	45	16	14	4	4	0	1	29	3	56	6	0	2	1	.667	0	1	1.89
1999 Calgary	AAA Fla	20	0	0	9	23.1	109	33	17	14	3	1	0	1	8	0	15	1	0	1	0	1.000	0	1	5.40
Portland	AA Fla	1	0	0	0	0.2	6	0	0	0	0	0	0	1	2	0	1	0	0	0	0	.000	0	0	0.00
El Paso	AA Ari	17	0	0	6	27	118	26	14	13	3	0	0	1	13	0	32	4	0	1	1	.500	0	1	4.33
5 Min. YEARS		137	31	1	41	344.1	1492	331	168	131	30	12	7	17	146	5	312	24	2	20	14	.588	0	8	3.42

Bats: Right **Throws:** Right **Pos:** 3B

Jamie Burke

Ht: 6'0" **Wt:** 195 **Born:** 9/24/71 **Age:** 28

				BATTING												BASERUNNING				PERCENTAGES		
Year Team	Lg Org	G	AB	H	2B	3B	HR	TB	R	RBI	TBB	IBB	SO	HBP	SH	SF	SB	CS	SB%	GDP	Avg	OBP	SLG
1993 Boise	A- Ana	66	226	68	11	1	1	84	32	30	39	3	28	5	2	2	2	3	.40	4	.301	.412	.372
1994 Cedar Rapds	A Ana	127	469	124	24	1	1	153	57	47	40	3	64	12	4	8	6	8	.43	15	.264	.333	.326
1995 Lk Elsinore	A+ Ana	106	365	100	15	6	2	133	47	56	32	1	53	9	11	4	6	4	.60	12	.274	.344	.364
1996 Midland	AA Ana	45	144	46	8	2	2	64	24	16	20	1	22	2	1	0	1	1	.50	1	.319	.410	.444
Vancouver	AAA Ana	41	156	39	5	0	1	47	12	14	7	0	18	1	1	2	2	1	.67	5	.250	.283	.301
1997 Midland	AA Ana	116	428	141	44	3	6	209	77	72	40	0	46	8	0	3	2	3	.40	12	.329	.395	.488
Vancouver	AAA Ana	8	27	8	1	0	0	9	4	3	3	0	2	1	0	0	0	0	.00	1	.296	.387	.333
1998 Vancouver	AAA Ana	61	162	35	6	0	2	47	16	14	13	0	25	6	2	2	0	0	.00	7	.216	.295	.290
Midland	AA Ana	12	41	10	1	0	0	11	7	4	7	0	4	0	0	0	0	0	.00	4	.244	.354	.268
1999 Edmonton	AAA Ana	46	149	50	9	0	3	68	29	16	23	0	18	3	2	0	0	1	.00	2	.336	.434	.456
7 Min. YEARS		628	2167	621	124	13	18	825	305	272	224	8	280	47	23	21	19	22	.46	63	.287	.363	.381

Lance Burkhart

Bats: Right **Throws:** Right **Pos:** C **Ht:** 5'9" **Wt:** 190 **Born:** 12/16/74 **Age:** 25

Year Team	Lg Org	G	AB	H	2B	3B	HR	TB	R	RBI	TBB	IBB	SO	HBP	SH	SF	SB	CS	SB%	GDP	Avg	OBP	SLG
1997 Vermont	A- Mon	38	143	24	6	1	0	32	15	12	17	0	40	1	0	0	3	3	.50	3	.168	.261	.224
1998 Vermont	A- Mon	16	44	13	4	1	0	19	13	5	13	0	13	1	1	1	0	0	.00	0	.295	.458	.432
Cape Fear	A Mon	17	50	12	3	1	1	20	10	11	16	1	17	2	1	1	1	3	.25	0	.240	.435	.400
1999 Cape Fear	A Mon	2	6	1	1	0	0	2	2	0	2	0	4	0	0	0	0	0	.00	0	.167	.375	.333
Ottawa	AAA Mon	2	8	1	0	0	0	1	1	0	0	0	5	0	0	0	0	0	.00	0	.125	.125	.125
Jupiter	A+ Mon	45	131	28	8	0	5	51	19	21	13	1	35	2	0	2	1	1	.50	1	.214	.291	.389
3 Min. YEARS		120	382	79	22	3	6	125	60	49	61	2	114	6	2	4	5	7	.42	4	.207	.322	.327

Morgan Burkhart

Bats: Both **Throws:** Left **Pos:** 1B-DH **Ht:** 5'11" **Wt:** 225 **Born:** 1/29/72 **Age:** 28

Year Team	Lg Org	G	AB	H	2B	3B	HR	TB	R	RBI	TBB	IBB	SO	HBP	SH	SF	SB	CS	SB%	GDP	Avg	OBP	SLG
1995 Richmond	IND —	70	282	93	28	1	9	150	58	70	41	4	24	7	0	7	16	7	.70	5	.330	.418	.532
1996 Richmond	IND —	74	266	95	27	1	17	175	60	64	49	4	24	14	0	6	22	4	.85	3	.357	.472	.658
1997 Richmond	IND —	80	285	92	22	0	24	186	76	74	73	8	47	8	0	5	8	4	.67	6	.323	.466	.653
1998 Richmond	IND —	80	280	113	18	1	36	241	97	98	85	9	38	13	0	1	13	1	.93	6	.404	.557	.861
1999 Sarasota	A+ Bos	68	245	89	18	0	23	176	56	67	37	6	33	6	0	7	5	2	.71	4	.363	.447	.718
Trenton	AA Bos	66	239	55	14	1	12	107	40	41	31	1	43	10	0	3	3	0	1.00	3	.230	.339	.448
5 Min. YEARS		438	1597	537	127	4	121	1035	387	414	316	32	209	58	0	29	67	18	.79	26	.336	.456	.648

Gary Burnham

Bats: Left **Throws:** Left **Pos:** 1B **Ht:** 5'11" **Wt:** 200 **Born:** 10/13/74 **Age:** 25

Year Team	Lg Org	G	AB	H	2B	3B	HR	TB	R	RBI	TBB	IBB	SO	HBP	SH	SF	SB	CS	SB%	GDP	Avg	OBP	SLG
1997 Batavia	A- Phi	73	289	94	22	4	5	139	44	45	30	0	47	5	1	2	3	1	.75	8	.325	.396	.481
1998 Clearwater	A+ Phi	139	513	152	33	10	8	229	93	70	63	8	76	14	0	7	10	4	.71	9	.296	.384	.446
1999 Reading	AA Phi	116	354	88	20	0	12	144	47	49	41	3	49	15	6	1	11	3	.79	16	.249	.350	.407
3 Min. YEARS		328	1156	334	75	14	25	512	184	164	134	11	172	34	7	10	24	8	.75	33	.289	.376	.443

Kevin Burns

Bats: Left **Throws:** Left **Pos:** 1B **Ht:** 6'5" **Wt:** 220 **Born:** 9/9/75 **Age:** 24

Year Team	Lg Org	G	AB	H	2B	3B	HR	TB	R	RBI	TBB	IBB	SO	HBP	SH	SF	SB	CS	SB%	GDP	Avg	OBP	SLG
1995 Astros	R Hou	42	136	34	4	1	3	49	17	23	12	1	24	0	0	1	8	3	.73	5	.250	.309	.360
1996 Auburn	A- Hou	71	269	71	19	3	11	129	27	55	15	1	77	4	0	5	2	1	.67	1	.264	.307	.480
1997 Quad City	A Hou	131	477	129	28	4	20	219	72	86	53	8	114	6	0	4	1	2	.33	12	.270	.348	.459
1998 Kissimmee	A+ Hou	128	470	127	24	4	19	216	69	81	69	5	124	5	0	3	11	3	.79	8	.270	.367	.460
1999 Jackson	AA Hou	113	352	99	21	2	12	160	55	58	42	4	74	4	0	4	6	3	.67	2	.281	.361	.455
5 Min. YEARS		485	1704	460	96	11	65	773	240	303	191	19	413	19	0	17	28	12	.70	28	.270	.347	.454

Pat Burrell

Bats: Right **Throws:** Right **Pos:** 1B **Ht:** 6'4" **Wt:** 230 **Born:** 10/10/76 **Age:** 23

Year Team	Lg Org	G	AB	H	2B	3B	HR	TB	R	RBI	TBB	IBB	SO	HBP	SH	SF	SB	CS	SB%	GDP	Avg	OBP	SLG
1998 Clearwater	A+ Phi	37	132	40	7	1	7	70	29	30	27	2	22	0	0	2	2	0	1.00	3	.303	.416	.530
1999 Reading	AA Phi	117	417	139	28	6	28	263	84	90	79	3	103	0	0	2	3	1	.75	13	.333	.438	.631
Scranton-WB	AAA Phi	10	33	5	0	0	0	8	4	4	4	0	8	1	0	0	0	1	.00	0	.152	.263	.242
2 Min. YEARS		164	582	184	35	7	36	341	117	124	110	5	133	1	0	4	5	2	.71	16	.316	.423	.586

Andy Burress

Bats: Right **Throws:** Right **Pos:** OF **Ht:** 6'0" **Wt:** 185 **Born:** 7/18/77 **Age:** 22

Year Team	Lg Org	G	AB	H	2B	3B	HR	TB	R	RBI	TBB	IBB	SO	HBP	SH	SF	SB	CS	SB%	GDP	Avg	OBP	SLG
1995 Billings	R+ Cin	35	103	27	9	2	2	46	17	18	6	0	16	3	0	1	0	2	.00	4	.262	.319	.447
1996 Billings	R+ Cin	27	107	34	5	2	5	58	23	25	7	0	16	1	0	1	4	1	.80	3	.318	.362	.542
1997 Chstn-WV	A Cin	38	87	18	0	0	2	24	12	14	4	0	26	0	0	2	1	0	1.00	3	.207	.237	.276
Billings	R+ Cin	27	102	31	7	0	5	53	13	18	6	0	20	0	0	0	1	1	.50	4	.304	.343	.520
1998 Burlington	A Cin	124	449	126	25	10	9	198	75	67	62	2	91	3	0	5	25	5	.83	12	.281	.368	.441
1999 Rockford	A Cin	72	270	82	24	2	4	122	45	32	17	1	45	2	1	3	17	6	.74	4	.304	.346	.452
Chattanooga	AA Cin	63	257	70	12	1	7	105	42	28	18	1	41	2	2	1	11	4	.73	6	.272	.324	.409
5 Min. YEARS		386	1375	388	82	17	34	606	227	202	120	4	255	11	3	13	59	19	.76	36	.282	.342	.441

Terry Burrows

Pitches: Left **Bats:** Left **Pos:** P **Ht:** 6'1" **Wt:** 190 **Born:** 11/28/68 **Age:** 31

Year Team	Lg Org	G	GS	CG	GF	IP	BFP	H	R	ER	HR	SH	SF	HB	TBB	IBB	SO	WP	Bk	W	L	Pct.	ShO	Sv	ERA
1990 Butte	R+ Tex	14	11	1	1	62.2	275	56	35	28	1	3	1	0	35	0	64	6	2	3	6	.333	0	0	4.02
1991 Gastonia	A Tex	27	26	0	0	147.2	614	107	79	73	11	3	0	5	78	0	151	6	6	12	8	.600	0	0	4.45
1992 Charlotte	A+ Tex	14	14	0	0	80	327	71	22	18	2	2	1	4	25	1	66	5	4	4	2	.667	0	0	2.03
Tulsa	AA Tex	14	13	1	0	76	314	66	22	18	3	0	0	0	35	0	59	4	0	6	3	.667	0	0	2.13
Okla City	AAA Tex	1	1	0	0	8	30	3	1	1	1	0	0	0	5	0	0	1	0	1.000	0	0	1.13
1993 Okla City	AAA Tex	27	25	1	0	138	645	171	107	98	19	8	7	2	76	0	74	8	5	7	15	.318	0	0	6.39
1994 Okla City	AAA Tex	44	5	0	15	82.1	353	75	43	39	9	4	3	4	37	3	57	4	5	3	5	.375	0	1	4.26

Year Team	Lg Org	G	GS	CG	GF	IP	BFP	H	R	ER	HR	SH	SF	HB	TBB	IBB	SO	WP	Bk	W	L	Pct.	ShO	Sv	ERA
		HOW MUCH HE PITCHED						**WHAT HE GAVE UP**												**THE RESULTS**					
1995 Okla City	AAA Tex	5	0	0	0	2.2	16	5	4	3	0	0	0	0	2	0	4	1	0	0	1	.000	0	0	10.13
1996 New Orleans	AAA Mil	18	0	0	9	28.2	108	19	9	8	1	0	1	0	8	0	17	1	1	3	0	1.000	0	6	2.51
Columbus	AAA NYY	23	0	0	5	22.2	102	24	16	15	1	1	1	0	11	0	20	1	0	1	0	1.000	0	0	5.96
1997 Las Vegas	AAA SD	31	1	0	10	33.2	160	44	24	24	3	1	0	1	19	3	26	1	1	1	5	.167	0	2	6.42
Edmonton	AAA Oak	13	0	0	3	27	127	35	18	17	2	1	2	0	15	2	24	2	0	2	2	.500	0	0	5.67
1998 Rochester	AAA Bal	29	15	1	3	132.1	531	104	49	43	8	1	7	2	42	0	112	2	1	9	6	.600	0	0	2.92
1999 Orioles	R Bal	2	2	0	0	5	17	0	1	0	0	0	0	1	1	0	4	0	1	0	0	.000	0	0	0.00
Rochester	AAA Bal	17	17	0	0	93	382	74	49	41	9	2	6	7	39	0	75	1	2	1	6	.143	0	0	3.97
1994 Texas	AL	1	0	0	0	1	5	1	1	1	1	0	0	0	1	0	0	0	0	0	0	.000	0	0	9.00
1995 Texas	AL	28	3	0	6	44.2	207	60	37	32	1	1	0	2	19	0	22	4	0	2	2	.500	0	1	6.45
1996 Milwaukee	AL	8	0	0	4	12.2	58	12	4	4	2	1	0	1	10	0	5	0	0	1	0	1.000	0	0	2.84
1997 San Diego	NL	13	0	0	4	10.1	52	12	13	12	1	1	0	1	8	1	8	0	0	0	2	.000	0	0	10.45
10 Min. YEARS		279	130	4	46	939.2	4001	854	479	426	70	26	29	28	428	9	753	42	28	53	59	.473	0	9	4.08
4 Maj. YEARS		50	3	0	14	68.2	322	85	55	49	5	2	0	4	38	1	35	4	0	4	4	.500	0	1	6.42

Darren Burton

Bats: Both **Throws:** Right **Pos:** OF   **Ht:** 6'1" **Wt:** 185 **Born:** 9/16/72 **Age:** 27

Year Team	Lg Org	G	AB	H	2B	3B	HR	TB	R	RBI	TBB	IBB	SO	HBP	SH	SF	SB	CS	SB%	GDP	Avg	OBP	SLG
		BATTING															**BASERUNNING**				**PERCENTAGES**		
1990 Royals	R KC	15	58	12	0	1	0	14	10	2	4	0	17	0	1	2	6	0	1.00	0	.207	.250	.241
1991 Appleton	A KC	134	532	143	32	6	2	193	78	51	45	4	122	1	3	6	37	12	.76	18	.269	.324	.363
1992 Baseball Cy	A+ KC	123	431	106	15	6	4	145	54	36	49	7	93	6	4	3	16	14	.53	7	.246	.329	.336
1993 Wilmington	A+ KC	134	549	152	23	5	10	215	82	45	48	1	111	1	13	4	30	10	.75	7	.277	.334	.392
1994 Memphis	AA KC	97	373	95	12	3	3	122	55	37	35	4	53	1	4	5	10	6	.63	5	.255	.316	.327
1995 Omaha	AAA KC	2	5	0	0	0	0	0	0	0	0	0	1	0	0	0	0	0	.00	0	.000	.000	.000
Wichita	AA KC	41	163	39	9	1	1	53	13	20	12	0	27	1	0	0	6	6	.50	2	.239	.295	.325
Orlando	AA ChC	62	222	68	16	2	4	100	40	21	27	2	42	0	0	0	7	4	.64	5	.306	.382	.450
1996 Omaha	AAA KC	129	463	125	28	5	15	208	75	67	59	6	82	6	9	4	7	7	.50	10	.270	.357	.449
1997 Scranton-WB	AAA Phi	70	253	63	16	3	8	109	34	39	19	1	40	3	1	4	3	0	1.00	6	.249	.305	.431
Reading	AA Phi	45	184	58	11	3	8	99	23	34	9	2	39	3	2	3	1	1	.50	1	.315	.352	.538
1998 Scranton-WB	AAA Phi	117	394	105	21	3	18	186	56	64	53	1	83	6	2	3	9	0	1.00	10	.266	.360	.472
1999 Scranton-WB	AAA Phi	118	409	107	30	3	13	182	61	63	44	2	96	5	3	4	7	2	.78	9	.262	.338	.445
10 Min. YEARS		1087	4036	1073	213	41	86	1626	581	479	404	30	806	33	51	38	139	62	.69	80	.266	.335	.403

Adam Butler

Pitches: Left **Bats:** Left **Pos:** P   **Ht:** 6'2" **Wt:** 225 **Born:** 8/17/73 **Age:** 26

Year Team	Lg Org	G	GS	CG	GF	IP	BFP	H	R	ER	HR	SH	SF	HB	TBB	IBB	SO	WP	Bk	W	L	Pct.	ShO	Sv	ERA
		HOW MUCH HE PITCHED						**WHAT HE GAVE UP**												**THE RESULTS**					
1995 Eugene	A- Atl	23	0	0	18	25.1	109	15	9	7	0	1	0	3	12	5	50	1	0	4	1	.800	0	8	2.49
1996 Macon	A Atl	12	0	0	12	14.2	53	5	3	2	1	0	0	1	3	0	23	1	0	1	0	.000	0	8	1.23
Durham	A+ Atl	9	0	0	9	11	41	2	0	0	0	0	0	1	7	0	14	0	0	0	0	.000	0	5	0.00
Greenville	AA Atl	38	0	0	31	35.1	161	36	22	20	6	5	3	2	16	3	31	3	0	1	4	.200	0	17	5.09
1997 Greenville	AA Atl	46	0	0	38	49	203	40	16	14	3	3	2	4	15	2	56	1	0	5	1	.833	0	22	2.57
1998 Richmond	AAA Atl	48	4	0	34	100	427	96	41	40	9	6	6	6	28	1	92	3	1	3	7	.300	0	14	3.60
1999 Richmond	AAA Atl	9	0	0	7	8	39	10	4	2	0	2	1	0	3	0	6	1	0	1	0	.000	0	3	2.25
Greenville	AA Atl	27	0	0	12	42.1	215	71	44	36	7	4	3	5	12	1	29	1	0	1	3	.250	0	1	7.65
1998 Atlanta	NL	8	0	0	1	5	28	5	7	6	1	2	1	1	6	1	7	1	0	1	0	.000	0	0	10.80
5 Min. YEARS		212	4	0	161	285.2	1248	275	139	121	26	21	15	22	96	12	301	11	1	14	18	.438	0	78	3.81

Brent Butler

Bats: Right **Throws:** Right **Pos:** SS   **Ht:** 6'0" **Wt:** 180 **Born:** 2/11/78 **Age:** 22

Year Team	Lg Org	G	AB	H	2B	3B	HR	TB	R	RBI	TBB	IBB	SO	HBP	SH	SF	SB	CS	SB%	GDP	Avg	OBP	SLG
		BATTING															**BASERUNNING**				**PERCENTAGES**		
1996 Johnson Cy	R+ StL	62	248	85	21	1	8	132	45	50	25	1	29	2	1	2	8	1	.89	11	.343	.404	.532
1997 Peoria	A StL	129	480	147	37	2	15	233	81	71	63	6	69	4	0	5	6	4	.60	9	.306	.388	.485
1998 Pr William	A+ StL	126	475	136	27	2	11	200	63	76	39	2	74	9	2	7	3	4	.43	12	.286	.347	.421
1999 Arkansas	AA StL	139	528	142	21	1	13	204	68	54	26	0	47	6	0	5	0	4	.00	16	.269	.308	.386
4 Min. YEARS		456	1731	510	106	6	47	769	257	251	153	9	219	21	3	19	17	13	.57	48	.295	.356	.444

Michael Byas

Bats: Both **Throws:** Right **Pos:** OF   **Ht:** 6'0" **Wt:** 170 **Born:** 4/21/76 **Age:** 24

Year Team	Lg Org	G	AB	H	2B	3B	HR	TB	R	RBI	TBB	IBB	SO	HBP	SH	SF	SB	CS	SB%	GDP	Avg	OBP	SLG
		BATTING															**BASERUNNING**				**PERCENTAGES**		
1997 Salem-Keizr	A- SF	71	290	80	9	1	0	91	68	16	48	0	44	2	1	0	51	9	.85	4	.276	.382	.314
1998 San Jose	A+ SF	135	521	131	10	2	1	148	87	36	81	1	98	0	2	5	30	22	.58	8	.251	.349	.284
1999 Shreveport	AA SF	129	487	132	9	1	0	143	76	41	68	0	79	1	3	0	31	15	.67	7	.271	.362	.294
Fresno	AAA SF	5	22	8	2	0	0	10	4	2	5	1	4	0	0	0	2	1	.67	0	.364	.481	.455
3 Min. YEARS		340	1320	351	30	4	1	392	235	95	202	2	225	3	6	5	114	47	.71	19	.266	.363	.297

Jimmie Byington

Bats: Right **Throws:** Right **Pos:** OF   **Ht:** 5'11" **Wt:** 175 **Born:** 8/22/73 **Age:** 26

Year Team	Lg Org	G	AB	H	2B	3B	HR	TB	R	RBI	TBB	IBB	SO	HBP	SH	SF	SB	CS	SB%	GDP	Avg	OBP	SLG
		BATTING															**BASERUNNING**				**PERCENTAGES**		
1993 Eugene	A- KC	53	170	44	5	0	8	73	23	32	14	0	45	3	1	1	9	1	.90	2	.259	.324	.429
1994 Rockford	A KC	105	328	82	14	3	1	105	44	48	26	0	64	5	0	5	14	7	.67	5	.250	.310	.320
1995 Wilmington	A+ KC	92	273	61	6	1	0	69	24	23	13	0	33	4	3	2	12	6	.67	3	.223	.267	.253

		BATTING															BASERUNNING				PERCENTAGES		
Year Team	Lg Org	G	AB	H	2B	3B	HR	TB	R	RBI	TBB	IBB	SO	HBP	SH	SF	SB	CS	SB%	GDP	Avg	OBP	SLG
1996 Wilmington	A+ KC	105	297	88	20	2	1	115	46	32	19	0	44	5	6	5	12	8	.60	4	.296	.344	.387
1997 Wichita	AA KC	92	196	46	8	0	2	60	30	16	15	0	39	4	3	2	5	6	.45	3	.235	.300	.306
1998 Wichita	AA KC	26	66	11	1	0	0	12	12	5	15	0	19	1	2	1	1	2	.33	2	.167	.325	.182
Wilmington	A+ KC	32	98	33	7	1	0	42	13	6	10	0	20	2	2	1	3	4	.43	0	.337	.405	.429
1999 Omaha	AAA KC	89	228	47	10	1	2	65	28	23	20	0	46	3	3	1	3	7	.30	6	.206	.278	.285
7 Min. YEARS		594	1656	412	71	8	14	541	220	185	132	0	310	27	20	18	59	41	.59	25	.249	.312	.327

Eric Byrnes

Bats: Right **Throws:** Right **Pos:** OF　　　　　　**Ht:** 6'2" **Wt:** 200 **Born:** 2/16/76 **Age:** 24

		BATTING															BASERUNNING				PERCENTAGES		
Year Team	Lg Org	G	AB	H	2B	3B	HR	TB	R	RBI	TBB	IBB	SO	HBP	SH	SF	SB	CS	SB%	GDP	Avg	OBP	SLG
1998 Sou Oregon	A- Oak	42	169	53	10	2	7	88	36	31	16	1	16	2	0	1	6	1	.86	3	.314	.378	.521
Visalia	A+ Oak	29	108	46	9	2	4	71	26	21	18	0	15	1	0	2	11	1	.92	2	.426	.504	.657
1999 Midland	AA Oak	43	164	39	14	0	1	56	25	22	17	0	32	3	2	3	6	3	.67	5	.238	.316	.341
Modesto	A+ Oak	96	365	123	28	1	6	171	86	66	58	2	37	9	0	7	28	8	.78	14	.337	.433	.468
2 Min. YEARS		210	806	261	61	5	18	386	173	140	109	3	100	15	2	13	51	13	.80	24	.324	.408	.479

Greg Cadaret

Pitches: Left **Bats:** Left **Pos:** P　　　　　　**Ht:** 6'3" **Wt:** 230 **Born:** 2/27/62 **Age:** 38

		HOW MUCH HE PITCHED						WHAT HE GAVE UP										THE RESULTS					
Year Team	Lg Org	G	GS	CG	GF	IP	BFP	H	R	ER	HR	SH	SF	HB	TBB	IBB	SO	WP	Bk	W	L	Pct.	ShO	Sv	ERA
1983 Medford	A- Oak	12	11	1	0	64	—	73	36	31	2	—	—	1	36	0	51	3	1	7	3	.700	1	0	4.36
1984 Modesto	A+ Oak	26	26	6	0	171.1	0	162	79	58	7	0	0	1	82	0	138	14	2	13	8	.619	2	0	3.05
1985 Huntsville	AA Oak	17	17	0	0	82.1	387	96	61	56	9	2	4	3	57	0	60	9	0	3	7	.300	0	0	6.12
Modesto	A+ Oak	12	12	1	0	61.1	0	59	50	40	4	0	0	1	54	0	43	10	0	3	9	.250	1	0	5.87
1986 Huntsville	AA Oak	28	28	1	0	141.1	666	166	106	85	6	1	4	1	98	0	113	15	0	12	5	.706	0	0	5.41
Tacoma	AAA Oak	7	0	0	4	13	57	5	6	5	1	2	0	0	13	1	12	0	0	1	2	.333	0	1	3.46
1987 Huntsville	AA Oak	24	0	0	21	40.1	172	31	16	13	1	1	0	0	20	3	48	6	1	5	2	.714	0	9	2.90
1995 Louisville	AAA StL	12	0	0	2	11.2	50	14	4	4	0	1	0	0	1	0	7	0	0	1	0	1.000	0	0	3.09
Las Vegas	AAA SD	28	4	0	6	52	234	56	40	34	6	2	3	0	22	0	52	10	0	3	5	.375	0	0	5.88
1996 Calgary	AAA Pit	9	0	0	3	12.1	69	20	18	10	2	2	0	1	12	2	10	4	0	0	3	.000	0	0	7.30
Buffalo	AAA Cle	32	3	0	9	64	274	59	28	26	3	3	2	2	29	2	44	4	0	1	5	.167	0	2	3.66
1997 Buffalo	AAA Cle	29	1	0	13	50	231	64	31	27	3	1	2	1	35	2	49	8	0	2	2	.500	0	4	4.86
Vancouver	AAA Ana	9	0	0	3	14.1	56	11	5	5	1	0	0	0	4	0	16	1	0	0	1	.000	0	3	3.14
1998 Vancouver	AAA Ana	9	0	0	3	10	36	4	2	0	0	1	0	0	3	0	12	1	0	2	1	.667	0	1	0.00
1999 Buffalo	AAA Cle	10	0	0	2	6.2	32	5	3	2	0	0	1	0	7	1	8	1	0	0	0	.000	0	0	2.70
1987 Oakland	AL	29	0	0	7	39.2	176	37	22	20	6	2	2	1	24	1	30	1	0	6	2	.750	0	0	4.54
1988 Oakland	AL	58	0	0	16	71.2	311	60	26	23	2	5	3	1	36	1	64	5	3	5	2	.714	0	3	2.89
1989 Oakland	AL	26	0	0	9	27.2	119	21	9	7	0	0	2	0	19	3	14	0	0	0	0	.000	0	0	2.28
New York	AL	20	13	3	1	92.1	412	109	53	47	7	3	3	2	38	1	66	6	2	5	5	.500	1	0	4.58
1990 New York	AL	54	6	0	9	121.1	525	120	62	56	8	9	4	1	64	5	80	14	0	5	4	.556	0	3	4.15
1991 New York	AL	68	5	0	17	121.2	517	110	52	49	8	6	3	2	59	6	105	3	1	8	6	.571	0	3	3.62
1992 New York	AL	46	11	1	9	103.2	471	104	53	49	12	3	3	2	74	7	73	5	1	4	8	.333	1	1	4.25
1993 Cincinnati	NL	34	0	0	15	32.2	158	40	19	18	3	3	0	1	23	5	23	2	0	2	1	.667	0	1	4.96
Kansas City	AL	13	0	0	3	15.1	62	14	5	5	0	4	0	1	7	0	2	0	0	1	1	.500	0	0	2.93
1994 Toronto	AL	21	0	0	8	20	100	24	15	13	4	0	0	0	17	2	15	6	0	0	1	.000	0	0	5.85
Detroit	AL	17	0	0	9	20	91	17	9	8	0	0	0	0	16	3	14	3	0	1	0	1.000	0	0	3.60
1997 Anaheim	AL	15	0	0	6	13.2	61	11	5	5	1	1	0	2	8	2	11	3	0	0	0	.000	0	0	3.29
1998 Anaheim	AL	39	0	0	11	37	167	38	17	17	6	1	0	3	15	0	37	5	0	1	2	.333	0	1	4.14
Texas	AL	11	0	0	3	7.2	36	11	4	4	1	1	0	0	3	0	5	3	0	0	0	.000	0	0	4.70
10 Min. YEARS		264	102	9	66	794.2	—	808	485	396	45	—	—	11	473	11	663	86	4	53	53	.500	4	20	4.48
10 Maj. YEARS		451	35	4	120	724.1	3206	716	351	321	58	35	21	16	403	36	539	56	7	38	32	.543	2	14	3.99

Cam Cairncross

Pitches: Left **Bats:** Left **Pos:** P　　　　　　**Ht:** 6'2" **Wt:** 212 **Born:** 5/11/72 **Age:** 28

		HOW MUCH HE PITCHED						WHAT HE GAVE UP										THE RESULTS					
Year Team	Lg Org	G	GS	CG	GF	IP	BFP	H	R	ER	HR	SH	SF	HB	TBB	IBB	SO	WP	Bk	W	L	Pct.	ShO	Sv	ERA
1991 Chston-SC	A SD	24	24	2	0	131.1	545	111	72	52	10	4	3	7	74	0	102	6	9	8	5	.615	1	0	3.56
1992 Waterloo	A SD	24	24	1	0	137	578	127	68	55	14	3	3	14	61	2	138	8	9	8	8	.500	1	0	3.61
1993 Rancho Cuca	A+ SD	29	26	0	0	154.2	706	182	112	88	10	5	6	13	81	1	122	8	9	10	11	.476	0	0	5.12
1994 Las Vegas	AAA SD	4	0	0	0	6.1	32	8	3	3	0	0	0	0	6	2	4	0	0	1	0	.000	0	0	4.26
Rancho Cuca	A+ SD	29	0	0	6	34.2	139	26	19	17	3	0	1	2	14	0	40	1	2	3	1	.750	0	3	4.41
Wichita	AA SD	31	0	0	13	37	162	37	19	15	5	0	2	1	15	1	33	6	1	2	3	.400	0	3	3.65
1997 Rancho Cuca	A+ SD	40	0	0	17	64	291	81	46	40	5	4	1	5	15	0	70	4	1	1	3	.250	0	1	5.63
1999 Kinston	A+ Cle	6	0	0	4	9.2	35	5	1	0	0	0	0	1	4	0	11	1	0	2	0	1.000	0	2	0.00
Buffalo	AAA Cle	19	0	0	5	19	86	22	13	11	1	2	4	2	6	0	13	1	0	0	3	.000	0	0	5.21
6 Min. YEARS		206	74	3	45	593.2	2574	599	353	281	48	18	20	45	276	6	533	35	31	34	35	.493	2	9	4.26

Kiko Calero

Pitches: Right **Bats:** Right **Pos:** P　　　　　　**Ht:** 6'1" **Wt:** 170 **Born:** 1/9/75 **Age:** 25

		HOW MUCH HE PITCHED						WHAT HE GAVE UP										THE RESULTS					
Year Team	Lg Org	G	GS	CG	GF	IP	BFP	H	R	ER	HR	SH	SF	HB	TBB	IBB	SO	WP	Bk	W	L	Pct.	ShO	Sv	ERA
1996 Spokane	A- KC	17	11	0	0	75	318	77	34	21	0	6	3	3	18	0	61	2	2	4	2	.667	0	1	2.52
1997 Wichita	AA KC	23	22	2	0	127.2	541	120	78	63	15	4	6	4	44	0	100	2	2	11	9	.550	0	0	4.44
1998 Lansing	A KC	4	4	0	0	16.2	76	19	7	7	1	0	0	2	7	0	10	1	1	1	0	1.000	0	0	3.78
Wichita	AA KC	3	3	0	0	14	72	23	16	15	2	1	0	1	6	0	5	0	0	1	1	.500	0	0	9.64
Wilmington	A+ KC	17	17	0	0	97.2	409	74	33	31	7	1	3	7	51	1	90	6	0	7	3	.700	0	0	2.86

Year Team	Lg Org	G	GS	CG	GF	IP	BFP	H	R	ER	HR	SH	SF	HB	TBB	IBB	SO	WP	Bk	W	L	Pct.	ShO	Sv	ERA
1999 Wichita	AA KC	26	23	1	1	129.1	579	143	67	59	14	2	2	6	57	3	92	7	2	9	3	.750	1	1	4.11
4 Min. YEARS		90	80	3	4	460.1	1995	456	235	196	44	8	17	23	183	4	358	18	7	33	17	.660	1	2	3.83

Jeremy Callier

Pitches: Right Bats: Right Pos: P   Ht: 6'0" Wt: 195 Born: 11/18/75 Age: 24

		HOW MUCH HE PITCHED						WHAT HE GAVE UP												THE RESULTS					
Year Team	Lg Org	G	GS	CG	GF	IP	BFP	H	R	ER	HR	SH	SF	HB	TBB	IBB	SO	WP	Bk	W	L	Pct.	ShO	Sv	ERA
1998 Butte	R+ Ana	19	11	2	1	101.2	433	102	51	40	7	1	2	8	26	0	78	3	2	3	9	.250	0	0	3.54
1999 Erie	AA Ana	1	0	0	1	1	7	2	2	2	0	0	0	0	2	0	2	0	0	0	0	.000	0	0	18.00
Lk Elsinore	A+ Ana	34	7	0	9	95.2	418	107	48	41	5	5	0	3	33	2	69	6	1	5	3	.625	0	0	3.86
2 Min. YEARS		54	18	2	11	198.1	858	211	101	83	12	6	2	11	61	2	149	9	3	8	12	.400	0	2	3.77

Ron Calloway

Bats: Left Throws: Left Pos: OF   Ht: 6'0" Wt: 195 Born: 9/6/76 Age: 23

		BATTING															BASERUNNING				PERCENTAGES		
Year Team	Lg Org	G	AB	H	2B	3B	HR	TB	R	RBI	TBB	IBB	SO	HBP	SH	SF	SB	CS	SB%	GDP	Avg	OBP	SLG
1997 Lethbridge	R+ Ari	43	148	37	5	0	0	42	23	9	14	0	29	3	0	2	5	8	.38	4	.250	.323	.284
South Bend	A Ari	9	25	7	1	0	0	8	3	1	2	0	8	0	0	0	1	0	1.00	1	.280	.333	.320
1998 High Desert	A+ Ari	44	156	44	8	2	3	65	30	27	12	0	38	2	2	2	2	4	.33	3	.282	.337	.417
South Bend	A Ari	69	251	66	12	2	3	91	29	33	25	1	50	2	1	3	7	5	.58	3	.263	.331	.363
1999 High Desert	A+ Ari	60	196	62	14	1	3	87	41	23	30	0	34	2	2	0	22	7	.76	3	.316	.412	.444
El Paso	AA Ari	11	32	7	0	0	0	7	4	1	7	0	7	0	0	0	1	2	.33	0	.219	.359	.219
Jupiter	A+ Mon	54	211	57	8	4	3	82	30	25	15	0	45	2	4	0	5	6	.45	9	.270	.325	.389
3 Min. YEARS		290	1019	280	48	9	12	382	160	119	105	1	211	11	9	7	43	32	.57	23	.275	.347	.375

Aaron Cames

Pitches: Right Bats: Right Pos: P   Ht: 6'1" Wt: 192 Born: 11/21/75 Age: 24

		HOW MUCH HE PITCHED						WHAT HE GAVE UP												THE RESULTS					
Year Team	Lg Org	G	GS	CG	GF	IP	BFP	H	R	ER	HR	SH	SF	HB	TBB	IBB	SO	WP	Bk	W	L	Pct.	ShO	Sv	ERA
1996 Utica	A- Fla	18	9	1	3	73.2	301	60	28	23	2	3	5	2	18	2	77	5	4	6	2	.750	0	0	2.81
1997 Kane County	A Fla	26	26	3	0	149.2	627	143	67	65	11	6	6	15	43	0	157	10	6	8	10	.444	3	0	3.91
1998 Brevard Cty	A+ Fla	27	25	1	1	152.2	657	134	73	53	11	3	3	15	59	0	161	6	3	10	10	.333	0	0	3.12
1999 Portland	AA Fla	23	16	1	2	95.2	435	110	64	50	17	0	3	9	46	1	66	3	1	3	6	.333	0	0	5.55
Brevard Cty	A+ Fla	4	4	0	0	23.1	92	17	3	2	0	1	0	3	5	0	23	0	0	2	0	1.000	0	0	0.77
4 Min. YEARS		98	80	6	6	495	2112	464	235	202	41	13	17	44	171	3	484	24	14	24	28	.462	3	0	3.67

Jason Camilli

Bats: Right Throws: Right Pos: 2B   Ht: 6'0" Wt: 178 Born: 10/18/75 Age: 24

		BATTING															BASERUNNING				PERCENTAGES		
Year Team	Lg Org	G	AB	H	2B	3B	HR	TB	R	RBI	TBB	IBB	SO	HBP	SH	SF	SB	CS	SB%	GDP	Avg	OBP	SLG
1994 Expos	R Mon	53	212	54	4	3	0	64	33	13	31	1	44	0	0	1	5	6	.45	4	.255	.348	.302
1995 Albany	A Mon	53	181	34	5	0	3	48	28	16	38	0	50	3	0	2	13	10	.57	0	.188	.335	.265
Vermont	A- Mon	63	243	59	10	2	1	76	37	21	30	1	52	2	3	2	17	10	.63	4	.243	.329	.313
1996 Delmarva	A Mon	119	426	95	13	2	3	121	53	36	63	1	89	5	9	2	26	17	.60	4	.223	.329	.284
1997 Cape Fear	A Mon	98	396	118	35	2	3	166	57	43	31	0	64	5	7	2	22	11	.67	7	.298	.355	.419
Wst Plm Bch	A+ Mon	15	47	6	3	0	0	9	1	1	2	0	12	0	1	0	0	1	.00	1	.128	.163	.191
1998 Jupiter	A+ Mon	89	314	81	15	1	2	104	45	33	35	2	55	2	1	1	9	10	.47	2	.258	.335	.331
Harrisburg	AA Mon	6	18	2	0	0	0	2	1	1	3	0	5	0	0	0	0	0	.00	0	.111	.238	.111
1999 Ottawa	AAA Mon	35	102	27	6	0	0	33	12	8	11	0	19	0	0	0	4	1	.80	3	.265	.336	.324
Harrisburg	AA Mon	63	154	33	7	0	4	52	26	16	23	0	31	2	0	1	2	2	.00	3	.214	.322	.338
6 Min. YEARS		594	2093	509	98	10	16	675	293	188	267	5	421	19	21	11	96	68	.59	28	.243	.333	.323

Eric Cammack

Pitches: Right Bats: Right Pos: P   Ht: 6'1" Wt: 175 Born: 8/14/75 Age: 24

		HOW MUCH HE PITCHED						WHAT HE GAVE UP												THE RESULTS					
Year Team	Lg Org	G	GS	CG	GF	IP	BFP	H	R	ER	HR	SH	SF	HB	TBB	IBB	SO	WP	Bk	W	L	Pct.	ShO	Sv	ERA
1997 Pittsfield	A- NYM	23	0	0	17	31.1	117	9	4	3	1	3	1	4	14	1	32	1	1	0	1	.000	0	0	0.86
1998 Capital City	A NYM	25	0	0	22	32	127	17	13	10	2	0	0	2	13	0	49	1	0	4	0	1.000	0	8	2.81
St. Lucie	A+ NYM	29	0	0	24	35.2	142	22	12	8	2	0	1	0	14	2	53	0	0	3	2	.600	0	11	2.02
1999 Binghamton	AA NYM	45	0	0	38	56.2	231	28	17	15	2	5	2	1	38	1	83	0	2	4	2	.667	0	15	2.38
Norfolk	AAA NYM	9	0	0	5	8.2	35	7	3	3	1	0	0	1	1	0	17	1	0	0	0	.000	0	4	3.12
3 Min. YEARS		131	0	0	106	164.1	652	83	49	39	8	8	4	5	80	4	234	3	3	11	5	.688	0	46	2.14

Jared Camp

Pitches: Right Bats: Right Pos: P   Ht: 6'2" Wt: 195 Born: 5/4/75 Age: 25

		HOW MUCH HE PITCHED						WHAT HE GAVE UP												THE RESULTS					
Year Team	Lg Org	G	GS	CG	GF	IP	BFP	H	R	ER	HR	SH	SF	HB	TBB	IBB	SO	WP	Bk	W	L	Pct.	ShO	Sv	ERA
1995 Helena	R+ Mil	8	8	0	0	34.1	166	44	39	33	1	1	3	3	20	0	26	6	2	1	4	.200	0	0	8.65
1996 Beloit	A Mil	11	11	0	0	53	251	56	42	32	4	3	9	2	39	0	47	10	1	3	5	.375	0	0	5.43
Watertown	A- Cle	15	15	1	0	95.2	380	68	29	18	2	1	1	7	30	0	99	6	0	10	2	.833	1	0	1.69
1997 Akron	AA Cle	12	12	1	0	64	293	79	49	44	13	4	1	1	26	1	39	4	0	2	8	.200	0	0	6.19
Kinston	A+ Cle	13	12	0	0	73.2	297	57	36	31	11	5	1	2	20	0	64	1	1	5	4	.556	0	0	3.79
1998 Akron	AA Cle	18	16	0	2	85.2	364	84	37	36	8	3	5	5	31	0	42	2	1	6	2	.750	0	0	3.78
1999 Kinston	A+ Cle	18	6	1	7	54.2	224	48	15	12	2	0	3	4	16	0	59	4	0	3	2	.600	0	4	1.98
Buffalo	AAA Cle	10	0	0	7	10.2	51	4	1	1	1	0	0	1	13	0	14	4	0	0	0	.000	0	1	0.84

		HOW MUCH HE PITCHED						WHAT HE GAVE UP												THE RESULTS					
Year Team	Lg Org	G	GS	CG	GF	IP	BFP	H	R	ER	HR	SH	SF	HB	TBB	IBB	SO	WP	Bk	W	L	Pct.	ShO	Sv	ERA
Akron	AA Cle	17	0	0	13	18	92	22	17	13	0	2	3	2	16	0	18	2	1	1	2	.333	0	7	6.50
5 Min. YEARS		122	80	3	29	489.2	2118	462	266	220	41	19	27	27	211	1	408	39	6	31	29	.517	1	12	4.04

Carlos Campusano

Bats: Right **Throws:** Right **Pos:** SS **Ht:** 5'11" **Wt:** 160 **Born:** 9/2/75 **Age:** 24

		BATTING														BASERUNNING				PERCENTAGES		
Year Team	Lg Org	G	AB	H	2B	3B	HR	TB	R	RBI	TBB	IBB	SO	HBP	SH	SF	SB	CS	SB%	GDP	Avg	OBP	SLG
1995 Brewers	R Mil	54	173	43	4	1	1	52	25	15	14	1	27	5	1	1	7	3	.70	6	.249	.321	.301
1996 Beloit	A Mil	108	337	83	17	4	1	111	33	20	10	0	63	5	5	1	4	3	.57	7	.246	.278	.329
1997 Bakersfield	A+ SF	61	191	38	8	3	1	55	17	15	7	0	49	4	3	2	2	0	1.00	3	.199	.240	.288
1998 San Jose	A+ SF	34	98	18	1	2	0	23	11	7	5	0	29	3	1	1	0	0	.00	3	.184	.243	.235
1999 San Jose	A+ SF	27	84	26	2	1	1	33	13	7	6	0	15	4	3	1	4	1	.80	1	.310	.379	.393
Shreveport	AA SF	15	39	6	0	2	1	13	5	6	3	0	10	0	0	0	1	0	1.00	1	.154	.214	.333
Bakersfield	A+ SF	14	51	18	2	0	1	23	7	4	1	0	13	2	0	0	2	2	.50	0	.353	.389	.451
Fresno	AAA SF	16	46	13	2	0	0	15	2	3	2	0	9	3	0	1	0	0	.00	4	.283	.346	.326
5 Min. YEARS		329	1019	245	36	13	6	325	113	77	48	1	215	26	13	7	20	9	.69	25	.240	.290	.319

Casey Candaele

Bats: Both **Throws:** Right **Pos:** 2B **Ht:** 5' 9" **Wt:** 165 **Born:** 1/12/61 **Age:** 39

		BATTING														BASERUNNING				PERCENTAGES		
Year Team	Lg Org	G	AB	H	2B	3B	HR	TB	R	RBI	TBB	IBB	SO	HBP	SH	SF	SB	CS	SB%	GDP	Avg	OBP	SLG
1983 Wst Plm Bch	A+ Mon	127	511	156	26	9	0	200	77	45	51	2	44	2	8	1	22	17	.56	—	.305	.370	.391
Memphis	A Mon	5	19	4	1	0	0	5	4	1	1	0	3	0	0	0	1	0	1.00	—	.211	.250	.263
1984 Jacksnville	AA Mon	132	532	145	23	2	2	178	68	53	30	1	35	1	5	6	26	18	.59	13	.273	.309	.335
1985 Indianpols	AAA Mon	127	390	101	13	5	0	124	55	35	44	2	33	0	11	1	13	10	.57	15	.259	.333	.318
1986 Indianpols	AAA Mon	119	480	145	32	6	2	195	77	42	46	6	29	1	11	2	16	10	.62	8	.302	.363	.406
1988 Indianpols	AAA Mon	60	239	63	11	6	2	92	23	36	12	0	20	0	1	7	5	1	.83	5	.264	.291	.385
Tucson	AAA Hou	17	66	17	3	0	0	20	8	5	4	0	6	0	0	0	4	2	.67	5	.258	.300	.303
1989 Tucson	AAA Hou	68	206	45	6	1	0	53	22	17	20	4	37	0	4	1	6	3	.67	7	.218	.286	.257
1990 Tucson	AAA Hou	7	28	6	1	0	0	7	2	2	3	1	2	1	1	0	1	2	.33	1	.214	.313	.250
1993 Tucson	AAA Hou	6	27	8	1	0	0	9	4	4	3	1	2	0	0	0	1	2	.33	2	.296	.367	.333
1994 Indianpols	AAA Cin	131	511	144	31	7	4	201	66	52	32	4	65	0	3	4	8	6	.57	21	.282	.322	.393
1995 Albuquerque	AAA LA	12	27	7	0	0	0	7	2	2	4	0	4	0	1	1	0	1	.00	1	.259	.344	.259
Buffalo	AAA Cle	97	364	90	10	7	4	126	50	38	22	1	42	2	4	7	9	2	.82	6	.247	.289	.346
1996 Buffalo	AAA Cle	94	392	122	22	2	6	166	66	37	27	2	35	1	3	3	3	5	.38	6	.311	.355	.423
1997 Buffalo	AAA Cle	79	311	71	21	0	7	113	39	38	31	2	43	1	4	4	1	6	.14	12	.228	.297	.363
1998 Nashville	AAA Pit	44	147	40	5	2	1	52	18	15	13	1	19	1	1	0	1	1	.50	3	.272	.335	.354
New Orleans	AAA Hou	66	221	64	11	2	1	82	36	25	18	2	34	0	0	2	2	0	1.00	12	.290	.340	.371
1999 New Orleans	AAA Hou	126	467	124	34	3	2	185	56	42	47	1	54	3	2	0	3	9	.25	7	.266	.337	.396
1986 Montreal	NL	30	104	24	4	1	0	30	9	6	5	0	15	0	0	1	3	5	.38	3	.231	.264	.288
1987 Montreal	NL	138	449	122	23	4	1	156	62	23	38	3	28	2	4	2	7	10	.41	5	.272	.330	.347
1988 Montreal	NL	36	116	20	5	1	0	27	9	4	10	1	11	0	2	0	1	0	1.00	7	.172	.238	.233
Houston	NL	21	31	5	3	0	0	8	2	1	1	0	6	0	1	0	1	0	.00	0	.161	.188	.258
1990 Houston	NL	130	262	75	8	6	3	104	30	22	31	5	42	1	4	0	7	5	.58	4	.286	.364	.397
1991 Houston	NL	151	461	121	20	7	4	167	44	50	40	7	49	0	1	3	9	3	.75	5	.262	.319	.362
1992 Houston	NL	135	320	68	12	1	1	85	19	18	24	3	36	3	7	6	7	1	.88	5	.213	.269	.266
1993 Houston	NL	75	121	29	8	0	1	40	18	7	10	0	14	0	0	0	2	3	.40	0	.240	.298	.331
1996 Cleveland	AL	24	44	11	2	0	1	16	8	4	1	0	9	0	0	0	0	0	.00	0	.250	.267	.364
1997 Cleveland	AL	14	26	8	1	0	0	9	5	4	1	0	1	0	0	0	1	0	1.00	0	.308	.333	.346
14 Min. YEARS		1317	4938	1352	251	52	36	1815	673	489	408	30	507	13	59	39	122	95	.56	—	.274	.328	.368
9 Maj. YEARS		754	1934	483	86	20	11	642	206	139	161	19	211	6	19	12	37	28	.57	29	.250	.308	.332

Ben Candelaria

Bats: Left **Throws:** Right **Pos:** OF **Ht:** 5'11" **Wt:** 167 **Born:** 1/29/75 **Age:** 25

		BATTING														BASERUNNING				PERCENTAGES		
Year Team	Lg Org	G	AB	H	2B	3B	HR	TB	R	RBI	TBB	IBB	SO	HBP	SH	SF	SB	CS	SB%	GDP	Avg	OBP	SLG
1992 Blue Jays	R Tor	29	77	12	2	1	0	16	10	3	6	0	16	0	1	1	4	3	.57	0	.156	.214	.208
1993 Medcine Hat	R+ Tor	62	208	55	7	1	5	79	24	34	27	1	49	3	5	4	3	3	.50	3	.264	.351	.380
1994 Hagerstown	A Tor	3	13	3	0	0	1	6	2	3	0	0	4	0	0	0	0	0	.00	0	.231	.231	.462
St.Cathrnes	A- Tor	71	250	66	15	1	2	89	36	37	35	1	55	1	3	1	8	4	.67	6	.264	.355	.356
1995 Dunedin	A+ Tor	125	471	122	21	5	5	168	66	49	53	1	98	0	3	5	11	4	.73	11	.259	.331	.357
1996 Knoxville	AA Tor	55	162	45	11	2	3	69	16	14	18	0	40	2	2	0	3	3	.50	7	.278	.357	.426
Dunedin	A+ Tor	39	125	25	5	0	1	33	13	6	12	0	25	1	0	1	1	4	.20	1	.200	.270	.264
1997 Knoxville	AA Tor	120	472	139	32	5	15	226	81	67	42	2	89	5	4	6	4	3	.57	9	.294	.354	.479
1998 Knoxville	AA Tor	36	156	52	8	3	10	96	33	31	9	0	31	1	1	1	0	3	.00	2	.333	.371	.615
Syracuse	AAA Tor	69	251	62	13	2	7	100	28	32	23	2	68	2	0	3	2	0	1.00	5	.247	.312	.398
1999 Jacksnville	AA Det	120	464	125	31	3	18	216	65	77	35	3	93	1	0	5	6	7	.46	13	.269	.319	.466
8 Min. YEARS		729	2649	706	145	23	67	1098	374	353	260	10	568	15	20	26	42	34	.55	57	.267	.333	.414

Javier Cardona

Bats: Right **Throws:** Right **Pos:** C **Ht:** 6'1" **Wt:** 185 **Born:** 9/15/75 **Age:** 24

		BATTING														BASERUNNING				PERCENTAGES		
Year Team	Lg Org	G	AB	H	2B	3B	HR	TB	R	RBI	TBB	IBB	SO	HBP	SH	SF	SB	CS	SB%	GDP	Avg	OBP	SLG
1994 Jamestown	A- Det	19	46	12	2	0	0	14	6	5	7	0	9	0	0	0	1	0	.00	2	.261	.358	.304
1995 Fayettevlle	A Det	51	165	34	8	0	3	51	18	19	13	0	30	1	0	0	1	0	1.00	1	.206	.268	.309
1996 Fayettevlle	A Det	97	348	98	21	0	4	131	42	28	28	1	53	2	3	3	1	5	.17	9	.282	.336	.376
1997 Lakeland	A+ Det	85	284	82	15	0	7	118	28	38	25	1	51	1	2	2	1	3	.25	8	.289	.346	.415

Year Team	Lg Org	G	AB	H	2B	3B	HR	TB	R	RBI	TBB	IBB	SO	HBP	SH	SF	SB	CS	SB%	GDP	Avg	OBP	SLG
																	BASERUNNING				PERCENTAGES		
1998 Jacksnville	AA Det	46	163	54	16	1	4	84	31	40	15	1	29	1	0	2	0	0	.00	6	.331	.387	.515
Toledo	AAA Det	47	162	31	4	0	5	50	12	16	9	1	32	1	0	0	0	0	.00	3	.191	.238	.309
1999 Jacksnville	AA Det	108	418	129	31	0	26	238	84	92	46	0	69	8	0	5	4	2	.67	16	.309	.384	.569
6 Min. YEARS		453	1586	440	97	1	49	686	221	238	143	4	273	14	9	12	7	10	.41	49	.277	.340	.433

Ken Carlyle

Pitches: Right **Bats:** Right **Pos:** P **Ht:** 6'1" **Wt:** 195 **Born:** 4/16/71 **Age:** 29

Year Team	Lg Org	G	GS	CG	GF	IP	BFP	H	R	ER	HR	SH	SF	HB	TBB	IBB	SO	WP	Bk	W	L	Pct.	ShO	Sv	ERA
1992 Niagara Fal	A- Det	1	1	0	0	6	26	6	1	1	0	0	0	0	1	0	9	1	1	1	0	1.000	0	0	1.50
Fayettevlle	A Det	14	14	1	0	79.2	319	64	21	17	3	0	1	4	24	0	59	6	1	8	4	.667	1	0	1.92
1993 Toledo	AAA Det	15	14	1	0	75.2	339	88	59	54	13	2	2	1	36	1	43	4	2	2	10	.167	0	0	6.42
London	AA Det	12	12	1	0	78	341	72	40	32	8	1	3	5	35	1	50	0	2	4	6	.400	0	0	3.69
1994 Trenton	AA Det	19	19	5	0	116.1	519	125	75	53	6	4	3	3	47	3	69	5	2	3	9	.250	1	0	4.10
Toledo	AAA Det	12	1	0	3	24.1	104	23	13	11	2	1	2	2	8	0	12	1	0	1	0	1.000	0	1	4.07
1995 Toledo	AAA Det	32	20	0	0	124.2	541	139	65	60	10	2	5	4	44	2	63	7	0	8	8	.500	0	0	4.33
1996 Jacksnville	AA Det	27	26	1	0	155.2	671	167	92	70	8	7	6	9	51	2	89	6	0	8	5	.615	1	0	4.05
1997 Richmond	AAA Atl	16	11	1	1	69.2	284	69	26	22	4	0	1	1	19	0	48	0	0	4	1	.800	1	0	2.84
1998 Richmond	AAA Atl	30	30	0	0	156.2	701	206	104	90	22	10	4	2	46	1	76	2	0	6	12	.333	0	0	5.17
1999 Greenville	AA Atl	17	12	0	2	71.1	346	89	60	47	11	1	1	4	42	4	33	5	0	1	6	.143	0	0	5.93
8 Min. YEARS		195	160	10	6	958	4191	1048	556	457	87	28	28	35	353	14	551	37	8	46	61	.430	4	1	4.29

Bubba Carpenter

Bats: Left **Throws:** Left **Pos:** OF **Ht:** 6'1" **Wt:** 195 **Born:** 7/23/68 **Age:** 31

Year Team	Lg Org	G	AB	H	2B	3B	HR	TB	R	RBI	TBB	IBB	SO	HBP	SH	SF	SB	CS	SB%	GDP	Avg	OBP	SLG
1991 Pr William	A+ NYY	69	236	66	10	3	6	100	33	34	40	3	50	2	1	3	4	1	.80	7	.280	.384	.424
1992 Albany-Colo	AA NYY	60	221	51	11	5	4	84	24	31	25	0	41	2	0	1	2	3	.40	8	.231	.313	.380
Pr William	A+ NYY	68	240	76	15	2	5	110	41	41	35	2	44	1	1	6	4	4	.50	4	.317	.397	.458
1993 Albany-Colo	AA NYY	14	53	17	4	0	2	27	8	14	7	0	4	0	0	1	2	2	.50	2	.321	.393	.509
Columbus	AAA NYY	70	199	53	9	0	5	77	29	17	29	3	35	3	0	1	2	2	.50	4	.266	.366	.387
1994 Albany-Colo	AA NYY	116	378	109	14	1	13	164	47	51	58	5	65	3	3	3	9	5	.64	3	.288	.385	.434
Columbus	AAA NYY	7	15	4	0	0	0	4	0	2	0	0	7	0	0	0	0	0	.00	1	.267	.267	.267
1995 Columbus	AAA NYY	116	374	92	12	3	11	143	57	40	40	2	70	1	2	3	13	6	.68	2	.246	.318	.382
1996 Columbus	AAA NYY	132	466	114	23	3	7	164	55	48	48	1	80	0	2	1	10	7	.59	7	.245	.315	.352
1997 Columbus	AAA NYY	85	271	76	12	4	6	114	47	39	48	0	46	0	3	1	4	8	.33	3	.280	.388	.421
1998 Yankees	R NYY	5	17	4	0	2	1	11	3	7	2	0	2	0	0	0	0	0	.00	0	.235	.316	.647
Columbus	AAA NYY	63	198	45	14	2	7	84	28	24	36	2	48	1	2	0	3	2	.60	9	.227	.349	.424
1999 Columbus	AAA NYY	101	325	92	20	2	22	182	78	81	75	7	68	4	1	4	7	3	.70	4	.283	.419	.560
9 Min. YEARS		906	2993	799	144	27	89	1264	450	438	443	25	560	17	15	24	60	43	.58	54	.267	.362	.422

Dustin Carr

Bats: Right **Throws:** Right **Pos:** 2B **Ht:** 6'0" **Wt:** 190 **Born:** 6/7/75 **Age:** 25

Year Team	Lg Org	G	AB	H	2B	3B	HR	TB	R	RBI	TBB	IBB	SO	HBP	SH	SF	SB	CS	SB%	GDP	Avg	OBP	SLG
1997 Hudson Val	A- TB	74	281	81	12	2	5	112	46	47	42	2	42	2	0	3	4	2	.67	10	.288	.381	.399
1998 St. Pete	A+ TB	138	516	132	23	5	6	183	85	52	70	4	86	11	8	3	11	4	.73	9	.256	.355	.355
1999 Orlando	AA TB	125	461	139	22	3	6	185	76	63	70	0	62	4	8	3	7	2	.78	12	.302	.396	.401
3 Min. YEARS		337	1258	352	57	10	17	480	207	162	182	6	190	17	16	9	22	8	.73	31	.280	.376	.382

Jeremy Carr

Bats: Right **Throws:** Right **Pos:** OF **Ht:** 5'9" **Wt:** 180 **Born:** 3/30/71 **Age:** 29

Year Team	Lg Org	G	AB	H	2B	3B	HR	TB	R	RBI	TBB	IBB	SO	HBP	SH	SF	SB	CS	SB%	GDP	Avg	OBP	SLG
1993 Eugene	A- KC	42	136	31	2	5	0	43	33	12	20	1	18	6	2	2	30	3	.91	4	.228	.348	.316
1994 Rockford	A KC	121	437	112	9	5	1	134	85	32	60	1	59	16	2	4	52	22	.70	8	.256	.364	.307
1995 Wilmington	A+ KC	5	13	3	1	0	0	4	1	0	1	0	3	0	0	0	0	1	.00	0	.231	.286	.308
Bakersfield	A+ KC	128	499	128	22	2	1	157	92	38	79	0	73	11	6	0	52	21	.71	9	.257	.370	.315
1996 Wichita	AA KC	129	453	118	23	2	6	163	68	40	47	1	64	12	3	3	41	9	.82	15	.260	.344	.360
1997 Wichita	AA KC	91	340	104	19	1	8	149	76	40	50	1	53	9	3	1	39	8	.83	4	.306	.408	.360
Omaha	AAA KC	35	120	32	3	2	2	45	17	9	15	0	17	3	1	0	12	3	.80	3	.267	.362	.375
1998 Omaha	AAA KC	49	178	52	14	3	5	87	40	23	19	1	31	1	2	2	19	5	.79	3	.292	.360	.489
1999 Omaha	AAA KC	73	275	72	12	1	4	98	47	25	42	1	58	5	9	0	15	8	.65	4	.262	.370	.356
7 Min. YEARS		673	2451	652	105	21	27	880	459	219	333	6	376	63	28	12	260	80	.76	50	.266	.367	.359

Giovanni Carrara

Pitches: Right **Bats:** Right **Pos:** P **Ht:** 6'2" **Wt:** 230 **Born:** 3/4/68 **Age:** 32

Year Team	Lg Org	G	GS	CG	GF	IP	BFP	H	R	ER	HR	SH	SF	HB	TBB	IBB	SO	WP	Bk	W	L	Pct.	ShO	Sv	ERA
1991 St.Cathrnes	A- Tor	15	13	2	0	89.2	363	66	26	16	5	0	4	8	21	0	83	4	2	5	2	.714	0	0	1.61
1992 Dunedin	A+ Tor	5	4	0	1	23.1	101	22	13	12	1	0	0	2	11	0	16	4	0	0	1	.000	0	0	4.63
Myrtle Bch	A Tor	22	16	1	2	100.1	416	86	40	35	12	0	2	4	36	0	100	9	3	11	7	.611	1	0	3.14
1993 Dunedin	A+ Tor	27	24	1	1	140.2	601	136	69	54	14	4	4	4	59	0	108	10	0	6	11	.353	0	0	3.45
1994 Knoxville	AA Tor	26	26	1	0	164.1	705	158	85	71	16	2	7	7	59	0	96	9	0	13	7	.650	0	0	3.89
1995 Syracuse	AAA Tor	21	21	0	0	131.2	565	116	72	58	11	3	2	4	56	2	81	3	0	7	7	.500	0	0	3.96
1996 Syracuse	AAA Tor	9	6	1	1	37.2	159	37	16	15	2	0	1	0	12	1	28	1	0	4	4	.500	0	0	3.58

48

		HOW MUCH HE PITCHED				WHAT HE GAVE UP								THE RESULTS					
Year Team	Lg Org	G	GS	CG	GF	IP	BFP	H	R	ER	HR	SH	SF	HB	TBB	IBB	SO	WP	Bk	W	L	Pct.	ShO	Sv	ERA
Indianapols	AAA Cin	9	6	1	2	47.2	177	25	6	4	2	0	1	3	9	0	45	0	1	4	0	1.000	1	1	0.76
1997 Rochester	AAA Bal	8	8	1	0	46.2	196	45	23	23	4	1	3	2	16	0	48	1	0	4	2	.667	0	0	4.44
Indianapols	AAA Cin	19	18	2	0	120.2	509	111	50	47	12	5	0	3	51	3	105	1	1	12	5	.706	0	0	3.51
1999 Indianapols	AAA Cin	39	21	2	7	158	660	144	68	61	20	7	2	7	58	3	114	3	1	12	7	.632	1	0	3.47
1995 Toronto	AL	12	7	1	2	48.2	229	64	46	39	10	1	2	1	25	1	27	1	0	2	4	.333	0	0	7.21
1996 Toronto	AL	11	0	0	3	15	76	23	19	19	5	0	0	0	12	2	10	1	0	0	1	.000	0	0	11.40
Cincinnati	NL	8	5	0	1	23	112	31	17	15	6	1	0	2	13	1	13	0	0	1	0	1.000	0	0	5.87
1997 Cincinnati	NL	2	2	0	0	10.1	49	14	9	9	4	1	0	0	6	1	5	0	0	0	1	.000	0	0	7.84
8 Min. YEARS		200	163	12	14	1060.2	4452	946	468	396	99	22	26	44	388	9	824	45	8	78	53	.595	5	1	3.36
3 Maj. YEARS		33	14	1	6	97	466	132	91	82	25	3	2	3	56	5	55	2	0	3	6	.333	0	0	7.61

Dave Carroll

Pitches: Left **Bats:** Right **Pos:** P   **Ht:** 6'3" **Wt:** 205 **Born:** 7/23/72 **Age:** 27

		HOW MUCH HE PITCHED				WHAT HE GAVE UP								THE RESULTS					
Year Team	Lg Org	G	GS	CG	GF	IP	BFP	H	R	ER	HR	SH	SF	HB	TBB	IBB	SO	WP	Bk	W	L	Pct.	ShO	Sv	ERA
1993 Johnson Cy	R+ StL	6	6	1	0	34.1	131	27	8	7	3	0	0	1	10	0	22	1	0	4	1	.800	0	0	1.83
1994 Madison	A StL	27	26	0	0	137	626	170	101	79	13	11	4	3	62	1	85	8	2	6	11	.353	0	0	5.19
1995 Peoria	A StL	24	6	0	5	51.1	230	53	33	25	3	2	0	3	24	0	41	6	1	2	2	.500	0	0	4.38
1997 St. Pete	A+ TB	47	0	0	9	50.2	218	50	15	10	1	1	2	2	20	3	34	2	0	4	1	.800	0	0	1.78
1998	A+ Oak	22	0	0	11	32.2	156	34	21	11	1	2	1	2	22	2	29	1	0	1	4	.200	0	4	3.03
Huntsville	AA Oak	20	0	0	7	34	141	26	9	9	0	0	2	3	13	1	34	0	0	1	0	1.000	0	3	2.38
Edmonton	AAA Oak	7	0	0	2	9.1	55	22	16	13	2	0	0	1	5	0	11	1	0	0	1	.000	0	0	12.54
1999 Tampa	A+ NYY	2	1	0	1	4.1	22	6	1	1	0	0	0	0	2	0	5	0	0	0	0	.000	0	0	2.08
Norwich	AA NYY	3	0	0	1	6	27	5	3	0	0	0	0	1	2	0	4	1	0	0	0	.000	0	1	0.00
Columbus	AAA NYY	1	0	0	0	1	5	1	2	1	0	0	0	0	0	0	0	0	0	0	0	.000	0	0	9.00
Salt Lake	AAA Min	36	0	0	9	34.1	152	34	25	25	5	0	1	3	19	1	26	6	0	0	1	.000	0	2	6.55
6 Min. YEARS		195	39	1	45	395	1763	428	234	181	28	16	10	19	179	8	292	27	3	18	21	.462	0	10	4.12

Jamey Carroll

Bats: Right **Throws:** Right **Pos:** 2B   **Ht:** 5'11" **Wt:** 165 **Born:** 2/18/75 **Age:** 25

		BATTING														BASERUNNING				PERCENTAGES		
Year Team	Lg Org	G	AB	H	2B	3B	HR	TB	R	RBI	TBB	IBB	SO	HBP	SH	SF	SB	CS	SB%	GDP	Avg	OBP	SLG
1996 Vermont	A- Mon	54	203	56	6	1	0	64	40	17	29	0	25	0	3	2	16	11	.59	1	.276	.363	.315
1997 Wst Plm Bch	A+ Mon	121	407	99	19	1	0	120	56	38	43	0	48	4	8	4	17	11	.61	4	.243	.319	.295
1998 Jupiter	A+ Mon	55	222	58	5	0	0	63	40	14	24	1	26	5	2	1	11	4	.73	2	.261	.345	.284
Harrisburg	AA Mon	75	261	66	11	3	0	83	43	20	41	0	29	5	5	0	11	5	.69	4	.253	.365	.318
1999 Harrisburg	AA Mon	141	561	164	34	5	5	223	78	63	48	2	58	5	5	4	21	10	.68	13	.292	.351	.398
4 Min. YEARS		446	1654	443	75	10	5	553	257	152	185	3	186	19	23	11	76	41	.65	24	.268	.346	.334

Mark Carroll

Bats: Right **Throws:** Right **Pos:** C   **Ht:** 6'0" **Wt:** 185 **Born:** 10/19/78 **Age:** 21

		BATTING														BASERUNNING				PERCENTAGES		
Year Team	Lg Org	G	AB	H	2B	3B	HR	TB	R	RBI	TBB	IBB	SO	HBP	SH	SF	SB	CS	SB%	GDP	Avg	OBP	SLG
1997 Mariners	R Sea	36	121	37	4	0	0	41	15	26	27	0	30	6	0	1	3	1	.75	1	.306	.452	.339
1998 Everett	A- Sea	1	3	0	0	0	0	0	0	0	0	0	0	0	0	0	0	0	.00	0	.000	.000	.000
Mariners	R Sea	31	89	16	5	1	0	23	13	5	18	0	24	1	0	3	1	0	1.00	4	.180	.315	.258
1999 Tacoma	AAA Sea	1	1	0	0	0	0	0	0	0	0	0	1	0	0	0	0	0	.00	0	.000	.000	.000
Everett	A- Sea	45	127	29	6	0	1	38	22	14	29	0	39	1	0	4	0	0	.00	3	.228	.366	.299
3 Min. YEARS		114	341	82	15	1	1	102	50	45	74	0	94	8	0	8	4	1	.80	8	.240	.381	.299

Mike Carter

Bats: Right **Throws:** Right **Pos:** OF   **Ht:** 5'9" **Wt:** 170 **Born:** 5/5/69 **Age:** 31

		BATTING														BASERUNNING				PERCENTAGES		
Year Team	Lg Org	G	AB	H	2B	3B	HR	TB	R	RBI	TBB	IBB	SO	HBP	SH	SF	SB	CS	SB%	GDP	Avg	OBP	SLG
1990 Helena	R+ Mil	61	241	74	11	3	0	91	45	30	16	0	20	6	2	3	22	7	.76	0	.307	.358	.378
1991 Beloit	A Mil	123	452	126	24	4	2	164	62	40	26	5	42	4	2	3	46	13	.78	5	.279	.322	.363
1992 Stockton	A+ Mil	67	252	66	9	1	3	86	38	26	17	1	26	2	3	5	31	8	.79	4	.262	.308	.341
El Paso	AA Mil	50	165	42	4	4	1	57	20	15	16	2	31	0	3	1	10	8	.56	3	.255	.319	.345
1993 El Paso	AA Mil	17	73	27	4	1	2	39	16	16	3	0	7	0	0	4	6	4	.60	1	.370	.395	.534
New Orleans	AAA Mil	104	369	102	18	5	3	139	49	31	17	0	52	4	11	4	20	11	.65	6	.276	.312	.377
1994 Iowa	AAA ChC	122	421	122	24	3	6	170	56	30	14	1	43	4	12	4	16	14	.53	7	.290	.316	.404
1995 Iowa	AAA ChC	107	421	137	16	3	8	183	57	40	14	3	46	6	3	3	12	12	.50	5	.325	.354	.435
1996 Iowa	AAA ChC	113	384	102	13	1	2	123	41	18	10	0	42	1	5	1	4	6	.40	5	.266	.285	.320
1997 Midland	AA Ana	15	65	18	3	1	0	23	9	2	2	0	8	0	1	0	5	2	.71	1	.277	.299	.354
1998 Sioux Falls	IND —	13	56	19	6	0	4	37	15	15	1	0	7	1	1	2	3	1	.75	2	.339	.350	.661
1999 Scranton-WB	AAA Phi	9	31	5	1	1	1	11	2	4	0	0	8	2	0	0	0	1	.00	0	.161	.212	.355
Sioux Falls	IND —	15	65	16	1	1	0	19	10	4	3	0	10	0	0	0	1	2	.33	1	.246	.279	.292
10 Min. YEARS		816	2995	856	134	28	32	1142	420	271	139	12	342	30	43	28	176	89	.66	40	.286	.321	.381

Shannon Carter

Bats: Left **Throws:** Left **Pos:** OF   **Ht:** 6'0" **Wt:** 170 **Born:** 3/23/79 **Age:** 21

		BATTING														BASERUNNING				PERCENTAGES		
Year Team	Lg Org	G	AB	H	2B	3B	HR	TB	R	RBI	TBB	IBB	SO	HBP	SH	SF	SB	CS	SB%	GDP	Avg	OBP	SLG
1997 Orioles	R Bal	50	159	31	3	2	0	38	22	11	12	0	45	4	0	0	13	5	.72	1	.195	.269	.239
1998 Bluefield	R+ Bal	36	150	37	2	0	1	42	23	10	9	0	35	0	0	0	14	3	.82	1	.247	.289	.280
St.Cathrnes	A- Tor	24	61	16	3	0	1	22	8	7	4	0	14	1	1	0	2	0	1.00	1	.262	.318	.361

Year Team	Lg Org	G	AB	H	2B	3B	HR	TB	R	RBI	TBB	IBB	SO	HBP	SH	SF	SB	CS	SB%	GDP	Avg	OBP	SLG
1999 St.Cathrnes	A- Tor	61	215	60	5	4	1	76	38	16	11	0	54	2	1	1	15	6	.71	1	.279	.319	.353
Syracuse	AAA Tor	2	9	1	0	0	0	1	0	0	0	0	2	0	0	0	0	0	.00	2	.111	.111	.111
3 Min. YEARS		173	594	145	13	6	3	179	91	44	36	0	150	7	2	1	44	14	.76	6	.244	.295	.301

Jhonny Carvajal

Bats: Right **Throws:** Right **Pos:** SS **Ht:** 5'10" **Wt:** 165 **Born:** 7/24/74 **Age:** 25

Year Team	Lg Org	G	AB	H	2B	3B	HR	TB	R	RBI	TBB	IBB	SO	HBP	SH	SF	SB	CS	SB%	GDP	Avg	OBP	SLG
1993 Princeton	R+ Cin	67	253	74	10	5	0	94	41	16	29	1	31	4	8	0	7	11	.39	3	.292	.374	.372
1994 Chstn-WV	A Cin	67	198	45	6	0	0	51	27	13	19	0	25	2	2	3	12	3	.80	3	.227	.297	.258
Princeton	R+ Cin	53	218	59	10	4	2	83	35	29	14	2	38	5	5	3	31	11	.74	0	.271	.325	.381
1995 Chstn-WV	A Cin	135	486	128	18	5	0	156	78	42	58	0	77	6	4	4	44	19	.70	4	.263	.347	.321
1996 Wst Plm Bch	A+ Mon	114	426	101	18	0	2	125	50	38	44	0	73	6	7	4	14	16	.47	9	.237	.315	.293
Harrisburg	AA Mon	16	60	18	3	2	0	25	7	4	5	0	10	1	1	0	1	1	.50	1	.300	.364	.417
1997 Harrisburg	AA Mon	116	378	98	12	1	1	115	36	31	27	3	66	4	4	3	10	7	.59	8	.259	.313	.304
1998 Harrisburg	AA Mon	112	338	88	12	4	0	108	37	21	34	5	69	6	8	1	4	6	.40	12	.260	.338	.320
1999 Ottawa	AAA Mon	106	355	82	20	4	0	110	28	34	21	2	67	5	3	6	7	3	.70	8	.231	.279	.310
7 Min. YEARS		786	2712	693	109	25	5	867	339	228	251	13	456	39	42	24	130	77	.63	48	.256	.325	.320

Jovino Carvajal

Bats: Both **Throws:** Right **Pos:** OF **Ht:** 6'2" **Wt:** 200 **Born:** 9/2/68 **Age:** 31

Year Team	Lg Org	G	AB	H	2B	3B	HR	TB	R	RBI	TBB	IBB	SO	HBP	SH	SF	SB	CS	SB%	GDP	Avg	OBP	SLG
1990 Oneonta	A- NYY	52	171	49	3	1	0	54	19	18	7	0	37	0	3	0	15	11	.58	1	.287	.315	.316
1991 Ft. Laud	A+ NYY	117	416	96	6	9	1	123	49	29	28	5	84	0	3	1	33	17	.66	7	.231	.279	.296
1992 Ft. Laud	A+ NYY	113	435	100	7	1	1	112	53	29	30	0	63	1	3	4	40	14	.74	6	.230	.279	.257
1993 Pr William	A+ NYY	120	445	118	20	9	1	159	52	42	21	1	69	1	8	3	17	13	.57	8	.265	.298	.357
1994 Cedar Rapds	A Ana	121	503	147	23	8	6	204	82	54	40	3	76	1	3	1	68	25	.73	5	.292	.345	.406
1995 Midland	AA Ana	79	348	109	13	5	2	138	58	23	18	2	42	1	5	2	39	21	.65	3	.313	.347	.397
Vancouver	AAA Ana	41	163	53	3	3	1	65	25	10	3	0	18	1	1	0	10	7	.59	6	.325	.341	.399
1996 Vancouver	AAA Ana	77	272	65	6	2	4	87	29	31	14	2	38	1	6	3	17	7	.71	8	.239	.276	.320
Midland	AA Ana	41	160	43	5	2	2	58	20	22	10	1	24	0	1	0	7	7	.50	4	.269	.312	.363
1997 Vancouver	AAA Ana	131	480	137	20	20	2	203	80	51	21	3	85	4	4	1	28	9	.76	10	.285	.320	.423
1998 Vancouver	AAA Ana	115	389	104	20	5	6	152	47	34	22	2	72	1	5	3	20	11	.65	8	.267	.303	.391
1999 Edmonton	AAA Ana	108	367	90	15	3	5	126	38	40	20	1	63	3	4	3	17	13	.57	7	.245	.288	.343
10 Min. YEARS		1115	4149	1111	141	68	31	1481	552	383	232	20	671	14	46	21	311	155	.67	73	.268	.307	.357

Steve Carver

Bats: Left **Throws:** Right **Pos:** 1B **Ht:** 6'3" **Wt:** 215 **Born:** 9/27/72 **Age:** 27

Year Team	Lg Org	G	AB	H	2B	3B	HR	TB	R	RBI	TBB	IBB	SO	HBP	SH	SF	SB	CS	SB%	GDP	Avg	OBP	SLG
1995 Batavia	A- Phi	56	217	66	13	2	7	104	35	41	17	1	29	0	1	1	2	1	.67	3	.304	.353	.479
1996 Clearwater	A+ Phi	117	436	121	32	0	17	204	59	79	52	7	89	1	0	4	1	1	.50	12	.278	.353	.468
1997 Reading	AA Phi	79	282	74	11	3	15	136	41	43	36	9	69	3	0	1	2	2	.50	8	.262	.351	.482
1998 Reading	AA Phi	127	458	119	17	0	21	199	63	88	64	8	108	2	0	4	0	3	.00	12	.260	.350	.434
Scranton-WB	AAA Phi	8	23	7	2	0	1	12	3	4	2	0	10	0	0	0	1	0	.00	0	.304	.360	.522
1999 Scranton-WB	AAA Phi	98	288	68	18	1	11	121	33	38	34	3	101	1	2	0	2	0	1.00	8	.236	.319	.420
5 Min. YEARS		485	1704	455	93	6	72	776	234	293	205	28	406	7	3	10	7	8	.47	43	.267	.346	.455

Raul Casanova

Bats: Both **Throws:** Right **Pos:** C **Ht:** 6'0" **Wt:** 195 **Born:** 8/23/72 **Age:** 27

Year Team	Lg Org	G	AB	H	2B	3B	HR	TB	R	RBI	TBB	IBB	SO	HBP	SH	SF	SB	CS	SB%	GDP	Avg	OBP	SLG
1990 Mets	R NYM	23	65	5	0	0	0	5	4	1	4	0	16	0	0	0	0	1	.00	2	.077	.130	.077
1991 Mets	R NYM	32	111	27	4	2	0	35	19	9	12	0	22	2	1	1	3	0	1.00	4	.243	.325	.315
Kingsport	R+ NYM	5	18	1	0	0	0	1	0	1	1	0	10	0	0	0	0	0	.00	0	.056	.105	.056
1992 Columbia	A NYM	5	18	3	0	0	0	3	2	1	1	0	4	0	0	0	0	0	.00	2	.167	.211	.167
Kingsport	R+ NYM	42	137	37	9	1	4	60	25	27	26	2	25	4	0	0	3	1	.75	7	.270	.401	.438
1993 Waterloo	A SD	76	227	58	12	0	6	88	32	30	21	2	46	1	5	0	0	1	.00	5	.256	.321	.388
1994 Rancho Cuca	A+ SD	123	471	160	27	2	23	260	83	120	43	2	97	9	0	3	1	4	.20	16	.340	.403	.552
1995 Memphis	AA SD	89	306	83	18	0	12	137	42	44	25	2	51	4	0	4	0	1	.00	7	.271	.330	.448
1996 Jacksnville	AA Det	8	30	10	2	0	4	24	5	9	7	0	7	0	0	0	0	0	.00	1	.333	.375	.800
Toledo	AAA Det	49	161	44	11	0	8	79	23	28	20	0	24	2	1	4	0	1	.00	11	.273	.353	.491
1997 Toledo	AAA Det	12	41	8	0	0	1	11	1	3	3	0	8	0	0	1	0	0	.00	0	.195	.244	.268
1998 Toledo	AAA Det	50	171	44	8	0	7	73	17	26	22	1	28	3	0	1	0	1	.00	6	.257	.350	.427
1999 Tigers	R Det	2	5	4	0	0	1	7	1	1	0	0	0	0	0	0	0	0	.00	0	.800	.800	1.400
Lakeland	A+ Det	4	12	6	2	0	1	11	3	6	0	0	1	1	0	0	0	0	.00	0	.500	.538	.917
Toledo	AAA Det	44	160	33	9	0	6	60	21	23	7	0	28	1	0	0	0	0	.00	8	.206	.243	.375
1996 Detroit	AL	25	85	16	1	0	4	29	6	9	6	0	18	0	0	0	0	0	.00	2	.188	.242	.341
1997 Detroit	AL	101	304	74	10	1	5	101	27	24	26	1	48	3	0	1	1	1	.50	10	.243	.308	.332
1998 Detroit	AL	16	42	6	2	0	1	11	4	3	5	0	10	1	0	0	0	0	.00	0	.143	.250	.262
10 Min. YEARS		564	1933	523	102	5	73	854	278	328	187	9	367	27	7	15	11	11	.50	70	.271	.341	.442
3 Maj. YEARS		142	431	96	13	1	10	141	37	36	37	1	76	4	0	1	1	1	.50	16	.223	.290	.327

Carlos Casimiro

Bats: Right **Throws:** Right **Pos:** 2B   **Ht:** 5'11" **Wt:** 175 **Born:** 11/8/76 **Age:** 23

								BATTING										BASERUNNING				PERCENTAGES		
Year Team	Lg Org	G	AB	H	2B	3B	HR	TB	R	RBI	TBB	IBB	SO	HBP	SH	SF	SB	CS	SB%	GDP	Avg	OBP	SLG
1995 Orioles	R Bal	32	107	27	4	2	2	41	14	11	10	0	22	1	1	2	1	3	.25	3	.252	.317	.383
1996 Bluefield	R+ Bal	62	239	66	16	0	10	112	51	33	20	1	52	2	2	2	22	9	.71	3	.276	.335	.469
1997 Delmarva	A Bal	122	457	111	21	8	9	175	54	51	26	1	108	5	4	2	20	13	.61	11	.243	.290	.383
1998 Frederick	A+ Bal	131	478	113	23	9	15	199	44	61	25	2	98	1	4	6	10	7	.59	16	.236	.273	.416
1999 Bowie	AA Bal	139	526	116	23	1	18	195	73	64	39	0	101	3	5	5	7	12	.37	10	.221	.276	.371
5 Min. YEARS		486	1807	433	87	20	54	722	236	220	120	4	381	12	16	17	60	44	.58	43	.240	.289	.400

Frank Castillo

Pitches: Right **Bats:** Right **Pos:** P   **Ht:** 6'2" **Wt:** 200 **Born:** 4/1/69 **Age:** 31

			HOW MUCH HE PITCHED					WHAT HE GAVE UP											THE RESULTS					
Year Team	Lg Org	G	GS	CG	GF	IP	BFP	H	R	ER	HR	SH	SF	HB	TBB	IBB	SO	WP	Bk	W	L	Pct.	ShO	Sv	ERA
1987 Wytheville	R+ ChC	12	12	5	0	90.1	372	86	31	23	4	3	2	5	21	0	83	2	1	10	1	.909	0	0	2.29
Geneva	A- ChC	1	1	0	0	6	23	3	1	0	0	0	0	0	1	0	6	0	0	1	0	1.000	0	0	0.00
1988 Peoria	A ChC	9	8	2	0	51	186	25	5	4	1	0	0	1	10	0	58	0	0	6	1	.857	2	0	0.71
1989 Winston-Sal	A+ ChC	18	18	8	0	129.1	521	118	42	36	5	2	1	3	24	1	114	1	1	9	6	.600	1	0	2.51
Charlotte	AA ChC	10	10	4	0	68	283	73	35	29	7	4	2	1	12	3	43	1	0	3	4	.429	0	0	3.84
1990 Charlotte	AA ChC	18	18	4	0	111.1	471	113	54	48	8	6	3	8	27	4	112	5	1	6	6	.500	1	0	3.88
1991 Iowa	AAA ChC	4	4	1	0	25	98	20	7	7	0	0	1	1	7	0	20	2	0	3	1	.750	1	0	2.52
1994 Daytona	A+ ChC	1	1	0	0	4	19	7	3	2	0	0	1	0	0	0	1	0	0	1	0	.000	0	0	4.50
Orlando	AA ChC	1	1	0	0	7	27	4	2	1	0	1	0	1	1	0	2	0	0	1	0	1.000	0	0	1.29
Iowa	AA ChC	11	11	0	0	66	266	57	30	24	9	0	1	5	10	0	64	3	2	4	2	.667	0	0	3.27
1998 Lakeland	A+ Det	1	1	0	0	5	18	2	0	0	0	1	0	1	0	0	4	0	0	1	0	1.000	0	0	0.00
1999 Nashville	AAA Pit	19	19	0	0	119.1	520	139	72	62	15	2	1	6	32	4	90	5	0	7	5	.583	0	0	4.68
1991 Chicago	NL	18	18	4	0	111.2	467	107	56	54	5	6	3	0	33	2	73	5	1	6	7	.462	0	0	4.35
1992 Chicago	NL	33	33	0	0	205.1	856	179	91	79	19	11	5	6	63	6	135	11	0	10	11	.476	0	0	3.46
1993 Chicago	NL	29	25	2	0	141.1	614	162	83	76	20	10	3	9	39	4	84	5	3	5	8	.385	0	0	4.84
1994 Chicago	NL	4	4	1	0	23	96	25	13	11	3	1	0	0	5	0	19	0	0	2	1	.667	0	0	4.30
1995 Chicago	NL	29	29	2	0	188	795	179	75	67	22	11	3	6	52	4	135	3	1	11	10	.524	2	0	3.21
1996 Chicago	NL	33	33	1	0	182.1	789	209	112	107	28	4	5	8	46	4	139	2	1	7	16	.304	1	0	5.28
1997 Chicago	NL	20	19	0	0	98	446	113	64	59	9	11	0	4	44	1	67	1	0	6	9	.400	1	0	5.42
Colorado	NL	14	14	0	0	86.1	384	107	57	52	16	6	2	4	25	3	59	2	0	6	3	.667	0	0	5.42
1998 Detroit	AL	27	19	0	4	116	531	150	91	88	17	2	6	5	44	0	81	0	0	3	9	.250	0	0	6.83
8 Min. YEARS		105	104	24	0	682.1	2804	647	282	236	49	19	11	32	145	12	597	19	5	51	27	.654	5	0	3.11
8 Maj. YEARS		207	194	10	4	1152	4978	1231	642	593	139	62	27	42	351	24	792	29	6	56	74	.431	3	1	4.63

Jose Castro

Bats: Both **Throws:** Right **Pos:** 2B-SS   **Ht:** 5'10" **Wt:** 160 **Born:** 10/15/74 **Age:** 25

								BATTING										BASERUNNING				PERCENTAGES		
Year Team	Lg Org	G	AB	H	2B	3B	HR	TB	R	RBI	TBB	IBB	SO	HBP	SH	SF	SB	CS	SB%	GDP	Avg	OBP	SLG
1994 Athletics	R Oak	42	150	42	5	3	1	56	27	11	22	0	34	4	0	0	17	7	.71	0	.280	.386	.373
1995 W Michigan	A Oak	113	409	98	20	2	2	128	76	40	76	2	94	11	13	0	51	20	.72	2	.240	.373	.313
1996 Modesto	A+ Oak	95	363	82	16	1	8	124	58	48	42	0	124	3	8	3	25	12	.68	4	.226	.309	.342
1997 Edmonton	AAA Oak	2	6	1	0	0	0	1	0	0	1	0	2	0	0	0	1	0	.00	0	.167	.286	.167
Modesto	A+ Oak	112	368	78	17	4	5	118	67	28	58	0	125	2	11	0	27	13	.68	2	.212	.322	.321
Huntsville	AA Oak	5	13	5	0	0	0	5	4	0	4	0	2	1	0	0	0	0	.00	0	.385	.556	.385
1998 Modesto	A+ Oak	57	197	43	11	5	1	67	23	18	28	1	66	3	0	1	10	3	.77	2	.218	.323	.340
Huntsville	AA Oak	55	147	24	4	2	2	38	24	16	25	0	48	2	2	0	12	1	.92	4	.163	.293	.259
1999 Midland	AA Oak	119	368	96	17	3	7	140	69	42	38	1	90	7	9	3	21	7	.75	5	.261	.339	.380
6 Min. YEARS		600	2021	469	90	20	26	677	348	203	294	4	585	33	43	7	163	64	.72	19	.232	.338	.335

Andujar Cedeno

Bats: Right **Throws:** Right **Pos:** 3B   **Ht:** 6'1" **Wt:** 170 **Born:** 8/21/69 **Age:** 30

								BATTING										BASERUNNING				PERCENTAGES		
Year Team	Lg Org	G	AB	H	2B	3B	HR	TB	R	RBI	TBB	IBB	SO	HBP	SH	SF	SB	CS	SB%	GDP	Avg	OBP	SLG
1988	R Hou	46	165	47	5	2	1	59	25	20	11	0	34	1	0	4	10	4	.71	1	.285	.326	.358
1989 Asheville	A Hou	126	487	146	23	6	14	223	76	93	29	0	124	1	2	5	23	10	.70	10	.300	.337	.458
1990 Columbus	AA Hou	132	495	119	21	11	19	219	57	64	33	1	135	6	7	5	6	10	.38	11	.240	.293	.442
1991 Tucson	AAA Hou	93	347	105	19	6	7	157	49	55	19	2	67	5	3	7	5	3	.63	9	.303	.341	.452
1992 Tucson	AAA Hou	74	280	82	18	4	6	126	27	56	18	3	49	1	1	6	6	4	.60	8	.293	.331	.450
1999 Columbus	AAA NYY	62	215	63	14	3	6	101	27	38	11	0	31	3	2	1	1	1	.50	11	.293	.335	.470
1990 Houston	NL	7	8	0	0	0	0	0	0	0	0	0	5	0	0	0	0	0	.00	0	.000	.000	.000
1991 Houston	NL	67	251	61	13	2	9	105	27	36	9	1	74	1	1	2	4	3	.57	3	.243	.270	.418
1992 Houston	NL	71	220	38	13	2	2	61	15	13	14	2	71	3	0	0	2	0	1.00	1	.173	.232	.277
1993 Houston	NL	149	505	143	24	4	11	208	69	56	48	9	97	3	4	5	9	7	.56	17	.283	.346	.412
1994 Houston	NL	98	342	90	26	0	9	143	38	49	29	15	79	8	0	1	1	1	.50	5	.263	.334	.418
1995 San Diego	NL	120	390	82	16	2	6	120	42	31	28	7	92	5	0	1	5	3	.63	12	.210	.271	.308
1996 San Diego	NL	49	154	36	2	1	3	49	10	18	9	2	32	1	0	1	3	2	.60	7	.234	.279	.318
Detroit	AL	52	179	35	4	2	7	64	19	20	4	0	37	0	3	0	2	1	.67	8	.196	.213	.358
Houston	NL	3	2	0	0	0	0	0	1	0	2	0	1	0	0	0	0	0	.00	0	.000	.500	.000
6 Min. YEARS		533	1989	562	100	32	53	885	261	326	121	6	440	17	15	28	51	32	.61	50	.283	.325	.445
7 Maj. YEARS		616	2051	485	98	13	47	750	221	223	143	36	488	21	8	10	26	17	.60	53	.236	.292	.366

Blas Cedeno

Pitches: Right Bats: Right Pos: P Ht: 6'0" Wt: 165 Born: 11/15/72 Age: 27

Year Team	Lg Org	G	GS	CG	GF	IP	BFP	H	R	ER	HR	SH	SF	HB	TBB	IBB	SO	WP	Bk	W	L	Pct.	ShO	Sv	ERA
1991 Bristol	R+ Det	14	2	0	6	45	202	47	36	19	7	0	3	2	18	1	37	3	4	1	4	.200	0	0	3.80
1992 Bristol	R+ Det	13	13	3	0	80.2	335	64	21	18	2	3	1	5	41	0	77	6	0	8	2	.800	2	0	2.01
Fayettevlle	A Det	2	1	1	1	9	32	3	3	3	0	0	0	0	4	0	12	0	0	0	1	.000	0	1	3.00
1993 Fayettevlle	A Det	28	22	1	3	148.2	621	145	64	52	11	5	3	11	55	0	103	6	0	6	6	.500	1	0	3.15
1994 Lakeland	A+ Det	5	0	0	3	14	52	9	3	2	1	1	1	0	4	0	16	1	0	1	0	1.000	0	0	1.29
Trenton	AA Det	34	0	0	18	52.1	228	50	18	15	5	4	0	2	27	2	40	4	0	1	3	.250	0	3	2.58
1995 Jacksonville	AA Det	48	5	0	13	80.2	329	71	34	31	7	1	1	1	36	1	53	2	1	3	2	.600	0	0	3.46
1996 Lakeland	A+ Det	10	0	0	5	16.1	72	17	10	10	3	0	0	1	7	0	11	2	0	1	1	.500	0	0	5.51
Jacksnville	AA Det	26	2	0	8	46.2	219	63	34	28	7	2	3	3	26	0	30	3	0	0	0	.000	0	0	5.40
1997 Rockford	A ChC	22	0	0	13	40.1	168	36	19	13	3	1	1	1	14	2	25	0	0	3	3	.500	0	0	2.90
1998 New Jersey	IND —	12	7	0	2	48.1	224	62	34	24	3	0	0	3	14	1	37	7	0	1	6	.143	0	1	4.47
1999 Clearwater	A+ Phi	34	0	0	8	57.2	243	63	33	27	5	2	4	1	17	1	42	4	0	4	4	.500	0	1	4.21
Reading	AA Phi	19	0	0	5	31.2	131	30	16	15	5	2	1	0	12	3	18	0	0	2	2	.500	0	0	4.26
9 Min. YEARS		267	52	5	85	671.1	2856	660	325	257	59	21	18	30	275	11	501	38	5	31	34	.477	3	6	3.45

Silvio Censale

Pitches: Left Bats: Left Pos: P Ht: 6'2" Wt: 195 Born: 11/21/71 Age: 28

Year Team	Lg Org	G	GS	CG	GF	IP	BFP	H	R	ER	HR	SH	SF	HB	TBB	IBB	SO	WP	Bk	W	L	Pct.	ShO	Sv	ERA
1993 Batavia	A- Phi	9	9	1	0	52	207	39	20	12	1	1	3	0	19	0	54	3	0	5	2	.714	0	0	2.08
1995 Piedmont	A Phi	22	21	0	0	120	507	96	54	42	6	5	4	5	54	0	123	10	3	10	6	.625	0	0	3.15
1996 Clearwater	A+ Phi	24	22	1	1	126.1	546	118	65	55	5	3	6	7	54	1	100	4	3	8	9	.471	1	0	3.92
1997 Reading	AA Phi	20	20	0	0	107.1	456	88	58	52	21	4	1	4	56	0	102	5	1	9	4	.692	0	0	4.36
1998 Reading	AA Phi	4	0	0	1	4.2	22	4	2	1	0	0	0	0	3	0	2	3	0	0	0	.000	0	1	1.93
1999 Reading	AA Phi	16	11	0	0	52	279	74	76	68	15	3	5	3	48	1	36	4	0	1	6	.143	0	0	11.77
6 Min. YEARS		95	83	2	2	462.1	2017	419	275	230	48	16	19	19	234	2	417	29	7	33	27	.550	1	1	4.48

Jose Cepeda

Bats: Right Throws: Right Pos: 2B Ht: 6'0" Wt: 185 Born: 8/1/74 Age: 25

Year Team	Lg Org	G	AB	H	2B	3B	HR	TB	R	RBI	TBB	IBB	SO	HBP	SH	SF	SB	CS	SB%	GDP	Avg	OBP	SLG
1995 Royals	R KC	54	187	65	6	4	0	79	32	21	15	0	5	2	1	4	2	2	.50	0	.348	.394	.422
1996 Lansing	A KC	135	558	161	29	3	3	205	87	81	38	0	44	11	9	8	10	3	.77	8	.289	.341	.367
1997 Wilmington	A+ KC	28	71	20	0	0	0	20	9	3	12	0	10	0	3	0	1	0	1.00	1	.282	.386	.282
Lansing	A KC	89	326	91	17	1	2	116	40	35	42	0	35	3	5	4	4	2	.67	10	.279	.363	.356
1998 Wilmington	A+ KC	115	391	110	20	5	1	143	46	38	36	3	55	11	10	5	19	3	.86	8	.281	.354	.366
1999 Wilmington	A+ KC	59	227	71	7	2	0	82	35	25	22	0	19	5	6	3	5	8	.38	9	.313	.381	.361
Myrtle Bch	A+ Atl	1	5	0	0	0	0	0	1	0	0	0	0	0	0	0	0	0	.00	0	.000	.000	.000
Greenville	AA Atl	58	196	54	8	2	1	69	19	17	13	0	15	1	2	3	2	3	.40	7	.276	.319	.352
5 Min. YEARS		539	1961	572	87	17	7	714	269	220	178	3	184	33	36	27	43	21	.67	43	.292	.356	.364

Dionys Cesar

Bats: Both Throws: Right Pos: 2B Ht: 5'10" Wt: 170 Born: 9/27/76 Age: 23

Year Team	Lg Org	G	AB	H	2B	3B	HR	TB	R	RBI	TBB	IBB	SO	HBP	SH	SF	SB	CS	SB%	GDP	Avg	OBP	SLG
1995 Athletics	R Oak	48	171	55	11	4	2	80	41	21	23	0	29	2	3	2	17	10	.63	0	.322	.404	.468
1996 Modesto	A+ Oak	22	60	12	2	0	0	14	5	4	7	0	19	0	6	0	1	3	.25	0	.200	.284	.233
Sou Oregon	A- Oak	52	203	55	7	4	1	73	37	12	19	0	46	4	7	1	18	6	.75	3	.271	.344	.360
1997 Visalia	A+ Oak	97	285	68	16	2	1	91	60	11	43	1	79	1	6	0	10	12	.45	5	.239	.340	.319
1998 Visalia	A+ Oak	130	501	141	34	8	7	212	87	54	56	2	98	1	6	3	31	12	.72	6	.281	.353	.423
1999 Midland	AA Oak	35	105	20	4	3	3	39	15	15	18	0	28	1	1	1	1	4	.20	0	.190	.312	.371
Visalia	A+ Oak	77	320	103	21	5	7	155	59	62	41	3	51	3	2	5	21	11	.66	8	.322	.398	.484
5 Min. YEARS		461	1645	454	95	26	21	664	304	179	207	6	350	12	31	12	99	58	.63	22	.276	.359	.404

Dan Cey

Bats: Right Throws: Right Pos: 2B Ht: 5'11" Wt: 168 Born: 11/8/75 Age: 24

Year Team	Lg Org	G	AB	H	2B	3B	HR	TB	R	RBI	TBB	IBB	SO	HBP	SH	SF	SB	CS	SB%	GDP	Avg	OBP	SLG
1996 Fort Wayne	A Min	27	85	22	4	0	0	26	8	6	8	0	11	0	0	0	2	1	.67	2	.259	.323	.306
1997 Fort Myers	A+ Min	127	521	148	34	5	7	213	84	60	34	1	85	5	3	4	23	9	.72	11	.284	.332	.409
1998 New Britain	AA Min	136	569	143	28	2	8	199	82	50	40	0	95	3	3	1	23	7	.77	13	.251	.303	.350
1999 Salt Lake	AAA Min	117	403	119	18	3	11	176	63	56	32	1	66	7	2	3	10	2	.83	12	.295	.355	.437
4 Min. YEARS		407	1578	432	84	10	26	614	237	172	114	2	257	15	8	8	58	19	.75	38	.274	.327	.389

Wes Chamberlain

Bats: Right Throws: Right Pos: 1B Ht: 6'2" Wt: 230 Born: 4/13/66 Age: 34

Year Team	Lg Org	G	AB	H	2B	3B	HR	TB	R	RBI	TBB	IBB	SO	HBP	SH	SF	SB	CS	SB%	GDP	Avg	OBP	SLG
1987 Watertown	A- Pit	66	258	67	13	4	5	103	50	35	25	2	48	1	0	3	22	7	.76	6	.260	.324	.399
1988 Augusta	A Pit	27	107	36	7	2	1	50	22	17	11	0	11	1	2	0	1	3	.25	4	.336	.403	.467
Salem	A+ Pit	92	365	100	15	1	11	150	66	50	38	2	59	0	0	2	14	4	.78	7	.274	.341	.411
1989 Harrisburg	AA Pit	129	471	144	26	3	21	239	65	87	32	4	82	2	0	7	11	10	.52	14	.306	.348	.507
1990 Buffalo	AAA Pit	123	416	104	24	2	6	150	43	52	34	0	58	8	2	5	14	19	.42	19	.250	.315	.361
1991 Scranton-WB	AAA Phi	39	144	37	7	2	2	54	12	20	8	1	13	0	0	4	7	4	.64	6	.257	.288	.375

(Batting leader — continued)

Year Team	Lg Org	G	AB	H	2B	3B	HR	TB	R	RBI	TBB	IBB	SO	HBP	SH	SF	SB	CS	SB%	GDP	Avg	OBP	SLG
1992 Scranton-WB	AAA Phi	34	127	42	6	2	4	64	16	26	11	0	13	2	1	2	6	2	.75	2	.331	.387	.504
1994 Clearwater	A+ Phi	6	25	9	1	0	3	19	5	6	1	1	1	1	0	0	0	1	.00	1	.360	.407	.760
1995 Pawtucket	AAA Bos	48	183	64	17	1	12	119	28	40	3	0	45	3	0	1	5	3	.63	3	.350	.368	.650
Omaha	AAA KC	16	64	14	3	0	1	20	2	6	2	0	15	2	0	0	0	0	.00	4	.219	.261	.313
1996 Syracuse	AAA Tor	37	131	45	5	0	10	80	20	37	19	2	19	0	0	1	2	1	.67	5	.344	.424	.611
1997 Calgary	AAA Pit	18	60	19	4	0	2	29	7	9	0	0	14	0	0	0	1	0	1.00	1	.317	.317	.483
Norfolk	AAA NYM	97	336	92	16	2	7	133	33	50	24	1	58	10	0	1	7	2	.78	13	.274	.340	.396
1998 Winnipeg	IND —	43	163	64	13	0	12	113	49	44	22	5	26	9	0	1	7	1	.88	8	.393	.487	.693
Oklahoma	AAA Tex	27	96	35	7	0	5	57	16	21	7	2	12	4	0	2	0	1	.00	1	.365	.422	.594
1999 Albuquerque	AAA LA	111	375	115	19	3	18	194	53	78	24	0	66	7	0	3	3	7	.30	8	.307	.357	.517
1990 Philadelphia	NL	18	46	13	3	0	2	22	9	4	1	0	9	0	0	0	4	0	1.00	0	.283	.298	.478
1991 Philadelphia	NL	101	383	92	16	3	13	153	51	50	31	0	73	2	1	0	9	4	.69	8	.240	.300	.399
1992 Philadelphia	NL	76	275	71	18	0	9	116	26	41	10	2	55	1	1	2	4	0	1.00	7	.258	.285	.422
1993 Philadelphia	NL	96	284	80	20	2	12	140	34	45	17	3	51	1	0	4	2	1	.67	8	.282	.320	.493
1994 Philadelphia	NL	24	69	19	5	0	2	30	7	6	3	0	12	0	0	0	0	0	.00	3	.275	.306	.435
Boston	AL	51	164	42	9	1	4	65	13	20	12	2	38	0	0	0	0	2	.00	6	.256	.307	.396
1995 Boston	AL	19	42	5	1	0	1	9	4	1	3	0	11	0	0	0	1	0	1.00	2	.119	.178	.214
12 Min. YEARS		913	3321	987	183	22	120	1574	487	578	261	20	540	50	5	33	100	65	.61	101	.297	.354	.474
6 Maj. YEARS		385	1263	322	72	6	43	535	144	167	77	7	249	4	2	6	20	7	.74	34	.255	.299	.424

Jim Chamblee

Bats: Right **Throws:** Right **Pos:** 2B   **Ht:** 6' 4" **Wt:** 176 **Born:** 5/6/75 **Age:** 25

Year Team	Lg Org	G	AB	H	2B	3B	HR	TB	R	RBI	TBB	IBB	SO	HBP	SH	SF	SB	CS	SB%	GDP	Avg	OBP	SLG
1995 Utica	A- Bos	62	200	51	9	1	2	68	36	16	23	0	45	6	1	1	9	7	.56	5	.255	.348	.340
1996 Michigan	A Bos	100	303	66	15	2	1	88	31	39	16	0	75	7	4	4	2	2	.50	1	.218	.270	.290
1997 Michigan	A Bos	133	487	146	29	5	22	251	112	73	53	3	107	17	0	5	18	4	.82	8	.300	.384	.515
1998 Trenton	AA Bos	136	489	118	33	3	17	208	71	65	62	1	144	16	6	4	9	5	.64	2	.241	.343	.425
1999 Pawtucket	AAA Bos	127	464	127	21	3	24	226	84	88	43	2	126	13	4	3	5	3	.63	4	.274	.350	.487
5 Min. YEARS		558	1943	508	107	14	66	841	334	281	197	6	497	59	15	17	43	21	.67	20	.261	.345	.433

Carlos Chantres

Pitches: Right **Bats:** Right **Pos:** P   **Ht:** 6'3" **Wt:** 175 **Born:** 4/1/76 **Age:** 24

Year Team	Lg Org	G	GS	CG	GF	IP	BFP	H	R	ER	HR	SH	SF	HB	TBB	IBB	SO	WP	Bk	W	L	Pct.	ShO	Sv	ERA
1994 White Sox	R CWS	16	2	0	3	35	150	28	21	14	2	1	0	3	13	0	29	6	1	0	1	.000	0	1	3.60
1995 White Sox	R CWS	11	11	2	0	61.2	257	65	32	22	2	1	1	1	14	0	47	1	2	2	3	.400	0	0	3.21
1996 Hickory	A CWS	18	18	0	0	119.2	497	108	63	50	10	6	3	1	38	0	93	8	5	6	7	.462	0	0	3.76
South Bend	A CWS	10	9	1	0	65	274	61	31	26	3	1	2	2	19	0	41	3	1	4	5	.444	0	0	3.60
1997 Winston-Sal	A+ CWS	26	26	2	0	164.2	712	152	94	86	21	6	5	4	71	1	158	10	2	9	11	.450	0	0	4.70
1998 Birmingham	AA CWS	20	5	0	7	52.2	251	58	35	34	5	6	6	0	42	1	49	3	0	2	4	.333	0	1	5.81
Winston-Sal	A+ CWS	13	13	1	0	88.1	370	71	43	37	10	3	6	8	41	0	86	5	0	5	5	.500	0	0	3.77
1999 Birmingham	AA CWS	28	21	1	5	141.1	596	122	64	55	13	1	7	7	61	0	105	9	1	6	8	.429	0	2	3.50
6 Min. YEARS		142	105	7	15	728.1	3107	665	383	324	66	25	30	26	299	2	608	45	12	34	44	.436	0	4	4.00

Jake Chapman

Pitches: Left **Bats:** Right **Pos:** P   **Ht:** 6'1" **Wt:** 175 **Born:** 1/11/74 **Age:** 26

Year Team	Lg Org	G	GS	CG	GF	IP	BFP	H	R	ER	HR	SH	SF	HB	TBB	IBB	SO	WP	Bk	W	L	Pct.	ShO	Sv	ERA
1996 Spokane	A- KC	19	0	0	3	68.1	274	44	19	18	2	2	2	6	20	1	71	3	1	7	1	.875	0	1	2.37
1997 Wilmington	A+ KC	27	26	0	0	154.1	673	163	83	66	7	3	5	5	59	5	122	4	0	8	9	.471	0	0	3.85
1998 Wilmington	A+ KC	27	26	1	0	162.1	665	158	72	59	4	6	3	6	37	1	113	5	2	13	9	.591	1	0	3.27
1999 Wichita	AA KC	52	0	0	13	69.2	316	87	38	34	3	5	0	3	29	6	53	4	0	3	0	1.000	0	3	4.39
4 Min. YEARS		125	59	1	16	454.2	1928	452	212	177	16	16	10	20	145	13	359	16	3	31	19	.620	1	4	3.50

Frank Charles

Bats: Right **Throws:** Right **Pos:** C   **Ht:** 6'4" **Wt:** 210 **Born:** 2/23/69 **Age:** 31

Year Team	Lg Org	G	AB	H	2B	3B	HR	TB	R	RBI	TBB	IBB	SO	HBP	SH	SF	SB	CS	SB%	GDP	Avg	OBP	SLG
1991 Everett	A- SF	62	239	76	17	1	9	122	31	49	21	0	55	1	0	1	1	2	.33	5	.318	.374	.510
1992 Clinton	A SF	2	5	0	0	0	0	0	1	0	0	0	3	0	0	0	0	0	.00	0	.000	.000	.000
San Jose	A+ SF	87	286	83	16	1	0	101	27	34	11	2	61	4	1	0	4	4	.50	12	.290	.326	.353
1993 St. Paul	IND —	58	216	59	13	0	2	78	27	37	11	0	33	3	5	1	5	3	.63	9	.273	.316	.361
1994 Charlotte	A+ Tex	79	254	67	17	1	2	92	23	33	16	1	52	3	5	2	2	3	.40	2	.264	.313	.362
1995 Tulsa	AA Tex	126	479	121	24	3	13	190	51	72	22	4	92	4	1	4	1	0	1.00	19	.253	.289	.397
1996 Okla City	AAA Tex	35	113	21	7	2	1	35	10	8	4	0	29	1	0	2	0	3	.00	3	.186	.217	.310
Tulsa	AA Tex	41	147	39	6	0	5	60	18	15	10	0	28	0	0	0	2	0	1.00	1	.265	.312	.408
1997 Tulsa	AA Tex	95	335	77	18	2	9	126	38	49	24	1	81	3	1	1	2	2	.50	9	.230	.287	.376
1998 Fresno	AAA SF	4	10	5	0	0	1	8	2	1	1	0	2	0	0	0	0	0	.00	0	.500	.545	.800
Shreveport	AA SF	108	411	118	39	1	12	195	49	66	18	0	93	6	0	5	0	2	.00	10	.287	.323	.474
1999 Las Vegas	AAA SD	80	272	67	19	2	2	96	25	28	10	2	61	3	0	2	2	0	1.00	16	.246	.279	.353
9 Min. YEARS		777	2767	733	176	13	56	1103	302	392	148	6	590	28	13	18	19	19	.50	86	.265	.307	.399

David Chavarria

Pitches: Right **Bats:** Left **Pos:** P **Ht:** 6'7" **Wt:** 235 **Born:** 5/19/73 **Age:** 27

Year Team	Lg Org	G	GS	CG	GF	IP	BFP	H	R	ER	HR	SH	SF	HB	TBB	IBB	SO	WP	Bk	W	L	Pct.	ShO	Sv	ERA
1991 Rangers	R Tex	8	7	0	0	29.2	132	36	19	14	1	0	1	0	11	0	26	3	2	0	6	.000	0	0	4.25
1992 Butte	R+ Tex	13	12	0	0	47.1	229	54	44	33	0	2	3	2	30	0	33	6	3	2	7	.222	0	0	6.27
1994 Hudson Val	A- Tex	14	0	0	6	17.1	82	17	11	5	0	0	2	2	17	0	14	3	1	0	1	.000	0	0	2.60
1995 Chston-SC	A Tex	52	0	0	22	62	277	55	33	27	5	2	5	1	38	3	68	16	0	3	5	.375	0	6	3.92
1996 Charlotte	A+ Tex	38	4	0	22	81.2	364	76	46	28	4	3	8	0	43	0	76	14	1	1	6	.143	0	7	3.09
1997 Arkansas	AA StL	28	14	0	4	90	394	85	56	45	10	4	5	3	41	1	62	13	2	3	6	.333	0	0	4.50
1999 San Jose	A+ SF	21	0	0	2	29.2	145	43	25	25	2	2	1	3	16	0	26	11	3	0	2	.000	0	0	7.58
Shreveport	AA SF	10	1	0	8	15.2	86	24	22	13	4	0	1	1	9	0	16	5	0	0	1	.000	0	0	7.47
7 Min. YEARS		184	38	0	64	373.1	1709	390	256	190	26	13	26	12	205	4	321	71	12	9	34	.209	0	15	4.58

Anthony Chavez

Pitches: Right **Bats:** Right **Pos:** P **Ht:** 5'10" **Wt:** 188 **Born:** 10/22/70 **Age:** 29

Year Team	Lg Org	G	GS	CG	GF	IP	BFP	H	R	ER	HR	SH	SF	HB	TBB	IBB	SO	WP	Bk	W	L	Pct.	ShO	Sv	ERA
1992 Boise	A- Ana	14	0	0	2	16	75	22	13	7	0	0	0	0	4	2	21	3	0	1	1	.500	0	0	3.94
1993 Cedar Rapds	A Ana	41	0	0	35	59.1	252	44	17	10	1	6	2	2	24	2	87	3	1	4	5	.444	0	16	1.52
Midland	AA Ana	5	0	0	3	8.2	41	11	5	4	1	0	1	0	4	1	9	3	0	0	0	.000	0	1	4.15
1994 Lk Elsinore	A+ Ana	12	0	0	7	13.1	75	21	19	15	0	2	1	2	11	2	12	2	0	0	5	.000	0	1	10.13
Cedar Rapds	A Ana	39	1	0	34	50	227	48	33	24	0	3	2	2	28	4	52	7	0	4	3	.571	0	16	4.32
1995 Vancouver	AAA Ana	8	0	0	5	12	46	7	4	2	0	1	0	0	4	0	8	0	0	2	0	1.000	0	1	1.50
Midland	AA Ana	7	0	0	6	9	42	13	9	8	1	0	0	1	1	0	4	1	0	0	1	.000	0	2	8.00
Lk Elsinore	A+ Ana	33	0	0	14	44.2	206	51	28	21	2	2	3	4	19	2	49	5	0	4	2	.667	0	4	4.23
1996 Lk Elsinore	A+ Ana	10	0	0	8	13.2	53	8	4	3	0	0	0	3	3	0	16	0	0	3	0	1.000	0	4	1.98
Midland	AA Ana	31	0	0	16	72.2	322	81	40	34	4	6	7	2	24	2	55	3	1	2	4	.333	0	1	4.21
1997 Midland	AA Ana	33	1	0	15	47	200	53	23	22	1	3	2	3	15	1	35	4	0	1	2	.333	0	6	4.21
Vancouver	AAA Ana	28	0	0	26	28.1	111	21	8	8	2	0	1	1	6	0	22	3	0	4	1	.800	0	15	2.54
1998 Vancouver	AAA Ana	53	0	0	51	51.1	218	44	20	15	5	4	2	6	17	0	42	0	0	1	4	.200	0	22	2.63
1999 Vancouver	AAA Oak	54	0	0	36	69	315	67	42	30	8	8	3	3	37	5	72	2	0	4	6	.400	0	14	3.91
1997 Anaheim	AL	7	0	0	2	9.2	41	7	1	1	1	1	1	0	5	1	10	0	0	0	0	.000	0	0	0.93
8 Min. YEARS		368	2	0	258	495	2183	491	265	203	25	35	24	29	197	21	484	36	2	30	34	.469	0	99	3.69

Carlos Chavez

Pitches: Right **Bats:** Right **Pos:** P **Ht:** 6'1" **Wt:** 210 **Born:** 8/25/72 **Age:** 27

Year Team	Lg Org	G	GS	CG	GF	IP	BFP	H	R	ER	HR	SH	SF	HB	TBB	IBB	SO	WP	Bk	W	L	Pct.	ShO	Sv	ERA
1992 Bluefield	R+ Bal	15	7	0	3	45.2	219	49	42	35	5	1	4	1	34	0	44	10	6	1	2	.333	0	1	6.90
1993 Albany	A Bal	20	0	0	13	34	155	33	20	20	3	3	0	3	18	0	28	6	2	1	3	.250	0	3	5.29
Bluefield	R+ Bal	14	13	0	0	82	356	80	43	34	15	1	2	3	37	1	71	14	1	6	3	.667	0	0	3.73
1994 Albany	A Bal	5	0	0	3	9.1	41	9	3	3	0	0	0	0	7	0	4	0	0	1	0	1.000	0	0	2.89
Bluefield	R+ Bal	13	13	2	0	85.2	346	58	38	28	11	2	5	6	32	0	92	12	1	7	5	.583	1	0	2.94
1995 Frederick	A Bal	43	1	0	16	81.1	342	62	38	23	4	1	0	2	40	2	107	16	1	5	5	.500	0	6	2.55
Rochester	AAA Bal	1	0	0	0	1.2	11	3	2	2	0	0	0	1	3	0	1	2	0	0	0	.000	0	0	10.80
Bowie	AA Bal	1	0	0	0	2	6	0	0	0	0	0	0	0	1	0	2	0	0	0	0	.000	0	0	0.00
1996 Bowie	AA Bal	56	1	0	27	83	369	69	44	40	8	1	3	6	52	0	80	19	0	4	6	.400	0	7	4.34
1997 Portland	AA Fla	30	0	0	13	39.1	169	35	23	23	4	1	1	3	16	1	32	9	0	2	1	.667	0	1	5.26
Sioux Falls	IND —	10	0	0	3	15	67	19	11	10	3	2	2	0	4	1	15	4	0	0	2	.000	0	0	6.00
Stockton	A+ Mil	4	0	0	1	3.1	15	5	2	2	1	0	0	0	0	0	5	0	0	0	0	.000	0	0	5.40
1998 El Paso	AA Mil	54	4	0	7	88.1	417	104	74	58	6	6	2	4	45	5	83	15	1	3	5	.375	0	0	5.91
1999 Huntsville	AA Mil	13	3	0	6	22	116	37	27	26	5	0	2	2	13	0	12	3	0	0	3	.000	0	0	10.64
8 Min. YEARS		279	42	2	92	592.2	2629	563	367	304	65	18	22	30	302	10	576	110	12	30	35	.462	1	18	4.62

Raul Chavez

Bats: Right **Throws:** Right **Pos:** C **Ht:** 5'11" **Wt:** 210 **Born:** 3/18/73 **Age:** 27

Year Team	Lg Org	G	AB	H	2B	3B	HR	TB	R	RBI	TBB	IBB	SO	HBP	SH	SF	SB	CS	SB%	GDP	Avg	OBP	SLG
1990 Astros	R Hou	48	155	50	8	1	0	60	23	23	7	0	12	2	2	1	5	3	.63	7	.323	.358	.387
1991 Burlington	A Hou	114	420	108	17	0	3	134	54	41	25	1	64	10	3	4	1	4	.20	13	.257	.312	.319
1992 Asheville	A Hou	95	348	99	22	1	2	129	37	40	16	1	39	4	1	4	1	0	1.00	7	.284	.320	.371
1993 Osceola	A+ Hou	58	197	45	5	1	0	52	13	16	8	0	19	1	1	1	1	1	.50	12	.228	.261	.264
1994 Jackson	AA Hou	89	251	55	7	0	1	65	17	22	17	3	41	2	2	1	1	0	1.00	5	.219	.273	.259
1995 Jackson	AA Hou	58	188	54	8	0	4	74	16	25	8	1	17	3	4	2	1	4	.00	7	.287	.323	.394
Tucson	AAA Hou	32	103	27	5	0	0	32	14	10	8	0	13	2	1	1	1	0	1.00	7	.262	.325	.311
1996 Ottawa	AAA Mon	60	198	49	10	0	2	65	15	24	11	0	31	1	4	0	0	2	.00	7	.247	.290	.328
1997 Ottawa	AAA Mon	92	310	76	17	0	4	105	31	46	18	1	42	4	3	3	1	3	.25	9	.245	.293	.339
1998 Ottawa	AAA Mon	11	31	7	0	0	0	7	2	1	5	0	5	0	1	0	0	0	.00	1	.226	.333	.226
Tacoma	AAA Sea	76	233	52	6	0	4	70	27	34	22	1	41	4	2	6	1	2	.33	7	.223	.294	.300
1999 Tacoma	AAA Sea	102	354	95	20	1	3	126	39	40	28	1	63	6	0	2	1	3	.25	11	.268	.331	.356
1996 Montreal	NL	4	5	1	0	0	0	1	1	0	1	0	1	0	0	0	1	1	1.00	1	.200	.333	.200
1997 Montreal	NL	13	26	7	0	0	0	7	0	2	0	0	5	0	0	0	1	1	1.00	1	.269	.259	.269
1998 Seattle	AL	1	1	0	0	0	0	0	0	0	0	0	0	0	0	0	0	0	.00	0	.000	.000	.000
10 Min. YEARS		835	2788	717	125	4	23	919	288	322	173	9	387	39	24	25	12	23	.34	97	.257	.307	.330
3 Maj. YEARS		18	32	8	0	0	0	8	1	2	1	0	6	0	0	0	2	0	1.00	1	.250	.265	.250

Virgil Chevalier

Bats: Right **Throws:** Right **Pos:** OF   **Ht:** 6'2" **Wt:** 240 **Born:** 10/31/73 **Age:** 26

					BATTING													BASERUNNING				PERCENTAGES		
Year Team	Lg Org	G	AB	H	2B	3B	HR	TB	R	RBI	TBB	IBB	SO	HBP	SH	SF	SB	CS	SB%	GDP	Avg	OBP	SLG
1995 Utica	A- Bos	64	250	77	12	2	7	114	34	46	11	0	35	3	0	3	15	6	.71	6	.308	.341	.456
Michigan	A Bos	2	6	4	1	0	0	5	2	0	1	0	0	0	0	0	1	0	1.00	0	.667	.714	.833
1996 Michigan	A Bos	126	483	120	31	3	8	181	61	62	33	1	69	1	1	5	11	4	.73	11	.248	.295	.375
1997 Sarasota	A+ Bos	94	289	60	13	1	6	93	31	37	19	0	43	3	2	3	8	7	.53	6	.208	.261	.322
1998 Sarasota	A+ Bos	81	327	107	22	4	8	161	59	59	27	3	59	1	1	6	13	4	.76	5	.327	.374	.492
Trenton	AA Bos	30	117	32	7	2	2	49	19	16	4	0	17	0	3	1	2	2	.50	2	.274	.295	.419
1999 Trenton	AA Bos	131	509	149	29	4	13	225	81	76	50	0	73	2	8	8	9	9	.50	11	.293	.353	.442
5 Min. YEARS		528	1981	549	115	16	44	828	287	296	145	4	296	10	15	26	59	32	.65	41	.277	.326	.418

Paul Chiaffredo

Bats: Right **Throws:** Right **Pos:** C   **Ht:** 6'2" **Wt:** 195 **Born:** 5/30/76 **Age:** 24

					BATTING													BASERUNNING				PERCENTAGES		
Year Team	Lg Org	G	AB	H	2B	3B	HR	TB	R	RBI	TBB	IBB	SO	HBP	SH	SF	SB	CS	SB%	GDP	Avg	OBP	SLG
1997 St.Cathrnes	A- Tor	48	163	39	8	1	2	55	20	15	9	0	42	9	1	1	5	2	.71	1	.239	.313	.337
1998 Dunedin	A+ Tor	89	290	68	19	0	4	99	34	41	16	0	68	6	6	3	1	3	.25	8	.234	.286	.341
1999 Knoxville	AA Tor	11	39	3	1	0	1	7	3	3	0	0	10	2	2	0	0	0	.00	2	.077	.122	.179
Dunedin	A+ Tor	88	261	66	22	2	3	101	39	21	17	0	44	12	4	4	1	4	.20	12	.253	.323	.387
3 Min. YEARS		236	753	176	50	3	10	262	96	80	42	0	164	29	13	8	7	9	.44	23	.234	.297	.348

Giuseppe Chiaramonte

Bats: Right **Throws:** Right **Pos:** C   **Ht:** 6'0" **Wt:** 200 **Born:** 2/19/76 **Age:** 24

					BATTING													BASERUNNING				PERCENTAGES		
Year Team	Lg Org	G	AB	H	2B	3B	HR	TB	R	RBI	TBB	IBB	SO	HBP	SH	SF	SB	CS	SB%	GDP	Avg	OBP	SLG
1997 San Jose	A+ SF	64	223	51	11	1	12	100	29	44	25	1	58	4	0	3	0	0	.00	7	.229	.314	.448
1998 San Jose	A+ SF	129	502	137	33	3	22	242	87	87	47	4	139	4	0	12	5	2	.71	7	.273	.333	.482
1999 Shreveport	AA SF	114	400	98	20	2	19	179	54	74	40	1	88	6	0	5	4	2	.67	5	.245	.319	.448
3 Min. YEARS		307	1125	286	64	6	53	521	170	205	112	6	285	14	0	20	9	4	.69	19	.254	.324	.463

German Chirinos

Bats: Right **Throws:** Right **Pos:** OF   **Ht:** 6'0" **Wt:** 170 **Born:** 8/29/78 **Age:** 21

					BATTING													BASERUNNING				PERCENTAGES		
Year Team	Lg Org	G	AB	H	2B	3B	HR	TB	R	RBI	TBB	IBB	SO	HBP	SH	SF	SB	CS	SB%	GDP	Avg	OBP	SLG
1999 Athletics	R Oak	54	199	54	9	5	6	91	34	56	28	1	47	2	0	1	13	4	.76	3	.271	.365	.457
Midland	AA Oak	4	14	3	1	0	0	4	1	0	3	0	3	0	0	0	1	0	1.00	0	.214	.353	.286
1 Min. YEARS		58	213	57	10	5	6	95	35	56	31	1	50	2	0	1	14	4	.78	3	.268	.364	.446

Eddie Christian

Bats: Both **Throws:** Left **Pos:** OF   **Ht:** 5'11" **Wt:** 180 **Born:** 8/26/71 **Age:** 28

					BATTING													BASERUNNING				PERCENTAGES		
Year Team	Lg Org	G	AB	H	2B	3B	HR	TB	R	RBI	TBB	IBB	SO	HBP	SH	SF	SB	CS	SB%	GDP	Avg	OBP	SLG
1992 Marlins	R Fla	59	219	61	10	3	0	77	33	29	31	2	35	1	0	3	14	5	.74	6	.279	.366	.352
1993 Kane County	A Fla	112	366	98	21	5	3	138	49	46	58	6	77	0	3	10	9	11	.45	7	.268	.359	.377
1994 Portland	AA Fla	65	228	53	11	0	1	67	27	21	19	0	52	1	3	2	1	4	.20	7	.232	.292	.294
Brevard Cty	A+ Fla	54	192	50	11	0	2	67	20	22	18	0	35	1	4	3	3	2	.60	5	.260	.322	.349
1995 Long Beach	IND —	83	333	113	27	2	1	147	66	50	48	1	39	0	9	1	27	11	.71	9	.339	.421	.441
1996 Lk Elsinore	A+ Ana	16	58	23	5	0	2	34	10	9	12	0	10	2	1	0	1	2	.33	0	.397	.514	.586
Midland	AA Ana	107	426	130	30	5	5	185	59	46	36	0	72	0	4	3	7	9	.44	8	.305	.357	.434
1997 Memphis	AA Sea	68	238	80	20	0	4	112	50	39	36	6	24	1	2	3	8	3	.73	11	.336	.421	.471
Tacoma	AAA Sea	35	135	43	5	1	1	53	16	9	14	0	24	0	3	0	3	2	.60	3	.319	.383	.393
1998 Midland	AA Ana	105	400	133	39	4	5	195	80	49	49	4	61	3	0	2	13	11	.54	6	.333	.407	.488
1999 Edmonton	AAA Ana	44	148	35	5	1	5	57	24	15	12	0	31	0	0	0	4	3	.57	6	.236	.294	.385
Erie	AA Ana	53	205	58	11	1	3	80	29	27	20	0	34	0	8	1	14	3	.82	5	.283	.345	.390
8 Min. YEARS		801	2948	877	195	22	32	1212	463	362	353	19	494	9	37	28	104	66	.61	73	.297	.371	.411

Eric Christopherson

Bats: Right **Throws:** Right **Pos:** C   **Ht:** 6'1" **Wt:** 190 **Born:** 4/25/69 **Age:** 31

					BATTING													BASERUNNING				PERCENTAGES		
Year Team	Lg Org	G	AB	H	2B	3B	HR	TB	R	RBI	TBB	IBB	SO	HBP	SH	SF	SB	CS	SB%	GDP	Avg	OBP	SLG
1990 San Jose	A+ SF	7	23	4	0	0	0	4	4	1	3	0	6	0	0	0	0	0	.00	0	.174	.269	.174
Everett	A- SF	48	162	43	8	1	1	56	20	22	31	1	28	0	1	2	7	2	.78	2	.265	.379	.346
1991 Clinton	A SF	110	345	93	18	0	5	126	45	58	68	1	54	1	1	6	10	7	.59	10	.270	.386	.365
1992 Shreveport	AA SF	80	270	68	10	1	6	98	36	34	37	0	44	1	0	2	1	6	.14	5	.252	.342	.363
1993 Giants	R SF	8	22	9	1	1	0	12	7	4	9	0	1	0	0	0	0	0	.00	0	.409	.581	.545
Shreveport	AA SF	15	46	7	2	0	0	9	5	9	10	0	10	0	0	0	1	1	.50	1	.152	.291	.196
1994 Shreveport	AA SF	88	267	67	22	0	6	107	30	39	42	4	55	0	1	2	5	1	.83	5	.251	.350	.401
1995 Phoenix	AAA SF	94	282	62	9	1	1	76	21	25	35	1	54	3	5	5	1	1	.50	12	.220	.308	.270
1996 Tucson	AAA Hou	67	223	64	15	3	6	103	31	36	21	2	47	1	1	4	2	0	1.00	1	.287	.345	.462
1997 New Orleans	AAA Hou	9	21	4	0	0	0	4	3	0	4	0	7	0	0	0	0	0	.00	0	.190	.320	.190
Tulsa	AA Tex	39	123	30	9	0	6	57	26	34	25	0	22	0	0	3	1	1	.50	4	.244	.364	.463
1998 Norfolk	AAA NYM	37	97	18	4	1	1	27	7	13	18	0	20	0	3	2	1	1	.50	1	.186	.308	.278
Calgary	AAA CWS	21	54	19	2	1	5	38	12	14	7	1	7	0	2	1	0	0	.00	0	.352	.419	.704
1999 Charlotte	AAA CWS	63	188	59	17	0	3	85	36	27	30	1	39	0	4	1	4	0	1.00	7	.314	.406	.452
10 Min. YEARS		686	2123	547	117	9	40	802	283	309	339	11	394	6	18	28	33	20	.62	45	.258	.357	.378

Stubby Clapp

Bats: Left **Throws:** Right **Pos:** 2B-OF   **Ht:** 5'8" **Wt:** 175 **Born:** 2/24/73 **Age:** 27

Year Team	Lg Org	G	AB	H	2B	3B	HR	TB	R	RBI	TBB	IBB	SO	HBP	SH	SF	SB	CS	SB%	GDP	Avg	OBP	SLG
1996 Johnson Cy	R+ StL	29	94	21	3	2	1	31	25	15	26	0	15	1	1	1	9	2	.82	2	.223	.393	.330
1997 Pr William	A+ StL	78	267	85	21	6	4	130	51	46	52	2	41	6	4	4	9	4	.69	2	.318	.435	.487
1998 Arkansas	AA StL	139	514	143	30	9	12	227	113	57	86	3	100	8	8	6	18	10	.64	10	.278	.386	.442
1999 Memphis	AAA StL	110	393	102	26	2	14	174	72	62	53	4	96	3	4	4	7	7	.50	9	.260	.349	.443
4 Min. YEARS		356	1268	351	80	19	31	562	261	180	217	9	252	18	17	15	43	23	.65	23	.277	.386	.443

Brady Clark

Bats: Right **Throws:** Right **Pos:** OF   **Ht:** 6'2" **Wt:** 195 **Born:** 4/18/73 **Age:** 27

Year Team	Lg Org	G	AB	H	2B	3B	HR	TB	R	RBI	TBB	IBB	SO	HBP	SH	SF	SB	CS	SB%	GDP	Avg	OBP	SLG
1997 Burlington	A Cin	126	459	149	29	7	11	225	108	63	76	3	71	4	1	3	31	18	.63	10	.325	.423	.490
1998 Chattanooga	AA Cin	64	222	60	13	1	2	81	41	16	31	0	34	4	1	0	12	4	.75	11	.270	.370	.365
1999 Chattanooga	AA Cin	138	506	165	37	4	17	261	103	75	89	6	58	2	5	5	25	17	.60	6	.326	.425	.516
3 Min. YEARS		328	1187	374	79	12	30	567	252	154	196	9	163	10	7	8	68	39	.64	27	.315	.414	.478

Chris Clark

Pitches: Right **Bats:** Right **Pos:** P   **Ht:** 6'1" **Wt:** 180 **Born:** 10/29/74 **Age:** 25

Year Team	Lg Org	G	GS	CG	GF	IP	BFP	H	R	ER	HR	SH	SF	HB	TBB	IBB	SO	WP	Bk	W	L	Pct.	ShO	Sv	ERA
1994 Padres	R SD	17	1	0	6	33.2	153	35	17	12	2	1	0	2	18	0	25	5	0	0	0	.000	0	1	3.21
1995 Padres	R SD	13	12	1	0	73	313	52	30	17	1	1	1	7	38	0	82	5	0	5	5	.500	0	0	2.10
Idaho Falls	R+ SD	1	1	0	0	6	24	3	3	3	1	0	0	0	4	0	9	1	0	0	0	.000	0	0	4.50
1996 Clinton	A SD	24	11	0	7	82	385	96	58	46	5	4	3	7	51	1	74	9	1	3	8	.273	0	1	5.05
1997 Clinton	A SD	32	11	0	5	89	395	89	50	41	5	0	3	6	46	0	91	15	0	5	5	.500	0	3	4.15
1998 Brevard Cty	A+ Fla	40	2	0	30	60.2	288	52	38	29	1	3	7	4	46	3	58	12	0	2	3	.400	0	9	4.30
1999 Portland	AA Fla	4	0	0	1	6	29	5	5	5	1	1	1	0	7	0	4	1	0	1	0	1.000	0	0	7.50
Brevard Cty	A+ Fla	28	12	0	10	86	395	93	60	53	5	3	5	6	48	1	48	12	0	3	8	.273	0	1	5.55
6 Min. YEARS		159	50	1	59	436.1	1982	425	261	206	21	13	17	29	258	5	391	60	1	19	29	.396	0	15	4.25

Dave Clark

Bats: Left **Throws:** Right **Pos:** OF   **Ht:** 6'2" **Wt:** 210 **Born:** 9/3/62 **Age:** 37

Year Team	Lg Org	G	AB	H	2B	3B	HR	TB	R	RBI	TBB	IBB	SO	HBP	SH	SF	SB	CS	SB%	GDP	Avg	OBP	SLG
1983 Waterloo	A Cle	58	159	44	8	1	4	66	20	20	19	3	32	3	0	1	2	2	.50	—	.277	.363	.415
1984 Waterloo	A Cle	110	363	112	16	3	15	179	74	63	57	4	68	10	4	4	20	5	.80	6	.309	.412	.493
Buffalo	AA Cle	17	56	10	1	0	3	20	12	10	9	0	13	1	0	2	1	1	.50	1	.179	.294	.357
1985 Waterbury	AA Cle	132	463	140	24	7	12	214	75	64	86	8	79	1	1	4	27	12	.69	11	.302	.410	.462
1986 Maine	AAA Cle	106	355	99	17	2	19	177	56	58	52	5	70	3	2	2	6	5	.55	8	.279	.374	.499
1987 Buffalo	AAA Cle	108	420	143	22	3	30	261	83	80	52	7	62	3	1	5	14	11	.56	13	.340	.413	.621
1988 Colo Sprngs	AAA KC	47	165	49	10	2	4	75	27	31	27	1	38	2	1	2	4	5	.44	5	.297	.398	.455
1991 Omaha	AAA KC	104	359	108	24	3	13	177	45	64	30	4	53	0	0	2	6	5	.55	13	.301	.353	.493
1992 Buffalo	AAA Pit	78	253	77	17	6	11	139	43	55	34	4	51	2	2	1	6	4	.60	4	.304	.390	.549
1999 Albuquerque	AAA LA	37	108	35	7	1	3	53	19	17	26	1	26	0	0	3	2	0	1.00	3	.324	.455	.491
1986 Cleveland	AL	18	58	16	1	0	3	26	10	9	7	0	11	0	0	2	1	0	1.00	1	.276	.348	.448
1987 Cleveland	AL	29	87	18	5	0	3	32	11	12	2	0	24	0	0	1	1	0	1.00	4	.207	.225	.368
1988 Cleveland	AL	63	156	41	4	1	3	56	11	18	17	2	28	0	0	2	0	0	.00	8	.263	.333	.359
1989 Cleveland	AL	102	253	60	12	0	8	96	21	29	30	5	63	0	1	1	0	2	.00	7	.237	.317	.379
1990 Chicago	NL	84	171	47	4	2	5	70	22	20	8	1	40	0	0	2	1	1	.88	4	.275	.304	.409
1991 Kansas City	AL	11	10	2	0	0	0	2	1	1	1	0	1	0	0	0	0	0	.00	0	.200	.273	.200
1992 Pittsburgh	NL	23	33	7	0	0	2	13	3	7	6	0	8	0	0	1	0	0	.00	0	.212	.325	.394
1993 Pittsburgh	NL	110	277	75	11	2	11	123	43	46	38	5	58	1	0	2	1	0	1.00	10	.271	.358	.444
1994 Pittsburgh	NL	86	223	66	11	1	10	109	37	46	22	0	48	0	1	3	2	2	.50	5	.296	.355	.489
1995 Pittsburgh	NL	77	196	55	6	0	4	73	30	24	24	1	38	1	0	0	3	3	.50	9	.281	.359	.372
1996 Pittsburgh	NL	92	211	58	12	2	8	98	28	35	31	3	51	0	0	1	2	1	.67	6	.275	.366	.464
Los Angeles	NL	15	15	3	0	0	0	3	0	1	3	0	2	0	0	0	0	0	.00	0	.200	.333	.200
1997 Chicago	NL	102	143	43	8	0	5	66	19	32	19	3	34	2	0	2	1	0	1.00	2	.301	.386	.462
1998 Houston	NL	93	131	27	7	0	0	34	12	4	14	1	45	0	1	0	1	1	.50	2	.206	.288	.260
9 Min. YEARS		797	2701	817	146	28	114	1361	454	462	392	37	492	25	11	23	88	50	.64	—	.302	.393	.504
13 Maj. YEARS		905	1964	518	81	8	62	801	248	284	222	21	451	5	4	16	19	12	.61	58	.264	.338	.408

Doug Clark

Bats: Left **Throws:** Right **Pos:** OF   **Ht:** 6'2" **Wt:** 205 **Born:** 3/5/76 **Age:** 24

Year Team	Lg Org	G	AB	H	2B	3B	HR	TB	R	RBI	TBB	IBB	SO	HBP	SH	SF	SB	CS	SB%	GDP	Avg	OBP	SLG
1998 Salem-Keizr	A- SF	59	227	76	8	6	3	105	49	41	32	0	31	1	1	1	12	8	.60	1	.335	.422	.463
1999 Bakersfield	A+ SF	118	420	137	17	2	11	191	67	58	59	4	89	5	0	1	17	11	.61	5	.326	.415	.455
Shreveport	AA SF	15	50	11	3	0	1	17	6	6	4	0	9	0	0	0	0	0	.00	2	.220	.278	.340
2 Min. YEARS		192	697	224	28	8	15	313	122	105	95	4	129	6	1	1	29	19	.60	8	.321	.408	.449

Howie Clark

Bats: Left **Throws:** Right **Pos:** OF   **Ht:** 5'10" **Wt:** 179 **Born:** 2/13/74 **Age:** 26

Year Team	Lg Org	G	AB	H	2B	3B	HR	TB	R	RBI	TBB	IBB	SO	HBP	SH	SF	SB	CS	SB%	GDP	Avg	OBP	SLG
1992 Orioles	R Bal	43	138	33	7	1	0	42	12	6	12	2	21	2	1	0	1	2	.33	2	.239	.309	.304

(continued)

Year Team	Lg Org	G	AB	H	2B	3B	HR	TB	R	RBI	TBB	IBB	SO	HBP	SH	SF	SB	CS	SB%	GDP	Avg	OBP	SLG
1993 Albany	A Bal	7	17	4	0	0	0	4	2	1	0	0	3	0	0	0	1	0	1.00	1	.235	.235	.235
Bluefield	R+ Bal	58	180	53	10	1	3	74	29	30	26	2	34	4	1	4	2	2	.50	4	.294	.388	.411
1994 Frederick	A+ Bal	2	7	1	1	0	0	2	1	0	0	0	2	0	0	0	0	0	.00	1	.143	.143	.286
Albany	A Bal	108	353	95	22	7	2	137	56	47	51	3	58	7	4	1	5	4	.56	7	.269	.371	.388
1995 High Desert	A+ Bal	100	329	85	20	2	5	124	50	40	32	0	51	4	3	3	12	6	.67	4	.258	.329	.377
1996 Bowie	AA Bal	127	449	122	29	3	4	169	55	52	59	1	54	2	10	7	2	8	.20	8	.272	.354	.376
1997 Bowie	AA Bal	105	314	90	16	0	9	133	39	37	32	2	38	1	1	3	2	2	.50	5	.287	.351	.424
1998 Rochester	AAA Bal	30	95	22	4	1	3	37	13	8	9	0	11	0	0	0	1	2	.33	2	.232	.298	.389
Bowie	AA Bal	88	276	79	16	0	9	122	37	45	29	2	42	3	0	1	1	1	.50	7	.286	.359	.442
1999 Bowie	AA Bal	39	126	37	6	0	2	49	17	12	10	0	12	3	0	0	2	0	1.00	0	.294	.360	.389
Rochester	AAA Bal	79	279	82	19	4	6	127	33	28	34	2	24	1	1	2	1	2	.33	8	.294	.370	.455
8 Min. YEARS		786	2563	703	150	19	43	1020	344	306	294	14	350	27	21	21	30	29	.51	49	.274	.352	.398

Kevin Clark

Bats: Right **Throws:** Right **Pos:** DH **Ht:** 6'1" **Wt:** 200 **Born:** 4/30/73 **Age:** 27

Year Team	Lg Org	G	AB	H	2B	3B	HR	TB	R	RBI	TBB	IBB	SO	HBP	SH	SF	SB	CS	SB%	GDP	Avg	OBP	SLG
1993 Red Sox	R Bos	40	137	28	9	0	1	40	14	19	16	1	24	3	0	4	1	1	.50	5	.204	.294	.292
1994 Utica	A- Bos	57	185	47	12	0	2	65	31	12	19	1	50	6	0	1	2	3	.40	2	.254	.341	.351
1995 Sarasota	A+ Bos	84	293	66	11	0	4	89	23	31	21	0	63	2	1	0	2	5	.29	9	.225	.282	.304
1996 Michigan	A Bos	126	474	131	32	3	10	199	53	56	30	2	94	12	1	4	4	5	.44	11	.276	.333	.420
1997 Sarasota	A+ Bos	3	5	3	0	0	0	3	0	1	0	0	2	1	0	0	0	0	.00	0	.600	.667	.600
Rio Grande	IND —	66	250	71	15	0	10	116	50	45	28	2	57	3	0	2	3	0	1.00	9	.284	.360	.464
High Desert	A+ Ari	13	47	11	4	0	1	18	4	3	3	0	13	0	1	0	0	0	.00	1	.234	.280	.383
1998 High Desert	A+ Ari	127	498	132	24	5	20	226	72	98	36	0	121	6	0	5	1	0	1.00	16	.265	.319	.454
1999 El Paso	AA Ari	106	373	111	24	3	8	165	44	64	21	4	75	3	0	2	0	2	.00	14	.298	.338	.442
7 Min. YEARS		622	2262	600	131	11	56	921	291	329	174	10	499	36	3	18	13	16	.45	67	.265	.325	.407

Terry Clark

Pitches: Right **Bats:** Right **Pos:** P **Ht:** 6'2" **Wt:** 195 **Born:** 10/10/60 **Age:** 39

Year Team	Lg Org	G	GS	CG	GF	IP	BFP	H	R	ER	HR	SH	SF	HB	TBB	IBB	SO	WP	Bk	W	L	Pct.	ShO	Sv	ERA
1979 Johnson Cy	R+ StL	23	0	0	20	32	134	31	10	7	1	3	2	0	11	0	22	0	1	4	2	.667	0	0	1.97
1980 Gastonia	A StL	49	0	0	38	88	365	82	34	31	8	8	4	5	22	0	50	3	0	4	7	.364	0	0	3.17
1981 Gastonia	A StL	53	0	0	51	75	304	56	23	18	4	2	1	1	25	0	66	2	1	4	5	.444	0	0	2.16
1982 St. Pete	A+ StL	58	0	0	51	88.1	385	81	32	25	1	11	4	3	34	0	61	6	0	10	7	.588	0	0	2.55
1983 Arkansas	AA StL	52	0	0	39	81.1	323	68	31	29	9	3	1	2	19	0	63	4	0	6	6	.500	0	15	3.21
1984 Louisville	AAA StL	18	1	0	9	34.1	156	41	19	18	5	0	1	1	12	2	24	2	0	1	3	.250	0	1	4.72
1985 Arkansas	AA StL	42	7	0	8	96.2	420	102	64	53	9	7	5	4	38	2	67	0	1	6	5	.545	0	2	4.93
1986 Midland	AA Ana	57	2	0	32	90.1	386	98	49	33	6	2	4	4	28	3	66	1	0	9	4	.692	0	3	3.29
1987 Edmonton	AAA Ana	33	20	5	6	154.2	654	140	79	66	13	6	2	7	56	8	88	4	4	8	9	.471	1	4	3.84
1988 Edmonton	AAA Ana	16	16	3	0	113.2	488	128	62	57	7	4	4	4	33	0	59	0	3	7	6	.538	0	0	4.51
1989 Edmonton	AAA Ana	21	20	4	1	138.1	569	130	62	55	7	5	3	6	33	5	90	8	1	11	5	.688	2	0	3.58
1990 Tucson	AAA Hou	29	22	3	2	155	657	172	73	61	9	9	8	8	41	2	80	3	5	11	4	.733	1	1	3.54
1991 Tucson	AAA Hou	26	26	2	0	164	705	199	104	85	5	4	5	6	37	0	97	9	2	14	7	.667	0	0	4.66
1992 Colo Sprngs	AAA Cle	9	9	2	0	59.2	248	62	30	25	3	1	3	1	13	0	33	3	0	4	4	.500	0	0	3.77
1993 Rancho Cuca	A+ SD	8	0	0	2	9.2	39	7	5	5	1	1	0	0	4	2	7	0	0	2	0	.000	0	0	4.66
Wichita	AA SD	19	0	0	3	29.2	125	27	10	8	2	1	2	1	7	0	30	2	0	3	0	1.000	0	0	2.43
1994 Richmond	AAA Atl	61	0	0	45	83.1	342	72	33	28	6	7	3	0	27	5	74	1	0	5	4	.556	0	26	3.02
1995 Rochester	AAA Bal	9	0	0	7	10	37	5	3	3	2	0	1	0	2	1	10	0	1	1	2	.333	0	5	2.70
1996 Omaha	AAA KC	16	2	0	4	45.2	190	42	15	13	5	1	2	4	13	1	36	1	0	3	1	.750	0	2	2.56
1997 Buffalo	AAA Cle	25	10	4	7	94.2	390	86	34	30	8	3	2	2	30	0	63	4	0	7	3	.700	1	3	2.85
1998 Oklahoma	AAA Tex	30	24	2	2	165.1	680	156	72	62	8	2	5	12	35	0	95	4	1	12	5	.706	0	1	3.38
1999 Vancouver	AAA Oak	14	7	0	1	41.1	180	47	25	22	3	1	1	3	14	0	17	3	0	3	4	.429	0	0	4.79
1988 California	AL	15	15	2	0	94	410	120	54	53	8	2	5	0	31	6	39	5	2	6	6	.500	1	0	5.07
1989 California	AL	4	2	0	2	11	48	13	8	6	0	2	1	0	3	0	7	2	1	0	2	.000	0	0	4.91
1990 Houston	NL	1	1	0	0	4	25	9	7	6	0	1	0	0	3	0	2	0	0	0	0	.000	0	0	13.50
1995 Atlanta	NL	3	0	0	1	3.2	18	3	2	2	0	0	0	0	5	0	2	1	0	0	0	.000	0	0	4.91
Baltimore	AL	38	0	0	12	39	166	40	15	15	3	4	1	1	15	5	18	1	0	2	5	.286	0	1	3.46
1996 Kansas City	AL	12	0	0	5	17.1	87	28	15	15	3	0	0	0	7	1	12	3	0	1	1	.500	0	0	7.79
Houston	NL	5	0	0	3	6.1	37	16	10	8	1	0	0	1	2	1	5	1	0	0	2	.000	0	0	11.37
1997 Cleveland	AL	4	4	0	0	26.1	118	29	21	18	3	1	2	0	13	1	13	0	0	0	3	.000	0	0	6.15
Texas	AL	9	5	0	2	30.2	138	41	20	20	3	0	0	2	10	0	11	1	0	1	4	.200	0	0	5.87
21 Min. YEARS		668	166	25	328	1851	7777	1832	869	734	122	81	63	74	534	31	1198	60	20	133	95	.583	5	64	3.57
6 Maj. YEARS		91	27	2	25	232.1	1047	299	152	143	21	10	9	4	89	14	109	14	3	10	23	.303	1	1	5.54

Chris Clemons

Pitches: Right **Bats:** Right **Pos:** P **Ht:** 6'4" **Wt:** 225 **Born:** 10/31/72 **Age:** 27

Year Team	Lg Org	G	GS	CG	GF	IP	BFP	H	R	ER	HR	SH	SF	HB	TBB	IBB	SO	WP	Bk	W	L	Pct	ShO	Sv	ERA
1994 White Sox	R CWS	2	2	0	0	7	27	5	3	3	0	0	0	1	1	0	5	0	0	0	1	.000	0	0	3.86
Hickory	A CWS	12	12	0	0	69.1	290	74	37	34	5	4	2	5	18	0	42	6	0	4	2	.667	0	0	4.41
1995 Pr William	A+ CWS	27	27	1	0	137	606	136	78	72	18	4	4	11	64	2	92	2	0	7	12	.368	0	0	4.73
1996 Pr William	A+ CWS	6	6	0	0	36	150	36	16	9	6	0	2	4	8	0	26	1	0	1	4	.200	0	0	2.25
Birmingham	AA CWS	19	16	1	2	94.1	400	91	39	33	7	0	1	6	40	2	69	1	1	5	2	.714	0	0	3.15
1997 Nashville	AAA CWS	22	21	1	1	124.2	543	115	73	63	15	2	3	4	65	0	70	6	1	5	5	.500	1	0	4.55
1998 Tucson	AAA Ari	20	19	0	1	86.1	410	103	69	59	13	2	4	9	44	0	79	2	0	3	9	.250	0	0	6.15
1999 Tucson	AAA Ari	45	3	0	11	68.1	329	77	53	45	11	6	4	4	44	3	75	4	0	6	4	.600	0	1	5.93

Year Team	Lg Org	HOW MUCH HE PITCHED						WHAT HE GAVE UP												THE RESULTS					
		G	GS	CG	GF	IP	BFP	H	R	ER	HR	SH	SF	HB	TBB	IBB	SO	WP	Bk	W	L	Pct.	ShO	Sv	ERA
1997 Chicago	AL	5	2	0	3	12.2	67	19	13	12	4	0	0	1	11	0	8	1	0	0	2	.000	0	0	8.53
6 Min. YEARS		153	106	3	15	623	2755	637	368	318	75	18	20	43	284	7	458	26	2	31	39	.443	1	1	4.59

Pat Cline

Bats: Right Throws: Right Pos: C   Ht: 6'3" Wt: 225 Born: 10/9/74 Age: 25

Year Team	Lg Org	BATTING															BASERUNNING				PERCENTAGES		
		G	AB	H	2B	3B	HR	TB	R	RBI	TBB	IBB	SO	HBP	SH	SF	SB	CS	SB%	GDP	Avg	OBP	SLG
1993 Huntington	R+ ChC	33	96	18	5	0	2	29	17	13	17	0	28	1	1	3	0	0	.00	1	.188	.308	.302
1994 Cubs	R ChC	3	0	0	0	0	0	0	0	0	0	0	0	0	0	0	0	0	.00	0	.000	.000	.000
1995 Rockford	A ChC	112	390	106	27	0	13	172	65	77	58	3	93	11	0	5	6	1	.86	6	.272	.377	.441
1996 Daytona	A+ ChC	124	434	121	30	2	17	206	75	76	54	2	79	12	0	2	10	2	.83	6	.279	.373	.475
1997 Iowa	AAA ChC	27	95	21	2	0	3	32	6	10	10	1	24	0	0	1	0	1	.00	4	.221	.292	.337
Orlando	AA ChC	78	271	69	19	0	7	109	39	37	27	1	78	5	0	2	2	2	.50	7	.255	.331	.402
1998 Iowa	AAA ChC	122	424	119	22	2	13	184	52	60	36	4	59	9	1	5	2	3	.40	14	.281	.346	.434
1999 Iowa	AAA ChC	98	290	66	20	1	6	106	27	42	26	0	73	4	0	1	1	2	.33	8	.228	.299	.366
7 Min. YEARS		597	2000	520	125	5	61	838	281	315	228	11	434	42	2	19	21	11	.66	46	.260	.345	.419

Trevor Cobb

Pitches: Left Bats: Left Pos: P   Ht: 6'2" Wt: 190 Born: 7/13/73 Age: 26

Year Team	Lg Org	HOW MUCH HE PITCHED						WHAT HE GAVE UP												THE RESULTS					
		G	GS	CG	GF	IP	BFP	H	R	ER	HR	SH	SF	HB	TBB	IBB	SO	WP	Bk	W	L	Pct.	ShO	Sv	ERA
1992 Twins	R Min	11	11	1	0	59.2	252	54	34	24	1	1	0	0	17	0	40	5	1	3	3	.500	0	0	3.62
1993 Elizabethtn	R+ Min	13	13	1	0	82.2	356	71	48	36	7	5	4	5	40	0	53	7	1	5	4	.556	0	0	3.92
1994 Elizabethtn	R+ Min	12	12	1	0	78.2	318	61	33	25	2	4	1	0	19	0	68	8	1	9	1	.900	1	0	2.86
1995 Twins	R Min	3	3	0	0	19	74	11	5	2	0	1	0	1	7	0	15	2	0	2	0	1.000	0	0	0.95
Fort Wayne	A Min	11	10	0	0	53.1	226	51	26	23	3	1	0	3	18	0	46	6	0	4	4	.500	0	0	3.88
1996 Fort Myers	A+ Min	31	14	1	5	126.1	520	101	44	37	1	4	6	5	43	0	98	12	1	7	3	.700	1	0	2.64
1997 Fort Myers	A+ Min	15	7	1	0	60.2	246	49	29	20	2	3	1	2	16	0	48	2	0	7	0	1.000	1	0	2.97
New Britain	AA Min	19	13	3	1	94.1	386	77	41	36	6	4	3	4	39	0	68	12	0	6	4	.600	0	1	3.43
1998 New Britain	AA Min	27	23	1	2	133.1	596	160	81	75	17	1	2	10	49	0	87	10	1	6	9	.400	0	0	5.06
1999 Tulsa	AA Tex	35	3	0	8	75.1	350	79	52	44	13	3	4	7	33	0	44	13	0	4	5	.444	0	1	5.26
8 Min. YEARS		177	109	9	16	783.1	3324	714	393	322	52	27	20	42	281	0	567	77	5	53	33	.616	3	2	3.70

Ivanon Coffie

Bats: Left Throws: Right Pos: 3B   Ht: 6'1" Wt: 170 Born: 5/16/77 Age: 23

Year Team	Lg Org	BATTING															BASERUNNING				PERCENTAGES		
		G	AB	H	2B	3B	HR	TB	R	RBI	TBB	IBB	SO	HBP	SH	SF	SB	CS	SB%	GDP	Avg	OBP	SLG
1996 Orioles	R Bal	56	193	42	8	4	0	58	29	20	23	1	26	2	0	0	6	2	.75	4	.218	.307	.301
1997 Delmarva	A Bal	90	305	84	14	5	3	117	41	48	23	1	45	4	1	6	19	10	.66	5	.275	.328	.384
1998 Frederick	A+ Bal	130	473	121	19	2	16	192	62	75	48	2	109	3	3	9	17	12	.59	11	.256	.323	.406
1999 Bowie	AA Bal	57	195	36	9	3	3	60	21	23	20	0	46	1	1	3	2	2	.50	3	.185	.260	.308
Frederick	A+ Bal	73	276	78	18	4	11	137	35	53	28	3	62	4	0	3	7	4	.64	5	.283	.354	.496
4 Min. YEARS		406	1442	361	68	18	33	564	188	219	142	7	288	14	5	21	51	30	.63	28	.250	.319	.391

Dave Coggin

Pitches: Right Bats: Right Pos: P   Ht: 6'4" Wt: 195 Born: 10/30/76 Age: 23

Year Team	Lg Org	HOW MUCH HE PITCHED						WHAT HE GAVE UP												THE RESULTS					
		G	GS	CG	GF	IP	BFP	H	R	ER	HR	SH	SF	HB	TBB	IBB	SO	WP	Bk	W	L	Pct.	ShO	Sv	ERA
1995 Martinsvlle	R+ Phi	11	11	0	0	48	209	45	25	16	1	1	1	5	31	0	37	8	1	5	3	.625	0	0	3.00
1996 Piedmont	A Phi	28	28	3	0	169.1	699	156	87	81	12	3	3	7	46	1	129	12	1	9	12	.429	3	0	4.31
1997 Clearwater	A+ Phi	27	27	3	0	155	697	160	96	81	12	5	7	9	86	0	110	24	1	11	8	.579	2	0	4.70
1998 Reading	AA Phi	20	20	0	0	108.2	477	106	58	50	8	2	2	8	62	1	65	14	0	4	8	.333	0	0	4.14
1999 Reading	AA Phi	9	9	0	0	42	203	55	37	35	8	0	0	3	20	0	21	6	0	2	5	.286	0	0	7.50
5 Min. YEARS		95	95	6	0	523	2285	522	303	263	41	11	13	32	245	2	362	64	3	31	36	.463	5	0	4.53

Eric Cole

Bats: Right Throws: Right Pos: OF   Ht: 6'0" Wt: 185 Born: 11/15/75 Age: 24

Year Team	Lg Org	BATTING															BASERUNNING				PERCENTAGES		
		G	AB	H	2B	3B	HR	TB	R	RBI	TBB	IBB	SO	HBP	SH	SF	SB	CS	SB%	GDP	Avg	OBP	SLG
1995 Astros	R Hou	39	122	33	3	1	0	38	17	12	7	0	21	2	3		5	7	.58	0	.270	.321	.311
1996 Auburn	A- Hou	46	151	26	4	0	1	33	9	10	6	0	46	3	1	4	3	1	.75	7	.172	.213	.219
1997 Auburn	A- Hou	71	222	61	20	3	8	111	29	34	19	1	46	5	2	3	4	4	.50	3	.275	.341	.500
1998 Quad City	A Hou	132	500	140	30	6	11	215	73	83	24	0	104	5	0	1	32	15	.68	4	.280	.319	.430
1999 Kissimmee	A+ Hou	120	460	122	27	5	13	198	62	67	39	3	120	7	0	4	23	13	.64	12	.265	.329	.430
Jackson	AA Hou	15	54	9	0	0	2	16	4	8	1	0	11	0	1		0	0	.00	3	.167	.182	.296
5 Min. YEARS		423	1509	391	85	15	35	611	194	214	96	4	348	22	7	12	69	38	.64	32	.259	.311	.405

Victor Cole

Pitches: Right Bats: Both Pos: P   Ht: 5'10" Wt: 160 Born: 1/23/68 Age: 32

Year Team	Lg Org	HOW MUCH HE PITCHED						WHAT HE GAVE UP												THE RESULTS					
		G	GS	CG	GF	IP	BFP	H	R	ER	HR	SH	SF	HB	TBB	IBB	SO	WP	Bk	W	L	Pct.	ShO	Sv	ERA
1988 Eugene	A- KC	15	0	0	13	23.2	94	16	6	4	0	0	0	2	8	0	39	3	0	1	0	1.000	0	9	1.52
Baseball Cy	A+ KC	10	5	0	2	35	149	27	9	8	0	1	1	1	21	0	29	2	0	5	0	1.000	0	1	2.06
1989 Memphis	AA KC	13	13	0	0	63.2	303	67	53	45	4	4	1	5	51	1	52	4	1	1	9	.100	0	0	6.36
Baseball Cy	A+ KC	9	9	0	0	42	186	43	23	18	2	1	1	1	22	0	30	2	1	3	1	.750	0	0	3.86

58

Year Team	Lg Org	G	GS	CG	GF	IP	BFP	H	R	ER	HR	SH	SF	HB	TBB	IBB	SO	WP	Bk	W	L	Pct.	ShO	Sv	ERA
1990 Memphis	AA KC	46	6	0	15	107.2	479	91	61	52	6	4	1	3	70	2	102	2	2	3	8	.273	0	4	4.35
1991 Omaha	AAA KC	6	0	0	1	13	54	9	6	6	1	0	0	0	9	1	12	0	0	1	1	.500	0	0	4.15
Carolina	AA Pit	20	0	0	17	28.1	116	13	8	6	1	0	1	2	19	1	32	3	2	0	2	.000	0	12	1.91
Buffalo	AAA Pit	19	1	0	9	24	115	23	11	10	2	0	1	1	20	0	23	3	0	1	2	.333	0	0	3.75
1992 Buffalo	AAA Pit	19	19	3	0	115.2	498	102	46	40	8	3	3	4	61	0	69	8	0	11	6	.647	1	0	3.11
1993 Buffalo	AAA Pit	6	6	0	0	26.1	134	35	25	25	5	2	1	0	24	0	14	1	0	1	3	.250	0	0	8.54
Carolina	AA Pit	27	0	0	13	41	189	39	30	27	5	1	0	2	31	2	35	6	0	0	4	.000	0	8	5.93
New Orleans	AAA Mil	6	1	0	0	6	34	9	7	7	0	0	1	1	7	0	5	0	0	0	2	.000	0	0	10.50
1994 El Paso	AA Mil	8	0	0	2	8	50	18	17	16	4	0	0	1	9	1	3	0	1	0	1	.000	0	0	18.00
Memphis	AA KC	6	6	0	0	35.2	162	32	22	19	3	0	4	0	23	0	22	2	0	2	1	.667	0	0	4.79
1995 Las Vegas	AAA SD	4	4	0	0	19.2	86	19	17	14	4	1	1	0	10	0	12	1	1	0	2	.000	0	0	6.41
Salinas	IND —	4	4	0	0	22.2	104	25	16	9	0	2	2	0	13	0	22	2	0	1	1	.500	0	0	3.57
Memphis	AA SD	8	2	0	3	20	81	15	5	3	0	0	0	0	8	1	17	0	0	1	0	1.000	0	0	1.35
1996 Pine Bluff	IND —	8	0	0	2	23.1	89	16	2	2	0	1	0	2	4	0	27	2	0	3	0	1.000	0	0	0.77
Memphis	AA SD	8	1	0	4	15	65	11	3	2	0	0	0	1	8	0	13	0	0	1	0	1.000	0	0	1.20
1998 West Tenn	AA ChC	19	0	0	2	30	127	26	12	8	1	1	1	1	11	1	31	2	0	2	2	.500	0	0	2.40
Iowa	AAA ChC	38	2	0	6	67.1	296	77	35	28	4	3	1	1	25	0	69	7	1	2	2	.500	0	3	3.74
1999 Iowa	AAA ChC	19	2	0	2	40.1	188	41	24	21	3	2	0	3	23	1	33	5	2	1	1	.667	0	0	4.69
West Tenn	AA ChC	17	0	0	8	23	103	21	11	10	2	0	1	0	18	0	17	2	0	3	1	.750	0	0	3.91
1992 Pittsburgh	NL	8	4	0	2	23	104	23	14	14	1	1	1	0	14	0	12	1	0	0	2	.000	0	0	5.48
11 Min. YEARS		335	81	3	99	831.1	3702	775	449	380	55	26	21	31	495	11	708	57	11	44	49	.473	1	35	4.11

Roberto Colina

Bats: Left **Throws:** Left **Pos:** DH   **Ht:** 6'0" **Wt:** 200 **Born:** 1/29/71 **Age:** 29

Year Team	Lg Org	G	AB	H	2B	3B	HR	TB	R	RBI	TBB	IBB	SO	HBP	SH	SF	SB	CS	SB%	GDP	Avg	OBP	SLG
1997 Devil Rays	R TB	1	2	0	0	0	0	0	0	0	1	0	0	0	0	0	0	0	.00	0	.000	.333	.000
St. Pete	A+ TB	96	351	87	13	3	5	121	48	49	45	3	40	5	1	2	4	5	.44	9	.248	.340	.345
1998 Devil Rays	R TB	3	11	4	1	0	0	5	0	2	0	0	1	0	0	0	0	0	.00	0	.364	.364	.455
St. Pete	A+ TB	94	360	108	22	2	6	152	44	46	44	5	50	3	0	2	2	3	.40	8	.300	.379	.422
1999 Orlando	AA TB	99	315	86	20	1	6	126	45	53	37	4	47	3	0	3	0	1	.00	8	.273	.352	.400
3 Min. YEARS		293	1039	285	56	6	17	404	137	150	127	12	138	11	1	7	6	9	.40	25	.274	.357	.389

Michael Collins

Bats: Right **Throws:** Right **Pos:** 2B   **Ht:** 5'9" **Wt:** 166 **Born:** 1/29/77 **Age:** 23

Year Team	Lg Org	G	AB	H	2B	3B	HR	TB	R	RBI	TBB	IBB	SO	HBP	SH	SF	SB	CS	SB%	GDP	Avg	OBP	SLG
1998 Yakima	A- LA	18	67	19	2	0	0	21	5	2	4	0	6	1	3	0	2	6	.25	0	.284	.333	.313
Great Falls	R+ LA	44	143	44	10	3	0	60	23	18	13	0	19	3	10	2	4	2	.67	2	.308	.373	.420
1999 San Antonio	AA LA	7	12	4	0	0	0	4	1	0	5	0	2	0	1	0	0	1	.00	0	.333	.529	.333
Vero Beach	A+ LA	101	356	95	10	2	3	118	37	31	34	0	68	1	9	3	8	12	.40	7	.267	.330	.331
2 Min. YEARS		170	578	162	22	5	3	203	66	51	56	0	95	5	23	5	14	21	.40	9	.280	.346	.351

Luis Colmenares

Pitches: Right **Bats:** Right **Pos:** P   **Ht:** 5'11" **Wt:** 189 **Born:** 11/25/76 **Age:** 23

Year Team	Lg Org	G	GS	CG	GF	IP	BFP	H	R	ER	HR	SH	SF	HB	TBB	IBB	SO	WP	Bk	W	L	Pct.	ShO	Sv	ERA
1994 Rockies	R Col	12	0	0	11	14.1	70	16	7	4	1	0	0	3	4	1	20	3	0	1	0	1.000	0	5	2.51
1995 Asheville	A Col	45	0	0	38	55	223	37	15	14	1	2	2	1	29	1	74	11	2	2	2	.500	0	21	2.29
1996 Salem	A+ Col	32	0	0	25	32.2	156	28	21	19	4	5	2	2	22	1	45	6	3	4	5	.444	0	12	5.23
Asheville	A Col	12	12	1	0	65	282	58	36	32	6	0	4	2	25	1	56	5	7	2	6	.250	0	0	4.43
1997 Salem	A+ Col	32	3	0	15	66.2	283	60	34	29	5	6	4	4	30	3	70	6	2	6	1	.857	0	2	3.92
1998 Salem	A+ Col	28	28	1	0	160.1	716	187	96	90	16	5	3	11	63	0	117	8	0	13	6	.684	0	5	5.05
1999 Carolina	AA Col	8	0	0	1	10	52	16	9	9	2	2	0	0	8	0	10	1	0	0	0	.000	0	0	8.10
Salem	A+ Col	26	7	0	7	75.2	341	80	43	39	6	2	3	3	34	0	65	5	0	5	3	.625	0	0	4.64
6 Min. YEARS		195	50	2	97	479.2	2123	482	261	236	41	22	18	26	215	7	457	45	14	33	23	.589	0	40	4.43

Kevin Connacher

Bats: Right **Throws:** Right **Pos:** 2B   **Ht:** 5'9" **Wt:** 175 **Born:** 4/6/75 **Age:** 25

Year Team	Lg Org	G	AB	H	2B	3B	HR	TB	R	RBI	TBB	IBB	SO	HBP	SH	SF	SB	CS	SB%	GDP	Avg	OBP	SLG
1997 Winston-Sal	A+ CWS	70	243	70	16	2	3	99	32	27	28	0	50	2	2	3	12	8	.60	2	.288	.362	.407
1998 Winston-Sal	A+ CWS	80	212	51	9	3	7	87	45	23	34	1	63	3	9	1	15	5	.75	1	.241	.352	.410
1999 Winston-Sal	A+ CWS	121	413	107	14	5	10	161	60	48	63	0	101	1	6	0	27	13	.68	7	.259	.358	.390
Birmingham	AA CWS	7	18	4	0	0	0	4	1	0	2	0	5	0	0	0	1	0	1.00	0	.222	.300	.222
3 Min. YEARS		278	886	232	39	10	20	351	138	98	127	1	219	6	17	4	55	26	.68	10	.262	.357	.396

Steve Connelly

Pitches: Right **Bats:** Right **Pos:** P   **Ht:** 6'4" **Wt:** 210 **Born:** 4/27/74 **Age:** 26

Year Team	Lg Org	G	GS	CG	GF	IP	BFP	H	R	ER	HR	SH	SF	HB	TBB	IBB	SO	WP	Bk	W	L	Pct.	ShO	Sv	ERA
1995 Sou Oregon	A- Oak	17	0	0	10	28.1	133	29	17	12	1	3	2	4	14	4	19	6	0	2	4	.333	0	2	3.81
1996 Modesto	A+ Oak	52	0	0	42	64.2	283	58	33	27	5	1	1	5	32	1	65	5	2	4	7	.364	0	14	3.76
1997 Huntsville	AA Oak	43	0	0	22	69.2	297	74	33	29	3	2	1	4	20	2	49	5	0	3	3	.500	0	7	3.75
1998 Edmonton	AAA Oak	55	0	0	27	76	310	64	34	32	7	1	2	2	24	2	62	5	0	6	0	1.000	0	13	3.79
1999 Fresno	AAA SF	54	0	0	20	72	338	93	58	42	8	2	2	5	32	3	47	14	1	6	4	.600	0	2	5.25

		HOW MUCH HE PITCHED			WHAT HE GAVE UP			THE RESULTS		
Year Team	Lg Org	G GS CG GF	IP BFP	H R ER HR SH SF HB	TBB IBB SO WP Bk	W L Pct ShO Sv ERA
1998 Oakland	AL	3 0 0 1	4.2 28	10 1 1 0 0 0 1	4 0 1 0 0	0 0 .000 0 0 1.93
5 Min. YEARS		221 0 0 121	310.2 1361	318 175 142 24 9 8 20	122 12 242 35 3	21 18 .538 0 38 4.11

Decomba Conner

Bats: Right **Throws:** Right **Pos:** OF   **Ht:** 5'10" **Wt:** 185 **Born:** 7/17/73 **Age:** 26

		BATTING														BASERUNNING				PERCENTAGES		
Year Team	Lg Org	G	AB	H	2B	3B	HR	TB	R	RBI	TBB	IBB	SO	HBP	SH	SF	SB	CS	SB%	GDP	Avg	OBP	SLG
1994 Princeton	R+ Cin	46	158	53	7	5	7	91	45	19	24	3	39	0	1	2	30	4	.88	0	.335	.418	.576
1995 Princeton	R+ Cin	6	16	2	2	0	0	4	2	5	3	0	3	0	0	1	2	0	1.00	0	.125	.250	.250
Chstn-WV	A Cin	91	308	81	10	7	5	120	55	40	39	1	77	3	4	6	22	5	.81	6	.263	.346	.390
1996 Winston-Sal	A+ Cin	129	512	144	18	5	20	232	77	64	43	1	117	2	5	4	33	11	.75	6	.281	.337	.453
1997 Jacksnville	AA Det	47	154	32	6	3	4	56	22	17	30	1	45	2	0	1	5	1	.83	4	.208	.342	.364
Lakeland	A+ Det	56	201	64	7	4	7	100	35	29	21	1	47	0	3	1	9	2	.82	1	.318	.381	.498
1998 Bowie	AA Bal	65	208	52	5	2	5	76	31	27	16	0	42	0	7	1	10	3	.77	1	.250	.302	.365
Frederick	A+ Bal	32	121	36	7	2	2	53	16	11	10	0	21	2	1	0	10	5	.67	2	.298	.361	.438
1999 Chattanooga	AA Cin	45	123	22	3	2	5	44	17	19	17	0	31	0	1	2	1	2	.33	1	.179	.275	.358
Wilmington	A+ KC	48	171	52	7	2	1	66	27	17	21	1	26	5	1	0	9	1	.90	2	.304	.396	.386
6 Min. YEARS		565	1972	538	72	32	56	842	327	248	224	8	448	14	23	18	131	34	.79	23	.273	.348	.427

Jason Conti

Bats: Left **Throws:** Right **Pos:** OF   **Ht:** 5'11" **Wt:** 180 **Born:** 1/27/75 **Age:** 25

		BATTING														BASERUNNING				PERCENTAGES		
Year Team	Lg Org	G	AB	H	2B	3B	HR	TB	R	RBI	TBB	IBB	SO	HBP	SH	SF	SB	CS	SB%	GDP	Avg	OBP	SLG
1996 Lethbridge	R+ Ari	63	226	83	15	1	4	112	63	49	30	0	29	6	0	3	30	7	.81	3	.367	.449	.496
1997 South Bend	A Ari	117	458	142	22	10	3	193	78	43	45	2	99	11	4	3	30	18	.63	10	.310	.383	.421
High Desert	A+ Ari	14	59	21	5	1	2	34	15	8	10	0	12	1	0	0	1	2	.33	0	.356	.457	.576
1998 Tulsa	AA Ari	130	530	167	31	12	15	267	125	67	63	4	96	9	1	2	19	13	.59	5	.315	.396	.504
1999 Tucson	AAA Ari	133	520	151	23	8	9	217	100	57	55	1	89	5	3	6	22	8	.73	8	.290	.360	.417
4 Min. YEARS		457	1793	564	96	32	33	823	381	224	203	7	325	32	8	14	102	48	.68	26	.315	.391	.459

Jim Converse

Pitches: Right **Bats:** Left **Pos:** P   **Ht:** 5'9" **Wt:** 180 **Born:** 8/17/71 **Age:** 28

		HOW MUCH HE PITCHED			WHAT HE GAVE UP			THE RESULTS		
Year Team	Lg Org	G GS CG GF	IP BFP	H R ER HR SH SF HB	TBB IBB SO WP Bk	W L Pct ShO Sv ERA
1990 Bellingham	A- Sea	12 12 0 0	66.2 281	50 31 29 1 0 1 2	32 0 75 2 9	2 4 .333 0 0 3.92
1991 Peninsula	A+ Sea	26 26 1 0	137.2 643	143 90 76 12 3 4 2	97 2 137 9 2	6 15 .286 0 0 4.97
1992 Jacksnville	AA Sea	27 26 4 0	159 677	134 61 47 9 3 4 5	82 1 157 8 1	12 7 .632 0 0 2.66
1993 Calgary	AAA Sea	23 22 4 0	121.2 565	144 86 73 6 2 7 3	64 1 78 8 0	7 8 .467 0 0 5.40
1994 Calgary	AAA Sea	14 14 0 0	74 334	105 48 42 7 5 2 1	21 0 53 2 0	5 3 .625 0 0 5.11
1995 Tacoma	AAA Sea	17 12 0 3	73.2 337	96 57 49 5 4 5 1	36 1 43 4 4	4 7 .364 0 0 5.99
Omaha	AAA KC	4 0 0 0	5 19	1 0 0 0 0 0 0	1 0 9 1 0	1 0 1.000 0 0 0.00
1997 Omaha	AAA KC	6 3 0 1	17.1 75	18 13 13 3 0 2 1	9 0 13 0 0	2 1 .667 0 0 6.75
Yankees	R NYY	3 3 0 0	4.2 21	5 1 1 0 0 0 0	1 0 8 0 0	0 0 .000 0 0 1.93
Columbus	AAA NYY	10 1 0 5	19 86	22 8 7 1 0 0 0	11 1 13 1 0	0 2 .000 0 1 3.32
1998 Bowie	AA Bal	1 1 0 0	5 23	9 4 4 0 1 1 0	1 0 2 0 0	0 0 .000 0 0 7.20
Rochester	AAA Bal	36 0 0 13	82.2 365	86 51 45 12 0 4 0	40 0 74 7 0	2 8 .200 0 1 4.90
Oklahoma	AAA Tex	4 0 0 2	7 31	8 5 4 3 0 0 0	2 0 4 0 0	0 0 .000 0 0 5.14
1999 Huntsville	AA Mil	16 0 0 15	22 87	14 8 7 2 0 2 1	7 0 25 1 0	1 1 .500 0 5 2.86
Louisville	AAA Mil	30 4 0 4	62 288	76 43 40 8 1 2 0	34 0 40 3 0	4 3 .571 0 0 5.81
1993 Seattle	AL	4 4 0 0	20.1 93	23 12 12 0 0 1 0	14 2 10 0 0	1 3 .250 0 0 5.31
1994 Seattle	AL	13 8 0 1	48.2 253	73 49 47 5 2 3 1	40 4 39 3 0	0 5 .000 0 0 8.69
1995 Seattle	AL	6 1 0 3	11 55	16 9 9 2 1 0 0	8 0 9 0 0	0 3 .000 0 1 7.36
Kansas City	AL	9 0 0 1	12.1 54	12 8 8 0 1 0 0	8 2 5 2 0	1 0 1.000 0 0 5.84
1997 Kansas City	AL	3 0 0 1	5 23	4 2 2 2 0 0 0	5 0 3 0 0	0 0 .000 0 0 3.60
9 Min. YEARS		226 130 7 43	857.1 3832	911 506 437 69 19 34 16	438 6 731 46 16	46 59 .438 0 8 4.59
4 Maj. YEARS		35 13 0 6	97.1 478	128 80 78 9 4 4 1	75 8 66 5 0	2 11 .154 0 1 7.21

Derrick Cook

Pitches: Right **Bats:** Right **Pos:** P   **Ht:** 6'3" **Wt:** 195 **Born:** 8/6/75 **Age:** 24

		HOW MUCH HE PITCHED			WHAT HE GAVE UP			THE RESULTS		
Year Team	Lg Org	G GS CG GF	IP BFP	H R ER HR SH SF HB	TBB IBB SO WP Bk	W L Pct ShO Sv ERA
1996 Rangers	R Tex	6 5 1 0	23 100	25 14 12 1 0 1 2	11 0 13 1 0	2 1 .667 1 0 4.70
1997 Pulaski	R+ Tex	6 6 0 0	33.2 141	32 15 14 1 0 1 2	12 0 32 4 0	2 2 .500 0 0 3.74
Charlotte	A+ Tex	8 8 2 0	58.2 243	54 21 15 5 0 1 2	15 0 35 4 0	5 2 .714 0 0 2.30
1998 Charlotte	A+ Tex	26 26 1 0	167.1 710	170 81 68 13 8 2 5	64 1 111 13 1	13 7 .650 1 0 3.66
1999 Tulsa	AA Tex	21 21 2 0	114.1 524	137 81 72 12 3 6 4	45 3 71 17 0	7 6 .538 0 0 5.67
4 Min. YEARS		67 66 6 0	397 1718	418 212 181 32 11 11 15	147 4 262 39 1	29 18 .617 2 0 4.10

Steve Cooke

Pitches: Left **Bats:** Right **Pos:** P   **Ht:** 6'6" **Wt:** 245 **Born:** 1/14/70 **Age:** 30

		HOW MUCH HE PITCHED			WHAT HE GAVE UP			THE RESULTS		
Year Team	Lg Org	G GS CG GF	IP BFP	H R ER HR SH SF HB	TBB IBB SO WP Bk	W L Pct ShO Sv ERA
1990 Welland	A- Pit	11 11 0 0	46 188	36 21 18 2 1 4 2	17 0 43 6 1	2 3 .400 0 0 3.52
1991 Augusta	A Pit	11 11 1 0	60.2 269	50 28 19 0 3 1 5	35 1 52 3 0	5 4 .556 0 0 2.82
Salem	A+ Pit	2 2 0 0	13 57	14 8 7 0 0 0 2	2 0 5 4 1	1 0 1.000 0 0 4.85
Carolina	AA Pit	9 9 1 0	55.2 223	39 21 14 2 1 4 1	19 0 46 5 0	3 3 .500 1 0 2.26

Year Team	Lg Org	G	GS	CG	GF	IP	BFP	H	R	ER	HR	SH	SF	HB	TBB	IBB	SO	WP	Bk	W	L	Pct.	ShO	Sv	ERA
1992 Carolina	AA Pit	6	6	0	0	36	143	31	13	12	1	0	1	3	12	1	38	1	0	2	2	.500	0	0	3.00
Buffalo	AAA Pit	13	13	0	0	74.1	325	71	35	31	2	5	3	4	36	2	52	5	1	6	3	.667	0	0	3.75
1995 Augusta	A Pit	1	1	0	0	5	19	2	0	0	0	0	0	0	1	0	6	0	0	1	0	1.000	0	0	0.00
Carolina	AA Pit	1	1	0	0	5	27	5	4	4	0	0	0	0	5	0	4	1	0	0	0	.000	0	0	7.20
1996 Carolina	AA Pit	12	12	0	0	53.2	240	56	34	26	3	4	1	3	26	3	45	3	1	1	5	.167	0	0	4.36
1998 Indianapolis	AAA Cin	2	2	0	0	1.2	13	3	7	7	0	0	0	0	5	0	0	0	0	0	1	.000	0	0	37.80
1999 Las Vegas	AAA SD	5	0	0	1	3	27	6	10	10	2	0	2	1	12	1	0	5	0	0	0	.000	0	0	30.00
Zion	IND —	8	8	0	0	41.2	206	47	43	37	5	1	5	7	42	0	11	10	0	2	2	.500	0	0	7.99
1992 Pittsburgh	NL	11	0	0	8	23	91	22	9	9	2	0	0	0	4	1	10	0	0	2	0	1.000	0	1	3.52
1993 Pittsburgh	NL	32	32	3	0	210.2	882	207	101	91	22	13	6	3	59	4	132	3	3	10	10	.500	1	0	3.89
1994 Pittsburgh	NL	25	23	2	1	134.1	590	157	79	75	21	9	3	5	46	7	74	3	0	4	11	.267	0	0	5.02
1996 Pittsburgh	NL	3	0	0	1	8.1	41	11	7	7	1	0	1	0	5	0	7	1	0	0	0	.000	0	0	7.56
1997 Pittsburgh	NL	32	32	0	0	167.1	756	184	95	80	15	18	5	9	77	11	109	8	1	9	15	.375	0	0	4.30
1998 Cincinnati	NL	1	1	0	0	6	23	4	1	1	0	0	0	0	3	0	0	3	0	1	0	1.000	0	0	1.50
7 Min. YEARS		81	76	2	1	395.2	1737	360	224	185	17	15	15	29	212	8	302	43	4	23	23	.500	1	0	4.21
6 Maj. YEARS		104	88	5	10	549.2	2383	585	292	263	61	40	15	18	191	23	335	15	4	26	36	.419	1	1	4.31

Mike Coolbaugh

Bats: Right Throws: Right Pos: 3B-OF Ht: 6'1" Wt: 185 Born: 6/5/72 Age: 28

Year Team	Lg Org	G	AB	H	2B	3B	HR	TB	R	RBI	TBB	IBB	SO	HBP	SH	SF	SB	CS	SB%	GDP	Avg	OBP	SLG
1990 Medcine Hat	R+ Tor	58	211	40	9	0	2	55	21	16	13	0	47	1	1	2	3	2	.60	8	.190	.238	.261
1991 St.Cathrnes	A- Tor	71	255	58	13	2	3	84	28	26	17	0	40	3	4	4	4	5	.44	1	.227	.280	.329
1992 St.Cathrnes	A- Tor	15	49	14	1	1	0	17	3	2	3	0	12	0	2	0	2		.00	1	.286	.327	.347
1993 Hagerstown	A Tor	112	389	94	23	1	16	167	58	62	32	5	94	3	4	4	4	3	.57	9	.242	.301	.429
1994 Dunedin	A+ Tor	122	456	120	33	3	16	207	53	66	28	3	94	7	3	4	3	4	.43	14	.263	.313	.454
1995 Knoxville	AA Tor	142	500	120	32	2	9	183	71	56	37	3	110	11	4	3	7	11	.39	13	.240	.305	.366
1996 Charlotte	A+ Tor	124	449	129	33	4	15	215	76	75	42	4	80	8	0	3	8	10	.44	10	.287	.357	.479
Tulsa	AA Tex	7	23	8	3	0	2	17	6	9	2	0	3	2	0	0	1	0	1.00	0	.348	.444	.739
1997 Huntsville	AA Oak	139	559	172	37	2	30	303	100	132	52	3	105	7	2	8	8	3	.73	17	.308	.369	.542
1998 Colo Spngs	AAA Col	108	386	107	35	2	16	194	62	75	32	0	93	1	2	4	0	3	.00	13	.277	.331	.503
1999 Columbus	AAA NYY	114	391	108	31	2	15	188	65	66	38	0	112	2	2	4	5	7	.42	5	.276	.340	.481
10 Min. YEARS		1012	3668	970	250	19	124	1630	543	585	296	18	790	45	24	36	43	50	.46	91	.264	.324	.444

Scott Coolbaugh

Bats: Right Throws: Right Pos: 3B Ht: 5'11" Wt: 195 Born: 6/13/66 Age: 34

Year Team	Lg Org	G	AB	H	2B	3B	HR	TB	R	RBI	TBB	IBB	SO	HBP	SH	SF	SB	CS	SB%	GDP	Avg	OBP	SLG
1987 Charlotte	A+ Tex	66	233	64	21	0	2	91	27	20	24	1	56	0	1	2	0	1	.00	5	.275	.340	.391
1988 Tulsa	AA Tex	136	470	127	15	4	13	189	52	75	76	4	79	1	2	8	2	4	.33	14	.270	.368	.402
1989 Okla City	AAA Tex	144	527	137	28	0	18	219	66	74	57	5	93	2	2	3	1	3	.33	13	.260	.333	.416
1990 Okla City	AAA Tex	76	293	66	17	2	6	105	39	30	27	2	62	1	0	3	0	1	.00	6	.225	.290	.358
1991 Las Vegas	AAA SD	60	209	60	9	2	7	94	29	29	34	2	53	0	0	2	2	2	.50	9	.287	.384	.450
1992 Las Vegas	AAA SD	65	199	48	13	2	8	89	30	39	19	1	52	3	1	1	0	0	.00	9	.241	.315	.447
Nashville	AAA Cin	59	188	48	8	3	5	77	25	23	32	0	50	0	2	5	3	2	.60	5	.255	.356	.410
1993 Rochester	AAA Bal	118	421	103	26	4	18	191	52	67	27	2	110	2	1	2	0	0	.00	9	.245	.292	.454
1994 Louisville	AAA StL	94	333	101	25	6	19	195	60	75	39	10	69	10	0	4	3	5	.38	10	.303	.389	.586
1996 Ottawa	AAA Mon	58	173	36	12	1	3	59	20	22	23	1	37	0	1	4	2	2	.50	7	.208	.295	.341
1997 Birmingham	AA CWS	68	235	68	18	0	11	119	35	50	37	3	60	4	0	4	0	0	.00	8	.289	.389	.506
1999 Tucson	AAA Ari	74	212	54	14	1	7	91	28	31	32	3	49	2	1	1	1	1	.50	4	.255	.352	.429
El Paso	AA Ari	18	61	17	3	0	3	29	12	17	13	1	9	0	0	0	2	0	1.00	2	.279	.405	.475
1989 Texas	AL	25	51	14	1	0	2	21	7	7	4	0	12	0	1	1	0	0	.00	2	.275	.321	.412
1990 Texas	AL	67	180	36	6	0	2	48	21	13	15	0	47	1	4	1	0	1	.00	2	.200	.264	.267
1991 San Diego	NL	60	180	39	8	1	2	55	12	15	19	2	45	1	4	1	3	0	.00	8	.217	.294	.306
1994 St. Louis	NL	15	21	4	0	0	2	10	4	6	1	0	4	0	0	1	0	0	.00	2	.190	.217	.476
11 Min. YEARS		1036	3554	929	209	25	120	1548	475	552	440	35	779	25	11	42	15	20	.43	95	.261	.343	.436
4 Maj. YEARS		167	432	93	15	1	8	134	44	41	39	2	108	2	9	4	3	1	.25	15	.215	.281	.310

Bryan Corey

Pitches: Right Bats: Right Pos: P Ht: 6'0" Wt: 170 Born: 10/21/73 Age: 26

Year Team	Lg Org	G	GS	CG	GF	IP	BFP	H	R	ER	HR	SH	SF	HB	TBB	IBB	SO	WP	Bk	W	L	Pct.	ShO	Sv	ERA
1995 Jamestown	A- Det	29	0	0	28	28	116	21	14	12	2	0	1	2	12	1	41	4	0	2	2	.500	0	10	3.86
1996 Fayettevlle	A Det	60	0	0	53	82	315	50	19	11	2	4	6	2	17	3	101	6	2	6	4	.600	0	34	1.21
1997 Jacksnville	A Det	52	0	0	36	68	298	74	42	36	8	5	3	1	21	3	37	4	0	3	8	.273	0	9	4.76
1998 Tucson	AAA Ari	39	10	0	14	87.2	401	116	61	53	14	1	2	6	24	0	50	2	2	4	6	.400	0	2	5.44
1999 Toledo	AAA Det	48	0	0	17	69.1	303	63	27	22	6	4	1	2	34	4	36	2	1	5	2	.714	0	2	2.86
1998 Arizona	NL	3	0	0	2	4	20	6	4	4	1	0	0	1	2	0	1	0	0	0	0	.000	0	0	9.00
5 Min. YEARS		228	10	0	148	335	1433	324	163	134	32	14	13	12	108	11	265	18	5	20	22	.476	0	57	3.60

Mark Corey

Pitches: Right Bats: Right Pos: P Ht: 6'2" Wt: 220 Born: 11/16/74 Age: 25

Year Team	Lg Org	G	GS	CG	GF	IP	BFP	H	R	ER	HR	SH	SF	HB	TBB	IBB	SO	WP	Bk	W	L	Pct.	ShO	Sv	ERA
1995 Princeton	R+ Cin	4	3	0	0	14.2	61	12	7	6	1	0	0	0	6	0	8	0	0	1	1	.500	0	0	3.68
1997 Chstn-WV	A Cin	26	26	1	0	136	602	169	87	69	7	8	5	4	42	3	97	14	0	8	13	.381	0	0	4.57
1998 Burlington	A Cin	20	20	6	0	140	577	125	55	38	9	3	6	6	36	0	109	10	1	12	6	.667	2	0	2.44

61

Year Team	Lg Org	G	GS	CG	GF	IP	BFP	H	R	ER	HR	SH	SF	HB	TBB	IBB	SO	WP	Bk	W	L	Pct.	ShO	Sv	ERA
		HOW MUCH HE PITCHED						**WHAT HE GAVE UP**												**THE RESULTS**					
Indianapols	AAA Cin	1	1	1	0	6	24	4	3	3	1	0	0	0	3	0	2	0	0	0	1	.000	0	0	4.50
Chattanooga	AA Cin	6	6	0	0	26.1	127	32	25	24	6	1	2	2	16	1	6	0	0	0	4	.000	0	0	8.20
1999 Binghamton	AA NYM	29	27	0	0	155	698	175	108	93	18	4	1	9	64	0	111	1	1	7	13	.350	0	0	5.40
4 Min. YEARS		86	83	8	0	478	2089	517	285	233	42	17	11	21	167	4	333	25	2	28	38	.424	2	0	4.39

Edwin Corps

Pitches: Right **Bats:** Right **Pos:** P **Ht:** 5'11" **Wt:** 190 **Born:** 11/3/72 **Age:** 27

Year Team	Lg Org	G	GS	CG	GF	IP	BFP	H	R	ER	HR	SH	SF	HB	TBB	IBB	SO	WP	Bk	W	L	Pct.	ShO	Sv	ERA
		HOW MUCH HE PITCHED						**WHAT HE GAVE UP**												**THE RESULTS**					
1994 San Jose	A+ SF	29	29	0	0	168.1	731	180	95	74	6	5	6	20	43	1	91	4	1	10	6	.625	0	0	3.96
1995 Shreveport	AA SF	27	27	2	0	165.2	712	195	80	71	16	2	6	8	41	2	53	4	2	13	6	.684	0	0	3.86
1996 Shreveport	AA SF	38	3	0	6	70.1	305	74	46	35	6	1	1	3	26	2	39	2	0	2	3	.400	0	1	4.48
1997 Phoenix	AAA SF	7	2	0	1	19	88	26	14	12	0	0	2	0	8	1	8	0	0	2	1	.667	0	0	5.68
Shreveport	AA SF	43	1	0	20	72.1	306	66	38	35	6	5	4	0	35	2	24	4	0	5	3	.625	0	6	4.35
1998 Shreveport	AA SF	46	5	0	11	92.1	396	94	47	40	13	5	4	2	32	4	42	8	0	2	5	.286	0	1	3.90
1999 Shreveport	AA SF	24	12	0	5	84.1	376	98	54	43	9	4	2	4	29	1	34	5	1	4	4	.500	0	2	4.59
Fresno	AAA SF	4	0	0	3	7	33	9	7	3	0	0	0	0	3	0	11	1	0	0	0	.000	0	0	3.86
6 Min. YEARS		218	79	2	46	679.1	2947	742	381	313	56	22	25	37	217	13	302	28	4	38	28	.576	0	8	4.15

Tim Cossins

Bats: Right **Throws:** Right **Pos:** C **Ht:** 6'1" **Wt:** 192 **Born:** 3/31/70 **Age:** 30

Year Team	Lg Org	G	AB	H	2B	3B	HR	TB	R	RBI	TBB	IBB	SO	HBP	SH	SF	SB	CS	SB%	GDP	Avg	OBP	SLG
		BATTING															**BASERUNNING**				**PERCENTAGES**		
1993 Erie	A- Tex	4	10	4	1	0	0	5	1	3	2	0	0	0	0	0	0	1	.00	0	.400	.500	.500
Chston-SC	A Tex	27	89	13	2	0	0	15	8	10	7	0	21	3	0	1	0	1	.00	3	.146	.230	.169
1994 Hudson Val	A- Tex	6	17	2	1	0	1	6	1	2	0	0	4	0	1	0	0	0	.00	0	.118	.118	.353
Charlotte	A+ Tex	10	28	3	0	0	0	3	2	2	4	0	6	0	1	0	1	0	1.00	1	.107	.219	.107
1995 Rangers	R Tex	2	4	0	0	0	0	0	0	0	0	0	1	0	0	0	0	0	.00	0	.000	.000	.000
Chston-SC	A Tex	22	59	12	5	0	1	20	8	8	9	0	13	1	0	0	2	0	1.00	0	.203	.319	.339
Charlotte	A+ Tex	7	17	1	0	0	0	1	1	0	4	1	5	0	0	0	0	1	.00	0	.059	.238	.059
1996 Tulsa	AA Tex	3	4	2	0	0	0	2	0	1	3	0	0	0	0	0	0	0	.00	0	.500	.714	.500
Charlotte	A+ Tex	67	233	56	16	0	3	81	34	32	13	0	44	2	3	2	1	1	.50	11	.240	.284	.348
1997 Tulsa	AA Tex	36	108	32	5	1	4	51	11	17	8	0	24	0	2	2	2	0	1.00	1	.296	.339	.472
1998 Tampa	A+ NYY	30	94	21	6	0	1	30	6	6	3	0	14	0	2	1	0	0	.00	4	.223	.245	.319
1999 Harrisburg	AA Mon	41	93	16	2	0	4	30	8	14	4	1	21	1	4	2	0	0	.00	4	.172	.210	.323
7 Min. YEARS		255	756	162	38	1	14	244	80	95	57	2	153	7	12	8	6	4	.60	26	.214	.273	.323

John Cotton

Bats: Left **Throws:** Right **Pos:** 3B **Ht:** 6'0" **Wt:** 190 **Born:** 10/30/70 **Age:** 29

Year Team	Lg Org	G	AB	H	2B	3B	HR	TB	R	RBI	TBB	IBB	SO	HBP	SH	SF	SB	CS	SB%	GDP	Avg	OBP	SLG
		BATTING															**BASERUNNING**				**PERCENTAGES**		
1989 Burlington	R+ Cle	64	227	47	5	1	2	60	36	22	22	0	56	3	4	1	20	3	.87	5	.207	.285	.264
1990 Watertown	A- Cle	73	286	60	9	4	2	83	53	27	40	3	71	2	2	1	24	7	.77	4	.210	.310	.290
1991 Columbus	A Cle	122	405	92	11	9	13	160	88	42	93	1	135	3	3	3	56	15	.79	6	.227	.373	.395
1992 Kinston	A+ Cle	103	360	72	7	3	11	118	67	39	48	1	106	2	1	2	23	7	.77	3	.200	.296	.328
1993 Kinston	A+ Cle	127	454	120	16	3	13	181	81	51	59	1	130	11	5	2	28	24	.54	3	.264	.361	.399
1994 Springfield	A SD	24	82	19	5	3	1	33	14	8	12	0	19	0	0	0	7	1	.88	0	.232	.330	.402
Wichita	AA SD	34	85	16	4	0	3	29	9	14	13	3	20	1	0	2	2	0	1.00	3	.188	.297	.341
Rancho Cuca	A+ SD	48	171	35	3	2	4	54	35	19	22	0	48	2	0	0	9	3	.75	3	.205	.303	.316
1995 Memphis	AA SD	121	407	103	19	8	12	174	60	47	38	0	101	4	6	4	15	6	.71	2	.253	.320	.428
1996 Toledo	AAA Det	50	171	32	7	1	4	53	14	19	7	0	64	2	2	0	4	4	.50	1	.187	.228	.310
Jacksnville	AA Det	63	217	52	7	4	13	106	34	39	19	2	66	2	0	1	15	3	.83	2	.240	.305	.488
1997 Birmingham	AA CWS	33	124	36	10	2	7	71	23	26	9	0	33	2	0	1	1	2	.33	3	.290	.346	.573
Nashville	AAA CWS	94	323	87	14	3	11	140	45	50	24	1	94	0	1	2	8	2	.80	7	.269	.318	.433
1998 Daytona	A+ ChC	12	48	14	4	0	3	27	8	11	3	0	8	1	0	0	0	0	.00	3	.292	.346	.563
West Tenn	AA ChC	90	319	93	14	3	13	152	46	53	19	1	68	4	0	5	10	3	.77	3	.292	.334	.476
1999 Carolina	AA Col	42	163	46	9	0	10	85	27	21	10	1	48	1	0	0	0	1	.00	3	.282	.328	.521
Colo Sprngs	AAA Col	70	235	74	18	1	15	139	50	48	14	4	64	2	1	3	4	2	.67	6	.315	.354	.591
11 Min. YEARS		1170	4077	998	162	47	137	1665	690	536	452	18	1131	42	25	27	226	83	.73	57	.245	.324	.408

Robbie Crabtree

Pitches: Right **Bats:** Right **Pos:** P **Ht:** 6'1" **Wt:** 175 **Born:** 11/25/72 **Age:** 27

Year Team	Lg Org	G	GS	CG	GF	IP	BFP	H	R	ER	HR	SH	SF	HB	TBB	IBB	SO	WP	Bk	W	L	Pct.	ShO	Sv	ERA
		HOW MUCH HE PITCHED						**WHAT HE GAVE UP**												**THE RESULTS**					
1996 Bellingham	A- SF	28	0	0	13	52	206	38	18	16	8	2	1	0	14	1	72	3	0	3	3	.500	0	4	2.77
1997 Bakersfield	A+ SF	45	9	1	9	112.1	506	124	77	64	10	1	0	5	59	1	116	12	1	7	7	.500	0	1	5.13
1998 San Jose	A+ SF	34	0	0	10	54.1	213	39	6	6	0	4	0	3	8	0	67	1	0	6	1	.857	0	2	0.99
Shreveport	AA SF	26	0	0	13	54	205	30	11	10	4	1	0	2	16	2	56	2	0	2	0	1.000	0	4	1.67
Fresno	AAA SF	3	1	0	2	4.2	26	8	7	6	1	0	0	1	2	0	10	0	0	0	0	.000	0	0	11.57
1999 Fresno	AAA SF	22	1	0	11	34.1	150	37	23	20	2	0	0	0	10	1	40	3	0	1	4	.200	0	1	5.24
Shreveport	AA SF	36	0	0	14	63.1	251	50	21	18	2	0	1	0	18	2	65	3	0	4	2	.667	0	2	2.56
4 Min. YEARS		184	11	1	72	375	1557	326	163	140	27	8	2	11	127	7	426	24	1	23	17	.575	0	14	3.36

Rickey Cradle

Bats: Right **Throws:** Right **Pos:** OF | **Ht:** 6' 2" **Wt:** 180 **Born:** 6/20/73 **Age:** 27

Year Team	Lg Org	G	AB	H	2B	3B	HR	TB	R	RBI	TBB	IBB	SO	HBP	SH	SF	SB	CS	SB%	GDP	Avg	OBP	SLG
1991 Blue Jays	R Tor	44	132	28	4	3	1	41	16	6	24	1	37	3	1	1	4	5	.44	0	.212	.344	.311
1992 Medcine Hat	R+ Tor	65	217	49	8	0	9	84	38	36	42	0	69	6	1	2	16	2	.89	5	.226	.363	.387
1993 Hagerstown	A Tor	129	441	112	26	4	13	185	72	62	68	2	125	11	1	4	19	14	.58	5	.254	.365	.420
1994 Dunedin	A+ Tor	114	344	88	14	3	10	138	65	39	59	0	87	9	0	1	20	10	.67	5	.256	.378	.401
1995 Knoxville	AA Tor	41	117	21	5	1	4	40	17	13	17	0	29	3	1	1	3	3	.50	3	.179	.297	.342
Dunedin	A+ Tor	50	178	49	10	3	7	86	33	27	28	0	49	2	1	2	6	2	.75	2	.275	.376	.483
1996 Knoxville	AA Tor	92	333	94	23	2	12	157	59	47	55	1	65	10	7	7	15	11	.58	2	.282	.393	.471
Syracuse	AAA Tor	40	130	26	5	3	8	61	22	22	14	1	39	1	0	2	1	0	1.00	1	.200	.279	.469
1997 Syracuse	AAA Tor	11	25	3	0	0	1	6	4	3	2	0	9	2	0	0	0	1	.00	0	.120	.241	.240
Knoxville	AA Tor	84	257	55	16	1	10	103	50	34	41	0	67	7	2	1	5	6	.45	5	.214	.337	.401
1998 Tacoma	AAA Sea	82	297	86	25	1	12	149	53	53	24	1	76	4	0	2	9	5	.64	4	.290	.349	.502
1999 Toledo	AAA Det	110	348	83	27	2	10	144	57	52	42	1	82	6	1	5	11	6	.65	6	.239	.327	.414
1998 Seattle	AL	5	7	1	0	0	0	1	0	2	1	0	5	0	0	0	1	0	1.00	0	.143	.250	.143
9 Min. YEARS		862	2819	694	163	23	97	1194	486	394	416	7	734	64	15	28	109	65	.63	39	.246	.353	.424

Kevin Crafton

Pitches: Right **Bats:** Right **Pos:** P | **Ht:** 6'1" **Wt:** 185 **Born:** 5/10/74 **Age:** 26

	HOW MUCH HE PITCHED						WHAT HE GAVE UP									THE RESULTS					
Year Team	Lg Org	G	GS	CG	GF	IP	BFP	H	R	ER	HR	SH	SF	HB	TBB	IBB	SO	WP	Bk	W	L	Pct.	ShO	Sv	ERA
1996 New Jersey	A- StL	23	0	0	10	33	132	28	8	8	1	3	1	1	6	2	43	2	0	2	3	.400	0	2	2.18
1997 Peoria	A StL	50	0	0	45	55	219	40	16	12	2	5	2	2	18	7	59	2	1	7	2	.778	0	29	1.96
1998 Arkansas	AA StL	46	0	0	13	55.2	227	52	23	20	8	3	2	0	7	0	44	2	0	5	1	.833	0	1	3.23
1999 Memphis	AAA StL	4	0	0	0	4.1	26	12	12	11	2	0	1	1	0	0	2	0	0	0	1	.000	0	0	22.85
Arkansas	AA StL	42	0	0	14	46.1	209	57	41	39	9	2	1	1	16	1	41	2	0	7	2	.778	0	2	7.58
4 Min. YEARS		165	0	0	82	194.1	813	189	100	90	22	13	7	5	47	10	189	8	1	21	9	.700	0	34	4.17

Joey Cranford

Bats: Right **Throws:** Right **Pos:** OF | **Ht:** 6'0" **Wt:** 192 **Born:** 2/10/75 **Age:** 25

Year Team	Lg Org	G	AB	H	2B	3B	HR	TB	R	RBI	TBB	IBB	SO	HBP	SH	SF	SB	CS	SB%	GDP	Avg	OBP	SLG
1996 Elizabethtn	R+ Min	32	121	34	6	3	4	58	20	18	13	0	28	0	0	0	2	1	.67	4	.281	.351	.479
Fort Myers	A+ Min	30	105	23	3	1	0	28	9	17	7	0	21	0	0	2	3	1	.75	0	.219	.265	.267
1997 Fort Myers	A+ Min	112	355	71	9	1	1	85	39	22	21	0	90	1	3	1	4	6	.40	4	.200	.246	.239
1998 Fort Myers	A+ Min	75	254	57	15	3	8	102	41	39	26	0	58	2	4	0	6	1	.86	3	.224	.301	.402
1999 Fort Myers	A+ Min	38	124	30	4	1	3	45	18	14	17	0	22	2	0	6	3	2	.60	4	.242	.329	.363
New Britain	AA Min	57	159	33	4	1	5	54	19	14	10	0	38	1	3	2	0	3	.00	1	.208	.256	.340
4 Min. YEARS		344	1118	248	41	10	21	372	146	124	94	0	257	6	12	10	18	14	.56	16	.222	.283	.333

Paxton Crawford

Pitches: Right **Bats:** Right **Pos:** P | **Ht:** 6'3" **Wt:** 193 **Born:** 8/4/77 **Age:** 22

	HOW MUCH HE PITCHED						WHAT HE GAVE UP									THE RESULTS					
Year Team	Lg Org	G	GS	CG	GF	IP	BFP	H	R	ER	HR	SH	SF	HB	TBB	IBB	SO	WP	Bk	W	L	Pct.	ShO	Sv	ERA
1995 Red Sox	R Bos	12	7	1	4	46	184	38	17	14	2	0	0	1	12	0	44	6	0	2	4	.333	0	2	2.74
1996 Michigan	A Bos	22	22	1	0	128.1	548	120	62	51	5	2	5	8	42	1	105	8	1	6	11	.353	0	0	3.58
1997 Sarasota	A+ Bos	12	11	2	0	65.1	289	69	42	33	6	4	2	1	27	2	56	3	0	4	8	.333	1	0	4.55
1998 Trenton	AA Bos	22	20	1	1	108	457	104	53	50	8	3	1	6	39	1	82	7	0	6	5	.545	0	0	4.17
1999 Trenton	AA Bos	28	28	1	0	163.1	696	151	81	74	12	7	4	10	59	1	111	10	1	7	8	.467	1	0	4.08
5 Min. YEARS		96	88	6	5	511	2174	482	255	222	33	16	12	26	179	5	398	34	2	25	36	.410	2	2	3.91

Joe Crede

Bats: Right **Throws:** Right **Pos:** 3B | **Ht:** 6'3" **Wt:** 195 **Born:** 4/26/78 **Age:** 22

Year Team	Lg Org	G	AB	H	2B	3B	HR	TB	R	RBI	TBB	IBB	SO	HBP	SH	SF	SB	CS	SB%	GDP	Avg	OBP	SLG
1996 White Sox	R CWS	56	221	66	17	1	4	97	30	32	9	0	41	2	1	4	1	1	.50	8	.299	.326	.439
1997 Hickory	A CWS	113	402	109	25	0	5	149	45	62	24	0	83	5	0	2	3	1	.75	6	.271	.319	.371
1998 Winston-Sal	A+ CWS	137	492	155	32	3	20	253	92	88	53	3	98	12	0	11	9	7	.56	10	.315	.387	.514
1999 Birmingham	AA CWS	74	291	73	14	1	4	101	37	42	22	1	47	1	0	3	2	6	.25	15	.251	.303	.347
4 Min. YEARS		380	1406	403	88	5	33	600	204	224	108	4	269	20	1	20	15	15	.50	39	.287	.342	.427

Ryan Creek

Pitches: Right **Bats:** Right **Pos:** P | **Ht:** 6'1" **Wt:** 180 **Born:** 9/24/72 **Age:** 27

	HOW MUCH HE PITCHED						WHAT HE GAVE UP									THE RESULTS					
Year Team	Lg Org	G	GS	CG	GF	IP	BFP	H	R	ER	HR	SH	SF	HB	TBB	IBB	SO	WP	Bk	W	L	Pct.	ShO	Sv	ERA
1993 Astros	R Hou	12	11	2	1	69.1	291	53	26	18	0	1	5	4	30	0	62	6	0	7	3	.700	1	1	2.34
1994 Quad City	A Hou	21	15	0	3	74	356	86	62	41	6	3	5	14	41	2	66	9	3	3	5	.375	0	0	4.99
1995 Jackson	AA Hou	26	24	1	1	143.2	622	137	74	58	11	6	8	6	64	0	120	12	2	9	7	.563	1	0	3.63
1996 Jackson	AA Hou	27	26	1	1	142	674	139	95	83	9	3	7	11	121	0	119	14	1	7	15	.318	0	0	5.26
1997 Jackson	AA Hou	19	19	0	0	105	471	95	57	48	10	5	1	3	74	1	88	14	0	10	5	.667	0	0	4.11
1999 Kissimmee	A+ Hou	7	7	0	0	35.1	153	36	19	16	4	1	2	4	12	0	23	0	0	2	4	.333	0	0	4.08
Jackson	AA Hou	8	7	0	0	43.1	199	47	25	22	4	1	0	2	25	0	32	2	0	4	3	.571	0	0	4.57
New Orleans	AAA Hou	6	5	0	0	31.2	141	30	17	14	4	4	0	2	16	0	20	2	0	1	2	.333	0	0	3.98
6 Min. YEARS		126	114	4	6	644.1	2907	623	371	300	48	24	28	46	383	3	530	59	6	43	44	.494	2	1	4.19

Felipe Crespo

Bats: Both **Throws:** Right **Pos:** 1B   **Ht:** 5'11" **Wt:** 200 **Born:** 3/5/73 **Age:** 27

Year Team	Lg Org	G	AB	H	2B	3B	HR	TB	R	RBI	TBB	IBB	SO	HBP	SH	SF	SB	CS	SB%	GDP	Avg	OBP	SLG
1991 Medcine Hat	R+ Tor	49	184	57	11	4	4	88	40	31	25	0	31	3	2	2	6	4	.60	2	.310	.397	.478
1992 Myrtle Bch	A Tor	81	263	74	14	3	1	97	43	29	58	2	38	4	2	5	7	7	.50	1	.281	.412	.369
1993 Dunedin	A+ Tor	96	345	103	16	8	6	153	51	39	47	3	40	4	5	2	18	5	.78	9	.299	.387	.443
1994 Knoxville	AA Tor	129	502	135	30	4	8	197	74	49	57	3	95	2	4	1	20	8	.71	5	.269	.345	.392
1995 Syracuse	AAA Tor	88	347	102	20	5	13	171	56	41	41	4	56	2	1	1	12	7	.63	5	.294	.371	.493
1996 Dunedin	A+ Tor	9	34	11	1	0	2	18	3	6	2	1	3	0	0	0	1	3	.25	1	.324	.361	.529
Syracuse	AAA Tor	98	355	100	25	0	8	149	53	58	56	2	39	9	2	4	10	11	.48	7	.282	.389	.420
1997 Syracuse	AAA Tor	80	290	75	12	0	12	123	53	26	46	0	38	4	2	2	7	7	.50	1	.259	.365	.424
1999 Fresno	AAA SF	112	385	128	27	5	24	237	98	84	78	6	73	7	5	7	17	8	.68	10	.332	.447	.616
1996 Toronto	AL	22	49	9	4	0	0	13	6	4	12	0	13	3	0	0	1	0	1.00	0	.184	.375	.265
1997 Toronto	AL	12	28	8	0	1	1	13	3	5	2	0	4	0	1	0	0	0	.00	1	.286	.333	.464
1998 Toronto	AL	66	130	34	8	1	1	47	11	15	15	1	27	2	4	2	4	3	.57	1	.262	.342	.362
8 Min. YEARS		742	2705	785	156	29	78	1233	471	363	410	21	413	35	23	24	98	60	.62	41	.290	.388	.456
3 Maj. YEARS		100	207	51	12	2	2	73	20	24	29	1	44	5	5	2	5	3	.63	2	.246	.350	.353

Jack Cressend

Pitches: Right **Bats:** Right **Pos:** P   **Ht:** 6'1" **Wt:** 185 **Born:** 5/13/75 **Age:** 25

Year Team	Lg Org	G	GS	CG	GF	IP	BFP	H	R	ER	HR	SH	SF	HB	TBB	IBB	SO	WP	Bk	W	L	Pct.	ShO	Sv	ERA
1996 Lowell	A- Bos	9	8	0	1	45.2	189	37	15	12	0	2	2	4	17	1	57	6	1	3	2	.600	0	0	2.36
1997 Sarasota	A+ Bos	28	25	2	1	165.2	718	163	98	70	15	8	6	2	56	1	149	14	4	8	11	.421	1	0	3.80
1998 Trenton	AA Bos	29	29	1	0	149.1	646	168	86	72	13	10	2	5	55	0	130	6	0	10	11	.476	1	0	4.34
1999 Trenton	AA Bos	3	3	0	0	15	71	19	12	12	3	0	1	0	7	0	11	2	0	1	0	1.000	0	0	7.20
New Britain	AA Min	25	24	2	0	145	629	152	79	70	10	3	5	5	50	0	125	4	2	7	10	.412	2	0	4.34
4 Min. YEARS		94	89	5	2	520.2	2253	539	290	236	41	23	16	16	185	2	472	32	7	29	34	.460	4	0	4.08

Jason Crews

Pitches: Right **Bats:** Right **Pos:** P   **Ht:** 6'2" **Wt:** 205 **Born:** 8/28/73 **Age:** 26

Year Team	Lg Org	G	GS	CG	GF	IP	BFP	H	R	ER	HR	SH	SF	HB	TBB	IBB	SO	WP	Bk	W	L	Pct.	ShO	Sv	ERA
1996 Lethbridge	R+ Ari	25	1	0	19	39.2	164	30	12	11	2	2	3	0	15	1	37	3	0	1	1	.500	0	5	2.50
1997 South Bend	A Ari	50	0	0	32	82	354	70	39	29	5	4	3	2	27	7	74	4	1	4	6	.400	0	9	3.18
1998 High Desert	A+ Ari	48	0	0	14	86.1	384	100	62	40	4	0	3	5	22	1	58	12	2	7	7	.500	0	2	4.17
1999 South Bend	A Ari	9	0	0	8	13	56	11	6	3	0	1	1	1	2	0	14	2	0	0	2	.000	0	1	2.08
El Paso	AA Ari	35	2	0	9	55.2	261	73	47	35	7	1	2	2	23	2	30	7	0	3	4	.429	0	0	5.66
4 Min. YEARS		167	3	0	82	276.2	1219	292	166	118	18	8	12	10	89	11	213	28	3	15	20	.429	0	17	3.84

Bobby Cripps

Bats: Left **Throws:** Right **Pos:** DH   **Ht:** 6'2" **Wt:** 200 **Born:** 5/9/77 **Age:** 23

Year Team	Lg Org	G	AB	H	2B	3B	HR	TB	R	RBI	TBB	IBB	SO	HBP	SH	SF	SB	CS	SB%	GDP	Avg	OBP	SLG
1996 Great Falls	R+ LA	49	139	43	4	3	2	59	23	28	9	0	19	2	1	5	6	5	.55	5	.309	.348	.424
1997 Great Falls	R+ LA	47	145	45	6	5	4	73	19	25	7	1	26	3	1	2	4	4	.50	3	.310	.350	.503
St.Cathrnes	A- Tor	14	40	5	0	1	1	10	4	3	4	0	11	2	0	0	0	0	.00	1	.125	.239	.250
1998 Hagerstown	A Tor	123	423	112	17	3	29	222	64	88	41	3	123	7	5	4	2	3	.40	7	.265	.337	.525
1999 Dunedin	A+ Tor	5	16	1	0	0	0	1	1	1	1	0	7	0	0	0	0	0	.00	1	.063	.118	.063
St.Cathrnes	A- Tor	10	31	9	0	0	2	15	3	7	2	0	9	0	0	1	0	0	.00	0	.290	.324	.484
Knoxville	AA Tor	25	87	15	6	0	2	27	13	9	6	0	37	2	0	1	0	0	.00	0	.172	.240	.310
4 Min. YEARS		273	881	230	33	12	40	407	127	161	70	4	232	16	7	13	12	12	.50	17	.261	.322	.462

Andy Croghan

Pitches: Right **Bats:** Right **Pos:** P   **Ht:** 6'5" **Wt:** 220 **Born:** 10/26/69 **Age:** 30

Year Team	Lg Org	G	GS	CG	GF	IP	BFP	H	R	ER	HR	SH	SF	HB	TBB	IBB	SO	WP	Bk	W	L	Pct.	ShO	Sv	ERA
1991 Oneonta	A- NYY	14	14	0	0	78.1	352	92	59	49	6	1	1	2	28	0	54	5	0	5	4	.556	0	0	5.63
1992 Greensboro	A NYY	33	19	1	3	122.1	544	128	78	61	11	2	9	3	57	0	98	9	0	10	8	.556	0	0	4.49
1993 Pr William	A NYY	39	14	1	19	105	455	117	66	56	9	4	4	3	27	0	80	6	0	5	11	.313	0	1	4.80
1994 Albany-Colo	AA NYY	36	0	0	33	36.2	153	33	7	7	1	2	1	0	14	0	38	1	0	0	1	.000	0	16	1.72
Columbus	AAA NYY	21	0	0	17	24	110	25	11	11	6	5	0	0	13	1	28	3	0	2	2	.500	0	8	4.13
1995 Columbus	AAA NYY	20	0	0	13	25	113	21	10	10	1	0	0	1	22	0	22	1	2	1	1	.500	0	4	3.60
1996 Columbus	AAA NYY	14	0	0	3	22.1	108	27	24	21	6	3	1	2	13	0	21	3	0	2	0	1.000	0	0	8.46
Norwich	AA NYY	35	0	0	19	41	181	41	23	14	4	2	0	1	16	3	49	5	0	9	5	.643	0	4	3.07
1997 Norwich	AA NYY	42	1	0	18	67.2	308	72	48	43	9	1	1	3	36	2	85	3	0	2	1	.667	0	4	5.72
1999 Syracuse	AAA LA	2	0	0	2	3.1	12	0	0	0	0	1	1	0	2	0	4	0	0	0	0	.000	0	2	0.00
Albuquerque	AAA LA	35	0	0	5	41.2	175	40	18	18	5	0	0	1	11	0	91	0	0	2	1	.667	0	3	2.81
8 Min. YEARS		291	48	2	131	567.1	2515	599	342	285	58	21	22	17	242	6	510	36	2	38	34	.528	0	51	4.52

Brandon Cromer

Bats: Left **Throws:** Right **Pos:** 2B   **Ht:** 6'2" **Wt:** 175 **Born:** 1/25/74 **Age:** 26

Year Team	Lg Org	G	AB	H	2B	3B	HR	TB	R	RBI	TBB	IBB	SO	HBP	SH	SF	SB	CS	SB%	GDP	Avg	OBP	SLG
1992 Blue Jays	R Tor	49	180	51	12	3	1	72	26	21	14	0	26	5	2	2	7	8	.47	2	.283	.348	.400
1993 St.Cathrnes	A- Tor	75	278	64	9	2	5	92	29	20	21	2	64	1	3	1	2	4	.33	1	.230	.286	.331
1994 Hagerstown	A Tor	80	259	35	8	5	6	71	25	26	25	0	98	0	2	3	0	2	.00	4	.135	.209	.274

Year Team	Lg Org	G	AB	H	2B	3B	HR	TB	R	RBI	TBB	IBB	SO	HBP	SH	SF	SB	CS	SB%	GDP	Avg	OBP	SLG
								BATTING									BASERUNNING				PERCENTAGES		
1995 Dunedin	A+ Tor	106	329	78	11	3	6	113	40	43	43	3	84	5	5	3	0	5	.00	6	.237	.332	.343
1996 Knoxville	AA Tor	98	318	88	15	8	7	140	56	32	60	3	84	2	2	3	3	6	.33	2	.277	.392	.440
1997 Carolina	A Pit	55	193	44	12	4	4	76	23	14	29	0	50	0	4	2	1	5	.17	0	.228	.326	.394
Calgary	AAA Pit	68	228	53	15	2	8	96	30	36	19	2	46	0	1	3	3	1	.75	5	.232	.288	.421
1998 Portland	AA Fla	122	391	87	13	5	15	155	51	47	43	0	89	0	1	4	3	2	.60	12	.223	.297	.396
1999 Louisville	AAA Mil	115	330	71	12	1	24	157	46	61	40	5	103	2	1	0	6	0	1.00	1	.215	.304	.476
8 Min. YEARS		768	2506	571	107	33	76	972	326	300	294	15	644	15	21	21	25	33	.43	33	.228	.310	.388

D.T. Cromer

Bats: Left **Throws:** Left **Pos:** OF-1B **Ht:** 6'2" **Wt:** 190 **Born:** 3/19/71 **Age:** 29

Year Team	Lg Org	G	AB	H	2B	3B	HR	TB	R	RBI	TBB	IBB	SO	HBP	SH	SF	SB	CS	SB%	GDP	Avg	OBP	SLG
								BATTING									BASERUNNING				PERCENTAGES		
1992 Sou Oregon	A- Oak	50	168	35	7	0	4	54	17	26	13	1	34	1	1	2	4	3	.57	2	.208	.266	.321
1993 Madison	A Oak	98	321	84	20	4	4	124	37	41	22	0	72	1	7	2	8	6	.57	1	.262	.309	.386
1994 W Michigan	A Oak	102	349	89	20	5	10	149	50	58	33	1	76	4	3	2	11	10	.52	5	.255	.325	.427
1995 Modesto	A+ Oak	108	378	98	18	5	14	168	59	52	36	1	66	4	6	6	5	7	.42	10	.259	.325	.444
1996 Modesto	A+ Oak	124	505	166	40	10	30	316	100	130	32	4	67	6	3	4	20	7	.74	5	.329	.373	.626
1997 Huntsville	AA Oak	134	545	176	40	6	15	273	100	121	60	4	102	3	0	6	12	7	.63	8	.323	.389	.501
1998 Edmonton	AAA Oak	125	504	148	30	3	16	232	75	85	32	3	93	4	0	4	12	6	.67	9	.294	.338	.460
1999 Indianapols	AAA Cin	136	535	166	37	4	30	301	83	107	44	3	98	3	0	7	4	2	.67	12	.310	.362	.563
8 Min. YEARS		877	3305	962	212	37	123	1617	521	620	272	17	608	26	20	33	76	48	.61	52	.291	.347	.489

Dean Crow

Pitches: Right **Bats:** Left **Pos:** P **Ht:** 6'4" **Wt:** 215 **Born:** 8/21/72 **Age:** 27

Year Team	Lg Org	G	GS	CG	GF	IP	BFP	H	R	ER	HR	SH	SF	HB	TBB	IBB	SO	WP	Bk	W	L	Pct.	ShO	Sv	ERA
				HOW MUCH HE PITCHED							WHAT HE GAVE UP											THE RESULTS			
1993 Bellingham	A- Sea	25	0	0	12	47.2	190	31	14	10	1	1	2	0	21	1	38	0	0	5	3	.625	0	4	1.89
1994 Appleton	A Sea	16	0	0	8	15.1	80	25	15	12	4	2	3	1	7	4	11	1	0	2	4	.333	0	2	7.04
1995 Riverside	A+ Sea	51	0	0	47	61.2	249	54	21	18	1	3	2	3	13	0	46	2	0	3	4	.429	0	22	2.63
1996 Port City	AA Sea	60	0	0	49	68	285	64	35	23	4	5	1	1	20	1	43	6	0	2	3	.400	0	26	3.04
1997 Tacoma	AAA Sea	33	0	0	23	43.1	200	56	25	23	3	2	3	1	19	1	36	3	0	4	2	.667	0	7	4.78
Toledo	AAA Det	18	0	0	10	18.1	90	26	16	16	1	2	1	2	10	1	10	0	0	2	0	1.000	0	2	7.85
1998 Toledo	AAA Det	24	0	0	21	24.1	97	21	8	4	1	1	1	1	3	0	12	0	0	2	0	1.000	0	10	1.48
1999 New Orleans	AAA Hou	34	0	0	11	46	217	71	36	36	4	5	6	2	12	4	22	2	1	2	6	.250	0	3	7.04
1998 Detroit	AL	32	0	0	15	45.2	192	55	22	20	6	2	1	2	16	6	18	0	0	2	2	.500	0	1	3.94
7 Min. YEARS		261	0	0	181	324.2	1408	348	170	142	19	21	19	11	105	12	218	14	1	23	22	.511	0	76	3.94

Jim Crowell

Pitches: Left **Bats:** Right **Pos:** P **Ht:** 6'4" **Wt:** 230 **Born:** 5/14/74 **Age:** 26

Year Team	Lg Org	G	GS	CG	GF	IP	BFP	H	R	ER	HR	SH	SF	HB	TBB	IBB	SO	WP	Bk	W	L	Pct.	ShO	Sv	ERA
				HOW MUCH HE PITCHED							WHAT HE GAVE UP											THE RESULTS			
1995 Watertown	A- Cle	12	9	0	0	56.2	241	50	22	18	1	0	2	1	27	1	48	2	1	5	2	.714	0	0	2.86
1996 Columbus	A Cle	28	28	3	0	165.1	710	163	89	76	16	9	5	9	69	0	104	12	0	7	10	.412	0	0	4.14
1997 Kinston	A+ Cle	17	17	0	0	114	461	96	41	30	4	3	2	8	26	0	94	3	0	9	4	.692	0	0	2.37
Akron	AA Cle	3	3	0	0	18	82	13	12	9	2	1	1	1	11	0	7	1	0	1	1	.000	0	0	4.50
Chattanooga	AA Cin	3	3	0	0	19	75	19	6	6	2	1	1	0	5	0	14	0	0	2	1	.667	0	0	2.84
Indianapols	AAA Cin	3	3	1	0	19.2	85	19	7	6	1	0	2	0	8	0	6	1	0	1	1	.500	1	0	2.75
1998 Chattanooga	AA Cin	5	5	0	0	24.1	129	38	27	23	2	0	3	0	17	0	10	2	2	0	4	.000	0	0	8.51
Chstn-WV	A Cin	5	5	0	0	15	83	28	23	22	1	0	2	2	9	0	9	1	0	0	4	.000	0	0	13.20
Indianapols	AAA Cin	1	1	0	0	4	19	7	3	3	0	0	0	0	0	0	2	0	0	0	0	.000	0	0	6.75
1999 Chattanooga	AA Cin	27	27	0	0	148.1	690	173	98	84	12	5	6	4	85	0	80	3	0	10	5	.667	1	0	5.10
1997 Cincinnati	NL	2	1	0	1	6.1	36	12	7	7	2	2	0	0	5	0	3	0	0	0	1	.000	0	0	9.95
5 Min. YEARS		104	101	4	0	584.1	2573	606	328	277	41	19	24	25	257	1	374	25	3	35	31	.530	2	0	4.27

Charlie Cruz

Pitches: Left **Bats:** Left **Pos:** P **Ht:** 5'10" **Wt:** 175 **Born:** 10/22/73 **Age:** 26

Year Team	Lg Org	G	GS	CG	GF	IP	BFP	H	R	ER	HR	SH	SF	HB	TBB	IBB	SO	WP	Bk	W	L	Pct.	ShO	Sv	ERA
				HOW MUCH HE PITCHED							WHAT HE GAVE UP											THE RESULTS			
1995 Eugene	A- Atl	15	15	0	0	81.1	348	68	34	23	2	2	3	4	36	2	90	2	1	6	7	.462	0	0	2.55
1996 Durham	A+ Atl	8	0	0	1	18.2	82	15	12	12	2	0	0	3	7	0	12	0	0	1	1	.500	0	0	5.79
Macon	A Atl	35	0	0	18	77.1	338	70	40	32	8	5	1	5	34	3	89	4	1	5	4	.556	0	4	3.72
1997 Durham	A+ Atl	49	0	0	23	85.1	379	80	37	30	5	7	4	5	44	3	76	6	0	5	0	1.000	0	1	3.16
1998 Greenville	AA Atl	49	1	0	16	73	315	80	33	27	6	4	3	1	31	3	57	5	1	3	3	.500	0	4	3.33
1999 Greenville	AA Atl	11	0	0	4	15.2	77	23	6	6	1	0	2	1	9	1	11	0	0	1	0	1.000	0	0	3.45
5 Min. YEARS		167	16	0	62	351.1	1539	336	162	130	24	18	13	19	161	12	335	17	3	21	15	.583	0	10	3.33

Cirilo Cruz

Bats: Right **Throws:** Right **Pos:** OF **Ht:** 6'0" **Wt:** 185 **Born:** 5/29/75 **Age:** 25

Year Team	Lg Org	G	AB	H	2B	3B	HR	TB	R	RBI	TBB	IBB	SO	HBP	SH	SF	SB	CS	SB%	GDP	Avg	OBP	SLG
								BATTING									BASERUNNING				PERCENTAGES		
1995 Mariners	R Sea	39	146	45	8	0	0	53	22	20	16	0	37	3	2	0	0	2	.00	2	.308	.388	.363
1996 Everett	A- Sea	44	163	44	6	0	0	50	12	21	8	0	34	2	0	1	1	5	.17	3	.270	.310	.307
1997 Wisconsin	A Sea	69	241	72	12	1	0	86	26	19	21	1	50	4	13	1	1	6	.14	7	.299	.363	.357
Lancaster	A+ Sea	43	152	41	10	1	1	56	22	25	24	0	33	6	0	1	0	3	.00	2	.270	.388	.368
1998 Lancaster	A+ Sea	134	546	170	40	1	7	233	86	104	56	3	122	8	1	7	2	2	.50	12	.311	.379	.427
1999 New Haven	AA Sea	18	57	9	3	0	0	12	5	9	10	0	13	2	0	0	0	0	.00	0	.158	.300	.211

Year Team	Lg Org	G	AB	H	2B	3B	HR	TB	R	RBI	TBB	IBB	SO	HBP	SH	SF	SB	CS	SB%	GDP	Avg	OBP	SLG
								BATTING									BASERUNNING				PERCENTAGES		
Lancaster	A+ Sea	94	342	85	12	1	12	135	51	44	28	1	73	4	3	1	1	1	.50	4	.249	.312	.395
5 Min. YEARS		441	1647	466	91	4	20	625	224	242	163	5	362	29	19	12	5	19	.21	32	.283	.355	.379

Luis Cruz

Bats: Right **Throws:** Right **Pos:** 2B **Ht:** 6'0" **Wt:** 180 **Born:** 1/21/77 **Age:** 23

Year Team	Lg Org	G	AB	H	2B	3B	HR	TB	R	RBI	TBB	IBB	SO	HBP	SH	SF	SB	CS	SB%	GDP	Avg	OBP	SLG
								BATTING									BASERUNNING				PERCENTAGES		
1997 Devil Rays	R TB	34	116	42	8	2	4	66	25	20	16	0	26	0	0	2	17	4	.81	3	.362	.433	.569
Princeton	R+ TB	18	78	22	2	0	3	33	16	14	5	0	16	0	0	3	2	2	.50	2	.282	.314	.423
1998 Chston-SC	A TB	34	137	36	5	1	1	36	15	11	11	0	28	0	1	0	4	1	.80	1	.190	.250	.263
Hudson Val	A- TB	63	230	51	4	3	7	82	36	32	19	1	46	2	6	1	4	5	.44	7	.222	.286	.357
1999 Orlando	AA TB	13	32	9	2	0	0	11	2	1	1	0	6	0	0	0	0	0	.00	1	.281	.303	.344
St. Pete	A+ TB	58	218	48	5	0	2	59	25	17	10	0	38	1	3	1	1	2	.33	5	.220	.257	.271
3 Min. YEARS		220	811	198	26	6	17	287	119	95	62	1	160	3	10	7	28	14	.67	19	.244	.298	.354

Trent Cuevas

Bats: Right **Throws:** Right **Pos:** 3B **Ht:** 5'11" **Wt:** 170 **Born:** 12/25/76 **Age:** 23

Year Team	Lg Org	G	AB	H	2B	3B	HR	TB	R	RBI	TBB	IBB	SO	HBP	SH	SF	SB	CS	SB%	GDP	Avg	OBP	SLG
								BATTING									BASERUNNING				PERCENTAGES		
1995 Yakima	A- LA	38	123	25	7	0	1	35	13	8	14	0	22	0	1	1	3	4	.43	3	.203	.283	.285
1996 Savannah	A LA	15	46	7	1	0	0	8	2	6	0	0	14	0	0	2	0	0	.00	0	.152	.146	.174
Great Falls	R+ LA	51	155	40	12	1	3	63	24	20	11	0	30	1	1	3	2	5	.29	2	.258	.306	.406
1997 Savannah	A LA	90	313	73	10	3	10	119	42	41	13	1	59	5	1	2	3	1	.75	10	.233	.273	.380
1998 Vero Beach	A+ LA	92	324	84	21	2	5	124	42	41	22	1	52	3	2	1	3	0	1.00	11	.259	.311	.383
Albuquerque	AAA LA	5	18	6	1	0	0	7	3	4	0	0	1	0	1	1	0	0	.00	0	.333	.316	.389
1999 San Antonio	AA LA	2	2	1	0	0	0	1	0	0	0	0	0	0	0	0	0	0	.00	0	.500	.500	.500
5 Min. YEARS		293	981	236	52	6	19	357	126	120	60	2	178	9	6	10	11	10	.52	26	.241	.288	.364

Chris Cumberland

Pitches: Left **Bats:** Right **Pos:** P **Ht:** 6'1" **Wt:** 189 **Born:** 1/15/73 **Age:** 27

Year Team	Lg Org	G	GS	CG	GF	IP	BFP	H	R	ER	HR	SH	SF	HB	TBB	IBB	SO	WP	Bk	W	L	Pct.	ShO	Sv	ERA
				HOW MUCH HE PITCHED							WHAT HE GAVE UP											THE RESULTS			
1993 Oneonta	A- NYY	15	15	0	0	89	393	109	43	33	2	1	5	0	28	0	62	6	2	4	4	.500	0	0	3.34
1994 Greensboro	A NYY	22	22	1	0	137.2	559	123	55	45	9	4	2	4	41	0	95	11	2	14	5	.737	1	0	2.94
1995 Yankees	R NYY	4	4	0	0	7	26	3	1	1	0	0	0	0	1	0	7	0	0	0	1	.000	0	0	1.29
Tampa	A+ NYY	5	5	0	0	24.2	104	28	10	5	1	1	0	1	5	0	10	1	0	1	2	.333	0	0	1.82
1996 Columbus	AAA NYY	12	12	1	0	58	272	86	45	42	9	4	1	4	23	0	35	3	0	2	7	.222	0	0	6.52
Norwich	AA NYY	16	16	2	0	95.2	427	112	73	56	13	2	5	4	37	2	44	4	0	5	7	.417	1	0	5.27
1997 Norwich	AA NYY	25	25	3	0	154.2	686	188	100	69	12	5	3	5	59	1	81	10	4	11	10	.524	1	0	4.02
1998 New Britain	AA Min	1	1	0	0	5.2	22	5	2	2	0	0	0	0	2	0	2	2	0	1	0	1.000	0	0	3.18
New Britain	AA Min	37	2	0	10	54.2	220	44	24	16	1	1	2	1	17	2	48	6	0	3	4	.429	0	1	2.63
Salt Lake	AAA Min	17	1	1	4	30.1	142	37	21	20	2	3	1	1	18	1	19	5	3	3	2	.600	0	0	5.93
1999 Trenton	AA Bos	14	0	0	6	21	84	12	1	1	0	1	1	0	13	1	18	1	0	2	0	1.000	0	1	0.43
Pawtucket	AAA Bos	36	1	0	16	62.2	266	56	33	31	4	2	3	2	30	0	35	4	0	4	3	.571	0	0	4.45
7 Min. YEARS		204	104	8	36	741	3201	803	408	321	53	24	23	21	274	7	456	53	11	50	45	.526	4	2	3.90

John Cummings

Pitches: Left **Bats:** Left **Pos:** P **Ht:** 6'3" **Wt:** 205 **Born:** 5/10/69 **Age:** 31

Year Team	Lg Org	G	GS	CG	GF	IP	BFP	H	R	ER	HR	SH	SF	HB	TBB	IBB	SO	WP	Bk	W	L	Pct.	ShO	Sv	ERA
				HOW MUCH HE PITCHED							WHAT HE GAVE UP											THE RESULTS			
1990 Bellingham	A- Sea	6	6	0	0	34	129	25	11	8	1	1	1	0	8	0	39	2	3	1	1	.500	0	0	2.12
San Berndno	A+ Sea	7	7	1	0	40.2	186	47	27	19	3	0	1	0	20	0	30	3	0	2	4	.333	0	0	4.20
1991 San Berndno	A+ Sea	29	20	0	2	124	567	129	79	56	7	1	6	3	61	1	120	15	4	4	10	.286	0	1	4.06
1992 Peninsula	A+ Sea	27	27	4	0	168.1	712	149	71	48	11	7	5	10	63	6	144	4	1	16	6	.727	1	0	2.57
1993 Jacksnville	AA Sea	7	7	1	0	45.2	194	50	24	16	1	2	0	1	9	0	35	1	2	2	2	.500	0	0	3.15
Calgary	AAA Sea	11	10	0	0	65.1	290	69	40	30	6	0	1	2	21	2	42	7	0	3	4	.429	0	0	4.13
1994 Appleton	A Sea	1	1	0	0	3	11	2	1	1	0	0	0	0	0	0	6	0	1	0	0	.000	0	0	3.00
Calgary	AAA Sea	1	1	0	0	6	23	3	1	1	1	0	0	0	2	0	4	0	0	1	0	1.000	0	0	1.50
Riverside	A+ Sea	1	1	0	0	2.2	14	5	2	2	0	0	0	0	1	0	2	0	0	0	1	.000	0	0	6.75
1995 Tacoma	AAA Sea	1	1	0	0	2.1	16	6	4	2	1	0	0	0	3	0	3	0	0	0	1	.000	0	0	7.71
San Antonio	AA LA	6	5	0	0	27.1	113	28	13	12	0	2	1	1	7	0	13	3	2	2	0	1.000	0	0	3.95
1996 Albuquerque	AAA LA	27	9	0	8	78.1	342	91	47	36	5	5	4	3	28	1	49	3	0	2	6	.250	0	2	4.14
1997 Toledo	AAA Det	19	0	0	5	16.1	70	13	6	5	2	2	2	1	6	1	7	0	0	2	1	.667	0	0	2.76
1998 Buffalo	AAA Cle	21	0	0	7	18.2	88	25	15	12	3	1	0	1	4	0	15	2	0	0	1	.000	0	0	5.79
Pawtucket	AAA Bos	10	8	0	1	38	170	46	28	26	3	1	0	3	12	0	17	2	0	0	5	.000	0	0	6.16
1999 Tucson	AAA Ari	11	1	0	2	21.2	103	33	24	20	5	0	2	0	9	0	18	1	1	1	1	.500	0	0	8.31
1993 Seattle	AL	10	8	1	0	46.1	207	59	34	31	6	0	2	2	16	2	19	1	1	0	6	.000	0	0	6.02
1994 Seattle	AL	17	8	0	2	64	283	66	43	40	7	1	0	0	27	2	00	0	1	0	1	.000	0	0	5.62
1995 Seattle	AL	4	0	0	0	5.1	30	8	8	7	0	1	2	0	7	2	4	4	1	0	0	.000	0	0	11.81
Los Angeles	NL	35	0	0	11	39	165	38	16	13	3	2	1	0	10	4	21	1	0	3	1	.750	0	0	3.00
1996 Los Angeles	NL	4	0	0	1	5.1	30	12	7	4	1	1	1	0	2	1	5	0	0	1	0	1.000	0	0	6.75
Detroit	AL	21	0	0	7	31.2	152	36	20	18	3	2	1	2	20	3	24	1	0	3	3	.500	0	0	5.12
1997 Detroit	AL	19	0	0	2	21.2	103	32	22	15	3	2	0	0	14	1	8	0	0	2	0	1.000	0	0	5.47
10 Min. YEARS		185	104	6	25	692.1	3018	721	393	294	49	22	23	25	254	11	544	43	14	34	45	.430	1	3	3.82
5 Maj. YEARS		110	16	1	23	216.1	988	251	150	128	23	9	10	4	106	15	114	13	3	10	15	.400	0	0	5.33

66

Ryan Cummings

Pitches: Right **Bats:** Right **Pos:** P   **Ht:** 6'2" **Wt:** 210 **Born:** 6/3/76 **Age:** 24

Year Team	Lg Org	G	GS	CG	GF	IP	BFP	H	R	ER	HR	SH	SF	HB	TBB	IBB	SO	WP	Bk	W	L	Pct.	ShO	Sv	ERA
1997 Boise	A- Ana	14	13	0	0	70	297	73	38	24	3	2	1	7	10	0	79	4	2	6	2	.750	0	0	3.09
1998 Lk Elsinore	A+ Ana	1	1	0	0	5	23	5	3	3	0	0	0	2	3	0	4	1	0	0	1	.000	0	0	5.40
1999 Cedar Rapds	A Ana	19	19	3	0	121	511	104	69	59	14	4	10	6	35	0	97	18	2	5	8	.385	1	0	4.39
Lk Elsinore	A+ Ana	7	7	0	0	46.2	203	43	19	17	3	1	0	4	15	1	41	1	0	3	1	.750	0	0	3.28
Erie	AA Ana	3	3	0	0	17.2	81	18	12	10	3	0	1	3	10	0	7	0	0	1	1	.500	0	0	5.09
3 Min. YEARS		44	43	3	0	260.1	1115	243	141	113	23	7	12	22	73	1	228	24	4	15	13	.536	1	0	3.91

John Curl

Bats: Left **Throws:** Right **Pos:** OF   **Ht:** 6'3" **Wt:** 205 **Born:** 11/10/72 **Age:** 27

Year Team	Lg Org	G	AB	H	2B	3B	HR	TB	R	RBI	TBB	IBB	SO	HBP	SH	SF	SB	CS	SB%	GDP	Avg	OBP	SLG
1995 Medicne Hat	R+ Tor	69	270	86	26	1	7	135	47	63	31	8	61	0	0	3	5	1	.83	11	.319	.385	.500
1996 Dunedin	A+ Tor	125	447	110	20	2	18	188	52	62	44	1	133	1	2	5	7	4	.64	6	.246	.312	.421
1997 Knoxville	AA Tor	10	29	6	1	0	0	7	0	1	3	0	6	0	0	0	0	0	.00	0	.207	.281	.241
Dunedin	A+ Tor	74	231	59	14	0	15	118	36	48	24	4	53	0	0	1	3	2	.60	4	.255	.324	.511
1998 Mobile	AA SD	104	363	100	22	2	16	174	47	66	40	1	108	0	0	1	6	1	.86	4	.275	.347	.479
1999 Mobile	AA SD	133	474	135	30	3	22	237	79	76	77	3	137	1	0	8	9	5	.64	0	.285	.380	.500
5 Min. YEARS		515	1814	496	113	8	78	859	261	316	219	17	498	2	2	18	30	13	.70	25	.273	.349	.474

Milt Cuyler

Bats: Both **Throws:** Right **Pos:** OF   **Ht:** 5'10" **Wt:** 185 **Born:** 10/7/68 **Age:** 31

Year Team	Lg Org	G	AB	H	2B	3B	HR	TB	R	RBI	TBB	IBB	SO	HBP	SH	SF	SB	CS	SB%	GDP	Avg	OBP	SLG
1986 Bristol	R+ Det	45	174	40	3	5	1	56	24	11	15	0	35	5	2	0	12	4	.75	1	.230	.309	.322
1987 Fayettevlle	A Det	94	366	107	8	4	2	129	65	34	34	4	78	7	17	2	27	13	.68	3	.292	.362	.352
1988 Lakeland	A+ Det	132	483	143	11	3	2	166	100	32	71	2	83	4	14	1	50	25	.67	3	.296	.390	.344
1989 Toledo	AAA Det	24	83	14	3	2	0	21	4	6	8	0	27	0	3	1	4	1	.80	1	.169	.239	.253
London	AA Det	98	366	96	8	7	7	139	69	34	47	2	74	4	4	0	32	5	.86	2	.262	.353	.380
1990 Toledo	AAA Det	124	461	119	11	8	2	152	77	42	60	1	77	5	7	2	52	14	.79	6	.258	.348	.330
1994 Toledo	AAA Det	15	64	22	4	1	0	28	8	2	3	0	11	1	0	0	4	4	.50	0	.344	.382	.438
1995 Toledo	AAA Det	54	203	62	10	4	6	98	33	28	20	0	40	5	0	4	6	7	.46	1	.305	.375	.483
1998 Nashua	IND —	73	249	77	18	6	6	125	62	33	39	1	42	6	7	1	21	8	.72	4	.309	.414	.502
Oklahoma	AAA Tex	2	6	0	0	0	0	0	0	0	2	0	4	0	0	0	0	1	.00	0	.000	.250	.000
1999 Tulsa	AA Tex	36	138	45	4	4	0	57	30	13	18	1	29	2	1	0	7	6	.54	2	.326	.411	.413
Oklahoma	AAA Tex	20	52	9	4	0	0	13	3	6	2	0	12	0	1	0	1	1	.50	0	.173	.204	.250
1990 Detroit	AL	19	51	13	3	1	0	18	8	8	5	0	10	0	2	1	1	2	.33	1	.255	.316	.353
1991 Detroit	AL	154	475	122	15	7	3	160	77	33	52	0	92	5	12	2	41	10	.80	4	.257	.335	.337
1992 Detroit	AL	89	291	70	11	1	3	92	39	28	10	0	62	4	8	0	8	5	.62	4	.241	.275	.316
1993 Detroit	AL	82	249	53	11	7	0	78	46	19	19	0	53	3	4	1	13	2	.87	2	.213	.276	.313
1994 Detroit	AL	48	116	28	3	1	1	36	20	11	13	0	21	1	2	2	5	3	.63	3	.241	.318	.310
1995 Detroit	AL	41	88	18	1	4	0	27	15	5	8	0	16	0	2	0	2	1	.67	0	.205	.271	.307
1996 Boston	AL	50	110	22	1	2	2	33	19	12	13	0	19	3	7	1	7	3	.70	1	.200	.299	.300
1998 Texas	AL	7	6	3	2	0	1	8	3	3	1	0	0	0	0	0	0	0	.00	0	.500	.571	1.333
9 Min. YEARS		717	2645	734	84	44	26	984	475	241	319	11	512	39	57	11	216	89	.71	23	.278	.362	.372
8 Maj. YEARS		490	1386	329	47	23	10	452	227	119	121	0	273	16	37	7	77	26	.75	15	.237	.305	.326

Derek Dace

Pitches: Left **Bats:** Left **Pos:** P   **Ht:** 6'7" **Wt:** 200 **Born:** 4/11/75 **Age:** 25

Year Team	Lg Org	G	GS	CG	GF	IP	BFP	H	R	ER	HR	SH	SF	HB	TBB	IBB	SO	WP	Bk	W	L	Pct.	ShO	Sv	ERA
1994 Astros	R Hou	11	11	1	0	59	245	55	26	22	2	5	2	1	21	0	52	2	3	2	3	.400	0	0	3.36
1995 Astros	R Hou	11	10	2	1	69.1	274	60	20	15	2	4	3	0	6	0	77	5	2	3	4	.429	1	0	1.95
Kissimmee	A+ Hou	1	1	0	0	2.2	17	4	5	5	0	0	1	0	5	0	1	0	0	0	1	.000	0	0	16.88
1996 Kissimmee	A+ Hou	12	0	0	3	18.1	73	19	6	6	0	0	0	0	7	0	11	1	0	0	0	.000	0	1	2.95
Jackson	AA Hou	1	1	0	0	4	21	5	1	1	1	0	0	0	5	0	0	0	0	0	0	.000	0	0	2.25
Auburn	A- Hou	15	15	0	0	97	400	89	41	35	7	2	1	2	35	2	87	1	0	9	4	.692	0	0	3.25
1997 Lakeland	A+ Det	2	0	0	1	2.1	9	2	1	1	1	0	0	0	1	0	0	0	0	0	0	.000	0	0	3.86
W Michigan	A Det	10	2	0	3	25	100	23	2	2	0	0	0	1	4	0	24	0	0	1	0	1.000	0	0	0.72
Toledo	AAA Det	5	0	0	3	10	48	13	8	4	0	1	0	1	6	0	6	1	0	0	0	.000	0	0	3.60
1998 Jacksnville	AA Det	40	0	0	15	67	277	51	32	31	8	0	2	2	29	0	48	2	0	5	3	.625	0	3	4.16
1999 El Paso	AA Ari	40	0	0	14	52	232	58	33	30	4	2	3	3	23	2	34	0	0	2	2	.500	0	0	5.19
6 Min. YEARS		148	40	3	40	406.2	1696	379	175	152	25	13	9	11	142	4	340	12	5	22	17	.564	1	6	3.36

Brian Dallimore

Bats: Right **Throws:** Right **Pos:** 2B   **Ht:** 6'1" **Wt:** 185 **Born:** 11/15/73 **Age:** 26

Year Team	Lg Org	G	AB	H	2B	3B	HR	TB	R	RBI	TBB	IBB	SO	HBP	SH	SF	SB	CS	SB%	GDP	Avg	OBP	SLG
1996 Auburn	A- Hou	74	290	77	17	3	5	115	50	30	18	0	38	10	0	4	7	5	.58	5	.266	.326	.397
1997 Quad City	A Hou	130	492	128	23	3	6	175	80	48	38	0	76	20	0	6	24	8	.75	19	.260	.335	.356
Kissimmee	A+ Hou	1	3	0	0	0	0	0	0	0	0	0	2	0	0	0	0	0	.00	0	.000	.000	.000
1998 Kissimmee	A+ Hou	62	240	61	11	1	0	74	34	19	19	0	42	5	4	1	7	5	.58	6	.254	.321	.308
1999 Kissimmee	A+ Hou	19	74	20	2	0	0	22	12	3	4	0	10	3	1	1	2	1	.67	1	.270	.329	.297
Jackson	AA Hou	70	251	67	13	1	5	97	38	19	16	0	44	10	2	1	13	3	.81	12	.267	.335	.386
4 Min. YEARS		356	1350	353	66	8	16	483	214	119	95	0	212	48	13	12	53	22	.71	43	.261	.330	.358

Jeff D'Amico

Pitches: Right Bats: Right Pos: P Ht: 6'3" Wt: 195 Born: 11/9/74 Age: 25

Year Team	Lg Org	G	GS	CG	GF	IP	BFP	H	R	ER	HR	SH	SF	HB	TBB	IBB	SO	WP	Bk	W	L	Pct.	ShO	Sv	ERA
1996 Athletics	R Oak	8	0	0	2	19	72	14	3	3	0	0	0	3	2	0	15	0	1	3	0	1.000	0	0	1.42
Modesto	A+ Oak	1	0	0	0	1	7	3	3	2	0	0	0	0	1	0	0	0	0	0	0	.000	0	0	18.00
1997 Modesto	A+ Oak	20	13	0	5	97	442	115	57	41	5	1	4	7	34	1	89	9	1	7	3	.700	0	1	3.80
Edmonton	AAA Oak	10	7	0	1	30.2	141	42	29	28	7	1	2	2	6	0	19	3	0	1	2	.333	0	1	8.22
1998 Athletics	R Oak	4	1	0	0	9.1	34	6	4	4	2	0	0	1	1	0	8	0	0	0	0	.000	0	0	3.86
Huntsville	AA Oak	24	8	0	4	61	295	77	57	52	12	1	6	3	34	0	46	6	5	5	5	.500	0	0	7.67
1999 Midland	AA Oak	32	0	0	18	45.1	207	53	31	25	4	3	3	3	16	2	38	3	0	1	2	.333	0	3	4.96
Vancouver	AAA Oak	14	0	0	11	17	75	16	6	5	1	1	0	0	10	1	10	2	0	2	2	.500	0	3	2.65
Omaha	AAA KC	12	0	0	10	18.2	88	29	13	9	1	0	0	1	3	0	12	3	1	1	3	.250	0	2	4.34
4 Min. YEARS		125	29	0	51	299	1361	355	203	169	32	7	15	21	106	4	237	26	8	20	17	.541	0	10	5.09

David Daniels

Pitches: Right Bats: Right Pos: P Ht: 6'2" Wt: 184 Born: 7/25/73 Age: 26

Year Team	Lg Org	G	GS	CG	GF	IP	BFP	H	R	ER	HR	SH	SF	HB	TBB	IBB	SO	WP	Bk	W	L	Pct.	ShO	Sv	ERA
1995 Johnstown	IND —	28	0	0	9	44	186	36	22	16	1	3	1	4	15	1	40	1	3	4	1	.800	0	3	3.27
1996 Augusta	A Pit	11	0	0	7	12.1	58	21	8	7	0	1	0	0	3	1	14	0	1	0	1	.000	0	3	5.11
Erie	A- Pit	31	0	0	19	36.1	150	33	13	11	3	3	1	4	5	3	45	0	0	1	3	.250	0	7	2.72
1997 Augusta	A Pit	44	0	0	39	55	231	51	22	16	0	1	0	1	13	3	51	0	1	6	3	.667	0	18	2.62
Lynchburg	A+ Pit	10	0	0	8	10	36	6	2	2	1	0	0	0	1	0	6	1	0	1	1	.500	0	4	1.80
1998 Lynchburg	A+ Pit	14	0	0	12	18.1	65	9	3	3	2	1	0	0	3	0	19	0	0	0	0	.000	0	3	1.47
Carolina	AA Pit	35	0	0	32	39.1	163	34	15	13	0	1	3	2	16	1	37	2	2	4	3	.571	0	16	2.97
Nashville	AAA Pit	2	0	0	1	1	4	0	0	0	0	0	0	0	2	0	1	0	0	0	0	.000	0	0	0.00
1999 Altoona	AA Pit	55	0	0	29	67.1	276	55	21	20	6	3	1	2	19	2	63	1	0	2	2	.500	0	8	2.67
5 Min. YEARS		230	0	0	155	283.2	1169	245	105	88	13	13	6	13	77	11	276	5	7	18	14	.563	0	68	2.79

John Daniels

Pitches: Right Bats: Both Pos: P Ht: 6'3" Wt: 185 Born: 2/7/74 Age: 26

Year Team	Lg Org	G	GS	CG	GF	IP	BFP	H	R	ER	HR	SH	SF	HB	TBB	IBB	SO	WP	Bk	W	L	Pct.	ShO	Sv	ERA
1993 Mariners	R Sea	13	8	0	0	53	222	46	30	20	0	1	4	5	13	0	50	8	2	3	4	.429	0	0	3.40
1994 Bellingham	A- Sea	20	2	0	3	41.1	196	49	22	17	4	2	2	4	21	0	42	3	2	2	2	.500	0	1	3.70
1995 Wisconsin	A Sea	39	0	0	19	74.1	315	63	28	22	5	0	2	6	22	2	60	2	0	4	5	.444	0	7	2.66
1996 Lancaster	A+ Sea	43	0	0	23	95.1	412	91	51	35	9	3	2	8	30	1	100	3	0	3	5	.375	0	8	3.30
1997 St. Pete	A+ TB	55	0	0	44	61.1	255	53	24	18	4	3	1	3	14	3	72	3	0	4	4	.500	0	29	2.64
1998 Durham	AAA TB	4	0	0	1	9.2	34	4	2	2	1	0	1	0	3	0	9	1	0	2	0	1.000	0	1	1.86
Orlando	AA TB	11	0	0	3	18.2	82	14	12	11	4	0	3	2	9	3	19	0	0	1	2	.333	0	5	5.30
St. Pete	A+ TB	34	0	0	33	40.2	170	31	12	8	3	3	1	4	11	1	46	4	1	4	2	.667	0	19	1.77
1999 Durham	AAA TB	21	0	0	8	35	154	37	19	19	2	1	1	4	9	0	25	2	0	2	0	1.000	0	0	4.89
Orlando	AA TB	38	0	0	30	52	208	33	14	11	2	1	3	4	15	3	40	3	1	3	2	.600	0	14	1.90
7 Min. YEARS		278	10	0	164	481.1	2048	421	214	163	34	14	20	40	147	13	463	29	6	28	26	.519	0	79	3.05

Tony Darden

Bats: Right Throws: Right Pos: 3B Ht: 6'0" Wt: 180 Born: 5/29/74 Age: 26

Year Team	Lg Org	G	AB	H	2B	3B	HR	TB	R	RBI	TBB	IBB	SO	HBP	SH	SF	SB	CS	SB%	GDP	Avg	OBP	SLG
1994 Elmira	A- Fla	50	175	46	8	5	1	67	34	20	18	0	30	6	1	0	6	3	.67	5	.263	.352	.383
1995 Kane County	A Fla	86	286	82	15	5	3	116	42	31	40	1	40	8	1	2	5	5	.50	6	.287	.387	.406
1996 Brevard Cty	A+ Fla	108	390	94	21	4	1	126	37	43	28	1	55	7	4	8	6	11	.35	7	.241	.298	.323
1997 Brevard Cty	A+ Fla	107	392	112	32	4	6	170	50	48	32	0	72	4	1	3	7	3	.70	12	.286	.343	.434
1998 Norfolk	AAA NYM	1	0	0	0	0	0	0	0	0	1	0	0	0	0	0	0	0	.000	0	.000	1.000	.000
Binghamton	AA NYM	107	320	92	19	4	3	128	38	36	25	2	57	10	0	6	5	6	.45	7	.288	.352	.400
1999 Norfolk	AAA NYM	18	33	4	1	0	0	5	4	3	7	1	4	0	0	1	2	2	.50	2	.121	.268	.152
Binghamton	AA NYM	49	164	58	8	1	5	83	25	23	19	2	30	8	0	0	5	4	.56	3	.354	.445	.506
6 Min. YEARS		526	1760	488	104	23	19	695	230	204	170	7	288	43	7	20	36	34	.51	42	.277	.352	.395

David Darwin

Pitches: Left Bats: Left Pos: P Ht: 6'0" Wt: 185 Born: 12/19/73 Age: 26

Year Team	Lg Org	G	GS	CG	GF	IP	BFP	H	R	ER	HR	SH	SF	HB	TBB	IBB	SO	WP	Bk	W	L	Pct.	ShO	Sv	ERA
1996 Fayetteville	A Det	17	9	0	0	59	234	54	22	21	2	0	1	2	12	1	49	5	3	5	2	.714	0	0	3.20
1997 W Michigan	A Det	21	4	0	10	40.1	164	23	7	4	2	0	2	2	20	2	31	0	1	1	0	1.000	0	3	0.89
Lakeland	A+ Det	12	12	1	0	82.2	326	70	23	23	2	3	2	0	18	0	41	1	1	10	1	.909	0	0	2.50
1998 Toledo	AAA Det	1	1	1	0	7	25	4	1	1	1	0	0	1	0	0	5	0	0	1	0	1.000	0	0	1.29
Jacksnville	AA Det	24	23	2	1	139.2	612	152	94	83	22	3	2	6	52	0	76	2	2	12	6	.667	1	0	3.35
1999 Jacksnville	AA Det	28	28	3	0	187.1	813	194	95	74	19	1	6	11	58	1	100	2	0	14	12	.538	1	0	3.56
4 Min. YEARS		103	77	7	11	516	2174	497	242	206	48	7	13	22	160	4	302	10	7	43	21	.672	2	3	3.59

Jeff Darwin

Pitches: Right Bats: Right Pos: P Ht: 6'3" Wt: 180 Born: 7/6/69 Age: 30

Year Team	Lg Org	G	GS	CG	GF	IP	BFP	H	R	ER	HR	SH	SF	HB	TBB	IBB	SO	WP	Bk	W	L	Pct.	ShO	Sv	ERA
1989 Bellingham	A- Sea	12	12	0	0	64	286	73	42	35	3	1	3	3	24	0	47	4	0	1	7	.125	0	0	4.92
1990 Peninsula	A+ Sea	25	25	1	0	150.1	651	153	86	67	12	6	2	4	57	0	89	6	9	8	14	.364	0	0	4.01

68

(continued)

Year Team	Lg Org	G	GS	CG	GF	IP	BFP	H	R	ER	HR	SH	SF	HB	TBB	IBB	SO	WP	Bk	W	L	Pct.	ShO	Sv	ERA
1991 San Berndno	A+ Sea	16	14	0	1	74	323	80	53	51	14	2	4	4	31	1	58	1	1	3	9	.250	0	0	6.20
1992 Peninsula	A+ Sea	32	20	4	9	139.2	583	132	58	52	13	5	3	4	40	5	122	6	5	5	11	.313	2	3	3.35
1993 Jacksnville	AA Sea	27	0	0	22	36.1	159	29	17	12	1	1	0	3	17	3	39	0	0	3	5	.375	0	7	2.97
Edmonton	AAA Fla	25	0	0	14	30.2	151	50	34	29	5	1	2	0	10	2	22	1	0	2	2	.500	0	2	8.51
1994 Calgary	AAA Sea	42	0	0	21	70.2	299	60	32	27	9	3	2	2	28	3	54	5	0	1	2	.333	0	11	3.44
1995 Tacoma	AAA Sea	46	0	0	31	63.1	256	51	21	19	2	3	3	1	21	5	51	0	0	7	2	.778	0	12	2.70
1996 Nashville	AAA CWS	25	6	0	11	63.1	256	52	31	25	8	0	1	1	17	1	33	5	0	5	2	.714	0	3	3.55
1997 Nashville	AAA CWS	47	0	0	36	53.2	244	60	32	27	8	3	1	2	24	4	44	6	0	4	3	.571	0	22	4.53
1998 Fresno	AAA SF	56	0	0	45	54.1	239	69	44	41	8	1	2	3	10	1	45	2	0	2	6	.250	0	24	6.79
1999 Las Vegas	AAA SD	8	0	0	5	10	55	19	17	15	2	0	1	0	5	0	9	1	0	1	1	.500	0	0	13.50
1994 Seattle	AL	2	0	0	1	4	22	7	6	6	1	0	0	1	3	1	1	0	0	0	0	.000	0	0	13.50
1996 Chicago	AL	22	0	0	9	30.2	124	26	10	10	5	1	0	2	9	1	15	0	0	0	1	.000	0	0	2.93
1997 Chicago	AL	14	0	0	6	13.2	65	17	8	8	1	0	1	0	7	0	9	3	0	0	1	.000	0	0	5.27
11 Min. YEARS		361	77	5	195	810.1	3502	828	467	400	85	26	24	27	284	25	613	37	15	42	64	.396	2	84	4.44
3 Maj. YEARS		38	0	0	16	48.1	211	50	24	24	7	1	1	3	19	2	25	3	0	0	2	.000	0	0	4.47

Allen Davis

Pitches: Left Bats: Left Pos: P Ht: 6'4" Wt: 195 Born: 10/1/75 Age: 24

Year Team	Lg Org	G	GS	CG	GF	IP	BFP	H	R	ER	HR	SH	SF	HB	TBB	IBB	SO	WP	Bk	W	L	Pct.	ShO	Sv	ERA
1998 Yakima	A- LA	4	2	0	1	16	61	10	4	2	0	0	0	0	3	0	14	1	0	2	0	1.000	0	0	1.13
San Berndno	A+ LA	5	5	0	0	31	127	30	13	10	2	1	1	0	7	0	34	1	2	1	2	.333	0	0	2.90
San Antonio	AA LA	6	5	0	0	31.1	132	31	13	11	2	1	0	1	9	0	33	0	1	2	2	.500	0	0	3.16
1999 San Antonio	AA LA	29	20	1	3	130	574	140	83	61	13	5	4	4	46	1	87	4	0	7	10	.412	1	0	4.22
2 Min. YEARS		44	32	1	4	208.1	894	211	113	84	17	7	5	5	65	1	168	6	3	12	14	.462	1	0	3.63

Glenn Davis

Bats: Both Throws: Left Pos: OF-1B Ht: 6'1" Wt: 200 Born: 11/25/75 Age: 24

Year Team	Lg Org	G	AB	H	2B	3B	HR	TB	R	RBI	TBB	IBB	SO	HBP	SH	SF	SB	CS	SB%	GDP	Avg	OBP	SLG
1997 San Berndno	A+ LA	64	228	56	16	0	9	99	44	36	46	0	77	2	0	0	7	3	.70	3	.246	.377	.434
1998 Vero Beach	A+ LA	102	376	89	14	2	20	167	63	70	70	1	106	2	0	5	13	4	.76	7	.237	.355	.444
San Antonio	AA LA	20	69	20	2	0	6	40	14	15	10	0	22	0	0	0	2	0	1.00	0	.290	.380	.580
1999 San Antonio	AA LA	134	492	128	33	4	10	199	72	63	69	4	130	0	1	2	6	7	.46	12	.260	.350	.404
3 Min. YEARS		320	1165	293	65	6	45	505	193	177	195	5	335	4	1	7	28	14	.67	24	.252	.359	.433

James Davis

Bats: Right Throws: Right Pos: C Ht: 6'4" Wt: 215 Born: 4/14/73 Age: 27

Year Team	Lg Org	G	AB	H	2B	3B	HR	TB	R	RBI	TBB	IBB	SO	HBP	SH	SF	SB	CS	SB%	GDP	Avg	OBP	SLG
1995 Princeton	R+ Cin	58	225	62	10	4	3	89	40	29	14	0	33	1	1	2	8	0	1.00	2	.276	.318	.396
1996 Chstn-WV	A Cin	84	313	90	14	1	3	115	42	38	32	0	57	1	1	3	8	3	.73	6	.288	.352	.367
1997 Burlington	A Cin	91	319	93	18	1	5	128	37	46	17	1	46	4	4	2	3	0	1.00	8	.292	.333	.401
1998 Chattanooga	AA Cin	37	126	37	5	0	2	48	11	12	8	0	21	2	2	0	0	0	.00	4	.294	.346	.381
Indianapols	AAA Cin	19	50	10	2	0	1	15	4	4	1	0	12	0	0	0	0	0	.00	0	.200	.216	.300
1999 Chattanooga	AA Cin	16	54	13	5	0	4	30	7	16	1	0	5	2	0	1	0	1	.00	3	.241	.276	.556
Clinton	A Cin	3	10	2	0	0	0	2	0	0	1	0	2	1	0	0	0	1	1.00	0	.200	.333	.200
Indianapols	AAA Cin	16	52	15	4	1	0	21	7	10	3	0	6	1	0	1	0	0	.00	3	.288	.333	.404
5 Min. YEARS		324	1149	322	58	7	18	448	148	155	77	1	182	12	8	9	20	4	.83	26	.280	.330	.390

Jason Davis

Pitches: Left Bats: Left Pos: P Ht: 6'3" Wt: 195 Born: 8/15/74 Age: 25

Year Team	Lg Org	G	GS	CG	GF	IP	BFP	H	R	ER	HR	SH	SF	HB	TBB	IBB	SO	WP	Bk	W	L	Pct.	ShO	Sv	ERA
1996 Piedmont	A Phi	19	0	0	10	24.2	100	16	6	5	1	0	2	4	5	1	22	1	1	6	1	.857	0	2	1.82
1997 Piedmont	A Phi	17	0	0	7	29.1	102	10	3	2	1	2	0	0	6	0	34	0	0	1	0	1.000	0	1	0.61
Clearwater	A+ Phi	24	0	0	6	42.1	169	31	11	7	0	2	0	1	17	0	36	4	1	2	1	.667	0	2	1.49
1998 Reading	AA Phi	45	10	0	11	104.2	488	116	68	56	8	5	1	8	55	3	81	6	2	6	8	.429	0	1	4.82
1999 Shreveport	AA SF	52	0	0	38	64	249	42	9	9	1	3	0	1	22	1	54	2	2	5	1	.833	0	21	1.27
4 Min. YEARS		157	10	0	72	265	1108	215	97	79	11	12	3	14	105	5	227	13	6	20	11	.645	0	27	2.68

Kane Davis

Pitches: Right Bats: Right Pos: P Ht: 6'3" Wt: 194 Born: 6/25/75 Age: 25

Year Team	Lg Org	G	GS	CG	GF	IP	BFP	H	R	ER	HR	SH	SF	HB	TBB	IBB	SO	WP	Bk	W	L	Pct.	ShO	Sv	ERA
1993 Pirates	R Pit	11	4	0	5	28	140	34	30	22	0	3	2	0	19	1	24	2	0	0	4	.000	0	0	7.07
1994 Welland	A- Pit	15	15	2	0	98.1	400	90	36	29	4	2	2	3	32	1	74	7	1	5	5	.500	0	0	2.65
1995 Augusta	A Pit	26	25	1	0	139.1	602	136	73	58	4	3	3	9	43	0	78	10	1	12	6	.667	0	0	3.75
1996 Lynchburg	A+ Pit	26	26	3	0	157.1	684	160	84	75	12	12	3	10	56	0	116	11	2	11	9	.550	1	0	4.29
1997 Carolina	AA Pit	6	6	0	0	28.2	128	22	17	12	2	2	1	3	16	1	23	2	0	0	3	.000	0	0	3.77
1998 Augusta	A Pit	2	2	0	0	9	36	8	6	6	0	1	0	1	3	0	6	0	0	0	0	.000	0	0	6.00
Carolina	AA Pit	18	16	0	0	74	362	102	84	76	12	4	0	7	38	2	39	10	1	1	11	.083	0	0	9.24
1999 Altoona	AA Pit	16	16	0	0	95.1	421	97	51	40	5	2	4	3	41	1	53	4	0	3	6	.400	0	0	3.78
Nashville	AAA Pit	12	9	0	1	49.1	224	65	38	37	8	2	1	3	17	1	31	2	0	3	2	.600	0	0	6.75
7 Min. YEARS		132	119	6	6	679.1	2997	714	419	355	47	31	18	38	265	7	444	48	7	36	46	.439	1	0	4.70

Tim Davis

Pitches: Left **Bats:** Left **Pos:** P **Ht:** 5'11" **Wt:** 165 **Born:** 7/14/70 **Age:** 29

Year Team	Lg Org	G	GS	CG	GF	IP	BFP	H	R	ER	HR	SH	SF	HB	TBB	IBB	SO	WP	Bk	W	L	Pct.	ShO	Sv	ERA
1993 Appleton	A Sea	16	10	3	4	77.2	313	54	20	16	5	1	2	2	33	0	89	4	2	10	2	.833	2	2	1.85
Riverside	A+ Sea	18	0	0	17	30.2	117	14	6	6	1	0	1	1	9	0	56	1	0	3	0	1.000	0	7	1.76
1994 Calgary	AAA Sea	6	6	1	0	39.2	161	35	13	8	1	1	1	0	8	0	43	0	0	3	1	.750	0	0	1.82
1995 Tacoma	AAA Sea	2	2	0	0	13.1	57	15	8	8	2	0	0	0	4	0	13	0	0	0	1	.000	0	0	5.40
1996 Everett	A- Sea	1	1	0	0	2	7	0	0	0	0	0	0	0	1	0	5	0	0	0	0	.000	0	0	0.00
Tacoma	AAA Sea	8	1	0	1	17	78	19	12	10	1	3	1	0	10	2	19	1	0	0	1	.000	0	0	5.29
1997 Tacoma	AAA Sea	1	1	0	0	5	22	4	2	2	0	1	0	0	3	0	5	0	0	1	0	1.000	0	0	3.60
1998 Orlando	AA Sea	14	5	0	2	22	86	18	9	6	2	0	2	1	4	0	19	3	0	1	1	.500	0	1	2.45
1999 Durham	AAA TB	3	0	0	1	2	11	2	2	2	0	0	0	2	1	0	1	0	0	0	0	.000	0	0	9.00
St. Pete	A+ TB	1	0	0	0	0.2	6	3	2	2	0	0	0	0	1	0	1	0	0	0	0	.000	0	0	27.00
1994 Seattle	AL	42	1	0	12	49.1	225	57	25	22	4	3	3	1	25	5	28	6	0	2	2	.500	0	2	4.01
1995 Seattle	AL	5	5	0	0	24	117	30	21	17	2	0	1	0	18	2	19	0	0	2	1	.667	0	0	6.38
1996 Seattle	AL	40	0	0	4	42.2	187	43	21	19	4	1	1	2	17	1	34	0	0	2	2	.500	0	0	4.01
1997 Seattle	AL	2	0	0	1	6.2	31	6	5	5	1	0	0	1	4	0	10	0	0	0	0	.000	0	0	6.75
7 Min. YEARS		70	26	4	25	210	858	164	74	60	12	6	7	6	74	2	251	10	2	18	6	.750	2	10	2.57
4 Maj. YEARS		89	6	0	17	122.2	560	136	72	63	11	4	5	4	64	8	91	6	0	6	5	.545	0	2	4.62

Joey Dawley

Pitches: Right **Bats:** Right **Pos:** P **Ht:** 6'4" **Wt:** 205 **Born:** 9/19/71 **Age:** 28

Year Team	Lg Org	G	GS	CG	GF	IP	BFP	H	R	ER	HR	SH	SF	HB	TBB	IBB	SO	WP	Bk	W	L	Pct.	ShO	Sv	ERA
1993 Bluefield	R+ Bal	20	0	0	15	30.2	143	34	16	12	1	2	1	1	14	3	30	3	1	3	1	.750	0	3	3.52
1994 Bluefield	R+ Bal	11	2	0	5	23.2	110	20	18	15	2	0	1	1	18	0	18	4	0	1	2	.333	0	2	5.70
Albany	A Bal	5	0	0	4	7.1	37	7	6	5	0	0	1	1	7	1	4	1	0	0	0	.000	0	0	6.14
1995 Frederick	A+ Bal	24	0	0	8	32.2	163	41	28	23	4	1	1	3	22	1	29	5	1	1	2	.333	0	1	6.34
Palm Spring	IND —	15	0	0	1	28	128	28	14	12	2	0	1	2	9	0	20	1	1	1	0	1.000	0	0	3.86
1996 Palm Spring	IND —	27	0	0	18	33.2	146	26	14	6	3	0	0	1	18	1	29	2	1	2	1	.667	0	4	1.60
1997 Chico	IND —	41	0	0	35	41.1	186	42	24	20	2	0	2	2	18	2	51	2	1	1	4	.200	0	14	4.35
1998 Chico	IND —	45	0	0	41	43	196	43	22	16	2	2	2	0	27	2	36	5	0	2	4	.333	0	26	3.35
1999 Greenville	AA Atl	26	11	0	2	91.2	387	76	54	41	5	3	4	3	37	3	89	3	2	5	3	.625	0	4	4.03
Richmond	AAA Atl	7	7	1	0	40	174	43	26	23	5	3	2	0	12	0	31	4	0	0	3	.000	0	0	5.18
7 Min. YEARS		221	20	1	129	372	1670	360	226	173	26	11	15	14	182	13	337	30	7	16	20	.444	0	50	4.19

Jason Dawsey

Pitches: Left **Bats:** Left **Pos:** P **Ht:** 5'8" **Wt:** 165 **Born:** 5/27/74 **Age:** 26

Year Team	Lg Org	G	GS	CG	GF	IP	BFP	H	R	ER	HR	SH	SF	HB	TBB	IBB	SO	WP	Bk	W	L	Pct.	ShO	Sv	ERA
1995 Helena	R+ Mil	9	8	0	0	42.2	183	40	15	13	1	0	3	2	23	0	47	5	1	3	0	1.000	0	0	2.74
1996 Beloit	A Mil	31	14	1	4	101.1	411	71	21	17	4	4	0	1	42	0	119	2	1	6	4	.600	1	2	1.51
1997 El Paso	AA Mil	8	7	0	0	38.1	182	50	30	29	3	0	1	2	23	0	14	4	1	2	2	.500	0	0	6.81
1998 El Paso	AA Mil	6	6	0	0	31.2	141	34	29	28	4	1	2	2	22	1	19	1	0	1	3	.250	0	0	7.96
Stockton	A+ Mil	19	9	0	3	62.1	263	54	28	22	3	4	1	0	27	1	79	7	0	4	2	.667	0	0	3.18
1999 Huntsville	AA Mil	4	4	0	0	18	83	22	18	18	6	0	0	0	10	0	8	0	0	1	0	1.000	0	0	9.00
Sacramento	IND —	20	5	0	6	49.2	245	57	37	30	5	1	3	2	38	0	43	5	0	3	3	.500	0	0	5.44
5 Min. YEARS		97	53	1	13	344	1514	328	178	157	26	10	10	9	185	2	329	24	3	20	14	.588	1	2	4.11

Tim DeCinces

Bats: Left **Throws:** Right **Pos:** C **Ht:** 6'2" **Wt:** 195 **Born:** 4/26/74 **Age:** 26

Year Team	Lg Org	G	AB	H	2B	3B	HR	TB	R	RBI	TBB	IBB	SO	HBP	SH	SF	SB	CS	SB%	GDP	Avg	OBP	SLG
1996 Bluefield	R+ Bal	39	128	38	8	0	7	67	24	32	24	0	28	2	0	5	3	1	.75	5	.297	.403	.523
1997 Delmarva	A Bal	127	416	107	20	0	13	166	65	70	97	1	117	0	1	3	3	4	.43	10	.257	.395	.399
1998 Rochester	AAA Bal	7	21	2	1	0	0	3	1	0	2	0	6	0	0	0	0	0	.00	0	.095	.174	.143
Frederick	A+ Bal	110	374	100	25	0	16	173	50	64	59	2	90	4	1	2	3	4	.43	5	.267	.371	.463
Bowie	AA Bal	5	18	6	1	0	1	10	5	4	1	0	5	0	0	0	0	0	.00	0	.333	.368	.556
1999 Bowie	AA Bal	84	258	67	15	0	12	118	38	36	54	3	52	0	0	1	0	2	.00	7	.264	.387	.457
Rochester	AAA Bal	16	53	14	5	0	2	25	7	8	0	0	12	0	0	0	0	0	.00	2	.264	.264	.472
4 Min. YEARS		388	1268	334	75	0	51	562	190	214	237	6	310	6	2	11	9	11	.45	32	.263	.379	.443

Billy Deck

Bats: Left **Throws:** Left **Pos:** 1B-OF **Ht:** 6'0" **Wt:** 180 **Born:** 9/16/76 **Age:** 23

Year Team	Lg Org	G	AB	H	2B	3B	HR	TB	R	RBI	TBB	IBB	SO	HBP	SH	SF	SB	CS	SB%	GDP	Avg	OBP	SLG
1995 Johnson Cy	R+ StL	59	205	53	12	0	1	68	27	30	30	0	52	7	1	2	4	6	.40	4	.259	.369	.332
1996 Johnson Cy	R+ StL	52	182	52	14	0	5	81	40	33	38	1	59	10	0	3	5	2	.71	4	.286	.429	.445
1997 Peoria	A StL	114	383	103	30	0	3	142	51	53	51	2	89	4	1	2	2	5	.29	11	.269	.359	.371
1998 Pr William	A+ StL	118	355	85	13	3	4	116	34	45	40	3	87	13	5	6	5	6	.45	11	.239	.333	.327
1999 Arkansas	AA StL	18	33	2	1	0	0	3	1	0	1	0	16	2	0	0	0	0	.00	1	.061	.139	.091
Potomac	A+ StL	71	235	61	12	4	3	90	35	32	31	1	54	11	3	2	4	2	.67	6	.260	.369	.383
5 Min. YEARS		432	1393	356	82	7	16	500	188	193	191	7	357	47	10	15	20	21	.49	34	.256	.361	.359

Jim Dedrick

Pitches: Right **Bats:** Both **Pos:** P   **Ht:** 6' 0" **Wt:** 185 **Born:** 4/4/68 **Age:** 32

		HOW MUCH HE PITCHED						WHAT HE GAVE UP										THE RESULTS					
Year Team	Lg Org	G	GS	CG	GF	IP	BFP	H	R	ER	HR	SH	SF	HB	TBB	IBB	SO	WP	Bk	W	L	Pct.	ShO	Sv	ERA
1990 Wausau	A Bal	3	1	0	1	10	41	6	4	3	0	0	0	0	4	0	8	0	3	0	1	.000	0	0	2.70
1991 Kane County	A Bal	16	15	0	0	88.1	380	84	38	29	2	1	2	5	38	1	71	5	2	4	5	.444	0	0	2.95
1992 Frederick	A+ Bal	38	5	1	19	108.2	454	94	41	37	5	5	0	5	42	4	86	4	3	8	4	.667	0	3	3.06
1993 Bowie	AA Bal	38	6	1	14	106.1	426	84	36	30	4	5	0	3	32	1	78	1	0	8	3	.727	1	3	2.54
Rochester	AAA Bal	1	1	0	0	7	27	6	2	2	2	0	0	0	0	0	3	0	0	1	0	1.000	0	0	2.57
1994 Rochester	AAA Bal	44	1	0	18	99	421	98	56	42	7	3	1	3	35	7	70	4	1	3	6	.333	0	1	3.82
1995 Bowie	AA Bal	10	10	0	0	60.1	267	59	24	20	7	2	2	5	25	2	48	5	1	4	2	.667	0	0	2.98
Rochester	AAA Bal	24	2	0	4	45.2	190	45	9	9	0	2	4	1	14	1	31	4	0	4	0	1.000	0	1	1.77
1996 Rochester	AAA Bal	39	3	0	20	66.1	316	88	59	48	14	2	4	1	41	0	37	5	1	6	3	.667	0	4	6.51
Bowie	AA Bal	13	0	0	4	26.2	116	28	10	10	3	1	0	0	14	1	21	1	0	1	1	.500	0	0	3.38
1997 Harrisburg	AA Mon	15	0	0	7	19.1	78	18	8	6	1	1	0	0	8	0	17	0	1	2	1	.667	0	1	2.79
Ottawa	AAA Mon	8	0	0	2	14	68	15	12	11	2	1	0	0	13	0	14	0	0	0	1	.000	0	0	7.07
Tulsa	AA Tex	12	0	0	2	23	100	26	9	6	0	0	1	0	9	0	16	5	0	1	0	1.000	0	0	2.35
Okla City	AAA Tex	8	0	0	4	10.2	57	16	7	7	0	0	0	0	10	0	2	1	0	0	0	.000	0	3	5.91
1998 Richmond	AAA Atl	26	0	0	17	37.1	160	36	24	22	4	0	2	0	15	3	27	2	0	2	3	.400	0	0	5.30
1999 Akron	AA Cle	2	0	0	1	3	13	4	3	3	2	0	0	0	0	0	0	0	0	1	0	1.000	0	0	9.00
Buffalo	AAA Cle	30	0	0	4	46.1	211	49	23	21	5	1	2	1	27	1	26	1	1	2	2	.500	0	0	4.08
1995 Baltimore	AL	6	0	0	1	7.2	35	8	2	2	1	0	2	1	6	0	3	0	0	0	0	.000	0	0	2.35
10 Min. YEARS		327	44	3	117	772	3325	756	365	306	58	24	18	24	327	21	555	38	13	47	32	.595	1	16	3.57

Kory DeHaan

Bats: Left **Throws:** Right **Pos:** OF   **Ht:** 6'2" **Wt:** 187 **Born:** 7/16/76 **Age:** 23

		BATTING															BASERUNNING				PERCENTAGES		
Year Team	Lg Org	G	AB	H	2B	3B	HR	TB	R	RBI	TBB	IBB	SO	HBP	SH	SF	SB	CS	SB%	GDP	Avg	OBP	SLG
1997 Erie	A- Pit	58	205	49	8	6	1	72	43	18	38	2	43	2	6	4	14	9	.61	4	.239	.357	.351
1998 Augusta	A Pit	132	475	149	39	8	8	228	85	75	69	3	114	8	8	7	33	13	.72	4	.314	.404	.480
1999 Lynchburg	A+ Pit	78	295	96	19	5	7	146	55	42	36	3	63	4	4	1	32	10	.76	4	.325	.405	.495
Altoona	AA Pit	47	190	51	13	2	3	77	26	24	11	0	46	2	5	3	14	6	.70	3	.268	.311	.405
3 Min. YEARS		315	1165	345	79	21	19	523	209	159	154	8	266	16	23	15	93	38	.71	15	.296	.381	.449

Francisco de la Cruz

Pitches: Right **Bats:** Right **Pos:** P   **Ht:** 6'2" **Wt:** 175 **Born:** 7/9/73 **Age:** 26

		HOW MUCH HE PITCHED						WHAT HE GAVE UP										THE RESULTS					
Year Team	Lg Org	G	GS	CG	GF	IP	BFP	H	R	ER	HR	SH	SF	HB	TBB	IBB	SO	WP	Bk	W	L	Pct.	ShO	Sv	ERA
1997 Norwich	AA NYY	2	2	0	0	8.1	39	8	3	3	0	1	0	2	7	0	0	0	0	0	1	.000	0	0	3.24
Tampa	A+ NYY	8	8	0	0	36.2	174	39	30	28	5	3	2	1	29	1	22	2	0	0	2	.000	0	0	6.87
Greensboro	A NYY	13	13	1	0	84.2	359	71	41	31	6	2	2	4	36	1	75	3	2	5	4	.556	0	0	3.30
1998 Norwich	AA NYY	2	2	0	0	4.2	31	8	13	4	2	0	1	1	4	0	5	0	0	0	2	.000	0	0	7.71
Yankees	R NYY	3	3	0	0	13.2	61	11	9	5	1	0	0	0	8	1	18	1	0	1	1	.500	0	0	3.29
Greensboro	A NYY	5	3	0	1	20.1	83	15	9	9	3	0	1	1	10	1	18	0	0	2	1	.667	0	0	3.98
Tampa	A+ NYY	19	12	0	5	75.1	344	81	55	38	5	4	1	3	36	1	66	5	0	5	6	.455	0	0	4.54
1999 Norwich	AA NYY	29	19	1	4	133.1	603	141	89	68	10	2	5	2	73	0	91	11	3	6	5	.545	0	0	4.59
3 Min. YEARS		81	62	2	10	377	1694	374	249	186	32	12	12	14	203	5	295	22	5	19	22	.463	0	0	4.44

Javier de la Hoya

Pitches: Right **Bats:** Right **Pos:** P   **Ht:** 6'2" **Wt:** 160 **Born:** 2/21/70 **Age:** 30

		HOW MUCH HE PITCHED						WHAT HE GAVE UP										THE RESULTS					
Year Team	Lg Org	G	GS	CG	GF	IP	BFP	H	R	ER	HR	SH	SF	HB	TBB	IBB	SO	WP	Bk	W	L	Pct.	ShO	Sv	ERA
1989 Dodgers	R LA	9	8	2	1	55.1	212	28	13	9	0	1	1	4	19	0	70	3	1	4	3	.571	1	0	1.46
1990 Vero Beach	A+ LA	4	4	0	0	21	100	14	14	13	0	1	1	1	20	2	22	0	0	1	2	.333	0	0	5.57
Bakersfield	A+ LA	9	7	0	0	39.1	190	50	30	26	5	0	1	1	24	0	37	6	0	4	1	.800	0	0	5.95
Yakima	A- LA	14	14	0	0	70.2	326	65	52	35	2	2	5	7	39	2	71	9	0	3	5	.375	0	0	4.46
1991 Bakersfield	A+ LA	27	11	1	7	98	425	92	47	40	6	2	3	1	44	1	102	3	3	6	4	.600	0	2	3.67
1992 Vero Beach	A+ LA	14	14	2	0	80	325	68	25	25	4	1	1	4	26	0	92	2	0	4	5	.444	2	0	2.81
San Antonio	AA LA	5	5	0	0	25.1	116	20	11	8	1	1	2	1	17	0	24	1	0	2	1	.667	0	0	2.84
1993 San Antonio	AA LA	21	21	1	0	125.1	537	122	61	51	14	4	3	8	42	0	107	2	1	8	10	.444	0	0	3.66
1994 Portland	AA Fla	22	11	1	5	73.2	328	81	56	53	11	2	1	2	29	4	60	3	0	0	7	.000	0	2	6.48
Brevard Cty	A+ Fla	9	7	0	1	50	201	39	17	14	2	1	2	3	12	1	45	1	0	4	3	.571	0	0	2.52
1995 Brevard Cty	A+ Fla	5	0	0	1	10.1	40	6	2	2	1	0	0	2	2	0	8	0	0	1	0	1.000	0	0	1.74
1996 Bend	IND —	2	2	0	0	5.1	25	9	4	4	1	0	1	0	1	0	2	0	0	0	0	.000	0	0	6.75
1998 Bowie	AA Bal	6	4	1	1	30.2	126	32	13	13	4	0	0	2	7	1	33	0	0	4	1	.800	0	0	3.82
1999 Bowie	AA Bal	12	12	1	0	77.2	310	64	29	29	12	2	1	1	18	0	68	4	0	9	1	.900	0	0	3.36
Rochester	AAA Bal	14	14	0	0	81.1	356	88	49	46	14	1	3	7	26	0	58	5	2	4	3	.571	0	0	5.09
10 Min. YEARS		173	134	9	16	844	3617	778	423	368	77	18	25	44	326	12	799	39	7	54	46	.540	3	4	3.92

Roland de la Maza

Pitches: Right **Bats:** Right **Pos:** P   **Ht:** 6' 2" **Wt:** 195 **Born:** 11/9/71 **Age:** 28

		HOW MUCH HE PITCHED						WHAT HE GAVE UP										THE RESULTS					
Year Team	Lg Org	G	GS	CG	GF	IP	BFP	H	R	ER	HR	SH	SF	HB	TBB	IBB	SO	WP	Bk	W	L	Pct.	ShO	Sv	ERA
1993 Watertown	A- Cle	15	15	1	0	100	402	90	39	28	8	2	1	3	14	0	81	0	1	10	3	.769	0	0	2.52
1994 Columbus	A Cle	21	21	1	0	112.2	473	102	59	37	13	5	4	6	25	0	97	3	2	13	2	.867	0	0	2.96
1995 Canton-Akrn	AA Cle	7	7	0	0	37.1	162	35	19	17	5	0	0	2	18	0	27	1	0	2	1	.667	0	0	4.10
Kinston	A+ Cle	26	12	0	5	110.1	445	99	31	29	13	7	0	3	28	3	100	3	0	6	0	1.000	0	0	2.37
1996 Canton-Akrn	AA Cle	40	14	0	9	139.2	587	122	75	68	15	6	1	1	49	3	132	3	2	9	7	.563	0	0	4.38
1997 Buffalo	AAA Cle	34	14	2	11	115	481	104	42	37	12	4	1	1	43	4	73	4	0	9	4	.692	0	0	2.90

71

Year Team	Lg Org	G	GS	CG	GF	IP	BFP	H	R	ER	HR	SH	SF	HB	TBB	IBB	SO	WP	Bk	W	L	Pct.	ShO	Sv	ERA
		HOW MUCH HE PITCHED						WHAT HE GAVE UP												THE RESULTS					
1998 Omaha	AAA KC	31	16	0	5	131	587	169	83	78	22	1	3	6	38	2	82	4	0	9	6	.600	0	0	5.36
1999 Vancouver	AAA Oak	4	0	0	1	3	16	5	4	4	1	0	0	0	4	0	4	0	0	0	0	.000	0	0	12.00
1997 Kansas City	AL	1	0	0	0	2	9	1	1	1	0	0	0	0	1	0	1	1	0	0	0	.000	0	0	4.50
7 Min. YEARS		178	99	4	31	749	3153	726	352	298	89	25	10	21	219	9	596	18	7	58	23	.716	0	4	3.58

Maximo de la Rosa

Pitches: Right **Bats:** Right **Pos:** P   Ht: 5'11" **Wt:** 170 **Born:** 7/12/71 **Age:** 28

Year Team	Lg Org	G	GS	CG	GF	IP	BFP	H	R	ER	HR	SH	SF	HB	TBB	IBB	SO	WP	Bk	W	L	Pct.	ShO	Sv	ERA
		HOW MUCH HE PITCHED						WHAT HE GAVE UP												THE RESULTS					
1993 Burlington	R+ Cle	14	14	2	0	76.1	319	53	38	32	3	3	2	5	37	2	69	3	2	7	2	.778	1	0	3.77
1994 Columbus	A Cle	14	14	0	0	75.1	310	49	33	28	2	1	1	10	38	0	71	5	2	4	2	.667	0	0	3.35
Kinston	A Cle	13	13	0	0	69.2	324	82	56	39	7	2	4	4	38	0	53	3	2	0	11	.000	0	0	5.04
1995 Canton-Akrn	AA Cle	1	0	0	0	0.1	3	1	2	2	1	0	0	0	1	0	0	0	0	0	0	.000	0	0	54.00
Kinston	A+ Cle	43	0	0	21	61.2	266	46	23	15	0	5	2	4	37	3	61	7	1	5	2	.714	0	8	2.19
1996 Canton-Akrn	AA Cle	40	15	0	17	119.2	530	104	60	52	7	2	4	3	81	3	109	12	2	11	5	.688	0	3	3.91
1997 Buffalo	AAA Cle	15	4	0	3	43	208	43	34	31	10	2	3	9	33	0	31	1	0	2	2	.500	0	0	6.49
Akron	AA Cle	17	13	5	2	97.1	435	112	63	48	11	8	4	5	32	3	70	2	4	4	9	.308	0	0	4.44
1998 Orlando	AA Sea	42	0	0	29	62.1	260	47	23	21	2	4	4	3	24	1	51	5	0	6	4	.600	0	8	3.03
Tacoma	AAA Sea	9	0	0	8	10.2	45	6	4	4	0	0	3	1	8	0	4	0	0	2	1	.667	0	0	3.38
1999 New Haven	AA Sea	10	0	0	9	10.2	45	9	4	3	1	0	0	1	3	0	7	2	0	0	1	.000	0	4	2.53
Tacoma	AAA Sea	15	0	0	5	22	112	34	18	15	3	0	2	3	10	1	24	2	0	0	2	.000	0	1	6.14
Colo Sprngs	AAA Col	8	0	0	2	11	48	12	3	3	1	1	0	2	4	1	5	2	0	0	1	.000	0	0	2.45
7 Min. YEARS		241	73	7	96	660	2905	598	361	293	48	28	29	50	346	14	555	44	13	41	42	.494	1	24	4.00

Tomas de la Rosa

Bats: Right **Throws:** Right **Pos:** SS   Ht: 5'10" **Wt:** 155 **Born:** 1/28/78 **Age:** 22

Year Team	Lg Org	G	AB	H	2B	3B	HR	TB	R	RBI	TBB	IBB	SO	HBP	SH	SF	SB	CS	SB%	GDP	Avg	OBP	SLG
		BATTING															BASERUNNING				PERCENTAGES		
1996 Expos	R Mon	53	184	46	7	1	0	55	34	21	22	0	25	2	4	1	8	5	.62	2	.250	.335	.299
Vermont	A- Mon	3	8	2	0	0	0	2	1	1	0	0	3	0	0	0	0	0	.00	1	.250	.250	.250
1997 Wst Plm Bch	A+ Mon	4	9	2	0	0	0	2	1	0	2	0	3	0	0	0	2	0	1.00	0	.222	.364	.222
Vermont	A- Mon	69	271	72	14	6	2	104	46	40	32	0	47	2	3	4	19	6	.76	1	.266	.343	.384
1998 Jupiter	A+ Mon	117	390	98	22	1	3	131	56	43	37	0	61	6	10	3	27	7	.79	5	.251	.323	.336
1999 Harrisburg	AA Mon	135	467	122	22	3	6	168	70	43	42	2	64	1	7	5	28	15	.65	10	.261	.320	.360
4 Min. YEARS		381	1329	342	65	11	11	462	208	148	135	2	203	11	24	13	84	33	.72	19	.257	.328	.348

Alex Delgado

Bats: Right **Throws:** Right **Pos:** C   Ht: 6' 0" **Wt:** 160 **Born:** 1/11/71 **Age:** 29

Year Team	Lg Org	G	AB	H	2B	3B	HR	TB	R	RBI	TBB	IBB	SO	HBP	SH	SF	SB	CS	SB%	GDP	Avg	OBP	SLG
		BATTING															BASERUNNING				PERCENTAGES		
1988 R.S./Marnrs	R Bos	34	111	39	10	0	0	49	11	22	6	0	5	1	3	2	2	4	.33	1	.351	.383	.441
1989 Winter Havn	A+ Bos	78	285	64	7	0	0	71	27	16	17	0	30	1	5	0	7	3	.70	9	.225	.271	.249
1990 New Britain	AA Bos	7	18	1	1	0	0	2	3	0	2	0	5	0	0	0	0	0	.00	1	.056	.150	.111
Winter Havn	A+ Bos	89	303	68	9	2	1	84	37	25	37	0	37	3	5	3	10	4	.71	7	.224	.312	.277
1991 Lynchburg	A+ Bos	61	179	38	8	0	0	46	21	17	16	0	19	2	1	1	2	1	.67	6	.212	.283	.257
1992 Winter Havn	A+ Bos	56	167	35	2	0	2	43	11	12	16	0	11	1	4	1	1	1	.50	6	.210	.281	.257
1993 Ft. Laud	A+ Bos	63	225	57	9	0	2	72	26	25	9	1	21	5	7	1	2	2	.50	4	.253	.296	.320
New Britain	AA Bos	33	87	16	2	0	1	21	10	9	4	0	11	4	4	2	1	1	.50	5	.184	.247	.241
1994 Red Sox	R Bos	7	24	4	1	0	0	5	3	7	2	1	2	2	0	1	0	0	.00	0	.167	.276	.208
New Britain	AA Bos	40	140	36	3	0	2	45	16	12	4	0	21	2	1	1	1	1	.50	7	.257	.286	.321
1995 Pawtucket	AAA Bos	44	107	27	3	0	5	45	14	12	6	0	12	1	0	0	0	0	.00	4	.252	.298	.421
Trenton	AA Bos	23	72	24	1	0	3	34	13	14	9	0	8	3	1	1	0	0	.00	2	.333	.424	.472
1996 Trenton	AA Bos	21	81	18	4	0	3	31	7	14	9	1	8	1	1	1	1	0	1.00	0	.222	.304	.383
Pawtucket	AAA Bos	27	88	19	3	0	1	25	15	6	7	0	11	0	0	0	0	0	.00	5	.216	.274	.284
1997 Charlotte	AAA Fla	14	38	8	1	0	0	9	1	6	3	0	7	0	3	1	0	0	.00	1	.211	.262	.237
1998 Syracuse	AAA Tor	82	286	67	14	0	6	99	22	28	25	3	39	4	3	1	2	0	1.00	15	.234	.304	.346
1999 Dunedin	A+ Tor	13	47	8	0	0	2	14	6	4	1	0	6	2	0	0	0	0	.00	2	.170	.220	.298
Syracuse	AAA Tor	37	107	22	7	0	2	35	11	12	14	0	14	4	1	0	0	0	.00	4	.206	.320	.327
1996 Boston	AL	26	20	5	0	0	0	5	5	1	3	0	3	0	1	0	0	0	.00	0	.250	.348	.250
12 Min. YEARS		729	2365	551	85	2	30	730	254	241	187	6	267	36	39	16	29	17	.63	79	.233	.297	.309

Danny Delgado

Pitches: Right **Bats:** Right **Pos:** P   Ht: 6'2" **Wt:** 180 **Born:** 2/10/78 **Age:** 22

Year Team	Lg Org	G	GS	CG	GF	IP	BFP	H	R	ER	HR	SH	SF	HB	TBB	IBB	SO	WP	Bk	W	L	Pct.	ShO	Sv	ERA
		HOW MUCH HE PITCHED						WHAT HE GAVE UP												THE RESULTS					
1997 Mariners	R Sea	6	0	0	1	8.2	44	11	5	5	2	0	0	0	7	0	8	0	0	0	0	.000	0	0	5.19
1998 Mariners	R Sea	5	0	0	2	13.1	55	12	9	7	3	0	0	1	2	0	15	0	0	2	1	.667	0	0	4.73
Everett	A- Sea	14	0	0	3	30	123	31	15	15	2	0	1	0	8	0	32	3	0	0	0	.000	0	0	4.50
Orlando	AA Sea	1	0	0	1	3	3	0	0	0	0	0	0	0	0	0	0	0	0	0	0	.000	0	0	0.00
1999 Tacoma	AAA Sea	2	0	0	2	3	14	4	2	2	0	1	0	2	2	1	2	0	0	0	1	.000	0	0	6.00
Everett	A- Sea	17	1	0	9	38.1	164	35	18	13	3	7	4	0	12	1	35	1	0	2	3	.400	0	3	3.05
3 Min. YEARS		45	1	0	18	94.1	403	93	49	42	10	8	5	1	31	2	92	4	0	4	5	.444	0	3	4.01

Ernie Delgado

Pitches: Right **Bats:** Right **Pos:** P | **Ht:** 6'2" **Wt:** 190 **Born:** 7/21/75 **Age:** 24

Year Team	Lg Org	G	GS	CG	GF	IP	BFP	H	R	ER	HR	SH	SF	HB	TBB	IBB	SO	WP	Bk	W	L	Pct.	ShO	Sv	ERA
1993 Marlins	R Fla	11	11	0	0	61.1	261	61	27	21	0	4	2	4	19	0	46	5	2	4	3	.571	0	0	3.08
1994 Brevard Cty	A+ Fla	1	1	0	0	6	25	3	3	2	0	1	2	0	4	0	1	1	0	0	1	.000	0	0	3.00
Marlins	R Fla	4	2	0	2	16	71	15	10	6	0	0	0	0	5	0	18	1	0	1	1	.500	0	1	3.38
1995 Brevard Cty	A+ Fla	18	10	0	4	62.1	308	74	51	49	4	1	4	7	59	0	36	7	2	1	6	.143	0	0	7.07
1996 Hagerstown	A Tor	35	2	0	16	85.1	386	89	50	34	2	5	3	7	45	1	70	12	2	4	7	.364	0	2	3.59
1997 Hagerstown	A Tor	32	17	0	5	134.1	618	163	96	78	10	6	6	10	56	0	103	12	0	5	10	.333	0	1	5.23
1998 Dunedin	A+ Tor	44	9	2	13	118.2	532	119	57	48	5	6	1	6	59	4	97	6	2	7	10	.412	1	1	3.64
1999 Knoxville	AA Tor	31	0	0	12	51.1	219	49	27	20	1	1	3	1	23	0	33	5	0	4	1	.800	0	0	3.51
Syracuse	AAA Tor	14	4	0	2	27.2	139	38	29	29	3	1	1	0	19	0	15	2	0	0	4	.000	0	0	9.43
7 Min. YEARS		190	56	2	54	563	2559	611	350	287	25	21	22	35	289	5	419	51	8	26	43	.377	1	5	4.59

Pete Della Ratta

Pitches: Right **Bats:** Right **Pos:** P | **Ht:** 6'4" **Wt:** 220 **Born:** 2/14/74 **Age:** 26

Year Team	Lg Org	G	GS	CG	GF	IP	BFP	H	R	ER	HR	SH	SF	HB	TBB	IBB	SO	WP	Bk	W	L	Pct.	ShO	Sv	ERA
1996 Sou Oregon	A- Oak	22	0	0	6	41.1	194	45	34	33	10	2	2	4	24	4	41	3	1	0	5	.000	0	2	7.19
1997 Modesto	A+ Oak	45	0	0	19	83.2	362	73	45	31	5	5	4	6	31	8	81	6	0	6	7	.462	0	3	3.33
1998 Huntsville	AA Oak	5	0	0	2	8	49	21	12	10	2	0	2	0	4	2	3	0	0	1	0	1.000	0	0	11.25
Visalia	A+ Oak	36	0	0	28	59	249	43	24	16	5	3	1	1	25	6	73	4	0	5	1	.833	0	13	2.44
1999 Binghamton	AA NYM	41	3	0	9	82.2	329	75	22	20	4	2	3	3	13	1	68	2	0	1	4	.200	0	0	2.18
4 Min. YEARS		149	3	0	64	274.2	1183	257	137	110	26	12	11	14	97	21	266	15	1	12	18	.400	0	18	3.60

Eddy de los Santos

Bats: Right **Throws:** Right **Pos:** SS | **Ht:** 6'2" **Wt:** 165 **Born:** 2/24/78 **Age:** 22

Year Team	Lg Org	G	AB	H	2B	3B	HR	TB	R	RBI	TBB	IBB	SO	HBP	SH	SF	SB	CS	SB%	GDP	Avg	OBP	SLG
1996 Devil Rays	R TB	50	196	48	6	1	0	56	18	20	13	0	58	3	2	0	1	3	.79	4	.245	.302	.286
Butte	R+ TB	16	59	16	0	0	0	16	15	12	6	0	17	0	2	2	1	1	.50	1	.271	.328	.271
1997 Chston-SC	A TB	127	432	101	11	2	2	122	46	40	20	0	101	2	5	4	8	9	.47	3	.234	.269	.282
1998 St. Pete	A+ TB	111	393	94	11	1	0	107	33	32	17	1	64	3	5	3	6	4	.60	7	.239	.274	.272
Durham	AAA TB	4	11	3	2	0	0	5	2	2	0	0	6	1	0	0	0	0	.00	0	.273	.333	.455
1999 Orlando	AA TB	128	448	123	24	4	3	164	53	49	29	0	69	2	5	7	3	2	.60	9	.275	.317	.366
4 Min. YEARS		436	1539	385	54	8	5	470	167	155	85	1	315	11	19	16	29	19	.60	24	.250	.291	.305

Luis de los Santos

Pitches: Right **Bats:** Right **Pos:** P | **Ht:** 6'2" **Wt:** 187 **Born:** 11/1/77 **Age:** 22

Year Team	Lg Org	G	GS	CG	GF	IP	BFP	H	R	ER	HR	SH	SF	HB	TBB	IBB	SO	WP	Bk	W	L	Pct.	ShO	Sv	ERA
1995 Yankees	R NYY	2	0	0	1	5	23	5	2	0	0	0	0	1	2	0	6	0	0	0	0	.000	0	0	0.00
1996 Greensboro	A NYY	7	6	0	0	31.2	141	39	17	17	4	0	1	0	11	0	21	0	0	4	1	.800	0	0	4.83
Oneonta	A- NYY	10	10	3	0	58	240	44	28	24	3	0	3	3	21	0	62	2	1	4	4	.500	2	0	3.72
1997 Greensboro	A NYY	14	14	1	0	88.2	377	91	45	30	3	3	6	7	13	0	62	4	0	5	6	.455	0	0	3.05
Tampa	A+ NYY	10	10	0	0	61.2	240	49	19	16	4	0	3	2	8	0	39	0	1	5	0	1.000	0	0	2.34
Norwich	AA NYY	4	4	0	0	25	104	23	9	7	1	4	1	0	7	0	15	0	1	1	1	.500	0	0	2.52
1998 Norwich	AA NYY	13	13	2	0	79	360	97	49	43	4	1	3	7	23	2	51	4	0	2	6	.250	0	0	4.90
Tampa	A+ NYY	10	10	1	0	66.2	280	69	40	31	2	3	2	3	11	0	33	5	1	4	2	.667	0	0	4.19
1999 Yankees	R NYY	2	2	0	0	8	28	5	0	0	0	0	1	0	0	0	7	0	0	0	0	.000	0	0	0.00
Columbus	AAA NYY	12	12	0	0	66	299	81	42	35	11	1	0	4	24	0	45	1	0	6	3	.667	0	0	4.77
5 Min. YEARS		84	81	7	1	489.2	2092	503	251	203	35	9	19	28	120	2	341	16	4	31	23	.574	2	0	3.73

Chris Demetral

Bats: Left **Throws:** Right **Pos:** 2B | **Ht:** 5'11" **Wt:** 175 **Born:** 12/8/69 **Age:** 30

Year Team	Lg Org	G	AB	H	2B	3B	HR	TB	R	RBI	TBB	IBB	SO	HBP	SH	SF	SB	CS	SB%	GDP	Avg	OBP	SLG
1991 Yakima	A- LA	65	226	64	11	0	2	81	43	41	34	2	32	1	6	0	4	3	.57	2	.283	.379	.358
1992 Bakersfield	A+ LA	90	306	84	14	1	4	112	38	36	33	7	45	1	4	3	7	8	.47	3	.275	.344	.366
1993 Vero Beach	A+ LA	122	437	142	22	3	5	185	63	48	69	2	47	2	6	3	6	6	.50	9	.325	.417	.423
1994 San Antonio	AA LA	108	368	96	26	3	6	146	44	39	34	5	44	1	11	2	5	2	.71	8	.261	.323	.397
1995 Albuquerque	AAA LA	87	187	52	7	1	3	70	34	19	24	2	28	0	3	0	1	6	.14	7	.278	.360	.374
1996 San Berndno	A+ LA	11	32	9	3	0	1	15	5	4	6	1	5	0	0	0	0	3	.00	0	.281	.395	.469
Albuquerque	AAA LA	99	209	55	8	0	4	75	30	26	40	5	35	0	5	5	4	3	.57	6	.263	.374	.359
1997 Albuquerque	AAA LA	12	24	6	2	0	1	11	1	1	6	0	3	0	0	0	0	1	.00	1	.250	.400	.458
Vero Beach	A+ LA	86	278	77	13	3	12	132	52	45	48	0	40	2	2	4	5	2	.71	6	.277	.383	.475
1998 Tulsa	AA Tex	45	147	40	9	3	4	67	22	18	33	0	24	1	2	0	2	3	.40	4	.272	.409	.456
Oklahoma	AAA Tex	57	157	47	6	0	4	65	26	16	20	0	31	0	4	2	3	2	.60	1	.299	.374	.414
1999 Oklahoma	AAA Tex	65	183	48	7	1	4	69	29	18	28	0	35	0	7	1	1	2	.33	3	.262	.358	.377
9 Min. YEARS		847	2554	720	128	15	50	1028	387	311	375	24	369	8	50	20	38	41	.48	50	.282	.373	.403

Les Dennis

Bats: Right **Throws:** Right **Pos:** SS | **Ht:** 6'0" **Wt:** 175 **Born:** 6/3/73 **Age:** 27

Year Team	Lg Org	G	AB	H	2B	3B	HR	TB	R	RBI	TBB	IBB	SO	HBP	SH	SF	SB	CS	SB%	GDP	Avg	OBP	SLG
1995 Oneonta	A- NYY	48	148	39	6	2	1	52	24	13	14	0	40	3	0	2	5	2	.71	4	.264	.335	.351
1996 Greensboro	A NYY	33	75	19	3	0	1	25	15	9	11	0	27	1	2	0	1	2	.33	2	.253	.356	.333

73

Year Team	Lg Org	G	AB	H	2B	3B	HR	TB	R	RBI	TBB	IBB	SO	HBP	SH	SF	SB	CS	SB%	GDP	Avg	OBP	SLG
Oneonta	A- NYY	72	276	67	3	2	0	74	36	43	33	1	76	1	5	6	20	9	.69	2	.243	.320	.268
1997 Norwich	AA NYY	10	30	10	1	0	0	11	4	2	5	0	11	0	2	0	1	1	.50	0	.333	.429	.367
Tampa	A+ NYY	85	177	46	4	0	0	50	24	17	16	0	36	1	6	1	1	6	.14	6	.260	.323	.282
1998 Tampa	A+ NYY	44	104	19	4	0	1	26	16	8	5	0	20	0	5	0	1	0	1.00	6	.183	.220	.250
Norwich	AA NYY	32	93	23	5	1	0	30	12	13	24	0	20	0	2	0	2	2	.50	5	.247	.402	.323
1999 Tampa	A+ NYY	23	89	27	3	1	0	32	20	7	15	0	20	0	1	1	0	1	.00	2	.303	.400	.360
Yankees	R NYY	3	8	2	0	0	0	2	2	1	0	0	0	0	0	0	1	0	1.00	0	.250	.333	.250
Norwich	AA NYY	53	176	44	10	0	0	54	27	12	27	0	50	3	2	1	0	2	.00	1	.250	.357	.307
5 Min. YEARS		403	1176	296	39	6	3	356	180	124	151	1	300	9	25	11	32	25	.56	32	.252	.339	.303

Shane Dennis

Pitches: Left Bats: Right Pos: P   Ht: 6'3" Wt: 200 Born: 7/3/71 Age: 28

Year Team	Lg Org	G	GS	CG	GF	IP	BFP	H	R	ER	HR	SH	SF	HB	TBB	IBB	SO	WP	Bk	W	L	Pct.	ShO	Sv	ERA
1994 Spokane	A- SD	12	12	1	0	77.1	322	76	38	35	5	4	3	3	25	0	80	2	2	1	7	.125	1	0	4.07
Springfield	A SD	3	3	0	0	17	61	5	2	2	1	0	0	0	8	0	10	0	0	1	0	1.000	0	0	1.06
1995 Clinton	A SD	14	14	3	0	86	364	68	51	37	5	4	0	2	35	3	80	5	0	3	9	.250	0	0	3.87
Rancho Cuca	A+ SD	11	11	2	0	79	316	63	27	22	8	3	2	0	22	1	77	1	0	8	2	.800	1	0	2.51
1006 Rancho Cuca	A+ SD	9	9	1	0	59	247	57	22	21	6	1	1	1	19	0	54	2	0	4	2	.667	0	0	3.20
Memphis	AA SD	19	19	1	0	115	471	83	35	29	11	4	2	5	45	0	131	8	1	9	1	.900	0	0	2.27
1999 Las Vegas	AAA SD	34	18	0	5	116	538	140	83	72	19	4	4	4	60	1	104	6	0	3	10	.231	0	0	5.59
4 Min. YEARS		102	86	8	5	549.1	2319	492	258	218	55	20	12	15	214	5	536	24	3	29	31	.483	2	0	3.57

Darrell Dent

Bats: Left Throws: Left Pos: OF   Ht: 6'2" Wt: 172 Born: 5/26/77 Age: 23

Year Team	Lg Org	G	AB	H	2B	3B	HR	TB	R	RBI	TBB	IBB	SO	HBP	SH	SF	SB	CS	SB%	GDP	Avg	OBP	SLG
1995 Orioles	R Bal	36	125	35	7	3	0	48	24	6	21	0	22	2	0	1	6	2	.75	2	.280	.389	.384
1996 Bluefield	R+ Bal	59	193	43	6	2	0	53	40	14	28	1	49	0	1	4	30	9	.77	2	.223	.316	.275
1997 Delmarva	A Bal	128	441	103	17	4	1	131	69	37	63	2	110	4	7	6	60	15	.80	4	.234	.331	.297
1998 Frederick	A+ Bal	131	456	112	19	1	0	133	65	24	43	1	95	4	13	3	33	16	.67	4	.246	.314	.292
1999 Bowie	AA Bal	108	250	53	9	2	0	66	41	17	37	0	58	2	12	4	24	5	.83	4	.212	.314	.264
Rochester	AAA Bal	9	30	4	0	0	2	10	3	5	3	0	8	0	1	1	4	0	1.00	0	.133	.206	.333
5 Min. YEARS		471	1495	350	50	12	3	441	243	103	105	4	342	12	34	19	157	47	.77	14	.234	.324	.295

Joe DePastino

Bats: Right Throws: Right Pos: C   Ht: 6'2" Wt: 210 Born: 9/4/73 Age: 26

Year Team	Lg Org	G	AB	H	2B	3B	HR	TB	R	RBI	TBB	IBB	SO	HBP	SH	SF	SB	CS	SB%	GDP	Avg	OBP	SLG
1992 Red Sox	R Bos	40	157	41	6	1	1	52	13	16	7	1	25	3	0	2	1	1	.50	7	.261	.302	.331
1993 Utica	A- Bos	62	221	56	9	1	2	73	28	32	16	0	51	4	1	5	3	2	.60	4	.253	.309	.330
1994 Utica	A- Bos	51	172	46	11	1	5	74	23	31	22	1	41	3	1	2	5	2	.71	1	.267	.357	.430
1995 Michigan	A Bos	98	325	90	20	4	10	148	47	53	30	1	70	8	0	5	3	3	.50	5	.277	.348	.455
1996 Sarasota	A+ Bos	97	344	90	16	2	6	128	35	44	29	1	71	3	0	4	2	3	.40	7	.262	.321	.372
1997 Trenton	AA Bos	79	276	70	14	1	17	137	51	55	32	0	63	7	0	1	1	2	.33	10	.254	.345	.496
1998 Red Sox	R Bos	6	17	5	1	1	1	11	2	1	5	0	3	0	0	0	0	0	.00	0	.294	.455	.647
Pawtucket	AAA Bos	9	33	8	1	0	0	9	1	4	0	0	8	1	0	0	1	1	.50	1	.242	.265	.273
Trenton	AA Bos	73	275	81	16	0	10	127	34	43	28	5	51	1	0	2	1	0	1.00	4	.295	.359	.462
1999 Trenton	AA Bos	6	23	5	1	0	2	12	5	5	3	0	3	1	0	0	1	0	1.00	1	.217	.333	.522
Pawtucket	AAA Bos	77	257	65	13	0	13	117	35	52	27	0	40	1	0	2	1	1	.50	4	.253	.324	.455
8 Min. YEARS		598	2100	557	108	11	67	888	274	336	199	9	426	32	2	23	21	15	.58	45	.265	.335	.423

Marc Deschenes

Pitches: Right Bats: Right Pos: P   Ht: 6'0" Wt: 175 Born: 1/6/73 Age: 27

Year Team	Lg Org	G	GS	CG	GF	IP	BFP	H	R	ER	HR	SH	SF	HB	TBB	IBB	SO	WP	Bk	W	L	Pct.	ShO	Sv	ERA
1996 Columbus	A Cle	16	16	0	0	76.2	343	70	38	29	7	1	3	1	41	0	67	6	0	5	2	.714	0	0	3.40
1997 Columbus	A Cle	40	0	0	39	42.2	180	31	11	9	2	0	1	1	21	0	69	3	0	2	2	.500	0	19	1.90
Kinston	A+ Cle	20	0	0	19	22.1	79	9	2	2	0	0	0	0	4	0	39	1	0	2	0	1.000	0	10	0.81
1998 Kinston	A+ Cle	1	0	0	1	1	4	0	0	0	0	0	0	0	0	0	2	0	0	0	0	.000	0	0	0.00
Akron	AA Cle	47	0	0	26	58.1	259	52	36	25	4	2	4	0	34	6	52	5	0	4	6	.400	0	5	3.86
1999 Akron	AA Cle	43	0	0	26	65.1	277	57	28	24	5	5	2	2	31	6	64	3	0	3	2	.600	0	3	3.31
4 Min. YEARS		167	16	0	111	266.1	1142	219	115	89	22	8	10	4	132	12	293	18	0	16	12	.571	0	37	3.01

John DeSilva

Pitches: Right Bats: Right Pos: P   Ht: 6'0" Wt: 195 Born: 9/30/67 Age: 32

Year Team	Lg Org	G	GS	CG	GF	IP	BFP	H	R	ER	HR	SH	SF	HB	TBB	IBB	SO	WP	Bk	W	L	Pct.	ShO	Sv	ERA
1989 Niagara Fal	A- Det	4	4	0	0	24	95	15	5	5	0	1	0	2	8	0	24	3	1	3	0	1.000	0	0	1.88
Fayetteville	A Det	9	9	1	0	52.2	215	40	23	16	4	1	2	0	21	0	54	2	3	2	2	.500	0	0	2.73
1990 Lakeland	A+ Det	14	14	0	0	91	349	54	18	15	4	1	2	4	25	0	113	3	1	8	1	.889	0	0	1.48
London	AA Det	14	14	1	0	89	372	87	47	37	4	1	4	2	27	0	76	3	0	5	6	.455	1	0	3.74
1991 London	AA Det	11	11	2	0	73.2	294	51	24	23	4	2	2	0	24	0	80	1	0	5	4	.556	1	0	2.81
Toledo	AAA Det	11	11	1	0	58.2	254	62	33	30	10	0	1	1	21	0	56	1	0	5	4	.556	0	0	4.60
1992 Toledo	AAA Det	7	2	0	3	19	89	26	18	18	5	1	0	0	8	0	21	0	0	0	3	.000	0	0	8.53
London	AA Det	9	9	1	0	52.1	216	51	24	24	4	1	2	1	13	0	53	1	0	2	4	.333	1	0	4.13

Year Team	Lg Org	G	GS	CG	GF	IP	BFP	H	R	ER	HR	SH	SF	HB	TBB	IBB	SO	WP	Bk	W	L	Pct.	ShO	Sv	ERA
1993 Toledo	AAA Det	25	24	1	0	161	675	145	73	66	13	2	5	0	60	2	136	3	1	7	10	.412	0	0	3.69
1994 Albuquerque	AAA LA	25	6	0	4	66.2	317	90	62	58	7	1	3	4	27	0	39	3	0	3	5	.375	0	1	7.83
San Antonio	AA LA	25	2	0	7	46	202	46	29	26	3	2	1	1	18	2	46	2	1	1	3	.250	0	2	5.09
1995 Rochester	AAA Bal	26	25	2	1	150.2	644	156	78	70	19	3	3	6	51	0	82	2	1	11	9	.550	0	0	4.18
1996 Palm Spring	IND —	1	1	0	0	5	18	1	2	2	1	0	0	0	2	0	7	0	0	1	0	1.000	0	0	3.60
Pawtucket	AAA Bos	16	16	0	0	84.2	373	99	55	49	12	2	1	0	27	0	68	1	0	4	3	.571	0	0	5.21
1998 New Jersey	IND —	11	11	4	0	80.2	315	53	17	14	4	5	0	3	24	2	90	8	0	8	1	.889	1	0	1.56
Ottawa	AAA Mon	7	7	0	0	48.1	191	42	15	14	5	1	2	2	12	0	25	1	1	4	2	.667	0	0	2.61
1999 Ottawa	AAA Mon	22	15	0	3	90.1	377	73	35	29	4	6	5	2	41	1	75	5	0	4	1	.800	0	0	2.89
1993 Detroit	AL	1	0	0	1	1	4	2	1	1	0	0	1	0	0	0	0	0	0	0	0	.000	0	0	9.00
Los Angeles	NL	3	0	0	2	5.1	23	6	4	4	0	0	0	0	1	0	6	0	0	0	0	.000	0	0	6.75
1995 Baltimore	AL	2	2	0	0	8.2	41	8	7	7	3	1	1	1	7	0	1	0	0	1	0	1.000	0	0	7.27
10 Min. YEARS		237	181	13	18	1193.2	4996	1091	558	496	103	30	33	28	409	7	1045	40	10	73	58	.557	4	3	3.74
2 Maj. YEARS		6	2	0	3	15	68	16	12	12	3	1	2	1	8	0	7	0	0	1	0	1.000	0	0	7.20

Kris Detmers

Pitches: Left Bats: Both Pos: P   Ht: 6'5" Wt: 215 Born: 6/22/74 Age: 26

Year Team	Lg Org	G	GS	CG	GF	IP	BFP	H	R	ER	HR	SH	SF	HB	TBB	IBB	SO	WP	Bk	W	L	Pct.	ShO	Sv	ERA
1994 Madison	A StL	16	16	0	0	90.1	380	88	45	34	4	1	1	4	31	0	74	0	1	5	7	.417	0	0	3.39
1995 St. Pete	A+ StL	25	25	1	0	146.2	606	120	64	53	12	3	7	2	57	0	150	3	2	10	9	.526	0	0	3.25
1996 Arkansas	AA StL	27	27	0	0	163.2	698	154	72	61	15	6	3	4	70	0	97	8	0	12	8	.600	0	0	3.35
1997 Louisville	AAA StL	10	5	0	0	35	164	43	28	28	3	0	2	2	17	0	22	1	0	3	3	.500	0	0	7.20
Arkansas	AA StL	15	15	0	0	78	346	99	54	50	11	3	2	2	27	0	44	1	0	5	7	.417	0	0	5.77
1998 Arkansas	AA StL	27	26	0	0	153.2	698	175	100	84	14	8	8	8	78	1	88	9	3	9	10	.474	0	0	4.92
1999 Memphis	AAA StL	23	22	0	0	125.1	544	135	74	71	17	5	5	2	44	2	90	2	0	6	8	.429	0	0	5.10
6 Min. YEARS		143	136	1	0	792.2	3436	814	437	381	76	26	28	24	324	3	565	24	6	50	52	.490	0	0	4.33

Cesar Devarez

Bats: Right Throws: Right Pos: C   Ht: 5'10" Wt: 175 Born: 9/22/69 Age: 30

Year Team	Lg Org	G	AB	H	2B	3B	HR	TB	R	RBI	TBB	IBB	SO	HBP	SH	SF	SB	CS	SB%	GDP	Avg	OBP	SLG
1989 Bluefield	R+ Bal	12	42	9	4	0	0	13	3	7	1	0	5	0	0	0	0	0	.00	3	.214	.233	.310
1990 Wausau	A Bal	56	171	34	4	1	3	49	7	19	7	0	28	0	0	2	2	3	.40	3	.199	.230	.287
1991 Frederick	A+ Bal	74	235	59	13	2	3	85	25	29	14	0	28	4	2	1	2	2	.50	9	.251	.303	.362
1992 Hagerstown	AA Bal	110	319	72	8	1	2	88	20	32	17	0	49	6	2	2	5	5	.29	3	.226	.276	.276
1993 Frederick	A+ Bal	38	124	36	8	0	2	50	15	16	12	1	18	1	1	0	1	4	.20	2	.290	.358	.403
Bowie	AA Bal	57	174	39	7	1	0	48	14	15	5	0	21	2	2	2	5	1	.83	6	.224	.251	.276
1994 Bowie	AA Bal	73	249	78	13	4	6	117	43	48	8	1	25	1	3	4	7	2	.78	10	.313	.332	.470
1995 Rochester	AAA Bal	67	240	60	12	1	1	77	32	21	7	0	25	0	1	1	2	2	.50	8	.250	.270	.321
1996 Rochester	AAA Bal	67	223	64	9	1	4	87	24	27	9	0	26	1	2	4	5	1	.83	7	.287	.312	.390
1997 Devil Rays	R TB	4	6	0	0	0	0	0	0	0	4	0	2	0	0	0	0	0	.00	0	.000	.400	.000
Orlando	AA TB	34	96	27	4	1	5	48	13	17	8	2	15	0	1	0	1	0	1.00	2	.281	.337	.500
1998 Durham	AAA TB	38	116	31	5	2	4	52	11	20	8	0	24	1	0	0	4	2	.67	3	.267	.320	.448
1999 Bowie	AA Bal	58	200	53	11	0	4	76	25	29	16	1	24	2	1	1	2	2	.50	5	.265	.324	.380
1995 Baltimore	AL	6	4	0	0	0	0	0	0	0	0	0	0	0	1	0	0	0	.00	0	.000	.000	.000
1996 Baltimore	AL	10	18	2	0	1	0	4	3	0	1	0	3	0	0	0	0	0	.00	0	.111	.158	.222
11 Min. YEARS		688	2195	562	98	14	34	790	232	280	116	5	290	18	17	15	33	24	.58	61	.256	.297	.360
2 Maj. YEARS		16	22	2	0	1	0	4	3	0	1	0	3	0	1	0	0	0	.00	0	.091	.130	.182

Jason Dewey

Bats: Right Throws: Right Pos: C   Ht: 6'1" Wt: 200 Born: 4/18/77 Age: 23

Year Team	Lg Org	G	AB	H	2B	3B	HR	TB	R	RBI	TBB	IBB	SO	HBP	SH	SF	SB	CS	SB%	GDP	Avg	OBP	SLG
1997 Boise	A- Ana	68	272	88	17	2	13	148	55	64	41	4	70	2	1	2	5	2	.71	2	.324	.413	.544
1998 Lk Elsinore	A+ Ana	111	391	115	30	3	15	196	64	66	66	0	118	0	0	2	8	8	.50	10	.294	.394	.501
1999 Erie	AA Ana	40	139	31	7	0	4	50	17	14	17	1	50	0	0	0	0	1	.00	2	.223	.308	.360
Lk Elsinore	A+ Ana	66	242	78	23	0	10	131	48	31	30	0	62	2	0	2	0	0	.00	8	.322	.399	.541
3 Min. YEARS		285	1044	312	77	5	42	525	184	175	154	5	300	4	1	6	13	11	.54	22	.299	.389	.503

Matt DeWitt

Pitches: Right Bats: Right Pos: P   Ht: 6'4" Wt: 220 Born: 9/4/77 Age: 22

Year Team	Lg Org	G	GS	CG	GF	IP	BFP	H	R	ER	HR	SH	SF	HB	TBB	IBB	SO	WP	Bk	W	L	Pct.	ShO	Sv	ERA
1995 Johnson Cy	R+ StL	13	12	0	0	62.2	288	84	56	49	10	0	3	1	32	0	45	5	0	2	6	.250	0	0	7.04
1996 Johnson Cy	R+ StL	14	14	0	0	79.2	353	96	53	48	17	1	0	3	26	0	58	7	0	5	5	.500	0	0	5.42
1997 Peoria	A StL	27	27	1	0	158.1	672	152	84	72	16	7	8	9	57	2	121	6	1	9	9	.500	0	0	4.09
1998 Pr William	A+ StL	24	24	1	0	148.1	588	132	65	60	13	3	3	7	18	0	118	6	1	6	9	.400	0	0	3.64
1999 Arkansas	AA StL	26	26	0	0	148.1	644	153	87	73	21	4	3	1	59	0	107	3	1	9	8	.529	0	0	4.43
5 Min. YEARS		104	103	2	0	597.1	2562	617	345	302	77	15	17	21	192	2	449	26	8	31	37	.456	0	0	4.55

Scott DeWitt

Pitches: Left Bats: Right Pos: P   Ht: 6'3" Wt: 210 Born: 10/6/74 Age: 25

Year Team	Lg Org	G	GS	CG	GF	IP	BFP	H	R	ER	HR	SH	SF	HB	TBB	IBB	SO	WP	Bk	W	L	Pct.	ShO	Sv	ERA
1995 Marlins	R Fla	11	10	1	0	63.2	245	48	15	14	1	3	2	2	9	0	70	1	1	5	3	.625	0	0	1.98

		HOW MUCH HE PITCHED						WHAT HE GAVE UP										THE RESULTS					
Year Team	Lg Org	G	GS	CG	GF	IP	BFP	H	R	ER	HR	SH	SF	HB	TBB	IBB	SO	WP	Bk	W	L	Pct.	ShO	Sv	ERA
Kane County	A Fla	1	1	0	0	3	10	0	0	0	0	0	0	1	1	0	2	0	0	0	0	.000	0	0	0.00
1996 Kane County	A Fla	27	27	1	0	148.2	667	151	96	78	8	5	4	19	59	0	119	2	2	10	11	.476	1	0	4.72
1997 Brevard Cty	A+ Fla	25	24	0	1	132	585	145	80	61	13	6	3	8	51	0	121	3	1	4	10	.286	0	0	4.16
1998 Portland	AA Fla	50	3	0	13	59.2	278	61	35	30	7	2	3	4	36	0	64	4	1	4	4	.500	0	1	4.53
1999 Carolina	AA Col	45	0	0	15	66.2	309	84	34	29	2	3	2	4	21	1	65	6	1	1	2	.333	0	2	3.92
5 Min. YEARS		159	65	2	29	473.2	2094	489	260	212	31	19	14	38	177	1	441	16	6	24	30	.444	1	3	4.03

Alejandro Diaz

Bats: Right **Throws:** Right **Pos:** OF **Ht:** 5'9" **Wt:** 175 **Born:** 7/9/78 **Age:** 21

		BATTING														BASERUNNING				PERCENTAGES		
Year Team	Lg Org	G	AB	H	2B	3B	HR	TB	R	RBI	TBB	IBB	SO	HBP	SH	SF	SB	CS	SB%	GDP	Avg	OBP	SLG
1999 Clinton	A Cin	55	221	63	14	3	6	101	39	41	12	1	35	2	0	4	28	11	.72	6	.285	.322	.457
Chattanooga	AA Cin	55	220	58	9	8	7	104	27	35	8	0	31	3	2	2	6	2	.75	3	.264	.296	.473
1 Min. YEARS		110	441	121	23	11	13	205	66	76	20	1	66	5	2	6	34	13	.72	9	.274	.309	.465

Freddie Diaz

Bats: Both **Throws:** Right **Pos:** SS **Ht:** 5'11" **Wt:** 190 **Born:** 9/10/72 **Age:** 27

		BATTING														BASERUNNING				PERCENTAGES		
Year Team	Lg Org	G	AB	H	2B	3B	HR	TB	R	RBI	TBB	IBB	SO	HBP	SH	SF	SB	CS	SB%	GDP	Avg	OBP	SLG
1992 Angels	R Ana	14	37	10	3	0	0	13	6	4	5	0	7	0	2	1	3	1	.75	0	.270	.349	.351
1993 Boise	A- Ana	26	75	22	4	1	2	34	13	14	9	0	11	0	3	0	1	3	.25	0	.293	.369	.453
1994 Lk Elsinore	A+ Ana	110	350	100	29	1	5	146	48	64	35	0	71	4	7	6	4	4	.50	5	.286	.352	.417
1995 Midland	AA Ana	8	25	6	3	0	0	9	3	4	0	0	12	0	2	0	0	0	.00	1	.240	.240	.360
Lk Elsinore	A+ Ana	49	149	35	12	2	1	54	25	25	11	0	54	0	3	6	1	1	.50	6	.235	.277	.362
1996 Midland	AA Ana	54	156	31	7	2	3	51	23	18	13	1	43	0	4	3	1	1	.50	3	.199	.256	.327
Vancouver	AAA Ana	34	123	32	9	2	3	54	19	23	14	0	25	0	3	3	0	0	.00	1	.260	.329	.439
1997 Midland	AA Ana	43	135	36	9	0	2	51	21	18	18	0	30	1	2	2	0	0	.00	6	.267	.353	.378
1998 Midland	AA Ana	4	11	2	0	0	0	2	3	2	3	0	4	0	0	0	0	0	.00	0	.182	.357	.182
Lk Elsinore	A+ Ana	75	273	83	23	0	5	121	36	29	25	4	59	0	0	2	0	1	.00	6	.304	.360	.443
1999 Tulsa	AA Tex	16	52	5	3	0	0	8	5	9	6	1	15	0	0	1	1	0	1.00	1	.096	.186	.154
Zion	IND —	33	120	26	6	1	2	40	18	24	17	0	17	0	3	1	1	1	.50	3	.217	.312	.333
8 Min. YEARS		466	1506	388	108	9	23	583	220	234	156	6	348	5	29	25	12	12	.50	29	.258	.324	.387

Juan Diaz

Bats: Right **Throws:** Right **Pos:** 1B **Ht:** 6'2" **Wt:** 228 **Born:** 2/19/76 **Age:** 24

		BATTING														BASERUNNING				PERCENTAGES		
Year Team	Lg Org	G	AB	H	2B	3B	HR	TB	R	RBI	TBB	IBB	SO	HBP	SH	SF	SB	CS	SB%	GDP	Avg	OBP	SLG
1997 Savannah	A LA	127	460	106	24	2	25	209	63	83	48	2	155	4	1	4	2	2	.50	0	.230	.306	.454
Vero Beach	A+ LA	1	3	2	0	0	1	5	2	3	0	0	1	1	0	0	0	0	.00	0	.667	.750	1.667
1998 Vero Beach	A+ LA	67	250	73	12	1	17	138	33	51	21	2	52	4	0	3	1	2	.33	4	.292	.353	.552
San Antonio	AA LA	56	188	50	13	0	13	102	26	30	15	1	45	2	0	0	0	0	.00	4	.266	.327	.543
1999 San Antonio	AA LA	66	254	77	21	1	9	127	42	52	26	1	77	3	0	4	0	0	.00	4	.303	.369	.500
3 Min. YEARS		317	1155	308	70	4	65	581	166	219	110	6	330	14	1	11	3	4	.43	22	.267	.335	.503

R.A. Dickey

Pitches: Right **Bats:** Right **Pos:** P **Ht:** 6'2" **Wt:** 205 **Born:** 10/29/74 **Age:** 25

		HOW MUCH HE PITCHED						WHAT HE GAVE UP										THE RESULTS					
Year Team	Lg Org	G	GS	CG	GF	IP	BFP	H	R	ER	HR	SH	SF	HB	TBB	IBB	SO	WP	Bk	W	L	Pct.	ShO	Sv	ERA
1997 Charlotte	A+ Tex	8	6	0	2	35	162	51	32	27	8	0	0	0	12	1	32	5	3	1	4	.200	0	0	6.94
1998 Charlotte	A+ Tex	57	0	0	54	60	260	58	31	22	9	4	1	0	22	3	53	3	2	1	5	.167	0	38	3.30
1999 Tulsa	AA Tex	35	11	0	21	95	419	105	60	48	13	1	4	2	40	1	59	9	0	6	7	.462	0	10	4.55
Oklahoma	AAA Tex	6	2	0	1	22.2	99	23	12	11	1	3	0	1	7	1	17	2	0	2	2	.500	0	0	4.37
3 Min. YEARS		106	19	0	78	212.2	940	237	135	108	31	8	5	3	81	6	161	19	5	10	18	.357	0	48	4.57

Juan Dilone

Bats: Both **Throws:** Right **Pos:** OF **Ht:** 6'1" **Wt:** 188 **Born:** 5/10/73 **Age:** 27

		BATTING														BASERUNNING				PERCENTAGES		
Year Team	Lg Org	G	AB	H	2B	3B	HR	TB	R	RBI	TBB	IBB	SO	HBP	SH	SF	SB	CS	SB%	GDP	Avg	OBP	SLG
1991 Athletics	R Oak	48	153	34	2	0	0	36	26	21	37	2	44	0	1	4	5	3	.63	4	.222	.366	.235
1992 Athletics	R Oak	48	151	35	5	0	0	40	30	13	39	0	42	0	2	3	12	3	.80	1	.232	.383	.265
1993 Sou Oregon	A- Oak	54	152	32	6	1	1	43	19	19	22	1	52	1	4	2	7	5	.58	0	.211	.311	.283
1994 W Michigan	A Oak	106	352	81	15	5	12	142	66	48	46	3	110	4	5	3	29	12	.71	3	.230	.323	.403
1996 Modesto	A+ Oak	111	404	107	17	1	14	168	78	66	45	0	138	6	8	5	31	10	.76	11	.265	.343	.416
1997 Modesto	A+ Oak	97	325	73	15	6	19	157	54	51	44	1	112	0	3	0	7	1	.88	6	.225	.317	.483
1998 San Jose	A+ SF	85	316	101	24	2	18	183	63	47	31	2	103	4	0	4	19	9	.68	3	.320	.383	.579
Shreveport	AA SF	36	111	23	8	2	4	47	13	10	10	2	35	3	1	1	3	1	.75	4	.207	.288	.423
1999 Shreveport	AA SF	112	340	86	19	6	5	132	52	44	46	3	87	8	1	1	11	7	.61	8	.253	.354	.388
8 Min. YEARS		697	2304	572	111	23	73	948	401	325	320	14	723	26	24	23	124	51	.71	40	.248	.343	.411

Doug Dimma

Pitches: Left **Bats:** Right **Pos:** P **Ht:** 5'11" **Wt:** 180 **Born:** 7/3/78 **Age:** 21

		HOW MUCH HE PITCHED						WHAT HE GAVE UP										THE RESULTS					
Year Team	Lg Org	G	GS	CG	GF	IP	BFP	H	R	ER	HR	SH	SF	HB	TBB	IBB	SO	WP	Bk	W	L	Pct.	ShO	Sv	ERA
1999 St.Cathrnes	A- Tor	17	2	0	5	47.2	214	48	29	20	1	1	0	3	28	1	42	4	2	3	1	.750	0	1	3.78
Syracuse	AAA Tor	1	0	0	0	1	4	2	1	1	1	0	0	0	0	0	1	0	0	0	0	.000	0	0	9.00
1 Min. YEARS		18	2	0	5	48.2	218	50	30	21	2	1	0	3	28	1	43	4	2	3	1	.750	0	1	3.88

Allen Dina

Bats: Right **Throws:** Right **Pos:** OF   **Ht:** 5'10" **Wt:** 180 **Born:** 9/28/73 **Age:** 26

				BATTING														BASERUNNING				PERCENTAGES		
Year Team	Lg Org	G	AB	H	2B	3B	HR	TB	R	RBI	TBB	IBB	SO	HBP	SH	SF	SB	CS	SB%	GDP	Avg	OBP	SLG
1998 Pittsfield	A- NYM	68	278	83	16	5	5	124	47	39	24	0	34	1	1	4	18	5	.78	1	.299	.352	.446
Capital Cty	A NYM	2	8	3	2	0	0	5	1	3	0	0	1	0	0	0	0	0	.00	0	.375	.375	.625
1999 St. Lucie	A+ NYM	85	343	118	16	4	12	178	65	47	25	0	54	6	4	3	34	10	.77	2	.344	.395	.519
Binghamton	AA NYM	49	192	44	10	3	0	60	25	15	9	0	46	1	0	2	9	3	.75	6	.229	.265	.313
2 Min. YEARS		204	821	248	44	12	17	367	138	104	58	0	135	8	5	9	61	18	.77	9	.302	.350	.447

Craig Dingman

Pitches: Right **Bats:** Right **Pos:** P   **Ht:** 6'4" **Wt:** 195 **Born:** 3/12/74 **Age:** 26

		HOW MUCH HE PITCHED						WHAT HE GAVE UP											THE RESULTS					
Year Team	Lg Org	G	GS	CG	GF	IP	BFP	H	R	ER	HR	SH	SF	HB	TBB	IBB	SO	WP	Bk	W	L	Pct.	ShO	Sv	ERA
1994 Yankees	R NYY	17	1	0	11	32	135	27	17	12	0	7	2	3	10	0	51	4	0	0	5	.000	0	1	3.38
1996 Oneonta	A- NYY	20	0	0	15	35.1	137	17	11	8	0	1	1	1	9	0	52	0	1	0	2	.000	0	9	2.04
1997 Tampa	A+ NYY	19	0	0	11	22.1	92	15	14	13	2	1	0	0	14	2	26	3	0	0	4	.000	0	6	5.24
Greensboro	A NYY	30	0	0	27	33	131	19	7	7	0	2	1	1	12	0	41	3	0	2	0	1.000	0	19	1.91
1998 Tampa	A+ NYY	50	0	0	28	70.2	293	48	29	25	8	3	2	1	39	9	95	2	0	5	4	.556	0	7	3.18
1999 Norwich	AA NYY	55	0	0	21	74.1	288	56	16	13	2	2	0	2	12	2	90	2	0	8	6	.571	0	9	1.57
5 Min. YEARS		191	1	0	113	267.2	1076	182	94	78	12	16	6	8	96	13	355	14	1	15	21	.417	0	51	2.62

Mike Diorio

Pitches: Right **Bats:** Right **Pos:** P   **Ht:** 6'2" **Wt:** 200 **Born:** 3/1/73 **Age:** 27

		HOW MUCH HE PITCHED						WHAT HE GAVE UP											THE RESULTS					
Year Team	Lg Org	G	GS	CG	GF	IP	BFP	H	R	ER	HR	SH	SF	HB	TBB	IBB	SO	WP	Bk	W	L	Pct.	ShO	Sv	ERA
1993 Auburn	A- Hou	15	15	0	0	79	356	98	57	45	6	2	2	3	27	0	57	6	0	3	7	.300	0	0	5.13
1994 Astros	R Hou	2	0	0	0	2.1	15	5	6	6	1	0	0	0	3	0	2	0	0	1	0	.000	0	0	23.14
Osceola	A+ Hou	13	7	0	0	44	191	48	24	14	4	1	2	0	11	0	27	2	0	3	2	.600	0	0	2.86
1995 Quad City	A Hou	33	11	0	4	91.2	391	82	39	33	6	4	0	4	36	1	81	13	2	6	4	.600	0	1	3.24
1997 Jackson	AA Hou	8	0	0	2	11.1	63	18	17	12	1	1	0	2	6	1	9	1	2	1	3	.250	0	1	9.53
Kissimmee	A+ Hou	36	0	0	30	39.1	161	33	15	13	1	1	0	1	10	1	30	1	1	3	2	.600	0	19	2.97
1998 Jackson	AA Hou	32	0	0	24	43	182	35	16	10	0	3	0	2	21	4	31	2	0	2	3	.400	0	11	2.09
New Orleans	AAA Hou	21	0	0	8	29.1	134	38	24	17	3	2	2	1	11	4	14	1	0	4	2	.667	0	2	5.22
1999 New Orleans	AAA Hou	50	0	0	14	70.1	333	85	59	50	10	2	2	7	31	6	32	6	0	2	3	.400	0	1	6.40
6 Min. YEARS		210	33	0	82	410.1	1826	442	257	200	32	16	8	20	156	17	283	32	5	24	27	.471	0	35	4.39

Dan DiPace

Bats: Left **Throws:** Right **Pos:** DH-OF   **Ht:** 6'2" **Wt:** 215 **Born:** 4/24/75 **Age:** 25

				BATTING														BASERUNNING				PERCENTAGES		
Year Team	Lg Org	G	AB	H	2B	3B	HR	TB	R	RBI	TBB	IBB	SO	HBP	SH	SF	SB	CS	SB%	GDP	Avg	OBP	SLG
1996 Lafayette	IND —	40	104	24	2	0	5	41	13	24	14	1	24	3	1	0	6	1	.86	1	.231	.339	.394
1997 Duluth-Sup	IND —	5	17	3	1	0	0	4	1	0	3	0	5	0	0	0	0	0	.00	1	.176	.300	.235
Tyler	IND —	42	115	33	6	0	5	54	22	24	16	0	31	2	1	1	4	3	.57	0	.287	.381	.470
1998 Lansing	A KC	20	49	13	1	0	1	17	11	7	11	1	14	2	0	2	1	0	1.00	1	.265	.406	.347
Wilmington	A+ KC	16	41	5	0	0	0	5	5	2	7	0	20	1	0	0	0	0	.00	2	.122	.265	.122
Spokane	A- KC	44	113	31	11	0	6	60	12	34	18	1	28	4	0	4	0	0	.00	1	.274	.381	.531
1999 Chstn-WV	A KC	65	192	43	11	0	2	60	23	19	34	1	67	6	1	0	8	3	.73	3	.224	.358	.313
Huntsville	AA Mil	11	26	3	1	0	0	4	2	2	3	0	9	0	0	0	0	0	.00	0	.115	.207	.154
4 Min. YEARS		243	657	155	33	0	19	245	89	112	106	4	198	18	3	7	19	7	.73	9	.236	.354	.373

Nate Dishington

Bats: Left **Throws:** Right **Pos:** OF   **Ht:** 6'3" **Wt:** 210 **Born:** 1/8/75 **Age:** 25

				BATTING														BASERUNNING				PERCENTAGES		
Year Team	Lg Org	G	AB	H	2B	3B	HR	TB	R	RBI	TBB	IBB	SO	HBP	SH	SF	SB	CS	SB%	GDP	Avg	OBP	SLG
1993 Johnson Cy	R+ StL	36	121	19	5	1	1	29	13	7	16	0	52	2	0	2	4	2	.67	3	.157	.262	.240
1994 Cardinals	R StL	51	179	51	15	3	4	84	36	36	22	2	58	5	0	2	1	1	.50	2	.285	.375	.469
1995 Savannah	A StL	124	444	95	17	5	11	155	56	44	62	4	154	17	0	6	13	7	.65	14	.214	.329	.349
1996 Peoria	A StL	75	208	47	12	3	3	74	22	30	25	0	73	7	0	4	1	1	.50	0	.226	.324	.356
1997 Pr William	A+ StL	133	448	122	20	6	28	238	75	106	81	11	121	7	1	6	8	5	.62	3	.272	.387	.531
1998 Arkansas	AA StL	75	237	60	6	1	17	119	40	49	40	1	91	3	0	1	6	1	.86	3	.253	.367	.502
Memphis	AAA StL	60	200	53	15	1	10	100	30	34	24	1	88	8	0	0	1	1	.50	2	.265	.366	.500
1999 Memphis	AAA StL	72	196	41	11	1	8	78	34	34	25	1	96	0	0	2	1	4	.20	1	.209	.296	.398
Akron	AA Cle	17	59	14	2	0	5	31	12	14	6	0	30	3	0	0	0	0	.00	1	.237	.338	.525
7 Min. YEARS		643	2092	502	103	21	87	908	318	352	301	20	763	52	1	23	35	22	.61	35	.240	.346	.434

Rich Dishman

Pitches: Right **Bats:** Right **Pos:** P   **Ht:** 6'5" **Wt:** 220 **Born:** 4/26/75 **Age:** 25

		HOW MUCH HE PITCHED						WHAT HE GAVE UP											THE RESULTS					
Year Team	Lg Org	G	GS	CG	GF	IP	BFP	H	R	ER	HR	SH	SF	HB	TBB	IBB	SO	WP	Bk	W	L	Pct.	ShO	Sv	ERA
1997 Eugene	A- Atl	19	1	0	6	51	213	47	19	17	2	1	0	7	13	0	60	5	1	2	2	.500	0	3	3.00
1998 Macon	A Atl	18	0	0	6	39.1	170	38	22	17	2	3	0	0	17	1	44	2	1	1	1	.500	0	1	3.89
Danville	A+ Atl	20	11	0	6	77.1	308	82	20	16	1	3	1	3	28	0	85	3	0	3	2	.600	0	1	1.86
1999 Greenville	AA Atl	30	24	1	1	139.2	613	146	76	65	19	6	4	7	58	0	131	5	0	6	13	.316	0	1	4.19
3 Min. YEARS		87	36	1	19	307.1	1304	285	137	115	24	13	5	17	116	1	320	15	2	12	18	.400	0	5	3.37

Tim Dixon

Pitches: Left   Bats: Left   Pos: P   Ht: 6'2"   Wt: 215   Born: 2/26/72   Age: 28

Year Team	Lg Org	G	GS	CG	GF	IP	BFP	H	R	ER	HR	SH	SF	HB	TBB	IBB	SO	WP	Bk	W	L	Pct.	ShO	Sv	ERA
1995 Vermont	A- Mon	18	9	0	2	69	287	58	20	14	0	3	0	8	16	0	58	5	7	7	2	.778	0	1	1.83
1996 Wst Plm Bch	A+ Mon	37	16	0	8	124	528	126	55	40	10	8	5	6	35	3	87	7	0	5	11	.313	0	2	2.90
1997 Ottawa	AAA Mon	5	0	0	0	9.1	45	12	10	10	2	1	1	0	5	1	8	2	0	1	1	.500	0	0	9.64
Harrisburg	AA Mon	37	2	0	6	69.1	296	66	34	26	6	4	3	4	24	2	75	4	0	5	2	.714	0	0	3.38
1998 Harrisburg	AA Mon	37	0	0	15	58	249	58	29	25	5	3	2	1	16	2	52	4	0	2	5	.286	0	2	3.88
Ottawa	AAA Mon	9	0	0	5	18.1	84	22	15	12	2	0	1	0	7	0	13	3	0	0	0	.000	0	0	5.89
1999 Harrisburg	AA Mon	2	0	0	0	4.2	20	4	4	3	1	0	1	0	2	0	4	1	0	0	1	.000	0	0	5.79
Ottawa	AAA Mon	2	0	0	1	1.1	6	3	1	1	1	0	0	0	0	0	1	0	0	0	0	.000	0	0	6.75
Pawtucket	AAA Bos	2	0	0	0	5	25	6	5	5	3	0	0	1	3	0	4	0	0	0	1	.000	0	0	9.00
Trenton	AA Bos	8	2	0	1	18.1	73	15	6	6	2	1	0	2	6	0	10	2	0	2	0	1.000	0	0	2.95
Huntsville	AA Mil	24	1	0	15	39.1	174	33	16	12	3	2	2	4	19	0	43	2	0	0	0	.000	0	6	2.75
5 Min. YEARS		181	30	0	54	416.2	1787	403	195	154	35	22	15	26	133	8	355	30	7	22	23	.489	0	11	3.33

Robert Dodd

Pitches: Left   Bats: Left   Pos: P   Ht: 6'3"   Wt: 195   Born: 3/14/73   Age: 27

Year Team	Lg Org	G	GS	CG	GF	IP	BFP	H	R	ER	HR	SH	SF	HB	TBB	IBB	SO	WP	Bk	W	L	Pct.	ShO	Sv	ERA
1994 Batavia	A- Phi	14	7	0	2	52	209	42	16	13	0	2	1	2	14	1	44	4	0	2	4	.333	0	1	2.26
1995 Clearwater	A+ Phi	26	26	0	0	151	636	144	64	53	4	3	6	1	58	0	110	3	7	8	7	.533	0	0	3.16
Reading	AA Phi	1	0	0	0	1.1	5	0	0	0	0	0	0	0	2	0	0	0	0	0	0	.000	0	0	0.00
1996 Reading	AA Phi	18	5	0	4	43	185	41	21	17	4	4	3	3	24	2	35	0	1	2	3	.400	0	0	3.56
Scranton-WB	AAA Phi	8	2	0	2	20	101	32	21	18	4	0	0	1	9	0	12	1	0	0	0	.000	0	0	8.10
1997 Reading	AA Phi	63	0	0	23	80.1	314	61	29	29	8	6	0	0	21	1	94	1	0	9	4	.692	0	8	3.25
1998 Scranton-WB	AAA Phi	42	0	0	16	41.2	177	37	15	15	4	2	1	1	19	2	41	0	0	4	1	.800	0	6	3.24
1999 Reading	AA Phi	42	0	0	18	80	335	78	38	34	8	2	2	3	23	1	79	1	2	10	2	.833	0	5	3.83
Scranton-WB	AAA Phi	6	4	1	1	29.2	114	19	5	3	1	1	1	1	6	0	23	0	0	4	0	1.000	0	1	0.91
1998 Philadelphia	NL	4	0	0	3	5	25	7	6	4	1	0	2	1	1	0	4	1	1	1	0	1.000	0	1	7.20
6 Min. YEARS		220	44	1	66	499	2076	454	209	182	33	20	14	12	176	7	438	10	10	39	21	.650	0	21	3.28

Jeremy Dodson

Bats: Left   Throws: Right   Pos: OF   Ht: 6'2"   Wt: 200   Born: 5/3/77   Age: 23

Year Team	Lg Org	G	AB	H	2B	3B	HR	TB	R	RBI	TBB	IBB	SO	HBP	SH	SF	SB	CS	SB%	GDP	Avg	OBP	SLG
1998 Spokane	A- KC	69	268	90	19	5	9	146	56	59	25	2	59	6	0	5	8	4	.67	5	.336	.398	.545
1999 Wichita	AA KC	133	452	116	20	1	21	201	63	58	51	2	95	2	1	0	9	5	.64	12	.257	.335	.445
2 Min. YEARS		202	720	206	39	6	30	347	119	117	76	4	154	8	1	5	17	9	.65	17	.286	.358	.482

Bo Donaldson

Pitches: Right   Bats: Right   Pos: P   Ht: 6'1"   Wt: 200   Born: 10/10/74   Age: 25

Year Team	Lg Org	G	GS	CG	GF	IP	BFP	H	R	ER	HR	SH	SF	HB	TBB	IBB	SO	WP	Bk	W	L	Pct.	ShO	Sv	ERA
1997 Boise	A- Ana	27	0	0	25	52	208	31	10	7	0	3	2	0	20	1	88	10	2	3	1	.750	0	15	1.21
1998 Lk Elsinore	A+ Ana	54	3	0	42	76.1	340	65	38	32	7	5	3	9	40	4	99	12	4	4	6	.400	0	20	3.77
1999 Rockford	A Cin	19	0	0	7	30	119	17	7	4	0	4	0	0	12	3	50	2	1	2	1	.667	0	1	1.20
Chattanooga	AA Cin	38	0	0	19	51.1	199	30	18	17	2	3	1	1	16	2	67	2	1	5	3	.625	0	2	2.98
3 Min. YEARS		138	3	0	93	209.2	866	143	73	60	9	15	5	12	88	10	304	26	8	14	11	.560	0	42	2.58

Brendan Donnelly

Pitches: Right   Bats: Right   Pos: P   Ht: 6'3"   Wt: 205   Born: 7/4/71   Age: 28

Year Team	Lg Org	G	GS	CG	GF	IP	BFP	H	R	ER	HR	SH	SF	HB	TBB	IBB	SO	WP	Bk	W	L	Pct.	ShO	Sv	ERA
1992 White Sox	R CWS	9	7	0	1	41.2	191	41	25	17	0	0	2	0	21	0	31	6	0	0	3	.000	0	1	3.67
1993 Geneva	A- ChC	21	3	0	7	43	198	39	34	30	4	1	1	6	29	0	29	7	3	4	0	1.000	0	1	6.28
1994 Ohio Valley	IND —	10	0	0	1	13.2	59	13	5	4	1	0	0	3	4	0	20	1	0	1	1	.500	0	0	2.63
1995 Chstn-WV	A Cin	24	0	0	22	30.1	112	14	4	4	0	1	2	1	7	1	33	1	0	1	1	.500	0	12	1.19
Winston-Sal	A Cin	23	0	0	14	35.1	138	20	6	4	1	2	0	2	14	2	32	0	1	1	2	.333	0	2	1.02
Indianapols	AAA Cin	3	0	0	0	2.2	18	7	8	7	2	0	1	1	2	0	1	2	0	1	1	.500	0	0	23.63
1996 Chattanooga	AA Cin	22	0	0	10	29.1	118	27	21	18	4	0	1	1	17	2	22	1	0	1	2	.333	0	0	5.52
1997 Chattanooga	AA Cin	62	0	0	21	82.2	359	71	43	30	6	4	3	4	37	4	64	9	0	6	4	.600	0	6	3.27
1998 Chattanooga	AA Cin	38	0	0	35	45.1	203	43	16	15	4	1	1	3	24	5	47	0	0	2	5	.286	0	13	2.98
Indianapols	AAA Cin	19	1	0	6	37.1	157	29	16	11	3	1	0	3	16	3	39	2	0	4	1	.800	0	0	2.65
1999 Nashua	IND —	3	0	0	3	3	11	1	1	1	1	0	0	0	3	0	4	0	0	0	0	.000	0	0	3.00
Durham	AAA TB	37	1	0	10	62	247	53	23	21	5	0	4	4	18	1	61	5	0	5	5	.500	0	2	3.05
Altoona	AA Pit	2	0	0	2	2.1	12	4	2	2	0	1	2	0	2	0	0	0	0	0	0	.000	0	1	7.71
Syracuse	AAA Tor	5	0	0	2	9.1	39	8	4	3	1	2	0	0	4	1	9	1	0	0	1	.000	0	0	2.89
8 Min. YEARS		278	12	0	134	438	1877	370	208	167	32	13	17	36	198	19	392	43	4	26	26	.500	0	38	3.43

John Dorman

Bats: Right   Throws: Right   Pos: 2B   Ht: 5'9"   Wt: 170   Born: 8/29/73   Age: 26

Year Team	Lg Org	G	AB	H	2B	3B	HR	TB	R	RBI	TBB	IBB	SO	HBP	SH	SF	SB	CS	SB%	GDP	Avg	OBP	SLG
1997 Winnipeg	IND —	78	268	83	11	4	8	126	50	56	31	0	55	7	10	1	15	4	.79	3	.310	.394	.470
1998 Kinston	A+ Cle	106	317	66	14	4	2	94	46	22	34	1	76	8	15	2	24	9	.73	10	.208	.299	.297
1999 Akron	AA Cle	3	7	1	0	0	0	0	0	0	0	0	1	0	0	0	0	0	.00	0	.143	.143	.143
3 Min. YEARS		187	592	150	25	8	10	221	96	78	65	1	132	15	25	3	39	13	.75	13	.253	.341	.373

Tony Dougherty

Pitches: Right Bats: Right Pos: P Ht: 6'2" Wt: 200 Born: 4/12/73 Age: 27

Year Team	Lg Org	G	GS	CG	GF	IP	BFP	H	R	ER	HR	SH	SF	HB	TBB	IBB	SO	WP	Bk	W	L	Pct.	ShO	Sv	ERA
1994 Watertown	A- Cle	26	0	0	13	40.2	178	33	20	13	0	3	0	4	19	2	37	3	2	6	1	.857	0	2	2.88
1995 Columbus	A Cle	27	10	0	3	87.2	405	85	61	46	5	2	4	8	50	4	78	4	1	4	4	.500	0	0	4.72
1996 Columbus	A Cle	19	1	0	8	49	202	30	16	16	3	2	2	4	22	0	44	4	1	3	1	.750	0	2	2.94
Canton-Akrn	AA Cle	3	0	0	0	5	26	3	5	5	1	0	0	0	8	1	6	0	0	0	0	.000	0	0	9.00
Kinston	A+ Cle	18	0	0	15	33.1	135	29	6	6	2	3	0	1	11	2	32	3	1	3	1	.750	0	8	1.62
1997 Akron	AA Cle	28	0	0	26	39	163	31	11	11	2	1	2	1	19	1	31	0	0	2	0	.000	0	8	2.54
Buffalo	AAA Cle	18	0	0	7	28.2	128	31	17	12	2	1	0	0	18	0	21	5	0	2	0	1.000	0	2	3.77
1998 Akron	AA Cle	43	0	0	25	76.1	328	68	29	26	5	7	1	2	36	3	60	4	0	6	5	.545	0	5	3.07
Buffalo	AAA Cle	1	0	0	0	3	15	4	4	1	0	0	0	0	2	0	1	0	0	0	0	.000	0	0	3.00
1999 Buffalo	AAA Cle	16	1	0	4	24	112	28	17	15	3	0	3	1	15	2	8	1	1	0	2	.000	0	0	5.63
Altoona	AA Pit	9	0	0	3	15.2	80	29	19	13	3	0	0	1	7	1	6	0	0	0	0	.000	0	0	7.47
Sarasota	A+ Bos	4	0	0	2	3	13	3	1	1	1	0	0	1	1	0	2	0	0	0	1	.000	0	0	3.00
Trenton	AA Bos	6	1	0	2	7.2	41	12	8	7	0	0	0	0	6	0	10	0	0	0	0	.000	0	1	8.22
6 Min. YEARS		218	13	0	108	413	1826	386	214	172	27	19	13	24	214	16	336	24	6	24	17	.585	0	28	3.75

Brian Doughty

Pitches: Right Bats: Right Pos: P Ht: 6'5" Wt: 235 Born: 9/21/74 Age: 25

Year Team	Lg Org	G	GS	CG	GF	IP	BFP	H	R	ER	HR	SH	SF	HB	TBB	IBB	SO	WP	Bk	W	L	Pct.	ShO	Sv	ERA
1992 Bellingham	A- Sea	11	5	1	3	38.2	157	32	16	11	2	2	1	1	9	0	27	3	0	3	1	.750	1	0	2.56
1993 Bellingham	A- Sea	14	14	1	0	76	331	65	30	21	4	3	1	0	42	1	39	9	0	5	4	.556	0	0	2.49
1994 Appleton	A Sea	12	7	1	2	38.2	173	44	32	25	8	1	0	1	19	0	14	6	1	1	5	.167	0	0	5.82
Mariners	R Sea	7	6	0	0	37	154	36	15	11	0	0	1	4	4	0	27	1	0	1	3	.250	0	0	2.68
1995 Wisconsin	A Sea	32	3	0	12	84.1	360	83	50	37	4	4	3	6	26	3	54	5	0	5	7	.417	0	4	3.95
1996 Reno —	IND —	18	18	4	0	132.2	575	143	71	63	12	6	2	8	44	0	73	8	0	11	3	.786	1	0	4.27
1997 Reno —	IND —	19	19	3	0	130.2	596	180	93	68	7	5	5	3	30	0	83	1	1	11	3	.786	0	0	4.68
1998 Rancho Cuca	A+ SD	16	2	0	3	31.2	134	29	14	9	2	1	1	3	8	0	23	2	2	2	1	.667	0	1	2.56
Mobile	AA SD	17	0	0	2	38	189	62	33	23	3	1	2	2	8	0	19	1	0	0	0	.000	0	0	5.45
1999 Mobile	AA SD	36	15	0	3	137.2	591	161	85	73	20	7	4	3	29	1	69	1	0	8	10	.444	0	1	4.77
8 Min. YEARS		182	89	10	25	745.1	3260	835	439	341	62	30	20	31	219	5	428	37	4	47	37	.560	2	6	4.12

Scott Downs

Pitches: Left Bats: Left Pos: P Ht: 6'2" Wt: 180 Born: 3/17/76 Age: 24

Year Team	Lg Org	G	GS	CG	GF	IP	BFP	H	R	ER	HR	SH	SF	HB	TBB	IBB	SO	WP	Bk	W	L	Pct.	ShO	Sv	ERA
1997 Williamsprt	A- ChC	5	5	0	0	23	93	15	11	7	0	1	1	0	7	0	28	0	2	0	2	.000	0	0	2.74
Rockford	A ChC	5	5	0	0	36	128	17	5	5	1	1	0	1	8	0	43	2	2	3	0	1.000	0	0	1.25
1998 Daytona	A+ ChC	27	27	2	0	161.2	713	179	83	70	12	7	7	4	55	0	117	12	4	8	9	.471	0	0	3.90
1999 New Britain	AA Min	6	3	0	1	19.2	99	33	21	19	5	0	0	1	10	1	22	0	0	0	0	.000	0	0	8.69
Fort Myers	A+ Min	2	2	0	0	9.2	45	7	3	0	0	0	1	0	6	0	9	2	0	1	0	1.000	0	0	0.00
Daytona	A+ ChC	7	7	1	0	48	185	41	12	10	2	0	0	1	11	0	41	3	1	5	0	1.000	1	0	1.88
West Tenn	AA ChC	13	12	1	0	80	319	56	13	12	2	1	0	1	28	0	101	1	0	8	1	.889	0	0	1.35
3 Min. YEARS		65	61	4	1	378	1582	348	148	123	22	10	9	8	125	1	361	20	9	24	13	.649	1	0	2.93

Matt Drews

Pitches: Right Bats: Right Pos: P Ht: 6'8" Wt: 230 Born: 8/29/74 Age: 25

Year Team	Lg Org	G	GS	CG	GF	IP	BFP	H	R	ER	HR	SH	SF	HB	TBB	IBB	SO	WP	Bk	W	L	Pct.	ShO	Sv	ERA
1994 Oneonta	A- NYY	14	14	0	0	90	369	76	31	21	1	1	2	8	19	0	69	3	0	7	6	.538	1	0	2.10
1995 Tampa	A+ NYY	28	28	3	0	182	748	142	73	46	5	5	5	17	58	0	140	8	2	15	7	.682	0	0	2.27
1996 Columbus	AAA NYY	7	7	0	0	20.1	113	18	27	19	4	1	5	7	27	0	7	8	0	0	4	.000	0	0	8.41
Tampa	A+ NYY	4	4	0	0	17.2	93	26	20	14	0	2	1	3	12	2	12	1	0	0	3	.000	0	0	7.13
Norwich	AA NYY	9	9	0	0	46	210	40	26	23	4	1	0	5	33	1	37	1	0	1	3	.250	0	0	4.50
Jacksnville	AA Det	6	6	1	0	31	138	26	18	15	3	0	0	4	19	0	40	2	1	0	4	.000	0	0	4.35
1997 Jacksnville	AA Det	24	24	4	0	144.1	652	160	109	88	23	1	6	16	50	0	85	3	0	8	11	.421	1	0	5.49
Toledo	AAA Det	3	3	0	0	15	72	14	11	11	2	2	0	0	14	1	7	2	0	0	2	.000	0	0	6.60
1998 Toledo	AAA Det	27	27	1	0	149.1	702	175	120	109	26	5	11	16	78	1	86	15	2	5	17	.227	0	0	6.57
1999 Toledo	AAA Det	28	22	0	3	136	668	171	136	125	21	1	10	14	91	2	70	16	2	2	14	.125	0	0	8.27
6 Min. YEARS		150	144	10	3	831.2	3765	848	571	471	89	19	40	90	401	7	553	59	7	38	71	.349	2	0	5.10

Travis Driskill

Pitches: Right Bats: Right Pos: P Ht: 6'0" Wt: 185 Born: 8/1/71 Age: 28

Year Team	Lg Org	G	GS	CG	GF	IP	BFP	H	R	ER	HR	SH	SF	HB	TBB	IBB	SO	WP	Bk	W	L	Pct.	ShO	Sv	ERA
1993 Watertown	A- Cle	21	8	0	7	63	276	62	38	29	4	3	6	5	21	0	53	6	0	5	4	.556	0	3	4.14
1994 Columbus	A Cle	62	0	0	59	64.1	267	51	25	18	2	5	2	1	30	4	88	6	0	5	5	.500	0	35	2.52
1995 Canton-Akrn	AA Cle	33	0	0	22	46.1	200	46	24	24	3	1	1	1	19	1	39	0	1	3	4	.429	0	4	4.66
Kinston	A+ Cle	15	0	0	9	23	90	17	7	7	2	0	3	1	5	1	24	1	0	2	0	.000	0	0	2.74
1996 Canton-Akrn	AA Cle	29	24	4	0	172	732	169	89	69	8	6	6	3	63	0	148	10	2	13	7	.650	2	0	3.61
1997 Buffalo	AAA Cle	29	24	1	1	147	645	159	86	76	22	2	6	3	60	0	102	15	1	8	7	.533	0	0	4.65
1998 Akron	AA Cle	5	4	0	1	26.1	109	27	12	10	4	0	1	1	7	0	16	0	0	3	0	1.000	0	0	3.42
Buffalo	AAA Cle	1	1	0	0	6	28	9	6	6	0	0	0	0	1	0	5	0	0	0	0	.000	0	0	9.00
1999 Buffalo	AAA Cle	31	18	0	3	132.1	561	146	78	71	21	5	5	6	32	2	90	4	1	9	8	.529	0	0	4.83
7 Min. YEARS		226	79	5	102	680.1	2908	686	365	310	66	22	30	21	238	8	565	42	5	46	37	.554	2	42	4.10

Al Drumheller

Pitches: Left Bats: Right Pos: P   Ht: 6'0" Wt: 185 Born: 7/31/71 Age: 28

Year Team	Lg Org	G	GS	CG	GF	IP	BFP	H	R	ER	HR	SH	SF	HB	TBB	IBB	SO	WP	Bk	W	L	Pct.	ShO	Sv	ERA
1993 Oneonta	A- NYY	16	0	0	7	30.1	132	28	18	17	2	2	1	2	11	0	28	2	1	3	1	.750	0	0	5.04
1994 Greensboro	A NYY	30	0	0	18	58	253	50	27	19	3	2	1	2	32	1	73	5	2	1	2	.333	0	2	2.95
1995 Tampa	A+ NYY	32	0	0	10	40.1	158	24	11	6	1	2	2	1	14	2	45	1	0	3	3	.500	0	1	1.34
1996 Tampa	A+ NYY	36	0	0	7	51.1	215	34	15	13	2	4	0	0	33	2	57	2	0	9	3	.750	0	1	2.28
1997 Rancho Cuca	A+ SD	38	6	0	8	81	355	76	48	41	5	5	1	0	37	2	107	4	1	5	6	.455	0	1	4.56
1998 Mobile	AA SD	50	6	0	21	97.1	412	75	43	38	5	5	5	2	49	0	118	4	0	5	4	.556	0	4	3.51
1999 Mobile	AA SD	12	12	0	0	68.2	304	78	40	33	7	4	3	2	29	2	55	4	0	5	2	.714	0	0	4.33
Las Vegas	AAA SD	20	7	0	6	60.2	266	72	36	33	7	1	6	2	22	0	46	6	0	6	4	.600	0	0	4.90
7 Min. YEARS		234	31	0	77	487.2	2095	437	238	200	32	25	19	11	227	9	529	28	4	37	25	.597	0	10	3.69

Mike Drumright

Pitches: Right Bats: Left Pos: P   Ht: 6' 4" Wt: 210 Born: 4/19/74 Age: 26

Year Team	Lg Org	G	GS	CG	GF	IP	BFP	H	R	ER	HR	SH	SF	HB	TBB	IBB	SO	WP	Bk	W	L	Pct.	ShO	Sv	ERA
1995 Lakeland	A+ Det	5	5	0	0	21	87	19	11	10	2	1	0	0	9	0	19	1	2	1	1	.500	0	0	4.29
Jacksonville	AA Det	5	5	0	0	31.2	137	30	13	13	4	0	0	2	15	1	34	1	5	0	1	.000	0	0	3.69
1996 Jacksnville	AA Det	18	18	1	0	99.2	418	80	51	44	11	1	3	3	48	0	109	10	6	6	4	.600	1	0	3.97
1997 Jacksnville	AA Det	5	5	0	0	28.2	112	16	7	5	0	1	1	3	13	0	24	2	0	1	1	.500	0	0	1.57
Toledo	AAA Det	23	23	0	0	133.1	612	134	78	75	22	8	4	4	91	1	115	5	4	5	10	.333	0	0	5.06
1998 Toledo	AAA Det	29	27	1	1	154	733	188	130	119	21	3	13	7	94	0	91	16	1	4	19	.174	0	0	6.95
1999 Toledo	AAA Det	21	21	1	0	120.2	535	116	88	80	17	2	7	7	59	2	76	8	0	6	10	.375	0	0	5.97
Calgary	AAA Fla	12	0	0	1	21	113	39	33	32	5	1	0	1	13	0	15	2	0	0	2	.000	0	0	13.71
5 Min. YEARS		118	104	3	2	610	2747	622	411	378	82	17	32	27	342	4	483	45	18	23	48	.324	1	0	5.58

Brian DuBose

Bats: Left Throws: Right Pos: 1B   Ht: 6'3" Wt: 208 Born: 5/17/71 Age: 29

Year Team	Lg Org	G	AB	H	2B	3B	HR	TB	R	RBI	TBB	IBB	SO	HBP	SH	SF	SB	CS	SB%	GDP	Avg	OBP	SLG
1990 Bristol	R+ Det	67	223	56	8	0	6	82	31	21	24	2	53	3	0	1	5	3	.63	1	.251	.331	.368
1991 Lakeland	A+ Det	15	35	7	2	0	1	12	7	6	10	0	12	1	0	0	1	0	1.00	0	.200	.391	.343
Niagara Fal	A- Det	44	164	42	7	1	7	72	26	32	17	0	32	1	0	0	3	1	.75	6	.256	.330	.439
1992 Fayetteville	A Det	122	404	92	20	6	12	158	49	73	64	1	100	4	2	4	19	12	.61	8	.228	.336	.391
1993 Lakeland	A+ Det	122	448	140	27	11	8	213	74	68	49	5	97	4	0	4	18	18	.50	11	.313	.382	.475
1994 Trenton	AA Det	108	378	85	10	3	9	128	48	41	32	0	96	6	1	1	12	10	.55	8	.225	.295	.339
1997 W Michigan	A Det	105	358	96	12	7	15	167	72	79	66	3	87	3	3	2	17	2	.89	5	.268	.385	.466
1998 Lakeland	A+ Det	69	258	81	7	3	14	136	45	48	39	2	51	2	0	4	8	3	.73	5	.314	.403	.527
Jacksnville	AA Det	46	165	39	10	1	7	72	30	25	13	1	39	1	0	0	4	0	1.00	3	.236	.296	.436
1999 Binghamton	AA NYM	30	69	12	3	0	0	15	8	4	14	0	19	0	0	1	5	1	.83	0	.174	.310	.217
Somerset	IND —	21	74	16	1	1	2	25	6	10	5	0	12	2	1	0	1	0	1.00	2	.216	.284	.338
San Antonio	AA LA	42	121	32	9	3	3	56	15	22	11	1	25	0	0	3	1	1	.00	4	.264	.319	.463
8 Min. YEARS		791	2697	698	116	35	84	1136	411	429	344	15	623	27	7	20	92	52	.64	50	.259	.346	.421

Eric DuBose

Pitches: Left Bats: Left Pos: P   Ht: 6'3" Wt: 215 Born: 5/15/76 Age: 24

Year Team	Lg Org	G	GS	CG	GF	IP	BFP	H	R	ER	HR	SH	SF	HB	TBB	IBB	SO	WP	Bk	W	L	Pct.	ShO	Sv	ERA
1997 Sou Oregon	A- Oak	3	1	0	0	10	39	5	0	0	0	0	0	0	6	0	15	0	0	1	0	1.000	0	0	0.00
Visalia	A+ Oak	10	9	0	0	38.1	194	43	37	30	4	2	0	5	28	0	39	6	3	1	3	.250	0	0	7.04
1998 Visalia	A+ Oak	17	10	0	4	72	307	56	34	27	5	1	2	5	35	0	85	8	2	6	1	.857	0	1	3.38
Huntsville	AA Oak	14	14	1	0	83.1	363	86	37	25	2	3	4	7	34	1	66	4	0	7	6	.538	1	0	2.70
1999 Midland	AA Oak	21	14	0	3	77	361	89	57	47	10	2	4	7	44	1	68	8	0	4	2	.667	0	1	5.49
3 Min. YEARS		65	48	1	7	280.2	1264	279	165	129	21	8	10	24	147	2	273	26	5	19	12	.613	1	2	4.14

Matt Duff

Pitches: Right Bats: Right Pos: P   Ht: 6'1" Wt: 192 Born: 10/6/74 Age: 25

Year Team	Lg Org	G	GS	CG	GF	IP	BFP	H	R	ER	HR	SH	SF	HB	TBB	IBB	SO	WP	Bk	W	L	Pct.	ShO	Sv	ERA
1997 Springfield	IND —	14	12	2	1	79.2	334	70	33	24	3	2	6	1	27	1	76	3	0	7	4	.636	0	0	2.71
Augusta	A Pit	2	1	0	1	6	26	6	1	1	0	0	0	1	2	0	6	0	0	0	1	.000	0	0	1.50
1998 Augusta	A Pit	10	0	0	9	9	42	8	3	3	1	0	0	1	4	0	12	0	0	1	0	1.000	0	3	3.00
Lynchburg	A+ Pit	40	0	0	25	62.2	257	52	26	23	4	3	3	1	20	2	61	4	0	4	5	.444	0	10	3.30
1999 Lynchburg	A+ Pit	7	7	0	0	39	169	41	22	22	6	1	1	0	13	0	40	0	1	2	3	.400	0	0	5.08
Altoona	AA Pit	44	0	0	29	52.2	241	43	19	18	5	4	2	2	35	4	59	4	1	2	4	.333	0	12	2.81
3 Min. YEARS		117	20	2	65	254	1069	220	104	91	19	10	12	8	101	7	254	11	2	16	17	.485	0	25	3.22

Jim Duffy

Bats: Right Throws: Right Pos: OF   Ht: 6'2" Wt: 195 Born: 7/18/74 Age: 25

Year Team	Lg Org	G	AB	H	2B	3B	HR	TB	R	RBI	TBB	IBB	SO	HBP	SH	SF	SB	CS	SB%	GDP	Avg	OBP	SLG
1997 Kissimmee	A+ Hou	19	41	6	1	0	0	7	1	4	4	0	9	0	1	0	0	2	.00	1	.146	.222	.171
Quad City	A Hou	12	44	11	3	0	0	14	4	7	3	0	9	0	0	1	0	0	.00	1	.250	.292	.318
Auburn	A- Hou	48	181	51	9	1	9	89	28	25	14	0	47	2	0	0	4	4	.50	4	.276	.333	.481
1998 Quad City	A Hou	37	123	32	8	0	3	49	16	17	9	1	34	1	1	0	5	0	1.00	3	.260	.316	.398
Jackson	AA Hou	12	32	5	1	0	0	6	1	0	1	0	9	0	0	0	0	0	.00	2	.156	.182	.188

Year Team	Lg Org	G	AB	H	2B	3B	HR	TB	R	RBI	TBB	IBB	SO	HBP	SH	SF	SB	CS	SB%	GDP	Avg	OBP	SLG
Kissimmee	A+ Hou	24	80	15	2	0	1	20	7	8	4	0	29	2	0	0	1	1	.50	1	.188	.244	.250
1999 Jackson	AA Hou	26	60	8	0	0	0	8	5	2	4	0	15	1	0	0	0	0	.00	1	.133	.200	.133
Kissimmee	A+ Hou	60	149	37	8	2	3	58	26	25	17	0	48	3	3	1	5	5	.50	3	.248	.335	.389
3 Min. YEARS		238	714	165	32	3	16	251	88	88	56	1	200	9	5	2	15	12	.56	16	.231	.294	.352

Matt Dunbar

Pitches: Left **Bats:** Left **Pos:** P   **Ht:** 6' 0" **Wt:** 160 **Born:** 10/15/68 **Age:** 31

	HOW MUCH HE PITCHED						WHAT HE GAVE UP										THE RESULTS					
Year Team	Lg Org	G	GS	CG	GF	IP	BFP	H	R	ER	HR	SH	SF	HB	TBB	IBB	SO	WP	Bk	W	L	Pct.	ShO	Sv	ERA
1990 Yankees	R NYY	3	0	0	2	6	24	4	2	2	0	1	0	2	3	0	7	0	1	0	0	.000	0	1	3.00
Oneonta	A- NYY	19	2	0	8	30.1	145	32	23	14	1	2	2	1	24	2	24	5	1	1	4	.200	0	0	4.15
1991 Greensboro	A NYY	24	2	1	14	44.2	184	36	14	11	1	0	1	3	15	0	40	2	0	2	2	.500	0	1	2.22
1992 Pr William	A+ NYY	44	0	0	21	81.2	350	68	37	26	5	7	4	6	33	2	68	7	1	5	4	.556	0	2	2.87
1993 Pr William	A+ NYY	49	0	0	20	73	292	50	21	14	0	6	0	3	30	1	66	6	0	6	2	.750	0	4	1.73
Albany-Colo	AA NYY	15	0	0	6	23.2	91	23	8	7	0	0	0	0	6	0	18	0	0	1	0	1.000	0	0	2.66
1994 Albany-Colo	AA NYY	34	0	0	12	39.2	163	30	10	9	1	2	2	4	14	0	41	1	0	2	1	.667	0	4	2.04
Columbus	AAA NYY	19	0	0	6	26	104	20	5	5	1	0	1	1	10	1	21	2	1	0	0	.000	0	2	1.73
1995 Columbus	AAA NYY	36	0	0	9	44.1	201	50	22	20	1	0	1	3	19	2	33	5	1	2	3	.400	0	0	4.06
1996 Greensboro	A NYY	2	2	0	0	14	56	6	3	3	1	0	0	1	4	0	19	1	0	1	1	.500	0	0	1.93
Norwich	AA NYY	33	6	0	11	70.2	306	59	33	14	3	6	4	5	28	3	59	2	0	4	2	.667	0	1	1.78
Columbus	AAA NYY	14	0	0	1	20.2	84	12	6	4	0	0	1	2	13	0	16	0	0	2	0	1.000	0	0	1.74
1997 Huntsville	AA Oak	5	0	0	2	5	23	8	3	3	0	0	0	0	1	0	7	0	0	1	0	1.000	0	0	5.40
Edmonton	AAA Oak	12	1	0	3	21.2	98	29	12	12	2	1	3	1	8	1	18	0	0	1	0	1.000	0	0	4.98
Vancouver	AAA Ana	2	0	0	1	2	14	3	6	6	2	0	0	0	6	0	2	2	0	0	0	.000	0	0	27.00
1998 Louisville	AAA Mil	50	0	0	18	55.2	281	74	47	38	6	1	1	7	32	1	45	5	1	1	3	.250	0	0	6.14
1999 Altoona	AA Pit	49	0	0	14	47.1	204	35	19	18	2	2	1	6	23	3	35	7	0	3	5	.375	0	2	3.42
Nashville	AAA Pit	11	0	0	1	10.1	46	13	6	5	1	2	0	0	4	1	9	0	0	1	0	1.000	0	0	4.35
1995 Florida	NL	8	0	0	1	7	45	12	9	9	0	2	0	1	11	3	5	1	0	0	1	.000	0	0	11.57
10 Min. YEARS		421	13	1	149	616.2	2666	552	277	211	27	30	21	45	273	17	528	45	6	33	28	.541	0	17	3.08

Courtney Duncan

Pitches: Right **Bats:** Left **Pos:** P   **Ht:** 6'0" **Wt:** 185 **Born:** 10/9/74 **Age:** 25

	HOW MUCH HE PITCHED						WHAT HE GAVE UP										THE RESULTS					
Year Team	Lg Org	G	GS	CG	GF	IP	BFP	H	R	ER	HR	SH	SF	HB	TBB	IBB	SO	WP	Bk	W	L	Pct.	ShO	Sv	ERA
1996 Williamsprt	A- ChC	15	15	1	0	90.1	360	58	28	22	6	3	0	5	34	0	91	8	0	11	1	.917	0	0	2.19
1997 Daytona	A+ ChC	19	19	1	0	121.2	489	90	35	22	3	6	1	8	35	0	120	8	1	8	4	.667	0	0	1.63
Orlando	AA ChC	8	8	0	0	45	196	37	28	17	2	1	2	1	29	5	45	4	0	2	2	.500	0	0	3.40
1998 West Tenn	AA ChC	29	29	0	0	162.2	730	141	89	77	7	9	7	14	108	5	157	9	2	7	9	.438	0	0	4.26
1999 West Tenn	AA ChC	11	8	0	2	41.2	210	44	42	33	3	2	6	2	42	4	42	8	0	1	7	.125	0	0	7.13
Daytona	A+ ChC	15	11	1	3	65	300	70	60	40	6	3	2	4	34	1	48	5	0	4	5	.444	1	1	5.54
4 Min. YEARS		97	90	3	5	526.1	2285	440	282	211	27	24	18	34	282	15	503	42	3	33	28	.541	1	1	3.61

Geoff Duncan

Pitches: Right **Bats:** Right **Pos:** P   **Ht:** 6'2" **Wt:** 185 **Born:** 4/1/75 **Age:** 25

	HOW MUCH HE PITCHED						WHAT HE GAVE UP										THE RESULTS					
Year Team	Lg Org	G	GS	CG	GF	IP	BFP	H	R	ER	HR	SH	SF	HB	TBB	IBB	SO	WP	Bk	W	L	Pct.	ShO	Sv	ERA
1996 Utica	A- Fla	24	1	0	8	40.1	191	46	23	17	3	0	1	4	19	5	52	5	3	2	5	.286	0	2	3.79
1997 Kane County	A Fla	44	2	0	13	86.1	375	85	46	39	7	7	2	5	30	5	96	4	0	7	2	.778	0	1	4.07
1998 Brevard Cty	A+ Fla	17	0	0	9	32	135	35	15	8	1	2	0	6	9	3	30	2	0	1	3	.250	0	2	2.25
Portland	AA Fla	42	0	0	29	57.1	242	39	21	18	2	1	1	6	31	5	74	5	1	9	2	.818	0	11	2.83
1999 Calgary	AAA Fla	5	0	0	2	9	39	4	4	4	0	0	0	2	10	0	5	2	0	1	0	1.000	0	1	4.00
Portland	AA Fla	43	0	0	22	66.1	276	59	24	21	8	1	0	2	26	2	59	3	1	2	3	.400	0	4	2.85
4 Min. YEARS		175	3	0	83	291.1	1258	268	133	107	21	11	4	21	125	20	316	20	5	22	15	.595	0	21	3.31

Mariano Duncan

Bats: Right **Throws:** Right **Pos:** 2B   **Ht:** 6' 0" **Wt:** 185 **Born:** 3/13/63 **Age:** 37

	BATTING																BASERUNNING				PERCENTAGES		
Year Team	Lg Org	G	AB	H	2B	3B	HR	TB	R	RBI	TBB	IBB	SO	HBP	SH	SF	SB	CS	SB%	GDP	Avg	OBP	SLG
1982 Lethbridge	R+ LA	30	55	13	3	1	1	21	9	8	8	0	21	1	0	1	1	2	.33	—	.236	.338	.382
1983 Vero Beach	A+ LA	109	384	102	10	15	0	142	73	42	44	4	87	8	5	2	56	13	.81	—	.266	.352	.370
1984 San Antonio	AA LA	125	502	127	14	11	2	169	80	44	41	0	110	5	4	2	41	13	.76	8	.253	.315	.337
1987 Albuquerque	AAA LA	6	22	6	0	0	0	6	6	0	2	0	5	0	0	0	3	0	1.00	0	.273	.333	.273
1988 Albuquerque	AAA LA	56	227	65	4	8	0	85	48	25	10	0	40	8	2	3	33	7	.83	0	.286	.335	.374
1996 Columbus	AAA NYY	2	5	1	0	0	0	1	0	2	0	0	2	0	0	0	0	0	.00	0	.200	.167	.200
1999 Bridgeport	IND —	22	87	31	7	2	0	42	12	20	3	0	15	1	0	2	0	1	.00	2	.356	.376	.483
Calgary	AAA Fla	2	5	1	1	0	0	2	0	0	0	0	2	1	0	0	0	0	.00	0	.200	.333	.400
1985 Los Angeles	NL	142	562	137	24	6	6	191	74	39	38	4	113	3	13	4	38	8	.83	9	.244	.293	.340
1986 Los Angeles	NL	109	407	93	7	0	8	124	47	30	30	1	78	2	5	1	48	13	.79	6	.229	.284	.305
1987 Los Angeles	NL	76	261	56	8	1	6	84	31	18	17	1	62	2	6	1	11	1	.92	4	.215	.267	.322
1989 Los Angeles	NL	49	84	21	5	1	0	28	9	8	0	0	15	2	1	0	3	3	.50	1	.250	.267	.333
Cincinnati	NL	45	174	43	10	1	3	64	23	13	8	0	36	3	1	0	6	2	.75	2	.247	.292	.368
1990 Cincinnati	NL	125	435	133	22	11	10	207	67	55	24	4	67	4	4	4	13	7	.65	10	.306	.345	.476
1991 Cincinnati	NL	100	333	86	7	4	12	137	46	40	12	0	57	3	5	5	5	5	.50	13	.258	.288	.411
1992 Philadelphia	NL	142	574	153	40	3	8	223	71	50	17	0	108	5	5	4	23	3	.88	15	.267	.292	.389
1993 Philadelphia	NL	124	496	140	26	4	11	207	68	73	12	0	88	4	4	2	6	5	.55	13	.282	.304	.417
1994 Philadelphia	NL	88	347	93	22	1	8	141	49	48	17	1	72	4	2	4	10	2	.83	10	.268	.306	.406
1995 Philadelphia	NL	52	196	56	12	1	3	79	20	23	0	0	43	1	0	3	1	2	.33	6	.286	.285	.403

Year Team	Lg Org	G	AB	H	2B	3B	HR	TB	R	RBI	TBB	IBB	SO	HBP	SH	SF	SB	CS	SB%	GDP	Avg	OBP	SLG
Cincinnati	NL	29	69	20	2	1	3	33	16	13	5	0	19	0	0	2	0	1	.00	1	.290	.329	.478
1996 New York	AL	109	400	136	34	3	8	200	62	56	9	1	77	1	2	5	4	3	.57	10	.340	.352	.500
1997 New York	AL	50	172	42	8	0	1	53	16	13	6	0	39	0	1	0	2	1	.67	2	.244	.270	.308
Toronto	AL	39	167	38	6	0	0	44	20	12	6	0	39	3	0	0	4	2	.67	4	.228	.267	.263
7 Min. YEARS		352	1287	346	39	37	3	468	228	141	108	4	282	24	11	11	134	36	.79	—	.269	.334	.364
12 Maj. YEARS		1279	4677	1247	233	37	87	1815	619	491	201	12	913	37	50	33	174	57	.75	93	.267	.300	.388

Pat Dunham

Pitches: Right **Bats:** Right **Pos:** P   **Ht:** 6'5" **Wt:** 200 **Born:** 3/16/76 **Age:** 24

Year Team	Lg Org	G	GS	CG	GF	IP	BFP	H	R	ER	HR	SH	SF	HB	TBB	IBB	SO	WP	Bk	W	L	Pct.	ShO	Sv	ERA
1997 Everett	A- Sea	17	0	0	10	28.1	127	26	19	13	3	1	0	1	12	1	39	5	3	0	3	.000	0	3	4.13
1998 Lancaster	A+ Sea	17	17	0	0	104	442	97	48	40	8	0	3	8	41	0	88	4	6	9	5	.643	0	0	3.46
Orlando	AA Sea	10	9	0	0	56.1	245	52	33	31	8	1	2	1	32	0	34	2	2	2	6	.250	0	0	4.95
1999 New Haven	AA Sea	3	0	0	2	7	37	1	2	2	0	2	1	0	16	3	5	1	0	0	1	.000	0	0	2.57
Wisconsin	A Sea	12	0	0	4	14.1	74	23	15	12	1	1	1	2	7	0	13	4	0	0	1	.000	0	1	7.53
Mariners	R Sea	7	0	0	5	10.1	50	13	11	11	0	0	0	1	7	0	11	1	0	0	2	.000	0	3	9.58
Lancaster	A+ Sea	9	8	0	0	39.1	193	49	40	34	5	0	2	2	28	0	33	6	2	1	4	.200	0	0	7.78
3 Min. YEARS		75	34	0	21	259.2	1168	261	168	143	25	5	9	15	143	4	223	23	13	12	22	.353	0	7	4.96

Todd Dunn

Bats: Right **Throws:** Right **Pos:** OF   **Ht:** 6' 5" **Wt:** 224 **Born:** 7/29/70 **Age:** 29

Year Team	Lg Org	G	AB	H	2B	3B	HR	TB	R	RBI	TBB	IBB	SO	HBP	SH	SF	SB	CS	SB%	GDP	Avg	OBP	SLG
1993 Helena	R+ Mil	43	150	46	11	2	10	91	33	42	22	1	52	6	1	2	5	2	.71	2	.307	.411	.607
1994 Beloit	A Mil	129	429	94	13	2	23	180	72	63	50	3	131	6	4	4	18	8	.69	6	.219	.307	.420
1995 Stockton	A+ Mil	67	249	73	20	2	7	118	44	40	19	2	67	2	1	1	14	3	.82	5	.293	.347	.474
1996 El Paso	AA Mil	98	359	122	24	5	19	213	72	78	45	1	84	2	2	4	13	4	.76	11	.340	.412	.593
1997 Tucson	AAA Mil	93	332	101	31	4	18	194	66	66	39	1	83	8	0	1	5	5	.50	11	.304	.389	.584
1998 Stockton	A+ Mil	3	13	2	1	0	0	3	2	0	0	0	4	0	0	0	0	0	.00	1	.154	.154	.231
El Paso	AA Mil	75	294	92	28	3	13	165	60	57	27	1	63	6	0	3	7	2	.78	6	.313	.379	.561
Louisville	AAA Mil	10	34	13	3	0	1	19	5	1	0	0	10	2	0	0	0	2	.00	1	.382	.417	.559
1999 Louisville	AAA Mil	40	106	23	1	1	5	41	14	16	14	0	32	2	0	0	2	1	.67	2	.217	.320	.387
Rochester	AAA Bal	30	98	17	5	0	2	28	8	15	0	0	35	2	1	1	1	2	.33	9	.173	.248	.286
Altoona	AA Pit	8	30	5	2	0	0	7	0	2	2	0	10	0	0	0	0	1	.00	0	.167	.219	.233
1996 Milwaukee	AL	6	10	3	1	0	0	4	2	1	0	0	3	0	0	0	0	0	.00	1	.300	.300	.400
1997 Milwaukee	AL	44	118	27	5	0	3	41	17	9	2	0	39	0	0	0	3	0	1.00	0	.229	.242	.347
7 Min. YEARS		596	2094	588	139	19	98	1059	376	380	226	9	571	36	9	16	65	30	.68	54	.281	.358	.506
2 Maj. YEARS		50	128	30	6	0	3	45	19	10	2	0	42	0	0	0	3	0	1.00	3	.234	.246	.352

Roberto Duran

Pitches: Left **Bats:** Left **Pos:** P   **Ht:** 6' 0" **Wt:** 205 **Born:** 3/6/73 **Age:** 27

Year Team	Lg Org	G	GS	CG	GF	IP	BFP	H	R	ER	HR	SH	SF	HB	TBB	IBB	SO	WP	Bk	W	L	Pct.	ShO	Sv	ERA
1992 Dodgers	R LA	9	8	0	0	38.2	166	22	17	12	1	1	1	2	31	0	57	6	0	4	3	.571	0	0	2.79
Vero Beach	A+ LA	2	1	0	0	5	24	6	5	5	1	0	0	0	4	0	5	1	0	0	0	.000	0	0	9.00
1993 Vero Beach	A+ LA	8	0	0	2	9.2	43	10	4	4	0	0	0	0	8	1	9	0	0	1	1	.500	0	0	3.72
Yakima	A- LA	20	3	0	6	40	201	37	34	31	3	1	2	6	42	0	50	10	0	2	2	.500	0	0	6.98
1994 Bakersfield	A+ LA	42	4	0	29	65.1	300	61	43	35	5	3	4	5	48	0	86	6	0	6	5	.545	0	10	4.82
1995 Vero Beach	A+ LA	23	22	0	0	101.1	446	82	42	38	8	3	1	1	70	0	114	12	2	7	4	.636	0	0	3.38
1996 Dunedin	A+ Tor	8	8	1	0	48.1	188	31	9	6	1	1	1	2	19	0	54	5	0	3	1	.750	1	0	1.12
Knoxville	AA Tor	19	16	0	1	80.2	366	72	52	46	8	1	1	3	61	1	74	13	2	4	6	.400	0	0	5.13
1997 Jacksonville	AA Det	50	0	0	34	60.2	265	41	19	16	2	2	5	2	39	0	95	11	0	4	2	.667	0	16	2.37
1998 Toledo	AAA Det	1	0	0	0	0.2	5	1	2	2	0	0	0	0	2	0	1	0	0	0	0	.000	0	0	27.00
Lakeland	A+ Det	8	0	0	2	8.2	46	4	5	4	0	1	1	2	13	1	9	1	0	0	0	.000	0	0	4.15
1999 Harrisburg	AA Mon	19	1	0	7	21.2	115	15	20	20	1	0	1	7	31	0	20	8	0	2	2	.500	0	1	8.31
Jupiter	A+ Mon	7	6	0	0	24	110	13	15	11	3	0	2	6	29	1	24	3	0	0	2	.000	0	0	4.13
Ottawa	AAA Mon	5	2	0	0	12	59	10	8	7	1	1	0	1	13	0	10	3	0	1	1	.500	0	0	5.25
1997 Detroit	AL	13	0	0	1	10.2	56	7	9	9	0	0	1	3	15	0	11	1	1	0	0	.000	0	0	7.59
1998 Detroit	AL	18	0	0	5	15.1	74	9	10	10	0	2	0	2	17	0	12	2	0	0	1	.000	0	0	5.87
8 Min. YEARS		221	71	1	81	516.2	2334	405	275	237	34	14	19	38	410	4	608	81	4	34	29	.540	1	27	4.13
2 Maj. YEARS		31	0	0	6	26	130	16	19	19	0	2	1	5	32	0	23	3	1	0	1	.000	0	0	6.58

Ariel Durango

Bats: Both **Throws:** Right **Pos:** 2B   **Ht:** 5'10" **Wt:** 150 **Born:** 4/5/79 **Age:** 21

Year Team	Lg Org	G	AB	H	2B	3B	HR	TB	R	RBI	TBB	IBB	SO	HBP	SH	SF	SB	CS	SB%	GDP	Avg	OBP	SLG
1998 Mariners	R Sea	24	67	18	3	1	2	29	16	10	6	0	18	3	3	0	7	5	.58	0	.269	.355	.433
1999 Mariners	R Sea	21	77	24	5	1	2	37	20	12	8	0	7	2	3	0	6	2	.75	0	.312	.391	.481
Tacoma	AAA Sea	1	4	0	0	0	0	0	0	0	0	0	0	0	0	0	0	0	.00	1	.000	.000	.000
Everett	A- Sea	25	93	25	5	1	2	38	19	9	9	0	25	1	0	0	11	5	.69	3	.269	.340	.409
2 Min. YEARS		71	241	67	13	3	6	104	55	31	23	0	50	6	6	0	24	12	.67	4	.278	.356	.432

Jayson Durocher

Pitches: Right **Bats:** Right **Pos:** P **Ht:** 6'3" **Wt:** 195 **Born:** 8/18/74 **Age:** 25

Year Team	Lg Org	G	GS	CG	GF	IP	BFP	H	R	ER	HR	SH	SF	HB	TBB	IBB	SO	WP	Bk	W	L	Pct.	ShO	Sv	ERA
1993 Expos	R Mon	7	7	3	0	39	150	32	23	15	0	2	0	3	13	0	21	3	1	2	3	.400	2	0	3.46
1994 Vermont	A- Mon	15	15	3	0	99	422	92	40	34	0	0	3	2	44	1	74	11	1	9	2	.818	1	0	3.09
1995 Albany	A Mon	24	22	1	1	122	526	105	67	53	5	4	11	5	56	1	88	11	1	3	7	.300	0	0	3.91
1996 Frederick	A+ Mon	23	23	1	0	129.1	557	118	65	48	5	4	3	7	44	0	101	15	3	7	6	.538	1	0	3.34
1997 Wst Plm Bch	A+ Mon	25	17	0	2	87	385	84	58	37	6	3	3	4	39	0	71	10	2	6	4	.600	0	0	3.83
1998 Jupiter	A+ Mon	23	0	0	12	36.1	162	47	21	17	3	1	2	1	8	0	27	4	0	2	1	.667	0	5	4.21
Harrisburg	AA Mon	10	0	0	4	11.1	48	10	8	5	0	1	1	0	6	0	12	1	0	0	1	.000	0	1	3.97
1999 Harrisburg	AA Mon	29	1	0	11	51.2	224	44	29	20	5	2	2	6	25	1	36	3	1	1	3	.250	0	1	3.48
Ottawa	AAA Mon	17	0	0	6	35.2	146	17	12	6	2	3	1	1	20	2	22	3	0	1	3	.250	0	4	1.51
7 Min. YEARS		173	85	8	36	611.1	2620	549	323	235	26	20	26	29	255	5	452	61	9	31	30	.508	4	14	3.46

Radhames Dykhoff

Pitches: Left **Bats:** Left **Pos:** P **Ht:** 6' 0" **Wt:** 200 **Born:** 9/27/74 **Age:** 25

Year Team	Lg Org	G	GS	CG	GF	IP	BFP	H	R	ER	HR	SH	SF	HB	TBB	IBB	SO	WP	Bk	W	L	Pct.	ShO	Sv	ERA
1993 Orioles	R Bal	14	3	0	1	45	184	37	22	17	2	3	3	2	11	0	29	3	0	1	2	.333	0	1	3.40
1994 Orioles	R Bal	12	12	1	0	73	307	69	34	27	2	0	5	0	17	0	67	4	1	3	6	.333	0	0	3.33
1995 High Desert	A+ Bal	34	2	0	10	80.2	389	95	68	45	8	7	7	0	44	2	88	0	2	1	5	.167	0	3	5.02
1996 Frederick	A+ Bal	33	0	0	15	62	290	77	45	39	7	4	4	1	22	2	75	0	0	2	6	.250	0	3	5.66
1997 Bowie	AA Bal	7	0	0	4	8.2	43	10	9	8	2	0	0	0	7	0	7	0	0	0	0	.000	0	0	8.31
Delmarva	A Bal	1	0	0	1	3	12	3	0	0	0	0	0	0	0	0	3	0	0	0	0	.000	0	1	0.00
Frederick	A+ Bal	31	0	0	18	67	282	48	19	18	4	6	1	0	38	3	98	0	1	3	3	.500	0	5	2.42
1998 Bowie	AA Bal	38	8	0	9	93.2	411	83	51	49	10	2	3	4	52	1	98	3	0	3	7	.300	0	1	4.71
1999 Rochester	AAA Bal	47	0	0	6	82.1	341	69	42	36	11	3	2	3	31	0	57	1	0	2	0	1.000	0	0	3.94
1998 Baltimore	AL	1	0	0	1	1	6	2	2	2	0	0	0	0	1	0	1	0	0	0	0	.000	0	0	18.00
7 Min. YEARS		217	25	1	64	515.1	2259	491	290	239	46	25	25	10	222	8	522	11	4	15	29	.341	0	15	4.17

Mike Eaglin

Bats: Right **Throws:** Right **Pos:** 2B **Ht:** 5'10" **Wt:** 170 **Born:** 4/25/73 **Age:** 27

									BATTING								BASERUNNING				PERCENTAGES		
Year Team	Lg Org	G	AB	H	2B	3B	HR	TB	R	RBI	TBB	IBB	SO	HBP	SH	SF	SB	CS	SB%	GDP	Avg	OBP	SLG
1992 Braves	R Atl	14	45	11	1	0	0	12	4	3	4	0	8	0	2	1	3	1	.75	0	.244	.300	.267
1993 Idaho Falls	R+ Atl	66	236	77	5	4	2	96	50	35	29	0	48	1	2	2	28	11	.72	1	.326	.399	.407
1994 Macon	A Atl	26	77	18	0	0	0	18	8	5	9	0	18	2	2	0	7	2	.78	1	.234	.330	.234
1995 Macon	A Atl	129	530	141	15	4	2	170	82	30	64	0	94	7	5	1	41	13	.76	8	.266	.352	.321
1996 Durham	A+ Atl	131	466	118	25	2	11	180	84	54	50	0	88	18	4	4	23	12	.66	1	.253	.346	.386
1997 Greenville	AA Atl	126	396	114	15	3	5	150	62	47	41	4	66	9	13	3	15	10	.60	5	.288	.365	.379
1998 Greenville	AA Atl	129	492	126	22	2	9	179	84	47	51	1	107	13	10	4	30	19	.61	11	.256	.339	.364
1999 Birmingham	AA CWS	27	75	17	2	0	0	19	7	8	4	0	17	1	0	2	1	2	.33	2	.227	.268	.253
8 Min. YEARS		648	2317	622	85	15	29	824	381	229	252	5	446	51	38	17	148	70	.68	29	.268	.351	.356

Clay Eason

Pitches: Right **Bats:** Right **Pos:** P **Ht:** 5'11" **Wt:** 175 **Born:** 11/18/75 **Age:** 24

Year Team	Lg Org	G	GS	CG	GF	IP	BFP	H	R	ER	HR	SH	SF	HB	TBB	IBB	SO	WP	Bk	W	L	Pct.	ShO	Sv	ERA
1997 Batavia	A- Phi	20	0	0	9	29.1	119	16	6	3	1	0	1	1	11	0	29	2	1	0	1	.000	0	1	0.92
1998 Piedmont	A Phi	34	2	0	11	65.1	271	53	32	27	8	0	5	2	22	0	67	4	0	3	1	.750	0	0	3.72
1999 Piedmont	A Phi	10	0	0	5	20.2	86	13	5	5	2	0	0	1	11	1	33	0	0	1	0	1.000	0	2	2.18
Clearwater	A+ Phi	18	0	0	3	27	125	26	18	12	3	3	2	0	17	3	31	4	1	1	1	.500	0	0	4.00
Reading	AA Phi	10	1	0	5	13	74	14	15	15	4	1	0	6	14	0	13	4	0	0	2	.000	0	1	10.38
3 Min. YEARS		92	3	0	33	155.1	675	122	76	62	18	4	8	10	75	4	173	14	2	4	6	.400	0	4	3.59

Adam Eaton

Pitches: Right **Bats:** Right **Pos:** P **Ht:** 6'2" **Wt:** 190 **Born:** 11/23/77 **Age:** 22

Year Team	Lg Org	G	GS	CG	GF	IP	BFP	H	R	ER	HR	SH	SF	HB	TBB	IBB	SO	WP	Bk	W	L	Pct.	ShO	Sv	ERA
1997 Piedmont	A Phi	14	14	0	0	71.1	318	81	38	33	2	0	2	4	30	0	57	4	2	5	6	.455	0	0	4.16
1998 Clearwater	A+ Phi	24	23	1	0	131.2	578	152	68	65	9	3	5	4	47	1	89	9	1	9	8	.529	0	0	4.44
1999 Clearwater	A+ Phi	13	13	0	0	69	308	81	39	30	2	2	2	4	24	0	50	1	2	5	5	.500	0	0	3.91
Reading	AA Phi	12	12	2	0	77	317	60	30	25	9	1	0	5	28	1	67	1	2	5	4	.556	0	0	2.92
Scranton-WB	AAA Phi	3	3	0	0	21	83	17	10	7	1	0	0	2	6	0	10	0	0	1	1	.500	0	0	3.00
3 Min. YEARS		66	65	3	0	370	1604	391	185	160	23	6	11	19	135	2	273	15	7	25	24	.510	0	0	3.89

Kevin Eberwein

Bats: Right **Throws:** Right **Pos:** 3B **Ht:** 6'4" **Wt:** 200 **Born:** 3/30/77 **Age:** 23

									BATTING								BASERUNNING				PERCENTAGES		
Year Team	Lg Org	G	AB	H	2B	3B	HR	TB	R	RBI	TBB	IBB	SO	HBP	SH	SF	SB	CS	SB%	GDP	Avg	OBP	SLG
1998 Clinton	A SD	65	247	73	20	3	10	129	42	38	26	0	66	6	2	2	4	2	.67	6	.296	.374	.522
1999 Mobile	AA SD	10	35	6	1	0	1	10	5	2	3	0	16	0	0	1	0	0	.00	0	.171	.231	.286
Rancho Cuca	A+ SD	110	417	108	30	4	18	200	69	69	42	0	139	12	2	2	7	5	.58	7	.259	.342	.480
2 Min. YEARS		185	699	187	51	7	29	339	116	109	71	0	221	18	4	5	11	7	.61	13	.268	.348	.485

Alex Eckelman

Bats: Right **Throws:** Right **Pos:** 3B   **Ht:** 5'11" **Wt:** 187 **Born:** 7/16/74 **Age:** 25

		BATTING														BASERUNNING				PERCENTAGES		
Year Team	Lg Org	G	AB	H	2B	3B	HR	TB	R	RBI	TBB	IBB	SO	HBP	SH	SF	SB	CS	SB%	GDP	Avg	OBP	SLG
1997 Johnson Cy	R+ StL	49	165	53	13	1	7	89	30	27	10	0	23	7	1	2	3	1	.75	3	.321	.380	.539
1998 Peoria	A StL	16	52	17	4	1	1	26	7	11	5	0	9	0	0	0	2	2	.00	0	.327	.386	.500
Pr William	A+ StL	38	89	26	1	1	2	35	15	9	9	0	14	0	1	1	2	2	.50	2	.292	.354	.393
1999 Potomac	A+ StL	52	161	31	5	2	4	52	20	14	13	0	39	5	1	0	3	3	.50	2	.193	.274	.323
Arkansas	AA StL	41	116	28	4	3	1	41	5	13	5	0	20	4	2	3	0	0	.00	4	.241	.289	.353
3 Min. YEARS		196	583	155	27	8	15	243	77	74	42	0	105	16	5	6	8	8	.50	11	.266	.329	.417

David Eckstein

Bats: Right **Throws:** Right **Pos:** 2B   **Ht:** 5'8" **Wt:** 168 **Born:** 1/20/75 **Age:** 25

		BATTING														BASERUNNING				PERCENTAGES		
Year Team	Lg Org	G	AB	H	2B	3B	HR	TB	R	RBI	TBB	IBB	SO	HBP	SH	SF	SB	CS	SB%	GDP	Avg	OBP	SLG
1997 Lowell	A- Bos	68	249	75	11	4	4	106	43	39	33	1	29	12	8	1	21	5	.81	2	.301	.407	.426
1998 Sarasota	A+ Bos	135	503	154	29	4	3	200	99	58	87	3	51	22	1	2	45	16	.74	8	.306	.428	.398
1999 Trenton	AA Bos	131	483	151	22	5	6	201	109	52	89	0	48	25	13	5	32	13	.71	6	.313	.440	.416
3 Min. YEARS		334	1235	380	62	13	13	507	251	149	209	4	128	59	22	8	98	34	.74	16	.308	.429	.411

Steve Eddie

Bats: Right **Throws:** Right **Pos:** 3B   **Ht:** 6'1" **Wt:** 190 **Born:** 1/6/71 **Age:** 29

		BATTING														BASERUNNING				PERCENTAGES		
Year Team	Lg Org	G	AB	H	2B	3B	HR	TB	R	RBI	TBB	IBB	SO	HBP	SH	SF	SB	CS	SB%	GDP	Avg	OBP	SLG
1993 Billings	R+ Cin	67	231	66	8	1	3	85	31	38	23	0	33	2	3	0	5	9	.36	4	.286	.355	.368
1994 Chstn-WV	A Cin	132	470	116	28	1	1	149	40	57	24	0	82	4	4	6	1	5	.17	11	.247	.286	.317
1995 Chstn-WV	A Cin	115	331	91	16	3	6	131	45	47	24	0	46	7	3	6	10	3	.77	9	.275	.332	.396
1996 Winston-Sal	A+ Cin	137	497	135	23	2	9	189	56	64	45	3	78	4	6	4	14	9	.61	14	.272	.335	.380
1997 Chattanooga	AA Cin	118	394	113	25	4	8	170	57	49	21	4	64	1	3	7	3	2	.60	10	.287	.319	.431
1998 Chattanooga	AA Cin	134	520	151	30	3	10	217	70	81	43	3	84	1	4	9	3	3	.50	16	.290	.340	.417
1999 Indianapolis	AAA Cin	10	24	9	2	0	0	11	3	3	1	0	1	0	0	0	0	0	.00	0	.375	.400	.458
Chattanooga	AA Cin	6	21	4	0	0	0	4	2	2	0	0	3	0	0	1	0	0	.00	1	.190	.182	.190
Nashua	IND —	2	8	2	1	0	0	3	1	1	0	0	0	0	0	0	0	0	.00	0	.250	.250	.375
Charlotte	AAA CWS	33	119	30	4	0	2	40	14	12	7	0	19	0	2	5	0	0	.00	5	.252	.282	.336
Birmingham	AA CWS	46	136	27	8	0	1	38	13	10	12	0	27	0	3	2	0	3	.00	6	.199	.260	.279
7 Min. YEARS		800	2751	744	145	14	40	1037	332	364	200	10	437	19	28	40	36	34	.51	75	.270	.320	.377

Geoff Edsell

Pitches: Right **Bats:** Right **Pos:** P   **Ht:** 6'2" **Wt:** 194 **Born:** 12/10/71 **Age:** 28

		HOW MUCH HE PITCHED						WHAT HE GAVE UP										THE RESULTS					
Year Team	Lg Org	G	GS	CG	GF	IP	BFP	H	R	ER	HR	SH	SF	HB	TBB	IBB	SO	WP	Bk	W	L	Pct.	ShO	Sv	ERA
1993 Boise	A- Ana	13	13	1	0	64	296	64	52	49	10	1	5	3	40	0	63	6	3	4	3	.571	0	0	6.89
1994 Cedar Rapids	A Ana	17	17	4	0	125.1	538	109	54	42	10	5	0	6	65	1	84	10	4	11	5	.688	1	0	3.02
Lk Elsinore	A+ Ana	9	7	0	1	40	174	38	21	18	3	0	0	2	24	1	26	3	2	2	2	.500	0	0	4.05
1995 Lk Elsinore	A+ Ana	23	22	1	0	139.2	600	127	81	57	11	7	3	7	67	0	134	6	1	8	12	.400	1	0	3.67
Midland	AA Ana	5	5	1	0	32	140	39	26	21	5	1	2	0	16	0	19	5	0	2	3	.400	0	0	5.91
1996 Midland	AA Ana	14	14	0	0	88	382	84	53	46	10	3	5	6	47	0	60	5	1	5	5	.500	0	0	4.70
Vancouver	AAA Ana	15	15	3	0	105	437	93	45	40	7	5	4	3	45	1	48	2	2	4	6	.400	2	0	3.43
1997 Vancouver	AAA Ana	30	29	6	1	183.1	826	196	121	105	11	5	6	12	96	1	95	8	0	14	11	.560	1	0	5.15
1998 Vancouver	AAA Ana	56	0	0	27	69	305	63	45	32	8	3	4	5	33	1	64	6	0	4	8	.333	0	4	4.17
1999 Erie	AA Ana	26	2	0	14	39	179	45	20	15	1	1	3	6	13	0	28	0	0	2	3	.400	0	2	3.46
Edmonton	AAA Ana	30	0	0	7	46.2	208	46	27	26	6	1	2	2	25	2	37	1	0	1	4	.200	0	0	5.01
7 Min. YEARS		238	124	16	50	932	4085	904	545	451	82	32	34	52	471	7	658	52	13	57	62	.479	5	6	4.36

Scott Eibey

Pitches: Left **Bats:** Left **Pos:** P   **Ht:** 6'4" **Wt:** 210 **Born:** 1/19/74 **Age:** 26

		HOW MUCH HE PITCHED						WHAT HE GAVE UP										THE RESULTS					
Year Team	Lg Org	G	GS	CG	GF	IP	BFP	H	R	ER	HR	SH	SF	HB	TBB	IBB	SO	WP	Bk	W	L	Pct.	ShO	Sv	ERA
1995 Bluefield	R+ Bal	14	6	0	3	43.2	196	51	32	27	4	2	0	2	24	0	26	6	1	3	1	.750	0	2	5.56
1996 High Desert	A+ Bal	11	0	0	1	11.2	65	17	16	11	0	0	1	0	10	2	7	2	0	1	0	1.000	0	0	8.49
Bluefield	R+ Bal	24	0	0	10	45	187	30	19	14	3	0	3	3	17	0	59	4	1	5	1	.833	0	2	2.80
1997 Delmarva	A Bal	47	0	0	19	93.1	371	65	25	19	3	7	0	2	33	5	82	4	0	10	4	.714	0	7	1.83
1998 Bowie	AA Bal	24	0	0	8	36.1	159	40	20	17	5	0	1	0	14	0	29	1	1	1	1	.500	0	0	4.21
Frederick	A+ Bal	21	0	0	5	35	152	47	17	15	3	4	1	0	8	0	20	3	0	1	2	.333	0	1	3.86
1999 Frederick	A+ Bal	15	0	0	6	29	120	26	14	12	2	0	1	0	10	1	27	0	0	0	2	.000	0	0	3.72
Bowie	AA Bal	27	4	0	3	51.1	222	49	17	15	2	1	1	1	25	2	29	5	2	2	0	1.000	0	0	2.63
5 Min. YEARS		183	10	0	55	345.1	1472	325	160	130	22	14	8	8	141	10	279	25	5	23	11	.676	0	12	3.39

Darrell Einertson

Pitches: Right **Bats:** Right **Pos:** P   **Ht:** 6'2" **Wt:** 190 **Born:** 9/4/72 **Age:** 27

		HOW MUCH HE PITCHED						WHAT HE GAVE UP										THE RESULTS					
Year Team	Lg Org	G	GS	CG	GF	IP	BFP	H	R	ER	HR	SH	SF	HB	TBB	IBB	SO	WP	Bk	W	L	Pct.	ShO	Sv	ERA
1995 Oneonta	A- NYY	25	0	0	8	38.1	167	32	20	8	1	1	0	3	15	1	35	0	1	0	4	.000	0	0	1.88
1996 Greensboro	A NYY	48	0	0	26	70	306	69	29	21	1	4	2	2	19	3	48	4	1	3	9	.250	0	8	2.70
1997 Tampa	A+ NYY	45	0	0	24	71	287	63	24	17	2	5	0	1	19	8	55	1	0	5	4	.556	0	2	2.15
1998 Norwich	AA NYY	17	0	0	5	35.1	142	23	7	4	1	3	0	1	10	3	33	2	0	3	1	.750	0	0	1.02
1999 Yankees	R NYY	1	0	0	1	2	11	3	3	0	0	0	0	0	1	0	4	0	0	0	0	.000	0	0	0.00
Tampa	A+ NYY	2	1	0	0	4.2	19	1	1	1	0	0	0	1	1	0	3	0	0	0	0	.000	0	1	1.93

Year Team	Lg Org	G	GS	CG	GF	IP	BFP	H	R	ER	HR	SH	SF	HB	TBB	IBB	SO	WP	Bk	W	L	Pct.	ShO	Sv	ERA
						HOW MUCH HE PITCHED					WHAT HE GAVE UP											THE RESULTS			
Norwich	AA NYY	21	0	0	6	29	141	39	23	16	2	4	0	1	10	5	16	1	0	2	2	.500	0	0	4.97
5 Min. YEARS		159	1	0	70	250.1	1073	230	107	67	7	17	2	9	75	20	194	11	2	13	21	.382	0	14	2.41

Joey Eischen

Pitches: Left Bats: Left Pos: P   Ht: 6' 1" Wt: 200 Born: 5/25/70 Age: 30

Year Team	Lg Org	G	GS	CG	GF	IP	BFP	H	R	ER	HR	SH	SF	HB	TBB	IBB	SO	WP	Bk	W	L	Pct.	ShO	Sv	ERA
1989 Butte	R+ Tex	12	12	0	0	52.2	248	50	45	31	4	1	0	6	38	0	57	13	11	3	7	.300	0	0	5.30
1990 Gastonia	A Tex	17	14	0	0	73.1	311	51	36	22	0	3	4	3	40	0	69	9	0	3	7	.300	0	0	2.70
1991 Charlotte	A+ Tex	18	18	1	0	108.1	467	99	59	40	5	6	3	4	55	1	80	8	1	4	10	.286	0	0	3.32
Wst Plm Bch	A+ Mon	8	8	1	0	38.1	177	34	27	22	3	3	1	2	24	0	26	3	0	4	2	.667	1	0	5.17
1992 Wst Plm Bch	A+ Mon	27	26	3	0	169.2	705	128	68	58	5	4	3	8	83	2	167	6	0	9	8	.529	2	0	3.08
1993 Harrisburg	AA Mon	20	20	0	0	119.1	533	122	62	48	11	3	6	4	60	0	110	9	1	14	4	.778	0	0	3.62
Ottawa	AAA Mon	6	6	0	0	40.2	166	34	18	16	3	1	2	0	15	0	29	1	0	2	2	.500	0	0	3.54
1994 Ottawa	AAA Mon	48	2	0	20	62	274	54	38	34	7	3	4	0	40	4	57	10	0	2	6	.250	0	2	4.94
1995 Ottawa	AAA Mon	11	0	0	3	15.2	61	9	4	3	0	1	0	0	8	1	13	0	0	2	1	.667	0	0	1.72
Albuquerque	AAA LA	13	0	0	6	16.1	59	8	0	0	0	0	0	1	3	0	14	1	0	3	0	1.000	0	2	0.00
1997 Indianapols	AAA Cin	26	5	0	7	42.2	173	41	7	6	1	2	0	1	13	1	26	2	0	1	0	1.000	0	2	1.27
1998 Indianapols	AAA Cin	61	0	0	18	73.1	326	73	42	37	9	7	3	4	29	3	60	7	0	2	5	.286	0	2	4.54
1999 Tucson	AAA Ari	27	1	0	8	41.2	209	63	47	42	7	1	1	1	26	3	36	6	0	1	3	.250	0	1	9.07
Adirondack	IND —	7	7	1	0	48	204	52	22	20	1	0	2	1	11	0	49	4	0	4	2	.667	0	0	3.75
1994 Montreal	NL	1	0	0	0	0.2	7	4	4	4	0	0	0	1	0	0	1	0	0	0	0	.000	0	0	54.00
1995 Los Angeles	NL	17	0	0	8	20.1	95	19	9	7	1	0	0	2	11	1	15	1	0	0	0	.000	0	0	3.10
1996 Los Angeles	NL	28	0	0	11	43.1	198	48	25	23	4	3	1	4	20	4	36	1	0	0	1	.000	0	0	4.78
Detroit	AL	24	0	0	3	25	110	27	11	9	3	0	1	0	14	3	15	3	0	1	1	.500	0	0	3.24
1997 Cincinnati	NL	1	0	0	0	1.1	7	2	2	1	0	0	0	0	1	0	2	1	0	0	0	.000	0	0	6.75
10 Min. YEARS		301	119	6	62	902	3913	818	475	379	56	35	29	35	445	15	793	79	13	54	57	.486	3	9	3.78
4 Maj. YEARS		71	0	0	22	90.2	417	100	51	44	8	3	2	7	46	8	69	6	0	1	2	.333	0	0	4.37

David Elder

Pitches: Right Bats: Right Pos: P   Ht: 6'0" Wt: 185 Born: 9/23/75 Age: 24

Year Team	Lg Org	G	GS	CG	GF	IP	BFP	H	R	ER	HR	SH	SF	HB	TBB	IBB	SO	WP	Bk	W	L	Pct.	ShO	Sv	ERA
1997 Pulaski	R+ Tex	20	0	0	17	32.1	127	18	8	7	2	0	0	0	12	0	57	4	0	2	2	.500	0	6	1.95
1999 Charlotte	A+ Tex	24	1	0	16	44.1	186	33	15	14	2	4	0	2	25	0	42	4	0	4	2	.667	0	4	2.84
Tulsa	AA Tex	3	0	0	1	6.2	32	8	7	6	0	0	0	0	6	1	7	0	0	1	0	1.000	0	0	8.10
2 Min. YEARS		47	1	0	34	83.1	345	59	30	27	4	4	0	2	43	1	106	8	0	7	4	.636	0	10	2.92

Dave Elliott

Bats: Right Throws: Right Pos: OF   Ht: 6'2" Wt: 205 Born: 8/10/73 Age: 26

Year Team	Lg Org	G	AB	H	2B	3B	HR	TB	R	RBI	TBB	IBB	SO	HBP	SH	SF	SB	CS	SB%	GDP	Avg	OBP	SLG
1995 Helena	R+ Mil	54	172	45	11	1	7	79	35	37	33	1	29	3	1	4	3	5	.38	3	.262	.382	.459
1996 Beloit	A Mil	112	365	98	12	3	12	152	65	58	62	4	80	7	0	4	17	10	.63	10	.268	.381	.416
1997 Stockton	A+ Mil	25	82	16	5	1	1	26	8	8	12	0	18	1	0	0	1	1	.50	6	.195	.305	.317
Beloit	A Mil	76	267	74	12	2	12	126	44	48	30	3	60	6	1	2	13	7	.65	3	.277	.361	.472
1998 Stockton	A+ Mil	96	317	89	22	3	8	141	52	44	30	3	56	4	2	5	12	8	.60	10	.281	.346	.445
1999 Huntsville	AA Mil	123	404	94	23	0	12	153	69	55	59	2	111	7	1	6	11	6	.65	5	.233	.336	.379
5 Min. YEARS		486	1607	416	85	10	52	677	273	250	226	13	354	28	5	21	57	37	.61	37	.259	.356	.421

Robert Ellis

Pitches: Right Bats: Right Pos: P   Ht: 6' 5" Wt: 220 Born: 12/15/70 Age: 29

Year Team	Lg Org	G	GS	CG	GF	IP	BFP	H	R	ER	HR	SH	SF	HB	TBB	IBB	SO	WP	Bk	W	L	Pct.	ShO	Sv	ERA
1991 Utica	A- CWS	15	15	1	0	87.2	407	87	66	45	4	6	5	6	61	0	66	13	0	3	9	.250	1	0	4.62
1992 White Sox	R CWS	1	1	0	0	5	24	10	6	6	0	0	0	0	1	0	4	0	0	1	0	1.000	0	0	10.80
South Bend	A CWS	18	18	1	0	123	481	90	46	32	3	4	2	4	35	0	97	7	2	6	5	.545	1	0	2.34
1993 Sarasota	A+ CWS	15	15	8	0	104	414	81	37	29	3	4	3	3	31	1	79	6	1	7	8	.467	2	0	2.51
Birmingham	AA CWS	12	12	2	0	81.1	336	68	33	28	2	1	1	4	21	0	77	6	0	6	3	.667	1	0	3.10
1994 Nashville	AAA CWS	19	19	1	0	105	483	126	77	71	19	5	6	2	55	1	76	1	4	4	10	.286	0	0	6.09
1995 Nashville	AAA CWS	4	4	0	0	20.2	85	16	7	5	2	0	1	1	10	0	9	1	0	1	1	.500	0	0	2.18
1996 Nashville	AAA CWS	19	13	1	2	70.1	327	78	49	47	6	5	3	7	45	3	35	8	0	3	8	.273	0	0	6.01
Birmingham	AA CWS	2	2	0	0	7.1	35	6	9	9	1	0	1	1	8	0	8	1	0	0	1	.000	0	0	11.05
Vancouver	AAA Ana	7	7	1	0	44.1	186	30	19	16	2	2	2	0	28	0	29	5	0	2	3	.400	0	0	3.25
1997 Vancouver	AAA Ana	29	23	3	1	149	698	185	108	98	15	6	6	7	83	1	70	15	1	9	10	.474	0	0	5.92
1998 Louisville	AAA Mil	30	28	0	0	150.1	693	171	103	94	21	2	8	8	78	1	79	13	0	10	10	.500	0	0	5.63
1999 New Orleans	AAA Hou	27	27	1	0	155.2	690	176	106	94	20	5	6	5	51	1	105	11	2	7	12	.368	0	0	5.43
1996 California	AL	3	0	0	3	5	19	0	0	0	0	0	0	0	4	0	5	1	0	0	0	.000	0	0	0.00
9 Min. YEARS		198	184	19	3	1103.2	4859	1124	666	574	98	45	38	48	507	8	734	87	10	59	80	.424	5	0	4.68

Scott Emmons

Bats: Right Throws: Right Pos: C   Ht: 6'4" Wt: 205 Born: 12/25/73 Age: 26

Year Team	Lg Org	G	AB	H	2B	3B	HR	TB	R	RBI	TBB	IBB	SO	HBP	SH	SF	SB	CS	SB%	GDP	Avg	OBP	SLG
1995 Oneonta	A- NYY	67	242	48	15	3	2	75	25	32	25	0	62	3	2	5	1	1	.50	5	.198	.276	.310
1996 Greensboro	A NYY	15	46	11	1	0	1	15	7	9	2	0	6	1	1	1	0	1	.00	0	.239	.280	.326

							BATTING										BASERUNNING				PERCENTAGES		
Year Team	Lg Org	G	AB	H	2B	3B	HR	TB	R	RBI	TBB	IBB	SO	HBP	SH	SF	SB	CS	SB%	GDP	Avg	OBP	SLG
Tampa	A+ NYY	36	98	20	2	1	1	27	6	10	10	1	26	2	3	0	0	1	.00	1	.204	.291	.276
1997 Tampa	A+ NYY	51	118	21	5	0	2	32	19	14	9	0	28	6	2	1	0	0	.00	2	.178	.269	.271
Greensboro	A NYY	3	7	2	1	0	0	3	1	0	1	0	1	0	0	0	0	0	.00	0	.286	.375	.429
1998 Tampa	A+ NYY	13	24	6	2	0	0	8	3	4	4	0	6	1	0	0	1	0	1.00	2	.250	.379	.333
Norwich	AA NYY	48	145	25	6	0	1	34	12	5	14	0	43	4	0	2	2	1	.67	4	.172	.261	.234
1999 Norwich	AA NYY	37	102	24	1	0	3	34	13	16	6	0	25	4	1	0	0	0	.00	4	.235	.304	.333
5 Min. YEARS		270	782	157	33	4	10	228	86	90	71	1	197	21	9	9	4	4	.50	18	.201	.282	.292

Angelo Encarnacion

Bats: Right **Throws:** Right **Pos:** C **Ht:** 5' 8" **Wt:** 190 **Born:** 4/18/73 **Age:** 27

							BATTING										BASERUNNING				PERCENTAGES		
Year Team	Lg Org	G	AB	H	2B	3B	HR	TB	R	RBI	TBB	IBB	SO	HBP	SH	SF	SB	CS	SB%	GDP	Avg	OBP	SLG
1991 Welland	A- Pit	50	181	46	3	2	0	53	21	15	5	0	27	1	0	0	4	3	.57	5	.254	.278	.293
1992 Augusta	A Pit	94	314	80	14	3	1	103	39	29	25	1	37	1	4	2	2	4	.33	5	.255	.310	.328
1993 Salem	A+ Pit	70	238	61	12	1	3	84	20	24	13	1	27	0	0	1	1	4	.20	5	.256	.294	.353
Buffalo	AAA Pit	3	9	3	0	0	0	3	1	2	0	0	0	0	0	0	0	0	.00	0	.333	.333	.333
1994 Carolina	AA Pit	67	227	66	17	0	3	92	26	32	11	1	28	2	0	4	2	2	.50	4	.291	.324	.405
1995 Calgary	AAA Pit	21	80	20	3	0	1	26	8	6	1	1	12	0	0	0	1	0	1.00	2	.250	.259	.325
1996 Calgary	AAA Pit	75	263	84	18	0	4	114	38	31	10	2	19	3	0	2	6	2	.75	10	.319	.349	.433
1997 Las Vegas	AAA SD	79	253	62	12	1	3	85	27	23	15	1	32	1	1	0	1	5	.17	9	.245	.290	.000
1998 Vancouver	AAA Ana	8	25	6	2	0	0	8	3	2	0	0	2	0	0	0	0	1	.00	1	.240	.240	.320
Midland	AA Ana	28	93	20	1	0	2	27	9	7	8	0	11	1	2	0	0	0	.00	2	.215	.284	.290
1999 Akron	AA Cle	34	127	27	7	0	1	37	9	21	6	0	19	0	1	1	1	1	.50	5	.213	.248	.291
West Tenn	AA ChC	30	101	26	6	1	1	37	11	10	4	0	12	1	0	0	2	0	1.00	1	.257	.292	.366
1995 Pittsburgh	NL	58	159	36	7	2	2	53	18	10	13	5	28	0	3	0	1	1	.50	3	.226	.285	.333
1996 Pittsburgh	NL	7	22	7	2	0	0	9	3	1	0	0	5	0	0	0	0	0	.00	0	.318	.318	.409
1997 Anaheim	AL	11	17	7	1	0	1	11	2	4	0	0	1	0	0	0	2	0	1.00	1	.412	.412	.647
9 Min. YEARS		559	1911	501	95	8	19	669	212	202	98	7	226	10	8	9	20	22	.48	49	.262	.300	.350
3 Maj. YEARS		76	198	50	10	2	3	73	23	15	13	5	34	0	3	0	3	1	.75	4	.253	.299	.369

Mario Encarnacion

Bats: Right **Throws:** Right **Pos:** OF **Ht:** 6'2" **Wt:** 187 **Born:** 9/24/77 **Age:** 22

							BATTING										BASERUNNING				PERCENTAGES		
Year Team	Lg Org	G	AB	H	2B	3B	HR	TB	R	RBI	TBB	IBB	SO	HBP	SH	SF	SB	CS	SB%	GDP	Avg	OBP	SLG
1996 W Michigan	A Oak	118	401	92	14	3	7	133	55	43	49	0	131	5	4	0	23	8	.74	12	.229	.321	.332
1997 Modesto	A+ Oak	111	364	108	17	9	18	197	70	78	42	1	121	6	0	1	14	11	.56	7	.297	.378	.541
1998 Huntsville	AA Oak	110	357	97	15	2	15	161	70	61	60	1	123	4	3	1	11	8	.58	9	.272	.382	.451
1999 Midland	AA Oak	94	353	109	21	4	18	192	69	71	47	4	86	1	0	2	9	9	.50	6	.309	.390	.544
Vancouver	AAA Oak	39	145	35	5	0	3	49	18	17	6	0	44	2	0	2	5	4	.56	7	.241	.277	.338
4 Min. YEARS		472	1620	441	72	18	61	732	282	270	204	6	505	18	7	6	62	40	.61	41	.272	.359	.452

Trevor Enders

Pitches: Left **Bats:** Right **Pos:** P **Ht:** 6'1" **Wt:** 205 **Born:** 12/22/74 **Age:** 25

			HOW MUCH HE PITCHED					WHAT HE GAVE UP											THE RESULTS					
Year Team	Lg Org	G	GS	CG	GF	IP	BFP	H	R	ER	HR	SH	SF	HB	TBB	IBB	SO	WP	Bk	W	L	Pct.	ShO	Sv	ERA
1996 Butte	R+ TB	19	0	0	6	27.2	132	34	22	15	1	2	2	2	13	1	24	2	0	0	1	.000	0	1	4.88
1997 Chston-SC	A TB	44	0	0	24	67	271	55	18	14	2	2	1	2	17	3	73	2	1	4	3	.571	0	2	1.88
1998 St. Pete	A+ TB	51	0	0	16	68.2	267	48	20	17	4	2	2	3	15	3	61	5	0	10	1	.909	0	1	2.23
1999 Orlando	AA TB	60	0	0	11	95.1	394	86	37	35	4	3	5	2	33	1	63	5	0	8	2	.800	0	1	3.30
4 Min. YEARS		174	0	0	57	258.2	1064	223	97	81	11	9	10	9	78	8	221	14	1	22	7	.759	0	5	2.82

Chris Enochs

Pitches: Right **Bats:** Right **Pos:** P **Ht:** 6'3" **Wt:** 225 **Born:** 10/11/75 **Age:** 24

			HOW MUCH HE PITCHED					WHAT HE GAVE UP											THE RESULTS					
Year Team	Lg Org	G	GS	CG	GF	IP	BFP	H	R	ER	HR	SH	SF	HB	TBB	IBB	SO	WP	Bk	W	L	Pct.	ShO	Sv	ERA
1997 Sou Oregon	A- Oak	3	3	0	0	12	4	4	0	0	0	1	2	0	10	1	0	0	0	.000	0	0	3.48
Modesto	A+ Oak	10	9	0	1	45.1	203	51	20	14	0	3	2	3	12	0	45	7	0	3	0	1.000	0	0	2.78
1998 Huntsville	AA Oak	26	26	0	0	148	660	159	101	78	12	2	6	9	64	2	100	5	0	9	10	.474	0	0	4.74
1999 Midland	AA Oak	13	11	0	0	45	238	69	57	50	9	0	5	2	34	1	33	11	0	3	5	.375	0	0	10.00
Visalia	A+ Oak	4	4	0	0	18.1	87	24	10	10	4	0	0	1	10	0	19	2	0	0	0	.000	0	0	4.91
3 Min. YEARS		56	53	0	1	267	1233	315	192	156	25	5	13	16	122	3	207	26	0	15	15	.500	0	0	5.26

Chad Epperson

Bats: Both **Throws:** Right **Pos:** DH **Ht:** 6'3" **Wt:** 221 **Born:** 3/26/72 **Age:** 28

							BATTING										BASERUNNING				PERCENTAGES		
Year Team	Lg Org	G	AB	H	2B	3B	HR	TB	R	RBI	TBB	IBB	SO	HBP	SH	SF	SB	CS	SB%	GDP	Avg	OBP	SLG
1992 Mets	R NYM	37	97	16	2	0	1	21	7	12	12	0	20	3	0	3	1	1	.50	2	.165	.270	.216
1993 Kingsport	R+ NYM	38	117	40	7	0	6	65	15	26	18	0	24	1	1	0	3	1	.75	4	.342	.434	.556
1994 St. Lucie	A+ NYM	50	148	32	7	0	2	45	15	10	16	2	42	0	1	2	1	2	.33	2	.216	.289	.304
1995 Binghamton	AA NYM	7	17	1	0	1	0	3	0	0	1	1	8	0	0	0	0	1	.00	0	.059	.111	.176
St. Lucie	A+ NYM	42	121	23	7	1	1	35	7	14	17	2	32	0	1	2	1	0	1.00	7	.190	.286	.289
1996 Lafayette	IND —	56	217	73	15	4	10	126	46	49	29	1	44	0	1	3	9	3	.75	4	.336	.410	.581
1997 Sarasota	A+ Bos	107	367	100	25	1	8	151	45	48	32	3	95	1	1	1	13	8	.62	8	.272	.332	.411
Trenton	AA Bos	3	9	3	1	0	0	4	2	1	0	0	2	0	0	0	1	0	1.00	0	.333	.333	.444
1998 Trenton	AA Bos	109	383	97	27	2	15	173	53	57	38	2	129	6	3	4	2	8	.20	6	.253	.327	.452
1999 Sarasota	A+ Bos	26	99	24	1	1	3	36	9	14	3	0	18	0	0	0	2	1	.67	2	.242	.265	.364

(continued)

Year Team	Lg Org	G	AB	H	2B	3B	HR	TB	R	RBI	TBB	IBB	SO	HBP	SH	SF	SB	CS	SB%	GDP	Avg	OBP	SLG
Trenton	AA Bos	55	188	37	10	1	2	55	24	15	31	1	46	0	0	0	1	2	.33	10	.197	.311	.293
8 Min. YEARS		530	1763	446	102	11	48	714	223	246	197	12	460	11	8	15	35	26	.57	45	.253	.329	.405

Matt Erickson

Bats: Left **Throws:** Right **Pos:** 2B   Ht: 5'11" Wt: 190 Born: 7/30/75 Age: 24

Year Team	Lg Org	G	AB	H	2B	3B	HR	TB	R	RBI	TBB	IBB	SO	HBP	SH	SF	SB	CS	SB%	GDP	Avg	OBP	SLG
1997 Utica	A- Fla	69	238	78	10	0	5	103	44	44	48	3	36	1	2	4	9	3	.75	7	.328	.455	.433
1998 Kane County	A Fla	124	441	143	32	2	4	191	83	64	72	1	62	18	7	3	17	7	.71	8	.324	.436	.433
1999 Portland	AA Fla	107	361	97	20	2	0	121	38	35	51	0	65	3	5	5	2	3	.40	9	.269	.360	.335
3 Min. YEARS		300	1040	318	62	4	9	415	165	143	171	4	163	32	14	12	28	13	.68	24	.306	.415	.399

Roman Escamilla

Bats: Right **Throws:** Right **Pos:** C   Ht: 5'10" Wt: 200 Born: 1/21/74 Age: 26

Year Team	Lg Org	G	AB	H	2B	3B	HR	TB	R	RBI	TBB	IBB	SO	HBP	SH	SF	SB	CS	SB%	GDP	Avg	OBP	SLG
1996 Spokane	A- KC	46	152	33	7	0	2	46	11	21	12	0	22	0	1	0	1	0	1.00	1	.217	.274	.303
1997 Wilmington	A+ KC	57	167	42	7	0	1	52	19	21	28	0	30	0	4	1	0	6	.00	4	.251	.357	.311
1998 Omaha	AAA KC	1	1	0	0	0	0	0	0	0	0	0	1	0	0	0	0	0	.00	0	.000	.000	.000
Wichita	AA KC	43	129	34	6	0	1	43	16	10	10	0	21	0	1	2	0	1	.00	7	.264	.312	.333
1999 Wichita	AA KC	60	201	49	13	0	1	65	21	28	13	1	46	0	0	4	3	0	1.00	6	.244	.284	.323
4 Min. YEARS		207	650	158	33	0	5	206	67	80	63	1	120	0	6	7	4	7	.36	18	.243	.307	.317

Emiliano Escandon

Bats: Left **Throws:** Right **Pos:** DH-2B   Ht: 5'10" Wt: 180 Born: 11/6/74 Age: 25

Year Team	Lg Org	G	AB	H	2B	3B	HR	TB	R	RBI	TBB	IBB	SO	HBP	SH	SF	SB	CS	SB%	GDP	Avg	OBP	SLG
1995 Spokane	A- KC	13	44	14	1	1	1	20	7	12	6	0	11	1	0	0	1	0	1.00	0	.318	.412	.455
1996 Lansing	A KC	107	372	101	18	5	4	141	50	52	46	3	47	3	6	2	8	5	.62	3	.272	.355	.379
1997 Wilmington	A+ KC	80	238	65	9	3	2	86	40	32	57	3	54	1	5	2	9	4	.69	3	.273	.413	.361
1998 Wilmington	A+ KC	116	353	92	23	1	5	132	50	58	74	5	64	3	1	5	5	9	.36	10	.261	.389	.374
1999 Wichita	AA KC	120	340	88	18	5	7	137	59	57	73	3	46	4	4	7	5	7	.42	9	.259	.389	.403
5 Min. YEARS		436	1347	360	69	15	19	516	206	211	256	14	222	12	16	16	28	25	.53	25	.267	.385	.383

Ruben Escobar

Pitches: Right **Bats:** Right **Pos:** P   Ht: 6'1" Wt: 185 Born: 6/8/76 Age: 24

Year Team	Lg Org	G	GS	CG	GF	IP	BFP	H	R	ER	HR	SH	SF	HB	TBB	IBB	SO	WP	Bk	W	L	Pct.	ShO	Sv	ERA
1998 Watertown	A- Cle	14	0	0	2	24.1	96	20	12	10	0	0	3	0	6	0	14	3	0	0	1	.000	0	0	3.70
1999 Mahoning Vy	A- Cle	17	0	0	8	41.2	175	47	20	17	5	4	2	0	5	0	22	2	0	2	1	1.000	0	1	3.67
Akron	AA Cle	1	0	0	0	1.2	11	5	3	3	1	0	0	0	0	0	0	0	1	0	0	.000	0	0	16.20
2 Min. YEARS		32	0	0	10	67.2	282	72	35	30	6	4	5	0	11	0	36	5	1	2	1	.667	0	1	3.99

Josue Espada

Bats: Right **Throws:** Right **Pos:** SS   Ht: 5'10" Wt: 175 Born: 8/30/75 Age: 24

Year Team	Lg Org	G	AB	H	2B	3B	HR	TB	R	RBI	TBB	IBB	SO	HBP	SH	SF	SB	CS	SB%	GDP	Avg	OBP	SLG
1996 Sou Oregon	A- Oak	15	54	12	1	0	1	16	7	5	5	0	10	1	1	0	0	0	.00	1	.222	.300	.296
W Michigan	A Oak	23	74	20	2	0	0	22	9	4	13	0	11	2	0	0	3	1	.75	2	.270	.393	.297
1997 Visalia	A+ Oak	118	445	122	7	3	3	144	90	39	72	1	69	9	7	3	46	17	.73	6	.274	.384	.324
1998 Huntsville	AA Oak	51	161	41	7	1	1	53	29	22	27	0	15	4	5	1	7	4	.64	4	.255	.373	.329
1999 Midland	AA Oak	113	435	147	15	2	6	184	85	51	62	0	51	2	2	3	22	16	.58	5	.338	.420	.423
Vancouver	AAA Oak	6	26	8	1	0	0	9	2	0	3	0	4	0	0	0	1	2	.33	0	.308	.379	.346
4 Min. YEARS		326	1195	350	33	6	11	428	222	121	182	1	160	18	15	7	79	40	.66	18	.293	.392	.358

Jose Espinal

Pitches: Right **Bats:** Right **Pos:** P   Ht: 6'3" Wt: 195 Born: 8/31/76 Age: 23

Year Team	Lg Org	G	GS	CG	GF	IP	BFP	H	R	ER	HR	SH	SF	HB	TBB	IBB	SO	WP	Bk	W	L	Pct.	ShO	Sv	ERA
1995 Cubs	R ChC	13	5	0	6	36	158	29	20	7	0		2	4	10	0	27	2	0	3	2	.600	0	1	1.75
1996 Cubs	R ChC	11	7	0	2	61	246	46	20	15	0	1	2	4	18	0	57	8	1	4	1	.800	0	0	2.21
1997 Rockford	A ChC	24	24	1	0	120.2	545	147	83	66	7	2	4	2	41	1	107	4	7	10	10	.500	0	0	4.92
1998 Daytona	A+ ChC	28	22	0	3	144.2	641	165	95	76	16	6	3	6	50	1	117	10	0	10	10	.500	0	0	4.73
1999 New Britain	AA Min	29	20	2	3	131.2	595	160	100	81	10	8	11	2	41	0	90	3	0	3	12	.200	0	0	5.54
5 Min. YEARS		105	78	3	14	494	2185	547	318	245	33	19	21	18	160	2	398	27	8	30	35	.462	0	1	4.46

Juan Espinal

Bats: Right **Throws:** Right **Pos:** 3B   Ht: 5'11" Wt: 165 Born: 4/15/75 Age: 25

Year Team	Lg Org	G	AB	H	2B	3B	HR	TB	R	RBI	TBB	IBB	SO	HBP	SH	SF	SB	CS	SB%	GDP	Avg	OBP	SLG
1993 Padres	R SD	37	136	41	11	1	2	60	23	19	15	1	40	1	0	1	3	3	.50	2	.301	.373	.441
1994 Springfield	A SD	118	386	95	27	3	14	170	66	50	36	1	102	3	4	5	0	2	.00	2	.246	.312	.440
1995 Clinton	A SD	116	336	70	11	0	7	102	28	46	47	2	79	4	6	7	3	3	.50	8	.208	.307	.304
1996 Bakersfield	A+ SD	137	522	143	38	0	26	259	81	98	74	2	126	6	1	6	1	4	.20	11	.274	.367	.496

Year Team	Lg Org	BATTING															BASERUNNING				PERCENTAGES		
		G	AB	H	2B	3B	HR	TB	R	RBI	TBB	IBB	SO	HBP	SH	SF	SB	CS	SB%	GDP	Avg	OBP	SLG
1997 Sarasota	A+ Bos	109	322	80	20	2	7	125	49	45	51	0	79	6	2	3	4	5	.44	2	.248	.359	.388
1998 Sarasota	A+ Bos	127	508	141	32	1	16	223	76	88	37	2	107	4	1	2	3	1	.75	20	.278	.330	.439
1999 Sarasota	A+ Bos	111	411	123	26	0	10	179	78	67	47	0	83	6	1	4	12	4	.75	9	.299	.376	.436
Trenton	AA Bos	17	65	12	1	0	2	19	11	7	5	0	19	1	0	2	0	1	.00	2	.185	.247	.292
7 Min. YEARS		772	2686	705	166	7	84	1137	412	420	312	8	635	31	15	30	26	23	.53	56	.262	.343	.423

Eric Estes

Pitches: Right **Bats:** Right **Pos:** P   Ht: 6'4" **Wt:** 185 **Born:** 9/4/72 **Age:** 27

Year Team	Lg Org	HOW MUCH HE PITCHED						WHAT HE GAVE UP												THE RESULTS					
		G	GS	CG	GF	IP	BFP	H	R	ER	HR	SH	SF	HB	TBB	IBB	SO	WP	Bk	W	L	Pct.	ShO	Sv	ERA
1997 Frederick	A+ Bal	26	25	1	1	148	608	142	70	57	8	2	2	6	30	0	124	4	0	9	8	.529	0	0	3.47
1998 Bowie	AA Bal	9	9	1	0	49.1	208	53	28	24	6	0	0	1	8	0	29	6	0	5	2	.714	0	0	4.38
Mobile	AA SD	17	16	0	0	88.1	403	117	61	52	8	1	2	3	31	1	72	4	0	7	4	.636	0	0	5.30
1999 Mobile	AA SD	8	2	0	5	17.1	93	33	22	21	5	1	2	0	9	0	4	4	0	0	1	.000	0	0	10.90
Atlantic Ct	IND —	3	0	0	1	4	23	6	7	5	2	0	1	0	5	0	3	1	0	1	0	1.000	0	0	11.25
3 Min. YEARS		63	52	2	7	307	1335	351	188	159	29	4	7	10	83	1	232	19	0	22	15	.595	0	0	4.66

Jake Esteves

Pitches: Right **Bats:** Right **Pos:** P   Ht: 6'1" **Wt:** 200 **Born:** 7/31/75 **Age:** 24

Year Team	Lg Org	HOW MUCH HE PITCHED						WHAT HE GAVE UP												THE RESULTS					
		G	GS	CG	GF	IP	BFP	H	R	ER	HR	SH	SF	HB	TBB	IBB	SO	WP	Bk	W	L	Pct.	ShO	Sv	ERA
1998 Salem-Keizr	A- SF	1	1	0	0	4	15	1	1	1	1	0	0	1	0	0	5	0	0	0	0	.000	0	0	2.25
Bakersfield	A+ SF	14	6	0	4	35.2	168	43	30	17	7	1	2	2	12	0	24	0	0	0	2	.000	0	1	4.29
1999 San Jose	A+ SF	12	11	1	1	71.2	281	59	21	16	1	4	1	2	17	0	56	3	1	6	1	.857	0	1	2.01
Shreveport	AA SF	15	14	0	0	91.2	373	76	40	37	7	2	5	4	23	1	53	3	2	8	2	.800	0	0	3.63
2 Min. YEARS		42	32	1	5	203	837	179	92	71	16	7	8	9	52	1	138	6	3	14	5	.737	0	2	3.15

Marco Estrada

Bats: Both **Throws:** Right **Pos:** SS   Ht: 6'0" **Wt:** 187 **Born:** 12/11/76 **Age:** 23

Year Team	Lg Org	BATTING															BASERUNNING				PERCENTAGES		
		G	AB	H	2B	3B	HR	TB	R	RBI	TBB	IBB	SO	HBP	SH	SF	SB	CS	SB%	GDP	Avg	OBP	SLG
1999 Madison	IND —	15	41	7	0	0	1	10	7	1	7	0	9	0	0	0	0	0	.00	1	.171	.292	.244
Lancaster	A+ Sea	13	35	7	2	0	0	9	3	3	2	0	8	1	0	0	1	0	1.00	1	.200	.263	.257
New Haven	AA Sea	8	20	3	1	0	0	4	3	1	3	0	8	0	0	0	0	0	.00	1	.150	.261	.200
1 Min. YEARS		36	96	17	3	0	1	23	13	5	12	0	25	1	0	0	1	0	1.00	3	.177	.275	.240

Luis Estrella

Pitches: Right **Bats:** Right **Pos:** P   Ht: 6'2" **Wt:** 220 **Born:** 10/7/74 **Age:** 25

Year Team	Lg Org	HOW MUCH HE PITCHED						WHAT HE GAVE UP												THE RESULTS					
		G	GS	CG	GF	IP	BFP	H	R	ER	HR	SH	SF	HB	TBB	IBB	SO	WP	Bk	W	L	Pct.	ShO	Sv	ERA
1996 Bellingham	A- SF	23	0	0	6	55.1	213	35	13	11	3	1	0	0	22	1	52	6	0	4	0	1.000	0	1	1.79
1997 San Jose	A+ SF	42	0	0	15	77	332	84	39	29	3	1	0	2	25	3	59	7	6	5	5	.500	0	2	3.39
1998 San Jose	A+ SF	36	2	0	12	72	315	79	41	38	5	3	1	2	27	0	57	9	1	5	6	.455	0	2	4.75
1999 Fresno	AAA SF	8	0	0	1	11.2	63	23	16	16	4	1	1	0	7	0	5	1	0	0	1	.000	0	0	12.34
Shreveport	AA SF	40	5	0	15	92.1	375	77	33	31	2	2	1	2	33	1	75	7	1	6	4	.600	0	4	3.02
4 Min. YEARS		149	7	0	55	308.1	1298	298	142	125	17	8	3	6	114	5	248	30	8	20	16	.556	0	9	3.65

Seth Etherton

Pitches: Right **Bats:** Right **Pos:** P   Ht: 6'1" **Wt:** 200 **Born:** 10/17/76 **Age:** 23

Year Team	Lg Org	HOW MUCH HE PITCHED						WHAT HE GAVE UP												THE RESULTS					
		G	GS	CG	GF	IP	BFP	H	R	ER	HR	SH	SF	HB	TBB	IBB	SO	WP	Bk	W	L	Pct.	ShO	Sv	ERA
1998 Midland	AA Ana	9	7	1	1	48.1	211	57	36	33	9	3	2	1	12	0	35	1	1	1	5	.167	0	0	6.14
1999 Erie	AA Ana	24	24	4	0	167.2	694	153	72	61	14	7	5	3	43	0	153	4	4	10	10	.500	1	0	3.27
Edmonton	AAA Ana	4	4	0	0	21.1	94	25	13	13	7	1	0	0	6	0	19	1	0	0	2	.000	0	0	5.48
2 Min. YEARS		37	35	5	1	237.1	999	235	121	107	30	11	8	4	61	0	207	6	5	11	17	.393	1	0	4.06

Todd Etler

Pitches: Right **Bats:** Right **Pos:** P   Ht: 6'0" **Wt:** 205 **Born:** 4/18/74 **Age:** 26

Year Team	Lg Org	HOW MUCH HE PITCHED						WHAT HE GAVE UP												THE RESULTS					
		G	GS	CG	GF	IP	BFP	H	R	ER	HR	SH	SF	HB	TBB	IBB	SO	WP	Bk	W	L	Pct.	ShO	Sv	ERA
1992 Princeton	R+ Cin	12	10	0	0	52	241	62	40	28	3	2	2	4	21	0	29	5	0	4	4	.500	0	0	4.85
1993 Billings	R+ Cin	15	15	1	0	89.2	359	75	33	27	4	2	4	7	30	0	55	4	0	8	1	.889	1	0	2.71
1994 Chstn-WV	A Cin	7	7	1	0	47.2	190	48	17	14	4	1	0	2	3	1	31	0	0	4	2	.667	1	0	2.64
Winston-Sal	A+ Cin	19	19	1	0	106	479	141	84	76	25	1	5	3	31	0	61	5	1	5	11	.313	1	0	6.45
1995 Winston-Sal	A+ Cin	24	23	3	0	153.2	628	148	71	63	13	4	5	2	49	2	78	3	2	6	12	.333	0	0	3.69
1996 Winston-Sal	A+ Cin	33	1	0	16	77.1	321	72	30	30	7	3	2	5	17	0	59	2	0	4	5	.444	0	2	3.49
1997 Burlington	A Cin	25	0	0	12	43	175	34	13	10	2	2	2	0	14	2	40	2	0	2	3	.400	0	3	2.09
Chattanooga	AA Cin	23	0	0	6	37	172	38	29	27	6	1	1	1	24	4	29	5	0	0	3	.000	0	0	6.57
1998 Chattanooga	AA Cin	46	0	0	21	65.2	276	61	21	14	1	2	1	3	21	2	58	3	0	6	0	1.000	0	5	1.92
1999 Erie	AA Cin	14	0	0	3	23	94	17	6	6	1	0	1	1	8	0	26	0	0	0	0	.000	0	0	2.35
Indianapls	AAA Cin	26	0	0	6	38	182	42	29	27	3	0	2	0	29	1	35	1	0	2	1	.667	0	0	6.39
8 Min. YEARS		244	75	6	64	733	3117	738	373	322	69	18	23	30	247	12	501	30	3	41	42	.494	3	10	3.95

Bart Evans

Pitches: Right **Bats:** Right **Pos:** P | **Ht:** 6' 2" **Wt:** 210 **Born:** 12/30/70 **Age:** 29

		HOW MUCH HE PITCHED						WHAT HE GAVE UP										THE RESULTS					
Year Team	Lg Org	G	GS	CG	GF	IP	BFP	H	R	ER	HR	SH	SF	HB	TBB	IBB	SO	WP	Bk	W	L	Pct.	ShO	Sv	ERA
1992 Eugene	A- KC	13	1	0	4	26	126	17	20	18	1	1	2	4	31	0	39	14	0	1	1	.500	0	0	6.23
1993 Rockford	A KC	27	16	0	4	99	439	95	52	48	5	1	2	4	60	0	120	10	1	10	4	.714	0	0	4.36
1994 Wilmington	A+ KC	26	26	0	0	145	587	107	53	48	7	1	0	4	61	0	145	10	0	10	3	.769	0	0	2.98
1995 Wichita	AA KC	7	7	0	0	22.1	123	22	28	26	3	1	0	1	45	0	13	7	1	0	4	.000	0	0	10.48
Wilmington	A+ KC	16	6	0	4	46.2	215	30	21	15	0	0	1	5	44	0	47	7	0	4	1	.800	0	2	2.89
1996 Wichita	AA KC	9	7	0	0	24.1	146	31	38	32	7	3	2	6	36	0	16	12	0	1	2	.333	0	0	11.84
1997 Wilmington	A+ KC	16	2	0	8	20.2	101	22	18	15	1	0	2	3	15	0	22	3	0	0	1	.000	0	0	6.53
Wichita	AA KC	32	0	0	22	33.1	148	45	20	17	4	2	1	0	8	2	28	1	0	1	2	.333	0	6	4.59
1998 Omaha	AAA KC	49	0	0	40	57	236	50	18	16	4	2	2	0	22	2	54	3	0	3	1	.750	0	27	2.53
1999 Omaha	AAA KC	30	0	0	12	33.1	172	33	34	30	5	1	1	9	36	2	34	6	0	4	5	.444	0	2	8.10
1998 Kansas City	AL	8	0	0	3	9	34	7	3	2	1	0	0	0	0	0	7	0	0	0	0	.000	0	0	2.00
8 Min. YEARS		225	65	0	94	507.2	2293	452	302	265	37	12	11	38	358	6	518	73	2	34	24	.586	0	37	4.70

Dave Evans

Pitches: Right **Bats:** Right **Pos:** P | **Ht:** 6'3" **Wt:** 205 **Born:** 1/1/68 **Age:** 32

		HOW MUCH HE PITCHED						WHAT HE GAVE UP										THE RESULTS					
Year Team	Lg Org	G	GS	CG	GF	IP	BFP	H	R	ER	HR	SH	SF	HB	TBB	IBB	SO	WP	Bk	W	L	Pct.	ShO	Sv	ERA
1990 San Berndno	A+ Sea	26	26	4	0	155	673	135	83	72	9	4	7	7	74	0	143	10	0	14	9	.609	0	0	4.18
1991 Jacksonville	AA Sea	21	20	1	0	115.2	507	118	74	67	15	2	7	9	49	0	76	12	0	9	5	.357	0	0	5.21
1993 Appleton	A Sea	5	5	0	0	27.2	117	21	9	7	0	0	0	2	15	0	23	5	2	2	1	.667	0	0	2.28
Riverside	A+ Sea	8	8	1	0	41.2	187	41	22	21	5	1	1	5	23	0	42	2	0	3	2	.600	1	0	4.54
1994 Jacksnville	AA Sea	31	6	0	8	81.1	354	86	59	50	11	3	4	5	31	2	62	4	0	3	5	.375	0	2	5.53
1995 Jackson	AA Hou	49	0	0	37	67.2	278	50	29	25	2	5	3	4	28	6	54	0	1	2	9	.182	0	18	3.33
Tucson	AAA Hou	2	0	0	0	3	12	2	0	0	0	0	0	0	1	0	4	0	0	0	0	.000	0	0	0.00
1996 Tucson	AAA Hou	43	15	0	12	111.2	511	120	77	65	8	8	3	12	47	3	80	11	0	6	12	.333	0	1	5.24
1998 Carolina	AA Pit	26	3	0	6	56.2	254	56	36	33	8	3	1	0	30	1	52	8	3	5	4	.556	0	0	5.24
Nashville	AAA Pit	7	1	0	4	11.2	67	19	12	11	2	2	0	3	8	1	8	4	0	0	2	.000	0	0	8.49
Bowie	AA Bal	14	0	0	6	18.1	84	17	9	4	1	1	1	5	6	0	26	2	0	1	1	.500	0	1	1.96
1999 Rochester	AAA Bal	60	0	0	32	70.2	309	70	48	42	11	5	2	5	27	2	65	9	1	2	11	.154	0	2	5.35
8 Min. YEARS		292	84	6	105	761	3353	735	458	397	72	34	29	57	339	15	635	67	7	43	65	.398	1	23	4.70

Keith Evans

Pitches: Right **Bats:** Right **Pos:** P | **Ht:** 6'5" **Wt:** 200 **Born:** 11/2/75 **Age:** 24

		HOW MUCH HE PITCHED						WHAT HE GAVE UP										THE RESULTS					
Year Team	Lg Org	G	GS	CG	GF	IP	BFP	H	R	ER	HR	SH	SF	HB	TBB	IBB	SO	WP	Bk	W	L	Pct.	ShO	Sv	ERA
1997 Cape Fear	A Mon	21	21	3	0	138	551	113	56	40	6	2	4	10	18	0	102	1	0	12	7	.632	1	0	2.61
Wst Plm Bch	A+ Mon	7	7	2	0	43.2	185	42	23	21	4	2	2	5	11	0	20	1	0	2	4	.333	2	0	4.33
1998 Jupiter	A+ Mon	8	8	1	0	50.1	194	45	18	16	1	0	1	3	5	0	25	1	0	5	2	.714	0	0	2.86
Harrisburg	AA Mon	20	20	1	0	124	520	133	59	49	13	6	2	8	30	2	76	2	0	8	9	.471	0	0	3.56
1999 Harrisburg	AA Mon	5	5	0	0	27	120	29	14	11	5	1	0	3	5	0	21	1	0	0	2	.000	0	0	3.67
Ottawa	AAA Mon	24	18	2	0	122	525	143	79	65	17	3	1	10	22	0	74	2	0	2	13	.133	0	0	4.80
3 Min. YEARS		85	79	9	0	505	2095	505	249	202	46	14	10	39	91	2	318	8	0	29	37	.439	3	0	3.60

Tom Evans

Bats: Right **Throws:** Right **Pos:** 3B | **Ht:** 6' 1" **Wt:** 200 **Born:** 7/9/74 **Age:** 25

		BATTING														BASERUNNING				PERCENTAGES		
Year Team	Lg Org	G	AB	H	2B	3B	HR	TB	R	RBI	TBB	IBB	SO	HBP	SH	SF	SB	CS	SB%	GDP	Avg	OBP	SLG
1992 Medcine Hat	R+ Tor	52	166	36	3	0	1	42	17	21	33	0	29	1	1	1	4	3	.57	4	.217	.348	.253
1993 Hagerstown	A Tor	119	389	100	25	1	7	148	47	54	53	2	61	3	0	4	9	2	.82	7	.257	.347	.380
1994 Hagerstown	A Tor	95	322	88	16	2	13	147	52	48	51	1	80	1	1	1	2	1	.67	3	.273	.373	.457
1995 Dunedin	A+ Tor	130	444	124	29	3	9	186	63	66	51	0	80	8	3	7	7	2	.78	10	.279	.359	.419
1996 Knoxville	AA Tor	120	394	111	27	1	17	191	87	65	115	0	113	9	0	2	4	0	1.00	7	.282	.452	.485
1997 Dunedin	A+ Tor	15	42	11	2	0	2	19	8	4	11	0	10	4	0	1	0	0	.00	0	.262	.448	.452
Syracuse	AAA Tor	107	376	99	17	1	15	163	60	65	53	1	104	9	1	3	1	2	.33	4	.263	.365	.434
1998 Syracuse	AAA Tor	109	400	120	32	1	15	199	57	55	50	1	74	8	0	1	11	7	.61	13	.300	.388	.498
1999 Oklahoma	AAA Tex	128	439	123	35	3	12	200	84	68	66	1	100	9	1	1	5	4	.56	10	.280	.384	.456
1997 Toronto	AL	12	38	11	2	0	1	16	7	2	2	0	10	1	0	0	0	1	.00	0	.289	.341	.421
1998 Toronto	AL	7	10	0	0	0	0	0	0	0	1	0	2	0	0	1	0	0	.00	1	.000	.091	.000
8 Min. YEARS		875	2972	812	186	12	91	1295	475	446	483	6	651	52	7	21	43	21	.67	58	.273	.382	.436
2 Maj. YEARS		19	48	11	2	0	1	16	7	2	3	0	12	1	0	1	0	1	.00	1	.229	.288	.333

Adam Everett

Bats: Right **Throws:** Right **Pos:** SS | **Ht:** 6'1" **Wt:** 167 **Born:** 2/6/77 **Age:** 23

		BATTING														BASERUNNING				PERCENTAGES		
Year Team	Lg Org	G	AB	H	2B	3B	HR	TB	R	RBI	TBB	IBB	SO	HBP	SH	SF	SB	CS	SB%	GDP	Avg	OBP	SLG
1998 Lowell	A- Bos	21	71	21	6	2	0	31	11	9	11	0	13	3	1	1	2	1	.67	2	.296	.407	.437
1999 Trenton	AA Bos	98	338	89	11	0	10	130	56	44	41	0	64	10	9	4	21	5	.81	3	.263	.356	.385
2 Min. YEARS		119	409	110	17	2	10	161	67	53	52	0	77	13	10	5	23	6	.79	5	.269	.365	.394

Bryan Eversgerd

Pitches: Left **Bats:** Right **Pos:** P | **Ht:** 6' 1" **Wt:** 190 **Born:** 2/11/69 **Age:** 31

		HOW MUCH HE PITCHED						WHAT HE GAVE UP										THE RESULTS					
Year Team	Lg Org	G	GS	CG	GF	IP	BFP	H	R	ER	HR	SH	SF	HB	TBB	IBB	SO	WP	Bk	W	L	Pct.	ShO	Sv	ERA
1989 Johnson Cy	R+ StL	16	1	0	5	29.2	127	30	16	12	1	2	6	0	12	1	19	2	0	2	3	.400	0	0	3.64

Year Team	Lg Org	G	GS	CG	GF	IP	BFP	H	R	ER	HR	SH	SF	HB	TBB	IBB	SO	WP	Bk	W	L	Pct.	ShO	Sv	ERA
		HOW MUCH HE PITCHED						**WHAT HE GAVE UP**												**THE RESULTS**					
1990 Springfield	A StL	20	15	2	2	104.1	457	123	60	48	6	5	4	4	26	1	55	2	0	6	8	.429	0	0	4.14
1991 Savannah	A StL	72	0	0	22	93.1	390	71	43	36	7	2	0	3	34	4	98	11	0	1	5	.167	0	1	3.47
1992 St. Pete	A+ StL	57	1	0	13	74	305	65	25	22	0	9	4	2	25	4	57	1	1	3	2	.600	0	0	2.68
Arkansas	AA StL	6	0	0	2	5.1	25	7	4	4	0	1	0	2	2	1	4	0	0	0	1	.000	0	0	6.75
1993 Arkansas	AA StL	62	0	0	32	66	269	60	24	16	3	2	1	1	19	4	68	7	1	4	4	.500	0	0	2.18
1994 Louisville	AAA StL	9	0	0	2	12	54	11	7	6	0	1	1	0	8	0	8	1	0	1	1	.500	0	0	4.50
1995 Ottawa	AAA Mon	38	0	0	9	53	232	49	21	14	1	2	3	1	26	1	45	2	0	6	2	.750	0	2	2.38
1996 Trenton	AA Bos	4	0	0	2	7	31	6	2	2	0	1	0	1	4	1	2	0	1	1	0	1.000	0	0	2.57
Okla City	AAA Tex	38	5	0	14	65.2	266	57	21	20	3	2	1	4	14	0	60	3	0	3	3	.500	0	4	2.74
1997 Okla City	AAA Tex	26	7	0	5	76.1	339	91	48	36	12	4	2	2	24	2	43	5	1	3	3	.250	0	0	4.24
1998 Memphis	AAA StL	49	0	0	17	56.2	238	51	25	21	9	1	0	1	20	1	50	2	1	2	5	.286	0	0	3.34
1999 Memphis	AAA StL	59	0	0	27	66	269	56	26	21	9	4	0	3	15	0	46	0	0	6	6	.500	0	2	2.86
1994 St. Louis	NL	40	1	0	8	67.2	283	75	36	34	8	5	2	2	20	1	47	3	1	2	3	.400	0	0	4.52
1995 Montreal	NL	25	0	0	5	21	95	22	13	12	2	1	2	1	9	2	8	1	0	0	0	.000	0	0	5.14
1997 Texas	AL	3	0	0	1	1.1	12	5	3	3	0	0	0	0	3	0	2	0	0	0	2	.000	0	0	20.25
1998 St. Louis	NL	8	0	0	2	6	31	9	7	6	1	0	2	1	2	0	4	0	0	0	0	.000	0	0	9.00
11 Min. YEARS		456	29	2	152	709.1	3002	677	322	258	51	36	22	22	229	20	555	36	5	36	43	.456	0	9	3.27
4 Maj. YEARS		76	1	0	16	96	421	111	59	55	11	6	6	4	34	3	61	4	1	2	5	.286	0	0	5.16

Ethan Faggett

Bats: Left **Throws:** Left **Pos:** OF **Ht:** 6'0" **Wt:** 190 **Born:** 8/21/74 **Age:** 25

Year Team	Lg Org	G	AB	H	2B	3B	HR	TB	R	RBI	TBB	IBB	SO	HBP	SH	SF	SB	CS	SB%	GDP	Avg	OBP	SLG
		BATTING															**BASERUNNING**				**PERCENTAGES**		
1992 Red Sox	R Bos	34	103	18	1	1	1	24	9	9	10	0	37	2	0	0	1	2	.33	1	.175	.261	.233
1993 Red Sox	R Bos	23	58	10	2	1	0	14	4	2	10	0	15	1	0	1	5	1	.83	0	.172	.300	.241
1994 Red Sox	R Bos	41	117	34	2	2	1	43	14	17	12	0	33	2	0	0	10	7	.59	2	.291	.366	.368
1995 Michigan	A Bos	115	399	97	11	7	8	146	56	47	37	3	112	4	3	2	23	7	.77	9	.243	.312	.366
1996 Sarasota	A+ Bos	110	408	112	12	8	4	152	48	35	35	0	118	6	7	1	24	10	.71	9	.275	.340	.373
1997 Sarasota	A+ Bos	114	410	120	19	9	3	166	56	46	43	4	87	7	4	4	23	12	.66	4	.293	.366	.405
Trenton	AA Bos	17	56	16	2	0	2	24	10	8	8	0	17	1	2	1	2	0	1.00	0	.286	.379	.429
1998 Sarasota	A+ Bos	62	233	65	12	1	4	91	42	25	25	1	55	3	7	3	13	5	.72	3	.279	.352	.391
Mobile	AA SD	54	162	40	2	1	3	53	22	25	16	1	40	3	3	2	7	1	.88	4	.247	.322	.327
1999 Mobile	AA SD	128	527	128	18	11	6	186	82	43	53	0	126	7	3	0	63	14	.82	6	.243	.320	.353
8 Min. YEARS		698	2473	640	81	41	32	899	343	257	249	9	640	36	29	14	171	59	.74	36	.259	.334	.364

Chad Faircloth

Bats: Left **Throws:** Right **Pos:** OF **Ht:** 6'0" **Wt:** 180 **Born:** 4/25/75 **Age:** 25

Year Team	Lg Org	G	AB	H	2B	3B	HR	TB	R	RBI	TBB	IBB	SO	HBP	SH	SF	SB	CS	SB%	GDP	Avg	OBP	SLG
		BATTING															**BASERUNNING**				**PERCENTAGES**		
1997 Salem-Keizr	A- SF	31	102	29	5	2	0	38	13	13	14	0	30	1	0	1	2	0	1.00	3	.284	.373	.373
Bakersfield	A+ SF	19	73	19	5	0	1	27	8	7	6	0	22	0	3	0	1	0	1.00	1	.260	.316	.370
1998 Bakersfield	A+ SF	84	288	74	13	3	3	102	39	30	16	0	78	2	1	1	12	2	.86	5	.257	.300	.354
San Jose	A+ SF	18	63	13	3	1	0	18	5	2	1	0	12	0	0	0	1	1	.50	0	.206	.219	.286
1999 Fresno	AAA SF	1	1	0	0	0	0	0	0	0	0	0	0	0	0	0	0	0	.00	0	.000	.000	.000
Shreveport	AA SF	23	37	8	2	0	0	10	4	3	2	0	14	0	0	0	0	0	.00	0	.216	.256	.270
Bakersfield	A+ SF	51	145	38	12	1	0	52	14	16	14	1	35	0	1	2	5	4	.56	2	.262	.323	.359
3 Min. YEARS		227	709	181	40	7	4	247	83	71	53	1	191	3	5	4	21	7	.75	13	.255	.308	.348

Cordell Farley

Bats: Right **Throws:** Right **Pos:** OF **Ht:** 6'0" **Wt:** 185 **Born:** 3/29/73 **Age:** 27

Year Team	Lg Org	G	AB	H	2B	3B	HR	TB	R	RBI	TBB	IBB	SO	HBP	SH	SF	SB	CS	SB%	GDP	Avg	OBP	SLG
		BATTING															**BASERUNNING**				**PERCENTAGES**		
1996 Johnson Cy	R+ StL	15	63	18	4	3	0	28	17	9	4	0	20	1	0	0	2	2	.50	1	.286	.338	.444
Peoria	A StL	29	82	19	1	1	0	22	10	7	4	0	23	0	0	0	1	4	.20	3	.232	.267	.268
St. Pete	A+ StL	5	4	0	0	0	0	0	1	0	1	0	1	1	0	0	0	0	.00	0	.000	.333	.000
1997 New Jersey	A- StL	6	19	7	0	0	0	7	6	1	2	0	6	1	0	0	1	0	1.00	0	.368	.455	.368
Pr William	A+ StL	61	211	55	9	3	3	79	34	32	15	1	46	1	3	1	24	7	.77	2	.261	.311	.374
1998 Pr William	A+ StL	134	546	159	28	11	11	242	92	59	27	1	145	7	4	0	50	17	.75	4	.291	.333	.443
1999 Arkansas	AA StL	122	421	109	16	8	8	165	43	41	19	0	97	2	5	3	24	16	.60	3	.259	.292	.392
4 Min. YEARS		372	1346	367	58	26	22	543	203	149	72	2	338	13	12	4	102	46	.69	13	.273	.315	.403

Mike Farmer

Pitches: Left **Bats:** Right **Pos:** P **Ht:** 6'1" **Wt:** 193 **Born:** 7/3/68 **Age:** 31

Year Team	Lg Org	G	GS	CG	GF	IP	BFP	H	R	ER	HR	SH	SF	HB	TBB	IBB	SO	WP	Bk	W	L	Pct.	ShO	Sv	ERA
		HOW MUCH HE PITCHED						**WHAT HE GAVE UP**												**THE RESULTS**					
1992 Clearwater	A+ Phi	11	9	1	2	53	209	33	16	11	1	1	1	1	13	1	41	2	5	3	3	.500	1	0	1.87
1993 Reading	AA Phi	22	18	0	3	102	455	125	62	57	18	5	5	1	34	2	64	8	4	5	10	.333	0	0	5.03
1994 Central Val	A+ Col	14	3	0	4	28.2	125	28	17	15	4	1	1	3	11	1	28	4	1	1	4	.200	0	1	4.71
New Haven	AA Col	10	0	0	4	14	54	7	2	2	1	1	1	0	5	0	13	0	0	0	0	.000	0	2	1.29
1995 New Haven	AA Col	40	12	0	7	110.1	475	117	63	60	8	6	2	5	35	4	77	5	3	10	5	.667	0	0	4.89
1996 Colo Sprngs	AAA Col	9	9	2	0	57.1	245	51	27	21	4	2	3	2	25	2	28	2	0	2	3	.400	0	0	3.30
1997 Colo Sprngs	AAA Col	18	8	0	3	54.2	243	70	42	41	14	3	1	5	18	0	29	4	1	5	5	.500	0	0	6.75
1998 Colo Sprngs	AAA Col	28	23	0	2	126.2	608	173	107	79	19	7	11	7	56	5	74	6	1	7	7	.500	0	0	5.61
1999 Colo Sprngs	AAA Col	25	20	2	1	113.1	532	170	111	99	24	11	1	2	44	3	75	1	3	8	10	.444	0	0	7.86
1996 Colorado	NL	7	4	0	1	28	127	32	25	24	8	2	0	0	13	0	16	1	0	0	1	.000	0	0	7.71
8 Min. YEARS		177	102	5	26	660	2946	774	447	385	93	37	26	26	241	18	429	32	18	42	47	.472	2	3	5.25

Jim Farrell

Pitches: Right **Bats:** Right **Pos:** P **Ht:** 6'1" **Wt:** 180 **Born:** 11/1/73 **Age:** 26

		HOW MUCH HE PITCHED						WHAT HE GAVE UP													THE RESULTS					
Year Team	Lg Org	G	GS	CG	GF	IP	BFP	H	R	ER	HR	SH	SF	HB	TBB	IBB	SO	WP	Bk	W	L	Pct.	ShO	Sv	ERA
1995 Red Sox	R Bos	1	1	0	0	6	20	2	1	1	1	0	0	0	1	0	3	0	0	1	0	1.000	0	0	1.50
Michigan	A Bos	13	13	1	0	69	291	62	34	28	10	1	1	5	23	0	70	3	1	3	2	.600	0	0	3.65
1996 Michigan	A Bos	7	7	2	0	44	185	39	15	12	2	1	0	1	17	1	32	1	0	6	1	.857	0	0	2.45
Sarasota	A+ Bos	21	21	3	0	133.1	539	116	58	52	11	4	5	4	34	0	92	9	0	9	8	.529	1	0	3.51
1997 Trenton	AA Bos	26	26	0	0	162.2	706	173	93	79	24	1	5	7	57	0	110	11	0	12	7	.632	0	0	4.37
Pawtucket	AAA Bos	1	1	0	0	5	21	4	0	0	0	1	0	0	2	0	6	1	0	0	0	.000	0	0	0.00
1998 Pawtucket	AAA Bos	28	25	2	0	163.1	709	176	106	100	31	2	5	5	52	0	142	8	1	14	8	.636	1	0	5.51
1999 Pawtucket	AAA Bos	14	5	0	2	43	191	45	25	20	7	2	3	1	16	0	35	2	0	2	3	.400	0	0	4.19
Trenton	AA Bos	7	5	0	0	27	116	26	13	10	1	0	1	0	9	1	26	1	0	2	2	.500	0	0	3.33
5 Min. YEARS		118	104	8	2	653.1	2778	643	345	302	87	12	20	24	211	2	516	36	2	49	31	.613	2	0	4.16

Adam Faurot

Bats: Right **Throws:** Right **Pos:** 3B **Ht:** 5'11" **Wt:** 175 **Born:** 8/7/74 **Age:** 25

		BATTING																BASERUNNING				PERCENTAGES		
Year Team	Lg Org	G	AB	H	2B	3B	HR	TB	R	RBI	TBB	IBB	SO	HBP	SH	SF	SB	CS	SB%	GDP	Avg	OBP	SLG
1996 Ogden	R+ Mil	67	238	56	9	0	2	71	41	18	26	0	35	11	6	1	18	10	.64	8	.235	.337	.298
1997 Beloit	A Mil	100	298	71	11	1	1	87	38	19	17	0	56	10	14	0	9	11	.45	4	.238	.302	.292
1998 El Paso	AA Mil	101	249	74	13	2	1	94	27	39	9	2	49	4	6	2	10	3	.77	5	.297	.330	.378
1999 Huntsville	AA Mil	22	50	13	2	0	0	15	5	7	1	0	7	0	0	1	1	0	1.00	3	.260	.269	.300
Trenton	AA Bos	33	108	27	4	1	0	33	11	8	6	0	20	0	1	0	1	1	.50	7	.250	.289	.306
4 Min. YEARS		323	943	241	39	4	4	300	122	91	59	2	167	25	27	4	39	25	.61	27	.256	.315	.318

Pedro Feliz

Bats: Right **Throws:** Right **Pos:** 3B **Ht:** 6'1" **Wt:** 180 **Born:** 4/27/77 **Age:** 23

		BATTING																BASERUNNING				PERCENTAGES		
Year Team	Lg Org	G	AB	H	2B	3B	HR	TB	R	RBI	TBB	IBB	SO	HBP	SH	SF	SB	CS	SB%	GDP	Avg	OBP	SLG
1994 Giants	R SF	38	119	23	0	0	0	23	7	3	2	0	20	2	3	0	2	3	.40	3	.193	.220	.193
1995 Bellingham	A- SF	43	113	31	2	1	0	35	14	16	7	0	33	0	2	2	1	1	.50	2	.274	.311	.310
1996 Burlington	A SF	93	321	85	12	2	5	116	36	36	18	0	65	1	0	3	5	2	.71	11	.265	.303	.361
1997 Bakersfield	A+ SF	135	515	140	25	4	14	215	59	56	23	0	90	7	3	3	5	7	.42	15	.272	.310	.417
1998 Shreveport	AA SF	100	364	96	23	2	12	159	39	50	9	0	62	2	0	4	1	0	1.00	15	.264	.282	.437
Fresno	AAA SF	3	7	3	1	0	1	7	1	3	1	0	0	0	0	0	0	0	.00	1	.429	.500	1.000
1999 Shreveport	AA SF	131	491	124	24	6	13	199	52	77	19	0	90	3	1	5	4	2	.67	18	.253	.282	.405
6 Min. YEARS		543	1930	502	87	15	45	754	208	241	79	0	360	15	9	17	17	16	.52	65	.260	.292	.391

Anthony Felston

Bats: Left **Throws:** Left **Pos:** OF **Ht:** 5'9" **Wt:** 180 **Born:** 11/26/74 **Age:** 25

		BATTING																BASERUNNING				PERCENTAGES		
Year Team	Lg Org	G	AB	H	2B	3B	HR	TB	R	RBI	TBB	IBB	SO	HBP	SH	SF	SB	CS	SB%	GDP	Avg	OBP	SLG
1996 Twins	R Min	2	4	2	0	0	0	2	2	0	2	0	0	0	0	0	0	0	.00	0	.500	.667	.500
Fort Wayne	A Min	62	201	63	4	1	0	69	53	18	43	0	36	4	2	1	22	4	.85	2	.313	.442	.343
1997 Fort Wayne	A Min	94	338	94	10	2	2	114	63	29	55	1	53	4	11	1	45	15	.75	6	.278	.384	.337
1998 Fort Myers	A+ Min	114	427	119	8	0	0	127	74	43	83	2	65	6	10	6	86	26	.77	5	.279	.398	.297
New Britain	AA Min	12	45	10	2	0	0	12	5	5	6	0	10	3	1	1	2	1	.67	0	.222	.345	.267
1999 New Britain	AA Min	36	135	28	3	2	0	35	17	12	13	1	15	0	1	3	12	2	.86	0	.207	.272	.259
Fort Myers	A+ Min	81	311	92	11	3	3	118	66	47	52	0	41	9	4	1	21	10	.68	2	.296	.410	.379
4 Min. YEARS		401	1461	408	38	8	5	477	280	154	254	4	220	26	29	13	188	58	.76	15	.279	.392	.326

Barry Fennell

Pitches: Left **Bats:** Right **Pos:** P **Ht:** 6'4" **Wt:** 225 **Born:** 9/30/76 **Age:** 23

		HOW MUCH HE PITCHED						WHAT HE GAVE UP													THE RESULTS					
Year Team	Lg Org	G	GS	CG	GF	IP	BFP	H	R	ER	HR	SH	SF	HB	TBB	IBB	SO	WP	Bk	W	L	Pct.	ShO	Sv	ERA
1994 Cubs	R ChC	11	11	0	0	47.2	224	59	39	33	2	5	3	0	21	0	39	5	1	0	6	.000	0	0	6.23
1995 Rockford	A ChC	4	4	0	0	23	94	19	8	6	2	0	2	1	8	0	13	1	1	2	1	.667	0	0	2.35
1996 Cubs	R ChC	10	7	0	2	42.2	179	37	19	14	0	4	0	2	12	0	42	2	0	0	4	.000	0	1	2.95
1997 Williamsprt	A- ChC	17	10	0	1	66.1	306	92	51	45	5	3	3	3	29	0	50	4	1	2	10	.167	0	0	6.11
1998 Rockford	A ChC	17	0	0	9	28.1	110	14	2	2	0	1	0	2	12	0	25	3	0	2	0	1.000	0	6	0.64
Daytona	A+ ChC	24	0	0	10	31.1	151	30	16	9	0	1	0	2	22	2	24	1	0	2	2	.500	0	2	2.59
1999 Daytona	A+ ChC	22	0	0	14	30.2	140	33	21	17	1	3	3	1	18	1	21	3	0	1	2	.333	0	5	4.99
West Tenn	AA ChC	1	0	0	0	1.1	6	2	0	0	0	0	0	0	1	1	0	0	0	0	0	.000	0	0	0.00
6 Min. YEARS		106	32	0	36	271.1	1210	286	156	126	10	17	11	11	123	4	214	19	3	9	25	.265	0	14	4.18

Derek Feramisco

Bats: Right **Throws:** Right **Pos:** OF **Ht:** 6'5" **Wt:** 195 **Born:** 11/7/74 **Age:** 25

		BATTING																BASERUNNING				PERCENTAGES		
Year Team	Lg Org	G	AB	H	2B	3B	HR	TB	R	RBI	TBB	IBB	SO	HBP	SH	SF	SB	CS	SB%	GDP	Avg	OBP	SLG
1997 Johnson Cy	R+ StL	53	184	63	12	3	6	99	34	36	16	0	37	4	0	0	8	2	.80	2	.342	.407	.538
1998 Peoria	A StL	26	85	17	4	0	1	24	18	5	8	0	23	4	1	1	1	0	1.00	0	.200	.296	.282
Pr William	A+ StL	72	256	76	23	3	2	111	39	30	20	2	78	2	2	2	6	3	.67	0	.297	.350	.434
1999 Arkansas	AA StL	57	121	22	5	0	2	33	10	9	19	0	27	1	0	0	1	2	.33	3	.182	.298	.273
Vero Beach	A+ LA	18	53	11	3	0	1	17	7	4	11	0	12	1	0	0	0	2	.00	0	.208	.354	.321
3 Min. YEARS		226	699	189	47	6	12	284	108	84	74	2	177	12	3	3	16	9	.64	5	.270	.349	.406

Jeff Ferguson

Bats: Right **Throws:** Right **Pos:** 3B-2B   **Ht:** 5'10" **Wt:** 184 **Born:** 6/18/73 **Age:** 27

										BATTING						BASERUNNING				PERCENTAGES		
Year Team	Lg Org	G	AB	H	2B	3B	HR	TB	R	RBI	TBB	IBB	SO	HBP	SH	SF	SB	CS	SB%	GDP	Avg	OBP	SLG
1994 Fort Wayne	A Min	22	89	23	7	1	1	35	15	6	11	0	18	1	0	0	4	1	.80	1	.258	.347	.393
1996 Hardware Cy	AA Min	89	284	81	16	2	5	116	46	20	37	2	67	3	0	1	5	4	.56	2	.285	.372	.408
1997 New Britain	AA Min	36	135	33	4	0	1	40	19	21	12	0	31	1	1	1	1	1	.50	2	.244	.309	.296
Salt Lake	AAA Min	65	241	68	19	2	8	115	51	35	24	0	48	6	1	1	4	2	.67	5	.282	.360	.477
1998 Salt Lake	AAA Min	81	223	46	6	1	3	63	35	20	24	0	42	13	3	0	7	2	.78	7	.206	.319	.283
1999 Salt Lake	AAA Min	95	298	79	16	2	4	111	44	48	28	0	39	8	5	3	7	5	.58	12	.265	.341	.372
5 Min. YEARS		388	1270	330	68	8	22	480	210	150	136	2	245	32	10	6	28	15	.65	29	.260	.345	.378

Jared Fernandez

Pitches: Right **Bats:** Right **Pos:** P   **Ht:** 6'2" **Wt:** 223 **Born:** 2/2/72 **Age:** 28

		HOW MUCH HE PITCHED						WHAT HE GAVE UP										THE RESULTS				
Year Team	Lg Org	G	GS	CG	GF	IP	BFP	H	R	ER	HR	SH	SF	HB	TBB	IBB	SO	WP	Bk	W	L	Pct.	ShO	Sv	ERA
1994 Utica	A- Bos	21	1	0	15	30	144	43	18	12	4	0	0	0	8	2	24	0	1	1	1	.500	0	4	3.60
1995 Utica	A- Bos	5	5	1	0	38	148	30	11	8	2	0	1	1	9	1	23	1	0	3	2	.600	0	0	1.89
Trenton	AA Bos	11	10	1	0	67	290	64	32	29	4	3	1	5	28	1	40	2	0	5	4	.556	0	0	3.90
1996 Trenton	AA Bos	30	29	3	0	179	798	185	115	101	19	5	9	10	83	5	94	10	0	9	9	.500	0	0	5.08
1997 Pawtucket	AAA Bos	11	11	0	0	60.2	281	76	45	39	7	2	2	5	28	1	33	4	0	0	3	.000	0	0	5.79
Trenton	AA Bos	21	18	1	4	121.1	500	100	90	73	12	2	2	0	66	0	73	14	0	4	6	.400	0	0	5.41
1998 Trenton	AA Bos	36	7	0	10	118.1	527	132	80	69	8	8	3	3	51	3	70	15	1	3	7	.300	0	1	5.25
Pawtucket	AAA Bos	5	2	0	2	24.2	107	26	16	13	5	0	2	3	7	0	15	4	0	1	1	.500	0	0	4.74
1999 Trenton	AA Bos	7	0	0	4	18.2	80	18	9	7	4	0	0	0	8	0	10	1	0	3	0	1.000	0	1	3.38
Pawtucket	AAA Bos	27	20	3	2	163.1	687	172	88	77	20	7	5	5	39	0	76	3	1	12	9	.571	0	0	4.24
6 Min. YEARS		174	101	9	37	821	3622	884	504	428	85	27	25	32	327	13	458	54	3	41	42	.494	0	6	4.69

Sean Fesh

Pitches: Left **Bats:** Left **Pos:** P   **Ht:** 6'2" **Wt:** 165 **Born:** 11/3/72 **Age:** 27

		HOW MUCH HE PITCHED						WHAT HE GAVE UP										THE RESULTS				
Year Team	Lg Org	G	GS	CG	GF	IP	BFP	H	R	ER	HR	SH	SF	HB	TBB	IBB	SO	WP	Bk	W	L	Pct.	ShO	Sv	ERA
1991 Astros	R Hou	6	0	0	2	12.1	53	5	4	3	0	0	0	0	11	0	7	4	0	0	0	.000	0	0	2.19
1992 Osceola	A+ Hou	3	0	0	2	5.1	24	5	3	1	0	0	0	0	1	0	5	3	0	0	1	.000	0	0	1.69
Astros	R Hou	18	0	0	12	36.1	142	25	7	7	0	3	0	4	8	0	35	4	0	1	0	1.000	0	6	1.73
1993 Asheville	A Hou	65	0	0	58	82.1	353	75	39	33	4	11	6	5	37	8	49	4	1	10	6	.625	0	20	3.61
1994 Osceola	A+ Hou	43	0	0	39	49.2	222	50	27	14	2	5	0	6	24	6	32	2	0	2	4	.333	0	11	2.54
Jackson	AA Hou	20	1	0	5	25.2	122	34	17	12	2	2	1	0	11	0	19	2	0	1	2	.333	0	0	4.21
1995 Tucson	AAA Hou	10	0	0	1	13.1	52	11	2	2	0	0	0	0	3	0	7	0	0	1	0	1.000	0	0	1.35
Las Vegas	AAA SD	30	0	0	11	38	185	53	21	14	2	4	0	3	16	5	18	1	1	2	1	.667	0	1	3.32
1996 Memphis	AAA SD	7	0	0	2	8	36	7	5	5	2	0	0	0	7	1	5	0	0	1	1	.500	0	0	5.63
1997 Rancho Cuca	A+ SD	4	0	0	1	4.2	28	10	7	6	2	1	0	1	3	0	5	0	0	0	1	.000	0	0	11.57
Binghamton	AA NYM	45	0	0	13	55.1	255	60	26	20	3	0	1	2	24	0	37	2	3	3	1	.750	0	4	3.25
1998 Scranton-WB	AAA Phi	8	0	0	1	6	25	3	2	2	0	0	0	1	4	1	4	0	0	0	0	.000	0	0	3.00
Reading	AA Phi	31	0	0	23	33	140	19	8	5	1	1	1	5	19	1	41	1	2	3	1	.750	0	9	1.36
1999 Scranton-WB	AAA Phi	45	0	0	16	53.1	235	50	29	26	5	4	1	0	31	5	38	4	0	4	3	.571	0	1	4.39
9 Min. YEARS		335	1	0	176	423.1	1872	407	197	150	23	31	10	27	199	27	302	27	7	28	21	.571	0	52	3.19

Dave Feuerstein

Bats: Right **Throws:** Right **Pos:** OF   **Ht:** 6'2" **Wt:** 200 **Born:** 7/19/73 **Age:** 26

										BATTING						BASERUNNING				PERCENTAGES		
Year Team	Lg Org	G	AB	H	2B	3B	HR	TB	R	RBI	TBB	IBB	SO	HBP	SH	SF	SB	CS	SB%	GDP	Avg	OBP	SLG
1995 Portland	A- Col	70	269	72	10	3	5	103	40	44	23	2	41	2	3	3	20	8	.71	9	.268	.327	.383
1996 Asheville	A Col	130	514	147	27	7	1	191	69	69	42	0	68	5	5	5	21	10	.68	7	.286	.343	.372
1997 Salem	A+ Col	94	327	76	13	3	1	98	47	34	21	3	45	4	7	2	20	6	.77	8	.232	.285	.300
New Haven	AA Col	26	104	27	4	3	0	37	8	10	7	0	20	0	0	0	2	1	.67	4	.260	.306	.356
1998 New Haven	AA Col	133	505	139	13	5	6	180	61	51	23	0	56	2	7	2	18	11	.62	15	.275	.308	.356
1999 Carolina	AA Col	101	287	63	9	3	1	81	27	18	18	1	43	3	1	2	6	2	.75	6	.220	.271	.282
5 Min. YEARS		554	2006	524	76	24	14	690	252	226	134	6	273	16	23	14	87	38	.70	49	.261	.311	.344

Nathan Field

Pitches: Right **Bats:** Right **Pos:** P   **Ht:** 6'2" **Wt:** 185 **Born:** 12/11/75 **Age:** 24

		HOW MUCH HE PITCHED						WHAT HE GAVE UP										THE RESULTS				
Year Team	Lg Org	G	GS	CG	GF	IP	BFP	H	R	ER	HR	SH	SF	HB	TBB	IBB	SO	WP	Bk	W	L	Pct.	ShO	Sv	ERA
1998 Vermont	A- Mon	25	0	0	16	35	150	32	16	12	1	1	0	3	11	0	39	5	1	3	1	.750	0	2	3.09
1999 Ottawa	AAA Mon	2	0	0	1	3	16	4	1	1	0	0	0	0	4	0	4	0	0	0	0	.000	0	0	3.00
Cape Fear	A Mon	42	0	0	21	65	300	75	49	39	8	2	3	7	22	2	55	4	0	4	8	.333	0	2	5.40
2 Min. YEARS		69	0	0	38	103	466	111	66	52	9	3	3	10	37	2	98	9	1	7	9	.438	0	4	4.54

Luis Figueroa

Bats: Both **Throws:** Right **Pos:** SS   **Ht:** 5'9" **Wt:** 146 **Born:** 2/16/74 **Age:** 26

										BATTING						BASERUNNING				PERCENTAGES		
Year Team	Lg Org	G	AB	H	2B	3B	HR	TB	R	RBI	TBB	IBB	SO	HBP	SH	SF	SB	CS	SB%	GDP	Avg	OBP	SLG
1997 Augusta	A Pit	71	248	56	8	0	0	64	38	21	35	0	29	1	9	2	22	6	.79	2	.226	.322	.258
Lynchburg	A+ Pit	26	89	25	5	0	0	30	12	2	7	0	6	0	0	0	1	2	.33	5	.281	.333	.337
1998 Carolina	AA Pit	117	350	87	9	3	0	102	54	24	71	3	46	2	10	2	6	5	.55	12	.249	.376	.291
1999 Altoona	AA Pit	131	418	110	15	5	3	144	61	50	52	0	44	3	16	3	9	9	.50	7	.263	.347	.344
3 Min. YEARS		345	1105	278	37	8	3	340	165	97	165	3	125	6	35	7	38	22	.63	26	.252	.350	.308

Nelson Figueroa

Pitches: Right Bats: Both Pos: P   Ht: 6'1" Wt: 155 Born: 5/18/74 Age: 26

Year Team	Lg Org	G	GS	CG	GF	IP	BFP	H	R	ER	HR	SH	SF	HB	TBB	IBB	SO	WP	Bk	W	L	Pct.	ShO	Sv	ERA
1995 Kingsport	R+ NYM	12	12	2	0	76.1	304	57	31	26	3	3	2	5	22	1	79	5	0	7	3	.700	2	0	3.07
1996 Capital Cty	A NYM	26	25	8	1	185.1	723	119	55	42	10	3	2	2	58	1	200	9	2	14	7	.667	4	0	2.04
1997 Binghamton	AA NYM	33	22	0	3	143	617	137	76	69	14	7	2	6	68	1	116	7	0	5	11	.313	0	0	4.34
1998 Binghamton	AA NYM	21	21	3	0	123.2	531	133	73	64	19	2	1	0	44	2	116	1	1	12	3	.800	2	0	4.66
Tucson	AAA Ari	7	7	0	0	41.1	180	46	22	17	8	0	2	2	16	1	29	1	0	2	2	.500	0	0	3.70
1999 Diamondbcks	R Ari	1	1	0	0	3	11	3	1	0	0	0	0	0	0	0	0	2	0	0	1	.000	0	0	0.00
Tucson	AAA Ari	24	21	1	0	128	541	128	59	56	16	3	1	5	41	0	106	6	0	11	6	.647	1	0	3.94
5 Min. YEARS		124	109	14	4	700.2	2907	623	317	274	70	18	10	20	249	6	648	29	3	51	33	.607	9	0	3.52

John Finn

Bats: Right Throws: Right Pos: SS   Ht: 5'8" Wt: 168 Born: 10/18/67 Age: 32

					BATTING													BASERUNNING				PERCENTAGES		
Year Team	Lg Org	G	AB	H	2B	3B	HR	TB	R	RBI	TBB	IBB	SO	HBP	SH	SF	SB	CS	SB%	GDP	Avg	OBP	SLG
1989 Beloit	A Mil	73	274	82	8	7	1	107	49	20	38	0	27	4	5	2	29	11	.73	3	.299	.390	.391
1990 Stockton	A+ Mil	95	290	60	4	0	1	67	48	23	52	0	50	1	6	6	29	15	.66	1	.207	.324	.231
1991 Stockton	A+ Mil	65	223	57	12	1	0	71	45	25	44	1	28	9	6	3	19	9	.68	5	.256	.394	.318
El Paso	AA Mil	63	230	69	12	2	2	91	48	24	16	0	27	2	5	2	8	4	.67	0	.300	.348	.396
1992 El Paso	AA Mil	124	439	121	12	6	1	148	83	47	71	3	44	11	9	7	30	12	.71	7	.276	.384	.337
1993 New Orleans	AAA Mil	117	335	94	13	2	1	114	47	37	33	1	36	6	9	0	27	9	.75	8	.281	.356	.340
1994 New Orleans	AAA Mil	76	229	66	12	0	2	84	36	24	35	1	21	7	6	4	15	10	.60	3	.288	.393	.367
1995 New Orleans	AAA Mil	35	117	38	4	1	3	53	20	19	13	2	7	2	4	0	9	2	.82	1	.325	.402	.453
1996 Calgary	AAA Pit	69	193	49	13	1	0	64	24	32	25	4	28	3	2	5	2	5	.29	4	.254	.341	.332
Iowa	AAA ChC	17	55	15	1	0	1	19	10	5	4	0	7	2	2	1	1	1	.50	2	.273	.339	.345
1997 Birmingham	AA CWS	73	246	68	15	0	0	83	49	27	39	0	28	8	4	1	13	2	.87	5	.276	.391	.337
1998 Birmingham	AA CWS	44	146	40	6	1	3	57	37	15	34	0	12	4	3	2	4	4	.50	3	.274	.419	.390
Calgary	AAA CWS	45	148	46	9	1	1	60	31	11	20	0	9	5	4	1	3	2	.60	6	.311	.408	.405
1999 Reading	AA Phi	40	115	24	8	1	0	34	15	9	20	0	16	1	3	0	7	1	.88	1	.209	.331	.296
Scranton-WB	AAA Phi	42	124	27	1	0	4	40	18	10	15	0	12	3	2	0	2	0	1.00	2	.218	.317	.323
11 Min. YEARS		978	3164	856	130	23	20	1092	560	328	459	12	352	68	70	34	198	87	.69	51	.271	.371	.345

Tony Fiore

Pitches: Right Bats: Right Pos: P   Ht: 6'4" Wt: 210 Born: 10/12/71 Age: 28

Year Team	Lg Org	G	GS	CG	GF	IP	BFP	H	R	ER	HR	SH	SF	HB	TBB	IBB	SO	WP	Bk	W	L	Pct.	ShO	Sv	ERA
1992 Martinsvlle	R+ Phi	17	2	0	9	32.1	161	32	20	15	0	2	1	3	31	1	30	11	0	2	3	.400	0	0	4.18
1993 Batavia	A- Phi	16	16	1	0	97.1	411	82	51	33	1	3	4	4	40	0	55	15	0	2	8	.200	0	0	3.05
1994 Spartanburg	A Phi	28	28	9	0	166.2	719	162	94	76	10	2	5	4	77	1	113	19	1	12	13	.480	1	0	4.10
1995 Clearwater	A+ Phi	24	10	0	3	70.1	323	70	41	29	4	3	5	2	44	2	45	9	3	6	2	.750	0	0	3.71
1996 Clearwater	A+ Phi	22	22	3	0	128	533	102	61	45	4	1	1	5	56	1	80	13	1	8	4	.667	1	0	3.16
Reading	AA Phi	5	5	0	0	31	146	32	21	15	2	0	1	1	18	0	19	6	0	1	2	.333	0	0	4.35
1997 Reading	AA Phi	17	16	0	0	104.2	434	89	47	35	6	8	4	5	40	0	64	10	1	8	3	.727	0	0	3.01
Scranton-WB	AAA Phi	9	9	1	0	60.2	268	60	34	26	3	3	1	0	26	1	56	6	1	3	5	.375	0	0	3.86
1998 Scranton-WB	AAA Phi	41	7	0	12	94.2	418	92	53	47	4	3	3	1	52	1	71	6	0	4	7	.364	0	1	4.47
1999 Scranton-WB	AAA Phi	13	0	0	2	20.1	102	28	19	15	0	0	1	0	15	1	13	4	0	0	0	.000	0	0	6.64
Salt Lake	AAA Min	40	0	0	35	46.2	205	45	21	18	1	2	2	2	26	3	38	3	1	2	1	.667	0	19	3.47
8 Min. YEARS		232	115	14	61	852.2	3720	794	462	354	35	27	28	27	425	11	584	102	8	48	48	.500	2	20	3.74

Brian Fitzgerald

Pitches: Left Bats: Left Pos: P   Ht: 5'11" Wt: 175 Born: 12/26/74 Age: 25

Year Team	Lg Org	G	GS	CG	GF	IP	BFP	H	R	ER	HR	SH	SF	HB	TBB	IBB	SO	WP	Bk	W	L	Pct.	ShO	Sv	ERA
1996 Everett	A- Sea	21	1	0	8	39	181	56	36	28	2	1	1	0	8	0	31	1	2	1	2	.333	0	1	6.46
1997 Wisconsin	A Sea	41	0	0	28	69.2	281	63	16	15	4	1	0	0	19	2	68	2	1	3	1	.750	0	10	1.94
1998 Lancaster	A+ Sea	41	0	0	18	70.2	315	79	39	33	5	2	1	2	24	2	48	1	0	1	2	.333	0	1	4.20
Orlando	AA Sea	2	0	0	1	4.1	18	5	1	1	0	0	0	0	1	0	4	0	0	0	0	.000	0	1	2.08
1999 Lancaster	A+ Sea	6	6	0	0	34	153	50	35	27	3	0	2	0	4	0	23	1	0	1	3	.250	0	0	7.15
New Haven	AA Sea	29	1	0	13	54	228	58	24	23	2	2	2	1	18	0	37	0	0	2	2	.500	0	3	3.83
4 Min. YEARS		140	8	0	68	271.2	1176	311	151	127	16	6	6	3	74	4	211	5	3	8	10	.444	0	16	4.21

Jason Flach

Pitches: Right Bats: Right Pos: P   Ht: 6'0" Wt: 165 Born: 11/25/73 Age: 26

Year Team	Lg Org	G	GS	CG	GF	IP	BFP	H	R	ER	HR	SH	SF	HB	TBB	IBB	SO	WP	Bk	W	L	Pct.	ShO	Sv	ERA
1996 Eugene	A- Atl	27	0	0	14	59.2	238	45	18	15	2	4	1	1	17	1	68	2	0	4	1	.800	0	11	2.26
1997 Eugene	A- Atl	23	0	0	18	39.1	180	40	18	13	2	4	1	1	24	5	51	2	0	4	3	.571	0	2	2.97
1998 Danville	A+ Atl	37	11	0	7	106	453	110	43	37	5	6	4	6	31	4	108	6	0	5	5	.500	0	1	3.14
Greenville	AA Atl	1	0	0	0	1.1	7	3	0	0	0	0	0	0	0	0	4	0	0	0	0	.000	0	0	0.00
1999 Myrtle Bch	A+ Atl	24	14	0	4	108.1	460	101	50	37	8	5	2	3	37	1	63	3	0	9	4	.692	0	0	3.07
Greenville	AA Atl	12	2	0	4	36.2	163	44	29	27	4	3	3	3	10	0	15	1	0	1	2	.333	0	1	6.63
4 Min. YEARS		124	27	0	47	351.1	1501	343	158	129	21	21	11	14	119	11	309	14	0	23	15	.605	0	18	3.30

Ben Fleetham

Pitches: Right **Bats:** Right **Pos:** P **Ht:** 6'1" **Wt:** 205 **Born:** 8/3/72 **Age:** 27

Year Team	Lg Org	G	GS	CG	GF	IP	BFP	H	R	ER	HR	SH	SF	HB	TBB	IBB	SO	WP	Bk	W	L	Pct.	ShO	Sv	ERA
1994 Vermont	A- Mon	17	0	0	2	28.2	125	23	13	8	0	2	2	1	16	1	29	2	2	0	0	.000	0	2	2.51
Burlington	A Mon	6	0	0	2	13.1	51	5	4	3	1	0	0	0	4	0	27	2	3	1	0	1.000	0	0	2.03
Harrisburg	AA Mon	2	0	0	2	3	14	2	0	0	0	0	0	1	2	0	0	1	1	0	0	.000	0	0	0.00
1995 Pueblo	IND —	2	0	0	2	2	8	1	0	0	0	0	0	0	2	0	0	0	0	0	0	.000	0	1	0.00
1996 Delmarva	A Mon	16	0	0	15	19.2	74	9	4	3	2	2	0	0	7	0	34	3	0	1	0	1.000	0	13	1.37
Wst Plm Bch	A+ Mon	31	0	0	29	30.2	122	15	8	7	0	0	1	0	15	0	48	9	2	0	1	.000	0	17	2.05
Harrisburg	AA Mon	4	0	0	3	6	23	2	0	0	0	0	0	0	5	0	6	0	0	0	0	.000	0	1	0.00
1997 Ottawa	AAA Mon	9	0	0	9	9	40	2	3	2	1	0	0	1	10	0	14	2	0	1	2	.333	0	1	2.00
Harrisburg	AA Mon	49	0	0	46	50.1	216	28	21	17	4	3	2	2	33	2	69	4	0	2	1	.667	0	30	3.04
1998 Ottawa	AAA Mon	55	0	0	56	56.2	258	49	26	22	3	3	0	0	42	0	65	5	0	4	2	.667	0	25	3.49
1999 Norfolk	AAA NYM	6	0	0	2	6.2	40	11	15	11	3	0	0	0	10	1	9	2	0	1	2	.333	0	0	14.85
Tacoma	AAA Sea	14	0	0	7	18.2	85	19	9	7	1	0	1	0	10	0	26	3	0	1	2	.333	0	1	3.38
Fargo-Mh	IND —	10	0	0	1	15.2	67	18	9	9	1	0	2	0	5	1	17	2	0	1	0	1.000	0	0	5.17
6 Min. YEARS		221	0	0	162	260.1	1123	184	112	89	16	10	8	5	159	5	346	35	8	12	10	.545	0	91	3.08

Huck Flener

Pitches: Left **Bats:** Both **Pos:** P **Ht:** 5'11" **Wt:** 180 **Born:** 2/25/69 **Age:** 31

Year Team	Lg Org	G	GS	CG	GF	IP	BFP	H	R	ER	HR	SH	SF	HB	TBB	IBB	SO	WP	Bk	W	L	Pct.	ShO	Sv	ERA
1990 St.Cathrnes	A- Tor	14	7	0	3	61.2	258	45	29	23	4	3	0	1	33	0	46	4	3	4	3	.571	0	1	3.36
1991 Myrtle Bch	A Tor	55	0	0	44	79.1	334	58	28	16	1	5	3	0	41	0	107	7	2	6	4	.600	0	13	1.82
1992 Dunedin	A+ Tor	41	8	0	19	112.1	451	70	35	28	4	5	2	7	50	2	93	2	1	7	3	.700	0	8	2.24
1993 Knoxville	AA Tor	38	16	2	10	136.1	556	130	56	50	9	6	4	3	39	1	114	9	8	13	6	.684	2	4	3.30
1994 Syracuse	AAA Tor	6	6	0	0	37	155	38	22	19	6	0	3	0	8	0	20	2	1	0	3	.000	0	0	4.62
1995 Syracuse	AAA Tor	30	23	1	3	134.2	572	131	70	59	20	1	6	6	41	2	83	2	2	6	11	.353	0	0	3.94
1996 Syracuse	AAA Tor	14	14	0	0	86.2	350	73	27	22	3	3	3	3	23	1	62	2	3	7	3	.700	0	0	2.28
1997 Syracuse	AAA Tor	20	20	1	0	124	524	126	71	57	14	3	3	2	43	1	58	6	2	6	6	.500	1	0	4.14
1998 Akron	AA Cle	12	10	3	1	73	289	57	18	15	2	2	0	3	22	0	51	5	3	3	3	.500	2	0	1.85
Buffalo	AAA Cle	14	8	0	3	60.2	278	73	52	45	12	3	1	0	26	1	35	2	0	7	3	.700	0	0	6.68
1999 Tacoma	AAA Sea	22	5	0	6	66	292	72	41	40	6	2	2	3	26	2	48	5	1	4	4	.500	0	1	5.45
1993 Toronto	AL	6	0	0	1	6.2	30	7	3	3	0	0	0	0	4	1	2	1	0	0	0	.000	0	0	4.05
1996 Toronto	AL	15	11	0	0	70.2	309	68	40	36	9	0	4	1	33	1	44	1	0	3	2	.600	0	0	4.58
1997 Toronto	AL	8	1	0	3	17.1	97	40	19	19	3	0	1	0	6	0	9	2	0	0	1	.000	0	0	9.87
10 Min. YEARS		266	117	7	89	971.2	4059	873	449	374	81	33	27	28	352	10	717	46	26	63	49	.563	5	27	3.46
3 Maj. YEARS		29	12	0	4	94.2	436	115	62	58	12	0	5	1	43	2	55	4	0	3	3	.500	0	0	5.51

Jose Flores

Bats: Right **Throws:** Right **Pos:** SS **Ht:** 5'11" **Wt:** 180 **Born:** 6/28/73 **Age:** 27

Year Team	Lg Org	G	AB	H	2B	3B	HR	TB	R	RBI	TBB	IBB	SO	HBP	SH	SF	SB	CS	SB%	GDP	Avg	OBP	SLG
1994 Batavia	A- Phi	68	229	58	7	3	0	71	41	16	41	0	31	6	2	2	23	8	.74	3	.253	.358	.310
1995 Clearwater	A+ Phi	49	185	41	4	3	1	54	25	19	15	0	27	4	7	1	12	5	.71	4	.222	.293	.292
Piedmont	A Phi	61	186	49	7	0	0	56	22	19	24	0	29	3	5	4	11	8	.58	6	.263	.350	.301
1996 Scranton-WB	AAA Phi	26	70	18	1	0	0	19	10	3	12	0	10	2	1	1	0	1	.00	2	.257	.376	.271
Clearwater	A+ Phi	84	281	64	6	5	1	83	39	39	34	0	42	3	5	1	15	2	.88	6	.228	.317	.295
1997 Scranton-WB	AAA Phi	71	204	51	14	1	1	70	32	18	28	1	51	2	5	2	3	1	.75	2	.250	.343	.343
1998 Scranton-WB	AAA Phi	98	345	104	18	2	6	144	53	34	49	1	45	2	7	2	12	6	.67	7	.301	.389	.417
1999 Scranton-WB	AAA Phi	64	228	56	6	2	0	66	35	18	37	1	43	7	4	0	13	3	.81	1	.246	.368	.289
Tacoma	AAA Sea	42	143	44	6	1	3	61	33	15	37	1	23	5	2	2	4	3	.57	2	.308	.460	.427
6 Min. YEARS		563	1871	485	69	17	12	624	290	181	277	4	301	34	38	15	93	37	.72	33	.259	.362	.334

Randy Flores

Pitches: Left **Bats:** Left **Pos:** P **Ht:** 6'0" **Wt:** 180 **Born:** 7/31/75 **Age:** 24

Year Team	Lg Org	G	GS	CG	GF	IP	BFP	H	R	ER	HR	SH	SF	HB	TBB	IBB	SO	WP	Bk	W	L	Pct.	ShO	Sv	ERA
1997 Oneonta	A- NYY	13	13	0	0	74.2	308	64	32	27	3	0	1	4	23	1	70	5	1	4	4	.500	1	0	3.25
1998 Tampa	A+ NYY	5	5	0	0	23.2	115	28	23	17	2	2	2	1	16	2	15	0	4	1	2	.333	0	0	6.46
Greensboro	A NYY	21	20	2	0	130.2	555	119	48	38	6	2	3	7	33	0	139	2	4	12	7	.632	1	0	2.62
1999 Norwich	AA NYY	4	4	0	0	25	120	32	20	18	0	2	0	1	11	1	19	1	1	0	1	.000	0	0	6.48
Tampa	A+ NYY	21	20	1	1	135	555	118	56	43	4	4	4	7	38	0	99	5	0	11	4	.733	1	0	2.87
3 Min. YEARS		64	62	5	1	389	1633	361	179	143	15	10	10	20	121	4	342	13	10	28	18	.609	3	0	3.31

Tim Florez

Bats: Right **Throws:** Right **Pos:** 3B-2B **Ht:** 5'10" **Wt:** 170 **Born:** 7/23/69 **Age:** 30

Year Team	Lg Org	G	AB	H	2B	3B	HR	TB	R	RBI	TBB	IBB	SO	HBP	SH	SF	SB	CS	SB%	GDP	Avg	OBP	SLG
1991 Everett	A- SF	59	193	48	8	4	0	64	33	25	12	1	33	1	2	1	7	1	.88	4	.249	.295	.332
1992 Clinton	A SF	81	292	68	12	2	2	90	39	25	30	2	53	3	0	2	20	5	.80	6	.233	.309	.308
San Jose	A+ SF	38	131	32	6	1	1	43	15	17	4	0	21	0	4	4	3	3	.50	2	.244	.259	.328
1993 Shreveport	AA SF	106	318	81	17	2	1	105	33	26	16	4	43	2	3	2	3	5	.38	9	.255	.293	.330
1994 Phoenix	AAA SF	13	24	6	1	0	1	10	5	2	1	0	4	0	0	0	0	0	.00	1	.250	.280	.417
Shreveport	AA SF	61	158	34	10	0	1	47	21	13	21	3	34	1	2	1	0	3	.00	4	.215	.309	.297
1995 Shreveport	AA SF	100	295	79	11	2	9	121	37	46	26	1	49	4	3	3	4	3	.57	7	.268	.332	.410
1996 Shreveport	AA SF	18	66	18	1	0	2	25	9	8	7	1	11	1	0	0	2	0	1.00	0	.273	.351	.379
Phoenix	AAA SF	113	366	106	31	3	4	155	42	39	34	0	56	10	0	3	0	5	.00	12	.290	.363	.423

Year Team	Lg Org	G	AB	H	2B	3B	HR	TB	R	RBI	TBB	IBB	SO	HBP	SH	SF	SB	CS	SB%	GDP	Avg	OBP	SLG
																	BASERUNNING				PERCENTAGES		
1997 Phoenix	AAA SF	114	402	121	24	4	7	174	57	61	32	2	68	8	5	1	6	3	.67	5	.301	.363	.433
1998 Tucson	AAA Ari	77	227	64	5	1	3	80	31	23	18	1	49	3	0	5	4	2	.67	10	.282	.336	.352
1999 Somerset	IND —	9	23	6	0	0	1	9	3	5	3	0	3	0	1	0	0	0	.00	1	.261	.346	.391
Nashua	IND —	47	180	48	8	1	1	61	25	12	10	0	22	1	5	1	5	3	.63	9	.267	.307	.339
Chattanooga	AA Cin	39	139	35	8	1	5	60	24	22	15	0	23	3	1	3	7	2	.78	6	.252	.331	.432
9 Min. YEARS		875	2814	746	142	21	38	1044	374	324	229	19	469	37	26	26	61	35	.64	76	.265	.326	.371

Pat Flury

Pitches: Right Bats: Right Pos: P   Ht: 6'1" Wt: 220 Born: 3/14/73 Age: 27

Year Team	Lg Org	G	GS	CG	GF	IP	BFP	H	R	ER	HR	SH	SF	HB	TBB	IBB	SO	WP	Bk	W	L	Pct.	ShO	Sv	ERA
1993 Eugene	A- KC	27	0	0	19	33	144	25	15	12	0	2	0	1	22	1	34	4	0	2	2	.500	0	7	3.27
1994 Rockford	A KC	34	0	0	18	55	254	61	27	24	3	2	2	5	33	2	41	3	2	1	3	.250	0	2	3.93
1995 Wilmington	A+ KC	15	0	0	6	22	89	18	6	6	2	0	1	1	9	1	14	1	1	1	0	1.000	0	1	2.45
Springfield	A KC	34	0	0	19	54.1	246	65	32	26	5	4	1	1	24	0	35	2	0	2	6	.250	0	1	4.31
1996 Wilmington	A+ KC	45	0	0	19	84.1	339	66	22	18	2	2	1	0	29	4	67	9	0	7	2	.778	0	5	1.92
1997 Wichita	AA KC	42	0	0	19	48	215	47	26	19	4	2	3	4	18	3	47	1	0	8	3	.727	0	5	3.56
Omaha	AAA KC	18	0	0	7	26.2	124	29	18	18	5	2	0	2	16	2	24	1	0	1	0	1.000	0	0	6.08
1998 Wichita	AA KC	8	0	0	2	11.2	59	14	11	7	0	1	0	3	7	1	13	1	0	1	1	.500	0	0	5.40
Trenton	AA Bos	26	0	0	24	30.2	122	24	6	6	2	0	0	0	11	1	37	3	0	0	0	.000	0	16	1.76
Pawtucket	AAA Bos	17	0	0	5	22.1	100	23	15	14	3	1	0	0	16	0	22	4	0	0	0	.000	0	0	5.64
1999 Chattanooga	AA Cin	43	0	0	21	53.1	221	36	20	17	2	5	0	1	31	0	69	4	1	1	1	.500	0	15	2.87
Indianapols	AAA Cin	23	0	0	14	23	115	27	18	18	4	0	1	1	20	0	20	6	0	1	1	.500	0	6	7.04
7 Min. YEARS		332	0	0	173	464.1	2028	435	216	185	32	21	9	19	236	14	423	39	4	25	19	.568	0	58	3.59

Josh Fogg

Pitches: Right Bats: Right Pos: P   Ht: 6'2" Wt: 205 Born: 12/13/76 Age: 23

Year Team	Lg Org	G	GS	CG	GF	IP	BFP	H	R	ER	HR	SH	SF	HB	TBB	IBB	SO	WP	Bk	W	L	Pct.	ShO	Sv	ERA
1998 White Sox	R CWS	2	0	0	0	4	13	0	0	0	0	1	0	0	1	0	5	1	0	1	0	1.000	0	0	0.00
Hickory	A CWS	8	8	0	0	41.1	173	36	17	10	4	1	0	1	13	0	29	1	1	1	3	.250	0	0	2.18
Winston-Sal	A+ CWS	1	0	0	1	1	6	2	2	0	0	0	0	0	0	0	2	1	0	1	0	1.000	0	0	0.00
1999 Winston-Sal	A+ CWS	17	17	1	0	103.1	441	93	44	34	3	1	1	11	33	0	109	2	0	10	5	.667	1	0	2.96
Birmingham	AA CWS	10	10	0	0	55	249	66	37	36	8	1	2	5	18	0	40	2	1	3	2	.600	0	0	5.89
2 Min. YEARS		38	35	1	1	204.2	882	197	100	80	15	4	3	17	65	0	185	7	2	15	11	.577	1	0	3.52

Franklin Font

Bats: Right Throws: Right Pos: SS   Ht: 5'10" Wt: 190 Born: 11/4/77 Age: 22

Year Team	Lg Org	G	AB	H	2B	3B	HR	TB	R	RBI	TBB	IBB	SO	HBP	SH	SF	SB	CS	SB%	GDP	Avg	OBP	SLG
1996 Cubs	R ChC	59	239	72	5	4	0	85	43	18	17	0	36	4	2	2	31	9	.78	0	.301	.355	.356
1997 Williamsprt	A- ChC	33	135	42	6	2	0	52	13	12	7	0	20	2	1	2	10	4	.71	2	.311	.349	.385
Orlando	AA ChC	10	20	6	0	0	0	6	3	2	2	0	1	0	0	0	0	1	.00	1	.300	.364	.300
Daytona	A+ ChC	19	59	13	2	1	0	17	8	2	4	0	13	0	1	0	2	1	.67	0	.220	.270	.288
1998 Rockford	A ChC	66	237	64	5	2	0	73	34	15	20	0	39	5	4	1	25	6	.81	5	.270	.338	.308
Daytona	A+ ChC	60	204	60	2	1	0	64	26	16	18	0	35	1	2	0	7	6	.54	3	.294	.354	.314
1999 Daytona	A+ ChC	87	315	93	7	4	2	114	48	33	21	0	38	2	4	3	14	6	.70	10	.295	.340	.362
West Tenn	AA ChC	25	96	33	2	1	1	40	14	17	8	1	14	1	1	1	4	4	.50	0	.344	.396	.417
4 Min. YEARS		359	1305	383	29	15	3	451	189	115	97	1	196	15	19	9	93	37	.72	21	.293	.347	.346

Joe Fontenot

Pitches: Right Bats: Right Pos: P   Ht: 6'2" Wt: 185 Born: 3/20/77 Age: 23

Year Team	Lg Org	G	GS	CG	GF	IP	BFP	H	R	ER	HR	SH	SF	HB	TBB	IBB	SO	WP	Bk	W	L	Pct.	ShO	Sv	ERA
1995 Bellingham	A- SF	6	6	0	0	18.2	77	14	5	4	0	0	0	0	10	0	14	0	2	0	3	.000	0	0	1.93
1996 San Jose	A+ SF	26	23	0	1	144	642	137	81	71	7	10	6	11	74	0	124	13	1	9	4	.692	0	0	4.44
1997 Shreveport	AA SF	26	26	1	0	151.1	688	171	105	93	12	8	1	12	65	0	103	10	0	10	11	.476	0	0	5.53
1998 Portland	AA Fla	7	7	0	0	38	167	37	16	13	1	2	1	4	13	1	31	3	0	3	1	.750	0	0	3.08
Charlotte	AAA Fla	1	1	0	0	3	15	4	4	4	1	0	0	0	2	0	0	0	0	0	1	.000	0	0	12.00
1999 Calgary	AAA Fla	8	8	1	0	44	193	52	26	25	2	4	3	3	19	0	18	1	1	3	2	.600	1	0	5.11
1998 Florida	NL	8	8	0	0	42.2	204	56	34	30	5	3	1	5	20	1	24	6	0	0	7	.000	0	0	6.33
5 Min. YEARS		74	71	2	1	399	1782	415	243	210	23	24	11	30	183	1	290	27	4	25	22	.532	1	0	4.74

P.J. Forbes

Bats: Right Throws: Right Pos: 2B-3B   Ht: 5'10" Wt: 160 Born: 9/22/67 Age: 32

Year Team	Lg Org	G	AB	H	2B	3B	HR	TB	R	RBI	TBB	IBB	SO	HBP	SH	SF	SB	CS	SB%	GDP	Avg	OBP	SLG
1990 Boise	A- Ana	43	170	42	9	1	0	53	29	19	23	1	21	0	7	1	11	4	.73	9	.247	.335	.312
1991 Palm Spring	A+ Ana	94	349	93	14	2	2	117	45	26	36	1	44	4	12	0	18	8	.69	7	.266	.342	.335
1992 Quad City	A Ana	105	376	106	16	5	2	138	53	46	44	1	51	2	24	5	15	6	.71	4	.282	.356	.367
1993 Midland	AA Ana	126	498	159	23	2	15	231	90	64	26	1	50	4	14	2	6	8	.43	13	.319	.357	.464
Vancouver	AAA Ana	5	16	4	2	0	0	6	1	3	0	0	3	0	1	0	0	0	.00	1	.250	.250	.375
1994 Angels	R Ana	2	6	0	0	0	0	0	1	0	0	0	1	0	0	0	0	0	.00	0	.000	.000	.000
Vancouver	AAA Ana	90	318	91	21	2	1	119	39	40	22	0	42	2	7	5	4	2	.67	6	.286	.331	.374
1995 Vancouver	AAA Ana	109	369	101	22	3	1	132	47	52	21	0	46	2	7	10	4	6	.40	4	.274	.308	.358
1996 Vancouver	AAA Ana	117	409	112	24	2	0	140	58	46	42	3	44	5	10	4	4	3	.57	13	.274	.346	.342

Year Team	Lg Org	BATTING																	BASERUNNING				PERCENTAGES		
		G	AB	H	2B	3B	HR	TB	R	RBI	TBB	IBB	SO	HBP	SH	SF		SB	CS	SB%	GDP		Avg	OBP	SLG
1997 Rochester	AAA Bal	116	434	118	22	2	8	168	67	54	35	0	42	6	8	3		15	4	.79	11		.272	.333	.387
1998 Rochester	AAA Bal	116	460	135	37	3	6	196	74	52	36	1	54	5	8	3		10	2	.83	15		.293	.349	.426
1999 Oklahoma	AAA Tex	22	67	7	1	0	0	8	4	2	5	0	12	1	2	0		0	0	.00	2		.104	.178	.119
Rochester	AAA Bal	88	349	92	16	1	0	110	49	19	26	0	40	3	11	2		5	0	1.00	1		.264	.318	.315
1998 Baltimore	AL	9	10	1	0	0	0	1	0	2	0	0	0	0	0	0		0	0	.00	0		.100	.100	.100
10 Min. YEARS		1033	3821	1060	207	23	35	1418	557	423	316	8	450	34	111	35		92	43	.68	82		.277	.335	.371

Pitches: Right **Bats:** Right **Pos:** P

Ben Ford

Ht: 6' 7" **Wt:** 200 **Born:** 8/15/75 **Age:** 24

Year Team	Lg Org	HOW MUCH HE PITCHED						WHAT HE GAVE UP											THE RESULTS					
		G	GS	CG	GF	IP	BFP	H	R	ER	HR	SH	SF	HB	TBB	IBB	SO	WP	Bk	W	L	Pct.	ShO	Sv	ERA
1994 Yankees	R NYY	18	0	0	11	34	143	27	13	9	0	0	0	6	8	0	31	3	0	2	2	.500	0	3	2.38
1995 Greensboro	A NYY	7	0	0	2	7	31	4	4	4	1	1	0	0	5	1	8	2	0	0	0	.000	0	0	5.14
Oneonta	A- NYY	29	0	0	10	52	224	39	23	5	1	0	2	5	16	0	50	8	0	5	0	1.000	0	0	0.87
1996 Greensboro	A NYY	43	0	0	16	82.1	359	75	48	39	3	4	1	11	33	6	84	9	0	2	6	.250	0	2	4.26
1997 Tampa	A+ NYY	32	0	0	30	37.1	155	27	8	8	1	2	0	6	14	1	37	4	0	4	0	1.000	0	18	1.93
Norwich	AA NYY	28	0	0	14	42.2	183	35	28	20	1	1	2	3	19	1	38	4	0	4	3	.571	0	1	4.22
1998 Tucson	AAA Ari	48	0	0	36	68.1	313	68	41	33	6	3	3	2	33	5	63	7	1	2	5	.286	0	13	4.35
1999 Columbus	AAA NYY	53	0	0	23	70.1	318	69	42	37	4	2	1	9	39	1	40	11	0	6	3	.667	0	3	4.73
1999 Arizona	NL	0	0	0	2	10	49	13	11	11	2	0	0	2	0	0	5	1	0	0	0	.000	0	0	9.90
6 Min. YEARS		258	0	0	142	394	1726	344	207	155	17	13	9	42	167	15	351	48	1	25	19	.568	0	40	3.54

Pitches: Left **Bats:** Left **Pos:** P

Tom Fordham

Ht: 6' 2" **Wt:** 205 **Born:** 2/20/74 **Age:** 26

Year Team	Lg Org	HOW MUCH HE PITCHED						WHAT HE GAVE UP											THE RESULTS					
		G	GS	CG	GF	IP	BFP	H	R	ER	HR	SH	SF	HB	TBB	IBB	SO	WP	Bk	W	L	Pct.	ShO	Sv	ERA
1993 White Sox	R CWS	3	0	0	1	10	41	9	2	2	0	0	0	0	3	0	12	1	0	1	1	.500	0	0	1.80
Sarasota	A+ CWS	2	0	0	1	5	21	3	1	0	0	0	0	0	3	2	5	1	1	0	0	.000	0	0	0.00
Hickory	A CWS	8	8	1	0	48.2	194	36	21	21	3	1	6	0	21	0	27	3	2	4	3	.571	0	0	3.88
1994 Hickory	A CWS	17	17	1	0	109	452	101	47	38	10	1	1	3	30	1	121	6	4	10	5	.667	1	0	3.14
South Bend	A CWS	11	11	1	0	74.2	315	82	46	36	4	4	3	0	14	0	48	4	0	4	4	.500	1	0	4.34
1995 Pr William	A+ CWS	13	13	1	0	84	340	66	20	19	7	2	1	2	35	2	78	1	0	9	0	1.000	1	0	2.04
Birmingham	AA CWS	14	14	2	0	82.2	348	79	35	31	9	2	2	0	28	2	61	3	0	6	3	.667	1	0	3.38
1996 Birmingham	AA CWS	6	6	0	0	37.1	147	26	13	11	4	0	2	0	14	1	37	2	0	2	1	.667	0	0	2.65
Nashville	AAA CWS	22	22	3	0	140.2	589	117	60	54	15	4	2	4	69	1	118	7	1	10	8	.556	2	0	3.45
1997 Nashville	AAA CWS	21	20	2	0	114	493	113	64	60	14	1	5	1	53	1	90	6	1	6	7	.462	0	0	4.74
1998 Calgary	AAA CWS	9	9	0	0	56.2	225	65	29	19	6	1	3	0	26	0	39	3	0	4	2	.667	0	0	3.02
1999 Charlotte	AAA CWS	29	21	0	2	112	538	144	101	91	25	2	4	3	66	0	101	10	0	4	7	.364	0	0	7.31
1997 Chicago	AL	7	1	0	1	17.1	78	17	13	12	2	1	2	1	10	2	10	0	0	0	1	.000	0	0	6.23
1998 Chicago	AL	29	5	0	5	48	228	51	36	36	7	1	1	1	42	0	23	1	0	1	2	.333	0	0	6.75
7 Min. YEARS		155	141	11	4	874.2	3703	814	431	382	97	18	29	13	362	10	737	46	9	60	41	.594	6	0	3.93
2 Maj. YEARS		36	6	0	6	65.1	306	68	49	48	9	2	3	2	52	2	33	1	0	1	3	.250	0	0	6.61

Pitches: Right **Bats:** Right **Pos:** P

Rick Forney

Ht: 6'4" **Wt:** 230 **Born:** 10/24/71 **Age:** 28

Year Team	Lg Org	HOW MUCH HE PITCHED						WHAT HE GAVE UP											THE RESULTS					
		G	GS	CG	GF	IP	BFP	H	R	ER	HR	SH	SF	HB	TBB	IBB	SO	WP	Bk	W	L	Pct.	ShO	Sv	ERA
1991 Orioles	R Bal	12	10	2	0	65.2	260	48	21	16	1	1	1	4	10	0	51	1	2	7	0	1.000	1	0	2.19
1992 Kane County	A Bal	20	18	2	0	123.1	513	114	40	34	4	4	2	9	26	1	104	9	2	3	6	.333	1	0	2.48
1993 Frederick	A+ Bal	27	27	2	0	165	704	156	64	51	11	4	4	7	64	0	175	12	2	14	8	.636	0	0	2.78
Bowie	AA Bal	1	1	0	0	7	24	1	1	1	0	0	1	1	1	0	4	0	0	0	0	.000	0	0	1.29
1994 Bowie	AA Bal	28	28	4	0	165.2	715	168	105	85	17	4	7	3	58	1	125	9	2	13	8	.619	2	0	4.62
1995 Rochester	AAA Bal	3	3	0	0	16	72	19	9	7	2	2	1	0	6	0	12	2	0	0	0	.000	0	0	3.94
Bowie	AA Bal	23	19	1	2	97	437	110	69	62	14	2	6	3	42	0	73	7	1	7	7	.500	1	0	5.75
1996 Lubbock	IND —	22	22	1	0	142	634	151	88	71	14	4	6	12	56	1	123	14	0	9	7	.563	0	0	4.50
1997 Winnipeg	IND —	17	17	1	0	113	480	113	54	46	12	3	2	5	39	0	106	10	0	11	4	.733	0	0	3.66
1998 Winnipeg	IND —	19	19	3	0	129.2	545	145	63	51	11	1	1	9	20	1	113	2	0	11	6	.647	1	0	3.54
1999 Greenville	AA Atl	12	12	0	0	72.1	291	67	27	24	5	4	1	2	19	1	70	0	0	3	3	.500	0	0	2.99
Winnipeg	IND —	13	12	0	1	84.1	351	93	30	20	5	2	1	3	13	0	62	4	0	9	3	.750	0	0	2.13
9 Min. YEARS		197	188	16	3	1181	5026	1185	571	468	97	31	32	58	354	5	1018	70	9	87	52	.626	6	0	3.57

Pitches: Left **Bats:** Right **Pos:** P

Scott Forster

Ht: 6'1" **Wt:** 194 **Born:** 10/27/71 **Age:** 28

Year Team	Lg Org	HOW MUCH HE PITCHED						WHAT HE GAVE UP											THE RESULTS					
		G	GS	CG	GF	IP	BFP	H	R	ER	HR	SH	SF	HB	TBB	IBB	SO	WP	Bk	W	L	Pct.	ShO	Sv	ERA
1994 Vermont	A- Mon	12	9	0	0	52.2	236	38	32	19	0	0	1	4	34	0	39	6	2	1	6	.143	0	0	3.25
1995 Wst Plm Bch	A+ Mon	26	26	1	0	146.2	643	129	78	66	6	5	4	7	80	1	92	16	0	6	11	.353	0	0	4.05
1996 Harrisburg	AA Mon	28	28	0	0	176.1	755	164	92	74	15	3	4	7	67	2	97	5	0	10	7	.588	0	0	3.78
1997 Harrisburg	AA Mon	17	15	0	2	79.1	366	77	45	20	7	7	6	6	48	0	71	4	0	3	6	.333	0	0	2.27
1998 Jupiter	A+ Mon	6	0	0	1	8	38	9	10	8	0	0	1	1	5	0	7	2	0	0	0	.000	0	0	9.00
Harrisburg	AA Mon	25	11	0	5	77.2	360	90	50	42	8	2	1	6	47	1	54	5	0	7	3	.700	0	0	4.87
1999 Harrisburg	AA Mon	2	0	0	1	5	16	3	0	0	0	0	0	0	1	0	1	0	0	0	0	.000	0	0	0.00
Ottawa	AAA Mon	53	0	0	27	52.1	249	49	32	30	3	2	1	3	47	2	32	8	0	0	4	.000	0	2	5.16
6 Min. YEARS		169	89	1	36	598	2662	559	339	259	39	19	18	34	328	6	393	46	2	27	37	.422	0	2	3.90

Jim Foster

Bats: Right **Throws:** Right **Pos:** C   **Ht:** 6'3" **Wt:** 220 **Born:** 8/18/71 **Age:** 28

					BATTING											BASERUNNING				PERCENTAGES		
Year Team	Lg Org	G	AB	H	2B	3B	HR	TB	R	RBI	TBB	IBB	SO	HBP	SH	SF	SB	CS	SB%	GDP	Avg	OBP	SLG
1993 Bluefield	R+ Bal	61	218	71	21	1	10	124	59	45	42	1	34	3	0	3	3	1	.75	4	.326	.436	.569
1994 Albany	A Bal	121	421	112	29	3	8	171	61	56	54	0	59	11	0	6	5	3	.63	13	.266	.360	.406
1995 Frederick	A+ Bal	128	429	112	27	3	6	163	44	56	51	5	63	8	0	5	2	3	.40	10	.261	.347	.380
1996 Frederick	A+ Bal	82	278	70	20	2	7	115	35	42	39	1	32	4	0	3	6	3	.67	7	.252	.349	.414
Bowie	AA Bal	9	33	10	0	1	2	18	7	9	7	0	6	0	0	1	0	0	.00	0	.303	.415	.545
1997 Rochester	AAA Bal	3	9	5	2	0	0	7	4	4	3	0	0	0	0	0	0	1	.00	0	.556	.667	.778
Frederick	A+ Bal	61	200	70	12	1	16	132	48	65	45	7	28	7	0	3	8	0	1.00	5	.350	.478	.660
Bowie	AA Bal	63	211	58	12	0	7	91	36	41	36	0	31	1	1	2	1	1	.50	6	.275	.380	.431
1998 Bowie	AA Bal	66	221	53	17	0	5	85	24	33	31	1	38	5	0	0	1	1	.50	6	.240	.346	.385
Rochester	AAA Bal	43	153	36	9	0	5	60	22	26	18	1	22	2	0	1	3	1	.75	5	.235	.322	.392
1999 Rochester	AAA Bal	35	118	27	3	1	0	32	6	11	12	1	19	0	0	0	0	0	.00	3	.229	.300	.271
Tucson	AAA Ari	11	26	7	1	0	0	8	4	3	4	0	2	0	0	0	0	0	.00	3	.269	.355	.308
Erie	AA Ana	4	16	4	1	0	1	8	2	3	2	0	0	0	0	0	0	0	.00	1	.250	.333	.500
Edmonton	AAA Ana	24	88	26	10	0	2	42	13	15	4	0	13	0	0	1	1	0	1.00	2	.295	.323	.477
7 Min. YEARS		711	2421	661	164	12	69	1056	365	409	348	17	347	41	1	26	34	16	.68	64	.273	.370	.436

Kris Foster

Pitches: Right **Bats:** Right **Pos:** P   **Ht:** 6'1" **Wt:** 200 **Born:** 8/30/74 **Age:** 25

		HOW MUCH HE PITCHED						WHAT HE GAVE UP										THE RESULTS					
Year Team	Lg Org	G	GS	CG	GF	IP	BFP	H	R	ER	HR	SH	SF	HB	TBB	IBB	SO	WP	Bk	W	L	Pct.	ShO	Sv	ERA
1993 Expos	R Mon	17	3	0	7	44.2	195	44	26	17	0	3	2	6	16	0	30	6	3	1	6	.143	0	1	3.43
1994 Expos	R Mon	18	5	0	5	52.1	229	34	21	9	1	0	1	5	32	0	65	3	2	4	2	.667	0	4	1.55
1995 Yakima	A- LA	15	10	0	5	56	241	38	27	18	2	2	4	2	38	3	55	8	1	2	3	.400	0	3	2.89
1996 San Berndno	A+ LA	30	8	0	9	81.2	355	66	46	35	5	3	4	3	54	3	78	10	4	3	5	.375	0	2	3.86
1997 Vero Beach	A+ LA	17	17	2	0	89.2	414	97	69	53	8	3	3	7	44	1	77	5	1	6	3	.667	0	0	5.32
1998 Vero Beach	A+ LA	24	6	0	7	53	249	59	45	40	8	2	1	1	27	0	52	6	5	3	5	.375	0	1	6.79
1999 Vero Beach	A+ LA	8	0	0	3	15.1	59	10	5	3	1	0	2	0	2	0	15	0	0	1	1	.500	0	1	1.76
San Antonio	AA LA	33	0	0	19	52.2	228	43	24	21	3	2	2	0	26	1	53	6	0	0	2	.000	0	4	3.59
7 Min. YEARS		162	49	2	55	445.1	1970	391	263	196	28	15	19	24	239	8	425	44	16	20	27	.426	0	15	3.96

Aaron France

Pitches: Right **Bats:** Left **Pos:** P   **Ht:** 6'3" **Wt:** 186 **Born:** 4/17/74 **Age:** 26

		HOW MUCH HE PITCHED						WHAT HE GAVE UP										THE RESULTS					
Year Team	Lg Org	G	GS	CG	GF	IP	BFP	H	R	ER	HR	SH	SF	HB	TBB	IBB	SO	WP	Bk	W	L	Pct.	ShO	Sv	ERA
1994 Welland	A- Pit	7	5	0	1	24	98	22	12	6	1	0	1	3	6	0	16	1	1	0	2	.000	0	0	2.25
1995 Augusta	A Pit	18	15	0	0	94.2	388	80	29	26	4	3	3	5	26	0	77	6	2	6	6	.500	0	0	2.47
1996 Lynchburg	A+ Pit	13	13	0	0	60.1	286	79	53	43	6	1	0	3	32	1	40	8	3	0	8	.000	0	0	6.41
Augusta	A Pit	5	5	0	0	25	105	23	9	7	2	2	0	1	7	0	24	0	1	2	1	.667	0	0	2.52
1997 Augusta	A Pit	26	17	1	2	107.1	458	98	48	42	5	0	2	8	44	0	89	6	3	7	4	.636	0	0	3.52
1998 Lynchburg	A+ Pit	26	20	0	2	129	529	99	51	39	9	3	1	12	45	0	110	7	0	6	5	.545	0	0	2.72
1999 Altoona	AA Pit	33	11	0	7	95.2	414	79	50	39	8	5	3	5	48	1	70	7	3	4	5	.444	0	0	3.67
6 Min. YEARS		128	86	1	12	536	2278	480	252	202	35	14	10	37	208	2	426	35	13	25	31	.446	0	0	3.39

David Francia

Bats: Left **Throws:** Left **Pos:** OF   **Ht:** 6'0" **Wt:** 167 **Born:** 4/16/75 **Age:** 25

					BATTING											BASERUNNING				PERCENTAGES		
Year Team	Lg Org	G	AB	H	2B	3B	HR	TB	R	RBI	TBB	IBB	SO	HBP	SH	SF	SB	CS	SB%	GDP	Avg	OBP	SLG
1996 Batavia	A- Phi	69	280	81	14	5	4	117	45	29	8	0	25	6	2	2	16	6	.73	1	.289	.321	.418
1997 Piedmont	A Phi	112	424	127	24	7	9	192	72	65	25	2	61	19	4	8	39	12	.76	5	.300	.359	.453
Clearwater	A+ Phi	21	75	21	3	1	0	26	5	10	6	0	7	1	3	0	5	2	.71	1	.280	.341	.347
1998 Clearwater	A+ Phi	48	194	54	13	0	6	85	33	23	12	0	30	7	2	2	13	4	.76	4	.278	.340	.438
Reading	AA Phi	68	269	64	12	4	3	93	29	20	13	0	41	2	3	2	6	7	.46	3	.238	.276	.346
1999 Reading	AA Phi	107	339	92	22	5	4	136	41	43	21	3	57	13	6	1	13	4	.76	5	.271	.337	.401
4 Min. YEARS		425	1581	439	88	22	26	649	225	190	85	5	221	48	20	15	92	35	.72	19	.278	.331	.410

Raul Franco

Bats: Right **Throws:** Right **Pos:** 2B   **Ht:** 5'11" **Wt:** 170 **Born:** 1/14/76 **Age:** 24

					BATTING											BASERUNNING				PERCENTAGES		
Year Team	Lg Org	G	AB	H	2B	3B	HR	TB	R	RBI	TBB	IBB	SO	HBP	SH	SF	SB	CS	SB%	GDP	Avg	OBP	SLG
1995 Marlins	R Fla	49	184	51	12	0	0	63	30	22	16	0	14	2	1	2	9	3	.75	5	.277	.338	.342
1996 Marlins	R Fla	59	238	66	14	2	0	84	39	15	13	0	29	3	9	1	15	7	.68	6	.277	.322	.353
1997 Utica	A- Fla	72	293	103	19	0	3	131	41	38	17	3	24	2	2	5	10	4	.71	11	.352	.385	.447
1998 Kane County	A Fla	132	551	158	24	0	2	188	81	51	24	2	52	2	12	7	15	12	.56	8	.287	.315	.341
1999 Calgary	AAA Fla	16	55	15	0	0	0	15	7	4	2	0	4	0	0	0	0	0	.00	7	.273	.298	.273
Brevard Cty	A+ Fla	111	426	102	17	1	1	124	41	43	13	0	48	3	3	10	4	6	.40	14	.239	.261	.291
5 Min. YEARS		439	1747	495	86	3	6	605	239	173	85	5	171	12	27	25	53	32	.62	51	.283	.317	.346

Mike Frank

Bats: Left **Throws:** Left **Pos:** OF   **Ht:** 6'2" **Wt:** 195 **Born:** 1/14/75 **Age:** 25

					BATTING											BASERUNNING				PERCENTAGES		
Year Team	Lg Org	G	AB	H	2B	3B	HR	TB	R	RBI	TBB	IBB	SO	HBP	SH	SF	SB	CS	SB%	GDP	Avg	OBP	SLG
1997 Billings	R+ Cin	69	266	100	22	6	10	164	62	62	35	5	24	2	0	3	18	8	.69	7	.376	.448	.617
1998 Indianaplos	AAA Cin	22	88	30	4	0	0	34	8	13	7	0	9	0	0	0	1	0	1.00	3	.341	.389	.386
Chattanooga	AA Cin	58	231	75	12	4	12	131	43	43	19	1	28	1	0	3	5	2	.71	3	.325	.374	.567

Year Team	Lg Org	G	AB	H	2B	3B	HR	TB	R	RBI	TBB	IBB	SO	HBP	SH	SF	SB	CS	SB%	GDP	Avg	OBP	SLG
1999 Indianapols	AAA Cin	121	433	128	36	7	9	205	73	62	36	2	55	8	2	3	10	6	.63	10	.296	.358	.473
1998 Cincinnati	NL	28	89	20	6	0	0	26	14	7	7	0	12	0	1	1	0	0	.00	3	.225	.278	.292
3 Min. YEARS		270	1018	333	74	17	31	534	186	180	97	8	116	11	2	9	34	16	.68	23	.327	.389	.525

Wayne Franklin

Pitches: Left **Bats:** Left **Pos:** P

Ht: 6'2" **Wt:** 195 **Born:** 3/9/74 **Age:** 26

		HOW MUCH HE PITCHED						WHAT HE GAVE UP										THE RESULTS					
Year Team	Lg Org	G	GS	CG	GF	IP	BFP	H	R	ER	HR	SH	SF	HB	TBB	IBB	SO	WP	Bk	W	L	Pct.	ShO	Sv	ERA
1996 Yakima	A- LA	20	0	0	5	25	115	32	10	7	2	0	0	0	12	3	22	3	1	1	0	1.000	0	1	2.52
1997 Savannah	A LA	28	7	1	10	82	362	79	41	29	10	1	1	4	35	0	58	2	1	5	3	.625	0	2	3.18
San Berndno	A+ LA	1	0	0	0	2	7	2	0	0	0	0	0	0	0	0	1	0	0	0	0	.000	0	0	0.00
1998 Vero Beach	A+ LA	48	0	0	26	86.2	369	81	43	34	7	3	5	2	26	0	78	3	2	9	3	.750	0	10	3.53
1999 Kissimmee	A+ Hou	12	0	0	17.2	69	11	4	3	0	1	0	1	6	0	22	0	0	3	0	1.000	0	1	1.53
Jackson	AA Hou	46	0	0	40	50.1	200	31	11	9	3	3	4	3	16	3	40	1	0	3	1	.750	0	20	1.61
4 Min. YEARS		155	7	1	88	263.2	1122	236	109	82	22	8	10	10	95	6	221	9	4	21	7	.750	0	34	2.80

Dan Fraraccio

Bats: Right **Throws:** Right **Pos:** OF

Ht: 5'11" **Wt:** 175 **Born:** 9/18/70 **Age:** 29

		BATTING															BASERUNNING				PERCENTAGES		
Year Team	Lg Org	G	AB	H	2B	3B	HR	TB	R	RBI	TBB	IBB	SO	HBP	SH	SF	SB	CS	SB%	GDP	Avg	OBP	SLG
1992 White Sox	R CWS	52	149	31	5	1	0	38	19	8	5	0	18	4	1	1	5	7	.42	1	.208	.252	.255
Sarasota	A+ CWS	1	3	1	0	0	0	1	0	0	0	0	1	0	0	0	0	0	.00	0	.333	.333	.333
1993 Hickory	A CWS	41	147	31	9	1	1	45	13	15	6	0	21	3	0	1	2	2	.50	2	.211	.255	.306
South Bend	A CWS	49	135	37	10	0	0	47	23	21	6	0	29	3	1	1	0	1	.00	4	.274	.317	.348
1994 Pr William	A+ CWS	26	80	19	1	1	1	25	10	7	3	0	19	0	1	1	1	0	1.00	1	.238	.262	.313
White Sox	R CWS	3	2	1	0	0	0	1	0	0	1	0	1	0	0	0	0	0	.00	0	.500	.667	.500
1995 Nashville	AAA CWS	10	28	7	0	0	0	7	2	3	1	0	6	0	1	0	2	0	1.00	1	.250	.276	.250
Pr William	A+ CWS	24	74	17	5	0	2	28	11	6	8	0	12	0	1	0	0	0	.00	1	.230	.305	.378
1996 Pr William	A+ CWS	44	149	41	9	0	0	50	16	20	12	0	20	1	2	0	1	0	1.00	5	.275	.333	.336
Thunder Bay	IND —	36	132	39	11	2	2	60	19	17	10	0	23	0	1	0	0	0	.00	6	.295	.338	.455
1997 St. Pete	A+ TB	129	463	137	34	3	1	180	67	63	53	0	50	14	5	6	7	7	.50	11	.296	.381	.389
1998 Bridgeport	IND —	87	305	84	19	2	6	125	53	42	44	1	25	9	3	4	9	5	.64	7	.275	.378	.410
1999 Orlando	AA TB	82	254	73	19	3	7	119	48	28	25	1	43	2	2	4	1	4	.20	7	.287	.351	.469
Durham	AAA TB	15	30	8	3	0	1	14	5	4	4	0	4	1	0	0	2	0	1.00	1	.267	.371	.467
8 Min. YEARS		599	1951	526	125	13	21	740	286	234	178	2	272	37	18	21	30	26	.54	47	.270	.339	.379

Lou Frazier

Bats: Both **Throws:** Right **Pos:** OF

Ht: 6' 2" **Wt:** 175 **Born:** 1/26/65 **Age:** 35

		BATTING															BASERUNNING				PERCENTAGES		
Year Team	Lg Org	G	AB	H	2B	3B	HR	TB	R	RBI	TBB	IBB	SO	HBP	SH	SF	SB	CS	SB%	GDP	Avg	OBP	SLG
1986 Astros	R Hou	51	178	51	7	2	1	65	39	23	32	0	25	1	3	1	17	8	.68	3	.287	.396	.365
1987 Asheville	A Hou	108	399	103	9	2	1	119	83	33	68	1	89	2	4	3	75	24	.76	3	.258	.367	.298
1988 Osceola	A+ Hou	130	468	110	11	3	0	127	79	34	90	5	104	4	5	1	87	16	.84	9	.235	.362	.271
1989 Columbus	AA Hou	135	460	106	10	1	4	130	65	31	76	2	101	1	2	2	43	14	.75	7	.230	.340	.283
1990 London	AA Det	81	242	53	4	1	0	59	29	15	27	0	52	0	1	1	20	3	.87	5	.219	.296	.244
1991 London	AA Det	122	439	105	9	4	3	131	69	40	77	5	86	1	3	1	42	17	.71	8	.239	.353	.298
1992 London	AA Det	129	477	120	16	3	0	142	85	34	95	1	107	0	2	2	58	23	.72	3	.252	.375	.298
1995 Ottawa	AAA Mon	31	110	24	3	0	1	30	11	10	13	0	20	1	1	1	10	1	.91	2	.218	.304	.273
1996 Okla City	AAA Tex	58	208	51	8	3	3	74	28	16	14	2	42	1	3	1	13	4	.76	3	.245	.295	.356
1997 Bowie	AA Bal	25	103	24	4	2	0	32	20	8	21	0	20	0	3	0	13	1	.93	2	.233	.363	.311
Rochester	AAA Bal	84	302	75	12	4	2	101	40	39	36	1	68	1	3	3	24	6	.80	9	.248	.327	.334
1998 Calgary	AAA CWS	101	397	107	26	3	14	181	81	50	57	1	84	3	2	2	42	8	.84	2	.270	.364	.456
1999 Scranton-WB	AAA Phi	89	308	76	16	7	6	124	54	32	44	1	79	2	4	1	21	3	.88	5	.247	.344	.403
1993 Montreal	NL	112	189	54	7	1	1	66	27	16	16	0	24	0	5	1	17	2	.89	3	.286	.340	.349
1994 Montreal	NL	76	140	38	3	1	0	43	25	14	18	0	23	1	1	0	20	4	.83	1	.271	.358	.307
1995 Montreal	NL	35	63	12	2	0	0	14	6	3	8	0	12	0	1	0	4	0	1.00	1	.190	.297	.222
Texas	AL	49	99	21	2	0	0	23	19	8	7	0	20	2	3	0	9	1	.90	2	.212	.278	.232
1996 Texas	AL	30	50	13	2	1	0	17	5	5	8	0	10	1	1	0	4	2	.67	2	.260	.373	.340
1998 Chicago	AL	7	7	0	0	0	0	0	0	0	2	0	0	0	0	0	1	0	1.00	0	.000	.222	.000
12 Min. YEARS		1144	4091	1005	135	35	35	1315	683	365	650	19	877	17	36	19	465	128	.78	61	.246	.350	.321
5 Maj. YEARS		309	548	138	16	3	1	163	82	46	59	0	95	6	11	2	58	9	.87	9	.252	.330	.297

Ryan Freel

Bats: Right **Throws:** Right **Pos:** OF

Ht: 5'10" **Wt:** 175 **Born:** 3/8/76 **Age:** 24

		BATTING															BASERUNNING				PERCENTAGES		
Year Team	Lg Org	G	AB	H	2B	3B	HR	TB	R	RBI	TBB	IBB	SO	HBP	SH	SF	SB	CS	SB%	GDP	Avg	OBP	SLG
1995 St.Cathrnes	A- Tor	65	243	68	10	5	3	97	30	29	22	0	49	7	7	5	12	7	.63	3	.280	.350	.399
1996 Dunedin	A+ Tor	104	381	97	23	3	4	138	64	41	33	0	76	5	14	2	19	15	.56	4	.255	.321	.362
1997 Knoxville	AA Tor	33	94	19	1	1	0	22	18	4	19	0	13	2	1	0	5	3	.63	3	.202	.348	.234
Dunedin	A+ Tor	61	181	51	8	2	3	72	42	17	46	2	28	9	6	1	24	5	.83	3	.282	.447	.398
1998 Knoxville	AA Tor	66	252	72	17	3	4	107	46	36	33	0	32	1	3	4	18	9	.67	3	.286	.366	.425
Syracuse	AAA Tor	37	118	27	4	0	2	37	19	12	26	0	16	4	0	3	9	4	.69	2	.229	.377	.314
1999 Knoxville	AA Tor	11	46	13	5	1	1	23	9	9	8	0	4	0	0	1	4	2	.67	0	.283	.382	.500
Syracuse	AAA Tor	20	77	23	3	2	1	33	15	11	8	0	13	4	1	0	10	3	.77	3	.299	.393	.429
5 Min. YEARS		397	1392	370	71	17	18	529	244	159	195	2	231	32	32	16	101	48	.68	22	.266	.365	.380

Ricky Freeman

Bats: Right **Throws:** Right **Pos:** 1B **Ht:** 6'4" **Wt:** 210 **Born:** 2/3/72 **Age:** 28

BATTING / BASERUNNING / PERCENTAGES

Year Team	Lg Org	G	AB	H	2B	3B	HR	TB	R	RBI	TBB	IBB	SO	HBP	SH	SF	SB	CS	SB%	GDP	Avg	OBP	SLG
1994 Huntington	R+ ChC	64	218	49	10	3	0	65	23	30	35	0	22	3	0	7	12	6	.67	6	.225	.331	.298
1995 Rockford	A ChC	131	466	127	33	5	11	203	89	67	61	3	57	7	0	1	8	3	.73	11	.273	.364	.436
1996 Daytona	A+ ChC	127	477	145	36	6	13	232	70	64	36	2	72	10	0	2	10	8	.56	9	.304	.364	.486
1997 Iowa	AAA ChC	31	77	13	0	0	1	16	7	4	8	0	20	3	0	0	1	0	1.00	4	.169	.273	.208
Orlando	AA ChC	81	308	96	19	2	16	167	58	73	29	6	51	5	0	2	8	5	.62	3	.312	.378	.542
1998 West Tenn	AA ChC	106	370	100	18	4	15	171	67	76	45	3	50	9	0	4	7	5	.58	7	.270	.360	.462
1999 Vancouver	AAA Oak	61	202	45	14	0	4	71	27	24	20	0	39	3	2	0	0	0	.00	4	.223	.302	.351
6 Min. YEARS		601	2118	575	130	20	60	925	341	338	234	14	311	40	2	16	46	27	.63	44	.271	.353	.437

Alejandro Freire

Bats: Right **Throws:** Right **Pos:** 1B-DH **Ht:** 6'2" **Wt:** 185 **Born:** 8/23/74 **Age:** 25

BATTING / BASERUNNING / PERCENTAGES

Year Team	Lg Org	G	AB	H	2B	3B	HR	TB	R	RBI	TBB	IBB	SO	HBP	SH	SF	SB	CS	SB%	GDP	Avg	OBP	SLG
1994 Astros	R Hou	29	83	25	4	0	1	32	8	13	5	0	17	3	2	2	5	1	.83	0	.301	.355	.386
1995 Quad City	A Hou	125	417	127	23	1	15	197	71	65	50	1	83	6	2	7	9	5	.64	9	.305	.381	.472
1996 Kissimmee	A+ Hou	115	384	98	24	1	12	160	40	42	24	1	66	7	1	2	11	7	.61	11	.255	.309	.417
1997 Lakeland	A+ Det	130	477	154	30	2	24	260	85	92	50	1	84	12	0	7	13	4	.76	10	.323	.396	.545
1998 Jacksnville	AA Det	129	494	136	30	0	16	214	79	78	33	1	83	17	1	9	3	1	.75	16	.275	.336	.433
1999 Lakeland	A+ Det	13	41	19	3	0	1	15	6	5	10	0	7	3	1	0	0	0	.00	1	.220	.400	.366
Jacksnville	AA Det	66	243	72	20	0	10	122	45	43	23	0	44	6	0	4	2	0	1.00	8	.296	.366	.502
6 Min. YEARS		607	2139	621	134	4	79	1000	334	338	195	4	384	54	7	32	43	18	.70	55	.290	.360	.468

Steve Frey

Pitches: Left **Bats:** Left **Pos:** P **Ht:** 5'9" **Wt:** 170 **Born:** 7/29/63 **Age:** 36

HOW MUCH HE PITCHED / WHAT HE GAVE UP / THE RESULTS

Year Team	Lg Org	G	GS	CG	GF	IP	BFP	H	R	ER	HR	SH	SF	HB	TBB	IBB	SO	WP	Bk	W	L	Pct.	ShO	Sv	ERA
1983 Oneonta	A- NYY	28	1	0	24	72.1		47	27	22	2	—	—	0	35	1	86	5	0	4	6	.400	0	9	2.74
1984 Ft. Laud	A+ NYY	47	0	0	25	64.2	281	46	26	15	2	1	3	0	34	2	66	4	0	4	2	.667	0	4	2.09
1985 Ft. Laud	A+ NYY	19	0	0	13	22.1	89	11	4	3	0	1	0	1	12	0	15	0	0	1	1	.500	0	7	1.21
Albany-Colo	AA NYY	40	0	0	14	61.1	261	53	30	26	4	2	0	3	25	5	54	0	0	4	7	.364	0	3	3.82
1986 Columbus	AAA NYY	11	0	0	2	19	93	29	17	17	3	0	2	0	10	1	11	0	0	0	2	.000	0	0	8.05
Albany-Colo	AA NYY	40	0	0	26	73	287	50	25	17	5	2	4	2	18	1	62	2	0	3	4	.429	0	4	2.10
1987 Albany-Colo	AA NYY	14	0	0	10	28	111	20	6	6	0	1	0	2	7	1	19	1	0	0	2	.000	0	1	1.93
Columbus	AAA NYY	23	0	0	11	47.1	196	45	19	16	2	1	3	0	10	0	35	4	0	2	1	.667	0	6	3.04
1988 Tidewater	AAA NYM	58	1	0	22	54.2	230	38	23	19	3	4	2	3	25	6	58	1	3	6	3	.667	0	3	3.13
1989 Indianapols	AAA Mon	21	0	0	8	25.1	97	18	7	5	1	2	0	0	6	1	23	0	0	2	1	.667	0	3	1.78
1990 Indianapols	AAA Mon	2	0	0	1	3	10	0	0	0	0	0	0	0	1	0	3	0	0	0	0	.000	0	1	0.00
1991 Indianapols	AAA Mon	30	0	0	15	35.2	145	25	6	6	1	1	0	1	15	2	45	1	1	3	1	.750	0	3	1.51
1995 Scranton-WB	AAA Phi	4	0	0	2	5	21	3	1	1	0	1	0	1	2	1	3	1	0	0	0	.000	0	0	1.80
1996 Scranton-WB	AAA Phi	10	0	0	2	13.1	57	11	8	8	1	1	0	0	8	0	9	0	0	2	2	.500	0	0	5.40
1997 Vancouver	AAA Ana	31	1	0	10	41.1	183	45	23	23	6	3	0	1	21	1	28	0	0	3	3	.500	0	4	5.01
1998 Pawtucket	AAA Bos	50	0	0	16	62.2	270	66	29	27	6	4	4	1	22	4	42	3	0	4	2	.667	0	2	3.88
1999 Oklahoma	AAA Tex	30	0	0	19	44.1	191	51	25	22	7	1	0	0	15	0	38	1	0	1	2	.333	0	9	4.47
1989 Montreal	NL	20	0	0	11	21.1	103	29	15	13	4	0	2	1	11	1	15	1	1	3	2	.600	0	0	5.48
1990 Montreal	NL	51	0	0	21	55.2	236	44	15	13	4	3	2	1	29	6	29	0	0	8	2	.800	0	9	2.10
1991 Montreal	NL	31	0	0	5	39.2	182	43	31	22	3	3	2	1	23	4	21	3	1	0	1	.000	0	1	4.99
1992 California	AL	51	0	0	20	45.1	193	39	18	18	6	2	3	2	22	3	24	1	0	4	2	.667	0	4	3.57
1993 California	AL	55	0	0	28	48.1	212	41	20	16	1	4	1	3	26	1	22	3	0	2	3	.400	0	13	2.98
1994 San Francisco	NL	44	0	0	12	31	137	37	17	17	6	1	4	2	15	3	20	1	0	1	0	1.000	0	0	4.94
1995 San Francisco	NL	9	0	0	1	6.1	29	7	6	3	1	1	1	0	2	0	5	0	0	1	0	.000	0	0	4.26
Seattle	AL	13	0	0	3	11.1	56	16	7	6	0	3	1	1	6	1	7	0	0	0	0	.000	0	0	4.76
Philadelphia	NL	9	0	0	3	10.2	36	3	1	1	1	0	2	0	1	0	2	0	0	0	0	.000	0	1	0.84
1996 Philadelphia	NL	31	0	0	12	34.1	151	38	19	18	4	2	2	0	18	3	12	0	0	0	1	.000	0	0	4.72
14 Min. YEARS		458	3	0	220	673.1	—	558	276	233	43	—	—	13	266	26	597	23	4	39	39	.500	0	62	3.11
8 Maj. YEARS		314	0	0	116	304	1335	297	149	127	30	20	18	11	154	23	157	9	2	18	15	.545	0	28	3.76

Brian Fuentes

Pitches: Left **Bats:** Left **Pos:** P **Ht:** 6'4" **Wt:** 220 **Born:** 8/9/75 **Age:** 24

HOW MUCH HE PITCHED / WHAT HE GAVE UP / THE RESULTS

Year Team	Lg Org	G	GS	CG	GF	IP	BFP	H	R	ER	HR	SH	SF	HB	TBB	IBB	SO	WP	Bk	W	L	Pct.	ShO	Sv	ERA
1996 Everett	A- Sea	13	2	0	3	26.2	114	23	14	13	2	0	1	0	13	0	26	5	0	0	1	.000	0	0	4.39
1997 Wisconsin	A Sea	22	22	0	0	118.2	486	84	54	47	6	3	3	8	59	0	153	11	3	6	7	.462	0	0	3.56
1998 Lancaster	A+ Sea	24	22	0	1	118.2	541	121	73	55	8	1	6	9	81	0	137	14	2	7	7	.500	0	0	4.17
1999 New Haven	AA Sea	15	14	0	0	60	272	53	36	33	5	2	5	11	46	0	66	1	1	3	3	.500	0	0	4.95
4 Min. YEARS		74	60	0	4	324	1413	281	175	148	21	6	15	28	199	0	382	31	6	16	18	.471	0	0	4.11

Aaron Fultz

Pitches: Left **Bats:** Left **Pos:** P **Ht:** 6'0" **Wt:** 196 **Born:** 9/4/73 **Age:** 26

HOW MUCH HE PITCHED / WHAT HE GAVE UP / THE RESULTS

Year Team	Lg Org	G	GS	CG	GF	IP	BFP	H	R	ER	HR	SH	SF	HB	TBB	IBB	SO	WP	Bk	W	L	Pct.	ShO	Sv	ERA
1992 Giants	R SF	14	14	0	0	67.2	282	51	24	16	0	4	1	4	33	0	72	7	0	3	2	.600	0	0	2.13
1993 Clinton	A SF	26	25	2	0	148	641	132	63	56	8	12	2	11	64	2	144	10	2	14	8	.636	0	0	3.41
Fort Wayne	A Min	1	1	0	0	21		10	4	4	0	0	0	0	0	0	8	0	0	0	0	.000	0	0	9.00
1994 Fort Myers	A+ Min	28	28	3	0	168.1	745	193	95	81	9	6	4	7	60	5	132	9	2	9	10	.474	0	0	4.33
1995 Hardware Cy	AA Min	3	3	0	0	15	64	11	12	11	0	1	1	2	9	0	12	0	0	0	2	.000	0	0	6.60

Year Team	Lg Org	G	GS	CG	GF	IP	BFP	H	R	ER	HR	SH	SF	HB	TBB	IBB	SO	WP	Bk	W	L	Pct.	ShO	Sv	ERA
		HOW MUCH HE PITCHED						WHAT HE GAVE UP												THE RESULTS					
Fort Myers	A+ Min	21	21	2	0	122	516	115	52	44	10	4	3	8	41	1	127	7	1	3	6	.333	2	0	3.25
1996 San Jose	A+ SF	36	12	0	11	104.2	460	101	52	46	7	9	3	8	54	2	103	13	0	9	5	.643	0	1	3.96
1997 Shreveport	AA SF	49	0	0	20	70	293	65	30	22	6	4	5	2	19	0	60	4	1	6	3	.667	0	1	2.83
1998 Shreveport	AA SF	54	0	0	34	62	273	58	40	26	4	8	3	3	29	10	61	5	1	5	7	.417	0	15	3.77
Fresno	AAA SF	10	0	0	3	16	68	22	10	9	2	0	0	0	2	1	13	1	0	0	0	.000	0	0	5.06
1999 Fresno	AAA SF	37	20	1	7	137.1	601	141	87	76	32	3	9	7	51	1	151	11	1	9	8	.529	0	0	4.98
8 Min. YEARS		279	124	8	75	915	3964	899	469	391	79	50	32	50	362	22	878	67	8	58	51	.532	3	17	3.85

Joe Funaro

Bats: Right Throws: Right Pos: 3B Ht: 5'9" Wt: 180 Born: 3/20/73 Age: 27

Year Team	Lg Org	G	AB	H	2B	3B	HR	TB	R	RBI	TBB	IBB	SO	HBP	SH	SF	SB	CS	SB%	GDP	Avg	OBP	SLG
		BATTING															BASERUNNING				PERCENTAGES		
1995 Elmira	A- Fla	56	189	50	10	3	2	72	24	16	17	1	21	0	1	2	5	2	.71	3	.265	.322	.381
1996 Kane County	A Fla	89	291	90	20	2	7	135	57	43	40	2	42	7	5	4	5	3	.63	5	.309	.401	.464
1997 Brevard Cty	A+ Fla	125	470	150	16	6	4	190	67	53	49	3	65	7	3	6	9	5	.64	5	.319	.387	.404
1998 Portland	AA Fla	95	340	97	10	4	5	130	54	28	32	1	44	3	2	2	9	6	.60	8	.285	.350	.382
1999 Portland	AA Fla	74	268	98	19	1	3	128	42	40	31	1	22	4	3	4	6	6	.50	6	.366	.433	.478
5 Min. YEARS		439	1558	485	75	16	21	655	244	180	169	8	194	21	14	18	34	22	.61	30	.311	.382	.420

Bryon Gainey

Bats: Left Throws: Right Pos: 1B Ht: 6'5" Wt: 215 Born: 1/23/76 Age: 24

Year Team	Lg Org	G	AB	H	2B	3B	HR	TB	R	RBI	TBB	IBB	SO	HBP	SH	SF	SB	CS	SB%	GDP	Avg	OBP	SLG
		BATTING															BASERUNNING				PERCENTAGES		
1994 Mets	R NYM	47	179	41	8	1	5	66	26	28	17	0	54	3	1	5	0	1	.00	1	.229	.299	.369
Kingsport	R+ NYM	10	32	5	0	0	3	14	4	7	4	1	16	0	0	0	0	2	.00	0	.156	.250	.438
1995 Capital City	A NYM	124	448	109	20	5	14	181	49	64	30	1	157	9	0	2	1	3	.25	7	.243	.303	.404
1996 Capital City	A NYM	122	446	97	23	0	14	162	53	62	41	3	169	5	0	3	5	2	.71	13	.217	.289	.363
1997 St. Lucie	A+ NYM	117	405	97	22	0	13	158	33	51	18	2	133	6	0	3	0	2	.00	7	.240	.280	.390
1998 Mets	R NYM	8	28	3	0	0	1	6	2	1	0	0	11	0	0	0	0	0	.00	0	.107	.107	.214
St. Lucie	A+ NYM	88	336	94	15	3	19	172	47	57	16	2	116	3	0	3	1	3	.25	9	.280	.316	.512
1999 Binghamton	AA NYM	137	502	119	28	6	25	234	68	78	40	2	184	6	0	5	1	2	.33	9	.237	.298	.466
6 Min. YEARS		653	2376	565	116	15	94	993	282	348	166	11	840	32	1	21	8	15	.35	45	.238	.294	.418

Steve Gajkowski

Pitches: Right Bats: Right Pos: P Ht: 6'3" Wt: 215 Born: 12/30/69 Age: 30

Year Team	Lg Org	G	GS	CG	GF	IP	BFP	H	R	ER	HR	SH	SF	HB	TBB	IBB	SO	WP	Bk	W	L	Pct.	ShO	Sv	ERA
		HOW MUCH HE PITCHED						WHAT HE GAVE UP												THE RESULTS					
1990 Burlington	R+ Cle	14	10	1	1	63.2	287	74	34	29	0	0	3	3	23	0	44	0	1	2	6	.250	0	0	4.10
1991 Columbus	A Cle	3	0	0	2	6	24	3	2	2	0	0	0	0	5	0	5	0	0	0	0	.000	0	0	3.00
Watertown	A- Cle	20	4	0	7	48	221	41	36	28	0	1	2	6	32	1	34	7	2	3	3	.500	0	0	5.25
1992 Utica	A- CWS	29	0	0	26	47	184	33	14	7	1	0	2	1	10	1	38	6	0	3	2	.600	0	0	1.34
1993 Sarasota	A+ CWS	43	0	0	38	69.2	273	52	21	16	1	3	3	4	17	5	45	5	1	3	3	.500	0	15	2.07
Birmingham	AA CWS	1	0	0	0	2.1	8	0	0	0	0	0	0	0	0	0	2	0	0	0	0	.000	0	0	0.00
1994 Nashville	AA CWS	58	0	0	32	82.1	355	78	35	28	0	6	3	5	26	1	44	2	0	11	5	.688	0	8	3.06
1995 Nashville	AAA CWS	15	0	0	5	24.2	113	26	15	7	2	0	1	1	8	1	12	1	0	0	1	.000	0	0	2.55
Birmingham	AA CWS	35	0	0	14	51.2	230	64	27	24	4	2	0	2	16	1	29	1	0	4	4	.500	0	2	4.18
1996 Nashville	AAA CWS	49	8	0	17	107.1	472	113	61	47	11	4	5	5	41	5	47	6	0	5	6	.455	0	2	3.94
1997 Tacoma	AAA Sea	44	3	0	10	93	394	100	43	40	11	2	1	5	24	0	48	3	1	5	3	.625	0	3	3.87
1998 Tacoma	AAA Sea	53	0	0	44	73.2	299	60	23	21	3	2	2	2	20	3	61	0	0	3	3	.500	0	24	2.57
1999 Iowa	AAA ChC	58	0	0	31	79.2	332	79	36	33	8	5	0	0	25	0	64	4	0	5	8	.385	0	9	3.73
1998 Seattle	AL	9	0	0	3	8.2	42	14	8	7	3	0	0	2	4	0	3	0	0	0	0	.000	0	0	7.27
10 Min. YEARS		422	25	1	227	749	3184	723	347	282	47	25	22	34	247	18	473	35	5	44	44	.500	0	76	3.39

Shawn Gallagher

Bats: Right Throws: Right Pos: 1B Ht: 6'0" Wt: 187 Born: 11/8/76 Age: 23

Year Team	Lg Org	G	AB	H	2B	3B	HR	TB	R	RBI	TBB	IBB	SO	HBP	SH	SF	SB	CS	SB%	GDP	Avg	OBP	SLG
		BATTING															BASERUNNING				PERCENTAGES		
1995 Rangers	R Tex	58	210	71	13	3	7	111	34	40	19	0	44	1	0	3	17	4	.81	7	.338	.391	.529
Hudson Val	A- Tex	5	20	3	2	0	0	5	1	4	1	0	4	1	0	0	0	0	.00	2	.150	.227	.250
1996 Chston-SC	A Tex	88	303	68	11	4	7	108	29	32	18	0	104	6	3	2	6	1	.86	6	.224	.280	.356
Hudson Val	A- Tex	44	176	48	10	2	4	74	15	29	7	0	48	2	0	1	8	5	.62	5	.273	.306	.420
1997 Charlotte	A+ Tex	27	99	14	4	0	0	18	7	8	5	0	35	1	0	1	0	0	.00	0	.141	.189	.182
Pulaski	R+ Tex	50	199	64	13	3	15	128	41	52	10	0	49	4	0	4	2	0	1.00	1	.322	.359	.643
1998 Charlotte	A+ Tex	137	520	160	37	4	26	283	111	121	66	3	116	7	0	10	18	6	.75	4	.308	.386	.544
1999 Tulsa	AA Tex	112	452	128	30	3	18	218	61	78	26	2	84	4	0	2	1	0	1.00	5	.283	.326	.482
5 Min. YEARS		521	1979	556	120	19	77	945	299	364	152	5	484	26	3	23	52	16	.76	34	.281	.337	.478

Gus Gandarillas

Pitches: Right Bats: Right Pos: P Ht: 6'1" Wt: 183 Born: 7/19/71 Age: 28

Year Team	Lg Org	G	GS	CG	GF	IP	BFP	H	R	ER	HR	SH	SF	HB	TBB	IBB	SO	WP	Bk	W	L	Pct.	ShO	Sv	ERA
		HOW MUCH HE PITCHED						WHAT HE GAVE UP												THE RESULTS					
1992 Elizabethtn	R+ Min	29	0	0	29	36	148	24	14	12	1	0	0	3	10	2	34	4	1	1	2	.333	0	13	3.00
1993 Fort Wayne	A Min	52	0	0	48	66.1	295	66	37	24	8	5	5	1	22	2	59	4	0	5	5	.500	0	25	3.26
1994 Fort Myers	A+ Min	37	0	0	34	46.2	190	37	7	4	0	3	2	2	13	4	39	5	0	4	1	.800	0	20	0.77
Nashville	AA Min	28	0	0	20	37	156	34	13	13	1	2	1	4	10	0	35	9	0	2	2	.500	0	8	3.16
1995 Salt Lake	AAA Min	22	0	0	13	29.1	135	34	23	21	5	3	1	1	19	4	17	5	0	2	3	.400	0	1	6.44

Year Team	Lg Org	G	GS	CG	GF	IP	BFP	H	R	ER	HR	SH	SF	HB	TBB	IBB	SO	WP	Bk	W	L	Pct.	ShO	Sv	ERA
						HOW MUCH HE PITCHED						**WHAT HE GAVE UP**									**THE RESULTS**				
Hardware Cy	AA Min	25	0	0	18	32.1	152	38	26	22	1	2	0	3	16	0	25	3	0	2	4	.333	0	7	6.12
1996 Twins	R Min	3	1	0	2	9	43	10	3	1	1	1	0	0	3	0	14	1	0	0	0	.000	0	2	1.00
Fort Myers	A+ Min	4	0	0	3	6	35	9	7	6	0	0	0	1	8	0	3	1	0	0	0	.000	0	1	9.00
1997 New Britain	AA Min	17	7	1	2	61.1	253	67	34	32	6	0	2	3	15	0	29	5	0	2	4	.333	0	0	4.70
Salt Lake	AAA Min	11	2	0	2	22.2	93	22	8	8	1	0	0	1	6	1	13	1	0	1	0	1.000	0	2	3.18
1998 Salt Lake	AAA Min	53	1	0	24	70	322	88	47	41	4	1	2	0	24	5	42	9	0	1	3	.444	0	4	5.27
1999 New Britain	AA Min	18	0	0	5	32.1	155	38	32	31	3	2	1	2	21	2	26	5	0	1	3	.250	0	1	8.63
Salt Lake	AAA Min	42	0	0	8	61.1	279	73	37	31	8	0	0	2	20	4	47	7	1	2	2	.500	0	2	4.55
8 Min. YEARS		341	11	1	208	510.1	2256	540	288	246	39	19	14	23	187	24	377	56	2	26	31	.456	0	87	4.34

Jamie Gann

Bats: Right **Throws:** Right **Pos:** OF **Ht:** 6'1" **Wt:** 197 **Born:** 5/1/75 **Age:** 25

Year Team	Lg Org	G	AB	H	2B	3B	HR	TB	R	RBI	TBB	IBB	SO	HBP	SH	SF	SB	CS	SB%	GDP	Avg	OBP	SLG
							BATTING											**BASERUNNING**			**PERCENTAGES**		
1996 Lethbridge	R+ Ari	49	129	37	10	1	2	55	19	22	10	0	42	2	0	1	3	3	.50	4	.287	.345	.426
1997 South Bend	A Ari	12	36	6	1	0	0	6	7	4	3	1	0	9	1	0	0	1	.00	1	.167	.189	.194
High Desert	A+ Ari	91	267	60	12	2	6	94	33	32	17	2	71	1	2	2	2	1	.67	6	.225	.272	.352
1998 Diamondbcks	R Ari	2	7	3	1	0	0	4	1	1	0	0	2	0	0	0	0	0	.00	0	.429	.429	.571
High Desert	A+ Ari	59	217	48	8	3	6	80	25	25	8	0	59	5	0	1	9	4	.69	4	.221	.264	.369
1999 El Paso	AA Ari	109	443	116	24	6	9	179	69	56	32	0	141	8	3	2	7	11	.39	8	.262	.322	.404
4 Min. YEARS		322	1099	270	56	12	23	419	151	139	68	2	324	16	6	6	21	20	.51	22	.246	.298	.381

Al Garcia

Pitches: Right **Bats:** Both **Pos:** P **Ht:** 6'4" **Wt:** 225 **Born:** 6/11/74 **Age:** 26

Year Team	Lg Org	G	GS	CG	GF	IP	BFP	H	R	ER	HR	SH	SF	HB	TBB	IBB	SO	WP	Bk	W	L	Pct.	ShO	Sv	ERA
						HOW MUCH HE PITCHED						**WHAT HE GAVE UP**									**THE RESULTS**				
1993 Cubs	R ChC	9	7	0	2	49.2	210	47	26	18	0	5	3	4	7	0	33	3	5	2	5	.286	0	0	3.26
Huntington	R+ ChC	3	3	0	0	20	86	23	11	11	2	0	2	2	1	0	11	0	0	1	2	.333	0	0	4.95
1994 Huntington	R+ ChC	8	4	0	3	30	129	35	23	15	3	0	0	1	6	0	28	0	0	1	4	.200	0	1	4.50
Williamsprt	A- ChC	8	7	3	1	45.1	190	41	16	15	1	1	3	1	17	1	39	4	1	3	3	.500	1	1	2.98
1995 Rockford	A ChC	27	27	1	0	177	755	176	94	74	13	4	4	15	43	0	120	10	0	14	9	.609	1	0	3.76
1996 Daytona	A+ ChC	7	7	0	0	47	187	48	20	15	1	3	1	2	5	0	28	2	0	4	1	.800	0	0	2.87
Orlando	AA ChC	23	16	1	3	118.2	528	149	71	64	17	6	5	7	32	1	66	4	0	6	7	.462	0	0	4.85
1997 Orlando	AA ChC	12	12	0	0	72.1	315	87	39	28	6	2	2	4	23	1	27	1	1	4	4	.500	0	0	3.48
1998 West Tenn	AA ChC	25	10	0	3	78	334	89	47	43	2	5	1	6	16	1	39	0	2	4	5	.444	0	0	4.96
1999 Altoona	AA Pit	2	0	0	1	4	22	6	4	2	0	2	0	0	3	0	1	1	0	0	0	.000	0	0	4.50
7 Min. YEARS		124	93	5	13	642	2756	701	351	285	45	28	21	42	153	4	392	25	9	39	40	.494	2	2	4.00

Apostol Garcia

Pitches: Right **Bats:** Right **Pos:** P **Ht:** 6'0" **Wt:** 155 **Born:** 8/3/76 **Age:** 23

Year Team	Lg Org	G	GS	CG	GF	IP	BFP	H	R	ER	HR	SH	SF	HB	TBB	IBB	SO	WP	Bk	W	L	Pct.	ShO	Sv	ERA
						HOW MUCH HE PITCHED						**WHAT HE GAVE UP**									**THE RESULTS**				
1997 W Michigan	A Det	33	5	0	10	65.2	275	48	26	22	2	1	0	4	31	0	52	10	2	7	2	.778	0	1	3.02
1998 Lakeland	A+ Det	34	16	1	6	119.1	560	155	89	72	14	2	2	10	52	0	56	8	1	5	8	.385	0	1	5.43
1999 Jacksnville	AA Det	3	0	0	2	4.1	14	0	0	0	0	0	0	0	1	0	0	0	0	0	0	.000	0	0	0.00
San Antonio	AA LA	32	11	0	8	101.2	455	110	57	38	5	5	4	7	45	3	50	7	2	7	5	.583	0	1	3.36
3 Min. YEARS		102	32	1	26	291	1304	313	172	132	21	8	6	21	129	3	158	25	5	19	15	.559	0	3	4.08

Neil Garcia

Bats: Both **Throws:** Right **Pos:** C **Ht:** 6'0" **Wt:** 185 **Born:** 4/6/73 **Age:** 27

Year Team	Lg Org	G	AB	H	2B	3B	HR	TB	R	RBI	TBB	IBB	SO	HBP	SH	SF	SB	CS	SB%	GDP	Avg	OBP	SLG
							BATTING											**BASERUNNING**			**PERCENTAGES**		
1995 Fayetteville	A Det	88	251	58	12	1	7	93	46	33	59	0	49	10	2	4	3	6	.33	5	.231	.392	.371
1997 St. Pete	A+ TB	75	195	44	10	2	0	58	33	21	31	3	20	2	5	5	2	3	.40	7	.226	.330	.297
1998 St. Pete	A+ TB	92	328	105	20	0	6	143	45	52	40	4	40	2	1	2	3	4	.43	6	.320	.395	.436
1999 Orlando	AA TB	31	95	27	6	0	1	36	13	11	10	0	16	1	3	3	0	1	.00	2	.284	.349	.379
Durham	AAA TB	12	33	3	1	0	1	7	1	2	8	0	8	0	0	1	1	0	1.00	1	.091	.139	.212
4 Min. YEARS		298	902	237	49	3	15	337	138	119	142	7	133	15	11	15	9	14	.39	21	.263	.367	.374

Ossie Garcia

Bats: Right **Throws:** Right **Pos:** OF **Ht:** 6'1" **Wt:** 180 **Born:** 10/14/73 **Age:** 26

Year Team	Lg Org	G	AB	H	2B	3B	HR	TB	R	RBI	TBB	IBB	SO	HBP	SH	SF	SB	CS	SB%	GDP	Avg	OBP	SLG
							BATTING											**BASERUNNING**			**PERCENTAGES**		
1993 Glens Falls	A- StL	57	168	36	6	0	0	42	27	13	7	0	38	1	10	0	7	4	.64	1	.214	.250	.250
1994 New Jersey	A- StL	71	264	71	8	2	1	86	54	29	26	0	35	8	1	3	24	7	.77	4	.269	.349	.326
1995 St. Pete	A+ StL	105	315	55	4	0	0	59	37	13	28	0	66	6	7	0	24	11	.69	8	.175	.255	.187
1996 Peoria	A StL	120	359	85	14	1	0	101	70	38	46	0	68	14	14	4	20	13	.61	6	.237	.343	.281
1997 Pr William	A+ StL	104	247	59	12	3	0	77	38	20	25	0	41	3	6	2	10	5	.67	9	.239	.314	.312
1998 Arkansas	AA StL	94	200	49	10	3	0	65	32	24	13	1	35	4	1	1	10	6	.63	5	.245	.301	.325
1999 Arkansas	AA StL	5	8	1	0	0	0	1	0	1	1	0	2	0	0	0	0	0	.00	0	.125	.222	.125
Elmira	IND —	39	139	42	11	1	0	55	19	19	11	0	25	3	0	2	7	6	.54	2	.302	.361	.396
7 Min. YEARS		595	1700	398	65	10	0	486	277	157	157	1	310	39	39	13	102	52	.66	35	.234	.311	.286

Lee Gardner

Pitches: Right Bats: Right Pos: P Ht: 6'0" Wt: 200 Born: 1/16/75 Age: 25

Year Team	Lg Org	G	GS	CG	GF	IP	BFP	H	R	ER	HR	SH	SF	HB	TBB	IBB	SO	WP	Bk	W	L	Pct.	ShO	Sv	ERA
1998 St. Pete	A+ TB	3	0	0	1	4	15	3	0	0	0	0	0	0	1	0	2	0	0	0	0	.000	0	0	0.00
Chston-SC	A TB	28	0	0	13	35.2	154	38	18	16	3	2	0	1	4	0	55	1	0	0	3	.000	0	3	4.04
1999 Orlando	AA TB	1	0	0	0	2	9	3	2	2	0	0	0	0	0	0	1	0	0	0	0	.000	0	0	9.00
St. Pete	A+ TB	20	0	0	13	23	96	20	7	5	1	1	1	2	5	0	22	0	0	2	0	1.000	0	7	1.96
2 Min. YEARS		52	0	0	27	64.2	274	64	27	23	4	3	1	3	11	0	80	1	0	2	3	.400	0	10	3.20

Jon Garland

Pitches: Right Bats: Right Pos: P Ht: 6'6" Wt: 205 Born: 9/27/79 Age: 20

Year Team	Lg Org	G	GS	CG	GF	IP	BFP	H	R	ER	HR	SH	SF	HB	TBB	IBB	SO	WP	Bk	W	L	Pct.	ShO	Sv	ERA
1997 Cubs	R ChC	10	7	0	0	40	161	37	14	12	3	0	0	1	10	0	39	3	3	3	2	.600	0	0	2.70
1998 Rockford	A ChC	19	19	1	0	107.1	467	124	69	60	11	1	1	8	45	0	70	5	1	4	7	.364	0	0	5.03
Hickory	A CWS	5	5	0	0	26.2	126	36	20	16	2	1	2	2	13	0	19	2	0	1	4	.200	0	0	5.40
1999 Winston-Sal	A+ CWS	19	19	2	0	119	502	109	57	44	7	4	5	8	39	2	84	7	0	5	7	.417	1	0	3.33
Birmingham	AA CWS	7	7	0	0	39	175	39	22	19	4	2	1	3	18	0	27	4	0	3	1	.750	0	0	4.38
3 Min. YEARS		60	57	3	0	332	1431	345	182	151	27	8	9	22	125	2	239	21	4	16	21	.432	1	0	4.09

Tim Garland

Bats: Right Throws: Right Pos: OF Ht: 6'0" Wt: 185 Born: 7/15/68 Age: 31

Year Team	Lg Org	G	AB	H	2B	3B	HR	TB	R	RBI	TBB	IBB	SO	HBP	SH	SF	SB	CS	SB%	GDP	Avg	OBP	SLG
1989 Yankees	R NYY	32	107	35	3	1	0	40	20	20	11	0	19	1	0	3	5	3	.63	1	.327	.385	.374
1990 Greensboro	A NYY	77	258	55	6	1	1	66	25	12	21	0	73	5	0	1	15	4	.79	3	.213	.284	.256
1991 Pr William	A+ NYY	27	80	12	1	1	0	15	4	7	7	0	22	0	0	1	3	0	1.00	2	.150	.216	.188
Ft. Laud	A+ NYY	44	129	31	4	1	0	37	11	12	7	0	37	1	0	2	7	3	.70	1	.240	.281	.287
1992 Pr William	A+ NYY	43	128	30	4	4	0	42	13	18	14	0	33	2	2	2	10	2	.83	3	.234	.315	.328
1994 San Antonio	IND —	74	291	85	6	4	4	111	52	33	20	—	46	—	—	—	28	8	.78	—	.292	.344	.381
1995 Rio Grande	IND —	96	376	113	20	0	9	160	85	44	45	1	54	5	6	2	37	11	.77	6	.301	.381	.426
1996 San Jose	A+ SF	132	550	171	18	7	5	218	96	61	54	1	77	10	5	6	51	18	.74	6	.311	.379	.396
1997 San Jose	A+ SF	135	577	172	28	9	3	227	106	39	34	1	88	14	3	3	65	15	.81	6	.298	.350	.393
1998 Shreveport	AA SF	55	194	51	6	2	1	64	24	16	15	1	24	4	2	2	15	5	.75	3	.263	.326	.330
Frederick	A+ Bal	11	38	10	1	0	0	11	4	5	3	0	5	2	1	1	6	1	.86	0	.263	.341	.289
Bowie	AA Bal	59	164	43	4	3	2	59	18	8	25	2	24	4	7	0	8	7	.53	8	.262	.373	.360
1999 Midland	AA Oak	119	463	134	23	10	6	195	84	55	29	1	59	9	5	1	28	13	.68	11	.289	.343	.421
10 Min. YEARS		904	3355	942	124	43	31	1245	542	330	285	—	561	—	—	—	278	90	.76	—	.281	.346	.371

Hal Garrett

Pitches: Right Bats: Right Pos: P Ht: 6'2" Wt: 175 Born: 4/27/75 Age: 25

Year Team	Lg Org	G	GS	CG	GF	IP	BFP	H	R	ER	HR	SH	SF	HB	TBB	IBB	SO	WP	Bk	W	L	Pct.	ShO	Sv	ERA
1993 Padres	R SD	14	14	0	0	72.1	317	64	40	26	2	0	1	5	31	2	83	6	0	6	5	.545	0	0	3.24
1994 Springfield	A SD	21	20	0	0	102.1	454	93	67	54	8	2	1	6	54	2	79	9	2	7	4	.636	0	0	4.75
1995 Clinton	A SD	11	11	1	0	58	268	58	43	36	4	5	2	4	34	3	41	5	0	3	8	.273	0	0	5.59
Rancho Cuca	A+ SD	23	1	0	5	42	196	40	21	13	2	2	5	2	25	0	43	7	1	0	0	.000	0	0	2.79
1996 Clinton	A SD	25	3	0	11	49.2	229	45	28	25	4	2	2	5	31	2	60	3	0	2	3	.400	0	1	4.53
Rancho Cuca	A+ SD	24	1	0	3	51	214	41	12	11	3	1	2	3	20	0	56	6	0	4	1	.800	0	0	1.94
1997 Carolina	AA Pit	6	0	0	2	13.1	64	19	14	13	6	1	0	0	6	1	7	2	0	1	2	.333	0	0	8.78
Lynchburg	A+ Pit	29	5	0	11	56	250	56	36	30	5	4	3	4	22	3	45	5	0	2	5	.286	0	0	4.82
Savannah	A LA	8	1	0	4	16	78	21	15	15	0	1	0	2	7	0	13	4	0	0	3	.000	0	0	8.44
1998 Vero Beach	A+ LA	20	20	1	0	112.1	506	111	75	62	11	1	3	7	57	0	86	10	0	6	6	.500	0	0	4.97
San Antonio	AA LA	11	2	0	6	22.1	95	21	9	9	1	0	0	0	13	0	13	2	0	1	1	.667	0	2	3.63
1999 San Antonio	AA LA	42	4	0	13	94.2	404	70	47	38	8	7	2	1	55	4	76	9	0	5	9	.357	0	2	3.61
Albuquerque	AAA LA	1	0	0	0	2.1	11	3	4	4	1	0	0	0	2	0	1	0	0	0	1	.000	0	0	15.43
7 Min. YEARS		235	82	2	55	692.1	3086	642	411	336	56	26	25	39	357	17	603	68	3	38	52	.422	0	10	4.37

Webster Garrison

Bats: Right Throws: Right Pos: 1B Ht: 5'11" Wt: 193 Born: 8/24/65 Age: 34

Year Team	Lg Org	G	AB	H	2B	3B	HR	TB	R	RBI	TBB	IBB	SO	HBP	SH	SF	SB	CS	SB%	GDP	Avg	OBP	SLG
1984 Florence	A Tor	129	502	120	14	0	0	134	80	33	57	0	44	1	2	2	16	7	.70	9	.239	.317	.267
1985 Kinston	A+ Tor	129	449	91	14	1	1	110	40	30	42	0	76	3	2	5	22	5	.81	6	.203	.273	.245
1986 Florence	A Tor	105	354	85	10	0	3	104	47	40	56	3	53	2	0	3	4	7	.36	7	.240	.345	.294
Knoxville	AA Tor	5	6	0	0	0	0	0	0	0	0	0	2	0	0	0	1	0	1.00	0	.000	.000	.000
1987 Dunedin	A+ Tor	128	477	135	14	4	0	157	70	44	57	0	53	0	0	5	27	9	.75	12	.283	.356	.329
1988 Knoxville	AA Tor	138	534	136	24	5	0	170	61	40	53	0	74	1	2	4	42	15	.74	7	.255	.321	.318
1989 Knoxville	AA Tor	54	203	55	6	2	4	77	38	14	33	0	38	0	4	1	8	6	.75	5	.271	.371	.379
Syracuse	AAA Tor	50	151	43	7	1	0	52	18	9	18	1	25	2	4	0	3	2	.60	5	.285	.368	.344
1990 Syracuse	AAA Tor	37	101	20	5	1	0	27	12	10	14	0	20	0	3	1	0	3	.00	3	.198	.293	.267
1991 Tacoma	AAA Oak	75	237	51	11	2	2	72	28	28	26	0	34	2	7	2	4	0	1.00	6	.215	.296	.304
Huntsville	AA Oak	31	110	29	9	0	2	44	18	10	16	0	21	1	0	1	5	2	.71	1	.264	.359	.400
1992 Tacoma	AAA Oak	33	116	28	5	1	2	41	15	17	2	0	12	0	1	2	1	1	.50	5	.241	.250	.353
Huntsville	AA Oak	91	348	96	25	4	8	153	50	30	30	0	59	0	3	5	8	6	.57	12	.276	.329	.440
1993 Tacoma	AAA Oak	138	544	165	29	5	7	225	91	73	58	2	64	2	2	5	17	9	.65	17	.303	.369	.414
1994 Colo Sprngs	AAA Col	128	514	155	32	5	13	236	94	68	46	2	65	0	1	4	18	5	.78	11	.302	.356	.459
1995 Colo Sprngs	AAA Col	126	460	135	32	6	12	215	83	77	46	2	74	3	1	5	12	4	.75	9	.293	.357	.467

Year Team	Lg Org	G	AB	H	2B	3B	HR	TB	R	RBI	TBB	IBB	SO	HBP	SH	SF	SB	CS	SB%	GDP	Avg	OBP	SLG
1996 Huntsville	AA Oak	47	178	50	12	2	7	87	28	31	22	0	33	1	0	1	1	1	.50	4	.281	.361	.489
Edmonton	AAA Oak	80	294	89	18	0	10	137	56	49	41	2	47	0	1	2	2	1	.67	11	.303	.386	.466
1997 Edmonton	AAA Oak	125	429	124	24	2	15	197	70	80	57	5	91	2	2	4	5	3	.63	6	.289	.372	.459
1998 Huntsville	AA Oak	104	295	80	15	0	11	128	47	51	51	0	56	1	1	4	1	3	.25	5	.271	.376	.434
1999 Midland	AA Oak	43	124	34	9	0	4	55	17	21	16	2	15	1	0	2	1	1	.50	3	.274	.357	.444
1996 Oakland	AL	5	9	0	0	0	0	0	0	0	1	0	0	0	0	0	0	0	.00	0	.000	.100	.000
16 Min. YEARS		1796	6426	1721	315	41	101	2421	963	786	741	19	956	22	38	59	208	90	.70	144	.268	.343	.377

Albert Garza

Pitches: Right Bats: Right Pos: P Ht: 6'3" Wt: 195 Born: 5/25/77 Age: 23

Year Team	Lg Org	G	GS	CG	GF	IP	BFP	H	R	ER	HR	SH	SF	HB	TBB	IBB	SO	WP	Bk	W	L	Pct.	ShO	Sv	ERA
1996 Burlington	R+ Cle	9	9	0	0	39.2	169	34	24	24	5	1	2	1	15	0	34	2	0	2	4	.333	0	0	5.45
1997 Columbus	A Cle	18	18	2	0	95	380	72	34	33	7	0	2	9	32	0	107	5	0	8	3	.727	1	0	3.13
Kinston	A+ Cle	1	1	0	0	8	33	5	3	3	0	0	0	0	4	1	4	1	0	1	0	1.000	0	0	3.38
1998 Kinston	A+ Cle	20	20	3	0	112.1	467	79	44	40	7	5	1	6	60	0	110	8	1	4	8	.333	0	0	3.20
Akron	AA Cle	4	4	1	0	21	95	24	12	9	1	0	1	1	9	0	19	0	0	3	0	1.000	0	0	3.86
1999 Kinston	A+ Cle	6	6	0	0	27.1	128	25	13	11	2	1	0	3	17	0	27	1	0	2	3	.400	0	0	3.62
Akron	AA Cle	10	9	0	0	42.1	216	54	46	44	5	2	0	3	41	0	38	4	0	3	5	.375	0	0	9.35
4 Min. YEARS		68	67	6	0	345.2	1488	293	176	164	27	9	6	23	178	1	339	21	1	23	23	.500	1	0	4.27

Chris Garza

Pitches: Left Bats: Left Pos: P Ht: 5'11" Wt: 187 Born: 7/23/75 Age: 24

Year Team	Lg Org	G	GS	CG	GF	IP	BFP	H	R	ER	HR	SH	SF	HB	TBB	IBB	SO	WP	Bk	W	L	Pct.	ShO	Sv	ERA
1996 Elizabethtn	R+ Min	22	0	0	12	36.1	145	26	8	8	3	1	1	2	12	0	44	3	3	4	0	1.000	0	5	1.98
1997 Fort Wayne	A Min	60	0	0	32	95	385	67	28	21	2	3	2	3	38	1	90	11	0	5	2	.714	0	15	1.99
1998 Fort Myers	A+ Min	58	0	0	43	82	358	73	33	25	3	9	4	4	46	3	63	9	0	5	5	.500	0	14	2.74
1999 Fort Myers	A+ Min	21	1	0	10	40.1	169	36	16	14	1	1	1	3	18	0	30	3	1	1	2	.333	0	2	3.12
New Britain	AA Min	31	0	0	8	30.1	129	14	10	7	0	2	1	4	19	0	40	4	0	1	0	1.000	0	0	2.08
4 Min. YEARS		192	1	0	105	284	1186	216	95	75	9	16	9	16	133	4	267	30	4	16	9	.640	0	36	2.38

Marty Gazarek

Bats: Right Throws: Right Pos: OF Ht: 6'2" Wt: 205 Born: 6/1/73 Age: 27

Year Team	Lg Org	G	AB	H	2B	3B	HR	TB	R	RBI	TBB	IBB	SO	HBP	SH	SF	SB	CS	SB%	GDP	Avg	OBP	SLG
1994 Williamsprt	A- ChC	45	181	68	13	0	2	87	22	18	6	0	17	2	3	0	14	7	.67	2	.376	.402	.481
Peoria	A ChC	23	89	29	6	0	1	38	18	12	2	0	14	3	0	2	2	3	.40	4	.326	.354	.427
1995 Rockford	A ChC	107	399	104	24	1	3	139	57	53	27	1	58	8	2	3	7	5	.58	3	.261	.318	.348
1996 Daytona	A+ ChC	129	472	131	31	4	11	203	68	77	28	0	52	12	0	5	15	13	.54	10	.278	.331	.430
1997 Orlando	AA ChC	76	290	96	23	0	10	149	55	52	20	2	31	5	0	2	10	3	.77	3	.331	.382	.514
1998 West Tenn	AA ChC	21	64	21	4	2	1	32	14	11	13	1	10	2	0	1	6	2	.75	3	.328	.450	.500
Iowa	AAA ChC	88	238	61	16	0	4	89	33	16	16	0	38	5	2	0	4	3	.57	5	.256	.317	.374
1999 Iowa	AAA ChC	40	128	41	12	0	5	68	13	16	5	1	13	1	0	1	0	1	.00	2	.320	.348	.531
West Tenn	AA ChC	35	128	38	9	1	6	67	16	27	4	1	7	3	0	1	2	5	.29	3	.297	.331	.523
6 Min. YEARS		564	1989	589	138	8	43	872	296	282	121	6	240	41	7	15	60	42	.59	40	.296	.347	.438

John Geis

Pitches: Left Bats: Left Pos: P Ht: 6'2" Wt: 191 Born: 12/21/73 Age: 26

Year Team	Lg Org	G	GS	CG	GF	IP	BFP	H	R	ER	HR	SH	SF	HB	TBB	IBB	SO	WP	Bk	W	L	Pct.	ShO	Sv	ERA
1996 Johnson Cy	R+ StL	5	1	0	0	10	41	8	5	5	2	1	0	0	4	1	12	3	0	1	0	1.000	0	0	4.50
1997 Johnson Cy	R+ StL	30	0	0	12	40.2	188	44	27	18	4	1	2	1	15	1	57	1	0	3	4	.429	0	0	3.98
New Jersey	A- StL	3	0	0	0	3	14	2	1	1	0	0	0	0	3	0	3	0	0	0	0	.000	0	0	3.00
1998 Peoria	A StL	23	0	0	6	27.1	115	21	15	9	2	3	1	1	10	0	21	2	0	0	2	.000	0	0	2.96
Pr William	A+ StL	32	0	0	9	39.1	170	49	24	19	3	5	4	0	10	1	27	2	0	3	1	.750	0	0	4.35
1999 Arkansas	AA StL	45	0	0	13	55.1	256	65	44	42	9	4	2	3	29	2	29	2	0	2	5	.286	0	0	6.83
4 Min. YEARS		138	1	0	40	175.2	784	189	116	94	20	14	9	5	71	5	149	10	0	9	12	.429	0	0	4.82

Scott Gentile

Pitches: Right Bats: Right Pos: P Ht: 5'10" Wt: 205 Born: 12/21/70 Age: 29

Year Team	Lg Org	G	GS	CG	GF	IP	BFP	H	R	ER	HR	SH	SF	HB	TBB	IBB	SO	WP	Bk	W	L	Pct.	ShO	Sv	ERA
1992 Jamestown	A- Mon	13	13	0	0	62.2	282	59	32	27	3	0	0	6	34	0	44	5	0	4	4	.500	0	0	3.88
1993 Wst Plm Bch	A+ Mon	25	25	0	0	138.1	592	132	72	62	8	4	5	7	54	0	108	6	0	8	9	.471	0	0	4.03
1994 Harrisburg	AA Mon	6	2	0	1	10.1	72	16	21	20	1	1	0	0	25	0	14	6	0	1	0	1.000	0	0	17.42
Wst Plm Bch	A+ Mon	53	1	0	40	65.1	255	44	16	14	0	3	0	1	19	0	90	4	2	5	2	.714	0	26	1.93
1995 Harrisburg	AA Mon	37	0	0	26	49.2	202	36	19	19	3	2	1	4	15	2	48	1	0	2	2	.500	0	11	3.44
1996 Expos	R Mon	5	1	0	2	7.1	30	5	4	4	0	0	0	0	4	0	5	0	1	1	1	.500	0	1	4.91
Harrisburg	AA Mon	7	0	0	5	10	39	8	0	0	0	0	0	0	2	0	5	1	0	0	0	.000	0	1	0.00
Wst Plm Bch	A+ Mon	15	0	0	6	24	100	14	8	7	2	2	0	0	14	1	23	0	0	2	2	.500	0	1	2.63
1997 Jacksnville	AA Det	43	0	0	27	63.2	273	69	41	37	8	3	3	0	21	0	52	2	0	1	5	.167	0	2	5.23
1999 Frederick	A+ Bal	2	0	0	0	2	6	0	0	0	0	0	0	0	0	0	4	0	0	0	0	.000	0	0	0.00
Bowie	AA Bal	10	0	0	4	14	68	15	13	13	5	0	1	1	9	0	12	1	0	1	2	.333	0	0	8.36
7 Min. YEARS		216	42	0	111	447.1	1919	398	226	203	30	16	10	22	197	3	405	26	3	24	28	.462	0	42	4.08

Ken Giard

Pitches: Right **Bats:** Right **Pos:** P   **Ht:** 6'3" **Wt:** 219 **Born:** 4/2/73 **Age:** 27

		HOW MUCH HE PITCHED						WHAT HE GAVE UP									THE RESULTS					
Year Team	Lg Org	G	GS	CG	GF	IP	BFP	H	R	ER	HR	SH	SF	HB	TBB	IBB	SO	WP	Bk	W	L	Pct.	ShO	Sv	ERA
1991 Braves	R Atl	11	10	0	0	38	167	42	21	16	3	0	0	0	13	0	24	2	1	0	2	.000	0	0	3.79
1992 Idaho Falls	R+ Atl	11	10	0	0	51	228	49	29	22	1	1	3	2	35	0	36	0	1	0	3	.000	0	0	3.88
1993 Macon	A Atl	41	1	0	16	68	287	59	37	29	2	5	3	1	27	0	58	5	0	1	7	.125	0	2	3.84
1994 Durham	A+ Atl	20	0	0	4	30.1	146	31	23	23	4	1	1	0	27	1	39	3	0	1	2	.333	0	0	6.82
1995 Eugene	A- Atl	25	0	0	7	34	137	31	9	9	3	2	0	1	5	1	44	3	0	3	0	1.000	0	2	2.38
Macon	A Atl	5	0	0	3	13.1	51	7	1	1	0	1	0	0	5	0	19	2	0	1	0	1.000	0	0	0.68
1996 Macon	A Atl	5	0	0	4	5.2	20	3	1	1	0	0	0	0	1	0	9	0	0	1	0	1.000	0	1	1.59
Durham	A+ Atl	42	0	0	15	68	310	69	44	39	9	4	2	1	43	3	93	5	0	3	5	.375	0	1	5.16
1997 Durham	A+ Atl	30	0	0	28	38.2	175	28	14	10	2	2	2	2	35	2	47	5	0	2	2	.500	0	12	2.33
Greenville	AA Atl	25	0	0	9	36.2	152	30	9	8	1	0	1	0	11	1	39	2	0	3	0	1.000	0	6	1.96
1998 Nashville	AAA Pit	15	0	0	5	17.1	82	17	12	11	3	0	1	0	12	0	16	0	0	1	2	.333	0	0	5.71
Carolina	AA Pit	42	0	0	25	58.1	246	33	24	17	4	8	3	3	37	4	56	4	0	6	5	.545	0	2	2.62
1999 Altoona	AA Pit	38	0	0	20	42	182	34	12	8	1	1	0	0	25	2	48	2	0	2	2	.500	0	6	1.71
Nashville	AAA Pit	14	0	0	4	16.2	76	16	10	8	1	1	1	0	11	0	21	1	0	0	0	.000	0	0	4.32
9 Min. YEARS		324	21	0	140	518	2259	449	246	202	34	26	17	10	287	14	549	34	2	24	30	.444	0	36	3.51

Kevin Gibbs

Bats: Both **Throws:** Right **Pos:** OF   **Ht:** 6'2" **Wt:** 162 **Born:** 4/3/74 **Age:** 26

		BATTING														BASERUNNING				PERCENTAGES		
Year Team	Lg Org	G	AB	H	2B	3B	HR	TB	R	RBI	TBB	IBB	SO	HBP	SH	SF	SB	CS	SB%	GDP	Avg	OBP	SLG
1995 Yakima	A- LA	52	182	57	6	4	1	74	36	18	36	1	46	5	2	3	38	5	.88	3	.313	.434	.407
Vero Beach	A+ LA	7	20	5	1	0	0	6	1	2	0	0	0	0	0	0	1	0	1.00	0	.250	.250	.300
San Berndno	A+ LA	5	13	3	1	0	0	4	1	0	0	0	2	0	0	0	1	0	1.00	0	.231	.231	.308
1996 Vero Beach	A+ LA	118	423	114	9	11	0	145	69	33	65	0	80	4	6	4	60	19	.76	6	.270	.369	.343
1997 San Antonio	AA LA	101	358	120	21	6	2	159	89	34	72	3	48	6	6	3	49	19	.72	2	.335	.451	.444
1998 Albuquerque	AAA LA	2	8	1	0	0	0	1	1	1	2	0	1	0	0	0	0	0	.00	0	.125	.300	.125
1999 Albuquerque	AAA LA	11	21	6	3	0	0	9	4	1	4	0	6	1	1	0	2	2	.50	0	.286	.423	.429
5 Min. YEARS		296	1025	306	41	21	3	398	201	89	179	4	183	16	15	10	151	45	.77	11	.299	.407	.388

David Gibralter

Bats: Right **Throws:** Right **Pos:** 1B   **Ht:** 6'3" **Wt:** 215 **Born:** 6/19/75 **Age:** 25

		BATTING														BASERUNNING				PERCENTAGES		
Year Team	Lg Org	G	AB	H	2B	3B	HR	TB	R	RBI	TBB	IBB	SO	HBP	SH	SF	SB	CS	SB%	GDP	Avg	OBP	SLG
1993 Red Sox	R Bos	48	177	48	14	0	3	71	23	27	11	1	34	6	1	2	1	1	.50	3	.271	.332	.401
1994 Sarasota	A+ Bos	51	184	35	5	1	4	54	20	18	6	1	41	1	0	0	1	2	.33	2	.190	.220	.293
Utica	A- Bos	62	222	57	11	0	5	83	31	32	14	2	40	5	1	2	3	1	.75	5	.257	.313	.374
1995 Michigan	A Bos	121	456	115	34	1	16	199	48	82	20	2	79	8	3	4	3	4	.43	7	.252	.293	.436
1996 Sarasota	A+ Bos	120	452	129	34	3	12	205	47	70	30	3	101	9	0	4	8	7	.53	9	.285	.339	.454
1997 Trenton	AA Bos	123	478	131	25	1	14	200	70	86	44	3	103	9	1	4	3	5	.38	10	.274	.344	.418
1998 Trenton	AA Bos	100	385	100	16	0	15	161	48	61	25	2	91	7	1	6	2	3	.40	5	.260	.312	.418
1999 Trenton	AA Bos	124	448	134	22	1	24	230	76	97	32	3	68	13	2	5	5	5	.50	13	.299	.359	.513
7 Min. YEARS		749	2802	749	161	7	93	1203	363	473	182	17	557	58	9	27	26	28	.48	54	.267	.322	.429

Steve Gibralter

Bats: Right **Throws:** Right **Pos:** OF   **Ht:** 6'0" **Wt:** 195 **Born:** 10/9/72 **Age:** 27

		BATTING														BASERUNNING				PERCENTAGES		
Year Team	Lg Org	G	AB	H	2B	3B	HR	TB	R	RBI	TBB	IBB	SO	HBP	SH	SF	SB	CS	SB%	GDP	Avg	OBP	SLG
1990 Reds	R Cin	52	174	45	11	3	4	74	26	27	23	1	30	3	3	1	8	2	.80	5	.259	.353	.425
1991 Chstn-WV	A Cin	140	544	145	36	7	6	213	72	71	31	2	117	5	2	6	11	13	.46	14	.267	.309	.392
1992 Cedar Rapds	A Cin	137	529	162	32	3	19	257	92	99	51	4	99	12	1	3	12	9	.57	8	.306	.378	.486
1993 Chattanooga	AA Cin	132	477	113	25	3	11	177	65	47	20	2	108	7	3	4	7	12	.37	6	.237	.276	.371
1994 Chattanooga	AA Cin	133	460	124	28	3	14	200	71	63	47	0	114	9	4	5	10	8	.56	5	.270	.345	.435
1995 Indianapols	AAA Cin	79	263	83	19	3	18	162	49	63	25	3	70	4	1	2	0	2	.00	6	.316	.381	.616
1996 Indianapols	AAA Cin	126	447	114	29	2	11	180	58	54	26	6	114	2	1	3	2	3	.40	10	.255	.297	.403
1997 Chattanooga	AA Cin	30	97	25	9	0	2	40	20	12	13	1	22	2	1	3	0	0	.00	4	.258	.348	.412
1998 Chattanooga	AA Cin	17	67	18	4	0	1	25	8	4	6	0	13	1	1	0	1	0	1.00	3	.269	.338	.373
Indianapols	AAA Cin	68	226	58	12	4	11	111	34	31	10	0	66	2	0	1	1	2	.33	9	.257	.293	.491
1999 Omaha	AAA KC	110	417	111	21	1	28	218	77	78	27	1	97	13	2	2	6	3	.67	9	.266	.329	.523
1995 Cincinnati	NL	4	3	1	0	0	0	1	0	0	0	0	0	0	0	0	0	0	.00	0	.333	.333	.333
1996 Cincinnati	NL	2	2	0	0	0	0	0	0	0	0	0	2	0	0	0	0	0	.00	0	.000	.000	.000
10 Min. YEARS		1024	3701	998	226	29	125	1657	572	549	279	20	850	60	19	30	58	54	.52	69	.270	.329	.448
2 Maj. YEARS		6	5	1	0	0	0	1	0	0	0	0	2	0	0	0	0	0	.00	0	.200	.200	.200

Benji Gil

Bats: Right **Throws:** Right **Pos:** SS   **Ht:** 6'2" **Wt:** 190 **Born:** 10/6/72 **Age:** 27

		BATTING														BASERUNNING				PERCENTAGES		
Year Team	Lg Org	G	AB	H	2B	3B	HR	TB	R	RBI	TBB	IBB	SO	HBP	SH	SF	SB	CS	SB%	GDP	Avg	OBP	SLG
1991 Butte	R+ Tex	32	129	37	4	3	2	53	25	15	14	1	36	0	0	1	9	3	.75	0	.287	.354	.411
1992 Gastonia	A Tex	132	482	132	21	1	9	182	75	55	50	0	106	3	3	4	26	13	.67	16	.274	.343	.378
1993 Tulsa	AA Tex	101	342	94	9	1	17	156	45	59	35	2	89	7	0	3	20	12	.63	9	.275	.351	.456
1994 Okla City	AAA Tex	139	487	121	20	6	10	183	62	55	33	2	120	4	7	6	14	8	.64	9	.248	.298	.376
1996 Charlotte	A+ Tex	11	31	8	6	0	1	17	2	7	3	0	7	0	0	0	0	0	.00	0	.258	.324	.548
Okla City	AAA Tex	84	292	65	15	1	6	100	32	28	21	0	90	2	4	3	4	6	.40	10	.223	.277	.342
1998 Calgary	AAA CWS	128	460	114	24	5	14	190	80	69	41	2	90	4	5	6	11	4	.73	9	.248	.311	.413
1999 Calgary	AAA Fla	116	412	115	29	1	17	197	74	64	27	1	101	7	4	3	17	5	.77	5	.279	.332	.478

Year Team	Lg Org	G	AB	H	2B	3B	HR	TB	R	RBI	TBB	IBB	SO	HBP	SH	SF	SB	CS	SB%	GDP	Avg	OBP	SLG
								BATTING										BASERUNNING			PERCENTAGES		
1993 Texas	AL	22	57	7	0	0	0	7	3	2	5	0	22	0	4	0	1	2	.33	0	.123	.194	.123
1995 Texas	AL	130	415	91	20	3	9	144	36	46	26	0	147	1	10	2	2	4	.33	5	.219	.266	.347
1996 Texas	AL	5	5	2	0	0	0	2	0	1	1	0	1	0	1	0	0	1	.00	0	.400	.500	.400
1997 Texas	AL	110	317	71	13	2	6	103	35	31	17	0	96	1	6	4	1	2	.33	3	.224	.263	.325
7 Min. YEARS		743	2635	686	128	18	76	1078	395	352	224	8	639	27	23	26	101	51	.66	58	.260	.322	.409
4 Maj. YEARS		267	794	171	33	5	14	256	74	80	49	0	266	2	21	6	4	9	.31	8	.215	.261	.322

Geronimo Gil

Bats: Right Throws: Right Pos: C   Ht: 6'2" Wt: 195 Born: 8/7/75 Age: 24

Year Team	Lg Org	G	AB	H	2B	3B	HR	TB	R	RBI	TBB	IBB	SO	HBP	SH	SF	SB	CS	SB%	GDP	Avg	OBP	SLG
								BATTING										BASERUNNING			PERCENTAGES		
1996 Savannah	A LA	79	276	67	13	1	7	103	29	38	8	3	69	5	1	3	0	2	.00	4	.243	.274	.373
1997 Vero Beach	A+ LA	66	213	53	13	1	6	86	30	24	15	0	41	4	1	0	3	0	1.00	5	.249	.310	.404
1998 San Antonio	AA LA	75	241	70	17	3	6	111	27	29	15	0	43	0	2	2	2	1	.67	2	.290	.329	.461
1999 San Antonio	AA LA	106	343	97	26	1	15	170	47	59	49	1	58	2	0	4	2	0	1.00	15	.283	.372	.496
4 Min. YEARS		326	1073	287	69	6	34	470	133	150	87	4	211	11	4	9	7	3	.70	32	.267	.326	.438

Shawn Gilbert

Bats: Right Throws: Right Pos: OF   Ht: 5'9" Wt: 185 Born: 3/12/68 Age: 32

Year Team	Lg Org	G	AB	H	2B	3B	HR	TB	R	RBI	TBB	IBB	SO	HBP	SH	SF	SB	CS	SB%	GDP	Avg	OBP	SLG
								BATTING										BASERUNNING			PERCENTAGES		
1987 Visalia	A+ Min	82	272	61	5	0	5	81	39	27	34	0	59	7	4	4	6	4	.60	8	.224	.322	.298
1988 Visalia	A+ Min	14	43	16	3	2	0	23	10	8	10	0	7	1	0	0	1	1	.50	0	.372	.500	.535
Kenosha	A Min	108	402	112	21	2	3	146	80	44	63	2	61	2	0	5	49	10	.83	6	.279	.375	.363
1989 Visalia	A+ Min	125	453	113	17	1	2	138	52	43	54	1	70	3	6	3	42	16	.72	11	.249	.331	.305
1990 Orlando	AA Min	123	433	110	18	2	4	144	68	44	61	0	69	5	4	3	31	9	.78	10	.254	.351	.333
1991 Orlando	AA Min	138	529	135	12	5	3	166	69	38	53	1	70	11	6	6	43	19	.69	18	.255	.332	.314
1992 Portland	AAA Min	138	444	109	17	2	3	139	60	52	36	2	55	4	5	2	31	8	.79	10	.245	.307	.313
1993 Nashville	AAA CWS	104	278	63	17	2	0	84	28	17	12	0	41	2	2	1	6	2	.75	4	.227	.263	.302
1994 Scranton-WB	AAA Phi	141	547	139	33	4	7	201	81	52	66	3	86	7	3	3	20	15	.57	9	.254	.340	.367
1995 Scranton-WB	AAA Phi	136	536	141	26	2	2	177	84	42	64	0	102	6	4	4	16	11	.59	8	.263	.346	.330
1996 Norfolk	AAA NYM	131	493	126	28	1	9	183	76	50	46	0	97	5	14	4	17	9	.65	5	.256	.323	.371
1997 Norfolk	AAA NYM	78	288	76	13	1	8	115	53	33	43	1	64	2	3	1	16	4	.80	2	.264	.362	.399
1998 Norfolk	AAA NYM	39	133	36	8	0	2	50	21	12	16	1	28	2	0	2	7	2	.78	2	.271	.353	.376
Memphis	AAA StL	62	216	58	15	2	7	98	37	32	29	1	53	6	0	3	7	4	.64	3	.269	.366	.454
1999 Albuquerque	AAA LA	114	421	128	35	3	10	199	88	52	62	0	84	4	8	4	25	8	.76	3	.304	.395	.473
1997 New York	NL	29	22	3	0	0	1	6	3	1	1	0	8	0	0	0	1	0	1.00	0	.136	.174	.273
1998 New York	NL	3	3	0	0	0	0	0	1	0	0	0	1	0	0	0	0	0	.00	0	.000	.000	.000
St. Louis	NL	4	2	1	0	0	0	1	0	0	0	0	1	0	0	0	1	0	1.00	0	.500	.500	.500
13 Min. YEARS		1533	5488	1423	268	29	65	1944	846	546	649	12	946	67	59	45	317	122	.72	99	.259	.342	.354
2 Maj. YEARS		36	27	4	0	0	1	7	4	1	1	0	10	0	0	0	2	0	1.00	0	.148	.179	.259

Tim Giles

Bats: Left Throws: Right Pos: 1B   Ht: 6'3" Wt: 215 Born: 9/12/75 Age: 24

Year Team	Lg Org	G	AB	H	2B	3B	HR	TB	R	RBI	TBB	IBB	SO	HBP	SH	SF	SB	CS	SB%	GDP	Avg	OBP	SLG
								BATTING										BASERUNNING			PERCENTAGES		
1996 Medcine Hat	R+ Tor	68	258	69	17	0	10	116	36	45	19	2	52	0	0	3	5	0	1.00	7	.267	.314	.450
1997 Hagerstown	A Tor	112	380	127	32	4	12	195	54	56	46	4	95	2	0	7	2	2	.50	4	.334	.402	.513
1998 Dunedin	A+ Tor	102	363	110	20	2	18	188	53	65	31	3	83	0	1	3	3	2	.60	4	.303	.355	.518
1999 Knoxville	AA Tor	133	505	157	24	2	18	239	76	114	56	5	93	6	1	10	0	2	.00	13	.311	.380	.473
4 Min. YEARS		415	1506	463	93	4	58	738	219	280	152	14	323	8	2	23	10	6	.63	32	.307	.369	.490

Eric Gillespie

Bats: Left Throws: Right Pos: OF   Ht: 5'10" Wt: 200 Born: 6/6/75 Age: 25

Year Team	Lg Org	G	AB	H	2B	3B	HR	TB	R	RBI	TBB	IBB	SO	HBP	SH	SF	SB	CS	SB%	GDP	Avg	OBP	SLG
								BATTING										BASERUNNING			PERCENTAGES		
1996 Boise	A- Ana	61	192	53	11	5	3	83	28	38	25	1	50	1	1	3	0	1	.00	4	.276	.357	.432
1997 Cedar Rapds	A Ana	122	421	107	26	7	18	201	78	72	55	0	80	4	0	4	8	0	1.00	7	.254	.343	.477
1998 Lk Elsinore	A+ Ana	30	98	31	12	0	3	52	10	3	14	1	21	1	0	0	2	1	.67	1	.316	.407	.531
1999 Jacksnville	AA Det	118	474	145	28	6	19	242	80	88	53	2	89	2	0	5	12	2	.86	12	.306	.375	.511
4 Min. YEARS		331	1185	336	77	18	43	578	199	209	147	4	240	8	1	12	22	4	.85	24	.284	.363	.488

Keith Ginter

Bats: Right Throws: Right Pos: 2B   Ht: 5'10" Wt: 190 Born: 5/5/76 Age: 24

Year Team	Lg Org	G	AB	H	2B	3B	HR	TB	R	RBI	TBB	IBB	SO	HBP	SH	SF	SB	CS	SB%	GDP	Avg	OBP	SLG
								BATTING										BASERUNNING			PERCENTAGES		
1998 Auburn	A- Hou	71	241	76	22	1	8	124	55	41	60	0	68	7	0	2	10	7	.59	1	.315	.461	.515
1999 Jackson	AA Hou	9	34	13	1	0	1	17	9	6	4	0	6	2	0	1	0	0	.00	0	.382	.463	.500
Kissimmee	A+ Hou	103	376	99	15	4	13	161	66	46	61	1	90	12	2	2	9	10	.47	7	.263	.381	.428
2 Min. YEARS		183	651	188	38	5	22	302	130	93	125	1	164	21	2	5	19	17	.53	8	.289	.416	.464

Isabel Giron

Pitches: Right Bats: Right Pos: P   Ht: 6'2" Wt: 170 Born: 11/17/77 Age: 22

Year Team	Lg Org	G	GS	CG	GF	IP	BFP	H	R	ER	HR	SH	SF	HB	TBB	IBB	SO	WP	Bk	W	L	Pct.	ShO	Sv	ERA
1998 Hagerstown	A Tor	21	21	4	0	126.1	517	110	57	35	11	6	3	7	27	1	129	7	2	10	9	.526	3	0	2.49
Knoxville	AA Tor	6	5	0	0	35.1	145	29	15	15	5	0	1	0	13	1	35	3	0	1	1	.500	0	0	3.82
1999 Knoxville	AA Tor	17	16	0	0	95.2	423	97	59	52	12	3	6	7	39	0	81	1	1	7	5	.583	0	0	4.89
Mobile	AA SD	11	11	0	0	62.2	273	71	49	44	17	1	3	1	15	1	45	2	0	4	7	.364	0	0	6.32
2 Min. YEARS		55	53	4	0	320	1358	307	180	146	45	10	13	15	94	3	290	13	3	22	22	.500	3	0	4.11

Chris Gissell

Pitches: Right Bats: Right Pos: P   Ht: 6'5" Wt: 200 Born: 1/4/78 Age: 22

Year Team	Lg Org	G	GS	CG	GF	IP	BFP	H	R	ER	HR	SH	SF	HB	TBB	IBB	SO	WP	Bk	W	L	Pct.	ShO	Sv	ERA
1996 Cubs	R ChC	11	10	0	0	61.1	246	54	23	16	1	0	1	4	8	0	64	1	3	4	2	.667	0	0	2.35
1997 Rockford	A ChC	26	24	3	1	143.2	646	155	89	71	7	5	4	11	62	1	105	11	3	6	11	.353	1	0	4.45
1998 Rockford	A ChC	5	5	0	0	33.2	138	27	8	3	0	1	1	1	15	0	23	1	0	3	0	1.000	0	0	0.80
Daytona	A+ ChC	22	21	1	0	136	597	149	80	63	12	3	5	11	38	1	123	7	0	7	6	.538	0	0	4.17
West Tenn	AA ChC	1	1	0	0	4	21	5	7	6	2	0	0	4	2	4	0	0	0	1	0	1.000	0	0	13.50
1999 West Tenn	AA ChC	20	18	0	0	97.2	470	121	76	65	10	4	6	10	62	3	57	9	2	3	8	.273	1	0	5.99
4 Min. YEARS		85	70	4	1	476.1	2118	511	283	224	32	13	17	37	189	7	376	29	8	23	28	.451	1	0	4.23

Chip Glass

Bats: Left Throws: Left Pos: OF   Ht: 5'11" Wt: 180 Born: 6/24/71 Age: 29

Year Team	Lg Org	G	AB	H	2B	3B	HR	TB	R	RBI	TBB	IBB	SO	HBP	SH	SF	SB	CS	SB%	GDP	Avg	OBP	SLG
1994 Watertown	A- Cle	60	237	73	8	6	2	99	51	22	26	1	34	0	1	1	12	10	.55	1	.308	.375	.418
1995 Columbus	A Cle	115	402	116	17	5	5	158	70	45	37	1	47	5	5	0	37	8	.82	4	.289	.356	.393
1996 Kinston	A+ Cle	134	479	128	18	9	5	179	64	52	40	2	67	4	5	1	11	6	.65	8	.267	.328	.374
1997 Akron	AA Cle	113	394	102	17	4	5	142	74	37	56	1	61	7	3	1	16	10	.62	11	.259	.360	.360
1998 Columbus	AAA NYY	8	15	3	1	0	0	4	2	2	0	0	1	0	0	0	0	0	.00	1	.200	.200	.267
Norwich	AA NYY	120	424	120	8	3	4	146	61	56	40	2	78	2	8	7	15	6	.71	5	.283	.342	.344
1999 Columbus	AAA NYY	53	159	44	7	3	2	63	32	30	22	1	32	1	3	1	5	4	.56	2	.277	.366	.396
Norwich	AA NYY	65	239	60	9	3	6	93	36	34	31	1	49	1	0	0	5	5	.50	6	.251	.339	.389
6 Min. YEARS		668	2349	646	85	33	29	884	390	278	252	9	369	20	25	11	101	49	.67	38	.275	.349	.376

Keith Glauber

Pitches: Right Bats: Right Pos: P   Ht: 6'2" Wt: 190 Born: 1/18/72 Age: 28

Year Team	Lg Org	G	GS	CG	GF	IP	BFP	H	R	ER	HR	SH	SF	HB	TBB	IBB	SO	WP	Bk	W	L	Pct.	ShO	Sv	ERA
1994 New Jersey	A- StL	17	10	0	3	68.2	289	67	36	32	3	4	2	2	26	1	51	8	0	4	6	.400	0	0	4.19
1995 Savannah	A StL	40	0	0	3	62.2	276	50	29	26	2	2	3	5	36	3	62	9	1	2	1	.667	0	0	3.73
1996 Peoria	A StL	54	0	0	36	64	276	54	31	22	2	2	5	1	26	2	80	2	1	3	3	.500	0	14	3.09
1997 Arkansas	AA StL	50	0	0	22	59	245	48	22	18	3	2	4	2	25	2	53	5	0	5	7	.417	0	3	2.75
Louisville	AAA StL	15	0	0	12	15.2	71	18	14	9	2	1	0	1	4	0	14	0	0	1	3	.250	0	5	5.17
1998 Burlington	A Cin	7	1	0	1	14	73	13	9	6	1	0	0	2	6	0	13	2	0	0	1	.000	0	0	3.86
Chattanooga	AA Cin	2	2	0	0	9	35	3	4	4	1	0	0	0	6	0	5	0	0	1	1	.500	0	0	4.00
Indianapols	AAA Cin	4	4	0	0	16	78	20	17	16	1	3	2	1	14	0	15	3	0	1	3	.250	0	0	9.00
1999 Chattanooga	AA Cin	7	7	0	0	50	193	42	12	11	0	1	1	2	8	0	26	3	1	5	0	1.000	0	0	1.98
Indianapols	AAA Cin	12	12	1	0	68	305	84	49	44	8	2	6	6	20	0	51	1	0	3	3	.500	1	0	5.82
1998 Cincinnati	NL	3	0	0	2	7.2	31	6	2	2	0	0	2	0	1	0	4	2	0	0	0	.000	0	0	2.35
6 Min. YEARS		208	36	1	77	427	1842	399	223	188	23	17	23	22	171	8	370	33	3	25	28	.472	1	22	3.96

Mike Glavine

Bats: Left Throws: Left Pos: 1B   Ht: 6'3" Wt: 210 Born: 1/24/73 Age: 27

Year Team	Lg Org	G	AB	H	2B	3B	HR	TB	R	RBI	TBB	IBB	SO	HBP	SH	SF	SB	CS	SB%	GDP	Avg	OBP	SLG
1995 Burlington	R+ Cle	46	155	38	10	0	11	81	28	28	22	0	37	1	0	2	1	0	1.00	1	.245	.339	.523
1996 Columbus	A Cle	38	119	33	5	0	6	56	17	16	28	2	33	1	0	1	0	0	.00	2	.277	.416	.471
1997 Columbus	A Cle	114	397	95	16	0	28	195	62	75	80	1	127	3	0	1	1	0	1.00	9	.239	.370	.491
1998 Kinston	A+ Cle	125	398	87	23	1	22	178	61	76	73	4	117	5	2	6	1	4	.20	9	.219	.342	.447
1999 Greenville	AA Atl	107	305	82	24	0	17	157	47	52	49	0	65	1	0	2	0	3	.00	3	.269	.370	.515
5 Min. YEARS		430	1374	335	78	1	84	667	215	247	252	7	379	11	2	12	2	8	.20	18	.244	.363	.485

Mike Glendenning

Bats: Right Throws: Right Pos: OF-DH   Ht: 6'0" Wt: 225 Born: 8/26/76 Age: 23

Year Team	Lg Org	G	AB	H	2B	3B	HR	TB	R	RBI	TBB	IBB	SO	HBP	SH	SF	SB	CS	SB%	GDP	Avg	OBP	SLG
1996 Bellingham	A- SF	73	265	69	19	4	12	132	54	48	39	0	80	1	1	2	4	6	.40	6	.260	.355	.498
1997 Bakersfield	A+ SF	134	503	130	27	0	33	256	95	100	63	1	150	4	0	7	1	4	.20	15	.258	.341	.509
1998 Shreveport	AA SF	78	254	62	12	2	7	99	27	33	35	1	57	4	0	1	0	0	.00	2	.244	.344	.390
San Jose	A+ SF	48	176	44	9	0	10	83	26	33	24	0	66	0	0	0	1	1	.50	5	.250	.340	.472
1999 San Jose	A+ SF	104	368	90	26	1	23	187	71	80	71	2	112	11	0	3	7	4	.64	10	.245	.380	.508
Shreveport	AA SF	32	106	28	6	0	5	49	14	19	12	0	30	1	0	1	1	1	.50	2	.264	.342	.462
4 Min. YEARS		469	1672	423	99	7	90	806	287	313	244	4	495	21	1	14	14	16	.47	40	.253	.353	.482

Gary Goldsmith

Pitches: Right **Bats:** Right **Pos:** P   **Ht:** 6'2" **Wt:** 205 **Born:** 7/4/71 **Age:** 28

		HOW MUCH HE PITCHED						WHAT HE GAVE UP											THE RESULTS					
Year Team	Lg Org	G	GS	CG	GF	IP	BFP	H	R	ER	HR	SH	SF	HB	TBB	IBB	SO	WP	Bk	W	L	Pct.	ShO	Sv	ERA
1993 Niagara Fal	A- Det	21	5	0	12	54.2	231	43	21	14	3	2	0	4	20	3	64	4	0	4	2	.667	0	0	2.30
1994 Lakeland	A+ Det	23	19	1	3	120.2	499	105	50	44	4	4	4	7	51	2	81	7	2	7	7	.500	0	0	3.28
Trenton	AA Det	4	4	2	0	25.2	103	23	12	11	3	1	0	0	9	1	27	3	0	0	4	.000	0	0	3.86
1995 Jacksnville	AA Det	15	15	0	0	82	347	78	52	42	14	1	4	2	31	1	42	5	0	4	7	.364	0	0	4.61
1996 Visalia	A+ Det	28	27	0	0	170	752	188	108	94	23	4	10	7	76	1	120	2	1	10	11	.476	0	0	4.98
1997 Toledo	AAA Det	1	0	0	1	2	8	2	1	1	1	0	0	0	0	0	1	0	0	0	0	.000	0	0	4.50
Jacksnville	AA Det	31	8	1	5	97.1	415	97	48	44	16	2	4	5	30	0	45	1	0	4	5	.444	1	1	4.07
1998 Toledo	AAA Det	46	0	0	14	78.2	339	83	47	46	16	1	4	3	29	2	50	5	0	1	0	.000	0	1	5.26
1999 Jacksnville	AA Det	33	5	0	10	79	337	84	35	34	8	3	4	6	24	0	30	4	0	3	4	.429	0	2	3.87
Toledo	AAA Det	6	5	0	1	22	100	29	21	17	5	0	0	1	9	1	14	1	0	0	3	.000	0	0	6.95
7 Min. YEARS		208	88	4	46	732	3131	732	395	347	93	18	30	35	279	11	474	32	3	32	44	.421	1	4	4.27

Ramon Gomez

Bats: Right **Throws:** Right **Pos:** OF   **Ht:** 6'2" **Wt:** 175 **Born:** 10/6/75 **Age:** 24

		BATTING													BASERUNNING				PERCENTAGES		
Year Team	Lg Org	G	AB	H	2B	3B	HR	TB	R	RBI	TBB	IBB	SO	HBP	SH	SF	SB	CS	SB%	GDP	Avg	OBP	SLG
1995 Yankees	A CWS	76	231	53	6	0	0	59	26	9	18	0	64	2	3	0	17	9	.65	5	.229	.291	.255
White Sox	R CWS	30	103	27	3	0	1	33	16	6	12	0	22	3	0	0	12	4	.75	2	.262	.356	.320
1996 Hickory	A CWS	116	418	104	8	3	1	121	73	30	44	0	99	2	11	2	57	19	.75	5	.249	.322	.289
1997 Winston-Sal	A+ CWS	118	477	132	23	12	2	185	78	42	42	0	132	3	8	2	53	21	.72	9	.277	.338	.388
1998 Winston-Sal	A+ CWS	43	124	27	5	2	0	36	21	10	12	1	36	2	3	0	13	3	.81	1	.218	.297	.290
1999 Birmingham	AA CWS	99	274	78	10	5	0	98	47	26	31	1	81	2	6	1	26	10	.72	1	.285	.360	.358
5 Min. YEARS		482	1627	421	55	22	4	532	261	123	159	2	434	14	31	5	178	66	.73	23	.259	.329	.327

Rudy Gomez

Bats: Right **Throws:** Right **Pos:** SS-3B   **Ht:** 5'11" **Wt:** 180 **Born:** 9/14/74 **Age:** 25

		BATTING													BASERUNNING				PERCENTAGES		
Year Team	Lg Org	G	AB	H	2B	3B	HR	TB	R	RBI	TBB	IBB	SO	HBP	SH	SF	SB	CS	SB%	GDP	Avg	OBP	SLG
1996 Yankees	R NYY	16	58	16	6	0	0	22	12	10	9	2	7	4	0	1	0	1	.00	1	.276	.403	.379
Tampa	A+ NYY	40	130	38	9	1	1	52	15	24	26	0	12	0	4	3	4	1	.80	8	.292	.403	.400
1997 Norwich	AA NYY	102	393	118	18	7	5	165	65	52	61	0	64	10	1	3	11	7	.61	8	.300	.405	.420
1998 Columbus	AAA NYY	67	234	48	6	2	6	76	34	25	26	0	37	7	1	4	5	5	.50	2	.205	.299	.325
Norwich	AA NYY	46	189	59	10	2	3	82	31	20	17	0	28	2	0	0	8	6	.57	9	.312	.375	.434
1999 Knoxville	AA Tor	122	427	120	26	3	17	203	74	92	75	0	63	6	5	8	10	4	.71	16	.281	.390	.475
4 Min. YEARS		393	1431	399	75	15	32	600	231	223	214	2	211	29	11	19	38	24	.61	44	.279	.379	.419

Rene Gonzales

Bats: Right **Throws:** Right **Pos:** 1B   **Ht:** 6'3" **Wt:** 215 **Born:** 9/3/60 **Age:** 39

		BATTING													BASERUNNING				PERCENTAGES		
Year Team	Lg Org	G	AB	H	2B	3B	HR	TB	R	RBI	TBB	IBB	SO	HBP	SH	SF	SB	CS	SB%	GDP	Avg	OBP	SLG
1982 Memphis	AA Mon	56	183	39	3	1	1	47	10	11	9	0	44	3	5	0	2	3	.40	—	.213	.262	.257
1983 Memphis	AA Mon	144	476	128	12	2	2	150	67	44	40	1	53	3	16	2	5	2	.71	—	.269	.328	.315
1984 Indianapols	AAA Mon	114	359	84	12	2	2	106	41	32	20	0	33	2	10	4	10	4	.71	9	.234	.275	.295
1985 Indianapols	AAA Mon	130	340	77	11	1	0	90	21	25	22	0	49	0	4	1	3	5	.38	4	.226	.273	.265
1986 Indianapols	AAA Mon	116	395	108	14	2	3	135	57	43	41	0	47	2	7	4	8	6	.57	7	.273	.342	.342
1987 Rochester	AAA Bal	42	170	51	9	3	0	66	20	24	13	2	17	1	4	4	4	2	.67	7	.300	.346	.388
1994 Charlotte	AAA Cle	42	133	30	4	0	2	40	26	17	38	1	21	3	1	1	1	2	.33	4	.226	.406	.301
1995 Midland	AA Ana	5	17	3	0	0	0	3	1	2	4	0	1	0	0	0	0	1	.00	1	.176	.333	.176
Vancouver	AAA Ana	50	165	45	12	0	4	69	27	18	24	1	25	2	0	1	0	0	.00	7	.273	.370	.418
1996 Okla City	AAA Tex	42	154	40	8	2	3	61	21	13	26	2	23	2	2	2	1	1	.50	5	.260	.370	.396
1997 Las Vegas	AAA SD	13	43	8	1	0	0	9	2	3	6	0	6	1	0	0	0	0	.00	4	.186	.300	.209
Colo Spnrgs	AAA Col	85	296	88	20	1	3	119	48	39	37	0	43	3	4	5	2	4	.33	6	.297	.375	.402
1998 Calgary	AAA CWS	15	44	9	1	0	0	10	4	1	11	0	8	1	1	0	0	0	.00	1	.205	.375	.227
Oklahoma	AAA Tex	62	196	43	9	0	4	64	24	22	36	0	30	2	2	2	1	3	.25	10	.219	.343	.327
1999 New Orleans	AAA Hou	27	79	20	4	0	0	24	9	11	11	0	11	0	0	1	1	0	1.00	3	.253	.341	.304
1984 Montreal	NL	29	30	7	1	0	0	8	5	2	2	0	5	1	0	0	0	0	.00	0	.233	.303	.267
1986 Montreal	NL	11	26	3	0	0	0	3	1	0	2	0	7	0	0	0	0	2	.00	0	.115	.179	.115
1987 Baltimore	AL	37	60	16	2	1	1	23	14	7	3	0	11	0	2	0	1	0	1.00	2	.267	.302	.383
1988 Baltimore	AL	92	237	51	6	0	2	63	13	15	13	0	32	3	5	2	2	0	1.00	5	.215	.263	.266
1989 Baltimore	AL	71	166	36	4	0	1	43	16	11	12	0	30	0	6	1	5	3	.63	6	.217	.268	.259
1990 Baltimore	AL	67	103	22	3	1	1	30	13	12	12	0	14	0	6	1	1	2	.33	4	.214	.296	.291
1991 Toronto	AL	71	118	23	3	0	1	29	16	6	12	0	22	4	6	1	0	0	.00	5	.195	.289	.246
1992 California	AL	104	329	91	17	1	7	131	47	38	41	1	46	4	5	1	7	4	.64	17	.277	.363	.398
1993 California	AL	118	335	84	17	0	2	107	34	31	49	2	45	1	2	2	5	5	.50	12	.251	.346	.319
1994 Cleveland	AL	22	23	8	1	1	1	14	6	5	5	0	3	0	1	1	2	0	1.00	0	.348	.448	.609
1995 California	AL	30	18	6	1	0	1	10	1	3	0	0	4	0	0	0	1	0	.00	1	.333	.333	.556
1996 Texas	AL	51	92	20	4	0	2	30	19	5	10	0	11	0	0	2	0	0	.00	3	.217	.288	.326
1997 Colorado	NL	2	2	1	0	0	0	1	0	1	0	0	0	0	0	0	0	0	.00	0	.500	.500	.500
12 Min. YEARS		943	3050	773	120	14	24	993	378	305	338	7	411	25	58	27	38	33	.54	—	.253	.330	.326
13 Maj. YEARS		705	1539	368	59	4	19	492	185	136	161	3	230	13	33	10	23	16	.59	54	.239	.315	.320

Dicky Gonzalez

Pitches: Right Bats: Right Pos: P Ht: 5'11" Wt: 170 Born: 10/21/78 Age: 21

Year Team	Lg Org	G	GS	CG	GF	IP	BFP	H	R	ER	HR	SH	SF	HB	TBB	IBB	SO	WP	Bk	W	L	Pct.	ShO	Sv	ERA
1996 Mets	R NYM	11	8	2	1	47.1	195	50	19	14	1	2	0	2	3	0	51	1	0	4	2	.667	1	0	2.66
Kingsport	R+ NYM	1	1	0	0	5	20	4	2	1	0	1	0	0	0	0	7	1	0	1	0	1.000	0	0	1.80
1997 Capital Cty	A NYM	10	7	1	2	47.1	204	50	28	26	8	2	1	1	15	0	49	2	0	1	4	.200	0	0	4.94
Kingsport	R+ NYM	12	12	1	0	66	282	70	38	32	7	4	2	4	10	0	76	0	0	3	6	.333	0	0	4.36
1998 St. Lucie	A+ NYM	8	8	0	0	46.2	193	46	22	16	8	1	0	1	13	0	23	1	0	2	1	.667	0	0	3.09
Capital Cty	A NYM	18	18	1	0	111.1	449	104	57	41	9	5	1	9	14	1	107	5	1	10	3	.769	0	0	3.31
1999 Norfolk	AAA NYM	1	1	0	0	6.2	23	5	2	2	0	0	0	0	1	0	3	0	0	0	1	.000	0	0	2.70
St. Lucie	A+ NYM	25	25	3	0	168.2	673	156	66	53	11	4	0	6	30	1	143	4	1	14	9	.609	0	0	2.83
4 Min. YEARS		86	80	8	3	499	2039	485	234	185	44	19	4	23	86	2	459	14	2	35	26	.574	1	0	3.34

Gabe Gonzalez

Pitches: Left Bats: Left Pos: P Ht: 6'1" Wt: 150 Born: 5/24/72 Age: 28

Year Team	Lg Org	G	GS	CG	GF	IP	BFP	H	R	ER	HR	SH	SF	HB	TBB	IBB	SO	WP	Bk	W	L	Pct.	ShO	Sv	ERA
1995 Kane County	A Fla	32	0	0	10	43.1	181	32	18	11	0	2	1	2	14	2	41	1	0	4	4	.500	0	1	2.28
1996 Huntington	AAA Fla	2	0	0	1	3	15	4	1	1	0	0	0	0	2	0	3	0	0	0	0	.000	0	0	3.00
Brovard Cty	A+ Fla	47	0	0	32	76.1	308	56	20	15	2	9	1	3	23	7	62	2	0	2	7	.222	0	9	1.77
1997 Portland	AA Fla	29	0	0	10	42.2	171	43	12	10	1	3	3	0	5	1	28	1	0	3	2	.600	0	3	2.11
Charlotte	AAA Fla	37	1	0	11	42.2	176	38	15	13	3	1	2	2	14	1	24	0	0	2	2	.500	0	3	2.74
1998 Charlotte	AAA Fla	57	4	0	13	87	412	101	67	53	3	8	7	1	53	5	41	2	1	3	9	.250	0	2	5.48
1999 Portland	AA Fla	26	0	0	11	38	161	38	19	15	2	4	1	3	8	1	34	2	0	2	4	.333	0	0	3.55
Calgary	AAA Fla	24	0	0	10	28	123	27	15	13	2	0	2	2	9	1	23	0	0	1	1	.500	0	0	4.18
1998 Florida	NL	3	0	0	1	1	5	1	1	1	0	0	0	1	1	0	0	0	0	0	0	.000	0	0	9.00
5 Min. YEARS		254	5	0	98	361	1547	339	167	131	13	27	17	13	128	18	256	8	1	17	29	.370	0	18	3.27

Jeremi Gonzalez

Pitches: Right Bats: Right Pos: P Ht: 6'2" Wt: 205 Born: 1/8/75 Age: 25

Year Team	Lg Org	G	GS	CG	GF	IP	BFP	H	R	ER	HR	SH	SF	HB	TBB	IBB	SO	WP	Bk	W	L	Pct.	ShO	Sv	ERA
1992 Rockies/Cub	R ChC	14	7	0	1	45	238	65	59	39	0	0	6	10	22	0	39	11	1	0	5	.000	0	0	7.80
1993 Huntington	R+ ChC	12	12	1	0	67.2	319	82	59	47	6	1	2	5	38	0	42	5	2	3	9	.250	0	0	6.25
1994 Peoria	A ChC	13	13	1	0	71.1	325	80	53	44	4	2	3	7	32	0	30	5	2	1	7	.125	0	0	5.55
Williamsprt	A- ChC	16	12	1	2	80.2	357	83	46	38	6	3	3	10	29	0	64	4	1	4	6	.400	1	1	4.24
1995 Rockford	A ChC	12	12	1	0	65.1	297	63	43	37	4	1	4	8	28	0	36	8	1	4	4	.500	0	0	5.10
1996 Orlando	AA ChC	17	14	0	2	97	415	95	39	36	6	1	2	4	28	1	85	2	0	6	3	.667	0	0	3.34
1997 Iowa	AAA ChC	10	10	1	0	62	249	47	27	24	8	1	1	1	21	0	58	2	0	2	2	.500	1	0	3.48
1999 Daytona	A+ ChC	2	2	0	0	4.2	16	2	0	0	0	0	0	0	0	0	4	0	0	0	0	.000	0	0	0.00
West Tenn	AA ChC	3	3	0	0	10.1	46	7	2	2	0	1	0	1	9	0	12	0	0	0	0	.000	0	0	1.74
Iowa	AAA ChC	3	3	0	0	10	45	10	8	5	1	1	0	1	6	0	10	1	0	0	1	.000	0	0	4.50
1997 Chicago	NL	23	23	1	0	144	613	126	73	68	16	4	5	2	69	5	93	1	1	11	9	.550	1	0	4.25
1998 Chicago	NL	20	20	1	0	110	493	124	72	65	13	5	2	3	41	5	70	2	3	7	7	.500	1	0	5.32
7 Min. YEARS		121	90	5	12	558.1	2485	574	351	278	35	12	23	48	226	2	419	42	9	25	38	.397	2	5	4.48
2 Maj. YEARS		43	43	2	0	254	1106	250	145	133	29	9	7	5	110	10	163	3	4	18	16	.529	2	0	4.71

Jimmy Gonzalez

Bats: Right Throws: Right Pos: C Ht: 6'3" Wt: 235 Born: 3/8/73 Age: 27

Year Team	Lg Org	G	AB	H	2B	3B	HR	TB	R	RBI	TBB	IBB	SO	HBP	SH	SF	SB	CS	SB%	GDP	Avg	OBP	SLG
1991 Astros	R Hou	34	103	21	3	0	0	24	7	3	7	0	33	0	1	0	3	5	.38	1	.204	.255	.233
1992 Burlington	A Hou	91	301	53	10	0	4	78	32	21	34	0	119	1	0	0	0	3	.00	6	.176	.262	.259
1993 Quad City	A Hou	47	154	35	9	1	0	46	20	15	14	1	36	4	1	1	2	2	.50	4	.227	.306	.299
Asheville	A Hou	43	149	33	5	0	4	50	16	15	7	0	37	0	2	1	3	1	.75	3	.221	.255	.336
1994 Jackson	AA Hou	4	6	0	0	0	0	0	0	0	0	0	0	0	0	0	0	0	.00	0	.000	.000	.000
Osceola	A+ Hou	99	321	74	18	0	5	107	33	38	20	0	80	4	2	2	2	0	1.00	10	.231	.278	.333
1995 Quad City	A Hou	35	78	19	3	1	1	27	4	14	8	0	13	1	0	1	1	2	.33	2	.244	.318	.346
1996 Jackson	AA Hou	2	5	1	0	0	0	1	1	0	1	0	1	0	0	0	0	0	.00	2	.200	.333	.200
Kissimmee	A+ Hou	73	208	35	4	1	6	59	19	17	25	0	59	3	2	3	1	0	1.00	8	.168	.264	.284
1997 Kissimmee	A+ Hou	12	44	15	6	2	2	31	7	6	1	0	9	1	0	0	0	0	.00	1	.341	.388	.705
Jackson	AA Hou	97	342	87	18	0	14	147	49	58	37	1	91	8	0	1	2	1	.67	7	.254	.338	.430
1998 Mobile	AA SD	26	85	25	8	0	6	51	14	17	13	0	22	0	0	0	0	0	.00	1	.294	.388	.600
Las Vegas	AAA SD	51	160	38	9	0	5	62	22	21	15	1	44	1	1	2	1	0	1.00	1	.238	.303	.388
1999 Mobile	AA SD	21	68	18	3	0	2	27	15	8	7	1	16	3	0	1	0	0	.00	2	.265	.354	.397
Las Vegas	AAA SD	40	112	33	9	1	3	53	10	19	14	1	29	0	0	3	1	0	1.00	1	.295	.364	.473
9 Min. YEARS		675	2136	487	108	6	52	763	249	252	203	5	589	28	9	18	15	14	.52	47	.228	.301	.357

Jose Gonzalez

Bats: Right Throws: Right Pos: 2B Ht: 5'10" Wt: 170 Born: 9/24/77 Age: 22

Year Team	Lg Org	G	AB	H	2B	3B	HR	TB	R	RBI	TBB	IBB	SO	HBP	SH	SF	SB	CS	SB%	GDP	Avg	OBP	SLG
1996 White Sox	R CWS	51	166	46	6	3	0	58	22	14	12	0	31	2	7	2	4	6	.40	3	.277	.330	.349
1997 Bristol	R+ CWS	24	85	26	5	1	0	33	10	8	8	0	19	1	1	0	1	1	.50	1	.306	.372	.388
1998 Winston-Sal	A+ CWS	14	30	8	2	0	0	10	3	5	1	0	8	0	1	0	0	2	.00	1	.267	.290	.333
Bristol	R+ CWS	51	205	64	14	0	1	81	39	24	18	0	35	4	3	1	16	5	.76	5	.312	.377	.395
1999 Charlotte	AAA CWS	9	14	4	1	0	0	5	3	1	0	0	3	0	0	1	1	0	1.00	1	.286	.286	.357

		BATTING																BASERUNNING				PERCENTAGES		
Year Team	Lg Org	G	AB	H	2B	3B	HR	TB	R	RBI	TBB	IBB	SO	HBP	SH	SF	SB	CS	SB%	GDP	Avg	OBP	SLG
Burlington	A CWS	70	266	74	11	2	3	98	36	28	19	0	52	7	2	3	13	8	.62	3	.278	.339	.368
4 Min. YEARS		219	766	222	39	6	4	285	113	80	58	0	148	14	15	6	35	22	.61	14	.290	.348	.372

Lariel Gonzalez

Pitches: Right **Bats:** Right **Pos:** P **Ht:** 6' 4" **Wt:** 228 **Born:** 5/25/76 **Age:** 24

		HOW MUCH HE PITCHED						WHAT HE GAVE UP											THE RESULTS					
Year Team	Lg Org	G	GS	CG	GF	IP	BFP	H	R	ER	HR	SH	SF	HB	TBB	IBB	SO	WP	Bk	W	L	Pct.	ShO	Sv	ERA
1995 Portland	A- Col	15	11	0	2	57.2	258	44	31	26	4	1	1	7	43	0	48	9	5	3	4	.429	0	2	4.06
1996 Asheville	A Col	35	0	0	24	45	208	37	21	18	2	0	0	1	37	0	53	4	2	1	1	.500	0	4	3.60
1997 Salem	A+ Col	44	0	0	25	57	237	42	19	16	3	2	2	3	23	1	79	4	0	5	0	1.000	0	8	2.53
1998 New Haven	AA Col	58	0	0	45	58	255	46	30	27	5	3	3	3	40	2	63	11	0	0	4	.000	0	22	4.19
1999 Colo Sprngs	AAA Col	11	0	0	4	13.1	66	18	16	15	2	1	1	0	12	2	9	1	0	0	0	.000	0	0	10.13
Carolina	AA Col	30	0	0	24	34	167	39	27	20	4	4	1	1	22	0	41	8	0	2	1	.667	0	14	5.29
1998 Colorado	NL	1	0	0	1	1	3	0	0	0	0	0	0	0	0	0	0	0	0	0	0	.000	0	0	0.00
5 Min. YEARS		193	11	0	124	265	1191	226	144	122	20	11	8	15	177	5	293	37	7	11	11	.500	0	50	4.14

Manny Gonzalez

Bats: Both **Throws:** Right **Pos:** OF **Ht:** 6'2" **Wt:** 190 **Born:** 5/5/76 **Age:** 24

		BATTING																BASERUNNING				PERCENTAGES		
Year Team	Lg Org	G	AB	H	2B	3B	HR	TB	R	RBI	TBB	IBB	SO	HBP	SH	SF	SB	CS	SB%	GDP	Avg	OBP	SLG
1995 Great Falls	R+ LA	59	197	71	9	3	4	98	35	30	9	1	27	0	1	3	16	7	.70	2	.360	.383	.497
1996 San Berndno	A+ LA	43	168	51	7	3	0	64	29	21	12	0	32	0	2	0	10	8	.56	2	.304	.350	.381
Savannah	A LA	65	231	53	10	2	1	70	30	19	20	0	52	1	1	2	15	8	.65	3	.229	.291	.303
1997 Hickory	A CWS	116	469	129	21	2	11	187	70	54	28	1	78	1	7	5	31	12	.72	11	.275	.314	.399
1998 Birmingham	AA CWS	102	371	112	24	2	2	146	51	35	23	0	52	4	8	1	9	7	.56	11	.302	.348	.394
1999 Charlotte	AAA CWS	48	129	40	6	1	1	51	14	25	5	1	20	0	8	0	1	4	.20	1	.310	.336	.395
St. Paul	IND —	18	83	24	4	1	2	36	13	12	5	0	9	1	0	0	5	4	.56	1	.289	.337	.434
5 Min. YEARS		451	1648	480	81	14	21	652	242	196	102	3	270	7	27	11	87	50	.64	31	.291	.333	.396

Mike Gonzalez

Pitches: Left **Bats:** Right **Pos:** P **Ht:** 6'2" **Wt:** 218 **Born:** 5/23/78 **Age:** 22

		HOW MUCH HE PITCHED						WHAT HE GAVE UP											THE RESULTS					
Year Team	Lg Org	G	GS	CG	GF	IP	BFP	H	R	ER	HR	SH	SF	HB	TBB	IBB	SO	WP	Bk	W	L	Pct.	ShO	Sv	ERA
1997 Pirates	R Pit	7	3	0	0	29	115	21	9	8	0	1	0	1	8	0	33	3	3	2	0	1.000	0	0	2.48
Augusta	A Pit	4	3	0	1	19.1	76	11	5	4	1	1	0	0	8	0	22	3	0	1	1	.500	0	0	1.86
1998 Lynchburg	A+ Pit	7	7	0	0	28.1	131	40	21	21	5	0	1	3	13	0	22	1	0	0	3	.000	0	0	6.67
Augusta	A Pit	11	9	0	0	50.2	221	43	24	16	2	1	1	7	26	0	72	3	4	4	2	.667	0	0	2.84
1999 Lynchburg	A+ Pit	20	20	0	0	112	478	98	55	50	10	2	1	4	63	0	119	10	0	10	4	.714	0	0	4.02
Altoona	AA Pit	7	5	0	0	26.2	133	34	25	24	4	2	1	2	19	0	31	3	3	2	3	.400	0	0	8.10
3 Min. YEARS		56	47	0	1	266	1154	247	139	123	22	7	4	17	137	0	299	23	10	19	13	.594	0	0	4.16

Raul Gonzalez

Bats: Right **Throws:** Right **Pos:** OF **Ht:** 5'8" **Wt:** 190 **Born:** 12/27/73 **Age:** 26

		BATTING																BASERUNNING				PERCENTAGES		
Year Team	Lg Org	G	AB	H	2B	3B	HR	TB	R	RBI	TBB	IBB	SO	HBP	SH	SF	SB	CS	SB%	GDP	Avg	OBP	SLG
1991 Royals	R KC	47	160	47	5	3	0	58	24	17	19	0	21	0	1	2	3	4	.43	4	.294	.365	.363
1992 Appleton	A KC	119	449	115	32	1	9	176	82	51	57	1	58	2	4	6	13	5	.72	4	.256	.339	.392
1993 Wilmington	A+ KC	127	461	124	30	3	11	193	59	55	54	1	58	4	1	4	13	5	.72	8	.269	.348	.419
1994 Wilmington	A+ KC	115	414	108	19	8	9	170	60	51	45	2	50	2	2	4	0	4	.00	8	.261	.333	.411
1995 Wichita	AA KC	22	79	23	3	2	2	36	14	11	8	0	13	0	0	0	4	0	1.00	1	.291	.356	.456
Wilmington	A+ KC	86	308	90	19	3	11	148	36	49	14	3	34	2	3	7	6	4	.60	3	.292	.320	.481
1996 Wichita	AA KC	23	84	24	5	1	1	34	17	9	5	0	12	1	0	0	1	2	.33	3	.286	.333	.405
1997 Wichita	AA KC	129	452	129	30	4	13	206	66	74	36	0	52	2	3	8	12	8	.60	12	.285	.335	.456
1998 Wichita	AA KC	118	455	148	31	1	17	232	84	86	58	3	53	2	1	4	12	8	.60	15	.325	.401	.510
1999 Trenton	AA Bos	127	505	169	33	4	18	264	80	103	51	3	71	3	1	7	12	3	.80	14	.335	.394	.523
9 Min. YEARS		913	3367	977	207	30	91	1517	522	506	347	13	422	18	16	42	76	43	.64	72	.290	.356	.451

Steve Goodell

Bats: Right **Throws:** Right **Pos:** 3B **Ht:** 6'3" **Wt:** 196 **Born:** 4/23/75 **Age:** 25

		BATTING																BASERUNNING				PERCENTAGES		
Year Team	Lg Org	G	AB	H	2B	3B	HR	TB	R	RBI	TBB	IBB	SO	HBP	SH	SF	SB	CS	SB%	GDP	Avg	OBP	SLG
1995 Elmira	A- Fla	69	253	64	14	4	7	107	42	30	36	0	50	14	1	2	4	5	.44	8	.253	.374	.423
Kane County	A Fla	2	7	2	0	0	0	2	0	1	2	0	2	0	0	0	0	0	.00	0	.286	.444	.286
1996 Brevard Cty	A+ Fla	1	4	1	0	0	0	1	0	0	0	0	0	0	0	0	0	0	.00	0	.250	.250	.250
Kane County	A Fla	86	282	79	17	2	9	127	34	39	30	2	68	13	2	5	1	1	.50	8	.280	.370	.450
1997 Brevard Cty	A+ Fla	117	381	103	18	2	11	158	48	61	60	0	67	14	6	7	1	1	.50	7	.270	.383	.415
1998 Portland	AA Fla	48	118	22	6	0	1	31	13	11	26	1	35	4	2	0	0	1	.00	3	.186	.351	.263
Danville	A+ Atl	54	198	59	14	2	5	92	21	20	17	1	42	6	4	3	3	4	.43	5	.298	.366	.465
Greenville	AA Atl	5	18	5	1	0	3	15	7	6	3	0	3	1	0	0	0	0	.00	1	.278	.409	.833
1999 Greenville	AA Atl	102	338	101	25	2	15	175	69	58	55	2	61	12	0	3	8	6	.57	5	.299	.412	.518
5 Min. YEARS		484	1599	436	95	12	51	708	234	226	229	6	328	64	15	20	17	18	.49	37	.273	.381	.443

Jason Gooding

Pitches: Left **Bats:** Right **Pos:** P   **Ht:** 5'11" **Wt:** 190 **Born:** 7/29/74 **Age:** 25

		HOW MUCH HE PITCHED						WHAT HE GAVE UP											THE RESULTS				
Year Team	Lg Org	G	GS	CG	GF	IP	BFP	H	R	ER	HR	SH	SF	HB	TBB	IBB	SO	WP	Bk	W	L	Pct.	ShO	Sv	ERA
1997 Spokane	A- KC	11	11	0	0	55.2	220	44	16	14	2	0	0	3	11	0	58	3	0	4	0	1.000	0	0	2.26
Lansing	A KC	1	1	0	0	4.2	24	6	5	3	0	0	1	1	1	0	3	2	0	0	1	.000	0	0	5.79
1998 Wichita	AA KC	25	23	0	1	129.1	593	171	93	75	15	9	9	10	43	1	68	8	2	5	7	.417	0	0	5.22
1999 Omaha	AAA KC	1	1	0	0	6	26	8	4	4	1	0	1	0	1	0	2	0	0	0	1	.000	0	0	6.00
Wichita	AA KC	23	23	0	0	139	599	176	80	73	16	3	2	2	39	5	63	3	0	13	7	.650	0	0	4.73
3 Min. YEARS		61	59	0	1	334.2	1462	405	198	169	34	12	13	16	95	6	194	16	2	22	16	.579	0	0	4.54

David Goodwin

Bats: Right **Throws:** Right **Pos:** 1B   **Ht:** 6'1" **Wt:** 205 **Born:** 3/26/75 **Age:** 25

		BATTING													BASERUNNING				PERCENTAGES		
Year Team	Lg Org	G	AB	H	2B	3B	HR	TB	R	RBI	TBB	IBB	SO	HBP	SH	SF	SB	CS	SB%	GDP	Avg	OBP	SLG
1998 Royals	R KC	48	177	65	20	0	4	97	26	33	20	1	33	5	1	2	0	0	.00	2	.367	.441	.548
1999 Chstn-WV	A KC	128	490	140	29	6	9	208	68	73	45	0	123	13	2	4	10	5	.67	10	.286	.359	.424
Wichita	AA KC	3	10	3	0	0	0	3	3	0	1	0	3	0	0	0	0	0	.00	0	.300	.364	.300
2 Min. YEARS		179	677	208	49	6	13	308	97	106	66	1	159	18	3	6	10	5	.67	12	.307	.381	.455

Joe Goodwin

Bats: Right **Throws:** Right **Pos:** C   **Ht:** 5'10" **Wt:** 180 **Born:** 4/19/74 **Age:** 26

		BATTING													BASERUNNING				PERCENTAGES		
Year Team	Lg Org	G	AB	H	2B	3B	HR	TB	R	RBI	TBB	IBB	SO	HBP	SH	SF	SB	CS	SB%	GDP	Avg	OBP	SLG
1995 Hudson Val	A- Tex	57	181	51	6	0	1	60	29	27	20	0	20	6	2	2	2	1	.67	7	.282	.368	.331
1996 Chston-SC	A Tex	80	252	65	13	1	0	80	25	31	32	1	34	5	3	3	3	5	.38	4	.258	.349	.317
1997 Charlotte	A+ Tex	61	185	44	9	1	2	61	18	22	20	0	18	5	2	0	2	2	.50	6	.238	.329	.330
1998 Charlotte	A+ Tex	10	26	10	3	0	0	13	5	4	4	0	2	1	0	0	1	0	.00	0	.385	.484	.500
Tulsa	AA Tex	10	31	3	1	0	0	4	3	3	1	0	7	1	0	1	0	0	.00	2	.097	.147	.129
1999 Tulsa	AA Tex	30	98	23	7	0	0	30	15	8	7	0	16	0	1	0	0	0	.00	1	.235	.286	.306
5 Min. YEARS		248	773	196	39	2	3	248	95	95	84	1	97	18	8	6	7	10	.41	20	.254	.338	.321

Mike Gordon

Pitches: Right **Bats:** Left **Pos:** P   **Ht:** 6'2" **Wt:** 210 **Born:** 11/30/72 **Age:** 27

		HOW MUCH HE PITCHED						WHAT HE GAVE UP											THE RESULTS				
Year Team	Lg Org	G	GS	CG	GF	IP	BFP	H	R	ER	HR	SH	SF	HB	TBB	IBB	SO	WP	Bk	W	L	Pct.	ShO	Sv	ERA
1992 Yankees	R NYY	11	10	0	1	53.1	223	33	21	18	1	2	3	5	33	0	55	5	4	3	4	.429	0	0	3.04
1993 Yankees	R NYY	11	9	0	1	64.2	266	43	23	12	0	2	1	0	27	0	61	6	1	4	2	.667	0	0	1.67
Oneonta	A- NYY	3	3	1	0	14.1	68	13	12	11	0	0	2	3	11	0	15	3	0	0	3	.000	0	0	6.91
1994 Greensboro	A NYY	23	22	0	0	107.1	501	128	88	77	15	1	3	8	54	0	116	11	1	2	10	.167	0	0	6.46
1995 Tampa	A+ NYY	21	21	1	0	124.1	521	111	54	42	6	3	1	4	49	0	96	9	2	4	6	.400	0	0	3.04
Dunedin	A+ Tor	7	6	0	0	36.2	179	44	32	24	6	2	0	3	24	0	36	2	0	1	2	.333	0	0	5.89
1996 Dunedin	A+ Tor	24	24	0	0	133.1	588	127	70	51	7	2	5	7	64	1	102	15	1	3	12	.200	0	0	3.44
1997 Akron	AA Cle	6	6	0	0	30.1	147	37	28	14	3	1	4	2	14	0	16	2	0	1	2	.333	0	0	4.15
Knoxville	AA Tor	33	6	0	7	72.2	341	91	46	43	5	3	2	1	40	3	64	6	0	2	3	.400	0	0	5.33
1998 Knoxville	AA Tor	44	12	0	11	113	521	123	82	63	13	1	5	3	64	5	95	7	0	8	2	.800	0	0	5.02
1999 Huntsville	AA Mil	7	0	0	6	6.1	35	8	8	0	0	0	0	0	3	2	5	0	0	0	1	.000	0	0	0.00
8 Min. YEARS		190	119	2	26	756.1	3390	758	464	355	56	17	22	35	387	11	661	66	9	28	47	.373	0	2	4.22

Chris Gorrell

Pitches: Right **Bats:** Right **Pos:** P   **Ht:** 6'2" **Wt:** 188 **Born:** 1/27/76 **Age:** 24

		HOW MUCH HE PITCHED						WHAT HE GAVE UP											THE RESULTS				
Year Team	Lg Org	G	GS	CG	GF	IP	BFP	H	R	ER	HR	SH	SF	HB	TBB	IBB	SO	WP	Bk	W	L	Pct.	ShO	Sv	ERA
1996 Athletics	R Oak	12	2	0	3	36.2	149	36	18	16	1	1	1	3	8	0	32	2	3	1	2	.333	0	1	3.93
1997 Sou Oregon	A- Oak	18	10	1	0	71.2	326	86	50	37	8	4	1	3	28	0	60	5	2	5	3	.625	0	0	4.65
1998 Visalia	A+ Oak	32	0	0	12	55.1	247	65	39	32	3	5	2	6	17	2	53	4	1	3	5	.375	0	2	5.20
1999 Midland	AA Oak	30	0	0	12	56.1	285	92	63	49	7	3	1	2	23	7	41	0	1	2	0	1.000	0	1	7.83
Visalia	A+ Oak	16	0	0	14	23	110	33	14	13	2	1	0	1	7	0	31	2	0	4	3	.571	0	4	5.09
4 Min. YEARS		108	12	1	41	243	1117	312	184	147	21	14	5	15	83	9	217	13	7	15	13	.536	0	8	5.44

Jason Grabowski

Bats: Left **Throws:** Right **Pos:** 3B   **Ht:** 6'3" **Wt:** 200 **Born:** 5/24/76 **Age:** 24

		BATTING													BASERUNNING				PERCENTAGES		
Year Team	Lg Org	G	AB	H	2B	3B	HR	TB	R	RBI	TBB	IBB	SO	HBP	SH	SF	SB	CS	SB%	GDP	Avg	OBP	SLG
1997 Pulaski	R+ Tex	50	174	51	14	0	4	77	36	24	40	2	32	0	1	1	6	1	.86	2	.293	.423	.443
1998 Savannah	A Tex	104	352	95	13	6	14	162	63	52	57	0	93	1	0	1	16	9	.64	7	.270	.372	.460
1999 Charlotte	A+ Tex	123	434	136	31	6	12	215	68	87	65	3	66	5	1	2	13	10	.57	8	.313	.407	.495
Tulsa	AA Tex	2	6	1	0	0	0	1	1	0	2	1	2	0	0	0	0	0	.00	0	.167	.375	.167
3 Min. YEARS		279	966	283	58	12	30	455	168	163	164	6	193	6	2	4	35	20	.64	17	.293	.397	.471

Jeff Granger

Pitches: Left **Bats:** Right **Pos:** P   **Ht:** 6'4" **Wt:** 200 **Born:** 12/16/71 **Age:** 28

		HOW MUCH HE PITCHED						WHAT HE GAVE UP											THE RESULTS				
Year Team	Lg Org	G	GS	CG	GF	IP	BFP	H	R	ER	HR	SH	SF	HB	TBB	IBB	SO	WP	Bk	W	L	Pct.	ShO	Sv	ERA
1993 Eugene	A- KC	8	7	0	0	36	146	28	17	12	2	1	0	1	10	1	56	1	0	3	3	.500	0	0	3.00
1994 Memphis	AA KC	25	25	0	0	139.2	615	155	72	60	8	3	3	0	61	0	112	14	3	7	7	.500	0	0	3.87
1995 Wichita	AA KC	18	18	0	0	95.2	439	122	76	63	9	3	4	1	40	0	81	10	0	4	7	.364	0	0	5.93

110

Year Team	Lg Org	G	GS	CG	GF	IP	BFP	H	R	ER	HR	SH	SF	HB	TBB	IBB	SO	WP	Bk	W	L	Pct.	ShO	Sv	ERA
1996 Omaha	AAA KC	45	0	0	25	77	314	65	24	20	10	2	2	2	29	2	68	3	0	5	3	.625	0	4	2.34
1997 Calgary	AAA Pit	30	12	0	7	82.2	387	111	63	51	7	3	1	3	33	5	68	6	0	1	7	.125	0	1	5.55
1998 Oklahoma	AAA Tex	32	19	0	6	129	574	160	80	67	10	4	7	2	38	1	94	10	0	4	8	.333	0	1	4.67
1999 Louisville	AAA Mil	56	1	0	21	59	271	72	40	31	8	5	2	3	25	3	50	0	0	1	6	.143	0	3	4.73
1993 Kansas City	AL	1	0	0	0	1	8	3	3	3	0	0	0	0	2	0	1	0	0	0	0	.000	0	0	27.00
1994 Kansas City	AL	2	2	0	0	9.1	47	13	8	7	2	0	1	0	6	0	3	0	0	0	1	.000	0	0	6.75
1996 Kansas City	AL	15	0	0	5	16.1	80	21	13	12	3	0	1	2	10	0	11	2	0	0	0	.000	0	0	6.61
1997 Pittsburgh	NL	9	0	0	1	5	32	10	10	10	3	0	0	0	8	1	4	2	0	0	0	.000	0	0	18.00
7 Min. YEARS		214	82	0	59	619	2746	713	372	304	54	21	19	12	236	12	529	44	3	25	41	.379	0	9	4.42
4 Maj. YEARS		27	2	0	6	31.2	167	47	34	32	8	0	2	2	26	1	19	4	0	0	1	.000	0	9	9.09

Bryan Graves

Bats: Right **Throws:** Right **Pos:** C — **Ht:** 5'11" **Wt:** 210 **Born:** 10/8/74 **Age:** 25

Year Team	Lg Org	G	AB	H	2B	3B	HR	TB	R	RBI	TBB	IBB	SO	HBP	SH	SF	SB	CS	SB%	GDP	Avg	OBP	SLG
1995 Boise	A- Ana	32	53	11	2	0	1	16	9	5	17	0	12	0	0	0	0	0	.00	0	.208	.400	.302
1996 Cedar Rapds	A Ana	83	228	51	5	2	4	72	27	27	46	0	59	5	1	3	4	2	.67	3	.224	.362	.316
1997 Cedar Rapds	A Ana	68	191	39	12	0	1	54	14	17	32	0	32	3	0	0	1	2	.33	4	.204	.327	.283
1998 Lk Elsinore	A+ Ana	8	20	4	1	0	0	5	1	1	1	0	7	0	0	0	0	0	.00	0	.200	.238	.250
Midland	AA Ana	29	85	19	3	0	1	25	8	6	16	0	18	2	1	1	0	1	.00	5	.224	.356	.294
1999 Lk Elsinore	A+ Ana	15	38	9	2	0	0	11	3	6	7	0	13	0	0	1	0	0	.00	1	.237	.348	.289
Edmonton	AAA Ana	2	5	2	1	0	0	3	2	1	1	0	2	1	0	0	0	0	.00	0	.400	.571	.600
Erie	AA Ana	37	103	20	2	1	1	27	22	8	32	0	32	2	3	0	1	0	1.00	1	.194	.394	.262
5 Min. YEARS		274	723	155	28	3	8	213	86	71	152	0	175	13	5	5	6	5	.55	14	.214	.358	.295

Chad Green

Bats: Both **Throws:** Right **Pos:** OF — **Ht:** 5'10" **Wt:** 180 **Born:** 6/28/75 **Age:** 25

Year Team	Lg Org	G	AB	H	2B	3B	HR	TB	R	RBI	TBB	IBB	SO	HBP	SH	SF	SB	CS	SB%	GDP	Avg	OBP	SLG
1996 Ogden	R+ Mil	21	81	29	4	1	3	44	22	8	15	0	23	1	1	2	12	3	.80	0	.358	.455	.543
1997 Stockton	A+ Mil	127	513	128	26	14	2	188	78	43	37	2	138	2	11	4	37	16	.70	3	.250	.300	.366
1998 Stockton	A+ Mil	40	151	52	13	2	0	69	30	17	12	3	22	1	1	1	22	5	.81	2	.344	.394	.457
El Paso	AA Mil	7	6	0	0	0	0	0	0	0	1	0	3	0	0	0	0	0	.00	0	.000	.143	.000
1999 Huntsville	AA Mil	116	422	104	22	3	10	162	56	46	46	2	109	2	2	3	28	13	.68	6	.246	.321	.384
4 Min. YEARS		311	1173	313	65	20	15	463	186	114	111	7	295	6	15	10	99	37	.73	11	.267	.331	.395

Jason Green

Pitches: Right **Bats:** Right **Pos:** P — **Ht:** 6'4" **Wt:** 190 **Born:** 6/5/75 **Age:** 25

Year Team	Lg Org	G	GS	CG	GF	IP	BFP	H	R	ER	HR	SH	SF	HB	TBB	IBB	SO	WP	Bk	W	L	Pct.	ShO	Sv	ERA
1994 Astros	R Hou	18	0	0	7	23	96	16	11	7	0	1	1	1	16	0	12	6	4	2	1	.667	0	1	2.74
1995 Auburn	A- Hou	14	14	2	0	82.2	365	82	48	35	1	4	0	10	29	0	48	5	0	8	2	.800	1	0	3.81
1997 Kissimmee	A+ Hou	8	0	0	4	8.2	50	11	12	5	0	0	0	0	10	1	3	2	0	0	3	.000	0	0	5.19
Quad City	A Hou	23	22	1	1	125.2	548	126	79	64	9	5	2	8	53	2	96	12	2	7	12	.368	0	0	4.58
1998 Kissimmee	A+ Hou	51	3	0	44	67.1	304	64	34	25	4	2	2	4	32	3	67	5	1	2	5	.286	0	14	3.34
1999 Jackson	AA Hou	33	0	0	18	42.1	187	41	20	16	2	0	0	0	20	2	50	0	1	3	3	.500	0	10	3.40
5 Min. YEARS		147	39	3	74	349.2	1550	340	204	152	16	12	5	23	160	8	276	30	8	22	26	.458	1	25	3.91

Steve Green

Pitches: Right **Bats:** Right **Pos:** P — **Ht:** 6'2" **Wt:** 195 **Born:** 1/26/78 **Age:** 22

Year Team	Lg Org	G	GS	CG	GF	IP	BFP	H	R	ER	HR	SH	SF	HB	TBB	IBB	SO	WP	Bk	W	L	Pct.	ShO	Sv	ERA
1998 Cedar Rapds	A Ana	18	10	1	5	83.1	356	86	49	42	9	3	3	3	25	0	61	9	1	2	6	.250	0	0	4.54
1999 Lk Elsinore	A+ Ana	19	19	4	0	120.2	526	130	70	53	9	4	1	6	37	2	91	1	3	7	6	.538	4	0	3.95
Erie	AA Ana	6	6	1	0	40.2	176	34	25	15	4	1	2	2	19	0	32	1	0	3	1	.750	0	0	3.32
2 Min. YEARS		43	35	6	5	244.2	1058	250	144	110	22	8	6	11	81	2	184	11	4	12	13	.480	4	0	4.05

Tyler Green

Pitches: Right **Bats:** Right **Pos:** P — **Ht:** 6'5" **Wt:** 207 **Born:** 2/18/70 **Age:** 30

Year Team	Lg Org	G	GS	CG	GF	IP	BFP	H	R	ER	HR	SH	SF	HB	TBB	IBB	SO	WP	Bk	W	L	Pct.	ShO	Sv	ERA
1991 Batavia	A- Phi	3	3	0	0	15	58	7	2	2	0	0	0	2	6	0	19	2	0	1	0	1.000	0	0	1.20
Clearwater	A+ Phi	2	2	0	0	13	50	3	2	2	0	0	0	0	8	0	20	2	0	2	0	1.000	0	0	1.38
1992 Reading	AA Phi	12	12	0	0	62.1	249	46	16	13	2	4	1	1	20	0	67	5	0	6	3	.667	0	0	1.88
Scranton-WB	AAA Phi	2	2	0	0	10.1	50	7	7	7	1	0	0	1	12	0	15	0	1	0	1	.000	0	0	6.10
1993 Scranton-WB	AAA Phi	28	14	4	6	118.1	496	102	62	52	8	3	4	5	43	2	87	8	2	6	10	.375	0	0	3.95
1994 Scranton-WB	AAA Phi	27	26	4	0	162	725	179	110	100	25	4	4	12	77	3	95	14	1	7	16	.304	0	0	5.56
1997 Scranton-WB	AAA Phi	12	12	3	0	72.1	322	80	54	49	13	1	0	1	29	3	40	4	0	4	8	.333	0	0	6.10
1999 Scranton-WB	AAA Phi	19	7	1	4	50.1	248	78	47	43	8	1	3	4	24	1	31	3	0	4	6	.400	0	0	7.69
1993 Philadelphia	NL	3	2	0	1	7.1	41	16	9	6	1	0	0	0	5	0	7	2	0	0	0	.000	0	0	7.36
1995 Philadelphia	NL	26	25	4	0	140.2	623	157	86	83	15	5	6	4	66	3	85	9	2	8	9	.471	2	0	5.31
1997 Philadelphia	NL	14	14	0	0	76.2	340	72	50	42	8	0	3	1	45	4	58	7	0	4	4	.500	0	0	4.93
1998 Philadelphia	NL	27	27	0	0	159.1	699	142	97	89	23	5	6	9	85	1	113	8	0	6	12	.333	0	0	5.03
6 Min. YEARS		105	78	12	10	503.2	2198	502	300	268	57	13	12	26	219	9	374	38	4	30	44	.405	0	0	4.79
4 Maj. YEARS		70	68	4	1	384	1703	387	242	220	47	10	15	14	201	8	263	26	2	18	25	.419	2	0	5.16

Kevin Gregg

Pitches: Right **Bats:** Right **Pos:** P **Ht:** 6'6" **Wt:** 200 **Born:** 6/20/78 **Age:** 22

Year Team	Lg Org	G	GS	CG	GF	IP	BFP	H	R	ER	HR	SH	SF	HB	TBB	IBB	SO	WP	Bk	W	L	Pct.	ShO	Sv	ERA
1996 Athletics	R Oak	11	9	0	0	40.2	169	30	14	14	1	1	1	2	21	0	48	11	0	3	3	.500	0	0	3.10
1997 Visalia	A+ Oak	25	24	0	0	115.1	534	116	81	73	8	2	3	5	74	0	136	28	0	6	8	.429	0	0	5.70
1998 Modesto	A+ Oak	30	24	0	3	144	640	139	72	61	7	9	2	6	76	2	141	7	0	8	7	.533	0	1	3.81
1999 Visalia	A+ Oak	13	11	1	2	64	271	60	34	27	3	1	2	4	23	0	48	7	1	4	4	.500	1	1	3.80
Midland	AA Det	16	16	2	0	91.1	380	75	45	38	7	0	3	6	31	1	66	6	0	4	7	.364	0	0	3.74
Vancouver	AAA Oak	1	1	0	0	5	21	6	2	2	0	0	0	0	2	0	4	2	0	1	0	1.000	0	0	3.60
4 Min. YEARS		96	85	3	5	460.1	2015	426	248	215	26	13	11	23	227	3	443	61	1	26	29	.473	1	2	4.20

Seth Greisinger

Pitches: Right **Bats:** Right **Pos:** P **Ht:** 6'3" **Wt:** 200 **Born:** 7/29/75 **Age:** 24

Year Team	Lg Org	G	GS	CG	GF	IP	BFP	H	R	ER	HR	SH	SF	HB	TBB	IBB	SO	WP	Bk	W	L	Pct.	ShO	Sv	ERA
1997 Jacksonville	AA Det	28	28	1	0	159.1	710	194	103	92	29	3	6	3	53	0	105	12	2	10	6	.625	0	0	5.20
1998 Toledo	AAA Det	10	10	0	0	58.2	247	50	21	19	5	1	1	5	22	0	37	3	2	3	4	.429	0	0	2.91
1999 Lakeland	A+ Det	1	1	0	0	4.2	17	2	2	2	1	0	0	0	1	0	2	0	0	0	0	.000	0	0	3.86
Toledo	AAA Det	2	2	0	0	7.2	34	9	5	5	0	1	0	0	3	0	4	1	0	0	1	.000	0	0	5.87
1990 Detroit	AL	21	21	0	0	130	562	142	79	74	17	2	5	4	48	2	66	3	0	6	9	.400	0	0	5.12
3 Min. YEARS		41	41	1	0	230.1	1008	255	131	118	35	5	7	8	79	0	148	16	4	13	11	.542	0	0	4.61

Pedro Grifol

Bats: Right **Throws:** Right **Pos:** C **Ht:** 6'1" **Wt:** 197 **Born:** 11/28/69 **Age:** 30

Year Team	Lg Org	G	AB	H	2B	3B	HR	TB	R	RBI	TBB	IBB	SO	HBP	SH	SF	SB	CS	SB%	GDP	Avg	OBP	SLG
1991 Elizabethtn	R+ Min	55	202	53	12	0	7	86	24	36	16	0	33	2	0	4	0	1	.00	6	.262	.317	.426
Orlando	AA Min	6	20	3	0	0	0	3	0	2	0	0	6	0	0	0	0	0	.00	0	.150	.150	.150
1992 Miracle	A+ Min	94	333	76	13	1	4	103	24	32	17	1	38	2	3	1	1	0	1.00	19	.228	.269	.309
Orlando	AA Min	14	40	11	2	0	0	13	2	5	2	0	9	0	0	1	0	0	.00	2	.275	.302	.325
1993 Nashville	AA Min	58	197	40	13	0	5	68	22	29	11	0	38	2	5	3	0	0	.00	6	.203	.249	.345
Portland	AAA Min	28	94	31	4	2	2	45	14	17	4	0	14	0	2	2	0	0	.00	5	.330	.350	.479
1994 Nashville	AA Min	20	55	7	0	0	1	10	4	4	10	0	7	1	0	1	0	0	.00	1	.127	.269	.182
1995 Hardware Cy	AA Min	77	226	40	9	0	3	58	23	21	23	1	33	1	1	1	1	0	1.00	8	.177	.255	.257
1996 Binghamton	AA NYM	64	202	48	3	0	7	72	22	28	13	2	29	0	0	0	0	0	.00	6	.238	.284	.356
1997 Binghamton	AA NYM	61	200	40	6	0	3	55	15	15	9	0	29	3	3	3	1	1	.50	9	.200	.242	.275
1998 Binghamton	AA NYM	116	394	88	18	0	3	115	34	57	28	4	72	1	2	5	2	2	.50	12	.223	.273	.292
1999 Norfolk	AAA NYM	59	177	46	5	0	4	63	11	27	12	1	33	0	3	4	1	1	.50	3	.260	.301	.356
9 Min. YEARS		652	2140	483	85	3	39	691	195	273	145	9	341	12	27	25	6	6	.50	77	.226	.276	.323

Kevin Grijak

Bats: Left **Throws:** Right **Pos:** OF **Ht:** 6'2" **Wt:** 215 **Born:** 8/6/70 **Age:** 29

Year Team	Lg Org	G	AB	H	2B	3B	HR	TB	R	RBI	TBB	IBB	SO	HBP	SH	SF	SB	CS	SB%	GDP	Avg	OBP	SLG
1991 Idaho Falls	R+ Atl	52	202	68	9	1	10	109	33	58	16	1	15	1	2	4	4	1	.80	5	.337	.381	.540
1992 Pulaski	R+ Atl	10	31	11	3	0	0	14	1	6	6	0	0	0	0	0	2	2	.50	1	.355	.459	.452
Macon	A Atl	47	157	41	13	0	5	69	20	21	15	2	16	3	0	2	3	0	1.00	3	.261	.333	.439
1993 Macon	A Atl	120	389	115	26	5	7	172	50	58	37	4	37	6	2	12	9	5	.64	9	.296	.356	.442
1994 Durham	A+ Atl	22	68	25	3	0	11	61	18	22	12	4	6	3	0	1	1	1	.50	1	.368	.476	.897
Greenville	AA Atl	100	348	94	19	1	11	148	40	58	20	1	40	6	0	7	2	3	.40	11	.270	.315	.425
1995 Greenville	AA Atl	21	74	32	5	0	2	43	14	11	7	0	9	2	0	2	0	1	.00	0	.432	.482	.581
Richmond	AAA Atl	106	309	92	16	5	12	154	35	56	25	4	47	4	0	4	1	3	.25	10	.298	.354	.498
1996 Richmond	AAA Atl	13	30	11	3	0	1	17	3	8	5	0	7	1	0	0	0	1	.00	1	.367	.472	.567
1997 Greenville	AA Atl	72	240	60	12	1	13	113	35	48	18	2	35	5	1	3	0	1	.00	8	.250	.312	.471
1998 Carolina	AA Pit	46	146	51	8	0	9	86	29	33	18	2	15	4	0	3	1	0	1.00	4	.349	.427	.589
Nashville	AAA Pit	67	227	65	17	0	15	127	32	40	23	0	34	3	1	1	1	4	.20	8	.286	.358	.559
1999 Albuquerque	AAA LA	119	401	127	28	1	18	211	58	80	19	2	50	3	2	3	2	6	.25	4	.317	.350	.526
9 Min. YEARS		795	2622	792	162	14	114	1324	368	499	221	22	311	41	8	42	26	28	.48	65	.302	.360	.505

Jason Grilli

Pitches: Right **Bats:** Right **Pos:** P **Ht:** 6'4" **Wt:** 185 **Born:** 11/11/76 **Age:** 23

Year Team	Lg Org	G	GS	CG	GF	IP	BFP	H	R	ER	HR	SH	SF	HB	TBB	IBB	SO	WP	Bk	W	L	Pct.	ShO	Sv	ERA
1998 Shreveport	AA SF	21	21	3	0	123.1	511	113	60	52	11	6	3	4	37	0	100	6	3	7	10	.412	0	0	3.79
Fresno	AAA SF	8	8	0	0	42	193	49	30	24	7	0	1	5	18	0	37	1	1	2	3	.400	0	0	5.14
1999 Fresno	AAA SF	19	19	1	0	100.2	461	124	69	62	22	2	3	6	39	0	76	3	0	7	5	.583	0	0	5.54
Calgary	AAA Fla	8	8	0	0	41	205	56	48	35	7	2	1	2	23	0	27	5	1	1	5	.167	0	0	7.68
2 Min. YEARS		56	56	4	0	307	1370	342	207	173	47	10	0	17	117	0	240	15	5	17	23	.425	0	0	5.07

Kevin Gryboski

Pitches: Right **Bats:** Right **Pos:** P **Ht:** 6'5" **Wt:** 220 **Born:** 11/15/73 **Age:** 26

Year Team	Lg Org	G	GS	CG	GF	IP	BFP	H	R	ER	HR	SH	SF	HB	TBB	IBB	SO	WP	Bk	W	L	Pct.	ShO	Sv	ERA
1995 Everett	A- Sea	25	0	0	14	36	156	27	18	14	2	3	1	3	18	2	25	3	0	1	5	.167	0	2	3.50
1996 Wisconsin	A Sea	32	21	3	5	138.2	630	146	90	72	9	6	12	12	62	2	100	12	0	10	5	.667	0	1	4.74
1997 Lancaster	A+ Sea	21	15	0	4	67.1	332	113	82	74	13	2	8	1	26	0	41	7	0	0	7	.000	0	0	9.89
1998 Orlando	AA Sea	2	0	0	0	5	23	8	5	5	1	0	0	0	1	0	4	2	0	0	0	.000	0	0	9.00

Year Team	Lg Org	G	GS	CG	GF	IP	BFP	H	R	ER	HR	SH	SF	HB	TBB	IBB	SO	WP	Bk	W	L	Pct.	ShO	Sv	ERA
Lancaster	A+ Sea	37	3	0	17	85	351	75	35	25	4	1	2	4	31	1	73	3	0	5	5	.500	0	8	2.65
1999 New Haven	AA Sea	47	0	0	32	62.1	267	67	27	20	5	5	2	3	20	4	41	3	0	2	5	.286	0	10	2.89
5 Min. YEARS		164	39	3	72	394.1	1759	436	257	211	32	20	19	23	158	9	284	30	0	18	27	.400	0	21	4.82

Mike Grzanich

Ht: 6' 1" **Wt:** 180 **Born:** 8/24/72 **Age:** 27

Pitches: Right **Bats:** Right **Pos:** P

Year Team	Lg Org	G	GS	CG	GF	IP	BFP	H	R	ER	HR	SH	SF	HB	TBB	IBB	SO	WP	Bk	W	L	Pct.	ShO	Sv	ERA
1992 Astros	R Hou	17	3	0	9	33.2	159	38	21	17	0	2	3	6	14	0	29	1	0	2	5	.286	0	3	4.54
1993 Auburn	A- Hou	16	14	4	1	93.1	409	106	63	50	11	3	3	3	27	0	71	7	1	5	8	.385	1	0	4.82
1994 Quad City	A Hou	23	22	3	1	142.2	598	145	55	49	5	2	1	11	43	2	101	5	0	11	7	.611	0	0	3.09
1995 Jackson	AA Hou	50	0	0	23	65.2	276	55	22	20	0	5	3	6	38	5	44	4	0	5	3	.625	0	8	2.74
1996 Jackson	AA Hou	57	0	0	19	72.1	316	60	47	32	10	4	2	8	43	2	80	6	0	5	4	.556	0	6	3.98
1997 Jackson	AA Hou	38	13	0	21	101.2	472	114	68	56	10	4	5	8	46	2	73	2	0	7	6	.538	0	12	4.96
1998 Kissimmee	A+ Hou	4	0	0	1	7.1	36	9	7	5	0	2	0	1	5	0	8	1	0	1	1	.500	0	0	6.14
New Orleans	AAA Hou	34	0	0	16	39.2	165	27	13	10	2	2	3	3	21	0	39	5	0	1	2	.333	0	5	2.27
1999 Toledo	AAA Det	14	0	0	8	21.1	109	21	24	22	4	0	3	5	25	0	17	1	0	1	0	1.000	0	1	9.28
1998 Houston	NL	1	0	0	0	1	6	1	2	2	0	0	1	0	2	0	1	0	0	0	0	.000	0	0	18.00
8 Min. YEARS		253	52	7	99	577.2	2540	575	320	261	42	24	23	51	262	11	462	32	1	38	36	.514	1	35	4.07

Mark Guerra

Ht: 6'2" **Wt:** 200 **Born:** 11/4/71 **Age:** 28

Pitches: Right **Bats:** Right **Pos:** P

Year Team	Lg Org	G	GS	CG	GF	IP	BFP	H	R	ER	HR	SH	SF	HB	TBB	IBB	SO	WP	Bk	W	L	Pct.	ShO	Sv	ERA
1994 Pittsfield	A- NYM	14	14	2	0	94	392	105	47	36	4	4	5	4	21	1	62	2	2	7	6	.538	0	0	3.45
1995 St. Lucie	A+ NYM	23	23	4	0	160	644	148	55	47	5	4	4	4	33	1	110	2	3	9	9	.500	3	0	2.64
Binghamton	AA NYM	6	5	1	0	32.2	139	35	24	21	6	1	0	0	9	1	24	0	0	2	1	.667	0	0	5.79
1996 Binghamton	AA NYM	27	20	1	3	140.1	577	143	60	55	23	5	2	2	34	3	84	1	1	7	6	.538	0	0	3.53
1997 Binghamton	AA NYM	48	7	1	17	94.2	403	96	46	34	10	3	2	1	30	1	74	2	0	4	8	.333	0	7	3.23
1998 Norfolk	AAA NYM	18	0	0	8	30.2	142	40	24	22	6	2	3	1	14	1	19	0	0	2	1	.667	0	6	6.46
Binghamton	AA NYM	30	2	0	21	41.1	171	38	17	13	5	1	3	0	11	1	30	0	0	3	3	.500	0	12	2.83
1999 Norfolk	AAA NYM	63	2	0	11	89	391	90	45	29	5	3	2	0	39	8	70	2	0	8	3	.727	0	0	2.93
6 Min. YEARS		229	73	9	60	682.2	2859	695	318	257	64	23	21	12	191	17	473	9	6	42	37	.532	3	19	3.39

Aaron Guiel

Ht: 5'10" **Wt:** 190 **Born:** 10/5/72 **Age:** 27

Bats: Left **Throws:** Right **Pos:** OF

Year Team	Lg Org	G	AB	H	2B	3B	HR	TB	R	RBI	TBB	IBB	SO	HBP	SH	SF	SB	CS	SB%	GDP	Avg	OBP	SLG
1993 Boise	A- Ana	35	104	31	6	4	2	51	24	12	26	1	21	4	2	0	3	0	1.00	1	.298	.455	.490
1994 Cedar Rapids	A Ana	127	454	122	30	1	18	208	84	82	64	2	93	6	5	3	21	7	.75	7	.269	.364	.458
1995 Lk Elsinore	A+ Ana	113	409	110	25	7	7	170	73	58	69	0	96	7	4	1	7	6	.54	7	.269	.380	.416
1996 Midland	AA Ana	129	439	118	29	7	10	191	72	48	56	0	71	10	2	1	11	7	.61	6	.269	.364	.435
1997 Midland	AA Ana	116	419	138	37	7	22	255	91	85	59	3	94	18	2	3	14	10	.58	9	.329	.431	.609
Mobile	AA SD	8	26	10	2	0	1	15	9	9	5	0	4	1	0	0	1	0	1.00	0	.385	.500	.577
1998 Padres	R SD	8	16	8	3	1	1	16	8	6	5	1	5	3	0	0	1	1	.50	0	.500	.667	1.000
Las Vegas	AAA SD	60	183	57	15	4	5	95	33	31	28	2	51	4	1	2	5	1	.83	6	.311	.410	.519
1999 Las Vegas	AAA SD	84	257	63	25	2	12	128	46	39	44	3	86	5	0	3	5	4	.56	6	.245	.362	.498
7 Min. YEARS		680	2307	657	172	33	78	1129	440	370	356	12	521	58	16	16	68	36	.65	40	.285	.391	.489

Jeff Guiel

Ht: 5'11" **Wt:** 195 **Born:** 1/12/74 **Age:** 26

Bats: Left **Throws:** Right **Pos:** OF

Year Team	Lg Org	G	AB	H	2B	3B	HR	TB	R	RBI	TBB	IBB	SO	HBP	SH	SF	SB	CS	SB%	GDP	Avg	OBP	SLG
1997 Cedar Rapids	A Ana	41	132	42	7	0	10	79	32	26	35	5	28	3	0	2	13	2	.87	0	.318	.465	.598
1998 Lk Elsinore	A+ Ana	101	315	85	24	7	16	171	64	60	83	5	87	8	0	3	19	9	.68	3	.270	.430	.543
1999 Lk Elsinore	A+ Ana	15	58	19	4	2	3	36	12	12	11	0	18	0	0	0	2	1	.67	0	.328	.435	.621
Erie	AA Ana	57	175	46	10	3	6	80	34	24	33	0	33	2	1	3	3	3	.50	3	.263	.380	.457
3 Min. YEARS		214	680	192	45	12	35	366	142	122	162	10	166	13	1	8	37	15	.71	6	.282	.425	.538

Matt Guiliano

Ht: 5'9" **Wt:** 180 **Born:** 10/7/72 **Age:** 27

Bats: Right **Throws:** Right **Pos:** SS

Year Team	Lg Org	G	AB	H	2B	3B	HR	TB	R	RBI	TBB	IBB	SO	HBP	SH	SF	SB	CS	SB%	GDP	Avg	OBP	SLG
1994 Martinsvlle	R+ Phi	58	190	42	5	0	5	62	33	16	24	0	57	7	3	2	16	3	.84	4	.221	.327	.326
1995 Piedmont	A Phi	129	451	102	22	12	4	160	67	59	51	1	114	7	9	6	6	8	.43	7	.226	.311	.355
1996 Reading	AA Phi	74	220	44	9	3	0	59	19	19	25	1	59	3	3	1	0	0	.00	4	.200	.289	.268
Clearwater	A+ Phi	55	166	37	8	2	1	52	12	14	6	0	46	6	6	3	2	3	.40	3	.223	.271	.313
1997 Reading	AA Phi	119	367	83	15	3	7	125	38	37	34	4	99	5	8	2	7	6	.54	8	.226	.299	.341
1998 Reading	AA Phi	126	439	99	15	2	12	154	47	44	45	4	102	4	6	1	2	4	.33	16	.226	.303	.351
1999 Scranton-WB	AAA Phi	71	216	41	15	0	2	62	20	24	17	0	61	2	5	2	3	2	.60	4	.190	.253	.287
6 Min. YEARS		632	2049	448	89	22	31	674	236	213	202	10	538	34	40	17	36	26	.58	46	.219	.297	.329

Mike Gulan

Bats: Right **Throws:** Right **Pos:** 3B   **Ht:** 6' 1" **Wt:** 190 **Born:** 12/18/70 **Age:** 29

Year Team	Lg Org	G	AB	H	2B	3B	HR	TB	R	RBI	TBB	IBB	SO	HBP	SH	SF	SB	CS	SB%	GDP	Avg	OBP	SLG
1992 Hamilton	A- StL	62	242	66	8	4	7	103	33	36	23	0	53	1	0	4	12	4	.75	7	.273	.333	.426
1993 Springfield	A StL	132	455	118	28	4	23	223	81	76	34	0	135	9	3	3	8	4	.67	4	.259	.321	.490
1994 St. Pete	A+ StL	120	466	113	30	2	8	171	39	56	26	2	108	2	0	6	2	8	.20	8	.242	.282	.367
1995 Arkansas	AA StL	64	242	76	16	3	12	134	47	48	11	1	52	6	0	1	4	2	.67	4	.314	.358	.554
Louisville	AAA StL	58	195	46	10	4	5	79	21	27	10	1	53	3	0	2	2	2	.50	6	.236	.281	.405
1996 Louisville	AAA StL	123	419	107	27	4	17	193	47	55	26	1	119	7	1	2	7	2	.78	10	.255	.308	.461
1997 Louisville	AAA StL	116	412	110	20	6	14	184	50	61	28	0	121	3	1	3	5	2	.71	12	.267	.316	.447
1998 Portland	AA Fla	46	160	49	16	2	5	84	24	23	10	0	40	1	0	1	3	2	.60	6	.306	.349	.525
1999 Calgary	AAA Fla	84	286	79	23	2	13	145	41	51	10	0	82	4	1	3	2	1	.67	9	.276	.307	.507
1997 St. Louis	NL	5	9	0	0	0	0	0	2	1	1	0	5	0	0	0	0	0	.00	0	.000	.100	.000
8 Min. YEARS		805	2877	764	178	31	104	1316	383	433	178	5	763	36	6	25	45	27	.63	66	.266	.314	.457

Mark Gulseth

Bats: Left **Throws:** Right **Pos:** DH   **Ht:** 6'4" **Wt:** 215 **Born:** 11/12/71 **Age:** 28

Year Team	Lg Org	G	AB	H	2B	3B	HR	TB	R	RBI	TBB	IBB	SO	HBP	SH	SF	SB	CS	SB%	GDP	Avg	OBP	SLG
1993 Everell	A- 3F	00	190	47	10	4	7	78	20	36	36	0	50	2	1	2	0	1	.00	3	.240	.360	.398
1994 Giants	R SF	7	20	5	2	0	0	7	7	2	8	0	3	0	0	0	0	1	.00	0	.250	.464	.350
Clinton	A SF	35	102	24	2	1	1	31	6	9	12	0	23	0	0	1	0	2	.00	1	.235	.313	.304
1995 San Jose	A+ SF	22	64	15	4	1	0	21	8	6	10	2	16	0	0	0	1	0	1.00	0	.234	.338	.328
Burlington	A SF	41	137	38	7	0	4	57	15	19	18	0	30	2	0	2	3	3	.50	4	.277	.365	.416
1996 Burlington	A SF	125	423	111	35	4	5	169	61	41	89	3	95	1	4	3	4	2	.67	11	.262	.390	.400
1997 San Jose	A+ SF	95	325	103	25	3	10	164	47	58	46	5	49	1	2	3	1	0	1.00	11	.317	.400	.505
1998 San Jose	A+ SF	119	467	132	38	2	9	201	72	75	50	2	67	6	1	3	2	2	.50	11	.283	.357	.430
1999 Shreveport	AA SF	62	145	33	6	0	1	42	13	17	18	0	26	0	1	2	1	0	1.00	6	.228	.309	.290
7 Min. YEARS		566	1879	508	129	11	37	770	258	262	287	12	359	12	9	16	12	11	.52	47	.270	.368	.410

Shane Gunderson

Bats: Right **Throws:** Right **Pos:** OF   **Ht:** 6'0" **Wt:** 216 **Born:** 10/16/73 **Age:** 26

Year Team	Lg Org	G	AB	H	2B	3B	HR	TB	R	RBI	TBB	IBB	SO	HBP	SH	SF	SB	CS	SB%	GDP	Avg	OBP	SLG
1995 Elizabethtn	H+ Min	37	139	43	11	2	7	79	32	30	20	0	24	2	0	1	4	0	1.00	3	.300	.401	.568
Fort Wayne	A Min	26	87	22	7	0	2	35	17	12	10	1	17	2	4	0	2	1	.67	0	.253	.343	.402
1996 Fort Myers	A+ Min	117	410	103	20	5	5	148	61	50	63	2	85	14	6	2	12	8	.60	5	.251	.368	.361
1997 New Britain	AA Min	33	117	30	7	3	2	49	17	10	19	0	31	1	4	0	7	2	.78	1	.256	.365	.419
Fort Wayne	A Min	13	45	12	1	0	0	13	3	7	3	0	3	0	1	1	1	1	.50	2	.267	.306	.289
Fort Myers	A+ Min	14	50	14	4	0	0	18	5	5	7	0	8	1	0	0	3	1	.75	2	.280	.379	.360
1998 New Britain	AA Min	23	62	10	0	0	3	19	8	14	12	0	11	2	1	1	0	0	.00	2	.161	.312	.306
Fort Myers	A+ Min	42	149	40	12	2	5	71	25	20	23	1	42	3	4	1	3	2	.60	1	.268	.375	.477
1999 New Britain	AA Min	46	154	39	11	1	3	61	15	16	7	0	37	2	2	0	1	1	.50	6	.253	.294	.396
5 Min. YEARS		351	1213	313	73	13	27	493	183	164	164	4	258	27	22	6	33	16	.67	22	.258	.357	.406

Chris Haas

Bats: Left **Throws:** Right **Pos:** 3B   **Ht:** 6'2" **Wt:** 210 **Born:** 10/15/76 **Age:** 23

Year Team	Lg Org	G	AB	H	2B	3B	HR	TB	R	RBI	TBB	IBB	SO	HBP	SH	SF	SB	CS	SB%	GDP	Avg	OBP	SLG
1995 Johnson Cy	R+ StL	67	242	65	15	3	7	107	43	50	52	0	93	1	0	0	1	3	.25	8	.269	.400	.442
1996 Peoria	A StL	124	421	101	19	1	11	155	56	65	64	3	169	7	1	3	3	2	.60	4	.240	.347	.368
1997 Peoria	A StL	36	115	36	11	0	5	62	23	22	22	1	38	3	0	2	3	0	1.00	4	.313	.430	.539
Pr William	A+ StL	100	361	86	10	2	14	142	58	54	42	2	144	4	1	2	1	1	.50	7	.238	.323	.393
1998 Arkansas	AA StL	132	445	122	27	4	20	217	75	83	73	5	129	8	0	5	1	2	.33	5	.274	.382	.488
1999 Memphis	AAA StL	114	397	91	19	2	18	168	63	73	66	3	155	2	3	5	4	4	.50	4	.229	.338	.423
5 Min. YEARS		573	1981	501	101	12	75	851	318	347	319	14	728	25	5	17	13	12	.52	32	.253	.361	.430

Steve Hacker

Bats: Right **Throws:** Right **Pos:** DH   **Ht:** 6'5" **Wt:** 230 **Born:** 9/6/74 **Age:** 25

Year Team	Lg Org	G	AB	H	2B	3B	HR	TB	R	RBI	TBB	IBB	SO	HBP	SH	SF	SB	CS	SB%	GDP	Avg	OBP	SLG
1995 Eugene	A- Atl	16	57	12	3	0	2	21	4	9	1	0	13	2	0	1	0	0	.00	1	.211	.246	.368
1996 Eugene	A- Atl	75	292	73	15	1	21	153	45	61	26	3	64	6	0	6	0	0	.00	2	.250	.318	.524
1997 Macon	A Atl	117	460	149	35	1	33	285	80	119	34	7	91	5	0	9	1	0	1.00	5	.324	.370	.620
1998 Twins	R Min	6	24	5	0	0	1	8	5	3	2	0	2	0	0	0	0	0	.00	0	.208	.269	.333
Fort Myers	A+ Min	62	251	62	11	0	11	106	29	38	17	0	40	2	0	2	0	1	.00	5	.247	.298	.422
1999 New Britain	AA Min	118	461	139	36	0	27	256	71	97	39	2	103	5	0	6	0	2	.00	13	.302	.358	.555
Salt Lake	AAA Min	8	20	3	0	0	2	9	2	3	5	1	7	1	0	0	0	1	.00	1	.150	.346	.450
5 Min. YEARS		402	1565	443	100	2	97	838	236	330	124	13	320	21	0	24	1	4	.20	31	.283	.339	.535

Jeff Hafer

Pitches: Right Bats: Right Pos: P   Ht: 6'1" Wt: 185 Born: 10/27/74 Age: 25

Year Team	Lg Org	G	GS	CG	GF	IP	BFP	H	R	ER	HR	SH	SF	HB	TBB	IBB	SO	WP	Bk	W	L	Pct.	ShO	Sv	ERA
1996 Kingsport	R+ NYM	24	0	0	14	33.2	137	29	9	8	1	1	0	1	8	1	43	7	0	0	2	.000	0	6	2.14
1997 Capital Cty	A NYM	37	2	0	18	69.1	284	59	29	23	2	3	1	2	21	3	74	10	1	6	5	.545	0	7	2.99
1998 Mets	R NYM	4	4	0	0	7.2	30	8	3	3	1	0	0	0	1	0	6	2	0	0	0	.000	0	0	3.52
St. Lucie	A+ NYM	24	0	0	11	41.2	200	63	42	37	7	1	4	2	11	1	37	3	0	3	3	.500	0	1	7.99
1999 St. Lucie	A+ NYM	36	2	0	21	67	306	74	43	24	3	3	3	2	16	4	51	3	2	4	2	.667	0	5	3.22
Binghamton	AA NYM	7	0	0	1	14.1	54	12	5	5	2	0	0	0	0	0	9	1	0	0	2	.000	0	0	3.14
4 Min. YEARS		132	8	0	65	233.2	1011	245	131	100	16	8	8	7	57	9	220	26	3	13	14	.481	0	19	3.85

Tom Hage

Bats: Left Throws: Right Pos: 1B   Ht: 6'3" Wt: 210 Born: 8/2/74 Age: 25

Year Team	Lg Org	G	AB	H	2B	3B	HR	TB	R	RBI	TBB	IBB	SO	HBP	SH	SF	SB	CS	SB%	GDP	Avg	OBP	SLG
1996 Elmira	IND —	37	129	38	3	2	0	45	10	12	3	0	5	0	1	1	0	2	.00	3	.295	.308	.349
1997 Allentown	IND —	74	302	105	17	1	4	136	44	43	27	0	23	3	0	5	2	1	.67	7	.348	.401	.450
1998 Bluefield	R+ Bal	28	107	39	8	1	10	79	26	37	15	0	9	2	0	4	1	0	1.00	4	.364	.438	.738
Frederick	A+ Bal	45	163	47	12	0	2	65	15	27	12	1	27	2	0	3	0	0	.00	1	.288	.339	.399
1999 Bowie	AA Bal	128	426	118	21	4	8	171	53	65	50	3	60	2	3	3	1	1	.50	8	.277	.353	.401
4 Min. YEARS		312	1127	347	61	8	24	496	148	184	107	4	124	9	4	16	4	4	.50	21	.308	.368	.440

Phil Haigler

Pitches: Right Bats: Right Pos: P   Ht: 6'3" Wt: 217 Born: 6/13/74 Age: 26

Year Team	Lg Org	G	GS	CG	GF	IP	BFP	H	R	ER	HR	SH	SF	HB	TBB	IBB	SO	WP	Bk	W	L	Pct.	ShO	Sv	ERA
1996 Fort Wayne	A Min	15	13	0	0	68.1	305	80	42	40	3	1	3	6	25	0	35	1	3	4	3	.571	0	0	5.27
1997 Fort Myers	A+ Min	25	25	4	0	158.1	652	172	57	50	7	3	4	2	32	0	80	2	0	11	9	.550	1	0	2.84
1998 Twins	R Min	3	1	0	0	11.2	41	9	2	2	0	0	0	0	3	0	6	0	0	0	0	.000	0	0	1.54
1999 New Britain	AA Min	19	6	0	7	52.2	252	74	53	37	6	2	3	5	20	0	18	0	0	1	4	.200	0	0	6.32
Fort Myers	A+ Min	11	9	1	2	53	228	68	27	25	3	2	0	2	10	1	24	1	0	6	3	.667	0	0	4.25
4 Min. YEARS		73	54	5	9	344	1478	403	181	154	19	8	10	15	87	1	163	4	3	22	19	.537	1	0	4.03

Dave Hajek

Bats: Right Throws: Right Pos: 2B   Ht: 5'10" Wt: 165 Born: 10/14/67 Age: 32

Year Team	Lg Org	G	AB	H	2B	3B	HR	TB	R	RBI	TBB	IBB	SO	HBP	SH	SF	SB	CS	SB%	GDP	Avg	OBP	SLG
1990 Asheville	A Hou	135	498	155	28	0	6	201	86	60	61	1	50	2	6	10	43	24	.64	16	.311	.382	.404
1991 Osceola	A+ Hou	63	232	61	9	4	0	78	35	20	23	0	30	1	4	1	8	5	.62	5	.263	.331	.336
Jackson	AA Hou	37	94	18	6	0	0	24	10	9	7	2	12	0	0	1	2	0	1.00	1	.191	.245	.255
1992 Osceola	A+ Hou	5	18	2	1	0	0	3	3	1	1	0	1	0	0	0	1	0	1.00	0	.111	.158	.167
Jackson	AA Hou	103	326	88	12	3	1	109	36	18	31	2	25	0	10	3	8	3	.73	5	.270	.331	.334
1993 Jackson	AA Hou	110	332	97	20	2	5	136	50	27	17	2	14	2	1	3	6	5	.55	10	.292	.328	.410
1994 Tucson	AAA Hou	129	484	157	29	5	7	217	71	70	29	5	23	2	5	5	12	7	.63	10	.324	.362	.448
1995 Tucson	AAA Hou	131	502	164	37	4	4	221	99	79	39	7	27	2	5	6	12	7	.63	11	.327	.373	.440
1996 Tucson	AAA Hou	121	508	161	31	5	4	214	81	64	25	5	36	1	1	4	9	6	.60	17	.317	.348	.421
1997 Toledo	AAA Det	72	253	55	14	2	4	85	27	32	21	0	18	0	2	2	0	2	.00	7	.217	.275	.336
Las Vegas	AAA SD	41	156	53	14	1	0	69	25	25	14	1	6	0	0	1	7	2	.78	7	.340	.392	.442
1998 Las Vegas	AAA SD	130	539	177	45	3	4	240	85	63	23	0	46	1	3	12	14	6	.70	13	.328	.350	.445
1999 Colo Sprngs	AAA Col	127	533	157	43	3	8	230	84	58	25	0	42	0	3	7	13	8	.62	12	.295	.322	.432
1995 Houston	NL	5	2	0	0	0	0	0	0	0	0	1	0	1	0	0	1	0	1.00	0	.000	.333	.000
1996 Houston	NL	8	10	3	1	0	0	4	3	0	2	0	0	0	0	0	0	0	.00	3	.300	.417	.400
10 Min. YEARS		1204	4475	1345	289	32	43	1827	692	526	316	25	330	11	40	55	135	75	.64	114	.301	.344	.408
2 Maj. YEARS		13	12	3	1	0	0	4	3	0	3	0	1	0	2	0	1	0	1.00	3	.250	.400	.333

Toby Hall

Bats: Right Throws: Right Pos: C   Ht: 6'3" Wt: 205 Born: 10/21/75 Age: 24

Year Team	Lg Org	G	AB	H	2B	3B	HR	TB	R	RBI	TBB	IBB	SO	HBP	SH	SF	SB	CS	SB%	GDP	Avg	OBP	SLG
1997 Hudson Val	A- TB	55	200	50	3	0	1	56	25	27	13	1	33	1	1	3	0	0	.00	3	.250	.295	.280
1998 Chston-SC	A TB	105	377	121	25	1	6	166	59	50	39	2	32	5	0	6	3	7	.30	15	.321	.386	.440
1999 St. Pete	A+ TB	56	212	63	13	1	4	90	24	36	17	0	9	2	1	4	0	2	.00	7	.297	.350	.425
Orlando	AA TB	46	173	44	7	0	9	78	20	34	4	1	10	1	1	4	1	1	.50	7	.254	.269	.451
3 Min. YEARS		262	962	278	48	2	20	390	128	147	73	4	84	9	3	16	4	10	.29	32	.289	.340	.405

Pat Hallmark

Bats: Right Throws: Right Pos: OF   Ht: 6'0" Wt: 170 Born: 12/31/73 Age: 26

Year Team	Lg Org	G	AB	H	2B	3B	HR	TB	R	RBI	TBB	IBB	SO	HBP	SH	SF	SB	CS	SB%	GDP	Avg	OBP	SLG
1995 Spokane	A- KC	56	227	69	11	0	4	92	36	25	13	0	37	2	2	2	5	3	.63	5	.304	.344	.405
1996 Lansing	A KC	118	453	127	23	5	1	163	68	53	34	2	80	3	6	1	33	9	.79	3	.280	.334	.360
1997 Lansing	A KC	88	306	87	13	6	0	112	49	39	28	0	43	7	1	5	22	5	.81	8	.284	.353	.366
Wilmington	A+ KC	27	100	30	5	0	2	41	22	11	12	0	16	3	1	2	8	3	.73	0	.300	.385	.410
1998 Wilmington	A+ KC	103	364	99	19	1	5	135	59	35	46	0	71	5	6	5	33	19	.63	6	.272	.357	.371
1999 Wichita	AA KC	75	242	69	7	2	5	95	35	24	21	0	62	5	3	2	14	7	.67	3	.285	.352	.393
5 Min. YEARS		467	1692	481	78	14	17	638	269	187	154	2	309	25	19	17	115	46	.71	25	.284	.350	.377

Garrick Haltiwanger

Bats: Right **Throws:** Left **Pos:** OF **Ht:** 6'2" **Wt:** 190 **Born:** 3/3/75 **Age:** 25

Year Team	Lg Org	G	AB	H	2B	3B	HR	TB	R	RBI	TBB	IBB	SO	HBP	SH	SF	SB	CS	SB%	GDP	Avg	OBP	SLG
1996 Pittsfield	A- NYM	60	203	52	9	2	9	92	36	37	24	3	55	4	1	2	9	4	.69	3	.256	.343	.453
1997 Capital Cty	A NYM	125	441	115	19	2	14	180	59	73	45	0	107	10	1	2	20	7	.74	4	.261	.341	.408
1998 St. Lucie	A+ NYM	108	344	64	11	1	11	110	35	42	34	0	69	7	5	3	7	6	.54	5	.186	.271	.320
1999 Binghamton	AA NYM	4	11	3	0	0	1	6	1	2	1	0	1	0	0	0	0	0	.00	0	.273	.333	.545
Norfolk	AAA NYM	6	13	0	0	0	0	0	2	0	0	0	8	0	0	0	0	0	.00	1	.000	.000	.000
St. Lucie	A+ NYM	111	423	112	18	6	10	172	67	71	31	3	77	13	0	5	20	12	.63	6	.265	.331	.407
4 Min. YEARS		414	1435	346	57	11	45	560	200	225	135	6	317	34	7	12	56	29	.66	19	.241	.319	.390

Jon Hamel

Bats: Right **Throws:** Right **Pos:** C **Ht:** 5'11" **Wt:** 195 **Born:** 1/11/77 **Age:** 23

Year Team	Lg Org	G	AB	H	2B	3B	HR	TB	R	RBI	TBB	IBB	SO	HBP	SH	SF	SB	CS	SB%	GDP	Avg	OBP	SLG
1999 Padres	R SD	27	80	14	2	0	0	16	9	7	18	0	23	7	0	2	2	2	.50	0	.175	.364	.200
Las Vegas	AAA SD	1	2	0	0	0	0	0	0	0	1	0	1	0	0	0	0	0	.00	0	.000	.500	.000
1 Min. YEARS		28	82	14	2	0	0	16	9	7	19	0	24	8	0	2	2	2	.50	0	.171	.369	.195

Bob Hamelin

Bats: Left **Throws:** Left **Pos:** DH **Ht:** 6'0" **Wt:** 235 **Born:** 11/29/67 **Age:** 32

Year Team	Lg Org	G	AB	H	2B	3B	HR	TB	R	RBI	TBB	IBB	SO	HBP	SH	SF	SB	CS	SB%	GDP	Avg	OBP	SLG
1988 Eugene	A- KC	70	235	70	19	1	17	142	42	61	56	4	67	5	0	5	9	1	.90	7	.298	.431	.604
1989 Memphis	AA KC	68	211	65	12	5	16	135	45	47	52	7	52	5	0	1	3	6	.33	2	.308	.454	.640
1990 Omaha	AAA KC	90	271	63	11	2	8	102	31	30	62	5	78	4	1	2	2	2	.50	1	.232	.381	.376
1991 Omaha	AAA KC	37	127	24	3	1	4	41	13	19	16	0	32	0	1	4	0	0	.00	4	.189	.272	.323
1992 Baseball Cy	A+ KC	11	44	12	0	1	1	17	7	6	2	0	11	0	0	0	0	0	.00	0	.273	.304	.386
Memphis	AA KC	35	120	40	8	0	6	66	23	22	26	2	17	0	0	0	0	1	.00	4	.333	.452	.550
Omaha	AAA KC	27	95	19	3	1	5	39	9	15	14	0	15	0	0	3	0	0	.00	1	.200	.295	.411
1993 Omaha	AAA KC	137	479	124	19	3	29	236	77	84	82	9	94	5	0	9	8	3	.73	8	.259	.367	.493
1995 Omaha	AAA KC	36	119	35	12	0	10	77	25	32	31	5	34	0	0	2	2	3	.40	1	.294	.434	.647
1996 Omaha	AAA KC	4	16	5	1	1	0	8	4	0	1	0	4	0	0	0	1	0	1.00	0	.313	.353	.500
1997 Toledo	AAA Det	27	91	22	7	0	6	47	14	24	27	2	24	0	0	0	0	0	.00	1	.242	.415	.516
1999 Toledo	AAA Det	46	149	33	9	0	5	57	20	20	24	2	29	3	0	2	4	1	.80	3	.221	.337	.383
1993 Kansas City	AL	16	49	11	3	0	2	20	2	5	6	0	15	0	0	0	0	0	.00	2	.224	.309	.408
1994 Kansas City	AL	101	312	88	25	1	24	187	64	65	56	3	62	1	0	5	4	3	.57	4	.282	.388	.599
1995 Kansas City	AL	72	208	35	7	1	7	65	20	25	26	1	56	6	0	1	0	1	.00	6	.168	.278	.313
1996 Kansas City	AL	89	239	61	14	1	9	104	31	40	54	2	58	2	0	4	5	2	.71	7	.255	.391	.435
1997 Detroit	AL	110	318	86	15	0	18	155	47	52	48	3	72	1	0	2	2	1	.67	8	.270	.366	.487
1998 Milwaukee	NL	109	146	32	6	0	7	59	15	22	16	1	30	1	1	3	0	1	.00	7	.219	.295	.404
10 Min. YEARS		588	1957	512	104	15	107	967	310	360	393	36	457	22	2	31	29	17	.63	30	.262	.386	.494
6 Maj. YEARS		497	1272	313	70	3	67	590	179	209	206	10	293	11	1	15	11	8	.58	34	.246	.352	.464

Jimmy Hamilton

Pitches: Left **Bats:** Left **Pos:** P **Ht:** 6'3" **Wt:** 190 **Born:** 8/1/75 **Age:** 24

Year Team	Lg Org	G	GS	CG	GF	IP	BFP	H	R	ER	HR	SH	SF	HB	TBB	IBB	SO	WP	Bk	W	L	Pct.	ShO	Sv	ERA
1996 Burlington	R+ Cle	10	10	0	0	45	193	45	22	20	7	1	2	3	16	0	50	8	0	1	3	.250	0	0	4.00
1997 Columbus	A Cle	22	22	0	0	123	547	123	68	61	10	3	2	0	66	0	137	11	0	5	7	.417	0	0	4.46
1998 Kinston	A+ Cle	44	0	0	15	75.1	305	61	25	23	5	8	3	4	21	5	83	4	0	6	4	.400	0	4	2.75
1999 Akron	AA Cle	25	0	0	10	31.1	134	19	14	13	1	1	1	1	24	2	27	4	0	0	2	.000	0	2	3.73
Buffalo	AAA Cle	26	0	0	4	24.1	122	24	22	14	3	1	3	1	27	0	25	1	0	1	2	.333	0	0	5.18
Rochester	AAA Bal	3	0	0	0	2	11	1	3	3	0	0	1	0	4	0	2	0	0	0	0	.000	0	0	13.50
4 Min. YEARS		130	32	0	29	301	1312	273	154	134	26	14	12	9	158	7	324	28	0	11	20	.355	0	6	4.01

Ryan Hancock

Pitches: Right **Bats:** Right **Pos:** P **Ht:** 6'2" **Wt:** 220 **Born:** 11/11/71 **Age:** 28

Year Team	Lg Org	G	GS	CG	GF	IP	BFP	H	R	ER	HR	SH	SF	HB	TBB	IBB	SO	WP	Bk	W	L	Pct.	ShO	Sv	ERA
1993 Boise	A- Ana	3	3	0	0	16.1	69	14	9	6	1	1	0	0	8	1	18	0	0	1	0	1.000	0	0	3.31
1994 Lk Elsinore	A+ Ana	18	18	3	0	116.1	494	113	62	49	10	1	5	5	36	1	95	2	5	9	6	.600	1	0	3.79
Midland	AA Ana	8	8	0	0	48	219	63	34	31	1	1	1	6	11	0	35	0	2	3	4	.429	0	0	5.81
1995 Midland	AA Ana	28	28	5	0	175.2	764	222	107	89	17	5	4	8	45	1	79	7	3	12	9	.571	1	0	4.56
1996 Vancouver	AAA Ana	19	11	1	1	80.1	347	69	38	33	7	7	0	5	38	0	65	1	1	4	6	.400	0	0	3.70
1997 Vancouver	AAA Ana	39	2	0	18	74.1	330	72	37	30	4	2	1	3	36	1	60	1	1	3	3	.500	0	2	3.63
Las Vegas	AAA SD	4	0	0	1	5	25	9	7	7	1	0	1	0	4	0	3	0	0	0	0	.000	0	0	12.60
1999 Zion	IND —	13	4	0	2	29.1	149	45	35	27	2	1	2	2	15	0	18	1	0	2	2	.500	0	1	8.28
Erie	AA Ana	8	0	0	3	13.2	63	23	8	8	2	0	1	0	2	0	6	1	0	0	1	.000	0	1	5.27
1996 California	AL	11	4	0	4	27.2	130	34	23	23	2	0	2	1	17	1	19	2	0	4	1	.800	0	0	7.48
6 Min. YEARS		140	74	9	25	559	2460	630	337	280	45	18	15	29	195	4	379	13	12	34	31	.523	2	3	4.51

Marcus Hanel

Bats: Right **Throws:** Right **Pos:** C **Ht:** 6'4" **Wt:** 205 **Born:** 10/19/71 **Age:** 28

Year Team	Lg Org	G	AB	H	2B	3B	HR	TB	R	RBI	TBB	IBB	SO	HBP	SH	SF	SB	CS	SB%	GDP	Avg	OBP	SLG
1989 Pirates	R Pit	28	78	18	3	1	0	23	11	8	6	0	18	0	4	0	2	1	.67	2	.231	.286	.295

116

Year Team	Lg Org	G	AB	H	2B	3B	HR	TB	R	RBI	TBB	IBB	SO	HBP	SH	SF	SB	CS	SB%	GDP	Avg	OBP	SLG
								BATTING										**BASERUNNING**				**PERCENTAGES**		
1990 Welland	A- Pit	40	98	15	2	0	0	17	5	8	5	2	26	1	0	0	1	2	.33	2	.153	.202	.173
1991 Augusta	A Pit	104	364	60	10	1	1	75	33	29	17	1	88	9	2	5	9	3	.75	8	.165	.218	.206
1992 Salem	A+ Pit	75	231	43	8	0	3	60	12	17	11	0	53	2	6	1	4	0	1.00	6	.186	.229	.260
1993 Salem	A+ Pit	69	195	36	6	2	2	52	18	16	18	2	65	4	9	2	5	3	.63	2	.185	.265	.267
1994 Salem	A+ Pit	87	286	70	9	1	5	96	36	27	14	0	54	6	5	3	3	2	.60	5	.245	.291	.336
1995 Carolina	AA Pit	21	60	11	1	0	0	12	1	3	4	0	18	1	1	1	0	1	.00	2	.183	.242	.200
Lynchburg	A+ Pit	40	135	25	4	1	3	40	14	8	4	0	33	1	2	0	0	1	.00	1	.185	.214	.296
Calgary	AAA Pit	2	8	1	0	0	0	1	1	0	0	0	1	0	0	0	0	0	.00	0	.125	.125	.125
1996 Carolina	AA Pit	101	332	59	19	1	5	95	22	36	16	4	57	7	3	4	2	2	.50	9	.178	.228	.286
1997 Carolina	AA Pit	56	173	41	5	0	2	52	15	12	9	3	39	2	3	0	0	0	.00	5	.237	.283	.301
1998 Richmond	AAA Atl	29	85	18	3	0	0	21	9	7	11	2	23	0	0	1	0	0	.00	0	.212	.299	.247
1999 Tucson	AAA Ari	6	15	1	0	0	0	1	0	0	4	0	2	0	0	0	0	0	.00	0	.067	.263	.067
11 Min. YEARS		658	2060	398	70	7	21	545	178	171	119	14	477	33	35	17	26	15	.63	42	.193	.247	.265

Todd Haney

Bats: Right **Throws:** Right **Pos:** 2B **Ht:** 5' 9" **Wt:** 165 **Born:** 7/30/65 **Age:** 34

Year Team	Lg Org	G	AB	H	2B	3B	HR	TB	R	RBI	TBB	IBB	SO	HBP	SH	SF	SB	CS	SB%	GDP	Avg	OBP	SLG
								BATTING										**BASERUNNING**				**PERCENTAGES**		
1987 Bellingham	A- Sea	66	252	64	11	2	5	94	57	27	44	0	33	2	1	2	18	10	.64	1	.254	.367	.373
1988 Wausau	A Sea	132	452	127	23	2	7	175	66	52	56	0	54	7	8	2	35	10	.78	7	.281	.368	.387
1989 San Berndno	A+ Sea	25	107	27	5	0	0	32	10	7	7	0	14	0	0	1	2	3	.40	2	.252	.296	.299
Williamsprt	AA Sea	115	401	108	20	4	2	142	59	31	49	2	43	5	7	3	13	8	.62	7	.269	.354	.354
1990 Williamsprt	AA Sea	1	2	1	1	0	0	2	0	0	1	0	0	0	0	0	0	0	.00	1	.500	.667	1.000
Calgary	AAA Sea	108	419	142	15	6	1	172	81	36	37	1	38	4	6	0	16	11	.59	11	.339	.398	.411
1991 Indianapols	AAA Mon	132	510	159	32	3	2	203	68	39	47	3	49	9	7	4	11	10	.52	7	.312	.377	.398
1992 Indianapols	AAA Mon	57	200	53	14	0	6	85	30	33	37	0	34	1	3	2	1	0	1.00	2	.265	.379	.425
1993 Ottawa	AAA Mon	136	506	147	30	4	3	194	69	46	36	1	56	3	5	2	11	8	.58	15	.291	.340	.383
1994 Iowa	AAA ChC	83	305	89	22	1	3	122	48	35	28	0	29	8	3	2	9	6	.60	8	.292	.364	.400
1995 Iowa	AAA ChC	90	326	102	20	2	4	138	38	30	28	0	21	6	4	2	2	2	.50	17	.313	.376	.423
1996 Iowa	AAA ChC	66	240	59	13	0	2	78	20	19	19	0	24	0	6	2	3	1	.75	6	.246	.299	.325
1997 Tacoma	AAA Sea	4	17	6	4	0	0	10	3	2	2	0	2	0	0	0	0	0	.00	0	.353	.421	.588
New Orleans	AAA Hou	115	454	128	25	0	2	159	63	63	43	0	50	3	10	7	5	2	.71	10	.282	.343	.350
1998 St. Lucie	A+ NYM	1	4	1	0	0	0	1	1	0	0	0	0	0	0	0	0	0	.00	0	.250	.250	.250
Norfolk	AAA NYM	117	440	152	33	4	3	202	84	51	55	1	44	5	5	1	11	2	.85	13	.345	.423	.459
1999 Norfolk	AAA NYM	122	447	139	25	6	5	191	82	48	73	1	43	3	0	6	7	9	.44	10	.311	.406	.427
1992 Montreal	NL	7	10	3	1	0	0	4	0	1	0	0	1	0	0	0	0	0	.00	1	.300	.300	.400
1994 Chicago	NL	17	37	6	0	0	1	9	6	2	3	0	3	1	1	1	2	1	.67	0	.162	.238	.243
1995 Chicago	NL	25	73	30	8	0	2	44	11	6	7	0	11	0	1	0	0	0	.00	0	.411	.463	.603
1996 Chicago	NL	49	82	11	1	0	0	12	11	3	7	0	15	0	2	1	1	0	1.00	1	.134	.200	.146
1998 New York	NL	3	3	0	0	0	0	0	0	0	1	0	0	0	0	0	0	0	.00	0	.000	.250	.000
13 Min. YEARS		1370	5082	1504	293	34	45	2000	779	519	562	9	534	56	65	36	144	82	.64	117	.296	.370	.394
5 Maj. YEARS		101	205	50	10	0	3	69	28	12	18	0	29	1	5	2	3	1	.75	2	.244	.305	.337

Erik Hanson

Pitches: Right **Bats:** Right **Pos:** P **Ht:** 6' 6" **Wt:** 215 **Born:** 5/18/65 **Age:** 35

Year Team	Lg Org	G	GS	CG	GF	IP	BFP	H	R	ER	HR	SH	SF	HB	TBB	IBB	SO	WP	Bk	W	L	Pct.	ShO	Sv	ERA
				HOW MUCH HE PITCHED							**WHAT HE GAVE UP**											**THE RESULTS**			
1986 Chattanooga	AA Sea	3	2	0	1	9.1	43	10	4	4	1	0	0	2	4	1	11	1	1	0	0	.000	0	0	3.86
1987 Chattanooga	AA Sea	21	21	1	0	131.1	538	102	56	38	10	1	2	3	43	0	131	11	1	8	10	.444	0	0	2.60
Calgary	AAA Sea	8	7	0	0	47.1	201	38	23	19	4	2	2	2	21	0	43	2	0	1	3	.250	0	0	3.61
1988 Calgary	AAA Sea	27	26	2	1	161.2	691	167	92	76	9	2	5	0	57	0	154	10	4	12	7	.632	1	0	4.23
1989 Calgary	AAA Sea	8	8	1	0	38	175	51	30	29	1	1	1	2	11	0	37	4	0	4	2	.667	0	0	6.87
1991 Calgary	AAA Sea	1	1	0	0	6	21	1	1	1	0	1	0	0	2	0	5	1	0	0	0	.000	0	0	1.50
1997 Dunedin	A+ Tor	2	2	0	0	7	28	7	5	1	1	0	0	0	1	0	5	0	0	0	0	.000	0	0	1.29
1998 Dunedin	A+ Tor	1	1	0	0	4	18	4	1	1	0	0	0	0	2	0	5	0	0	0	0	.000	0	0	2.25
Vancouver	AAA Ana	14	14	2	0	82	353	82	43	41	7	4	2	3	36	0	60	6	0	5	5	.500	1	0	4.50
1999 Calgary	AAA Fla	10	9	0	0	47.2	229	68	43	40	4	3	1	2	26	0	42	1	0	1	6	.143	0	0	7.55
Omaha	AAA KC	14	10	0	3	60.2	255	58	32	31	11	3	2	3	22	0	43	5	1	4	3	.571	0	0	4.60
1988 Seattle	AL	6	6	0	0	41.2	168	35	17	15	4	3	0	1	12	1	36	2	2	2	3	.400	0	0	3.24
1989 Seattle	AL	17	17	1	0	113.1	466	103	44	40	7	4	1	5	32	1	75	3	0	9	5	.643	0	0	3.18
1990 Seattle	AL	33	33	5	0	236	964	205	88	85	15	5	6	2	68	6	211	10	1	18	9	.667	1	0	3.24
1991 Seattle	AL	27	27	2	0	174.2	744	182	82	74	16	2	8	2	56	2	143	14	1	8	8	.500	1	0	3.81
1992 Seattle	AL	31	30	6	0	186.2	809	209	110	100	14	8	9	7	57	1	112	6	0	8	17	.320	1	0	4.82
1993 Seattle	AL	31	30	7	0	215	898	215	91	83	17	10	4	5	60	6	163	8	0	11	12	.478	0	0	3.47
1994 Cincinnati	NL	22	21	0	1	122.2	519	137	60	56	10	5	4	3	23	3	101	8	1	5	5	.500	0	0	4.11
1995 Boston	AL	29	29	1	0	186.2	800	187	94	88	17	6	8	1	59	0	139	5	0	15	5	.750	1	0	4.24
1996 Toronto	AL	35	35	4	0	214.2	955	243	143	129	26	4	5	2	102	2	156	13	0	13	17	.433	1	0	5.41
1997 Toronto	AL	3	2	0	1	15	65	16	13	13	3	0	0	0	6	0	18	1	0	0	0	.000	0	0	7.80
1998 Toronto	AL	11	8	0	3	49	243	73	34	34	10	3	0	1	29	1	21	1	1	0	3	.000	0	0	6.24
8 Min. YEARS		109	101	6	5	595	2552	588	330	281	48	17	15	17	225	1	536	41	7	35	36	.493	2	0	4.25
11 Maj. YEARS		245	238	26	5	1555.1	6630	1604	776	717	139	50	45	29	504	23	1175	71	6	89	84	.514	5	0	4.15

Mike Hardge

Bats: Right **Throws:** Right **Pos:** OF **Ht:** 5'11" **Wt:** 183 **Born:** 1/27/72 **Age:** 28

Year Team	Lg Org	G	AB	H	2B	3B	HR	TB	R	RBI	TBB	IBB	SO	HBP	SH	SF	SB	CS	SB%	GDP	Avg	OBP	SLG
								BATTING										**BASERUNNING**				**PERCENTAGES**		
1990 Expos	R Mon	53	176	39	5	0	1	47	33	13	15	0	43	2	0	2	5	2	.71	1	.222	.287	.267
1991 Expos	R Mon	60	237	60	17	3	3	92	44	30	23	0	41	2	0	4	20	7	.74	3	.253	.320	.388

BATTING

Year Team	Lg Org	G	AB	H	2B	3B	HR	TB	R	RBI	TBB	IBB	SO	HBP	SH	SF	SB	CS	SB%	GDP	Avg	OBP	SLG
1992 Rockford	A Mon	127	448	97	21	2	12	158	63	49	47	0	141	4	3	4	44	13	.77	7	.217	.294	.353
Wst Plm Bch	A+ Mon	4	15	5	1	0	0	6	3	0	2	0	5	0	0	0	2	0	1.00	0	.333	.412	.400
1993 Wst Plm Bch	A+ Mon	27	92	21	2	1	1	28	14	12	14	0	16	0	4	3	5	6	.45	1	.228	.321	.304
Harrisburg	AA Mon	99	386	94	14	10	6	146	70	35	37	0	97	3	3	1	27	8	.77	3	.244	.314	.378
1994 Harrisburg	AA Mon	121	453	101	10	2	6	133	60	42	56	0	109	0	8	1	30	18	.63	8	.223	.308	.294
1995 Pawtucket	AAA Bos	29	91	23	3	0	1	29	9	5	8	0	16	0	0	0	3	3	.25	2	.253	.313	.319
Trenton	AA Bos	40	127	31	4	1	0	37	18	12	11	0	26	0	1	2	3	4	.43	7	.244	.300	.291
1996 Lubbock	IND —	98	393	119	24	7	8	181	77	64	35	2	57	4	4	1	26	5	.84	5	.303	.365	.461
1997 Lubbock	IND —	87	361	122	27	4	8	181	75	54	26	0	43	3	3	4	22	11	.67	12	.338	.383	.501
1998 Arkansas	AA StL	106	355	104	24	2	8	156	60	66	43	2	78	3	1	5	8	8	.50	7	.293	.369	.439
1999 Arkansas	AA StL	54	141	32	3	1	5	52	15	11	25	1	43	4	0	0	3	3	.50	2	.227	.359	.369
10 Min. YEARS		905	3275	848	155	33	59	1246	541	393	342	5	715	24	28	25	196	88	.69	58	.259	.331	.380

Jason Hardtke

Bats: Both **Throws:** Right **Pos:** 2B-3B **Ht:** 5'10" **Wt:** 175 **Born:** 9/15/71 **Age:** 28

BATTING

Year Team	Lg Org	G	AB	H	2B	3B	HR	TB	R	RBI	TBB	IBB	SO	HBP	SH	SF	SB	CS	SB%	GDP	Avg	OBP	SLG
1990 Burlington	R+ Cle	39	142	38	7	0	4	57	18	16	23	0	19	2	0	0	11	1	.92	3	.268	.377	.401
1991 Columbus	A Cle	139	534	155	26	8	12	233	104	81	75	5	48	7	6	6	22	4	.85	6	.290	.381	.436
1992 Kinston	A+ Cle	6	19	4	0	0	0	4	3	1	4	0	4	0	0	0	0	0	.00	0	.211	.348	.211
Waterloo	A SD	110	411	125	27	4	8	184	75	47	38	3	33	5	1	5	9	7	.56	9	.304	.366	.448
High Desert	A+ SD	10	41	11	1	0	2	18	9	8	4	0	4	1	0	1	1	1	.50	1	.268	.340	.439
1993 Rancho Cuca	A+ SD	130	523	167	38	7	11	252	98	85	61	2	54	2	2	6	7	8	.47	12	.319	.389	.482
1994 Wichita	AA SD	75	255	60	15	1	5	92	26	29	21	1	44	0	2	4	1	2	.33	4	.235	.289	.361
Rancho Cuca	A+ SD	4	13	4	0	0	0	4	2	0	3	0	2	0	0	0	0	1	.00	0	.308	.438	.308
1995 Norfolk	AAA NYM	4	7	2	1	0	0	3	1	0	2	0	0	0	0	0	0	1	.00	0	.286	.444	.429
Binghamton	AA NYM	121	455	130	42	4	4	192	65	52	66	1	58	4	2	9	6	8	.43	7	.286	.375	.422
1996 Binghamton	AA NYM	35	137	36	11	0	3	56	23	16	16	1	16	0	1	0	0	1	.00	3	.263	.340	.409
Norfolk	AAA NYM	71	257	77	17	2	9	125	49	35	29	1	29	0	4	2	4	6	.40	4	.300	.368	.486
1997 Norfolk	AAA NYM	97	388	107	23	3	11	169	46	45	40	1	54	0	4	1	3	6	.33	9	.276	.343	.436
Binghamton	AA NYM	6	26	10	2	0	1	15	3	4	2	0	2	0	0	0	0	0	.00	0	.385	.429	.577
1998 Iowa	AAA ChC	91	333	96	20	1	11	151	67	53	35	1	46	4	1	2	7	7	.50	7	.288	.361	.453
1999 Indianapols	AAA Cin	101	416	137	37	2	12	214	74	61	35	1	43	2	1	4	7	4	.64	7	.329	.381	.514
1996 New York	NL	19	57	11	5	0	0	16	3	6	2	0	12	1	0	0	0	0	.00	1	.193	.233	.281
1997 New York	NL	30	56	15	2	0	2	23	9	8	4	1	6	1	0	1	1	1	.50	3	.268	.323	.411
1998 Chicago	NL	18	21	5	0	0	0	5	2	2	2	0	6	0	0	0	0	0	.00	0	.238	.304	.238
10 Min. YEARS		1039	3957	1159	267	32	93	1769	663	533	454	17	456	27	24	40	79	57	.58	72	.293	.366	.447
3 Maj. YEARS		67	134	31	7	0	2	44	14	16	8	1	24	2	0	1	1	1	.50	4	.231	.283	.328

Brett Haring

Pitches: Left **Bats:** Right **Pos:** P **Ht:** 5'11" **Wt:** 180 **Born:** 2/7/75 **Age:** 25

		HOW MUCH HE PITCHED						WHAT HE GAVE UP												THE RESULTS				
Year Team	Lg Org	G	GS	CG	GF	IP	BFP	H	R	ER	HR	SH	SF	HB	TBB	IBB	SO	WP	Bk	W	L	Pct.	ShO	Sv	ERA
1997 Billings	R+ Cin	14	0	0	4	23.1	106	30	14	12	2	0	0	2	9	0	16	1	0	0	2	.000	0	0	4.63
1998 Chstn-WV	A Cin	38	13	2	15	108.1	457	123	48	40	6	8	3	2	26	1	91	5	0	2	9	.182	0	4	3.32
1999 Rockford	A Cin	25	18	3	1	124	516	113	53	46	7	4	3	4	42	0	94	5	0	10	3	.769	1	2	3.34
Chattanooga	AA Cin	7	4	0	0	36.1	159	46	18	15	1	3	0	0	12	0	15	2	0	2	1	.667	0	0	3.72
3 Min. YEARS		84	35	5	20	292	1238	312	133	113	16	15	6	8	89	1	216	13	0	14	15	.483	3	5	3.48

Travis Harper

Pitches: Right **Bats:** Right **Pos:** P **Ht:** 6'4" **Wt:** 190 **Born:** 5/21/76 **Age:** 24

		HOW MUCH HE PITCHED						WHAT HE GAVE UP												THE RESULTS				
Year Team	Lg Org	G	GS	CG	GF	IP	BFP	H	R	ER	HR	SH	SF	HB	TBB	IBB	SO	WP	Bk	W	L	Pct.	ShO	Sv	ERA
1998 Hudson Val	A- TB	13	10	0	1	56.1	228	38	14	12	2	1	1	8	20	0	81	4	0	6	2	.750	0	0	1.92
1999 St. Pete	A+ TB	14	14	0	0	81.1	347	82	36	31	4	1	4	10	23	0	79	8	0	5	4	.556	0	0	3.43
Orlando	AA TB	14	14	1	0	72	319	73	45	43	10	0	5	10	26	0	68	7	0	6	3	.667	1	0	5.38
2 Min. YEARS		41	38	1	1	209.2	894	193	95	86	16	2	10	28	69	0	228	19	0	17	9	.654	1	0	3.69

Denny Harriger

Pitches: Right **Bats:** Right **Pos:** P **Ht:** 5'11" **Wt:** 185 **Born:** 7/21/69 **Age:** 30

		HOW MUCH HE PITCHED						WHAT HE GAVE UP												THE RESULTS				
Year Team	Lg Org	G	GS	CG	GF	IP	BFP	H	R	ER	HR	SH	SF	HB	TBB	IBB	SO	WP	Bk	W	L	Pct.	ShO	Sv	ERA
1987 Kingsport	R+ NYM	12	7	0	2	43.2	198	43	31	21	3	4	1	4	22	0	24	1	0	2	5	.286	0	0	4.33
1988 Kingsport	R+ NYM	13	13	2	0	92.1	375	83	35	22	3	1	1	0	24	1	59	2	1	7	2	.778	1	0	2.14
1989 Pittsfield	A- NYM	3	3	1	0	21	84	20	4	4	0	2	0	1	0	0	17	0	0	2	0	1.000	1	0	1.71
St. Lucie	A+ NYM	11	11	0	0	67.2	284	72	33	24	6	0	0	2	17	0	17	1	0	5	3	.625	0	0	3.19
1990 St. Lucie	A+ NYM	27	7	1	9	71.2	293	73	36	28	0	0	0	1	20	0	47	2	1	5	3	.625	0	2	3.52
1991 Columbia	A NYM	2	2	1	0	11	37	5	0	0	0	1	0	0	2	0	13	0	0	2	0	1.000	1	0	0.00
St. Lucie	A+ NYM	14	11	2	1	71.1	286	67	20	18	2	4	2	1	12	0	37	1	0	6	1	.857	2	0	2.27
1992 Binghamton	AA NYM	11	0	0	5	21.1	88	22	11	9	2	2	0	1	7	0	8	0	0	2	2	.500	0	0	3.80
St. Lucie	A+ NYM	27	10	0	9	88.1	372	89	30	22	1	6	0	3	14	1	65	5	1	7	3	.700	0	3	2.24
1993 Binghamton	AA NYM	35	24	4	0	170.2	716	174	69	56	8	6	2	7	40	0	89	9	1	13	10	.565	1	0	2.95
1994 Las Vegas	AAA SD	30	25	3	0	157.1	720	216	122	104	16	6	5	4	44	0	87	3	1	6	11	.353	0	0	5.95
1995 Las Vegas	AAA SD	29	28	1	0	177	776	187	94	80	12	6	5	4	60	2	97	4	1	9	9	.500	2	0	4.07
1996 Las Vegas	AAA SD	26	25	1	0	164.1	711	183	91	77	12	3	8	7	51	1	102	4	1	10	7	.588	0	0	4.22
1997 Toledo	AAA Det	27	27	2	0	167	717	159	87	74	19	5	1	5	63	2	109	3	0	11	8	.579	1	0	3.99
1998 Toledo	AAA Det	22	22	1	0	142.1	603	151	78	72	15	4	0	2	48	0	87	2	0	5	12	.294	1	0	4.55

118

Year Team	Lg Org	G	GS	CG	GF	IP	BFP	H	R	ER	HR	SH	SF	HB	TBB	IBB	SO	WP	Bk	W	L	Pct.	ShO	Sv	ERA
1999 Indianapols	AAA Cin	27	27	1	0	172	717	183	82	78	15	2	5	4	36	2	110	6	0	14	6	.700	0	0	4.08
1998 Detroit	AL	4	2	0	2	12	61	17	12	9	1	1	0	0	8	2	3	0	0	0	3	.000	0	0	6.75
13 Min. YEARS		316	242	29	30	1639	6977	1727	823	689	114	52	35	46	460	9	968	43	7	106	82	.564	12	6	3.78

Mark Harriger

Pitches: Right Bats: Right Pos: P Ht: 6'2" Wt: 196 Born: 4/29/75 Age: 25

Year Team	Lg Org	G	GS	CG	GF	IP	BFP	H	R	ER	HR	SH	SF	HB	TBB	IBB	SO	WP	Bk	W	L	Pct.	ShO	Sv	ERA
1996 Boise	A- Ana	7	0	0	1	4.1	26	9	5	4	1	1	0	0	3	0	3	1	1	0	0	.000	0	0	8.31
1997 Cedar Rapds	A Ana	12	11	1	1	50.2	251	70	50	44	4	3	3	1	33	1	50	10	4	1	6	.143	1	0	7.82
Boise	A- Ana	13	12	0	0	51	243	51	52	45	2	1	5	1	36	1	42	15	0	3	4	.429	0	0	7.94
1998 Cedar Rapds	A Ana	16	16	3	0	117	472	86	37	29	3	3	2	4	38	0	105	14	1	8	4	.667	1	0	2.23
Lk Elsinore	A+ Ana	13	12	3	0	81.1	350	86	43	37	5	3	2	2	23	0	68	6	0	5	5	.500	1	0	4.09
1999 Erie	AA Ana	6	6	0	0	30.2	135	31	16	16	4	0	0	0	15	0	13	4	0	2	1	.667	0	0	4.70
4 Min. YEARS		67	57	7	2	335	1477	333	203	175	19	11	12	8	148	2	281	50	6	19	20	.487	3	0	4.70

Brian Harris

Bats: Both Throws: Right Pos: 2B Ht: 5'10" Wt: 180 Born: 4/28/75 Age: 25

Year Team	Lg Org	G	AB	H	2B	3B	HR	TB	R	RBI	TBB	IBB	SO	HBP	SH	SF	SB	CS	SB%	GDP	Avg	OBP	SLG
1997 Batavia	A- Phi	51	148	46	7	1	0	55	31	19	31	0	27	4	3	1	11	6	.65	1	.311	.440	.372
1998 Clearwater	A+ Phi	118	437	121	17	6	5	165	55	65	47	2	56	9	6	9	20	13	.61	13	.277	.353	.378
Reading	AA Phi	11	40	10	0	1	0	12	5	4	5	0	7	0	0	1	0	1	.00	0	.250	.326	.300
1999 Reading	AA Phi	119	380	84	13	3	5	118	42	41	46	1	58	1	7	6	9	5	.64	10	.221	.303	.311
3 Min. YEARS		299	1005	261	37	11	10	350	133	129	129	3	148	14	16	17	40	25	.62	24	.260	.347	.348

D.J. Harris

Pitches: Right Bats: Right Pos: P Ht: 5'10" Wt: 190 Born: 4/11/71 Age: 29

Year Team	Lg Org	G	GS	CG	GF	IP	BFP	H	R	ER	HR	SH	SF	HB	TBB	IBB	SO	WP	Bk	W	L	Pct.	ShO	Sv	ERA
1993 Pocatello	R+ —	5	0	0	4	7	40	14	10	5	0	0	0	0	3	0	10	7	0	0	0	.000	0	1	6.43
1994 Winnipeg	IND —	9	0	0	4	16.1	81	22	15	14	1	0	3	2	11	0	10	2	1	0	0	.000	0	1	7.71
1995 Dunedin	A+ Tor	42	0	0	16	67	294	54	29	24	6	3	3	6	41	1	56	2	0	3	3	.500	0	2	3.22
1996 Dunedin	A+ Tor	35	0	0	19	43.1	203	49	30	25	3	3	3	4	19	1	31	3	0	4	3	.571	0	6	5.19
1997 Dunedin	A+ Tor	42	3	0	24	78.1	344	64	41	28	5	1	2	4	45	4	66	7	4	8	4	.667	0	5	3.22
Knoxville	AA Tor	2	2	0	0	11	43	6	2	2	1	0	0	0	6	0	8	1	0	1	1	.500	0	0	1.64
1998 Knoxville	AA Tor	22	0	0	8	48.2	203	52	17	15	1	1	1	0	24	1	31	3	0	4	2	.667	0	2	2.77
Syracuse	AAA Tor	25	1	0	11	40.2	172	40	20	18	6	1	1	1	21	1	25	2	0	1	4	.200	0	0	3.98
1999 Syracuse	AAA Tor	7	0	0	0	14	73	20	15	12	4	0	0	0	10	0	6	2	0	0	0	.000	0	0	7.71
Knoxville	AA Tor	25	4	0	6	60	283	73	50	47	9	0	3	2	31	0	36	3	0	2	4	.333	0	0	7.05
7 Min. YEARS		214	10	0	92	386.1	1736	394	229	190	36	9	16	19	211	8	279	32	5	23	21	.523	0	17	4.43

Jeff Harris

Pitches: Right Bats: Right Pos: P Ht: 6'0" Wt: 195 Born: 7/4/74 Age: 25

Year Team	Lg Org	G	GS	CG	GF	IP	BFP	H	R	ER	HR	SH	SF	HB	TBB	IBB	SO	WP	Bk	W	L	Pct.	ShO	Sv	ERA
1995 Elizabethtn	R+ Min	21	0	0	10	33	154	42	15	14	2	1	0	4	13	1	27	6	1	1	3	.250	0	0	3.82
1996 Fort Wayne	A Min	42	0	0	15	89.2	387	90	35	31	4	3	8	4	33	1	85	10	1	8	3	.727	0	3	3.11
1997 Fort Myers	A+ Min	24	0	0	6	42	164	30	11	10	4	3	4	0	15	2	32	1	0	4	.333	0	1	2.14
New Britain	AA Min	28	0	0	14	42.1	175	30	15	11	2	3	2	3	16	0	44	3	0	2	1	.667	0	3	2.34
1998 New Britain	AA Min	26	0	0	11	38	148	21	7	7	3	1	1	0	5	0	40	0	1	1	0	1.000	0	5	1.66
Salt Lake	AAA Min	25	0	0	18	32	148	38	24	21	4	3	3	0	19	4	24	3	0	8	0	1.000	0	3	5.91
1999 Salt Lake	AAA Min	36	0	0	7	45.2	220	61	38	35	7	3	4	3	26	1	20	2	0	4	3	.571	0	0	6.90
New Britain	AA Min	20	0	0	6	24.1	106	21	5	4	0	3	0	1	14	2	12	1	0	3	1	.750	0	1	1.48
5 Min. YEARS		222	0	0	87	347	1492	333	150	133	26	20	19	15	141	11	284	26	3	29	15	.659	0	15	3.45

Adonis Harrison

Bats: Left Throws: Right Pos: 2B Ht: 5'9" Wt: 165 Born: 9/28/76 Age: 23

Year Team	Lg Org	G	AB	H	2B	3B	HR	TB	R	RBI	TBB	IBB	SO	HBP	SH	SF	SB	CS	SB%	GDP	Avg	OBP	SLG
1995 Mariners	R Sea	45	155	45	7	5	1	65	31	14	37	0	37	3	0	4	7	9	.44	0	.290	.427	.419
1996 Lancaster	A+ Sea	16	40	14	4	0	0	18	7	5	8	0	13	0	0	0	4	1	.80	0	.350	.458	.450
Wisconsin	A Sea	54	196	52	15	2	1	74	29	24	19	0	36	1	1	0	5	3	.63	3	.265	.333	.378
1997 Wisconsin	A Sea	125	412	131	26	6	7	190	61	62	55	2	74	6	5	3	25	18	.58	11	.318	.403	.461
1998 Lancaster	A+ Sea	69	258	87	21	4	2	122	63	35	49	0	48	2	1	2	24	14	.63	4	.337	.444	.473
Orlando	AA Sea	58	191	44	6	2	3	63	35	21	30	0	30	3	1	1	6	4	.60	2	.230	.342	.330
1999 New Haven	AA Sea	120	449	122	16	0	2	144	54	45	38	0	75	6	1	4	22	17	.56	12	.272	.334	.321
5 Min. YEARS		487	1701	495	95	19	16	676	280	206	236	2	313	21	9	14	93	66	.58	32	.291	.381	.397

Tommy Harrison

Pitches: Right Bats: Right Pos: P Ht: 6'2" Wt: 185 Born: 9/30/71 Age: 28

Year Team	Lg Org	G	GS	CG	GF	IP	BFP	H	R	ER	HR	SH	SF	HB	TBB	IBB	SO	WP	Bk	W	L	Pct.	ShO	Sv	ERA
1995 Durham	A+ Atl	7	6	0	0	37.2	145	22	5	4	1	0	0	1	13	1	25	0	0	3	1	.750	0	0	0.96
Greenville	AA Atl	14	14	1	0	88.1	370	87	50	43	9	7	1	2	27	3	57	5	0	6	4	.600	0	0	4.38

Year Team	Lg Org	HOW MUCH HE PITCHED						WHAT HE GAVE UP												THE RESULTS					
		G	GS	CG	GF	IP	BFP	H	R	ER	HR	SH	SF	HB	TBB	IBB	SO	WP	Bk	W	L	Pct.	ShO	Sv	ERA
Richmond	AAA Atl	9	6	0	1	42	182	34	17	15	2	4	3	2	20	1	16	0	1	2	1	.667	0	1	3.21
1996 Richmond	AAA Atl	10	0	0	3	19	87	16	12	11	5	0	2	2	12	0	12	3	0	0	0	.000	0	0	5.21
Greenville	AA Atl	20	16	0	3	99.1	421	88	55	52	11	2	6	3	34	0	82	7	1	8	4	.667	0	0	4.71
1997 Richmond	AAA Atl	22	22	1	0	122	519	118	64	57	21	2	4	5	40	2	92	3	0	9	7	.563	0	0	4.20
1998 Richmond	AAA Atl	2	2	0	0	10	41	9	5	5	0	0	0	0	3	0	11	0	0	2	0	1.000	0	0	4.50
1999 Greenville	AA Atl	16	12	0	0	63.1	311	75	59	52	11	2	3	7	43	1	42	5	2	3	7	.300	0	0	7.39
Richmond	AAA Atl	4	0	0	1	10	52	17	9	9	2	0	0	0	6	1	6	1	0	0	1	.000	0	0	8.10
5 Min. YEARS		104	78	2	8	491.2	2128	466	276	248	62	17	19	22	198	9	343	24	4	33	25	.569	0	1	4.54

Robin Harriss

Bats: Right **Throws:** Right **Pos:** C   **Ht:** 6'1" **Wt:** 205 **Born:** 8/7/71 **Age:** 28

Year Team	Lg Org	BATTING														BASERUNNING				PERCENTAGES		
		G	AB	H	2B	3B	HR	TB	R	RBI	TBB	IBB	SO	HBP	SH	SF	SB	CS	SB%	GDP	Avg	OBP	SLG
1994 Watertown	A- Cle	49	168	41	5	0	4	58	19	25	16	0	16	1	3	4	1	0	1.00	5	.244	.307	.345
1995 Kinston	A+ Cle	15	49	12	3	1	2	23	8	6	3	0	8	0	1	1	0	0	.00	1	.245	.283	.469
Columbus	A Cle	51	179	40	6	0	2	52	18	18	11	0	30	3	3	0	0	3	.00	8	.223	.280	.291
1996 Kinston	A+ Cle	89	262	57	7	1	5	81	25	32	16	1	57	5	12	3	1	2	.33	8	.218	.273	.309
1997 Akron	AA Cle	49	146	39	8	0	1	50	24	17	20	0	36	0	7	2	0	1	.00	8	.267	.351	.342
1998 Kinston	A+ Cle	44	132	30	6	0	0	36	19	11	16	1	36	2	3	1	1	3	.25	4	.227	.318	.273
Akron	AA Cle	15	45	5	2	0	0	7	3	2	9	1	21	0	2	0	1	0	1.00	2	.111	.259	.156
1999 Buffalo	AAA Cle	2	3	0	0	0	0	0	0	0	1	0	1	0	1	0	0	0	.00	0	.000	.250	.000
Akron	AA Cle	17	48	8	1	0	2	15	9	6	1	0	12	2	1	0	1	0	1.00	0	.167	.216	.313
6 Min. YEARS		331	1032	232	38	2	16	322	125	117	93	3	217	13	33	11	5	9	.36	36	.225	.294	.312

Len Hart

Pitches: Left **Bats:** Left **Pos:** P   **Ht:** 5'11" **Wt:** 190 **Born:** 10/8/73 **Age:** 26

Year Team	Lg Org	HOW MUCH HE PITCHED						WHAT HE GAVE UP												THE RESULTS					
		G	GS	CG	GF	IP	BFP	H	R	ER	HR	SH	SF	HB	TBB	IBB	SO	WP	Bk	W	L	Pct.	ShO	Sv	ERA
1996 Williamsprt	A- ChC	28	0	0	13	31.1	129	15	6	5	0	2	0	0	24	1	26	1	0	2	3	.400	0	2	1.44
1997 Rockford	A ChC	27	0	0	5	47.1	194	30	11	11	0	1	0	2	28	1	55	5	0	2	1	.667	0	0	2.09
Daytona	A+ ChC	8	0	0	0	9.1	44	10	6	6	0	1	0	1	7	0	12	1	0	1	2	.333	0	0	5.79
1998 Daytona	A+ ChC	37	0	0	11	50.2	221	52	28	20	4	1	3	2	20	1	46	2	0	3	3	.500	0	2	3.55
1999 Rancho Cuca	A+ SD	33	0	0	12	43.1	166	19	5	4	1	0	0	1	18	0	54	3	0	2	1	.667	0	3	0.83
Mobile	AA SD	2	0	0	0	2.2	14	4	1	1	0	0	0	0	2	0	4	0	0	0	0	.000	0	0	3.38
4 Min. YEARS		135	0	0	41	184.2	768	130	57	47	5	5	3	6	99	3	197	12	0	10	10	.500	0	7	2.29

Ron Hartman

Bats: Right **Throws:** Right **Pos:** 3B   **Ht:** 6'1" **Wt:** 200 **Born:** 12/12/74 **Age:** 25

Year Team	Lg Org	BATTING														BASERUNNING				PERCENTAGES		
		G	AB	H	2B	3B	HR	TB	R	RBI	TBB	IBB	SO	HBP	SH	SF	SB	CS	SB%	GDP	Avg	OBP	SLG
1996 Lethbridge	R+ Ari	66	258	84	23	0	16	155	69	72	36	0	42	6	0	8	5	2	.71	6	.326	.409	.601
1997 South Bend	A Ari	53	197	50	17	2	3	80	25	37	25	1	35	1	0	2	1	0	1.00	12	.254	.338	.406
High Desert	A+ Ari	75	291	85	22	0	14	149	43	65	30	0	57	4	0	8	0	2	.00	3	.292	.357	.512
1998 Tucson	AAA Ari	126	438	118	21	0	9	166	54	55	22	0	53	3	3	3	1	3	.25	11	.269	.307	.379
1999 High Desert	A+ Ari	33	124	31	6	0	2	43	13	22	7	1	13	3	0	1	0	0	.00	7	.250	.304	.347
El Paso	AA Ari	24	82	16	3	1	0	21	6	7	5	0	8	1	0	2	0	0	.00	0	.195	.244	.256
4 Min. YEARS		377	1390	384	92	3	44	614	210	258	125	2	208	18	3	24	7	7	.50	39	.276	.338	.442

Pete Hartmann

Pitches: Left **Bats:** Left **Pos:** P   **Ht:** 6'2" **Wt:** 200 **Born:** 5/13/71 **Age:** 29

Year Team	Lg Org	HOW MUCH HE PITCHED						WHAT HE GAVE UP												THE RESULTS					
		G	GS	CG	GF	IP	BFP	H	R	ER	HR	SH	SF	HB	TBB	IBB	SO	WP	Bk	W	L	Pct.	ShO	Sv	ERA
1993 Erie	A- Tex	15	15	1	0	88.1	380	74	51	41	5	1	0	3	43	0	98	6	1	7	7	.462	0	0	4.18
1994 Charlotte	A+ Tex	26	24	0	1	128.1	575	132	70	65	8	4	5	4	77	0	107	15	6	5	11	.313	0	0	4.56
1995 Charlotte	A+ Tex	15	2	0	9	35.2	180	46	34	29	7	4	2	0	26	0	30	3	4	2	4	.333	0	2	7.32
Stockton	A+ Mil	12	0	0	5	14	61	9	7	7	1	1	0	0	11	0	9	1	1	2	0	1.000	0	0	4.50
1996 Grays Harbr	IND —	5	5	0	0	25.1	125	33	23	22	0	1	1	0	22	1	10	0	0	0	3	.000	0	0	7.82
1997 New Jersey	IND —	17	17	5	0	119.2	519	120	60	46	8	2	1	1	55	2	118	7	4	8	6	.571	1	0	3.46
1998 New Jersey	IND —	7	7	2	0	47.2	185	34	11	9	2	1	1	1	15	2	41	2	0	4	0	1.000	0	0	1.70
1999 Bowie	AA Bal	11	0	0	1	15.2	66	11	4	3	1	2	0	0	8	0	12	2	1	1	1	.500	0	1	1.72
Rochester	AAA Bal	34	3	0	8	44.1	215	56	45	44	14	0	1	3	27	1	43	7	0	1	5	.167	0	0	8.93
7 Min. YEARS		142	73	8	24	519	2306	515	305	266	46	20	12	12	284	6	468	43	17	29	37	.439	1	3	4.61

Ty Hartshorn

Pitches: Right **Bats:** Right **Pos:** P   **Ht:** 6'5" **Wt:** 190 **Born:** 8/3/74 **Age:** 25

Year Team	Lg Org	HOW MUCH HE PITCHED						WHAT HE GAVE UP												THE RESULTS					
		G	GS	CG	GF	IP	BFP	H	R	ER	HR	SH	SF	HB	TBB	IBB	SO	WP	Bk	W	L	Pct.	ShO	Sv	ERA
1993 Blue Jays	R Tor	9	4	0	4	26.2	124	36	26	18	0	2	1	0	7	0	18	0	1	0	0	.000	0	0	6.08
1994 Blue Jays	R Tor	10	10	0	0	54.1	209	38	15	11	0	1	0	1	17	1	52	2	0	2	3	.400	0	0	1.82
1995 Hagerstown	A Tor	12	7	0	1	48.2	224	59	37	29	8	1	1	5	20	0	26	6	0	3	4	.429	0	0	5.36
St.Cathrnes	A- Tor	13	13	1	0	69.2	307	83	45	33	6	3	1	3	25	0	25	6	1	3	4	.429	1	0	4.26
1996 Hagerstown	A Tor	26	26	1	0	147	648	153	86	75	15	5	6	9	64	1	109	22	1	5	11	.313	0	0	4.59
1997 Dunedin	A+ Tor	26	24	2	1	160	711	197	102	79	19	3	4	12	40	3	101	1	0	5	13	.278	1	0	4.44
1998 Dunedin	A+ Tor	9	9	1	0	63	252	52	16	9	1	2	0	1	17	0	54	0	0	8	0	1.000	1	0	1.29
Knoxville	AA Tor	19	19	0	0	107.2	483	133	74	62	15	3	1	2	43	0	55	2	0	7	6	.538	0	0	5.18
1999 Knoxville	AA Tor	10	7	0	0	47	206	60	32	25	4	0	3	4	15	0	24	0	1	4	1	.800	0	0	4.79

120

		HOW MUCH HE PITCHED						WHAT HE GAVE UP									THE RESULTS				
Year Team	Lg Org	G	GS	CG	GF	IP	BFP	H	R	ER	HR	SH	SF	HB	TBB	IBB	SO	WP	Bk	W	L	Pct.	ShO	Sv	ERA
Dunedin	A+ Tor	7	7	0	0	31	150	43	25	23	3	0	3	2	16	0	30	1	0	3	1	.750	0	0	6.68
7 Min. YEARS		141	126	5	6	755	3314	854	458	364	71	20	20	39	264	5	496	42	3	40	47	.460	3	1	4.34

Chad Hartvigson

Pitches: Left **Bats:** Left **Pos:** P   **Ht:** 6'1" **Wt:** 170 **Born:** 12/15/70 **Age:** 29

		HOW MUCH HE PITCHED						WHAT HE GAVE UP									THE RESULTS				
Year Team	Lg Org	G	GS	CG	GF	IP	BFP	H	R	ER	HR	SH	SF	HB	TBB	IBB	SO	WP	Bk	W	L	Pct.	ShO	Sv	ERA
1994 Everett	A- SF	12	1	0	1	40.2	168	34	16	15	5	1	0	0	14	3	51	4	2	2	2	.500	0	0	3.32
1995 San Jose	A+ SF	32	7	0	8	84	357	85	38	33	4	6	3	0	24	1	63	3	1	4	4	.500	0	4	3.54
1996 San Jose	A+ SF	36	10	0	7	103	427	94	46	37	10	1	4	1	30	0	114	4	0	4	7	.364	0	2	3.23
1997 Bakersfield	A+ SF	5	4	0	0	27	103	22	9	9	2	1	1	1	5	0	22	1	0	1	1	.500	0	0	3.00
Shreveport	AA SF	4	1	1	1	12.2	53	11	8	5	3	0	0	0	5	0	9	2	0	1	0	1.000	0	0	3.55
Phoenix	AAA SF	17	4	0	4	53.2	238	63	34	32	4	1	1	2	17	0	52	2	1	2	2	.500	0	0	5.37
Okla City	AAA Tex	14	1	0	6	25.2	121	35	21	19	5	1	1	0	9	0	22	0	0	2	2	.500	0	2	6.66
1998 Sioux Falls	IND —	32	7	0	21	78	324	70	36	34	10	5	4	1	25	2	88	6	0	2	5	.286	0	10	3.92
1999 Carolina	AA Col	30	0	0	17	43	193	48	35	30	6	2	3	0	11	1	32	1	0	0	5	.000	0	1	6.28
6 Min. YEARS		182	35	1	65	467.2	1984	462	243	214	49	18	17	5	140	7	453	23	4	18	28	.391	0	19	4.12

Derek Hasselhoff

Pitches: Right **Bats:** Right **Pos:** P   **Ht:** 6'2" **Wt:** 185 **Born:** 10/10/73 **Age:** 26

		HOW MUCH HE PITCHED						WHAT HE GAVE UP									THE RESULTS				
Year Team	Lg Org	G	GS	CG	GF	IP	BFP	H	R	ER	HR	SH	SF	HB	TBB	IBB	SO	WP	Bk	W	L	Pct.	ShO	Sv	ERA
1995 Bristol	R+ CWS	12	11	0	1	66.1	281	66	32	27	4	1	1	2	14	0	46	2	2	7	3	.700	0	0	3.66
1996 South Bend	A CWS	35	0	0	29	47.2	205	46	19	17	4	4	1	2	17	0	39	5	0	6	3	.667	0	10	3.21
Pr William	A+ CWS	5	0	0	4	10.1	49	14	7	6	1	0	0	0	6	2	9	0	0	0	1	.000	0	1	5.23
1997 Winston-Sal	A+ CWS	20	0	0	11	34.2	138	22	10	6	1	2	1	0	15	3	41	4	0	3	2	.600	0	3	1.56
Birmingham	AA CWS	18	0	0	10	33.2	141	35	10	9	3	0	1	1	11	0	22	1	0	5	2	.714	0	3	2.41
Nashville	AAA CWS	6	0	0	1	7.1	37	9	8	8	2	0	0	0	7	0	2	0	0	1	1	.500	0	0	9.82
1998 Calgary	AAA CWS	13	0	0	5	19	89	23	15	14	3	1	1	1	8	0	24	0	1	2	0	1.000	0	0	6.63
White Sox	R CWS	6	1	0	1	10	36	6	1	0	0	0	0	0	0	0	16	0	0	0	0	.000	0	0	0.00
Winston-Sal	A+ CWS	1	0	0	0	2	9	3	0	0	0	0	0	0	0	0	3	0	0	0	0	.000	0	0	0.00
1999 Charlotte	AAA CWS	49	0	0	18	71	311	83	46	38	7	1	0	0	25	1	65	3	0	6	0	1.000	0	4	4.82
5 Min. YEARS		165	12	0	80	302	1296	307	148	125	25	9	5	6	103	6	267	15	3	30	12	.714	0	21	3.73

Lionel Hastings

Bats: Right **Throws:** Right **Pos:** C   **Ht:** 5'9" **Wt:** 165 **Born:** 1/26/73 **Age:** 27

		BATTING													BASERUNNING				PERCENTAGES		
Year Team	Lg Org	G	AB	H	2B	3B	HR	TB	R	RBI	TBB	IBB	SO	HBP	SH	SF	SB	CS	SB%	GDP	Avg	OBP	SLG
1994 Elmira	A- Fla	73	282	77	17	0	5	109	39	43	28	0	48	4	3	4	4	5	.44	3	.273	.343	.387
1995 Brevard Cty	A+ Fla	120	469	128	20	0	7	169	60	45	44	0	64	3	5	2	3	3	.50	14	.273	.338	.360
1996 Portland	AA Fla	97	293	68	12	1	6	100	30	44	15	2	50	8	10	1	5	2	.71	8	.232	.287	.341
1997 Portland	AA Fla	93	279	96	21	0	10	147	55	35	39	1	53	3	3	3	6	3	.67	6	.344	.426	.527
1998 Charlotte	AAA Fla	104	265	64	10	2	1	81	40	21	19	0	55	3	2	0	4	3	.57	4	.242	.300	.306
1999 Calgary	AAA Fla	34	75	20	4	1	1	29	8	4	5	1	13	0	2	1	2	0	1.00	4	.267	.309	.387
Portland	AA Fla	61	197	45	5	1	3	61	26	14	32	0	45	2	1	0	2	2	.50	6	.228	.342	.310
6 Min. YEARS		582	1860	498	89	5	33	696	258	206	182	4	328	23	26	11	26	18	.59	45	.268	.339	.374

Chris Hatcher

Bats: Right **Throws:** Right **Pos:** OF   **Ht:** 6'3" **Wt:** 235 **Born:** 1/7/69 **Age:** 31

		BATTING													BASERUNNING				PERCENTAGES		
Year Team	Lg Org	G	AB	H	2B	3B	HR	TB	R	RBI	TBB	IBB	SO	HBP	SH	SF	SB	CS	SB%	GDP	Avg	OBP	SLG
1990 Auburn	A- Hou	72	259	64	10	0	9	101	37	45	27	3	86	5	0	5	8	2	.80	4	.247	.324	.390
1991 Burlington	A Hou	129	497	117	23	6	13	191	69	65	46	4	180	9	0	4	10	5	.67	6	.235	.309	.384
1992 Osceola	A+ Hou	97	367	103	19	6	17	185	49	68	20	1	97	5	0	5	11	0	1.00	5	.281	.322	.504
1993 Jackson	AA Hou	101	367	95	15	3	15	161	45	64	11	0	104	11	0	3	5	8	.38	8	.259	.298	.439
1994 Tucson	AAA Hou	108	349	104	28	4	12	176	55	73	19	0	90	4	0	6	5	1	.83	6	.298	.336	.504
1995 Jackson	AA Hou	11	39	12	1	0	1	16	5	3	4	0	6	1	0	1	0	2	.00	1	.308	.378	.410
Tucson	AAA Hou	94	290	83	19	2	14	148	59	50	42	2	107	4	1	2	7	3	.70	9	.286	.382	.510
1996 Jackson	AA Hou	41	156	48	9	1	13	98	29	36	9	2	39	4	0	1	2	1	.67	5	.308	.359	.628
Tucson	AAA Hou	95	348	105	21	4	18	188	53	61	14	1	87	5	0	5	10	8	.56	9	.302	.333	.540
1997 Wichita	AA KC	11	42	11	0	0	5	26	7	7	4	0	16	1	0	0	1	0	1.00	0	.262	.340	.619
Omaha	AAA KC	68	222	51	9	0	11	93	34	24	17	2	68	6	0	3	1	0	.00	4	.230	.298	.419
1998 Omaha	AAA KC	126	485	150	21	2	46	313	84	106	25	3	125	3	0	3	8	6	.57	9	.309	.345	.645
1999 Colo Spngs	AAA Col	98	334	115	24	2	21	206	63	69	23	1	89	10	0	5	12	4	.75	12	.344	.398	.617
1998 Kansas City	AL	8	15	1	0	0	0	1	0	1	1	0	7	0	0	0	0	0	.00	0	.067	.125	.067
10 Min. YEARS		1051	3755	1058	199	30	195	1902	589	671	261	19	1094	68	1	43	79	41	.66	78	.282	.336	.507

Kevin Haverbusch

Bats: Right **Throws:** Right **Pos:** 3B   **Ht:** 6'3" **Wt:** 197 **Born:** 6/16/76 **Age:** 24

		BATTING													BASERUNNING				PERCENTAGES		
Year Team	Lg Org	G	AB	H	2B	3B	HR	TB	R	RBI	TBB	IBB	SO	HBP	SH	SF	SB	CS	SB%	GDP	Avg	OBP	SLG
1997 Erie	A- Pit	67	241	75	15	2	10	124	37	55	13	1	37	4	2	4	4	4	.50	6	.311	.351	.515
1998 Lynchburg	A+ Pit	49	181	60	12	1	8	98	25	39	9	0	33	6	0	2	4	2	.67	5	.331	.379	.541
Carolina	AA Pit	46	168	63	10	0	3	82	28	29	13	1	20	3	0	0	1	3	.25	3	.375	.429	.488
1999 Altoona	AA Pit	93	332	95	22	2	14	163	57	61	12	0	60	19	1	9	6	3	.67	9	.286	.339	.491
3 Min. YEARS		255	922	293	59	5	35	467	147	184	47	2	150	32	3	15	15	12	.56	23	.318	.366	.507

Ryan Hawblitzel

Pitches: Right **Bats:** Right **Pos:** P **Ht:** 6' 2" **Wt:** 185 **Born:** 4/30/71 **Age:** 29

Year Team	Lg Org	G	GS	CG	GF	IP	BFP	H	R	ER	HR	SH	SF	HB	TBB	IBB	SO	WP	Bk	W	L	Pct.	ShO	Sv	ERA
1990 Huntington	R+ ChC	14	14	2	0	75.2	322	72	38	33	8	0	0	6	25	0	71	2	0	6	5	.545	1	0	3.93
1991 Winston-Sal	A+ ChC	20	20	5	0	134	552	110	40	34	7	5	7	7	47	0	103	8	1	15	2	.882	2	0	2.28
Charlotte	AA ChC	5	5	1	0	33.2	141	31	14	12	2	5	2	3	12	3	25	0	0	1	2	.333	1	0	3.21
1992 Charlotte	AA ChC	28	28	3	0	174.2	727	180	84	73	18	5	5	4	38	3	119	8	0	12	8	.600	1	0	3.76
1993 Colo Sprngs	AAA Col	29	28	2	0	165.1	764	221	129	113	16	10	9	4	49	0	90	3	0	8	13	.381	0	0	6.15
1994 Colo Sprngs	AAA Col	28	28	3	0	163	732	200	119	111	21	6	2	10	53	2	103	5	0	10	10	.500	1	0	6.13
1995 Colo Sprngs	AAA Col	21	14	0	1	83	352	88	47	42	7	3	5	3	17	1	40	2	0	5	3	.625	0	0	4.55
1996 Colo Sprngs	AAA Col	26	18	0	5	117	501	131	76	65	17	4	4	5	27	2	75	2	0	7	6	.538	0	1	5.00
1997 Scranton-WB	AAA Phi	34	15	1	9	115.1	498	132	65	64	16	3	4	4	33	3	80	1	0	6	9	.400	1	2	4.99
1998 Charlotte	AAA Fla	20	19	0	0	103	437	133	68	64	20	2	2	2	14	0	72	3	0	8	5	.615	0	0	5.59
1999 Edmonton	AAA Ana	24	7	0	2	64	295	81	47	38	8	2	2	4	24	1	37	0	0	4	4	.500	0	0	5.34
1996 Colorado	NL	8	0	0	3	15	69	18	12	10	2	0	1	0	6	0	7	1	0	0	1	.000	0	0	6.00
10 Min. YEARS		249	196	17	17	1228.2	5321	1379	727	649	140	45	42	52	339	15	815	34	1	82	67	.550	7	3	4.75

Al Hawkins

Pitches: Right **Bats:** Right **Pos:** P **Ht:** 6'3" **Wt:** 210 **Born:** 1/1/78 **Age:** 22

Year Team	Lg Org	G	GS	CG	GF	IP	BFP	H	R	ER	HR	SH	SF	HB	TBB	IBB	SO	WP	Bk	W	L	Pct.	ShO	Sv	ERA
1996 Ogden	R+ Mil	9	5	0	1	33.2	144	31	16	12	1	0	0	6	13	0	23	1	3	3	3	.500	0	0	3.21
1997 Beloit	A Mil	6	6	0	0	24.2	133	46	33	29	8	0	1	5	12	0	17	2	1	1	4	.200	0	0	10.58
Ogden	R+ Mil	14	14	0	0	81	394	113	74	53	8	0	2	4	24	0	47	5	0	2	8	.200	0	0	5.89
1998 Beloit	A Mil	15	14	1	0	88	382	94	52	35	4	7	2	7	20	0	64	3	1	6	3	.667	0	0	3.58
Stockton	A+ Mil	9	9	0	0	55.1	252	60	37	28	7	1	4	3	26	0	32	4	1	3	4	.429	0	0	4.55
1999 Stockton	A+ Mil	4	4	0	0	25	105	26	12	10	2	1	0	1	6	0	11	2	0	3	0	1.000	0	0	3.60
Huntsville	AA Mil	19	19	0	0	99.2	447	126	71	59	10	1	6	10	29	2	56	14	1	8	9	.471	0	0	5.33
4 Min. YEARS		76	71	1	1	407.1	1857	496	295	226	40	10	15	30	130	2	250	31	7	26	31	.456	0	0	4.99

Kraig Hawkins

Bats: Right **Throws:** Right **Pos:** OF **Ht:** 6'2" **Wt:** 170 **Born:** 12/4/71 **Age:** 28

Year Team	Lg Org	G	AB	H	2B	3B	HR	TB	R	RBI	TBB	IBB	SO	HBP	SH	SF	SB	CS	SB%	GDP	Avg	OBP	SLG
1992 Oneonta	A- NYY	70	227	50	1	0	0	51	24	18	26	0	67	1	7	0	14	5	.74	1	.220	.303	.225
1993 Greensboro	A NYY	131	418	106	13	1	0	121	66	45	67	1	112	1	9	3	07	10	.79	0	.254	.356	.289
1994 Tampa	A+ NYY	108	437	104	7	1	0	113	72	29	61	0	105	2	3	0	37	19	.66	4	.238	.334	.259
1995 Norwich	AA NYY	12	45	10	0	0	0	10	5	3	7	0	11	0	2	0	7	2	.78	0	.222	.327	.222
Tampa	A+ NYY	111	432	105	9	3	1	123	56	19	66	0	95	2	11	1	28	14	.67	6	.243	.345	.285
1996 Tampa	A+ NYY	75	268	80	2	5	1	95	41	21	35	0	41	2	9	1	13	6	.68	2	.299	.382	.354
1997 Norwich	AA NYY	51	188	49	6	1	0	57	36	16	26	0	37	1	1	3	12	2	.86	1	.261	.350	.303
Tampa	A+ NYY	9	30	9	1	0	0	10	2	4	8	0	2	0	0	0	3	2	.60	1	.300	.447	.333
1998 St. Pete	A+ TB	30	96	19	1	1	0	22	15	4	11	0	12	1	1	0	9	4	.69	2	.198	.287	.229
Durham	AAA TB	6	23	6	0	0	0	6	2	1	0	0	2	0	0	0	1	0	1.00	1	.261	.261	.261
Orlando	AA TB	51	184	52	3	2	0	59	37	13	39	1	31	1	1	0	12	5	.71	1	.283	.411	.321
1999 Orlando	AA TB	94	296	89	10	1	0	101	41	27	38	1	45	1	4	2	19	10	.66	9	.301	.380	.341
8 Min. YEARS		748	2644	679	53	15	2	768	397	200	384	3	560	12	50	9	222	87	.72	37	.257	.353	.290

Chris Hayes

Bats: Right **Throws:** Right **Pos:** 3B **Ht:** 6'2" **Wt:** 190 **Born:** 12/23/73 **Age:** 26

Year Team	Lg Org	G	AB	H	2B	3B	HR	TB	R	RBI	TBB	IBB	SO	HBP	SH	SF	SB	CS	SB%	GDP	Avg	OBP	SLG
1995 St.Cathrnes	A- Tor	70	271	83	17	3	2	112	39	36	24	0	50	7	1	1	8	7	.53	2	.306	.376	.413
1996 Hagerstown	A Tor	88	315	78	15	4	5	116	48	51	32	2	59	9	0	4	7	6	.54	6	.248	.331	.368
Dunedin	A+ Tor	32	106	25	6	0	1	34	14	12	11	0	21	5	4	1	1	2	.33	6	.236	.333	.321
1997 Dunedin	A+ Tor	60	139	32	5	1	2	45	20	20	15	0	27	4	2	0	2	1	.67	4	.230	.323	.324
1998 Hagerstown	A Tor	63	207	61	17	1	8	104	41	33	23	0	41	9	3	1	6	2	.75	2	.295	.388	.502
1999 Dunedin	A+ Tor	60	190	58	15	2	6	95	42	41	26	1	37	9	4	1	12	4	.75	3	.305	.412	.500
Knoxville	AA Tor	36	129	37	11	1	2	56	25	16	18	0	29	5	0	0	4	4	.50	3	.287	.395	.434
5 Min. YEARS		409	1357	374	86	12	26	562	229	209	149	3	264	48	14	8	40	26	.61	26	.276	.366	.414

Heath Hayes

Bats: Right **Throws:** Right **Pos:** C **Ht:** 6'3" **Wt:** 195 **Born:** 2/29/72 **Age:** 28

Year Team	Lg Org	G	AB	H	2B	3B	HR	TB	R	RBI	TBB	IBB	SO	HBP	SH	SF	SB	CS	SB%	GDP	Avg	OBP	SLG
1994 Watertown	A- Cle	46	147	38	5	1	4	57	31	27	22	0	31	1	0	3	3	1	.75	4	.259	.353	.388
1995 Watertown	A- Cle	15	52	11	3	0	0	14	4	6	7	0	14	0	0	1	1	1	.50	1	.212	.300	.269
1996 Columbus	A Cle	104	348	81	14	0	22	161	51	57	36	0	106	6	0	5	2	1	.67	2	.233	.311	.463
1997 Kinston	A+ Cle	100	370	96	22	0	24	190	51	60	10	0	107	0	0	0	0	0	.40	7	.261	.297	.502
1998 Akron	AA Cle	91	329	68	14	1	11	117	36	46	24	1	95	2	2	3	2	3	.40	7	.207	.263	.356
1999 Akron	AA Cle	119	418	111	15	2	16	178	51	68	41	1	111	7	1	5	2	1	.67	8	.266	.338	.426
6 Min. YEARS		478	1672	405	73	4	77	717	227	263	170	5	464	18	3	19	12	10	.55	29	.242	.316	.429

122

Nathan Haynes

Bats: Left **Throws:** Left **Pos:** OF **Ht:** 5'9" **Wt:** 170 **Born:** 9/7/79 **Age:** 20

Year Team	Lg Org	G	AB	H	2B	3B	HR	TB	R	RBI	TBB	IBB	SO	HBP	SH	SF	SB	CS	SB%	GDP	Avg	OBP	SLG
1997 Athletics	R Oak	17	54	15	1	0	0	16	8	6	7	0	9	2	1	0	5	1	.83	3	.278	.381	.296
Sou Oregon	A- Oak	24	82	23	1	1	0	26	18	9	26	0	21	2	0	1	19	3	.86	1	.280	.459	.317
1998 Modesto	A+ Oak	125	507	128	13	7	1	158	89	41	54	2	139	4	6	2	42	18	.70	10	.252	.328	.312
1999 Visalia	A+ Oak	35	145	45	7	1	1	57	28	14	17	0	27	3	2	1	12	10	.55	1	.310	.392	.393
Lk Elsinore	A+ Ana	26	110	36	5	5	1	54	19	15	12	0	19	1	0	1	10	5	.67	2	.327	.395	.491
Erie	AA Ana	5	19	3	1	0	0	4	3	0	5	0	5	1	0	0	0	0	.00	2	.158	.360	.211
3 Min. YEARS		232	917	250	28	14	3	315	165	85	121	2	220	13	9	5	88	37	.70	19	.273	.364	.344

Andy Hazlett

Pitches: Left **Bats:** Left **Pos:** P **Ht:** 6'3" **Wt:** 195 **Born:** 8/27/75 **Age:** 24

Year Team	Lg Org	G	GS	CG	GF	IP	BFP	H	R	ER	HR	SH	SF	HB	TBB	IBB	SO	WP	Bk	W	L	Pct.	ShO	Sv	ERA
1997 Lowell	A- Bos	19	3	0	12	50.1	206	44	16	9	1	0	1	0	7	0	66	0	0	5	0	1.000	0	4	1.61
Michigan	A Bos	2	2	0	0	12	50	15	7	7	2	0	0	0	1	0	12	0	0	1	0	1.000	0	0	5.25
1998 Sarasota	A+ Bos	30	22	4	1	160.2	662	154	76	57	4	2	7	3	25	2	135	3	1	11	7	.611	2	1	3.19
1999 Trenton	AA Bos	27	26	2	1	164.1	674	155	84	76	15	5	2	8	41	0	123	7	3	9	9	.500	1	1	4.16
3 Min. YEARS		78	53	6	14	387.1	1592	368	183	149	22	7	10	11	74	2	336	10	4	26	16	.619	3	6	3.46

Mike Heathcott

Pitches: Right **Bats:** Right **Pos:** P **Ht:** 6' 3" **Wt:** 180 **Born:** 5/16/69 **Age:** 31

Year Team	Lg Org	G	GS	CG	GF	IP	BFP	H	R	ER	HR	SH	SF	HB	TBB	IBB	SO	WP	Bk	W	L	Pct.	ShO	Sv	ERA
1991 Utica	A- CWS	6	6	0	0	33	138	26	19	13	4	1	1	1	14	0	14	1	0	3	1	.750	0	0	3.55
1992 South Bend	A CWS	15	14	0	1	82	340	67	28	14	3	5	2	0	32	0	49	8	0	9	5	.643	0	0	1.54
1993 Sarasota	A+ CWS	26	26	6	0	179.1	739	174	90	72	5	12	10	4	62	7	83	16	1	11	10	.524	1	0	3.61
1994 Birmingham	AA CWS	17	17	0	0	98	449	126	71	63	11	1	6	2	44	4	44	9	0	3	7	.300	0	0	5.79
Pr William	A+ CWS	9	8	1	1	43	193	51	28	19	7	1	0	1	23	0	27	6	0	1	2	.333	0	0	3.98
1995 Pr William	A+ CWS	27	14	1	4	88.2	387	96	56	46	8	2	7	2	36	3	68	18	0	4	9	.308	0	3	4.67
1996 Birmingham	AA CWS	23	23	1	0	147.2	625	138	72	66	9	5	5	4	55	3	108	5	0	11	8	.579	0	0	4.02
1997 Nashville	AAA CWS	17	0	0	7	27	129	39	23	22	5	1	0	0	12	0	23	6	0	2	3	.400	0	0	7.33
Birmingham	AA CWS	30	1	0	12	59	247	50	20	12	2	3	1	1	25	0	47	3	0	3	1	.750	0	7	1.83
1998 Calgary	AAA CWS	39	13	1	10	109	483	113	65	61	12	2	4	5	51	2	77	8	0	9	6	.600	0	0	5.04
1999 Charlotte	AAA CWS	32	21	1	5	139.1	632	177	89	80	14	6	4	4	64	1	77	9	0	10	8	.556	0	0	5.17
1998 Chicago	AL	1	0	0	0	3	12	2	1	1	0	0	0	0	1	0	3	2	0	0	0	.000	0	0	3.00
9 Min. YEARS		241	143	11	40	1006	4362	1057	561	468	80	39	39	24	418	20	617	89	1	66	60	.524	1	11	4.19

Andy Heckman

Pitches: Left **Bats:** Right **Pos:** P **Ht:** 6'3" **Wt:** 185 **Born:** 10/17/71 **Age:** 28

Year Team	Lg Org	G	GS	CG	GF	IP	BFP	H	R	ER	HR	SH	SF	HB	TBB	IBB	SO	WP	Bk	W	L	Pct.	ShO	Sv	ERA
1992 Everett	A- SF	22	2	0	12	40.1	158	26	12	12	6	1	1	2	14	2	41	1	0	2	3	.400	0	2	2.68
1993 Clinton	A SF	11	1	0	5	20.2	88	18	6	4	2	1	0	2	4	0	24	0	0	2	1	.667	0	0	1.74
San Jose	A+ SF	30	0	0	19	59	242	45	20	16	3	2	4	2	23	0	40	2	0	5	1	.833	0	7	2.44
1994 San Jose	A+ SF	7	0	0	3	10	38	3	3	3	0	0	0	0	6	0	11	4	0	0	0	.000	0	0	2.70
Shreveport	AA SF	20	14	0	4	97.2	398	84	30	27	9	2	1	5	25	1	59	1	0	7	1	.875	0	0	2.49
1998 Newburgh	IND —	23	15	2	3	93	418	106	54	48	10	2	1	5	36	2	63	8	0	4	4	.500	0	0	4.65
1999 Shreveport	AA SF	23	23	1	0	132.1	572	142	67	60	11	6	5	2	43	1	70	3	0	10	6	.625	1	0	4.08
5 Min. YEARS		136	55	3	46	453	1914	424	192	170	41	14	12	18	151	6	308	19	0	30	16	.652	1	9	3.38

Jon Heinrichs

Bats: Right **Throws:** Right **Pos:** OF **Ht:** 6'0" **Wt:** 195 **Born:** 11/18/74 **Age:** 25

Year Team	Lg Org	G	AB	H	2B	3B	HR	TB	R	RBI	TBB	IBB	SO	HBP	SH	SF	SB	CS	SB%	GDP	Avg	OBP	SLG
1997 Kane County	A Fla	60	235	63	12	2	1	82	35	36	19	1	34	0	3	1	8	5	.62	7	.268	.322	.349
1998 Brevard Cty	A+ Fla	128	470	134	17	2	12	191	63	64	50	3	68	6	0	8	21	6	.78	6	.285	.356	.406
1999 Portland	AA Fla	49	176	40	11	1	3	62	25	17	16	0	23	3	1	0	4	0	1.00	7	.227	.303	.352
Brevard Cty	A+ Fla	67	252	63	12	0	6	93	40	44	22	1	34	1	0	4	7	2	.78	6	.250	.308	.369
3 Min. YEARS		304	1133	300	52	5	22	428	163	161	107	5	159	10	4	13	40	13	.75	26	.265	.330	.378

Chad Helmer

Pitches: Right **Bats:** Right **Pos:** P **Ht:** 6'4" **Wt:** 210 **Born:** 9/12/75 **Age:** 24

Year Team	Lg Org	G	GS	CG	GF	IP	BFP	H	R	ER	HR	SH	SF	HB	TBB	IBB	SO	WP	Bk	W	L	Pct.	ShO	Sv	ERA
1997 Helena	R+ Mil	14	0	0	4	30.1	132	27	12	7	2	2	2	4	9	0	33	1	0	0	2	.000	0	2	2.08
Stockton	A+ Mil	7	0	0	3	11.2	50	12	4	4	0	0	0	1	4	0	10	2	0	2	0	1.000	0	0	3.09
1998 Stockton	A+ Mil	46	0	0	31	65	283	45	35	29	6	4	2	4	42	0	76	9	0	6	7	.462	0	6	4.02
1999 Huntsville	AA Mil	7	0	0	3	9.2	56	15	12	9	1	0	1	0	9	0	7	2	0	1	0	1.000	0	0	8.38
Stockton	A+ Mil	20	4	0	11	34.2	157	35	18	11	3	2	3	3	18	2	33	5	0	1	4	.200	0	6	2.86
3 Min. YEARS		94	4	0	52	151.1	678	134	81	60	12	8	8	12	82	2	159	19	0	10	13	.435	0	15	3.57

Wes Helms

Bats: Right **Throws:** Right **Pos:** 1B — **Ht:** 6' 4" **Wt:** 230 **Born:** 5/12/76 **Age:** 24

Year Team	Lg Org	G	AB	H	2B	3B	HR	TB	R	RBI	TBB	IBB	SO	HBP	SH	SF	SB	CS	SB%	GDP	Avg	OBP	SLG
1994 Braves	R Atl	56	184	49	15	1	4	78	22	29	22	0	36	4	0	1	6	1	.86	3	.266	.355	.424
1995 Macon	A Atl	136	539	149	32	1	11	216	89	85	50	0	107	10	0	3	2	2	.50	8	.276	.347	.401
1996 Durham	A+ Atl	67	258	83	19	2	13	145	40	54	12	0	51	7	0	1	1	1	.50	7	.322	.367	.562
Greenville	AA Atl	64	231	59	13	2	4	88	24	22	13	2	48	4	1	0	2	1	.67	6	.255	.306	.381
1997 Richmond	AAA Atl	32	110	21	4	0	3	34	11	15	10	1	34	5	0	1	1	1	.50	4	.191	.286	.309
Greenville	AA Atl	86	314	93	14	1	11	142	50	44	33	2	50	6	0	3	3	4	.43	14	.296	.371	.452
1998 Richmond	AAA Atl	125	451	124	27	1	13	192	56	75	35	2	103	13	0	4	6	2	.75	11	.275	.342	.426
1999 Braves	R Atl	9	33	15	2	0	0	17	1	10	5	0	4	1	0	0	0	1	.00	1	.455	.538	.515
Greenville	AA Atl	30	113	34	6	0	8	64	15	26	7	1	34	1	0	0	1	0	1.00	3	.301	.347	.566
1998 Atlanta	NL	7	13	4	1	0	1	8	2	2	0	0	4	0	0	0	0	0	.00	0	.308	.308	.615
6 Min. YEARS		605	2233	627	132	8	67	976	308	360	187	8	467	51	1	13	22	13	.63	57	.281	.348	.437

Rod Henderson

Pitches: Right **Bats:** Right **Pos:** P — **Ht:** 6' 4" **Wt:** 195 **Born:** 3/11/71 **Age:** 29

Year Team	Lg Org	G	GS	CG	GF	IP	BFP	H	R	ER	HR	SH	SF	HB	TBB	IBB	SO	WP	Bk	W	L	Pct.	ShO	Sv	ERA
1992 Jamestown	A- Mon	1	1	0	0	3	13	2	3	2	0	0	0	0	5	0	2	0	0	0	0	.000	0	0	6.00
1993 Wst Plm Bch	A+ Mon	22	22	1	0	143	580	110	50	46	3	4	5	8	44	0	127	8	8	12	7	.032	1	0	2.90
Harrisburg	AA Mon	5	5	0	0	29.2	125	20	10	6	0	1	0	0	15	0	25	2	1	5	0	1.000	0	0	1.82
1994 Harrisburg	AA Mon	2	2	0	0	12	44	5	2	2	1	0	0	0	4	0	16	0	0	2	0	1.000	0	0	1.50
Ottawa	AAA Mon	23	21	0	1	122.2	545	123	67	63	16	2	5	2	67	3	100	1	0	6	9	.400	0	1	4.62
1995 Harrisburg	AA Mon	12	12	0	0	56.1	240	51	28	27	4	0	1	5	18	0	53	1	0	3	6	.333	0	0	4.31
1996 Ottawa	AAA Mon	25	23	3	0	121.1	528	117	75	70	12	1	4	4	52	1	83	2	0	4	11	.267	1	0	5.19
1997 Ottawa	AAA Mon	26	20	2	3	123.2	542	136	72	68	18	4	2	6	49	3	103	6	0	5	9	.357	1	1	4.95
1998 Ottawa	AAA Mon	6	0	0	1	11	66	23	17	11	3	1	0	0	12	0	12	0	0	0	1	.000	0	0	9.00
El Paso	AA Mil	1	0	0	0	1.2	10	4	1	1	0	0	0	0	1	0	0	0	0	0	0	.000	0	0	5.40
Louisville	AAA Mil	22	19	1	1	121.1	493	100	45	40	4	2	1	4	39	0	68	1	0	11	5	.688	0	0	2.97
1999 Louisville	AAA Mil	28	22	0	1	120.2	550	119	109	85	20	5	5	7	64	0	76	6	0	7	11	.389	0	0	6.34
1994 Montreal	NL	3	2	0	0	6.2	37	9	9	7	1	3	0	0	7	0	3	0	0	0	1	.000	0	0	9.45
1998 Milwaukee	NL	2	0	0	0	3.2	17	5	4	4	2	0	0	1	0	0	1	0	0	0	0	.000	0	0	9.82
8 Min. YEARS		173	147	7	7	866.1	3736	810	479	421	81	20	23	34	370	7	665	27	7	55	59	.482	3	2	4.37
2 Maj. YEARS		5	2	0	0	10.1	54	14	13	11	3	3	0	1	7	0	4	0	0	0	1	.000	0	0	9.58

Ryan Henderson

Pitches: Right **Bats:** Right **Pos:** P — **Ht:** 6'1" **Wt:** 190 **Born:** 9/30/69 **Age:** 30

Year Team	Lg Org	G	GS	CG	GF	IP	BFP	H	R	ER	HR	SH	SF	HB	TBB	IBB	SO	WP	Bk	W	L	Pct.	ShO	Sv	ERA
1992 Great Falls	R+ LA	11	11	1	0	55	228	37	22	13	0	3	0	2	25	0	54	5	6	5	1	.833	1	0	2.13
Bakersfield	A+ LA	3	3	0	0	16	72	17	10	9	1	0	0	0	9	1	15	0	0	0	2	.000	0	0	5.06
1993 Vero Beach	A+ LA	30	0	0	25	34	158	29	24	15	2	4	1	0	28	4	34	4	1	0	3	.000	0	10	3.97
San Antonio	AA LA	23	0	0	20	25	110	19	10	7	0	3	1	0	16	2	22	1	1	0	0	.000	0	5	2.52
1994 Bakersfield	A+ LA	29	0	0	27	31.1	145	26	14	10	1	2	0	1	26	0	38	8	1	0	1	.000	0	14	2.87
San Antonio	AA LA	11	1	0	0	21.2	105	25	18	17	2	0	1	1	18	1	15	3	1	1	2	.333	0	0	7.06
1995 Vero Beach	A+ LA	39	6	0	10	104.1	453	98	53	45	1	6	1	5	58	3	86	9	2	11	5	.688	0	2	3.88
1996 Albuquerque	AAA LA	3	0	0	1	5.2	31	5	9	5	0	0	1	0	6	0	7	1	2	0	0	.000	0	0	7.94
San Antonio	AA LA	39	0	0	19	63.2	275	59	29	27	2	2	4	5	29	0	46	4	0	3	3	.500	0	6	3.82
1997 Albuquerque	AAA LA	13	0	0	4	17.1	87	20	14	12	0	3	0	1	14	3	17	1	0	1	3	.250	0	0	6.23
Colo Sprngs	AAA Col	6	1	0	2	13	67	22	18	18	3	0	0	1	9	1	12	0	0	1	1	.500	0	0	12.46
New Haven	AA Col	24	4	0	7	50.2	228	54	29	27	2	2	2	3	27	2	46	6	0	2	5	.286	0	0	4.80
1998 Binghamton	AA NYM	29	0	0	16	40.1	173	34	18	15	2	1	1	0	20	3	39	3	1	0	3	.000	0	4	3.35
Norfolk	AAA NYM	3	0	0	0	4	23	6	5	5	0	0	0	0	6	0	2	0	0	0	0	.000	0	0	11.25
El Paso	AA Mil	20	0	0	11	22	105	22	14	9	0	0	0	3	13	2	20	2	0	2	0	1.000	0	5	3.68
1999 Huntsville	AA Mil	12	0	0	10	14.1	59	12	2	1	0	1	0	0	6	1	13	2	0	2	0	1.000	0	6	0.63
Louisville	AAA Mil	21	0	0	7	35.1	168	35	32	25	2	0	1	3	25	3	34	7	0	1	0	1.000	0	0	6.37
Norfolk	AAA NYM	7	2	0	1	13.1	63	14	13	12	2	0	0	1	9	0	12	2	0	0	2	.000	0	0	8.10
Binghamton	AA NYM	5	2	0	1	7.2	35	9	6	6	1	0	0	1	6	0	8	2	0	0	2	.000	0	0	7.04
8 Min. YEARS		328	30	1	161	574.2	2585	541	340	278	21	27	13	27	350	26	520	60	18	29	33	.468	1	52	4.35

Scott Henderson

Pitches: Right **Bats:** Right **Pos:** P — **Ht:** 6'3" **Wt:** 195 **Born:** 2/27/75 **Age:** 25

Year Team	Lg Org	G	GS	CG	GF	IP	BFP	H	R	ER	HR	SH	SF	HB	TBB	IBB	SO	WP	Bk	W	L	Pct.	ShO	Sv	ERA
1997 Utica	A- Fla	15	1	0	6	39.2	151	28	11	10	1	2	1	1	7	0	51	3	0	5	1	.833	0	4	2.27
1998 Kane County	A Fla	40	1	0	19	81.1	337	64	29	27	2	4	2	4	27	1	96	2	0	10	7	.588	0	4	2.99
1999 Portland	AA Fla	46	1	0	21	85	343	67	32	28	4	4	2	8	26	4	83	7	0	6	3	.667	0	7	2.96
3 Min. YEARS		101	3	0	46	206	831	159	72	65	7	10	5	13	60	11	230	12	0	21	11	.656	0	15	2.84

Mark Hendrickson

Pitches: Left **Bats:** Left **Pos:** P — **Ht:** 6'9" **Wt:** 230 **Born:** 6/23/74 **Age:** 26

Year Team	Lg Org	G	GS	CG	GF	IP	BFP	H	R	ER	HR	SH	SF	HB	TBB	IBB	SO	WP	Bk	W	L	Pct.	ShO	Sv	ERA
1998 Dunedin	A+ Tor	16	5	0	1	49.1	207	44	16	13	2	2	2	0	26	1	38	2	0	4	3	.571	0	1	2.37
1999 Knoxville	AA Tor	12	11	0	0	55.2	254	73	46	41	4	2	0	2	21	0	39	2	1	2	7	.222	0	0	6.63
2 Min. YEARS		28	16	0	1	105	461	117	62	54	6	4	2	2	47	1	77	4	1	6	10	.375	0	1	4.63

124

Oscar Henriquez

Pitches: Right **Bats:** Right **Pos:** P **Ht:** 6' 6" **Wt:** 220 **Born:** 1/28/74 **Age:** 26

Year Team	Lg Org	G	GS	CG	GF	IP	BFP	H	R	ER	HR	SH	SF	HB	TBB	IBB	SO	WP	Bk	W	L	Pct.	ShO	Sv	ERA
1993 Asheville	A Hou	27	26	2	0	150	679	154	95	74	12	6	5	10	70	2	117	7	3	9	10	.474	1	0	4.44
1995 Kissimmee	A+ Hou	20	0	0	7	44.2	207	40	29	25	2	2	2	6	30	0	36	3	0	3	4	.429	0	1	5.04
1996 Kissimmee	A+ Hou	37	0	0	33	34	162	28	18	15	0	1	1	3	29	2	40	4	0	0	4	.000	0	15	3.97
1997 New Orleans	AAA Hou	60	0	0	37	74	313	65	28	23	4	6	3	5	27	3	80	7	1	4	5	.444	0	12	2.80
1998 Charlotte	AAA Fla	26	0	0	19	31.2	134	29	12	9	3	0	1	2	12	0	37	4	0	1	0	1.000	0	11	2.56
1999 Norfolk	AAA NYM	53	0	0	41	54	254	54	31	24	8	4	3	3	38	4	65	8	1	3	4	.429	0	23	4.00
1997 Houston	NL	4	0	0	1	4	17	2	2	2	0	1	0	1	3	0	3	0	0	0	1	.000	0	0	4.50
1998 Florida	NL	15	0	0	4	20	100	26	22	19	4	0	2	1	12	0	19	1	0	0	0	.000	0	0	8.55
6 Min. YEARS		223	26	2	137	388.1	1749	370	213	170	29	19	15	29	206	11	375	33	5	20	27	.426	1	62	3.94
2 Maj. YEARS		19	0	0	5	24	117	28	24	21	4	1	2	2	15	0	22	1	0	0	1	.000	0	0	7.88

Russ Herbert

Pitches: Right **Bats:** Right **Pos:** P **Ht:** 6'3" **Wt:** 195 **Born:** 4/21/72 **Age:** 28

Year Team	Lg Org	G	GS	CG	GF	IP	BFP	H	R	ER	HR	SH	SF	HB	TBB	IBB	SO	WP	Bk	W	L	Pct.	ShO	Sv	ERA
1994 White Sox	R CWS	4	2	0	1	13	46	6	3	3	0	0	0	1	2	0	19	0	0	1	0	.000	0	0	2.08
Hickory	A CWS	8	7	0	1	36.2	154	33	14	14	3	1	0	2	15	0	34	1	2	2	1	.667	0	0	3.44
1995 Hickory	A CWS	18	18	1	0	114.2	474	83	48	34	9	3	3	8	46	0	115	5	2	3	8	.273	1	0	2.67
South Bend	A CWS	9	9	0	0	53.2	224	46	25	21	3	1	0	3	27	0	48	1	2	2	4	.333	0	0	3.52
1996 Pr William	A+ CWS	25	25	1	0	144	609	129	73	54	12	8	11	6	62	3	148	3	2	6	10	.375	0	0	3.38
1997 Birmingham	AA CWS	27	26	3	0	158.2	681	136	72	64	14	3	6	14	80	0	126	7	0	13	5	.722	1	0	3.63
1998 Calgary	AAA CWS	28	28	2	0	163.2	728	182	100	92	25	3	6	10	74	0	147	5	1	9	10	.474	0	0	5.06
1999 Reading	AA Phi	26	9	0	7	83.1	369	90	53	44	7	3	6	8	32	1	55	1	3	3	5	.375	0	3	4.75
6 Min. YEARS		145	124	7	9	767.2	3285	705	388	326	73	22	32	52	338	4	692	23	12	38	44	.463	2	3	3.82

Brett Herbison

Pitches: Right **Bats:** Right **Pos:** P **Ht:** 6'5" **Wt:** 180 **Born:** 6/13/77 **Age:** 23

Year Team	Lg Org	G	GS	CG	GF	IP	BFP	H	R	ER	HR	SH	SF	HB	TBB	IBB	SO	WP	Bk	W	L	Pct.	ShO	Sv	ERA
1995 Mets	R NYM	9	9	0	0	41	170	31	13	10	3	1	2	0	16	0	31	4	0	3	0	1.000	0	0	2.20
Kingsport	R+ NYM	1	1	0	0	5	23	6	4	4	2	1	0	0	2	0	4	1	0	1	0	1.000	0	0	7.20
1996 Kingsport	R+ NYM	13	12	0	0	76.2	297	43	18	11	4	0	1	3	31	0	86	6	0	6	2	.750	0	0	1.29
Pittsfield	A- NYM	1	1	0	0	2	15	4	6	5	0	0	0	0	4	0	1	1	0	0	0	.000	0	0	22.50
1997 Capital Cty	A NYM	28	27	2	0	160	690	166	86	71	13	7	2	9	63	0	146	11	2	7	14	.333	0	0	3.99
1998 St. Lucie	A+ NYM	26	25	0	0	146.2	649	165	93	84	10	7	7	9	52	2	94	10	0	7	13	.350	0	0	5.15
1999 Binghamton	AA NYM	27	26	1	0	149.1	689	161	115	97	20	5	9	14	81	0	60	7	0	5	13	.278	0	0	5.85
5 Min. YEARS		105	101	3	0	580.2	2533	576	335	282	52	21	21	35	249	2	422	40	2	29	43	.403	0	0	4.37

Maximo Heredia

Pitches: Right **Bats:** Right **Pos:** P **Ht:** 6'0" **Wt:** 163 **Born:** 9/27/76 **Age:** 23

Year Team	Lg Org	G	GS	CG	GF	IP	BFP	H	R	ER	HR	SH	SF	HB	TBB	IBB	SO	WP	Bk	W	L	Pct.	ShO	Sv	ERA
1996 Orioles	R Bal	17	0	0	7	34.1	143	22	15	11	1	1	0	4	12	0	25	2	0	3	1	.750	0	4	2.88
1997 Delmarva	A Bal	37	6	0	13	114	441	97	29	27	4	3	3	0	20	0	73	2	0	10	5	.667	0	1	2.13
1998 Bowie	AA Bal	5	4	0	0	13	56	18	9	9	2	0	0	1	2	0	7	0	0	1	1	.500	0	0	6.23
Frederick	A+ Bal	29	3	0	8	64	279	71	44	35	8	5	3	2	19	3	36	3	0	1	3	.250	0	3	4.92
1999 Bowie	AA Bal	50	0	0	17	76.1	341	80	42	36	12	1	1	5	33	4	56	3	1	6	4	.600	0	0	4.24
4 Min. YEARS		138	13	0	45	301.2	1260	288	139	118	27	10	7	12	86	7	197	10	1	21	14	.600	0	8	3.52

Juan Hernaiz

Bats: Right **Throws:** Right **Pos:** DH **Ht:** 5'10" **Wt:** 192 **Born:** 2/15/75 **Age:** 25

									BATTING								BASERUNNING				PERCENTAGES		
Year Team	Lg Org	G	AB	H	2B	3B	HR	TB	R	RBI	TBB	IBB	SO	HBP	SH	SF	SB	CS	SB%	GDP	Avg	OBP	SLG
1992 Dodgers	R LA	35	104	13	3	0	0	16	10	4	4	0	41	2	2	1	3	2	.60	2	.125	.171	.154
1993 Great Falls	R+ LA	52	186	65	7	2	3	85	24	19	3	0	42	0	1	1	8	5	.62	3	.349	.358	.457
1994 Vero Beach	A+ LA	2	1	0	0	0	0	0	0	0	0	0	1	1	0	0	0	0	.00	0	.000	.500	.000
1995 Vero Beach	A+ LA	50	156	33	1	1	2	42	17	9	9	1	39	1	4	0	5	1	.83	4	.212	.259	.269
Yakima	A- LA	50	158	44	9	2	0	57	23	16	6	0	30	1	1	1	9	3	.75	1	.278	.307	.361
1996 Savannah	A LA	132	492	137	19	8	14	214	68	73	21	3	96	8	3	3	42	15	.74	5	.278	.317	.435
1997 Lakeland	A+ Det	118	438	122	13	6	12	183	58	56	22	1	107	3	1	1	29	13	.69	0	.279	.317	.418
1998 Jacksnville	AA Det	99	382	96	21	2	11	154	60	58	16	0	93	3	1	6	8	2	.80	4	.251	.283	.403
1999 Akron	AA Cle	7	21	4	0	0	1	7	3	1	0	0	7	0	0	0	0	0	.00	1	.190	.190	.333
8 Min. YEARS		545	1938	514	73	21	43	758	263	236	81	5	456	19	13	13	104	41	.72	20	.265	.299	.391

Alex Hernandez

Bats: Left **Throws:** Left **Pos:** OF **Ht:** 6'4" **Wt:** 186 **Born:** 5/28/77 **Age:** 23

									BATTING								BASERUNNING				PERCENTAGES		
Year Team	Lg Org	G	AB	H	2B	3B	HR	TB	R	RBI	TBB	IBB	SO	HBP	SH	SF	SB	CS	SB%	GDP	Avg	OBP	SLG
1995 Pirates	R Pit	49	186	50	5	3	1	64	24	17	17	1	33	1	1	2	4	4	.50	3	.269	.330	.344
1996 Erie	A- Pit	61	225	65	13	4	4	98	38	30	20	1	47	0	1	2	7	8	.47	1	.289	.344	.436
1997 Lynchburg	A+ Pit	131	520	151	37	4	5	211	75	68	27	2	140	2	2	7	13	8	.62	6	.290	.324	.406
1998 Carolina	AA Pit	115	452	117	22	7	8	177	62	48	41	2	81	0	5	6	11	4	.73	12	.259	.317	.392
1999 Altoona	AA Pit	126	475	122	26	3	15	199	76	63	54	1	110	2	3	3	11	8	.58	3	.257	.333	.419
5 Min. YEARS		482	1858	505	103	21	33	749	275	226	159	7	411	5	12	20	46	32	.59	25	.272	.328	.403

125

Elvin Hernandez

Pitches: Right **Bats:** Right **Pos:** P   **Ht:** 6'1" **Wt:** 195 **Born:** 8/20/77 **Age:** 22

		HOW MUCH HE PITCHED						WHAT HE GAVE UP										THE RESULTS					
Year Team	Lg Org	G	GS	CG	GF	IP	BFP	H	R	ER	HR	SH	SF	HB	TBB	IBB	SO	WP	Bk	W	L	Pct.	ShO	Sv	ERA
1995 Erie	A- Pit	14	14	2	0	90.1	377	82	40	29	8	5	3	4	22	0	54	2	1	6	1	.857	1	0	2.89
1996 Augusta	A Pit	27	27	2	0	157.2	624	140	60	55	13	0	2	5	16	2	171	7	0	17	5	.773	1	0	3.14
1997 Carolina	AA Pit	17	17	0	0	92.2	409	104	67	59	11	2	2	3	26	2	66	4	0	2	7	.222	0	0	5.73
Lynchburg	A+ Pit	3	0	0	2	5	20	4	1	1	0	0	0	0	1	0	5	0	0	0	0	.000	0	1	1.80
1998 Carolina	AA Pit	27	13	0	2	102.1	462	127	73	65	14	0	3	2	31	0	67	5	0	3	6	.333	0	0	5.72
1999 West Tenn	AA ChC	29	25	1	1	151.1	672	174	100	83	16	4	7	6	50	3	98	10	0	9	9	.500	1	1	4.94
5 Min. YEARS		117	96	5	5	599.1	2564	631	341	292	62	11	17	20	146	7	461	28	1	37	28	.569	3	2	4.38

Fernando Hernandez

Pitches: Right **Bats:** Right **Pos:** P   **Ht:** 6'2" **Wt:** 185 **Born:** 6/16/71 **Age:** 29

		HOW MUCH HE PITCHED						WHAT HE GAVE UP										THE RESULTS					
Year Team	Lg Org	G	GS	CG	GF	IP	BFP	H	R	ER	HR	SH	SF	HB	TBB	IBB	SO	WP	Bk	W	L	Pct.	ShO	Sv	ERA
1990 Indians	R Cle	11	11	2	0	69.2	289	61	36	31	3	2	2	1	30	0	43	2	7	4	4	.500	0	0	4.00
1991 Burlington	R+ Cle	14	13	0	1	77	326	74	33	25	4	2	0	7	19	0	86	12	1	4	4	.500	0	0	2.92
1992 Columbus	A Cle	11	11	1	0	68.2	268	42	16	12	4	1	0	6	33	1	70	4	1	4	5	.444	1	0	1.57
Kinston	A+ Cle	8	8	1	0	41.2	177	36	23	21	2	3	3	1	22	0	32	3	0	1	3	.250	0	0	4.54
1993 Kinston	A+ Cle	8	8	0	0	51	200	34	15	10	1	2	1	2	18	0	53	1	0	2	3	.400	0	0	1.76
Canton-Akrn	AA Cle	2	2	0	0	7.2	40	14	11	10	1	0	1	1	5	0	8	0	0	0	1	.000	0	0	11.74
Rancho Cuca	A+ SD	17	17	1	0	99.2	441	90	54	46	8	3	4	2	67	0	121	4	1	7	5	.583	0	0	4.15
1994 Wichita	AA SD	23	23	0	0	131.1	595	124	82	70	12	8	9	10	77	6	95	8	0	7	9	.438	1	0	4.80
1995 Las Vegas	AAA SD	8	8	0	0	37.2	186	43	32	32	3	0	2	3	31	3	40	4	0	1	6	.143	0	0	7.65
Memphis	AA SD	12	12	0	0	66.1	303	72	46	38	4	0	0	3	42	1	74	8	1	4	6	.400	0	0	5.16
1996 Memphis	AA SD	27	27	0	0	147.1	655	128	83	76	8	3	8	8	85	4	161	11	1	11	10	.524	1	0	4.64
1997 Toledo	AAA Det	55	1	0	18	76.2	350	71	44	35	5	4	2	1	51	1	98	1	1	6	5	.545	0	4	4.11
1998 Tucson	AAA Ari	3	2	0	0	10	55	23	17	17	5	1	1	0	1	0	13	2	0	0	1	.000	0	0	15.30
1999 Tucson	AAA Ari	5	1	0	1	16	75	22	16	15	3	1	0	1	4	0	14	0	0	0	2	.000	0	0	8.44
1997 Detroit	AL	2	0	0	0	1.1	13	5	6	6	0	0	0	0	3	1	2	0	0	0	0	.000	0	0	40.50
10 Min. YEARS		204	144	6	20	900.2	3960	834	508	438	63	30	33	46	485	16	908	60	13	51	64	.443	2	4	4.38

Santos Hernandez

Pitches: Right **Bats:** Right **Pos:** P   **Ht:** 6'1" **Wt:** 172 **Born:** 11/3/72 **Age:** 27

		HOW MUCH HE PITCHED						WHAT HE GAVE UP										THE RESULTS					
Year Team	Lg Org	G	GS	CG	GF	IP	BFP	H	R	ER	HR	SH	SF	HB	TBB	IBB	SO	WP	Bk	W	L	Pct.	ShO	Sv	ERA
1994 Clinton	A SF	32	0	0	11	48	201	47	23	20	5	6	2	4	10	1	48	4	4	5	7	.417	0	4	3.75
1995 Burlington	A SF	44	0	0	28	64.1	274	54	27	19	3	4	4	2	20	2	85	1	0	5	8	.385	0	9	2.66
1996 Burlington	A SF	61	0	0	58	66.2	249	39	15	14	4	3	1	2	13	0	79	7	1	3	3	.500	0	35	1.89
1997 San Jose	A+ SF	47	0	0	39	57	237	51	26	22	7	4	0	1	14	2	87	4	0	2	6	.250	0	15	3.47
Shreveport	AA SF	11	0	0	11	15.2	62	13	4	4	1	0	0	1	3	0	14	3	0	1	1	.500	0	6	2.30
1998 Durham	AAA TB	53	0	0	10	80	343	88	45	43	11	2	3	2	21	2	60	8	0	2	0	1.000	0	2	4.84
1999 Durham	AAA TB	6	4	0	0	18.1	98	34	25	22	9	0	0	1	11	0	12	1	1	0	2	.000	0	0	10.80
Orlando	AA TB	35	4	0	13	56	228	43	31	23	5	3	1	2	15	0	47	1	0	5	4	.556	0	5	3.70
6 Min. YEARS		289	8	0	170	406	1692	369	196	167	45	22	11	15	107	7	432	29	6	23	31	.426	0	76	3.70

Junior Herndon

Pitches: Right **Bats:** Right **Pos:** P   **Ht:** 6'1" **Wt:** 190 **Born:** 9/11/78 **Age:** 21

		HOW MUCH HE PITCHED						WHAT HE GAVE UP										THE RESULTS					
Year Team	Lg Org	G	GS	CG	GF	IP	BFP	H	R	ER	HR	SH	SF	HB	TBB	IBB	SO	WP	Bk	W	L	Pct.	ShO	Sv	ERA
1997 Padres	R SD	14	14	0	0	77.1	348	80	51	38	2	3	3	5	32	0	65	6	2	3	2	.600	0	0	4.42
Idaho Falls	R+ SD	1	1	0	0	5	20	5	0	0	0	0	0	0	1	0	3	0	0	0	0	.000	0	0	0.00
1998 Clinton	A SD	21	21	3	0	132.1	543	119	59	44	3	4	5	8	34	0	101	2	0	10	8	.556	1	0	2.99
Rancho Cuca	A+ SD	6	6	0	0	39.2	165	37	18	15	5	2	2	2	13	0	29	1	0	3	2	.600	0	0	3.40
1999 Mobile	AA SD	26	26	2	0	163	706	172	96	85	24	9	1	8	52	3	87	10	0	10	9	.526	2	0	4.69
3 Min. YEARS		68	68	5	0	417.1	1782	413	224	182	34	18	11	23	132	3	285	19	2	26	21	.553	3	0	3.92

Jose Herrera

Bats: Left **Throws:** Left **Pos:** OF   **Ht:** 6'0" **Wt:** 165 **Born:** 8/30/72 **Age:** 27

		BATTING															BASERUNNING				PERCENTAGES		
Year Team	Lg Org	G	AB	H	2B	3B	HR	TB	R	RBI	TBB	IBB	SO	HBP	SH	SF	SB	CS	SB%	GDP	Avg	OBP	SLG
1991 Medcine Hat	R+ Tor	40	143	35	5	1	1	45	21	11	6	1	38	3	1	0	6	7	.46	0	.245	.289	.315
St.Cathrnes	A- Tor	3	9	3	1	0	0	4	3	2	1	0	2	1	0	0	1	0	1.00	0	.333	.455	.444
1992 Medcine Hat	R+ Tor	72	265	72	9	2	0	85	45	21	32	1	62	6	7	0	32	8	.80	4	.272	.363	.321
1993 Hagerstown	A Tor	95	388	123	22	5	5	170	60	42	26	1	63	7	5	4	36	20	.64	3	.317	.367	.438
Madison	A Oak	4	14	3	0	0	0	3	1	0	0	0	6	0	1	0	1	1	.50	0	.214	.214	.214
1994 Modesto	A+ Oak	103	370	106	20	3	11	165	59	56	38	3	76	10	5	6	21	12	.64	5	.286	.363	.446
1995 Huntsville	AA Oak	92	358	101	11	4	6	138	37	45	27	2	58	2	2	2	9	8	.53	8	.282	.334	.385
1996 Huntsville	AA Oak	23	84	24	4	0	1	31	18	7	14	1	15	0	0	2	3	2	.60	2	.286	.380	.369
1997 Edmonton	AAA Oak	122	421	125	21	2	4	162	64	41	42	2	64	1	7	2	7	5	.58	12	.297	.361	.385
1998 Syracuse	AAA Tor	118	473	129	21	6	12	198	72	40	32	1	60	1	6	4	27	12	.69	11	.273	.318	.419
1999 Rochester	AAA Bal	39	127	26	7	1	2	41	11	16	2	0	20	0	2	1	3	1	.75	4	.205	.215	.323
1995 Oakland	AL	33	70	17	1	2	0	22	9	2	6	0	11	0	0	1	1	3	.25	1	.243	.299	.314
1996 Oakland	AL	108	320	86	15	1	6	121	44	30	20	1	59	3	3	0	8	2	.80	5	.269	.318	.378
9 Min. YEARS		711	2652	747	121	24	42	1042	391	281	220	12	464	31	34	21	145	77	.65	49	.282	.341	.393
2 Maj. YEARS		141	390	103	16	3	6	143	53	32	26	1	70	3	3	1	9	5	.64	6	.264	.314	.367

Jason Herrick

Bats: Left Throws: Left Pos: OF Ht: 6'0" Wt: 175 Born: 7/29/73 Age: 26

Year Team	Lg Org	G	AB	H	2B	3B	HR	TB	R	RBI	TBB	IBB	SO	HBP	SH	SF	SB	CS	SB%	GDP	Avg	OBP	SLG
1992 Angels	R Ana	8	30	12	3	0	0	15	7	6	5	0	4	1	0	0	2	1	.67	0	.400	.500	.500
1993 Angels	R Ana	56	196	59	9	4	3	85	34	36	41	2	51	2	1	2	5	4	.56	6	.301	.423	.434
1994 Cedar Rapds	A Ana	109	339	85	18	5	7	134	62	51	42	2	92	3	2	6	10	3	.77	8	.251	.333	.395
1995 Cedar Rapds	A Ana	104	358	102	21	4	11	164	54	57	38	2	84	2	3	3	19	3	.86	7	.285	.354	.458
1996 Lk Elsinore	A+ Ana	58	210	67	13	2	6	102	35	30	25	2	52	0	2	2	5	4	.56	5	.319	.388	.486
1997 Midland	AA Ana	118	416	105	27	4	20	200	60	67	34	3	141	2	6	2	9	6	.60	7	.252	.311	.481
1998 Midland	AA Ana	71	274	91	20	7	18	179	61	73	20	2	75	2	1	4	5	5	.50	1	.332	.377	.653
Vancouver	AAA Ana	59	207	45	8	3	6	77	17	19	4	0	65	2	2	1	0	4	.00	2	.217	.238	.372
1999 Edmonton	AAA Ana	25	72	15	3	0	1	21	6	7	1	0	27	0	0	0	0	2	.00	0	.208	.219	.292
Erie	AA Ana	25	78	13	5	1	2	26	9	6	8	0	28	0	1	1	1	0	1.00	2	.167	.241	.333
El Paso	AA Ari	49	173	52	18	1	6	90	23	20	14	1	45	2	0	0	2	5	.29	5	.301	.360	.520
8 Min. YEARS		682	2353	646	145	31	80	1093	368	372	232	14	664	16	18	21	58	37	.61	43	.275	.341	.465

Phil Hiatt

Bats: Right Throws: Right Pos: 1B Ht: 6'3" Wt: 200 Born: 5/1/69 Age: 31

Year Team	Lg Org	G	AB	H	2B	3B	HR	TB	R	RBI	TBB	IBB	SO	HBP	SH	SF	SB	CS	SB%	GDP	Avg	OBP	SLG
1990 Eugene	A- KC	73	289	85	18	5	2	119	33	44	17	1	69	1	1	4	15	4	.79	1	.294	.331	.412
1991 Baseball Cy	A+ KC	81	315	94	21	6	5	142	41	33	22	4	70	3	1	2	28	14	.67	8	.298	.348	.451
Memphis	AA KC	56	206	47	7	1	6	74	29	33	9	1	63	3	0	6	6	1	.86	3	.228	.263	.359
1992 Memphis	AA KC	129	487	119	20	5	27	230	71	83	25	1	157	5	1	3	5	10	.33	11	.244	.287	.472
Omaha	AAA KC	5	14	3	0	0	2	9	3	4	2	0	3	0	0	0	1	0	1.00	0	.214	.313	.643
1993 Omaha	AAA KC	12	51	12	2	0	3	23	8	10	4	0	20	1	0	0	0	0	.00	0	.235	.304	.451
1994 Omaha	AAA KC	6	22	4	1	0	1	8	2	2	0	0	4	1	0	0	1	0	1.00	2	.182	.217	.364
Memphis	AA KC	108	400	120	26	4	17	205	57	66	40	4	116	13	2	2	12	8	.60	4	.300	.380	.513
1995 Omaha	AAA KC	20	76	12	5	0	2	23	7	8	2	0	25	0	0	1	0	0	.00	0	.158	.177	.303
1996 Toledo	AAA Det	142	555	145	27	3	42	304	99	119	50	3	180	2	0	4	17	6	.74	13	.261	.322	.548
1998 Buffalo	AAA Cle	119	453	112	19	0	31	224	81	74	41	1	146	4	2	3	4	1	.80	16	.247	.313	.494
1999 Indianapols	AAA Cin	78	311	74	11	0	18	139	46	54	30	0	103	2	0	3	0	0	.00	8	.238	.306	.447
1993 Kansas City	AL	81	238	52	12	1	7	87	30	36	16	0	82	7	0	2	6	3	.67	8	.218	.285	.366
1995 Kansas City	AL	52	113	23	6	0	4	41	11	12	9	0	37	0	2	0	1	0	1.00	3	.204	.262	.363
1996 Detroit	AL	7	21	4	0	1	0	6	3	1	2	0	11	0	0	0	0	0	.00	1	.190	.261	.286
9 Min. YEARS		829	3179	827	157	24	156	1500	477	530	242	15	956	35	8	28	89	44	.67	66	.260	.317	.472
3 Maj. YEARS		140	372	79	18	2	11	134	44	49	27	0	130	7	2	2	7	3	.70	12	.212	.277	.360

Billy Hibbard

Pitches: Right Bats: Right Pos: P Ht: 6'3" Wt: 198 Born: 6/24/76 Age: 24

Year Team	Lg Org	G	GS	CG	GF	IP	BFP	H	R	ER	HR	SH	SF	HB	TBB	IBB	SO	WP	Bk	W	L	Pct.	ShO	Sv	ERA
1994 Blue Jays	R Tor	19	0	0	12	32.1	137	32	14	8	1	2	0	0	8	1	23	1	1	3	5	.375	0	3	2.23
1995 Hagerstown	A Tor	16	0	0	5	34.2	149	42	16	15	1	0	1	1	6	1	20	2	0	2	1	.667	0	0	3.89
Medcine Hat	R+ Tor	4	3	0	0	17.2	70	14	8	7	1	0	1	0	4	0	15	0	0	1	1	.500	0	0	3.57
1997 Hagerstown	A Tor	11	0	0	5	17.1	75	23	10	10	1	0	0	0	3	0	13	2	0	0	0	.000	0	0	5.19
1998 Dunedin	A+ Tor	2	0	0	0	4	16	4	0	0	0	1	0	0	2	0	1	0	0	0	0	.000	0	0	0.00
Amarillo	IND —	26	0	0	17	40.1	193	63	31	27	2	3	0	1	12	2	27	1	0	3	2	.600	0	2	6.02
1999 Knoxville	AA Tor	3	0	0	0	3.1	18	7	3	3	1	0	0	0	1	0	0	0	0	0	0	.000	0	0	8.10
Dunedin	A+ Tor	31	1	0	4	55.1	235	54	29	29	4	4	2	2	18	0	34	2	0	3	2	.600	0	0	4.72
5 Min. YEARS		112	4	0	43	205	893	239	111	99	11	10	4	4	54	4	133	8	1	12	11	.522	0	5	4.35

Jason Hill

Pitches: Left Bats: Right Pos: P Ht: 5'11" Wt: 175 Born: 4/14/72 Age: 28

Year Team	Lg Org	G	GS	CG	GF	IP	BFP	H	R	ER	HR	SH	SF	HB	TBB	IBB	SO	WP	Bk	W	L	Pct.	ShO	Sv	ERA
1994 Boise	A- Ana	23	0	0	8	29.2	135	31	14	10	2	0	1	1	16	3	37	2	2	4	3	.571	0	2	3.03
1995 Cedar Rapds	A Ana	48	0	0	17	59.1	276	59	38	30	4	8	1	5	41	6	49	2	1	2	1	.667	0	2	4.55
1996 Cedar Rapds	A Ana	18	6	0	2	43.2	197	38	19	15	2	3	1	5	31	1	26	4	0	2	2	.500	0	1	3.09
Lk Elsinore	A+ Ana	32	0	0	8	39.2	167	39	16	11	4	1	0	2	14	0	28	0	2	4	3	.571	0	0	2.50
1997 Lk Elsinore	A+ Ana	54	0	0	37	66	313	71	43	31	2	10	1	5	34	4	73	4	0	3	7	.300	0	15	4.23
1998 Midland	AA Ana	48	0	0	17	66	311	68	44	36	5	4	0	7	38	1	53	2	1	1	1	.500	0	2	4.91
1999 Erie	AA Ana	23	0	0	7	28	151	37	37	31	4	3	1	4	24	1	14	1	0	1	2	.333	0	0	9.96
Lk Elsinore	A+ Ana	10	0	0	5	10.1	61	16	19	15	3	2	0	3	12	0	12	2	0	0	2	.000	0	2	13.06
6 Min. YEARS		256	6	0	101	342.2	1611	359	230	179	26	31	5	32	210	16	292	17	6	17	21	.447	0	24	4.70

Shea Hillenbrand

Bats: Right Throws: Right Pos: C Ht: 6'1" Wt: 200 Born: 7/27/75 Age: 24

Year Team	Lg Org	G	AB	H	2B	3B	HR	TB	R	RBI	TBB	IBB	SO	HBP	SH	SF	SB	CS	SB%	GDP	Avg	OBP	SLG
1996 Lowell	A- Bos	72	279	88	18	2	2	116	33	38	18	1	32	8	0	2	4	3	.57	6	.315	.371	.416
1997 Michigan	A Bos	64	224	65	13	3	3	93	28	39	9	1	20	1	0	4	1	3	.25	2	.290	.315	.415
Sarasota	A+ Bos	57	220	65	12	0	2	83	25	28	7	1	29	2	1	2	9	8	.53	4	.295	.320	.377
1998 Michigan	A Bos	129	498	174	33	4	19	272	80	92	19	2	49	10	1	3	13	7	.65	11	.349	.383	.546
1999 Trenton	AA Bos	69	282	73	15	0	7	109	41	36	14	3	27	3	0	3	6	5	.55	6	.259	.298	.387
4 Min. YEARS		391	1503	465	91	9	33	673	207	233	67	8	157	24	2	14	33	26	.56	29	.309	.346	.448

Rich Hills

Bats: Right **Throws:** Right **Pos:** 3B **Ht:** 6'0" **Wt:** 195 **Born:** 7/28/73 **Age:** 26

Year Team	Lg Org	G	AB	H	2B	3B	HR	TB	R	RBI	TBB	IBB	SO	HBP	SH	SF	SB	CS	SB%	GDP	Avg	OBP	SLG
1995 Idaho Falls	R+ SD	61	224	69	14	1	7	106	49	48	31	0	27	11	0	5	4	1	.80	5	.308	.410	.473
1996 Clinton	A SD	124	433	108	34	0	7	163	42	58	50	2	69	12	0	3	4	4	.50	11	.249	.341	.376
1997 Rancho Cuca	A+ SD	40	128	35	8	1	0	45	19	15	18	0	31	2	1	1	1	1	.50	2	.273	.369	.352
Mobile	AA SD	71	216	54	12	1	5	83	37	30	25	1	34	3	0	3	2	0	1.00	8	.250	.332	.384
1998 Orlando	AA Sea	124	440	104	19	0	3	132	54	51	56	1	66	7	2	9	1	2	.33	16	.236	.326	.300
1999 Tacoma	AAA Sea	1	4	0	0	0	0	0	0	0	0	0	0	0	0	0	0	0	.00	0	.000	.000	.000
New Haven	AA Sea	83	282	74	15	0	4	101	30	29	40	0	47	7	0	2	1	3	.25	6	.262	.366	.358
5 Min. YEARS		504	1727	444	102	3	26	630	231	231	220	4	274	42	3	23	13	11	.54	48	.257	.351	.365

Eric Hinske

Bats: Left **Throws:** Right **Pos:** 3B-1B **Ht:** 6'2" **Wt:** 225 **Born:** 8/5/77 **Age:** 22

Year Team	Lg Org	G	AB	H	2B	3B	HR	TB	R	RBI	TBB	IBB	SO	HBP	SH	SF	SB	CS	SB%	GDP	Avg	OBP	SLG
1998 Williamsprt	A- ChC	68	248	74	20	0	9	121	46	57	35	3	61	2	0	4	19	3	.86	2	.298	.384	.488
Rockford	A ChC	6	20	9	4	0	1	16	8	4	5	0	6	0	0	1	1	0	1.00	0	.450	.538	.800
1999 Daytona	A+ ChC	130	445	132	28	6	19	229	76	79	62	7	90	5	1	5	16	10	.62	5	.297	.385	.515
Iowa	AAA ChC	4	15	4	0	1	1	9	3	2	1	0	4	0	0	0	0	0	.00	0	.267	.313	.600
2 Min. YEARS		208	728	219	52	7	30	375	133	142	103	10	161	7	1	10	36	13	.73	7	.301	.388	.515

Kevin Hite

Pitches: Right **Bats:** Right **Pos:** P **Ht:** 6'1" **Wt:** 155 **Born:** 7/23/74 **Age:** 25

| | HOW MUCH HE PITCHED | | | | | | WHAT HE GAVE UP | | | | | | | | | | THE RESULTS | | | | | |
Year Team	Lg Org	G	GS	CG	GF	IP	BFP	H	R	ER	HR	SH	SF	HB	TBB	IBB	SO	WP	Bk	W	L	Pct.	ShO	Sv	ERA
1996 Padres	R SD	13	12	2	0	77	326	86	44	31	1	3	0	1	15	0	65	4	2	5	5	.500	1	0	3.62
1997 Clinton	A SD	38	4	1	17	87	354	86	38	32	6	0	4	1	11	0	85	2	1	5	5	.500	0	1	3.31
1998 Rancho Cuca	A+ SD	30	0	0	25	41.2	166	36	16	14	2	0	3	0	8	1	45	4	0	4	0	1.000	0	12	3.02
1999 Rancho Cuca	A+ SD	7	0	0	7	6.2	27	6	3	3	0	1	0	0	1	0	8	0	0	0	1	.000	0	4	4.05
Mobile	AA SD	51	0	0	39	58.1	256	71	30	28	6	1	4	3	17	4	52	2	1	2	4	.333	0	15	4.32
4 Min. YEARS		139	16	3	88	270.2	1129	285	131	108	15	5	11	5	52	5	255	12	4	16	15	.516	1	32	3.59

Kevin Hodges

Pitches: Right **Bats:** Right **Pos:** P **Ht:** 6'4" **Wt:** 200 **Born:** 6/24/73 **Age:** 27

| | HOW MUCH HE PITCHED | | | | | | WHAT HE GAVE UP | | | | | | | | | | THE RESULTS | | | | | |
Year Team	Lg Org	G	GS	CG	GF	IP	BFP	H	R	ER	HR	SH	SF	HB	TBB	IBB	SO	WP	Bk	W	L	Pct.	ShO	Sv	ERA
1991 Royals	R KC	9	3	0	0	23	104	22	14	11	0	1	1	4	11	0	13	2	0	1	2	.333	0	0	4.30
1992 Royals	R KC	11	9	0	0	49.2	232	60	30	26	1	2	2	4	25	0	24	1	1	5	3	.625	0	0	4.71
1993 Royals	R KC	12	10	0	2	71	299	52	25	16	0	5	0	7	25	0	40	3	0	7	2	.778	0	0	2.03
Wilmington	A+ KC	3	0	0	1	4.2	18	2	0	0	0	1	0	1	3	0	1	0	0	1	0	1.000	0	0	0.00
1994 Rockford	A KC	24	17	2	6	114.1	466	96	53	43	5	3	0	9	35	1	83	7	3	9	6	.600	1	3	3.38
1995 Wilmington	A+ KC	12	10	0	1	53.2	232	53	31	27	1	1	1	3	25	1	27	4	0	2	3	.400	0	0	4.53
1996 Lansing	A KC	9	9	0	0	48.1	208	47	32	25	3	2	1	6	19	0	23	3	1	1	2	.333	0	0	4.66
Wilmington	A+ KC	8	8	0	0	38.2	172	45	30	23	2	0	3	1	18	0	15	5	1	2	4	.333	0	0	5.35
1997 Wilmington	A+ KC	28	20	0	4	124.2	563	150	78	62	11	3	6	5	44	7	63	5	2	8	11	.421	0	1	4.48
1998 Jackson	AA Hou	29	15	0	4	107.1	462	108	55	43	8	5	2	7	38	3	70	6	2	4	5	.444	0	0	3.61
1999 Jackson	AA Hou	8	8	0	0	49	211	48	22	16	0	2	2	3	16	0	21	0	0	1	4	.200	0	0	2.94
New Orleans	AAA Hou	5	5	0	0	27.1	126	34	23	22	6	0	2	1	11	1	16	0	0	1	3	.250	0	0	7.24
Tacoma	AAA Sea	14	12	0	1	83	358	88	31	30	3	3	1	9	27	1	42	3	0	3	3	.500	0	1	3.25
9 Min. YEARS		172	126	2	19	794.2	3451	805	424	344	40	28	21	60	297	14	438	39	10	45	48	.484	1	5	3.90

Todd Hogan

Bats: Right **Throws:** Right **Pos:** OF **Ht:** 6'2" **Wt:** 180 **Born:** 9/18/75 **Age:** 24

Year Team	Lg Org	G	AB	H	2B	3B	HR	TB	R	RBI	TBB	IBB	SO	HBP	SH	SF	SB	CS	SB%	GDP	Avg	OBP	SLG
1996 Johnson Cy	R+ StL	47	183	63	7	3	0	76	38	32	20	0	41	6	1	2	18	6	.75	5	.344	.422	.415
St. Pete	A+ StL	2	6	2	0	0	0	2	1	0	0	0	3	0	0	0	0	0	.00	0	.333	.333	.333
1997 Peoria	A StL	112	449	111	18	3	6	153	57	37	26	2	104	11	3	3	28	16	.64	7	.247	.303	.341
1998 Pr William	A+ StL	123	485	135	24	3	2	171	79	45	20	1	116	7	4	7	26	19	.58	7	.278	.312	.353
1999 Arkansas	AA StL	91	280	56	7	6	4	87	36	21	21	0	68	5	4	2	8	7	.53	6	.200	.266	.311
4 Min. YEARS		375	1403	367	56	15	12	489	211	135	87	3	332	29	12	14	80	48	.63	25	.262	.315	.349

Aaron Holbert

Bats: Right **Throws:** Right **Pos:** 2B **Ht:** 6'0" **Wt:** 160 **Born:** 1/9/73 **Age:** 27

Year Team	Lg Org	G	AB	H	2B	3B	HR	TB	R	RBI	TBB	IBB	SO	HBP	SH	SF	SB	CS	SB%	GDP	Avg	OBP	SLG
1990 Johnson Cy	R+ StL	54	176	30	4	1	1	39	27	18	24	1	33	3	1	1	3	5	.38	2	.170	.279	.222
1991 Springfield	A StL	59	215	48	5	1	1	58	22	24	15	0	26	6	1	2	5	8	.38	3	.223	.290	.270
1992 Savannah	A StL	119	438	117	17	4	1	145	53	34	40	0	57	8	6	3	62	25	.71	4	.267	.337	.331
1993 St. Pete	A+ StL	121	457	121	18	3	2	151	60	31	28	2	61	4	15	1	45	22	.67	6	.265	.312	.330
1994 Cardinals	R StL	5	12	2	0	0	0	2	3	0	2	0	2	0	0	0	2	0	1.00	0	.167	.286	.167
Arkansas	AA StL	59	233	69	10	6	2	97	41	19	14	0	25	2	4	1	9	7	.56	5	.296	.340	.416
1995 Louisville	AAA StL	112	401	103	16	4	9	154	57	40	20	1	60	5	3	5	14	6	.70	10	.257	.297	.384
1996 Louisville	AAA StL	112	436	115	16	6	4	155	54	30	21	0	61	2	4	3	20	14	.59	8	.264	.298	.356
1997 Louisville	AAA StL	93	314	80	14	3	4	112	32	32	15	1	56	2	3	4	9	5	.64	9	.255	.290	.357
1998 Orlando	AA Sea	68	251	72	13	5	3	104	46	34	22	0	41	5	4	1	10	14	.42	3	.287	.355	.414

	BATTING																BASERUNNING				PERCENTAGES		
Year Team	Lg Org	G	AB	H	2B	3B	HR	TB	R	RBI	TBB	IBB	SO	HBP	SH	SF	SB	CS	SB%	GDP	Avg	OBP	SLG
Tacoma	AAA Sea	56	229	72	12	0	9	111	38	31	12	0	40	3	2	1	6	6	.50	3	.314	.355	.485
1999 Durham	AAA TB	100	347	108	18	4	12	170	77	56	25	0	56	5	8	5	14	5	.74	4	.311	.361	.490
1996 St. Louis	NL	1	3	0	0	0	0	0	0	0	0	0	0	0	0	0	0	0	.00	0	.000	.000	.000
10 Min. YEARS		958	3509	937	143	37	48	1298	510	351	238	5	518	45	52	28	199	117	.63	57	.267	.319	.370

David Holdridge

Pitches: Right **Bats:** Right **Pos:** P ·   **Ht:** 6' 3" **Wt:** 190 **Born:** 2/5/69 **Age:** 31

	HOW MUCH HE PITCHED						WHAT HE GAVE UP											THE RESULTS					
Year Team	Lg Org	G	GS	CG	GF	IP	BFP	H	R	ER	HR	SH	SF	HB	TBB	IBB	SO	WP	Bk	W	L	Pct.	ShO	Sv	ERA
1988 Quad City	A Ana	28	28	0	0	153.2	686	151	92	66	4	5	4	13	79	1	110	8	4	6	12	.333	0	0	3.87
1989 Clearwater	A+ Phi	24	24	3	0	132.1	610	147	100	84	11	2	6	8	77	0	77	16	1	7	10	.412	0	0	5.71
1990 Reading	AA Phi	24	24	1	0	127.2	571	114	74	64	13	3	5	6	79	0	78	8	0	8	12	.400	0	0	4.51
1991 Reading	AA Phi	7	7	0	0	26.1	135	26	24	16	3	2	3	1	34	0	19	3	0	0	2	.000	0	0	5.47
Clearwater	A+ Phi	15	0	0	4	25	126	34	23	21	2	0	2	1	21	0	23	4	0	0	0	.000	0	1	7.56
1992 Palm Spring	A+ Ana	28	27	3	0	159	726	169	99	75	5	5	3	5	87	4	135	21	0	12	12	.500	2	0	4.25
1993 Midland	AA Ana	27	27	1	0	151	700	202	117	102	13	4	2	11	55	0	123	13	1	8	10	.444	1	0	6.08
1994 Vancouver	AAA Ana	4	0	0	1	7	36	12	7	4	1	0	1	1	4	0	4	0	0	0	0	.000	0	0	5.14
Midland	AA Ana	38	2	0	17	66.1	286	66	33	29	4	1	3	5	23	0	59	2	0	7	4	.636	0	2	3.93
1995 Lk Elsinore	A+ Ana	12	0	0	8	18.1	74	13	3	2	0	1	1	2	5	1	24	3	0	3	0	1.000	0	0	0.98
Midland	AA Ana	14	0	0	11	25.1	100	20	8	5	1	1	0	1	8	0	23	2	0	1	0	1.000	0	1	1.78
Vancouver	AAA Ana	11	0	0	6	13.2	68	18	10	7	0	2	0	1	7	1	13	3	0	0	2	.000	0	1	4.61
1996 Vancouver	AAA Ana	29	0	0	17	35	163	39	19	18	4	0	2	2	23	2	26	3	0	2	1	.667	0	1	4.63
Lk Elsinore	A+ Ana	12	0	0	12	13	53	11	3	3	1	0	0	1	2	0	21	0	0	0	0	.000	0	6	2.08
1997 Memphis	AA Sea	30	0	0	27	35	149	31	14	13	2	1	1	2	17	1	37	2	0	0	3	.000	0	17	3.34
Tacoma	AAA Sea	15	0	0	8	24.1	105	21	9	8	0	1	1	1	13	0	24	0	0	1	1	.500	0	1	2.96
1998 Tacoma	AAA Sea	42	0	0	17	70.2	299	55	28	26	2	6	2	7	34	5	73	3	1	7	5	.583	0	7	3.31
1999 Tacoma	AAA Sea	41	0	0	26	66.1	297	67	38	32	3	3	2	9	23	2	68	7	0	5	6	.455	0	10	4.34
1998 Seattle	AL	7	0	0	3	6.2	31	6	3	3	0	0	1	0	4	0	6	3	0	0	0	.000	0	0	4.05
12 Min. YEARS		401	139	8	154	1150	5184	1196	701	575	69	37	38	77	591	17	937	98	7	67	80	.456	3	47	4.50

Damon Hollins

Bats: Right **Throws:** Left **Pos:** OF   **Ht:** 5'11" **Wt:** 180 **Born:** 6/12/74 **Age:** 26

	BATTING																BASERUNNING				PERCENTAGES		
Year Team	Lg Org	G	AB	H	2B	3B	HR	TB	R	RBI	TBB	IBB	SO	HBP	SH	SF	SB	CS	SB%	GDP	Avg	OBP	SLG
1992 Braves	R Atl	49	179	41	12	1	1	58	35	15	30	0	22	2	2	0	15	2	.88	3	.229	.346	.324
1993 Danville	R+ Atl	62	240	77	15	2	7	117	37	51	19	0	30	1	0	3	10	2	.83	5	.321	.369	.488
1994 Durham	A+ Atl	131	485	131	28	0	23	228	76	88	45	0	115	4	2	3	12	7	.63	9	.270	.335	.470
1995 Greenville	AA Atl	129	466	115	26	2	18	199	64	77	44	6	120	4	0	6	6	6	.50	7	.247	.313	.427
1996 Richmond	AAA Atl	42	146	29	9	0	0	38	16	8	16	1	37	0	1	0	2	3	.40	2	.199	.278	.260
1997 Richmond	AAA Atl	134	498	132	31	3	20	229	73	63	45	4	84	3	6	1	7	2	.78	18	.265	.329	.460
1998 Richmond	AAA Atl	119	436	115	26	3	13	186	61	48	45	2	85	0	1	4	10	2	.83	16	.264	.330	.427
1999 Indianapolis	AAA Cin	106	328	86	19	0	9	132	58	43	31	1	44	1	1	0	11	2	.85	13	.262	.328	.402
1998 Atlanta	NL	3	6	1	0	0	0	1	0	0	0	0	1	0	0	0	0	0	.00	0	.167	.167	.167
Los Angeles	NL	5	9	2	0	0	0	2	1	2	0	0	0	0	0	0	0	1	.00	0	.222	.222	.222
8 Min. YEARS		772	2778	726	166	11	91	1187	420	393	275	14	537	15	13	17	73	26	.74	73	.261	.329	.427

Mark Holzemer

Pitches: Left **Bats:** Left **Pos:** P   **Ht:** 6' 0" **Wt:** 185 **Born:** 8/20/69 **Age:** 30

	HOW MUCH HE PITCHED						WHAT HE GAVE UP											THE RESULTS					
Year Team	Lg Org	G	GS	CG	GF	IP	BFP	H	R	ER	HR	SH	SF	HB	TBB	IBB	SO	WP	Bk	W	L	Pct.	ShO	Sv	ERA
1988 Bend	A- Ana	13	13	1	0	68.2	311	59	51	40	3	0	1	6	47	1	72	8	6	4	6	.400	1	0	5.24
1989 Quad City	A Ana	25	25	3	0	139.1	603	122	68	52	4	3	5	5	64	1	131	12	4	12	7	.632	1	0	3.36
1990 Midland	AA Ana	15	15	1	0	77	363	92	55	45	10	2	1	6	41	0	54	6	0	1	7	.125	0	0	5.26
1991 Midland	AA Ana	2	2	0	0	6.1	28	3	2	1	0	1	0	1	5	0	7	2	0	0	0	.000	0	0	1.42
1992 Palm Spring	A+ Ana	5	5	2	0	30	124	23	10	10	2	1	0	3	13	0	32	0	0	3	2	.600	0	0	3.00
Midland	AA Ana	7	7	2	0	44.2	188	45	22	19	4	0	1	1	13	0	36	3	1	2	5	.286	0	0	3.83
Edmonton	AAA Ana	17	16	4	1	89	416	114	69	66	12	2	6	7	55	1	49	6	1	7	5	.417	0	0	6.67
1993 Vancouver	AAA Ana	24	23	2	0	145.2	642	158	94	78	9	6	4	4	70	2	80	5	5	9	6	.600	0	0	4.82
1994 Vancouver	AAA Ana	29	17	0	5	117.1	540	144	93	86	19	4	5	6	58	1	77	15	0	5	10	.333	0	0	6.60
1995 Vancouver	AAA Ana	28	4	0	11	54.2	228	45	18	15	2	5	0	3	24	4	35	2	0	3	2	.600	0	2	2.47
1996 Lk Elsinore	A+ Ana	9	3	0	2	11.1	47	10	3	3	0	0	0	1	4	0	10	0	0	0	1	.000	0	0	2.38
1997 Tacoma	AAA Sea	37	0	0	26	41	165	32	10	10	1	0	2	0	10	3	38	1	0	1	0	1.000	0	13	2.20
1998 Edmonton	AAA Oak	30	0	0	8	39	168	41	15	14	2	3	4	3	11	1	27	2	0	1	1	.500	0	0	3.23
1999 Colo Sprngs	AAA Col	41	1	0	11	55.1	268	77	39	35	10	2	2	6	24	1	49	2	0	3	2	.600	0	1	5.69
1993 California	AL	5	4	0	1	23.1	117	34	24	23	2	1	0	3	13	0	10	1	0	0	3	.000	0	0	8.87
1995 California	AL	12	0	0	5	8.1	45	11	6	5	1	1	0	1	7	1	5	0	0	0	1	.000	0	0	5.40
1996 California	AL	25	0	0	3	24.2	119	35	28	24	7	0	1	3	8	1	20	0	0	1	0	1.000	0	0	8.76
1997 Seattle	AL	14	0	0	2	9	44	9	6	6	0	0	0	0	8	0	7	0	0	0	0	.000	0	1	6.00
1998 Oakland	AL	13	0	0	4	9.2	44	13	6	6	1	0	1	1	3	0	3	1	0	1	0	1.000	0	0	5.59
12 Min. YEARS		282	131	15	64	919.1	4091	965	549	474	78	29	31	52	439	15	697	64	17	49	56	.467	2	22	4.64
5 Maj. YEARS		69	4	0	15	75	369	102	70	64	11	2	2	8	39	2	45	2	0	2	4	.333	0	1	7.68

David Hooten

Pitches: Right **Bats:** Right **Pos:** P   **Ht:** 6'0" **Wt:** 182 **Born:** 5/8/75 **Age:** 25

	HOW MUCH HE PITCHED						WHAT HE GAVE UP											THE RESULTS					
Year Team	Lg Org	G	GS	CG	GF	IP	BFP	H	R	ER	HR	SH	SF	HB	TBB	IBB	SO	WP	Bk	W	L	Pct.	ShO	Sv	ERA
1996 Elizabethtn	R+ Min	6	0	0	5	8.1	37	6	4	4	0	0	2	1	5	0	15	0	2	1	0	1.000	0	1	4.32

Year Team	Lg Org	G	GS	CG	GF	IP	BFP	H	R	ER	HR	SH	SF	HB	TBB	IBB	SO	WP	Bk	W	L	Pct.	ShO	Sv	ERA
						HOW MUCH HE PITCHED				WHAT HE GAVE UP												THE RESULTS			
Fort Wayne	A Min	21	0	0	14	37.1	155	30	11	10	0	2	4	2	13	1	39	3	1	4	1	.800	0	2	2.41
1997 Fort Wayne	A Min	28	27	2	0	165.2	675	134	57	48	5	4	2	9	54	1	138	4	6	11	8	.579	2	0	2.61
1998 Fort Myers	A+ Min	28	28	0	0	158.1	714	185	94	79	7	0	10	11	57	0	136	4	0	9	11	.450	0	0	4.49
1999 New Britain	AA Min	52	5	0	17	103.2	450	94	55	41	10	3	6	1	49	2	89	3	0	6	6	.500	0	1	3.56
4 Min. YEARS		135	60	2	36	473.1	2031	449	221	182	22	9	24	24	178	3	417	14	9	31	26	.544	2	4	3.46

Jeff Horn

Bats: Right **Throws:** Right **Pos:** C   **Ht:** 6'1" **Wt:** 213 **Born:** 8/23/70 **Age:** 29

Year Team	Lg Org	G	AB	H	2B	3B	HR	TB	R	RBI	TBB	IBB	SO	HBP	SH	SF	SB	CS	SB%	GDP	Avg	OBP	SLG
								BATTING									BASERUNNING				PERCENTAGES		
1992 Elizabethtn	R+ Min	41	144	35	6	0	1	44	20	26	25	1	25	4	0	2	2	0	1.00	5	.243	.366	.306
1993 Fort Wayne	A Min	66	200	39	7	0	5	61	19	23	18	0	51	4	1	4	1	2	.33	3	.195	.270	.305
1994 Fort Myers	A+ Min	34	100	28	3	0	0	31	10	9	8	1	11	3	0	1	0	2	.00	6	.280	.348	.310
1995 Salt Lake	AAA Min	3	10	5	1	0	0	6	0	2	0	0	1	0	0	0	0	0	.00	0	.500	.500	.600
Fort Myers	A+ Min	66	199	53	5	1	0	60	25	20	38	1	30	4	1	3	2	3	.40	4	.266	.389	.302
1996 Salt Lake	AAA Min	25	83	28	5	0	3	42	14	13	12	1	5	2	2	2	0	1	.00	4	.337	.424	.506
Hardware Cy	AA Min	12	45	12	2	0	0	14	4	3	6	1	7	0	0	0	0	1	.00	0	.267	.353	.311
1997 New Britain	AA Min	56	184	47	10	0	4	69	17	26	19	0	24	7	2	2	2	4	.33	7	.255	.344	.375
Salt Lake	AAA Min	23	78	26	6	0	1	35	16	13	11	0	22	1	0	0	0	0	.00	0	.333	.422	.449
1998 Salt Lake	AAA Min	24	72	22	5	0	1	30	14	0	12	0	18	1	2	0	1	2	.33	0	.306	.412	.417
1999 Greenville	AA Atl	66	166	38	6	0	2	50	19	27	16	0	28	4	0	3	0	1	.00	4	.229	.307	.301
8 Min. YEARS		416	1281	333	56	1	17	442	158	168	165	5	222	30	8	17	8	16	.33	33	.260	.354	.345

Tyrone Horne

Bats: Left **Throws:** Right **Pos:** OF   **Ht:** 5'10" **Wt:** 185 **Born:** 11/2/70 **Age:** 29

Year Team	Lg Org	G	AB	H	2B	3B	HR	TB	R	RBI	TBB	IBB	SO	HBP	SH	SF	SB	CS	SB%	GDP	Avg	OBP	SLG
								BATTING									BASERUNNING				PERCENTAGES		
1989 Expos	R Mon	24	68	14	3	2	0	21	7	13	11	0	29	0	0	0	4	4	.50	1	.206	.316	.309
1990 Gate City	R+ Mon	56	202	57	11	2	1	75	26	13	24	1	62	2	2	2	23	8	.74	1	.282	.361	.371
Jamestown	A- Mon	7	23	7	2	1	0	11	1	5	4	0	5	0	0	0	3	0	1.00	1	.304	.407	.478
1991 Sumter	A Mon	118	428	114	20	3	10	170	69	49	42	1	133	2	1	4	23	12	.66	4	.266	.332	.397
1992 Rockford	A Mon	129	480	134	27	4	12	205	71	48	62	5	141	1	2	2	23	13	.64	1	.279	.361	.427
Harrisburg	AA Mon	1	1	1	0	0	0	1	0	0	0	0	0	0	0	0	0	0	.00	0	1.000	1.000	1.000
1993 Wst Plm Bch	A+ Mon	82	288	85	19	2	10	138	43	44	40	1	72	0	1	3	11	10	.52	1	.295	.378	.479
Harrisburg	AA Mon	35	128	46	8	1	4	68	22	22	22	0	37	1	1	0	3	2	.60	3	.359	.457	.531
1994 Expos	R Mon	7	29	7	1	0	1	11	3	7	4	0	9	0	0	0	1	0	1.00	0	.241	.333	.379
Harrisburg	AA Mon	90	311	89	15	0	9	131	56	48	50	1	92	1	1	2	11	13	.46	7	.286	.385	.421
1995 Harrisburg	AA Mon	87	294	87	17	4	14	154	59	47	58	2	65	1	3	3	14	8	.64	3	.296	.410	.524
Norwich	AA NYY	46	166	47	16	1	2	71	23	22	26	1	36	0	0	3	4	2	.67	4	.283	.374	.428
1996 Edmonton	AAA Oak	67	204	47	7	2	4	70	28	16	32	1	53	1	0	2	5	3	.63	6	.230	.335	.343
Binghamton	AA NYM	43	125	34	10	0	3	53	17	19	15	4	39	1	0	0	3	0	1.00	1	.272	.355	.424
1997 Kane County	A Fla	133	468	143	24	2	21	234	89	91	104	18	88	3	0	1	18	7	.72	13	.306	.434	.500
1998 Arkansas	AA StL	123	443	138	13	3	37	268	94	139	70	7	97	1	0	8	18	7	.72	8	.312	.402	.605
Memphis	AAA StL	3	11	4	1	0	0	5	1	1	1	0	4	0	0	0	0	0	.00	0	.364	.417	.455
1999 Reading	AA Phi	80	262	70	13	2	5	102	37	37	43	1	64	0	0	2	13	8	.62	4	.267	.368	.389
11 Min. YEARS		1131	3931	1124	207	29	133	1788	646	621	608	43	1026	14	11	30	177	97	.65	60	.286	.381	.455

Jim Horner

Bats: Right **Throws:** Right **Pos:** C   **Ht:** 6'0" **Wt:** 210 **Born:** 11/11/73 **Age:** 26

Year Team	Lg Org	G	AB	H	2B	3B	HR	TB	R	RBI	TBB	IBB	SO	HBP	SH	SF	SB	CS	SB%	GDP	Avg	OBP	SLG
								BATTING									BASERUNNING				PERCENTAGES		
1996 Everett	A- Sea	18	60	9	2	0	2	17	6	5	10	1	16	1	0	0	0	0	.00	1	.150	.282	.283
1997 Wisconsin	A Sea	47	161	40	10	1	5	67	19	24	17	0	53	5	1	1	0	1	.00	4	.248	.337	.416
Lancaster	A+ Sea	45	163	42	6	0	9	75	26	27	16	0	48	2	0	1	2	0	1.00	4	.258	.330	.460
1998 Orlando	AA Sea	73	247	54	9	1	9	92	29	36	33	0	59	3	1	5	2	1	.67	5	.219	.313	.372
1999 New Haven	AA Sea	76	278	75	17	0	6	110	29	50	17	0	51	4	1	2	1	1	.50	10	.270	.319	.396
4 Min. YEARS		259	909	220	44	2	31	361	109	142	93	1	227	15	3	9	5	3	.63	24	.242	.320	.397

Dwayne Hosey

Bats: Both **Throws:** Right **Pos:** OF   **Ht:** 5'10" **Wt:** 180 **Born:** 3/11/67 **Age:** 33

Year Team	Lg Org	G	AB	H	2B	3B	HR	TB	R	RBI	TBB	IBB	SO	HBP	SH	SF	SB	CS	SB%	GDP	Avg	OBP	SLG
								BATTING									BASERUNNING				PERCENTAGES		
1987 White Sox	R CWS	41	129	36	2	1	1	43	26	10	18	1	22	3	0	2	19	4	.83	1	.279	.375	.333
1988 South Bend	A CWS	95	311	71	11	0	2	88	53	24	28	2	55	5	4	2	36	15	.71	5	.228	.301	.283
Utica	A- CWS	3	7	1	0	0	0	1	0	0	2	0	1	0	0	0	1	0	1.00	0	.143	.333	.143
1989 Madison	A Oak	123	470	115	16	6	11	176	72	51	44	3	82	8	2	2	33	18	.65	9	.245	.319	.374
1990 Modesto	A+ Oak	113	453	133	21	5	16	212	77	61	50	5	70	8	8	2	30	23	.57	2	.294	.372	.468
1991 Huntsville	AA Oak	28	102	25	6	0	1	34	16	7	9	1	19	1	1	1	3	4	.50	1	.245	.310	.333
Stockton	A+ Mil	85	356	97	12	7	15	168	55	62	31	1	58	3	1	9	22	8	.73	4	.272	.328	.472
1992 Wichita	AA SD	125	427	108	23	5	9	168	56	68	40	3	70	10	1	9	16	11	.59	3	.253	.326	.393
1993 Wichita	AA SD	86	326	95	19	2	18	172	52	61	25	4	44	2	0	4	13	4	.76	4	.291	.342	.528
Las Vegas	AAA SD	32	110	29	4	4	3	50	21	12	11	1	17	4	0	0	7	4	.64	0	.264	.352	.455
1994 Omaha	AAA KC	112	406	135	23	8	27	255	95	80	61	10	85	8	0	6	27	12	.69	3	.333	.424	.628
1995 Omaha	AAA KC	75	271	80	21	4	12	145	59	50	29	2	45	1	1	1	15	6	.71	1	.295	.363	.535
1996 Pawtucket	AAA Bos	93	367	109	25	4	14	184	77	53	40	2	67	3	0	5	20	7	.74	5	.297	.366	.501
1999 Ottawa	AAA Mon	33	94	17	3	1	1	25	16	11	15	1	26	4	1	3	6	4	.60	1	.181	.310	.266
Winnipeg	IND —	58	206	68	18	2	6	108	47	46	41	1	27	2	0	4	8	8	.43	3	.330	.439	.524

Year Team	Lg Org	G	AB	H	2B	3B	HR	TB	R	RBI	TBB	IBB	SO	HBP	SH	SF	SB	CS	SB%	GDP	Avg	OBP	SLG
1995 Boston	AL	24	68	23	8	1	3	42	20	7	8	0	16	0	1	0	6	0	1.00	0	.333	.422	.618
1996 Boston	AL	28	78	17	2	2	1	26	13	3	7	0	17	0	2	0	6	3	.67	0	.218	.282	.333
11 Min. YEARS		1102	4035	1119	204	49	136	1829	722	596	444	37	684	62	19	49	256	128	.67	40	.277	.354	.453
2 Maj. YEARS		52	146	40	10	3	4	68	33	10	15	0	33	0	3	0	12	3	.80	0	.274	.342	.466

Matt Howard

Bats: Right Throws: Right Pos: 2B   Ht: 5'10" Wt: 170 Born: 9/22/67 Age: 32

Year Team	Lg Org	G	AB	H	2B	3B	HR	TB	R	RBI	TBB	IBB	SO	HBP	SH	SF	SB	CS	SB%	GDP	Avg	OBP	SLG
1989 Great Falls	R+ LA	59	186	62	8	2	3	83	39	34	21	0	14	9	5	2	23	8	.74	3	.333	.422	.446
1990 Bakersfield	A+ LA	137	551	144	22	3	1	175	75	54	37	1	39	13	4	6	47	10	.82	8	.261	.320	.318
1991 Vero Beach	A+ LA	128	441	115	21	3	3	151	79	39	56	2	49	10	14	6	50	18	.74	6	.261	.353	.342
1992 San Antonio	AA LA	95	345	93	12	5	2	121	40	34	28	1	38	4	16	1	18	15	.55	12	.270	.331	.351
Albuquerque	AAA LA	36	116	34	3	0	0	37	14	8	9	0	7	0	2	0	1	2	.33	2	.293	.344	.319
1993 Albuquerque	AAA LA	18	26	4	0	1	0	6	3	4	3	0	2	0	1	1	1	1	.50	1	.154	.233	.231
San Antonio	AA LA	41	122	35	5	1	0	42	12	5	16	1	14	3	2	0	4	5	.44	4	.287	.383	.344
1994 Albuquerque	AAA LA	88	267	79	12	6	1	106	44	33	14	0	13	6	4	1	15	8	.65	12	.296	.344	.397
1995 Bowie	AA Bal	70	251	76	8	2	1	91	42	15	29	1	27	5	3	1	22	4	.85	6	.303	.385	.363
1996 Columbus	AAA NYY	51	202	70	12	2	2	92	36	16	18	0	9	1	3	1	9	3	.75	5	.347	.401	.455
1997 Columbus	AAA NYY	122	478	149	28	7	6	209	90	67	54	1	33	10	3	3	22	7	.76	12	.312	.391	.437
1998 Fresno	AAA SF	117	407	113	21	0	2	140	70	36	40	3	34	10	6	2	10	6	.63	8	.278	.355	.344
1999 Nashville	AAA Pit	114	399	117	17	2	2	144	41	44	25	0	24	4	4	5	13	10	.57	15	.293	.337	.361
1996 New York	AL	35	54	11	1	0	1	15	9	9	2	0	8	0	2	1	1	0	1.00	2	.204	.228	.278
11 Min. YEARS		1076	3791	1091	169	34	23	1397	585	389	350	10	303	75	67	29	235	97	.71	94	.288	.357	.369

Mike Hubbard

Bats: Right Throws: Right Pos: C   Ht: 6'1" Wt: 205 Born: 2/16/71 Age: 29

Year Team	Lg Org	G	AB	H	2B	3B	HR	TB	R	RBI	TBB	IBB	SO	HBP	SH	SF	SB	CS	SB%	GDP	Avg	OBP	SLG
1992 Geneva	A- ChC	50	183	44	4	4	3	65	25	25	7	0	29	3	4	4	6	4	.60	2	.240	.274	.355
1993 Daytona	A+ ChC	68	245	72	10	3	1	91	25	20	18	0	41	5	2	5	10	6	.63	4	.294	.348	.371
1994 Orlando	AA ChC	104	357	102	13	3	11	154	52	39	29	4	58	8	2	2	7	7	.50	5	.286	.351	.431
1995 Iowa	AAA ChC	75	254	66	6	3	5	93	28	23	26	1	60	0	6	3	6	1	.86	6	.260	.325	.366
1996 Iowa	AAA ChC	67	232	68	12	0	7	101	38	33	10	1	56	3	3	1	2	0	1.00	6	.293	.329	.435
1997 Iowa	AAA ChC	50	186	52	15	1	6	87	24	26	11	0	23	0	1	2	2	0	1.00	2	.280	.317	.468
1998 Ottawa	AAA Mon	20	70	16	5	0	0	21	9	8	3	0	13	0	0	1	0	0	.00	3	.229	.257	.300
1999 Oklahoma	AAA Tex	110	392	111	19	0	9	157	48	49	25	1	70	3	2	5	4	1	.80	13	.283	.327	.401
1995 Chicago	NL	15	23	4	0	0	0	4	2	1	2	0	2	0	0	0	0	0	.00	1	.174	.240	.174
1996 Chicago	NL	21	38	4	0	0	1	7	1	4	0	0	15	0	0	1	0	0	.00	1	.105	.103	.184
1997 Chicago	NL	29	64	13	0	0	1	16	4	2	2	1	21	0	0	0	0	0	.00	1	.203	.227	.250
1998 Montreal	NL	32	55	8	1	0	1	12	3	3	0	0	17	1	0	0	0	0	.00	1	.145	.161	.218
8 Min. YEARS		544	1919	531	84	14	42	769	249	223	129	7	350	22	20	23	37	19	.66	40	.277	.326	.401
4 Maj. YEARS		97	180	29	1	0	3	39	10	10	4	1	55	1	0	1	0	0	.00	4	.161	.183	.217

Dan Hubbs

Pitches: Right Bats: Right Pos: P   Ht: 6'2" Wt: 200 Born: 1/23/71 Age: 29

Year Team	Lg Org	G	GS	CG	GF	IP	BFP	H	R	ER	HR	SH	SF	HB	TBB	IBB	SO	WP	Bk	W	L	Pct.	ShO	Sv	ERA
1993 Great Falls	R+ LA	3	0	0	1	7.2	29	3	1	1	0	0	0	2	2	0	12	0	1	1	1	.500	0	0	1.17
Bakersfield	A+ LA	19	1	0	8	44.2	181	36	12	9	4	1	2	0	15	1	44	3	1	2	1	.667	0	1	1.81
1994 Bakersfield	A+ LA	13	0	0	6	35.1	145	29	17	15	3	3	0	1	10	0	51	0	0	3	1	.750	0	2	3.82
San Antonio	AA LA	38	1	0	13	80	340	82	34	28	3	1	6	4	27	7	75	5	0	5	5	.500	0	1	3.15
1995 San Antonio	AA LA	31	0	0	6	61	248	58	25	24	3	3	1	1	16	0	52	0	1	2	1	.667	0	0	3.54
1996 Albuquerque	AAA LA	49	0	0	15	75.2	356	89	51	40	4	0	3	3	47	12	82	2	0	7	1	.875	0	2	4.76
1997 Albuquerque	AAA LA	62	3	0	19	94.2	411	103	45	41	11	4	5	4	38	2	87	2	0	6	4	.600	0	3	3.90
1998 Albuquerque	AAA LA	13	0	0	4	19.2	92	23	16	15	4	1	0	0	12	2	25	3	0	1	2	.333	0	0	6.86
1999 Reading	AA Phi	3	1	0	0	8	37	10	5	5	2	0	0	0	5	0	8	0	0	0	0	.000	0	0	5.63
7 Min. YEARS		231	6	0	72	426.2	1839	433	206	178	34	13	17	15	172	24	436	15	3	27	16	.628	0	9	3.75

Ken Huckaby

Bats: Right Throws: Right Pos: C   Ht: 6'1" Wt: 205 Born: 1/27/71 Age: 29

Year Team	Lg Org	G	AB	H	2B	3B	HR	TB	R	RBI	TBB	IBB	SO	HBP	SH	SF	SB	CS	SB%	GDP	Avg	OBP	SLG
1991 Great Falls	R+ LA	57	213	55	16	0	3	80	39	37	17	0	38	4	1	3	3	2	.60	4	.258	.321	.376
1992 Vero Beach	A+ LA	73	261	63	9	0	0	72	14	21	7	0	42	1	2	2	1	1	.50	5	.241	.262	.276
1993 Vero Beach	A+ LA	79	281	75	14	1	4	103	22	41	11	1	35	2	3	2	2	1	.67	3	.267	.297	.367
San Antonio	AA LA	28	82	18	1	0	0	19	4	5	2	1	7	2	0	1	0	1	.00	2	.220	.253	.232
1994 San Antonio	AA LA	11	41	11	1	0	1	15	3	9	1	1	1	0	0	0	1	0	1.00	1	.268	.286	.366
Bakersfield	A+ LA	77	270	81	18	1	2	107	29	37	10	0	37	0	2	0	2	3	.40	7	.300	.329	.396
1995 Albuquerque	AAA LA	89	278	90	16	2	1	113	30	40	12	1	26	4	3	1	3	1	.75	16	.324	.359	.406
1996 Albuquerque	AAA LA	103	286	79	16	2	3	108	37	41	17	1	35	2	3	1	0	0	.00	10	.276	.320	.378
1997 Albuquerque	AAA LA	69	201	40	5	1	0	47	14	18	9	1	36	0	0	2	1	0	1.00	5	.199	.231	.234
1998 Tacoma	AAA Sea	16	49	11	2	0	0	13	4	1	5	0	6	0	0	0	0	0	.00	2	.224	.296	.265
Columbus	AAA NYY	36	101	21	3	1	1	29	13	10	11	0	14	0	3	0	0	2	.00	3	.208	.286	.287
1999 Tucson	AAA Ari	107	355	107	20	1	2	135	44	42	13	2	33	2	4	5	0	0	.00	11	.301	.325	.380
9 Min. YEARS		745	2418	651	121	9	17	841	253	295	115	8	310	19	22	18	13	10	.57	67	.269	.305	.348

Joe Hudson

Pitches: Right **Bats:** Right **Pos:** P **Ht:** 6' 1" **Wt:** 180 **Born:** 9/29/70 **Age:** 29

		HOW MUCH HE PITCHED						WHAT HE GAVE UP										THE RESULTS					
Year Team	Lg Org	G	GS	CG	GF	IP	BFP	H	R	ER	HR	SH	SF	HB	TBB	IBB	SO	WP	Bk	W	L	Pct.	ShO	Sv	ERA
1992 Elmira	A- Bos	19	7	0	6	72	320	76	46	35	2	3	0	2	33	0	38	4	2	3	3	.500	0	0	4.38
1993 Lynchburg	A+ Bos	49	1	0	30	84.1	372	97	49	38	1	2	2	2	38	2	62	10	2	8	6	.571	0	6	4.06
1994 Sarasota	A+ Bos	30	0	0	21	48.1	215	42	20	12	0	1	1	2	27	0	33	6	0	3	1	.750	0	7	2.23
New Britain	AA Bos	23	0	0	11	39	183	49	18	17	0	3	1	2	18	1	24	1	1	5	3	.625	0	0	3.92
1995 Trenton	AA Bos	22	0	0	17	31.2	133	20	8	6	0	1	0	1	17	3	24	2	1	0	1	.000	0	8	1.71
1996 Pawtucket	AAA Bos	25	0	0	15	33.1	151	29	19	13	0	0	1	1	21	0	18	4	0	1	1	.500	0	5	3.51
1997 Pawtucket	AAA Bos	29	0	0	17	32	148	25	22	8	1	2	2	2	23	3	14	3	0	2	1	.667	0	7	2.25
1998 Pawtucket	AAA Bos	46	0	0	26	47.2	222	57	32	24	3	2	2	0	23	3	32	4	0	2	2	.500	0	10	4.53
Louisville	AAA Mil	9	0	0	1	12.1	57	13	7	7	1	0	1	2	5	1	4	0	0	1	0	1.000	0	0	5.11
1999 Oklahoma	AAA Tex	5	0	0	3	9	42	15	6	5	1	0	1	0	4	0	4	1	0	1	1	.500	0	0	5.00
1995 Boston	AL	39	0	0	11	46	205	53	21	21	2	3	1	2	23	1	29	6	0	0	1	.000	0	1	4.11
1996 Boston	AL	36	0	0	16	45	214	57	35	27	4	1	2	0	32	4	19	0	0	3	5	.375	0	1	5.40
1997 Boston	AL	26	0	0	9	35.2	154	39	16	14	1	1	0	4	14	2	14	1	0	3	1	.750	0	0	3.53
1998 Milwaukee	NL	1	0	0	0	0.1	7	2	6	6	0	0	1	0	4	1	0	0	0	0	0	.000	0	0	162.00
8 Min. YEARS		257	8	0	147	409.2	1843	423	227	165	9	14	11	15	209	13	253	35	6	26	19	.578	0	43	3.62
4 Maj. YEARS		102	0	0	36	127	580	151	78	68	7	5	4	6	73	8	62	7	0	6	7	.462	0	2	4.82

Mike Huelsmann

Bats: Both **Throws:** Right **Pos:** OF **Ht:** 5'11" **Wt:** 165 **Born:** 11/21/74 **Age:** 25

		BATTING														BASERUNNING				PERCENTAGES		
Year Team	Lg Org	G	AB	H	2B	3B	HR	TB	R	RBI	TBB	IBB	SO	HBP	SH	SF	SB	CS	SB%	GDP	Avg	OBP	SLG
1996 Watertown	A- Cle	41	130	34	5	1	0	41	21	21	17	0	14	2	3	0	14	4	.78	0	.262	.356	.315
1997 Kinston	A+ Cle	90	289	71	9	4	2	94	50	19	48	0	56	4	4	0	12	4	.75	8	.246	.357	.325
1998 Akron	AA Cle	9	20	2	0	0	1	5	4	1	4	0	9	1	1	0	1	0	1.00	0	.100	.280	.250
Kinston	A+ Cle	114	425	121	19	4	5	163	63	47	70	5	67	6	6	2	21	16	.57	3	.285	.392	.384
1999 Kinston	A+ Cle	58	177	54	6	4	2	74	35	22	29	0	19	1	8	0	14	3	.82	0	.305	.406	.418
Akron	AA Cle	43	177	49	5	1	1	59	20	10	15	0	30	0	3	0	12	3	.80	0	.277	.333	.333
4 Min. YEARS		355	1218	331	44	14	11	436	193	120	183	5	195	12	25	2	74	30	.71	11	.272	.372	.358

Aubrey Huff

Bats: Left **Throws:** Right **Pos:** 3B **Ht:** 6'4" **Wt:** 220 **Born:** 12/20/76 **Age:** 23

		BATTING														BASERUNNING				PERCENTAGES		
Year Team	Lg Org	G	AB	H	2B	3B	HR	TB	R	RBI	TBB	IBB	SO	HBP	SH	SF	SB	CS	SB%	GDP	Avg	OBP	SLG
1998 Chston-SC	A TB	69	265	85	19	1	13	145	38	54	24	0	40	0	0	5	3	1	.75	5	.321	.371	.547
1999 Orlando	AA TB	133	491	148	40	3	22	260	85	78	64	4	77	4	0	2	2	3	.40	14	.301	.385	.530
2 Min. YEARS		202	756	233	59	4	35	405	123	132	88	4	117	4	0	7	5	4	.56	19	.308	.380	.536

B.J. Huff

Bats: Right **Throws:** Right **Pos:** OF **Ht:** 6'1" **Wt:** 195 **Born:** 8/1/75 **Age:** 24

		BATTING														BASERUNNING				PERCENTAGES		
Year Team	Lg Org	G	AB	H	2B	3B	HR	TB	R	RBI	TBB	IBB	SO	HBP	SH	SF	SB	CS	SB%	GDP	Avg	OBP	SLG
1996 Pittsfield	A- NYM	42	138	27	4	2	2	41	19	14	7	0	36	1	1	1	3	1	.75	2	.196	.238	.297
1997 Capital Cty	A NYM	99	363	92	20	5	7	143	49	41	19	1	78	4	1	2	11	3	.79	8	.253	.296	.394
1998 St. Lucie	A+ NYM	118	451	117	23	3	11	179	60	60	25	0	108	7	1	6	8	10	.44	14	.259	.305	.397
1999 Binghamton	AA NYM	57	205	51	9	1	7	83	26	32	19	1	46	1	0	2	9	2	.82	4	.249	.313	.405
4 Min. YEARS		316	1157	287	56	11	27	446	154	147	70	2	268	13	3	11	31	16	.66	28	.248	.296	.385

Larry Huff

Bats: Right **Throws:** Right **Pos:** 3B **Ht:** 6'0" **Wt:** 175 **Born:** 1/24/72 **Age:** 28

		BATTING														BASERUNNING				PERCENTAGES		
Year Team	Lg Org	G	AB	H	2B	3B	HR	TB	R	RBI	TBB	IBB	SO	HBP	SH	SF	SB	CS	SB%	GDP	Avg	OBP	SLG
1994 Martinsvlle	R+ Phi	39	143	36	2	1	1	43	24	7	29	0	20	6	1	0	17	4	.81	3	.252	.399	.301
Batavia	A- Phi	20	67	15	1	0	0	16	13	2	12	1	10	0	2	0	5	0	1.00	1	.224	.342	.239
1995 Piedmont	A Phi	130	481	131	26	4	1	168	86	51	74	5	64	10	7	4	26	8	.76	9	.272	.378	.349
1996 Clearwater	A+ Phi	128	483	132	17	5	0	159	73	37	60	1	65	6	10	4	37	11	.77	4	.273	.358	.329
1997 Reading	AA Phi	124	425	112	21	3	5	154	58	41	36	3	57	6	6	0	24	7	.77	10	.264	.330	.362
1998 Reading	AA Phi	40	136	46	7	2	7	78	26	25	19	0	15	5	1	1	10	2	.83	4	.338	.435	.574
1999 Reading	AA Phi	121	427	111	28	3	3	154	72	54	60	1	69	10	6	8	28	6	.82	11	.260	.358	.361
Scranton-WB	AAA Phi	9	17	4	2	0	0	6	4	1	5	0	2	1	0	0	0	0	.00	0	.235	.435	.353
6 Min. YEARS		611	2179	587	104	18	17	778	356	218	295	11	302	44	33	17	147	38	.79	42	.269	.365	.357

Rick Huisman

Pitches: Right **Bats:** Right **Pos:** P **Ht:** 6' 3" **Wt:** 210 **Born:** 5/17/69 **Age:** 31

		HOW MUCH HE PITCHED						WHAT HE GAVE UP										THE RESULTS					
Year Team	Lg Org	G	GS	CG	GF	IP	BFP	H	R	ER	HR	SH	SF	HB	TBB	IBB	SO	WP	Bk	W	L	Pct.	ShO	Sv	ERA
1990 Everett	A- SF	1	0	0	0	2	10	3	1	1	0	0	0	0	2	0	2	1	0	0	0	.000	0	0	4.50
Clinton	A SF	14	13	0	0	79	315	57	19	18	2	1	2	0	33	0	103	5	4	6	5	.545	0	0	2.05
1991 San Jose	A+ SF	26	26	7	0	182.1	720	126	45	37	5	11	3	3	73	1	216	13	3	16	4	.800	4	0	1.83
1992 Shreveport	AA SF	17	16	1	0	103.1	403	79	33	27	3	2	0	5	31	1	100	3	1	7	4	.636	1	0	2.35
Phoenix	AAA SF	9	8	0	0	56	230	45	16	15	3	1	1	1	24	0	44	1	0	3	2	.600	0	0	2.41
1993 San Jose	A+ SF	4	4	1	0	23.1	97	19	6	6	0	2	1	2	12	0	15	1	0	2	1	.667	0	0	2.31
Phoenix	AAA SF	14	14	0	0	72.1	333	78	54	48	5	1	1	1	45	0	59	8	4	3	4	.429	0	0	5.97
Tucson	AAA Hou	2	0	0	0	3.2	18	6	5	3	0	0	0	0	1	0	4	5	0	1	0	1.000	0	0	7.36
1994 Jackson	AA Hou	49	0	0	46	50.1	204	32	10	9	1	1	1	2	24	2	63	1	0	3	0	1.000	0	31	1.61

HOW MUCH HE PITCHED / WHAT HE GAVE UP / THE RESULTS

Year Team	Lg Org	G	GS	CG	GF	IP	BFP	H	R	ER	HR	SH	SF	HB	TBB	IBB	SO	WP	Bk	W	L	Pct.	ShO	Sv	ERA
1995 Tucson	AAA Hou	42	0	0	28	54.2	246	58	33	27	1	0	3	1	28	3	47	3	1	6	1	.857	0	6	4.45
Omaha	AAA KC	5	0	0	3	5	19	3	1	1	1	0	0	0	1	0	13	0	0	0	0	.000	0	1	1.80
1996 Omaha	AAA KC	27	4	0	6	57.1	243	54	32	31	9	0	1	2	24	0	50	0	1	2	4	.333	0	0	4.87
1997 Omaha	AAA KC	37	1	0	8	59.2	268	59	29	24	7	1	3	3	35	1	57	7	0	1	5	.167	0	2	3.62
1998 Fresno	AAA SF	44	0	0	17	72	309	65	43	43	18	0	2	1	34	2	80	4	0	2	6	.250	0	0	5.38
1999 New Orleans	AAA Hou	35	0	0	15	52.1	217	42	23	21	6	0	1	1	16	2	67	0	0	3	1	.750	0	3	3.61
1995 Kansas City	AL	7	0	0	2	9.2	44	14	8	8	2	1	0	0	1	0	12	0	0	0	0	.000	0	0	7.45
1996 Kansas City	AL	22	0	0	5	29.1	130	25	15	15	4	2	2	0	18	2	23	0	0	2	1	.667	0	1	4.60
10 Min. YEARS		326	86	9	123	873.1	3632	726	350	311	61	20	19	22	383	12	920	52	14	55	37	.598	5	43	3.20
2 Maj. YEARS		29	0	0	7	39	174	39	23	23	6	3	2	0	19	2	35	0	0	2	1	.667	0	1	5.31

Steve Huls

Bats: Right **Throws:** Right **Pos:** 3B **Ht:** 6'0" **Wt:** 178 **Born:** 10/11/74 **Age:** 25

Year Team	Lg Org	G	AB	H	2B	3B	HR	TB	R	RBI	TBB	IBB	SO	HBP	SH	SF	SB	CS	SB%	GDP	Avg	OBP	SLG
1996 Fort Wayne	A Min	60	201	43	3	1	1	51	21	11	12	1	53	1	6	2	2	2	.50	3	.214	.259	.254
1997 Fort Wayne	A Min	56	158	30	7	0	0	37	20	16	12	0	37	0	2	1	2	1	.67	2	.190	.246	.234
1998 Fort Myers	A+ Min	74	223	47	3	0	1	53	30	25	20	0	43	2	4	3	3	5	.38	7	.211	.278	.238
1999 New Britain	AA Min	56	152	33	1	0	0	34	13	10	23	0	32	3	3	1	4	2	.67	5	.217	.330	.224
Salt Lake	AAA Min	17	30	7	0	0	0	7	6	2	3	0	7	0	0	0	0	1	.00	2	.233	.303	.233
4 Min. YEARS		263	764	160	14	1	2	182	90	64	70	1	172	6	15	7	11	11	.50	19	.209	.279	.238

David Hulse

Bats: Left **Throws:** Left **Pos:** OF **Ht:** 5'11" **Wt:** 195 **Born:** 2/25/68 **Age:** 32

Year Team	Lg Org	G	AB	H	2B	3B	HR	TB	R	RBI	TBB	IBB	SO	HBP	SH	SF	SB	CS	SB%	GDP	Avg	OBP	SLG
1990 Butte	R+ Tex	64	257	92	12	2	2	114	54	36	25	1	31	2	2	0	24	5	.83	4	.358	.419	.444
1991 Charlotte	A+ Tex	88	310	86	4	5	0	100	41	17	36	2	75	1	6	0	44	7	.86	4	.277	.354	.323
1992 Tulsa	AA Tex	88	354	101	14	3	3	130	40	20	20	2	86	3	1	0	17	10	.63	2	.285	.329	.367
Okla City	AAA Tex	8	30	7	1	1	0	10	7	3	1	0	4	1	1	0	2	2	.50	0	.233	.281	.333
1994 Okla City	AAA Tex	25	99	28	5	2	0	37	10	6	6	1	21	1	0	0	6	0	1.00	1	.283	.330	.374
1996 New Orleans	AAA Mil	8	29	8	2	0	0	10	2	1	1	0	6	0	0	0	0	0	.00	1	.276	.300	.345
1998 Nashua	IND —	62	230	81	16	2	8	125	43	42	10	3	29	0	0	3	10	3	.77	1	.352	.374	.543
1999 Pawtucket	AAA Bos	21	85	28	6	2	1	41	9	13	2	0	18	0	0	0	3	1	.75	4	.329	.345	.482
Memphis	AAA StL	74	200	67	13	2	4	96	37	31	9	1	39	3	0	3	4	2	.67	3	.335	.367	.480
1992 Texas	AL	32	92	28	4	0	0	32	14	2	3	0	18	0	2	0	3	1	.75	0	.304	.326	.348
1993 Texas	AL	114	407	118	9	10	1	150	71	29	26	1	57	1	5	2	29	9	.76	9	.290	.333	.369
1994 Texas	AL	77	310	79	8	4	1	98	58	19	21	0	53	2	7	1	18	2	.90	1	.255	.305	.316
1995 Milwaukee	AL	119	339	85	11	6	3	117	46	47	18	2	60	0	2	5	15	3	.83	3	.251	.285	.345
1996 Milwaukee	AL	81	117	26	3	0	0	29	18	6	8	0	16	0	2	0	4	1	.80	2	.222	.272	.248
7 Min. YEARS		438	1594	498	73	19	18	663	243	169	110	10	309	11	10	6	110	30	.79	19	.312	.360	.416
5 Maj. YEARS		423	1265	336	35	20	5	426	207	103	76	3	204	3	18	8	69	16	.81	15	.266	.307	.337

Scott Hunter

Bats: Right **Throws:** Right **Pos:** OF **Ht:** 6'1" **Wt:** 210 **Born:** 12/17/75 **Age:** 24

Year Team	Lg Org	G	AB	H	2B	3B	HR	TB	R	RBI	TBB	IBB	SO	HBP	SH	SF	SB	CS	SB%	GDP	Avg	OBP	SLG
1994 Great Falls	R+ LA	64	237	75	12	4	2	101	45	28	25	1	40	5	4	3	17	5	.77	1	.316	.389	.426
1995 San Berndno	A+ LA	113	379	108	19	3	11	166	68	59	36	1	83	6	4	1	27	8	.77	0	.285	.355	.438
Capital Cty	A NYM	12	40	10	0	0	0	10	2	1	2	0	13	1	1	1	2	1	.67	2	.250	.295	.250
1996 St. Lucie	A+ NYM	127	475	122	19	1	2	149	71	38	38	4	68	8	3	3	49	12	.80	6	.257	.321	.314
1997 Binghamton	AA NYM	80	289	74	12	2	10	120	45	31	25	1	52	4	1	4	24	9	.73	6	.256	.320	.415
1998 Norfolk	AAA NYM	7	21	3	0	0	0	3	2	3	3	0	5	2	1	0	1	2	.33	1	.143	.308	.143
Binghamton	AA NYM	130	487	153	25	3	14	226	80	65	47	2	75	7	1	8	39	15	.72	6	.314	.377	.464
1999 Norfolk	AAA NYM	50	180	41	4	0	8	69	20	23	8	0	42	3	1	2	6	6	.50	2	.228	.269	.383
Ottawa	AAA Mon	78	280	63	13	0	8	100	22	41	21	0	64	3	2	5	2	5	.29	1	.225	.282	.357
6 Min. YEARS		661	2388	649	104	13	55	944	355	289	205	9	442	39	18	27	167	63	.73	25	.272	.336	.395

Scott Huntsman

Pitches: Right **Bats:** Right **Pos:** P **Ht:** 6'2" **Wt:** 235 **Born:** 10/28/72 **Age:** 27

Year Team	Lg Org	G	GS	CG	GF	IP	BFP	H	R	ER	HR	SH	SF	HB	TBB	IBB	SO	WP	Bk	W	L	Pct.	ShO	Sv	ERA
1994 Brewers	R Mil	4	0	0	4	3.2	12	1	0	0	0	0	0	0	0	0	3	0	0	0	0	.000	0	1	0.00
Helena	R+ Mil	17	0	0	11	20	99	28	19	15	2	3	1	1	11	1	22	1	0	1	0	1.000	0	5	6.75
1995 Beloit	A Mil	43	0	0	14	49.2	229	42	17	15	3	2	1	5	34	2	49	5	0	4	3	.571	0	2	2.72
1996 Stockton	A+ Mil	43	0	0	29	48.1	213	37	21	15	3	0	3	2	27	0	56	2	0	4	3	.571	0	12	2.79
1997 El Paso	AA Mil	42	0	0	13	55	272	76	56	44	5	0	5	4	21	2	37	4	2	4	4	.500	0	3	7.20
1998 El Paso	AA Mil	52	0	0	12	74.1	353	106	71	69	12	1	4	4	31	2	49	5	1	4	3	.571	0	3	8.35
1999 Huntsville	AA Mil	47	0	0	20	69.1	300	72	33	28	8	2	2	3	25	3	31	1	0	1	4	.200	0	5	3.63
6 Min. YEARS		248	0	0	103	320.1	1478	362	217	186	33	8	16	19	149	10	247	18	3	18	17	.514	0	30	5.23

Jimmy Hurst

Bats: Right **Throws:** Right **Pos:** OF **Ht:** 6'6" **Wt:** 225 **Born:** 3/1/72 **Age:** 28

Year Team	Lg Org	G	AB	H	2B	3B	HR	TB	R	RBI	TBB	IBB	SO	HBP	SH	SF	SB	CS	SB%	GDP	Avg	OBP	SLG
1991 White Sox	R CWS	36	121	31	4	0	0	35	14	12	13	0	32	1	0	0	6	1	.86	3	.256	.333	.289

Year Team	Lg Org	G	AB	H	2B	3B	HR	TB	R	RBI	TBB	IBB	SO	HBP	SH	SF	SB	CS	SB%	GDP	Avg	OBP	SLG
1992 Utica	A- CWS	68	220	50	8	5	6	86	31	35	27	1	78	4	2	5	11	3	.79	4	.227	.316	.391
1993 South Bend	A CWS	123	464	113	26	0	20	199	79	79	37	3	141	8	0	5	15	2	.88	9	.244	.307	.429
1994 Pr William	A+ CWS	127	455	126	31	6	25	244	90	91	72	4	128	4	0	5	15	8	.65	9	.277	.377	.536
1995 Birmingham	AA CWS	91	301	57	11	0	12	104	47	34	33	0	95	1	0	2	12	5	.71	5	.189	.270	.346
1996 Birmingham	AA CWS	126	472	125	23	1	18	204	62	88	53	2	128	3	0	8	19	11	.63	10	.265	.338	.432
Nashville	AAA CWS	3	6	2	1	0	1	6	2	2	1	0	3	0	0	0	0	0	.00	0	.333	.429	1.000
1997 Jacksnville	AA Det	5	17	8	2	0	2	16	5	6	3	0	6	0	0	1	0	0	.00	0	.471	.524	.941
Toledo	AAA Det	110	377	102	11	3	18	173	51	58	47	1	115	0	1	4	14	5	.74	11	.271	.348	.459
1998 Pawtucket	AAA Bos	103	360	103	11	1	20	176	61	67	59	1	98	1	1	0	22	9	.71	17	.286	.388	.489
1999 Syracuse	AAA Tor	29	103	29	3	0	3	41	18	10	15	0	32	0	0	2	4	3	.57	3	.282	.367	.398
1997 Detroit	AL	13	17	3	1	0	1	7	1	1	2	0	6	0	0	0	0	0	.00	0	.176	.263	.412
9 Min. YEARS		821	2896	746	131	16	125	1284	460	482	360	12	856	22	4	32	118	47	.72	71	.258	.341	.443

Norm Hutchins

Bats: Both Throws: Left Pos: OF Ht: 5'11" Wt: 198 Born: 11/20/75 Age: 24

Year Team	Lg Org	G	AB	H	2B	3B	HR	TB	R	RBI	TBB	IBB	SO	HBP	SH	SF	SB	CS	SB%	GDP	Avg	OBP	SLG
1994 Angels	R Ana	43	136	26	4	1	0	32	8	7	3	0	44	1	1	1	5	2	.71	0	.191	.213	.235
1995 Angels	R Ana	14	59	16	1	1	0	19	9	7	4	0	10	1	2	1	8	4	.67	1	.271	.323	.322
Boioo	A Ana	45	176	44	6	2	2	60	34	11	15	0	44	2	4	1	10	6	.63	2	.250	.314	.341
1996 Cedar Rapds	A Ana	126	466	105	13	16	3	156	59	52	28	0	110	6	8	2	22	8	.73	5	.225	.277	.335
1997 Lk Elsinore	A+ Ana	132	564	163	31	12	15	263	82	69	23	4	147	6	8	6	39	17	.70	2	.289	.321	.466
1998 Midland	AA Ana	89	394	123	20	10	10	193	74	50	14	0	84	4	0	1	32	10	.76	8	.312	.341	.490
Vancouver	AAA Ana	7	29	6	0	0	1	9	4	3	2	0	9	1	0	1	1	2	.33	0	.207	.273	.310
1999 Edmonton	AAA Ana	126	521	130	27	6	7	190	80	51	40	1	127	8	4	4	25	17	.60	8	.250	.311	.365
6 Min. YEARS		582	2345	613	102	48	37	922	350	250	129	5	575	29	24	17	142	66	.68	26	.261	.306	.393

Chad Hutchinson

Pitches: Right Bats: Right Pos: P Ht: 6'5" Wt: 220 Born: 2/21/77 Age: 23

Year Team	Lg Org	G	GS	CG	GF	IP	BFP	H	R	ER	HR	SH	SF	HB	TBB	IBB	SO	WP	Bk	W	L	Pct.	ShO	Sv	ERA
1998 New Jersey	A- StL	3	3	0	0	15.1	67	15	7	6	0	0	0	2	4	0	20	0	0	0	1	.000	0	0	3.52
Pr William	A+ StL	5	5	0	0	29	118	20	12	9	4	1	0	1	11	0	31	0	2	2	0	1.000	0	0	2.79
1999 Arkansas	AA StL	25	25	0	0	141	624	127	79	74	12	8	5	4	85	0	150	20	3	7	11	.389	0	0	4.72
Memphis	AAA StL	2	2	0	0	12.1	48	4	3	3	2	0	0	0	8	0	16	0	0	2	0	1.000	0	0	2.19
2 Min. YEARS		35	35	0	0	197.2	857	166	101	92	18	9	5	7	108	0	217	20	5	11	12	.478	0	0	4.19

Brandon Hyde

Bats: Right Throws: Right Pos: DH-C Ht: 6'3" Wt: 210 Born: 10/3/73 Age: 26

Year Team	Lg Org	G	AB	H	2B	3B	HR	TB	R	RBI	TBB	IBB	SO	HBP	SH	SF	SB	CS	SB%	GDP	Avg	OBP	SLG
1997 White Sox	R CWS	28	77	15	4	0	1	22	10	14	11	0	24	2	1	1	0	0	.00	2	.195	.308	.286
1998 Bristol	R+ CWS	27	94	35	9	0	5	59	21	26	21	0	20	8	0	0	0	1	.00	0	.372	.520	.628
1999 Birmingham	AA CWS	7	18	5	3	0	0	8	4	2	3	0	4	0	0	0	0	1	.00	0	.278	.381	.444
Burlington	A CWS	65	210	60	15	0	6	93	33	40	33	0	60	6	1	3	1	1	.50	4	.286	.393	.443
3 Min. YEARS		127	399	115	31	0	12	182	68	82	68	0	108	16	2	4	1	3	.25	9	.288	.409	.456

Adam Hyzdu

Bats: Right Throws: Right Pos: OF Ht: 6'2" Wt: 210 Born: 12/6/71 Age: 28

Year Team	Lg Org	G	AB	H	2B	3B	HR	TB	R	RBI	TBB	IBB	SO	HBP	SH	SF	SB	CS	SB%	GDP	Avg	OBP	SLG
1990 Everett	A- SF	69	253	62	16	1	6	98	31	34	28	1	78	2	0	5	2	4	.33	4	.245	.319	.387
1991 Clinton	A SF	124	410	96	14	5	5	135	47	50	64	1	131	3	7	2	4	5	.44	10	.234	.340	.329
1992 San Jose	A+ SF	128	457	127	25	5	9	189	60	60	55	4	134	1	1	8	10	5	.67	6	.278	.351	.414
1993 San Jose	A+ SF	44	165	48	11	3	13	104	35	38	29	0	53	0	1	2	1	1	.50	3	.291	.393	.630
Shreveport	AA SF	86	302	61	17	0	6	96	30	25	20	2	82	1	1	1	0	5	.00	5	.202	.253	.318
1994 Winston-Sal	A+ Cin	55	210	58	11	1	15	116	30	39	18	0	33	2	0	1	1	5	.17	3	.276	.336	.552
Chattanooga	AA Cin	38	133	35	10	0	3	54	17	9	8	0	21	1	1	0	0	2	.00	1	.263	.310	.406
Indianapols	AAA Cin	12	25	3	2	0	0	5	3	3	1	0	5	0	0	2	0	0	.00	0	.120	.143	.200
1995 Chattanooga	AA Cin	102	312	82	14	1	13	137	55	48	45	2	56	4	2	1	3	2	.60	4	.263	.362	.439
1996 Trenton	AA Bos	109	374	126	24	3	25	231	71	80	56	6	75	2	0	2	8	1	.89	7	.337	.424	.618
1997 Pawtucket	AAA Bos	119	413	114	21	4	23	206	77	84	72	0	113	4	1	0	10	6	.63	6	.276	.387	.499
1998 Tucson	AAA Ari	34	100	34	7	1	4	55	21	14	15	0	23	0	1	2	1	0	.00	2	.340	.419	.550
1999 Pawtucket	AAA Bos	12	35	8	0	0	1	11	4	6	4	0	13	0	0	0	0	0	.00	1	.229	.308	.314
Altoona	AA Pit	91	345	109	26	2	24	211	64	78	40	1	62	3	0	0	8	4	.67	0	.316	.392	.612
Nashville	AAA Pit	14	44	11	1	0	5	27	6	13	4	0	11	0	0	0	0	0	.00	2	.250	.313	.614
10 Min. YEARS		1037	3578	974	199	23	152	1675	551	581	459	17	890	23	15	29	40	48	.45	56	.272	.356	.468

Anthony Iapoce

Bats: Both Throws: Left Pos: OF Ht: 5'10" Wt: 178 Born: 8/23/73 Age: 26

Year Team	Lg Org	G	AB	H	2B	3B	HR	TB	R	RBI	TBB	IBB	SO	HBP	SH	SF	SB	CS	SB%	GDP	Avg	OBP	SLG
1994 Brewers	R Mil	55	222	55	7	2	0	66	37	25	15	0	43	5	3	1	16	3	.84	1	.248	.309	.297
1995 Brewers	R Mil	3	3	1	0	0	0	1	2	0	1	0	1	0	0	0	1	0	1.00	0	.333	.500	.333
Helena	R+ Mil	39	146	44	7	0	0	51	43	13	28	0	24	2	2	2	19	3	.86	2	.301	.416	.349
1996 Beloit	A Mil	77	266	78	6	3	1	93	62	11	35	0	53	7	3	0	23	13	.64	4	.293	.405	.350

Year Team	Lg Org	BATTING															BASERUNNING				PERCENTAGES		
		G	AB	H	2B	3B	HR	TB	R	RBI	TBB	IBB	SO	HBP	SH	SF	SB	CS	SB%	GDP	Avg	OBP	SLG
1997 Tucson	AAA Mil	7	21	7	4	0	0	11	5	3	1	0	4	0	0	0	0	0	.00	1	.333	.364	.524
Stockton	A+ Mil	99	387	103	13	4	1	127	48	27	30	0	71	6	9	2	22	12	.65	3	.266	.327	.328
1998 El Paso	AA Mil	133	576	181	23	6	2	222	97	53	33	1	67	11	9	2	35	20	.64	4	.314	.362	.385
1999 Louisville	AAA Mil	26	83	14	2	0	0	16	6	0	7	1	30	0	1	0	6	3	.67	3	.169	.233	.193
Huntsville	AA Mil	50	133	35	7	0	0	42	17	5	12	0	25	1	0	0	2	2	.50	0	.263	.329	.316
6 Min. YEARS		489	1837	518	69	15	4	629	317	137	170	2	318	32	27	7	124	56	.69	18	.282	.352	.342

Jesse Ibarra

Bats: Both Throws: Right Pos: DH   Ht: 6'3" Wt: 195 Born: 7/12/72 Age: 27

Year Team	Lg Org	BATTING															BASERUNNING				PERCENTAGES		
		G	AB	H	2B	3B	HR	TB	R	RBI	TBB	IBB	SO	HBP	SH	SF	SB	CS	SB%	GDP	Avg	OBP	SLG
1994 Everett	A- SF	67	252	57	15	1	10	104	32	37	34	0	82	1	0	0	0	0	.00	5	.226	.321	.413
1995 Burlington	A SF	129	437	144	30	1	34	278	72	96	77	6	94	4	0	1	1	2	.33	8	.330	.434	.636
San Jose	A+ SF	3	9	3	2	0	0	5	1	4	1	0	1	0	0	0	0	0	.00	2	.333	.400	.556
1996 San Jose	A+ SF	126	498	141	38	0	17	230	74	95	63	3	108	3	0	2	5	1	.83	12	.283	.366	.462
1997 Jacksnville	AA Det	115	441	125	24	1	25	226	73	91	55	4	85	3	0	5	3	2	.60	9	.283	.363	.512
1998 Toledo	AAA Det	81	271	62	9	1	9	100	22	38	30	0	65	0	0	2	1	1	.50	9	.229	.304	.369
Jacksnville	AA Det	10	30	3	1	0	0	4	1	1	5	1	14	0	0	1	0	0	.00	1	.100	.229	.133
1999 Jacksnville	AA Det	18	70	11	1	0	1	15	9	6	10	1	20	0	0	1	0	0	.00	1	.157	.259	.214
Tulsa	AA Tex	90	325	72	10	1	11	117	32	49	41	4	88	5	1	3	0	0	.00	10	.222	.316	.360
6 Min. YEARS		639	2333	618	130	5	107	1079	316	417	316	19	557	16	1	14	10	6	.63	57	.265	.355	.462

Luis Iglesias

Bats: Right Throws: Right Pos: 3B   Ht: 6'3" Wt: 210 Born: 2/3/67 Age: 33

Year Team	Lg Org	BATTING															BASERUNNING				PERCENTAGES		
		G	AB	H	2B	3B	HR	TB	R	RBI	TBB	IBB	SO	HBP	SH	SF	SB	CS	SB%	GDP	Avg	OBP	SLG
1984 Johnson Cy	R+ StL	31	82	19	6	2	1	32	11	4	8	0	9	0	0	1	0	2	.00	3	.232	.297	.390
1985 Erie	A- StL	4	14	4	0	0	1	7	3	1	1	1	4	2	0	0	1	0	1.00	1	.286	.412	.500
Savannah	A StL	21	63	13	3	0	0	16	11	3	8	0	14	2	0	1	0	0	.00	3	.206	.311	.254
Johnson Cy	R+ StL	59	166	52	17	0	9	96	33	41	34	1	32	3	1	4	3	0	1.00	1	.313	.430	.578
1986 Savannah	A StL	102	310	71	14	2	7	110	37	34	39	0	72	8	2	0	12	4	.75	4	.229	.331	.355
1987 Spartanbrg	A Phi	134	457	125	20	1	18	201	73	82	62	1	69	8	2	7	10	9	.53	11	.274	.365	.440
1988 Clearwater	A+ Phi	66	219	49	10	0	4	71	18	34	21	1	37	7	3	3	2	1	.00	4	.224	.308	.324
1989 Miami	A+ —	97	293	68	18	1	10	118	37	40	50	0	61	7	3	2	7	7	.50	8	.232	.355	.403
1999 Altoona	AA Pit	31	89	25	6	0	6	49	13	16	14	0	26	1	0	0	0	1	.00	1	.281	.385	.551
7 Min. YEARS		545	1693	426	94	6	56	700	236	255	237	4	324	38	11	18	35	23	.60	36	.252	.353	.413

Mario Iglesias

Pitches: Right Bats: Both Pos: P   Ht: 6'3" Wt: 195 Born: 6/2/74 Age: 26

Year Team	Lg Org	HOW MUCH HE PITCHED						WHAT HE GAVE UP												THE RESULTS					
		G	GS	CG	GF	IP	BFP	H	R	ER	HR	SH	SF	HB	TBB	IBB	SO	WP	Bk	W	L	Pct.	ShO	Sv	ERA
1996 Bristol	R+ CWS	3	0	0	1	8.1	29	6	2	2	1	0	1	0	1	0	2	1	0	0	0	.000	0	1	2.16
Hickory	A CWS	10	5	0	2	34.2	155	45	19	19	4	0	0	6	6	0	31	1	1	2	3	.400	0	1	4.93
1997 Hickory	A CWS	36	0	0	27	68.2	289	64	29	26	4	3	2	1	26	5	64	7	2	8	4	.667	0	10	3.41
1998 Winston-Sal	A+ CWS	35	0	0	18	78	305	51	24	20	5	4	2	6	19	0	90	3	0	13	1	.929	0	5	2.31
1999 Birmingham	AA CWS	23	2	0	4	50	216	51	29	26	8	2	1	2	21	1	29	3	0	5	3	.625	0	0	4.68
Bowie	AA Bal	14	2	0	3	26.1	123	28	23	22	6	3	0	1	16	2	27	0	0	1	4	.200	0	0	7.52
4 Min. YEARS		121	9	0	55	266	1117	245	126	115	28	12	6	14	89	8	243	15	3	29	15	.659	0	17	3.89

Mike Iglesias

Pitches: Right Bats: Right Pos: P   Ht: 6'5" Wt: 223 Born: 11/9/72 Age: 27

Year Team	Lg Org	HOW MUCH HE PITCHED						WHAT HE GAVE UP												THE RESULTS					
		G	GS	CG	GF	IP	BFP	H	R	ER	HR	SH	SF	HB	TBB	IBB	SO	WP	Bk	W	L	Pct.	ShO	Sv	ERA
1991 Dodgers	R LA	8	6	0	1	23	108	26	13	12	1	1	1	0	17	0	17	2	3	1	1	.500	0	0	4.70
1992 Great Falls	R+ LA	12	12	0	0	56	272	69	56	38	4	0	1	4	26	0	37	10	1	3	6	.333	0	0	6.11
1993 Bakersfield	A+ LA	6	3	0	0	19.1	93	26	16	12	2	1	0	1	12	0	10	3	1	1	2	.333	0	0	5.59
Yakima	A- LA	10	5	0	0	30.2	150	42	29	26	1	0	5	2	21	1	24	5	1	0	3	.000	0	0	7.63
1994 Vero Beach	A+ LA	19	14	1	3	89.2	376	87	46	42	9	2	4	1	29	2	50	4	1	3	6	.333	0	0	4.22
1995 Bakersfield	A+ LA	24	23	2	0	143.2	609	124	65	52	11	5	3	11	38	0	108	7	0	7	10	.412	1	0	3.26
San Berndno	A+ LA	4	3	0	0	15	74	26	14	11	1	0	0	2	2	0	12	3	0	1	2	.333	0	0	6.60
1996 Vero Beach	A+ LA	31	16	0	14	104	463	112	68	59	9	1	4	5	37	1	101	6	1	5	8	.385	0	7	5.11
1997 San Antonio	AA LA	42	0	0	20	59.1	247	51	25	24	7	2	1	0	26	1	55	5	1	6	2	.750	0	3	3.64
1998 Albuquerque	AAA LA	39	9	0	6	95.2	419	112	43	39	9	4	4	2	29	2	57	2	0	7	1	.875	0	3	3.67
1999 Richmond	AAA Atl	3	0	0	0	4	22	6	7	7	0	0	1	0	4	1	7	0	0	0	2	.000	0	0	15.75
Greenville	AA Atl	4	4	0	0	14	66	19	11	11	2	0	1	0	6	0	5	1	1	0	3	.000	0	0	7.07
9 Min. YEARS		202	95	3	44	654.1	2877	700	393	333	56	16	24	28	247	8	483	48	10	34	46	.425	1	15	4.58

Pete Incaviglia

Bats: Right Throws: Right Pos: OF   Ht: 6'1" Wt: 230 Born: 4/2/64 Age: 36

Year Team	Lg Org	BATTING															BASERUNNING				PERCENTAGES		
		G	AB	H	2B	3B	HR	TB	R	RBI	TBB	IBB	SO	HBP	SH	SF	SB	CS	SB%	GDP	Avg	OBP	SLG
1997 Columbus	AAA NYY	3	13	4	1	0	0	5	1	2	0	0	4	0	0	0	0	0	.00	0	.308	.308	.385
1998 New Orleans	AAA Hou	76	281	91	10	1	23	172	57	66	34	0	63	9	0	2	11	3	.79	9	.324	.411	.612
1999 Tucson	AAA Ari	8	32	5	4	0	0	9	3	7	1	0	11	0	0	0	1	0	1.00	0	.156	.182	.281
New Orleans	AAA Hou	18	62	12	3	1	1	20	6	6	8	0	15	1	0	1	1	2	.33	0	.194	.292	.323
1986 Texas	AL	153	540	135	21	2	30	250	82	88	55	2	185	4	0	7	3	2	.60	9	.250	.320	.463

135

BATTING | **BASERUNNING** | **PERCENTAGES**

Year Team	Lg Org	G	AB	H	2B	3B	HR	TB	R	RBI	TBB	IBB	SO	HBP	SH	SF	SB	CS	SB%	GDP	Avg	OBP	SLG
1987 Texas	AL	139	509	138	26	4	27	253	85	80	48	1	168	1	0	5	9	3	.75	8	.271	.332	.497
1988 Texas	AL	116	418	104	19	3	22	195	59	54	39	3	153	7	0	3	6	4	.60	6	.249	.321	.467
1989 Texas	AL	133	453	107	27	4	21	205	48	81	32	0	136	6	0	4	5	7	.42	12	.236	.293	.453
1990 Texas	AL	153	529	123	27	0	24	222	59	85	45	5	146	9	0	4	3	4	.43	18	.233	.302	.420
1991 Detroit	AL	97	337	72	12	1	11	119	38	38	36	0	92	1	1	2	1	3	.25	6	.214	.290	.353
1992 Houston	NL	113	349	93	22	1	11	150	31	44	25	2	99	3	0	2	2	2	.50	6	.266	.319	.430
1993 Philadelphia	NL	116	368	101	16	3	24	195	60	89	21	1	82	6	0	7	1	1	.50	9	.274	.318	.530
1994 Philadelphia	NL	80	244	56	10	1	13	107	28	32	16	3	71	1	0	2	1	0	1.00	3	.230	.278	.439
1996 Philadelphia	NL	99	269	63	7	2	16	122	33	42	30	2	82	3	0	0	2	0	1.00	6	.234	.318	.454
Baltimore	AL	12	33	10	2	0	2	18	4	8	0	0	7	1	0	1	0	0	.00	0	.303	.314	.545
1997 Baltimore	AL	48	138	34	4	0	5	53	18	12	11	2	43	3	0	1	0	0	.00	1	.246	.314	.384
New York	AL	5	16	4	0	0	0	4	1	0	1	0	3	0	0	0	0	0	.00	0	.250	.250	.250
1998 Detroit	AL	7	14	1	0	0	0	1	0	0	1	0	6	0	0	0	0	0	.00	0	.071	.133	.071
Houston	NL	13	16	2	1	0	0	3	1	1	1	0	4	0	0	1	0	0	.00	1	.125	.176	.188
3 Min. YEARS		105	388	112	18	2	24	206	67	81	43	0	93	10	0	3	13	5	.72	10	.289	.372	.531
12 Maj. YEARS		1284	4233	1043	194	21	206	1897	546	655	360	21	1277	45	1	38	33	26	.56	85	.246	.310	.448

Jeff Inglin

Bats: Right **Throws:** Right **Pos:** OF **Ht:** 5'11" **Wt:** 185 **Born:** 10/8/75 **Age:** 24

BATTING | **BASERUNNING** | **PERCENTAGES**

Year Team	Lg Org	G	AB	H	2B	3B	HR	TB	R	RBI	TBB	IBB	SO	HBP	SH	SF	SB	CS	SB%	GDP	Avg	OBP	SLG
1996 Bristol	R+ CWS	50	193	56	10	0	8	90	27	24	11	0	25	9	0	0	9	6	.60	8	.290	.357	.466
Hickory	A CWS	22	83	30	6	2	2	46	12	15	4	0	11	1	0	1	2	1	.67	3	.361	.393	.554
1997 Hickory	A CWS	135	536	179	34	6	16	273	100	102	49	4	87	4	0	9	31	8	.79	12	.334	.388	.509
1998 Birmingham	AA CWS	139	494	121	22	6	24	227	75	100	78	3	101	4	0	9	3	2	.60	12	.245	.347	.460
1999 Charlotte	AAA CWS	14	39	8	0	0	3	17	8	8	4	0	9	1	0	0	0	1	.00	0	.205	.295	.436
Birmingham	AA CWS	117	432	126	26	4	15	205	63	63	58	3	62	6	2	2	20	2	.91	13	.292	.382	.475
4 Min. YEARS		477	1777	520	98	18	68	858	285	312	204	10	295	25	2	21	65	20	.76	48	.293	.370	.483

Darron Ingram

Bats: Right **Throws:** Right **Pos:** OF **Ht:** 6'3" **Wt:** 226 **Born:** 6/7/76 **Age:** 24

BATTING | **BASERUNNING** | **PERCENTAGES**

Year Team	Lg Org	G	AB	H	2B	3B	HR	TB	R	RBI	TBB	IBB	SO	HBP	SH	SF	SB	CS	SB%	GDP	Avg	OBP	SLG
1994 Princeton	R+ Cin	46	131	26	5	1	2	39	13	11	19	0	50	1	3	1	1	4	.20	2	.198	.303	.298
1995 Princeton	R+ Cin	60	233	64	6	3	14	118	37	53	11	0	78	1	0	2	3	1	.75	5	.275	.308	.506
1996 Chstn-WV	A Cin	15	48	9	3	0	1	15	5	6	8	1	19	0	0	0	0	0	.00	0	.188	.298	.313
Billings	R+ Cin	65	251	74	13	0	17	138	49	56	34	2	88	2	0	1	7	3	.70	1	.295	.382	.550
1997 Burlington	A Cin	134	510	135	25	4	29	255	74	97	46	1	195	0	0	3	8	5	.62	9	.265	.324	.500
1998 Chattanooga	AA Cin	125	466	108	21	9	17	198	62	65	43	1	169	0	0	7	4	3	.57	6	.232	.293	.425
1999 Chattanooga	AA Cin	85	267	59	11	3	11	109	42	40	28	1	95	0	0	1	5	7	.42	5	.221	.294	.408
Clinton	A Cin	22	76	27	5	0	5	47	15	18	14	0	20	0	0	0	1	1	.50	0	.355	.456	.618
6 Min. YEARS		552	1982	502	89	20	96	919	297	346	203	6	714	4	3	16	29	24	.55	30	.253	.322	.464

Garey Ingram

Bats: Right **Throws:** Right **Pos:** OF **Ht:** 5'11" **Wt:** 195 **Born:** 7/25/70 **Age:** 29

BATTING | **BASERUNNING** | **PERCENTAGES**

Year Team	Lg Org	G	AB	H	2B	3B	HR	TB	R	RBI	TBB	IBB	SO	HBP	SH	SF	SB	CS	SB%	GDP	Avg	OBP	SLG
1990 Great Falls	R+ LA	56	198	68	12	8	2	102	43	21	22	0	37	3	0	1	10	6	.63	3	.343	.415	.515
1991 Bakersfield	A+ LA	118	445	132	16	4	9	183	75	61	52	4	70	14	5	6	30	13	.70	5	.297	.383	.411
San Antonio	AA LA	1	1	0	0	0	0	0	0	1	0	0	1	0	0	1	0	0	.00	0	.000	.000	.000
1992 San Antonio	AA LA	65	198	57	9	5	2	82	34	17	28	2	43	12	2	1	11	6	.65	4	.288	.406	.414
1993 San Antonio	AA LA	84	305	82	14	5	6	124	43	33	31	0	50	5	2	2	19	6	.76	3	.269	.344	.407
1994 San Antonio	AA LA	99	345	89	24	3	8	143	68	28	43	3	61	9	2	0	19	5	.79	5	.258	.355	.414
Albuquerque	AAA LA	2	8	2	0	0	0	2	2	0	0	0	1	0	0	0	1	0	1.00	1	.250	.250	.250
1995 Albuquerque	AAA LA	63	232	57	11	4	1	79	28	30	21	1	40	3	0	3	10	4	.71	4	.246	.313	.341
1996 Albuquerque	AAA LA	6	10	1	0	0	0	1	1	0	1	0	2	0	0	0	1	0	.00	1	.100	.182	.100
1997 San Antonio	AA LA	92	348	104	28	7	12	182	68	52	37	1	50	4	1	2	16	6	.73	5	.299	.371	.523
1998 Albuquerque	AAA LA	108	377	114	25	5	8	173	60	58	30	1	69	5	7	2	20	6	.77	7	.302	.360	.459
1999 Pawtucket	AAA Bos	85	296	73	15	3	9	121	49	39	17	0	52	3	7	2	11	2	.85	5	.247	.292	.409
1994 Los Angeles	NL	26	78	22	1	0	3	32	10	8	7	3	22	0	1	0	5	0	.00	3	.282	.341	.410
1995 Los Angeles	NL	44	55	11	2	0	0	13	5	3	9	0	8	0	2	0	3	0	1.00	0	.200	.313	.236
1997 Los Angeles	NL	12	9	4	0	0	0	4	2	1	1	0	3	0	0	0	1	0	1.00	0	.444	.500	.444
10 Min. YEARS		779	2763	779	154	44	57	1192	471	340	282	12	476	58	26	20	147	54	.73	43	.282	.358	.431
3 Maj. YEARS		82	142	37	3	0	3	49	17	12	17	3	33	0	3	0	9	0	1.00	3	.261	.340	.345

Eric Ireland

Pitches: Right **Bats:** Right **Pos:** P **Ht:** 6'1" **Wt:** 170 **Born:** 3/11/77 **Age:** 23

HOW MUCH HE PITCHED | **WHAT HE GAVE UP** | **THE RESULTS**

Year Team	Lg Org	G	GS	CG	GF	IP	BFP	H	R	ER	HR	SH	SF	HB	TBB	IBB	SO	WP	Bk	W	L	Pct.	ShO	Sv	ERA
1996 Astros	R Hou	12	11	0	1	53.2	235	54	33	28	1	3	1	3	23	1	43	13	1	3	4	.429	0	0	4.70
1997 Auburn	A- Hou	16	16	2	0	107	458	111	55	44	4	2	0	12	21	1	78	3	0	5	7	.417	0	0	3.70
1998 Quad City	A Hou	29	28	6	1	206	860	172	80	66	15	5	4	15	71	2	191	7	3	14	9	.609	2	0	2.88
1999 Jackson	AA Hou	3	3	0	0	14.2	64	19	9	7	1	1	0	0	2	1	15	2	0	0	1	.000	0	0	4.30
Kissimmee	A+ Hou	24	24	5	0	170.1	684	145	59	39	12	7	1	8	30	1	133	13	2	10	7	.588	2	0	2.06
4 Min. YEARS		84	82	13	2	551.2	2301	501	236	184	33	18	6	38	147	6	460	38	6	32	28	.533	4	0	3.00

Johnny Isom

Bats: Right Throws: Right Pos: OF Ht: 5'11" Wt: 210 Born: 8/9/73 Age: 26

Year Team	Lg Org	G	AB	H	2B	3B	HR	TB	R	RBI	TBB	IBB	SO	HBP	SH	SF	SB	CS	SB%	GDP	Avg	OBP	SLG
1995 Bluefield	R+ Bal	59	212	73	14	4	6	113	47	56	25	0	27	1	2	7	9	2	.82	5	.344	.404	.533
1996 Frederick	A+ Bal	124	486	141	27	3	18	228	69	104	40	4	87	7	0	6	8	6	.57	15	.290	.349	.469
1997 Bowie	AA Bal	135	518	142	28	4	20	238	70	91	44	4	121	11	2	4	1	5	.17	12	.274	.341	.459
1998 Rochester	AAA Bal	39	142	32	4	0	2	42	13	13	18	0	31	2	0	0	2	0	1.00	1	.225	.321	.296
Bowie	AA Bal	93	325	78	12	1	13	131	47	39	29	0	72	4	2	2	1	3	.25	18	.240	.308	.403
1999 Bowie	AA Bal	38	127	29	6	0	2	41	19	16	12	1	25	1	0	0	0	1	.00	5	.228	.300	.323
Rochester	AAA Bal	34	119	41	12	0	2	59	19	10	10	0	28	0	0	0	1	1	.50	6	.345	.395	.496
5 Min. YEARS		522	1929	536	103	12	63	852	284	329	178	9	391	26	6	19	22	18	.55	62	.278	.344	.442

Gavin Jackson

Bats: Right Throws: Right Pos: SS Ht: 5'10" Wt: 170 Born: 7/19/73 Age: 26

Year Team	Lg Org	G	AB	H	2B	3B	HR	TB	R	RBI	TBB	IBB	SO	HBP	SH	SF	SB	CS	SB%	GDP	Avg	OBP	SLG
1993 Red Sox	R Bos	42	160	50	7	2	0	61	29	11	14	0	18	11	2	0	11	5	.69	2	.313	.405	.381
1994 Sarasota	A+ Bos	108	321	77	6	1	0	85	46	27	33	0	40	7	12	0	9	10	.47	1	.240	.324	.265
1995 Sarasota	A+ Bos	100	342	91	19	1	0	112	61	36	40	3	43	6	8	4	11	12	.48	8	.266	.349	.327
1996 Trenton	AA Bos	6	20	5	2	0	0	7	2	3	2	0	3	0	0	0	0	1	.00	0	.250	.318	.350
Pawtucket	AAA Bos	15	44	11	2	0	0	13	5	1	3	0	8	0	1	0	0	1	.00	0	.250	.298	.295
Sarasota	A+ Bos	87	276	66	13	2	0	83	26	24	33	0	47	7	8	3	4	6	.40	6	.239	.332	.301
1997 Trenton	AA Bos	100	301	82	12	0	1	97	46	46	48	0	36	6	12	2	2	6	.25	11	.272	.381	.322
1998 Trenton	AA Bos	50	168	41	7	1	0	50	12	17	18	0	21	0	1	2	3	1	.75	5	.244	.314	.298
Pawtucket	AAA Bos	67	206	49	4	1	3	64	21	24	27	0	40	3	2	4	3	2	.60	5	.238	.329	.311
1999 Trenton	AA Bos	27	71	15	1	0	0	16	11	5	15	0	12	4	3	1	2	1	.67	1	.211	.374	.225
Pawtucket	AAA Bos	49	140	23	3	0	0	26	17	5	27	0	32	0	1	0	2	0	1.00	4	.164	.299	.186
7 Min. YEARS		651	2049	510	76	8	4	614	276	199	260	3	300	44	50	16	47	45	.51	43	.249	.344	.300

Russell Jacob

Pitches: Right Bats: Right Pos: P Ht: 6'6" Wt: 240 Born: 1/2/75 Age: 25

Year Team	Lg Org	G	GS	CG	GF	IP	BFP	H	R	ER	HR	SH	SF	HB	TBB	IBB	SO	WP	Bk	W	L	Pct.	ShO	Sv	ERA
1994 Mariners	R Sea	8	2	0	2	13.1	52	9	4	4	0	0	1	0	5	0	12	1	0	0	0	.000	0	0	2.70
1995 Mariners	R Sea	12	11	0	1	56.1	248	47	29	18	0	0	1	3	31	0	54	6	2	6	2	.750	0	0	2.88
1996 Wisconsin	A Sea	24	10	0	4	68.1	313	67	48	40	2	2	3	2	53	0	63	13	2	4	4	.500	0	2	5.27
1997 Wisconsin	A Sea	21	9	0	2	77	339	62	41	38	7	3	4	3	58	1	76	14	1	4	2	.667	0	1	4.44
1998 High Desert	A+ Ari	31	7	0	4	67.1	310	78	42	33	2	2	1	2	26	0	64	7	0	3	2	.600	0	1	4.41
1999 El Paso	AA Ari	3	0	0	2	2.2	16	5	4	2	1	0	0	0	2	0	3	0	0	0	0	.000	0	0	6.75
6 Min. YEARS		99	39	0	15	285	1278	268	168	135	12	7	10	10	175	1	272	41	5	17	10	.630	0	4	4.26

Ryan Jacobs

Pitches: Left Bats: Right Pos: P Ht: 6'2" Wt: 175 Born: 2/3/74 Age: 26

Year Team	Lg Org	G	GS	CG	GF	IP	BFP	H	R	ER	HR	SH	SF	HB	TBB	IBB	SO	WP	Bk	W	L	Pct.	ShO	Sv	ERA
1992 Braves	R Atl	12	2	0	6	35	148	30	18	10	1	2	2	1	8	2	40	2	0	1	3	.250	0	1	2.57
1993 Danville	R+ Atl	10	10	0	0	42.2	188	35	24	19	5	1	2	1	25	0	32	6	0	4	3	.571	0	0	4.01
1994 Macon	A Atl	27	18	1	2	121.2	532	105	54	39	9	4	2	3	62	2	81	6	1	8	7	.533	1	1	2.88
1995 Durham	A+ Atl	29	25	1	3	148.2	640	145	72	58	12	6	5	3	57	3	99	10	0	11	6	.647	0	0	3.51
1996 Greenville	AA Atl	21	21	0	0	99.2	468	127	83	74	19	3	4	4	57	1	64	8	0	3	9	.250	0	0	6.68
1997 Greenville	AA Atl	28	6	0	3	68.2	328	84	61	55	8	1	5	2	43	1	52	6	0	1	8	.111	0	1	7.21
1998 Richmond	AAA Atl	2	0	0	0	4.1	28	9	9	9	1	0	0	0	6	0	1	1	0	0	0	.000	0	0	18.69
Greenville	AA Atl	35	15	0	7	101	478	104	73	60	14	3	8	2	72	3	74	12	1	6	9	.400	0	0	5.35
1999 Carolina	AA Col	28	21	1	2	114	535	120	76	67	10	6	4	8	68	1	89	5	0	6	12	.333	0	0	5.29
8 Min. YEARS		192	118	3	23	735.2	3345	759	470	391	79	27	32	24	398	13	532	56	2	40	57	.412	1	3	4.78

Buck Jacobsen

Bats: Right Throws: Right Pos: OF Ht: 6'4" Wt: 220 Born: 8/30/75 Age: 24

Year Team	Lg Org	G	AB	H	2B	3B	HR	TB	R	RBI	TBB	IBB	SO	HBP	SH	SF	SB	CS	SB%	GDP	Avg	OBP	SLG
1997 Ogden	R+ Mil	67	238	78	17	2	8	123	57	52	41	0	44	3	0	4	6	6	.50	4	.328	.427	.517
1998 Beloit	A Mil	135	499	146	31	1	27	260	96	100	83	3	133	8	0	4	5	2	.71	10	.293	.399	.521
1999 Huntsville	AA Mil	47	150	29	6	1	3	46	20	19	20	0	32	0	0	5	4	1	.80	4	.193	.292	.307
Stockton	A+ Mil	46	156	39	8	0	5	62	22	22	21	1	40	4	0	1	3	3	.50	4	.250	.352	.397
3 Min. YEARS		295	1043	292	62	4	43	491	195	193	165	4	249	18	0	14	18	12	.60	22	.280	.383	.471

Joe Jacobsen

Pitches: Right Bats: Right Pos: P Ht: 6'3" Wt: 225 Born: 12/26/71 Age: 28

Year Team	Lg Org	G	GS	CG	GF	IP	BFP	H	R	ER	HR	SH	SF	HB	TBB	IBB	SO	WP	Bk	W	L	Pct.	ShO	Sv	ERA
1992 Dodgers	R LA	6	3	0	2	26	100	17	7	5	0	0	0	0	6	0	25	2	2	1	1	.500	0	0	1.73
Great Falls	R+ LA	6	6	1	0	32.1	143	37	22	19	2	0	1	1	9	0	24	3	0	2	2	.500	0	0	5.29
1993 Yakima	A- LA	25	0	0	7	37.2	174	27	16	10	0	2	3	1	28	2	55	1	0	1	0	1.000	0	3	2.39
Bakersfield	A+ LA	6	0	0	3	19.2	88	22	16	10	1	1	0	0	8	0	23	3	0	1	0	1.000	0	2	4.58
1994 Bakersfield	A+ LA	3	0	0	1	7.1	26	2	1	1	1	1	0	0	1	0	5	0	0	1	0	1.000	0	0	1.23
San Antonio	AA LA	18	0	0	12	25	108	21	9	7	0	2	2	2	12	2	15	2	1	2	1	.667	0	1	2.52
Vero Beach	A+ LA	37	0	0	34	43	193	40	15	13	1	3	0	2	23	2	44	3	0	0	5	.000	0	15	2.72

Year Team	Lg Org	HOW MUCH HE PITCHED						WHAT HE GAVE UP												THE RESULTS					
		G	GS	CG	GF	IP	BFP	H	R	ER	HR	SH	SF	HB	TBB	IBB	SO	WP	Bk	W	L	Pct.	ShO	Sv	ERA
1995 Vero Beach	A+ LA	47	0	0	44	49	215	42	22	20	2	5	2	2	23	2	54	10	1	1	3	.250	0	32	3.67
San Berndno	A+ LA	4	0	0	3	3.2	17	4	2	0	0	0	0	0	2	0	5	1	0	0	0	.000	0	2	0.00
1996 San Antonio	AA LA	38	0	0	23	58	256	62	33	27	4	4	3	1	24	2	39	7	0	1	4	.200	0	5	4.19
1997 Portland	AA Fla	47	1	0	29	58.1	270	76	44	33	7	1	2	2	23	4	48	5	0	5	5	.500	0	11	5.09
1998 Portland	AA Fla	3	0	0	2	5.1	19	4	1	1	1	0	0	0	0	0	3	0	0	1	0	1.000	0	0	1.69
Charlotte	AAA Fla	9	8	0	0	42.1	191	64	29	28	8	3	0	0	7	0	17	1	0	1	3	.250	0	0	5.95
Vancouver	AAA Ana	2	0	0	0	3.1	14	3	1	1	1	0	0	1	0	0	0	0	0	0	0	.000	0	0	2.70
Midland	AA Ana	26	1	0	19	35.2	148	34	13	6	1	4	0	1	7	0	19	5	0	2	1	.667	0	5	1.51
1999 Edmonton	AAA Ana	12	0	0	7	15	75	24	13	12	2	0	1	0	5	1	6	1	0	0	1	.000	0	0	7.20
Nashua	IND —	26	0	0	23	25.1	118	35	16	15	4	1	0	2	9	0	24	2	0	0	2	.000	0	11	5.33
Atlantic Ct	IND —	7	0	0	3	10.1	58	19	14	8	2	2	1	3	5	0	8	1	0	0	0	.000	0	1	6.97
Somerset	IND —	8	0	0	3	13.2	53	7	4	4	0	1	0	1	5	1	2	0	0	0	0	.000	0	3	2.63
8 Min. YEARS		330	19	1	215	511	2266	540	278	220	37	30	15	19	197	16	416	47	4	19	28	.404	0	91	3.87

Tom Jacquez

Pitches: Left **Bats:** Left **Pos:** P   **Ht:** 6'2" **Wt:** 195 **Born:** 12/29/75 **Age:** 24

Year Team	Lg Org	HOW MUCH HE PITCHED						WHAT HE GAVE UP												THE RESULTS					
		G	GS	CG	GF	IP	BFP	H	R	ER	HR	SH	SF	HB	TBB	IBB	SO	WP	Bk	W	L	Pct.	ShO	Sv	ERA
1997 Batavia	A- Phi	4	4	0	0	22.1	93	20	6	6	0	0	2	3	2	0	20	0	0	2	1	.667	0	0	2.42
Piedmont	A Phi	8	8	0	0	41.2	183	45	20	23	2	2	3	0	13	0	26	1	0	2	4	.333	0	0	4.07
1998 Clearwater	A+ Phi	29	28	2	0	169.2	740	215	102	81	12	6	9	3	31	3	108	5	4	9	11	.450	0	0	4.30
1999 Reading	AA Phi	38	14	0	8	122.2	555	149	84	72	20	3	2	11	32	1	68	1	0	6	5	.545	0	1	5.28
Scranton-WB	AAA Phi	3	0	0	0	3.2	15	4	1	1	0	0	0	0	0	0	4	0	0	0	1	.000	0	0	2.45
3 Min. YEARS		82	54	2	9	360	1586	433	222	183	34	11	16	20	78	4	226	7	4	19	22	.463	1	1	4.58

Kenny James

Bats: Both **Throws:** Right **Pos:** OF   **Ht:** 6'0" **Wt:** 198 **Born:** 10/9/76 **Age:** 23

Year Team	Lg Org	BATTING															BASERUNNING				PERCENTAGES		
		G	AB	H	2B	3B	HR	TB	R	RBI	TBB	IBB	SO	HBP	SH	SF	SB	CS	SB%	GDP	Avg	OBP	SLG
1995 Expos	R Mon	43	156	33	1	0	0	34	20	3	20	0	43	3	0	0	11	8	.58	1	.212	.313	.218
1996 Expos	R Mon	44	165	35	5	2	0	44	24	12	15	1	33	3	2	0	4	3	.57	0	.212	.290	.267
1997 Vermont	A- Mon	71	301	70	4	5	2	90	61	23	13	1	52	11	2	1	37	4	.90	0	.233	.288	.299
1998 Cape Fear	A Mon	114	451	114	10	3	2	136	73	32	21	0	68	11	12	1	41	6	.87	6	.253	.302	.302
1999 Harrisburg	AA Mon	29	102	26	4	2	0	34	8	6	1	0	19	1	5	0	7	3	.70	1	.255	.269	.333
Jupiter	A+ Mon	99	372	88	9	1	2	105	68	32	31	2	57	6	8	1	37	7	.84	8	.237	.305	.282
5 Min. YEARS		400	1547	366	33	13	6	443	254	108	101	4	272	35	29	3	137	31	.82	16	.237	.298	.286

Mike James

Pitches: Right **Bats:** Right **Pos:** P   **Ht:** 6'3" **Wt:** 200 **Born:** 8/15/67 **Age:** 32

Year Team	Lg Org	HOW MUCH HE PITCHED						WHAT HE GAVE UP												THE RESULTS					
		G	GS	CG	GF	IP	BFP	H	R	ER	HR	SH	SF	HB	TBB	IBB	SO	WP	Bk	W	L	Pct.	ShO	Sv	ERA
1988 Great Falls	R+ LA	14	12	0	0	67	299	61	36	28	7	3	2	7	41	0	59	2	5	7	1	.875	0	0	3.76
1989 Bakersfield	A+ LA	27	27	1	0	159.2	706	144	82	67	11	3	3	12	78	1	127	13	0	11	8	.579	1	0	3.78
1990 San Antonio	AA LA	26	26	3	0	157	681	144	73	58	14	4	7	9	78	1	97	10	0	11	4	.733	0	0	3.32
1991 San Antonio	AA LA	15	15	2	0	89.1	402	88	54	45	10	2	1	4	51	1	74	5	0	9	5	.643	1	0	4.53
Albuquerque	AAA LA	13	8	0	3	45	208	51	36	33	7	0	3	2	30	0	39	5	1	1	3	.250	0	0	6.60
1992 San Antonio	AA LA	8	8	0	0	54	214	39	16	16	3	2	0	1	20	0	52	1	1	2	1	.667	0	0	2.67
Albuquerque	AAA LA	18	6	0	3	46.2	211	55	35	29	4	3	2	2	22	0	33	4	0	2	1	.667	0	1	5.59
1993 San Antonio	AA LA	16	0	0	5	31.1	154	38	28	26	5	1	2	4	19	3	32	2	0	1	0	1.000	0	2	7.47
Vero Beach	A+ LA	30	1	0	15	60.1	271	54	37	33	2	2	2	5	33	5	60	5	1	2	3	.400	0	4	4.92
1994 Vancouver	AAA Ana	37	10	0	18	91.1	402	101	56	53	15	1	3	6	34	1	66	3	0	5	3	.625	0	8	5.22
1995 Lk Elsinore	A+ Ana	5	1	0	1	5.2	29	9	6	6	1	0	0	0	3	0	6	0	0	0	0	.000	0	0	9.53
1999 Lk Elsinore	A+ Ana	3	3	0	0	9.1	41	12	6	6	0	0	0	1	0	0	6	0	0	0	0	.000	0	0	5.79
Edmonton	AAA Ana	8	1	0	0	8.1	43	16	14	8	3	0	0	1	2	0	3	1	0	1	2	.333	0	0	8.64
1995 California	AL	46	0	0	11	55.2	237	49	27	24	6	2	0	3	26	2	36	1	0	3	0	1.000	0	1	3.88
1996 California	AL	69	0	0	23	81	353	62	27	24	7	6	5	10	42	7	65	5	0	5	5	.500	0	1	2.67
1997 Anaheim	AL	58	0	0	22	62.2	284	69	32	30	3	6	1	5	28	4	57	1	0	5	5	.500	0	7	4.31
1998 Anaheim	AL	11	0	0	3	14	55	10	3	3	0	0	0	0	7	0	12	0	0	0	0	.000	0	0	1.93
9 Min. YEARS		220	118	6	45	825	3661	812	479	408	82	20	26	49	411	12	656	51	8	52	31	.627	2	16	4.45
4 Maj. YEARS		184	0	0	59	213.1	929	190	89	81	16	14	6	18	103	13	170	7	0	13	10	.565	0	9	3.42

Marty Janzen

Pitches: Right **Bats:** Right **Pos:** P   **Ht:** 6'3" **Wt:** 197 **Born:** 5/31/73 **Age:** 27

Year Team	Lg Org	HOW MUCH HE PITCHED						WHAT HE GAVE UP												THE RESULTS					
		G	GS	CG	GF	IP	BFP	H	R	ER	HR	SH	SF	HB	TBB	IBB	SO	WP	Bk	W	L	Pct.	ShO	Sv	ERA
1992 Yankees	R NYY	12	11	0	0	68.2	277	55	21	18	0	3	2	5	15	0	73	3	3	7	2	.778	0	0	2.36
Greensboro	A NYY	2	2	0	0	5	20	5	2	2	0	0	0	0	1	0	5	2	0	0	0	.000	0	1	3.60
1993 Yankees	R NYY	5	5	0	0	22.1	93	20	5	3	0	0	0	1	3	0	19	0	0	0	1	.000	0	0	1.21
1994 Greensboro	A NYY	17	17	0	0	104	431	98	57	45	8	0	0	2	25	1	92	2	2	7	3	.700	0	0	3.89
1995 Tampa	A+ NYY	18	18	1	0	113.2	461	102	38	33	4	1	2	4	30	0	104	3	4	10	3	.769	0	0	2.61
Norwich	AA NYY	3	3	0	0	20	85	17	11	11	2	0	0	2	7	0	16	2	0	1	2	.333	0	0	4.95
Knoxville	AA Tor	7	7	2	0	48	188	35	14	14	2	0	1	1	14	0	44	1	1	5	1	.833	1	0	2.63
1996 Syracuse	AAA Tor	10	10	0	0	55.2	257	74	54	48	12	1	4	0	24	2	34	2	0	3	4	.429	0	0	7.76
1997 Syracuse	AAA Tor	22	9	0	6	65	304	76	58	52	12	3	3	3	36	0	56	8	0	5	5	.000	0	1	7.20
1998 Columbus	AAA NYY	16	12	1	0	68.2	318	78	48	44	8	0	3	1	38	0	54	6	0	5	6	.455	0	0	5.77
Yankees	R NYY	1	1	0	0	3	10	1	0	0	0	0	0	0	0	0	5	0	0	0	0	.000	0	0	0.00
Norwich	AA NYY	11	7	1	0	34.2	168	42	28	15	3	2	4	2	19	1	38	2	0	1	7	.125	0	0	3.89

Year Team	Lg Org	G	GS	CG	GF	IP	BFP	H	R	ER	HR	SH	SF	HB	TBB	IBB	SO	WP	Bk	W	L	Pct.	ShO	Sv	ERA
		HOW MUCH HE PITCHED						WHAT HE GAVE UP												THE RESULTS					
1999 Indianapolis	AAA Cin	9	1	0	3	16.2	73	16	9	9	0	1	1	2	8	2	8	1	0	1	1	.500	0	0	4.86
Chattanooga	AA Cin	30	4	0	7	54.2	246	54	32	30	6	4	1	7	29	4	41	5	0	1	3	.250	0	0	4.94
1996 Toronto	AL	15	11	0	3	73.2	344	95	65	60	16	1	3	2	38	3	47	7	0	4	6	.400	0	0	7.33
1997 Toronto	AL	12	0	0	6	25	105	23	11	10	4	0	0	0	13	0	17	0	0	2	1	.667	0	0	3.60
8 Min. YEARS		163	105	5	20	680	2931	673	377	324	57	15	21	32	249	10	589	37	10	37	42	.468	1	2	4.29
2 Maj. YEARS		27	11	0	9	98.2	449	118	76	70	20	1	3	2	51	3	64	7	0	6	7	.462	0	0	6.39

Matt Jarvis
Pitches: Left Bats: Right Pos: P Ht: 6'4" Wt: 185 Born: 2/22/72 Age: 28

Year Team	Lg Org	G	GS	CG	GF	IP	BFP	H	R	ER	HR	SH	SF	HB	TBB	IBB	SO	WP	Bk	W	L	Pct.	ShO	Sv	ERA
		HOW MUCH HE PITCHED						WHAT HE GAVE UP												THE RESULTS					
1991 Orioles	R Bal	11	5	0	2	37.1	163	44	22	18	2	1	2	0	17	0	30	2	1	3	1	.750	0	1	4.34
1992 Kane County	A Bal	34	7	0	8	71.1	327	84	53	36	3	2	1	1	35	2	43	7	3	4	4	.500	0	1	4.54
1993 Albany	A Bal	29	29	8	0	185.1	797	173	82	63	7	5	2	5	82	4	118	10	1	11	13	.458	1	0	3.06
1994 Frederick	A+ Bal	31	14	0	3	103.2	459	92	58	48	7	5	2	9	48	0	67	3	0	10	4	.714	0	1	4.17
1995 Bowie	AA Bal	26	21	0	1	118	531	154	71	67	11	4	4	4	42	1	60	5	3	9	8	.529	0	0	5.11
1996 Bowie	AA Bal	6	4	0	0	19.1	91	31	17	16	2	0	2	1	7	0	13	4	1	1	3	.250	0	0	7.45
Winnipeg	IND —	17	15	2	1	103	454	99	46	41	11	3	2	6	55	1	63	3	3	11	3	.786	0	0	3.58
1997 Arkansas	AA StL	50	4	0	16	80	344	70	24	17	0	9	1	3	45	4	52	4	0	8	5	.615	0	2	1.91
1998 Arkansas	AA StL	56	0	0	32	59.1	258	55	30	27	2	2	0	3	30	2	46	3	0	6	1	.857	0	15	4.10
1999 San Antonio	AA LA	3	0	0	0	3	20	10	10	9	0	0	0	0	3	1	1	0	0	0	1	.000	0	0	27.00
9 Min. YEARS		263	99	10	63	780.1	3444	812	413	342	45	31	16	32	364	15	493	41	12	63	43	.594	1	19	3.94

Jason Jensen
Pitches: Left Bats: Left Pos: P Ht: 6'2" Wt: 175 Born: 11/4/75 Age: 24

Year Team	Lg Org	G	GS	CG	GF	IP	BFP	H	R	ER	HR	SH	SF	HB	TBB	IBB	SO	WP	Bk	W	L	Pct.	ShO	Sv	ERA
		HOW MUCH HE PITCHED						WHAT HE GAVE UP												THE RESULTS					
1997 Lethbridge	R+ Ari	14	14	0	0	63.1	282	73	43	35	3	2	1	3	23	0	46	0	0	4	3	.571	0	0	4.97
1998 South Bend	A Ari	28	26	1	0	153	684	174	91	71	8	9	2	6	59	0	115	12	0	4	11	.267	0	0	4.18
1999 South Bend	A Ari	18	2	0	6	44.1	179	26	19	13	1	1	2	1	21	0	22	1	0	2	3	.400	0	2	2.64
Tucson	AAA Ari	1	1	0	0	4.2	24	6	6	2	0	0	0	0	4	1	3	0	0	0	1	.000	0	0	3.86
El Paso	AA Ari	4	2	0	0	11.2	62	20	11	11	0	1	1	0	9	0	8	3	0	1	0	1.000	0	0	8.49
High Desert	A+ Ari	9	9	0	0	44.1	194	43	24	22	8	0	1	1	22	0	24	2	0	2	2	.500	0	0	4.47
3 Min. YEARS		74	54	1	6	321.1	1425	342	194	154	20	13	7	11	138	1	218	18	0	12	21	.364	0	2	4.31

Ryan Jensen
Pitches: Right Bats: Right Pos: P Ht: 6'0" Wt: 205 Born: 9/17/75 Age: 24

Year Team	Lg Org	G	GS	CG	GF	IP	BFP	H	R	ER	HR	SH	SF	HB	TBB	IBB	SO	WP	Bk	W	L	Pct.	ShO	Sv	ERA
		HOW MUCH HE PITCHED						WHAT HE GAVE UP												THE RESULTS					
1996 Bellingham	A- SF	13	11	0	0	47	208	35	30	26	4	1	0	1	38	0	31	7	0	2	4	.333	0	0	4.98
1997 Bakersfield	A+ SF	1	1	0	0	1.1	7	3	2	2	1	0	1	0	0	0	2	0	0	0	0	.000	0	0	13.50
Salem-Keizr	A- SF	16	16	0	0	80.1	353	87	55	46	10	2	4	4	32	0	67	2	1	7	3	.700	0	0	5.15
1998 Bakersfield	A+ SF	29	27	0	1	168.1	726	162	89	63	14	6	1	8	61	3	164	10	2	11	12	.478	0	0	3.37
Fresno	AAA SF	2	1	0	0	5.2	25	4	5	3	2	0	0	1	4	0	6	0	0	0	0	.000	0	0	4.76
1999 Fresno	AAA SF	27	27	0	0	156.1	688	160	96	89	17	6	6	6	68	1	150	13	0	11	10	.524	0	0	5.12
4 Min. YEARS		88	83	0	1	459	2007	451	277	229	48	15	11	19	203	4	420	32	3	31	29	.517	0	0	4.49

Todd Johannes
Bats: Right Throws: Right Pos: C Ht: 6'3" Wt: 185 Born: 10/25/76 Age: 23

Year Team	Lg Org	G	AB	H	2B	3B	HR	TB	R	RBI	TBB	IBB	SO	HBP	SH	SF	SB	CS	SB%	GDP	Avg	OBP	SLG
		BATTING															BASERUNNING				PERCENTAGES		
1999 Harrisburg	AA Mon	1	4	1	0	0	0	1	0	0	0	0	2	0	0	0	0	0	.00	0	.250	.250	.250
Vermont	A- Mon	24	84	25	2	0	0	27	5	11	10	0	15	0	0	2	1	0	1.00	2	.298	.365	.321
1 Min. YEARS		25	88	26	2	0	0	28	5	11	10	0	17	0	0	2	1	0	1.00	2	.295	.360	.318

Keith Johns
Bats: Right Throws: Right Pos: SS Ht: 6'1" Wt: 175 Born: 7/19/71 Age: 28

Year Team	Lg Org	G	AB	H	2B	3B	HR	TB	R	RBI	TBB	IBB	SO	HBP	SH	SF	SB	CS	SB%	GDP	Avg	OBP	SLG
		BATTING															BASERUNNING				PERCENTAGES		
1992 Hamilton	A- StL	70	275	78	11	1	1	94	36	28	27	0	42	1	1	3	15	10	.60	5	.284	.346	.342
1993 Springfield	A StL	132	467	121	24	1	2	153	74	40	70	0	68	4	9	5	40	20	.67	8	.259	.357	.328
1994 St. Pete	A+ StL	122	464	106	20	0	3	135	52	47	37	1	49	2	12	4	18	9	.67	7	.228	.286	.291
1995 Arkansas	AA StL	111	396	111	13	2	2	134	69	28	55	0	53	2	11	2	14	7	.67	11	.280	.369	.338
Louisville	AAA StL	5	10	0	0	0	0	0	0	0	0	0	2	0	0	0	0	0	.00	0	.000	.000	.000
1996 Arkansas	AA StL	127	447	110	17	1	1	132	52	40	47	0	61	4	7	1	8	9	.47	17	.246	.323	.295
1997 Tucson	AAA Mil	112	333	88	21	3	5	130	45	36	46	0	61	2	6	2	4	2	.67	7	.264	.350	.390
Rochester	AAA Bal	1	1	0	0	0	0	0	0	0	0	0	0	1	0	0	0	0	.00	0	.000	.500	.000
1998 Pawtucket	AAA Bos	96	329	75	12	1	8	113	31	38	28	0	82	4	1	5	2	6	.25	10	.228	.292	.343
1999 Edmonton	AAA Ana	81	236	49	9	2	3	71	32	26	26	0	38	2	1	2	2	0	1.00	8	.208	.289	.301
1998 Boston	AL	2	0	0	0	0	0	0	0	0	0	1	0	0	0	0	0	0	.00	5	.000	1.000	.000
8 Min. YEARS		857	2958	738	127	11	25	962	391	283	333	1	456	22	48	24	103	63	.62	73	.249	.328	.325

A.J. Johnson

Bats: Right **Throws:** Right **Pos:** OF **Ht:** 6'3" **Wt:** 210 **Born:** 2/17/73 **Age:** 27

Year Team	Lg Org	G	AB	H	2B	3B	HR	TB	R	RBI	TBB	IBB	SO	HBP	SH	SF	SB	CS	SB%	GDP	Avg	OBP	SLG
1995 Lethbridge	R+ —	61	229	68	10	3	2	90	30	41	18	2	33	6	1	2	6	8	.43	9	.297	.361	.393
1996 Chstn-WV	A Cin	9	26	6	1	0	1	10	3	5	6	0	9	1	0	0	1	2	.33	0	.231	.394	.385
Duluth-Sup	IND —	80	315	103	29	2	20	196	59	65	28	0	60	3	0	5	6	1	.86	4	.327	.382	.622
1997 Kingsport	R+ NYM	15	45	15	3	0	3	27	10	9	9	0	17	0	0	0	1	1	.50	1	.333	.444	.600
Duluth-Sup	IND —	83	333	100	19	5	7	150	63	57	24	1	54	14	1	3	12	5	.71	8	.300	.369	.450
1998 Rancho Cuca	A+ SD	134	539	166	33	5	24	281	94	94	28	2	98	6	2	5	15	10	.60	15	.308	.346	.521
1999 Jackson	AA Hou	63	187	45	7	0	4	64	21	16	9	0	38	8	1	2	4	2	.67	3	.241	.301	.342
Mobile	AA SD	44	136	33	7	0	4	52	12	16	6	0	35	2	0	0	1	3	.25	4	.243	.285	.382
5 Min. YEARS		489	1810	536	109	15	65	870	292	305	128	5	344	40	5	17	46	32	.59	44	.296	.353	.481

Adam Johnson

Bats: Left **Throws:** Left **Pos:** OF **Ht:** 6'0" **Wt:** 185 **Born:** 7/18/75 **Age:** 24

Year Team	Lg Org	G	AB	H	2B	3B	HR	TB	R	RBI	TBB	IBB	SO	HBP	SH	SF	SB	CS	SB%	GDP	Avg	OBP	SLG
1996 Eugene	A- Atl	76	318	100	22	9	7	161	58	56	19	3	32	4	1	2	4	1	.80	4	.314	.359	.506
1997 Durham	A+ Atl	133	502	141	39	3	26	264	80	92	50	9	94	4	0	16	18	8	.69	10	.281	.341	.526
1998 Greenville	AA Atl	121	411	104	21	3	19	188	67	77	42	6	71	4	0	7	7	7	.50	10	.253	.323	.457
1999 Richmond	AAA Atl	14	42	14	2	0	1	19	7	6	2	0	5	1	1	0	1	1	.50	0	.333	.378	.452
Greenville	AA Atl	104	394	114	27	2	14	187	50	72	31	1	74	4	0	5	1	6	.14	11	.289	.343	.475
4 Min. YEARS		448	1667	473	111	17	67	819	262	303	144	19	276	17	2	30	31	23	.57	35	.284	.341	.491

Barry Johnson

Pitches: Right **Bats:** Right **Pos:** P **Ht:** 6'4" **Wt:** 200 **Born:** 8/21/69 **Age:** 30

Year Team	Lg Org	G	GS	CG	GF	IP	BFP	H	R	ER	HR	SH	SF	HB	TBB	IBB	SO	WP	Bk	W	L	Pct.	ShO	Sv	ERA
1991 Expos	R Mon	7	1	0	3	12.2	55	10	9	5	0	0	0	4	6	0	10	2	0	0	2	.000	0	0	3.55
1992 South Bend	A CWS	16	16	5	0	109.1	463	111	56	46	5	1	5	6	23	0	74	8	1	7	5	.583	1	0	3.79
1993 Sarasota	A+ CWS	18	1	0	7	54.1	205	33	5	4	1	5	2	2	8	0	40	1	1	5	0	1.000	0	1	0.66
Birmingham	AA CWS	13	1	0	8	21.2	97	27	11	8	2	1	0	0	6	0	16	2	1	2	0	1.000	0	1	3.32
1994 Birmingham	AA CWS	51	4	0	12	97.2	427	100	51	35	7	8	3	2	30	3	67	2	0	6	2	.750	0	1	3.23
1995 Birmingham	AA CWS	47	0	0	10	78	308	64	21	16	1	4	1	2	15	1	53	2	1	7	4	.636	0	0	1.85
1996 Birmingham	AA CWS	9	0	0	7	10.2	35	2	0	0	0	1	0	0	1	0	15	0	0	0	0	.000	0	0	0.00
Nashville	AAA CWS	38	8	0	8	103	403	93	38	32	11	2	3	1	39	3	68	4	0	7	2	.778	0	0	2.80
1997 Nashville	AAA CWS	14	0	0	5	25.1	108	24	10	10	1	1	1	0	11	1	10	3	0	4	1	.800	0	0	3.55
Calgary	AAA Pit	34	1	0	12	56.2	247	55	30	26	7	1	3	1	23	2	51	3	0	5	2	.714	0	0	4.13
1998 Oklahoma	AAA Tex	31	7	1	10	77.1	343	96	66	57	13	2	1	3	21	0	54	3	0	2	8	.200	0	1	6.63
Tucson	AAA Ari	5	1	0	0	11.2	56	16	12	9	2	0	0	1	5	1	10	1	0	0	1	.000	0	0	6.94
Norwich	AA NYY	7	0	0	3	12	53	13	6	5	1	1	1	0	5	0	12	1	0	1	0	1.000	0	0	3.75
1999 Scranton-WB	AAA Phi	31	18	1	5	136.1	602	157	83	76	12	1	5	1	49	2	88	7	0	6	10	.375	1	0	5.02
9 Min. YEARS		321	58	7	90	806.2	3429	801	398	329	63	26	26	23	242	13	568	39	4	52	37	.584	2	11	3.67

Earl Johnson

Bats: Both **Throws:** Right **Pos:** OF **Ht:** 5'10" **Wt:** 165 **Born:** 10/3/71 **Age:** 28

Year Team	Lg Org	G	AB	H	2B	3B	HR	TB	R	RBI	TBB	IBB	SO	HBP	SH	SF	SB	CS	SB%	GDP	Avg	OBP	SLG
1992 Padres	R SD	35	101	17	1	0	0	18	20	1	10	0	28	1	0	0	19	5	.79	0	.168	.250	.178
1993 Spokane	A- SD	63	199	49	3	1	0	54	33	14	16	0	49	1	5	1	19	3	.86	2	.246	.304	.271
1994 Springfield	A SD	136	533	149	11	3	1	169	80	43	37	0	94	3	13	4	80	25	.76	2	.280	.328	.317
1995 Rancho Cuca	A+ SD	81	341	100	11	3	0	117	51	25	25	0	51	1	5	0	34	12	.74	5	.293	.343	.343
Memphis	AA SD	2	10	2	0	0	0	2	0	1	0	0	0	0	0	0	0	1	.00	0	.200	.273	.200
1996 Memphis	AA SD	82	337	85	10	6	2	113	50	33	18	1	59	1	5	3	15	13	.54	5	.252	.290	.335
1997 Mobile	AA SD	78	307	78	11	3	1	98	52	22	21	0	56	0	6	2	35	13	.73	3	.254	.300	.319
Jacksnville	AA Det	36	146	33	3	1	2	44	24	13	9	0	19	1	3	2	7	1	.88	3	.226	.272	.301
1998 Toledo	AAA Det	105	362	91	10	8	1	120	44	24	19	0	65	0	7	1	20	6	.77	4	.251	.288	.331
1999 Tacoma	AAA Sea	17	55	13	2	0	0	15	6	4	8	0	6	0	0	1	5	1	.83	1	.236	.328	.273
New Haven	AA Sea	37	139	34	3	0	0	37	18	10	8	0	31	0	2	2	11	3	.79	1	.245	.282	.266
8 Min. YEARS		672	2530	651	65	25	7	787	378	189	172	1	458	8	46	16	245	83	.75	26	.257	.305	.311

Greg Johnson

Pitches: Left **Bats:** Left **Pos:** P **Ht:** 6'0" **Wt:** 185 **Born:** 4/28/74 **Age:** 26

Year Team	Lg Org	G	GS	CG	GF	IP	BFP	H	R	ER	HR	SH	SF	HB	TBB	IBB	SO	WP	Bk	W	L	Pct.	ShO	Sv	ERA
1996 Boise	A- Ana	8	0	0	5	9.2	47	17	11	11	2	0	1	0	2	1	6	0	0	0	0	.000	0	0	10.24
1997 Lk Elsinore	A+ Ana	34	0	0	8	44.2	197	46	21	17	2	2	3	5	9	2	35	1	0	1	0	1.000	0	0	3.43
1998 Midland	AA Ana	2	0	0	0	1.2	10	4	2	2	0	0	1	0	2	0	1	1	0	0	0	.000	0	0	10.80
Lk Elsinore	A+ Ana	37	1	0	13	75.2	323	78	40	36	9	5	1	1	23	3	63	5	1	3	3	.500	0	0	4.28
1999 Lk Elsinore	A+ Ana	39	5	1	12	81.1	337	83	36	29	5	6	1	0	15	2	63	7	1	4	4	.500	0	1	3.21
Erie	AA Ana	2	0	0	1	3	17	8	4	4	0	0	1	0	1	0	4	0	0	0	0	.000	0	0	12.00
4 Min. YEARS		122	6	1	39	216	931	236	114	99	18	13	8	6	52	8	172	14	2	8	7	.533	0	1	4.13

J.J. Johnson

Bats: Right Throws: Right Pos: OF   Ht: 6'0" Wt: 204 Born: 8/31/73 Age: 26

| | | BATTING | | | | | | | | | | | | | | | BASERUNNING | | | | PERCENTAGES | | |
Year Team	Lg Org	G	AB	H	2B	3B	HR	TB	R	RBI	TBB	IBB	SO	HBP	SH	SF	SB	CS	SB%	GDP	Avg	OBP	SLG
1991 Red Sox	R Bos	31	110	19	1	0	0	20	14	9	10	0	15	2	0	2	3	1	.75	2	.173	.250	.182
1992 Elmira	A- Bos	30	114	26	3	1	1	34	8	12	4	0	32	1	4	1	8	0	1.00	2	.228	.258	.298
1993 Utica	A- Bos	43	170	49	17	4	2	80	33	27	9	1	34	7	2	3	5	3	.63	2	.288	.344	.471
Lynchburg	A+ Bos	25	94	24	3	0	4	39	10	17	7	0	20	2	2	2	1	2	.33	3	.255	.314	.415
1994 Lynchburg	A+ Bos	131	515	120	28	4	14	198	66	51	36	3	132	4	1	1	4	7	.36	9	.233	.288	.384
1995 Sarasota	A+ Bos	107	391	108	16	4	10	162	49	43	26	0	74	6	2	2	7	8	.47	9	.276	.329	.414
Trenton	AA Bos	2	6	3	0	0	0	3	1	1	0	0	0	0	0	0	0	0	.00	0	.500	.500	.500
1996 Hardware Cy	AA Min	119	440	120	23	3	16	197	62	59	40	3	90	7	2	3	10	11	.48	4	.273	.341	.448
Salt Lake	AAA Min	13	56	19	3	1	1	27	8	13	1	0	11	1	1	0	0	1	.00	1	.339	.362	.482
1997 Salt Lake	AAA Min	26	82	12	1	1	0	15	6	5	4	0	24	1	1	0	2	2	.50	2	.146	.195	.183
New Britain	AA Min	103	356	84	11	3	3	110	60	42	38	1	94	4	3	6	13	1	.93	6	.236	.312	.309
1998 New Britain	AA Min	101	371	95	19	3	13	159	54	48	25	0	103	2	1	1	5	5	.50	7	.256	.306	.429
1999 Jackson	AA Hou	131	437	110	28	2	18	196	57	69	47	1	119	5	6	2	11	11	.50	7	.252	.330	.449
9 Min. YEARS		862	3142	789	153	26	82	1240	428	396	247	9	748	42	25	23	69	52	.57	54	.251	.312	.395

Keith Johnson

Bats: Right Throws: Right Pos: 2B   Ht: 5'11" Wt: 200 Born: 4/17/71 Age: 29

| | | BATTING | | | | | | | | | | | | | | | BASERUNNING | | | | PERCENTAGES | | |
Year Team	Lg Org	G	AB	H	2B	3B	HR	TB	R	RBI	TBB	IBB	SO	HBP	SH	SF	SB	CS	SB%	GDP	Avg	OBP	SLG
1992 Yakima	A- LA	57	197	40	6	0	1	49	27	17	16	0	37	10	1	1	5	1	.83	4	.203	.295	.249
1993 Vero Beach	A+ LA	111	404	96	22	0	4	130	37	48	18	0	71	4	6	5	13	13	.50	8	.238	.274	.322
1994 Bakersfield	A+ LA	64	210	42	12	1	2	62	19	19	16	0	49	5	3	2	13	7	.65	3	.200	.270	.295
1995 San Berndno	A+ LA	111	417	101	26	1	17	180	64	68	17	0	83	4	11	2	20	12	.63	4	.242	.277	.432
1996 San Antonio	AA LA	127	521	143	28	6	10	213	74	57	17	1	82	4	9	3	15	8	.65	15	.274	.301	.409
Albuquerque	AAA LA	4	16	4	1	0	0	5	2	2	1	0	1	0	0	0	0	0	.00	0	.250	.294	.313
1997 San Antonio	AA LA	96	298	80	9	3	9	122	43	52	17	0	48	4	8	3	7	6	.54	4	.268	.314	.409
1998 Albuquerque	AAA LA	82	254	59	5	1	6	84	32	26	10	0	51	4	6	1	5	3	.67	4	.232	.271	.331
San Antonio	AA LA	40	154	46	10	1	3	67	20	16	10	2	26	3	6	1	10	5	.67	3	.299	.351	.435
1999 El Paso	AA Ari	17	70	21	10	1	3	42	17	15	4	0	17	0	1	1	0	1	.00	4	.300	.333	.600
Tucson	AAA Ari	107	356	102	19	0	12	157	61	46	30	2	71	8	4	4	2	4	.33	11	.287	.352	.441
8 Min. YEARS		816	2897	734	148	14	67	1111	396	366	156	5	536	46	55	23	91	60	.60	60	.253	.300	.384

Mark Johnson

Pitches: Right Bats: Right Pos: P   Ht: 6'3" Wt: 226 Born: 5/2/75 Age: 25

| | | HOW MUCH HE PITCHED | | | | | | WHAT HE GAVE UP | | | | | | | | | | | | THE RESULTS | | | | |
Year Team	Lg Org	G	GS	CG	GF	IP	BFP	H	R	ER	HR	SH	SF	HB	TBB	IBB	SO	WP	Bk	W	L	Pct.	ShO	Sv	ERA
1997 Kissimmee	A+ Hou	26	26	3	0	155.1	652	150	67	53	7	5	6		39	1	127	4	6	8	9	.471	1	0	3.07
1998 Portland	AA Fla	26	26	2	0	142.1	615	147	89	73	12	8	2	4	60	4	120	7	0	5	14	.263	0	0	4.62
1999 Yankees	R NYY	3	2	0	0	11	53	15	11	10	1	1	1	0	5	1	10	0	0	0	3	.000	0	0	8.18
Tampa	A+ NYY	1	1	0	0	6	22	4	1	1	1	0	0	0	1	0	6	0	0	1	0	1.000	0	0	1.50
Norwich	AA NYY	16	15	0	0	88	393	88	51	36	7	1	5	4	39	0	52	6	0	9	3	.750	0	0	3.68
3 Min. YEARS		72	70	5	0	402.2	1735	404	219	173	29	17	13	14	144	6	315	17	6	23	29	.442	1	0	3.87

Nick Johnson

Bats: Left Throws: Left Pos: 1B   Ht: 6'3" Wt: 195 Born: 9/19/78 Age: 21

| | | BATTING | | | | | | | | | | | | | | | BASERUNNING | | | | PERCENTAGES | | |
Year Team	Lg Org	G	AB	H	2B	3B	HR	TB	R	RBI	TBB	IBB	SO	HBP	SH	SF	SB	CS	SB%	GDP	Avg	OBP	SLG
1996 Yankees	R NYY	47	157	45	11	1	2	64	31	33	30	0	35	9	0	3	0	0	.00	5	.287	.422	.408
1997 Greensboro	A NYY	127	433	118	23	1	16	191	77	75	76	1	99	18	0	6	16	3	.84	5	.273	.398	.441
1998 Tampa	A+ NYY	92	303	96	14	1	17	163	69	58	68	3	76	19	0	3	1	4	.20	5	.317	.466	.538
1999 Norwich	AA NYY	132	420	145	33	5	14	230	114	87	123	6	88	37	0	1	8	6	.57	9	.345	.525	.548
4 Min. YEARS		398	1313	404	81	8	49	648	291	253	297	10	298	83	0	13	25	13	.66	24	.308	.460	.494

Ric Johnson

Bats: Right Throws: Right Pos: OF   Ht: 6'2" Wt: 185 Born: 3/18/74 Age: 26

| | | BATTING | | | | | | | | | | | | | | | BASERUNNING | | | | PERCENTAGES | | |
Year Team	Lg Org	G	AB	H	2B	3B	HR	TB	R	RBI	TBB	IBB	SO	HBP	SH	SF	SB	CS	SB%	GDP	Avg	OBP	SLG
1996 Quad City	A Hou	95	318	75	9	3	3	99	36	39	16	0	47	8	4	6	10	4	.71	12	.236	.284	.311
1997 Kissimmee	A+ Hou	121	453	127	11	4	1	149	47	40	21	0	67	6	3	4	21	8	.72	8	.280	.318	.329
1998 Jackson	AA Hou	23	80	16	2	0	0	18	5	2	3	0	9	1	0	0	0	1	.00	2	.200	.238	.225
Kissimmee	A+ Hou	103	381	103	17	2	6	142	67	45	34	0	48	5	2	1	20	8	.71	5	.270	.337	.373
1999 Jackson	AA Hou	99	323	79	19	1	1	103	28	27	13	2	44	2	4	2	5	5	.50	6	.245	.276	.319
4 Min. YEARS		441	1555	400	58	10	11	511	183	153	87	2	215	22	13	13	56	26	.68	33	.257	.304	.329

Doug Johnston

Pitches: Right Bats: Right Pos: P   Ht: 6'5" Wt: 180 Born: 3/16/78 Age: 22

| | | HOW MUCH HE PITCHED | | | | | | WHAT HE GAVE UP | | | | | | | | | | | | THE RESULTS | | | | |
Year Team	Lg Org	G	GS	CG	GF	IP	BFP	H	R	ER	HR	SH	SF	HB	TBB	IBB	SO	WP	Bk	W	L	Pct.	ShO	Sv	ERA
1997 Helena	R+ Mil	13	13	0	0	74.1	318	64	39	36	5	1	1	6	34	0	66	5	0	6	2	.750	0	0	4.36
1998 Beloit	A Mil	14	14	2	0	91	379	77	30	25	6	1	0	7	28	1	71	3	1	8	2	.800	1	0	2.47
Stockton	A+ Mil	9	9	1	0	60.1	240	47	20	18	3	0	1	5	26	0	54	1	2	5	1	.833	0	0	2.69
1999 Huntsville	AA Mil	21	21	1	0	118.2	516	128	72	66	17	5	3	9	43	3	80	5	1	7	11	.389	0	0	5.01
3 Min. YEARS		57	57	4	0	344.1	1453	316	161	145	31	7	5	27	131	4	271	14	4	26	16	.619	1	0	3.79

Chris Jones

Bats: Right **Throws:** Right **Pos:** DH
Ht: 6' 1" **Wt:** 219 **Born:** 12/16/65 **Age:** 34

Year Team	Lg Org	G	AB	H	2B	3B	HR	TB	R	RBI	TBB	IBB	SO	HBP	SH	SF	SB	CS	SB%	GDP	Avg	OBP	SLG
1984 Billings	R+ Cin	21	73	11	2	0	2	19	8	13	2	0	24	0	0	1	4	0	1.00	0	.151	.171	.260
1985 Billings	R+ Cin	63	240	62	12	5	4	96	43	33	19	0	72	1	1	1	13	0	1.00	3	.258	.314	.400
1986 Cedar Rapds	A Cin	128	473	117	13	9	20	208	65	78	20	1	126	3	0	4	23	17	.58	7	.247	.280	.440
1987 Vermont	AA Cin	113	383	88	11	4	10	137	50	39	23	4	99	4	2	3	13	10	.57	12	.230	.278	.358
1988 Chattanooga	AA Cin	116	410	111	20	7	4	157	50	61	29	1	102	2	0	7	11	9	.55	4	.271	.317	.383
1989 Nashville	AAA Cin	21	49	8	1	0	2	15	8	5	0	0	16	0	1	0	2	0	1.00	0	.163	.163	.306
Chattanooga	AA Cin	103	378	95	18	2	10	147	47	54	23	1	68	3	0	1	10	2	.83	13	.251	.299	.389
1990 Nashville	AAA Cin	134	436	114	23	3	10	173	53	52	23	3	86	2	5	1	12	8	.60	18	.261	.301	.397
1991 Nashville	AAA Cin	73	267	65	5	4	9	105	29	33	19	1	65	2	0	1	10	5	.67	6	.243	.298	.393
1992 Tucson	AAA Hou	45	170	55	9	8	3	89	25	28	18	2	34	0	1	2	7	1	.88	7	.324	.384	.524
1993 Colo Sprngs	AAA Col	46	168	47	5	5	12	98	41	40	19	2	47	2	0	4	8	2	.80	2	.280	.352	.583
1994 Colo Sprngs	AAA Col	98	386	124	22	4	20	214	77	75	35	3	72	2	0	1	12	2	.86	9	.321	.380	.554
1995 Norfolk	AAA NYM	33	114	38	12	1	3	61	20	19	11	1	20	1	0	3	5	2	.71	2	.333	.388	.535
1998 Fresno	AAA SF	25	60	16	1	3	3	32	11	8	6	0	12	0	1	0	2	1	.67	0	.267	.333	.533
1999 Syracuse	AAA Tor	81	279	66	12	3	6	108	45	40	19	0	74	0	1	0	11	3	.79	12	.237	.285	.387
1991 Cincinnati	NL	52	89	26	1	2	2	37	14	6	2	0	31	0	0	1	2	1	.67	2	.292	.304	.416
1992 Houston	NL	54	63	12	2	1	1	19	7	4	7	0	21	0	3	0	3	0	1.00	1	.190	.271	.302
1993 Colorado	NL	86	209	57	11	4	6	94	29	31	10	1	48	0	5	1	9	4	.69	6	.273	.305	.450
1994 Colorado	NL	21	40	12	2	1	0	16	6	2	2	1	14	0	0	0	1	0	1.00	1	.300	.333	.400
1995 New York	NL	79	182	51	6	2	8	85	33	31	13	1	45	1	2	3	2	1	.67	2	.280	.327	.467
1996 New York	NL	89	149	36	7	0	4	55	22	18	12	1	42	2	0	0	1	0	1.00	3	.242	.307	.369
1997 San Diego	NL	92	152	37	9	0	7	67	24	25	16	0	45	2	1	1	7	2	.78	4	.243	.322	.441
1998 Arizona	NL	20	31	6	1	0	0	7	3	3	3	0	9	0	0	0	0	0	.00	2	.194	.265	.226
San Francisco	NL	43	90	17	2	1	2	27	14	10	8	0	28	0	0	2	2	1	.67	0	.189	.250	.300
14 Min. YEARS		1100	3886	1017	166	58	120	1659	572	578	266	19	917	22	12	29	143	62	.70	95	.262	.310	.427
8 Maj. YEARS		536	1005	254	41	11	30	407	152	130	73	4	283	5	11	8	26	10	.72	21	.253	.304	.405

Jaime Jones

Bats: Left **Throws:** Left **Pos:** OF
Ht: 6'3" **Wt:** 190 **Born:** 8/2/76 **Age:** 23

Year Team	Lg Org	G	AB	H	2B	3B	HR	TB	R	RBI	TBB	IBB	SO	HBP	SH	SF	SB	CS	SB%	GDP	Avg	OBP	SLG
1995 Marlins	R Fla	5	18	4	0	0	0	4	2	3	5	1	4	0	0	0	0	0	.00	0	.222	.391	.222
Elmira	A- Fla	31	116	33	6	2	4	55	21	11	9	0	30	0	0	0	5	4	.56	2	.284	.336	.474
1996 Kane County	A Fla	62	237	59	17	1	8	102	29	45	19	0	74	0	0	5	7	2	.78	6	.249	.299	.430
1997 Brevard Cty	A+ Fla	95	373	101	27	4	10	166	63	60	44	2	86	1	0	4	4	1	.86	7	.271	.346	.445
1998 Portland	AA Fla	123	438	123	27	4	20	180	58	63	55	3	118	3	0	3	4	1	.80	11	.281	.363	.411
1999 Calgary	AAA Fla	41	138	34	6	0	0	40	12	7	10	1	30	0	0	0	1	3	.25	5	.246	.297	.290
Portland	AA Fla	73	244	62	16	0	7	99	39	31	47	1	81	2	0	2	2	0	1.00	3	.254	.376	.406
5 Min. YEARS		430	1564	416	99	7	39	646	224	220	189	8	423	6	0	14	25	11	.69	34	.266	.345	.413

Marcus Jones

Pitches: Right **Bats:** Right **Pos:** P
Ht: 6'5" **Wt:** 235 **Born:** 3/29/75 **Age:** 25

Year Team	Lg Org	G	GS	CG	GF	IP	BFP	H	R	ER	HR	SH	SF	HB	TBB	IBB	SO	WP	Bk	W	L	Pct.	ShO	Sv	ERA
1997 Sou Oregon	A- Oak	14	10	0	0	56	246	58	37	28	4	0	3	2	22	0	49	4	0	3	3	.500	0	0	4.50
1998 Visalia	A+ Oak	29	20	0	8	131	587	155	79	68	8	2	4	7	45	3	112	2	3	7	9	.438	0	4	4.67
Edmonton	AAA Oak	2	2	0	0	10.2	50	14	7	3	1	0	0	0	5	0	4	1	0	1	0	1.000	0	0	2.53
1999 Visalia	A+ Oak	18	15	0	0	91	401	103	56	45	7	3	3	4	32	1	82	3	1	6	4	.600	0	0	4.45
Vancouver	AAA Oak	3	3	0	0	15	73	23	11	4	1	0	0	0	5	0	5	1	0	2	1	.667	0	0	2.40
Modesto	A+ Oak	7	5	0	0	32	137	29	18	10	5	2	0	3	14	0	36	1	0	2	1	.667	0	0	2.81
3 Min. YEARS		73	55	0	8	335.2	1494	382	208	158	26	7	10	16	123	4	288	12	4	22	18	.550	0	4	4.24

Ryan Jones

Bats: Right **Throws:** Right **Pos:** 1B
Ht: 6'3" **Wt:** 225 **Born:** 11/5/74 **Age:** 25

Year Team	Lg Org	G	AB	H	2B	3B	HR	TB	R	RBI	TBB	IBB	SO	HBP	SH	SF	SB	CS	SB%	GDP	Avg	OBP	SLG
1993 Medcine Hat	R+ Tor	47	171	42	5	0	3	56	20	27	12	0	46	3	0	1	1	1	.50	9	.246	.305	.327
1994 Hagerstown	A Tor	115	402	96	29	0	18	179	60	72	45	0	124	6	0	5	1	0	1.00	6	.239	.321	.445
1995 Dunedin	A+ Tor	127	478	119	28	0	18	201	65	78	41	3	92	7	0	5	1	1	.50	7	.249	.315	.421
1996 Knoxville	AA Tor	134	506	137	26	3	20	229	70	97	60	6	88	6	0	6	2	2	.50	6	.271	.351	.453
1997 Syracuse	AAA Tor	41	123	17	5	1	3	33	8	16	15	0	28	3	0	4	0	2	.00	2	.138	.241	.268
Knoxville	AA Tor	86	328	84	19	3	12	145	41	51	27	1	63	3	0	4	0	1	.00	5	.256	.315	.442
1998 Knoxville	AA Tor	109	408	102	21	0	11	156	50	51	44	0	79	5	0	3	4	4	.50	6	.250	.328	.382
1999 Jacksnville	AA Det	125	487	123	21	3	19	207	66	73	50	0	115	3	0	3	1	1	.50	7	.253	.324	.425
7 Min. YEARS		784	2903	720	154	10	104	1206	380	465	294	10	635	36	0	31	10	12	.45	48	.248	.322	.415

Ricardo Jordan

Pitches: Left **Bats:** Left **Pos:** P
Ht: 6' 0" **Wt:** 160 **Born:** 6/27/70 **Age:** 30

Year Team	Lg Org	G	GS	CG	GF	IP	BFP	H	R	ER	HR	SH	SF	HB	TBB	IBB	SO	WP	Bk	W	L	Pct.	ShO	Sv	ERA
1990 Dunedin	A+ Tor	13	2	0	4	22.2	103	15	9	6	0	1	1	1	19	3	16	1	5	0	2	.000	0	1	2.38
1991 Myrtle Bch	A Tor	29	23	3	3	144.2	606	100	58	44	3	3	4	6	79	0	152	3	5	9	8	.529	1	1	2.74
1992 Dunedin	A+ Tor	45	0	0	32	47	208	44	26	20	3	3	0	2	28	3	49	7	2	0	5	.000	0	15	3.83
1993 Dunedin	A+ Tor	15	0	0	3	24.2	104	20	13	12	0	1	0	1	15	1	24	3	0	2	0	1.000	0	1	4.38
Knoxville	AA Tor	25	0	0	8	36.2	158	33	17	10	2	5	1	0	18	1	35	0	0	1	4	.200	0	2	2.45

142

Year Team	Lg Org	G	GS	CG	GF	IP	BFP	H	R	ER	HR	SH	SF	HB	TBB	IBB	SO	WP	Bk	W	L	Pct.	ShO	Sv	ERA
						HOW MUCH HE PITCHED					WHAT HE GAVE UP											THE RESULTS			
1994 Knoxville	AA Tor	53	0	0	40	64.1	273	54	25	19	2	4	2	4	23	2	70	4	0	4	3	.571	0	17	2.66
1995 Syracuse	AAA Tor	13	0	0	5	12.1	59	15	9	9	1	0	0	1	7	1	17	2	0	0	0	.000	0	0	6.57
1996 Scranton-WB	AAA Phi	32	0	0	15	39.1	180	40	30	23	5	3	0	1	22	1	40	2	0	3	3	.500	0	1	5.26
1997 Norfolk	AAA NYM	34	0	0	10	29	128	20	11	9	1	0	1	2	24	2	34	1	0	0	1	.000	0	1	2.79
1998 Indianapolis	AAA Cin	37	6	0	6	69.2	309	70	39	27	8	2	3	2	33	2	52	1	0	2	4	.333	0	0	3.49
Columbus	AAA NYY	5	5	0	0	26	119	28	15	14	4	0	1	1	17	0	22	0	0	2	0	1.000	0	0	4.85
1999 Albuquerque	AAA LA	37	0	0	10	30	142	33	26	24	5	0	3	4	21	1	35	0	0	4	1	.800	0	2	7.20
Somerset	IND —	18	0	0	4	32.2	137	29	19	14	4	3	0	0	13	0	29	2	0	2	3	.400	0	1	3.86
1995 Toronto	AL	15	0	0	3	15	76	18	11	11	3	0	2	2	13	1	10	1	0	1	0	1.000	0	1	6.60
1996 Philadelphia	NL	26	0	0	2	25	103	18	6	5	0	1	1	0	12	0	17	1	0	2	2	.500	0	0	1.80
1997 New York	NL	22	0	0	4	27	123	31	17	16	1	2	2	2	15	2	19	0	0	1	2	.333	0	0	5.33
1998 Cincinnati	NL	6	0	0	0	3.1	21	4	9	9	2	0	1	0	7	0	1	0	0	1	0	1.000	0	0	24.30
10 Min. YEARS		356	36	3	140	579	2526	501	297	231	38	25	16	25	319	17	575	26	12	29	34	.460	1	41	3.59
4 Maj. YEARS		69	0	0	9	70.1	323	71	43	41	6	3	6	4	47	3	47	2	0	5	4	.556	0	1	5.25

Randy Jorgensen

Bats: Left **Throws:** Left **Pos:** 1B   **Ht:** 6'2" **Wt:** 195 **Born:** 4/3/72 **Age:** 28

Year Team	Lg Org	G	AB	H	2B	3B	HR	TB	R	RBI	TBB	IBB	SO	HBP	SH	SF	SB	CS	SB%	GDP	Avg	OBP	SLG
					BATTING												BASERUNNING				PERCENTAGES		
1993 Bellingham	A- Sea	67	228	60	13	0	5	88	42	22	37	2	33	3	2	4	7	4	.64	6	.263	.368	.386
1994 Riverside	A+ Sea	110	368	97	13	1	3	121	45	42	39	2	63	5	5	2	1	2	.33	19	.264	.341	.329
1995 Riverside	A+ Sea	133	495	148	32	2	12	220	78	97	46	1	74	15	0	8	4	2	.67	13	.299	.371	.444
1996 Port City	AA Sea	137	460	129	32	1	8	187	61	81	58	10	75	7	5	5	2	1	.67	15	.280	.366	.407
1997 Memphis	AA Sea	129	477	139	28	3	11	206	66	70	38	2	58	8	0	7	1	2	.33	10	.291	.349	.432
1998 Orlando	AA Sea	7	26	10	3	0	0	13	4	10	4	0	3	1	0	0	0	0	.00	2	.385	.484	.500
Tacoma	AAA Sea	81	253	59	13	1	3	83	27	26	21	4	42	0	3	3	0	0	.00	7	.233	.289	.328
1999 St. Pete	A+ TB	26	96	21	6	0	1	30	6	5	5	1	11	0	0	1	0	0	.00	1	.219	.255	.313
Duluth-Sup	IND —	15	59	17	4	0	1	24	9	8	7	1	13	0	0	1	0	0	.00	1	.288	.368	.407
Mobile	AA SD	72	252	81	15	0	7	117	41	54	36	0	46	5	1	3	2	2	.50	6	.321	.412	.464
7 Min. YEARS		777	2714	761	159	8	51	1089	379	415	291	23	418	44	16	34	17	13	.57	86	.280	.355	.401

Tim Jorgensen

Bats: Left **Throws:** Right **Pos:** 3B   **Ht:** 6'3" **Wt:** 200 **Born:** 11/30/72 **Age:** 27

Year Team	Lg Org	G	AB	H	2B	3B	HR	TB	R	RBI	TBB	IBB	SO	HBP	SH	SF	SB	CS	SB%	GDP	Avg	OBP	SLG
					BATTING												BASERUNNING				PERCENTAGES		
1995 Watertown	A- Cle	73	295	96	19	9	8	157	44	52	32	4	63	2	1	1	4	1	.80	4	.325	.394	.532
1996 Kinston	A+ Cle	119	412	89	24	0	17	164	56	64	41	2	103	6	1	3	1	2	.33	7	.216	.294	.398
1997 Kinston	A+ Cle	91	334	95	19	2	18	172	49	65	28	0	47	1	0	6	0	1	.00	9	.284	.336	.515
1999 Lynchburg	A+ Pit	64	230	64	21	3	4	103	32	34	26	2	47	3	0	2	0	1	.00	6	.278	.356	.448
Altoona	AA Pit	7	23	3	1	0	0	4	1	2	0	0	6	0	0	0	0	0	.00	1	.130	.130	.174
4 Min. YEARS		354	1294	347	84	14	47	600	182	217	127	8	266	12	2	12	5	5	.50	27	.268	.336	.464

Kevin Joseph

Pitches: Right **Bats:** Right **Pos:** P   **Ht:** 6'4" **Wt:** 200 **Born:** 8/1/76 **Age:** 23

Year Team	Lg Org	G	GS	CG	GF	IP	BFP	H	R	ER	HR	SH	SF	HB	TBB	IBB	SO	WP	Bk	W	L	Pct.	ShO	Sv	ERA
						HOW MUCH HE PITCHED					WHAT HE GAVE UP											THE RESULTS			
1997 Salem-Keizr	A- SF	17	6	0	5	45	208	44	35	27	4	1	2	2	26	0	45	10	3	3	5	.375	0	1	5.40
1998 Bakersfield	A+ SF	6	6	0	0	21	120	35	26	19	3	1	1	2	20	0	17	7	0	0	4	.000	0	0	8.14
Salem-Keizr	A+ SF	23	0	0	0	43.1	194	36	25	21	3	1	3	5	27	0	37	8	1	1	1	.500	0	0	4.36
1999 San Jose	A+ SF	20	0	0	9	30.2	122	17	9	8	1	3	0	0	13	0	30	2	1	1	2	.333	0	2	2.35
Shreveport	AA SF	7	0	0	3	12.2	52	8	4	2	0	1	0	1	5	0	16	0	0	0	2	.000	0	0	1.42
3 Min. YEARS		73	12	0	17	152.2	696	140	99	77	11	7	6	10	91	0	145	27	5	5	14	.263	0	3	4.54

Jarod Juelsgaard

Pitches: Right **Bats:** Right **Pos:** P   **Ht:** 6'3" **Wt:** 205 **Born:** 6/27/68 **Age:** 32

Year Team	Lg Org	G	GS	CG	GF	IP	BFP	H	R	ER	HR	SH	SF	HB	TBB	IBB	SO	WP	Bk	W	L	Pct.	ShO	Sv	ERA
						HOW MUCH HE PITCHED					WHAT HE GAVE UP											THE RESULTS			
1991 Everett	A- SF	20	6	0	8	62	270	62	36	30	3	1	1	2	27	2	46	16	4	3	5	.375	0	3	4.35
1992 Clinton	A SF	35	9	1	11	76.2	368	86	58	45	2	4	4	3	52	6	60	12	1	6	9	.400	0	2	5.28
1993 Kane County	A Fla	11	2	1	3	26	101	21	11	11	0	0	0	1	7	0	18	2	2	3	0	1.000	0	0	3.81
High Desert	A+ Fla	17	16	0	1	79.1	359	81	57	49	8	1	1	1	58	0	58	4	1	6	5	.545	0	0	5.56
1994 Portland	AA Fla	36	12	0	13	92.2	443	115	74	68	9	4	5	4	55	4	55	7	2	4	9	.308	0	0	6.60
1995 Portland	AA Fla	48	0	0	13	71.2	313	65	35	31	3	1	2	2	44	2	44	5	0	3	1	.750	0	2	3.89
1996 Charlotte	AAA Fla	26	5	0	9	44	192	63	43	17	1	1	2	0	21	0	29	3	0	4	2	.667	0	1	3.48
1997 Charlotte	AAA Fla	21	6	0	0	50.2	251	65	41	34	5	2	1	2	39	3	31	3	0	1	3	.250	0	0	6.04
1998 Tacoma	AAA Sea	28	21	0	0	125.1	574	131	91	78	13	4	4	9	73	0	89	5	1	5	5	.500	0	0	5.60
1999 Iowa	AAA ChC	23	12	2	3	83.2	372	92	57	52	12	3	4	7	26	1	54	0	2	4	7	.364	1	0	5.59
9 Min. YEARS		265	89	4	67	712	3243	761	483	415	56	21	24	31	402	18	484	57	13	39	46	.459	1	8	5.25

Jason Karnuth

Pitches: Right **Bats:** Right **Pos:** P   **Ht:** 6'2" **Wt:** 190 **Born:** 5/15/76 **Age:** 24

Year Team	Lg Org	G	GS	CG	GF	IP	BFP	H	R	ER	HR	SH	SF	HB	TBB	IBB	SO	WP	Bk	W	L	Pct.	ShO	Sv	ERA
						HOW MUCH HE PITCHED					WHAT HE GAVE UP											THE RESULTS			
1997 New Jersey	A- StL	7	7	0	0	38.2	158	33	8	8	0	1	1	2	9	0	23	2	0	4	1	.800	0	0	1.86
Peoria	A StL	4	4	0	0	23	102	29	19	17	1	1	1	1	7	1	12	2	1	0	3	.000	0	0	6.65
1998 Pr William	A+ StL	16	15	2	1	108	411	86	26	20	3	6	0	7	14	0	53	4	0	8	1	.889	2	0	1.67

		HOW MUCH HE PITCHED			WHAT HE GAVE UP			THE RESULTS		
Year Team	Lg Org	G GS CG GF	IP	BFP	H R ER HR SH SF HB	TBB IBB	SO WP Bk	W L	Pct. ShO Sv	ERA
1999 Arkansas	AA StL	26 26 2 0	160.1	696	175 105 93 16 5 7 11	55 0	71 2 0	7 11	.389 0 0	5.22
3 Min. YEARS		53 52 4 1	330	1367	323 158 138 20 13 9 21	85 1	159 10 1	19 16	.543 2 0	3.76

Ryan Karp

Pitches: Left **Bats:** Left **Pos:** P   **Ht:** 6'4" **Wt:** 214 **Born:** 4/5/70 **Age:** 30

		HOW MUCH HE PITCHED			WHAT HE GAVE UP			THE RESULTS		
Year Team	Lg Org	G GS CG GF	IP	BFP	H R ER HR SH SF HB	TBB IBB	SO WP Bk	W L	Pct. ShO Sv	ERA
1992 Oneonta	A- NYY	14 13 1 0	70.1	300	66 38 32 2 1 1 3	30 0	58 2 0	6 4	.600 1 0	4.09
1993 Greensboro	A NYY	17 17 0 0	109.1	436	73 26 22 2 0 2 2	40 0	132 6 1	13 1	.929 1 0	1.81
Pr William	A+ NYY	8 8 1 0	49	189	35 17 12 4 2 2 2	12 0	34 5 1	3 2	.600 1 0	2.20
Albany-Colo	AA NYY	3 3 0 0	13	60	13 7 6 1 0 1 0	9 0	10 1 0	0 0	.000 0 0	4.15
1994 Reading	AA Phi	21 21 0 0	121.1	528	123 67 60 12 0 4 3	54 3	96 4 0	4 11	.267 0 0	4.45
1995 Reading	AA Phi	7 7 0 0	47	190	44 18 16 4 3 0 0	15 0	37 1 2	1 2	.333 0 0	3.06
Scranton-WB	AAA Phi	13 13 0 0	81.1	357	81 43 38 6 2 2 4	31 0	73 2 0	7 1	.875 0 0	4.20
1996 Scranton-WB	AAA Phi	7 7 0 0	41	168	35 14 14 1 1 0 0	14 1	30 3 0	1 1	.500 0 0	3.07
1997 Scranton-WB	AAA Phi	32 5 0 8	73	326	72 35 34 9 4 1 2	42 6	55 5 0	4 3	.571 0 1	4.19
1998 Durham	AAA TB	36 5 1 11	73	314	76 44 43 9 2 1 1	31 2	64 6 0	2 6	.250 0 1	5.30
1999 Bridgeport	IND —	2 2 0 0	10	40	9 2 2 0 1 0 0	1 0	12 0 0	1 0	1.000 0 0	1.80
Oklahoma	AAA Tex	8 6 1 0	39.2	190	62 34 33 5 1 1 3	14 0	28 2 0	2 2	.500 0 0	7.49
Tulsa	AA Tex	11 9 1 0	64.2	259	50 21 20 5 4 2 3	21 0	49 2 0	2 2	.500 0 0	2.78
1995 Philadelphia	NL	1 0 0 0	2	10	1 1 1 0 0 0 0	3 0	2 1 0	0 0	.000 0 0	4.50
1997 Philadelphia	NL	15 1 0 1	15	67	12 12 9 2 1 0 2	9 0	18 1 0	1 1	.500 0 0	5.40
8 Min. YEARS		179 116 5 17	792.2	3357	739 366 332 60 21 17 23	314 12	678 39 4	46 35	.568 2 2	3.77
2 Maj. YEARS		16 1 0 1	17	77	13 13 10 2 1 0 2	12 0	20 2 0	1 1	.500 0 0	5.29

Brad Kaufman

Pitches: Right **Bats:** Right **Pos:** P   **Ht:** 6'2" **Wt:** 210 **Born:** 4/26/72 **Age:** 28

		HOW MUCH HE PITCHED			WHAT HE GAVE UP			THE RESULTS		
Year Team	Lg Org	G GS CG GF	IP	BFP	H R ER HR SH SF HB	TBB IBB	SO WP Bk	W L	Pct. ShO Sv	ERA
1993 Spokane	A- SD	25 8 1 11	53.2	264	56 56 41 8 0 3 3	41 2	48 4 2	5 4	.556 0 4	6.88
1994 Springfield	A SD	31 20 3 4	145.1	602	124 62 54 9 5 3 4	63 6	122 14 1	10 9	.526 0 0	3.34
1995 Memphis	AA SD	27 27 0 0	148.1	676	142 112 95 17 6 5 14	90 4	119 10 0	11 10	.524 0 0	5.76
1996 Memphis	AA SD	29 29 3 0	178.1	768	161 84 72 18 8 4 4	83 4	163 8 0	12 10	.545 1 0	3.63
1997 Las Vegas	AAA SD	6 6 0 0	32.1	151	40 37 29 9 0 1 1	15 0	19 1 0	0 5	.000 0 0	8.07
Mobile	AA SD	22 22 1 0	125.1	585	138 97 86 10 9 11 5	66 0	103 3 0	5 13	.278 0 0	6.18
1998 Mobile	AA SD	5 5 0 0	24.1	96	18 3 3 0 2 0 2	8 0	21 1 0	1 0	1.000 0 0	1.11
Las Vegas	AAA SD	23 22 0 0	118.1	559	148 90 84 12 2 3 6	65 0	83 8 0	9 9	.500 0 0	6.39
Columbus	AAA NYY	3 3 0 0	15	72	17 15 12 3 1 0 0	12 0	13 0 0	1 2	.333 0 0	7.20
1999 Norwich	AA NYY	40 5 0 9	83	361	76 45 38 6 2 3 2	38 5	81 7 0	3 2	.600 0 1	4.12
7 Min. YEARS		211 147 8 24	924	4134	920 601 514 92 35 33 41	481 21	772 56 3	57 64	.471 1 5	5.01

John Kaufman

Pitches: Left **Bats:** Left **Pos:** P   **Ht:** 5'10" **Wt:** 170 **Born:** 10/23/74 **Age:** 25

		HOW MUCH HE PITCHED			WHAT HE GAVE UP			THE RESULTS		
Year Team	Lg Org	G GS CG GF	IP	BFP	H R ER HR SH SF HB	TBB IBB	SO WP Bk	W L	Pct. ShO Sv	ERA
1996 Butte	R+ TB	13 12 0 0	46.1	214	53 36 24 2 3 3 0	24 0	55 7 2	2 3	.400 0 0	4.66
1997 St. Pete	A+ TB	26 26 2 0	149.2	649	138 62 56 9 4 3 7	66 1	121 3 1	9 5	.643 1 0	3.37
1998 St. Pete	A+ TB	18 17 0 0	102	430	92 40 36 6 2 3 1	33 0	93 5 1	7 5	.583 0 0	3.18
Orlando	AA TB	7 6 0 0	24.1	115	34 25 18 6 0 0 1	9 0	17 1 0	0 5	.000 0 0	6.66
1999 Orlando	AA TB	21 2 0 5	35.2	172	54 39 35 3 2 3 0	14 0	22 0 0	1 3	.250 0 0	8.83
St. Pete	A+ TB	16 0 0 5	22.2	101	29 10 9 3 2 0 2	6 2	22 0 0	1 2	.333 0 0	3.57
4 Min. YEARS		101 63 2 10	380.2	1681	400 212 178 29 13 12 11	152 3	330 16 4	20 23	.465 1 0	4.21

Kyle Kawabata

Pitches: Right **Bats:** Right **Pos:** P   **Ht:** 6'0" **Wt:** 195 **Born:** 1/2/74 **Age:** 26

		HOW MUCH HE PITCHED			WHAT HE GAVE UP			THE RESULTS		
Year Team	Lg Org	G GS CG GF	IP	BFP	H R ER HR SH SF HB	TBB IBB	SO WP Bk	W L	Pct. ShO Sv	ERA
1995 Batavia	A- Phi	18 0 0 4	32.2	140	34 16 13 3 2 1 3	5 1	30 2 1	2 0	1.000 0 0	3.58
1996 Batavia	A- Phi	25 0 0 25	28	115	21 7 6 2 2 0 1	7 1	24 2 0	1 2	.333 0 20	1.93
1997 Piedmont	A Phi	44 0 0 41	62.2	242	45 14 10 2 6 0 2	13 2	75 5 0	9 5	.643 0 16	1.44
1998 Reading	AA Phi	7 0 0 3	7.1	37	14 8 3 1 0 0 0	2 0	2 1 0	1 0	1.000 0 0	3.68
Clearwater	A+ Phi	53 0 0 50	64.2	270	63 25 19 3 6 1 4	16 2	49 3 1	4 3	.571 0 33	2.64
1999 Clearwater	A+ Phi	33 0 0 18	47	191	36 11 6 2 2 1 2	10 0	37 3 0	3 1	.750 0 7	1.15
Reading	AA Phi	8 0 0 3	12	58	20 9 8 2 1 1 0	2 0	7 0 0	0 0	.000 0 0	6.00
5 Min. YEARS		188 0 0 144	254.1	1053	233 90 65 15 19 4 12	55 6	224 16 2	20 11	.645 0 76	2.30

Greg Keagle

Pitches: Right **Bats:** Right **Pos:** P   **Ht:** 6'2" **Wt:** 195 **Born:** 6/28/71 **Age:** 29

		HOW MUCH HE PITCHED			WHAT HE GAVE UP			THE RESULTS		
Year Team	Lg Org	G GS CG GF	IP	BFP	H R ER HR SH SF HB	TBB IBB	SO WP Bk	W L	Pct. ShO Sv	ERA
1993 Spokane	A- SD	15 15 1 0	83	368	80 37 30 2 4 4 7	40 2	77 4 4	3 3	.500 0 0	3.25
1994 Rancho Cuca	A+ SD	14 14 1 0	92	377	62 23 21 2 1 3 5	41 1	91 0 0	11 1	.917 1 0	2.05
Wichita	AA SD	13 13 0 0	70.1	321	84 53 49 5 5 2 2	32 1	57 3 1	3 9	.250 0 0	6.27
1995 Memphis	AA SD	15 15 1 0	81	365	82 52 46 11 1 3 6	41 2	82 8 3	4 9	.308 0 0	5.11
Rancho Cuca	A+ SD	2 2 0 0	14	59	14 9 7 1 0 1 2	2 0	11 1 0	0 0	.000 0 0	4.50
Las Vegas	AAA SD	14 13 0 1	75.2	351	76 47 36 3 6 5 6	42 2	49 2 0	7 6	.538 0 0	4.28

Year Team	Lg Org	G	GS	CG	GF	IP	BFP	H	R	ER	HR	SH	SF	HB	TBB	IBB	SO	WP	Bk	W	L	Pct.	ShO	Sv	ERA
		HOW MUCH HE PITCHED						WHAT HE GAVE UP												THE RESULTS					
1996 Toledo	AAA Det	6	6	0	0	27	135	42	32	30	7	1	2	4	11	0	24	0	1	2	3	.400	0	0	10.00
1997 Toledo	AAA Det	23	23	3	0	151.1	645	136	68	64	8	4	2	10	61	0	140	4	1	11	7	.611	1	0	3.81
1998 Toledo	AAA Det	15	14	0	1	81.2	365	94	48	42	12	1	2	6	32	0	61	1	2	5	3	.625	0	0	4.63
1999 Lakeland	A+ Det	6	6	0	0	36	153	35	19	18	5	2	2	4	13	0	26	1	3	1	3	.250	0	0	4.50
Jacksnville	AA Det	9	9	1	0	53.2	238	58	22	17	4	0	1	1	22	0	28	1	2	4	2	.667	0	0	2.85
Toledo	AAA Det	7	7	0	0	32.2	158	50	29	26	3	1	2	4	13	0	19	1	1	1	4	.200	0	0	7.16
1996 Detroit	AL	26	6	0	5	87.2	435	104	76	72	13	2	7	9	68	5	70	2	0	3	6	.333	0	0	7.39
1997 Detroit	AL	11	10	0	0	45.1	214	58	33	33	9	2	1	5	18	0	33	1	0	3	5	.375	0	0	6.55
1998 Detroit	AL	9	7	0	0	38.2	180	46	26	24	5	0	4	4	20	0	25	2	0	0	5	.000	0	0	5.59
7 Min. YEARS		139	137	7	2	798.1	3535	813	439	386	63	26	29	57	350	8	665	27	18	52	50	.510	2	0	4.35
3 Maj. YEARS		46	23	0	5	171.2	829	208	135	129	27	4	8	18	106	5	128	5	0	6	16	.273	0	0	6.76

Brian Keck

Bats: Right   Throws: Right   Pos: 3B   Ht: 6'3"   Wt: 185   Born: 1/15/74   Age: 26

Year Team	Lg Org	G	AB	H	2B	3B	HR	TB	R	RBI	TBB	IBB	SO	HBP	SH	SF	SB	CS	SB%	GDP	Avg	OBP	SLG
		BATTING															BASERUNNING				PERCENTAGES		
1996 Portland	A- Col	43	156	41	1	2	0	46	29	20	22	0	23	1	3	1	7	2	.78	1	.263	.356	.295
1997 Asheville	A Col	37	124	29	3	0	0	32	8	8	9	0	22	0	7	0	5	2	.71	5	.234	.286	.258
Salem	A+ Col	48	121	34	4	0	0	38	22	11	11	1	21	3	5	2	17	3	.85	3	.281	.350	.314
1998 Salem	A+ Col	85	263	72	8	3	1	89	30	24	24	0	39	1	11	2	10	11	.48	8	.274	.334	.338
1999 Salem	A+ Col	103	347	84	10	3	3	109	54	30	37	1	53	1	14	5	14	2	.88	9	.242	.313	.314
Carolina	AA Col	5	15	3	0	1	0	5	0	2	4	0	3	0	0	0	2	1	.67	1	.200	.368	.333
4 Min. YEARS		321	1026	263	26	9	4	319	143	95	107	2	161	6	40	10	55	21	.72	27	.256	.327	.311

Randy Keisler

Pitches: Left   Bats: Left   Pos: P   Ht: 6'3"   Wt: 190   Born: 2/24/76   Age: 24

Year Team	Lg Org	G	GS	CG	GF	IP	BFP	H	R	ER	HR	SH	SF	HB	TBB	IBB	SO	WP	Bk	W	L	Pct.	ShO	Sv	ERA
		HOW MUCH HE PITCHED						WHAT HE GAVE UP												THE RESULTS					
1998 Oneonta	A- NYY	6	2	0	1	9.2	51	14	10	8	0	0	3	0	7	1	11	0	0	1	1	.500	0	1	7.45
1999 Greensboro	A NYY	4	4	0	0	22.2	91	12	6	6	1	0	0	1	10	0	42	0	0	1	1	.500	0	0	2.38
Tampa	A+ NYY	15	15	1	0	90	375	67	43	33	2	3	1	3	40	0	77	4	1	10	3	.769	0	0	3.30
Norwich	AA NYY	8	8	0	0	43.1	189	45	24	22	2	1	3	3	17	0	33	2	0	3	4	.429	0	0	4.57
2 Min. YEARS		33	29	1	1	165.2	706	138	83	69	5	4	7	7	74	1	163	6	1	15	9	.625	0	1	3.75

Rich Kelley

Pitches: Left   Bats: Left   Pos: P   Ht: 6'3"   Wt: 210   Born: 5/27/70   Age: 30

Year Team	Lg Org	G	GS	CG	GF	IP	BFP	H	R	ER	HR	SH	SF	HB	TBB	IBB	SO	WP	Bk	W	L	Pct.	ShO	Sv	ERA
		HOW MUCH HE PITCHED						WHAT HE GAVE UP												THE RESULTS					
1991 Niagara Fal	A- Det	15	13	0	1	81.1	341	76	38	30	7	0	2	1	33	1	78	4	0	4	8	.333	0	0	3.32
1992 Fayettevlle	A Det	28	26	2	0	162.2	664	140	62	51	15	2	4	6	63	0	117	12	9	13	5	.722	0	0	2.82
1993 Lakeland	A+ Det	26	9	0	10	85.2	350	78	31	29	2	2	2	4	31	1	45	5	4	4	5	.444	0	2	3.05
London	AA Det	7	0	0	0	5	25	7	5	5	1	0	0	0	5	0	3	3	1	0	0	.000	0	0	9.00
1994 Lakeland	A+ Det	13	0	0	10	38	156	32	15	10	2	2	5	0	15	1	23	0	0	4	2	.667	0	1	2.37
Trenton	AA Det	16	4	0	2	42.1	178	46	28	27	8	1	1	0	20	0	29	3	1	1	2	.333	0	0	5.74
1995 Jacksnville	AA Det	7	0	0	1	6	24	9	3	3	1	1	1	0	2	0	6	1	1	1	0	1.000	0	0	4.50
1998 Rochester	AAA Bal	15	3	0	4	38	156	34	28	23	6	0	1	1	17	0	24	2	1	1	3	.250	0	0	5.45
Bowie	AA Bal	18	13	0	1	85	355	80	38	35	12	1	3	2	34	2	56	2	2	8	2	.800	0	0	3.71
1999 Huntsville	AA Mil	25	0	0	12	28.1	123	30	19	18	3	2	0	3	8	0	26	1	1	1	3	.250	0	0	5.72
7 Min. YEARS		170	68	2	41	572.1	2372	532	267	231	57	11	19	17	226	5	403	32	20	37	30	.552	0	7	3.63

Nathan Kent

Pitches: Right   Bats: Right   Pos: P   Ht: 6'6"   Wt: 210   Born: 8/16/78   Age: 21

Year Team	Lg Org	G	GS	CG	GF	IP	BFP	H	R	ER	HR	SH	SF	HB	TBB	IBB	SO	WP	Bk	W	L	Pct.	ShO	Sv	ERA
		HOW MUCH HE PITCHED						WHAT HE GAVE UP												THE RESULTS					
1999 Jamestown	A- Atl	14	11	0	1	52.1	225	57	31	24	2	0	0	0	11	0	49	1	0	3	3	.500	0	1	4.13
Greenville	AA Atl	1	0	0	0	1	6	1	2	2	1	0	0	0	2	0	2	0	0	0	0	.000	0	0	18.00
1 Min. YEARS		15	11	0	1	53.1	231	58	33	26	3	0	0	0	13	0	51	1	0	3	3	.500	0	1	4.39

Robbie Kent

Bats: Right   Throws: Right   Pos: 2B   Ht: 5'10"   Wt: 185   Born: 1/8/74   Age: 26

Year Team	Lg Org	G	AB	H	2B	3B	HR	TB	R	RBI	TBB	IBB	SO	HBP	SH	SF	SB	CS	SB%	GDP	Avg	OBP	SLG
		BATTING															BASERUNNING				PERCENTAGES		
1996 Idaho Falls	R+ SD	47	181	56	14	0	2	76	40	25	21	0	28	4	1	1	4	1	.80	5	.309	.391	.420
1997 Rancho Cuca	A+ SD	81	295	73	18	4	2	103	35	32	22	0	65	4	3	4	0	2	.00	4	.247	.305	.349
1998 Rancho Cuca	A+ SD	116	457	123	22	3	7	172	65	59	33	0	81	7	8	5	2	1	.67	15	.269	.325	.376
1999 Mobile	AA SD	109	336	91	17	3	8	138	48	56	44	3	71	2	2	3	2	0	1.00	8	.271	.356	.411
4 Min. YEARS		353	1269	343	71	6	21	489	188	172	120	3	245	17	14	13	8	4	.67	32	.270	.338	.385

Al Kermode

Pitches: Right   Bats: Right   Pos: P   Ht: 6'4"   Wt: 185   Born: 12/10/70   Age: 29

Year Team	Lg Org	G	GS	CG	GF	IP	BFP	H	R	ER	HR	SH	SF	HB	TBB	IBB	SO	WP	Bk	W	L	Pct.	ShO	Sv	ERA
		HOW MUCH HE PITCHED						WHAT HE GAVE UP												THE RESULTS					
1992 Jamestown	A- Mon	4	4	0	0	16.2	73	22	9	9	3	0	0	0	1	1	16	1	0	0	2	.000	0	0	4.86
Albany	A Mon	22	0	0	21	26	107	19	7	6	1	0	0	0	8	1	29	2	0	0	3	.000	0	12	2.08
1993 Expos	R Mon	4	0	0	1	6	23	5	2	2	0	0	0	0	1	0	5	0	0	0	0	.000	0	1	3.00

145

Year Team	Lg Org	G	GS	CG	GF	IP	BFP	H	R	ER	HR	SH	SF	HB	TBB	IBB	SO	WP	Bk	W	L	Pct.	ShO	Sv	ERA
Burlington	A Mon	19	0	0	10	27	117	29	11	11	2	0	1	1	9	1	32	2	0	0	1	.000	0	3	3.67
1994 Burlington	A Mon	39	17	1	19	128.2	553	123	72	59	10	4	9	4	47	3	88	8	1	6	7	.462	1	6	4.13
1995 Amarillo	IND —	22	22	5	0	151	638	171	81	69	9	10	6	4	26	0	92	4	0	14	4	.778	2	0	4.11
1996 Amarillo	IND —	24	23	4	0	155.2	675	174	93	77	15	7	6	9	27	0	107	7	0	8	12	.400	1	0	4.45
1997 Amarillo	IND —	21	19	4	0	132.2	590	171	82	63	14	3	2	4	25	2	69	5	1	10	3	.769	0	0	4.27
1998 Amarillo	IND —	20	19	2	1	132.2	563	145	66	58	7	10	5	8	20	0	118	11	0	12	3	.800	0	0	3.93
1999 Amarillo	IND —	11	10	3	0	75.1	307	69	33	28	6	1	0	3	15	0	61	3	0	6	2	.750	0	0	3.35
El Paso	AA Ari	12	11	1	0	71.2	293	68	31	24	7	4	4	2	12	0	56	7	0	4	4	.500	1	0	3.01
8 Min. YEARS		198	125	20	52	923.1	3939	996	487	406	74	39	33	35	191	8	673	45	2	60	41	.594	5	22	3.96

Jason Kershner

Pitches: Left   Bats: Left   Pos: P   Ht: 6'2"   Wt: 165   Born: 12/19/76   Age: 23

Year Team	Lg Org	G	GS	CG	GF	IP	BFP	H	R	ER	HR	SH	SF	HB	TBB	IBB	SO	WP	Bk	W	L	Pct.	ShO	Sv	ERA
1995 Martinsvlle	R+ Phi	13	13	0	0	63	278	67	42	36	10	0	2	5	29	0	64	6	0	4	2	.667	0	0	5.14
1996 Piedmont	A Phi	28	28	2	0	168	703	154	81	70	12	5	4	3	59	0	156	12	1	11	9	.550	1	0	3.75
1997 Clearwater	A+ Phi	22	16	0	3	99.1	417	113	49	43	9	2	4	4	21	0	51	2	0	5	10	.333	0	1	3.90
1998 Clearwater	A+ Phi	41	8	0	11	94.1	405	108	57	42	8	1	3	6	25	0	65	8	0	3	3	.500	0	3	4.01
1999 Reading	AA Phi	57	2	0	30	92.2	412	99	67	59	14	3	6	5	40	3	86	5	0	4	4	.500	0	8	5.73
5 Min. YEARS		161	67	2	44	517.1	2215	541	296	250	53	11	19	23	174	3	422	33	1	27	28	.491	1	12	4.35

Tim Kester

Pitches: Right   Bats: Right   Pos: P   Ht: 6'4"   Wt: 190   Born: 12/1/71   Age: 28

Year Team	Lg Org	G	GS	CG	GF	IP	BFP	H	R	ER	HR	SH	SF	HB	TBB	IBB	SO	WP	Bk	W	L	Pct.	ShO	Sv	ERA
1993 Auburn	A- Hou	15	13	4	1	96.1	398	78	40	22	2	2	0	10	19	1	83	5	2	4	6	.400	1	0	2.06
1994 Osceola	A+ Hou	24	22	2	0	134	580	159	85	73	7	8	5	8	30	5	71	3	0	5	12	.294	0	0	4.90
1995 Quad City	A Hou	28	23	2	3	160.2	665	158	80	53	8	5	6	10	20	1	111	4	0	12	5	.706	0	0	2.97
1996 Tucson	AAA Hou	1	1	0	0	1.2	15	8	8	8	1	1	1	0	1	0	1	0	0	0	1	.000	0	0	43.20
Jackson	AA Hou	48	4	0	7	103.2	435	105	52	43	8	4	4	6	16	0	55	8	0	2	4	.333	0	1	3.73
1997 Jackson	AA Hou	47	4	0	18	82.2	375	107	53	48	9	2	4	8	26	3	50	2	0	4	6	.400	0	2	5.23
1998 Jackson	AA Hou	55	0	0	26	86	364	90	47	40	13	5	2	6	19	5	51	0	0	5	5	.500	0	6	4.19
1999 Jackson	AA Hou	43	2	0	13	75	342	91	43	31	9	8	2	10	19	2	51	4	0	8	5	.615	0	1	3.72
7 Min. YEARS		261	69	8	68	740	3174	796	408	318	57	35	24	58	150	17	473	26	2	40	44	.476	1	10	3.87

Brooks Kieschnick

Bats: Left   Throws: Right   Pos: DH   Ht: 6'4"   Wt: 230   Born: 6/6/72   Age: 28

Year Team	Lg Org	G	AB	H	2B	3B	HR	TB	R	RBI	TBB	IBB	SO	HBP	SH	SF	SB	CS	SB%	GDP	Avg	OBP	SLG
1993 Cubs	R ChC	3	9	2	1	0	0	3	0	0	0	0	1	0	0	0	0	0	.00	0	.222	.222	.333
Daytona	A+ ChC	6	22	4	2	0	0	6	1	2	1	0	4	0	0	0	0	1	.00	1	.182	.217	.273
Orlando	AA ChC	25	91	31	8	0	2	45	12	10	7	1	19	0	0	0	1	2	.33	0	.341	.388	.495
1994 Orlando	AA ChC	126	468	132	25	3	14	205	57	55	33	3	78	4	0	4	3	5	.38	10	.282	.332	.438
1995 Iowa	AAA ChC	138	505	149	30	1	23	250	61	73	58	7	91	4	0	3	2	3	.40	11	.295	.370	.495
1996 Iowa	AAA ChC	117	441	114	21	0	18	190	47	64	37	4	108	0	0	2	0	1	.00	8	.259	.315	.431
1997 Iowa	AAA ChC	97	360	93	21	0	21	177	57	66	36	4	89	1	0	5	0	2	.00	8	.258	.323	.492
1998 Durham	AAA TB	7	23	3	1	0	1	7	4	2	4	0	8	0	0	0	0	1	.00	2	.130	.259	.304
Devil Rays	R TB	4	12	6	1	0	2	13	4	8	1	0	0	0	0	0	0	0	.00	0	.500	.538	1.083
St. Pete	A+ TB	28	105	26	6	0	5	47	15	18	11	0	18	0	0	1	0	0	.00	4	.248	.316	.448
1999 Durham	AAA TB	23	75	15	5	0	1	23	6	5	5	0	14	0	0	0	0	0	.00	3	.200	.250	.307
Edmonton	AAA TB	77	296	93	20	3	23	188	54	73	19	1	60	2	0	2	0	0	.00	5	.314	.357	.635
1996 Chicago	NL	25	29	10	2	0	1	15	6	3	0	0	8	0	0	0	0	0	.00	0	.345	.406	.517
1997 Chicago	NL	39	90	18	2	0	4	32	9	12	12	0	21	0	0	0	1	0	1.00	0	.200	.294	.356
7 Min. YEARS		651	2407	668	140	8	110	1154	318	376	212	20	490	11	0	17	6	16	.27	52	.278	.337	.479
2 Maj. YEARS		64	119	28	4	0	5	47	15	18	12	0	29	0	0	0	1	0	1.00	0	.235	.321	.395

Joe Kilburg

Bats: Left   Throws: Right   Pos: OF   Ht: 5'11"   Wt: 180   Born: 12/20/75   Age: 24

Year Team	Lg Org	G	AB	H	2B	3B	HR	TB	R	RBI	TBB	IBB	SO	HBP	SH	SF	SB	CS	SB%	GDP	Avg	OBP	SLG
1997 Burlington	R+ Cle	52	182	61	8	7	3	92	59	30	39	0	46	7	3	2	29	5	.85	1	.335	.465	.505
Kinston	A+ Cle	9	30	7	2	0	1	12	5	5	5	0	6	0	0	0	1	0	1.00	0	.233	.343	.400
1998 Columbus	A Cle	121	446	112	19	4	7	160	81	44	67	0	93	4	11	0	24	10	.71	8	.251	.354	.359
1999 Kinston	A+ Cle	42	137	41	8	1	3	60	34	17	29	1	19	4	3	0	3	3	.50	1	.299	.435	.438
Akron	AA Cle	42	144	39	8	0	1	50	20	14	23	1	28	5	1	0	1	2	.33	3	.271	.390	.347
3 Min. YEARS		266	939	260	45	12	15	374	199	110	163	2	192	20	18	2	58	20	.74	13	.277	.394	.398

Sun Kim

Pitches: Right   Bats: Right   Pos: P   Ht: 6'2"   Wt: 180   Born: 9/4/77   Age: 22

Year Team	Lg Org	G	GS	CG	GF	IP	BFP	H	R	ER	HR	SH	SF	HB	TBB	IBB	SO	WP	Bk	W	L	Pct.	ShO	Sv	ERA
1998 Sarasota	A+ Bos	26	24	5	0	153	655	159	88	82	18	2	8	2	40	1	132	11	0	12	8	.600	0	0	4.82
1999 Trenton	AA Bos	26	26	1	0	149	641	160	86	81	16	2	5	9	44	2	130	4	0	9	8	.529	1	0	4.89
2 Min. YEARS		52	50	6	0	302	1296	319	174	163	34	4	13	11	84	3	262	15	0	21	16	.568	1	0	4.86

Andy Kimball

Pitches: Right Bats: Right Pos: P   Ht: 6'0" Wt: 190 Born: 8/23/75 Age: 24

Year Team	Lg Org	G	GS	CG	GF	IP	BFP	H	R	ER	HR	SH	SF	HB	TBB	IBB	SO	WP	Bk	W	L	Pct.	ShO	Sv	ERA
1997 Sou Oregon	A- Oak	13	7	0	0	54.2	230	37	29	22	4	1	1	3	17	0	75	8	2	3	2	.600	0	0	3.62
1998 Modesto	A+ Oak	42	8	0	24	97.1	440	113	62	48	7	3	8	6	29	5	96	6	2	5	6	.455	0	12	4.44
1999 Midland	AA Oak	47	0	0	15	89.1	412	112	64	54	14	2	4	2	40	4	87	13	4	9	5	.643	0	2	5.44
3 Min. YEARS		102	15	0	39	241.1	1082	262	155	124	25	6	13	11	86	9	258	27	8	17	13	.567	0	14	4.62

Bill King

Pitches: Right Bats: Right Pos: P   Ht: 6'5" Wt: 215 Born: 2/18/73 Age: 27

Year Team	Lg Org	G	GS	CG	GF	IP	BFP	H	R	ER	HR	SH	SF	HB	TBB	IBB	SO	WP	Bk	W	L	Pct.	ShO	Sv	ERA
1994 Sou Oregon	A- Oak	1	1	0	0	3	10	1	0	0	0	0	0	0	1	0	2	0	0	0	0	.000	0	0	0.00
W Michigan	A Oak	17	1	0	8	44.2	183	35	11	9	2	2	0	1	19	1	25	0	1	2	1	.667	0	4	1.81
1995 W Michigan	A Oak	30	18	0	3	148.1	633	152	75	55	6	5	1	5	41	0	95	6	5	9	7	.563	0	2	3.34
1996 Modesto	A+ Oak	29	27	0	1	163	716	193	102	86	11	3	8	8	40	0	100	8	2	16	4	.800	0	1	4.75
1997 Huntsville	AA Oak	28	27	1	0	176	762	216	99	82	18	8	3	10	28	0	103	7	0	9	7	.563	0	0	4.19
1998 Edmonton	AAA Oak	24	22	0	1	120.2	553	162	95	88	20	1	3	7	42	0	57	4	2	8	13	.381	0	0	6.56
1999 Vancouver	AAA Oak	45	7	0	14	98	414	105	52	38	11	3	4	4	22	2	60	5	0	9	6	.600	0	4	3.49
6 Min. YEARS		174	103	1	27	753.2	3271	864	434	358	68	22	19	35	193	3	442	30	10	53	38	.582	0	11	4.28

Brad King

Bats: Right Throws: Right Pos: C   Ht: 6'2" Wt: 205 Born: 12/3/74 Age: 25

Year Team	Lg Org	G	AB	H	2B	3B	HR	TB	R	RBI	TBB	IBB	SO	HBP	SH	SF	SB	CS	SB%	GDP	Avg	OBP	SLG
1996 Williamsprt	A- ChC	23	70	12	2	1	0	16	7	8	4	0	20	4	0	1	0	1	.00	0	.171	.253	.229
1997 Rockford	A ChC	68	204	51	14	1	7	88	31	29	19	2	35	8	2	4	4	4	.50	5	.250	.332	.431
1998 Daytona	A+ ChC	84	276	81	17	0	1	101	49	37	30	0	37	7	2	2	5	6	.45	11	.293	.375	.366
1999 West Tenn	AA ChC	92	232	53	10	0	0	63	29	25	38	5	34	9	2	6	2	1	.67	7	.228	.351	.272
4 Min. YEARS		267	782	197	43	2	8	268	116	99	91	7	126	28	6	13	11	12	.48	23	.252	.346	.343

Brett King

Bats: Right Throws: Right Pos: SS   Ht: 6'1" Wt: 190 Born: 7/20/72 Age: 27

Year Team	Lg Org	G	AB	H	2B	3B	HR	TB	R	RBI	TBB	IBB	SO	HBP	SH	SF	SB	CS	SB%	GDP	Avg	OBP	SLG
1993 Everett	A- SF	69	243	55	10	0	2	71	43	24	40	2	63	5	9	0	26	11	.70	2	.226	.347	.292
1994 San Jose	A+ SF	48	188	47	8	2	1	62	24	11	19	1	62	4	1	0	6	8	.43	0	.250	.332	.330
Clinton	A SF	68	261	57	13	2	5	89	45	30	23	1	86	2	3	2	12	3	.80	2	.218	.285	.341
1995 San Jose	A+ SF	107	394	108	29	4	3	154	61	41	41	1	86	5	5	6	28	8	.78	8	.274	.345	.391
1996 Shreveport	AA SF	127	459	107	23	4	7	159	61	48	49	0	116	6	17	1	19	9	.68	5	.233	.315	.346
1997 Shreveport	AA SF	79	193	42	6	1	6	68	28	20	30	1	55	1	1	1	4	5	.44	3	.218	.324	.352
1998 Shreveport	AA SF	85	257	44	9	2	3	66	29	19	27	1	64	3	2	2	4	2	.67	4	.171	.256	.257
1999 West Tenn	AA ChC	54	142	31	6	0	3	46	27	13	39	1	49	4	2	2	7	6	.54	0	.218	.396	.324
Iowa	AAA ChC	32	112	22	6	0	4	40	16	10	17	0	27	1	2	1	6	1	.86	2	.196	.305	.357
7 Min. YEARS		669	2249	513	110	15	34	755	334	216	285	8	608	31	42	15	112	53	.68	26	.228	.321	.336

Cesar King

Bats: Right Throws: Right Pos: C   Ht: 6'0" Wt: 175 Born: 2/28/78 Age: 22

Year Team	Lg Org	G	AB	H	2B	3B	HR	TB	R	RBI	TBB	IBB	SO	HBP	SH	SF	SB	CS	SB%	GDP	Avg	OBP	SLG
1996 Chston-SC	A Tex	84	276	69	10	1	7	102	35	28	21	0	58	1	0	2	8	5	.62	5	.250	.303	.370
1997 Charlotte	A+ Tex	91	307	91	14	4	6	131	51	37	35	0	58	1	3	4	8	6	.57	5	.296	.366	.427
Tulsa	AA Tex	14	45	16	1	0	1	20	6	8	5	0	3	0	0	0	0	1	.00	2	.356	.420	.444
1998 Tulsa	AA Tex	90	316	70	16	2	3	99	40	39	30	2	68	2	3	6	1	1	.50	10	.222	.288	.313
1999 Tulsa	AA Tex	95	321	73	19	2	11	129	41	45	32	1	70	2	3	1	2	1	.67	7	.227	.301	.402
4 Min. YEARS		374	1265	319	60	9	28	481	173	157	123	3	257	6	9	13	19	14	.58	29	.252	.318	.380

Brendan Kingman

Bats: Right Throws: Right Pos: 1B   Ht: 6'1" Wt: 235 Born: 5/22/73 Age: 27

Year Team	Lg Org	G	AB	H	2B	3B	HR	TB	R	RBI	TBB	IBB	SO	HBP	SH	SF	SB	CS	SB%	GDP	Avg	OBP	SLG
1992 Marlins	R Fla	42	121	28	2	1	0	32	8	13	22	0	29	2	2	0	2	2	.50	5	.231	.359	.264
1993 Marlins	R Fla	57	203	51	14	1	2	73	34	37	25	0	36	2	0	4	0	0	.00	5	.251	.333	.360
1994 Kane County	A Fla	93	334	81	15	3	3	111	41	38	24	0	67	4	4	0	2	3	.40	4	.243	.301	.332
1995 Brevard Cty	A+ Fla	95	348	88	19	4	8	139	37	47	31	3	45	1	0	4	1	0	1.00	21	.253	.313	.399
1998 Lancaster	A+ Sea	112	456	155	30	3	16	239	91	78	40	6	55	6	1	4	6	7	.46	20	.340	.397	.524
1999 New Haven	AA Sea	130	509	142	20	0	10	192	58	56	26	2	71	5	1	4	0	0	.00	18	.279	.318	.377
6 Min. YEARS		529	1971	545	100	12	39	786	269	269	168	11	303	20	8	16	11	12	.48	73	.277	.337	.399

Matt Kinney

Pitches: Right Bats: Right Pos: P   Ht: 6'4" Wt: 200 Born: 12/16/76 Age: 23

Year Team	Lg Org	G	GS	CG	GF	IP	BFP	H	R	ER	HR	SH	SF	HB	TBB	IBB	SO	WP	Bk	W	L	Pct.	ShO	Sv	ERA
1995 Red Sox	R Bos	8	2	0	4	27.2	119	29	13	9	0	1	2	2	10	0	11	5	0	1	3	.250	0	2	2.93
1996 Lowell	A- Bos	15	15	0	0	87.1	387	68	51	26	0	3	3	9	44	2	72	13	1	3	9	.250	0	0	2.68
1997 Michigan	A Bos	22	22	2	0	117.1	514	93	59	46	4	5	2	0	78	2	123	6	0	8	5	.615	1	0	3.53

147

		HOW MUCH HE PITCHED						WHAT HE GAVE UP												THE RESULTS					
Year Team	Lg Org	G	GS	CG	GF	IP	BFP	H	R	ER	HR	SH	SF	HB	TBB	IBB	SO	WP	Bk	W	L	Pct.	ShO	Sv	ERA
1998 Sarasota	A+ Bos	22	20	2	1	121.1	536	109	70	54	5	5	2	2	75	3	96	19	2	9	6	.600	1	1	4.01
Fort Myers	A+ Min	7	7	0	0	37.1	162	31	18	13	0	2	1	0	18	0	39	6	0	3	2	.600	0	0	3.13
1999 Twins	R Min	3	3	0	0	5.2	24	6	4	3	0	0	0	0	3	0	8	0	0	0	1	.000	0	0	4.76
New Britain	AA Min	14	13	0	0	60.2	284	69	54	48	8	2	3	4	36	0	50	6	1	4	7	.364	0	0	7.12
5 Min. YEARS		91	82	4	5	457.1	2026	405	269	199	17	18	13	17	264	7	399	55	4	28	33	.459	2	3	3.92

Wayne Kirby

Bats: Left **Throws:** Right **Pos:** OF   **Ht:** 5'10" **Wt:** 185 **Born:** 1/22/64 **Age:** 36

		BATTING														BASERUNNING				PERCENTAGES		
Year Team	Lg Org	G	AB	H	2B	3B	HR	TB	R	RBI	TBB	IBB	SO	HBP	SH	SF	SB	CS	SB%	GDP	Avg	OBP	SLG
1983 Dodgers	R LA	60	216	63	7	1	0	72	43	13	34	0	19	1	4	1	23	8	.74	—	.292	.389	.333
1984 Vero Beach	A+ LA	76	224	61	6	3	0	73	39	21	21	2	30	6	5	2	11	9	.55	3	.272	.348	.326
Great Falls	R+ LA	20	84	26	2	2	1	35	19	11	12	2	9	0	1	1	19	3	.86	2	.310	.392	.417
Bakersfield	A+ LA	23	84	23	3	0	0	26	14	10	4	0	5	0	2	1	8	3	.73	0	.274	.303	.310
1985 Vero Beach	A+ LA	122	437	123	9	3	0	138	70	28	41	1	41	3	4	3	31	14	.69	3	.281	.345	.316
1986 Vero Beach	A+ LA	114	387	101	9	4	2	124	60	31	37	3	30	1	2	2	28	17	.62	5	.261	.326	.320
1987 San Antonio	AA LA	24	80	19	1	2	1	27	7	9	4	0	7	0	3	0	6	4	.60	0	.238	.274	.338
Bakersfield	A+ LA	105	416	112	14	3	0	132	77	34	49	1	41	3	5	2	56	21	.73	3	.269	.349	.317
1988 Bakersfield	A+ LA	12	47	13	0	1	0	15	12	4	11	0	4	0	0	0	9	2	.82	0	.277	.414	.319
San Antonio	AA LA	100	334	80	9	2	0	93	50	21	21	2	42	3	10	1	26	10	.72	5	.240	.290	.270
1989 San Antonio	AA LA	44	140	30	3	1	0	35	14	7	18	0	17	1	2	1	11	6	.65	4	.214	.306	.250
1990 Albuquerque	AAA LA	78	310	106	18	8	0	140	62	30	26	1	27	1	5	1	29	14	.67	2	.342	.393	.452
Albuquerque	AAA LA	119	342	95	14	5	0	119	56	30	28	1	36	3	4	3	29	7	.81	2	.278	.335	.348
1991 Colo Sprngs	AAA Cle	118	385	113	14	4	1	138	66	39	34	2	36	2	5	3	29	14	.67	8	.294	.351	.358
1992 Colo Sprngs	AAA Cle	123	470	162	18	16	11	245	101	74	36	4	28	2	4	2	51	20	.72	7	.345	.392	.521
1993 Charlotte	AAA Cle	17	76	22	6	2	3	41	10	7	3	0	10	0	0	1	4	2	.67	1	.289	.316	.539
1997 Albuquerque	AAA LA	68	269	90	16	5	10	146	57	43	26	0	33	1	1	2	18	5	.78	5	.335	.393	.543
1998 Memphis	AAA StL	58	227	64	15	3	5	100	36	32	15	1	33	0	2	0	10	2	.83	2	.282	.326	.441
Norfolk	AAA NYM	42	162	50	8	3	5	79	32	23	21	1	18	2	1	0	11	5	.69	1	.309	.395	.488
1999 Las Vegas	AAA SD	66	160	48	7	3	10	91	29	31	28	0	36	0	1	1	2	4	.33	1	.300	.402	.569
1991 Cleveland	AL	21	43	9	2	0	0	11	4	5	2	0	6	0	1	1	1	2	.33	2	.209	.239	.256
1992 Cleveland	AL	21	18	3	1	0	1	7	9	1	3	0	2	0	0	0	0	3	.00	1	.167	.286	.389
1993 Cleveland	AL	131	458	123	19	5	6	170	71	60	37	2	58	3	7	6	17	5	.77	8	.269	.323	.371
1994 Cleveland	AL	78	191	56	6	0	5	77	33	23	13	0	30	1	2	0	11	4	.73	1	.293	.341	.403
1995 Cleveland	AL	101	188	39	10	2	1	56	29	14	13	0	32	1	1	2	10	3	.77	4	.207	.260	.298
1996 Cleveland	AL	27	16	4	1	0	0	5	3	1	2	0	2	0	0	0	0	1	.00	1	.250	.333	.313
Los Angeles	NL	65	188	51	10	1	1	66	23	11	17	1	17	1	1	0	4	2	.67	3	.271	.333	.351
1997 Los Angeles	NL	46	65	11	2	0	0	13	6	4	10	0	12	0	0	0	0	0	.00	1	.169	.280	.200
1998 New York	NL	26	31	6	0	1	0	8	5	0	1	0	9	0	1	0	1	1	.50	1	.194	.219	.258
14 Min. YEARS		1389	4850	1401	179	71	49	1869	854	498	469	21	502	29	61	26	411	170	.71	—	.289	.353	.385
8 Maj. YEARS		516	1198	302	51	9	14	413	183	119	98	3	168	6	13	10	44	21	.68	21	.252	.309	.345

Chris Kirgan

Bats: Right **Throws:** Right **Pos:** 1B   **Ht:** 6'4" **Wt:** 235 **Born:** 6/29/73 **Age:** 27

		BATTING														BASERUNNING				PERCENTAGES		
Year Team	Lg Org	G	AB	H	2B	3B	HR	TB	R	RBI	TBB	IBB	SO	HBP	SH	SF	SB	CS	SB%	GDP	Avg	OBP	SLG
1994 Bluefield	R+ Bal	58	209	58	8	3	7	93	34	29	27	1	53	0	0	4	4	0	1.00	4	.278	.354	.445
1995 Frederick	A+ Bal	124	378	76	18	2	11	131	25	47	25	3	107	3	1	3	2	2	.60	7	.201	.254	.347
1996 High Desert	A+ Bal	136	529	157	23	1	35	287	96	131	54	3	162	5	1	2	2	3	.40	9	.297	.366	.543
1997 Bowie	AA Bal	139	504	116	25	0	19	198	72	71	60	1	141	2	0	3	0	0	.00	13	.230	.313	.393
1998 New Haven	AA Col	114	427	116	32	0	22	214	63	79	44	8	105	3	0	5	2	1	.67	9	.272	.340	.501
Colo Sprngs	AAA Col	26	87	28	6	0	3	43	12	15	3	1	16	0	0	0	0	0	.00	4	.322	.344	.494
1999 Carolina	AA Col	133	474	105	27	2	13	175	55	84	60	4	115	2	0	4	1	0	1.00	17	.222	.309	.369
6 Min. YEARS		730	2608	656	139	8	110	1141	357	456	273	21	699	15	2	21	12	6	.67	63	.252	.324	.438

Daron Kirkreit

Pitches: Right **Bats:** Right **Pos:** P   **Ht:** 6'6" **Wt:** 225 **Born:** 8/7/72 **Age:** 27

		HOW MUCH HE PITCHED						WHAT HE GAVE UP												THE RESULTS					
Year Team	Lg Org	G	GS	CG	GF	IP	BFP	H	R	ER	HR	SH	SF	HB	TBB	IBB	SO	WP	Bk	W	L	Pct.	ShO	Sv	ERA
1993 Watertown	A- Cle	7	7	1	0	36.1	156	33	14	9	1	1	0	0	11	0	44	1	1	4	1	.800	0	0	2.23
1994 Kinston	A+ Cle	20	19	4	1	127.2	510	92	48	38	9	3	1	7	40	0	116	6	0	8	7	.533	0	0	2.68
Canton-Akrn	AA Cle	9	9	0	0	46.1	217	53	35	32	5	2	1	0	25	2	54	4	0	3	5	.375	0	0	6.22
1995 Canton-Akrn	AA Cle	14	14	1	0	80.2	360	74	54	51	13	5	5	6	46	1	67	2	0	2	9	.182	0	0	5.69
Kinston	A+ Cle	3	3	0	0	13.2	63	14	9	9	1	1	1	2	6	0	14	1	0	0	1	.000	0	0	5.93
1996 Kinston	A+ Cle	6	6	0	0	32.2	125	23	7	7	3	0	1	2	10	0	19	3	0	2	0	1.000	0	0	1.93
1997 Buffalo	AAA Cle	1	1	1	0	7	23	3	0	0	0	0	0	0	1	0	2	0	0	1	0	1.000	1	0	0.00
Akron	AA Cle	26	20	1	3	117.2	562	131	96	68	15	9	4	13	69	3	83	10	1	8	9	.471	0	0	5.20
1998 Wichita	AA KC	10	7	0	0	38	184	52	34	28	4	3	2	3	16	1	23	5	0	1	3	.250	0	0	6.63
El Paso	AA Mil	18	13	0	2	73.2	348	103	57	51	6	4	3	2	39	0	31	6	1	1	6	.143	0	0	6.23
1999 Nashua	IND —	7	7	0	0	39.2	194	53	36	26	5	0	1	1	18	0	24	3	0	1	2	.333	0	0	5.90
New Haven	AA Sea	5	4	0	1	24	107	33	8	7	1	0	1	0	7	0	15	3	0	2	2	.500	0	0	2.63
Lancaster	A+ Sea	9	9	0	0	47	212	65	34	28	5	0	1	1	17	0	35	4	1	4	4	.500	0	0	5.36
7 Min. YEARS		135	119	8	7	684.1	3061	729	432	354	67	29	21	37	305	7	527	48	6	37	49	.430	1	0	4.66

Stacy Kleiner

Bats: Right **Throws:** Right **Pos:** C **Ht:** 6'0" **Wt:** 185 **Born:** 1/12/75 **Age:** 25

Year Team	Lg Org	G	AB	H	2B	3B	HR	TB	R	RBI	TBB	IBB	SO	HBP	SH	SF	SB	CS	SB%	GDP	Avg	OBP	SLG
1996 New Jersey	A- StL	56	177	52	10	2	2	72	24	23	9	0	32	1	2	0	2	1	.67	5	.294	.332	.407
1997 Pr William	A+ StL	91	310	97	22	4	4	139	37	32	28	2	69	4	1	1	1	1	.50	11	.313	.376	.448
Arkansas	AA StL	16	55	14	4	2	1	25	7	10	2	0	14	0	0	0	0	0	.00	2	.255	.281	.455
1998 Arkansas	AA StL	99	333	86	28	1	6	134	44	57	33	2	79	3	3	1	1	2	.33	5	.258	.330	.402
1999 Arkansas	AA StL	85	235	52	8	2	2	70	23	16	24	0	60	3	2	1	2	1	.67	10	.221	.300	.298
4 Min. YEARS		347	1110	301	72	11	15	440	135	138	96	4	254	11	8	3	6	5	.55	33	.271	.334	.396

Larry Kleinz

Bats: Right **Throws:** Right **Pos:** 3B **Ht:** 6'1" **Wt:** 205 **Born:** 3/3/74 **Age:** 26

Year Team	Lg Org	G	AB	H	2B	3B	HR	TB	R	RBI	TBB	IBB	SO	HBP	SH	SF	SB	CS	SB%	GDP	Avg	OBP	SLG
1996 Utica	A- Fla	73	256	62	14	1	0	78	21	34	20	0	44	13	2	3	1	0	1.00	6	.242	.325	.305
1997 Kane County	A Fla	107	364	88	16	1	11	139	50	44	48	2	63	4	2	3	1	2	.33	8	.242	.334	.382
1998 Brevard Cty	A+ Fla	88	320	92	23	1	7	138	48	34	46	0	51	7	1	5	1	0	1.00	8	.288	.384	.431
1999 Brevard Cty	A+ Fla	11	44	10	3	0	0	13	8	6	4	0	8	1	0	0	0	0	.00	0	.227	.306	.295
Portland	AA Fla	94	276	72	21	1	5	110	30	43	39	2	50	5	3	0	2	3	.40	12	.261	.363	.399
4 Min. YEARS		373	1260	324	77	4	23	478	157	161	157	4	216	30	8	11	5	5	.50	34	.257	.350	.379

Josh Klimek

Bats: Left **Throws:** Right **Pos:** 3B **Ht:** 6'1" **Wt:** 175 **Born:** 2/2/74 **Age:** 26

Year Team	Lg Org	G	AB	H	2B	3B	HR	TB	R	RBI	TBB	IBB	SO	HBP	SH	SF	SB	CS	SB%	GDP	Avg	OBP	SLG
1996 Helena	R+ Mil	67	253	75	17	0	6	110	56	51	42	5	39	0	0	3	5	1	.83	4	.296	.393	.435
1997 Beloit	A Mil	121	443	118	31	3	12	191	62	66	39	1	56	5	2	6	4	8	.33	8	.266	.329	.431
1998 Stockton	A+ Mil	124	440	125	27	6	9	191	61	56	36	7	60	4	1	6	4	2	.67	6	.284	.340	.434
1999 Huntsville	AA Mil	123	431	103	28	0	14	173	46	71	33	6	78	4	2	8	3	2	.60	5	.239	.294	.401
4 Min. YEARS		435	1567	421	103	9	41	665	225	244	150	19	233	13	5	23	16	13	.55	23	.269	.333	.424

Scott Klingenbeck

Pitches: Right **Bats:** Right **Pos:** P **Ht:** 6'2" **Wt:** 205 **Born:** 2/3/71 **Age:** 29

Year Team	Lg Org	G	GS	CG	GF	IP	BFP	H	R	ER	HR	SH	SF	HB	TBB	IBB	SO	WP	Bk	W	L	Pct.	ShO	Sv	ERA
1992 Kane County	A Bal	11	11	0	0	68.1	283	50	31	20	3	2	0	1	28	1	64	4	8	3	4	.429	0	0	2.63
1993 Frederick	A+ Bal	23	23	0	0	139	593	151	62	46	7	2	2	2	35	1	146	5	2	13	4	.765	0	0	2.98
1994 Bowie	AA Bal	25	25	3	0	143.2	613	151	76	58	15	2	4	5	37	2	120	6	3	7	5	.583	0	0	3.63
1995 Rochester	AAA Bal	8	7	0	0	43	177	46	14	13	2	3	2	1	10	0	29	2	0	3	1	.750	0	0	2.72
1996 Salt Lake	AAA Min	22	22	5	0	150.2	635	159	64	52	8	4	6	3	41	2	100	9	1	9	3	.750	2	0	3.11
1997 Salt Lake	AAA Min	1	1	0	0	7	26	6	1	1	1	0	0	0	0	0	6	0	0	0	0	.000	0	0	1.29
Indianapols	AAA Cin	27	27	2	0	170.2	727	180	85	75	23	5	6	5	41	0	119	2	2	12	8	.600	0	0	3.96
1998 Indianapols	AAA Cin	10	10	0	0	63	249	57	26	20	7	1	2	0	10	0	50	0	0	2	6	.250	0	0	2.86
Nashville	AAA Pit	6	6	0	0	29.1	137	45	24	20	3	2	2	2	7	0	15	0	1	2	2	.500	0	0	6.14
1999 Indianapols	AAA Cin	14	12	0	1	74.2	328	89	44	40	8	5	5	2	26	1	53	3	0	4	4	.500	0	1	4.82
1994 Baltimore	AL	1	1	0	0	7	31	6	4	3	1	0	1	1	4	1	5	0	0	1	0	1.000	0	0	3.86
1995 Baltimore	AL	6	5	0	0	31.1	137	32	17	17	6	0	0	0	18	0	15	2	0	2	2	.500	0	0	4.88
Minnesota	AL	18	4	0	4	48.1	236	69	48	46	16	3	1	4	24	0	27	5	0	0	2	.000	0	0	8.57
1996 Minnesota	AL	10	3	0	2	28.2	137	42	28	25	5	1	1	1	10	0	15	1	0	1	1	.500	0	0	7.85
1998 Cincinnati	NL	4	4	0	0	22.2	102	26	17	15	6	2	1	1	7	0	13	0	0	1	3	.250	0	0	5.96
8 Min. YEARS		147	144	10	1	889.1	3768	934	427	345	77	26	29	21	235	7	702	31	17	59	33	.641	2	1	3.49
4 Maj. YEARS		39	17	0	6	138	643	175	114	106	34	6	4	7	63	1	75	8	0	5	8	.385	0	0	6.91

Brandon Knight

Pitches: Right **Bats:** Left **Pos:** P **Ht:** 6'0" **Wt:** 170 **Born:** 10/1/75 **Age:** 24

Year Team	Lg Org	G	GS	CG	GF	IP	BFP	H	R	ER	HR	SH	SF	HB	TBB	IBB	SO	WP	Bk	W	L	Pct.	ShO	Sv	ERA
1995 Rangers	R Tex	3	2	0	0	12	54	12	7	7	0	0	1	0	6	0	11	2	0	2	1	.667	0	0	5.25
Chston-SC	A Tex	9	9	0	0	54.2	218	37	22	19	5	0	4	0	21	0	52	4	1	4	2	.667	0	0	3.13
1996 Hudson Val	A- Tex	9	9	0	0	53	236	59	29	26	1	2	1	1	21	0	52	2	1	2	2	.500	0	0	4.42
Charlotte	A+ Tex	19	17	2	0	102	463	118	65	58	9	4	7	2	45	0	74	6	0	4	10	.286	0	0	5.12
1997 Charlotte	A+ Tex	14	12	3	1	92.2	380	82	33	23	9	3	2	1	22	0	91	0	2	7	4	.636	1	0	2.23
Tulsa	AA Tex	14	14	0	0	90	383	83	52	45	12	0	4	2	35	0	84	9	4	6	4	.600	1	0	4.50
1998 Tulsa	AA Tex	14	14	0	0	86.1	379	94	54	49	11	1	3	0	37	0	87	12	0	6	6	.500	0	0	5.11
Oklahoma	AAA Tex	16	12	0	0	64.2	315	100	75	70	16	0	2	1	29	0	52	9	1	0	7	.000	0	0	9.74
1999 Oklahoma	AAA Tex	27	26	5	0	163	706	173	96	89	23	1	3	10	47	2	97	9	3	9	8	.529	0	0	4.91
5 Min. YEARS		125	115	12	1	718.1	3134	758	433	386	86	11	27	17	263	2	600	53	12	40	44	.476	2	0	4.84

Brian Knoll

Pitches: Right **Bats:** Right **Pos:** P **Ht:** 6'3" **Wt:** 200 **Born:** 8/4/73 **Age:** 26

Year Team	Lg Org	G	GS	CG	GF	IP	BFP	H	R	ER	HR	SH	SF	HB	TBB	IBB	SO	WP	Bk	W	L	Pct.	ShO	Sv	ERA
1995 Bellingham	A- SF	22	2	0	5	57	232	44	22	13	1	4	1	3	17	0	35	2	1	5	2	.714	0	0	2.05
1996 Burlington	A SF	52	2	0	16	79	342	76	43	32	5	6	2	4	34	2	56	4	0	3	8	.273	0	1	3.65
1997 Bakersfield	A+ SF	49	0	0	23	68	323	88	50	43	6	3	1	2	25	3	66	10	0	0	0	.000	0	2	3.09
1998 San Jose	A+ SF	42	6	1	15	114.2	490	135	47	44	4	3	5	5	21	0	109	5	0	7	7	.500	1	3	3.45
1999 Shreveport	AA SF	33	17	1	6	128.1	530	117	54	50	15	5	4	11	34	0	91	6	0	9	7	.563	1	1	3.51
5 Min. YEARS		198	25	2	65	447	1917	460	216	182	31	21	11	25	141	5	347	27	1	27	30	.474	2	7	3.66

149

Eric Knott

Pitches: Left Bats: Left Pos: P   Ht: 6'0" Wt: 188 Born: 9/23/74 Age: 25

Year Team	Lg Org	G	GS	CG	GF	IP	BFP	H	R	ER	HR	SH	SF	HB	TBB	IBB	SO	WP	Bk	W	L	Pct.	ShO	Sv	ERA
1997 Lethbridge	R+ Ari	21	3	0	7	47	195	41	21	15	4	2	1	0	9	1	62	2	0	0	4	.000	0	3	2.87
1998 High Desert	A+ Ari	28	22	1	3	143.1	616	175	84	72	16	3	4	1	28	1	96	3	3	12	7	.632	0	0	4.52
1999 El Paso	AA Ari	27	27	3	0	161.1	711	198	95	82	11	4	5	5	42	0	83	3	2	7	11	.389	0	0	4.57
3 Min. YEARS		76	52	4	10	351.2	1522	414	200	169	31	9	10	6	79	2	241	8	5	19	22	.463	0	3	4.33

Gary Knotts

Pitches: Right Bats: Right Pos: P   Ht: 6'4" Wt: 200 Born: 2/12/77 Age: 23

Year Team	Lg Org	G	GS	CG	GF	IP	BFP	H	R	ER	HR	SH	SF	HB	TBB	IBB	SO	WP	Bk	W	L	Pct.	ShO	Sv	ERA
1996 Marlins	R Fla	12	9	1	2	57.1	227	35	16	13	0	2	2	6	17	0	46	5	0	4	2	.667	1	0	2.04
1997 Kane County	A Fla	7	7	0	0	20	113	33	34	29	2	2	0	3	17	0	19	8	1	1	5	.167	0	0	13.05
Utica	A- Fla	12	12	1	0	69.2	304	70	34	28	3	1	2	8	27	1	65	3	0	3	5	.375	0	0	3.62
1998 Kane County	A Fla	27	27	3	0	158.1	686	144	84	68	11	4	6	11	66	1	148	7	0	8	8	.500	0	0	3.87
1999 Brevard Cty	A+ Fla	16	16	3	0	94	402	101	52	48	7	1	3	8	29	0	65	1	0	9	6	.600	2	0	4.60
Portland	AA Fla	12	12	1	0	81.2	358	79	39	34	12	4	3	8	33	0	63	4	0	6	3	.667	1	0	3.75
4 Min. YEARS		86	83	9	2	481	2090	462	259	220	35	14	16	44	189	2	406	28	1	31	29	.517	4	0	4.12

Ramsey Koeyers

Bats: Right Throws: Right Pos: C   Ht: 6'1" Wt: 187 Born: 8/7/74 Age: 25

Year Team	Lg Org	G	AB	H	2B	3B	HR	TB	R	RBI	TBB	IBB	SO	HBP	SH	SF	SB	CS	SB%	GDP	Avg	OBP	SLG
1992 Expos	R Mon	42	125	21	2	0	0	23	7	16	8	1	28	0	0	6	1	0	1.00	1	.168	.209	.184
1993 Wst Plm Bch	A+ Mon	4	12	2	0	0	0	2	0	3	0	0	3	0	1	0	0	0	.00	0	.167	.167	.167
Jamestown	A- Mon	65	233	52	9	2	4	77	25	29	10	0	69	2	0	2	1	1	.50	5	.223	.259	.330
1994 Wst Plm Bch	A+ Mon	79	241	62	11	1	3	84	27	31	21	0	61	1	3	0	3	3	.50	9	.257	.319	.349
1995 Wst Plm Bch	A+ Mon	77	244	46	6	1	0	54	19	18	9	0	64	0	5	3	2	1	.67	10	.189	.215	.221
1996 Harrisburg	AA Mon	25	77	16	3	0	1	22	6	9	2	0	27	1	3	1	0	0	.00	4	.208	.235	.286
Expos	R Mon	7	19	3	1	0	0	4	2	0	3	0	6	0	0	0	0	0	.00	0	.158	.273	.211
Wst Plm Bch	A+ Mon	10	33	4	2	0	0	6	2	2	0	0	8	0	0	0	0	0	.00	4	.121	.121	.182
1997 Portland	AA Fla	83	286	74	14	1	12	126	37	50	15	2	67	2	1	1	0	3	.00	5	.259	.299	.441
1998 Tulsa	AA Ari	55	164	41	2	0	4	55	25	18	13	1	45	4	0	0	1	0	1.00	8	.250	.320	.335
1999 High Desert	A+ Ari	5	17	4	0	0	1	7	3	2	1	0	3	0	1	0	0	0	.00	1	.235	.278	.412
Tucson	AAA Ari	15	39	5	1	0	0	6	6	1	4	0	7	0	1	0	0	0	.00	0	.128	.209	.154
El Paso	AA Ari	26	77	16	9	0	1	28	6	10	4	0	20	1	0	0	0	0	.00	2	.208	.256	.364
8 Min. YEARS		493	1567	346	60	5	26	494	165	189	90	4	408	11	15	13	8	9	.47	46	.221	.266	.315

Ryan Kohlmeier

Pitches: Right Bats: Right Pos: P   Ht: 6'2" Wt: 195 Born: 6/25/77 Age: 23

Year Team	Lg Org	G	GS	CG	GF	IP	BFP	H	R	ER	HR	SH	SF	HB	TBB	IBB	SO	WP	Bk	W	L	Pct.	ShO	Sv	ERA
1997 Delmarva	A Bal	50	0	0	41	74.2	276	48	22	22	8	2	2	1	17	1	99	2	1	2	2	.500	0	24	2.65
Bowie	AA Bal	2	0	0	1	2.2	9	0	0	0	0	0	0	0	2	0	5	0	1	0	0	.000	0	1	0.00
1998 Bowie	AA Bal	42	0	0	28	50	219	52	37	34	13	1	1	3	16	1	56	2	1	4	4	.500	0	7	6.12
Frederick	A+ Bal	9	0	0	9	9.2	44	10	9	8	1	0	2	1	3	0	15	0	1	1	2	.333	0	5	7.45
1999 Bowie	AA Bal	55	0	0	49	62.2	256	44	23	22	10	4	2	1	29	1	78	2	1	3	7	.300	0	23	3.16
3 Min. YEARS		158	0	0	128	199.2	804	154	91	86	32	7	7	6	67	3	253	6	5	10	15	.400	0	60	3.88

Brandon Kolb

Pitches: Right Bats: Right Pos: P   Ht: 6'1" Wt: 190 Born: 11/20/73 Age: 26

Year Team	Lg Org	G	GS	CG	GF	IP	BFP	H	R	ER	HR	SH	SF	HB	TBB	IBB	SO	WP	Bk	W	L	Pct.	ShO	Sv	ERA
1995 Idaho Falls	R+ SD	9	8	0	0	38.1	181	42	33	30	1	2	2	2	29	0	21	5	0	2	3	.400	0	0	7.04
Padres	R SD	4	4	1	0	23	100	13	10	3	0	0	0	3	13	0	21	4	0	1	1	.500	1	0	1.17
1996 Clinton	A SD	27	27	3	0	181.1	776	170	84	69	7	6	7	8	76	1	138	19	0	16	9	.640	0	0	3.42
1997 Rancho Cuca	A+ SD	10	10	0	0	63	261	60	29	21	0	1	1	2	22	0	49	5	0	3	2	.600	0	0	3.00
1998 Rancho Cuca	A+ SD	4	4	0	0	20.2	92	14	8	7	3	0	0	1	18	0	16	0	1	0	2	.000	0	0	3.05
Mobile	AA SD	21	6	0	4	62	291	46	33	31	4	3	3	1	40	0	58	6	0	4	3	.571	0	1	4.50
1999 Mobile	AA SD	7	0	0	6	11.1	52	8	4	1	0	1	0	1	4	0	14	1	0	0	2	.000	0	2	0.79
Las Vegas	AAA SD	42	0	0	16	61.2	281	72	36	27	3	1	3	3	29	1	63	7	0	2	1	.667	0	4	3.94
5 Min. YEARS		124	59	4	26	461.1	2017	425	237	189	18	14	16	21	231	2	380	47	1	28	23	.549	1	7	3.69

Toby Kominek

Bats: Right Throws: Right Pos: OF-1B   Ht: 6'1" Wt: 200 Born: 6/13/73 Age: 27

Year Team	Lg Org	G	AB	H	2B	3B	HR	TB	R	RBI	TBB	IBB	SO	HBP	SH	SF	SB	CS	SB%	GDP	Avg	OBP	SLG
1995 Helena	R+ Mil	13	48	16	1	1	3	28	7	18	3	0	9	1	0	1	2	1	.67	0	.333	.377	.583
Beloit	A Mil	55	187	52	14	2	7	91	38	30	18	1	56	10	0	3	12	2	.86	1	.278	.369	.487
1996 Stockton	A+ Mil	100	358	106	17	7	7	158	76	47	49	1	97	8	4	3	10	7	.59	7	.296	.390	.441
1997 Stockton	A+ Mil	128	476	143	28	7	15	230	83	72	50	3	107	24	1	2	22	14	.61	8	.300	.393	.483
1998 El Paso	AA Mil	135	496	150	33	4	17	242	114	83	73	4	120	22	0	4	21	16	.57	5	.302	.412	.488
1999 Huntsville	AA Mil	128	456	106	20	3	12	168	56	59	52	2	118	18	1	3	7	10	.41	9	.232	.333	.368
5 Min. YEARS		559	2021	573	113	24	61	917	374	309	245	11	507	83	6	15	74	50	.60	30	.284	.381	.454

Scott Krause

Bats: Right Throws: Right Pos: OF   Ht: 6'1" Wt: 195 Born: 8/16/73 Age: 26

BATTING / BASERUNNING / PERCENTAGES

Year Team	Lg Org	G	AB	H	2B	3B	HR	TB	R	RBI	TBB	IBB	SO	HBP	SH	SF	SB	CS	SB%	GDP	Avg	OBP	SLG
1994 Helena	R+ Mil	63	252	90	18	3	4	126	51	52	18	2	49	9	1	2	13	6	.68	2	.357	.416	.500
1995 Beloit	A Mil	134	481	119	30	4	13	196	83	76	50	5	126	12	3	7	24	10	.71	7	.247	.329	.407
1996 El Paso	AA Mil	24	85	27	5	2	3	45	16	11	2	0	19	1	1	0	2	0	1.00	1	.318	.341	.529
Stockton	A+ Mil	108	427	128	22	4	19	215	82	83	32	0	101	16	1	3	25	6	.81	9	.300	.368	.504
1997 El Paso	AA Mil	125	474	171	33	11	16	274	97	88	20	3	108	7	4	7	13	4	.76	7	.361	.390	.578
1998 Louisville	AAA Mil	117	390	114	25	2	26	221	71	82	46	3	104	15	3	1	11	4	.73	16	.292	.387	.567
1999 Louisville	AAA Mil	133	499	138	26	7	15	223	57	89	33	2	104	13	7	8	10	6	.63	13	.277	.333	.447
6 Min. YEARS		704	2608	787	159	33	96	1300	457	481	201	15	611	73	20	28	98	36	.73	55	.302	.365	.498

Rick Krivda

Pitches: Left Bats: Right Pos: P   Ht: 6'1" Wt: 185 Born: 1/19/70 Age: 30

HOW MUCH HE PITCHED / WHAT HE GAVE UP / THE RESULTS

Year Team	Lg Org	G	GS	CG	GF	IP	BFP	H	R	ER	HR	SH	SF	HB	TBB	IBB	SO	WP	Bk	W	L	Pct.	ShO	Sv	ERA
1991 Bluefield	R+ Bal	15	8	0	2	67	265	48	20	14	0	2	1	0	24	0	79	1	4	7	1	.875	0	1	1.88
1992 Kane County	A Bal	18	18	2	0	121.2	502	108	53	41	6	0	3	1	41	0	124	5	1	12	5	.706	0	0	3.03
Frederick	A+ Bal	9	9	1	0	57.1	236	51	23	19	7	0	0	1	15	0	64	1	1	5	1	.833	1	0	2.98
1993 Bowie	AA Bal	22	22	0	0	125.2	522	114	46	43	10	2	1	2	50	0	108	1	2	7	5	.583	0	0	3.08
Rochester	AAA Bal	5	5	0	0	33.1	133	20	7	7	2	1	0	1	16	0	23	1	0	3	0	1.000	0	0	1.89
1994 Rochester	AAA Bal	28	26	3	2	163	688	149	75	64	12	1	6	4	73	4	122	9	1	9	10	.474	2	0	3.53
1995 Rochester	AAA Bal	16	16	1	0	101.2	429	96	44	36	11	6	4	2	32	0	74	3	3	6	5	.545	0	0	3.19
1996 Rochester	AAA Bal	8	8	0	0	44	191	51	24	21	6	0	1	1	15	0	34	2	2	3	1	.750	0	0	4.30
1997 Rochester	AAA Bal	22	21	6	0	146	589	122	61	55	13	0	2	5	34	0	128	2	2	14	2	.875	3	0	3.39
1999 Omaha	AAA KC	21	18	0	0	115.1	541	154	94	73	17	2	3	5	41	0	70	3	3	6	8	.429	0	0	5.70
1995 Baltimore	AL	13	13	1	0	75.1	319	76	40	38	9	0	4	4	25	1	53	2	2	2	7	.222	0	0	4.54
1996 Baltimore	AL	22	11	0	4	81.2	359	89	48	45	14	2	2	1	39	2	54	3	1	3	5	.375	0	0	4.96
1997 Baltimore	AL	10	10	0	0	50	225	67	36	35	7	1	2	0	18	1	29	0	2	4	2	.667	0	0	6.30
1998 Cleveland	AL	11	1	0	5	25	112	24	10	9	2	0	0	0	16	1	10	1	1	2	0	1.000	0	0	3.24
Cincinnati	NL	16	1	0	1	26.1	138	41	34	33	7	3	1	3	19	1	19	1	1	0	2	.000	0	0	11.28
8 Min. YEARS		164	151	13	4	975	4096	913	447	373	84	14	21	22	341	4	826	28	19	72	38	.655	6	1	3.44
4 Maj. YEARS		72	36	1	10	258.1	1153	297	168	160	39	6	9	8	117	6	165	7	7	11	16	.407	0	0	5.57

Marc Kroon

Pitches: Right Bats: Right Pos: P   Ht: 6'2" Wt: 195 Born: 4/2/73 Age: 27

HOW MUCH HE PITCHED / WHAT HE GAVE UP / THE RESULTS

Year Team	Lg Org	G	GS	CG	GF	IP	BFP	H	R	ER	HR	SH	SF	HB	TBB	IBB	SO	WP	Bk	W	L	Pct.	ShO	Sv	ERA
1991 Mets	R NYM	12	10	1	2	47.2	208	39	33	24	1	0	1	4	22	0	39	10	5	2	3	.400	0	0	4.53
1992 Kingsport	R+ NYM	12	12	0	0	68	307	52	41	31	3	0	3	1	57	0	60	13	2	3	5	.375	0	0	4.10
1993 Capital Cty	A NYM	29	19	0	8	124.1	542	123	65	48	6	1	8	5	70	0	122	10	2	2	11	.154	0	2	3.47
1994 Rancho Cuca	A+ SD	26	26	0	0	143.1	655	143	86	77	14	4	9	11	81	1	153	9	3	11	6	.647	0	0	4.83
1995 Memphis	AA SD	22	19	0	2	115.1	497	90	49	45	12	2	2	6	61	1	123	16	1	7	5	.583	0	2	3.51
1996 Memphis	AA SD	44	0	0	43	46.2	208	33	19	15	4	1	4	3	28	1	56	6	1	2	4	.333	0	22	2.89
1997 Las Vegas	AAA SD	46	0	0	33	41.2	175	34	22	21	5	2	2	3	22	0	53	6	0	1	3	.250	0	15	4.54
1998 Indianapols	AAA Cin	39	0	0	9	46.1	219	39	29	29	6	1	2	5	47	0	36	14	0	3	2	.600	0	1	5.63
1999 Mariners	R Sea	4	4	0	0	7	27	5	3	3	2	0	0	0	0	0	12	0	0	0	0	.000	0	0	3.86
Tacoma	AAA Sea	13	5	0	1	35.1	161	31	24	24	5	0	1	4	21	0	38	1	1	3	2	.600	0	0	6.11
1995 San Diego	NL	2	0	0	1	1.2	7	1	2	2	0	0	0	0	2	0	2	0	0	0	1	.000	0	0	10.80
1997 San Diego	NL	12	0	0	2	11.1	56	14	9	9	2	0	0	1	5	0	12	1	0	0	0	.000	0	0	7.15
1998 San Diego	NL	2	0	0	2	2.1	8	6	2	0	0	0	0	0	1	0	6	0	0	0	0	.000	0	0	0.00
Cincinnati	NL	4	0	0	2	5.1	30	7	8	8	0	0	0	1	8	0	4	2	1	0	0	.000	0	0	13.50
9 Min. YEARS		247	95	1	98	675.2	2999	589	371	317	58	11	32	42	409	3	692	85	15	34	41	.453	0	42	4.22
3 Maj. YEARS		20	0	0	7	20.2	101	22	19	19	2	0	0	2	16	0	20	3	1	0	2	.000	0	0	8.27

Hector Kuilan

Bats: Right Throws: Right Pos: C   Ht: 5'11" Wt: 190 Born: 4/3/76 Age: 24

BATTING / BASERUNNING / PERCENTAGES

Year Team	Lg Org	G	AB	H	2B	3B	HR	TB	R	RBI	TBB	IBB	SO	HBP	SH	SF	SB	CS	SB%	GDP	Avg	OBP	SLG
1994 Marlins	R Fla	40	141	22	7	0	0	29	11	17	6	0	15	0	2	2	0	1	.00	4	.156	.188	.206
1995 Marlins	R Fla	48	153	38	8	0	0	46	14	27	17	1	20	1	2	2	4	1	.80	4	.248	.324	.301
Kane County	A Fla	2	7	0	0	0	0	0	0	0	0	0	1	0	0	0	0	0	.00	0	.000	.000	.000
1996 Kane County	A Fla	94	308	62	12	1	6	94	28	30	22	0	52	3	3	2	1	3	.25	7	.201	.260	.305
1997 Brevard Cty	A+ Fla	77	265	60	16	0	0	76	18	25	7	0	41	4	3	3	0	1	.00	12	.226	.254	.287
Charlotte	AAA Fla	14	39	4	0	0	0	4	3	3	2	0	8	0	0	0	0	0	.00	2	.103	.146	.103
1998 Portland	AA Fla	31	107	27	4	0	2	37	8	14	2	0	9	0	3	2	0	0	.00	2	.252	.261	.346
Brevard Cty	A+ Fla	61	208	47	11	0	6	76	13	28	12	0	29	2	2	1	2	1	.67	3	.226	.274	.365
1999 Portland	AA Fla	76	245	64	11	0	2	81	22	32	11	0	42	2	3	4	0	0	.00	9	.261	.294	.331
6 Min. YEARS		443	1473	324	69	1	16	443	117	176	79	1	217	12	18	16	7	7	.50	43	.220	.263	.301

Steve Lackey

Bats: Right Throws: Right Pos: SS   Ht: 5'11" Wt: 159 Born: 9/25/74 Age: 25

BATTING / BASERUNNING / PERCENTAGES

Year Team	Lg Org	G	AB	H	2B	3B	HR	TB	R	RBI	TBB	IBB	SO	HBP	SH	SF	SB	CS	SB%	GDP	Avg	OBP	SLG
1992 Mets	R NYM	12	47	9	1	0	0	10	6	3	3	0	7	1	1	0	0	0	.00	0	.191	.255	.213
Kingsport	R+ NYM	38	148	26	2	0	0	28	16	10	17	0	22	3	0	0	3	4	.43	5	.176	.274	.189
1993 Kingsport	R+ NYM	53	172	25	4	0	0	29	14	9	14	0	30	0	1	1	3	4	.43	4	.145	.209	.169
1994 Pittsfield	A- NYM	3	4	1	0	0	0	1	1	0	0	0	2	0	0	0	0	0	.00	0	.250	.500	.250

Year Team	Lg Org	G	AB	H	2B	3B	HR	TB	R	RBI	TBB	IBB	SO	HBP	SH	SF	SB	CS	SB%	GDP	Avg	OBP	SLG
								BATTING										BASERUNNING			PERCENTAGES		
Kingsport	R+ NYM	56	187	37	6	1	0	45	22	7	24	1	31	3	3	0	2	2	.50	2	.198	.299	.241
1995 Pittsfield	A- NYM	21	75	18	5	0	0	23	7	6	2	0	16	1	1	1	1	0	1.00	1	.240	.266	.307
Capital Cty	A NYM	67	178	34	8	0	1	45	21	21	11	1	42	2	5	3	9	2	.82	2	.191	.242	.253
1996 Fayettevlle	A Det	82	310	67	13	0	4	92	38	43	28	0	58	3	5	5	24	6	.80	4	.216	.283	.297
Visalia	A+ Det	46	184	49	11	1	4	74	27	29	16	0	44	1	2	2	7	1	.88	7	.266	.325	.402
1997 Jacksnville	AA Det	5	13	1	0	0	0	1	1	0	0	0	1	0	1	0	1	0	1.00	0	.077	.077	.077
Lakeland	A+ Det	71	247	55	14	0	0	69	24	22	10	0	58	1	6	2	5	4	.56	3	.223	.254	.279
1998 Jacksnville	AA Det	12	34	11	1	0	0	12	6	3	5	0	5	0	0	0	0	0	.00	0	.324	.410	.353
Lakeland	A+ Det	102	415	118	14	3	3	147	68	39	31	0	73	4	9	5	19	7	.73	7	.284	.336	.354
1999 Myrtle Bch	A+ Atl	53	216	59	10	2	0	73	24	16	15	0	33	4	1	2	13	4	.76	1	.273	.329	.338
Greenville	AA Atl	80	315	92	18	3	4	128	50	38	21	0	55	0	6	3	9	8	.53	7	.292	.333	.406
8 Min. YEARS		701	2545	602	107	10	16	777	325	246	199	2	475	23	43	24	96	43	.69	45	.237	.295	.305

Kerry Lacy

Pitches: Right **Bats:** Right **Pos:** P **Ht:** 6' 2" **Wt:** 215 **Born:** 8/7/72 **Age:** 27

Year Team	Lg Org	G	GS	CG	GF	IP	BFP	H	R	ER	HR	SH	SF	HB	TBB	IBB	SO	WP	Bk	W	L	Pct.	ShO	Sv	ERA
		HOW MUCH HE PITCHED						WHAT HE GAVE UP												THE RESULTS					
1991 Butte	R+ Tex	24	2	0	6	48	221	47	34	30	5	0	2	6	36	0	45	15	4	2	1	.667	0	1	5.63
1992 Gastonia	A Tex	49	1	0	32	55.2	262	55	35	24	2	2	0	1	42	2	57	9	2	3	7	.300	0	17	3.88
1993 Chston-SC	A Tex	58	0	0	57	60	267	40	25	21	1	3	5	5	32	5	54	6	2	0	6	.000	0	36	3.15
Charlotte	A+ Tex	4	0	0	3	4.2	21	2	2	1	0	0	0	1	3	0	3	1	0	0	0	.000	0	2	1.93
1994 Tulsa	AA Tex	41	0	0	35	63.2	270	49	30	26	4	3	2	3	37	4	46	3	1	2	6	.250	0	12	3.68
1995 Tulsa	AA Tex	28	7	0	16	82	363	94	47	39	5	3	3	3	39	7	49	7	0	2	7	.222	0	9	4.28
Okla City	AAA Tex	1	0	0	1	2.1	7	0	0	0	0	0	0	0	0	0	1	0	0	0	0	.000	0	0	0.00
1996 Tulsa	AA Tex	2	0	0	2	4	15	3	0	0	0	1	0	2	0	0	1	0	0	0	0	.000	0	2	0.00
Okla City	AAA Tex	37	0	0	28	56	232	48	21	18	2	2	0	0	15	2	31	2	0	3	3	.500	0	6	2.89
Pawtucket	AAA Bos	7	0	0	6	8	26	1	0	0	0	0	0	0	2	0	8	0	0	0	0	.000	0	4	0.00
1997 Pawtucket	AAA Bos	23	0	0	19	32.1	144	36	18	17	4	1	0	2	11	1	21	1	0	5	3	.625	0	8	4.73
1999 Iowa	AAA ChC	49	5	0	14	92.2	422	105	65	56	5	4	4	3	44	2	69	7	1	3	8	.273	0	0	5.44
1996 Boston	AL	11	0	0	3	10.2	54	15	5	4	2	0	0	1	8	0	9	0	0	2	0	1.000	0	0	3.38
1997 Boston	AL	33	0	0	12	45.2	215	60	34	31	7	0	2	0	22	4	18	0	0	1	1	.500	0	1	6.11
8 Min. YEARS		323	15	0	219	509.1	2250	489	277	232	28	19	16	26	261	23	385	51	10	20	41	.328	0	98	4.10
2 Maj. YEARS		44	0	0	15	56.1	269	75	39	35	9	0	2	1	30	4	27	0	0	3	1	.750	0	3	5.59

Denny Lail

Pitches: Right **Bats:** Right **Pos:** P **Ht:** 6'1" **Wt:** 172 **Born:** 9/10/74 **Age:** 25

Year Team	Lg Org	G	GS	CG	GF	IP	BFP	H	R	ER	HR	SH	SF	HB	TBB	IBB	SO	WP	Bk	W	L	Pct.	ShO	Sv	ERA
		HOW MUCH HE PITCHED						WHAT HE GAVE UP												THE RESULTS					
1995 Oneonta	A- NYY	13	13	0	0	68	309	66	38	30	3	1	4	5	31	0	59	1	0	5	6	.455	0	0	3.97
1996 Greensboro	A NYY	11	0	0	1	23	100	19	16	12	2	0	0	2	11	1	24	4	0	1	0	1.000	0	0	4.70
Tampa	A+ NYY	31	0	0	8	35.1	152	37	11	10	0	1	0	1	14	2	21	2	0	4	0	1.000	0	1	2.55
1997 Tampa	A+ NYY	44	1	0	13	62.1	267	67	38	27	2	1	5	0	23	7	40	4	0	3	5	.375	0	1	3.90
1998 Norwich	AA NYY	8	0	0	0	10	49	15	6	6	1	0	0	0	7	2	9	0	0	0	0	.000	0	0	5.40
Tampa	A+ NYY	31	0	0	13	48.2	211	44	24	22	3	1	2	1	25	0	46	4	1	4	0	1.000	0	1	4.07
1999 Tampa	A+ NYY	22	4	0	6	60.2	237	45	17	14	2	0	1	1	16	0	53	1	0	1	3	.250	0	0	2.08
Norwich	AA NYY	6	6	0	0	41.1	156	24	12	8	1	1	0	0	11	0	29	1	1	5	0	1.000	0	0	1.74
5 Min. YEARS		166	24	0	41	349.1	1481	317	162	129	14	5	12	10	138	12	281	17	2	23	14	.622	0	5	3.32

Jason Lakman

Pitches: Right **Bats:** Right **Pos:** P **Ht:** 6'4" **Wt:** 220 **Born:** 10/17/76 **Age:** 23

Year Team	Lg Org	G	GS	CG	GF	IP	BFP	H	R	ER	HR	SH	SF	HB	TBB	IBB	SO	WP	Bk	W	L	Pct.	ShO	Sv	ERA
		HOW MUCH HE PITCHED						WHAT HE GAVE UP												THE RESULTS					
1995 White Sox	R CWS	9	5	0	1	41.1	181	44	17	15	2	0	2	5	12	0	23	2	2	3	0	1.000	0	0	3.27
1996 Hickory	A CWS	13	13	0	0	63.2	302	66	55	48	7	0	1	4	43	0	43	7	3	0	6	.000	0	0	6.79
Bristol	R+ CWS	13	13	1	0	66.2	312	70	48	42	5	0	3	6	38	0	64	13	1	4	4	.500	0	0	5.67
1997 Hickory	A CWS	27	27	3	0	154.2	667	139	82	67	11	5	1	4	70	0	168	24	1	10	9	.526	0	0	3.90
1998 Winston-Sal	A+ CWS	13	13	1	0	86	363	62	37	36	0	2	2	17	30	0	98	3	0	3	2	.600	0	0	3.77
Birmingham	AA CWS	15	15	0	0	72.1	352	89	70	64	15	1	3	8	40	0	79	6	2	0	10	.000	0	0	7.96
1999 Birmingham	AA CWS	3	0	0	2	3	22	5	5	5	0	0	0	2	9	0	3	1	0	0	0	.000	0	0	15.00
Winston-Sal	A+ CWS	20	20	2	0	119.2	531	108	69	58	4	3	4	8	55	1	110	14	0	9	8	.529	0	0	4.36
5 Min. YEARS		113	106	7	3	607.1	2730	581	383	335	44	11	16	54	297	1	588	74	9	29	39	.426	0	0	4.96

Mike Lamb

Bats: Left **Throws:** Right **Pos:** 3B **Ht:** 6'1" **Wt:** 185 **Born:** 8/9/75 **Age:** 24

Year Team	Lg Org	G	AB	H	2B	3B	HR	TB	R	RBI	TBB	IBB	SO	HBP	SH	SF	SB	CS	SB%	GDP	Avg	OBP	SLG
								BATTING										BASERUNNING			PERCENTAGES		
1997 Pulaski	R+ Tex	60	233	78	19	3	9	130	59	47	31	2	18	4	2	6	7	2	.78	5	.335	.412	.558
1998 Charlotte	A+ Tex	135	536	162	35	3	9	230	83	93	45	5	80	1	2	9	19	7	.70	10	.302	.356	.429
1999 Tulsa	AA Tex	137	544	176	51	5	21	300	98	100	53	5	65	7	1	8	4	3	.57	11	.324	.386	.551
Oklahoma	AAA Tex	2	2	1	0	0	0	1	0	0	1	1	0	1	0	0	0	1	.00	0	.500	.750	.500
3 Min. YEARS		334	1315	417	105	11	39	661	240	240	130	13	146	16	5	22	29	13	.69	26	.317	.380	.503

Ryan Lane

Bats: Right **Throws:** Right **Pos:** DH   **Ht:** 6'1" **Wt:** 185 **Born:** 7/6/74 **Age:** 25

Year Team	Lg Org	G	AB	H	2B	3B	HR	TB	R	RBI	TBB	IBB	SO	HBP	SH	SF	SB	CS	SB%	GDP	Avg	OBP	SLG
1993 Twins	R Min	43	138	20	3	2	0	27	15	5	15	0	38	2	3	1	3	1	.75	2	.145	.237	.196
1994 Elizabethtn	R+ Min	59	202	48	13	0	3	70	32	18	26	0	47	2	3	2	4	3	.57	4	.238	.328	.347
1995 Fort Wayne	A Min	115	432	115	37	1	6	172	69	56	65	0	92	7	6	4	17	9	.65	9	.266	.368	.398
1996 Fort Myers	A+ Min	106	404	110	20	7	9	171	74	62	60	0	96	6	6	9	21	9	.70	2	.272	.367	.423
Hardware Cy	AA Min	33	117	26	5	1	2	39	13	12	8	0	29	0	2	1	3	4	.43	1	.222	.270	.333
1997 New Britain	AA Min	128	444	115	26	2	5	160	63	56	43	0	79	1	8	7	18	7	.72	5	.259	.321	.360
1998 Twins	R Min	18	65	19	5	1	2	32	9	10	4	0	13	0	1	0	2	1	.67	1	.292	.333	.492
1999 New Britain	AA Min	17	49	14	0	1	3	25	6	6	7	1	10	2	0	0	2	2	.50	1	.286	.397	.510
Tulsa	AA Tex	77	264	72	23	5	9	132	38	48	26	0	47	1	0	4	5	2	.71	9	.273	.336	.500
7 Min. YEARS		596	2115	539	132	20	39	828	319	273	254	1	451	21	29	28	75	38	.66	34	.255	.337	.391

Selwyn Langaigne

Bats: Left **Throws:** Left **Pos:** OF   **Ht:** 6'0" **Wt:** 185 **Born:** 3/22/76 **Age:** 24

Year Team	Lg Org	G	AB	H	2B	3B	HR	TB	R	RBI	TBB	IBB	SO	HBP	SH	SF	SB	CS	SB%	GDP	Avg	OBP	SLG
1996 Medcine Hat	R+ Tor	32	100	26	4	1	2	38	19	11	17	0	20	1	2	0	8	2	.80	4	.260	.373	.380
Hagerstown	A Tor	4	14	2	0	0	0	2	1	1	1	0	5	0	0	0	2	0	1.00	0	.143	.200	.143
Dunedin	A+ Tor	31	117	26	2	3	0	34	16	4	9	0	30	2	4	0	1	3	.25	5	.222	.289	.291
1997 Dunedin	A+ Tor	42	90	17	3	0	1	23	9	7	10	0	26	0	4	0	4	1	.80	4	.189	.270	.256
St.Cathrnes	A- Tor	74	266	85	15	4	1	111	50	39	48	1	46	2	0	3	19	9	.68	5	.320	.423	.417
1998 Dunedin	A+ Tor	128	475	124	7	0	0	131	52	38	37	0	73	2	7	2	21	17	.55	12	.261	.316	.276
1999 Knoxville	AA Tor	40	123	30	4	1	0	36	18	10	10	0	25	0	2	0	3	4	.43	10	.244	.301	.293
Dunedin	A+ Tor	62	201	59	9	1	2	76	35	25	16	0	29	0	3	3	5	5	.50	2	.294	.341	.378
4 Min. YEARS		413	1386	369	44	10	6	451	200	135	148	1	254	7	22	8	63	41	.61	42	.266	.338	.325

Yovanny Lara

Pitches: Right **Bats:** Right **Pos:** P   **Ht:** 6'4" **Wt:** 180 **Born:** 9/20/75 **Age:** 24

Year Team	Lg Org	G	GS	CG	GF	IP	BFP	H	R	ER	HR	SH	SF	HB	TBB	IBB	SO	WP	Bk	W	L	Pct.	ShO	Sv	ERA
1995 Expos	R Mon	11	4	0	1	30	139	35	21	17	4	0	3	2	19	0	16	0	1	1	2	.333	0	0	5.10
1996 Vermont	A- Mon	15	15	2	0	92.1	392	95	54	48	5	3	3	4	27	0	63	7	1	6	3	.667	0	0	4.68
1997 Cape Fear	A Mon	28	27	1	0	170	742	199	107	86	13	9	9	9	45	0	100	13	1	9	12	.429	0	0	4.55
1998 Cape Fear	A Mon	22	9	0	3	54.2	281	61	51	43	5	2	4	7	48	0	31	15	0	2	5	.286	0	0	7.08
1999 Harrisburg	AA Mon	9	0	0	6	13.2	71	19	12	12	2	1	0	0	8	0	10	0	0	0	0	.000	0	0	7.90
Jupiter	A+ Mon	33	0	0	15	65.1	264	59	24	20	1	7	2	0	18	2	42	2	1	3	1	.750	0	0	2.76
5 Min. YEARS		118	55	3	25	426	1889	468	269	226	30	22	21	22	165	2	262	37	4	21	23	.477	0	0	4.77

Jason LaRiviere

Bats: Right **Throws:** Right **Pos:** OF   **Ht:** 5'10" **Wt:** 180 **Born:** 9/30/73 **Age:** 26

Year Team	Lg Org	G	AB	H	2B	3B	HR	TB	R	RBI	TBB	IBB	SO	HBP	SH	SF	SB	CS	SB%	GDP	Avg	OBP	SLG
1995 New Jersey	A- StL	33	100	28	3	1	0	33	13	9	14	0	10	0	2	0	8	2	.80	2	.280	.368	.330
1996 Peoria	A StL	64	225	56	13	1	1	74	33	36	25	0	31	0	2	3	6	5	.55	5	.249	.320	.329
St. Pete	A+ StL	41	140	42	6	0	3	57	27	18	18	1	19	0	4	1	1	1	.50	1	.300	.377	.407
1997 Arkansas	AA StL	118	372	102	24	5	6	154	50	60	33	1	69	0	3	4	4	3	.57	16	.274	.330	.414
1998 Arkansas	AA StL	132	435	111	29	5	8	174	69	58	50	1	58	2	2	4	14	6	.70	18	.255	.332	.400
1999 Memphis	AAA StL	133	497	142	35	3	9	210	90	47	47	0	64	7	4	3	18	4	.82	10	.286	.354	.423
5 Min. YEARS		521	1769	481	110	15	27	702	282	228	187	3	251	9	17	15	51	21	.71	52	.272	.342	.397

Andy Larkin

Pitches: Right **Bats:** Right **Pos:** P   **Ht:** 6'4" **Wt:** 190 **Born:** 6/27/74 **Age:** 26

Year Team	Lg Org	G	GS	CG	GF	IP	BFP	H	R	ER	HR	SH	SF	HB	TBB	IBB	SO	WP	Bk	W	L	Pct.	ShO	Sv	ERA
1992 Marlins	R Fla	14	4	0	2	41.1	187	41	26	24	0	1	1	7	19	0	20	4	0	1	2	.333	0	2	5.23
1993 Elmira	A- Fla	14	14	4	0	88	368	74	43	29	1	1	3	12	23	0	89	9	1	5	7	.417	1	0	2.97
1994 Kane County	A Fla	21	21	3	0	140	577	125	53	44	6	3	3	19	27	0	125	4	0	9	7	.563	1	0	2.83
1995 Portland	AA Fla	9	9	0	0	49.1	216	29	16	15	5	4	0	6	11	2	23	1	0	1	2	.333	0	0	3.38
1996 Brevard Cty	A+ Fla	6	6	0	0	27.2	126	34	20	13	0	0	1	7	7	0	18	3	0	0	4	.000	0	0	4.23
Portland	AA Fla	8	8	0	0	49.1	195	45	18	17	6	2	0	2	10	0	40	3	0	4	1	.800	0	0	3.10
1997 Charlotte	AAA Fla	28	27	3	0	144.1	669	166	109	97	23	3	3	15	76	2	103	4	1	6	11	.353	0	0	6.05
1998 Charlotte	AAA Fla	11	10	0	0	53.2	246	55	39	38	8	2	0	4	32	2	41	2	0	4	1	.800	0	0	6.37
1999 Brevard Cty	A+ Fla	4	4	0	0	15	66	16	5	4	0	0	2	3	3	0	7	0	0	1	0	1.000	0	0	2.40
Portland	AA Fla	7	1	0	3	12.2	57	16	10	10	2	0	0	0	4	0	7	1	0	1	1	.500	0	0	7.11
1996 Florida	NL	1	1	0	0	5	22	3	1	1	0	0	0	1	4	0	2	0	0	0	0	.000	0	0	1.80
1998 Florida	NL	17	14	0	0	74.2	373	101	87	80	12	5	2	4	55	3	43	3	0	3	8	.273	0	0	9.64
8 Min. YEARS		122	104	10	5	612	2651	601	339	291	51	16	13	75	212	6	473	31	2	31	37	.456	2	2	4.28
2 Maj. YEARS		18	15	0	0	79.2	395	104	88	81	12	5	2	5	59	3	45	3	0	3	8	.273	0	0	9.15

Stephen Larkin

Bats: Left **Throws:** Left **Pos:** 1B   **Ht:** 6'0" **Wt:** 190 **Born:** 7/24/73 **Age:** 26

Year Team	Lg Org	G	AB	H	2B	3B	HR	TB	R	RBI	TBB	IBB	SO	HBP	SH	SF	SB	CS	SB%	GDP	Avg	OBP	SLG
1994 Hudson Val	A- Tex	66	237	47	10	1	2	65	26	22	30	1	47	1	0	3	10	5	.67	3	.198	.288	.274
1995 Chston-SC	A Tex	113	369	94	19	1	5	130	50	45	54	2	80	1	3	5	18	10	.64	7	.255	.347	.352

Year Team	Lg Org	G	AB	H	2B	3B	HR	TB	R	RBI	TBB	IBB	SO	HBP	SH	SF	SB	CS	SB%	GDP	Avg	OBP	SLG
Winston-Sal	A+ Cin	13	50	11	1	0	0	12	2	4	3	1	12	0	0	1	2	2	.50	0	.220	.259	.240
1996 Winston-Sal	A+ Cin	39	117	21	2	0	3	32	13	6	14	2	25	0	1	1	6	1	.86	6	.179	.265	.274
Chstn-WV	A Cin	58	203	55	7	2	5	81	30	33	35	1	40	4	1	1	5	4	.56	2	.271	.387	.399
1997 Chstn-WV	A Cin	129	464	129	23	10	13	211	88	79	52	1	83	5	0	5	28	9	.76	6	.278	.354	.455
1998 Chattanooga	AA Cin	80	267	61	22	1	3	94	33	31	23	0	52	1	1	4	3	4	.43	7	.228	.288	.352
1999 Chattanooga	AA Cin	104	264	79	16	2	4	111	34	42	31	3	44	0	3	6	7	3	.70	3	.299	.365	.420
1998 Cincinnati	NL	1	3	1	0	0	0	1	0	0	0	0	1	0	0	0	0	0	.00	0	.333	.333	.333
6 Min. YEARS		602	1971	497	100	17	35	736	276	262	242	11	383	12	9	26	79	38	.68	34	.252	.334	.373

Greg LaRocca

Bats: Right **Throws:** Right **Pos:** 3B-SS **Ht:** 5'11" **Wt:** 185 **Born:** 11/10/72 **Age:** 27

Year Team	Lg Org	G	AB	H	2B	3B	HR	TB	R	RBI	TBB	IBB	SO	HBP	SH	SF	SB	CS	SB%	GDP	Avg	OBP	SLG
1994 Spokane	A- SD	42	158	46	9	2	0	59	20	14	14	0	18	2	2	0	7	2	.78	4	.291	.356	.373
Rancho Cuca	A+ SD	28	85	14	5	1	1	24	7	8	7	0	11	2	1	1	3	1	.75	2	.165	.242	.282
1995 Rancho Cuca	A+ SD	125	466	150	36	5	8	220	77	74	44	0	77	12	0	2	15	4	.79	13	.322	.393	.472
Memphis	AA SD	2	7	1	0	0	0	1	0	0	0	0	1	0	0	0	0	1	.00	1	.143	.143	.143
1996 Memphis	AA SD	128	445	122	22	5	6	172	66	42	51	4	58	10	5	5	5	9	.36	9	.274	.358	.387
1997 Mobile	AA SD	76	300	80	16	2	3	109	44	31	26	0	46	8	0	5	8	3	.73	4	.267	.336	.363
1998 Las Vegas	AAA SD	95	304	94	22	5	8	150	55	39	19	0	48	12	2	2	7	4	.04	0	.309	.371	.403
1999 Las Vegas	AAA SD	14	51	14	2	0	0	16	3	2	2	0	10	4	0	1	2	2	.50	3	.275	.345	.314
6 Min. YEARS		510	1816	521	112	20	26	751	272	210	163	4	269	50	10	16	47	26	.64	39	.287	.359	.414

Brandon Larson

Bats: Right **Throws:** Right **Pos:** 3B **Ht:** 6'0" **Wt:** 205 **Born:** 5/24/76 **Age:** 24

Year Team	Lg Org	G	AB	H	2B	3B	HR	TB	R	RBI	TBB	IBB	SO	HBP	SH	SF	SB	CS	SB%	GDP	Avg	OBP	SLG
1997 Chattanooga	AA Cin	11	41	11	5	1	0	18	4	6	1	0	10	0	0	1	0	0	.00	1	.268	.279	.439
1998 Burlington	A Cin	18	68	15	3	0	2	24	5	9	4	0	16	0	0	0	2	1	.67	1	.221	.264	.353
1999 Rockford	A Cin	69	250	75	18	1	13	134	38	52	25	1	67	3	0	3	12	2	.86	7	.300	.367	.536
Chattanooga	AA Cin	43	172	49	10	0	12	95	28	42	10	1	51	3	0	2	4	5	.44	3	.285	.332	.552
3 Min. YEARS		141	531	150	36	2	27	271	75	109	40	2	144	6	0	6	18	8	.69	12	.282	.336	.510

Joe Lawrence

Bats: Right **Throws:** Right **Pos:** 3B **Ht:** 6'2" **Wt:** 190 **Born:** 2/13/77 **Age:** 23

Year Team	Lg Org	G	AB	H	2B	3B	HR	TB	R	RBI	TBB	IBB	SO	HBP	SH	SF	SB	CS	SB%	GDP	Avg	OBP	SLG
1996 St.Cathrnes	A- Tor	27	92	20	7	2	0	31	22	11	14	1	16	2	1	3	1	1	.50	1	.217	.324	.337
1997 Hagerstown	A Tor	116	446	102	24	1	8	152	63	38	49	0	107	5	3	2	10	12	.45	3	.229	.311	.341
1998 Dunedin	A+ Tor	125	454	140	31	6	11	216	102	44	105	2	88	4	5	1	15	12	.56	11	.308	.441	.476
1999 Knoxville	AA Tor	70	250	66	16	2	7	107	52	24	56	0	48	3	0	2	7	6	.54	10	.264	.402	.428
4 Min. YEARS		338	1242	328	78	11	26	506	239	117	224	3	259	14	9	8	33	31	.52	25	.264	.380	.407

Sean Lawrence

Pitches: Left **Bats:** Left **Pos:** P **Ht:** 6'4" **Wt:** 215 **Born:** 9/2/70 **Age:** 29

Year Team	Lg Org	G	GS	CG	GF	IP	BFP	H	R	ER	HR	SH	SF	HB	TBB	IBB	SO	WP	Bk	W	L	Pct.	ShO	Sv	ERA
1992 Welland	A- Pit	15	15	0	0	74	330	75	55	43	10	2	2	2	34	1	71	6	3	3	6	.333	0	0	5.23
1993 Augusta	A Pit	22	22	0	0	121	516	108	59	42	9	7	4	4	50	1	96	6	0	6	8	.429	0	0	3.12
Salem	A+ Pit	4	4	0	0	15	77	25	19	17	1	2	1	0	9	0	14	2	0	1	3	.250	0	0	10.20
1994 Salem	A+ Pit	12	12	0	0	72	312	76	38	21	8	1	2	3	18	0	66	2	0	4	2	.667	0	0	2.63
1995 Carolina	AA Pit	12	3	0	3	21.1	96	27	13	13	2	0	1	0	8	1	19	0	0	0	0	.000	0	0	5.48
Lynchburg	A+ Pit	20	19	0	0	111	465	115	56	52	16	3	3	1	25	0	82	3	0	5	8	.385	0	0	4.22
1996 Carolina	AA Pit	37	9	0	13	82	362	80	40	36	11	2	1	3	36	1	81	0	1	3	5	.375	0	2	3.95
1997 Calgary	AAA Pit	26	26	2	0	143.1	641	154	83	67	17	9	6	3	57	3	116	6	0	8	9	.471	0	0	4.21
1998 Nashville	AAA Pit	26	26	0	0	147	634	153	86	82	20	7	2	6	57	1	126	4	1	12	9	.571	0	0	5.02
1999 Vancouver	AAA Oak	25	2	0	7	39.1	188	51	25	21	4	2	1	1	21	1	37	1	0	2	2	.500	0	0	4.81
1998 Pittsburgh	NL	7	3	0	0	19.2	92	25	16	16	4	0	2	0	10	0	12	1	0	2	1	.667	0	0	7.32
8 Min. YEARS		199	138	2	23	826	3621	864	474	394	98	35	22	24	315	9	708	30	5	44	54	.449	0	2	4.29

Tony Lawrence

Bats: Right **Throws:** Right **Pos:** C **Ht:** 6'1" **Wt:** 205 **Born:** 3/7/75 **Age:** 25

Year Team	Lg Org	G	AB	H	2B	3B	HR	TB	R	RBI	TBB	IBB	SO	HBP	SH	SF	SB	CS	SB%	GDP	Avg	OBP	SLG
1997 Idaho Falls	R+ SD	56	210	56	8	2	5	89	40	36	34	3	48	2	0	3	7	3	.70	2	.267	.369	.424
1998 Clinton	A SD	86	296	69	16	3	7	112	35	40	35	1	93	1	2	4	5	4	.56	8	.233	.313	.378
1999 Fort Wayne	A SD	46	142	28	8	1	0	38	11	8	21	0	45	4	2	0	1	1	.50	2	.197	.317	.268
Rockford	A Cin	10	35	6	2	0	0	8	2	5	2	0	12	0	0	0	0	0	.00	2	.171	.216	.229
Chattanooga	AA Cin	4	8	1	0	0	0	1	0	1	1	0	4	1	0	0	0	0	.00	0	.125	.300	.125
3 Min. YEARS		202	691	160	34	6	14	248	88	90	93	4	202	8	4	7	13	8	.62	16	.232	.327	.359

Jason Layne

Bats: Left **Throws:** Right **Pos:** 1B   **Ht:** 6'2" **Wt:** 215 **Born:** 5/17/73 **Age:** 27

Year Team	Lg Org	G	AB	H	2B	3B	HR	TB	R	RBI	TBB	IBB	SO	HBP	SH	SF	SB	CS	SB%	GDP	Avg	OBP	SLG
1996 Spokane	A- KC	41	126	36	9	3	5	66	24	27	17	1	34	5	0	0	0	0	.00	0	.286	.392	.524
Lansing	A KC	25	91	23	4	0	1	30	11	16	13	0	23	0	0	0	1	0	1.00	1	.253	.346	.330
1997 Lansing	A KC	98	337	93	22	3	9	148	54	68	54	3	85	9	0	3	0	0	.00	5	.276	.387	.439
1998 Wilmington	A+ KC	108	357	97	28	8	10	171	54	71	45	2	108	9	2	5	1	0	1.00	5	.272	.363	.479
1999 Wichita	AA KC	30	92	20	4	0	2	30	13	12	15	0	24	1	1	0	1	2	.33	3	.217	.333	.326
4 Min. YEARS		302	1003	269	67	14	27	445	156	194	144	6	274	24	3	8	3	2	.60	14	.268	.371	.444

Jalal Leach

Bats: Left **Throws:** Left **Pos:** OF   **Ht:** 6'2" **Wt:** 200 **Born:** 3/14/69 **Age:** 31

Year Team	Lg Org	G	AB	H	2B	3B	HR	TB	R	RBI	TBB	IBB	SO	HBP	SH	SF	SB	CS	SB%	GDP	Avg	OBP	SLG
1990 Oneonta	A- NYY	69	257	74	7	1	2	89	41	18	37	3	52	0	4	0	33	13	.72	1	.288	.378	.346
1991 Ft. Laud	A+ NYY	122	468	119	13	9	2	156	48	42	44	3	122	0	3	3	28	12	.70	5	.254	.317	.333
1992 Pr William	A+ NYY	128	462	122	22	7	5	173	61	65	47	2	114	0	3	5	18	9	.67	8	.264	.329	.374
1993 Albany-Colo	AA NYY	125	457	129	19	9	14	208	64	79	47	3	113	1	0	4	16	12	.57	5	.282	.348	.455
1994 Columbus	AAA NYY	132	444	116	18	9	6	170	56	56	39	3	106	1	3	4	14	12	.54	8	.261	.320	.383
1995 Columbus	AAA NYY	88	272	66	12	5	6	106	37	31	22	1	60	2	1	4	11	4	.73	5	.243	.300	.390
1996 Harrisburg	AA Mon	83	268	88	22	3	6	134	38	48	21	4	55	0	2	4	3	7	.30	6	.328	.372	.500
Ottawa	AAA Mon	37	101	32	4	0	3	45	12	9	8	1	17	0	0	0	0	0	.00	1	.317	.367	.446
1997 Tacoma	AAA Sea	115	415	128	26	3	9	187	56	55	32	2	74	1	2	3	6	6	.50	11	.308	.357	.451
1998 Shreveport	AA SF	72	253	87	17	2	10	138	43	45	36	3	35	0	0	5	10	2	.83	6	.344	.418	.545
Fresno	AAA SF	35	130	46	8	2	9	85	23	26	8	1	26	0	0	1	3	2	.60	1	.354	.388	.654
1999 Fresno	AAA SF	116	371	109	19	5	15	183	58	75	27	2	67	0	2	4	8	7	.53	8	.294	.338	.493
10 Min. YEARS		1122	3898	1116	187	55	87	1674	537	549	368	28	841	5	20	37	150	86	.64	65	.286	.346	.429

Eric LeBlanc

Pitches: Right **Bats:** Left **Pos:** P   **Ht:** 6'0" **Wt:** 195 **Born:** 7/6/73 **Age:** 26

| | | HOW MUCH HE PITCHED | | | | | | WHAT HE GAVE UP | | | | | | | | | | THE RESULTS | | | | | |
Year Team	Lg Org	G	GS	CG	GF	IP	BFP	H	R	ER	HR	SH	SF	HB	TBB	IBB	SO	WP	Bk	W	L	Pct.	ShO	Sv	ERA
1996 Princeton	R+ Cin	9	6	0	3	45.2	198	39	29	23	0	0	1	2	16	0	51	2	1	4	1	.800	0	1	4.53
Chstn-WV	A Cin	6	5	0	0	29	129	33	18	16	2	0	2	0	13	0	28	0	0	1	2	.333	0	0	4.97
1997 Chstn-WV	A Cin	24	13	2	2	107	440	98	51	40	7	0	5	6	29	1	77	7	2	10	7	.588	0	1	3.36
Chattanooga	AA Cin	8	8	0	0	50	216	53	35	31	3	2	3	1	21	0	25	2	2	2	4	.333	0	0	5.58
1998 Burlington	A Cin	19	6	0	5	56.2	237	51	25	19	1	1	3	4	20	0	41	6	0	3	3	.500	0	0	3.02
Chattanooga	AA Cin	23	7	0	6	66.1	286	56	33	29	5	1	4	1	38	0	49	7	1	4	3	.571	0	0	3.93
1999 Rockford	A Cin	2	1	0	1	9.2	38	5	2	2	0	0	0	1	4	0	9	0	0	0	0	.000	0	1	1.86
Chattanooga	AA Cin	15	9	0	2	65.2	271	63	33	28	7	4	1	1	20	1	37	2	0	3	3	.500	0	0	3.84
Indianapolis	AAA Cin	14	3	0	1	44.1	209	57	43	35	4	1	5	4	19	1	26	3	0	1	2	.333	0	1	7.11
4 Min. YEARS		120	58	2	20	474.1	2024	455	269	223	29	9	24	20	180	3	343	29	6	28	25	.528	0	4	4.23

Matthew LeCroy

Bats: Right **Throws:** Right **Pos:** C   **Ht:** 6'2" **Wt:** 225 **Born:** 12/13/75 **Age:** 24

Year Team	Lg Org	G	AB	H	2B	3B	HR	TB	R	RBI	TBB	IBB	SO	HBP	SH	SF	SB	CS	SB%	GDP	Avg	OBP	SLG
1998 Fort Wayne	A Min	64	225	62	17	1	9	108	33	40	34	1	45	8	0	2	0	0	.00	6	.276	.387	.480
Fort Myers	A+ Min	51	200	61	9	1	12	108	32	51	21	1	35	4	0	6	2	1	.67	6	.305	.372	.540
Salt Lake	AAA Min	3	13	4	1	0	2	11	2	4	0	0	7	0	0	0	0	0	.00	0	.308	.308	.846
1999 Fort Myers	A+ Min	89	333	93	20	1	20	175	54	69	42	3	51	3	0	1	0	1	.00	10	.279	.364	.526
Salt Lake	AAA Min	29	119	36	4	1	10	72	23	30	5	0	22	1	0	2	0	1	.00	8	.303	.331	.605
2 Min. YEARS		236	890	256	51	4	53	474	144	194	102	5	160	16	0	11	2	3	.40	33	.288	.367	.533

Derek Lee

Pitches: Left **Bats:** Left **Pos:** P   **Ht:** 6'4" **Wt:** 185 **Born:** 8/20/74 **Age:** 25

| | | HOW MUCH HE PITCHED | | | | | | WHAT HE GAVE UP | | | | | | | | | | THE RESULTS | | | | | |
Year Team	Lg Org	G	GS	CG	GF	IP	BFP	H	R	ER	HR	SH	SF	HB	TBB	IBB	SO	WP	Bk	W	L	Pct.	ShO	Sv	ERA
1997 Ogden	R+ Mil	14	13	0	0	74.1	325	89	49	32	3	2	6	3	20	0	71	8	1	4	4	.500	0	0	3.87
1998 Stockton	A+ Mil	30	18	1	2	136	583	134	70	63	9	4	5	5	48	1	141	8	0	5	9	.357	1	1	4.17
1999 Huntsville	AA Mil	26	21	4	0	140	604	143	70	60	16	6	2	8	51	4	77	5	1	8	8	.500	2	0	3.86
3 Min. YEARS		70	52	5	2	350.1	1512	366	189	155	28	12	13	16	119	5	289	21	2	17	21	.447	3	1	3.98

Brandon Leese

Pitches: Right **Bats:** Right **Pos:** P   **Ht:** 6'4" **Wt:** 205 **Born:** 10/8/75 **Age:** 24

| | | HOW MUCH HE PITCHED | | | | | | WHAT HE GAVE UP | | | | | | | | | | THE RESULTS | | | | | |
Year Team	Lg Org	G	GS	CG	GF	IP	BFP	H	R	ER	HR	SH	SF	HB	TBB	IBB	SO	WP	Bk	W	L	Pct.	ShO	Sv	ERA
1996 Bellingham	A- SF	16	15	0	0	80.1	341	59	39	29	6	0	2	5	37	0	90	8	0	5	6	.455	0	0	3.25
1997 San Jose	A+ SF	19	19	0	0	112	475	99	44	38	11	1	0	4	46	2	99	15	0	7	5	.583	0	0	3.05
Kane County	A Fla	7	6	0	0	42.1	171	27	18	18	0	1	2	3	18	0	32	3	1	3	1	.750	0	0	3.83
1998 Brevard Cty	A+ Fla	8	8	0	0	47.1	209	63	36	30	3	1	1	2	7	0	30	2	0	1	5	.167	0	0	5.70
Portland	AA Fla	20	20	0	0	126.1	544	137	70	58	16	11	1	5	37	1	94	2	0	7	4	.364	0	0	4.13
1999 Portland	AA Fla	20	11	0	2	81.2	370	110	66	52	8	2	0	7	20	0	52	2	2	4	4	.500	0	0	5.73
4 Min. YEARS		90	79	0	2	490	2110	495	273	225	44	16	6	26	165	3	397	32	3	24	28	.462	0	0	4.13

Adam Leggett

Bats: Both **Throws:** Right **Pos:** 2B **Ht:** 6'0" **Wt:** 190 **Born:** 4/3/76 **Age:** 24

Year Team	Lg Org	G	AB	H	2B	3B	HR	TB	R	RBI	TBB	IBB	SO	HBP	SH	SF	SB	CS	SB%	GDP	Avg	OBP	SLG
1997 Boise	A- Ana	62	219	49	16	2	1	72	47	32	34	1	54	6	0	3	8	1	.89	7	.224	.340	.329
1998 Cedar Rapds	A Ana	125	443	121	26	3	11	186	83	50	80	3	83	8	8	3	24	14	.63	9	.273	.391	.420
1999 Lk Elsinore	A+ Ana	57	185	45	14	0	3	68	19	25	20	1	30	2	2	2	6	3	.67	3	.243	.321	.368
Erie	AA Ana	24	72	12	0	0	1	15	8	6	21	1	14	0	1	1	2	3	.40	2	.167	.351	.208
3 Min. YEARS		268	919	227	56	5	16	341	157	113	155	6	181	16	11	9	40	21	.66	21	.247	.362	.371

Chris Lemonis

Bats: Left **Throws:** Right **Pos:** 2B **Ht:** 5'11" **Wt:** 185 **Born:** 8/21/73 **Age:** 26

Year Team	Lg Org	G	AB	H	2B	3B	HR	TB	R	RBI	TBB	IBB	SO	HBP	SH	SF	SB	CS	SB%	GDP	Avg	OBP	SLG
1995 Jamestown	A- Det	57	191	45	7	2	0	56	19	21	18	0	32	2	3	1	5	1	.83	4	.236	.307	.293
1996 Visalia	A+ Det	126	482	134	27	3	14	209	69	82	35	1	99	6	2	4	12	5	.71	12	.278	.332	.434
1997 W Michigan	A Det	48	158	48	10	1	3	69	27	30	9	1	31	1	0	0	2	5	.29	3	.304	.345	.437
1998 Lakeland	A+ Det	93	327	92	17	1	3	120	45	48	27	3	46	2	0	3	1	1	.50	10	.281	.337	.367
1999 Jacksnville	AA Det	75	265	75	16	1	5	108	35	38	19	0	45	6	0	0	1	2	.33	6	.283	.345	.408
5 Min. YEARS		399	1423	394	77	8	25	562	195	219	108	5	253	17	5	8	21	14	.60	35	.277	.334	.395

Donny Leon

Bats: Both **Throws:** Right **Pos:** 3B **Ht:** 6'2" **Wt:** 185 **Born:** 5/7/76 **Age:** 24

Year Team	Lg Org	G	AB	H	2B	3B	HR	TB	R	RBI	TBB	IBB	SO	HBP	SH	SF	SB	CS	SB%	GDP	Avg	OBP	SLG
1995 Yankees	R NYY	16	41	7	1	0	0	8	3	5	3	0	14	0	0	0	0	1	1.00	0	.171	.227	.195
1996 Yankees	R NYY	53	191	69	14	4	6	109	30	46	9	2	30	4	1	4	1	2	.33	2	.361	.394	.571
1997 Greensboro	A NYY	137	516	131	32	1	12	201	45	74	15	2	106	5	2	7	6	4	.60	13	.254	.278	.390
1998 Tampa	A+ NYY	100	385	112	24	1	10	168	54	59	23	1	64	7	1	2	0	0	.00	9	.291	.341	.436
1999 Norwich	AA NYY	118	457	138	34	2	21	239	69	100	34	2	102	3	1	7	0	0	.00	10	.302	.349	.523
5 Min. YEARS		424	1590	457	105	8	49	725	201	284	84	7	316	19	5	20	7	7	.50	34	.287	.327	.456

Jose Leon

Bats: Right **Throws:** Right **Pos:** 3B **Ht:** 6'0" **Wt:** 175 **Born:** 12/8/76 **Age:** 23

Year Team	Lg Org	G	AB	H	2B	3B	HR	TB	R	RBI	TBB	IBB	SO	HBP	SH	SF	SB	CS	SB%	GDP	Avg	OBP	SLG
1994 Cardinals	R StL	46	161	37	3	2	0	44	16	17	11	0	51	3	1	4	1	4	.20	4	.230	.285	.273
1995 Savannah	A StL	41	133	22	4	1	0	28	15	11	10	1	46	1	1	0	0	1	.00	6	.165	.229	.211
1996 Johnson Cy	R+ StL	59	222	55	9	3	10	100	29	36	17	0	92	2	2	1	5	3	.63	1	.248	.306	.450
New Jersey	A- StL	7	28	8	3	1	1	16	4	3	0	0	7	2	0	0	0	0	.00	0	.286	.333	.571
1997 Peoria	A StL	118	399	92	21	2	20	177	50	54	32	1	122	9	2	2	6	5	.55	10	.231	.301	.444
1998 Pr William	A+ StL	124	436	127	31	3	21	227	77	74	53	4	137	9	2	4	5	3	.63	6	.291	.376	.521
1999 Arkansas	AA StL	112	335	78	17	0	18	149	37	54	25	0	114	6	1	1	3	3	.50	5	.233	.297	.445
6 Min. YEARS		507	1714	419	88	12	70	741	228	249	148	6	569	32	9	12	20	19	.51	32	.244	.314	.432

John LeRoy

Pitches: Right **Bats:** Right **Pos:** P **Ht:** 6'3" **Wt:** 175 **Born:** 4/19/75 **Age:** 25

Year Team	Lg Org	G	GS	CG	GF	IP	BFP	H	R	ER	HR	SH	SF	HB	TBB	IBB	SO	WP	Bk	W	L	Pct.	ShO	Sv	ERA
1993 Braves	R Atl	10	2	0	4	26.1	107	21	9	6	1	1	1	0	8	1	32	2	0	2	2	.500	0	1	2.05
1994 Macon	A Atl	10	9	0	0	40.1	173	36	21	20	4	2	1	0	20	0	44	1	5	3	3	.500	0	0	4.46
1995 Durham	A+ Atl	24	22	1	0	125.2	545	128	82	76	17	2	5	5	57	1	77	5	1	6	9	.400	0	0	5.44
1996 Durham	A+ Atl	19	19	0	0	110.2	463	91	47	43	6	4	5	2	52	0	94	10	2	7	4	.636	0	0	3.50
Greenville	AA Atl	8	8	0	0	45.1	193	43	18	15	5	2	2	2	18	1	38	4	1	1	1	.500	0	0	2.98
1997 Greenville	AA Atl	29	14	0	9	98.1	444	105	59	55	20	1	2	5	43	1	84	15	1	5	5	.500	0	1	5.03
1998 Durham	AAA TB	4	0	0	1	4	27	11	12	12	1	0	0	0	5	0	1	0	1	0	1	.000	0	0	27.00
St. Pete	A+ TB	11	0	0	3	17.2	75	18	9	9	1	3	0	2	6	0	17	0	0	1	1	.500	0	0	4.58
Orlando	AA TB	12	0	0	3	22.1	97	22	17	16	5	0	0	0	10	0	12	1	0	1	0	1.000	0	0	6.45
1999 Orlando	AA TB	4	0	0	2	6	30	7	3	3	2	0	0	0	5	0	5	0	0	0	0	.000	0	0	4.50
1997 Atlanta	NL	2	0	0	0	2	10	1	0	0	0	0	0	0	3	1	3	0	0	1	0	1.000	0	0	0.00
7 Min. YEARS		131	74	1	22	496.2	2154	482	277	255	62	15	16	16	224	4	404	38	11	26	26	.500	0	2	4.62

Brian Lesher

Bats: Right **Throws:** Left **Pos:** 1B-OF **Ht:** 6'5" **Wt:** 222 **Born:** 3/5/71 **Age:** 29

Year Team	Lg Org	G	AB	H	2B	3B	HR	TB	R	RBI	TBB	IBB	SO	HBP	SH	SF	SB	CS	SB%	GDP	Avg	OBP	SLG
1992 Sou Oregon	A- Oak	46	136	26	7	1	3	44	21	18	12	0	35	2	0	1	3	7	.30	3	.191	.265	.324
1993 Madison	A Oak	119	394	108	13	5	5	146	63	47	46	0	102	9	6	6	20	9	.69	13	.274	.358	.371
1994 Modesto	A+ Oak	117	393	114	21	0	14	177	76	68	81	5	84	8	0	8	11	11	.50	8	.290	.414	.450
1995 Huntsville	AA Oak	127	471	123	23	2	19	207	78	71	64	2	110	2	0	1	7	8	.47	7	.261	.351	.439
1996 Edmonton	AAA Oak	109	414	119	29	2	18	206	57	75	36	0	108	7	2	3	6	5	.55	9	.287	.352	.498
1997 Edmonton	AAA Oak	110	415	134	27	5	21	234	85	78	64	3	86	3	0	2	14	3	.82	14	.323	.415	.564
1998 Edmonton	AAA Oak	99	360	108	31	1	11	174	62	60	46	1	96	2	0	2	3	4	.43	11	.300	.380	.483
1999 Vancouver	AAA Oak	103	387	113	29	2	14	188	66	64	41	0	71	6	2	5	8	2	.80	16	.292	.364	.486
1996 Oakland	AL	26	82	19	3	0	5	37	11	16	5	0	17	1	1	0	0	0	.00	2	.232	.281	.451
1997 Oakland	AL	46	131	30	4	1	4	48	17	16	9	0	30	0	0	2	4	1	.80	4	.229	.275	.366
1998 Oakland	AL	7	7	1	1	0	0	2	0	1	0	0	3	0	0	0	0	0	.00	0	.143	.143	.286
8 Min. YEARS		830	2970	845	180	18	105	1376	508	481	390	11	692	39	10	28	72	49	.60	81	.285	.372	.463
3 Maj. YEARS		79	220	50	8	1	9	87	28	33	14	0	50	1	1	2	4	1	.80	6	.227	.273	.395

Allen Levrault

Pitches: Right **Bats:** Right **Pos:** P   **Ht:** 6'3" **Wt:** 238 **Born:** 8/15/77 **Age:** 22

Year Team	Lg Org	G	GS	CG	GF	IP	BFP	H	R	ER	HR	SH	SF	HB	TBB	IBB	SO	WP	Bk	W	L	Pct.	ShO	Sv	ERA
				HOW MUCH HE PITCHED						WHAT HE GAVE UP											THE RESULTS			
1996 Helena	R+ Mil	18	11	0	2	71	302	70	43	42	9	0	0	8	22	0	68	4	3	4	3	.571	0	1	5.32
1997 Beloit	A Mil	24	24	1	0	131.1	561	141	89	77	18	1	2	6	40	1	112	3	12	3	10	.231	0	0	5.28
1998 Stockton	A+ Mil	16	15	4	0	97.1	388	76	33	31	8	4	3	2	27	0	86	2	1	9	3	.750	1	0	2.87
El Paso	AA Mil	11	11	0	0	62.2	281	77	51	41	7	2	2	1	17	0	46	1	1	1	5	.167	0	0	5.89
1999 Huntsville	AA Mil	16	16	2	0	99.2	404	77	44	38	11	3	2	5	33	0	82	3	3	9	2	.818	1	0	3.43
Louisville	AAA Mil	9	5	0	1	34.1	169	48	37	33	9	1	2	3	16	0	33	1	0	1	3	.250	0	0	8.65
4 Min. YEARS		94	82	7	3	496.1	2105	489	297	262	62	11	11	25	155	1	427	14	20	27	26	.509	2	1	4.75

Marc Lewis

Bats: Right **Throws:** Right **Pos:** OF   **Ht:** 6'2" **Wt:** 185 **Born:** 5/20/75 **Age:** 25

Year Team	Lg Org	G	AB	H	2B	3B	HR	TB	R	RBI	TBB	IBB	SO	HBP	SH	SF	SB	CS	SB%	GDP	Avg	OBP	SLG
				BATTING												BASERUNNING				PERCENTAGES		
1994 Red Sox	R Bos	50	197	64	13	2	3	90	32	32	10	0	19	1	2	4	16	3	.84	4	.325	.354	.457
Lynchburg	A+ Bos	8	32	6	1	0	1	10	3	5	3	0	4	0	0	0	0	2	.00	0	.188	.257	.313
1995 Michigan	A Bos	36	92	14	2	1	1	21	14	5	9	0	16	0	2	0	10	3	.77	1	.152	.228	.228
Utica	A- Bos	69	272	82	15	5	5	122	47	39	17	0	32	0	2	3	24	9	.73	6	.301	.339	.449
1996 Macon	A Atl	66	241	76	14	3	5	111	36	28	21	1	31	1	1	6	25	8	.76	6	.315	.364	.461
Durham	A+ Atl	68	262	78	12	2	6	112	43	26	24	2	37	2	3	1	25	9	.74	5	.298	.360	.427
1997 Greenville	AA Atl	135	512	140	17	3	17	214	64	67	25	3	84	8	4	2	21	14	.60	9	.273	.316	.418
1998 Salt Lake	AAA Min	119	444	130	31	1	14	205	61	68	23	0	64	1	3	2	10	11	.48	15	.293	.328	.462
1999 New Britain	AA Min	101	384	100	27	0	9	154	38	52	38	1	79	4	0	2	6	4	.60	12	.260	.332	.401
6 Min. YEARS		652	2436	690	132	17	61	1039	338	322	170	7	366	17	17	20	137	63	.69	58	.283	.332	.427

Richie Lewis

Pitches: Right **Bats:** Right **Pos:** P   **Ht:** 5'10" **Wt:** 175 **Born:** 1/25/66 **Age:** 34

Year Team	Lg Org	G	GS	CG	GF	IP	BFP	H	R	ER	HR	SH	SF	HB	TBB	IBB	SO	WP	Bk	W	L	Pct.	ShO	Sv	ERA
				HOW MUCH HE PITCHED						WHAT HE GAVE UP											THE RESULTS			
1987 Indianapols	AAA Mon	2	0	0	2	3.2	19	6	4	4	2	0	0	0	2	0	3	0	0	0	1	.000	0	0	9.82
1988 Jacksnville	AA Mon	12	12	1	0	61.1	275	37	32	23	2	0	3	3	56	0	60	7	4	5	3	.625	0	0	3.38
1989 Jacksnville	AA Mon	17	17	0	0	94.1	414	80	37	27	2	7	1	2	55	0	105	8	2	5	4	.556	0	0	2.58
1990 Wst Plm Bch	A+ Mon	10	0	0	6	15	68	12	8	5	0	1	0	0	11	0	14	1	0	0	1	.000	0	2	3.00
Jacksnville	AA Mon	11	0	0	8	14.1	54	7	2	2	0	1	0	0	5	0	14	3	0	0	0	.000	0	5	1.26
1991 Harrisburg	AA Mon	34	6	0	16	74.2	318	67	33	31	2	3	2	2	40	1	82	5	2	6	5	.545	0	5	3.74
Indianapols	AAA Mon	5	4	0	0	27.2	131	35	12	11	1	0	1	0	20	1	22	2	0	1	0	1.000	0	0	3.58
Rochester	AAA Bal	2	2	0	0	16	62	13	5	5	1	0	0	0	7	0	18	1	0	1	0	1.000	0	0	2.81
1992 Rochester	AAA Bal	24	23	6	1	159.1	668	136	63	58	15	1	4	3	61	2	154	13	2	10	9	.526	1	0	3.28
1995 Charlotte	AAA Fla	17	8	1	4	59	243	50	22	21	5	2	4	0	20	0	45	4	2	5	2	.714	0	0	3.20
1996 Toledo	AAA Det	2	0	0	0	4	13	1	1	1	1	0	0	0	1	0	4	0	0	0	0	.000	0	0	2.25
1997 Edmonton	AAA Oak	11	1	0	4	20	96	24	13	13	2	1	1	1	14	1	25	3	0	1	1	.500	0	1	5.85
Indianapols	AAA Cin	27	0	0	17	29.2	120	22	7	5	0	1	2	2	7	2	33	3	0	1	0	1.000	0	9	1.52
1998 Rochester	AAA Bal	21	21	2	0	124	526	107	77	69	17	1	3	7	42	0	131	10	0	5	7	.417	0	0	5.01
1999 Norfolk	AAA NYM	20	20	3	0	122.2	542	128	82	69	19	6	2	5	49	7	101	4	2	7	8	.467	1	0	5.06
1992 Baltimore	AL	2	2	0	0	6.2	40	13	8	8	1	0	1	0	7	0	4	0	0	1	1	.500	0	0	10.80
1993 Florida	NL	57	0	0	14	77.1	341	68	37	28	7	8	4	1	43	6	65	9	1	6	3	.667	0	0	3.26
1994 Florida	NL	45	0	0	9	54	261	62	44	34	7	3	1	1	38	9	45	10	1	1	4	.200	0	0	5.67
1995 Florida	NL	21	1	0	6	36	152	30	15	15	9	2	0	1	15	5	32	1	2	0	1	.000	0	0	3.75
1996 Detroit	AL	72	0	0	19	90.1	412	78	45	42	9	5	10	4	65	9	78	14	2	4	6	.400	0	2	4.18
1997 Oakland	AL	14	0	0	5	18.2	94	24	21	20	7	1	1	1	15	0	12	2	0	2	0	1.000	0	0	9.64
Cincinnati	NL	4	0	0	0	5.2	25	4	5	4	3	2	0	0	3	0	4	0	0	0	0	.000	0	0	6.35
1998 Baltimore	AL	2	1	0	0	4.2	25	8	8	8	2	0	1	0	5	0	4	1	0	0	0	.000	0	0	15.43
11 Min. YEARS		215	114	13	58	825.2	3549	725	398	344	69	23	24	25	390	14	811	64	14	46	41	.529	2	22	3.75
7 Maj. YEARS		217	4	0	53	293.1	1350	287	183	159	45	21	18	8	191	29	244	37	6	14	15	.483	0	2	4.88

Julian Leyva

Pitches: Right **Bats:** Left **Pos:** P   **Ht:** 6'0" **Wt:** 200 **Born:** 2/11/78 **Age:** 22

Year Team	Lg Org	G	GS	CG	GF	IP	BFP	H	R	ER	HR	SH	SF	HB	TBB	IBB	SO	WP	Bk	W	L	Pct.	ShO	Sv	ERA
				HOW MUCH HE PITCHED						WHAT HE GAVE UP											THE RESULTS			
1996 Athletics	R Oak	1	0	0	0	2	8	1	0	0	0	0	0	0	1	0	2	0	0	0	0	.000	0	0	0.00
1997 Modesto	A+ Oak	28	19	0	6	139	596	148	99	76	21	3	3	6	38	1	90	5	1	4	9	.308	0	2	4.92
1998 Edmonton	AAA Oak	1	0	0	0	3	13	3	3	0	1	0	0	0	0	0	3	0	0	1	0	1.000	0	0	0.00
Modesto	A+ Oak	28	21	1	3	137.2	577	156	70	55	9	4	3	5	25	2	92	1	0	11	7	.611	0	1	3.60
1999 Visalia	A+ Oak	15	14	0	1	82.2	366	87	50	39	9	1	4	4	25	0	67	0	0	7	3	.700	0	1	4.25
Midland	AA Oak	12	11	1	1	62.2	274	86	46	42	10	0	1	0	12	1	39	0	0	3	4	.429	1	0	6.03
4 Min. YEARS		85	65	2	11	427	1834	481	268	212	50	8	11	15	101	4	293	6	1	25	24	.510	1	4	4.47

Kevin Lidle

Bats: Right **Throws:** Right **Pos:** C   **Ht:** 5'11" **Wt:** 170 **Born:** 3/22/72 **Age:** 28

Year Team	Lg Org	G	AB	H	2B	3B	HR	TB	R	RBI	TBB	IBB	SO	HBP	SH	SF	SB	CS	SB%	GDP	Avg	OBP	SLG
				BATTING												BASERUNNING				PERCENTAGES		
1992 Niagara Fal	A- Det	58	140	34	6	2	1	47	21	18	8	0	42	1	6	3	3	2	.60	1	.243	.283	.336
1993 Fayetteville	A Det	58	197	42	14	1	5	73	29	25	34	0	42	1	0	1	2	0	1.00	0	.213	.330	.371
1994 Lakeland	A+ Det	56	187	49	13	2	6	84	26	30	19	0	46	4	1	1	1	1	.50	2	.262	.341	.449
1995 Jacksnville	AA Det	36	80	13	7	0	1	23	12	5	1	0	21	0	1	0	1	0	1.00	1	.163	.173	.288
Fayetteville	A Det	36	113	16	4	1	4	34	15	13	16	0	44	1	3	2	0	1	.00	1	.142	.250	.301
1996 Lakeland	A+ Det	97	320	69	18	1	8	113	37	41	30	0	90	3	0	1	1	1	.50	4	.216	.288	.353

Year Team	Lg Org	G	AB	H	2B	3B	HR	TB	R	RBI	TBB	IBB	SO	HBP	SH	SF	SB	CS	SB%	GDP	Avg	OBP	SLG
Jacksnville	AA Det	4	8	2	0	0	1	5	2	2	1	0	2	0	0	0	1	0	1.00	0	.250	.333	.625
1997 Jacksnville	AA Det	59	186	28	7	0	1	38	18	16	17	0	77	2	3	2	0	0	.00	4	.151	.227	.204
1998 Salem	A+ Col	31	59	7	4	0	2	17	6	7	3	0	14	0	0	0	0	0	.00	2	.119	.161	.288
New Haven	AA Col	11	35	5	2	0	2	13	5	5	3	0	13	0	1	0	0	0	.00	0	.143	.211	.371
Colo Sprngs	AAA Col	5	15	4	1	1	0	7	2	1	1	0	8	1	0	0	0	0	.00	0	.267	.353	.467
1999 Mobile	AA SD	63	180	40	8	0	6	66	23	26	30	2	40	5	2	2	1	3	.25	4	.222	.346	.367
Las Vegas	AAA SD	10	29	8	3	0	2	17	5	5	3	0	8	0	0	1	0	0	.00	2	.276	.333	.586
8 Min. YEARS		524	1549	317	87	8	39	537	201	194	166	2	457	18	17	13	10	8	.56	21	.205	.287	.347

Bats: Right Throws: Right Pos: OF

Tal Light

Ht: 6'3" Wt: 205 Born: 11/28/73 Age: 26

Year Team	Lg Org	G	AB	H	2B	3B	HR	TB	R	RBI	TBB	IBB	SO	HBP	SH	SF	SB	CS	SB%	GDP	Avg	OBP	SLG
1995 Asheville	A Col	23	63	17	4	0	4	33	13	13	18	0	17	0	0	3	0	0	.00	0	.270	.417	.524
1996 Asheville	A Col	52	205	67	15	0	12	118	34	51	21	0	58	1	0	2	8	4	.67	3	.327	.389	.576
Salem	A+ Col	64	234	55	10	0	13	104	29	36	19	0	59	5	0	1	3	1	.75	6	.235	.305	.444
1997 New Haven	AA Col	25	83	20	6	0	5	41	10	11	5	0	36	0	1	0	0	1	.00	1	.241	.284	.494
Salem	A+ Col	104	373	99	19	2	15	167	57	65	59	2	144	4	0	4	0	1	.00	6	.265	.368	.448
1998 New Haven	AA Col	57	181	30	9	1	4	53	15	24	13	1	62	0	3	2	1	4	.20	5	.166	.219	.293
1999 Carolina	AA Col	80	259	48	18	0	9	93	20	30	10	0	121	7	1	1	0	3	.00	1	.185	.251	.359
Stockton	A+ Mil	4	17	2	0	0	0	2	1	2	0	0	13	0	0	0	0	0	.00	1	.118	.118	.118
5 Min. YEARS		409	1415	338	81	3	62	611	185	232	151	3	510	17	5	13	12	14	.46	26	.239	.317	.432

Bats: Right Throws: Right Pos: OF

Rod Lindsey

Ht: 5'8" Wt: 175 Born: 1/28/76 Age: 24

Year Team	Lg Org	G	AB	H	2B	3B	HR	TB	R	RBI	TBB	IBB	SO	HBP	SH	SF	SB	CS	SB%	GDP	Avg	OBP	SLG
1994 Padres	R SD	48	172	46	3	0	0	49	29	19	11	0	59	9	0	0	15	8	.65	2	.267	.344	.285
1995 Idaho Falls	R+ SD	35	155	41	4	4	0	53	30	14	13	0	37	4	0	1	21	7	.75	1	.265	.335	.342
1996 Clinton	A SD	23	87	14	2	0	0	16	11	4	11	0	30	3	0	1	12	8	.60	2	.161	.275	.184
Idaho Falls	R+ SD	48	185	56	4	6	5	87	45	17	23	0	53	2	0	0	16	3	.84	1	.303	.386	.470
1997 Clinton	A SD	130	502	107	15	8	6	156	80	49	62	0	161	7	3	2	70	23	.75	8	.213	.307	.311
1998 Clinton	A SD	40	155	42	4	4	4	66	32	17	17	1	54	3	1	1	36	4	.90	2	.271	.352	.426
W Michigan	A Det	45	158	43	7	4	3	67	37	17	22	1	42	10	0	1	24	8	.75	1	.272	.393	.424
1999 Jacksnville	AA Det	7	27	5	1	0	0	6	3	2	1	0	6	0	1	0	0	0	.00	0	.185	.214	.222
Lakeland	A+ Det	120	485	129	20	8	7	186	81	51	25	0	129	18	4	5	61	20	.75	6	.266	.323	.384
6 Min. YEARS		496	1926	483	60	34	25	686	348	190	185	2	571	56	9	11	255	81	.76	23	.251	.332	.356

Bats: Right Throws: Right Pos: C

David Lindstrom

Ht: 5'10" Wt: 185 Born: 8/6/74 Age: 25

Year Team	Lg Org	G	AB	H	2B	3B	HR	TB	R	RBI	TBB	IBB	SO	HBP	SH	SF	SB	CS	SB%	GDP	Avg	OBP	SLG
1996 Jamestown	A- Det	52	165	41	10	0	5	66	19	13	10	0	29	2	5	0	1	0	1.00	3	.248	.299	.400
1997 Lakeland	A+ Det	76	213	44	8	0	3	61	25	14	24	0	25	3	5	2	1	0	1.00	9	.207	.293	.286
1998 Toledo	AAA Det	1	3	0	0	0	0	0	0	0	0	0	1	0	0	0	0	0	.00	0	.000	.000	.000
Lakeland	A+ Det	103	337	83	20	2	5	122	52	42	50	1	46	11	3	7	0	3	.00	8	.246	.356	.362
1999 Jacksnville	AA Det	66	214	58	17	1	7	98	30	35	24	0	35	6	1	5	1	3	.25	9	.271	.353	.458
4 Min. YEARS		298	932	226	55	3	20	347	126	104	108	1	136	22	14	14	3	6	.33	29	.242	.331	.372

Pitches: Right Bats: Right Pos: P

Scott Linebrink

Ht: 6'3" Wt: 185 Born: 8/4/76 Age: 23

Year Team	Lg Org	G	GS	CG	GF	IP	BFP	H	R	ER	HR	SH	SF	HB	TBB	IBB	SO	WP	Bk	W	L	Pct.	ShO	Sv	ERA
1997 Salem-Keizr	A- SF	3	3	0	0	10	42	7	5	5	1	0	0	0	6	0	6	1	0	0	0	.000	0	0	4.50
San Jose	A+ SF	6	6	0	0	28.1	120	29	11	10	2	0	0	0	10	0	40	2	0	2	1	.667	0	0	3.18
1998 Shreveport	AA SF	21	21	0	0	113	494	101	66	63	12	6	5	7	58	1	128	8	0	10	8	.556	0	0	5.02
1999 Shreveport	AA SF	10	10	0	0	43.1	190	48	31	31	7	0	4	0	14	0	33	1	0	1	8	.111	0	0	6.44
3 Min. YEARS		40	40	0	0	194.2	846	185	113	109	22	6	9	7	88	1	207	12	0	13	17	.433	0	0	5.04

Pitches: Right Bats: Right Pos: P

Aaron Lineweaver

Ht: 6'0" Wt: 210 Born: 7/26/73 Age: 26

Year Team	Lg Org	G	GS	CG	GF	IP	BFP	H	R	ER	HR	SH	SF	HB	TBB	IBB	SO	WP	Bk	W	L	Pct.	ShO	Sv	ERA
1996 Spokane	A- KC	21	5	0	5	49	227	62	43	41	6	1	3	2	23	0	34	3	4	3	4	.429	0	1	7.53
1997 Lansing	A KC	21	9	0	3	83.2	359	89	38	31	4	2	2	3	28	1	73	6	1	7	1	.875	0	0	3.33
1998 Wilmington	A+ KC	26	26	5	0	168	685	136	62	52	5	12	3	14	54	3	116	8	1	13	5	.722	2	0	2.79
1999 Omaha	AAA KC	1	1	0	0	6	25	6	4	4	0	1	0	3	3	0	3	0	0	0	1	.000	0	0	0.00
Wilmington	A+ KC	17	16	0	0	101.1	425	96	45	40	5	6	2	4	36	0	75	4	0	8	6	.571	0	0	3.55
Wichita	AA KC	9	7	0	1	44.1	205	49	32	26	5	1	2	6	15	0	20	1	0	4	3	.571	0	1	5.28
4 Min. YEARS		95	64	5	9	452.1	1926	438	224	194	25	22	13	29	159	4	321	22	6	35	20	.636	2	2	3.86

158

Bob Lisanti

Bats: Right **Throws:** Right **Pos:** C **Ht:** 5'10" **Wt:** 180 **Born:** 5/28/73 **Age:** 27

Year Team	Lg Org	G	AB	H	2B	3B	HR	TB	R	RBI	TBB	IBB	SO	HBP	SH	SF	SB	CS	SB%	GDP	Avg	OBP	SLG
1996 Williamsprt	A- ChC	43	119	23	7	0	0	30	10	15	13	0	27	1	3	0	0	3	.00	2	.193	.278	.252
1997 Rockford	A ChC	66	182	43	8	0	0	51	18	21	15	0	42	5	1	4	1	3	.25	0	.236	.306	.280
Iowa	AAA ChC	4	11	4	0	0	0	4	2	1	2	0	5	0	0	0	0	0	.00	0	.364	.462	.364
1998 Daytona	A+ ChC	12	10	1	0	0	0	1	1	1	1	0	4	0	0	0	0	0	.00	0	.100	.182	.100
Rockford	A ChC	26	75	17	7	0	1	27	7	14	14	0	18	1	2	3	2	0	1.00	1	.227	.344	.360
1999 Iowa	AAA ChC	31	52	9	3	0	0	12	5	1	1	0	14	0	1	0	0	0	.00	1	.173	.189	.231
4 Min. YEARS		182	449	97	25	0	1	125	43	53	46	0	110	7	7	7	3	6	.33	4	.216	.295	.278

Joe Lisio

Pitches: Right **Bats:** Right **Pos:** P **Ht:** 6'2" **Wt:** 205 **Born:** 8/5/73 **Age:** 26

Year Team	Lg Org	G	GS	CG	GF	IP	BFP	H	R	ER	HR	SH	SF	HB	TBB	IBB	SO	WP	Bk	W	L	Pct.	ShO	Sv	ERA
1994 Kingsport	R+ NYM	21	0	0	19	23.1	100	22	9	7	3	1	0	2	7	0	22	1	0	2	3	.400	0	9	2.70
1995 Pittsfield	A- NYM	28	0	0	23	33.1	141	27	8	6	0	2	5	1	14	1	24	2	0	2	2	.500	0	12	1.62
1996 Capital Cty	A NYM	40	0	0	37	44.1	186	40	16	10	0	3	2	1	15	1	42	3	2	2	5	.286	0	18	2.03
1997 St. Lucie	A+ NYM	48	0	0	44	47.1	209	48	27	24	4	4	0	4	19	5	42	3	2	2	6	.250	0	16	4.56
1998 High Desert	A+ Ari	11	0	0	3	15.1	79	19	11	10	1	1	0	2	11	1	17	1	0	1	2	.333	0	0	5.87
Tulsa	AA Tex	9	0	0	3	13.1	67	21	13	12	1	0	1	0	8	0	13	0	0	0	0	.000	0	0	8.10
Norwich	AA NYY	1	0	0	1	5		1	0	0	0	1	0	0	1	0	1	0	0	1	0	1.000	0	0	0.00
Tampa	A+ NYY	31	0	0	28	32.2	135	19	13	9	2	4	0	3	16	2	43	2	0	2	3	.400	0	15	2.48
1999 Norwich	AA NYY	59	0	0	56	56.2	245	58	27	26	4	2	1	1	27	1	49	2	0	2	6	.250	0	33	4.13
6 Min. YEARS		248	0	0	213	267.1	1167	255	124	104	15	18	9	14	118	11	253	14	4	14	27	.341	0	103	3.50

Mark Little

Bats: Right **Throws:** Right **Pos:** OF **Ht:** 6' 0" **Wt:** 195 **Born:** 7/11/72 **Age:** 27

Year Team	Lg Org	G	AB	H	2B	3B	HR	TB	R	RBI	TBB	IBB	SO	HBP	SH	SF	SB	CS	SB%	GDP	Avg	OBP	SLG
1994 Hudson Val	A- Tex	54	208	61	15	5	3	95	33	27	22	1	38	1	0	4	14	5	.74	4	.293	.357	.457
1995 Charlotte	A+ Tex	115	438	112	31	8	9	186	75	50	51	1	108	14	2	2	20	14	.59	4	.256	.350	.425
1996 Tulsa	AA Tex	101	409	119	24	2	13	186	69	50	48	0	88	10	5	3	22	10	.69	5	.291	.377	.455
1997 Okla City	AAA Tex	121	415	109	23	4	15	185	72	45	39	1	100	8	8	0	21	9	.70	8	.263	.338	.446
1998 Oklahoma	AAA Tex	69	274	81	20	4	8	133	58	46	16	0	60	10	0	5	9	6	.60	4	.296	.351	.485
Memphis	AAA StL	19	63	17	3	3	0	26	9	6	6	1	10	2	0	2	0	3	.00	0	.270	.342	.413
1999 Memphis	AAA StL	51	196	58	11	5	3	88	40	22	10	1	48	6	1	1	12	5	.71	3	.296	.347	.449
1998 St. Louis	NL	7	12	1	0	0	0	1	0	0	2	0	5	0	1	0	1	0	1.00	0	.083	.214	.083
6 Min. YEARS		530	2003	557	127	31	51	899	356	246	192	5	452	51	16	17	98	52	.65	28	.278	.354	.449

Doug Livingston

Bats: Right **Throws:** Right **Pos:** 2B **Ht:** 5'8" **Wt:** 160 **Born:** 4/9/74 **Age:** 26

Year Team	Lg Org	G	AB	H	2B	3B	HR	TB	R	RBI	TBB	IBB	SO	HBP	SH	SF	SB	CS	SB%	GDP	Avg	OBP	SLG
1996 Portland	A- Col	57	224	67	18	4	5	108	36	34	23	1	45	3	6	2	6	0	1.00	4	.299	.369	.482
1997 Asheville	A Col	128	468	123	30	3	3	168	53	61	45	1	82	5	15	0	8	5	.62	12	.263	.334	.359
1998 Salem	A+ Col	131	514	139	31	1	2	178	87	58	50	0	98	3	7	5	27	5	.84	12	.270	.336	.346
1999 Carolina	AA Col	43	119	24	2	1	1	31	11	9	13	4	24	0	3	2	4	2	.67	1	.202	.276	.261
Salem	A+ Col	64	233	60	13	2	0	77	33	24	30	0	39	3	6	4	10	2	.83	6	.258	.344	.330
4 Min. YEARS		423	1558	413	94	11	11	562	220	186	161	6	288	14	37	13	55	14	.80	35	.265	.337	.361

Scott Livingstone

Bats: Left **Throws:** Right **Pos:** 1B **Ht:** 6' 0" **Wt:** 190 **Born:** 7/15/65 **Age:** 34

Year Team	Lg Org	G	AB	H	2B	3B	HR	TB	R	RBI	TBB	IBB	SO	HBP	SH	SF	SB	CS	SB%	GDP	Avg	OBP	SLG
1988 Lakeland	A+ Det	53	180	51	8	1	2	67	28	25	11	3	25	3	2	2	1	1	.50	3	.283	.332	.372
1989 London	AA Det	124	452	98	18	1	14	160	46	71	52	4	67	2	0	6	1	1	.50	4	.217	.297	.354
1990 Toledo	AAA Det	103	345	94	19	0	6	131	44	36	21	0	40	1	0	1	1	5	.17	7	.272	.315	.380
1991 Toledo	AAA Det	92	331	100	13	3	3	128	48	62	40	3	52	2	3	6	2	1	.67	9	.302	.375	.387
1997 Rancho Cuca	A+ SD	3	8	2	0	0	0	2	2	0	3	0	0	0	1	0	0	1	.00	0	.250	.455	.250
Louisville	AAA StL	9	25	9	1	0	0	10	4	2	2	0	3	0	0	1	0	0	.00	0	.360	.393	.400
1999 Albuquerque	AAA LA	28	78	16	1	0	1	20	11	4	9	1	12	0	0	0	2	1	.67	1	.205	.287	.256
Rochester	AAA Bal	14	43	16	4	0	0	20	5	7	7	2	4	0	0	1	1	0	1.00	5	.372	.451	.465
Norfolk	AAA NYM	36	114	34	7	0	1	44	10	20	7	0	9	0	1	1	2	0	1.00	6	.298	.336	.386
1991 Detroit	AL	44	127	37	5	0	2	48	19	11	10	0	25	0	1	1	2	1	.67	0	.291	.341	.378
1992 Detroit	AL	117	354	100	21	0	4	133	43	46	21	1	36	0	3	4	1	3	.25	8	.282	.319	.376
1993 Detroit	AL	98	304	89	10	2	2	109	39	39	19	1	32	0	1	6	1	3	.25	8	.293	.328	.359
1994 Detroit	AL	15	23	5	1	0	0	6	0	1	1	0	4	0	0	0	0	0	.00	0	.217	.250	.261
San Diego	NL	57	180	49	12	1	2	69	11	10	6	0	22	0	0	1	2	2	.50	5	.272	.294	.383
1995 San Diego	NL	99	196	66	15	0	5	96	26	32	15	1	22	0	0	2	2	1	.67	3	.337	.380	.490
1996 San Diego	NL	102	172	51	4	1	2	63	20	20	9	0	22	0	0	0	0	1	.00	6	.297	.331	.366
1997 San Diego	NL	23	26	4	1	0	0	5	1	3	2	0	1	0	0	0	0	0	.00	0	.154	.214	.192
St. Louis	NL	42	41	7	1	0	0	8	3	3	1	0	10	0	0	2	1	0	1.00	1	.171	.182	.195
1998 Montreal	NL	76	110	23	6	0	0	29	7	12	5	2	15	0	0	3	1	1	.50	2	.209	.237	.264
6 Min. YEARS		462	1576	420	71	5	27	582	198	227	152	13	212	8	7	18	10	10	.50	35	.266	.331	.369
9 Maj. YEARS		675	1533	431	76	4	17	566	163	177	89	5	189	0	5	19	10	12	.45	29	.281	.317	.369

159

Jose Lobaton

Bats: Right **Throws:** Right **Pos:** SS **Ht:** 5'11" **Wt:** 154 **Born:** 3/29/74 **Age:** 26

								BATTING									BASERUNNING				PERCENTAGES		
Year Team	Lg Org	G	AB	H	2B	3B	HR	TB	R	RBI	TBB	IBB	SO	HBP	SH	SF	SB	CS	SB%	GDP	Avg	OBP	SLG
1993 Yankees	R NYY	44	165	57	8	6	1	80	30	16	19	0	28	2	1	2	24	2	.92	2	.345	.415	.485
1994 Oneonta	A- NYY	66	239	54	9	2	0	67	34	15	22	0	55	3	3	2	14	7	.67	7	.226	.297	.280
1995 Greensboro	A NYY	60	185	45	6	5	0	61	26	23	22	0	58	2	11	2	11	6	.65	3	.243	.327	.330
Oneonta	A- NYY	41	145	32	11	3	1	52	23	11	13	0	30	2	1	0	4	1	.80	2	.221	.294	.359
1996 Tampa	A+ NYY	113	375	87	16	5	5	128	39	37	34	1	74	8	11	4	11	7	.61	6	.232	.306	.341
1997 Tampa	A+ NYY	7	23	3	0	0	0	3	0	5	2	0	6	0	1	1	0	0	.00	2	.130	.192	.130
Norwich	AA NYY	68	197	38	6	0	1	47	16	15	12	0	60	2	5	2	2	3	.40	4	.193	.244	.239
1998 Tampa	A+ NYY	33	130	33	4	1	4	51	21	15	4	0	32	2	3	1	4	1	.80	2	.254	.285	.392
Norwich	AA NYY	52	177	45	14	1	1	64	16	21	10	0	36	2	3	4	2	2	.50	2	.254	.295	.362
Columbus	AAA NYY	6	7	1	1	0	0	2	0	0	0	0	2	0	0	0	0	0	.00	1	.143	.143	.286
1999 Huntsville	AA Mil	45	128	36	6	0	2	48	23	18	13	1	34	1	3	3	2	0	1.00	0	.281	.345	.375
Portland	AA Fla	13	32	8	2	0	0	10	2	0	2	0	13	0	3	0	1	0	1.00	1	.250	.294	.313
Calgary	AAA Fla	36	90	17	6	0	0	23	9	4	6	0	26	2	2	0	2	2	.50	5	.189	.255	.256
7 Min. YEARS		584	1893	456	89	23	15	636	239	180	159	2	454	26	47	21	77	31	.71	36	.241	.305	.336

Kyle Lohse

Pitches: Right **Bats:** Right **Pos:** P **Ht:** 6'2" **Wt:** 190 **Born:** 10/4/78 **Age:** 21

		HOW MUCH HE PITCHED						WHAT HE GAVE UP												THE RESULTS				
Year Team	Lg Org	G	GS	CG	GF	IP	BFP	H	R	ER	HR	SH	SF	HB	TBB	IBB	SO	WP	Bk	W	L	Pct.	ShO	Sv	ERA
1997 Cubs	R ChC	12	11	0	0	47.2	210	46	22	16	0	1	1	1	22	0	49	3	0	2	2	.500	0	0	3.02
1998 Rockford	A ChC	28	26	3	1	170.2	712	158	76	61	8	8	5	11	45	1	121	13	1	13	8	.619	1	0	3.22
1999 Daytona	A+ ChC	9	9	0	0	53	217	48	21	17	4	2	1	0	16	0	41	1	0	5	3	.625	1	0	2.89
Fort Myers	A+ Min	7	7	0	0	41.2	180	47	28	24	5	2	4	4	9	0	33	1	0	2	3	.400	0	0	5.18
New Britain	AA Min	11	11	1	0	70.1	311	87	49	46	9	3	4	5	23	0	41	2	0	3	4	.429	0	0	5.89
3 Min. YEARS		67	64	5	1	383.1	1630	386	196	164	26	16	15	21	115	1	285	20	1	25	20	.556	2	0	3.85

Kevin Lomon

Pitches: Right **Bats:** Right **Pos:** P **Ht:** 6'1" **Wt:** 195 **Born:** 11/20/71 **Age:** 28

		HOW MUCH HE PITCHED						WHAT HE GAVE UP												THE RESULTS				
Year Team	Lg Org	G	GS	CG	GF	IP	BFP	H	R	ER	HR	SH	SF	HB	TBB	IBB	SO	WP	Bk	W	L	Pct.	ShO	Sv	ERA
1991 Pulaski	R+ Atl	10	5	1	1	44	168	17	9	3	0	0	1	4	13	0	70	4	6	6	0	1.000	1	1	0.61
Macon	A Atl	1	0	0	1	5	17	2	1	1	0	0	0	0	1	0	2	0	1	1	0	1.000	0	0	1.80
1992 Durham	A+ Atl	27	27	0	0	135	609	147	83	74	13	5	3	11	63	1	113	16	3	8	9	.471	0	0	4.93
1993 Durham	A+ Atl	14	14	1	0	85	358	80	36	35	6	0	1	2	30	1	68	5	3	4	2	.667	0	0	3.71
Greenville	AA Atl	13	13	1	0	79.1	338	76	41	34	4	3	3	4	31	2	68	4	0	3	4	.429	1	0	3.86
1994 Richmond	AAA Atl	28	26	0	0	147	628	159	69	63	12	1	2	3	53	2	97	9	0	10	8	.556	0	0	3.86
1995 Richmond	AAA Atl	32	3	0	8	60	261	62	23	20	2	4	4	0	32	4	52	4	0	1	2	.333	0	1	3.00
1996 Richmond	AAA Atl	26	26	2	0	141.1	607	151	82	68	11	5	4	4	44	2	102	6	1	9	8	.529	0	0	4.33
1997 Columbus	AAA NYY	3	3	0	0	14.1	71	21	12	10	2	1	1	2	7	0	14	1	0	1	1	.500	0	0	6.28
Norwich	AA NYY	18	18	2	0	115	487	104	51	41	5	1	5	6	50	0	117	5	1	9	7	.563	1	0	3.21
1998 Las Vegas	AAA SD	30	17	0	3	124	551	128	78	71	13	4	3	8	62	2	118	19	1	2	9	.182	0	0	5.15
1999 Edmonton	AAA Ana	23	17	0	0	123.2	560	170	86	79	23	2	7	5	35	0	91	11	2	7	8	.467	0	0	5.75
1995 New York	NL	6	0	0	1	9.1	47	17	8	7	0	0	0	0	5	1	6	0	0	0	1	.000	0	0	6.75
1996 Atlanta	NL	6	0	0	1	7.1	31	7	4	4	0	0	0	1	3	0	1	0	1	0	0	.000	0	0	4.91
9 Min. YEARS		225	169	7	13	1073.2	4655	1117	571	499	91	26	34	49	421	14	912	84	17	61	58	.513	3	2	4.18
2 Maj. YEARS		12	0	0	2	16.2	78	24	12	11	0	0	0	1	8	1	7	0	1	0	1	.000	0	0	5.94

Garrett Long

Bats: Right **Throws:** Right **Pos:** OF-1B **Ht:** 6'3" **Wt:** 205 **Born:** 10/5/76 **Age:** 23

								BATTING									BASERUNNING				PERCENTAGES		
Year Team	Lg Org	G	AB	H	2B	3B	HR	TB	R	RBI	TBB	IBB	SO	HBP	SH	SF	SB	CS	SB%	GDP	Avg	OBP	SLG
1995 Pirates	R Pit	20	63	22	2	1	1	29	13	8	17	0	10	0	0	0	0	1	.00	3	.349	.488	.460
Erie	A- Pit	29	108	30	4	0	2	40	17	16	15	0	25	1	0	2	2	2	.50	6	.278	.365	.370
1996 Erie	A- Pit	20	70	20	2	1	0	24	5	7	9	0	17	1	1	1	1	2	.33	3	.286	.370	.343
1997 Augusta	A Pit	83	280	84	10	2	7	119	50	41	61	2	78	1	0	1	5	2	.71	3	.300	.424	.425
Lynchburg	A+ Pit	9	29	6	3	0	1	12	1	5	3	0	10	0	0	0	0	0	.00	3	.207	.281	.414
1998 Lynchburg	A+ Pit	91	309	87	29	1	7	139	46	43	49	2	83	3	0	3	7	2	.78	8	.282	.382	.450
Carolina	AA Pit	28	98	29	3	0	0	32	14	8	11	1	27	1	0	0	1	0	1.00	6	.296	.373	.327
1999 Altoona	AA Pit	109	355	87	12	4	18	161	61	56	63	1	100	7	4	2	6	6	.50	7	.245	.368	.454
5 Min. YEARS		389	1312	365	65	9	36	556	207	184	228	6	350	14	5	9	22	15	.59	39	.278	.388	.424

Joey Long

Pitches: Left **Bats:** Right **Pos:** P **Ht:** 6'2" **Wt:** 215 **Born:** 7/15/70 **Age:** 29

		HOW MUCH HE PITCHED						WHAT HE GAVE UP												THE RESULTS				
Year Team	Lg Org	G	GS	CG	GF	IP	BFP	H	R	ER	HR	SH	SF	HB	TBB	IBB	SO	WP	Bk	W	L	Pct.	ShO	Sv	ERA
1991 Spokane	A- SD	13	11	0	0	56.2	282	78	57	44	2	1	3	2	39	0	40	8	4	1	9	.100	0	0	6.99
1993 Waterloo	A SD	33	7	0	7	96.1	415	96	56	52	7	3	3	3	36	2	90	8	3	4	3	.571	0	0	4.86
1994 Rancho Cuca	A+ SD	46	0	0	17	52	248	69	36	27	3	6	2	1	22	1	52	8	0	2	4	.333	0	3	4.67
1995 Las Vegas	AAA SD	25	0	0	9	31.1	143	38	22	16	1	0	4	0	16	2	13	0	0	1	3	.250	0	0	4.60
Memphis	AA SD	25	0	0	3	21.2	104	28	15	8	0	1	1	1	10	2	18	0	0	2	0	1.000	0	0	3.32
1996 Memphis	AA SD	10	0	0	1	18	79	16	4	4	0	1	0	1	11	1	14	3	0	2	0	1.000	0	0	2.00
Las Vegas	AAA SD	32	0	0	13	34	156	39	21	16	2	2	3	0	23	3	23	5	0	3	3	.500	0	1	4.24
1997 Las Vegas	AAA SD	16	0	0	2	18.2	83	17	10	10	3	0	0	0	12	2	13	2	0	0	0	.000	0	0	4.82
1998 Ottawa	AAA Mon	34	1	0	12	47	216	53	27	23	6	3	0	3	24	2	41	4	0	2	4	.333	0	0	4.40
1999 Nashville	AAA Pit	35	0	0	10	36	164	39	25	18	5	0	4	0	22	2	37	6	1	2	1	.667	0	0	4.50

		HOW MUCH HE PITCHED						WHAT HE GAVE UP									THE RESULTS					
Year Team	Lg Org	G	GS	CG	GF	IP	BFP	H	R	ER	HR	SH	SF	HB	TBB	IBB	SO	WP	Bk	W	L	Pct.	ShO	Sv	ERA
Altoona	AA Pit	8	0	0	4	10.2	50	16	8	7	3	0	0	0	4	0	5	0	0	0	0	.000	0	0	5.91
1997 San Diego	NL	10	0	0	4	11	60	17	11	10	1	1	0	1	8	1	8	1	0	0	0	.000	0	0	8.18
8 Min. YEARS		277	19	0	78	422.1	1940	489	281	225	32	17	18	10	219	17	346	44	8	17	29	.370	0	4	4.79

Ryan Long

Bats: Right **Throws:** Right **Pos:** OF **Ht:** 6' 2" **Wt:** 215 **Born:** 2/3/73 **Age:** 27

		BATTING														BASERUNNING				PERCENTAGES		
Year Team	Lg Org	G	AB	H	2B	3B	HR	TB	R	RBI	TBB	IBB	SO	HBP	SH	SF	SB	CS	SB%	GDP	Avg	OBP	SLG
1991 Royals	R KC	48	177	54	2	2	0	60	17	20	10	0	20	2	0	1	5	4	.56	3	.305	.347	.339
1992 Eugene	A- KC	54	183	42	5	2	0	51	19	18	3	0	33	4	2	1	7	5	.58	4	.230	.257	.279
1993 Rockford	A KC	107	396	115	27	6	8	178	46	68	16	3	76	18	2	5	16	6	.73	6	.290	.343	.449
1994 Wilmington	A+ KC	123	494	130	25	5	11	198	69	68	16	0	72	8	3	3	7	3	.70	4	.263	.296	.401
1995 Wichita	AA KC	102	342	79	26	0	5	120	36	34	10	1	48	5	1	0	4	4	.50	9	.231	.263	.351
1996 Wichita	AA KC	122	442	125	29	1	20	216	64	78	17	0	71	5	1	2	6	5	.55	9	.283	.315	.489
1997 Omaha	AAA KC	113	411	109	26	0	19	192	48	56	18	2	98	7	3	3	2	4	.33	14	.265	.305	.467
1998 Omaha	AAA KC	18	59	12	2	0	4	26	6	8	8	0	13	2	0	0	0	0	.00	0	.203	.319	.441
Wichita	AA KC	67	248	63	14	1	7	100	32	29	17	1	51	3	1	1	2	2	.50	10	.254	.309	.403
1999 Orlando	AA TB	8	30	7	1	0	0	8	2	4	1	0	3	0	0	0	0	0	.00	3	.233	.258	.267
Newark	IND —	67	205	44	10	2	6	76	24	21	22	0	38	2	0	1	1	1	.50	5	.215	.296	.371
Lehigh Vly	IND —	33	121	34	9	0	4	55	15	23	7	0	28	1	0	2	0	0	.00	3	.281	.321	.455
1997 Kansas City	AL	6	9	2	0	0	0	2	2	2	0	0	3	1	0	0	0	0	.00	1	.222	.300	.222
9 Min. YEARS		862	3108	814	176	19	84	1280	378	427	145	7	551	57	13	19	50	34	.60	70	.262	.305	.412

Brian Looney

Pitches: Left **Bats:** Left **Pos:** P **Ht:** 5'10" **Wt:** 180 **Born:** 9/26/69 **Age:** 30

		HOW MUCH HE PITCHED						WHAT HE GAVE UP										THE RESULTS					
Year Team	Lg Org	G	GS	CG	GF	IP	BFP	H	R	ER	HR	SH	SF	HB	TBB	IBB	SO	WP	Bk	W	L	Pct.	ShO	Sv	ERA
1991 Jamestown	A- Mon	11	11	0	0	62.1	246	42	12	8	0	2	0	0	28	0	64	6	0	7	1	.875	1	0	1.16
1992 Rockford	A Mon	17	0	0	5	31.1	141	28	13	11	0	2	0	1	23	0	34	1	0	3	1	.750	0	0	3.16
Albany	A Mon	11	11	1	0	67.1	265	51	22	16	1	1	3	0	30	0	56	4	0	3	2	.600	1	0	2.14
1993 Wst Plm Bch	A+ Mon	18	16	0	1	106	451	108	48	37	2	7	3	5	29	0	109	2	1	4	6	.400	0	0	3.14
Harrisburg	AA Mon	8	8	1	0	56.2	221	36	15	15	2	1	1	1	17	1	76	0	0	3	2	.600	1	0	2.38
1994 Ottawa	AAA Mon	27	16	0	2	124.2	565	134	71	60	10	3	6	3	67	4	90	2	0	7	7	.500	0	0	4.33
1995 Pawtucket	AAA Bos	18	18	1	0	100.2	438	106	44	39	9	2	0	3	33	0	78	7	2	4	7	.364	0	0	3.49
1996 Pawtucket	AAA Bos	27	9	1	7	82.1	357	78	55	44	14	0	2	4	27	2	78	3	0	5	6	.455	1	1	4.81
1997 Salt Lake	AAA Min	17	0	0	6	24.2	103	20	7	6	4	1	0	0	10	2	21	2	0	0	2	.000	0	1	2.19
1998 Columbus	AAA NYY	41	10	0	7	92.2	424	97	52	46	13	3	5	1	52	2	63	3	0	4	4	.500	0	0	4.47
1999 Toledo	AAA Det	47	1	0	11	55	255	51	38	38	7	5	4	2	44	0	52	7	0	3	0	1.000	0	2	6.22
Scranton-WB	AAA Phi	3	3	0	0	16	74	19	9	7	3	0	0	1	6	0	12	1	1	1	0	1.000	0	0	3.94
1993 Montreal	NL	3	1	0	1	6	28	8	2	2	0	0	0	0	2	0	7	0	1	0	0	.000	0	0	3.00
1994 Montreal	NL	1	0	0	0	2	11	4	5	5	1	0	0	1	0	0	2	0	0	0	0	.000	0	0	22.50
1995 Boston	AL	3	1	0	0	4.2	29	12	9	9	1	1	2	0	4	1	2	0	0	0	1	.000	0	0	17.36
9 Min. YEARS		245	103	6	39	819.2	3540	770	386	327	65	27	26	21	366	11	733	38	4	44	38	.537	4	4	3.59
3 Maj. YEARS		7	2	0	1	12.2	68	24	16	16	2	1	2	1	6	1	11	0	1	0	1	.000	0	0	11.37

Johan Lopez

Pitches: Right **Bats:** Right **Pos:** P **Ht:** 6'2" **Wt:** 200 **Born:** 4/4/75 **Age:** 25

		HOW MUCH HE PITCHED						WHAT HE GAVE UP										THE RESULTS					
Year Team	Lg Org	G	GS	CG	GF	IP	BFP	H	R	ER	HR	SH	SF	HB	TBB	IBB	SO	WP	Bk	W	L	Pct.	ShO	Sv	ERA
1992 Astros	R Hou	17	0	0	4	34	160	42	28	17	2	4	1	0	13	0	19	7	4	1	1	.500	0	0	4.50
1994 Auburn	A- Hou	14	14	2	0	76.2	339	86	49	41	4	2	4	4	24	0	74	7	3	7	5	.583	1	0	4.81
1995 Kissimmee	A+ Hou	18	12	0	3	69	283	55	30	20	3	1	2	3	25	0	67	5	3	5	5	.500	0	1	2.61
1996 Kissimmee	A+ Hou	19	19	2	0	98.1	434	114	50	41	5	0	5	1	35	1	70	9	3	3	10	.231	1	0	3.75
1997 Jackson	AA Hou	35	19	0	5	133.2	586	131	79	65	18	7	2	6	57	3	109	11	4	6	8	.429	0	1	4.38
1998 New Orleans	AAA Hou	45	6	0	7	80.1	357	84	52	50	11	6	1	2	28	1	77	3	0	7	2	.778	0	0	5.60
1999 Binghamton	AA NYM	2	0	0	1	2	11	3	3	3	0	1	0	0	3	0	1	0	0	0	0	.000	0	0	13.50
Norfolk	AAA NYM	33	8	0	6	102	438	98	49	47	13	6	0	2	44	6	84	10	1	3	5	.375	0	1	4.15
7 Min. YEARS		183	78	4	26	596	2608	613	340	284	55	24	14	21	229	11	501	52	18	32	36	.471	2	3	4.29

Jose Lopez

Bats: Right **Throws:** Right **Pos:** OF-3B **Ht:** 6'1" **Wt:** 175 **Born:** 8/4/75 **Age:** 24

		BATTING														BASERUNNING				PERCENTAGES		
Year Team	Lg Org	G	AB	H	2B	3B	HR	TB	R	RBI	TBB	IBB	SO	HBP	SH	SF	SB	CS	SB%	GDP	Avg	OBP	SLG
1994 Mets	R NYM	45	164	53	10	1	2	71	34	31	13	0	30	2	1	8	2	1	.67	1	.323	.364	.433
Kingsport	R+ NYM	4	15	4	3	0	1	10	1	1	0	0	0	0	0	0	0	0	.00	1	.267	.267	.667
1995 Capital City	A NYM	82	280	65	17	4	5	105	37	38	35	3	76	4	2	7	7	2	.78	7	.232	.319	.375
St. Lucie	A+ NYM	1	2	2	0	0	0	2	0	1	2	0	0	0	0	0	0	0	.00	0	1.000	1.000	1.000
1996 St. Lucie	A+ NYM	121	419	122	17	5	11	182	63	60	39	2	103	9	1	2	18	10	.64	7	.291	.362	.434
1997 Norfolk	AAA NYM	2	6	2	0	0	0	2	1	0	0	0	2	0	0	0	0	0	.00	0	.333	.333	.333
Binghamton	AA NYM	66	207	51	10	1	6	81	31	26	13	1	63	0	0	0	4	2	.67	4	.246	.290	.464
St. Lucie	A+ NYM	23	87	17	3	1	4	34	14	13	3	0	25	1	0	1	2	0	1.00	1	.195	.231	.391
1998 Binghamton	AA NYM	92	327	90	23	1	10	145	47	51	18	2	91	8	0	3	7	3	.70	8	.275	.326	.443
1999 Binghamton	AA NYM	20	55	8	2	0	0	10	2	6	2	0	24	0	0	0	2	1	.67	2	.145	.175	.182
6 Min. YEARS		456	1562	414	85	13	44	657	230	227	125	8	414	24	4	21	42	19	.69	31	.265	.325	.421

161

Luis Lopez

Bats: Right **Throws:** Right **Pos:** 1B   **Ht:** 6'0" **Wt:** 200 **Born:** 10/5/73 **Age:** 26

Year Team	Lg Org	G	AB	H	2B	3B	HR	TB	R	RBI	TBB	IBB	SO	HBP	SH	SF	SB	CS	SB%	GDP	Avg	OBP	SLG
1996 St.Cathrnes	A- Tor	74	260	74	17	2	7	116	36	40	27	1	31	7	4	3	2	3	.40	4	.285	.364	.446
1997 Hagerstown	A Tor	136	503	180	47	4	11	268	96	99	60	4	45	8	0	6	5	8	.38	14	.358	.430	.533
1998 Syracuse	AAA Tor	11	41	9	0	0	1	12	6	3	6	0	6	0	0	1	0	0	.00	2	.220	.313	.293
Knoxville	AA Tor	119	450	141	27	1	15	215	70	85	58	3	55	3	0	8	0	2	.00	18	.313	.389	.478
1999 Syracuse	AAA Tor	136	531	171	35	2	4	222	76	69	40	2	58	1	2	8	1	0	1.00	22	.322	.366	.418
4 Min. YEARS		476	1785	575	126	9	38	833	284	296	191	10	195	19	6	26	8	13	.38	60	.322	.388	.467

Mickey Lopez

Bats: Both **Throws:** Right **Pos:** 2B   **Ht:** 5'10" **Wt:** 165 **Born:** 11/17/73 **Age:** 26

Year Team	Lg Org	G	AB	H	2B	3B	HR	TB	R	RBI	TBB	IBB	SO	HBP	SH	SF	SB	CS	SB%	GDP	Avg	OBP	SLG
1995 Helena	R+ Mil	57	225	73	19	2	1	99	66	41	38	3	20	5	2	4	12	8	.60	1	.324	.426	.440
1996 Beloit	A Mil	61	236	64	10	2	0	78	35	14	28	0	36	1	10	0	12	8	.60	8	.271	.351	.331
Stockton	A+ Mil	64	217	61	10	1	0	73	30	25	23	0	36	4	9	1	6	4	.60	0	.281	.359	.336
1997 El Paso	AA Mil	134	483	145	21	10	3	195	79	58	48	2	60	5	9	5	20	10	.67	10	.300	.366	.404
1998 El Paso	AA Mil	120	459	127	24	9	2	175	81	64	46	1	61	2	4	5	12	10	.55	11	.277	.342	.381
Louisville	AAA Mil	3	4	1	0	0	0	1	1	0	2	1	0	0	0	0	0	0	.00	0	.250	.500	.250
1999 Huntsville	AA Mil	83	315	94	16	5	5	135	58	40	46	2	46	5	3	4	31	4	.89	9	.298	.392	.429
Louisville	AAA Mil	49	181	58	17	2	5	94	43	31	37	0	25	2	2	1	11	7	.61	1	.320	.439	.519
5 Min. YEARS		571	2120	623	117	31	16	850	393	273	268	9	284	24	39	20	104	51	.67	40	.294	.376	.401

Pedro Lopez

Bats: Right **Throws:** Right **Pos:** C   **Ht:** 6'1" **Wt:** 200 **Born:** 3/29/69 **Age:** 31

Year Team	Lg Org	G	AB	H	2B	3B	HR	TB	R	RBI	TBB	IBB	SO	HBP	SH	SF	SB	CS	SB%	GDP	Avg	OBP	SLG
1988 Padres	R SD	42	156	44	4	6	1	63	18	22	10	0	24	0	0	0	9	4	.69	2	.282	.325	.404
1989 Waterloo	A SD	97	319	61	13	1	2	82	32	26	25	1	61	4	6	1	4	4	.50	12	.191	.258	.257
1990 Chston-SC	A SD	32	101	20	2	0	0	22	9	5	7	0	18	4	0	2	0	1	.00	2	.198	.272	.218
1991 Waterloo	A SD	102	342	97	13	1	8	136	49	57	47	5	66	2	2	4	3	3	.50	4	.284	.370	.398
1992 Wichita	AA SD	96	319	78	8	4	6	112	35	48	13	0	68	7	2	6	4	3	.57	7	.245	.284	.351
1993 Rancho Cuca	A+ SD	37	103	26	10	0	1	39	25	9	24	1	19	2	0	0	1	1	.00	3	.252	.403	.379
Wichita	AA SD	50	142	29	7	0	4	48	12	14	22	2	24	1	1	0	3	0	1.00	2	.204	.315	.338
1994 Wichita	AA SD	42	131	33	7	0	1	43	15	12	15	0	16	3	1	2	0	2	.00	2	.252	.338	.328
Rancho Cuca	A+ SD	7	20	5	2	0	0	7	1	1	1	0	2	0	0	1	0	0	.00	1	.250	.286	.350
Las Vegas	AAA SD	17	47	10	2	0	1	15	3	4	1	0	7	0	1	1	0	0	.00	1	.213	.224	.319
1995 El Paso	AA Mil	84	218	68	15	2	4	99	32	28	18	1	45	4	3	0	0	3	.00	8	.312	.375	.454
New Orleans	AAA Mil	3	8	0	0	0	0	0	0	0	0	0	3	0	0	0	0	0	.00	0	.000	.000	.000
1996 El Paso	AA Mil	46	144	44	10	1	2	62	22	20	17	1	24	0	3	2	2	2	.50	2	.306	.374	.431
New Orleans	AAA Mil	34	87	19	4	0	0	23	7	3	13	1	22	0	0	0	0	0	.00	5	.218	.320	.264
1997 Kissimmee	A+ Hou	25	69	14	4	1	0	20	7	8	4	0	11	0	0	1	0	1	.00	2	.203	.243	.290
Jackson	AA Hou	27	88	26	5	0	2	37	9	13	4	0	16	1	0	0	0	1	.00	2	.295	.333	.420
1998 Jackson	AA Hou	60	178	51	14	0	9	92	29	28	17	0	27	8	1	1	2	0	1.00	6	.287	.373	.517
1999 New Orleans	AAA Hou	19	60	16	4	0	2	26	11	11	7	1	8	0	2	0	0	0	.00	0	.267	.343	.433
Jackson	AA Hou	81	255	47	11	0	6	76	20	28	12	0	52	2	4	2	1	1	.50	2	.184	.225	.298
12 Min. YEARS		901	2787	688	135	16	49	1002	336	337	257	13	513	38	26	22	28	26	.52	65	.247	.317	.360

Rafael Lopez

Bats: Right **Throws:** Right **Pos:** C   **Ht:** 6'0" **Wt:** 195 **Born:** 10/22/76 **Age:** 23

Year Team	Lg Org	G	AB	H	2B	3B	HR	TB	R	RBI	TBB	IBB	SO	HBP	SH	SF	SB	CS	SB%	GDP	Avg	OBP	SLG
1996 Kingsport	R+ NYM	65	250	79	22	4	7	130	53	58	31	1	25	4	0	2	0	1	.00	4	.316	.397	.520
Pittsfield	A- NYM	5	14	6	0	1	0	8	2	3	1	0	1	0	0	0	0	0	.00	0	.429	.467	.571
1997 St. Lucie	A+ NYM	113	375	93	19	0	3	121	40	30	39	3	56	0	1	1	3	2	.60	10	.248	.318	.323
1998 Mariners	R Sea	5	15	5	2	0	0	7	1	2	1	0	2	0	0	0	0	0	.00	4	.333	.375	.467
Wisconsin	A Sea	35	121	27	5	1	1	37	11	12	9	0	18	1	0	0	0	0	.00	4	.223	.282	.306
1999 New Haven	AA Sea	8	32	6	1	0	0	7	1	1	1	0	5	0	0	0	0	0	.00	2	.188	.188	.219
Lancaster	A+ Sea	72	247	71	10	3	5	102	37	28	15	0	36	5	2	1	5	4	.56	11	.287	.340	.413
4 Min. YEARS		303	1054	287	59	9	16	412	145	134	96	4	143	10	3	4	8	7	.53	31	.272	.338	.391

Rodrigo Lopez

Pitches: Right **Bats:** Right **Pos:** P   **Ht:** 6'1" **Wt:** 180 **Born:** 12/14/75 **Age:** 24

Year Team	Lg Org	G	GS	CG	GF	IP	BFP	H	R	ER	HR	SH	SF	HB	TBB	IBB	SO	WP	Bk	W	L	Pct.	ShO	Sv	ERA
1995 Padres	R SD	11	7	0	3	34.2	162	41	29	21	0	1	2	2	14	0	33	3	1	1	1	.500	0	1	5.45
1996 Idaho Falls	R+ SD	16	11	0	1	71	311	76	52	45	7	2	4	4	34	0	72	8	4	4	4	.500	0	1	5.70
1997 Clinton	A SD	37	14	2	19	121.2	508	103	49	43	6	7	4	3	42	1	123	3	4	6	8	.429	0	9	3.18
1998 Mobile	AA SD	4	4	2	0	25.2	101	21	11	4	1	0	1	0	4	0	20	0	0	3	0	1.000	1	0	1.40
1999 Mobile	AA SD	28	28	2	0	169.1	728	187	91	83	14	4	6	7	58	3	138	5	1	10	8	.556	1	0	4.41
5 Min. YEARS		95	67	6	23	422.1	1813	428	232	196	24	16	16	16	152	4	386	19	10	24	21	.533	2	11	4.18

Mike Lopez-Cao

Bats: Left **Throws:** Right **Pos:** C   **Ht:** 5'6" **Wt:** 180 **Born:** 8/14/75 **Age:** 24

Year Team	Lg Org	G	AB	H	2B	3B	HR	TB	R	RBI	TBB	IBB	SO	HBP	SH	SF	SB	CS	SB%	GDP	Avg	OBP	SLG
1997 Hudson Val	A- TB	14	44	13	3	0	1	19	6	7	3	0	10	0	0	1	2	0	1.00	2	.295	.333	.432
Princeton	R+ TB	17	53	12	0	1	1	17	7	7	5	0	8	0	0	1	0	0	.00	0	.226	.288	.321
1998 Chston-SC	A TB	14	24	6	0	0	0	6	2	4	4	0	4	1	0	1	2	0	1.00	0	.250	.367	.250
1999 Delmarva	A Bal	2	6	1	0	0	1	4	2	3	1	0	0	0	0	1	0	0	.00	0	.167	.250	.667
Frederick	A+ Bal	29	88	21	4	0	2	31	12	11	9	0	16	0	1	1	1	0	1.00	1	.239	.306	.352
Bowie	AA Bal	16	47	12	1	0	2	19	5	7	2	0	8	0	0	0	0	0	.00	1	.255	.286	.404
3 Min. YEARS		92	262	65	8	1	7	96	34	39	24	0	46	1	1	5	5	0	1.00	4	.248	.308	.366

Luis Lorenzana

Bats: Right **Throws:** Right **Pos:** 3B-2B   **Ht:** 6'0" **Wt:** 180 **Born:** 11/9/78 **Age:** 21

Year Team	Lg Org	G	AB	H	2B	3B	HR	TB	R	RBI	TBB	IBB	SO	HBP	SH	SF	SB	CS	SB%	GDP	Avg	OBP	SLG
1996 Pirates	R Pit	18	53	8	1	0	0	9	4	5	12	0	8	1	1	1	0	1	.00	1	.151	.313	.170
Erie	A- Pit	44	128	25	8	1	0	35	19	12	16	0	26	3	4	3	1	4	.20	1	.195	.293	.273
1997 Augusta	A Pit	92	288	68	11	1	0	81	36	20	31	0	66	2	4	1	4	5	.44	5	.236	.314	.281
1998 Lynchburg	A+ Pit	95	283	67	7	2	2	84	27	24	35	1	62	5	9	2	2	2	.50	8	.237	.329	.297
1999 Lynchburg	A+ Pit	49	156	40	7	0	2	53	15	14	11	0	37	4	0	1	2	3	.40	2	.256	.320	.340
Altoona	AA Pit	34	74	16	2	1	2	26	9	8	14	0	17	4	1	3	0	0	.00	2	.216	.358	.351
4 Min. YEARS		332	982	224	36	5	6	288	110	83	119	1	216	19	19	11	9	15	.38	25	.228	.320	.293

Kevin Lovingier

Pitches: Left **Bats:** Left **Pos:** P   **Ht:** 6'1" **Wt:** 190 **Born:** 8/29/71 **Age:** 28

Year Team	Lg Org	G	GS	CG	GF	IP	BFP	H	R	ER	HR	SH	SF	HB	TBB	IBB	SO	WP	Bk	W	L	Pct.	ShO	Sv	ERA
1994 New Jersey	A- StL	35	0	0	5	52.1	211	36	13	9	3	3	0	2	19	1	71	3	0	1	0	1.000	0	1	1.55
1995 Savannah	A StL	38	0	0	18	47	195	35	14	7	1	3	1	1	21	5	54	3	0	6	3	.667	0	1	1.34
St. Pete	A+ StL	22	0	0	6	21.2	82	9	4	4	0	1	1	2	10	1	14	1	0	1	0	1.000	0	0	1.66
1996 Arkansas	AA StL	60	0	0	19	63.2	295	60	30	29	4	6	2	1	48	6	73	3	0	2	3	.400	0	1	4.10
1997 Arkansas	AA StL	59	0	0	22	74.1	314	68	27	21	4	3	0	1	26	2	82	5	1	4	3	.571	0	3	2.54
1998 Arkansas	AA StL	19	0	0	6	24	104	20	9	7	2	0	0	0	13	1	26	3	0	1	0	1.000	0	0	2.63
Memphis	AAA StL	39	0	0	8	59	245	38	22	20	7	3	0	0	33	0	63	2	1	5	1	.833	0	0	3.05
1999 Memphis	AAA StL	51	0	0	11	78	338	66	44	42	8	1	1	0	40	0	66	4	0	3	4	.429	0	0	4.85
6 Min. YEARS		323	0	0	95	420	1784	332	163	139	29	20	5	9	210	16	449	24	2	23	14	.622	0	6	2.98

Benny Lowe

Pitches: Left **Bats:** Left **Pos:** P   **Ht:** 5'10" **Wt:** 185 **Born:** 6/13/74 **Age:** 26

Year Team	Lg Org	G	GS	CG	GF	IP	BFP	H	R	ER	HR	SH	SF	HB	TBB	IBB	SO	WP	Bk	W	L	Pct.	ShO	Sv	ERA
1994 Blue Jays	R Tor	22	1	0	5	22.1	104	20	16	11	0	4	0	2	14	1	27	1	1	2	1	.667	0	1	4.43
1995 St.Cathrnes	A- Tor	15	15	0	0	78.2	358	89	43	38	3	3	3	9	40	0	61	10	1	4	5	.444	0	0	4.35
1996 Hagerstown	A Tor	46	1	0	34	65.2	289	40	24	17	2	2	1	7	52	0	89	2	0	2	3	.400	0	9	2.33
1997 Knoxville	AA Tor	18	0	0	8	26	124	33	21	16	6	1	1	2	14	1	29	2	2	3	1	.750	0	0	5.54
Dunedin	A+ Tor	13	0	0	13	14.2	57	7	3	3	0	0	1	1	3	0	19	1	0	2	1	.667	0	5	1.84
Hagerstown	A Tor	2	0	0	2	2	10	3	3	0	0	0	0	0	0	0	4	0	0	0	0	.000	0	0	0.00
1998 Dunedin	A+ Tor	9	0	0	2	9.1	46	8	5	2	0	1	1	2	6	0	13	1	0	0	0	.000	0	1	1.93
1999 Knoxville	AA Tor	58	0	0	19	68.1	309	68	44	39	8	6	4	3	40	0	70	7	0	4	6	.400	0	3	5.14
6 Min. YEARS		183	17	0	83	287	1297	268	159	126	19	17	11	26	169	2	312	24	4	17	17	.500	0	18	3.95

Brian Loyd

Bats: Right **Throws:** Right **Pos:** C   **Ht:** 6'2" **Wt:** 210 **Born:** 12/3/73 **Age:** 26

Year Team	Lg Org	G	AB	H	2B	3B	HR	TB	R	RBI	TBB	IBB	SO	HBP	SH	SF	SB	CS	SB%	GDP	Avg	OBP	SLG
1996 Clinton	A SD	10	37	11	2	0	0	13	3	2	0	0	6	2	0	0	0	0	.00	0	.297	.333	.351
1997 Clinton	A SD	73	259	71	10	0	2	87	35	33	25	2	41	8	4	5	6	4	.60	12	.274	.350	.336
1998 Rancho Cuca	A+ SD	87	318	97	19	1	4	130	55	35	42	1	45	10	2	2	1	4	.20	8	.305	.401	.409
Dunedin	A+ Tor	16	49	10	0	0	1	13	8	5	5	0	10	1	1	2	1	0	1.00	3	.204	.281	.265
1999 Knoxville	AA Tor	104	364	102	18	1	11	155	53	65	46	3	57	4	4	6	9	2	.82	11	.280	.362	.426
4 Min. YEARS		290	1027	291	49	2	18	398	154	140	118	6	159	25	11	15	17	10	.63	34	.283	.366	.388

Matt Lubozynski

Pitches: Left **Bats:** Right **Pos:** P   **Ht:** 6'4" **Wt:** 190 **Born:** 11/9/76 **Age:** 23

Year Team	Lg Org	G	GS	CG	GF	IP	BFP	H	R	ER	HR	SH	SF	HB	TBB	IBB	SO	WP	Bk	W	L	Pct.	ShO	Sv	ERA
1998 Boise	A- Ana	9	0	0	2	27.2	103	17	5	5	1	1	0	2	7	0	21	0	0	2	1	.667	0	1	1.63
Cedar Rapds	A Ana	19	0	0	6	21.1	80	17	10	6	6	0	0	1	5	0	12	0	0	2	0	1.000	0	0	2.53
1999 Lk Elsinore	A+ Ana	30	0	0	15	39	164	35	12	10	1	2	0	0	17	2	18	4	1	1	1	.500	0	3	2.31
Edmonton	AAA Ana	1	0	0	1	2	8	1	0	0	0	0	0	0	1	0	1	0	0	0	0	.000	0	0	0.00
2 Min. YEARS		59	0	0	24	90	355	70	27	21	8	3	1	1	30	2	52	6	1	5	2	.714	0	5	2.10

Lou Lucca

Bats: Right **Throws:** Right **Pos:** 3B   **Ht:** 5'11" **Wt:** 210 **Born:** 10/13/70 **Age:** 29

Year Team	Lg Org	G	AB	H	2B	3B	HR	TB	R	RBI	TBB	IBB	SO	HBP	SH	SF	SB	CS	SB%	GDP	Avg	OBP	SLG
1992 Erie	A- Fla	76	263	74	16	1	13	131	51	44	33	0	40	5	0	2	6	3	.67	8	.281	.370	.498
1993 Kane County	A Fla	127	419	116	25	2	6	163	52	53	60	0	58	9	2	7	4	10	.29	9	.277	.374	.389
1994 Brevard Cty	A+ Fla	130	441	125	29	1	8	180	62	76	72	2	73	4	0	6	3	7	.30	18	.283	.384	.408
1995 Portland	AA Fla	112	388	107	28	1	9	164	57	64	59	5	77	5	0	2	4	4	.50	18	.276	.377	.423
1996 Charlotte	AAA Fla	87	273	71	14	1	7	108	26	35	11	0	62	4	0	3	0	3	.00	11	.260	.296	.396
1997 Charlotte	AAA Fla	96	292	83	22	1	18	161	40	51	22	4	56	2	0	3	5	4	.56	7	.284	.335	.551
1998 Charlotte	AAA Fla	112	397	115	32	0	11	180	47	51	13	2	75	5	0	2	2	6	.25	10	.290	.319	.453
1999 Scranton-WB	AAA Phi	136	533	143	33	2	12	216	61	70	22	0	94	9	0	5	4	6	.40	15	.268	.306	.405
8 Min. YEARS		876	3006	834	199	9	84	1303	396	444	292	13	535	43	2	30	28	43	.39	96	.277	.347	.433

Robert Luce

Pitches: Right **Bats:** Both **Pos:** P   **Ht:** 6'0" **Wt:** 168 **Born:** 7/19/74 **Age:** 25

Year Team	Lg Org	G	GS	CG	GF	IP	BFP	H	R	ER	HR	SH	SF	HB	TBB	IBB	SO	WP	Bk	W	L	Pct.	ShO	Sv	ERA
1996 Everett	A- Sea	23	0	0	16	41	187	45	26	20	6	3	1	1	16	1	47	6	1	3	4	.429	0	7	4.39
1997 Lancaster	A+ Sea	14	14	0	0	86.1	372	100	43	27	8	0	2	5	24	0	57	4	0	10	1	.909	0	0	2.81
Memphis	AA Sea	13	13	1	0	75.2	315	90	40	33	5	2	0	1	14	0	41	3	0	5	2	.714	0	0	3.93
1998 Orlando	AA Sea	27	26	1	1	168	741	218	103	95	20	2	2	6	49	0	73	1	0	12	7	.632	0	0	5.09
1999 New Haven	AA Sea	2	0	0	0	7.1	35	11	10	7	2	2	0	1	3	0	3	1	0	0	0	.000	0	0	8.59
Tacoma	AAA Sea	3	3	0	0	16	73	22	15	15	4	1	1	0	7	0	6	0	0	0	3	.000	0	0	8.44
4 Min. YEARS		82	56	2	17	394.1	1723	486	237	197	45	8	6	14	113	1	227	15	1	30	17	.638	0	7	4.50

Brian Luderer

Bats: Right **Throws:** Right **Pos:** C   **Ht:** 5'11" **Wt:** 195 **Born:** 8/19/78 **Age:** 21

Year Team	Lg Org	G	AB	H	2B	3B	HR	TB	R	RBI	TBB	IBB	SO	HBP	SH	SF	SB	CS	SB%	GDP	Avg	OBP	SLG
1996 Athletics	R Oak	6	13	4	0	0	0	4	1	2	0	0	1	0	1	0	0	0	.00	0	.308	.308	.308
1997 Athletics	R Oak	39	123	33	4	0	3	46	21	26	17	0	12	6	1	1	3	4	.43	6	.268	.381	.374
1998 Modesto	A+ Oak	19	45	6	2	2	0	12	3	3	4	0	6	0	2	0	0	0	.00	0	.133	.204	.267
Sou Oregon	A- Oak	10	37	11	2	1	2	21	9	7	2	0	7	0	0	0	0	0	.00	0	.297	.333	.568
Huntsville	AA Oak	17	38	11	1	1	0	14	4	5	3	0	7	1	1	0	0	0	.00	1	.289	.357	.368
1999 Vancouver	AAA Oak	10	28	9	1	0	0	10	6	4	4	0	2	1	0	0	0	0	.00	0	.321	.424	.357
Modesto	A+ Oak	55	182	52	13	2	1	72	22	22	16	1	25	2	2	2	3	3	.50	5	.286	.347	.396
4 Min. YEARS		156	466	126	23	6	6	179	66	69	46	1	60	10	7	3	6	7	.46	12	.270	.347	.384

Julio Lugo

Bats: Right **Throws:** Right **Pos:** SS   **Ht:** 6'0" **Wt:** 165 **Born:** 11/16/75 **Age:** 24

Year Team	Lg Org	G	AB	H	2B	3B	HR	TB	R	RBI	TBB	IBB	SO	HBP	SH	SF	SB	CS	SB%	GDP	Avg	OBP	SLG
1995 Auburn	A- Hou	59	230	67	8	3	1	82	36	16	26	0	31	2	2	0	17	7	.71	7	.291	.368	.357
1996 Quad City	A Hou	101	393	116	18	2	10	168	60	50	32	0	75	3	4	4	24	11	.69	7	.295	.350	.427
1997 Kissimmee	A+ Hou	125	505	135	22	14	7	206	89	61	46	1	99	2	8	4	35	8	.81	8	.267	.329	.408
1998 Kissimmee	A+ Hou	128	509	154	20	14	7	223	81	62	49	3	72	4	6	2	51	18	.74	13	.303	.367	.438
1999 Jackson	AA Hou	116	445	142	24	5	10	206	77	42	44	0	53	3	1	4	25	11	.69	6	.319	.381	.463
5 Min. YEARS		529	2082	614	90	38	35	885	343	231	197	4	330	14	21	14	152	55	.73	41	.295	.358	.425

Mark Lukasiewicz

Pitches: Left **Bats:** Left **Pos:** P   **Ht:** 6'5" **Wt:** 230 **Born:** 3/8/73 **Age:** 27

Year Team	Lg Org	G	GS	CG	GF	IP	BFP	H	R	ER	HR	SH	SF	HB	TBB	IBB	SO	WP	Bk	W	L	Pct.	ShO	Sv	ERA
1994 Hagerstown	A Tor	29	17	0	5	98	449	108	70	52	8	6	4	7	51	0	84	8	0	3	6	.333	0	0	4.78
1995 Dunedin	A+ Tor	31	13	0	11	88.1	383	80	62	55	13	1	2	7	42	0	71	7	0	3	6	.333	0	1	5.60
1996 Dunedin	A+ Tor	23	0	0	5	31.1	144	28	20	16	1	1	1	4	22	1	31	1	0	2	1	.667	0	1	4.60
Bakersfield	A+ Tor	7	0	0	3	12.2	66	17	14	13	2	1	0	1	11	0	9	1	0	0	2	.000	0	0	9.24
Hagerstown	A Tor	9	1	0	4	15.2	63	8	5	4	0	0	0	1	7	0	20	1	0	2	0	1.000	0	0	2.30
1997 Knoxville	AA Tor	27	0	0	8	37	149	26	17	15	2	1	1	1	14	1	43	4	0	2	0	1.000	0	7	3.65
Syracuse	AAA Tor	30	0	0	9	31.1	146	37	22	18	7	1	2	2	13	1	31	1	0	2	3	.400	0	0	5.17
1998 Knoxville	A+ Tor	9	0	0	1	10.2	42	7	2	1	0	0	1	0	4	0	8	0	0	1	1	.500	0	0	0.84
Knoxville	AA Tor	5	0	0	2	9.1	33	6	2	2	0	0	0	1	1	0	16	0	0	0	0	.000	0	1	1.93
Syracuse	AAA Tor	22	4	0	3	47.2	201	38	18	18	8	0	0	3	24	1	30	3	0	2	2	.500	0	1	3.40
1999 Syracuse	AAA Tor	37	9	1	6	97.2	431	109	59	58	20	1	2	0	40	1	77	5	1	4	4	.500	0	3	5.34
6 Min. YEARS		229	44	1	57	479.2	2107	464	291	252	61	12	13	26	229	5	420	31		21	25	.457	0	14	4.73

Fernando Lunar

Bats: Right **Throws:** Right **Pos:** C   **Ht:** 6'1" **Wt:** 190 **Born:** 5/25/77 **Age:** 23

Year Team	Lg Org	G	AB	H	2B	3B	HR	TB	R	RBI	TBB	IBB	SO	HBP	SH	SF	SB	CS	SB%	GDP	Avg	OBP	SLG
1994 Braves	R Atl	33	100	24	5	0	2	35	9	12	1	0	13	3	1	1	0	0	.00	1	.240	.267	.350
1995 Macon	A Atl	39	134	24	2	0	0	26	13	9	10	0	38	3	3	0	1	0	1.00	3	.179	.252	.194
Eugene	A- Atl	38	131	32	6	0	2	44	13	16	9	0	28	0	2	0	0	1	.00	2	.244	.293	.336
1996 Macon	A Atl	104	343	63	9	0	7	93	33	33	20	0	65	12	3	2	3	2	.60	11	.184	.252	.271
1997 Macon	A Atl	105	380	99	26	2	7	150	41	37	18	1	42	5	2	1	0	1	.00	11	.261	.302	.395
1998 Danville	A+ Atl	91	286	63	9	0	3	81	19	28	6	0	52	12	2	0	1	1	.50	8	.220	.266	.283
1999 Greenville	AA Atl	105	343	77	15	1	3	103	33	35	12	5	64	12	0	0			.00		.224	.275	.300
6 Min. YEARS		515	1717	382	72	3	24	532	161	170	76	6	302	47	13	4	5	6	.45	43	.222	.274	.310

Keith Luuloa

Bats: Right Throws: Right Pos: 2B   Ht: 6'0" Wt: 185 Born: 12/24/74 Age: 25

Year Team	Lg Org	G	AB	H	2B	3B	HR	TB	R	RBI	TBB	IBB	SO	HBP	SH	SF	SB	CS	SB%	GDP	Avg	OBP	SLG
1994 Angels	R Ana	28	97	29	4	1	1	38	14	10	8	0	14	4	1	3	3	4	.43	0	.299	.366	.392
1995 Lk Elsinore	A+ Ana	102	380	100	22	7	5	151	50	53	24	0	47	6	7	1	1	5	.17	9	.263	.316	.397
1996 Midland	AA Ana	134	531	138	24	2	7	187	80	44	47	0	54	6	8	3	4	6	.40	14	.260	.325	.352
1997 Midland	AA Ana	120	421	115	29	5	9	181	67	59	36	0	59	5	10	6	7	4	.64	18	.273	.333	.430
1998 Midland	AA Ana	130	479	160	43	10	17	274	85	102	75	5	54	7	2	16	6	5	.55	15	.334	.419	.572
Vancouver	AAA Ana	8	30	10	1	0	0	11	4	3	4	0	3	0	0	1	1	1	.50	1	.333	.400	.367
1999 Edmonton	AAA Ana	115	396	113	23	1	4	150	54	46	44	0	53	5	4	2	7	7	.50	14	.285	.362	.379
6 Min. YEARS		637	2334	665	146	26	43	992	354	317	238	5	284	33	32	32	29	32	.48	71	.285	.355	.425

Ryan Luzinski

Bats: Right Throws: Right Pos: C   Ht: 6'1" Wt: 215 Born: 8/22/73 Age: 26

Year Team	Lg Org	G	AB	H	2B	3B	HR	TB	R	RBI	TBB	IBB	SO	HBP	SH	SF	SB	CS	SB%	GDP	Avg	OBP	SLG
1992 Great Falls	R+ LA	61	227	57	14	4	4	91	26	29	22	2	47	2	0	1	2	1	.67	1	.251	.321	.401
1993 Bakersfield	A+ LA	48	147	41	10	1	3	62	18	9	13	0	24	5	0	0	2	2	.50	3	.279	.358	.422
Yakima	A- LA	69	237	61	10	3	4	89	32	46	41	4	44	4	3	3	6	1	.86	2	.257	.372	.376
1994 Vero Beach	A+ LA	112	379	99	18	3	11	156	48	61	33	1	91	5	1	5	2	1	.67	11	.261	.325	.412
1995 San Antonio	AA LA	44	144	33	5	0	1	41	18	9	13	1	32	3	2	1	1	1	.50	6	.229	.304	.285
Vero Beach	A+ LA	38	134	45	12	0	5	72	15	23	9	3	21	0	0	1	1	0	1.00	4	.336	.375	.537
1996 Albuquerque	AAA LA	9	14	2	0	0	0	2	0	1	0	0	6	0	0	0	0	0	.00	0	.143	.143	.143
San Antonio	AA LA	32	103	30	6	0	0	36	12	10	12	0	19	1	1	0	2	0	1.00	6	.291	.365	.350
San Berndno	A+ LA	30	118	41	10	0	5	66	24	21	11	0	33	0	2	1	6	1	.86	2	.347	.400	.559
1997 Frederick	A+ Bal	1	3	2	0	0	0	2	1	0	1	0	0	0	0	0	0	0	.00	0	.667	.750	.667
Bowie	AA Bal	30	81	23	4	0	5	42	12	15	10	1	17	0	0	0	3	0	1.00	1	.284	.363	.519
Rochester	AAA Bal	42	125	26	7	1	2	41	12	16	19	0	49	3	1	1	1	0	1.00	5	.208	.324	.328
1998 Bowie	AA Bal	72	233	56	3	0	7	80	25	25	20	0	72	2	1	0	3	3	.50	5	.240	.306	.343
Rochester	AAA Bal	4	12	0	0	0	0	0	0	1	0	0	3	0	0	1	0	0	.00	1	.000	.000	.000
1999 Chattanooga	AA Cin	55	171	42	10	0	2	58	17	26	24	2	43	1	1	1	1	2	.33	4	.246	.340	.339
Mobile	AA SD	22	62	23	10	0	0	33	11	4	13	0	15	1	1	1	0	0	.00	2	.371	.481	.532
8 Min. YEARS		669	2190	581	119	12	49	871	271	296	240	14	516	27	13	16	29	13	.69	53	.265	.343	.398

Scott Lydy

Bats: Right Throws: Right Pos: OF   Ht: 6'5" Wt: 195 Born: 10/26/68 Age: 31

Year Team	Lg Org	G	AB	H	2B	3B	HR	TB	R	RBI	TBB	IBB	SO	HBP	SH	SF	SB	CS	SB%	GDP	Avg	OBP	SLG
1990 Madison	A Oak	54	174	33	6	2	4	55	33	19	25	1	62	1	0	2	7	5	.58	1	.190	.292	.316
Athletics	R Oak	18	50	17	6	0	2	29	8	11	10	0	14	0	0	0	0	0	.00	1	.340	.450	.580
1991 Madison	A Oak	127	464	120	26	2	12	186	64	69	66	5	109	5	0	4	24	9	.73	10	.259	.354	.401
1992 Reno	A+ Oak	33	124	49	13	2	2	72	29	27	26	2	30	0	0	0	9	4	.69	1	.395	.500	.581
Huntsville	AA Oak	109	387	118	20	3	9	171	64	65	67	5	95	4	0	4	16	5	.76	4	.305	.409	.442
1993 Tacoma	AAA Oak	95	341	100	22	6	9	161	70	41	50	3	87	1	2	3	12	4	.75	8	.293	.382	.472
1994 Tacoma	AAA Oak	135	508	160	37	3	17	254	98	73	58	1	108	6	1	6	22	6	.79	14	.315	.388	.500
1995 Edmonton	AAA Oak	104	400	116	29	7	16	207	78	65	33	3	66	6	3	5	15	4	.79	11	.290	.349	.518
1998 Rochester	AAA Bal	20	66	9	5	0	1	17	3	8	4	0	15	1	0	1	1	0	1.00	2	.136	.194	.258
Winnipeg	IND —	3	10	1	0	0	0	2	1	2	1	0	7	1	0	0	0	0	.00	0	.100	.250	.200
1999 Charlotte	AAA CWS	19	66	14	2	0	2	22	11	13	8	0	15	0	0	2	1	0	1.00	2	.212	.289	.333
Birmingham	AA CWS	111	400	106	25	1	20	193	74	65	67	3	61	3	1	1	18	3	.86	5	.265	.374	.483
1993 Oakland	AL	41	102	23	5	0	2	34	11	7	8	0	39	1	0	0	2	0	1.00	1	.225	.288	.333
8 Min. YEARS		828	2990	843	192	26	94	1369	533	458	415	23	669	28	7	28	125	40	.76	59	.282	.372	.458

Ryan Lynch

Pitches: Left Bats: Left Pos: P   Ht: 6'4" Wt: 220 Born: 8/10/74 Age: 25

Year Team	Lg Org	G	GS	CG	GF	IP	BFP	H	R	ER	HR	SH	SF	HB	TBB	IBB	SO	WP	Bk	W	L	Pct.	ShO	Sv	ERA
1996 Elizabethtn	R+ Min	11	9	0	0	45	197	43	19	17	2	1	1	3	22	0	35	2	0	3	2	.600	0	0	3.40
1997 Fort Wayne	A Min	15	2	0	5	34.1	155	38	20	12	2	1	1	3	10	0	39	2	0	2	2	.500	0	1	3.15
1998 Clinton	A SD	17	0	0	5	20	86	14	8	4	1	4	2	2	10	1	28	2	0	0	0	.000	0	2	1.80
Rancho Cuca	A+ SD	21	2	0	11	42.2	179	34	17	14	2	0	2	3	19	0	35	1	0	3	3	.500	0	1	2.95
1999 Mobile	AA Bal	9	0	0	5	15.2	85	23	15	12	1	0	1	2	16	1	11	1	0	1	0	1.000	0	1	6.89
Frederick	A+ Bal	12	1	0	3	20.1	104	18	12	11	2	4	1	2	20	2	23	4	0	1	1	.500	0	0	4.87
4 Min. YEARS		85	14	0	29	178	806	170	91	70	10	10	8	15	97	4	171	10	0	10	10	.500	0	4	3.54

Mike Lyons

Pitches: Right Bats: Right Pos: P   Ht: 6'3" Wt: 195 Born: 5/20/75 Age: 25

Year Team	Lg Org	G	GS	CG	GF	IP	BFP	H	R	ER	HR	SH	SF	HB	TBB	IBB	SO	WP	Bk	W	L	Pct.	ShO	Sv	ERA
1996 Kingsport	R+ NYM	25	0	0	15	38	157	27	14	8	1	1	0	3	14	1	52	1	1	3	2	.600	0	5	1.89
1997 Capital Cty	A NYM	44	0	0	32	58	228	40	15	12	3	4	0	1	20	4	55	2	0	6	2	.750	0	14	1.86
1998 St. Lucie	A+ NYM	28	0	0	23	40.2	172	28	12	4	0	2	1	3	14	2	27	2	2	3	2	.600	0	9	0.89
Binghamton	AA NYM	29	0	0	9	38.1	166	37	16	14	2	1	1	2	15	2	32	2	0	4	1	.800	0	5	3.29
1999 Norfolk	AAA NYM	2	0	0	2	3	19	7	7	7	1	0	0	0	3	0	5	0	0	0	0	.000	0	0	21.00
Binghamton	AA NYM	53	0	0	29	79.1	358	76	41	30	6	6	2	12	37	2	70	4	0	4	7	.364	0	5	3.40
4 Min. YEARS		181	0	0	108	257.1	1100	215	105	75	13	14	4	21	103	11	241	11	3	20	14	.588	0	38	2.62

Jon Macalutas

Bats: Right **Throws:** Right **Pos:** 1B **Ht:** 6'0" **Wt:** 200 **Born:** 1/3/74 **Age:** 26

							BATTING										BASERUNNING				PERCENTAGES		
Year Team	Lg Org	G	AB	H	2B	3B	HR	TB	R	RBI	TBB	IBB	SO	HBP	SH	SF	SB	CS	SB%	GDP	Avg	OBP	SLG
1996 Salinas	IND —	2	5	1	0	0	0	1	2	0	0	0	1	0	0	0	0	0	.00	0	.200	.200	.200
Ogden	R+ Mil	54	178	61	10	0	3	80	41	24	18	0	21	7	0	3	8	2	.80	4	.343	.417	.449
1997 Beloit	A Mil	59	211	66	13	1	10	111	45	36	24	1	19	11	1	1	6	5	.55	6	.313	.409	.526
Stockton	A+ Mil	42	164	44	10	2	4	70	18	35	9	0	13	3	0	2	2	2	.50	6	.268	.315	.427
1998 Stockton	A+ Mil	138	527	150	31	0	6	199	72	59	40	3	52	18	2	5	6	8	.43	16	.285	.353	.378
1999 Stockton	A+ Mil	32	121	34	7	0	2	47	12	20	15	0	16	2	0	3	2	2	.50	3	.281	.362	.388
Huntsville	AA Mil	93	306	81	20	1	5	118	50	45	38	2	32	11	0	0	4	3	.57	11	.265	.366	.386
4 Min. YEARS		420	1512	437	91	4	30	626	240	219	144	6	154	52	3	14	28	22	.56	46	.289	.368	.414

Rob Mackowiak

Bats: Left **Throws:** Right **Pos:** 2B **Ht:** 5'10" **Wt:** 165 **Born:** 6/20/76 **Age:** 24

							BATTING										BASERUNNING				PERCENTAGES		
Year Team	Lg Org	G	AB	H	2B	3B	HR	TB	R	RBI	TBB	IBB	SO	HBP	SH	SF	SB	CS	SB%	GDP	Avg	OBP	SLG
1996 Pirates	R Pit	27	86	23	6	1	0	31	8	14	13	1	11	1	0	1	3	1	.75	3	.267	.366	.360
1997 Erie	A- Pit	61	203	58	14	2	1	79	26	25	21	0	47	7	3	1	1	7	.13	5	.286	.371	.389
1998 Augusta	A Pit	25	70	17	4	0	1	24	16	8	13	0	19	1	1	0	4	2	.67	2	.243	.369	.343
Lynchburg	A+ Pit	86	292	80	24	6	3	125	30	31	17	0	65	4	4	2	6	3	.67	4	.274	.321	.428
1999 Lynchburg	A+ Pit	74	263	80	7	4	7	116	51	30	18	0	57	6	4	0	9	4	.69	5	.304	.362	.441
Altoona	AA Pit	53	195	51	15	3	3	81	21	27	8	1	34	7	2	4	0	2	.00	6	.262	.308	.415
4 Min. YEARS		326	1109	309	70	16	15	456	152	135	90	2	233	26	14	8	23	19	.55	25	.279	.345	.411

Scott MacRae

Pitches: Right **Bats:** Right **Pos:** P **Ht:** 6'3" **Wt:** 205 **Born:** 8/13/74 **Age:** 25

		HOW MUCH HE PITCHED						WHAT HE GAVE UP												THE RESULTS				
Year Team	Lg Org	G	GS	CG	GF	IP	BFP	H	R	ER	HR	SH	SF	HB	TBB	IBB	SO	WP	Bk	W	L	Pct.	ShO	Sv	ERA
1995 Billings	R+ Cin	18	0	0	4	27	135	32	24	17	0	0	5	3	20	4	9	2	1	0	1	.000	0	1	5.67
1996 Chstn-WV	A Cin	29	20	1	2	123.2	530	118	61	46	3	4	3	7	53	0	82	8	0	8	7	.533	0	0	3.35
1997 Burlington	A Cin	27	26	4	0	160.1	694	159	76	68	9	7	4	9	57	0	89	18	1	11	4	.733	1	0	3.82
1998 Chattanooga	AA Cin	49	5	0	6	113.2	492	105	70	56	5	3	2	3	56	2	67	10	0	9	4	.692	0	0	4.43
1999 Chattanooga	AA Cin	39	17	0	2	128.1	555	139	76	63	18	3	2	5	49	1	81	6	0	8	7	.533	0	0	4.42
5 Min. YEARS		162	68	5	14	553	2406	553	307	250	35	17	16	27	235	7	328	44	2	36	23	.610	1	1	4.07

Garry Maddox

Bats: Left **Throws:** Right **Pos:** OF **Ht:** 6'3" **Wt:** 180 **Born:** 10/24/74 **Age:** 25

							BATTING										BASERUNNING				PERCENTAGES		
Year Team	Lg Org	G	AB	H	2B	3B	HR	TB	R	RBI	TBB	IBB	SO	HBP	SH	SF	SB	CS	SB%	GDP	Avg	OBP	SLG
1997 High Desert	A+ Ari	101	409	125	22	12	7	192	89	44	52	2	94	0	3	0	25	8	.76	8	.306	.384	.469
1998 High Desert	A+ Ari	2	8	5	2	0	1	10	3	4	1	0	1	0	0	1	1	0	1.00	0	.625	.600	1.250
Jackson	AA Hou	25	94	33	3	2	3	49	20	14	5	0	20	0	0	1	3	2	.60	0	.351	.384	.521
Tucson	AAA Ari	81	269	71	13	4	4	104	36	18	15	0	57	3	0	1	4	3	.57	6	.264	.309	.387
1999 El Paso	AA Ari	127	492	145	35	9	15	243	80	75	31	2	106	8	1	4	22	5	.81	5	.295	.344	.494
3 Min. YEARS		336	1272	379	75	27	30	598	228	155	104	4	278	11	4	6	55	18	.75	19	.298	.355	.470

Calvin Maduro

Pitches: Right **Bats:** Right **Pos:** P **Ht:** 6'0" **Wt:** 188 **Born:** 9/5/74 **Age:** 25

		HOW MUCH HE PITCHED						WHAT HE GAVE UP												THE RESULTS				
Year Team	Lg Org	G	GS	CG	GF	IP	BFP	H	R	ER	HR	SH	SF	HB	TBB	IBB	SO	WP	Bk	W	L	Pct.	ShO	Sv	ERA
1992 Orioles	R Bal	13	12	1	1	71.1	289	56	29	18	2	2	3	1	26	0	66	4	3	1	4	.200	1	0	2.27
1993 Bluefield	R+ Bal	14	14	3	0	91	378	90	46	40	4	0	2	3	17	0	83	4	1	9	4	.692	0	0	3.96
1994 Frederick	A+ Bal	27	26	0	1	152.1	636	132	86	72	18	3	3	4	59	0	137	10	4	9	8	.529	0	0	4.25
1995 Frederick	A+ Bal	20	20	2	0	122.1	499	109	43	40	16	3	2	6	34	0	120	2	0	8	5	.615	2	0	2.94
Bowie	AA Bal	7	7	0	0	35.1	165	39	28	20	3	1	2	0	27	0	26	3	0	0	6	.000	0	0	5.09
1996 Bowie	AA Bal	19	19	4	0	124.1	507	116	50	45	8	4	1	2	36	0	87	4	2	9	7	.563	3	0	3.26
Rochester	AAA Bal	8	8	0	0	43.2	197	49	25	23	8	1	1	3	18	0	40	2	0	3	5	.375	0	0	4.74
1997 Scranton-WB	AAA Phi	13	13	2	0	79.1	354	71	48	44	10	5	2	1	57	1	53	6	0	6	4	.600	0	0	4.99
1998 Scranton-WB	AAA Phi	28	27	4	0	177.2	799	211	123	118	28	4	6	2	68	1	120	3	1	12	9	.571	1	0	5.98
1999 Scranton-WB	AAA Phi	29	28	2	0	169	735	179	88	75	23	1	7	5	60	0	149	4	1	11	11	.500	1	0	3.99
1996 Philadelphia	NL	4	2	0	0	15.1	62	13	6	6	1	1	0	2	3	0	11	1	0	0	1	.000	0	0	3.52
1997 Philadelphia	NL	15	13	0	0	71	331	83	59	57	12	1	4	3	41	5	31	6	2	3	7	.300	0	0	7.23
8 Min. YEARS		178	174	18	2	1066.1	4559	1052	566	495	120	24	29	27	402	2	881	42	12	68	63	.519	8	0	4.18
2 Maj. YEARS		19	15	0	0	86.1	393	96	65	63	13	2	4	5	44	5	42	7	2	3	8	.273	0	0	6.57

Kats Maeda

Pitches: Right **Bats:** Right **Pos:** P **Ht:** 6'2" **Wt:** 215 **Born:** 6/23/71 **Age:** 29

		HOW MUCH HE PITCHED						WHAT HE GAVE UP												THE RESULTS				
Year Team	Lg Org	G	GS	CG	GF	IP	BFP	H	R	ER	HR	SH	SF	HB	TBB	IBB	SO	WP	Bk	W	L	Pct.	ShO	Sv	ERA
1996 Yankees	R NYY	2	2	1	0	9	35	4	3	3	1	0	1	1	2	0	7	0	0	1	1	.500	1	0	3.00
Tampa	A+ NYY	2	2	0	0	10.2	50	11	5	5	0	1	1	2	6	0	8	0	0	0	0	.000	0	0	4.22
Norwich	AA NYY	9	9	1	0	53.1	221	49	25	24	4	1	2	1	21	0	30	4	0	3	2	.600	1	0	4.05
1997 Norwich	AA NYY	25	21	1	2	124.1	545	117	75	63	14	4	2	8	62	1	76	11	2	8	10	.444	1	0	4.56
1998 Columbus	AAA NYY	13	0	0	9	14.1	62	13	5	4	1	1	0	0	8	1	16	2	0	0	1	.000	0	0	2.51
Norwich	AA NYY	28	0	0	10	37.1	186	44	36	32	4	1	0	0	31	2	27	5	0	1	3	.250	0	1	7.71
1999 Norwich	AA NYY	25	7	1	11	76.2	345	82	41	37	7	0	5	3	40	0	48	10	0	3	2	.600	0	1	4.34
4 Min. YEARS		104	41	4	32	325.2	1444	320	190	168	31	8	10	15	170	4	212	32	2	16	19	.457	3	2	4.64

Ricky Magdaleno

Bats: Right Throws: Right Pos: SS Ht: 6'0" Wt: 185 Born: 7/6/74 Age: 25

BATTING / BASERUNNING / PERCENTAGES

Year Team	Lg Org	G	AB	H	2B	3B	HR	TB	R	RBI	TBB	IBB	SO	HBP	SH	SF	SB	CS	SB%	GDP	Avg	OBP	SLG
1993 Chstn-WV	A Cin	131	447	107	15	4	3	139	49	25	37	0	103	1	6	1	8	8	.50	15	.239	.298	.311
1994 Winston-Sal	A+ Cin	127	437	114	22	2	13	179	52	49	49	1	80	0	2	4	7	9	.44	9	.261	.333	.410
1995 Chattanooga	AA Cin	11	40	7	2	0	1	12	2	2	4	0	13	0	0	0	0	0	.00	3	.175	.250	.300
Winston-Sal	A+ Cin	91	309	69	13	1	7	105	30	40	15	0	69	2	3	3	3	1	.75	4	.223	.261	.340
Indianaplis	AAA Cin	4	8	1	0	0	1	4	1	1	0	0	3	0	1	0	0	0	.00	0	.125	.125	.500
1996 Chattanooga	AA Cin	132	424	94	21	1	17	168	60	63	64	4	135	1	5	4	2	7	.22	8	.222	.323	.396
1997 Chattanooga	AA Cin	61	187	49	13	1	8	88	33	34	42	1	51	1	1	1	1	1	.50	11	.262	.398	.471
Indianaplis	AAA Cin	56	155	32	11	0	4	55	20	14	16	0	48	0	1	2	1	0	.00	4	.206	.277	.355
1998 Richmond	AAA Atl	73	249	73	11	1	5	101	32	29	23	1	63	0	1	2	1	3	.25	3	.293	.350	.406
1999 Charlotte	AAA CWS	27	81	19	5	1	0	26	7	7	7	1	20	0	2	1	0	1	.00	0	.235	.292	.321
Lancaster	A+ Sea	23	89	31	4	2	1	42	12	14	11	0	12	1	0	2	2	1	.67	1	.348	.417	.472
New Haven	AA Sea	68	258	70	13	1	1	88	30	24	21	0	45	1	2	2	1	3	.25	6	.271	.326	.341
7 Min. YEARS		804	2684	666	130	14	61	1007	328	302	289	8	642	7	24	22	25	35	.42	64	.248	.320	.375

Chris Magruder

Bats: Both Throws: Right Pos: OF Ht: 5'11" Wt: 200 Born: 4/26/77 Age: 23

BATTING / BASERUNNING / PERCENTAGES

Year Team	Lg Org	G	AB	H	2B	3B	HR	TB	R	RBI	TBB	IBB	SO	HBP	SH	SF	SB	CS	SB%	GDP	Avg	OBP	SLG
1998 Bakersfield	A+ SF	22	92	28	7	0	1	38	21	4	13	1	16	0	0	0	3	0	1.00	2	.304	.390	.413
Salem-Keizr	A- SF	47	177	59	8	5	3	86	43	18	37	1	21	8	2	2	14	7	.67	2	.333	.464	.486
1999 Shreveport	AA SF	133	476	122	21	4	6	169	78	60	69	4	85	8	2	3	17	12	.59	15	.256	.358	.355
2 Min. YEARS		202	745	209	36	9	10	293	142	82	119	6	122	16	4	5	34	19	.64	19	.281	.389	.393

Alan Mahaffey

Pitches: Left Bats: Left Pos: P Ht: 6'1" Wt: 199 Born: 2/2/74 Age: 26

HOW MUCH HE PITCHED / WHAT HE GAVE UP / THE RESULTS

Year Team	Lg Org	G	GS	CG	GF	IP	BFP	H	R	ER	HR	SH	SF	HB	TBB	IBB	SO	WP	Bk	W	L	Pct.	ShO	Sv	ERA
1995 Elizabethtn	R+ Min	13	12	1	0	70	308	66	42	27	4	6	2	3	21	0	73	4	5	5	6	.455	0	0	3.47
1996 Fort Wayne	A Min	30	19	2	1	126.1	545	139	84	68	13	8	6	3	35	1	75	4	7	7	10	.412	0	0	4.84
1997 Fort Myers	A+ Min	38	0	0	11	48.1	200	46	27	22	2	3	2	1	8	0	55	1	0	1	2	.333	0	1	4.10
New Britain	AA Min	13	1	0	5	22.2	98	19	11	9	2	1	3	0	10	0	29	4	0	1	2	.333	0	1	3.57
1998 New Britain	AA Min	34	1	0	13	52.1	236	62	27	26	6	3	1	0	17	1	61	0	0	2	3	.400	0	0	4.47
1999 Salt Lake	AAA Min	7	5	0	0	21.1	106	28	17	13	1	1	0	1	15	1	11	1	1	1	2	.333	0	0	5.48
New Britain	AA Min	33	12	1	7	98.1	435	109	47	45	15	3	5	6	34	0	89	3	2	8	6	.571	0	1	4.12
5 Min. YEARS		168	50	4	37	439.1	1928	469	255	210	43	25	19	14	140	3	393	17	18	25	31	.446	0	3	4.30

Mike Mahoney

Bats: Right Throws: Right Pos: C Ht: 6'1" Wt: 200 Born: 12/5/72 Age: 27

BATTING / BASERUNNING / PERCENTAGES

Year Team	Lg Org	G	AB	H	2B	3B	HR	TB	R	RBI	TBB	IBB	SO	HBP	SH	SF	SB	CS	SB%	GDP	Avg	OBP	SLG
1995 Eugene	A- Atl	43	112	27	6	0	1	36	14	15	15	1	17	3	1	1	6	2	.75	5	.241	.344	.321
1996 Durham	A+ Atl	101	363	94	24	2	9	149	52	46	23	0	64	7	4	4	4	3	.57	8	.259	.312	.410
1997 Greenville	AA Atl	87	298	68	17	0	8	109	46	46	28	1	75	3	5	2	1	0	1.00	10	.228	.299	.366
1998 Greenville	AA Atl	20	74	16	5	0	1	24	3	6	1	0	20	2	0	2	1	1	.50	1	.216	.241	.324
Richmond	AAA Atl	71	208	44	10	0	5	69	26	28	24	3	49	5	6	5	1	1	.50	10	.212	.302	.332
1999 Richmond	AAA Atl	55	145	33	7	0	2	46	10	20	6	1	25	1	2	3	0	1	.00	2	.228	.258	.317
5 Min. YEARS		377	1200	282	69	2	26	433	151	161	97	6	250	21	18	17	13	8	.62	36	.235	.300	.361

Oswaldo Mairena

Pitches: Left Bats: Left Pos: P Ht: 5'11" Wt: 165 Born: 7/30/75 Age: 24

HOW MUCH HE PITCHED / WHAT HE GAVE UP / THE RESULTS

Year Team	Lg Org	G	GS	CG	GF	IP	BFP	H	R	ER	HR	SH	SF	HB	TBB	IBB	SO	WP	Bk	W	L	Pct.	ShO	Sv	ERA
1997 Tampa	A+ NYY	3	0	0	0	4.1	19	6	2	2	1	0	0	0	6	0	6	0	0	0	0	.000	0	0	4.15
Greensboro	A NYY	49	0	0	20	60.1	241	43	24	17	2	3	1	1	16	3	75	0	3	6	1	.857	0	8	2.54
1998 Tampa	A+ NYY	52	0	0	11	54	238	52	24	19	5	2	2	3	23	3	50	0	2	1	5	.167	0	0	3.17
1999 Norwich	AA NYY	49	0	0	16	57.1	252	48	24	17	3	4	4	1	27	4	47	4	0	4	3	.571	0	2	2.67
3 Min. YEARS		153	0	0	47	176	750	150	74	55	11	9	7	5	66	10	178	4	5	11	9	.550	0	10	2.81

Jaime Malave

Bats: Right Throws: Right Pos: C-DH Ht: 6'0" Wt: 196 Born: 3/22/75 Age: 25

BATTING / BASERUNNING / PERCENTAGES

Year Team	Lg Org	G	AB	H	2B	3B	HR	TB	R	RBI	TBB	IBB	SO	HBP	SH	SF	SB	CS	SB%	GDP	Avg	OBP	SLG
1995 Yakima	A- LA	44	137	37	13	2	1	57	12	15	6	0	41	1	1	2	1	1	.50	1	.270	.301	.416
1996 Savannah	A LA	6	16	4	0	0	0	4	2	5	0	0	3	1	0	1	0	0	.00	0	.250	.278	.250
Yakima	A- LA	40	108	22	6	0	5	43	14	16	6	0	33	0	1	0	0	0	.00	2	.204	.246	.398
1997 Savannah	A LA	58	206	52	11	1	9	92	23	32	4	0	54	1	1	1	2	1	.67	2	.252	.269	.447
San Berndno	A+ LA	1	4	1	0	0	0	1	0	0	0	0	0	0	0	0	0	0	.00	0	.250	.250	.250
1998 Vero Beach	A+ LA	28	89	24	6	1	4	44	12	9	10	0	16	0	0	0	1	0	1.00	1	.270	.343	.494
San Antonio	AA LA	28	55	14	5	0	1	22	3	4	6	1	10	0	2	0	0	0	.00	2	.255	.328	.400
1999 Waterbury	IND —	19	72	19	2	0	3	30	12	9	10	0	17	1	0	0	0	0	.00	1	.264	.361	.417
Jupiter	A+ Mon	3	10	4	2	0	0	6	2	2	2	0	1	0	0	1	0	0	.00	0	.400	.462	.600
Ottawa	AAA Mon	3	8	2	0	0	0	2	2	0	0	0	4	0	0	0	0	0	.00	0	.250	.333	.250
Harrisburg	AA Mon	12	18	4	0	0	3	13	4	4	2	0	4	0	0	1	0	0	.00	0	.222	.300	.722
5 Min. YEARS		242	723	183	45	4	26	314	86	96	47	1	183	4	6	5	4	2	.67	9	.253	.300	.434

Jose Malave

Bats: Right **Throws:** Right **Pos:** OF **Ht:** 6' 2" **Wt:** 212 **Born:** 5/31/71 **Age:** 29

Year Team	Lg Org	G	AB	H	2B	3B	HR	TB	R	RBI	TBB	IBB	SO	HBP	SH	SF	SB	CS	SB%	GDP	Avg	OBP	SLG
1990 Elmira	A- Bos	13	29	4	1	0	0	5	4	3	2	0	12	0	0	1	1	0	1.00	0	.138	.188	.172
1991 Red Sox	R Bos	37	146	47	4	2	2	61	24	28	10	0	23	1	0	3	6	0	1.00	3	.322	.363	.418
1992 Winter Havn	A+ Bos	8	25	4	0	0	0	4	1	0	0	0	11	0	1	0	0	0	.00	0	.160	.160	.160
Elmira	A- Bos	65	268	87	9	1	12	134	44	46	14	3	48	3	0	1	8	3	.73	2	.325	.364	.500
1993 Lynchburg	A+ Bos	82	312	94	27	1	8	147	42	54	36	3	54	3	0	5	2	3	.40	8	.301	.374	.471
1994 New Britain	AA Bos	122	465	139	37	7	24	262	87	92	52	1	81	4	0	7	4	7	.36	12	.299	.369	.563
1995 Pawtucket	AAA Bos	91	318	86	12	1	23	169	55	57	30	1	67	2	0	0	0	1	.00	4	.270	.337	.531
1996 Pawtucket	AAA Bos	41	155	42	6	0	8	72	30	29	12	1	37	2	0	1	2	1	.67	5	.271	.329	.465
1997 Pawtucket	AAA Bos	115	427	127	24	2	17	206	87	70	55	1	78	2	0	5	12	4	.75	12	.297	.376	.482
1999 Nashua	IND —	56	210	67	19	1	6	102	30	34	19	0	21	2	0	2	5	0	1.00	2	.160	.365	.493
Carolina	AA Col	44	146	40	10	1	10	82	21	26	16	0	28	2	0	2	0	1	.00	3	.274	.349	.562
1996 Boston	AL	41	102	24	3	0	4	39	12	17	2	0	25	1	0	0	0	0	.00	0	.235	.257	.382
1997 Boston	AL	4	4	0	0	0	0	0	0	0	0	0	2	0	0	1	0	0	.00	1	.000	.000	.000
9 Min. YEARS		674	2498	733	149	16	110	1244	425	439	246	10	460	21	1	27	40	20	.67	51	.293	.358	.498
2 Maj. YEARS		45	106	24	3	0	4	39	12	17	2	0	27	1	0	0	0	0	.00	1	.226	.248	.368

Randi Mallard

Pitches: Right **Bats:** Right **Pos:** P **Ht:** 0'1" **Wt:** 180 **Born:** 0/11/75 **Age:** 24

		HOW MUCH HE PITCHED						WHAT HE GAVE UP										THE RESULTS				
Year Team	Lg Org	G	GS	CG	GF	IP	BFP	H	R	ER	HR	SH	SF	HB	TBB	IBB	SO	WP	Bk	W	L	Pct.	ShO	Sv	ERA
1996 Princeton	R+ Cin	13	11	1	1	66	302	66	42	27	2	0	3	4	38	0	72	16	1	2	7	.222	0	0	3.68
1997 Chstn-WV	A Cin	13	12	0	0	56.1	238	51	25	24	0	2	3	5	23	0	61	8	0	3	3	.500	0	0	3.83
1998 Burlington	A Cin	14	13	2	0	82.2	356	79	41	31	3	2	1	1	32	0	71	6	1	9	3	.750	0	0	3.38
Chattanooga	AA Cin	13	12	0	0	60.1	294	65	37	29	3	1	1	3	58	1	34	7	1	1	4	.200	0	0	4.33
1999 Chattanooga	AA Cin	14	14	0	0	71.2	342	92	61	54	7	2	2	2	45	0	45	15	2	4	5	.444	0	0	6.78
Clinton	A Cin	6	1	0	1	15.2	70	18	12	12	0	0	0	3	3	0	21	4	0	0	1	.000	0	0	6.89
4 Min. YEARS		73	63	3	2	352.2	1602	371	218	177	15	7	10	18	199	1	304	56	5	19	23	.452	0	0	4.52

Bill Malloy

Pitches: Right **Bats:** Right **Pos:** P **Ht:** 6'2" **Wt:** 225 **Born:** 5/22/75 **Age:** 25

		HOW MUCH HE PITCHED						WHAT HE GAVE UP										THE RESULTS				
Year Team	Lg Org	G	GS	CG	GF	IP	BFP	H	R	ER	HR	SH	SF	HB	TBB	IBB	SO	WP	Bk	W	L	Pct.	ShO	Sv	ERA
1996 Bellingham	A- SF	15	7	0	3	34	155	34	27	22	0	2	3	3	15	0	41	7	4	2	3	.400	0	0	5.82
1997 Bakersfield	A+ SF	29	29	0	0	167.1	755	184	106	89	11	5	3	7	83	1	124	23	1	7	9	.438	0	0	4.79
1998 San Jose	A+ SF	41	15	0	10	125.1	550	132	81	68	10	5	4	4	42	1	103	10	8	11	7	.611	0	4	4.88
1999 Shreveport	AA SF	17	0	0	6	27.1	125	31	20	19	3	0	1	1	15	0	16	2	0	2	0	1.000	0	1	6.26
San Jose	A+ SF	17	13	0	1	79.2	348	87	45	37	4	1	0	3	37	0	66	7	4	5	4	.556	0	0	4.18
4 Min. YEARS		119	64	0	20	433.2	1933	468	279	235	28	13	11	18	192	2	350	49	17	27	23	.540	0	5	4.88

Marty Malloy

Bats: Left **Throws:** Right **Pos:** 2B **Ht:** 5'10" **Wt:** 165 **Born:** 7/6/72 **Age:** 27

Year Team	Lg Org	G	AB	H	2B	3B	HR	TB	R	RBI	TBB	IBB	SO	HBP	SH	SF	SB	CS	SB%	GDP	Avg	OBP	SLG
1992 Idaho Falls	R+ Atl	62	251	79	18	1	2	105	45	28	11	0	43	2	0	1	8	4	.67	2	.315	.347	.418
1993 Macon	A Atl	109	376	110	19	3	2	141	55	36	39	3	70	2	3	3	24	8	.75	4	.293	.360	.375
1994 Durham	A+ Atl	118	428	113	22	1	6	155	53	35	52	2	69	2	2	3	18	12	.60	9	.264	.344	.362
1995 Greenville	AA Atl	124	461	128	20	3	10	184	73	59	39	1	58	0	7	8	11	12	.48	6	.278	.329	.399
1996 Richmond	AAA Atl	18	64	13	2	1	0	17	7	8	5	1	7	0	2	1	3	0	1.00	1	.203	.257	.266
Greenville	AA Atl	111	429	134	27	2	4	177	82	36	54	6	50	4	6	2	11	10	.52	11	.312	.393	.413
1997 Richmond	AAA Atl	108	414	118	19	5	2	153	66	25	41	1	61	1	5	0	17	7	.71	6	.285	.351	.370
1998 Richmond	AAA Atl	124	483	140	25	3	7	192	75	54	51	2	65	5	5	4	20	7	.74	12	.290	.361	.398
1999 Richmond	AAA Atl	114	407	119	23	1	7	165	58	36	53	2	52	2	4	3	19	15	.56	2	.292	.374	.405
1998 Atlanta	NL	11	28	5	1	0	1	9	3	1	2	0	2	0	0	0	0	0	.00	0	.179	.233	.321
8 Min. YEARS		888	3313	954	175	20	40	1289	514	317	345	18	475	18	34	25	131	75	.64	53	.288	.356	.389

Sean Maloney

Pitches: Right **Bats:** Right **Pos:** P **Ht:** 6' 7" **Wt:** 210 **Born:** 5/25/71 **Age:** 29

		HOW MUCH HE PITCHED						WHAT HE GAVE UP										THE RESULTS				
Year Team	Lg Org	G	GS	CG	GF	IP	BFP	H	R	ER	HR	SH	SF	HB	TBB	IBB	SO	WP	Bk	W	L	Pct.	ShO	Sv	ERA
1993 Helena	R+ Mil	17	3	1	10	47.2	209	55	31	23	2	3	2	2	11	1	35	3	0	2	2	.500	0	0	4.34
1994 Beloit	A Mil	51	0	0	41	59	272	73	42	36	3	2	5	4	10	5	53	6	1	2	6	.250	0	22	5.49
1995 El Paso	AA Mil	43	0	0	27	64.2	292	69	41	30	4	4	4	3	28	9	54	5	0	7	5	.583	0	15	4.18
1996 El Paso	AA Mil	51	0	0	49	56.2	230	49	11	9	1	2	1	1	12	1	57	6	1	3	2	.600	0	38	1.43
1997 Tucson	AAA Mil	15	0	0	10	18.2	82	24	10	10	3	5	0	0	3	3	21	1	0	0	2	.000	0	5	4.82
1998 Albuquerque	AAA LA	26	0	0	23	35	190	38	21	18	5	1	0	1	8	1	00	4	0	0	2	.000	0	0	4.63
1999 Orioles	R Bal	1	0	0	0	2	7	1	0	0	0	0	0	0	1	0	3	0	0	0	0	.000	0	0	0.00
Frederick	A+ Bal	15	0	0	8	25.1	109	21	10	4	2	0	1	1	10	1	22	0	0	1	0	1.000	0	2	1.42
Bowie	AA Bal	4	0	0	1	10.2	46	10	4	4	1	0	0	0	3	0	17	1	0	0	0	.000	0	0	3.38
1997 Milwaukee	AL	3	0	0	2	7	29	7	4	4	1	0	2	2	2	0	5	2	0	0	0	.000	0	0	5.14
1998 Los Angeles	NL	11	0	0	2	12.2	57	13	7	7	2	1	0	2	5	0	11	1	0	0	1	.000	0	0	4.97
7 Min. YEARS		223	3	1	169	319.2	1397	340	170	134	22	17	13	12	86	21	300	26	2	18	19	.486	0	91	3.77
2 Maj. YEARS		14	0	0	4	19.2	86	20	11	11	3	1	2	4	7	0	16	3	0	0	1	.000	0	0	5.03

168

Dwight Maness

Bats: Right **Throws:** Right **Pos:** OF **Ht:** 6'3" **Wt:** 188 **Born:** 4/3/74 **Age:** 26

Year Team	Lg Org	G	AB	H	2B	3B	HR	TB	R	RBI	TBB	IBB	SO	HBP	SH	SF	SB	CS	SB%	GDP	Avg	OBP	SLG
1992 Dodgers	R LA	44	139	35	6	3	0	47	24	12	14	0	36	8	3	3	18	9	.67	1	.252	.348	.338
1993 Vero Beach	A+ LA	118	409	106	21	4	6	153	57	42	32	0	105	15	8	7	22	13	.63	3	.259	.330	.374
1994 San Antonio	AA LA	57	215	47	5	5	5	77	32	20	25	0	54	6	2	0	15	16	.48	1	.219	.317	.358
Bakersfield	A+ LA	74	248	62	13	1	3	86	38	26	29	3	67	11	5	5	21	9	.70	1	.250	.348	.347
1995 San Antonio	AA LA	57	179	40	2	3	5	63	29	24	20	0	44	5	5	2	4	6	.40	2	.223	.316	.352
Vero Beach	A+ LA	43	143	33	3	0	3	45	16	23	11	0	29	6	2	5	13	5	.72	2	.231	.303	.315
St. Lucie	A+ NYM	14	44	9	4	0	0	13	4	5	7	0	6	0	1	0	1	2	.33	0	.205	.314	.295
1996 Binghamton	AA NYM	130	399	97	14	7	6	143	65	47	52	2	80	8	7	5	25	8	.76	2	.243	.338	.358
1997 St. Lucie	A+ NYM	45	179	53	9	2	3	75	29	19	12	0	29	3	0	0	12	6	.67	1	.296	.351	.419
Binghamton	AA NYM	74	259	49	13	3	5	83	33	31	24	1	73	5	4	2	4	4	.50	2	.189	.269	.320
1998 Binghamton	AA NYM	27	93	22	3	0	3	34	15	10	14	0	28	2	1	0	3	5	.38	4	.237	.349	.366
Norfolk	AAA NYM	6	10	1	0	0	0	1	1	0	0	0	4	0	0	0	2	0	1.00	0	.100	.100	.100
Trenton	AA Bos	85	313	77	12	5	11	132	48	32	37	0	80	8	8	3	15	6	.71	4	.246	.338	.422
1999 Somerset	IND —	75	282	75	17	2	12	132	48	42	27	1	49	7	0	2	21	9	.70	1	.266	.343	.468
New Haven	AA Sea	27	87	21	2	1	5	40	11	12	11	0	18	1	0	0	9	5	.64	3	.241	.333	.460
8 Min. YEARS		876	2999	727	124	36	67	1124	450	345	315	7	702	85	46	34	185	103	.64	28	.242	.328	.375

James Manias

Pitches: Left **Bats:** Left **Pos:** P **Ht:** 6'4" **Wt:** 190 **Born:** 10/21/74 **Age:** 25

Year Team	Lg Org	G	GS	CG	GF	IP	BFP	H	R	ER	HR	SH	SF	HB	TBB	IBB	SO	WP	Bk	W	L	Pct.	ShO	Sv	ERA
1996 Butte	R+ TB	16	13	0	1	72	336	98	64	42	8	2	4	5	22	0	55	5	1	5	4	.556	0	0	5.25
1997 St. Pete	A+ TB	28	28	2	0	171.1	710	163	84	72	16	3	4	11	40	0	119	6	0	13	5	.722	2	0	3.78
1998 St. Pete	A+ TB	30	21	0	3	137	618	167	99	85	27	3	11	9	37	0	79	7	0	6	13	.316	0	0	5.58
1999 Chattanooga	AA Cin	1	0	0	0	0.2	2	0	0	0	0	0	0	0	0	0	0	0	0	0	0	.000	0	0	0.00
Rockford	A Cin	30	10	4	1	90.2	391	84	46	37	5	1	1	2	36	2	103	5	0	9	7	.563	1	0	3.67
4 Min. YEARS		105	72	6	5	471.2	2057	512	293	236	56	9	21	25	135	2	356	23	1	33	29	.532	3	0	4.50

Jim Mann

Pitches: Right **Bats:** Right **Pos:** P **Ht:** 6'3" **Wt:** 225 **Born:** 11/17/74 **Age:** 25

Year Team	Lg Org	G	GS	CG	GF	IP	BFP	H	R	ER	HR	SH	SF	HB	TBB	IBB	SO	WP	Bk	W	L	Pct.	ShO	Sv	ERA
1994 Blue Jays	R Tor	11	9	0	0	53	236	54	28	22	1	3	3		26	1	41	0	1	3	2	.600	0	0	3.74
1995 Medcine Hat	R+ Tor	14	14	1	0	77.2	347	78	47	37	5	3	2	7	37	0	66	6	0	4	5	.556	1	0	4.29
1996 St.Cathrnes	A- Tor	26	0	0	23	27.1	117	22	12	11	3	2	2	3	10	1	37	0	1	2	1	.667	0	17	3.62
1997 Hagerstown	A Tor	19	0	0	16	26.2	122	35	18	15	4	0	1	1	11	0	30	2	0	1	0	1.000	0	4	5.06
Dunedin	A+ Tor	12	0	0	4	18	88	27	12	12	2	0	1		6	1	13	1	0	1	0	1.000	0	0	6.00
1998 Dunedin	A+ Tor	51	0	0	47	50.1	206	31	19	17	4	0	2	0	24	1	59	2	0	2	0	.000	0	25	3.04
1999 Knoxville	AA Tor	6	0	0	4	9.2	39	6	2	1	1	3	1	2	1	0	12	0	0	1	2	.333	0	0	0.93
Syracuse	AAA Tor	47	0	0	20	66	287	53	35	34	11	1	1	2	39	1	72	6	0	6	5	.545	0	5	4.64
6 Min. YEARS		186	23	1	114	328.2	1442	306	173	149	31	12	11	19	154	5	330	17	2	18	17	.514	1	51	4.08

David Manning

Pitches: Right **Bats:** Right **Pos:** P **Ht:** 6'3" **Wt:** 215 **Born:** 8/14/72 **Age:** 27

Year Team	Lg Org	G	GS	CG	GF	IP	BFP	H	R	ER	HR	SH	SF	HB	TBB	IBB	SO	WP	Bk	W	L	Pct.	ShO	Sv	ERA
1992 Butte	R+ Tex	8	7	0	0	25.1	143	50	41	31	4	1	0	3	15	0	13	6	5	0	4	.000	0	0	11.01
Rangers	R Tex	5	3	0	0	16.1	75	22	13	11	0	1	1		4	0	9	1	0	1	1	.500	0	0	6.06
1993 Chston-SC	A Tex	37	10	0	8	116	495	112	54	39	3	5	5		39	4	83	11	3	6	7	.462	0	2	3.03
1994 Charlotte	A+ Tex	20	20	0	0	97	438	119	69	60	5	4	3	6	39	0	46	8	3	4	11	.267	0	0	5.57
1995 Charlotte	A+ Tex	26	20	0	2	128.2	545	127	56	50	7	3	3	3	46	0	66	0	5	9	5	.643	0	0	3.50
1996 Okla City	AAA Tex	1	1	0	0	5	21	6	3	3	0	0	1	0	2	0	1	0	0	0	0	.000	0	0	5.40
Tulsa	AA Tex	39	5	0	13	91	394	89	36	33	5	3	5	2	45	6	48	5	0	6	5	.545	0	3	3.26
1997 Tulsa	AA Tex	13	12	1	1	75.2	324	77	46	41	8	2	3	0	27	0	55	5	0	4	7	.364	0	0	4.88
Okla City	AAA Tex	5	5	1	0	28.2	130	33	17	14	6	0	0	2	9	0	15	1	0	1	3	.250	0	0	4.40
Charlotte	A+ Tex	1	1	0	0	6	26	4	1	1	1	0	0	0	4	0	4	0	0	0	0	.000	0	0	1.50
1998 Tulsa	AA Tex	6	0	0	1	13	61	13	7	7	2	0	1	0	11	0	15	2	0	2	0	1.000	0	0	4.85
Rangers	R Tex	3	3	0	0	5	22	6	3	3	0	1	1	0	1	0	2	1	0	0	0	.000	0	0	5.40
Charlotte	A+ Tex	7	0	0	2	8.1	36	4	4	0	1	0	0	0	6	0	11	0	0	0	0	.000	0	0	0.00
Oklahoma	AAA Tex	6	0	0	4	9	36	11	1	1	1	0	0	0	9	0	9	0	0	0	0	.000	0	1	1.00
1999 Iowa	AAA ChC	7	0	0	2	9.2	44	9	6	5	2	0	3	0	8	0	7	0	0	0	0	.000	0	0	4.66
West Tenn	AA ChC	23	18	6	0	123.1	518	113	59	54	7	5	4	3	51	1	78	7	0	8	5	.615	2	0	3.94
8 Min. YEARS		207	105	8	33	758	3308	795	416	353	52	25	29	27	307	11	462	47	16	41	48	.461	2	6	4.19

Nate Manning

Bats: Right **Throws:** Right **Pos:** 3B **Ht:** 6'2" **Wt:** 215 **Born:** 12/20/73 **Age:** 26

Year Team	Lg Org	G	AB	H	2B	3B	HR	TB	R	RBI	TBB	IBB	SO	HBP	SH	SF	SB	CS	SB%	GDP	Avg	OBP	SLG
1996 Williamsprt	A- ChC	62	240	76	14	1	4	104	28	32	14	2	62	2	0	2	4	0	1.00	3	.317	.357	.433
1997 Daytona	A+ ChC	120	454	111	29	0	7	161	51	54	14	0	93	6	0	6	5	4	.56	12	.244	.273	.355
1998 West Tenn	AA ChC	16	57	11	1	0	0	12	5	6	2	0	14	1	0	0	0	2	.00	2	.193	.233	.211
Daytona	A+ ChC	108	427	115	23	1	16	188	61	71	26	5	89	10	2	4	2	4	.33	13	.269	.323	.440
1999 West Tenn	AA ChC	13	27	6	2	0	0	8	0	5	2	0	8	2	0	0	1	0	1.00	0	.222	.323	.296
Daytona	A+ ChC	110	393	99	23	3	11	161	48	57	33	1	83	7	2	4	2	2	.50	10	.252	.318	.410
4 Min. YEARS		429	1598	418	92	5	38	634	193	225	91	8	349	28	4	16	14	12	.54	40	.262	.310	.397

Julio Manon

Pitches: Right **Bats:** Right **Pos:** P **Ht:** 6'1" **Wt:** 183 **Born:** 7/10/73 **Age:** 26

Year Team	Lg Org	G	GS	CG	GF	IP	BFP	H	R	ER	HR	SH	SF	HB	TBB	IBB	SO	WP	Bk	W	L	Pct.	ShO	Sv	ERA
1993 Cardinals	R StL	15	4	0	1	33.1	151	44	21	19	2	0	3	0	12	0	22	5	4	2	3	.400	0	0	5.13
1994 Johnson Cy	R+ StL	5	0	0	2	8.2	43	11	8	8	2	0	0	0	5	0	7	0	0	1	2	.333	0	0	8.31
Cardinals	R StL	14	0	0	4	16	69	20	9	9	0	0	0	0	1	0	18	1	2	0	1	.000	0	1	5.06
1995 Huntington	R+ StL	16	8	2	3	74	319	75	34	30	4	0	3	2	30	2	77	10	0	3	4	.429	0	1	3.65
1997 Chston-SC	A TB	27	9	0	4	88.2	392	95	53	44	8	5	3	3	22	1	98	7	0	3	5	.375	0	0	4.47
1998 Orlando	AA TB	13	0	0	5	20.2	96	22	19	14	3	0	1	0	9	0	22	3	0	0	2	.000	0	0	6.10
St. Pete	A+ TB	38	0	0	14	55.2	219	41	25	23	7	0	0	2	19	1	73	4	1	5	5	.500	0	1	3.72
1999 Orlando	AA TB	30	5	0	8	67	303	80	43	38	9	0	1	2	23	0	53	3	0	3	3	.500	0	0	5.10
St. Paul	IND —	4	3	0	0	20.1	85	18	9	5	0	0	1	0	7	0	21	1	0	1	1	.500	0	0	2.21
6 Min. YEARS		162	29	2	41	384.1	1677	406	221	190	35	5	12	9	128	4	391	34	7	18	26	.409	0	3	4.45

Tim Manwiller

Pitches: Right **Bats:** Right **Pos:** P **Ht:** 6'2" **Wt:** 205 **Born:** 9/5/74 **Age:** 25

Year Team	Lg Org	G	GS	CG	GF	IP	BFP	H	R	ER	HR	SH	SF	HB	TBB	IBB	SO	WP	Bk	W	L	Pct.	ShO	Sv	ERA
1997 Sou Oregon	A- Oak	12	3	0	5	29	115	19	8	6	0	2	1	0	10	0	30	1	2	2	0	1.000	0	2	1.86
Modesto	A+ Oak	7	0	0	0	20.2	85	21	8	7	1	2	3	0	7	2	18	1	1	1	1	.500	0	0	3.05
1998 Modesto	A+ Oak	30	21	1	2	156.1	650	150	69	55	8	1	5	3	46	1	129	3	2	13	6	.684	0	1	3.17
Edmonton	AAA Oak	2	0	0	1	11	39	8	1	1	0	0	1	0	2	0	10	0	0	1	0	1.000	0	0	0.82
1999 Midland	AA Oak	17	13	0	1	84.2	366	95	43	33	6	4	2	4	24	2	58	3	0	6	2	.750	0	0	3.51
Vancouver	AAA Oak	11	11	0	0	54.1	247	72	42	39	9	2	4	4	14	0	30	1	0	4	2	.667	0	0	6.46
3 Min. YEARS		79	48	1	9	356	1502	365	171	141	24	11	16	11	103	5	275	9	5	27	11	.711	0	3	3.56

Adrian Manzano

Pitches: Right **Bats:** Right **Pos:** P **Ht:** 5'9" **Wt:** 185 **Born:** 11/27/78 **Age:** 21

Year Team	Lg Org	G	GS	CG	GF	IP	BFP	H	R	ER	HR	SH	SF	HB	TBB	IBB	SO	WP	Bk	W	L	Pct.	ShO	Sv	ERA
1998 Greenville	AA Atl	39	5	0	24	64	293	72	43	35	7	6	4	1	29	5	57	3	0	1	5	.167	0	8	4.92
1999 Greenville	AA Atl	42	0	0	6	61.2	267	61	24	22	6	4	2	2	22	6	51	1	0	5	2	.714	0	2	3.21
2 Min. YEARS		81	5	0	30	125.2	560	133	67	57	13	10	6	3	51	11	108	4	0	6	7	.462	0	10	4.08

T.R. Marcinczyk

Bats: Right **Throws:** Right **Pos:** 1B **Ht:** 6'2" **Wt:** 195 **Born:** 10/11/73 **Age:** 26

Year Team	Lg Org	G	AB	H	2B	3B	HR	TB	R	RBI	TBB	IBB	SO	HBP	SH	SF	SB	CS	SB%	GDP	Avg	OBP	SLG
1996 Sou Oregon	A- Oak	63	216	48	13	2	7	86	29	38	22	0	57	5	5	4	3	3	.50	3	.222	.304	.398
1997 Modesto	A+ Oak	133	463	128	41	2	23	242	89	91	71	5	107	11	1	6	4	4	.50	7	.276	.381	.523
1998 Huntsville	AA Oak	131	501	135	25	2	26	242	90	88	51	3	127	9	0	7	2	6	.25	15	.269	.343	.483
1999 Midland	AA Oak	127	477	133	39	1	23	243	87	111	62	2	109	12	0	7	2	1	1.00	12	.279	.371	.509
4 Min. YEARS		454	1657	444	118	7	79	813	295	328	206	10	400	37	6	24	11	13	.46	37	.268	.357	.491

Kevin Marn

Bats: Right **Throws:** Right **Pos:** OF **Ht:** 6'4" **Wt:** 205 **Born:** 3/23/74 **Age:** 26

Year Team	Lg Org	G	AB	H	2B	3B	HR	TB	R	RBI	TBB	IBB	SO	HBP	SH	SF	SB	CS	SB%	GDP	Avg	OBP	SLG
1996 Billings	R+ Cin	66	271	75	11	1	1	91	48	38	24	0	49	3	1	4	19	3	.86	5	.277	.338	.336
1998 Chstn-WV	A Cin	96	344	89	19	1	4	122	40	39	28	0	63	5	2	4	15	6	.71	9	.259	.320	.355
Chattanooga	AA Cin	20	36	13	3	0	0	16	8	4	5	0	8	0	0	1	2	1	1.00	0	.361	.429	.444
1999 New Haven	AA Sea	2	7	2	0	0	0	2	0	1	1	0	3	0	0	0	1	0	1.00	0	.286	.375	.286
3 Min. YEARS		184	658	179	33	2	5	231	96	82	58	0	123	8	3	9	37	9	.80	14	.272	.334	.351

Mike Maroth

Pitches: Left **Bats:** Left **Pos:** P **Ht:** 6'0" **Wt:** 180 **Born:** 8/17/77 **Age:** 22

Year Team	Lg Org	G	GS	CG	GF	IP	BFP	H	R	ER	HR	SH	SF	HB	TBB	IBB	SO	WP	Bk	W	L	Pct.	ShO	Sv	ERA
1998 Red Sox	R Bos	4	2	0	1	12.2	49	9	3	0	0	0	0	0	2	0	14	0	0	1	1	.500	0	0	0.00
Lowell	A- Bos	6	6	0	0	31	127	22	13	10	1	0	1	3	13	0	34	3	0	2	3	.400	0	0	2.90
1999 Sarasota	A+ Bos	20	19	0	0	111.1	497	124	65	50	8	3	6	4	35	1	64	11	2	11	6	.647	0	0	4.04
Lakeland	A+ Det	3	3	0	0	16.2	71	18	7	6	1	1	0	0	7	0	11	2	0	2	1	.667	0	0	3.24
Jacksnville	AA Det	4	4	0	0	20.2	96	27	15	11	2	1	1	0	7	0	10	1	0	1	2	.333	0	0	4.79
2 Min. YEARS		37	34	0	1	192.1	840	200	103	77	7	8	6	13	64	1	133	17	2	17	13	.567	0	0	3.60

Robert Marquez

Pitches: Right **Bats:** Right **Pos:** P **Ht:** 6'0" **Wt:** 180 **Born:** 4/21/73 **Age:** 27

Year Team	Lg Org	G	GS	CG	GF	IP	BFP	H	R	ER	HR	SH	SF	HB	TBB	IBB	SO	WP	Bk	W	L	Pct.	ShO	Sv	ERA
1995 Vermont	A- Mon	29	0	0	29	32	122	15	5	3	0	1	0	1	11	0	32	1	0	1	1	.500	0	21	0.84
1996 Wst Plm Bch	A+ Mon	11	0	0	7	11	54	14	10	9	0	0	0	4	5	0	8	0	0	1	1	.500	0	6	7.36
Delmarva	A Mon	29	0	0	14	46.2	210	44	23	19	4	2	5	3	22	0	49	5	0	1	2	.333	0	3	3.66
1997 Cape Fear	A Mon	12	0	0	5	18.1	71	15	6	6	0	0	0	1	12	0	18	0	0	0	0	.000	0	2	2.95
Wst Plm Bch	A+ Mon	21	0	0	13	28	117	28	12	8	3	0	2	0	3	0	22	0	0	1	1	.500	0	6	2.57
1998 Jupiter	A+ Mon	39	0	0	14	51.1	234	60	28	22	4	4	0	7	16	0	46	0	0	5	4	.556	0	3	3.86
Harrisburg	AA Mon	4	0	0	3	6	22	4	2	2	0	0	0	0	1	0	5	0	0	0	0	.000	0	0	3.00

		HOW MUCH HE PITCHED					WHAT HE GAVE UP											THE RESULTS					
Year Team	Lg Org	G	GS	CG	GF	IP	BFP	H	R	ER	HR	SH	SF	HB	TBB	IBB	SO	WP	Bk	W	L	Pct.	ShO	Sv	ERA
1999 Jupiter	A+ Mon	13	0	0	9	15.2	60	5	2	0	0	2	0	1	6	0	15	0	1	3	0	1.000	0	3	0.00
Harrisburg	AA Mon	18	0	0	11	25.2	116	31	15	13	3	1	1	2	8	1	22	0	0	2	2	.500	0	1	4.56
Ottawa	AAA Mon	18	0	0	7	27.2	131	33	19	15	3	1	1	1	14	2	16	1	1	1	1	.500	0	1	4.88
5 Min. YEARS		194	0	0	112	262.1	1147	249	122	97	19	12	7	20	99	3	233	7	4	15	12	.556	0	45	3.33

Jason Marquis

Pitches: Right **Bats:** Left **Pos:** P   **Ht:** 6'1" **Wt:** 185 **Born:** 8/21/78 **Age:** 21

		HOW MUCH HE PITCHED					WHAT HE GAVE UP											THE RESULTS					
Year Team	Lg Org	G	GS	CG	GF	IP	BFP	H	R	ER	HR	SH	SF	HB	TBB	IBB	SO	WP	Bk	W	L	Pct.	ShO	Sv	ERA
1996 Danville	R+ Atl	7	4	0	0	23.1	113	30	18	12	0	0	0	1	7	0	24	2	0	1	1	.500	0	0	4.63
1997 Macon	A Atl	28	28	0	0	141.2	627	156	78	69	10	2	7	2	55	1	121	8	2	14	10	.583	0	0	4.38
1998 Danville	A+ Atl	22	22	1	0	114.2	500	120	65	62	3	4	3	6	41	0	135	7	0	2	12	.143	0	0	4.87
1999 Myrtle Bch	A+ Atl	6	6	0	0	32	134	22	2	1	0	0	1	1	17	0	41	2	0	3	0	1.000	0	0	0.28
Greenville	AA Atl	12	12	1	0	55	248	52	33	28	7	0	1	2	29	0	35	1	0	3	4	.429	0	0	4.58
4 Min. YEARS		75	72	2	0	366.2	1622	380	196	172	20	6	12	12	149	1	356	20	2	23	27	.460	0	0	4.22

Oreste Marrero

Bats: Left **Throws:** Left **Pos:** 1B   **Ht:** 6'0" **Wt:** 195 **Born:** 10/31/69 **Age:** 30

		BATTING														BASERUNNING				PERCENTAGES		
Year Team	Lg Org	G	AB	H	2B	3B	HR	TB	R	RBI	TBB	IBB	SO	HBP	SH	SF	SB	CS	SB%	GDP	Avg	OBP	SLG
1987 Helena	R+ Mil	51	154	50	8	2	7	83	30	34	18	3	31	1	1	0	2	1	.67	1	.325	.399	.539
1988 Beloit	A Mil	19	52	9	2	0	1	14	5	7	3	0	16	0	0	0	0	1	.00	0	.173	.218	.269
Helena	R+ Mil	67	240	85	15	0	16	148	52	44	42	2	48	0	0	1	3	4	.43	4	.354	.449	.617
1989 Beloit	A Mil	14	40	5	1	0	0	6	1	3	3	0	20	0	0	1	1	0	1.00	0	.125	.182	.150
Brewers	R Mil	10	44	18	0	1	3	29	13	16	2	0	5	0	0	1	2	2	.50	0	.409	.426	.659
Boise	A- Mil	54	203	56	8	1	11	99	38	43	30	3	60	0	0	4	1	2	.33	3	.276	.363	.488
1990 Beloit	A Mil	119	400	110	25	1	16	185	59	55	45	3	107	0	0	1	8	4	.67	12	.275	.348	.463
1991 Stockton	A+ Mil	123	438	110	15	2	13	168	63	61	57	8	98	0	1	7	4	5	.44	5	.251	.333	.384
1992 El Paso	AA Mil	18	54	10	2	1	1	17	8	4	0		13	0	0	1	1	0	1.00	0	.185	.237	.315
Stockton	A+ Mil	76	243	67	17	0	7	105	35	51	44	6	49	1	1	1	3	2	.60	0	.276	.388	.432
1993 Harrisburg	AA Mon	85	255	85	18	1	10	135	39	49	22	2	46	0	3	4	3	3	.50	2	.333	.381	.529
1994 Ottawa	AAA Mon	88	254	62	14	7	7	111	41	31	29	1	56	0	1	2	1	1	.50	5	.244	.319	.437
1995 San Antonio	AA LA	125	445	115	25	3	21	209	60	86	64	5	98	3	0	3	5	2	.71	4	.258	.353	.470
Albuquerque	AAA LA	7	23	8	2	0	2	16	5	6	1	0	5	0	0	0	0	0	.00	0	.348	.375	.696
1996 Albuquerque	AAA LA	121	441	125	29	1	13	195	50	76	36	1	119	1	0	4	2	6	.25	12	.283	.336	.442
1997 Albuquerque	AAA LA	96	263	69	20	0	9	116	38	42	24	2	70	0	0	1	1	1	.50	8	.262	.323	.441
1999 Huntsville	AA Mil	15	37	8	3	0	1	14	2	7	1	0	8	0	0	1	0	0	.00	0	.216	.237	.378
Madison	IND —	24	92	22	7	0	2	35	14	12	8	1	21	2	0	1	3	1	.75	3	.239	.311	.380
1993 Montreal	NL	32	81	17	5	1	1	27	10	4	14	0	16	0	0	0	1	3	.25	0	.210	.326	.333
1996 Los Angeles	NL	10	8	3	1	0	0	4	2	1	1	0	3	0	0	0	0	0	.00	0	.375	.444	.500
12 Min. YEARS		1112	3678	1014	211	20	140	1685	553	631	433	37	870	8	8	32	40	35	.53	61	.276	.351	.458
2 Maj. YEARS		42	89	20	6	1	1	31	12	5	15	0	19	0	0	0	1	3	.25	0	.225	.337	.348

Brandon Marsters

Bats: Right **Throws:** Right **Pos:** C   **Ht:** 5'11" **Wt:** 190 **Born:** 3/14/75 **Age:** 25

		BATTING														BASERUNNING				PERCENTAGES		
Year Team	Lg Org	G	AB	H	2B	3B	HR	TB	R	RBI	TBB	IBB	SO	HBP	SH	SF	SB	CS	SB%	GDP	Avg	OBP	SLG
1996 Batavia	A- Phi	42	151	35	8	2	1	50	15	13	8	0	46	1	0	0	1	0	1.00	1	.232	.275	.331
1997 Piedmont	A Phi	61	212	43	8	0	2	57	25	20	22	2	51	0	2	0	0	0	.00	4	.203	.278	.269
Clearwater	A+ Phi	44	141	26	3	0	0	29	10	18	15	0	26	4	1	2	1	0	1.00	3	.184	.278	.206
1998 Clearwater	A+ Phi	76	265	75	12	1	6	107	33	39	16	0	41	2	4	2	2	1	.67	4	.283	.326	.404
Reading	AA Phi	38	143	33	4	2	1	44	9	7	11	0	34	1	0	1	0	1	.00	5	.231	.288	.308
1999 Salt Lake	AAA Min	11	25	5	1	0	1	9	4	8	2	0	6	0	0	0	0	0	.00	0	.200	.259	.360
Fort Myers	A+ Min	54	173	41	11	0	2	58	18	28	19	0	33	1	0	5	1	0	1.00	7	.237	.308	.335
4 Min. YEARS		326	1110	258	47	5	13	354	114	133	93	2	237	9	7	10	5	2	.71	25	.232	.295	.319

Chandler Martin

Pitches: Right **Bats:** Right **Pos:** P   **Ht:** 6'1" **Wt:** 180 **Born:** 10/23/73 **Age:** 26

		HOW MUCH HE PITCHED					WHAT HE GAVE UP											THE RESULTS					
Year Team	Lg Org	G	GS	CG	GF	IP	BFP	H	R	ER	HR	SH	SF	HB	TBB	IBB	SO	WP	Bk	W	L	Pct.	ShO	Sv	ERA
1995 Portland	A- Col	7	7	0	0	38	153	20	10	7	0	2	0	2	21	0	34	3	3	4	1	.800	0	0	1.66
Asheville	A Col	8	8	0	0	49.1	216	48	23	21	0	2	0	3	27	0	32	6	1	4	3	.571	0	0	3.83
1996 New Haven	AA Col	1	1	0	0	5	22	6	4	4	2	0	1	1	3	0	4	0	0	1	0	1.000	0	0	7.20
Asheville	A Col	14	14	0	0	86	347	65	26	21	2	1	0	3	30	1	73	11	0	9	0	1.000	0	0	2.20
Salem	A+ Col	13	13	1	0	69	333	80	56	45	5	0	2	5	53	1	59	12	0	2	8	.200	1	0	5.87
1997 Salem	A+ Col	16	5	0	8	45.1	205	46	25	20	1	1	0	3	25	0	30	7	0	1	5	.167	0	1	3.97
1998 Salem	A+ Col	24	24	7	0	160	641	136	54	44	9	5	1	4	43	0	104	14	0	12	7	.632	0	0	2.48
1999 Carolina	AA Col	27	27	2	0	164.1	707	153	82	69	14	6	4	14	63	0	130	11	6	13	8	.619	1	0	3.78
5 Min. YEARS		110	99	10	8	617	2624	554	280	231	33	17	8	35	266	1	466	64	10	46	32	.590	2	1	3.37

Chris Martin

Bats: Right **Throws:** Right **Pos:** SS   **Ht:** 6'1" **Wt:** 170 **Born:** 1/25/68 **Age:** 32

		BATTING														BASERUNNING				PERCENTAGES		
Year Team	Lg Org	G	AB	H	2B	3B	HR	TB	R	RBI	TBB	IBB	SO	HBP	SH	SF	SB	CS	SB%	GDP	Avg	OBP	SLG
1990 Wst Plm Bch	A+ Mon	59	222	62	17	1	3	90	31	31	27	6	37	1	1	2	7	5	.58	4	.279	.357	.405
1991 Harrisburg	AA Mon	87	294	66	10	0	6	94	30	36	22	0	61	4	2	5	1	4	.20	8	.224	.283	.320

Year Team	Lg Org	G	AB	H	2B	3B	HR	TB	R	RBI	TBB	IBB	SO	HBP	SH	SF	SB	CS	SB%	GDP	Avg	OBP	SLG
1992 Harrisburg	AA Mon	125	383	87	22	1	5	126	39	31	49	1	67	2	1	3	8	6	.57	15	.227	.316	.329
1993 Harrisburg	AA Mon	116	395	116	23	1	7	162	68	54	40	2	48	6	7	3	16	6	.73	13	.294	.365	.410
1994 Ottawa	AAA Mon	113	374	89	24	0	3	122	44	40	35	0	46	2	7	5	5	4	.56	17	.238	.303	.326
1995 Ottawa	AAA Mon	126	412	106	19	1	3	136	55	40	46	1	59	4	8	3	30	5	.86	12	.257	.335	.330
1996 Ottawa	AAA Mon	122	451	119	30	1	8	175	68	54	33	0	54	7	6	5	25	12	.68	16	.264	.321	.388
1997 St. Pete	A+ TB	105	393	102	20	0	9	149	72	49	62	1	66	7	5	4	23	7	.77	13	.260	.367	.379
1998 Durham	AAA TB	131	448	116	26	2	8	170	71	49	62	1	80	8	7	5	19	11	.63	9	.259	.356	.379
1999 Durham	AAA TB	120	399	109	20	1	9	158	64	53	48	3	61	7	9	7	14	2	.88	15	.273	.356	.396
10 Min. YEARS		1104	3771	972	211	8	61	1382	542	437	424	15	579	48	53	42	148	62	.70	122	.258	.337	.366

Jared Martin

Bats: Both **Throws:** Right **Pos:** 3B   **Ht:** 5'10" **Wt:** 180 **Born:** 3/3/75 **Age:** 25

Year Team	Lg Org	G	AB	H	2B	3B	HR	TB	R	RBI	TBB	IBB	SO	HBP	SH	SF	SB	CS	SB%	GDP	Avg	OBP	SLG
1997 Lethbridge	R+ Ari	25	78	18	3	3	0	27	12	5	15	1	19	2	0	1	1	0	1.00	1	.231	.365	.346
South Bend	A Ari	34	97	24	6	1	0	32	13	10	9	0	30	1	2	2	1	1	.67	0	.247	.312	.330
1998 South Bend	A Ari	15	47	11	0	0	0	11	8	4	8	0	6	0	1	2	1	0	1.00	0	.234	.333	.234
High Desert	A+ Ari	50	168	41	7	5	3	67	30	21	19	0	37	1	6	1	3	3	.50	4	.244	.323	.399
1999 El Paso	AA Ari	19	62	16	4	0	1	23	9	5	4	0	13	0	0	1	0	0	.00	0	.258	.299	.371
High Desert	A+ Ari	89	283	68	12	2	2	90	38	30	29	0	46	2	3	1	2	4	.33	2	.240	.314	.318
3 Min. YEARS		232	735	178	32	11	6	250	110	75	84	1	151	6	12	8	9	8	.53	7	.242	.322	.340

Chris Martine

Bats: Right **Throws:** Right **Pos:** C   **Ht:** 6'2" **Wt:** 190 **Born:** 7/10/75 **Age:** 24

Year Team	Lg Org	G	AB	H	2B	3B	HR	TB	R	RBI	TBB	IBB	SO	HBP	SH	SF	SB	CS	SB%	GDP	Avg	OBP	SLG
1997 New Jersey	A- StL	47	142	30	5	0	0	35	22	12	22	0	37	2	0	3	0	0	.00	3	.211	.320	.246
1998 Pr William	A+ StL	96	279	52	13	0	2	71	29	25	38	0	77	4	5	3	2	6	.25	4	.186	.290	.254
1999 Potomac	A+ StL	42	136	28	7	2	1	42	11	14	16	0	42	2	3	2	1	2	.33	3	.206	.295	.309
Arkansas	AA StL	18	40	6	1	0	0	7	3	1	2	0	12	4	2	0	0	0	.00	1	.150	.261	.175
3 Min. YEARS		203	597	116	26	2	3	155	65	52	78	0	168	12	10	8	3	8	.27	11	.194	.296	.260

Gabby Martinez

Bats: Right **Throws:** Right **Pos:** SS   **Ht:** 6'2" **Wt:** 170 **Born:** 1/7/74 **Age:** 26

Year Team	Lg Org	G	AB	H	2B	3B	HR	TB	R	RBI	TBB	IBB	SO	HBP	SH	SF	SB	CS	SB%	GDP	Avg	OBP	SLG
1992 Brewers	R Mil	48	165	43	7	2	0	54	29	24	12	0	19	3	2	2	7	5	.58	3	.261	.319	.327
1993 Beloit	A Mil	94	285	69	14	5	0	93	40	24	14	0	52	1	15	4	22	10	.69	2	.242	.276	.326
1994 Stockton	A+ Mil	112	364	90	18	3	0	114	37	32	17	1	66	4	4	4	19	11	.63	8	.247	.285	.313
1995 Stockton	A+ Mil	64	213	55	13	3	1	77	25	20	10	0	25	2	9	3	13	6	.68	6	.258	.294	.362
El Paso	AA Mil	44	133	37	3	2	0	44	13	11	2	0	22	2	3	1	5	1	.83	2	.278	.297	.331
1997 Yankees	R NYY	2	5	2	0	0	1	5	3	2	1	0	0	0	0	0	2	0	1.00	0	.400	.500	1.000
Norwich	AA NYY	77	312	100	12	5	6	140	49	54	11	0	44	5	10	3	21	6	.78	5	.321	.350	.449
1998 Columbus	AAA NYY	36	131	31	3	1	0	36	17	8	4	0	22	1	2	1	5	3	.63	6	.237	.263	.275
Tampa	A+ NYY	44	166	53	8	1	5	78	26	24	5	2	20	3	1	0	21	6	.78	6	.319	.351	.470
1999 Charlotte	AAA CWS	16	49	14	1	0	4	27	8	5	5	0	6	0	3	0	3	3	.50	2	.286	.352	.551
7 Min. YEARS		537	1823	494	79	22	17	668	247	204	81	3	276	21	49	18	118	51	.70	37	.271	.307	.366

Greg Martinez

Bats: Both **Throws:** Right **Pos:** OF   **Ht:** 5'10" **Wt:** 168 **Born:** 1/27/72 **Age:** 28

Year Team	Lg Org	G	AB	H	2B	3B	HR	TB	R	RBI	TBB	IBB	SO	HBP	SH	SF	SB	CS	SB%	GDP	Avg	OBP	SLG
1993 Brewers	R Mil	5	19	12	0	0	0	12	6	3	4	0	1	0	1	0	7	1	.88	0	.632	.708	.632
Helena	R+ Mil	52	183	53	4	2	0	61	45	19	30	0	26	6	3	5	30	6	.83	0	.290	.397	.333
1994 Beloit	A Mil	81	224	62	8	1	0	72	39	20	25	1	32	3	6	1	27	11	.71	4	.277	.356	.321
1995 Stockton	A+ Mil	114	410	113	8	2	0	125	80	43	69	1	64	2	10	1	55	9	.86	7	.276	.382	.305
1996 Stockton	A+ Mil	73	286	82	5	1	0	89	51	26	29	0	34	0	8	2	30	9	.77	3	.287	.350	.311
El Paso	AA Mil	41	166	52	2	2	1	61	27	21	13	0	19	3	6	1	14	4	.78	4	.313	.372	.367
1997 El Paso	AA Mil	95	381	111	10	10	1	144	75	29	32	0	55	3	9	2	39	7	.85	5	.291	.349	.378
Tucson	AAA Mil	3	12	5	2	0	0	7	2	3	0	0	1	0	0	0	0	0	.00	0	.417	.417	.583
1998 Louisville	AAA Mil	115	376	98	4	11	4	136	65	25	51	0	80	0	10	0	43	7	.86	3	.261	.349	.362
1999 Huntsville	AA Mil	25	98	27	3	2	0	34	18	6	12	1	13	0	1	0	8	2	.80	2	.276	.355	.347
Louisville	AAA Mil	107	419	111	13	4	4	144	79	29	53	0	50	4	5	1	48	7	.87	10	.265	.352	.344
1998 Milwaukee	NL	13	3	0	0	0	0	0	2	0	1	0	2	0	0	0	2	0	1.00	0	.000	.250	.000
7 Min. YEARS		711	2574	726	59	35	10	885	487	224	318	3	374	22	58	13	301	63	.83	38	.282	.364	.344

Javier Martinez

Pitches: Right **Bats:** Right **Pos:** P   **Ht:** 6'2" **Wt:** 235 **Born:** 2/5/77 **Age:** 23

Year Team	Lg Org	G	GS	CG	GF	IP	BFP	H	R	ER	HR	SH	SF	HB	TBB	IBB	SO	WP	Bk	W	L	Pct.	ShO	Sv	ERA
1994 Huntington	R+ ChC	9	8	0	1	35	147	24	20	15	1	1	2	3	21	0	31	9	2	2	1	.667	0	0	3.86
1995 Rockford	A ChC	18	18	1	0	104.2	455	100	56	46	6	5	4	12	39	0	53	15	2	6	6	.500	0	0	3.96
1996 Cubs	R ChC	3	3	0	0	15	62	11	4	1	0	0	0	1	6	0	15	1	0	2	1	.667	0	0	0.60
Rockford	A ChC	10	10	3	0	59	250	49	26	22	5	2	2	1	30	0	53	9	0	4	3	.571	0	0	3.36
1997 Daytona	A+ ChC	9	9	2	0	51.1	238	65	40	33	8	1	3	3	26	0	34	3	2	2	6	.250	0	0	5.79
Rockford	A ChC	17	17	1	0	79	369	85	61	50	7	3	2	3	50	0	70	10	0	1	7	.125	0	0	5.70

Year Team	Lg Org	G	GS	CG	GF	IP	BFP	H	R	ER	HR	SH	SF	HB	TBB	IBB	SO	WP	Bk	W	L	Pct.	ShO	Sv	ERA
1999 Hickory	A Pit	6	0	0	0	7.2	36	6	6	3	0	1	0	0	6	0	13	1	0	0	0	.000	0	0	3.52
Altoona	AA Pit	10	0	0	3	10.1	55	11	8	7	1	0	1	0	14	0	16	0	0	0	0	.000	0	0	6.10
1998 Pittsburgh	NL	37	0	0	13	41	199	39	32	22	5	1	3	4	34	1	42	5	0	0	1	.000	0	0	4.83
5 Min. YEARS		82	65	7	4	362	1612	351	221	177	28	13	14	23	192	1	285	48	6	17	24	.415	0	0	4.40

Jose Martinez

Pitches: Right **Bats:** Right **Pos:** P **Ht:** 6'0" **Wt:** 165 **Born:** 2/4/75 **Age:** 25

Year Team	Lg Org	G	GS	CG	GF	IP	BFP	H	R	ER	HR	SH	SF	HB	TBB	IBB	SO	WP	Bk	W	L	Pct.	ShO	Sv	ERA
1996 Chston-SC	A Tex	11	1	0	3	21	105	34	24	23	7	0	1	2	7	1	17	6	2	1	2	.333	0	0	9.86
Hudson Val	A- Tex	16	5	0	4	54.2	233	56	35	23	3	3	2	0	11	0	38	6	3	2	3	.400	0	0	3.79
1997 Charlotte	A+ Tex	26	0	0	13	57.2	229	52	25	24	6	3	0	0	13	0	48	4	1	3	1	.750	0	2	3.75
1998 Tulsa	AA Tex	7	7	0	0	34.1	160	46	34	29	6	1	2	2	14	0	21	3	2	2	2	.500	0	0	7.60
Charlotte	A+ Tex	19	19	2	0	123.2	521	120	55	38	12	3	3	5	28	3	86	5	3	7	5	.583	0	0	2.77
1999 Tulsa	AA Tex	33	9	0	10	98	441	112	69	59	16	2	6	2	36	0	70	2	1	4	4	.500	0	3	5.42
4 Min. YEARS		112	41	2	30	389.1	1689	420	242	196	50	12	14	11	109	4	280	26	12	19	17	.528	0	5	4.53

Pablo Martinez

Bats: Both **Throws:** Right **Pos:** SS **Ht:** 5'10" **Wt:** 155 **Born:** 6/29/69 **Age:** 31

Year Team	Lg Org	G	AB	H	2B	3B	HR	TB	R	RBI	TBB	IBB	SO	HBP	SH	SF	SB	CS	SB%	GDP	Avg	OBP	SLG
1989 Spokane	A- SD	2	8	2	0	0	0	2	3	0	0	0	0	0	0	0	1	0	1.00	1	.250	.250	.250
Padres	R SD	45	178	42	3	1	0	47	31	12	22	1	25	2	0	0	29	4	.88	1	.236	.327	.264
Chston-SC	A SD	31	80	14	2	0	0	16	13	4	11	0	21	0	3	1	0	1	.00	2	.175	.272	.200
1990 Chston-SC	A SD	136	453	100	12	6	0	124	51	33	41	0	104	4	7	2	16	10	.62	6	.221	.290	.274
1991 Chston-SC	A SD	121	442	118	17	6	3	156	62	36	42	1	64	0	6	2	39	19	.67	8	.267	.329	.353
1992 High Desert	A+ SD	126	427	102	8	4	0	118	60	39	50	0	74	1	2	4	19	14	.58	16	.239	.317	.276
1993 Wichita	AA SD	45	130	36	5	1	2	49	19	14	11	1	24	1	1	1	8	5	.62	2	.277	.336	.377
Las Vegas	AAA SD	76	251	58	4	1	2	70	24	20	18	3	46	3	10	2	8	2	.80	5	.231	.288	.279
1994 Norfolk	AAA NYM	34	80	12	1	0	0	13	8	5	4	0	22	0	3	0	1	1	.50	0	.150	.190	.163
Binghamton	AA NYM	13	48	9	2	2	0	15	3	4	5	0	12	0	2	0	0	1	.00	3	.188	.264	.313
St. Lucie	A+ NYM	49	177	42	5	0	1	50	19	10	13	0	29	0	3	1	7	7	.50	4	.237	.288	.282
1995 Greenville	AA Atl	120	462	118	22	4	5	163	70	29	37	0	89	2	8	1	12	12	.50	7	.255	.313	.353
Richmond	AAA Atl	14	48	11	0	2	0	15	5	4	2	0	7	0	0	1	1	1	.50	3	.229	.260	.313
1996 Greenville	AA Atl	9	37	12	2	2	1	21	7	11	2	0	6	0	1	1	3	0	1.00	1	.324	.350	.568
Richmond	AAA Atl	77	263	71	12	3	1	92	29	18	12	0	58	1	11	1	14	7	.67	3	.270	.303	.350
1997 Richmond	AAA Atl	96	296	76	14	1	4	104	32	20	26	0	77	0	8	2	9	11	.45	3	.257	.315	.351
1998 Louisville	AAA Mil	63	186	44	4	1	2	56	22	9	18	3	31	1	2	2	6	3	.67	5	.237	.304	.301
Allentown	IND —	10	34	9	4	0	0	13	6	2	4	0	4	0	0	0	4	1	.80	1	.265	.342	.382
Richmond	AAA Atl	15	36	10	1	0	0	11	3	3	2	0	10	0	0	0	1	2	.33	0	.278	.316	.306
1999 Greenville	AA Atl	57	228	54	9	3	1	72	28	19	20	0	41	0	2	3	6	8	.43	6	.237	.295	.316
Richmond	AAA Atl	63	186	36	7	3	1	52	18	18	25	1	42	3	7	1	13	3	.81	1	.194	.298	.280
1996 Atlanta	NL	4	2	1	0	0	0	1	1	0	0	0	0	0	0	0	0	0	.00	0	.500	.500	.500
11 Min. YEARS		1202	4050	976	134	40	23	1259	513	310	365	10	786	18	76	24	197	112	.64	78	.241	.305	.311

Romulo Martinez

Pitches: Right **Bats:** Right **Pos:** P **Ht:** 6'1" **Wt:** 170 **Born:** 12/5/76 **Age:** 23

Year Team	Lg Org	G	GS	CG	GF	IP	BFP	H	R	ER	HR	SH	SF	HB	TBB	IBB	SO	WP	Bk	W	L	Pct.	ShO	Sv	ERA
1995 Tigers	R Det	16	0	0	3	24	115	27	22	20	0	1	0	1	13	3	14	3	5	0	0	.000	0	1	7.50
1996 Tigers	R Det	12	12	0	0	62.2	261	67	28	19	1	3	1	2	9	0	51	4	3	1	6	.143	0	0	2.73
1997 W Michigan	A Det	36	0	0	12	79	329	73	28	21	3	6	0	0	21	0	51	4	3	6	4	.600	0	2	2.39
1998 Lakeland	A+ Det	49	0	0	35	65	276	63	32	19	6	2	1	0	20	3	34	2	1	6	3	.667	0	16	2.63
1999 Jacksnville	AA Det	52	0	0	16	72.1	325	85	48	40	5	6	2	3	21	2	46	2	0	3	7	.300	0	1	4.98
Toledo	AAA Det	6	0	0	3	6.2	32	7	5	4	0	0	0	0	6	0	2	0	0	0	0	.000	0	0	5.40
5 Min. YEARS		171	12	0	69	309.2	1338	322	163	123	15	18	4	6	90	8	198	15	12	16	20	.444	0	20	3.57

Victor Martinez

Bats: Right **Throws:** Right **Pos:** 2B **Ht:** 5'11" **Wt:** 180 **Born:** 3/12/78 **Age:** 22

Year Team	Lg Org	G	AB	H	2B	3B	HR	TB	R	RBI	TBB	IBB	SO	HBP	SH	SF	SB	CS	SB%	GDP	Avg	OBP	SLG
1997 Everett	A- Sea	20	58	14	2	1	0	18	10	9	8	0	16	0	1	0	0	1	.00	2	.241	.334	.310
Wisconsin	A Sea	30	95	19	2	1	0	23	9	6	4	0	19	1	6	0	3	3	.50	4	.200	.240	.242
1998 Everett	A- Sea	67	288	99	13	2	5	131	60	32	28	0	48	2	2	2	21	8	.72	8	.344	.403	.455
Wisconsin	A Sea	5	22	3	0	0	0	3	2	2	0	0	5	0	0	0	1	0	1.00	1	.136	.136	.136
1999 Wisconsin	A Sea	69	254	57	10	3	3	82	41	28	21	0	37	6	3	4	3	2	.60	7	.224	.295	.323
New Haven	AA Sea	2	4	0	0	0	0	0	0	0	1	0	3	1	0	0	0	0	.00	0	.000	.333	.000
Everett	A- Sea	28	113	24	2	1	1	31	9	15	4	0	24	1	1	2	1	3	.25	0	.212	.242	.274
3 Min. YEARS		221	834	216	29	8	9	288	131	92	66	0	152	11	13	8	29	17	.63	22	.259	.319	.345

Willie Martinez

Pitches: Right **Bats:** Right **Pos:** P **Ht:** 6'2" **Wt:** 180 **Born:** 1/4/78 **Age:** 22

Year Team	Lg Org	G	GS	CG	GF	IP	BFP	H	R	ER	HR	SH	SF	HB	TBB	IBB	SO	WP	Bk	W	L	Pct.	ShO	Sv	ERA
1995 Burlington	R+ Cle	11	11	0	0	40	208	64	50	42	1	2	2	4	25	0	36	6	3	0	7	.000	0	0	9.45
1996 Watertown	A- Cle	14	14	1	0	90	358	79	25	24	5	2	0	0	21	2	92	6	0	6	5	.545	1	0	2.40

Year Team	Lg Org	G	GS	CG	GF	IP	BFP	H	R	ER	HR	SH	SF	HB	TBB	IBB	SO	WP	Bk	W	L	Pct.	ShO	Sv	ERA
						HOW MUCH HE PITCHED					WHAT HE GAVE UP											THE RESULTS			
1997 Kinston	A+ Cle	23	23	1	0	137	568	125	61	47	13	4	3	4	42	2	120	4	0	8	2	.800	0	0	3.09
1998 Akron	AA Cle	26	26	2	0	154	661	169	92	75	15	6	2	6	44	0	117	10	1	9	7	.563	1	0	4.38
1999 Akron	AA Cle	24	24	0	0	147.1	639	163	83	67	20	5	2	3	45	0	91	8	0	9	8	.529	0	0	4.09
Buffalo	AAA Cle	4	4	0	0	22.1	101	28	17	17	3	1	0	2	7	1	12	0	0	2	2	.500	0	0	6.85
5 Min. YEARS		102	102	4	0	590.2	2535	628	328	272	57	20	9	19	184	5	468	34	4	34	31	.523	2	0	4.14

Eric Martins

Bats: Right **Throws:** Right **Pos:** 2B   **Ht:** 5'9" **Wt:** 170 **Born:** 11/19/72 **Age:** 27

Year Team	Lg Org	G	AB	H	2B	3B	HR	TB	R	RBI	TBB	IBB	SO	HBP	SH	SF	SB	CS	SB%	GDP	Avg	OBP	SLG
					BATTING													BASERUNNING			PERCENTAGES		
1994 Sou Oregon	A- Oak	56	236	78	16	3	4	112	47	34	23	1	36	5	2	0	17	10	.63	4	.331	.402	.475
W Michigan	A Oak	18	71	22	4	1	0	28	11	7	5	0	12	0	1	2	1	2	.33	2	.310	.346	.394
1995 Modesto	A+ Oak	106	407	118	17	5	1	148	71	54	62	0	74	4	18	4	7	8	.47	8	.290	.386	.364
1996 Huntsville	AA Oak	111	388	99	23	2	1	129	61	34	47	0	77	5	8	1	7	7	.50	6	.255	.342	.332
1997 Huntsville	AA Oak	61	205	53	10	3	3	78	33	31	23	0	31	2	3	2	2	1	.67	9	.259	.336	.380
Edmonton	AAA Oak	27	82	23	7	1	1	35	17	8	11	0	19	1	2	0	0	0	.00	3	.280	.372	.427
1998 Huntsville	AA Oak	70	234	71	15	1	3	97	45	24	34	1	32	6	10	1	6	4	.60	8	.303	.404	.415
Edmonton	AAA Oak	39	129	36	8	0	3	53	14	16	9	1	22	0	0	1	1	0	1.00	2	.279	.324	.411
1999 Vancouver	AAA Oak	97	301	72	15	5	3	106	39	33	31	2	47	4	3	2	2	1	.67	9	.239	.317	.352
6 Min. YEARS		585	2053	572	115	21	19	786	338	241	245	5	350	27	47	13	43	33	.57	50	.279	.361	.383

Raul Marval

Bats: Right **Throws:** Right **Pos:** SS   **Ht:** 6'0" **Wt:** 170 **Born:** 12/13/75 **Age:** 24

Year Team	Lg Org	G	AB	H	2B	3B	HR	TB	R	RBI	TBB	IBB	SO	HBP	SH	SF	SB	CS	SB%	GDP	Avg	OBP	SLG
					BATTING													BASERUNNING			PERCENTAGES		
1993 Giants	R SF	19	47	11	2	0	0	13	8	3	3	0	4	0	0	1	3	1	.75	2	.234	.275	.277
1994 Everett	A- SF	29	99	21	5	0	1	29	9	12	4	0	22	1	1	3	4	4	.50	3	.212	.243	.293
Clinton	A SF	81	273	60	9	3	0	75	27	28	16	0	75	2	4	6	4	5	.44	5	.220	.263	.275
1995 San Jose	A+ SF	10	36	10	0	0	0	10	1	3	1	0	5	0	2	0	1	1	.50	0	.278	.297	.278
Burlington	A SF	88	296	79	8	2	1	94	42	19	10	0	32	6	3	1	4	6	.40	9	.267	.304	.318
1996 Burlington	A SF	44	159	32	10	0	0	42	13	9	6	0	12	3	4	2	3	1	.75	7	.201	.241	.264
San Jose	A+ SF	39	137	32	6	0	0	38	19	19	9	0	13	1	4	1	0	0	.00	3	.234	.284	.277
1997 Bakersfield	A+ SF	115	437	112	15	3	2	139	41	42	11	0	66	2	6	3	8	6	.57	8	.256	.276	.318
1998 Shreveport	AA SF	96	296	70	6	1	1	81	14	21	13	0	35	1	4	3	2	2	.50	9	.236	.268	.274
1999 Shreveport	AA SF	2	4	1	0	0	0	1	0	0	0	0	1	0	0	0	0	1	.00	0	.250	.250	.250
Fresno	AAA SF	97	280	84	15	1	7	122	42	46	16	1	48	3	9	5	2	3	.40	4	.300	.339	.436
7 Min. YEARS		620	2064	512	76	10	12	644	216	202	89	1	313	19	37	25	31	30	.51	50	.248	.282	.312

John Marzano

Bats: Right **Throws:** Right **Pos:** C   **Ht:** 5'11" **Wt:** 195 **Born:** 2/14/63 **Age:** 37

Year Team	Lg Org	G	AB	H	2B	3B	HR	TB	R	RBI	TBB	IBB	SO	HBP	SH	SF	SB	CS	SB%	GDP	Avg	OBP	SLG
					BATTING													BASERUNNING			PERCENTAGES		
1985 New Britain	AA Bos	103	350	86	14	6	4	124	36	51	19	0	43	3	7	9	4	3	.57	14	.246	.283	.354
1986 New Britain	AA Bos	118	445	126	28	2	10	188	55	62	24	2	66	12	0	6	2	0	1.00	10	.283	.333	.422
1987 Pawtucket	AAA Bos	70	255	72	22	0	10	124	46	35	21	0	50	5	2	1	2	3	.40	10	.282	.348	.486
1988 Pawtucket	AAA Bos	33	111	22	2	1	0	26	7	5	8	0	17	0	2	1	1	1	.50	4	.198	.250	.234
New Britain	AA Bos	35	112	23	6	1	0	31	11	5	10	2	13	3	1	1	1	0	1.00	6	.205	.286	.277
1989 Pawtucket	AAA Bos	106	322	68	11	0	8	103	27	36	15	1	53	4	4	2	1	4	.20	7	.211	.254	.320
1990 Pawtucket	AAA Bos	26	75	24	4	1	2	36	16	8	11	0	9	0	0	0	6	3	.67	2	.320	.407	.480
1992 Pawtucket	AAA Bos	18	62	18	1	0	2	25	5	12	3	0	11	2	0	0	0	0	.00	1	.290	.343	.403
1993 Charlotte	AAA Cle	3	9	1	0	0	0	1	0	0	1	0	1	0	0	0	0	0	.00	1	.111	.200	.111
1994 Scranton-WB	AAA Phi	88	280	59	19	2	1	85	25	19	24	2	32	5	1	2	2	3	.40	4	.211	.283	.304
1995 Okla City	AAA Tex	120	427	132	41	3	9	206	55	56	33	2	54	8	0	6	3	4	.43	17	.309	.365	.482
1999 Charlotte	A+ Tex	1	4	0	0	0	0	0	0	0	0	0	0	0	0	0	0	0	.00	1	.000	.000	.000
Oklahoma	AAA Tex	44	160	39	10	0	2	55	15	16	8	0	19	2	1	0	0	1	.00	2	.244	.288	.344
1987 Boston	AL	52	168	41	11	0	5	67	20	24	7	0	41	3	2	2	0	1	.00	3	.244	.283	.399
1988 Boston	AL	10	29	4	1	0	0	5	3	1	1	0	3	0	0	0	0	0	.00	1	.138	.167	.172
1989 Boston	AL	7	18	8	3	0	1	14	5	3	0	0	2	0	0	1	0	0	.00	1	.444	.421	.778
1990 Boston	AL	32	83	20	4	0	0	24	8	6	5	0	10	0	2	1	0	0	.00	0	.241	.281	.289
1991 Boston	AL	49	114	30	8	0	0	38	10	9	1	0	16	1	1	2	0	0	.00	5	.263	.271	.333
1992 Boston	AL	19	50	4	2	1	0	8	4	1	2	0	12	1	1	0	0	0	.00	5	.080	.132	.160
1995 Texas	AL	2	6	2	0	0	0	2	1	0	0	0	0	0	0	0	0	0	.00	0	.333	.333	.333
1996 Seattle	AL	41	106	26	6	0	0	32	8	6	7	0	15	4	3	0	0	0	.00	2	.245	.316	.302
1997 Seattle	AL	39	87	25	3	0	1	31	7	10	7	0	15	0	2	0	0	0	.00	2	.287	.340	.356
1998 Seattle	AL	50	133	31	7	1	4	52	13	12	9	1	24	2	2	0	0	0	.00	3	.233	.325	.391
11 Min. YEARS		765	2612	670	158	16	48	1004	298	305	177	9	368	44	18	28	22	22	.50	83	.257	.311	.384
10 Maj. YEARS		301	794	191	45	2	11	273	79	72	39	1	138	18	14	6	0	2	.00	17	.241	.289	.344

Damon Mashore

Bats: Right **Throws:** Right **Pos:** OF   **Ht:** 5'11" **Wt:** 209 **Born:** 10/31/69 **Age:** 30

Year Team	Lg Org	G	AB	H	2B	3B	HR	TB	R	RBI	TBB	IBB	SO	HBP	SH	SF	SB	CS	SB%	GDP	Avg	OBP	SLG
					BATTING													BASERUNNING			PERCENTAGES		
1991 Sou Oregon	A- Oak	73	264	72	17	6	6	119	48	31	34	1	94	2	2	3	15	5	.75	6	.273	.356	.451
1992 Modesto	A+ Oak	124	471	133	22	3	18	215	91	64	73	3	136	6	5	1	29	17	.63	6	.282	.385	.456
1993 Huntsville	AA Oak	70	253	59	7	2	3	79	35	20	25	0	64	4	1	2	18	4	.82	5	.233	.310	.312
1994 Athletics	R Oak	11	34	14	2	0	0	16	6	6	4	0	3	1	0	1	1	1	.50	3	.412	.475	.471
Huntsville	AA Oak	59	210	47	11	2	3	71	24	21	13	1	53	0	1	3	6	1	.86	3	.224	.265	.338

174

Year Team	Lg Org	G	AB	H	2B	3B	HR	TB	R	RBI	TBB	IBB	SO	HBP	SH	SF	SB	CS	SB%	GDP	Avg	OBP	SLG
1995 Edmonton	AAA Oak	117	337	101	19	5	1	133	50	37	42	0	77	5	3	3	17	5	.77	9	.300	.382	.395
1996 Edmonton	AAA Oak	50	183	49	9	1	8	84	32	29	19	0	48	5	2	2	6	2	.75	3	.268	.349	.459
1998 Vancouver	AAA Ana	42	143	39	7	0	2	52	19	15	18	0	28	1	2	0	1	1	.50	2	.273	.358	.364
1999 Fresno	AAA SF	110	347	91	20	1	20	173	62	69	38	0	98	4	4	2	7	3	.70	15	.262	.340	.499
1996 Oakland	AL	50	105	28	7	1	3	46	20	12	16	0	31	1	1	1	4	0	1.00	2	.267	.366	.438
1997 Oakland	AL	92	279	69	10	2	3	92	55	18	50	1	82	5	7	1	5	4	.56	5	.247	.370	.330
1998 Anaheim	AL	43	98	23	6	0	2	35	13	11	9	0	22	3	1	0	1	0	1.00	3	.235	.318	.357
8 Min. YEARS		656	2242	605	114	20	61	942	367	292	266	5	601	28	20	17	100	39	.72	52	.270	.352	.420
3 Maj. YEARS		185	482	120	23	3	8	173	88	41	75	1	135	9	9	2	10	4	.71	10	.249	.359	.359

Justin Mashore

Bats: Right **Throws:** Right **Pos:** OF   **Ht:** 5'9" **Wt:** 190 **Born:** 2/14/72 **Age:** 28

Year Team	Lg Org	G	AB	H	2B	3B	HR	TB	R	RBI	TBB	IBB	SO	HBP	SH	SF	SB	CS	SB%	GDP	Avg	OBP	SLG
1991 Bristol	R+ Det	58	177	36	3	0	3	48	29	11	28	1	65	0	2	0	17	6	.74	1	.203	.312	.271
1992 Fayettevlle	A Det	120	401	96	18	3	4	132	54	43	36	2	117	3	9	1	31	8	.79	3	.239	.306	.329
1993 Lakeland	A+ Det	118	442	113	11	4	3	141	64	30	37	4	92	6	16	5	26	13	.67	9	.256	.318	.319
1994 Trenton	AA Det	131	450	100	13	5	7	144	63	45	36	0	120	3	8	3	31	7	.82	9	.222	.283	.320
1995 Toledo	AAA Det	72	223	49	4	3	4	71	32	21	14	1	62	3	9	2	12	9	.57	1	.220	.273	.318
Jacksnville	AA Det	40	148	36	8	2	4	60	26	15	6	0	41	3	3	0	5	1	.83	2	.243	.287	.405
1996 Jacksnville	AA Det	120	453	129	27	8	7	193	67	50	33	1	97	4	7	2	17	13	.57	10	.285	.337	.426
1997 Mobile	AA SD	90	281	67	10	5	11	120	53	41	32	2	70	5	3	3	11	8	.58	8	.238	.324	.427
1998 Chico	IND —	87	369	107	18	5	14	177	88	69	31	3	91	5	4	2	45	15	.75	6	.290	.351	.480
1999 Trenton	AA Bos	5	16	6	2	2	0	12	3	5	1	1	4	0	1	0	1	0	1.00	1	.375	.412	.750
Sarasota	A+ Bos	17	49	8	3	0	2	17	6	4	5	0	13	0	1	0	1	0	1.00	1	.163	.241	.347
St. Lucie	A+ NYM	28	104	22	4	2	1	33	13	10	7	1	25	2	0	1	1	4	.20	2	.212	.272	.317
Binghamton	AA NYM	13	42	9	2	0	1	14	4	3	0	0	13	1	1	0	1	0	1.00	1	.214	.233	.333
9 Min. YEARS		899	3155	778	123	39	61	1162	502	347	266	16	810	35	63	19	199	84	.70	55	.247	.311	.368

Del Mathews

Pitches: Left **Bats:** Left **Pos:** P   **Ht:** 6'4" **Wt:** 224 **Born:** 10/31/74 **Age:** 25

		HOW MUCH HE PITCHED						WHAT HE GAVE UP										THE RESULTS					
Year Team	Lg Org	G	GS	CG	GF	IP	BFP	H	R	ER	HR	SH	SF	HB	TBB	IBB	SO	WP	Bk	W	L	Pct.	ShO	Sv	ERA
1993 Braves	R Atl	14	12	0	0	62	282	65	42	31	4	3	1	8	26	0	59	4	2	2	4	.333	0	0	4.50
1994 Macon	A Atl	26	18	0	2	117.2	540	133	73	59	9	2	7	8	50	2	92	6	0	10	7	.588	0	0	4.51
1995 Durham	A+ Atl	33	16	1	8	112	478	117	53	44	6	4	1	10	38	2	77	6	0	7	8	.467	0	1	3.54
1996 Durham	A+ Atl	42	2	0	26	65	292	74	39	32	9	1	3	6	26	0	46	6	0	4	3	.571	0	5	4.43
1997 Lynchburg	A+ Pit	18	5	0	6	48.2	209	48	25	19	3	4	1	3	13	3	48	3	0	2	5	.286	0	1	3.51
Carolina	AA Pit	21	1	0	5	50.1	225	53	25	17	5	4	2	1	20	1	51	2	1	5	2	.714	0	1	3.04
1998 Carolina	AA Pit	22	0	0	8	42.1	180	36	14	11	2	3	0	3	17	0	36	1	0	2	0	1.000	0	1	2.34
Nashville	AAA Pit	4	0	0	0	6	33	8	8	7	1	0	1	0	6	0	4	2	0	1	0	1.000	0	0	10.50
1999 Altoona	AA Pit	9	0	0	2	12	66	21	15	8	2	0	0	0	6	2	8	1	0	1	1	.500	0	0	6.00
7 Min. YEARS		189	54	1	57	516	2305	555	294	228	41	21	16	39	202	10	421	31	3	34	30	.531	0	9	3.98

Jared Mathis

Bats: Right **Throws:** Right **Pos:** SS   **Ht:** 5'10" **Wt:** 175 **Born:** 8/8/75 **Age:** 24

Year Team	Lg Org	G	AB	H	2B	3B	HR	TB	R	RBI	TBB	IBB	SO	HBP	SH	SF	SB	CS	SB%	GDP	Avg	OBP	SLG
1997 Lubbock	IND —	36	133	39	7	0	0	46	24	20	26	1	16	1	1	3	1	0	1.00	1	.293	.405	.346
1998 Modesto	A Mil	24	90	24	5	0	0	29	12	3	1	0	8	1	4	0	0	1	.00	4	.267	.283	.322
Stockton	A+ Mil	69	204	59	6	0	0	65	24	17	4	0	17	4	8	3	8	0	1.00	3	.289	.308	.319
1999 Stockton	A+ Mil	23	61	14	1	0	0	15	7	10	2	0	3	2	0	1	1	3	.25	1	.230	.273	.246
Huntsville	AA Mil	74	218	49	5	1	2	62	23	24	8	0	32	1	9	1	2	3	.40	2	.225	.254	.284
3 Min. YEARS		226	706	185	24	1	2	217	90	74	40	1	76	9	22	8	12	7	.63	11	.262	.307	.307

Joe Mathis

Bats: Left **Throws:** Right **Pos:** OF   **Ht:** 5'11" **Wt:** 180 **Born:** 8/10/74 **Age:** 25

Year Team	Lg Org	G	AB	H	2B	3B	HR	TB	R	RBI	TBB	IBB	SO	HBP	SH	SF	SB	CS	SB%	GDP	Avg	OBP	SLG
1993 Mariners	R Sea	36	84	21	4	1	0	27	14	9	5	0	26	1	0	0	7	1	.88	1	.250	.300	.321
1994 Bellingham	A- Sea	53	158	39	4	3	2	55	21	17	16	0	45	2	3	0	13	5	.72	0	.247	.324	.348
1995 Wisconsin	A Sea	117	376	100	17	3	6	141	59	43	43	1	91	0	5	2	26	6	.81	7	.266	.340	.375
1996 Wisconsin	A Sea	126	473	135	19	8	5	185	79	47	36	0	75	4	3	2	19	6	.76	4	.285	.340	.391
1997 Lancaster	A+ Sea	134	562	159	28	15	14	259	94	82	38	1	94	7	3	5	25	16	.61	3	.283	.333	.461
1998 Orlando	AA Sea	103	395	99	18	5	4	139	49	41	27	0	84	3	2	4	12	11	.52	6	.251	.301	.352
1999 New Haven	AA Sea	67	240	65	13	5	2	94	29	30	15	0	45	3	8	1	9	5	.64	3	.271	.320	.392
Tacoma	AAA Sea	26	92	23	5	1	0	30	8	7	6	1	25	0	2	1	3	0	1.00	0	.250	.293	.326
7 Min. YEARS		662	2380	641	108	41	33	930	353	276	186	3	485	20	26	15	114	50	.70	24	.269	.326	.391

Francisco Matos

Bats: Right **Throws:** Right **Pos:** 2B   **Ht:** 6'1" **Wt:** 160 **Born:** 7/23/69 **Age:** 30

Year Team	Lg Org	G	AB	H	2B	3B	HR	TB	R	RBI	TBB	IBB	SO	HBP	SH	SF	SB	CS	SB%	GDP	Avg	OBP	SLG
1989 Modesto	A+ Oak	65	200	41	5	1	1	51	14	23	12	0	41	0	0	1	6	5	.55	5	.205	.249	.255
1990 Modesto	A+ Oak	83	321	88	12	1	1	105	46	20	15	0	65	5	7	2	26	5	.84	2	.274	.315	.327
Huntsville	AA Oak	45	180	41	3	3	0	50	18	12	9	1	18	1	2	1	7	4	.64	3	.228	.267	.278

175

		BATTING														BASERUNNING				PERCENTAGES		
Year Team	Lg Org	G	AB	H	2B	3B	HR	TB	R	RBI	TBB	IBB	SO	HBP	SH	SF	SB	CS	SB%	GDP	Avg	OBP	SLG
1991 Huntsville	AA Oak	55	191	37	1	2	0	42	18	19	17	1	28	2	5	0	12	2	.86	8	.194	.267	.220
Modesto	A+ Oak	50	189	53	4	0	1	60	32	22	30	1	24	1	4	1	19	8	.70	5	.280	.380	.317
1992 Huntsville	AA Oak	44	150	33	5	1	1	43	11	14	11	0	27	2	1	1	4	4	.50	4	.220	.280	.287
1993 Huntsville	AA Oak	123	461	127	12	3	1	148	69	32	22	1	54	4	4	3	16	6	.73	6	.275	.312	.321
1994 Tacoma	AAA Oak	86	336	103	10	1	0	115	40	30	14	0	32	0	4	3	16	9	.64	13	.307	.331	.342
1995 Calgary	AAA Pit	100	341	110	11	6	3	142	36	40	5	0	25	2	3	1	9	2	.82	11	.323	.335	.416
1996 Ottawa	AAA Mon	100	307	73	15	3	2	100	30	23	16	0	35	3	3	2	4	5	.44	14	.238	.280	.326
1997 Rochester	AAA Bal	101	389	126	17	4	4	163	51	51	9	0	42	4	9	3	8	2	.80	15	.324	.343	.419
1998 Durham	AAA TB	32	114	27	2	3	0	35	13	14	1	0	15	1	2	1	2	1	.67	4	.237	.248	.307
Columbus	AAA NYY	76	293	99	18	2	2	127	42	33	20	0	26	2	0	1	3	2	.60	13	.338	.383	.433
1999 Tacoma	AAA Sea	100	393	122	24	3	3	161	43	33	18	0	41	2	5	5	4	6	.40	10	.310	.340	.410
1994 Oakland	AL	14	28	7	1	0	0	8	1	2	1	0	2	0	0	1	1	0	1.00	1	.250	.267	.286
11 Min. YEARS		1060	3865	1080	139	33	19	1342	463	366	199	4	473	29	49	25	136	66	.69	113	.279	.318	.347

Julius Matos

Bats: Right **Throws:** Right **Pos:** SS   **Ht:** 5'11" **Wt:** 175 **Born:** 12/12/74 **Age:** 25

		BATTING															BASERUNNING				PERCENTAGES		
Year Team	Lg Org	G	AB	H	2B	3B	HR	TB	R	RBI	TBB	IBB	SO	HBP	SH	SF	SB	CS	SB%	GDP	Avg	OBP	SLG
1004 Watertown	A Cle	43	138	34	2	2	0	40	13	18	13	0	33	0	0	2	3	2	.60	9	.246	.307	.290
1995 Columbus	A Cle	52	155	38	7	3	0	51	16	13	11	1	21	3	1	0	2	2	.50	8	.245	.308	.329
1996 Thunder Bay	IND —	82	295	81	13	0	3	103	33	32	14	0	48	2	5	1	8	7	.53	9	.275	.311	.349
1997 Sioux City	IND —	83	353	94	12	3	6	130	64	44	20	0	38	4	1	2	8	7	.53	9	.266	.311	.368
1998 High Desert	A+ Ari	111	439	132	27	4	4	179	70	60	23	0	40	2	7	8	19	13	.59	9	.301	.333	.408
1999 El Paso	AA Ari	120	425	119	17	5	5	161	54	41	13	0	37	1	4	3	5	2	.71	10	.280	.301	.379
6 Min. YEARS		491	1805	498	78	17	18	664	250	208	94	1	217	12	18	16	45	33	.58	46	.276	.313	.368

Luis Matos

Bats: Right **Throws:** Right **Pos:** OF   **Ht:** 6'0" **Wt:** 155 **Born:** 10/30/78 **Age:** 21

		BATTING															BASERUNNING				PERCENTAGES		
Year Team	Lg Org	G	AB	H	2B	3B	HR	TB	R	RBI	TBB	IBB	SO	HBP	SH	SF	SB	CS	SB%	GDP	Avg	OBP	SLG
1996 Orioles	R Bal	43	130	38	2	0	0	40	21	13	15	0	18	2	4	0	12	7	.63	3	.292	.374	.308
1997 Delmarva	A Bal	36	119	25	1	2	0	30	10	13	9	0	21	2	2	1	8	5	.62	2	.210	.275	.252
Bluefield	R+ Bal	61	240	66	7	3	2	85	37	35	20	0	36	4	1	1	26	4	.87	5	.275	.340	.354
1998 Delmarva	A Bal	133	503	137	26	6	7	196	73	62	38	0	90	7	6	7	42	14	.75	9	.272	.328	.390
Bowie	AA Bal	5	19	5	0	0	1	8	2	3	1	0	1	0	0	0	1	1	.50	0	.263	.300	.421
1999 Frederick	A+ Bal	68	273	81	15	1	7	119	40	41	20	1	35	2	2	5	27	6	.82	6	.297	.343	.436
Bowie	AA Bal	66	283	67	11	1	9	107	41	36	15	0	39	1	5	6	14	4	.78	6	.237	.272	.378
4 Min. YEARS		412	1567	419	62	13	26	585	224	203	118	1	240	18	20	20	130	41	.76	31	.267	.322	.373

Troy Mattes

Pitches: Right **Bats:** Right **Pos:** P   **Ht:** 6'7" **Wt:** 185 **Born:** 8/26/75 **Age:** 24

		HOW MUCH HE PITCHED						WHAT HE GAVE UP											THE RESULTS					
Year Team	Lg Org	G	GS	CG	GF	IP	BFP	H	R	ER	HR	SH	SF	HB	TBB	IBB	SO	WP	Bk	W	L	Pct.	ShO	Sv	ERA
1994 Expos	R Mon	12	11	1	0	55.2	221	35	25	21	2	0	0	3	21	0	51	7	0	3	2	.600	1	0	3.40
1995 Albany	A Mon	4	4	0	0	19.2	90	21	12	11	0	2	0	0	12	1	15	1	1	0	2	.000	0	0	5.03
Vermont	A- Mon	10	10	0	0	46	209	51	34	19	3	5	4	5	25	0	23	7	0	3	4	.429	0	0	3.72
Expos	R Mon	2	2	0	0	12	43	7	0	0	0	0	0	0	3	0	8	0	0	2	0	1.000	0	0	0.00
1996 Delmarva	A Mon	27	27	5	0	173.1	714	142	77	55	14	6	4	14	50	0	151	17	1	10	9	.526	3	0	2.86
1997 Wst Plm Bch	A+ Mon	20	16	2	3	102	441	123	61	56	8	3	5	5	20	0	61	11	1	6	9	.400	2	1	4.94
1998 Jupiter	A+ Mon	17	10	0	2	73.1	307	73	33	25	4	2	1	3	19	0	42	2	1	7	6	.538	0	0	3.07
1999 Jupiter	A+ Mon	5	5	0	0	24.1	103	27	11	10	2	1	1	3	7	0	12	0	0	3	0	1.000	0	0	3.70
Harrisburg	AA Mon	20	19	0	0	97.1	433	114	67	58	12	8	4	7	38	0	58	3	0	5	8	.385	0	0	5.36
6 Min. YEARS		117	104	8	5	603.2	2561	593	320	255	45	27	19	40	195	1	421	48	4	39	40	.494	6	1	3.80

Mike Matthews

Pitches: Left **Bats:** Left **Pos:** P   **Ht:** 6'2" **Wt:** 175 **Born:** 10/24/73 **Age:** 26

		HOW MUCH HE PITCHED						WHAT HE GAVE UP											THE RESULTS					
Year Team	Lg Org	G	GS	CG	GF	IP	BFP	H	R	ER	HR	SH	SF	HB	TBB	IBB	SO	WP	Bk	W	L	Pct.	ShO	Sv	ERA
1992 Burlington	R+ Cle	10	10	0	0	62.1	245	33	13	7	1	2	1	3	27	0	55	3	1	7	0	1.000	0	0	1.01
Watertown	A- Cle	2	2	0	0	11	47	10	4	4	0	0	1	0	8	0	5	1	0	1	0	1.000	0	0	3.27
1994 Columbus	A Cle	23	23	0	0	119.2	502	120	53	41	8	3	3	7	44	1	99	7	3	6	8	.429	0	0	3.08
1995 Canton-Akrn	AA Cle	15	15	1	0	74.1	345	82	62	49	6	2	8	2	43	1	37	8	1	5	8	.385	0	0	5.93
1996 Canton-Akrn	AA Cle	27	27	3	0	162.1	713	178	96	84	13	6	7	5	74	3	112	6	1	9	11	.450	0	0	4.66
1997 Buffalo	AAA Cle	5	5	0	0	21	106	32	19	18	7	0	2	0	10	0	17	1	0	0	2	.000	0	0	7.71
Akron	AA Cle	19	19	3	0	113	492	116	62	48	13	3	0	7	57	0	69	5	4	6	8	.429	1	0	3.82
1998 Buffalo	AAA Cle	24	23	0	1	130.1	577	137	79	67	19	4	1	5	68	1	86	5	2	9	6	.600	0	0	4.63
1999 Buffalo	AAA Cle	13	6	0	0	21.1	55	13	10	10	3	1	2	2	10	0	0	0	1	2	.000	0	0	7.53
Akron	AA Cle	6	6	0	0	25.2	127	36	30	25	7	0	3	2	15	0	10	0	2	0	5	.000	0	0	8.77
Trenton	AA Bos	3	3	0	0	11.2	52	11	7	6	1	1	1	0	9	0	10	0	0	0	0	.000	0	0	4.63
Arkansas	AA StL	2	2	1	0	12	39	3	0	0	0	0	0	0	0	0	10	0	0	2	0	1.000	1	0	0.00
7 Min. YEARS		161	135	8	9	764.2	3344	781	443	367	78	22	29	33	374	6	524	36	15	46	50	.479	2	0	4.32

Dave Maurer

Pitches: Left **Bats:** Right **Pos:** P **Ht:** 6'2" **Wt:** 205 **Born:** 2/23/75 **Age:** 25

Year Team	Lg Org	HOW MUCH HE PITCHED						WHAT HE GAVE UP										THE RESULTS					
		G	GS	CG	GF	IP	BFP	H	R	ER	HR	SH	SF	HB	TBB	IBB	SO	WP	Bk	W	L	Pct.	ShO	Sv	ERA
1997 Clinton	A SD	25	0	0	10	34.1	142	24	15	11	1	2	1	0	15	0	43	3	1	0	4	.000	0	3	2.88
1998 Rancho Cuca	A+ SD	48	0	0	14	83.1	348	56	27	25	1	1	1	1	46	1	93	8	2	5	2	.714	0	5	2.70
1999 Mobile	AA SD	54	0	0	33	72	301	59	30	29	7	1	4	3	26	5	59	6	0	4	4	.500	0	3	3.63
3 Min. YEARS		127	0	0	57	189.2	791	139	72	65	9	8	6	4	87	6	195	17	3	9	10	.474	0	11	3.08

Brian Maxcy

Pitches: Right **Bats:** Right **Pos:** P **Ht:** 6'1" **Wt:** 170 **Born:** 5/4/71 **Age:** 29

Year Team	Lg Org	HOW MUCH HE PITCHED						WHAT HE GAVE UP										THE RESULTS					
		G	GS	CG	GF	IP	BFP	H	R	ER	HR	SH	SF	HB	TBB	IBB	SO	WP	Bk	W	L	Pct.	ShO	Sv	ERA
1992 Bristol	R+ Det	14	7	2	7	49.1	204	41	24	19	4	0	2	0	17	1	43	3	1	4	2	.667	2	3	3.47
1993 Fayetteville	A Det	39	12	1	20	113.2	501	111	51	37	2	5	3	13	42	3	101	5	0	12	4	.750	1	9	2.93
1994 Trenton	AA Det	5	0	0	2	10.2	45	6	1	0	0	0	0	1	4	0	5	0	0	0	0	.000	0	1	0.00
Toledo	AAA Det	24	1	0	6	44.1	182	31	12	8	1	2	1	2	18	1	43	1	0	2	3	.400	0	3	1.62
1995 Toledo	AAA Det	20	0	0	9	25.2	120	32	20	15	3	4	0	1	11	1	11	3	0	1	3	.250	0	2	5.26
1996 Toledo	AAA Det	15	0	0	6	22.2	97	24	11	10	2	3	2	0	9	2	8	2	0	3	1	.750	0	0	3.97
Louisville	AAA StL	36	3	0	8	62	274	63	34	33	5	2	3	4	32	6	52	5	0	4	2	.667	0	1	4.79
1997 Louisville	AAA StL	30	0	0	20	38.1	176	36	18	16	4	3	2	4	24	3	22	2	0	2	2	.500	0	9	3.76
1998 Memphis	AAA StL	3	0	0	0	4	21	8	8	8	1	0	0	1	1	0	4	0	0	1	1	.500	0	0	18.00
Norfolk	AAA NYM	28	0	0	5	49.1	228	49	25	15	3	1	1	4	27	0	39	4	0	3	0	1.000	0	0	2.74
1999 New Orleans	AAA Hou	4	1	0	3	8	39	12	11	11	2	1	0	1	2	0	6	0	0	0	0	.000	0	0	12.38
1995 Detroit	AL	41	0	0	14	52.1	247	61	48	40	6	3	3	2	31	7	20	6	2	4	5	.444	0	0	6.88
1996 Detroit	AL	2	0	0	0	3.1	19	8	5	5	2	0	0	0	2	0	1	0	0	0	0	.000	0	0	13.50
8 Min. YEARS		218	24	3	86	428	1887	413	215	172	27	21	14	31	187	17	334	25	1	32	18	.640	3	28	3.62
2 Maj. YEARS		43	0	0	14	55.2	266	69	53	45	8	3	3	2	33	7	21	6	2	4	5	.444	0	0	7.28

Jason Maxwell

Bats: Right **Throws:** Right **Pos:** SS **Ht:** 6'1" **Wt:** 185 **Born:** 3/26/72 **Age:** 28

Year Team	Lg Org	BATTING														BASERUNNING				PERCENTAGES		
		G	AB	H	2B	3B	HR	TB	R	RBI	TBB	IBB	SO	HBP	SH	SF	SB	CS	SB%	GDP	Avg	OBP	SLG
1993 Huntington	R+ ChC	61	179	52	7	2	7	84	50	38	35	0	39	4	2	1	6	5	.55	0	.291	.416	.469
1994 Daytona	A+ ChC	116	368	85	18	2	10	137	71	32	55	0	96	8	6	2	7	7	.50	6	.231	.342	.372
1995 Daytona	A+ ChC	117	388	102	13	3	10	151	66	58	63	1	68	6	1	8	12	7	.63	6	.263	.368	.389
1996 Orlando	AA ChC	126	433	115	20	1	9	164	64	45	56	3	77	6	4	3	19	4	.83	5	.266	.355	.379
1997 Orlando	AA ChC	122	409	114	22	6	14	190	87	58	82	1	72	4	5	9	12	9	.57	6	.279	.397	.465
1998 Iowa	AAA ChC	124	483	144	40	3	15	235	86	60	52	1	93	8	1	4	8	1	.89	5	.298	.373	.487
1999 Toledo	AAA Det	119	419	99	17	2	15	165	60	62	53	0	87	2	4	4	6	3	.67	4	.236	.322	.394
1998 Chicago	NL	7	3	1	0	0	1	4	2	2	0	0	2	0	1	0	0	0	.00	0	.333	.333	1.333
7 Min. YEARS		785	2679	711	137	19	80	1126	484	353	396	6	532	38	23	31	70	36	.66	33	.265	.364	.420

Craig Mayes

Bats: Left **Throws:** Right **Pos:** C **Ht:** 5'10" **Wt:** 195 **Born:** 5/8/70 **Age:** 30

Year Team	Lg Org	BATTING														BASERUNNING				PERCENTAGES		
		G	AB	H	2B	3B	HR	TB	R	RBI	TBB	IBB	SO	HBP	SH	SF	SB	CS	SB%	GDP	Avg	OBP	SLG
1992 Everett	A- SF	38	110	38	3	0	0	41	17	10	10	1	13	0	0	0	3	3	.50	5	.345	.400	.373
1993 Clinton	A SF	75	226	67	12	1	3	90	25	37	10	0	52	0	3	3	1	0	1.00	6	.296	.322	.398
1994 Clinton	A SF	49	155	32	5	1	1	42	13	14	11	1	33	0	2	1	0	2	.00	4	.206	.257	.271
San Berndno	A+ SF	50	191	48	5	0	2	59	20	21	17	1	35	1	0	0	2	2	.50	3	.251	.316	.309
1995 Shreveport	AA SF	3	9	2	1	0	0	3	0	0	2	0	2	0	0	0	0	0	.00	0	.222	.222	.333
San Jose	A+ SF	90	318	80	17	4	0	105	34	39	27	1	50	0	1	2	3	1	.75	7	.252	.308	.330
1996 Shreveport	AA SF	10	40	16	2	0	0	18	5	3	5	1	2	0	0	0	0	1	.00	0	.400	.467	.450
San Jose	A+ SF	114	472	155	26	4	3	198	56	68	29	2	43	0	2	4	6	8	.43	5	.328	.364	.419
1997 Shreveport	AA SF	86	293	80	8	5	2	104	27	38	14	1	29	1	0	3	1	0	1.00	17	.273	.305	.355
Phoenix	AAA SF	7	21	2	1	0	0	3	2	0	1	0	5	0	0	0	0	0	.00	2	.095	.136	.143
1998 San Jose	A+ SF	3	11	4	1	0	1	8	1	4	0	0	1	0	0	0	0	0	.00	0	.364	.364	.727
Shreveport	AA SF	29	88	21	2	0	3	32	11	16	4	0	9	0	1	1	0	0	.00	1	.239	.269	.364
Fresno	AAA SF	34	101	28	4	0	2	38	14	16	9	2	14	0	1	1	0	1	.00	1	.277	.333	.376
1999 Fresno	AAA SF	62	169	44	12	0	3	65	19	16	8	1	26	0	2	1	1	1	.50	9	.260	.292	.385
8 Min. YEARS		650	2204	617	99	15	20	806	244	285	145	11	314	2	12	16	17	19	.47	62	.280	.323	.366

Blake Mayo

Pitches: Right **Bats:** Right **Pos:** P **Ht:** 6'2" **Wt:** 210 **Born:** 12/18/72 **Age:** 27

Year Team	Lg Org	HOW MUCH HE PITCHED						WHAT HE GAVE UP										THE RESULTS					
		G	GS	CG	GF	IP	BFP	H	R	ER	HR	SH	SF	HB	TBB	IBB	SO	WP	Bk	W	L	Pct.	ShO	Sv	ERA
1996 Yakima	A- LA	20	6	0	8	67.1	256	44	15	9	1	0	1	0	12	0	68	5	1	5	2	.714	0	1	1.20
1997 San Berndno	A+ LA	20	0	0	5	29.2	141	36	18	17	0	1	1	1	17	2	29	6	0	1	1	.500	0	0	5.16
1998 Vero Beach	A+ LA	32	7	0	21	82.2	356	70	35	27	7	8	2	1	48	4	53	4	0	4	7	.364	0	5	2.94
San Antonio	AA LA	13	0	0	5	18.1	73	13	3	3	0	0	0	0	6	0	15	3	1	2	1	.667	0	1	1.47
1999 San Antonio	AA LA	41	0	0	17	51	230	63	40	33	5	2	2	2	20	2	31	2	0	2	2	.500	0	3	5.82
El Paso	AA Ari	15	1	0	1	25	127	41	16	15	0	1	0	1	13	1	18	6	0	1	1	.500	0	1	5.40
4 Min. YEARS		141	14	0	57	274	1183	267	127	104	13	12	6	5	116	9	214	26	2	15	14	.517	0	11	3.42

177

Rod McCall

Bats: Left **Throws:** Right **Pos:** 1B   **Ht:** 6'7" **Wt:** 235 **Born:** 11/4/71 **Age:** 28

Year Team	Lg Org	G	AB	H	2B	3B	HR	TB	R	RBI	TBB	IBB	SO	HBP	SH	SF	SB	CS	SB%	GDP	Avg	OBP	SLG
1990 Indians	R Cle	10	36	10	2	0	0	12	5	6	5	1	10	0	0	0	0	0	.00	0	.278	.366	.333
Burlington	R+ Cle	31	92	15	5	0	1	23	8	11	10	0	43	2	0	2	0	1	.00	1	.163	.255	.250
1991 Columbus	A Cle	103	323	70	14	1	5	101	34	35	61	3	128	3	0	1	2	2	.50	5	.217	.345	.313
1992 Columbus	A Cle	116	404	97	15	0	20	172	55	80	68	4	121	4	0	6	1	1	.50	9	.240	.351	.426
1993 Kinston	A+ Cle	71	245	51	13	0	9	91	32	33	32	2	85	3	0	4	3	1	.75	3	.208	.303	.371
1994 Kinston	A+ Cle	58	205	44	14	0	11	91	32	27	26	1	75	7	1	0	1	1	.50	2	.215	.324	.444
High Desert	A+ Cle	48	183	51	14	0	17	116	40	43	20	0	63	5	0	1	2	1	.67	4	.279	.364	.634
Canton-Akrn	AA Cle	20	66	13	4	0	3	26	8	9	2	0	27	2	1	1	0	0	.00	1	.197	.239	.394
1995 Bakersfield	A+ Cle	96	345	114	19	1	20	195	61	70	40	7	90	8	2	4	2	5	.29	6	.330	.408	.565
Canton-Akrn	AA Cle	26	95	26	5	0	9	58	16	18	12	3	21	1	0	0	1	1	.50	3	.274	.361	.611
1996 Canton-Akrn	AA Cle	120	440	132	29	2	27	246	80	85	52	4	118	6	0	0	2	0	1.00	4	.300	.382	.559
1997 Buffalo	AAA Cle	36	107	25	5	0	6	48	12	20	9	1	37	2	0	2	0	0	.00	3	.234	.300	.449
Orlando	AA ChC	19	70	21	2	0	6	41	11	20	10	0	24	2	0	1	0	0	.00	1	.300	.398	.586
Iowa	AAA ChC	49	148	42	5	0	14	89	26	35	22	2	53	2	0	1	0	0	.00	1	.284	.382	.601
1998 Iowa	AAA ChC	114	361	91	19	0	30	200	78	70	64	5	151	4	0	2	0	2	.00	4	.252	.369	.554
1999 Indianapolis	AAA Cin	47	139	36	7	0	6	61	21	28	32	0	49	1	0	3	1	0	1.00	4	.259	.394	.439
Zion	IND —	40	145	38	5	1	13	84	34	42	35	0	52	1	0	2	0	1	.00	4	.262	.404	.579
10 Min. YEARS		1004	3404	876	177	5	197	1654	553	632	500	33	1147	53	4	30	15	16	.48	51	.257	.358	.486

Greg McCarthy

Pitches: Left **Bats:** Left **Pos:** P   **Ht:** 6'2" **Wt:** 215 **Born:** 10/30/68 **Age:** 31

		HOW MUCH HE PITCHED						WHAT HE GAVE UP												THE RESULTS				
Year Team	Lg Org	G	GS	CG	GF	IP	BFP	H	R	ER	HR	SH	SF	HB	TBB	IBB	SO	WP	Bk	W	L	Pct.	ShO	Sv	ERA
1987 Utica	A- Phi	20	0	0	13	29.2	130	14	9	3	0	2	1	2	23	2	40	1	2	4	1	.800	0	3	0.91
1988 Spartanburg	A Phi	34	1	0	20	64.2	297	52	36	29	3	3	3	10	52	0	65	8	3	4	2	.667	0	2	4.04
1989 Spartanburg	A Phi	24	15	2	4	112	499	90	58	52	3	3	5	9	80	0	115	8	2	5	8	.385	1	0	4.18
1990 Clearwater	A+ Phi	42	1	0	19	59.2	265	47	32	22	4	2	2	1	38	1	67	5	2	1	3	.250	0	5	3.32
1992 Kinston	A+ Cle	23	0	0	21	27.1	105	14	0	0	0	1	0	5	9	0	37	8	0	3	0	1.000	0	12	0.00
1993 Kinston	A+ Cle	9	0	0	6	10.2	51	8	4	2	0	0	0	0	13	0	14	2	0	0	0	.000	0	2	1.69
Canton-Akrn	AA Cle	33	0	0	19	34.1	156	28	18	18	1	0	3	2	37	2	39	5	0	2	3	.400	0	4	4.72
1994 Canton-Akrn	AA Cle	22	0	0	19	32	133	19	12	8	0	0	1	0	23	2	39	2	0	2	3	.400	0	9	2.25
Charlotte	AAA Cle	18	0	0	11	23.1	118	17	22	18	1	1	2	6	28	1	21	5	0	1	0	1.000	0	0	6.94
1995 Birmingham	AA CWS	38	0	0	13	44.2	195	37	28	25	4	4	2	2	29	3	48	3	1	3	3	.500	0	0	5.04
1996 Tacoma	AAA Sea	39	0	0	14	68.1	317	58	31	25	2	3	1	5	53	2	90	11	2	4	2	.667	0	4	3.29
1997 Tacoma	AAA Sea	22	0	0	10	22	103	21	8	8	3	1	0	2	16	2	34	1	0	2	1	.667	0	3	3.27
1998 Tacoma	AAA Sea	19	0	0	6	19.1	95	15	14	9	2	1	1	2	22	0	24	4	0	1	2	.333	0	1	4.19
1999 Tacoma	AAA Sea	18	0	0	6	22	94	18	6	5	0	0	1	2	13	1	14	3	0	0	1	.000	0	2	2.05
Columbus	AAA NYY	29	0	0	17	35	150	24	19	15	4	0	2	1	19	0	21	3	0	2	1	.667	0	1	3.86
1996 Seattle	AL	10	0	0	1	9.2	45	8	2	2	0	1	1	4	4	0	7	0	0	0	0	.000	0	0	1.86
1997 Seattle	AL	37	0	0	4	29.2	130	26	21	18	4	0	0	1	16	0	34	4	0	1	1	.500	0	0	5.46
1998 Seattle	AL	29	0	0	5	23.1	106	18	13	13	6	2	0	3	17	2	25	1	0	1	2	.333	0	0	5.01
12 Min. YEARS		390	17	2	198	605	2708	462	297	239	27	21	23	50	455	16	668	69	12	34	30	.531	1	51	3.56
3 Maj. YEARS		76	0	0	10	62.2	281	52	36	33	10	3	1	8	37	2	66	5	0	2	3	.400	0	0	4.74

Dave McCarty

Bats: Right **Throws:** Left **Pos:** 1B   **Ht:** 6'5" **Wt:** 215 **Born:** 11/23/69 **Age:** 30

Year Team	Lg Org	G	AB	H	2B	3B	HR	TB	R	RBI	TBB	IBB	SO	HBP	SH	SF	SB	CS	SB%	GDP	Avg	OBP	SLG
1991 Visalia	A+ Min	15	50	19	3	0	3	31	16	8	13	0	7	3	0	0	3	1	.75	0	.380	.530	.620
Orlando	AA Min	28	88	23	4	0	3	36	18	11	10	0	20	2	0	0	0	0	.00	1	.261	.350	.409
1992 Orlando	AA Min	129	456	124	16	2	18	198	75	79	55	5	89	8	1	6	6	6	.50	8	.272	.356	.434
Portland	AAA Min	7	26	13	2	0	1	18	7	8	5	0	3	1	1	0	1	0	1.00	1	.500	.594	.692
1993 Portland	AAA Min	40	143	55	11	0	8	90	42	31	27	2	25	1	0	3	5	2	.71	3	.385	.477	.629
1994 Salt Lake	AAA Min	55	186	47	9	3	3	71	32	19	35	0	34	4	1	2	1	3	.25	9	.253	.379	.382
1995 Indianapolis	AAA Cin	37	140	47	10	1	8	83	31	32	15	0	30	1	1	1	0	0	.00	5	.336	.401	.593
Phoenix	AAA SF	37	151	53	19	2	4	88	31	19	17	1	27	6	0	1	1	1	.50	6	.351	.434	.583
1996 Phoenix	AAA SF	6	25	10	1	1	1	16	4	7	2	0	4	0	0	1	0	0	.00	0	.400	.429	.640
1997 Phoenix	AAA SF	121	434	153	27	5	22	256	85	92	49	5	75	2	1	2	9	4	.69	18	.353	.419	.590
1998 Tacoma	AAA Sea	108	398	126	30	2	11	193	73	52	59	3	85	6	1	2	9	6	.60	15	.317	.411	.485
1999 Toledo	AAA Det	132	466	125	24	3	31	248	85	77	70	5	110	4	0	3	6	6	.50	9	.268	.366	.532
1993 Minnesota	AL	98	350	75	15	2	2	100	36	21	19	0	80	1	1	0	2	6	.25	13	.214	.257	.286
1994 Minnesota	AL	44	131	34	8	2	1	49	21	12	7	1	32	5	0	0	2	1	.67	3	.260	.322	.374
1995 Minnesota	NL	25	55	12	3	1	0	17	10	4	4	0	18	1	0	1	0	1	.00	1	.218	.279	.309
San Francisco	NL	12	20	5	1	0	0	6	1	2	2	0	4	0	0	0	1	0	1.00	0	.250	.318	.300
1996 San Francisco	NL	91	175	38	3	0	6	59	16	24	18	0	43	2	0	2	1	0	.67	5	.217	.294	.337
1998 Seattle	AL	8	18	5	0	0	0	5	2	0	4	0	6	0	0	0	0	0	1.00	0	.278	.435	.444
9 Min. YEARS		715	2563	795	156	19	113	1328	499	435	357	21	509	38	6	21	41	30	.58	75	.310	.399	.518
5 Maj. YEARS		278	749	169	30	5	10	239	85	65	55	1	181	9	1	3	8	9	.47	22	.226	.286	.319

Scott McClain

Bats: Right **Throws:** Right **Pos:** 3B   **Ht:** 6'4" **Wt:** 220 **Born:** 5/19/72 **Age:** 28

Year Team	Lg Org	G	AB	H	2B	3B	HR	TB	R	RBI	TBB	IBB	SO	HBP	SH	SF	SB	CS	SB%	GDP	Avg	OBP	SLG
1990 Bluefield	R+ Bal	40	107	21	2	0	4	35	20	15	22	0	35	2	0	1	2	3	.40	1	.196	.333	.327
1991 Kane County	A Bal	25	81	18	0	0	0	18	9	4	17	0	25	0	1	0	1	1	.50	4	.222	.357	.222
Bluefield	R+ Bal	41	149	39	5	0	0	44	16	24	14	0	39	3	0	1	5	3	.63	3	.262	.335	.295

	BATTING																BASERUNNING				PERCENTAGES		
Year Team	Lg Org	G	AB	H	2B	3B	HR	TB	R	RBI	TBB	IBB	SO	HBP	SH	SF	SB	CS	SB%	GDP	Avg	OBP	SLG
1992 Kane County	A Bal	96	316	84	12	2	3	109	43	30	48	1	62	6	6	1	7	4	.64	5	.266	.372	.345
1993 Frederick	A+ Bal	133	427	111	22	2	9	164	65	54	70	0	88	6	3	2	10	6	.63	8	.260	.370	.384
1994 Bowie	AA Bal	133	427	103	29	1	11	167	71	58	72	2	89	1	2	7	6	3	.67	14	.241	.347	.391
1995 Rochester	AAA Bal	61	199	50	9	1	8	85	32	22	23	0	34	1	1	2	0	1	.00	5	.251	.329	.427
Bowie	AA Bal	70	259	72	14	1	13	127	41	61	25	1	44	3	0	4	2	1	.67	13	.278	.344	.490
1996 Rochester	AAA Bal	131	463	130	23	4	17	212	76	69	61	1	109	1	0	7	8	6	.57	6	.281	.361	.458
1997 Norfolk	AAA NYM	127	429	120	29	2	21	216	71	64	64	5	93	2	1	8	1	3	.25	8	.280	.370	.503
1998 Durham	AAA TB	126	472	141	35	0	34	278	91	109	66	5	113	2	1	3	6	2	.75	9	.299	.385	.589
1999 Durham	AAA TB	137	533	134	33	1	28	253	106	104	73	1	156	3	0	6	4	2	.67	11	.251	.341	.475
1998 Tampa Bay	AL	9	20	2	0	0	0	2	2	0	2	0	6	1	0	0	0	0	.00	0	.100	.217	.100
10 Min. YEARS		1120	3862	1023	213	14	148	1708	641	614	555	16	887	30	15	45	52	35	.60	87	.265	.358	.442

Tim McClaskey

Pitches: Right Bats: Right Pos: P   Ht: 6'1" Wt: 180 Born: 1/11/76 Age: 24

	HOW MUCH HE PITCHED						WHAT HE GAVE UP												THE RESULTS					
Year Team	Lg Org	G	GS	CG	GF	IP	BFP	H	R	ER	HR	SH	SF	HB	TBB	IBB	SO	WP	Bk	W	L	Pct.	ShO	Sv	ERA
1996 Marlins	R Fla	12	12	2	0	73	288	58	28	21	3	5	3	2	13	0	63	2	0	4	3	.571	2	0	2.59
1997 Utica	A- Fla	1	0	0	1	5	16	1	0	0	0	0	0	0	0	0	8	0	0	1	0	1.000	0	0	0.00
Kane County	A Fla	18	2	0	7	37	151	29	18	13	3	1	2	3	8	2	38	3	1	2	1	.667	0	0	3.16
1998 Kane County	A Fla	34	2	0	18	74	326	87	45	35	5	3	4	5	16	3	70	4	0	5	2	.714	0	2	4.26
1999 New Haven	AA Sea	4	0	0	2	8	27	4	2	2	1	0	0	1	1	0	7	0	0	0	0	.000	0	0	2.25
Lancaster	A+ Sea	30	0	0	9	58	260	83	51	41	9	1	1	6	11	0	54	3	0	3	3	.500	0	0	6.36
4 Min. YEARS		99	16	2	37	255	1068	262	144	112	21	10	10	16	49	5	240	12	1	15	9	.625	2	3	3.95

Sean McClellan

Pitches: Right Bats: Right Pos: P   Ht: 6'2" Wt: 215 Born: 4/26/73 Age: 27

	HOW MUCH HE PITCHED						WHAT HE GAVE UP												THE RESULTS					
Year Team	Lg Org	G	GS	CG	GF	IP	BFP	H	R	ER	HR	SH	SF	HB	TBB	IBB	SO	WP	Bk	W	L	Pct.	ShO	Sv	ERA
1996 Medcine Hat	R+ Tor	12	8	0	2	51.2	228	52	38	35	5	0	0	4	19	0	61	2	2	3	3	.500	0	1	6.10
1997 Dunedin	A+ Tor	3	0	0	2	3.1	20	5	4	4	0	0	1	0	5	0	4	0	0	0	0	.000	0	0	10.80
Hagerstown	A Tor	35	0	0	26	65	271	49	21	12	3	5	3	1	26	1	80	4	0	3	2	.600	0	11	1.66
1998 Dunedin	A+ Tor	24	0	0	8	57	223	34	14	14	3	1	0	3	20	0	73	2	0	4	0	1.000	0	5	2.21
Knoxville	AA Tor	24	3	0	10	49.2	209	31	23	20	5	1	2	1	33	0	44	2	1	3	5	.375	0	4	3.62
1999 Syracuse	AAA Tor	8	0	0	5	7	34	6	4	3	1	0	0	0	4	0	5	1	0	0	0	.000	0	0	3.86
Dunedin	A+ Tor	3	0	0	0	3	11	1	2	2	1	0	0	0	1	0	5	0	0	0	0	.000	0	0	6.00
Knoxville	AA Tor	14	0	0	4	20.2	88	18	8	8	1	1	1	0	11	0	24	0	0	1	0	1.000	0	0	3.48
4 Min. YEARS		123	11	0	57	257.1	1084	196	114	98	19	8	7	9	119	1	296	11	3	14	10	.583	0	24	3.43

Brian McClure

Bats: Left Throws: Right Pos: 2B   Ht: 6'0" Wt: 170 Born: 1/15/74 Age: 26

	BATTING																BASERUNNING				PERCENTAGES		
Year Team	Lg Org	G	AB	H	2B	3B	HR	TB	R	RBI	TBB	IBB	SO	HBP	SH	SF	SB	CS	SB%	GDP	Avg	OBP	SLG
1996 Idaho Falls	R+ SD	72	308	99	18	6	6	147	62	45	38	0	63	3	0	4	10	2	.83	6	.321	.397	.477
1997 Clinton	A SD	118	416	115	18	11	4	167	75	55	90	4	64	1	3	6	12	11	.52	7	.276	.402	.401
1998 Rancho Cuca	A+ SD	129	492	130	25	11	9	204	89	57	66	2	98	7	5	4	4	3	.57	8	.264	.357	.415
1999 Rancho Cuca	A+ SD	36	116	26	5	1	2	39	26	15	26	0	22	1	3	2	4	1	.80	1	.224	.366	.336
Mobile	AA SD	51	169	35	10	3	1	54	17	27	17	1	34	2	1	2	0	0	.00	4	.207	.284	.320
4 Min. YEARS		406	1501	405	76	32	22	611	269	199	237	7	281	14	12	18	30	17	.64	26	.270	.371	.407

Jason McCommon

Pitches: Right Bats: Right Pos: P   Ht: 6'0" Wt: 190 Born: 8/9/71 Age: 28

	HOW MUCH HE PITCHED						WHAT HE GAVE UP												THE RESULTS					
Year Team	Lg Org	G	GS	CG	GF	IP	BFP	H	R	ER	HR	SH	SF	HB	TBB	IBB	SO	WP	Bk	W	L	Pct.	ShO	Sv	ERA
1994 Vermont	A- Mon	24	3	0	13	48	196	47	20	19	0	1	3	0	15	2	47	7	1	3	4	.429	0	4	3.56
1995 Wst Plm Bch	A+ Mon	26	26	3	0	156	650	153	75	65	13	7	6	10	38	0	94	6	7	7	11	.389	1	0	3.75
1996 Harrisburg	AA Mon	30	24	1	2	153	663	169	88	67	13	2	8	7	44	1	92	5	0	10	10	.500	1	0	3.94
1997 Harrisburg	AA Mon	29	8	0	7	82.2	358	81	50	46	13	0	0	3	39	0	58	4	1	3	6	.667	0	5	5.01
1998 Harrisburg	AA Mon	6	0	0	3	9.2	40	8	4	4	1	0	0	0	6	1	7	1	0	1	0	1.000	0	1	3.72
Bowie	AA Bal	23	19	2	1	124	518	113	63	59	17	4	5	4	42	0	73	5	0	8	8	.500	0	0	4.28
1999 Rochester	AAA Bal	29	18	1	1	124.2	550	143	73	69	21	4	3	1	50	1	68	2	2	7	10	.412	1	0	4.98
6 Min. YEARS		167	98	7	27	698	2975	714	373	329	78	18	25	25	234	5	439	30	11	42	46	.477	2	6	4.24

Sam McConnell

Pitches: Left Bats: Left Pos: P   Ht: 6'5" Wt: 212 Born: 12/31/75 Age: 24

	HOW MUCH HE PITCHED						WHAT HE GAVE UP												THE RESULTS					
Year Team	Lg Org	G	GS	CG	GF	IP	BFP	H	R	ER	HR	SH	SF	HB	TBB	IBB	SO	WP	Bk	W	L	Pct.	ShO	Sv	ERA
1997 Erie	A- Pit	17	10	0	0	58.2	261	56	38	33	7	1	3	3	24	0	45	6	0	2	2	.500	0	0	5.06
1998 Augusta	A Pit	8	8	1	0	45	183	36	22	16	2	1	0	1	13	1	35	1	1	4	3	.571	0	0	3.20
Lynchburg	A+ Pit	19	19	3	0	121	483	118	48	39	4	2	1	1	20	0	80	2	0	8	5	.615	1	0	2.90
Carolina	AA Pit	2	1	0	0	12	53	15	7	6	2	1	1	0	3	0	5	0	0	0	1	.000	0	0	4.50
1999 Altoona	A+ Pit	15	15	4	0	101.2	402	84	41	36	8	3	5	5	27	1	70	6	0	7	3	.700	2	0	3.19
Altoona	AA Pit	13	12	1	0	62.1	299	82	52	46	7	6	3	4	33	1	40	5	1	1	7	.125	0	0	6.64
3 Min. YEARS		74	65	9	0	400.2	1681	391	208	176	30	14	13	14	120	3	275	20	2	22	21	.512	3	0	3.95

Scott McCrary

Pitches: Right Bats: Right Pos: P Ht: 6'4" Wt: 204 Born: 1/8/74 Age: 26

Year Team	Lg Org	G	GS	CG	GF	IP	BFP	H	R	ER	HR	SH	SF	HB	TBB	IBB	SO	WP	Bk	W	L	Pct.	ShO	Sv	ERA
1997 Mets	R NYM	5	0	0	4	9	36	5	3	0	0	0	0	1	2	0	15	2	1	1	0	1.000	0	2	0.00
Capital Cty	A NYM	13	0	0	5	28	104	20	4	3	1	1	1	0	5	1	24	2	0	3	2	.600	0	0	0.96
1998 Binghamton	AA NYM	1	1	0	0	6	21	1	0	0	0	0	0	1	1	0	8	0	0	1	0	1.000	0	0	0.00
St. Lucie	A+ NYM	37	4	0	14	92.1	373	78	40	30	9	3	2	2	18	2	75	7	1	8	4	.667	0	6	2.92
1999 Binghamton	AA NYM	17	6	0	3	53.2	247	72	34	29	8	4	4	1	21	0	29	1	0	1	5	.167	0	0	4.86
3 Min. YEARS		73	11	0	26	189	781	176	81	62	18	8	7	5	47	3	151	12	2	14	11	.560	0	8	2.95

Mike McCutcheon

Pitches: Left Bats: Left Pos: P Ht: 5'11" Wt: 158 Born: 7/5/77 Age: 22

Year Team	Lg Org	G	GS	CG	GF	IP	BFP	H	R	ER	HR	SH	SF	HB	TBB	IBB	SO	WP	Bk	W	L	Pct.	ShO	Sv	ERA
1996 Diamondbcks	R Ari	14	0	0	11	18.1	70	9	3	1	0	0	0	0	7	0	18	1	0	0	1	.000	0	2	0.49
1997 South Bend	A Ari	31	17	0	6	105.2	464	104	55	40	5	3	5	5	49	1	67	9	2	7	5	.583	0	1	3.41
1998 South Bend	A Ari	13	6	0	4	49.1	214	53	30	20	2	2	1	0	22	0	32	8	2	3	3	.500	0	0	3.65
Lethbridge	R+ Ari	17	10	0	0	64.2	291	66	45	39	4	2	1	3	34	0	40	6	3	5	3	.625	0	0	5.43
1999 El Paso	AA Ari	3	1	0	0	8.2	41	7	8	6	1	1	0	0	9	0	8	1	0	1	1	.500	0	0	6.23
South Bend	A Ari	28	8	0	6	87.2	384	87	48	39	5	2	2	1	36	0	74	3	1	6	2	.750	0	0	4.00
4 Min. YEARS		106	42	0	27	334.1	1464	326	189	145	17	11	9	11	157	1	239	28	8	22	15	.595	0	3	3.90

Allen McDill

Pitches: Left Bats: Left Pos: P Ht: 6'0" Wt: 170 Born: 8/23/71 Age: 28

Year Team	Lg Org	G	GS	CG	GF	IP	BFP	H	R	ER	HR	SH	SF	HB	TBB	IBB	SO	WP	Bk	W	L	Pct.	ShO	Sv	ERA
1992 Kingsport	R+ NYM	1	0	0	0	0.1	3	0	0	0	0	0	0	0	2	0	0	0	0	0	0	.000	0	0	0.00
Mets	R NYM	10	9	0	0	53.1	216	36	23	16	3	0	0	4	15	0	60	3	0	3	4	.429	0	0	2.70
1993 Kingsport	R+ NYM	9	9	0	0	53.1	224	52	19	13	1	1	2	0	14	0	42	2	2	5	2	.714	0	0	2.19
Pittsfield	A- NYM	5	5	0	0	28.1	132	31	22	17	0	2	2	1	15	0	24	3	0	2	3	.400	0	0	5.40
1994 Capital Cty	A NYM	19	19	1	0	111.2	461	101	52	44	11	5	2	4	38	2	102	9	0	9	6	.600	0	0	3.55
1995 St. Lucie	A+ NYM	7	7	1	0	49.1	190	36	11	9	2	1	0	1	13	0	28	3	0	4	2	.667	1	0	1.64
Binghamton	AA NYM	12	12	1	0	73	324	69	42	37	5	1	4	3	38	2	44	3	1	3	5	.375	0	0	4.56
Wichita	AA KC	12	1	0	5	21.1	85	16	7	5	2	0	0	1	5	0	20	1	0	1	0	1.000	0	1	2.11
1996 Omaha	AAA KC	2	0	0	0	0.1	5	3	2	2	0	0	0	0	1	0	1	2	0	0	1	.000	0	0	54.00
Wichita	AA KC	54	0	0	30	65	288	79	43	40	10	2	4	4	21	3	62	7	0	1	5	.167	0	11	5.54
1997 Omaha	AAA KC	23	6	0	5	64.1	295	80	42	42	10	2	1	5	26	2	51	2	0	5	2	.714	0	2	5.88
Wichita	AA KC	16	0	0	7	17.1	72	18	7	6	1	0	1	0	7	1	14	1	0	0	0	.000	0	3	3.12
1998 Omaha	AAA KC	61	0	0	22	60.1	246	54	22	16	4	3	0	0	24	3	62	0	1	6	4	.600	0	4	2.39
1999 Oklahoma	AAA Tex	42	0	0	35	48.1	207	45	22	20	6	1	1	2	17	0	46	4	0	1	3	.250	0	18	3.72
1997 Kansas City	AL	3	0	0	1	4	24	6	6	6	1	1	0	1	8	0	2	0	0	0	0	.000	0	0	13.50
1998 Kansas City	AL	7	0	0	1	6	29	9	7	7	3	0	0	0	2	0	3	0	0	0	0	.000	0	0	10.50
8 Min. YEARS		273	68	3	104	646.1	2748	620	314	267	54	19	16	25	236	13	556	40	4	40	38	.513	1	39	3.72
2 Maj. YEARS		10	0	0	2	10	53	12	13	13	4	1	0	1	10	0	5	0	0	0	0	.000	0	0	11.70

Donzell McDonald

Bats: Both Throws: Right Pos: OF Ht: 5'11" Wt: 165 Born: 2/20/75 Age: 25

Year Team	Lg Org	G	AB	H	2B	3B	HR	TB	R	RBI	TBB	IBB	SO	HBP	SH	SF	SB	CS	SB%	GDP	Avg	OBP	SLG
1995 Yankees	R NYY	28	110	26	5	1	0	33	23	9	16	0	24	2	0	1	11	2	.85	1	.236	.341	.300
1996 Oneonta	A- NYY	74	282	78	8	10	2	112	57	30	43	0	62	2	3	2	54	4	.93	1	.277	.374	.397
1997 Tampa	A+ NYY	77	297	88	23	8	3	136	69	23	48	0	75	4	1	1	39	18	.68	3	.296	.400	.458
1998 Norwich	AA NYY	134	495	125	20	7	6	177	80	36	55	1	127	4	4	7	35	22	.61	7	.253	.330	.358
Tampa	A+ NYY	5	18	6	1	2	0	11	6	2	2	0	7	1	1	0	2	0	1.00	0	.333	.429	.611
1999 Norwich	AA NYY	137	533	145	19	10	4	196	95	33	90	0	110	6	11	1	54	20	.73	5	.272	.383	.368
5 Min. YEARS		455	1735	468	76	38	15	665	330	133	254	1	405	19	23	9	195	66	.75	17	.270	.367	.383

Keith McDonald

Bats: Right Throws: Right Pos: C Ht: 6'2" Wt: 215 Born: 2/8/73 Age: 27

Year Team	Lg Org	G	AB	H	2B	3B	HR	TB	R	RBI	TBB	IBB	SO	HBP	SH	SF	SB	CS	SB%	GDP	Avg	OBP	SLG
1994 Johnson Cy	R+ StL	59	199	49	12	0	6	79	32	31	27	3	36	5	2	3	3	1	.75	9	.246	.346	.397
1995 Peoria	A StL	65	179	48	6	0	1	57	22	20	22	0	38	6	4	0	1	0	.00	2	.268	.367	.318
1996 St. Pete	A+ StL	114	410	111	25	0	2	142	30	52	34	1	65	5	1	5	1	3	.25	18	.271	.330	.346
1997 Arkansas	AA StL	79	233	56	16	0	5	87	32	30	31	0	56	3	1	0	1	0	.00	4	.240	.337	.373
1998 Memphis	AAA StL	58	170	54	8	0	7	83	21	22	10	2	30	2	2	0	1	1	.50	2	.318	.363	.488
1999 Arkansas	AA StL	49	163	50	10	0	2	66	21	14	15	0	35	3	0	2	1	1	1.00	1	.307	.372	.405
Memphis	AAA StL	39	119	34	7	0	6	66	30	27	20	0	25	0	1	2	1	0	1.00	1	.301	.400	.496
6 Min. YEARS		463	1467	402	84	0	28	570	178	196	159	6	285	24	11	12	7	7	.50	37	.274	.352	.389

Mike McDougal

Pitches: Right Bats: Left Pos: P Ht: 6'4" Wt: 210 Born: 3/22/75 Age: 25

Year Team	Lg Org	G	GS	CG	GF	IP	BFP	H	R	ER	HR	SH	SF	HB	TBB	IBB	SO	WP	Bk	W	L	Pct.	ShO	Sv	ERA
1995 Johnson Cy	R+ StL	1	0	0	0	0	1	0	0	0	0	0	0	0	1	0	0	0	0	0	0	.000	0	0	0.00
1996 New Jersey	A- StL	14	0	0	4	20.1	87	20	17	16	4	1	1	1	4	0	25	1	0	1	1	.500	0	0	7.08
1997 New Jersey	A- StL	13	11	2	0	68.2	272	62	24	19	1	3	0	2	9	0	63	1	0	4	4	.500	2	0	2.49

180

		HOW MUCH HE PITCHED						WHAT HE GAVE UP												THE RESULTS					
Year Team	Lg Org	G	GS	CG	GF	IP	BFP	H	R	ER	HR	SH	SF	HB	TBB	IBB	SO	WP	Bk	W	L	Pct.	ShO	Sv	ERA
1998 Pr William	A+ StL	17	2	0	3	32	132	38	11	10	4	1	0	1	2	0	28	1	0	3	0	1.000	0	0	2.81
Arkansas	AA StL	24	0	0	8	31	143	45	21	17	7	0	2	2	5	1	16	1	0	2	3	.400	0	1	4.94
1999 Delmarva	A Bal	1	0	0	0	2	9	3	0	0	0	0	0	0	0	0	3	0	0	1	0	1.000	0	0	0.00
Bowie	AA Bal	48	0	0	22	61.1	285	70	34	29	10	7	0	4	31	6	47	2	0	5	7	.417	0	8	4.26
5 Min. YEARS		118	13	2	37	215.1	929	238	107	91	26	12	3	10	52	7	182	6	0	16	15	.516	2	9	3.80

Ethan McEntire

Pitches: Left **Bats:** Left **Pos:** P **Ht:** 6'1" **Wt:** 194 **Born:** 7/19/75 **Age:** 24

		HOW MUCH HE PITCHED						WHAT HE GAVE UP												THE RESULTS					
Year Team	Lg Org	G	GS	CG	GF	IP	BFP	H	R	ER	HR	SH	SF	HB	TBB	IBB	SO	WP	Bk	W	L	Pct.	ShO	Sv	ERA
1993 Mets	R NYM	10	7	0	0	42.2	165	36	12	12	0	0	1	2	14	0	41	7	0	4	1	.800	0	0	2.53
1994 Kingsport	R+ NYM	13	13	3	0	87.1	352	62	38	25	4	5	2	6	29	0	69	7	4	4	4	.500	2	0	2.58
1995 Capital Cty	A NYM	6	6	1	0	32.1	146	26	14	12	4	3	0	0	23	0	31	3	0	3	2	.600	1	0	3.34
Pittsfield	A- NYM	13	13	0	0	69.1	325	81	43	39	2	1	2	5	46	0	41	7	0	4	2	.667	0	0	5.06
1996 Capital Cty	A NYM	27	27	1	0	174	689	123	51	43	10	2	0	4	61	0	190	6	0	9	6	.600	1	0	2.22
1997 St. Lucie	A+ NYM	3	3	0	0	11.2	54	16	9	8	0	0	1	0	7	0	8	0	0	0	1	.000	0	0	6.17
1998 Capital Cty	A NYM	1	1	0	0	5	22	3	0	0	0	0	0	0	4	0	2	0	0	1	0	1.000	0	0	0.00
St. Lucie	A+ NYM	22	12	0	3	85.2	388	85	38	28	5	4	0	1	58	1	52	1	0	5	4	.556	0	0	2.94
1999 Binghamton	AA NYM	4	3	0	1	13.2	75	26	23	20	5	0	0	0	8	0	7	1	0	0	2	.000	0	0	13.17
St. Lucie	A+ NYM	22	21	0	0	129	562	130	68	55	8	5	6	5	62	0	63	4	0	8	10	.444	0	0	3.84
7 Min. YEARS		121	106	5	4	650.2	2778	588	296	242	38	20	12	23	312	1	504	36	4	38	32	.543	4	0	3.35

Cody McKay

Bats: Left **Throws:** Right **Pos:** C **Ht:** 6'0" **Wt:** 190 **Born:** 1/11/74 **Age:** 26

		BATTING													BASERUNNING				PERCENTAGES		
Year Team	Lg Org	G	AB	H	2B	3B	HR	TB	R	RBI	TBB	IBB	SO	HBP	SH	SF	SB	CS	SB%	GDP	Avg	OBP	SLG
1996 Sou Oregon	A- Oak	69	254	68	13	0	3	90	33	30	25	0	42	6	1	3	0	5	.00	7	.268	.344	.354
1997 Modesto	A+ Oak	125	390	97	20	1	7	140	47	50	46	2	69	16	3	4	4	2	.67	9	.249	.349	.359
1998 Huntsville	AA Oak	9	21	6	0	0	1	9	5	1	6	0	5	2	0	0	0	0	.00	0	.286	.483	.429
Edmonton	AAA Oak	19	57	13	3	0	0	16	6	5	7	0	5	3	2	0	1	0	1.00	2	.228	.343	.281
Modesto	A+ Oak	107	402	114	25	1	6	159	59	58	40	1	62	17	3	3	2	4	.33	12	.284	.370	.396
1999 Midland	AA Oak	94	333	98	21	1	6	139	59	43	38	5	40	8	1	5	1	2	.33	11	.294	.375	.417
4 Min. YEARS		423	1457	396	82	3	23	553	209	187	162	8	223	52	10	15	8	13	.38	41	.272	.362	.380

Walt McKeel

Bats: Right **Throws:** Right **Pos:** C **Ht:** 6'0" **Wt:** 200 **Born:** 1/17/72 **Age:** 28

		BATTING													BASERUNNING				PERCENTAGES		
Year Team	Lg Org	G	AB	H	2B	3B	HR	TB	R	RBI	TBB	IBB	SO	HBP	SH	SF	SB	CS	SB%	GDP	Avg	OBP	SLG
1990 Red Sox	R Bos	13	44	11	3	0	0	14	2	6	3	0	8	0	0	1	0	2	.00	2	.250	.292	.318
1991 Red Sox	R Bos	35	113	15	0	1	2	23	10	12	17	0	20	1	0	4	0	0	.00	5	.133	.244	.204
1992 Lynchburg	A+ Bos	96	288	64	11	0	12	111	33	33	22	0	77	3	5	1	2	1	.67	3	.222	.283	.385
1993 Lynchburg	A+ Bos	80	247	59	17	2	5	95	28	32	26	0	40	3	4	6	0	1	.00	6	.239	.315	.385
1994 Sarasota	A+ Bos	37	137	38	8	1	2	54	15	15	8	1	19	1	0	0	0	1	1.00	1	.277	.322	.394
New Britain	AA Bos	50	164	30	6	1	1	41	10	17	7	1	35	3	1	2	0	0	.00	5	.183	.227	.250
1995 Trenton	AA Bos	29	84	20	3	1	2	31	11	11	8	0	15	0	0	2	2	1	.67	1	.238	.298	.369
Sarasota	A+ Bos	62	198	66	14	0	8	104	26	35	25	0	28	3	0	5	6	3	.67	4	.333	.407	.525
1996 Trenton	AA Bos	128	464	140	19	1	16	209	86	78	60	3	52	7	5	7	2	4	.33	13	.302	.385	.450
1997 Pawtucket	AAA Bos	66	237	60	15	0	6	93	34	30	34	3	39	1	1	2	0	1	.00	8	.253	.347	.392
Trenton	AA Bos	7	25	4	2	0	0	6	0	4	1	0	2	0	1	0	0	0	.00	1	.160	.192	.240
1998 Red Sox	R Bos	13	36	9	2	0	1	14	1	4	4	0	8	0	0	1	0	0	.00	0	.250	.317	.389
Pawtucket	AAA Bos	48	170	49	10	1	4	73	26	26	21	0	27	1	0	0	1	2	.33	8	.288	.370	.429
1999 Toledo	AAA Det	67	215	52	9	1	7	84	21	37	26	0	32	4	1	2	2	2	.50	6	.242	.332	.391
Sonoma Cty	IND —	2	9	4	0	0	1	7	1	1	0	0	3	0	0	0	0	0	.00	0	.444	.444	.778
1996 Boston	AL	1	0	0	0	0	0	0	0	0	0	0	0	0	0	0	0	0	.00	0	.000	.000	.000
1997 Boston	AL	5	3	0	0	0	0	0	0	0	0	0	1	0	0	0	0	0	.00	0	.000	.000	.000
10 Min. YEARS		733	2431	621	119	9	67	959	304	341	262	8	405	27	20	30	16	17	.48	63	.255	.331	.394
2 Maj. YEARS		6	3	0	0	0	0	0	0	0	0	0	1	0	0	0	0	0	.00	0	.000	.000	.000

Dan McKinley

Bats: Left **Throws:** Right **Pos:** OF **Ht:** 6'0" **Wt:** 180 **Born:** 5/15/76 **Age:** 24

		BATTING													BASERUNNING				PERCENTAGES		
Year Team	Lg Org	G	AB	H	2B	3B	HR	TB	R	RBI	TBB	IBB	SO	HBP	SH	SF	SB	CS	SB%	GDP	Avg	OBP	SLG
1998 Shreveport	AA SF	33	112	20	3	3	0	29	16	11	11	1	30	3	0	1	2	3	.40	3	.179	.268	.259
Bakersfield	A+ SF	94	379	114	16	4	6	156	58	44	30	2	84	10	4	2	19	6	.76	8	.301	.366	.412
1999 San Jose	A+ SF	15	53	12	2	1	1	19	7	3	7	1	13	1	1	0	2	0	1.00	1	.226	.328	.358
Akron	AA Cle	111	463	119	20	6	3	160	70	37	24	0	87	4	8	3	3	5	.38	8	.257	.298	.346
2 Min. YEARS		253	1007	265	41	14	10	364	151	95	72	4	214	18	13	6	26	14	.65	20	.263	.322	.361

Sandy McKinnon

Bats: Right **Throws:** Right **Pos:** OF **Ht:** 5'8" **Wt:** 175 **Born:** 9/20/72 **Age:** 27

		BATTING													BASERUNNING				PERCENTAGES		
Year Team	Lg Org	G	AB	H	2B	3B	HR	TB	R	RBI	TBB	IBB	SO	HBP	SH	SF	SB	CS	SB%	GDP	Avg	OBP	SLG
1993 White Sox	R CWS	6	11	2	0	0	0	2	2	0	3	0	2	2	1	0	4	0	1.00	0	.182	.438	.182
Hickory	A CWS	64	263	66	10	3	0	82	29	21	21	0	47	1	1	2	17	12	.59	1	.251	.307	.312
1994 South Bend	A CWS	117	462	111	9	4	3	137	64	28	32	0	83	4	7	3	36	14	.72	7	.240	.293	.297
1995 Pr William	A+ CWS	125	494	125	19	5	2	160	64	23	39	0	93	3	3	1	35	17	.67	6	.253	.311	.324

Year Team	Lg Org	G	AB	H	2B	3B	HR	TB	R	RBI	TBB	IBB	SO	HBP	SH	SF	SB	CS	SB%	GDP	Avg	OBP	SLG
1996 Pr William	A+ CWS	113	410	108	28	5	8	170	56	60	23	0	68	2	9	2	20	10	.67	4	.263	.304	.415
1997 Birmingham	AA CWS	96	332	90	20	1	4	124	58	31	31	1	68	2	5	3	13	6	.68	3	.271	.334	.373
1998 Winston-Sal	A+ CWS	45	149	39	8	1	1	52	18	15	12	0	37	2	3	0	3	2	.60	2	.262	.325	.349
Birmingham	AA CWS	57	200	40	8	0	1	51	21	18	19	1	41	2	6	3	11	3	.79	1	.200	.272	.255
1999 El Paso	AA Ari	3	12	3	0	0	0	3	1	2	0	0	2	0	0	0	0	0	.00	0	.250	.250	.250
High Desert	A+ Ari	1	3	2	0	0	0	2	0	1	0	0	0	0	0	0	1	0	1.00	0	.667	.667	.667
7 Min. YEARS		627	2336	586	102	19	19	783	313	199	180	2	441	18	35	14	140	64	.69	24	.251	.308	.335

Tony McKnight

Pitches: Right **Bats:** Left **Pos:** P **Ht:** 6'5" **Wt:** 205 **Born:** 6/29/77 **Age:** 23

Year Team	Lg Org	G	GS	CG	GF	IP	BFP	H	R	ER	HR	SH	SF	HB	TBB	IBB	SO	WP	Bk	W	L	Pct.	ShO	Sv	ERA
1995 Astros	R Hou	3	3	0	0	11.2	48	14	5	5	0	0	2	0	2	0	8	1	0	1	1	.500	0	0	3.86
1996 Astros	R Hou	8	5	0	0	21.2	108	28	21	15	1	0	2	3	7	0	15	3	0	2	1	.667	0	0	6.23
1997 Quad City	A Hou	20	20	0	0	115.1	504	116	71	60	7	6	3	5	55	5	92	6	3	4	9	.308	0	0	4.68
1998 Kissimmee	A+ Hou	28	28	0	0	154.1	701	191	101	80	12	4	3	9	50	2	104	12	2	11	13	.458	0	0	4.67
1999 Jackson	AA Hou	24	24	0	0	160.1	653	134	60	49	15	1	0	4	44	0	118	6	1	9	9	.500	0	0	2.75
5 Min. YEARS		83	80	0	0	463.1	2014	483	258	209	35	11	10	21	158	7	337	28	6	27	33	.450	0	0	4.06

Brian McLamb

Bats: Both **Throws:** Right **Pos:** 3B **Ht:** 6'3" **Wt:** 185 **Born:** 12/13/72 **Age:** 27

Year Team	Lg Org	G	AB	H	2B	3B	HR	TB	R	RBI	TBB	IBB	SO	HBP	SH	SF	SB	CS	SB%	GDP	Avg	OBP	SLG
1993 Oneonta	A- NYY	54	194	44	7	2	0	55	20	18	19	0	61	3	0	1	4	3	.57	2	.227	.304	.284
1994 Greensboro	A NYY	32	110	30	7	0	0	37	13	14	6	0	31	3	1	2	3	3	.50	2	.273	.322	.336
Oneonta	A- NYY	71	262	48	10	2	1	65	31	20	12	0	59	5	2	5	8	3	.73	9	.183	.229	.248
1995 Greensboro	A NYY	81	252	57	11	0	6	86	34	32	25	2	61	6	2	0	11	4	.73	9	.226	.311	.341
1996 Tampa	A+ NYY	85	266	56	13	0	2	75	31	25	23	1	62	4	4	3	7	5	.58	5	.211	.280	.282
1998 Norwich	AA NYY	62	196	35	10	0	1	48	18	11	10	0	67	2	1	0	2	3	.40	2	.179	.226	.245
1999 Norwich	AA NYY	48	126	20	5	0	2	31	11	14	4	0	46	5	0	0	1	1	.50	6	.159	.215	.246
6 Min. YEARS		433	1406	290	63	4	12	397	158	134	99	3	387	28	10	11	36	22	.62	35	.206	.270	.282

Billy McMillon

Bats: Left **Throws:** Left **Pos:** OF **Ht:** 5'11" **Wt:** 179 **Born:** 11/17/71 **Age:** 28

Year Team	Lg Org	G	AB	H	2B	3B	HR	TB	R	RBI	TBB	IBB	SO	HBP	SH	SF	SB	CS	SB%	GDP	Avg	OBP	SLG
1993 Elmira	A- Fla	57	227	69	14	2	6	105	38	35	30	4	44	4	0	0	5	4	.56	3	.304	.395	.463
1994 Kane County	A Fla	137	496	125	25	3	17	207	88	101	84	2	99	10	1	9	7	3	.70	13	.252	.366	.417
1995 Portland	AA Fla	141	518	162	29	3	14	239	92	93	96	5	90	7	1	5	15	9	.63	10	.313	.423	.461
1996 Charlotte	AAA Fla	97	347	122	32	2	17	209	72	70	36	0	76	5	0	2	5	3	.63	8	.352	.418	.602
1997 Charlotte	AAA Fla	57	204	57	18	0	8	99	34	26	32	1	51	1	0	1	8	0	1.00	3	.279	.378	.485
Scranton-WB	AAA Phi	26	92	27	8	1	4	49	18	21	12	0	24	0	0	0	2	0	1.00	1	.293	.375	.533
1998 Scranton-WB	AAA Phi	77	267	69	16	1	13	126	42	38	34	1	59	3	0	3	6	3	.67	6	.258	.345	.472
1999 Scranton-WB	AAA Phi	132	464	141	38	4	16	235	97	85	65	4	79	6	1	10	11	2	.85	10	.304	.389	.506
1996 Florida	NL	28	51	11	0	0	0	11	4	4	5	1	14	0	0	0	0	0	.00	1	.216	.286	.216
1997 Florida	NL	13	18	2	1	0	0	3	0	1	0	0	7	0	0	0	0	0	.00	0	.111	.111	.167
Philadelphia	NL	24	72	21	4	1	2	33	10	13	6	0	17	0	0	3	2	1	.67	1	.292	.333	.458
7 Min. YEARS		724	2615	772	180	16	95	1269	481	469	389	17	522	36	3	30	59	24	.71	54	.295	.390	.485
2 Maj. YEARS		65	141	34	5	1	2	47	14	18	11	1	38	0	0	3	2	1	.67	2	.241	.290	.333

Jerry McMullen

Pitches: Left **Bats:** Left **Pos:** P **Ht:** 6'2" **Wt:** 190 **Born:** 10/13/73 **Age:** 26

Year Team	Lg Org	G	GS	CG	GF	IP	BFP	H	R	ER	HR	SH	SF	HB	TBB	IBB	SO	WP	Bk	W	L	Pct.	ShO	Sv	ERA
1995 Eugene	A- Atl	22	0	0	8	30.2	128	28	7	5	0	4	0	1	8	2	31	3	0	1	1	.500	0	1	1.47
1996 Tri-City	IND —	32	0	0	8	48.1	211	41	18	14	2	2	1	2	24	3	46	8	0	1	2	.333	0	0	2.61
1997 Sarasota	A+ Bos	33	0	0	18	51.2	243	61	33	30	5	2	3	3	28	0	37	6	0	2	4	.333	0	2	5.23
1998 Sarasota	A+ Bos	39	0	0	10	62.2	273	53	23	19	3	6	3	3	36	1	60	5	2	3	1	.750	0	2	2.73
1999 Trenton	AA Bos	3	0	0	1	3	15	4	2	2	0	0	0	0	2	0	2	1	0	1	0	1.000	0	0	6.00
Sarasota	A+ Bos	41	0	0	15	47.1	206	47	21	15	4	0	0	1	19	0	56	4	0	1	3	.250	0	2	2.85
5 Min. YEARS		170	0	0	60	243.2	1076	234	104	85	14	14	7	10	117	6	232	26	2	9	11	.450	0	7	3.14

Mike McMullen

Pitches: Right **Bats:** Right **Pos:** P **Ht:** 6'2" **Wt:** 185 **Born:** 10/13/73 **Age:** 26

Year Team	Lg Org	G	GS	CG	GF	IP	BFP	H	R	ER	HR	SH	SF	HB	TBB	IBB	SO	WP	Bk	W	L	Pct.	ShO	Sv	ERA
1993 Giants	R SF	14	14	0	0	64	306	70	60	45	1	3	2	5	53	0	44	12	0	1	6	.143	0	0	6.33
1994 Clinton	A SF	14	1	0	5	24.1	122	34	25	17	5	1	1	1	14	0	22	4	2	1	3	.250	0	0	6.29
Giants	R SF	10	9	0	0	49	205	47	21	18	2	2	3	3	15	1	40	3	0	3	3	.500	0	0	3.31
1995 Burlington	A SF	29	11	2	6	83.2	410	98	76	51	5	2	4	9	54	3	53	9	2	4	10	.286	0	0	5.49
1996 Burlington	A SF	38	0	0	7	56.1	241	47	22	18	3	4	2	5	28	0	33	5	0	2	0	.000	0	0	2.88
1997 San Jose	A+ SF	56	0	0	23	91	377	85	37	27	1	9	4	5	33	3	71	6	0	6	4	.600	0	7	2.67
1998 Shreveport	AA SF	52	0	0	37	67.2	296	47	23	16	1	5	1	6	41	9	76	5	0	6	4	.600	0	9	2.13
Fresno	AAA SF	2	0	0	0	3.1	14	2	2	2	0	0	0	0	2	0	2	0	0	1	0	1.000	0	0	5.40
1999 Fresno	AAA SF	41	0	0	13	66	290	52	36	32	5	1	1	10	41	2	56	4	2	2	2	.500	0	0	4.36
7 Min. YEARS		256	35	2	91	505.1	2261	482	302	226	23	27	18	44	281	18	397	48	6	24	34	.414	0	16	4.03

Buck McNabb

Bats: Left **Throws:** Right **Pos:** OF **Ht:** 6'0" **Wt:** 180 **Born:** 1/17/73 **Age:** 27

					BATTING												BASERUNNING				PERCENTAGES		
Year Team	Lg Org	G	AB	H	2B	3B	HR	TB	R	RBI	TBB	IBB	SO	HBP	SH	SF	SB	CS	SB%	GDP	Avg	OBP	SLG
1991 Astros	R Hou	48	174	51	3	3	0	60	34	9	12	0	33	4	3	2	23	8	.74	0	.293	.349	.345
1992 Burlington	A Hou	123	456	118	12	3	1	139	82	34	60	0	80	10	3	2	56	19	.75	4	.259	.356	.305
1993 Osceola	A+ Hou	125	487	139	15	7	1	171	69	35	52	2	66	6	4	1	28	15	.65	8	.285	.361	.351
1994 Jackson	AA Hou	125	454	124	25	7	0	163	67	27	26	0	63	1	4	2	15	17	.47	10	.273	.313	.359
1995 Jackson	AA Hou	15	50	13	1	0	0	14	4	3	5	0	11	0	0	0	1	0	1.00	1	.260	.327	.280
Canton-Akrn	AA Cle	19	48	8	0	0	0	8	3	1	6	0	14	1	2	0	0	1	.00	0	.167	.273	.167
Bakersfield	A+ Cle	63	237	71	8	1	0	81	34	27	38	1	38	0	4	2	11	1	.92	5	.300	.394	.342
1996 Kissimmee	A+ Hou	7	26	9	1	0	0	10	4	3	3	1	5	0	0	0	3	0	1.00	0	.346	.414	.385
Jackson	AA Hou	88	279	84	15	5	0	109	38	26	41	1	37	2	1	2	10	6	.63	3	.301	.392	.391
1997 New Orleans	AAA Hou	11	19	3	0	1	0	5	2	0	1	0	6	0	0	0	0	0	.00	0	.158	.200	.263
Jackson	AA Hou	112	395	102	16	2	1	125	65	30	42	0	58	4	7	0	10	9	.53	9	.258	.336	.316
1998 West Tenn	AA ChC	124	385	113	21	5	6	162	62	48	51	4	61	6	1	3	22	13	.63	10	.294	.382	.421
1999 Greenville	AA Atl	25	93	30	4	0	0	34	9	5	5	0	18	0	0	0	2	2	.50	2	.323	.357	.366
Richmond	AAA Atl	17	48	11	0	0	1	14	8	6	1	0	9	0	0	0	0	1	.00	3	.229	.315	.292
9 Min. YEARS		902	3151	876	121	34	10	1095	481	256	348	10	499	34	29	14	181	92	.66	55	.278	.355	.348

Sean McNally

Bats: Right **Throws:** Right **Pos:** 3B **Ht:** 6'4" **Wt:** 210 **Born:** 12/14/72 **Age:** 27

					BATTING												BASERUNNING				PERCENTAGES		
Year Team	Lg Org	G	AB	H	2B	3B	HR	TB	R	RBI	TBB	IBB	SO	HBP	SH	SF	SB	CS	SB%	GDP	Avg	OBP	SLG
1994 Eugene	A- KC	74	278	69	16	2	3	98	44	30	24	1	66	4	2	2	4	7	.36	5	.248	.315	.353
1995 Springfield	A KC	132	479	130	28	8	12	210	60	79	35	6	119	8	0	6	6	3	.67	10	.271	.328	.438
1996 Wilmington	A+ KC	126	428	118	27	1	8	171	49	63	57	2	83	5	1	8	3	3	.50	8	.276	.361	.400
1997 Wichita	AA KC	18	53	13	4	0	0	17	9	2	11	0	12	0	0	0	1	2	.33	2	.245	.375	.321
Wilmington	A+ KC	95	323	86	22	2	17	163	51	68	40	4	98	2	3	1	2	1	.67	6	.266	.350	.505
1998 Wichita	AA KC	98	319	84	21	3	6	129	43	44	39	0	86	1	2	5	2	4	.33	9	.263	.341	.404
1999 Wichita	AA KC	129	440	124	24	2	36	260	97	109	93	2	132	6	1	3	7	3	.70	12	.282	.411	.591
6 Min. YEARS		672	2320	624	142	18	82	1048	353	395	299	15	596	26	9	25	25	23	.52	52	.269	.355	.452

Rusty McNamara

Bats: Right **Throws:** Right **Pos:** 3B **Ht:** 5'9" **Wt:** 185 **Born:** 1/23/75 **Age:** 25

					BATTING												BASERUNNING				PERCENTAGES		
Year Team	Lg Org	G	AB	H	2B	3B	HR	TB	R	RBI	TBB	IBB	SO	HBP	SH	SF	SB	CS	SB%	GDP	Avg	OBP	SLG
1997 Batavia	A- Phi	72	295	92	17	0	6	127	55	54	15	0	33	10	0	6	3	3	.50	4	.312	.359	.431
1998 Clearwater	A+ Phi	134	529	154	36	1	9	219	78	94	23	1	44	14	3	9	14	7	.67	20	.291	.332	.414
1999 Clearwater	A+ Phi	69	274	88	12	2	3	113	40	43	29	1	22	9	2	2	5	3	.63	8	.321	.401	.412
Reading	AA Phi	50	177	44	9	1	5	70	26	20	17	0	22	4	4	0	0	2	.00	6	.249	.328	.395
3 Min. YEARS		325	1275	378	74	4	23	529	199	211	84	2	121	37	9	17	22	15	.59	38	.296	.353	.415

Josh McNatt

Pitches: Left **Bats:** Both **Pos:** P **Ht:** 6'4" **Wt:** 200 **Born:** 7/23/77 **Age:** 22

		HOW MUCH HE PITCHED					WHAT HE GAVE UP											THE RESULTS				
Year Team	Lg Org	G	GS	CG	GF	IP	BFP	H	R	ER	HR	SH	SF	HB	TBB	IBB	SO	WP	Bk	W	L	Pct.	ShO	Sv	ERA
1996 Orioles	R Bal	12	8	0	2	53.2	206	36	15	13	1	1	2	0	12	0	42	1	0	3	2	.600	0	0	2.18
Bluefield	R+ Bal	2	1	0	0	6.1	33	10	6	6	1	0	0	0	6	0	7	1	0	0	1	.000	0	0	8.53
1997 Delmarva	A Bal	28	11	0	2	96.2	425	97	48	39	4	2	6	1	45	1	73	4	0	6	2	.750	0	1	3.63
1998 Frederick	A+ Bal	27	26	3	0	157.1	661	141	78	55	10	8	4	5	70	2	118	17	3	11	8	.579	1	0	3.15
1999 Orioles	R Bal	1	0	0	0	2	7	1	0	0	0	1	0	0	0	0	2	0	0	1	0	1.000	0	0	0.00
Frederick	A+ Bal	19	6	0	3	45	219	41	36	30	5	2	5	3	44	2	29	12	0	2	3	.400	0	0	6.00
Bowie	AA Bal	2	1	0	0	7	32	8	5	4	0	1	0	0	6	0	1	2	0	0	1	.000	0	0	5.14
4 Min. YEARS		91	53	3	7	368	1583	334	188	147	21	14	17	10	183	5	272	37	3	23	17	.575	1	1	3.60

Rusty Meacham

Pitches: Right **Bats:** Right **Pos:** P **Ht:** 6'3" **Wt:** 180 **Born:** 1/27/68 **Age:** 32

		HOW MUCH HE PITCHED					WHAT HE GAVE UP											THE RESULTS				
Year Team	Lg Org	G	GS	CG	GF	IP	BFP	H	R	ER	HR	SH	SF	HB	TBB	IBB	SO	WP	Bk	W	L	Pct.	ShO	Sv	ERA
1988 Fayettevlle	A Det	6	5	0	0	24.2	117	37	19	17	3	0	1	2	6	1	16	2	5	0	3	.000	0	0	6.20
Bristol	R+ Det	13	9	2	1	75.1	303	55	14	12	2	1	1	7	22	0	85	5	1	9	1	.900	2	0	1.43
1989 Fayettevlle	A Det	16	15	2	1	102	413	103	33	26	4	1	4	1	23	0	74	2	3	10	3	.769	0	0	2.29
Lakeland	A+ Det	11	9	4	1	64.2	259	59	15	14	3	3	0	2	12	2	39	0	0	5	4	.556	2	0	1.95
1990 London	AA Det	26	26	9	0	178	722	160	70	62	11	3	7	4	36	0	123	5	1	15	9	.625	3	0	3.13
1991 Toledo	AAA Det	26	17	3	4	125.1	517	117	53	43	8	2	5	1	40	3	70	6	0	9	7	.563	1	2	3.09
1993 Omaha	AAA KC	7	0	0	2	9.1	37	10	5	5	1	0	0	0	1	0	10	0	0	0	0	.000	0	0	4.82
1994 Omaha	AAA KC	8	0	0	5	9	40	9	7	7	0	0	1	0	3	0	16	1	1	1	1	.500	0	1	7.00
1996 Omaha	AAA KC	23	4	0	8	52.1	233	56	30	28	6	4	2	1	18	0	39	2	1	3	3	.500	0	2	4.82
Tacoma	AAA Sea	7	2	0	2	19.2	78	13	7	5	0	0	0	1	5	0	20	1	0	2	1	.667	0	2	2.29
1997 Pawtucket	AAA Bos	28	2	0	9	43.1	196	54	23	23	6	2	2	2	15	2	42	5	0	3	3	.500	0	1	4.78
1998 Memphis	AAA StL	38	0	0	10	52.1	235	68	30	30	9	1	3	3	15	3	56	3	0	1	2	.333	0	2	5.16
Nashville	AAA Pit	15	2	0	6	29.2	131	35	14	11	2	1	0	0	8	3	25	2	0	2	1	.667	0	3	3.34
1999 Indianaplis	AAA Cin	16	1	0	6	29.2	142	38	27	23	6	2	3	0	15	3	19	2	0	1	3	.250	0	1	6.98
New Orleans	AAA Hou	17	5	0	7	47.1	205	56	26	26	6	1	2	1	9	0	47	1	1	3	4	.429	0	1	4.94
1991 Detroit	AL	10	4	0	1	27.2	126	35	17	16	4	1	3	0	11	0	14	0	1	2	1	.667	0	0	5.20
1992 Kansas City	AL	64	0	0	20	101.2	412	88	39	31	5	3	9	1	21	5	64	4	0	10	4	.714	0	2	2.74
1993 Kansas City	AL	15	0	0	11	21	104	31	15	13	2	0	1	3	5	1	13	0	0	2	2	.500	0	0	5.57
1994 Kansas City	AL	36	0	0	15	50.2	213	51	23	21	7	1	4	2	12	1	36	4	0	3	3	.500	0	4	3.73

183

Year Team	Lg Org	G	GS	CG	GF	IP	BFP	H	R	ER	HR	SH	SF	HB	TBB	IBB	SO	WP	Bk	W	L	Pct.	ShO	Sv	ERA
		HOW MUCH HE PITCHED						**WHAT HE GAVE UP**												**THE RESULTS**					
1995 Kansas City	AL	49	0	0	26	59.2	262	72	36	33	6	1	4	1	19	5	30	0	0	4	3	.571	0	2	4.98
1996 Seattle	AL	15	5	0	3	42.1	192	57	28	27	9	0	1	4	13	1	25	1	0	1	1	.500	0	1	5.74
10 Min. YEARS		257	97	20	62	862.2	3628	870	373	332	67	21	31	27	228	17	681	37	13	64	45	.587	8	15	3.46
6 Maj. YEARS		189	9	0	76	303	1309	334	158	141	33	6	22	11	81	13	182	9	1	22	14	.611	0	9	4.19

Carlos Medina

Pitches: Left **Bats:** Left **Pos:** P **Ht:** 6'2" **Wt:** 160 **Born:** 5/16/77 **Age:** 23

Year Team	Lg Org	G	GS	CG	GF	IP	BFP	H	R	ER	HR	SH	SF	HB	TBB	IBB	SO	WP	Bk	W	L	Pct.	ShO	Sv	ERA
		HOW MUCH HE PITCHED						**WHAT HE GAVE UP**												**THE RESULTS**					
1996 Marlins	R Fla	4	1	0	1	9.2	48	16	7	4	0	1	0	2	1	0	9	3	0	0	1	.000	0	0	3.72
1998 Delmarva	A Bal	22	11	0	5	80.2	343	70	41	34	7	10	3	6	39	1	85	5	3	4	6	.400	0	0	3.79
Bowie	AA Bal	1	1	0	0	5	16	1	0	0	0	0	0	0	0	0	6	1	0	1	0	1.000	0	0	0.00
1999 Frederick	A+ Bal	5	5	0	0	31.1	127	22	6	6	1	2	0	3	13	0	30	1	1	4	0	1.000	0	0	1.72
Bowie	AA Bal	15	15	0	0	78	350	86	52	48	6	2	2	7	37	0	70	6	4	3	6	.333	0	0	5.54
3 Min. YEARS		47	33	0	6	204.2	884	195	106	92	14	15	5	18	90	1	200	16	8	12	13	.480	0	0	4.05

Tony Medrano

Bats: Right **Throws:** Right **Pos:** 2B **Ht:** 5'10" **Wt:** 175 **Born:** 12/8/74 **Age:** 25

Year Team	Lg Org	G	AB	H	2B	3B	HR	TB	R	RBI	TBB	IBB	SO	HBP	SH	SF	SB	CS	SB%	GDP	Avg	OBP	SLG
		BATTING															**BASERUNNING**				**PERCENTAGES**		
1993 Blue Jays	R Tor	39	158	42	9	0	0	51	20	9	10	0	9	3	0	0	6	2	.75	1	.266	.322	.323
1994 Blue Jays	R Tor	6	22	8	4	0	1	15	2	5	1	0	0	0	0	0	0	0	.00	2	.364	.391	.682
Dunedin	A+ Tor	60	199	47	6	4	4	73	20	21	12	0	26	3	3	1	3	3	.50	4	.236	.288	.367
1995 KC	AA KC	1	5	0	0	0	0	0	0	0	0	0	3	0	0	0	0	0	.00	0	.000	.000	.000
Wilmington	A+ KC	123	460	131	20	6	3	172	69	43	34	2	42	5	15	4	11	6	.65	10	.285	.338	.374
1996 Wichita	AA KC	125	474	130	26	1	8	182	59	55	18	0	36	2	7	2	10	8	.56	8	.274	.302	.384
1997 Wichita	AA KC	108	349	86	9	1	4	109	45	42	26	1	32	1	9	4	8	2	.80	10	.246	.297	.312
Omaha	AAA KC	17	59	12	0	0	4	24	10	9	4	1	5	0	0	3	0	1	.00	1	.203	.242	.407
1998 Wichita	AA KC	95	301	92	14	2	10	140	48	46	28	0	36	9	8	3	3	3	.50	7	.306	.378	.465
1999 Wichita	AA KC	73	257	87	15	1	5	119	45	32	21	0	23	4	5	6	4	2	.67	3	.339	.389	.463
Omaha	AAA KC	33	112	35	6	1	2	49	14	23	10	0	15	1	3	2	0	1	.00	3	.313	.368	.438
7 Min. YEARS		680	2396	670	109	16	41	934	332	285	164	4	227	28	50	25	45	28	.62	49	.280	.330	.390

Mike Meggers

Bats: Right **Throws:** Right **Pos:** OF **Ht:** 6'2" **Wt:** 200 **Born:** 7/6/70 **Age:** 29

Year Team	Lg Org	G	AB	H	2B	3B	HR	TB	R	RBI	TBB	IBB	SO	HBP	SH	SF	SB	CS	SB%	GDP	Avg	OBP	SLG
		BATTING															**BASERUNNING**				**PERCENTAGES**		
1992 Billings	R+ Cin	73	257	69	16	3	12	127	47	48	48	1	72	3	1	2	10	7	.59	4	.268	.387	.494
1993 Chstn-WV	A Cin	116	388	80	14	2	12	134	43	49	33	1	118	3	2	5	5	3	.38	2	.206	.270	.345
1994 Winston-Sal	A+ Cin	114	418	95	25	2	25	199	62	80	31	0	139	1	0	7	6	2	.75	8	.227	.278	.476
1995 Winston-Sal	A+ Cin	76	272	67	18	1	20	147	45	54	32	5	69	1	0	4	7	3	.70	5	.246	.324	.540
1996 Chattanooga	AA Cin	38	111	22	6	0	5	43	13	18	16	0	33	1	0	2	1	2	.33	1	.198	.300	.387
Madison	IND —	57	215	64	15	1	14	123	40	39	25	0	70	1	2	1	0	0	.00	4	.298	.372	.572
1997 Winnipeg	IND —	40	172	50	10	0	16	108	38	57	17	0	54	4	0	2	5	0	1.00	4	.291	.364	.628
Duluth-Sup	IND —	41	166	53	7	1	16	110	39	42	16	1	48	1	0	2	3	1	.75	1	.319	.378	.663
1998 Duluth-Sup	IND —	24	82	30	9	1	12	77	20	34	22	3	26	2	0	2	0	1	.00	0	.366	.500	.939
1999 Binghamton	AA NYM	18	56	9	4	0	1	16	6	6	7	1	29	0	0	0	0	0	.00	0	.161	.254	.286
8 Min. YEARS		597	2137	539	124	11	133	1084	353	427	247	12	658	17	5	27	35	21	.63	29	.252	.331	.507

Roberto Mejia

Bats: Right **Throws:** Right **Pos:** 3B **Ht:** 5'11" **Wt:** 165 **Born:** 4/14/72 **Age:** 28

Year Team	Lg Org	G	AB	H	2B	3B	HR	TB	R	RBI	TBB	IBB	SO	HBP	SH	SF	SB	CS	SB%	GDP	Avg	OBP	SLG
		BATTING															**BASERUNNING**				**PERCENTAGES**		
1991 Great Falls	R+ LA	23	84	22	6	2	2	38	17	14	7	0	22	1	0	1	3	1	.75	0	.262	.323	.452
1992 Vero Beach	A+ LA	96	330	82	17	1	12	137	42	40	37	4	60	2	0	5	14	10	.58	6	.248	.324	.415
1993 Colo Sprngs	AAA Col	77	291	87	15	2	14	148	51	48	18	0	56	1	0	3	12	5	.71	6	.299	.339	.509
1994 Colo Sprngs	AAA Col	73	283	80	24	2	6	126	54	37	21	2	49	4	4	2	7	4	.64	5	.283	.339	.445
1995 Colo Sprngs	AAA Col	38	143	42	10	2	2	62	18	14	7	2	29	1	2	0	0	2	.00	6	.294	.331	.434
1996 Indianapols	AAA Cin	101	374	109	24	9	13	190	55	58	29	1	79	1	1	5	13	5	.72	7	.291	.340	.508
Pawtucket	AAA Bos	21	74	19	4	0	0	23	9	4	5	0	18	1	0	1	4	1	.80	3	.257	.309	.311
1997 Louisville	AAA StL	6	21	7	1	0	1	11	3	2	0	0	4	1	0	0	0	2	.00	0	.333	.364	.524
1998 Memphis	AAA StL	49	175	42	5	2	8	75	23	25	5	0	42	2	1	2	10	5	.67	3	.240	.266	.429
1999 Albuquerque	AAA LA	16	41	6	0	0	1	9	6	5	1	0	8	0	0	1	0	1	.00	0	.146	.167	.220
1993 Colorado	NL	65	229	53	14	5	5	92	31	20	13	1	63	1	4	1	4	1	.80	2	.231	.275	.402
1994 Colorado	NL	38	116	28	8	1	4	50	11	14	15	2	33	0	0	1	3	1	.75	1	.241	.326	.431
1995 Colorado	NL	23	52	8	1	0	1	12	5	4	0	0	17	1	0	1	0	1	.00	1	.154	.167	.231
1997 St. Louis	NL	7	14	1	0	0	0	2	0	2	0	0	5	0	1	1	0	0	.00	0	.071	.067	.143
9 Min. YEARS		500	1816	496	106	20	59	819	278	247	130	9	367	14	8	19	63	36	.64	36	.273	.323	.451
4 Maj. YEARS		133	411	90	24	6	10	156	47	40	28	3	118	2	5	4	7	3	.70	4	.219	.270	.380

Adam Melhuse

Bats: Both **Throws:** Right **Pos:** OF **Ht:** 6'2" **Wt:** 185 **Born:** 3/27/72 **Age:** 28

Year Team	Lg Org	G	AB	H	2B	3B	HR	TB	R	RBI	TBB	IBB	SO	HBP	SH	SF	SB	CS	SB%	GDP	Avg	OBP	SLG
		BATTING															**BASERUNNING**				**PERCENTAGES**		
1993 St.Cathrnes	A- Tor	73	266	68	14	2	5	101	40	32	45	4	61	0	2	3	4	0	1.00	4	.256	.360	.380
1994 Hagerstown	A Tor	118	422	109	16	3	11	164	61	58	53	1	77	1	1	6	6	8	.43	13	.258	.338	.389

Year Team	Lg Org	G	AB	H	2B	3B	HR	TB	R	RBI	TBB	IBB	SO	HBP	SH	SF	SB	CS	SB%	GDP	Avg	OBP	SLG
1995 Dunedin	A+ Tor	123	428	92	20	0	4	124	43	41	61	1	87	1	1	4	6	1	.86	7	.215	.312	.290
1996 Dunedin	A+ Tor	97	315	78	23	2	13	144	50	51	69	2	68	3	1	4	3	1	.75	5	.248	.384	.457
Knoxville	AA Tor	32	94	20	3	0	1	26	13	6	14	1	29	0	1	1	0	1	.00	3	.213	.312	.277
1997 Knoxville	AA Tor	31	87	20	3	0	3	32	14	10	19	1	19	0	1	1	0	0	.00	1	.230	.364	.368
Syracuse	AAA Tor	38	118	28	5	1	2	41	7	9	12	0	18	1	0	1	1	1	.50	2	.237	.311	.347
1998 Syracuse	AAA Tor	12	38	11	3	0	1	17	4	7	7	0	6	0	0	1	0	0	.00	0	.289	.391	.447
Knoxville	AA Tor	76	240	72	22	0	15	139	56	43	70	1	39	0	0	0	4	4	.50	6	.300	.458	.579
1999 Syracuse	AAA Tor	21	71	20	5	0	2	31	15	16	10	0	20	0	0	0	1	1	.50	1	.282	.370	.437
Knoxville	AA Tor	107	374	110	25	0	19	192	79	69	108	7	76	4	0	3	5	6	.45	10	.294	.454	.513
7 Min. YEARS		728	2453	628	139	8	76	1011	382	342	468	20	500	10	6	24	30	23	.57	52	.256	.374	.412

Juan Melo

Bats: Both **Throws:** Right **Pos:** SS **Ht:** 6'1" **Wt:** 180 **Born:** 11/5/76 **Age:** 23

Year Team	Lg Org	G	AB	H	2B	3B	HR	TB	R	RBI	TBB	IBB	SO	HBP	SH	SF	SB	CS	SB%	GDP	Avg	OBP	SLG
1994 Spokane	A- SD	3	11	4	1	0	1	8	4	2	1	0	3	0	0	0	0	0	.00	1	.364	.417	.727
Las Vegas	AAA SD	1	0	0	0	0	0	0	0	0	0	0	0	0	0	0	0	0	.00	0	.000	.000	.000
Padres	R SD	37	145	41	3	3	0	50	20	15	10	0	36	6	0	1	3	2	.60	5	.283	.352	.345
1995 Clinton	A SD	134	479	135	32	1	5	184	65	46	33	0	88	5	5	2	12	10	.55	11	.282	.333	.384
1996 Rancho Cuca	A+ SD	128	503	153	27	6	8	216	75	75	22	0	102	10	0	1	6	8	.43	10	.304	.345	.429
1997 Las Vegas	AAA SD	12	48	13	4	0	1	20	6	6	1	0	10	1	0	1	0	0	.00	0	.271	.294	.417
Mobile	AA SD	113	456	131	22	2	7	178	52	67	29	4	90	0	0	2	7	9	.44	16	.287	.329	.390
1998 Las Vegas	AAA SD	130	467	127	26	1	6	173	61	47	24	2	91	4	2	3	9	8	.53	15	.272	.311	.370
1999 Las Vegas	AAA SD	45	169	34	3	2	2	47	17	13	7	0	34	2	0	0	1	1	.50	5	.201	.242	.278
Syracuse	AAA Tor	41	141	33	9	1	3	53	21	13	10	0	31	1	0	1	8	4	.67	2	.234	.288	.376
Indianapols	AAA Cin	3	9	3	0	0	0	6	2	3	0	0	2	0	0	0	1	0	1.00	0	.333	.333	.667
6 Min. YEARS		647	2428	674	127	16	34	935	323	287	137	6	487	29	7	11	47	42	.53	65	.278	.322	.385

Carlos Mendez

Bats: Right **Throws:** Right **Pos:** 1B **Ht:** 6'0" **Wt:** 210 **Born:** 6/18/74 **Age:** 26

Year Team	Lg Org	G	AB	H	2B	3B	HR	TB	R	RBI	TBB	IBB	SO	HBP	SH	SF	SB	CS	SB%	GDP	Avg	OBP	SLG
1992 Royals	R KC	49	200	61	16	1	3	88	34	33	8	2	13	2	0	3	2	1	.67	2	.305	.333	.440
1993 Royals	R KC	50	163	51	10	0	4	73	18	27	4	1	15	2	0	4	6	1	.86	2	.313	.329	.448
1994 Rockford	A KC	104	363	129	26	2	5	174	45	51	13	2	50	5	4	4	0	2	.00	11	.355	.382	.479
1995 Wilmington	A+ KC	107	396	108	19	2	7	152	46	61	18	1	36	0	1	5	0	4	.00	17	.273	.301	.384
1996 Wilmington	A+ KC	109	406	119	25	3	4	162	40	59	22	4	39	3	3	7	3	1	.75	6	.293	.329	.399
1997 Wichita	AA KC	129	507	165	32	1	12	235	72	90	19	2	43	1	0	8	4	7	.36	19	.325	.346	.464
1998 Omaha	AAA KC	50	173	47	13	0	2	66	23	18	10	0	24	1	0	2	3	0	1.00	4	.272	.312	.382
Wichita	AA KC	52	207	66	14	0	9	107	37	39	7	1	20	0	1	5	4	1	.80	10	.319	.333	.517
1999 Omaha	AAA KC	84	293	82	25	0	10	137	38	37	6	0	32	0	3	3	4	3	.57	8	.280	.291	.468
8 Min. YEARS		734	2708	828	180	9	56	1194	353	415	107	13	272	14	12	41	26	20	.57	79	.306	.331	.441

Carlos Mendoza

Bats: Left **Throws:** Left **Pos:** OF **Ht:** 5'11" **Wt:** 165 **Born:** 11/14/74 **Age:** 25

Year Team	Lg Org	G	AB	H	2B	3B	HR	TB	R	RBI	TBB	IBB	SO	HBP	SH	SF	SB	CS	SB%	GDP	Avg	OBP	SLG
1995 Kingsport	R+ NYM	51	192	63	9	0	1	75	56	24	27	0	24	3	4	2	28	6	.82	3	.328	.415	.391
1996 Capital Cty	A NYM	85	300	101	10	2	0	115	61	37	57	1	46	8	11	2	31	13	.70	2	.337	.452	.383
1997 Binghamton	AA NYM	59	228	87	12	2	1	106	36	13	14	1	25	4	7	0	14	12	.54	4	.382	.427	.465
Norfolk	AAA NYM	10	35	5	0	1	0	7	3	0	3	0	4	1	1	0	1	0	1.00	1	.143	.231	.200
1998 Durham	AAA TB	51	201	54	8	0	0	62	32	11	16	0	29	1	5	1	9	9	.50	5	.269	.324	.308
St. Pete	A+ TB	8	32	10	2	0	0	12	6	8	4	0	3	1	2	1	4	2	.67	0	.313	.395	.375
Devil Rays	R TB	6	18	8	1	0	0	9	6	4	5	0	3	1	0	1	3	1	.75	1	.444	.560	.500
Orlando	AA TB	35	139	47	3	3	1	59	27	19	19	0	18	4	4	0	16	2	.89	6	.338	.432	.424
1999 Durham	AAA TB	75	266	78	8	3	1	95	57	25	32	0	38	7	9	0	9	8	.53	5	.293	.384	.357
1997 New York	NL	15	12	3	0	0	0	3	6	1	4	0	2	2	0	0	0	0	.00	0	.250	.500	.250
5 Min. YEARS		380	1411	453	53	11	4	540	284	141	177	2	190	30	43	7	115	53	.68	27	.321	.406	.383

Carlos Mendoza

Bats: Both **Throws:** Right **Pos:** SS **Ht:** 6'0" **Wt:** 175 **Born:** 11/27/79 **Age:** 20

Year Team	Lg Org	G	AB	H	2B	3B	HR	TB	R	RBI	TBB	IBB	SO	HBP	SH	SF	SB	CS	SB%	GDP	Avg	OBP	SLG
1997 Salem-Keizr	A- SF	33	106	22	0	0	0	22	10	6	11	0	19	1	4	0	6	0	1.00	3	.208	.288	.208
1998 San Jose	A+ SF	110	365	78	7	3	0	91	36	20	19	0	64	1	12	0	11	8	.58	10	.214	.255	.249
1999 Shreveport	AA SF	111	332	67	16	4	3	100	35	34	36	3	65	6	8	4	1	4	.20	3	.202	.288	.301
3 Min. YEARS		254	803	167	23	7	3	213	81	60	66	3	148	8	24	4	18	12	.60	16	.208	.274	.265

Paul Menhart

Pitches: Right **Bats:** Right **Pos:** P **Ht:** 6'2" **Wt:** 190 **Born:** 3/25/69 **Age:** 31

Year Team	Lg Org	G	GS	CG	GF	IP	BFP	H	R	ER	HR	SH	SF	HB	TBB	IBB	SO	WP	Bk	W	L	Pct.	ShO	Sv	ERA
1990 St.Cathrnes	A- Tor	8	8	0	0	40	180	34	27	18	2	1	1	5	19	0	38	6	0	0	5	.000	0	0	4.05
Myrtle Bch	A Tor	5	4	1	1	30.2	113	18	5	2	1	1	0	0	5	0	18	1	0	3	0	1.000	0	0	0.59
1991 Dunedin	A+ Tor	20	20	3	0	128.1	521	114	42	38	3	2	2	3	34	0	114	4	1	10	6	.625	0	0	2.66
1992 Knoxville	AA Tor	28	28	2	0	177.2	735	181	85	76	14	2	6	11	38	0	104	12	1	10	11	.476	1	0	3.85

Year Team	Lg Org	G	GS	CG	GF	IP	BFP	H	R	ER	HR	SH	SF	HB	TBB	IBB	SO	WP	Bk	W	L	Pct.	ShO	Sv	ERA
1993 Syracuse	AAA Tor	25	25	4	0	151	646	143	74	61	16	4	3	7	67	4	108	8	1	9	10	.474	0	0	3.64
1995 Syracuse	AAA Tor	10	10	0	0	51.1	234	62	42	36	5	2	3	0	25	0	30	3	1	2	4	.333	0	0	6.31
1996 Tacoma	AAA Sea	6	6	0	0	26	142	53	33	32	4	0	3	1	16	0	12	3	0	0	3	.000	0	0	11.08
1997 Tacoma	AAA Sea	15	10	0	2	61.1	285	76	46	42	11	2	1	4	34	1	51	4	1	4	7	.364	1	0	6.16
Las Vegas	AAA SD	11	11	1	0	66.1	294	78	46	44	7	7	3	2	21	1	44	2	1	0	7	.000	0	0	5.97
1998 Las Vegas	AAA SD	49	2	0	16	64	310	79	45	38	10	4	3	5	39	6	50	3	2	7	6	.538	0	4	5.34
1999 Edmonton	AAA Ana	9	9	0	0	42.1	190	58	34	32	10	1	0	1	14	1	21	0	0	3	3	.500	0	0	6.80
Buffalo	AAA Cle	7	0	0	0	13	60	18	7	7	0	0	0	1	4	0	10	2	0	2	1	.667	0	0	4.85
Calgary	AAA Fla	8	8	0	0	38.2	185	48	26	21	0	0	3	0	23	0	30	2	0	2	2	.500	0	0	4.89
1995 Toronto	AL	21	9	1	6	78.2	350	72	49	43	9	3	4	6	47	4	50	6	0	1	4	.200	0	0	4.92
1996 Seattle	AL	11	6	0	4	42	196	55	36	34	9	1	0	2	25	0	18	1	0	2	2	.500	0	0	7.29
1997 San Diego	NL	9	8	0	0	44	180	42	23	23	6	2	1	0	13	0	22	4	0	2	3	.400	0	0	4.70
9 Min. YEARS		201	141	11	19	890.2	3895	962	512	447	83	26	28	40	339	13	630	50	10	52	65	.444	1	5	4.52
3 Maj. YEARS		41	23	1	10	164.2	726	169	108	100	24	6	5	8	85	4	90	11	0	5	9	.357	0	0	5.47

Hector Mercado

Pitches: Left   Bats: Left   Pos: P   Ht: 6'3"   Wt: 205   Born: 4/29/74   Age: 26

Year Team	Lg Org	G	GS	CG	GF	IP	BFP	H	R	ER	HR	SH	SF	HB	TBB	IBB	SO	WP	Bk	W	L	Pct.	ShO	Sv	ERA
1992 Astros	R Hou	13	3	0	4	30	140	22	17	11	0	1	0	3	25	0	36	7	6	1	2	.333	0	0	4.20
1993 Osceola	A+ Hou	2	2	0	0	8.2	39	9	7	5	0	0	0	0	6	1	5	0	0	1	1	.500	0	0	5.19
Astros	R Hou	11	11	1	0	67	278	49	26	18	1	0	3	1	29	0	59	10	2	5	4	.556	1	0	2.42
1994 Osceola	A+ Hou	25	25	1	0	136.2	601	123	75	60	5	11	4	1	79	4	88	9	3	6	13	.316	1	0	3.95
1995 Kissimmee	A+ Hou	19	17	2	0	104	433	96	50	40	2	2	3	3	37	0	75	4	1	6	8	.429	0	0	3.46
Jackson	AA Hou	8	7	0	0	30	157	36	33	26	5	2	1	2	32	1	20	4	0	1	4	.200	0	0	7.80
1996 Kissimmee	A+ Hou	56	0	0	18	80	353	78	43	37	4	3	1	4	48	1	68	6	0	3	5	.375	0	3	4.16
1997 Charlotte	AAA Fla	1	1	0	0	5	25	5	5	5	2	0	0	0	5	0	1	1	0	0	1	.000	0	0	9.00
Portland	AA Fla	31	17	1	6	129.2	565	129	66	57	10	6	1	3	54	5	125	16	2	11	3	.786	1	0	3.96
1999 Norfolk	AAA NYM	2	2	0	0	6	22	3	1	1	1	0	0	1	1	0	2	0	0	0	0	.000	0	0	1.50
7 Min. YEARS		168	85	5	28	597	2613	550	323	263	30	25	13	18	316	12	479	57	14	34	41	.453	3	3	3.96

Henry Mercedes

Bats: Right   Throws: Right   Pos: C   Ht: 6' 1"   Wt: 210   Born: 7/23/69   Age: 30

Year Team	Lg Org	G	AB	H	2B	3B	HR	TB	R	RBI	TBB	IBB	SO	HBP	SH	SF	SB	CS	SB%	GDP	Avg	OBP	SLG
1988 Athletics	R Oak	2	5	2	0	0	0	2	1	0	0	0	0	0	0	0	0	0	.00	0	.400	.400	.400
1989 Madison	A Oak	51	152	32	3	0	2	41	11	13	22	1	46	1	3	0	0	0	.00	1	.211	.314	.270
Modesto	A+ Oak	16	37	3	0	0	1	6	6	3	7	0	22	0	0	0	0	0	.00	2	.081	.227	.162
Sou Oregon	A- Oak	22	61	10	0	1	0	12	6	1	10	0	24	1	0	0	2	0	.00	0	.164	.292	.197
1990 Tacoma	AAA Oak	12	31	6	1	0	0	7	3	2	3	0	7	0	2	0	0	1	.00	2	.194	.265	.226
Madison	A Oak	90	282	64	13	2	3	90	29	38	30	0	100	1	6	2	6	0	1.00	5	.227	.302	.319
1991 Modesto	A+ Oak	116	388	100	17	3	4	135	55	61	68	1	110	2	3	3	5	8	.38	6	.258	.369	.348
1992 Tacoma	AAA Oak	85	246	57	9	2	0	70	36	20	26	0	60	0	4	0	1	3	.25	8	.232	.305	.285
1993 Tacoma	AAA Oak	85	256	61	13	1	4	88	37	32	31	2	53	1	3	7	1	2	.33	8	.238	.315	.344
1994 Tacoma	AAA Oak	66	205	39	5	1	1	49	16	17	13	0	60	0	5	3	1	2	.33	6	.190	.235	.239
1995 Omaha	AAA KC	86	275	59	12	0	11	104	37	37	22	0	90	3	6	1	2	0	1.00	7	.215	.279	.378
1996 Omaha	AAA KC	72	223	48	9	1	8	83	28	35	28	0	60	0	6	2	0	0	.00	4	.215	.300	.372
1997 Okla City	AAA Tex	16	57	14	3	0	1	20	6	4	9	0	12	0	0	0	0	0	.00	0	.246	.348	.351
1998 Fresno	AAA SF	27	88	19	5	2	2	34	17	11	15	0	28	1	3	0	0	0	.00	1	.216	.337	.386
Indianapols	AAA Cin	8	16	2	0	0	0	2	1	1	1	0	5	0	0	0	0	0	.00	1	.125	.176	.125
1999 Omaha	AAA KC	69	193	47	8	0	6	73	27	32	27	0	63	2	3	1	4	1	.80	2	.244	.341	.378
1992 Oakland	AL	9	5	4	0	1	0	6	1	1	0	0	1	0	0	0	0	0	.00	0	.800	.800	1.200
1993 Oakland	AL	20	47	10	2	0	0	12	5	3	2	0	15	1	0	0	1	1	.50	0	.213	.260	.255
1995 Kansas City	AL	23	43	11	2	0	0	13	7	9	8	0	13	1	1	2	0	0	.00	0	.256	.370	.302
1996 Kansas City	AL	4	4	1	0	0	0	1	1	0	0	0	1	0	0	0	0	0	.00	0	.250	.250	.250
1997 Texas	AL	23	47	10	4	0	0	14	4	4	6	0	25	0	3	0	1	0	.50	0	.213	.302	.298
12 Min. YEARS		823	2515	563	98	13	43	816	316	307	312	4	740	12	44	19	20	19	.51	61	.224	.310	.324
5 Maj. YEARS		79	146	36	8	1	0	46	18	17	16	0	55	2	4	2	1	1	.50	0	.247	.325	.315

Jose Mercedes

Pitches: Right   Bats: Right   Pos: P   Ht: 6' 1"   Wt: 208   Born: 3/5/71   Age: 29

Year Team	Lg Org	G	GS	CG	GF	IP	BFP	H	R	ER	HR	SH	SF	HB	TBB	IBB	SO	WP	Bk	W	L	Pct.	ShO	Sv	ERA
1992 Orioles	R Bal	8	5	2	1	35.1	143	31	12	7	0	0	1	1	13	0	21	5	1	2	3	.400	0	0	1.78
Kane County	A Bal	8	8	2	0	47.1	199	40	26	14	1	2	0	0	15	0	45	6	2	3	2	.600	2	0	2.66
1993 Bowie	AA Bal	26	23	3	0	147	659	170	86	78	13	6	3	2	65	0	75	9	1	6	8	.429	0	0	4.78
1994 El Paso	AA Mil	3	0	0	0	9.2	44	13	6	5	1	0	1	0	4	0	8	1	0	2	0	1.000	0	0	4.66
New Orleans	AAA Mil	3	3	0	0	18.1	81	19	10	10	1	0	0	2	8	0	7	1	0	0	0	.000	0	0	4.91
1996 New Orleans	AAA Mil	25	15	0	3	101	439	109	58	40	14	3	5	7	28	1	47	4	1	3	7	.300	0	1	3.56
1998 El Paso	AA Mil	1	1	0	0	3.1	18	4	4	2	0	1	2	1	0	0	0	0	0	0	0	.000	0	0	10.80
1999 Las Vegas	AAA SD	15	14	0	0	88	396	110	57	42	14	5	2	2	20	0	57	1	1	2	6	.250	0	0	4.30
Calgary	AAA Fla	4	4	0	0	26	112	30	13	9	2	1	0	0	3	0	13	0	0	1	2	.333	0	0	3.12
Norfolk	AAA NYM	6	6	0	0	32	146	36	15	9	2	4	2	2	11	1	19	0	0	2	1	.667	0	0	2.53
1994 Milwaukee	AL	19	0	0	5	31	120	22	9	8	4	0	0	2	16	1	11	0	1	2	0	1.000	0	0	2.32
1995 Milwaukee	AL	12	0	0	0	7.1	42	12	9	8	1	0	2	0	8	0	6	1	0	0	1	.000	0	0	9.82
1996 Milwaukee	AL	11	0	0	4	16.2	74	20	18	17	6	0	1	0	5	0	6	2	0	0	2	.000	0	0	9.18
1997 Milwaukee	AL	29	23	2	1	159	667	146	76	67	24	3	4	5	53	2	80	1	1	7	10	.412	1	0	3.79
1998 Milwaukee	NL	7	5	0	0	32	146	42	25	24	5	1	2	1	9	1	11	0	0	2	2	.500	0	0	6.75
6 Min. YEARS		99	79	7	4	508	2237	567	287	218	50	21	15	16	167	2	292	27	6	21	29	.420	2	1	3.86
5 Maj. YEARS		71	28	2	10	246	1035	242	137	124	40	4	9	8	91	4	114	4	2	11	15	.423	1	0	4.54

Phil Merrell

Pitches: Right Bats: Right Pos: P   Ht: 6'3" Wt: 190 Born: 3/11/78 Age: 22

		HOW MUCH HE PITCHED						WHAT HE GAVE UP										THE RESULTS					
Year Team	Lg Org	G	GS	CG	GF	IP	BFP	H	R	ER	HR	SH	SF	HB	TBB	IBB	SO	WP	Bk	W	L	Pct.	ShO	Sv	ERA
1996 Billings	R+ Cin	14	13	1	1	69	339	83	63	54	11	1	4	5	48	0	54	11	2	4	7	.364	0	1	7.04
1997 Billings	R+ Cin	14	14	0	0	72.2	313	72	51	35	6	3	1	2	27	1	62	2	0	2	6	.250	0	0	4.33
1998 Chstn-WV	A Cin	26	25	4	0	149.1	656	169	91	77	11	8	4	9	43	0	117	14	1	5	15	.250	0	0	4.64
1999 Clinton	A Cin	16	16	3	0	102.1	402	75	32	25	3	3	1	5	31	0	87	10	0	8	3	.727	3	0	2.20
Indianapols	AAA Cin	3	3	0	0	11	59	21	21	18	4	0	1	1	4	0	6	3	1	0	3	.000	0	0	14.73
Chattanooga	AA Cin	7	7	0	0	35.1	166	47	32	26	3	3	2	2	14	1	15	6	0	2	2	.500	0	0	6.62
4 Min. YEARS		80	78	8	1	439.2	1935	467	290	235	38	18	13	24	167	2	341	46	4	21	36	.368	3	1	4.81

Mike Metcalfe

Bats: Right Throws: Right Pos: SS   Ht: 5'10" Wt: 175 Born: 1/2/73 Age: 27

		BATTING															BASERUNNING				PERCENTAGES		
Year Team	Lg Org	G	AB	H	2B	3B	HR	TB	R	RBI	TBB	IBB	SO	HBP	SH	SF	SB	CS	SB%	GDP	Avg	OBP	SLG
1994 Bakersfield	A+ LA	69	275	78	10	0	0	88	44	18	28	0	34	1	4	2	41	13	.76	6	.284	.350	.320
1995 San Antonio	AA LA	10	41	10	1	0	0	11	10	2	7	0	2	0	1	1	1	2	.33	0	.244	.347	.268
Vero Beach	A+ LA	120	435	131	13	3	3	159	86	35	60	2	37	3	6	5	60	27	.69	8	.301	.386	.366
1996 Vero Beach	A+ LA	2	5	0	0	0	0	0	0	0	0	0	0	0	0	0	0	0	.00	0	.000	.000	.000
1997 San Berndno	A+ LA	132	519	147	28	7	3	198	83	47	55	0	79	4	6	1	67	32	.68	5	.283	.356	.382
1998 San Antonio	AA LA	57	213	60	5	5	3	84	35	19	30	1	24	1	3	2	19	15	.56	3	.282	.370	.394
1999 San Antonio	AA LA	123	461	135	25	3	3	175	78	57	65	1	47	3	9	4	57	21	.73	3	.293	.381	.380
1998 Los Angeles	NL	4	1	0	0	0	0	0	0	0	0	0	1	0	0	0	2	0	1.00	0	.000	.000	.000
6 Min. YEARS		513	1949	561	82	18	12	715	336	178	245	4	223	12	29	15	245	110	.69	25	.288	.368	.367

Rod Metzler

Bats: Both Throws: Right Pos: 2B   Ht: 5'11" Wt: 185 Born: 11/19/74 Age: 25

		BATTING															BASERUNNING				PERCENTAGES		
Year Team	Lg Org	G	AB	H	2B	3B	HR	TB	R	RBI	TBB	IBB	SO	HBP	SH	SF	SB	CS	SB%	GDP	Avg	OBP	SLG
1997 Spokane	A- KC	62	224	51	5	5	3	75	37	31	18	0	48	1	5	2	9	2	.82	1	.228	.286	.335
1998 Lansing	A KC	88	323	81	17	4	2	112	45	34	36	0	77	3	4	0	17	6	.74	2	.251	.331	.347
1999 Chstn-WV	A KC	130	462	122	23	7	7	180	64	60	48	0	98	9	5	1	29	14	.67	7	.264	.344	.390
Wichita	AA KC	3	10	5	2	0	2	13	5	4	0	0	3	1	1	0	0	0	.00	0	.500	.545	1.300
3 Min. YEARS		283	1019	259	47	16	14	380	151	129	102	0	226	14	15	3	55	22	.71	10	.254	.330	.373

Jake Meyer

Pitches: Right Bats: Right Pos: P   Ht: 6'1" Wt: 195 Born: 1/7/75 Age: 25

		HOW MUCH HE PITCHED						WHAT HE GAVE UP										THE RESULTS					
Year Team	Lg Org	G	GS	CG	GF	IP	BFP	H	R	ER	HR	SH	SF	HB	TBB	IBB	SO	WP	Bk	W	L	Pct.	ShO	Sv	ERA
1997 Bristol	R+ CWS	17	0	0	15	20	84	15	7	5	3	1	0	0	7	0	25	4	0	1	1	.500	0	5	2.25
1998 Hickory	A CWS	35	0	0	24	56	244	58	30	20	5	2	1	0	22	1	47	7	1	0	6	.000	0	11	3.21
Winston-Sal	A+ CWS	11	0	0	10	12.1	51	12	6	4	1	0	0	0	3	2	13	2	0	0	1	.000	0	2	2.92
1999 Rockford	A Cin	33	0	0	31	46	197	40	16	13	1	4	0	3	18	4	51	2	0	3	2	.600	0	16	2.54
Chattanooga	AA Cin	20	0	0	10	22.2	102	24	17	15	1	0	1	0	14	0	16	4	0	2	2	.500	0	0	5.96
3 Min. YEARS		116	0	0	90	157	678	149	76	57	11	7	2	3	64	7	152	19	1	6	12	.333	0	34	3.27

Mike Meyers

Pitches: Right Bats: Right Pos: P   Ht: 6'2" Wt: 210 Born: 10/18/77 Age: 22

		HOW MUCH HE PITCHED						WHAT HE GAVE UP										THE RESULTS					
Year Team	Lg Org	G	GS	CG	GF	IP	BFP	H	R	ER	HR	SH	SF	HB	TBB	IBB	SO	WP	Bk	W	L	Pct.	ShO	Sv	ERA
1997 Cubs	R ChC	12	2	0	4	38.1	166	34	15	6	2	1	1	2	13	0	45	0	0	3	1	.750	0	3	1.41
Williamsprt	A- ChC	1	1	0	0	4	15	3	0	0	1	0	0	0	1	0	2	0	0	0	0	.000	0	0	0.00
1998 Rockford	A ChC	17	16	0	0	85.2	363	75	37	32	3	2	0	3	32	2	86	5	1	7	5	.583	0	0	3.36
1999 Daytona	A+ ChC	19	17	2	2	107.1	436	68	30	23	9	2	3	9	40	0	122	4	0	10	3	.769	0	0	1.93
West Tenn	AA ChC	5	5	0	0	33	128	21	5	4	1	1	1	0	10	1	51	1	0	4	0	1.000	0	0	1.09
3 Min. YEARS		54	41	2	6	268.1	1108	201	87	65	15	7	5	14	96	3	306	10	1	24	9	.727	0	3	2.18

Bart Miadich

Pitches: Right Bats: Right Pos: P   Ht: 6'4" Wt: 205 Born: 2/3/76 Age: 24

		HOW MUCH HE PITCHED						WHAT HE GAVE UP										THE RESULTS					
Year Team	Lg Org	G	GS	CG	GF	IP	BFP	H	R	ER	HR	SH	SF	HB	TBB	IBB	SO	WP	Bk	W	L	Pct.	ShO	Sv	ERA
1998 Sarasota	A+ Bos	22	0	0	15	48.2	199	40	20	17	1	3	0	1	15	4	64	2	1	3	2	.600	0	7	3.14
Trenton	AA Bos	22	8	0	4	54.1	253	66	39	36	4	1	2	5	26	1	33	3	0	1	6	.143	0	1	5.96
1999 El Paso	AA Ari	12	0	0	2	20	104	37	22	18	3	1	1	2	7	1	16	0	0	0	2	.000	0	1	8.10
High Desert	A+ Ari	21	16	0	1	98	448	125	71	59	9	2	4	12	40	0	85	1	1	3	8	.273	0	0	5.42
2 Min. YEARS		77	24	0	22	221	1004	268	152	130	17	7	7	20	88	6	198	6	2	7	18	.280	0	9	5.29

Chris Michalak

Pitches: Left Bats: Left Pos: P   Ht: 6'2" Wt: 195 Born: 1/4/71 Age: 29

		HOW MUCH HE PITCHED						WHAT HE GAVE UP										THE RESULTS					
Year Team	Lg Org	G	GS	CG	GF	IP	BFP	H	R	ER	HR	SH	SF	HB	TBB	IBB	SO	WP	Bk	W	L	Pct.	ShO	Sv	ERA
1993 Sou Oregon	A- Oak	16	15	0	0	79	346	77	41	25	2	2	5	6	36	0	57	4	3	7	3	.700	0	0	2.85
1994 W Michigan	A Oak	15	10	0	0	67	291	66	32	29	3	4	2	8	28	0	38	2	3	5	3	.625	0	0	3.90
Modesto	A+ Oak	17	10	1	3	77.1	310	67	28	25	13	2	3	3	20	1	46	4	3	5	3	.625	0	2	2.91
1995 Huntsville	AA Oak	7	0	0	4	5.2	32	10	7	7	1	1	0	1	5	0	4	2	0	1	1	.500	0	1	11.12
Modesto	A+ Oak	44	0	0	16	65.1	266	56	26	19	3	4	3	4	27	1	49	2	1	3	2	.600	0	2	2.62

187

Year Team	Lg Org	G	GS	CG	GF	IP	BFP	H	R	ER	HR	SH	SF	HB	TBB	IBB	SO	WP	Bk	W	L	Pct.	ShO	Sv	ERA
1996 Modesto	A+ Oak	21	0	0	13	38.2	173	37	21	13	4	0	2	2	17	0	39	6	0	2	2	.500	0	4	3.03
Huntsville	AA Oak	21	0	0	4	23.1	123	32	29	20	2	1	1	1	26	4	15	4	0	4	0	1.000	0	0	7.71
1997 High Desert	A+ Ari	49	0	0	17	85	362	76	36	25	3	0		9	31	1	74	6	1	3	7	.300	0	4	2.65
1998 Tulsa	AA Ari	10	0	0	3	19.2	73	10	4	4	2	2	0	2	2	0	15	0	2	1	2	.333	0	0	1.83
Tucson	AAA Ari	29	9	0	6	73.1	326	91	47	41	11	2	5	4	29	3	50	4	3	3	8	.273	0	0	5.03
1999 Edmonton	AAA Ana	24	0	0	7	28.1	125	28	20	18	3	0	2	1	14	0	25	1	0	1	0	1.000	0	0	5.72
Tucson	AAA Ari	21	6	0	7	64	275	64	30	26	6	2	2	6	26	2	41	1	1	5	0	1.000	0	3	3.66
1998 Arizona	NL	5	0	0	2	5.1	29	9	7	7	1	0	1	0	4	0	5	0	0	0	0	.000	0	0	11.81
7 Min. YEARS		274	50	1	82	626.2	2702	614	321	252	54	23	25	47	261	12	453	30	19	40	31	.563	0	16	3.62

Mike Micucci

Bats: Left **Throws:** Right **Pos:** C   **Ht:** 5'11" **Wt:** 190 **Born:** 12/15/72 **Age:** 27

Year Team	Lg Org	G	AB	H	2B	3B	HR	TB	R	RBI	TBB	IBB	SO	HBP	SH	SF	SB	CS	SB%	GDP	Avg	OBP	SLG
1994 Williamsprt	A- ChC	43	105	20	2	0	0	22	16	8	8	0	16	4	5	3	3	2	.60	1	.190	.267	.210
1995 Daytona	A+ ChC	23	41	8	2	0	0	10	4	3	4	0	9	0	2	0	0	0	.00	0	.195	.267	.244
1996 Daytona	A+ ChC	39	82	15	0	0	0	15	6	3	5	0	16	1	1	0	0	3	.00	3	.183	.239	.183
1997 Orlando	AA ChC	4	6	0	0	0	0	0	0	0	0	0	1	0	0	0	0	0	.00	0	.000	.000	.000
Daytona	A+ ChC	54	140	35	5	0	1	43	15	24	12	1	27	1	1	0	1	4	.20	3	.250	.314	.307
1998 West Tenn	AA ChC	53	138	40	11	1	0	53	20	21	17	3	18	1	0	0	0	0	.00	3	.290	.372	.384
1999 West Tenn	AA ChC	52	124	21	1	0	0	22	7	7	7	1	32	0	1	1	0	1	1.00	0	.169	.212	.177
6 Min. YEARS		268	636	139	21	1	1	165	68	66	53	5	119	7	10	4	5	9	.36	14	.219	.284	.259

Jason Middlebrook

Pitches: Right **Bats:** Right **Pos:** P   **Ht:** 6'3" **Wt:** 215 **Born:** 6/26/75 **Age:** 25

Year Team	Lg Org	G	GS	CG	GF	IP	BFP	H	R	ER	HR	SH	SF	HB	TBB	IBB	SO	WP	Bk	W	L	Pct.	ShO	Sv	ERA
1997 Rancho Cuca	A+ SD	6	6	0	0	22.1	105	29	15	10	1	1	3	0	12	1	18	2	1	0	2	.000	0	0	4.03
Clinton	A SD	14	14	2	0	81.1	353	76	46	36	4	3	1	1	39	0	86	6	5	6	4	.600	1	0	3.98
1998 Rancho Cuca	A+ SD	28	28	0	0	150	665	162	99	82	10	1	9	4	63	0	132	17	4	10	12	.455	0	0	4.92
1999 Padres	R SD	1	1	0	0	5	25	9	5	4	0	0	0	0	1	0	3	0	0	1	0	1.000	0	0	7.20
Mobile	AA SD	13	13	0	0	63.2	302	78	59	57	9	1	5	8	30	1	38	5	0	4	6	.400	0	0	8.06
3 Min. YEARS		62	62	2	0	322.1	1450	354	224	189	24	6	18	13	145	2	277	30	10	21	24	.467	1	0	5.28

Bob Milacki

Pitches: Right **Bats:** Right **Pos:** P   **Ht:** 6'4" **Wt:** 230 **Born:** 7/28/64 **Age:** 35

Year Team	Lg Org	G	GS	CG	GF	IP	BFP	H	R	ER	HR	SH	SF	HB	TBB	IBB	SO	WP	Bk	W	L	Pct.	ShO	Sv	ERA
1984 Hagerstown	A+ Bal	15	13	1	1	77.2	339	69	35	29	2	1	2	0	48	0	62	6	0	4	5	.444	0	0	3.36
1985 Daytona Bch	A+ Bal	8	6	2	1	38.1	167	32	23	17	0	2	3	0	26	1	24	7	1	1	4	.200	0	0	3.99
Hagerstown	A Bal	7	7	1	0	40.2	174	32	16	12	1	0	0	2	22	0	37	0	0	3	2	.600	0	0	2.66
1986 Hagerstown	A+ Bal	13	12	1	0	60.2	292	69	59	32	4	1	4	1	37	2	46	6	1	4	5	.444	1	0	4.75
Miami	A+ Bal	12	11	0	0	67.1	297	70	36	28	1	2	4	2	27	2	41	6	0	4	4	.500	0	0	3.74
Charlotte	AA Bal	1	1	0	0	5.1	28	7	4	4	0	1	0	0	4	0	6	2	0	0	1	.000	0	0	6.75
1987 Charlotte	AA Bal	29	24	2	2	148	662	168	86	75	10	2	3	3	66	0	101	10	0	11	9	.550	0	1	4.56
1988 Charlotte	AA Bal	5	5	1	0	37.2	150	26	11	10	1	1	1	3	12	1	29	1	1	3	1	.750	0	0	2.39
Rochester	AAA Bal	24	24	11	0	176.2	747	174	62	53	8	2	2	1	65	1	103	6	1	12	8	.600	3	0	2.70
1991 Hagerstown	AA Bal	3	3	0	0	17	67	14	3	2	1	0	0	0	3	0	18	0	0	3	0	1.000	0	0	1.06
1992 Rochester	AAA Bal	9	9	3	0	61	253	57	33	31	9	1	4	2	21	0	35	3	0	7	1	.875	0	0	4.57
1993 Charlotte	AAA Cle	21	7	0	8	71.2	288	59	31	27	6	2	2	0	19	1	46	4	0	4	3	.571	0	0	3.39
1994 Omaha	AAA KC	16	14	1	1	86	386	91	54	48	11	5	5	6	42	0	59	2	0	4	3	.571	0	0	5.02
1995 Omaha	AAA KC	15	15	2	0	105.1	421	90	42	39	8	1	0	2	31	0	63	3	0	8	3	.727	2	0	3.33
Tacoma	AAA Sea	12	12	1	0	71.2	322	94	50	42	5	2	3	0	23	1	31	0	0	6	4	.600	0	0	5.27
1996 Tacoma	AAA Sea	23	23	5	0	164.1	653	131	62	50	12	3	1	4	39	1	117	4	1	13	3	.813	2	0	2.74
1998 Memphis	AAA StL	1	0	0	0	1.1	4	0	0	0	0	0	0	0	0	0	1	0	0	0	0	.000	0	0	0.00
New Orleans	AAA Hou	29	28	2	0	189.2	804	199	96	81	18	1	6	8	51	1	104	5	0	10	8	.556	0	0	3.84
1999 Nashville	AAA Pit	22	20	0	0	111	480	130	82	60	14	12	4	4	43	5	79	10	0	6	8	.429	0	0	4.86
1988 Baltimore	AL	3	3	1	0	25	91	9	2	2	1	0	0	0	9	0	18	0	0	2	0	1.000	1	0	0.72
1989 Baltimore	AL	37	36	3	1	243	1022	233	105	101	21	7	6	2	88	4	113	1	1	14	12	.538	2	0	3.74
1990 Baltimore	AL	27	24	1	0	135.1	594	143	73	67	18	5	5	0	61	2	60	2	1	5	8	.385	1	0	4.46
1991 Baltimore	AL	31	26	3	0	184	758	175	86	82	17	7	5	1	53	3	108	1	0	10	9	.526	1	0	4.01
1992 Baltimore	AL	23	20	0	1	115.2	525	140	78	75	16	3	3	2	44	2	51	7	1	6	8	.429	0	1	5.84
1993 Cleveland	AL	5	2	0	0	16	74	19	8	6	3	0	0	0	11	0	7	0	0	1	1	.500	0	0	3.38
1994 Kansas City	AL	10	10	0	0	55.2	254	68	43	38	6	1	4	1	20	3	17	2	0	0	5	.000	0	0	6.14
1996 Seattle	AL	7	4	0	1	21	106	30	20	16	3	0	0	0	15	3	13	0	0	1	2	.200	0	0	6.86
13 Min. YEARS		265	234	33	13	1531.1	6564	1512	785	640	111	39	44	38	579	16	1002	75	5	103	72	.589	8	5	3.76
8 Maj. YEARS		143	125	8	4	795.2	3424	817	415	387	85	23	23	6	301	17	387	13	5	39	47	.453	5	1	4.38

Adam Milburn

Pitches: Left **Bats:** Right **Pos:** P   **Ht:** 6'1" **Wt:** 195 **Born:** 4/27/74 **Age:** 26

Year Team	Lg Org	G	GS	CG	GF	IP	BFP	H	R	ER	HR	SH	SF	HB	TBB	IBB	SO	WP	Bk	W	L	Pct.	ShO	Sv	ERA
1996 Eugene	A- Atl	24	0	0	16	42.1	176	28	17	14	1	2	3	1	21	4	33	4	1	3	1	.750	0	7	2.98
1997 Macon	A Atl	46	0	0	18	70	301	71	29	26	6	2	1	3	23	2	51	2	0	4	1	.800	0	4	3.34
1998 Danville	A+ Atl	45	0	0	16	53.1	248	62	32	24	5	3	4	1	27	8	33	3	0	0	2	.000	0	2	4.05
1999 Myrtle Bch	A+ Atl	39	0	0	32	45	195	53	27	21	5	4	6	1	14	6	27	0	0	2	4	.333	0	15	4.20
Greenville	AA Atl	14	0	0	9	19	85	23	10	10	2	0	1	1	7	1	10	1	1	1	0	1.000	0	0	4.74

	HOW MUCH HE PITCHED						WHAT HE GAVE UP												THE RESULTS					
Year Team	Lg Org	G	GS	CG	GF	IP	BFP	H	R	ER	HR	SH	SF	HB	TBB	IBB	SO	WP	Bk	W	L	Pct.	ShO	Sv	ERA
4 Min. YEARS		168	0	0	91	229.2	1005	237	115	95	19	11	14	7	92	21	154	10	2	10	8	.556	0	28	3.72

Chad Miles

Pitches: Left   Bats: Both   Pos: P   Ht: 6'3"   Wt: 195   Born: 2/26/73   Age: 27

	HOW MUCH HE PITCHED						WHAT HE GAVE UP												THE RESULTS					
Year Team	Lg Org	G	GS	CG	GF	IP	BFP	H	R	ER	HR	SH	SF	HB	TBB	IBB	SO	WP	Bk	W	L	Pct.	ShO	Sv	ERA
1994 Elmira	A- Fla	11	9	0	1	42	207	46	32	23	1	1	4	4	33	0	14	10	1	0	6	.000	0	0	4.93
1995 Kane County	A Fla	19	0	0	4	27.1	145	35	33	22	3	4	4	4	23	1	14	2	1	1	1	.500	0	0	7.24
Elmira	A- Fla	14	0	0	4	21.2	105	29	18	16	2	1	1	1	10	0	10	5	1	1	1	.500	0	0	6.65
1996 Brevard Cty	A+ Fla	27	7	0	12	70.2	328	90	57	43	8	4	4	3	31	3	37	7	1	1	5	.167	0	0	5.48
1997 Brevard Cty	A+ Fla	42	0	0	18	64	291	63	46	32	4	2	1	2	31	4	59	6	0	3	4	.429	0	5	4.50
1998 Lakeland	A+ Det	42	1	0	17	61.2	297	67	43	38	9	2	3	3	38	2	65	4	1	1	8	.111	0	2	5.55
1999 Jacksnville	AA Det	45	0	0	23	58.2	285	78	49	40	9	0	3	2	30	0	50	7	0	3	2	.600	0	0	6.14
6 Min. YEARS		200	17	0	79	346	1658	408	278	214	36	14	20	19	196	10	249	41	5	10	27	.270	0	7	5.57

Adan Millan

Bats: Right   Throws: Right   Pos: C   Ht: 6'0"   Wt: 195   Born: 3/26/72   Age: 28

	BATTING															BASERUNNING				PERCENTAGES		
Year Team	Lg Org	G	AB	H	2B	3B	HR	TB	R	RBI	TBB	IBB	SO	HBP	SH	SF	SB	CS	SB%	GDP	Avg	OBP	SLG
1994 Batavia	A- Phi	17	53	17	4	0	0	21	10	11	10	0	6	1	0	1	0	0	.00	1	.321	.431	.396
Spartanburg	A Phi	48	153	41	12	0	4	65	20	29	33	1	21	1	0	1	1	1	.50	6	.268	.399	.425
1995 Reading	AA Phi	10	20	7	3	0	1	13	3	7	4	0	3	1	0	1	0	0	.00	1	.350	.462	.650
Piedmont	A Phi	107	394	116	25	2	10	175	69	64	44	3	45	7	1	3	1	4	.20	15	.294	.373	.444
1996 Clearwater	A+ Phi	101	348	94	21	1	11	150	55	55	52	2	52	3	0	6	1	2	.33	15	.270	.364	.431
1997 Clearwater	A+ Phi	13	55	16	3	1	1	24	7	8	5	0	8	0	0	1	1	0	1.00	1	.291	.344	.436
Scranton-WB	AAA Phi	1	2	1	0	0	0	1	0	1	1	1	0	0	0	0	0	0	.00	0	.500	.667	.500
Reading	AA Phi	95	266	65	10	0	9	102	43	43	44	0	52	2	2	4	0	0	.00	5	.244	.351	.383
1998 Reading	AA Phi	61	195	58	18	1	9	105	18	42	28	0	36	0	0	3	1	1	.50	6	.297	.381	.538
Scranton-WB	AAA Phi	8	23	3	1	0	1	7	5	3	5	0	7	1	0	0	0	0	.00	0	.130	.310	.304
1999 Scranton-WB	AAA Phi	1	2	0	0	0	0	0	0	0	1	0	2	0	0	0	0	0	.00	0	.000	.333	.000
Lehigh Vly	IND —	102	302	73	10	0	10	113	50	39	80	1	61	0	4	1	4	5	.44	3	.242	.399	.374
6 Min. YEARS		564	1813	491	107	5	56	776	280	302	307	8	293	16	7	21	9	13	.41	53	.271	.377	.428

Corky Miller

Bats: Right   Throws: Right   Pos: C   Ht: 6'1"   Wt: 215   Born: 3/18/76   Age: 24

	BATTING															BASERUNNING				PERCENTAGES		
Year Team	Lg Org	G	AB	H	2B	3B	HR	TB	R	RBI	TBB	IBB	SO	HBP	SH	SF	SB	CS	SB%	GDP	Avg	OBP	SLG
1998 Billings	R+ Cin	45	129	35	8	0	5	58	28	24	24	0	24	21	2	2	1	4	.20	2	.271	.455	.450
1999 Rockford	A Cin	66	195	56	10	1	10	98	43	40	33	1	42	20	1	1	3	6	.33	5	.287	.438	.503
Chattanooga	AA Cin	33	104	23	10	0	4	45	20	16	11	0	30	11	0	1	0	0	.00	3	.221	.354	.433
2 Min. YEARS		144	428	114	28	1	19	201	91	80	68	1	96	52	3	4	4	10	.29	10	.266	.424	.470

David Miller

Bats: Left   Throws: Left   Pos: OF   Ht: 6'4"   Wt: 200   Born: 12/9/73   Age: 26

	BATTING															BASERUNNING				PERCENTAGES		
Year Team	Lg Org	G	AB	H	2B	3B	HR	TB	R	RBI	TBB	IBB	SO	HBP	SH	SF	SB	CS	SB%	GDP	Avg	OBP	SLG
1996 Kinston	A+ Cle	129	488	124	23	1	7	170	71	54	38	4	94	0	2	5	14	7	.67	7	.254	.305	.348
1997 Akron	AA Cle	134	509	153	27	9	4	210	84	61	48	2	77	2	6	4	22	11	.67	5	.301	.361	.413
1998 Buffalo	AAA Cle	115	415	111	19	2	9	161	56	54	61	3	72	2	4	3	6	8	.43	10	.267	.362	.388
1999 Buffalo	AAA Cle	101	325	78	21	3	2	111	37	37	33	2	57	0	1	1	12	5	.71	8	.240	.309	.342
4 Min. YEARS		479	1737	466	90	15	22	652	248	206	180	11	300	4	13	13	54	31	.64	30	.268	.336	.375

Matt Miller

Pitches: Left   Bats: Left   Pos: P   Ht: 6'3"   Wt: 175   Born: 8/2/74   Age: 25

	HOW MUCH HE PITCHED						WHAT HE GAVE UP												THE RESULTS					
Year Team	Lg Org	G	GS	CG	GF	IP	BFP	H	R	ER	HR	SH	SF	HB	TBB	IBB	SO	WP	Bk	W	L	Pct.	ShO	Sv	ERA
1996 Jamestown	A- Det	6	6	0	0	25.1	115	33	16	13	0	1	0	3	13	0	21	6	2	1	3	.250	0	0	4.62
1998 W Michigan	A Det	14	14	3	0	95	366	59	20	16	1	5	0	4	26	0	102	4	1	7	4	.636	1	0	1.52
Jacksnville	AA Det	13	13	0	0	61.1	297	70	49	48	6	0	2	2	50	1	49	3	1	3	7	.300	0	0	7.04
1999 Lakeland	A+ Det	19	19	1	0	108.1	473	108	58	50	9	5	2	2	45	0	82	0	1	4	9	.308	0	0	4.15
Jacksnville	AA Det	7	7	0	0	40.2	176	43	23	20	3	3	1	2	12	0	25	0	0	4	1	.800	0	0	4.43
3 Min. YEARS		59	59	4	0	330.2	1427	313	166	147	19	14	5	13	146	1	279	13	5	19	24	.442	1	0	4.00

Matt Miller

Pitches: Right   Bats: Right   Pos: P   Ht: 6'2"   Wt: 215   Born: 11/23/71   Age: 28

	HOW MUCH HE PITCHED						WHAT HE GAVE UP												THE RESULTS					
Year Team	Lg Org	G	GS	CG	GF	IP	BFP	H	R	ER	HR	SH	SF	HB	TBB	IBB	SO	WP	Bk	W	L	Pct.	ShO	Sv	ERA
1996 Greenville	IND —	19	6	0	5	69.2	331	77	51	47	2	1	3	8	50	0	54	3	2	5	2	.714	0	1	6.07
1997 Greenville	IND —	15	15	5	0	107.1	433	76	34	27	0	3	2	4	49	0	129	10	1	12	3	.800	3	0	2.26
1998 Greenville	IND —	8	8	4	0	53.2	228	46	26	17	1	6	2	1	19	1	49	2	0	1	7	.125	0	0	2.85
Savannah	A Tex	17	0	0	10	35.1	137	25	9	9	0	2	0	2	10	0	46	2	0	3	1	.750	0	3	2.29
1999 Charlotte	A+ Tex	22	0	0	20	29.2	132	27	12	10	0	1	1	1	13	1	39	2	0	1	2	.333	0	8	3.03
Tulsa	AA Tex	34	0	0	25	56	235	42	24	21	2	4	5	1	28	2	83	5	0	6	4	.600	0	7	3.38
4 Min. YEARS		115	29	9	60	351.2	1496	293	156	131	5	16	13	17	169	4	400	24	3	28	19	.596	3	19	3.35

189

Orlando Miller

Bats: Right **Throws:** Right **Pos:** SS **Ht:** 6' 3" **Wt:** 205 **Born:** 1/13/69 **Age:** 31

Year Team	Lg Org	G	AB	H	2B	3B	HR	TB	R	RBI	TBB	IBB	SO	HBP	SH	SF	SB	CS	SB%	GDP	Avg	OBP	SLG
1988 Ft. Laud	A+ NYY	3	11	3	0	0	0	3	0	1	0	0	1	0	0	0	0	0	.00	1	.273	.273	.273
Yankees	R NYY	14	44	8	1	0	0	9	5	5	3	1	10	0	0	0	1	0	1.00	0	.182	.234	.205
1989 Oneonta	A- NYY	58	213	62	5	2	1	74	29	25	6	0	38	3	3	1	8	2	.80	3	.291	.318	.347
1990 Asheville	A Hou	121	438	137	29	6	4	190	60	62	25	2	52	10	2	4	12	5	.71	12	.313	.361	.434
1991 Jackson	AA Hou	23	70	13	6	0	1	22	5	5	5	1	13	2	2	0	0	0	.00	2	.186	.260	.314
Osceola	A+ Hou	74	272	81	11	2	0	96	27	36	13	0	30	8	2	3	1	3	.25	5	.298	.345	.353
1992 Jackson	AA Hou	115	379	100	26	5	5	151	51	53	16	0	75	4	2	4	7	5	.58	5	.264	.298	.398
Tucson	AAA Hou	10	37	9	0	0	2	15	4	8	1	0	2	0	0	1	0	0	.00	1	.243	.256	.405
1993 Tucson	AAA Hou	122	471	143	29	16	16	252	86	89	20	0	95	7	1	4	2	4	.33	12	.304	.339	.535
1994 Tucson	AAA Hou	93	338	87	16	6	10	145	54	55	16	1	77	6	3	7	3	3	.50	8	.257	.297	.429
1997 Lakeland	A+ Det	5	21	4	1	1	0	7	1	0	1	0	4	0	0	0	0	0	.00	1	.190	.227	.333
Jacksnville	AA Det	3	11	4	1	0	1	8	2	3	1	0	1	1	0	0	0	0	.00	0	.364	.462	.727
Toledo	AAA Det	8	30	8	1	0	1	12	3	5	2	0	5	0	0	0	2	1	.67	1	.267	.313	.400
1998 Omaha	AAA KC	39	114	28	10	0	2	44	16	15	15	1	32	1	0	2	1	0	1.00	5	.246	.333	.386
Rochester	AAA Bal	37	143	42	4	1	5	63	21	25	9	0	31	5	0	0	3	1	.75	1	.294	.357	.441
New Orleans	AAA Hou	29	98	29	6	2	0	39	15	9	10	0	25	1	0	1	1	0	1.00	2	.296	.364	.398
1999 Buffalo	AAA Cle	68	233	60	17	0	7	98	27	33	12	1	52	5	1	0	5	0	1.00	6	.258	.308	.421
1994 Houston	NL	16	40	13	0	1	2	21	3	9	2	2	12	2	0	0	1	0	1.00	0	.325	.386	.525
1995 Houston	NL	92	324	85	20	1	5	122	36	36	22	8	71	5	4	0	3	4	.43	7	.262	.310	.377
1996 Houston	NL	139	468	120	26	2	15	195	43	58	14	4	116	10	1	3	3	7	.30	14	.256	.291	.417
1997 Detroit	AL	50	111	26	7	1	2	41	13	10	5	0	24	4	1	1	1	0	1.00	1	.234	.289	.369
10 Min. YEARS		822	2923	818	163	41	55	1228	406	429	155	7	543	53	16	27	46	24	.66	65	.280	.325	.420
4 Maj. YEARS		297	943	244	53	5	24	379	95	113	43	14	223	21	6	4	8	11	.42	22	.259	.305	.402

Ryan Miller

Bats: Right **Throws:** Right **Pos:** 2B **Ht:** 6'0" **Wt:** 175 **Born:** 10/22/72 **Age:** 27

Year Team	Lg Org	G	AB	H	2B	3B	HR	TB	R	RBI	TBB	IBB	SO	HBP	SH	SF	SB	CS	SB%	GDP	Avg	OBP	SLG
1994 Pittsfield	A- NYM	68	277	71	11	1	1	87	37	23	16	1	37	4	3	2	3	3	.50	0	.256	.304	.314
1995 St. Lucie	A+ NYM	89	279	68	10	3	2	90	32	23	13	0	42	7	8	2	5	3	.63	7	.244	.292	.323
Binghamton	AA NYM	9	19	1	0	0	0	1	3	0	2	0	4	0	1	0	1	0	1.00	0	.053	.143	.053
1996 St. Lucie	A+ NYM	86	310	79	8	3	2	99	32	23	22	1	51	3	13	1	8	5	.62	5	.255	.310	.319
1997 St. Lucie	A+ NYM	61	193	49	12	1	2	69	27	28	11	0	38	1	2	2	5	5	.50	3	.254	.295	.358
Kissimmee	A+ Hou	13	34	9	0	0	0	9	5	1	5	0	3	0	2	0	1	0	1.00	0	.265	.359	.265
Jackson	AA Hou	20	55	11	0	2	1	18	6	8	5	0	10	0	1	1	1	0	1.00	1	.200	.262	.327
1998 New Orleans	AAA Hou	8	17	5	1	0	0	6	4	3	1	0	3	1	0	0	1	0	1.00	0	.294	.368	.353
Jackson	AA Hou	102	293	90	20	0	3	119	36	26	9	0	43	9	3	4	6	4	.60	10	.307	.343	.406
1999 Jackson	AA Hou	27	75	11	0	1	0	13	5	4	2	0	11	2	0	0	5	0	1.00	4	.147	.190	.173
New Orleans	AAA Hou	64	174	48	8	0	1	59	19	25	5	0	29	1	0	1	0	2	.00	3	.276	.298	.339
6 Min. YEARS		547	1726	442	70	11	12	570	206	164	91	2	271	28	33	13	36	22	.62	33	.256	.302	.330

Ralph Milliard

Bats: Right **Throws:** Right **Pos:** SS **Ht:** 5'11" **Wt:** 175 **Born:** 12/30/73 **Age:** 26

Year Team	Lg Org	G	AB	H	2B	3B	HR	TB	R	RBI	TBB	IBB	SO	HBP	SH	SF	SB	CS	SB%	GDP	Avg	OBP	SLG
1993 Marlins	R Fla	53	192	45	15	0	0	60	35	25	30	0	17	6	0	1	11	5	.69	8	.234	.354	.313
1994 Kane County	A Fla	133	515	153	34	2	8	215	97	67	68	2	63	9	4	7	10	10	.50	6	.297	.384	.417
1995 Portland	AA Fla	128	464	124	22	3	11	185	104	40	85	3	83	14	13	4	22	10	.69	5	.267	.389	.399
1996 Charlotte	AAA Fla	69	250	69	15	2	6	106	47	26	38	0	43	5	1	1	8	4	.67	5	.276	.381	.424
Portland	AA Fla	6	20	4	0	1	0	6	2	2	1	0	5	0	0	0	1	0	1.00	0	.200	.238	.300
1997 Charlotte	AAA Fla	33	132	35	5	1	4	54	19	18	9	0	21	3	4	0	5	3	.63	1	.265	.326	.409
Portland	AA Fla	19	69	19	1	2	0	24	13	5	7	0	8	1	3	0	3	2	.60	2	.275	.351	.348
1998 Norfolk	AAA NYM	127	417	108	24	4	15	185	73	52	79	0	59	8	5	2	17	6	.74	4	.259	.385	.444
1999 Chattanooga	AA Cin	32	102	30	3	1	4	47	19	23	20	1	13	3	1	2	2	3	.40	1	.294	.417	.461
1996 Florida	NL	24	62	10	2	0	0	12	7	1	14	1	16	0	1	0	2	0	1.00	1	.161	.312	.194
1997 Florida	NL	8	30	6	0	0	0	6	2	2	3	0	3	2	1	0	1	1	.50	2	.200	.314	.200
1998 New York	NL	10	1	0	0	0	0	0	3	0	0	0	1	0	0	0	0	0	.00	0	.000	.000	.000
7 Min. YEARS		600	2161	587	119	16	48	882	409	258	337	6	312	49	31	17	79	43	.65	32	.272	.379	.408
3 Maj. YEARS		42	93	16	2	0	0	18	12	3	17	1	20	2	1	1	3	1	.75	3	.172	.310	.194

Blas Minor

Pitches: Right **Bats:** Right **Pos:** P **Ht:** 6' 3" **Wt:** 200 **Born:** 3/20/66 **Age:** 34

Year Team	Lg Org	G	GS	CG	GF	IP	BFP	H	R	ER	HR	SH	SF	HB	TBB	IBB	SO	WP	Bk	W	L	Pct.	ShO	Sv	ERA
1988 Princeton	R+ Pit	15	0	0	14	16.1	77	18	10	8	2	0	0	0	5	0	23	0	0	0	1	.000	0	7	4.41
1989 Salem	A+ Pit	39	4	0	25	86.2	377	91	43	35	6	4	1	2	31	6	62	3	1	3	5	.375	0	0	3.63
1990 Harrisburg	AA Pit	38	6	0	23	94	391	81	41	32	5	8	4	0	29	7	98	3	1	6	4	.600	0	5	3.06
Buffalo	AAA Pit	1	0	0	0	2.2	12	2	1	1	0	0	0	0	2	0	2	0	0	0	1	.000	0	0	3.38
1991 Buffalo	AAA Pit	17	3	0	3	36	168	46	27	23	7	2	1	0	15	0	25	1	0	2	2	.500	0	0	5.75
Carolina	AA Pit	3	2	0	1	12.2	52	9	4	4	0	1	0	0	7	0	18	1	0	0	0	.000	0	0	2.84
1992 Buffalo	AAA Pit	45	7	0	29	96.1	379	72	30	26	7	4	2	1	26	2	60	1	1	5	4	.556	0	18	2.43
1994 Buffalo	AAA Pit	33	3	0	20	51.1	212	47	17	17	6	2	0	1	12	0	61	1	0	1	2	.333	0	11	2.98
1996 Tacoma	AAA Sea	7	0	0	6	9.2	45	15	11	9	1	0	1	0	3	1	8	0	1	1	2	.333	0	1	8.38
1997 New Orleans	AAA Hou	23	0	0	15	31.2	122	20	8	8	1	3	2	0	9	3	27	3	0	3	3	.500	0	6	2.27
Tucson	AAA Mil	12	3	0	4	29	137	36	21	13	3	1	0	2	15	1	21	2	0	2	2	.500	0	1	4.03
1998 Ogden	R+ Mil	2	2	0	0	4	18	4	2	2	0	0	0	1	1	0	4	0	0	0	0	.000	0	0	4.50

(pitcher — continued)

Year Team	Lg Org	HOW MUCH HE PITCHED						WHAT HE GAVE UP												THE RESULTS					
		G	GS	CG	GF	IP	BFP	H	R	ER	HR	SH	SF	HB	TBB	IBB	SO	WP	Bk	W	L	Pct.	ShO	Sv	ERA
El Paso	AA Mil	8	2	0	2	25.1	108	30	14	13	5	1	0	0	3	1	26	2	0	1	3	.250	0	1	4.62
Louisville	AAA Mil	3	1	0	0	9	39	11	6	5	0	0	1	0	2	0	9	0	0	1	0	1.000	0	0	5.00
1999 Huntsville	AA Mil	2	2	0	0	7.2	39	11	12	8	3	0	0	0	5	0	6	1	0	1	0	.000	0	0	9.39
Louisville	AAA Mil	21	17	0	0	108	466	118	59	55	13	1	2	4	32	2	77	1	0	4	4	.500	0	0	4.58
1992 Pittsburgh	NL	1	0	0	0	2	9	3	2	1	0	0	0	0	0	0	0	1	0	0	0	.000	0	0	4.50
1993 Pittsburgh	NL	65	0	0	18	94.1	398	94	43	43	8	6	4	4	26	3	84	5	0	8	6	.571	0	2	4.10
1994 Pittsburgh	NL	17	0	0	2	19	90	27	17	17	4	2	1	1	9	2	17	0	0	1	0	1.000	0	1	8.05
1995 New York	NL	35	0	0	10	46.2	192	44	21	19	6	4	0	1	13	1	43	3	0	4	2	.667	0	1	3.66
1996 New York	NL	17	0	0	4	25.2	104	23	11	10	4	0	1	0	6	2	20	1	0	0	0	.000	0	0	3.51
Seattle	AL	11	0	0	6	25.1	109	27	14	14	6	0	0	0	11	0	14	2	0	0	1	.000	0	0	4.97
1997 Houston	NL	11	0	0	5	12	55	13	7	6	1	1	1	1	5	0	6	4	0	1	0	1.000	0	0	4.50
10 Min. YEARS		269	52	0	142	620.1	2642	611	306	259	59	27	14	11	197	23	529	21	4	29	34	.460	0	50	3.76
6 Maj. YEARS		157	0	0	45	225	957	231	115	110	29	13	7	7	70	8	184	16	0	13	10	.565	0	5	4.40

Damon Minor

Bats: Left Throws: Left Pos: 1B Ht: 6'7" Wt: 230 Born: 1/5/74 Age: 26

Year Team	Lg Org	BATTING															BASERUNNING				PERCENTAGES		
		G	AB	H	2B	3B	HR	TB	R	RBI	TBB	IBB	SO	HBP	SH	SF	SB	CS	SB%	GDP	Avg	OBP	SLG
1996 Bellingham	A- SF	75	269	65	11	1	12	114	44	55	47	4	86	5	1	1	0	2	.00	5	.242	.363	.424
1997 Bakersfield	A+ SF	140	532	154	34	1	31	283	98	99	87	8	143	5	0	5	2	1	.67	6	.289	.391	.532
1998 Shreveport	AA SF	81	289	69	11	1	14	124	39	52	30	1	51	6	0	2	1	0	1.00	3	.239	.321	.429
San Jose	A+ SF	48	176	50	10	1	7	83	26	36	28	0	40	2	0	1	0	1	.00	1	.284	.386	.472
1999 Shreveport	AA SF	136	473	129	33	4	20	230	76	82	80	6	115	8	0	3	1	0	1.00	10	.273	.385	.486
4 Min. YEARS		480	1739	467	99	8	84	834	283	324	272	19	435	26	1	12	4	4	.50	25	.269	.373	.480

Marc Mirizzi

Bats: Both Throws: Right Pos: SS-3B Ht: 6'1" Wt: 190 Born: 6/17/75 Age: 25

Year Team	Lg Org	BATTING															BASERUNNING				PERCENTAGES		
		G	AB	H	2B	3B	HR	TB	R	RBI	TBB	IBB	SO	HBP	SH	SF	SB	CS	SB%	GDP	Avg	OBP	SLG
1997 Oneonta	A- NYY	74	245	64	5	1	1	74	40	33	38	0	36	3	3	3	12	7	.63	4	.261	.363	.302
1998 Greensboro	A NYY	103	373	104	29	1	11	168	57	44	31	1	85	5	1	2	4	5	.44	10	.279	.341	.450
1999 Greensboro	A NYY	9	34	9	0	1	1	14	5	3	5	0	9	1	0	0	0	0	.00	1	.265	.375	.412
Norwich	AA NYY	15	47	5	0	0	1	8	6	6	5	0	13	1	0	3	0	0	.00	1	.106	.196	.170
Tampa	A+ NYY	90	330	79	16	3	6	119	40	30	37	1	87	5	4	2	1	0	1.00	8	.239	.324	.361
3 Min. YEARS		291	1029	261	50	6	20	383	148	116	116	2	230	15	8	10	17	12	.59	24	.254	.335	.372

Dean Mitchell

Pitches: Right Bats: Right Pos: P Ht: 5'11" Wt: 175 Born: 3/19/74 Age: 26

Year Team	Lg Org	HOW MUCH HE PITCHED						WHAT HE GAVE UP												THE RESULTS					
		G	GS	CG	GF	IP	BFP	H	R	ER	HR	SH	SF	HB	TBB	IBB	SO	WP	Bk	W	L	Pct.	ShO	Sv	ERA
1996 Yakima	A- LA	15	5	0	3	52.1	233	53	25	20	4	1	5	0	25	1	61	3	1	2	2	.500	0	2	3.44
1997 Savannah	A LA	52	7	1	38	122	499	110	50	39	6	5	3	1	25	1	118	2	1	11	5	.688	0	16	2.88
San Berndno	A+ LA	1	0	0	1	1	4	0	0	0	0	0	0	0	1	0	1	0	0	0	0	.000	0	0	0.00
1998 San Antonio	AA LA	46	3	0	29	79	331	74	31	29	8	5	1	3	22	2	76	4	0	2	5	.286	0	14	3.30
1999 Albuquerque	AAA LA	31	0	0	15	47.2	232	61	41	39	9	1	3	1	28	2	42	6	0	2	1	.667	0	0	7.36
San Antonio	AA LA	10	7	0	2	31.2	144	36	20	11	2	0	2	0	14	0	28	3	0	1	2	.333	0	0	3.13
4 Min. YEARS		155	22	1	88	333.2	1443	334	167	138	29	12	14	5	115	6	326	18	2	18	15	.545	0	32	3.72

Derek Mitchell

Bats: Right Throws: Right Pos: SS Ht: 6'2" Wt: 170 Born: 3/9/75 Age: 25

Year Team	Lg Org	BATTING															BASERUNNING				PERCENTAGES		
		G	AB	H	2B	3B	HR	TB	R	RBI	TBB	IBB	SO	HBP	SH	SF	SB	CS	SB%	GDP	Avg	OBP	SLG
1996 Jamestown	A- Det	56	184	45	10	2	2	65	25	25	18	0	38	2	7	2	7	4	.64	1	.245	.316	.353
1997 W Michigan	A Det	110	353	70	14	2	1	91	47	31	50	1	91	5	8	3	11	8	.58	5	.198	.304	.258
1998 Jacksnville	AA Det	128	421	93	21	2	2	124	58	54	68	1	94	6	4	8	6	3	.67	9	.221	.332	.295
1999 Jacksnville	AA Det	124	422	102	17	1	7	142	56	49	53	0	117	2	4	5	4	2	.67	3	.242	.326	.336
4 Min. YEARS		418	1380	310	62	7	12	422	186	159	189	2	340	15	23	18	28	17	.62	18	.225	.321	.306

Keith Mitchell

Bats: Right Throws: Right Pos: OF-DH Ht: 5'10" Wt: 195 Born: 8/6/69 Age: 30

Year Team	Lg Org	BATTING															BASERUNNING				PERCENTAGES		
		G	AB	H	2B	3B	HR	TB	R	RBI	TBB	IBB	SO	HBP	SH	SF	SB	CS	SB%	GDP	Avg	OBP	SLG
1987 Braves	R Atl	57	208	50	12	1	2	70	24	21	29	0	50	2	0	2	7	2	.78	4	.240	.336	.337
1988 Sumter	A Atl	98	341	85	16	1	5	118	35	33	41	0	50	4	3	2	9	6	.60	8	.249	.335	.346
1989 Burlington	A Atl	127	448	117	23	0	10	170	64	49	70	1	65	5	0	4	12	7	.63	9	.261	.364	.379
1990 Durham	A+ Atl	129	456	134	24	3	6	182	81	48	92	2	48	4	1	7	18	17	.51	16	.294	.411	.399
1991 Greenville	AA Atl	60	214	70	15	3	10	121	46	47	29	0	29	1	3	5	12	8	.60	5	.327	.402	.565
Richmond	AAA Atl	25	95	31	6	1	2	45	16	17	9	0	13	1	2	3	0	2	.00	3	.326	.380	.474
1992 Richmond	AAA Atl	121	403	91	19	1	4	124	45	50	66	2	55	4	2	4	14	9	.61	6	.226	.338	.308
1993 Richmond	AAA Atl	110	353	82	23	1	4	119	59	44	44	0	48	2	3	3	9	5	.64	11	.232	.318	.337
1994 Calgary	AAA Sea	9	39	10	0		4	22	6	12	2	0	4	0	0	1	0	0	.00		.256	.286	.564
1995 Indianapols	AAA Cin	70	213	52	11	2	11	100	40	36	40	3	40	1	1	1	4	4	.50	7	.244	.360	.469
1996 Indianapols	AAA Cin	112	357	107	21	3	16	182	60	66	64	2	68	1	0	6	9	1	.90	7	.300	.402	.510
1997 Indianapols	AAA Cin	124	407	108	24	1	15	179	72	60	72	1	65	1	1	6	10	4	.71	11	.265	.372	.440
1998 Trenton	AA Bos	12	41	8	2	0	2	16	4	7	8	0	5	0	0	1	0	0	.00	1	.195	.320	.390
Pawtucket	AAA Bos	63	211	66	15	0	12	117	55	45	44	2	37	1	0	4	3	3	.50	5	.313	.427	.555

BATTING

Year Team	Lg Org	G	AB	H	2B	3B	HR	TB	R	RBI	TBB	IBB	SO	HBP	SH	SF	SB	CS	SB%	GDP	Avg	OBP	SLG
1999 Pawtucket	AAA Bos	117	431	111	32	4	12	187	71	52	78	0	69	0	1	4	9	1	.90	11	.258	.368	.434
1991 Atlanta	NL	48	66	21	0	0	2	27	11	5	8	0	12	0	0	0	3	1	.75	1	.318	.392	.409
1994 Seattle	AL	46	128	29	2	0	5	46	21	15	18	0	22	1	1	1	0	0	.00	2	.227	.324	.359
1996 Cincinnati	NL	11	15	4	1	0	1	8	2	3	1	0	3	0	0	0	0	0	.00	0	.267	.313	.533
1998 Boston	AL	23	33	9	2	0	0	11	4	6	7	1	5	0	0	0	1	0	1.00	0	.273	.400	.333
13 Min. YEARS		1234	4217	1122	243	21	115	1752	678	587	688	13	646	27	17	56	116	69	.63	104	.266	.368	.415
4 Maj. YEARS		128	242	63	5	0	8	92	38	29	34	1	42	1	1	1	4	1	.80	3	.260	.353	.380

Mike Mitchell

Bats: Left Throws: Right Pos: 1B   Ht: 6'3" Wt: 205 Born: 4/5/73 Age: 27

BATTING

Year Team	Lg Org	G	AB	H	2B	3B	HR	TB	R	RBI	TBB	IBB	SO	HBP	SH	SF	SB	CS	SB%	GDP	Avg	OBP	SLG
1994 Oneonta	A- NYY	28	104	31	6	0	2	43	13	12	10	0	9	1	0	1	0	0	.00		.298	.362	.413
Greensboro	A NYY	39	133	35	5	1	3	51	15	19	14	1	19	1	0	1	0	1	.00		.263	.336	.383
Albany-Colo	AA NYY	8	24	8	2	0	0	10	3	2	4	1	5	0	0	0	0	0	.00		.333	.429	.417
1995 Tampa	A+ NYY	102	368	98	16	1	8	140	40	61	29	1	52	2	1	6	1	0	1.00	10	.266	.319	.380
1997 Rancho Cuca	A+ SD	109	440	154	36	1	17	243	78	106	35	0	83	6	0	5	2	0	1.00	8	.350	.401	.552
1998 Mobile	AA SD	134	509	162	32	2	15	243	72	97	61	1	95	1	0	3	0	0	.00	7	.318	.390	.477
1999 Las Vegas	AAA SD	27	87	21	5	0	1	29	7	11	12	0	20	0	1	0	0	0	.00	3	.241	.330	.333
5 Min. YEARS		447	1665	509	102	5	46	759	228	308	165	4	283	11	1	17	3	1	.75	35	.306	.369	.456

Scott Mitchell

Pitches: Right Bats: Right Pos: P   Ht: 5'11" Wt: 170 Born: 3/19/73 Age: 27

		HOW MUCH HE PITCHED						WHAT HE GAVE UP											THE RESULTS					
Year Team	Lg Org	G	GS	CG	GF	IP	BFP	H	R	ER	HR	SH	SF	HB	TBB	IBB	SO	WP	Bk	W	L	Pct.	ShO	Sv	ERA
1995 Vermont	A- Mon	18	1	0	5	40.1	171	35	18	10	1	2	2	4	15	0	30	2	4	3	1	.750	0	1	2.23
1996 Delmarva	A Mon	33	5	1	10	76.2	320	69	29	20	7	3	1	5	24	1	76	3	3	5	6	.455	0	1	2.35
1997 Wst Plm Bch	A+ Mon	39	3	0	15	73.2	291	61	21	21	4	3	1	3	18	0	56	4	0	5	3	.625	0	3	2.57
Harrisburg	AA Mon	4	3	0	0	17.1	67	11	7	7	3	1	0	1	3	0	13	1	0	1	0	1.000	0	0	3.63
1998 Harrisburg	AA Mon	32	17	2	5	135	558	136	58	57	13	3	6	6	37	1	81	0	0	9	3	.750	1	2	3.80
1999 Harrisburg	AA Mon	3	3	1	0	19	74	16	9	9	5	0	1	0	3	0	10	1	1	2	0	1.000	0	0	4.26
Ottawa	AAA Mon	18	9	0	1	62.1	282	78	43	39	11	1	3	3	25	0	28	0	1	4	4	.500	0	0	5.63
5 Min. YEARS		147	41	4	36	424.1	1763	406	185	163	44	13	14	22	125	2	294	11	9	29	17	.630	1	7	3.46

Greg Mix

Pitches: Right Bats: Right Pos: P   Ht: 6'4" Wt: 225 Born: 8/21/71 Age: 28

		HOW MUCH HE PITCHED						WHAT HE GAVE UP											THE RESULTS					
Year Team	Lg Org	G	GS	CG	GF	IP	BFP	H	R	ER	HR	SH	SF	HB	TBB	IBB	SO	WP	Bk	W	L	Pct.	ShO	Sv	ERA
1993 Elmira	A- Fla	17	1	0	8	45.1	205	51	26	21	4	0	1	4	17	0	38	4	0	3	3	.500	0	2	4.17
1994 Brevard Cty	A+ Fla	44	0	0	22	78	314	65	29	27	2	4	4	2	20	2	51	1	0	6	2	.750	0	4	3.12
1995 Brevard Cty	A+ Fla	5	4	1	0	29.2	119	27	13	13	1	0	0	3	10	0	17	1	1	3	1	.750	0	0	3.94
Portland	AA Fla	24	13	0	1	92.1	401	98	53	48	9	2	4	4	25	5	56	3	0	6	4	.600	0	0	4.68
1996 Charlotte	AAA Fla	4	4	0	0	18.1	87	27	15	14	4	2	0	2	7	1	9	1	0	1	3	.250	0	0	6.87
Portland	AA Fla	25	5	0	8	65.2	296	80	40	33	8	4	5	5	19	5	57	6	2	3	0	1.000	0	1	4.52
1997 Portland	AA Fla	30	13	0	4	102.2	461	121	70	54	16	7	5	8	32	0	74	5	0	7	7	.500	0	0	4.73
1998 Greenville	AA Atl	22	0	0	9	25	119	32	19	14	2	0	3	0	11	0	18	3	0	1	1	.500	0	2	5.04
Richmond	AAA Atl	28	2	0	13	64.2	268	52	24	21	8	1	2	4	19	0	59	1	0	2	4	.333	0	2	2.92
1999 Pawtucket	AAA Bos	46	4	0	13	85.1	388	89	45	35	9	3	5	4	40	0	79	9	1	4	4	.500	0	1	3.69
7 Min. YEARS		245	46	1	78	607	2658	642	332	280	63	23	29	36	200	13	458	34	4	36	29	.554	0	12	4.15

Doug Mlicki

Pitches: Right Bats: Right Pos: P   Ht: 6'3" Wt: 175 Born: 4/12/71 Age: 29

		HOW MUCH HE PITCHED						WHAT HE GAVE UP											THE RESULTS					
Year Team	Lg Org	G	GS	CG	GF	IP	BFP	H	R	ER	HR	SH	SF	HB	TBB	IBB	SO	WP	Bk	W	L	Pct.	ShO	Sv	ERA
1992 Auburn	A- Hou	14	13	0	0	81.1	330	50	35	27	4	1	3	6	30	0	83	9	2	1	6	.143	0	0	2.99
1993 Osceola	A+ Hou	26	23	0	0	158.2	668	158	81	69	16	5	6	5	65	1	111	9	0	11	10	.524	0	0	3.91
1994 Jackson	AA Hou	23	23	1	0	138.2	575	107	62	52	20	5	2	8	54	5	130	13	3	13	7	.650	0	0	3.38
1995 Jackson	AA Hou	16	16	2	0	96.2	393	73	41	30	6	1	2	4	33	0	72	5	0	8	3	.727	0	0	2.79
Tucson	AAA Hou	6	6	0	0	34	155	44	27	21	3	2	1	2	6	0	22	1	0	2	2	.333	0	0	5.56
1996 Tucson	AAA Hou	26	26	0	0	137.1	624	171	89	72	9	4	9	4	41	2	98	12	0	5	11	.313	0	0	4.72
1997 Kissimmee	A+ Hou	1	1	0	0	4	17	4	0	0	0	0	0	0	0	0	2	0	0	0	0	.000	0	0	0.00
Jackson	AA Hou	9	9	0	0	48.2	229	69	36	29	7	0	1	3	20	0	35	3	0	4	4	.500	0	0	5.36
New Orleans	AAA Hou	14	3	0	4	30	124	27	12	12	4	0	0	1	10	0	18	1	0	4	3	.571	0	0	3.60
1998 Omaha	AAA KC	7	2	0	2	12.2	51	15	6	6	3	0	0	0	2	0	9	0	0	1	1	.500	0	0	4.26
Memphis	AAA StL	24	8	0	2	54	238	62	36	31	9	3	2	1	24	4	21	1	1	1	5	.167	0	0	5.17
1999 Memphis	AAA StL	38	0	0	12	67	299	78	48	43	16	1	1	1	26	2	26	6	0	3	1	.750	0	0	5.78
8 Min. YEARS		204	130	3	20	863	3700	858	473	392	97	23	26	32	311	14	627	60	6	52	53	.495	0	0	4.09

Chad Moeller

Bats: Right Throws: Right Pos: C   Ht: 6'3" Wt: 207 Born: 2/18/75 Age: 25

BATTING

Year Team	Lg Org	G	AB	H	2B	3B	HR	TB	R	RBI	TBB	IBB	SO	HBP	SH	SF	SB	CS	SB%	GDP	Avg	OBP	SLG
1996 Elizabethtn	R+ Min	17	59	21	4	0	4	37	17	13	18	0	9	2	0	0	1	2	.33	3	.356	.519	.627
1997 Fort Wayne	A Min	108	384	111	18	3	9	162	58	39	48	0	76	13	2	1	11	8	.58	8	.289	.386	.422
1998 Fort Myers	A+ Min	66	254	83	24	1	6	127	37	39	31	4	37	3	0	0	2	3	.40	8	.327	.406	.500
New Britain	AA Min	58	187	44	10	0	6	72	21	23	24	0	41	3	1	0	2	1	.67	4	.235	.332	.385

Year Team	Lg Org	G	AB	H	2B	3B	HR	TB	R	RBI	TBB	IBB	SO	HBP	SH	SF	SB	CS	SB%	GDP	Avg	OBP	SLG
1999 New Britain	AA Min	89	250	62	11	3	4	91	29	24	21	1	44	6	1	4	0	0	.00	7	.248	.317	.364
4 Min. YEARS		338	1134	321	67	7	29	489	162	138	142	5	207	27	4	5	16	14	.53	30	.283	.375	.431

Dustan Mohr

Bats: Right **Throws:** Right **Pos:** OF **Ht:** 6'2" **Wt:** 210 **Born:** 6/19/76 **Age:** 24

Year Team	Lg Org	G	AB	H	2B	3B	HR	TB	R	RBI	TBB	IBB	SO	HBP	SH	SF	SB	CS	SB%	GDP	Avg	OBP	SLG
1997 Watertown	A- Cle	74	275	80	20	2	7	125	52	53	31	1	76	4	0	4	3	6	.33	1	.291	.366	.455
1998 Kinston	A+ Cle	134	491	119	23	9	19	217	60	65	39	3	146	9	2	2	8	4	.67	7	.242	.309	.442
1999 Akron	AA Cle	12	42	7	2	1	0	11	3	2	5	0	7	0	1	0	0	1	.00	1	.167	.255	.262
Kinston	A+ Cle	112	429	120	29	3	8	179	46	60	26	2	104	1	1	1	6	6	.50	13	.280	.322	.417
3 Min. YEARS		332	1237	326	74	15	34	532	161	180	101	6	333	14	4	7	17	17	.50	22	.264	.325	.430

Izzy Molina

Bats: Right **Throws:** Right **Pos:** C **Ht:** 6'1" **Wt:** 224 **Born:** 6/3/71 **Age:** 29

Year Team	Lg Org	G	AB	H	2B	3B	HR	TB	R	RBI	TBB	IBB	SO	HBP	SH	SF	SB	CS	SB%	GDP	Avg	OBP	SLG
1990 Athletics	R Oak	38	122	43	12	2	0	59	19	18	9	1	21	2	1	3	5	0	1.00	0	.352	.397	.484
1991 Madison	A Oak	95	316	89	16	1	3	116	35	45	15	1	40	6	1	4	6	4	.60	9	.282	.323	.367
1992 Reno	A+ Oak	116	436	113	17	2	10	164	71	75	39	0	57	7	7	6	8	7	.53	20	.259	.326	.376
Tacoma	AAA Oak	10	36	7	0	1	0	9	3	5	2	0	6	0	0	0	1	0	1.00	1	.194	.237	.250
1993 Modesto	A+ Oak	125	444	116	26	5	6	170	61	69	44	0	85	3	4	11	2	8	.20	11	.261	.325	.383
1994 Huntsville	AA Oak	116	388	84	17	2	8	129	31	50	16	0	47	5	7	7	5	1	.83	10	.216	.252	.332
1995 Edmonton	AAA Oak	2	6	1	0	0	0	1	0	0	0	0	2	0	0	0	0	0	.00	0	.167	.167	.167
Huntsville	AA Oak	83	301	78	16	1	8	120	38	26	26	0	62	8	0	2	3	4	.43	6	.259	.332	.399
1996 Edmonton	AAA Oak	98	342	90	12	3	12	144	45	56	25	4	55	3	5	2	2	5	.29	9	.263	.317	.421
1997 Edmonton	AAA Oak	61	218	57	11	3	6	92	33	34	12	0	27	0	1	0	2	0	1.00	4	.261	.300	.422
1998 Edmonton	AAA Oak	86	303	73	15	2	8	116	29	38	17	0	60	4	1	3	3	0	1.00	16	.241	.287	.383
1999 Columbus	AAA NYY	97	338	83	16	1	4	113	44	51	18	0	47	1	2	6	4	2	.67	9	.246	.281	.334
1996 Oakland	AL	14	25	5	2	0	0	7	0	1	1	0	3	0	0	0	0	0	.00	0	.200	.231	.280
1997 Oakland	AL	48	111	22	3	1	3	36	6	7	3	0	17	0	1	0	0	0	.00	1	.198	.219	.324
1998 Oakland	AL	6	2	1	0	0	0	1	1	0	0	0	0	0	0	0	0	0	.00	0	.500	.500	.500
10 Min. YEARS		927	3250	834	158	23	65	1233	409	467	223	6	509	39	29	44	41	31	.57	95	.257	.308	.379
3 Maj. YEARS		68	138	28	5	1	3	44	7	8	4	0	20	0	1	0	0	0	.00	1	.203	.225	.319

Wonderful Monds

Bats: Right **Throws:** Right **Pos:** OF **Ht:** 6'3" **Wt:** 190 **Born:** 1/11/73 **Age:** 27

Year Team	Lg Org	G	AB	H	2B	3B	HR	TB	R	RBI	TBB	IBB	SO	HBP	SH	SF	SB	CS	SB%	GDP	Avg	OBP	SLG
1993 Idaho Falls	R+ Atl	60	214	64	13	8	4	105	47	35	25	1	43	2	2	0	16	4	.80	4	.299	.378	.491
1994 Durham	A+ Atl	18	53	11	2	0	2	19	7	10	2	1	11	0	0	1	5	0	1.00	3	.208	.232	.358
Macon	A Atl	104	365	106	23	12	10	183	70	41	22	0	82	9	8	2	42	9	.82	6	.290	.344	.501
1995 Braves	R Atl	4	15	2	0	0	0	2	1	1	1	0	8	0	0	0	2	1	.67	0	.133	.188	.133
Durham	A+ Atl	81	297	83	17	0	6	118	44	33	17	1	63	1	1	1	28	7	.80	7	.279	.320	.397
1996 Braves	R Atl	3	5	2	0	0	2	8	3	3	2	0	1	0	0	0	0	0	.00	0	.400	.500	1.600
Greenville	AA Atl	32	110	33	9	1	2	50	17	14	9	0	17	0	1	0	7	3	.70	2	.300	.350	.455
1997 Greenville	AA Atl	27	89	28	5	0	8	57	21	15	20	0	23	0	1	1	6	3	.67	1	.315	.436	.640
Braves	R Atl	2	4	1	0	0	1	4	2	1	1	0	1	0	0	0	1	0	.00	0	.250	.400	1.000
1998 New Haven	AA Col	122	453	127	32	3	9	192	76	58	33	1	105	4	5	3	41	12	.77	5	.280	.333	.424
1999 Chattanooga	AA Cin	75	311	81	14	2	11	132	48	32	17	0	49	1	5	1	14	8	.64	8	.260	.300	.424
7 Min. YEARS		528	1916	538	115	26	55	870	336	243	149	4	403	17	22	11	161	47	.77	36	.281	.336	.454

Craig Monroe

Bats: Right **Throws:** Right **Pos:** OF **Ht:** 6'1" **Wt:** 195 **Born:** 2/27/77 **Age:** 23

Year Team	Lg Org	G	AB	H	2B	3B	HR	TB	R	RBI	TBB	IBB	SO	HBP	SH	SF	SB	CS	SB%	GDP	Avg	OBP	SLG
1995 Rangers	R Tex	54	193	48	6	2	0	58	22	33	18	0	25	2	1	2	13	2	.87	1	.249	.316	.301
1996 Chston-SC	A Tex	49	153	23	11	1	0	36	11	9	18	0	48	3	0	0	2	2	.50	3	.150	.253	.235
Hudson Val	A- Tex	67	268	74	16	6	5	117	53	29	23	0	63	2	0	2	21	7	.75	4	.276	.336	.437
1997 Charlotte	A+ Tex	92	328	77	23	1	7	123	54	41	44	1	80	0	0	6	24	1	.96	5	.235	.320	.375
1998 Charlotte	A+ Tex	132	472	114	26	7	17	205	74	76	66	0	102	3	0	7	50	13	.79	15	.242	.334	.434
1999 Charlotte	A+ Tex	130	480	125	21	1	17	199	77	81	42	2	102	4	3	7	40	16	.71	8	.260	.321	.415
Oklahoma	AAA Tex	6	16	4	1	0	0	5	2	1	1	0	4	0	1	0	0	0	.00	0	.250	.294	.313
5 Min. YEARS		530	1910	465	104	18	46	743	292	270	212	3	424	14	5	24	150	41	.79	36	.243	.320	.389

Ivan Montane

Pitches: Right **Bats:** Right **Pos:** P **Ht:** 6'2" **Wt:** 195 **Born:** 6/3/73 **Age:** 27

		HOW MUCH HE PITCHED						WHAT HE GAVE UP										THE RESULTS					
Year Team	Lg Org	G	GS	CG	GF	IP	BFP	H	R	ER	HR	SH	SF	HB	TBB	IBB	SO	WP	Bk	W	L	Pct.	ShO	Sv	ERA
1992 Mariners	R Sea	13	1	0	1	46	224	44	39	29	0	0	0	3	41	0	48	18	4	1	3	.250	0	0	5.67
1993 Bellingham	A- Sea	15	15	1	0	73.1	305	55	36	32	7	2	1	3	37	0	53	9	3	5	4	.556	0	0	3.93
1994 Appleton	A Sea	29	26	1	0	159	680	132	79	68	13	4	6	12	82	0	155	19	2	8	9	.471	1	0	3.85
1995 Riverside	A+ Sea	24	16	0	6	92.2	442	101	67	58	3	4	3	6	71	0	79	19	0	5	5	.500	0	0	5.63
1996 Lancaster	A+ Sea	11	11	0	0	59.1	273	57	37	24	2	5	3	2	43	0	54	9	0	2	2	.500	0	0	3.64
Port City	AA Sea	18	18	0	0	100.1	461	96	67	57	6	1	2	9	75	0	81	16	2	3	8	.273	0	0	5.11
1997 Memphis	AA Sea	22	12	0	6	71.2	347	83	70	60	16	1	5	6	51	0	63	11	0	0	8	.000	0	0	7.53

Year Team	Lg Org	HOW MUCH HE PITCHED						WHAT HE GAVE UP										THE RESULTS				
		G	GS	CG	GF	IP	BFP	H	R	ER	HR	SH	SF	HB	TBB	IBB	SO	WP	Bk	W	L	Pct.	ShO	Sv	ERA
Lancaster	A+ Sea	6	6	0	0	32.1	150	40	25	19	2	1	2	2	13	1	34	8	1	1	2	.333	0	0	5.29
1998 Orlando	AA Sea	2	0	0	0	2.1	12	3	3	3	0	0	0	0	2	0	0	0	0	0	0	.000	0	0	11.57
1999 Wisconsin	A Sea	10	0	0	9	12.2	49	5	1	1	0	0	0	0	5	0	18	2	0	0	0	.000	0	3	0.71
New Haven	AA Sea	41	0	0	25	54.2	219	38	16	15	2	3	0	2	22	2	70	5	0	4	2	.667	0	10	2.47
8 Min. YEARS		191	115	2	47	704.1	3162	654	440	366	51	20	25	49	442	3	655	116	12	29	43	.403	1	13	4.68

Matt Montgomery

Pitches: Right Bats: Right Pos: P   Ht: 6'4" Wt: 210 Born: 5/13/76 Age: 24

Year Team	Lg Org	HOW MUCH HE PITCHED						WHAT HE GAVE UP										THE RESULTS				
		G	GS	CG	GF	IP	BFP	H	R	ER	HR	SH	SF	HB	TBB	IBB	SO	WP	Bk	W	L	Pct.	ShO	Sv	ERA
1997 Yakima	A- LA	11	9	0	0	55.1	229	48	23	15	3	2	0	1	17	0	38	2	2	2	2	.500	0	0	2.44
Great Falls	R+ LA	4	4	0	0	23	92	24	11	10	1	0	0	0	3	0	6	1	0	1	1	.500	0	0	3.91
1998 San Berndno	A+ LA	63	0	0	58	79	331	69	31	28	6	4	3	1	27	4	81	5	1	4	6	.400	0	26	3.19
Albuquerque	AAA LA	3	0	0	3	3	11	5	0	0	0	1	0		2	0	3	0	0	0	0	.000	0	2	0.00
1999 San Antonio	AA LA	58	0	0	56	55.1	254	65	35	16	1	3	2	3	17	2	39	5	1	5	6	.455	0	26	2.60
3 Min. YEARS		139	13	0	117	215.2	917	206	100	69	11	10	5	6	66	6	167	13	4	12	15	.444	0	54	2.88

Ray Montgomery

Bats: Right Throws: Right Pos: OF   Ht: 6'3" Wt: 225 Born: 8/8/70 Age: 29

Year Team	Lg Org	BATTING															BASERUNNING				PERCENTAGES		
		G	AB	H	2B	3B	HR	TB	R	RBI	TBB	IBB	SO	HBP	SH	SF	SB	CS	SB%	GDP	Avg	OBP	SLG
1990 Auburn	A- Hou	61	193	45	8	1	0	55	19	13	23	1	32	1	4	1	11	5	.69	5	.233	.317	.285
1991 Burlington	A Hou	120	433	109	24	3	3	148	60	57	37	1	66	8	11	2	17	14	.55	10	.252	.321	.342
1992 Jackson	AA Hou	51	148	31	4	1	1	40	13	10	7	2	27	0	1	1	4	1	.80	5	.209	.244	.270
1993 Tucson	AAA Hou	15	50	17	3	1	2	28	9	6	5	0	7	1	1	0	1	2	.33	1	.340	.411	.560
Jackson	AA Hou	100	338	95	16	3	10	147	50	59	36	1	54	6	1	6	12	6	.67	7	.281	.355	.435
1994 Tucson	AAA Hou	103	332	85	19	6	7	137	51	51	35	6	54	2	2	3	5	3	.63	9	.256	.328	.413
1995 Jackson	AA Hou	35	127	38	8	1	10	78	24	24	13	2	13	5	0	1	6	3	.67	3	.299	.384	.614
Tucson	AAA Hou	88	291	88	19	0	11	140	48	68	24	1	58	2	1	8	5	3	.63	3	.302	.351	.481
1996 Tucson	AAA Hou	100	360	110	20	0	22	196	70	75	59	7	54	3	0	1	7	1	.88	12	.306	.407	.544
1997 New Orleans	AAA Hou	20	73	21	5	0	6	44	17	13	11	0	15	0	0	0	1	1	.50	2	.288	.381	.603
1998 New Orleans	AAA Hou	75	272	79	18	1	9	126	42	45	26	0	48	3	0	4	4	2	.67	8	.290	.354	.463
1999 Nashville	AAA Pit	90	272	90	23	2	16	165	57	52	24	0	49	5	1	5	5	3	.63	5	.331	.389	.607
1996 Houston	NL	12	14	3	1	0	1	7	4	4	1	0	5	0	0	0	0	0	.00	0	.214	.267	.500
1997 Houston	NL	29	68	16	4	1	0	22	8	4	5	0	18	0	0	3	0	0	.00	2	.235	.276	.324
1998 Houston	NL	6	5	2	0	0	0	2	2	0	0	0	0	0	0	0	0	0	.00	0	.400	.400	.400
10 Min. YEARS		858	2889	808	167	19	97	1304	460	473	300	21	477	36	22	32	78	44	.64	70	.280	.351	.451
3 Maj. YEARS		47	87	21	5	1	1	31	14	8	6	0	23	0	0	3	0	0	.00	2	.241	.281	.356

Norm Montoya

Pitches: Left Bats: Left Pos: P   Ht: 6'2" Wt: 215 Born: 9/24/70 Age: 29

Year Team	Lg Org	HOW MUCH HE PITCHED						WHAT HE GAVE UP										THE RESULTS				
		G	GS	CG	GF	IP	BFP	H	R	ER	HR	SH	SF	HB	TBB	IBB	SO	WP	Bk	W	L	Pct.	ShO	Sv	ERA
1990 Angels	R Ana	10	6	1	2	47	199	49	20	11	1	1	0	1	7	0	28	0	0	3	3	.500	0	1	2.11
Quad City	A Ana	4	4	1	0	28.2	117	30	12	10	0	1	1	0	6	0	13	0	1	3	1	.750	0	0	3.14
1991 Quad City	A Ana	8	8	0	0	40.1	186	55	27	23	2	1	1	0	12	0	22	4	1	4	1	.800	0	0	5.13
Palm Spring	A+ Ana	17	17	1	0	105	455	117	64	48	10	3	4	2	26	4	45	3	1	4	7	.364	0	0	4.11
1992 Palm Spring	A+ Ana	14	6	2	6	43.2	194	42	21	18	3	4	2	1	19	1	46	2	1	2	3	.400	0	0	3.71
1993 Palm Spring	A+ Ana	28	4	0	8	63.2	286	83	38	34	0	3	4	3	21	5	35	6	0	1	3	.250	0	0	4.81
1994 Stockton	A+ Mil	11	0	0	3	16.1	65	12	6	4	1	2	0	1	3	0	15	0	0	0	1	.000	0	1	2.20
El Paso	AA Mil	9	0	0	4	12.1	48	10	5	4	0	1	0	0	4	2	8	0	0	1	1	.500	0	1	2.92
1995 El Paso	AA Mil	51	0	0	9	76.1	330	88	36	29	3	5	2	2	18	5	43	4	0	2	5	.286	0	2	3.42
1996 New Orleans	AAA Mil	11	0	0	6	12.2	63	23	16	12	3	0	0	0	5	1	8	0	0	0	0	.000	0	2	8.53
El Paso	AA Mil	24	17	1	4	125.1	545	153	74	65	6	3	2	2	28	2	73	4	1	9	8	.529	0	1	4.67
1997 Tucson	AAA Mil	27	24	0	2	131	589	175	100	91	16	5	4	4	38	0	75	6	2	6	10	.375	0	0	6.25
1998 Midland	AA Ana	9	5	0	0	36.2	156	46	21	19	3	3	0	1	6	0	15	5	0	2	3	.400	0	0	4.66
1999 Edmonton	AAA Ana	38	3	0	14	67.1	296	92	49	42	5	3	3	3	17	2	30	2	0	4	1	.800	0	0	5.61
10 Min. YEARS		261	94	6	58	806.1	3529	975	489	410	53	35	21	20	210	22	456	36	7	41	47	.466	0	8	4.58

Eric Moody

Pitches: Right Bats: Right Pos: P   Ht: 6'6" Wt: 185 Born: 1/6/71 Age: 29

Year Team	Lg Org	HOW MUCH HE PITCHED						WHAT HE GAVE UP										THE RESULTS				
		G	GS	CG	GF	IP	BFP	H	R	ER	HR	SH	SF	HB	TBB	IBB	SO	WP	Bk	W	L	Pct.	ShO	Sv	ERA
1993 Erie	A- Tex	17	7	0	4	54	229	54	30	23	2	1	0	2	13	1	33	3	1	3	3	.500	0	0	3.83
1994 Hudson Val	A- Tex	15	12	1	1	89	355	82	32	28	2	2	3	2	18	1	68	3	4	7	3	.700	0	0	2.83
1995 Charlotte	A+ Tex	13	13	2	0	88.1	353	84	30	27	2	3	1	5	13	0	57	0	0	5	5	.500	2	0	2.75
1996 Tulsa	AA Tex	44	5	0	29	95.2	395	92	40	38	4	1	3	1	23	2	80	4	0	6	3	.667	0	16	3.57
1997 Okla City	AAA Tex	35	10	1	10	112	469	114	49	43	13	5	1	4	21	1	72	1	0	5	6	.455	1	1	3.46
1998 Oklahoma	AAA Tex	45	6	0	29	101.1	436	112	51	38	9	2	4	6	23	4	73	4	1	6	6	.500	0	12	3.38
1999 Charlotte	A+ Tex	1	1	0	0	2	9	2	2	2	0	0	1	0	0	0	1	0	0	0	0	.000	0	0	9.00
Oklahoma	AAA Tex	39	1	0	20	73.2	309	78	33	28	5	3	3	4	13	3	31	3	0	7	4	.636	0	4	3.42
1997 Texas	AL	10	1	0	3	19	82	26	10	9	4	0	1	0	2	0	12	0	0	0	1	.000	0	0	4.26
7 Min. YEARS		209	55	4	93	616	2555	618	267	227	38	16	17	24	124	12	415	18	6	41	31	.569	3	33	3.32

Brandon Moore

Bats: Right **Throws:** Right **Pos:** SS **Ht:** 5'11" **Wt:** 175 **Born:** 8/23/72 **Age:** 27

								BATTING										BASERUNNING				PERCENTAGES		
Year Team	Lg Org	G	AB	H	2B	3B	HR	TB	R	RBI	TBB	IBB	SO	HBP	SH	SF	SB	CS	SB%	GDP	Avg	OBP	SLG
1994 White Sox	R CWS	4	10	1	0	0	0	1	1	0	1	0	1	0	0	0	0	0	.00	0	.100	.182	.100
Hickory	A CWS	60	230	57	5	2	1	69	43	26	33	1	28	1	7	3	10	6	.63	7	.248	.341	.300
1995 South Bend	A CWS	132	510	131	9	3	0	146	75	37	48	1	49	3	7	5	34	8	.81	15	.257	.322	.286
1996 Pr William	A+ CWS	125	439	106	13	2	1	126	56	41	82	1	70	3	2	3	4	11	.45	14	.241	.362	.287
1997 Birmingham	AA CWS	125	414	106	15	1	1	126	58	47	45	0	48	1	21	4	7	7	.36	11	.256	.328	.304
1998 Calgary	AAA CWS	86	244	51	4	1	2	63	37	19	20	1	30	2	3	1	5	3	.63	6	.209	.273	.258
1999 Birmingham	AA CWS	36	119	23	3	2	0	30	11	13	17	0	20	0	2	1	4	2	.67	9	.193	.292	.252
Charlotte	AAA CWS	90	299	85	21	2	1	113	44	41	21	1	41	2	13	4	3	2	.60	6	.284	.331	.378
6 Min. YEARS		658	2265	560	70	13	6	674	325	224	267	5	287	12	55	21	69	39	.64	68	.247	.327	.298

Kenderick Moore

Bats: Right **Throws:** Right **Pos:** OF **Ht:** 5'10" **Wt:** 175 **Born:** 5/17/73 **Age:** 27

								BATTING										BASERUNNING				PERCENTAGES		
Year Team	Lg Org	G	AB	H	2B	3B	HR	TB	R	RBI	TBB	IBB	SO	HBP	SH	SF	SB	CS	SB%	GDP	Avg	OBP	SLG
1996 Spokane	A- KC	52	204	53	6	1	2	67	37	25	23	0	29	3	5	2	19	3	.86	4	.260	.341	.328
1997 Lansing	A KC	112	456	130	16	8	6	180	105	42	45	0	78	14	2	5	43	14	.75	5	.285	.370	.395
1998 Wilmington	A+ KC	121	387	105	17	4	5	145	54	41	45	0	51	12	6	4	22	19	.54	6	.271	.362	.375
1999 Wichita	AA KC	80	243	61	11	0	0	72	36	27	20	0	55	11	3	2	19	10	.66	4	.251	.333	.296
4 Min. YEARS		365	1290	349	50	13	13	464	232	135	133	0	213	45	16	13	103	46	.69	19	.271	.356	.360

Marcus Moore

Pitches: Right **Bats:** Both **Pos:** P **Ht:** 6'5" **Wt:** 204 **Born:** 11/2/70 **Age:** 29

		HOW MUCH HE PITCHED						WHAT HE GAVE UP												THE RESULTS					
Year Team	Lg Org	G	GS	CG	GF	IP	BFP	H	R	ER	HR	SH	SF	HB	TBB	IBB	SO	WP	Bk	W	L	Pct.	ShO	Sv	ERA
1989 Bend	A- Ana	14	14	1	0	81.2	373	84	55	41	2	3	4	5	51	1	74	14	6	2	5	.286	0	0	4.52
1990 Quad City	A Ana	27	27	2	0	160.1	717	150	83	59	6	2	7	3	106	0	160	13	9	16	5	.762	1	0	3.31
1991 Dunedin	A+ Tor	27	25	2	1	160.2	694	139	78	66	3	9	5	4	99	3	115	12	9	6	13	.316	0	0	3.70
1992 Knoxville	AA Tor	36	14	1	18	106.1	493	110	82	66	10	3	7	5	79	0	85	17	5	5	10	.333	0	0	5.59
1993 Central Val	A+ Col	8	0	0	8	12	53	7	3	1	0	1	0	0	9	0	15	1	0	1	0	1.000	0	2	0.75
Colo Sprngs	AAA Col	30	0	0	14	44.1	209	54	26	22	3	3	1	1	29	0	38	4	0	1	5	.167	0	4	4.47
1994 Colo Sprngs	AAA Col	19	8	0	5	54	283	67	59	48	5	1	1	1	61	0	54	2	0	3	4	.429	0	0	8.00
1995 Indianapols	AAA Cin	7	1	0	2	12.2	62	13	8	7	0	1	0	0	14	2	6	0	0	1	0	1.000	0	1	4.97
Chattanooga	AA Cin	36	0	0	8	43.1	192	31	24	24	6	2	2	2	34	1	57	3	1	6	1	.857	0	2	4.98
1996 Indianapols	AAA Cin	15	15	0	0	88.2	369	72	41	34	8	1	2	3	38	1	70	2	0	4	7	.364	0	0	3.45
1997 Akron	AA Cle	13	10	1	0	71	323	84	50	39	9	5	3	1	32	1	63	4	1	3	5	.375	0	0	4.94
Buffalo	AAA Cle	10	10	3	0	71	291	54	26	20	6	1	0	0	31	1	72	0	0	5	3	.625	1	0	2.54
1998 Buffalo	AAA Cle	11	7	0	3	47.2	220	41	35	30	9	1	2	2	41	1	43	2	0	3	5	.375	0	0	5.66
Akron	AA Tor	23	12	0	10	82	370	78	49	41	10	4	1	2	54	2	90	6	2	5	2	.286	0	6	4.50
1999 Syracuse	AAA Tor	7	0	0	5	12	62	14	15	15	2	1	0	1	13	0	12	1	0	0	1	.000	0	0	11.25
Zion	IND —	17	15	1	0	100	457	95	58	43	6	1	1	5	64	0	114	1	0	8	3	.727	0	0	3.87
1993 Colorado	NL	27	0	0	8	26.1	128	30	25	20	4	0	4	1	20	0	13	4	0	3	1	.750	0	0	6.84
1994 Colorado	NL	29	0	0	13	33.2	158	33	26	23	4	1	0	5	21	2	33	4	1	1	1	.500	0	0	6.15
1996 Cincinnati	NL	23	0	0	11	26.1	129	26	21	17	3	3	3	3	22	1	27	1	0	3	5	.500	0	2	5.81
11 Min. YEARS		300	158	11	74	1147.2	5168	1093	692	556	85	39	36	35	755	13	1068	82	33	66	72	.478	2	15	4.36
3 Maj. YEARS		79	0	0	32	86.1	415	89	72	60	11	4	7	8	63	3	73	9	1	7	5	.583	0	2	6.25

David Moraga

Pitches: Left **Bats:** Left **Pos:** P **Ht:** 6'0" **Wt:** 184 **Born:** 7/8/75 **Age:** 24

		HOW MUCH HE PITCHED						WHAT HE GAVE UP												THE RESULTS					
Year Team	Lg Org	G	GS	CG	GF	IP	BFP	H	R	ER	HR	SH	SF	HB	TBB	IBB	SO	WP	Bk	W	L	Pct.	ShO	Sv	ERA
1994 Expos	R Mon	14	0	0	7	23.2	100	23	11	4	0	3	1	0	8	1	13	4	2	3	5	.375	0	0	1.52
1995 Wst Plm Bch	A+ Mon	3	3	0	0	16	75	20	7	7	0	0	0	0	10	0	10	0	0	1	1	.500	0	0	3.94
Albany	A Mon	25	24	1	0	147.2	620	136	63	44	6	6	4	1	46	0	109	10	0	8	8	.500	0	0	2.68
1996 Wst Plm Bch	A+ Mon	29	20	1	1	125.2	560	138	74	64	6	4	7	4	50	0	96	12	0	7	10	.412	0	0	4.58
1997 Wst Plm Bch	A+ Mon	13	7	0	3	47.2	207	50	27	26	3	1	2	1	18	0	37	6	0	1	4	.200	0	0	4.91
1998 Jupiter	A+ Mon	25	0	0	11	45	180	37	16	14	2	5	2	1	9	0	38	3	0	5	2	.714	0	0	2.80
Harrisburg	AA Mon	19	4	0	5	40	182	42	27	22	3	2	1	3	22	2	23	5	0	1	4	.200	0	0	4.95
1999 Ottawa	AAA Mon	4	3	0	0	16	76	24	14	11	4	1	2	0	5	0	10	1	0	1	2	.333	0	0	6.19
Jupiter	A+ Mon	23	23	2	0	137.2	575	124	63	56	8	4	0	4	44	0	91	6	0	8	6	.571	2	0	3.66
Harrisburg	AA Mon	1	0	0	0	3	11	1	0	0	0	0	0	1	0	0	0	0	0	1	0	1.000	0	0	0.00
6 Min. YEARS		156	84	4	27	602.1	2586	595	302	248	32	26	19	15	212	3	427	47	2	36	42	.462	2	3	3.71

Francisco Morales

Bats: Right **Throws:** Right **Pos:** C **Ht:** 6'3" **Wt:** 180 **Born:** 1/31/73 **Age:** 27

								BATTING										BASERUNNING				PERCENTAGES		
Year Team	Lg Org	G	AB	H	2B	3B	HR	TB	R	RBI	TBB	IBB	SO	HBP	SH	SF	SB	CS	SB%	GDP	Avg	OBP	SLG
1992 Huntington	R+ ChC	13	39	7	1	0	1	11	4	9	10	0	13	1	1	0	1	2	.33	1	.179	.360	.282
Geneva	A- ChC	19	49	11	2	0	0	13	3	0	7	1	21	0	4	0	0	0	.00	0	.224	.321	.265
1993 Peoria	A ChC	19	49	10	1	1	3	22	9	11	9	0	16	0	4	0	1	0	1.00	2	.204	.328	.449
Geneva	A- ChC	45	123	24	4	0	2	34	12	20	15	0	41	1	0	2	1	1	.50	2	.195	.284	.276
1994 Orlando	AA ChC	22	58	12	0	0	2	18	3	10	7	0	21	0	0	0	1	0	1.00	1	.207	.292	.310
Daytona	A+ ChC	38	120	29	7	1	1	41	9	10	9	0	37	1	0	1	1	0	1.00	2	.242	.298	.342
1995 Orlando	AA ChC	2	6	1	0	0	0	1	0	0	1	0	2	0	0	0	0	0	.00	0	.167	.286	.167
Daytona	A+ ChC	36	101	26	6	0	6	50	17	23	16	0	28	3	0	2	1	1	.50	2	.257	.369	.495
Savannah	A StL	19	75	11	3	0	2	20	3	4	4	0	23	1	0	1	0	2	.00	2	.147	.198	.267

Year Team	Lg Org	G	AB	H	2B	3B	HR	TB	R	RBI	TBB	IBB	SO	HBP	SH	SF	SB	CS	SB%	GDP	Avg	OBP	SLG
St. Pete	A+ StL	28	87	17	5	0	2	28	10	10	11	0	29	1	0	0	1	0	1.00	3	.195	.293	.322
1996 St. Pete	A+ StL	21	67	14	5	1	1	24	6	6	5	0	25	2	0	1	0	0	.00	1	.209	.280	.358
Wst Plm Bch	A+ Mon	75	259	71	20	2	3	104	32	42	19	0	79	5	3	1	3	1	.75	5	.274	.335	.402
1997 Ottawa	AAA Mon	7	18	2	0	1	1	7	2	4	1	0	6	0	0	0	0	0	.00	0	.111	.158	.389
Wst Plm Bch	A+ Mon	45	127	36	7	1	4	57	15	13	10	1	37	0	1	0	0	0	.00	2	.283	.336	.449
Harrisburg	AA Mon	16	49	10	1	0	2	17	5	4	3	1	22	1	0	1	0	0	.00	0	.204	.259	.347
1998 Harrisburg	AA Mon	96	311	67	11	1	9	107	25	45	30	4	86	5	0	2	1	1	.50	12	.215	.293	.344
1999 Ottawa	AAA Mon	99	345	79	11	1	10	122	43	44	31	1	93	5	1	5	1	1	.50	10	.229	.298	.354
8 Min. YEARS		600	1883	427	84	9	49	676	198	255	188	8	579	26	10	16	10	11	.48	47	.227	.303	.359

Willie Morales

Bats: Right Throws: Right Pos: C   Ht: 5'10" Wt: 182 Born: 9/7/72 Age: 27

Year Team	Lg Org	G	AB	H	2B	3B	HR	TB	R	RBI	TBB	IBB	SO	HBP	SH	SF	SB	CS	SB%	GDP	Avg	OBP	SLG
1993 Sou Oregon	A- Oak	60	208	56	16	0	1	75	34	27	19	2	36	4	1	4	0	3	.00	2	.269	.336	.361
1994 W Michigan	A Oak	111	380	101	26	0	13	166	47	51	36	4	64	3	3	2	3	5	.38	12	.266	.333	.437
1995 Modesto	A+ Oak	109	419	116	32	0	4	160	49	60	28	1	75	7	2	4	1	4	.20	13	.277	.330	.382
1996 Huntsville	AA Oak	108	377	110	24	0	18	188	54	73	38	2	67	7	4	6	0	2	.00	11	.292	.362	.499
1997 Huntsville	AA Oak	36	136	37	11	0	3	57	19	24	17	0	24	0	0	3	1	0	1.00	1	.272	.346	.419
Edmonton	AAA Oak	56	179	52	12	0	5	79	23	35	11	0	27	0	3	3	0	2	.00	4	.291	.320	.441
1998 Edmonton	AAA Oak	73	242	47	13	0	5	75	25	30	17	0	47	1	1	1	0	1	.00	8	.194	.249	.310
1999 Vancouver	AAA Oak	5	14	2	1	0	0	3	2	2	1	0	4	0	1	1	0	0	.00	2	.143	.188	.214
Midland	AA Oak	102	343	96	27	0	16	171	43	71	24	0	54	6	2	4	2	0	1.00	8	.280	.334	.499
7 Min. YEARS		660	2298	617	162	0	65	974	296	373	191	9	398	28	17	28	7	17	.29	62	.268	.328	.424

Juan Moreno

Pitches: Left Bats: Left Pos: P   Ht: 6'1" Wt: 190 Born: 2/28/75 Age: 25

Year Team	Lg Org	G	GS	CG	GF	IP	BFP	H	R	ER	HR	SH	SF	HB	TBB	IBB	SO	WP	Bk	W	L	Pct.	ShO	Sv	ERA
1995 Athletics	R Oak	20	0	0	8	44.2	181	36	10	6	1	1	1	0	20	0	49	2	5	6	2	.750	0	1	1.21
1996 W Michigan	A Oak	38	11	0	5	107	475	98	60	52	6	6	6	2	69	5	97	6	2	4	6	.400	0	0	4.37
1999 Tulsa	AA Tex	42	0	0	27	62.2	255	33	20	16	5	2	3	3	32	2	83	6	0	4	3	.571	0	3	2.30
3 Min. YEARS		100	11	0	40	214.1	911	167	90	74	12	9	10	5	121	7	229	14	7	14	11	.560	0	3	3.11

Julio Moreno

Pitches: Right Bats: Right Pos: P   Ht: 6'1" Wt: 165 Born: 10/23/75 Age: 24

Year Team	Lg Org	G	GS	CG	GF	IP	BFP	H	R	ER	HR	SH	SF	HB	TBB	IBB	SO	WP	Bk	W	L	Pct.	ShO	Sv	ERA
1994 Orioles	R Bal	4	2	0	0	8.1	14	14	14	11	2	0	2	0	1	0	6	0	0	0	2	.000	0	0	11.88
1995 Orioles	R Bal	5	5	1	0	34	131	17	9	6	0	1	2	1	7	0	29	1	1	2	0	.600	1	0	1.59
Bluefield	R+ Bal	9	8	0	1	49.1	214	61	31	23	3	1	3	0	12	0	36	3	1	4	3	.571	0	0	4.20
1996 Frederick	A+ Bal	28	26	0	1	162	682	167	80	63	14	8	0	9	38	0	147	9	3	9	10	.474	0	0	3.50
1997 Bowie	AA Bal	27	25	1	0	138.2	596	141	76	59	20	2	3	6	64	4	106	6	3	9	6	.600	0	0	3.83
1999 Bowie	R Bal	4	2	0	0	10	39	8	4	2	1	0	1	0	5	0	5	0	0	1	0	1.000	0	0	1.80
Bowie	AA Bal	10	10	0	0	44.1	202	46	29	26	9	1	2	1	27	0	25	4	0	2	2	.500	0	0	5.28
5 Min. YEARS		87	78	2	2	446.2	1905	454	243	190	49	13	13	17	150	4	354	23	8	28	25	.528	1	0	3.83

Shea Morenz

Bats: Left Throws: Right Pos: DH-OF   Ht: 6'2" Wt: 205 Born: 1/22/74 Age: 26

Year Team	Lg Org	G	AB	H	2B	3B	HR	TB	R	RBI	TBB	IBB	SO	HBP	SH	SF	SB	CS	SB%	GDP	Avg	OBP	SLG
1995 Oneonta	A- NYY	33	116	32	5	3	1	46	11	20	15	0	27	3	0	1	1	4	.20	4	.276	.370	.397
1996 Greensboro	A NYY	91	338	84	14	4	2	112	40	48	38	4	92	12	2	3	13	3	.81	2	.249	.343	.331
1997 Tampa	A+ NYY	117	403	95	14	1	7	132	43	44	18	3	101	7	6	5	2	3	.40	7	.236	.277	.328
1998 Norwich	AA NYY	116	409	103	18	3	15	172	51	52	31	4	109	10	2	6	7	5	.58	7	.252	.316	.421
Las Vegas	AAA SD	13	37	11	5	0	1	19	5	6	1	0	9	2	0	0	0	0	.00	2	.297	.350	.514
1999 Mobile	AA SD	21	57	15	5	0	0	20	6	7	4	0	27	1	0	1	1	1	.50	0	.263	.317	.351
Padres	R SD	4	12	5	2	1	0	9	5	3	3	0	2	0	0	0	0	0	.00	0	.417	.500	.750
5 Min. YEARS		395	1372	345	63	12	26	510	161	180	110	11	367	35	10	17	24	16	.60	22	.251	.319	.372

Ramon Moreta

Bats: Right Throws: Right Pos: OF   Ht: 5'11" Wt: 185 Born: 9/5/75 Age: 24

Year Team	Lg Org	G	AB	H	2B	3B	HR	TB	R	RBI	TBB	IBB	SO	HBP	SH	SF	SB	CS	SB%	GDP	Avg	OBP	SLG
1997 Great Falls	R+ LA	68	265	89	6	2	1	102	45	20	18	0	38	1	6	0	29	17	.63	5	.336	.380	.385
1998 San Berndno	A+ LA	134	536	138	19	7	1	174	67	24	44	1	109	2	11	0	46	23	.67	8	.257	.316	.325
Albuquerque	AAA LA	8	27	10	1	2	0	15	5	3	1	0	9	0	0	0	2	2	.50	0	.370	.379	.556
1999 San Antonio	AA LA	117	397	121	13	3	2	146	56	42	18	0	66	0	11	2	26	16	.62	12	.305	.333	.368
3 Min. YEARS		327	1225	358	39	14	4	437	173	89	81	1	222	3	28	3	103	58	.64	25	.292	.337	.357

Scott Morgan

Bats: Right Throws: Right Pos: OF   Ht: 6'7" Wt: 230 Born: 7/19/73 Age: 26

Year Team	Lg Org	G	AB	H	2B	3B	HR	TB	R	RBI	TBB	IBB	SO	HBP	SH	SF	SB	CS	SB%	GDP	Avg	OBP	SLG
1995 Watertown	A- Cle	66	244	64	18	0	2	88	42	33	26	0	63	8	0	4	6	5	.55	11	.262	.348	.361

Year Team	Lg Org	G	AB	H	2B	3B	HR	TB	R	RBI	TBB	IBB	SO	HBP	SH	SF	SB	CS	SB%	GDP	Avg	OBP	SLG
1996 Columbus	A Cle	87	305	95	25	1	22	188	62	80	46	0	70	11	0	4	9	5	.64	5	.311	.415	.616
1997 Kinston	A+ Cle	95	368	116	32	3	23	223	86	67	47	3	87	5	0	4	4	2	.67	8	.315	.396	.606
Akron	AA Cle	21	69	12	3	0	2	21	11	6	8	0	20	1	0	1	1	0	1.00	0	.174	.266	.304
1998 Akron	AA Cle	119	456	134	31	4	25	248	95	89	56	1	124	8	0	4	4	5	.44	9	.294	.378	.544
1999 Akron	AA Cle	88	344	97	26	2	26	205	72	70	38	5	96	2	0	1	6	1	.86	4	.282	.356	.596
Buffalo	AAA Cle	48	171	44	9	0	8	77	32	31	18	0	38	3	0	3	2	3	.40	2	.257	.333	.450
5 Min. YEARS		524	1957	562	144	10	108	1050	400	376	239	9	498	38	0	21	32	21	.60	39	.287	.372	.537

Mike Moriarty

Bats: Right **Throws:** Right **Pos:** SS **Ht:** 6'0" **Wt:** 190 **Born:** 3/8/74 **Age:** 26

Year Team	Lg Org	G	AB	H	2B	3B	HR	TB	R	RBI	TBB	IBB	SO	HBP	SH	SF	SB	CS	SB%	GDP	Avg	OBP	SLG
1995 Fort Wayne	A Min	62	203	46	6	3	4	70	26	26	27	1	44	2	2	3	8	0	1.00	1	.227	.319	.345
1996 Fort Myers	A+ Min	133	428	107	18	2	3	138	76	39	59	0	67	8	5	4	14	15	.48	2	.250	.349	.322
1997 New Britain	AA Min	135	421	93	22	5	6	143	60	48	53	1	68	3	10	5	12	5	.71	10	.221	.309	.340
1998 New Britain	AA Min	38	112	32	8	0	4	52	22	15	17	0	16	3	3	1	0	4	.00	1	.286	.391	.464
Salt Lake	AAA Min	64	161	36	8	2	3	57	21	19	22	0	39	1	2	1	2	1	.67	1	.224	.319	.354
1999 Salt Lake	AAA Min	128	380	98	21	7	4	145	63	51	56	1	62	6	11	5	6	4	.60	9	.258	.358	.382
5 Min. YEARS		560	1705	412	83	19	24	605	268	198	234	3	296	23	33	19	42	29	.59	24	.242	.338	.355

Russ Morman

Bats: Right **Throws:** Right **Pos:** 1B **Ht:** 6'4" **Wt:** 225 **Born:** 4/28/62 **Age:** 38

Year Team	Lg Org	G	AB	H	2B	3B	HR	TB	R	RBI	TBB	IBB	SO	HBP	SH	SF	SB	CS	SB%	GDP	Avg	OBP	SLG
1983 Glens Falls	AA CWS	71	233	57	9	1	3	77	29	32	40	0	65	5	0	3	8	3	.73	—	.245	.363	.330
1984 Appleton	A CWS	122	424	111	17	7	7	163	68	80	80	3	93	8	4	4	29	6	.83	17	.262	.386	.384
1985 Glens Falls	A CWS	119	422	131	24	5	17	216	64	81	65	3	51	5	1	3	11	10	.52	8	.310	.406	.512
Buffalo	AAA CWS	21	64	19	3	1	7	45	16	14	10	0	16	2	0	0	2	0	1.00	2	.297	.408	.703
1986	AAA CWS	106	365	97	17	2	13	157	52	57	54	4	58	5	0	3	3	1	.75	5	.266	.365	.430
1987 Hawaii	AAA CWS	89	294	79	19	2	9	129	52	53	60	3	56	1	0	3	5	3	.63	4	.269	.391	.439
1988 Vancouver	AAA CWS	69	257	77	8	1	5	102	40	45	32	2	48	1	0	2	4	3	.57	3	.300	.377	.397
1989 Vancouver	AAA CWS	61	216	60	14	1	1	79	18	23	18	2	41	1	0	1	1	6	.14	5	.278	.335	.366
1990 Omaha	AAA KC	121	436	130	14	9	13	201	67	81	51	2	78	3	0	5	21	5	.81	7	.298	.372	.461
1991 Omaha	AAA KC	88	316	83	15	3	7	125	46	50	43	1	53	2	1	6	10	6	.63	12	.263	.349	.396
1992 Nashville	AAA Cin	101	384	119	31	2	14	196	53	63	36	3	60	1	0	2	5	2	.71	6	.310	.369	.510
1993 Buffalo	AAA Pit	119	409	131	34	2	22	235	79	77	48	4	59	2	0	5	0	3	.00	7	.320	.390	.574
1994 Edmonton	AAA Fla	114	406	142	30	2	19	233	69	82	36	0	62	1	0	4	0	1	1.00	6	.350	.400	.574
1995 Charlotte	AAA Fla	44	169	53	7	1	6	80	28	36	14	3	22	1	0	3	2	2	.50	4	.314	.364	.473
1996 Charlotte	AAA Fla	80	289	96	18	1	18	170	59	77	29	2	51	1	0	4	2	4	.33	10	.332	.390	.588
1997 Charlotte	AAA Fla	117	395	126	17	2	33	246	82	99	58	11	89	4	0	5	3	2	.60	6	.319	.407	.623
1998 Durham	AAA TB	98	367	104	26	1	10	162	48	67	32	0	65	3	0	3	0	1	.00	13	.283	.343	.441
1999 Calgary	AAA Fla	21	52	17	1	0	3	27	10	12	7	0	6	0	0	0	1	0	1.00	1	.327	.407	.519
1986 Chicago	AL	49	159	40	5	0	4	57	18	17	16	0	36	2	1	2	1	0	1.00	5	.252	.324	.358
1988 Chicago	AL	40	75	18	2	0	0	20	8	3	3	0	17	0	2	0	0	0	.00	5	.240	.269	.267
1989 Chicago	AL	37	58	13	2	0	0	15	5	8	6	1	16	0	2	1	1	0	1.00	1	.224	.292	.259
1990 Kansas City	AL	12	37	10	4	2	1	21	5	3	3	0	3	0	0	1	0	0	.00	0	.270	.317	.568
1991 Kansas City	AL	12	23	6	0	0	0	6	1	1	1	1	5	0	0	0	0	0	.00	0	.261	.292	.261
1994 Florida	NL	13	33	7	0	1	1	12	2	2	2	0	9	1	0	0	0	0	.00	1	.212	.278	.364
1995 Florida	NL	34	72	20	2	1	3	33	9	7	3	0	12	1	0	0	0	0	.00	5	.278	.316	.458
1996 Florida	NL	6	6	1	1	0	0	2	0	0	1	0	2	0	0	0	0	0	.00	0	.167	.286	.333
1997 Florida	NL	4	7	2	1	0	0	6	3	2	0	0	2	0	0	0	1	0	1.00	0	.286	.286	.857
17 Min. YEARS		1561	5498	1632	304	43	207	2643	880	1029	713	43	973	46	6	56	116	57	.67	—	.297	.379	.481
9 Maj. YEARS		207	470	117	17	4	10	172	51	43	35	2	102	4	5	4	3	0	1.00	17	.249	.304	.366

Bobby Morris

Bats: Left **Throws:** Right **Pos:** DH **Ht:** 6'0" **Wt:** 175 **Born:** 11/22/72 **Age:** 27

Year Team	Lg Org	G	AB	H	2B	3B	HR	TB	R	RBI	TBB	IBB	SO	HBP	SH	SF	SB	CS	SB%	GDP	Avg	OBP	SLG
1993 Huntington	R+ ChC	50	170	49	8	3	1	66	29	24	24	0	29	1	2	3	6	7	.46	2	.288	.374	.388
1994 Peoria	A ChC	101	362	128	33	1	7	184	61	64	53	4	63	7	10	2	7	7	.50	10	.354	.443	.508
1995 Daytona	A+ ChC	95	344	106	18	2	2	134	44	55	38	6	46	8	2	5	22	8	.73	5	.308	.385	.390
1996 Orlando	AA ChC	131	465	122	29	3	8	181	72	62	65	4	73	6	0	8	12	14	.46	12	.262	.355	.389
1997 Orlando	AA ChC	4	16	5	1	0	0	6	3	1	2	0	3	0	0	0	0	0	.00	0	.313	.389	.375
Kinston	A+ Cle	10	32	5	1	0	2	12	6	10	4	0	6	2	0	1	0	0	.00	1	.156	.282	.375
Akron	AA Cle	42	119	30	9	1	1	44	17	15	22	0	21	2	2	3	1	2	.33	3	.252	.375	.370
1998 Kinston	A+ Cle	25	65	17	2	1	2	27	11	14	6	0	12	3	3	1	2	1	.67	1	.262	.347	.415
1999 Tulsa	AA Tex	6	21	7	2	0	0	9	0	2	4	0	1	1	0	0	0	0	.00	0	.333	.462	.429
7 Min. YEARS		464	1594	469	103	11	23	663	243	247	218	14	254	30	19	21	50	39	.56	36	.294	.385	.416

Jeremy Morris

Bats: Right **Throws:** Right **Pos:** DH **Ht:** 6'3" **Wt:** 225 **Born:** 10/7/74 **Age:** 25

Year Team	Lg Org	G	AB	H	2B	3B	HR	TB	R	RBI	TBB	IBB	SO	HBP	SH	SF	SB	CS	SB%	GDP	Avg	OBP	SLG
1997 Oneonta	A- NYY	68	239	67	19	1	2	94	44	28	29	0	47	5	0	3	10	3	.77	0	.280	.366	.393
1998 Tampa	A+ NYY	124	445	134	25	1	13	200	69	72	48	1	96	1	2	6	11	3	.79	8	.301	.366	.449
1999 Yankees	R NYY	5	15	6	0	0	2	12	7	7	6	0	5	1	0	0	0	0	.00	0	.400	.591	.800
Norwich	AA NYY	111	392	97	16	1	9	142	50	52	31	0	91	2	2	2	8	2	.80	7	.247	.304	.362
3 Min. YEARS		308	1091	304	60	3	26	448	170	159	114	1	239	9	4	11	29	8	.78	16	.279	.349	.411

Robbie Morrison

Pitches: Right Bats: Right Pos: P
Ht: 6'0" Wt: 215 Born: 12/7/76 Age: 23

Year Team	Lg Org	G	GS	CG	GF	IP	BFP	H	R	ER	HR	SH	SF	HB	TBB	IBB	SO	WP	Bk	W	L	Pct.	ShO	Sv	ERA
1998 Spokane	A- KC	26	0	0	22	25.1	111	15	8	6	2	2	1	1	18	2	33	1	0	3	0	1.000	0	13	2.13
1999 Wilmington	A+ KC	28	0	0	22	43.2	173	31	13	11	2	2	1	4	13	1	47	0	1	2	5	.286	0	6	2.27
Wichita	AA KC	15	0	0	11	22.1	97	26	7	5	0	0	0	1	7	1	21	3	0	2	0	1.000	0	5	2.01
2 Min. YEARS		69	0	0	55	91.1	381	72	28	22	4	4	2	6	38	4	101	4	1	7	5	.583	0	24	2.17

Paul Morse

Pitches: Right Bats: Right Pos: P
Ht: 6'2" Wt: 185 Born: 2/27/73 Age: 27

Year Team	Lg Org	G	GS	CG	GF	IP	BFP	H	R	ER	HR	SH	SF	HB	TBB	IBB	SO	WP	Bk	W	L	Pct.	ShO	Sv	ERA
1994 Elizabethtn	R+ Min	7	0	0	5	7.1	35	8	7	6	2	0	1	2	3	0	8	0	0	0	0	.000	0	0	7.36
Fort Wayne	A Min	16	0	0	11	20.1	97	27	15	13	2	1	0	2	10	0	17	0	0	0	3	.000	0	3	5.75
1995 Fort Myers	A+ Min	35	0	0	29	61.1	247	57	30	26	3	1	4	3	12	0	56	4	1	3	1	.750	0	15	3.82
1996 Fort Myers	A+ Min	13	0	0	12	14	50	8	4	4	1	0	0	0	5	0	10	0	0	1	0	1.000	0	9	2.57
Hardware Cy	AA Min	35	1	0	23	55.2	249	55	36	33	5	4	4	1	26	2	48	4	1	6	4	.600	0	4	5.34
1997 New Britain	AA Min	37	17	0	9	111.1	508	124	91	74	16	4	2	6	70	2	75	11	0	3	11	.214	0	1	5.98
1998 San Berndno	AA LA	30	26	0	2	153.2	696	160	110	90	13	6	9	6	77	0	116	17	2	7	14	.333	0	0	5.27
Albuquerque	AAA LA	2	2	0	0	15	59	8	5	5	1	0	1	3	6	0	11	0	0	1	1	.500	0	0	3.00
1999 Edmonton	AAA Ana	10	9	0	1	49.1	232	64	44	39	10	1	1	1	34	0	30	6	1	1	5	.167	0	0	7.11
Erie	AA Ana	15	14	2	0	97.1	419	83	44	36	9	5	1	5	54	0	52	10	1	8	6	.571	0	0	3.33
6 Min. YEARS		200	69	2	92	585.1	2592	594	386	326	62	22	23	29	297	4	423	52	6	30	45	.400	0	32	5.01

Mark Mortimer

Bats: Right Throws: Right Pos: C
Ht: 6'1" Wt: 215 Born: 9/15/75 Age: 24

Year Team	Lg Org	G	AB	H	2B	3B	HR	TB	R	RBI	TBB	IBB	SO	HBP	SH	SF	SB	CS	SB%	GDP	Avg	OBP	SLG
1997 Danville	R+ Atl	5	13	1	0	0	0	1	1	3	4	0	1	0	1	1	0	0	.00	1	.077	.278	.077
Eugene	A- Atl	53	174	53	7	2	2	70	25	21	16	0	24	0	2	2	1	1	.50	3	.305	.366	.402
1998 Macon	A Atl	28	94	28	7	0	5	50	21	26	18	0	11	2	0	0	1	0	1.00	2	.298	.421	.532
Danville	A+ Atl	98	338	80	11	2	6	113	32	33	41	4	53	5	0	2	0	4	.00	12	.237	.326	.334
1999 Greenville	AA Atl	11	30	7	1	0	0	8	4	5	3	0	7	0	0	1	0	0	.00	0	.233	.294	.267
Myrtle Bch	A+ Atl	73	250	69	13	0	3	91	29	31	28	0	48	5	3	4	1	0	1.00	6	.276	.355	.364
3 Min. YEARS		268	899	238	39	4	16	333	112	119	110	4	144	14	4	10	3	5	.38	24	.265	.350	.370

Julio Mosquera

Bats: Right Throws: Right Pos: C
Ht: 6'0" Wt: 190 Born: 1/29/72 Age: 28

Year Team	Lg Org	G	AB	H	2B	3B	HR	TB	R	RBI	TBB	IBB	SO	HBP	SH	SF	SB	CS	SB%	GDP	Avg	OBP	SLG
1993 Blue Jays	R Tor	35	108	28	3	2	0	35	9	15	8	0	16	1	2	1	3	2	.60	3	.259	.314	.324
1994 Medcine Hat	R+ Tor	59	229	78	17	1	2	103	33	44	18	3	35	3	0	2	3	3	.50	4	.341	.393	.450
1995 Hagerstown	A Tor	108	406	118	22	5	3	159	64	46	29	2	53	13	3	5	5	5	.50	13	.291	.353	.392
1996 Knoxville	AA Tor	92	318	73	17	0	2	96	36	31	29	1	55	4	3	1	6	5	.55	16	.230	.301	.302
Syracuse	AAA Tor	23	72	18	1	0	0	19	6	5	6	0	14	1	0	0	0	0	.00	1	.250	.316	.264
1997 Syracuse	AAA Tor	10	35	8	1	0	0	9	5	1	2	0	5	1	0	0	0	0	.00	2	.229	.289	.257
Knoxville	AA Tor	87	309	90	23	1	5	130	47	50	22	0	56	5	2	3	3	4	.43	10	.291	.345	.421
1998 Syracuse	AAA Tor	28	94	20	6	0	2	32	10	4	5	0	12	4	1	1	1	0	1.00	2	.213	.279	.340
Knoxville	AA Tor	12	43	12	1	0	0	13	4	8	4	0	7	0	0	1	0	1	.00	2	.279	.333	.302
1999 Orlando	AA TB	80	259	79	13	1	4	106	36	37	15	2	40	3	1	4	1	0	1.00	14	.305	.345	.409
1996 Toronto	AL	8	22	5	2	0	0	7	2	2	0	0	3	1	0	0	0	1	.00	0	.227	.261	.318
1997 Toronto	AL	3	8	2	1	0	0	3	0	0	0	0	2	0	0	0	0	0	.00	0	.250	.250	.375
7 Min. YEARS		534	1873	524	104	10	18	702	250	241	138	8	293	35	12	18	22	19	.54	65	.280	.338	.375
2 Maj. YEARS		11	30	7	3	0	0	10	2	2	0	0	5	1	0	0	0	1	.00	0	.233	.258	.333

Damian Moss

Pitches: Left Bats: Right Pos: P
Ht: 6'0" Wt: 187 Born: 11/24/76 Age: 23

Year Team	Lg Org	G	GS	CG	GF	IP	BFP	H	R	ER	HR	SH	SF	HB	TBB	IBB	SO	WP	Bk	W	L	Pct.	ShO	Sv	ERA
1994 Danville	R+ Atl	12	12	1	0	60.1	265	30	28	24	1	1	0	14	55	0	77	12	3	2	5	.286	1	0	3.58
1995 Macon	A Atl	27	27	0	0	149.1	653	134	73	59	13	0	2	12	70	0	177	14	5	9	10	.474	0	0	3.56
1996 Durham	A+ Atl	14	14	0	0	84	333	52	25	21	9	3	3	2	40	0	89	7	2	9	1	.900	0	0	2.25
Greenville	AA Atl	11	10	0	0	58	262	57	41	32	5	0	3	3	35	0	48	12	0	2	5	.286	0	0	4.97
1997 Greenville	AA Atl	21	19	1	0	112.2	498	111	73	67	13	1	8	9	58	0	116	14	2	6	8	.429	0	0	5.35
1999 Macon	A Atl	12	12	0	0	41.2	172	33	20	20	8	1	0	4	15	0	49	2	1	0	3	.000	0	0	4.32
Greenville	AA Atl	7	7	0	0	32.2	171	50	33	31	6	0	3	2	21	0	22	8	0	1	3	.250	0	0	8.54
5 Min. YEARS		104	101	2	0	538.2	2354	467	293	254	55	6	19	46	294	0	578	69	13	29	35	.453	1	0	4.24

Rick Moss

Bats: Left Throws: Right Pos: 3B
Ht: 6'2" Wt: 197 Born: 9/18/75 Age: 24

Year Team	Lg Org	G	AB	H	2B	3B	HR	TB	R	RBI	TBB	IBB	SO	HBP	SH	SF	SB	CS	SB%	GDP	Avg	OBP	SLG
1996 Twins	R Min	28	107	37	8	2	0	49	18	23	7	1	7	3	0	1	2	2	.50	2	.346	.398	.458
Elizabethtn	R+ Min	32	116	41	10	0	5	66	21	18	14	0	17	0	0	0	3	1	.75	3	.353	.423	.569
1997 Fort Wayne	A Min	133	508	141	28	4	3	186	76	77	61	4	57	2	2	8	3	3	.50	10	.278	.352	.366
1998 Fort Myers	A+ Min	41	160	50	7	0	1	60	18	19	24	0	17	3	1	0	0	0	.00	3	.313	.412	.375
New Britain	AA Min	65	193	54	9	0	2	69	17	25	20	0	20	0	4	0	0	0	.00	4	.280	.347	.358

					BATTING												BASERUNNING				PERCENTAGES		
Year Team	Lg Org	G	AB	H	2B	3B	HR	TB	R	RBI	TBB	IBB	SO	HBP	SH	SF	SB	CS	SB%	GDP	Avg	OBP	SLG
1999 New Britain	AA Min	90	252	68	13	0	4	93	28	29	24	1	37	2	1	0	0	5	.00	5	.270	.338	.369
4 Min. YEARS		389	1336	391	75	6	15	523	178	191	150	6	155	10	8	9	8	11	.42	27	.293	.366	.391

Danny Mota

Pitches: Right **Bats:** Right **Pos:** P   **Ht:** 6'0" **Wt:** 180 **Born:** 10/9/75 **Age:** 24

		HOW MUCH HE PITCHED						WHAT HE GAVE UP												THE RESULTS					
Year Team	Lg Org	G	GS	CG	GF	IP	BFP	H	R	ER	HR	SH	SF	HB	TBB	IBB	SO	WP	Bk	W	L	Pct.	ShO	Sv	ERA
1995 Yankees	R NYY	14	0	0	9	32.2	133	27	9	8	2	4	0	2	4	0	35	6	3	2	3	.400	0	0	2.20
1996 Oneonta	A- NYY	10	0	0	8	10	42	10	5	5	0	0	0	0	2	0	11	0	1	0	1	.000	0	7	4.50
1997 Greensboro	A NYY	20	0	0	9	29.2	111	17	6	6	1	0	0	0	11	1	30	0	0	2	0	1.000	0	1	1.82
Oneonta	A- NYY	27	0	0	25	28.1	119	21	8	7	0	1	0	0	16	0	40	0	0	1	0	1.000	0	17	2.22
1998 Fort Wayne	A Min	25	0	0	20	32	135	24	14	8	2	3	0	2	8	1	39	0	1	4	3	.571	0	7	2.25
Fort Myers	A+ Min	19	4	0	9	47.1	206	45	21	15	3	1	3	0	22	0	49	6	1	3	5	.375	0	0	2.85
1999 Fort Myers	A+ Min	11	0	0	3	18.2	79	19	5	5	0	1	1	0	5	0	22	0	0	1	1	.500	0	0	2.41
New Britain	AA Min	6	0	0	5	12.2	52	11	5	5	2	1	0	0	5	1	12	0	0	1	0	.000	0	0	3.55
5 Min. YEARS		132	4	0	88	211.1	877	174	73	59	10	11	4	4	73	3	238	12	6	13	14	.481	0	32	2.51

Tony Mota

Bats: Both **Throws:** Right **Pos:** OF   **Ht:** 6'1" **Wt:** 170 **Born:** 10/31/77 **Age:** 22

					BATTING												BASERUNNING				PERCENTAGES		
Year Team	Lg Org	G	AB	H	2B	3B	HR	TB	R	RBI	TBB	IBB	SO	HBP	SH	SF	SB	CS	SB%	GDP	Avg	OBP	SLG
1996 Yakima	A- LA	60	225	62	11	3	3	88	29	29	13	0	37	1	3	1	13	7	.65	0	.276	.317	.391
1997 San Berndno	A+ LA	111	420	101	14	13	4	153	53	49	30	2	97	4	6	2	11	8	.58	9	.240	.296	.364
1998 Vero Beach	A+ LA	61	254	81	18	5	7	130	45	35	18	3	27	2	0	0	13	8	.62	6	.319	.369	.512
San Antonio	AA LA	59	222	54	10	6	2	82	20	22	12	1	36	0	2	3	16	8	.67	6	.243	.278	.369
1999 San Antonio	AA LA	98	345	112	31	2	15	192	65	75	41	6	56	0	4	2	13	5	.72	14	.325	.394	.557
4 Min. YEARS		389	1466	410	84	29	31	645	212	210	114	12	253	7	15	8	66	36	.65	35	.280	.333	.440

Chad Mottola

Bats: Right **Throws:** Right **Pos:** OF   **Ht:** 6'3" **Wt:** 215 **Born:** 10/15/71 **Age:** 28

					BATTING												BASERUNNING				PERCENTAGES		
Year Team	Lg Org	G	AB	H	2B	3B	HR	TB	R	RBI	TBB	IBB	SO	HBP	SH	SF	SB	CS	SB%	GDP	Avg	OBP	SLG
1992 Billings	R+ Cin	57	213	61	8	3	12	111	53	37	25	0	43	0	0	0	12	3	.80	4	.286	.361	.521
1993 Winston-Sal	A+ Cin	137	493	138	25	3	21	232	76	91	62	2	109	2	0	3	13	7	.65	9	.280	.361	.471
1994 Chattanooga	AA Cin	118	402	97	19	1	7	139	44	41	30	1	68	1	2	2	9	12	.43	12	.241	.294	.346
1995 Chattanooga	AA Cin	51	181	53	13	1	10	98	32	39	13	0	32	1	0	1	2	3	.40	2	.293	.342	.541
Indianapols	AAA Cin	69	239	62	11	1	8	99	40	37	20	0	50	0	0	1	8	1	.89	6	.259	.315	.414
1996 Indianapolis	AAA Cin	103	362	95	24	3	9	152	45	47	21	3	93	4	0	4	9	6	.60	10	.262	.307	.420
1997 Chattanooga	AA Cin	46	174	63	9	3	5	93	35	32	16	1	23	1	1	5	7	1	.88	3	.362	.408	.534
Indianapolis	AAA Cin	83	284	82	10	6	7	125	33	45	16	2	43	4	0	2	12	4	.75	6	.289	.333	.440
1998 Indianapolis	AAA Cin	5	12	5	0	0	1	8	2	2	4	0	0	0	0	0	2	0	.00	0	.417	.563	.667
Tulsa	AA Tex	8	26	13	1	0	1	17	9	7	10	1	1	0	0	0	3	0	1.00	0	.500	.639	.654
Oklahoma	AAA Tex	74	257	68	13	1	2	89	29	22	18	1	49	1	0	2	8	3	.73	7	.265	.313	.346
1999 Charlotte	AAA CWS	140	511	164	32	4	20	264	95	94	60	1	83	3	0	7	18	6	.75	7	.321	.391	.517
1996 Cincinnati	NL	35	79	17	3	0	3	29	10	6	6	1	16	0	0	0	2	2	.50	0	.215	.271	.367
8 Min. YEARS		891	3154	901	165	26	103	1427	493	494	295	12	594	17	4	27	100	47	.68	66	.286	.347	.452

Tony Mounce

Pitches: Left **Bats:** Left **Pos:** P   **Ht:** 6'2" **Wt:** 175 **Born:** 2/8/75 **Age:** 25

		HOW MUCH HE PITCHED						WHAT HE GAVE UP												THE RESULTS					
Year Team	Lg Org	G	GS	CG	GF	IP	BFP	H	R	ER	HR	SH	SF	HB	TBB	IBB	SO	WP	Bk	W	L	Pct.	ShO	Sv	ERA
1994 Astros	R Hou	11	11	0	0	59.2	246	56	24	18	1	2	1	1	18	0	72	2	2	4	2	.667	0	0	2.72
1995 Quad City	A Hou	25	25	3	0	159	649	118	55	43	6	6	6	3	57	2	143	6	2	16	8	.667	1	0	2.43
1996 Kissimmee	A+ Hou	25	25	4	0	155.2	675	139	65	39	7	6	3	10	68	1	102	7	0	9	9	.500	2	0	2.25
1997 New Orleans	AAA Hou	1	1	0	0	4.2	21	2	1	1	1	0	0	0	6	0	6	0	0	0	0	.000	0	0	1.93
Jackson	AA Hou	25	25	1	0	145	645	165	91	81	18	6	5	2	66	3	116	7	0	8	9	.471	0	0	5.03
1998 Jackson	AA Hou	32	17	1	3	109.2	498	128	73	62	14	3	5	2	48	0	82	5	0	6	6	.500	0	0	5.09
Kissimmee	A+ Hou	5	5	0	0	26	122	35	22	20	2	2	0	2	13	1	15	1	0	1	2	.333	0	0	6.92
1999 New Orleans	AAA Hou	14	0	0	2	11	55	10	3	3	0	0	1	1	13	0	10	2	0	0	1	.000	0	0	2.45
Jackson	AA Hou	31	6	0	11	68.1	300	64	33	28	6	1	1	2	30	0	80	5	0	5	2	.714	0	0	3.69
6 Min. YEARS		169	115	9	16	739	3211	717	367	295	55	26	22	22	319	7	626	35	4	49	39	.557	3	0	3.59

Kelcey Mucker

Bats: Left **Throws:** Right **Pos:** OF   **Ht:** 6'4" **Wt:** 250 **Born:** 2/17/75 **Age:** 25

					BATTING												BASERUNNING				PERCENTAGES		
Year Team	Lg Org	G	AB	H	2B	3B	HR	TB	R	RBI	TBB	IBB	SO	HBP	SH	SF	SB	CS	SB%	GDP	Avg	OBP	SLG
1993 Twins	R Min	9	29	4	0	0	0	4	6	2	4	0	10	0	0	0	2	0	1.00	1	.138	.242	.138
1994 Elizabethtn	R+ Min	64	240	57	10	0	6	85	23	31	22	1	65	2	0	3	5	2	.50	9	.238	.303	.354
1995 Fort Wayne	A Min	109	405	93	16	1	7	132	48	47	27	1	59	4	1	2	12	4	.75	8	.230	.283	.326
1996 Fort Myers	A+ Min	100	331	79	9	3	2	100	34	32	36	4	66	2	1	1	5	2	.71	11	.239	.316	.302
1997 Fort Myers	A+ Min	114	389	93	26	3	3	134	43	48	33	1	80	4	4	7	1	5	.17	5	.239	.300	.344
1998 Fort Myers	A+ Min	21	71	24	6	0	2	36	11	9	5	0	10	2	0	5	1	0	1.00	1	.338	.397	.507
New Britain	AA Min	71	226	67	14	0	5	96	22	27	23	0	31	3	2	5	1	0	1.00	10	.296	.362	.425
1999 New Britain	AA Min	100	000	100	10	0	1	110	20	20	02	1	37	3	0	3	3	00	.00	10	.212	.333	.323
7 Min. YEARS		597	2059	517	97	7	26	706	213	221	182	8	378	20	9	21	24	16	.60	55	.251	.315	.343

199

Mark Mulder

Pitches: Left **Bats:** Left **Pos:** P **Ht:** 6'6" **Wt:** 200 **Born:** 8/5/77 **Age:** 22

Year Team	Lg Org	G	GS	CG	GF	IP	BFP	H	R	ER	HR	SH	SF	HB	TBB	IBB	SO	WP	Bk	W	L	Pct.	ShO	Sv	ERA
		HOW MUCH HE PITCHED						WHAT HE GAVE UP												THE RESULTS					
1999 Vancouver	AAA Oak	22	22	1	0	128.2	549	152	69	58	13	4	5	3	31	0	81	6	0	6	7	.462	0	0	4.06

Scott Mullen

Pitches: Left **Bats:** Right **Pos:** P **Ht:** 6'2" **Wt:** 190 **Born:** 1/17/75 **Age:** 25

Year Team	Lg Org	G	GS	CG	GF	IP	BFP	H	R	ER	HR	SH	SF	HB	TBB	IBB	SO	WP	Bk	W	L	Pct.	ShO	Sv	ERA
		HOW MUCH HE PITCHED						WHAT HE GAVE UP												THE RESULTS					
1996 Spokane	A- KC	15	15	0	0	80.1	352	78	45	35	6	1	2	8	29	0	78	1	0	5	6	.455	0	0	3.92
1997 Lansing	A KC	16	16	0	0	92.1	391	90	46	38	14	0	3	4	31	0	78	2	1	5	2	.714	0	0	3.70
Wilmington	A+ KC	11	11	0	0	59.1	260	64	35	30	5	1	2	1	26	4	43	5	2	4	4	.500	0	0	4.55
1998 Wilmington	A+ KC	14	14	1	0	85.2	344	68	28	21	4	3	1	7	25	0	56	3	1	8	4	.667	1	0	2.21
Wichita	AA KC	12	12	0	0	70	289	66	34	32	7	0	3	1	26	0	42	7	0	8	2	.800	0	0	4.11
1999 Wichita	AA KC	9	9	0	0	49.1	216	47	28	22	2	1	4	1	18	1	30	3	0	4	3	.571	0	0	4.01
Omaha	AAA KC	20	20	0	0	119.1	543	150	91	83	24	4	6	2	53	2	87	7	1	6	7	.462	0	0	6.26
4 Min. YEARS		97	97	1	0	556.1	2395	563	307	261	62	10	21	24	208	7	414	28	5	40	28	.588	1	0	4.22

Rob Mummau

Bats: Right **Throws:** Right **Pos:** 2B **Ht:** 5'11" **Wt:** 185 **Born:** 8/21/71 **Age:** 28

Year Team	Lg Org	G	AB	H	2B	3B	HR	TB	R	RBI	TBB	IBB	SO	HBP	SH	SF	SB	CS	SB%	GDP	Avg	OBP	SLG
		BATTING															BASERUNNING				PERCENTAGES		
1993 St.Cathrnes	A- Tor	75	257	62	9	3	3	86	35	21	23	1	44	5	2	0	7	12	.37	3	.241	.316	.335
1994 Dunedin	A+ Tor	21	50	11	1	0	0	12	5	6	4	0	15	0	1	0	0	2	.00	0	.220	.278	.240
Hagerstown	A Tor	46	169	50	10	2	1	67	20	24	10	0	32	2	0	3	2	2	.50	4	.296	.337	.396
1995 Hagerstown	A Tor	107	366	94	17	3	5	132	63	42	42	1	74	14	6	3	6	1	.86	7	.257	.353	.361
1996 Dunedin	A+ Tor	36	106	22	3	0	0	25	10	10	12	0	22	0	7	0	2	4	.33	2	.208	.288	.236
Syracuse	AAA Tor	4	3	0	0	0	0	0	1	0	0	0	1	0	0	0	0	0	.00	0	.000	.000	.000
Knoxville	AA Tor	47	154	43	11	0	2	60	23	22	15	1	25	3	3	2	1	4	.20	6	.279	.351	.390
1997 Syracuse	AAA Tor	103	333	85	17	2	8	130	47	40	35	3	60	7	5	2	2	3	.40	3	.255	.337	.390
1998 Knoxville	AA Tor	39	141	41	5	2	3	59	28	28	11	0	24	2	3	3	4	1	.80	5	.291	.344	.418
Syracuse	AAA Tor	3	7	3	1	0	0	4	0	2	0	0	1	0	0	0	0	0	.00	0	.429	.429	.571
1999 Syracuse	AAA Tor	123	433	105	29	3	5	155	52	58	28	1	61	6	6	7	2	1	.67	7	.242	.293	.358
7 Min. YEARS		604	2019	516	103	15	27	730	284	253	180	7	359	39	33	20	26	30	.46	35	.256	.326	.362

Bobby Munoz

Pitches: Right **Bats:** Right **Pos:** P **Ht:** 6' 8" **Wt:** 260 **Born:** 3/3/68 **Age:** 32

Year Team	Lg Org	G	GS	CG	GF	IP	BFP	H	R	ER	HR	SH	SF	HB	TBB	IBB	SO	WP	Bk	W	L	Pct.	ShO	Sv	ERA
		HOW MUCH HE PITCHED						WHAT HE GAVE UP												THE RESULTS					
1989 Yankees	R NYY	2	2	0	0	10.1	41	5	4	4	0	0	0	0	4	0	13	1	1	1	1	.500	0	0	3.48
Ft. Laud	A+ NYY	3	3	0	0	13.1	58	16	8	7	2	0	0	0	7	0	2	0	1	1	2	.333	0	0	4.73
1990 Greensboro	A NYY	25	24	0	0	132.2	581	134	70	55	4	2	2	5	58	1	100	4	6	5	12	.294	0	0	3.73
1991 Ft. Laud	A+ NYY	19	19	4	0	108	443	91	45	28	4	2	4	4	40	0	53	6	2	5	8	.385	2	0	2.33
Columbus	AAA NYY	1	1	0	0	3	21	8	8	8	0	0	0	0	3	0	2	0	0	0	1	.000	0	0	24.00
1992 Albany-Colo	AA NYY	22	22	0	0	112.1	491	96	55	41	2	2	4	4	70	0	66	8	0	7	5	.583	0	0	3.28
1993 Columbus	AAA NYY	22	1	0	18	31.1	124	24	6	5	0	1	0	0	8	0	16	1	0	3	1	.750	0	5	1.44
1994 Scranton-WB	AAA Phi	6	5	0	0	34	138	27	9	8	2	0	1	0	14	1	24	3	0	2	3	.400	0	0	2.12
1995 Reading	AA Phi	4	4	0	0	15	74	28	19	18	4	0	0	0	3	0	8	1	0	0	4	.000	0	0	10.80
Scranton-WB	AAA Phi	2	2	1	0	16	57	8	2	1	0	0	0	0	3	1	10	1	0	1	0	1.000	1	0	0.56
1996 Clearwater	A+ Phi	2	2	0	0	14	58	15	4	3	0	1	0	0	2	0	7	0	0	1	1	.500	0	0	1.93
Scranton-WB	AAA Phi	8	8	0	0	50.2	220	50	24	22	6	1	1	0	7	0	34	2	0	4	2	.667	0	0	3.91
Reading	AA Phi	4	4	0	0	27.2	113	24	13	9	3	1	0	1	8	0	29	2	1	0	1	.000	0	0	2.93
1997 Las Vegas	AAA SD	17	1	0	6	22.2	108	30	26	25	2	0	2	0	11	0	13	1	0	0	0	.000	0	0	9.93
Albuquerque	AAA LA	18	0	0	6	31	145	43	17	15	2	0	1	0	15	3	20	1	0	0	3	.000	0	0	4.35
1998 Rochester	AAA Bal	44	0	0	34	59.1	228	40	9	7	5	1	1	5	13	0	46	4	0	3	1	.750	0	19	1.06
1999 Durham	AAA TB	39	3	0	11	55.1	251	55	35	27	5	2	3	1	31	1	50	7	0	3	3	.500	0	5	4.39
1993 New York	AL	38	0	0	12	45.2	208	48	27	27	1	1	3	0	26	5	33	2	0	3	3	.500	0	0	5.32
1994 Philadelphia	NL	21	14	1	1	104.1	447	101	40	31	8	5	5	1	35	0	59	5	1	7	5	.583	0	1	2.67
1995 Philadelphia	NL	3	3	0	0	15.2	70	15	13	10	2	0	2	3	9	0	6	0	0	0	2	.000	0	0	5.74
1996 Philadelphia	NL	6	6	0	0	25.1	123	42	28	22	5	2	1	1	7	1	8	0	0	0	3	.000	0	0	7.82
1997 Philadelphia	NL	8	7	0	1	33.1	161	47	35	33	4	2	3	2	15	1	20	3	1	1	5	.167	0	0	8.91
1998 Baltimore	AL	9	1	0	5	12	58	18	13	13	4	1	3	1	6	0	6	0	1	0	0	.000	0	0	9.75
11 Min. YEARS		238	101	5	76	736.2	3138	694	354	283	41	13	19	22	297	7	493	42	11	36	50	.419	3	34	3.46
6 Maj. YEARS		85	31	1	19	236.1	1067	271	156	136	24	11	17	8	98	7	132	10	3	11	18	.379	0	1	5.18

Juan Munoz

Bats: Left **Throws:** Left **Pos:** DH-OF **Ht:** 5'9" **Wt:** 170 **Born:** 3/27/74 **Age:** 26

Year Team	Lg Org	G	AB	H	2B	3B	HR	TB	R	RBI	TBB	IBB	SO	HBP	SH	SF	SB	CS	SB%	GDP	Avg	OBP	SLG
		BATTING															BASERUNNING				PERCENTAGES		
1995 Johnson Cy	R+ StL	57	190	66	12	1	7	101	43	31	27	0	17	0	0	2	13	2	.87	1	.347	.425	.532
1996 Peoria	A StL	31	111	38	9	0	0	47	19	19	14	0	14	1	0	3	4	1	.80	2	.342	.411	.423
St. Pete	A+ StL	90	330	80	12	3	1	101	41	46	38	0	35	1	3	3	6	5	.55	8	.242	.320	.306
1997 Pr William	A+ StL	66	256	80	16	7	4	122	41	48	19	3	25	0	0	4	3	1	.75	5	.313	.355	.477
Arkansas	AA StL	58	215	60	9	2	6	91	28	31	16	0	26	1	2	1	6	10	.38	2	.279	.330	.423
1998 Arkansas	AA StL	28	119	32	9	0	0	41	16	18	3	0	15	0	0	0	0	0	.00	4	.269	.280	.345
Memphis	AAA StL	117	399	107	17	5	4	146	54	44	29	5	58	0	5	2	9	4	.69	9	.268	.316	.366
1999 Arkansas	AA StL	2	3	2	0	0	0	2	1	0	0	0	0	0	0	0	0	0	.00	0	.667	.667	.667
5 Min. YEARS		449	1623	465	84	18	22	651	243	237	146	8	190	3	10	18	41	23	.64	31	.287	.343	.401

Mike Murphy

Bats: Right **Throws:** Right **Pos:** OF — **Ht:** 6'2" **Wt:** 185 **Born:** 1/23/72 **Age:** 28

Year Team	Lg Org	G	AB	H	2B	3B	HR	TB	R	RBI	TBB	IBB	SO	HBP	SH	SF	SB	CS	SB%	GDP	Avg	OBP	SLG
1990 Martinsvlle	R+ Phi	9	31	3	0	0	0	3	4	1	7	0	17	0	0	0	1	2	.33	1	.097	.263	.097
1991 Martinsvlle	R+ Phi	44	156	34	3	0	0	37	15	7	11	1	40	1	2	0	9	2	.82	5	.218	.274	.237
1992 Batavia	A- Phi	63	228	58	6	2	2	74	32	27	21	0	48	4	3	0	15	8	.65	6	.254	.328	.325
1993 Spartanburg	A Phi	133	509	147	29	6	3	197	70	60	35	1	91	9	9	2	33	14	.70	15	.289	.344	.387
1994 Dunedin	A+ Tor	125	469	129	11	4	1	151	57	34	55	3	106	9	4	3	31	10	.76	9	.275	.360	.322
1995 Canton-Akrn	AA Cle	10	23	1	0	0	0	1	3	0	4	0	3	0	0	0	0	1	.00	0	.043	.185	.043
Kinston	A+ Cle	67	177	41	6	0	1	50	26	15	15	1	30	3	1	1	13	4	.76	2	.232	.301	.282
1996 Charlotte	A+ Tex	87	358	119	20	7	7	174	73	52	32	1	94	3	3	0	22	9	.71	5	.332	.392	.486
Tulsa	AA Tex	34	121	28	7	2	4	51	22	16	21	0	29	3	1	1	1	0	1.00	2	.231	.356	.421
1997 Tulsa	AA Tex	46	156	40	10	1	4	64	30	19	35	0	45	4	0	0	6	3	.67	3	.256	.405	.410
Okla City	AAA Tex	73	243	80	13	5	5	118	37	25	38	1	66	4	4	2	14	5	.74	1	.329	.425	.486
1998 Charlotte	A+ Tex	3	7	2	1	0	0	3	4	1	3	0	1	0	0	0	1	0	1.00	0	.286	.500	.429
Tulsa	AA Tex	58	196	49	8	2	4	73	26	22	27	1	56	2	0	2	6	2	.75	8	.250	.344	.372
Oklahoma	AAA Tex	24	74	16	1	0	0	17	10	5	6	0	23	0	1	0	3	1	.75	1	.216	.275	.230
Rochester	AAA Bal	8	29	11	0	0	1	14	3	2	3	0	7	0	0	0	1	1	.50	0	.379	.438	.483
1999 Rochester	AAA Bal	70	217	49	6	3	1	64	35	21	34	0	63	1	3	3	7	3	.70	6	.226	.329	.295
Tacoma	AAA Sea	38	129	38	7	3	2	57	22	22	13	0	36	2	1	1	10	4	.71	2	.295	.361	.442
10 Min. YEARS		892	3123	845	128	35	35	1148	469	329	360	9	755	45	32	17	173	69	.71	66	.271	.353	.368

Nate Murphy

Bats: Left **Throws:** Left **Pos:** OF — **Ht:** 6'1" **Wt:** 210 **Born:** 4/15/75 **Age:** 25

Year Team	Lg Org	G	AB	H	2B	3B	HR	TB	R	RBI	TBB	IBB	SO	HBP	SH	SF	SB	CS	SB%	GDP	Avg	OBP	SLG
1996 Boise	A- Ana	67	266	76	18	1	7	117	58	41	41	1	63	1	0	1	12	4	.75	4	.286	.382	.440
1997 Cedar Rapds	A Ana	51	149	33	4	2	0	41	21	13	19	1	43	1	0	1	4	2	.67	2	.221	.312	.275
1998 Lk Elsinore	A+ Ana	40	120	20	2	0	5	37	15	10	9	1	46	0	1	0	5	2	.71	2	.167	.225	.308
1999 Lk Elsinore	A+ Ana	28	107	38	8	1	5	63	21	20	11	1	27	2	0	1	9	4	.69	0	.355	.421	.589
Erie	AA Ana	104	359	96	17	8	14	171	48	56	54	3	85	3	4	2	6	5	.55	7	.267	.366	.476
4 Min. YEARS		290	1001	263	49	12	31	429	163	140	134	7	264	7	5	5	36	17	.68	15	.263	.352	.429

Adrian Myers

Bats: Right **Throws:** Right **Pos:** OF — **Ht:** 5'10" **Wt:** 175 **Born:** 5/10/75 **Age:** 25

Year Team	Lg Org	G	AB	H	2B	3B	HR	TB	R	RBI	TBB	IBB	SO	HBP	SH	SF	SB	CS	SB%	GDP	Avg	OBP	SLG
1996 Hudson Val	A- Tex	54	142	24	5	4	1	40	22	15	17	0	44	8	0	2	19	2	.90	2	.169	.290	.282
1997 Charlotte	A+ Tex	90	287	71	7	4	0	86	40	21	36	0	73	3	1	1	18	15	.55	5	.247	.336	.300
1998 Charlotte	A+ Tex	122	454	122	20	7	6	174	84	64	55	1	98	3	7	9	51	23	.69	11	.269	.345	.383
1999 Tulsa	AA Tex	99	357	84	12	4	1	107	60	28	44	0	63	3	1	1	33	7	.83	14	.235	.323	.300
4 Min. YEARS		365	1240	301	44	19	8	407	206	128	152	1	278	17	9	13	121	47	.72	32	.243	.331	.328

Jimmy Myers

Pitches: Right **Bats:** Right **Pos:** P — **Ht:** 6'1" **Wt:** 190 **Born:** 4/28/69 **Age:** 31

Year Team	Lg Org	G	GS	CG	GF	IP	BFP	H	R	ER	HR	SH	SF	HB	TBB	IBB	SO	WP	Bk	W	L	Pct.	ShO	Sv	ERA
1987 Pocatello	R+ SF	10	2	0	4	19.2	92	29	21	19	1	1	1	1	16	1	12	5	2	0	2	.000	0	0	8.69
1988 Pocatello	R+ SF	12	12	0	0	58.1	283	72	50	35	3	2	1	1	32	1	39	7	1	4	5	.444	0	0	5.40
1989 Clinton	A SF	32	21	0	5	137.2	592	139	71	57	6	8	5	9	58	5	63	11	0	4	12	.250	0	0	3.73
1990 San Jose	A+ SF	60	0	0	50	84	361	80	44	30	2	3	3	2	34	6	61	3	1	5	8	.385	0	25	3.21
1991 Shreveport	AA SF	62	0	0	55	76.1	325	71	22	21	2	6	0	2	30	5	51	4	0	6	4	.600	0	24	2.48
1992 Phoenix	AAA SF	25	0	0	19	23.2	114	32	20	15	1	2	1	0	13	5	11	0	0	0	4	.000	0	10	5.70
Shreveport	AA SF	33	0	0	32	32	141	39	17	17	0	2	2	2	10	1	15	1	0	2	4	.333	0	18	4.78
1993 Shreveport	AA SF	29	0	0	14	49.1	210	50	14	11	1	2	0	2	19	3	23	4	0	2	2	.500	0	1	2.01
Phoenix	AAA SF	31	3	0	5	58.2	259	69	.35	24	2	3	0	3	22	2	20	5	0	2	5	.286	0	6	3.68
1994 Memphis	AA KC	33	2	0	12	64.1	286	68	38	35	3	7	2	4	32	4	35	7	1	4	4	.500	0	3	4.90
Carolina	AA Pit	44	2	0	17	76	335	85	41	38	3	7	3	7	39	5	42	8	1	5	5	.500	0	7	4.50
1995 Rochester	AAA Bal	55	0	0	28	64.2	289	72	28	22	2	3	2	1	29	1	31	1	0	0	4	.000	0	6	3.06
1996 Rochester	AAA Bal	39	0	0	35	53	220	53	19	17	1	8	0	2	12	4	21	5	0	7	5	.583	0	12	2.89
1997 Norfolk	AAA NYM	45	0	0	14	69	288	57	23	14	1	2	1	4	33	5	31	4	2	2	4	.333	0	2	1.83
1998 Oklahoma	AAA Tex	41	0	0	22	62.1	252	56	20	14	4	2	1	3	20	3	24	0	1	7	1	.875	0	9	2.02
1999 Norfolk	AAA NYM	3	0	0	1	3.2	14	11	8	7	0	0	0	0	2	0	2	0	0	0	0	.000	0	0	17.18
Scranton-WB	AAA Phi	11	0	0	2	14.1	60	15	6	6	1	0	1	1	3	0	6	2	0	1	0	1.000	0	1	3.77
1996 Baltimore	AL	11	0	0	5	14	64	18	13	11	4	0	2	0	3	1	6	1	0	0	0	.000	0	0	7.07
13 Min. YEARS		565	42	0	315	947	4131	988	477	382	33	58	23	44	404	51	487	67	9	51	69	.425	0	118	3.63

Rod Myers

Bats: Left **Throws:** Left **Pos:** OF — **Ht:** 6'1" **Wt:** 190 **Born:** 1/14/73 **Age:** 27

Year Team	Lg Org	G	AB	H	2B	3B	HR	TB	R	RBI	TBB	IBB	SO	HBP	SH	SF	SB	CS	SB%	GDP	Avg	OBP	SLG
1991 Royals	R KC	44	133	37	2	3	1	48	14	18	6	1	27	5	0	1	12	2	.86	1	.278	.331	.361
Baseball Cy	A+ KC	4	11	2	0	0	0	2	1	0	0	0	5	0	0	0	1	1	.50	1	.182	.182	.182
1992 Appleton	A KC	71	218	48	10	2	4	74	31	30	39	1	67	2	4	4	25	6	.81	3	.220	.338	.339
1993 Rockford	A KC	129	474	123	24	5	9	184	69	68	58	6	117	5	6	4	49	16	.75	7	.259	.344	.388
1994 Wilmington	A+ KC	126	457	120	20	4	12	184	76	65	67	3	93	6	12	1	31	11	.74	4	.263	.363	.403
1995 Wichita	AA KC	131	499	153	22	6	7	208	71	62	34	3	77	4	8	3	29	16	.64	7	.307	.354	.417
1996 Omaha	AAA KC	112	411	120	27	1	16	197	68	54	49	6	106	9	9	3	37	8	.82	6	.292	.377	.479

(Batting — continued)

Year Team	Lg Org	BATTING															BASERUNNING				PERCENTAGES		
		G	AB	H	2B	3B	HR	TB	R	RBI	TBB	IBB	SO	HBP	SH	SF	SB	CS	SB%	GDP	Avg	OBP	SLG
1997 Wichita	AA KC	4	16	5	2	0	0	7	3	3	3	0	3	0	0	0	0	1	.00	0	.313	.421	.438
Omaha	AAA KC	38	142	36	10	0	2	52	21	10	15	0	37	0	4	1	6	4	.60	0	.254	.323	.366
1998 Wichita	AA KC	41	143	32	11	0	4	55	19	10	30	1	31	0	3	2	8	1	.89	0	.224	.354	.385
Omaha	AAA KC	30	101	22	4	1	0	28	15	10	12	0	25	0	1	2	4	4	.50	3	.218	.296	.277
1999 San Antonio	AA LA	46	147	37	11	0	2	54	21	16	18	0	35	1	3	2	2	2	.50	2	.252	.333	.367
1996 Kansas City	AL	22	63	18	7	0	1	28	9	11	7	0	16	0	0	0	3	2	.60	1	.286	.357	.444
1997 Kansas City	AL	31	101	26	7	0	2	39	14	9	17	0	22	1	2	0	4	0	1.00	0	.257	.370	.386
9 Min. YEARS		776	2752	735	143	22	57	1093	409	357	331	21	623	32	50	23	204	72	.74	34	.267	.350	.397
2 Maj. YEARS		53	164	44	14	0	3	67	23	20	24	0	38	1	2	0	7	2	.78	3	.268	.365	.409

Tyrone Narcisse

Pitches: Right Bats: Right Pos: P   Ht: 6'6" Wt: 220 Born: 2/4/72 Age: 28

Year Team	Lg Org	HOW MUCH HE PITCHED						WHAT HE GAVE UP												THE RESULTS					
		G	GS	CG	GF	IP	BFP	H	R	ER	HR	SH	SF	HB	TBB	IBB	SO	WP	Bk	W	L	Pct.	ShO	Sv	ERA
1990 Padres	R SD	7	1	0	3	10.2	52	13	11	6	0	0	0	2	6	0	6	3	2	0	0	.000	0	0	5.06
1991 Padres	R SD	11	10	0	0	37.1	193	43	41	31	1	1	1	4	37	0	23	5	3	2	3	.400	0	0	7.47
1992 Astros	R Hou	11	6	0	2	34.2	158	31	25	19	0	1	3	2	24	0	32	5	1	3	2	.600	0	0	4.93
1993 Asheville	A Hou	29	29	2	0	160.1	702	173	95	78	11	4	8	12	66	0	114	9	5	6	12	.333	0	0	4.38
1994 Osceola	A+ Hou	26	26	2	0	146	633	153	91	79	7	5	5	11	57	2	86	9	4	7	11	.389	0	0	4.87
1995 Jackson	AA Hou	27	27	2	0	163.2	686	140	76	59	8	10	8	10	60	5	93	8	0	5	14	.203	0	0	3.24
1996 Jackson	AA Hou	27	26	0	0	126.2	572	151	92	78	15	9	4	6	55	2	88	9	1	7	12	.368	0	0	5.54
1997 Rancho Cuca	A+ SD	22	0	0	9	34.1	140	21	13	13	3	2	2	2	22	0	38	4	0	2	0	1.000	0	0	3.41
1998 Tampa	A+ NYY	4	0	0	1	5	23	4	1	1	0	0	0	1	3	0	7	0	0	0	0	.000	0	0	1.80
Norwich	AA NYY	29	0	0	16	53.1	247	61	38	31	6	0	2	4	26	1	43	11	0	1	0	1.000	0	1	5.23
1999 Jackson	AA Hou	10	0	0	2	12.1	59	14	12	10	4	1	1	2	7	1	8	2	0	0	2	.000	0	0	7.30
Kissimmee	A+ Hou	4	0	0	3	5.1	29	10	4	4	0	0	1	1	2	0	3	0	0	0	0	.000	0	0	6.75
10 Min. YEARS		207	125	6	36	789.2	3494	814	499	409	55	33	35	57	365	11	541	65	16	33	56	.371	0	1	4.66

Mike Neal

Bats: Right Throws: Right Pos: OF   Ht: 6'1" Wt: 180 Born: 11/5/71 Age: 28

Year Team	Lg Org	BATTING															BASERUNNING				PERCENTAGES		
		G	AB	H	2B	3B	HR	TB	R	RBI	TBB	IBB	SO	HBP	SH	SF	SB	CS	SB%	GDP	Avg	OBP	SLG
1993 Watertown	A- Cle	67	234	68	15	3	4	101	47	43	55	4	45	6	1	3	7	1	.88	2	.291	.433	.432
1994 Kinston	A+ Cle	101	378	99	21	1	5	137	51	38	40	1	94	3	3	1	8	12	.40	6	.262	.336	.362
1995 Canton-Akrn	AA Cle	134	419	112	24	2	5	155	64	46	71	3	79	9	4	8	5	6	.45	7	.267	.379	.370
1996 Canton-Akrn	AA Cle	94	254	57	9	3	4	84	42	32	39	0	53	5	2	6	2	3	.40	3	.224	.332	.331
1997 Akron	AA Cle	126	457	129	24	2	17	208	77	69	55	0	103	12	5	3	8	7	.53	7	.282	.372	.455
1998 Jackson	AA Hou	103	341	111	27	2	17	193	53	70	39	0	80	4	1	1	4	4	.50	7	.326	.400	.566
New Orleans	AAA Hou	30	91	21	4	1	0	27	13	6	2	0	16	6	1	1	0	0	.00	1	.231	.290	.297
1999 New Orleans	AAA Hou	94	243	49	10	1	6	79	33	28	27	0	61	2	0	2	3	0	1.00	3	.202	.285	.325
7 Min. YEARS		749	2417	646	134	15	58	984	380	332	328	8	531	47	17	25	37	33	.53	36	.267	.362	.407

Richard Negrette

Pitches: Right Bats: Right Pos: P   Ht: 6'2" Wt: 175 Born: 3/6/76 Age: 24

Year Team	Lg Org	HOW MUCH HE PITCHED						WHAT HE GAVE UP												THE RESULTS					
		G	GS	CG	GF	IP	BFP	H	R	ER	HR	SH	SF	HB	TBB	IBB	SO	WP	Bk	W	L	Pct.	ShO	Sv	ERA
1995 Watertown	A- Cle	18	5	0	0	45.2	203	42	30	28	5	2	2	7	23	2	35	6	1	3	3	.500	0	3	5.52
1996 Burlington	R+ Cle	14	13	0	0	59.1	283	57	50	34	3	1	3	5	36	0	52	12	0	2	6	.250	0	0	5.16
Kinston	A+ Cle	1	1	0	0	2.1	20	9	7	6	0	0	0	0	4	0	0	0	0	0	1	.000	0	0	23.14
1997 Columbus	A Cle	16	0	0	8	36.1	155	24	23	18	2	2	1	6	16	0	21	5	0	2	1	.667	0	1	4.46
Watertown	A- Cle	17	0	0	7	39.1	171	25	17	16	0	5	2	3	29	2	30	6	1	2	3	.400	0	1	3.66
1998 Columbus	A Cle	21	0	0	10	40.2	181	39	24	23	4	0	0	5	22	1	35	6	2	1	3	.250	0	2	5.09
Kinston	A+ Cle	28	0	0	11	50	208	32	22	16	3	3	3	4	27	1	41	5	0	3	5	.375	0	0	2.88
1999 Akron	AA Cle	33	0	0	10	47	230	49	35	32	2	1	2	3	47	0	34	7	0	1	3	.250	0	1	6.13
West Tenn	AA ChC	3	0	0	2	3.1	15	3	2	2	1	0	0	0	2	0	2	1	0	1	0	1.000	0	0	5.40
5 Min. YEARS		151	19	0	54	324	1466	280	210	175	20	14	13	33	206	6	250	48	4	15	25	.375	0	8	4.86

Mike Neill

Bats: Left Throws: Left Pos: OF   Ht: 6'2" Wt: 200 Born: 4/27/70 Age: 30

Year Team	Lg Org	BATTING															BASERUNNING				PERCENTAGES		
		G	AB	H	2B	3B	HR	TB	R	RBI	TBB	IBB	SO	HBP	SH	SF	SB	CS	SB%	GDP	Avg	OBP	SLG
1991 Sou Oregon	A- Oak	63	240	84	14	0	5	113	42	42	35	3	54	0	4	1	9	3	.75	1	.350	.431	.471
1992 Reno	A+ Oak	130	473	159	26	7	5	214	101	76	81	2	96	5	6	2	23	11	.68	15	.336	.437	.452
Huntsville	AA Oak	5	16	5	0	0	0	5	4	2	2	0	7	0	1	1	1	0	1.00	0	.313	.368	.313
1993 Huntsville	AA Oak	54	179	44	8	0	1	55	30	15	34	0	45	1	0	1	3	4	.43	4	.246	.367	.307
Modesto	A+ Oak	17	62	12	3	0	0	15	4	4	12	0	12	0	1	0	0	1	.00	0	.194	.324	.242
1994 Tacoma	AAA Oak	7	22	5	1	0	0	6	1	2	3	0	7	0	0	0	0	0	.00	2	.227	.320	.273
Modesto	A+ Oak	47	165	48	4	1	2	60	22	18	26	1	50	1	2	1	1	1	.50	4	.291	.389	.364
1995 Modesto	A+ Oak	71	257	71	17	1	6	108	39	36	34	2	65	2	5	1	4	4	.50	6	.276	.364	.420
Huntsville	AA Oak	33	107	32	6	1	2	46	11	16	12	1	29	0	1	1	1	0	1.00	1	.299	.367	.430
1996 Edmonton	AAA Oak	7	20	3	1	0	1	7	4	2	3	0	7	0	0	0	0	0	.00	0	.150	.227	.350
Modesto	A+ Oak	114	442	150	20	6	19	239	101	78	68	4	123	4	2	2	28	7	.80	3	.339	.430	.541
1997 Edmonton	AAA Oak	7	21	4	0	0	0	4	3	3	7	0	7	0	0	2	1	1	.50	1	.190	.393	.190
Huntsville	AA Oak	122	486	165	30	2	14	241	129	80	72	0	113	4	3	3	16	7	.70	8	.340	.427	.496
1998 Edmonton	AAA Oak	99	371	112	18	4	10	168	72	48	65	0	91	2	6	1	6	5	.55	12	.302	.408	.453
Huntsville	AA Oak	12	35	9	5	0	0	14	1	2	4	1	13	0	1	0	0	0	.00	0	.257	.333	.400
1999 Vancouver	AAA Oak	96	365	108	23	2	6	165	61	61	57	3	97	2	1	0	10	5	.67	11	.296	.390	.452

Year Team	Lg Org	BATTING															BASERUNNING				PERCENTAGES		
		G	AB	H	2B	3B	HR	TB	R	RBI	TBB	IBB	SO	HBP	SH	SF	SB	CS	SB%	GDP	Avg	OBP	SLG
1998 Oakland	AL	6	15	4	1	0	0	5	2	0	2	0	4	0	0	0	0	0	.00	0	.267	.353	.333
9 Min. YEARS		883	3261	1011	176	24	75	1460	625	487	514	17	812	21	36	18	103	49	.68	68	.310	.405	.448

Bry Nelson

Bats: Both Throws: Right Pos: 3B   Ht: 5'10" Wt: 205 Born: 1/27/74 Age: 26

Year Team	Lg Org	BATTING															BASERUNNING				PERCENTAGES		
		G	AB	H	2B	3B	HR	TB	R	RBI	TBB	IBB	SO	HBP	SH	SF	SB	CS	SB%	GDP	Avg	OBP	SLG
1994 Quad City	A Hou	45	156	38	6	0	1	47	20	6	11	0	15	0	0	0	3	5	.38	3	.244	.293	.301
Auburn	A- Hou	65	261	84	16	7	6	132	53	35	11	0	13	1	3	1	2	1	.67	9	.322	.350	.506
1995 Kissimmee	A+ Hou	105	395	129	34	5	3	182	47	52	20	0	37	1	1	6	14	10	.58	8	.327	.355	.461
Quad City	A Hou	6	26	1	1	0	0	2	1	2	0	0	3	0	0	0	0	0	.00	2	.038	.038	.077
1996 Kissimmee	A+ Hou	89	345	87	21	6	3	129	38	52	19	3	27	1	1	4	8	2	.80	13	.252	.290	.374
1997 Orlando	AA ChC	110	382	110	33	2	8	171	51	58	45	4	43	1	1	6	5	7	.42	15	.288	.359	.448
1998 West Tenn	AA ChC	32	102	29	6	2	2	45	10	18	12	2	12	0	0	1	4	2	.67	5	.284	.357	.441
1999 West Tenn	AA ChC	129	471	126	24	5	16	208	66	78	42	4	52	2	1	4	10	7	.59	13	.268	.328	.442
6 Min. YEARS		581	2138	604	141	27	39	916	286	301	160	13	202	6	7	22	46	34	.58	68	.283	.331	.428

Chris Nelson

Pitches: Right Bats: Both Pos: P   Ht: 6'2" Wt: 180 Born: 1/26/73 Age: 27

Year Team	Lg Org	HOW MUCH HE PITCHED						WHAT HE GAVE UP											THE RESULTS					
		G	GS	CG	GF	IP	BFP	H	R	ER	HR	SH	SF	HB	TBB	IBB	SO	WP	Bk	W	L	Pct.	ShO	Sv	ERA
1995 Sou Oregon	A- Oak	16	6	0	3	54.1	218	43	25	21	5	3	3	3	13	1	52	1	1	2	3	.400	0	1	3.48
Modesto	A+ Oak	2	2	0	0	10	37	4	1	1	0	0	0	0	4	0	8	1	0	2	0	1.000	0	0	0.90
1996 W Michigan	A Oak	16	9	0	3	70.2	275	53	19	19	3	3	1	1	20	0	79	4	8	3	1	.750	0	1	2.42
Modesto	A+ Oak	14	13	0	0	63.1	292	86	50	38	7	1	3	4	17	0	62	6	1	3	5	.375	0	0	5.40
1997 Modesto	A+ Oak	8	8	0	0	47	198	55	23	20	4	0	1	1	7	0	53	2	2	3	3	.500	0	0	3.83
Huntsville	AA Oak	20	15	1	0	99.2	430	116	60	55	10	3	3	1	25	1	71	4	2	9	3	.750	1	0	4.97
1998 Edmonton	AAA Oak	4	1	0	0	9.1	51	16	16	15	2	2	2	0	8	1	4	0	0	0	1	.000	0	0	14.46
Huntsville	AA Oak	28	10	0	6	83.2	397	111	70	60	21	1	3	4	39	1	62	7	3	3	4	.429	0	0	6.45
1999 Midland	AA Oak	19	0	0	8	30.2	157	45	30	27	5	0	4	1	22	0	24	3	0	1	1	.500	0	0	7.92
5 Min. YEARS		127	64	1	20	468.2	2055	529	294	256	57	13	20	15	155	4	415	28	17	26	21	.553	1	2	4.92

Joe Nelson

Pitches: Right Bats: Right Pos: P   Ht: 6'2" Wt: 185 Born: 10/25/74 Age: 25

Year Team	Lg Org	HOW MUCH HE PITCHED						WHAT HE GAVE UP											THE RESULTS					
		G	GS	CG	GF	IP	BFP	H	R	ER	HR	SH	SF	HB	TBB	IBB	SO	WP	Bk	W	L	Pct.	ShO	Sv	ERA
1996 Eugene	A- Atl	14	13	0	0	70	309	69	43	34	5	3	1	5	29	1	67	6	0	5	3	.625	0	0	4.37
1997 Durham	A+ Atl	25	24	0	0	124.2	543	114	74	66	17	5	4	12	61	1	99	5	0	10	6	.625	0	0	4.76
1998 Greenville	AA Atl	45	12	1	15	108.1	506	124	76	60	9	4	8	5	69	2	74	11	1	6	9	.400	1	2	4.98
1999 Greenville	AA Atl	25	0	0	15	30.1	130	19	15	8	2	2	1	3	14	2	37	0	0	1	1	.500	0	8	2.37
Richmond	AAA Atl	12	3	0	2	33.2	150	33	18	17	2	4	1	0	15	0	31	3	0	2	3	.400	0	1	4.54
4 Min. YEARS		121	52	1	32	367	1638	359	226	185	35	22	11	25	188	6	308	25	1	24	22	.522	1	11	4.54

Adam Neubart

Bats: Right Throws: Right Pos: OF   Ht: 5'11" Wt: 165 Born: 7/23/77 Age: 22

Year Team	Lg Org	BATTING															BASERUNNING				PERCENTAGES		
		G	AB	H	2B	3B	HR	TB	R	RBI	TBB	IBB	SO	HBP	SH	SF	SB	CS	SB%	GDP	Avg	OBP	SLG
1998 Diamondbcks	R Ari	6	19	3	2	0	0	5	6	0	3	0	2	1	0	0	1	0	1.00	0	.158	.304	.263
High Desert	A+ Ari	39	141	46	7	4	2	67	24	21	9	0	35	5	2	2	4	2	.67	3	.326	.382	.475
1999 South Bend	A Ari	27	91	21	3	1	1	29	14	9	6	0	20	6	0	2	4	4	.50	2	.231	.314	.319
El Paso	AA Ari	13	43	9	3	0	1	15	7	4	5	0	14	0	2	0	1	0	.00	0	.209	.292	.349
High Desert	A+ Ari	55	212	68	9	6	8	113	47	38	20	1	52	10	2	3	10	10	.50	3	.321	.400	.533
2 Min. YEARS		140	506	147	24	11	12	229	98	72	43	1	123	22	6	7	19	17	.53	8	.291	.367	.453

Garrett Neubart

Bats: Right Throws: Right Pos: OF   Ht: 5'10" Wt: 160 Born: 11/7/73 Age: 26

Year Team	Lg Org	BATTING															BASERUNNING				PERCENTAGES		
		G	AB	H	2B	3B	HR	TB	R	RBI	TBB	IBB	SO	HBP	SH	SF	SB	CS	SB%	GDP	Avg	OBP	SLG
1995 Portland	A- Col	39	128	34	8	0	0	42	23	8	21	0	24	7	0	2	12	3	.80	0	.266	.392	.328
1996 Asheville	A Col	71	282	79	11	3	0	96	60	22	31	0	45	3	1	3	34	5	.87	2	.280	.354	.340
Salem	A+ Col	24	85	31	2	2	0	37	16	6	12	0	13	4	1	0	8	6	.57	0	.365	.465	.435
1997 Salem	A+ Col	133	527	135	23	3	0	164	66	34	39	0	90	12	10	2	50	18	.74	3	.256	.321	.311
1998 Binghamton	AA NYM	109	363	100	10	3	3	125	58	37	34	0	65	12	7	5	29	8	.78	4	.275	.353	.344
1999 Norfolk	AAA NYM	13	38	6	0	0	0	6	6	2	6	0	7	3	0	0	5	1	.83	2	.158	.319	.158
Binghamton	AA NYM	83	260	75	14	4	3	106	36	21	22	0	40	8	8	1	17	5	.77	6	.288	.361	.408
5 Min. YEARS		472	1683	460	68	15	6	576	265	130	165	0	284	49	27	13	155	46	.77	17	.273	.353	.342

Tom Nevers

Bats: Right Throws: Right Pos: SS   Ht: 6'1" Wt: 175 Born: 9/13/71 Age: 28

Year Team	Lg Org	BATTING															BASERUNNING				PERCENTAGES		
		G	AB	H	2B	3B	HR	TB	R	RBI	TBB	IBB	SO	HBP	SH	SF	SB	CS	SB%	GDP	Avg	OBP	SLG
1990 Astros	R Hou	50	185	44	10	5	2	70	23	32	27	0	38	3	0	3	13	3	.81	3	.238	.339	.378
1991 Asheville	A Hou	129	441	111	26	2	16	189	59	71	53	0	124	3	2	5	10	12	.45	11	.252	.333	.429
1992 Osceola	A+ Hou	125	455	114	24	6	8	174	49	55	22	1	124	3	2	1	6	2	.75	10	.251	.289	.382
1993 Jackson	AA Hou	55	184	50	8	2	1	65	21	10	16	2	36	1	1	1	7	2	.78	5	.272	.335	.353

BATTING

Year Team	Lg Org	G	AB	H	2B	3B	HR	TB	R	RBI	TBB	IBB	SO	HBP	SH	SF	SB	CS	SB%	GDP	Avg	OBP	SLG
1994 Jackson	AA Hou	125	449	120	25	2	8	173	54	62	31	2	101	4	1	7	10	5	.67	8	.267	.316	.385
1995 Jackson	AA Hou	83	298	72	7	3	8	109	36	35	24	2	58	2	0	1	5	2	.71	10	.242	.301	.366
Stockton	A+ Mil	4	14	4	0	0	0	4	2	3	0	0	6	2	0	0	1	0	1.00	0	.286	.375	.286
El Paso	AA Mil	35	118	30	5	1	1	40	19	12	11	0	21	3	0	0	2	1	.67	6	.254	.333	.339
1996 Hardware Cy	A+ Mil	127	459	121	27	7	7	183	65	44	46	1	87	3	2	3	3	10	.23	18	.264	.333	.399
1997 Louisville	AAA StL	71	227	53	9	0	8	86	22	27	12	0	48	2	2	2	1	3	.25	12	.233	.276	.379
1998 Vancouver	AAA Ana	30	89	18	0	0	1	21	7	4	5	0	18	0	0	1	1	0	1.00	3	.202	.242	.236
Chattanooga	AA Cin	58	221	48	9	4	7	86	30	31	17	3	53	2	4	1	1	0	1.00	6	.217	.278	.389
1999 Chattanooga	AA Cin	111	380	112	23	2	17	190	61	65	15	0	74	2	2	2	3	5	.38	14	.295	.323	.500
10 Min. YEARS		1003	3520	897	173	34	84	1390	448	451	279	11	788	31	16	28	63	45	.58	106	.255	.313	.395

Bats: Right **Throws:** Right **Pos:** OF

Marc Newfield

Ht: 6' 4" **Wt:** 226 **Born:** 10/19/72 **Age:** 27

BATTING

Year Team	Lg Org	G	AB	H	2B	3B	HR	TB	R	RBI	TBB	IBB	SO	HBP	SH	SF	SB	CS	SB%	GDP	Avg	OBP	SLG
1990 Mariners	R Sea	49	185	60	13	2	6	95	34	38	23	0	20	2	0	2	4	4	.50	3	.324	.401	.514
1991 San Berndno	A+ Sea	125	440	132	22	3	11	193	64	68	59	9	90	10	0	5	12	6	.67	14	.300	.391	.439
Jacksnville	AA Sea	6	26	6	3	0	0	9	4	2	0	0	8	1	0	0	0	0	.00	0	.231	.259	.346
1992 Jacksnville	AA Sea	45	162	40	12	0	4	64	15	19	12	0	34	3	1	1	1	5	.17	3	.247	.309	.395
1993 Jacksnville	AA Sea	91	330	103	10	0	19	170	40	51	30	1	35	5	0	3	1	1	.50	12	.307	.374	.530
1994 Calgary	AAA Sea	107	430	150	44	2	19	255	89	83	42	2	58	7	0	3	0	0	.00	13	.349	.413	.593
1995 Tacoma	AAA Sea	53	198	55	11	0	5	81	30	30	19	1	30	5	0	0	1	0	1.00	6	.278	.356	.409
Las Vegas	AAA SD	20	70	24	5	1	3	40	10	12	3	0	11	1	1	1	2	0	1.00	1	.343	.373	.571
1997 Tucson	AAA Mil	8	31	10	1	0	1	14	4	3	4	1	6	0	0	0	0	0	.00	1	.323	.400	.452
1999 Vancouver	AAA Oak	7	28	4	0	0	0	4	1	1	1	0	2	0	0	0	0	0	.00	1	.143	.172	.143
Trenton	AA Bos	4	13	2	1	0	1	6	3	2	1	0	3	2	0	0	1	0	1.00	0	.154	.313	.462
1993 Seattle	AL	22	66	15	3	0	1	21	5	7	2	0	8	1	0	1	0	1	.00	2	.227	.257	.318
1994 Seattle	AL	12	38	7	1	0	1	11	3	4	2	0	4	0	0	0	0	0	.00	2	.184	.225	.289
1995 Seattle	AL	24	85	16	3	0	3	28	7	14	3	1	16	1	0	0	0	0	.00	2	.188	.225	.329
San Diego	NL	21	55	17	5	1	1	27	6	7	2	0	8	0	0	0	0	0	.00	3	.309	.333	.491
1996 San Diego	NL	84	191	48	11	0	5	74	27	26	16	1	44	2	0	3	1	1	.50	7	.251	.311	.387
Milwaukee	AL	49	179	55	15	0	7	91	21	31	11	1	26	4	0	4	0	1	.00	7	.307	.354	.508
1997 Milwaukee	AL	50	157	36	8	0	1	47	14	18	14	0	27	2	0	3	0	0	.00	4	.229	.295	.299
1998 Milwaukee	NL	93	186	44	7	0	3	60	15	25	19	1	29	1	0	3	0	1	.00	7	.237	.306	.323
8 Min. YEARS		515	1919	586	130	8	69	939	302	309	197	14	297	36	2	15	22	19	.54	54	.305	.378	.489
6 Maj. YEARS		355	957	238	53	1	22	359	98	132	69	4	102	11	0	14	1	4	.20	28	.249	.303	.375

Pitches: Right **Bats:** Right **Pos:** P

Eric Newman

Ht: 6'4" **Wt:** 220 **Born:** 8/27/72 **Age:** 27

		HOW MUCH HE PITCHED						WHAT HE GAVE UP												THE RESULTS					
Year Team	Lg Org	G	GS	CG	GF	IP	BFP	H	R	ER	HR	SH	SF	HB	TBB	IBB	SO	WP	Bk	W	L	Pct.	ShO	Sv	ERA
1995 Clinton	A SD	11	10	1	0	42.1	212	52	41	36	5	1	2	2	38	2	31	3	3	1	7	.125	0	0	7.65
Idaho Falls	R+ SD	15	14	0	0	81.2	365	91	49	40	3	5	4	7	35	0	65	3	1	8	4	.667	0	0	4.41
1996 Clinton	A SD	34	14	0	6	113.1	501	101	71	54	9	3	7	7	67	0	108	13	1	5	7	.417	0	1	4.29
1997 Rancho Cuca	A+ SD	35	15	0	3	123.2	542	104	64	57	12	1	3	7	73	1	141	12	0	13	6	.684	0	0	4.15
1998 Mobile	AA SD	27	25	1	0	140	632	152	100	87	14	5	9	6	71	1	120	17	0	9	12	.429	1	0	5.59
1999 West Tenn	AA ChC	58	0	0	15	84.1	359	61	37	30	5	5	2	5	49	6	90	8	0	5	3	.625	0	8	3.20
5 Min. YEARS		180	78	2	24	585.1	2611	561	362	304	48	20	27	34	333	10	555	56	5	41	39	.513	1	9	4.67

Bats: Left **Throws:** Left **Pos:** OF

Warren Newson

Ht: 5' 7" **Wt:** 202 **Born:** 7/3/64 **Age:** 35

BATTING

Year Team	Lg Org	G	AB	H	2B	3B	HR	TB	R	RBI	TBB	IBB	SO	HBP	SH	SF	SB	CS	SB%	GDP	Avg	OBP	SLG
1986 Spokane	A- SD	54	159	37	8	1	2	53	29	31	47	1	37	0	1	1	3	1	.75	5	.233	.406	.333
1987 Chston-SC	A SD	58	191	66	12	2	7	103	50	32	52	1	35	0	2	2	13	7	.65	5	.346	.484	.539
Reno	A+ SD	51	165	51	7	2	6	80	44	28	39	0	34	0	2	1	2	6	.25	1	.309	.439	.485
1988 Riverside	A+ SD	130	438	130	23	7	22	233	99	91	107	3	102	0	0	3	36	19	.65	11	.297	.432	.532
1989 Wichita	AA SD	128	427	130	20	6	18	216	94	70	103	10	99	0	0	1	20	9	.69	6	.304	.436	.506
1990 Las Vegas	AAA SD	123	404	123	20	3	13	188	80	58	83	3	110	0	1	4	13	5	.72	10	.304	.420	.465
1991 Vancouver	AAA CWS	33	111	41	12	1	2	61	19	19	30	1	26	0	0	2	4	5	.56	2	.369	.497	.550
1992 Vancouver	AAA CWS	19	59	15	0	0	0	15	7	9	16	1	21	1	0	0	3	2	.60	0	.254	.421	.254
1993 Nashville	AAA CWS	61	176	60	8	2	4	84	40	21	38	4	38	1	0	3	5	2	.71	4	.341	.454	.477
1997 Tulsa	AA Tex	2	7	1	0	0	1	4	1	2	2	0	1	0	0	0	0	0	.00	0	.143	.333	.571
1998 Oklahoma	AAA Tex	111	398	122	21	1	21	208	75	75	66	4	106	0	1	5	7	5	.58	11	.307	.401	.523
1999 Albuquerque	AAA LA	95	285	74	22	0	8	120	42	38	44	1	70	2	0	4	4	8	.33	9	.260	.363	.421
1991 Chicago	AL	71	132	39	5	0	4	56	20	25	28	1	34	0	0	0	2	2	.50	4	.295	.419	.424
1992 Chicago	AL	63	136	30	3	0	1	36	19	11	37	2	38	0	0	0	3	0	1.00	4	.221	.387	.265
1993 Chicago	AL	26	40	12	0	0	2	18	9	6	9	1	12	0	0	0	1	0	.00	2	.300	.429	.450
1994 Chicago	AL	63	102	20	3	0	2	07	10	7	14	1	20	0	0	0	1	0	1.00	2	.055	.316	.???
1995 Chicago	AL	51	85	20	0	2	3	33	19	9	23	0	27	1	0	0	1	1	.50	2	.235	.404	.388
Seattle	AL	33	72	21	2	0	2	29	15	6	16	0	18	0	0	0	1	0	1.00	1	.292	.420	.403
1996 Texas	AL	91	235	60	14	1	10	106	34	31	37	1	82	0	0	1	3	0	1.00	5	.255	.355	.451
1997 Texas	AL	81	169	36	10	1	10	78	23	23	31	2	53	0	0	1	3	0	1.00	4	.213	.333	.462
1998 Texas	AL	10	21	4	1	0	0	5	1	2	4	0	9	0	0	0	0	0	.00	1	.190	.227	.238
11 Min. YEARS		865	2820	850	153	25	104	1365	580	474	627	29	679	4	8	25	109	64	.63	67	.301	.426	.484
8 Maj. YEARS		489	992	248	40	4	34	398	156	120	196	9	292	1	2	2	14	3	.82	24	.250	.374	.401

204

Doug Newstrom

Bats: Left **Throws:** Right **Pos:** C **Ht:** 6'1" **Wt:** 195 **Born:** 9/18/71 **Age:** 28

Year Team	Lg Org	G	AB	H	2B	3B	HR	TB	R	RBI	TBB	IBB	SO	HBP	SH	SF	SB	CS	SB%	GDP	Avg	OBP	SLG
1993 Yakima	A- LA	75	279	83	16	2	2	109	51	36	53	4	44	1	1	3	11	1	.92	7	.297	.408	.391
1994 Vero Beach	A+ LA	119	405	117	22	5	2	155	47	46	59	3	51	2	0	5	4	5	.44	5	.289	.378	.383
1995 San Berndno	A+ LA	97	316	92	22	1	6	134	53	58	40	0	58	2	6	3	19	9	.68	7	.291	.371	.424
1996 High Desert	A+ Bal	122	403	126	30	3	11	195	84	75	72	0	62	0	2	6	15	8	.65	9	.313	.412	.484
1997 New Haven	AA Col	95	244	65	10	1	1	80	29	43	39	1	32	1	2	4	9	5	.64	8	.266	.365	.328
1998 New Haven	AA Col	102	331	94	21	1	5	132	38	24	41	4	53	0	3	2	7	5	.58	7	.284	.361	.399
1999 Birmingham	AA CWS	82	253	72	11	1	3	94	30	23	29	2	42	0	0	2	3	4	.43	8	.285	.356	.372
7 Min. YEARS		692	2231	649	132	14	30	899	332	305	333	14	342	6	14	25	68	37	.65	51	.291	.381	.403

Geronimo Newton

Pitches: Left **Bats:** Left **Pos:** P **Ht:** 6'0" **Wt:** 165 **Born:** 12/31/73 **Age:** 26

Year Team	Lg Org	G	GS	CG	GF	IP	BFP	H	R	ER	HR	SH	SF	HB	TBB	IBB	SO	WP	Bk	W	L	Pct.	ShO	Sv	ERA
1993 Mariners	R Sea	21	1	0	12	40.1	182	31	27	10	0	6	1	1	23	2	39	7	0	1	4	.200	0	1	2.23
1994 Riverside	A+ Sea	2	1	0	0	8	32	5	4	4	2	0	0	0	3	0	4	0	1	0	0	.000	0	0	4.50
Bellingham	A- Sea	21	8	0	4	60	255	43	19	14	1	2	2	2	36	3	43	8	3	3	4	.429	0	0	2.10
1995 Riverside	A+ Sea	46	0	0	11	71.1	307	74	35	25	1	3	3	4	24	3	42	2	4	4	4	.500	0	2	3.15
1996 Port City	AA Sea	33	1	0	9	45.2	195	45	16	14	6	2	1	1	22	4	25	0	1	4	1	.800	0	0	2.76
1997 Mariners	R Sea	4	0	0	3	4	12	0	0	0	0	0	0	0	0	0	6	0	0	0	0	.000	0	3	0.00
1998 Orlando	AA Sea	21	1	0	2	40.2	188	45	27	25	3	2	2	3	22	1	28	0	0	4	1	.800	0	0	5.53
Lancaster	A+ Sea	19	0	0	10	31.2	141	30	15	11	2	1	0	0	21	0	30	5	0	3	0	1.000	0	2	3.13
1999 San Antonio	AA LA	11	0	0	3	14	67	17	6	5	1	1	0	0	10	1	14	0	1	0	1	.000	0	0	3.21
New Haven	AA Sea	31	2	0	8	59	254	60	32	26	8	1	1	0	26	0	48	1	0	2	1	.667	0	0	3.97
7 Min. YEARS		209	14	0	62	374.2	1633	350	181	134	24	18	10	11	187	14	279	23	10	21	16	.568	0	8	3.22

Darrell Nicholas

Bats: Right **Throws:** Right **Pos:** OF **Ht:** 5'11" **Wt:** 180 **Born:** 5/26/72 **Age:** 28

Year Team	Lg Org	G	AB	H	2B	3B	HR	TB	R	RBI	TBB	IBB	SO	HBP	SH	SF	SB	CS	SB%	GDP	Avg	OBP	SLG
1994 Helena	R+ Mil	15	61	23	3	2	0	30	18	13	10	0	10	1	0	0	11	3	.79	0	.377	.472	.492
Beloit	A Mil	59	221	63	8	3	1	80	33	35	22	1	54	1	2	4	17	4	.81	4	.285	.347	.362
1995 El Paso	AA Mil	15	39	8	0	1	0	10	4	2	0	0	11	0	1	0	4	0	1.00	6	.205	.205	.256
Stockton	A+ Mil	87	350	112	16	3	5	149	54	39	23	1	75	1	1	1	26	8	.76	6	.320	.363	.426
1996 El Paso	AA Mil	70	237	65	12	4	2	91	46	24	27	2	57	1	4	1	9	7	.44	6	.274	.350	.384
1997 El Paso	AA Mil	127	518	163	47	5	14	262	79	68	27	1	116	2	6	3	17	6	.74	14	.315	.349	.506
1998 Louisville	AAA Mil	130	497	146	28	8	12	226	87	64	40	0	113	5	0	6	31	13	.70	4	.294	.349	.455
1999 Salt Lake	AAA Min	106	348	102	19	2	5	140	55	44	33	0	76	4	7	1	14	7	.67	6	.293	.360	.402
6 Min. YEARS		609	2271	682	133	28	39	988	376	289	182	5	512	15	31	16	127	50	.72	40	.300	.354	.435

Kevin Nicholson

Bats: Both **Throws:** Right **Pos:** SS **Ht:** 5'10" **Wt:** 190 **Born:** 3/29/76 **Age:** 24

Year Team	Lg Org	G	AB	H	2B	3B	HR	TB	R	RBI	TBB	IBB	SO	HBP	SH	SF	SB	CS	SB%	GDP	Avg	OBP	SLG
1997 Padres	R SD	7	34	9	1	0	2	16	7	8	2	0	5	0	0	0	0	2	.00	2	.265	.306	.471
Rancho Cuca	A+ SD	17	65	21	5	0	1	29	7	9	4	0	15	2	2	0	2	1	.67	1	.323	.380	.446
1998 Mobile	AA SD	132	488	105	27	3	5	153	64	52	47	7	114	3	5	6	9	5	.64	10	.215	.285	.314
1999 Mobile	AA SD	127	489	141	38	3	13	224	84	81	46	1	92	5	1	6	16	5	.76	15	.288	.352	.458
3 Min. YEARS		283	1076	276	71	6	21	422	162	150	99	8	226	10	8	12	27	13	.68	28	.257	.322	.392

Chris Nichting

Pitches: Right **Bats:** Right **Pos:** P **Ht:** 6'1" **Wt:** 205 **Born:** 5/13/66 **Age:** 34

Year Team	Lg Org	G	GS	CG	GF	IP	BFP	H	R	ER	HR	SH	SF	HB	TBB	IBB	SO	WP	Bk	W	L	Pct.	ShO	Sv	ERA
1988 Vero Beach	A+ LA	21	19	5	2	138	545	90	40	32	7	0	2	2	51	0	151	7	0	11	4	.733	1	1	2.09
1989 San Antonio	AA LA	26	26	2	0	154	698	160	96	86	13	9	6	6	101	6	136	14	4	4	14	.222	0	0	5.03
1992 Albuquerque	AAA LA	10	9	0	0	42	205	64	42	37	2	2	0	0	23	1	25	5	1	1	3	.250	0	0	7.93
San Antonio	AA LA	13	13	0	0	78.2	309	58	25	22	3	4	0	1	37	0	81	4	0	4	5	.444	0	0	2.52
1993 Vero Beach	A+ LA	4	4	0	0	17.1	75	18	9	8	2	0	0	0	6	0	18	1	0	1	0	1.000	0	0	4.15
1994 Albuquerque	AAA LA	10	7	0	1	41.1	209	61	39	34	5	0	0	3	28	1	25	6	0	2	2	.500	0	0	7.40
San Antonio	AA LA	21	8	0	8	65.2	277	47	21	12	1	4	1	2	34	1	74	7	1	3	4	.429	0	1	1.64
1995 Okla City	AAA Tex	23	7	3	8	67.2	275	58	19	16	4	4	2	2	19	0	72	2	0	5	5	.500	2	1	2.13
1996 Okla City	AAA Tex	4	1	0	1	9	37	9	1	1	0	0	0	0	3	0	7	0	0	1	0	1.000	0	0	1.00
1997 Edmonton	AAA Oak	33	24	3	3	131	602	170	120	113	21	0	7	3	46	2	90	8	1	7	13	.350	0	1	7.76
1998 Buffalo	AAA Cle	43	5	0	17	96.1	428	104	54	47	9	6	4	3	37	4	97	11	1	8	6	.571	0	1	4.39
1999 Columbus	AAA NYY	25	21	2	0	127.2	552	135	80	75	22	2	4	7	47	0	110	6	0	8	5	.615	0	0	5.29
1995 Texas	AL	13	0	0	3	24.1	122	36	19	19	1	1	2	1	13	1	6	3	0	0	0	.000	0	0	7.03
10 Min. YEARS		233	144	15	40	968.2	4212	974	546	483	89	31	26	25	432	15	886	71	8	54	62	.466	3	5	4.49

Ruben Niebla

Pitches: Left **Bats:** Left **Pos:** P **Ht:** 5'10" **Wt:** 175 **Born:** 12/19/71 **Age:** 28

Year Team	Lg Org	G	GS	CG	GF	IP	BFP	H	R	ER	HR	SH	SF	HB	TBB	IBB	SO	WP	Bk	W	L	Pct.	ShO	Sv	ERA
1995 Laredo	IND —	2	1	0	1	9	37	11	3	3	1	0	0	0	1	0	10	1	0	1	0	1.000	0	0	3.00
Corp.Chrsti	IND —	13	0	0	2	17	84	24	13	10	2	0	1	0	11	0	16	1	0	0	0	.000	0	0	5.29

205

Year Team	Lg Org	G	GS	CG	GF	IP	BFP	H	R	ER	HR	SH	SF	HB	TBB	IBB	SO	WP	Bk	W	L	Pct.	ShO	Sv	ERA
		HOW MUCH HE PITCHED						WHAT HE GAVE UP												THE RESULTS					
1996 Palm Spring	IND —	24	18	2	2	140.2	608	166	74	61	10	3	4	10	38	0	68	3	3	8	9	.471	0	0	3.90
1997 Tri-City	IND —	20	15	1	1	112	463	108	45	38	8	4	4	3	36	1	76	0	2	8	6	.571	0	0	3.05
1998 Jupiter	A+ Mon	13	0	0	3	22.2	90	15	8	3	1	0	1	1	5	0	22	1	0	0	1	.000	0	0	1.19
Harrisburg	AA Mon	24	1	0	3	43	178	45	23	22	5	1	6	1	6	0	30	4	0	0	2	.000	0	1	4.60
Ottawa	AAA Mon	6	0	0	3	12.1	58	20	12	7	4	0	0	0	4	0	7	0	0	0	1	.000	0	0	5.11
1999 Harrisburg	AA Mon	29	0	0	12	30.2	142	31	22	19	2	0	2	1	22	0	23	2	1	2	0	1.000	0	1	5.58
Reno	IND —	3	3	0	0	18.2	83	21	19	14	5	3	1	0	5	0	15	0	0	0	1	.000	0	0	6.75
San Berndno	A+ LA	3	0	0	1	5.2	25	9	3	3	1	0	0	0	1	0	6	0	0	0	1	.000	0	0	4.76
Vero Beach	A+ LA	1	0	0	0	2	7	1	0	0	0	0	0	0	0	0	4	0	0	0	0	.000	0	0	0.00
San Antonio	AA LA	12	0	0	4	14.1	65	19	7	6	0	1	0	0	5	1	12	0	0	2	1	.667	0	0	3.77
5 Min. YEARS		150	38	3	32	428	1840	470	229	186	39	12	19	16	134	2	289	12	6	21	22	.488	0	2	3.91

Brad Niedermaier

Pitches: Right Bats: Right Pos: P Ht: 6'2" Wt: 209 Born: 2/9/73 Age: 27

Year Team	Lg Org	G	GS	CG	GF	IP	BFP	H	R	ER	HR	SH	SF	HB	TBB	IBB	SO	WP	Bk	W	L	Pct.	ShO	Sv	ERA
		HOW MUCH HE PITCHED						WHAT HE GAVE UP												THE RESULTS					
1995 Elizabethtn	R+ Min	7	7	0	0	40.2	171	33	14	10	1	0	1	0	17	0	47	9	0	2	0	1.000	0	0	2.21
1996 Fort Wayne	A Min	32	3	0	14	69.1	295	64	39	25	3	3	4	0	29	2	72	11	0	6	4	.600	0	2	3.25
1997 Fort Myers	A+ Min	32	0	0	29	36.2	154	27	15	6	2	2	4	0	12	2	47	4	0	2	3	.400	0	17	1.47
Salt Lake	AAA Min	10	0	0	5	20	118	20	22	17	7	2	0	0	13	2	20	1	0	2	1	.667	0	0	5.88
1998 Fort Myers	A+ Min	25	0	0	13	40	202	59	39	35	3	2	0	1	21	1	44	13	0	4	2	.667	0	3	7.88
New Britain	AA Min	8	1	0	2	9	45	14	5	5	1	0	0	0	4	0	8	1	0	0	0	.000	0	0	5.00
1999 New Britain	AA Min	41	0	0	23	49.2	222	50	29	24	6	2	1	1	27	0	47	7	0	2	2	.500	0	9	4.35
5 Min. YEARS		161	11	0	86	271.1	1207	276	163	122	23	11	10	2	123	7	285	46	0	18	12	.600	0	31	4.05

Drew Niles

Bats: Both Throws: Right Pos: SS Ht: 6'1" Wt: 175 Born: 3/17/77 Age: 23

Year Team	Lg Org	G	AB	H	2B	3B	HR	TB	R	RBI	TBB	IBB	SO	HBP	SH	SF	SB	CS	SB%	GDP	Avg	OBP	SLG
		BATTING															BASERUNNING				PERCENTAGES		
1998 Kane County	A Fla	26	87	24	4	0	0	28	12	9	12	1	20	0	0	4	2	1	.67	1	.276	.350	.322
Charlotte	AAA Fla	16	49	13	1	0	1	17	5	5	6	0	12	1	0	1	0	1	.00	1	.265	.351	.347
1999 Brevard Cty	A+ Fla	40	117	20	1	1	1	26	12	12	15	0	30	1	0	2	0	0	.00	1	.171	.267	.222
Utica	A- Fla	18	66	15	3	0	0	18	4	7	9	0	15	0	2	0	0	3	.00	1	.227	.320	.273
Portland	AA Fla	46	135	31	3	0	0	34	12	9	21	0	34	0	3	2	2	2	.00	7	.230	.329	.252
2 Min. YEARS		146	454	103	12	1	2	123	45	42	63	1	111	2	5	9	2	7	.22	12	.227	.318	.271

Randy Niles

Pitches: Right Bats: Right Pos: P Ht: 6'2" Wt: 200 Born: 8/28/75 Age: 24

Year Team	Lg Org	G	GS	CG	GF	IP	BFP	H	R	ER	HR	SH	SF	HB	TBB	IBB	SO	WP	Bk	W	L	Pct.	ShO	Sv	ERA
		HOW MUCH HE PITCHED						WHAT HE GAVE UP												THE RESULTS					
1997 Sou Oregon	A- Oak	7	4	0	0	22.2	98	14	12	5	0	1	1	4	12	0	15	4	5	0	1	.000	0	0	1.99
Modesto	A+ Oak	7	5	0	0	34.2	148	32	13	10	3	1	0	6	9	0	20	0	0	4	0	1.000	0	0	2.60
1998 Visalia	A+ Oak	31	22	0	2	148.1	648	144	92	67	12	11	4	11	54	3	103	9	5	6	12	.333	0	0	4.07
1999 Modesto	A+ Oak	8	4	0	3	34.1	144	39	13	12	2	1	0	3	8	1	35	4	0	3	0	1.000	0	2	3.15
Midland	AA Oak	23	14	0	2	88	435	126	78	56	7	2	5	1	47	0	46	6	0	4	6	.400	0	0	5.73
3 Min. YEARS		76	49	0	7	328	1473	355	208	150	24	16	10	25	130	4	219	23	10	17	19	.472	0	2	4.12

Elvin Nina

Pitches: Right Bats: Right Pos: P Ht: 6'0" Wt: 185 Born: 11/25/75 Age: 24

Year Team	Lg Org	G	GS	CG	GF	IP	BFP	H	R	ER	HR	SH	SF	HB	TBB	IBB	SO	WP	Bk	W	L	Pct.	ShO	Sv	ERA
		HOW MUCH HE PITCHED						WHAT HE GAVE UP												THE RESULTS					
1997 Sou Oregon	A- Oak	18	2	0	8	31	150	36	24	18	4	0	0	2	18	1	26	2	2	1	3	.250	0	1	5.23
1998 Visalia	A+ Oak	30	21	1	5	130.1	583	135	77	65	9	2	6	5	62	1	131	13	2	8	8	.500	1	0	4.49
Edmonton	AAA Oak	1	0	0	0	0.1	4	1	0	0	0	1	0	0	2	1	0	1	0	0	0	.000	0	0	0.00
1999 Modesto	A+ Oak	17	12	0	0	73.1	319	59	31	17	2	3	0	6	41	1	74	5	0	5	2	.714	0	0	2.09
Midland	AA Oak	7	4	0	2	30	140	36	21	16	0	0	1	2	18	0	18	2	0	3	2	.600	0	0	4.80
Erie	AA Ana	4	4	0	0	24.1	103	20	12	11	2	1	1	0	15	0	19	1	0	3	0	1.000	0	0	4.07
3 Min. YEARS		77	43	1	15	289.1	1299	287	165	127	17	7	8	15	156	4	268	24	4	20	15	.571	1	1	3.95

Les Norman

Bats: Right Throws: Right Pos: OF Ht: 6'1" Wt: 185 Born: 2/25/69 Age: 31

Year Team	Lg Org	G	AB	H	2B	3B	HR	TB	R	RBI	TBB	IBB	SO	HBP	SH	SF	SB	CS	SB%	GDP	Avg	OBP	SLG
		BATTING															BASERUNNING				PERCENTAGES		
1991 Eugene	A- KC	30	102	25	4	1	2	37	14	18	9	0	18	1	2	1	2	1	.67	4	.245	.310	.363
1992 Appleton	A KC	59	218	82	17	1	4	113	38	47	22	0	18	1	2	3	8	6	.57	5	.376	.430	.518
Memphis	AA KC	72	271	74	14	5	3	107	32	20	22	0	37	2	1	1	4	4	.50	2	.273	.331	.395
1993 Memphis	AA KC	133	484	141	32	5	17	234	78	81	50	3	88	14	7	2	11	9	.55	8	.291	.373	.483
1994 Omaha	AAA KC	10	00	7	0	0	1	10	4	4	6	0	11	1	1	0	0	1	.00	2	.184	.311	.342
Memphis	AA KC	106	383	101	19	4	13	167	53	55	36	1	44	7	3	2	7	7	.50	6	.264	.336	.436
1995 Omaha	AAA KC	83	313	89	19	3	9	141	46	33	18	2	48	4	3	2	5	3	.63	3	.284	.329	.450
1996 Omaha	AAA KC	24	77	20	6	0	1	29	8	13	6	0	8	1	0	1	0	1	.00	2	.260	.318	.377
1997 Buffalo	AAA Cle	118	428	111	20	1	17	184	71	56	43	2	80	8	6	4	7	6	.54	5	.259	.335	.430
1998 Oklahoma	AAA Tex	100	380	116	32	2	10	182	64	51	17	0	79	9	5	3	6	2	.75	8	.305	.347	.479
1999 Omaha	AAA KC	89	333	91	20	2	13	154	53	40	14	0	45	5	3	5	7	3	.70	6	.273	.308	.462
1995 Kansas City	AL	24	40	9	0	1	0	11	6	4	6	0	6	0	1	0	1	1	.00	0	.225	.326	.275
1996 Kansas City	AL	54	49	6	0	0	0	6	9	0	6	0	14	1	0	0	1	1	.50	0	.122	.232	.122
9 Min. YEARS		827	3027	857	186	24	90	1361	461	418	243	8	476	53	33	24	57	43	.57	45	.283	.344	.450
2 Maj. YEARS		78	89	15	0	1	0	17	15	4	12	0	20	1	1	0	2	2	.33	0	.169	.275	.191

Ben Norris

Pitches: Left **Bats:** Left **Pos:** P   Ht: 6'3"   Wt: 185   Born: 12/6/77   **Age:** 22

		HOW MUCH HE PITCHED						WHAT HE GAVE UP											THE RESULTS					
Year Team	Lg Org	G	GS	CG	GF	IP	BFP	H	R	ER	HR	SH	SF	HB	TBB	IBB	SO	WP	Bk	W	L	Pct.	ShO	Sv	ERA
1996 Diamondbcks	R Ari	8	7	0	0	31.1	133	33	21	16	3	3	0	4	4	0	37	2	0	2	2	.500	0	0	4.60
Lethbridge	R+ Ari	3	3	0	0	11.1	54	14	9	8	0	0	2	0	5	0	12	2	1	0	0	.000	0	0	6.35
1997 South Bend	A Ari	14	13	0	0	60.1	291	69	44	27	7	2	2	6	31	0	40	2	1	1	8	.111	0	0	4.03
Lethbridge	R+ Ari	14	14	0	0	83.1	373	93	61	45	6	1	3	8	23	0	54	4	0	7	3	.700	0	0	4.86
1998 South Bend	A Ari	15	15	0	0	89.1	389	98	44	33	6	1	5	10	27	0	53	7	0	1	5	.167	0	0	3.32
High Desert	A+ Ari	9	6	0	2	40.2	180	48	27	25	7	2	0	0	18	0	17	1	0	2	2	.500	0	0	5.53
1999 High Desert	A+ Ari	8	8	0	0	40.2	181	39	27	20	4	0	3	4	24	0	45	0	0	2	2	.500	0	0	4.43
El Paso	AA Ari	20	20	0	0	119	535	132	61	55	13	3	2	8	53	0	87	6	2	10	6	.625	0	0	4.16
4 Min. YEARS		91	86	0	2	476	2136	526	294	229	46	12	17	40	185	0	345	24	4	25	28	.472	0	1	4.33

Dax Norris

Bats: Right **Throws:** Right **Pos:** 1B   Ht: 5'10"   Wt: 190   Born: 1/14/73   **Age:** 27

		BATTING														BASERUNNING				PERCENTAGES		
Year Team	Lg Org	G	AB	H	2B	3B	HR	TB	R	RBI	TBB	IBB	SO	HBP	SH	SF	SB	CS	SB%	GDP	Avg	OBP	SLG
1996 Eugene	A- Atl	60	232	67	17	0	7	105	31	37	18	0	32	3	3	1	2	0	1.00	4	.289	.346	.453
1997 Greenville	AA Atl	2	9	3	0	0	1	6	3	3	0	0	1	0	0	0	0	0	.00	0	.333	.333	.667
Durham	A+ Atl	95	338	80	19	0	7	120	29	45	32	1	49	4	0	3	2	5	.29	10	.237	.308	.355
1998 Danville	A+ Atl	28	92	30	12	1	3	53	9	21	7	1	15	2	0	3	1	2	.33	1	.326	.375	.576
Greenville	AA Atl	64	199	46	15	0	6	79	30	26	15	0	43	4	1	1	2	2	.33	7	.231	.297	.397
1999 Greenville	AA Atl	120	403	112	27	0	15	184	59	66	41	2	59	7	0	4	2	1	.67	10	.278	.352	.457
4 Min. YEARS		369	1273	338	90	1	39	547	161	198	113	4	199	20	4	12	8	10	.44	32	.266	.332	.430

Chris Norton

Bats: Right **Throws:** Right **Pos:** DH   Ht: 6'2"   Wt: 215   Born: 9/21/70   **Age:** 29

		BATTING														BASERUNNING				PERCENTAGES		
Year Team	Lg Org	G	AB	H	2B	3B	HR	TB	R	RBI	TBB	IBB	SO	HBP	SH	SF	SB	CS	SB%	GDP	Avg	OBP	SLG
1992 Watertown	A- Cle	1	4	0	0	0	0	0	1	0	0	0	2	0	0	0	0	0	.00	0	.000	.000	.000
Burlington	R+ Cle	4	12	3	0	0	0	3	2	2	1	0	4	0	0	1	0	0	.00	0	.250	.286	.250
Jamestown	A- Mon	60	207	42	4	1	4	60	15	27	15	0	64	2	0	2	3	0	1.00	3	.203	.261	.290
1993 Cardinals	R StL	27	83	19	5	3	0	30	10	11	11	1	23	1	0	0	0	0	.00	2	.229	.326	.361
1994 Savannah	A StL	126	439	116	11	2	26	209	75	82	73	4	144	4	3	2	6	4	.60	11	.264	.373	.476
1995 Arkansas	AA StL	10	25	6	2	0	0	8	6	6	11	2	5	0	0	1	0	0	.00	0	.240	.459	.320
Lubbock	IND —	97	327	95	16	3	21	180	61	61	75	7	87	1	0	2	6	2	.75	5	.291	.422	.550
1996 Lubbock	IND —	51	187	71	13	1	15	131	39	54	27	3	27	4	0	2	6	0	1.00	3	.380	.464	.701
Norwich	AA NYY	47	172	48	12	1	7	83	24	28	15	0	43	1	0	0	3	2	.60	3	.279	.340	.483
1997 Lk Elsinore	A+ Ana	37	138	38	7	2	11	82	34	35	22	1	41	2	0	1	0	1	.00	2	.275	.380	.594
Midland	AA Ana	58	200	53	8	1	16	111	40	47	35	0	57	0	0	2	2	1	.67	8	.265	.371	.555
Vancouver	AAA Ana	1	5	1	0	0	1	4	1	1	0	0	2	0	0	0	0	0	.00	0	.200	.200	.800
1998 Midland	AA Ana	17	60	19	1	0	4	32	10	12	9	0	23	1	0	0	0	0	.00	1	.317	.414	.533
Vancouver	AAA Ana	43	148	31	11	0	5	57	14	17	18	0	46	1	0	1	0	0	.00	4	.209	.298	.385
Portland	AA Fla	22	68	24	4	1	6	48	12	19	12	0	17	0	0	0	0	0	.00	0	.353	.450	.706
1999 Portland	AA Fla	120	406	118	25	0	38	257	74	97	71	2	124	1	0	1	1	2	.33	15	.291	.397	.633
8 Min. YEARS		721	2481	684	119	15	154	1295	418	499	395	20	709	18	3	15	27	12	.69	62	.276	.377	.522

Phillip Norton

Pitches: Left **Bats:** Right **Pos:** P   Ht: 6'1"   Wt: 185   Born: 2/1/76   **Age:** 24

		HOW MUCH HE PITCHED						WHAT HE GAVE UP											THE RESULTS					
Year Team	Lg Org	G	GS	CG	GF	IP	BFP	H	R	ER	HR	SH	SF	HB	TBB	IBB	SO	WP	Bk	W	L	Pct.	ShO	Sv	ERA
1996 Cubs	R ChC	1	0	0	1	3	10	1	0	0	0	0	0	0	0	0	6	0	1	0	0	.000	0	0	0.00
Williamsprt	A- ChC	15	13	2	1	85	364	68	33	24	1	3	2	3	33	2	77	7	3	7	4	.636	1	0	2.54
1997 Rockford	A ChC	18	18	3	0	109	460	92	51	39	4	3	3	1	44	1	114	12	1	9	3	.750	0	0	3.22
Daytona	A+ ChC	7	6	3	0	42.1	171	40	11	11	5	1	0	0	12	0	44	0	0	3	2	.600	0	0	2.34
Orlando	AA ChC	2	1	0	1	7	28	8	2	2	0	0	0	0	2	1	7	0	0	1	0	1.000	0	0	2.57
1998 Daytona	A+ ChC	10	10	0	0	66	275	57	30	24	4	1	1	2	26	1	54	4	1	4	3	.571	0	0	3.27
West Tenn	AA ChC	19	19	1	0	120.1	515	118	60	47	11	4	3	5	50	1	119	6	1	6	6	.500	1	0	3.52
1999 West Tenn	AA ChC	14	13	0	0	86.2	365	72	32	23	5	3	4	3	42	4	81	9	0	7	4	.636	0	0	2.39
Iowa	AAA ChC	14	14	0	0	79.2	361	98	63	59	20	0	2	5	33	0	61	3	1	5	6	.455	0	0	6.67
4 Min. YEARS		100	94	9	3	599	2549	554	282	229	50	15	15	19	242	10	563	41	8	42	28	.600	2	0	3.44

Maximo Nunez

Pitches: Right **Bats:** Right **Pos:** P   Ht: 6'5"   Wt: 165   Born: 1/15/73   **Age:** 27

		HOW MUCH HE PITCHED						WHAT HE GAVE UP											THE RESULTS					
Year Team	Lg Org	G	GS	CG	GF	IP	BFP	H	R	ER	HR	SH	SF	HB	TBB	IBB	SO	WP	Bk	W	L	Pct.	ShO	Sv	ERA
1994 Blue Jays	R Tor	20	0	0	15	24.2	119	32	23	11	0	1	1	1	10	0	17	2	2	1	5	.167	0	2	4.01
1995 Hagerstown	A Tor	22	0	0	11	37.1	172	40	29	23	4	3	2	3	20	0	21	8	0	1	1	.500	0	0	5.54
St.Cathrnes	A- Tor	7	0	0	4	7.2	42	11	10	8	1	2	0	1	7	0	6	1	0	1	0	1.000	0	0	9.39
1996 Hickory	A CWS	31	24	3	3	152.1	660	173	93	79	12	3	9	7	45	0	105	5	3	5	16	.238	1	0	4.67
1997 Winston-Sal	A+ CWS	28	0	0	19	52	210	35	15	10	5	3	2	1	21	1	53	2	0	0	8	.000	0	1	1.73
Birmingham	AA CWS	14	0	0	3	17.2	85	19	18	15	1	0	1	1	13	0	14	3	2	0	0	.000	0	0	7.64
1998 Orlando	AA TB	6	0	0	5	11.2	45	5	1	1	0	1	1	0	4	1	14	2	0	2	0	1.000	0	2	0.77
Durham	AAA TB	58	0	0	32	63	292	67	39	35	9	5	1	5	40	7	53	5	1	3	6	.333	0	5	5.00
1999 Durham	AAA TB	21	0	0	9	31.2	147	25	20	19	2	1	0	5	28	0	31	6	0	1	0	1.000	0	9	5.40
Orlando	AA TB	26	0	0	18	26	121	23	11	10	2	1	1	3	17	0	19	0	0	0	2	.000	0	9	3.46
6 Min. YEARS		233	24	3	119	424	1891	430	259	211	36	20	18	27	205	9	333	34	8	14	32	.304	1	28	4.48

207

Talmadge Nunnari

Bats: Left   Throws: Left   Pos: 1B   Ht: 6'1"   Wt: 205   Born: 4/9/75   Age: 25

Year Team	Lg Org	G	AB	H	2B	3B	HR	TB	R	RBI	TBB	IBB	SO	HBP	SH	SF	SB	CS	SB%	GDP	Avg	OBP	SLG
1997 Vermont	A- Mon	62	236	75	11	3	4	104	30	42	31	4	37	3	0	4	6	3	.67	4	.318	.398	.441
Cape Fear	A Mon	9	35	13	1	1	1	19	8	6	1	0	5	0	0	0	2	0	1.00	0	.371	.389	.543
1998 Cape Fear	A Mon	79	289	88	18	0	2	112	51	51	42	2	44	1	0	0	4	4	.50	5	.304	.395	.388
Jupiter	A+ Mon	56	201	59	14	0	2	79	18	34	30	1	39	0	0	6	1	2	.33	2	.294	.376	.393
1999 Jupiter	A+ Mon	71	261	93	17	1	5	127	41	44	27	1	36	3	1	0	10	0	1.00	5	.356	.423	.487
Harrisburg	AA Mon	63	239	79	17	1	6	116	45	29	39	3	46	1	2	2	7	2	.78	1	.331	.423	.485
3 Min. YEARS		340	1261	407	78	6	20	557	193	206	170	11	207	8	3	12	30	11	.73	19	.323	.403	.442

Mark Nussbeck

Pitches: Right   Bats: Left   Pos: P   Ht: 6'4"   Wt: 180   Born: 5/25/74   Age: 26

Year Team	Lg Org	G	GS	CG	GF	IP	BFP	H	R	ER	HR	SH	SF	HB	TBB	IBB	SO	WP	Bk	W	L	Pct.	ShO	Sv	ERA
1996 New Jersey	A- StL	16	14	0	1	79.2	301	72	31	26	4	2	2	4	16	0	74	3	3	6	3	.667	0	0	2.94
1997 Peoria	A StL	27	27	2	0	151.1	683	181	92	77	14	4	8	3	56	3	132	6	4	12	12	.400	2	0	4.58
1998 Pr William	A+ StL	14	13	0	0	86	349	75	40	34	10	2	1	1	16	0	65	0	0	3	6	.333	0	0	3.56
Arkansas	AA StL	10	8	0	0	42.1	192	44	30	24	7	2	2	1	18	1	21	2	0	4	2	.667	0	0	5.10
1999 Arkansas	AA StL	2	2	0	0	11.2	54	12	8	8	1	0	0	0	9	0	11	2	0	0	1	.000	0	0	6.17
Memphis	AAA StL	36	16	0	6	101.2	481	145	100	93	23	7	4	3	37	1	82	5	1	6	10	.375	0	0	8.23
4 Min. YEARS		105	80	2	7	472.2	2084	529	301	262	59	17	17	12	152	5	385	18	8	27	34	.443	2	0	4.99

Ryan Nye

Pitches: Right   Bats: Right   Pos: P   Ht: 6'2"   Wt: 212   Born: 6/24/73   Age: 27

Year Team	Lg Org	G	GS	CG	GF	IP	BFP	H	R	ER	HR	SH	SF	HB	TBB	IBB	SO	WP	Bk	W	L	Pct.	ShO	Sv	ERA
1994 Batavia	A- Phi	13	12	1	0	71.2	301	64	27	21	3	1	0	6	15	0	71	2	1	7	2	.778	0	0	2.64
1995 Clearwater	A+ Phi	27	27	5	0	167	681	164	71	63	8	5	5	6	33	1	116	4	3	12	7	.632	1	0	3.40
1996 Reading	AA Phi	14	14	0	0	86.2	365	76	41	37	9	1	3	6	30	1	90	3	1	8	2	.800	0	0	3.84
Scranton-WB	AAA Phi	14	14	0	0	80.2	362	97	52	45	10	0	2	3	30	0	51	1	1	5	2	.714	0	0	5.02
1997 Scranton-WB	AAA Phi	17	17	0	0	109.1	465	117	70	67	20	2	2	2	32	1	85	2	1	4	10	.286	0	0	5.52
1998 Scranton-WB	AAA Phi	23	22	3	0	140	595	139	73	63	8	4	2	7	49	2	118	7	2	9	6	.600	2	0	4.05
1999 Scranton-WB	AAA Phi	14	10	0	1	65.1	283	69	41	37	8	2	1	2	20	1	63	2	0	5	4	.556	0	0	5.10
1997 Philadelphia	NL	4	2	0	1	12	65	20	11	11	2	1	2	2	9	0	7	0	0	0	2	.000	0	0	8.25
1998 Philadelphia	NL	1	0	0	1	1	6	3	3	3	1	0	0	0	0	0	3	0	0	0	0	.000	0	0	27.00
6 Min. YEARS		122	116	9	1	720.2	3052	726	375	333	66	15	15	32	209	6	594	21	9	50	33	.602	3	0	4.16
2 Maj. YEARS		5	2	0	2	13	71	23	14	14	3	1	2	2	9	0	10	0	0	0	2	.000	0	0	9.69

Brian O'Connor

Pitches: Left   Bats: Left   Pos: P   Ht: 6'2"   Wt: 190   Born: 1/4/77   Age: 23

Year Team	Lg Org	G	GS	CG	GF	IP	BFP	H	R	ER	HR	SH	SF	HB	TBB	IBB	SO	WP	Bk	W	L	Pct.	ShO	Sv	ERA
1995 Pirates	R Pit	14	5	0	5	43	183	33	22	9	1	0	1	0	13	0	43	4	2	2	2	.500	0	1	1.88
1996 Augusta	A Pit	19	0	0	5	35.1	147	33	13	12	2	3	1	1	8	0	37	6	0	0	1	.000	0	1	3.06
Erie	A- Pit	15	15	0	0	67.2	329	75	60	44	4	3	2	3	47	0	60	10	1	4	10	.286	0	0	5.85
1997 Augusta	A Pit	25	14	0	3	85.2	385	90	54	42	6	4	1	2	39	1	91	11	0	2	7	.222	0	0	4.41
Lynchburg	A+ Pit	11	0	0	6	13	55	11	5	5	0	0	0	1	6	1	14	3	0	2	1	.667	0	2	3.46
1998 Lynchburg	A+ Pit	14	14	1	0	86.2	371	86	34	25	3	3	1	1	22	1	84	7	0	6	2	.750	0	0	2.60
Carolina	AA Pit	14	13	0	0	64.1	318	86	65	59	11	3	2	3	53	1	41	12	0	2	4	.333	0	0	8.25
1999 Altoona	AA Pit	28	27	1	0	153.1	698	152	98	77	10	11	3	6	92	2	106	21	0	7	11	.389	0	0	4.52
5 Min. YEARS		140	88	2	19	549	2486	566	351	273	37	27	11	17	280	6	476	74	3	25	38	.397	0	4	4.48

Jake O'Dell

Pitches: Right   Bats: Right   Pos: P   Ht: 6'1"   Wt: 205   Born: 9/22/73   Age: 26

Year Team	Lg Org	G	GS	CG	GF	IP	BFP	H	R	ER	HR	SH	SF	HB	TBB	IBB	SO	WP	Bk	W	L	Pct.	ShO	Sv	ERA
1996 Sou Oregon	A- Oak	13	10	0	0	48.2	205	41	25	18	2	1	3	1	16	1	46	2	1	2	3	.400	0	0	3.33
Modesto	A+ Oak	1	1	0	0	5	22	6	4	3	1	0	0	1	0	0	4	0	1	1	0	1.000	0	0	5.40
1997 Visalia	A+ Oak	27	27	1	0	150.2	648	159	86	76	17	4	2	11	47	0	117	10	0	8	5	.615	1	0	4.54
1998 Visalia	A+ Oak	9	5	0	3	41	164	34	13	10	0	0	1	1	9	0	36	2	1	3	1	.750	0	1	2.20
Huntsville	AA Oak	27	9	0	6	78.1	347	84	54	45	8	3	6	3	30	3	69	2	0	2	5	.286	0	1	5.17
1999 Modesto	A+ Oak	3	0	0	0	7	31	7	2	2	0	0	0	0	3	0	10	0	0	1	0	1.000	0	0	2.57
Midland	AA Oak	9	3	0	2	24.2	125	36	31	31	8	0	2	2	15	1	16	3	0	0	2	.000	0	0	11.31
4 Min. YEARS		89	55	1	11	355.1	1542	367	215	185	36	8	14	19	120	5	298	19	3	17	16	.515	1	1	4.69

Kevin Ohme

Pitches: Left   Bats: Left   Pos: P   Ht: 6'1"   Wt: 185   Born: 4/13/71   Age: 29

Year Team	Lg Org	G	GS	CG	GF	IP	BFP	H	R	ER	HR	SH	SF	HB	TBB	IBB	SO	WP	Bk	W	L	Pct.	ShO	Sv	ERA
1993 Fort Wayne	A Min	15	4	0	6	46.1	184	38	16	13	1	2	2	1	15	1	45	4	1	3	2	.600	0	0	2.53
1994 Fort Wayne	A Min	2	2	0	0	7	29	7	2	2	0	0	0	1	0	0	8	0	0	0	1	.000	0	0	2.57
1995 Hardware Cy	AA Min	35	11	0	7	101.1	427	89	51	39	5	7	7	3	45	1	52	7	0	3	4	.429	0	0	3.46
1996 Hardware Cy	AA Min	51	0	0	22	81	363	83	49	39	7	6	4	6	33	5	42	5	2	5	6	.455	0	3	4.33
1997 Salt Lake	AAA Min	56	0	0	34	73.2	324	70	49	46	6	5	1	6	34	4	45	4	1	2	5	.286	0	11	5.62
1998 Salt Lake	AAA Min	51	0	0	23	82.2	361	90	48	46	5	3	4	6	31	3	47	3	1	4	3	.571	0	6	5.01
1999 Salt Lake	AAA Min	51	3	0	15	82.1	368	94	44	35	8	1	6	8	31	2	48	4	1	5	3	.625	0	2	3.83
7 Min. YEARS		261	20	0	107	474.1	2056	471	262	220	32	24	24	31	189	16	287	27	6	22	24	.478	0	22	4.17

Augie Ojeda

Bats: Both   Throws: Right   Pos: SS   **Ht:** 5'9" **Wt:** 165 **Born:** 12/20/74 **Age:** 25

		BATTING															BASERUNNING				PERCENTAGES		
Year Team	Lg Org	G	AB	H	2B	3B	HR	TB	R	RBI	TBB	IBB	SO	HBP	SH	SF	SB	CS	SB%	GDP	Avg	OBP	SLG
1997 Frederick	A+ Bal	34	128	44	11	1	1	60	25	20	18	1	18	1	4	0	2	5	.29	1	.344	.429	.469
Bowie	AA Bal	58	204	60	9	1	2	77	33	23	31	1	17	3	4	3	7	0	1.00	6	.294	.390	.377
Rochester	AAA Bal	15	47	11	3	1	0	16	5	6	8	0	4	0	3	0	1	2	.33	2	.234	.345	.340
1998 Orioles	R Bal	4	15	6	2	0	0	8	6	2	3	0	1	2	0	0	3	0	1.00	0	.400	.550	.533
Bowie	AA Bal	73	254	65	10	2	1	82	36	19	36	0	30	3	5	1	0	3	.00	5	.256	.354	.323
1999 Rochester	AAA Bal	1	1	0	0	0	0	0	1	0	0	0	0	0	0	0	0	0	.00	0	.000	.000	.000
Bowie	AA Bal	134	460	123	18	4	10	179	73	60	57	0	47	11	25	4	6	2	.75	7	.267	.359	.389
3 Min. YEARS		319	1109	309	53	9	14	422	179	130	153	2	117	20	41	8	19	12	.61	21	.279	.374	.381

Jason Olsen

Pitches: Right   Bats: Right   Pos: P   **Ht:** 6'4" **Wt:** 210 **Born:** 3/16/75 **Age:** 25

		HOW MUCH HE PITCHED						WHAT HE GAVE UP										THE RESULTS				
Year Team	Lg Org	G	GS	CG	GF	IP	BFP	H	R	ER	HR	SH	SF	HB	TBB	IBB	SO	WP	Bk	W	L	Pct.	ShO	Sv	ERA
1996 South Bend	A CWS	9	9	0	0	56.2	220	39	16	11	3	2	1	2	13	0	55	3	0	4	1	.800	0	0	1.75
Hickory	A CWS	4	4	1	0	26.1	101	19	5	4	1	0	0	0	6	0	32	0	0	2	1	.667	0	0	1.37
Pr William	A+ CWS	12	12	0	0	79	343	74	39	34	5	0	2	5	31	1	55	3	0	6	4	.600	0	0	3.87
1997 Birmingham	AA CWS	28	27	1	0	160.1	709	183	101	87	14	11	5	3	58	2	121	9	0	9	14	.391	1	0	4.88
1998 Birmingham	AA CWS	28	28	4	0	159.1	709	188	95	83	19	4	3	5	53	3	134	6	1	8	10	.444	0	0	4.69
1999 Charlotte	AAA CWS	22	10	0	2	62	296	84	59	49	12	1	5	5	29	0	49	3	0	2	4	.333	0	0	7.11
Birmingham	AA CWS	9	4	1	3	33	138	33	15	14	2	1	0	1	10	0	25	3	0	1	3	.250	0	0	3.82
4 Min. YEARS		112	94	7	5	576.2	2516	620	330	282	56	19	16	21	200	6	471	27	1	32	37	.464	1	0	4.40

Dan Olson

Bats: Left   Throws: Left   Pos: DH   **Ht:** 6'2" **Wt:** 210 **Born:** 4/10/75 **Age:** 25

		BATTING															BASERUNNING				PERCENTAGES		
Year Team	Lg Org	G	AB	H	2B	3B	HR	TB	R	RBI	TBB	IBB	SO	HBP	SH	SF	SB	CS	SB%	GDP	Avg	OBP	SLG
1996 White Sox	R CWS	3	11	4	3	0	0	7	4	5	4	0	4	0	0	0	0	0	.00	0	.364	.533	.636
Hickory	A CWS	57	193	48	8	2	2	66	25	19	31	3	65	0	0	0	2	3	.40	1	.249	.353	.342
1997 Hickory	A CWS	98	350	100	31	3	9	164	59	47	36	1	120	3	1	5	4	1	.80	4	.286	.353	.469
1998 Winston-Sal	A+ CWS	117	404	105	33	5	18	202	73	68	41	2	152	7	1	4	5	6	.45	2	.260	.336	.500
1999 Winston-Sal	AA CWS	33	97	16	4	0	6	38	14	13	15	0	44	0	0	0	1	1	.50	0	.165	.277	.392
Winston-Sal	A+ CWS	64	216	69	16	0	9	112	36	41	39	4	80	6	0	1	1	1	.50	0	.319	.435	.519
4 Min. YEARS		372	1271	342	95	10	44	589	211	193	166	10	465	16	2	10	13	12	.52	7	.269	.358	.463

Paul O'Malley

Pitches: Right   Bats: Right   Pos: P   **Ht:** 6'2" **Wt:** 190 **Born:** 12/20/72 **Age:** 27

		HOW MUCH HE PITCHED						WHAT HE GAVE UP										THE RESULTS				
Year Team	Lg Org	G	GS	CG	GF	IP	BFP	H	R	ER	HR	SH	SF	HB	TBB	IBB	SO	WP	Bk	W	L	Pct.	ShO	Sv	ERA
1994 Auburn	A- Hou	9	9	1	0	44.2	205	51	30	27	3	1	1	5	18	0	38	7	2	3	4	.429	0	0	5.44
1995 Kissimmee	A+ Hou	27	27	0	0	147	661	148	86	59	7	3	3	18	62	0	80	13	2	8	10	.444	0	0	3.61
1996 Quad City	A Hou	26	26	1	0	178	753	173	80	66	10	7	9	11	51	0	111	15	2	11	9	.550	0	0	3.34
1997 Jackson	AA Hou	28	0	0	7	44.2	211	53	32	32	4	1	5	5	21	1	25	4	0	0	2	.000	0	0	6.45
Kissimmee	A+ Hou	24	0	0	13	35.1	145	24	12	11	3	1	2	1	19	3	20	1	0	2	0	.000	0	5	2.80
1998 Jackson	AA Hou	29	28	1	1	152	695	162	112	92	22	6	7	23	70	2	89	6	4	11	10	.524	0	0	5.45
1999 Jackson	AA Hou	36	7	0	11	70.2	329	75	53	44	10	2	3	5	48	0	65	10	0	1	3	.250	0	0	5.60
6 Min. YEARS		179	97	3	32	672.1	2999	686	405	331	59	21	30	68	289	6	428	56	10	36	40	.474	0	5	4.43

Steve Ontiveros

Pitches: Right   Bats: Right   Pos: P   **Ht:** 6' 0" **Wt:** 190 **Born:** 3/5/61 **Age:** 39

		HOW MUCH HE PITCHED						WHAT HE GAVE UP										THE RESULTS				
Year Team	Lg Org	G	GS	CG	GF	IP	BFP	H	R	ER	HR	SH	SF	HB	TBB	IBB	SO	WP	Bk	W	L	Pct.	ShO	Sv	ERA
1982 Medford	A- Oak	4	0	0	3	8	—	3	0	0	0	—	—	0	4	0	9	0	0	1	0	1.000	0	0	0.00
West Haven	AA Oak	16	2	0	5	27	—	34	26	19	4	—	—	3	12	0	28	1	0	2	2	.500	0	0	6.33
1983 Albany	AA Oak	32	13	5	12	129.2	—	131	62	54	11	—	—	0	36	2	91	3	0	8	4	.667	0	5	3.75
1984 Tacoma	AAA Oak	2	2	0	0	11.1	0	18	11	10	3	0	0	1	5	0	6	0	0	1	1	.500	0	0	7.94
Madison	A Oak	5	5	2	0	30.2	122	23	10	7	0	1	1	1	6	0	26	1	0	3	1	.750	0	0	2.05
1985 Tacoma	AAA Oak	15	0	0	7	33.2	0	26	13	11	1	0	0	2	21	2	30	1	0	3	0	1.000	0	2	2.94
1987 Tacoma	AAA Oak	1	1	0	0	3	12	1	1	1	0	0	1	0	2	0	1	1	0	0	0	.000	0	0	3.00
1989 Scranton-WB	AAA Phi	1	1	0	0	3.1	15	3	0	0	0	0	0	0	3	0	5	0	0	0	0	.000	0	0	0.00
1990 Clearwater	A+ Phi	3	3	0	0	7.2	29	4	2	2	0	0	0	0	2	0	8	0	1	0	2	.000	0	0	2.35
Reading	AA Phi	2	2	0	0	6	29	7	6	6	0	0	0	2	2	0	8	0	0	0	2	.000	0	0	9.00
1991 Scranton-WB	AAA Phi	7	7	0	0	31	127	29	11	10	2	0	1	0	10	0	21	2	0	2	1	.667	0	0	2.90
1993 Portland	AAA Min	20	16	2	2	103.1	418	90	40	33	5	2	6	4	20	0	73	5	2	7	6	.538	0	0	2.87
1996 Lk Elsinore	A+ Ana	2	2	0	0	8	35	12	3	2	0	0	0	0	0	0	8	1	0	1	1	.500	0	0	2.25
1997 Lk Elsinore	A+ Ana	1	1	0	0	0.1	2	0	1	1	0	0	0	0	0	0	0	0	0	0	0	.000	0	0	27.00
1998 Memphis	AAA StL	3	3	0	0	9.2	45	14	11	9	1	0	0	0	2	0	10	0	1	0	0	.000	0	0	8.38
Rochester	AAA Bal	16	14	0	2	80.2	333	77	35	33	10	2	2	2	25	0	64	1	0	5	1	.833	0	1	3.68
1999 Louisville	AAA Mil	8	8	0	0	48.2	203	47	26	24	5	3	1	0	12	1	33	1	0	5	1	.833	0	0	4.44
1985 Oakland	AL	39	0	0	18	74.2	284	45	17	16	4	2	2	2	19	2	36	1	0	1	3	.250	0	8	1.93
1986 Oakland	AL	46	0	0	27	72.2	305	72	40	38	10	1	6	1	25	3	54	4	0	2	2	.500	0	10	4.71
1987 Oakland	AL	35	22	2	6	150.2	645	141	78	67	19	6	2	4	50	3	97	4	1	10	8	.556	1	0	4.00
1988 Oakland	AL	10	10	0	0	54.2	241	57	32	28	4	5	0	0	21	1	30	5	5	3	4	.429	0	0	4.61
1989 Philadelphia	NL	6	5	0	0	30.2	134	34	15	13	2	1	0	0	15	1	12	2	0	2	2	.667	0	0	3.82
1990 Philadelphia	NL	5	0	0	1	10	43	9	3	3	1	0	0	0	3	0	6	0	0	0	0	.000	0	0	2.70
1993 Seattle	AL	14	0	0	8	18	72	18	3	2	1	0	0	0	6	2	13	1	0	0	2	.000	0	0	1.00

209

		HOW	MUCH	HE	PITCHED			WHAT	HE	GAVE	UP									THE	RESULTS			
Year Team	Lg Org	G	GS	CG	GF	IP	BFP	H	R	ER	HR	SH	SF	HB	TBB	IBB	SO	WP	Bk	W	L	Pct.	ShO	Sv	ERA
1994 Oakland	AL	27	13	2	5	115.1	463	93	39	34	7	2	1	6	26	1	56	5	0	6	4	.600	0	0	2.65
1995 Oakland	AL	22	22	2	0	129.2	558	144	75	63	12	2	6	4	38	0	77	5	0	9	6	.600	1	0	4.37
13 Min. YEARS		138	80	9	31	542	—	519	258	222	42	—	—	15	164	5	410	17	4	38	22	.633	0	8	3.69
9 Maj. YEARS		204	72	6	65	656.1	2745	613	302	264	59	20	17	17	203	13	381	27	6	33	30	.524	2	19	3.62

Mario Opipari

Pitches: Right Bats: Both Pos: P Ht: 6'2" Wt: 185 Born: 1/24/75 Age: 25

		HOW	MUCH	HE	PITCHED			WHAT	HE	GAVE	UP									THE	RESULTS			
Year Team	Lg Org	G	GS	CG	GF	IP	BFP	H	R	ER	HR	SH	SF	HB	TBB	IBB	SO	WP	Bk	W	L	Pct.	ShO	Sv	ERA
1996 Twins	R Min	4	0	0	3	6	23	2	0	0	0	0	0	0	3	0	6	0	0	0	0	.000	0	1	0.00
Elizabethtn	R+ Min	19	1	0	16	32.1	135	26	10	7	2	0	0	1	9	0	36	2	0	3	1	.750	0	6	1.95
1997 Fort Wayne	A Min	53	2	0	27	70.2	307	71	45	27	2	5	3	3	24	3	61	7	1	6	7	.462	0	8	3.44
1998 Fort Myers	A+ Min	17	0	0	4	34	152	38	19	15	2	1	1	3	13	1	18	1	0	1	0	1.000	0	0	3.97
Pr William	A+ StL	32	2	0	19	54	221	47	17	13	1	6	3	0	9	3	26	1	0	5	5	.500	0	3	2.17
1999 Potomac	A+ StL	7	0	0	4	8.2	41	12	7	3	0	1	1	0	3	0	9	0	0	0	1	.000	0	0	3.12
Memphis	AAA StL	3	0	0	0	2.2	11	2	3	3	0	0	0	0	3	0	1	0	0	0	0	.000	0	0	10.13
Arkansas	AA StL	20	0	0	8	25.2	112	30	11	10	1	1	3	1	11	2	16	2	0	1	0	1.000	0	0	3.51
4 Min. YEARS		155	5	0	81	234	1002	228	112	78	8	14	11	8	75	9	172	14	1	15	15	.500	0	18	3.00

Eddie Oropesa

Pitches: Left Bats: Left Pos: P Ht: 6'3" Wt: 215 Born: 11/23/71 Age: 28

		HOW	MUCH	HE	PITCHED			WHAT	HE	GAVE	UP									THE	RESULTS			
Year Team	Lg Org	G	GS	CG	GF	IP	BFP	H	R	ER	HR	SH	SF	HB	TBB	IBB	SO	WP	Bk	W	L	Pct.	ShO	Sv	ERA
1994 Vero Beach	A+ LA	19	10	1	3	72	285	54	24	17	2	3	2	4	25	2	67	2	0	4	3	.571	1	0	2.13
1995 San Antonio	AA LA	16	0	0	7	17.1	87	22	8	6	2	1	2	3	12	1	16	0	1	1	1	.500	0	1	3.12
Vero Beach	A+ LA	19	1	0	7	28.1	120	25	12	12	0	1	2	3	10	0	23	4	2	3	1	.750	0	1	3.81
San Berndno	A+ LA	1	0	0	1	1	3	0	0	0	0	0	0	0	0	0	0	0	0	0	0	.000	0	1	0.00
1996 San Berndno	A+ LA	33	19	0	2	156.1	669	133	74	58	8	1	3	6	77	1	133	8	4	11	6	.647	0	1	3.34
1997 Shreveport	AA SF	43	9	1	12	124	531	122	58	54	7	7	4	4	64	0	65	6	6	7	7	.500	0	0	3.92
1998 Shreveport	AA SF	32	20	2	3	143	623	143	71	60	6	7	5	7	67	3	104	15	2	7	11	.389	0	0	3.78
1999 Bakersfield	A+ SF	2	1	0	0	10	41	13	5	4	2	0	0	0	1	0	10	2	0	2	0	1.000	0	0	3.60
Fresno	AAA SF	21	18	1	0	102	460	113	69	55	15	3	1	3	49	0	61	13	4	6	5	.545	0	0	4.85
6 Min. YEARS		186	78	5	35	654	2819	625	321	266	42	23	19	30	305	7	479	50	19	41	34	.547	1	4	3.66

Bill Ortega

Bats: Right Throws: Right Pos: OF Ht: 6'4" Wt: 205 Born: 7/24/75 Age: 24

		BATTING														BASERUNNING				PERCENTAGES		
Year Team	Lg Org	G	AB	H	2B	3B	HR	TB	R	RBI	TBB	IBB	SO	HBP	SH	SF	SB	CS	SB%	GDP	Avg	OBP	SLG
1997 Pr William	A+ StL	73	249	57	14	0	0	71	15	21	1	42	0	1	0		1	2	.33	10	.229	.289	.285
1998 Peoria	A StL	105	398	110	23	2	2	143	57	60	39	0	69	5	3	2	4	8	.33	14	.276	.347	.359
1999 Potomac	A+ StL	110	421	129	27	4	9	191	66	74	38	2	69	4	6	3	7	7	.50	17	.306	.367	.454
Arkansas	AA StL	20	69	26	9	0	2	41	10	10	10	0	9	0	1	0	0	0	.00	4	.377	.456	.594
3 Min. YEARS		308	1137	322	73	6	13	446	156	159	108	3	189	9	11	5	12	17	.41	45	.283	.349	.392

Pablo Ortega

Pitches: Right Bats: Both Pos: P Ht: 6'2" Wt: 170 Born: 11/7/76 Age: 23

		HOW	MUCH	HE	PITCHED			WHAT	HE	GAVE	UP									THE	RESULTS			
Year Team	Lg Org	G	GS	CG	GF	IP	BFP	H	R	ER	HR	SH	SF	HB	TBB	IBB	SO	WP	Bk	W	L	Pct.	ShO	Sv	ERA
1996 Devil Rays	R TB	13	13	1	0	82.1	330	61	24	18	1	2	0	3	12	0	86	7	4	4	6	.400	0	0	1.97
1997 Chston-SC	A TB	29	29	3	0	188.2	778	173	87	60	10	7	6	10	30	0	142	4	1	12	10	.545	0	0	2.86
1998 St. Pete	A+ TB	28	25	2	2	155.1	685	187	104	76	13	3	7	6	39	1	111	3	1	5	9	.357	0	0	4.40
1999 St. Pete	A+ TB	4	1	0	0	9.1	39	9	6	2	1	0	0	1	1	0	5	1	0	1	2	.333	0	0	1.93
Durham	AAA TB	1	1	0	0	2.1	16	10	9	9	0	0	0	0	0	0	2	1	0	0	1	.000	0	0	34.71
Orlando	AA TB	22	22	1	0	130.1	567	147	77	56	14	3	9	8	47	3	74	4	3	8	10	.444	1	0	3.87
4 Min. YEARS		97	91	7	2	568.1	2415	587	307	221	39	15	22	28	129	4	420	20	9	30	38	.441	1	0	3.50

Hector Ortiz

Bats: Right Throws: Right Pos: C Ht: 6'0" Wt: 205 Born: 10/14/69 Age: 30

		BATTING														BASERUNNING				PERCENTAGES		
Year Team	Lg Org	G	AB	H	2B	3B	HR	TB	R	RBI	TBB	IBB	SO	HBP	SH	SF	SB	CS	SB%	GDP	Avg	OBP	SLG
1988 Salem	A- LA	32	77	11	1	0	0	12	5	4	5	0	16	1	1	0	0	2	.00	5	.143	.205	.156
1989 Vero Beach	A+ LA	42	85	12	0	1	0	14	5	4	6	0	15	2	4	0	0	0	.00	1	.141	.215	.165
Salem	A- LA	44	140	32	3	1	0	37	13	12	4	0	24	1	2	0	2	1	.67	6	.229	.255	.264
1990 Yakima	A- LA	52	173	47	3	1	0	52	16	12	5	0	15	1	1	0	1	1	.50	6	.272	.296	.301
1991 Vero Beach	A+ LA	42	123	28	2	0	0	30	3	8	5	0	8	3	0	0	0	0	.00	2	.228	.275	.244
1992 Bakersfield	A+ LA	63	206	58	8	1	1	71	19	31	21	0	16	5	3	2	2	3	.40	8	.282	.359	.345
San Antonio	AA LA	26	59	12	1	0	0	13	1	5	11	0	13	1	1	0	0	0	.00	2	.203	.338	.220
1993 San Antonio	AA LA	49	131	28	5	0	1	36	6	6	9	2	17	0	3	0	0	2	.00	3	.214	.264	.275
Albuquerque	AAA LA	18	44	8	1	1	0	11	6	0	3	0	6	1	2	0	0	0	.00	1	.182	.200	.250
1994 Albuquerque	AAA LA	34	93	28	1	1	0	31	7	10	3	0	12	0	0	1	0	0	.00	7	.301	.320	.333
San Antonio	AA LA	24	75	9	0	0	0	9	4	4	2	0	7	1	0	2	0	0	.00	6	.120	.150	.120
1995 Orlando	AA ChC	96	299	70	12	0	0	82	13	18	20	0	39	1	1	4	0	5	.00	10	.234	.281	.274
1996 Orlando	AA ChC	78	216	47	8	0	0	55	16	15	26	2	23	0	1	3	1	2	.33	12	.218	.298	.255
Iowa	AAA ChC	27	79	19	2	0	0	21	6	3	3	1	16	0	0	1	0	0	.00	1	.241	.265	.266
1997 Omaha	AAA KC	21	63	12	3	0	0	15	7	3	13	0	15	0	0	0	0	0	.00	1	.190	.329	.238
Wichita	AA KC	59	180	45	3	0	1	51	20	25	21	0	15	1	4	2	0	2	.33	10	.250	.332	.283

(continued)

Year Team	Lg Org	G	AB	H	2B	3B	HR	TB	R	RBI	TBB	IBB	SO	HBP	SH	SF	SB	CS	SB%	GDP	Avg	OBP	SLG
1998 Wichita	AA KC	4	13	2	0	0	0	2	1	0	2	0	1	0	0	0	0	1	.00	0	.154	.267	.154
Omaha	AAA KC	63	191	43	7	0	0	50	17	12	9	0	26	1	2	0	0	0	.00	10	.225	.264	.262
1999 San Antonio	AA LA	40	121	29	4	0	0	33	10	13	10	0	17	0	0	3	0	1	.00	2	.240	.291	.273
Albuquerque	AAA LA	55	164	50	9	0	6	77	21	20	7	1	27	1	0	3	2	3	.40	8	.305	.331	.470
1998 Kansas City	AL	4	4	0	0	0	0	0	1	0	0	0	0	0	0	0	0	0	.00	0	.000	.000	.000
12 Min. YEARS		869	2532	590	73	6	9	702	190	208	182	6	328	21	25	21	9	23	.28	103	.233	.288	.277

Jose Ortiz

Bats: Right Throws: Right Pos: SS Ht: 5'9" Wt: 160 Born: 6/13/77 Age: 23

Year Team	Lg Org	G	AB	H	2B	3B	HR	TB	R	RBI	TBB	IBB	SO	HBP	SH	SF	SB	CS	SB%	GDP	Avg	OBP	SLG
1996 Athletics	R Oak	52	200	66	12	8	4	106	43	25	20	2	34	1	1	1	16	5	.76	1	.330	.392	.530
Modesto	A+ Oak	1	4	1	0	0	0	1	0	0	0	0	1	0	0	0	0	0	.00	0	.250	.250	.250
1997 Modesto	A+ Oak	128	497	122	25	7	16	209	92	58	60	2	107	6	3	4	22	14	.61	7	.245	.332	.421
1998 Huntsville	AA Oak	94	354	98	24	2	6	144	70	55	48	0	63	5	6	2	22	8	.73	6	.277	.369	.407
1999 Vancouver	AAA Oak	107	377	107	29	2	9	167	66	45	29	1	50	9	3	4	13	4	.76	8	.284	.346	.443
4 Min. YEARS		382	1432	394	90	19	35	627	271	183	157	5	255	21	13	11	73	31	.70	22	.275	.353	.438

Luis Ortiz

Bats: Right Throws: Right Pos: DH Ht: 6'0" Wt: 195 Born: 5/25/70 Age: 30

Year Team	Lg Org	G	AB	H	2B	3B	HR	TB	R	RBI	TBB	IBB	SO	HBP	SH	SF	SB	CS	SB%	GDP	Avg	OBP	SLG
1991 Red Sox	R Bos	42	153	51	11	2	4	78	21	29	7	0	9	2	1	1	2	1	.67	1	.333	.368	.510
1992 Lynchburg	A+ Bos	94	355	103	27	1	10	162	43	61	22	3	55	2	0	5	4	2	.67	8	.290	.331	.456
1993 Pawtucket	AAA Bos	102	402	118	28	1	18	202	45	81	13	3	74	2	0	4	1	1	.50	10	.294	.316	.502
1994 Pawtucket	AAA Bos	81	317	99	15	3	6	138	47	36	29	5	29	0	0	4	1	4	.20	9	.312	.370	.435
1995 Okla City	AAA Tex	47	170	52	10	5	2	78	19	20	8	2	20	0	1	3	1	1	.50	7	.306	.331	.459
1996 Okla City	AAA Tex	124	501	159	25	0	14	226	70	73	22	2	36	4	0	6	0	5	.00	17	.317	.347	.451
1997 Okla City	AAA Tex	22	82	25	5	0	1	33	9	11	5	0	7	0	0	3	1	1	.50	2	.305	.333	.402
1998 Omaha	AAA KC	44	138	42	13	0	5	70	27	22	10	1	11	0	0	0	0	2	.00	6	.304	.351	.507
1999 Louisville	AAA Mil	96	304	80	11	0	11	124	36	33	23	0	41	0	0	4	0	2	.00	4	.263	.311	.408
1993 Boston	AL	9	12	3	0	0	0	3	0	1	0	0	2	0	0	0	0	0	.00	0	.250	.250	.250
1994 Boston	AL	7	18	3	2	0	0	5	3	6	1	0	5	0	1	3	0	0	.00	0	.167	.182	.278
1995 Texas	AL	41	108	25	5	2	1	37	10	18	6	0	18	0	0	1	0	1	.00	7	.231	.270	.343
1996 Texas	AL	3	7	2	0	1	1	7	1	1	0	0	1	0	0	0	0	0	.00	0	.286	.286	1.000
9 Min. YEARS		652	2422	729	145	12	71	1111	317	366	139	16	282	10	2	26	10	19	.34	68	.301	.338	.459
4 Maj. YEARS		60	145	33	7	3	2	52	14	26	7	0	26	0	1	4	0	1	.00	7	.228	.256	.359

Nicky Ortiz

Bats: Right Throws: Right Pos: SS Ht: 6'0" Wt: 160 Born: 7/9/73 Age: 26

Year Team	Lg Org	G	AB	H	2B	3B	HR	TB	R	RBI	TBB	IBB	SO	HBP	SH	SF	SB	CS	SB%	GDP	Avg	OBP	SLG
1991 Red Sox	R Bos	35	100	26	3	1	0	31	16	13	22	0	24	4	1	0	1	2	.33	1	.260	.413	.310
1992 Red Sox	R Bos	50	163	43	9	3	0	58	25	15	28	0	36	0	2	1	3	2	.60	4	.264	.370	.356
Elmira	A- Bos	9	28	5	3	0	0	8	2	1	5	0	13	0	0	0	0	0	.00	0	.179	.303	.286
1993 Ft. Laud	A+ Bos	36	112	23	9	1	1	37	9	14	9	0	39	0	4	0	2	1	.67	4	.205	.264	.330
Utica	A- Bos	63	197	53	14	1	2	75	31	26	19	0	56	6	1	2	4	1	.80	3	.269	.348	.381
1994 Sarasota	A+ Bos	81	283	76	18	3	2	106	34	40	21	1	57	3	6	3	7	2	.78	11	.269	.323	.375
1995 Sarasota	A+ Bos	91	304	75	20	1	5	112	38	38	27	0	68	4	1	1	6	4	.60	3	.247	.315	.368
1996 Michigan	A Bos	73	242	73	14	4	2	101	37	25	20	1	44	5	1	1	1	1	.50	4	.302	.366	.417
Trenton	AA Bos	38	130	29	4	0	3	42	20	13	13	2	28	0	1	0	2	2	.50	3	.223	.294	.323
1997 Trenton	AA Bos	87	288	81	17	2	8	126	47	53	27	1	55	5	6	5	3	2	.60	8	.281	.348	.438
1998 Ottawa	AAA Mon	12	32	3	1	0	0	4	1	0	6	0	10	0	1	0	0	0	.00	0	.094	.237	.125
Harrisburg	AA Mon	56	163	44	11	2	6	77	18	24	18	0	37	2	7	2	2	3	.40	7	.270	.346	.472
Trenton	AA Bos	39	131	30	6	0	1	39	17	9	14	0	27	1	3	0	0	0	.00	3	.229	.308	.298
1999 Buffalo	AAA Cle	22	51	13	4	0	0	17	7	1	3	0	10	0	0	0	0	0	.00	2	.255	.296	.333
Akron	AA Cle	55	195	52	15	2	2	77	24	13	17	0	40	4	0	3	1	2	.33	5	.267	.333	.395
San Antonio	AA LA	14	40	7	1	0	0	8	4	2	3	0	7	0	0	0	0	0	.00	2	.175	.233	.200
9 Min. YEARS		761	2459	633	149	20	32	918	330	287	252	5	551	34	34	18	32	22	.59	60	.257	.333	.373

Gavin Osteen

Pitches: Left Bats: Right Pos: P Ht: 6'0" Wt: 195 Born: 11/27/69 Age: 30

Year Team	Lg Org	G	GS	CG	GF	IP	BFP	H	R	ER	HR	SH	SF	HB	TBB	IBB	SO	WP	Bk	W	L	Pct.	ShO	Sv	ERA
1989 Sou Oregon	A- Oak	16	6	0	3	46.1	211	44	24	18	3	4	1	3	29	0	42	9	0	2	2	.500	0	0	3.50
1990 Madison	A Oak	27	27	1	0	154	659	126	69	53	6	5	6	3	80	0	120	10	4	10	10	.500	1	0	3.10
1991 Huntsville	AA Oak	28	28	2	0	173	742	176	82	68	4	6	7	4	65	2	105	4	2	13	9	.591	1	0	3.54
1992 Tacoma	AAA Oak	4	4	0	0	14.1	77	21	18	16	4	2	3	2	13	0	7	1	1	0	2	.000	0	0	10.05
Huntsville	AA Oak	16	16	1	0	102.1	425	106	45	41	9	5	5	1	27	0	56	2	2	5	5	.500	0	0	3.61
1993 Huntsville	AA Oak	11	11	2	0	70.1	288	56	21	18	1	1	1	2	25	1	46	2	0	7	3	.700	0	0	2.30
Tacoma	AAA Oak	16	15	0	0	83.1	356	89	51	47	4	4	5	1	31	1	46	0	1	7	7	.500	0	0	5.08
1994 Tacoma	AAA Oak	24	24	2	0	138.1	618	169	95	81	17	3	12	4	39	0	71	0	0	8	9	.471	1	0	5.27
1995 Athletics	R Oak	1	1	0	0	2	7	1	0	0	0	0	0	0	0	0	1	0	0	0	0	.000	0	0	0.00
1997 Bowie	AA Bal	18	2	0	0	30.2	119	20	7	7	1	0	0	0	11	0	22	2	0	1	1	.500	0	0	2.05
1998 Rochester	AAA Bal	44	0	0	18	72.2	310	74	37	32	10	1	2	3	25	0	46	4	2	1	2	.333	0	2	3.96
1999 Albuquerque	AAA LA	34	12	0	10	103.2	464	127	64	59	10	2	1	6	33	4	65	3	0	6	8	.429	0	2	5.12
10 Min. YEARS		239	146	8	33	991	4276	1009	513	440	69	33	45	30	378	8	627	37	12	60	58	.508	3	4	4.00

211

Ricky Otero

Bats: Both **Throws:** Right **Pos:** OF **Ht:** 5' 5" **Wt:** 153 **Born:** 4/15/72 **Age:** 28

Year Team	Lg Org	G	AB	H	2B	3B	HR	TB	R	RBI	TBB	IBB	SO	HBP	SH	SF	SB	CS	SB%	GDP	Avg	OBP	SLG
1991 Kingsport	R+ NYM	66	235	81	16	3	7	124	47	52	35	5	32	2	1	6	12	4	.75	4	.345	.424	.528
Pittsfield	A- NYM	6	24	7	0	0	0	7	4	2	2	0	1	0	0	0	4	0	1.00	0	.292	.346	.292
1992 Columbia	A NYM	96	353	106	24	4	8	162	57	60	38	0	53	3	4	6	39	13	.75	4	.300	.368	.459
St. Lucie	A+ NYM	40	151	48	8	4	0	64	20	19	9	1	11	2	3	2	10	5	.67	1	.318	.360	.424
1993 Binghamton	AA NYM	124	503	133	21	10	2	180	63	54	38	2	57	7	7	4	28	15	.65	5	.264	.322	.358
1994 Binghamton	AA NYM	128	531	156	31	9	7	226	96	57	50	1	49	3	4	4	33	16	.67	7	.294	.355	.426
1995 Norfolk	AAA NYM	72	295	79	8	6	1	102	37	23	27	0	33	1	2	0	16	13	.55	2	.268	.331	.346
1996 Scranton-WB	AAA Phi	46	177	53	9	8	1	81	38	9	28	1	13	0	2	1	15	6	.71	2	.299	.393	.458
1997 Scranton-WB	AAA Phi	38	160	53	10	5	1	76	24	15	13	0	13	0	0	3	5	4	.56	1	.331	.375	.475
1998 Rochester	AAA Bal	87	354	102	25	6	4	151	53	45	21	1	30	3	0	3	10	5	.67	4	.288	.331	.427
1999 Rochester	AAA Bal	53	199	46	11	4	4	77	16	21	16	1	23	1	4	2	5	5	.50	3	.231	.289	.387
Zion	IND —	74	323	114	25	6	8	175	81	47	36	5	24	1	0	3	31	8	.79	2	.353	.416	.542
1995 New York	NL	35	51	7	2	0	0	9	5	1	3	0	10	0	1	0	2	1	.67	1	.137	.185	.176
1996 Philadelphia	NL	104	411	112	11	7	2	143	54	32	34	0	30	2	0	2	16	10	.62	3	.273	.330	.348
1997 Philadelphia	NL	50	151	38	6	2	0	48	20	3	19	0	15	1	3	0	0	3	.00	2	.252	.339	.318
9 Min. YEARS		830	3305	978	188	65	43	1425	536	404	313	17	339	23	27	34	208	94	.69	35	.296	.358	.431
3 Maj. YEARS		189	613	157	19	9	2	200	79	36	56	0	55	3	4	2	18	14	.56	6	.256	.320	.326

Paul Ottavinia

Bats: Left **Throws:** Left **Pos:** OF **Ht:** 6'1" **Wt:** 190 **Born:** 4/22/73 **Age:** 27

Year Team	Lg Org	G	AB	H	2B	3B	HR	TB	R	RBI	TBB	IBB	SO	HBP	SH	SF	SB	CS	SB%	GDP	Avg	OBP	SLG
1994 Burlington	A Mon	49	187	38	8	0	2	52	17	21	7	0	28	0	0	2	5	1	.83	2	.203	.230	.278
1995 Wst Plm Bch	A+ Mon	112	395	93	20	2	1	120	35	37	34	2	44	2	5	2	13	6	.68	10	.235	.298	.304
1996 Expos	R Mon	3	10	4	0	0	0	4	1	1	2	0	1	0	0	0	0	0	.00	0	.400	.500	.400
Wst Plm Bch	A+ Mon	45	141	30	2	1	1	37	15	10	12	0	20	0	3	1	2	1	.67	2	.213	.273	.262
1997 Fargo-Mh	IND —	42	168	56	16	3	0	78	45	22	16	0	16	2	0	0	12	4	.75	2	.333	.398	.464
1998 Fargo-Mh	IND —	10	44	18	4	3	1	31	11	19	1	0	6	0	0	0	1	1	.50	0	.409	.422	.705
Tampa	A+ NYY	57	174	44	13	3	5	78	25	28	14	2	20	0	0	5	2	0	1.00	3	.253	.301	.448
1999 Norwich	AA NYY	59	191	55	11	3	7	93	26	31	14	1	40	1	0	1	5	3	.63	5	.288	.338	.487
6 Min. YEARS		377	1310	338	74	15	17	493	175	169	100	5	175	5	8	11	40	16	.71	24	.258	.311	.376

Jayhawk Owens

Bats: Right **Throws:** Right **Pos:** C **Ht:** 6' 1" **Wt:** 213 **Born:** 2/10/69 **Age:** 31

Year Team	Lg Org	G	AB	H	2B	3B	HR	TB	R	RBI	TBB	IBB	SO	HBP	SH	SF	SB	CS	SB%	GDP	Avg	OBP	SLG
1990 Kenosha	A Min	66	216	51	9	2	5	79	31	30	39	0	59	13	1	1	15	7	.68	8	.236	.383	.366
1991 Visalia	A+ Min	65	233	57	16	1	6	93	33	33	35	1	70	8	0	2	14	6	.70	4	.245	.360	.399
1992 Orlando	AA Min	102	330	88	24	0	4	124	50	30	36	0	67	11	0	5	10	2	.83	5	.267	.353	.376
1993 Colo Sprngs	AAA Col	55	174	54	11	3	6	89	24	43	21	0	56	5	0	3	5	3	.63	4	.310	.394	.511
1994 Colo Sprngs	AAA Col	77	257	69	11	7	6	112	43	44	32	2	66	6	3	3	3	3	.50	7	.268	.359	.436
1995 Colo Sprngs	AAA Col	70	221	65	13	5	12	124	47	48	20	2	61	7	1	2	2	1	.67	2	.294	.368	.561
1996 Colo Sprngs	AAA Col	6	22	5	3	0	0	8	6	3	0	0	6	0	1	0	0	0	.00	1	.227	.320	.364
1997 Colo Sprngs	AAA Col	95	289	75	17	0	10	122	57	34	55	4	98	11	1	2	4	1	.80	3	.260	.395	.422
1998 Salt Lake	AAA Min	52	161	33	9	0	3	51	19	16	13	0	63	2	2	1	1	2	.33	1	.205	.271	.317
Indianapols	AAA Cin	16	37	11	4	0	2	21	5	8	4	1	17	0	0	0	0	0	.00	1	.297	.366	.568
1999 Chattanooga	AA Cin	47	153	34	6	1	6	60	24	21	31	1	45	2	0	2	3	0	1.00	9	.222	.356	.392
Indianapols	AAA Cin	18	53	11	1	0	4	24	7	10	4	0	18	3	0	0	0	0	.00	0	.208	.300	.453
1993 Colorado	NL	33	86	18	5	0	3	32	12	6	6	1	30	2	0	0	1	0	1.00	1	.209	.277	.372
1994 Colorado	NL	6	12	3	0	1	0	5	4	1	3	0	3	0	0	0	0	0	.00	1	.250	.400	.417
1995 Colorado	NL	18	45	11	2	0	4	25	7	12	2	0	15	1	0	1	0	0	.00	0	.244	.286	.556
1996 Colorado	NL	73	180	43	9	1	4	66	31	17	27	0	56	1	3	2	4	1	.80	1	.239	.338	.367
10 Min. YEARS		669	2146	553	124	19	64	907	346	323	293	11	626	68	9	21	57	25	.70	45	.258	.362	.423
4 Maj. YEARS		130	323	75	16	2	11	128	54	36	38	1	104	4	3	3	5	1	.83	3	.232	.318	.396

Ryan Owens

Bats: Right **Throws:** Right **Pos:** 3B **Ht:** 6'2" **Wt:** 200 **Born:** 3/18/78 **Age:** 22

Year Team	Lg Org	G	AB	H	2B	3B	HR	TB	R	RBI	TBB	IBB	SO	HBP	SH	SF	SB	CS	SB%	GDP	Avg	OBP	SLG
1999 El Paso	AA Ari	31	113	36	5	1	4	46	11	18	8	0	36	2	0	1	1	2	.33	1	.319	.371	.407
High Desert	A+ Ari	26	103	41	7	3	4	66	19	28	9	0	30	1	1	1	1	2	.33	0	.398	.447	.641
1 Min. YEARS		57	216	77	12	4	5	112	30	46	17	0	66	3	1	2	2	4	.33	1	.356	.408	.519

Pablo Ozuna

Bats: Right **Throws:** Right **Pos:** SS **Ht:** 6'0" **Wt:** 160 **Born:** 8/25/78 **Age:** 21

Year Team	Lg Org	G	AB	H	2B	3B	HR	TB	R	RBI	TBB	IBB	SO	HBP	SH	SF	SB	CS	SB%	GDP	Avg	OBP	SLG
1997 Johnson Cy	R+ StL	56	232	75	13	1	5	105	40	24	10	0	24	1	6	2	23	5	.82	2	.323	.351	.453
1998 Peoria	A StL	133	538	192	27	10	9	266	122	62	29	3	56	11	12	2	62	26	.70	6	.357	.400	.494
1999 Portland	AA Fla	117	502	141	25	7	7	201	62	46	13	0	50	13	7	3	31	15	.67	8	.281	.315	.400
3 Min. YEARS		306	1272	408	65	18	21	572	224	132	52	3	130	25	25	7	116	46	.72	16	.321	.358	.450

John Pachot

Bats: Right Throws: Right Pos: C   Ht: 6'2" Wt: 168 Born: 11/11/74 Age: 25

Year Team	Lg Org	G	AB	H	2B	3B	HR	TB	R	RBI	TBB	IBB	SO	HBP	SH	SF	SB	CS	SB%	GDP	Avg	OBP	SLG
					BATTING												BASERUNNING				PERCENTAGES		
1993 Expos	R Mon	35	121	37	4	1	0	43	13	16	2	0	7	0	4	2	0	1	.00	0	.306	.312	.355
1994 Burlington	A Mon	100	351	89	17	0	1	109	37	26	13	1	46	3	5	4	1	2	.33	12	.254	.283	.311
1995 Wst Plm Bch	A+ Mon	67	227	57	10	0	0	67	17	23	12	0	38	2	3	1	1	2	.33	4	.251	.293	.295
1996 Expos	R Mon	8	30	9	1	1	0	12	3	3	1	0	0	1	1	0	0	0	.00	0	.300	.344	.400
Wst Plm Bch	A+ Mon	44	163	31	9	0	0	40	8	19	2	0	19	0	1	0	0	1	.00	1	.190	.200	.245
1997 Harrisburg	AA Mon	94	323	90	23	3	7	140	40	50	22	0	42	3	2	5	6	6	.50	10	.279	.326	.433
1998 Ottawa	AAA Mon	100	344	78	18	1	2	104	33	39	15	1	45	3	3	3	2	2	.50	13	.227	.263	.302
1999 Ottawa	AAA Mon	17	56	12	4	0	0	16	7	6	6	1	9	0	1	1	0	0	.00	2	.214	.286	.286
Tucson	AAA Ari	35	102	27	4	0	1	34	10	11	3	0	10	0	0	0	1	0	1.00	5	.265	.286	.333
7 Min. YEARS		500	1717	430	90	6	11	565	168	193	76	3	216	12	20	16	11	14	.44	47	.250	.284	.329

Pete Paciorek

Bats: Left Throws: Left Pos: 1B   Ht: 6'3" Wt: 195 Born: 5/19/76 Age: 24

Year Team	Lg Org	G	AB	H	2B	3B	HR	TB	R	RBI	TBB	IBB	SO	HBP	SH	SF	SB	CS	SB%	GDP	Avg	OBP	SLG
					BATTING												BASERUNNING				PERCENTAGES		
1995 SD	R SD	54	183	47	11	3	5	79	32	24	33	1	58	1	1	0	6	4	.60	1	.257	.373	.432
1996 Idaho Falls	R+ SD	72	283	84	15	2	15	148	56	69	36	1	64	4	0	6	6	1	.86	6	.297	.377	.523
1997 Clinton	A SD	126	435	102	19	11	7	164	70	52	70	5	113	4	1	5	10	4	.71	6	.234	.342	.377
1998 Rancho Cuca	A+ SD	137	481	133	28	6	17	224	82	86	63	3	135	4	6	6	8	7	.53	4	.277	.361	.466
1999 Mobile	AA SD	83	226	50	9	2	4	75	38	17	38	1	60	4	0	0	2	3	.40	6	.221	.343	.332
5 Min. YEARS		472	1608	416	82	24	48	690	278	248	240	11	430	17	8	17	32	19	.63	23	.259	.358	.429

Juan Padilla

Pitches: Right Bats: Right Pos: P   Ht: 6'0" Wt: 188 Born: 2/17/77 Age: 23

Year Team	Lg Org	G	GS	CG	GF	IP	BFP	H	R	ER	HR	SH	SF	HB	TBB	IBB	SO	WP	Bk	W	L	Pct.	ShO	Sv	ERA
			HOW MUCH HE PITCHED						WHAT HE GAVE UP											THE RESULTS					
1998 Twins	R Min	17	0	0	14	25.2	100	19	4	4	1	1	0	2	1	0	27	1	0	1	1	.500	0	10	1.40
1999 Quad City	A Min	12	0	0	4	15	69	18	8	4	0	0	1	0	6	2	16	4	1	0	2	.000	0	0	2.40
New Britain	AA Min	11	0	0	3	19	92	31	15	14	3	2	1	1	7	0	12	2	0	1	1	.500	0	0	6.63
Fort Myers	A+ Min	22	0	0	11	33.2	146	32	14	13	1	3	2	1	17	2	28	3	0	2	2	.500	0	2	3.48
2 Min. YEARS		62	0	0	32	93.1	407	100	41	35	5	6	4	4	31	4	83	10	1	4	6	.400	0	12	3.38

Mick Pageler

Pitches: Right Bats: Right Pos: P   Ht: 6'2" Wt: 205 Born: 4/30/76 Age: 24

Year Team	Lg Org	G	GS	CG	GF	IP	BFP	H	R	ER	HR	SH	SF	HB	TBB	IBB	SO	WP	Bk	W	L	Pct.	ShO	Sv	ERA
			HOW MUCH HE PITCHED						WHAT HE GAVE UP											THE RESULTS					
1996 Bellingham	A- SF	30	0	0	25	34.1	137	22	9	6	2	2	2	0	10	0	55	2	1	2	0	1.000	0	12	1.57
1997 Bakersfield	A+ SF	61	0	0	53	65.1	291	69	39	34	8	2	1	5	26	3	68	4	0	2	5	.286	0	29	4.68
1998 Portland	AA Fla	60	0	0	32	76	336	73	40	39	8	2	2	6	32	5	67	5	1	5	5	.500	0	13	4.62
1999 Portland	AA Fla	31	1	0	12	51	237	70	33	27	4	1	2	3	13	1	44	4	0	4	2	.667	0	1	4.76
4 Min. YEARS		182	1	0	122	226.2	1001	234	121	106	22	7	7	14	81	9	234	15	2	13	12	.520	0	55	4.21

Vicente Palacios

Pitches: Right Bats: Right Pos: P   Ht: 6'3" Wt: 208 Born: 7/19/63 Age: 36

Year Team	Lg Org	G	GS	CG	GF	IP	BFP	H	R	ER	HR	SH	SF	HB	TBB	IBB	SO	WP	Bk	W	L	Pct.	ShO	Sv	ERA
			HOW MUCH HE PITCHED						WHAT HE GAVE UP											THE RESULTS					
1984 Glens Falls	AA CWS	5	5	0	0	25.1	110	23	12	7	0	0	0	0	11	0	10	1	0	1	2	.333	0	0	2.49
1985 Glens Falls	AA CWS	8	4	0	1	39.2	185	44	25	21	1	0	3	2	29	1	20	5	4	1	1	.500	0	1	4.76
1987 Vancouver	AAA Pit	27	26	7	0	185	765	140	63	53	10	11	1	5	85	1	148	5	6	13	5	.722	5	0	2.58
1988 Buffalo	AAA Pit	5	5	1	0	31.2	126	26	7	7	0	0	1	1	5	0	23	2	1	3	0	1.000	1	0	1.99
1989 Buffalo	AAA Pit	2	2	0	0	10	45	9	8	8	2	0	2	1	8	0	8	1	1	0	2	.000	0	0	7.20
1990 Buffalo	AAA Pit	28	28	5	0	183.2	762	173	77	70	8	6	4	1	53	2	137	9	2	13	7	.650	2	0	3.43
1991 Buffalo	AAA Pit	3	0	0	2	6.1	27	7	1	1	0	0	0	0	2	0	7	2	0	0	0	.000	0	0	1.42
1999 Norfolk	AAA NYM	7	0	0	2	9.2	42	9	2	2	1	1	1	2	4	0	9	0	0	2	1	.667	0	1	1.86
1987 Pittsburgh	NL	6	4	0	0	29.1	120	27	14	14	1	2	0	1	9	1	13	0	2	1	0	.667	0	0	4.30
1988 Pittsburgh	NL	7	3	0	0	24.1	113	28	18	18	3	2	1	0	15	1	15	2	3	1	2	.333	0	0	6.66
1990 Pittsburgh	NL	7	0	0	4	15	50	4	0	0	0	0	0	0	2	0	8	2	0	0	0	.000	0	3	0.00
1991 Pittsburgh	NL	36	7	1	8	81.2	347	69	34	34	12	4	1	1	38	2	64	6	2	6	3	.667	1	3	3.75
1992 Pittsburgh	NL	20	8	0	4	53	232	56	25	25	1	4	1	0	27	1	33	7	0	3	2	.600	0	0	4.25
1994 St. Louis	NL	31	17	1	5	117.2	484	104	60	58	16	7	6	3	43	2	95	4	0	3	8	.273	1	0	4.44
1995 St. Louis	NL	20	5	0	3	40.1	184	48	29	26	7	2	1	2	19	1	34	1	0	2	3	.400	0	0	5.80
8 Min. YEARS		85	70	13	5	491.1	2062	431	195	169	22	18	12	12	197	4	362	25	14	33	18	.647	8	4	3.10
7 Maj. YEARS		127	44	2	24	361.1	1530	336	180	175	40	21	11	7	153	8	262	22	7	17	19	.472	2	7	4.36

Donn Pall

Pitches: Right Bats: Right Pos: P   Ht: 6'1" Wt: 180 Born: 1/11/62 Age: 38

Year Team	Lg Org	G	GS	CG	GF	IP	BFP	H	R	ER	HR	SH	SF	HB	TBB	IBB	SO	WP	Bk	W	L	Pct.	ShO	Sv	ERA
			HOW MUCH HE PITCHED						WHAT HE GAVE UP											THE RESULTS					
1985 White Sox	R CWS	13	13	4	0	86	342	68	34	16	2	3	5	2	10	0	63	3	3	7	5	.583	2	0	1.67
1986 Appleton	A CWS	11	11	3	0	78	317	71	29	20	2	2	0	4	14	1	51	4	0	5	5	.500	1	0	2.31
Birmingham	AA CWS	21	9	0	6	73	313	77	38	36	9	3	2	2	27	3	41	5	2	3	4	.429	0	1	4.44
1987 Birmingham	AA CWS	30	23	3	0	158	718	173	100	75	18	3	8	8	63	4	139	9	2	8	11	.421	0	0	4.27
1988 Vancouver	AAA CWS	44	0	0	25	72.2	293	61	21	18	2	2	1	3	20	2	41	2	1	5	2	.714	0	10	2.23
1989 South Bend	A CWS	2	0	0	0	3.1	12	1	0	0	0	0	0	0	0	0	4	0	0	0	0	.000	0	0	0.00

213

Year Team	Lg Org	G	GS	CG	GF	IP	BFP	H	R	ER	HR	SH	SF	HB	TBB	IBB	SO	WP	Bk	W	L	Pct.	ShO	Sv	ERA
1995 Nashville	AAA CWS	44	0	0	13	86	365	89	40	38	10	5	3	4	20	7	79	3	0	4	3	.571	0	3	3.98
1996 Charlotte	AAA Fla	38	0	0	33	51.2	208	42	21	17	3	1	4	4	12	0	53	2	0	3	3	.500	0	17	2.96
1997 Charlotte	AAA Fla	59	0	0	28	79.2	334	82	40	30	10	2	1	5	11	2	70	3	0	4	7	.364	0	8	3.39
1998 Charlotte	AAA Fla	29	0	0	25	34.2	147	33	17	16	1	2	2	0	10	0	33	1	0	1	2	.333	0	14	4.15
1999 Indianapolis	AAA Cin	4	0	0	1	5.1	26	9	7	5	2	1	0	0	1	0	1	0	0	1	0	1.000	0	0	8.44
1988 Chicago	AL	17	0	0	6	28.2	130	39	11	11	1	2	1	0	8	1	16	1	0	0	2	.000	0	0	3.45
1989 Chicago	AL	53	0	0	27	87	370	90	35	32	9	8	2	8	19	3	58	4	1	4	5	.444	0	6	3.31
1990 Chicago	AL	56	0	0	11	76	306	63	33	28	7	4	2	4	24	8	39	2	0	3	5	.375	0	2	3.32
1991 Chicago	AL	51	0	0	7	71	282	59	22	19	7	4	0	3	20	3	40	2	0	7	2	.778	0	4	2.41
1992 Chicago	AL	39	0	0	12	73	323	79	43	40	9	1	3	2	27	8	27	1	2	5	2	.714	0	1	4.93
1993 Chicago	AL	39	0	0	9	58.2	251	62	25	21	5	6	1	2	11	3	29	3	0	2	3	.400	0	1	3.22
Philadelphia	NL	8	0	0	2	17.2	69	15	7	5	1	1	0	0	3	0	11	0	1	1	0	1.000	0	0	2.55
1994 New York	AL	26	0	0	7	35	157	43	18	14	3	0	1	1	9	0	21	2	0	1	2	.333	0	0	3.60
Chicago	NL	2	0	0	0	4	19	8	2	2	1	0	0	0	1	0	2	0	0	0	0	.000	0	0	4.50
1996 Florida	NL	12	0	0	2	18.2	80	16	15	12	3	1	1	0	9	1	9	1	0	1	1	.500	0	0	5.79
1997 Florida	NL	2	0	0	1	2.1	11	3	1	1	1	0	0	0	1	0	0	0	0	0	0	.000	0	0	3.86
1998 Florida	NL	23	0	0	11	33.1	141	42	19	19	5	3	1	1	7	2	26	2	0	0	1	.000	0	0	5.13
10 Min. YEARS		295	56	10	134	728.1	3075	706	347	271	59	24	26	32	188	19	575	32	8	41	42	.494	3	53	3.35
10 Maj. YEARS		328	0	0	94	505.1	2139	519	231	204	52	30	12	21	139	29	278	18	4	24	23	.511	0	10	3.63

Roberto Paredes

Pitches: Right **Bats:** Right **Pos:** P **Ht:** 6'3" **Wt:** 170 **Born:** 10/16/73 **Age:** 26

Year Team	Lg Org	G	GS	CG	GF	IP	BFP	H	R	ER	HR	SH	SF	HB	TBB	IBB	SO	WP	Bk	W	L	Pct.	ShO	Sv	ERA
1996 Helena	R+ Mil	25	0	0	16	30.1	131	23	13	9	1	3	2	1	16	0	41	6	0	3	1	.750	0	6	2.67
1997 Beloit	A Mil	46	0	0	44	50.1	225	36	19	16	2	2	4	4	33	2	49	5	0	5	4	.556	0	15	2.86
1998 Stockton	A+ Mil	43	0	0	27	46.2	222	54	30	20	1	2	2	2	27	1	47	16	0	1	3	.250	0	11	3.86
1999 Stockton	A+ Mil	12	6	0	3	34	159	31	28	28	7	0	3	2	27	0	30	1	1	1	3	.250	0	0	7.41
Huntsville	AA Mil	28	0	0	7	52.1	237	48	26	23	4	1	1	5	29	1	35	8	0	2	3	.400	0	1	3.96
4 Min. YEARS		154	6	0	97	213.2	974	192	116	96	15	8	11	15	132	4	202	36	1	12	14	.462	0	33	4.04

Christian Parker

Pitches: Right **Bats:** Right **Pos:** P **Ht:** 6'1" **Wt:** 200 **Born:** 7/3/75 **Age:** 24

Year Team	Lg Org	G	GS	CG	GF	IP	BFP	H	R	ER	HR	SH	SF	HB	TBB	IBB	SO	WP	Bk	W	L	Pct.	ShO	Sv	ERA
1996 Vermont	A- Mon	14	14	2	0	80	322	63	26	22	1	2	1	4	22	0	61	8	3	7	1	.875	1	0	2.48
1997 Cape Fear	A Mon	25	25	0	0	153	640	146	72	53	5	9	6	7	49	0	106	9	2	11	10	.524	0	0	3.12
Wst Plm Bch	A+ Mon	3	3	0	0	19	81	22	7	7	0	0	0	0	5	0	10	2	0	1	0	1.000	0	0	3.32
1998 Harrisburg	AA Mon	36	16	0	8	126.2	550	124	66	49	9	6	2	10	47	3	73	8	0	6	6	.500	0	5	3.48
1999 Ottawa	AAA Mon	7	0	0	2	10.2	49	10	9	9	0	1	1	2	7	0	5	0	0	0	1	.000	0	0	7.59
Harrisburg	AA Mon	36	6	0	16	88.2	386	86	39	36	11	5	0	15	37	2	45	10	2	8	5	.615	0	3	3.65
4 Min. YEARS		121	64	2	26	478	2028	451	219	176	26	23	10	38	167	5	300	37	7	32	24	.571	1	8	3.31

Chad Paronto

Pitches: Right **Bats:** Right **Pos:** P **Ht:** 6'5" **Wt:** 250 **Born:** 7/28/75 **Age:** 24

Year Team	Lg Org	G	GS	CG	GF	IP	BFP	H	R	ER	HR	SH	SF	HB	TBB	IBB	SO	WP	Bk	W	L	Pct.	ShO	Sv	ERA
1996 Frederick	A+ Bal	8	1	0	2	15	63	11	9	8	0	2	0	0	8	0	6	2	0	0	1	.000	0	0	4.80
Bluefield	R+ Bal	9	2	0	1	21.1	82	16	4	4	0	0	0	0	5	0	24	0	1	1	1	.500	0	1	1.69
1997 Delmarva	A Bal	28	23	0	0	127.1	569	133	95	67	9	5	5	1	56	1	93	6	0	6	9	.400	0	0	4.74
1998 Frederick	A+ Bal	18	18	0	0	103.2	451	116	44	36	4	3	2	3	39	0	87	8	0	7	6	.538	0	3	3.13
Bowie	AA Bal	8	7	0	1	35.2	165	38	30	23	1	0	1	3	23	0	28	4	0	1	3	.250	0	1	5.80
1999 Bowie	AA Bal	15	9	0	0	41	209	59	39	37	3	1	1	4	32	1	27	3	0	0	4	.000	0	0	8.12
Frederick	A+ Bal	13	13	1	0	72.1	323	81	46	38	7	2	1	5	26	1	55	2	0	3	5	.375	0	0	4.73
4 Min. YEARS		99	73	1	6	416.1	1862	454	267	213	24	13	10	16	189	3	320	25	1	18	29	.383	0	2	4.60

John Parrish

Pitches: Left **Bats:** Left **Pos:** P **Ht:** 5'11" **Wt:** 165 **Born:** 11/26/77 **Age:** 22

Year Team	Lg Org	G	GS	CG	GF	IP	BFP	H	R	ER	HR	SH	SF	HB	TBB	IBB	SO	WP	Bk	W	L	Pct.	ShO	Sv	ERA
1996 Orioles	R Bal	11	0	0	6	19.1	83	13	5	4	0	0	0	0	11	0	33	2	0	2	0	1.000	0	2	1.86
Bluefield	R+ Bal	8	0	0	5	13.1	60	11	6	4	0	1	2	0	9	1	18	2	0	2	1	.667	0	1	2.70
1997 Bowie	AA Bal	1	1	0	0	5	20	3	1	1	0	0	0	0	2	0	3	0	0	1	0	1.000	0	0	1.80
Frederick	A+ Bal	5	5	0	0	22.1	103	23	18	15	3	1	0	2	16	0	17	3	0	1	3	.250	0	0	6.04
Delmarva	A Bal	23	10	0	5	72.2	315	69	39	31	7	2	3	2	32	3	76	9	0	3	3	.500	0	1	3.84
1998 Frederick	A+ Bal	16	16	1	0	82.2	352	77	39	30	5	3	4	5	27	1	81	9	0	4	4	.500	0	0	3.27
1999 Delmarva	A Bal	4	0	0	1	10	47	9	8	8	1	0	0	1	6	1	10	3	0	0	1	.000	0	0	7.20
Frederick	A+ Bal	6	6	0	0	36.2	151	34	17	17	4	1	2	2	12	0	44	5	0	2	2	.500	0	0	4.17
Bowie	AA Bal	12	10	0	2	55.2	248	49	28	25	4	7	5	3	43	1	42	3	1	0	2	.000	0	0	4.04
4 Min. YEARS		86	48	1	19	317.2	1379	288	161	135	24	15	16	13	158	7	324	36	1	15	16	.484	0	4	3.82

Brian Passini

Pitches: Left **Bats:** Left **Pos:** P **Ht:** 6'3" **Wt:** 195 **Born:** 1/24/75 **Age:** 25

Year Team	Lg Org	G	GS	CG	GF	IP	BFP	H	R	ER	HR	SH	SF	HB	TBB	IBB	SO	WP	Bk	W	L	Pct.	ShO	Sv	ERA
1996 Helena	R+ Mil	15	14	1	0	77.2	343	91	37	30	5	0	2	6	27	0	71	7	3	7	2	.778	0	0	3.48

Year Team	Lg Org	G	GS	CG	GF	IP	BFP	H	R	ER	HR	SH	SF	HB	TBB	IBB	SO	WP	Bk	W	L	Pct.	ShO	Sv	ERA
1997 Beloit	A Mil	19	19	1	0	123	505	114	48	44	14	2	1	4	35	0	116	3	3	9	5	.643	0	0	3.22
Stockton	A+ Mil	8	8	1	0	45.1	185	40	28	24	7	3	1	3	21	0	34	1	0	1	5	.167	0	0	4.76
1998 Stockton	A+ Mil	15	15	1	0	90	375	83	39	36	7	4	1	3	21	0	91	4	0	5	6	.455	0	0	3.60
El Paso	AA Mil	12	12	1	0	80.1	334	69	35	26	5	2	2	2	28	0	51	5	0	5	4	.556	1	0	2.91
1999 Louisville	AAA Mil	6	6	0	0	27.2	132	34	23	23	4	1	2	0	17	1	14	0	0	2	3	.400	0	0	7.48
Huntsville	AA Mil	8	8	0	0	37.1	160	33	19	15	2	1	3	2	19	1	22	4	0	0	4	.000	0	0	3.62
4 Min. YEARS		83	82	5	0	481.1	2034	464	229	198	44	13	12	20	178	2	399	24	6	29	29	.500	1	0	3.70

Jarrod Patterson

Bats: Left **Throws:** Right **Pos:** 3B **Ht:** 6'1" **Wt:** 195 **Born:** 9/7/73 **Age:** 26

Year Team	Lg Org	G	AB	H	2B	3B	HR	TB	R	RBI	TBB	IBB	SO	HBP	SH	SF	SB	CS	SB%	GDP	Avg	OBP	SLG
1993 Mets	R NYM	46	166	40	9	1	2	57	27	25	24	1	28	0	1	4	1	3	.25	5	.241	.330	.343
1994 Kingsport	R+ NYM	36	112	29	5	2	5	53	12	18	12	2	39	1	0	0	2	0	1.00	1	.259	.336	.473
Pittsfield	A- NYM	29	106	19	6	1	1	30	8	15	10	0	34	0	0	2	0	1	.00	1	.179	.246	.283
1995 Kingsport	R+ NYM	64	240	67	17	3	13	129	45	57	28	2	50	0	0	3	3	1	.75	2	.279	.351	.538
1996 St. Lucie	A+ NYM	17	61	11	2	0	1	16	6	6	3	0	19	1	0	1	1	0	1.00	0	.180	.227	.262
Capital Cty	A NYM	70	213	49	9	1	3	69	26	37	33	3	65	2	0	4	1	1	.50	3	.230	.333	.324
1997 Regina	IND —	65	240	87	24	2	7	136	52	50	38	2	47	2	2	1	7	3	.70	1	.363	.452	.567
1998 High Desert	A+ Ari	131	492	165	34	9	18	271	89	102	66	4	97	2	0	3	9	2	.82	8	.335	.414	.551
1999 El Paso	AA Ari	67	249	95	27	3	8	152	63	51	51	6	45	1	0	3	3	2	.60	3	.382	.484	.610
Tucson	AAA Ari	75	274	92	25	3	11	156	46	47	36	0	37	3	0	3	4	1	.80	9	.336	.415	.569
7 Min. YEARS		600	2153	654	158	25	69	1069	374	408	301	20	461	12	3	24	31	14	.69	33	.304	.388	.497

John Patterson

Pitches: Right **Bats:** Right **Pos:** P **Ht:** 6'6" **Wt:** 197 **Born:** 1/30/78 **Age:** 22

Year Team	Lg Org	G	GS	CG	GF	IP	BFP	H	R	ER	HR	SH	SF	HB	TBB	IBB	SO	WP	Bk	W	L	Pct.	ShO	Sv	ERA
1997 South Bend	A Ari	18	18	0	0	78	327	63	32	28	3	1	2	5	34	0	95	8	0	1	9	.100	0	0	3.23
1998 High Desert	A+ Ari	25	25	0	0	127	519	102	54	40	12	0	3	4	42	0	148	5	0	8	7	.533	0	0	2.83
1999 El Paso	AA Ari	18	18	2	0	100	429	98	61	53	16	3	1	0	42	0	117	3	0	8	6	.571	0	0	4.77
Tucson	AAA Ari	7	6	0	0	30.2	148	43	26	24	3	0	0	0	18	0	29	0	0	1	5	.167	0	0	7.04
3 Min. YEARS		68	67	2	0	335.2	1423	306	173	145	34	4	6	9	136	0	389	16	0	18	27	.400	0	0	3.89

Jeff Patzke

Bats: Both **Throws:** Right **Pos:** 2B **Ht:** 6'0" **Wt:** 190 **Born:** 11/19/73 **Age:** 26

Year Team	Lg Org	G	AB	H	2B	3B	HR	TB	R	RBI	TBB	IBB	SO	HBP	SH	SF	SB	CS	SB%	GDP	Avg	OBP	SLG
1992 Blue Jays	R Tor	6	21	2	0	0	0	2	3	1	3	0	2	0	0	0	0	1	.00	0	.095	.208	.095
Medcine Hat	R+ Tor	59	193	42	4	0	2	52	19	17	17	0	42	0	3	0	3	1	.75	4	.218	.281	.269
1993 Medcine Hat	R+ Tor	71	273	80	11	2	1	98	45	22	34	1	31	2	3	1	5	7	.42	5	.293	.374	.359
1994 Hagerstown	A Tor	80	271	55	10	1	4	79	43	22	36	1	57	3	2	3	7	3	.70	4	.203	.300	.292
1995 Dunedin	A+ Tor	129	470	124	32	6	11	201	68	75	85	8	81	2	1	2	5	3	.63	10	.264	.377	.428
1996 Knoxville	AA Tor	124	429	130	31	4	4	181	70	66	80	6	103	6	0	2	6	5	.55	2	.303	.418	.422
1997 Syracuse	AAA Tor	96	316	90	25	2	2	125	38	29	51	3	66	1	3	2	0	3	.00	4	.285	.384	.396
1998 Dunedin	A+ Tor	20	62	18	0	0	0	18	10	4	9	0	18	0	0	0	0	1	.00	0	.290	.380	.290
Nashville	AAA Pit	104	361	108	16	0	7	145	48	48	48	0	74	9	2	1	5	6	.45	6	.299	.394	.402
1999 Altoona	AA Pit	53	198	59	12	1	2	79	31	25	33	1	45	2	0	2	4	2	.67	4	.298	.400	.399
Nashville	AAA Pit	59	173	38	5	1	2	51	20	14	32	1	29	2	1	2	2	3	.40	2	.220	.344	.295
8 Min. YEARS		801	2767	746	146	17	35	1031	395	323	428	21	548	27	15	15	37	35	.51	41	.270	.371	.373

Dave Pavlas

Pitches: Right **Bats:** Right **Pos:** P **Ht:** 6'7" **Wt:** 205 **Born:** 8/12/62 **Age:** 37

Year Team	Lg Org	G	GS	CG	GF	IP	BFP	H	R	ER	HR	SH	SF	HB	TBB	IBB	SO	WP	Bk	W	L	Pct.	ShO	Sv	ERA
1985 Peoria	A ChC	17	15	3	2	110	452	90	40	32	7	3	1	3	32	0	86	6	1	8	3	.727	1	1	2.62
1986 Winston-Sal	A+ ChC	28	26	5	0	173.1	739	172	91	74	8	6	4	6	57	2	143	11	1	14	6	.700	2	0	3.84
1987 Pittsfield	AA ChC	7	7	0	0	45	199	49	25	19	6	0	3	3	17	0	27	1	1	6	1	.857	0	0	3.80
Tulsa	AA Tex	13	12	0	1	59.2	280	79	51	51	9	1	0	3	27	0	46	7	0	1	6	.143	0	0	7.69
1988 Tulsa	AA Tex	26	5	1	9	77.1	299	52	26	17	3	6	2	5	18	1	69	4	6	5	2	.714	0	2	1.98
Okla City	AAA Tex	13	8	0	2	52.1	237	59	29	26	1	1	2	3	28	0	40	2	1	3	1	.750	0	0	4.47
1989 Okla City	AAA Tex	29	21	4	4	143.2	652	175	89	75	7	6	7	7	67	4	94	8	1	2	14	.125	0	0	4.70
1990 Iowa	AAA ChC	53	3	0	22	99.1	421	84	38	36	4	4	3	10	48	6	96	8	1	8	3	.727	0	8	3.26
1991 Iowa	AAA ChC	61	0	0	29	97.1	418	92	49	43	5	10	5	5	43	9	54	13	0	5	6	.455	0	7	3.98
1992 Iowa	AAA ChC	12	4	0	6	37.1	166	43	20	14	5	2	0	1	8	0	34	0	0	3	3	.500	0	0	3.38
1995 Columbus	AAA NYY	48	0	0	32	58.2	233	43	19	17	2	4	1	1	20	2	51	4	0	3	3	.500	0	18	2.61
1996 Columbus	AAA NYY	57	0	0	46	77	306	64	20	17	5	1	0	0	13	1	65	3	0	8	2	.800	0	26	1.99
1997 Columbus	AAA NYY	26	0	0	25	25.1	116	33	14	13	3	2	1	0	4	2	34	0	0	1	3	.250	0	12	4.62
1998 Tucson	AAA Ari	9	0	0	8	8.1	46	15	11	8	3	0	1	1	6	0	9	0	0	0	2	.000	0	1	8.64
Edmonton	AAA Oak	26	3	0	10	58	239	51	23	20	4	0	3	1	12	1	41	2	0	2	2	.500	0	1	3.10
1999 Columbus	AAA NYY	38	2	0	13	62.1	256	60	30	28	5	0	3	2	9	1	49	1	0	4	2	.667	0	1	4.04
1990 Chicago	NL	13	0	0	3	21.1	93	23	7	5	2	0	2	0	6	2	12	3	0	2	0	1.000	0	0	2.11
1991 Chicago	NL	1	0	0	1	1	5	3	2	2	1	1	0	0	0	0	0	0	0	0	0	.000	0	0	18.00
1995 New York	AL	5	0	0	1	5.2	24	8	2	2	0	0	0	0	2	0	6	0	0	0	0	.000	0	0	3.18
1996 New York	AL	16	0	0	8	23	97	23	7	6	0	2	0	1	7	2	18	3	0	0	0	.000	0	1	2.35
13 Min. YEARS		463	106	13	209	1185	5059	1170	577	490	77	46	36	51	408	30	937	70	12	73	59	.553	3	77	3.72
4 Maj. YEARS		34	0	0	13	51	219	57	18	15	3	3	2	1	13	4	33	6	0	2	0	1.000	0	2	2.65

Richard Paz

Bats: Right **Throws:** Right **Pos:** 3B **Ht:** 5'8" **Wt:** 130 **Born:** 7/30/77 **Age:** 22

							BATTING										BASERUNNING				PERCENTAGES		
Year Team	Lg Org	G	AB	H	2B	3B	HR	TB	R	RBI	TBB	IBB	SO	HBP	SH	SF	SB	CS	SB%	GDP	Avg	OBP	SLG
1996 High Desert	A+ Bal	7	17	3	1	0	0	4	2	0	1	0	4	0	2	0	0	0	.00	1	.176	.222	.235
Bluefield	R+ Bal	50	170	50	7	0	1	60	42	21	42	0	24	3	1	4	9	4	.69	1	.294	.434	.353
1997 Delmarva	A Bal	111	389	94	14	4	2	122	60	48	38	1	60	5	15	4	15	5	.75	8	.242	.314	.314
1998 Orioles	R Bal	1	0	0	0	0	0	0	0	0	0	0	0	0	0	0	0	0	.00	0	.000	.000	.000
Delmarva	A Bal	98	325	104	10	4	5	137	55	56	75	2	42	8	2	5	22	7	.76	6	.320	.453	.422
Frederick	A+ Bal	40	143	35	10	0	3	54	31	8	21	0	22	4	3	0	6	3	.67	3	.245	.357	.378
1999 Frederick	A+ Bal	54	163	41	9	0	0	50	27	18	47	0	27	2	3	5	15	6	.71	2	.252	.415	.307
Bowie	AA Bal	79	273	78	12	2	2	100	39	20	51	0	35	6	8	2	11	3	.79	4	.286	.407	.366
4 Min. YEARS		440	1480	405	63	10	13	527	256	171	275	3	214	28	34	20	78	28	.74	25	.274	.393	.356

J.J. Pearsall

Pitches: Left **Bats:** Left **Pos:** P **Ht:** 6'2" **Wt:** 202 **Born:** 9/9/73 **Age:** 26

			HOW MUCH HE PITCHED						WHAT HE GAVE UP										THE RESULTS					
Year Team	Lg Org	G	GS	CG	GF	IP	BFP	H	R	ER	HR	SH	SF	HB	TBB	IBB	SO	WP	Bk	W	L	Pct.	ShO	Sv	ERA
1995 San Berndno	A+ LA	6	0	0	2	10.2	54	15	10	10	3	0	0	0	7	0	5	1	0	0	1	.000	0	0	8.44
Yakima	A- LA	20	1	0	8	38.2	167	39	18	14	1	1	2	2	14	0	26	5	0	2	3	.400	0	1	3.26
1996 Savannah	A LA	45	2	0	13	87.2	394	76	48	32	6	3	2	7	46	3	88	8	3	6	5	.545	0	3	3.29
1997 San Berndno	A+ LA	31	28	0	1	160.2	698	145	91	81	12	4	4	0	93	0	112	0	2	11	11	.660	0	0	4.54
1998 San Antonio	AA LA	46	4	0	11	72	320	71	38	35	8	0	2	2	37	2	63	5	0	6	5	.545	0	0	4.38
Albuquerque	AAA LA	8	0	0	4	13	62	16	10	9	1	1	1	1	8	0	8	1	0	1	1	.500	0	1	6.23
1999 San Antonio	AA LA	10	0	0	3	16	75	14	11	8	1	0	1	1	8	0	13	0	0	0	0	.000	0	0	4.50
Chattanooga	AA Cin	32	0	0	7	39.2	184	40	31	26	5	0	1	0	28	3	36	2	0	3	1	.750	0	0	5.90
5 Min. YEARS		198	35	0	49	438.1	1952	416	257	215	37	12	13	21	241	8	351	31	5	32	27	.542	0	5	4.41

Alex Pelaez

Bats: Right **Throws:** Right **Pos:** DH-3B **Ht:** 5'9" **Wt:** 190 **Born:** 4/6/76 **Age:** 24

							BATTING										BASERUNNING				PERCENTAGES		
Year Team	Lg Org	G	AB	H	2B	3B	HR	TB	R	RBI	TBB	IBB	SO	HBP	SH	SF	SB	CS	SB%	GDP	Avg	OBP	SLG
1998 Idaho Falls	R+ SD	63	262	89	17	1	8	132	52	51	29	0	32	1	0	2	3	1	.75	10	.340	.405	.504
1999 Las Vegas	AAA SD	5	13	4	0	0	0	4	1	0	0	0	2	0	0	0	0	0	.00	1	.308	.308	.308
Rancho Cuca	A+ SD	117	443	132	21	4	4	173	62	54	35	3	53	1	1	2	7	3	.70	24	.298	.349	.391
2 Min. YEARS		185	718	225	38	5	12	309	115	105	64	3	87	2	1	4	10	4	.71	35	.313	.369	.430

Kit Pellow

Bats: Right **Throws:** Right **Pos:** 3B **Ht:** 6'1" **Wt:** 205 **Born:** 8/28/73 **Age:** 26

							BATTING										BASERUNNING				PERCENTAGES		
Year Team	Lg Org	G	AB	H	2B	3B	HR	TB	R	RBI	TBB	IBB	SO	HBP	SH	SF	SB	CS	SB%	GDP	Avg	OBP	SLG
1996 Spokane	A- KC	71	279	80	18	2	18	156	48	66	20	0	52	8	1	7	8	3	.73	5	.287	.344	.559
1997 Lansing	A KC	65	256	76	17	2	11	130	39	52	24	1	74	6	0	4	2	0	1.00	5	.297	.366	.508
Wichita	AA KC	68	241	60	12	1	10	104	40	41	21	1	72	2	2	3	5	2	.71	5	.249	.311	.432
1998 Wichita	AA KC	103	374	100	24	3	29	217	70	73	27	2	107	6	1	3	4	3	.57	2	.267	.324	.580
Omaha	AAA KC	14	54	10	3	0	2	19	8	6	2	0	19	0	0	2	2	0	1.00	1	.185	.207	.352
1999 Omaha	AAA KC	131	475	136	28	4	35	277	88	99	26	1	117	18	1	7	6	5	.55	11	.286	.335	.583
4 Min. YEARS		452	1679	462	102	12	105	903	293	337	114	7	441	40	5	26	27	13	.68	29	.275	.331	.538

Rudy Pemberton

Bats: Right **Throws:** Right **Pos:** DH **Ht:** 6'1" **Wt:** 185 **Born:** 12/17/69 **Age:** 30

							BATTING										BASERUNNING				PERCENTAGES		
Year Team	Lg Org	G	AB	H	2B	3B	HR	TB	R	RBI	TBB	IBB	SO	HBP	SH	SF	SB	CS	SB%	GDP	Avg	OBP	SLG
1988 Bristol	R+ Det	6	5	0	0	0	0	0	2	0	1	0	3	2	0	0	0	0	.00	1	.000	.375	.000
1989 Bristol	R+ Det	56	214	58	9	2	6	89	40	39	14	0	43	4	0	1	19	3	.86	3	.271	.326	.416
1990 Fayetteville	A Det	127	454	126	14	5	6	168	60	61	42	1	91	12	1	9	12	9	.57	12	.278	.348	.370
1991 Lakeland	A+ Det	111	375	86	15	2	3	114	40	36	25	2	51	9	6	2	25	15	.63	5	.229	.292	.304
1992 Lakeland	A+ Det	104	343	91	16	5	3	126	41	43	21	2	37	13	2	3	25	10	.71	4	.265	.329	.367
1993 London	AA Det	124	471	130	22	4	15	205	70	67	24	1	80	12	0	3	14	12	.54	11	.276	.325	.435
1994 Toledo	AAA Det	99	360	109	13	3	12	164	49	58	18	3	62	6	0	0	30	9	.77	8	.303	.341	.456
1995 Toledo	AAA Det	67	224	77	15	3	7	119	31	23	15	2	36	5	0	3	8	4	.67	5	.344	.393	.531
1996 Okla City	AAA Tex	17	71	18	3	0	2	27	6	11	1	0	10	1	0	1	1	4	.20	0	.254	.270	.380
Pawtucket	AAA Bos	102	396	129	28	3	27	244	77	92	18	0	63	14	0	1	16	7	.70	12	.326	.375	.616
1999 Memphis	AAA StL	25	73	19	7	0	2	32	13	11	6	1	13	6	0	0	1	0	1.00	1	.260	.365	.438
Birmingham	AA CWS	85	307	85	14	3	18	159	49	60	27	2	55	11	0	3	8	3	.73	8	.277	.353	.518
1995 Detroit	AL	12	30	9	3	1	0	14	3	3	1	0	5	1	0	0	0	0	.00	3	.300	.344	.467
1996 Boston	AL	13	41	21	8	0	1	32	11	10	2	0	4	2	0	0	3	1	.75	0	.512	.556	.780
1997 Boston	AL	27	63	15	2	0	2	23	8	10	4	0	13	3	0	0	0	0	.00	0	.238	.314	.365
10 Min. YEARS		923	3293	928	156	30	101	1447	478	501	212	14	544	95	9	32	159	76	.68	70	.282	.340	.439
0 Maj. YEARS		52	134	45	13	1	3	69	22	23	7	0	22	6	0	0	3	1	.75	3	.336	.395	.515

Alex Pena

Pitches: Right **Bats:** Right **Pos:** P **Ht:** 6'2" **Wt:** 175 **Born:** 9/9/77 **Age:** 22

			HOW MUCH HE PITCHED						WHAT HE GAVE UP										THE RESULTS					
Year Team	Lg Org	G	GS	CG	GF	IP	BFP	H	R	ER	HR	SH	SF	HB	TBB	IBB	SO	WP	Bk	W	L	Pct.	ShO	Sv	ERA
1998 Augusta	A Pit	1	0	0	1	1	8	2	2	2	0	0	1	0	3	0	1	1	0	0	0	.000	0	0	18.00
1999 Hickory	A Pit	22	7	0	7	46.1	244	68	42	34	6	1	2	8	31	2	37	7	0	0	4	.000	0	0	6.60
Altoona	AA Pit	9	0	0	2	21	93	22	12	9	2	0	0	3	9	0	20	2	1	1	0	1.000	0	0	3.86
2 Min. YEARS		32	7	0	10	68.1	345	92	56	45	8	1	3	11	43	2	58	10	1	1	4	.200	0	0	5.93

Elvis Pena

Bats: Both **Throws:** Right **Pos:** 2B **Ht:** 5'11" **Wt:** 155 **Born:** 9/15/76 **Age:** 23

Year Team	Lg Org	G	AB	H	2B	3B	HR	TB	R	RBI	TBB	IBB	SO	HBP	SH	SF	SB	CS	SB%	GDP	Avg	OBP	SLG
1994 Rockies	R Col	49	171	39	5	2	0	48	31	9	35	0	47	6	1	0	20	12	.63	1	.228	.377	.281
1995 Asheville	A Col	48	145	33	2	0	0	35	27	4	28	0	32	4	3	0	23	6	.79	1	.228	.367	.241
Portland	A- Col	58	215	54	6	3	0	66	29	18	26	0	45	1	3	0	28	7	.80	2	.251	.335	.307
1996 Salem	A+ Col	102	341	76	9	4	0	93	48	28	61	2	70	3	13	1	30	16	.65	12	.223	.345	.273
1997 Salem	A+ Col	93	279	62	9	2	1	78	41	30	37	0	53	2	14	3	16	6	.73	1	.222	.315	.280
1998 Asheville	A Col	115	428	123	24	4	6	173	93	48	70	2	85	14	7	2	41	12	.77	5	.287	.403	.404
1999 Colo Sprngs	AAA Col	13	43	7	1	0	0	8	5	1	3	0	7	1	0	0	4	1	.80	0	.163	.234	.186
Carolina	AA Col	110	356	107	24	6	2	149	57	31	48	2	64	6	8	2	21	6	.78	6	.301	.391	.419
6 Min. YEARS		588	1978	501	80	21	9	650	331	169	308	6	403	37	49	8	183	66	.73	28	.253	.363	.329

Tyrone Pendergrass

Bats: Both **Throws:** Right **Pos:** OF **Ht:** 6'1" **Wt:** 180 **Born:** 7/31/76 **Age:** 23

Year Team	Lg Org	G	AB	H	2B	3B	HR	TB	R	RBI	TBB	IBB	SO	HBP	SH	SF	SB	CS	SB%	GDP	Avg	OBP	SLG
1995 Braves	R Atl	52	188	34	4	0	1	41	19	7	15	0	51	1	0	0	8	4	.67	5	.181	.245	.218
1996 Danville	R+ Atl	54	220	68	8	7	3	99	50	23	24	0	39	4	2	2	40	6	.87	4	.309	.384	.450
Macon	A Atl	12	45	12	1	1	1	18	8	3	4	0	12	1	0	0	5	3	.63	0	.267	.340	.400
1997 Macon	A Atl	127	489	127	16	5	6	171	81	37	60	0	101	4	8	3	70	15	.82	5	.260	.344	.350
1998 Danville	A+ Atl	132	518	143	23	10	4	198	74	35	43	0	91	7	5	1	39	18	.68	7	.276	.339	.382
Greenville	AA Atl	5	16	2	0	0	0	2	3	0	2	0	4	0	0	0	1	0	1.00	0	.125	.222	.125
1999 Greenville	AA Atl	100	344	90	12	3	6	126	60	31	37	0	61	2	5	3	19	14	.58	3	.262	.334	.366
5 Min. YEARS		482	1820	476	64	26	21	655	295	136	185	0	359	19	20	9	182	60	.75	24	.262	.334	.360

Brad Pennington

Pitches: Left **Bats:** Left **Pos:** P **Ht:** 6'6" **Wt:** 215 **Born:** 4/14/69 **Age:** 31

Year Team	Lg Org	G	GS	CG	GF	IP	BFP	H	R	ER	HR	SH	SF	HB	TBB	IBB	SO	WP	Bk	W	L	Pct.	ShO	Sv	ERA
1989 Bluefield	R+ Bal	15	14	0	0	64.1	319	50	58	47	2	1	3	6	74	0	81	14	8	2	7	.222	0	0	6.58
1990 Wausau	A Bal	32	18	1	7	106	523	81	89	61	12	6	4	4	121	1	142	10	1	4	9	.308	0	0	5.18
1991 Kane County	A Bal	23	0	0	19	23	112	16	17	15	1	0	0	0	25	0	43	6	0	0	2	.000	0	4	5.87
Frederick	A+ Bal	36	0	0	27	43.2	203	32	23	19	4	3	2	2	44	0	58	4	0	1	4	.200	0	13	3.92
1992 Frederick	A+ Bal	8	0	0	6	9	38	5	3	2	0	1	1	1	4	0	16	1	0	1	0	1.000	0	2	2.00
Hagerstown	AA Bal	19	0	0	16	28.1	121	20	9	8	0	4	3	3	17	0	33	4	0	1	2	.333	0	7	2.54
Rochester	AAA Bal	29	0	0	17	39	158	12	10	9	2	4	1	1	33	2	56	2	0	1	3	.250	0	5	2.08
1993 Rochester	AAA Bal	17	0	0	14	15.2	73	12	11	6	0	0	0	0	13	0	19	1	1	1	2	.333	0	8	3.45
1994 Rochester	AAA Bal	35	9	0	17	86.1	396	68	59	51	11	2	5	4	74	1	89	7	0	6	8	.429	0	3	5.32
1995 Indianapols	AAA Cin	11	2	0	1	14	79	17	19	16	3	0	1	0	21	1	11	2	0	0	0	.000	0	0	10.29
1996 Lk Elsinore	A+ Ana	2	2	0	0	3	11	0	0	0	0	0	0	0	2	0	5	0	0	0	0	.000	0	0	0.00
Vancouver	AAA Ana	11	2	0	1	27.2	124	20	20	13	2	0	1	0	22	0	43	1	0	3	0	1.000	0	1	4.23
1997 Wichita	AA KC	12	0	0	8	12	50	7	1	1	0	0	0	0	8	0	14	3	0	0	0	.000	0	3	0.75
Omaha	AAA KC	35	1	0	6	50	230	41	28	24	6	3	4	3	41	0	48	4	0	2	1	.667	0	4	4.32
1998 Durham	AAA TB	45	6	0	11	100	442	77	55	54	12	0	3	6	65	0	125	8	1	4	4	.500	0	1	4.86
1999 Syracuse	AAA Tor	27	0	0	12	34	158	30	20	16	3	0	5	2	30	0	34	4	1	3	0	1.000	0	1	4.24
1993 Baltimore	AL	34	0	0	16	33	158	34	25	24	7	2	1	2	25	0	39	3	0	3	2	.600	0	4	6.55
1994 Baltimore	AL	8	0	0	3	6	35	9	8	8	2	1	0	0	8	0	7	2	0	0	1	.000	0	0	12.00
1995 Baltimore	AL	8	0	0	2	6.2	33	3	7	6	1	0	0	0	11	1	10	1	0	0	1	.000	0	0	8.10
Cincinnati	NL	6	0	0	2	9.2	47	9	8	6	0	0	2	1	11	0	7	3	0	0	0	.000	0	0	5.59
1996 Boston	AL	14	0	0	6	13	59	6	5	4	1	0	1	0	15	1	13	1	0	0	2	.000	0	0	2.77
California	AL	8	0	0	2	7.1	43	5	10	10	1	0	0	0	16	0	7	1	0	0	0	.000	0	0	12.27
1998 Tampa Bay	AL	1	0	0	0	0	4	1	1	1	0	0	0	0	3	0	0	1	0	0	0	.000	0	0	0.00
11 Min. YEARS		357	54	1	162	656	3037	488	422	342	58	24	33	32	594	5	817	71	12	29	42	.408	0	48	4.69
5 Maj. YEARS		79	0	0	31	75.2	379	67	64	59	12	3	4	3	89	2	83	11	0	3	6	.333	0	4	7.02

Brad Penny

Pitches: Right **Bats:** Right **Pos:** P **Ht:** 6'4" **Wt:** 200 **Born:** 5/24/78 **Age:** 22

Year Team	Lg Org	G	GS	CG	GF	IP	BFP	H	R	ER	HR	SH	SF	HB	TBB	IBB	SO	WP	Bk	W	L	Pct.	ShO	Sv	ERA
1996 Diamondbcks	R Ari	11	8	0	1	49.2	201	36	18	13	1	0	1	3	14	0	52	3	2	2	2	.500	0	0	2.36
1997 South Bend	A Ari	25	25	0	0	118.2	489	91	44	36	4	5	0	4	43	2	116	10	2	10	5	.667	0	0	2.73
1998 High Desert	A+ Ari	28	28	1	0	164	661	138	65	54	15	3	2	9	35	0	207	4	0	14	5	.737	0	0	2.96
1999 El Paso	AA Ari	17	17	0	0	90	391	109	56	48	9	1	2	4	25	0	100	4	2	2	7	.222	0	0	4.80
Portland	AA Fla	6	6	0	0	32.1	139	28	15	14	3	0	1	3	14	0	35	3	2	1	0	1.000	0	0	3.90
4 Min. YEARS		87	84	1	1	454.2	1881	402	198	165	32	9	6	23	131	2	510	24	8	29	19	.604	0	0	3.27

William Pennyfeather

Bats: Right **Throws:** Right **Pos:** OF **Ht:** 6'2" **Wt:** 215 **Born:** 5/25/68 **Age:** 32

Year Team	Lg Org	G	AB	H	2B	3B	HR	TB	R	RBI	TBB	IBB	SO	HBP	SH	SF	SB	CS	SB%	GDP	Avg	OBP	SLG
1988 Pirates	R Pit	17	74	18	2	1	1	25	6	7	2	0	18	0	0	1	3	3	.50	0	.243	.260	.338
Princeton	R+ Pit	16	57	19	2	0	1	24	11	5	6	0	15	0	0	0	7	2	.78	0	.333	.397	.421
1989 Welland	A- Pit	75	289	55	10	1	3	76	34	26	12	1	75	2	1	6	18	5	.78	6	.190	.223	.263
1990 Augusta	A Pit	122	465	122	14	4	4	156	69	48	23	0	85	3	3	3	21	10	.68	7	.262	.300	.335
1991 Salem	A+ Pit	81	319	85	17	3	8	132	35	46	8	0	52	1	1	2	11	8	.58	9	.266	.285	.414
Carolina	AA Pit	42	149	41	5	0	0	46	13	7	7	0	17	1	1	1	3	2	.60	8	.275	.310	.309
1992 Carolina	AA Pit	51	199	67	13	1	6	100	28	25	9	1	34	0	0	5	7	6	.54	5	.337	.360	.503

BATTING

Year Team	Lg Org	G	AB	H	2B	3B	HR	TB	R	RBI	TBB	IBB	SO	HBP	SH	SF	SB	CS	SB%	GDP	Avg	OBP	SLG
Buffalo	AAA Pit	55	160	38	6	2	1	51	19	12	2	0	24	3	2	0	3	2	.60	4	.238	.261	.319
1993 Buffalo	AAA Pit	112	457	114	18	3	14	180	54	41	18	2	92	0	8	1	10	12	.45	3	.249	.277	.394
1994 Buffalo	AAA Pit	10	36	9	2	0	0	11	2	3	3	0	9	0	1	0	0	0	.00	1	.250	.308	.306
Indianapols	AAA Cin	93	361	98	25	3	7	150	52	45	23	1	58	1	4	5	14	4	.78	5	.271	.313	.416
1995 Princeton	R+ Cin	1	3	0	0	0	0	0	0	0	0	0	1	0	0	0	0	0	.00	0	.000	.000	.000
1996 Vancouver	AAA Ana	108	413	117	36	3	5	174	56	63	19	0	71	1	5	2	19	10	.66	7	.283	.315	.421
1997 Albuquerque	AAA LA	115	402	102	21	4	17	182	59	54	26	1	73	1	2	2	11	11	.50	9	.254	.299	.453
1998 Atlantic Ct	IND —	100	376	112	25	2	16	189	81	69	51	2	65	2	2	5	13	2	.87	4	.298	.380	.503
1999 Atlantic Ct	IND —	42	175	53	9	2	2	72	26	20	10	0	26	0	1	0	4	0	1.00	1	.303	.341	.411
Erie	AA Ana	11	39	8	1	0	0	9	4	4	5	0	13	0	0	1	1	2	.33	0	.205	.289	.231
Edmonton	AAA Ana	34	99	21	5	1	2	34	16	10	5	0	21	0	0	1	3	0	1.00	1	.212	.250	.343
1992 Pittsburgh	NL	15	9	2	0	0	0	2	2	0	0	0	0	0	1	0	0	0	.00	0	.222	.222	.222
1993 Pittsburgh	NL	21	34	7	1	0	0	8	4	2	0	0	6	0	0	0	0	1	.00	1	.206	.206	.235
1994 Pittsburgh	NL	4	3	0	0	0	0	0	0	0	0	0	0	0	0	0	0	0	.00	0	.000	.000	.000
12 Min. YEARS		1085	4073	1079	211	30	87	1611	565	487	229	8	749	15	32	32	148	79	.65	73	.265	.304	.396
3 Maj. YEARS		40	46	9	1	0	0	10	6	2	0	0	6	0	1	0	0	1	.00	2	.196	.196	.217

Danny Peoples

Bats: Right **Throws:** Right **Pos:** 1B   **Ht:** 6'1" **Wt:** 207 **Born:** 1/20/75 **Age:** 25

BATTING

Year Team	Lg Org	G	AB	H	2B	3B	HR	TB	R	RBI	TBB	IBB	SO	HBP	SH	SF	SB	CS	SB%	GDP	Avg	OBP	SLG
1996 Watertown	A- Cle	35	117	28	7	0	3	44	20	26	28	2	36	2	0	1	3	1	.75	2	.239	.392	.376
1997 Kinston	A+ Cle	121	409	102	21	1	34	227	82	84	84	4	145	6	0	6	8	1	.89	6	.249	.380	.555
1998 Akron	AA Cle	60	222	62	19	0	8	105	30	32	29	1	61	1	0	2	1	1	.50	7	.279	.362	.473
1999 Akron	AA Cle	127	494	124	23	3	21	216	75	78	55	1	142	4	0	2	2	1	.67	9	.251	.330	.437
4 Min. YEARS		343	1242	316	70	4	66	592	207	220	196	8	384	13	0	11	14	4	.78	24	.254	.359	.477

Dario Perez

Pitches: Right **Bats:** Right **Pos:** P   **Ht:** 6'1" **Wt:** 150 **Born:** 6/27/70 **Age:** 30

Year Team	Lg Org	HOW MUCH HE PITCHED						WHAT HE GAVE UP												THE RESULTS					
		G	GS	CG	GF	IP	BFP	H	R	ER	HR	SH	SF	HB	TBB	IBB	SO	WP	Bk	W	L	Pct.	ShO	Sv	ERA
1990 Royals	R KC	10	10	0	0	50.2	206	43	20	11	0	1	1	1	11	0	37	4	3	2	4	.333	0	0	1.95
1991 Appleton	A KC	34	9	0	6	100	418	86	45	36	7	0	5	4	41	0	73	10	5	7	5	.583	0	0	3.24
Memphis	AA KC	3	2	0	1	12.2	57	15	12	12	5	0	0	0	5	0	12	2	0	0	1	.000	0	0	8.53
1992 Baseball Cy	A+ KC	28	16	2	4	118	495	107	46	40	7	0	6	9	36	0	82	8	4	8	4	.667	1	0	3.05
1993 Wilmington	A+ KC	33	3	0	13	68.2	294	77	41	31	8	5	1	4	14	0	56	4	1	3	9	.250	0	1	4.06
1994 Wilmington	A+ KC	31	4	0	12	61	259	63	38	36	9	0	2	2	15	2	56	3	0	3	3	.500	0	2	5.31
1999 Calgary	AAA Fla	28	21	0	2	132	563	150	94	84	22	7	3	7	31	0	66	3	0	7	13	.350	0	0	5.73
6 Min. YEARS		167	65	2	38	543	2292	541	296	250	58	13	18	27	153	2	382	34	13	30	39	.435	1	3	4.14

Jhonny Perez

Bats: Right **Throws:** Right **Pos:** 2B   **Ht:** 5'10" **Wt:** 180 **Born:** 10/23/76 **Age:** 23

BATTING

Year Team	Lg Org	G	AB	H	2B	3B	HR	TB	R	RBI	TBB	IBB	SO	HBP	SH	SF	SB	CS	SB%	GDP	Avg	OBP	SLG
1994 Astros	R Hou	36	144	46	12	2	1	65	37	27	15	1	16	1	1	1	18	3	.86	4	.319	.385	.451
1995 Kissimmee	A+ Hou	65	214	58	12	0	4	82	34	31	22	1	37	7	0	0	23	7	.77	5	.271	.358	.383
1996 Kissimmee	A+ Hou	90	322	87	20	2	12	147	54	49	26	1	70	2	3	0	16	16	.50	3	.270	.329	.457
1997 Kissimmee	A+ Hou	69	273	72	16	5	3	107	40	22	12	0	38	1	2	3	8	6	.57	5	.264	.294	.392
Jackson	AA Hou	48	154	39	7	0	3	55	16	17	12	0	26	1	1	0	4	3	.57	2	.253	.311	.357
1998 Jackson	AA Hou	130	439	125	20	0	10	175	65	39	45	4	72	1	6	0	22	11	.67	6	.285	.353	.399
1999 Jackson	AA Hou	76	276	69	16	4	4	105	37	25	19	0	44	1	6	2	7	8	.47	8	.250	.299	.380
6 Min. YEARS		514	1822	496	103	13	37	736	273	210	151	7	303	14	19	6	98	54	.64	36	.272	.332	.404

Juan Perez

Pitches: Left **Bats:** Left **Pos:** P   **Ht:** 6'0" **Wt:** 155 **Born:** 3/28/73 **Age:** 27

Year Team	Lg Org	HOW MUCH HE PITCHED						WHAT HE GAVE UP												THE RESULTS					
		G	GS	CG	GF	IP	BFP	H	R	ER	HR	SH	SF	HB	TBB	IBB	SO	WP	Bk	W	L	Pct.	ShO	Sv	ERA
1993 Athletics	R Oak	12	0	0	1	35	145	34	12	9	2	1	1	1	9	0	31	4	1	4	1	.800	0	0	2.31
1994 Athletics	R Oak	14	4	0	7	47.1	216	66	30	23	1	0	3	0	14	0	41	3	0	3	2	.600	0	1	4.37
1995 W Michigan	A Oak	30	19	1	3	141	610	129	73	57	4	1	2	8	55	0	117	5	1	11	8	.579	0	1	3.64
1996 Modesto	A+ Oak	38	8	0	15	98.2	445	120	68	55	12	5	3	2	34	0	89	5	1	4	8	.333	0	4	5.02
1997 Visalia	A+ Oak	53	0	0	25	64.2	266	47	30	20	6	2	6	1	24	4	66	7	1	3	6	.333	0	2	2.78
1998 Huntsville	AA Oak	27	0	0	19	36.2	157	29	13	10	3	3	2	1	16	4	37	2	1	3	2	.600	0	8	2.45
Edmonton	AAA Oak	24	0	0	9	40.1	168	35	17	14	3	0	1	1	18	2	37	0	0	3	4	.429	0	1	3.12
1999 Vancouver	AAA Oak	20	1	0	7	32.1	151	42	25	25	3	2	2	2	15	3	22	3	0	0	4	.000	0	0	6.96
Midland	AA Oak	23	0	0	11	35	167	47	29	27	2	3	2	1	18	3	30	2	2	2	2	.500	0	3	6.94
7 Min. YEARS		241	32	1	97	531	2325	549	297	240	36	17	22	17	203	16	470	31	7	31	33	.484	0	26	4.07

Santiago Perez

Bats: Both **Throws:** Right **Pos:** SS   **Ht:** 6'2" **Wt:** 150 **Born:** 12/30/75 **Age:** 24

BATTING

Year Team	Lg Org	G	AB	H	2B	3B	HR	TB	R	RBI	TBB	IBB	SO	HBP	SH	SF	SB	CS	SB%	GDP	Avg	OBP	SLG
1995 Fayetteville	A Det	130	425	101	15	1	4	130	54	44	30	0	98	1	7	7	10	9	.53	6	.238	.285	.306
1996 Lakeland	A+ Det	122	418	105	18	2	1	130	33	27	16	1	88	3	7	2	6	5	.55	9	.251	.282	.311
1997 Lakeland	A+ Det	111	445	122	20	12	4	178	66	46	20	1	98	2	8	5	21	9	.70	6	.274	.305	.400
1998 El Paso	AA Mil	107	454	139	20	13	11	218	73	64	28	3	70	4	4	5	21	11	.66	7	.306	.348	.480

Year Team	Lg Org	G	AB	H	2B	3B	HR	TB	R	RBI	TBB	IBB	SO	HBP	SH	SF	SB	CS	SB%	GDP	Avg	OBP	SLG
Louisville	AAA Mil	36	133	36	4	3	3	55	18	14	6	0	31	0	2	1	6	3	.67	3	.271	.300	.414
1999 Louisville	AAA Mil	108	407	107	23	8	7	167	57	38	31	1	94	2	2	5	21	4	.84	7	.263	.315	.410
5 Min. YEARS		614	2282	610	100	39	30	878	301	233	131	6	479	12	30	25	85	41	.67	38	.267	.307	.385

Tomas Perez

Bats: Right **Throws:** Right **Pos:** SS   **Ht:** 5'11" **Wt:** 177 **Born:** 12/29/73 **Age:** 26

Year Team	Lg Org	G	AB	H	2B	3B	HR	TB	R	RBI	TBB	IBB	SO	HBP	SH	SF	SB	CS	SB%	GDP	Avg	OBP	SLG
1993 Expos	R Mon	52	189	46	3	1	2	57	27	21	23	0	25	0	4	2	7	3	.70	5	.243	.322	.302
1994 Burlington	A Mon	119	465	122	22	1	8	170	76	47	48	3	78	1	4	5	8	10	.44	2	.262	.329	.366
1996 Syracuse	AAA Tor	40	123	34	10	1	1	49	15	13	7	0	19	0	3	1	8	1	.89	2	.276	.313	.398
1997 Syracuse	AAA Tor	89	303	68	13	0	1	84	32	20	37	1	67	0	14	1	3	4	.43	9	.224	.308	.277
1998 Syracuse	AAA Tor	116	404	102	15	4	3	134	40	37	18	0	67	0	4	4	4	7	.36	10	.252	.284	.332
1999 Edmonton	AAA Ana	83	296	77	17	1	4	108	31	40	19	0	43	2	2	3	2	2	.50	1	.260	.306	.365
1995 Toronto	AL	41	98	24	3	1	1	32	12	8	7	0	18	0	0	1	0	1	.00	6	.245	.292	.327
1996 Toronto	AL	91	295	74	13	4	1	98	24	19	25	0	29	1	6	1	1	2	.33	10	.251	.311	.332
1997 Toronto	AL	40	123	24	3	2	0	31	9	9	11	0	28	1	3	0	1	1	.50	2	.195	.267	.252
1998 Toronto	AL	6	9	1	0	0	0	1	1	0	1	0	3	0	1	0	0	0	.00	1	.111	.200	.111
6 Min. YEARS		499	1780	449	80	8	19	602	221	178	152	4	299	3	31	12	32	27	.54	29	.252	.310	.338
4 Maj. YEARS		178	525	123	19	7	2	162	46	36	44	0	78	2	10	2	2	4	.33	19	.234	.295	.309

Chan Perry

Bats: Right **Throws:** Right **Pos:** 1B   **Ht:** 6'2" **Wt:** 200 **Born:** 9/13/72 **Age:** 27

Year Team	Lg Org	G	AB	H	2B	3B	HR	TB	R	RBI	TBB	IBB	SO	HBP	SH	SF	SB	CS	SB%	GDP	Avg	OBP	SLG
1994 Burlington	R+ Cle	52	185	58	16	1	5	91	28	32	18	0	28	1	0	4	6	0	1.00	9	.314	.370	.492
1995 Columbus	A Cle	113	411	117	30	4	9	182	64	50	53	1	49	2	2	4	7	2	.78	6	.285	.366	.443
1996 Kinston	A+ Cle	96	358	104	27	1	10	163	44	62	36	3	33	2	3	3	2	3	.40	9	.291	.356	.455
1997 Akron	AA Cle	119	476	150	34	2	20	248	74	96	28	0	61	5	1	6	3	3	.50	14	.315	.355	.521
1998 Buffalo	AAA Cle	13	49	11	4	0	0	15	8	3	6	0	10	2	0	0	1	0	1.00	0	.224	.333	.306
Akron	AA Cle	54	203	57	17	2	5	93	36	27	23	1	43	0	0	1	3	2	.60	2	.281	.352	.458
1999 Akron	AA Cle	37	154	43	14	0	7	78	24	30	11	0	27	1	0	1	1	0	1.00	3	.279	.329	.506
Buffalo	AAA Cle	79	273	77	17	0	10	124	44	59	19	0	34	3	3	7	5	1	.83	9	.282	.328	.454
6 Min. YEARS		563	2109	617	159	10	66	994	322	359	194	5	285	16	9	26	28	11	.72	52	.293	.353	.471

Mark Persails

Pitches: Right **Bats:** Right **Pos:** P   **Ht:** 6'3" **Wt:** 190 **Born:** 10/25/75 **Age:** 24

Year Team	Lg Org	G	GS	CG	GF	IP	BFP	H	R	ER	HR	SH	SF	HB	TBB	IBB	SO	WP	Bk	W	L	Pct.	ShO	Sv	ERA
1995 Tigers	R Det	11	10	0	0	51	237	50	37	25	4	5	3	4	25	0	30	8	1	1	4	.200	0	0	4.41
1996 Jamestown	A- Det	13	13	0	0	63.2	275	53	35	30	6	1	0	6	29	0	37	6	0	1	4	.200	0	0	4.24
1997 Jamestown	A- Det	15	14	2	1	84.2	384	103	64	54	5	1	3	3	33	1	56	13	0	3	7	.300	0	0	5.74
1998 W Michigan	A Det	39	3	0	15	92.1	372	75	33	29	7	7	1	3	29	0	64	4	0	11	5	.688	0	2	2.83
1999 Kissimmee	A+ Hou	10	0	0	2	20.1	92	26	9	5	1	0	0	1	4	0	15	3	0	1	1	.500	0	0	2.21
Jackson	AA Hou	12	0	0	2	19.2	82	15	5	3	1	1	0	0	10	0	20	2	0	1	0	1.000	0	0	1.37
5 Min. YEARS		100	40	2	20	331.2	1442	322	183	146	24	15	7	17	130	1	222	36	1	18	21	.462	0	2	3.96

Tommy Peterman

Bats: Left **Throws:** Left **Pos:** 1B   **Ht:** 6'0" **Wt:** 228 **Born:** 5/5/75 **Age:** 25

Year Team	Lg Org	G	AB	H	2B	3B	HR	TB	R	RBI	TBB	IBB	SO	HBP	SH	SF	SB	CS	SB%	GDP	Avg	OBP	SLG
1996 Elizabethtn	R+ Min	3	10	3	0	0	1	6	5	4	5	0	1	0	0	0	0	0	.00	0	.300	.533	.600
Fort Wayne	A Min	58	176	45	11	0	3	65	17	28	10	3	30	2	0	3	0	1	.00	1	.256	.298	.369
1997 Fort Wayne	A Min	113	417	122	22	0	7	165	46	57	28	4	69	1	1	5	0	4	.00	9	.293	.335	.396
1998 Fort Myers	A+ Min	135	519	162	36	2	20	262	71	110	63	13	86	4	1	6	2	0	1.00	11	.312	.387	.505
1999 New Britain	AA Min	140	538	141	28	0	20	229	68	84	61	5	84	3	0	4	1	2	.33	10	.262	.338	.426
4 Min. YEARS		449	1660	473	97	2	51	727	207	283	167	25	270	10	2	18	3	7	.30	31	.285	.350	.438

Don Peters

Pitches: Right **Bats:** Right **Pos:** P   **Ht:** 6'0" **Wt:** 190 **Born:** 10/7/69 **Age:** 30

Year Team	Lg Org	G	GS	CG	GF	IP	BFP	H	R	ER	HR	SH	SF	HB	TBB	IBB	SO	WP	Bk	W	L	Pct.	ShO	Sv	ERA
1990 Sou Oregon	A- Oak	11	7	0	3	35.2	147	20	7	3	0	1	0	1	17	1	34	5	0	1	1	.500	0	0	0.76
1991 Huntsville	AA Oak	33	20	0	3	126	567	131	89	70	14	6	8	2	70	1	59	10	4	4	11	.267	0	0	5.00
1995 San Jose	A+ SF	20	13	0	5	68	284	68	33	32	6	1	3	4	24	0	38	1	1	3	3	.500	0	2	4.24
1997 South Bend	A Ari	13	0	0	5	15.1	65	19	7	5	0	1	0	1	4	0	8	1	0	0	2	.000	0	0	2.93
High Desert	A+ Ari	21	0	0	15	33.1	134	20	10	6	2	1	0	1	13	0	25	3	0	1	2	.333	0	7	1.62
1998 Tucson	AAA Ari	13	0	0	5	21.1	96	27	18	18	8	1	2	0	7	1	4	3	0	1	1	.500	0	1	7.59
1999 Tucson	AAA Ari	3	0	0	2	4.2	17	1	2	2	0	1	1	1	2	0	2	0	0	1	0	1.000	0	0	3.86
El Paso	AA Ari	32	0	0	18	41	199	57	36	26	3	3	3	3	16	1	29	2	0	3	3	.500	0	4	5.71
6 Min. YEARS		167	40	0	75	365.2	1603	367	213	167	35	15	18	12	160	5	219	25	5	13	25	.342	0	21	4.11

Dan Petroff

Pitches: Right **Bats:** Right **Pos:** P   **Ht:** 6'4" **Wt:** 220 **Born:** 4/5/74 **Age:** 26

			HOW	MUCH	HE	PITCHED		WHAT	HE	GAVE	UP								THE	RESULTS			
Year Team	Lg Org	G	GS	CG	GF	IP	BFP	H	R	ER	HR	SH	SF	HB	TBB	IBB	SO	WP	Bk	W	L	Pct.	ShO	Sv	ERA
1994 Boise	A- Ana	8	8	0	0	44.1	183	35	18	14	1	3	0	3	19	2	41	0	2	3	2	.600	0	0	2.84
1995 Cedar Rapds	A Ana	27	27	2	0	146	635	153	86	75	9	5	4	14	47	0	98	9	2	9	10	.474	0	0	4.62
1996 Cedar Rapds	A Ana	9	9	2	0	49.2	227	44	34	21	3	2	3	4	34	0	29	5	1	2	3	.400	0	0	3.81
1999 Johnstown	IND —	3	3	0	0	14	71	21	12	11	1	0	2	2	6	1	10	2	0	0	1	.000	0	0	7.07
Erie	AA Ana	8	0	0	4	13.1	66	21	17	14	1	1	3	1	4	0	8	0	1	0	0	.000	0	0	9.45
4 Min. YEARS		55	47	4	4	267.1	1182	274	167	135	15	11	12	24	110	3	186	16	6	14	16	.467	0	0	4.54

Adam Pettyjohn

Pitches: Left **Bats:** Right **Pos:** P   **Ht:** 6'3" **Wt:** 190 **Born:** 6/11/77 **Age:** 23

			HOW	MUCH	HE	PITCHED		WHAT	HE	GAVE	UP								THE	RESULTS			
Year Team	Lg Org	G	GS	CG	GF	IP	BFP	H	R	ER	HR	SH	SF	HB	TBB	IBB	SO	WP	Bk	W	L	Pct.	ShO	Sv	ERA
1998 Jamestown	A- Det	4	4	0	0	22	93	21	10	7	0	1	2	2	4	0	24	1	1	2	2	.500	0	0	2.86
W Michigan	A Det	8	8	1	0	50.1	210	46	15	11	3	3	0	4	9	0	64	1	0	4	2	.667	1	0	1.97
1999 Lakeland	A+ Det	9	9	2	0	59.2	255	62	35	25	2	2	0	1	11	0	51	2	0	3	4	.429	0	0	3.77
Jacksonville	AA Det	20	20	0	0	126.2	548	134	75	66	13	3	5	8	35	0	92	4	0	9	5	.643	0	0	4.69
2 Min. YEARS		41	41	3	0	258.2	1106	263	135	109	18	9	7	15	59	0	231	8	1	18	13	.581	1	0	3.79

Tommy Phelps

Pitches: Left **Bats:** Left **Pos:** P   **Ht:** 6'3" **Wt:** 192 **Born:** 3/4/74 **Age:** 26

			HOW	MUCH	HE	PITCHED		WHAT	HE	GAVE	UP								THE	RESULTS			
Year Team	Lg Org	G	GS	CG	GF	IP	BFP	H	R	ER	HR	SH	SF	HB	TBB	IBB	SO	WP	Bk	W	L	Pct.	ShO	Sv	ERA
1993 Burlington	A Mon	8	8	0	0	41	173	36	18	17	4	1	1	1	13	0	33	2	0	2	4	.333	0	0	3.73
Jamestown	A- Mon	16	15	1	0	92.1	416	102	62	47	4	4	3	5	37	1	74	7	1	3	8	.273	0	0	4.58
1994 Burlington	A Mon	23	23	1	0	118.1	534	143	91	73	9	7	7	5	48	1	82	7	0	8	8	.500	1	0	5.55
1995 Wst Plm Bch	A+ Mon	2	2	0	0	5	33	10	10	9	0	0	0	0	11	0	5	2	0	0	2	.000	0	0	16.20
Albany	A Mon	24	24	1	0	135.1	597	142	76	50	6	6	0	4	45	0	119	5	1	10	9	.526	0	0	3.33
1996 Wst Plm Bch	A+ Mon	18	18	1	0	112	468	105	42	36	5	4	1	2	35	0	71	8	0	10	2	.833	1	0	2.89
Harrisburg	AA Mon	8	8	2	0	47.1	195	43	16	13	3	2	0	1	19	2	23	0	0	2	2	.500	2	0	2.47
1997 Harrisburg	AA Mon	18	18	0	0	101.1	462	115	68	53	14	8	5	5	39	1	86	3	1	10	6	.625	0	0	4.71
1998 Jupiter	A+ Mon	7	7	0	0	41	181	42	21	20	3	0	2	2	15	0	21	1	0	2	2	.500	0	0	4.39
Harrisburg	AA Mon	12	10	0	0	59.2	247	57	29	24	5	4	3	0	26	0	26	2	0	5	4	.556	0	0	3.62
1999 Harrisburg	AA Mon	13	13	1	0	64.2	306	76	53	41	13	3	6	7	26	0	36	2	0	3	6	.333	0	0	5.71
7 Min. YEARS		149	146	7	0	818	3612	871	486	383	66	33	32	33	314	5	576	39	3	55	53	.509	4	0	4.21

Jason Phillips

Bats: Right **Throws:** Right **Pos:** C   **Ht:** 6'1" **Wt:** 171 **Born:** 9/27/76 **Age:** 23

				BATTING													BASERUNNING				PERCENTAGES		
Year Team	Lg Org	G	AB	H	2B	3B	HR	TB	R	RBI	TBB	IBB	SO	HBP	SH	SF	SB	CS	SB%	GDP	Avg	OBP	SLG
1997 Pittsfield	A NYM	48	155	32	9	0	2	47	15	17	13	0	24	4	1	2	4	0	1.00	6	.206	.282	.303
1998 St. Lucie	A+ NYM	8	28	13	2	0	0	15	4	2	2	0	1	0	1	0	0	0	.00	1	.464	.500	.536
Capital Cty	A NYM	69	251	68	15	1	5	100	36	37	23	1	35	5	1	1	5	2	.71	3	.271	.343	.398
1999 Binghamton	AA NYM	39	141	32	5	0	7	58	13	23	13	0	20	3	2	1	0	0	.00	4	.227	.304	.411
St. Lucie	A+ NYM	81	283	73	12	1	9	114	36	48	23	0	28	3	0	4	0	1	.00	10	.258	.327	.403
3 Min. YEARS		245	858	218	43	2	23	334	104	127	74	1	108	20	5	8	9	3	.75	20	.254	.325	.389

Paul Phillips

Bats: Right **Throws:** Right **Pos:** C   **Ht:** 5'11" **Wt:** 175 **Born:** 4/15/77 **Age:** 23

				BATTING													BASERUNNING				PERCENTAGES		
Year Team	Lg Org	G	AB	H	2B	3B	HR	TB	R	RBI	TBB	IBB	SO	HBP	SH	SF	SB	CS	SB%	GDP	Avg	OBP	SLG
1998 Spokane	A- KC	59	234	72	12	2	4	100	55	25	18	0	19	4	0	1	12	1	.92	2	.308	.366	.427
Wilmington	A+ KC	2	5	2	0	0	0	2	0	2	0	0	1	0	0	1	0	0	.00	0	.400	.333	.400
1999 Wichita	AA KC	108	393	105	20	2	3	138	58	56	26	0	38	2	3	3	8	9	.47	8	.267	.314	.351
2 Min. YEARS		169	632	179	32	4	7	240	113	83	44	0	58	6	3	5	20	10	.67	10	.283	.333	.380

Wynter Phoenix

Bats: Left **Throws:** Left **Pos:** OF   **Ht:** 6'2" **Wt:** 208 **Born:** 12/7/74 **Age:** 25

				BATTING													BASERUNNING				PERCENTAGES		
Year Team	Lg Org	G	AB	H	2B	3B	HR	TB	R	RBI	TBB	IBB	SO	HBP	SH	SF	SB	CS	SB%	GDP	Avg	OBP	SLG
1997 Yakima	A- LA	56	186	47	14	2	3	74	29	17	23	2	36	3	5	1	11	4	.73	1	.253	.343	.398
1998 San Berndno	A+ LA	110	318	79	16	3	7	122	38	47	35	2	67	3	3	2	20	11	.65	2	.248	.327	.384
1999 Vero Beach	A+ LA	62	202	70	10	2	5	99	43	31	42	4	30	8	1	1	6	5	.55	1	.347	.474	.490
San Antonio	AA LA	60	169	42	6	1	5	65	22	22	21	1	41	2	4	2	1	2	.33	3	.249	.335	.385
3 Min. YEARS		288	875	238	46	8	20	360	132	117	121	9	174	16	13	6	38	22	.63	7	.272	.368	.411

Adam Piatt

Bats: Right **Throws:** Right **Pos:** 3B   **Ht:** 6'2" **Wt:** 195 **Born:** 2/8/76 **Age:** 24

				BATTING													BASERUNNING				PERCENTAGES		
Year Team	Lg Org	G	AB	H	2B	3B	HR	TB	R	RBI	TBB	IBB	SO	HBP	SH	SF	SB	CS	SB%	GDP	Avg	OBP	SLG
1997 Sou Oregon	A- Oak	57	216	63	9	1	13	113	63	35	35	1	58	1	0	1	19	4	.83	4	.292	.391	.523
1998 Modesto	A+ Oak	133	500	144	40	3	20	250	91	107	80	1	99	0	1	8	20	6	.77	15	.288	.381	.500
1999 Midland	AA Oak	129	476	164	48	3	39	335	128	135	93	10	101	7	0	9	7	3	.70	11	.345	.451	.704
Vancouver	AAA Oak	6	18	4	1	0	0	5	1	3	6	0	2	0	0	0	0	0	.00	2	.222	.417	.278
3 Min. YEARS		325	1210	375	98	7	72	703	283	280	214	12	260	8	1	18	46	13	.78	32	.310	.412	.581

220

Ricky Pickett

Pitches: Left Bats: Left Pos: P Ht: 6' 1" Wt: 200 Born: 1/19/70 Age: 30

Year Team	Lg Org	G	GS	CG	GF	IP	BFP	H	R	ER	HR	SH	SF	HB	TBB	IBB	SO	WP	Bk	W	L	Pct.	ShO	Sv	ERA
1992 Billings	R+ Cin	20	4	0	4	53.2	225	35	21	14	2	1	2	5	28	0	41	3	1	1	2	.333	0	2	2.35
1993 Chstn-WV	A Cin	44	1	0	5	43.2	227	42	40	33	1	1	1	5	48	0	65	6	3	1	2	.333	0	0	6.80
1994 Chstn-WV	A Cin	28	0	0	19	27.1	121	14	8	6	1	0	1	2	20	0	48	4	0	1	1	.500	0	13	1.98
Winston-Sal	A+ Cin	21	0	0	17	24	112	16	11	10	0	1	1	2	23	1	33	2	0	2	1	.667	0	4	3.75
1995 Chattanooga	AA Cin	40	0	0	19	46.2	203	22	20	17	3	2	0	0	44	3	69	1	0	4	5	.444	0	9	3.28
Shreveport	AA SF	14	0	0	9	21	82	9	5	4	1	0	1	0	9	0	23	2	0	2	0	1.000	0	3	1.71
1996 Phoenix	AAA SF	8	0	0	2	8.1	43	12	8	8	1	0	0	1	5	0	7	1	0	0	3	.000	0	0	8.64
Shreveport	AA SF	29	0	0	12	48.2	214	35	21	15	4	3	2	3	35	3	51	2	0	4	1	.800	0	2	2.77
1997 Phoenix	AAA SF	61	0	0	29	67.2	302	52	27	24	2	4	1	4	49	3	85	4	0	3	3	.500	0	12	3.19
1998 Fresno	AAA SF	5	0	0	3	7	42	6	4	3	1	3	0	0	14	1	11	0	0	1	1	.500	0	0	3.86
Tucson	AAA Ari	5	0	0	1	4.2	29	7	8	8	1	0	0	0	9	0	5	1	0	0	0	.000	0	0	15.43
Oklahoma	AAA Tex	24	10	2	5	80	349	69	39	33	7	2	1	0	52	0	78	3	0	6	6	.500	2	1	3.71
1999 Oklahoma	AAA Tex	29	3	0	11	55.1	281	77	53	50	12	2	3	2	43	0	55	4	0	3	4	.429	0	2	8.13
1998 Arizona	NL	2	0	0	0	0.2	9	3	6	6	0	0	0	0	4	0	2	1	0	0	0	.000	0	0	81.00
8 Min. YEARS		328	18	2	136	488	2230	396	265	225	36	19	13	24	379	11	571	33	4	28	29	.491	2	48	4.15

Jeff Pickler

Bats: Left Throws: Right Pos: 2B Ht: 5'10" Wt: 185 Born: 1/6/76 Age: 24

Year Team	Lg Org	G	AB	H	2B	3B	HR	TB	R	RBI	TBB	IBB	SO	HBP	SH	SF	SB	CS	SB%	GDP	Avg	OBP	SLG
1998 Ogden	R+ Mil	71	280	102	22	0	4	136	55	49	39	0	25	2	4	2	20	8	.71	4	.364	.443	.486
1999 Stockton	A+ Mil	80	311	105	14	3	1	128	40	42	23	2	29	0	1	1	7	6	.54	6	.338	.382	.412
Huntsville	AA Mil	51	183	51	8	1	1	64	20	23	15	0	25	0	2	2	9	4	.69	11	.279	.330	.350
2 Min. YEARS		202	774	258	44	4	6	328	115	114	77	2	79	2	7	5	36	18	.67	21	.333	.393	.424

Kirk Pierce

Bats: Right Throws: Right Pos: C Ht: 6'3" Wt: 200 Born: 5/26/73 Age: 27

Year Team	Lg Org	G	AB	H	2B	3B	HR	TB	R	RBI	TBB	IBB	SO	HBP	SH	SF	SB	CS	SB%	GDP	Avg	OBP	SLG
1995 Batavia	A- Phi	30	101	22	5	1	0	29	18	7	10	0	23	6	1	0	0	0	.00	4	.218	.325	.287
1996 Piedmont	A Phi	67	198	50	12	0	2	68	22	28	22	0	43	12	1	2	0	1	.00	6	.253	.359	.343
1997 Clearwater	A+ Phi	24	68	18	1	1	1	24	9	5	3	0	13	3	1	0	0	0	.00	3	.265	.324	.353
1998 Reading	AA Phi	80	265	67	12	0	6	97	31	29	41	2	63	4	2	1	0	0	.00	6	.253	.360	.366
Scranton-WB	AAA Phi	4	13	1	0	0	0	1	2	0	3	0	2	1	2	0	0	0	.00	0	.077	.294	.077
1999 Reading	AA Phi	83	255	66	10	0	9	103	37	40	42	1	56	10	0	5	4	3	.57	9	.259	.378	.404
5 Min. YEARS		288	900	224	40	2	18	322	119	109	121	3	200	36	7	8	4	4	.50	28	.249	.358	.358

Chris Piersoll

Pitches: Right Bats: Right Pos: P Ht: 6'4" Wt: 195 Born: 9/25/77 Age: 22

Year Team	Lg Org	G	GS	CG	GF	IP	BFP	H	R	ER	HR	SH	SF	HB	TBB	IBB	SO	WP	Bk	W	L	Pct.	ShO	Sv	ERA
1997 Cubs	R ChC	14	0	0	3	31.2	130	21	11	8	0	0	0	2	9	0	35	2	4	4	0	1.000	0	2	2.27
1998 Rockford	A ChC	27	4	1	11	59.2	251	52	28	26	8	1	0	4	20	0	55	3	0	2	0	1.000	0	2	3.92
1999 Daytona	A+ ChC	33	0	0	20	67.2	296	68	30	28	7	1	0	7	24	2	74	9	0	7	3	.700	0	5	3.72
West Tenn	AA ChC	8	1	0	4	14.1	57	12	1	1	0	1	0	0	3	0	14	2	0	0	0	.000	0	0	0.63
3 Min. YEARS		82	5	1	38	173.1	734	153	70	63	15	3	0	13	56	2	178	16	4	13	3	.813	0	10	3.27

Anthony Pigott

Bats: Right Throws: Right Pos: OF Ht: 6'1" Wt: 195 Born: 6/13/76 Age: 24

Year Team	Lg Org	G	AB	H	2B	3B	HR	TB	R	RBI	TBB	IBB	SO	HBP	SH	SF	SB	CS	SB%	GDP	Avg	OBP	SLG
1997 Hudson Val	A- TB	1	4	0	0	0	0	0	0	1	0	0	1	0	0	0	0	0	.00	0	.000	.000	.000
Princeton	R+ TB	46	151	35	4	1	0	41	20	14	8	0	34	1	1	1	2	1	.67	3	.232	.273	.272
1998 Hudson Val	A- TB	9	16	4	1	0	0	5	3	3	1	0	2	0	0	1	1	0	1.00	1	.250	.294	.313
Chston-SC	A TB	29	100	17	3	1	2	28	9	11	2	0	26	0	0	1	0	1	.00	4	.170	.184	.280
1999 St. Pete	A+ TB	105	339	91	9	4	2	114	41	33	11	0	84	4	3	1	16	8	.67	5	.268	.299	.336
Orlando	AA TB	4	8	2	1	0	0	3	0	0	0	0	2	0	0	0	0	0	.00	0	.250	.250	.375
3 Min. YEARS		194	618	149	18	6	4	191	73	62	22	0	149	5	4	3	19	10	.66	13	.241	.272	.309

Jose Pimentel

Bats: Right Throws: Right Pos: OF-3B Ht: 6'0" Wt: 160 Born: 12/3/74 Age: 25

Year Team	Lg Org	G	AB	H	2B	3B	HR	TB	R	RBI	TBB	IBB	SO	HBP	SH	SF	SB	CS	SB%	GDP	Avg	OBP	SLG
1996 Savannah	A LA	123	461	128	21	4	7	178	66	54	28	1	100	10	5	4	50	19	.72	9	.278	.330	.386
1997 Vero Beach	A+ LA	110	344	89	13	1	5	119	56	40	17	0	67	2	2	1	41	19	.68	8	.259	.297	.346
1998 San Antonio	AA LA	90	271	55	4	4	4	79	34	24	17	0	59	6	11	1	16	7	.70	6	.203	.264	.292
1999 Greenville	AA Atl	106	364	78	18	1	8	122	55	45	24	3	80	5	4	4	20	10	.67	9	.214	.270	.335
4 Min. YEARS		429	1440	350	56	10	24	498	211	163	86	4	306	23	22	10	127	55	.70	32	.243	.294	.346

Rafael Pina

Pitches: Right **Bats:** Right **Pos:** P **Ht:** 6'1" **Wt:** 170 **Born:** 8/16/71 **Age:** 28

		HOW MUCH HE PITCHED					WHAT HE GAVE UP											THE RESULTS					
Year Team	Lg Org	G	GS	CG	GF	IP	BFP	H	R	ER	HR	SH	SF	HB	TBB	IBB	SO	WP	Bk	W	L	Pct.	ShO	Sv	ERA
1991 Elizabethtn	R+ Min	16	13	3	1	89.1	394	79	42	25	1	3	2	5	44	0	64	8	10	4	5	.444	1	0	2.52
1992 Elizabethtn	R+ Min	11	10	1	0	66	292	68	39	27	2	3	0	2	22	0	43	7	1	6	2	.750	0	0	3.68
1999 Rochester	AAA Bal	48	10	0	18	111.1	488	113	60	54	15	1	3	2	48	2	88	7	1	8	10	.444	0	5	4.37
3 Min. YEARS		75	33	4	19	266.2	1174	260	141	106	18	7	5	9	114	2	195	22	12	18	17	.514	1	5	3.58

Joel Pineiro

Pitches: Right **Bats:** Right **Pos:** P **Ht:** 6'1" **Wt:** 180 **Born:** 9/25/78 **Age:** 21

		HOW MUCH HE PITCHED					WHAT HE GAVE UP											THE RESULTS					
Year Team	Lg Org	G	GS	CG	GF	IP	BFP	H	R	ER	HR	SH	SF	HB	TBB	IBB	SO	WP	Bk	W	L	Pct.	ShO	Sv	ERA
1997 Mariners	R Sea	1	0	0	0	3	11	1	0	0	0	0	0	1	0	0	4	0	0	1	0	1.000	0	0	0.00
Everett	A- Sea	18	6	0	9	49	223	54	33	29	2	0	0	3	18	1	59	3	2	4	2	.667	0	2	5.33
1998 Wisconsin	A Sea	16	16	1	0	96	401	92	40	34	8	3	2	3	28	1	84	3	1	8	4	.667	0	0	3.19
Lancaster	A+ Sea	9	9	1	0	45	217	58	40	39	6	0	0	6	22	0	48	2	3	2	0	1.000	1	0	7.80
Orlando	AA Sea	1	1	0	0	5	22	7	4	3	0	0	1	0	2	0	2	0	0	1	0	1.000	0	0	5.40
1999 New Haven	AA Sea	28	25	4	0	166	724	190	105	87	18	6	5	5	52	0	116	11	0	10	15	.400	0	0	4.72
3 Min. YEARS		73	57	6	9	364	1598	402	222	192	34	9	8	18	122	2	313	19	6	26	21	.553	1	2	4.75

Juan Piniella

Bats: Right **Throws:** Right **Pos:** OF **Ht:** 5'10" **Wt:** 160 **Born:** 3/13/78 **Age:** 22

		BATTING															BASERUNNING				PERCENTAGES		
Year Team	Lg Org	G	AB	H	2B	3B	HR	TB	R	RBI	TBB	IBB	SO	HBP	SH	SF	SB	CS	SB%	GDP	Avg	OBP	SLG
1996 Rangers	R Tex	55	223	53	6	2	0	63	38	18	15	0	54	5	4	2	19	5	.79	1	.238	.298	.283
1997 Pulaski	R+ Tex	33	126	34	4	3	1	47	20	17	8	0	22	0	3	2	9	4	.69	1	.270	.309	.373
1998 Savannah	A Tex	72	255	87	13	6	3	121	51	39	30	0	48	4	7	2	28	11	.72	0	.341	.416	.475
Charlotte	A+ Tex	61	222	68	8	3	2	88	37	23	25	0	38	1	1	0	23	6	.79	0	.306	.379	.396
1999 Tulsa	AA Tex	124	458	121	23	2	9	175	69	46	61	0	120	7	1	8	15	6	.71	6	.264	.354	.382
4 Min. YEARS		345	1284	363	54	16	15	494	215	143	139	0	282	17	16	14	94	32	.75	8	.283	.357	.385

Erik Plantenberg

Pitches: Left **Bats:** Both **Pos:** P **Ht:** 6'1" **Wt:** 187 **Born:** 10/30/68 **Age:** 31

		HOW MUCH HE PITCHED					WHAT HE GAVE UP											THE RESULTS					
Year Team	Lg Org	G	GS	CG	GF	IP	BFP	H	R	ER	HR	SH	SF	HB	TBB	IBB	SO	WP	Bk	W	L	Pct.	ShO	Sv	ERA
1990 Elmira	A- Bos	16	5	0	4	40.1	186	44	26	18	2	6	1	0	19	0	36	4	1	2	3	.400	0	1	4.02
1991 Lynchburg	A+ Bos	20	20	0	0	103	461	116	59	43	3	4	2	4	51	1	73	8	0	11	5	.688	0	0	3.76
1992 Lynchburg	A+ Bos	21	12	0	4	81.2	384	112	69	47	7	2	4	5	36	0	62	6	0	2	3	.400	0	0	5.18
1993 Jacksnville	AA Sea	34	0	0	13	44.2	182	38	11	10	0	1	0	0	14	1	49	1	0	2	1	.667	0	1	2.01
1994 Jacksnville	AA Sea	14	0	0	7	20.1	85	19	6	3	0	1	0	0	8	2	23	0	0	1	0	1.000	0	1	1.33
Calgary	AAA Sea	19	19	1	0	101.2	480	122	82	66	10	2	3	2	62	1	69	14	0	6	7	.462	1	0	5.84
1995 Las Vegas	AAA SD	2	0	0	0	0.1	5	3	3	3	0	0	0	1	0	0	1	0	0	0	0	.000	0	0	81.00
Memphis	AA SD	20	0	0	9	21.2	80	19	4	4	2	1	0	1	2	1	16	1	0	2	1	.000	0	2	1.66
1996 Canton-Akrn	AA Cle	19	0	0	9	21	84	21	7	7	3	1	0	0	2	1	26	2	0	0	0	.000	0	0	3.00
Buffalo	AAA Cle	17	1	0	7	33.2	148	35	16	14	2	0	1	0	14	0	29	0	0	2	2	.500	0	1	3.74
1997 Scranton-WB	AAA Phi	18	0	0	8	14.1	74	22	12	12	1	1	1	0	9	2	12	1	0	0	2	.000	0	0	7.53
1998 Fresno	AAA SF	53	1	0	17	77.1	356	78	45	38	6	6	3	5	43	4	67	10	2	4	5	.444	0	1	4.42
1999 Durham	AAA TB	23	7	0	5	58.1	270	75	43	39	19	1	0	1	28	0	51	3	1	5	4	.556	0	0	6.02
Rochester	AAA Bal	17	0	0	7	22.1	101	25	16	14	1	0	0	0	13	0	21	5	0	2	1	.667	0	0	5.64
1993 Seattle	AL	20	0	0	4	9.2	48	11	7	7	0	1	0	1	12	1	3	1	0	0	0	.000	0	1	6.52
1994 Seattle	AL	6	0	0	2	7	31	4	0	0	0	1	0	1	7	0	1	0	0	0	0	.000	0	0	0.00
1997 Philadelphia	NL	35	0	0	9	25.2	113	25	14	14	1	1	1	1	12	0	12	2	0	0	0	.000	0	0	4.91
10 Min. YEARS		293	65	1	90	640.2	2896	729	399	318	56	26	16	19	301	13	535	55	4	38	34	.528	1	10	4.47
3 Maj. YEARS		61	0	0	15	42.1	197	40	21	21	1	2	1	3	31	1	16	3	0	0	0	.000	0	1	4.46

Kinnis Pledger

Bats: Left **Throws:** Right **Pos:** 1B **Ht:** 6'4" **Wt:** 220 **Born:** 7/17/68 **Age:** 31

		BATTING															BASERUNNING				PERCENTAGES		
Year Team	Lg Org	G	AB	H	2B	3B	HR	TB	R	RBI	TBB	IBB	SO	HBP	SH	SF	SB	CS	SB%	GDP	Avg	OBP	SLG
1987 White Sox	R CWS	37	127	32	6	3	1	47	18	13	13	3	46	0	0	1	20	5	1.00	1	.252	.319	.370
1988 South Bend	A CWS	107	371	75	13	4	3	105	42	34	39	2	106	0	4	3	18	10	.64	2	.202	.276	.283
1989 South Bend	A CWS	89	293	78	13	5	3	110	49	39	56	3	79	0	4	4	26	14	.65	0	.266	.380	.375
1990 Sarasota	A+ CWS	131	460	114	18	4	3	149	72	40	94	3	134	8	6	3	26	14	.65	10	.248	.382	.324
Vancouver	AAA CWS	1	1	0	0	0	0	0	0	0	0	0	0	0	0	0	0	0	.000	0	.000	.000	.000
1991 Birmingham	AA CWS	117	363	79	16	8	9	138	53	51	60	3	104	4	4	1	15	10	.60	2	.218	.334	.380
1992 Sarasota	A+ CWS	59	217	70	11	2	7	106	42	38	28	4	47	3	0	1	13	9	.59	6	.323	.406	.488
Birmingham	AA CWS	60	191	34	5	2	1	46	18	14	19	3	65	0	5	3	2	4	.33	5	.178	.249	.241
1993 Birmingham	AA CWS	125	393	95	10	6	14	159	70	56	74	0	120	3	5	4	19	6	.76	9	.242	.363	.405
1994 Daytona	A+ ChC	11	37	8	1	1	1	14	5	3	10	0	12	0	0	0	0	0	.00	0	.216	.383	.378
Orlando	AA ChC	23	70	19	3	1	2	30	4	8	7	1	17	1	0	0	3	1	.75	4	.271	.346	.429
Iowa	AAA ChC	69	230	65	17	3	8	112	47	34	24	1	54	1	6	3	2	5	.29	2	.283	.349	.487
1995 Iowa	AAA ChC	11	24	2	0	0	0	2	1	0	2	0	12	0	0	0	1	0	.00	1	.083	.154	.083
Mobile	IND —	85	299	80	17	3	21	166	57	61	53	4	76	2	1	4	14	7	.67	2	.268	.377	.555
1996 Norwich	AA NYY	131	445	118	27	6	19	214	80	67	65	7	123	2	1	0	20	5	.80	4	.265	.361	.481
1997 Wichita	AA KC	12	37	3	1	1	0	6	3	0	5	0	14	0	0	0	0	0	.00	0	.081	.190	.162
New Haven	AA Col	61	201	51	10	2	10	95	35	26	30	2	53	1	2	1	2	2	.50	7	.254	.352	.473
1998 Bridgeport	IND —	97	348	116	21	1	26	217	91	91	64	4	84	3	1	9	14	4	.78	5	.333	.432	.624
1999 Bridgeport	IND —	60	225	67	15	2	16	134	46	63	31	3	54	0	1	5	6	4	.60	2	.298	.377	.596

222

Year Team	Lg Org	G	AB	H	2B	3B	HR	TB	R	RBI	TBB	IBB	SO	HBP	SH	SF	SB	CS	SB%	GDP	Avg	OBP	SLG
Tacoma	AAA Sea	43	153	42	8	1	8	76	20	30	19	1	37	2	1	5	0	2	.00	4	.275	.352	.497
13 Min. YEARS		1327	4485	1148	212	55	152	1926	753	668	693	44	1237	30	41	46	200	97	.67	71	.256	.356	.429

Scott Podsednik

Bats: Left **Throws:** Left **Pos:** OF **Ht:** 6'0" **Wt:** 170 **Born:** 3/18/76 **Age:** 24

Year Team	Lg Org	G	AB	H	2B	3B	HR	TB	R	RBI	TBB	IBB	SO	HBP	SH	SF	SB	CS	SB%	GDP	Avg	OBP	SLG
1994 Rangers	R Tex	60	211	48	7	1	1	60	34	17	41	0	34	3	2	3	18	5	.78	1	.227	.357	.284
1995 Hudson Val	A- Tex	65	252	67	3	0	0	70	42	20	35	3	31	1	1	2	20	6	.77	9	.266	.355	.278
1996 Brevard Cty	A+ Fla	108	383	100	9	2	0	113	39	30	45	0	65	3	7	0	20	10	.67	8	.261	.343	.295
1997 Kane County	A Fla	135	531	147	23	4	3	187	80	49	60	2	72	3	14	3	28	11	.72	5	.277	.352	.352
1998 Tulsa	AA Tex	17	75	18	4	1	0	24	9	4	6	0	11	0	0	0	5	2	.71	3	.240	.296	.320
Charlotte	A+ Tex	81	302	86	12	4	4	118	55	39	44	0	32	0	4	6	26	8	.76	2	.285	.369	.391
1999 Rangers	R Tex	5	17	7	2	0	0	9	6	5	2	0	3	0	0	0	1	0	1.00	1	.412	.474	.529
Tulsa	AA Tex	37	116	18	4	0	0	22	10	1	5	0	13	0	2	0	6	2	.75	3	.155	.190	.190
6 Min. YEARS		508	1887	491	64	12	8	603	275	165	238	5	261	10	30	14	124	44	.74	32	.260	.344	.320

Ike Pohle

Bats: Right **Throws:** Right **Pos:** C **Ht:** 6'3" **Wt:** 210 **Born:** 6/3/77 **Age:** 23

Year Team	Lg Org	G	AB	H	2B	3B	HR	TB	R	RBI	TBB	IBB	SO	HBP	SH	SF	SB	CS	SB%	GDP	Avg	OBP	SLG
1999 St.Cathrnes	A- Tor	46	142	34	10	0	4	56	19	20	21	0	47	4	1	2	0	1	.00	2	.239	.349	.394
Syracuse	AAA Tor	2	5	1	0	0	0	1	0	0	0	0	2	1	0	0	0	0	.00	0	.200	.333	.200
1 Min. YEARS		48	147	35	10	0	4	57	19	20	21	0	49	5	1	2	0	1	.00	2	.238	.349	.388

Enohel Polanco

Bats: Right **Throws:** Right **Pos:** SS **Ht:** 5'11" **Wt:** 165 **Born:** 8/11/75 **Age:** 24

Year Team	Lg Org	G	AB	H	2B	3B	HR	TB	R	RBI	TBB	IBB	SO	HBP	SH	SF	SB	CS	SB%	GDP	Avg	OBP	SLG
1995 Kingsport	R+ NYM	62	205	47	5	2	2	62	28	21	18	0	60	2	3	3	7	6	.54	5	.229	.294	.302
1996 Capital Cty	A NYM	92	299	65	12	1	1	82	34	24	18	0	78	5	9	1	6	3	.67	5	.217	.272	.274
1997 St. Lucie	A+ NYM	43	131	33	9	1	0	44	20	12	10	0	33	1	4	1	2	5	.29	4	.252	.308	.336
Binghamton	AA NYM	82	263	79	13	4	3	109	34	32	17	2	59	5	5	0	7	5	.58	3	.300	.354	.414
1998 Binghamton	AA NYM	26	79	19	4	0	0	23	10	5	7	2	27	0	1	1	1	1	.50	1	.241	.302	.291
St. Lucie	A+ NYM	75	239	63	8	1	2	79	35	19	11	0	38	5	5	2	6	2	.75	2	.264	.307	.331
1999 West Tenn	AA ChC	116	354	85	21	5	3	125	44	30	20	2	89	4	5	3	12	8	.60	9	.240	.286	.353
5 Min. YEARS		496	1570	391	72	14	11	524	205	143	101	6	384	22	32	10	41	30	.58	29	.249	.302	.332

Trey Poland

Pitches: Left **Bats:** Left **Pos:** P **Ht:** 6'1" **Wt:** 190 **Born:** 4/3/75 **Age:** 25

Year Team	Lg Org	G	GS	CG	GF	IP	BFP	H	R	ER	HR	SH	SF	HB	TBB	IBB	SO	WP	Bk	W	L	Pct.	ShO	Sv	ERA
1997 Pulaski	R+ Tex	13	13	3	0	85.1	333	57	29	19	9	2	0	3	18	0	106	4	3	7	3	.700	2	0	2.00
1998 Charlotte	A+ Tex	26	25	1	0	148.2	645	150	82	64	15	2	4	4	60	0	138	7	2	8	5	.615	0	0	3.87
1999 Charlotte	A+ Tex	5	5	1	0	32.1	120	16	4	3	1	0	1	0	9	0	28	0	0	2	2	.500	1	0	0.84
Tulsa	AA Tex	21	21	2	0	118.2	546	139	74	65	11	3	3	5	56	0	80	9	2	5	8	.385	1	0	4.93
3 Min. YEARS		65	64	7	0	385	1644	362	189	151	36	7	8	12	143	0	352	20	7	22	18	.550	4	0	3.53

Kevin Polcovich

Bats: Right **Throws:** Right **Pos:** SS **Ht:** 5'9" **Wt:** 182 **Born:** 6/28/70 **Age:** 30

Year Team	Lg Org	G	AB	H	2B	3B	HR	TB	R	RBI	TBB	IBB	SO	HBP	SH	SF	SB	CS	SB%	GDP	Avg	OBP	SLG
1992 Carolina	AA Pit	13	35	6	0	0	0	6	1	1	4	0	4	2	0	0	0	0	.00	1	.171	.293	.171
Augusta	A Pit	46	153	40	6	2	0	50	24	10	18	0	30	8	3	0	7	7	.50	1	.261	.369	.327
1993 Augusta	A Pit	14	48	13	2	0	0	15	9	4	7	0	8	0	2	1	2	1	.67	1	.271	.357	.313
Carolina	AA Pit	4	11	3	0	0	0	3	1	1	1	0	1	0	2	0	0	0	.00	1	.273	.333	.273
Salem	A+ Pit	94	282	72	10	3	1	91	44	25	49	0	42	12	6	3	13	6	.68	7	.255	.384	.323
1994 Carolina	AA Pit	125	406	95	14	2	2	119	46	33	38	4	70	11	10	8	9	4	.69	6	.234	.311	.293
1995 Carolina	AA Pit	64	221	70	8	0	3	87	27	18	14	1	29	5	3	1	10	5	.67	3	.317	.369	.394
Calgary	AAA Pit	62	213	60	8	1	3	79	31	27	11	0	32	8	2	3	5	6	.45	7	.282	.336	.371
1996 Calgary	AAA Pit	104	336	92	21	3	1	122	53	46	18	3	49	14	5	2	7	6	.54	9	.274	.335	.363
1997 Carolina	AA Pit	17	50	16	5	0	3	30	13	7	10	0	4	2	2	0	4	2	.67	1	.320	.452	.600
Calgary	AAA Pit	17	62	19	4	0	1	26	7	9	1	0	7	1	0	1	0	0	.00	1	.306	.323	.419
1999 Nashville	AAA Pit	80	233	56	10	1	3	77	37	25	20	1	52	4	7	4	6	4	.60	4	.240	.307	.330
1997 Pittsburgh	NL	84	245	67	16	1	4	97	37	21	21	4	45	9	2	2	2	2	.50	11	.273	.350	.396
1998 Pittsburgh	NL	81	212	40	12	0	0	52	18	14	15	2	33	5	3	3	4	3	.57	7	.189	.255	.245
7 Min. YEARS		640	2050	542	88	12	17	705	293	206	191	9	328	67	42	23	63	43	.59	42	.264	.343	.344
2 Maj. YEARS		165	457	107	28	1	4	149	55	35	36	6	78	14	5	5	6	5	.55	18	.234	.307	.326

Joe Pomierski

Bats: Left **Throws:** Right **Pos:** OF **Ht:** 6'2" **Wt:** 192 **Born:** 4/15/74 **Age:** 26

Year Team	Lg Org	G	AB	H	2B	3B	HR	TB	R	RBI	TBB	IBB	SO	HBP	SH	SF	SB	CS	SB%	GDP	Avg	OBP	SLG
1992 Mariners	R Sea	32	103	24	4	1	0	30	19	13	14	0	26	2	2	0	2	1	.67	0	.233	.336	.291
1993 Mariners	R Sea	48	173	39	8	4	2	61	19	29	19	0	39	2	1	3	4	1	.80	2	.225	.305	.353

(Batting — top player, continued)

Year Team	Lg Org	G	AB	H	2B	3B	HR	TB	R	RBI	TBB	IBB	SO	HBP	SH	SF	SB	CS	SB%	GDP	Avg	OBP	SLG
1994 Bellingham	A- Sea	55	152	27	4	0	4	43	20	25	16	2	46	1	1	3	2	3	.40	2	.178	.256	.283
1995 Everett	A- Sea	59	217	48	15	3	11	102	31	38	26	0	58	4	0	0	4	2	.67	2	.221	.316	.470
1996 Hudson Val	A- TB	74	285	74	25	3	8	129	45	54	35	1	91	4	0	6	2	4	.33	6	.260	.342	.453
1997 St. Pete	A+ TB	119	422	112	25	5	11	180	64	49	43	4	78	4	2	3	4	3	.57	5	.265	.337	.427
1998 St. Pete	A+ TB	112	390	92	28	1	12	158	47	67	40	1	90	0	2	5	3	1	.75	9	.236	.303	.405
1999 Orlando	AA TB	62	188	49	10	3	9	92	31	33	22	0	44	5	2	2	1	1	.50	2	.261	.350	.489
8 Min. YEARS		561	1930	465	119	20	57	795	276	308	215	8	472	22	10	22	22	16	.58	28	.241	.321	.412

Dan Pontes

Pitches: Right **Bats:** Right **Pos:** P **Ht:** 6'3" **Wt:** 200 **Born:** 4/27/71 **Age:** 29

Year Team	Lg Org	G	GS	CG	GF	IP	BFP	H	R	ER	HR	SH	SF	HB	TBB	IBB	SO	WP	Bk	W	L	Pct.	ShO	Sv	ERA
1993 Glens Falls	A- StL	20	6	0	2	44.2	202	49	26	19	0	1	3	1	18	2	40	3	2	2	3	.400	0	0	3.83
1994 Savannah	A StL	17	14	0	0	91.2	369	80	43	30	8	0	3	5	17	0	81	9	1	6	6	.500	0	0	2.95
1995 Peoria	A StL	34	6	0	9	67.2	267	47	19	12	1	4	1	4	15	1	88	1	0	2	5	.286	0	1	1.60
1996 St. Pete	A+ StL	27	22	1	2	120.1	495	120	56	51	8	3	5	3	34	0	73	3	1	7	8	.467	0	0	3.81
1997 Elmira	IND —	12	11	1	1	64.2	266	47	20	17	1	2	0	1	28	0	68	1	2	5	2	.714	0	0	2.37
1998 Binghamton	AA NYM	49	0	0	21	55.1	245	52	20	18	5	2	6	4	24	0	48	3	0	3	2	.600	0	5	2.93
1999 St. Lucie	A+ NYM	4	0	0	0	6.2	28	7	2	2	0	0	0	0	2	0	7	1	0	0	0	.000	0	0	2.70
Norfolk	AAA NYM	14	0	0	1	23	116	36	25	24	5	1	0	1	11	0	14	2	0	0	0	.000	0	0	9.39
Binghamton	AA NYM	19	0	0	5	32.1	141	29	18	18	7	0	0	2	15	1	37	1	0	3	1	.750	0	1	5.01
7 Min. YEARS		196	59	2	41	506.1	2129	467	229	191	35	13	18	21	164	4	456	24	6	28	27	.509	0	7	3.39

Dave Post

Bats: Right **Throws:** Right **Pos:** 2B **Ht:** 5'11" **Wt:** 170 **Born:** 9/3/73 **Age:** 26

Year Team	Lg Org	G	AB	H	2B	3B	HR	TB	R	RBI	TBB	IBB	SO	HBP	SH	SF	SB	CS	SB%	GDP	Avg	OBP	SLG
1992 Great Falls	R+ LA	41	138	40	8	0	1	51	23	25	23	0	16	4	3	2	10	5	.67	4	.290	.401	.370
1993 Yakima	A- LA	60	210	53	8	1	1	66	34	22	35	1	27	4	3	3	7	4	.64	3	.252	.365	.314
1994 Bakersfield	A+ LA	31	106	25	5	1	0	32	16	9	13	0	9	3	0	0	6	4	.60	2	.236	.336	.302
Yakima	A- LA	70	263	77	14	1	1	96	46	27	56	3	42	5	1	5	18	5	.78	3	.293	.419	.365
1995 Vero Beach	A+ LA	52	114	27	2	1	0	31	16	11	23	0	11	2	3	1	3	0	1.00	5	.237	.371	.272
1996 Expos	R Mon	8	25	2	0	0	1	5	3	1	4	1	6	0	1	0	1	0	1.00	0	.080	.207	.200
Wst Plm Bch	A+ Mon	79	258	72	15	6	5	114	42	35	37	1	32	5	5	4	8	4	.67	6	.279	.375	.442
1997 Harrisburg	AA Mon	48	156	41	10	0	3	60	20	10	24	0	24	5	3	1	5	1	.83	1	.263	.376	.385
1998 Harrisburg	AA Mon	19	58	20	3	1	1	28	9	9	7	0	3	1	0	0	1	1	.50	0	.345	.424	.483
Ottawa	AAA Mon	93	330	99	23	2	6	144	59	35	28	1	50	6	1	0	7	7	.50	5	.300	.365	.436
1999 Harrisburg	AA Mon	5	21	8	1	0	1	12	5	3	1	0	2	0	1	0	0	0	.00	0	.381	.409	.571
Ottawa	AAA Mon	108	375	97	17	2	10	148	49	36	34	3	56	8	2	3	12	8	.60	9	.259	.331	.395
8 Min. YEARS		614	2054	561	106	15	30	787	328	231	285	10	278	43	26	19	78	39	.67	38	.273	.370	.383

Alonzo Powell

Bats: Right **Throws:** Right **Pos:** DH **Ht:** 6'2" **Wt:** 190 **Born:** 12/12/64 **Age:** 35

Year Team	Lg Org	G	AB	H	2B	3B	HR	TB	R	RBI	TBB	IBB	SO	HBP	SH	SF	SB	CS	SB%	GDP	Avg	OBP	SLG
1983 Clinton	A SF	36	113	22	5	1	0	29	14	9	15	1	27	0	0	1	2	1	.67	—	.195	.287	.257
Great Falls	R+ SF	51	149	33	2	2	1	42	13	16	12	1	34	1	2	0	10	4	.71	—	.221	.284	.282
1984 Everett	A- SF	6	17	3	1	0	1	7	2	4	1	0	3	0	0	2	0	0	.00	1	.176	.200	.412
Clinton	A SF	47	149	37	3	2	1	47	22	10	19	0	31	0	0	2	0	0	.00	3	.248	.333	.315
1985 San Jose	A+ SF	136	473	122	27	6	9	188	79	62	71	0	118	3	3	6	34	11	.76	11	.258	.354	.397
1986 Wst Plm Bch	A+ Mon	23	76	25	7	1	4	46	20	18	22	0	16	0	0	1	5	1	.83	2	.329	.475	.605
Jacksonville	AA Mon	105	402	121	21	5	15	197	67	80	49	3	78	4	2	3	15	11	.58	10	.301	.380	.490
1987 Indianapols	AAA Mon	90	331	99	14	10	19	190	64	74	32	1	68	1	3	3	12	8	.60	7	.299	.360	.574
1988 Indianapols	AAA Mon	88	282	74	18	3	4	110	31	39	28	0	72	0	2	4	10	8	.56	7	.262	.326	.390
1989 Wst Plm Bch	A+ Mon	12	41	13	4	3	1	26	7	8	7	2	3	0	0	1	1	1	.50	1	.317	.408	.634
Indianapols	AAA Mon	121	423	98	26	5	13	173	50	59	38	2	106	2	1	3	9	6	.60	6	.232	.296	.409
1990 Portland	AAA Min	107	376	121	25	3	8	176	56	62	40	1	79	4	0	3	23	11	.68	9	.322	.390	.468
1991 Calgary	AAA Sea	53	192	72	18	7	7	125	45	43	31	2	33	0	0	5	2	6	.25	3	.375	.452	.651
1992 Calgary	AAA Sea	10	35	12	1	1	1	18	7	7	5	0	10	1	0	0	0	1	.00	2	.343	.439	.514
1998 Syracuse	AAA Tor	15	48	11	1	0	3	21	8	9	7	0	12	1	0	0	0	1	.00	2	.229	.339	.438
1999 Columbus	AAA NYY	130	470	148	23	1	24	245	97	90	82	3	110	2	0	6	1	3	.25	14	.315	.414	.521
1987 Montreal	NL	14	41	8	3	0	0	11	3	4	5	0	17	0	0	0	0	0	.00	0	.195	.283	.268
1991 Seattle	AL	57	111	24	6	1	3	41	16	12	11	0	24	1	0	2	0	2	.00	1	.216	.288	.369
12 Min. YEARS		1030	3577	1011	196	50	111	1640	582	590	459	16	800	19	15	37	124	73	.63	—	.283	.364	.458
2 Maj. YEARS		71	152	32	9	1	3	52	19	16	16	0	41	1	0	2	0	2	.00	—	.211	.287	.342

Brian Powell

Pitches: Right **Bats:** Right **Pos:** P **Ht:** 6'2" **Wt:** 205 **Born:** 10/10/73 **Age:** 26

Year Team	Lg Org	G	GS	CG	GF	IP	BFP	H	R	ER	HR	SH	SF	HB	TBB	IBB	SO	WP	Bk	W	L	Pct.	ShO	Sv	ERA
1995 Jamestown	A- Det	5	5	0	0	26.1	108	19	12	9	1	0	1	5	8	0	15	3	0	2	1	.667	0	0	3.08
Fayetteville	A Det	5	5	0	0	28	111	15	5	5	0	1	1	2	11	0	37	2	0	4	0	1.000	0	0	1.61
1996 Lakeland	A+ Det	29	27	5	2	174.1	746	195	106	95	12	9	2	7	47	0	84	1	2	8	13	.381	0	0	4.90
1997 Lakeland	A+ Det	27	27	8	0	183.1	732	153	70	51	9	4	5	6	35	2	122	5	0	13	9	.591	2	0	2.50
1998 Jacksonville	AA Det	14	14	2	0	93.2	379	84	37	32	5	0	3	4	24	0	51	3	2	10	2	.833	1	0	3.07
Toledo	AAA Det	1	1	0	0	7	27	7	3	0	0	0	0	0	0	0	7	0	0	0	0	.000	0	0	0.00
1999 New Orleans	AAA Hou	9	9	0	0	48	214	54	39	33	5	3	0	0	21	0	36	5	1	4	4	.500	0	0	6.19

		HOW MUCH HE PITCHED		WHAT HE GAVE UP		THE RESULTS	
Year Team	Lg Org	G GS CG GF	IP BFP	H R ER HR SH SF HB	TBB IBB SO WP Bk	W L Pct. ShO Sv	ERA
1998 Detroit	AL	18 16 0 1	83.2 383	101 67 59 17 1 1 2	36 2 46 3 0	3 8 .273 1 0	6.35
5 Min. YEARS		90 88 15 2	560.2 2317	525 269 225 32 17 12 24	146 2 352 19 5	41 29 .586 3 0	3.61

Nick Presto

Bats: Right Throws: Right Pos: SS   Ht: 5'10" Wt: 175 Born: 7/8/74 Age: 25

		BATTING				BASERUNNING	PERCENTAGES
Year Team	Lg Org	G AB H	2B 3B HR TB	R RBI TBB IBB SO HBP SH SF	SB CS SB% GDP	Avg OBP SLG
1996 Princeton	R+ Cin	12 42 11	2 1 0 15	12 1 6 0 4 0 0 0	1 2 .33 1	.262 .354 .357
Billings	R+ Cin	4 16 2	0 0 0 2	2 1 2 0 6 0 0 1	0 1 .00 0	.125 .211 .125
1997 Chstn-WV	A Cin	83 300 86	19 2 3 118	57 44 26 0 60 3 9 8	16 2 .89 0	.287 .341 .393
Chattanooga	AA Cin	9 31 7	1 0 0 8	2 6 2 0 7 1 0 1	1 0 1.00 1	.226 .286 .258
Burlington	A Cin	27 94 20	7 0 0 27	14 8 7 0 15 1 0 0	3 2 .60 1	.213 .275 .287
1998 Chattanooga	AA Cin	128 481 120	22 0 4 154	75 35 74 1 52 0 9 2	20 18 .53 5	.249 .348 .320
1999 Reds	R Cin	3 8 3	2 0 0 5	2 0 1 0 1 0 0 0	1 0 1.00 0	.375 .444 .625
Chattanooga	AA Cin	73 224 60	8 0 2 94	34 28 38 0 34 6 2 2	5 7 .42 6	.268 .385 .330
4 Min. YEARS		339 1196 309	61 3 9 403	198 123 156 1 179 11 20 14	47 32 .59 14	.258 .346 .337

Brian Preston

Bats: Right Throws: Right Pos: C   Ht: 5'10" Wt: 190 Born: 12/11/76 Age: 23

		BATTING				BASERUNNING	PERCENTAGES
Year Team	Lg Org	G AB H	2B 3B HR TB	R RBI TBB IBB SO HBP SH SF	SB CS SB% GDP	Avg OBP SLG
1999 Harrisburg	AA Mon	6 15 1	0 0 0 1	1 2 1 0 4 0 0 0	0 0 .00 1	.067 .125 .067
Vermont	A- Mon	28 103 22	8 0 2 36	14 16 13 0 25 2 0 4	2 0 1.00 2	.214 .303 .350
1 Min. YEARS		34 118 23	8 0 2 37	15 18 14 0 29 2 0 4	2 0 1.00 3	.195 .283 .314

Kevin Priebe

Pitches: Left Bats: Right Pos: P   Ht: 6'2" Wt: 225 Born: 1/1/75 Age: 25

		HOW MUCH HE PITCHED		WHAT HE GAVE UP		THE RESULTS	
Year Team	Lg Org	G GS CG GF	IP BFP	H R ER HR SH SF HB	TBB IBB SO WP Bk	W L Pct. ShO Sv	ERA
1997 Helena	R+ Mil	19 0 0 12	28 115	24 7 5 0 2 0 0	9 0 25 0 0	2 1 .667 0 6	1.61
1998 Beloit	A Mil	43 0 0 15	54.1 241	43 17 13 3 8 0 2	37 4 63 2 0	1 3 .250 0 2	2.15
1999 Stockton	A+ Mil	34 0 0 24	42.1 185	40 20 13 1 4 0 0	22 4 46 6 1	3 2 .600 0 6	2.76
Huntsville	AA Mil	3 0 0 1	7 29	7 2 2 1 1 0 1	2 0 4 0 0	0 0 .000 0 0	2.57
3 Min. YEARS		99 0 0 52	131.2 570	114 46 33 5 15 0 3	70 8 138 8 1	6 6 .500 0 14	2.26

Matt Priess

Bats: Right Throws: Right Pos: C   Ht: 6'2" Wt: 200 Born: 11/24/74 Age: 25

		BATTING				BASERUNNING	PERCENTAGES
Year Team	Lg Org	G AB H	2B 3B HR TB	R RBI TBB IBB SO HBP SH SF	SB CS SB% GDP	Avg OBP SLG
1997 Salem-Keizr	A- SF	46 172 47	8 2 3 68	22 31 12 0 30 1 0 3	0 1 .00 3	.273 .319 .395
1998 Shreveport	AA SF	2 1 0	0 0 0 0	0 0 0 1 0 0 0 0	0 0 .00 0	.000 .500 .000
Bakersfield	A+ SF	52 188 54	11 0 4 77	23 19 19 0 30 4 1 2	0 0 .00 11	.287 .362 .410
1999 San Jose	A+ SF	86 293 67	11 2 1 85	35 28 38 1 38 2 4 4	1 2 .33 11	.229 .318 .290
Shreveport	AA SF	5 12 2	0 0 0 5	1 1 1 0 3 0 0 0	0 0 .00 0	.167 .231 .417
3 Min. YEARS		191 666 170	30 4 9 235	81 79 71 1 101 7 5 9	1 3 .25 25	.255 .329 .353

Eddie Priest

Pitches: Left Bats: Right Pos: P   Ht: 6'1" Wt: 200 Born: 4/8/74 Age: 26

		HOW MUCH HE PITCHED		WHAT HE GAVE UP		THE RESULTS	
Year Team	Lg Org	G GS CG GF	IP BFP	H R ER HR SH SF HB	TBB IBB SO WP Bk	W L Pct. ShO Sv	ERA
1994 Billings	R+ Cin	13 13 2 0	85 333	74 31 24 3 1 0 1	14 0 82 2 1	7 4 .636 0 0	2.54
1995 Winston-Sal	A+ Cin	12 12 1 0	67 275	60 32 27 7 2 2 0	22 0 60 2 0	5 5 .500 1 0	3.63
1996 Winston-Sal	A+ Cin	4 4 0 0	12.1 48	5 2 1 1 0 0 0	6 0 9 1 0	1 0 1.000 0 0	0.73
1997 Chstn-WV	A Cin	14 14 0 0	77 321	79 38 31 6 2 3 2	10 0 70 5 0	5 3 .625 0 0	3.62
Chattanooga	AA Cin	14 14 1 0	91.2 379	101 39 35 7 2 2 0	17 1 63 3 1	4 6 .400 0 0	3.44
1998 Chattanooga	AA Cin	4 4 0 0	26 105	15 6 5 1 1 0 0	10 1 29 1 0	1 2 .333 0 0	1.73
Indianapols	AAA Cin	6 6 0 0	34 147	36 19 18 6 2 0 1	7 0 21 2 0	4 1 .800 0 0	4.76
Buffalo	AAA Cle	16 16 0 0	88 390	103 56 48 10 2 1 2	28 1 44 2 0	3 5 .375 0 0	4.91
1999 Indianapols	AAA Cin	18 12 0 2	69 303	86 41 41 10 3 3 2	20 1 35 3 1	6 5 .545 0 2	5.35
Chattanooga	AA Cin	12 12 0 0	77 337	99 42 34 6 3 1 3	14 0 60 1 2	4 3 .571 0 0	3.97
1998 Cincinnati	NL	2 2 0 0	6 29	12 8 7 2 0 1 0	1 0 1 0 0	0 1 .000 0 0	10.50
6 Min. YEARS		113 107 4 2	627 2638	658 306 264 57 18 12 11	148 4 473 22 5	40 34 .541 1 2	3.79

Alejandro Prieto

Bats: Right Throws: Right Pos: SS-2B   Ht: 5'11" Wt: 175 Born: 6/19/76 Age: 24

		BATTING				BASERUNNING	PERCENTAGES
Year Team	Lg Org	G AB H	2B 3B HR TB	R RBI TBB IBB SO HBP SH SF	SB CS SB% GDP	Avg OBP SLG
1993 Royals	R KC	45 114 28	3 0 0 31	14 6 9 1 13 0 4 0	4 2 .67 1	.246 .301 .272
1994 Royals	R KC	18 60 18	5 0 2 29	15 17 2 1 5 4 0 1	1 0 1.00 0	.300 .358 .483
1995 Springfield	A KC	124 431 108	9 3 2 129	61 44 40 1 69 6 12 2	11 7 .61 10	.251 .322 .299
1996 Wilmington	A+ KC	119 447 127	19 6 1 161	65 40 31 0 66 3 8 5	26 15 .63 7	.284 .331 .360
1997 Wilmington	A+ KC	129 437 94	13 3 3 122	52 38 41 1 59 2 11 6	20 8 .71 6	.215 .282 .279
1998 Wichita	AA KC	113 384 101	18 7 2 139	61 35 31 0 54 2 8 1	4 8 .33 13	.263 .321 .362
1999 Wichita	AA KC	114 360 106	23 4 6 155	56 41 35 1 47 1 13 3	12 6 .67 10	.294 .356 .431
7 Min. YEARS		662 2233 582	90 23 16 766	324 221 189 5 313 18 56 17	78 46 .63 47	.261 .321 .343

Chris Prieto

Bats: Left   Throws: Left   Pos: OF   Ht: 5'11"   Wt: 180   Born: 8/24/72   Age: 27

							BATTING											BASERUNNING				PERCENTAGES		
Year Team	Lg Org	G	AB	H	2B	3B	HR	TB	R	RBI	TBB	IBB	SO	HBP	SH	SF	SB	CS	SB%	GDP	Avg	OBP	SLG
1993 Spokane	A- SD	73	280	81	17	5	1	111	64	28	47	0	30	5	0	3	36	3	.92	4	.289	.397	.396
1994 Rancho Cuca	A+ SD	102	353	87	10	3	1	106	64	29	52	1	49	5	6	4	29	11	.73	3	.246	.348	.300
1995 Rancho Cuca	A+ SD	114	366	100	12	6	2	130	80	35	64	2	55	5	8	5	39	14	.74	10	.273	.384	.355
1996 Rancho Cuca	A+ SD	55	217	52	11	2	2	73	36	23	39	1	36	0	1	0	23	8	.74	2	.240	.355	.336
Las Vegas	AAA SD	5	7	0	0	0	0	0	1	0	0	0	0	0	0	0	0	0	.00	0	.000	.000	.000
Memphis	AA SD	7	12	4	0	1	0	6	1	0	1	0	2	0	0	0	2	0	1.00	0	.333	.385	.500
1997 Rancho Cuca	A+ SD	22	82	23	4	0	4	39	21	12	19	1	16	0	3	0	4	3	.57	0	.280	.416	.476
Mobile	AA SD	109	388	124	22	9	2	170	80	58	59	0	55	10	1	5	26	6	.81	2	.320	.418	.438
1998 Las Vegas	AAA SD	92	352	107	18	6	2	143	65	35	40	1	48	1	1	0	20	11	.65	4	.304	.377	.406
1999 Las Vegas	AAA SD	108	348	84	14	6	6	128	66	29	46	0	51	6	2	2	21	6	.78	2	.241	.338	.368
7 Min. YEARS		687	2405	662	108	38	20	906	478	249	367	6	342	32	22	19	200	62	.76	27	.275	.376	.377

Rick Prieto

Bats: Both   Throws: Right   Pos: OF   Ht: 5'10"   Wt: 175   Born: 8/24/72   Age: 27

							BATTING											BASERUNNING				PERCENTAGES		
Year Team	Lg Org	G	AB	H	2B	3B	HR	TB	R	RBI	TBB	IBB	SO	HBP	SH	SF	SB	CS	SB%	GDP	Avg	OBP	SLG
1993 Watertown	A- Cle	68	219	64	15	4	4	99	53	40	39	2	61	8	1	1	11	1	.92	3	.292	.416	.452
1994 Columbus	A Cle	124	378	81	14	8	8	135	64	39	65	3	87	15	4	0	21	10	.68	8	.214	.352	.357
1995 Kinston	A+ Cle	26	88	17	2	1	1	24	12	10	13	0	20	0	1	0	3	1	.75	2	.193	.297	.273
Bakersfield	A+ Cle	74	248	55	12	2	2	77	34	22	29	0	46	3	6	0	15	2	.88	1	.222	.311	.310
Columbus	A Cle	4	18	4	0	0	1	7	1	2	0	0	4	0	0	0	0	0	.00	0	.222	.222	.389
1996 Salinas	IND —	88	364	123	27	10	5	185	83	49	38	1	42	7	1	0	30	1	.97	6	.338	.410	.508
1997 Salinas	IND —	22	98	35	6	2	1	48	14	10	5	0	12	2	0	1	15	0	1.00	1	.357	.396	.490
Rancho Cuca	A+ SD	68	281	82	12	3	5	115	47	31	44	0	45	6	2	0	11	6	.65	0	.292	.399	.409
1998 Las Vegas	AAA SD	32	79	21	6	1	0	29	15	8	12	0	22	2	0	1	4	2	.67	0	.266	.372	.367
Mobile	AA SD	72	218	52	9	2	4	77	30	25	21	1	49	3	0	0	9	2	.82	0	.239	.314	.353
1999 Mobile	AA SD	118	359	103	14	4	6	143	61	43	57	0	55	5	5	1	28	5	.85	6	.287	.391	.398
7 Min. YEARS		696	2350	637	117	37	37	939	417	279	323	7	443	51	19	5	147	30	.83	25	.271	.370	.400

Steve Prihoda

Pitches: Left   Bats: Right   Pos: P   Ht: 6'6"   Wt: 215   Born: 12/7/72   Age: 27

		HOW MUCH HE PITCHED						WHAT HE GAVE UP												THE RESULTS				
Year Team	Lg Org	G	GS	CG	GF	IP	BFP	H	R	ER	HR	SH	SF	HB	TBB	IBB	SO	WP	Bk	W	L	Pct.	ShO	Sv	ERA
1995 Spokane	A- KC	14	13	1	0	69.1	293	65	36	25	7	3	1	5	18	0	63	4	0	1	6	.143	0	0	3.25
1996 Wilmington	A+ KC	47	0	0	40	79.1	313	50	17	13	1	6	1	3	22	4	89	3	0	6	6	.500	0	25	1.47
1997 Wichita	AA KC	70	0	0	32	89	391	87	34	32	3	9	1	4	40	8	68	3	1	3	0	.000	0	10	3.24
1998 Wichita	AA KC	58	3	0	16	122	528	140	76	64	18	9	7	9	23	7	85	7	1	11	8	.579	0	3	4.72
1999 Wichita	AA KC	49	0	0	15	78.2	343	91	43	35	8	4	2	4	15	4	51	3	0	6	3	.667	0	2	4.00
5 Min. YEARS		238	16	1	103	438.1	1868	433	206	169	37	31	12	25	118	23	356	20	2	24	26	.480	0	40	3.47

Alan Probst

Bats: Right   Throws: Right   Pos: C   Ht: 6'4"   Wt: 215   Born: 10/24/70   Age: 29

							BATTING											BASERUNNING				PERCENTAGES		
Year Team	Lg Org	G	AB	H	2B	3B	HR	TB	R	RBI	TBB	IBB	SO	HBP	SH	SF	SB	CS	SB%	GDP	Avg	OBP	SLG
1992 Auburn	A- Hou	66	224	53	14	1	5	84	24	34	23	1	48	3	1	2	1	0	1.00	5	.237	.313	.375
1993 Asheville	A Hou	40	124	32	4	0	5	51	14	21	12	0	34	0	0	1	0	2	.00	5	.258	.321	.411
Quad City	A Hou	49	176	48	9	2	3	70	18	28	16	1	48	3	0	3	2	0	1.00	1	.273	.338	.398
1994 Quad City	A Hou	113	375	87	14	1	9	130	50	41	37	3	98	2	3	3	2	5	.29	8	.232	.302	.347
1995 Quad City	A Hou	52	151	39	12	1	7	74	23	27	13	0	28	1	1	1	2	0	1.00	3	.258	.319	.490
Jackson	AA Hou	28	89	21	5	0	1	29	11	8	7	0	25	1	0	2	0	0	.00	3	.236	.293	.326
1996 Tucson	AAA Hou	2	7	2	1	0	0	3	0	1	1	0	3	0	0	0	0	0	.00	0	.286	.375	.429
Jackson	AA Hou	63	180	44	9	1	7	76	20	33	16	1	43	2	2	2	1	0	1.00	1	.244	.310	.422
1997 Jackson	AA Hou	8	24	8	2	0	1	13	2	7	3	0	7	0	0	0	0	0	.00	0	.333	.407	.542
New Orleans	AAA Hou	46	112	25	6	0	2	37	8	10	9	0	27	0	1	2	0	0	.00	4	.223	.276	.330
1998 Knoxville	AA Tor	79	261	68	22	0	10	120	53	44	35	0	81	2	1	3	2	1	.67	7	.261	.349	.460
Syracuse	AAA Tor	12	33	11	1	0	1	15	2	4	2	0	6	0	0	0	0	0	.00	1	.333	.371	.455
1999 Syracuse	AAA Tor	23	59	13	2	0	1	18	6	5	4	0	18	0	0	1	0	0	.00	0	.220	.266	.305
Knoxville	AA Tor	21	66	14	3	0	1	20	5	7	5	0	23	0	1	2	0	0	.00	3	.212	.260	.303
8 Min. YEARS		602	1881	465	104	6	53	740	236	270	183	6	489	14	10	22	10	8	.56	43	.247	.315	.393

Luke Prokopec

Pitches: Right   Bats: Left   Pos: P   Ht: 5'11"   Wt: 166   Born: 2/23/78   Age: 22

		HOW MUCH HE PITCHED						WHAT HE GAVE UP												THE RESULTS				
Year Team	Lg Org	G	GS	CG	GF	IP	BFP	H	R	ER	HR	SH	SF	HB	TBB	IBB	SO	WP	Bk	W	L	Pct.	ShO	Sv	ERA
1997 Savannah	A LA	13	6	0	5	42	175	37	21	19	8	1	3	1	12	0	45	1	0	3	1	.750	0	0	4.07
1998 San Berndno	A+ LA	20	20	0	0	110.1	460	98	43	33	11	3	2	3	33	1	148	5	1	8	5	.615	0	0	2.69
San Antonio	AA LA	5	5	0	0	26	106	16	5	4	1	0	0	1	13	0	25	2	1	3	1	1.000	0	0	1.38
1999 San Antonio	AA LA	27	27	0	0	157.2	685	172	113	95	18	7	8	7	46	0	128	3	1	8	12	.400	0	0	5.42
3 Min. YEARS		65	58	0	5	336	1426	323	182	151	37	11	14	12	104	1	346	11	3	22	18	.550	0	0	4.04

Denis Pujals

Pitches: Right **Bats:** Right **Pos:** P | Ht: 6'4" **Wt:** 215 **Born:** 2/5/73 **Age:** 27

Year Team	Lg Org	G	GS	CG	GF	IP	BFP	H	R	ER	HR	SH	SF	HB	TBB	IBB	SO	WP	Bk	W	L	Pct.	ShO	Sv	ERA
1996 Butte	R+ TB	15	15	0	0	87.1	392	110	65	49	9	1	0	5	19	0	82	6	3	2	7	.222	0	0	5.05
1997 St. Pete	A+ TB	24	24	2	0	140.1	588	156	74	69	14	6	8	8	27	1	69	1	0	9	4	.692	1	0	4.43
1998 St. Pete	A+ TB	42	0	0	9	72.2	308	73	30	23	1	2	1	2	22	2	46	2	0	5	2	.714	0	1	2.85
1999 Orlando	AA TB	42	0	0	9	72.1	316	82	35	31	6	2	6	6	19	3	39	6	0	5	3	.625	0	0	3.86
4 Min. YEARS		123	39	2	18	372.2	1604	421	204	172	30	11	15	21	87	6	236	15	3	21	16	.568	1	1	4.15

Ken Pumphrey

Pitches: Right **Bats:** Right **Pos:** P | Ht: 6'6" **Wt:** 208 **Born:** 9/10/76 **Age:** 23

Year Team	Lg Org	G	GS	CG	GF	IP	BFP	H	R	ER	HR	SH	SF	HB	TBB	IBB	SO	WP	Bk	W	L	Pct.	ShO	Sv	ERA
1994 Mets	R NYM	10	8	0	0	57.1	244	51	27	23	6	1	4	3	16	0	42	6	3	1	3	.250	0	0	3.61
1995 Kingsport	R+ NYM	12	12	0	0	65.1	283	50	32	28	3	3	0	6	42	0	76	7	0	7	3	.700	0	0	3.86
1996 Pittsfield	A- NYM	14	14	1	0	87	373	68	41	31	1	1	2	4	41	0	61	10	2	7	2	.778	1	0	3.21
1997 Capital Cty	A NYM	27	27	3	0	165.2	708	137	70	57	11	7	3	20	72	0	133	11	1	12	6	.667	2	0	3.10
1998 St. Lucie	A+ NYM	25	25	1	0	142.1	606	126	66	50	7	2	6	7	57	0	99	9	1	10	6	.625	0	0	3.16
Binghamton	AA NYM	3	2	0	0	8	36	10	4	4	0	0	0	0	3	0	6	0	0	1	0	1.000	0	0	4.50
1999 Binghamton	AA NYM	25	23	0	0	131.1	617	146	95	70	10	4	4	15	71	0	84	5	0	6	9	.400	0	0	4.80
6 Min. YEARS		116	111	5	1	657	2867	588	335	263	38	18	19	55	302	0	501	48	7	44	29	.603	3	0	3.60

David Pyc

Pitches: Left **Bats:** Left **Pos:** P | Ht: 6'3" **Wt:** 235 **Born:** 2/11/71 **Age:** 29

Year Team	Lg Org	G	GS	CG	GF	IP	BFP	H	R	ER	HR	SH	SF	HB	TBB	IBB	SO	WP	Bk	W	L	Pct.	ShO	Sv	ERA
1992 Great Falls	R+ LA	25	0	0	19	34.2	155	32	15	11	0	3	1	1	16	5	34	1	0	2	3	.400	0	9	2.86
1993 Vero Beach	A+ LA	23	15	1	2	113.1	469	97	41	30	1	6	3	1	47	2	78	5	4	7	8	.467	0	0	2.38
1994 San Antonio	AA LA	25	25	0	0	154.2	656	165	77	64	2	9	4	3	47	5	120	3	0	4	11	.267	0	0	3.72
1995 San Antonio	AA LA	26	26	1	0	157	676	170	72	59	6	6	4	3	49	1	78	3	1	12	6	.667	0	0	3.38
Albuquerque	AAA LA	1	1	0	0	7	31	7	5	3	1	0	1	0	2	1	3	0	0	0	1	.000	0	0	3.86
1996 Albuquerque	AAA LA	13	4	0	2	35.1	179	53	39	36	4	1	1	5	19	3	27	2	0	2	3	.400	0	0	9.17
San Antonio	AA LA	14	14	1	0	96.2	415	106	45	32	5	10	1	2	24	0	62	4	0	7	5	.583	1	0	2.98
1997 Albuquerque	AAA LA	31	23	3	1	152	671	181	104	90	18	4	6	5	50	2	106	5	1	12	12	.500	2	1	5.33
1999 Clearwater	A+ Phi	7	0	0	5	10	35	7	0	0	0	1	0	0	1	0	9	0	0	3	0	1.000	0	0	0.00
Reading	AA Phi	17	13	1	1	81	351	95	44	39	9	2	2	6	15	0	51	1	0	5	2	.714	0	0	4.33
7 Min. YEARS		182	121	7	30	841.2	3642	913	442	364	46	41	23	26	270	19	568	24	6	54	51	.514	3	10	3.89

Rob Quarnstrom

Pitches: Left **Bats:** Right **Pos:** P | Ht: 5'11" **Wt:** 200 **Born:** 10/30/76 **Age:** 23

Year Team	Lg Org	G	GS	CG	GF	IP	BFP	H	R	ER	HR	SH	SF	HB	TBB	IBB	SO	WP	Bk	W	L	Pct.	ShO	Sv	ERA
1998 Rangers	R Tex	23	0	0	21	34.2	120	16	6	6	1	1	0	1	3	0	37	1	1	4	1	.800	0	12	1.56
1999 Tulsa	AA Tex	10	0	0	8	13.2	58	12	3	3	2	1	0	0	4	0	7	0	0	1	0	1.000	0	0	1.98
Charlotte	A+ Tex	30	0	0	16	59	260	68	30	23	3	2	5	2	16	0	38	3	1	2	2	.500	0	4	3.51
2 Min. YEARS		63	0	0	45	107.1	438	96	39	32	6	4	5	3	23	0	82	4	2	7	3	.700	0	16	2.68

Matt Quatraro

Bats: Right **Throws:** Right **Pos:** C | Ht: 6'2" **Wt:** 205 **Born:** 11/14/73 **Age:** 26

Year Team	Lg Org	G	AB	H	2B	3B	HR	TB	R	RBI	TBB	IBB	SO	HBP	SH	SF	SB	CS	SB%	GDP	Avg	OBP	SLG
1996 Butte	R+ TB	59	244	84	16	4	1	111	53	59	25	0	29	8	0	3	3	1	.75	4	.344	.418	.455
1997 Chston-SC	A TB	78	294	88	18	2	7	131	55	59	42	0	55	2	1	5	15	5	.75	7	.299	.339	.446
1998 St. Pete	A+ TB	73	270	67	14	2	4	97	36	31	31	1	67	2	1	3	4	0	1.00	12	.248	.327	.359
1999 Orlando	AA TB	1	4	1	0	0	0	1	1	2	0	0	2	0	1	0	0	0	0		.250	.250	1.000
St. Pete	A+ TB	73	218	57	14	2	3	84	20	23	14	1	47	1	2	0	3	1	.75	6	.261	.309	.385
4 Min. YEARS		284	1030	297	62	10	16	427	145	157	88	2	200	13	5	11	25	7	.78	29	.288	.349	.415

Ruben Quevedo

Pitches: Right **Bats:** Right **Pos:** P | Ht: 6'1" **Wt:** 180 **Born:** 1/5/79 **Age:** 21

Year Team	Lg Org	G	GS	CG	GF	IP	BFP	H	R	ER	HR	SH	SF	HB	TBB	IBB	SO	WP	Bk	W	L	Pct.	ShO	Sv	ERA
1996 Braves	R Atl	10	10	0	0	55	221	50	19	14	1	4	1	1	9	0	49	3	2	2	6	.250	0	0	2.29
1997 Danville	R+ Atl	13	11	0	0	68.1	286	46	37	27	6	3	5	4	27	0	78	3	1	1	5	.167	0	0	3.56
1998 Macon	A Atl	25	15	1	0	112	470	114	50	39	13	3	4	1	31	0	117	5	1	11	3	.786	0	0	3.13
Danville	A+ Atl	6	6	0	0	32.2	143	28	22	13	2	1	2	3	13	1	35	2	0	0	2	.000	0	0	3.58
1999 Richmond	AAA Atl	21	21	0	0	105.2	444	112	65	63	26	2	2	1	34	0	98	4	0	6	5	.545	0	0	5.37
Iowa	AAA ChC	7	7	1	0	44.1	185	34	18	17	1	2	3	0	21	0	50	0	0	3	1	.750	0	0	3.45
4 Min. YEARS		82	70	2	0	418	1749	384	211	173	49	15	17	10	135	1	427	17	4	23	22	.511	1	0	3.72

Edward Quezada

Pitches: Right **Bats:** Right **Pos:** P | Ht: 6'2" **Wt:** 150 **Born:** 1/15/75 **Age:** 25

Year Team	Lg Org	G	GS	CG	GF	IP	BFP	H	R	ER	HR	SH	SF	HB	TBB	IBB	SO	WP	Bk	W	L	Pct.	ShO	Sv	ERA
1995 Expos	R Mon	12	10	0	2	52.1	221	52	36	29	2	1	1	5	10	0	36	10	1	0	7	.000	0	0	4.99
1996 Vermont	A- Mon	14	14	2	0	92.2	378	82	32	24	3	3	1	7	20	0	79	7	0	6	5	.545	0	0	2.33

		HOW MUCH HE PITCHED					WHAT HE GAVE UP											THE RESULTS					
Year Team	Lg Org	G	GS	CG	GF	IP	BFP	H	R	ER	HR	SH	SF	HB	TBB	IBB	SO	WP	Bk	W	L	Pct.	ShO	Sv	ERA
1997 Cape Fear	A Mon	30	19	0	5	141.1	589	143	73	67	12	1	1	11	31	0	87	4	0	8	6	.571	0	2	4.27
1998 Cape Fear	A Mon	30	19	2	1	138.1	592	136	72	63	12	5	9	12	51	0	82	5	1	8	8	.500	1	0	4.10
1999 Harrisburg	AA Mon	3	0	0	2	5	18	2	1	1	1	0	0	0	1	0	4	0	0	0	0	.000	0	0	1.80
Jupiter	A+ Mon	34	1	0	14	63.2	273	64	34	31	4	1	1	7	17	0	25	6	1	2	6	.250	0	0	4.38
5 Min. YEARS		123	63	4	24	493.1	2071	479	248	215	34	11	13	42	130	0	313	32	3	24	32	.429	1	2	3.92

Tom Quinlan

Bats: Right **Throws:** Right **Pos:** 3B   **Ht:** 6' 3" **Wt:** 214 **Born:** 3/27/68 **Age:** 32

		BATTING														BASERUNNING				PERCENTAGES		
Year Team	Lg Org	G	AB	H	2B	3B	HR	TB	R	RBI	TBB	IBB	SO	HBP	SH	SF	SB	CS	SB%	GDP	Avg	OBP	SLG
1987 Myrtle Bch	A Tor	132	435	97	20	3	5	138	42	51	34	0	130	6	3	6	0	2	.00	4	.223	.285	.317
1988 Knoxville	AA Tor	98	326	71	19	1	8	116	33	47	35	1	99	5	3	2	4	9	.31	5	.218	.302	.356
1989 Knoxville	AA Tor	139	452	95	21	3	16	170	62	57	41	0	118	9	3	4	6	4	.60	11	.210	.287	.376
1990 Knoxville	AA Tor	141	481	124	24	6	15	205	70	51	49	2	157	14	7	1	8	9	.47	5	.258	.343	.426
1991 Syracuse	AAA Tor	132	466	112	24	6	10	178	56	49	72	3	163	5	3	2	9	4	.69	7	.240	.347	.382
1992 Syracuse	AAA Tor	107	349	75	17	1	6	112	43	36	43	0	112	10	1	2	1	3	.25	11	.215	.317	.321
1993 Syracuse	AAA Tor	141	461	109	20	5	16	187	63	53	56	2	156	19	2	6	6	1	.86	7	.236	.339	.406
1994 Scranton-WB	AAA Phi	76	262	63	12	2	9	106	38	23	28	0	91	4	1	1	4	2	.67	7	.240	.322	.405
1995 Salt Lake	AAA Min	130	466	130	22	6	17	215	78	88	39	2	124	15	1	6	6	3	.67	12	.279	.350	.461
1996 Salt Lake	AAA Min	121	491	139	38	1	15	224	81	81	38	2	121	15	0	8	4	8	.33	8	.283	.348	.456
1997 Colo Sprngs	AAA Col	134	509	145	36	2	23	254	85	113	50	4	117	12	1	8	1	1	.50	15	.285	.358	.499
1998 Oklahoma	AAA Tex	137	539	150	33	3	16	237	75	97	43	0	155	19	1	6	4	0	1.00	14	.278	.349	.440
1999 Iowa	AAA ChC	133	472	118	26	1	17	197	62	58	41	0	159	13	1	2	1	1	.50	6	.250	.326	.417
1990 Toronto	AL	1	2	1	0	0	0	1	0	0	0	0	1	1	0	0	0	0	.00	0	.500	.667	.500
1992 Toronto	AL	13	15	1	1	0	0	2	2	2	2	0	9	0	0	0	0	0	.00	0	.067	.176	.133
1994 Philadelphia	NL	24	35	7	2	0	1	12	6	3	3	1	13	0	1	0	0	0	.00	0	.200	.263	.343
1996 Minnesota	AL	4	6	0	0	0	0	0	0	0	0	0	3	0	0	0	0	0	.00	0	.000	.000	.000
13 Min. YEARS		1621	5709	1428	312	40	173	2339	788	804	569	16	1702	146	27	54	54	47	.53	112	.250	.331	.410
4 Maj. YEARS		42	58	9	3	0	1	15	8	5	5	1	26	1	1	0	0	0	.00	0	.155	.234	.259

Brian Raabe

Bats: Right **Throws:** Right **Pos:** 2B   **Ht:** 5' 9" **Wt:** 170 **Born:** 11/5/67 **Age:** 32

		BATTING														BASERUNNING				PERCENTAGES		
Year Team	Lg Org	G	AB	H	2B	3B	HR	TB	R	RBI	TBB	IBB	SO	HBP	SH	SF	SB	CS	SB%	GDP	Avg	OBP	SLG
1990 Visalia	A+ Min	42	138	34	3	2	0	41	11	17	10	0	9	1	1	0	5	1	.83	6	.246	.302	.297
1991 Visalia	A+ Min	85	311	80	3	1	1	88	36	22	40	0	14	4	3	2	15	5	.75	8	.257	.347	.283
1992 Miracle	A+ Min	102	361	104	16	2	2	130	52	32	48	1	17	8	1	3	7	6	.54	3	.288	.381	.360
Orlando	AA Min	32	108	30	6	0	2	42	12	6	2	0	2	0	3	0	0	4	.00	2	.278	.291	.389
1993 Nashville	AA Min	134	524	150	23	2	6	195	80	52	56	1	28	10	10	4	18	8	.69	9	.286	.364	.372
1994 Salt Lake	AAA Min	123	474	152	26	3	3	193	78	49	50	1	11	1	0	8	9	8	.53	19	.321	.381	.407
1995 Salt Lake	AAA Min	112	440	134	32	6	3	187	88	60	45	2	14	3	2	7	15	0	1.00	12	.305	.368	.425
1996 Salt Lake	AAA Min	116	482	169	39	4	18	270	103	69	47	2	19	4	2	4	8	8	.50	12	.351	.410	.560
1997 Tacoma	AAA Sea	135	543	191	35	4	14	276	101	80	38	5	20	16	1	9	1	6	.14	12	.352	.404	.508
1999 Columbus	AAA NYY	130	493	161	35	5	11	239	93	77	48	2	19	14	0	8	5	7	.42	18	.327	.396	.485
1995 Minnesota	AL	6	14	3	0	0	0	3	4	1	1	0	0	0	0	0	0	0	.00	0	.214	.267	.214
1996 Minnesota	AL	7	9	2	0	0	0	2	0	1	0	0	1	0	0	1	0	0	.00	0	.222	.200	.222
1997 Seattle	AL	2	3	0	0	0	0	0	0	0	1	0	2	0	0	0	0	0	.00	0	.000	.250	.000
Colorado	NL	2	3	1	0	0	0	1	0	0	0	0	1	0	0	0	0	0	.00	0	.333	.333	.333
9 Min. YEARS		1011	3874	1205	218	29	60	1661	654	464	384	14	153	61	23	45	83	53	.61	101	.311	.378	.429
3 Maj. YEARS		17	29	6	0	0	0	6	4	2	2	0	4	0	0	1	0	0	.00	0	.207	.250	.207

Ryan Radmanovich

Bats: Left **Throws:** Right **Pos:** OF   **Ht:** 6' 2" **Wt:** 200 **Born:** 8/9/71 **Age:** 28

		BATTING														BASERUNNING				PERCENTAGES		
Year Team	Lg Org	G	AB	H	2B	3B	HR	TB	R	RBI	TBB	IBB	SO	HBP	SH	SF	SB	CS	SB%	GDP	Avg	OBP	SLG
1993 Fort Wayne	A Min	62	204	59	7	5	8	100	36	38	30	2	60	7	2	2	8	2	.80	4	.289	.395	.490
1994 Fort Myers	A+ Min	26	85	16	4	0	2	26	11	9	7	0	19	2	0	0	3	1	.75	0	.188	.266	.306
Fort Wayne	A Min	101	383	105	20	6	19	194	64	69	45	3	98	3	1	1	19	14	.58	7	.274	.354	.507
1995 Fort Myers	A+ Min	12	41	13	2	0	0	15	3	5	2	0	8	1	0	0	0	0	.00	0	.317	.364	.366
1996 Hardware Cy	AA Min	125	453	127	31	2	25	237	77	86	49	6	122	3	3	2	4	11	.27	12	.280	.353	.523
1997 Salt Lake	AAA Min	133	485	128	25	4	28	245	92	78	67	7	138	4	1	5	11	4	.73	4	.264	.355	.505
1998 Tacoma	AAA Sea	110	397	119	33	2	15	201	73	65	46	3	83	1	5	7	2	4	.33	6	.300	.368	.506
1999 Tacoma	AAA Sea	109	420	120	24	3	17	201	69	80	53	5	83	4	3	6	10	4	.71	8	.286	.366	.479
1998 Seattle	AL	25	69	15	4	0	2	25	5	10	4	1	25	0	2	0	1	1	.50	0	.217	.260	.362
7 Min. YEARS		678	2468	687	146	22	114	1219	425	430	299	26	611	25	15	23	57	40	.59	41	.278	.359	.494

Brady Raggio

Pitches: Right **Bats:** Right **Pos:** P   **Ht:** 6' 4" **Wt:** 210 **Born:** 9/17/72 **Age:** 27

		HOW MUCH HE PITCHED						WHAT HE GAVE UP												THE RESULTS					
Year Team	Lg Org	G	GS	CG	GF	IP	BFP	H	R	ER	HR	SH	SF	HB	TBB	IBB	SO	WP	Bk	W	L	Pct.	ShO	Sv	ERA
1992 Cardinals	R StL	14	6	3	4	48.1	207	51	26	19	1	2	2	3	7	1	48	5	0	4	3	.571	0	1	3.54
1994 New Jersey	A- StL	4	4	0	0	27	115	28	7	5	0	0	1	0	4	0	20	1	0	3	0	1.000	0	0	1.67
Madison	A StL	11	11	1	0	67.1	277	63	31	24	8	3	2	3	14	1	66	3	0	4	3	.571	0	0	3.21
1995 Peoria	A StL	8	8	3	0	48.2	181	42	13	10	1	1	1	0	2	0	34	0	0	3	0	1.000	2	0	1.85
St. Pete	A+ StL	20	3	0	4	47.1	195	43	24	20	2	3	1	1	13	2	35	2	1	2	3	.400	0	0	3.80
1996 Arkansas	AA StL	26	24	4	0	162.1	667	160	68	58	17	8	2	3	40	2	123	3	2	9	10	.474	1	0	3.22
1997 Louisville	AAA StL	22	22	2	0	138	576	145	68	64	18	5	3	6	32	0	91	3	1	8	11	.421	0	0	4.17

Year Team	Lg Org	G	GS	CG	GF	IP	BFP	H	R	ER	HR	SH	SF	HB	TBB	IBB	SO	WP	Bk	W	L	Pct.	ShO	Sv	ERA
		HOW MUCH HE PITCHED						**WHAT HE GAVE UP**												**THE RESULTS**					
1998 Memphis	AAA StL	24	23	2	0	152.1	616	156	57	52	11	3	3	4	31	0	100	4	1	8	9	.471	1	0	3.07
1999 Oklahoma	AAA Tex	30	24	4	4	168	732	193	100	96	16	3	8	7	49	1	114	8	0	6	11	.353	2	1	5.14
1997 St. Louis	NL	15	4	0	5	31.1	151	44	24	24	1	1	2	1	16	0	21	3	0	1	2	.333	0	0	6.89
1998 St. Louis	NL	4	1	0	2	7	43	22	12	12	1	0	1	1	3	0	3	0	0	1	1	.500	0	0	15.43
7 Min. YEARS		159	125	19	12	859.1	3566	881	394	348	74	28	23	27	192	7	631	29	5	47	50	.485	6	2	3.64
2 Maj. YEARS		19	5	0	7	38.1	194	66	36	36	2	1	3	2	19	0	24	3	0	2	3	.400	0	0	8.45

Matt Raleigh

Bats: Right **Throws:** Right **Pos:** 1B   **Ht:** 5'11" **Wt:** 235 **Born:** 7/18/70 **Age:** 29

Year Team	Lg Org	G	AB	H	2B	3B	HR	TB	R	RBI	TBB	IBB	SO	HBP	SH	SF	SB	CS	SB%	GDP	Avg	OBP	SLG
		BATTING															**BASERUNNING**				**PERCENTAGES**		
1992 Jamestown	A- Mon	77	261	57	14	2	11	108	41	44	45	2	101	0	0	2	14	2	.88	3	.218	.331	.414
1993 Jamestown	A- Mon	77	263	62	17	0	15	124	51	42	39	0	99	1	0	4	5	2	.71	3	.236	.332	.471
1994 Burlington	A Mon	114	398	109	18	2	34	233	78	83	75	3	138	5	0	3	6	2	.75	8	.274	.393	.585
1995 Wst Plm Bch	A+ Mon	66	179	37	11	0	2	54	29	18	54	1	64	6	1	3	4	2	.67	4	.207	.401	.302
1996 Frederick	A+ Bal	21	57	13	0	1	1	18	8	8	12	0	22	2	0	2	3	0	1.00	0	.228	.370	.316
High Desert	A+ Bal	27	84	24	6	0	7	51	17	13	14	0	33	0	0	1	2	0	1.00	2	.286	.384	.607
Bowie	AA Bal	4	8	2	1	0	0	3	0	2	1	0	3	0	0	0	0	0	.00	0	.250	.333	.375
1997 Binghamton	AA NYM	122	398	78	15	0	37	204	71	74	79	6	169	1	0	1	0	2	.00	7	.196	.330	.513
1998 Norfolk	AAA NYM	4	4	0	0	0	0	0	0	0	0	0	3	0	0	0	0	0	.00	0	.000	.000	.000
Binghamton	AA NYM	47	140	28	6	0	6	52	22	28	29	0	60	1	0	2	1	4	.20	1	.200	.337	.371
1999 Lehigh Vly	IND —	60	215	56	11	0	16	115	38	45	44	1	79	0	0	3	3	0	1.00	1	.260	.382	.535
Carolina	AA Col	48	115	24	8	0	4	44	13	12	23	1	60	1	1	0	0	0	.00	2	.209	.345	.383
8 Min. YEARS		667	2122	490	107	5	133	1006	368	369	415	14	831	17	2	21	38	14	.73	31	.231	.358	.474

Dan Ramirez

Bats: Right **Throws:** Right **Pos:** OF   **Ht:** 6'0" **Wt:** 180 **Born:** 2/22/74 **Age:** 26

Year Team	Lg Org	G	AB	H	2B	3B	HR	TB	R	RBI	TBB	IBB	SO	HBP	SH	SF	SB	CS	SB%	GDP	Avg	OBP	SLG
		BATTING															**BASERUNNING**				**PERCENTAGES**		
1994 Mets	R NYM	44	176	50	10	2	0	64	26	29	11	0	23	3	0	0	7	5	.58	4	.284	.337	.364
1995 Kingsport	R+ NYM	62	226	56	6	2	2	72	30	32	15	1	44	1	9	0	21	10	.68	5	.248	.298	.319
1996 Capital Cty	A NYM	47	143	33	5	0	1	41	20	13	11	0	30	1	6	0	6	4	.60	2	.231	.290	.287
Pittsfield	A- NYM	70	260	73	5	5	1	91	28	22	14	0	45	4	4	2	24	9	.73	3	.281	.325	.350
1997 Capital Cty	A NYM	130	478	146	24	4	1	181	82	42	44	0	104	4	3	3	51	25	.67	4	.305	.367	.379
1998 St. Lucie	A+ NYM	123	469	127	17	2	5	163	65	50	32	0	93	3	10	6	27	19	.59	9	.271	.318	.348
1999 Birmingham	AA CWS	32	127	25	5	0	0	30	16	10	3	0	31	1	0	1	6	4	.60	0	.197	.220	.236
Winston-Sal	A+ CWS	85	360	96	4	3	1	109	56	19	29	0	58	2	2	1	44	17	.72	7	.267	.324	.303
Charlotte	AAA CWS	6	14	2	1	0	0	3	2	2	1	0	3	1	1	1	1	0	1.00	1	.143	.235	.214
6 Min. YEARS		599	2253	608	77	18	11	754	325	219	160	1	431	20	35	14	187	93	.67	35	.270	.322	.335

Jose Ramirez

Pitches: Left **Bats:** Left **Pos:** P   **Ht:** 6'1" **Wt:** 170 **Born:** 9/1/75 **Age:** 24

Year Team	Lg Org	G	GS	CG	GF	IP	BFP	H	R	ER	HR	SH	SF	HB	TBB	IBB	SO	WP	Bk	W	L	Pct.	ShO	Sv	ERA
		HOW MUCH HE PITCHED						**WHAT HE GAVE UP**												**THE RESULTS**					
1996 Fayetteville	A Det	15	1	0	5	26	126	35	14	14	2	1	0	1	14	1	30	3	0	1	1	.500	0	0	4.15
Tigers	R Det	13	11	0	2	59.2	280	69	49	26	0	4	1	3	23	0	47	7	5	2	7	.222	0	0	3.92
1997 Jamestown	A- Det	15	15	1	0	94.2	398	84	49	41	4	4	4	4	38	0	75	5	2	3	4	.429	0	0	3.90
1998 Tigers	R Det	2	0	0	0	7	30	7	3	3	1	0	0	0	4	0	8	0	0	1	0	1.000	0	0	3.86
Jamestown	A- Det	1	0	0	0	4	15	4	0	0	0	0	0	0	1	0	5	1	0	1	0	1.000	0	0	0.00
W Michigan	A Det	22	10	1	4	72.1	315	69	49	40	5	2	3	2	31	1	60	7	0	4	5	.444	0	0	4.98
1999 Lakeland	A+ Det	29	6	0	7	84.2	370	79	53	47	9	1	2	2	46	2	62	5	1	5	5	.500	0	0	5.00
Toledo	AAA Det	1	1	0	0	5	23	3	1	1	0	0	0	1	4	1	3	0	0	0	0	.000	0	0	1.80
4 Min. YEARS		98	44	2	18	353.1	1557	350	219	170	21	12	10	13	161	5	290	28	8	17	22	.436	0	0	4.33

Omar Ramirez

Bats: Right **Throws:** Right **Pos:** OF   **Ht:** 5'9" **Wt:** 170 **Born:** 11/2/70 **Age:** 29

Year Team	Lg Org	G	AB	H	2B	3B	HR	TB	R	RBI	TBB	IBB	SO	HBP	SH	SF	SB	CS	SB%	GDP	Avg	OBP	SLG
		BATTING															**BASERUNNING**				**PERCENTAGES**		
1990 Indians	R Cle	18	58	10	0	0	0	10	6	2	11	0	11	0	0	0	2	4	.33	2	.172	.304	.172
1991 Watertown	A- Cle	56	210	56	17	0	2	79	30	17	30	0	30	1	3	1	12	2	.86	2	.267	.360	.376
1992 Kinston	A+ Cle	110	411	123	20	5	13	192	73	49	38	1	53	3	8	2	19	12	.61	5	.299	.361	.467
1993 Canton-Akrn	AA Cle	125	516	162	24	6	7	219	116	53	53	2	49	5	4	1	24	6	.80	9	.314	.383	.424
1994 Charlotte	AAA Cle	134	419	97	20	2	8	145	66	45	54	0	43	1	2	3	15	7	.68	11	.232	.319	.346
1995 Canton-Akrn	AA Cle	10	34	11	0	0	0	11	6	3	3	0	3	0	1	0	0	0	.00	0	.324	.378	.324
1996 Kinston	A+ Cle	2	5	2	0	0	1	5	1	3	1	0	0	0	0	0	0	0	.00	1	.400	.500	1.000
1998 Rio Grande	IND —	71	284	96	18	4	12	158	66	58	37	1	24	3	1	2	26	3	.90	10	.338	.417	.556
1999 New Orleans	AAA Hou	110	379	96	15	2	6	133	56	51	30	2	49	2	2	2	8	3	.73	13	.253	.310	.351
9 Min. YEARS		636	2316	653	114	19	49	952	420	281	257	6	262	15	21	11	106	37	.74	53	.282	.356	.411

Scott Randall

Pitches: Right **Bats:** Right **Pos:** P   **Ht:** 6'3" **Wt:** 178 **Born:** 10/29/75 **Age:** 24

Year Team	Lg Org	G	GS	CG	GF	IP	BFP	H	R	ER	HR	SH	SF	HB	TBB	IBB	SO	WP	Bk	W	L	Pct.	ShO	Sv	ERA
		HOW MUCH HE PITCHED						**WHAT HE GAVE UP**												**THE RESULTS**					
1995 Portland	A- Col	15	11	0	5	95	391	76	35	21	2	2	2	8	28	1	78	7	2	7	3	.700	0	0	1.99
1996 Asheville	A Col	24	24	1	0	154.1	615	121	53	47	11	5	1	7	50	3	136	4	0	14	4	.778	1	0	2.74
1997 Salem	A+ Col	27	26	2	1	176	763	167	93	75	8	8	6	11	66	3	128	14	0	9	10	.474	1	0	3.84

(continued)

Year Team	Lg Org	G	GS	CG	GF	IP	BFP	H	R	ER	HR	SH	SF	HB	TBB	IBB	SO	WP	Bk	W	L	Pct.	ShO	Sv	ERA
1998 New Haven	AA Col	29	29	7	0	202	863	210	102	86	14	9	10	9	62	1	135	10	1	10	14	.417	2	0	3.83
1999 Colo Sprngs	AAA Col	9	9	0	0	42	205	62	41	37	5	3	1	1	22	1	25	5	1	1	4	.200	0	0	7.93
Carolina	AA Col	16	16	3	0	99.2	432	101	52	38	6	3	5	8	34	2	102	3	0	5	8	.385	1	0	3.43
5 Min. YEARS		120	119	14	1	769	3269	737	376	304	46	30	25	44	262	11	604	43	4	46	43	.517	5	0	3.56

Steve Randolph

Pitches: Left **Bats:** Left **Pos:** P **Ht:** 6'3" **Wt:** 185 **Born:** 5/1/74 **Age:** 26

Year Team	Lg Org	G	GS	CG	GF	IP	BFP	H	R	ER	HR	SH	SF	HB	TBB	IBB	SO	WP	Bk	W	L	Pct.	ShO	Sv	ERA
1995 Yankees	R NYY	8	3	0	1	24.1	94	11	7	6	1	0	0	1	16	0	34	3	1	4	0	1.000	0	0	2.22
Oneonta	A- NYY	6	6	0	0	21.2	109	19	22	18	0	0	2	1	23	0	31	5	0	0	3	.000	0	0	7.48
1996 Greensboro	A NYY	32	17	0	7	100.1	451	64	46	42	8	4	5	5	96	1	111	13	3	4	7	.364	0	0	3.77
1997 Tampa	A+ NYY	34	13	1	6	95.1	417	74	55	41	8	7	3	3	63	5	108	4	1	4	7	.364	0	1	3.87
1998 High Desert	A+ Ari	17	17	0	0	85.1	357	71	44	34	6	3	2	3	42	0	104	0	0	4	4	.500	0	0	3.59
Tucson	AAA Ari	17	1	0	3	22.2	99	16	11	8	1	0	2	0	19	2	23	3	0	1	3	.250	0	0	3.18
1999 El Paso	AA Ari	8	8	0	0	44.1	186	39	14	13	1	2	0	1	20	2	38	1	1	2	2	.500	0	0	2.64
Diamondbcks	R Ari	2	2	0	0	6	25	5	3	3	0	0	0	0	2	0	7	0	0	0	0	.000	0	0	4.50
Tucson	AAA Ari	11	10	1	0	41.2	204	47	37	32	7	1	2	2	32	1	26	1	0	0	7	.000	0	0	6.91
5 Min. YEARS		135	77	2	17	441.2	1942	346	239	197	32	17	16	16	316	9	482	30	6	19	33	.365	0	1	4.01

Cody Ransom

Bats: Right **Throws:** Right **Pos:** SS **Ht:** 6'2" **Wt:** 190 **Born:** 2/17/76 **Age:** 24

Year Team	Lg Org	G	AB	H	2B	3B	HR	TB	R	RBI	TBB	IBB	SO	HBP	SH	SF	SB	CS	SB%	GDP	Avg	OBP	SLG
1998 Salem-Keizr	A- SF	71	236	55	12	7	6	99	52	27	43	1	56	2	3	4	19	6	.76	4	.233	.269	.419
1999 Bakersfield	A+ SF	99	356	98	12	6	11	155	69	47	54	0	108	8	1	1	15	8	.65	2	.275	.382	.435
Shreveport	AA SF	14	41	5	0	0	2	11	6	4	4	0	22	1	1	2	0	0	.00	0	.122	.208	.268
2 Min. YEARS		184	633	158	24	13	19	265	127	78	101	1	186	11	5	7	34	14	.71	6	.250	.359	.419

Travis Rapp

Bats: Right **Throws:** Right **Pos:** C **Ht:** 6'2" **Wt:** 205 **Born:** 1/28/75 **Age:** 25

Year Team	Lg Org	G	AB	H	2B	3B	HR	TR	R	RRI	TRR	IRR	SO	HBP	SH	SF	SB	CS	SB%	GDP	Avg	OBP	SLG
1997 Bristol	R+ CWS	26	81	15	4	0	2	25	9	12	9	0	33	1	1	2	0	1	.00	1	.185	.269	.309
1998 White Sox	R CWS	18	37	9	5	0	0	14	5	3	6	1	15	1	1	0	0	1	.00	0	.243	.364	.378
1999 Cedar Rapds	A Ana	14	37	7	3	0	1	13	6	8	2	0	16	2	0	1	0	0	.00	0	.189	.262	.351
Erie	AA Ana	3	8	2	1	0	0	3	1	0	2	0	4	0	0	0	0	0	.00	0	.250	.400	.375
Lk Elsinore	A+ Ana	12	34	6	2	0	0	8	2	1	2	0	14	1	0	0	0	0	.00	0	.176	.243	.235
3 Min. YEARS		73	197	39	15	0	3	63	23	24	21	1	82	5	2	3	0	2	.00	1	.198	.288	.320

Fred Rath

Pitches: Right **Bats:** Right **Pos:** P **Ht:** 6'3" **Wt:** 220 **Born:** 1/5/73 **Age:** 27

Year Team	Lg Org	G	GS	CG	GF	IP	BFP	H	R	ER	HR	SH	SF	HB	TBB	IBB	SO	WP	Bk	W	L	Pct.	ShO	Sv	ERA
1995 Elizabethtn	R+ Min	27	0	0	25	33.1	134	20	8	5	2	2	0	1	11	1	50	3	0	1	1	.500	0	12	1.35
1996 Fort Wayne	A Min	32	0	0	29	41.2	163	26	12	7	1	0	2	0	10	0	63	3	0	1	2	.333	0	14	1.51
Fort Myers	A+ Min	22	0	0	16	29	123	25	10	9	1	1	0	2	10	0	29	3	0	2	5	.286	0	4	2.79
1997 Fort Myers	A+ Min	17	0	0	11	22	87	18	4	4	2	1	1	0	3	1	22	1	0	4	0	1.000	0	2	1.64
New Britain	AA Min	33	0	0	23	50.1	200	43	17	15	1	1	3	1	13	0	33	3	0	3	3	.500	0	12	2.68
1998 Salt Lake	AAA Min	10	0	0	9	11	46	11	2	2	1	0	0	0	2	0	11	0	0	1	0	1.000	0	3	1.64
Colo Sprngs	AAA Col	27	0	0	22	31.2	132	35	16	16	4	1	0	2	8	0	15	3	0	1	2	.333	0	8	4.55
1999 Salt Lake	AAA Min	56	0	0	18	82.2	350	88	41	36	9	3	5	6	24	0	36	6	0	7	5	.583	0	3	3.92
1998 Colorado	NL	2	0	0	1	5.1	23	6	1	1	0	0	1	0	2	0	2	0	0	0	0	.000	0	0	1.69
5 Min. YEARS		247	0	0	167	330	1368	303	127	110	23	10	13	14	96	3	279	26	0	24	20	.545	0	62	3.00

Jon Ratliff

Pitches: Right **Bats:** Right **Pos:** P **Ht:** 6'4" **Wt:** 195 **Born:** 12/22/71 **Age:** 28

Year Team	Lg Org	G	GS	CG	GF	IP	BFP	H	R	ER	HR	SH	SF	HB	TBB	IBB	SO	WP	Bk	W	L	Pct.	ShO	Sv	ERA
1993 Geneva	A- ChC	3	3	0	0	14	65	12	8	5	0	0	0	0	8	0	7	0	0	1	1	.500	0	0	3.21
Daytona	A+ ChC	8	8	0	0	41	194	50	29	18	0	2	3	5	23	0	15	3	1	2	4	.333	0	0	3.95
1994 Daytona	A+ ChC	8	8	1	0	54	227	64	23	21	5	2	1	4	5	0	17	4	0	3	2	.600	0	0	3.50
Iowa	AAA ChC	5	4	0	0	28.1	131	39	19	17	7	1	1	2	7	0	10	3	0	1	3	.250	0	0	5.40
Orlando	AA ChC	12	12	1	0	62.1	292	78	44	39	4	4	5	8	26	1	19	5	0	1	9	.100	0	0	5.63
1995 Orlando	AA ChC	26	25	1	1	140	599	143	67	54	9	2	8	10	42	1	94	13	0	5	5	.667	1	0	3.47
1996 Iowa	AAA ChC	32	13	0	5	93.2	419	107	63	55	10	3	6	6	31	2	59	3	0	4	8	.333	0	0	5.28
1997 Iowa	AAA ChC	9	4	0	1	32.1	134	30	20	20	6	1	2	2	7	0	25	2	0	1	3	.250	0	0	5.57
Orlando	AA ChC	18	15	0	1	101.1	443	112	59	49	10	5	2	1	32	3	68	12	1	6	4	.600	0	0	4.35
1998 Richmond	AAA Atl	29	29	2	0	151.1	671	167	90	83	18	4	9	4	65	0	143	9	0	12	13	.480	0	0	4.94
1999 Richmond	AAA Atl	27	27	0	0	157.2	660	154	88	78	24	3	6	3	44	2	129	5	0	5	12	.294	0	0	4.45
7 Min. YEARS		177	148	5	8	876	3835	956	510	439	93	27	41	47	290	9	586	59	2	46	64	.418	1	2	4.51

Luis Raven

Bats: Right **Throws:** Right **Pos:** DH **Ht:** 6'4" **Wt:** 230 **Born:** 11/19/68 **Age:** 31

BATTING / BASERUNNING / PERCENTAGES

Year Team	Lg Org	G	AB	H	2B	3B	HR	TB	R	RBI	TBB	IBB	SO	HBP	SH	SF	SB	CS	SB%	GDP	Avg	OBP	SLG
1989 Angels	R Ana	43	145	30	6	2	1	43	15	20	8	0	43	1	0	3	3	0	1.00	3	.207	.248	.297
1991 Boise	A- Ana	38	84	23	2	0	2	31	13	13	9	0	19	1	0	0	1	1	.50	6	.274	.351	.369
1992 Palm Spring	A+ Ana	107	378	109	16	2	9	156	59	55	24	2	81	2	0	4	18	7	.72	5	.288	.331	.413
1993 Midland	AA Ana	43	167	43	12	1	2	63	21	30	5	1	45	1	1	0	4	2	.67	4	.257	.283	.377
Palm Spring	A+ Ana	85	343	95	20	2	7	140	38	52	22	0	84	3	1	2	15	11	.58	6	.277	.324	.408
1994 Midland	AA Ana	47	191	58	8	5	18	130	41	57	5	2	51	3	0	3	4	1	.80	9	.304	.327	.681
Vancouver	AAA Ana	85	328	100	13	4	13	160	66	59	22	1	88	2	0	8	7	0	1.00	6	.305	.344	.488
1995 Lk Elsinore	A+ Ana	6	24	10	2	1	2	20	5	6	5	0	7	1	0	0	1	0	1.00	0	.417	.533	.833
Vancouver	AAA Ana	37	135	33	11	1	5	61	18	26	15	0	35	0	1	1	3	1	.75	6	.244	.318	.452
Midland	AA Ana	21	86	23	2	1	5	42	9	15	4	0	30	1	0	1	1	1	.50	2	.267	.304	.488
1996 Canton-Akrn	AA Cle	74	268	81	17	0	21	161	57	64	38	6	73	1	0	2	0	0	.00	6	.302	.388	.601
1997 Birmingham	AA CWS	117	456	153	30	3	30	279	88	112	46	7	126	5	0	7	4	3	.57	5	.336	.397	.612
1999 Charlotte	AAA CWS	139	532	150	32	4	33	289	97	125	50	0	127	3	1	6	5	0	1.00	19	.282	.343	.543
9 Min. YEARS		842	3137	908	171	26	148	1575	527	634	253	19	809	24	4	37	66	27	.71	77	.289	.343	.502

Kevin Rawitzer

Pitches: Left **Bats:** Left **Pos:** P **Ht:** 5'9" **Wt:** 180 **Born:** 2/28/71 **Age:** 29

HOW MUCH HE PITCHED / WHAT HE GAVE UP / THE RESULTS

Year Team	Lg Org	G	GS	CG	GF	IP	BFP	H	R	ER	HR	SH	SF	HB	TBB	IBB	SO	WP	Bk	W	L	Pct.	ShO	Sv	ERA
1993 Eugene	A- KC	6	4	0	0	18	69	13	1	1	0	0	0	1	5	0	20	0	0	1	0	1.000	0	0	0.50
Rockford	A KC	5	5	0	0	30	126	23	7	5	0	0	0	1	11	0	34	0	0	3	0	1.000	0	0	1.50
1994 Rockford	A KC	15	15	0	0	76.1	329	80	27	21	5	0	4	3	27	1	75	6	1	5	2	.714	0	0	2.48
Wilmington	A+ KC	7	1	0	2	17.2	79	18	10	9	0	1	0	0	11	0	13	1	0	0	1	.000	0	1	4.58
1995 Wilmington	A+ KC	15	1	0	7	27	111	21	8	7	0	1	0	3	8	1	22	1	0	2	0	1.000	0	3	2.33
Wichita	AA KC	28	3	0	7	48	209	48	30	28	4	0	2	1	19	0	42	1	0	6	4	.600	0	1	5.25
1996 Wichita	AA KC	42	0	0	17	68.1	314	77	52	36	8	2	2	5	39	1	48	3	0	0	6	.000	0	3	4.74
1997 Wichita	AA KC	44	9	0	6	97	457	125	66	62	10	2	1	6	44	4	75	1	1	5	1	.833	0	0	5.75
1998 Wichita	AA KC	14	14	2	0	85	379	94	52	48	13	3	5	3	28	0	54	4	1	7	4	.636	0	0	5.08
Omaha	AAA KC	10	10	0	0	60	269	72	42	32	7	1	3	2	25	1	37	4	0	4	5	.444	0	0	4.80
1999 Carolina	AA Col	33	4	0	8	70	304	73	33	28	5	3	2	4	26	0	54	3	1	3	2	.600	0	1	3.60
7 Min. YEARS		219	66	2	47	597.1	2646	644	330	277	52	13	19	29	243	8	474	24	4	36	25	.590	0	9	4.17

Mark Raynor

Bats: Right **Throws:** Right **Pos:** 2B **Ht:** 6'0" **Wt:** 180 **Born:** 4/1/73 **Age:** 27

BATTING / BASERUNNING / PERCENTAGES

Year Team	Lg Org	G	AB	H	2B	3B	HR	TB	R	RBI	TBB	IBB	SO	HBP	SH	SF	SB	CS	SB%	GDP	Avg	OBP	SLG
1995 Batavia	A- Phi	66	267	70	10	6	3	101	49	37	38	1	42	2	1	1	13	4	.76	1	.262	.357	.378
1996 Clearwater	A+ Phi	18	55	11	1	1	0	14	8	4	17	0	9	0	1	2	2	1	.67	1	.200	.378	.255
Piedmont	A Phi	111	428	130	21	2	4	167	73	62	50	0	67	3	5	6	16	10	.62	7	.304	.376	.390
1997 Clearwater	A+ Phi	136	469	110	12	2	3	135	54	45	60	1	58	9	3	2	8	6	.57	10	.235	.331	.288
1998 Clearwater	A+ Phi	23	93	23	1	1	1	29	19	10	7	0	12	0	0	1	1	1	.50	2	.247	.297	.312
Reading	AA Phi	100	379	111	9	4	0	128	43	31	38	0	33	0	4	3	7	2	.78	7	.293	.355	.338
1999 Reading	AA Phi	14	43	9	0	1	0	11	4	3	6	0	4	1	1	0	0	1	.00	6	.209	.320	.256
5 Min. YEARS		468	1734	464	54	17	11	585	250	192	216	2	225	15	15	15	47	25	.65	34	.268	.351	.337

Bobby Rector

Pitches: Right **Bats:** Right **Pos:** P **Ht:** 6'1" **Wt:** 170 **Born:** 9/24/74 **Age:** 25

HOW MUCH HE PITCHED / WHAT HE GAVE UP / THE RESULTS

Year Team	Lg Org	G	GS	CG	GF	IP	BFP	H	R	ER	HR	SH	SF	HB	TBB	IBB	SO	WP	Bk	W	L	Pct.	ShO	Sv	ERA
1994 Giants	R SF	9	5	0	0	30.1	117	19	8	4	0	1	1	1	8	0	37	2	0	1	2	.333	0	0	1.19
1995 Burlington	A SF	27	24	0	0	135.2	589	135	78	62	7	4	5	6	59	3	102	6	2	9	11	.450	0	0	4.11
1996 San Jose	A+ SF	28	26	1	1	165.1	694	161	77	66	14	4	5	8	43	0	145	4	0	12	8	.600	0	0	3.59
1997 Bakersfield	A+ SF	8	8	0	0	48.1	199	52	27	22	8	1	1	1	12	1	32	1	1	2	4	.333	0	0	4.10
Kane County	A Fla	3	3	1	0	21	76	11	2	2	1	1	0	0	4	0	24	0	0	1	0	1.000	1	0	0.86
Portland	AA Fla	6	6	0	0	33.2	155	45	20	18	7	2	1	1	11	0	23	2	0	2	2	.500	0	0	4.81
1998 Portland	AA Fla	14	1	0	6	20.2	105	31	27	24	6	4	0	2	10	2	15	2	0	1	1	.500	0	0	10.45
1999 Portland	AA Fla	13	4	0	1	42.2	187	43	23	17	3	7	0	2	14	0	19	0	0	0	4	.000	0	0	3.59
6 Min. YEARS		108	77	2	8	497.2	2122	497	262	215	46	24	13	21	161	6	397	20	3	28	32	.467	1	0	3.89

Tike Redman

Bats: Left **Throws:** Left **Pos:** OF **Ht:** 5'11" **Wt:** 166 **Born:** 3/10/77 **Age:** 23

BATTING / BASERUNNING / PERCENTAGES

Year Team	Lg Org	G	AB	H	2B	3B	HR	TB	R	RBI	TBB	IBB	SO	HBP	SH	SF	SB	CS	SB%	GDP	Avg	OBP	SLG
1996 Pirates	R Pit	26	104	31	4	1	1	40	20	16	12	1	12	0	0	1	15	3	.83	0	.298	.368	.385
Erie	A- Pit	43	170	50	4	6	2	72	31	21	17	0	30	0	2	3	7	3	.70	2	.294	.353	.424
1997 Lynchburg	A+ Pit	125	415	104	18	5	4	144	55	45	45	0	82	7	8	1	21	8	.72	8	.251	.333	.347
1998 Lynchburg	A+ Pit	131	525	135	26	10	6	199	70	46	32	2	73	1	3	6	36	16	.69	5	.257	.298	.379
1999 Altoona	AA Pit	136	532	143	20	12	3	196	84	60	52	1	52	3	6	10	29	16	.64	6	.269	.332	.368
4 Min. YEARS		461	1746	463	72	34	16	651	260	188	158	4	249	11	19	20	108	46	.70	21	.265	.327	.373

Dana Reece

Pitches: Left **Bats:** Left **Pos:** P **Ht:** 5'11" **Wt:** 180 **Born:** 6/12/77 **Age:** 23

Year Team	Lg Org	HOW MUCH HE PITCHED						WHAT HE GAVE UP										THE RESULTS					
		G	GS	CG	GF	IP	BFP	H	R	ER	HR	SH	SF	HB	TBB	IBB	SO	WP	Bk	W	L	Pct.	ShO	Sv	ERA
1999 Medcine Hat	R+ Tor	13	0	0	4	11.2	66	19	11	10	4	0	0	0	8	0	14	1	0	2	1	.667	0	0	7.71
St.Cathrnes	A- Tor	5	0	0	3	6.2	27	4	2	2	1	0	0	1	3	0	7	0	0	1	0	1.000	0	0	2.70
Syracuse	AAA Tor	1	0	0	0	2	9	1	0	0	0	0	0	0	2	0	1	0	0	0	0	.000	0	0	0.00
1 Min. YEARS		19	0	0	7	20.1	102	24	13	12	5	0	0	1	13	0	22	1	0	3	1	.750	0	0	5.31

Brandon Reed

Pitches: Right **Bats:** Right **Pos:** P **Ht:** 6'4" **Wt:** 185 **Born:** 12/18/74 **Age:** 25

Year Team	Lg Org	HOW MUCH HE PITCHED						WHAT HE GAVE UP										THE RESULTS					
		G	GS	CG	GF	IP	BFP	H	R	ER	HR	SH	SF	HB	TBB	IBB	SO	WP	Bk	W	L	Pct.	ShO	Sv	ERA
1994 Bristol	R+ Det	13	13	0	0	78	337	82	41	31	3	1	3	9	10	0	68	4	0	3	5	.375	0	0	3.58
1995 Fayettevlle	A Det	55	0	0	53	64.2	252	40	11	7	1	1	0	3	18	1	78	8	0	3	0	1.000	0	41	0.97
1996 Tigers	R Det	1	1	0	0	2	6	0	0	0	0	0	0	0	1	0	2	0	0	0	0	.000	0	0	0.00
Jacksnville	AA Det	7	3	0	1	26	94	18	6	6	1	0	1	1	3	0	18	0	0	1	0	1.000	0	0	2.08
1997 Jacksnville	AA Det	27	27	2	0	176	754	190	100	89	25	6	10	8	54	0	90	9	0	11	9	.550	0	0	4.55
1998 Toledo	AAA Det	39	17	0	6	117.1	540	159	84	78	17	4	4	5	46	1	70	2	0	5	7	.417	0	0	5.98
1999 Toledo	AAA Det	44	6	1	21	91.1	401	101	53	42	6	1	7	5	26	3	59	1	0	8	5	.615	0	3	4.14
6 Min. YEARS		186	67	3	81	555.1	2384	590	295	253	53	13	25	32	157	5	385	24	0	31	26	.544	0	45	4.10

Steve Reed

Pitches: Right **Bats:** Right **Pos:** P **Ht:** 6'2" **Wt:** 205 **Born:** 9/24/75 **Age:** 24

Year Team	Lg Org	HOW MUCH HE PITCHED						WHAT HE GAVE UP										THE RESULTS					
		G	GS	CG	GF	IP	BFP	H	R	ER	HR	SH	SF	HB	TBB	IBB	SO	WP	Bk	W	L	Pct.	ShO	Sv	ERA
1994 Cardinals	R StL	12	0	0	2	13	59	16	8	8	2	2	2	1	4	0	10	1	1	0	0	.000	0	0	5.54
1995 Johnson Cy	R+ StL	31	0	0	19	42.2	194	48	24	21	2	0	1	0	15	0	41	3	2	2	2	.500	0	1	4.43
1996 Johnson Cy	R+ StL	31	0	0	15	40	170	39	21	18	4	1	2	3	12	1	38	0	0	5	1	.833	0	4	4.05
1997 Peoria	A StL	38	6	0	7	75.2	349	107	56	50	7	4	1	5	16	0	64	4	2	4	3	.571	0	0	5.95
Pr William	A+ StL	7	7	0	0	39.2	176	45	24	19	6	0	1	0	12	0	25	2	2	2	2	.500	0	0	4.31
1998 Arkansas	AA StL	32	17	0	6	116.1	529	163	92	78	18	5	8	3	31	1	53	6	2	4	7	.364	0	0	6.03
1999 Arkansas	AA StL	36	9	0	10	81.1	355	87	59	49	15	1	7	2	28	1	45	5	2	4	8	.333	0	0	5.42
6 Min. YEARS		187	39	0	59	408.2	1832	505	284	243	54	13	22	14	118	3	276	21	11	21	23	.477	0	5	5.35

Cory Reeder

Bats: Right **Throws:** Right **Pos:** C **Ht:** 6'2" **Wt:** 220 **Born:** 3/17/71 **Age:** 29

Year Team	Lg Org	BATTING														BASERUNNING				PERCENTAGES		
		G	AB	H	2B	3B	HR	TB	R	RBI	TBB	IBB	SO	HBP	SH	SF	SB	CS	SB%	GDP	Avg	OBP	SLG
1994 Lancaster	IND —	1	0	0	0	0	0	0	0	0	1	0	0	0	0	0	0	0	.00	0	.000	1.000	.000
1995 Surrey	IND —	42	114	21	0	0	3	30	14	13	7	0	22	3	1	1	0	0	.00	2	.184	.248	.263
1996 Regina	IND —	34	125	24	6	0	4	42	20	19	9	0	44	2	3	3	0	0	.00	4	.192	.252	.336
Minot	IND —	27	102	39	7	0	7	67	23	22	2	0	14	2	0	1	1	1	.50	3	.382	.402	.657
1997 Peoria	IND —	65	222	52	12	1	16	114	31	54	26	1	57	5	1	2	1	0	1.00	7	.234	.325	.514
1998 Stockton	A+ Mil	44	116	26	5	0	4	43	12	10	11	0	41	0	0	1	0	0	.00	3	.224	.289	.371
1999 Oklahoma	AAA Tex	8	21	4	2	0	0	6	3	1	0	0	6	2	0	0	0	0	.00	0	.190	.261	.286
Somerset	IND —	60	178	36	6	0	7	63	21	27	17	0	59	2	1	3	1	1	.50	3	.202	.275	.354
6 Min. YEARS		281	878	202	38	1	41	365	124	146	73	1	243	16	6	11	3	2	.60	22	.230	.298	.416

Nate Reese

Bats: Right **Throws:** Right **Pos:** C-DH **Ht:** 5'11" **Wt:** 215 **Born:** 10/17/74 **Age:** 25

Year Team	Lg Org	BATTING														BASERUNNING				PERCENTAGES		
		G	AB	H	2B	3B	HR	TB	R	RBI	TBB	IBB	SO	HBP	SH	SF	SB	CS	SB%	GDP	Avg	OBP	SLG
1997 Marlins	R Fla	11	29	7	1	0	0	8	3	3	3	0	9	1	0	0	0	1	.00	1	.241	.333	.276
Utica	A- Fla	13	44	9	2	0	0	11	5	5	2	0	14	0	0	0	0	0	.00	1	.205	.234	.250
1998 Brevard Cty	A+ Fla	11	40	7	2	0	2	15	3	7	3	0	9	0	0	0	0	0	.00	2	.175	.233	.375
Kane County	A Fla	13	40	10	1	0	1	14	3	7	5	0	12	2	0	0	0	0	.00	2	.250	.362	.350
Charlotte	AAA Fla	3	8	3	0	0	1	6	1	1	1	0	3	0	0	0	0	0	.00	0	.375	.444	.750
1999 Portland	AA Fla	3	0	0	0	0	0	0	0	0	0	0	1	0	0	0	0	0	.00	0	.000	.000	.000
Brevard Cty	A+ Fla	70	237	63	12	0	7	96	25	38	18	0	44	2	2	5	0	0	.00	7	.266	.317	.405
Calgary	AAA Fla	9	20	5	1	0	0	6	4	2	1	0	5	0	0	0	0	0	.00	1	.250	.286	.300
3 Min. YEARS		133	421	104	19	0	11	156	44	63	33	0	97	5	3	6	0	1	.00	14	.247	.305	.371

Glenn Reeves

Bats: Right **Throws:** Right **Pos:** OF **Ht:** 6'0" **Wt:** 195 **Born:** 1/19/74 **Age:** 26

Year Team	Lg Org	BATTING														BASERUNNING				PERCENTAGES		
		G	AB	H	2B	3B	HR	TB	R	RBI	TBB	IBB	SO	HBP	SH	SF	SB	CS	SB%	GDP	Avg	OBP	SLG
1993 Marlins	R Fla	48	177	50	6	2	0	60	36	19	22	0	29	2	3	1	0	3	.07	1	.282	.360	.339
1994 Kane County	A Fla	102	370	95	15	3	3	125	65	34	66	0	76	2	5	0	5	4	.56	15	.257	.372	.338
1995 Brevard Cty	A+ Fla	117	415	112	22	2	1	141	68	33	78	0	78	6	2	3	6	7	.46	12	.270	.390	.340
1996 Brevard Cty	A+ Fla	123	478	143	29	4	6	198	72	41	63	0	82	5	4	4	8	5	.62	6	.299	.384	.414
1997 Portland	AA Fla	66	222	78	14	2	6	114	53	35	39	0	43	4	0	2	9	4	.69	3	.351	.453	.514
1998 Portland	AA Fla	53	190	48	7	2	1	62	40	18	37	1	42	5	1	5	5	3	.63	3	.253	.380	.326
1999 Portland	AA Fla	6	9	0	0	0	0	0	0	0	0	0	6	0	0	0	0	0	.00	0	.000	.000	.000
Calgary	AAA Fla	91	236	51	8	1	2	67	33	21	37	0	42	4	0	1	3	6	.33	10	.216	.331	.284
7 Min. YEARS		606	2097	577	101	16	19	767	367	201	342	1	398	28	15	16	42	32	.57	50	.275	.381	.366

232

Jason Regan

Bats: Right **Throws:** Right **Pos:** 3B   **Ht:** 5'9" **Wt:** 175 **Born:** 6/30/76 **Age:** 24

Year Team	Lg Org	G	AB	H	2B	3B	HR	TB	R	RBI	TBB	IBB	SO	HBP	SH	SF	SB	CS	SB%	GDP	Avg	OBP	SLG
1996 Everett	A- Sea	40	124	26	11	0	3	46	17	22	25	0	47	4	2	2	3	3	.50	1	.210	.355	.371
1997 Wisconsin	A Sea	51	177	45	14	1	9	88	31	23	23	0	55	4	0	3	2	0	1.00	1	.254	.348	.497
Lancaster	A+ Sea	69	260	73	20	2	22	163	50	54	45	2	79	6	0	0	2	2	.50	2	.281	.399	.627
1998 Lancaster	A+ Sea	124	416	124	26	6	19	219	105	82	106	1	123	11	0	6	9	3	.75	7	.298	.447	.526
1999 New Haven	AA Sea	45	150	32	9	1	3	52	12	13	17	1	46	2	1	0	2	1	.67	1	.213	.302	.347
Lancaster	A+ Sea	64	231	59	17	1	15	123	50	45	33	2	77	6	1	2	4	1	.80	6	.255	.360	.532
4 Min. YEARS		393	1358	359	97	11	71	691	265	239	249	6	427	33	4	13	22	10	.69	18	.264	.388	.509

Mike Rennhack

Bats: Both **Throws:** Right **Pos:** OF   **Ht:** 6'3" **Wt:** 200 **Born:** 8/25/74 **Age:** 25

Year Team	Lg Org	G	AB	H	2B	3B	HR	TB	R	RBI	TBB	IBB	SO	HBP	SH	SF	SB	CS	SB%	GDP	Avg	OBP	SLG
1992 Astros	R Hou	35	126	26	2	4	0	36	11	16	14	2	18	0	0	1	6	4	.60	8	.206	.284	.286
1993 Asheville	A Hou	118	441	120	30	3	10	186	57	52	37	0	90	3	2	3	16	10	.62	8	.272	.331	.422
1994 Quad City	A Hou	127	449	102	14	1	10	148	54	48	50	2	83	2	8	5	12	5	.71	14	.227	.304	.330
1995 Quad City	A Hou	100	299	81	14	1	1	100	46	47	39	1	37	1	4	8	15	4	.79	3	.271	.349	.334
1996 Stockton	A+ Mil	121	456	146	32	4	17	237	67	103	53	1	66	4	2	7	8	10	.44	11	.320	.390	.520
1997 El Paso	AA Mil	106	369	102	28	7	9	171	59	64	38	1	81	2	2	6	4	3	.57	5	.276	.342	.463
1998 El Paso	AA Mil	82	256	74	19	3	4	111	55	38	33	0	52	0	0	4	1	2	.33	2	.289	.365	.434
New Haven	AA Col	52	182	56	15	1	3	82	27	32	23	0	31	0	0	3	4	3	.57	8	.308	.380	.451
1999 Iowa	AAA ChC	49	146	33	7	1	2	48	8	11	20	2	40	0	0	0	2	1	.67	1	.226	.319	.329
West Tenn	AA ChC	66	189	48	11	0	5	74	29	21	34	0	46	2	0	0	4	0	1.00	6	.254	.373	.392
8 Min. YEARS		856	2913	788	172	25	61	1193	413	432	341	9	544	14	18	37	72	42	.63	66	.271	.346	.410

Greg Resz

Pitches: Right **Bats:** Left **Pos:** P   **Ht:** 6'5" **Wt:** 215 **Born:** 12/25/71 **Age:** 28

Year Team	Lg Org	G	GS	CG	GF	IP	BFP	H	R	ER	HR	SH	SF	HB	TBB	IBB	SO	WP	Bk	W	L	Pct.	ShO	Sv	ERA
1993 Oneonta	A- NYY	24	0	0	18	26.1	117	18	14	11	2	1	1	4	16	1	16	4	0	3	0	1.000	0	9	3.76
1994 Greensboro	A NYY	7	0	0	7	7.2	32	6	3	3	0	0	0	0	2	0	14	1	0	0	0	.000	0	2	3.52
Tampa	A+ NYY	18	0	0	18	18.2	79	21	8	3	0	0	1	1	4	0	20	0	0	0	2	.000	0	6	1.45
1995 Tampa	A+ NYY	12	0	0	13.1		61	10	9	5	0	0	0	1	9	2	16	3	0	1	0	1.000	0	1	3.38
1996 Norwich	AA NYY	19	2	0	9	39	172	38	17	11	1	1	0	1	18	1	37	3	0	1	1	.500	0	2	2.54
Tampa	A+ NYY	20	0	0	9	25	108	20	11	7	0	1	2	0	12	1	31	2	0	0	1	.000	0	4	2.52
1997 Tampa	A+ NYY	1	1	0	0	5.2	23	5	2	2	1	0	0	1	2	0	5	0	0	1	0	1.000	0	0	3.18
Norwich	AA NYY	25	13	0	6	90	410	94	59	47	9	3	6	3	43	0	75	17	0	5	4	.556	0	0	4.70
1998 Columbus	AAA NYY	12	9	0	0	53	235	53	35	29	4	2	3	2	23	0	31	0	0	3	3	.500	0	0	4.92
Norwich	AA NYY	19	3	0	3	47.2	200	46	20	15	4	1	1	2	11	1	47	0	1	4	0	1.000	0	0	2.83
1999 Norwich	AA NYY	20	5	0	4	43.1	190	40	25	21	1	1	1	1	20	2	45	2	0	3	2	.600	0	0	4.36
7 Min. YEARS		177	33	0	77	369.2	1627	351	203	154	22	10	15	16	160	8	337	32	1	20	14	.588	0	24	3.75

Jackie Rexrode

Bats: Left **Throws:** Right **Pos:** 2B   **Ht:** 5'11" **Wt:** 175 **Born:** 9/16/78 **Age:** 21

Year Team	Lg Org	G	AB	H	2B	3B	HR	TB	R	RBI	TBB	IBB	SO	HBP	SH	SF	SB	CS	SB%	GDP	Avg	OBP	SLG
1996 Diamondbcks	R Ari	48	140	46	2	0	1	51	28	17	44	0	27	0	0	4	8	5	.62	1	.329	.479	.364
1997 South Bend	A Ari	92	330	93	10	5	2	119	60	27	55	0	47	2	5	3	15	5	.75	3	.282	.385	.361
Lethbridge	R+ Ari	26	89	30	2	2	1	39	29	14	29	0	17	1	2	1	7	3	.70	0	.337	.500	.438
1998 South Bend	A Ari	50	175	51	7	2	0	62	33	7	45	1	31	1	3	1	22	3	.88	1	.291	.437	.354
High Desert	A+ Ari	53	208	71	5	4	1	87	51	23	46	0	42	0	0	3	19	1	.95	2	.341	.455	.418
1999 Birmingham	AA Ari	70	213	57	7	5	0	74	34	25	28	0	30	0	5	4	14	4	.78	1	.268	.347	.347
El Paso	AA Ari	37	144	46	7	2	2	63	30	11	29	0	16	0	2	1	7	3	.70	0	.319	.431	.438
4 Min. YEARS		376	1299	394	40	20	7	495	265	124	276	1	210	4	17	17	92	24	.79	8	.303	.422	.381

Eddy Reyes

Pitches: Right **Bats:** Right **Pos:** P   **Ht:** 6'4" **Wt:** 200 **Born:** 4/24/76 **Age:** 24

Year Team	Lg Org	G	GS	CG	GF	IP	BFP	H	R	ER	HR	SH	SF	HB	TBB	IBB	SO	WP	Bk	W	L	Pct.	ShO	Sv	ERA
1997 Hudson Val	A- TB	31	0	0	29	32.2	144	24	12	10	1	2	0	4	18	0	29	0	5	0	2	.000	0	14	2.76
1998 Chston-SC	A TB	56	0	0	52	61.2	255	60	23	15	2	2	1	3	12	1	49	6	0	4	6	.400	0	24	2.19
1999 St. Pete	A+ TB	37	0	0	33	38.1	172	31	13	8	0	4	1	6	23	1	30	0	0	0	2	.000	0	25	1.88
Orlando	AA TB	18	0	0	11	28.2	133	31	16	13	3	1	1	6	11	2	25	2	3	1	3	.250	0	2	4.08
3 Min. YEARS		142	0	0	125	161.1	704	146	64	46	6	9	3	19	64	4	133	8	8	5	13	.278	0	65	2.57

Dan Ricabal

Pitches: Right **Bats:** Right **Pos:** P   **Ht:** 6'1" **Wt:** 185 **Born:** 7/8/72 **Age:** 27

Year Team	Lg Org	G	GS	CG	GF	IP	BFP	H	R	ER	HR	SH	SF	HB	TBB	IBB	SO	WP	Bk	W	L	Pct.	ShO	Sv	ERA
1994 Yakima	A- LA	27	0	0	27	29	111	17	4	1	0	1	1	1	10	2	32	1	1	5	1	.833	0	12	0.31
1995 San Berndo	A+ LA	43	0	0	13	72	315	63	35	31	7	0	4	5	33	1	62	2	1	4	1	.800	0	2	3.88
1996 Vero Beach	A+ LA	13	1	0	8	30	119	14	7	4	1	3	0	0	17	4	36	0	1	0	2	.000	0	1	1.20
Savannah	A LA	40	0	0	37	55.1	225	32	19	14	4	4	1	2	17	2	78	2	1	2	4	.333	0	24	2.28
1997 Vero Beach	A+ LA	75	0	0	71	84.2	373	78	44	40	1	4	4	7	39	5	79	5	2	4	5	.444	0	28	4.25
1998 San Antonio	AA LA	54	1	0	38	78	355	78	59	53	7	2	7	6	40	1	61	10	0	2	9	.182	0	15	6.12

		HOW MUCH HE PITCHED						WHAT HE GAVE UP										THE RESULTS					
Year Team	Lg Org	G	GS	CG	GF	IP	BFP	H	R	ER	HR	SH	SF	HB	TBB	IBB	SO	WP	Bk	W	L	Pct.	ShO	Sv	ERA
1999 San Jose	A+ SF	7	0	0	5	7.1	39	13	7	4	0	0	0	0	5	0	1	0	0	1	0	1.000	0	1	4.91
Shreveport	AA SF	8	0	0	6	11	49	15	6	6	1	1	0	0	5	0	4	2	0	2	0	1.000	0	0	4.91
6 Min. YEARS		267	2	0	205	367.1	1586	310	181	153	21	15	15	24	166	15	353	22	7	20	22	.476	0	83	3.75

Bats: Left Throws: Left Pos: 1B

Chris Richard

Ht: 6'2" Wt: 185 Born: 6/7/74 Age: 26

		BATTING														BASERUNNING				PERCENTAGES		
Year Team	Lg Org	G	AB	H	2B	3B	HR	TB	R	RBI	TBB	IBB	SO	HBP	SH	SF	SB	CS	SB%	GDP	Avg	OBP	SLG
1995 New Jersey	A- StL	75	284	80	14	3	3	109	36	43	47	3	31	6	0	2	6	6	.50	3	.282	.392	.384
1996 St. Pete	A+ StL	129	460	130	28	6	14	212	65	82	57	6	50	9	0	5	7	3	.70	11	.283	.369	.461
1997 Arkansas	AA StL	113	390	105	24	3	11	168	62	58	60	1	59	5	0	3	6	4	.60	8	.269	.371	.431
1998 Pr William	A+ StL	8	30	8	2	0	0	10	5	1	1	0	5	0	0	0	1	0	1.00	2	.267	.290	.333
Arkansas	AA StL	28	89	18	5	1	2	31	7	17	9	0	10	1	0	1	0	1	.00	1	.202	.280	.348
1999 Arkansas	AA StL	133	442	130	26	3	29	249	78	94	43	5	75	8	0	6	7	7	.50	14	.294	.363	.563
Memphis	AAA StL	4	17	7	2	0	1	12	3	4	1	0	2	0	0	0	0	0	.00	1	.412	.444	.706
5 Min. YEARS		490	1712	478	101	16	60	791	256	299	218	15	232	29	0	17	27	21	.56	40	.279	.367	.462

Bats: Right Throws: Right Pos: 3B

Brian Richardson

Ht: 6'2" Wt: 215 Born: 8/31/75 Age: 24

		BATTING														BASERUNNING				PERCENTAGES		
Year Team	Lg Org	G	AB	H	2B	3B	HR	TB	R	RBI	TBB	IBB	SO	HBP	SH	SF	SB	CS	SB%	GDP	Avg	OBP	SLG
1992 Dodgers	R LA	37	122	26	6	2	0	36	8	15	11	0	27	0	0	2	3	0	1.00	2	.213	.274	.295
1993 Great Falls	R+ LA	54	178	40	11	0	0	51	16	13	14	1	47	3	1	2	1	2	.33	7	.225	.289	.287
1994 Vero Beach	A+ LA	19	52	12	0	1	0	14	3	3	4	0	15	0	0	2	3	0	1.00	2	.231	.276	.269
Yakima	A- LA	70	266	62	15	0	5	92	35	44	35	1	82	1	0	0	12	4	.75	3	.233	.325	.346
1995 San Berndno	A+ LA	127	462	131	18	1	12	187	68	58	35	2	122	7	6	3	17	16	.52	11	.284	.341	.405
1996 San Antonio	AA LA	19	62	20	1	1	0	23	10	7	2	0	10	2	0	0	0	2	.00	0	.323	.364	.371
Albuquerque	AAA LA	105	355	87	17	2	9	135	52	43	32	6	89	3	4	4	4	1	.80	5	.245	.310	.380
1997 San Antonio	AA LA	133	484	144	23	13	13	232	73	90	42	0	97	8	2	5	3	6	.33	12	.298	.360	.479
1998 Albuquerque	AAA LA	11	41	6	0	0	1	9	5	5	3	0	10	0	0	0	0	0	.00	1	.146	.205	.220
New Haven	AA Col	6	20	2	0	0	0	2	1	2	1	0	4	0	0	0	1	0	1.00	0	.100	.143	.100
1999 Salt Lake	AAA Min	130	451	125	23	4	18	210	77	73	54	0	104	6	2	8	0	0	.00	10	.277	.356	.466
8 Min. YEARS		711	2493	655	114	24	58	991	348	353	233	10	607	30	15	26	44	31	.59	55	.263	.330	.398

Pitches: Right Bats: Right Pos: P

Ray Ricken

Ht: 6'5" Wt: 225 Born: 8/11/73 Age: 26

		HOW MUCH HE PITCHED						WHAT HE GAVE UP										THE RESULTS					
Year Team	Lg Org	G	GS	CG	GF	IP	BFP	H	R	ER	HR	SH	SF	HB	TBB	IBB	SO	WP	Bk	W	L	Pct.	ShO	Sv	ERA
1994 Oneonta	A- NYY	10	10	0	0	50.1	206	45	25	20	1	1	1	2	17	1	55	6	3	2	3	.400	0	0	3.58
Greensboro	A NYY	5	5	0	0	25	109	27	13	13	1	0	1	0	12	0	19	3	0	1	2	.333	0	0	4.68
1995 Greensboro	A NYY	10	10	0	0	64.2	245	42	20	16	2	1	1	0	16	1	77	3	0	3	2	.600	0	0	2.23
Tampa	A+ NYY	11	11	1	0	75.1	291	47	25	18	3	2	1	1	27	0	58	1	2	3	4	.429	0	0	2.15
Norwich	AA NYY	8	8	1	0	53	217	44	21	16	2	2	0	1	24	2	43	3	0	4	2	.667	1	0	2.72
1996 Norwich	AA NYY	8	8	1	0	46.1	201	42	26	23	7	1	3	1	20	0	42	5	0	5	2	.714	1	0	4.47
Columbus	AAA NYY	20	11	1	2	68	301	62	44	36	4	1	3	3	37	2	58	8	0	4	5	.444	0	1	4.76
1997 Norwich	AA NYY	2	2	0	0	10.2	48	12	8	8	0	2	0	0	5	0	13	0	0	0	2	.000	0	0	6.75
Columbus	AAA NYY	26	26	0	0	152.2	701	172	104	94	12	3	3	6	81	2	99	16	1	11	7	.611	0	0	5.54
1998 Columbus	AAA NYY	14	14	0	0	87	374	90	46	44	9	1	1	4	35	2	95	11	0	5	4	.556	0	0	4.55
Las Vegas	AAA SD	4	3	1	1	19.2	88	24	17	16	5	0	2	0	11	0	17	1	0	0	3	.000	0	1	7.32
1999 Mobile	AA SD	3	3	0	0	14.1	71	18	17	16	3	0	1	0	10	0	16	2	0	0	1	.000	0	0	10.05
1999 Mobile	AA SD	20	19	3	0	110.2	496	122	73	66	15	2	2	0	55	0	67	5	0	7	7	.500	1	0	5.37
6 Min. YEARS		141	130	8	3	777.2	3348	747	439	386	64	16	19	18	350	10	659	64	6	45	44	.506	3	2	4.47

Pitches: Right Bats: Right Pos: P

Chad Ricketts

Ht: 6'5" Wt: 225 Born: 2/12/75 Age: 25

		HOW MUCH HE PITCHED						WHAT HE GAVE UP										THE RESULTS					
Year Team	Lg Org	G	GS	CG	GF	IP	BFP	H	R	ER	HR	SH	SF	HB	TBB	IBB	SO	WP	Bk	W	L	Pct.	ShO	Sv	ERA
1995 ChC	R ChC	2	2	0	0	9	32	1	1	0	0	0	0	1	1	0	5	0	0	1	0	1.000	0	0	0.00
Williamsprt	A- ChC	12	12	0	0	68.2	312	89	46	32	4	0	3	8	16	0	37	1	3	4	5	.444	0	0	4.19
1996 Rockford	A ChC	37	9	0	17	87.2	389	89	60	49	8	5	2	7	29	2	70	5	1	3	8	.273	0	4	5.03
1997 Rockford	A ChC	16	0	0	10	29	116	19	9	8	1	1	1	1	11	2	32	1	0	4	0	1.000	0	3	2.48
Daytona	A+ ChC	20	0	0	17	20.1	82	13	4	1	0	0	0	1	6	0	18	1	0	3	1	.750	0	8	0.44
Orlando	AA ChC	2	0	0	0	2	15	7	4	4	0	0	0	0	2	0	3	0	0	0	0	.000	0	0	18.00
1998 Daytona	A+ ChC	47	0	0	41	49	204	41	15	10	0	3	0	3	11	1	59	2	0	2	1	.667	0	19	1.84
West Tenn	AA ChC	13	0	0	11	15.1	65	19	7	6	0	0	1	1	4	2	13	1	0	0	2	.000	0	4	3.52
1999 West Tenn	AA ChC	57	0	0	26	67	275	55	25	23	8	3	1	2	21	4	80	1	0	6	4	.600	0	8	3.09
5 Min. YEARS		206	23	0	122	348	1490	333	171	133	21	12	8	24	101	11	317	12	4	23	21	.523	0	48	3.44

Pitches: Right Bats: Right Pos: P

John Riedling

Ht: 5'11" Wt: 190 Born: 8/29/75 Age: 24

		HOW MUCH HE PITCHED						WHAT HE GAVE UP										THE RESULTS					
Year Team	Lg Org	G	GS	CG	GF	IP	BFP	H	R	ER	HR	SH	SF	HB	TBB	IBB	SO	WP	Bk	W	L	Pct.	ShO	Sv	ERA
1994 Billings	R+ Cin	15	5	0	2	44.1	221	62	36	27	0	2	2	3	28	0	27	7	0	4	1	.800	0	0	5.48
1995 Billings	R+ Cin	13	7	0	2	38.1	192	51	38	30	4	0	3	1	21	2	28	8	0	2	2	.500	0	1	7.04
1996 Chstn-WV	A Cin	26	26	0	0	140	615	135	85	62	2	10	6	10	66	6	90	6	1	6	10	.375	0	0	3.99
1997 Burlington	A Cin	35	16	0	11	102.2	461	101	70	60	8	3	5	7	47	0	104	10	0	7	6	.538	0	0	5.26

Year Team	Lg Org	G	GS	CG	GF	IP	BFP	H	R	ER	HR	SH	SF	HB	TBB	IBB	SO	WP	Bk	W	L	Pct.	ShO	Sv	ERA
						HOW MUCH HE PITCHED						WHAT HE GAVE UP								THE RESULTS					
1998 Chattanooga	AA Cin	24	20	0	1	102.2	475	112	70	57	10	1	5	4	60	5	86	5	0	3	10	.231	0	0	5.00
1999 Chattanooga	AA Cin	40	0	0	23	42	186	41	23	16	2	1	2	1	20	3	38	7	0	9	5	.643	0	5	3.43
Indianapols	AAA Cin	24	0	0	6	35	142	19	9	6	1	2	0	3	18	2	26	2	0	1	0	1.000	0	1	1.54
6 Min. YEARS		177	74	0	45	505	2292	521	331	258	27	19	23	29	260	18	399	45	1	32	34	.485	0	7	4.60

Paul Rigdon

Ht: 6'5" **Wt:** 210 **Born:** 11/2/75 **Age:** 24

Pitches: Right **Bats:** Right **Pos:** P

Year Team	Lg Org	G	GS	CG	GF	IP	BFP	H	R	ER	HR	SH	SF	HB	TBB	IBB	SO	WP	Bk	W	L	Pct.	ShO	Sv	ERA
						HOW MUCH HE PITCHED						WHAT HE GAVE UP								THE RESULTS					
1996 Watertown	A- Cle	22	0	0	21	39.2	174	41	24	18	4	1	0	2	10	0	46	1	1	2	2	.500	0	6	4.08
1998 Kinston	A+ Cle	24	24	0	0	127.1	532	126	65	57	9	2	6	9	35	1	97	3	0	11	7	.611	0	4	4.03
1999 Akron	AA Cle	8	7	0	0	50	177	20	5	5	2	0	1	2	10	0	25	1	0	7	0	1.000	0	0	0.90
Buffalo	AAA Cle	19	19	0	0	103.1	451	114	60	52	11	3	2	1	28	0	60	4	2	7	4	.636	0	0	4.53
3 Min. YEARS		73	50	0	21	320.1	1334	301	154	132	26	6	9	14	83	1	228	9	3	27	13	.675	0	6	3.71

Adam Riggs

Ht: 6'0" **Wt:** 190 **Born:** 10/4/72 **Age:** 27

Bats: Right **Throws:** Right **Pos:** 2B

Year Team	Lg Org	G	AB	H	2B	3B	HR	TB	R	RBI	TBB	IBB	SO	HBP	SH	SF	SB	CS	SB%	GDP	Avg	OBP	SLG
						BATTING												BASERUNNING				PERCENTAGES	
1994 Great Falls	R+ LA	62	234	73	20	3	5	114	55	44	31	1	38	4	2	2	19	8	.70	2	.312	.399	.487
Yakima	A- LA	4	7	2	1	0	0	3	1	0	0	0	1	0	0	0	0	0	.00	0	.286	.286	.429
1995 San Berndno	A+ LA	134	542	196	39	5	24	317	106	106	37	1	93	10	7	4	31	10	.76	9	.362	.431	.585
1996 San Antonio	AA LA	134	506	143	31	6	14	228	68	66	37	1	82	9	5	5	16	6	.73	13	.283	.339	.451
1997 Albuquerque	AAA LA	57	227	69	8	3	13	122	59	28	29	1	39	3	0	0	12	2	.86	2	.304	.390	.537
1998 Albuquerque	AAA LA	44	170	63	13	3	4	94	30	25	21	1	29	3	1	1	12	6	.67	1	.371	.446	.553
1999 Albuquerque	AAA LA	133	513	150	29	7	13	232	87	81	54	0	114	10	2	5	25	17	.60	8	.292	.368	.452
1997 Los Angeles	NL	9	20	4	1	0	0	5	3	1	4	1	3	0	0	0	1	0	1.00	0	.200	.333	.250
6 Min. YEARS		568	2199	696	141	27	73	1110	411	350	231	5	396	39	17	17	115	49	.70	35	.317	.389	.505

Marquis Riley

Ht: 5'10" **Wt:** 170 **Born:** 12/27/70 **Age:** 29

Bats: Both **Throws:** Right **Pos:** OF

Year Team	Lg Org	G	AB	H	2B	3B	HR	TB	R	RBI	TBB	IBB	SO	HBP	SH	SF	SB	CS	SB%	GDP	Avg	OBP	SLG
						BATTING												BASERUNNING				PERCENTAGES	
1992 Boise	A- Ana	52	201	48	12	1	0	62	47	12	37	0	29	2	2	0	7	4	.64	3	.239	.363	.308
1993 Palm Spring	A+ Ana	130	508	134	10	2	1	151	93	42	90	1	117	0	5	2	69	25	.73	3	.264	.373	.297
1994 Midland	AA Ana	93	374	107	12	4	1	130	68	29	35	3	57	6	7	4	32	5	.86	10	.286	.353	.348
Vancouver	AAA Ana	4	14	3	0	0	0	3	3	1	3	0	3	0	0	0	1	0	1.00	1	.214	.353	.214
1995 Vancouver	AAA Ana	120	477	125	6	6	0	143	70	43	49	3	69	1	2	4	29	10	.74	11	.262	.330	.300
1996 Vancouver	AAA Ana	12	47	11	2	0	0	13	8	0	3	0	12	0	0	0	3	0	1.00	2	.234	.280	.277
Charlotte	AAA Fla	92	300	68	10	0	0	78	43	13	26	1	31	1	4	2	16	5	.76	8	.227	.289	.260
1997 Vancouver	AAA Ana	65	242	64	6	0	0	70	33	8	36	0	27	1	6	2	27	7	.79	4	.264	.359	.289
1999 Jacksnville	AA Det	54	161	41	4	0	0	45	30	16	30	0	29	0	1	1	16	3	.84	1	.255	.370	.280
7 Min. YEARS		622	2324	601	62	13	2	695	395	164	309	8	374	11	26	15	200	59	.77	43	.259	.346	.299

Michael Riley

Ht: 6'2" **Wt:** 165 **Born:** 1/2/75 **Age:** 25

Pitches: Left **Bats:** Left **Pos:** P

Year Team	Lg Org	G	GS	CG	GF	IP	BFP	H	R	ER	HR	SH	SF	HB	TBB	IBB	SO	WP	Bk	W	L	Pct.	ShO	Sv	ERA
						HOW MUCH HE PITCHED						WHAT HE GAVE UP								THE RESULTS					
1996 Bellingham	A- SF	17	3	0	2	36.2	181	38	26	17	3	1	1	2	29	0	38	5	2	1	3	.250	0	0	4.17
1997 Bakersfield	A+ SF	6	4	0	0	20.1	94	25	20	19	4	0	1	0	8	0	17	0	0	1	2	.333	0	0	8.41
Salem-Keizr	A- SF	15	15	1	0	88.1	375	76	39	34	9	2	2	4	28	0	96	6	1	9	2	.818	0	0	3.46
1998 Bakersfield	A+ SF	40	15	2	7	128	555	130	73	64	8	3	3	3	58	1	110	9	1	6	12	.333	0	2	4.50
1999 Shreveport	AA SF	30	13	1	4	111	456	80	35	26	6	2	2	1	53	0	107	2	1	8	3	.727	1	1	2.11
4 Min. YEARS		108	50	4	13	384.1	1661	349	193	160	30	8	9	10	176	1	368	22	5	25	22	.532	1	3	3.75

Danny Rios

Ht: 6'2" **Wt:** 195 **Born:** 11/11/72 **Age:** 27

Pitches: Right **Bats:** Right **Pos:** P

Year Team	Lg Org	G	GS	CG	GF	IP	BFP	H	R	ER	HR	SH	SF	HB	TBB	IBB	SO	WP	Bk	W	L	Pct.	ShO	Sv	ERA
						HOW MUCH HE PITCHED						WHAT HE GAVE UP								THE RESULTS					
1993 Yankees	R NYY	24	0	0	17	38.1	170	34	18	15	0	2	1	5	16	0	29	9	3	2	1	.667	0	6	3.52
1994 Greensboro	A NYY	37	0	0	34	41.1	164	32	4	4	1	2	0	3	13	1	36	3	0	3	2	.600	0	17	0.87
Tampa	A+ NYY	9	0	0	8	10.1	41	6	2	0	0	0	1	1	4	0	11	0	0	0	0	.000	0	2	0.00
1995 Tampa	A+ NYY	57	0	0	52	67.1	296	67	24	15	1	5	2	8	20	4	72	2	0	4	4	.000	0	24	2.00
1996 Norwich	AA NYY	38	0	0	29	43	183	34	14	10	2	0		3	21	1	38	3	2	3	1	.750	0	17	2.09
Columbus	AAA NYY	24	0	0	6	27.2	111	22	7	6	1	0	2	4	6	0	22	1	0	4	1	.800	0	3	1.95
1997 Columbus	AAA NYY	58	0	0	14	84.2	351	73	37	29	8	3	4	1	31	1	53	5	0	7	4	.636	0	3	3.08
1998 Omaha	AAA KC	25	18	2	4	123	563	159	90	77	14	2	4	6	41	0	51	6	0	6	7	.462	0	1	5.63
1999 Omaha	AAA KC	47	5	0	20	89	417	111	64	60	13	3	4	8	39	4	44	6	1	10	4	.714	0	4	6.07
1997 New York	AL	2	0	0	0	2.1	19	9	5	5	3	0	0	1	2	0	1	0	0	0	0	.000	0	0	19.29
1998 Kansas City	AL	5	0	0	1	7.1	38	9	5	5	1	0	1	0	6	0	6	1	0	0	1	.000	0	0	6.14
7 Min. YEARS		319	23	2	184	524.2	2296	538	260	216	38	19	18	39	191	11	356	35	6	35	24	.593	0	74	3.71
2 Maj. YEARS		7	0	0	1	9.2	57	18	10	10	4	0	1	2	8	0	7	1	0	0	1	.000	0	0	9.31

Eduardo Rios

Bats: Right **Throws:** Right **Pos:** 2B 　　　　**Ht:** 5'10" **Wt:** 178 **Born:** 10/13/72 **Age:** 27

						BATTING										BASERUNNING				PERCENTAGES		
Year Team	Lg Org	G	AB	H	2B	3B	HR	TB	R	RBI	TBB	IBB	SO	HBP	SH	SF	SB	CS	SB%	GDP	Avg	OBP	SLG
1993 Great Falls	R+ LA	26	107	29	4	3	2	45	18	12	10	1	11	1	0	1	2	4	.33	1	.271	.336	.421
Bakersfield	A+ LA	29	113	32	4	0	7	57	19	17	8	0	17	2	2	0	2	3	.40	1	.283	.341	.504
1994 Vero Beach	A+ LA	133	529	139	28	8	13	222	70	79	24	1	85	8	2	6	2	5	.29	15	.263	.302	.420
1995 San Antonio	AA LA	98	365	104	22	4	5	149	43	53	20	2	47	1	1	5	2	4	.33	8	.285	.320	.408
1996 Albuquerque	AAA LA	15	29	2	0	0	0	2	3	1	3	1	6	1	0	1	1	0	1.00	1	.069	.176	.069
San Antonio	AA LA	75	242	67	11	2	5	97	29	37	20	0	32	0	0	1	2	2	.50	7	.277	.331	.401
1997 Saskatoon	IND —	66	283	81	21	2	7	127	58	30	21	1	37	3	1	1	2	1	.67	6	.286	.341	.449
1998 Thunder Bay	IND —	66	248	68	16	1	8	110	34	49	10	0	38	2	0	5	2	1	.67	12	.274	.302	.444
1999 Quebec	IND —	2	9	3	1	0	0	4	1	2	0	0	1	0	0	0	0	0	.00	1	.333	.333	.444
Tucson	AAA Ari	3	8	3	1	0	1	7	1	2	0	0	3	0	0	1	0	0	.00	0	.375	.333	.875
El Paso	AA Ari	16	60	17	3	0	0	20	8	10	4	0	8	0	0	0	0	0	.00	1	.283	.328	.333
7 Min. YEARS		529	1993	545	111	20	48	840	284	292	120	6	285	18	6	21	15	20	.43	53	.273	.317	.421

Luis Rivas

Bats: Right **Throws:** Right **Pos:** SS 　　　　**Ht:** 5'10" **Wt:** 175 **Born:** 8/30/79 **Age:** 20

						BATTING										BASERUNNING				PERCENTAGES		
Year Team	Lg Org	G	AB	H	2B	3B	HR	TB	R	RBI	TBB	IBB	SO	HBP	SH	SF	SB	CS	SB%	GDP	Avg	OBP	SLG
1996 Twins	R Min	53	201	52	12	1	1	69	29	13	18	0	37	0	1	0	35	10	.78	2	.259	.320	.343
1997 Fort Wayne	A Min	121	419	100	20	6	1	135	61	30	33	1	90	5	6	2	28	18	.61	5	.239	.301	.322
1998 Fort Myers	A+ Min	126	463	130	21	5	4	173	58	51	14	0	75	3	4	6	34	8	.81	11	.281	.302	.374
1999 New Britain	AA Min	132	527	134	30	7	7	199	78	49	41	1	92	2	8	2	31	14	.69	16	.254	.309	.378
4 Min. YEARS		432	1610	416	83	19	13	576	226	143	106	2	294	10	19	10	128	50	.72	34	.258	.306	.358

Mike Rivera

Bats: Right **Throws:** Right **Pos:** C 　　　　**Ht:** 6'0" **Wt:** 190 **Born:** 9/8/76 **Age:** 23

						BATTING										BASERUNNING				PERCENTAGES		
Year Team	Lg Org	G	AB	H	2B	3B	HR	TB	R	RBI	TBB	IBB	SO	HBP	SH	SF	SB	CS	SB%	GDP	Avg	OBP	SLG
1997 Tigers	R Det	47	154	44	9	2	10	87	34	36	18	2	25	3	0	2	0	0	.00	2	.286	.367	.565
1998 W Michigan	A Det	108	403	111	34	3	9	178	40	67	15	0	68	2	1	5	0	2	.00	8	.275	.301	.442
1999 Jacksnville	AA Det	7	23	4	1	0	2	11	3	6	2	0	5	0	0	0	0	0	.00	0	.174	.240	.478
Lakeland	A+ Det	104	370	103	20	2	14	169	44	72	20	0	59	3	0	8	1	1	.50	10	.278	.314	.457
3 Min. YEARS		266	950	262	64	7	35	445	121	181	55	2	157	8	1	15	1	3	.25	20	.276	.316	.468

Roberto Rivera

Bats: Both **Throws:** Right **Pos:** OF 　　　　**Ht:** 6'2" **Wt:** 160 **Born:** 11/25/76 **Age:** 23

						BATTING										BASERUNNING				PERCENTAGES		
Year Team	Lg Org	G	AB	H	2B	3B	HR	TB	R	RBI	TBB	IBB	SO	HBP	SH	SF	SB	CS	SB%	GDP	Avg	OBP	SLG
1995 Orioles	R Bal	42	150	44	7	3	3	66	21	26	10	0	38	2	0	2	6	3	.67	5	.293	.341	.440
1996 Orioles	R Bal	4	8	5	1	1	0	8	7	2	3	0	1	0	0	1	3	0	1.00	0	.625	.667	1.000
Bluefield	R+ Bal	46	158	34	8	0	5	57	20	26	10	0	54	0	0	0	14	4	.78	3	.215	.262	.361
1997 Delmarva	A Bal	17	59	9	0	1	2	17	6	5	1	0	20	0	0	0	1	2	.33	0	.153	.167	.288
Frederick	A+ Bal	16	53	12	1	0	1	16	8	3	0	0	16	1	0	0	1	1	.50	1	.226	.281	.302
Bluefield	R+ Bal	50	192	61	20	2	3	94	28	27	13	1	43	1	2	1	6	6	.50	3	.318	.362	.490
1998 Frederick	A+ Bal	3	6	2	0	0	1	5	1	1	1	1	1	0	0	0	0	0	.00	0	.333	.429	.833
Delmarva	A Bal	110	390	93	21	5	7	145	55	50	25	1	99	4	3	5	17	4	.81	5	.238	.288	.372
1999 Frederick	A+ Bal	118	460	126	21	4	12	191	70	53	39	3	89	3	0	3	18	9	.67	4	.274	.333	.415
Bowie	AA Bal	9	36	8	0	0	0	8	0	1	1	0	9	0	0	0	2	0	1.00	1	.222	.243	.222
5 Min. YEARS		415	1512	394	79	16	34	607	216	199	106	3	370	11	5	12	68	29	.70	21	.261	.311	.401

Jon Rivers

Bats: Right **Throws:** Right **Pos:** OF 　　　　**Ht:** 6'3" **Wt:** 205 **Born:** 8/17/74 **Age:** 25

						BATTING										BASERUNNING				PERCENTAGES		
Year Team	Lg Org	G	AB	H	2B	3B	HR	TB	R	RBI	TBB	IBB	SO	HBP	SH	SF	SB	CS	SB%	GDP	Avg	OBP	SLG
1992 Blue Jays	R Tor	32	72	16	2	0	2	24	12	9	4	0	20	2	0	0	5	1	.83	2	.222	.282	.333
1993 Blue Jays	R Tor	51	178	34	5	2	0	43	13	19	16	0	31	1	1	0	7	2	.78	5	.191	.262	.242
1994 Medcine Hat	R+ Tor	55	190	46	3	1	3	60	26	23	24	0	42	4	1	0	7	5	.58	0	.242	.339	.316
1995 Hagerstown	A Tor	123	429	126	16	6	6	172	54	48	40	0	104	6	1	4	18	5	.78	9	.294	.359	.401
1996 Dunedin	A+ Tor	97	333	83	14	3	6	121	46	43	38	3	67	1	1	1	8	9	.47	10	.249	.327	.363
1997 Dunedin	A+ Tor	132	457	123	21	3	13	189	62	75	53	0	107	5	0	7	24	8	.75	8	.269	.347	.414
1998 Dunedin	A+ Tor	5	20	4	2	0	0	6	0	4	1	0	5	0	0	0	2	1	.67	1	.200	.238	.300
Knoxville	AA Tor	91	302	81	19	4	9	135	51	49	47	1	62	8	3	1	20	13	.61	8	.268	.380	.447
1999 West Tenn	AA ChC	35	88	16	3	0	1	22	10	6	8	0	20	1	0	0	5	0	1.00	2	.182	.258	.250
8 Min. YEARS		621	2069	529	85	19	40	772	274	276	231	4	458	28	7	13	96	44	.69	45	.256	.337	.373

Scott Rivette

Pitches: Right **Bats:** Both **Pos:** P 　　　　**Ht:** 6'2" **Wt:** 200 **Born:** 2/8/74 **Age:** 26

		HOW MUCH HE PITCHED					WHAT HE GAVE UP											THE RESULTS					
Year Team	Lg Org	G	GS	CG	GF	IP	BFP	H	R	ER	HR	SH	SF	HB	TBB	IBB	SO	WP	Bk	W	L	Pct.	ShO	Sv	ERA
1995 Sou Oregon	A- Oak	9	1	0	3	19	83	16	5	2	0	1	1	1	11	2	22	1	0	2	0	1.000	0	2	0.95
W Michigan	A Oak	8	0	0	4	15.1	65	12	5	5	0	0	2	0	7	0	15	1	0	1	0	1.000	0	2	2.93
1996 W Michigan	A Oak	32	29	0	1	153.1	667	145	80	60	7	2	3	12	51	0	142	9	2	8	9	.471	0	0	3.52
1997 Modesto	A+ Oak	20	20	3	0	126	533	147	65	50	12	3	2	7	31	1	96	8	1	9	9	.500	0	0	3.57
Huntsville	AA Oak	7	6	0	0	39	180	52	29	29	3	2	3	0	19	0	33	3	1	3	1	.750	0	0	6.69
1998 Huntsville	AA Oak	35	0	0	9	68.1	309	75	46	35	7	4	5	1	32	0	53	5	0	6	4	.600	0	2	4.61

236

Year Team	Lg Org	G	GS	CG	GF	IP	BFP	H	R	ER	HR	SH	SF	HB	TBB	IBB	SO	WP	Bk	W	L	Pct.	ShO	Sv	ERA
Knoxville	AA Tor	7	0	0	2	9.1	44	7	4	4	0	1	2	0	7	1	4	1	0	0	1	.000	0	0	3.86
1999 Knoxville	AA Tor	56	0	0	33	78	341	85	40	33	2	1	3	5	29	4	74	7	2	4	7	.364	0	10	3.81
5 Min. YEARS		174	56	3	52	508.1	2222	539	274	218	31	10	20	30	187	8	439	35	6	33	31	.516	0	17	3.86

Petie Roach

Pitches: Left **Bats:** Left **Pos:** P **Ht:** 6'2" **Wt:** 175 **Born:** 9/19/70 **Age:** 29

		HOW MUCH HE PITCHED						WHAT HE GAVE UP												THE RESULTS					
Year Team	Lg Org	G	GS	CG	GF	IP	BFP	H	R	ER	HR	SH	SF	HB	TBB	IBB	SO	WP	Bk	W	L	Pct.	ShO	Sv	ERA
1994 Yakima	A- LA	8	4	0	2	40	147	24	5	3	0	0	0	1	6	0	32	0	1	3	1	.750	0	0	0.68
Vero Beach	A+ LA	7	6	0	0	36.2	157	41	20	18	0	0	1	1	12	0	19	1	1	2	3	.400	0	0	4.42
1995 San Berndno	A+ LA	30	0	0	14	33	143	28	16	11	2	2	2	1	14	1	38	5	0	1	2	.333	0	8	3.00
1996 Vero Beach	A+ LA	17	10	0	2	69	273	56	30	28	6	1	1	1	17	1	52	3	2	3	4	.429	0	0	3.65
San Antonio	AA LA	13	13	1	0	75.1	336	81	41	32	5	3	3	5	34	0	40	5	4	6	3	.667	0	0	3.82
1997 San Antonio	AA LA	13	13	1	0	82	351	76	39	34	14	3	2	1	35	0	56	7	0	7	4	.636	0	0	3.73
Albuquerque	AAA LA	31	0	0	6	49.1	232	56	31	29	6	3	4	6	27	3	33	8	0	0	5	.000	0	1	5.29
1998 Albuquerque	AAA LA	19	0	0	5	15.1	73	20	17	14	3	3	0	0	10	0	12	2	0	0	0	.000	0	0	8.22
1999 Chico	IND —	18	12	0	1	65.1	298	82	51	44	5	3	4	6	28	1	50	8	1	4	2	.667	0	0	6.06
Toledo	AAA Det	4	0	0	0	8	29	6	4	4	2	0	1	0	2	0	5	0	0	1	1	.500	0	0	4.50
6 Min. YEARS		160	58	2	30	474	2039	470	254	217	43	18	18	23	185	6	337	39	9	27	25	.519	0	9	4.12

Jake Robbins

Pitches: Right **Bats:** Right **Pos:** P **Ht:** 6'5" **Wt:** 190 **Born:** 5/23/76 **Age:** 24

		HOW MUCH HE PITCHED						WHAT HE GAVE UP												THE RESULTS					
Year Team	Lg Org	G	GS	CG	GF	IP	BFP	H	R	ER	HR	SH	SF	HB	TBB	IBB	SO	WP	Bk	W	L	Pct.	ShO	Sv	ERA
1994 Yankees	R NYY	8	3	0	0	23	102	21	16	13	2	1	3	1	15	0	14	2	1	0	2	.000	0	0	5.09
1995 Yankees	R NYY	14	3	0	3	37.1	159	32	26	23	2	2	1	1	18	1	17	4	0	2	3	.400	0	0	5.54
Oneonta	A- NYY	1	0	0	1	1	3	0	0	0	0	0	0	0	0	0	1	0	0	0	0	.000	0	0	0.00
1996 Greensboro	A NYY	18	12	0	2	74	349	80	59	53	5	4	5	7	49	0	50	10	4	1	8	.111	0	0	6.45
Oneonta	A- NYY	11	11	0	0	66	298	64	42	33	3	5	1	2	35	1	47	6	1	3	4	.429	0	0	4.50
1997 Greensboro	A NYY	20	19	0	0	101.1	462	114	81	65	6	2	3	2	55	1	72	7	0	6	4	.600	0	0	5.77
Tampa	A+ NYY	3	3	0	0	16	73	18	14	9	2	2	0	0	10	1	5	2	0	1	1	.500	0	0	5.06
1998 Tampa	A+ NYY	26	25	2	0	152.1	674	167	83	65	5	5	6	1	72	2	87	4	1	11	6	.647	2	0	3.84
1999 Norwich	AA NYY	20	19	2	0	111	508	118	80	67	7	4	8	3	60	3	63	2	2	3	12	.200	1	0	5.43
Tampa	A+ NYY	7	7	0	0	41.2	187	44	30	22	3	1	2	2	19	2	31	5	0	3	3	.500	0	0	4.75
6 Min. YEARS		128	102	4	6	623.2	2815	658	431	350	35	24	31	19	333	11	387	42	9	30	43	.411	3	0	5.05

J.P. Roberge

Bats: Right **Throws:** Right **Pos:** 2B **Ht:** 6'0" **Wt:** 177 **Born:** 9/12/72 **Age:** 27

		BATTING															BASERUNNING				PERCENTAGES		
Year Team	Lg Org	G	AB	H	2B	3B	HR	TB	R	RBI	TBB	IBB	SO	HBP	SH	SF	SB	CS	SB%	GDP	Avg	OBP	SLG
1994 Great Falls	R+ LA	63	256	82	17	1	1	104	55	42	20	0	22	5	2	5	24	4	.86	7	.320	.374	.406
Yakima	A- LA	4	8	3	1	0	0	4	1	0	0	0	3	1	0	0	0	1	.00	0	.375	.444	.500
1995 Vero Beach	A+ LA	3	9	0	0	0	0	0	1	0	0	0	2	0	0	0	0	0	.00	0	.000	.000	.000
San Berndno	A+ LA	116	450	129	22	1	17	204	92	59	34	0	62	8	2	3	31	8	.79	9	.287	.345	.453
1996 San Antonio	A+ LA	12	44	16	3	1	1	24	8	6	3	0	9	2	0	1	1	2	.33	0	.364	.420	.545
San Antonio	AA LA	62	232	68	14	2	6	104	28	27	14	1	39	2	2	2	9	3	.75	5	.293	.336	.448
Albuquerque	AAA LA	53	156	50	6	1	4	70	17	17	14	1	28	1	3	0	3	0	1.00	1	.321	.380	.449
1997 San Antonio	AA LA	134	516	166	26	4	17	251	94	105	39	3	70	7	2	5	18	9	.67	13	.322	.374	.486
1998 Albuquerque	AAA LA	136	475	144	30	1	10	206	83	67	31	1	64	5	2	5	22	6	.79	17	.303	.349	.434
1999 Omaha	AAA KC	116	437	137	31	3	13	213	77	66	26	0	59	5	5	0	16	5	.76	15	.314	.359	.487
6 Min. YEARS		699	2583	795	150	14	69	1180	456	389	181	6	358	36	18	21	124	38	.77	67	.308	.359	.457

Chris Roberts

Pitches: Left **Bats:** Right **Pos:** P **Ht:** 5'10" **Wt:** 185 **Born:** 6/25/71 **Age:** 29

		HOW MUCH HE PITCHED						WHAT HE GAVE UP												THE RESULTS					
Year Team	Lg Org	G	GS	CG	GF	IP	BFP	H	R	ER	HR	SH	SF	HB	TBB	IBB	SO	WP	Bk	W	L	Pct.	ShO	Sv	ERA
1993 St. Lucie	A+ NYM	25	25	3	0	173.1	703	162	64	53	3	2	4	7	36	0	111	2	1	13	5	.722	2	0	2.75
1994 Binghamton	AA NYM	27	27	4	0	175.1	751	164	77	64	11	8	6	5	77	1	128	12	1	13	8	.619	2	0	3.29
1995 Norfolk	AAA NYM	25	25	2	0	150	676	197	99	92	24	6	4	8	58	0	88	5	0	7	13	.350	0	0	5.52
1996 Norfolk	R NYM	3	3	0	0	13	48	11	2	2	0	0	0	1	0	0	12	1	0	0	0	.000	0	0	1.38
St. Lucie	A+ NYM	1	1	0	0	6	21	1	0	0	0	0	0	0	3	0	2	0	0	1	0	1.000	0	0	0.00
Binghamton	AA NYM	9	9	1	0	46	225	55	40	37	6	6	2	1	37	0	30	1	0	2	7	.222	0	0	7.24
1997 Binghamton	AA NYM	19	19	1	0	105.1	448	103	69	58	18	6	2	8	33	0	66	1	1	5	8	.385	0	0	4.96
Norfolk	AAA NYM	7	6	0	1	37.1	164	38	17	12	2	2	1	2	17	0	21	0	1	0	4	.000	0	0	2.89
1998 Edmonton	AAA Oak	18	8	0	2	50.2	234	55	39	33	5	3	3	5	28	0	44	5	1	0	5	.000	0	0	5.86
Newburgh	IND —	9	9	2	0	53.1	230	58	28	27	4	0	1	3	19	1	37	1	0	5	2	.714	1	0	4.56
1999 Carolina	AA Col	43	1	0	17	81	360	76	46	34	10	5	2	6	36	0	52	3	0	5	4	.556	0	1	3.78
7 Min. YEARS		186	133	11	20	891.1	3860	920	481	412	83	38	24	47	344	2	591	31	5	51	55	.481	5	1	4.16

Grant Roberts

Pitches: Right **Bats:** Right **Pos:** P **Ht:** 6'3" **Wt:** 205 **Born:** 9/13/77 **Age:** 22

		HOW MUCH HE PITCHED						WHAT HE GAVE UP												THE RESULTS					
Year Team	Lg Org	G	GS	CG	GF	IP	BFP	H	R	ER	HR	SH	SF	HB	TBB	IBB	SO	WP	Bk	W	L	Pct.	ShO	Sv	ERA
1995 Mets	R NYM	11	3	0	4	29.1	121	19	13	7	1	1	3		14	1	24	4	1	2	1	.667	0	0	2.15
1996 Kingsport	R+ NYM	13	13	2	0	68.2	285	43	18	16	3	1	0	7	37	1	92	4	0	9	1	.900	2	0	2.10
1997 Capital Cty	A NYM	22	22	2	0	129.2	530	98	37	34	1	3	3	8	44	0	122	5	0	11	3	.786	1	0	2.36

Year Team	Lg Org	G	GS	CG	GF	IP	BFP	H	R	ER	HR	SH	SF	HB	TBB	IBB	SO	WP	Bk	W	L	Pct.	ShO	Sv	ERA
						HOW MUCH HE PITCHED				WHAT HE GAVE UP												THE RESULTS			
1998 St. Lucie	A+ NYM	17	17	0	0	72.1	323	72	37	34	11	1	1	5	37	0	70	2	0	4	5	.444	0	0	4.23
1999 Binghamton	AA NYM	23	23	0	0	131.1	576	135	81	71	9	6	3	12	49	0	94	8	0	7	6	.538	0	0	4.87
Norfolk	AAA NYM	5	5	0	0	28	122	32	15	14	1	0	1	0	11	2	30	3	0	2	1	.667	0	0	4.50
5 Min. YEARS		91	83	4	4	459.1	1957	399	201	176	26	12	9	35	192	4	432	26	1	35	17	.673	3	0	3.45

Lonell Roberts

Bats: Both **Throws:** Right **Pos:** OF **Ht:** 6'0" **Wt:** 172 **Born:** 6/7/71 **Age:** 29

Year Team	Lg Org	G	AB	H	2B	3B	HR	TB	R	RBI	TBB	IBB	SO	HBP	SH	SF	SB	CS	SB%	GDP	Avg	OBP	SLG
				BATTING													BASERUNNING				PERCENTAGES		
1989 Medcine Hat	R+ Tor	29	78	11	1	0	0	12	2	6	7	0	27	1	1	0	3	3	.50	1	.141	.221	.154
1990 Medcine Hat	R+ Tor	38	118	25	2	0	0	27	14	8	5	0	29	0	0	0	8	1	.89	3	.212	.244	.229
1991 Myrtle Bch	A Tor	110	388	86	7	2	2	103	39	27	27	1	84	2	10	2	35	14	.71	0	.222	.274	.265
1992 St.Cathrnes	A- Tor	62	244	50	3	1	0	55	37	11	19	1	75	3	4	0	33	13	.72	0	.205	.271	.225
Knoxville	AA Tor	5	14	0	0	0	0	0	1	0	1	0	4	0	0	0	1	0	1.00	0	.000	.067	.000
1993 Hagerstown	A Tor	131	501	120	21	4	3	158	78	46	53	1	103	4	2	3	54	15	.78	8	.240	.316	.315
1994 Dunedin	A+ Tor	118	490	132	18	3	3	165	74	31	32	3	104	3	2	4	61	12	.84	4	.269	.316	.337
1995 Knoxville	AA Tor	116	454	107	12	3	1	128	66	29	27	1	97	3	4	4	57	18	.76	1	.236	.281	.282
1996 Knoxville	AA Tor	58	237	69	1	0	1	73	35	12	32	1	39	0	3	0	24	14	.63	1	.291	.375	.308
1997 Knoxville	AA Tor	7	21	4	0	1	0	6	5	0	2	0	3	2	2	0	0	2	.00	1	.190	.320	.286
Syracuse	AAA Tor	77	173	27	4	0	3	40	17	10	19	0	50	0	2	0	6	7	.46	1	.156	.240	.231
1998 Greenville	AA Atl	47	182	53	9	5	2	78	26	17	11	0	42	0	0	2	4	4	.50	2	.291	.328	.429
1999 Richmond	AAA Atl	119	442	116	19	5	3	154	66	41	33	1	95	0	0	8	17	9	.65	5	.262	.308	.348
11 Min. YEARS		917	3342	800	97	24	18	999	460	238	268	9	752	18	30	23	303	112	.73	32	.239	.297	.299

Mark Roberts

Pitches: Right **Bats:** Right **Pos:** P **Ht:** 6'2" **Wt:** 205 **Born:** 9/29/75 **Age:** 24

Year Team	Lg Org	G	GS	CG	GF	IP	BFP	H	R	ER	HR	SH	SF	HB	TBB	IBB	SO	WP	Bk	W	L	Pct.	ShO	Sv	ERA
						HOW MUCH HE PITCHED				WHAT HE GAVE UP												THE RESULTS			
1996 Hickory	A CWS	13	13	0	0	72	298	70	42	39	12	3	2	3	19	0	62	4	3	4	6	.400	0	0	4.88
1997 Hickory	A CWS	4	4	0	0	22	96	23	12	9	3	1	1	0	9	0	14	1	0	0	2	.000	0	0	3.68
Winston-Sal	A+ CWS	14	14	3	0	91.1	379	78	48	41	10	1	3	3	45	0	64	4	0	5	9	.357	0	0	4.04
1998 Winston-Sal	A+ CWS	27	25	2	0	165.1	706	165	88	72	15	6	8	10	50	1	142	6	0	9	9	.500	1	0	3.92
1999 Birmingham	AA CWS	33	17	0	7	124.1	525	108	64	47	11	3	7	3	41	0	84	3	0	5	8	.385	0	2	3.40
4 Min. YEARS		91	73	5	7	475	2004	444	254	208	51	14	21	19	164	1	366	18	3	23	34	.404	1	2	3.94

Jeromie Robertson

Pitches: Left **Bats:** Left **Pos:** P **Ht:** 6'1" **Wt:** 190 **Born:** 3/30/77 **Age:** 23

Year Team	Lg Org	G	GS	CG	GF	IP	BFP	H	R	ER	HR	SH	SF	HB	TBB	IBB	SO	WP	Bk	W	L	Pct.	ShO	Sv	ERA
						HOW MUCH HE PITCHED				WHAT HE GAVE UP												THE RESULTS			
1996 Astros	R Hou	13	13	1	0	78.1	304	51	20	15	2	3	0	4	15	0	98	6	2	5	3	.625	1	0	1.72
Kissimmee	A+ Hou	1	1	0	0	7	27	4	4	2	0	0	0	0	1	0	2	0	0	0	0	.000	0	0	2.57
1997 Quad City	A Hou	26	25	2	1	146	647	151	86	66	12	1	4	8	56	1	135	5	3	11	8	.579	1	1	4.07
1998 Kissimmee	A+ Hou	28	28	2	0	175	740	185	83	72	13	3	5	7	53	3	131	5	6	10	10	.500	0	0	3.70
1999 Jackson	AA Hou	28	28	1	0	191	791	184	81	65	22	6	4	8	45	2	133	5	7	15	7	.682	0	0	3.06
4 Min. YEARS		96	95	6	1	597.1	2509	575	274	220	49	13	13	27	170	6	499	21	18	41	28	.594	2	1	3.31

Mike Robertson

Bats: Left **Throws:** Left **Pos:** 1B **Ht:** 6'0" **Wt:** 189 **Born:** 10/9/70 **Age:** 29

Year Team	Lg Org	G	AB	H	2B	3B	HR	TB	R	RBI	TBB	IBB	SO	HBP	SH	SF	SB	CS	SB%	GDP	Avg	OBP	SLG
				BATTING													BASERUNNING				PERCENTAGES		
1991 Utica	A- CWS	13	54	9	2	1	0	13	6	8	5	0	10	0	0	0	2	1	.67	0	.167	.237	.241
South Bend	A CWS	54	210	69	16	2	1	92	30	26	18	3	24	3	3	3	6	5	.54	5	.329	.385	.438
1992 Sarasota	A+ CWS	106	395	99	21	3	10	156	50	59	50	3	55	7	1	3	5	7	.42	8	.251	.343	.395
Birmingham	AA CWS	27	90	17	8	1	1	30	6	9	10	1	19	0	1	1	0	1	.00	2	.189	.267	.333
1993 Birmingham	AA CWS	138	511	138	31	3	11	208	73	73	59	4	97	3	0	8	10	5	.67	10	.270	.344	.407
1994 Birmingham	AA CWS	53	196	62	20	2	3	95	32	30	31	4	34	2	0	2	6	3	.67	5	.316	.411	.485
Nashville	AAA CWS	67	213	48	8	1	8	82	21	21	15	4	27	3	0	0	0	5	.00	4	.225	.286	.385
1995 Nashville	AAA CWS	139	499	124	17	4	19	206	55	52	50	7	72	11	3	2	2	4	.33	8	.248	.329	.413
1996 Nashville	AAA CWS	138	450	116	16	4	21	203	64	74	38	4	83	5	9	2	1	2	.33	10	.258	.321	.451
1997 Scranton-WB	AAA Phi	121	416	124	17	3	12	183	61	72	58	4	67	4	1	6	0	2	.00	5	.298	.384	.440
1998 Tucson	AAA Ari	111	411	112	14	3	13	171	49	70	33	1	56	7	0	1	1	0	1.00	15	.273	.335	.416
1999 Altoona	AA Pit	46	175	49	12	0	9	88	31	28	24	2	26	1	3	0	1	0	.00	5	.280	.370	.503
Nashville	AAA Pit	74	220	68	16	1	9	113	34	31	10	1	32	3	1	2	2	1	.67	5	.309	.343	.514
1996 Chicago	AL	6	7	1	1	0	0	2	0	0	0	0	1	0	0	0	0	0	.00	0	.143	.143	.286
1997 Philadelphia	NL	22	38	8	2	1	0	12	3	4	0	0	6	3	0	0	1	0	1.00	0	.211	.268	.316
1998 Arizona	NL	11	13	2	0	0	0	2	0	0	0	0	2	0	0	0	0	0	.00	0	.154	.154	.154
0 Min. YEARS		1087	3840	1035	198	28	117	1640	512	553	401	38	602	49	22	33	36	38	.49	82	.270	.344	.427
3 Maj. YEARS		39	58	11	3	1	0	16	3	4	0	0	9	3	0	0	1	0	1.00	0	.190	.230	.276

Rich Robertson

Pitches: Left **Bats:** Left **Pos:** P **Ht:** 6'4" **Wt:** 182 **Born:** 9/15/68 **Age:** 31

Year Team	Lg Org	G	GS	CG	GF	IP	BFP	H	R	ER	HR	SH	SF	HB	TBB	IBB	SO	WP	Bk	W	L	Pct.	ShO	Sv	ERA
						HOW MUCH HE PITCHED				WHAT HE GAVE UP												THE RESULTS			
1990 Welland	A- Pit	16	13	0	0	64.1	293	51	34	22	4	1	2	1	55	2	80	6	2	3	4	.429	0	0	3.08
1991 Salem	A+ Pit	12	11	0	0	45.2	210	34	32	25	2	1	0	3	42	0	32	4	0	2	4	.333	0	0	4.93
Augusta	A Pit	13	12	1	1	74	348	73	52	41	4	2	1	1	51	0	62	3	1	4	7	.364	0	0	4.99

Year Team	Lg Org	HOW MUCH HE PITCHED						WHAT HE GAVE UP								THE RESULTS						
		G	GS	CG	GF	IP	BFP	H	R	ER	HR	SH	SF	HB	TBB	IBB	SO	WP	Bk	W	L	Pct.	ShO	Sv	ERA
1992 Salem	A+ Pit	6	6	0	0	37	152	29	18	14	6	0	1	1	10	0	27	1	1	3	0	1.000	0	0	3.41
Carolina	AA Pit	20	20	1	0	124.2	534	127	51	42	7	1	2	4	41	2	107	4	1	6	7	.462	1	0	3.03
1993 Buffalo	AAA Pit	23	23	2	0	132.1	569	141	67	63	9	3	5	2	52	2	71	10	1	9	8	.529	0	0	4.28
1994 Buffalo	AAA Pit	18	17	0	0	118.2	487	112	47	41	6	3	5	3	36	0	71	0	0	5	10	.333	0	0	3.11
1995 Salt Lake	AAA Min	7	7	1	0	44.1	172	31	13	12	2	2	0	0	12	1	40	1	0	5	0	1.000	0	0	2.44
1998 Vancouver	AAA Ana	27	27	2	0	175	744	171	85	74	14	5	5	8	68	0	123	9	0	11	12	.478	0	0	3.81
1999 Oklahoma	AAA Tex	3	0	0	0	4.2	24	7	5	4	0	0	1	0	3	0	4	0	0	0	1	.000	0	0	7.71
Nashville	AAA Pit	7	6	0	0	29.1	148	39	27	26	3	3	1	4	20	1	29	4	0	2	3	.400	0	0	7.98
Indianapols	AAA Cin	9	0	0	1	7.1	42	17	9	8	0	0	0	0	4	1	7	0	1	0	0	.000	0	0	9.82
Carolina	AA Col	11	7	0	0	47.2	201	48	20	17	3	1	2	4	16	0	42	2	0	3	2	.600	0	0	3.21
1993 Pittsburgh	NL	9	0	0	2	9	44	15	6	6	0	1	0	0	4	0	5	0	0	0	1	.000	0	0	6.00
1994 Pittsburgh	NL	8	0	0	1	15.2	76	20	12	12	2	1	1	0	10	4	8	0	0	0	0	.000	0	0	6.89
1995 Minnesota	AL	25	4	1	8	51.2	228	48	28	22	4	5	2	0	31	4	38	0	1	2	0	1.000	0	0	3.83
1996 Minnesota	AL	36	31	5	1	186.1	853	197	113	106	22	2	4	9	116	2	114	7	0	7	17	.292	3	0	5.12
1997 Minnesota	AL	31	26	0	2	147	666	169	105	93	19	3	8	6	70	3	69	10	0	8	12	.400	0	0	5.69
1998 Anaheim	AL	5	0	0	0	5.2	31	11	11	10	3	0	1	0	2	0	3	0	0	0	0	.000	0	0	15.88
8 Min. YEARS		172	149	7	4	905	3924	880	460	389	60	22	25	31	410	9	695	44	7	53	58	.477	1	0	3.87
6 Maj. YEARS		114	61	6	14	415.1	1898	460	275	249	50	12	16	15	233	13	237	17	1	17	30	.362	3	0	5.40

Ryan Robertson

Bats: Left **Throws:** Right **Pos:** C **Ht:** 6'4" **Wt:** 210 **Born:** 9/30/72 **Age:** 27

Year Team	Lg Org	BATTING															BASERUNNING				PERCENTAGES		
		G	AB	H	2B	3B	HR	TB	R	RBI	TBB	IBB	SO	HBP	SH	SF	SB	CS	SB%	GDP	Avg	OBP	SLG
1995 Thunder Bay	IND —	47	141	27	8	0	0	35	9	17	17	0	27	1	3	1	0	1	.00	3	.191	.281	.248
1996 Kane County	A Fla	55	160	37	8	0	3	54	21	16	37	1	31	1	2	3	0	1	.00	3	.231	.373	.338
1997 Kane County	A Fla	116	376	107	22	1	11	164	64	71	85	4	69	3	0	7	0	3	.00	8	.285	.414	.436
1998 Portland	AA Fla	98	308	80	14	0	7	115	31	47	44	2	62	2	0	4	0	1	.00	8	.260	.352	.373
1999 Portland	AA Fla	44	130	32	6	0	2	44	15	10	22	0	17	1	1	0	0	0	.00	5	.246	.359	.338
Calgary	AAA Fla	59	169	51	10	0	1	64	16	19	26	0	29	0	0	1	0	2	.00	2	.302	.393	.379
5 Min. YEARS		419	1284	334	68	1	24	476	156	180	231	7	235	8	6	16	0	8	.00	30	.260	.372	.371

Adam Robinson

Bats: Right **Throws:** Right **Pos:** 2B-SS **Ht:** 6'0" **Wt:** 185 **Born:** 6/28/75 **Age:** 25

Year Team	Lg Org	BATTING															BASERUNNING				PERCENTAGES		
		G	AB	H	2B	3B	HR	TB	R	RBI	TBB	IBB	SO	HBP	SH	SF	SB	CS	SB%	GDP	Avg	OBP	SLG
1997 Sou Oregon	A- Oak	68	250	68	13	2	3	94	41	27	28	0	68	6	2	3	13	11	.54	8	.272	.355	.376
1998 Visalia	A+ Oak	82	296	69	13	3	0	88	54	26	43	0	89	3	3	3	14	4	.78	4	.233	.333	.297
Kinston	A+ Cle	24	91	15	3	0	3	27	9	8	11	0	22	1	2	0	4	1	.80	2	.165	.262	.297
1999 Akron	AA Cle	66	238	66	12	4	5	101	37	30	20	0	49	2	2	0	4	1	.80	5	.277	.338	.424
3 Min. YEARS		240	875	218	41	9	11	310	141	91	102	0	228	12	9	6	35	17	.67	19	.249	.334	.354

Bobby Rodgers

Pitches: Right **Bats:** Right **Pos:** P **Ht:** 6'3" **Wt:** 225 **Born:** 7/22/74 **Age:** 25

Year Team	Lg Org	HOW MUCH HE PITCHED						WHAT HE GAVE UP								THE RESULTS						
		G	GS	CG	GF	IP	BFP	H	R	ER	HR	SH	SF	HB	TBB	IBB	SO	WP	Bk	W	L	Pct.	ShO	Sv	ERA
1996 Lowell	A- Bos	14	14	2	0	90	363	60	33	19	3	2	2	3	31	0	108	9	2	7	4	.636	1	0	1.90
1997 Kane County	A Fla	27	27	2	0	165.2	699	154	81	71	9	6	4	14	61	0	138	7	1	8	10	.444	0	0	3.86
1998 Brevard Cty	A+ Fla	7	7	0	0	35.1	143	34	17	16	2	2	1	1	7	0	35	1	0	1	1	.500	0	0	4.08
Portland	AA Fla	14	14	2	0	82	339	68	37	34	8	5	3	3	28	0	72	2	1	6	5	.545	1	0	3.73
1999 Portland	AA Fla	26	22	0	1	122.2	576	147	85	74	13	4	3	6	70	0	109	8	0	5	10	.333	0	0	5.43
4 Min. YEARS		88	84	6	1	495.2	2120	463	253	214	35	19	13	27	197	0	462	27	4	27	30	.474	2	0	3.89

Jose Rodriguez

Pitches: Left **Bats:** Left **Pos:** P **Ht:** 6'1" **Wt:** 205 **Born:** 12/18/74 **Age:** 25

Year Team	Lg Org	HOW MUCH HE PITCHED						WHAT HE GAVE UP								THE RESULTS						
		G	GS	CG	GF	IP	BFP	H	R	ER	HR	SH	SF	HB	TBB	IBB	SO	WP	Bk	W	L	Pct.	ShO	Sv	ERA
1997 Johnson Cy	R+ StL	4	0	0	1	6.2	27	4	3	3	1	1	0	1	3	1	8	1	0	0	0	.000	0	0	4.05
1998 Peoria	A StL	40	0	0	12	39.1	191	47	32	20	0	6	1	2	19	1	30	3	0	2	4	.333	0	0	4.58
1999 Arkansas	AA StL	30	0	0	9	36	173	38	16	13	6	2	0	0	25	0	30	4	0	1	2	.333	0	0	3.25
Peoria	A StL	15	0	0	2	16.1	74	14	7	6	1	3	0	0	8	0	15	0	0	2	3	.400	0	0	3.31
3 Min. YEARS		89	0	0	24	98.1	465	103	58	42	8	12	1	3	55	2	83	8	0	5	9	.357	0	0	3.84

Luis Rodriguez

Bats: Right **Throws:** Right **Pos:** C **Ht:** 5'9" **Wt:** 160 **Born:** 1/3/74 **Age:** 26

Year Team	Lg Org	BATTING															BASERUNNING				PERCENTAGES		
		G	AB	H	2B	3B	HR	TB	R	RBI	TBB	IBB	SO	HBP	SH	SF	SB	CS	SB%	GDP	Avg	OBP	SLG
1995 St.Cathrnes	A- Tor	66	257	71	16	2	1	94	22	20	10	1	49	1	2	1	2	4	.33	7	.276	.305	.366
1996 Hagerstown	A Tor	79	256	53	8	1	1	66	19	25	24	0	58	1	5	1	6	4	.60	3	.207	.277	.258
1997 Syracuse	AAA Tor	3	2	0	0	0	0	0	0	0	0	0	0	0	0	0	0	0	.00	0	.000	.000	.000
Hagerstown	A Tor	27	94	25	6	0	2	37	13	14	2	0	20	1	3	2	3	0	1.00	2	.266	.283	.394
Knoxville	AA Tor	24	78	21	3	1	0	26	6	6	3	0	20	1	0	0	1	0	.00	1	.269	.305	.333
1998 Syracuse	AAA Tor	5	15	2	0	0	0	2	1	2	0	0	6	0	1	1	0	0	.00	0	.133	.125	.133
Dunedin	A+ Tor	67	196	57	15	0	4	84	34	41	10	0	39	2	5	4	11	2	.85	3	.291	.325	.429
Knoxville	AA Tor	8	17	7	0	1	0	9	6	1	7	0	5	0	0	0	1	0	1.00	1	.412	.583	.529
1999 Pawtucket	AAA Bos	2	3	0	0	0	0	0	0	0	0	0	1	0	0	0	0	0	.00	0	.000	.000	.000
Sarasota	A+ Bos	31	114	33	8	0	3	50	19	14	8	0	17	1	1	2	5	1	.83	2	.289	.336	.439

			BATTING													BASERUNNING				PERCENTAGES		
Year Team	Lg Org	G	AB	H	2B	3B	HR	TB	R	RBI	TBB	IBB	SO	HBP	SH	SF	SB	CS	SB%	GDP	Avg	OBP	SLG
Trenton	AA Bos	32	114	31	7	0	4	50	10	14	3	0	25	1	0	0	2	1	.67	4	.272	.297	.439
5 Min. YEARS		344	1146	300	63	5	15	418	130	137	67	1	242	8	17	11	30	13	.70	23	.262	.304	.365

Sammy Rodriguez

Bats: Right **Throws:** Right **Pos:** C **Ht:** 5'9" **Wt:** 185 **Born:** 8/20/75 **Age:** 24

			BATTING													BASERUNNING				PERCENTAGES		
Year Team	Lg Org	G	AB	H	2B	3B	HR	TB	R	RBI	TBB	IBB	SO	HBP	SH	SF	SB	CS	SB%	GDP	Avg	OBP	SLG
1995 Mets	R NYM	6	18	5	0	0	0	5	1	1	2	0	4	0	0	0	0	1	.00	0	.278	.350	.278
Butte	R+ NYM	17	57	14	1	0	1	18	7	6	4	0	13	0	0	0	2	1	.67	0	.246	.295	.316
1996 Pittsfield	A- NYM	32	93	18	3	0	1	24	8	10	11	0	25	1	0	1	1	0	1.00	3	.194	.283	.258
1997 Pittsfield	A- NYM	36	110	27	6	2	5	52	15	20	21	1	33	2	1	2	2	1	.67	1	.245	.370	.473
1998 Binghamton	AA NYM	3	8	1	0	0	0	1	2	1	1	0	0	0	0	0	0	0	.00	0	.125	.222	.125
St. Lucie	A+ NYM	53	152	39	9	1	2	56	20	24	20	0	36	2	4	2	3	1	.75	1	.257	.347	.368
1999 Norfolk	AAA NYM	5	9	2	0	0	2	8	2	4	3	0	2	0	0	0	0	0	.00	0	.222	.417	.889
Binghamton	AA NYM	69	203	46	10	0	3	65	15	24	21	0	49	3	2	0	2	2	.50	2	.227	.308	.320
5 Min. YEARS		221	650	152	29	3	14	229	70	90	83	1	162	8	7	5	10	6	.63	7	.234	.326	.352

Victor Rodriguez

Bats: Right **Throws:** Right **Pos:** 3D **Ht:** 6'1" **Wt:** 190 **Born:** 10/25/76 **Age:** 23

			BATTING													BASERUNNING				PERCENTAGES		
Year Team	Lg Org	G	AB	H	2B	3B	HR	TB	R	RBI	TBB	IBB	SO	HBP	SH	SF	SB	CS	SB%	GDP	Avg	OBP	SLG
1994 Marlins	R Fla	24	96	31	2	0	0	33	13	17	7	0	7	0	0	3	2	0	1.00	3	.323	.358	.344
1995 Kane County	A Fla	127	472	111	9	1	0	122	65	43	40	0	47	2	16	4	18	6	.75	17	.235	.295	.258
1996 Brevard Cty	A+ Fla	114	438	120	14	4	0	142	54	26	32	0	42	2	8	3	20	7	.74	13	.274	.324	.324
1997 Portland	AA Fla	113	401	111	18	4	3	146	63	38	30	0	43	0	10	3	13	7	.65	15	.277	.325	.364
1998 Portland	AA Fla	66	222	63	9	1	4	86	28	19	18	0	26	5	4	0	5	4	.56	7	.284	.351	.387
1999 Portland	AA Fla	38	97	20	3	1	1	28	13	12	10	0	9	2	3	1	0	1	.00	3	.206	.291	.289
6 Min. YEARS		482	1726	456	55	11	8	557	236	155	137	0	174	11	41	14	58	25	.70	58	.264	.320	.323

Jason Rogers

Pitches: Left **Bats:** Left **Pos:** P **Ht:** 6'6" **Wt:** 220 **Born:** 4/5/73 **Age:** 27

		HOW MUCH HE PITCHED						WHAT HE GAVE UP										THE RESULTS					
Year Team	Lg Org	G	GS	CG	GF	IP	BFP	H	R	ER	HR	SH	SF	HB	TBB	IBB	SO	WP	Bk	W	L	Pct.	ShO	Sv	ERA
1994 Bluefield	R+ Bal	9	8	0	1	39	158	39	14	10	0	1	0	0	10	0	30	7	1	1	2	.333	0	0	2.31
1995 Frederick	A+ Bal	15	14	1	0	66.2	309	64	38	32	1	2	2	3	45	3	39	6	2	1	3	.250	0	0	4.32
High Desert	A+ Bal	5	5	0	0	23	121	32	26	20	0	1	2	0	18	0	10	5	0	1	3	.250	0	0	7.83
1996 Frederick	A+ Bal	31	18	1	1	115	540	136	87	70	8	8	3	4	62	0	87	5	2	7	8	.467	0	0	5.48
1997 Frederick	A+ Bal	36	5	0	8	70.2	320	68	46	45	6	1	2	5	48	1	57	2	3	5	3	.625	0	0	5.73
1998 Frederick	A+ Bal	17	0	0	3	20.1	87	19	12	9	2	1	0	2	7	0	19	2	0	0	3	.000	0	0	3.98
Bowie	AA Bal	38	0	0	17	56.1	223	40	22	20	2	2	1	4	20	0	46	3	1	4	3	.571	0	3	3.20
1999 Rochester	AAA Bal	9	0	0	3	10	50	15	9	9	3	1	0	0	6	1	7	2	0	0	2	.000	0	0	8.10
Bowie	AA Bal	7	0	0	2	11.2	53	11	5	2	0	2	1	0	9	1	9	0	1	0	1	.000	0	0	1.54
6 Min. YEARS		167	50	2	35	412.2	1861	424	259	217	22	19	11	18	225	6	304	32	10	19	28	.404	0	3	4.73

Nate Rolison

Bats: Left **Throws:** Right **Pos:** 1B **Ht:** 6'6" **Wt:** 240 **Born:** 3/27/77 **Age:** 23

			BATTING													BASERUNNING				PERCENTAGES		
Year Team	Lg Org	G	AB	H	2B	3B	HR	TB	R	RBI	TBB	IBB	SO	HBP	SH	SF	SB	CS	SB%	GDP	Avg	OBP	SLG
1995 Marlins	R Fla	37	134	37	10	2	1	54	22	19	15	1	34	8	0	1	0	0	.00	1	.276	.380	.403
1996 Kane County	A Fla	131	474	115	28	1	14	187	63	75	66	9	170	8	1	0	3	3	.50	9	.243	.345	.395
1997 Brevard Cty	A+ Fla	122	473	121	22	0	16	191	59	65	38	1	143	2	0	1	3	1	.75	16	.256	.313	.404
1998 Portland	AA Fla	131	484	134	35	2	16	221	80	83	64	6	150	7	0	6	5	0	1.00	9	.277	.365	.457
1999 Portland	AA Fla	124	438	131	20	1	17	204	71	69	68	3	112	6	0	2	0	1	.00	16	.299	.399	.466
5 Min. YEARS		545	2003	538	115	6	64	857	295	311	251	20	609	31	1	10	11	5	.69	51	.269	.357	.428

Jimmy Rollins

Bats: Both **Throws:** Right **Pos:** SS **Ht:** 5'8" **Wt:** 160 **Born:** 11/27/78 **Age:** 21

			BATTING													BASERUNNING				PERCENTAGES		
Year Team	Lg Org	G	AB	H	2B	3B	HR	TB	R	RBI	TBB	IBB	SO	HBP	SH	SF	SB	CS	SB%	GDP	Avg	OBP	SLG
1996 Martinsvlle	R+ Phi	49	172	41	3	1	1	49	22	16	28	1	20	2	1	0	11	5	.69	2	.238	.351	.285
1997 Piedmont	A Phi	139	560	151	22	8	6	207	94	59	52	2	80	0	9	3	46	6	.88	4	.270	.330	.370
1998 Clearwater	A+ Phi	119	495	121	18	9	6	175	72	35	41	1	62	4	4	3	23	9	.72	9	.244	.306	.354
1999 Reading	AA Phi	133	532	145	21	8	11	215	81	56	51	1	47	1	12	2	24	12	.67	8	.273	.336	.404
Scranton-WB	AAA Phi	4	13	1	1	0	0	2	0	0	1	0	1	0	1	0	1	0	1.00	0	.077	.143	.154
4 Min. YEARS		444	1772	459	65	26	24	648	269	166	173	5	210	7	27	8	105	32	.77	23	.259	.326	.366

Mandy Romero

Bats: Both **Throws:** Right **Pos:** C **Ht:** 5'11" **Wt:** 196 **Born:** 10/29/67 **Age:** 32

			BATTING													BASERUNNING				PERCENTAGES		
Year Team	Lg Org	G	AB	H	2B	3B	HR	TB	R	RBI	TBB	IBB	SO	HBP	SH	SF	SB	CS	SB%	GDP	Avg	OBP	SLG
1988 Princeton	R+ Pit	30	71	22	6	0	2	34	7	11	13	0	15	1	0	0	1	0	1.00	0	.310	.424	.479
1989 Augusta	A Pit	121	388	87	26	3	4	131	58	55	67	4	74	6	3	6	8	5	.62	10	.224	.343	.338
1990 Salem	A+ Pit	124	460	134	31	3	17	222	62	90	55	3	68	5	2	4	0	2	.00	10	.291	.370	.483
1991 Carolina	AA Pit	98	323	70	12	0	3	91	28	31	45	4	53	1	2	2	1	2	.33	9	.217	.313	.282
1992 Carolina	AA Pit	80	269	58	16	0	3	83	28	27	29	0	39	1	1	2	0	3	.00	10	.216	.292	.309

(Batting)

Year Team	Lg Org	G	AB	H	2B	3B	HR	TB	R	RBI	TBB	IBB	SO	HBP	SH	SF	SB	CS	SB%	GDP	Avg	OBP	SLG
1993 Buffalo	AAA Pit	42	136	31	6	1	2	45	11	14	6	1	12	0	1	1	1	0	1.00	5	.228	.259	.331
1994 Buffalo	AAA Pit	7	23	3	0	0	0	3	3	1	2	0	1	0	0	0	0	0	.00	2	.130	.200	.130
1995 Wichita	AA KC	121	440	133	32	1	21	230	73	82	69	10	60	5	0	1	1	3	.25	15	.302	.402	.523
1996 Memphis	AA SD	88	297	80	15	0	10	125	40	46	41	2	52	1	1	2	3	1	.75	15	.269	.358	.421
1997 Mobile	AA SD	61	222	71	22	0	13	132	50	52	38	3	31	2	0	1	0	1	.00	4	.320	.422	.595
Las Vegas	AAA SD	33	91	28	4	1	3	43	19	13	11	1	19	1	0	1	0	0	.00	4	.308	.385	.473
1998 Las Vegas	AAA SD	40	131	38	8	0	8	70	25	22	20	1	25	1	1	0	0	1	.00	9	.290	.388	.534
Pawtucket	AAA Bos	45	139	46	5	0	8	75	20	27	24	6	15	0	2	4	0	0	.00	1	.331	.419	.540
1999 Pawtucket	AAA Bos	46	143	31	7	0	3	47	8	22	13	0	26	0	2	1	0	0	.00	6	.217	.280	.329
Norfolk	AAA NYM	28	97	25	6	0	1	34	7	9	9	0	18	1	1	1	0	0	.00	5	.258	.324	.351
1997 San Diego	NL	21	48	10	0	0	2	16	7	4	2	0	18	0	0	0	1	0	1.00	1	.208	.240	.333
1998 San Diego	NL	6	9	0	0	0	0	0	1	0	1	0	3	0	0	0	0	0	.00	0	.000	.100	.000
Boston	AL	12	13	3	1	0	0	4	2	1	3	0	3	0	0	0	0	0	.00	0	.231	.375	.308
12 Min. YEARS		964	3230	857	196	9	98	1365	439	502	442	35	508	25	17	26	15	18	.45	105	.265	.356	.423
2 Maj. YEARS		39	70	13	1	0	2	20	10	5	6	0	24	0	0	0	1	0	1.00	2	.186	.250	.286

Greg Romo

Pitches: Right **Bats:** Left **Pos:** P   **Ht:** 6'2" **Wt:** 165 **Born:** 5/14/75 **Age:** 25

Year Team	Lg Org	G	GS	CG	GF	IP	BFP	H	R	ER	HR	SH	SF	HB	TBB	IBB	SO	WP	Bk	W	L	Pct.	ShO	Sv	ERA
1995 Tigers	R Det	5	5	0	0	27.1	110	25	9	8	0	0	2	0	5	0	25	3	0	3	1	.750	0	0	2.63
1996 Tigers	R Det	8	1	0	7	23	93	19	7	4	0	0	1	2	4	0	29	1	0	1		1.000	0	0	1.57
Jamestown	A- Det	6	6	1	0	38.1	155	35	17	10	3	0	1	1	6	0	39	3	0	4	2	.667	0	0	2.35
1997 W Michigan	A Det	24	24	0	0	139.2	595	128	65	55	7	3	5	0	51	0	124	14	3	12	6	.667	0	0	3.54
1998 W Michigan	A Det	16	16	0	0	95.2	390	78	42	31	6	1	0	1	25	0	105	3	0	7	4	.636	0	0	2.92
Lakeland	A+ Det	12	12	3	0	76.1	325	72	46	34	4	1	2	1	30	0	53	9	0	5	5	.500	0	0	4.01
1999 Lakeland	A+ Det	25	15	1	4	105.2	445	90	46	41	8	1	1	4	46	1	89	3	0	4	4	.667	1	2	3.49
Jacksnville	AA Det	8	3	0	2	20.2	94	29	20	19	4	0	0	0	7	1	15	3	0	2	2	.500	0	0	8.27
5 Min. YEARS		104	82	5	13	526.2	2207	476	252	202	32	6	12	9	174	2	479	39	3	42	24	.636	1	3	3.45

Marc Ronan

Bats: Left **Throws:** Right **Pos:** C   **Ht:** 6'2" **Wt:** 190 **Born:** 9/19/69 **Age:** 30

Year Team	Lg Org	G	AB	H	2B	3B	HR	TB	R	RBI	TBB	IBB	SO	HBP	SH	SF	SB	CS	SB%	GDP	Avg	OBP	SLG
1990 Hamilton	A- StL	56	167	38	6	0	1	47	14	15	15	0	37	1	0	3	1	2	.33	3	.228	.290	.281
1991 Savannah	A StL	108	343	81	10	1	0	93	41	45	37	1	54	4	3	1	11	2	.85	13	.236	.317	.271
1992 Springfield	A StL	110	376	81	19	2	6	122	45	48	23	2	58	1	0	4	4	5	.44	11	.215	.260	.324
1993 St. Pete	A+ StL	25	87	27	5	0	0	32	13	6	6	0	10	0	3	2	0	0	.00	1	.310	.347	.368
Arkansas	AA StL	96	281	60	16	1	7	99	33	34	26	2	47	2	3	3	1	3	.25	4	.214	.282	.352
1994 Louisville	AAA StL	84	269	64	11	2	2	85	32	21	12	2	43	2	2	2	3	1	.75	9	.238	.274	.316
1995 Louisville	AAA StL	78	225	48	8	0	0	56	15	8	14	2	42	0	2	0	4	3	.57	10	.213	.259	.249
1996 Charlotte	AAA Fla	79	220	67	10	0	4	89	23	20	16	2	37	2	0	2	3	4	.43	4	.305	.354	.405
1997 Columbus	AAA NYY	55	156	43	12	0	1	58	16	19	27	3	24	1	0	0	1	3	.25	9	.276	.386	.372
1998 New Orleans	AAA Hou	51	123	30	5	0	1	38	7	10	17	2	25	1	0	0	0	0	.00	3	.244	.340	.309
1999 Scranton-WB	AAA Phi	38	115	19	5	0	2	30	14	10	8	1	28	1	0	1	1	2	.33	4	.165	.224	.261
1993 St. Louis	NL	6	12	1	0	0	0	1	0	0	0	0	5	0	0	0	0	0	.00	0	.083	.083	.083
10 Min. YEARS		780	2362	558	107	6	24	749	253	236	201	17	405	15	13	18	29	25	.54	71	.236	.298	.317

Joe Ronca

Bats: Right **Throws:** Right **Pos:** DH-OF   **Ht:** 6'2" **Wt:** 200 **Born:** 7/3/71 **Age:** 28

Year Team	Lg Org	G	AB	H	2B	3B	HR	TB	R	RBI	TBB	IBB	SO	HBP	SH	SF	SB	CS	SB%	GDP	Avg	OBP	SLG
1989 Pirates	R Pit	45	179	39	6	1	1	50	21	18	8	0	19	0	0	1	7	4	.64	7	.218	.250	.279
1990 Welland	A- Pit	63	140	30	2	0	1	35	21	4	8	1	26	0	0	0	15	5	.75	2	.214	.257	.250
1991 Augusta	A Pit	105	381	89	13	4	1	113	35	49	21	0	81	1	0	2	14	9	.61	5	.234	.274	.297
1992 Salem	A+ Pit	47	152	35	6	0	4	53	11	17	6	0	39	1	1	2	3	1	.75	7	.230	.261	.349
Augusta	A Pit	27	96	20	4	0	0	24	5	10	9	0	21	0	1	0	6	0	1.00	1	.208	.276	.250
1993 Salem	A+ Pit	92	290	83	13	2	12	136	41	51	26	0	60	1	0	3	5	7	.42	5	.286	.344	.469
1994 Alexandria	IND —	78	305	103	18	1	10	153	58	68	22	—	41	—	—	—	5	0	1.00	—	.338	.380	.502
1995 Alexandria	IND —	99	412	134	24	1	14	202	67	82	34	5	55	2	0	5	3	0	1.00	13	.325	.375	.490
1996 Alexandria	IND —	99	397	126	24	1	13	191	62	77	34	2	66	3	0	2	8	2	.80	10	.317	.374	.481
1997 Springfield	IND —	77	293	100	23	6	17	186	54	72	31	3	56	2	0	4	4	0	1.00	10	.341	.403	.635
1998 Springfield	IND —	76	317	109	21	0	16	178	56	77	33	1	58	3	1	0	1	0	1.00	14	.344	.411	.562
1999 Bowie	AA Bal	46	153	37	12	1	5	66	12	25	13	2	43	1	0	1	1	3	.25	2	.242	.304	.431
11 Min. YEARS		854	3115	905	166	17	94	1387	443	550	245	—	565	—	—	—	72	31	.70		.291	.343	.445

Mike Rooney

Pitches: Right **Bats:** Right **Pos:** P   **Ht:** 6'1" **Wt:** 175 **Born:** 10/6/75 **Age:** 24

Year Team	Lg Org	G	GS	CG	GF	IP	BFP	H	R	ER	HR	SH	SF	HB	TBB	IBB	SO	WP	Bk	W	L	Pct.	ShO	Sv	ERA
1997 Lethbridge	R+ Ari	13	13	1	0	62.1	282	72	42	38	4	2	3	5	24	0	40	3	0	5	2	.714	0	0	5.49
1998 South Bend	A Ari	21	20	1	1	105.2	474	122	75	61	6	2	7	7	35	0	72	2	1	4	9	.308	0	0	5.20
Tucson	AAA Ari	3	3	0	0	15.2	74	20	10	8	3	2	0	2	9	1	6	0	0	0	2	.000	0	0	4.60
1999 Tucson	AAA Ari	1	0	0	0	0	4	2	3	1	1	0	0	0	2	0	0	0	0	0	0	.000	0	0	0.00
3 Min. YEARS		38	36	2	1	183.2	834	216	130	108	14	6	10	14	70	1	118	5	1	9	13	.409	0	0	5.29

241

Derek Root

Pitches: Left Bats: Left Pos: P Ht: 6'5" Wt: 215 Born: 5/26/75 Age: 25

Year Team	Lg Org	G	GS	CG	GF	IP	BFP	H	R	ER	HR	SH	SF	HB	TBB	IBB	SO	WP	Bk	W	L	Pct.	ShO	Sv	ERA
1995 Kissimmee	A+ Hou	5	0	0	1	6	29	10	3	3	0	0	0	0	2	0	3	0	0	0	0	.000	0	0	4.50
Auburn	A- Hou	17	3	0	5	38.1	165	28	14	14	0	2	1	2	24	0	37	4	1	2	0	1.000	0	1	3.29
1996 Quad City	A Hou	40	2	0	22	63	272	55	25	21	1	4	4	4	26	4	47	6	0	5	3	.625	0	7	3.00
1997 Kissimmee	A+ Hou	26	22	2	0	129	555	131	76	60	10	4	7	7	42	1	68	7	5	4	14	.222	0	0	4.19
1998 Kissimmee	A+ Hou	29	9	2	13	80.1	323	69	28	21	3	2	1	4	20	2	79	4	1	5	4	.556	2	4	2.35
Jackson	AA Hou	7	6	0	0	44	192	46	24	19	4	1	1	1	17	1	31	1	0	4	1	.800	0	0	3.89
New Orleans	AAA Hou	1	1	0	0	6.1	24	3	2	2	1	0	0	0	3	0	4	1	0	1	0	1.000	0	0	2.84
1999 Jackson	AA Hou	28	26	0	0	156.2	711	167	103	81	17	5	3	11	79	2	129	14	2	7	16	.304	0	0	4.65
5 Min. YEARS		153	69	4	41	523.2	2271	509	275	221	36	18	17	29	213	10	398	37	9	28	38	.424	2	12	3.80

Mel Rosario

Bats: Both Throws: Right Pos: C Ht: 6'0" Wt: 200 Born: 5/25/73 Age: 27

Year Team	Lg Org	G	AB	H	2B	3B	HR	TB	R	RBI	TBB	IBB	SO	HBP	SH	SF	SB	CS	SB%	GDP	Avg	OBP	SLG
1992 Spokane	A- SD	66	237	54	13	1	10	99	38	40	20	2	62	4	0	4	5	3	.63	6	.228	.294	.418
1993 Waterloo	A SD	32	105	22	6	2	5	47	15	15	7	1	37	2	0	0	5	2	.71	0	.210	.272	.448
Spokane	A- SD	41	140	31	5	0	4	40	17	10	8	2	36	0	0	0	2	1	.67	1	.220	.270	.360
1995 South Bend	A CWS	118	450	123	30	6	15	210	58	57	30	7	109	4	1	3	1	8	.11	0	.273	.322	.467
1996 Rancho Cuca	A+ SD	10	33	9	3	0	3	21	7	10	3	0	8	0	0	0	1	0	1.00	0	.273	.333	.636
High Desert	A+ Bal	42	163	52	9	1	10	93	35	34	21	0	45	9	0	0	4	0	1.00	3	.319	.425	.571
Bowie	AA Bal	47	162	34	10	0	2	50	14	17	6	1	43	5	1	2	3	2	.60	4	.210	.257	.309
Rochester	AAA Bal	3	2	0	0	0	0	0	0	0	0	0	1	0	0	0	0	0	.00	0	.000	.000	.000
1997 Bowie	AA Bal	123	430	113	26	1	12	177	68	60	27	2	106	9	1	4	4	7	.36	5	.263	.317	.412
1998 Rochester	AAA Bal	34	113	28	4	0	3	41	10	10	6	0	24	1	0	1	5	2	.71	1	.248	.289	.363
Bowie	AA Bal	39	130	35	5	4	5	63	22	25	9	0	31	3	1	2	2	1	.67	3	.269	.326	.485
1999 Altoona	AA Pit	26	87	21	9	0	1	33	11	11	6	0	15	0	0	1	0	0	.00	6	.241	.287	.379
Oklahoma	AAA Tex	7	26	5	1	0	0	6	2	3	0	0	8	0	0	0	1	0	1.00	1	.192	.192	.231
Tulsa	AA Tex	28	96	20	3	0	8	47	12	19	3	0	28	1	1	1	1	0	1.00	0	.208	.238	.490
1997 Baltimore	AL	4	3	0	0	0	0	0	0	0	0	0	1	0	0	0	0	0	.00	0	.000	.000	.000
7 Min. YEARS		616	2174	548	124	15	78	936	309	320	146	15	553	38	5	18	34	26	.57	30	.252	.308	.431

Mike Rose

Bats: Both Throws: Right Pos: C Ht: 6'1" Wt: 185 Born: 8/25/76 Age: 23

Year Team	Lg Org	G	AB	H	2B	3B	HR	TB	R	RBI	TBB	IBB	SO	HBP	SH	SF	SB	CS	SB%	GDP	Avg	OBP	SLG
1995 Astros	R Hou	35	89	23	2	1	1	30	13	9	11	0	18	3	0	0	2	1	.67	1	.258	.359	.337
1996 Kissimmee	A+ Hou	2	1	0	0	0	0	0	0	0	0	0	1	0	0	0	0	0	.00	0	.000	.000	.000
Auburn	A- Hou	61	180	45	5	1	2	58	20	11	30	0	41	1	4	0	9	3	.75	5	.250	.360	.322
1997 Quad City	A Hou	79	234	60	6	1	3	77	22	27	28	0	62	4	8	3	3	1	.75	1	.256	.342	.329
1998 Kissimmee	A+ Hou	18	62	14	4	0	3	27	9	9	8	0	14	0	1	0	1	0	1.00	3	.226	.314	.435
Quad City	A Hou	88	267	81	13	2	7	119	48	40	52	3	56	1	3	1	10	8	.56	5	.303	.417	.446
1999 Jackson	AA Hou	15	45	11	0	0	3	20	8	8	13	1	10	0	1	0	2	0	.00	1	.244	.414	.444
Kissimmee	A+ Hou	95	303	84	16	2	11	137	61	32	59	0	64	3	0	2	12	6	.67	7	.277	.398	.452
5 Min. YEARS		393	1181	318	46	7	30	468	181	136	201	4	266	12	17	6	37	21	.64	22	.269	.379	.396

Ted Rose

Pitches: Right Bats: Left Pos: P Ht: 6'2" Wt: 185 Born: 8/23/73 Age: 26

Year Team	Lg Org	G	GS	CG	GF	IP	BFP	H	R	ER	HR	SH	SF	HB	TBB	IBB	SO	WP	Bk	W	L	Pct.	ShO	Sv	ERA
1996 Princeton	R+ Cin	11	11	1	0	59.1	262	70	44	41	9	2	3	3	21	0	53	9	2	3	5	.375	1	0	6.22
1997 Chstn-WV	A Cin	38	13	2	9	129.1	525	108	44	36	7	9	3	6	27	0	132	3	2	11	6	.647	2	4	2.51
1998 Chattanooga	AA Cin	29	29	1	0	168.1	745	191	97	86	12	1	6	6	66	3	108	6	4	11	10	.524	0	0	4.60
1999 Reds	R Cin	1	0	0	1	2	11	4	2	2	0	0	0	0	1	0	3	0	0	0	0	.000	0	0	9.00
Chattanooga	AA Cin	13	0	0	4	17	75	17	8	8	2	0	1	2	9	1	23	0	0	2	0	1.000	0	2	4.24
4 Min. YEARS		92	53	4	14	376	1618	390	195	173	30	12	13	17	124	4	319	18	8	27	21	.563	3	6	4.14

Terry Rosenkranz

Pitches: Left Bats: Left Pos: P Ht: 6'4" Wt: 205 Born: 11/5/70 Age: 29

Year Team	Lg Org	G	GS	CG	GF	IP	BFP	H	R	ER	HR	SH	SF	HB	TBB	IBB	SO	WP	Bk	W	L	Pct.	ShO	Sv	ERA
1992 Butte	R+ Tex	14	0	0	8	26.2	127	34	22	17	4	1	3	1	12	0	23	2	1	0	0	.000	0	0	5.74
1993 Rangers	R Tex	8	0	0	1	10.1	52	16	12	11	2	0	3	0	4	0	6	0	0	0	0	.000	0	0	9.58
1995 Beloit	A Mil	4	0	0	2	8	30	2	2	0	0	0	0	0	2	0	4	0	0	0	0	.000	0	0	0.00
Stockton	A+ Mil	35	1	0	14	49.1	234	44	34	34	4	5	4	1	49	2	43	4	0	1	2	.333	0	0	6.20
1996 Green Bay	IND —	17	16	1	5	115.2	540	132	85	73	12	4	6	3	65	1	104	7	0	8	6	.571	0	0	5.68
1997 Saskatoon	IND —	14	12	1	0	73	342	85	58	48	5	4	2	3	47	0	53	1	0	4	5	.444	0	0	5.92
1998 Bridgeport	IND —	39	0	0	6	58.2	237	31	17	14	3	1	2	1	27	0	61	3	0	8	2	.800	0	1	2.15
1999 Bridgeport	IND —	14	0	0	4	19.1	82	14	4	3	1	0	1	0	10	0	22	2	0	1	0	1.000	0	0	1.40
Bowie	AA Bal	26	0	0	9	43	186	36	20	19	5	3	3	0	26	0	36	4	0	3	1	.750	0	0	3.98
7 Min. YEARS		171	29	9	45	404	1830	394	254	219	36	18	23	10	242	3	352	23	1	25	16	.610	0	1	4.88

Mike Rossiter

Pitches: Right **Bats:** Right **Pos:** P **Ht:** 6'6" **Wt:** 230 **Born:** 6/20/73 **Age:** 27

					HOW MUCH HE PITCHED			WHAT HE GAVE UP										THE RESULTS				
Year Team	Lg Org	G	GS	CG	GF	IP	BFP	H	R	ER	HR	SH	SF	HB	TBB	IBB	SO	WP	Bk	W	L	Pct.	ShO	Sv	ERA
1991 Athletics	R Oak	10	9	0	0	38.1	179	43	24	17	3	1	0	2	22	0	35	6	0	3	4	.429	0	0	3.99
1992 Madison	A Oak	27	27	2	0	154.2	651	135	83	68	17	2	5	4	68	1	135	4	3	8	14	.364	0	0	3.96
1993 Modesto	A+ Oak	20	17	2	0	112	491	120	62	54	14	4	1	1	45	0	96	5	0	8	6	.571	0	0	4.34
1994 Athletics	R Oak	2	0	0	0	3.2	20	8	6	2	0	1	0	0	0	0	3	1	0	0	1	.000	0	0	4.91
1995 Modesto	A+ Oak	18	7	0	3	68.2	290	68	33	32	5	2	2	2	19	0	70	1	1	7	2	.778	0	0	4.19
1996 Huntsville	AA Oak	27	25	2	1	145	636	167	92	78	15	2	10	7	44	4	116	5	0	8	9	.471	1	0	4.84
1997 Stockton	A+ Mil	34	8	0	9	86	368	83	31	26	6	2	1	15	27	0	79	3	0	8	1	.889	0	0	2.72
El Paso	AA Mil	8	0	0	4	20.2	87	22	6	6	0	1	1	1	8	0	11	1	0	1	0	1.000	0	0	2.61
1998 Mobile	AA SD	22	0	0	3	45.1	185	34	10	9	2	1	0	1	11	0	46	1	0	2	0	1.000	0	0	1.79
Las Vegas	AAA SD	31	0	0	13	41	185	44	20	20	2	1	2	7	17	3	34	0	0	2	2	.500	0	2	4.39
1999 Colo Sprngs	AAA Col	24	0	0	5	37	166	37	16	16	3	2	5	20	0	31	3	0	2	0	1.000	0	0	3.89
Rockies	R Col	1	0	0	0	2	6	0	0	0	0	0	0	0	0	0	5	0	0	0	0	.000	0	0	0.00
Carolina	AA Col	16	0	0	8	21.2	80	11	5	5	0	1	0	1	9	0	24	2	0	0	1	.000	0	2	2.08
9 Min. YEARS		240	93	6	46	776	3344	772	388	333	67	20	25	46	290	8	685	32	4	49	40	.551	1	4	3.86

Rico Rossy

Bats: Right **Throws:** Right **Pos:** SS **Ht:** 5'10" **Wt:** 175 **Born:** 2/16/64 **Age:** 36

				BATTING													BASERUNNING				PERCENTAGES		
Year Team	Lg Org	G	AB	H	2B	3B	HR	TB	R	RBI	TBB	IBB	SO	HBP	SH	SF	SB	CS	SB%	GDP	Avg	OBP	SLG
1985 Newark	A- Bal	73	246	53	14	2	3	80	38	25	32	1	22	1	3	1	17	7	.71	13	.215	.307	.325
1986 Miami	A+ Bal	38	134	34	7	1	1	46	26	9	24	0	8	1	6	1	10	6	.63	4	.254	.369	.343
Charlotte	AA Bal	77	232	68	16	2	3	97	40	25	26	0	19	2	8	1	13	5	.72	2	.293	.368	.418
1987 Charlotte	AA Bal	127	471	135	22	3	4	175	69	50	43	0	38	3	3	1	20	9	.69	20	.287	.349	.372
1988 Buffalo	AAA Pit	68	187	46	4	0	1	53	12	20	13	0	17	0	0	1	1	5	.17	4	.246	.294	.283
1989 Harrisburg	AA Pit	78	238	60	16	1	2	84	20	25	27	0	19	3	0	2	2	4	.33	5	.252	.333	.353
Buffalo	AAA Pit	38	109	21	5	0	0	26	11	10	18	1	11	1	1	2	4	0	1.00	4	.193	.308	.239
1990 Buffalo	AAA Pit	8	17	3	0	1	0	5	3	2	4	0	2	0	1	1	1	0	1.00	0	.176	.318	.294
Greenville	AA Atl	5	21	4	1	0	0	5	4	0	1	0	2	0	0	0	0	2	.00	1	.190	.227	.238
Richmond	AAA Atl	107	380	88	13	0	4	113	58	32	69	1	43	3	7	2	11	6	.65	12	.232	.352	.297
1991 Richmond	AAA Atl	139	482	124	25	1	2	157	58	48	67	1	46	5	13	3	4	8	.33	12	.257	.352	.326
1992 Omaha	AAA KC	48	174	55	10	1	4	79	29	17	34	0	14	0	2	3	3	5	.38	5	.316	.422	.454
1993 Omaha	AAA KC	37	131	39	10	1	5	66	25	21	20	1	19	3	0	1	3	2	.60	1	.298	.400	.504
1994 Omaha	AAA KC	120	412	97	23	0	11	153	49	63	61	1	60	5	5	4	9	10	.47	14	.235	.338	.371
1995 Las Vegas	AAA SD	98	316	95	11	2	1	113	44	45	55	2	36	2	2	6	3	7	.30	13	.301	.401	.358
1996 Las Vegas	AAA SD	130	413	104	21	2	4	141	56	35	70	7	63	6	9	5	6	6	.50	11	.252	.364	.341
1997 Ottawa	AAA Mon	117	375	94	23	0	10	147	56	52	37	2	64	4	8	4	5	0	1.00	14	.251	.321	.392
1998 Tacoma	AAA Sea	56	210	60	18	0	8	102	33	36	26	2	36	0	2	0	1	1	.50	7	.286	.364	.486
1999 Las Vegas	AAA SD	93	259	66	12	0	10	108	42	29	41	3	27	2	4	2	4	1	.80	5	.255	.359	.417
1991 Atlanta	NL	5	1	0	0	0	0	0	0	0	0	0	1	0	0	0	0	0	.00	0	.000	.000	.000
1992 Kansas City	AL	59	149	32	8	1	1	45	21	12	20	1	20	1	7	1	0	3	.00	6	.215	.310	.302
1993 Kansas City	AL	46	86	19	4	0	2	29	10	12	9	0	11	1	1	0	0	0	.00	4	.221	.302	.337
1998 Seattle	AL	37	81	16	6	0	1	25	12	4	6	0	13	0	2	0	0	0	.00	1	.198	.253	.309
15 Min. YEARS		1457	4807	1246	251	17	73	1750	673	544	668	22	546	41	74	40	117	84	.58	147	.259	.352	.364
4 Maj. YEARS		147	317	67	18	1	4	99	43	28	35	1	45	2	10	1	0	3	.00	6	.211	.293	.312

Aaron Royster

Bats: Right **Throws:** Right **Pos:** OF **Ht:** 6'1" **Wt:** 220 **Born:** 11/30/72 **Age:** 27

				BATTING													BASERUNNING				PERCENTAGES		
Year Team	Lg Org	G	AB	H	2B	3B	HR	TB	R	RBI	TBB	IBB	SO	HBP	SH	SF	SB	CS	SB%	GDP	Avg	OBP	SLG
1994 Martinsvlle	R+ Phi	54	168	46	11	2	7	82	31	39	28	1	47	2	0	1	7	4	.64	2	.274	.382	.488
1995 Piedmont	A Phi	126	489	129	23	3	8	182	73	58	39	1	106	7	0	4	22	9	.71	16	.264	.325	.372
1996 Clearwater	A+ Phi	72	289	81	10	2	11	128	35	60	23	1	56	3	3	2	4	3	.57	7	.280	.338	.443
Reading	AA Phi	65	230	59	11	0	4	82	42	20	30	2	56	5	3	1	4	5	.44	3	.257	.353	.357
1997 Reading	AA Phi	112	412	106	18	5	15	179	59	62	53	0	104	1	0	2	2	3	.40	12	.257	.342	.434
1998 Reading	AA Phi	112	430	110	27	4	7	166	67	55	57	1	117	2	0	0	3	1	.75	13	.256	.346	.386
1999 Clearwater	A+ Phi	11	41	13	2	2	0	19	6	5	3	0	10	0	0	0	1	0	1.00	3	.317	.364	.463
Reading	AA Phi	91	310	90	17	2	8	135	53	48	48	2	90	3	2	3	11	5	.69	3	.290	.387	.435
6 Min. YEARS		643	2369	634	119	20	60	973	366	347	281	8	586	23	8	13	54	30	.64	59	.268	.349	.411

Matt Ruebel

Pitches: Left **Bats:** Left **Pos:** P **Ht:** 6'2" **Wt:** 180 **Born:** 10/16/69 **Age:** 30

					HOW MUCH HE PITCHED			WHAT HE GAVE UP										THE RESULTS				
Year Team	Lg Org	G	GS	CG	GF	IP	BFP	H	R	ER	HR	SH	SF	HB	TBB	IBB	SO	WP	Bk	W	L	Pct.	ShO	Sv	ERA
1991 Welland	A- Pit	6	6	0	0	27.2	113	16	9	6	3	0	1	4	11	0	27	2	3	1	1	.500	0	0	1.95
Augusta	A Pit	8	8	2	0	47	202	43	26	20	2	1	0	2	25	0	35	3	0	3	4	.429	1	0	3.83
1992 Augusta	A Pit	12	10	1	1	64.2	268	53	26	20	1	3	0	5	19	0	65	2	1	5	2	.714	0	0	2.78
Salem	A+ Pit	13	13	1	0	78.1	344	77	49	41	13	6	5	3	43	0	46	6	1	1	6	.143	0	0	4.71
1993 Salem	A+ Pit	19	1	0	4	33.1	168	34	31	22	6	3	0	3	32	3	29	8	2	1	4	.200	0	0	5.94
Augusta	A Pit	23	7	1	6	63.1	276	51	28	17	2	1	3	5	34	4	50	1	0	5	5	.500	1	0	2.42
1994 Carolina	AA Pit	6	3	0	0	16.1	78	28	15	12	3	1	1	1	3	0	14	0	0	1	1	.500	0	0	6.61
Salem	A+ Pit	21	13	0	0	86.1	374	87	49	33	9	2	3	7	27	0	72	4	1	6	6	.500	0	0	3.44
1995 Carolina	AA Pit	27	27	4	0	169.1	699	150	68	52	7	4	7	7	45	1	136	7	1	13	5	.722	3	0	2.76
1996 Calgary	AAA Pit	13	13	1	0	76.1	338	89	43	39	8	4	3	3	28	2	48	0	0	5	3	.625	0	0	4.60
1998 Durham	AAA TB	24	23	1	0	129	569	141	73	68	17	0	3	5	45	1	87	2	0	9	6	.600	1	0	4.74
1999 Tucson	AAA Ari	6	2	0	0	27	120	32	26	21	6	0	2	1	10	0	19	2	0	1	3	.250	0	0	7.00
Binghamton	AA NYM	6	5	0	0	26.1	114	24	13	8	2	0	1	1	8	0	25	1	0	2	0	1.000	0	0	2.73

Year Team	Lg Org	G	GS	CG	GF	IP	BFP	H	R	ER	HR	SH	SF	HB	TBB	IBB	SO	WP	Bk	W	L	Pct.	ShO	Sv	ERA
Norfolk	AAA NYM	7	7	0	0	40	174	40	20	20	6	0	2	3	17	0	23	0	0	3	0	1.000	0		4.50
1996 Pittsburgh	NL	26	7	0	3	58.2	265	64	38	30	7	0	3	6	25	0	22	2	0	1	1	.500	0	1	4.60
1997 Pittsburgh	NL	44	0	0	9	62.2	296	77	50	44	8	3	5	5	27	3	50	4	0	3	2	.600	0	0	6.32
1998 Tampa Bay	AL	7	1	0	1	8.2	39	11	7	6	3	0	0	0	4	0	6	0	0	0	2	.000	0	0	6.23
8 Min. YEARS		191	138	11	11	885	3837	865	476	379	85	25	30	50	347	11	676	38	9	56	46	.549	6	0	3.85
3 Maj. YEARS		77	8	0	13	130	600	152	95	80	18	3	8	11	56	3	78	6	0	4	5	.444	0	1	5.54

Scott Ruffcorn

Pitches: Right Bats: Right Pos: P Ht: 6' 4" Wt: 210 Born: 12/29/69 Age: 30

Year Team	Lg Org	G	GS	CG	GF	IP	BFP	H	R	ER	HR	SH	SF	HB	TBB	IBB	SO	WP	Bk	W	L	Pct.	ShO	Sv	ERA
1991 White Sox	R CWS	4	2	0	1	11.1	49	8	7	4	0	0	0	0	5	0	15	1	0	0	0	.000	0	0	3.18
South Bend	A CWS	9	9	0	0	43.2	193	35	26	19	1	2	1	2	25	0	45	1	2	1	3	.250	0	0	3.92
1992 Sarasota	A+ CWS	25	24	2	0	160.1	642	122	53	39	7	4	5	3	39	0	140	3	1	14	5	.737	0	0	2.19
1993 Birmingham	AA CWS	20	20	3	0	135	563	108	47	41	6	5	0	4	52	0	141	7	0	9	4	.692	3	0	2.73
Nashville	AAA CWS	7	6	1	0	45	172	30	16	14	5	2	1	0	8	1	44	3	0	2	2	.500	0	0	2.80
1994 Nashville	AAA CWS	24	24	3	0	165.2	672	139	57	50	5	3	6	6	40	1	144	6	0	15	3	.833	3	0	2.72
1995 Nashville	AAA CWS	2	2	0	0	0.1	9	3	4	4	0	0	0	2	3	0	0	1	0	0	0	.000	0	0	108.00
White Sox	R CWS	3	3	0	0	10	46	7	4	1	0	1	0	0	5	0	7	1	0	0	0	.000	0	0	0.90
Birmingham	AA CWS	3	3	0	0	16	71	17	11	10	0	0	0	0	10	0	13	2	0	0	2	.000	0	0	5.63
1996 Nashville	AAA CWS	24	24	2	0	149	649	142	71	64	18	6	4	5	61	1	129	7	0	13	4	.765	1	0	3.87
1997 Scranton-WB	AAA Phi	5	5	2	0	31	126	22	6	4	0	2	0	1	10	0	20	0	0	2	0	1.000	2	0	1.16
1998 Chattanooga	AA Cin	10	0	0	5	13	51	8	3	2	2	1	0	0	6	0	9	1	0	3	0	1.000	0	0	1.38
Indianapolis	AAA Cin	23	0	0	2	34.1	186	44	35	33	7	3	2	8	37	2	28	7	0	6	2	.750	0	0	8.65
1999 St. Paul	IND —	10	10	1	0	60	268	62	35	32	9	1	0	6	26	0	40	3	0	2	5	.286	0	0	4.80
Omaha	AAA KC	8	0	0	0	14.1	63	14	10	8	4	0	1	0	10	0	8	1	0	1	0	1.000	0	0	5.02
1993 Chicago	AL	3	2	0	1	10	46	9	11	9	2	1	1	0	10	0	2	1	0	0	2	.000	0	0	8.10
1994 Chicago	AL	2	2	0	0	6.1	39	15	11	9	1	0	1	0	5	0	3	0	0	0	2	.000	0	0	12.79
1995 Chicago	AL	4	0	0	0	8	46	10	7	7	0	1	0	2	13	0	5	0	0	0	0	.000	0	0	7.88
1996 Chicago	AL	3	1	0	1	6.1	34	10	8	8	1	1	0	0	6	0	3	2	0	1	0	1.000	0	0	11.37
1997 Philadelphia	NL	18	4	0	3	39.2	202	42	40	34	4	1	5	7	36	1	33	6	1	0	3	.000	0	0	7.71
9 Min. YEARS		177	132	14	9	889	3760	761	385	325	64	30	20	37	337	5	783	44	4	68	30	.694	9	0	3.29
5 Maj. YEARS		30	9	0	5	70.1	367	86	77	67	8	4	7	9	70	1	46	9	1	0	8	.000	0	0	8.57

Johnny Ruffin

Pitches: Right Bats: Right Pos: P Ht: 6' 3" Wt: 170 Born: 7/29/71 Age: 28

Year Team	Lg Org	G	GS	CG	GF	IP	BFP	H	R	ER	HR	SH	SF	HB	TBB	IBB	SO	WP	Bk	W	L	Pct.	ShO	Sv	ERA
1988 White Sox	R CWS	13	11	1	1	58.2	246	43	27	15	3	1	2	4	22	0	31	9	2	4	2	.667	0	0	2.30
1989 Utica	A- CWS	15	15	0	0	88.1	376	67	43	33	3	5	1	1	46	0	92	8	0	4	8	.333	0	0	3.36
1990 South Bend	A CWS	24	24	0	0	123	568	117	86	57	7	1	5	3	82	0	92	17	4	7	6	.538	0	0	4.17
1991 Sarasota	A+ CWS	26	26	6	0	158.2	655	126	68	57	9	3	5	5	62	0	117	10	2	11	4	.733	2	0	3.23
1992 Birmingham	AA CWS	10	10	0	0	47.2	228	51	48	32	3	1	5	1	34	0	44	9	0	0	7	.000	0	0	6.04
Sarasota	A+ CWS	23	8	0	6	62.2	290	56	46	41	5	2	1	4	41	0	61	10	2	3	7	.300	0	0	5.89
1993 Birmingham	AA CWS	11	0	0	10	22.1	92	16	9	7	2	2	1	0	9	1	23	0	0	0	4	.000	0	2	2.82
Nashville	AAA CWS	29	0	0	11	60	242	48	24	22	5	2	2	1	16	4	69	10	0	3	4	.429	0	1	3.30
Indianapolis	AAA Cin	5	0	0	3	6.2	25	3	1	1	0	1	0	0	2	1	6	0	0	1	1	.500	0	1	1.35
1995 Indianapolis	AAA Cin	36	1	0	4	49.2	213	27	19	16	3	2	1	0	37	2	58	7	0	3	1	.750	0	0	2.90
1997 Pawtucket	AAA Bos	6	1	0	2	14	60	5	7	7	0	0	0	0	16	0	16	4	0	1	0	1.000	0	0	4.50
1998 Louisville	AAA Mil	35	2	0	11	60	262	40	27	20	4	2	0	1	48	2	57	7	0	5	3	.625	0	0	3.00
Norfolk	AAA NYM	17	3	0	2	39	161	31	15	12	2	2	2	0	20	1	40	1	0	1	0	1.000	0	0	2.77
1999 Albuquerque	AAA LA	46	0	0	28	54	222	41	21	19	7	3	2	0	26	0	66	5	0	1	1	.500	0	10	3.17
1993 Cincinnati	NL	21	0	0	5	37.2	159	36	16	15	4	1	0	1	11	1	30	2	0	2	1	.667	0	0	3.58
1994 Cincinnati	NL	51	0	0	13	70	287	57	26	24	7	2	2	0	27	3	44	5	1	7	2	.778	0	1	3.09
1995 Cincinnati	NL	10	0	0	6	13.1	54	4	3	2	0	0	0	0	11	0	11	3	0	0	0	.000	0	0	1.35
1996 Cincinnati	NL	49	0	0	13	62.1	289	71	42	38	10	4	3	2	37	5	69	8	0	1	3	.250	0	0	5.49
10 Min. YEARS		294	101	7	78	844.2	3640	671	441	339	53	27	27	20	461	11	772	97	10	43	49	.467	2	14	3.61
4 Maj. YEARS		131	0	0	37	183.1	789	168	87	79	21	7	5	3	86	9	154	18	1	10	6	.625	0	3	3.88

Toby Rumfield

Bats: Right Throws: Right Pos: C-1B Ht: 6'3" Wt: 190 Born: 9/4/72 Age: 27

Year Team	Lg Org	G	AB	H	2B	3B	HR	TB	R	RBI	TBB	IBB	SO	HBP	SH	SF	SB	CS	SB%	GDP	Avg	OBP	SLG
1991 Princeton	R+ Cin	59	226	62	13	3	3	90	22	30	9	0	43	5	2	3	1	7	.13	6	.274	.313	.398
1992 Billings	R+ Cin	66	253	68	15	3	4	101	34	50	7	0	34	4	0	4	5	2	.71	4	.269	.295	.399
1993 Chstn-WV	A Cin	97	333	75	20	1	5	112	36	50	26	1	74	3	0	4	6	4	.60	7	.225	.284	.336
1994 Winston-Sal	A+ Cin	123	462	115	11	4	29	221	79	88	48	1	107	2	0	7	2	3	.40	9	.249	.318	.478
1995 Chattanooga	AA Cin	92	273	72	12	1	8	110	32	53	26	2	47	3	3	5	0	3	.00	14	.264	.329	.403
1996 Chattanooga	AA Cin	113	304	102	23	1	3	150	40	50	07	1	51	0	0	0	2	1	.07	10	.000	.061	.100
1997 Chattanooga	AA Cin	101	331	95	22	1	5	134	35	38	18	3	32	2	4	2	0	1	.00	12	.287	.326	.405
1998 Greenville	AA Atl	125	462	134	32	0	10	196	61	66	43	1	67	3	1	8	9	4	.69	17	.290	.349	.424
1999 Richmond	AAA Atl	111	383	105	23	1	15	175	57	62	31	1	57	6	2	2	1	2	.33	13	.274	.336	.457
9 Min. YEARS		887	3087	828	173	15	88	1295	405	490	245	10	512	34	15	41	26	27	.49	94	.268	.325	.420

244

Tony Runion

Pitches: Right **Bats:** Right **Pos:** P   **Ht:** 6'3" **Wt:** 229 **Born:** 12/6/71 **Age:** 28

Year Team	Lg Org	G	GS	CG	GF	IP	BFP	H	R	ER	HR	SH	SF	HB	TBB	IBB	SO	WP	Bk	W	L	Pct.	ShO	Sv	ERA
		HOW MUCH HE PITCHED						WHAT HE GAVE UP												THE RESULTS					
1993 Watertown	A- Cle	4	1	0	0	8	38	7	9	6	0	1	1	0	9	0	8	4	1	0	1	.000	0	0	6.75
Burlington	R+ Cle	3	2	0	0	12	47	10	4	4	1	1	0	0	6	0	6	2	0	0	0	.000	0	0	3.00
1994 Columbus	A Cle	35	8	1	7	119	486	89	40	33	5	4	0	11	39	3	140	10	0	8	6	.571	0	2	2.50
1995 Kinston	A+ Cle	28	24	0	2	143	599	131	70	65	9	2	6	13	57	0	84	10	0	7	11	.389	0	0	4.09
1996 Kinston	A+ Cle	6	1	0	2	14	71	16	10	9	0	1	0	3	14	0	11	3	0	1	1	.500	0	0	5.79
Bakersfield	A+ Cle	7	6	1	0	35.2	197	61	56	45	5	2	2	3	27	0	20	9	0	0	6	.000	0	0	11.36
1997 Fargo-Mh	IND —	11	0	0	3	21.1	90	25	9	9	2	2	1	0	5	1	22	0	0	1	1	.500	0	1	3.80
Sioux Falls	IND —	26	0	0	15	33.2	151	36	16	15	3	4	0	2	12	0	26	1	0	7	2	.778	0	2	4.01
1998 Lynchburg	A+ Pit	36	0	0	15	57	239	49	21	19	5	4	1	6	20	2	72	7	0	5	8	.385	0	4	3.00
Carolina	AA Pit	7	0	0	6	9.1	47	11	7	5	0	1	0	0	7	1	11	1	1	1	2	.333	0	0	4.82
1999 Altoona	AA Pit	31	0	0	8	42.2	184	52	23	17	3	2	3	1	9	0	39	4	1	1	4	.200	0	2	3.59
7 Min. YEARS		194	42	2	58	495.2	2149	487	265	227	33	24	14	39	205	7	439	51	3	31	42	.425	0	11	4.12

Chad Rupp

Bats: Right **Throws:** Right **Pos:** OF   **Ht:** 6'2" **Wt:** 225 **Born:** 9/30/71 **Age:** 28

Year Team	Lg Org	G	AB	H	2B	3B	HR	TB	R	RBI	TBB	IBB	SO	HBP	SH	SF	SB	CS	SB%	GDP	Avg	OBP	SLG
		BATTING															BASERUNNING				PERCENTAGES		
1993 Elizabethtn	R+ Min	67	228	56	14	1	10	102	54	36	44	2	79	9	1	4	0	1	.00	2	.246	.382	.447
1994 Fort Wayne	A Min	85	257	63	20	0	15	128	46	50	50	0	79	4	0	7	2	0	1.00	5	.245	.368	.498
1995 Fort Myers	A+ Min	107	376	100	23	1	12	161	44	52	38	1	77	2	0	3	14	3	.82	10	.266	.334	.428
1996 Hardware Cy	A+ Min	77	278	70	14	0	18	138	38	48	13	0	56	4	3	5	3	2	.60	8	.252	.290	.496
1997 Salt Lake	AAA Min	117	426	116	19	7	32	245	77	94	49	1	112	7	3	6	2	1	.67	10	.272	.352	.575
1998 Salt Lake	AAA Min	115	413	120	25	3	20	211	78	89	61	4	105	6	1	8	8	3	.73	3	.291	.383	.511
1999 Salt Lake	AAA Min	37	119	23	3	0	7	47	18	18	17	0	48	2	0	3	3	0	1.00	4	.193	.298	.395
Dunedin	A+ Tor	4	13	4	2	0	1	9	4	7	5	0	4	0	0	0	0	0	.00	0	.308	.500	.692
Knoxville	AA Tor	67	241	62	19	2	16	133	49	44	44	0	73	2	0	0	7	2	.78	1	.257	.376	.552
7 Min. YEARS		676	2351	614	139	14	131	1174	408	438	321	8	633	36	8	36	39	12	.76	38	.261	.354	.499

Paul Russo

Bats: Right **Throws:** Right **Pos:** 1B   **Ht:** 5'11" **Wt:** 215 **Born:** 8/26/69 **Age:** 30

Year Team	Lg Org	G	AB	H	2B	3B	HR	TB	R	RBI	TBB	IBB	SO	HBP	SH	SF	SB	CS	SB%	GDP	Avg	OBP	SLG
		BATTING															BASERUNNING				PERCENTAGES		
1990 Elizabethtn	R+ Min	62	221	74	9	3	22	155	58	67	38	5	56	1	0	2	4	1	.80	3	.335	.431	.701
1991 Kenosha	A Min	125	421	114	20	3	20	200	60	100	64	4	105	7	0	10	4	1	.80	5	.271	.369	.475
1992 Orlando	AA Min	126	420	107	13	2	22	190	63	74	48	0	122	1	2	5	0	0	.00	17	.255	.329	.452
1993 Portland	AAA Min	83	288	81	24	2	10	139	43	47	29	0	69	0	0	6	0	1	.00	10	.281	.341	.483
1994 Salt Lake	AAA Min	35	115	34	7	0	3	50	18	17	12	0	28	2	0	3	0	3	.00	4	.296	.364	.435
Nashville	AA Min	82	299	68	14	3	10	118	43	40	31	1	77	3	3	0	1	0	1.00	11	.227	.306	.395
1995 Memphis	AA SD	45	122	38	9	1	6	67	19	18	22	1	33	1	0	0	1	0	1.00	3	.311	.421	.549
Las Vegas	AAA SD	44	148	44	10	0	4	66	17	19	9	2	31	0	1	2	0	1	.00	4	.297	.333	.446
1996 Las Vegas	AAA SD	80	226	57	15	2	4	88	16	33	23	1	53	1	0	2	2	1	.67	7	.252	.321	.389
1997 Columbus	AAA NYY	9	22	3	0	0	2	9	3	4	5	0	6	0	0	0	0	0	.00	2	.136	.296	.409
1998 New Orleans	AAA Hou	93	268	68	15	1	12	121	33	44	30	1	55	4	3	4	0	0	.00	10	.254	.333	.451
1999 New Orleans	AAA Hou	48	133	35	6	0	4	53	19	18	21	0	28	0	0	0	1	0	1.00	8	.263	.364	.398
10 Min. YEARS		832	2683	723	142	17	119	1256	392	481	332	15	663	20	9	34	13	8	.62	84	.269	.350	.468

Brian Rust

Bats: Right **Throws:** Right **Pos:** 1B-3B   **Ht:** 6'2" **Wt:** 205 **Born:** 8/1/74 **Age:** 25

Year Team	Lg Org	G	AB	H	2B	3B	HR	TB	R	RBI	TBB	IBB	SO	HBP	SH	SF	SB	CS	SB%	GDP	Avg	OBP	SLG
		BATTING															BASERUNNING				PERCENTAGES		
1995 Eugene	A- Atl	53	157	32	7	1	4	53	18	19	7	0	43	2	2	2	2	1	.67	2	.204	.244	.338
1996 Macon	A Atl	7	9	1	0	0	0	1	2	2	2	0	2	0	0	0	0	0	.00	0	.111	.273	.111
Eugene	A- Atl	71	275	79	24	3	10	139	52	43	20	2	74	3	0	0	4	2	.67	4	.287	.342	.505
1997 Durham	A+ Atl	122	430	111	29	2	12	180	67	71	43	0	104	3	1	5	10	4	.71	8	.258	.326	.419
1998 Greenville	AA Atl	95	265	68	19	1	9	116	43	39	35	2	93	4	1	2	10	1	.91	5	.257	.350	.438
1999 Delmarva	A Bal	21	77	20	9	1	1	34	11	16	6	1	27	0	1	3	0	0	.00	5	.260	.302	.442
Frederick	A+ Bal	9	27	4	1	0	0	5	7	1	5	0	7	2	0	0	0	0	.00	0	.148	.324	.185
Bowie	AA Bal	52	149	46	11	0	4	69	24	21	17	0	29	3	2	3	2	0	1.00	3	.309	.384	.463
Rochester	AAA Bal	1	3	0	0	0	0	0	0	1	0	0	0	0	0	1	0	0	.00	0	.000	.000	.000
5 Min. YEARS		431	1392	361	100	8	40	597	224	213	135	5	379	17	7	16	28	8	.78	27	.259	.329	.429

Mark Rutherford

Pitches: Right **Bats:** Right **Pos:** P   **Ht:** 6'2" **Wt:** 211 **Born:** 11/9/74 **Age:** 25

Year Team	Lg Org	G	GS	CG	GF	IP	BFP	H	R	ER	HR	SH	SF	HB	TBB	IBB	SO	WP	Bk	W	L	Pct.	ShO	Sv	ERA
		HOW MUCH HE PITCHED						WHAT HE GAVE UP												THE RESULTS					
1997 Batavia	A- Phi	3	2	0	0	12	47	10	5	1	0	0	1	0	3	0	11	3	0	2	1	.667	0	0	0.75
Piedmont	A Phi	9	9	0	0	58.1	225	42	17	16	4	2	0	1	9	0	47	3	0	1	4	.200	0	0	2.47
1998 Clearwater	A+ Phi	18	18	0	0	119	452	94	40	35	11	3	3	5	20	0	71	3	1	8	5	.615	0	0	2.65
1999 Clearwater	A+ Phi	9	9	0	0	46	228	64	57	47	6	2	6	2	25	3	23	1	1	0	4	.000	0	0	9.20
Reading	AA Phi	4	4	0	0	18.1	72	11	3	2	1	0	0	0	9	0	10	1	0	1	0	1.000	0	0	0.98
3 Min. YEARS		43	42	0	0	253.2	1024	221	122	101	22	7	10	8	66	3	162	11	2	12	14	.462	0	0	3.58

Matt Ryan

Pitches: Right Bats: Right Pos: P
Ht: 6'5" Wt: 190 Born: 3/20/72 Age: 28

Year Team	Lg Org	G	GS	CG	GF	IP	BFP	H	R	ER	HR	SH	SF	HB	TBB	IBB	SO	WP	Bk	W	L	Pct.	ShO	Sv	ERA
1993 Pirates	R Pit	9	0	0	5	19.1	81	17	8	5	0	1	0	1	9	0	20	0	0	1	1	.500	0	2	2.33
Welland	A- Pit	16	0	0	12	17.1	84	11	10	3	0	0	1	1	12	1	25	5	0	0	1	.000	0	5	1.56
1994 Augusta	A Pit	34	0	0	31	41	174	33	14	6	0	1	0	4	7	1	49	0	0	2	1	.667	0	13	1.32
Salem	A+ Pit	25	0	0	16	28.1	120	27	12	6	0	3	0	2	8	1	13	2	0	2	2	.500	0	7	1.91
1995 Calgary	AAA Pit	5	0	0	4	4.2	20	5	1	1	0	0	0	1	1	1	2	0	0	0	0	.000	0	1	1.93
Carolina	AA Pit	44	0	0	38	46	188	33	10	8	0	4	0	2	19	2	23	3	0	2	1	.667	0	26	1.57
1996 Calgary	AAA Pit	51	0	0	44	52.2	259	70	39	31	4	3	1	6	28	8	35	6	0	2	6	.250	0	24	5.30
1997 Carolina	AA Pit	48	0	0	39	52.2	229	32	18	13	2	4	1	12	21	4	43	9	0	4	3	.571	0	14	2.22
1998 Nashville	AAA Pit	51	6	0	10	86.1	384	85	50	40	2	5	1	6	36	8	41	17	1	4	3	.571	0	3	4.17
1999 Nashville	AAA Pit	48	6	0	20	79.1	357	87	48	39	7	1	2	6	35	1	52	2	0	6	5	.545	0	8	4.42
7 Min. YEARS		331	12	0	219	427.2	1896	400	210	152	15	22	6	41	176	27	303	44	1	23	23	.500	0	99	3.20

Derek Ryder

Bats: Right Throws: Right Pos: C
Ht: 6'1" Wt: 190 Born: 3/30/73 Age: 27

Year Team	Lg Org	G	AB	H	2B	3B	HR	TB	R	RBI	TBB	IBB	SO	HBP	SH	SF	SB	CS	SB%	GDP	Avg	OBP	SLG
1995 Cedar Rapds	A Ana	17	21	2	0	0	0	2	1	2	5	0	7	0	3	0	0	1	.00	1	.095	.269	.095
1996 Cedar Rapds	A Ana	62	153	36	5	2	0	45	11	11	21	0	31	2	6	1	0	2	.00	5	.235	.333	.294
1997 Lk Elsinore	A+ Ana	36	91	21	5	2	1	33	12	13	8	0	17	0	3	1	1	2	.33	1	.231	.290	.363
Midland	AA Ana	25	78	18	2	0	0	20	4	6	2	0	6	0	1	1	1	0	1.00	2	.231	.247	.256
1998 Newburgh	IND —	1	4	2	0	0	0	2	0	0	0	0	1	0	0	0	0	0	.00	0	.500	.500	.500
Newburgh	IND —	91	299	69	6	2	1	82	26	28	15	0	33	1	8	2	3	2	.60	5	.231	.268	.274
1999 Birmingham	AA CWS	12	27	4	1	0	0	5	4	2	2	0	3	1	1	0	0	0	.00	0	.148	.233	.185
Winston-Sal	A+ CWS	39	120	25	4	0	0	29	11	8	5	0	17	1	3	2	0	3	.00	2	.208	.242	.242
5 Min. YEARS		283	793	177	23	6	2	218	69	70	58	0	115	5	25	7	5	10	.33	16	.223	.278	.275

Matt Sachse

Bats: Left Throws: Left Pos: OF
Ht: 6'4" Wt: 205 Born: 6/29/76 Age: 24

Year Team	Lg Org	G	AB	H	2B	3B	HR	TB	R	RBI	TBB	IBB	SO	HBP	SH	SF	SB	CS	SB%	GDP	Avg	OBP	SLG
1995 Everett	A- Sea	59	191	44	6	0	1	53	34	14	29	1	76	4	2	1	5	4	.56	3	.230	.342	.277
1996 Everett	A- Sea	67	237	56	9	1	5	82	24	27	14	2	94	2	1	1	4	2	.67	6	.236	.282	.346
1997 Wisconsin	A Sea	110	373	100	21	3	6	145	37	51	26	1	110	2	1	2	5	3	.63	10	.268	.318	.389
1998 Lancaster	A+ Sea	86	285	76	16	4	8	124	51	45	41	1	77	0	2	4	4	4	.50	6	.267	.355	.435
1999 New Haven	AA Sea	27	97	11	1	0	1	15	12	4	10	0	36	0	1	0	1	2	.33	3	.113	.196	.155
Tacoma	AAA Sea	11	35	7	1	0	0	8	2	0	4	0	13	0	2	0	1	0	1.00	0	.200	.282	.229
Lancaster	A+ Sea	69	236	72	18	2	7	115	40	41	33	0	67	1	1	1	5	4	.56	1	.305	.391	.487
5 Min. YEARS		429	1454	366	72	10	28	542	200	182	157	5	473	9	10	10	25	19	.57	29	.252	.326	.373

A.J. Sager

Pitches: Right Bats: Right Pos: P
Ht: 6'4" Wt: 220 Born: 3/3/65 Age: 35

Year Team	Lg Org	G	GS	CG	GF	IP	BFP	H	R	ER	HR	SH	SF	HB	TBB	IBB	SO	WP	Bk	W	L	Pct.	ShO	Sv	ERA
1988 Spokane	A- SD	15	15	2	0	98.2	443	123	67	56	3	2	5	4	27	1	74	3	2	8	3	.727	0	0	5.11
1989 Chston-SC	A SD	26	25	6	0	167.2	708	166	77	63	4	4	5	7	40	1	105	10	1	14	9	.609	2	0	3.38
1990 Wichita	AA SD	26	26	2	0	154.1	686	200	105	94	7	8	4	3	29	0	79	3	3	11	12	.478	1	0	5.48
1991 Wichita	AA SD	10	10	1	0	65.1	275	69	35	30	5	3	2	0	16	0	31	1	0	4	3	.571	0	0	4.13
Las Vegas	AAA SD	18	13	3	0	109	458	127	63	57	5	1	4	1	20	3	61	4	1	7	5	.583	2	0	4.71
1992 Las Vegas	AAA SD	30	3	0	7	60	282	89	57	53	8	0	4	1	17	3	40	3	2	1	7	.125	0	1	7.95
1993 Wichita	AA SD	11	11	2	0	73.1	298	69	30	26	5	3	3	1	16	0	49	1	0	5	3	.625	1	0	3.19
Las Vegas	AAA SD	21	11	2	3	90	379	91	49	37	7	5	2	5	18	1	58	5	2	6	5	.545	1	1	3.70
1994 Las Vegas	AAA SD	23	2	0	13	40.2	180	57	24	20	3	1	0	1	8	3	23	1	0	1	4	.200	0	5	4.43
1995 Colo Sprngs	AAA Col	23	22	1	0	133.2	564	153	61	52	14	4	3	2	23	1	60	0	0	8	5	.615	1	0	3.50
1996 Toledo	AAA Det	18	2	0	6	37.2	149	38	14	11	5	0	0	1	3	0	24	0	1	1	0	1.000	0	0	2.63
1998 Toledo	AAA Det	14	0	0	5	24	107	27	8	8	1	1	1	0	13	1	16	0	0	1	2	.333	0	1	3.00
1999 Reds	R Cin	1	1	0	0	2	9	4	1	1	0	0	0	0	0	0	1	0	0	0	1	.000	0	0	4.50
Indianapolis	AAA Cin	24	7	0	6	52	254	79	45	27	5	3	4	1	25	1	18	0	1	6	3	.667	0	0	4.67
1994 San Diego	NL	22	3	0	4	46.2	217	62	34	31	4	6	2	2	16	5	26	0	0	1	4	.200	0	0	5.98
1995 Colorado	NL	10	0	0	2	14.2	70	19	16	12	1	2	0	0	7	1	10	0	0	0	0	.000	0	0	7.36
1996 Detroit	AL	22	9	0	1	79	347	91	46	44	10	3	3	2	29	2	52	1	0	4	5	.444	0	0	5.01
1997 Detroit	AL	38	1	0	8	84	350	81	43	39	10	5	6	1	24	6	53	0	0	3	4	.429	0	3	4.18
1998 Detroit	AL	31	3	0	7	59.1	274	79	47	43	7	5	1	1	23	4	23	4	0	4	2	.667	0	2	6.52
11 Min. YEARS		260	153	19	40	1108.1	4792	1292	636	535	72	35	37	27	255	15	659	31	13	73	62	.541	8	8	4.34
5 Maj. YEARS		123	16	0	22	283.2	1258	332	186	169	32	21	13	6	99	18	164	5	0	12	15	.444	0	5	5.36

Marc Sagmoen

Bats: Left Throws: Left Pos: OF
Ht: 5'11" Wt: 185 Born: 4/16/71 Age: 29

Year Team	Lg Org	G	AB	H	2B	3B	HR	TB	R	RBI	TBB	IBB	SO	HBP	SH	SF	SB	CS	SB%	GDP	Avg	OBP	SLG
1993 Erie	A- Tex	6	23	1	1	0	0	10	6	2	3	0	7	1	0	1	0	0	.00	0	.304	.393	.435
Chston-SC	A Tex	63	234	69	13	4	6	108	44	34	23	0	39	3	3	3	16	4	.80	2	.295	.361	.462
1994 Charlotte	A+ Tex	122	475	139	25	10	3	193	74	47	37	2	56	3	1	3	15	10	.60	15	.293	.346	.406
1995 Okla City	AAA Tex	56	188	42	11	3	3	68	20	25	16	0	31	2	1	4	5	2	.71	2	.223	.286	.362
Tulsa	AA Tex	63	242	56	8	5	6	92	36	22	23	0	23	4	1	2	5	4	.56	2	.231	.306	.380
1996 Tulsa	AA Tex	96	387	109	21	6	10	172	58	62	33	4	58	0	0	7	5	8	.38	7	.282	.336	.444

246

			BATTING															BASERUNNING				PERCENTAGES		
Year Team	Lg Org	G	AB	H	2B	3B	HR	TB	R	RBI	TBB	IBB	SO	HBP	SH	SF	SB	CS	SB%	GDP	Avg	OBP	SLG
Okla City	AAA Tex	32	116	34	6	0	5	55	16	16	4	0	20	1	0	1	1	0	1.00	0	.293	.320	.474
1997 Okla City	AAA Tex	111	418	110	32	6	5	169	47	44	26	4	95	1	1	2	4	3	.57	10	.263	.306	.404
1998 Oklahoma	AAA Tex	113	403	108	26	6	14	188	61	65	35	0	86	4	3	3	6	2	.75	7	.268	.330	.467
1999 Oklahoma	AAA Tex	83	268	73	11	3	13	129	42	43	24	3	58	0	1	1	3	2	.60	7	.272	.331	.481
1997 Texas	AL	21	43	6	2	0	1	11	2	4	2	0	13	0	0	1	0	0	.00	1	.140	.174	.256
7 Min. YEARS		745	2754	747	154	44	65	1184	404	360	224	13	473	21	11	27	60	35	.63	52	.271	.328	.430

Matt Saier

Pitches: Right **Bats:** Right **Pos:** P   **Ht:** 6'2" **Wt:** 190 **Born:** 1/29/73 **Age:** 27

		HOW MUCH HE PITCHED						WHAT HE GAVE UP										THE RESULTS					
Year Team	Lg Org	G	GS	CG	GF	IP	BFP	H	R	ER	HR	SH	SF	HB	TBB	IBB	SO	WP	Bk	W	L	Pct.	ShO	Sv	ERA
1995 Spokane	A- KC	16	0	0	9	35.1	138	24	14	13	2	2	1	2	12	0	41	4	0	1	2	.333	0	4	3.31
1996 Wilmington	A+ KC	26	26	0	0	134	585	136	74	60	9	4	0	6	52	2	129	9	2	9	9	.500	0	0	4.03
1997 Wilmington	A+ KC	9	9	0	0	42.2	173	31	11	8	4	0	2	0	15	0	47	2	0	2	2	.500	0	0	1.69
Wichita	AA KC	17	17	0	0	101	452	112	66	55	6	5	4	7	48	4	53	7	0	7	5	.583	0	0	4.90
1998 Omaha	AAA KC	9	9	0	0	48.2	232	73	46	45	13	1	2	2	16	0	25	0	0	2	4	.333	0	0	8.32
Wichita	AA KC	18	18	0	0	103	463	127	70	59	14	3	3	5	28	1	80	8	1	9	5	.643	0	0	5.16
1999 Wichita	AA KC	19	19	0	0	109.2	484	137	64	61	11	4	6	3	34	2	61	6	0	9	7	.563	0	0	5.01
Omaha	AAA KC	9	9	1	0	58.1	255	69	37	33	13	0	1	1	8	0	44	1	0	4	4	.500	0	0	5.09
5 Min. YEARS		123	107	1	9	632.2	2782	709	382	334	72	19	19	26	213	9	480	37	3	43	38	.531	0	4	4.75

Bobby St. Pierre

Pitches: Right **Bats:** Right **Pos:** P   **Ht:** 6'1" **Wt:** 190 **Born:** 4/11/74 **Age:** 26

		HOW MUCH HE PITCHED						WHAT HE GAVE UP										THE RESULTS					
Year Team	Lg Org	G	GS	CG	GF	IP	BFP	H	R	ER	HR	SH	SF	HB	TBB	IBB	SO	WP	Bk	W	L	Pct.	ShO	Sv	ERA
1995 Oneonta	A- NYY	15	15	0	0	89	368	83	39	28	4	1	4	2	24	0	91	4	2	5	3	.625	0	0	2.83
1996 Tampa	A+ NYY	29	22	0	3	140	579	133	69	50	8	5	3	6	38	1	107	7	2	12	6	.667	0	1	3.21
1997 Tampa	A+ NYY	27	3	0	7	51.1	225	66	27	22	5	3	1	1	18	4	37	0	0	3	5	.375	0	1	3.86
1998 Norwich	AA NYY	24	0	0	6	38	175	46	23	17	1	1	3	3	15	1	26	1	0	4	2	.667	0	0	4.03
Tampa	A+ NYY	16	0	0	4	30	146	46	26	23	4	0	2	2	12	2	21	2	0	0	0	.000	0	0	6.90
1999 Akron	AA Cle	4	0	0	3	4	25	9	8	8	1	0	0	0	4	0	2	0	0	0	0	.000	0	0	18.00
Newark	IND —	20	17	5	0	122.2	510	112	57	49	20	3	3	4	41	0	71	1	0	8	6	.571	0	0	3.60
5 Min. YEARS		135	57	5	23	475	2028	495	249	197	43	13	16	18	152	8	355	15	4	32	22	.593	0	2	3.73

Mike Saipe

Pitches: Right **Bats:** Right **Pos:** P   **Ht:** 6' 1" **Wt:** 188 **Born:** 9/10/73 **Age:** 26

		HOW MUCH HE PITCHED						WHAT HE GAVE UP										THE RESULTS					
Year Team	Lg Org	G	GS	CG	GF	IP	BFP	H	R	ER	HR	SH	SF	HB	TBB	IBB	SO	WP	Bk	W	L	Pct.	ShO	Sv	ERA
1994 Bend	A- Col	16	16	0	0	84.1	363	73	52	39	7	3	4	7	34	0	74	6	2	3	7	.300	0	0	4.16
1995 Salem	A+ Col	21	9	0	7	85.1	347	68	35	33	7	1	1	2	32	4	90	9	1	4	5	.444	0	3	3.48
1996 New Haven	AA Col	32	19	1	5	138	562	114	53	47	12	4	3	4	42	6	126	4	4	10	7	.588	1	3	3.07
1997 New Haven	AA Col	19	19	4	0	136.2	550	127	57	47	18	3	1	5	29	2	123	4	1	8	5	.615	2	0	3.10
Colo Sprngs	AAA Col	10	10	1	0	60.1	278	74	42	37	10	1	0	4	24	3	40	2	3	4	3	.571	0	0	5.52
1998 Colo Sprngs	AAA Col	24	24	2	0	139.2	632	167	96	80	19	3	5	8	51	1	124	4	0	5	11	.313	0	0	5.16
1999 Colo Sprngs	AAA Col	11	11	0	0	54	232	62	36	29	11	0	4	1	20	0	39	3	0	1	5	.167	0	0	4.83
1998 Colorado	NL	2	2	0	0	10	54	22	12	12	5	1	0	2	0	0	2	0	0	0	1	.000	0	0	10.80
6 Min. YEARS		133	108	8	12	698.1	2964	685	371	312	84	15	18	31	232	16	616	32	13	35	43	.449	3	6	4.02

Rich Saitta

Bats: Right **Throws:** Right **Pos:** SS   **Ht:** 5'10" **Wt:** 170 **Born:** 7/28/75 **Age:** 24

			BATTING															BASERUNNING				PERCENTAGES		
Year Team	Lg Org	G	AB	H	2B	3B	HR	TB	R	RBI	TBB	IBB	SO	HBP	SH	SF	SB	CS	SB%	GDP	Avg	OBP	SLG
1996 Yakima	A- LA	44	165	41	5	0	1	49	17	17	11	0	34	2	2	1	7	5	.58	5	.248	.302	.297
1997 Yakima	A- LA	44	183	57	13	2	1	77	37	15	14	0	27	2	1	1	6	2	.75	0	.311	.365	.421
Great Falls	R+ LA	16	58	14	3	0	0	17	4	4	2	0	9	0	0	0	0	1	.00	0	.241	.267	.293
1998 San Berndno	A+ LA	121	446	132	17	7	5	178	62	51	52	1	92	3	4	4	23	17	.58	6	.296	.370	.399
Albuquerque	AAA LA	5	16	1	0	0	0	1	1	0	0	0	5	0	0	0	0	0	.00	0	.063	.063	.063
1999 San Antonio	AA LA	91	254	74	11	4	2	99	25	34	8	0	43	1	1	2	7	4	.64	3	.291	.313	.390
4 Min. YEARS		321	1122	319	49	13	9	421	146	121	87	1	210	8	8	8	43	29	.60	14	.284	.338	.375

Jim Sak

Pitches: Right **Bats:** Right **Pos:** P   **Ht:** 6'1" **Wt:** 195 **Born:** 8/18/73 **Age:** 26

		HOW MUCH HE PITCHED						WHAT HE GAVE UP										THE RESULTS					
Year Team	Lg Org	G	GS	CG	GF	IP	BFP	H	R	ER	HR	SH	SF	HB	TBB	IBB	SO	WP	Bk	W	L	Pct.	ShO	Sv	ERA
1995 Idaho Falls	R+ SD	13	0	0	0	32.2	123	15	9	6	1	1	0	0	12	1	55	1	1	3	1	.750	0	1	1.65
Clinton	A SD	7	7	3	0	50	200	42	12	11	2	1	2	0	14	0	37	0	3	6	1	.857	0	0	1.98
1996 Rancho Cuca	A+ SD	4	4	0	0	15.2	78	21	13	11	2	1	0	2	12	0	14	0	0	0	3	.000	0	0	6.32
Clinton	A SD	21	7	0	6	65.2	291	46	31	26	2	4	2	4	45	1	72	4	0	3	4	.429	0	0	3.56
1997 Rancho Cuca	A+ SD	57	3	0	50	70.2	286	42	28	23	5	1	3	5	30	2	113	4	1	6	3	.667	0	27	2.93
1998 Mobile	AA SD	45	0	0	43	49	212	33	29	28	3	0	2	1	36	3	56	5	0	2	5	.286	0	16	5.14
1999 Mobile	AA SD	18	0	0	5	26.2	106	15	11	5	1	0	2	0	15	0	37	1	0	4	1	.800	0	2	1.69
Las Vegas	AAA SD	23	0	0	17	27.2	121	22	11	11	5	0	1	3	17	0	32	2	0	2	2	.500	0	6	3.58
5 Min. YEARS		188	21	3	124	338	1417	236	144	121	21	8	12	15	181	7	416	17	5	26	20	.565	0	52	3.22

John Salamon

Pitches: Right **Bats:** Right **Pos:** P **Ht:** 6'1" **Wt:** 220 **Born:** 3/30/72 **Age:** 28

Year Team	Lg Org	G	GS	CG	GF	IP	BFP	H	R	ER	HR	SH	SF	HB	TBB	IBB	SO	WP	Bk	W	L	Pct.	ShO	Sv	ERA
1993 Augusta	A Pit	47	0	0	14	61	282	43	37	24	1	5	5	9	42	2	59	5	2	1	2	.333	0	1	3.54
1994 Beloit	A Mil	33	0	0	17	48	219	27	17	14	2	2	3	4	52	0	54	5	1	3	1	.750	0	6	2.63
1995 New Haven	AA Col	6	0	0	0	10.1	54	9	7	7	0	1	2	0	16	1	9	1	0	1	0	1.000	0	0	6.10
Salem	A+ Col	8	0	0	4	14.2	60	13	10	10	5	0	0	0	5	0	9	0	0	1	0	1.000	0	1	6.14
1996 Madison	IND —	37	0	0	28	50.2	230	47	13	13	1	5	1	4	38	2	40	4	0	3	1	.750	0	7	2.31
1997 Madison	IND —	26	0	0	20	37.1	173	37	31	28	9	5	1	0	22	2	42	4	1	3	4	.429	0	7	6.75
Winnipeg	IND —	12	0	0	12	13.2	64	14	9	9	3	0	0	1	8	1	14	4	0	3	1	.750	0	2	5.93
1998 New Haven	AA Col	53	0	0	17	72	351	65	48	45	8	4	2	7	66	2	72	22	0	2	3	.400	0	1	5.63
1999 Greenville	AA Atl	28	1	0	5	42.1	207	42	41	39	7	4	3	2	42	2	41	6	2	2	4	.333	0	1	8.29
Lehigh Vly	IND —	8	0	0	1	11.1	52	11	6	4	1	0	1	0	8	0	9	1	0	1	0	1.000	0	0	3.18
Tampa	A+ NYY	2	0	0	1	1.2	11	3	2	0	0	0	0	0	2	0	2	0	0	0	0	.000	0	0	0.00
7 Min. YEARS		260	1	0	119	363	1703	311	221	193	37	26	18	27	301	12	351	52	6	20	16	.556	0	26	4.79

Roger Salkeld

Pitches: Right **Bats:** Right **Pos:** P **Ht:** 6' 5" **Wt:** 215 **Born:** 3/6/71 **Age:** 29

Year Team	Lg Org	G	GS	CG	GF	IP	BFP	H	R	ER	HR	SH	SF	HB	TBB	IBB	SO	WP	Bk	W	L	Pct.	ShO	Sv	ERA
1909 Dellingham	A Sea	8	6	0	1	42	168	27	17	6	0	0	1	4	10	0	55	3	3	2	2	.500	0	0	1.29
1990 San Berndno	A+ Sea	25	25	2	0	153.1	677	140	77	58	3	7	1	3	83	0	167	9	2	11	5	.688	0	0	3.40
1991 Jacksnville	AA Sea	23	23	5	0	153.2	634	131	56	52	9	5	5	10	55	1	159	12	2	8	8	.500	0	0	3.05
Calgary	AAA Sea	4	4	0	0	19.1	90	18	16	11	2	1	0	4	13	0	21	1	0	2	1	.667	0	0	5.12
1993 Jacksnville	AA Sea	14	14	0	0	77	334	71	39	28	8	3	5	5	29	1	56	2	1	4	3	.571	0	0	3.27
1994 Calgary	AAA Sea	13	13	0	0	67.1	315	74	54	46	11	0	5	4	39	2	54	5	0	3	7	.300	0	0	6.15
1995 Tacoma	AAA Sea	4	3	0	1	15	59	8	4	3	0	0	0	0	7	0	11	0	0	1	0	1.000	0	1	1.80
Indianapls	AAA Cin	20	20	1	0	119.1	497	96	60	56	13	3	4	2	57	1	86	3	0	12	2	.857	0	0	4.22
1997 Indianapls	AAA Cin	36	11	0	7	88	421	91	75	66	16	2	2	5	60	2	88	6	0	4	8	.333	0	1	6.75
1998 New Orleans	AAA Hou	37	11	0	9	82.1	391	82	57	53	8	4	6	3	64	1	79	9	0	3	6	.333	0	2	5.79
1999 Calgary	AAA Fla	27	2	0	10	35	159	37	21	18	5	0	3	2	20	1	32	4	0	1	1	.500	0	1	4.63
1993 Seattle	AL	3	2	0	0	14.1	61	13	4	4	0	0	0	1	4	0	13	0	0	0	0	.000	0	0	2.51
1994 Seattle	AL	13	13	0	0	59	291	76	47	47	7	0	3	1	45	1	46	2	0	2	5	.286	0	0	7.17
1996 Cincinnati	NL	29	19	1	2	116	509	114	69	67	18	10	3	6	54	2	82	7	1	8	5	.615	1	0	5.20
9 Min. YEARS		211	132	8	28	852.1	3745	775	476	397	75	25	32	42	437	9	808	54	8	51	43	.543	0	5	4.19
3 Maj. YEARS		45	34	1	2	189.1	861	203	120	118	25	10	6	8	103	3	141	9	1	10	10	.500	1	0	5.61

Cody Salter

Pitches: Right **Bats:** Right **Pos:** P **Ht:** 6'4" **Wt:** 200 **Born:** 10/8/75 **Age:** 24

Year Team	Lg Org	G	GS	CG	GF	IP	BFP	H	R	ER	HR	SH	SF	HB	TBB	IBB	SO	WP	Bk	W	L	Pct.	ShO	Sv	ERA
1998 Butte	R+ Ana	9	5	3	2	48.2	209	48	21	19	3	0	0	3	10	0	31	0	0	4	2	.667	0	0	3.51
1999 Lk Elsinore	A+ Ana	7	2	0	0	22	98	27	12	12	0	0	0	2	8	1	9	3	1	1	0	1.000	0	0	4.91
Erie	AA Ana	27	3	0	8	52.2	238	65	29	24	2	2	1	4	14	0	16	3	1	6	2	.750	0	0	4.10
2 Min. YEARS		43	10	3	10	123.1	545	140	62	55	5	2	1	9	32	1	56	6	2	11	4	.733	0	0	4.01

Jeremy Salyers

Pitches: Right **Bats:** Right **Pos:** P **Ht:** 6'3" **Wt:** 205 **Born:** 1/31/76 **Age:** 24

Year Team	Lg Org	G	GS	CG	GF	IP	BFP	H	R	ER	HR	SH	SF	HB	TBB	IBB	SO	WP	Bk	W	L	Pct.	ShO	Sv	ERA
1996 Expos	R Mon	11	9	2	1	57	246	47	36	27	4	3	1	8	26	0	30	1	0	1	4	.200	0	1	4.26
1997 Vermont	A- Mon	16	14	0	0	77.1	346	87	53	43	4	3	6	5	31	0	32	6	2	3	4	.429	0	0	5.00
1998 Cape Fear	A Mon	42	2	0	18	71.2	310	70	41	30	8	5	1	8	23	0	32	8	2	4	4	.500	0	3	3.77
1999 Cape Fear	A Mon	22	7	0	6	63	257	62	22	16	3	3	2	3	18	0	37	2	0	2	3	.400	0	1	2.29
Ottawa	AAA Mon	1	1	0	0	6	24	6	2	1	0	1	0	0	2	0	2	1	0	0	0	.000	0	0	1.50
Harrisburg	AA Mon	12	1	0	8	25.2	105	20	9	8	1	1	0	2	11	0	9	1	0	1	0	1.000	0	0	2.81
4 Min. YEARS		104	34	2	33	300.2	1288	292	163	125	20	16	10	26	111	0	142	19	4	11	15	.423	0	5	3.74

Jerry Salzano

Bats: Right **Throws:** Right **Pos:** 3B **Ht:** 6'0" **Wt:** 175 **Born:** 10/27/74 **Age:** 25

Year Team	Lg Org	G	AB	H	2B	3B	HR	TB	R	RBI	TBB	IBB	SO	HBP	SH	SF	SB	CS	SB%	GDP	Avg	OBP	SLG
1992 Brewers	R Mil	51	177	43	5	0	0	48	18	20	23	0	31	4	2	3	1	3	.25	4	.243	.338	.271
1993 Helena	R+ Mil	66	227	59	12	2	1	78	30	18	25	0	39	3	4	2	6	3	.67	2	.260	.339	.344
1994 Beloit	A Mil	19	57	10	2	0	0	12	10	1	7	0	12	4	0	0	1	3	.25	2	.175	.309	.211
Williamsprt	A- ChC	75	283	80	15	3	2	107	37	15	15	0	44	8	1	2	5	5	.50	4	.283	.334	.378
1995 Williamsprt	A- ChC	62	218	65	13	2	0	82	28	23	22	0	28	4	0	1	4	3	.57	6	.298	.371	.376
Rockford	A ChC	6	21	6	1	1	0	9	0	2	1	0	1	0	0	0	0	1	.00	1	.286	.318	.429
1996 Lakeland	A+ Det	128	420	110	20	1	9	167	59	50	38	0	66	9	2	4	7	46	10	.265	.335	.392
1997 Lakeland	A+ Det	40	135	30	4	1	2	42	20	8	22	2	27	2	1	0	1	1	.50	1	.222	.340	.311
Durham	A+ Atl	68	226	63	20	0	1	86	29	24	26	2	42	12	2	1	6	4	.60	10	.279	.381	.381
1998 Greenville	AA Atl	101	324	98	19	3	7	144	48	49	46	1	67	8	2	2	14	8	.64	8	.302	.400	.444
1999 Indianapols	AAA Cin	7	11	1	0	0	0	1	0	2	0	0	6	0	0	1	0	0	.00	0	.091	.083	.091
Chattanooga	AA Cin	72	263	86	19	1	4	119	44	38	39	1	38	5	2	4	14	10	.58	5	.327	.418	.452
8 Min. YEARS		690	2368	654	138	17	23	895	312	282	264	6	401	59	16	20	58	48	.55	53	.276	.360	.378

248

Nelson Samboy

Bats: Right **Throws:** Right **Pos:** OF-2B **Ht:** 5'10" **Wt:** 165 **Born:** 9/4/76 **Age:** 23

								BATTING										BASERUNNING				PERCENTAGES		
Year Team	Lg Org	G	AB	H	2B	3B	HR	TB	R	RBI	TBB	IBB	SO	HBP	SH	SF	SB	CS	SB%	GDP	Avg	OBP	SLG
1995 Astros	R Hou	55	192	60	12	2	1	79	39	22	26	0	19	3	4	1	21	8	.72	4	.313	.401	.411
1996 Kissimmee	A+ Hou	105	372	94	20	2	0	118	43	21	20	1	61	1	3	1	17	7	.71	7	.253	.292	.317
1997 Kissimmee	A+ Hou	48	190	60	9	2	1	76	20	13	7	0	34	2	2	0	9	6	.60	5	.316	.347	.400
Astros	R Hou	2	5	2	0	0	0	2	1	1	1	0	0	0	0	0	0	0	.00	0	.400	.500	.400
Quad City	A Hou	14	51	18	3	0	0	21	2	8	2	0	8	0	1	0	1	1	.50	0	.353	.377	.412
1998 Kissimmee	A+ Hou	124	527	150	31	4	3	198	73	45	37	0	71	1	0	3	40	15	.73	10	.285	.331	.376
1999 Jackson	AA Hou	45	170	51	9	0	0	60	20	14	11	0	14	0	1	1	6	5	.55	1	.300	.341	.353
5 Min. YEARS		393	1507	435	84	10	5	554	198	124	104	1	207	7	11	6	94	42	.69	27	.289	.336	.368

Alex Sanchez

Bats: Left **Throws:** Left **Pos:** OF **Ht:** 5'10" **Wt:** 179 **Born:** 8/26/76 **Age:** 23

								BATTING										BASERUNNING				PERCENTAGES		
Year Team	Lg Org	G	AB	H	2B	3B	HR	TB	R	RBI	TBB	IBB	SO	HBP	SH	SF	SB	CS	SB%	GDP	Avg	OBP	SLG
1996 Devil Rays	R TB	56	227	64	7	6	1	86	36	22	10	0	35	6	1	1	20	12	.63	2	.282	.328	.379
1997 Chston-SC	A TB	131	537	155	15	6	0	182	73	34	37	2	72	3	12	4	92	40	.70	7	.289	.336	.339
1998 St. Pete	A+ TB	128	545	180	17	9	1	218	77	50	31	1	70	1	4	12	66	33	.67	5	.330	.360	.400
1999 Orlando	AA TB	121	500	127	12	4	2	153	68	29	26	1	88	0	10	2	48	27	.64	8	.254	.290	.306
Durham	AAA TB	3	10	2	1	0	0	3	2	1	0	0	0	0	0	0	0	0	.00	0	.200	.273	.300
4 Min. YEARS		439	1819	528	52	25	4	642	256	135	105	4	265	10	27	19	226	112	.67	22	.290	.329	.353

Martin Sanchez

Pitches: Right **Bats:** Right **Pos:** P **Ht:** 6'2" **Wt:** 180 **Born:** 1/19/77 **Age:** 23

				HOW MUCH HE PITCHED						WHAT HE GAVE UP									THE RESULTS				
Year Team	Lg Org	G	GS	CG	GF	IP	BFP	H	R	ER	HR	SH	SF	HB	TBB	IBB	SO	WP	Bk	W	L	Pct.	ShO	Sv	ERA
1996 Macon	A Atl	31	13	0	6	106.2	483	109	60	47	8	3	4	9	53	1	92	10	0	5	5	.500	0	1	3.97
1997 Kane County	A Fla	51	0	0	44	54	237	40	31	27	2	4	0	5	32	2	57	11	0	3	5	.375	0	22	4.50
1998 High Desert	A+ Ari	35	0	0	32	44.1	189	36	16	15	7	3	1	3	21	1	35	7	1	3	0	1.000	0	11	3.05
South Bend	A Ari	9	0	0	8	11.1	53	14	11	11	3	1	0	0	3	0	14	2	0	1	0	1.000	0	4	8.74
1999 El Paso	AA Ari	42	9	0	21	97	434	95	57	42	10	4	4	6	41	1	73	7	0	4	4	.500	0	6	3.90
4 Min. YEARS		168	22	0	111	313.1	1396	294	175	142	30	15	9	23	150	5	271	40	1	16	14	.533	0	42	4.08

Victor Sanchez

Bats: Right **Throws:** Right **Pos:** 1B **Ht:** 5'10" **Wt:** 180 **Born:** 9/20/71 **Age:** 28

								BATTING										BASERUNNING				PERCENTAGES		
Year Team	Lg Org	G	AB	H	2B	3B	HR	TB	R	RBI	TBB	IBB	SO	HBP	SH	SF	SB	CS	SB%	GDP	Avg	OBP	SLG
1994 Auburn	A- Hou	58	219	63	15	0	3	87	33	35	13	1	40	4	0	1	0	1	.00	7	.288	.338	.397
1995 Quad City	A Hou	13	34	8	0	0	0	8	3	1	6	0	10	0	0	0	1	0	1.00	2	.235	.350	.235
Kissimmee	A+ Hou	78	272	73	11	0	7	105	34	38	23	1	69	8	1	4	6	3	.67	6	.268	.339	.386
1996 Jackson	AA Hou	86	210	46	9	0	13	94	30	34	15	0	58	4	0	0	4	1	.80	7	.219	.284	.448
1997 Jackson	AA Hou	69	175	37	4	0	8	65	22	35	23	1	42	2	1	1	1	2	.33	5	.211	.308	.371
1998 Jackson	AA Hou	117	439	121	29	1	23	221	65	80	21	1	100	4	1	4	4	3	.57	12	.276	.312	.503
1999 Jackson	AA Hou	125	407	102	18	0	17	171	61	68	40	3	93	7	0	3	11	9	.55	17	.251	.326	.420
6 Min. YEARS		546	1756	450	86	1	71	751	248	291	141	7	412	29	3	13	27	19	.59	56	.256	.320	.428

Yuri Sanchez

Bats: Left **Throws:** Right **Pos:** SS **Ht:** 6'1" **Wt:** 165 **Born:** 11/11/73 **Age:** 26

								BATTING										BASERUNNING				PERCENTAGES		
Year Team	Lg Org	G	AB	H	2B	3B	HR	TB	R	RBI	TBB	IBB	SO	HBP	SH	SF	SB	CS	SB%	GDP	Avg	OBP	SLG
1992 Bristol	R+ Det	36	102	18	2	2	0	24	11	5	21	0	41	0	1	0	5	3	.63	1	.176	.317	.235
1993 Fayetteville	A Det	111	340	69	7	6	0	88	53	30	73	0	125	2	7	3	20	9	.69	3	.203	.344	.259
1994 Lakeland	A+ Det	89	254	59	5	5	1	77	41	19	39	0	75	4	5	1	21	8	.72	6	.232	.342	.303
Trenton	AA Det	28	78	16	2	2	0	22	7	2	11	0	25	0	2	0	4	1	.80	0	.205	.303	.282
1995 Jacksnville	AA Det	121	342	73	8	7	6	113	52	26	38	0	116	1	15	0	15	6	.71	3	.213	.294	.330
1996 Visalia	A+ Det	18	59	14	1	0	3	24	9	6	7	0	19	0	3	0	1	1	.50	0	.237	.318	.407
Winston-Sal	A+ Cin	100	353	76	15	3	5	112	48	39	43	0	103	0	10	3	9	6	.60	10	.215	.298	.317
Indianapols	AAA Cin	1	4	0	0	0	0	0	0	0	0	0	0	0	0	0	0	0	.00	0	.000	.000	.000
1997 Burlington	A Cin	101	364	93	12	12	13	168	66	48	35	0	116	0	2	1	7	3	.70	9	.255	.320	.462
1998 Binghamton	AA NYM	93	316	82	14	7	3	119	47	26	35	1	95	4	11	0	11	7	.61	4	.259	.341	.377
1999 Binghamton	AA NYM	116	381	88	10	1	5	115	43	30	37	3	135	2	5	4	6	5	.55	3	.231	.300	.302
8 Min. YEARS		814	2593	588	76	45	36	862	377	231	339	4	852	13	61	12	99	49	.67	39	.227	.318	.332

Frankie Sanders

Pitches: Right **Bats:** Right **Pos:** P **Ht:** 5'11" **Wt:** 165 **Born:** 8/27/75 **Age:** 24

				HOW MUCH HE PITCHED						WHAT HE GAVE UP									THE RESULTS				
Year Team	Lg Org	G	GS	CG	GF	IP	BFP	H	R	ER	HR	SH	SF	HB	TBB	IBB	SO	WP	Bk	W	L	Pct.	ShO	Sv	ERA
1995 Burlington	R+ Cle	12	12	0	0	70	292	48	31	23	2	1	0	3	32	0	80	2	1	3	5	.375	0	0	2.96
Columbus	A Cle	2	0	0	1	9	39	9	3	3	0	1	0	1	4	0	9	1	0	1	1	.500	0	0	3.00
1996 Columbus	A Cle	22	22	0	0	121.1	508	103	52	34	8	3	2	6	37	1	109	13	4	9	3	.750	0	0	2.52
1997 Kinston	A+ Cle	25	25	2	0	146.1	611	130	72	66	10	6	2	2	66	1	127	8	0	11	5	.688	0	0	4.06
1998 Akron	AA Cle	29	29	2	0	186.1	781	175	82	72	15	8	6	11	71	0	108	6	0	11	8	.579	1	0	3.48
1999 Buffalo	AAA Cle	1	1	0	0	5	25	6	5	5	2	0	0	0	0	0	3	0	0	0	1	.000	0	0	9.00
Akron	AA Cle	33	13	0	6	120.2	546	139	72	65	12	6	7	6	51	2	72	9	0	6	6	.500	0	2	4.85
5 Min. YEARS		124	102	7	7	658.2	2802	610	317	268	49	25	17	29	265	4	508	39	5	41	29	.586	1	2	3.66

Jhensy Sandoval

Bats: Right Throws: Right Pos: OF Ht: 6'0" Wt: 200 Born: 9/11/78 Age: 21

Year Team	Lg Org	G	AB	H	2B	3B	HR	TB	R	RBI	TBB	IBB	SO	HBP	SH	SF	SB	CS	SB%	GDP	Avg	OBP	SLG
1996 Diamondbcks	R Ari	38	149	43	11	0	2	60	22	26	7	0	41	1	0	2	1	1	.50	5	.289	.321	.403
1997 South Bend	A Ari	19	72	19	3	0	1	25	9	4	2	0	19	1	0	0	4	3	.57	0	.264	.293	.347
Lethbridge	R+ Ari	40	160	60	14	1	8	100	33	37	8	1	36	3	1	1	7	3	.70	1	.375	.413	.625
1998 High Desert	A+ Ari	107	398	110	20	2	5	149	49	53	15	0	129	4	1	3	10	10	.50	7	.276	.307	.374
1999 El Paso	AA Ari	34	126	28	6	1	1	39	10	23	7	0	42	1	1	1	1	1	.50	3	.222	.267	.310
4 Min. YEARS		238	905	260	54	4	17	373	123	143	39	1	267	10	3	7	23	18	.56	16	.287	.322	.412

Pedro Santana

Bats: Right Throws: Right Pos: 2B Ht: 5'11" Wt: 160 Born: 9/21/76 Age: 23

Year Team	Lg Org	G	AB	H	2B	3B	HR	TB	R	RBI	TBB	IBB	SO	HBP	SH	SF	SB	CS	SB%	GDP	Avg	OBP	SLG
1996 Astros	R Hou	56	207	56	6	5	1	75	40	20	21	1	44	4	2	0	33	4	.89	3	.271	.349	.362
1997 W Michigan	A Det	74	287	75	10	6	3	106	36	28	14	0	55	6	3	0	20	3	.87	8	.261	.309	.369
1998 W Michigan	A Det	118	438	115	21	7	4	162	79	45	28	0	93	9	4	5	64	7	.90	4	.263	.317	.370
1999 Jacksnville	AA Det	120	512	143	35	6	5	205	89	49	34	0	98	3	8	5	34	9	.79	8	.279	.325	.400
4 Min. YEARS		368	1444	389	72	24	13	548	244	142	97	1	290	22	17	10	151	23	.87	23	.269	.323	.380

Victor Santos

Pitches: Right Bats: Right Pos: P Ht: 6'3" Wt: 175 Born: 10/2/76 Age: 23

Year Team	Lg Org	G	GS	CG	GF	IP	BFP	H	R	ER	HR	SH	SF	HB	TBB	IBB	SO	WP	Bk	W	L	Pct.	ShO	Sv	ERA
1996 Tigers	R Det	9	9	0	0	50	199	44	12	11	1	3	1	7	13	0	39	3	0	3	2	.600	0	0	1.98
Lakeland	A+ Det	5	4	0	0	28.1	114	19	11	7	2	2	1	4	9	0	25	2	0	1	1	.500	0	0	2.22
1997 Lakeland	A+ Det	26	26	4	0	145	623	136	74	52	10	4	6	6	59	1	108	12	1	10	5	.667	2	0	3.23
1998 Toledo	AAA Det	5	3	0	1	14.2	80	24	22	18	5	0	0	1	10	0	12	0	0	1	2	.333	0	0	11.05
Jacksnville	AA Det	16	15	0	1	100.1	408	88	38	28	9	5	2	3	24	1	74	3	0	5	2	.714	0	1	2.51
Lakeland	A+ Det	6	6	0	0	36.2	159	40	20	17	2	1	3	1	15	1	37	1	0	4	2	.667	0	0	4.17
1999 Jacksnville	AA Det	28	28	2	0	173	722	150	86	67	16	1	5	7	58	2	146	3	0	12	6	.667	1	0	3.49
4 Min. YEARS		95	91	6	2	548	2305	501	263	200	45	16	18	29	188	5	441	24	1	37	21	.638	3	1	3.28

Rob Sasser

Bats: Right Throws: Right Pos: 3B Ht: 6'3" Wt: 205 Born: 3/9/75 Age: 25

Year Team	Lg Org	G	AB	H	2B	3B	HR	TB	R	RBI	TBB	IBB	SO	HBP	SH	SF	SB	CS	SB%	GDP	Avg	OBP	SLG
1993 Braves	R Atl	33	113	27	4	0	0	31	19	7	6	0	25	4	0	2	2	1	.67	1	.239	.296	.274
1994 Idaho Falls	R+ Atl	58	219	50	9	6	2	77	32	26	19	3	58	1	0	1	13	1	.93	3	.228	.292	.352
1995 Danville	R+ Atl	12	47	15	2	1	0	19	8	7	4	1	7	0	0	1	5	1	.83	1	.319	.365	.404
Eugene	A- Atl	57	216	58	9	1	9	96	40	32	23	1	51	3	0	2	14	4	.78	2	.269	.344	.444
1996 Macon	A Atl	135	465	122	35	3	8	187	64	64	65	4	108	5	3	6	38	8	.83	4	.262	.355	.402
1997 Cedar Rapds	A Ana	134	497	135	26	5	17	222	103	77	69	6	92	8	0	3	37	13	.74	11	.272	.367	.447
1998 Charlotte	A+ Tex	4	13	4	2	0	0	6	1	3	3	0	5	0	0	0	1	0	1.00	1	.308	.438	.462
Tulsa	AA Tex	111	417	117	25	2	8	170	57	62	60	0	98	3	1	4	18	12	.60	11	.281	.372	.408
1999 Tulsa	AA Tex	5	19	5	2	0	0	7	3	0	1	0	2	0	0	0	0	0	.00	0	.263	.300	.368
Jacksnville	AA Det	117	424	120	38	1	7	181	60	61	57	1	101	3	0	3	9	5	.64	5	.283	.370	.427
1998 Texas	AL	1	1	0	0	0	0	0	0	0	0	0	0	0	0	0	0	0	.00	0	.000	.000	.000
7 Min. YEARS		666	2430	653	152	19	51	996	387	339	307	16	547	27	4	22	137	45	.75	39	.269	.354	.410

Luis Saturria

Bats: Right Throws: Right Pos: OF Ht: 6'2" Wt: 165 Born: 7/21/76 Age: 23

Year Team	Lg Org	G	AB	H	2B	3B	HR	TB	R	RBI	TBB	IBB	SO	HBP	SH	SF	SB	CS	SB%	GDP	Avg	OBP	SLG
1996 Johnson Cy	R+ StL	57	227	58	7	1	5	82	43	40	24	0	61	7	1	0	12	1	.92	11	.256	.345	.361
1997 Peoria	A StL	122	445	122	19	5	11	184	81	51	44	3	95	3	3	3	23	10	.70	5	.274	.341	.413
1998 Pr William	A+ StL	129	462	136	25	9	12	215	70	73	28	1	104	8	1	7	26	15	.63	12	.294	.341	.465
1999 Arkansas	AA StL	139	484	118	30	4	16	204	66	61	35	1	134	5	2	5	16	8	.67	12	.244	.299	.421
4 Min. YEARS		447	1618	434	81	19	44	685	260	225	131	5	394	23	7	15	77	34	.69	40	.268	.329	.423

Chris Saunders

Bats: Right Throws: Right Pos: 1B Ht: 6'1" Wt: 203 Born: 7/19/70 Age: 29

Year Team	Lg Org	G	AB	H	2B	3B	HR	TB	R	RBI	TBB	IBB	SO	HBP	SH	SF	SB	CS	SB%	GDP	Avg	OBP	SLG
1992 Pittsfield	A- NYM	72	254	64	11	2	2	85	34	32	34	0	50	1	1	5	5	2	.71	5	.252	.337	.335
1993 St. Lucie	A+ NYM	123	456	115	14	4	4	149	45	64	40	4	89	1	1	4	6	7	.46	10	.252	.311	.327
1994 Binghamton	AA NYM	132	499	134	29	0	10	193	68	70	43	0	96	4	2	7	6	6	.50	12	.269	.327	.387
1995 Norfolk	AAA NYM	16	56	13	3	1	3	27	9	10	9	0	19	0	0	0	1	1	.50	1	.000	.000	.100
Binghamton	AA NYM	122	441	114	22	5	8	170	58	66	45	1	98	5	5	7	3	6	.33	7	.259	.329	.385
1996 Binghamton	AA NYM	141	510	152	27	3	17	236	82	105	73	3	88	8	2	11	5	4	.56	11	.298	.387	.463
1997 Binghamton	AA NYM	30	111	36	13	0	3	58	16	22	12	1	20	2	0	4	3	1	.75	2	.324	.388	.523
Norfolk	AAA NYM	68	173	43	9	0	0	52	24	24	37	2	37	2	2	1	2	2	.50	6	.249	.385	.301
1998 Ottawa	AAA Mon	131	478	131	26	2	9	188	58	58	46	1	98	7	0	5	1	1	.50	10	.274	.343	.393
1999 Chattanooga	AA Cin	58	216	68	13	1	7	104	31	35	34	1	42	0	0	5	0	1	.00	6	.315	.400	.481
8 Min. YEARS		893	3194	870	167	18	63	1262	425	483	373	13	633	30	13	49	32	31	.51	70	.272	.349	.395

Rich Sauveur

Pitches: Left   **Bats:** Left   **Pos:** P   **Ht:** 6' 4"   **Wt:** 185   **Born:** 11/23/63   **Age:** 36

Year Team	Lg Org	G	GS	CG	GF	IP	BFP	H	R	ER	HR	SH	SF	HB	TBB	IBB	SO	WP	Bk	W	L	Pct.	ShO	Sv	ERA
1983 Watertown	A- Pit	16	12	1	0	93.2	—	80	41	24	6	—	—	1	31	0	73	2	4	7	5	.583	0	0	2.31
1984 Pr William	A+ Pit	10	10	0	0	54.2	240	43	22	19	5	2	1	1	31	0	54	3	0	3	3	.500	0	0	3.13
Nashua	AA Pit	10	10	2	0	70.2	291	54	27	23	4	4	1	3	34	1	48	2	4	5	3	.625	2	0	2.93
1985 Nashua	AA Pit	25	25	4	0	157.1	666	146	73	62	7	9	6	3	78	2	85	7	4	9	10	.474	2	0	3.55
1986 Nashua	AA Pit	5	5	2	0	38	141	21	5	5	1	1	0	1	11	0	28	1	1	3	1	.750	1	0	1.18
Hawaii	AAA Pit	14	14	6	0	92	391	73	40	31	3	2	0	6	45	1	68	4	8	7	6	.538	1	0	3.03
1987 Harrisburg	AA Pit	30	27	7	0	195	825	174	71	62	9	7	9	9	96	3	160	9	7	13	6	.684	1	0	2.86
1988 Jacksnville	AA Mon	8	0	4	4	6.2	32	7	5	3	0	0	0	0	5	0	8	0	0	0	2	.000	0	1	4.05
Indianapols	AAA Mon	43	3	0	18	81.1	318	60	26	22	8	5	1	1	28	5	58	3	3	7	4	.636	0	10	2.43
1989 Indianapols	AAA Mon	8	0	0	4	9.2	44	10	8	8	1	0	1	0	6	0	8	0	0	0	1	.000	0	1	7.45
1990 Miami	A+ —	11	6	1	2	40.2	178	41	16	15	2	2	0	4	17	0	34	0	3	0	4	.000	0	0	3.32
Indianapols	AAA Mon	14	7	0	0	56	232	45	14	12	1	2	2	3	25	0	24	1	3	2	2	.500	0	0	1.93
1991 Tidewater	AAA NYM	42	0	0	21	45.1	188	31	14	12	0	4	0	0	23	5	49	3	3	2	2	.500	0	6	2.38
1992 Omaha	AAA KC	34	13	1	7	117.1	467	93	54	42	8	3	5	2	39	1	88	4	4	7	6	.538	0	0	3.22
1993 Indianapols	AAA Cin	5	5	0	0	34.2	146	41	10	7	2	2	0	2	7	2	21	0	0	2	0	1.000	0	0	1.82
1994 Indianapols	AAA Cin	53	1	0	30	67	268	47	25	21	7	4	0	1	23	4	65	1	0	3	3	.500	0	12	2.82
1995 Indianapols	AAA Cin	52	0	0	43	57	228	43	17	13	3	1	1	2	18	3	47	3	0	5	2	.714	0	15	2.05
1996 Nashville	AAA CWS	61	3	0	20	73	311	63	34	30	8	2	3	3	28	4	69	3	0	4	3	.571	0	8	3.70
1997 Iowa	AAA ChC	39	1	0	19	45.1	198	46	19	17	4	2	1	3	21	5	37	0	0	1	3	.250	0	2	3.38
1998 Indianapols	AAA Cin	7	0	0	2	9	40	9	8	3	2	0	0	1	4	0	6	0	0	0	0	.000	0	1	3.00
Nashville	AAA Pit	46	0	0	20	44.2	178	34	15	9	0	2	2	1	17	4	43	2	0	1	4	.200	0	10	1.81
1999 Nashville	AAA Pit	53	3	0	18	64.2	272	62	21	14	6	1	0	0	16	5	61	1	0	5	2	.714	0	7	1.95
1986 Pittsburgh	NL	3	3	0	0	12	57	17	8	8	3	1	0	2	6	0	6	0	2	0	0	.000	0	0	6.00
1988 Montreal	NL	4	0	0	0	3	14	3	2	2	1	0	0	0	2	0	3	0	0	0	0	.000	0	0	6.00
1991 New York	NL	6	0	0	0	3.1	19	7	4	4	1	2	0	0	2	0	4	0	0	0	0	.000	0	0	10.80
1992 Kansas City	AL	8	0	0	2	14.1	65	15	7	7	1	0	0	2	8	1	7	0	1	0	1	.000	0	0	4.40
1996 Chicago	AL	3	0	0	0	3	15	3	5	5	1	0	0	1	5	0	1	0	0	0	0	.000	0	0	15.00
17 Min. YEARS		586	145	24	208	1453.2	—	1223	565	454	87	—	—	47	603	45	1134	49	44	86	72	.544	7	73	2.81
5 Maj. YEARS		24	3	0	2	35.2	170	45	26	26	7	3	0	5	23	1	21	0	3	0	1	.000	0	0	6.56

Jamie Saylor

Bats: Left   **Throws:** Right   **Pos:** OF   **Ht:** 5'11"   **Wt:** 185   **Born:** 9/11/74   **Age:** 25

Year Team	Lg Org	G	AB	H	2B	3B	HR	TB	R	RBI	TBB	IBB	SO	HBP	SH	SF	SB	CS	SB%	GDP	Avg	OBP	SLG
1993 Astros	R Hou	51	162	38	5	2	0	47	29	14	23	0	28	0	1	0	5	3	.63	1	.235	.330	.290
1994 Quad City	A Hou	92	321	84	16	2	2	110	57	22	28	2	65	7	7	1	14	5	.74	0	.262	.333	.343
1995 Kissimmee	A+ Hou	89	289	66	4	1	2	78	38	19	22	1	58	6	0	2	13	6	.68	5	.228	.295	.270
1996 Kissimmee	A+ Hou	59	181	37	3	3	1	49	17	6	10	0	43	0	3	2	8	6	.57	3	.204	.244	.271
Quad City	A Hou	23	58	7	1	0	0	8	8	5	3	0	13	2	2	2	4	2	.67	0	.121	.185	.138
1997 Quad City	A Hou	20	61	15	5	0	0	20	10	2	11	1	16	0	1	0	3	2	.60	3	.246	.361	.328
New Orleans	AAA Hou	2	0	0	0	0	0	0	0	0	0	0	0	0	0	0	0	0	.00	0	.000	.000	.000
Jackson	AA Hou	63	205	52	12	3	5	85	23	21	18	1	43	3	3	0	3	2	.60	1	.254	.323	.415
1998 New Orleans	AAA Hou	4	11	4	0	1	1	9	3	3	0	0	0	0	0	0	0	0	.00	0	.364	.364	.818
Jackson	AA Hou	122	462	135	21	6	17	219	80	66	39	1	91	5	7	3	15	10	.60	4	.292	.352	.474
1999 New Orleans	AAA Hou	113	330	74	14	5	4	110	38	36	34	1	83	3	2	4	8	10	.44	6	.224	.299	.333
7 Min. YEARS		638	2080	512	81	23	32	735	303	194	188	7	440	26	27	14	73	46	.61	23	.246	.315	.353

Ryan Saylor

Pitches: Right   **Bats:** Left   **Pos:** P   **Ht:** 5'10"   **Wt:** 175   **Born:** 5/20/75   **Age:** 25

Year Team	Lg Org	G	GS	CG	GF	IP	BFP	H	R	ER	HR	SH	SF	HB	TBB	IBB	SO	WP	Bk	W	L	Pct.	ShO	Sv	ERA
1997 Vermont	A- Mon	16	0	0	14	19	82	17	7	5	0	1	1	1	8	0	29	2	0	3	0	1.000	0	2	2.37
Cape Fear	A Mon	10	0	0	7	14.2	70	17	9	7	2	1	0	0	9	0	19	2	0	2	1	.667	0	1	4.30
1998 Cape Fear	A Mon	24	0	0	22	36.2	143	26	10	10	2	1	1	2	7	0	50	1	0	4	1	.800	0	6	2.45
Jupiter	A+ Mon	27	0	0	20	46	176	32	15	13	3	0	1	1	15	0	45	1	0	2	4	.333	0	7	2.54
1999 Jupiter	A+ Mon	21	0	0	21	22.1	92	15	1	1	1	0	0	0	6	0	21	0	0	1	0	1.000	0	10	0.40
Harrisburg	AA Mon	28	3	0	12	59.2	250	50	28	24	7	3	3	2	24	3	55	3	0	6	1	.857	0	7	3.62
3 Min. YEARS		126	3	0	96	198.1	813	157	70	60	15	6	6	6	69	3	219	9	0	18	7	.720	0	33	2.72

Bob Scanlan

Pitches: Right   **Bats:** Right   **Pos:** P   **Ht:** 6' 7"   **Wt:** 215   **Born:** 8/9/66   **Age:** 33

Year Team	Lg Org	G	GS	CG	GF	IP	BFP	H	R	ER	HR	SH	SF	HB	TBB	IBB	SO	WP	Bk	W	L	Pct.	ShO	Sv	ERA
1984 Phillies	R Phi	13	6	0	2	33.1	173	43	31	24	0	3	2	0	30	0	17	4	1	0	2	.000	0	0	6.48
1985 Spartanburg	A Phi	26	25	4	0	152.1	669	160	95	70	7	3	6	4	53	0	108	8	0	8	12	.400	1	0	4.14
1986 Clearwater	A+ Phi	24	22	5	0	125.2	559	146	73	58	1	6	4	5	45	4	51	4	1	8	12	.400	0	0	4.15
1987 Reading	AA Phi	27	26	3	0	164	718	187	98	93	12	9	9	11	55	3	91	4	1	15	5	.750	1	0	5.10
1988 Maine	AAA Phi	28	27	4	0	161	713	181	110	100	10	13	7	8	50	7	79	17	8	5	18	.217	1	0	5.59
1989 Reading	AA Phi	31	17	4	8	118.1	531	124	88	76	9	3	5	5	58	1	63	12	1	6	10	.375	1	0	5.78
1990 Scranton-WB	AAA Phi	23	23	1	0	130	565	128	79	70	11	3	4	7	59	3	74	3	0	8	11	.421	0	0	4.85
1991 Iowa	AAA ChC	4	3	0	1	18.1	79	14	8	6	0	2	0	0	10	1	15	3	0	2	0	1.000	0	0	2.95
1995 New Orleans	AAA Mil	3	3	0	0	11.2	51	17	7	7	0	0	0	1	3	0	5	1	0	0	1	.000	0	0	5.40
1996 Lakeland	A+ Det	2	2	0	0	9	39	9	6	5	0	1	0	0	3	0	4	2	0	0	1	.000	0	0	5.00
Toledo	AAA Det	14	5	0	3	36	171	46	35	30	5	2	1	3	15	0	18	5	0	1	3	.250	0	0	7.50
Omaha	AAA KC	12	0	0	12	12.1	45	10	2	1	0	0	0	0	3	0	9	0	0	0	0	.000	0	5	0.73
1997 Las Vegas	AAA SD	36	1	0	11	51	218	51	34	20	5	1	0	6	17	1	20	1	0	3	1	.750	0	0	3.53

		HOW MUCH HE PITCHED				WHAT HE GAVE UP								THE RESULTS					
Year Team	Lg Org	G GS CG GF	IP	BFP	H	R	ER	HR	SH	SF	HB	TBB	IBB	SO	WP	Bk	W	L	Pct.	ShO	Sv	ERA
1998 New Orleans	AAA Hou	14 12 1 0	61.1	295	90	50	44	6	3	5	2	24	0	35	2	0	5	4	.556	0	0	6.46
1999 New Orleans	AAA Hou	28 28 2 0	163.2	748	208	116	102	12	6	10	12	55	0	78	11	2	8	15	.348	0	0	5.61
1991 Chicago	NL	40 13 0 16	111	482	114	60	48	5	8	6	3	40	3	44	5	1	7	8	.467	0	1	3.89
1992 Chicago	NL	69 0 0 41	87.1	360	76	32	28	4	4	2	1	30	6	42	6	4	3	6	.333	0	14	2.89
1993 Chicago	NL	70 0 0 13	75.1	323	79	41	38	6	2	6	3	28	7	44	0	2	4	5	.444	0	0	4.54
1994 Milwaukee	AL	30 12 0 9	103	441	117	53	47	11	1	2	4	28	2	65	3	1	2	6	.250	0	2	4.11
1995 Milwaukee	AL	17 14 0 1	83.1	389	101	66	61	9	0	6	7	44	3	29	3	0	4	7	.364	0	0	6.59
1996 Detroit	AL	8 0 0 2	11	57	16	15	13	1	1	0	1	9	1	3	1	0	0	0	.000	0	0	10.64
Kansas City	AL	9 0 0 2	11.1	48	13	4	4	1	0	0	1	3	1	3	0	0	0	1	.000	0	0	3.18
1998 Houston	NL	27 0 0 9	26.1	118	24	12	9	4	3	3	1	13	0	9	5	0	0	1	.000	0	0	3.08
13 Min. YEARS		285 200 24 37	1248	5574	1414	822	706	77	55	53	64	480	20	667	77	14	69	95	.421	4	6	5.09
7 Maj. YEARS		270 39 0 93	508.2	2218	540	283	248	41	19	25	21	195	23	239	23	8	20	34	.370	0	17	4.39

Trevor Schaffer

Pitches: Right **Bats:** Right **Pos:** P **Ht:** 6'3" **Wt:** 210 **Born:** 1/13/74 **Age:** 26

		HOW MUCH HE PITCHED				WHAT HE GAVE UP								THE RESULTS					
Year Team	Lg Org	G GS CG GF	IP	BFP	H	R	ER	HR	SH	SF	HB	TBB	IBB	SO	WP	Bk	W	L	Pct.	ShO	Sv	ERA
1996 Williamsprt	A- ChC	25 0 0 19	32	134	25	6	6	0	3	3	1	16	1	29	0	2	2	0	1.000	0	8	1.69
1997 Rockford	A ChC	46 0 0 42	47.1	206	44	16	13	3	2	0	5	19	2	46	7	0	2	3	.400	0	21	2.47
1998 Dunedin	A+ Tor	47 0 0 21	69.2	325	58	48	36	5	3	6	13	48	4	45	4	0	1	0	1.000	0	2	4.65
1999 Dunedin	A+ Tor	8 0 0 4	13.2	51	8	3	3	0	1	0	0	6	0	10	2	0	3	1	.750	0	1	1.90
Knoxville	AA Tor	38 0 0 19	54	265	69	43	34	10	0	5	3	38	2	23	6	0	1	3	.250	0	1	5.67
4 Min. YEARS		164 0 0 105	216.2	981	204	116	92	18	9	14	22	127	9	153	19	2	8	8	.500	0	32	3.82

Gene Schall

Bats: Right **Throws:** Right **Pos:** 1B **Ht:** 6'3" **Wt:** 201 **Born:** 6/5/70 **Age:** 30

		BATTING														BASERUNNING				PERCENTAGES		
Year Team	Lg Org	G	AB	H	2B	3B	HR	TB	R	RBI	TBB	IBB	SO	HBP	SH	SF	SB	CS	SB%	GDP	Avg	OBP	SLG
1991 Batavia	A- Phi	13	44	15	1	0	2	22	5	8	3	2	16	0	0	0	0	1	.00	1	.341	.383	.500
1992 Spartanburg	A Phi	77	276	74	13	1	8	113	44	41	29	0	52	3	2	2	3	2	.60	8	.268	.342	.409
Clearwater	A+ Phi	40	133	33	4	2	4	53	16	19	14	0	29	4	1	3	1	2	.33	2	.248	.331	.398
1993 Reading	AA Phi	82	285	93	12	4	15	158	51	60	24	0	56	10	0	3	2	1	.67	15	.326	.394	.554
Scranton-WB	AAA Phi	40	139	33	6	1	4	53	16	16	19	1	38	7	1	1	4	2	.67	2	.237	.355	.381
1994 Scranton-WB	AAA Phi	127	463	132	35	4	16	223	54	89	50	5	86	6	0	6	9	1	.90	11	.285	.358	.482
1995 Scranton-WB	AAA Phi	92	320	100	25	4	12	169	52	63	49	2	54	10	0	4	3	3	.50	14	.313	.415	.528
1996 Scranton-WB	AAA Phi	104	371	107	16	5	17	184	66	67	48	2	92	9	0	5	1	0	1.00	9	.288	.379	.496
1997 Nashville	AAA CWS	33	112	22	0	1	5	39	11	17	11	0	32	1	1	0	1	1	.50	1	.196	.274	.348
1998 Richmond	AAA Atl	100	340	102	22	0	22	190	60	73	37	3	80	9	0	6	1	3	.25	5	.300	.378	.559
1999 Richmond	AAA Atl	100	355	104	25	1	12	167	49	53	35	1	84	8	1	3	0	1	.00	7	.293	.367	.470
1995 Philadelphia	NL	24	65	15	2	0	0	17	2	5	6	1	16	1	0	0	0	0	.00	1	.231	.306	.262
1996 Philadelphia	NL	28	66	18	5	1	2	31	7	10	12	0	15	1	0	0	0	0	.00	2	.273	.392	.470
9 Min. YEARS		808	2838	815	159	23	117	1371	424	506	319	16	619	67	6	33	25	17	.60	75	.287	.369	.483
2 Maj. YEARS		52	131	33	7	1	2	40	9	15	18	1	31	2	0	0	0	0	.00	3	.252	.351	.366

Tony Schifano

Bats: Right **Throws:** Right **Pos:** SS **Ht:** 6'1" **Wt:** 195 **Born:** 11/11/74 **Age:** 25

		BATTING														BASERUNNING				PERCENTAGES		
Year Team	Lg Org	G	AB	H	2B	3B	HR	TB	R	RBI	TBB	IBB	SO	HBP	SH	SF	SB	CS	SB%	GDP	Avg	OBP	SLG
1997 Brevard Cty	A+ Fla	1	1	0	0	0	0	0	0	0	0	0	1	0	0	0	0	0	.00	0	.000	.000	.000
Utica	A- Fla	48	153	40	7	0	1	50	26	14	11	0	28	2	8	1	5	5	.50	3	.261	.317	.327
1998 Brevard Cty	A+ Fla	91	304	71	3	4	1	85	28	14	14	0	46	6	4	0	8	1	.89	9	.234	.281	.280
1999 Brevard Cty	A+ Fla	45	141	35	3	1	2	46	21	15	12	0	36	2	3	2	2	2	.50	1	.248	.312	.326
Portland	AA Fla	29	67	16	1	1	0	19	9	6	5	0	9	1	1	0	0	0	.00	3	.239	.301	.284
Knoxville	AA Tor	27	92	25	4	1	0	31	12	15	3	0	15	1	1	1	5	3	.63	3	.272	.299	.337
3 Min. YEARS		241	758	187	18	7	4	231	96	64	45	0	135	12	17	4	20	11	.65	19	.247	.298	.305

Brian Schmack

Pitches: Right **Bats:** Right **Pos:** P **Ht:** 6'2" **Wt:** 195 **Born:** 12/7/73 **Age:** 26

		HOW MUCH HE PITCHED				WHAT HE GAVE UP								THE RESULTS					
Year Team	Lg Org	G GS CG GF	IP	BFP	H	R	ER	HR	SH	SF	HB	TBB	IBB	SO	WP	Bk	W	L	Pct.	ShO	Sv	ERA
1995 Newark	IND —	7 4 0 2	30.1	135	40	21	18	3	5	0	2	10	0	16	1	0	2	1	.667	0	0	5.34
1996 Hickory	A CWS	43 0 0 25	62.1	264	61	24	16	4	9	0	4	16	5	56	3	1	6	4	.600	0	5	2.31
1997 Winston-Sal	A+ CWS	42 0 0 18	75.1	325	65	32	23	0	5	3	2	36	4	71	6	1	5	2	.286	0	6	2.75
1998 Winston-Sal	A+ CWS	42 0 0 34	61.1	256	48	23	15	3	5	0	9	17	0	52	2	1	5	5	.500	0	10	2.20
1999 Birmingham	AA CWS	43 0 0 26	63	270	60	31	24	3	2	1	8	18	0	56	6	0	4	4	.500	0	6	3.43
5 Min. YEARS		177 4 0 105	292.1	1250	274	131	96	13	26	4	25	97	9	251	18	3	19	19	.500	0	27	2.96

Bryan Schmidl

Bats: Right **Throws:** Right **Pos:** 2B **Ht:** 6'2" **Wt:** 180 **Born:** 6/28/75 **Age:** 25

		BATTING														BASERUNNING				PERCENTAGES		
Year Team	Lg Org	G	AB	H	2B	3B	HR	TB	R	RBI	TBB	IBB	SO	HBP	SH	SF	SB	CS	SB%	GDP	Avg	OBP	SLG
1998 Padres	R SD	47	194	56	12	0	0	68	29	22	19	2	28	4	1	4	6	3	.67	3	.289	.357	.351
Idaho Falls	R+ SD	4	14	5	0	0	0	5	5	2	1	0	1	1	0	1	4	0	1.00	0	.357	.412	.357
1999 Mobile	AA SD	17	32	6	1	0	0	7	7	3	5	0	8	0	0	0	0	0	.00	1	.188	.297	.219
Fort Wayne	A SD	67	227	54	7	1	0	63	23	13	20	0	49	5	6	1	2	4	.33	8	.238	.312	.278
2 Min. YEARS		135	467	121	20	1	0	143	64	40	45	2	86	10	7	6	12	7	.63	12	.259	.333	.306

Dave Schmidt

Bats: Left **Throws:** Right **Pos:** C **Ht:** 6'1" **Wt:** 195 **Born:** 10/11/73 **Age:** 26

Year Team	Lg Org	G	AB	H	2B	3B	HR	TB	R	RBI	TBB	IBB	SO	HBP	SH	SF	SB	CS	SB%	GDP	Avg	OBP	SLG
1996 New Jersey	A- StL	57	189	48	9	2	1	64	17	23	16	0	55	0	3	2	1	1	.50	2	.254	.309	.339
1997 Pr William	A+ StL	82	231	45	9	0	0	54	23	19	28	0	66	9	3	1	2	2	.50	9	.195	.305	.234
1998 Arkansas	AA StL	66	183	49	11	1	3	71	23	15	26	5	47	2	2	1	0	0	.00	6	.268	.363	.388
1999 Arkansas	AA StL	48	113	25	4	0	3	38	6	15	11	0	34	2	1	4	1	1	.50	4	.221	.292	.336
4 Min. YEARS		253	716	167	33	3	7	227	69	72	81	5	202	13	9	8	4	4	.50	21	.233	.319	.317

Brian Schneider

Bats: Left **Throws:** Right **Pos:** C **Ht:** 6'1" **Wt:** 180 **Born:** 11/26/76 **Age:** 23

Year Team	Lg Org	G	AB	H	2B	3B	HR	TB	R	RBI	TBB	IBB	SO	HBP	SH	SF	SB	CS	SB%	GDP	Avg	OBP	SLG
1995 Expos	R Mon	30	97	22	3	0	0	25	7	4	14	0	23	1	0	0	2	4	.33	1	.227	.330	.258
1996 Expos	R Mon	52	164	44	5	2	0	53	26	23	24	3	15	3	2	0	2	3	.40	3	.268	.372	.323
Delmarva	A Mon	5	9	3	0	0	0	3	0	1	1	0	1	1	0	0	0	0	.00	1	.333	.455	.333
1997 Cape Fear	A Mon	113	381	96	20	1	4	130	46	49	53	2	45	4	6	5	3	6	.33	9	.252	.345	.341
1998 Cape Fear	A Mon	38	134	40	7	2	7	72	33	30	16	1	9	3	4	2	6	3	.67	3	.299	.381	.537
Jupiter	A+ Mon	82	302	82	12	1	3	105	32	30	22	1	38	1	0	2	4	4	.50	9	.272	.321	.348
1999 Harrisburg	AA Mon	121	421	111	19	1	17	183	48	66	32	2	56	2	3	1	2	2	.50	6	.264	.318	.435
5 Min. YEARS		441	1508	398	66	7	31	571	192	203	162	9	187	15	15	10	19	22	.46	32	.264	.339	.379

Scott Schroeffel

Pitches: Right **Bats:** Both **Pos:** P **Ht:** 6'0" **Wt:** 190 **Born:** 12/30/73 **Age:** 26

		HOW MUCH HE PITCHED						WHAT HE GAVE UP										THE RESULTS				
Year Team	Lg Org	G	GS	CG	GF	IP	BFP	H	R	ER	HR	SH	SF	HB	TBB	IBB	SO	WP	Bk	W	L	Pct.	ShO	Sv	ERA
1996 Portland	A- Col	16	6	0	7	59.2	235	36	15	11	1	2	2	4	17	0	61	4	1	1	1	.500	0	1	1.66
Asheville	A Col	2	2	0	0	11.2	52	10	7	5	0	0	3	1	6	1	15	4	0	1	0	1.000	0	0	3.86
1997 Salem	A+ Col	16	3	0	6	28.2	140	34	27	26	3	1	2	5	17	1	24	0	0	1	4	.200	0	0	8.16
Asheville	A Col	19	2	0	5	45.2	185	31	23	19	5	2	1	4	20	1	40	5	0	2	3	.400	0	0	3.74
1998 Colo Sprngs	AAA Col	1	0	0	0	3.2	16	4	3	3	1	0	1	0	3	0	3	1	0	0	0	.000	0	0	7.36
Salem	A+ Col	38	1	0	12	81.2	368	86	53	43	11	3	3	5	31	1	91	6	1	7	5	.583	0	2	4.74
1999 El Paso	AA Ari	41	1	0	13	64.1	305	75	55	48	9	1	4	6	34	2	52	18	1	5	4	.556	0	2	6.72
4 Min. YEARS		133	15	0	43	295.1	1301	276	183	155	30	9	16	25	128	6	286	38	3	17	17	.500	0	5	4.72

Carl Schutz

Pitches: Left **Bats:** Left **Pos:** P **Ht:** 5'11" **Wt:** 200 **Born:** 8/22/71 **Age:** 28

		HOW MUCH HE PITCHED						WHAT HE GAVE UP										THE RESULTS				
Year Team	Lg Org	G	GS	CG	GF	IP	BFP	H	R	ER	HR	SH	SF	HB	TBB	IBB	SO	WP	Bk	W	L	Pct.	ShO	Sv	ERA
1993 Danville	R+ Atl	13	0	0	9	14.2	57	6	1	1	0	1	0	0	6	0	25	1	0	1	0	1.000	0	4	0.61
Greenville	AA Atl	22	0	0	16	21.1	101	17	17	12	3	2	3	1	22	1	19	2	0	2	1	.667	0	3	5.06
1994 Durham	A+ Atl	53	0	0	47	53.1	240	35	30	29	6	4	1	2	46	1	81	10	0	3	3	.500	0	20	4.89
1995 Greenville	AA Atl	51	0	0	46	58.1	258	53	36	32	4	2	2	1	36	3	56	3	0	3	7	.300	0	26	4.94
1996 Richmond	AAA Atl	41	7	0	13	69.2	320	86	46	41	4	7	4	0	26	3	52	8	0	4	3	.571	0	3	5.30
1997 Richmond	AAA Atl	27	10	0	7	79.1	366	83	56	47	12	1	2	2	51	2	66	6	0	4	6	.400	0	0	5.33
1998 Greenville	AA Atl	33	0	0	13	37	182	41	29	23	3	3	2	0	32	2	33	6	0	1	3	.250	0	4	5.59
West Tenn	AA ChC	13	0	0	3	15	65	6	7	2	0	1	0	0	18	1	10	3	0	1	1	.500	0	1	1.20
1999 West Tenn	AA ChC	40	0	0	12	51.1	239	54	30	25	4	1	4	4	30	2	46	6	0	3	1	.750	0	1	4.38
1996 Atlanta	NL	3	0	0	1	3.1	13	3	1	1	0	0	0	0	2	1	5	0	0	0	0	.000	0	0	2.70
7 Min. YEARS		293	17	0	166	400	1828	381	252	212	36	22	18	10	267	15	388	45	0	22	25	.468	0	61	4.77

Chris Schwab

Bats: Right **Throws:** Left **Pos:** OF **Ht:** 6'3" **Wt:** 215 **Born:** 7/25/74 **Age:** 25

Year Team	Lg Org	G	AB	H	2B	3B	HR	TB	R	RBI	TBB	IBB	SO	HBP	SH	SF	SB	CS	SB%	GDP	Avg	OBP	SLG
1993 Expos	R Mon	56	218	48	12	1	0	62	21	20	22	0	53	0	0	0	0	2	.00	2	.220	.292	.284
1994 Burlington	A Mon	45	163	22	0	0	3	31	6	10	14	0	74	0	0	1	2	0	1.00	6	.135	.202	.190
Expos	R Mon	38	144	29	8	1	3	48	19	22	21	2	44	0	0	1	0	0	.00	0	.201	.301	.333
Vermont	A- Mon	28	103	22	3	0	1	28	14	12	12	0	32	0	1	2	2	1	.67	1	.214	.291	.272
1995 Albany	A Mon	122	484	110	22	3	5	153	60	43	48	1	173	1	0	4	6	4	.60	4	.227	.296	.316
1996 Delmarva	A Mon	119	428	96	30	3	9	159	52	64	45	6	135	1	0	6	3	4	.43	9	.224	.296	.371
1997 Cape Fear	A Mon	54	209	56	19	2	11	112	29	42	26	2	70	1	0	2	3	3	.50	3	.268	.349	.536
Wst Plm Bch	A+ Mon	58	207	39	7	0	9	73	22	28	22	0	82	1	0	3	3	1	.75	1	.188	.266	.353
1998 Jupiter	A+ Mon	120	433	93	19	1	23	183	56	48	40	0	175	1	2	2	7	6	.54	6	.215	.282	.423
Harrisburg	AA Mon	3	4	0	0	0	0	0	0	0	1	0	3	0	0	0	0	0	.00	0	.000	.200	.000
1999 Columbus	A Cle	54	177	51	10	1	9	90	25	26	26	2	54	0	0	0	13	6	.68	4	.288	.379	.508
Akron	AA Cle	2	6	0	0	0	0	0	0	0	1	0	3	0	0	0	0	0	.00	0	.000	.143	.000
Fargo-Mh	IND —	55	197	63	13	0	11	109	36	40	30	1	54	0	0	5	9	4	.69	4	.320	.401	.553
7 Min. YEARS		754	2773	629	143	12	84	1048	340	355	308	14	952	5	3	26	46	33	.58	40	.227	.303	.378

Darryl Scott

Pitches: Right **Bats:** Right **Pos:** P **Ht:** 6'1" **Wt:** 185 **Born:** 8/6/68 **Age:** 31

		HOW MUCH HE PITCHED						WHAT HE GAVE UP										THE RESULTS				
Year Team	Lg Org	G	GS	CG	GF	IP	BFP	H	R	ER	HR	SH	SF	HB	TBB	IBB	SO	WP	Bk	W	L	Pct.	ShO	Sv	ERA
1990 Boise	A- Ana	27	0	0	11	53.2	221	40	11	8	3	0	1	0	19	1	57	5	0	2	1	.667	0	5	1.34
1991 Quad City	A Ana	47	0	0	36	75.1	285	35	18	13	2	2	0	1	26	4	123	9	1	4	3	.571	0	19	1.55
1992 Midland	AA Ana	27	0	0	22	29.2	126	20	9	6	0	2	2	2	14	1	35	4	0	1	1	.500	0	9	1.82

		HOW MUCH HE PITCHED						WHAT HE GAVE UP												THE RESULTS					
Year Team	Lg Org	G	GS	CG	GF	IP	BFP	H	R	ER	HR	SH	SF	HB	TBB	IBB	SO	WP	Bk	W	L	Pct.	ShO	Sv	ERA
Edmonton	AAA Ana	31	0	0	17	36.1	164	41	21	21	1	0	3	0	21	1	48	4	2	0	2	.000	0	6	5.20
1993 Vancouver	AAA Ana	46	0	0	33	51.2	206	35	12	12	4	2	1	1	19	2	57	3	0	7	1	.875	0	15	2.09
1995 Colo Sprngs	AAA Col	59	1	0	27	95.2	429	113	63	50	7	4	7	3	41	1	77	7	0	4	10	.286	0	4	4.70
1996 Buffalo	AAA Cle	50	1	0	30	81	323	61	29	26	11	4	2	0	24	4	73	2	0	3	5	.375	0	9	2.89
1997 Buffalo	AAA Cle	48	0	0	35	65.2	272	52	24	21	10	4	1	0	28	2	29	4	0	5	6	.455	0	12	2.88
1998 Ottawa	AAA Mon	8	0	0	2	11.2	53	12	6	4	1	1	1	0	5	0	7	0	0	0	1	.000	0	2	3.09
Reading	AA Phi	8	0	0	5	11	43	7	4	4	2	1	0	0	2	0	13	1	0	0	1	.000	0	2	3.27
Scranton-WB	AAA Phi	33	0	0	23	39.1	172	37	24	22	8	1	2	1	15	1	37	3	0	4	5	.444	0	10	5.03
1999 Scranton-WB	AAA Phi	57	4	0	30	105.2	456	100	53	48	11	4	2	2	47	4	91	7	0	7	6	.538	0	10	4.09
1993 California	AL	16	0	0	2	20	90	19	13	13	1	0	2	1	11	1	13	2	0	1	2	.333	0	0	5.85
9 Min. YEARS		441	6	0	271	656.2	2750	553	284	235	60	25	22	10	261	27	647	49	3	37	42	.468	0	103	3.22

Tim Scott

Pitches: Right Bats: Right Pos: P Ht: 6' 2" Wt: 205 Born: 11/16/66 Age: 33

		HOW MUCH HE PITCHED						WHAT HE GAVE UP												THE RESULTS					
Year Team	Lg Org	G	GS	CG	GF	IP	BFP	H	R	ER	HR	SH	SF	HB	TBB	IBB	SO	WP	Bk	W	L	Pct.	ShO	Sv	ERA
1984 Great Falls	R+ LA	13	13	3	0	78	0	90	58	38	4	0	0	2	38	1	44	5	2	5	4	.556	2	0	4.38
1985 Bakersfield	A+ LA	12	10	2	1	63.2	0	84	46	41	4	0	0	1	28	0	31	2	4	3	4	.429	0	0	5.80
1986 Vero Beach	A+ LA	20	13	3	2	95.1	418	113	44	36	2	4	9	2	34	2	37	5	5	5	4	.556	1	0	3.40
1987 San Antonio	AA LA	2	2	0	0	5.1	33	14	10	10	2	0	1	1	2	0	6	1	0	0	1	.000	0	0	16.88
Bakersfield	A+ LA	7	5	1	1	32.1	137	33	19	16	2	0	1	1	10	1	29	2	0	2	3	.400	0	0	4.45
1988 Bakersfield	A+ LA	36	2	0	25	64.1	272	52	34	26	3	4	4	2	26	5	59	2	0	4	7	.364	0	7	3.64
1989 San Antonio	AA LA	48	0	0	28	68	308	71	30	28	3	5	3	0	36	5	64	1	4	4	2	.667	0	4	3.71
1990 Albuquerque	AAA LA	17	0	0	8	15	73	14	9	7	1	0	0	0	14	2	15	0	0	2	1	.667	0	0	4.20
San Antonio	AA LA	30	0	0	20	47.1	186	35	17	15	5	0	1	1	14	0	52	0	0	3	3	.500	0	7	2.85
1991 Las Vegas	AAA SD	41	11	0	9	111	497	133	78	64	8	5	2	1	39	8	74	1	0	8	8	.500	0	0	5.19
1992 Las Vegas	AAA SD	24	0	0	23	28	106	20	8	7	1	1	1	1	3	0	28	2	0	1	2	.333	0	15	2.25
1997 Colo Sprngs	AAA Col	12	0	0	9	14.2	52	7	2	2	1	1	1	0	3	0	18	1	1	0	0	.000	0	3	1.23
1998 San Berndno	A+ LA	2	2	0	0	4	15	4	2	2	1	0	0	0	1	0	2	0	0	0	1	.000	0	0	4.50
1999 Sacramento	IND —	17	0	0	17	17	65	11	3	3	1	2	0	0	3	0	23	0	0	1	1	.500	0	6	1.59
Nashville	AAA Pit	19	0	0	7	23	105	29	14	13	3	0	0	2	7	1	21	0	0	1	3	.250	0	0	5.09
1991 San Diego	NL	2	0	0	0	1	5	2	2	1	0	0	0	0	0	0	1	0	0	0	0	.000	0	0	9.00
1992 San Diego	NL	34	0	0	16	37.2	173	39	24	22	4	4	1	1	21	6	30	0	1	4	1	.800	0	0	5.26
1993 San Diego	NL	24	0	0	2	37.2	169	38	13	10	1	2	2	4	15	0	30	1	1	2	0	1.000	0	0	2.39
Montreal	NL	32	0	0	16	34	148	31	15	14	3	1	0	0	19	2	35	1	0	5	2	.714	0	1	3.71
1994 Montreal	NL	40	0	0	8	53.1	223	51	17	16	0	0	0	2	18	3	37	1	1	5	2	.714	0	1	2.70
1995 Montreal	NL	62	0	0	15	63.1	268	52	30	28	6	4	1	6	23	2	57	4	0	2	0	1.000	0	2	3.98
1996 Montreal	NL	45	0	0	14	46.1	198	41	18	16	3	1	2	2	21	2	37	1	0	3	5	.375	0	1	3.11
San Francisco	NL	20	0	0	2	19.2	90	24	18	18	5	3	1	1	9	0	10	2	0	2	2	.500	0	0	8.24
1997 San Diego	NL	14	0	0	2	18.1	87	25	17	16	2	0	1	3	5	0	14	0	0	1	1	.500	0	0	7.85
Colorado	NL	3	0	0	0	2.2	14	5	3	3	0	1	0	0	2	0	2	0	0	0	0	.000	0	0	10.13
12 Min. YEARS		300	58	9	150	667	2267	710	374	308	41	22	22	14	258	25	503	22	16	39	44	.470	3	45	4.16
7 Maj. YEARS		276	0	0	75	314	1375	308	157	144	24	16	8	19	133	15	253	10	3	24	13	.649	0	5	4.13

Marcos Scutaro

Bats: Right Throws: Right Pos: 2B Ht: 5'10" Wt: 170 Born: 10/30/75 Age: 24

		BATTING															BASERUNNING				PERCENTAGES		
Year Team	Lg Org	G	AB	H	2B	3B	HR	TB	R	RBI	TBB	IBB	SO	HBP	SH	SF	SB	CS	SB%	GDP	Avg	OBP	SLG
1996 Columbus	A Cle	85	315	79	12	3	10	127	66	45	38	0	86	4	4	5	6	3	.67	6	.251	.334	.403
1997 Buffalo	AAA Cle	21	57	15	3	0	1	21	8	6	6	0	8	0	1	1	0	1	.00	4	.263	.328	.368
Kinston	A+ Cle	97	378	103	17	6	10	162	58	59	35	0	72	9	2	3	23	7	.77	3	.272	.346	.429
1998 Buffalo	AAA Cle	8	26	6	3	0	0	9	3	4	0	0	2	1	0	0	0	0	.00	0	.231	.231	.346
Akron	AA Cle	124	462	146	27	6	11	218	68	62	47	0	71	10	4	6	33	16	.67	3	.316	.387	.472
1999 Buffalo	AAA Cle	129	462	126	24	2	8	178	76	51	61	2	69	6	6	4	21	6	.78	5	.273	.362	.385
4 Min. YEARS		464	1700	475	86	17	40	715	279	227	187	2	308	29	18	19	83	33	.72	26	.279	.357	.421

Scot Sealy

Bats: Right Throws: Right Pos: C Ht: 6'4" Wt: 225 Born: 2/10/71 Age: 29

		BATTING															BASERUNNING				PERCENTAGES		
Year Team	Lg Org	G	AB	H	2B	3B	HR	TB	R	RBI	TBB	IBB	SO	HBP	SH	SF	SB	CS	SB%	GDP	Avg	OBP	SLG
1992 Gastonia	A Tex	56	175	42	8	0	3	59	16	16	14	0	46	0	0	2	1	2	.33	4	.240	.293	.337
1993 Chston-SC	A Tex	2	7	1	0	0	0	1	0	0	0	0	4	0	0	0	0	0	.00	0	.143	.143	.143
1994 Mobile	IND —	68	203	37	7	0	3	53	24	20	19	—	58	—	—	0	3	2	.60	—	.182	.258	.261
1995 Tacoma	AAA Sea	4	10	3	0	0	0	3	1	0	0	0	0	0	0	0	0	0	.00	0	.300	.300	.300
Riverside	A+ Sea	58	206	50	5	0	2	61	23	30	16	0	36	1	1	1	2	2	.50	0	.243	.299	.296
1996 Lancaster	A+ Sea	75	254	69	22	3	9	124	47	49	41	0	63	8	2	1	3	2	.60	7	.272	.388	.488
Port City	AA Sea	18	59	5	1	0	0	6	2	1	8	0	24	0	1	1	0	2	.00	1	.085	.191	.102
1997 Memphis	AA Sea	45	143	34	9	0	6	61	17	20	15	0	33	4	1	0	1	2	.33	2	.238	.327	.427
Tacoma	AAA Sea	10	55	15	2	0	2	27	8	10	5	0	13	2	0	1	0	1	.00	2	.273	.349	.491
1998 Tacoma	AAA Sea	62	178	48	10	0	5	73	18	28	17	0	54	8	1	2	0	2	.00	4	.270	.356	.410
1999 Tacoma	AAA Sea	67	201	37	4	0	6	59	22	24	20	—	56	6	2	4	0	0	.00	2	.184	.273	.294
8 Min. YEARS		473	1491	341	69	3	37	527	178	198	155	—	387	—	—	—	10	15	.40	—	.229	.312	.353

Bobby Seay

Pitches: Left Bats: Left Pos: P   Ht: 6'2" Wt: 190 Born: 6/20/78 Age: 22

Year Team	Lg Org	G	GS	CG	GF	IP	BFP	H	R	ER	HR	SH	SF	HB	TBB	IBB	SO	WP	Bk	W	L	Pct.	ShO	Sv	ERA
1997 Chston-SC	A TB	13	13	0	0	61.1	269	56	35	31	2	2	2	3	37	0	64	6	0	3	4	.429	0	0	4.55
1998 Chston-SC	A TB	15	15	0	0	69	289	59	40	33	10	3	2	5	29	0	74	7	2	1	7	.125	0	0	4.30
1999 St. Pete	A+ TB	12	11	0	1	57	238	56	25	19	0	2	2	4	23	0	45	2	0	2	6	.250	0	0	3.00
Orlando	AA TB	6	6	0	0	17	85	22	15	15	2	0	1	0	15	0	16	4	2	1	2	.333	0	0	7.94
3 Min. YEARS		46	45	0	1	204.1	881	193	115	98	14	7	7	12	104	0	199	19	4	7	19	.269	0	0	4.32

Jason Secoda

Pitches: Right Bats: Right Pos: P   Ht: 6'1" Wt: 195 Born: 9/2/74 Age: 25

Year Team	Lg Org	G	GS	CG	GF	IP	BFP	H	R	ER	HR	SH	SF	HB	TBB	IBB	SO	WP	Bk	W	L	Pct.	ShO	Sv	ERA
1995 Bristol	R+ CWS	13	12	0	0	65.2	307	78	57	39	3	1	3	1	33	0	63	8	1	2	8	.200	0	0	5.35
1996 South Bend	A CWS	32	22	0	6	133.2	605	132	84	59	9	2	3	3	75	0	94	18	1	6	12	.333	0	1	3.97
1997 Winston-Sal	A+ CWS	29	15	1	5	119.2	525	118	67	55	11	3	5	4	57	1	85	16	1	7	4	.636	0	2	4.14
1998 Winston-Sal	A+ CWS	6	0	0	4	11.1	43	8	2	2	0	1	0	0	2	1	8	1	0	2	0	1.000	0	1	1.59
Birmingham	AA CWS	39	0	0	20	65.1	307	78	50	46	6	2	4	2	39	2	45	7	1	2	3	.400	0	1	6.34
1999 Birmingham	AA CWS	22	17	1	0	115	477	100	49	44	7	2	4	8	39	0	94	8	1	8	7	.533	1	0	3.44
Charlotte	AAA CWS	7	7	3	0	44.1	201	54	35	26	10	0	1	3	10	0	33	4	0	2	5	.286	0	0	5.28
5 Min. YEARS		148	73	5	35	555	2465	568	344	271	46	11	20	21	255	4	422	62	5	29	39	.426	1	4	4.39

Reed Secrist

Bats: Left Throws: Right Pos: C   Ht: 6'1" Wt: 210 Born: 5/7/70 Age: 30

Year Team	Lg Org	G	AB	H	2B	3B	HR	TB	R	RBI	TBB	IBB	SO	HBP	SH	SF	SB	CS	SB%	GDP	Avg	OBP	SLG
1992 Welland	A- Pit	42	117	25	6	0	1	34	16	13	19	0	36	2	2	1	4	3	.57	2	.214	.331	.291
1993 Augusta	A Pit	90	266	71	16	3	6	111	38	47	27	1	43	1	2	4	4	1	.80	10	.267	.332	.417
1994 Salem	A+ Pit	80	221	54	12	0	10	96	29	35	22	0	58	1	1	2	2	2	.50	4	.244	.314	.434
1995 Lynchburg	A+ Pit	112	380	107	18	3	19	188	60	75	54	7	88	3	1	4	3	4	.43	6	.282	.372	.495
1996 Calgary	AAA Pit	128	420	129	30	0	17	210	68	66	52	11	105	4	3	5	2	4	.33	8	.307	.385	.500
1997 Calgary	AAA Pit	40	121	32	7	3	5	60	19	18	14	0	32	0	1	0	0	1	.00	3	.264	.341	.496
1998 Memphis	AAA StL	75	214	46	10	0	6	74	34	29	31	1	57	1	0	3	1	2	.33	3	.215	.313	.346
Knoxville	AA Tor	15	50	12	4	1	2	24	9	8	4	1	14	0	0	0	0	0	.00	2	.240	.296	.480
1999 Altoona	AA Pit	36	95	16	5	0	0	21	9	10	13	1	23	1	1	1	0	0	.00	6	.168	.273	.221
Nashville	AAA Pit	46	102	27	8	1	2	43	12	15	8	1	22	2	1	1	1	1	.50	1	.265	.327	.422
8 Min. YEARS		664	1986	519	116	11	68	861	294	316	244	23	478	15	13	20	17	18	.49	45	.261	.343	.434

Chris Seelbach

Pitches: Right Bats: Right Pos: P   Ht: 6'4" Wt: 180 Born: 12/18/72 Age: 27

Year Team	Lg Org	G	GS	CG	GF	IP	BFP	H	R	ER	HR	SH	SF	HB	TBB	IBB	SO	WP	Bk	W	L	Pct.	ShO	Sv	ERA
1991 Braves	R Atl	4	4	0	0	15	65	13	7	7	3	1	0	0	6	0	19	3	1	0	1	.000	0	0	4.20
1992 Macon	A Atl	27	27	1	0	157.1	662	134	65	58	11	3	5	9	68	0	144	5	1	9	11	.450	0	0	3.32
1993 Durham	A+ Atl	25	25	0	0	131.1	590	133	85	72	15	4	4	7	74	1	112	10	0	9	9	.500	0	0	4.93
1994 Greenville	AA Atl	15	15	2	0	92.2	363	64	26	24	3	5	3	4	38	2	79	5	0	4	6	.400	0	0	2.33
Richmond	AAA Atl	12	11	0	0	61.1	273	68	37	33	6	2	3	0	36	2	35	3	0	3	5	.375	0	0	4.84
1995 Greenville	AA Atl	9	9	1	0	60.1	249	38	15	11	2	5	3	4	30	0	65	3	1	6	0	1.000	1	0	1.64
Richmond	AAA Atl	14	14	1	0	73.1	314	64	39	38	7	0	3	2	39	0	65	3	0	4	6	.400	0	0	4.66
1996 Charlotte	AAA Fla	25	25	1	0	138.1	650	167	123	113	26	2	5	5	76	3	98	9	1	6	13	.316	0	0	7.35
1997 Charlotte	AAA Fla	16	6	0	1	50.1	241	58	36	35	7	3	3	1	34	2	50	3	0	5	0	1.000	0	0	6.26
1998 Tacoma	AAA Sea	6	0	0	4	11.2	57	13	9	8	5	0	0	0	2	0	10	0	0	1	0	1.000	0	0	6.17
Orlando	AA Sea	23	21	0	0	116	500	103	63	52	5	4	6	4	52	0	106	6	1	8	3	.727	0	0	4.03
1999 Greenville	AA Atl	8	6	1	0	39.1	170	31	18	17	5	1	1	2	19	2	47	2	0	3	2	.600	0	0	3.89
Richmond	AAA Atl	13	8	1	2	57.2	255	51	34	33	4	1	1	2	34	1	48	3	0	6	1	.857	0	0	5.15
9 Min. YEARS		197	171	8	7	1004.2	4385	937	557	501	99	31	37	40	508	13	878	55	5	64	57	.529	1	0	4.49

Ryan Seifert

Pitches: Right Bats: Right Pos: P   Ht: 6'5" Wt: 215 Born: 8/14/75 Age: 24

Year Team	Lg Org	G	GS	CG	GF	IP	BFP	H	R	ER	HR	SH	SF	HB	TBB	IBB	SO	WP	Bk	W	L	Pct.	ShO	Sv	ERA
1997 Portland	A- Col	16	15	0	0	74.1	337	89	49	40	8	0	4	4	31	0	52	3	0	1	7	.125	0	0	4.84
1998 Asheville	A Col	36	0	0	19	87.1	363	66	44	40	8	12	4	6	37	0	90	1	0	7	6	.538	0	5	4.12
1999 Colo Sprngs	AAA Col	1	1	0	0	4	18	4	2	2	1	0	0	0	2	0	2	0	0	0	0	.000	0	0	4.50
Salem	A+ Col	24	0	0	5	46.1	196	40	24	18	0	2	2	3	21	0	51	0	0	3	5	.375	0	0	3.50
3 Min. YEARS		77	16	0	24	212	914	199	119	100	17	14	10	13	91	0	195	4	0	11	18	.379	0	5	4.25

Brad Seitzer

Bats: Right Throws: Right Pos: 3B   Ht: 6'2" Wt: 195 Born: 2/2/70 Age: 30

Year Team	Lg Org	G	AB	H	2B	3B	HR	TB	R	RBI	TBB	IBB	SO	HBP	SH	SF	SB	CS	SB%	GDP	Avg	OBP	SLG
1991 Bluefield	R+ Bal	12	45	13	2	0	3	24	5	5	5	0	10	0	0	0	1	1	.50	1	.289	.360	.533
Kane County	A Bal	58	197	55	11	1	2	74	34	28	36	3	36	1	1	1	1	0	1.00	3	.279	.391	.376
1992 Frederick	A+ Bal	129	459	114	21	3	14	183	59	61	38	2	111	7	4	3	2	4	.33	9	.248	.314	.399
1993 Frederick	A+ Bal	130	439	111	24	3	10	171	44	68	58	1	95	5	3	9	3	3	.50	6	.253	.341	.390
1994 Beloit	A Mil	102	343	86	13	0	11	132	45	53	58	1	78	3	6	4	2	2	.50	7	.251	.360	.385
1995 Stockton	A+ Mil	127	428	132	28	3	6	184	66	56	72	2	68	3	2	2	7	4	.64	10	.308	.410	.430

Year Team	Lg Org	G	AB	H	2B	3B	HR	TB	R	RBI	TBB	IBB	SO	HBP	SH	SF	SB	CS	SB%	GDP	Avg	OBP	SLG
1996 El Paso	AA Mil	115	433	138	31	1	17	222	78	87	51	0	67	7	2	5	6	4	.60	9	.319	.395	.513
1997 Tucson	AAA Mil	62	234	74	13	3	9	120	50	42	22	0	33	3	0	4	0	1	1.00	9	.316	.376	.513
Ottawa	AAA Mon	18	56	14	1	0	1	18	4	7	8	0	11	1	0	0	1	2	.33	2	.250	.354	.321
Omaha	AAA KC	21	63	12	3	0	0	15	4	4	5	0	10	0	0	1	0	0	.00	4	.190	.246	.238
Memphis	AA KC	17	70	23	8	1	2	39	14	13	6	0	13	1	0	1	1	0	1.00	4	.329	.385	.557
1998 Tacoma	AAA Sea	129	474	142	35	1	14	221	74	68	68	5	65	9	2	6	4	3	.57	13	.300	.393	.466
1999 Tacoma	AAA Sea	130	474	136	34	1	9	199	80	66	89	2	86	1	2	8	1	2	.33	14	.287	.395	.420
9 Min. YEARS		1050	3715	1050	224	17	98	1602	557	558	516	16	683	41	22	44	29	26	.53	92	.283	.372	.431

Jason Sekany

Pitches: Right Bats: Right Pos: P Ht: 6'4" Wt: 200 Born: 7/20/75 Age: 24

Year Team	Lg Org	G	GS	CG	GF	IP	BFP	H	R	ER	HR	SH	SF	HB	TBB	IBB	SO	WP	Bk	W	L	Pct.	ShO	Sv	ERA
1996 Red Sox	R Bos	5	2	0	2	11.2	50	14	3	3	1	0	0	1	3	0	16	2	0	0	0	.000	0	1	2.31
1997 Michigan	A Bos	16	16	3	0	106	448	92	55	48	5	2	4	4	41	1	103	14	0	5	6	.455	0	0	4.08
Sarasota	A+ Bos	10	9	0	1	64.2	290	56	43	40	8	2	2	2	41	0	32	3	2	4	4	.500	0	0	5.57
1998 Trenton	AA Bos	28	28	1	0	148.2	643	151	101	86	21	4	5	5	57	0	113	14	0	10	10	.500	0	0	5.21
1999 Pawtucket	AAA Bos	1	1	0	0	5.2	27	7	4	3	2	0	0	0	4	0	1	0	0	0	1	.000	0	0	4.76
Trenton	AA Bos	27	22	3	1	161.1	674	143	65	60	8	3	4	6	64	0	116	10	1	14	4	.778	2	0	3.35
4 Min. YEARS		87	78	7	4	498	2132	463	271	240	45	11	15	18	210	1	381	43	3	33	25	.569	2	1	4.34

Bill Selby

Bats: Left Throws: Right Pos: DH Ht: 5' 9" Wt: 190 Born: 6/11/70 Age: 30

Year Team	Lg Org	G	AB	H	2B	3B	HR	TB	R	RBI	TBB	IBB	SO	HBP	SH	SF	SB	CS	SB%	GDP	Avg	OBP	SLG
1992 Elmira	A- Bos	73	275	72	16	1	10	120	38	41	31	6	53	2	2	2	4	4	.50	3	.262	.339	.436
1993 Lynchburg	A+ Bos	113	394	99	22	1	7	144	57	38	24	2	66	3	2	7	1	2	.33	6	.251	.294	.365
1994 Lynchburg	A+ Bos	97	352	109	20	2	19	190	58	69	28	0	62	5	2	2	3	1	.75	7	.310	.367	.540
New Britain	AA Bos	35	107	28	5	0	1	36	15	18	15	0	16	0	0	6	0	1	.00	2	.262	.336	.336
1995 Trenton	AA Bos	117	451	129	29	2	13	201	64	68	46	3	52	3	2	8	4	6	.40	14	.286	.350	.446
1996 Pawtucket	AAA Bos	71	260	66	14	5	11	123	39	47	22	0	39	2	0	4	0	3	.00	5	.254	.313	.473
1998 Akron	AA Cle	20	77	30	7	1	3	48	15	10	3	1	11	1	0	1	0	0	.00	0	.390	.415	.623
Buffalo	AAA Cle	97	334	85	23	0	14	150	45	52	38	7	50	0	0	3	3	0	1.00	6	.254	.328	.449
1999 Buffalo	AAA Cle	122	447	132	32	5	20	234	75	85	51	3	63	2	0	8	4	3	.57	11	.295	.372	.523
1996 Boston	AL	40	95	26	4	0	3	39	12	6	9	1	11	0	1	0	1	1	.50	3	.274	.337	.411
7 Min. YEARS		745	2697	750	168	17	98	1246	406	428	264	22	412	18	8	41	19	20	.49	54	.278	.342	.462

Chip Sell

Bats: Left Throws: Right Pos: OF Ht: 6'2" Wt: 205 Born: 6/19/71 Age: 29

Year Team	Lg Org	G	AB	H	2B	3B	HR	TB	R	RBI	TBB	IBB	SO	HBP	SH	SF	SB	CS	SB%	GDP	Avg	OBP	SLG
1994 Yakima	A- LA	54	172	52	12	3	3	79	29	21	16	1	37	0	1	0	12	3	.00	6	.302	.362	.459
1995 Vero Beach	A+ LA	80	222	60	6	1	1	71	21	23	18	0	33	4	2	2	1	3	.25	5	.270	.333	.320
1996 San Berndno	A+ LA	95	321	90	12	0	1	105	47	23	27	2	68	5	3	1	13	5	.72	6	.280	.345	.327
1997 Vero Beach	A+ LA	111	342	97	21	7	7	153	50	46	29	2	67	4	2	3	25	8	.76	4	.284	.344	.447
1998 Albuquerque	AAA LA	37	136	43	2	2	0	49	22	10	11	0	23	0	1	1	9	6	.60	1	.316	.365	.360
San Antonio	AA LA	64	218	55	12	6	3	88	36	37	22	1	40	3	3	4	6	0	1.00	6	.252	.324	.404
1999 El Paso	AA Ari	92	329	101	16	1	8	143	50	35	20	0	66	3	0	4	19	6	.76	5	.307	.348	.435
Tucson	AAA Ari	30	84	30	5	2	1	42	12	18	3	0	14	3	2	0	4	3	.57	2	.357	.400	.500
6 Min. YEARS		563	1824	528	86	22	24	730	267	213	146	6	348	22	14	15	89	34	.72	35	.289	.347	.400

Tom Sergio

Bats: Left Throws: Right Pos: 2B Ht: 5'9" Wt: 175 Born: 6/27/75 Age: 25

Year Team	Lg Org	G	AB	H	2B	3B	HR	TB	R	RBI	TBB	IBB	SO	HBP	SH	SF	SB	CS	SB%	GDP	Avg	OBP	SLG
1997 Pulaski	R+ Tex	58	226	74	14	4	9	123	57	40	38	0	42	4	1	1	25	6	.81	1	.327	.431	.544
1998 Tulsa	AA Tex	11	39	10	1	1	0	13	7	0	4	0	1	0	0	0	0	0	.00	0	.256	.326	.333
Charlotte	A+ Tex	112	453	133	30	7	5	192	90	39	46	1	59	10	4	3	33	10	.77	6	.294	.364	.424
1999 Tulsa	AA Tex	128	512	149	38	6	10	229	88	72	58	3	59	5	5	4	19	5	.79	6	.291	.366	.447
3 Min. YEARS		309	1230	366	83	18	24	557	242	151	146	4	161	19	10	9	77	21	.79	13	.298	.378	.453

Wascar Serrano

Pitches: Right Bats: Right Pos: P Ht: 6'2" Wt: 178 Born: 7/2/78 Age: 21

Year Team	Lg Org	G	GS	CG	GF	IP	BFP	H	R	ER	HR	SH	SF	HB	TBB	IBB	SO	WP	Bk	W	L	Pct.	ShO	Sv	ERA
1997 Idaho Falls	R+ SD	2	2	0	0	8.1	43	13	12	11	2	0	0	1	4	0	13	0	0	0	1	.000	0	0	11.88
Padres	R SD	12	11	0	1	70.2	001	00	10	0C	1	0	1	1	22	0	75	8	3	6	3	.667	0	1	3.18
Clinton	A SD	1	1	1	0	6	24	6	5	4	0	0	0	0	2	1	2	1	0	1	0	1.000	0	0	6.00
1998 Clinton	A SD	26	26	0	0	156.2	663	150	74	56	6	6	4	6	54	1	143	7	0	9	7	.563	0	0	3.22
1999 Rancho Cuca	A+ SD	21	21	1	0	132.1	537	110	53	49	10	1	5	1	43	0	129	8	5	9	8	.529	1	0	3.33
Mobile	AA SD	7	7	0	0	42.1	196	48	27	26	5	1	3	6	17	1	29	1	1	2	3	.400	0	0	5.53
3 Min. YEARS		69	68	2	1	416.1	1764	387	219	171	27	8	16	18	142	3	391	25	9	26	23	.531	1	1	3.70

Jeff Sexton

Pitches: Right **Bats:** Right **Pos:** P 　　　　**Ht:** 6'2" **Wt:** 190 **Born:** 10/4/71 **Age:** 28

Year Team	Lg Org	G	GS	CG	GF	IP	BFP	H	R	ER	HR	SH	SF	HB	TBB	IBB	SO	WP	Bk	W	L	Pct.	ShO	Sv	ERA
1993 Watertown	A- Cle	17	1	1	9	33.2	145	35	15	10	1	1	0	1	10	3	30	3	0	1	1	.500	1	2	2.67
1994 Watertown	A- Cle	10	0	0	5	23	95	19	3	1	0	1	0	0	7	2	16	3	1	1	0	1.000	0	3	0.39
Columbus	A Cle	14	2	0	6	30	121	17	13	12	2	1	0	3	9	2	35	1	0	1	0	1.000	0	1	3.60
1995 Columbus	A Cle	14	13	2	0	82.1	318	66	27	20	2	1	1	3	16	0	71	1	0	6	2	.750	2	0	2.19
Kinston	A+ Cle	8	8	2	0	57	226	52	17	16	3	0	0	2	7	0	41	6	1	5	1	.833	1	0	2.53
1996 Canton-Akrn	AA Cle	9	9	0	0	49.1	210	45	29	28	6	2	0	2	23	1	34	1	0	2	4	.333	0	0	5.11
1997 Akron	AA Cle	16	3	0	5	47.1	215	55	27	25	4	4	4	5	15	1	38	1	2	2	0	1.000	0	1	4.75
Buffalo	AAA Cle	15	0	0	11	23.2	100	17	14	14	3	1	0	0	12	0	15	2	0	2	1	.667	0	0	5.32
1998 Akron	AA Cle	27	0	0	19	57.1	232	41	12	10	2	2	0	3	19	3	49	2	0	4	2	.667	0	11	1.57
Buffalo	AAA Cle	21	0	0	5	24.1	111	25	16	11	1	2	3	1	15	1	15	3	2	0	0	.000	0	1	4.07
1999 Akron	AA Cle	15	0	0	11	20	89	24	10	8	1	2	1	1	9	0	16	1	0	1	0	1.000	0	2	3.60
Buffalo	AAA Cle	23	1	0	11	29	149	47	24	21	3	1	2	1	14	3	22	3	0	0	1	.000	0	0	6.52
7 Min. YEARS		189	37	5	82	477	2011	443	207	176	28	18	15	22	156	16	382	27	6	25	12	.676	4	21	3.32

Chris Sheff

Bats: Right **Throws:** Right **Pos:** OF 　　　　**Ht:** 6'3" **Wt:** 215 **Born:** 2/4/71 **Age:** 29

Year Team	Lg Org	G	AB	H	2B	3B	HR	TB	R	RBI	TBB	IBB	SO	HBP	SH	SF	SB	CS	SB%	GDP	Avg	OBP	SLG
1992 Erie	A- Fla	57	193	46	8	2	3	67	29	16	32	1	47	1	1	1	15	2	.88	8	.238	.348	.347
1993 Kane County	A Fla	129	456	124	22	5	5	171	79	50	58	2	100	2	3	5	33	10	.77	11	.272	.353	.375
1994 Brevard Cty	A+ Fla	32	118	44	8	3	1	61	21	19	17	0	23	0	0	1	7	2	.78	2	.373	.449	.517
Portland	AA Fla	106	395	101	19	1	5	137	50	30	31	0	76	0	3	2	18	4	.82	13	.256	.308	.347
1995 Portland	AA Fla	131	471	130	25	7	12	205	85	91	72	6	84	5	1	8	23	6	.79	10	.276	.372	.435
1996 Portland	AA Fla	27	105	31	12	2	2	53	16	17	13	3	23	0	0	0	3	2	.60	3	.295	.373	.505
Charlotte	AAA Fla	92	284	75	15	1	12	128	41	49	21	1	55	0	0	1	7	1	.88	10	.264	.314	.451
1997 Charlotte	AAA Fla	120	322	82	23	1	11	140	54	43	43	1	76	1	2	3	16	4	.80	5	.255	.341	.435
1998 Edmonton	AAA Oak	120	402	120	24	4	10	182	74	55	67	0	82	5	0	1	17	5	.77	13	.299	.404	.453
1999 Vancouver	AAA Oak	118	421	121	24	1	15	192	62	70	45	1	87	1	3	3	9	6	.60	15	.287	.355	.456
8 Min. YEARS		932	3167	874	180	27	76	1336	511	440	399	15	653	15	13	25	148	42	.78	90	.276	.357	.422

Scot Shields

Pitches: Right **Bats:** Right **Pos:** P 　　　　**Ht:** 6'1" **Wt:** 175 **Born:** 7/22/75 **Age:** 24

Year Team	Lg Org	G	GS	CG	GF	IP	BFP	H	R	ER	HR	SH	SF	HB	TBB	IBB	SO	WP	Bk	W	L	Pct.	ShO	Sv	ERA
1997 Boise	A- Ana	30	0	0	13	52	225	45	20	17	1	3	2	3	24	4	61	9	1	7	2	.778	0	2	2.94
1998 Cedar Rapds	A Ana	58	0	0	38	74	311	62	33	30	5	5	2	8	29	0	81	9	1	6	5	.545	0	7	3.65
1999 Lk Elsinore	A+ Ana	24	9	2	6	107.1	443	91	37	30	1	4	4	5	39	4	113	6	1	10	3	.769	1	1	2.52
Erie	AA Ana	10	10	1	0	74.2	300	57	26	24	10	4	0	6	26	0	81	2	0	4	4	.500	1	0	2.89
3 Min. YEARS		122	19	3	57	308	1279	255	116	101	17	16	8	22	118	8	336	26	3	27	14	.659	2	10	2.95

Stephen Shoemaker

Pitches: Right **Bats:** Left **Pos:** P 　　　　**Ht:** 6'1" **Wt:** 195 **Born:** 2/3/73 **Age:** 27

Year Team	Lg Org	G	GS	CG	GF	IP	BFP	H	R	ER	HR	SH	SF	HB	TBB	IBB	SO	WP	Bk	W	L	Pct.	ShO	Sv	ERA
1994 Oneonta	A- NYY	12	12	0	0	58.2	262	62	32	28	7	2	1	3	28	0	46	5	1	3	5	.375	0	0	4.30
1995 Greensboro	A NYY	17	17	0	0	81	347	62	33	28	5	2	2	4	52	0	82	4	0	4	4	.500	0	0	3.11
Tampa	A+ NYY	3	2	0	0	16.2	73	9	5	2	1	2	1	0	13	0	12	2	0	1	0	1.000	0	0	1.08
1996 Salem	A+ Col	25	13	0	5	86.1	371	63	49	45	6	1	5	4	63	0	105	1	1	2	7	.222	0	1	4.69
1997 Salem	A+ Col	9	9	1	0	52	215	31	21	16	3	2	1	5	25	0	76	2	3	3	3	.500	0	0	2.77
New Haven	AA Col	14	14	1	0	95.1	389	64	36	32	6	7	3	5	53	3	111	5	1	6	4	.600	0	0	3.02
Colo Sprngs	AAA Col	5	4	0	0	20.1	101	23	19	19	5	0	1	3	17	0	27	1	0	1	1	.500	0	0	8.41
1998 Colo Sprngs	AAA Col	15	12	0	1	62.2	325	80	68	63	7	1	4	2	63	1	56	6	1	2	7	.222	0	0	9.05
New Haven	AA Col	15	15	0	0	84.2	390	69	60	46	7	6	3	5	63	0	85	4	0	3	5	.375	0	0	4.89
1999 Colo Sprngs	AAA Col	16	16	2	0	81	382	100	59	54	8	1	5	5	47	1	46	8	0	4	6	.400	0	0	6.00
6 Min. YEARS		131	114	4	6	638.2	2855	563	382	333	55	22	25	34	424	5	646	38	7	28	43	.394	0	1	4.69

Barry Short

Pitches: Right **Bats:** Right **Pos:** P 　　　　**Ht:** 6'3" **Wt:** 182 **Born:** 12/15/73 **Age:** 26

Year Team	Lg Org	G	GS	CG	GF	IP	BFP	H	R	ER	HR	SH	SF	HB	TBB	IBB	SO	WP	Bk	W	L	Pct.	ShO	Sv	ERA
1994 Mets	R NYM	10	7	0	1	62.1	252	49	21	17	3	1	0	1	19	0	49	9	0	5	2	.714	0	0	2.45
Kingsport	R+ NYM	1	1	0	0	5.1	22	5	0	0	0	0	0	0	3	0	3	0	0	1	0	1.000	0	0	0.00
1995 Pittsfield	A- NYM	2	0	0	1	2	10	4	1	1	0	0	0	0	0	0	3	1	0	0	0	.000	0	0	4.50
Capital Cty	A NYM	40	1	0	15	77.2	319	63	22	17	1	2	0	2	22	2	56	5	2	4	3	.571	0	4	1.97
1996 St. Lucie	A+ NYM	58	0	0	24	88.1	350	70	28	23	5	4	1	1	18	1	70	1	0	6	2	.750	0	10	2.34
1997 Binghamton	AA NYM	6	0	0	2	10.1	45	9	3	3	1	1	0	0	4	0	6	0	0	2	0	1.000	0	0	2.61
1998 St. Lucie	A+ NYM	22	0	0	6	42.2	198	52	24	20	1	3	1	2	23	4	25	4	0	2	3	.400	0	0	4.22
1999 St. Lucie	A+ NYM	10	0	0	4	16.2	72	19	8	8	0	0	0	0	4	1	9	1	0	2	2	.500	0	0	4.32
Binghamton	AA NYM	24	0	0	12	41.1	187	43	29	16	3	5	2	2	16	2	22	2	1	0	7	.000	0	0	3.48
6 Min. YEARS		173	9	0	65	346.2	1455	314	136	105	14	16	4	8	109	10	243	23	3	22	19	.537	0	15	2.73

257

Rick Short

Bats: Right Throws: Right Pos: OF Ht: 6'0" Wt: 190 Born: 12/6/72 Age: 27

Year Team	Lg Org	G	AB	H	2B	3B	HR	TB	R	RBI	TBB	IBB	SO	HBP	SH	SF	SB	CS	SB%	GDP	Avg	OBP	SLG
1994 Bluefield	R+ Bal	64	229	69	8	0	4	89	39	35	22	1	23	2	0	2	4	6	.40	3	.301	.365	.389
1995 Frederick	A+ Bal	5	13	1	0	0	0	1	1	2	1	0	2	1	0	0	1	0	1.00	0	.077	.143	.077
Bluefield	R+ Bal	11	39	11	2	0	2	19	9	12	2	0	1	1	0	1	2	1	.67	2	.282	.326	.487
High Desert	A+ Bal	29	98	41	3	0	4	56	14	12	10	0	5	2	0	0	1	2	.33	2	.418	.482	.571
1996 Frederick	A+ Bal	126	474	148	33	0	3	190	68	54	29	2	44	5	5	4	12	7	.63	14	.312	.355	.401
1997 Frederick	A+ Bal	126	480	153	29	1	10	214	73	72	38	2	44	12	7	1	10	7	.59	20	.319	.382	.446
1998 Frederick	A+ Bal	59	221	68	14	0	6	100	36	28	18	1	29	8	1	3	3	2	.60	12	.308	.376	.452
Bowie	AA Bal	34	87	20	4	0	2	30	12	18	13	0	18	0	1	4	0	0	.00	2	.230	.317	.345
Rochester	AAA Bal	13	34	6	1	0	1	10	3	4	4	0	4	1	0	1	0	0	.00	0	.176	.275	.294
1999 Bowie	AA Bal	112	392	123	19	0	16	190	60	62	43	2	48	9	0	5	6	0	1.00	9	.314	.390	.485
6 Min. YEARS		579	2067	640	113	1	48	899	315	299	180	8	218	40	14	21	39	25	.61	64	.310	.373	.435

Brian Shouse

Pitches: Left Bats: Left Pos: P Ht: 5'11" Wt: 180 Born: 9/26/68 Age: 31

Year Team	Lg Org	G	GS	CG	GF	IP	BFP	H	R	ER	HR	SH	SF	HB	TBB	IBB	SO	WP	Bk	W	L	Pct.	ShO	Sv	ERA
1990 Welland	A- Pit	17	1	0	7	39.2	177	50	27	23	2	3	2	3	7	0	39	1	2	4	3	.571	0	2	5.22
1991 Augusta	A Pit	26	0	0	25	31	124	22	13	11	1	1	0	0	1	0	32	6	0	2	3	.400	0	8	3.19
Salem	A+ Pit	17	0	0	9	33.2	147	35	12	11	2	2	0	0	15	2	25	1	0	2	1	.667	0	3	2.94
1992 Carolina	AA Pit	59	0	0	33	77.1	323	71	31	21	3	8	2	2	28	4	79	4	1	5	6	.455	0	4	2.44
1993 Buffalo	AAA Pit	48	0	0	14	51.2	218	54	24	22	7	0	3	2	17	2	25	1	0	1	0	1.000	0	2	3.83
1994 Buffalo	AAA Pit	43	0	0	20	52	212	44	22	21	6	4	2	1	15	4	31	0	0	3	4	.429	0	0	3.63
1995 Calgary	AAA Pit	8	8	1	0	39.1	185	62	35	27	2	1	1	1	7	0	17	3	0	4	4	.500	0	0	6.18
Carolina	AA Pit	21	20	0	0	114.2	480	126	64	57	14	5	3	4	19	2	76	1	1	7	6	.538	0	0	4.47
1996 Calgary	AAA Pit	12	1	0	2	12.2	65	22	15	15	4	0	1	0	4	1	12	1	0	1	0	1.000	0	0	10.66
Rochester	AAA Bal	32	0	0	10	50	217	53	27	25	6	2	2	1	16	1	45	5	0	1	2	.333	0	2	4.50
1997 Rochester	AAA Bal	54	0	0	29	71.1	282	48	21	18	6	5	1	3	21	4	81	2	0	6	2	.750	0	5	2.27
1998 Pawtucket	AAA Bos	22	1	0	15	31	121	21	11	10	7	1	1	0	7	0	25	0	0	2	0	1.000	0	6	2.90
1999 Tucson	AAA Ari	30	0	0	8	44.2	213	63	35	31	4	6	2	1	18	3	32	2	0	3	4	.429	0	0	6.25
1993 Pittsburgh	NL	6	0	0	1	4	22	7	4	4	1	0	1	0	2	0	3	1	0	0	0	.000	0	0	9.00
1998 Boston	AL	7	0	0	4	8	36	9	5	5	2	0	0	0	4	0	5	0	0	0	1	.000	0	0	5.63
10 Min. YEARS		389	31	1	172	649	2764	671	337	292	64	38	21	21	183	24	519	26	4	41	35	.539	0	36	4.05
2 Maj. YEARS		13	0	0	5	12	58	16	9	9	3	0	1	0	6	0	8	1	0	0	1	.000	0	0	6.75

Jacob Shumate

Pitches: Right Bats: Right Pos: P Ht: 6'2" Wt: 190 Born: 1/22/76 Age: 24

Year Team	Lg Org	G	GS	CG	GF	IP	BFP	H	R	ER	HR	SH	SF	HB	TBB	IBB	SO	WP	Bk	W	L	Pct.	ShO	Sv	ERA
1994 Danville	R+ Atl	12	7	0	1	31.2	175	30	34	29	0	1	5	8	52	0	29	15	0	0	4	.000	0	0	8.24
1995 Macon	A Atl	17	14	0	0	56	296	38	56	45	7	1	3	9	87	0	57	19	2	0	8	.000	0	0	7.23
Danville	R+ Atl	7	2	0	2	13.1	80	6	21	16	1	0	2	2	32	0	16	14	0	1	2	.333	0	0	10.80
1996 Macon	A Atl	1	1	0	0	3	16	5	5	4	0	0	1	0	2	0	2	1	0	0	0	.000	0	0	12.00
1997 Eugene	A- Atl	19	0	0	7	20.2	126	19	32	25	1	0	0	2	43	0	23	7	0	0	2	.000	0	0	10.89
1998 Macon	A Atl	44	0	0	10	50.2	280	44	54	38	5	2	3	13	75	0	65	39	1	5	4	.556	0	0	6.75
Greenville	AA Atl	2	0	0	0	2.1	13	3	4	4	0	0	0	0	4	0	1	1	0	0	1	.000	0	0	15.43
1999 Myrtle Bch	A+ Atl	20	0	0	6	22.2	116	15	19	18	0	3	1	1	33	0	31	8	0	3	3	.500	0	0	7.15
Greenville	AA Atl	14	12	0	1	57	270	43	30	30	6	1	3	5	61	1	48	9	1	3	4	.429	0	0	4.74
6 Min. YEARS		136	36	0	27	257.1	1372	203	255	209	20	8	18	40	389	1	272	113	4	12	28	.300	0	0	7.31

Derek Shumpert

Bats: Both Throws: Right Pos: OF-DH Ht: 6'2" Wt: 185 Born: 9/30/75 Age: 24

Year Team	Lg Org	G	AB	H	2B	3B	HR	TB	R	RBI	TBB	IBB	SO	HBP	SH	SF	SB	CS	SB%	GDP	Avg	OBP	SLG
1993 Yankees	R NYY	43	131	20	1	0	0	21	9	5	16	0	57	2	1	0	7	2	.78	2	.153	.255	.160
1994 Oneonta	A- NYY	75	239	54	7	1	0	63	21	22	26	0	86	1	4	1	10	11	.48	5	.226	.303	.264
1995 Greensboro	A NYY	56	153	33	3	1	0	38	21	14	18	0	41	2	1	0	4	2	.67	2	.216	.306	.248
Oneonta	A- NYY	62	196	41	7	3	0	54	25	11	29	0	58	2	2	0	13	3	.81	6	.209	.317	.276
1996 Greensboro	A NYY	141	522	132	20	10	3	181	76	45	57	0	144	14	4	4	28	18	.61	6	.253	.340	.347
1997 Tampa	A+ NYY	44	169	44	6	1	1	55	24	6	20	0	49	3	3	0	6	8	.43	1	.260	.349	.325
Greensboro	A NYY	86	322	97	22	6	6	149	49	39	27	1	91	7	0	1	12	6	.67	3	.301	.367	.463
1998 Tampa	A+ NYY	21	66	13	2	0	0	15	8	3	7	0	25	0	1	0	0	2	.00	2	.197	.274	.227
Yankees	R NYY	6	16	2	0	1	0	4	3	0	4	0	11	0	0	0	1	0	1.00	0	.125	.300	.250
1999 Norwich	AA NYY	54	166	36	8	0	7	65	25	15	13	0	63	6	3	3	3	2	.60	5	.217	.293	.392
7 Min. YEARS		588	1980	472	76	23	17	645	261	160	217	1	625	37	25	9	84	54	.61	32	.238	.324	.326

Joe Siddall

Bats: Left Throws: Right Pos: C Ht: 6'1" Wt: 200 Born: 10/25/67 Age: 32

Year Team	Lg Org	G	AB	H	2B	3B	HR	TB	R	RBI	TBB	IBB	SO	HBP	SH	SF	SB	CS	SB%	GDP	Avg	OBP	SLG
1988 Jamestown	A- Mon	53	178	38	5	3	1	52	18	16	14	1	29	1	4	2	5	4	.56	3	.213	.272	.292
1989 Rockford	A Mon	98	313	74	15	2	4	105	36	38	26	2	56	6	5	4	8	5	.62	3	.236	.304	.335
1990 Wst Plm Bch	A+ Mon	106	348	78	12	1	0	92	29	32	20	0	55	1	10	2	6	7	.46	7	.224	.267	.264
1991 Harrisburg	AA Mon	76	235	54	6	1	1	65	28	23	23	2	53	1	2	3	8	3	.73	7	.230	.298	.277
1992 Harrisburg	AA Mon	95	288	68	12	0	2	86	26	27	29	1	55	3	1	3	4	4	.50	7	.236	.310	.299
1993 Ottawa	AAA Mon	48	136	29	6	0	1	38	14	16	19	5	33	0	3	2	2	2	.50	6	.213	.306	.279

		BATTING															BASERUNNING				PERCENTAGES		
Year Team	Lg Org	G	AB	H	2B	3B	HR	TB	R	RBI	TBB	IBB	SO	HBP	SH	SF	SB	CS	SB%	GDP	Avg	OBP	SLG
1994 Ottawa	AAA Mon	38	110	19	2	1	3	32	9	13	10	2	21	2	7	2	1	1	.50	3	.173	.250	.291
1995 Ottawa	AAA Mon	83	248	53	14	2	1	74	26	23	23	0	42	4	2	0	3	3	.50	6	.214	.291	.298
1996 Charlotte	AAA Fla	65	189	53	13	1	3	77	22	20	11	1	36	3	2	0	1	2	.33	2	.280	.330	.407
1997 Ottawa	AAA Mon	57	164	45	12	1	1	62	18	16	21	3	42	1	0	0	1	2	.33	2	.274	.360	.378
1998 Toledo	AAA Det	43	129	31	5	0	4	48	16	16	11	0	42	2	2	0	2	1	.67	2	.240	.310	.372
1999 Toledo	AAA Det	84	244	47	15	0	8	86	29	33	34	0	74	2	4	1	4	1	.80	6	.193	.295	.352
1993 Montreal	NL	19	20	2	1	0	0	3	0	1	1	1	5	0	0	0	0	0	.00	0	.100	.143	.150
1995 Montreal	NL	7	10	3	0	0	0	3	4	1	3	0	3	1	0	0	0	0	.00	0	.300	.500	.300
1996 Florida	NL	18	47	7	1	0	0	8	0	3	2	0	8	0	0	0	0	0	.00	0	.149	.184	.170
1998 Detroit	AL	29	65	12	3	0	1	18	3	6	7	0	25	0	2	0	0	0	.00	1	.185	.264	.277
12 Min. YEARS		846	2582	589	117	12	29	817	271	273	241	17	538	26	42	19	45	35	.56	54	.228	.298	.316
4 Maj. YEARS		73	142	24	5	0	1	32	7	11	13	1	41	1	2	0	0	0	.00	1	.169	.244	.225

Mark Sievert

Pitches: Right **Bats:** Left **Pos:** P **Ht:** 6'4" **Wt:** 195 **Born:** 2/16/73 **Age:** 27

		HOW MUCH HE PITCHED						WHAT HE GAVE UP												THE RESULTS					
Year Team	Lg Org	G	GS	CG	GF	IP	BFP	H	R	ER	HR	SH	SF	HB	TBB	IBB	SO	WP	Bk	W	L	Pct.	ShO	Sv	ERA
1993 Medcine Hat	R+ Tor	15	15	0	0	63	280	63	40	35	2	2	2	3	30	0	52	1	0	6	3	.667	0	0	5.00
1994 St.Cathrnes	A- Tor	14	14	1	0	81.2	319	59	30	28	4	1	3	1	28	0	82	4	0	7	4	.636	1	0	3.09
1995 Hagerstown	A Tor	27	27	3	0	160.2	644	126	59	52	14	5	1	2	46	0	140	2	0	12	6	.667	0	0	2.91
1996 Knoxville	AA Tor	17	17	0	0	101.1	415	79	32	29	6	2	0	3	51	0	75	3	0	9	2	.818	0	0	2.58
Syracuse	AAA Tor	10	10	1	0	54.2	256	62	40	36	6	4	1	1	33	0	46	4	0	2	5	.286	0	0	5.93
1997 Syracuse	AAA Tor	1	1	0	0	5.1	23	5	3	2	0	0	0	0	2	0	5	0	0	0	0	.000	0	0	3.38
Dunedin	A+ Tor	3	2	0	0	11	44	10	5	4	0	0	0	1	5	0	7	2	1	1	0	1.000	0	0	3.27
1998 Syracuse	AAA Tor	21	18	0	3	96	423	92	48	44	8	1	4	4	59	2	37	7	1	7	6	.538	0	1	4.13
1999 Oklahoma	AAA Tex	7	0	0	5	11.1	57	17	13	13	4	0	0	1	8	0	5	1	0	0	0	.000	0	0	10.32
7 Min. YEARS		115	104	5	8	585	2461	513	270	243	44	15	11	16	262	2	449	35	2	44	26	.629	1	1	3.74

Brian Sikorski

Pitches: Right **Bats:** Right **Pos:** P **Ht:** 6'1" **Wt:** 190 **Born:** 7/27/73 **Age:** 26

		HOW MUCH HE PITCHED						WHAT HE GAVE UP												THE RESULTS					
Year Team	Lg Org	G	GS	CG	GF	IP	BFP	H	R	ER	HR	SH	SF	HB	TBB	IBB	SO	WP	Bk	W	L	Pct.	ShO	Sv	ERA
1995 Auburn	A- Hou	23	0	0	19	34.1	137	22	8	8	1	0	1	0	14	2	35	1	0	1	2	.333	0	12	2.10
Quad City	A Hou	2	0	0	1	3	11	1	1	0	0	0	0	0	0	0	4	0	0	1	0	1.000	0	0	3.00
1996 Quad City	A Hou	26	25	1	0	166.2	704	140	79	58	12	4	7	10	70	2	150	7	9	11	8	.579	0	0	3.13
1997 Kissimmee	A+ Hou	11	11	0	0	67.2	279	69	23	23	2	0	1	6	16	0	46	0	3	8	2	.800	0	0	3.06
Jackson	AA Hou	17	17	0	0	93.1	402	91	55	48	8	5	2	4	31	2	74	0	2	5	5	.500	0	0	4.63
1998 Jackson	AA Hou	15	15	0	0	97.1	419	83	50	44	13	3	2	6	44	1	80	3	1	6	4	.600	0	0	4.07
New Orleans	AAA Hou	15	14	1	0	84	371	86	57	54	9	2	4	6	32	1	64	2	1	5	8	.385	0	0	5.79
1999 New Orleans	AAA Hou	28	27	2	0	158.1	699	169	92	87	25	8	1	9	58	1	122	6	2	7	10	.412	1	0	4.95
5 Min. YEARS		137	109	4	20	704.2	3022	656	371	322	70	22	18	41	265	9	575	19	18	44	39	.530	1	12	4.11

Ted Silva

Pitches: Right **Bats:** Right **Pos:** P **Ht:** 6'0" **Wt:** 170 **Born:** 8/4/74 **Age:** 25

		HOW MUCH HE PITCHED						WHAT HE GAVE UP												THE RESULTS					
Year Team	Lg Org	G	GS	CG	GF	IP	BFP	H	R	ER	HR	SH	SF	HB	TBB	IBB	SO	WP	Bk	W	L	Pct.	ShO	Sv	ERA
1995 Chston-SC	A Tex	11	11	0	0	66.2	276	59	26	25	4	1	3	7	12	2	66	5	2	5	4	.556	0	0	3.38
1996 Charlotte	A+ Tex	16	16	4	0	113.1	463	98	39	36	9	2	3	3	27	1	95	3	1	10	2	.833	0	0	2.86
Tulsa	AA Tex	11	11	2	0	75.1	314	72	27	25	5	4	2	2	16	0	27	0	0	7	2	.778	0	0	2.99
1997 Tulsa	AA Tex	26	25	4	1	171.2	728	178	88	78	21	9	7	3	42	1	121	7	1	13	10	.565	0	0	4.09
1999 Tulsa	AA Tex	13	11	0	0	72	295	64	34	32	10	1	0	6	14	0	48	3	0	6	3	.667	0	0	4.00
4 Min. YEARS		77	74	10	1	499	2076	471	214	196	49	16	14	21	111	4	357	18	4	41	21	.661	1	0	3.54

Mitch Simons

Bats: Right **Throws:** Right **Pos:** 2B-3B **Ht:** 5'9" **Wt:** 172 **Born:** 12/13/68 **Age:** 31

		BATTING															BASERUNNING				PERCENTAGES		
Year Team	Lg Org	G	AB	H	2B	3B	HR	TB	R	RBI	TBB	IBB	SO	HBP	SH	SF	SB	CS	SB%	GDP	Avg	OBP	SLG
1991 Jamestown	A- Mon	41	153	47	12	0	1	62	38	16	39	1	20	0	2	2	23	5	.82	1	.307	.443	.405
Wst Plm Bch	A+ Mon	15	50	9	2	1	0	13	3	4	5	0	8	0	0	0	1	0	1.00	0	.180	.255	.260
1992 Albany	A Mon	130	481	136	26	5	1	175	57	61	60	0	47	7	2	10	34	12	.74	6	.283	.364	.364
1993 Wst Plm Bch	A+ Mon	45	156	40	4	1	1	49	24	13	19	0	9	3	1	2	14	8	.64	3	.256	.344	.314
Harrisburg	AA Mon	29	77	18	1	1	0	21	5	5	7	0	14	0	2	1	2	0	1.00	1	.234	.294	.273
1994 Nashville	AA Min	102	391	124	26	0	3	159	46	48	39	0	38	6	3	5	30	9	.77	6	.317	.383	.407
1995 Salt Lake	AAA Min	130	480	156	34	4	3	207	87	46	47	2	45	10	4	2	32	16	.67	9	.325	.395	.431
1996 Salt Lake	AAA Min	129	512	135	27	8	5	193	76	59	43	3	59	8	3	4	35	11	.76	7	.264	.328	.377
1997 Salt Lake	AAA Min	115	462	138	34	10	5	207	87	59	47	4	48	5	9	5	26	5	.84	7	.299	.366	.448
1998 Rochester	AAA Bal	59	190	41	8	2	1	56	21	16	20	0	16	1	1	1	7	2	.78	4	.216	.292	.295
Tacoma	AAA Sea	47	100	42	6	2	2	58	27	21	15	0	23	4	2	1	10	1	.91	5	.233	.305	.322
1999 Charlotte	AAA CWS	119	474	137	32	1	7	192	85	52	45	0	67	11	6	2	22	6	.79	10	.289	.363	.405
9 Min. YEARS		961	3606	1023	212	35	29	1392	556	400	386	10	394	55	35	35	236	75	.76	59	.284	.359	.386

Benji Simonton

Bats: Right **Throws:** Right **Pos:** OF **Ht:** 6'1" **Wt:** 236 **Born:** 5/12/72 **Age:** 28

		BATTING															BASERUNNING				PERCENTAGES		
Year Team	Lg Org	G	AB	H	2B	3B	HR	TB	R	RBI	TBB	IBB	SO	HBP	SH	SF	SB	CS	SB%	GDP	Avg	OBP	SLG
1992 Everett	A- SF	68	225	55	10	0	6	83	37	34	39	0	78	3	2	3	9	4	.69	1	.244	.359	.369

Year Team	Lg Org	G	AB	H	2B	3B	HR	TB	R	RBI	TBB	IBB	SO	HBP	SH	SF	SB	CS	SB%	GDP	Avg	OBP	SLG
			BATTING														BASERUNNING				PERCENTAGES		
1993 Clinton	A SF	100	310	79	18	4	12	141	52	49	40	2	112	6	0	2	8	7	.53	3	.255	.349	.455
1994 Clinton	A SF	67	237	64	16	4	14	130	47	57	52	3	73	5	1	0	10	3	.77	7	.270	.412	.549
San Jose	A+ SF	68	259	77	20	0	14	139	41	51	32	0	86	5	1	1	0	2	.00	5	.297	.384	.537
1995 San Jose	A+ SF	61	225	65	9	6	8	110	38	37	40	2	78	10	0	4	7	0	1.00	5	.289	.412	.489
Shreveport	AA SF	38	108	33	9	3	4	60	18	30	11	0	32	2	1	1	3	1	.75	1	.306	.377	.556
1996 Shreveport	AA SF	137	469	117	25	1	23	213	86	76	101	4	144	6	1	0	6	4	.60	12	.249	.389	.454
Phoenix	AAA SF	1	4	3	0	0	1	6	1	2	1	0	0	0	0	0	0	0	.00	0	.750	.800	1.500
1997 Shreveport	AA SF	116	387	99	15	2	20	178	73	79	81	1	120	6	0	5	7	5	.58	14	.256	.388	.460
1998 San Jose	A+ SF	89	300	96	28	4	16	180	59	69	53	0	100	4	0	2	4	2	.67	4	.320	.466	.600
Shreveport	AA SF	45	161	45	7	1	5	69	19	19	19	1	44	1	0	1	5	0	1.00	3	.280	.357	.429
1999 Erie	AA Ana	62	182	44	10	1	1	59	13	19	28	0	55	2	2	1	4	3	.57	6	.242	.347	.324
Lk Elsinore	A+ Ana	49	184	68	14	2	8	110	39	48	29	0	52	2	0	2	0	0	.00	3	.370	.456	.598
8 Min. YEARS		901	3051	845	181	28	132	1478	523	570	526	13	974	52	8	22	63	31	.67	64	.277	.390	.484

Steve Sisco

Bats: Right Throws: Right Pos: 2B   Ht: 5'10" Wt: 190 Born: 12/2/69 Age: 30

Year Team	Lg Org	G	AB	H	2B	3B	HR	TB	R	RBI	TBB	IBB	SO	HBP	SH	SF	SB	CS	SB%	GDP	Avg	OBP	SLG
			BATTING														BASERUNNING				PERCENTAGES		
1992 Eugene	A- KC	67	261	86	7	1	0	95	41	30	26	0	32	4	2	2	22	12	.65	7	.330	.396	.364
Appleton	A KC	1	4	1	0	0	0	1	1	0	0	0	1	0	0	0	0	0	.00	0	.250	.250	.250
1993 Rockford	A KC	124	460	132	22	4	2	168	62	57	42	2	65	2	4	5	25	10	.71	14	.287	.346	.365
1994 Wilmington	A+ KC	76	270	74	11	4	3	102	41	32	37	0	39	2	6	4	5	6	.45	2	.274	.361	.378
1995 Omaha	AAA KC	7	24	5	1	0	0	6	4	0	2	0	8	0	1	0	0	0	.00	0	.208	.269	.250
Wichita	AA KC	54	209	63	12	1	3	86	29	23	15	0	31	1	1	1	3	1	.75	5	.301	.350	.411
1996 Wichita	AA KC	122	462	137	24	1	13	202	80	74	40	0	69	3	5	5	4	2	.67	14	.297	.353	.437
1997 Wichita	AA KC	55	182	52	8	2	3	73	34	24	24	0	29	0	1	2	3	1	.75	5	.286	.365	.401
Omaha	AAA KC	54	188	49	8	0	3	66	23	12	8	0	34	0	3	1	2	1	.67	4	.261	.289	.351
1998 Omaha	AAA KC	109	371	104	20	0	20	184	58	58	26	1	58	0	5	3	4	6	.40	11	.280	.325	.496
1999 Richmond	AAA Atl	128	495	154	36	2	18	248	80	76	38	0	74	1	3	8	13	7	.65	7	.311	.356	.501
8 Min. YEARS		797	2926	857	149	15	65	1231	453	386	258	3	440	13	31	31	81	46	.64	69	.293	.349	.421

Andy Skeels

Bats: Left Throws: Right Pos: DH   Ht: 5'11" Wt: 195 Born: 7/25/65 Age: 34

Year Team	Lg Org	G	AB	H	2B	3B	HR	TB	R	RBI	TBB	IBB	SO	HBP	SH	SF	SB	CS	SB%	GDP	Avg	OBP	SLG
			BATTING														BASERUNNING				PERCENTAGES		
1987 Spokane	A- SD	72	270	78	23	1	5	118	48	64	58	5	46	5	0	5	1	1	.50	5	.289	.417	.437
1988 Riverside	A+ SD	123	396	92	20	2	3	125	56	57	57	3	84	2	3	2	8	5	.62	10	.232	.330	.316
1989 Riverside	A+ SD	126	432	104	18	4	4	142	52	52	64	3	104	3	0	5	4	0	1.00	10	.241	.339	.329
1990 Albany-Colo	AA NYY	75	215	58	7	0	1	68	18	21	23	4	29	0	2	2	1	1	.50	3	.270	.338	.316
1991 Albany-Colo	AA NYY	65	197	50	9	0	2	65	25	26	33	2	31	1	3	4	0	1	.00	4	.254	.357	.330
Columbus	AAA NYY	14	43	6	1	1	0	9	0	5	5	2	10	0	0	0	0	1	.00	1	.140	.178	.209
1992 Salinas	A+ —	20	45	11	1	0	0	12	6	3	2	0	11	0	0	0	1	0	1.00	1	.244	.277	.267
1993 Rancho Cuca	A+ SD	32	66	21	9	0	0	30	11	10	15	0	14	1	1	0	1	0	1.00	0	.318	.451	.455
1994 Duluth-Sup	IND —	5	20	3	2	0	0	5	2	1	0	0	6	0	0	0	0	0	.00	0	.150	.150	.250
1995 Mobile	IND —	76	220	47	7	1	6	74	34	20	54	2	31	3	0	3	0	3	.00	5	.214	.371	.336
1997 Lubbock	IND —	70	254	70	12	3	4	100	40	35	39	1	37	1	2	6	8	3	.73	7	.276	.367	.394
1998 Bayou	IND —	17	51	18	5	0	0	23	11	7	8	0	10	1	0	0	5	1	.83	1	.353	.450	.451
Somerset	IND —	45	138	35	10	1	0	47	20	14	35	2	26	2	1	2	4	1	.80	3	.254	.407	.341
1999 San Antonio	AA LA	1	1	1	0	0	0	1	0	0	0	0	0	0	0	0	0	0	.00	0	1.000	1.000	1.000
12 Min. YEARS		741	2348	594	124	13	25	819	323	317	390	22	439	19	12	29	32	18	.64	51	.253	.360	.349

David Skeels

Bats: Right Throws: Right Pos: C   Ht: 6'2" Wt: 195 Born: 6/23/73 Age: 27

Year Team	Lg Org	G	AB	H	2B	3B	HR	TB	R	RBI	TBB	IBB	SO	HBP	SH	SF	SB	CS	SB%	GDP	Avg	OBP	SLG
			BATTING														BASERUNNING				PERCENTAGES		
1995 Mobile	IND —	1	4	1	0	0	0	1	0	1	0	0	0	0	0	0	0	0	.00	0	.250	.250	.250
Corp.Chrsti	IND —	35	119	35	4	0	2	45	18	20	10	0	20	2	3	1	1	0	1.00	4	.294	.356	.378
1996 Everett	A- Sea	25	77	22	3	0	1	28	8	8	3	0	13	1	0	0	2	1	.67	3	.286	.321	.364
1997 Lancaster	A+ Sea	59	180	50	7	1	0	59	26	21	9	0	40	3	3	0	0	2	.00	10	.278	.323	.328
1998 Visalia	A+ Oak	78	222	50	14	1	1	69	19	35	18	0	42	3	8	1	0	1	.00	7	.225	.291	.311
1999 Midland	AA Oak	23	66	18	5	0	1	26	6	12	6	0	15	0	1	1	2	0	1.00	0	.273	.329	.394
5 Min. YEARS		221	668	176	33	2	5	228	77	97	46	0	130	9	15	3	5	4	.56	24	.263	.318	.341

Matt Skrmetta

Pitches: Right Bats: Both Pos: P   Ht: 6'3" Wt: 220 Born: 11/6/72 Age: 27

Year Team	Lg Org	G	GS	CG	GF	IP	BFP	H	R	ER	HR	SH	SF	HB	TBB	IBB	SO	WP	Bk	W	L	Pct.	ShO	Sv	ERA
			HOW MUCH HE PITCHED						WHAT HE GAVE UP											THE RESULTS				
1993 Bristol	R+ Det	8	5	0	1	35	158	30	23	19	1	0	3	3	22	1	29	6	3	2	3	.400	0	0	4.89
1994 Jamestown	A- Det	17	15	1	1	93.2	389	74	42	33	4	2	3	7	37	0	56	2	3	5	3	.625	0	0	3.17
1995 Fayettevlle	A Det	44	2	0	15	89.2	371	66	36	27	9	6	1	3	35	2	105	2	0	9	4	.692	0	2	2.71
1996 Jacksnville	AA Det	4	0	0	1	6	27	4	3	3	0	1	0	1	5	1	7	1	0	0	0	.000	0	0	4.50
Lakeland	A+ Det	40	0	0	20	52.2	223	44	23	21	5	2	0	2	19	1	52	2	1	5	5	.500	0	1	3.59
1997 Mobile	AA SD	21	0	0	7	32.2	154	32	21	19	4	0	1	2	21	3	30	3	0	2	3	.400	0	1	5.23
Rancho Cuca	A+ SD	17	0	0	8	28.1	122	27	7	5	2	0	0	1	10	0	36	4	0	1	0	1.000	0	1	1.59
1998 Mobile	AA SD	51	0	0	16	78	323	66	32	29	9	5	2	2	31	1	77	1	3	9	2	.818	0	0	3.35
1999 Mobile	AA SD	25	1	0	9	37.1	181	42	28	26	3	1	2	3	24	1	45	0	1	3	3	.250	0	1	6.27
Las Vegas	AAA SD	20	0	0	11	28.2	117	20	13	11	4	0	1	1	11	0	25	2	1	2	1	.667	0	1	3.45
7 Min. YEARS		247	23	1	89	482	2065	405	228	193	41	17	14	24	215	10	462	28	10	35	25	.583	0	10	3.60

Aaron Small

Pitches: Right **Bats:** Right **Pos:** P **Ht:** 6'5" **Wt:** 235 **Born:** 11/23/71 **Age:** 28

Year Team	Lg Org	G	GS	CG	GF	IP	BFP	H	R	ER	HR	SH	SF	HB	TBB	IBB	SO	WP	Bk	W	L	Pct.	ShO	Sv	ERA
1989 Medcine Hat	R+ Tor	15	14	0	0	70.2	326	80	55	46	2	3	2	3	31	1	40	9	5	1	7	.125	0	0	5.86
1990 Myrtle Bch	A Tor	27	27	1	0	147.2	643	150	72	46	6	2	7	4	56	2	96	16	5	9	9	.500	0	0	2.80
1991 Dunedin	A+ Tor	24	23	1	0	148.1	595	129	51	45	5	5	5	5	42	1	92	7	0	8	7	.533	0	0	2.73
1992 Knoxville	AA Tor	27	24	2	0	135	610	152	94	79	13	2	4	6	61	0	79	14	0	5	12	.294	1	0	5.27
1993 Knoxville	AA Tor	48	9	0	32	93	408	99	44	35	5	3	0	2	40	4	44	8	0	4	4	.500	0	16	3.39
1994 Syracuse	AAA Tor	13	0	0	6	24.1	99	19	8	6	2	2	0	1	9	2	15	2	0	3	2	.600	0	0	2.22
Knoxville	AA Tor	29	11	1	13	96.1	405	92	37	32	4	3	5	3	38	0	75	5	1	5	5	.500	1	5	2.99
1995 Syracuse	AAA Tor	1	0	0	0	1.2	9	3	1	1	1	0	0	0	1	0	2	0	0	0	0	.000	0	0	5.40
Charlotte	AAA Fla	33	0	0	17	40.2	170	36	15	13	2	0	1	2	10	1	31	3	0	2	1	.667	0	10	2.88
1996 Edmonton	AAA Oak	25	19	1	4	119.2	492	111	65	57	9	2	2	5	28	0	83	9	0	8	6	.571	1	1	4.29
1997 Edmonton	AAA Oak	1	1	0	0	5	16	1	0	0	0	0	0	0	0	0	4	0	0	1	0	1.000	0	0	0.00
1999 Louisville	AAA Mil	11	0	0	3	21	111	38	23	22	3	1	0	0	15	1	11	4	0	1	1	.500	0	0	9.43
Durham	AAA TB	21	18	0	0	99.1	444	118	81	70	16	1	8	3	32	2	52	4	0	4	6	.400	0	0	6.34
1994 Toronto	AL	1	0	0	1	2	13	5	2	2	1	0	1	0	2	0	0	0	0	0	0	.000	0	0	9.00
1995 Florida	NL	7	0	0	1	6.1	32	7	2	1	1	0	0	0	6	0	5	0	0	1	0	1.000	0	0	1.42
1996 Oakland	AL	12	3	0	4	28.2	144	37	28	26	3	0	1	1	22	1	17	2	0	1	3	.250	0	0	8.16
1997 Oakland	AL	71	0	0	22	96.2	425	109	50	46	6	5	6	3	40	6	57	4	0	9	5	.643	0	4	4.28
1998 Oakland	AL	24	0	0	4	36	174	51	34	29	3	3	1	3	14	3	19	4	0	1	1	.500	0	0	7.25
Arizona	NL	23	0	0	9	31.2	130	32	14	13	5	2	0	1	8	1	14	0	0	3	1	.750	0	0	3.69
10 Min. YEARS		275	146	6	75	1002.2	4328	1028	546	452	68	24	34	34	363	14	624	81	11	51	60	.459	3	32	4.06
5 Maj. YEARS		138	3	0	41	201.1	918	241	130	117	19	10	9	8	92	11	112	10	0	15	10	.600	0	4	5.23

Mark Small

Pitches: Right **Bats:** Right **Pos:** P **Ht:** 6'3" **Wt:** 205 **Born:** 11/12/67 **Age:** 32

Year Team	Lg Org	G	GS	CG	GF	IP	BFP	H	R	ER	HR	SH	SF	HB	TBB	IBB	SO	WP	Bk	W	L	Pct.	ShO	Sv	ERA
1989 Auburn	A- Hou	10	3	0	4	19.2	87	17	13	11	3	0	1	1	11	0	23	3	0	1	0	.000	0	2	5.03
1990 Asheville	A Hou	34	0	0	16	52	252	54	36	24	2	4	3	4	37	5	34	9	0	3	4	.429	0	6	4.15
1991 Osceola	A+ Hou	26	0	0	10	44.2	172	30	10	8	2	1	0	1	19	1	44	2	0	3	0	1.000	0	2	1.61
1992 Osceola	A+ Hou	22	20	1	2	105	435	97	56	45	8	3	3	3	38	0	69	5	1	5	9	.357	0	0	3.86
1993 Jackson	AA Hou	51	0	0	18	84.2	361	71	34	30	8	8	3	3	41	6	64	8	2	7	2	.778	0	0	3.19
1994 Jackson	AA Hou	16	0	0	9	21	97	22	16	9	1	1	2	1	10	2	14	4	0	3	1	.750	0	3	3.86
Tucson	AAA Hou	41	0	0	12	70	321	88	48	41	9	3	3	2	34	2	30	13	0	8	5	.615	0	4	5.27
1995 Tucson	AAA Hou	51	0	0	40	66	285	74	32	30	5	1	2	1	19	2	51	8	0	3	3	.500	0	19	4.09
1996 Tucson	AAA Hou	32	0	0	20	39	166	32	17	9	3	3	0	0	18	4	36	4	1	3	3	.500	0	7	2.08
1997 New Orleans	AAA Hou	7	0	0	4	9.1	43	11	9	6	1	0	1	0	3	1	7	1	0	1	1	.500	0	0	5.79
Jackson	AA Hou	37	0	0	25	43	196	46	20	15	1	4	1	1	19	2	40	0	1	3	4	.429	0	9	3.14
1998 Oklahoma	AAA Tex	15	6	0	4	47	206	53	30	24	4	1	3	4	13	1	42	8	0	4	4	.500	0	0	4.60
1999 Ottawa	AAA Mon	42	0	0	10	66.2	309	85	50	41	9	4	0	1	32	0	43	6	0	4	5	.444	0	2	5.54
1996 Houston	NL	16	0	0	4	24.1	122	33	24	16	1	1	0	1	13	3	16	1	0	1	0	1.000	0	0	5.92
11 Min. YEARS		384	29	1	174	668	2930	680	371	293	56	33	22	19	294	26	497	71	5	47	42	.528	0	54	3.95

Steve Smetana

Pitches: Left **Bats:** Left **Pos:** P **Ht:** 6'0" **Wt:** 205 **Born:** 4/14/73 **Age:** 27

Year Team	Lg Org	G	GS	CG	GF	IP	BFP	H	R	ER	HR	SH	SF	HB	TBB	IBB	SO	WP	Bk	W	L	Pct.	ShO	Sv	ERA
1996 Lowell	A- Bos	19	0	0	9	31	116	22	5	5	1	2	1	0	3	0	33	1	0	5	0	1.000	0	2	1.45
1997 Michigan	A Bos	18	0	0	6	30.2	132	23	16	8	1	1	3	1	12	0	29	2	0	2	1	.667	0	2	2.35
Trenton	AA Bos	18	0	0	10	21.1	97	25	9	7	2	2	1	2	7	1	16	1	0	1	2	.333	0	3	2.95
Sarasota	A+ Bos	10	1	0	3	21	90	25	12	11	1	0	1	0	7	0	20	2	0	1	0	1.000	0	0	4.71
1998 Trenton	AA Bos	49	0	0	30	76.2	336	88	40	38	9	2	1	1	23	4	51	1	0	2	3	.400	0	12	4.46
1999 Trenton	AA Bos	39	3	0	12	85.2	359	90	39	38	8	1	4	3	26	1	61	3	1	4	5	.556	0	1	3.99
4 Min. YEARS		153	4	0	70	266.1	1130	273	121	107	22	8	11	7	78	6	210	10	1	15	11	.577	0	20	3.62

Brian Smith

Pitches: Right **Bats:** Right **Pos:** P **Ht:** 5'11" **Wt:** 185 **Born:** 7/19/72 **Age:** 27

Year Team	Lg Org	G	GS	CG	GF	IP	BFP	H	R	ER	HR	SH	SF	HB	TBB	IBB	SO	WP	Bk	W	L	Pct.	ShO	Sv	ERA
1994 Medcine Hat	R+ Tor	20	5	0	11	64	268	58	36	24	3	2	4	5	20	0	53	6	3	5	4	.556	0	4	3.38
1995 Hagerstown	A Tor	47	0	0	36	104	402	77	18	10	1	5	0	5	16	1	101	2	2	9	1	.900	0	21	0.87
1996 Knoxville	AA Tor	54	0	0	43	75.2	333	76	42	32	7	6	3	4	31	6	58	4	0	3	5	.375	0	16	3.81
1997 Knoxville	AA Tor	1	0	0	0	1	4	0	0	0	0	0	0	0	1	0	1	0	0	0	0	.000	0	0	0.00
Syracuse	AAA Tor	31	21	0	2	137.1	619	169	89	82	12	2	6	8	51	1	73	4	3	7	11	.389	0	0	5.37
1998 Dunedin	A+ Tor	4	0	0	2	10.2	42	8	4	4	0	0	0	1	3	1	9	0	0	1	0	1.000	0	2	3.38
Knoxville	AA Tor	42	0	0	15	71	307	72	39	32	7	2	4	3	25	3	50	2	0	4	2	.667	0	7	4.06
1999 Knoxville	AA Tor	29	0	0	21	35	154	42	25	20	4	0	1	3	20	4	27	2	1	1	2	.333	0	13	5.14
Syracuse	AAA Tor	29	0	0	23	46.1	210	45	22	18	7	5	1	2	24	4	46	2	0	7	4	.636	0	7	3.50
6 Min. YEARS		257	26	0	153	545	2339	547	275	222	41	22	19	31	177	16	418	22	9	37	29	.561	0	70	3.67

Cam Smith

Pitches: Right **Bats:** Right **Pos:** P **Ht:** 6'3" **Wt:** 190 **Born:** 9/20/73 **Age:** 26

Year Team	Lg Org	G	GS	CG	GF	IP	BFP	H	R	ER	HR	SH	SF	HB	TBB	IBB	SO	WP	Bk	W	L	Pct.	ShO	Sv	ERA
1993 Bristol	R+ Det	9	7	1	0	37.2	162	25	22	15	5	0	0	6	22	0	33	2	3	3	1	.750	0	0	3.58
Niagara Fal	A- Det	2	2	0	0	5	31	12	11	10	0	0	2	0	6	0	2	0	0	0	0	.000	0	0	18.00

Year Team	Lg Org	G	GS	CG	GF	IP	BFP	H	R	ER	HR	SH	SF	HB	TBB	IBB	SO	WP	Bk	W	L	Pct.	ShO	Sv	ERA
1994 Fayettevlle	A Det	26	26	1	0	133.2	619	133	100	90	10	6	5	18	86	0	128	17	1	5	13	.278	0	0	6.06
1995 Fayettevlle	A Det	29	29	2	0	149	652	110	75	63	6	3	3	18	87	0	166	21	1	13	8	.619	2	0	3.81
1996 Lakeland	A+ Det	22	21	0	1	113.2	500	93	64	58	10	1	5	7	71	0	114	8	0	5	8	.385	0	0	4.59
1997 Mobile	AA SD	26	15	0	4	79.1	390	85	70	62	5	1	1	3	73	0	88	14	0	3	5	.375	0	1	7.03
1998 Lancaster	A+ Sea	8	0	0	3	18	81	11	7	5	1	0	0	3	13	0	32	4	0	1	1	.500	0	2	2.50
Orlando	AA Sea	32	0	1	8	39	186	32	27	20	6	3	3	6	32	0	49	9	0	1	3	.250	0	0	4.62
1999 New Haven	AA Sea	41	0	0	10	55	267	42	39	31	3	1	5	9	61	0	59	20	0	1	4	.200	0	0	5.07
7 Min. YEARS		186	101	4	26	630.1	2888	543	415	354	46	15	24	70	451	0	669	97	5	32	43	.427	2	3	5.05

Chuck Smith

Pitches: Right Bats: Right Pos: P
Ht: 6'1" Wt: 175 Born: 10/21/69 Age: 30

Year Team	Lg Org	G	GS	CG	GF	IP	BFP	H	R	ER	HR	SH	SF	HB	TBB	IBB	SO	WP	Bk	W	L	Pct.	ShO	Sv	ERA
1991 Astros	R Hou	15	7	1	2	59.1	272	56	36	23	2	3	0	7	37	0	64	7	5	4	3	.571	0	0	3.49
1992 Asheville	A Hou	28	20	1	3	132	596	128	93	76	14	5	4	4	78	1	117	4	7	9	9	.500	0	1	5.18
1993 Quad City	A Hou	22	17	2	3	110.2	488	109	73	57	16	3	2	6	52	0	103	7	4	7	5	.583	0	0	4.64
1994 Jackson	AA Hou	2	0	0	0	6	30	6	6	3	0	2	0	0	5	0	7	0	1	0	0	.000	0	0	4.50
Osceola	A+ Hou	35	2	0	11	84.2	376	73	41	35	2	2	2	2	49	3	60	7	3	4	4	.500	0	0	3.72
1995 South Bend	A CWS	26	25	4	1	167	688	128	70	50	8	7	2	13	61	0	145	21	11	10	10	.500	2	0	2.69
1996 Pr William	A+ CWS	20	20	2	0	123.1	545	125	65	55	7	3	2	10	49	1	99	13	1	6	6	.500	1	0	4.01
Birmingham	AA CWS	7	3	0	2	30.2	124	25	11	9	1	0	0	1	15	2	30	0	1	2	1	.667	0	1	2.64
Nashville	AAA CWS	1	0	0	0	0.2	5	2	2	2	0	0	0	0	1	0	1	0	0	0	0	.000	0	0	27.00
1997 Birmingham	AA CWS	25	0	0	6	62.2	280	63	35	22	4	1	2	5	27	5	57	8	3	2	2	.500	0	0	3.16
Nashville	AAA CWS	20	1	0	12	31.2	156	39	33	31	8	2	3	2	23	2	29	8	2	0	3	.000	0	0	8.81
1998 Sioux Falls	IND —	8	8	2	0	55	226	44	18	16	1	0	0	3	21	1	70	1	0	5	3	.625	1	0	2.62
1999 Oklahoma	AAA Tex	32	4	2	13	85	341	73	31	28	7	1	3	1	28	0	76	5	0	5	4	.556	0	4	2.96
9 Min. YEARS		241	107	14	53	948.2	4127	871	514	407	70	29	20	54	446	15	858	81	38	54	50	.519	4	6	3.86

Danny Smith

Pitches: Left Bats: Left Pos: P
Ht: 6'5" Wt: 205 Born: 4/20/69 Age: 31

Year Team	Lg Org	G	GS	CG	GF	IP	BFP	H	R	ER	HR	SH	SF	HB	TBB	IBB	SO	WP	Bk	W	L	Pct.	ShO	Sv	ERA
1990 Butte	R+ Tex	5	5	0	0	24.2	102	23	10	10	3	2	0	2	6	0	27	3	1	2	0	1.000	0	0	3.65
Tulsa	AA Tex	7	7	0	0	38.1	151	27	16	16	2	0	3	0	16	0	32	0	0	3	2	.600	0	0	3.76
1991 Okla City	AAA Tex	28	27	3	1	151.2	713	195	114	93	10	6	8	4	75	1	85	5	5	4	17	.190	0	0	5.52
1992 Tulsa	AA Tex	24	23	4	0	146.1	571	110	48	41	4	9	3	6	34	0	122	3	3	11	7	.611	3	0	2.52
1993 Charlotte	A+ Tex	1	1	0	0	7	24	3	0	0	0	0	0	0	0	0	5	1	0	1	0	1.000	0	0	0.00
Okla City	AAA Tex	3	3	0	0	15.1	66	16	11	8	2	1	1	1	5	0	12	0	0	1	2	.333	0	0	4.70
1994 Charlotte	A+ Tex	2	0	0	0	3.2	13	2	0	0	0	1	1	0	2	0	3	0	0	0	0	.000	0	0	0.00
Okla City	AAA Tex	10	2	0	3	25.1	110	27	9	8	2	0	2	2	9	0	15	0	0	2	1	.667	0	2	2.84
1996 Okla City	AAA Tex	5	5	0	0	15	78	27	19	15	4	0	1	1	7	0	12	1	0	0	2	.000	0	0	9.00
Charlotte	A+ Tex	5	5	0	0	23	92	21	7	7	1	0	0	0	8	0	16	1	1	0	1	.000	0	0	2.74
Tulsa	AA Tex	9	9	0	0	50.1	227	53	27	24	6	3	3	1	21	0	29	0	0	2	3	.400	0	0	4.29
1997 Tulsa	AA Tex	5	5	0	0	29.2	128	25	18	12	3	0	2	0	15	0	27	1	0	1	1	.500	0	0	3.64
Okla City	AAA Tex	23	23	0	0	129.1	574	154	88	81	11	2	5	5	42	0	67	3	1	3	14	.176	1	0	5.64
1998 St. Paul	IND —	19	18	3	0	112	488	119	64	57	9	3	2	9	55	1	107	1	2	8	9	.471	0	0	4.58
1999 West Tenn	AA ChC	56	0	0	21	74.2	321	70	38	35	9	4	4	1	31	0	78	2	0	5	3	.625	0	0	4.22
1992 Texas	AL	4	2	0	1	14.1	67	18	8	8	1	2	1	0	8	1	5	0	0	0	3	.000	0	0	5.02
1994 Texas	AL	13	0	0	2	14.2	76	18	11	7	2	0	0	0	12	0	9	2	0	1	2	.333	0	0	4.30
9 Min. YEARS		202	133	13	25	846.1	3658	872	469	407	66	31	35	32	326	2	637	21	13	43	62	.410	4	4	4.33
2 Maj. YEARS		17	2	0	3	29	143	36	19	15	3	2	1	0	20	1	14	2	0	1	5	.167	0	0	4.66

Demond Smith

Bats: Both Throws: Right Pos: OF
Ht: 5'11" Wt: 170 Born: 11/6/72 Age: 27

Year Team	Lg Org	G	AB	H	2B	3B	HR	TB	R	RBI	TBB	IBB	SO	HBP	SH	SF	SB	CS	SB%	GDP	Avg	OBP	SLG
1990 Mets	R NYM	46	153	40	9	2	1	56	19	7	20	0	34	0	1	2	16	10	.62	2	.261	.343	.366
1991 Kingsport	R+ NYM	35	116	29	3	4	1	43	28	12	12	0	25	6	0	1	16	7	.70	0	.250	.348	.371
1992 Pittsfield	A- NYM	66	233	58	10	4	1	79	39	24	23	0	42	7	1	3	21	15	.58	0	.249	.331	.339
1993 Capital Cty	A NYM	1	2	0	0	0	0	0	0	0	1	0	0	0	0	0	2	0	1.00	0	.000	.333	.000
1994 Lk Elsinore	A+ Ana	12	26	3	0	1	0	5	1	1	4	0	8	0	1	0	0	4	.00	1	.115	.233	.192
Boise	A- Ana	71	279	78	9	7	5	116	60	45	43	2	57	2	7	4	26	9	.74	0	.280	.375	.416
1995 Cedar Rapids	A Ana	79	317	108	25	7	7	168	64	41	32	2	61	6	5	1	37	12	.76	3	.341	.410	.530
Lk Elsinore	A+ Ana	34	148	52	8	2	7	85	32	26	11	0	36	2	0	1	14	3	.82	1	.351	.401	.574
W Michigan	A Oak	8	32	10	1	1	2	19	6	3	2	1	8	1	1	0	3	2	.60	0	.313	.371	.594
1996 Huntsville	AA Oak	123	447	116	17	14	8	188	75	62	55	1	89	11	8	5	30	15	.67	6	.260	.351	.421
Edmonton	AAA Oak	2	3	1	0	0	0	1	0	0	0	0	2	0	0	0	0	0	.00	0	.333	.333	.333
1997 Edmonton	AAA Oak	42	151	33	3	4	5	59	22	22	23	0	31	3	1	4	10	3	.77	3	.219	.326	.391
Huntsville	AA Oak	87	323	90	20	6	8	146	79	39	65	0	76	4	3	2	31	9	.78	3	.279	.404	.452
1998 Calgary	AAA CWS	5	17	1	0	0	0	1	0	0	1	0	6	0	0	0	0	0	.00	0	.059	.111	.059
Birmingham	AA CWS	84	321	99	23	7	5	151	75	30	48	1	67	6	4	4	25	14	.64	2	.308	.404	.470
1999 Greenville	AA Atl	132	416	127	20	7	9	188	70	59	55	1	72	7	8	5	31	13	.70	5	.305	.391	.452
10 Min. YEARS		827	2984	845	148	66	60	1305	570	371	395	8	614	55	40	32	262	116	.69	26	.283	.374	.437

Jeff Smith

Bats: Left **Throws:** Right **Pos:** C **Ht:** 6'3" **Wt:** 216 **Born:** 6/17/74 **Age:** 26

		BATTING													BASERUNNING				PERCENTAGES		
Year Team	Lg Org	G	AB	H	2B	3B	HR	TB	R	RBI	TBB	IBB	SO	HBP	SH	SF	SB	CS	SB%	GDP	Avg	OBP	SLG
1996 Fort Wayne	A Min	63	208	49	6	0	2	61	20	26	22	0	32	0	1	2	2	1	.67	4	.236	.306	.293
1997 Fort Myers	A+ Min	49	121	34	5	0	4	51	17	26	12	0	18	0	0	6	0	2	.00	4	.281	.331	.421
New Britain	AA Min	5	18	4	1	0	0	5	1	3	2	0	4	0	0	0	0	0	.00	0	.222	.300	.278
Salt Lake	AAA Min	7	12	3	2	0	0	5	2	2	1	0	3	0	0	0	0	0	.00	0	.250	.308	.417
1998 Fort Myers	A+ Min	6	23	8	2	0	0	10	4	1	1	0	2	1	0	0	1	0	1.00	1	.348	.400	.435
Salt Lake	AAA Min	23	67	17	3	0	0	20	9	2	4	0	13	0	2	0	0	0	.00	2	.254	.296	.299
New Britain	AA Min	27	84	23	11	0	1	37	11	12	5	2	21	1	1	2	0	0	.00	3	.274	.315	.440
1999 New Britain	AA Min	79	265	67	13	0	6	98	25	31	23	0	40	3	3	4	1	0	1.00	4	.253	.315	.370
Salt Lake	AAA Min	5	18	7	3	0	1	13	5	3	0	0	1	0	0	0	0	0	.00	1	.389	.389	.722
4 Min. YEARS		264	816	212	46	0	14	300	94	106	70	2	134	5	7	14	4	3	.57	19	.260	.317	.368

Keilan Smith

Pitches: Right **Bats:** Right **Pos:** P **Ht:** 6'4" **Wt:** 175 **Born:** 12/20/73 **Age:** 26

		HOW MUCH HE PITCHED						WHAT HE GAVE UP										THE RESULTS					
Year Team	Lg Org	G	GS	CG	GF	IP	BFP	H	R	ER	HR	SH	SF	HB	TBB	IBB	SO	WP	Bk	W	L	Pct.	ShO	Sv	ERA
1993 Blue Jays	R Tor	1	0	0	0	3.2	15	4	1	1	0	0	0	0	1	0	4	0	0	0	0	.000	0	0	2.45
Medcine Hat	R+ Tor	15	4	0	5	38	151	28	14	12	3	1	0	1	11	0	37	2	0	1	1	.500	0	1	2.84
1994 St.Cathrnes	A- Tor	15	15	2	0	94	396	81	43	33	5	3	8	5	38	0	56	8	0	3	4	.429	2	0	3.16
1995 Dunedin	A+ Tor	26	24	1	1	149	663	164	83	68	11	6	2	15	53	1	85	16	3	11	6	.647	0	0	4.11
1996 Hagerstown	A Tor	19	1	0	13	29	129	32	19	12	1	0	2	1	8	1	21	5	1	2	3	.400	0	2	3.72
Dunedin	A+ Tor	23	1	0	9	44.2	205	50	32	25	3	3	4	2	22	4	37	5	0	0	3	.000	0	2	5.04
1997 Lakeland	A+ Det	40	3	0	24	77	314	65	23	22	2	4	3	2	27	2	46	7	0	9	2	.818	0	7	2.57
1998 Jacksnville	AA Det	39	1	0	10	71.2	316	69	34	29	6	4	3	1	40	1	54	8	0	4	3	.571	0	0	3.64
1999 Jacksnville	AA Det	19	0	0	5	31.1	156	35	25	23	5	1	3	4	23	0	24	2	0	1	2	.333	0	0	6.61
7 Min. YEARS		197	49	3	67	538.1	2345	528	274	225	36	24	23	31	223	9	364	53	4	31	24	.564	2	12	3.76

Pete Smith

Pitches: Right **Bats:** Right **Pos:** P **Ht:** 6'2" **Wt:** 210 **Born:** 2/27/66 **Age:** 34

		HOW MUCH HE PITCHED						WHAT HE GAVE UP										THE RESULTS					
Year Team	Lg Org	G	GS	CG	GF	IP	BFP	H	R	ER	HR	SH	SF	HB	TBB	IBB	SO	WP	Bk	W	L	Pct.	ShO	Sv	ERA
1984 Phillies	R Phi	8	8	0	0	37	155	29	11	6	0	3	1	0	16	0	35	2	0	1	2	.333	0	0	1.46
1985 Clearwater	A+ Phi	26	25	4	0	153	663	135	68	56	2	1	7	2	80	1	86	3	6	12	10	.545	1	0	3.29
1986 Greenville	AA Atl	24	19	0	1	104.2	499	117	88	68	11	7	8	4	78	0	64	4	2	1	8	.111	0	0	5.85
1987 Greenville	AA Atl	29	25	5	2	177.1	744	162	76	66	10	1	4	3	67	0	119	11	2	9	9	.500	1	1	3.35
1990 Greenville	AA Atl	2	2	0	0	3.1	12	1	0	0	0	0	0	0	0	0	2	0	0	0	0	.000	0	0	0.00
1991 Macon	A Atl	3	3	0	0	9.2	45	15	11	9	1	0	0	0	2	0	14	2	0	0	0	.000	0	0	8.38
Richmond	AAA Atl	10	10	1	0	51	239	66	44	41	10	1	5	0	24	0	41	2	1	3	3	.500	0	0	7.24
1992 Richmond	AAA Atl	15	15	4	0	109.1	415	75	27	26	6	2	1	4	24	0	93	1	0	7	4	.636	1	0	2.14
1995 Charlotte	AAA Fla	10	8	0	1	49	206	51	21	21	5	1	2	1	17	0	20	2	2	2	1	.667	0	0	3.86
1996 Las Vegas	AAA SD	26	26	2	0	169	723	192	106	93	17	5	10	3	42	8	95	5	2	11	9	.550	1	0	4.95
1997 Las Vegas	AAA SD	6	6	0	0	33.2	138	38	16	16	5	2	0	0	6	0	24	0	1	3	2	.600	0	0	4.28
1999 Memphis	AAA StL	8	8	0	0	38	182	53	35	29	7	1	3	1	16	0	35	1	1	2	3	.400	0	0	6.87
Las Vegas	AAA SD	13	12	2	1	71.2	301	77	40	29	7	2	2	1	13	0	47	3	1	4	5	.444	0	0	3.64
1987 Atlanta	NL	6	6	0	0	31.2	143	39	21	17	3	0	2	0	14	0	11	3	1	1	2	.333	0	0	4.83
1988 Atlanta	NL	32	32	5	0	195.1	837	183	89	80	15	12	4	1	88	3	124	5	7	7	15	.318	3	0	3.69
1989 Atlanta	NL	28	27	1	0	142	613	144	83	75	13	4	5	0	57	2	115	3	7	5	14	.263	0	0	4.75
1990 Atlanta	NL	13	13	3	0	77	327	77	45	41	4	3	4	0	24	2	56	2	1	5	6	.455	0	0	4.79
1991 Atlanta	NL	14	10	0	2	48	211	48	33	27	5	2	4	0	22	3	29	1	4	1	3	.250	0	0	5.06
1992 Atlanta	NL	12	11	2	0	79	323	63	19	18	3	4	1	0	28	2	43	2	1	7	0	1.000	1	0	2.05
1993 Atlanta	NL	20	14	0	2	90.2	390	92	45	44	15	6	5	2	36	3	53	1	4	4	8	.333	0	0	4.37
1994 New York	NL	21	21	1	0	131.1	565	145	83	81	25	5	7	2	42	4	62	3	1	4	10	.286	0	0	5.55
1995 Cincinnati	NL	11	2	0	3	24.1	106	30	19	18	8	1	3	1	7	1	14	1	0	1	2	.333	0	0	6.66
1997 San Diego	NL	37	15	0	7	118	511	120	66	63	16	7	2	1	52	2	68	0	3	7	6	.538	0	1	4.81
1998 San Diego	NL	10	8	0	2	43.1	193	45	23	23	5	1	2	3	18	1	36	2	0	3	2	.600	0	0	4.78
Baltimore	AL	27	4	0	3	45	204	57	31	31	7	3	2	0	16	1	29	6	1	2	3	.400	0	0	6.20
11 Min. YEARS		180	167	18	5	1006.2	4322	1010	543	460	81	26	43	19	385	9	675	36	18	55	56	.495	4	1	4.11
11 Maj. YEARS		231	163	12	19	1025.2	4423	1043	557	518	126	49	40	10	404	24	640	29	27	47	71	.398	4	1	4.55

Rod Smith

Bats: Both **Throws:** Right **Pos:** 2B **Ht:** 6'0" **Wt:** 185 **Born:** 9/2/75 **Age:** 24

		BATTING													BASERUNNING				PERCENTAGES		
Year Team	Lg Org	G	AB	H	2B	3B	HR	TB	R	RBI	TBB	IBB	SO	HBP	SH	SF	SB	CS	SB%	GDP	Avg	OBP	SLG
1994 Yankees	R NYY	56	196	56	7	4	1	74	41	18	41	1	51	1	2	0	20	4	.83	2	.286	.412	.378
Greensboro	A NYY	7	20	1	0	0	0	1	2	0	3	0	7	0	0	0	1	0	1.00	0	.050	.174	.050
1995 Greensboro	A NYY	62	235	57	5	6	0	74	31	9	34	1	41	2	2	0	17	12	.59	4	.243	.343	.315
Oneonta	A- NYY	49	187	44	8	3	0	58	34	10	30	0	49	2	0	1	24	7	.77	1	.235	.345	.310
1996 Greensboro	A NYY	132	481	102	15	8	4	145	71	32	64	0	128	7	10	0	57	13	.81	5	.212	.313	.301
1997 Greensboro	A NYY	137	528	131	25	6	13	207	96	50	69	0	148	5	2	1	54	20	.73	5	.248	.340	.392
1998 Tampa	A+ NYY	86	327	80	15	2	6	117	57	35	39	1	70	5	6	2	40	14	.74	5	.245	.332	.358
1999 Tampa	A+ NYY	126	507	134	33	8	6	201	92	45	69	0	102	11	3	1	38	18	.68	1	.264	.364	.396
Norwich	AA NYY	1	5	3	0	0	0	3	1	1	0	0	1	0	0	0	2	0	1.00	0	.600	.600	.600
6 Min. YEARS		656	2486	608	108	37	30	880	425	200	349	3	597	33	25	5	253	88	.74	23	.245	.345	.354

263

Toby Smith

Pitches: Right Bats: Right Pos: P   Ht: 6'6" Wt: 225 Born: 11/16/71 Age: 28

		HOW MUCH HE PITCHED						WHAT HE GAVE UP										THE RESULTS				
Year Team	Lg Org	G	GS	CG	GF	IP	BFP	H	R	ER	HR	SH	SF	HB	TBB	IBB	SO	WP	Bk	W	L	Pct.	ShO	Sv	ERA
1993 Eugene	A- KC	14	0	0	8	23	90	14	8	6	1	2	0	1	7	0	31	0	1	1	1	.500	0	4	2.35
1994 Rockford	A KC	29	16	0	12	121	489	104	50	44	8	3	3	4	31	1	91	14	2	11	9	.550	0	4	3.27
1995 Wilmington	A+ KC	30	7	0	13	79	320	67	32	27	9	2	1	3	20	2	65	6	2	5	7	.417	0	4	3.08
1996 Wichita	AA KC	42	0	0	30	52.1	221	46	25	24	7	4	2	2	19	4	44	7	0	4	2	.667	0	8	4.13
1997 Omaha	AAA KC	17	0	0	12	20.2	96	24	19	18	6	1	1	0	15	2	11	3	1	1	3	.250	0	3	7.84
Wichita	AA KC	8	8	0	0	44	195	49	30	24	7	1	2	2	11	0	29	4	2	2	3	.400	0	0	4.91
1999 Chstn-WV	A KC	2	1	0	0	4.1	18	1	4	1	0	0	0	0	3	0	4	0	0	0	1	.000	0	0	2.08
Wichita	AA KC	22	13	0	5	79.2	336	86	30	26	6	1	1	3	18	1	40	3	0	5	2	.714	0	1	2.94
6 Min. YEARS		164	45	0	80	424	1765	391	198	170	44	14	10	15	124	10	315	37	8	29	28	.509	0	24	3.61

Travis Smith

Pitches: Right Bats: Right Pos: P   Ht: 5'10" Wt: 165 Born: 11/7/72 Age: 27

		HOW MUCH HE PITCHED						WHAT HE GAVE UP										THE RESULTS				
Year Team	Lg Org	G	GS	CG	GF	IP	BFP	H	R	ER	HR	SH	SF	HB	TBB	IBB	SO	WP	Bk	W	L	Pct.	ShO	Sv	ERA
1995 Helena	R+ Mil	20	7	0	11	56	224	41	16	15	4	0	0	7	19	0	63	4	2	4	2	.667	0	5	2.41
1996 Stockton	A+ Mil	14	6	0	3	58.2	241	56	17	12	4	1	0	4	21	0	48	2	4	6	1	.857	0	1	1.84
El Paso	AA Mil	17	17	3	0	107.2	478	119	58	50	6	4	5	6	39	0	68	2	0	7	4	.636	1	0	4.18
1997 El Paso	AA Mil	28	28	5	0	184.1	805	210	106	85	12	7	5	7	58	2	107	7	3	16	3	.842	1	0	4.15
1998 Louisville	AAA Mil	12	11	0	0	67.2	296	77	44	40	9	3	4	2	25	1	36	3	0	4	6	.400	0	0	5.32
1999 Ogden	R+ Mil	1	1	0	0	1	5	0	1	0	0	0	0	0	0	0	3	0	0	0	0	.000	0	0	0.00
Stockton	A+ Mil	3	3	0	0	7.1	35	9	6	5	1	1	0	1	3	0	8	0	0	0	2	.000	0	0	6.14
Huntsville	AA Mil	7	7	0	0	38.1	171	40	27	25	3	2	2	0	18	0	23	6	1	3	2	.600	0	0	5.87
1998 Milwaukee	NL	1	0	0	0	2	7	1	0	0	0	0	0	0	0	0	1	0	0	0	0	.000	0	0	0.00
5 Min. YEARS		102	80	8	14	521	2255	552	273	232	39	18	16	28	183	3	356	24	10	40	20	.667	2	6	4.01

John Sneed

Pitches: Right Bats: Left Pos: P   Ht: 6'6" Wt: 235 Born: 6/30/76 Age: 24

		HOW MUCH HE PITCHED						WHAT HE GAVE UP										THE RESULTS				
Year Team	Lg Org	G	GS	CG	GF	IP	BFP	H	R	ER	HR	SH	SF	HB	TBB	IBB	SO	WP	Bk	W	L	Pct.	ShO	Sv	ERA
1997 Medcine Hat	R+ Tor	15	10	2	1	69.2	275	42	19	10	5	2	1	7	20	0	79	2	0	6	1	.857	0	1	1.29
1998 Hagerstown	A Tor	27	27	2	0	161.2	660	123	59	46	9	4	0	11	58	0	210	5	2	16	2	.889	1	0	2.56
1999 Dunedin	A+ Tor	21	20	0	0	125.1	511	107	53	48	10	3	4	6	36	1	143	5	0	11	2	.846	0	0	3.45
Knoxville	AA Tor	6	6	0	0	28.1	131	33	17	16	2	1	1	2	21	0	28	1	0	3	1	.750	0	0	5.08
3 Min. YEARS		69	63	4	1	385	1577	305	148	120	26	10	6	26	135	1	460	13	2	36	6	.857	1	0	2.81

Clay Snellgrove

Bats: Right Throws: Right Pos: 2B-SS   Ht: 6'0" Wt: 180 Born: 11/22/74 Age: 25

		BATTING													BASERUNNING				PERCENTAGES		
Year Team	Lg Org	G	AB	H	2B	3B	HR	TB	R	RBI	TBB	IBB	SO	HBP	SH	SF	SB	CS	SB%	GDP	Avg	OBP	SLG
1997 Idaho Falls	R+ SD	66	281	97	19	7	2	136	52	48	18	2	39	3	2	6	3	2	.60	7	.345	.383	.484
1998 Clinton	A SD	104	368	88	14	2	2	112	42	30	27	0	32	6	4	1	11	9	.55	7	.239	.301	.304
1999 Las Vegas	AAA SD	1	3	2	2	0	0	4	1	0	0	0	0	0	0	0	0	0	.00	0	.667	.667	1.333
Rancho Cuca	A+ SD	116	426	125	20	2	3	158	62	43	19	0	42	7	4	5	8	7	.53	14	.293	.330	.371
3 Min. YEARS		287	1078	312	55	11	7	410	157	121	64	2	113	16	10	12	22	18	.55	28	.289	.335	.380

Chris Snopek

Bats: Right Throws: Right Pos: SS   Ht: 6'1" Wt: 185 Born: 9/20/70 Age: 29

		BATTING													BASERUNNING				PERCENTAGES		
Year Team	Lg Org	G	AB	H	2B	3B	HR	TB	R	RBI	TBB	IBB	SO	HBP	SH	SF	SB	CS	SB%	GDP	Avg	OBP	SLG
1992 Birmingham	A- CWS	73	245	69	15	1	2	92	49	29	52	4	44	2	1	4	14	4	.78	4	.282	.406	.376
1993 South Bend	A CWS	22	72	28	8	1	5	53	20	18	15	0	13	3	0	2	1	1	.50	1	.389	.500	.736
Sarasota	A+ CWS	107	371	91	21	4	10	150	61	50	65	2	67	1	3	6	3	2	.60	2	.245	.354	.404
1994 Birmingham	AA CWS	106	365	96	25	3	6	145	58	54	58	3	49	5	3	5	9	4	.69	7	.263	.367	.397
1995 Nashville	AAA CWS	113	393	127	23	4	12	194	56	55	50	1	72	4	6	3	2	5	.29	5	.323	.402	.494
1996 Nashville	AAA CWS	40	153	38	8	0	2	52	18	12	21	1	24	1	1	0	2	2	.50	0	.248	.343	.340
1997 Nashville	AAA CWS	20	73	17	4	0	3	30	8	8	7	0	13	0	0	0	0	0	.00	4	.233	.300	.411
1999 Pawtucket	AAA Bos	24	81	20	7	0	3	36	10	10	5	0	15	0	1	0	2	0	1.00	2	.247	.291	.444
Indianapols	AAA Cin	103	381	107	24	3	9	164	66	64	42	0	51	4	2	5	17	6	.74	10	.281	.354	.430
1995 Chicago	AL	22	68	22	4	0	1	29	12	7	9	0	12	0	0	0	1	0	1.00	1	.324	.403	.426
1996 Chicago	AL	46	104	27	6	1	6	53	18	18	6	0	16	1	1	1	0	1	.00	5	.260	.304	.510
1997 Chicago	AL	86	298	65	15	0	5	95	27	35	18	0	51	1	4	2	3	2	.60	4	.218	.263	.319
1998 Chicago	AL	53	125	26	2	0	1	31	17	4	14	0	24	1	0	1	3	0	1.00	4	.208	.291	.248
Boston	AL	8	12	2	0	0	0	2	2	2	1	0	5	0	0	0	0	0	.00	0	.167	.286	.167
7 Min. YEARS		608	2134	593	135	16	52	916	346	300	315	11	348	20	17	25	50	24	.68	35	.278	.372	.429
4 Maj. YEARS		215	607	142	27	1	13	210	76	66	49	0	108	3	5	4	7	3	.70	15	.234	.293	.346

Bert Snow

Pitches: Right Bats: Right Pos: P   Ht: 6'1" Wt: 190 Born: 3/23/77 Age: 23

		HOW MUCH HE PITCHED						WHAT HE GAVE UP										THE RESULTS				
Year Team	Lg Org	G	GS	CG	GF	IP	BFP	H	R	ER	HR	SH	SF	HB	TBB	IBB	SO	WP	Bk	W	L	Pct.	ShO	Sv	ERA
1998 Sou Oregon	A- Oak	11	8	0	1	44.2	215	52	38	28	2	5	3	6	18	1	35	5	1	1	3	.250	0	0	5.64
Modesto	A+ Oak	2	2	0	0	8.2	46	12	8	3	1	0	0	1	6	0	12	1	0	1	1	.500	0	0	3.12
1999 Visalia	A+ Oak	31	3	0	14	64.2	298	55	43	37	4	4	4	4	40	3	90	10	1	3	2	.600	0	5	5.15
Midland	AA Oak	21	0	0	21	21	84	14	4	4	3	0	0	0	9	3	32	1	0	1	1	.500	0	13	1.71

264

HOW MUCH HE PITCHED / WHAT HE GAVE UP / THE RESULTS

Year Team	Lg Org	G	GS	CG	GF	IP	BFP	H	R	ER	HR	SH	SF	HB	TBB	IBB	SO	WP	Bk	W	L	Pct.	ShO	Sv	ERA
Vancouver AAA Oak		2	0	0	0	2.1	11	3	1	1	0	1	0	0	1	0	3	0	0	1	0	1.000	0	0	3.86
2 Min. YEARS		67	13	0	36	141.1	654	136	94	73	10	10	7	11	74	7	172	17	2	7	7	.500	0	18	4.65

Casey Snow

Bats: Both **Throws:** Right **Pos:** C   **Ht:** 5'10" **Wt:** 185 **Born:** 12/8/74 **Age:** 25

BATTING / BASERUNNING / PERCENTAGES

Year Team	Lg Org	G	AB	H	2B	3B	HR	TB	R	RBI	TBB	IBB	SO	HBP	SH	SF	SB	CS	SB%	GDP	Avg	OBP	SLG
1996 Great Falls	R+ LA	43	130	35	6	0	2	47	19	23	13	0	33	5	0	3	1	4	.20	0	.269	.351	.362
1997 San Berndno	A+ LA	43	132	26	5	3	1	40	10	10	4	0	35	2	1	0	2	3	.40	1	.197	.232	.303
Great Falls	R+ LA	17	53	17	3	0	2	26	5	9	8	1	10	1	3	0	2	0	1.00	0	.321	.419	.491
1998 San Berndno	A+ LA	99	335	94	24	2	4	134	44	42	34	6	75	4	3	3	5	6	.45	2	.281	.351	.400
Albuquerque	AAA LA	7	20	4	2	0	0	6	2	2	4	0	7	1	0	1	0	0	.00	0	.200	.346	.300
1999 San Antonio	AA LA	61	170	43	8	2	4	67	21	16	13	1	45	2	2	3	0	0	.00	4	.253	.309	.394
4 Min. YEARS		270	840	219	48	7	13	320	101	102	76	8	205	15	9	10	10	13	.43	7	.261	.329	.381

Chris Snusz

Bats: Right **Throws:** Right **Pos:** C   **Ht:** 6'0" **Wt:** 190 **Born:** 11/8/72 **Age:** 27

BATTING / BASERUNNING / PERCENTAGES

Year Team	Lg Org	G	AB	H	2B	3B	HR	TB	R	RBI	TBB	IBB	SO	HBP	SH	SF	SB	CS	SB%	GDP	Avg	OBP	SLG
1995 Batavia	A- Phi	21	66	15	1	0	1	19	9	5	6	0	6	0	0	0	1	1	.50	4	.227	.292	.288
1996 Batavia	A- Phi	13	31	5	0	0	0	5	6	0	6	0	4	0	1	0	0	0	.00	0	.161	.297	.161
Piedmont	A Phi	4	11	1	0	0	0	1	2	0	2	0	1	0	0	0	0	1	.00	0	.091	.231	.091
1997 Clearwater	A+ Phi	36	105	21	7	0	0	28	12	3	2	0	22	0	0	3	0	0	.00	1	.200	.215	.267
1998 Scranton-WB	AAA Phi	3	9	1	1	0	0	2	0	0	0	0	2	0	0	0	0	0	.00	1	.111	.111	.222
Clearwater	A+ Phi	19	56	11	1	0	0	12	6	6	1	0	9	1	1	1	0	0	.00	0	.196	.220	.214
Reading	AA Phi	12	28	9	2	0	0	11	6	1	3	0	6	0	0	0	0	0	.00	0	.321	.387	.393
1999 Chattanooga	AA Cin	2	6	3	1	0	0	4	0	2	1	0	0	0	0	0	0	0	.00	0	.500	.571	.667
Clinton	A Cin	4	21	4	1	1	0	7	2	3	1	0	8	0	0	0	0	0	.00	0	.190	.227	.333
Rockford	A Cin	19	53	9	1	0	1	13	6	2	3	0	13	1	1	0	1	0	1.00	1	.170	.228	.245
Harrisburg	AA Mon	5	13	4	1	0	0	5	2	3	1	0	3	0	0	0	0	0	.00	0	.308	.357	.385
Ottawa	AAA Mon	21	63	18	3	0	3	30	6	9	1	0	18	0	1	0	0	0	.00	2	.286	.297	.476
5 Min. YEARS		159	462	101	19	1	5	137	57	34	27	0	92	2	7	1	2	2	.50	12	.219	.264	.297

Bill Snyder

Pitches: Right **Bats:** Right **Pos:** P   **Ht:** 6'0" **Wt:** 190 **Born:** 1/29/75 **Age:** 25

HOW MUCH HE PITCHED / WHAT HE GAVE UP / THE RESULTS

Year Team	Lg Org	G	GS	CG	GF	IP	BFP	H	R	ER	HR	SH	SF	HB	TBB	IBB	SO	WP	Bk	W	L	Pct.	ShO	Sv	ERA
1997 Jamestown	A- Det	25	0	0	25	29	126	19	8	7	1	2	0	2	20	2	42	1	1	1	3	.250	0	9	2.17
1998 W Michigan	A Det	42	0	0	20	59.1	236	40	17	12	2	1	1	3	18	2	84	1	0	3	1	.750	0	2	1.82
1999 Lakeland	A+ Det	47	0	0	42	51.2	197	34	13	11	0	4	2	1	18	0	39	0	0	4	1	.800	0	16	1.92
Jacksnville	AA Det	14	0	0	8	18	80	16	6	5	0	1	0	3	5	1	17	0	0	1	0	1.000	0	2	2.50
3 Min. YEARS		128	0	0	95	158	639	109	44	35	3	8	3	9	61	5	182	2	1	9	5	.643	0	29	1.99

Matt Snyder

Pitches: Right **Bats:** Right **Pos:** P   **Ht:** 5'11" **Wt:** 190 **Born:** 7/7/74 **Age:** 25

HOW MUCH HE PITCHED / WHAT HE GAVE UP / THE RESULTS

Year Team	Lg Org	G	GS	CG	GF	IP	BFP	H	R	ER	HR	SH	SF	HB	TBB	IBB	SO	WP	Bk	W	L	Pct.	ShO	Sv	ERA
1995 Bluefield	R+ Bal	17	0	0	15	34.2	150	35	9	4	1	0	0	3	13	0	46	1	0	0	0	.000	0	8	1.04
1996 High Desert	A+ Bal	58	0	0	49	72	317	60	34	30	6	5	2	1	38	2	93	9	1	6	2	.750	0	20	3.75
1997 Bowie	AA Bal	67	0	0	45	80	366	89	48	37	11	8	4	4	42	5	68	10	0	7	5	.583	0	19	4.16
1998 Rochester	AAA Bal	12	0	0	5	19.2	77	17	9	8	3	0	0	1	6	0	13	0	0	2	1	.667	0	0	3.66
Bowie	AA Bal	22	20	4	0	120	510	127	66	58	14	1	3	4	30	0	116	6	3	9	6	.600	1	0	4.35
1999 Rochester	AAA Bal	48	3	0	15	84.2	380	95	60	49	14	3	4	4	30	4	59	6	0	6	6	.500	0	1	5.21
5 Min. YEARS		224	23	4	129	411	1800	423	226	186	49	17	13	17	159	11	395	32	4	30	20	.600	1	48	4.07

Steve Soderstrom

Pitches: Right **Bats:** Right **Pos:** P   **Ht:** 6'3" **Wt:** 205 **Born:** 4/3/72 **Age:** 28

HOW MUCH HE PITCHED / WHAT HE GAVE UP / THE RESULTS

Year Team	Lg Org	G	GS	CG	GF	IP	BFP	H	R	ER	HR	SH	SF	HB	TBB	IBB	SO	WP	Bk	W	L	Pct.	ShO	Sv	ERA
1994 San Jose	A+ SF	8	8	0	0	40.2	179	34	20	19	2	2	1	4	26	0	40	4	1	2	3	.400	0	0	4.20
1995 Shreveport	AA SF	22	22	0	0	116	508	106	53	44	6	5	2	10	51	0	91	12	2	9	5	.643	0	0	3.41
1996 Phoenix	AAA SF	29	29	0	0	171.1	728	178	94	84	13	8	4	7	58	1	80	9	5	7	8	.467	0	0	4.41
1997 Phoenix	AAA SF	31	15	0	8	105.2	498	141	81	76	12	2	2	6	52	1	78	10	1	4	8	.333	0	1	6.47
1998 Fresno	AAA SF	25	23	2	1	137.2	580	133	94	62	20	2	3	7	39	0	96	4	0	11	4	.733	0	1	4.05
1999 Fresno	AAA SF	22	13	0	3	71.2	355	90	64	54	16	4	4	8	35	0	58	8	0	2	8	.200	0	0	6.78
1996 San Francisco	NL	3	3	0	0	13.2	63	16	11	8	1	0	2	2	6	0	9	0	0	2	0	1.000	0	0	5.27
6 Min. YEARS		137	110	2	12	643	2848	682	383	339	69	23	16	42	261	2	443	47	9	35	36	.493	0	2	4.74

Danny Solano

Bats: Right **Throws:** Right **Pos:** SS   **Ht:** 5'9" **Wt:** 155 **Born:** 12/3/78 **Age:** 21

BATTING / BASERUNNING / PERCENTAGES

Year Team	Lg Org	G	AB	H	2B	3B	HR	TB	R	RBI	TBB	IBB	SO	HBP	SH	SF	SB	CS	SB%	GDP	Avg	OBP	SLG
1998 Charlotte	A+ Tex	84	262	68	15	0	1	86	46	30	42	0	54	2	9	4	9	6	.60	2	.260	.361	.328
1999 Oklahoma	AAA Tex	3	6	0	0	0	0	0	0	1	0	0	4	0	0	0	0	0	.00	0	.000	.000	.000
Charlotte	A+ Tex	116	421	114	18	4	7	161	64	44	74	0	74	6	12	0	21	13	.62	3	.271	.387	.382
2 Min. YEARS		203	689	182	33	4	8	247	110	75	116	0	132	8	21	5	30	19	.61	5	.264	.374	.358

Fausto Solano

Bats: Right **Throws:** Right **Pos:** SS   **Ht:** 5'9" **Wt:** 144 **Born:** 6/19/74 **Age:** 26

Year Team	Lg Org	G	AB	H	2B	3B	HR	TB	R	RBI	TBB	IBB	SO	HBP	SH	SF	SB	CS	SB%	GDP	Avg	OBP	SLG
1994 St.Cathrnes	A- Tor	73	288	77	11	3	2	100	49	19	32	0	47	1	6	1	19	10	.66	4	.267	.342	.347
1995 Dunedin	A+ Tor	41	144	30	5	2	1	42	19	10	17	0	30	1	5	0	3	2	.60	4	.208	.296	.292
Blue Jays	R Tor	11	44	13	5	0	2	24	12	7	3	0	6	2	3	1	2	1	.67	4	.295	.360	.545
St.Cathrnes	A- Tor	57	207	59	17	1	2	84	28	24	30	1	28	3	4	1	14	4	.78	2	.285	.382	.406
1996 Hagerstown	A Tor	134	514	132	32	5	3	183	89	36	89	2	72	7	3	4	35	25	.58	8	.257	.371	.356
1997 Knoxville	AA Tor	115	378	100	24	4	10	162	52	56	37	2	47	1	4	4	8	14	.36	11	.265	.329	.429
1998 Knoxville	AA Tor	85	288	69	22	2	10	125	49	38	34	0	53	3	4	2	4	4	.50	5	.240	.324	.434
1999 Syracuse	AAA Tor	9	28	6	0	0	1	9	4	3	1	0	2	1	0	1	0	1	.00	3	.214	.258	.321
Knoxville	AA Tor	104	348	106	18	0	14	166	62	61	57	1	54	6	1	3	11	15	.42	9	.305	.408	.477
6 Min. YEARS		629	2239	592	134	17	45	895	364	254	300	6	339	25	30	17	96	76	.56	50	.264	.355	.400

Steve Soliz

Bats: Right **Throws:** Right **Pos:** C   **Ht:** 5'10" **Wt:** 180 **Born:** 1/27/71 **Age:** 29

Year Team	Lg Org	G	AB	H	2B	3B	HR	TB	R	RBI	TBB	IBB	SO	HBP	SH	SF	SB	CS	SB%	GDP	Avg	OBP	SLG
1993 Watertown	A- Cle	56	209	62	12	0	0	74	30	35	15	0	41	1	2	3	2	0	1.00	3	.297	.342	.354
1994 Kinston	A+ Cle	51	163	40	7	1	3	61	26	10	16	0	32	1	2	1	3	0	1.00	0	.264	.331	.374
Canton-Akrn	AA Cle	18	54	10	1	0	0	11	4	0	2	0	9	1	1	0	0	0	.00	4	.185	.228	.204
1995 Bakersfield	A+ LA	44	159	39	5	0	1	47	9	11	15	0	34	2	0	0	2	1	.67	6	.245	.318	.296
Canton-Akrn	AA Cle	32	81	14	3	0	2	23	9	7	13	0	16	0	1	1	0	0	.00	3	.173	.284	.284
1996 Canton-Akrn	AA Cle	46	143	37	4	2	2	51	18	15	11	0	28	2	0	2	1	2	.33	1	.259	.316	.357
1997 Buffalo	AAA Cle	62	151	29	5	0	1	37	12	13	10	0	40	0	5	3	0	1	.00	2	.192	.238	.245
1998 Buffalo	AAA Cle	39	112	25	6	0	0	31	14	9	11	0	23	3	1	1	0	1	.50	6	.223	.307	.277
1999 Akron	AA Cle	7	23	3	0	0	0	3	1	3	1	0	4	0	0	0	0	0	.00	1	.130	.167	.130
Buffalo	AAA Cle	40	112	29	6	0	2	41	15	14	6	0	24	2	0	1	0	0	.00	1	.259	.306	.366
7 Min. YEARS		395	1207	291	49	3	11	379	138	126	100	0	251	12	12	12	9	5	.64	27	.241	.303	.314

Gabe Sollecito

Pitches: Right **Bats:** Both **Pos:** P   **Ht:** 6'1" **Wt:** 190 **Born:** 3/3/72 **Age:** 28

Year Team	Lg Org	G	GS	CG	GF	IP	BFP	H	R	ER	HR	SH	SF	HB	TBB	IBB	SO	WP	Bk	W	L	Pct.	ShO	Sv	ERA
1993 Niagara Fal	A- Det	23	0	0	21	26.2	111	18	4	1	0	2	0	3	10	1	23	3	1	0	1	.000	0	14	0.34
1994 Fayettevle	A Det	46	0	0	45	57	238	47	21	18	1	2	2	10	15	2	52	1	0	4	3	.571	0	18	2.84
1996 Salinas	IND —	1	0	0	0	0.2		0	0	0	0	0	0	0	0	0	0	0	0	0	0	.000	0	0	0.00
1997 Sioux Falls	IND —	13	0	0	8	13	65	19	12	11	0	0	0	1	8	2	9	1	0	0	4	.000	0	0	7.62
Salinas	IND —	24	0	0	19	32.1	132	23	6	5	1	0	2	2	9	2	37	2	0	4	1	.800	0	5	1.39
1998 Charlotte	A+ Tex	37	0	0	18	60	251	54	13	6	1	1	3	6	14	2	50	0	0	5	2	.714	0	2	0.90
Tulsa	AA Tex	5	0	0	3	9.1	39	5	3	2	0	0	1	0	4	0	10	2	0	1	0	1.000	0	1	1.93
1999 Tulsa	AA Tex	53	0	0	23	96.1	400	85	28	26	6	3	3	8	29	1	80	3	1	5	4	.556	0	11	2.43
6 Min. YEARS		202	0	0	137	295.1	1237	251	87	69	9	8	10	31	89	10	261	12	2	21	15	.583	0	51	2.10

Scott Sollmann

Bats: Left **Throws:** Left **Pos:** OF   **Ht:** 5'10" **Wt:** 167 **Born:** 5/2/75 **Age:** 25

Year Team	Lg Org	G	AB	H	2B	3B	HR	TB	R	RBI	TBB	IBB	SO	HBP	SH	SF	SB	CS	SB%	GDP	Avg	OBP	SLG
1996 Jamestown	A- Det	67	253	71	5	5	0	86	49	19	34	1	47	7	6	2	35	14	.71	2	.281	.378	.340
1997 W Michigan	A Det	121	460	144	13	4	0	165	89	33	79	5	81	11	8	3	40	14	.74	1	.313	.423	.359
1998 Jacksnville	AA Det	10	26	2	0	0	0	2	4	1	7	0	4	1	2	0	1	1	.50	0	.077	.294	.077
Lakeland	A+ Det	104	401	101	11	4	2	126	81	35	62	0	52	3	7	3	59	17	.78	1	.252	.354	.314
1999 Stockton	A+ Mil	67	249	87	10	5	0	107	61	33	52	3	38	1	1	1	32	14	.70	1	.349	.462	.430
Huntsville	AA Mil	55	191	60	4	5	1	77	34	9	34	0	31	3	0	0	17	8	.68	3	.314	.425	.403
4 Min. YEARS		424	1580	465	43	23	3	563	318	130	268	9	253	26	24	9	184	68	.73	8	.294	.403	.356

Alfonso Soriano

Bats: Right **Throws:** Right **Pos:** SS   **Ht:** 6'1" **Wt:** 160 **Born:** 1/7/78 **Age:** 22

Year Team	Lg Org	G	AB	H	2B	3B	HR	TB	R	RBI	TBB	IBB	SO	HBP	SH	SF	SB	CS	SB%	GDP	Avg	OBP	SLG
1999 Norwich	AA NYY	89	361	110	20	3	15	181	57	68	32	1	67	4	0	5	24	16	.60	9	.305	.363	.501
Yankees	R NYY	5	19	5	2	0	1	10	7	5	1	0	3	1	0	1	0	0	.00	1	.263	.318	.526
Columbus	AAA NYY	20	82	15	5	1	2	28	8	11	5	0	18	0	0	2	1	1	.50	1	.183	.225	.341
1 Min. YEARS		114	462	130	27	4	18	219	72	84	38	1	88	5	0	8	25	17	.60	11	.281	.337	.474

Fred Soriano

Bats: Right **Throws:** Right **Pos:** 3B   **Ht:** 5'9" **Wt:** 160 **Born:** 8/5/74 **Age:** 25

Year Team	Lg Org	G	AB	H	2B	3B	HR	TB	R	RBI	TBB	IBB	SO	HBP	SH	SF	SB	CS	SB%	GDP	Avg	OBP	SLG
1993 Tacoma	AAA Oak	2	6	1	1	0	0	2	3	3	2	0	3	0	0	0			.00	0	.167	.375	.333
Athletics	R Oak	41	131	34	5	4	5	62	34	19	21	0	41	1	2	1	7	2	.78	0	.260	.364	.473
Modesto	A+ Oak	11	40	10	2	1	0	14	6	5	1	0	12	1	1	0	1	0	1.00	0	.250	.286	.350
1994 Modesto	A+ Oak	22	53	3	0	0	0	3	8	1	7	0	21	3	1	0	2	1	.67	2	.057	.206	.057
W Michigan	A Oak	78	201	45	2	1	1	52	30	16	21	0	70	12	12	0	23	7	.77	3	.224	.333	.259
1995 W Michigan	A Oak	107	305	80	7	3	13	102	68	32	51	1	72	8	18	2	40	6	.87	0	.262	.380	.334
1996 Modesto	A+ Oak	33	126	33	3	0	2	42	21	19	14	0	33	0	4	1	14	3	.82	1	.262	.326	.333
1997 Knoxville	AA Tor	7	17	1	0	0	0	1	3	0	2	0	4	2	0	0	1	1	.50	0	.059	.273	.059

Year Team	Lg Org	G	AB	H	2B	3B	HR	TB	R	RBI	TBB	IBB	SO	HBP	SH	SF	SB	CS	SB%	GDP	Avg	OBP	SLG
Dunedin	A+ Tor	26	78	24	5	1	2	37	18	12	8	0	17	4	3	1	3	0	1.00	1	.308	.396	.474
Hagerstown	A Tor	38	120	29	9	0	0	38	18	6	5	0	27	2	2	0	8	2	.80	5	.242	.283	.317
Syracuse	AAA Tor	17	44	5	1	1	0	8	3	4	1	0	7	1	2	0	2	0	1.00	0	.114	.152	.182
1998 Bakersfield	A+ SF	72	242	59	9	2	4	84	38	23	22	1	71	5	2	0	9	4	.69	3	.244	.320	.347
1999 Syracuse	AAA Tor	5	18	7	0	0	0	7	3	2	0	0	4	0	0	0	0	0	.00	1	.389	.389	.389
Dunedin	A+ Tor	46	136	29	5	0	4	46	21	17	9	0	35	1	3	0	3	4	.43	5	.213	.267	.338
7 Min. YEARS		505	1517	360	49	13	21	498	274	159	165	2	417	40	50	8	113	30	.79	21	.237	.327	.328

Jose Soriano

Bats: Right **Throws:** Right **Pos:** OF   **Ht:** 6'0" **Wt:** 165 **Born:** 4/20/74 **Age:** 26

Year Team	Lg Org	G	AB	H	2B	3B	HR	TB	R	RBI	TBB	IBB	SO	HBP	SH	SF	SB	CS	SB%	GDP	Avg	OBP	SLG
1993 Athletics	R Oak	48	181	48	7	5	3	74	30	31	12	1	51	0	1	2	8	3	.73	2	.265	.308	.409
1994 Sou Oregon	A- Oak	60	176	38	8	2	3	59	34	23	11	0	48	3	4	4	12	5	.71	3	.216	.268	.335
1995 W Michigan	A Oak	123	413	88	12	2	6	122	64	43	33	3	103	8	15	5	35	12	.74	7	.213	.281	.295
1996 W Michigan	A Oak	126	434	107	20	3	4	145	57	44	31	1	86	5	2	4	20	11	.65	15	.247	.302	.334
1997 Modesto	A+ Oak	124	360	82	13	3	5	116	51	44	37	0	95	5	6	7	28	11	.72	5	.228	.303	.322
1998 Visalia	A+ Oak	86	290	87	13	5	5	125	55	28	35	1	49	3	2	3	26	17	.60	2	.300	.378	.431
1999 Augusta	A Bos	38	148	51	7	5	5	83	28	28	10	0	37	2	0	3	12	5	.71	5	.345	.387	.561
Trenton	AA Bos	61	166	42	9	1	2	59	38	20	12	1	31	2	1	1	15	6	.71	3	.253	.309	.355
7 Min. YEARS		666	2168	543	89	26	33	783	357	261	181	7	500	28	31	29	156	70	.69	42	.250	.313	.361

Dorian Speed

Bats: Right **Throws:** Right **Pos:** OF   **Ht:** 6'3" **Wt:** 205 **Born:** 3/1/74 **Age:** 26

Year Team	Lg Org	G	AB	H	2B	3B	HR	TB	R	RBI	TBB	IBB	SO	HBP	SH	SF	SB	CS	SB%	GDP	Avg	OBP	SLG
1995 Williamsprt	A- ChC	60	204	44	8	3	2	64	30	23	28	0	56	1	1	3	18	5	.78	3	.216	.309	.314
1997 Rockford	A ChC	44	157	39	7	1	1	51	27	18	18	0	45	4	3	1	18	4	.82	5	.248	.339	.325
1998 Daytona	A+ ChC	85	250	67	11	5	6	106	43	34	20	0	56	2	3	1	13	5	.72	2	.268	.326	.424
1999 West Tenn	AA ChC	121	415	111	21	8	14	190	70	57	27	0	106	8	2	1	22	11	.67	6	.267	.324	.458
4 Min. YEARS		310	1026	261	47	17	23	411	170	132	93	0	263	15	9	6	71	25	.74	16	.254	.324	.401

Cam Spence

Pitches: Right **Bats:** Right **Pos:** P   **Ht:** 6'3" **Wt:** 195 **Born:** 10/11/74 **Age:** 25

| | | HOW MUCH HE PITCHED | | | | | | WHAT HE GAVE UP | | | | | | | | | | | | THE RESULTS | | | | |
Year Team	Lg Org	G	GS	CG	GF	IP	BFP	H	R	ER	HR	SH	SF	HB	TBB	IBB	SO	WP	Bk	W	L	Pct.	ShO	Sv	ERA
1996 Tampa	A+ NYY	8	8	0	0	40.1	181	51	31	26	3	0	2	3	12	0	20	2	1	2	4	.333	0	0	5.80
Greensboro	A NYY	19	19	0	0	114.2	492	108	66	49	8	5	3	4	38	1	89	7	0	6	6	.500	0	0	3.85
1997 Tampa	A+ NYY	15	5	0	2	49.1	191	42	16	13	2	2	0	1	10	0	31	1	2	1	2	.333	0	0	2.37
Greensboro	A NYY	8	7	0	0	48	195	43	23	18	4	3	3	3	10	0	35	0	0	2	2	.500	0	0	3.38
1998 Greensboro	A NYY	8	7	0	0	39.1	151	34	10	9	1	0	0	0	5	0	41	3	0	3	2	.600	0	0	2.06
Tampa	A+ NYY	21	20	2	0	127.1	542	125	66	53	7	5	4	2	38	1	105	3	4	9	5	.643	0	0	3.75
1999 Norwich	AA NYY	19	16	0	2	91.2	421	118	75	59	7	3	8	6	32	3	62	3	2	5	5	.500	0	0	5.79
Tampa	A+ NYY	7	7	1	0	46.2	185	32	13	10	2	0	1	1	11	0	36	1	0	3	0	1.000	0	0	1.93
Columbus	AAA NYY	1	1	0	0	7	30	8	4	4	1	0	1	0	4	0	4	0	0	0	1	.000	0	0	5.14
4 Min. YEARS		106	90	3	4	564.1	2388	561	304	241	35	18	22	20	157	5	423	20	9	31	27	.534	0	0	3.84

Corey Spiers

Pitches: Left **Bats:** Left **Pos:** P   **Ht:** 6'0" **Wt:** 204 **Born:** 6/19/75 **Age:** 25

| | | HOW MUCH HE PITCHED | | | | | | WHAT HE GAVE UP | | | | | | | | | | | | THE RESULTS | | | | |
Year Team	Lg Org	G	GS	CG	GF	IP	BFP	H	R	ER	HR	SH	SF	HB	TBB	IBB	SO	WP	Bk	W	L	Pct.	ShO	Sv	ERA
1996 Elizabethtn	R+ Min	17	8	0	2	59.1	289	69	45	22	3	0	3	2	26	0	67	9	1	6	5	.545	0	0	3.34
Fort Wayne	A Min	2	1	0	0	4	23	6	3	3	0	0	0	0	5	0	2	0	0	0	1	.000	0	0	6.75
1997 Fort Wayne	A Min	24	23	0	0	120.1	530	154	83	65	5	4	5	2	33	0	94	12	1	5	9	.357	0	0	4.86
1998 Fort Wayne	A Min	5	5	0	0	27	103	15	7	2	0	0	0	0	13	0	20	0	0	2	0	1.000	0	0	0.67
Fort Myers	A+ Min	24	24	1	0	151.1	650	172	70	56	7	2	5	6	38	0	98	7	1	9	8	.529	0	0	3.33
1999 New Britain	AA Min	8	8	1	0	46.2	192	50	21	18	3	0	3	1	12	0	21	3	0	5	2	.714	1	0	3.47
4 Min. YEARS		80	69	2	3	408.2	1787	466	229	166	18	6	16	11	127	0	302	31	3	27	25	.519	1	0	3.66

Junior Spivey

Bats: Right **Throws:** Right **Pos:** 2B   **Ht:** 6'0" **Wt:** 185 **Born:** 1/28/75 **Age:** 25

Year Team	Lg Org	G	AB	H	2B	3B	HR	TB	R	RBI	TBB	IBB	SO	HBP	SH	SF	SB	CS	SB%	GDP	Avg	OBP	SLG
1996 Diamondbcks	R Ari	20	69	23	0	0	0	23	13	3	12	0	16	4	1	1	11	2	.85	0	.333	.453	.333
Lethbridge	R+ Ari	31	107	36	3	4	2	53	30	25	23	0	24	3	1	2	8	3	.73	2	.336	.459	.495
1997 High Desert	A+ Ari	136	491	134	24	6	6	188	88	53	69	2	115	11	2	3	14	9	.61	9	.273	.373	.383
1998 High Desert	A+ Ari	79	285	80	14	5	5	119	64	35	64	0	61	3	0	1	34	12	.74	4	.281	.416	.418
Tulsa	AA Ari	34	119	37	10	1	3	58	26	16	28	1	25	3	1	1	8	4	.67	1	.311	.450	.487
1999 El Paso	AA Ari	44	164	48	10	4	3	75	40	19	36	0	27	2	1	1	14	10	.58	5	.293	.424	.457
4 Min. YEARS		344	1235	358	61	20	19	516	261	151	232	3	268	26	6	9	89	40	.69	21	.290	.410	.418

Scott Stahoviak

Bats: Left **Throws:** Right **Pos:** 1B **Ht:** 6' 5" **Wt:** 220 **Born:** 3/6/70 **Age:** 30

Year Team	Lg Org	G	AB	H	2B	3B	HR	TB	R	RBI	TBB	IBB	SO	HBP	SH	SF	SB	CS	SB%	GDP	Avg	OBP	SLG
1991 Visalia	A+ Min	43	158	44	9	1	1	58	29	25	22	2	28	3	2	0	9	3	.75	3	.278	.377	.367
1992 Visalia	A+ Min	110	409	126	26	3	5	173	62	68	82	2	66	3	0	2	17	6	.74	6	.308	.425	.423
1993 Nashville	AA Min	93	331	90	25	1	12	153	40	56	56	2	95	1	1	4	10	2	.83	5	.272	.375	.462
1994 Salt Lake	AAA Min	123	437	139	41	6	13	231	96	94	70	5	90	5	0	6	6	8	.43	12	.318	.413	.529
1995 Salt Lake	AAA Min	9	33	10	1	0	0	11	6	5	6	0	3	0	0	0	2	0	1.00	0	.303	.410	.333
1997 Salt Lake	AAA Min	8	28	6	0	0	2	12	5	10	5	0	8	1	0	0	0	0	.00	1	.214	.353	.429
1998 Salt Lake	AAA Min	111	399	126	33	6	18	225	71	82	45	4	94	1	0	7	5	2	.71	9	.316	.381	.564
1999 Iowa	AAA ChC	83	274	65	16	1	14	125	51	44	44	2	88	1	2	3	4	1	.80	3	.237	.342	.456
1993 Minnesota	AL	20	57	11	4	0	0	15	1	1	3	0	22	0	0	0	0	2	.00	2	.193	.233	.263
1995 Minnesota	AL	94	263	70	19	0	3	98	28	23	30	1	61	1	0	2	5	1	.83	3	.266	.341	.373
1996 Minnesota	AL	130	405	115	30	3	13	190	72	61	59	7	114	2	1	2	3	3	.50	9	.284	.376	.469
1997 Minnesota	AL	91	275	63	17	0	10	110	33	33	24	1	73	6	0	4	5	2	.71	7	.229	.301	.400
1998 Minnesota	AL	9	19	2	0	0	1	5	1	1	0	0	7	0	0	0	0	0	.00	0	.105	.105	.263
8 Min. YEARS		580	2069	606	151	18	65	988	360	384	330	17	472	15	5	22	53	22	.71	39	.293	.390	.478
5 Maj. YEARS		344	1019	261	70	3	27	418	135	119	116	9	277	9	1	8	13	8	.62	21	.256	.335	.410

Rob Stanifer

Pitches: Right **Bats:** Right **Pos:** P **Ht:** 6' 3" **Wt:** 205 **Born:** 3/10/72 **Age:** 20

Year Team	Lg Org	G	GS	CG	GF	IP	BFP	H	R	ER	HR	SH	SF	HB	TBB	IBB	SO	WP	Bk	W	L	Pct.	ShO	Sv	ERA
1994 Elmira	A- Fla	9	8	1	0	49	211	54	17	14	2	0	1	2	12	1	38	2	3	2	1	.667	0	0	2.57
Brevard Cty	A+ Fla	5	5	0	0	24.1	115	32	20	17	2	1	1	3	10	0	12	2	1	1	2	.333	0	0	6.29
1995 Brevard Cty	A+ Fla	18	13	0	0	82.2	360	97	47	38	4	4	5	7	15	0	45	2	0	3	6	.333	0	0	4.14
1996 Brevard Cty	A+ Fla	22	0	0	4	49	206	54	17	13	3	0	1	1	9	0	32	1	0	4	2	.667	0	0	2.39
Portland	AA Fla	18	0	0	10	34.1	137	27	15	6	3	1	2	1	9	0	33	2	0	3	1	.750	0	2	1.57
1997 Charlotte	AAA Fla	22	0	0	16	27.2	123	34	16	15	3	1	1	1	7	0	25	2	0	4	0	1.000	0	1	4.88
1998 Charlotte	AAA Fla	21	1	0	10	39.2	166	39	20	19	1	1	5	1	13	2	29	1	0	4	2	.667	0	4	4.31
1999 Calgary	AAA Fla	16	0	0	8	16	87	32	23	22	7	1	1	4	6	0	15	0	0	1	2	.333	0	0	12.38
Trenton	AA Bos	5	0	0	3	9	36	6	0	0	0	1	0	0	4	2	11	0	0	0	0	.000	0	1	0.00
Pawtucket	AAA Bos	31	0	0	20	39.2	168	34	21	9	5	0	0	0	15	1	29	4	0	3	1	.750	0	3	2.04
1997 Florida	NL	36	0	0	10	45	188	43	23	23	9	4	0	3	16	0	28	1	0	1	2	.333	0	0	4.60
1998 Florida	NL	38	0	0	11	48	222	54	33	30	5	2	3	0	22	2	30	1	0	2	4	.333	0	1	5.63
6 Min. YEARS		167	27	1	71	371.1	1609	409	196	153	30	10	17	20	100	6	209	16	4	25	17	.595	0	15	3.71
2 Maj. YEARS		74	0	0	21	93	410	97	56	53	14	6	3	3	38	2	58	2	0	3	6	.333	0	2	5.13

Andy Stankiewicz

Bats: Right **Throws:** Right **Pos:** 2B **Ht:** 5' 9" **Wt:** 165 **Born:** 8/10/64 **Age:** 35

Year Team	Lg Org	G	AB	H	2B	3B	HR	TB	R	RBI	TBB	IBB	SO	HBP	SH	SF	SB	CS	SB%	GDP	Avg	OBP	SLG
1986 Oneonta	A- NYY	59	216	64	8	3	0	78	51	17	38	0	41	5	4	4	14	3	.82	2	.296	.407	.361
1987 Ft. Laud	A+ NYY	119	456	140	18	7	2	178	80	47	62	1	84	4	7	1	26	13	.67	9	.307	.394	.390
1988 Albany-Colo	AA NYY	109	414	111	20	2	1	138	63	33	39	0	53	9	9	2	15	10	.60	6	.268	.343	.333
Columbus	AAA NYY	29	114	25	0	0	0	25	4	4	6	0	25	0	1	0	2	0	1.00	1	.219	.258	.219
1989 Albany-Colo	AA NYY	133	498	133	26	2	4	175	74	49	57	2	59	8	3	11	41	9	.82	8	.267	.345	.351
1990 Columbus	AAA NYY	135	446	102	14	4	1	127	68	48	71	1	63	10	7	4	25	8	.76	11	.229	.345	.285
1991 Columbus	AAA NYY	125	372	101	12	4	1	124	47	41	29	0	45	8	8	5	29	16	.64	9	.272	.333	.333
1993 Columbus	AAA NYY	90	331	80	12	5	0	102	45	32	29	0	46	3	4	3	12	8	.60	5	.242	.306	.308
1994 Jackson	AA Hou	5	12	5	0	0	0	5	1	3	0	0	4	0	0	0	0	0	.00	1	.417	.385	.417
1995 Tucson	AAA Hou	25	87	24	4	0	1	31	16	15	14	0	8	0	2	1	3	1	.75	3	.276	.373	.356
1998 Diamondbcks	R Ari	3	10	3	0	0	0	3	2	3	0	0	0	0	0	0	0	0	.00	0	.300	.300	.300
Tucson	AAA Ari	5	20	6	0	0	0	6	1	2	0	0	1	0	0	0	0	0	.00	1	.300	.333	.300
1999 Columbus	AAA NYY	50	163	45	8	3	1	62	34	20	23	0	27	3	4	1	6	1	.86	3	.276	.374	.380
1992 New York	AL	116	400	107	22	2	2	139	52	25	38	0	42	5	7	1	9	5	.64	13	.268	.338	.348
1993 New York	AL	16	9	0	0	0	0	0	5	0	1	0	1	0	0	0	0	0	.00	0	.000	.100	.000
1994 Houston	NL	37	54	14	3	0	1	20	10	5	12	0	12	1	2	0	1	1	.50	2	.259	.403	.370
1995 Houston	NL	43	52	6	1	0	0	7	6	7	12	2	19	0	1	0	4	2	.67	1	.115	.281	.135
1996 Montreal	NL	64	77	22	5	1	0	29	12	9	6	1	12	3	1	1	1	0	1.00	1	.286	.356	.377
1997 Montreal	NL	76	107	24	9	0	1	36	11	5	4	0	22	0	7	1	1	1	.50	1	.224	.250	.336
1998 Arizona	NL	77	145	30	5	0	0	40	8	7	0	0	33	0	1	0	1	0	1.00	3	.207	.252	.241
11 Min. YEARS		887	3139	839	122	30	11	1054	486	314	368	4	451	51	49	33	173	69	.71	62	.267	.350	.336
7 Maj. YEARS		429	844	203	45	3	4	266	105	59	80	3	141	11	18	4	17	9	.65	21	.241	.313	.315

T.J. Staton

Bats: Left **Throws:** Left **Pos:** OF **Ht:** 6'3" **Wt:** 210 **Born:** 2/17/75 **Age:** 25

Year Team	Lg Org	G	AB	H	2B	3B	HR	TB	R	RBI	TBB	IBB	SO	HBP	SH	SF	SB	CS	SB%	GDP	Avg	OBP	SLG
1993 Pirates	R Pit	32	115	41	9	2	1	57	23	18	8	0	14	0	0	0	10	2	.83	1	.357	.398	.496
1994 Welland	A- Pit	12	45	8	3	0	0	11	4	4	0	0	7	0	0	0	5	0	1.00	1	.178	.178	.244
Pirates	R Pit	11	39	10	1	0	1	16	3	5	1	0	8	1	0	0	0	0	.00	0	.256	.293	.410
Augusta	A Pit	37	125	27	6	1	0	35	9	5	10	0	38	0	1	1	6	1	.86	5	.216	.272	.280
1995 Augusta	A Pit	112	391	114	21	5	5	160	43	53	27	5	97	2	0	2	27	13	.68	6	.292	.340	.409
1996 Carolina	AA Pit	112	386	119	24	3	15	194	72	57	58	1	99	6	0	4	17	7	.71	4	.308	.403	.503
1997 Calgary	AAA Pit	65	199	47	14	0	2	67	30	22	22	0	51	2	1	1	3	3	.50	6	.236	.317	.337
Carolina	AA Pit	58	207	60	11	2	6	93	33	33	12	1	60	5	3	2	4	4	.67	3	.290	.341	.449
1998 Carolina	AA Pit	63	223	67	17	1	7	107	37	48	25	1	52	0	1	0	6	4	.60	5	.300	.375	.480
Nashville	AAA Pit	62	186	45	8	0	6	71	28	21	15	0	55	0	1	0	5	4	.56	1	.242	.307	.382

Year Team	Lg Org	G	AB	H	2B	3B	HR	TB	R	RBI	TBB	IBB	SO	HBP	SH	SF	SB	CS	SB%	GDP	Avg	OBP	SLG
1999 Ottawa	AAA Mon	14	42	8	3	1	0	13	5	5	10	0	11	0	0	1	2	0	1.00	1	.190	.340	.310
7 Min. YEARS		578	1958	546	119	15	43	824	287	271	188	8	492	22	5	13	89	38	.70	34	.279	.347	.421

Gene Stechschulte

Pitches: Right **Bats:** Right **Pos:** P **Ht:** 6'5" **Wt:** 210 **Born:** 8/12/73 **Age:** 26

		HOW MUCH HE PITCHED					WHAT HE GAVE UP										THE RESULTS					
Year Team	Lg Org	G	GS	CG	GF	IP	BFP	H	R	ER	HR	SH	SF	HB	TBB	IBB	SO	WP	Bk	W	L	Pct.	ShO	Sv	ERA
1996 New Jersey	A- StL	20	1	0	6	33	159	41	17	12	0	2	1	2	16	2	27	4	0	1	2	.333	0	0	3.27
1997 New Jersey	A- StL	30	0	0	9	36.1	164	45	16	13	2	0	2	1	16	0	28	3	0	1	1	.500	0	1	3.22
1998 Peoria	A StL	57	0	0	51	66	279	58	26	19	1	5	2	2	21	2	70	2	0	4	8	.333	0	33	2.59
1999 Memphis	AAA Mon	2	0	0	0	2.1	14	2	2	2	0	0	1	0	5	0	2	0	0	0	0	.000	0	0	7.71
Arkansas	AA StL	39	0	0	33	42.1	191	41	26	16	4	4	1	4	20	1	41	3	0	2	6	.250	0	19	3.40
4 Min. YEARS		148	1	0	99	180	807	187	87	62	7	11	7	9	78	5	168	12	0	8	17	.320	0	53	3.10

Dave Steed

Bats: Right **Throws:** Right **Pos:** 1B **Ht:** 6'1" **Wt:** 205 **Born:** 2/25/73 **Age:** 27

		BATTING															BASERUNNING				PERCENTAGES		
Year Team	Lg Org	G	AB	H	2B	3B	HR	TB	R	RBI	TBB	IBB	SO	HBP	SH	SF	SB	CS	SB%	GDP	Avg	OBP	SLG
1994 Yakima	A- LA	48	147	37	5	2	5	61	21	24	28	0	43	5	1	0	1	2	.33	4	.252	.389	.415
1995 Vero Beach	A+ LA	59	195	49	16	0	0	65	11	24	18	0	53	3	1	1	0	0	.00	5	.251	.323	.333
San Antonio	AA LA	40	123	31	10	1	3	52	13	16	11	0	32	1	0	2	0	1	.00	2	.252	.314	.423
1996 San Berndno	A+ LA	28	87	26	6	0	1	35	11	13	14	0	19	1	0	1	2	3	.40	1	.299	.398	.402
Vero Beach	A+ LA	23	73	21	3	0	1	27	6	10	6	0	15	0	1	0	1	0	1.00	1	.288	.342	.370
San Antonio	AA LA	7	17	2	1	0	0	3	0	2	1	0	6	0	0	0	0	0	.00	1	.118	.167	.176
1997 Albuquerque	AAA LA	25	47	10	4	0	1	17	8	4	4	1	19	0	0	0	0	0	.00	0	.213	.275	.362
1998 Albuquerque	AAA LA	57	151	42	7	1	4	63	18	21	11	0	39	2	0	2	0	1	.00	5	.278	.331	.417
1999 Albuquerque	AAA LA	30	62	13	4	0	0	17	8	5	7	1	17	0	4	1	0	1	.00	3	.210	.286	.274
6 Min. YEARS		317	902	231	56	4	15	340	96	119	100	2	243	12	7	7	4	8	.33	22	.256	.336	.377

Kennie Steenstra

Pitches: Right **Bats:** Right **Pos:** P **Ht:** 6' 5" **Wt:** 215 **Born:** 10/13/70 **Age:** 29

		HOW MUCH HE PITCHED					WHAT HE GAVE UP										THE RESULTS					
Year Team	Lg Org	G	GS	CG	GF	IP	BFP	H	R	ER	HR	SH	SF	HB	TBB	IBB	SO	WP	Bk	W	L	Pct.	ShO	Sv	ERA
1992 Geneva	A- ChC	3	3	1	0	20	76	11	4	2	0	0	0	0	3	0	12	0	1	3	0	1.000	0	0	0.90
Peoria	A ChC	12	12	4	0	89.2	364	79	29	21	5	2	1	3	21	1	68	4	3	6	3	.667	2	0	2.11
1993 Daytona	A+ ChC	13	13	1	0	81.1	317	64	26	23	2	3	2	8	12	1	57	2	1	5	3	.625	1	0	2.55
Iowa	AAA ChC	1	1	0	0	6.2	32	9	5	5	2	0	0	0	4	0	6	0	0	1	0	1.000	0	0	6.75
Orlando	AA ChC	14	14	2	0	100.1	427	103	47	40	4	4	2	9	25	0	60	5	2	8	3	.727	2	0	3.59
1994 Iowa	AAA ChC	3	3	0	0	13	68	24	21	19	2	0	2	2	4	0	10	0	0	1	2	.333	0	0	13.15
Orlando	AA ChC	23	23	2	0	158.1	654	146	55	46	12	9	3	9	39	4	83	4	1	9	7	.563	1	0	2.61
1995 Iowa	AAA ChC	29	26	6	1	171.1	722	174	85	74	15	6	6	8	48	3	96	6	0	9	12	.429	1	0	3.89
1996 Iowa	AAA ChC	26	26	1	0	158	686	170	96	88	24	5	9	9	47	4	101	2	0	8	12	.400	0	0	5.01
1997 Iowa	AAA ChC	25	25	4	0	160.2	663	161	85	70	15	4	9	0	41	4	111	7	0	5	10	.333	0	0	3.92
1998 Iowa	AAA ChC	25	24	1	0	148	639	171	84	72	16	6	3	1	36	1	104	0	0	11	5	.688	1	0	4.38
1999 Tacoma	AAA Sea	13	10	0	1	51.2	231	60	40	32	5	1	7	3	15	0	24	1	0	1	4	.200	0	0	5.57
Greenville	AA Atl	8	0	0	1	19	80	25	8	8	1	0	1	0	1	0	12	2	0	2	1	.667	0	0	3.79
1998 Chicago	NL	4	0	0	1	3.1	18	7	4	4	2	0	0	0	1	0	4	0	0	0	0	.000	0	0	10.80
8 Min. YEARS		195	180	22	3	1178	4959	1197	585	500	103	40	45	52	296	18	744	33	8	69	62	.527	9	0	3.82

Mike Stefanski

Bats: Right **Throws:** Right **Pos:** C **Ht:** 6' 2" **Wt:** 202 **Born:** 9/12/69 **Age:** 30

		BATTING															BASERUNNING				PERCENTAGES		
Year Team	Lg Org	G	AB	H	2B	3B	HR	TB	R	RBI	TBB	IBB	SO	HBP	SH	SF	SB	CS	SB%	GDP	Avg	OBP	SLG
1991 Brewers	R Mil	56	206	76	5	5	0	91	43	43	22	0	22	5	0	6	3	2	.60	4	.369	.431	.442
1992 Beloit	A Mil	116	385	105	12	0	4	129	66	45	55	1	81	4	3	3	9	4	.69	11	.273	.367	.335
1993 Stockton	A+ Mil	97	345	111	22	2	10	167	58	57	49	2	45	5	1	2	6	1	.86	15	.322	.411	.484
1994 El Paso	AA Mil	95	312	82	7	6	8	125	59	56	32	0	80	0	2	5	4	3	.57	5	.263	.327	.401
1995 El Paso	AA Mil	6	27	11	3	0	1	17	5	6	0	0	3	0	0	0	1	0	1.00	0	.407	.407	.630
New Orleans	AAA Mil	78	228	56	10	2	2	76	30	24	14	0	28	1	5	5	2	0	1.00	8	.246	.286	.333
1996 Louisville	AAA StL	53	126	26	7	1	2	41	11	9	11	1	11	1	1	2	1	2	.33	4	.206	.271	.325
1997 Arkansas	AA StL	1	4	1	0	1	0	3	1	0	0	0	0	0	0	0	0	0	.00	1	.250	.250	.750
Louisville	AAA StL	57	197	60	10	0	6	88	26	22	12	0	20	1	2	1	0	1	.00	0	.305	.346	.447
1998 Memphis	AAA StL	95	298	79	19	1	6	118	34	44	23	4	42	4	5	2	1	2	.33	11	.265	.324	.396
1999 Memphis	AAA StL	64	201	60	12	0	4	84	27	22	17	0	28	4	1	2	3	0	1.00	8	.299	.362	.418
9 Min. YEARS		718	2329	667	107	18	43	939	360	328	235	8	360	25	20	28	30	15	.67	73	.286	.354	.403

Randy Stegall

Bats: Right **Throws:** Right **Pos:** 3B **Ht:** 6'3" **Wt:** 190 **Born:** 2/16/75 **Age:** 25

		BATTING															BASERUNNING				PERCENTAGES		
Year Team	Lg Org	G	AB	H	2B	3B	HR	TB	R	RBI	TBB	IBB	SO	HBP	SH	SF	SB	CS	SB%	GDP	Avg	OBP	SLG
1998 Billings	R+ Cin	66	269	85	19	1	5	121	46	40	20	0	44	5	6	2	2	1	.67	15	.316	.372	.450
1999 Clinton	A Cin	71	252	63	12	4	4	95	39	44	27	0	64	4	2	2	3	2	.60	3	.250	.330	.377
Chattanooga	AA Cin	13	29	6	0	0	0	6	0	1	2	0	5	0	1	1	0	0	.00	1	.207	.250	.207
Rockford	A Cin	26	99	31	4	1	0	37	14	18	3	0	20	1	0	0	3	4	.43	3	.313	.340	.374
2 Min. YEARS		176	649	185	35	6	9	259	99	103	52	0	133	10	9	5	8	7	.53	22	.285	.345	.399

269

Earl Steinmetz

Pitches: Right **Bats:** Right **Pos:** P **Ht:** 6'3" **Wt:** 175 **Born:** 5/17/71 **Age:** 29

		HOW MUCH HE PITCHED						WHAT HE GAVE UP												THE RESULTS					
Year Team	Lg Org	G	GS	CG	GF	IP	BFP	H	R	ER	HR	SH	SF	HB	TBB	IBB	SO	WP	Bk	W	L	Pct.	ShO	Sv	ERA
1989 Braves	R Atl	10	8	1	0	47.2	184	30	12	11	2	0	1	4	16	0	54	5	1	3	2	.600	0	0	2.08
1990 Sumter	A Atl	25	24	2	0	144.2	605	148	67	55	11	1	2	7	34	3	105	5	6	11	8	.579	1	0	3.42
1991 Durham	A+ Atl	16	15	0	1	72	308	74	38	32	7	2	5	3	24	1	58	0	0	3	7	.300	0	0	4.00
1992 Durham	A+ Atl	26	8	0	5	73.1	319	70	48	41	11	1	6	2	36	0	49	4	3	2	5	.286	0	0	5.03
Macon	A Atl	6	6	0	0	35	148	37	16	14	0	1	2	0	10	0	17	1	1	2	2	.500	0	0	3.60
1993 Durham	A+ Atl	6	0	0	3	11	64	21	15	15	4	0	1	1	10	0	12	0	0	0	0	.000	0	0	12.27
Stockton	A+ Mil	28	3	0	2	59.2	270	73	36	26	2	2	4	3	22	0	41	1	0	4	1	.800	0	0	3.92
1994 San Antonio	IND —	5	3	0		24.2		29	19	15	2	—	—		13	—	12	—		2	2	.000	0	0	5.47
1995 Abilene	IND —	23	21	6	1	139	629	155	84	68	6	11	4	7	62	3	77	10	0	5	13	.278	1	0	4.40
1997 Kissimmee	A+ Hou	4	0	0	2	6	28	8	8	8	0	0	1	0	3	0	4	1	0	0	0	.000	0	0	12.00
Tyler	IND —	4	4	1	0	28.1	114	24	8	7	1	0	0	0	11	1	18	2	0	2	0	1.000	0	0	2.22
1998 Newburgh	IND —	4	4	0	0	23.1	98	22	15	12	1	0	0	0	9	0	18	0	0	0	0	.000	0	0	4.63
Bowie	AA Bal	1	0	0	0	0.1	4	2	0	0	0	0	0	0	1	0	0	0	0	0	0	.000	0	0	0.00
Frederick	A+ Bal	13	0	0	5	23	101	23	13	8	3	1	0	1	6	1	20	2	0	1	1	.500	0	0	3.13
1999 Greenville	AA Atl	6	2	0	2	10.2	57	13	9	8	1	0	1	1	16	1	6	1	0	2	2	.000	0	0	6.75
Winnipeg	IND —	5	5	0	0	30.2	139	35	20	15	1	2	0	2	11	1	29	1	0	2	1	.667	0	0	4.40
10 Min. YEARS		182	103	10	21	729.1	—	764	408	335	52	—	—	—	284	—	520	—		35	46	.432	2	0	4.13

Dernell Stenson

Bats: Left **Throws:** Left **Pos:** 1B **Ht:** 6'1" **Wt:** 230 **Born:** 6/17/78 **Age:** 22

		BATTING														BASERUNNING				PERCENTAGES		
Year Team	Lg Org	G	AB	H	2B	3B	HR	TB	R	RBI	TBB	IBB	SO	HBP	SH	SF	SB	CS	SB%	GDP	Avg	OBP	SLG
1996 Red Sox	R Bos	32	97	21	3	1	2	32	16	15	16	0	26	7	0	3	4	3	.57	0	.216	.358	.330
1997 Michigan	A Bos	131	471	137	35	2	15	221	79	80	72	6	105	19	0	8	6	4	.60	10	.291	.400	.469
1998 Trenton	AA Bos	138	505	130	21	1	24	225	90	71	84	3	135	14	1	4	5	3	.63	6	.257	.376	.446
1999 Red Sox	R Bos	6	23	5	0	0	2	11	2	7	3	0	5	0	0	0	0	0	.00	0	.217	.308	.478
Pawtucket	AAA Bos	121	440	119	28	2	18	205	64	82	55	5	119	6	2	5	2	1	.67	7	.270	.356	.466
4 Min. YEARS		428	1536	412	87	6	61	694	251	255	230	14	390	46	3	20	17	11	.61	23	.268	.376	.452

Brent Stentz

Pitches: Right **Bats:** Right **Pos:** P **Ht:** 6'5" **Wt:** 230 **Born:** 7/24/75 **Age:** 24

		HOW MUCH HE PITCHED						WHAT HE GAVE UP												THE RESULTS					
Year Team	Lg Org	G	GS	CG	GF	IP	BFP	H	R	ER	HR	SH	SF	HB	TBB	IBB	SO	WP	Bk	W	L	Pct.	ShO	Sv	ERA
1995 Tigers	R Det	24	0	0	24	26.2	66	21	7	7	1	1	1	1	12	2	28	4	1	2	1	.667	0	16	2.36
Lakeland	A+ Det	2	0	0	1	2	6	0	0	0	0	0	0	0	0	0	4	0	0	0	0	.000	0	0	0.00
1996 Fayetteville	A Det	45	8	0	7	98	413	91	51	38	4	4	1	6	27	1	92	5	2	7	8	.467	0	2	3.49
1997 Fort Myers	A+ Min	49	1	0	30	69.1	285	53	20	19	4	2	3	2	24	3	70	5	2	7	2	.778	0	17	2.47
1998 New Britain	AA Min	57	0	0	53	59	244	44	13	13	3	2	1	1	28	2	65	1	0	1	2	.333	0	43	1.98
1999 Salt Lake	AAA Min	23	0	0	15	25.2	139	43	34	32	6	2	2	0	21	1	23	3	1	0	3	.000	0	3	11.22
New Britain	AA Min	32	0	0	28	31.1	125	23	13	13	3	0	0	0	12	2	44	0	0	0	1	.000	0	9	3.73
5 Min. YEARS		232	9	0	158	312	1319	275	138	122	21	11	8	10	124	11	326	18	6	17	17	.500	0	90	3.52

Jason Stevenson

Pitches: Right **Bats:** Right **Pos:** P **Ht:** 6'3" **Wt:** 180 **Born:** 8/11/74 **Age:** 25

		HOW MUCH HE PITCHED						WHAT HE GAVE UP												THE RESULTS					
Year Team	Lg Org	G	GS	CG	GF	IP	BFP	H	R	ER	HR	SH	SF	HB	TBB	IBB	SO	WP	Bk	W	L	Pct.	ShO	Sv	ERA
1994 Huntington	R+ ChC	5	1	0	1	10.2	47	12	5	5	2	3	1	0	6	0	5	1	0	1	1	.500	0	1	4.22
Cubs	R ChC	25	5	0	0	25	112	31	12	7	1	3	1	0	4	0	19	3	0	1	1	.500	0	0	2.52
1995 Rockford	A ChC	33	5	0	9	77.1	333	85	50	48	9	1	4	1	31	0	54	5	5	4	3	.571	0	2	5.59
Daytona	A+ ChC	8	0	0	3	18.1	71	11	6	6	0	1	0	1	6	0	15	1	0	2	0	1.000	0	1	2.95
1996 Daytona	A+ ChC	27	17	2	5	122	519	136	56	48	7	6	5	5	22	2	86	8	1	8	5	.615	1	0	3.54
1997 Knoxville	AA Tor	26	26	2	0	149.2	640	166	88	71	18	5	5	7	43	1	101	7	1	12	9	.571	2	0	4.27
1998 Knoxville	AA Tor	33	22	1	6	134.1	600	159	88	81	16	7	2	6	51	4	98	9	3	6	10	.375	0	0	5.43
1999 Knoxville	AA Tor	21	19	1	0	92.1	429	99	69	64	8	2	5	2	57	0	73	4	4	7	7	.364	0	0	6.24
Syracuse	AAA Tor	7	7	0	0	38.2	180	52	30	26	7	0	2	1	21	0	15	2	1	1	2	.333	0	0	6.05
6 Min. YEARS		165	102	6	25	668.1	2931	751	404	356	68	28	25	23	241	7	466	40	15	39	38	.506	3	4	4.79

Rod Stevenson

Pitches: Right **Bats:** Right **Pos:** P **Ht:** 6'2" **Wt:** 210 **Born:** 3/21/74 **Age:** 26

		HOW MUCH HE PITCHED						WHAT HE GAVE UP												THE RESULTS					
Year Team	Lg Org	G	GS	CG	GF	IP	BFP	H	R	ER	HR	SH	SF	HB	TBB	IBB	SO	WP	Bk	W	L	Pct.	ShO	Sv	ERA
1996 Vermont	A- Mon	22	0	0	5	31.2	133	24	11	10	1	1	0	1	13	0	46	2	2	5	2	.714	0	1	2.84
1997 Cape Fear	A Mon	16	0	0	15	17	66	7	3	1	0	0	0	0	6	1	20	1	0	1	1	.500	0	5	0.53
Wst Plm Bch	A+ Mon	26	0	0	12	35.1	158	31	13	7	2	2	1	1	16	0	39	0	0	3	3	.500	0	2	1.78
Harrisburg	AA Mon	4	0	0	2	1	33	9	0	3	1	0	0	0	5	1	0	1	0	0	0	.000	0	0	2.96
1998 Jupiter	A+ Mon	19	0	0	14	23.2	91	13	7	7	2	1	0	0	6	0	21	1	0	1	0	.000	0	10	2.66
Harrisburg	AA Mon	37	0	0	23	39.1	168	32	19	19	3	2	2	2	18	5	47	1	0	5	0	1.000	0	8	4.35
1999 Ottawa	AAA Mon	17	0	0	11	18.1	76	15	9	8	4	0	3	2	7	0	12	1	0	2	1	.667	0	2	3.93
Harrisburg	AA Mon	37	0	0	25	51.1	224	54	32	25	8	2	5	1	21	1	34	5	0	2	9	.182	0	4	4.38
4 Min. YEARS		178	0	0	107	223.2	949	185	99	80	21	8	12	7	92	8	225	12	2	18	17	.514	0	32	3.22

270

Andy Stewart

Bats: Right **Throws:** Right **Pos:** C   **Ht:** 5'11" **Wt:** 205 **Born:** 12/5/70 **Age:** 29

Year Team	Lg Org	G	AB	H	2B	3B	HR	TB	R	RBI	TBB	IBB	SO	HBP	SH	SF	SB	CS	SB%	GDP	Avg	OBP	SLG
1990 Royals	R KC	21	52	10	4	0	0	14	5	1	9	1	13	3	3	0	3	0	1.00	0	.192	.344	.269
1991 Baseball Cy	A+ KC	78	276	64	16	1	3	91	30	36	7	1	59	4	4	2	6	4	.60	6	.232	.260	.330
1992 Baseball Cy	A+ KC	94	283	73	13	1	4	100	31	38	21	1	45	2	4	1	3	8	.27	4	.258	.313	.353
1993 Wilmington	A+ KC	110	361	100	20	3	8	150	54	42	26	0	88	8	0	1	7	1	.88	6	.277	.338	.416
1994 Wilmington	A+ KC	94	360	114	24	3	17	195	53	66	30	4	56	13	2	4	0	2	.00	11	.317	.386	.542
Memphis	AA KC	20	72	17	1	0	0	18	10	5	3	1	5	4	1	1	0	0	.00	3	.236	.300	.250
1995 Wichita	AA KC	60	216	56	18	0	3	83	28	32	11	0	31	4	0	2	1	2	.33	9	.259	.305	.384
Omaha	AAA KC	44	156	47	11	0	3	67	24	21	12	1	18	8	0	0	0	1	.00	4	.301	.381	.429
1996 Omaha	AAA KC	50	181	39	10	2	2	59	23	13	15	0	25	5	0	1	0	2	.00	9	.215	.292	.326
Wichita	AA KC	58	202	61	17	3	3	93	29	32	14	1	25	4	2	2	3	2	.60	9	.302	.356	.460
1997 Omaha	AAA KC	86	288	79	10	1	6	109	38	24	18	0	43	9	5	1	1	1	.50	11	.274	.335	.378
1998 Wichita	AA KC	85	305	103	26	0	12	165	45	58	19	0	33	5	2	4	0	2	.00	11	.338	.381	.541
Omaha	AAA KC	8	29	10	4	0	1	17	5	6	1	0	1	1	0	0	0	1	.00	3	.345	.387	.586
1999 Reading	AA Phi	54	190	57	19	0	7	97	23	40	16	1	18	7	3	4	0	3	.00	8	.300	.369	.511
1997 Kansas City	AL	5	8	2	1	0	0	3	1	0	0	0	0	0	0	0	0	0	.00	1	.250	.250	.375
10 Min. YEARS		862	2971	830	193	14	69	1258	398	414	202	11	460	77	26	23	24	29	.45	94	.279	.339	.423

Scott Stewart

Pitches: Left **Bats:** Right **Pos:** P   **Ht:** 6'2" **Wt:** 224 **Born:** 8/14/75 **Age:** 24

Year Team	Lg Org	G	GS	CG	GF	IP	BFP	H	R	ER	HR	SH	SF	HB	TBB	IBB	SO	WP	Bk	W	L	Pct.	ShO	Sv	ERA
1994 Rangers	R Tex	14	8	0	3	54.1	221	47	22	17	1	1	0	2	12	0	62	7	9	4	1	.800	0	1	2.82
1995 Chston-SC	A Tex	11	11	1	0	75.2	302	76	38	31	6	1	4	0	14	1	47	3	5	1	7	.125	0	0	3.69
Twins	R Min	3	1	0	0	5.2	29	7	4	4	0	0	0	1	4	0	9	0	1	0	0	.000	0	0	6.35
1996 St. Paul	IND —	19	18	0	0	86.1	417	121	70	56	13	5	3	1	42	2	54	14	1	6	8	.429	0	0	5.84
1997 St. Lucie	A+ NYM	22	18	4	1	123.1	496	114	62	55	8	3	7	4	18	1	64	4	7	5	10	.333	0	0	4.01
1998 Norfolk	AAA NYM	9	9	0	0	51.2	235	60	43	38	12	3	2	1	22	0	32	0	0	0	6	.000	0	0	6.62
Binghamton	AA NYM	24	13	0	3	90	382	91	44	37	12	4	2	1	29	2	65	2	4	8	5	.615	0	2	3.70
1999 Binghamton	AA NYM	1	1	0	0	5	18	3	0	0	0	0	0	0	0	0	5	0	0	1	0	1.000	0	0	0.00
Norfolk	AAA NYM	35	14	0	3	99.2	442	109	55	49	9	5	2	2	36	1	85	5	3	6	4	.600	0	0	4.42
6 Min. YEARS		138	93	5	10	591.2	2542	628	338	287	61	22	20	12	177	7	423	35	30	31	41	.431	0	3	4.37

Alex Stoffels

Bats: Right **Throws:** Right **Pos:** C   **Ht:** 5'10" **Wt:** 190 **Born:** 6/12/77 **Age:** 23

Year Team	Lg Org	G	AB	H	2B	3B	HR	TB	R	RBI	TBB	IBB	SO	HBP	SH	SF	SB	CS	SB%	GDP	Avg	OBP	SLG
1998 Kingsport	R+ NYM	41	137	40	7	1	0	49	23	18	13	0	29	0	3	1	4	5	.44	3	.292	.351	.358
1999 Pittsfield	A- NYM	26	70	8	1	0	0	9	5	9	6	0	19	3	0	0	6	2	.75	3	.114	.215	.129
Binghamton	AA NYM	3	8	0	0	0	0	0	0	0	2	0	4	1	0	0	0	0	.00	0	.000	.273	.000
2 Min. YEARS		70	215	48	8	1	0	58	28	27	21	0	52	4	3	1	10	7	.59	6	.223	.303	.270

Ricky Stone

Pitches: Right **Bats:** Right **Pos:** P   **Ht:** 6'1" **Wt:** 168 **Born:** 2/28/75 **Age:** 25

Year Team	Lg Org	G	GS	CG	GF	IP	BFP	H	R	ER	HR	SH	SF	HB	TBB	IBB	SO	WP	Bk	W	L	Pct.	ShO	Sv	ERA
1994 Great Falls	R+ LA	13	7	0	4	50.2	232	55	40	25	5	0	1	2	24	0	48	9	0	2	2	.500	0	2	4.44
1995 San Berndno	A+ LA	12	12	0	0	58	273	79	50	42	7	6	3	2	25	0	31	5	0	3	5	.375	0	0	6.52
Yakima	A- LA	16	6	0	7	48	213	54	31	28	5	2	2	2	20	0	28	4	1	4	4	.500	0	2	5.25
1996 Savannah	A LA	5	5	0	0	31.2	130	34	15	14	2	2	1	0	9	0	31	5	0	2	1	.667	0	0	3.98
Vero Beach	A+ LA	21	21	1	0	112.2	488	115	58	48	9	4	3	3	46	0	74	10	0	8	6	.571	0	0	3.83
1997 San Antonio	AA LA	25	5	0	10	52.2	245	63	33	32	4	4	1	3	30	0	46	3	0	0	3	.000	0	3	5.47
San Berndno	A+ LA	8	8	0	0	53.2	206	40	22	20	4	2	1	2	10	0	40	2	0	3	3	.500	0	0	3.35
1998 San Antonio	AA LA	13	13	1	0	82	336	76	40	35	7	5	1	1	26	0	69	6	0	7	2	.778	1	0	3.84
Albuquerque	AAA LA	18	16	0	0	105.1	465	120	69	63	13	2	1	3	41	0	85	9	1	5	5	.500	0	0	5.38
1999 Albuquerque	AAA LA	27	27	2	0	167	764	205	123	102	23	8	7	8	71	4	132	11	1	6	10	.375	0	0	5.50
6 Min. YEARS		158	120	4	21	761.2	3352	841	481	409	79	35	21	26	302	4	584	64	3	40	41	.494	1	7	4.83

Mike Stoner

Bats: Right **Throws:** Right **Pos:** OF-DH   **Ht:** 6'0" **Wt:** 200 **Born:** 5/23/73 **Age:** 27

Year Team	Lg Org	G	AB	H	2B	3B	HR	TB	R	RBI	TBB	IBB	SO	HBP	SH	SF	SB	CS	SB%	GDP	Avg	OBP	SLG
1996 Lethbridge	R+ Ari	24	78	25	1	2	1	33	13	13	12	0	13	2	1	2	1	0	1.00	1	.321	.415	.423
Bakersfield	A+ Ari	36	147	43	6	1	6	69	25	22	8	0	18	0	0	1	1	1	.50	4	.293	.327	.469
1997 High Desert	A+ Ari	136	567	203	44	5	33	356	115	142	36	4	91	3	1	11	6	4	.60	17	.358	.392	.628
1998 Tucson	AAA Ari	106	394	123	22	3	5	166	46	49	27	4	52	4	0	3	3	0	1.00	10	.312	.360	.421
1999 Tucson	AAA Ari	14	21	9	1	0	0	10	2	6	2	0	3	0	0	1	0	0	.00	0	.429	.458	.476
El Paso	AA Ari	1	0	0	0	0	0	0	1	0	1	0	0	0	0	0	0	0	.00	0	.000	1.000	.000
Erie	AA Ana	14	62	21	4	0	3	34	10	15	2	1	8	0	0	0	0	1	.00	0	.339	.359	.548
Edmonton	AAA Ana	22	81	28	5	1	3	44	12	12	4	0	11	0	0	0	0	1	.00	2	.346	.376	.543
4 Min. YEARS		353	1350	452	83	12	51	712	224	259	92	9	196	9	2	18	11	7	.61	34	.335	.376	.527

271

Jim Stoops

Pitches: Right **Bats:** Right **Pos:** P **Ht:** 6' 2" **Wt:** 180 **Born:** 6/30/72 **Age:** 28

		HOW MUCH HE PITCHED						WHAT HE GAVE UP										THE RESULTS					
Year Team	Lg Org	G	GS	CG	GF	IP	BFP	H	R	ER	HR	SH	SF	HB	TBB	IBB	SO	WP	Bk	W	L	Pct.	ShO	Sv	ERA
1995 Bellingham	A- SF	24	0	0	14	42	178	32	23	16	1	2	1	5	17	0	58	2	0	6	5	.545	0	4	3.43
1996 Burlington	A SF	46	0	0	18	60.2	262	43	24	17	2	4	1	6	40	4	69	6	1	3	3	.500	0	5	2.52
1997 San Jose	A+ SF	50	0	0	16	91.2	401	92	56	53	3	2	3	7	45	2	114	7	1	2	5	.286	0	4	5.20
1998 San Jose	A+ SF	45	0	0	43	55.1	222	28	7	6	0	0	0	3	25	0	96	1	0	2	1	.667	0	31	0.98
Salem	A+ Col	3	0	0	1	4.1	16	2	0	0	0	1	0	0	1	0	8	0	0	0	0	.000	0	0	0.00
Colo Sprngs	AAA Col	11	0	0	6	14.2	58	6	6	2	0	0	2	1	8	0	17	0	0	1	0	1.000	0	1	1.23
1999 Colo Sprngs	AAA Col	55	5	0	22	88.2	400	93	54	51	11	6	6	4	56	2	57	7	0	3	7	.300	0	3	5.18
1998 Colorado	NL	3	0	0	0	4	17	5	1	1	0	0	1	0	3	0	0	0	0	1	0	1.000	0	0	2.25
5 Min. YEARS		234	5	0	120	357.1	1537	296	170	145	17	15	13	26	192	8	419	23	2	17	21	.447	0	48	3.65

DaRond Stovall

Bats: Both **Throws:** Left **Pos:** OF **Ht:** 6' 1" **Wt:** 185 **Born:** 1/3/73 **Age:** 27

		BATTING														BASERUNNING				PERCENTAGES		
Year Team	Lg Org	G	AB	H	2B	3B	HR	TB	R	RBI	TBB	IBB	SO	HBP	SH	SF	SB	CS	SB%	GDP	Avg	OBP	SLG
1991 Johnson Cy	R+ StL	48	134	19	2	2	0	25	16	5	23	1	63	0	0	0	8	3	.73	1	.142	.268	.187
1992 Savannah	A StL	135	450	92	13	7	7	140	51	40	63	0	138	0	1	1	20	14	.59	13	.204	.302	.311
1993 Springfield	A StL	135	460	118	19	4	20	205	73	81	53	2	140	0	2	1	18	12	.60	5	.257	.333	.446
1994 St. Pete	A+ StL	134	507	113	20	6	15	190	68	69	62	4	154	0	1	2	24	8	.75	10	.223	.305	.375
1995 Wst Plm Bch	A+ Mon	121	461	107	22	2	4	145	52	51	44	2	117	0	0	3	18	12	.60	4	.232	.297	.315
1996 Expos	R Mon	9	34	15	3	2	0	22	5	7	3	0	6	0	0	0	3	0	1.00	1	.441	.486	.647
Wst Plm Bch	A+ Mon	8	31	14	4	0	1	21	8	8	6	0	7	0	0	0	2	2	.50	1	.452	.541	.677
1997 Harrisburg	AA Mon	74	272	60	7	1	10	99	38	36	32	1	86	2	4	0	10	5	.67	5	.221	.307	.364
Harrisburg	AA Mon	45	169	48	4	1	9	81	29	39	23	1	30	0	0	3	4	0	1.00	3	.284	.364	.479
Ottawa	AAA Mon	98	342	83	23	2	4	122	40	48	31	3	114	2	3	4	10	13	.43	6	.243	.306	.357
1998 Ottawa	AAA Mon	44	150	34	7	1	8	67	15	22	21	1	51	0	1	1	6	2	.75	6	.227	.320	.447
1999 Calgary	AAA Fla	37	106	20	3	3	3	38	10	13	11	1	44	0	1	1	0	0	.00	1	.189	.263	.358
San Antonio	AA LA	12	49	18	3	0	4	33	9	11	7	0	10	0	0	0	1	1	.50	0	.367	.446	.673
Albuquerque	AAA LA	46	160	35	12	0	7	68	30	21	22	0	65	0	0	3	8	4	.67	2	.219	.308	.425
1998 Montreal	NL	62	78	16	2	1	2	26	11	6	6	0	29	0	0	0	1	0	1.00	1	.205	.262	.333
9 Min. YEARS		946	3325	776	142	31	92	1256	444	451	401	16	1028	4	16	22	132	76	.63	56	.233	.315	.378

Doug Strange

Bats: Both **Throws:** Right **Pos:** 2B **Ht:** 6' 1" **Wt:** 188 **Born:** 4/13/64 **Age:** 36

		BATTING														BASERUNNING				PERCENTAGES		
Year Team	Lg Org	G	AB	H	2B	3B	HR	TB	R	RBI	TBB	IBB	SO	HBP	SH	SF	SB	CS	SB%	GDP	Avg	OBP	SLG
1985 Bristol	R+ Det	65	226	69	16	1	6	105	43	45	22	1	30	3	4	3	6	0	1.00	6	.305	.370	.465
1986 Lakeland	A+ Det	126	466	119	29	4	2	162	59	63	65	5	59	2	7	6	18	6	.75	18	.255	.345	.348
1987 Glens Falls	AA Det	115	431	130	31	1	13	202	63	70	31	3	53	3	0	5	5	11	.31	17	.302	.349	.469
Toledo	AAA Det	16	45	11	2	0	1	16	7	5	4	0	7	0	1	1	3	2	.60	1	.244	.300	.356
1988 Toledo	AAA Det	82	278	56	8	2	6	86	23	19	8	0	38	2	2	2	9	7	.56	8	.201	.228	.309
Glens Falls	AA Det	57	218	61	11	1	1	77	32	36	16	2	28	0	1	8	11	1	.92	5	.280	.318	.353
1989 Toledo	AAA Det	83	304	75	15	2	8	118	38	42	34	2	49	2	2	2	8	3	.73	11	.247	.325	.388
1990 Tucson	AAA Hou	37	98	22	3	0	0	25	7	7	8	0	23	0	2	0	0	0	.00	4	.224	.283	.255
Iowa	AAA ChC	82	269	82	17	1	5	116	31	35	28	2	42	1	3	1	6	3	.67	8	.305	.371	.431
1991 Iowa	AAA ChC	131	509	149	35	5	8	218	76	56	49	9	75	1	7	7	10	5	.67	12	.293	.352	.428
1992 Iowa	AAA ChC	55	212	65	16	1	4	95	32	26	9	0	32	1	1	4	3	3	.50	4	.307	.332	.448
1997 Ottawa	AAA Mon	2	7	3	1	0	0	4	3	0	1	0	1	0	0	0	0	0	.00	2	.429	.500	.571
1998 Carolina	AA Pit	4	14	5	0	0	0	5	4	0	2	0	1	0	0	0	0	0	.00	0	.357	.438	.357
1999 Nashville	AAA Pit	5	13	1	1	0	0	2	2	0	0	0	2	1	0	0	0	0	.00	1	.077	.143	.154
1989 Detroit	AL	64	196	42	4	1	1	51	16	14	17	0	36	1	3	0	3	3	.50	6	.214	.280	.260
1991 Chicago	NL	3	9	4	1	0	0	5	0	1	0	0	1	0	1	0	1	0	1.00	0	.444	.455	.556
1992 Chicago	NL	52	94	15	1	0	1	19	7	5	10	2	15	0	2	0	1	0	1.00	2	.160	.240	.202
1993 Texas	AL	145	484	124	29	0	7	174	58	60	43	3	69	3	8	4	6	4	.60	12	.256	.318	.360
1994 Texas	AL	73	226	48	12	1	5	77	26	26	15	0	38	3	4	2	1	3	.25	6	.212	.268	.341
1995 Seattle	AL	74	155	42	9	2	2	61	19	21	10	0	25	2	1	0	0	3	.00	3	.271	.323	.394
1996 Seattle	AL	88	183	43	7	1	3	61	19	23	14	0	31	1	0	2	1	0	1.00	3	.235	.290	.333
1997 Montreal	NL	118	327	84	16	2	12	140	40	47	36	9	76	2	5	2	0	2	.00	4	.257	.332	.428
1998 Pittsburgh	NL	90	185	32	8	0	0	40	9	14	10	1	39	1	3	2	1	0	1.00	5	.173	.217	.216
11 Min. YEARS		860	3090	848	185	18	54	1231	420	404	277	24	440	16	30	39	79	41	.66	97	.274	.333	.398
9 Maj. YEARS		707	1859	434	87	7	31	628	194	211	155	15	330	14	26	13	14	15	.48	41	.233	.295	.338

Mike Strange

Bats: Right **Throws:** Right **Pos:** 2B **Ht:** 6'0" **Wt:** 172 **Born:** 4/21/74 **Age:** 26

		BATTING														BASERUNNING				PERCENTAGES		
Year Team	Lg Org	G	AB	H	2B	3B	HR	TB	R	RBI	TBB	IBB	SO	HBP	SH	SF	SB	CS	SB%	GDP	Avg	OBP	SLG
1994 Medcine Hat	H+ Tor	55	177	44	7	3	1	60	30	20	22	0	58	0	2	0	1	0	.67	2	.249	.349	.339
1995 Hagerstown	A Tor	96	290	68	9	2	1	84	51	27	61	0	92	4	2	0	13	3	.81	7	.234	.375	.290
1996 Dunedin	A+ Tor	51	154	49	4	2	0	57	25	13	26	0	42	0	5	0	5	5	.50	3	.318	.417	.370
1997 Knoxville	AA Tor	12	21	2	0	1	0	4	1	0	3	0	4	0	0	0	0	0	.00	0	.095	.208	.190
Dunedin	A+ Tor	48	106	28	5	1	0	35	15	7	14	0	39	1	3	0	1	1	.50	0	.264	.355	.330
1998 Hagerstown	A Tor	76	186	42	11	0	1	56	33	12	45	0	59	5	2	0	9	5	.64	4	.226	.390	.301
1999 Dunedin	A+ Tor	3	8	3	0	0	1	6	2	3	1	0	3	0	0	0	0	0	.00	0	.375	.444	.750
Syracuse	AAA Tor	15	32	5	3	0	0	8	4	2	8	0	13	1	3	0	1	0	1.00	0	.156	.341	.250
Knoxville	AA Tor	29	54	5	0	0	0	5	10	4	26	0	24	1	0	0	1	0	1.00	3	.093	.395	.093
6 Min. YEARS		385	1028	246	39	9	4	315	171	88	206	0	326	18	17	2	34	16	.68	20	.239	.375	.306

272

Mark Strittmatter

Bats: Right **Throws:** Right **Pos:** C **Ht:** 6' 1" **Wt:** 210 **Born:** 4/4/69 **Age:** 31

Year Team	Lg Org	G	AB	H	2B	3B	HR	TB	R	RBI	TBB	IBB	SO	HBP	SH	SF	SB	CS	SB%	GDP	Avg	OBP	SLG
1992 Bend	A- Col	35	101	26	6	0	2	38	17	13	12	0	28	3	0	0	0	4	.00	2	.257	.353	.376
1993 Central Val	A+ Col	59	179	47	8	0	2	61	21	15	31	0	29	2	2	3	3	0	1.00	8	.263	.372	.341
Colo Sprngs	AAA Col	5	10	2	1	0	0	3	1	2	0	0	2	1	0	0	0	0	.00	2	.200	.273	.300
1994 New Haven	AA Col	73	215	49	8	0	2	63	20	26	33	1	39	9	3	4	1	2	.33	7	.228	.349	.293
1995 Colo Sprngs	AAA Col	5	17	5	2	0	0	7	1	3	0	0	3	0	0	0	0	0	.00	0	.294	.294	.412
New Haven	AA Col	90	288	70	12	1	7	105	44	42	47	1	51	6	1	2	1	0	1.00	5	.243	.359	.365
1996 Colo Sprngs	AAA Col	58	159	37	8	1	2	53	21	18	17	3	30	7	1	0	2	1	.67	5	.233	.333	.333
1997 Colo Sprngs	AAA Col	45	114	28	8	0	2	42	16	12	11	3	21	5	4	1	0	1	.00	4	.246	.336	.368
1998 Colo Sprngs	AAA Col	87	255	71	15	3	6	110	32	38	30	1	48	12	2	2	0	0	.00	6	.278	.378	.431
1999 Colo Sprngs	AAA Col	71	195	42	10	1	4	66	16	31	20	0	45	9	1	4	0	0	.00	2	.215	.311	.338
1998 Colorado	NL	4	4	0	0	0	0	0	0	0	0	0	3	0	0	0	0	0	.00	0	.000	.000	.000
8 Min. YEARS		528	1533	377	78	6	27	548	189	200	201	9	296	54	14	16	7	8	.47	41	.246	.350	.357

Ryan Stromsborg

Bats: Right **Throws:** Right **Pos:** OF **Ht:** 6'3" **Wt:** 185 **Born:** 12/19/74 **Age:** 25

Year Team	Lg Org	G	AB	H	2B	3B	HR	TB	R	RBI	TBB	IBB	SO	HBP	SH	SF	SB	CS	SB%	GDP	Avg	OBP	SLG
1996 Medcine Hat	R+ Tor	55	216	67	10	3	8	107	34	38	16	0	42	5	5	3	8	2	.80	4	.310	.367	.495
1997 Hagerstown	A Tor	56	184	53	10	4	4	75	22	24	13	0	37	2	1	3	5	1	.83	2	.288	.337	.408
1998 Knoxville	AA Tor	81	283	67	9	2	7	101	44	28	27	1	65	1	2	1	7	5	.58	4	.237	.304	.357
Dunedin	A+ Tor	30	108	27	5	0	2	38	12	12	5	0	28	1	2	1	1	0	1.00	1	.250	.287	.352
1999 Dunedin	A+ Tor	20	76	17	10	0	1	30	5	9	3	0	17	0	0	1	1	1	.50	1	.224	.250	.395
Knoxville	AA Tor	99	377	94	17	3	9	144	54	45	28	0	91	0	1	2	5	4	.56	6	.249	.300	.382
4 Min. YEARS		341	1244	325	61	8	31	495	171	156	92	1	280	9	11	11	27	13	.68	19	.261	.314	.398

Joe Strong

Pitches: Right **Bats:** Both **Pos:** P **Ht:** 6'0" **Wt:** 200 **Born:** 9/9/62 **Age:** 37

Year Team	Lg Org	G	GS	CG	GF	IP	BFP	H	R	ER	HR	SH	SF	HB	TBB	IBB	SO	WP	Bk	W	L	Pct.	ShO	Sv	ERA
1993 Las Vegas	AAA SD	21	0	0	5	27	129	37	23	17	4	1	2	2	10	1	18	0	1	1	3	.250	0	0	5.67
Rancho Cuca	A+ SD	7	0	0	6	10	42	10	3	3	0	0	0	0	2	0	13	2	0	1	0	1.000	0	1	2.70
Wichita	AA SD	4	3	0	1	14.2	68	13	13	11	2	2	1	0	11	0	13	0	1	1	0	1.000	0	0	6.75
1994 San Berndno	A+ —	12	11	0	0	53.2	246	60	46	40	11	0	4	3	27	0	43	6	2	2	3	.400	0	0	6.71
1995 Surrey	IND —	20	19	9	0	131	555	120	55	40	7	1	1	7	48	1	129	3	1	8	9	.471	2	0	2.75
1999 Orlando	AA TB	11	7	2	3	38	163	40	24	24	6	1	1	0	18	1	34	0	1	1	4	.200	0	0	5.68
Durham	AAA TB	6	1	0	1	14.2	71	20	13	13	4	0	0	0	8	0	12	0	0	0	1	.000	0	1	7.98
4 Min. YEARS		81	41	11	16	289	1274	300	177	148	34	5	9	12	124	3	262	11	6	14	20	.412	2	2	4.61

Eric Stuckenschneider

Bats: Right **Throws:** Right **Pos:** OF **Ht:** 6' 0" **Wt:** 200 **Born:** 8/24/71 **Age:** 28

Year Team	Lg Org	G	AB	H	2B	3B	HR	TB	R	RBI	TBB	IBB	SO	HBP	SH	SF	SB	CS	SB%	GDP	Avg	OBP	SLG
1994 Yakima	A- LA	58	190	57	13	4	3	87	40	39	45	3	43	5	3	0	22	4	.85	2	.300	.446	.458
1995 San Berndno	A+ LA	8	20	5	1	0	0	6	2	2	7	0	6	2	0	1	1	0	1.00	0	.250	.467	.300
Great Falls	R+ LA	40	118	37	8	2	4	61	32	16	32	0	26	5	0	1	10	7	.59	2	.314	.474	.517
1996 Savannah	A LA	140	470	130	28	6	16	218	111	63	111	5	96	12	2	4	50	18	.74	4	.277	.424	.464
1997 Vero Beach	A+ LA	131	452	126	25	3	6	175	100	45	101	1	79	12	4	5	40	11	.78	4	.279	.419	.387
1998 San Antonio	AA LA	72	282	78	16	7	3	117	60	22	44	1	47	9	2	3	16	3	.84	3	.277	.388	.415
Albuquerque	AAA LA	71	269	83	13	10	7	137	50	28	44	0	50	4	5	4	18	7	.72	2	.309	.408	.509
1999 Midland	AA Oak	29	92	15	4	2	0	23	17	16	17	0	22	1	0	0	6	1	.86	2	.163	.295	.250
6 Min. YEARS		549	1893	531	108	34	39	824	412	231	401	10	369	50	16	20	163	51	.76	19	.281	.415	.435

Brendan Sullivan

Pitches: Right **Bats:** Right **Pos:** P **Ht:** 6'3" **Wt:** 190 **Born:** 12/15/74 **Age:** 25

Year Team	Lg Org	G	GS	CG	GF	IP	BFP	H	R	ER	HR	SH	SF	HB	TBB	IBB	SO	WP	Bk	W	L	Pct.	ShO	Sv	ERA
1996 Idaho Falls	R+ SD	33	0	0	15	43	190	41	25	25	6	1	0	1	27	0	41	1	0	2	1	.667	0	5	5.23
1997 Clinton	A SD	47	0	0	35	62.1	283	55	33	27	1	4	3	7	34	2	54	2	0	7	5	.583	0	6	3.90
1998 Rancho Cuca	A+ SD	35	0	0	31	41.2	168	23	7	5	0	1	0	4	19	2	37	1	0	3	2	.600	0	8	1.08
Mobile	AA SD	35	0	0	29	39	153	28	8	8	1	1	3	3	16	1	24	2	0	1	2	.333	0	13	1.85
1999 Las Vegas	AAA SD	45	0	0	14	66.1	332	88	60	56	6	3	5	12	38	3	50	2	0	2	4	.333	0	0	7.60
4 Min. YEARS		195	0	0	124	252.1	1126	235	133	121	14	10	9	27	134	8	206	8	0	15	14	.517	0	32	4.32

Pedro Swann

Bats: Left **Throws:** Right **Pos:** OF **Ht:** 6'0" **Wt:** 195 **Born:** 10/27/70 **Age:** 29

Year Team	Lg Org	G	AB	H	2B	3B	HR	TB	R	RBI	TBB	IBB	SO	HBP	SH	SF	SB	CS	SB%	GDP	Avg	OBP	SLG
1991 Idaho Falls	R+ Atl	55	174	48	6	1	3	65	35	28	33	0	45	2	1	2	8	5	.62	4	.276	.393	.374
1992 Pulaski	R+ Atl	59	203	61	18	1	5	96	36	34	32	3	33	7	0	1	13	6	.68	6	.300	.412	.473
1993 Durham	A+ Atl	61	182	63	8	2	6	93	27	27	19	0	38	1	0	0	6	12	.33	2	.346	.411	.511
Greenville	AA Atl	44	157	48	9	2	3	70	19	21	9	0	23	1	1	0	2	2	.50	5	.306	.347	.446
1994 Greenville	AA Atl	126	428	121	25	2	10	180	55	49	46	2	85	4	0	2	16	9	.64	14	.283	.356	.421
1995 Richmond	AAA Atl	15	38	8	1	0	0	9	2	3	1	0	2	1	0	0	0	2	.00	0	.211	.250	.237
Greenville	AA Atl	102	339	110	24	2	11	171	57	64	45	2	63	3	0	3	14	11	.56	8	.324	.405	.504

273

	BATTING																	BASERUNNING				PERCENTAGES		
Year Team	Lg Org	G	AB	H	2B	3B	HR	TB	R	RBI	TBB	IBB	SO	HBP	SH	SF	SB	CS	SB%	GDP	Avg	OBP	SLG
1996 Greenville	AA Atl	35	129	40	5	0	3	54	15	20	18	2	23	3	1	1	4	4	.50	3	.310	.404	.419
Richmond	AAA Atl	93	296	74	11	4	4	105	42	35	22	2	56	4	2	3	7	7	.50	5	.250	.308	.355
1997 Greenville	AA Atl	124	465	133	29	2	24	238	78	83	49	5	75	4	0	1	5	5	.50	14	.286	.358	.512
1998 Toledo	AAA Det	120	419	122	28	2	15	199	56	66	41	4	74	3	1	4	6	3	.67	11	.291	.355	.475
1999 Toledo	AAA Det	103	332	86	14	2	10	134	51	37	36	0	67	6	0	5	3	1	.75	7	.259	.338	.404
9 Min. YEARS		937	3162	914	178	20	94	1414	473	467	351	20	584	39	6	22	84	67	.56	79	.289	.365	.447

Dave Swartzbaugh

Pitches: Right **Bats:** Right **Pos:** P   **Ht:** 6' 2" **Wt:** 210 **Born:** 2/11/68 **Age:** 32

	HOW MUCH HE PITCHED							WHAT HE GAVE UP												THE RESULTS					
Year Team	Lg Org	G	GS	CG	GF	IP	BFP	H	R	ER	HR	SH	SF	HB	TBB	IBB	SO	WP	Bk	W	L	Pct.	ShO	Sv	ERA
1989 Geneva	A- ChC	18	10	0	1	75	338	81	59	41	5	0	3	1	35	1	77	8	1	2	3	.400	0	0	4.92
1990 Peoria	A ChC	29	29	5	0	169.2	736	147	88	72	11	1	3	7	89	1	129	10	4	8	11	.421	2	0	3.82
1991 Peoria	A ChC	5	5	1	0	34.1	145	21	16	7	0	2	1	2	15	1	31	2	2	0	5	.000	0	0	1.83
Winston-Sal	A+ ChC	15	15	2	0	93.2	379	71	22	19	3	5	1	1	42	1	73	4	0	10	4	.714	1	0	1.83
Charlotte	AA ChC	1	1	0	0	5.1	25	6	7	6	1	0	0	0	3	1	5	1	0	1	1	.000	0	0	10.13
1992 Charlotte	AA ChC	27	27	5	0	165	689	134	78	67	13	5	10	9	62	2	111	5	1	7	10	.412	2	0	3.65
1993 Iowa	AAA ChC	26	9	0	5	86.2	385	90	57	51	16	6	4	5	44	1	69	6	0	4	6	.400	0	1	5.30
Orlando	AA ChC	10	9	1	0	00	200	52	00	01	5	2	1	0	10	0	50	2	0	1	3	.260	0	0	4.23
1994 Iowa	AAA ChC	10	0	0	1	19.1	94	24	18	18	8	1	2	1	15	1	14	2	0	1	0	1.000	0	0	8.38
Orlando	AA ChC	42	1	0	11	79	327	70	36	29	7	5	3	4	19	2	70	0	0	2	4	.333	0	2	3.30
1995 Orlando	AA ChC	16	0	0	3	29	111	18	10	8	1	1	1	2	7	0	37	1	1	4	0	1.000	0	0	2.48
Iowa	AAA ChC	30	0	0	9	47	187	33	10	8	1	2	0	1	18	1	38	1	0	3	0	1.000	0	0	1.53
1996 Iowa	AAA ChC	44	13	0	11	118.1	491	106	61	51	22	5	4	3	33	1	103	5	0	8	11	.421	0	0	3.88
1997 Iowa	AAA ChC	24	20	1	1	134	561	129	55	42	12	4	5	1	48	1	97	3	1	8	7	.533	1	1	2.82
1998 Iowa	AAA ChC	42	14	0	5	137.2	571	114	61	57	16	8	8	3	50	1	109	7	0	14	5	.737	0	0	3.73
1999 Jacksnville	AA Det	6	5	0	0	26.1	127	36	31	30	7	0	0	1	12	1	22	0	0	0	4	.000	0	0	10.25
Tucson	AAA Ari	13	0	0	5	21.2	105	27	16	15	4	1	1	1	14	0	20	2	0	0	0	.000	0	0	6.23
1995 Chicago	NL	7	0	0	2	7.1	27	5	2	0	0	0	0	0	3	1	5	0	0	0	0	.000	0	0	0.00
1996 Chicago	NL	6	5	0	0	24	110	26	17	17	3	2	0	0	14	1	13	2	0	0	2	.000	0	0	6.38
1997 Chicago	NL	2	2	0	0	8	42	12	8	8	1	0	1	1	7	0	4	0	0	0	1	.000	0	0	9.00
11 Min. YEARS		358	158	15	52	1308	5539	1159	658	552	132	48	47	45	524	16	1064	59	10	72	74	.493	6	5	3.80
3 Maj. YEARS		15	7	0	2	39.1	179	43	27	25	4	2	1	1	24	2	22	2	0	0	3	.000	0	0	5.72

Brian Sweeney

Pitches: Right **Bats:** Right **Pos:** P   **Ht:** 6'2" **Wt:** 185 **Born:** 6/13/74 **Age:** 26

	HOW MUCH HE PITCHED							WHAT HE GAVE UP												THE RESULTS					
Year Team	Lg Org	G	GS	CG	GF	IP	BFP	H	R	ER	HR	SH	SF	HB	TBB	IBB	SO	WP	Bk	W	L	Pct.	ShO	Sv	ERA
1997 Lancaster	A+ Sea	40	0	0	13	85.1	358	83	39	36	11	2	4	2	21	1	73	8	0	6	3	.667	0	1	3.80
1998 Lancaster	A+ Sea	17	4	0	3	52	211	41	26	21	6	0	1	1	21	1	48	2	1	6	0	1.000	0	0	3.63
1999 Lancaster	A+ Sea	5	0	0	1	9.1	44	14	7	7	4	0	0	0	3	0	14	1	0	0	0	.000	0	0	6.75
Tacoma	AAA Sea	5	1	0	2	16	75	26	17	12	5	2	0	0	2	0	10	1	0	0	2	.000	0	0	6.75
New Haven	AA Sea	23	18	0	3	111.1	478	125	65	58	18	1	3	4	31	1	83	4	0	4	6	.400	0	0	4.69
3 Min. YEARS		90	23	0	22	274	1166	289	154	134	44	5	8	7	78	3	228	16	1	16	11	.593	0	2	4.40

Jon Sweet

Bats: Left **Throws:** Right **Pos:** C   **Ht:** 6'0" **Wt:** 182 **Born:** 11/10/71 **Age:** 28

	BATTING																	BASERUNNING				PERCENTAGES		
Year Team	Lg Org	G	AB	H	2B	3B	HR	TB	R	RBI	TBB	IBB	SO	HBP	SH	SF	SB	CS	SB%	GDP	Avg	OBP	SLG
1994 Welland	A- Pit	51	154	39	8	0	0	47	17	17	17	1	20	5	1	1	0	3	.00	3	.253	.345	.305
1995 Augusta	A Pit	87	267	76	9	1	1	90	28	22	18	2	31	5	2	2	2	4	.56	6	.285	.339	.337
1996 Lynchburg	A+ Pit	72	212	58	10	0	0	68	16	35	17	1	26	2	5	3	2	4	.33	0	.274	.329	.321
Carolina	AA Pit	20	40	4	2	0	0	6	2	1	0	0	3	0	2	0	0	0	.00	5	.100	.100	.150
1997 Carolina	AA Pit	82	273	67	15	1	1	87	22	27	15	2	20	1	1	1	1	1	.50	8	.245	.286	.319
1998 Nashville	AAA Pit	17	43	7	1	0	1	11	4	4	2	0	9	2	1	1	0	0	.00	0	.163	.229	.256
Carolina	AA Pit	77	238	54	11	1	2	73	24	44	20	0	18	7	4	8	1	2	.33	6	.227	.297	.307
1999 Altoona	AA Pit	37	105	27	5	1	2	40	15	13	11	0	15	1	1	3	0	1	.00	3	.257	.325	.381
6 Min. YEARS		443	1332	332	61	4	7	422	128	163	100	6	142	23	17	19	9	15	.38	31	.249	.309	.317

Tom Szymborski

Pitches: Right **Bats:** Right **Pos:** P   **Ht:** 6'3" **Wt:** 210 **Born:** 3/7/75 **Age:** 25

	HOW MUCH HE PITCHED							WHAT HE GAVE UP												THE RESULTS					
Year Team	Lg Org	G	GS	CG	GF	IP	BFP	H	R	ER	HR	SH	SF	HB	TBB	IBB	SO	WP	Bk	W	L	Pct.	ShO	Sv	ERA
1996 Idaho Falls	R+ SD	16	14	0	2	80	348	80	39	35	6	1	4	6	30	0	65	11	5	7	3	.700	0	1	3.94
1997 Clinton	A SD	22	22	1	0	134.2	591	141	67	58	11	3	4	12	46	0	74	7	1	5	7	.417	1	0	3.88
1998 Rancho Cuca	A+ SD	15	1	0	4	29	147	48	24	18	2	4	3	2	14	0	8	2	1	0	2	.000	0	0	5.59
1999 Rancho Cuca	A+ SD	28	0	0	6	43.1	191	48	26	23	5	2	0	3	23	2	33	3	0	1	2	.333	0	0	4.70
Mobile	AA SD	6	0	0	3	6.2	37	10	9	4	1	0	1	0	5	0	3	0	0	1	0	1.000	0	0	5.40
4 Min. YEARS		87	37	1	15	293.2	1314	327	165	138	25	10	11	24	118	2	183	25	7	14	14	.500	1	1	4.23

Jeff Taglienti

Pitches: Right **Bats:** Right **Pos:** P   **Ht:** 6'0" **Wt:** 208 **Born:** 11/13/75 **Age:** 24

	HOW MUCH HE PITCHED							WHAT HE GAVE UP												THE RESULTS					
Year Team	Lg Org	G	GS	CG	GF	IP	BFP	H	R	ER	HR	SH	SF	HB	TBB	IBB	SO	WP	Bk	W	L	Pct.	ShO	Sv	ERA
1997 Lowell	A- Bos	17	4	0	11	36.2	150	30	22	20	2	0	0	0	13	0	34	3	2	3	4	.429	0	6	4.91
1998 Michigan	A Bos	57	0	0	49	76.1	303	54	19	16	0	3	2	3	17	2	111	3	0	4	2	.667	0	30	1.89

		HOW MUCH HE PITCHED						WHAT HE GAVE UP												THE RESULTS					
Year Team	Lg Org	G	GS	CG	GF	IP	BFP	H	R	ER	HR	SH	SF	HB	TBB	IBB	SO	WP	Bk	W	L	Pct.	ShO	Sv	ERA
1999 Sarasota	A+ Bos	14	0	0	5	30	128	26	12	10	1	2	2	2	12	1	27	4	0	1	1	.500	0	3	3.00
Trenton	AA Bos	10	0	0	4	19.1	72	9	6	6	2	1	1	0	5	0	17	0	0	0	0	.000	0	2	2.79
3 Min. YEARS		98	4	0	69	162.1	653	119	59	52	5	6	5	5	47	3	189	10	2	8	7	.533	0	41	2.88

John Tamargo

Bats: Both Throws: Right Pos: 3B   Ht: 5'9" Wt: 172 Born: 5/3/75 Age: 25

		BATTING														BASERUNNING				PERCENTAGES		
Year Team	Lg Org	G	AB	H	2B	3B	HR	TB	R	RBI	TBB	IBB	SO	HBP	SH	SF	SB	CS	SB%	GDP	Avg	OBP	SLG
1996 Pittsfield	A- NYM	55	184	41	5	3	0	52	26	19	35	0	34	2	1	3	5	3	.63	5	.223	.348	.283
1997 Capital Cty	A NYM	113	393	98	17	2	1	122	44	47	45	2	72	2	5	1	13	7	.65	9	.249	.329	.310
1998 St. Lucie	A+ NYM	105	347	84	24	1	0	110	40	33	41	2	60	3	9	2	14	7	.67	3	.242	.326	.317
Norfolk	AAA NYM	3	8	0	0	0	0	0	0	0	1	0	3	0	0	0	0	0	.00	0	.000	.111	.000
1999 Binghamton	AA NYM	112	363	78	13	3	4	109	27	37	40	1	55	4	5	3	7	5	.58	8	.215	.298	.300
4 Min. YEARS		388	1295	301	59	9	5	393	137	136	162	5	224	11	20	9	39	22	.64	25	.232	.321	.303

Ramon Tatis

Pitches: Left Bats: Left Pos: P   Ht: 6'3" Wt: 205 Born: 5/2/73 Age: 27

		HOW MUCH HE PITCHED						WHAT HE GAVE UP												THE RESULTS					
Year Team	Lg Org	G	GS	CG	GF	IP	BFP	H	R	ER	HR	SH	SF	HB	TBB	IBB	SO	WP	Bk	W	L	Pct.	ShO	Sv	ERA
1992 Mets	R NYM	11	5	0	5	36	184	56	40	34	2	0	1	4	15	0	25	7	1	1	3	.250	0	0	8.50
1993 Kingsport	R+ NYM	13	3	0	5	42.2	204	51	42	29	1	3	1	5	23	0	25	4	0	0	2	.000	0	1	6.12
1994 Kingsport	R+ NYM	13	4	0	8	40.2	187	35	25	15	2	2	1	3	31	0	36	5	2	1	3	.250	0	0	3.32
1995 Pittsfield	A- NYM	13	13	1	0	79.1	341	88	40	32	2	1	1	3	27	0	69	8	3	4	5	.444	1	0	3.63
Capital Cty	A NYM	18	2	0	9	32	141	34	27	20	1	2	1	1	14	0	27	5	0	2	3	.400	0	0	5.63
1996 St. Lucie	A+ NYM	46	1	0	20	74.1	325	71	35	28	4	7	2	2	38	8	46	14	1	4	2	.667	0	6	3.39
1998 Durham	AAA TB	19	9	0	4	61.1	267	66	29	25	5	1	2	3	24	2	44	4	1	1	3	.250	0	2	3.67
1999 Durham	AAA TB	28	28	0	0	155.1	692	178	100	95	19	2	4	4	74	0	97	9	9	12	8	.600	0	0	5.50
1997 Chicago	NL	56	0	0	12	55.2	255	66	36	33	13	6	3	3	29	6	33	4	2	1	1	.500	0	0	5.34
1998 Tampa Bay	AL	22	0	0	7	11.2	72	23	19	18	2	0	0	1	16	1	5	1	1	0	0	.000	0	0	13.89
7 Min. YEARS		161	65	1	46	521.2	2341	579	338	278	36	18	13	24	246	10	369	56	17	25	29	.463	1	9	4.80
2 Maj. YEARS		78	0	0	19	67.1	327	89	55	51	15	6	3	4	45	7	38	5	3	1	1	.500	0	0	6.82

Jimmy Tatum

Bats: Right Throws: Right Pos: 3B   Ht: 6'2" Wt: 205 Born: 10/9/67 Age: 32

		BATTING														BASERUNNING				PERCENTAGES		
Year Team	Lg Org	G	AB	H	2B	3B	HR	TB	R	RBI	TBB	IBB	SO	HBP	SH	SF	SB	CS	SB%	GDP	Avg	OBP	SLG
1985 Spokane	A- SD	74	281	64	9	1	1	78	21	32	20	0	60	5	4	1	0	1	.00	7	.228	.290	.278
1986 Chston-SC	A SD	120	431	112	19	2	10	165	55	62	41	2	83	2	4	5	2	4	.33	11	.260	.324	.383
1987 Chston-SC	A SD	128	468	131	22	2	9	184	52	72	46	2	65	8	4	9	8	5	.62	16	.280	.348	.393
1988 Wichita	AA SD	118	402	105	26	1	8	157	38	54	30	2	73	5	6	3	2	3	.40	5	.261	.318	.391
1990 Canton-Akrn	AA Cle	30	106	19	6	0	2	31	6	11	6	1	19	1	0	2	1	0	1.00	2	.179	.226	.292
Stockton	A+ Mil	70	260	68	16	0	12	120	41	59	13	0	49	8	0	4	4	5	.44	7	.262	.312	.462
1991 El Paso	AA Mil	130	493	158	27	8	18	255	99	128	63	5	79	15	2	20	5	7	.42	21	.320	.399	.517
1992 Denver	AAA Mil	130	492	162	36	3	19	261	74	101	40	3	87	9	4	11	8	9	.47	11	.329	.382	.530
1993 Colo Sprngs	AAA Col	13	45	10	2	0	2	18	5	7	2	0	9	1	0	0	0	1	.00	3	.222	.271	.400
1994 Colo Sprngs	AAA Col	121	439	154	43	1	21	262	76	97	44	4	84	5	1	10	2	2	.50	6	.351	.408	.597
1995 Colo Sprngs	AAA Col	27	93	30	7	0	6	55	17	18	6	0	21	1	0	2	0	1	.00	2	.323	.363	.591
1996 Pawtucket	AAA Bos	19	66	18	2	0	5	35	11	16	7	0	12	1	0	0	2	0	1.00	3	.273	.351	.530
Las Vegas	AAA SD	64	233	80	20	1	12	138	40	56	23	6	53	3	0	1	4	0	1.00	9	.343	.408	.592
1997 Las Vegas	AAA SD	44	161	51	12	1	9	92	21	25	8	0	39	1	0	2	1	2	.33	1	.317	.349	.571
1999 Colo Sprngs	AAA Col	109	396	124	23	1	14	191	57	64	33	0	85	3	1	8	1	2	.33	14	.313	.364	.482
1992 Milwaukee	AL	5	8	1	0	0	0	1	0	0	1	0	2	0	0	0	0	0	.00	0	.125	.222	.125
1993 Colorado	NL	92	98	20	5	0	1	28	7	12	5	0	27	1	0	2	0	0	.00	0	.204	.245	.286
1995 Colorado	NL	34	34	8	1	1	0	11	4	4	1	0	7	0	0	0	0	0	.00	0	.235	.257	.324
1996 Boston	AL	2	8	1	0	0	0	1	0	0	0	0	2	0	0	0	0	0	.00	0	.125	.125	.125
San Diego	NL	5	3	0	0	0	0	0	0	0	0	0	1	0	0	0	0	0	.00	0	.000	.000	.000
1998 New York	NL	35	50	9	1	2	2	20	4	13	3	0	19	0	0	4	0	0	.00	1	.180	.211	.400
13 Min. YEARS		1197	4366	1286	270	21	148	2042	613	802	382	25	818	68	26	78	40	42	.49	118	.295	.355	.468
5 Maj. YEARS		173	201	39	7	3	3	61	16	29	10	0	58	1	0	6	0	0	.00	1	.194	.229	.303

Jesus Tavarez

Bats: Both Throws: Right Pos: 1B   Ht: 6'0" Wt: 170 Born: 3/26/71 Age: 29

		BATTING														BASERUNNING				PERCENTAGES		
Year Team	Lg Org	G	AB	H	2B	3B	HR	TB	R	RBI	TBB	IBB	SO	HBP	SH	SF	SB	CS	SB%	GDP	Avg	OBP	SLG
1990 Peninsula	A+ Sea	108	379	90	10	1	0	102	39	32	20	0	79	0	2	2	40	12	.77	4	.237	.274	.269
1991 San Berndno	A+ Sea	124	466	132	11	3	5	164	80	41	39	1	77	4	13	1	69	20	.78	4	.283	.343	.352
1992 Jacksnville	AA Sea	105	392	101	9	2	3	123	38	25	23	0	54	1	4	4	29	14	.67	9	.258	.298	.314
1993 High Desert	A+ Fla	109	444	130	21	8	7	188	104	71	57	0	66	4	3	5	47	14	.77	6	.293	.375	.423
1994 Portland	AA Fla	99	353	101	11	8	1	134	60	32	35	2	63	1	7	1	20	8	.71	4	.286	.351	.380
1995 Charlotte	AAA Fla	39	140	42	6	2	1	55	15	8	9	0	19	0	0	2	7	7	.50	1	.300	.338	.393
1997 Pawtucket	AAA Bos	59	229	61	6	3	4	82	43	20	27	1	31	1	6	0	22	9	.71	3	.266	.346	.358
1998 Rochester	AAA Bal	102	364	102	17	6	1	134	62	30	27	0	59	2	5	3	22	3	.88	4	.280	.331	.368
1999 Fresno	AAA SF	2	6	1	0	0	0	1	0	0	0	0	0	0	0	0	0	0	.00	0	.167	.167	.167
1994 Florida	NL	17	39	7	0	0	0	7	4	4	1	0	5	0	1	0	1	1	.50	0	.179	.200	.179
1995 Florida	NL	63	190	55	6	2	2	71	31	13	16	1	27	1	3	1	7	5	.58	4	.289	.346	.374
1996 Florida	NL	98	114	25	3	0	0	28	14	6	7	0	18	0	3	0	5	1	.83	2	.219	.264	.246
1997 Boston	AL	42	69	12	3	1	0	17	12	9	4	0	9	0	0	1	0	0	.00	1	.174	.216	.246

Year Team	Lg Org	G	AB	H	2B	3B	HR	TB	R	RBI	TBB	IBB	SO	HBP	SH	SF	SB	CS	SB%	GDP	Avg	OBP	SLG
					BATTING												BASERUNNING				PERCENTAGES		
1998 Baltimore	AL	8	11	2	0	0	1	5	2	1	2	0	3	0	0	0	0	1	.00	0	.182	.308	.455
9 Min. YEARS		737	2773	760	91	33	22	983	441	259	237	4	448	13	40	18	256	87	.75	32	.274	.332	.354
5 Maj. YEARS		228	423	101	12	3	3	128	63	33	30	1	62	1	7	2	13	8	.62	5	.239	.289	.303

Frank Taveras

Bats: Left **Throws:** Right **Pos:** 3B   **Ht:** 6'1" **Wt:** 158 **Born:** 9/6/75 **Age:** 24

Year Team	Lg Org	G	AB	H	2B	3B	HR	TB	R	RBI	TBB	IBB	SO	HBP	SH	SF	SB	CS	SB%	GDP	Avg	OBP	SLG
1996 Burlington	R+ Cle	46	161	38	4	0	3	51	18	15	6	0	50	0	2	1	6	3	.67	4	.236	.262	.317
1997 Burlington	R+ Cle	56	194	51	10	3	2	73	29	34	16	0	56	0	1	4	11	8	.58	1	.263	.313	.376
1998 Columbus	A Cle	84	281	73	12	2	5	104	31	33	10	0	71	3	1	2	1	5	.17	5	.260	.291	.370
Akron	AA Cle	2	4	2	0	0	0	2	2	0	1	0	1	0	0	0	0	0	.00	0	.500	.600	.500
1999 Akron	AA Cle	16	42	8	1	0	1	12	6	4	4	0	17	0	0	1	0	0	.00	0	.190	.255	.286
Kinston	A+ Cle	31	107	25	7	1	1	37	11	11	6	0	27	1	0	0	0	0	.00	4	.234	.281	.346
4 Min. YEARS		235	789	197	34	6	12	279	97	97	43	0	222	4	4	8	18	16	.53	14	.250	.289	.354

Reggie Taylor

Bats: Left **Throws:** Right **Pos:** OF   **Ht:** 6'1" **Wt:** 175 **Born:** 1/12/77 **Age:** 23

Year Team	Lg Org	G	AB	H	2B	3B	HR	TB	R	RBI	TBB	IBB	SO	HBP	SH	SF	SB	CS	SB%	GDP	Avg	OBP	SLG
1995 Martinsvlle	R+ Phi	64	239	53	4	6	2	75	36	32	23	0	58	6	0	4	18	7	.72	5	.222	.301	.314
1996 Piedmont	A Phi	128	499	131	20	6	0	163	68	31	29	0	136	3	2	3	36	17	.68	10	.263	.305	.327
1997 Clearwater	A+ Phi	134	545	133	18	6	12	199	73	47	30	4	130	4	5	6	40	23	.63	3	.244	.285	.365
1998 Reading	AA Phi	79	337	92	14	6	5	133	49	22	12	0	73	2	0	2	22	10	.69	2	.273	.300	.395
1999 Reading	AA Phi	127	526	140	17	10	15	222	75	61	18	1	79	3	3	3	38	20	.66	11	.266	.293	.422
5 Min. YEARS		532	2146	549	73	34	34	792	301	193	112	5	476	18	10	18	154	77	.67	31	.256	.296	.369

Nate Tebbs

Bats: Both **Throws:** Right **Pos:** OF   **Ht:** 5'10" **Wt:** 170 **Born:** 12/14/72 **Age:** 27

Year Team	Lg Org	G	AB	H	2B	3B	HR	TB	R	RBI	TBB	IBB	SO	HBP	SH	SF	SB	CS	SB%	GDP	Avg	OBP	SLG
1993 Red Sox	R Bos	43	146	38	4	1	0	44	21	4	15	1	16	0	7	0	7	1	.88	1	.260	.329	.301
1994 Utica	A- Bos	70	219	44	5	0	0	49	18	23	11	0	34	1	4	1	9	4	.69	1	.201	.241	.224
1995 Sarasota	A+ Bos	118	440	128	15	4	2	157	58	52	39	0	80	3	4	1	25	15	.63	7	.291	.352	.357
1996 Sarasota	A+ Bos	116	420	105	11	2	1	123	44	34	24	1	68	3	10	1	17	4	.81	7	.250	.295	.293
1997 Sarasota	A+ Bos	111	375	98	14	3	5	133	52	39	27	3	65	0	2	3	15	9	.63	9	.261	.309	.355
Trenton	AA Bos	5	16	5	0	0	0	5	2	0	2	0	1	0	0	0	0	1	.00	0	.313	.389	.313
1998 Trenton	AA Bos	104	394	101	21	2	2	132	44	31	36	0	63	3	3	1	14	13	.52	10	.256	.323	.335
Pawtucket	AAA Bos	17	57	16	2	0	0	18	7	4	3	0	13	0	2	0	5	2	.71	0	.281	.317	.316
1999 Pawtucket	AAA Bos	4	5	3	1	0	0	4	1	1	2	0	1	1	0	0	0	1	.00	0	.600	.750	.800
Trenton	AA Bos	107	365	99	14	1	4	127	49	35	29	1	67	5	11	7	21	10	.68	7	.271	.328	.348
7 Min. YEARS		695	2437	637	87	13	14	792	296	223	188	6	408	16	43	14	113	60	.65	42	.261	.317	.325

Fausto Tejero

Bats: Right **Throws:** Right **Pos:** C   **Ht:** 6'2" **Wt:** 205 **Born:** 10/26/68 **Age:** 31

Year Team	Lg Org	G	AB	H	2B	3B	HR	TB	R	RBI	TBB	IBB	SO	HBP	SH	SF	SB	CS	SB%	GDP	Avg	OBP	SLG
1990 Boise	A- Ana	39	74	16	2	0	0	18	14	7	23	1	23	2	3	3	1	0	1.00	0	.216	.402	.243
1991 Quad City	A Ana	83	244	42	7	0	1	52	16	18	14	0	52	4	3	1	1	0	.00	5	.172	.228	.213
1992 Edmonton	AAA Ana	8	17	4	1	0	0	5	0	0	4	0	2	1	2	0	0	2	.00	0	.235	.409	.294
Midland	AA Ana	84	266	50	11	0	2	67	21	30	11	0	63	4	5	3	1	2	.33	6	.188	.229	.252
1993 Palm Spring	A+ Ana	7	20	6	2	0	0	8	2	1	2	0	1	0	1	0	0	1	.00	0	.300	.364	.400
Vancouver	AAA Ana	20	59	9	0	0	0	9	2	2	4	1	12	1	2	1	1	1	.50	0	.153	.215	.153
Midland	AA Ana	26	69	9	1	1	1	15	3	7	8	0	17	2	1	1	0	0	.00	3	.130	.238	.217
1994 Midland	AA Ana	50	150	32	3	0	5	50	17	24	15	0	31	1	1	2	2	2	.50	6	.213	.286	.333
Vancouver	AAA Ana	16	45	9	2	0	0	11	6	6	4	0	9	0	2	1	1	1	.50	1	.200	.260	.244
1995 Lk Elsinore	A+ Ana	8	21	5	1	0	0	6	5	3	5	0	6	0	0	1	1	0	1.00	1	.238	.370	.286
Vancouver	AAA Ana	37	96	25	3	0	0	28	10	8	10	1	22	0	1	0	2	0	1.00	1	.260	.330	.292
Midland	AA Ana	16	53	12	3	0	1	18	7	11	1	0	13	1	0	1	0	1	.00	1	.226	.250	.340
1996 Vancouver	AAA Ana	54	155	31	4	1	1	40	21	12	22	0	41	1	6	0	0	1	.00	6	.200	.303	.258
1997 Richmond	AAA Atl	76	225	52	11	0	6	81	31	28	23	2	41	4	2	2	0	1	.00	6	.231	.311	.360
1998 Richmond	AAA Atl	77	223	50	14	0	4	76	19	26	21	2	48	3	1	2	1	2	.33	6	.224	.297	.341
1999 Edmonton	AAA Ana	5	17	5	0	0	1	8	3	2	3	0	3	0	0	0	0	0	.00	0	.294	.400	.471
Erie	AA Ana	62	211	45	9	0	3	63	19	18	13	0	38	3	4	0	0	2	.00	7	.213	.269	.299
10 Min. YEARS		668	1945	402	74	2	25	555	196	203	183	7	422	27	34	18	10	17	.37	48	.207	.282	.285

Dave Telgheder

Pitches: Right **Bats:** Right **Pos:** P   **Ht:** 6'3" **Wt:** 223 **Born:** 11/11/66 **Age:** 33

Year Team	Lg Org	G	GS	CG	GF	IP	BFP	H	R	ER	HR	SH	SF	HB	TBB	IBB	SO	WP	Bk	W	L	Pct.	ShO	Sv	ERA
1989 Pittsfield	A- NYM	13	7	4	4	58.2	233	43	18	16	2	1	1	2	9	1	65	2	2	5	3	.625	1	2	2.45
1990 Columbia	A NYM	14	13	5	1	99.1	380	79	22	17	2	0	0	0	10	0	81	0	1	9	3	.750	1	0	1.54
St. Lucie	A+ NYM	14	14	3	0	96	382	84	38	32	3	3	4	3	14	0	77	3	0	9	4	.692	0	0	3.00
1991 Williamsprt	AA NYM	28	26	1	1	167.2	711	185	81	67	7	7	11	5	33	3	90	4	1	13	11	.542	1	0	3.60
1992 Tidewater	AAA NYM	28	27	3	1	169	698	173	87	79	16	4	7	0	36	4	118	1	1	6	14	.300	2	0	4.21
1993 Norfolk	AAA NYM	13	12	0	1	76.1	313	81	29	25	6	3	0	3	19	1	52	1	0	7	3	.700	0	1	2.95

Year Team	Lg Org	G	GS	CG	GF	IP	BFP	H	R	ER	HR	SH	SF	HB	TBB	IBB	SO	WP	Bk	W	L	Pct.	ShO	Sv	ERA
1994 Norfolk	AAA NYM	23	23	3	0	158.2	643	156	65	60	14	3	3	3	26	0	83	5	2	8	10	.444	2	0	3.40
1995 Norfolk	AAA NYM	29	11	0	8	92.1	356	77	34	23	7	5	2	1	8	0	75	0	2	5	4	.556	0	3	2.24
1996 Edmonton	AAA Oak	17	17	1	0	101.1	421	102	53	47	7	0	4	2	23	1	59	1	0	8	6	.571	0	0	4.17
Modesto	A+ Oak	1	1	0	0	6	24	4	3	1	0	0	0	0	1	0	3	0	0	1	0	1.000	0	0	1.50
1997 Modesto	A+ Oak	2	2	0	0	5.1	21	3	2	2	0	0	0	0	2	0	4	0	0	0	0	.000	0	0	3.38
1998 Edmonton	AAA Oak	3	3	0	0	16	74	26	14	13	2	0	1	0	3	0	9	0	1	1	2	.333	0	0	7.31
1999 Buffalo	AAA Cle	29	14	1	3	107	451	109	56	47	8	3	6	3	21	2	60	3	1	8	8	.500	0	0	3.95
1993 New York	NL	24	7	0	7	75.2	325	82	40	40	10	2	1	4	21	2	35	1	0	6	2	.750	0	0	4.76
1994 New York	NL	6	0	0	0	10	48	11	8	8	2	1	0	0	8	2	4	0	0	0	1	.000	0	0	7.20
1995 New York	NL	7	4	0	2	25.2	118	34	18	16	4	3	1	0	7	3	16	0	1	1	2	.333	0	0	5.61
1996 Oakland	AL	16	14	1	1	79.1	348	92	42	41	12	3	3	1	26	1	43	2	0	4	7	.364	1	0	4.65
1997 Oakland	AL	20	19	0	0	101	458	134	71	68	15	0	7	2	35	1	55	4	0	4	6	.400	0	0	6.06
1998 Oakland	AL	8	2	0	4	20	91	19	12	8	4	2	0	2	6	0	5	2	1	0	1	.000	0	0	3.60
11 Min. YEARS		214	170	21	19	1153.2	4707	1122	502	429	74	29	39	22	205	12	776	20	11	80	68	.541	6	6	3.35
6 Maj. YEARS		81	46	1	14	311.2	1388	372	191	181	47	11	12	9	103	9	158	9	2	15	19	.441	1	0	5.23

Marcus Thames

Bats: Right **Throws:** Right **Pos:** OF　　　　**Ht:** 6'2" **Wt:** 205 **Born:** 3/6/77 **Age:** 23

													BATTING		BASERUNNING				PERCENTAGES		
Year Team	Lg Org	G	AB	H	2B	3B	HR	TB	R	RBI	TBB	IBB	SO	HBP	SH	SF	SB	CS	SB%	GDP	Avg	OBP	SLG
1997 Yankees	R NYY	57	195	67	17	4	7	113	51	36	16	0	26	3	1	4	6	4	.60	3	.344	.394	.579
Greensboro	A NYY	14	16	5	1	0	0	6	2	2	0	0	3	0	0	0	1	0	1.00	0	.313	.313	.375
1998 Tampa	A+ NYY	122	457	130	18	3	11	187	62	59	24	1	78	8	1	5	13	6	.68	5	.284	.328	.409
1999 Norwich	AA NYY	51	182	41	6	2	4	63	25	26	22	0	40	3	1	2	0	1	.00	2	.225	.316	.346
Tampa	A+ NYY	69	266	65	12	4	11	118	47	38	33	1	58	3	1	2	3	0	1.00	1	.244	.332	.444
3 Min. YEARS		303	1116	308	54	13	33	487	187	161	95	2	205	17	4	13	23	11	.68	11	.276	.338	.436

Robert Theodile

Pitches: Right **Bats:** Right **Pos:** P　　　　**Ht:** 6'3" **Wt:** 190 **Born:** 9/16/72 **Age:** 27

Year Team	Lg Org	G	GS	CG	GF	IP	BFP	H	R	ER	HR	SH	SF	HB	TBB	IBB	SO	WP	Bk	W	L	Pct.	ShO	Sv	ERA
1992 White Sox	R CWS	4	1	0	0	13	45	7	1	1	0	0	0	0	4	0	12	0	0	2	0	1.000	0	0	0.69
1993 White Sox	R CWS	10	8	1	1	66	265	45	24	19	2	1	0	6	23	0	42	2	2	5	2	.714	1	1	2.59
Hickory	A CWS	8	8	0	0	45.1	211	63	40	34	1	0	2	1	21	0	23	5	0	0	4	.000	0	0	6.75
1994 Hickory	A CWS	18	16	2	1	86.1	383	81	53	46	7	1	2	2	47	0	68	11	1	7	4	.636	0	0	4.80
1995 South Bend	A CWS	7	4	0	0	26	130	45	30	22	1	1	1	1	13	0	16	5	0	1	2	.333	0	0	7.62
Hickory	A CWS	20	17	1	1	107	470	103	61	45	8	3	5	5	53	2	77	13	4	6	9	.400	1	0	3.79
1996 Pr William	A+ CWS	25	22	1	1	132	571	133	73	63	5	6	5	7	56	3	91	8	1	7	9	.438	1	1	4.30
1997 Birmingham	AA CWS	19	9	0	3	57.1	272	72	43	35	2	0	5	2	35	0	41	5	0	2	0	1.000	0	1	5.49
Winston-Sal	A+ CWS	13	12	0	1	82.2	344	66	34	27	6	2	4	6	33	0	75	5	0	7	3	.700	0	0	2.94
1998 Birmingham	AA CWS	8	0	0	4	16.2	85	18	18	14	1	2	1	2	16	0	17	0	0	0	1	.000	0	0	7.56
Calgary	AAA CWS	17	5	0	5	38.2	178	36	35	33	7	0	1	1	31	0	24	4	0	0	2	.000	0	0	7.68
1999 Huntsville	AA Mil	47	3	0	18	92.1	449	118	71	59	9	7	4	9	56	1	60	8	2	3	7	.300	0	0	5.75
8 Min. YEARS		196	105	5	35	763.1	3403	787	483	398	49	23	30	42	388	6	546	68	10	40	43	.482	3	3	4.69

Dave Therneau

Pitches: Right **Bats:** Right **Pos:** P　　　　**Ht:** 6'5" **Wt:** 195 **Born:** 12/23/75 **Age:** 24

Year Team	Lg Org	G	GS	CG	GF	IP	BFP	H	R	ER	HR	SH	SF	HB	TBB	IBB	SO	WP	Bk	W	L	Pct.	ShO	Sv	ERA
1998 Billings	R+ Cin	9	9	0	0	51	219	52	27	22	2	4	0	1	16	0	59	1	1	3	1	.750	0	0	3.88
Burlington	A Cin	7	6	0	1	39.2	166	36	17	17	3	2	0	0	17	0	42	4	0	2	3	.400	0	0	3.86
1999 Rockford	A Cin	16	16	2	0	100.1	422	95	41	38	6	2	3	4	33	1	106	5	2	12	3	.800	2	0	3.41
Chattanooga	AA Cin	3	3	0	0	21	88	22	7	6	2	0	0	1	8	0	11	0	0	2	0	1.000	0	0	2.57
Indianapolis	AAA Cin	7	7	0	0	36.1	172	52	36	33	9	1	2	1	14	0	22	4	1	0	2	.000	0	0	8.17
2 Min. YEARS		42	41	2	1	248.1	1067	257	128	116	22	9	5	7	88	1	240	14	4	19	9	.679	2	0	4.20

E.J. t'Hoen

Bats: Right **Throws:** Right **Pos:** 2B-3B　　　　**Ht:** 6'2" **Wt:** 185 **Born:** 11/8/75 **Age:** 24

													BATTING		BASERUNNING				PERCENTAGES		
Year Team	Lg Org	G	AB	H	2B	3B	HR	TB	R	RBI	TBB	IBB	SO	HBP	SH	SF	SB	CS	SB%	GDP	Avg	OBP	SLG
1996 Boise	A- Ana	18	60	12	1	0	2	19	6	4	4	0	17	1	1	0	0	0	.00	2	.200	.262	.317
1997 Cedar Rapds	A Ana	123	384	78	19	3	3	112	41	46	31	0	114	7	7	3	2	3	.40	7	.203	.273	.292
1998 Cedar Rapds	A Ana	130	441	96	22	1	18	174	57	55	50	2	129	7	3	2	10	5	.67	5	.218	.306	.395
1999 Edmonton	AAA Ana	9	29	4	0	0	0	4	2	0	2	0	7	0	1	0	0	0	.00	0	.138	.194	.138
Erie	AA Ana	56	187	38	12	1	2	58	18	21	13	0	52	3	5	1	6	2	.75	4	.203	.265	.310
4 Min. YEARS		336	1101	228	54	5	25	367	124	126	100	2	319	18	17	6	18	10	.64	18	.207	.282	.333

Evan Thomas

Pitches: Right **Bats:** Right **Pos:** P　　　　**Ht:** 5'10" **Wt:** 171 **Born:** 6/14/74 **Age:** 26

Year Team	Lg Org	G	GS	CG	GF	IP	BFP	H	R	ER	HR	SH	SF	HB	TBB	IBB	SO	WP	Bk	W	L	Pct.	ShO	Sv	ERA
1996 Batavia	A- Phi	13	13	0	0	81	321	60	29	25	3	1	3	5	23	0	75	6	0	10	2	.833	0	0	2.78
1997 Clearwater	A+ Phi	13	12	2	0	84.2	340	68	30	23	7	1	1	3	23	0	89	3	2	5	5	.500	0	0	2.44
Reading	AA Phi	15	15	0	0	83	377	98	51	38	10	5	2	7	32	1	83	3	2	3	6	.333	0	0	4.12
1998 Scranton-WB	AAA Phi	2	2	0	0	9	42	9	8	8	1	0	1	0	6	0	5	0	0	0	1	.000	0	0	8.00
Reading	AA Phi	24	24	3	0	158.1	676	180	66	59	12	3	5	4	44	2	134	3	1	8	5	.615	3	0	3.35

		HOW MUCH HE PITCHED			WHAT HE GAVE UP			THE RESULTS		
Year Team	Lg Org	G GS CG GF	IP	BFP	H R ER HR SH SF HB	TBB IBB SO WP Bk		W L Pct. ShO Sv ERA		
1999 Reading	AA Phi	36 15 1 8	127.1	545	123 53 46 7 3 7 5	50 2 127 2 0		9 5 .643 0 3 3.25		
4 Min. YEARS		103 81 6 8	543.1	2301	538 237 199 40 13 19 24	178 5 513 17 5		35 24 .593 3 3 3.30		

Juan Thomas

Bats: Right Throws: Right Pos: DH-1B   Ht: 6'5" Wt: 270 Born: 4/17/72 Age: 28

		BATTING													BASERUNNING				PERCENTAGES		
Year Team	Lg Org	G	AB	H	2B	3B	HR	TB	R	RBI	TBB	IBB	SO	HBP	SH	SF	SB	CS	SB%	GDP	Avg	OBP	SLG
1992 White Sox	R CWS	55	189	42	6	1	6	68	30	29	18	0	76	3	0	2	8	1	.89	4	.222	.297	.360
1993 White Sox	R CWS	20	59	18	3	2	1	28	12	9	12	0	12	1	0	0	5	4	.56	1	.305	.431	.475
Hickory	A CWS	90	328	75	14	6	12	137	51	46	35	1	124	7	1	3	2	4	.33	7	.229	.314	.418
1994 South Bend	A CWS	119	446	112	20	6	18	198	57	79	27	2	143	9	0	5	3	4	.43	13	.251	.304	.444
1995 Pr William	A+ CWS	132	464	109	20	4	26	215	64	69	40	4	156	8	1	2	4	5	.44	16	.235	.305	.463
1996 Pr William	A+ CWS	134	495	148	28	6	20	248	88	71	54	3	129	5	0	2	9	3	.75	15	.299	.372	.501
1997 Winston-Sal	A+ CWS	45	164	43	7	0	13	89	28	28	17	0	61	1	0	0	1	1	.50	5	.262	.335	.543
Birmingham	AA CWS	80	311	94	16	2	10	144	50	55	23	1	92	4	0	4	1	2	.33	4	.302	.354	.463
1998 Atlantic Ct	IND —	99	395	100	18	0	33	217	64	103	35	2	119	1	0	5	6	3	.67	6	.253	.312	.549
1999 Atlantic Ct	IND —	41	154	48	12	0	10	90	30	35	14	1	50	1	0	5	2	1	.67	3	.312	.362	.584
New Haven	AA Sea	71	267	65	13	0	16	126	47	51	14	1	92	6	0	1	0	0	.00	6	.243	.295	.472
8 Min. YEARS		886	3272	854	157	27	165	1560	521	575	289	15	1054	46	2	29	41	28	.59	80	.261	.327	.477

Andy Thompson

Bats: Right Throws: Right Pos: OF   Ht: 6'3" Wt: 210 Born: 10/8/75 Age: 24

		BATTING													BASERUNNING				PERCENTAGES		
Year Team	Lg Org	G	AB	H	2B	3B	HR	TB	R	RBI	TBB	IBB	SO	HBP	SH	SF	SB	CS	SB%	GDP	Avg	OBP	SLG
1995 Hagerstown	A Tor	124	461	110	19	2	6	151	48	57	29	2	108	8	1	3	2	3	.40	15	.239	.293	.328
1996 Dunedin	A+ Tor	129	425	120	26	5	11	189	64	50	60	1	108	1	1	3	16	4	.80	5	.282	.370	.445
1997 Knoxville	AA Tor	124	448	128	25	3	15	204	75	71	63	3	76	6	1	4	0	5	.00	18	.286	.378	.455
1998 Knoxville	AA Tor	125	481	137	33	2	14	216	74	88	54	2	69	3	0	5	8	3	.73	10	.285	.357	.449
1999 Knoxville	AA Tor	67	254	62	16	3	15	129	56	53	34	2	55	8	0	5	7	3	.70	2	.244	.346	.508
Syracuse	AAA Tor	62	229	67	17	2	16	136	42	42	21	0	45	2	0	0	5	0	1.00	4	.293	.357	.594
5 Min. YEARS		631	2298	624	136	17	77	1025	359	361	261	10	461	28	3	20	38	18	.68	54	.272	.350	.446

Chris Thompson

Pitches: Right Bats: Right Pos: P   Ht: 6'2" Wt: 202 Born: 9/29/72 Age: 27

		HOW MUCH HE PITCHED			WHAT HE GAVE UP		THE RESULTS		
Year Team	Lg Org	G GS CG GF	IP	BFP	H R ER HR SH SF HB	TBB IBB SO WP Bk	W L Pct. ShO Sv ERA		
1996 Lowell	A- Bos	25 0 0 12	47	214	43 34 23 2 1 4 5	20 1 51 8 1	2 5 .286 0 0 4.40		
1997 Michigan	A Bos	9 0 0 3	15.2	62	11 7 2 1 1 0 0	1 1 13 1 0	0 1 .000 0 0 1.15		
Sarasota	A+ Bos	29 6 0 8	61	289	68 35 25 7 1 3 1	29 2 36 6 0	5 2 .714 0 0 3.69		
1998 Pawtucket	AAA Bos	2 0 0 1	3	12	3 1 1 1 0 0 1	1 0 3 1 0	0 0 .000 0 0 3.00		
Sarasota	A+ Bos	30 0 0 16	45.1	194	48 19 16 1 2 1 1	17 5 28 8 0	5 2 .714 0 4 3.18		
1999 Trenton	AA Bos	1 0 0 1	1	6	2 1 1 0 0 0 0	1 0 1 1 0	0 0 .000 0 0 9.00		
Sarasota	A+ Bos	28 2 0 15	43.1	202	48 33 27 3 1 0 6	22 3 41 7 0	2 5 .286 0 1 5.61		
4 Min. YEARS		123 8 0 56	216.1	979	223 130 95 15 6 8 14	91 12 173 32 1	14 15 .483 0 5 3.95		

Jake Thrower

Bats: Both Throws: Right Pos: 2B   Ht: 5'11" Wt: 180 Born: 11/19/75 Age: 24

		BATTING													BASERUNNING				PERCENTAGES		
Year Team	Lg Org	G	AB	H	2B	3B	HR	TB	R	RBI	TBB	IBB	SO	HBP	SH	SF	SB	CS	SB%	GDP	Avg	OBP	SLG
1997 Idaho Falls	R+ SD	35	141	48	10	4	3	75	37	28	31	2	16	4	0	1	10	1	.91	2	.340	.469	.532
Clinton	A SD	19	63	16	3	0	0	19	8	12	14	0	15	2	1	0	1	3	.25	0	.254	.397	.302
1998 Clinton	A SD	43	145	42	11	1	5	70	25	27	22	0	22	4	0	0	11	3	.79	5	.290	.398	.483
Rancho Cuca	A+ SD	37	127	34	7	0	1	44	24	10	19	0	19	1	0	2	4	1	.80	2	.268	.362	.346
1999 Mobile	AA SD	40	149	36	9	2	3	58	15	26	21	1	26	1	0	1	3	3	.50	3	.242	.337	.389
Las Vegas	AAA SD	72	267	77	17	4	4	114	40	30	27	2	56	2	3	2	4	4	.50	6	.288	.356	.427
3 Min. YEARS		246	892	253	57	11	16	380	149	133	133	5	154	14	4	6	33	15	.69	17	.284	.383	.426

Jerrey Thurston

Bats: Right Throws: Right Pos: C   Ht: 6'4" Wt: 200 Born: 4/17/72 Age: 28

		BATTING													BASERUNNING				PERCENTAGES		
Year Team	Lg Org	G	AB	H	2B	3B	HR	TB	R	RBI	TBB	IBB	SO	HBP	SH	SF	SB	CS	SB%	GDP	Avg	OBP	SLG
1990 Padres	R SD	42	144	33	6	1	0	41	22	16	14	0	37	0	2	0	4	1	.80	1	.229	.297	.285
1991 Chston-SC	A SD	42	137	14	2	0	0	16	5	4	9	0	50	0	1	1	1	1	.50	3	.102	.156	.117
Spokane	A- SD	60	201	43	9	0	1	55	26	20	20	1	61	2	2	2	2	2	.50	2	.214	.289	.274
1992 Waterloo	A SD	96	263	37	7	0	0	44	20	14	12	0	73	2	6	2	1	0	1.00	4	.141	.183	.167
1993 Wichita	AA SD	78	197	48	10	0	2	64	22	22	14	0	62	6	3	0	2	0	1.00	3	.244	.313	.325
1994 Wichita	AA SD	77	238	51	10	2	4	77	30	28	19	1	73	8	2	1	4	1	.20	8	.214	.293	.324
1995 Las Vegas	AAA SD	5	20	4	1	0	0	5	2	0	0	0	5	1	0	0	0	0	.00	0	.200	.238	.250
Rancho Cuca	A+ SD	76	200	44	9	0	1	56	24	13	21	0	64	7	4	3	1	0	1.00	2	.220	.312	.280
1996 Orlando	AA ChC	67	177	37	6	1	3	54	16	23	14	0	57	0	3	0	0	0	.00	5	.209	.267	.305
1997 Lk Elsinore	A+ Ana	2	6	3	1	0	0	4	1	1	0	0	2	0	0	0	0	0	.00	0	.500	.500	.667
Vancouver	AAA Ana	65	195	46	3	1	4	63	17	19	8	0	59	4	8	2	3	2	.60	2	.236	.278	.323
1998 Midland	AA Ana	29	95	30	4	0	2	40	20	22	8	0	24	2	0	1	0	0	.00	2	.316	.377	.421
Vancouver	AAA Ana	9	25	4	1	0	0	5	0	1	3	0	8	0	0	0	0	0	.00	0	.160	.250	.200
Ottawa	AAA Mon	13	30	1	0	0	0	1	2	0	4	0	15	0	0	0	0	0	.00	0	.033	.147	.033
1999 New Orleans	AAA Hou	21	59	13	0	0	0	13	7	4	4	0	15	2	1	0	0	1	.00	3	.220	.292	.220
10 Min. YEARS		682	1987	408	69	5	17	538	214	187	150	2	605	34	32	12	15	11	.58	35	.205	.271	.271

Luis Tinoco

Bats: Right **Throws:** Right **Pos:** OF   **Ht:** 6'2" **Wt:** 215 **Born:** 7/24/74 **Age:** 25

Year Team	Lg Org	G	AB	H	2B	3B	HR	TB	R	RBI	TBB	IBB	SO	HBP	SH	SF	SB	CS	SB%	GDP	Avg	OBP	SLG
1993 Mariners	R Sea	39	112	29	4	2	1	40	20	20	31	1	41	1	1	1	4	1	.80	2	.259	.421	.357
1994 Mariners	R Sea	14	41	8	0	0	0	8	4	2	9	0	11	2	0	1	0	0	.00	0	.195	.358	.195
1995 Everett	A- Sea	62	203	58	10	2	9	99	34	31	35	1	41	3	0	1	9	3	.75	6	.286	.397	.488
1996 Wisconsin	A Sea	120	431	135	31	5	12	212	71	71	53	1	85	18	1	6	4	9	.31	14	.313	.406	.492
1997 Lancaster	A+ Sea	12	43	7	2	0	2	15	9	5	5	0	12	1	0	0	0	1	.00	3	.163	.265	.349
1998 Lancaster	A+ Sea	108	412	117	20	6	6	167	61	69	38	2	79	5	3	2	5	1	.83	15	.284	.350	.405
Orlando	AA Sea	20	75	20	3	0	1	26	9	12	11	0	8	0	0	0	0	0	.00	3	.267	.360	.347
1999 Reading	AA Phi	39	96	26	4	0	1	33	18	10	22	1	23	2	0	1	2	2	.50	3	.271	.413	.344
Clearwater	A+ Phi	32	110	20	3	0	0	23	15	6	8	0	23	4	0	1	1	0	1.00	1	.182	.260	.209
7 Min. YEARS		446	1523	420	77	15	32	623	241	226	212	6	323	36	5	13	25	17	.60	47	.276	.374	.409

Lee Tinsley

Bats: Both **Throws:** Right **Pos:** OF   **Ht:** 5'10" **Wt:** 198 **Born:** 3/4/69 **Age:** 31

Year Team	Lg Org	G	AB	H	2B	3B	HR	TB	R	RBI	TBB	IBB	SO	HBP	SH	SF	SB	CS	SB%	GDP	Avg	OBP	SLG
1987 Medford	A- Oak	45	132	23	3	2	0	30	22	13	35	0	57	2	1	4	9	3	.75	1	.174	.347	.227
1988 Sou Oregon	A- Oak	72	256	64	8	2	3	85	56	28	66	1	106	5	1	1	42	10	.81	1	.250	.412	.332
1989 Madison	A Oak	123	397	72	10	2	6	104	51	31	67	1	177	9	3	1	19	11	.63	6	.181	.312	.262
1990 Madison	A Oak	132	482	121	14	11	12	193	88	59	78	7	175	5	3	2	44	11	.80	3	.251	.360	.400
1991 Huntsville	AA Oak	92	303	68	7	6	2	93	47	24	52	1	97	3	1	4	36	14	.72	6	.224	.340	.307
Canton-Akrn	AA Cle	38	139	41	7	2	3	61	26	8	18	2	37	4	2	0	18	5	.78	2	.295	.391	.439
1992 Colo Sprngs	AAA Cle	27	81	19	2	1	0	23	19	4	16	0	19	1	1	1	3	3	.50	3	.235	.364	.284
Canton-Akrn	AA Cle	96	349	100	9	8	5	140	65	38	42	4	82	2	5	2	18	5	.78	13	.287	.365	.401
1993 Calgary	AAA Sea	111	450	136	25	18	10	227	94	63	50	5	98	2	3	4	34	11	.76	3	.302	.372	.504
1995 Trenton	AA Bos	4	18	7	1	0	0	8	3	3	1	0	5	0	0	0	1	0	1.00	0	.389	.421	.444
1996 Clearwater	A+ Phi	4	17	5	0	1	0	7	4	3	2	0	4	0	0	0	2	0	1.00	0	.294	.368	.412
1997 Tacoma	AAA Sea	31	105	19	2	1	2	29	15	7	12	0	34	0	0	0	1	4	.20	0	.181	.265	.276
1998 Ottawa	AAA Mon	51	185	40	9	2	2	59	25	19	16	0	43	1	3	2	13	2	.87	2	.216	.279	.319
Midland	AA Ana	11	42	11	4	1	0	17	2	5	2	0	7	0	0	0	3	1	.75	0	.262	.295	.405
Vancouver	AAA Ana	24	89	16	4	1	1	25	5	8	10	0	28	2	1	1	6	1	.86	4	.180	.275	.281
1999 Indianapols	AAA Cin	30	76	16	2	2	1	25	5	6	5	0	14	0	2	0	1	4	.20	0	.211	.259	.329
1993 Seattle	AL	11	19	3	1	0	1	7	2	2	2	0	9	0	0	0	0	0	.00	1	.158	.238	.368
1994 Boston	AL	78	144	32	4	0	2	42	27	14	19	1	36	1	3	1	13	0	1.00	2	.222	.315	.292
1995 Boston	AL	100	341	97	17	1	7	137	61	41	39	1	74	1	9	1	18	8	.69	8	.284	.359	.402
1996 Philadelphia	NL	31	52	7	0	0	0	7	1	2	4	0	22	0	1	0	2	4	.33	1	.135	.196	.135
Boston	AL	92	192	47	6	1	3	64	28	14	13	0	56	2	1	1	6	8	.43	5	.245	.298	.333
1997 Seattle	AL	49	122	24	6	2	0	34	12	6	11	0	34	0	0	0	2	0	1.00	1	.197	.263	.279
12 Min. YEARS		891	3121	758	107	60	47	1126	527	319	472	21	983	36	26	22	250	85	.75	44	.243	.347	.361
5 Maj. YEARS		361	870	210	34	4	13	291	131	79	88	2	231	4	14	3	41	20	.67	21	.241	.313	.334

Brian Tokarse

Pitches: Right **Bats:** Right **Pos:** P   **Ht:** 6'3" **Wt:** 180 **Born:** 2/28/75 **Age:** 25

Year Team	Lg Org	G	GS	CG	GF	IP	BFP	H	R	ER	HR	SH	SF	HB	TBB	IBB	SO	WP	Bk	W	L	Pct.	ShO	Sv	ERA
1997 Butte	R+ Ana	8	7	0	0	36.2	162	44	33	28	1	3	4	2	8	0	34	2	0	2	4	.333	0	0	6.87
1998 Lk Elsinore	A+ Ana	22	22	2	0	125.1	553	150	93	80	7	1	2	9	42	0	97	6	4	9	9	.500	0	0	5.74
Hickory	A CWS	2	2	0	0	3.2	17	3	3	3	1	0	0	2	3	0	3	1	0	0	1	.000	0	0	7.36
1999 Winston-Sal	A+ CWS	40	0	0	37	46.2	201	37	15	12	2	4	1	3	22	3	55	2	0	5	4	.556	0	14	2.31
Birmingham	AA CWS	6	0	0	0	10.2	46	12	7	6	1	1	0	0	3	0	11	1	0	0	1	.000	0	0	5.06
3 Min. YEARS		78	31	2	37	223	979	246	151	129	14	7	7	16	78	3	200	12	4	16	19	.457	0	14	5.21

Kevin Tolar

Pitches: Left **Bats:** Right **Pos:** P   **Ht:** 6'3" **Wt:** 225 **Born:** 1/28/71 **Age:** 29

Year Team	Lg Org	G	GS	CG	GF	IP	BFP	H	R	ER	HR	SH	SF	HB	TBB	IBB	SO	WP	Bk	W	L	Pct.	ShO	Sv	ERA
1989 White Sox	R CWS	13	12	1	0	60	256	29	16	11	0	1	1	1	54	0	58	10	0	6	2	.750	0	0	1.65
1990 Utica	A- CWS	15	15	1	0	90.1	407	80	44	33	2	1	3	4	61	1	69	9	1	4	6	.400	0	0	3.29
1991 South Bend	A CWS	30	19	0	6	114.2	510	87	54	35	3	5	5	8	85	0	87	6	0	8	5	.615	0	1	2.75
1992 Salinas	A+ CWS	14	8	3	3	53.1	255	55	43	36	4	1	7	5	46	0	24	6	0	1	8	.111	0	0	6.08
South Bend	A CWS	18	10	0	6	81.1	339	59	34	26	5	7	4	2	41	0	81	5	1	6	5	.545	0	2	2.88
1993 Sarasota	A+ CWS	23	11	0	8	77.1	358	75	55	46	1	5	7	6	51	1	60	8	0	2	6	.250	0	1	5.35
1995 Lynchburg	A+ Pit	18	0	0	4	19.1	77	13	7	6	1	0	1	1	6	0	19	3	0	2	0	1.000	0	0	2.79
Carolina	AA Pit	12	0	0	3	12.1	59	16	5	5	0	0	2	0	7	0	9	2	0	1	0	1.000	0	0	3.65
1996 Canton-Akrn	AA Cle	50	0	0	15	44.2	201	42	19	13	1	4	2	3	26	2	39	5	0	1	3	.250	0	1	2.62
1997 Binghamton	AA NYM	22	0	0	9	31.2	157	38	20	18	3	4	1	2	22	1	26	6	0	1	1	.500	0	1	5.12
St. Lucie	A+ NYM	9	0	0	3	13.1	54	9	3	3	0	0	0	0	6	0	8	1	0	0	0	.000	0	1	2.03
1998 Nashville	AAA Pit	1	0	0	0	3	14	2	2	2	0	0	0	0	4	0	1	1	0	0	0	.000	0	0	6.00
Carolina	AA Pit	42	0	0	15	48.2	211	35	12	12	1	4	1	2	33	0	48	1	0	1	2	.333	0	1	2.22
Indianapols	AAA Cin	19	0	0	3	14.2	82	21	18	17	3	1	0	0	17	1	19	3	0	0	1	.000	0	0	10.43
1999 Chattanooga	AA Cin	47	1	0	16	54.1	262	61	32	30	2	2	2	0	45	4	60	4	0	4	4	.500	0	1	4.97
Indianapols	AAA Cin	8	1	0	1	13	53	8	4	3	1	0	1	0	7	1	18	1	0	0	1	.000	0	0	2.08
10 Min. YEARS		341	77	5	92	732	3295	630	368	296	27	35	37	34	511	11	626	71	2	38	43	.469	0	6	3.64

Juan Tolentino

Bats: Right **Throws:** Right **Pos:** OF   **Ht:** 6'0" **Wt:** 165 **Born:** 3/12/76 **Age:** 24

		BATTING															BASERUNNING				PERCENTAGES		
Year Team	Lg Org	G	AB	H	2B	3B	HR	TB	R	RBI	TBB	IBB	SO	HBP	SH	SF	SB	CS	SB%	GDP	Avg	OBP	SLG
1996 Angels	R Ana	49	170	48	9	6	2	75	30	14	11	0	33	1	0	0	21	2	.91	4	.282	.330	.441
1997 Butte	R+ Ana	61	213	64	16	4	10	118	44	53	24	0	53	2	0	4	21	2	.91	2	.300	.370	.554
1998 Cedar Rapds	A Ana	133	495	129	27	6	11	201	82	57	51	1	135	6	3	2	49	25	.66	6	.261	.336	.406
1999 Erie	AA Ana	136	489	123	19	5	9	179	61	61	47	0	116	2	8	2	47	14	.77	7	.252	.319	.366
4 Min. YEARS		379	1367	364	71	21	32	573	217	185	133	1	337	11	11	8	138	43	.76	19	.266	.334	.419

Brian Tollberg

Pitches: Right **Bats:** Right **Pos:** P   **Ht:** 6'3" **Wt:** 195 **Born:** 9/16/72 **Age:** 27

		HOW MUCH HE PITCHED						WHAT HE GAVE UP												THE RESULTS					
Year Team	Lg Org	G	GS	CG	GF	IP	BFP	H	R	ER	HR	SH	SF	HB	TBB	IBB	SO	WP	Bk	W	L	Pct.	ShO	Sv	ERA
1994 Chillicothe	IND —	13	13	4	0	94.2	402	90	34	30	5	2	2	8	27	2	69	8	0	7	4	.636	0	0	2.85
1995 Beloit	A Mil	22	22	1	0	132	529	119	59	50	10	2	5	6	27	0	110	5	4	13	4	.765	1	0	3.41
1996 El Paso	AA Mil	26	26	0	0	154.1	663	183	90	84	15	2	3	10	23	0	109	4	1	7	5	.583	0	0	4.90
1997 Mobile	AA SD	31	13	1	5	123.1	512	123	60	51	15	2	1	4	24	2	108	4	0	6	3	.667	0	0	3.72
1998 Mobile	AA SD	6	6	1	0	41	152	31	11	11	3	1	0	1	4	0	45	0	1	3	2	.600	0	0	2.41
Las Vegas	AAA SD	33	15	1	7	110	492	138	85	78	21	2	2	12	27	2	109	0	1	6	6	.500	0	3	6.38
1999 Las Vegas	AAA SD	5	5	0	0	29.2	123	34	17	16	3	1	0	2	6	0	23	1	0	1	2	.333	0	0	4.85
Padres	H SD	2	2	0	0	4	10	4	2	2	0	0	0	0	0	0	6	0	0	0	0	.000	0	0	4.50
6 Min. YEARS		138	102	8	12	689	2889	722	358	322	72	12	13	43	138	6	579	22	7	43	26	.623	1	3	4.21

Andy Tomberlin

Bats: Left **Throws:** Left **Pos:** OF   **Ht:** 5'11" **Wt:** 185 **Born:** 11/7/66 **Age:** 33

		BATTING															BASERUNNING				PERCENTAGES		
Year Team	Lg Org	G	AB	H	2B	3B	HR	TB	R	RBI	TBB	IBB	SO	HBP	SH	SF	SB	CS	SB%	GDP	Avg	OBP	SLG
1986 Sumter	A Atl	13	1	0	0	0	0	0	0	0	1	0	1	0	0	0	0	0	.00	0	.000	.500	.000
Pulaski	R+ Atl	3	4	1	0	0	0	1	2	0	2	0	1	0	0	0	0	0	.00	0	.250	.500	.250
1987 Pulaski	R+ Atl	14	7	2	0	0	0	2	1	1	0	0	0	0	0	0	0	0	.00	0	.286	.286	.286
1988 Burlington	A Atl	43	134	46	7	3	3	68	24	18	22	2	33	2	1	1	7	4	.64	0	.343	.440	.507
Durham	A+ Atl	83	256	77	16	3	6	117	43	35	49	3	42	1	2	1	16	8	.67	2	.301	.414	.457
1989 Durham	A+ Atl	119	363	102	13	2	16	167	63	61	54	7	82	5	3	1	35	12	.74	4	.281	.381	.460
1990 Greenville	AA Atl	60	196	61	9	1	4	84	31	25	20	0	35	5	4	1	9	4	.69	1	.311	.387	.429
Richmond	AAA Atl	80	283	86	19	3	4	123	36	31	39	7	43	1	4	2	11	4	.73	7	.304	.388	.435
1991 Richmond	AAA Atl	93	329	77	13	2	2	100	47	24	41	3	85	8	9	1	10	6	.63	6	.234	.332	.304
1992 Richmond	AAA Atl	118	406	110	16	5	9	163	69	47	41	1	102	8	10	2	12	12	.50	2	.271	.348	.401
1993 Buffalo	AAA Pit	68	221	63	11	6	12	122	41	45	18	3	48	4	1	2	3	0	1.00	5	.285	.347	.552
1994 Pawtucket	AAA Bos	54	189	63	12	2	13	118	38	39	22	1	60	3	1	2	11	1	.92	1	.333	.407	.624
1995 Edmonton	AAA Oak	14	52	13	3	0	2	22	9	7	5	0	15	1	1	0	0	0	.00	1	.250	.328	.423
1996 Edmonton	AAA Oak	17	60	17	2	1	0	21	12	5	8	0	15	2	0	0	1	0	1.00	0	.283	.386	.350
Norfolk	AAA NYM	38	129	42	6	1	8	74	17	18	8	1	29	2	3	0	1	3	.25	2	.326	.374	.574
1997 Mets	R NYM	7	22	7	0	0	2	13	6	7	3	0	7	0	0	0	1	0	1.00	1	.318	.400	.591
St. Lucie	A+ NYM	1	3	0	0	0	0	0	0	1	1	0	2	0	0	0	0	0	.00	0	.000	.250	.000
1998 Toledo	AAA Det	14	47	16	2	1	2	26	13	4	8	0	15	4	0	0	1	1	.50	0	.340	.475	.553
Richmond	AAA Atl	39	104	27	3	0	4	42	12	15	15	1	29	7	0	1	1	1	.50	3	.260	.386	.404
1999 St. Lucie	A+ NYM	9	29	11	1	0	1	15	4	4	4	0	8	2	0	0	2	0	1.00	0	.379	.486	.517
Norfolk	AAA NYM	97	303	94	21	1	16	165	60	61	40	5	74	7	0	2	1	1	.67	4	.310	.401	.545
1993 Pittsburgh	NL	27	42	12	0	1	1	17	4	5	2	0	14	1	0	0	0	0	.00	0	.286	.333	.405
1994 Boston	AL	18	36	7	0	1	1	12	1	1	6	0	12	0	0	0	1	0	1.00	0	.194	.310	.333
1995 Oakland	AL	46	85	18	0	0	4	30	15	10	5	0	22	0	2	0	4	1	.80	2	.212	.256	.353
1996 New York	NL	63	66	17	4	0	3	30	12	10	9	0	27	1	0	0	0	0	.00	0	.258	.355	.455
1997 New York	NL	6	7	2	0	0	0	2	0	1	3	0	3	0	0	0	0	0	.00	0	.286	.375	.286
1998 Detroit	AL	32	69	15	2	0	2	23	8	12	3	1	25	3	0	0	1	0	1.00	3	.217	.280	.333
14 Min. YEARS		984	3138	915	154	31	104	1443	528	448	401	34	726	62	39	16	123	57	.68	39	.292	.381	.460
6 Maj. YEARS		192	305	71	6	2	11	114	40	38	26	1	103	5	2	0	6	1	.86	5	.233	.304	.374

Goefrey Tomlinson

Bats: Left **Throws:** Left **Pos:** OF   **Ht:** 6'1" **Wt:** 190 **Born:** 8/19/76 **Age:** 23

		BATTING															BASERUNNING				PERCENTAGES		
Year Team	Lg Org	G	AB	H	2B	3B	HR	TB	R	RBI	TBB	IBB	SO	HBP	SH	SF	SB	CS	SB%	GDP	Avg	OBP	SLG
1997 Spokane	A- KC	58	210	71	16	0	4	99	49	28	32	0	20	8	4	2	19	1	.95	1	.338	.440	.471
1998 Lansing	A KC	68	274	78	16	7	7	129	55	39	39	2	34	5	0	0	21	6	.78	4	.285	.384	.471
Wilmington	A+ KC	38	136	38	8	1	0	48	15	16	14	2	26	0	2	0	2	2	.50	3	.279	.347	.353
1999 Wichita	AA KC	128	479	134	31	4	4	185	100	46	72	4	82	4	8	5	24	19	.56	5	.280	.375	.386
3 Min. YEARS		292	1099	321	71	12	15	461	219	129	157	8	162	17	14	7	66	28	.70	13	.292	.387	.419

Yorvit Torrealba

Bats: Right **Throws:** Right **Pos:** C   **Ht:** 5'11" **Wt:** 180 **Born:** 7/19/78 **Age:** 21

		BATTING															BASERUNNING				PERCENTAGES		
Year Team	Lg Org	G	AB	H	2B	3B	HR	TB	R	RBI	TBB	IBB	SO	HBP	SH	SF	SB	CS	SB%	GDP	Avg	OBP	SLG
1995 Bellingham	A- SF	26	71	11	3	0	0	14	2	8	2	0	14	1	0	1	0	1	.00	1	.155	.187	.197
1996 San Jose	A+ SF	2	5	0	0	0	0	0	0	0	1	0	1	0	0	0	0	0	.00	0	.000	.167	.000
Burlington	A SF	1	4	0	0	0	0	0	0	0	0	0	0	0	0	0	0	0	.00	0	.000	.000	.000
Bellingham	A- SF	48	150	40	4	0	1	47	23	10	9	0	27	0	4	2	4	1	.80	7	.267	.304	.313
1997 Bakersfield	A+ SF	119	446	122	15	3	4	155	52	40	31	0	58	5	1	3	4	2	.67	8	.274	.326	.348
1998 San Jose	A+ SF	21	70	20	2	0	0	22	10	10	1	0	6	0	2	1	2	2	.50	2	.286	.292	.314
Shreveport	AA SF	59	196	46	7	0	0	53	18	13	18	3	30	4	3	1	0	5	.00	3	.235	.311	.270

Year Team	Lg Org	G	AB	H	2B	3B	HR	TB	R	RBI	TBB	IBB	SO	HBP	SH	SF	SB	CS	SB%	GDP	Avg	OBP	SLG
Fresno	AAA SF	4	11	2	1	0	0	3	1	1	1	1	4	0	0	0	0	0	.00	0	.182	.250	.273
1999 Fresno	AAA SF	17	63	16	2	0	2	24	9	10	4	0	11	2	0	0	0	1	.00	2	.254	.319	.381
Shreveport	AA SF	65	217	53	10	1	4	77	25	19	9	0	34	2	2	2	0	2	.00	6	.244	.278	.355
San Jose	A+ SF	19	73	23	3	0	2	32	10	14	6	0	15	1	0	1	0	0	.00	2	.315	.370	.438
5 Min. YEARS		381	1306	333	47	4	13	427	150	125	82	4	201	15	12	11	10	14	.42	32	.255	.304	.327

Bats: Right **Throws:** Right **Pos:** C

Dave Toth

Ht: 6'2" **Wt:** 208 **Born:** 12/8/69 **Age:** 30

Year Team	Lg Org	G	AB	H	2B	3B	HR	TB	R	RBI	TBB	IBB	SO	HBP	SH	SF	SB	CS	SB%	GDP	Avg	OBP	SLG
1990 Pulaski	R+ Atl	26	82	22	0	0	0	22	9	10	12	1	12	1	1	2	2	0	1.00	0	.268	.354	.268
1991 Idaho Falls	R+ Atl	47	160	34	3	0	4	49	27	22	18	1	21	4	1	2	1	0	1.00	6	.213	.304	.306
1992 Macon	A Atl	87	310	80	15	2	3	108	32	41	21	0	44	4	0	2	3	3	.50	6	.258	.312	.348
1993 Macon	A Atl	104	353	87	22	0	4	121	38	40	28	1	53	7	5	3	6	5	.55	11	.246	.312	.343
1994 Durham	A+ Atl	72	165	40	11	0	2	57	23	20	19	0	28	1	1	1	1	0	1.00	4	.242	.323	.345
1995 Richmond	AAA Atl	7	13	3	0	0	0	3	1	1	1	0	2	0	0	0	0	1	.00	1	.231	.286	.231
Durham	A+ Atl	85	257	63	6	0	6	87	20	26	25	1	42	6	0	1	3	3	.50	6	.245	.325	.339
1996 Greenville	AA Atl	120	376	100	31	1	10	163	63	55	58	0	61	11	1	4	2	3	.40	4	.266	.376	.434
1997 Richmond	AAA Atl	14	46	9	3	0	0	12	6	5	4	0	8	0	0	0	0	0	.00	3	.196	.260	.261
Greenville	AA Atl	58	184	45	9	0	7	75	23	24	25	0	35	4	0	0	2	2	.50	7	.245	.347	.408
1998 Calgary	AAA CWS	72	246	57	12	0	6	87	31	30	24	0	44	3	4	4	3	2	.60	11	.232	.303	.354
1999 Charlotte	AAA CWS	79	261	64	14	0	6	96	36	33	24	0	38	3	1	0	1	2	.33	6	.245	.316	.368
10 Min. YEARS		771	2453	604	126	3	48	880	309	307	258	3	388	44	14	19	24	21	.53	65	.246	.327	.359

Pitches: Right **Bats:** Right **Pos:** P

Josh Towers

Ht: 6'1" **Wt:** 150 **Born:** 2/26/77 **Age:** 23

Year Team	Lg Org	G	GS	CG	GF	IP	BFP	H	R	ER	HR	SH	SF	HB	TBB	IBB	SO	WP	Bk	W	L	Pct.	ShO	Sv	ERA
1996 Bluefield	R+ Bal	14	9	0	1	55	234	63	35	32	9	0	1	1	5	0	61	4	1	4	1	.800	0	0	5.24
1997 Delmarva	A Bal	9	1	0	5	18.1	73	18	8	7	1	1	1	0	2	0	16	0	0	0	0	.000	0	1	3.44
Frederick	A+ Bal	25	3	0	8	53.2	252	74	36	29	4	1	1	3	18	0	64	2	1	6	2	.750	0	1	4.86
1998 Frederick	A+ Bal	25	20	3	3	145.1	583	137	58	54	11	6	3	11	9	0	122	5	2	8	7	.533	0	1	3.34
Bowie	AA Bal	5	2	0	1	18	80	20	9	7	1	0	0	2	4	0	7	1	0	2	1	.667	0	0	3.50
1999 Bowie	AA Bal	29	28	5	1	189	786	204	86	79	26	12	4	5	26	1	106	5	3	12	7	.632	2	0	3.76
4 Min. YEARS		107	63	8	19	479.1	2008	516	232	208	52	20	10	22	64	1	376	17	7	32	18	.640	2	3	3.91

Bats: Left **Throws:** Right **Pos:** 3B

Andy Tracy

Ht: 6'3" **Wt:** 220 **Born:** 12/11/73 **Age:** 26

Year Team	Lg Org	G	AB	H	2B	3B	HR	TB	R	RBI	TBB	IBB	SO	HBP	SH	SF	SB	CS	SB%	GDP	Avg	OBP	SLG
1996 Vermont	A- Mon	57	175	47	11	1	4	72	26	24	32	2	37	2	1	2	1	1	.50	8	.269	.384	.411
1997 Cape Fear	A Mon	59	210	63	9	2	8	100	31	43	21	4	47	3	0	2	6	1	.86	4	.300	.369	.476
1998 Jupiter	A+ Mon	71	251	67	16	1	11	118	37	53	39	3	69	3	0	5	6	4	.60	3	.267	.366	.470
Harrisburg	AA Mon	62	211	48	12	3	10	96	33	33	24	3	62	4	0	3	1	2	.33	5	.227	.314	.455
1999 Harrisburg	AA Mon	134	493	135	26	2	37	276	96	128	70	4	139	6	1	3	6	1	.86	10	.274	.369	.560
4 Min. YEARS		383	1340	360	74	9	70	662	223	281	186	16	354	18	2	15	20	9	.69	30	.269	.362	.494

Pitches: Right **Bats:** Right **Pos:** P

Jody Treadwell

Ht: 6'0" **Wt:** 190 **Born:** 12/14/68 **Age:** 31

Year Team	Lg Org	G	GS	CG	GF	IP	BFP	H	R	ER	HR	SH	SF	HB	TBB	IBB	SO	WP	Bk	W	L	Pct.	ShO	Sv	ERA
1990 Vero Beach	A+ LA	16	8	2	5	80.1	316	59	17	16	2	3	1	1	22	6	80	2	3	9	1	.900	1	1	1.79
1991 San Antonio	AA LA	10	10	1	0	61	271	73	41	32	7	2	4	4	22	1	43	0	2	3	3	.500	0	0	4.72
Bakersfield	A+ LA	17	14	0	0	91.1	392	92	46	38	8	2	0	4	34	2	84	7	1	5	4	.556	0	0	3.74
1992 San Antonio	AA LA	29	4	2	4	76	331	74	40	35	3	2	3	4	40	4	68	6	2	3	5	.375	1	1	4.14
1993 Albuquerque	AAA LA	39	10	0	6	105.1	481	119	58	55	7	3	2	7	52	7	102	11	2	5	4	.556	0	0	4.70
1994 Albuquerque	AAA LA	33	24	0	4	158.2	676	151	78	75	11	5	2	10	59	3	114	7	1	10	6	.625	0	2	4.25
1995 Albuquerque	AAA LA	30	15	1	4	125	510	121	61	55	15	2	5	2	32	4	79	9	1	7	5	.583	1	1	3.96
1996 Albuquerque	AAA LA	5	3	0	0	18.1	93	30	18	16	4	0	3	0	10	1	16	0	0	1	1	.500	0	0	7.85
1997 Albuquerque	AAA LA	27	21	2	2	128.1	575	143	80	73	16	4	2	4	54	2	108	3	0	10	5	.667	0	1	5.12
1999 Norfolk	AAA NYM	11	3	0	2	22.2	115	27	25	25	5	1	2	2	18	1	19	1	0	1	2	.333	0	0	9.93
9 Min. YEARS		217	112	8	27	867	3760	889	464	420	78	24	21	38	343	31	713	46	12	54	36	.600	3	6	4.36

Bats: Left **Throws:** Left **Pos:** OF

Joe Trippy

Ht: 5'10" **Wt:** 185 **Born:** 7/31/73 **Age:** 26

Year Team	Lg Org	G	AB	H	2B	3B	HR	TB	R	RBI	TBB	IBB	SO	HBP	SH	SF	SB	CS	SB%	GDP	Avg	OBP	SLG
1995 Eugene	A- Atl	75	259	80	16	0	2	102	48	38	24	0	31	13	2	2	29	13	.69	1	.309	.393	.394
1996 Macon	A Atl	128	439	119	22	8	4	169	78	42	55	7	48	8	4	4	47	20	.70	6	.271	.360	.385
Durham	A+ Atl	5	20	5	0	0	1	8	3	3	2	0	3	0	0	0	1	2	.33	2	.250	.318	.400
1997 Durham	A+ Atl	120	437	119	24	4	4	163	62	45	61	0	76	9	10	4	34	20	.63	8	.272	.370	.373
1998 Greenville	AA Atl	64	175	38	4	0	1	45	19	9	27	0	33	3	3	0	2	8	.20	7	.217	.332	.257
Danville	A+ Atl	31	106	20	2	0	0	22	8	5	11	1	22	4	4	1	10	4	.71	2	.189	.287	.208
1999 Greenville	AA Atl	79	131	29	5	0	2	40	26	15	30	0	25	6	2	1	6	7	.46	1	.221	.387	.305
5 Min. YEARS		502	1567	410	73	12	14	549	244	157	210	8	238	43	25	12	129	74	.64	27	.262	.362	.350

281

Keith Troutman

Pitches: Right **Bats:** Right **Pos:** P   **Ht:** 6'1" **Wt:** 200 **Born:** 5/29/73 **Age:** 27

		HOW MUCH HE PITCHED						WHAT HE GAVE UP									THE RESULTS				
Year Team	Lg Org	G	GS	CG	GF	IP	BFP	H	R	ER	HR	SH	SF	HB	TBB	IBB	SO	WP	Bk	W	L	Pct.	ShO	Sv	ERA
1992 Yakima	A- LA	26	0	0	19	37.1	163	33	19	14	2	2	2	1	15	3	43	2	2	4	1	.800	0	3	3.38
1993 Great Falls	R+ LA	27	0	0	23	42	166	26	12	8	2	1	3	2	12	1	48	2	0	1	1	.500	0	16	1.71
1994 Vero Beach	A+ LA	43	0	0	10	78.1	328	69	39	34	6	3	2	1	35	5	66	5	1	3	2	.600	0	0	3.91
1995 San Antonio	AA LA	38	0	0	22	65.2	268	64	24	23	3	1	3	1	18	1	50	3	0	1	2	.333	0	2	3.15
1996 Scranton-WB	AAA Phi	8	0	0	4	14	65	19	9	8	1	1	0	1	5	1	9	1	0	1	1	.500	0	0	5.14
Reading	AA Phi	52	1	0	13	73.1	323	62	36	27	7	3	2	3	40	3	73	3	1	6	3	.667	0	1	3.31
1997 Reading	AA Phi	57	3	0	19	107.1	440	94	48	45	17	8	4	2	34	6	103	4	0	6	5	.545	0	7	3.77
1998 Scranton-WB	AAA Phi	43	0	0	10	80.2	351	80	44	38	13	2	5	3	31	3	78	6	0	6	3	.667	0	0	4.24
1999 Erie	AA Ana	38	0	0	26	59	257	66	32	27	8	7	0	0	19	0	49	3	0	5	4	.556	0	6	4.12
Edmonton	AAA Ana	6	3	0	1	20.1	88	23	12	8	4	0	1	3	2	0	22	2	0	1	0	1.000	0	0	3.54
8 Min. YEARS		338	7	0	147	578	2449	536	275	232	63	28	22	17	211	23	541	31	4	34	22	.607	0	35	3.61

Chris Truby

Bats: Right **Throws:** Right **Pos:** 3B   **Ht:** 6'2" **Wt:** 190 **Born:** 12/9/73 **Age:** 26

		BATTING														BASERUNNING				PERCENTAGES		
Year Team	Lg Org	G	AB	H	2B	3B	HR	TB	R	RBI	TBB	IBB	SO	HBP	SH	SF	SB	CS	SB%	GDP	Avg	OBP	SLG
1993 Astros	R Hou	57	215	49	10	2	1	66	30	24	22	0	30	1	2	1	16	1	.94	5	.228	.301	.307
Osceola	A+ Hou	3	13	0	0	0	0	0	0	0	0	0	2	0	0	0	0	0	.00	0	.000	.000	.000
1994 Quad City	A Hou	36	111	24	4	1	2	36	12	19	3	0	29	2	0	2	1	1	.50	3	.216	.246	.324
Auburn	A- Hou	73	282	91	17	6	7	141	56	61	23	0	48	3	1	8	20	4	.83	8	.323	.370	.500
1995 Quad City	A Hou	118	400	93	23	4	9	151	68	64	41	0	66	3	3	3	27	8	.77	11	.233	.306	.378
1996 Quad City	A Hou	109	362	91	15	3	8	136	45	37	28	1	74	2	6	5	6	10	.38	8	.251	.305	.376
1997 Quad City	A Hou	68	268	75	14	1	7	112	34	46	22	0	32	1	1	2	13	4	.76	8	.280	.334	.418
Kissimmee	A+ Hou	57	199	49	11	0	2	66	23	29	8	0	40	2	4	3	8	3	.73	4	.246	.278	.332
1998 Kissimmee	A+ Hou	52	212	66	16	1	14	126	36	48	19	3	30	3	0	2	6	1	.86	2	.311	.373	.594
Jackson	AA Hou	80	308	89	20	5	16	167	46	63	20	0	50	4	0	5	8	3	.73	5	.289	.335	.542
New Orleans	AAA Hou	5	17	7	1	1	1	13	6	1	1	0	3	0	0	0	1	0	1.00	0	.412	.444	.765
1999 Jackson	AA Hou	124	465	131	21	3	28	242	78	87	36	1	88	3	0	12	20	8	.71	11	.282	.329	.520
7 Min. YEARS		782	2852	765	152	27	95	1256	434	479	223	5	492	24	17	43	126	43	.75	65	.268	.322	.440

Pete Tucci

Bats: Right **Throws:** Right **Pos:** OF   **Ht:** 6'2" **Wt:** 205 **Born:** 10/8/75 **Age:** 24

		BATTING														BASERUNNING				PERCENTAGES		
Year Team	Lg Org	G	AB	H	2B	3B	HR	TB	R	RBI	TBB	IBB	SO	HBP	SH	SF	SB	CS	SB%	GDP	Avg	OBP	SLG
1996 St.Cathrnes	A- Tor	54	205	52	8	7	7	95	28	33	23	1	58	1	2	3	5	3	.63	1	.254	.328	.463
1997 Hagerstown	A Tor	127	466	123	28	5	10	191	60	75	35	1	95	5	1	6	9	5	.64	9	.264	.318	.410
1998 Dunedin	A+ Tor	92	356	117	30	3	23	222	72	76	29	0	97	5	2	2	8	5	.62	6	.329	.385	.624
Knoxville	AA Tor	38	141	41	7	4	7	77	25	36	13	0	29	2	0	2	3	2	.60	2	.291	.354	.546
1999 Mobile	AA SD	83	312	78	15	0	11	126	45	35	26	3	83	4	0	1	11	6	.65	7	.250	.315	.404
4 Min. YEARS		394	1480	411	88	19	58	711	230	255	126	5	362	17	5	14	36	21	.63	25	.278	.338	.480

Ben Tucker

Pitches: Right **Bats:** Right **Pos:** P   **Ht:** 6'4" **Wt:** 220 **Born:** 11/6/73 **Age:** 26

		HOW MUCH HE PITCHED						WHAT HE GAVE UP									THE RESULTS				
Year Team	Lg Org	G	GS	CG	GF	IP	BFP	H	R	ER	HR	SH	SF	HB	TBB	IBB	SO	WP	Bk	W	L	Pct.	ShO	Sv	ERA
1995 Bellingham	A- SF	12	10	0	1	56.2	249	53	21	12	4	2	2	4	19	0	48	2	1	2	1	.667	0	0	1.91
1996 San Jose	A+ SF	13	13	0	0	67.2	301	71	54	47	8	3	3	1	36	0	30	6	4	1	4	.200	0	0	6.25
1998 San Jose	A+ SF	29	14	0	5	112.2	467	97	54	47	10	4	2	9	33	1	69	3	2	5	5	.500	0	1	3.75
1999 Shreveport	AA SF	18	0	0	8	28	128	37	19	13	1	4	1	1	12	1	12	1	0	3	3	.500	0	1	4.18
San Jose	A+ SF	16	15	0	0	82.2	380	106	46	42	7	1	1	12	26	0	65	5	0	4	6	.400	0	0	4.57
4 Min. YEARS		88	52	0	14	347.2	1525	364	194	161	30	14	9	27	126	2	224	17	7	15	19	.441	0	2	4.17

Jon Tucker

Bats: Left **Throws:** Left **Pos:** 1B   **Ht:** 6'4" **Wt:** 200 **Born:** 12/17/76 **Age:** 23

		BATTING														BASERUNNING				PERCENTAGES		
Year Team	Lg Org	G	AB	H	2B	3B	HR	TB	R	RBI	TBB	IBB	SO	HBP	SH	SF	SB	CS	SB%	GDP	Avg	OBP	SLG
1995 Yakima	A- LA	41	115	19	3	0	1	25	6	5	13	0	35	1	0	1	0	0	.00	4	.165	.254	.217
1996 Great Falls	R+ LA	48	174	60	12	1	12	110	39	54	15	1	30	2	0	3	13	5	.72	0	.345	.397	.632
Savannah	A LA	14	47	15	2	1	1	22	8	12	6	0	7	1	1	1	0	1	1.00	0	.319	.400	.468
1997 Vero Beach	A+ LA	121	422	123	27	0	13	189	59	78	35	1	85	3	0	10	5	3	.63	7	.291	.343	.448
1998 San Antonio	AA LA	100	360	107	34	2	10	175	46	64	41	2	74	3	1	3	3	5	.38	6	.297	.371	.486
Harrisburg	AA Mon	25	79	22	7	0	3	38	13	16	18	0	18	0	1	0	0	0	.00	1	.278	.412	.481
1999 Jupiter	A+ Mon	3	10	4	0	0	0	4	0	1	0	1	0	0	0	0	0	0	.00	0	.400	.455	.400
Harrisburg	AA Mon	112	362	93	21	2	13	157	53	55	50	0	85	3	1	5	4	4	.50	8	.257	.348	.434
5 Min. YEARS		464	1569	443	106	6	53	720	224	284	179	4	335	13	4	23	26	19	.58	26	.282	.356	.459

Julien Tucker

Pitches: Right **Bats:** Left **Pos:** P   **Ht:** 6'7" **Wt:** 200 **Born:** 4/19/73 **Age:** 27

		HOW MUCH HE PITCHED						WHAT HE GAVE UP									THE RESULTS				
Year Team	Lg Org	G	GS	CG	GF	IP	BFP	H	R	ER	HR	SH	SF	HB	TBB	IBB	SO	WP	Bk	W	L	Pct.	ShO	Sv	ERA
1993 Astros	R Hou	11	10	1	1	54.2	251	55	36	24	2	0	1	8	22	0	33	5	3	2	3	.400	1	0	3.95
1994 Auburn	A- Hou	14	14	3	0	84.1	355	72	30	21	4	1	3	5	30	0	63	13	0	8	3	.727	1	0	2.24
1995 Kissimmee	A+ Hou	19	15	0	0	68.1	327	86	61	38	3	1	6	5	27	0	28	5	3	2	11	.154	0	0	5.00
1996 Kissimmee	A+ Hou	32	16	0	6	116	525	131	79	55	8	4	6	12	41	1	55	9	1	4	8	.333	0	1	4.27

Year Team	Lg Org	G	GS	CG	GF	IP	BFP	H	R	ER	HR	SH	SF	HB	TBB	IBB	SO	WP	Bk	W	L	Pct.	ShO	Sv	ERA
1997 Kissimmee	A+ Hou	33	8	0	7	69	324	79	48	40	1	0	3	5	42	3	49	2	1	8	7	.533	0	0	5.22
Hickory	A CWS	4	0	0	1	7.1	35	11	7	3	1	0	1	1	2	0	7	0	0	0	0	.000	0	0	3.68
1998 Birmingham	AA CWS	34	5	0	7	66	318	77	66	50	2	1	3	5	45	0	47	10	1	4	6	.400	0	3	6.82
1999 Birmingham	AA CWS	37	0	0	22	49	222	52	30	29	6	1	0	5	22	0	32	6	0	2	1	.667	0	5	5.33
7 Min. YEARS		184	68	4	44	514.2	2357	563	357	260	27	8	23	46	231	4	314	50	9	30	39	.435	1	9	4.55

T.J. Tucker

Pitches: Right **Bats:** Right **Pos:** P   **Ht:** 6'3" **Wt:** 245 **Born:** 8/20/78 **Age:** 21

Year Team	Lg Org	G	GS	CG	GF	IP	BFP	H	R	ER	HR	SH	SF	HB	TBB	IBB	SO	WP	Bk	W	L	Pct.	ShO	Sv	ERA
1997 Expos	R Mon	3	2	0	0	4.2	19	5	1	1	0	0	0	0	1	0	11	0	0	1	0	1.000	0	0	1.93
1998 Expos	R Mon	7	7	0	0	36	134	23	5	3	1	0	0	0	5	0	40	0	0	1	0	1.000	0	0	0.75
Vermont	A- Mon	6	6	0	0	33	135	24	9	8	0	1	0	2	15	0	34	3	0	3	1	.750	0	0	2.18
Jupiter	A+ Mon	2	1	0	1	9	32	5	1	1	0	1	1	0	0	0	10	1	0	1	1	.500	0	0	1.00
1999 Jupiter	A+ Mon	7	7	0	0	44	171	24	7	6	2	0	1	0	16	0	35	1	0	5	1	.833	0	0	1.23
Harrisburg	AA Mon	19	19	1	0	116.1	489	110	55	53	12	4	1	4	38	0	85	5	1	8	5	.615	1	0	4.10
3 Min. YEARS		44	42	1	1	243	980	191	78	72	15	6	3	6	75	0	215	10	1	19	8	.704	1	0	2.67

Mark Turnbow

Pitches: Right **Bats:** Right **Pos:** P   **Ht:** 6'3" **Wt:** 205 **Born:** 11/26/78 **Age:** 21

Year Team	Lg Org	G	GS	CG	GF	IP	BFP	H	R	ER	HR	SH	SF	HB	TBB	IBB	SO	WP	Bk	W	L	Pct.	ShO	Sv	ERA
1997 Burlington	R+ Cle	13	13	0	0	74.1	297	49	25	23	1	4	2	4	18	0	53	2	0	8	2	.800	0	0	2.78
1998 Columbus	A Cle	16	16	1	0	90.2	386	94	47	41	9	4	1	3	26	1	73	6	1	6	5	.545	0	0	4.07
1999 Kinston	A+ Cle	12	12	0	0	60.1	279	76	48	43	5	2	4	4	25	0	42	1	0	5	4	.556	0	0	6.41
Columbus	A Cle	13	13	1	0	72.2	304	78	38	30	7	0	3	3	13	0	75	4	2	3	4	.429	0	0	3.72
Akron	AA Cle	1	1	0	0	6	25	4	3	2	0	0	0	0	3	0	4	0	0	1	0	1.000	0	0	3.00
3 Min. YEARS		55	55	2	0	304	1291	301	161	139	22	10	10	14	85	1	247	13	3	23	15	.605	0	0	4.12

Rich Turrentine

Pitches: Right **Bats:** Right **Pos:** P   **Ht:** 6'0" **Wt:** 220 **Born:** 5/21/71 **Age:** 29

Year Team	Lg Org	G	GS	CG	GF	IP	BFP	H	R	ER	HR	SH	SF	HB	TBB	IBB	SO	WP	Bk	W	L	Pct.	ShO	Sv	ERA
1992 Yankees	R NYY	2	0	0	2	2	6	0	0	0	0	0	0	0	0	0	6	0	0	0	0	.000	0	1	0.00
Oneonta	A- NYY	1	0	0	0	2	2	1	2	2	0	0	0	0	1	0	0	0	0	0	0	.000	0	0	0.00
1994 Yankees	R NYY	6	0	0	1	8.2	40	10	8	7	1	1	0	1	4	0	11	2	0	0	0	.000	0	0	7.27
Tampa	A+ NYY	10	0	0	2	14.2	70	14	10	10	0	0	1	2	13	0	10	3	0	1	0	1.000	0	0	6.14
1995 Capital Cty	A NYM	26	14	0	8	104	437	70	38	29	3	6	4	6	60	1	111	16	1	4	4	.500	0	2	2.51
St. Lucie	A+ NYM	4	4	0	0	19.1	92	17	14	13	3	1	0	2	17	0	14	3	0	0	3	.000	0	0	6.05
1996 St. Lucie	A+ NYM	45	0	0	40	51.1	232	31	18	13	0	4	1	2	45	1	63	9	0	4	4	.500	0	21	2.28
Binghamton	AA NYM	8	0	0	7	9.1	43	12	3	3	0	0	1	0	5	0	10	0	0	1	1	.500	0	3	2.89
1997 Binghamton	AA NYM	61	0	0	45	62	292	66	38	36	3	4	1	2	54	2	58	17	0	2	4	.333	0	13	5.23
1998 Binghamton	AA NYM	28	0	0	23	30.2	125	15	10	10	3	2	0	1	17	0	55	5	1	1	2	.333	0	10	2.93
Norfolk	AAA NYM	5	0	0	5	6.1	22	4	1	1	0	0	0	0	2	0	9	0	0	0	0	.000	0	1	1.42
1999 Norfolk	AAA NYM	2	0	0	2	2.2	14	6	2	2	1	1	0	0	1	1	3	0	0	0	1	.000	0	0	6.75
Mets	R NYM	5	0	0	1	8	30	4	2	1	0	0	0	0	2	0	7	0	0	0	0	.000	0	0	1.13
Binghamton	AA NYM	17	0	0	4	19.1	97	20	13	10	0	0	0	1	20	2	16	2	0	0	2	.000	0	0	4.66
7 Min. YEARS		220	18	0	140	338.1	1502	270	159	137	14	19	8	17	241	7	373	57	2	13	21	.382	0	51	3.64

Dave Tuttle

Pitches: Right **Bats:** Right **Pos:** P   **Ht:** 6'3" **Wt:** 190 **Born:** 9/29/69 **Age:** 30

Year Team	Lg Org	G	GS	CG	GF	IP	BFP	H	R	ER	HR	SH	SF	HB	TBB	IBB	SO	WP	Bk	W	L	Pct.	ShO	Sv	ERA
1992 Chstn-WV	A Cin	17	16	0	0	97.1	416	87	46	42	5	0	6	1	53	1	93	4	0	3	5	.375	0	0	3.88
1993 Chstn-WV	A Cin	13	13	0	0	81.1	343	66	37	32	3	1	1	3	36	1	74	6	1	8	3	.727	0	0	3.54
Winston-Sal	A+ Cin	15	15	2	0	86.1	388	98	61	53	8	3	2	1	39	0	58	6	0	7	7	.500	1	0	5.53
1994 Chattanooga	AA Cin	14	14	0	0	84	377	82	60	42	8	4	2	7	48	5	54	10	0	2	9	.182	0	0	4.50
Winston-Sal	A+ Cin	13	13	2	0	76.2	315	58	26	18	8	0	0	3	27	0	64	2	0	5	2	.714	0	0	2.11
1995 Chattanooga	AA Cin	8	7	0	1	34.2	165	40	29	27	2	1	1	1	21	0	20	4	0	1	6	.143	0	0	7.01
Winston-Sal	A+ Cin	10	10	2	0	62.1	248	49	28	22	5	0	2	3	19	0	54	3	0	3	3	.500	1	0	3.18
Lakeland	A+ Det	6	4	1	1	31	132	31	11	10	1	0	3	2	12	0	28	1	0	1	4	.200	0	0	2.90
1996 Visalia	A+ Det	55	0	0	52	70.1	308	71	39	29	3	3	1	3	33	5	56	1	0	7	9	.438	0	21	3.71
1997 High Desert	A+ Ari	50	0	0	42	63	262	54	22	17	4	3	3	0	23	3	57	5	0	4	3	.571	0	19	2.43
1998 Tulsa	AA Ari	36	2	0	13	73.2	316	73	30	22	4	0	2	5	29	0	47	2	0	1	2	.333	0	4	2.69
Tucson	AAA Ari	10	3	0	3	26.1	125	32	20	20	2	2	1	2	16	1	8	0	0	1	2	.333	0	0	6.84
1999 Tucson	AAA Ari	35	9	0	11	84.1	385	100	62	61	8	3	6	4	48	2	55	4	1	2	5	.286	0	0	6.51
8 Min. YEARS		282	106	7	123	871.1	3780	841	471	395	65	21	30	35	404	18	668	48	2	45	60	.429	2	44	4.08

Brad Tweedlie

Pitches: Right **Bats:** Right **Pos:** P   **Ht:** 6'2" **Wt:** 210 **Born:** 12/9/71 **Age:** 28

Year Team	Lg Org	G	GS	CG	GF	IP	BFP	H	R	ER	HR	SH	SF	HB	TBB	IBB	SO	WP	Bk	W	L	Pct.	ShO	Sv	ERA
1993 Billings	R+ Cin	11	8	0	1	44	187	28	22	21	2	0	2	3	31	1	31	8	2	3	3	.500	0	1	4.30
1994 Winston-Sal	A+ Cin	10	5	0	1	29.1	161	48	47	40	7	1	3	3	19	0	18	4	0	1	4	.200	0	0	12.27
Chstn-WV	A Cin	8	8	0	0	38	173	42	27	24	4	2	0	2	20	0	30	9	2	3	4	.429	0	0	5.68
1995 Chstn-WV	A Cin	19	7	0	4	49.2	226	46	36	34	3	0	4	3	34	0	40	5	1	2	4	.333	0	0	6.16

Year Team	Lg Org	G	GS	CG	GF	IP	BFP	H	R	ER	HR	SH	SF	HB	TBB	IBB	SO	WP	Bk	W	L	Pct.	ShO	Sv	ERA
1996 Winston-Sal	A+ Cin	33	0	0	30	29.2	144	35	23	22	6	1	2	1	22	0	22	6	0	1	5	.167	0	11	6.67
Sarasota	A+ Bos	11	0	0	11	11.1	45	6	1	1	0	0	0	1	3	1	9	0	0	2	0	1.000	0	7	0.79
1997 Trenton	AA Bos	41	0	0	26	57.2	275	62	41	37	10	1	2	6	44	3	30	1	0	4	6	.400	0	5	5.77
1998 Trenton	AA Bos	35	0	0	12	41	197	47	33	27	6	1	2	4	27	2	29	3	0	1	2	.333	0	2	5.93
1999 Trenton	AA Bos	44	0	0	20	56.2	253	59	28	23	3	1	5	2	21	1	31	5	0	6	0	1.000	0	3	3.65
7 Min. YEARS		212	28	0	105	357.1	1661	373	258	229	41	7	20	25	221	8	240	41	5	23	28	.451	0	29	5.77

Brad Tyler

Bats: Left **Throws:** Right **Pos:** OF **Ht:** 6'2" **Wt:** 180 **Born:** 3/3/69 **Age:** 31

										BATTING						BASERUNNING				PERCENTAGES		
Year Team	Lg Org	G	AB	H	2B	3B	HR	TB	R	RBI	TBB	IBB	SO	HBP	SH	SF	SB	CS	SB%	GDP	Avg	OBP	SLG
1990 Wausau	A Bal	56	187	44	4	3	2	60	31	24	44	2	45	2	1	2	11	4	.73	2	.235	.383	.321
1991 Kane County	A Bal	60	199	54	10	3	3	79	35	29	44	1	25	1	1	2	5	3	.63	0	.271	.402	.397
Frederick	A+ Bal	56	187	48	6	0	4	66	26	26	33	3	33	2	1	1	3	2	.60	0	.257	.372	.353
1992 Frederick	A+ Bal	54	185	47	11	2	3	71	34	22	43	2	34	2	1	4	9	3	.75	2	.254	.393	.384
Hagerstown	AA Bal	83	256	57	9	1	2	74	41	21	34	2	45	2	1	0	23	5	.82	5	.223	.318	.289
1993 Bowie	AA Bal	129	437	103	23	17	10	190	85	44	84	2	89	1	1	3	24	11	.69	2	.236	.358	.435
1994 Rochester	AAA Bal	101	314	82	15	8	7	134	38	43	38	2	69	2	1	0	7	4	.64	4	.261	.345	.427
1995 Rochester	AAA Bal	114	361	93	17	3	17	167	60	52	71	4	63	4	0	5	10	5	.67	3	.258	.381	.463
1996 Rochester	AAA Bal	118	382	103	18	10	13	180	68	52	67	2	95	5	1	3	19	7	.73	2	.270	.383	.471
1997 Richmond	AAA Atl	129	383	101	15	10	19	190	09	77	55	2	110	3	3	7	13	6	.68	4	.264	.355	.496
1998 Edmonton	AAA Oak	131	430	115	24	4	18	201	68	75	62	1	107	0	0	6	10	1	.91	1	.267	.355	.467
1999 Richmond	AAA Atl	122	413	118	20	2	21	205	73	79	69	1	99	4	2	2	18	3	.86	4	.286	.391	.496
10 Min. YEARS		1153	3734	965	172	63	118	1617	628	544	644	24	814	28	13	35	152	54	.74	29	.258	.369	.433

Josh Tyler

Bats: Right **Throws:** Right **Pos:** OF **Ht:** 6'1" **Wt:** 185 **Born:** 9/6/73 **Age:** 26

										BATTING						BASERUNNING				PERCENTAGES		
Year Team	Lg Org	G	AB	H	2B	3B	HR	TB	R	RBI	TBB	IBB	SO	HBP	SH	SF	SB	CS	SB%	GDP	Avg	OBP	SLG
1994 Brewers	R Mil	54	193	52	4	3	0	62	35	24	30	0	34	6	0	4	8	4	.67	6	.269	.378	.321
1995 Beloit	A Mil	77	186	44	5	0	2	55	24	27	36	0	40	2	7	3	3	6	.33	4	.237	.361	.296
1996 Stockton	A+ Mil	75	273	88	14	2	2	112	42	33	25	0	35	11	7	2	4	8	.33	6	.322	.399	.410
1997 Tucson	AAA Mil	1	0	0	0	0	0	0	0	0	0	0	0	0	0	0	0	0	.00	0	.000	.000	.000
Stockton	A+ Mil	114	416	129	28	4	4	177	63	46	20	0	54	10	5	3	21	7	.75	7	.310	.354	.425
1998 San Jose	A+ SF	50	194	48	10	2	1	65	24	21	10	0	29	0	3	2	7	8	.47	8	.247	.282	.335
Shreveport	AA SF	14	39	8	0	0	0	8	5	3	1	1	4	1	0	1	0	0	.00	1	.205	.238	.205
Fresno	AAA SF	3	3	0	0	0	0	0	0	0	1	0	1	0	0	0	0	0	.00	0	.000	.250	.000
Bakersfield	A+ SF	53	220	59	14	1	6	93	27	43	11	0	32	3	3	2	12	2	.86	2	.268	.309	.423
1999 Shreveport	AA SF	105	331	87	17	0	3	113	41	39	30	1	53	4	3	2	14	5	.74	10	.263	.330	.341
6 Min. YEARS		546	1855	515	92	12	18	685	261	236	164	2	282	37	28	19	69	40	.63	44	.278	.345	.369

Jason Tyner

Bats: Left **Throws:** Left **Pos:** OF **Ht:** 6'1" **Wt:** 170 **Born:** 4/23/77 **Age:** 23

										BATTING						BASERUNNING				PERCENTAGES		
Year Team	Lg Org	G	AB	H	2B	3B	HR	TB	R	RBI	TBB	IBB	SO	HBP	SH	SF	SB	CS	SB%	GDP	Avg	OBP	SLG
1998 St. Lucie	A+ NYM	50	201	61	2	3	0	69	30	16	17	0	20	1	3	0	15	11	.58	3	.303	.361	.343
1999 Binghamton	AA NYM	129	518	162	19	5	0	191	91	33	62	0	46	1	8	1	49	15	.77	8	.313	.387	.369
Norfolk	AAA NYM	3	8	0	0	0	0	0	0	0	0	0	5	0	0	0	0	0	.00	0	.000	.000	.000
2 Min. YEARS		182	727	223	21	8	0	260	121	49	79	0	71	2	11	1	64	26	.71	11	.307	.376	.358

Jeff Urban

Pitches: Left **Bats:** Right **Pos:** P **Ht:** 6'8" **Wt:** 215 **Born:** 1/25/77 **Age:** 23

Year Team	Lg Org	G	GS	CG	GF	IP	BFP	H	R	ER	HR	SH	SF	HB	TBB	IBB	SO	WP	Bk	W	L	Pct.	ShO	Sv	ERA
1998 Salem-Keizr	A- SF	5	3	.0	0	21.2	95	21	14	12	1	2	0	0	8	0	22	2	0	1	2	.333	0	0	4.98
San Jose	A+ SF	4	4	0	0	23	103	27	13	9	2	2	1	3	5	0	23	2	0	4	0	1.000	0	0	3.52
1999 Shreveport	AA SF	14	14	0	0	69.2	319	100	54	45	8	5	0	1	19	0	54	3	0	2	7	.222	0	0	5.81
San Jose	A+ SF	15	13	0	2	81.1	336	78	41	34	7	0	2	4	18	0	89	0	0	8	5	.615	0	0	3.76
2 Min. YEARS		38	34	0	2	195.2	853	226	122	100	18	9	3	8	50	0	188	7	0	15	14	.517	0	0	4.60

Sal Urso

Pitches: Left **Bats:** Right **Pos:** P **Ht:** 5'11" **Wt:** 195 **Born:** 1/19/72 **Age:** 28

Year Team	Lg Org	G	GS	CG	GF	IP	BFP	H	R	ER	HR	SH	SF	HB	TBB	IBB	SO	WP	Bk	W	L	Pct.	ShO	Sv	ERA
1990 Mariners	R Sea	20	0	0	6	50.2	219	38	25	13	2	2	6	5	23	1	63	5	0	3	2	.600	0	1	2.31
1991 Peninsula	A+ Sea	46	0	0	29	61.2	290	74	36	21	1	3	4	5	30	7	44	6	0	3	0	.000	0	8	3.06
1992 San Berndno	A+ Sea	37	0	0	21	51.1	239	66	34	29	2	2	5	1	32	0	40	4	1	0	1	.000	0	1	5.08
1993 Appleton	A Sea	30	1	0	10	50.0	220	67	01	00	2	1	3	0	24	1	50	7	1	4	4	.500	0	2	3.35
1994 Riverside	A+ Sea	30	1	0	12	34.2	156	44	27	23	4	1	2	3	14	0	26	3	0	1	2	.333	0	1	5.97
1995 Port City	AA Sea	51	0	0	8	45.2	185	41	13	11	0	0	0	0	21	0	44	7	1	2	0	1.000	0	1	2.17
1996 Tacoma	AAA Sea	46	0	0	19	72.2	302	69	22	19	5	4	1	1	32	1	45	2	6	6	2	.750	0	3	2.35
1997 Columbus	AAA NYY	24	2	0	9	45.2	211	59	29	24	4	3	1	3	19	0	44	5	4	0	3	.000	0	0	4.73
Norwich	AA NYY	7	2	0	3	14.1	59	14	2	2	0	0	0	0	5	0	13	1	1	1	1	.500	0	1	1.26
1998 Trenton	AA Bos	69	0	0	18	83.1	354	86	45	38	7	2	0	2	32	8	86	8	0	8	6	.571	0	3	4.10
1999 Pawtucket	AAA Bos	4	0	0	0	7.2	36	10	4	3	0	0	1	0	5	0	6	2	0	1	0	1.000	0	0	3.52
Trenton	AA Bos	22	0	0	13	29	123	25	11	6	2	1	0	0	14	0	39	2	2	2	0	.500	0	5	1.86
10 Min. YEARS		392	6	0	156	550.1	2400	583	272	209	30	22	22	21	251	18	500	50	16	28	26	.519	0	25	3.42

284

Marc Valdes

Pitches: Right **Bats:** Right **Pos:** P — **Ht:** 6' 0" **Wt:** 185 **Born:** 12/20/71 **Age:** 28

Year Team	Lg Org	G	GS	CG	GF	IP	BFP	H	R	ER	HR	SH	SF	HB	TBB	IBB	SO	WP	Bk	W	L	Pct.	ShO	Sv	ERA
1993 Elmira	A- Fla	3	3	0	0	9.2	46	8	9	6	0	0	0	3	7	0	15	0	0	0	2	.000	0	0	5.59
1994 Kane County	A Fla	11	11	2	0	76.1	315	62	30	25	3	4	1	8	21	0	68	3	0	7	4	.636	0	0	2.95
Portland	AA Fla	15	15	0	0	99	411	77	31	28	5	3	1	8	39	1	70	4	3	8	4	.667	0	0	2.55
1995 Charlotte	AAA Fla	27	27	3	0	170.1	728	189	98	92	19	3	5	12	59	1	104	2	1	9	13	.409	2	0	4.86
1996 Portland	AA Fla	10	10	1	0	64.1	263	60	25	19	5	1	2	3	12	2	49	2	0	6	2	.750	0	0	2.66
Charlotte	AAA Fla	8	8	1	0	51	229	66	32	29	10	3	0	6	15	1	24	3	0	2	4	.333	0	0	5.12
1999 Orlando	AA TB	2	2	0	0	7.2	32	7	5	5	2	1	0	2	2	0	5	0	0	0	1	.000	0	0	5.87
Durham	AAA TB	9	9	0	0	40	171	39	25	23	3	2	0	4	12	0	23	0	0	1	2	.333	0	0	5.18
1995 Florida	NL	3	3	0	0	7	49	17	13	11	1	1	1	1	9	0	2	1	0	0	0	.000	0	0	14.14
1996 Florida	NL	11	8	0	0	48.2	228	63	32	26	5	1	3	1	23	0	13	3	2	1	3	.250	0	0	4.81
1997 Montreal	NL	48	7	0	9	95	407	84	36	33	2	5	5	8	39	5	54	2	0	4	4	.500	0	2	3.13
1998 Montreal	NL	20	4	0	3	36.1	169	41	34	30	6	1	2	1	21	2	28	4	0	1	3	.250	0	0	7.43
5 Min. YEARS		85	85	7	0	518.1	2195	508	255	227	47	17	9	46	167	5	358	14	4	33	32	.508	2	0	3.94
4 Maj. YEARS		82	22	0	12	187	853	205	115	100	14	8	11	11	92	7	97	10	2	6	10	.375	0	2	4.81

Pedro Valdes

Bats: Left **Throws:** Left **Pos:** DH — **Ht:** 6' 1" **Wt:** 180 **Born:** 6/29/73 **Age:** 27

Year Team	Lg Org	G	AB	H	2B	3B	HR	TB	R	RBI	TBB	IBB	SO	HBP	SH	SF	SB	CS	SB%	GDP	Avg	OBP	SLG
1991 Huntington	R+ ChC	50	157	45	11	1	0	58	18	16	17	3	31	2	1	5	5	1	.83	7	.287	.354	.369
1992 Peoria	A ChC	33	112	26	7	0	0	33	8	20	7	3	32	0	0	4	0	0	.00	1	.232	.268	.295
Geneva	A- ChC	66	254	69	10	0	5	94	27	24	3	1	33	3	2	2	4	5	.44	2	.272	.286	.370
1993 Peoria	A ChC	65	234	74	11	1	7	108	33	36	10	4	40	0	5	4	2	2	.50	3	.316	.339	.462
Daytona	A+ ChC	60	230	66	16	1	8	108	27	49	9	1	30	2	0	5	3	4	.43	8	.287	.313	.470
1994 Orlando	AA ChC	116	365	103	14	4	1	128	39	37	20	3	45	2	2	1	2	6	.25	10	.282	.322	.351
1995 Orlando	AA ChC	114	426	128	28	3	7	183	57	68	37	3	77	5	0	6	3	6	.33	7	.300	.359	.430
1996 Iowa	AAA ChC	103	397	117	23	0	15	185	61	60	31	1	57	1	1	5	2	0	1.00	12	.295	.343	.466
1997 Iowa	AAA ChC	125	464	132	30	1	14	206	65	60	48	5	67	2	1	6	9	2	.82	13	.284	.350	.444
1998 Iowa	AAA ChC	65	229	72	12	0	17	135	49	40	27	3	38	0	0	2	2	1	.67	6	.314	.384	.590
1999 Tulsa	AA Tex	11	34	12	4	0	1	19	3	4	8	0	6	0	0	0	0	0	.00	0	.353	.476	.559
Oklahoma	AAA Tex	110	394	129	27	1	21	221	72	72	52	6	60	6	0	4	1	2	.33	6	.327	.410	.561
1996 Chicago	NL	9	8	1	1	0	0	2	2	1	1	0	5	0	0	0	0	0	.00	0	.125	.222	.250
1998 Chicago	NL	14	23	5	1	1	0	8	1	2	1	0	3	0	0	0	0	1	.00	1	.217	.250	.348
9 Min. YEARS		918	3296	973	193	12	96	1478	459	486	269	33	516	23	12	44	33	29	.53	75	.295	.348	.448
2 Maj. YEARS		23	31	6	2	1	0	10	3	3	2	0	8	0	0	0	0	1	.00	1	.194	.242	.323

Mario Valdez

Bats: Left **Throws:** Right **Pos:** 1B — **Ht:** 6' 2" **Wt:** 190 **Born:** 11/19/74 **Age:** 25

Year Team	Lg Org	G	AB	H	2B	3B	HR	TB	R	RBI	TBB	IBB	SO	HBP	SH	SF	SB	CS	SB%	GDP	Avg	OBP	SLG
1994 White Sox	R CWS	53	157	37	11	2	2	58	20	25	30	0	28	2	0	1	0	6	.00	3	.236	.363	.369
1995 Hickory	A CWS	130	441	120	30	5	11	193	65	56	67	2	107	5	0	3	9	7	.56	5	.272	.372	.438
1996 South Bend	A CWS	61	202	76	19	0	10	125	46	43	36	2	42	6	0	2	2	4	.33	3	.376	.480	.619
Birmingham	AA CWS	51	168	46	10	2	3	69	22	28	32	2	34	5	0	3	0	0	.00	3	.274	.399	.411
1997 Nashville	AAA CWS	81	282	79	20	1	15	146	44	61	43	3	77	9	1	4	1	1	.50	4	.280	.388	.518
1998 Calgary	AAA CWS	123	448	148	32	0	20	240	86	81	60	3	102	12	0	4	1	2	.33	14	.330	.420	.536
1999 Charlotte	AAA CWS	121	402	110	17	2	26	209	78	76	76	4	91	12	0	1	1	0	1.00	8	.274	.403	.520
1997 Chicago	AL	54	115	28	7	0	1	38	11	13	17	0	39	3	0	2	1	0	1.00	3	.243	.350	.330
6 Min. YEARS		620	2100	616	139	12	87	1040	361	370	344	16	481	51	1	18	14	20	.41	44	.293	.402	.495

Victor Valencia

Bats: Right **Throws:** Right **Pos:** C — **Ht:** 6'2" **Wt:** 185 **Born:** 5/13/77 **Age:** 23

Year Team	Lg Org	G	AB	H	2B	3B	HR	TB	R	RBI	TBB	IBB	SO	HBP	SH	SF	SB	CS	SB%	GDP	Avg	OBP	SLG
1995 Yankees	R NYY	25	58	14	1	0	1	18	5	8	6	0	22	0	0	0	0	0	.00	1	.241	.313	.310
1996 Oneonta	A- NYY	72	261	51	8	0	3	68	30	25	21	0	86	0	3	3	3	0	1.00	4	.195	.253	.261
1997 Greensboro	A NYY	107	353	78	12	1	13	131	42	43	43	0	116	7	2	1	2	1	.67	6	.221	.317	.371
1998 Tampa	A+ NYY	122	411	92	18	1	16	160	53	43	26	2	139	3	5	4	0	1	.00	4	.224	.273	.389
1999 Norwich	AA NYY	119	396	88	18	0	22	172	57	72	45	0	142	5	4	3	0	0	.00	4	.222	.307	.434
5 Min. YEARS		445	1479	323	57	2	55	549	187	191	141	2	505	15	14	11	5	2	.71	19	.218	.291	.371

Yohanny Valera

Bats: Right **Throws:** Right **Pos:** C — **Ht:** 6'1" **Wt:** 196 **Born:** 8/17/76 **Age:** 23

Year Team	Lg Org	G	AB	H	2B	3B	HR	TB	R	RBI	TBB	IBB	SO	HBP	SH	SF	SB	CS	SB%	GDP	Avg	OBP	SLG
1995 Kingsport	R+ NYM	56	204	60	13	0	3	82	30	36	11	0	33	5	2	1	2	1	.67	6	.294	.344	.402
1996 Capital Cty	A NYM	108	372	79	18	0	6	115	38	38	17	3	78	13	1	7	2	4	.33	0	.212	.267	.309
1997 Capital Cty	A NYM	94	293	56	14	0	8	94	32	33	21	0	101	5	2	1	2	0	1.00	4	.191	.256	.321
1998 St. Lucie	A+ NYM	91	298	61	21	1	14	126	37	42	21	0	92	7	1	1	1	1	.50	7	.205	.272	.423
1999 Norfolk	AAA NYM	23	65	10	2	0	1	15	3	6	4	0	16	1	1	0	0	0	.00	0	.154	.214	.231
Binghamton	AA NYM	57	204	59	14	3	9	106	33	39	17	1	57	2	0	2	2	1	.67	6	.289	.347	.520
5 Min. YEARS		429	1436	325	82	4	41	538	173	194	91	4	377	33	7	12	9	7	.56	35	.226	.286	.375

Tim VanEgmond

Pitches: Right   **Bats:** Right   **Pos:** P   **Ht:** 6' 2"   **Wt:** 180   **Born:** 5/31/69   **Age:** 31

Year Team	Lg Org	G	GS	CG	GF	IP	BFP	H	R	ER	HR	SH	SF	HB	TBB	IBB	SO	WP	Bk	W	L	Pct.	ShO	Sv	ERA
1991 Red Sox	R Bos	3	2	0	1	15	54	6	1	1	0	0	0	1	1	0	20	2	2	2	0	1.000	0	1	0.60
Winter Havn	A+ Bos	13	10	4	2	68.1	292	69	32	23	2	1	0	2	23	1	47	2	1	4	5	.444	2	2	3.03
1992 Lynchburg	A+ Bos	28	27	2	0	173.2	727	161	73	66	12	4	1	8	52	0	140	18	1	12	4	.750	1	0	3.42
1993 New Britain	AA Bos	29	29	1	0	190.1	794	182	99	84	18	3	2	14	44	1	163	11	3	6	12	.333	1	0	3.97
1994 Pawtucket	AAA Bos	20	20	1	0	119.1	510	110	58	50	9	0	3	7	42	2	87	5	0	9	5	.643	0	0	3.77
1995 Pawtucket	AAA Bos	12	12	0	0	66.2	279	66	32	29	10	1	2	4	21	1	47	5	0	5	3	.625	0	0	3.92
1996 Pawtucket	AAA Bos	11	11	1	0	61.2	262	66	37	30	9	0	2	3	24	1	46	1	1	5	3	.625	0	0	4.38
New Orleans	AAA Mil	7	7	0	0	48	180	28	8	8	2	2	0	1	11	0	32	1	0	5	1	.833	0	0	1.50
1997 Tucson	AAA Mil	1	0	0	0	1	6	3	1	1	0	0	0	0	0	0	0	0	0	1	0	1.000	0	0	9.00
1998 Louisville	AAA Mil	24	20	0	1	131.2	569	132	72	65	23	5	2	9	45	2	99	6	1	6	11	.353	0	0	4.44
1999 Huntsville	AA Mil	3	3	0	0	11	52	11	6	4	3	1	0	0	6	0	9	0	0	0	1	.000	0	0	3.27
Louisville	AAA Mil	8	7	0	0	26.2	130	28	25	15	5	0	2	4	17	0	15	5	0	0	5	.000	0	0	5.06
1994 Boston	AL	7	7	1	0	38.1	173	38	27	27	7	0	3	0	21	3	22	1	0	2	3	.400	0	0	6.34
1995 Boston	AL	4	1	0	1	6.2	35	9	7	7	2	0	0	0	6	0	5	1	0	0	1	.000	0	0	9.45
1996 Milwaukee	AL	12	9	0	1	54.2	242	58	35	32	6	3	3	1	23	2	33	0	1	3	5	.375	0	0	5.27
9 Min. YEARS		159	148	9	4	913.1	3855	862	444	376	93	17	14	53	286	8	705	56	9	55	50	.524	4	3	3.71
3 Maj. YEARS		23	17	1	2	99.2	450	105	69	66	15	3	6	1	50	5	60	2	1	5	9	.357	0	0	5.96

Todd Van Poppel

Pitches: Right   **Bats:** Right   **Pos:** P   **Ht:** 6' 5"   **Wt:** 241   **Born:** 12/9/71   **Age:** 28

Year Team	Lg Org	G	GS	CG	GF	IP	BFP	H	R	ER	HR	SH	SF	HB	TBB	IBB	SO	WP	Bk	W	L	Pct.	ShO	Sv	ERA
1990 Sou Oregon	A- Oak	5	5	0	0	24	92	10	5	3	1	0	1	2	9	0	32	0	0	1	1	.500	0	0	1.13
Madison	A Oak	3	3	0	0	13.2	61	8	11	6	0	0	1	1	10	0	17	0	0	2	1	.667	0	0	3.95
1991 Huntsville	AA Oak	24	24	1	0	132.1	607	118	69	51	2	4	6	6	90	0	115	12	1	6	13	.316	1	0	3.47
1992 Tacoma	AAA Oak	9	9	0	0	45.1	202	44	22	20	1	3	4	1	35	0	29	1	1	4	2	.667	0	0	3.97
1993 Tacoma	AAA Oak	16	16	0	0	78.2	355	67	53	51	5	3	3	4	54	0	71	2	0	4	8	.333	0	0	5.83
1997 Omaha	AAA KC	11	6	0	1	37	188	50	36	33	10	2	3	3	24	0	27	2	0	1	5	.167	0	0	8.03
Charlotte	A+ Tex	6	6	2	0	35.2	152	36	19	16	3	2	2	1	10	0	33	2	0	0	4	.000	0	0	4.04
Tulsa	AA Tex	7	7	0	0	42.2	197	53	27	24	2	3	3	1	15	0	26	2	1	3	3	.500	0	0	5.06
1998 Tulsa	AA Tex	1	1	0	0	4	17	2	2	2	1	0	0	0	4	0	2	0	0	0	0	.000	0	0	4.50
Oklahoma	AAA Tex	15	13	2	0	87	370	88	44	36	11	0	2	1	25	0	69	3	1	5	5	.500	0	0	3.72
1999 Nashville	AAA Pit	27	27	0	0	163.2	716	173	95	90	23	7	4	5	62	1	157	5	1	10	6	.625	0	0	4.95
1991 Oakland	AL	1	1	0	0	4.2	21	7	5	5	1	0	0	0	2	0	6	0	0	0	0	.000	0	0	9.64
1993 Oakland	AL	16	16	0	0	84	380	76	50	47	10	1	2	2	62	0	47	3	0	6	6	.500	0	0	5.04
1994 Oakland	AL	23	23	0	0	116.2	532	108	80	79	20	4	4	3	89	2	83	3	1	7	10	.412	0	0	6.09
1995 Oakland	AL	36	14	1	10	138.1	582	125	77	75	16	3	6	4	56	1	122	4	0	4	8	.333	0	0	4.88
1996 Oakland	AL	28	6	0	8	63	301	86	56	54	13	3	5	2	33	3	37	4	0	1	5	.167	0	0	7.71
Detroit	AL	9	9	1	0	36.1	190	53	51	46	11	1	2	1	29	0	16	3	0	2	4	.333	1	0	11.39
1998 Texas	AL	4	4	0	0	19.1	95	26	20	19	5	0	1	1	10	0	10	2	0	1	2	.333	0	0	8.84
Pittsburgh	NL	18	7	0	3	47	208	53	32	28	4	3	2	0	18	3	32	5	3	1	2	.333	0	0	5.36
7 Min. YEARS		124	117	7	1	664	2957	649	383	332	59	24	29	25	338	1	578	29	5	36	48	.429	1	0	4.50
6 Maj. YEARS		135	80	2	21	509.1	2309	534	371	353	80	15	22	13	299	9	353	24	4	22	37	.373	1	1	6.24

Chris Van Rossum

Bats: Left   **Throws:** Left   **Pos:** OF   **Ht:** 6'2"   **Wt:** 180   **Born:** 2/15/74   **Age:** 26

										BATTING						BASERUNNING				PERCENTAGES		
Year Team	Lg Org	G	AB	H	2B	3B	HR	TB	R	RBI	TBB	IBB	SO	HBP	SH	SF	SB	CS	SB%	GDP	Avg	OBP	SLG
1996 Bellingham	A- SF	23	42	6	0	0	0	6	3	4	3	0	12	2	0	2	5	1	.83	0	.143	.224	.143
San Jose	A+ SF	11	31	8	2	0	0	10	7	4	6	0	10	1	0	0	1	2	.33	0	.258	.395	.323
1997 Bakersfield	A+ SF	125	441	115	17	5	2	148	72	40	57	1	98	15	5	3	9	12	.43	6	.261	.362	.336
1998 San Jose	A+ SF	65	214	53	9	3	2	74	33	15	17	0	55	4	1	1	10	2	.83	6	.248	.314	.346
Shreveport	AA SF	23	62	10	2	1	0	14	5	3	9	0	15	0	1	0	2	2	.50	1	.161	.268	.226
1999 High Desert	A+ Ari	28	90	28	5	1	4	47	13	16	9	0	27	2	0	2	2	1	.67	1	.311	.379	.522
Diamondbcks	R Ari	6	16	4	0	0	0	4	1	0	1	0	3	0	0	0	1	0	1.00	0	.250	.294	.250
South Bend	A Ari	2	6	1	0	0	0	1	2	1	3	0	1	0	0	0	0	0	.00	0	.167	.444	.167
El Paso	AA Ari	26	75	21	5	0	3	35	11	9	8	0	21	2	0	1	1	0	1.00	1	.280	.360	.467
4 Min. YEARS		309	977	246	40	10	11	339	147	92	113	1	242	26	7	9	31	20	.61	15	.252	.342	.347

Ben VanRyn

Pitches: Left   **Bats:** Left   **Pos:** P   **Ht:** 6' 5"   **Wt:** 195   **Born:** 8/9/71   **Age:** 28

Year Team	Lg Org	G	GS	CG	GF	IP	BFP	H	R	ER	HR	SH	SF	HB	TBB	IBB	SO	WP	Bk	W	L	Pct.	ShO	Sv	ERA
1990 Expos	R Mon	10	9	0	0	51.2	205	44	13	10	0	0	2	15	0	56	0	0	5	3	.625	0	0	1.74
1991 Sumter	A Mon	20	20	0	0	109.1	506	122	96	79	14	3	7	6	61	0	77	10	4	2	13	.133	0	0	6.50
Jamestown	A- Mon	6	6	1	0	32.1	143	37	19	18	1	0	0	2	12	0	23	4	0	3	3	.500	0	0	5.01
1992 Vero Beach	A+ LA	26	25	1	0	137.2	583	125	58	49	4	5	8	2	54	1	108	4	5	10	7	.588	1	0	3.20
1993 San Antonio	AA LA	21	21	1	0	134.1	557	118	43	33	5	4	1	3	38	1	144	2	4	14	4	.778	0	0	2.21
Albuquerque	AAA LA	6	6	0	0	24.1	102	35	30	29	1	1	2	0	17	0	9	0	0	1	4	.200	0	0	10.73
1994 Albuquerque	AAA LA	12	9	0	1	50.2	251	75	42	36	6	3	1	0	24	1	44	0	1	4	1	.800	0	0	6.39
San Antonio	AA LA	17	17	0	0	102.1	418	93	42	34	5	3	1	0	35	0	72	2	0	8	3	.727	0	0	2.99
1995 Chattanooga	AA Cin	5	3	0	0	12.2	69	22	18	13	2	0	2	1	6	0	6	0	0	1	0	1.000	0	0	9.24
Vancouver	AAA Ana	11	5	0	2	29.1	123	29	10	10	1	2	2	0	9	1	20	2	0	2	0	1.000	0	0	3.07
Midland	AA Ana	19	0	0	8	32.1	133	33	10	10	4	0	0	2	10	0	24	2	0	1	1	.500	0	0	2.78
1996 Vancouver	AAA Ana	18	1	0	0	34.2	154	35	17	15	2	3	1	1	13	1	28	3	0	3	3	.500	0	0	3.89
Louisville	AAA StL	19	10	0	4	66.1	288	69	43	36	9	2	3	0	27	0	42	0	0	4	6	.400	0	0	4.88

286

Year Team	Lg Org	G	GS	CG	GF	IP	BFP	H	R	ER	HR	SH	SF	HB	TBB	IBB	SO	WP	Bk	W	L	Pct.	ShO	Sv	ERA
1997 Iowa	AAA ChC	51	5	0	12	80.1	343	88	43	41	10	5	3	1	25	2	64	5	0	2	2	.500	0	3	4.59
1998 Syracuse	AAA Tor	30	0	0	7	41	164	34	16	16	3	1	3	0	13	1	30	0	0	2	1	.667	0	2	3.51
1999 Charlotte	AAA CWS	47	8	0	13	68.1	314	83	47	45	9	1	6	1	30	0	54	4	0	3	2	.600	0	5	5.93
1996 California	AL	1	0	0	1	1	5	1	0	0	0	0	0	0	1	0	0	0	0	0	0	.000	0	0	0.00
1998 Chicago	NL	9	0	0	2	8	39	9	3	3	0	0	1	1	6	0	6	0	0	0	0	.000	0	0	3.38
San Diego	NL	6	0	0	1	2.2	16	3	3	3	0	0	0	1	4	0	1	1	0	0	1	.000	0	0	10.13
Toronto	AL	10	0	0	3	4	17	6	4	4	0	0	0	0	2	0	3	0	0	0	1	.000	0	0	9.00
10 Min. YEARS		318	145	3	51	1007.2	4371	1042	547	474	76	33	40	21	391	8	801	40	14	64	54	.542	1	12	4.23
2 Maj. YEARS		26	0	0	7	15.2	77	19	10	10	0	0	1	2	13	0	10	1	0	0	2	.000	0	0	5.74

Dan Vardijan

Pitches: Right **Bats:** Right **Pos:** P · **Ht:** 6'4" **Wt:** 205 **Born:** 12/1/76 **Age:** 23

Year Team	Lg Org	G	GS	CG	GF	IP	BFP	H	R	ER	HR	SH	SF	HB	TBB	IBB	SO	WP	Bk	W	L	Pct.	ShO	Sv	ERA
1995 Marlins	R Fla	9	8	0	1	44	164	21	11	8	2	0	1	5	10	0	34	2	0	5	0	1.000	0	0	1.64
Kane County	A Fla	1	1	0	0	3	17	5	3	2	0	0	0	1	2	0	2	1	0	0	0	.000	0	0	6.00
1996 Kane County	A Fla	25	25	2	0	145	603	128	71	54	5	5	2	16	55	4	92	13	0	7	7	.500	1	0	3.35
1998 Brevard Cty	A+ Fla	8	0	0	5	12	56	15	4	4	0	1	1	2	4	0	8	2	0	2	0	1.000	0	0	3.00
Portland	AA Fla	19	0	0	3	28.2	143	34	26	25	4	2	1	2	22	3	15	7	0	1	1	.500	0	0	7.85
1999 Portland	AA Fla	5	0	0	0	4.1	37	12	15	14	1	0	1	2	8	1	5	3	0	0	1	.000	0	0	29.08
Brevard Cty	A+ Fla	34	0	0	27	45	198	43	14	13	1	4	1	5	20	4	33	4	0	3	1	.750	0	7	2.60
4 Min. YEARS		101	34	2	36	282	1218	258	144	120	13	12	7	33	121	12	189	32	0	18	10	.643	1	7	3.83

Leo Vasquez

Pitches: Left **Bats:** Left **Pos:** P · **Ht:** 6'4" **Wt:** 196 **Born:** 7/1/73 **Age:** 26

Year Team	Lg Org	G	GS	CG	GF	IP	BFP	H	R	ER	HR	SH	SF	HB	TBB	IBB	SO	WP	Bk	W	L	Pct.	ShO	Sv	ERA
1996 Aberdeen	IND —	19	16	2	1	105.1	429	79	39	26	7	2	0	1	39	0	106	4	0	11	2	.846	2	0	2.22
1997 Binghamton	AA NYM	1	1	0	0	5.1	26	7	6	6	3	1	2	0	2	0	2	0	0	1	0	1.000	0	0	10.13
Capital Cty	A NYM	22	8	0	8	56	250	63	37	32	4	1	2	3	22	1	49	7	1	4	5	.444	0	1	5.14
1998 Binghamton	AA NYM	14	2	0	2	29.1	140	28	16	15	1	2	1	2	25	0	28	3	0	1	1	.500	0	1	4.60
St. Lucie	A+ NYM	24	6	0	10	69	264	44	20	17	3	3	4	3	24	0	46	5	0	3	2	.600	0	4	2.22
1999 Binghamton	AA NYM	27	0	0	7	42.1	190	39	18	18	4	0	1	2	28	0	43	2	1	3	1	.333	0	1	3.83
Midland	AA Oak	13	0	0	5	23.1	103	18	11	8	2	1	1	2	13	1	24	1	1	3	1	.750	0	1	3.09
Vancouver	AAA Oak	1	0	0	0	1.2	8	2	1	1	0	0	0	0	2	0	0	0	0	0	0	.000	0	0	5.40
4 Min. YEARS		121	33	2	33	332.1	1410	280	148	123	24	10	11	13	155	2	298	22	3	23	14	.622	2	8	3.33

Mike Vavrek

Pitches: Left **Bats:** Left **Pos:** P · **Ht:** 6'2" **Wt:** 185 **Born:** 4/23/74 **Age:** 26

Year Team	Lg Org	G	GS	CG	GF	IP	BFP	H	R	ER	HR	SH	SF	HB	TBB	IBB	SO	WP	Bk	W	L	Pct.	ShO	Sv	ERA
1995 Portland	A- Col	3	3	0	0	14	52	8	0	0	0	0	0	0	3	0	14	0	0	0	0	.000	0	0	0.00
Asheville	A Col	12	12	1	0	76.2	322	64	24	17	3	0	1	5	25	0	54	4	5	5	4	.556	0	0	2.00
1996 Salem	A+ Col	26	25	2	0	149.2	658	167	92	81	15	6	8	5	59	0	103	10	0	10	8	.556	1	0	4.87
1997 Salem	A+ Col	10	9	0	0	62.2	255	55	21	15	3	1	4	3	18	0	48	3	0	2	2	.500	0	0	2.15
New Haven	AA Col	17	17	2	0	122.2	491	94	38	35	7	8	4	1	34	0	101	4	0	12	3	.800	0	0	2.57
1998 Colo Sprngs	AAA Col	10	9	0	1	44.2	227	62	50	41	8	3	4	1	34	0	41	5	0	2	6	.250	0	0	8.26
New Haven	AA Col	19	19	0	0	114.2	530	142	83	70	24	3	4	4	49	0	70	11	0	5	12	.294	0	0	5.49
1999 Carolina	AA Col	10	9	0	0	46.1	230	71	42	38	11	3	1	0	19	0	41	8	0	1	5	.167	0	0	7.38
Salem	A+ Col	10	5	0	3	48.2	191	32	10	10	2	1	1	2	13	0	38	1	0	3	1	.750	0	0	1.85
5 Min. YEARS		117	108	5	4	680	2956	695	360	307	73	25	27	21	254	0	510	46	5	40	41	.494	1	0	4.06

Roberto Vaz

Bats: Left **Throws:** Left **Pos:** OF-DH · **Ht:** 5'9" **Wt:** 195 **Born:** 3/15/75 **Age:** 25

Year Team	Lg Org	G	AB	H	2B	3B	HR	TB	R	RBI	TBB	IBB	SO	HBP	SH	SF	SB	CS	SB%	GDP	Avg	OBP	SLG
1997 Sou Oregon	A- Oak	22	78	25	6	0	3	40	11	15	7	1	4	1	0	1	5	3	.63	6	.321	.379	.513
Visalia	A+ Oak	19	73	26	5	0	3	40	9	13	8	0	10	0	2	2	2	5	.29	4	.356	.420	.548
1998 Huntsville	AA Oak	131	457	135	18	5	8	187	54	62	56	4	63	3	4	10	23	16	.59	14	.295	.369	.409
1999 Midland	AA Oak	10	32	13	3	0	1	19	4	12	8	0	5	0	1	2	0	1	.00	1	.406	.500	.594
Vancouver	AAA Oak	109	367	97	18	4	7	144	54	38	51	3	72	2	5	2	7	5	.58	8	.264	.355	.392
3 Min. YEARS		291	1007	296	50	9	22	430	132	140	130	8	154	6	12	15	37	30	.55	33	.294	.373	.427

Ramon Vazquez

Bats: Left **Throws:** Right **Pos:** SS · **Ht:** 5'11" **Wt:** 170 **Born:** 8/21/76 **Age:** 23

Year Team	Lg Org	G	AB	H	2B	3B	HR	TB	R	RBI	TBB	IBB	SO	HBP	SH	SF	SB	CS	SB%	GDP	Avg	OBP	SLG
1995 Mariners	R Sea	39	141	29	3	1	0	34	20	11	19	0	27	2	0	0	4	3	.57	2	.206	.309	.241
1996 Everett	A- Sea	33	126	35	5	2	1	47	25	18	26	0	26	1	2	5	7	2	.78	3	.278	.392	.373
Tacoma	AAA Sea	18	49	11	2	1	0	15	7	4	4	0	12	1	0	0	0	0	.00	2	.224	.296	.306
Wisconsin	A Sea	3	10	3	1	0	0	4	1	1	2	0	2	0	0	0	0	0	.00	1	.300	.417	.400
1997 Wisconsin	A Sea	131	479	129	25	5	8	188	79	49	78	2	93	3	4	3	16	10	.62	8	.269	.373	.392
1998 Lancaster	A+ Sea	121	468	129	26	4	2	169	77	72	81	5	66	2	4	1	15	11	.58	6	.276	.384	.361
1999 New Haven	AA Sea	127	438	113	27	3	5	161	58	45	62	4	77	5	6	3	8	1	.89	11	.258	.354	.368
5 Min. YEARS		472	1711	449	89	16	16	618	267	200	272	11	303	14	16	12	50	27	.65	33	.262	.366	.361

Dario Veras

Pitches: Right **Bats:** Right **Pos:** P **Ht:** 6' 1" **Wt:** 155 **Born:** 3/13/73 **Age:** 27

Year Team	Lg Org	G	GS	CG	GF	IP	BFP	H	R	ER	HR	SH	SF	HB	TBB	IBB	SO	WP	Bk	W	L	Pct.	ShO	Sv	ERA
1993 Bakersfield	A+ LA	7	0	0	1	13.1	61	13	11	11	1	0	1	0	8	2	11	0	0	1	0	1.000	0	0	7.43
Vero Beach	A+ LA	24	0	0	8	54.2	229	59	23	17	2	3	1	1	14	5	31	3	0	2	2	.500	0	2	2.80
1994 Rancho Cuca	A+ SD	59	0	0	13	79	332	66	28	18	7	7	0	6	25	9	56	2	0	9	2	.818	0	3	2.05
1995 Memphis	AA SD	58	0	0	22	82.2	360	81	38	35	8	3	1	7	27	11	70	5	1	7	3	.700	0	1	3.81
1996 Memphis	AA SD	29	0	0	8	42.2	172	38	14	11	4	1	2	1	9	2	47	2	1	3	1	.750	0	1	2.32
Las Vegas	AAA SD	19	1	0	9	40.1	165	41	17	13	1	3	1	0	6	2	30	2	0	6	2	.750	0	1	2.90
1997 Mobile	AA SD	5	2	0	2	5	25	8	5	5	1	0	0	0	3	0	5	0	0	0	0	.000	0	0	9.00
Rancho Cuca	A+ SD	2	0	0	1	3	13	3	3	2	1	1	0	0	1	0	3	1	0	0	0	.000	0	1	6.00
Las Vegas	AAA SD	12	0	0	5	14.1	59	14	8	8	1	0	0	0	6	0	13	3	0	0	2	.000	0	2	5.02
1998 Las Vegas	AAA SD	31	0	0	27	35.2	153	36	15	15	5	0	0	2	11	0	29	4	0	2	1	.667	0	9	3.79
Pawtucket	AAA Bos	23	0	0	21	29	124	30	12	12	4	1	1	0	11	3	27	0	0	2	0	1.000	0	7	3.72
1999 Royals	R KC	3	2	0	0	4	15	3	0	0	0	0	0	0	0	0	3	0	0	0	0	.000	0	0	0.00
Omaha	AAA KC	12	0	0	3	20.2	81	19	10	10	5	1	0	1	3	0	17	0	0	1	2	.333	0	0	4.35
1996 San Diego	NL	23	0	0	6	29	117	24	10	9	3	1	1	1	10	4	23	1	0	3	1	.750	0	0	2.79
1997 San Diego	NL	23	0	0	7	24.2	114	28	18	14	5	0	0	2	12	3	21	0	0	2	1	.667	0	0	5.11
1998 Boston	AL	7	0	0	4	8	43	12	9	9	0	0	0	1	7	0	2	2	0	0	1	.000	0	0	10.13
7 Min. YEARS		284	5	0	120	424.1	1789	411	184	157	40	20	7	18	124	34	342	22	2	33	15	.688	0	27	3.33
3 Maj. YEARS		53	0	0	17	61.2	274	64	37	32	8	1	1	4	29	7	46	3	0	5	3	.625	0	0	4.67

Jason Verdugo

Pitches: Right **Bats:** Right **Pos:** P **Ht:** 6'2" **Wt:** 195 **Born:** 3/28/75 **Age:** 25

Year Team	Lg Org	G	GS	CG	GF	IP	BFP	H	R	ER	HR	SH	SF	HB	TBB	IBB	SO	WP	Bk	W	L	Pct.	ShO	Sv	ERA
1997 Salem-Keizr	A- SF	16	14	0	0	78.1	347	85	48	42	7	5	1	6	25	1	82	1	1	4	8	.333	0	0	4.83
1998 Bakersfield	A+ SF	28	11	0	17	80.1	329	79	35	29	4	1	3	2	15	0	59	0	0	6	6	.500	0	3	3.25
San Jose	A+ SF	1	0	0	1	1	5	2	0	0	0	0	0	0	0	0	1	0	0	0	0	.000	0	0	0.00
Shreveport	AA SF	9	1	0	2	19.1	81	17	9	8	4	1	1	0	6	2	27	0	0	1	2	.333	0	1	3.72
1999 Shreveport	AA SF	40	0	0	22	62.2	261	58	34	21	7	4	4	1	12	0	46	4	2	2	3	.400	0	8	3.02
Fresno	AAA SF	9	2	0	2	20.1	89	19	14	11	5	0	0	0	9	0	29	1	0	1	0	1.000	0	0	4.87
3 Min. YEARS		103	28	0	44	262	1112	260	140	111	27	11	9	9	67	3	244	6	3	14	19	.424	0	12	3.81

Joe Verplancke

Pitches: Right **Bats:** Right **Pos:** P **Ht:** 6'2" **Wt:** 200 **Born:** 5/11/75 **Age:** 25

Year Team	Lg Org	G	GS	CG	GF	IP	BFP	H	R	ER	HR	SH	SF	HB	TBB	IBB	SO	WP	Bk	W	L	Pct.	ShO	Sv	ERA
1996 Lethbridge	R+ Ari	12	12	0	0	48	209	44	22	16	4	0	1	4	25	0	63	4	0	3	3	.500	0	0	3.00
1997 South Bend	A Ari	2	0	0	0	4.2	20	3	1	1	0	0	0	0	3	0	3	1	0	1	0	1.000	0	0	1.93
High Desert	A+ Ari	17	17	0	0	74.1	345	91	53	48	15	1	2	12	30	0	64	4	2	7	2	.778	0	0	5.81
1998 Tucson	AAA Ari	1	0	0	0	3.1	14	2	2	0	0	1	0	0	2	0	3	1	0	1	0	1.000	0	0	0.00
High Desert	A+ Ari	42	2	0	14	81.1	344	65	41	33	9	3	4	3	40	0	87	4	2	10	4	.714	0	1	3.65
1999 Tucson	AAA Ari	2	0	0	0	2.1	9	1	0	0	0	0	0	0	1	0	4	0	0	0	0	.000	0	0	0.00
High Desert	A+ Ari	3	0	0	0	4.1	22	5	5	5	1	1	1	0	4	0	5	0	0	1	0	1.000	0	0	10.38
El Paso	AA Ari	1	0	0	0	0.1	6	5	5	5	2	0	0	0	1	0	0	0	0	0	1	.000	0	0	135.00
South Bend	A Ari	18	0	0	6	33.2	145	16	22	18	4	2	3	4	24	0	43	4	0	2	2	.500	0	0	4.81
4 Min. YEARS		98	31	0	20	252.1	1114	232	151	126	35	8	11	23	129	0	272	18	4	25	12	.676	0	1	4.49

Gilbert Vidal

Bats: Right **Throws:** Right **Pos:** C **Ht:** 5'10" **Wt:** 188 **Born:** 4/21/75 **Age:** 25

Year Team	Lg Org	G	AB	H	2B	3B	HR	TB	R	RBI	TBB	IBB	SO	HBP	SH	SF	SB	CS	SB%	GDP	Avg	OBP	SLG
1995 Rockies	R Col	39	136	39	11	1	1	55	19	20	23	0	20	1	0	3	3	3	.50	9	.287	.387	.404
1996 Portland	A- Col	32	106	24	8	1	1	37	16	11	18	2	20	0	0	0	0	1	.00	3	.226	.333	.349
1997 Salem	A+ Col	80	226	54	21	0	6	93	20	30	19	1	54	0	2	5	1	2	.33	4	.239	.292	.412
1998 Asheville	A Col	76	275	82	21	0	7	124	42	42	26	0	63	2	0	2	3	1	.75	9	.298	.359	.451
1999 Salem	A+ Col	13	46	9	3	0	1	15	6	6	7	1	12	1	1	0	1	0	1.00	1	.196	.315	.326
Carolina	AA Col	45	129	31	8	0	2	45	10	12	8	0	30	1	3	1	0	0	.00	2	.240	.288	.349
5 Min. YEARS		285	918	239	72	2	18	369	113	121	100	4	199	5	6	13	8	7	.53	31	.260	.332	.402

Scott Vieira

Bats: Right **Throws:** Right **Pos:** OF **Ht:** 5'11" **Wt:** 185 **Born:** 8/17/73 **Age:** 26

Year Team	Lg Org	G	AB	H	2B	3B	HR	TB	R	RBI	TBB	IBB	SO	HBP	SH	SF	SB	CS	SB%	GDP	Avg	OBP	SLG
1995 Williamsprt	A- ChC	61	214	68	8	2	6	98	35	46	25	1	37	9	0	4	3	1	.75	3	.318	.405	.458
1996 Rockford	A ChC	134	442	143	30	4	8	205	81	81	84	7	89	26	2	9	9	8	.53	6	.324	.451	.464
1997 Daytona	A+ ChC	134	476	131	27	3	18	218	84	80	70	1	125	17	1	7	9	7	.56	5	.275	.382	.458
1998 Cubs	R ChC	4	12	6	1	0	1	10	2	4	2	0	0	0	0	0	0	0	.00	0	.500	.571	.833
Daytona	A+ ChC	15	54	20	6	0	1	29	11	13	9	0	12	3	0	1	3	0	1.00	1	.370	.478	.537
1999 West Tenn	AA ChC	126	455	133	44	4	10	215	63	58	53	4	126	12	0	3	10	6	.63	4	.292	.379	.473
5 Min. YEARS		474	1653	501	116	13	44	775	276	282	243	13	389	67	3	24	34	22	.61	19	.303	.408	.469

Brandon Villafuerte

Pitches: Right Bats: Right Pos: P | Ht: 5'11" Wt: 165 Born: 12/17/75 Age: 24

Year Team	Lg Org	G	GS	CG	GF	IP	BFP	H	R	ER	HR	SH	SF	HB	TBB	IBB	SO	WP	Bk	W	L	Pct.	ShO	Sv	ERA
1995 Kingsport	R+ NYM	20	0	0	6	32	144	28	21	20	0	1	1	1	26	0	42	8	0	5	1	.833	0	0	5.63
1996 Pittsfield	A- NYM	18	7	1	4	62.2	267	53	21	21	5	2	3	6	27	0	59	4	0	8	3	.727	0	1	3.02
1997 Capital Cty	A NYM	47	3	0	31	75.2	308	58	23	20	6	2	1	4	33	0	88	12	0	3	1	.750	0	7	2.38
1998 Brevard Cty	A+ Fla	3	0	0	0	9.2	34	7	3	1	0	0	0	0	1	0	6	0	0	1	0	1.000	0	1	0.93
Portland	AA Fla	30	0	0	11	54.1	262	68	35	30	3	6	0	4	33	2	52	3	0	0	2	.000	0	1	4.97
Charlotte	AAA Fla	10	0	0	1	11.1	55	15	8	8	2	1	0	1	8	0	9	1	0	1	0	1.000	0	0	6.35
1999 Portland	AA Fla	22	12	0	4	100.1	422	97	45	39	11	4	2	5	40	3	85	2	1	6	8	.429	0	0	3.50
Jacksnville	AA Det	15	0	0	10	24	101	17	6	5	0	2	1	1	12	0	20	1	0	0	2	.000	0	5	1.88
5 Min. YEARS		165	22	1	67	370	1593	343	162	144	27	18	8	22	180	5	361	31	1	24	17	.585	0	14	3.50

Carlos Villalobos

Bats: Right Throws: Right Pos: 3B | Ht: 6'0" Wt: 170 Born: 4/5/74 Age: 26

Year Team	Lg Org	G	AB	H	2B	3B	HR	TB	R	RBI	TBB	IBB	SO	HBP	SH	SF	SB	CS	SB%	GDP	Avg	OBP	SLG
1994 Mariners	R Sea	51	175	51	6	2	4	73	17	29	11	1	34	2	2	2	6	0	1.00	8	.291	.337	.417
1995 Wisconsin	A Sea	110	389	101	16	4	9	152	64	53	35	1	76	3	4	5	16	4	.80	3	.260	.322	.391
1996 Lancaster	A+ Sea	111	415	121	21	5	5	167	69	63	50	0	89	4	2	3	9	4	.69	9	.292	.371	.402
1997 Lancaster	A+ Sea	86	296	101	22	2	11	160	71	53	60	0	42	7	2	0	4	6	.40	3	.341	.463	.541
Lakeland	A+ Det	39	147	37	5	0	1	45	19	15	11	0	25	2	1	0	0	1	.00	3	.252	.313	.306
1998 Jacksnville	AA Det	128	497	159	34	2	18	251	96	80	55	2	85	3	0	6	8	0	1.00	6	.320	.387	.505
1999 New Orleans	AAA Hou	133	499	141	33	1	9	203	82	50	54	0	100	2	5	4	11	3	.79	11	.283	.352	.407
6 Min. YEARS		658	2418	711	137	16	57	1051	418	343	276	4	451	23	16	20	54	18	.75	57	.294	.369	.435

Mike Villano

Pitches: Right Bats: Right Pos: P | Ht: 6'0" Wt: 200 Born: 8/10/71 Age: 28

Year Team	Lg Org	G	GS	CG	GF	IP	BFP	H	R	ER	HR	SH	SF	HB	TBB	IBB	SO	WP	Bk	W	L	Pct.	ShO	Sv	ERA
1995 Burlington	A SF	16	0	0	7	25.1	120	20	12	8	1	2	1	4	21	0	29	5	0	3	1	.750	0	1	2.84
San Jose	A+ SF	21	0	0	16	32.2	137	27	7	6	2	0	1	3	11	0	42	3	0	0	0	.000	0	1	1.65
1996 San Jose	A+ SF	39	2	0	21	88	341	48	12	7	2	1	1	0	33	4	133	7	1	7	1	.875	0	8	0.72
Shreveport	AA SF	2	2	0	0	12	47	6	4	4	0	0	0	0	8	0	7	0	0	2	0	1.000	0	0	3.00
1997 Shreveport	AA SF	30	0	0	15	34.1	158	41	25	24	5	2	0	0	20	2	26	4	1	3	1	.750	0	2	6.29
Phoenix	AAA SF	13	11	0	1	71.1	309	75	36	33	7	3	2	2	27	1	41	2	0	5	3	.625	0	0	4.16
1998 Charlotte	AAA Fla	13	10	0	1	59.2	277	82	55	51	14	1	4	3	18	0	47	3	2	3	5	.375	0	0	7.69
1999 Calgary	AAA Fla	36	1	0	11	58	273	87	43	40	18	1	0	5	17	0	48	7	1	1	5	.167	0	2	6.21
Norfolk	AAA NYM	2	0	0	2	2	10	3	1	1	0	0	0	0	2	0	1	0	0	0	0	.000	0	0	4.50
5 Min. YEARS		172	26	0	74	383.1	1672	389	195	174	49	10	9	17	157	7	374	31	5	24	17	.585	0	14	4.09

Ismael Villegas

Pitches: Right Bats: Right Pos: P | Ht: 6'0" Wt: 188 Born: 8/12/76 Age: 23

Year Team	Lg Org	G	GS	CG	GF	IP	BFP	H	R	ER	HR	SH	SF	HB	TBB	IBB	SO	WP	Bk	W	L	Pct.	ShO	Sv	ERA
1995 Cubs	R ChC	11	10	0	0	41.1	168	33	17	11	1	2	6	2	11	0	26	3	2	3	2	.600	0	0	2.40
1996 Rockford	A ChC	10	10	1	0	47.1	223	63	40	27	5	1	2	3	25	0	30	3	1	2	5	.286	0	0	5.13
Williamsprt	A- ChC	2	2	0	0	7	31	7	3	2	0	0	0	0	4	0	5	1	0	0	0	.000	0	0	2.57
Danville	R+ Atl	1	0	0	0	3	11	2	1	1	0	0	0	0	1	0	4	1	0	0	0	.000	0	0	3.00
Macon	A Atl	12	12	2	0	72	313	80	46	40	8	2	4	1	19	1	60	6	0	3	7	.300	1	0	5.00
1997 Durham	A+ Atl	30	1	0	5	55	255	60	33	31	5	2	2	4	32	0	44	5	0	2	5	.286	0	1	5.07
1998 Greenville	AA Atl	40	17	1	11	124.1	567	134	78	73	11	3	3	3	71	1	120	11	2	7	6	.538	0	3	5.28
1999 Richmond	AAA Atl	44	2	0	8	92	400	93	51	45	7	6	3	2	39	3	61	8	0	6	7	.462	0	1	4.40
5 Min. YEARS		150	54	4	24	442	1968	472	269	230	37	16	20	15	202	5	350	38	5	23	32	.418	1	5	4.68

Julio Vinas

Bats: Right Throws: Right Pos: DH | Ht: 6'1" Wt: 205 Born: 2/14/73 Age: 27

Year Team	Lg Org	G	AB	H	2B	3B	HR	TB	R	RBI	TBB	IBB	SO	HBP	SH	SF	SB	CS	SB%	GDP	Avg	OBP	SLG
1991 White Sox	R CWS	50	187	42	9	0	3	60	21	29	19	0	40	2	0	2	2	3	.40	5	.225	.300	.321
1992 South Bend	A CWS	33	94	16	3	0	0	19	7	10	9	0	17	1	0	2	1	3	.25	1	.170	.245	.202
Utica	A- CWS	47	151	37	6	4	0	51	22	24	11	0	29	2	1	5	1	2	.33	2	.245	.296	.338
1993 South Bend	A CWS	55	188	60	15	1	9	104	24	37	12	1	29	1	2	2	1	1	.50	2	.319	.360	.553
Sarasota	A+ CWS	18	65	16	2	1	1	23	5	7	5	0	13	0	0	0	0	0	.00	2	.246	.300	.354
1994 South Bend	A CWS	121	466	118	31	1	9	178	68	75	43	4	75	4	6	6	0	2	.00	9	.253	.318	.382
1995 Birmingham	AA CWS	102	372	100	16	2	6	138	47	61	37	1	80	5	0	7	3	3	.50	6	.269	.337	.371
1996 Nashville	AAA CWS	104	338	80	18	2	11	135	48	52	36	2	63	2	0	4	1	4	.20	8	.237	.311	.399
1997 Nashville	AAA CWS	91	314	73	12	2	11	122	39	41	25	2	72	2	3	5	4	4	.50	4	.232	.289	.389
1998 Rochester	AAA Bal	62	199	70	15	4	6	111	26	40	12	0	30	1	1	2	2	1	.67	3	.352	.388	.558
1999 Rochester	AAA Bal	126	484	151	32	2	20	247	67	83	25	1	73	1	0	7	4	3	.57	13	.312	.342	.510
9 Min. YEARS		809	2858	763	159	19	76	1188	374	459	234	11	521	21	13	42	19	26	.42	57	.267	.323	.416

Ken Vining

Pitches: Left Bats: Left Pos: P | Ht: 6'0" Wt: 180 Born: 12/5/74 Age: 25

Year Team	Lg Org	G	GS	CG	GF	IP	BFP	H	R	ER	HR	SH	SF	HB	TBB	IBB	SO	WP	Bk	W	L	Pct.	ShO	Sv	ERA
1996 Bellingham	A- SF	12	11	0	0	60.1	238	45	16	14	4	1	0	1	23	0	69	5	0	4	2	.667	0	0	2.09

		HOW MUCH HE PITCHED						WHAT HE GAVE UP												THE RESULTS					
Year Team	Lg Org	G	GS	CG	GF	IP	BFP	H	R	ER	HR	SH	SF	HB	TBB	IBB	SO	WP	Bk	W	L	Pct.	ShO	Sv	ERA
1997 San Jose	A+ SF	23	23	1	0	136.2	592	140	77	64	9	1	6	5	60	0	142	3	1	9	6	.600	1	0	4.21
Winston-Sal	A+ SF	5	5	0	0	34.2	153	36	17	11	2	3	0	0	11	0	38	2	0	2	2	.500	0	0	2.86
1998 Birmingham	AA CWS	29	28	1	0	172.2	793	187	103	78	8	5	5	4	91	1	133	16	0	10	12	.455	0	0	4.07
1999 Birmingham	AA CWS	3	3	0	0	11.2	62	20	16	12	1	0	1	1	9	0	8	0	1	0	2	.000	0	0	9.26
4 Min. YEARS		72	70	2	0	416	1838	428	229	179	24	10	12	11	194	1	390	26	2	25	24	.510	1	0	3.87

Adam Virchis

Pitches: Right Bats: Right Pos: P   Ht: 6'3" Wt: 185 Born: 10/15/73 Age: 26

		HOW MUCH HE PITCHED						WHAT HE GAVE UP												THE RESULTS					
Year Team	Lg Org	G	GS	CG	GF	IP	BFP	H	R	ER	HR	SH	SF	HB	TBB	IBB	SO	WP	Bk	W	L	Pct.	ShO	Sv	ERA
1995 Bristol	R+ CWS	10	10	1	0	56	239	69	39	33	5	2	3	3	7	0	33	2	2	0	7	.000	0	0	5.30
1996 Hickory	A CWS	26	3	0	13	82.2	348	82	38	30	10	7	5	6	25	5	42	3	3	8	6	.571	0	0	3.27
1997 Winston-Sal	A+ CWS	14	9	1	1	58.1	265	62	44	31	12	1	2	2	19	1	42	6	2	3	7	.300	0	0	4.78
Hickory	A CWS	15	2	0	4	44.1	183	42	20	19	3	0	1	3	11	0	34	3	1	2	3	.400	0	1	3.86
1998 Hickory	A CWS	9	0	0	4	18.2	72	16	8	7	1	1	1	0	5	0	19	0	1	1	3	.250	0	1	3.38
Winston-Sal	A+ CWS	22	13	1	3	103.2	434	104	54	39	9	6	1	10	20	0	73	3	0	5	6	.455	0	0	3.39
1999 Birmingham	AA CWS	1	0	0	0	3	12	3	0	0	1	0	0	0	1	0	0	1	0	0	0	.000	0	0	0.00
Winston-Sal	A+ CWS	33	7	0	7	78	347	82	50	41	9	5	3	4	33	0	59	4	0	3	5	.375	0	0	4.73
Charlotte	AAA CWS	3	0	0	3	6.1	27	6	1	1	1	0	0	0	1	0	4	0	0	0	0	.000	0	0	1.42
5 Min. YEARS		133	44	3	35	451	1927	462	254	201	50	22	17	28	121	6	307	21	9	22	37	.373	0	3	4.01

Ryan Vogelsong

Pitches: Right Bats: Right Pos: P   Ht: 6'3" Wt: 195 Born: 7/22/77 Age: 22

		HOW MUCH HE PITCHED						WHAT HE GAVE UP												THE RESULTS					
Year Team	Lg Org	G	GS	CG	GF	IP	BFP	H	R	ER	HR	SH	SF	HB	TBB	IBB	SO	WP	Bk	W	L	Pct.	ShO	Sv	ERA
1998 San Jose	A+ SF	4	4	0	0	19	83	23	16	16	3	1	2	1	4	0	26	2	4	0	0	.000	0	0	7.58
Salem-Keizr	A- SF	10	10	0	0	56	221	37	15	11	5	3	2	1	16	0	66	2	2	6	1	.857	0	0	1.77
1999 San Jose	A+ SF	13	13	0	0	69.2	274	37	26	19	3	1	2	3	27	0	86	3	0	4	4	.500	0	0	2.45
Shreveport	AA SF	6	6	0	0	28.1	137	40	25	23	7	0	1	2	15	0	23	1	0	0	2	.000	0	0	7.31
2 Min. YEARS		33	33	0	0	173	715	137	82	69	18	5	7	7	62	0	201	8	7	10	7	.588	0	0	3.59

Jack Voigt

Bats: Right Throws: Right Pos: 1B   Ht: 6'1" Wt: 178 Born: 5/17/66 Age: 34

		BATTING															BASERUNNING				PERCENTAGES		
Year Team	Lg Org	G	AB	H	2B	3B	HR	TB	R	RBI	TBB	IBB	SO	HBP	SH	SF	SB	CS	SB%	GDP	Avg	OBP	SLG
1987 Newark	A- Bal	63	219	70	10	1	11	115	41	52	33	0	45	0	1	1	1	3	.25	3	.320	.407	.525
Hagerstown	A+ Bal	2	9	1	0	0	0	1	0	1	1	0	4	0	0	0	0	0	.00	0	.111	.200	.111
1988 Hagerstown	A+ Bal	115	367	83	18	2	12	141	62	42	66	2	92	6	3	2	5	2	.71	7	.226	.351	.384
1989 Frederick	A+ Bal	127	406	107	26	5	10	173	61	77	62	4	106	4	2	5	17	2	.89	5	.264	.363	.426
1990 Hagerstown	AA Bal	126	418	106	26	2	12	172	55	70	59	1	97	5	6	11	5	3	.63	7	.254	.345	.411
1991 Hagerstown	AA Bal	29	90	22	3	0	0	25	15	6	15	1	19	2	1	0	6	0	1.00	2	.244	.364	.278
Rochester	AAA Bal	83	267	72	11	4	6	109	46	35	40	2	53	1	5	2	9	1	.90	8	.270	.365	.408
1992 Rochester	AAA Bal	129	443	126	23	4	16	205	74	64	58	3	102	4	3	0	9	2	.82	10	.284	.372	.463
1993 Rochester	AAA Bal	18	61	22	6	1	3	39	16	11	9	0	14	0	0	0	1	0	1.00	1	.361	.443	.639
1994 Bowie	AA Bal	41	154	48	9	1	6	77	26	35	26	1	26	2	0	2	5	5	.50	2	.312	.413	.500
1995 Tulsa	AA Tex	4	16	3	0	0	1	6	1	3	2	0	5	0	0	0	1	0	1.00	1	.188	.278	.375
1996 Charlotte	A+ Tex	7	27	11	3	0	1	17	7	8	3	0	3	1	0	0	0	0	.00	0	.407	.484	.630
Okla City	AAA Tex	127	445	132	26	1	21	223	77	80	76	4	103	1	2	6	5	5	.50	11	.297	.396	.501
1997 Tucson	AAA Mil	66	235	64	20	0	5	99	36	40	43	1	57	1	0	2	4	3	.57	4	.272	.384	.421
1998 Edmonton	AAA Oak	18	68	22	6	0	4	40	10	11	8	0	15	0	0	0	1	2	.33	0	.324	.395	.588
Oklahoma	AAA Tex	20	70	24	6	0	2	36	10	11	14	0	19	1	0	1	1	0	1.00	1	.343	.453	.514
1999 Fresno	AAA SF	23	67	13	4	1	1	22	12	5	17	0	21	1	0	1	1	0	1.00	1	.194	.360	.328
Schaumburg	IND —	42	138	42	10	1	7	75	33	27	42	0	27	5	0	0	0	3	.00	5	.304	.481	.543
1992 Baltimore	AL	1	0	0	0	0	0	0	0	0	0	0	0	0	0	0	0	0	.00	0	.000	.000	.000
1993 Baltimore	AL	64	152	45	11	1	6	76	32	23	25	0	33	0	0	0	1	0	1.00	1	.296	.395	.500
1994 Baltimore	AL	59	141	34	5	0	3	48	15	20	18	1	25	1	1	2	0	0	.00	0	.241	.327	.340
1995 Baltimore	AL	3	1	1	0	0	0	1	1	0	0	0	0	0	0	0	0	0	.00	0	1.000	1.000	1.000
Texas	AL	33	62	10	3	0	2	19	8	8	10	0	14	0	0	1	0	0	.00	2	.161	.274	.306
1996 Texas	AL	5	9	1	0	0	0	1	1	0	0	0	2	0	0	0	0	0	.00	0	.111	.111	.111
1997 Milwaukee	AL	72	151	37	9	2	8	74	20	22	19	2	36	1	1	1	1	2	.33	5	.245	.331	.490
1998 Oakland	AL	57	72	10	4	0	1	17	7	10	6	0	19	0	0	0	5	1	.83	1	.139	.205	.236
13 Min. YEARS		1040	3500	968	207	23	118	1575	582	578	574	19	808	34	23	33	69	33	.68	68	.277	.381	.450
7 Maj. YEARS		294	588	138	32	3	20	236	84	83	78	3	129	2	4	4	7	3	.70	11	.235	.324	.401

Terrell Wade

Pitches: Left Bats: Left Pos: P   Ht: 6'3" Wt: 250 Born: 1/25/73 Age: 27

		HOW MUCH HE PITCHED						WHAT HE GAVE UP												THE RESULTS					
Year Team	Lg Org	G	GS	CG	GF	IP	BFP	H	R	ER	HR	SH	SF	HB	TBB	IBB	SO	WP	Bk	W	L	Pct.	ShO	Sv	ERA
1991 Braves	R Atl	10	2	0	0	23	112	29	17	16	0	1	2	0	15	0	22	3	2	2	0	1.000	0	0	6.26
1992 Idaho Falls	R+ Atl	13	11	0	0	50.1	257	59	46	36	5	4	5	2	42	0	54	5	0	1	4	.200	0	0	6.44
1993 Macon	A Atl	14	14	0	0	83.1	336	57	16	16	1	0	1	1	36	0	121	11	0	8	2	.800	0	0	1.73
Durham	A+ Atl	5	5	0	0	33	137	26	13	12	3	0	0	1	18	0	47	0	1	2	1	.667	0	0	3.27
Greenville	AA Atl	8	8	1	0	42	179	32	16	15	6	1	0	1	29	0	40	2	0	2	1	.667	1	0	3.21
1994 Greenville	AA Atl	21	21	0	0	105.2	444	87	49	45	7	3	2	0	58	0	105	8	0	9	3	.750	0	0	3.83
Richmond	AAA Atl	4	4	0	0	24	103	23	9	7	1	0	1	0	15	0	26	1	0	2	2	.500	0	0	2.63
1995 Richmond	AAA Atl	24	23	1	0	142	600	137	76	72	10	3	5	1	63	1	124	5	1	10	9	.526	0	0	4.56
1997 Greenville	AA Atl	8	6	0	0	12.2	60	15	10	7	3	0	0	0	8	0	14	1	0	0	2	.000	0	0	4.97

Year Team	Lg Org	G	GS	CG	GF	IP	BFP	H	R	ER	HR	SH	SF	HB	TBB	IBB	SO	WP	Bk	W	L	Pct.	ShO	Sv	ERA
1998 St. Pete	A+ TB	3	3	0	0	15	66	12	8	6	2	0	1	1	7	0	16	1	0	0	1	.000	0	0	3.60
Durham	AAA TB	4	4	0	0	19.2	92	21	12	10	1	0	0	1	12	1	14	0	0	1	1	.500	0	0	4.58
1999 Durham	AAA TB	34	19	0	4	98.2	501	140	112	104	21	1	8	2	80	0	61	5	0	1	7	.125	0	0	9.49
1995 Atlanta	NL	3	0	0	0	4	18	3	2	2	1	0	0	0	4	0	3	1	0	0	1	.000	0	0	4.50
1996 Atlanta	NL	44	8	0	13	69.2	305	57	28	23	9	5	1	1	47	6	79	2	0	5	0	1.000	0	1	2.97
1997 Atlanta	NL	12	9	0	1	42	197	60	31	25	6	2	5	2	16	1	35	1	0	2	3	.400	0	0	5.36
1998 Tampa Bay	AL	2	2	0	0	10.2	46	14	6	6	3	0	0	0	2	0	8	1	0	1	1	.500	0	0	5.06
8 Min. YEARS		148	120	2	4	649.1	2887	638	384	346	60	13	25	10	383	2	644	42	4	38	33	.535	1	0	4.80
4 Maj. YEARS		61	19	0	14	126.1	566	134	67	56	19	7	6	3	69	7	125	5	0	8	5	.615	0	0	3.99

Denny Wagner

Pitches: Right **Bats:** Right **Pos:** P **Ht:** 6'0" **Wt:** 205 **Born:** 11/8/76 **Age:** 23

Year Team	Lg Org	G	GS	CG	GF	IP	BFP	H	R	ER	HR	SH	SF	HB	TBB	IBB	SO	WP	Bk	W	L	Pct.	ShO	Sv	ERA
1997 Sou Oregon	A- Oak	10	4	0	1	14	86	29	27	24	3	0	0	1	14	0	11	8	1	1	1	.500	0	0	15.43
1998 Athletics	R Oak	3	1	0	0	7	28	4	4	3	0	0	1	1	3	0	11	1	0	2	1	.667	0	0	3.86
Sou Oregon	A- Oak	2	2	0	0	4	26	11	9	8	0	0	0	0	3	0	5	1	0	0	1	.000	0	0	18.00
1999 Modesto	A+ Oak	27	15	0	5	113.2	502	116	57	45	7	0	3	10	42	2	99	7	3	7	4	.636	0	3	3.56
Midland	AA Oak	5	5	0	0	27.2	127	28	22	13	1	0	2	2	14	1	12	3	0	1	2	.333	0	0	4.23
3 Min. YEARS		47	27	0	6	166.1	769	188	119	93	11	0	6	14	76	3	138	20	4	11	9	.550	0	3	5.03

Chris Wakeland

Bats: Left **Throws:** Left **Pos:** OF **Ht:** 6'0" **Wt:** 185 **Born:** 6/15/74 **Age:** 26

Year Team	Lg Org	G	AB	H	2B	3B	HR	TB	R	RBI	TBB	IBB	SO	HBP	SH	SF	SB	CS	SB%	GDP	Avg	OBP	SLG
1996 Jamestown	A- Det	70	220	68	14	5	10	122	38	49	43	0	83	4	1	3	8	3	.73	1	.309	.426	.555
1997 W Michigan	A Det	111	414	118	38	2	7	181	64	75	43	5	120	4	0	7	20	6	.77	3	.285	.353	.437
1998 Lakeland	A+ Det	131	487	147	26	5	18	237	82	89	66	4	111	5	4	5	19	13	.59	4	.302	.387	.487
1999 Tigers	R Det	4	14	1	0	0	0	1	2	1	0	0	4	0	0	0	0	0	.00	0	.071	.071	.071
Lakeland	A+ Det	4	17	7	1	0	0	8	3	7	0	0	0	0	0	0	1	0	1.00	0	.412	.412	.471
Jacksnville	AA Det	55	212	68	16	3	13	129	42	36	35	1	53	4	0	2	6	5	.55	2	.321	.423	.608
4 Min. YEARS		375	1364	409	95	15	48	678	231	257	187	10	371	17	5	17	54	27	.67	10	.300	.387	.497

Jamie Walker

Pitches: Left **Bats:** Left **Pos:** P **Ht:** 6'2" **Wt:** 190 **Born:** 7/1/71 **Age:** 28

Year Team	Lg Org	G	GS	CG	GF	IP	BFP	H	R	ER	HR	SH	SF	HB	TBB	IBB	SO	WP	Bk	W	L	Pct.	ShO	Sv	ERA
1992 Auburn	A- Hou	15	14	0	0	83.1	341	75	35	29	4	4	1	6	21	0	67	4	1	4	6	.400	0	0	3.13
1993 Quad City	A Hou	25	24	1	1	131.2	585	140	92	75	12	10	5	6	48	1	121	12	0	3	11	.214	1	0	5.13
1994 Quad City	A Hou	32	18	0	4	125	569	133	80	58	10	14	3	16	42	2	104	5	1	8	10	.444	0	0	4.18
1995 Jackson	AA Hou	50	0	0	19	58	250	59	29	29	6	3	2	2	24	5	38	4	1	4	2	.667	0	2	4.50
1996 Jackson	AA Hou	45	7	0	13	101	424	94	34	28	7	3	1	8	35	2	79	2	0	5	1	.833	0	2	2.50
1997 Wichita	AA KC	5	0	0	0	6.2	32	6	8	7	1	1	1	2	5	0	6	0	0	0	1	.000	0	0	9.45
1998 Omaha	AAA KC	7	7	0	0	46.2	198	57	15	14	3	2	1	2	11	1	21	1	0	5	1	.833	0	0	2.70
1999 Royals	R KC	2	2	0	0	8	35	10	3	3	1	0	0	0	0	0	9	1	0	1	0	1.000	0	0	3.38
Omaha	AAA KC	4	4	0	0	17.1	79	22	12	9	1	1	2	2	4	0	11	0	0	1	0	1.000	0	0	4.67
1997 Kansas City	AL	50	0	0	15	43	197	46	28	26	6	2	2	3	20	3	24	2	0	3	3	.500	0	0	5.44
1998 Kansas City	AL	6	2	0	2	17.1	86	30	20	19	5	1	1	2	3	0	15	0	0	1	1	.000	0	0	9.87
8 Min. YEARS		185	76	1	37	577.2	2513	596	308	252	45	38	16	44	190	11	456	29	3	30	33	.476	1	5	3.93
2 Maj. YEARS		56	2	0	17	60.1	283	76	48	45	11	3	3	5	23	3	39	2	0	3	4	.429	0	0	6.71

Mike Walker

Pitches: Right **Bats:** Right **Pos:** P **Ht:** 6'1" **Wt:** 205 **Born:** 10/4/66 **Age:** 33

Year Team	Lg Org	G	GS	CG	GF	IP	BFP	H	R	ER	HR	SH	SF	HB	TBB	IBB	SO	WP	Bk	W	L	Pct.	ShO	Sv	ERA
1986 Burlington	R+ Cle	14	13	1	0	70.1	339	75	65	46	9	2	5	4	45	0	42	1	0	4	6	.400	0	0	5.89
1987 Waterloo	A Cle	23	23	8	0	145.1	637	133	74	58	11	4	3	13	68	1	144	14	0	11	7	.611	1	0	3.59
Kinston	A+ Cle	3	3	0	0	20.2	91	17	7	6	0	2	0	1	14	0	19	2	0	1	0	1.000	0	0	2.61
1988 Williamsprt	AA Cle	28	27	3	1	164.1	717	162	82	68	11	5	3	9	74	1	144	17	2	15	7	.682	0	0	3.72
1989 Colo Sprngs	AAA Cle	28	28	4	0	168	772	193	124	108	21	8	7	14	93	0	97	12	0	6	15	.286	0	0	5.79
1990 Colo Sprngs	AAA Cle	18	12	0	2	79	374	96	62	49	6	3	9	7	36	5	50	6	0	2	7	.222	0	1	5.58
Canton-Akrn	AA Cle	1	1	0	0	7	29	4	0	0	0	0	0	0	4	0	3	0	0	1	0	1.000	0	0	0.00
1991 Canton-Akrn	AA Cle	45	1	0	34	77.1	347	68	36	24	2	5	1	7	45	6	42	13	0	9	4	.692	0	11	2.79
1992 Toledo	AAA Det	42	1	0	16	78.2	384	102	62	51	5	3	2	8	44	6	44	7	1	2	8	.200	0	4	5.83
1993 Orlando	AA ChC	16	2	0	6	28.1	138	42	26	23	4	3	0	6	9	4	21	5	1	2	3	.400	0	1	7.31
Iowa	AAA ChC	12	0	0	3	23.1	97	22	8	7	1	0	2	2	9	0	11	3	0	1	1	.500	0	0	2.70
1994 Iowa	AAA ChC	56	0	0	37	87.1	367	80	33	29	2	4	3	4	34	8	56	8	1	6	2	.750	0	8	2.99
1995 Iowa	AAA ChC	16	1	0	3	26.1	122	22	13	12	3	1	1	3	19	4	13	0	0	1	1	.500	0	4	4.10
1996 Toledo	AAA Det	28	0	0	14	44.2	194	37	23	19	4	3	0	1	27	1	37	8	0	3	2	.600	0	0	3.83
1997 Indianapolis	AAA Cin	55	5	0	19	102.2	431	80	35	34	7	4	1	6	44	4	80	13	0	9	6	.600	0	7	2.98
1998 Indianapolis	AAA Cin	78	3	0	40	102.1	448	86	49	36	6	9	3	13	48	2	63	6	0	4	8	.333	0	6	3.17
1999 Buffalo	AAA Cle	29	0	0	11	35.1	179	43	29	22	4	3	2	1	26	5	15	5	0	2	1	.667	0	2	5.60
1988 Cleveland	AL	3	1	0	0	8.2	42	8	7	7	0	1	0	0	10	0	7	0	0	0	1	.000	0	0	7.27
1990 Cleveland	AL	18	11	0	2	75.2	350	82	49	41	6	4	2	6	42	4	34	3	1	2	6	.250	0	0	4.88
1991 Cleveland	AL	5	0	0	3	4.1	22	6	1	1	0	0	0	1	2	1	2	0	0	0	1	.000	0	0	2.08
1995 Chicago	NL	42	0	0	12	44.2	206	45	22	16	2	4	0	0	24	3	20	3	1	1	3	.250	0	1	3.22
1996 Detroit	AL	20	0	0	12	27.2	135	40	26	26	10	1	2	1	17	1	13	2	0	0	0	1	.000	0	8.46
14 Min. YEARS		492	120	16	186	1261	5666	1262	728	592	96	57	44	98	641	47	881	120	5	81	78	.509	1	46	4.23
5 Maj. YEARS		88	12	0	29	161	755	181	105	91	18	10	6	8	95	9	76	8	2	3	11	.214	0	2	5.09

Pete Walker

Pitches: Right **Bats:** Right **Pos:** P **Ht:** 6' 2" **Wt:** 195 **Born:** 4/8/69 **Age:** 31

Year Team	Lg Org	G	GS	CG	GF	IP	BFP	H	R	ER	HR	SH	SF	HB	TBB	IBB	SO	WP	Bk	W	L	Pct.	ShO	Sv	ERA
1990 Pittsfield	A- NYM	16	13	1	1	80	346	74	43	37	2	0	4	3	46	0	73	1	0	5	7	.417	0	0	4.16
1991 St. Lucie	A+ NYM	26	25	1	0	151.1	641	145	77	54	9	9	5	4	52	2	95	7	3	10	12	.455	0	0	3.21
1992 Binghamton	AA NYM	24	23	4	1	139.2	605	159	77	64	9	3	2	3	46	0	72	5	2	7	12	.368	0	0	4.12
1993 Binghamton	AA NYM	45	10	0	33	99.1	423	89	45	38	6	6	1	5	46	1	89	5	0	4	9	.308	0	19	3.44
1994 St. Lucie	A+ NYM	3	0	0	2	4	16	3	2	1	0	0	0	0	1	0	5	0	0	0	0	.000	0	0	2.25
Norfolk	AAA NYM	37	0	0	19	47.2	207	48	22	21	3	3	2	0	24	2	42	3	0	2	4	.333	0	3	3.97
1995 Norfolk	AAA NYM	34	1	0	25	48.1	207	51	24	21	4	3	1	1	16	1	39	2	1	5	2	.714	0	8	3.91
1996 Padres	R SD	2	2	0	0	4	17	4	1	1	0	1	0	0	0	0	5	0	0	1	0	1.000	0	0	2.25
Las Vegas	AAA SD	26	0	0	8	27.2	129	37	22	21	7	1	4	0	14	2	23	0	0	5	1	.833	0	0	6.83
1997 Red Sox	R Bos	4	3	0	0	9.1	36	5	1	1	0	0	0	1	1	0	14	0	0	0	0	.000	0	0	0.96
Trenton	AA Bos	8	0	0	3	13.1	61	14	6	6	1	3	0	0	7	0	13	0	0	0	0	.000	0	0	4.05
Pawtucket	AAA Bos	7	0	0	2	11.2	57	14	8	7	2	0	0	0	7	1	8	1	0	0	0	.000	0	3	5.40
1998 Pawtucket	AAA Bos	22	0	0	6	33.1	145	34	26	22	8	2	1	0	17	1	19	1	0	1	4	.200	0	0	5.94
1999 Colo Sprngs	AAA Col	48	0	0	23	62.1	273	64	37	31	9	2	2	2	28	3	57	2	1	8	4	.667	0	5	4.48
1995 New York	NL	13	0	0	10	17.2	79	24	9	9	3	0	1	0	5	0	5	0	0	1	0	1.000	0	0	4.58
1996 San Diego	NL	1	0	0	0	0.2	5	0	0	0	0	0	0	0	3	0	1	0	0	0	0	.000	0	0	0.00
10 Min. YEARS		302	77	6	123	732	3163	741	391	325	61	33	22	19	305	13	554	27	7	47	56	.456	0	38	4.00
2 Maj. YEARS		14	0	0	10	18.1	84	24	9	9	3	0	1	0	8	0	6	0	0	1	0	1.000	0	0	4.42

Ron Walker

Bats: Right **Throws:** Right **Pos:** 3B **Ht:** 6'2" **Wt:** 215 **Born:** 12/29/75 **Age:** 24

								BATTING									BASERUNNING				PERCENTAGES		
Year Team	Lg Org	G	AB	H	2B	3B	HR	TB	R	RBI	TBB	IBB	SO	HBP	SH	SF	SB	CS	SB%	GDP	Avg	OBP	SLG
1997 Williamsprt	A- ChC	54	189	66	10	1	9	105	30	39	17	7	48	5	0	2	0	1	.00	6	.349	.413	.556
Rockford	A ChC	4	15	5	0	0	1	8	1	5	3	0	2	0	0	0	0	0	.00	0	.333	.444	.533
1998 Daytona	A+ ChC	100	357	102	20	1	24	196	57	78	46	1	80	7	0	0	5	2	.71	11	.286	.378	.549
1999 West Tenn	AA ChC	105	302	66	20	1	9	115	42	42	39	2	86	7	0	5	2	0	1.00	6	.219	.317	.381
3 Min. YEARS		263	863	239	50	3	43	424	130	164	105	10	216	19	0	7	7	3	.70	23	.277	.365	.491

Tyler Walker

Pitches: Right **Bats:** Right **Pos:** P **Ht:** 6'3" **Wt:** 250 **Born:** 5/15/76 **Age:** 24

Year Team	Lg Org	G	GS	CG	GF	IP	BFP	H	R	ER	HR	SH	SF	HB	TBB	IBB	SO	WP	Bk	W	L	Pct.	ShO	Sv	ERA
1997 Mets	R NYM	5	0	0	5	9	37	8	1	1	0	1	0	0	2	1	9	0	0	0	0	.000	0	3	1.00
Pittsfield	A- NYM	1	0	0	0	0.2	6	2	2	1	1	0	0	0	1	0	1	1	0	0	0	.000	0	0	13.50
1998 Capital Cty	A NYM	34	13	0	3	115.2	503	122	63	53	9	3	4	3	38	0	110	8	1	5	5	.500	0	1	4.12
1999 St. Lucie	A+ NYM	13	13	2	0	79.2	329	64	31	26	6	3	2	3	29	2	64	4	1	6	5	.545	0	0	2.94
Binghamton	AA NYM	13	13	0	0	68	306	78	49	47	11	3	2	2	32	0	59	4	3	6	4	.600	0	0	6.22
3 Min. YEARS		66	39	2	8	273	1181	274	146	128	27	10	8	8	102	3	243	17	5	17	14	.548	0	4	4.22

Kent Wallace

Pitches: Right **Bats:** Left **Pos:** P **Ht:** 6'3" **Wt:** 192 **Born:** 8/22/70 **Age:** 29

Year Team	Lg Org	G	GS	CG	GF	IP	BFP	H	R	ER	HR	SH	SF	HB	TBB	IBB	SO	WP	Bk	W	L	Pct.	ShO	Sv	ERA
1992 Oneonta	A- NYY	14	14	1	0	81.1	336	76	32	23	2	1	3	0	11	0	55	3	0	8	4	.667	1	0	2.55
1993 Greensboro	A NYY	13	10	2	2	66	277	63	31	22	2	0	2	2	12	0	49	3	2	4	2	.667	1	2	3.00
1994 Tampa	A+ NYY	39	0	0	17	77.2	310	60	23	18	2	2	3	3	22	4	61	2	0	6	3	.667	0	7	2.09
1995 Norwich	AA NYY	18	16	0	1	94.2	395	93	41	37	9	2	2	1	24	0	72	2	1	7	6	.538	0	0	3.52
Columbus	AAA NYY	9	9	0	0	50.2	200	44	19	17	8	0	0	0	11	0	31	3	0	4	1	.800	0	0	3.02
1996 Yankees	R NYY	1	1	0	0	5	18	3	1	1	0	0	0	0	0	0	5	0	0	1	0	1.000	0	0	1.80
Norwich	AA NYY	1	1	0	0	6	28	10	4	4	2	0	1	0	0	0	1	0	0	0	0	.000	0	0	6.00
Columbus	AAA NYY	13	12	2	0	67.1	284	69	37	35	15	1	1	2	15	0	34	1	0	4	2	.667	0	0	4.68
1998 Grays Harbr	IND —	3	3	0	0	22.2	86	17	5	4	1	0	0	0	2	0	20	0	0	3	0	1.000	0	0	1.59
Jackson	AA Hou	29	0	0	19	49.2	195	37	17	14	4	2	2	2	11	0	51	2	0	3	2	.600	0	11	2.54
New Orleans	AAA Hou	7	0	0	1	7.2	41	16	10	9	2	0	0	0	1	0	7	0	0	0	0	.000	0	0	10.57
1999 Jackson	AA Hou	13	0	0	12	58.2	248	13	4	4	1	1	1	0	6	0	16	1	0	0	1	.000	0	3	2.30
New Orleans	AAA Hou	36	1	0	11	58.2	248	61	30	27	9	1	2	1	13	3	43	1	0	2	2	.500	0	1	4.14
7 Min. YEARS		196	67	5	63	603	2482	562	254	215	57	10	17	11	128	7	445	18	3	42	23	.646	2	24	3.21

Doug Walls

Pitches: Right **Bats:** Left **Pos:** P **Ht:** 6'3" **Wt:** 200 **Born:** 3/21/74 **Age:** 26

Year Team	Lg Org	G	GS	CG	GF	IP	BFP	H	R	ER	HR	SH	SF	HB	TBB	IBB	SO	WP	Bk	W	L	Pct.	ShO	Sv	ERA
1993 Rockies	R Col	10	10	0	0	47.1	218	51	40	24	2	0	1	2	26	0	50	11	2	2	7	.222	0	0	4.56
1994 Asheville	A Col	21	21	1	0	106.1	470	81	66	53	8	0	7	0	71	1	111	18	5	6	10	.375	0	0	4.99
1995 Salem	A+ Col	15	15	0	0	79.2	344	61	39	34	10	1	3	3	49	1	79	5	2	5	5	.500	0	0	3.84
1996 Salem	A+ Col	5	3	0	1	14	70	17	12	11	3	0	3	0	10	0	17	3	0	0	0	.000	0	0	7.07
1997 Portland	A- Col	5	5	0	0	22	92	19	3	3	0	0	1	0	10	0	23	1	0	1	0	1.000	0	0	1.23
Asheville	A Col	10	9	0	1	51.2	227	50	23	17	4	0	1	2	22	0	62	2	1	4	2	.667	0	0	2.96
1998 Salem	A+ Col	27	26	2	0	159	677	145	91	79	10	11	5	9	63	0	169	7	2	6	13	.316	0	0	4.47
1999 Carolina	AA Col	26	26	2	0	150.1	642	159	74	61	14	10	4	4	44	0	140	6	1	10	9	.526	1	0	3.65
7 Min. YEARS		119	115	5	3	630.1	2740	583	350	288	49	25	21	29	295	2	651	51	13	34	46	.425	1	1	4.11

Mike Walter

Pitches: Right Bats: Right Pos: P   Ht: 6'1" Wt: 190 Born: 10/23/74 Age: 25

Year Team	Lg Org	G	GS	CG	GF	IP	BFP	H	R	ER	HR	SH	SF	HB	TBB	IBB	SO	WP	Bk	W	L	Pct.	ShO	Sv	ERA
1993 Astros	R Hou	17	0	0	16	19.1	88	15	10	6	0	1	1	4	12	0	16	3	0	0	1	.000	0	8	2.79
1994 Quad City	A Hou	23	0	0	10	28.1	134	27	18	13	0	2	2	1	20	1	28	4	1	2	2	.500	0	3	4.13
1995 Kissimmee	A+ Hou	41	0	0	21	71.1	338	78	58	44	4	5	9	10	42	1	42	9	2	4	3	.571	0	5	5.55
1996 Quad City	A Hou	52	0	0	48	61.2	261	37	20	14	3	2	1	7	34	1	85	7	1	3	6	.333	0	21	2.04
1997 Jackson	AA Hou	34	0	0	14	44.2	204	38	20	18	6	4	0	3	30	1	41	4	1	2	3	.400	0	7	3.63
1998 Astros	R Hou	3	0	0	1	4	15	2	0	0	0	0	0	0	1	0	6	0	0	0	0	.000	0	1	0.00
Jackson	AA Hou	38	0	0	23	48.1	223	48	31	25	7	3	2	5	22	3	55	4	0	1	7	.125	0	3	4.66
1999 Jackson	AA Hou	34	0	0	20	48.2	221	35	32	26	2	0	1	13	31	0	44	6	0	2	1	.667	0	4	4.81
7 Min. YEARS		242	0	0	153	326.1	1484	280	189	146	22	17	16	43	192	7	317	37	5	14	23	.378	0	47	4.03

Brett Walters

Pitches: Right Bats: Right Pos: P   Ht: 6'0" Wt: 185 Born: 9/30/74 Age: 25

Year Team	Lg Org	G	GS	CG	GF	IP	BFP	H	R	ER	HR	SH	SF	HB	TBB	IBB	SO	WP	Bk	W	L	Pct.	ShO	Sv	ERA
1994 Spokane	A- SD	2	0	0	1	1.2	9	4	1	1	0	1	0	0	0	0	2	1	0	0	0	.000	0	0	5.40
Padres	R SD	14	6	0	8	45.1	175	28	15	11	1	2	0	0	8	0	45	3	0	2	2	.500	0	6	2.18
1995 Clinton	A SD	32	19	4	4	146	598	133	58	44	9	6	1	10	27	3	122	4	2	8	7	.533	0	1	2.71
1996 Rancho Cuca	A+ SD	24	24	0	0	135.1	575	150	73	65	16	10	6	7	39	0	89	1	0	9	9	.500	0	0	4.32
1997 Mobile	AA SD	31	19	0	1	145	625	169	85	72	17	6	2	11	30	0	98	3	1	10	7	.588	0	0	4.47
1998 Mobile	AA SD	14	13	0	1	77	329	86	43	42	9	5	4	2	23	0	51	0	0	7	3	.700	0	0	4.91
1999 Mobile	AA SD	9	0	0	2	13.1	64	13	8	8	3	1	0	1	9	2	12	1	0	0	1	.000	0	0	5.40
Reno	IND —	11	10	0	0	51.1	243	75	42	36	2	1	4	4	15	0	30	6	0	3	3	.500	0	0	6.31
6 Min. YEARS		137	91	4	17	615	2618	658	325	279	57	32	17	35	151	5	449	19	3	39	32	.549	0	7	4.08

Chris Walther

Bats: Right Throws: Right Pos: 1B-3B   Ht: 6'2" Wt: 200 Born: 8/28/76 Age: 23

Year Team	Lg Org	G	AB	H	2B	3B	HR	TB	R	RBI	TBB	IBB	SO	HBP	SH	SF	SB	CS	SB%	GDP	Avg	OBP	SLG
1995 Brewers	R Mil	50	174	45	3	2	0	52	28	19	10	0	9	1	1	0	4	3	.57	5	.259	.303	.299
1996 Ogden	R+ Mil	63	239	84	16	4	6	126	47	54	14	0	21	1	3	2	3	2	.60	7	.351	.387	.527
1997 Beloit	A Mil	113	437	131	25	4	0	164	55	38	28	0	41	5	3	1	5	7	.42	16	.300	.348	.375
1998 Stockton	A+ Mil	115	419	117	20	4	3	154	52	50	21	2	41	8	6	2	2	2	.50	7	.279	.324	.368
1999 Lk Elsinore	A+ Ana	100	380	112	26	2	3	151	48	60	27	3	31	0	1	6	3	3	.50	15	.295	.337	.397
Erie	AA Ana	9	31	11	2	1	1	18	5	6	4	0	4	0	0	0	0	0	.00	3	.355	.429	.581
5 Min. YEARS		450	1680	500	92	17	13	665	235	227	104	5	147	15	14	11	17	17	.50	53	.298	.342	.396

Jerome Walton

Bats: Right Throws: Right Pos: OF   Ht: 6'1" Wt: 200 Born: 7/8/65 Age: 34

Year Team	Lg Org	G	AB	H	2B	3B	HR	TB	R	RBI	TBB	IBB	SO	HBP	SH	SF	SB	CS	SB%	GDP	Avg	OBP	SLG
1986 Wytheville	R+ ChC	62	229	66	7	4	5	96	48	34	28	0	40	6	3	3	21	3	.88	3	.288	.376	.419
1987 Peoria	A ChC	128	472	158	24	11	6	222	102	38	91	2	91	11	5	1	49	25	.66	9	.335	.452	.470
1988 Pittsfield	AA ChC	120	414	137	26	2	3	176	64	49	41	1	69	8	4	3	42	13	.76	6	.331	.399	.425
1989 Iowa	AAA ChC	4	18	6	1	0	1	10	4	3	1	0	5	0	0	0	2	1	.67	0	.333	.368	.556
1990 Iowa	AAA ChC	4	16	3	0	0	1	6	3	1	2	0	4	0	0	0	0	0	.00	0	.188	.278	.375
1992 Iowa	AAA ChC	7	27	8	2	1	0	12	8	3	4	0	6	0	0	0	1	1	.50	0	.296	.387	.444
1993 Vancouver	AAA Ana	54	176	55	11	1	2	74	34	20	16	0	24	1	8	1	5	4	.56	6	.313	.371	.420
1996 Greenville	AA Atl	3	5	1	0	1	0	3	0	0	3	0	1	0	0	0	0	0	.00	1	.200	.500	.600
Richmond	AA Atl	6	18	8	2	1	1	15	3	5	1	0	5	1	0	0	0	0	.00	0	.444	.500	.833
1997 Frederick	A+ Bal	7	19	4	0	0	1	7	1	2	5	0	0	0	0	0	1	1	.50	0	.211	.375	.368
1999 Somerset	IND —	17	53	20	3	0	2	29	12	7	17	0	8	0	0	1	6	2	.75	2	.377	.521	.547
Calgary	AAA Fla	26	84	27	8	1	0	37	12	12	5	0	12	2	0	1	5	1	.83	1	.321	.370	.440
1989 Chicago	NL	116	475	139	23	3	5	183	64	46	27	1	77	6	2	5	24	7	.77	6	.293	.335	.385
1990 Chicago	NL	101	392	103	16	2	2	129	63	21	50	1	70	4	1	2	14	7	.67	4	.263	.350	.329
1991 Chicago	NL	123	270	59	13	1	5	89	42	17	19	0	55	3	3	3	7	3	.70	7	.219	.275	.330
1992 Chicago	NL	30	55	7	0	1	0	9	7	1	9	0	13	2	3	0	1	2	.33	1	.127	.273	.164
1993 California	AL	5	2	0	0	0	0	0	2	0	1	0	2	0	0	0	0	0	1.00	0	.000	.333	.000
1994 Cincinnati	NL	46	68	21	4	0	1	28	10	9	4	0	12	0	1	0	1	3	.25	2	.309	.347	.412
1995 Cincinnati	NL	102	162	47	12	1	8	85	32	22	17	0	25	4	3	2	10	7	.59	0	.290	.368	.525
1996 Atlanta	NL	37	47	16	5	0	1	24	9	4	5	0	10	0	1	2	0	0	.00	1	.340	.389	.511
1997 Baltimore	AL	26	68	20	1	0	3	30	8	9	4	0	10	0	2	0	0	0	.00	3	.294	.333	.441
1998 Tampa Bay	AL	12	34	11	3	0	0	14	4	3	2	0	6	0	0	0	0	0	.00	1	.324	.361	.412
10 Min. YEARS		438	1531	493	84	22	22	687	291	174	214	3	265	29	20	10	132	51	.72	28	.322	.413	.449
10 Maj. YEARS		598	1573	423	77	8	25	591	241	132	138	2	280	19	16	14	58	29	.67	25	.269	.333	.376

Jeremy Ward

Pitches: Right Bats: Right Pos: P   Ht: 6'3" Wt: 220 Born: 2/24/78 Age: 22

Year Team	Lg Org	G	GS	CG	GF	IP	BFP	H	R	ER	HR	SH	SF	HB	TBB	IBB	SO	WP	Bk	W	L	Pct.	ShO	Sv	ERA
1999 High Desert	A+ Ari	4	4	0	0	8.2	35	5	2	2	0	0	0	1	3	0	12	0	4	0	0	.000	0	0	2.08
El Paso	AA Ari	19	0	0	17	25.2	101	18	7	7	1	0	1	0	9	1	26	1	0	1	1	.500	0	7	2.45
Tucson	AAA Ari	1	0	0	0	1.2	8	2	0	0	0	0	0	0	2	0	1	1	0	0	0	.000	0	0	0.00
1 Min. YEARS		24	4	0	17	36	144	25	9	9	1	0	1	1	14	1	39	2	4	1	1	.500	0	7	2.25

Jeremy Ware

Bats: Right Throws: Right Pos: OF Ht: 6'1" Wt: 190 Born: 10/23/75 Age: 24

Year Team	Lg Org	G	AB	H	2B	3B	HR	TB	R	RBI	TBB	IBB	SO	HBP	SH	SF	SB	CS	SB%	GDP	Avg	OBP	SLG
1995 Expos	R Mon	38	116	28	4	2	2	42	18	15	18	0	28	3	0	1	5	4	.56	2	.241	.355	.362
1996 Expos	R Mon	15	44	16	3	3	0	25	10	17	9	0	4	0	2	0	6	1	.86	0	.364	.472	.568
Vermont	A- Mon	32	94	18	2	0	0	20	12	6	15	0	25	0	1	0	5	3	.63	1	.191	.303	.213
1997 Cape Fear	A Mon	138	529	139	32	5	16	229	84	77	43	2	114	6	0	6	32	7	.82	8	.263	.322	.433
1998 Jupiter	A+ Mon	127	492	121	35	3	10	192	51	64	23	1	102	7	4	7	21	5	.81	16	.246	.285	.390
1999 Jupiter	A+ Mon	7	25	8	2	0	2	16	5	11	2	0	5	0	0	0	3	0	1.00	0	.320	.370	.640
Harrisburg	AA Mon	111	381	100	23	2	9	154	57	56	41	2	79	2	2	5	12	5	.71	19	.262	.333	.404
5 Min. YEARS		468	1681	430	101	15	39	678	237	246	151	5	357	18	9	19	84	25	.77	46	.256	.320	.403

Mike Warner

Bats: Left Throws: Left Pos: OF Ht: 5'10" Wt: 170 Born: 5/9/71 Age: 29

Year Team	Lg Org	G	AB	H	2B	3B	HR	TB	R	RBI	TBB	IBB	SO	HBP	SH	SF	SB	CS	SB%	GDP	Avg	OBP	SLG
1992 Idaho Falls	R+ Atl	10	33	9	3	0	1	15	4	6	3	0	5	0	0	0	1	0	1.00	0	.273	.333	.455
Macon	A Atl	50	180	50	7	2	1	64	40	8	34	0	28	0	3	0	21	4	.84	2	.278	.393	.356
1993 Durham	A+ Atl	77	263	84	18	4	5	125	55	32	50	3	45	2	3	3	29	12	.71	4	.319	.428	.475
Greenville	AA Atl	5	20	7	0	2	0	11	4	3	2	0	4	0	0	0	2	1	.67	0	.350	.409	.550
1994 Durham	A+ Atl	88	321	103	23	8	13	181	80	44	51	1	50	2	1	1	24	10	.71	3	.321	.416	.564
Greenville	AA Atl	16	55	18	5	0	1	26	13	3	9	0	5	1	0	0	3	0	1.00	0	.327	.431	.473
1995 Richmond	AAA Atl	28	97	20	4	1	2	32	10	8	10	0	21	1	2	0	0	3	.00	0	.206	.287	.330
Greenville	AA Atl	53	173	41	12	0	0	53	31	7	47	0	36	1	2	2	12	4	.75	1	.237	.399	.306
1996 Durham	A+ Atl	3	9	1	1	0	0	2	1	2	2	0	2	1	0	0	1	0	1.00	0	.111	.333	.222
Richmond	AAA Atl	7	29	6	1	0	0	7	4	1	1	0	8	0	0	0	1	2	.33	0	.207	.233	.241
Greenville	AA Atl	64	205	53	19	2	6	94	39	33	47	0	45	4	3	0	10	7	.59	4	.259	.406	.459
1997 Greenville	AA Atl	91	303	97	22	3	7	146	58	35	61	6	61	1	3	3	12	9	.57	1	.320	.432	.482
1998 Richmond	AAA Atl	96	322	71	16	5	6	115	42	27	47	1	85	0	1	0	7	5	.58	2	.220	.320	.357
Greenville	AA Atl	23	78	20	6	1	2	34	12	5	17	2	19	1	1	0	3	3	.50	1	.256	.396	.436
1999 San Antonio	AA LA	62	191	63	16	5	3	98	35	25	34	1	29	2	1	1	12	6	.67	2	.330	.434	.513
8 Min. YEARS		673	2279	643	153	33	47	1003	428	239	415	14	443	16	20	10	138	66	.68	20	.282	.395	.440

Ron Warner

Bats: Right Throws: Right Pos: OF Ht: 6'3" Wt: 185 Born: 12/2/68 Age: 31

Year Team	Lg Org	G	AB	H	2B	3B	HR	TB	R	RBI	TBB	IBB	SO	HBP	SH	SF	SB	CS	SB%	GDP	Avg	OBP	SLG
1991 Hamilton	A- StL	71	219	66	11	3	1	86	31	20	28	0	43	3	4	1	9	2	.82	4	.301	.386	.393
1992 Savannah	A StL	85	242	53	8	1	0	63	30	12	29	2	63	1	5	2	2	3	.40	5	.219	.303	.260
1993 St. Pete	A+ StL	103	311	90	8	3	4	116	42	37	31	2	39	5	7	4	5	1	.83	9	.289	.359	.373
1994 Arkansas	AA StL	95	233	56	14	1	4	84	28	25	39	5	57	1	2	0	1	1	.50	4	.240	.352	.361
1995 Arkansas	AA StL	47	98	24	3	0	0	27	9	8	16	1	15	1	3	2	0	0	.00	3	.245	.350	.276
1996 Arkansas	AA StL	84	233	70	22	4	6	118	36	39	38	1	25	1	2	2	5	1	.83	4	.300	.398	.506
1997 Louisville	AAA StL	101	276	64	16	0	7	101	43	30	42	0	45	1	6	1	4	1	.80	8	.232	.334	.366
1998 Memphis	AAA StL	116	370	100	29	1	7	152	57	38	42	0	68	4	1	2	3	5	.38	5	.270	.349	.411
1999 Memphis	AAA StL	90	245	71	14	1	11	120	35	33	32	2	70	3	0	2	8	2	.80	3	.290	.376	.490
9 Min. YEARS		792	2227	594	125	14	40	867	311	242	297	13	425	20	30	16	37	16	.70	46	.267	.356	.389

B.J. Waszgis

Bats: Right Throws: Right Pos: C Ht: 6'2" Wt: 215 Born: 8/24/70 Age: 29

Year Team	Lg Org	G	AB	H	2B	3B	HR	TB	R	RBI	TBB	IBB	SO	HBP	SH	SF	SB	CS	SB%	GDP	Avg	OBP	SLG
1991 Bluefield	R+ Bal	12	35	8	1	0	3	18	8	8	5	0	11	1	0	0	3	0	1.00	1	.229	.341	.514
1992 Kane County	A Bal	111	340	73	18	1	11	126	39	47	54	2	94	4	3	2	3	2	.60	8	.215	.328	.371
1993 Frederick	A+ Bal	31	109	27	4	0	3	40	12	9	9	0	30	2	0	1	1	1	.50	2	.248	.314	.367
Albany	A Bal	86	300	92	25	3	8	147	45	52	27	0	55	6	0	5	4	0	1.00	8	.307	.370	.490
1994 Frederick	A+ Bal	122	426	120	16	3	21	205	76	100	65	2	94	5	3	4	6	1	.86	9	.282	.380	.481
1995 Bowie	AA Bal	130	438	111	22	0	10	163	53	50	70	1	91	9	1	3	2	4	.33	5	.253	.365	.372
1996 Rochester	AAA Bal	96	304	81	16	0	11	130	37	48	41	0	87	4	1	1	2	3	.40	7	.266	.360	.428
1997 Rochester	AAA Bal	100	315	82	15	1	13	138	61	48	56	1	78	9	4	4	1	1	.50	5	.260	.383	.438
1998 Pawtucket	AAA Bos	66	208	42	9	0	9	78	31	41	26	0	52	0	4	3	2	4	.33	7	.202	.287	.375
1999 Columbus	AAA NYY	63	191	53	12	0	6	83	36	31	27	2	55	6	2	1	4	2	.67	4	.277	.382	.435
9 Min. YEARS		817	2666	689	138	8	95	1128	398	434	380	8	647	46	18	24	28	18	.61	50	.258	.358	.423

Dusty Wathan

Bats: Right Throws: Right Pos: C Ht: 6'4" Wt: 215 Born: 8/22/73 Age: 26

Year Team	Lg Org	G	AB	H	2B	3B	HR	TB	R	RBI	TBB	IBB	SO	HBP	SH	SF	SB	CS	SB%	GDP	Avg	OBP	SLG
1994 Mariners	R Sea	35	86	18	2	0	1	23	14	7	11	0	13	3	0	0	0	0	.00	0	.209	.320	.267
1995 Wisconsin	A Sea	5	11	1	0	0	1	4	1	3	0	0	3	1	0	0	0	0	.00	0	.091	.167	.364
Everett	A- Sea	53	181	49	9	1	6	78	32	25	17	0	26	7	1	0	2	1	.67	4	.271	.356	.431
1996 Lancaster	A+ Sea	74	246	64	10	1	8	100	41	40	26	0	65	6	3	1	1	1	.50	5	.260	.344	.407
1997 Lancaster	A+ Sea	56	202	60	17	0	4	89	27	35	21	0	51	7	1	1	0	1	.00	7	.297	.381	.441
Memphis	AA Sea	49	149	40	4	1	4	58	20	19	19	0	28	5	0	1	1	1	.50	4	.268	.368	.389
1998 Tacoma	AAA Sea	19	51	15	1	0	0	18	6	8	6	0	10	2	2	0	0	0	.00	4	.294	.390	.353
Orlando	AA Sea	69	234	60	10	0	2	76	32	21	28	2	39	15	2	2	3	1	.75	8	.256	.369	.325
1999 New Haven	AA Sea	96	333	93	16	2	4	125	37	37	24	1	60	12	4	1	4	1	.80	11	.279	.349	.375
6 Min. YEARS		456	1493	400	69	6	30	571	210	195	152	3	295	58	13	6	11	6	.65	43	.268	.357	.382

Scott Watkins

Pitches: Left **Bats:** Left **Pos:** P **Ht:** 6' 3" **Wt:** 180 **Born:** 5/15/70 **Age:** 30

		HOW MUCH HE PITCHED						WHAT HE GAVE UP											THE RESULTS				
Year Team	Lg Org	G	GS	CG	GF	IP	BFP	H	R	ER	HR	SH	SF	HB	TBB	IBB	SO	WP	Bk	W	L	Pct.	ShO	Sv	ERA
1992 Kenosha	A Min	27	0	0	11	46.1	196	43	21	19	4	2	1	3	14	0	58	1	0	2	5	.286	0	1	3.69
1993 Fort Wayne	A Min	15	0	0	8	30.1	124	26	13	11	0	1	2	1	9	0	31	0	1	2	0	1.000	0	1	3.26
Fort Myers	A+ Min	20	0	0	10	27.2	125	27	14	9	0	2	0	0	12	0	41	2	1	2	2	.500	0	3	2.93
Nashville	AA Min	13	0	0	3	16.2	75	19	15	11	2	0	1	1	7	0	17	2	1	0	1	.000	0	0	5.94
1994 Nashville	AA Min	11	0	0	8	13.2	60	13	9	7	1	1	2	0	4	0	11	1	0	1	0	1.000	0	3	4.61
Salt Lake	AAA Min	46	0	0	26	57.1	269	73	46	43	10	4	5	1	28	5	47	1	1	2	6	.250	0	4	6.75
1995 Salt Lake	AAA Min	45	0	0	33	54.2	217	45	18	17	4	1	3	1	13	1	57	1	0	4	2	.667	0	20	2.80
1996 Salt Lake	AAA Min	47	0	0	29	50.1	244	60	46	43	6	5	3	2	34	5	43	3	1	4	6	.400	0	1	7.69
1997 Omaha	AAA KC	9	0	0	4	15.1	72	19	13	11	4	0	1	0	6	0	15	2	1	0	0	.000	0	0	6.46
New Haven	AA Col	13	0	0	8	15.1	58	9	6	6	1	1	1	1	3	0	8	3	0	2	0	1.000	0	0	3.52
1998 Tulsa	AA Tex	10	1	0	4	21	80	14	5	5	1	0	0	0	2	0	25	1	0	1	0	1.000	0	1	2.14
Oklahoma	AAA Tex	38	0	0	22	49.2	214	44	19	18	6	2	1	3	22	1	50	5	0	6	1	.857	0	2	3.26
1999 Iowa	AAA ChC	47	3	0	10	63	287	71	47	43	11	3	3	2	33	1	54	7	0	1	2	.333	0	0	6.14
1995 Minnesota	AL	27	0	0	7	21.2	94	22	14	13	2	1	3	0	11	1	11	0	0	0	0	.000	0	0	5.40
8 Min. YEARS		341	4	0	176	461.1	2021	463	272	243	50	22	23	15	187	13	457	29	6	27	25	.519	0	35	4.74

Mark Watson

Pitches: Left **Bats:** Right **Pos:** P **Ht:** 6'4" **Wt:** 215 **Born:** 1/23/74 **Age:** 26

		HOW MUCH HE PITCHED						WHAT HE GAVE UP											THE RESULTS				
Year Team	Lg Org	G	GS	CG	GF	IP	BFP	H	R	ER	HR	SH	SF	HB	TBB	IBB	SO	WP	Bk	W	L	Pct.	ShO	Sv	ERA
1996 Helena	R+ Mil	13	13	0	0	60.1	262	59	43	32	2	1	2	1	28	0	68	7	0	5	2	.714	0	0	4.77
1997 Beloit	A Mil	8	7	0	0	32.1	153	40	33	24	3	0	3	1	20	0	33	3	0	0	3	.000	0	0	6.68
Ogden	R+ Mil	10	10	1	0	47.2	202	44	26	22	4	1	2	0	19	0	49	2	0	4	3	.571	0	0	4.15
1998 Columbus	A Cle	31	12	1	8	97.2	408	95	53	44	10	3	3	3	32	0	77	6	2	3	4	.429	0	0	4.05
Kinston	A+ Cle	1	1	0	0	6.1	26	3	4	0	0	0	1	0	2	0	8	0	0	0	1	.000	0	0	0.00
1999 Kinston	A+ Cle	11	4	0	1	43.1	163	28	7	5	1	0	0	0	10	0	40	1	1	6	0	1.000	0	0	1.04
Akron	AA Cle	19	17	0	1	110	500	143	64	53	9	6	7	6	38	0	57	6	2	9	8	.529	0	0	4.34
4 Min. YEARS		93	64	2	10	397.2	1714	412	230	180	29	11	18	11	149	0	332	25	5	27	21	.563	0	0	4.07

Alan Webb

Pitches: Left **Bats:** Left **Pos:** P **Ht:** 5'10" **Wt:** 165 **Born:** 9/26/79 **Age:** 20

		HOW MUCH HE PITCHED						WHAT HE GAVE UP											THE RESULTS				
Year Team	Lg Org	G	GS	CG	GF	IP	BFP	H	R	ER	HR	SH	SF	HB	TBB	IBB	SO	WP	Bk	W	L	Pct.	ShO	Sv	ERA
1997 Tigers	R Det	9	8	0	0	33.2	139	27	17	14	3	1	0	2	11	0	46	4	4	3	1	.750	0	0	3.74
1998 W Michigan	A Det	27	27	3	0	172	690	110	69	56	9	4	0	18	58	1	202	10	1	10	7	.588	2	0	2.93
1999 Jacksnville	AA Det	26	22	0	1	140	605	140	88	77	17	1	3	8	64	0	88	4	3	9	9	.500	0	0	4.95
3 Min. YEARS		62	57	3	1	345.2	1434	277	174	147	29	6	3	28	133	1	336	18	8	22	17	.564	2	0	3.83

Ben Weber

Pitches: Right **Bats:** Right **Pos:** P **Ht:** 6'4" **Wt:** 180 **Born:** 11/17/69 **Age:** 30

		HOW MUCH HE PITCHED						WHAT HE GAVE UP											THE RESULTS				
Year Team	Lg Org	G	GS	CG	GF	IP	BFP	H	R	ER	HR	SH	SF	HB	TBB	IBB	SO	WP	Bk	W	L	Pct.	ShO	Sv	ERA
1991 St.Cathrnes	A- Tor	16	14	1	2	97.1	417	105	43	35	3	4	2	4	24	2	60	7	2	6	3	.667	0	0	3.24
1992 Myrtle Bch	A Tor	41	1	0	23	98.2	406	83	27	18	1	2	3	7	29	3	65	7	0	4	7	.364	0	6	1.64
1993 Dunedin	A+ Tor	55	0	0	36	83.1	355	87	36	27	4	9	0	7	25	5	45	7	1	8	3	.727	0	12	2.92
1994 Dunedin	A+ Tor	18	0	0	14	26.1	110	25	8	8	1	6	0	1	5	3	19	1	0	3	2	.600	0	3	2.73
Knoxville	AA Tor	25	10	0	6	95.2	400	103	49	40	8	3	1	6	16	0	55	4	0	4	3	.571	0	0	3.76
1995 Knoxville	AA Tor	12	1	0	6	25.1	104	26	12	11	3	0	0	6	6	0	16	0	0	4	1	.800	0	0	3.91
Syracuse	AAA Tor	25	15	0	3	91.2	403	111	62	55	10	2	1	3	27	1	38	5	0	4	5	.444	1	0	5.40
1996 Salinas	IND —	22	22	2	0	148.1	618	138	68	57	11	11	1	8	42	1	102	15	0	12	6	.667	0	0	3.46
1999 Fresno	AAA SF	51	0	0	19	86.1	358	78	34	32	6	3	3	5	28	2	67	9	0	2	4	.333	0	8	3.34
7 Min. YEARS		265	63	3	109	753	3171	756	339	283	47	40	11	37	202	17	467	55	3	47	34	.580	0	30	3.38

Jake Weber

Bats: Left **Throws:** Right **Pos:** OF **Ht:** 5'11" **Wt:** 188 **Born:** 4/22/76 **Age:** 24

		BATTING														BASERUNNING				PERCENTAGES		
Year Team	Lg Org	G	AB	H	2B	3B	HR	TB	R	RBI	TBB	IBB	SO	HBP	SH	SF	SB	CS	SB%	GDP	Avg	OBP	SLG
1998 Everett	A- Sea	75	275	93	20	2	11	150	75	52	67	3	42	5	2	3	14	7	.67	3	.338	.471	.545
1999 New Haven	AA Sea	136	489	125	22	2	11	184	64	59	66	2	73	3	1	2	5	7	.42	7	.256	.346	.376
2 Min. YEARS		211	764	218	42	4	22	334	139	111	133	5	115	8	3	5	19	14	.58	10	.285	.395	.437

Neil Weber

Pitches: Left **Bats:** Left **Pos:** P **Ht:** 6' 5" **Wt:** 215 **Born:** 12/6/72 **Age:** 27

		HOW MUCH HE PITCHED						WHAT HE GAVE UP											THE RESULTS				
Year Team	Lg Org	G	GS	CG	GF	IP	BFP	H	R	ER	HR	SH	SF	HB	TBB	IBB	SO	WP	Bk	W	L	Pct.	ShO	Sv	ERA
1993 Jamestown	A- Mon	16	16	2	0	94.1	398	84	46	29	3	0	4	4	36	0	80	3	3	6	5	.545	1	0	2.77
1994 Wst Plm Bch	A+ Mon	25	24	1	0	135	566	113	58	48	8	4	4	4	62	0	134	7	5	9	7	.563	0	0	3.20
1995 Harrisburg	AA Mon	28	28	0	0	152.2	696	157	98	85	16	11	7	8	90	1	119	7	1	6	11	.353	0	0	5.01
1996 Harrisburg	AA Mon	18	18	1	0	107	440	90	37	36	8	3	3	5	44	0	74	5	0	7	4	.636	0	0	3.03
1997 Ottawa	AAA Mon	9	9	0	0	39.2	204	46	46	35	7	2	1	2	40	0	27	2	0	2	5	.286	0	0	7.94
Harrisburg	AA Mon	18	18	1	0	112.2	477	93	56	48	17	6	1	8	51	1	121	6	0	7	6	.538	1	0	3.83
1998 Tucson	AAA Ari	46	11	1	6	112.2	508	116	82	64	17	5	3	4	55	0	79	12	1	5	9	.357	0	1	5.11
1999 Tucson	AAA Ari	9	0	0	3	12.2	65	23	16	15	2	0	0	1	4	1	16	0	0	1	1	.500	0	0	10.66
San Antonio	AA LA	12	11	0	0	55	253	62	39	32	3	2	3	6	24	0	31	4	0	4	2	.667	0	0	5.24

295

Year Team	Lg Org	G	GS	CG	GF	IP	BFP	H	R	ER	HR	SH	SF	HB	TBB	IBB	SO	WP	Bk	W	L	Pct.	ShO	Sv	ERA
Albuquerque	AAA LA	9	0	0	4	16.2	87	30	19	19	6	2	1	1	9	0	14	3	0	0	1	.000	0	0	10.26
1998 Arizona	NL	4	0	0	0	2.1	15	5	3	3	0	0	0	0	3	0	4	0	0	0	0	.000	0	0	11.57
7 Min. YEARS		190	135	6	13	838.1	3694	814	497	411	87	35	27	43	415	3	695	49	10	47	51	.480	2	1	4.41

Clint Weibl

Pitches: Right **Bats:** Right **Pos:** P   **Ht:** 6'3" **Wt:** 180 **Born:** 3/17/75 **Age:** 25

Year Team	Lg Org	G	GS	CG	GF	IP	BFP	H	R	ER	HR	SH	SF	HB	TBB	IBB	SO	WP	Bk	W	L	Pct.	ShO	Sv	ERA
1996 Johnson Cy	R+ StL	7	7	0	0	44	172	27	12	10	1	0	0	1	12	0	51	0	0	4	1	.800	0	0	2.05
Peoria	A StL	5	5	0	0	29.2	122	27	16	16	2	0	1	2	7	0	21	0	0	1	2	.333	0	0	4.85
1997 Pr William	A+ StL	29	29	0	0	163	718	185	90	84	18	5	2	9	62	2	135	3	1	12	11	.522	0	0	4.64
1998 Memphis	AAA StL	1	1	0	0	5.2	24	6	5	4	0	0	0	0	2	0	2	2	0	1	0	.000	0	0	6.35
Arkansas	AA StL	25	23	0	0	139	616	161	86	83	22	4	9	5	53	2	85	3	0	12	10	.545	0	0	5.37
1999 Arkansas	AA StL	28	17	1	2	110	483	121	59	57	11	3	0	3	49	1	75	4	1	4	9	.308	0	0	4.66
Memphis	AAA StL	5	0	0	1	8.1	36	10	9	5	2	1	1	0	2	0	8	0	0	1	0	1.000	0	0	5.40
4 Min. YEARS		100	82	1	3	499.2	2171	537	277	259	56	13	13	20	187	5	377	12	2	34	34	.500	0	0	4.67

Mike Welch

Pitches: Right **Bats:** Left **Pos:** P   **Ht:** 6'2" **Wt:** 205 **Born:** 8/25/72 **Age:** 27

Year Team	Lg Org	G	GS	CG	GF	IP	BFP	H	R	ER	HR	SH	SF	HB	TBB	IBB	SO	WP	Bk	W	L	Pct.	ShO	Sv	ERA
1993 Pittsfield	A- NYM	17	0	0	14	31	126	23	9	5	0	2	4	0	6	1	34	3	1	3	1	.750	0	9	1.45
1994 Capital Cty	A NYM	24	24	5	0	159.2	667	151	81	64	14	7	5	11	33	0	127	5	0	7	11	.389	2	0	3.61
1995 St. Lucie	A+ NYM	44	6	0	33	70	322	96	50	42	7	4	3	6	18	4	51	4	0	4	4	.500	0	15	5.40
Binghamton	AA NYM	1	0	0	1	1	3	0	0	0	0	0	0	0	0	0	2	0	0	0	0	.000	0	0	0.00
1996 Binghamton	AA NYM	46	0	0	37	51	216	55	29	26	4	3	1	3	10	0	53	0	0	4	2	.667	0	27	4.59
Norfolk	AAA NYM	10	0	0	5	8.2	36	8	4	4	0	0	0	0	2	0	6	0	0	0	1	.000	0	2	4.15
1997 Norfolk	AAA NYM	46	0	0	38	51.2	216	53	21	21	6	2	2	1	16	2	35	0	0	2	2	.500	0	20	3.66
1998 Scranton-WB	AAA Phi	31	6	0	9	75.1	342	98	56	50	5	8	3	6	17	6	32	1	0	3	4	.429	0	2	5.97
1999 Scranton-WB	AAA Phi	13	5	0	2	34	156	45	30	30	4	0	3	1	13	0	11	1	0	1	2	.333	0	0	7.94
Norfolk	AAA NYM	24	0	0	14	32.2	142	33	17	13	4	1	1	2	13	1	17	3	0	2	2	.500	0	3	3.58
1998 Philadelphia	NL	10	2	0	0	20.2	94	26	19	19	7	1	0	2	7	0	15	0	0	0	2	.000	0	0	8.27
7 Min. YEARS		256	41	5	153	515	2226	562	297	255	44	27	22	30	128	14	368	17	1	26	29	.473	2	75	4.46

Jayson Werth

Bats: Right **Throws:** Right **Pos:** C   **Ht:** 6'6" **Wt:** 191 **Born:** 5/20/79 **Age:** 21

Year Team	Lg Org	G	AB	H	2B	3B	HR	TB	R	RBI	TBB	IBB	SO	HBP	SH	SF	SB	CS	SB%	GDP	Avg	OBP	SLG
1997 Orioles	R Bal	32	88	26	6	0	1	35	16	8	22	0	22	0	0	1	7	1	.88	0	.295	.432	.398
1998 Delmarva	A Bal	120	408	108	20	3	8	158	71	53	50	0	92	15	1	2	21	6	.78	14	.265	.364	.387
Bowie	AA Bal	5	19	3	2	0	0	5	2	1	2	0	6	0	0	0	1	0	1.00	0	.158	.238	.263
1999 Frederick	A+ Bal	66	236	72	10	1	3	93	41	30	37	2	37	3	1	2	16	3	.84	4	.305	.403	.394
Bowie	AA Bal	35	121	33	5	1	1	43	18	11	17	0	26	2	1	3	7	1	.88	1	.273	.364	.355
3 Min. YEARS		258	872	242	43	5	13	334	148	103	128	2	183	20	3	8	52	11	.83	19	.278	.379	.383

David West

Pitches: Left **Bats:** Left **Pos:** P   **Ht:** 6'6" **Wt:** 247 **Born:** 9/1/64 **Age:** 35

Year Team	Lg Org	G	GS	CG	GF	IP	BFP	H	R	ER	HR	SH	SF	HB	TBB	IBB	SO	WP	Bk	W	L	Pct.	ShO	Sv	ERA
1983 Mets	R NYM	12	10	0	2	53.2	—	41	28	17	1	—	—	1	52	1	56	10	1	2	4	.333	0	0	2.85
1984 Columbia	A NYM	12	12	0	0	60.2	288	41	47	42	2	4	2	2	68	1	60	14	1	3	5	.375	0	0	6.23
Little Fall	A- NYM	13	11	0	1	62	290	43	35	23	1	3	4	1	62	0	79	16	2	6	4	.600	0	0	3.34
1985 Columbia	A NYM	26	25	5	0	150	677	105	97	76	6	3	4	9	111	0	194	23	3	10	9	.526	2	0	4.56
1986 Lynchburg	A+ NYM	13	13	1	0	75	343	76	50	43	3	5	3	3	53	0	70	4	1	1	6	.143	0	0	5.16
Columbia	A NYM	13	13	3	0	92.2	403	74	41	30	4	3	3	3	56	1	101	14	2	10	3	.769	1	0	2.91
1987 Jackson	AA NYM	25	25	4	0	166.2	730	152	67	52	5	4	4	4	81	1	186	5	3	10	7	.588	2	0	2.81
1988 Tidewater	AAA NYM	23	23	7	0	160.1	675	106	42	32	5	11	3	9	97	1	143	5	3	12	4	.750	1	0	1.80
1989 Tidewater	AAA NYM	12	12	5	0	87.1	343	60	31	23	9	6	4	2	29	0	69	3	1	7	4	.636	1	0	2.37
1991 Orlando	AA Min	1	1	0	0	0.1	1	0	0	0	0	0	0	0	0	0	0	0	0	0	0	.000	0	0	0.00
Portland	AAA Min	4	4	0	0	15.2	68	12	11	11	3	1	1	0	12	0	15	0	0	1	1	.500	0	0	6.32
1992 Portland	AAA Min	19	18	1	0	101.2	444	88	51	50	6	4	2	2	65	1	87	7	1	7	6	.538	0	0	4.43
1995 Scranton-WB	AAA Phi	1	1	1	0	7	22	2	0	0	0	0	0	0	0	0	6	0	0	1	0	1.000	1	0	0.00
Reading	AA Phi	1	1	0	0	6	23	2	1	1	1	0	0	0	3	0	8	0	0	1	0	1.000	0	0	1.50
1996 Clearwater	A+ Phi	5	5	0	0	23	99	21	8	8	1	0	0	1	11	0	17	3	0	1	0	1.000	0	0	3.13
Scranton-WB	AAA Phi	2	2	0	0	12	52	14	8	7	3	0	0	0	2	0	12	2	0	1	0	1.000	0	0	5.25
1998 New Orleans	AAA Hou	19	2	0	3	31.2	136	26	11	9	2	0	0	1	22	0	33	3	0	1	1	.500	0	0	2.56
Pawtucket	AAA Bos	17	0	0	11	14	100	13	4	0	1	0	0	0	19	1	20	1	0	5	0	1.000	0	3	1.13
1999 Lehigh Vly	IND —	6	5	0	0	27.1	106	19	9	9	4	1	1	1	6	0	33	0	0	2	0	1.000	0	0	2.96
Albuquerque	AAA LA	2	1	0	1	7	29	9	5	5	1	0	1	0	0	0	7	1	0	0	1	.000	0	0	6.43
1988 New York	NL	2	1	0	0	6	25	6	2	2	0	0	0	0	3	0	3	0	0	1	0	1.000	0	0	3.00
1989 New York	NL	11	2	0	0	24.1	112	25	20	20	4	0	1	1	14	2	19	1	0	0	2	.000	0	0	7.40
Minnesota	AL	10	5	0	4	39.1	182	48	28	25	5	2	2	2	19	1	31	1	0	3	2	.600	0	0	6.41
1990 Minnesota	AL	29	27	2	0	146.1	646	142	88	83	21	6	4	4	78	1	92	4	1	7	9	.438	0	0	5.10
1991 Minnesota	AL	15	12	0	0	71.1	305	66	37	36	13	2	3	1	28	0	52	0	0	4	4	.500	0	0	4.54
1992 Minnesota	AL	9	3	0	1	28.1	129	32	24	22	3	2	0	0	20	0	19	2	0	1	3	.250	0	0	6.99
1993 Philadelphia	NL	76	0	0	27	86.1	375	60	37	28	6	8	2	5	51	4	87	3	0	6	4	.600	0	3	2.92
1994 Philadelphia	NL	31	14	0	7	99	429	74	44	39	7	4	2	1	61	2	83	0	0	4	10	.286	0	0	3.55

Year Team	Lg Org	G	GS	CG	GF	IP	BFP	H	R	ER	HR	SH	SF	HB	TBB	IBB	SO	WP	Bk	W	L	Pct.	ShO	Sv	ERA
						HOW MUCH HE PITCHED				WHAT HE GAVE UP												THE RESULTS			
1995 Philadelphia	NL	8	8	0	0	38	163	34	17	16	5	2	0	1	19	0	25	1	0	3	2	.600	0	0	3.79
1996 Philadelphia	NL	7	6	0	0	28.1	126	31	17	15	0	1	0	0	11	0	22	1	1	2	2	.500	0	0	4.76
1998 Boston	AL	6	0	0	0	2	20	7	6	6	1	0	0	0	7	0	4	1	0	0	0	.000	0	0	27.00
13 Min. YEARS		226	184	27	18	1164	—	910	546	441	58	—	—	41	742	8	1199	111	18	80	55	.593	8	3	3.41
10 Maj. YEARS		204	78	2	39	569.1	2522	525	321	295	65	25	16	16	311	10	437	26	4	31	38	.449	0	3	4.66

Jake Westbrook

Pitches: Right Bats: Right Pos: P   Ht: 6'3" Wt: 180 Born: 9/29/77 Age: 22

				HOW MUCH HE PITCHED						WHAT HE GAVE UP											THE RESULTS			
Year Team	Lg Org	G	GS	CG	GF	IP	BFP	H	R	ER	HR	SH	SF	HB	TBB	IBB	SO	WP	Bk	W	L	Pct.	ShO	Sv	ERA
1996 Rockies	R Col	11	11	0	0	62.2	271	66	33	20	0	3	1	8	14	0	57	4	0	4	2	.667	0	0	2.87
Portland	A- Col	4	4	0	0	24.2	99	22	8	7	1	0	0	1	5	0	19	2	0	1	1	.500	0	0	2.55
1997 Asheville	A Col	28	27	3	0	170	736	176	93	81	16	5	6	15	55	0	92	3	0	14	11	.560	2	0	4.29
1998 Jupiter	A+ Mon	27	27	0	0	171	720	169	70	62	11	5	3	11	60	0	79	4	0	11	6	.647	0	0	3.26
1999 Harrisburg	AA Mon	27	27	2	0	174.2	748	180	88	76	14	12	3	13	63	1	90	2	1	11	5	.688	2	0	3.92
4 Min. YEARS		97	96	7	0	603	2574	613	292	246	42	25	13	48	197	1	337	15	1	41	25	.621	4	0	3.67

Gabe Whatley

Bats: Left Throws: Right Pos: OF   Ht: 6'0" Wt: 180 Born: 12/29/71 Age: 28

							BATTING										BASERUNNING				PERCENTAGES		
Year Team	Lg Org	G	AB	H	2B	3B	HR	TB	R	RBI	TBB	IBB	SO	HBP	SH	SF	SB	CS	SB%	GDP	Avg	OBP	SLG
1993 Huntington	R+ ChC	51	175	46	12	1	5	75	30	25	26	0	32	5	1	1	3	2	.60	3	.263	.372	.429
1994 Williamsprt	A- ChC	71	230	56	9	3	2	77	35	25	36	3	32	4	1	1	10	4	.71	6	.243	.354	.335
1995 Rockford	A ChC	95	339	87	23	2	7	135	54	54	45	3	58	6	0	6	11	3	.79	6	.257	.348	.398
Daytona	A+ ChC	15	42	11	3	0	1	17	8	5	7	0	5	0	0	0	2	0	1.00	6	.262	.367	.405
1996 Daytona	A+ ChC	56	186	42	14	1	2	64	24	25	26	1	27	1	0	2	9	1	.90	2	.226	.321	.344
Durham	A+ Atl	49	160	53	11	0	3	73	29	26	32	1	23	1	2	0	7	6	.54	2	.331	.446	.456
1997 Durham	A+ Atl	43	154	42	16	0	8	82	37	30	28	0	33	3	0	2	9	1	.90	2	.273	.390	.532
Greenville	AA Atl	95	310	94	17	5	15	166	60	57	50	0	42	6	4	6	5	5	.50	9	.303	.403	.535
1998 Richmond	AAA Atl	135	475	126	36	4	10	200	64	54	53	2	93	5	3	3	11	4	.73	15	.265	.343	.421
1999 Richmond	AAA Atl	82	251	68	14	2	8	110	35	34	38	1	65	4	1	3	8	4	.67	3	.271	.372	.438
7 Min. YEARS		692	2322	625	155	18	61	999	376	335	341	11	410	35	12	24	75	30	.71	48	.269	.368	.430

Chad Whitaker

Bats: Left Throws: Right Pos: OF   Ht: 6'2" Wt: 190 Born: 9/16/76 Age: 23

							BATTING										BASERUNNING				PERCENTAGES		
Year Team	Lg Org	G	AB	H	2B	3B	HR	TB	R	RBI	TBB	IBB	SO	HBP	SH	SF	SB	CS	SB%	GDP	Avg	OBP	SLG
1996 Columbus	A Cle	66	234	55	10	1	12	103	32	29	25	1	80	1	0	1	2	2	.50	4	.235	.310	.440
1997 Columbus	A Cle	109	432	118	25	2	12	183	48	72	23	1	144	5	0	2	3	0	1.00	6	.273	.316	.424
1998 Kinston	A+ Cle	127	455	98	25	0	10	153	46	48	34	1	148	1	0	4	16	10	.62	6	.215	.271	.336
1999 Kinston	A+ Cle	76	280	67	14	0	9	108	34	36	21	1	62	1	0	2	2	3	.40	14	.239	.293	.386
Akron	AA Cle	41	149	48	12	2	5	79	18	38	15	0	40	0	0	2	0	1	.00	3	.322	.380	.530
4 Min. YEARS		419	1550	386	86	5	48	626	178	223	118	6	474	8	0	7	23	16	.59	33	.249	.304	.404

Derrick White

Bats: Right Throws: Right Pos: OF-1B   Ht: 6'1" Wt: 225 Born: 10/12/69 Age: 30

							BATTING										BASERUNNING				PERCENTAGES		
Year Team	Lg Org	G	AB	H	2B	3B	HR	TB	R	RBI	TBB	IBB	SO	HBP	SH	SF	SB	CS	SB%	GDP	Avg	OBP	SLG
1991 Jamestown	A- Mon	72	271	89	10	4	6	125	46	49	40	0	46	7	0	2	8	3	.73	8	.328	.425	.461
1992 Harrisburg	AA Mon	134	495	137	19	2	13	199	63	81	40	3	73	7	0	2	17	3	.85	16	.277	.338	.402
1993 Wst Plm Bch	A+ Mon	6	25	5	0	0	0	5	1	1	1	0	2	0	0	0	2	0	1.00	0	.200	.231	.200
Ottawa	AAA Mon	67	249	70	15	1	4	99	32	29	20	2	52	3	0	1	10	7	.59	10	.281	.341	.398
Harrisburg	AA Mon	21	79	18	1	0	2	25	14	12	5	0	17	2	0	1	2	0	1.00	2	.228	.287	.316
1994 Ottawa	AAA Mon	47	99	21	4	0	0	25	13	9	8	1	25	1	1	1	4	1	.80	3	.212	.275	.253
Portland	AA Fla	74	264	71	13	2	4	100	39	34	28	1	52	3	0	1	14	7	.67	5	.269	.343	.379
1995 Toledo	AAA Det	87	309	82	15	3	14	145	50	49	29	3	65	4	0	4	6	6	.50	12	.265	.332	.469
1996 W Michigan	A Oak	73	263	69	17	0	10	116	49	43	44	2	63	6	0	4	12	3	.80	7	.262	.375	.441
Modesto	A+ Oak	54	197	58	15	1	7	96	45	39	29	1	41	4	0	3	8	3	.73	1	.294	.391	.487
1997 Midland	AA Ana	10	37	7	2	0	0	9	2	3	5	0	6	1	0	0	1	0	1.00	1	.189	.302	.243
Vancouver	AAA Ana	116	414	134	35	2	11	206	64	65	44	2	73	7	1	2	11	7	.61	12	.324	.396	.498
1998 Iowa	AAA ChC	66	251	91	17	2	18	166	57	76	38	3	48	4	0	2	4	5	.44	4	.363	.451	.661
Colo Sprngs	AAA Col	22	81	23	5	0	2	34	15	10	10	0	14	2	0	2	2	1	.67	3	.284	.368	.420
1999 Iowa	AAA ChC	132	503	132	31	0	13	202	75	77	47	5	94	7	0	6	10	8	.56	11	.262	.330	.402
1993 Montreal	NL	17	49	11	3	0	2	20	6	4	2	1	12	1	0	0	2	0	1.00	1	.224	.269	.408
1995 Detroit	AL	39	48	9	2	0	0	11	3	2	1	0	7	0	0	0	1	0	1.00	1	.188	.188	.229
1998 Chicago	NL	11	10	1	0	0	1	4	1	2	0	0	5	0	0	0	0	0	.00	0	.100	.100	.400
Colorado	NL	9	9	0	0	0	0	0	0	0	0	0	4	0	0	0	0	0	.00	0	.000	.000	.000
9 Min. YEARS		981	3537	1007	199	17	104	1552	565	577	388	23	671	58	2	32	111	54	.67	95	.285	.362	.439
3 Maj. YEARS		76	116	21	5	0	3	35	10	8	2	1	28	1	0	0	3	0	1.00	2	.181	.202	.302

Walt White

Bats: Right Throws: Right Pos: 2B   Ht: 6'0" Wt: 195 Born: 12/12/71 Age: 28

							BATTING										BASERUNNING				PERCENTAGES		
Year Team	Lg Org	G	AB	H	2B	3B	HR	TB	R	RBI	TBB	IBB	SO	HBP	SH	SF	SB	CS	SB%	GDP	Avg	OBP	SLG
1994 Elmira	A- Fla	70	215	57	7	0	0	64	41	19	27	0	45	4	2	1	0	2	.00	4	.265	.356	.298
1995 Kane County	A Fla	63	207	59	18	2	1	84	30	23	32	0	52	3	5	3	3	2	.60	3	.285	.384	.406

Year Team	Lg Org	G	AB	H	2B	3B	HR	TB	R	RBI	TBB	IBB	SO	HBP	SH	SF	SB	CS	SB%	GDP	Avg	OBP	SLG
1996 Kane County	A Fla	95	308	54	15	3	1	78	26	24	35	0	90	4	5	1	1	4	.20	3	.175	.267	.253
1997 Brevard Cty	A+ Fla	54	163	33	8	0	1	44	18	15	14	1	41	1	0	1	0	0	.00	4	.202	.268	.270
1998 Brevard Cty	A+ Fla	13	39	6	0	0	0	6	6	4	7	0	9	0	0	0	0	2	.00	2	.154	.283	.154
Portland	AA Fla	70	203	55	9	2	6	86	23	25	16	0	53	4	2	2	1	1	.50	5	.271	.333	.424
1999 El Paso	AA Ari	13	50	6	3	0	0	9	4	1	2	0	13	0	0	0	0	0	.00	1	.120	.154	.180
Tucson	AAA Ari	54	153	31	8	1	3	50	18	13	14	1	39	0	1	1	0	0	.00	6	.203	.268	.327
6 Min. YEARS		432	1338	301	68	8	12	421	166	124	147	2	342	16	15	9	5	11	.31	28	.225	.307	.315

Curtis Whitley

Pitches: Left Bats: Left Pos: P
Ht: 6'4" Wt: 240 Born: 1/9/74 Age: 26

Year Team	Lg Org	G	GS	CG	GF	IP	BFP	H	R	ER	HR	SH	SF	HB	TBB	IBB	SO	WP	Bk	W	L	Pct.	ShO	Sv	ERA
1997 White Sox	R CWS	3	0	0	1	4.1	21	7	4	3	0	0	0	0	2	0	6	0	0	1	1	.500	0	0	6.23
Hickory	A CWS	9	0	0	6	12.1	58	11	7	5	1	0	0	1	5	0	8	2	0	0	1	.000	0	0	3.65
1998 Hickory	A CWS	22	17	1	1	112.1	498	111	70	52	7	6	5	3	58	0	87	7	0	4	8	.333	1	1	4.17
Winston-Sal	A+ CWS	10	0	0	1	14.1	61	11	2	1	0	0	0	1	6	0	21	1	0	1	0	.000	0	0	0.63
1999 Winston-Sal	A+ CWS	9	0	0	3	8	34	9	4	4	3	0	1	0	4	0	8	0	0	0	0	.000	0	2	4.50
Birmingham	AA CWS	36	0	0	14	50.1	228	58	31	28	4	1	1	0	25	0	24	5	0	4	2	.667	0	1	5.01
3 Min. YEARS		89	17	1	26	201.2	900	207	118	93	15	7	7	5	100	0	154	15	0	9	13	.409	1	4	4.15

Darrell Whitmore

Bats: Left Throws: Right Pos: OF
Ht: 6'1" Wt: 210 Born: 11/18/68 Age: 31

Year Team	Lg Org	G	AB	H	2B	3B	HR	TB	R	RBI	TBB	IBB	SO	HBP	SH	SF	SB	CS	SB%	GDP	Avg	OBP	SLG
1990 Burlington	R+ Cle	30	112	27	3	2	0	34	18	13	9	0	30	2	0	1	9	5	.64	0	.241	.306	.304
1991 Watertown	A- Cle	6	19	7	2	1	0	11	2	3	3	0	2	0	0	0	0	0	.00	0	.368	.455	.579
1992 Kinston	A+ Cle	121	443	124	22	2	10	180	71	52	56	5	92	5	0	5	17	9	.65	8	.280	.363	.406
1993 Edmonton	AAA Fla	73	273	97	24	2	9	152	52	62	22	0	53	0	0	3	11	8	.58	12	.355	.399	.557
1994 Edmonton	AAA Fla	115	421	119	24	5	20	213	72	61	41	3	76	2	0	3	14	3	.82	12	.283	.347	.506
1996 Charlotte	AAA Fla	55	204	62	13	0	11	108	27	36	7	2	43	1	0	2	2	5	.29	2	.304	.327	.529
1997 Syracuse	AAA Tor	58	195	50	15	0	4	77	23	21	24	3	54	1	0	2	7	4	.64	4	.256	.338	.395
Carolina	AA Pit	2	9	3	2	0	0	5	1	2	0	0	2	0	0	0	0	0	.00	0	.333	.333	.556
1998 Nashville	AAA Pit	105	311	96	19	1	21	180	58	50	36	1	87	6	0	2	3	4	.43	5	.309	.389	.579
1999 Indianapolo	AAA Cin	83	238	67	17	1	10	116	39	42	24	2	64	3	0	3	2	1	.67	8	.282	.351	.487
1993 Florida	NL	76	250	51	8	2	4	75	24	19	10	0	72	5	2	0	4	2	.67	8	.204	.249	.300
1994 Florida	NL	9	22	5	1	0	0	6	1	0	3	0	5	0	0	0	1	0	.00	0	.227	.320	.273
1995 Florida	NL	27	58	11	2	0	1	16	6	2	5	0	15	0	0	1	0	0	.00	1	.190	.250	.276
9 Min. YEARS		648	2225	652	141	14	85	1076	363	342	222	16	503	20	0	21	65	39	.63	51	.293	.359	.484
3 Maj. YEARS		112	330	67	11	2	5	97	31	21	18	0	92	5	3	1	4	3	.57	9	.203	.254	.294

Luke Wilcox

Bats: Left Throws: Right Pos: OF
Ht: 6'4" Wt: 190 Born: 11/15/73 Age: 26

Year Team	Lg Org	G	AB	H	2B	3B	HR	TB	R	RBI	TBB	IBB	SO	HBP	SH	SF	SB	CS	SB%	GDP	Avg	OBP	SLG
1995 Oneonta	A- NYY	59	223	73	16	7	1	106	25	28	20	3	28	1	0	2	9	3	.75	4	.327	.382	.475
1996 Tampa	A+ NYY	119	470	133	32	5	11	208	72	76	40	1	71	3	4	6	14	10	.58	14	.283	.339	.443
1997 Tampa	A+ NYY	12	40	12	4	0	0	16	7	4	7	2	6	1	0	1	1	1	.50	0	.300	.408	.400
Norwich	AA NYY	74	300	83	13	1	6	116	45	34	18	1	36	3	1	1	13	3	.81	6	.277	.323	.387
1998 Orlando	AA TB	88	331	95	23	3	17	175	57	69	39	5	54	5	0	6	2	3	.40	6	.287	.365	.529
Durham	AAA TB	43	151	34	11	0	2	51	17	17	16	0	27	1	0	1	0	0	.00	6	.225	.302	.338
1999 Orlando	AA TB	90	333	90	24	1	20	176	60	64	35	0	54	3	0	4	3	2	.60	9	.270	.341	.529
Durham	AAA TB	39	134	44	12	5	9	93	32	34	22	4	18	1	1	0	1	3	.25	2	.328	.427	.694
5 Min. YEARS		524	1982	564	135	22	66	941	315	326	197	16	294	18	6	21	43	25	.63	47	.285	.351	.475

Brad Wilkerson

Bats: Left Throws: Left Pos: OF
Ht: 6'0" Wt: 190 Born: 6/1/77 Age: 23

Year Team	Lg Org	G	AB	H	2B	3B	HR	TB	R	RBI	TBB	IBB	SO	HBP	SH	SF	SB	CS	SB%	GDP	Avg	OBP	SLG
1999 Harrisburg	AA Mon	138	422	99	21	3	8	150	66	49	88	3	100	7	1	5	3	5	.38	3	.235	.372	.355

Eddie Williams

Bats: Right Throws: Right Pos: DH
Ht: 6'0" Wt: 215 Born: 11/1/64 Age: 35

Year Team	Lg Org	G	AB	H	2B	3B	HR	TB	R	RBI	TBB	IBB	SO	HBP	SH	SF	SB	CS	SB%	GDP	Avg	OBP	SLG
1983 Little Fall	A- NYM	50	190	50	6	2	6	78	30	28	19	0	41	6	0	0	3	1	.75	0	.263	.349	.411
1984 Columbia	A NYM	10	160	29	4	2	2	45	17	24	15	2	31	4	1	0	1	0	1.00	13	.184	.275	.296
Tampa	A+ Cin	50	138	35	8	0	2	49	20	16	25	0	23	5	0	1	0	1	.00	4	.254	.385	.355
1985 Cedar Rapds	A Cin	119	406	106	13	3	20	185	71	83	62	4	101	15	0	5	5	4	.56	14	.261	.375	.456
1986 Waterbury	AA Cle	62	214	51	10	0	7	82	24	30	28	1	41	4	0	4	3	6	.33	4	.238	.332	.383
1987 Buffalo	AAA Cle	131	488	142	29	2	22	241	90	85	55	5	117	15	0	6	6	2	.75	10	.291	.379	.494
1988 Colo Sprngs	AAA Cle	101	365	110	24	3	12	176	53	58	18	4	51	12	0	6	0	2	.00	6	.301	.349	.482
1989 Vancouver	AAA CWS	35	114	28	8	0	1	39	12	13	15	0	18	2	0	1	1	1	.50	1	.246	.344	.342
1990 Las Vegas	AAA SD	93	348	110	29	2	17	194	59	75	42	3	47	8	0	8	0	0	.00	7	.316	.394	.557
1992 Richmond	AAA Atl	24	74	15	3	0	1	21	8	5	3	0	9	1	0	0	0	0	.00	2	.203	.244	.284
1993 New Orleans	AAA Mil	8	27	7	0	1	1	12	2	4	7	0	4	0	0	0	0	0	.00	1	.259	.400	.444
1994 Las Vegas	AAA SD	59	219	77	12	1	20	151	48	54	24	2	34	0	0	0	0	0	.00	12	.352	.417	.689

Year Team	Lg Org	G	AB	H	2B	3B	HR	TB	R	RBI	TBB	IBB	SO	HBP	SH	SF	SB	CS	SB%	GDP	Avg	OBP	SLG
1997 Albuquerque	AAA LA	76	279	102	17	0	29	206	73	76	37	4	45	8	0	2	0	2	.00	9	.366	.451	.738
1998 Las Vegas	AAA SD	90	307	103	24	0	20	187	69	77	33	7	66	6	0	7	1	1	.50	6	.336	.402	.609
1999 Salt Lake	AAA Min	97	345	109	24	0	17	184	56	57	35	1	68	5	0	2	0	1	.00	13	.316	.385	.533
1986 Cleveland	AL	5	7	1	0	0	0	1	2	1	0	0	3	0	0	0	0	0	.00	0	.143	.143	.143
1987 Cleveland	AL	22	64	11	4	0	1	18	9	4	9	0	19	1	0	1	0	0	.00	2	.172	.280	.281
1988 Cleveland	AL	10	21	4	0	0	0	4	3	1	0	0	3	1	1	0	0	0	.00	1	.190	.227	.190
1989 Chicago	AL	66	201	55	8	0	3	72	25	10	18	3	31	4	3	3	1	2	.33	4	.274	.341	.358
1990 San Diego	NL	14	42	12	3	0	3	24	5	4	5	2	6	0	0	0	0	1	.00	1	.286	.362	.571
1994 San Diego	NL	49	175	58	11	1	11	104	32	42	15	1	26	3	2	1	0	1	.00	10	.331	.392	.594
1995 San Diego	NL	97	296	77	11	1	12	126	35	47	23	0	47	4	0	2	0	0	.00	21	.260	.320	.426
1996 Detroit	AL	77	215	43	5	0	6	66	22	26	18	0	50	2	0	1	0	2	.00	8	.200	.267	.307
1997 Los Angeles	NL	8	7	1	0	0	0	1	0	1	1	1	1	0	0	0	0	0	.00	0	.143	.250	.143
Pittsburgh	NL	30	89	22	5	0	3	36	12	11	10	1	24	2	1	1	1	0	1.00	2	.247	.333	.404
1998 San Diego	NL	17	28	4	0	0	0	4	1	3	2	0	6	0	0	1	0	0	.00	1	.143	.194	.143
14 Min. YEARS		1038	3666	1073	211	16	178	1850	632	685	418	33	696	93	1	40	20	21	.49	102	.293	.376	.505
10 Maj. YEARS		395	1145	288	47	2	39	456	146	150	101	8	216	17	7	10	2	6	.25	50	.252	.319	.398

George Williams

Bats: Both **Throws:** Right **Pos:** C　　　**Ht:** 5'10" **Wt:** 214 **Born:** 4/22/69 **Age:** 31

Year Team	Lg Org	G	AB	H	2B	3B	HR	TB	R	RBI	TBB	IBB	SO	HBP	SH	SF	SB	CS	SB%	GDP	Avg	OBP	SLG
1991 Sou Oregon	A- Oak	55	174	41	10	0	2	57	24	24	38	0	36	5	3	1	9	4	.69	1	.236	.385	.328
1992 Madison	A Oak	115	349	106	18	2	5	143	56	42	76	6	53	8	5	1	9	5	.64	10	.304	.438	.410
1993 Huntsville	AA Oak	124	434	128	26	2	14	200	80	77	67	0	66	14	1	6	6	3	.67	10	.295	.401	.461
1994 W Michigan	A Oak	63	221	67	20	1	8	113	40	48	44	3	47	8	1	0	6	3	.67	3	.303	.436	.511
1995 Edmonton	AAA Oak	81	290	90	20	0	13	149	53	55	50	6	52	2	3	2	0	4	.00	9	.310	.413	.514
1996 Edmonton	AAA Oak	14	57	23	5	0	5	43	10	18	6	0	11	2	0	1	0	1	.00	2	.404	.470	.754
1997 Edmonton	AAA Oak	3	7	0	0	0	0	0	0	0	1	0	1	0	0	0	0	0	.00	0	.000	.125	.000
Modesto	A+ Oak	13	44	14	4	0	1	21	8	6	7	2	14	0	0	1	0	1	.00	2	.318	.404	.477
1998 Athletics	R Oak	1	2	1	0	0	0	1	0	0	1	0	0	0	0	0	0	0	.00	0	.500	.667	.500
1999 Salt Lake	AAA Min	74	228	69	16	1	6	105	38	31	42	2	51	6	0	0	0	3	.00	9	.303	.424	.461
New Orleans	AAA Hou	29	100	24	5	0	3	38	18	14	13	2	19	2	0	1	1	1	.50	6	.240	.336	.380
1995 Oakland	AL	29	79	23	5	1	3	39	13	14	11	2	21	2	0	2	0	0	.00	1	.291	.383	.494
1996 Oakland	AL	56	132	20	5	0	3	34	17	10	28	1	32	3	2	1	0	0	.00	2	.152	.311	.258
1997 Oakland	AL	76	201	58	9	1	3	78	30	22	35	0	46	2	2	1	1	0	.00	6	.289	.397	.388
9 Min. YEARS		572	1906	563	124	6	57	870	327	315	345	21	350	47	13	13	31	25	.55	50	.295	.413	.456
3 Maj. YEARS		161	412	101	19	2	9	151	60	46	74	3	99	7	4	4	1	0	.00	6	.245	.366	.367

Glenn Williams

Bats: Right **Throws:** Right **Pos:** 2B　　　**Ht:** 6'2" **Wt:** 170 **Born:** 7/18/77 **Age:** 22

Year Team	Lg Org	G	AB	H	2B	3B	HR	TB	R	RBI	TBB	IBB	SO	HBP	SH	SF	SB	CS	SB%	GDP	Avg	OBP	SLG
1994 Braves	R Atl	24	89	18	2	0	2	26	8	7	9	0	32	0	0	1	4	1	.80	0	.202	.273	.292
Danville	R+ Atl	24	79	20	2	0	1	25	11	9	8	0	20	3	0	0	2	4	.33	4	.253	.344	.316
1995 Macon	A Atl	38	120	21	4	0	0	25	13	14	16	0	42	1	1	3	2	1	.67	3	.175	.271	.208
Eugene	A- Atl	71	268	60	11	4	7	100	39	36	21	1	71	5	0	2	7	4	.64	4	.224	.291	.373
1996 Macon	A Atl	51	181	35	7	3	3	57	14	18	18	2	47	2	1	2	4	2	.67	3	.193	.271	.315
1997 Macon	A Atl	77	297	79	18	2	14	143	52	52	24	1	105	5	1	4	9	6	.60	1	.266	.327	.481
1998 Danville	A+ Atl	134	470	101	26	1	9	156	40	44	37	3	132	6	3	3	1	3	.25	5	.215	.279	.332
1999 Greenville	AA Atl	57	204	46	11	0	4	69	19	15	7	1	58	4	1	1	1	4	.20	2	.225	.264	.338
6 Min. YEARS		476	1708	380	81	10	40	601	196	195	140	8	507	26	7	16	30	25	.55	25	.222	.289	.352

Jason Williams

Bats: Right **Throws:** Right **Pos:** 2B　　　**Ht:** 5'8" **Wt:** 180 **Born:** 12/18/73 **Age:** 26

Year Team	Lg Org	G	AB	H	2B	3B	HR	TB	R	RBI	TBB	IBB	SO	HBP	SH	SF	SB	CS	SB%	GDP	Avg	OBP	SLG
1997 Burlington	A Cin	68	256	83	17	1	7	123	49	41	21	0	40	5	6	3	9	6	.60	6	.324	.382	.480
Chattanooga	AA Cin	69	271	84	21	1	5	122	38	28	18	0	35	6	0	3	5	5	.50	7	.310	.349	.450
1998 Indianapolis	AAA Cin	119	406	108	25	1	2	141	60	45	70	2	63	6	5	7	5	2	.71	10	.266	.376	.347
1999 Chattanooga	AA Cin	87	332	106	27	2	7	158	65	45	46	2	40	6	1	4	3	4	.43	9	.319	.407	.476
Indianapolis	AAA Cin	40	160	61	18	2	2	89	30	19	14	1	25	5	1	1	4	1	.80	4	.381	.444	.556
3 Min. YEARS		383	1425	442	108	7	23	633	242	178	169	5	203	22	14	18	26	18	.59	36	.310	.387	.444

Keith Williams

Bats: Right **Throws:** Right **Pos:** OF　　　**Ht:** 6' 0" **Wt:** 190 **Born:** 4/21/72 **Age:** 28

Year Team	Lg Org	G	AB	H	2B	3B	HR	TB	R	RBI	TBB	IBB	SO	HBP	SH	SF	SB	CS	SB%	GDP	Avg	OBP	SLG
1993 Everett	A- SF	75	288	87	21	5	12	154	57	49	48	4	73	3	2	0	21	7	.75	5	.302	.407	.535
1994 San Jose	A+ SF	128	504	151	30	8	21	260	91	97	60	2	102	4	0	8	4	3	.57	8	.300	.373	.516
1995 Shreveport	AA SF	75	275	84	20	1	9	133	39	55	23	3	39	0	0	7	5	3	.63	5	.305	.351	.484
Phoenix	AAA SF	24	83	25	4	1	2	37	7	14	5	0	11	1	4	2	0	0	.00	4	.301	.341	.446
1996 Phoenix	AAA SF	108	398	109	25	3	13	179	63	63	52	4	96	0	1	5	2	2	.50	9	.274	.354	.450
1997 Phoenix	AAA SF	3	5	1	0	0	0	1	0	0	0	0	2	0	0	0	0	0	.00	0	.200	.200	.200
Shreveport	AA SF	131	493	158	37	7	22	275	83	106	46	3	94	3	0	7	3	0	1.00	12	.320	.377	.558
1998 Fresno	AAA SF	113	353	103	23	2	19	187	47	68	18	1	74	2	1	4	0	1	.00	4	.292	.326	.530
1999 Fresno	AAA SF	89	294	83	23	3	11	145	46	50	34	1	50	2	2	3	4	2	.67	8	.282	.357	.493
1996 San Francisco	NL	9	20	5	0	0	0	5	0	0	0	0	6	0	0	0	0	0	.00	0	.250	.250	.250
7 Min. YEARS		746	2693	801	183	30	109	1371	433	502	286	18	541	15	10	36	39	18	.68	55	.297	.364	.509

Matt Williams

Pitches: Left   Bats: Both   Pos: P   Ht: 6'0"   Wt: 175   Born: 4/12/71   Age: 29

Year Team	Lg Org	G	GS	CG	GF	IP	BFP	H	R	ER	HR	SH	SF	HB	TBB	IBB	SO	WP	Bk	W	L	Pct.	ShO	Sv	ERA
1992 Watertown	A- Cle	6	6	0	0	32.2	130	22	15	8	2	0	4	3	9	0	29	1	2	1	0	1.000	0	0	2.20
1993 Kinston	A+ Cle	27	27	2	0	153.1	672	125	65	54	4	7	5	8	100	0	134	12	6	12	12	.500	1	0	3.17
1994 Canton-Akrn	AA Cle	5	4	0	1	23.2	112	30	22	20	3	1	3	1	14	0	9	1	0	0	3	.000	0	1	7.61
High Desert	A+ Cle	5	5	0	0	18	101	33	29	26	7	2	3	1	13	1	10	2	0	1	4	.200	0	1	13.00
Kinston	A+ Cle	15	15	1	0	81.1	358	86	63	55	17	0	2	2	33	0	67	4	2	4	6	.400	0	0	6.09
1995 Bakersfield	A+ Cle	7	7	0	0	34.1	150	34	9	9	1	3	2	3	14	0	30	1	1	2	0	1.000	0	0	2.36
Kissimmee	A+ Hou	19	18	2	0	101	446	115	60	52	7	5	3	2	44	1	71	5	1	4	6	.400	0	0	4.63
1996 Lynchburg	A+ Pit	23	0	0	5	41.1	189	40	27	24	9	0	1	2	28	1	45	3	1	0	0	.000	0	0	5.23
1997 St. Pete	A+ TB	43	0	0	15	63.2	267	57	26	21	4	2	0	2	24	3	50	3	3	9	5	.643	0	0	2.97
1998 Norwich	AA NYY	31	28	2	0	160.1	719	186	93	82	14	3	7	4	66	2	112	8	2	8	11	.421	0	0	4.60
1999 Norwich	AA NYY	22	0	0	5	30	128	22	9	8	3	0	1	1	18	3	44	3	0	1	1	.500	0	0	2.40
Columbus	AAA NYY	13	1	0	3	21	87	15	9	9	1	0	0	0	11	0	22	0	1	0	2	.000	0	0	3.86
8 Min. YEARS		216	111	7	29	760.2	3359	765	427	368	74	23	31	29	374	11	623	43	19	42	50	.457	1	2	4.35

Shad Williams

Pitches: Right   Bats: Right   Pos: P   Ht: 6'0"   Wt: 198   Born: 3/10/71   Age: 29

Year Team	Lg Org	G	GS	CG	GF	IP	BFP	H	R	ER	HR	SH	SF	HB	TBB	IBB	SO	WP	Bk	W	L	Pct.	ShO	Sv	ERA
1992 Quad City	A Ana	27	26	7	0	179.1	748	161	81	65	14	6	6	7	55	0	152	9	1	13	11	.542	0	0	3.26
1993 Midland	AA Ana	27	27	2	0	175.2	758	192	100	92	16	6	6	3	65	1	91	9	1	7	10	.412	0	0	4.71
1994 Midland	AA Ana	5	5	1	0	32.1	112	13	4	4	1	0	0	1	4	0	29	2	0	3	0	1.000	1	0	1.11
Vancouver	AAA Ana	16	16	1	0	86	386	100	61	44	14	3	2	3	30	0	42	6	0	4	6	.400	1	0	4.60
1995 Vancouver	AAA Ana	25	25	3	0	149.2	627	142	65	56	16	3	3	4	48	2	114	7	1	9	7	.563	1	0	3.37
1996 Vancouver	AAA Ana	15	13	1	1	75	321	73	36	33	8	4	0	2	28	0	57	2	0	6	2	.750	1	0	3.96
1997 Vancouver	AAA Ana	40	10	0	7	99	424	98	52	42	13	0	4	5	41	2	52	5	0	6	2	.750	0	0	3.82
1998 Columbus	AAA NYY	5	1	0	0	12	66	24	19	17	1	0	1	1	8	0	10	0	0	0	1	.000	0	0	12.75
Norwich	AA NYY	9	8	0	0	42	188	55	22	20	4	2	0	2	11	0	18	2	0	4	2	.667	0	0	4.29
Vancouver	AAA Ana	14	10	1	0	68	281	65	30	24	9	2	0	1	18	0	29	2	1	1	4	.200	0	0	3.18
1999 Scranton-WB	AAA Phi	2	2	0	0	5	33	17	11	11	0	0	2	1	3	0	2	0	0	0	2	.000	0	0	19.80
Reading	AA Phi	16	2	0	5	31.2	133	30	17	11	3	3	2	0	10	0	19	1	0	2	2	.500	0	2	3.13
Edmonton	AAA Ana	16	11	1	1	75	303	73	36	31	9	1	3	1	19	0	35	2	0	5	3	.625	0	0	3.72
1996 California	AL	13	2	0	3	28.1	150	42	34	28	7	3	1	2	21	4	26	2	0	0	2	.000	0	0	8.89
1997 Anaheim	AL	1	0	0	1	1	5	1	0	0	0	0	0	0	1	0	0	0	0	0	0	.000	0	0	0.00
8 Min. YEARS		217	156	17	15	1030.2	4380	1043	534	450	108	30	29	31	340	5	650	47	4	60	52	.536	4	2	3.93
2 Maj. YEARS		14	2	0	4	29.1	155	43	34	28	7	3	1	2	22	4	26	2	0	0	2	.000	0	0	8.59

Antone Williamson

Bats: Left   Throws: Right   Pos: DH   Ht: 6'1"   Wt: 195   Born: 7/18/73   Age: 26

Year Team	Lg Org	G	AB	H	2B	3B	HR	TB	R	RBI	TBB	IBB	SO	HBP	SH	SF	SB	CS	SB%	GDP	Avg	OBP	SLG
1994 Helena	R+ Mil	6	26	11	2	1	0	15	5	4	2	0	4	0	0	0	0	0	.00	1	.423	.464	.577
Stockton	A+ Mil	23	85	19	4	0	3	32	6	13	7	0	19	0	1	3	0	1	.00	1	.224	.274	.376
El Paso	AA Mil	14	48	12	3	0	1	18	8	9	7	0	8	0	0	1	0	0	.00	1	.250	.339	.375
1995 El Paso	AA Mil	104	392	121	30	6	7	184	62	90	47	3	57	3	0	4	3	1	.75	10	.309	.383	.469
1996 New Orleans	AAA Mil	55	199	52	10	1	5	79	23	23	19	1	40	1	0	2	1	0	1.00	6	.261	.326	.397
1997 Tucson	AAA Mil	83	304	87	20	5	5	132	53	41	49	3	41	3	0	1	3	1	.75	12	.286	.389	.434
1998 Louisville	AAA Mil	29	103	21	8	1	2	37	11	19	13	0	19	0	0	1	0	0	.00	4	.204	.291	.359
1999 Huntsville	AA Mil	12	38	13	3	0	0	16	5	6	7	0	6	1	0	0	3	0	1.00	1	.342	.457	.421
Louisville	AAA Mil	68	184	44	7	0	5	66	21	20	30	0	29	2	0	2	0	1	.00	5	.239	.349	.359
1997 Milwaukee	AL	24	54	11	3	0	0	14	2	6	4	0	8	0	1	1	0	1	.00	2	.204	.254	.259
6 Min. YEARS		394	1379	380	87	14	28	579	194	225	181	7	223	10	1	14	10	4	.71	44	.276	.360	.420

Justin Willoughby

Pitches: Left   Bats: Left   Pos: P   Ht: 6'3"   Wt: 170   Born: 4/9/78   Age: 22

Year Team	Lg Org	G	GS	CG	GF	IP	BFP	H	R	ER	HR	SH	SF	HB	TBB	IBB	SO	WP	Bk	W	L	Pct.	ShO	Sv	ERA
1997 Braves	R Atl	13	6	0	5	42	177	40	24	19	0	0	3	1	12	0	45	1	0	0	2	.000	0	1	4.07
1998 Danville	R+ Atl	13	13	0	0	73.2	320	87	42	33	5	0	2	1	20	0	53	7	2	4	5	.444	0	0	4.03
1999 Jamestown	A- Atl	19	5	0	2	47.2	222	55	35	28	5	2	1	2	16	1	49	8	0	5	3	.625	0	0	5.29
Richmond	AAA Atl	1	0	0	1	1	6	3	1	1	0	0	0	0	0	1	1	1	0	0	0	.000	0	0	9.00
3 Min. YEARS		46	24	0	8	164.1	725	185	102	81	10	2	6	4	48	1	148	17	2	9	10	.474	0	1	4.44

Brandon Wilson

Bats: Right   Throws: Right   Pos: 2B   Ht: 6'1"   Wt: 190   Born: 2/26/69   Age: 31

Year Team	Lg Org	G	AB	H	2B	3B	HR	TB	R	RBI	TBB	IBB	SO	HBP	SH	SF	SB	CS	SB%	GDP	Avg	OBP	SLG
1990 White Sox	R CWS	11	41	11	1	0	0	12	4	5	4	0	5	0	1	1	3	1	.75	1	.268	.326	.293
Utica	A- CWS	53	165	41	1	0	0	43	31	14	28	0	45	0	3	2	14	5	.74	1	.248	.354	.261
1991 South Bend	A CWS	125	463	145	18	6	2	181	75	49	61	2	70	2	7	4	41	11	.79	3	.313	.392	.391
Birmingham	AA CWS	2	10	4	1	0	0	5	3	2	0	0	2	0	0	0	2	0	.00	0	.400	.400	.500
1992 Sarasota	A+ CWS	103	399	118	22	6	4	164	68	54	45	2	64	4	5	2	30	16	.65	4	.296	.371	.411
Birmingham	AA CWS	27	107	29	4	0	0	33	10	4	4	0	16	0	0	0	5	0	1.00	1	.271	.297	.308
1993 Birmingham	AA CWS	137	500	135	19	5	2	170	76	48	52	0	77	3	4	3	43	10	.81	7	.270	.341	.340
1994 Nashville	AAA CWS	114	370	83	16	3	5	120	42	26	30	3	10	2	13	5	.72	4	.224	.286	.324
1995 Nashville	AAA CWS	27	85	25	5	0	1	33	8	10	4	0	11	0	0	3	1	.75	3	.294	.326	.388

Year Team	Lg Org	G	AB	H	2B	3B	HR	TB	R	RBI	TBB	IBB	SO	HBP	SH	SF	SB	CS	SB%	GDP	Avg	OBP	SLG
Indianapols	AAA Cin	4	12	2	0	0	0	2	3	0	2	0	1	0	0	0	0	0	.00	0	.167	.286	.167
Chattanooga	AA Cin	75	308	101	29	1	9	159	56	50	28	0	52	3	2	2	12	6	.67	7	.328	.387	.516
1996 Indianapols	AAA Cin	95	305	71	7	3	4	96	48	31	39	0	53	0	1	2	10	6	.63	8	.233	.318	.315
1997 Indianapols	AAA Cin	68	180	41	3	4	1	55	24	14	18	2	38	1	6	0	5	4	.56	3	.228	.302	.306
Iowa	AAA ChC	19	62	16	2	0	0	18	4	3	2	0	10	0	1	0	3	2	.60	1	.258	.281	.290
1998 Buffalo	AAA Cle	98	337	92	19	2	7	136	53	53	32	0	56	4	2	3	15	5	.75	5	.273	.340	.404
1999 Iowa	AAA ChC	123	472	131	28	6	12	207	82	49	34	1	76	6	8	4	31	5	.86	10	.278	.331	.439
10 Min. YEARS		1081	3816	1045	176	36	47	1434	587	412	383	7	643	26	51	25	228	77	.75	58	.274	.342	.376

Craig Wilson

Bats: Right **Throws:** Right **Pos:** DH   **Ht:** 6'2" **Wt:** 220 **Born:** 11/30/76 **Age:** 23

Year Team	Lg Org	G	AB	H	2B	3B	HR	TB	R	RBI	TBB	IBB	SO	HBP	SH	SF	SB	CS	SB%	GDP	Avg	OBP	SLG
1995 Medcine Hat	R+ Tor	49	184	52	14	1	7	89	33	35	24	1	41	3	0	4	8	2	.80	1	.283	.367	.484
1996 Hagerstown	A Tor	131	495	129	21	5	11	199	66	70	32	1	120	10	0	4	17	11	.61	12	.261	.316	.402
1997 Lynchburg	A+ Pit	117	401	106	26	1	19	191	54	69	39	6	98	15	1	2	6	5	.55	3	.264	.350	.476
1998 Lynchburg	A+ Pit	61	219	59	12	2	12	111	26	45	22	1	53	5	0	1	2	1	.67	3	.269	.348	.507
Carolina	AA Pit	45	148	49	11	0	5	75	20	21	14	0	32	4	0	2	4	1	.80	2	.331	.399	.507
1999 Altoona	AA Pit	111	362	97	21	3	20	184	57	69	40	0	104	19	1	4	1	3	.25	8	.268	.367	.508
5 Min. YEARS		514	1809	492	111	12	74	849	256	309	171	9	448	56	2	17	38	23	.62	29	.272	.350	.469

Desi Wilson

Bats: Left **Throws:** Left **Pos:** 1B   **Ht:** 6'7" **Wt:** 230 **Born:** 5/9/69 **Age:** 31

Year Team	Lg Org	G	AB	H	2B	3B	HR	TB	R	RBI	TBB	IBB	SO	HBP	SH	SF	SB	CS	SB%	GDP	Avg	OBP	SLG
1991 Rangers	R Tex	8	25	4	2	0	0	6	1	7	3	0	2	0	0	1	0	0	.00	0	.160	.241	.240
1992 Butte	R+ Tex	72	253	81	9	4	5	113	45	42	31	1	45	1	0	0	13	11	.54	1	.320	.396	.447
1993 Charlotte	A+ Tex	131	511	156	21	7	3	200	83	70	50	4	90	7	0	2	29	11	.73	18	.305	.374	.391
1994 Tulsa	AA Tex	129	493	142	27	0	6	187	69	55	40	5	115	2	0	1	16	14	.53	14	.288	.343	.379
1995 Shreveport	AA SF	122	482	138	27	3	5	186	77	72	40	2	68	1	0	7	11	9	.55	18	.286	.338	.386
1996 Phoenix	AAA SF	113	407	138	26	7	5	193	56	59	18	3	80	3	0	3	15	4	.79	9	.339	.369	.474
1997 Phoenix	AAA SF	121	451	155	27	6	7	215	76	53	44	5	73	4	0	3	16	3	.84	11	.344	.404	.477
1999 Tucson	AAA Ari	130	452	146	27	7	6	205	65	62	34	2	76	2	0	3	2	3	.40	18	.323	.371	.454
1996 San Francisco	NL	41	118	32	2	0	2	40	10	12	12	2	27	0	0	0	2	0	.00	2	.271	.338	.339
8 Min. YEARS		826	3074	960	166	34	37	1305	472	420	260	22	549	20	0	20	102	55	.65	89	.312	.368	.425

Kris Wilson

Pitches: Right **Bats:** Right **Pos:** P   **Ht:** 6'4" **Wt:** 225 **Born:** 8/6/76 **Age:** 23

Year Team	Lg Org	G	GS	CG	GF	IP	BFP	H	R	ER	HR	SH	SF	HB	TBB	IBB	SO	WP	Bk	W	L	Pct.	ShO	Sv	ERA
1997 Spokane	A- KC	15	15	0	0	73.2	345	101	50	37	6	0	3	5	21	1	72	1	2	5	3	.625	0	0	4.52
1998 Wilmington	A+ KC	10	2	0	4	24	96	19	10	10	0	2	2	3	6	1	20	1	0	0	3	.000	0	1	3.75
Lansing	A KC	18	18	1	0	117.1	470	119	50	46	7	3	3	3	15	0	74	2	0	10	5	.667	0	0	3.53
1999 Wilmington	A+ KC	14	4	0	1	48	169	25	7	6	0	0	0		11	0	45	1	0	8	1	.889	0	0	1.13
Omaha	AAA KC	1	1	0	0	5.1	23	8	5	5	3	0	0	0	0	0	3	0	0	1	0	.000	0	0	8.44
Wichita	AA KC	23	10	0	2	74.1	323	91	51	45	11	2	2	3	14	0	45	1	2	5	7	.417	0	0	5.45
3 Min. YEARS		81	50	1	7	342.2	1426	363	173	149	27	7	10	14	67	2	259	6	4	28	20	.583	0	1	3.91

Tom Wilson

Bats: Right **Throws:** Right **Pos:** C   **Ht:** 6'3" **Wt:** 210 **Born:** 12/19/70 **Age:** 29

Year Team	Lg Org	G	AB	H	2B	3B	HR	TB	R	RBI	TBB	IBB	SO	HBP	SH	SF	SB	CS	SB%	GDP	Avg	OBP	SLG
1991 Oneonta	A- NYY	70	243	59	12	2	4	87	38	42	34	2	71	3	0	5	4	4	.50	6	.243	.337	.358
1992 Greensboro	A NYY	117	395	83	22	0	6	123	50	48	68	0	128	3	1	8	2	1	.67	8	.210	.325	.311
1993 Greensboro	A NYY	120	394	98	20	1	10	150	55	63	91	0	112	4	3	8	2	5	.29	5	.249	.388	.381
1994 Albany-Colo	AA NYY	123	408	100	20	1	7	143	54	42	58	2	100	6	4	4	4	6	.40	5	.245	.345	.350
1995 Columbus	AAA NYY	22	62	16	3	1	0	21	11	9	9	0	10	0	2	0	0	0	.00	0	.258	.352	.339
Tampa	A+ NYY	17	48	8	0	0	0	8	3	2	11	0	13	0	1	1	1	0	1.00	0	.167	.317	.167
Norwich	AA NYY	28	84	12	4	0	0	16	6	4	17	0	22	0	0	0	0	0	.00	3	.143	.287	.190
1996 Columbus	AAA NYY	1	1	0	0	0	0	0	0	0	1	0	0	0	0	0	0	0	.00	0	.000	.000	.000
Buffalo	AAA Cle	72	208	56	14	2	9	101	28	30	35	0	66	6	1	0	0	1	.00	0	.269	.390	.486
1997 Columbus	AAA NYY	3	3	0	0	0	0	0	0	0	1	0	0	0	0	0	0	0	.00	0	.000	.250	.000
Norwich	AA NYY	124	419	124	21	4	21	216	88	80	86	0	126	4	0	5	1	4	.20	10	.296	.416	.516
1998 Tucson	AAA Ari	111	370	112	17	3	12	171	59	54	41	3	81	7	0	3	3	1	.75	10	.303	.380	.462
1999 Orlando	AA TB	30	104	30	2	0	7	53	12	23	18	0	34	3	0	1	0	0	.00	2	.288	.405	.510
Durham	AAA TB	67	215	60	19	0	16	127	41	44	49	1	59	0	1	1	0	2	.00	9	.279	.411	.591
9 Min. YEARS		903	2954	758	154	14	92	1216	445	441	519	8	822	36	13	36	17	24	.41	61	.257	.370	.412

Trevor Wilson

Pitches: Left **Bats:** Left **Pos:** P   **Ht:** 6'0" **Wt:** 192 **Born:** 6/7/66 **Age:** 34

Year Team	Lg Org	G	GS	CG	GF	IP	BFP	H	R	ER	HR	SH	SF	HB	TBB	IBB	SO	WP	Bk	W	L	Pct.	ShO	Sv	ERA
1985 Everett	A- SF	17	7	0	8	55.1	0	67	36	26	2	0	0	1	26	0	50	6	2	2	4	.333	0	3	4.23
1986 Clinton	A SF	34	21	0	7	130.2	569	126	70	62	6	3	3	6	64	1	84	5	2	6	11	.353	0	2	4.27
1987 Clinton	A SF	26	26	3	0	161.1	668	130	60	36	3	2	6	6	77	0	146	9	2	10	6	.625	2	0	2.01
1988 Shreveport	AA SF	12	11	0	0	72.2	291	55	19	15	0	2	3	0	23	1	53	1	13	5	4	.556	0	0	1.86

		HOW MUCH HE PITCHED						WHAT HE GAVE UP											THE RESULTS				
Year Team	Lg Org	G	GS	CG	GF	IP	BFP	H	R	ER	HR	SH	SF	HB	TBB	IBB	SO	WP	Bk	W	L	Pct.	ShO	Sv	ERA
Phoenix	AAA SF	11	9	0	0	51.2	233	49	35	29	3	3	1	0	33	2	49	1	4	2	3	.400	0	0	5.05
1989 Phoenix	AAA SF	23	20	2	2	115.1	504	109	49	40	5	5	4	2	76	1	77	5	7	7	7	.500	0	0	3.12
1990 Phoenix	AAA SF	11	10	2	0	66	290	63	31	28	2	4	3	0	44	2	45	1	3	5	5	.500	1	0	3.82
1993 San Jose	A+ SF	2	2	0	0	10	35	4	0	0	0	0	0	0	3	0	8	0	0	1	0	1.000	0	0	0.00
1995 San Jose	A+ SF	2	2	0	0	6.2	29	5	4	1	0	1	0	0	3	0	5	0	0	0	1	.000	0	0	1.35
1998 Vancouver	AAA Ana	21	21	4	0	141.2	604	130	67	57	14	1	2	11	59	0	94	6	4	5	9	.357	1	0	3.62
1999 Columbus	AAA NYY	19	4	0	4	48	207	47	25	19	5	1	1	6	12	0	41	2	3	3	2	.600	0	1	3.56
1988 San Francisco	NL	4	4	0	0	22	96	25	14	10	1	3	1	0	8	0	15	0	1	0	2	.000	0	0	4.09
1989 San Francisco	NL	14	4	0	2	39.1	167	28	20	19	2	3	1	4	24	0	22	0	1	2	3	.400	0	0	4.35
1990 San Francisco	NL	27	17	3	3	110.1	457	87	52	49	11	6	2	1	49	3	66	5	2	8	7	.533	2	0	4.00
1991 San Francisco	NL	44	29	2	6	202	841	173	87	80	13	14	5	5	77	4	139	5	3	13	11	.542	1	0	3.56
1992 San Francisco	NL	26	26	1	0	154	661	152	82	72	18	11	6	6	64	5	88	2	7	8	14	.364	1	0	4.21
1993 San Francisco	NL	22	18	1	1	110	455	110	45	44	8	6	3	6	40	3	57	0	0	7	5	.583	0	0	3.60
1995 San Francisco	NL	17	17	0	0	82.2	354	82	42	36	8	5	2	4	38	1	38	0	1	3	4	.429	0	0	3.92
1998 Anaheim	AL	15	0	0	2	7.2	37	8	4	3	0	0	1	1	5	2	6	0	0	0	0	.000	0	0	3.52
10 Min. YEARS		178	133	11	21	859.1	3430	785	396	313	40	22	23	32	420	7	652	36	40	46	52	.469	4	6	3.28
8 Maj. YEARS		169	115	7	14	728	3068	665	346	313	61	48	21	27	305	18	431	12	15	41	46	.471	4	0	3.87

Chris Wimmer

Bats: Right **Throws:** Right **Pos:** 2B **Ht:** 5'11" **Wt:** 175 **Born:** 9/25/70 **Age:** 20

		BATTING														BASERUNNING				PERCENTAGES		
Year Team	Lg Org	G	AB	H	2B	3B	HR	TB	R	RBI	TBB	IBB	SO	HBP	SH	SF	SB	CS	SB%	GDP	Avg	OBP	SLG
1993 San Jose	A+ SF	123	493	130	21	4	3	168	76	53	42	1	72	8	7	6	49	12	.80	6	.264	.328	.341
1994 Shreveport	AA SF	126	462	131	21	3	4	170	63	49	25	2	56	8	5	4	21	13	.62	7	.284	.329	.368
1995 Phoenix	AAA SF	132	449	118	23	4	2	155	55	44	31	1	49	13	5	5	13	7	.65	10	.263	.325	.345
1996 Louisville	AAA StL	112	345	86	11	2	2	107	40	23	16	0	41	6	3	2	11	3	.79	11	.249	.293	.310
1997 Louisville	AAA StL	5	12	2	0	0	0	2	0	1	0	0	1	0	0	0	0	0	.00	0	.167	.167	.167
Orlando	AA ChC	102	371	102	15	3	2	129	62	28	23	0	37	10	7	1	23	4	.85	13	.275	.333	.348
1998 Carolina	AA Pit	59	218	59	7	1	1	71	28	20	20	0	32	4	1	6	15	8	.65	6	.271	.335	.326
Nashville	AAA Pit	47	135	46	6	0	1	55	18	14	5	1	19	1	1	1	5	2	.71	5	.341	.366	.407
1999 Altoona	AA Pit	27	107	27	5	2	1	39	9	6	8	1	12	4	1	0	5	2	.71	3	.252	.328	.364
7 Min. YEARS		733	2592	701	109	19	16	896	351	238	170	6	319	54	30	25	142	51	.74	61	.270	.326	.346

Matt Wise

Pitches: Right **Bats:** Right **Pos:** P **Ht:** 6'4" **Wt:** 190 **Born:** 11/18/75 **Age:** 24

		HOW MUCH HE PITCHED						WHAT HE GAVE UP											THE RESULTS				
Year Team	Lg Org	G	GS	CG	GF	IP	BFP	H	R	ER	HR	SH	SF	HB	TBB	IBB	SO	WP	Bk	W	L	Pct.	ShO	Sv	ERA
1997 Boise	A- Ana	15	15	0	0	83	342	62	37	30	5	0	1	2	34	0	86	7	3	9	1	.900	0	0	3.25
1998 Midland	AA Ana	27	27	3	0	167.2	735	195	111	101	23	4	5	6	46	0	131	9	0	9	10	.474	0	0	5.42
1999 Erie	AA Ana	16	16	3	0	98	416	102	48	41	10	4	3	4	24	0	72	1	0	8	5	.615	0	0	3.77
3 Min. YEARS		58	58	6	0	348.2	1493	359	196	172	38	8	9	12	104	0	289	17	3	26	16	.619	1	0	4.44

Bryan Wolff

Pitches: Right **Bats:** Right **Pos:** P **Ht:** 6'1" **Wt:** 195 **Born:** 3/16/72 **Age:** 28

		HOW MUCH HE PITCHED						WHAT HE GAVE UP											THE RESULTS				
Year Team	Lg Org	G	GS	CG	GF	IP	BFP	H	R	ER	HR	SH	SF	HB	TBB	IBB	SO	WP	Bk	W	L	Pct.	ShO	Sv	ERA
1993 Spokane	A- SD	25	8	0	7	57	269	52	50	35	4	4	1	5	44	0	48	10	2	3	9	.250	0	1	5.53
1994 Springfield	A SD	60	0	0	47	63.2	298	46	43	38	3	7	1	0	58	4	99	11	4	3	8	.273	0	24	5.37
1995 Rancho Cuca	A+ SD	54	0	0	43	57	262	39	23	21	4	4	3	3	54	0	77	15	0	2	7	.222	0	18	3.32
1996 Wilmington	A+ KC	42	0	0	28	62.1	280	49	35	25	2	3	1	3	38	1	56	6	0	1	2	.333	0	4	3.61
1997 Wichita	AA KC	12	0	0	8	9.2	50	18	7	7	2	1	1	1	5	1	8	1	0	1	1	.500	0	1	6.52
Rancho Cuca	A+ SD	9	2	0	3	33.1	125	19	6	6	2	0	0	3	6	0	39	2	1	3	0	1.000	0	1	1.62
Mobile	AA SD	20	0	0	5	30	141	34	18	16	6	0	1	0	19	1	37	4	1	1	2	.333	0	0	4.80
1998 Las Vegas	AAA SD	9	0	0	5	10.2	50	14	8	8	5	2	0	0	5	0	8	0	0	0	0	.000	0	1	6.75
Mobile	AA SD	33	14	3	7	133.2	527	90	40	34	7	5	2	4	43	2	134	4	1	9	3	.750	2	0	2.29
1999 Las Vegas	AAA SD	28	27	2	0	177.2	770	199	99	92	22	10	6	8	57	0	151	8	1	8	12	.400	0	0	4.66
7 Min. YEARS		292	51	5	153	635	2772	560	329	282	57	36	16	27	329	9	657	61	10	31	44	.413	2	50	4.00

Mike Wolff

Bats: Right **Throws:** Right **Pos:** DH **Ht:** 6'1" **Wt:** 195 **Born:** 12/19/70 **Age:** 29

		BATTING														BASERUNNING				PERCENTAGES		
Year Team	Lg Org	G	AB	H	2B	3B	HR	TB	R	RBI	TBB	IBB	SO	HBP	SH	SF	SB	CS	SB%	GDP	Avg	OBP	SLG
1992 Boise	A- Ana	68	244	66	12	1	11	113	49	39	32	1	60	6	1	2	5	5	.50	0	.270	.366	.463
1993 Cedar Rapids	A Ana	120	407	100	18	5	17	179	63	72	74	1	104	2	5	5	8	8	.50	4	.246	.361	.440
1994 Midland	AA Ana	113	397	115	30	4	13	186	64	58	54	3	91	6	5	6	10	9	.53	4	.290	.378	.469
1995 Midland	AA Ana	127	445	135	28	3	14	211	76	70	65	3	83	3	4	7	10	9	.53	10	.303	.390	.474
1996 Lk Elsinore	A+ Ana	12	42	12	0	0	2	21	12	7	0	0	10	0	0	0	0	0	1.00	1	.286	.413	.500
Vancouver	AAA Ana	71	256	64	15	3	10	115	46	38	34	2	69	4	3	6	6	4	.60	3	.250	.340	.449
1997 Vancouver	AAA Ana	91	266	75	15	0	21	153	58	64	53	3	75	11	4	3	6	4	.60	1	.282	.417	.575
1999 Erie	AA Ana	91	307	76	21	3	10	133	43	40	63	2	85	5	1	0	4	6	.40	6	.248	.384	.433
7 Min. YEARS		693	2364	643	142	16	98	1111	411	388	384	15	577	37	23	29	52	45	.54	29	.272	.378	.470

Mike Wolff

Bats: Left **Throws:** Left **Pos:** 1B   **Ht:** 6'3" **Wt:** 205 **Born:** 2/17/73 **Age:** 27

				BATTING														BASERUNNING				PERCENTAGES		
Year Team	Lg Org	G	AB	H	2B	3B	HR	TB	R	RBI	TBB	IBB	SO	HBP	SH	SF	SB	CS	SB%	GDP	Avg	OBP	SLG
1994 Albany	A Bal	55	185	54	11	0	1	68	26	19	12	0	23	9	1	2	5	1	.83	5	.292	.361	.368
1995 High Desert	A+ Bal	94	292	79	17	3	5	117	32	44	16	1	53	9	1	6	3	5	.38	5	.271	.322	.401
1996 Frederick	A+ Bal	105	352	89	21	0	7	131	44	50	16	5	32	1	2	3	6	3	.67	12	.253	.285	.372
1997 Frederick	A+ Bal	112	321	81	12	0	8	117	50	34	45	4	47	6	11	2	4	4	.50	10	.252	.353	.364
1998 Modesto	A+ Oak	102	320	93	21	1	6	134	46	46	35	2	38	7	0	3	3	1	.75	6	.291	.370	.419
1999 South Bend	A Ari	66	237	69	18	1	5	104	31	45	20	2	28	4	0	4	1	4	.20	5	.291	.351	.439
El Paso	AA Ari	52	155	35	8	1	1	48	14	17	11	0	23	4	0	2	0	0	.00	5	.226	.291	.310
6 Min. YEARS		586	1862	500	108	6	33	719	243	255	155	14	244	40	15	22	22	18	.55	48	.269	.334	.386

Hank Woodman

Pitches: Right **Bats:** Both **Pos:** P   **Ht:** 6'1" **Wt:** 185 **Born:** 11/16/72 **Age:** 27

		HOW MUCH HE PITCHED						WHAT HE GAVE UP												THE RESULTS					
Year Team	Lg Org	G	GS	CG	GF	IP	BFP	H	R	ER	HR	SH	SF	HB	TBB	IBB	SO	WP	Bk	W	L	Pct.	ShO	Sv	ERA
1993 Twins	R Min	13	0	0	8	26.1	117	14	7	4	0	2	0	0	23	0	19	3	0	0	1	.000	0	0	1.37
1998 Springfield	IND —	12	11	1	0	69.2	317	71	56	38	8	2	4	4	41	1	64	6	0	5	5	.500	0	0	4.91
1999 Richmond	IND —	5	5	1	0	38.1	161	34	12	7	0	1	0	1	18	0	37	0	0	1	3	.250	0	0	1.64
Charlotte	A+ Tex	6	6	2	0	30.2	137	33	19	14	1	0	2	1	14	0	19	1	0	2	2	.500	0	0	4.11
Tulsa	AA Tex	6	6	0	0	29.2	133	27	24	18	4	0	0	1	19	0	25	0	0	0	4	.000	0	0	5.46
3 Min. YEARS		42	28	4	8	194.2	865	179	118	81	13	5	6	7	115	1	164	10	0	8	15	.348	0	0	3.74

Ken Woods

Bats: Right **Throws:** Right **Pos:** 3B   **Ht:** 5'10" **Wt:** 175 **Born:** 8/2/70 **Age:** 29

				BATTING														BASERUNNING				PERCENTAGES		
Year Team	Lg Org	G	AB	H	2B	3B	HR	TB	R	RBI	TBB	IBB	SO	HBP	SH	SF	SB	CS	SB%	GDP	Avg	OBP	SLG
1992 Everett	A- SF	64	257	65	9	1	0	76	50	31	35	1	46	7	1	0	20	17	.54	2	.253	.358	.296
1993 Clinton	A SF	108	320	90	10	1	4	114	56	44	41	1	55	4	7	2	30	5	.86	13	.281	.368	.356
1994 San Jose	A+ SF	90	336	100	18	3	6	142	58	49	45	0	43	4	3	3	15	7	.68	9	.298	.384	.423
1995 Shreveport	AA SF	89	209	53	11	0	3	73	30	23	23	2	29	1	2	1	4	5	.44	4	.254	.329	.349
1996 Shreveport	AA SF	83	287	80	17	1	1	102	36	29	29	0	35	4	4	6	14	10	.58	11	.279	.347	.355
Phoenix	AAA SF	56	208	58	12	1	2	78	32	13	19	0	29	1	0	3	3	4	.43	6	.279	.338	.375
1997 Phoenix	AAA SF	1	1	1	0	0	0	1	0	1	0	0	0	0	0	0	0	0	.00	0	1.000	1.000	1.000
Shreveport	AA SF	104	293	88	14	2	2	112	41	32	28	0	40	3	4	3	6	4	.60	6	.300	.364	.382
1998 Shreveport	AA SF	94	335	103	20	2	4	139	44	33	28	1	31	2	0	3	8	9	.47	8	.307	.361	.415
Fresno	AAA SF	23	44	16	5	0	0	21	9	5	2	1	8	1	1	0	0	0	.00	1	.364	.404	.477
1999 Fresno	AAA SF	124	469	152	23	4	6	201	77	73	33	0	45	3	2	9	19	4	.83	8	.324	.366	.429
8 Min. YEARS		836	2759	806	139	15	28	1059	433	333	283	6	361	30	24	30	119	65	.65	68	.292	.361	.384

Finley Woodward

Pitches: Right **Bats:** Right **Pos:** P   **Ht:** 5'11" **Wt:** 200 **Born:** 8/15/75 **Age:** 24

		HOW MUCH HE PITCHED						WHAT HE GAVE UP												THE RESULTS					
Year Team	Lg Org	G	GS	CG	GF	IP	BFP	H	R	ER	HR	SH	SF	HB	TBB	IBB	SO	WP	Bk	W	L	Pct.	ShO	Sv	ERA
1997 New Jersey	A- StL	29	0	0	20	32.1	137	30	14	12	3	0	1	2	10	1	39	3	1	2	1	.667	0	1	3.34
1990 Peoria	A StL	34	21	0	2	137.2	616	156	91	81	13	4	4	11	63	1	88	9	0	6	5	.545	0	0	5.30
1999 Potomac	A+ StL	24	18	1	1	120.2	511	126	61	55	14	4	6	1	28	0	82	5	0	6	7	.462	0	0	4.10
Arkansas	AA StL	5	5	0	0	27.1	124	36	19	15	4	0	0	2	10	0	15	1	0	0	2	.000	0	0	4.94
3 Min. YEARS		92	44	1	23	318	1388	348	185	163	34	8	11	16	111	2	224	18	1	14	15	.483	0	1	4.61

Jason Woolf

Bats: Both **Throws:** Right **Pos:** SS   **Ht:** 6'1" **Wt:** 170 **Born:** 6/6/77 **Age:** 23

				BATTING														BASERUNNING				PERCENTAGES		
Year Team	Lg Org	G	AB	H	2B	3B	HR	TB	R	RBI	TBB	IBB	SO	HBP	SH	SF	SB	CS	SB%	GDP	Avg	OBP	SLG
1995 Johnson Cy	R+ StL	31	111	31	7	1	0	40	16	14	8	0	21	1	1	3	6	3	.67	0	.279	.325	.360
1996 Peoria	A StL	108	362	93	12	8	1	124	68	27	57	1	87	2	3	1	28	12	.70	3	.257	.360	.343
1997 Pr William	A+ StL	70	251	62	11	3	6	97	59	18	55	1	75	5	1	1	26	5	.84	0	.247	.391	.386
1998 Arkansas	AA StL	76	294	78	22	5	4	122	63	16	34	0	84	9	2	1	28	5	.85	2	.265	.358	.415
1999 Arkansas	AA StL	86	320	87	18	4	8	137	46	15	28	0	86	8	6	1	11	3	.79	3	.272	.345	.428
5 Min. YEARS		371	1338	351	70	21	19	520	252	90	182	2	353	25	13	7	99	28	.78	8	.262	.360	.389

Shawn Wooten

Bats: Right **Throws:** Right **Pos:** 3B   **Ht:** 5'10" **Wt:** 205 **Born:** 7/24/72 **Age:** 27

				BATTING														BASERUNNING				PERCENTAGES		
Year Team	Lg Org	G	AB	H	2B	3B	HR	TB	R	RBI	TBB	IBB	SO	HBP	SH	SF	SB	CS	SB%	GDP	Avg	OBP	SLG
1993 Bristol	R+ Det	52	177	62	12	2	8	102	26	39	24	2	20	3	0	2	1	2	.33	7	.350	.432	.576
Fayettevlle	A Det	5	16	4	0	0	1	7	2	5	3	0	3	0	0	0	0	0	.00	1	.250	.368	.438
1994 Fayettevlle	A Det	121	439	118	25	1	3	154	45	61	27	0	84	11	3	4	1	3	.25	11	.269	.324	.351
1995 Jacksnville	AA Det	20	70	9	1	0	2	16	4	7	1	0	17	1	0	1	0	0	.00	3	.129	.151	.229
Lakeland	A+ Det	38	135	31	10	1	2	49	11	11	10	0	28	2	0	1	0	1	.00	2	.230	.291	.363
1996 Moose Jaw	IND —	77	292	89	17	0	12	142	44	57	18	2	46	2	0	1	2	0	1.00	8	.305	.348	.486
1997 Cedar Rapds	A Ana	108	353	102	23	1	15	172	43	75	49	0	71	6	3	6	0	1	.00	8	.289	.379	.487
1998 Midland	AA Ana	8	28	9	4	0	1	16	3	6	3	0	4	0	0	0	0	0	.00	0	.321	.387	.571
Lk Elsinore	A+ Ana	105	395	116	31	0	16	195	56	74	38	3	82	3	0	4	0	2	.00	9	.294	.357	.494
1999 Erie	AA Ana	137	518	151	27	1	19	237	70	88	50	1	102	10	1	8	3	1	.75	12	.292	.360	.458
7 Min. YEARS		671	2423	691	150	6	79	1090	304	423	223	8	457	38	7	27	7	10	.41	61	.285	.351	.450

Widd Workman

Pitches: Right **Bats:** Right **Pos:** P **Ht:** 6'1" **Wt:** 195 **Born:** 5/23/74 **Age:** 26

		HOW MUCH HE PITCHED					WHAT HE GAVE UP									THE RESULTS				
Year Team	Lg Org	G	GS	CG	GF	IP	BFP	H	R	ER	HR	SH	SF	HB	TBB	IBB	SO	WP	Bk	W	L	Pct.	ShO	Sv	ERA
1996 Idaho Falls	R+ SD	14	13	0	0	55.2	271	77	48	42	3	2	9	5	31	0	42	6	2	4	5	.444	0	0	6.79
1997 Clinton	A SD	25	25	1	0	144	663	161	91	79	17	1	8	12	72	0	107	17	5	9	10	.474	0	0	4.94
1998 Rancho Cuca	A+ SD	20	20	0	0	108	494	109	84	56	7	4	7	8	52	0	71	10	1	8	8	.500	0	0	4.67
San Berndno	A+ LA	1	1	0	0	5	27	10	7	7	0	0	1	0	2	0	1	0	0	0	1	.000	0	0	12.60
1999 San Antonio	AA LA	9	9	0	0	50.1	249	73	48	39	9	3	5	6	27	0	27	4	0	1	5	.167	0	0	6.97
Vero Beach	A+ LA	25	3	0	10	56.1	275	79	53	46	9	3	7	5	25	1	32	6	0	1	1	.500	0	0	7.35
4 Min. YEARS		94	71	1	10	419.1	1979	509	331	269	45	13	37	36	209	1	280	43	8	23	30	.434	0	0	5.77

Ron Wright

Bats: Right **Throws:** Right **Pos:** DH-1B **Ht:** 6'1" **Wt:** 230 **Born:** 1/21/76 **Age:** 24

		BATTING														BASERUNNING				PERCENTAGES		
Year Team	Lg Org	G	AB	H	2B	3B	HR	TB	R	RBI	TBB	IBB	SO	HBP	SH	SF	SB	CS	SB%	GDP	Avg	OBP	SLG
1994 Braves	R Atl	45	169	29	9	0	1	41	10	16	10	0	21	0	0	0	1	0	1.00	3	.172	.218	.243
1995 Macon	A Atl	135	527	143	23	1	32	264	93	104	62	1	118	2	0	3	2	0	1.00	11	.271	.348	.501
1996 Durham	A+ Atl	66	240	66	15	2	20	145	47	62	37	2	71	0	0	7	1	0	1.00	5	.275	.363	.604
Greenville	AA Atl	63	232	59	11	1	16	120	39	52	38	5	73	2	0	3	1	0	1.00	2	.254	.360	.517
Carolina	AA Atl	4	14	2	0	0	0	2	1	0	2	0	7	0	0	0	0	1	.00	0	.143	.250	.143
1997 Calgary	AAA Pit	91	336	102	31	0	16	181	50	63	24	2	81	2	0	6	0	2	.00	4	.304	.348	.539
1998 Nashville	AAA Pit	17	56	12	3	0	0	15	6	9	9	0	18	1	0	1	0	0	.00	2	.214	.328	.268
Pirates	R Pit	3	10	6	0	0	2	12	4	5	2	0	0	0	0	1	0	0	.00	0	.600	.615	1.200
1999 Altoona	AA Pit	24	80	17	6	0	0	23	2	4	9	0	27	1	0	0	0	0	.00	1	.213	.300	.288
6 Min. YEARS		448	1664	436	98	4	87	803	252	315	193	10	416	8	0	21	5	3	.63	28	.262	.338	.483

Kelly Wunsch

Pitches: Left **Bats:** Left **Pos:** P **Ht:** 6'5" **Wt:** 192 **Born:** 7/12/72 **Age:** 27

		HOW MUCH HE PITCHED						WHAT HE GAVE UP										THE RESULTS				
Year Team	Lg Org	G	GS	CG	GF	IP	BFP	H	R	ER	HR	SH	SF	HB	TBB	IBB	SO	WP	Bk	W	L	Pct.	ShO	Sv	ERA
1993 Beloit	A Mil	12	12	0	0	63.1	282	58	39	34	5	4	1	1	39	1	61	5	2	1	5	.167	0	0	4.83
1994 Beloit	A Mil	17	17	0	0	83.1	400	88	69	57	11	4	3	13	47	1	77	6	0	3	10	.231	0	0	6.16
Helena	R+ Mil	9	9	1	0	51	238	52	39	29	7	1	2	10	30	0	37	6	1	4	2	.667	0	0	5.12
1995 Beloit	A Mil	14	14	3	0	85.2	364	90	47	40	7	2	0	3	37	0	66	6	0	4	7	.364	1	0	4.20
Stockton	A+ Mil	14	13	1	0	74.1	349	89	51	44	4	8	1	7	39	0	62	6	0	5	6	.455	1	0	5.33
1997 Stockton	A+ Mil	24	22	2	0	143	627	141	65	55	11	10	4	14	62	0	98	9	2	7	9	.438	2	0	3.46
1998 El Paso	AA Mil	17	17	1	0	101.1	469	127	81	67	11	4	3	9	31	0	70	7	0	5	6	.455	1	0	5.95
Louisville	AAA Mil	9	8	0	0	51.2	220	53	23	22	6	0	1	3	15	0	36	2	0	3	1	.750	0	0	3.83
1999 Huntsville	AA Mil	22	3	0	7	50.2	204	40	13	11	1	1	4	1	23	1	35	0	0	4	1	.800	0	1	1.95
Louisville	AAA Mil	16	2	0	3	41.2	189	52	33	22	4	0	2	6	14	0	30	3	0	2	1	.667	0	0	4.75
6 Min. YEARS		154	117	8	10	746	3342	790	450	381	67	34	18	70	337	3	562	50	5	38	48	.442	5	1	4.60

L.J. Yankosky

Pitches: Right **Bats:** Right **Pos:** P **Ht:** 6'2" **Wt:** 208 **Born:** 2/1/75 **Age:** 25

		HOW MUCH HE PITCHED						WHAT HE GAVE UP										THE RESULTS				
Year Team	Lg Org	G	GS	CG	GF	IP	BFP	H	R	ER	HR	SH	SF	HB	TBB	IBB	SO	WP	Bk	W	L	Pct.	ShO	Sv	ERA
1998 Macon	A Atl	20	0	0	11	47	192	33	22	15	3	2	0	1	18	1	37	2	0	4	1	.800	0	4	2.87
1999 Greenville	AA Atl	20	20	1	0	108.1	489	122	70	51	5	1	4	3	43	3	62	3	1	5	8	.385	0	0	4.24
2 Min. YEARS		40	22	1	11	155.1	681	155	92	66	8	3	4	4	61	4	99	5	1	9	9	.500	0	4	3.82

Jay Yennaco

Pitches: Right **Bats:** Right **Pos:** P **Ht:** 6'4" **Wt:** 238 **Born:** 11/17/75 **Age:** 24

		HOW MUCH HE PITCHED						WHAT HE GAVE UP										THE RESULTS				
Year Team	Lg Org	G	GS	CG	GF	IP	BFP	H	R	ER	HR	SH	SF	HB	TBB	IBB	SO	WP	Bk	W	L	Pct.	ShO	Sv	ERA
1996 Michigan	A Bos	28	28	4	0	169.2	763	195	112	87	13	2	7	6	68	0	117	20	1	10	10	.500	1	0	4.61
1997 Sarasota	A+ Bos	7	7	2	0	44.1	179	30	12	11	3	1	0	1	19	1	41	2	1	4	0	1.000	1	0	2.23
Trenton	AA Bos	21	21	0	0	122.1	557	146	89	86	8	3	10	8	54	0	73	5	0	5	11	.313	0	0	6.33
1998 Trenton	AA Bos	9	9	0	0	53.2	217	50	30	29	8	1	3	2	19	1	23	3	0	3	3	.500	0	0	4.86
Pawtucket	AAA Bos	11	11	1	0	60.1	266	77	43	39	6	1	1	0	16	1	34	5	0	3	2	.600	0	0	5.82
Syracuse	AAA Tor	7	6	1	0	38.2	174	55	27	23	4	1	1	3	10	2	27	0	0	0	3	.000	0	0	5.35
1999 Syracuse	AAA Tor	15	15	0	0	80	373	107	68	61	11	2	2	1	42	1	45	2	0	2	6	.250	0	0	6.86
Dunedin	A+ Tor	3	2	0	0	11	44	10	2	1	0	1	0	2	0	0	11	0	0	2	0	1.000	0	0	0.82
Knoxville	AA Tor	8	8	1	0	43.2	193	52	34	32	9	2	0	0	17	0	30	0	0	3	4	.429	0	0	6.60
4 Min. YEARS		109	107	9	0	623.2	2766	722	417	369	62	14	24	23	245	6	401	37	2	32	39	.451	2	0	5.32

Nate Yeskie

Pitches: Right **Bats:** Right **Pos:** P **Ht:** 6'3" **Wt:** 201 **Born:** 8/13/74 **Age:** 25

		HOW MUCH HE PITCHED						WHAT HE GAVE UP										THE RESULTS				
Year Team	Lg Org	G	GS	CG	GF	IP	BFP	H	R	ER	HR	SH	SF	HB	TBB	IBB	SO	WP	Bk	W	L	Pct.	ShO	Sv	ERA
1996 Elizabethtn	R+ Min	7	6	0	0	32.2	141	38	27	19	3	0	0	0	8	0	28	2	0	3	3	.500	0	0	5.23
1997 Fort Wayne	A Min	27	27	2	0	165.1	718	190	99	89	12	3	3	5	41	1	111	7	3	11	7	.611	0	0	4.84
1998 Fort Myers	A+ Min	14	11	1	2	62.2	273	74	27	23	4	2	0	5	16	0	39	3	0	4	2	.667	0	0	3.30
New Britain	AA Min	1	1	0	0	1.2	10	4	3	3	0	0	0	0	2	0	1	0	0	0	0	.000	0	0	16.20
1999 New Britain	AA Min	25	23	0	2	129.2	574	157	83	76	15	3	3	3	47	0	102	3	0	5	11	.313	0	0	5.28
4 Min. YEARS		74	68	3	4	392	1716	463	239	210	34	8	6	13	114	1	281	15	3	23	23	.500	0	0	4.82

Jeff Yoder

Pitches: Right **Bats:** Left **Pos:** P   **Ht:** 6'2" **Wt:** 210 **Born:** 2/16/76 **Age:** 24

Year Team	Lg Org	G	GS	CG	GF	IP	BFP	H	R	ER	HR	SH	SF	HB	TBB	IBB	SO	WP	Bk	W	L	Pct.	ShO	Sv	ERA
1996 Rockford	A ChC	25	24	2	0	154.1	640	139	70	59	10	2	4	10	48	1	124	12	5	12	5	.706	0	0	3.44
1998 Daytona	A+ ChC	26	24	1	1	143	645	158	97	80	16	3	6	6	47	0	128	10	2	7	9	.438	0	0	5.03
1999 Daytona	A+ ChC	5	0	0	2	10.2	44	8	2	1	0	0	1	0	5	0	11	0	0	0	0	.000	0	1	0.84
West Tenn	AA ChC	29	22	0	1	134.1	574	115	54	46	10	2	6	5	70	5	109	5	1	10	5	.667	0	0	3.08
3 Min. YEARS		85	70	3	4	442.1	1903	420	223	186	36	7	17	21	170	6	372	27	8	29	19	.604	0	1	3.78

Danny Young

Pitches: Left **Bats:** Right **Pos:** P   **Ht:** 6'4" **Wt:** 210 **Born:** 11/3/71 **Age:** 28

Year Team	Lg Org	G	GS	CG	GF	IP	BFP	H	R	ER	HR	SH	SF	HB	TBB	IBB	SO	WP	Bk	W	L	Pct.	ShO	Sv	ERA
1991 Astros	R Hou	13	7	0	0	32.2	170	32	33	29	1	0	1	2	39	0	41	12	1	1	4	.200	0	0	7.99
1992 Asheville	A Hou	20	20	0	0	94.2	438	106	65	45	5	2	1	2	70	1	64	11	3	3	10	.231	0	0	4.28
1993 Asheville	A Hou	32	24	2	0	142.2	679	174	114	97	13	6	7	7	95	1	101	16	3	5	14	.263	1	0	6.12
1994 Salem	A+ Pit	10	0	0	2	18.2	94	32	17	16	2	0	1	0	9	0	12	3	0	2	0	1.000	0	0	7.71
Augusta	A Pit	21	9	0	3	66.2	290	58	32	25	2	2	3	2	33	0	73	6	1	2	5	.286	0	0	3.38
1995 Augusta	A Pit	6	2	0	1	14.1	66	9	6	4	0	0	1	0	16	0	11	2	0	1	0	1.000	0	0	2.51
Lynchburg	A+ Pit	24	2	0	7	41.1	196	52	37	34	3	1	2	2	27	1	34	5	0	2	4	.333	0	0	7.40
1996 Augusta	A Pit	22	1	0	6	33.2	171	36	33	22	1	2	3	3	29	2	36	12	2	0	4	.000	0	2	5.88
1997 Lynchburg	A+ Pit	15	0	0	8	24.1	113	27	17	16	2	1	1	1	14	0	22	0	0	0	0	.000	0	0	5.92
Augusta	A Pit	3	2	0	0	7.1	42	16	15	8	1	0	0	2	2	0	5	0	0	0	1	.000	0	0	9.82
1998 Daytona	A+ ChC	7	0	0	3	8.2	42	9	5	5	0	0	0	2	8	0	6	1	0	1	1	.500	0	0	5.19
West Tenn	AA ChC	23	1	0	4	27	114	22	13	11	1	2	0	1	15	0	20	2	0	0	2	.000	0	0	3.67
Iowa	AAA ChC	2	0	0	0	2	7	1	0	0	0	0	0	0	1	0	1	0	0	0	0	.000	0	0	0.00
1999 West Tenn	AA ChC	27	8	0	2	60.1	258	48	25	22	2	1	2	0	38	0	67	5	3	3	5	.375	0	0	3.28
9 Min. YEARS		225	76	2	36	574.1	2680	622	412	334	33	17	22	22	396	5	493	75	13	20	51	.282	1	2	5.23

Tim Young

Pitches: Left **Bats:** Left **Pos:** P   **Ht:** 5'9" **Wt:** 170 **Born:** 10/15/73 **Age:** 26

Year Team	Lg Org	G	GS	CG	GF	IP	BFP	H	R	ER	HR	SH	SF	HB	TBB	IBB	SO	WP	Bk	W	L	Pct.	ShO	Sv	ERA
1996 Vermont	A- Mon	27	0	0	26	29.1	106	14	1	1	1	2	1	2	4	0	46	0	1	1	0	1.000	0	18	0.31
1997 Cape Fear	A Mon	45	0	0	41	54	214	33	12	9	0	1	2	2	15	0	66	8	0	1	1	.500	0	18	1.50
Wst Plm Bch	A+ Mon	11	0	0	8	15.2	56	8	1	1	0	2	0	1	4	0	13	0	0	0	0	.000	0	5	0.57
Harrisburg	AA Mon	1	0	0	0	2	7	1	0	0	0	0	0	0	0	0	3	0	0	0	0	.000	0	0	0.00
1998 Harrisburg	AA Mon	26	0	0	19	35.2	146	28	17	15	3	5	0	1	10	0	52	1	0	3	3	.500	0	3	3.79
Ottawa	AAA Mon	20	0	0	10	26.2	119	26	14	6	1	0	0	1	12	2	34	0	0	1	1	.500	0	2	2.03
1999 Trenton	AA Bos	31	0	0	12	45.1	204	38	26	22	1	6	1	5	26	0	52	4	0	4	4	.500	0	2	4.37
1998 Montreal	NL	10	0	0	6	6	29	6	4	4	0	1	0	0	4	0	7	0	0	0	0	.000	0	0	6.00
4 Min. YEARS		161	0	0	116	208.2	852	148	71	54	6	16	4	12	71	2	266	13	1	10	9	.526	0	48	2.33

Travis Young

Bats: Right **Throws:** Right **Pos:** 2B   **Ht:** 6'1" **Wt:** 185 **Born:** 9/8/74 **Age:** 25

		BATTING															BASERUNNING				PERCENTAGES		
Year Team	Lg Org	G	AB	H	2B	3B	HR	TB	R	RBI	TBB	IBB	SO	HBP	SH	SF	SB	CS	SB%	GDP	Avg	OBP	SLG
1997 Salem-Keizr	A- SF	76	320	107	11	6	1	133	80	34	30	0	50	5	1	3	40	8	.83	3	.334	.397	.416
1998 San Jose	A+ SF	133	517	126	21	2	4	163	79	63	61	2	101	8	11	6	27	12	.69	14	.244	.329	.315
1999 Fresno	AAA SF	26	92	23	1	1	2	32	15	11	9	1	23	3	1	1	3	2	.60	1	.250	.333	.348
Shreveport	AA SF	108	416	110	28	2	5	157	68	38	33	0	75	8	7	2	16	11	.59	11	.264	.329	.377
3 Min. YEARS		343	1345	366	61	11	12	485	242	146	133	3	249	24	20	12	86	33	.72	29	.272	.345	.361

Mark Zamarripa

Pitches: Right **Bats:** Right **Pos:** P   **Ht:** 6'0" **Wt:** 175 **Born:** 7/28/74 **Age:** 25

Year Team	Lg Org	G	GS	CG	GF	IP	BFP	H	R	ER	HR	SH	SF	HB	TBB	IBB	SO	WP	Bk	W	L	Pct.	ShO	Sv	ERA
1995 Newark	IND —	7	2	0	1	20	98	24	22	17	0	1	0	1	13	0	16	2	1	2	1	.667	0	0	7.65
1996 Jamestown	A- Det	29	0	0	22	48.2	187	25	13	11	4	3	0	2	14	0	61	4	0	4	2	.667	0	4	2.03
1997 W Michigan	A Det	20	0	0	9	29.2	128	13	17	7	0	2	1	2	18	2	41	3	4	3	1	.750	0	2	2.12
Lakeland	A+ Det	11	0	0	8	12.1	59	16	12	11	0	0	0	0	11	0	9	1	0	2	1	.667	0	1	8.03
Tigers	R Det	4	0	0	1	8.1	35	6	6	6	2	0	0	0	6	0	11	2	1	0	0	.000	0	1	6.48
1998 W Michigan	A Det	35	1	0	12	72.2	299	59	19	18	3	6	3	3	34	2	88	2	3	6	2	.750	0	1	2.23
1999 Columbus	A Cle	15	0	0	7	28.2	120	26	13	11	3	0	2	2	12	1	31	2	0	4	0	1.000	0	1	3.45
Schaumburg	IND —	5	5	1	0	39.1	161	26	9	8	2	2	0	2	26	1	25	3	0	2	0	1.000	0	0	1.83
Carolina	AA Col	5	4	0	0	20.1	93	20	11	10	0	0	2	1	14	0	12	1	2	2	1	.667	0	0	4.43
5 Min. YEARS		131	12	1	60	280	1180	215	122	99	14	13	7	13	148	6	294	20	11	25	8	.758	0	10	3.18

Victor Zambrano

Pitches: Right **Bats:** Right **Pos:** P   **Ht:** 6'1" **Wt:** 170 **Born:** 8/6/74 **Age:** 25

Year Team	Lg Org	G	GS	CG	GF	IP	BFP	H	R	ER	HR	SH	SF	HB	TBB	IBB	SO	WP	Bk	W	L	Pct.	ShO	Sv	ERA
1996 Devil Rays	R TB	1	0	0	0	3.1	16	4	4	3	0	0	0	0	0	0	6	0	0	0	0	.000	0	0	8.10
1997 Devil Rays	R TB	2	0	0	0	3	10	1	0	0	0	0	0	0	0	0	2	0	0	0	0	.000	0	0	0.00
Princeton	R+ TB	20	0	0	6	29.2	126	18	13	6	1	0	0	4	9	1	36	2	1	0	2	.000	0	0	1.82
1998 Chston-SC	A TB	48	2	0	15	77.1	330	72	32	29	5	5	0	12	20	1	89	7	1	6	4	.600	0	0	3.38
1999 St. Pete	A+ TB	7	0	0	0	9	43	10	6	4	1	0	1	1	5	0	15	1	0	0	2	.000	0	0	4.00

Year Team	Lg Org	G	GS	CG	GF	IP	BFP	H	R	ER	HR	SH	SF	HB	TBB	IBB	SO	WP	Bk	W	L	Pct.	ShO	Sv	ERA
Orlando	AA TB	40	4	0	12	82.1	379	92	55	42	5	1	2	9	38	2	81	6	1	7	2	.778	0	1	4.59
4 Min. YEARS		118	6	0	34	204.2	904	197	110	84	12	6	3	26	72	4	229	16	3	13	10	.565	0	1	3.69

Junior Zamora

Bats: Right **Throws:** Right **Pos:** 3B — **Ht:** 6'2" **Wt:** 193 **Born:** 5/3/76 **Age:** 24

		BATTING															BASERUNNING				PERCENTAGES		
Year Team	Lg Org	G	AB	H	2B	3B	HR	TB	R	RBI	TBB	IBB	SO	HBP	SH	SF	SB	CS	SB%	GDP	Avg	OBP	SLG
1995 Mets	R NYM	20	56	13	2	2	0	19	9	4	5	0	10	1	1	1	0	0	.00	2	.232	.302	.339
1996 Kingsport	R+ NYM	60	227	55	13	0	7	89	37	41	11	0	59	7	0	3	2	1	.67	3	.242	.294	.392
Capital Cty	A NYM	1	4	0	0	0	0	0	0	0	0	0	3	0	0	0	0	0	.00	0	.000	.000	.000
1997 Capital Cty	A NYM	36	124	31	5	0	8	60	16	19	10	0	29	0	0	0	0	1	.00	2	.250	.306	.484
1998 Mets	R NYM	2	5	1	0	1	0	3	1	2	1	0	0	0	0	0	0	0	.00	1	.200	.333	.600
St. Lucie	A+ NYM	99	368	105	17	4	10	160	58	53	25	1	60	5	0	0	4	3	.57	9	.285	.339	.435
1999 Binghamton	AA NYM	67	255	61	17	0	10	108	28	33	12	1	62	3	0	2	1	1	.67	13	.239	.279	.424
5 Min. YEARS		285	1039	266	54	7	35	439	149	152	64	2	223	16	1	6	8	6	.57	30	.256	.308	.423

Pete Zamora

Pitches: Left **Bats:** Left **Pos:** P — **Ht:** 6'3" **Wt:** 185 **Born:** 8/13/75 **Age:** 24

		HOW MUCH HE PITCHED						WHAT HE GAVE UP												THE RESULTS					
Year Team	Lg Org	G	GS	CG	GF	IP	BFP	H	R	ER	HR	SH	SF	HB	TBB	IBB	SO	WP	Bk	W	L	Pct.	ShO	Sv	ERA
1997 Great Falls	R+ LA	13	10	1	2	69.2	289	59	27	20	3	1	1	3	30	0	73	3	1	2	5	.286	0	2	2.58
1998 San Berndno	A+ LA	25	5	0	15	81.2	321	43	21	19	1	5	1	4	33	0	77	3	2	4	1	.800	0	6	2.09
San Antonio	AA LA	12	12	0	0	66.2	299	71	52	33	6	4	3	1	27	0	47	1	1	3	8	.273	0	0	4.46
1999 San Antonio	AA LA	35	0	0	8	63.2	292	79	48	43	5	3	5	4	30	2	41	4	1	2	1	.667	0	3	6.08
3 Min. YEARS		85	27	1	25	281.2	1201	252	148	115	15	13	10	12	120	2	238	11	5	11	15	.423	0	11	3.67

Dave Zancanaro

Pitches: Left **Bats:** Left **Pos:** P — **Ht:** 6'1" **Wt:** 185 **Born:** 1/8/69 **Age:** 31

		HOW MUCH HE PITCHED						WHAT HE GAVE UP												THE RESULTS					
Year Team	Lg Org	G	GS	CG	GF	IP	BFP	H	R	ER	HR	SH	SF	HB	TBB	IBB	SO	WP	Bk	W	L	Pct.	ShO	Sv	ERA
1990 Sou Oregon	A- Oak	10	8	0	0	44.1	188	44	22	19	2	1	0	1	13	0	42	3	4	3	0	1.000	0	0	3.86
Modesto	A+ Oak	4	2	0	0	13	64	13	9	9	1	0	2	0	14	0	7	0	0	1	2	.333	0	0	6.23
1991 Huntsville	AA Oak	29	28	0	1	165	727	151	87	62	7	3	4	6	92	0	104	8	4	5	10	.333	0	0	3.38
1992 Tacoma	AAA Oak	23	19	0	0	105.2	486	108	61	50	3	5	7	2	75	0	47	7	2	2	11	.154	0	0	4.26
1995 W Michigan	A Oak	16	16	0	0	32.2	132	19	8	8	1	2	0	3	15	0	42	1	2	0	0	.000	0	0	2.20
1996 Modesto	A+ Oak	20	3	0	6	77.1	331	61	38	29	9	4	2	3	37	0	66	5	1	7	3	.700	0	3	3.38
Huntsville	AA Oak	10	10	0	0	43.1	206	54	32	27	4	0	1	2	26	1	36	3	0	3	3	.500	0	0	5.61
1997 Las Vegas	AAA SD	3	3	0	0	13.1	77	27	24	23	3	0	0	2	8	0	9	0	0	0	3	.000	0	0	15.53
Mobile	AA SD	27	19	3	3	133.2	581	140	69	66	15	5	3	4	57	0	66	10	1	10	8	.556	0	1	4.44
1998 Norwich	AA NYY	16	13	0	2	69	300	80	42	36	9	2	1	3	23	0	49	3	0	3	4	.429	0	0	4.70
1999 Norwich	AA NYY	15	11	1	1	79	327	64	25	20	4	5	1	2	32	1	61	2	0	6	1	.857	0	0	2.28
Columbus	AAA NYY	13	13	1	0	77.2	336	85	40	36	11	0	1	0	28	0	45	1	2	7	2	.778	0	0	4.17
8 Min. YEARS		186	145	5	13	854	3755	846	457	385	69	27	20	28	420	2	574	43	16	47	49	.490	0	4	4.06

Scott Zech

Bats: Right **Throws:** Right **Pos:** 3B-2B — **Ht:** 5'11" **Wt:** 175 **Born:** 6/6/74 **Age:** 26

		BATTING															BASERUNNING				PERCENTAGES		
Year Team	Lg Org	G	AB	H	2B	3B	HR	TB	R	RBI	TBB	IBB	SO	HBP	SH	SF	SB	CS	SB%	GDP	Avg	OBP	SLG
1997 Vermont	A- Mon	63	204	54	11	0	1	68	31	20	27	1	36	7	5	6	17	7	.71	4	.265	.361	.333
1998 Cape Fear	A Mon	102	304	87	20	2	3	120	53	45	43	0	48	13	9	4	13	8	.62	3	.286	.393	.395
1999 Cape Fear	A Mon	3	10	3	0	0	0	3	1	1	3	0	1	0	0	0	1	0	1.00	0	.300	.462	.300
Harrisburg	AA Mon	22	72	20	4	1	1	29	8	10	4	0	13	0	2	2	3	2	.60	0	.278	.308	.403
Jupiter	A+ Mon	68	203	57	13	0	1	73	28	18	29	0	30	5	10	3	15	5	.75	1	.281	.379	.360
3 Min. YEARS		258	793	221	48	3	6	293	121	94	106	1	128	25	26	15	49	22	.69	8	.279	.375	.369

Chad Zerbe

Pitches: Left **Bats:** Left **Pos:** P — **Ht:** 6'0" **Wt:** 190 **Born:** 4/27/72 **Age:** 28

		HOW MUCH HE PITCHED						WHAT HE GAVE UP												THE RESULTS					
Year Team	Lg Org	G	GS	CG	GF	IP	BFP	H	R	ER	HR	SH	SF	HB	TBB	IBB	SO	WP	Bk	W	L	Pct.	ShO	Sv	ERA
1991 Dodgers	R LA	16	1	0	4	32.2	145	31	19	8	1	0	3	1	15	0	23	6	3	0	2	.000	0	0	2.20
1992 Great Falls	R+ LA	15	15	1	0	92.1	378	75	27	22	2	1	1	5	26	0	70	5	0	8	3	.727	1	0	2.14
1993 Bakersfield	A+ LA	14	12	1	0	67	326	83	60	44	2	1	2	2	47	0	41	2	2	0	10	.000	0	0	5.91
Vero Beach	A+ LA	10	0	0	1	12.1	60	12	10	9	0	0	2	2	13	1	11	3	1	1	0	1.000	0	0	6.57
1994 Vero Beach	A+ LA	18	18	1	0	98.1	412	88	50	37	6	0	4	2	32	0	68	6	0	5	5	.500	0	0	3.39
1995 San Berndno	A+ LA	28	27	1	0	163.1	718	168	103	83	15	10	5	3	64	0	94	4	0	11	7	.611	0	0	4.57
1996 San Antonio	AA LA	17	11	1	1	80	384	98	52	40	0	5	2	2	37	2	29	1	1	4	6	.400	0	1	4.50
1997 High Desert	A+ Ari	9	8	0	0	36.1	192	61	49	30	7	0	3	1	15	0	26	1	0	1	6	.143	0	0	7.43
Sonoma Cty	IND —	14	13	2	0	89.2	417	117	70	54	7	5	4	3	36	1	52	1	0	4	5	.444	0	0	5.42
1998 Shreveport	AA SF	0	0	0	0	0	0	0	0	0	0	0	0	0	0	0	0	0	0	0	0	.000	0	0	0.00
San Jose	A+ SF	23	0	0	12	37.2	159	37	16	14	3	0	1	3	12	0	28	1	0	2	0	1.000	0	1	3.35
1999 Bakersfield	A+ SF	21	21	0	0	126	533	124	66	51	4	0	5	2	33	0	81	6	0	7	7	.500	0	0	3.64
Shreveport	AA SF	7	6	0	0	41.1	164	32	13	9	2	1	2	3	10	0	16	0	1	1	3	.250	0	0	1.96
9 Min. YEARS		193	132	7	20	883	3892	926	535	404	58	23	34	29	340	2	548	39	7	44	54	.449	1	2	4.12

Alan Zinter

Bats: Both **Throws:** Right **Pos:** 1B-C **Ht:** 6'2" **Wt:** 200 **Born:** 5/19/68 **Age:** 32

Year Team	Lg Org	G	AB	H	2B	3B	HR	TB	R	RBI	TBB	IBB	SO	HBP	SH	SF	SB	CS	SB%	GDP	Avg	OBP	SLG
1989 Pittsfield	A- NYM	12	41	15	2	1	2	25	11	12	12	0	4	0	0	1	0	1	.00	0	.366	.500	.610
St. Lucie	A+ NYM	48	159	38	10	0	3	57	17	32	18	2	31	1	1	5	0	1	.00	5	.239	.311	.358
1990 St. Lucie	A+ NYM	98	333	97	19	6	7	149	63	63	54	1	70	1	0	6	8	1	.89	10	.291	.386	.447
Jackson	AA NYM	6	20	4	1	0	0	5	2	1	3	0	11	0	0	0	1	0	1.00	1	.200	.304	.250
1991 Williamsprt	AA NYM	124	422	93	13	6	9	145	44	54	59	1	106	3	2	2	3	3	.50	10	.220	.319	.344
1992 Binghamton	AA NYM	128	431	96	13	5	16	167	63	50	70	5	117	4	0	0	0	0	.00	7	.223	.337	.387
1993 Binghamton	AA NYM	134	432	113	24	4	24	217	68	87	90	7	105	1	0	5	1	0	1.00	4	.262	.386	.502
1994 Toledo	AAA Det	134	471	112	29	5	21	214	66	58	69	4	185	7	0	0	13	5	.72	3	.238	.344	.454
1995 Toledo	AAA Det	101	334	74	15	4	13	136	42	48	36	1	102	2	2	5	4	1	.80	5	.222	.297	.407
1996 Pawtucket	AAA Bos	108	357	96	19	5	26	203	78	69	58	2	123	4	0	5	5	1	.83	3	.269	.373	.569
1997 Tacoma	AAA Sea	110	404	116	19	4	20	203	69	70	64	3	113	3	1	1	3	1	.75	7	.287	.388	.502
1998 Iowa	AAA ChC	129	419	130	23	1	23	224	82	81	75	1	116	3	0	3	3	5	.38	10	.310	.416	.535
1999 Iowa	AAA ChC	14	51	13	2	0	3	24	7	8	5	0	13	0	0	0	0	0	.00	0	.255	.321	.471
11 Min. YEARS		1146	3874	997	189	41	167	1769	612	633	613	33	1096	29	6	33	41	19	.68	65	.257	.360	.457

Barry Zito

Pitches: Left **Bats:** Left **Pos:** P **Ht:** 6'4" **Wt:** 205 **Born:** 5/13/78 **Age:** 22

		HOW MUCH HE PITCHED						WHAT HE GAVE UP										THE RESULTS					
Year Team	Lg Org	G	GS	CG	GF	IP	BFP	H	R	ER	HR	SH	SF	HB	TBB	IBB	SO	WP	Bk	W	L	Pct.	ShO	Sv	ERA
1999 Visalia	A+ Oak	8	8	0	0	40.1	157	21	13	11	3	0	1	0	22	0	62	3	0	3	0	1.000	0	0	2.45
Midland	AA Oak	4	4	0	0	22	99	22	15	12	1	0	0	1	11	0	29	2	0	2	1	.667	0	0	4.91
Vancouver	AAA Oak	1	1	0	0	6	24	5	1	1	0	0	0	0	2	0	6	2	0	1	0	1.000	0	0	1.50
1 Min. YEARS		13	13	0	0	68.1	280	48	29	24	4	0	1	1	35	0	97	7	0	6	1	.857	0	0	3.16

Jon Zuber

Bats: Left **Throws:** Left **Pos:** 1B **Ht:** 6'0" **Wt:** 185 **Born:** 12/10/69 **Age:** 30

Year Team	Lg Org	G	AB	H	2B	3B	HR	TB	R	RBI	TBB	IBB	SO	HBP	SH	SF	SB	CS	SB%	GDP	Avg	OBP	SLG
1992 Batavia	A- Phi	22	88	30	6	3	1	45	14	21	9	1	11	1	0	1	1	1	.50	1	.341	.404	.511
Spartanburg	A Phi	54	206	59	13	1	3	83	24	36	33	1	31	1	0	1	3	1	.75	6	.286	.386	.403
1993 Clearwater	A+ Phi	129	494	152	37	5	5	214	70	69	49	5	47	0	3	4	6	6	.50	15	.308	.367	.433
1994 Reading	AA Phi	138	498	146	29	5	9	212	81	70	71	4	71	1	1	5	2	4	.33	11	.293	.379	.426
1995 Scranton-WB	AAA Phi	119	418	120	19	5	3	158	53	50	49	2	68	0	1	2	1	2	.33	12	.287	.360	.378
1996 Scranton-WB	AAA Phi	118	412	128	22	5	4	172	62	59	58	3	50	1	2	4	4	2	.67	15	.311	.394	.417
1997 Scranton-WB	AAA Phi	126	435	137	37	2	6	196	85	64	79	0	53	3	1	3	3	4	.43	11	.315	.421	.451
1998 Scranton-WB	AAA Phi	80	280	91	23	4	4	134	47	56	45	7	34	2	1	6	0	0	.00	8	.325	.414	.479
1999 Scranton-WB	AAA Phi	111	387	114	24	2	6	160	69	54	86	6	48	1	0	4	7	1	.88	9	.295	.421	.413
1996 Philadelphia	NL	30	91	23	4	0	1	30	7	10	6	1	11	0	1	1	1	0	1.00	3	.253	.296	.330
1998 Philadelphia	NL	38	45	11	3	1	2	22	6	6	6	0	9	1	0	0	0	0	.00	1	.244	.346	.489
8 Min. YEARS		897	3218	977	210	32	41	1374	505	479	479	29	413	10	9	30	27	21	.56	88	.304	.392	.427
2 Maj. YEARS		68	136	34	7	1	3	52	13	16	12	1	20	1	1	1	1	0	1.00	4	.250	.313	.382

Julio Zuleta

Bats: Right **Throws:** Right **Pos:** 1B **Ht:** 6'6" **Wt:** 230 **Born:** 3/28/75 **Age:** 25

Year Team	Lg Org	G	AB	H	2B	3B	HR	TB	R	RBI	TBB	IBB	SO	HBP	SH	SF	SB	CS	SB%	GDP	Avg	OBP	SLG
1993 ChC	R ChC	17	53	13	0	1	0	15	3	6	3	0	12	3	0	0	0	0	.00	3	.245	.322	.283
1994 Huntington	R+ ChC	6	15	1	0	0	0	1	0	2	4	0	4	0	0	0	0	0	.00	1	.067	.263	.067
Cubs	R ChC	30	100	31	1	0	0	32	11	8	8	0	18	2	0	0	5	1	.83	0	.310	.373	.320
1995 Williamsprt	A- ChC	30	75	13	3	1	0	18	9	6	11	1	12	2	0	0	0	1	.00	4	.173	.295	.240
1996 Williamsprt	A- ChC	62	221	57	12	2	1	76	35	29	19	2	36	8	0	2	7	4	.64	8	.258	.336	.344
1997 Rockford	A ChC	119	430	124	30	5	6	182	59	77	35	6	88	12	3	8	5	5	.50	7	.288	.353	.423
1998 Daytona	A+ ChC	94	366	126	25	1	16	201	69	86	35	1	59	15	1	5	6	3	.67	12	.344	.418	.549
West Tenn	AA ChC	40	139	41	9	0	2	56	18	20	10	0	30	3	0	3	0	1	.00	3	.295	.348	.403
1999 West Tenn	AA ChC	133	482	142	37	4	21	250	75	97	35	6	122	20	0	8	4	3	.57	11	.295	.361	.519
7 Min. YEARS		531	1881	548	117	14	46	831	279	331	160	16	381	65	4	26	27	18	.60	49	.291	.363	.442

Mike Zywica

Bats: Right **Throws:** Right **Pos:** OF **Ht:** 6'4" **Wt:** 190 **Born:** 9/14/74 **Age:** 25

Year Team	Lg Org	G	AB	H	2B	3B	HR	TB	R	RBI	TBB	IBB	SO	HBP	SH	SF	SB	CS	SB%	GDP	Avg	OBP	SLG
1996 Rangers	R Tex	33	110	30	7	1	3	48	18	22	14	1	24	8	0	0	3	0	1.00	1	.273	.394	.436
Chston-SC	A Tex	20	67	9	1	1	2	18	5	4	7	0	13	1	0	0	3	1	.75	2	.134	.227	.269
1997 Charlotte	A+ Tex	126	462	119	25	5	12	190	75	64	50	0	116	12	0	6	19	19	.50	10	.258	.342	.411
1998 Charlotte	A+ Tex	68	252	96	21	3	11	156	67	49	34	2	40	6	0	4	16	5	.76	4	.381	.459	.619
Tulsa	AA Tex	58	214	60	15	4	5	98	40	45	19	0	56	5	0	4	7	3	.70	3	.280	.347	.458
1999 Oklahoma	AAA Tex	135	495	131	31	3	9	195	80	79	33	0	119	7	1	7	4	1	.80	13	.265	.315	.394
4 Min. YEARS		440	1600	445	100	17	42	705	285	263	157	3	368	39	1	21	52	29	.64	33	.278	.353	.441

1999 Class-A and Rookie Statistics

Any player who appeared in Class-A or Rookie ball without reaching Double-A or Triple-A has his 1999 statistics in this section. Class-A (A+, A, A-) and Rookie (R+, R) have subclassifications to distinguish the level of competition. Ages are as of June 30, 2000. A complete list of statistical abbreviations can be found in the introduction to the Career Register section on page 2.

Beginning with this edition, the handedness and position of each player is provided. An asterisk (*) identifies a lefthanded-hitting player or lefthanded pitcher. A player who switch-hits is noted with a pound sign (#).

A number of players in this section will be well-known prospects a year from now. Last year, three young pitchers—Rick Ankiel of the Cardinals, Detroit's Jeff Weaver and Ryan Rupe of the Devil Rays—were found in these pages. All three showed promise in the major leagues in 1999. Players who are in this section and may emerge as top-flight prospects in 2000 include Taiwanese import Chin-Feng Chen of the Dodgers, future Cubs center fielder Corey Patterson and third baseman Mike Cuddyer of the Twins.

Very few players reach Double-A or higher in their first pro season, so nearly all future major leaguers will be found in this section before reaching the majors. There are plenty of gems hidden away in these pages.

1999 Batting — Single-A and Rookie Leagues

BATTING																					BASERUNNING				PERCENTAGES		
Player	Pos	Team	Org	Lg	A	G	AB	H	2B	3B	HR	TB	R	RBI	TBB	IBB	SO	HBP	SH	SF	SB	CS	SB%	GDP	Avg	OBP	SLG
Aaron, Oginga	2b	Princeton	TB	R+	20	2	4	0	0	0	0	0	0	0	0	0	2	0	0	0	0	0	.00	0	.000	.000	.000
Abate, Mike	of	Everett	Sea	A-	21	57	185	47	15	0	5	77	34	23	17	1	57	2	2	0	1	2	.33	2	.254	.324	.416
Abreu, Cesar	1b	Reds	Cin	R	21	26	76	15	2	0	1	20	4	6	5	1	23	2	0	0	2	1	.67	1	.197	.265	.263
Abreu, David#	2b-3b	Mets	NYM	R	21	32	98	32	3	1	0	37	25	9	20	0	10	3	3	0	13	2	.87	1	.327	.455	.378
		Kingsport	NYM	R+	21	5	16	7	0	0	0	7	5	1	8	0	2	0	1	0	3	1	.75	0	.438	.625	.438
Abreu, Dennis	2b	Daytona	ChC	A+	22	105	374	96	10	2	2	116	44	30	13	0	69	3	2	1	29	9	.76	10	.257	.286	.310
Acevas, Jonathan	c	Burlington	CWS	A	22	65	202	38	9	2	4	63	28	23	35	3	52	8	5	1	3	2	.60	9	.188	.329	.312
Acevedo, Carlos	of	Clearwater	Phi	A+	19	12	42	12	2	1	0	16	4	6	3	0	7	0	0	0	2	1	.67	0	.286	.333	.381
		Piedmont	Phi	A	19	56	188	53	10	0	1	66	22	19	11	0	30	0	0	2	7	2	.78	3	.282	.318	.351
Acevedo, Inocencio	ss-2b	Charlotte	Tex	A+	21	1	3	0	0	0	0	0	1	0	0	0	0	1	0	0	1	0	1.00	0	.000	.250	.000
		Rangers	Tex	R	21	27	115	25	4	3	0	35	23	9	8	0	18	2	0	0	16	1	.94	2	.217	.280	.304
Acevedo, Luis	3b	Pulaski	Tex	R+	22	9	23	2	0	0	0	2	4	1	9	0	9	0	0	0	4	0	1.00	0	.087	.344	.087
		Savannah	Tex	A	22	6	15	0	0	0	0	0	1	0	3	0	5	0	0	0	0	0	.00	0	.000	.167	.000
Ackerman, Scott	c	Cape Fear	Mon	A	21	67	224	60	14	0	6	92	30	31	16	1	58	2	1	3	5	2	.71	4	.268	.318	.411
Acosta, Emilio	c	Johnson Cy	StL	R+	20	36	107	26	6	2	1	39	11	16	8	2	16	5	1	0	2	0	1.00	3	.243	.325	.364
Acuna, Ronald	of	Mets	NYM	R	21	5	20	5	1	0	0	6	1	3	1	0	4	0	0	0	2	0	1.00	1	.250	.286	.300
		Kingsport	NYM	R+	21	38	123	35	8	0	1	46	26	24	14	0	32	3	2	1	15	5	.75	3	.285	.369	.374
		Pittsfield	NYM	A-	21	22	71	16	3	0	0	19	7	6	8	0	26	1	2	1	8	6	.57	0	.225	.309	.268
Adams, John	of	South Bend	Ari	A	23	74	285	82	19	1	10	133	38	38	11	1	66	0	0	3	10	5	.67	5	.288	.311	.467
Aguila, Chris	of	Kane County	Fla	A	21	122	430	105	21	7	15	185	74	78	40	2	127	9	3	2	14	4	.78	9	.244	.320	.430
Aguirregaviria, Fran.	3b	Bristol	CWS	R+	22	17	46	11	2	0	1	16	3	3	3	0	16	0	0	0	0	0	.00	1	.239	.286	.348
Ahlers, Steve	ss	Cedar Rapds	Ana	A	21	74	260	69	5	1	1	79	27	29	30	0	44	1	3	3	15	9	.63	6	.265	.340	.304
Ahumada, Alex	ss	Augusta	Bos	A	21	125	455	118	24	4	10	180	72	57	41	0	107	16	5	4	9	7	.56	16	.259	.339	.396
Alamo, Efrain	of	Chston-SC	TB	A	23	97	346	85	14	8	10	145	46	53	16	0	96	7	4	2	4	6	.40	6	.246	.291	.419
		St. Pete	TB	A+	23	8	29	4	1	0	0	5	1	0	0	0	9	0	0	0	0	0	.00	0	.138	.138	.172
Albert, Rashad	of	Winston-Sal	CWS	A+	24	21	54	6	1	1	0	9	3	1	4	0	23	0	0	0	0	2	.00	1	.111	.172	.167
		Jupiter	Mon	A+	24	76	245	55	3	5	1	71	25	21	34	2	74	3	9	1	14	16	.47	6	.224	.325	.290
Albertson, Justin	of	Johnson Cy	StL	R+	20	41	128	30	1	1	5	48	17	16	17	0	60	1	0	0	11	2	.85	4	.234	.329	.375
Aldridge, Cory*	of	Macon	Atl	A	21	124	443	111	19	4	12	174	48	65	33	2	123	6	1	5	9	6	.60	9	.251	.308	.393
Aldrup, Morey	of	Eugene	ChC	A-	21	31	65	11	1	0	1	15	6	4	2	0	17	0	1	0	2	0	1.00	1	.169	.194	.231
Alevras, Chad	c	Sarasota	Bos	A+	25	2	7	1	0	0	1	4	2	2	0	0	0	0	1	0	0	0	.00	1	.143	.143	.571
		Augusta	Bos	A	25	5	17	5	1	0	0	6	2	3	2	0	6	0	0	0	0	0	.00	0	.294	.368	.353
Alfaro, Jason	ss	Michigan	Hou	A	22	118	473	128	25	4	5	176	74	50	23	0	62	1	5	7	5	5	.50	10	.271	.302	.372
Alfieri, Frank	3b	Auburn	Hou	A-	23	23	76	18	4	0	4	34	9	12	7	0	22	0	2	0	2	0	1.00	1	.237	.301	.447
Alfonzo, Eliezer	dh-c	New Jersey	StL	A-	21	46	178	58	12	2	3	83	14	28	3	0	39	4	1	1	3	4	.43	5	.326	.349	.466
Allen, Jeff	of	Bakersfield	SF	A+	24	130	480	127	32	3	10	195	80	65	47	0	130	10	0	4	24	5	.83	12	.265	.340	.406
Allen, Shane	of	Yakima	LA	A-	21	33	111	27	10	0	0	37	15	11	6	0	25	4	3	0	4	2	.67	1	.243	.306	.333
Alleyne, Roberto	of	Michigan	Hou	A	23	95	323	94	25	3	8	149	61	60	25	2	59	5	1	7	9	2	.82	4	.291	.344	.461
Allison, Cody*	1b	Kinston	Cle	A+	25	43	121	26	4	0	1	33	15	11	17	0	32	1	4	0	1	0	1.00	3	.215	.317	.273
Almonte, Claudio	of	Quad City	Min	A	21	46	150	32	4	2	0	40	19	12	19	0	41	1	3	1	4	3	.57	4	.213	.304	.267
		Elizabethtn	Min	R+	21	45	172	54	15	2	2	79	32	23	21	0	41	2	0	2	4	6	.40	1	.314	.391	.459
Almonte, Erick	ss	Yankees	NYY	R	22	9	30	9	2	0	2	17	5	9	3	0	10	0	0	2	1	0	1.00	1	.300	.343	.567
		Tampa	NYY	A+	22	61	230	59	8	2	5	86	36	25	18	0	49	2	5	2	3	1	.75	6	.257	.313	.374
Alou, Felipe	of	Chstn-WV	KC	A	21	57	185	36	8	1	0	46	18	13	13	0	50	2	2	2	11	4	.73	1	.195	.252	.249
		Spokane	KC	A-	21	17	42	10	1	1	0	13	4	4	5	0	12	0	0	0	2	0	1.00	1	.238	.319	.310
Altagen, Matt	dh	Tigers	Det	R	20	3	8	2	0	0	0	2	0	2	1	0	4	2	0	0	2	0	1.00	0	.250	.455	.250
Alvarez, Aaron	c	Marlins	Fla	R	20	24	74	19	5	0	0	24	7	4	3	0	12	0	0	1	0	1	.00	1	.257	.282	.324
		Brevard Cty	Fla	A+	20	1	3	2	0	0	1	5	1	1	0	0	0	0	0	0	0	0	.00	0	.667	.667	1.667
Alvarez, Antonio	3b	Williamsprt	Pit	A-	21	58	196	63	14	1	7	100	44	45	21	1	36	16	1	6	38	9	.81	2	.321	.418	.510
Alvarez, Carlos	of	Columbus	Cle	A	24	96	319	82	18	2	14	146	56	49	33	0	70	16	0	6	9	7	.56	5	.257	.350	.458
Alvarez, Henrry	c	Royals	KC	R	20	29	104	19	8	2	0	31	10	11	1	0	37	5	0	1	2	0	1.00	1	.183	.225	.298
Alvarez, Jimmy#	ss	Quad City	Min	A	20	121	435	110	20	1	6	150	69	48	81	3	112	6	7	5	15	10	.60	9	.253	.374	.345
Alvarez, Nell	c	Kingsport	NYM	R+	21	53	159	43	5	2	7	73	32	27	17	0	43	7	6	1	9	7	.56	5	.270	.364	.459
Alviso, Jerome#	2b	Salem	Col	A+	24	128	491	123	16	3	2	151	48	43	28	0	67	3	12	4	5	6	.45	4	.251	.293	.308
Amador, Jerry	of	Everett	Sea	A-	20	14	58	17	3	0	2	26	10	12	6	1	12	2	0	0	3	1	.75	3	.293	.379	.448
		Lancaster	Sea	A+	20	19	74	20	3	1	1	28	12	9	3	0	24	2	2	0	2	1	.67	0	.270	.316	.378
Ambres, Chip	of	Marlins	Fla	R	20	37	139	49	13	3	1	71	29	15	25	0	19	2	0	2	22	3	.88	0	.353	.452	.511
		Utica	Fla	A-	20	28	105	28	3	6	5	58	24	15	21	0	25	1	0	2	11	4	.73	1	.267	.388	.552
Ambrosini, Dom.*	of	Expos	Mon	R	19	19	62	10	1	0	0	11	5	0	8	0	19	0	1	0	1	0	1.00	4	.161	.257	.177
Amezaga, Alfredo	2b	Butte	Ana	R+	22	8	34	10	2	0	0	12	11	5	5	0	5	1	0	0	6	2	.75	0	.294	.400	.353
		Boise	Ana	A-	22	48	205	66	6	4	2	86	52	29	23	2	29	5	3	1	14	3	.82	7	.322	.402	.420
Amrhein, Mike	1b-c	Daytona	ChC	A+	25	127	449	125	27	1	10	184	55	58	31	1	67	13	3	6	1	1	.50	14	.278	.339	.410
Anderson, Dennis	c	Utica	Fla	A-	22	30	96	18	1	1	1	24	10	8	7	0	28	1	3	1	2	0	1.00	1	.188	.248	.250
Anderson, Frank	c	Hickory	Pit	A	24	38	129	25	4	0	4	41	15	11	8	1	52	3	1	0	0	2	.00	4	.194	.257	.318
		Lynchburg	Pit	A+	24	12	35	6	0	0	0	6	4	3	3	0	12	0	2	1	0	1	.00	0	.171	.231	.171
Anderson, Jon#	2b	Red Sox	Bos	R	23	3	11	2	1	0	0	3	1	1	1	0	3	0	0	0	0	1	.00	0	.182	.250	.273
		Lowell	Bos	A-	23	35	124	33	5	0	0	38	20	11	13	0	10	0	2	2	7	4	.64	1	.266	.331	.306
Anderson, Nat*	1b	Tigers	Det	R	18	19	46	6	2	0	0	8	6	3	11	0	16	0	1	1	5	0	1.00	2	.130	.293	.174
Anderson, Syketo*	of	Cubs	ChC	R	21	37	139	41	11	3	0	58	16	14	5	0	22	1	0	0	8	9	.47	2	.295	.324	.417
Andrianoff, Jon	ss	Martinsvlle	Hou	R+	19	24	55	12	1	0	0	13	8	6	9	0	29	2	1	1	4	2	.67	0	.218	.343	.236
Angell, Rick	of	Rangers	Tex	R	23	60	203	51	12	2	2	73	35	32	20	3	30	5	1	3	14	3	.82	5	.251	.329	.360
Araujo, Danilo	2b	Peoria	StL	A	23	105	361	100	10	2	1	117	53	30	43	0	73	3	8	3	21	16	.57	9	.277	.356	.324
Araujo, Victor	3b	Pirates	Pit	R	19	51	199	57	8	0	4	77	30	32	8	0	29	2	0	2	13	5	.72	4	.286	.318	.387
Argento, Shaun	c	Danville	Atl	R+	24	16	43	10	3	0	0	13	5	8	2	0	10	0	0	1	0	0	.00	1	.233	.261	.302
Arias, Jeison	of	Hudson Val	TB	A-	21	17	49	7	1	0	0	8	5	2	3	0	20	0	0	0	0	1	.00	0	.143	.192	.163
		Chston-SC	TB	A	21	30	81	12	2	2	0	18	9	6	7	0	34	1	0	0	1	0	1.00	3	.148	.225	.222
Arias, Leandro#	2b	Mets	NYM	R	19	47	173	52	14	6	5	93	38	33	23	1	30	3	2	0	10	9	.53	6	.301	.392	.538

1999 Batting — Single-A and Rookie Leagues

BATTING																					BASERUNNING				PERCENTAGES		
Player	Pos	Team	Org	Lg	A	G	AB	H	2B	3B	HR	TB	R	RBI	TBB	IBB	SO	HBP	SH	SF	SB	CS	SB%	GDP	Avg	OBP	SLG
Arias, Rogelio	c	Salem	Col	A+	24	76	263	68	11	2	0	83	28	24	15	2	33	0	6	0	3	0	1.00	12	.259	.299	.316
Armstrong, Chris	dh	Auburn	Hou	A-	23	22	77	25	4	1	0	31	17	11	4	0	9	4	0	0	7	1	.88	3	.325	.388	.403
Asche, Kirk	of	Sou Oregon	Oak	A-	22	66	260	75	14	3	17	146	53	67	34	3	56	6	0	2	10	0	1.00	7	.288	.381	.562
August, Brian	3b	Tampa	NYY	A+	24	92	318	86	21	1	5	124	40	42	41	0	72	2	4	10	1	0	1.00	9	.270	.348	.390
Auterson, Jeff	of	Vero Beach	LA	A+	22	104	349	72	19	2	2	101	39	27	34	0	118	10	7	3	5	18	.22	6	.206	.293	.289
Avila, Rob	dh-c	Phillies	Phi	R	21	16	58	19	3	0	2	28	6	5	4	0	10	2	0	0	2	0	1.00	1	.328	.391	.483
		Batavia	Phi	A-	21	10	27	4	3	0	0	7	3	2	6	0	6	2	0	0	0	0	.00	0	.148	.343	.259
		Piedmont	Phi	A	21	3	9	2	1	0	0	3	1	0	0	0	4	0	0	0	0	0	.00	0	.222	.222	.333
Ayala, Elio	2b	Ogden	Mil	R+	21	66	240	64	14	0	1	81	41	19	20	0	27	4	2	1	8	3	.73	5	.267	.332	.338
Ayres, Yancy	c	Chstn-WV	KC	A	24	25	65	11	0	0	0	11	4	2	7	0	17	0	0	0	0	0	.00	2	.169	.250	.169
Backe, Brandon	of	Chston-SC	TB	A	22	84	272	63	11	2	9	105	43	40	35	1	81	6	6	3	3	5	.38	8	.232	.329	.386
		St. Pete	TB	A+	22	41	132	26	6	1	1	37	21	11	21	0	34	3	6	2	0	3	.00	4	.197	.316	.280
Baderdeen, Kevin	3b	Clinton	Cin	A	23	113	405	102	22	4	9	159	47	49	35	0	128	2	0	2	9	6	.60	9	.252	.313	.393
Baez, Ernie#	of	Savannah	Tex	A	22	3	3	0	0	0	0	0	1	0	1	0	2	0	0	0	0	0	.00	0	.000	.250	.000
		Pulaski	Tex	R+	22	8	26	5	0	0	2	11	3	5	4	0	6	0	0	0	1	0	1.00	1	.192	.300	.423
		Rangers	Tex	R	22	12	42	12	1	0	1	16	4	8	3	0	15	1	2	0	2	1	.67	0	.286	.348	.381
Baez, Fleming	dh-c	Rangers	Tex	R	19	4	9	0	0	0	0	0	0	0	0	0	5	0	0	0	0	0	.00	0	.000	.000	.000
Bagley, Lorenzo	of	Dunedin	Tor	A+	24	90	275	77	11	2	12	128	46	44	35	1	70	6	0	5	9	7	.56	6	.280	.368	.465
Bailey, Jeff	dh	Kane County	Fla	A	21	76	277	77	19	1	10	128	49	53	34	2	77	6	0	5	1	1	.50	8	.278	.363	.462
Bailey, Travis	1b	New Jersey	StL	A-	23	66	241	55	9	8	8	104	37	31	17	1	81	4	1	1	6	2	.75	2	.228	.289	.432
Baker, Casey	2b	Yankees	NYY	R	19	35	104	20	3	0	0	23	12	9	18	0	20	1	1	1	4	2	.67	3	.192	.315	.221
Baker, Derek*	dh	Charlotte	Tex	A+	24	119	419	109	16	2	7	150	69	55	58	7	83	12	0	4	3	2	.60	9	.260	.363	.358
Baker, Jacob	1b	Spokane	KC	A-	24	65	234	66	15	2	3	94	34	39	32	2	46	1	0	2	9	4	.69	14	.282	.368	.402
Banez, Marco*	1b-p	Johnson Cy	StL	R+	20	2	5	1	0	0	0	1	1	0	0	0	1	0	0	0	0	0	.00	0	.200	.200	.200
Barnett, Nathan*	1b	Everett	Sea	A-	23	18	40	9	4	0	0	13	4	5	3	0	12	1	1	0	0	0	.00	0	.225	.295	.325
Barnowski, Bryan	c	Red Sox	Bos	R	19	32	88	20	5	1	0	27	13	4	10	0	23	2	1	0	3	1	.75	0	.227	.320	.307
Barns, B.J.*	of	Williamsprt	Pit	A-	22	14	50	20	4	0	1	27	10	11	12	0	11	3	0	0	0	2	.00	0	.400	.538	.540
		Hickory	Pit	A	22	52	174	40	8	4	6	74	16	25	25	0	47	2	1	0	5	3	.63	5	.230	.333	.425
Barr, Clint	c	Yankees	NYY	R	23	11	22	3	1	0	0	4	2	2	2	0	8	1	0	0	0	0	.00	0	.136	.240	.182
		Tampa	NYY	A+	23	7	13	2	0	0	0	2	1	0	2	0	6	1	0	0	0	0	.00	0	.154	.313	.154
Barrow, Corey	of	Reds	Cin	R	20	54	175	30	7	3	2	49	19	19	26	1	56	5	1	1	10	1	.91	3	.171	.295	.280
Barski, Chris*	dh	Boise	Ana	A-	22	53	184	64	14	0	6	96	39	39	30	1	44	4	0	3	1	0	1.00	3	.348	.443	.522
Basabe, Jesus	of	Modesto	Oak	A+	23	95	310	73	21	1	15	141	45	51	36	0	97	16	1	3	12	5	.71	5	.235	.342	.455
Bass, Kevin#	of	Eugene	ChC	A-	21	59	188	36	8	2	8	72	23	30	25	0	79	5	1	3	4	4	.50	1	.191	.299	.383
Bastardo, Angel	c	Burlington	Cle	R+	21	17	61	16	3	0	0	19	7	4	4	0	13	0	0	0	1	0	1.00	1	.262	.308	.311
		Columbus	Cle	A	21	19	53	13	0	2	3	26	6	9	5	0	13	1	0	0	0	0	.00	3	.245	.322	.491
Batcheller, Chris	of	Pirates	Pit	R	22	6	23	6	1	0	0	7	3	3	2	0	4	0	1	0	1	0	1.00	0	.261	.320	.304
		Williamsprt	Pit	A-	22	23	81	12	1	0	1	16	2	9	1	0	31	2	1	1	1	0	1.00	3	.148	.176	.198
Batista, Angel*	of	Hudson Val	TB	A-	20	53	164	30	5	0	0	35	19	12	22	0	46	1	3	3	8	4	.67	1	.183	.279	.213
		Princeton	TB	R+	20	7	29	4	1	0	0	5	4	1	1	0	8	0	0	0	0	0	.00	0	.138	.167	.172
		St. Pete	TB	A+	20	6	16	4	0	0	0	4	4	0	1	0	0	0	1	0	0	1	.00	0	.250	.294	.250
Batista, Carlos	1b	Burlington	Cle	R+	20	45	171	40	8	0	3	57	16	29	8	0	49	0	0	1	0	2	.00	6	.234	.267	.333
Batson, Tom	2b-3b	Batavia	Phi	A-	23	65	245	73	10	4	8	115	52	33	35	1	36	3	2	3	11	5	.69	3	.298	.388	.469
Battersby, Eric	1b	Burlington	CWS	A	24	132	472	137	27	2	18	222	78	93	83	1	90	4	0	9	13	2	.87	8	.290	.394	.470
Bautista, Jorge	dh	Kane County	Fla	A	23	61	186	41	12	0	3	62	30	30	21	0	54	4	1	4	2	1	.67	4	.220	.307	.333
Bautista, Rayner	ss	Lakeland	Det	A+	20	96	303	69	11	4	1	91	35	32	21	0	75	3	4	2	7	3	.70	10	.228	.283	.300
Bazzani, Matt	c	San Jose	SF	A+	26	34	93	22	4	1	7	49	18	12	8	0	29	1	0	0	0	0	.00	1	.237	.304	.527
Beam, Dusty	ss	Oneonta	Det	A-	23	50	165	28	5	0	0	33	20	3	17	0	45	0	2	0	2	1	.67	3	.170	.247	.200
Beatriz, Ramy*	of	Beloit	Mil	A	21	70	243	72	14	2	3	99	43	26	29	3	39	0	1	0	5	3	.63	5	.296	.371	.407
		Stockton	Mil	A+	21	41	149	36	7	2	1	50	21	10	7	0	24	1	0	2	3	5	.38	1	.242	.277	.336
Beattie, Andrew#	2b	Clinton	Cin	A	22	108	335	77	11	3	6	112	58	41	60	1	75	3	8	5	18	4	.82	6	.230	.347	.334
Beinbrink, Andrew	3b	Hudson Val	TB	A-	23	76	292	99	24	2	11	160	46	51	39	2	49	8	0	4	13	4	.76	4	.339	.426	.548
Bell, Josh	3b	Mets	NYM	R	20	31	90	20	0	0	0	20	14	7	11	0	27	3	6	0	4	3	.57	0	.222	.327	.222
Bell, Ricky	2b	Vero Beach	LA	A+	21	100	376	88	26	1	5	131	37	46	27	0	81	4	4	4	1	3	.25	13	.234	.290	.348
Belliard, Fernando	dh	St. Pete	TB	A+	19	6	12	2	0	0	0	2	1	0	0	0	6	0	0	0	0	0	.00	0	.167	.167	.167
Benham, David	c-1b	Augusta	Bos	A	24	3	9	0	0	0	0	0	0	0	0	0	7	0	0	0	0	0	.00	0	.000	.000	.000
		Sarasota	Bos	A+	24	33	105	25	5	0	3	39	10	11	5	0	18	3	0	1	0	0	.00	3	.238	.289	.371
		Potomac	StL	A+	24	9	26	4	1	0	0	5	2	1	1	0	7	2	1	0	0	0	.00	2	.154	.241	.192
Benham, Jason*	3b	Frederick	Bal	A+	24	16	27	4	0	0	0	4	3	2	2	0	2	0	1	1	0	0	.00	1	.148	.200	.148
		Delmarva	Bal	A	24	7	21	2	2	0	0	4	1	3	3	1	6	0	0	0	0	0	.00	0	.095	.208	.190
Benjamin, Al	of	Cape Fear	Mon	A	22	128	488	157	38	2	10	229	66	77	27	2	110	7	0	5	14	17	.45	9	.322	.362	.469
Berger, Brandon	of	Wilmington	KC	A+	25	119	450	132	27	4	16	215	73	73	45	0	93	8	6	6	29	7	.81	3	.293	.363	.478
Berger, Matt	1b	Winston-Sal	CWS	A+	25	90	329	74	17	0	10	121	41	49	34	1	86	2	1	6	1	3	.25	4	.225	.296	.368
Bernard, Dagoberto	ss-2b	Rockies	Col	R	20	34	117	38	5	0	0	43	14	21	6	1	17	3	0	2	7	6	.54	5	.325	.367	.368
Bernhardt, Jos.	3b	St.Cathrnes	Tor	A-	19	70	267	65	10	1	5	92	20	35	8	1	67	1	1	7	2	1	.67	3	.243	.261	.345
Berns, Robert	1b	St. Pete	TB	A+	25	14	43	9	3	0	0	12	4	7	3	0	2	2	0	2	0	1	.00	1	.209	.280	.279
Berrien, Sam*	1b	Bluefield	Bal	R+	21	30	92	22	3	1	0	27	13	9	18	0	22	4	0	0	1	1	.50	1	.239	.386	.293
Berroa, Cristian#	ss	Fort Wayne	SD	A	21	119	442	106	12	3	4	136	49	40	14	0	71	3	5	5	25	11	.69	9	.240	.265	.308
Bertrand, Ben	c	Bakersfield	SF	A+	24	12	21	4	1	0	0	5	3	0	3	0	7	1	0	0	0	0	.00	1	.190	.320	.238
Besco, Derek	of	Lakeland	Det	A+	24	122	456	131	28	4	9	194	70	66	37	4	88	3	1	3	10	7	.59	12	.287	.343	.425
Betemit, Wilson#	ss	Danville	Atl	R+	19	67	259	83	18	2	5	120	39	53	27	1	63	1	1	3	6	3	.67	4	.320	.383	.463
Betts, DeWayne	of	Athletics	Oak	R	20	34	70	9	3	0	0	12	13	6	8	0	25	1	0	1	0	0	.00	2	.129	.225	.171
Beverly, Shomari	of	Piedmont	Phi	A	22	50	173	34	7	0	6	59	18	12	11	0	62	2	1	0	4	2	.67	1	.197	.253	.341
		Batavia	Phi	A-	22	65	267	65	13	7	3	101	35	34	16	0	75	2	0	1	19	4	.83	2	.243	.290	.378
Bevins, Andy	dh-of	Potomac	StL	A+	24	138	513	142	30	2	25	251	92	97	44	2	128	11	3	4	6	2	.75	11	.277	.344	.489
Bigbie, Larry*	of	Bluefield	Bal	R+	22	8	30	8	0	0	0	8	3	4	3	0	8	1	0	1	1	3	.25	1	.267	.343	.267
		Delmarva	Bal	A	22	43	165	46	7	3	2	65	18	27	29	0	42	0	0	3	3	1	.75	4	.279	.381	.394

1999 Batting — Single-A and Rookie Leagues

BATTING																					BASERUNNING				PERCENTAGES		
Player	Pos	Team	Org	Lg	A	G	AB	H	2B	3B	HR	TB	R	RBI	TBB	IBB	SO	HBP	SH	SF	SB	CS	SB%	GDP	Avg	OBP	SLG
Bikowski, Scott*	of	Boise	Ana	A-	23	65	246	73	22	0	2	101	59	45	46	1	42	5	3	1	11	4	.73	3	.297	.416	.411
Bishop, Bennie	of	Phillies	Phi	R	21	28	82	19	4	1	0	25	9	9	7	0	23	0	0	1	4	1	.80	3	.232	.289	.305
Blair, James	3b	San Berndno	LA	A+	23	25	78	20	2	1	2	30	13	7	16	0	15	1	0	1	3	2	.60	4	.256	.385	.385
Blakely, Darren#	of	Lk Elsinore	Ana	A+	23	124	510	128	38	10	12	222	88	63	36	1	159	20	1	4	23	13	.64	3	.251	.323	.435
Blalock, Hank*	3b	Rangers	Tex	R	19	51	191	69	17	6	3	107	34	38	25	4	23	1	0	5	3	2	.60	7	.361	.428	.560
		Savannah	Tex	A	19	7	25	6	1	0	1	10	3	2	1	0	3	1	0	1	0	0	.00	0	.240	.286	.400
Blankenship, Tony	2b	White Sox	CWS	R	23	9	23	8	0	2	0	12	7	4	4	0	4	0	0	0	1	1	.50	1	.348	.444	.522
		Bristol	CWS	R+	23	12	29	3	0	0	0	3	4	1	5	0	16	0	0	0	0	1	.00	0	.103	.235	.103
Bledsoe, Hunter	dh	San Berndno	LA	A+	24	45	166	44	10	1	2	62	17	13	9	0	27	2	0	1	3	0	1.00	6	.265	.309	.373
Bloomquist, William	2b	Everett	Sea	A-	22	42	178	51	10	3	2	73	35	27	22	0	25	1	0	1	17	5	.77	1	.287	.366	.410
Bly, Derrick	1b	Lansing	ChC	A	25	63	220	65	14	4	4	99	36	29	9	0	48	3	0	2	1	1	.50	8	.295	.329	.450
		Daytona	ChC	A+	25	41	149	35	13	0	4	60	22	15	16	1	34	3	1	1	1	1	.50	2	.235	.320	.403
Boeth, Tim	2b	Boise	Ana	A-	23	51	169	50	11	2	2	71	36	22	24	0	21	4	0	4	9	6	.60	3	.296	.388	.420
Boitel, Rafael#	of	Twins	Min	R	19	45	161	46	6	2	0	56	23	14	18	3	39	1	1	1	6	4	.60	1	.286	.359	.348
Bolivar, Papo	of-dh	Fort Myers	Min	A+	21	114	433	132	21	3	3	168	54	37	27	1	56	4	3	1	8	9	.47	10	.305	.351	.388
Bolling, Kirk	3b	South Bend	Ari	A	23	16	49	9	5	0	1	17	6	6	6	0	18	1	0	0	1	0	1.00	0	.184	.286	.347
Bone, Billy	3b-2b	Pirates	Pit	R	24	7	24	3	1	0	0	4	4	3	2	0	3	0	1	1	0	0	.00	2	.125	.185	.167
		Hickory	Pit	A	24	7	20	4	2	0	1	9	7	3	7	0	6	1	1	0	0	0	.00	1	.200	.429	.450
		Lynchburg	Pit	A+	24	38	104	26	5	0	1	34	17	13	22	0	35	1	2	1	3	1	.75	1	.250	.383	.327
Bonifay, Josh	2b	Williamsprt	Pit	A-	21	52	200	52	10	2	4	78	42	17	25	0	55	2	1	0	2	2	.50	1	.260	.348	.390
Bonilla, Juan	1b	Delmarva	Bal	A	22	6	11	3	0	0	0	3	1	0	1	0	4	0	0	0	0	0	.00	1	.273	.333	.273
		Bluefield	Bal	R+	22	34	100	24	5	0	1	32	12	17	12	0	23	1	0	1	0	0	.00	2	.240	.325	.320
Bookout, Casey*	1b	Billings	Cin	R+	23	50	204	74	14	1	13	129	49	63	26	1	37	3	0	1	0	1	.00	5	.363	.440	.632
Boone, Matt	3b	W Michigan	Det	A	20	116	421	102	24	1	9	155	46	56	29	0	119	3	1	5	8	7	.53	8	.242	.293	.368
Bordenick, Ryan	c	Beloit	Mil	A	24	73	248	67	19	1	6	106	40	36	25	1	60	2	3	3	2	0	1.00	7	.270	.338	.427
Borjas, Henry#	1b	Red Sox	Bos	R	21	49	152	29	5	3	0	40	18	11	16	0	26	4	0	1	3	4	.43	5	.191	.283	.263
Borrego, Ramon#	of	Fort Myers	Min	A+	22	27	86	19	3	0	0	22	9	6	7	0	15	1	0	0	4	0	1.00	1	.221	.287	.256
Boscan, Jean	c	Macon	Atl	A	20	105	368	83	17	0	4	112	40	38	26	0	94	2	2	3	2	4	.33	10	.226	.278	.304
Bost, Tom*	dh-of	Mahoning Vy	Cle	A-	24	23	70	13	0	1	5	30	11	13	11	0	35	1	0	1	0	0	.00	0	.186	.301	.429
Boughton, Mike#	ss	Charlotte	Tex	A+	25	14	39	7	0	0	0	7	5	4	3	0	9	0	0	1	2	1	.67	1	.179	.233	.179
		Savannah	Tex	A	25	26	90	24	4	0	0	28	7	3	12	0	22	0	1	0	1	2	.33	4	.267	.353	.311
Bowen, Rob#	c	Twins	Min	R	19	29	77	20	4	0	0	24	10	11	20	0	15	0	1	3	2	2	.50	0	.260	.400	.312
Bowers, Jason	ss	Peoria	StL	A	22	112	414	109	14	8	2	145	53	49	32	1	78	9	5	1	10	9	.53	6	.263	.329	.350
Boyer, Cletis	2b	Expos	Mon	R	19	32	93	16	1	0	0	17	6	8	6	0	20	0	0	0	6	1	.86	3	.172	.222	.183
Boykin, Paul*	of	Idaho Falls	SD	R+	22	45	140	37	6	1	1	48	30	10	14	0	44	0	0	0	24	9	.73	3	.248	.313	.322
Bradley, Wade*	of	Phillies	Phi	R	21	2	5	0	0	0	0	0	0	0	0	0	3	0	0	0	0	0	.00	0	.000	.000	.000
Brazeal, Spencer	c	Staten Ilnd	NYY	A-	23	8	10	1	0	0	0	1	3	1	1	0	4	1	0	0	0	0	.00	0	.100	.250	.100
		Yankees	NYY	R	23	26	68	14	3	0	0	17	13	5	17	0	19	1	2	0	1	1	.50	0	.206	.372	.250
Brazell, Craig*	1b-dh	Kingsport	NYM	R+	20	59	221	85	16	1	6	121	27	39	7	4	34	8	2	1	6	5	.55	5	.385	.422	.548
Brazoban, Jose	of	Helena	Mil	R+	21	45	158	37	5	1	1	47	28	18	18	0	43	4	1	1	18	5	.78	2	.234	.326	.297
Brazoban, Yhency	of	Yankees	NYY	R	19	56	200	64	14	5	1	91	33	26	12	0	47	4	1	2	7	3	.70	2	.320	.367	.455
Brett, Jason	ss-2b	Capital Cty	NYM	A	23	32	95	23	3	0	0	26	11	1	12	0	25	1	3	0	4	2	.67	2	.242	.333	.274
		Pittsfield	NYM	A-	23	42	109	23	3	0	0	26	20	7	10	0	20	5	4	0	12	2	.86	0	.211	.306	.239
Brignac, Junior	of	Macon	Atl	A	22	69	268	80	18	3	7	125	35	38	11	0	68	2	0	2	17	5	.77	2	.299	.329	.466
		Myrtle Bch	Atl	A+	22	64	254	58	7	2	7	90	32	35	24	3	84	4	2	4	11	10	.52	6	.228	.301	.354
Briones, Chris	c-dh	Rancho Cuca	SD	A+	27	27	76	14	3	0	1	20	3	6	3	0	23	1	2	0	0	0	.00	2	.184	.225	.263
Brito, Justo	c	Mets	NYM	R	21	43	128	28	4	0	3	41	18	20	15	0	26	5	1	2	0	1	.00	6	.219	.320	.320
Brito, Obispo	c	Beloit	Mil	A	22	101	364	85	24	1	7	132	44	48	13	1	76	3	4	3	7	0	1.00	7	.234	.264	.363
Britt, Bryan	1b	Potomac	StL	A+	25	11	26	5	0	0	1	8	1	3	1	0	11	0	0	0	0	0	.00	2	.192	.222	.308
Bronowicz, Scott*	c	Myrtle Bch	Atl	A+	24	21	56	8	1	1	0	11	9	4	6	0	12	1	0	0	0	0	.00	0	.143	.238	.196
Brooks, Jeff	3b	Missoula	Ari	R+	20	73	295	100	18	4	12	162	48	60	17	0	77	5	0	0	6	2	.75	10	.339	.385	.549
Brown, Andy*	of	Greensboro	NYY	A	20	29	108	19	5	1	5	41	14	15	10	0	49	0	0	0	0	1	.00	0	.176	.246	.380
		Staten Ilnd	NYY	A-	20	67	215	46	8	5	7	85	38	22	27	0	97	2	0	2	5	2	.71	1	.214	.305	.395
Brown, Billy	of	Greensboro	NYY	A	24	134	520	153	28	6	19	250	102	62	71	0	144	12	2	1	21	10	.68	9	.294	.391	.481
Brown, Jason	dh	San Berndno	LA	A+	26	68	234	51	11	2	6	84	28	28	23	1	64	7	3	0	1	2	.33	9	.218	.307	.359
Brown, Matt	3b	Expos	Mon	R	19	31	99	16	1	0	3	26	11	8	11	0	38	1	0	0	3	0	1.00	1	.162	.252	.263
Brown, Tonayne	of	Augusta	Bos	A	22	135	541	141	24	7	4	191	82	45	46	0	89	8	8	4	25	22	.53	14	.261	.326	.353
Bryan, Jason	of	Rangers	Tex	R	18	6	20	7	2	0	0	9	3	1	3	0	9	0	0	0	1	1	.50	0	.350	.435	.450
Buccheri, Joe	2b	Helena	Mil	R+	21	21	65	13	2	0	0	15	6	13	3	0	15	2	1	0	4	4	.50	3	.200	.257	.231
		Ogden	Mil	R+	21	10	21	4	0	0	0	4	3	1	6	0	5	0	0	0	0	1	.00	0	.190	.370	.190
Buck, John	c	Auburn	Hou	A-	19	63	233	57	17	0	3	83	36	29	25	1	48	5	1	2	7	1	.88	7	.245	.328	.356
		Michigan	Hou	A	19	4	10	1	1	0	0	2	1	0	2	0	3	0	0	0	0	0	.00	0	.100	.250	.200
Buckley, Brandon	c	Kissimmee	Hou	A+	23	51	146	29	5	0	1	37	13	11	11	1	29	0	3	1	1	3	.25	4	.199	.253	.253
Buckley, Chris	dh-of	Johnson Cy	StL	R+	23	47	171	43	8	2	3	64	19	23	13	0	68	1	1	0	10	3	.77	0	.251	.308	.374
Bultmann, Kurt	2b	Hickory	Pit	A	23	13	45	16	2	0	0	18	4	9	6	0	4	0	2	1	1	1	.50	3	.356	.423	.400
		Lynchburg	Pit	A+	23	30	87	17	3	1	0	22	7	3	17	0	15	3	3	0	0	0	.00	3	.195	.346	.253
Bundy, Ryan	c	Hagerstown	Tor	A	22	46	153	34	5	1	5	56	19	17	18	0	62	5	3	0	5	3	.63	0	.222	.324	.366
Bunkley, Antuan	1b	Lakeland	Det	A+	24	133	493	134	26	0	4	172	52	69	49	2	69	8	0	4	1	1	.50	14	.272	.345	.349
Burford, Kevin*	dh	Portland	Col	A-	22	64	216	66	22	2	7	113	55	33	52	3	45	5	0	2	9	6	.60	3	.306	.447	.523
Burke, Paul	1b-c	Jamestown	Atl	A-	22	34	101	18	5	0	0	23	5	9	9	0	27	0	3	2	1	0	1.00	0	.178	.241	.228
Burnett, Mark*	2b	Billings	Cin	R+	23	60	224	73	13	2	4	102	56	29	46	0	32	4	3	2	12	9	.57	3	.326	.446	.455
Burns, Kevan*	of	Missoula	Ari	R+	23	16	55	20	2	2	1	29	15	14	6	0	10	0	0	0	3	0	1.00	2	.364	.426	.527
		South Bend	Ari	A	23	43	157	50	8	1	2	66	22	25	14	0	27	0	0	0	3	4	.43	3	.318	.374	.420
Burns, Pat#	1b	St. Lucie	NYM	A+	22	133	488	116	26	2	6	164	54	54	50	3	122	2	1	1	6	3	.67	15	.238	.311	.336
Burns, Xavier	3b	Bakersfield	SF	A+	25	80	229	50	9	3	3	74	28	29	19	1	70	11	0	6	10	9	.53	6	.218	.302	.323
Burroughs, Sean*	3b	Fort Wayne	SD	A	19	122	426	153	30	3	5	204	65	80	74	7	59	14	2	5	17	15	.53	10	.359	.464	.479
		Rancho Cuca	SD	A+	19	6	23	10	3	0	1	16	3	5	3	0	3	1	0	0	0	1	.00	1	.435	.519	.696

1999 Batting — Single-A and Rookie Leagues

BATTING																					BASERUNNING				PERCENTAGES		
Player	Pos	Team	Org	Lg	A	G	AB	H	2B	3B	HR	TB	R	RBI	TBB	IBB	SO	HBP	SH	SF	SB	CS	SB%	GDP	Avg	OBP	SLG
Bush, Brian	of	Piedmont	Phi	A	23	38	129	30	3	0	0	33	12	7	7	0	32	5	1	0	4	5	.44	0	.233	.298	.256
Bush, Darren*	of	Rancho Cuca	SD	A+	26	77	238	67	9	1	8	102	35	36	36	1	51	1	2	0	7	4	.64	7	.282	.378	.429
Bush, Ron	2b-ss	W Michigan	Det	A	23	118	444	113	23	4	1	147	56	60	44	0	57	5	10	3	14	10	.58	15	.255	.327	.331
Butler, Allen*	1b	Fort Myers	Min	A+	25	137	491	124	36	2	14	206	73	73	65	4	121	3	3	3	3	3	.50	8	.253	.342	.420
Butler, Garrett#	of	St. Pete	TB	A+	24	94	329	82	14	3	2	108	36	31	17	0	61	2	5	1	16	6	.73	3	.249	.289	.328
Byrd, Marlon	of	Batavia	Phi	A-	22	65	243	72	7	6	13	130	40	50	28	1	70	5	0	3	8	2	.80	3	.296	.376	.535
Bystrowski, Robby	of	Idaho Falls	SD	R+	23	44	155	46	8	3	3	69	37	19	27	0	44	6	1	0	19	5	.79	1	.297	.420	.445
Caballero, Antonio*	of	Hickory	Pit	A	21	13	38	3	0	0	0	3	3	2	3	0	13	0	0	0	0	1	.00	0	.079	.146	.079
Cabrera, Ray	of	Bluefield	Bal	R+	21	31	117	32	9	0	2	47	21	9	6	0	14	3	0	1	1	3	.25	3	.274	.323	.402
		Orioles	Bal	R	21	16	58	18	3	2	0	25	8	12	1	0	6	2	0	1	4	0	1.00	1	.310	.339	.431
Cabrera, Yoelmis	of	Pirates	Pit	R	19	27	78	22	7	0	0	29	17	6	10	0	15	3	0	1	8	0	1.00	2	.282	.380	.372
Caceres, Wilmy#	ss	Reds	Cin	R	21	2	9	3	0	0	0	3	2	0	0	0	1	0	0	0	0	0	.00	0	.333	.333	.333
		Clinton	Cin	A	21	117	476	124	18	5	1	155	77	30	30	1	65	2	2	2	52	22	.70	6	.261	.306	.326
Cadiente, Brett*	of	Pulaski	Tex	R+	23	68	274	97	16	7	7	148	69	49	38	1	51	3	1	3	18	2	.90	3	.354	.434	.540
Caiazzo, Nick	1b	Stockton	Mil	A+	25	114	430	129	21	4	8	182	51	56	25	0	85	8	1	4	2	3	.40	12	.300	.347	.423
Calais, Ian	ss	Jamestown	Atl	A-	23	68	224	47	8	1	0	57	19	20	23	0	47	2	4	1	4	5	.44	6	.210	.288	.254
Calderon, Henry	ss	Chstn-WV	KC	A	22	130	459	104	29	1	7	156	49	56	21	1	106	9	9	4	33	14	.70	9	.227	.272	.340
Callahan, David*	1b	Kane County	Fla	A	20	124	457	112	22	4	2	148	65	53	51	0	105	4	1	2	2	1	.67	7	.245	.325	.324
Calzado, Napolean	3b-ss	Bluefield	Bal	R+	20	52	199	58	11	2	6	91	46	31	20	1	32	3	0	1	9	1	.90	2	.291	.363	.457
		Delmarva	Bal	A	20	6	18	5	1	0	0	6	2	1	0	0	4	0	0	1	0	0	.00	1	.278	.263	.333
Camarero, Rafael	1b	Reds	Cin	R	18	31	81	17	2	0	1	22	4	10	9	0	17	0	0	2	1	2	.33	1	.210	.283	.272
Cameron, Troy#	3b	Macon	Atl	A	21	130	462	110	28	2	22	208	71	77	68	0	161	6	0	6	7	9	.44	6	.238	.339	.450
Camilo, Juan*	of	Visalia	Oak	A+	22	82	285	81	17	2	17	153	58	52	34	0	89	4	0	1	7	6	.54	8	.284	.367	.537
Campana, Wandel	ss	Reds	Cin	R	20	17	71	17	5	1	1	27	12	10	1	0	12	1	1	0	1	1	.50	1	.239	.260	.380
		Billings	Cin	R+	20	45	157	42	10	2	1	59	27	20	7	0	22	1	5	0	6	4	.60	3	.268	.303	.376
Campbell, Sean*	c	Fort Wayne	SD	A	23	102	343	91	17	4	7	137	48	54	27	2	71	3	4	4	10	4	.71	6	.265	.321	.399
Campbell, Wylie#	ss-2b	Wilmington	KC	A+	25	45	137	33	4	0	1	40	22	17	25	1	29	2	2	0	6	5	.55	3	.241	.366	.292
Candela, Frank	dh-of	Beloit	Mil	A	21	30	107	32	4	0	0	36	15	5	9	0	12	2	3	0	14	6	.70	1	.299	.364	.336
Candelario, Luis	of-dh	Princeton	TB	R+	18	13	54	7	1	0	1	11	3	8	1	0	18	0	0	1	1	0	1.00	4	.130	.143	.204
Cantu, Jorge	ss	Hudson Val	TB	A-	18	72	281	73	17	2	1	97	33	33	20	0	59	2	4	1	3	4	.43	8	.260	.313	.345
Capellan, Rene	ss-2b	Lakeland	Det	A+	22	34	113	20	2	0	1	25	14	9	3	0	10	1	2	0	2	2	.50	4	.177	.205	.221
Capista, Aaron#	ss	Sarasota	Bos	A+	21	130	518	137	18	3	5	176	64	47	45	2	60	3	8	4	25	10	.71	9	.264	.325	.340
Caracciolo, Anthony	ss	Vermont	Mon	A-	20	7	15	3	1	0	0	4	2	3	6	0	5	2	0	0	1	0	1.00	0	.200	.478	.267
Caradonna, Brett*	of	Winston-Sal	CWS	A+	21	128	505	127	28	4	9	190	68	62	48	2	108	2	4	5	18	7	.72	5	.251	.316	.376
Cardona, Raynier#	c	Pirates	Pit	R	19	14	37	8	3	0	0	11	2	7	9	0	9	0	0	0	1	0	1.00	1	.216	.370	.297
Caridi, Tony#	1b-c	Red Sox	Bos	R	20	25	72	12	2	0	0	14	9	3	9	0	19	0	0	1	1	0	1.00	2	.167	.256	.194
Carnes, Shayne*	1b	Piedmont	Phi	A	23	106	396	106	28	0	10	164	45	55	26	1	78	2	0	2	1	1	.50	18	.268	.315	.414
Carreno, Jose	c	Cape Fear	Mon	A	22	41	140	31	2	0	0	33	11	10	5	0	16	1	1	1	4	3	.57	3	.221	.252	.236
		Jupiter	Mon	A+	22	2	6	0	0	0	0	0	0	0	0	0	2	0	0	0	0	0	.00	0	.000	.000	.000
Carrillo, Robert	1b	Martinsvlle	Hou	R+	21	49	174	39	7	0	7	67	21	28	15	0	56	7	0	3	5	2	.71	5	.224	.307	.385
Carter, Charley	1b	Kissimmee	Hou	A+	24	115	416	114	19	2	12	173	62	56	28	2	77	3	0	4	0	3	.00	7	.274	.322	.416
Carter, Quincy	of	Daytona	ChC	A+	22	1	3	0	0	0	0	0	0	0	0	0	1	0	0	0	0	0	.00	0	.000	.000	.000
Caruso, Joe	2b-of	Wilmington	KC	A+	25	102	361	85	13	6	5	125	60	37	34	0	68	8	6	3	6	4	.60	7	.235	.313	.346
Carvajal, Ramon#	2b	New Jersey	StL	A-	19	65	240	60	9	8	6	103	35	30	13	0	59	1	4	1	12	7	.63	3	.250	.290	.429
Cash, Lavalroe	of	Cubs	ChC	R	20	49	194	52	10	1	9	91	29	29	10	0	46	2	0	2	4	3	.57	0	.268	.308	.469
Casillas, Uriel	3b-ss	Piedmont	Phi	A	24	73	225	51	11	2	0	66	30	20	48	0	33	7	2	1	4	5	.44	7	.227	.377	.293
		Clearwater	Phi	A+	24	32	113	32	5	0	0	37	23	24	17	0	10	9	4	1	4	2	.67	2	.283	.414	.327
Casper, Brett	of	San Jose	SF	A+	24	121	436	116	22	2	16	190	71	77	56	2	135	6	4	3	20	10	.67	12	.266	.355	.436
Castaneda, Cesar	3b	Savannah	Tex	A	23	103	331	67	13	2	12	120	33	47	29	0	105	5	0	1	2	4	.33	8	.202	.276	.363
Castellano, John	c	Vero Beach	LA	A+	22	6	18	8	0	0	0	8	3	0	2	0	0	0	1	0	0	0	.00	1	.444	.500	.444
		Great Falls	LA	R+	22	37	134	33	6	1	1	44	13	25	9	0	8	2	0	4	3	2	.60	4	.246	.295	.328
Castellano, Jose	of	Braves	Atl	R	19	23	70	16	3	1	1	24	11	11	8	0	18	4	1	0	1	1	.50	1	.229	.341	.343
Castillo, Carlos	c	Athletics	Oak	R	19	31	88	18	4	1	1	27	9	13	3	0	23	2	0	1	0	0	.00	2	.205	.245	.307
Castillo, Geramel#	of	Savannah	Tex	A	22	114	405	122	21	4	3	160	42	40	19	0	94	2	2	2	4	4	.50	7	.301	.334	.395
Castillo, Jose	ss-2b	Pirates	Pit	R	19	47	173	46	9	0	4	67	27	30	11	1	23	3	3	3	8	0	1.00	4	.266	.316	.387
Castillo, Ruben	ss	Wisconsin	Sea	A	19	20	44	9	0	0	0	9	7	4	5	0	9	0	0	0	1	1	.50	3	.205	.286	.205
		Everett	Sea	A-	19	62	226	65	10	2	2	85	38	27	19	0	48	2	3	1	11	2	.85	3	.288	.347	.376
Castillo, Victor	2b	Yankees	NYY	R	19	42	153	48	8	1	0	58	24	16	22	0	38	5	2	1	9	8	.53	1	.314	.414	.379
Castri, Andrea	1b	Greensboro	NYY	A	26	78	264	63	14	1	6	97	35	33	25	0	91	12	2	1	2	3	.40	1	.239	.331	.367
Castro, Martires	of	Expos	Mon	R	23	11	38	9	2	1	1	16	5	7	1	0	9	1	0	0	1	0	1.00	1	.237	.275	.421
		Cape Fear	Mon	A	23	9	31	9	2	1	0	13	1	3	0	0	7	0	0	0	1	0	1.00	0	.290	.290	.419
Castro, Nelson	ss	Lk Elsinore	Ana	A+	24	125	444	111	16	12	1	154	68	50	36	1	75	3	5	4	53	19	.74	5	.250	.308	.347
Castro, Ramon#	2b	Macon	Atl	A	20	105	350	91	12	4	3	120	32	33	24	0	55	2	7	2	13	5	.72	4	.260	.310	.343
Castro, Vicente	of	Pirates	Pit	R	20	43	161	45	9	0	3	63	21	21	6	0	30	2	0	1	3	0	1.00	1	.280	.312	.391
Catalanott, Greg#	of	Portland	Col	A-	23	68	245	69	8	2	14	123	38	47	30	2	75	2	1	3	4	2	.67	1	.282	.361	.502
Cates, Gary	2b	Orioles	Bal	R	18	45	127	34	7	0	1	44	20	20	15	1	20	5	5	4	11	2	.85	0	.268	.358	.346
Cedeno, Jesus	of	W Michigan	Det	A	24	47	157	37	9	0	3	55	14	18	6	0	34	3	1	1	3	3	.50	3	.236	.275	.350
Celli, Mike#	of	Jamestown	Atl	A-	23	72	246	67	16	1	2	91	39	33	32	1	55	5	1	6	8	0	1.00	6	.272	.360	.370
Centeno, Edwin#	of	Bluefield	Bal	R+	22	5	8	2	0	0	0	2	1	0	0	0	2	0	0	0	1	0	1.00	0	.250	.250	.250
		Orioles	Bal	R	22	33	92	25	4	3	2	41	22	15	4	0	26	1	1	1	12	3	.80	0	.272	.306	.446
Centile, Raul#	ss	Burlington	Cle	R+	21	9	24	4	0	0	0	4	2	1	4	0	7	0	0	0	1	0	1.00	0	.167	.286	.167
		Mahoning Vy	Cle	A-	21	25	88	21	5	2	1	33	15	13	5	0	17	0	1	1	3	1	.75	2	.239	.277	.375
Cepeda, Ali	of	Salem-Keizr	SF	A-	23	24	44	11	2	0	0	13	0	5	11	0	15	0	0	0	4	2	.67	1	.250	.400	.295
		San Jose	SF	A+	23	9	13	1	0	0	0	1	0	0	0	0	4	0	0	0	0	0	.00	0	.077	.077	.077
Cepicky, Matt*	of	Vermont	Mon	A-	22	74	323	99	15	5	12	160	50	53	20	1	49	1	0	0	10	9	.53	6	.307	.349	.495
Ceriani, Matt	c	Helena	Mil	R+	23	57	162	49	11	0	1	63	22	25	15	0	23	4	2	1	4	0	1.00	5	.302	.374	.389
Chambliss, Russ*	of	Tampa	NYY	A+	25	5	6	0	0	0	0	0	0	0	0	0	2	0	0	0	0	0	.00	0	.000	.000	.000

1999 Batting — Single-A and Rookie Leagues

BATTING																					BASERUNNING				PERCENTAGES		
Player	Pos	Team	Org	Lg	A	G	AB	H	2B	3B	HR	TB	R	RBI	TBB	IBB	SO	HBP	SH	SF	SB	CS	SB%	GDP	Avg	OBP	SLG
Chapman, Scott	c	Michigan	Hou	A	22	64	226	61	17	1	11	113	37	36	14	0	32	7	0	1	1	2	.33	7	.270	.331	.500
Chatman, Karl	of	San Berndno	LA	A+	25	79	300	80	13	2	4	109	40	37	29	2	87	4	1	2	13	9	.59	9	.267	.337	.363
Chavera, Arnie*	dh	Kissimmee	Hou	A+	26	62	213	59	13	0	14	114	29	43	26	3	59	7	0	0	1	0	1.00	2	.277	.374	.535
Chavez, Endy*	of	Capital Cty	NYM	A	22	73	253	64	8	1	0	74	40	15	34	0	36	0	2	1	20	12	.63	3	.253	.340	.292
		St. Lucie	NYM	A+	22	45	183	57	8	3	2	77	33	18	22	2	22	0	2	1	9	3	.75	5	.311	.383	.421
Cheek, Shawn	c	Augusta	Bos	A	26	5	16	6	2	0	0	8	3	2	0	0	1	0	0	0	0	0	.00	0	.375	.375	.500
		Sarasota	Bos	A+	26	15	25	2	0	0	0	2	1	1	2	0	10	1	0	1	0	0	.00	0	.080	.172	.080
Chen, Chin-Feng	of	San Berndno	LA	A+	22	131	510	161	22	10	31	296	98	123	75	6	129	5	0	7	31	7	.82	7	.316	.404	.580
Choi, Hee*	1b	Lansing	ChC	A	21	79	290	93	18	6	18	177	71	70	50	0	68	2	0	2	2	1	.67	8	.321	.422	.610
Christensen, Mike	3b	Cedar Rapds	Ana	A	24	127	504	142	36	2	18	236	68	71	42	3	102	5	0	4	1	2	.33	12	.282	.341	.468
Christians, Ryan	dh-c	Mariners	Sea	R	19	11	38	10	8	0	0	18	3	7	2	0	12	0	0	0	2	0	1.00	0	.263	.300	.474
		Everett	Sea	A-	19	30	107	30	7	0	8	61	19	17	14	1	31	3	0	0	3	1	.75	1	.280	.379	.570
Chwan, Brian*	c	Chston-SC	TB	A	23	49	136	30	8	0	3	47	16	9	10	0	29	1	0	3	0	0	.00	2	.221	.273	.346
Ciarrachi, Kevin	dh	Kingsport	NYM	R+	22	2	1	0	0	0	0	0	0	0	0	0	1	1	0	0	0	0	.00	0	.000	.500	.000
Cintron, Alex#	ss	High Desert	Ari	A+	21	128	499	153	25	4	3	195	78	64	19	0	65	3	17	4	15	8	.65	14	.307	.333	.391
Cisneros, Ventura#	c-1b	Mexico	—	R	—	46	172	60	9	6	2	87	24	27	12	1	26	2	2	2	3	2	.60	3	.349	.394	.506
Clark, Chivas*	of	Medcine Hat	Tor	R+	21	70	267	72	18	3	6	114	56	29	38	1	78	6	1	1	12	5	.71	1	.270	.372	.427
Clark, Greg	c	Peoria	StL	A	23	68	229	49	11	0	3	69	20	23	20	0	76	2	1	4	0	4	.00	6	.214	.303	.301
Clark, Jamie*	of	Mariners	Sea	R	21	26	96	33	3	3	3	51	26	17	17	1	29	1	2	0	5	2	.71	2	.344	.447	.531
Clark, Jermaine*	2b	Lancaster	Sea	A+	23	126	502	158	27	8	6	219	112	61	58	2	80	2	8	3	33	15	.69	10	.315	.386	.436
Clark, Tommy	of	Braves	Atl	R	20	38	112	19	8	0	4	39	18	13	30	1	46	3	0	1	5	3	.63	3	.170	.356	.348
Clarke, Jason#	2b-ss	Daytona	ChC	A+	24	81	254	61	6	1	2	75	24	29	25	0	27	1	2	3	8	3	.73	2	.240	.307	.295
Clay, Michael	3b	Spokane	KC	A-	23	31	87	13	4	0	1	20	9	4	4	0	15	2	0	1	1	0	1.00	4	.149	.202	.230
Clements, Jason#	ss	Sou Oregon	Oak	A-	22	36	105	19	2	0	1	24	20	8	13	0	32	2	2	1	0	3	.00	1	.181	.281	.229
Cleto, Ambioris	ss	Hickory	Pit	A	20	24	66	7	1	0	0	8	6	6	17	0	23	0	1	0	0	2	.00	1	.106	.289	.121
Cleveland, Russ	c	Tigers	Det	R	20	37	132	41	5	0	0	46	13	13	5	0	33	2	0	3	2	2	.50	4	.311	.338	.348
Clifton, Rodney	of	Visalia	Oak	A+	23	110	371	97	30	4	9	162	67	56	63	1	81	4	2	6	12	5	.71	6	.261	.369	.437
Close, James	of	Utica	Fla	A-	22	59	188	34	7	1	3	52	23	26	16	0	60	0	1	3	6	7	.46	3	.181	.242	.277
Closser, J.D.#	c	South Bend	Ari	A	20	52	174	42	8	0	3	59	29	27	34	0	37	1	0	3	0	1	.00	3	.241	.363	.339
		Missoula	Ari	R+	20	76	275	89	22	0	10	141	73	54	71	2	57	2	1	6	9	3	.75	8	.324	.458	.513
Cochrane, Mark	c	White Sox	CWS	R	20	29	82	18	5	1	0	25	13	2	10	0	19	2	2	0	0	0	.00	4	.220	.319	.305
Cody, Ryan	c	Piedmont	Phi	A	22	1	3	1	0	0	0	1	1	0	1	0	1	0	0	0	0	0	.00	0	.333	.500	.333
		Batavia	Phi	A-	22	3	9	1	1	0	0	2	1	0	1	0	4	0	0	0	0	0	.00	0	.111	.200	.222
Cohens, Derrick	of	Eugene	ChC	A-	25	43	118	25	5	0	0	30	14	11	15	0	29	1	0	0	3	5	.38	4	.212	.306	.254
Cole, Brian	of	Capital Cty	NYM	A	21	125	500	158	41	4	18	261	97	71	37	0	77	2	1	5	50	16	.76	8	.316	.362	.522
Colina, Javier	2b	Asheville	Col	A	21	124	516	156	37	3	6	217	70	81	26	0	101	6	2	6	12	11	.52	12	.302	.339	.421
Collazo, Julio	ss	Phillies	Phi	R	19	52	176	45	3	0	0	48	34	7	33	0	36	6	3	0	25	1	.96	5	.256	.391	.273
		Batavia	Phi	A-	19	5	16	4	0	0	0	4	0	2	2	0	6	0	1	0	1	0	1.00	0	.250	.333	.250
Collier, Lamonte	3b	Clearwater	Phi	A+	25	104	318	84	11	3	0	101	50	28	49	1	60	5	6	5	4	3	.57	12	.264	.366	.318
Collura, Todd	c	Elizabethtn	Min	R+	21	23	67	21	4	0	2	31	13	18	7	0	20	3	0	1	0	0	.00	0	.313	.397	.463
Colmenter, Jesus#	ss	Burlington	Cle	R+	18	36	140	34	6	0	0	40	15	12	6	0	39	0	0	1	4	1	.80	1	.243	.272	.286
Colon, Jose	of	Stockton	Mil	A+	24	97	264	68	9	2	3	90	49	28	23	0	62	6	1	2	15	6	.71	3	.258	.329	.341
Condon, Mike	2b	Cedar Rapds	Ana	A	26	13	41	5	0	0	0	5	2	1	3	0	7	1	0	0	0	0	.00	0	.122	.200	.122
Conley, Brian	2b	Rockford	Cin	A	25	89	285	65	7	3	2	84	39	22	19	0	69	4	6	2	13	8	.62	3	.228	.284	.295
Connally, Chris	dh-of	Daytona	ChC	A+	24	29	90	21	3	0	0	24	10	9	5	0	19	1	0	0	2	1	.67	0	.233	.281	.267
Connell, Jerry	of-dh	Clearwater	Phi	A+	22	25	90	26	4	1	2	38	11	18	8	0	27	1	0	2	2	0	1.00	3	.289	.347	.422
		Piedmont	Phi	A	22	31	109	26	9	1	3	46	9	15	10	0	46	1	0	1	1	1	.50	0	.239	.306	.422
Connors, Greg	c	Lancaster	Sea	A+	25	117	448	120	20	7	16	202	72	84	40	2	91	6	1	5	10	7	.59	3	.268	.333	.451
Conyer, Darryl*	of	Missoula	Ari	R+	20	49	190	50	9	2	3	72	55	23	43	0	56	5	6	1	20	7	.74	0	.263	.410	.379
Cook, Jon	of	Fort Wayne	SD	A	23	107	315	67	12	1	2	87	60	32	54	0	94	0	4	3	39	11	.78	3	.213	.325	.276
Cook, Josh	2b	Salem-Keizr	SF	A-	22	35	112	27	9	0	1	39	16	16	11	0	24	5	0	1	5	6	.45	2	.241	.333	.348
Copeland, Brandon	of	Capital Cty	NYM	A	23	33	101	20	4	0	5	39	14	17	15	0	39	5	1	1	5	1	.83	2	.198	.328	.386
		St. Lucie	NYM	A+	23	16	39	5	1	0	1	9	3	4	4	1	18	0	1	0	2	0	1.00	1	.128	.209	.231
Copley, Travis*	dh	Reds	Cin	R	24	7	24	5	2	0	0	7	5	1	4	0	6	0	0	0	0	0	.00	0	.208	.321	.292
		Clinton	Cin	A	24	4	15	3	0	0	0	3	3	0	3	0	0	0	0	0	0	0	.00	1	.200	.333	.200
Cordero, Willy	ss	Savannah	Tex	A	21	101	366	90	20	4	6	136	51	37	27	0	70	4	7	2	11	6	.65	4	.246	.303	.372
Cordido, Julio	3b	Salem-Keizr	SF	A-	19	70	242	64	10	2	1	81	36	28	29	0	44	4	2	1	8	4	.67	3	.264	.351	.335
Cordova, Alfredo*	dh-ss	Mexico	—	R	—	14	42	3	1	0	0	4	2	0	5	0	17	0	0	0	0	0	.00	1	.071	.170	.095
Cordova, Ben*	of	Royals	KC	R	20	52	168	48	9	2	5	76	36	26	51	0	50	1	2	1	12	3	.80	2	.286	.452	.452
		Spokane	KC	A-	20	4	16	4	0	1	2	12	4	7	3	0	5	0	0	0	0	0	.00	0	.250	.368	.750
Cornett, Robert	dh-1b	Medcine Hat	Tor	R+	23	49	166	48	9	3	3	72	26	36	25	0	31	4	0	3	1	1	.50	9	.289	.389	.434
Corporan, Elvis#	3b	Yankees	NYY	R	20	56	212	59	13	3	4	90	29	30	19	1	41	1	0	1	3	1	.75	6	.278	.339	.425
Correa, Dominic	dh	Staten Ilnd	NYY	A-	23	56	144	30	8	0	4	50	17	22	14	1	36	4	3	0	1	2	.33	3	.208	.296	.347
Correa, Miguel#	of	Salem	Col	A+	28	100	373	95	19	6	11	159	48	79	25	1	72	2	1	6	11	12	.48	5	.255	.300	.426
Correa, Nelson*	1b	Ogden	Mil	R+	22	50	156	45	9	2	9	85	25	34	17	0	30	6	0	2	2	2	.50	2	.288	.376	.545
Cortes, Jorge*	of	Pirates	Pit	R	19	32	93	28	4	1	0	34	14	14	14	0	19	0	0	2	2	1	.67	2	.301	.385	.366
Cortez, Sonny	of	Lynchburg	Pit	A+	25	48	161	36	6	0	1	45	19	10	8	0	34	3	4	1	1	3	.25	4	.224	.272	.280
Cosbey, Chris*	of	Modesto	Oak	A+	25	39	90	18	4	0	0	22	16	7	9	0	23	1	1	1	9	4	.69	1	.200	.277	.244
Cosby, Robert#	3b	Medcine Hat	Tor	R+	19	46	178	48	9	1	3	68	22	25	12	0	29	0	0	4	10	3	.77	3	.270	.309	.382
Cosentino, Tony	c-dh	Idaho Falls	SD	R+	21	20	88	33	5	2	2	48	14	30	6	1	11	0	0	2	0	0	.00	5	.375	.406	.545
		Fort Wayne	SD	A	21	37	127	31	5	0	0	36	11	11	22	0	33	1	0	1	1	1	.50	3	.244	.358	.283
Cosme, Caonabo	ss	Modesto	Oak	A+	21	100	444	95	21	2	2	126	55	47	45	1	148	4	3	3	14	7	.67	12	.214	.290	.284
Cota, Humberto	c	Chston-SC	TB	A	21	85	336	94	21	1	9	144	42	61	20	1	51	2	1	5	1	1	.50	9	.280	.320	.429
		Hickory	Pit	A	21	37	133	36	11	2	2	57	28	20	21	1	20	0	0	2	3	1	.75	0	.271	.365	.429
Cotten, Jeremy	1b	Williamsprt	Pit	A-	19	50	175	35	13	1	1	53	16	24	18	0	67	1	0	1	0	0	.00	4	.200	.277	.303
Covington, Kevin	of	Yakima	LA	A-	22	43	169	51	13	1	2	72	24	23	7	1	37	0	2	3	3	4	.43	4	.302	.324	.426
Craig, Benny#	of-dh	Kissimmee	Hou	A+	25	4	13	1	0	0	0	1	0	0	0	0	6	0	0	0	0	0	.00	1	.077	.077	.077

1999 Batting — Single-A and Rookie Leagues

BATTING																					BASERUNNING				PERCENTAGES		
Player	Pos	Team	Org	Lg	A	G	AB	H	2B	3B	HR	TB	R	RBI	TBB	IBB	SO	HBP	SH	SF	SB	CS	SB%	GDP	Avg	OBP	SLG
Crawford, Carl*	of	Princeton	TB	R+	18	60	260	83	14	4	0	105	62	25	13	0	47	1	1	3	17	3	.85	5	.319	.350	.404
Crespo, Cesar#	2b	Brevard Cty	Fla	A+	21	115	427	122	17	2	6	161	63	40	62	2	86	1	7	2	22	8	.73	4	.286	.376	.377
Cridland, Mark*	of	Stockton	Mil	A+	25	124	437	114	26	5	13	189	51	87	33	3	64	6	5	16	14	7	.67	6	.261	.311	.432
Crisp, Covelli#	2b	Johnson Cy	StL	R+	20	65	229	59	5	4	3	81	55	22	44	0	41	2	8	2	27	6	.82	0	.258	.379	.354
Crocker, Nick*	1b	Danville	Atl	R+	22	63	242	62	15	3	3	92	52	32	31	0	56	6	0	2	5	4	.56	4	.256	.352	.380
Crosby, Bubba*	of	San Berndno	LA	A+	23	96	371	110	21	3	1	140	53	37	42	3	71	6	4	1	19	8	.70	6	.296	.376	.377
Croud, Will#	of	Cedar Rapds	Ana	A	24	87	281	65	11	5	2	92	39	31	46	0	44	2	3	5	5	5	.50	8	.231	.338	.327
Cruz, Edgar	c	Kinston	Cle	A+	21	35	133	20	11	0	2	37	13	14	9	0	46	2	1	0	0	0	.00	1	.150	.215	.278
		Columbus	Cle	A	21	62	232	50	10	0	4	72	22	23	20	1	54	0	0	1	0	0	.00	3	.216	.277	.310
Cruz, Enrique	ss-3b	Mets	NYM	R	18	54	183	56	14	2	4	86	34	24	28	0	41	1	0	1	0	0	.00	3	.306	.399	.470
Cruz, Hector#	2b	High Desert	Ari	A+	21	14	41	9	1	0	0	10	8	3	2	0	11	1	0	0	0	1	.00	0	.220	.273	.244
		Diamondbcks	Ari	R	21	24	85	15	1	1	0	18	9	8	11	0	23	0	0	1	2	0	1.00	1	.176	.268	.212
		Missoula	Ari	R+	21	15	49	9	1	0	0	10	10	4	8	0	13	0	0	0	2	2	.50	0	.184	.298	.204
Cruz, Israel	dh	Mariners	Sea	R	20	13	28	8	1	0	0	9	4	4	2	0	6	0	1	0	1	0	1.00	1	.286	.333	.321
Cruz, Orlando	of	Rangers	Tex	R	18	46	136	25	5	2	0	34	12	11	15	0	44	5	5	1	0	2	.00	1	.184	.287	.250
Cruz, Rafael	c	Savannah	Tex	A	21	23	62	4	1	0	0	5	0	3	7	0	30	1	0	0	1	1	.50	1	.065	.171	.081
		Pulaski	Tex	R+	21	15	54	12	3	0	0	15	7	8	4	0	18	1	1	0	0	0	.00	2	.222	.288	.278
Cubillan, Jose#	dh	Pulaski	Tex	R+	21	5	10	1	0	0	0	1	4	1	2	0	8	2	0	1	0	0	.00	0	.100	.333	.100
Cuddyer, Michael	3b	Fort Myers	Min	A+	21	130	466	139	24	4	16	219	87	82	76	0	91	10	2	6	14	4	.78	20	.298	.403	.470
Cuntz, Casey	3b	High Desert	Ari	A+	25	86	257	68	11	1	10	111	46	39	38	1	61	2	3	1	0	2	.00	6	.265	.362	.432
Curry, Chris	c	Eugene	ChC	A-	22	41	132	30	6	0	2	42	18	9	5	0	35	3	0	0	0	2	.00	3	.227	.271	.318
Curry, Jesse*	1b	Idaho Falls	SD	R+	21	47	159	42	12	5	7	85	28	35	22	0	53	1	0	0	5	0	1.00	2	.264	.357	.535
Curry, Mike*	of	Chstn-WV	KC	A	23	85	318	99	13	3	0	118	70	25	48	0	58	9	6	3	61	13	.82	4	.311	.413	.371
		Wilmington	KC	A+	23	54	200	46	4	2	1	57	31	16	34	1	39	1	3	2	24	9	.73	2	.230	.342	.285
Curry, Zane	c	Great Falls	LA	R+	23	27	90	22	3	0	0	25	10	8	15	0	16	1	0	1	1	3	.25	0	.244	.355	.278
Curtis, Bill#	of-dh	Butte	Ana	R+	22	66	238	76	18	1	6	114	40	46	35	4	58	5	0	2	0	2	.00	4	.319	.414	.479
Curtis, Matt#	1b-dh	Lk Elsinore	Ana	A+	25	126	460	120	26	2	17	201	72	76	68	3	84	2	0	6	2	2	.50	8	.261	.354	.437
Cust, Jack*	of	High Desert	Ari	A+	21	125	455	152	42	3	32	296	107	112	96	2	145	2	0	3	1	4	.20	5	.334	.450	.651
Cutshall, Pat	3b	Michigan	Hou	A	25	8	21	5	0	0	0	5	3	2	2	0	3	0	1	0	0	1	.00	0	.238	.304	.238
Da Luz, Craig	1b-3b	W Michigan	Det	A	25	87	314	83	14	5	3	116	36	49	20	0	46	3	2	4	3	1	.75	6	.264	.311	.369
Daedelow, Craig	2b	Delmarva	Bal	A	24	45	160	50	3	2	0	57	28	21	35	0	26	3	2	3	1	3	.25	3	.313	.438	.356
		Frederick	Bal	A+	24	16	50	5	1	0	0	6	6	2	4	0	7	0	2	0	0	0	.00	0	.100	.167	.120
Daggett, Jesse	c-dh	Williamsprt	Pit	A-	21	5	18	4	3	0	0	7	1	1	4	0	3	0	0	0	0	0	.00	0	.222	.364	.389
Daigle, Leo	1b	W Michigan	Det	A	20	108	406	112	36	1	5	165	59	60	33	0	121	7	1	6	3	0	1.00	9	.276	.336	.406
Dalton, David	2b	Jamestown	Atl	A-	24	27	104	33	1	4	1	45	23	15	9	0	20	0	2	1	14	3	.82	1	.317	.368	.433
		Macon	Atl	A	24	39	132	38	7	1	3	56	19	12	14	0	34	4	0	1	3	3	.50	0	.288	.371	.424
Dalton, Josh#	2b	Yakima	LA	A-	23	59	203	51	12	0	1	66	33	28	42	3	45	5	6	3	11	5	.69	2	.251	.387	.325
Daly, Sean	1b	Rockies	Col	R	19	25	77	14	3	0	0	17	12	8	12	0	35	0	0	0	3	0	1.00	1	.182	.292	.221
Damato, Gabriel	c	Reds	Cin	R	23	5	10	2	0	0	0	2	0	0	1	0	0	2	0	0	0	1	.00	0	.200	.385	.200
Dampeer, Kelly	2b	Columbus	Cle	A	25	94	299	77	13	5	5	115	37	39	25	0	52	3	5	3	10	4	.71	12	.258	.318	.385
Darjean, John	of	Greensboro	NYY	A	24	113	398	99	18	4	2	131	47	43	19	0	80	8	7	3	20	11	.65	4	.249	.294	.329
Darula, Bobby*	of-dh	Beloit	Mil	A	25	120	438	133	24	8	4	185	63	75	62	4	57	7	1	4	19	5	.79	7	.304	.395	.422
Davies, Justin*	of	Hagerstown	Tor	A	23	127	396	78	6	1	0	86	69	23	86	1	55	2	7	1	36	15	.71	7	.197	.342	.217
Davis, Daniel*	of	Tigers	Det	R	19	45	147	27	6	0	1	36	14	11	23	1	59	1	0	0	2	2	.50	3	.184	.298	.245
Davis, J.J.	of-dh	Hickory	Pit	A	21	86	317	84	26	1	19	169	58	65	44	3	99	4	0	2	2	5	.29	3	.265	.360	.533
Davis, Jermaine	of	St.Cathrnes	Tor	A-	21	33	101	16	5	1	2	29	7	11	2	0	36	3	0	0	1	2	.33	0	.158	.198	.287
Davis, Quian	1b	Marlins	Fla	R	19	26	47	9	1	1	0	12	1	4	2	0	13	3	1	0	1	0	1.00	0	.191	.269	.255
Davison, Ashanti	of	Orioles	Bal	R	21	8	31	8	3	0	0	11	5	3	3	0	7	1	0	0	6	1	.86	0	.258	.343	.355
		Delmarva	Bal	A	21	53	170	27	5	0	1	35	20	13	31	0	45	7	2	0	8	6	.57	7	.159	.313	.206
Day, Paul	dh	Mahoning Vy	Cle	A-	23	9	32	7	1	1	0	10	4	5	5	0	6	0	0	1	0	0	.00	2	.219	.316	.313
DeAza, Modesto	2b	Auburn	Hou	A-	21	61	223	49	7	4	2	70	38	18	11	0	73	8	0	2	34	10	.77	5	.220	.279	.314
DeCaster, Yurendell	2b	Princeton	TB	R+	20	48	183	47	12	0	11	92	37	36	20	0	65	6	1	2	4	1	.80	4	.257	.346	.503
Dealey, Scott	of	Salem-Keizr	SF	A-	23	69	268	66	12	1	0	80	42	22	43	0	29	1	6	3	29	9	.76	3	.246	.349	.299
		San Jose	SF	A+	23	2	9	2	0	0	0	2	1	0	0	0	2	0	0	0	1	0	1.00	0	.222	.222	.222
Dean, Mike	c	San Jose	SF	A+	22	23	81	23	4	2	1	34	16	12	11	0	15	1	1	2	13	3	.81	1	.284	.368	.420
Deardorff, Jeff	3b	Stockton	Mil	A+	21	126	436	116	22	2	10	172	59	47	40	1	150	6	1	2	2	7	.22	5	.266	.335	.394
Declet, Miguel	ss	Sou Oregon	Oak	A-	20	14	50	19	7	0	2	32	13	6	3	0	16	1	0	1	1	0	1.00	0	.380	.418	.640
Dees, Charlie	of-1b	Orioles	Bal	R	22	56	186	40	12	1	9	81	21	32	20	0	41	1	0	3	5	6	.45	6	.215	.290	.435
DeGroote, Casey*	3b	Staten Ilnd	NYY	A-	20	7	21	2	1	0	0	3	3	0	2	0	12	0	0	0	0	0	.00	0	.095	.174	.143
		Yankees	NYY	R	20	7	20	3	0	0	0	3	1	2	3	0	6	0	0	0	1	0	1.00	0	.150	.261	.150
Dehner, Matt	3b-ss	Billings	Cin	R+	23	61	225	69	11	1	3	91	34	25	23	0	73	10	3	2	7	2	.78	5	.307	.392	.404
Deitrick, Jeremy	c	Phillies	Phi	R	23	5	17	6	2	1	0	10	3	3	0	0	2	0	0	0	0	1	.00	0	.353	.353	.588
		Batavia	Phi	A-	23	26	83	22	10	0	2	38	16	13	5	0	21	2	0	1	0	0	.00	0	.265	.319	.458
de la Cruz, Erickson	of	Beloit	Mil	A	21	95	260	56	8	0	0	64	19	13	19	0	35	3	8	0	1	4	.20	7	.215	.277	.246
de la Cruz, Henry	of	Lansing	ChC	A	23	71	209	45	14	0	6	77	26	31	29	0	75	3	1	1	7	4	.64	6	.215	.318	.368
de la Cruz, Jose	c	Visalia	Oak	A+	22	43	115	24	5	1	4	43	17	17	12	0	32	2	0	2	3	1	.75	4	.209	.290	.374
		Sou Oregon	Oak	A-	22	18	51	8	4	0	1	15	7	8	9	0	16	1	0	0	0	0	.00	1	.157	.295	.294
de la Cruz, Ruddi	2b	Kingsport	NYM	R+	20	54	160	36	6	2	2	52	30	12	25	0	47	7	3	1	10	4	.71	4	.225	.352	.325
DeLeon, Jorge	2b	Sarasota	Bos	A+	25	66	219	60	11	2	1	78	33	18	24	0	33	0	5	0	3	2	.60	5	.274	.346	.356
de los Santos, Hec.	of-ss	Red Sox	Bos	R	20	56	218	53	8	0	3	70	36	21	15	0	38	1	4	3	11	8	.58	1	.243	.291	.321
de los Santos, Nel.#	c	Ogden	Mil	R+	21	48	131	33	4	2	4	53	27	23	16	0	39	3	1	1	9	3	.75	3	.252	.344	.405
de los Santos, San.	ss	Johnson Cy	StL	R+	19	55	159	34	2	2	1	43	22	10	16	0	58	4	6	1	3	5	.38	2	.214	.300	.270
del Rosario, Em.#	2b	Orioles	Bal	R	18	40	123	30	2	0	0	32	19	8	22	0	10	2	4	1	10	5	.67	2	.244	.365	.260
Delgado, Ariel*	1b	Cedar Rapds	Ana	A	23	102	359	93	27	1	3	131	52	47	29	0	63	5	4	5	14	1	.93	8	.259	.319	.365
Delgado, Chris	1b	Bristol	CWS	R+	22	61	217	65	10	1	14	119	36	54	33	2	64	3	1	3	1	0	1.00	7	.300	.395	.548
Delgado, Dario	1b	Phillies	Phi	R	20	19	71	23	3	1	2	34	12	17	5	0	16	2	0	1	1	2	.33	0	.324	.380	.479
Delgado, Jorge	c	Diamondbcks	Ari	R	19	20	68	20	5	1	1	30	11	6	6	0	14	2	0	0	1	0	1.00	1	.294	.368	.441

1999 Batting — Single-A and Rookie Leagues

BATTING																					BASERUNNING				PERCENTAGES		
Player	Pos	Team	Org	Lg	A	G	AB	H	2B	3B	HR	TB	R	RBI	TBB	IBB	SO	HBP	SH	SF	SB	CS	SB%	GDP	Avg	OBP	SLG
DeMarco, Matt*	1b	Marlins	Fla	R	20	46	156	34	8	0	0	42	12	10	11	0	19	2	1	0	1	3	.25	5	.218	.278	.269
DePippo, Jeff	c	Kinston	Cle	A+	24	68	174	37	8	1	2	53	33	19	29	0	51	17	8	3	3	1	.75	1	.213	.372	.305
DeRosso, Tony	dh-1b	Red Sox	Bos	R	24	5	18	5	3	0	1	11	3	7	2	0	2	0	0	1	0	1	.00	1	.278	.333	.611
		Augusta	Bos	A	24	36	128	38	7	1	6	65	19	27	16	0	21	1	0	2	0	0	.00	3	.297	.374	.508
Deschaine, James	dh-of	Eugene	ChC	A-	22	73	272	81	12	0	10	123	49	48	29	0	59	0	1	0	7	7	.50	8	.298	.365	.452
Deschenes, Pat*	1b-3b	Mets	NYM	R	22	24	79	30	3	0	1	36	16	12	15	0	8	2	0	2	4	2	.67	3	.380	.480	.456
		Kingsport	NYM	R+	22	40	151	57	8	3	3	80	30	30	25	0	18	5	1	1	6	2	.75	4	.377	.478	.530
		Pittsfield	NYM	A-	22	5	16	5	0	0	1	8	7	3	4	0	2	0	0	1	0	0	.00	1	.313	.429	.500
DeShetler, Chris*	2b	Tigers	Det	R	23	33	114	34	5	2	2	49	17	21	15	1	15	2	0	1	1	1	.50	2	.298	.386	.430
Detienne, Dave	ss	Great Falls	LA	R+	20	47	153	33	3	0	1	39	22	16	11	0	34	5	2	2	9	5	.64	5	.216	.287	.255
Devanez, Noel	of	Mets	NYM	R	18	44	147	42	8	1	4	64	31	26	15	0	41	2	0	1	2	2	.50	2	.286	.358	.435
Devore, Doug*	of	Missoula	Ari	R+	22	32	115	27	4	4	3	48	22	22	14	0	36	4	0	2	2	0	1.00	2	.235	.333	.417
Diaz, Aneuris	3b	Johnson Cy	StL	R+	19	56	205	47	9	2	4	72	30	27	10	0	55	4	2	1	6	2	.75	3	.229	.277	.351
Diaz, Angel	c-dh	Cedar Rapds	Ana	A	23	81	281	68	11	1	10	111	43	42	34	0	85	6	0	0	0	3	.00	4	.242	.336	.395
Diaz, David	c	Pirates	Pit	R	19	17	38	7	2	0	0	9	4	1	1	0	10	0	0	0	0	0	.00	1	.184	.205	.237
Diaz, Diogenes	c	Williamsprt	Pit	A-	21	9	30	9	3	0	1	15	3	3	4	0	7	1	0	0	1	2	.33	1	.300	.400	.500
		Hickory	Pit	A	21	13	39	8	2	0	0	10	1	1	1	0	12	0	1	0	0	0	.00	1	.205	.225	.256
Diaz, Johnny	3b	Johnson Cy	StL	R+	19	3	9	1	0	0	0	1	0	1	0	0	0	1	0	1	0	0	.00	0	.111	.182	.111
Diaz, Jose	c	Mariners	Sea	R	20	23	66	12	2	0	0	14	7	7	5	0	16	0	4	1	0	2	.00	4	.182	.236	.212
Diaz, Maikell	ss	Delmarva	Bal	A	21	91	322	89	8	3	2	109	45	34	42	0	68	11	5	1	31	15	.67	9	.276	.378	.339
Diaz, Matt	of	Hudson Val	TB	A-	22	54	208	51	15	2	1	73	22	20	6	0	43	6	2	2	6	2	.75	5	.245	.284	.351
Diaz, Michael*	of	Butte	Ana	R+	23	14	49	16	1	0	0	17	22	2	15	0	7	1	0	0	11	2	.85	1	.327	.492	.347
		Cedar Rapds	Ana	A	23	25	72	13	1	0	0	14	12	6	14	0	22	0	1	3	3	1	.75	1	.181	.303	.194
Diaz, Miguel	of	Jupiter	Mon	A+	22	2	4	0	0	0	0	0	0	0	0	0	2	0	0	0	0	0	.00	0	.000	.000	.000
		Peoria	StL	A	22	105	343	87	18	6	3	126	44	34	8	0	59	7	6	1	10	6	.63	6	.254	.284	.367
Diaz, Miguel	c	Cape Fear	Mon	A	19	1	2	0	0	0	0	0	0	0	1	0	2	0	0	0	0	0	.00	0	.000	.333	.000
		Expos	Mon	R	19	20	56	10	2	1	0	14	7	5	6	0	12	1	0	0	2	0	1.00	1	.179	.270	.250
Dillard, Thomas	c	Elizabethtn	Min	R+	23	34	110	29	6	1	1	40	17	17	4	0	28	4	1	1	4	2	.67	2	.264	.311	.364
Dillon, Joe	3b	Wilmington	KC	A+	24	134	503	133	31	2	16	216	73	90	59	4	124	7	2	5	9	6	.60	12	.264	.347	.429
Dimmick, Josh#	c	Michigan	Hou	A	24	53	180	55	11	2	4	82	27	28	17	0	25	1	0	3	2	1	.67	5	.306	.363	.456
		Quad City	Min	A	24	24	84	22	5	1	2	35	9	12	10	2	12	1	0	0	0	0	.00	3	.262	.347	.417
Dito, Robert	c	Jupiter	Mon	A+	22	1	2	0	0	0	0	0	0	0	0	0	2	0	0	0	0	0	.00	0	.000	.000	.000
		Expos	Mon	R	22	18	48	11	0	0	1	14	5	9	5	0	13	1	0	0	0	0	.00	1	.229	.315	.292
Doakes, Schuyler#	2b	Mariners	Sea	R	23	34	138	35	7	3	0	48	21	11	13	0	30	1	0	1	9	1	.90	2	.254	.320	.348
Dolton, Odis	of	Reds	Cin	R	20	32	96	17	2	1	1	24	11	12	5	0	43	4	0	0	3	0	1.00	4	.177	.248	.250
Dominguez, Luis	3b	Auburn	Hou	A-	20	63	218	65	11	2	0	80	34	27	33	0	28	0	2	3	6	3	.67	4	.298	.386	.367
Dominique, Bubba	dh-c	Clearwater	Phi	A+	24	130	487	124	29	5	14	205	77	92	69	4	84	10	3	8	3	3	.50	13	.255	.354	.421
Donato, Gregorio	2b	Danville	Atl	R+	19	53	215	62	15	3	2	89	30	37	19	0	45	1	2	5	13	6	.68	6	.288	.342	.414
Donovan, Todd	of	Idaho Falls	SD	R+	21	53	198	59	11	3	1	79	57	22	25	1	39	6	1	3	40	5	.89	1	.298	.388	.399
Dorsett, Chris	c	Lansing	ChC	A	25	57	130	30	8	0	2	44	20	19	37	0	24	1	1	4	2	2	.50	7	.231	.395	.338
Dorsey, Ryan	ss	Pirates	Pit	R	18	14	40	7	1	1	0	10	4	2	6	0	18	0	0	0	0	0	.00	0	.175	.283	.250
Doucet, Brandon	of	Helena	Mil	R+	23	48	134	32	7	0	0	39	20	11	15	0	31	1	1	1	4	0	1.00	2	.239	.318	.291
Doudt, Anthony	c	Boise	Ana	A-	23	23	62	15	4	0	2	25	9	12	6	0	17	0	0	3	0	0	.00	2	.242	.296	.403
Dougherty, Jeb	of	Lk Elsinore	Ana	A+	24	115	381	99	13	4	7	141	66	45	54	0	68	10	4	3	35	13	.73	11	.260	.364	.370
Douglas, Mo*	of	Pirates	Pit	R	23	26	87	14	2	1	1	21	6	7	8	0	33	1	2	0	1	0	1.00	3	.161	.240	.241
Doumit, Ryan#	dh-c	Pirates	Pit	R	19	29	85	24	5	0	1	32	17	7	15	0	14	4	0	1	4	2	.67	0	.282	.410	.376
Downing, Brad*	of	Cedar Rapds	Ana	A	24	13	47	11	3	0	2	20	7	7	3	0	10	1	0	0	0	0	.00	1	.234	.294	.426
Downing, Lance*	3b	South Bend	Ari	A	21	118	439	127	18	5	1	158	65	51	35	3	69	3	0	7	7	3	.70	9	.289	.341	.360
Downs, Brian	1b-c	Winston-Sal	CWS	A+	25	20	61	11	1	0	1	15	7	5	2	0	13	0	0	0	1	0	1.00	3	.180	.206	.246
Driggers, Richard	of	Phillies	Phi	R	18	17	48	11	2	0	0	13	6	3	1	0	11	0	1	0	1	0	1.00	0	.229	.245	.271
Drobiak, Jayson*	3b	Oneonta	Det	A-	21	31	102	23	8	1	0	33	10	14	4	1	23	0	0	1	2	3	.40	2	.225	.252	.324
Duarte, Justin	1b	Batavia	Phi	A-	23	45	140	35	8	0	1	46	15	20	8	0	36	3	1	2	0	0	.00	4	.250	.301	.329
Duck, Kevin*	1b	Asheville	Col	A	22	105	338	76	15	0	8	115	37	36	42	0	98	1	2	1	0	2	.00	10	.225	.312	.340
Duenas, Manuel	2b	Padres	SD	R	20	45	156	30	8	2	1	45	28	20	15	0	60	2	1	3	4	0	1.00	1	.192	.267	.288
Dunaway, Jason	2b	Fort Wayne	SD	A	23	85	255	55	10	2	1	72	34	17	27	0	58	6	1	1	12	6	.67	11	.216	.304	.282
Duncan, Carlos	3b-ss	Piedmont	Phi	A	23	73	276	60	15	3	11	114	41	40	19	0	88	8	1	4	15	4	.79	4	.217	.283	.413
Duncan, Chris*	1b	Johnson Cy	StL	R+	19	55	201	43	8	1	6	71	23	34	25	0	62	1	0	3	3	1	.75	4	.214	.300	.353
Dunn, Adam*	of	Rockford	Cin	A	20	93	313	96	16	2	11	149	62	44	46	3	64	10	0	3	21	10	.68	6	.307	.409	.476
Dunn, Casey	c-dh	Spokane	KC	A-	23	58	218	64	7	1	11	106	34	49	19	2	28	4	1	3	0	0	.00	5	.294	.357	.486
Duplissea, William	c	Yakima	LA	A-	22	13	33	5	2	0	1	10	5	4	5	0	7	3	0	1	2	1	.67	1	.152	.310	.303
Duran, Francisco	2b	Butte	Ana	R+	21	53	209	52	6	1	2	66	39	43	26	0	40	3	3	6	8	4	.67	1	.249	.332	.316
Durham, Chad	of	Bristol	CWS	R+	22	68	278	90	12	2	0	106	66	36	33	2	44	4	2	3	57	13	.81	1	.324	.399	.381
		Burlington	CWS	A	22	7	25	5	1	0	0	6	3	0	4	0	6	0	0	0	2	3	.40	1	.200	.310	.240
Dusan, Joe*	1b	Fort Wayne	SD	A	22	53	184	54	10	2	5	83	29	37	29	0	50	2	1	4	1	3	.25	4	.293	.388	.451
		Hagerstown	Tor	A	22	69	243	58	14	0	8	96	26	37	28	0	82	2	0	1	3	1	.75	3	.239	.321	.395
Duverge, Alcides	c	Butte	Ana	R+	20	26	89	19	3	2	1	29	12	7	5	0	28	2	1	0	1	1	.50	1	.213	.271	.326
Dwyer, Mike*	1b	Lowell	Bos	A-	22	71	271	67	12	0	3	88	24	41	34	3	50	2	1	3	3	2	.60	6	.247	.332	.325
Dyer, Matt	c	Pittsfield	NYM	A-	23	2	4	2	0	0	0	2	0	2	0	0	1	0	0	0	0	0	.00	0	.500	.500	.500
		Mets	NYM	R	23	2	1	0	0	0	0	0	0	0	1	0	0	1	0	0	0	0	.00	0	.000	.667	.000
		Kingsport	NYM	R+	23	22	40	8	2	0	0	10	2	3	3	0	10	0	0	0	0	0	.00	1	.200	.256	.250
Dyt, Darren*	dh	Peoria	StL	A	24	81	253	60	15	1	1	80	30	24	24	0	55	1	1	0	4	2	.67	13	.237	.306	.316
Dzurilla, Mike	2b	Eugene	ChC	A-	22	70	278	81	14	2	5	114	43	44	16	0	33	3	2	1	12	4	.75	0	.291	[illegible]	.410
Eady, Gerald	of	Lancaster	Sea	A+	24	52	151	37	4	3	1	50	20	18	27	0	57	8	3	1	7	12	.37	2	.245	.385	.331
Eagle, Todd	dh-c	Phillies	Phi	R	19	14	39	5	1	0	0	6	1	3	1	0	5	1	0	0	1	0	1.00	1	.128	.171	.154
Eberly, Rod*	1b-3b	Phillies	Phi	R	23	7	26	5	1	0	0	6	4	3	4	0	5	0	0	0	1	0	1.00	2	.192	.300	.231
		Batavia	Phi	A-	23	50	171	35	5	0	2	46	17	18	15	0	26	2	1	5	0	0	.00	4	.205	.269	.269
Edge, Michael	of	Burlington	Cle	R+	20	29	92	19	1	0	0	20	9	9	9	0	26	1	3	2	1	1	.50	0	.207	.279	.217

1999 Batting — Single-A and Rookie Leagues

BATTING																					BASERUNNING				PERCENTAGES		
Player	Pos	Team	Org	Lg	A	G	AB	H	2B	3B	HR	TB	R	RBI	TBB	IBB	SO	HBP	SH	SF	SB	CS	SB%	GDP	Avg	OBP	SLG
Edwards, John	c	Twins	Min	R	22	33	100	23	2	0	2	31	17	16	9	1	20	3	1	2	3	1	.75	4	.230	.307	.310
Edwards, Mike	3b	Kinston	Cle	A+	23	133	456	132	25	4	16	213	76	89	93	6	117	9	0	9	8	3	.73	12	.289	.413	.467
Egly, John#	1b	Diamondbcks	Ari	R	20	51	197	50	8	1	1	63	25	20	12	1	54	1	0	0	1	1	.50	5	.254	.300	.320
Elder, Rick*	1b-dh	Orioles	Bal	R	20	3	10	6	2	0	2	14	2	4	2	0	1	0	0	0	0	0	.00	0	.600	.667	1.400
		Bluefield	Bal	R+	20	46	158	52	8	4	10	98	35	40	30	1	57	3	0	3	2	0	1.00	2	.329	.438	.620
		Delmarva	Bal	A	20	11	36	3	0	0	2	9	7	4	10	1	15	0	1	0	0	0	.00	0	.083	.283	.250
Elliott, Dawan*	dh-of	Rockford	Cin	A	23	19	30	4	0	0	1	7	3	6	4	0	10	0	0	1	0	1	.00	0	.133	.229	.233
Ellis, Alvyn	1b	Athletics	Oak	R	20	34	102	22	5	2	0	31	13	12	8	0	45	8	1	2	0	0	.00	0	.216	.317	.304
Ellis, John	c	Charlotte	Tex	A+	24	48	152	41	7	1	0	50	15	17	11	0	21	1	1	0	0	1	.00	2	.270	.323	.329
Ellis, Mark	ss	Spokane	KC	A-	23	71	281	92	14	0	7	127	67	47	47	3	40	3	5	4	21	7	.75	1	.327	.424	.452
Elwood, Brad	c	Greensboro	NYY	A	24	81	259	60	11	2	3	84	35	30	24	1	72	5	2	3	3	2	.60	2	.232	.306	.324
Elzy, Steve	c	Pittsfield	NYM	A-	22	40	131	32	10	1	0	44	16	18	9	0	15	2	2	1	2	0	1.00	4	.244	.301	.336
Encarnacion, Ar.	of	Marlins	Fla	R	20	46	151	42	9	2	0	55	21	14	3	0	24	4	3	0	5	6	.45	4	.278	.310	.364
Encarnacion, Bi.	ss-2b	Cedar Rapds	Ana	A	22	57	206	54	3	2	1	64	28	23	11	0	33	0	6	2	4	2	.67	8	.262	.297	.311
Encarnacion, San.	1b	Padres	SD	R	20	52	187	53	2	4	0	63	31	23	21	1	40	1	1	0	22	2	.92	2	.283	.359	.337
Ensberg, Morgan	3b	Kissimmee	Hou	A+	24	123	427	102	25	2	15	176	72	69	68	0	90	9	1	3	17	6	.74	9	.239	.353	.412
Erickson, Corey	2b	Capital Cty	NYM	A	23	129	424	100	21	1	23	192	64	57	46	0	120	14	0	6	9	3	.75	4	.236	.327	.453
Ernster, Mark	2b	Ogden	Mil	R+	22	5	22	5	1	1	0	8	3	2	1	0	1	1	1	0	1	0	1.00	1	.227	.292	.364
Escalante, Jaime#	c	Frederick	Bal	A+	23	5	3	1	1	0	0	2	0	1	0	0	1	0	0	0	0	0	.00	0	.333	.333	.667
		Delmarva	Bal	A	23	45	141	27	4	0	2	37	15	14	20	0	45	3	0	0	0	0	.00	3	.191	.305	.262
Escalera, Jose	of	Great Falls	LA	R+	19	32	114	29	4	0	2	39	14	10	6	0	20	0	2	0	1	2	.33	4	.254	.292	.342
Escalona, Felix	2b	Michigan	Hou	A	21	116	396	114	29	4	6	169	78	47	29	0	60	17	7	3	7	7	.50	4	.288	.360	.427
Escobar, Alex	of	Mets	NYM	R	21	2	8	3	2	0	0	5	1	1	1	0	2	0	0	0	0	0	.00	0	.375	.444	.625
		St. Lucie	NYM	A+	21	1	3	2	0	0	1	5	1	3	1	0	1	0	0	1	1	1	.50	0	.667	.600	1.667
Escobar, Gustavo	3b	New Jersey	StL	A-	20	31	96	26	2	3	0	34	17	12	7	0	22	1	0	0	5	2	.71	2	.271	.327	.354
		Peoria	StL	A	20	24	94	30	2	3	0	38	11	18	6	0	14	0	2	1	2	2	.50	5	.319	.356	.404
Espino, Fernando	of	Wisconsin	Sea	A	23	130	481	141	29	0	11	203	71	69	38	0	91	9	1	3	5	8	.38	16	.293	.354	.422
Espino, Jose	of	New Jersey	StL	A-	20	42	136	27	4	2	0	35	12	10	9	0	44	0	0	2	5	4	.56	3	.199	.245	.257
Espinoza, Andres	of	Vermont	Mon	A-	21	29	71	15	3	0	0	18	9	2	4	0	15	1	0	0	1	1	.50	1	.211	.263	.254
Espinoza, Efren	dh	Mexico	—	R	19	48	183	56	9	5	4	87	32	30	12	1	41	2	1	2	8	2	.80	2	.306	.352	.475
Espy, Nate	1b	Piedmont	Phi	A	22	83	295	75	18	2	11	130	37	38	48	2	56	1	0	1	3	1	.75	7	.254	.359	.441
Esquerra, Marques#	3b	Columbus	Cle	A	24	122	403	103	14	4	3	134	53	44	32	1	65	8	7	3	9	8	.53	14	.256	.321	.333
Essian, Jim#	1b	Royals	KC	R	21	30	71	14	4	1	0	20	13	8	24	0	26	1	2	0	3	1	.75	1	.197	.406	.282
Estevez, Domingo#	2b	St.Cathrnes	Tor	A-	22	61	212	54	21	2	3	88	31	28	21	0	32	6	2	4	12	9	.57	1	.255	.333	.415
Estrada, Johnny#	c	Clearwater	Phi	A+	24	98	346	96	15	0	9	138	35	52	14	3	26	2	6	8	1	0	1.00	12	.277	.303	.399
Estrella, Gorky	3b-1b	Everett	Sea	A-	23	28	84	21	4	1	1	30	15	11	31	3	22	0	0	0	2	2	.50	1	.250	.452	.357
Evans, Lee#	c	Lynchburg	Pit	A+	22	117	413	93	18	2	11	148	44	58	37	2	129	5	2	8	3	6	.33	4	.225	.292	.358
Evans, Mitch	c	Yankees	NYY	R	19	24	44	8	0	0	0	8	11	4	16	0	10	0	2	1	1	1	.50	2	.182	.393	.182
Evans, Pat#	dh	Frederick	Bal	A+	27	1	3	1	1	0	0	2	2	1	1	0	0	0	0	0	0	0	.00	0	.333	.500	.667
Ewan, Bry	1b	Jamestown	Atl	A-	21	31	109	21	3	0	1	27	9	15	13	0	33	2	1	2	0	0	.00	1	.193	.286	.248
Ewing, Byron	1b	Mahoning Vy	Cle	A-	23	15	44	12	2	0	1	17	7	6	9	0	9	0	0	0	1	0	1.00	2	.273	.396	.386
		Columbus	Cle	A	23	47	173	42	11	0	3	62	19	19	16	0	41	2	0	0	10	1	.91	2	.243	.314	.358
Ewing, Chris	of	New Jersey	StL	A-	24	26	54	7	1	1	0	10	5	0	9	0	25	2	0	0	1	1	.50	0	.130	.277	.185
Fafard, Mathias	3b	Mets	NYM	R	23	5	11	2	0	0	1	5	4	2	1	0	0	2	0	0	0	0	.00	0	.182	.357	.455
		Kingsport	NYM	R+	23	9	17	6	1	0	1	10	4	6	1	0	3	2	1	0	0	0	.00	0	.353	.450	.588
Faison, Vince*	of	Padres	SD	R	19	44	178	55	6	6	4	85	40	28	18	0	45	3	0	2	30	4	.88	0	.309	.378	.478
		Fort Wayne	SD	A	19	11	48	10	2	0	0	12	10	1	6	0	18	1	1	0	7	1	.88	0	.208	.309	.250
Fajardo, Alex	2b	Piedmont	Phi	A	24	118	444	108	16	6	6	154	66	43	52	0	91	6	10	3	44	10	.81	7	.243	.329	.347
Farnsworth, Troy	3b	Peoria	StL	A	24	134	500	125	33	3	19	221	76	78	55	4	124	12	0	4	3	2	.60	10	.250	.336	.442
Fatheree, Danny	c	Michigan	Hou	A	21	38	118	24	5	2	1	36	13	18	11	0	19	1	0	1	2	1	.67	3	.203	.275	.305
Feliciano, Jesus*	of	Vero Beach	LA	A+	21	98	370	94	13	0	0	107	44	21	29	1	38	4	2	2	20	10	.67	4	.254	.314	.289
Felix, Hersy	c	Chstn-WV	KC	A	22	23	80	23	7	0	1	33	6	4	3	0	17	0	0	0	2	0	1.00	2	.288	.313	.413
Felix, Osvaldo	of	Mexico	—	R	22	50	196	47	5	2	1	59	29	16	23	1	64	3	1	0	3	5	.38	2	.240	.329	.301
Feliz, Joselyn	c	Brevard Cty	Fla	A+	24	11	25	5	2	0	0	7	0	2	1	0	8	1	0	0	0	0	.00	0	.200	.259	.280
		Utica	Fla	A-	24	25	87	20	4	1	2	32	7	18	2	0	19	0	0	0	1	0	1.00	1	.230	.247	.368
Fennell, Jason#	dh-of	Burlington	CWS	A	22	114	398	111	28	7	6	171	78	79	75	5	56	5	1	8	22	6	.79	8	.279	.393	.430
Fera, Aaron	of	Medcine Hat	Tor	R+	22	61	213	47	10	1	6	77	26	29	18	0	58	5	1	1	3	2	.60	6	.221	.295	.362
Fernandez, Alej.	dh	Yankees	NYY	R	19	12	28	6	3	0	0	9	2	3	6	0	8	0	0	0	0	0	.00	0	.214	.353	.321
Fernandez, Alex*	of	Lancaster	Sea	A+	19	118	426	120	29	2	14	195	63	62	21	1	83	4	5	2	21	11	.66	13	.282	.320	.458
Fernandez, Med.#	of	Marlins	Fla	R	21	39	134	41	6	2	0	51	20	16	15	0	30	2	1	0	10	3	.77	1	.306	.384	.381
Ferrand, Francisco*	of	Kane County	Fla	A	20	16	51	13	4	0	0	17	6	4	7	0	8	0	0	0	0	2	.00	0	.255	.345	.333
		Utica	Fla	A-	20	63	229	67	16	0	2	89	26	27	15	0	38	1	5	3	3	1	.75	7	.293	.335	.389
Fierro, Robert	c	Medcine Hat	Tor	R+	22	22	59	14	2	0	0	16	10	10	16	0	9	3	0	1	0	0	.00	0	.237	.418	.271
Figgins, Chone#	ss	Salem	Col	A+	22	123	444	106	12	3	0	124	65	22	41	0	86	3	14	2	27	13	.68	5	.239	.306	.279
Figueroa, Carlos	ss	Rockies	Col	R	19	49	181	40	10	2	0	54	29	28	23	0	30	5	0	2	10	5	.67	2	.221	.322	.298
Figueroa, Eduardo*	1b-dh	Beloit	Mil	A	23	70	233	59	19	0	7	99	38	43	29	1	72	3	2	7	0	0	.00	7	.253	.335	.425
Figueroa, Franky	1b	Frederick	Bal	A+	23	132	527	132	20	3	17	209	59	78	32	0	138	7	0	5	2	3	.40	21	.250	.299	.397
Figueroa, Luis	3b	Lancaster	Sea	A+	23	39	146	52	8	1	4	74	21	20	18	2	8	2	0	2	2	2	.50	10	.356	.429	.507
		Mariners	Sea	R	23	3	10	5	1	0	0	6	2	1	0	0	0	0	0	0	0	0	.00	1	.500	.500	.600
Finnerty, Francis#	3b	Burlington	Cle	R+	19	37	131	31	2	0	1	36	12	15	12	0	34	1	0	2	0	2	.00	3	.237	.301	.275
Fiore, Curt	3b	Danville	Atl	R+	22	53	198	66	13	0	3	88	35	24	22	1	39	7	0	1	0	5	.00	4	.333	.417	.444
Fischer, Mark	of	Sarasota	Bos	A+	24	106	359	91	14	3	5	126	42	40	28	0	85	1	4	1	11	6	.65	11	.253	.308	.351
Fitzgerald, Jason*	dh	Kinston	Cle	A+	24	82	310	74	17	3	4	109	26	39	22	1	77	1	1	3	15	7	.68	5	.239	.289	.352
Flaherty, Tim	1b	San Jose	SF	A+	23	132	490	131	33	3	25	245	82	88	69	3	168	9	0	5	11	3	.79	5	.267	.365	.500
Fleming, Ryan*	of	Dunedin	Tor	A+	24	51	123	28	7	1	0	37	17	9	10	1	19	4	3	1	4	3	.57	3	.228	.304	.301
		Hagerstown	Tor	A	24	61	227	76	9	2	4	101	34	35	23	1	26	0	2	4	7	6	.54	4	.335	.390	.445
Flores, Javier	c	Visalia	Oak	A+	24	103	362	107	22	1	5	146	48	63	27	0	59	9	2	6	6	3	.67	8	.296	.354	.403

1999 Batting — Single-A and Rookie Leagues

BATTING																					BASERUNNING				PERCENTAGES		
Player	Pos	Team	Org	Lg	A	G	AB	H	2B	3B	HR	TB	R	RBI	TBB	IBB	SO	HBP	SH	SF	SB	CS	SB%	GDP	Avg	OBP	SLG
Flores, Ralph	ss	White Sox	CWS	R	20	55	193	65	9	7	0	88	30	30	23	0	26	2	3	1	10	5	.67	6	.337	.411	.456
Floyd, Mike	of	New Jersey	StL	A-	22	38	137	30	8	0	1	41	17	16	4	0	40	2	2	1	4	1	.80	1	.219	.250	.299
Folkers, Brandon*	1b	Peoria	StL	A	24	86	257	64	15	2	7	104	35	36	45	2	96	6	2	1	6	3	.67	5	.249	.372	.405
Foltynowic, Roger	c	Reds	Cin	R	23	22	68	17	5	0	0	22	1	7	4	0	11	2	0	0	2	0	1.00	4	.250	.311	.324
Forbes, Matt	of	Sou Oregon	Oak	A-	22	63	258	72	17	6	4	113	50	34	34	0	77	0	1	1	13	6	.68	0	.279	.362	.438
Forbes, Michael*	3b-dh	Danville	Atl	R+	20	58	207	58	11	4	1	80	47	34	53	0	47	5	0	0	1	4	.20	1	.280	.438	.386
Forbush, Nate#	1b-c	Lakeland	Det	A+	24	84	250	72	14	0	5	101	38	28	43	2	62	0	0	2	1	3	.25	7	.288	.390	.404
Ford, Lew	of	Lowell	Bos	A-	23	62	250	70	17	4	7	116	48	34	19	1	35	5	0	3	15	2	.88	6	.280	.339	.464
Ford, Will*	of	Ogden	Mil	R+	23	53	179	61	14	4	5	98	38	46	22	1	27	2	0	3	5	5	.50	6	.341	.413	.547
Forelli, Anthony	1b	Ogden	Mil	R+	23	64	228	67	17	0	3	93	22	37	18	0	51	5	1	2	3	3	.50	5	.294	.356	.408
Foster, Brian	c	Helena	Mil	R+	18	20	46	7	0	0	0	7	4	2	5	0	16	2	1	0	0	0	.00	3	.152	.264	.152
Foster, Quincy*	of	Brevard Cty	Fla	A+	25	134	568	167	13	6	3	201	78	54	36	1	96	8	2	2	56	23	.71	4	.294	.344	.354
Fowler, Ben#	c	Mahoning Vy	Cle	A-	23	17	62	13	3	0	3	25	5	15	2	0	21	0	0	1	0	1	.00	1	.210	.231	.403
		Columbus	Cle	A	23	28	97	25	4	0	3	38	12	11	5	0	23	0	1	0	2	2	.50	0	.258	.294	.392
Fowler, David	of	Yankees	NYY	R	20	57	187	47	9	2	4	72	28	25	27	0	63	10	1	0	6	5	.55	2	.251	.375	.385
Fox, Jason#	of	Stockton	Mil	A+	23	70	248	58	8	3	1	75	34	18	14	0	63	2	10	2	15	4	.79	7	.234	.278	.302
		Boloit	Mil	A	23	41	163	36	3	1	1	44	18	6	11	0	34	1	1	0	8	3	.73	2	.221	.274	.270
Francisco, Joe	of	Jamestown	Atl	A-	22	42	146	29	10	0	2	45	17	10	9	0	37	2	0	0	9	1	.90	3	.199	.255	.308
Franco, Pascual	c-dh	Johnson Cy	StL	R+	21	18	58	18	2	0	2	26	12	14	3	0	22	2	0	1	1	0	1.00	0	.310	.359	.448
Frank, Nick	3b	Ogden	Mil	R+	24	59	203	61	13	0	4	86	35	40	25	0	44	7	3	1	13	5	.72	5	.300	.394	.424
Frazier, Charlie	of	Marlins	Fla	R	19	35	125	36	6	0	0	42	12	9	13	0	31	4	0	0	5	1	.83	3	.288	.373	.336
Freeman, Brad	ss	Potomac	StL	A+	24	109	342	80	17	2	2	107	36	37	45	1	75	15	3	3	9	13	.41	3	.234	.346	.313
Freeman, Choo	of	Asheville	Col	A	20	131	485	133	22	4	14	205	82	66	39	1	132	7	1	2	16	4	.80	3	.274	.336	.423
Freeman, Corey	ss	Mariners	Sea	R	20	28	103	28	9	0	0	37	20	13	8	0	25	2	0	0	8	2	.80	1	.272	.336	.359
		Wisconsin	Sea	A	20	18	63	12	6	0	0	18	6	9	1	0	18	1	2	0	0	0	.00	1	.190	.215	.286
Freeman, T.J.*	dh	Missoula	Ari	R+	22	16	42	10	1	2	0	15	3	6	7	0	15	1	0	0	1	1	.50	0	.238	.360	.357
Freeman, Terr.#	2b	Lakeland	Det	A+	25	101	381	106	19	2	0	129	64	47	43	0	59	7	3	3	37	12	.76	2	.278	.359	.339
Freitas, Jeremy*	dh	Chstn-WV	KC	A	25	85	300	74	20	2	13	137	38	52	37	1	80	4	1	2	3	0	1.00	3	.247	.335	.457
Freitas, Joe	dh	Lk Elsinore	Ana	A+	26	3	9	1	1	0	0	2	1	1	1	0	3	0	0	0	0	0	.00	0	.111	.200	.222
French, Ron	dh	Rancho Cuca	SD	A+	22	7	20	3	0	1	0	5	2	3	1	0	5	4	1	0	0	0	.00	0	.150	.320	.250
		Fort Wayne	SD	A	22	65	219	59	11	0	4	82	24	31	23	1	58	7	4	4	0	3	.00	3	.269	.352	.374
Frese, Nate	ss	Lansing	ChC	A	22	107	373	99	27	4	4	146	68	49	58	2	67	5	1	8	10	4	.71	13	.265	.365	.391
Frick, Matt	c	Kane County	Fla	A	24	21	80	22	5	0	3	36	14	10	9	0	27	1	0	2	0	1	.00	1	.275	.348	.450
		Brevard Cty	Fla	A+	24	35	113	25	5	0	0	30	8	12	11	0	27	2	1	1	0	1	.00	2	.221	.299	.265
Fuentes, Javier	3b	Augusta	Bos	A	25	39	130	33	4	1	1	42	16	13	22	0	13	4	1	1	6	1	.86	0	.254	.376	.323
		Sarasota	Bos	A+	25	64	176	51	4	0	0	55	28	13	33	0	17	6	3	3	6	1	.86	2	.290	.413	.313
Fuentes, Joel#	2b	Bakersfield	SF	A+	24	64	162	32	5	0	0	37	20	16	19	0	38	0	1	2	5	1	.83	1	.198	.279	.228
Fuentes, Omar	c	Tampa	NYY	A+	20	19	57	14	0	0	0	14	4	8	3	0	7	1	0	1	0	0	.00	1	.246	.290	.246
		Staten Ilnd	NYY	A-	20	50	129	36	7	1	3	54	15	21	19	0	18	3	2	1	0	1	.00	2	.279	.382	.419
Fukuhara, Pete	of	Lansing	ChC	A	24	60	235	73	19	2	11	129	39	40	24	1	31	5	3	2	7	5	.58	3	.311	.383	.549
Fulse, Sheldon#	of	Mariners	Sea	R	18	31	97	24	11	0	0	35	15	9	22	0	34	0	0	0	12	8	.60	1	.247	.387	.361
Furcal, Rafael#	ss	Macon	Atl	A	19	83	335	113	15	1	1	133	73	29	41	1	36	5	1	0	73	22	.77	4	.337	.417	.397
		Myrtle Bch	Atl	A+	19	43	184	54	9	3	0	69	32	12	14	0	42	0	6	0	23	8	.74	3	.293	.343	.375
Furniss, Eddy*	1b	Lynchburg	Pit	A+	24	128	444	116	33	1	23	220	96	87	94	5	113	6	0	5	5	4	.56	13	.261	.393	.495
Gajewski, Matt#	1b	Rangers	Tex	R	22	52	162	34	7	1	4	55	31	26	34	2	41	9	2	0	1	0	1.00	3	.210	.376	.340
Gallaher, T.T.	of	Mahoning Vy	Cle	A-	22	6	19	6	1	1	1	12	7	5	5	0	0	0	0	0	2	0	1.00	0	.316	.458	.632
Gallegos, Al.*	of	Mexico	—	R	—	44	136	22	5	2	1	34	14	16	25	0	57	2	4	1	2	2	.50	1	.162	.299	.250
Gallo, Ismael*	ss-2b	San Berndno	LA	A+	23	104	338	106	15	3	2	133	66	42	40	2	30	7	12	4	3	1	.75	4	.314	.393	.393
Garabito, Eddy#	2b	Frederick	Bal	A+	21	132	539	138	24	4	6	188	76	77	52	1	68	4	8	10	38	18	.68	7	.256	.321	.349
Garabito, Vianney	3b	Reds	Cin	R	20	35	141	40	4	0	3	53	11	16	1	0	9	1	1	0	7	2	.78	2	.284	.294	.376
Garbe, B.J.	of	Elizabethtn	Min	R+	19	41	171	54	8	0	3	71	33	32	20	0	34	1	0	0	4	1	.80	3	.316	.391	.415
Garcia, Alex	2b	Fort Wayne	SD	A	21	71	201	42	9	1	2	59	27	26	25	0	62	0	2	4	5	2	.71	2	.209	.291	.294
Garcia, Douglas*	of	Charlotte	Tex	A+	21	112	386	115	14	5	0	139	57	34	26	0	69	3	3	1	14	8	.64	4	.298	.346	.360
Garcia, Hector	1b	Helena	Mil	R+	20	68	264	81	10	2	16	143	48	62	12	0	46	8	0	1	8	1	.89	3	.307	.354	.542
Garcia, Kenji	1b	Mets	NYM	R	19	32	72	6	2	0	1	11	9	6	17	0	46	2	0	0	0	0	.00	2	.083	.275	.153
Garcia, Kevys	3b	Martinsvlle	Hou	R+	19	50	192	49	9	3	2	70	36	18	20	0	65	4	1	0	16	4	.80	2	.255	.338	.365
Garcia, Luis	of	Mexico	—	R	21	50	188	62	9	6	13	122	35	40	22	1	31	0	0	1	1	2	.33	2	.330	.398	.649
Garcia, Nick	ss	Orioles	Bal	R	20	21	70	16	5	0	3	30	12	15	4	0	10	2	0	3	1	2	.33	1	.229	.278	.429
Garcia, Oscar	ss	Burlington	Cle	R+	19	56	194	56	9	1	5	82	39	41	33	0	42	8	1	6	17	4	.81	6	.289	.402	.423
		Columbus	Cle	A	19	8	29	7	2	0	0	9	3	1	4	0	11	0	0	0	1	1	.50	0	.241	.333	.310
Garcia, Tony	c	Burlington	CWS	A	22	73	230	54	10	0	2	70	35	20	22	0	76	13	5	1	3	4	.43	4	.235	.335	.304
Garcia, Yosnel	c	Bristol	CWS	R+	21	29	83	21	2	1	0	25	9	11	9	0	12	1	2	0	4	1	.80	1	.253	.333	.301
Garrett, Scott	c	Rockford	Cin	A	26	8	20	4	1	0	0	5	4	1	3	0	7	1	0	0	0	0	.00	0	.200	.333	.250
Garrett, Shawn#	1b	Idaho Falls	SD	R+	21	53	192	59	14	1	7	96	46	33	21	0	46	4	0	2	5	3	.63	11	.307	.384	.500
Garrick, Matt	c	Potomac	StL	A+	24	70	216	36	10	1	3	57	17	17	32	0	57	0	3	1	1	5	.17	4	.167	.273	.264
Garza, Rolando	1b	Burlington	CWS	A	20	40	148	31	4	0	1	38	13	8	12	0	30	0	3	1	4	3	.57	5	.209	.267	.257
		Bristol	CWS	R+	20	61	197	50	10	0	1	63	30	17	21	0	32	3	0	3	3	3	.50	5	.254	.330	.320
Gasparino, Billy	3b	Portland	Col	A-	23	62	242	63	9	2	6	94	48	23	40	1	57	4	5	1	10	8	.56	4	.260	.373	.388
Gastelum, Carlos	ss	Cedar Rapds	Ana	A	18	19	66	15	1	0	0	16	8	8	6	0	5	0	1	0	2	2	.50	1	.227	.292	.242
		Butte	Ana	R+	18	58	211	55	12	2	0	71	37	28	22	0	28	4	4	3	11	5	.69	6	.261	.338	.336
Gauch, Barry	c	White Sox	CWS	R	23	26	61	14	3	0	0	17	7	11	11	0	7	4	1	0	1	0	1.00	2	.230	.382	.279
Gay, Curtis*	1b	Mahoning Vy	Cle	A-	22	65	234	54	13	2	2	77	34	24	24	0	98	4	1	2	3	2	.60	0	.231	.311	.329
Gay, Dennis	2b	Boise	Ana	A-	23	10	33	8	2	0	0	10	5	5	3	0	6	1	0	1	0	0	.00	0	.242	.316	.303
		Cedar Rapds	Ana	A	23	16	47	9	3	0	0	12	4	8	4	0	14	2	1	1	0	0	.00	0	.191	.278	.255
Gearlds, Aaron	of	Rockies	Col	R	20	51	180	56	4	4	1	71	37	29	18	0	43	6	0	5	22	2	.92	3	.311	.383	.394
Geisbush, David	dh	Braves	Atl	R	23	23	78	18	4	0	2	28	12	11	8	0	21	4	1	0	1	1	.50	1	.231	.333	.359
		Jamestown	Atl	A-	23	26	69	16	2	1	3	29	11	12	5	0	25	0	1	0	2	0	1.00	1	.232	.284	.420

1999 Batting — Single-A and Rookie Leagues

BATTING																					BASERUNNING				PERCENTAGES		
Player	Pos	Team	Org	Lg	A	G	AB	H	2B	3B	HR	TB	R	RBI	TBB	IBB	SO	HBP	SH	SF	SB	CS	SB%	GDP	Avg	OBP	SLG
Gentry, Aaron	3b	Potomac	StL	A+	25	66	138	22	4	1	1	31	13	8	13	0	54	1	1	2	4	3	.57	4	.159	.234	.225
Gentry, Garett*	c-dh	Martinsvlle	Hou	R+	19	33	117	28	4	2	2	42	16	14	9	0	26	2	0	0	4	0	1.00	0	.239	.305	.359
Geraldo, Anulfo	2b	Helena	Mil	R+	20	45	161	42	8	0	2	56	28	22	20	0	26	0	4	1	2	3	.40	7	.261	.341	.348
German, Esteban	2b	Modesto	Oak	A+	21	128	501	156	16	12	4	208	107	52	102	0	128	5	5	7	40	16	.71	3	.311	.428	.415
German, Franklin	of	Lansing	ChC	A	20	84	281	68	12	2	5	99	49	31	23	0	75	7	1	3	12	4	.75	3	.242	.312	.352
Gerut, Jody*	of	Salem	Col	A+	22	133	499	144	33	11	11	232	80	63	61	4	65	3	1	3	25	12	.68	10	.289	.367	.465
Gettis, Byron	of	Royals	KC	R	20	28	95	30	6	2	5	55	20	21	17	0	21	3	0	3	3	2	.60	2	.316	.424	.579
		Chstn-WV	KC	A	20	43	149	44	7	2	2	61	19	13	10	0	36	6	4	1	10	3	.77	3	.295	.361	.409
Gibbons, Jay*	1b	Hagerstown	Tor	A	23	71	292	89	20	2	16	161	53	69	32	1	56	1	0	5	3	0	1.00	12	.305	.370	.551
		Dunedin	Tor	A+	23	60	212	66	14	0	9	107	34	39	25	0	38	0	0	1	2	1	.67	4	.311	.382	.505
Gil, Eric#	2b	Mexico	—	R	19	22	62	12	1	1	0	15	8	4	8	0	24	0	2	0	0	1	.00	3	.194	.286	.242
Giles, Marcus	2b	Myrtle Bch	Atl	A+	22	126	497	162	40	7	13	255	80	73	54	5	89	4	0	5	9	6	.60	9	.326	.393	.513
Giron, Alejandro	of	Piedmont	Phi	A	21	99	387	111	15	6	8	162	43	59	15	0	75	3	2	3	12	6	.67	8	.287	.316	.419
Glassey, Josh*	c	Yakima	LA	A-	23	28	92	21	4	0	2	31	13	14	19	0	24	0	4	1	0	1	.00	5	.228	.357	.337
Gload, Ross*	1b	Brevard Cty	Fla	A+	24	133	490	146	26	3	10	208	80	74	53	3	76	5	2	5	3	1	.75	8	.298	.369	.424
Godbolt, Keith	of	Great Falls	LA	R+	19	43	150	40	7	1	1	52	26	18	12	0	24	3	3	1	2	3	.40	5	.267	.331	.347
Godfrey, Tim#	2b	Rockford	Cin	A	22	34	77	19	2	0	1	24	10	7	9	0	23	0	2	1	3	3	.50	1	.247	.322	.312
Goelz, Jim	2b	Yakima	LA	A-	24	42	142	40	3	1	1	48	19	17	12	0	22	2	3	2	2	5	.29	4	.282	.342	.338
Goldbach, Jeff	c	Lansing	ChC	A	20	112	399	108	27	3	18	195	82	72	64	2	66	7	0	5	1	4	.20	5	.271	.377	.489
Goldfield, Josh*	of	Diamondbcks	Ari	R	20	2	3	1	0	0	0	1	3	0	2	0	0	0	0	0	0	0	.00	0	.333	.600	.333
		High Desert	Ari	A+	20	5	5	2	0	0	0	2	2	0	1	0	0	0	0	0	0	0	.00	0	.400	.500	.400
		Missoula	Ari	R+	20	35	122	31	4	0	0	35	15	23	13	0	31	2	1	0	2	0	1.00	2	.254	.336	.287
Gomez, Alexis*	of	Royals	KC	R	19	56	214	59	12	1	5	88	44	31	32	0	48	1	1	1	13	5	.72	1	.276	.371	.411
Gomez, Jose	3b	Utica	Fla	A-	21	25	75	13	3	1	0	18	6	6	5	0	27	2	2	0	2	0	1.00	1	.173	.244	.240
Gomez, Richard	of	W Michigan	Det	A	22	130	479	145	26	12	8	219	89	81	54	1	122	10	0	1	66	10	.87	1	.303	.384	.457
Gonzales, Jose	c	Salem	Col	A+	25	44	141	24	6	0	0	30	9	18	12	0	35	0	3	3	1	0	1.00	1	.170	.231	.213
Gonzalez, Felix	of	Expos	Mon	R	20	44	115	24	4	1	0	30	11	12	14	0	13	3	2	2	5	3	.63	4	.209	.306	.261
Gonzalez, Jimmy	3b-2b	San Berndno	LA	A+	21	111	471	149	28	6	5	204	78	53	20	2	55	5	5	4	9	9	.50	8	.316	.348	.433
Gonzalez, Julian	of	Spokane	KC	A-	23	16	52	13	2	1	1	20	5	6	9	0	17	0	0	0	1	3	.25	0	.250	.361	.385
Gonzalez, Luis	ss	Kinston	Cle	A+	21	1	1	0	0	0	0	0	0	0	0	0	0	0	0	0	0	0	.00	0	.000	.000	.000
		Columbus	Cle	A	21	83	299	88	18	2	7	131	41	50	26	0	40	5	4	5	6	5	.55	5	.294	.355	.438
Gonzalez, Reggie	ss-2b	Twins	Min	R	20	44	143	43	6	3	1	58	17	14	7	0	20	1	5	2	3	3	.50	2	.301	.333	.406
Gonzalez, Santos#	ss	St.Cathrnes	Tor	A-	23	42	150	35	3	1	3	49	14	14	13	0	41	0	1	1	9	2	.82	1	.233	.293	.327
Goodeill, Harold	dh-of	Hudson Val	TB	A-	22	8	23	4	1	1	0	7	3	2	2	0	6	1	0	0	0	0	.00	0	.174	.269	.304
Goodman, Scott*	of	Utica	Fla	A-	22	68	221	58	15	1	7	96	38	29	43	2	43	11	0	0	4	7	.36	10	.262	.407	.434
Goolsby, Kevin	of	White Sox	CWS	R	25	45	155	39	5	1	2	52	28	17	22	0	35	2	4	2	7	1	.88	3	.252	.348	.335
Gordnier, Aaron	of	Columbus	Cle	A	25	64	177	45	10	2	8	83	30	29	23	0	49	2	0	1	3	2	.60	5	.254	.345	.469
Gordon, Alex*	of	Orioles	Bal	R	20	36	125	45	7	6	6	82	25	34	14	2	37	0	0	1	12	2	.86	1	.360	.421	.656
		Bluefield	Bal	R+	20	27	105	35	4	4	9	74	26	32	13	1	35	2	0	1	4	1	.80	0	.333	.413	.705
Gordon, Brian*	of	South Bend	Ari	A	21	48	184	39	9	3	0	54	21	17	9	0	35	1	0	1	8	3	.73	3	.212	.251	.293
Gordon, Johnny*	of	Oneonta	Det	A-	23	44	110	17	4	3	0	27	13	5	14	0	30	0	0	0	4	1	.80	1	.155	.250	.245
Gorr, Robb	1b	San Berndno	LA	A+	23	132	546	174	22	6	11	241	67	106	30	5	59	5	3	7	5	2	.71	14	.319	.355	.441
Gosewisch, Chip	c	Butte	Ana	R+	23	55	207	51	10	2	1	68	29	30	12	0	43	1	1	3	0	2	.00	6	.246	.287	.329
Goudie, Jaime	2b	Reds	Cin	R	21	1	2	1	0	0	0	1	0	1	0	0	0	0	0	0	0	0	.00	0	.500	.500	.500
		Clinton	Cin	A	21	84	340	109	20	4	3	146	56	50	21	2	46	2	0	2	16	6	.73	8	.321	.362	.429
Gould, Elliotte	of	Padres	SD	R	22	21	56	11	1	0	0	12	7	4	5	0	19	4	2	0	6	3	.67	1	.196	.308	.214
Graham, Jess*	of	Sarasota	Bos	A+	24	129	462	124	33	5	7	188	66	65	49	3	77	19	6	2	5	4	.56	8	.268	.361	.407
Graham, Justin	of	High Desert	Ari	A+	22	4	10	1	0	0	0	1	0	1	0	0	4	0	0	0	0	0	.00	0	.100	.100	.100
		Missoula	Ari	R+	22	23	62	14	2	1	1	21	12	5	10	0	19	1	0	1	0	0	.00	0	.226	.338	.339
Green, Jason	c	Staten Ilnd	NYY	A-	23	25	25	5	1	0	0	6	6	1	7	0	3	1	0	0	0	0	.00	1	.200	.394	.240
Green, Kevin	2b	Danville	Atl	R+	21	44	149	26	8	0	5	49	24	16	13	0	68	11	2	2	4	2	.67	1	.174	.286	.329
Green, Kevin	of	Brevard Cty	Fla	A+	24	11	24	4	0	0	0	4	1	2	1	0	10	0	1	0	0	1	.00	0	.167	.200	.167
Green, Nick	2b	Jamestown	Atl	A-	21	73	273	81	15	0	11	129	52	41	26	0	66	4	0	3	14	4	.78	4	.297	.363	.473
		Macon	Atl	A	21	3	10	2	0	0	1	5	1	3	0	0	4	0	0	0	1	0	1.00	0	.200	.200	.500
Green, Ricky	c	Orioles	Bal	R	21	2	1	0	0	0	0	0	0	0	0	0	1	0	0	0	0	0	.00	0	.000	.000	.000
Greene, Claude#	of	Greensboro	NYY	A	23	115	437	108	16	5	16	182	74	68	26	2	118	17	0	6	7	2	.78	10	.247	.311	.416
Greene, Clay	of	Bakersfield	SF	A+	25	46	148	38	2	0	0	40	19	17	18	0	44	1	3	0	16	4	.80	2	.257	.341	.270
Gregg, Mitch*	1b	Athletics	Oak	R	23	37	118	28	9	1	1	42	21	16	32	1	40	1	0	1	4	2	.67	3	.237	.401	.356
Gregg, Neal*	1b	Greensboro	NYY	A	24	11	24	5	0	0	0	5	1	2	0	0	7	1	0	0	0	0	.00	0	.208	.240	.208
		Staten Ilnd	NYY	A-	24	17	33	7	3	0	1	13	4	8	5	0	14	3	0	1	0	0	.00	1	.212	.357	.394
Gregorio, Thomas	c	Boise	Ana	A-	23	52	186	55	10	1	5	82	29	36	11	0	33	2	0	2	0	1	.00	3	.296	.338	.441
Griffin, Justin	of	Burlington	Cle	R+	23	14	39	7	2	0	0	9	7	1	1	0	13	2	0	0	0	1	.00	0	.179	.238	.231
		Mahoning Vy	Cle	A-	23	5	9	1	0	0	0	1	2	0	2	0	5	0	0	0	0	0	.00	0	.111	.273	.111
Griffin, Matt	1b	Lansing	ChC	A	24	5	11	2	1	0	0	3	0	1	1	0	4	0	0	0	0	0	.00	0	.182	.250	.273
Grimmett, Ryan	of	Lakeland	Det	A+	25	50	133	27	4	1	3	42	32	16	25	0	41	5	1	1	24	4	.86	1	.203	.348	.316
Grindell, Nate	3b	Mahoning Vy	Cle	A-	23	71	267	84	20	2	5	123	42	47	24	1	39	4	0	4	6	5	.55	3	.315	.375	.461
Gripp, Ryan	3b	Eugene	ChC	A-	22	73	266	82	18	1	12	138	40	48	27	0	65	10	0	3	2	1	.67	7	.308	.389	.519
Griswold, Matt*	of	Orioles	Bal	R	22	10	26	9	3	0	0	12	4	4	6	0	4	1	1	2	0	1	.00	0	.346	.457	.462
		Bluefield	Bal	R+	22	40	149	41	8	1	6	69	30	26	32	1	50	2	0	1	2	1	.67	0	.275	.408	.463
Grochol, Bryan*	dh	Salem-Keizr	SF	A-	21	28	79	19	1	0	1	23	9	10	7	1	15	0	0	0	2	3	.40	2	.241	.302	.291
Grummitt, Dan	1b	Chston-SC	TB	A	24	8	30	4	1	0	1	8	6	4	1	0	12	2	0	0	0	0	.00	0	.133	.212	.267
		Hudson Val	TB	A-	24	73	287	73	13	1	22	154	44	58	30	1	78	5	0	2	3	1	.75	4	.254	.333	.537
Gsell, Tony	ss	Eugene	ChC	A-	23	76	276	69	21	1	12	128	50	43	23	1	69	11	0	2	12	5	.71	3	.250	.330	.464
Guerrero, Cristian	of	Ogden	Mil	R+	19	65	226	70	7	3	5	98	51	28	23	0	59	2	0	1	26	2	.93	3	.310	.377	.434
Guerrero, James	1b	Red Sox	Bos	R	18	23	50	11	1	0	0	12	4	4	7	0	21	1	0	0	0	2	.00	2	.220	.328	.240
Guerrero, Julio	of	Red Sox	Bos	R	19	31	112	22	1	1	0	25	16	11	10	0	17	2	1	1	8	4	.67	2	.196	.272	.223
Guerrero, Pedro	2b	Savannah	Tex	A	20	42	131	24	2	3	3	41	20	12	11	0	39	1	11	2	11	0	1.00	4	.183	.248	.313

1999 Batting — Single-A and Rookie Leagues

BATTING																					BASERUNNING				PERCENTAGES		
Player	Pos	Team	Org	Lg	A	G	AB	H	2B	3B	HR	TB	R	RBI	TBB	IBB	SO	HBP	SH	SF	SB	CS	SB%	GDP	Avg	OBP	SLG
		Pulaski	Tex	R+	20	63	218	47	7	2	5	73	57	22	49	1	59	6	6	3	19	7	.73	2	.216	.370	.335
Guillen, Jose#	ss	Beloit	Mil	A	20	76	228	61	7	4	1	79	45	20	48	0	65	2	7	2	12	4	.75	5	.268	.396	.346
Guilliams, Earl	c	Braves	Atl	R	19	18	35	4	1	0	0	5	1	0	4	0	7	0	0	0	0	0	.00	1	.114	.205	.143
Gundrum, Kris*	1b	Everett	Sea	A-	23	29	91	27	4	0	2	37	13	15	10	1	27	1	0	2	5	0	1.00	0	.297	.365	.407
Gutierrez, Derrick	ss	Delmarva	Bal	A	21	30	103	27	6	0	1	36	12	14	3	0	28	2	0	0	1	1	.50	3	.262	.296	.350
		Bluefield	Bal	R+	21	34	123	25	2	3	2	39	18	15	20	0	44	1	3	0	3	1	.75	0	.203	.319	.317
Gutierrez, Fernando	c	Bluefield	Bal	R+	19	23	78	21	7	0	0	28	5	11	4	0	19	1	0	0	0	1	.00	0	.269	.313	.359
Gutierrez, Roberto	3b	Medcine Hat	Tor	R+	19	7	20	3	0	1	0	5	1	1	2	0	2	0	0	0	0	0	.00	2	.150	.227	.250
Gutierrez, Said	c	Padres	SD	R	20	7	19	6	0	0	1	9	2	6	2	0	0	0	0	1	0	0	.00	0	.316	.364	.474
		Idaho Falls	SD	R+	20	26	87	27	5	0	1	35	10	11	3	0	14	3	0	0	0	1	.00	2	.310	.355	.402
Gutierrez, Victor	ss	Lynchburg	Pit	A+	22	114	428	100	11	8	1	130	55	33	37	0	68	3	11	0	23	9	.72	10	.234	.299	.304
Guyton, Eric	3b	Kingsport	NYM	R+	23	59	186	49	11	1	2	68	17	28	11	0	39	2	3	1	6	1	.86	2	.263	.310	.366
Guzman, Alexis#	ss	Medcine Hat	Tor	R+	20	47	149	32	8	1	0	42	28	10	18	0	39	1	1	3	3	1	.75	3	.215	.298	.282
Guzman, Carlos*	of	Piedmont	Phi	A	22	16	49	8	2	0	0	10	5	5	3	0	17	0	0	0	2	0	1.00	0	.163	.212	.204
Guzman, Elpidio*	of	Cedar Rapds	Ana	A	21	130	526	144	26	13	4	208	74	48	41	4	84	2	5	3	52	17	.75	11	.274	.327	.395
Guzman, Javier#	of	Rockies	Col	R	20	13	49	18	4	2	2	32	11	11	1	0	12	0	0	0	5	0	1.00	1	.367	.380	.653
Guzman, Jonathan	of	Royals	KC	R	19	43	141	34	4	1	2	46	23	14	21	0	46	1	2	2	11	2	.85	5	.241	.339	.326
Guzman, Juan#	ss	Royals	KC	R	20	30	96	16	4	0	0	20	11	7	10	0	36	1	3	3	7	0	1.00	2	.167	.245	.208
Haas, Danny*	of	Sarasota	Bos	A+	24	87	241	58	8	5	0	76	18	24	22	1	54	6	2	2	4	3	.57	5	.241	.317	.315
Hafner, Travis*	1b	Savannah	Tex	A	23	134	480	140	30	4	28	262	94	111	67	6	151	11	0	5	5	4	.56	11	.292	.387	.546
Hagins, Steve	c	Lk Elsinore	Ana	A+	25	40	141	37	14	1	4	65	21	22	5	0	39	5	0	1	2	1	.67	3	.262	.309	.461
Halgren, Chris	c	Athletics	Oak	R	21	10	22	4	0	0	0	4	4	0	3	0	11	1	1	0	0	0	.00	1	.182	.308	.182
Hall, Bill	ss	Ogden	Mil	R+	20	69	280	81	15	2	6	118	41	31	15	1	61	2	2	1	19	8	.70	6	.289	.329	.421
Hall, Doug*	of-dh	Lansing	ChC	A	25	33	90	25	8	0	2	39	16	18	16	1	23	0	0	2	3	2	.60	3	.278	.380	.433
		Daytona	ChC	A+	25	31	101	25	8	0	0	33	9	8	2	0	11	0	2	1	2	0	1.00	1	.248	.260	.327
Hall, Justin	ss	Athletics	Oak	R	23	7	20	7	1	0	0	8	5	4	5	0	5	2	0	1	0	1	.00	0	.350	.500	.400
		Sou Oregon	Oak	A-	23	5	20	6	3	0	0	9	2	2	1	0	4	1	1	1	1	0	1.00	0	.300	.348	.450
Hall, Noah	of	Jupiter	Mon	A+	23	119	398	94	10	3	8	134	57	49	49	1	60	8	6	7	32	11	.74	12	.236	.327	.337
Hall, Victor*	of	Diamondbcks	Ari	R	19	27	104	38	2	1	0	42	19	14	13	0	25	2	3	1	10	5	.67	1	.365	.442	.404
		Missoula	Ari	R+	19	34	147	41	4	0	0	45	27	11	15	0	30	4	1	1	18	7	.72	1	.279	.359	.306
Halloran, Matt	ss	Rancho Cuca	SD	A+	22	95	309	67	11	2	0	82	39	22	17	0	75	7	4	1	15	9	.63	17	.217	.272	.265
Haman, Mack	of	Delmarva	Bal	A	24	68	246	54	9	4	3	80	27	37	14	1	67	7	1	1	4	2	.67	6	.220	.280	.325
Hambrick, Marcus*	of	Danville	Atl	R+	21	38	120	31	4	1	1	40	21	9	14	0	39	0	1	1	9	3	.75	0	.258	.333	.333
Hamilton, Jon*	of	Kincton	Cle	A+	22	131	473	132	29	5	13	210	74	65	61	1	114	1	5	4	9	4	.69	3	.279	.360	.444
Hamilton, Josh*	of	Princeton	TB	R+	19	56	236	82	20	4	10	140	49	48	13	0	43	0	1	2	18	3	.86	0	.347	.378	.593
		Hudson Val	TB	A-	19	16	72	14	3	0	0	17	7	7	1	0	14	1	0	1	1	1	.50	2	.194	.213	.236
Hamlin, Mark	of	Salem	Col	A+	26	103	363	90	20	3	7	137	45	48	35	2	111	8	3	2	4	3	.57	5	.248	.326	.377
Hammock, Robert	c	High Desert	Ari	A+	23	114	379	126	20	7	9	187	80	72	47	2	63	2	0	6	3	6	.33	8	.332	.403	.493
Hammond, Derry	of	Beloit	Mil	A	20	107	380	87	17	2	17	159	65	50	43	0	141	5	0	5	1	1	.50	7	.229	.312	.418
Hammond, Joey	3b	Delmarva	Bal	A	22	21	81	21	1	2	1	29	10	7	13	0	22	0	0	0	0	0	.00	4	.259	.362	.358
		Frederick	Bal	A+	22	79	245	71	14	1	3	96	41	37	57	0	66	0	5	2	3	3	.50	8	.290	.421	.392
Hamn, Larnell	of	Mets	NYM	R	20	32	60	7	2	0	0	9	6	4	3	0	22	2	0	0	0	2	.00	0	.117	.185	.150
Hankins, Ryan	3b	Burlington	CWS	A	24	129	487	143	36	4	15	232	93	74	91	1	118	3	2	8	11	6	.65	8	.294	.402	.476
Hannahan, Buzz	3b	Piedmont	Phi	A	24	22	65	8	0	0	0	8	5	3	6	0	12	0	0	0	3	1	.75	0	.123	.197	.123
Hargreaves, Brad	c	Daytona	ChC	A+	22	39	101	17	3	0	0	20	6	6	4	0	27	0	2	0	1	0	1.00	8	.168	.200	.198
Hargrove, Harvey	of	Lancaster	Sea	A+	24	130	510	150	20	2	11	207	83	80	51	0	116	3	4	5	17	16	.52	5	.294	.359	.406
Harper, Brandon	c	Brevard Cty	Fla	A+	24	81	280	75	9	0	4	96	35	40	30	2	31	3	4	3	1	1	.50	4	.268	.342	.343
Harper, Shaun	of	Braves	Atl	R	20	51	191	47	8	0	2	61	20	16	9	0	61	2	1	1	6	1	.86	1	.246	.286	.319
Harrell, Ken	c	Tampa	NYY	A+	25	1	1	1	0	0	0	1	1	1	0	0	0	0	0	0	0	0	.00	0	1.000	1.000	1.000
		Yankees	NYY	R	25	1	5	3	1	0	0	4	0	0	0	0	0	0	0	0	0	0	.00	0	.600	.600	.800
Harrelson, Casey*	1b-dh	Bristol	CWS	R+	22	18	40	6	1	0	0	7	3	1	5	0	11	1	0	0	0	1	.00	0	.150	.261	.175
Harris, Corey	of	Mets	NYM	R	20	49	185	48	11	6	1	74	26	28	18	0	27	0	1	1	6	0	1.00	5	.259	.324	.400
Harris, Karl	1b	Expos	Mon	R	19	28	89	18	4	0	0	22	4	6	4	0	19	1	1	0	0	1	.00	2	.202	.245	.247
Harris, Kevin	of	Savannah	Tex	A	22	59	180	29	5	2	3	47	15	11	3	0	72	3	3	0	8	6	.57	0	.161	.188	.261
Harris, Willie*	2b	Bluefield	Bal	R+	22	5	22	6	1	0	0	7	3	3	4	0	2	0	0	1	1	0	1.00	1	.273	.370	.318
		Delmarva	Bal	A	22	66	272	72	13	3	2	97	42	32	20	0	41	1	4	4	17	11	.61	4	.265	.313	.357
Harrison, Jamal	dh	Fort Myers	Min	A+	22	30	95	18	1	0	2	25	6	11	16	0	24	1	0	2	0	2	.00	1	.189	.307	.263
Hart, Bo	ss-2b	New Jersey	StL	A-	23	50	163	30	3	3	3	48	23	15	10	0	38	12	3	0	4	2	.67	1	.184	.281	.294
Hart, Corey#	3b	Chstn-WV	KC	A	24	92	295	56	16	3	0	78	43	39	58	1	62	3	4	5	13	7	.65	3	.190	.324	.264
Hart, Dickie	2b	Boise	Ana	A-	23	4	2	0	0	0	0	0	0	0	0	0	2	0	0	0	0	0	.00	0	.000	.000	.000
Hart, Jason	1b	Modesto	Oak	A+	22	135	550	168	48	2	19	277	96	123	56	1	105	4	0	7	2	5	.29	18	.305	.370	.504
Hart, Keith	1b	Augusta	Bos	A	24	86	336	88	14	2	5	121	29	50	12	0	72	5	0	5	2	0	1.00	15	.262	.293	.360
Hartley, Will#	dh	Burlington	Cle	R+	19	48	151	24	3	0	4	39	19	14	41	0	51	5	0	0	3	0	1.00	0	.159	.355	.258
Harts, Jeremy#	of	Pirates	Pit	R	20	28	122	36	3	2	2	49	20	15	8	0	21	2	0	1	8	3	.73	5	.295	.346	.402
		Hickory	Pit	A	20	22	68	9	1	0	0	10	8	1	10	0	24	1	1	0	1	0	1.00	1	.132	.253	.147
Harvey, Kenneth	1b	Spokane	KC	A-	22	56	204	81	17	0	8	122	49	41	23	4	30	8	0	0	7	1	.88	3	.397	.477	.598
Hattig, John#	3b	Red Sox	Bos	R	20	50	163	44	7	3	1	60	28	17	16	1	20	1	0	3	1	1	.50	8	.270	.333	.368
Haver, Lance	c	Billings	Cin	R+	23	11	35	12	4	0	0	16	5	4	0	0	15	2	1	1	0	1	.00	0	.343	.368	.457
Hawes, B.J.	ss	Reds	Cin	R	21	45	162	49	11	5	0	70	23	18	13	1	22	1	1	1	11	2	.85	4	.302	.356	.432
Hawthorne, Kyle	ss	Quad City	Min	A	22	84	315	75	14	2	2	99	44	31	27	1	61	5	4	4	14	5	.74	6	.238	.305	.314
Haynes, Larry	of	Wisconsin	Sea	A	22	67	176	46	5	5	6	79	36	23	18	0	58	1	4	0	9	3	.75	0	.261	.333	.449
Hazelton, Justin	of	Savannah	Tex	A	21	4	13	2	1	0	0	3	0	1	1	0	6	0	0	0	0	0	.00	0	.154	.214	.231
Hazen, Mike	of	Fort Wayne	SD	A	24	72	222	45	8	0	3	62	23	24	37	0	62	6	1	3	6	5	.55	8	.203	.328	.279
Healy, Liam	of-1b	Spokane	KC	A-	23	17	50	12	2	0	3	23	8	12	6	0	12	2	2	0	0	1	.00	1	.240	.345	.460
Heffernan, Chris*	of	Danville	Atl	R+	22	23	55	6	0	2	0	10	10	2	11	0	25	0	1	0	4	0	1.00	0	.109	.258	.182
Heine, Kyle	c	Greensboro	NYY	A	24	19	59	15	5	0	0	20	5	7	5	0	14	1	2	0	0	1	.00	1	.254	.323	.339
Heintz, Chris	c	Winston-Sal	CWS	A+	25	118	417	122	33	2	7	180	55	60	40	1	72	4	3	2	6	3	.67	7	.293	.359	.432

1999 Batting — Single-A and Rookie Leagues

BATTING																					BASERUNNING				PERCENTAGES		
Player	Pos	Team	Org	Lg	A	G	AB	H	2B	3B	HR	TB	R	RBI	TBB	IBB	SO	HBP	SH	SF	SB	CS	SB%	GDP	Avg	OBP	SLG
Helena, Roberto	of	Princeton	TB	R+	18	61	223	60	7	0	1	70	31	14	10	0	44	1	1	1	4	5	.44	1	.269	.302	.314
Helquist, Jon	ss-3b	Martinsvlle	Hou	R+	19	49	173	52	15	3	4	85	33	17	18	0	50	2	0	0	5	4	.56	0	.301	.373	.491
Hemme, Justin*	1b	Salem	Col	A+	24	22	78	15	4	0	2	25	8	4	7	1	22	0	2	1	0	1	.00	1	.192	.256	.321
		Portland	Col	A-	24	71	275	76	16	1	14	136	48	59	29	1	56	3	1	3	2	1	.67	3	.276	.348	.495
Hemmings, Scot	of-dh	Fort Wayne	SD	A	23	12	36	4	1	0	0	5	3	4	5	0	18	1	0	0	1	0	1.00	1	.111	.238	.139
Henderson, Brad	2b	Sou Oregon	Oak	A-	23	57	197	53	9	1	5	79	30	36	27	0	33	5	0	7	3	1	.75	4	.269	.360	.401
Hendricks, Jason	of	Cape Fear	Mon	A	24	82	270	71	13	2	11	121	42	38	26	0	84	10	0	2	8	4	.67	0	.263	.347	.448
Henley, Bob	dh-c	Expos	Mon	R	27	2	4	1	0	0	0	1	0	1	1	0	1	0	0	1	0	0	.00	0	.250	.333	.250
Henson, Drew	3b	Tampa	NYY	A+	20	69	254	71	12	0	13	122	37	37	26	0	71	1	0	3	3	1	.75	6	.280	.345	.480
Herbert, Keith	2b	Marlins	Fla	R	19	29	79	17	3	3	1	29	8	8	7	0	20	1	0	0	1	0	1.00	0	.215	.287	.367
Hernandez, Ar.*	1b	Orioles	Bal	R	19	39	118	21	3	0	2	30	10	15	9	1	20	1	3	0	0	1	.00	3	.178	.242	.254
Hernandez, Carlos	3b	Kingsport	NYM	R+	21	5	4	0	0	0	0	0	1	0	1	0	2	0	0	0	0	0	.00	0	.000	.200	.000
Hernandez, Jesus*	of	Columbus	Cle	A	23	70	255	78	22	3	12	142	43	56	30	3	53	4	0	2	8	2	.80	6	.306	.385	.557
Hernandez, John	c	San Berndno	LA	A+	20	61	199	52	17	0	7	90	31	25	21	1	44	3	4	0	0	1	.00	8	.261	.341	.452
Hernandez, John.#	of	Johnson Cy	StL	R+	20	60	225	59	12	3	1	80	45	32	38	3	45	2	0	5	23	7	.77	9	.262	.367	.356
		New Jersey	StL	A-	20	10	33	13	1	0	0	14	4	2	10	0	9	0	0	0	1	4	.20	0	.394	.535	.424
Hernandez, Jose	c	Williamsprt	Pit	A-	19	35	118	28	4	0	0	32	5	9	3	0	20	2	2	0	1	1	.50	7	.237	.268	.271
Hernandez, Michel	c	Tampa	NYY	A+	21	82	281	69	10	1	2	87	26	23	18	0	49	3	3	2	2	2	.50	8	.246	.296	.310
Hernandez, Nic.#	of	Expos	Mon	R	20	4	7	1	0	0	0	1	0	1	1	0	0	0	0	0	0	0	.00	3	.143	.250	.143
Hernandez, Orlando	of	Mariners	Sea	R	21	27	106	26	7	1	1	38	17	19	5	0	17	1	1	1	1	2	.33	2	.245	.283	.358
		Wisconsin	Sea	A	21	15	26	6	1	0	0	7	3	1	0	0	8	1	0	0	0	0	.00	1	.231	.259	.269
Herrera, Elvis	2b	Pirates	Pit	R	19	7	18	2	0	0	0	2	5	1	4	0	6	0	0	1	0	0	.00	0	.111	.261	.111
Hertel, Brian	1b	Everett	Sea	A-	22	5	14	5	1	0	0	6	5	0	3	0	3	0	0	0	0	0	.00	0	.357	.471	.429
		Mariners	Sea	R	22	33	125	35	5	1	3	51	22	19	6	0	20	2	1	2	1	0	1.00	2	.280	.319	.408
Hessman, Mike	3b	Myrtle Bch	Atl	A+	22	103	365	90	25	0	23	184	62	54	47	3	135	11	0	3	0	3	.00	3	.247	.347	.504
Hill, Bobby*	ss	Capital Cty	NYM	A	21	86	278	68	12	3	3	95	31	14	16	0	57	2	5	4	12	3	.80	5	.245	.287	.342
Hill, Jason	c	Cedar Rapds	Ana	A	23	111	390	112	22	0	9	161	59	52	36	4	59	12	4	5	3	2	.60	5	.287	.361	.413
Hill, Jeremy	c	Wilmington	KC	A+	22	92	304	71	12	1	4	97	37	27	38	0	75	6	8	2	2	0	1.00	15	.234	.329	.319
Hill, Mike	of	Auburn	Hou	A-	23	69	269	80	11	2	6	113	44	39	29	1	65	3	0	2	22	6	.79	2	.297	.370	.420
Hill, Nakia	2b	Vero Beach	LA	A+	24	19	50	9	0	3	0	15	6	4	4	0	12	0	1	0	0	1	.00	0	.180	.241	.300
Hill, Steve#	2b	Bakersfield	SF	A+	24	135	522	139	16	6	0	167	78	60	40	0	99	6	10	2	39	13	.75	7	.266	.325	.320
Hill, Willy*	of	Kane County	Fla	A	23	127	535	162	19	6	2	199	85	57	44	0	56	8	10	8	38	24	.61	4	.303	.360	.372
Hills, Chris	of	Butte	Ana	R+	22	31	92	20	3	0	0	23	15	13	8	0	30	5	2	2	2	1	.67	0	.217	.308	.250
Hines, Derek	of	Cubs	ChC	R	23	36	123	29	4	5	0	43	14	9	11	0	39	2	1	1	6	1	.86	1	.236	.307	.350
Hitchcox, Brian*	ss	Batavia	Phi	A-	21	54	166	37	5	1	2	50	22	18	19	0	14	8	1	3	7	1	.88	2	.223	.327	.301
Hlousek, Robert	2b	Oneonta	Det	A-	22	36	109	24	3	0	0	27	15	3	12	1	11	1	3	1	9	1	.90	3	.220	.301	.248
Hobbs, Jay*	of	Hickory	Pit	A	25	124	409	103	22	1	21	190	60	73	75	0	116	3	5	6	5	5	.50	8	.252	.367	.465
Hoch, Corey	ss	Delmarva	Bal	A	24	36	115	24	2	0	0	26	7	12	23	0	27	3	1	0	0	2	.00	2	.209	.355	.226
Hochgesang, Josh	dh-3b	Sou Oregon	Oak	A-	23	21	71	11	2	0	1	16	10	8	14	0	23	4	1	0	0	1	.00	1	.155	.326	.225
Hodge, Kevin	3b	Quad City	Min	A	23	125	425	102	30	3	13	177	65	73	78	1	85	7	1	8	6	6	.50	12	.240	.361	.416
Hodges, Scott*	3b	Cape Fear	Mon	A	21	127	449	116	31	2	8	175	62	59	45	2	105	3	1	9	8	15	.35	11	.258	.324	.390
Holliday, Josh#	dh	St.Cathrnes	Tor	A-	23	71	216	55	13	1	10	100	50	37	63	2	57	11	5	4	1	2	.33	2	.255	.439	.463
Holliday, Matt	3b	Asheville	Col	A	20	121	444	117	28	0	16	193	76	64	53	0	116	9	0	5	10	3	.77	8	.264	.350	.435
Holst, Micah	of	Salem-Keizr	SF	A-	23	57	204	59	8	2	4	83	37	28	6	1	32	3	0	3	20	5	.80	1	.289	.315	.407
Holt, Todd	of	Bristol	CWS	R+	22	36	113	33	8	0	1	44	14	13	8	0	33	1	3	0	4	5	.44	2	.292	.344	.389
Honeycutt, Heath	3b	Brevard Cty	Fla	A+	23	103	376	107	18	8	5	156	58	50	25	1	78	9	0	3	6	1	.86	10	.285	.341	.415
Hood, Jay	2b	Lk Elsinore	Ana	A+	23	102	374	88	14	5	3	121	48	43	24	0	81	2	5	6	8	9	.47	7	.235	.281	.324
Hook, Kevin	ss	Cape Fear	Mon	A	23	5	16	1	0	0	0	1	1	0	2	0	4	0	0	0	0	0	.00	0	.063	.167	.063
		Jupiter	Mon	A+	23	34	88	21	5	0	1	29	16	6	16	0	21	4	3	1	3	1	.75	1	.239	.376	.330
Hooper, Daren	dh	Delmarva	Bal	A	23	24	90	22	7	2	0	33	13	5	3	0	30	2	0	0	0	1	.00	6	.244	.284	.367
Hooper, Kevin	2b	Utica	Fla	A-	23	73	289	81	18	6	0	111	52	22	39	0	35	4	2	3	14	8	.64	2	.280	.370	.384
Hoover, Paul	c	St. Pete	TB	A+	24	118	408	111	13	6	8	160	66	54	54	3	81	16	0	4	23	7	.77	13	.272	.376	.392
Hoover, Steve	of	Auburn	Hou	A-	22	32	94	19	2	2	1	28	4	5	8	0	18	4	0	0	2	2	.50	0	.202	.292	.298
Hopper, Norris	2b	Royals	KC	R	21	46	179	46	3	2	0	53	33	13	19	0	20	0	2	4	22	5	.81	2	.257	.322	.296
		Chstn-WV	KC	A	21	5	22	11	0	2	0	15	3	2	0	0	1	0	0	0	1	0	1.00	0	.500	.500	.682
House, J.R.	1b-c	Pirates	Pit	R	20	33	113	37	9	3	5	67	13	23	11	0	23	2	0	1	1	0	1.00	1	.327	.394	.593
		Williamsprt	Pit	A-	20	26	100	30	6	0	1	39	11	13	9	0	21	0	0	0	0	1	.00	2	.300	.358	.390
		Hickory	Pit	A	20	4	11	3	0	0	0	3	1	0	0	0	3	0	0	0	0	0	.00	0	.273	.273	.273
Howard, Jason	c	Billings	Cin	R+	23	6	21	4	1	0	0	5	2	3	1	0	7	1	0	0	0	0	.00	0	.190	.261	.238
		Clinton	Cin	A	23	25	68	11	3	0	0	14	5	6	3	0	17	0	0	0	0	0	.00	2	.162	.197	.206
Howe, Matt	3b	Visalia	Oak	A+	23	42	120	24	3	1	1	32	14	11	18	0	27	3	0	2	3	4	.43	3	.200	.315	.267
		Sou Oregon	Oak	A-	23	64	229	69	12	2	14	127	44	45	48	2	49	4	0	2	9	2	.82	3	.301	.428	.555
Hudnall, Josh	ss	Pirates	Pit	R	20	25	82	16	3	0	0	19	6	6	4	0	28	0	1	1	1	2	.33	0	.195	.230	.232
Hudson, Danny	of	Pirates	Pit	R	22	7	19	4	1	1	0	7	5	3	3	0	3	3	0	0	4	1	.80	1	.211	.400	.368
		Williamsprt	Pit	A-	22	37	117	25	6	2	0	35	14	9	22	0	41	1	1	1	5	3	.63	1	.214	.340	.299
Hudson, Orlando#	3b	Hagerstown	Tor	A	22	132	513	137	36	6	7	206	66	74	42	3	85	2	1	5	8	6	.57	10	.267	.322	.402
Huff, Jake	c	Idaho Falls	SD	R+	22	30	108	34	7	0	4	53	25	29	17	0	25	2	0	1	0	0	.00	1	.315	.414	.491
Huffman, Royce	3b	Martinsvlle	Hou	R+	23	53	196	58	16	7	2	94	39	36	31	0	29	4	0	4	18	2	.90	2	.296	.396	.480
Hughes, Brian	of	Frederick	Bal	A+	24	90	272	67	14	3	2	93	38	26	45	0	67	2	4	1	5	4	.56	12	.246	.356	.342
Huisman, Jason	3b	Lk Elsinore	Ana	A+	24	91	346	95	17	3	3	127	50	43	24	0	64	8	0	4	10	5	.67	8	.275	.332	.367
Hunter, David*	1b	Kingsport	NYM	R+	20	19	32	8	1	0	2	15	5	4	2	0	10	0	1	0	0	0	.00	0	.250	.294	.469
		Mets	NYM	R	20	25	82	18	2	1	0	22	12	8	5	0	20	0	0	1	1	1	.50	0	.220	.261	.268
Hurtado, Omar	of	Billings	Cin	R+	21	60	223	58	18	4	4	96	33	35	19	0	56	0	0	5	3	1	.75	4	.260	.312	.430
Huth, Jason#	3b	Billings	Cin	R+	23	59	251	70	12	9	1	103	52	29	25	0	53	1	4	1	3	3	.50	4	.279	.345	.410
Ide, Antoine	of	Bluefield	Bal	R+	21	24	85	19	2	2	0	25	17	8	7	0	10	2	1	0	2	1	.67	1	.224	.298	.294
		Orioles	Bal	R	21	15	50	14	2	0	1	19	12	5	5	0	12	0	2	1	8	2	.80	0	.280	.339	.380
Ienni, Greg	of	Idaho Falls	SD	R+	22	53	193	44	13	0	6	75	34	29	12	0	58	7	2	0	10	6	.63	2	.228	.297	.389

1999 Batting — Single-A and Rookie Leagues

BATTING																					BASERUNNING				PERCENTAGES		
Player	Pos	Team	Org	Lg	A	G	AB	H	2B	3B	HR	TB	R	RBI	TBB	IBB	SO	HBP	SH	SF	SB	CS	SB%	GDP	Avg	OBP	SLG
Illig, Brett	3b-2b	San Berndno	LA	A+	22	75	276	65	11	2	2	86	33	25	23	0	74	5	2	3	7	3	.70	9	.236	.303	.312
Infante, Juan#	2b-ss	Expos	Mon	R	18	26	67	17	0	0	0	17	5	3	10	0	11	1	2	0	2	3	.40	1	.254	.359	.254
Infante, Omar	ss	Tigers	Det	R	18	21	75	20	0	0	0	20	9	4	3	0	9	0	0	1	4	0	1.00	1	.267	.291	.267
Inge, Brandon	c	W Michigan	Det	A	23	100	352	86	25	2	9	142	54	46	39	0	87	3	2	6	15	3	.83	7	.244	.320	.403
Isenia, Chairon	c	Princeton	TB	R+	21	30	101	28	7	2	2	45	19	12	8	0	15	2	0	1	5	2	.71	2	.277	.339	.446
		Hudson Val	TB	A-	21	33	118	31	9	0	3	49	17	16	4	0	22	1	0	2	0	1	.00	4	.263	.288	.415
Ishida, Takehito	2b	Piedmont	Phi	A	21	10	33	8	1	1	0	11	2	0	1	0	7	0	0	0	0	1	.00	0	.242	.265	.333
		Phillies	Phi	R	21	27	85	27	11	0	1	41	8	14	9	0	11	1	0	1	1	1	.50	1	.318	.385	.482
Isturiz, Maicer#	ss	Columbus	Cle	A	19	57	220	66	5	3	4	89	46	23	20	0	28	1	1	3	14	2	.88	2	.300	.357	.405
Izturis, Cesar#	ss	Dunedin	Tor	A+	20	131	536	165	28	12	3	226	77	77	22	4	58	6	17	9	32	16	.67	9	.308	.337	.422
Jackson, Brandon	of	Butte	Ana	R+	23	22	68	19	2	1	3	32	16	13	10	0	28	3	2	0	3	1	.75	1	.279	.395	.471
Jackson, Brandon	ss	St.Cathrnes	Tor	A-	24	62	214	71	13	1	2	92	37	25	28	0	45	8	0	5	3	8	.27	4	.332	.420	.430
Jackson, Chris	c-of	Burlington	Cle	R+	21	22	59	9	2	0	0	11	8	5	10	0	16	2	0	0	0	0	.00	1	.153	.296	.186
Jackson, Jeremy*	of	Salem	Col	A+	24	36	122	30	7	1	0	39	12	5	5	0	36	1	3	0	4	1	.80	1	.246	.281	.320
		Asheville	Col	A	24	17	52	13	4	0	0	17	6	3	3	0	14	1	0	0	2	0	1.00	0	.250	.304	.327
Jackson, Kevin	1b	Oneonta	Det	A-	22	38	125	27	5	0	3	41	11	20	11	0	48	0	0	4	2	0	1.00	0	.216	.271	.328
Jacobs, John	3b	Princeton	TB	R+	20	65	241	62	10	1	4	86	30	36	29	3	72	8	0	0	15	6	.71	4	.257	.356	.394
Jacobs, Mike*	c-dh	Mets	NYM	R	19	44	147	49	12	0	4	73	18	30	14	2	30	1	0	5	2	0	1.00	3	.333	.383	.497
Jaile, Chris	c	Rangers	Tex	R	19	39	139	24	5	0	2	35	16	14	22	1	32	1	1	2	0	0	.00	6	.173	.287	.252
James, Drue	c	Macon	Atl	A	23	40	119	22	2	0	1	27	10	8	15	0	37	2	1	0	0	0	.00	3	.185	.287	.227
James, Tony	2b	Augusta	Bos	A	24	55	170	38	8	0	2	52	17	19	10	0	35	5	1	1	3	3	.50	7	.224	.285	.306
Jaramillo, Frank	3b-ss	Charlotte	Tex	A+	25	12	37	8	0	0	0	8	1	4	1	1	9	0	0	0	1	1	.50	0	.216	.237	.216
		Beloit	Mil	A	25	65	244	75	12	2	12	127	48	40	24	0	41	1	1	2	6	2	.75	9	.307	.369	.520
Jaramillo, Lee	c	Stockton	Mil	A+	23	23	48	11	2	1	1	18	4	10	5	0	13	1	0	0	1	2	.33	2	.229	.315	.375
		Ogden	Mil	R+	23	43	143	44	11	2	3	68	20	18	21	1	27	3	1	3	2	3	.40	1	.308	.400	.476
Jaramillo, Milko#	ss	Vero Beach	LA	A+	20	99	320	65	4	1	1	74	26	31	14	1	67	8	10	1	15	5	.75	4	.203	.254	.231
Jaramillo, Tony*	2b	Pulaski	Tex	R+	21	25	81	15	4	0	0	19	10	11	11	1	25	0	1	1	0	0	.00	1	.185	.280	.235
Jaroncyk, Ryan#	of	Yakima	LA	A-	23	8	31	11	4	0	0	15	6	4	5	0	10	0	2	0	2	1	.67	1	.355	.444	.484
Jarvais, Kregg	c	Lowell	Bos	A-	23	36	109	21	6	1	0	29	13	6	8	0	31	1	0	0	3	0	1.00	1	.193	.254	.266
Jaworowski, Aaron*	3b	Staten Ilnd	NYY	A-	24	11	30	6	2	0	0	8	2	4	3	1	8	2	0	0	0	0	.00	0	.200	.314	.267
Jenkins, Brian	of	Capital Cty	NYM	A	21	107	400	116	15	7	20	205	69	79	30	2	69	4	4	6	19	7	.73	7	.290	.341	.513
Jenkins, Corey	of	Burlington	CWS	A	23	32	113	22	5	0	3	36	8	12	16	0	51	1	0	0	1	0	1.00	4	.195	.300	.319
Jenkins, Neil	3b	Tigers	Det	R	19	33	111	33	13	3	2	58	18	15	16	0	37	2	1	0	2	1	.67	1	.297	.395	.523
Jenkins, Robert	of	Reds	Cin	R	24	6	17	1	0	0	0	1	1	1	1	0	11	0	0	1	0	0	.00	0	.059	.105	.059
Jester, Joe	ss-2b	Salem-Keizr	SF	A-	21	72	263	79	19	1	8	124	67	40	50	3	57	7	7	2	13	6	.68	2	.300	.422	.471
Jewson, Ben	3b	Phillies	Phi	R	21	31	101	24	3	0	0	27	5	11	9	0	32	2	0	0	1	0	1.00	3	.238	.313	.267
Jimenez, Carlos	ss	W Michigan	Det	A	20	87	272	62	12	2	3	87	57	24	49	0	78	2	2	1	14	5	.74	3	.228	.349	.320
Jimenez, Felipe	of	Daytona	ChC	A+	23	18	51	10	0	0	0	10	5	7	4	0	13	2	0	0	2	1	.67	2	.196	.281	.196
Jimenez, Jonathan	3b	Pulaski	Tex	R+	21	61	213	51	11	1	3	73	25	27	17	0	65	5	1	2	3	2	.60	2	.239	.308	.343
Joffrion, Jack	ss	Chston-SC	TB	A	24	83	292	61	15	1	5	93	32	28	9	0	89	2	1	4	7	3	.70	3	.209	.235	.318
Johnerson, Ryan	of	Reds	Cin	R	23	7	23	11	1	0	0	12	7	3	6	0	3	1	1	1	3	1	.75	0	.478	.581	.522
		Clinton	Cin	A	23	40	120	25	5	1	2	38	17	16	9	0	37	2	1	1	3	3	.50	2	.208	.273	.317
Johnson, Ben	of	Johnson Cy	StL	R+	19	57	203	67	9	1	10	108	38	51	29	1	57	5	1	2	14	6	.70	0	.330	.423	.532
Johnson, Brian	c	Spokane	KC	A-	23	41	137	34	7	0	1	44	18	22	12	0	20	9	1	3	4	3	.57	0	.248	.342	.321
Johnson, Eric	of	Delmarva	Bal	A	25	11	47	11	5	0	0	16	5	7	6	0	15	1	0	0	1	2	.33	1	.234	.333	.340
Johnson, Eric	of	Burlington	Cle	R+	22	39	147	34	9	1	3	54	26	22	25	0	29	7	0	1	14	1	.93	3	.231	.367	.367
		Mahoning Vy	Cle	A-	22	28	105	27	4	1	1	36	23	10	18	0	17	2	0	0	12	1	.92	3	.257	.376	.343
Johnson, Erik	c-dh	Asheville	Col	A	23	87	311	91	20	2	9	142	40	43	18	0	34	4	1	1	7	2	.78	6	.293	.338	.457
Johnson, Gabe	c-dh	New Jersey	StL	A-	20	35	124	24	5	2	5	48	12	14	9	0	49	1	1	1	1	1	.50	4	.194	.252	.387
Johnson, Gary	of	Daytona	ChC	A+	23	108	323	74	16	1	7	113	46	38	39	1	53	10	3	5	4	6	.40	10	.229	.326	.350
Johnson, Gerald*	of	Boise	Ana	A-	24	71	264	83	17	1	2	108	56	48	34	3	44	2	0	3	6	2	.75	6	.314	.393	.409
Johnson, Jason	of	Piedmont	Phi	A	22	111	447	118	21	5	1	152	51	31	22	0	61	8	5	2	27	11	.71	7	.264	.309	.340
Johnson, Kareem	of	Twins	Min	R	19	40	128	34	2	2	0	40	20	15	13	0	39	2	2	0	5	1	.83	3	.266	.343	.313
Johnson, Patrick	c	Lk Elsinore	Ana	A+	25	26	78	16	0	0	1	19	7	6	10	0	26	0	2	0	0	0	.00	1	.205	.295	.244
		High Desert	Ari	A+	25	37	99	31	6	0	2	43	15	15	19	0	27	0	1	1	0	2	.00	1	.313	.420	.434
Johnson, Reed	of	St.Cathrnes	Tor	A-	23	60	191	46	8	2	2	64	24	23	24	1	31	2	4	4	5	5	.50	4	.241	.326	.335
Johnson, Rontrez	of	Sarasota	Bos	A+	23	132	494	148	30	4	8	210	97	59	74	0	63	8	8	7	18	15	.55	7	.300	.395	.425
Johnson, Tom	of	St. Lucie	NYM	A+	24	56	199	51	12	0	1	66	25	10	21	0	57	1	2	4	12	5	.71	1	.256	.324	.332
		Asheville	Col	A	24	2	9	3	0	0	0	3	1	1	0	0	4	0	0	0	1	1	.50	0	.333	.333	.333
Johnson, Tony#	of	Pittsfield	NYM	A-	22	63	178	36	8	4	5	67	31	28	39	1	59	4	2	1	14	2	.88	2	.202	.356	.376
Johnstone, Ben	of	Cubs	ChC	R	22	2	7	3	0	0	0	3	1	1	0	0	2	0	0	0	0	0	.00	0	.429	.429	.429
		Eugene	ChC	A-	22	54	186	62	9	0	1	74	34	11	9	0	30	10	3	0	16	14	.53	1	.333	.395	.398
Jones, A.J.	of	Twins	Min	R	22	33	73	11	0	0	0	11	11	4	5	0	18	3	1	0	4	1	.80	3	.151	.235	.151
Jones, Aaron*	1b	Tampa	NYY	A+	24	132	454	126	25	11	4	185	50	57	76	3	92	4	1	2	6	5	.55	18	.278	.384	.407
Jones, Damien*	of	Danville	Atl	R+	20	68	284	84	6	5	1	103	56	29	37	0	58	3	6	0	27	11	.71	4	.296	.383	.363
Jones, Garrett*	1b	Braves	Atl	R	19	46	170	41	3	0	3	53	17	18	16	0	47	1	0	1	1	2	.33	1	.241	.309	.312
Jones, Jason#	1b	Pulaski	Tex	R+	23	69	262	93	24	1	11	152	65	58	33	1	55	7	0	5	1	2	.33	5	.355	.433	.580
Jones, Jason*	of-dh	Rangers	Tex	R	22	11	34	7	2	0	0	9	1	3	2	0	12	1	0	0	1	0	1.00	0	.206	.270	.265
Jones, Jay*	c	Asheville	Col	A	25	43	148	44	8	0	4	64	22	20	8	0	16	2	0	0	2	0	1.00	1	.297	.342	.432
		Salem	Col	A+	25	18	60	9	3	0	0	12	4	8	4	0	9	1	0	2	0	0	.00	0	.150	.209	.200
Jones, Jeremy	c	Charlotte	Tex	A+	22	11	31	6	1	0	1	10	4	4	4	0	10	0	0	0	1	0	1.00	1	.194	.286	.323
		Savannah	Tex	A	22	43	133	32	6	2	0	42	18	16	15	0	27	1	2	3	0	1	.00	2	.241	.316	.316
Jones, Tim*	of	Visalia	Oak	A+	22	72	185	38	8	2	5	65	31	31	40	1	76	2	0	2	9	1	.90	3	.205	.349	.351
Jordan, Kevin	of	Michigan	Hou	A	23	116	413	104	21	2	11	162	60	66	18	1	98	8	1	3	17	6	.74	8	.252	.294	.392
Jordan, Yustin	1b-of	Elizabethtn	Min	R+	21	11	35	13	5	0	3	27	7	8	5	0	7	0	0	0	0	0	.00	1	.371	.450	.771
		Quad City	Min	A	21	47	150	30	11	0	7	62	28	30	26	0	42	4	1	1	0	1	.00	8	.200	.331	.413
Jorgenson, Chris*	dh	Diamondbcks	Ari	R	19	3	3	0	0	0	0	0	1	0	2	0	2	0	0	0	0	0	.00	0	.000	.400	.000
Joyce, Jesse	dh	Auburn	Hou	A-	24	18	70	21	5	2	2	36	11	10	4	0	13	2	0	0	1	2	.33	1	.300	.355	.514

1999 Batting — Single-A and Rookie Leagues

BATTING																					BASERUNNING				PERCENTAGES		
Player	Pos	Team	Org	Lg	A	G	AB	H	2B	3B	HR	TB	R	RBI	TBB	IBB	SO	HBP	SH	SF	SB	CS	SB%	GDP	Avg	OBP	SLG
		Michigan	Hou	A	24	8	24	4	1	1	1	10	4	1	2	0	5	0	0	0	0	1	.00	0	.167	.231	.417
		Kissimmee	Hou	A+	24	4	7	1	0	0	0	1	2	0	0	0	2	0	0	0	0	0	.00	0	.143	.143	.143
Juarez, Jonny*	of	Medcine Hat	Tor	R+	22	29	102	26	1	0	1	30	11	10	8	0	14	0	7	2	8	2	.80	2	.255	.304	.294
Kail, Tom	of	Diamondbcks	Ari	R	20	55	220	67	15	3	5	103	33	41	16	0	48	3	0	4	1	0	1.00	8	.305	.354	.468
Kalczynski, Joe	dh	Missoula	Ari	R+	22	23	61	12	4	0	1	19	12	8	11	0	17	2	0	0	2	0	1.00	2	.197	.338	.311
Kanaya, Takeshi	c	Red Sox	Bos	R	21	14	32	10	1	0	1	14	6	9	3	0	4	1	1	0	1	0	1.00	2	.313	.389	.438
Kane, Pat	2b	Martinsvlle	Hou	R+	23	35	98	20	5	0	1	28	15	8	16	0	33	5	0	0	4	3	.57	0	.204	.345	.286
Kashirsky, Michael	1b	White Sox	CWS	R	22	15	32	4	0	0	0	4	5	1	9	0	7	0	0	0	0	2	.00	3	.125	.317	.125
Kasper, Todd*	c	South Bend	Ari	A	23	34	101	19	1	0	0	20	7	9	12	0	37	0	0	1	1	1	.50	2	.188	.272	.198
Kata, Matt#	ss	South Bend	Ari	A	22	78	318	83	14	5	3	116	40	33	28	0	46	4	1	1	5	6	.45	5	.261	.328	.365
Katz, Glenn	of	Chston-SC	TB	A	23	55	179	44	7	0	0	51	18	17	6	0	24	2	4	1	6	7	.46	2	.246	.277	.285
Kawabata, Ken.#	of	Red Sox	Bos	R	21	46	145	43	4	4	1	58	35	15	31	1	34	6	0	3	15	4	.79	1	.297	.432	.400
Kearns, Austin	of	Rockford	Cin	A	20	124	426	110	36	5	13	195	72	48	50	3	120	9	0	3	21	8	.72	9	.258	.346	.458
Keaveney, Jeff	1b	Augusta	Bos	A	24	23	78	16	3	0	4	31	10	18	10	0	31	4	0	0	0	0	.00	1	.205	.326	.397
Keith, Rusty	of	Visalia	Oak	A+	22	124	448	140	28	3	10	204	87	62	82	1	59	7	3	4	10	8	.56	13	.313	.423	.455
Kelleher, Pat*	of	Boise	Ana	A-	23	9	17	3	2	0	0	5	4	2	8	0	4	0	2	0	3	0	1.00	0	.176	.440	.294
Keller, G.W.	3b-of	Sou Oregon	Oak	A-	23	28	95	23	5	0	0	28	10	13	17	0	10	6	2	2	5	1	.83	2	.242	.383	.295
Kelley, Casey*	1b	Boise	Ana	A-	23	61	205	63	12	4	7	104	45	37	32	0	60	1	0	1	2	1	.67	3	.307	.402	.507
Kellner, Ryan	c	Vero Beach	LA	A+	22	54	179	37	1	1	2	46	21	14	10	0	51	2	3	0	1	1	.50	5	.207	.257	.257
Kelly, Chris	1b-dh	Peoria	StL	A	23	18	59	10	1	0	0	11	5	7	7	0	18	1	0	0	0	0	.00	0	.169	.269	.186
Kelly, Heath	2b-ss	Kane County	Fla	A	24	69	189	47	8	2	1	62	34	31	36	1	69	4	1	3	7	3	.70	6	.249	.375	.328
Kelly, Kenny	of	St. Pete	TB	A+	21	51	206	57	10	4	3	84	39	21	18	0	46	4	0	0	14	5	.74	1	.277	.346	.408
Kelton, Dave	3b	Lansing	ChC	A	20	124	509	137	17	4	13	201	75	68	39	1	121	2	0	3	22	9	.71	11	.269	.322	.395
Kennedy, Gus	of	Lk Elsinore	Ana	A+	26	29	93	19	5	0	3	33	13	13	15	0	25	0	0	1	4	2	.67	3	.204	.312	.355
Kenney, Jeff	ss	Helena	Mil	R+	22	48	153	40	8	2	4	64	40	29	37	0	33	9	1	2	8	4	.67	3	.261	.428	.418
Kent, Mat*	c	Mariners	Sea	R	19	34	119	27	3	3	3	45	18	15	5	0	28	4	0	0	1	0	1.00	3	.227	.281	.378
Kerrigan, Joseph*	2b	Lowell	Bos	A-	22	63	242	76	6	3	0	88	38	19	43	1	52	2	1	1	5	6	.45	3	.314	.420	.364
		Augusta	Bos	A	22	9	35	7	1	0	0	8	7	1	6	0	6	0	0	0	1	2	.33	1	.200	.317	.229
Kessick, Jonathan	c	Bluefield	Bal	R+	22	28	93	19	3	0	4	34	13	14	4	0	33	3	0	1	0	0	.00	0	.204	.257	.366
Key, Jeff*	1b	Augusta	Bos	A	25	78	255	54	9	3	4	81	32	27	29	1	61	10	0	1	11	1	.92	2	.212	.315	.318
		Sarasota	Bos	A+	25	25	77	18	6	1	1	29	9	13	10	1	12	0	0	1	4	2	.67	4	.234	.318	.377
Kidd, Scott	2b	Greensboro	NYY	A	26	115	463	127	31	4	15	211	74	84	25	0	103	6	0	5	4	2	.67	17	.274	.317	.456
Kidwell, Tommy	2b-3b	Peoria	StL	A	23	50	167	43	6	2	0	53	23	15	5	0	27	2	2	1	2	1	.67	2	.257	.286	.317
Kielty, Bobby#	of	Quad City	Min	A	23	69	245	72	13	1	13	126	52	43	43	1	56	3	2	3	12	3	.80	7	.294	.401	.514
Kiil, Skip	of	Clearwater	Phi	A+	26	86	305	91	15	8	14	164	74	55	70	0	101	7	5	3	24	5	.83	2	.298	.436	.538
Kim, Dave	of	Potomac	StL	A+	24	123	440	114	23	1	19	196	68	72	42	1	107	6	2	6	7	6	.54	16	.259	.328	.445
King, Brennan	3b	Great Falls	LA	R+	19	61	247	72	13	1	2	93	37	30	24	0	45	4	6	3	9	6	.60	7	.291	.360	.377
King, Jason	3b	Braves	Atl	R	20	45	168	33	4	3	1	46	15	11	13	0	40	1	2	1	5	2	.71	3	.196	.257	.274
Kirby, Scott	3b	Beloit	Mil	A	22	68	247	75	14	1	17	142	54	47	47	0	59	3	0	3	3	1	.75	5	.304	.417	.575
		Stockton	Mil	A+	22	60	202	58	15	3	10	109	35	36	25	2	59	7	0	4	3	3	.50	7	.287	.378	.540
Kison, Robbie	2b	Reds	Cin	R	23	7	11	3	0	0	0	3	2	2	0	0	0	0	0	0	1	0	1.00	0	.273	.273	.273
		Billings	Cin	R+	23	9	27	4	0	0	0	4	4	2	6	0	4	1	0	0	0	0	.00	1	.148	.324	.148
		Rockford	Cin	A	23	7	15	3	0	0	0	3	3	1	4	0	4	2	0	0	0	0	.00	0	.200	.429	.200
		Clinton	Cin	A	23	20	55	13	2	1	1	20	7	5	8	0	12	2	0	1	0	1	.00	2	.236	.348	.364
Klatt, Jason	2b	Padres	SD	R	24	47	174	51	7	3	4	76	34	38	25	0	19	2	0	5	12	9	.57	7	.293	.379	.437
Klee, Chuck	ss	Winston-Sal	CWS	A+	23	73	199	42	11	0	4	65	19	24	14	0	50	2	1	0	3	0	1.00	4	.211	.270	.327
Kluver, Hayden*	of-dh	Yakima	LA	A-	20	25	79	16	2	0	1	21	9	9	6	0	26	0	2	1	0	1	.00	1	.203	.256	.266
Knight, Marcus#	of	Cedar Rapds	Ana	A	21	132	462	100	20	7	9	161	69	52	61	2	97	6	1	2	21	8	.72	5	.216	.315	.348
Knorr, Mario*	of	Diamondbcks	Ari	R	20	50	193	45	5	2	0	54	16	21	6	0	32	1	0	2	2	0	1.00	5	.233	.257	.280
Knox, Ryan	of	Helena	Mil	R+	23	72	275	96	17	1	2	121	58	25	25	1	27	4	3	4	44	11	.80	1	.349	.406	.440
Knupfer, Jason	2b	Clearwater	Phi	A+	25	15	45	13	2	0	0	15	13	3	12	0	5	0	3	0	1	0	1.00	0	.289	.439	.333
Koen, Nate	c	Eugene	ChC	A-	23	23	27	5	3	0	0	8	1	3	4	0	6	0	0	0	0	0	.00	1	.185	.290	.296
Kofler, Eric*	dh	Yankees	NYY	R	24	1	3	2	1	0	1	6	1	4	1	0	0	0	0	0	0	0	.00	0	.667	.750	2.000
		Tampa	NYY	A+	24	15	53	19	6	2	0	29	7	14	5	1	10	1	0	1	1	0	1.00	2	.358	.417	.547
Koonce, Gray*	1b	Rancho Cuca	SD	A+	25	132	474	135	16	1	19	210	76	79	76	5	110	11	0	6	4	1	.80	12	.285	.392	.443
Kopitzke, Casey	c	Eugene	ChC	A-	22	37	110	23	3	0	0	26	19	12	15	0	25	4	0	2	3	3	.50	6	.209	.321	.236
Kraus, Jake	1b	Stockton	Mil	A+	26	25	72	17	4	1	0	23	4	11	6	0	11	0	0	1	0	1	.00	2	.236	.291	.319
Kremblas, Mike	c	Hagerstown	Tor	A	24	58	165	34	7	0	0	41	22	7	15	0	28	14	1	1	2	0	1.00	5	.206	.323	.248
Kuzmic, Craig#	3b	Lancaster	Sea	A+	23	32	108	22	4	0	5	41	19	15	20	1	43	1	0	1	3	1	.75	1	.204	.331	.380
		Wisconsin	Sea	A	23	91	323	77	18	1	10	127	48	55	61	0	84	2	2	2	7	4	.64	10	.238	.361	.393
Laflair, Jay	c	Mahoning Vy	Cle	A-	24	16	30	6	3	0	0	9	8	3	5	0	6	3	1	0	2	0	1.00	2	.200	.368	.300
LaForest, Pete*	3b	Chston-SC	TB	A	22	125	445	114	21	3	13	180	64	53	55	6	97	5	6	3	9	3	.75	11	.256	.343	.404
Lagana, Shawn	ss	Diamondbcks	Ari	R	19	39	159	41	8	1	0	51	28	21	10	0	33	1	0	3	5	3	.63	5	.258	.301	.321
Laidlaw, Jake	3b	Marlins	Fla	R	18	56	201	53	9	4	3	79	24	32	22	0	49	5	1	3	3	4	.43	3	.264	.346	.393
Laird, Gerald	c	Sou Oregon	Oak	A-	20	60	228	65	7	2	2	82	45	39	28	0	43	2	2	5	10	5	.67	4	.285	.361	.360
Lama, Jesus	dh-of	Princeton	TB	R+	20	20	65	17	5	1	4	36	16	13	12	0	26	0	0	0	4	1	.80	1	.262	.377	.554
Landaeta, Luis*	of	Asheville	Col	A	23	117	453	127	22	1	4	163	61	51	20	1	80	2	5	1	9	7	.56	9	.280	.313	.360
Landreth, Jason	of-1b	Williamsprt	Pit	A-	24	62	210	66	14	1	6	100	35	37	34	0	35	2	0	2	5	5	.50	3	.314	.411	.476
Landry, Jacques	3b	Modesto	Oak	A+	26	133	508	158	46	6	27	297	92	111	47	2	128	10	3	12	18	4	.82	6	.311	.373	.585
Lane, Jason	1b	Auburn	Hou	A-	23	74	283	79	18	5	13	146	46	59	38	2	46	3	0	4	6	4	.60	2	.279	.366	.516
Lane, Richard*	of	Expos	Mon	R	20	41	144	32	5	0	1	40	16	14	10	0	30	4	0	0	4	2	.67	6	.222	.291	.278
Langerhans, Ryan*	of	Macon	Atl	A	20	121	448	120	30	1	9	179	66	49	52	2	99	7	2	2	19	11	.63	8	.268	.352	.400
Langlois, Jean	of	Jamestown	Atl	A-	21	59	220	54	7	2	3	74	24	20	25	1	54	3	0	0	10	2	.83	4	.245	.331	.336
Langston, James#	of	Williamsprt	Pit	A-	22	54	200	55	8	1	1	68	15	20	6	1	40	1	0	0	2	1	.67	6	.275	.300	.340
Lankford, Derrick*	of	Lynchburg	Pit	A+	25	123	456	133	28	8	20	237	80	88	52	1	124	7	0	6	4	0	1.00	7	.292	.369	.520
Lantigua, Denys	c	Burlington	Cle	R+	20	14	45	6	1	0	0	7	7	2	4	0	8	0	0	0	1	0	1.00	0	.133	.204	.156
Lara, Balmes	of	Oneonta	Det	A-	22	63	232	64	10	4	7	103	30	37	14	1	63	4	2	3	9	1	.90	5	.276	.324	.444

1999 Batting — Single-A and Rookie Leagues

BATTING																					BASERUNNING				PERCENTAGES		
Player	Pos	Team	Org	Lg	A	G	AB	H	2B	3B	HR	TB	R	RBI	TBB	IBB	SO	HBP	SH	SF	SB	CS	SB%	GDP	Avg	OBP	SLG
Lara, Eddie	ss	Visalia	Oak	A+	24	105	358	107	20	6	9	166	67	56	44	0	45	11	6	5	25	16	.61	17	.299	.388	.464
Lara, Franklin	3b	Mariners	Sea	R	20	30	104	30	4	1	0	36	17	6	9	0	13	3	0	0	1	2	.33	6	.288	.362	.346
Larned, Andrew	c	Augusta	Bos	A	24	34	93	24	4	0	1	31	8	13	12	0	18	2	2	0	1	1	.50	4	.258	.355	.333
Lauterhahn, Dan	ss	Lakeland	Det	A+	24	63	152	41	7	1	2	56	19	14	13	0	22	0	2	1	4	3	.57	1	.270	.325	.368
Lawson, Forrest	of	Mets	NYM	R	19	37	116	29	3	1	0	34	15	11	17	1	36	5	0	1	1	1	.50	4	.250	.367	.293
Layton, Blane*	of	Clinton	Cin	A	23	42	109	32	6	2	2	48	19	12	25	3	31	1	3	0	5	2	.71	1	.294	.430	.440
		Rockford	Cin	A	23	34	110	30	10	3	2	52	19	20	6	0	27	0	0	2	4	3	.57	2	.273	.305	.473
Leach, Nick*	1b	Vero Beach	LA	A+	22	128	449	127	21	0	20	208	58	74	62	3	73	6	0	3	10	5	.67	6	.283	.375	.463
Leal, Jaeme	1b	Jamestown	Atl	A-	21	33	99	27	5	0	8	56	16	28	8	0	37	3	0	3	0	0	.00	3	.273	.336	.566
Leatherman, Dan*	1b	Quad City	Min	A	24	74	255	66	12	0	2	84	41	31	35	3	28	3	4	1	2	5	.29	5	.259	.354	.329
Leaumont, Jeff*	1b	Staten Ilnd	NYY	A-	23	67	212	51	12	1	0	65	35	20	21	0	61	1	1	5	7	4	.64	4	.241	.305	.307
Lebron, Francisco	1b	Capital Cty	NYM	A	25	10	36	8	0	0	2	14	4	2	6	0	9	0	0	0	0	0	.00	1	.222	.333	.389
		Pittsfield	NYM	A-	25	75	266	77	17	0	9	121	46	43	46	1	53	1	0	0	6	1	.86	8	.289	.396	.455
Lebron, Hector*	1b	Hudson Val	TB	A-	22	17	56	14	3	0	1	20	3	6	3	0	13	0	0	1	0	0	.00	1	.250	.283	.357
		Chston-SC	TB	A	22	57	188	43	3	2	1	53	26	21	8	0	42	6	3	2	7	2	.78	5	.229	.279	.282
Lebron, Jesus	of	St.Cathrnes	Tor	A-	22	65	218	52	11	1	6	83	37	29	27	0	90	2	1	4	15	4	.79	2	.239	.323	.381
Ledesma, Luis	of	Martinsville	Hou	R+	20	26	93	17	3	0	0	20	10	7	5	0	20	0	0	0	1	2	.33	2	.183	.224	.215
Ledesma, Phil	of	Lowell	Bos	A-	25	30	74	20	3	2	1	30	19	12	16	0	15	5	2	1	8	2	.80	1	.270	.427	.405
Lee, Jason*	of	Peoria	StL	A	23	66	224	52	14	0	2	72	31	26	24	1	58	4	1	3	5	3	.63	2	.232	.314	.321
		Potomac	StL	A+	23	44	113	24	4	0	1	31	15	9	18	0	35	3	2	1	11	0	1.00	1	.212	.333	.274
Lee, Monte	of	New Jersey	StL	A-	23	38	121	27	4	0	0	31	20	10	18	0	25	5	0	0	14	6	.70	1	.223	.347	.256
Leed, Adam	of	Rangers	Tex	R	23	12	44	12	2	0	2	20	5	8	3	0	12	0	0	1	1	1	.50	1	.273	.313	.455
Leer, David	of	Tigers	Det	R	23	32	107	29	3	2	0	36	12	12	7	0	26	5	1	1	11	4	.73	3	.271	.342	.336
Leflore, Ron	of	Billings	Cin	R+	19	2	6	0	0	0	0	0	0	0	0	0	1	1	0	0	0	0	.00	2	.000	.143	.000
		Reds	Cin	R	19	19	63	11	1	1	0	14	5	2	8	0	24	0	1	0	5	2	.71	2	.175	.268	.222
Lehr, Ryan	1b-dh	Myrtle Bch	Atl	A+	21	109	423	108	18	4	14	176	59	68	45	1	63	5	0	1	3	2	.60	15	.255	.333	.416
Lemon, Tim	of	New Jersey	StL	A-	19	72	242	48	5	3	4	71	25	29	22	0	62	6	4	2	16	16	.50	4	.198	.279	.293
Lentz, Ryan*	3b	Jupiter	Mon	A+	23	114	362	75	16	1	6	111	39	35	50	2	84	17	4	3	1	3	.25	5	.207	.329	.307
Leon, Alfredo	3b	Orioles	Bal	R	20	29	107	35	6	3	1	50	18	15	6	1	11	3	0	0	11	3	.79	2	.327	.379	.467
		Frederick	Bal	A+	20	6	14	3	0	0	0	3	3	1	1	0	3	0	1	0	1	0	1.00	1	.214	.267	.214
Leon, Carlos#	2b	Sarasota	Bos	A+	20	47	154	24	1	1	0	27	16	14	12	0	16	3	5	0	9	1	.90	3	.156	.231	.175
		Augusta	Bos	A	20	60	210	49	7	0	1	59	34	19	23	0	42	10	0	1	13	4	.76	2	.233	.336	.281
Leon, Richy	2b	Asheville	Col	A	24	62	212	52	10	0	5	77	28	31	6	0	29	5	9	2	2	3	.40	5	.245	.280	.363
Leonardo, Santos	of	Tigers	Det	R	18	38	120	31	6	1	0	39	16	13	14	0	31	1	1	0	12	7	.63	1	.258	.341	.325
Leone, Justin	3b	Everett	Sea	A-	23	62	205	54	14	2	6	90	34	35	32	0	49	2	1	5	5	3	.63	5	.263	.361	.439
Ligons, Merrell#	of	Chstn-WV	KC	A	23	87	232	47	10	2	4	73	37	18	45	0	82	1	3	0	17	6	.74	6	.203	.335	.315
Lincoln, Justin	ss	Portland	Col	A-	21	68	253	61	14	2	6	97	36	44	28	0	102	4	0	2	6	1	.86	6	.241	.324	.383
Lindsey, Cordell	3b	Butte	Ana	R+	22	63	255	87	23	7	10	154	72	58	23	0	46	4	0	1	13	5	.72	5	.341	.403	.604
Lindsey, John	1b-dh	Salem	Col	A+	23	75	260	54	15	1	4	83	32	35	20	1	69	7	3	1	2	1	.67	3	.208	.281	.319
Liriano, Ruddy	3b	Reds	Cin	R	19	22	69	14	2	1	0	18	10	9	4	0	9	1	1	2	4	0	1.00	0	.203	.250	.261
		Billings	Cin	R+	19	17	54	19	2	0	1	24	10	8	6	0	12	1	1	0	1	0	1.00	1	.352	.426	.444
Llamas, Juan	3b	Yankees	NYY	R	20	4	4	2	0	0	0	2	1	0	2	0	1	0	0	0	0	0	.00	0	.500	.667	.500
Llanos, Alex*	dh-2b	Chston-SC	TB	A	23	5	13	0	0	0	0	0	1	0	2	0	4	0	0	0	1	0	1.00	1	.000	.133	.000
Lockwood, Mike*	of	Sou Oregon	Oak	A-	23	69	255	92	18	5	7	141	48	51	39	1	49	8	0	6	6	5	.55	5	.361	.451	.553
Logan, Kyle*	of	Kissimmee	Hou	A+	24	113	399	116	33	7	7	184	57	62	33	4	62	3	1	3	16	5	.76	5	.291	.347	.461
Logan, Matt*	1b	Hagerstown	Tor	A	20	119	453	110	21	1	9	160	55	57	32	1	130	2	2	4	3	2	.60	6	.243	.293	.353
Loggins, Josh	of	Fort Wayne	SD	A	23	136	522	155	29	7	14	240	75	85	60	4	119	12	2	5	24	12	.67	13	.297	.379	.460
Lombardi, Dominick	c	Boise	Ana	A-	24	6	24	7	2	0	0	9	1	5	2	0	3	0	0	0	0	0	.00	1	.292	.346	.375
Londono, Alex	of	Rockies	Col	R	20	38	142	38	7	3	4	63	29	28	11	2	46	10	1	1	10	3	.77	0	.268	.360	.444
Longmire, Marcel	c	Eugene	ChC	A-	22	1	2	0	0	0	0	0	0	1	0	0	1	0	0	0	0	0	.00	0	.000	.000	.000
Lopez, Aristides	of	Martinsvlle	Hou	R+	21	41	132	29	4	1	0	35	13	8	5	0	31	0	0	0	9	6	.60	2	.220	.248	.265
Lopez, Felipe#	ss	Hagerstown	Tor	A	20	134	537	149	27	4	14	226	87	80	61	0	157	3	0	6	21	14	.60	7	.277	.351	.421
Lopez, Guillermo	c	Danville	Atl	R+	21	14	36	3	1	0	0	4	6	2	14	0	15	1	0	0	0	0	.00	0	.083	.353	.111
Lopez, Jose	c	Missoula	Ari	R+	21	5	14	8	4	1	1	17	5	3	2	0	1	1	0	1	0	0	.00	0	.571	.611	1.214
		South Bend	Ari	A	21	26	91	15	3	0	1	21	5	8	3	0	19	1	0	0	0	0	.00	2	.165	.200	.231
Lopez, Luis	of	Michigan	Hou	A	22	95	335	89	22	3	14	159	55	48	33	0	96	4	3	1	7	5	.58	9	.266	.338	.475
Lopez, Manny	of	Fort Myers	Min	A+	22	86	291	71	7	2	2	88	44	26	30	1	58	2	5	2	7	5	.58	11	.244	.317	.302
Lopez, Miguel	c	High Desert	Ari	A+	21	9	20	4	1	0	0	5	1	3	0	0	7	1	0	1	0	0	.00	2	.200	.227	.250
Lopez, Norberto	c	Butte	Ana	R+	23	8	17	2	0	0	0	2	1	0	0	0	8	1	0	0	0	0	.00	0	.118	.167	.118
		Boise	Ana	A-	23	5	13	3	1	0	0	4	1	0	2	0	5	0	0	0	0	0	.00	0	.231	.333	.308
		Lk Elsinore	Ana	A+	23	2	4	0	0	0	0	0	0	0	0	0	2	0	0	0	0	0	.00	0	.000	.000	.000
		Cedar Rapds	Ana	A	23	2	6	1	0	0	0	1	0	1	1	0	2	0	0	0	0	0	.00	0	.167	.286	.167
Lopez, Orlando	of	Mariners	Sea	R	19	42	138	35	6	2	0	45	18	10	16	0	27	1	3	0	11	7	.61	4	.254	.335	.326
Lopez, Sam	2b	Pittsfield	NYM	A-	22	2	7	3	0	0	0	3	0	0	0	0	3	0	0	0	0	0	.00	0	.429	.429	.429
Lopez, Youanny	of	Red Sox	Bos	R	20	51	181	44	10	2	3	67	18	26	21	1	41	2	0	1	3	5	.38	7	.243	.327	.370
Lora, Thomas#	2b	Royals	KC	R	21	47	175	48	3	4	1	62	31	17	31	0	37	3	3	1	20	2	.91	2	.274	.390	.354
Lorenzo, Juan#	ss	Fort Myers	Min	A+	22	119	421	108	11	1	3	130	51	48	9	0	68	6	4	4	8	3	.73	8	.257	.280	.309
Lotterhos, Chris	ss	Mahoning Vy	Cle	A-	23	41	124	26	7	2	1	40	21	9	23	0	33	2	0	1	5	6	.45	2	.210	.340	.323
Lough, Aaron	c	Fort Myers	Min	A+	23	5	14	2	0	0	0	2	0	0	0	0	3	0	0	0	0	0	.00	0	.143	.143	.143
		Quad City	Min	A	23	3	12	3	0	0	0	3	1	1	1	0	4	0	0	0	0	0	.00	0	.250	.308	.250
		Elizabethtn	Min	R+	20	[illegible]	100	[illegible]	[illegible]	0	0	[illegible]	11	9	10	1	[illegible]	[illegible]	0	0	0	0	.00	3	.220	[illegible]	.350
Louwsma, Chris	1b-3b	Marlins	Fla	R	21	55	182	32	7	1	1	44	20	8	24	1	56	3	0	2	3	3	.50	7	.176	.280	.242
Lowe, Ernesto	of	White Sox	CWS	R	21	50	181	58	8	3	0	72	29	23	11	0	42	9	1	2	7	4	.64	2	.320	.384	.398
Lowe, Steve	ss	Mahoning Vy	Cle	A-	23	33	95	22	3	0	2	31	19	11	12	0	26	9	1	1	4	3	.57	0	.232	.368	.326
Lucas, Kevin	of	Spokane	KC	A-	22	38	121	31	3	1	0	36	28	11	4	0	12	5	5	0	5	1	.83	2	.256	.308	.298
Lucca, Tony*	1b	Utica	Fla	A-	25	67	240	77	20	1	7	120	35	47	36	3	47	7	0	2	7	2	.78	6	.321	.421	.500
Ludvigsen, Marc*	of	Pittsfield	NYM	A-	23	30	100	22	5	1	2	35	11	13	5	0	43	0	2	1	0	1	.00	0	.220	.255	.350

1999 Batting — Single-A and Rookie Leagues

BATTING																					BASERUNNING				PERCENTAGES		
Player	Pos	Team	Org	Lg	A	G	AB	H	2B	3B	HR	TB	R	RBI	TBB	IBB	SO	HBP	SH	SF	SB	CS	SB%	GDP	Avg	OBP	SLG
Ludwick, Ryan	of	Modesto	Oak	A+	21	43	171	47	11	3	4	76	28	34	19	0	45	3	0	5	2	1	.67	0	.275	.348	.444
Lugo, Carlos	of	Burlington	Cle	R+	20	25	71	10	0	1	0	12	5	5	1	0	31	3	2	0	1	1	.50	1	.141	.187	.169
Lugo, Felix#	3b	Expos	Mon	R	19	6	19	7	2	1	1	14	6	4	3	0	4	0	0	1	2	0	1.00	0	.368	.435	.737
		Vermont	Mon	A-	19	46	170	35	6	3	5	62	19	25	12	0	67	3	2	1	3	2	.60	3	.206	.269	.365
Lugo, Roberto*	1b	Mets	NYM	R	20	14	21	6	2	0	0	8	1	2	1	0	3	0	4	0	0	1	.00	3	.286	.318	.381
		Kingsport	NYM	R+	20	25	39	7	1	0	1	11	5	4	2	0	8	1	0	0	0	0	.00	1	.179	.238	.282
Lundquist, Ryan	dh	Reds	Cin	R	23	1	3	2	0	0	0	2	1	2	1	0	0	0	0	0	1	0	1.00	0	.667	.750	.667
Luster, Jeremy#	1b	Bakersfield	SF	A+	23	52	184	37	4	3	0	47	26	19	22	1	54	0	0	1	9	4	.69	6	.201	.285	.255
		Salem-Keizr	SF	A-	23	39	146	32	7	1	1	44	22	14	16	0	48	3	1	0	7	1	.88	0	.219	.309	.301
Luther, Ryan	c	Salem-Keizr	SF	A-	23	61	220	66	12	1	4	92	34	38	18	1	35	9	0	2	12	4	.75	5	.300	.373	.418
Lutz, David*	1b	Expos	Mon	R	18	44	154	49	8	1	0	59	21	15	14	0	14	3	0	1	4	1	.80	4	.318	.384	.383
Lutz, Manuel*	of	Lakeland	Det	A+	24	46	177	51	15	0	3	75	19	23	9	0	45	1	0	1	0	2	.00	6	.288	.324	.424
Lydon, Wayne	of	Mets	NYM	R	19	37	60	11	3	0	0	14	13	5	7	0	13	1	1	0	0	1	.00	1	.183	.279	.233
Lynn, Brody#	3b	Burlington	Cle	R+	19	37	121	17	0	0	2	23	17	9	19	0	56	2	1	2	2	4	.33	5	.140	.264	.190
Machado, Albenis#	ss	Cape Fear	Mon	A	21	124	434	107	16	5	2	139	84	34	102	2	77	6	7	1	19	28	.40	1	.247	.396	.320
Machado, Alejandro	2b	Braves	Atl	R	18	56	223	62	11	0	0	73	45	14	20	1	22	5	2	2	19	6	.76	3	.278	.348	.327
Machado, And.#	2b-ss	Clearwater	Phi	A+	19	1	2	0	0	0	0	0	0	0	0	0	1	0	0	0	0	0	.00	0	.000	.000	.000
		Phillies	Phi	R	19	43	143	37	6	3	2	55	26	12	15	1	38	2	7	1	6	3	.67	5	.259	.335	.385
		Piedmont	Phi	A	19	20	60	14	4	2	0	22	7	7	7	0	20	1	1	0	2	1	.67	0	.233	.324	.367
Mack, Antonio	of	Orioles	Bal	R	21	48	170	42	6	1	0	50	36	5	17	0	46	0	5	0	20	7	.74	1	.247	.316	.294
Mackiewitz, Rich.*	1b	Beloit	Mil	A	24	102	355	93	19	1	8	138	44	57	28	2	57	3	2	3	1	0	1.00	9	.262	.319	.389
MacMillan, Chris	3b	Mahoning Vy	Cle	A-	24	7	24	4	1	0	0	5	2	4	4	0	5	0	0	0	0	0	.00	1	.167	.286	.208
Macrory, Bob	2b	Potomac	StL	A+	25	114	434	101	15	2	2	126	52	29	24	0	70	5	5	1	27	10	.73	8	.233	.280	.290
Maduro, Jorge	c	Princeton	TB	R+	19	24	83	20	4	0	0	24	5	6	4	0	20	1	1	0	1	2	.33	0	.241	.284	.289
Maduro, Remy*	of	Brevard Cty	Fla	A+	23	29	91	21	5	0	2	32	14	8	8	0	17	3	0	2	1	0	1.00	2	.231	.308	.352
Mahoney, Ricardo	3b	Portland	Col	A-	21	63	226	57	13	2	4	86	31	28	17	0	33	1	1	3	4	2	.67	4	.252	.304	.381
Mahoney, Sean	of	St. Pete	TB	A+	24	35	112	17	6	0	1	26	8	8	13	0	32	3	1	2	2	0	1.00	2	.152	.254	.232
Maier, T.J.	3b	Potomac	StL	A+	25	102	353	93	15	0	2	114	53	38	55	0	61	3	0	4	12	7	.63	6	.263	.364	.323
Malave, Dennis*	of	Mahoning Vy	Cle	A-	20	12	41	10	0	0	1	13	11	8	7	0	9	1	0	1	1	1	.50	0	.244	.360	.317
		Columbus	Cle	A	20	44	150	40	6	1	3	57	16	15	14	0	44	1	2	0	8	8	.50	5	.267	.333	.380
Maldonado, Carlos	c	Wisconsin	Sea	A	21	92	302	93	13	0	0	106	35	33	43	1	32	0	2	2	4	6	.40	10	.308	.392	.351
Malinowski, Scott*	3b	Capital Cty	NYM	A	23	100	313	65	2	2	1	74	30	20	15	0	51	0	3	1	3	3	.50	7	.208	.243	.236
Mallory, Mike	of	Cubs	ChC	R	19	42	149	36	6	0	4	54	20	15	12	0	48	6	0	1	2	2	.50	5	.242	.321	.362
Malone, Nick	ss	Lowell	Bos	A-	27	6	16	4	2	0	0	6	3	1	1	0	5	0	1	1	1	0	1.00	0	.250	.278	.375
		Red Sox	Bos	R	27	12	25	3	2	0	0	5	4	1	3	0	8	1	1	0	2	1	.67	0	.120	.241	.200
		Sarasota	Bos	A+	27	15	32	5	2	0	0	7	3	2	4	0	5	0	0	0	0	0	.00	3	.156	.250	.219
Maloney, Jeff#	of	Hagerstown	Tor	A	23	88	305	71	17	1	7	111	36	37	26	0	70	4	2	2	8	4	.67	6	.233	.300	.364
Maluchnik, Gregg	c-1b	Macon	Atl	A	23	57	131	27	3	0	1	33	18	9	21	0	35	5	3	1	2	3	.40	2	.206	.335	.252
Mann, Derek*	2b	Chston-SC	TB	A	22	124	449	127	20	1	5	164	86	45	71	0	88	9	12	4	22	10	.69	6	.283	.388	.365
Manning, Brian	of	Winston-Sal	CWS	A+	25	106	350	84	20	4	5	127	45	47	32	1	55	10	3	5	24	4	.86	7	.240	.317	.363
Manning, Pat	ss	Braves	Atl	R	20	24	89	37	9	1	4	60	21	19	14	0	14	1	1	0	4	1	.80	2	.416	.500	.674
		Macon	Atl	A	20	43	170	44	11	2	4	71	25	19	14	1	42	3	4	0	3	1	.75	3	.259	.326	.418
Manning, Ricky*	of	Twins	Min	R	19	19	51	10	0	0	0	10	12	7	14	0	13	3	3	0	5	1	.83	1	.196	.397	.196
Mansfield, Doug*	of	Princeton	TB	R+	20	22	69	10	2	0	0	12	9	8	5	0	30	3	0	0	0	0	.00	2	.145	.234	.174
Manuel, Marcellous*	of	Bristol	CWS	R+	24	66	240	72	13	1	6	105	38	48	23	0	37	4	1	5	8	3	.73	7	.300	.364	.438
Mapes, Jake	c	Salem-Keizr	SF	A-	21	12	29	5	2	0	0	7	2	4	2	0	11	1	0	0	0	2	.00	0	.172	.250	.241
		Bakersfield	SF	A+	21	11	17	3	2	0	0	5	3	3	1	0	7	0	0	0	0	0	.00	0	.176	.222	.294
Marbury, Ben	of	Red Sox	Bos	R	21	20	53	9	3	0	1	15	5	6	4	0	20	3	1	0	1	1	.50	0	.170	.267	.283
Marchiano, Mike	of	Lancaster	Sea	A+	25	47	182	57	11	1	3	79	25	29	16	1	28	3	0	3	4	1	.80	5	.313	.373	.434
		Mariners	Sea	R	25	3	9	4	0	0	1	7	2	5	2	0	0	0	0	1	1	1	.50	0	.444	.500	.778
Marciante, Frank#	dh	Savannah	Tex	A	21	84	286	83	12	1	5	112	36	37	16	0	50	3	0	4	1	2	.33	8	.290	.330	.392
Marciniak, Dave	dh	Quad City	Min	A	23	47	165	43	7	0	3	59	20	19	20	0	19	5	1	0	2	1	.67	3	.261	.358	.358
Markray, Thad	3b	Clinton	Cin	A	20	3	10	1	0	0	0	1	1	0	1	0	2	0	0	0	0	0	.00	0	.100	.182	.100
		Rockford	Cin	A	20	59	180	35	6	0	4	53	21	22	21	0	47	1	3	4	3	4	.43	6	.194	.277	.294
Marquez, Eduardo	of	Eugene	ChC	A-	23	32	74	16	2	1	0	20	9	8	1	0	15	5	1	0	3	1	.75	2	.216	.275	.270
Marsh, Roy	of	Sarasota	Bos	A+	26	7	24	9	0	1	0	11	6	3	1	0	5	0	0	0	3	0	1.00	0	.375	.400	.458
Martin, Billy	3b	Capital Cty	NYM	A	24	64	220	52	19	1	8	97	38	30	24	0	82	6	0	3	1	1	.50	3	.236	.324	.441
Martin, Brandon*	of	Butte	Ana	R+	20	45	142	35	4	4	1	50	22	21	23	0	40	1	2	1	11	4	.73	3	.246	.353	.352
Martin, Brian	of	Chston-SC	TB	A	20	40	145	25	1	2	3	39	9	13	9	0	70	1	0	1	1	2	.33	5	.172	.224	.269
		Hudson Val	TB	A-	20	70	262	51	7	6	5	85	34	27	40	1	107	5	2	2	12	5	.71	4	.195	.311	.324
Martin, Justin#	2b	Williamsprt	Pit	A-	24	31	109	27	2	0	0	29	26	8	21	0	26	0	2	1	16	1	.94	1	.248	.366	.266
		Hickory	Pit	A	24	23	85	25	1	0	0	26	14	5	17	0	19	1	1	0	12	2	.86	0	.294	.417	.306
Martin, Kyle	c	Orioles	Bal	R	20	29	82	22	4	1	0	28	11	8	9	1	20	2	0	0	3	2	.60	2	.268	.355	.341
Martinez, Al.#	dh	Helena	Mil	R+	23	38	128	37	7	0	2	50	14	16	18	1	20	0	0	0	1	0	1.00	3	.289	.377	.391
Martinez, Belvani	2b	High Desert	Ari	A+	21	109	477	159	23	9	8	224	84	55	18	1	69	9	3	4	35	30	.54	7	.333	.366	.470
Martinez, Candido	of	Great Falls	LA	R+	20	69	265	62	8	3	4	88	43	42	22	0	87	6	2	1	11	2	.85	3	.234	.306	.332
Martinez, Dionnar#	ss	Cubs	ChC	R	19	41	126	32	5	0	0	37	13	11	15	1	20	1	1	1	5	2	.71	3	.254	.336	.294
Martinez, Eddy	ss	Frederick	Bal	A+	22	127	416	121	21	1	2	150	68	55	52	1	99	13	5	5	8	4	.67	6	.291	.383	.361
Martinez, Edgar	c	Red Sox	Bos	R	18	33	113	27	3	0	1	33	12	20	9	0	13	1	0	0	1	2	.33	1	.239	.301	.292
Martinez, Guill.#	ss	Mariners	Sea	R	20	42	160	49	7	0	1	59	24	19	4	0	33	3	3	2	3	6	.33	5	.306	.331	.369
Martinez, Hipolito	of	Visalia	Oak	A+	23	113	431	115	24	3	21	208	93	77	59	1	119	5	1	5	8	4	.67	8	.267	.358	.483
Martinez, Louis	3b	Braves	Atl	R	23	23	87	28	4	1	0	34	8	14	8	0	13	1	2	0	0	2	.00	1	.322	.385	.391
		Myrtle Bch	Atl	A+	23	5	15	2	1	0	0	3	1	0	1	0	2	0	0	0	0	0	.00	0	.133	.188	.200
Martinez, Octavio	c	Orioles	Bal	R	20	36	114	27	8	1	0	37	11	15	4	0	11	2	0	2	8	1	.89	5	.237	.270	.325
Martinez, Orlando	of	Reds	Cin	R	21	4	13	4	1	1	0	7	4	1	0	0	2	1	0	0	0	0	.00	0	.308	.357	.538
Martinez, Victor#	c	Mahoning Vy	Cle	A-	21	64	235	65	9	0	4	86	37	36	27	0	31	1	0	6	0	1	.00	4	.277	.346	.366
Massucco, Scott	c	Yankees	NYY	R	20	6	13	2	0	0	0	2	1	1	2	0	0	0	0	0	0	1	.00	1	.154	.267	.154

1999 Batting — Single-A and Rookie Leagues

						BATTING															BASERUNNING				PERCENTAGES		
Player	Pos	Team	Org	Lg	A	G	AB	H	2B	3B	HR	TB	R	RBI	TBB	IBB	SO	HBP	SH	SF	SB	CS	SB%	GDP	Avg	OBP	SLG
		Greensboro	NYY	A	20	3	4	0	0	0	0	0	0	0	0	0	2	0	0	0	0	0	.00	1	.000	.000	.000
Matan, James	dh-1b	Rockford	Cin	A	24	116	393	100	17	0	10	147	39	56	38	2	90	5	0	6	5	6	.45	10	.254	.324	.374
Mateo, Henry#	2b	Jupiter	Mon	A+	23	118	447	116	27	7	4	169	69	58	44	3	112	10	17	6	32	16	.67	4	.260	.335	.378
Matos, Angel	c	Rangers	Tex	R	20	36	122	34	12	2	2	56	21	22	18	0	36	0	0	1	2	1	.67	3	.279	.369	.459
Matranga, David	ss	Kissimmee	Hou	A+	23	124	472	109	20	4	6	155	70	48	68	0	118	12	9	2	17	10	.63	3	.231	.341	.328
Mattern, Erik	2b	Salem-Keizr	SF	A-	24	17	41	9	1	1	1	15	11	6	16	0	9	4	2	0	1	1	.50	1	.220	.475	.366
Matthews, Lamont*	of	Yakima	LA	A-	22	66	249	56	11	2	17	122	46	52	34	1	87	2	2	2	4	4	.50	1	.225	.321	.490
		San Berndno	LA	A+	22	4	15	4	1	0	1	8	2	3	2	0	7	0	0	0	0	1	.00	0	.267	.353	.533
Mauck, Matt*	1b	Lansing	ChC	A	21	107	298	66	9	4	8	107	37	59	45	0	100	7	1	1	2	1	.67	5	.221	.336	.359
Maule, Jason*	2b	Auburn	Hou	A-	22	35	86	19	3	0	0	22	12	11	21	0	20	1	0	1	10	1	.91	3	.221	.376	.256
Maxwell, Keith	1b-of	Hickory	Pit	A	25	62	206	54	11	1	8	91	26	39	19	0	49	9	0	0	2	2	.50	3	.262	.350	.442
		Lynchburg	Pit	A+	25	35	132	33	6	1	3	50	10	16	6	0	29	4	0	0	0	2	.00	9	.250	.303	.379
Maxwell, Vernon	of	Tampa	NYY	A+	23	23	47	4	0	0	0	4	4	1	3	0	14	1	0	0	0	0	.00	1	.085	.157	.085
		Yankees	NYY	R	23	1	4	2	0	0	0	2	0	0	0	0	1	0	0	0	0	0	.00	0	.500	.500	.500
May, Freddy*	of	Lynchburg	Pit	A+	24	126	441	130	20	4	8	182	61	56	85	0	105	3	0	5	17	11	.61	12	.295	.408	.413
Maya, Johan#	2b-ss	Martinsvlle	Hou	R+	20	42	138	33	7	1	1	45	22	12	7	0	15	5	1	1	9	5	.64	3	.239	.298	.326
Maynard, Scott	c	Lancaster	Sea	A+	22	8	27	7	4	0	1	14	6	3	4	0	8	0	0	0	0	0	.00	0	.259	.355	.519
		Wisconsin	Sea	A	22	50	135	27	4	0	2	37	16	15	10	0	29	0	1	1	1	3	.25	3	.200	.253	.274
Mayo, Terry	of	Helena	Mil	R+	18	36	104	17	3	0	1	23	5	12	6	0	47	1	2	0	0	3	.00	0	.163	.216	.221
Maza, Luis	ss	Twins	Min	R	20	25	61	16	4	0	0	20	11	10	10	0	15	3	1	0	1	1	.50	1	.262	.392	.328
McAffee, Josh	c	South Bend	Ari	A	22	68	232	57	16	0	5	88	32	24	35	0	76	5	0	2	0	1	.00	3	.246	.354	.379
McArthur, Joe	c	Batavia	Phi	A-	20	31	103	20	10	0	2	36	13	4	5	0	31	4	0	0	0	0	.00	1	.194	.259	.350
McAuley, James	c	Spokane	KC	A-	22	12	35	5	1	0	1	9	7	6	9	0	10	1	1	0	2	0	1.00	0	.143	.333	.257
McBride, Gator	of	Sarasota	Bos	A+	26	36	136	49	10	3	9	92	25	29	7	3	13	2	1	0	2	1	.67	1	.360	.400	.676
McCall, Gerard	c-dh	White Sox	CWS	R	20	46	168	45	12	5	3	76	33	26	20	0	36	1	2	0	6	3	.67	5	.268	.349	.452
McCarty, Brock	of	Diamondbcks	Ari	R	20	53	191	61	5	2	1	73	28	18	7	0	41	2	1	0	5	3	.63	4	.319	.350	.382
McClure, Trey	1b	Cubs	ChC	R	24	47	164	44	9	2	7	78	30	25	21	0	25	3	0	0	3	0	1.00	6	.268	.362	.476
McConnell, Jason#	ss	Quad City	Min	A	24	27	99	21	1	1	0	24	12	3	7	0	24	0	1	2	3	3	.50	1	.212	.259	.242
		Fort Myers	Min	A+	24	48	151	36	6	0	0	42	23	13	20	0	24	0	3	2	5	0	1.00	2	.238	.324	.278
McCorkle, Shawn*	1b	Lancaster	Sea	A+	22	83	302	83	22	1	9	134	45	52	35	4	97	1	0	2	1	1	.50	3	.275	.350	.444
McCrotty, Will	c	San Berndno	LA	A+	21	93	319	81	12	3	4	111	43	43	27	0	49	1	4	6	0	2	.00	11	.254	.309	.348
McDonald, Darnell	of	Frederick	Bal	A+	21	130	507	135	23	5	6	186	81	73	61	0	92	5	7	7	26	9	.74	13	.266	.347	.367
McDowell, Arturo*	of	Bakersfield	SF	A+	20	121	441	98	16	10	2	140	66	37	49	0	140	11	3	6	28	23	.55	1	.222	.312	.317
McGee, Tom	c	Frederick	Bal	A+	25	7	30	6	1	0	0	7	2	3	1	0	6	0	0	1	0	0	.00	2	.200	.219	.233
		Delmarva	Bal	A	25	71	218	59	16	2	4	91	37	27	34	2	52	4	2	5	0	4	.00	5	.271	.372	.417
McGowan, Sean	dh-1b	Salem-Keizr	SF	A-	23	63	257	86	12	1	15	145	40	62	20	4	56	1	0	0	3	1	.75	6	.335	.385	.564
		San Jose	SF	A+	23	2	8	3	1	0	0	4	1	1	0	0	3	0	0	0	0	1	.00	0	.375	.375	.500
McGrath, Sean	2b	St. Lucie	NYM	A+	24	35	72	16	1	0	0	17	7	6	3	0	17	1	3	1	0	0	.00	1	.222	.260	.236
		Capital Cty	NYM	A	24	30	95	17	6	1	0	25	13	13	1	0	31	3	0	5	0	0	.00	2	.179	.202	.263
McIntyre, Robert	ss	Mets	NYM	R	19	32	102	31	2	0	0	33	18	15	15	0	19	2	2	3	7	2	.78	1	.304	.393	.324
McKinley, Josh#	ss	Cape Fear	Mon	A	20	48	168	44	12	0	0	56	18	17	16	0	38	0	0	1	9	6	.60	3	.262	.324	.333
		Vermont	Mon	A-	20	69	283	71	12	3	4	101	47	32	33	0	52	1	3	3	9	5	.64	7	.251	.328	.357
McKinney, Antonio	of	Oneonta	Det	A-	22	68	229	57	9	1	2	74	36	20	18	0	60	8	1	1	26	4	.87	1	.249	.324	.323
McMillan, Drew	c	Expos	Mon	R	19	31	100	21	4	0	0	25	11	2	8	0	19	2	1	0	2	1	.67	1	.210	.282	.250
McMillin, Brian	of	Quad City	Min	A	23	116	414	110	21	3	19	194	69	74	53	3	75	4	4	3	19	4	.83	18	.266	.352	.469
McNaughton, Troy*	of-dh	Peoria	StL	A	25	125	484	132	25	6	14	211	57	84	37	1	123	4	0	4	5	4	.56	11	.273	.327	.436
McNeal, Aaron	1b	Michigan	Hou	A	22	133	536	166	29	3	38	315	95	131	40	4	121	2	0	3	7	1	.88	13	.310	.358	.588
McQueen, Eric	c	Portland	Col	A-	23	46	153	39	8	1	1	52	14	14	10	0	52	3	0	3	0	1	.00	3	.255	.308	.340
Meadows, Mike	dh	Pittsfield	NYM	A-	21	48	134	35	10	0	5	60	23	24	21	1	57	1	0	1	3	0	1.00	0	.261	.363	.448
Meadows, Randy	3b	Vermont	Mon	A-	23	9	30	6	0	0	0	6	4	2	3	0	7	0	1	0	1	2	.33	0	.200	.273	.200
		Cape Fear	Mon	A	23	50	141	32	5	1	0	39	18	9	7	0	35	5	4	0	2	5	.29	2	.227	.288	.277
Meadows, Tydus	of	Lansing	ChC	A	22	126	449	135	32	6	17	230	80	74	66	2	85	11	0	4	18	10	.64	13	.301	.400	.512
Medina, Luis	1b	Eugene	ChC	A-	21	56	202	68	6	0	3	83	30	31	11	0	21	2	1	0	2	1	.67	7	.337	.377	.411
Medosch, Keith	2b	Cedar Rapds	Ana	A	25	20	40	5	0	0	0	5	4	0	9	0	15	1	0	0	0	1	.00	0	.125	.300	.125
Medrano, Jesus	2b	Kane County	Fla	A	21	118	445	122	26	5	5	173	64	46	36	1	92	4	1	5	42	11	.79	3	.274	.331	.389
Medrano, Steve#	ss	Wilmington	KC	A+	22	98	362	91	4	3	0	101	41	24	30	1	66	1	8	1	12	10	.55	5	.251	.310	.279
Meier, Dan*	1b	High Desert	Ari	A+	22	129	418	112	25	4	24	217	85	89	70	3	138	9	1	1	0	0	.00	6	.268	.384	.519
Mejia, Max	of	Vero Beach	LA	A+	22	28	87	19	4	0	1	26	14	20	8	0	25	2	2	1	4	2	.67	1	.218	.296	.299
Mejias, Aureliano#	of	Johnson Cy	StL	R+	19	33	75	17	3	1	0	22	9	5	10	0	29	2	0	1	2	2	.50	3	.227	.330	.293
Mejias, Erick#	2b	Charlotte	Tex	A+	19	1	4	2	0	0	0	2	0	1	0	0	1	0	0	0	0	0	.00	0	.500	.500	.500
		Rangers	Tex	R	19	56	194	50	7	1	1	62	35	23	22	0	36	8	2	1	11	3	.79	3	.258	.356	.320
Melconian, Alex	of	Brevard Cty	Fla	A+	25	58	205	54	6	1	4	74	26	20	24	0	48	9	4	1	11	9	.55	9	.263	.364	.361
Melendez, Angel	of	San Jose	SF	A+	24	101	370	82	17	1	5	116	32	41	24	1	100	9	4	3	10	8	.56	13	.222	.283	.314
Meliah, David*	2b	Savannah	Tex	A	23	93	358	106	21	3	8	157	53	49	16	0	80	3	0	2	3	6	.33	8	.296	.330	.439
Melian, Jackson	of	Tampa	NYY	A+	20	128	467	132	17	13	6	193	65	61	49	1	98	10	1	8	11	8	.58	8	.283	.358	.413
Melo, Ramon	ss-of	Chstn-WV	KC	A	20	3	11	3	0	0	0	3	0	1	1	0	4	0	0	0	0	0	.00	0	.273	.333	.273
Melucci, Lou	2b	Vermont	Mon	A-	22	33	123	24	3	1	0	29	13	7	10	0	34	1	1	0	6	1	.86	2	.195	.261	.236
Mench, Kevin	of	Pulaski	Tex	R+	22	65	260	94	22	1	16	166	63	60	28	0	48	2	0	5	12	2	.86	2	.362	.420	.638
		Savannah	Tex	A	22	6	23	7	1	1	2	16	4	8	2	0	4	0	0	0	0	0	.00	1	.304	.360	.696
Mendez, Donaldo	ss	Auburn	Hou	A-	22	25	86	18	1	1	0	21	9	10	2	0	23	4	0	2	10	5	.67	3	.209	.255	.244
Mendez, Hector	2b	Mexico		R		7	15	1	0	0	0	1	0	0	0	0	0	0	0	0	0	0	.00	0	.067	.067	.067
Mendieta, Enrique	of	Marlins	Fla	R	20	30	49	8	3	0	0	11	2	6	9	0	14	1	0	1	1	1	.50	0	.163	.300	.224
Mendoza, Angel	of	Augusta	Bos	A	21	119	429	113	7	8	7	157	58	46	34	0	97	7	1	2	19	8	.70	8	.263	.326	.366
Mensik, Todd*	1b-dh	Visalia	Oak	A+	25	134	505	147	29	4	29	271	93	123	79	11	114	9	0	3	5	1	.83	8	.291	.394	.537
Mento, Alfredo	of	St. Lucie	NYM	A+	22	1	1	0	0	0	0	0	0	0	0	0	1	0	0	0	0	0	.00	0	.000	.000	.000
		Pittsfield	NYM	A-	22	72	275	69	12	3	2	93	42	23	24	0	55	5	5	2	24	11	.69	2	.251	.320	.338
		Capital Cty	NYM	A	22	3	12	4	1	0	0	5	5	2	0	0	2	0	0	0	2	0	1.00	0	.333	.333	.417

1999 Batting — Single-A and Rookie Leagues

BATTING																					BASERUNNING				PERCENTAGES		
Player	Pos	Team	Org	Lg	A	G	AB	H	2B	3B	HR	TB	R	RBI	TBB	IBB	SO	HBP	SH	SF	SB	CS	SB%	GDP	Avg	OBP	SLG
Meran, Jorge	c	W Michigan	Det	A	23	44	152	30	9	4	2	53	18	23	7	0	38	1	1	2	1	3	.25	1	.197	.235	.349
Mercado, Wilkins	3b	Royals	KC	R	21	41	128	34	5	1	3	50	17	15	17	0	23	1	0	1	1	0	1.00	7	.266	.354	.391
Merhoff, Aaron	of	Batavia	Phi	A-	24	16	51	7	2	1	0	11	3	6	6	0	16	0	0	0	0	0	.00	0	.137	.228	.216
		Phillies	Phi	R	24	22	78	25	6	2	1	38	10	12	10	1	15	0	1	2	2	1	.67	2	.321	.389	.487
Merriman, Terrell*	of	Burlington	CWS	A	22	109	382	117	18	9	15	198	77	85	70	3	84	2	2	6	27	4	.87	2	.306	.411	.518
Messner, Jake*	of-dh	Salem-Keizr	SF	A-	23	8	19	5	0	0	1	8	4	5	5	0	4	0	0	0	0	0	.00	0	.263	.417	.421
		Bakersfield	SF	A+	23	55	172	50	11	6	7	94	33	35	16	1	45	1	0	2	2	2	.50	1	.291	.351	.547
Michaels, Jason	of	Clearwater	Phi	A+	24	122	451	138	31	6	14	223	91	65	68	2	103	3	1	6	10	7	.59	7	.306	.396	.494
Miles, Aaron#	2b	Michigan	Hou	A	23	112	470	149	28	8	10	223	72	71	28	3	33	2	6	7	17	12	.59	8	.317	.353	.474
Miley, Perry	of	Lowell	Bos	A-	22	46	147	36	6	1	2	50	19	19	18	0	29	3	4	1	9	3	.75	4	.245	.337	.340
Miller, Josh*	dh-of	Pirates	Pit	R	21	6	22	2	2	0	0	4	0	0	0	0	6	0	0	0	0	0	.00	0	.091	.091	.182
Miller, Kenny	3b-ss	St. Lucie	NYM	A+	24	93	304	72	13	1	3	96	32	24	18	0	50	6	5	1	3	5	.38	6	.237	.292	.316
Milton, Prinz	of	Danville	Atl	R+	21	36	127	22	4	1	0	28	20	15	9	0	31	5	0	0	6	1	.86	5	.173	.255	.220
Minges, Tyler	of	Columbus	Cle	A	20	127	492	119	25	11	10	196	64	62	19	0	113	4	3	6	23	7	.77	12	.242	.273	.398
Minus, Steve	3b	Lowell	Bos	A-	23	66	237	59	13	2	5	91	32	26	39	2	67	1	0	2	6	1	.86	6	.249	.355	.384
Mitchell, Andres	of	Salem	Col	A+	24	33	109	20	3	1	1	28	10	11	11	0	35	2	2	1	7	2	.78	3	.183	.268	.257
Mitchell, Brian	2b-of	Medcine Hat	Tor	R+	23	30	84	19	4	1	2	31	13	11	12	0	20	2	1	0	1	3	.25	2	.226	.337	.369
Mitchell, Todd	2b	Staten Ilnd	NYY	A-	21	65	248	67	13	1	1	85	34	23	21	1	39	1	1	0	11	2	.85	3	.270	.330	.343
Mize, Matt#	2b	Pittsfield	NYM	A-	23	69	281	74	15	2	3	102	32	27	22	0	78	1	3	0	22	7	.76	2	.263	.319	.363
Moncrief, Kyle*	1b	Reds	Cin	R	20	39	97	17	3	1	1	25	11	7	22	0	41	2	1	0	3	1	.75	2	.175	.339	.258
Montas, Ricardo	dh	Wilmington	KC	A+	23	98	349	86	15	0	2	107	46	31	47	0	60	3	5	2	4	2	.67	7	.246	.339	.307
Montenegro, Jose	c	Ogden	Mil	R+	24	18	54	14	3	0	0	17	8	4	2	0	8	1	0	0	0	0	.00	3	.259	.298	.315
		Beloit	Mil	A	24	2	6	2	1	1	0	5	1	1	2	0	1	0	0	0	0	0	.00	0	.333	.500	.833
		Stockton	Mil	A+	24	21	55	9	0	0	1	12	1	5	2	0	8	1	1	0	0	1	.00	0	.164	.207	.218
Montilla, Mike#	ss	Tampa	NYY	A+	26	12	33	4	0	0	0	4	2	0	8	0	10	1	0	0	0	0	.00	0	.121	.310	.121
Monzon, Francisco	c	Bluefield	Bal	R+	20	24	82	20	4	0	1	27	14	7	9	0	20	1	0	0	1	1	.50	3	.244	.326	.329
Moon, Brian#	c	Stockton	Mil	A+	22	116	385	102	14	2	2	126	52	30	37	4	40	7	2	4	6	6	.50	9	.265	.337	.327
Moore, Chris*	2b	Portland	Col	A-	23	63	260	69	19	2	4	104	39	38	15	2	64	1	3	2	0	2	.00	1	.265	.306	.400
Moore, Frank*	2b	Hudson Val	TB	A-	21	74	319	97	12	5	2	125	53	20	21	1	68	2	2	2	24	9	.73	1	.304	.349	.392
Moore, Griffin	3b	Wilmington	KC	A+	24	6	17	1	1	0	0	2	1	4	1	0	7	1	0	0	0	0	.00	0	.059	.158	.118
		Chstn-WV	KC	A	24	40	106	23	3	1	0	28	10	6	8	0	13	3	1	1	2	2	.50	4	.217	.288	.264
Moore, Jason#	ss	Idaho Falls	SD	R+	22	64	252	68	16	3	6	108	54	43	43	0	54	6	1	3	16	1	.94	6	.270	.385	.429
Moore, Kevin#	of	Vero Beach	LA	A+	25	2	6	3	0	0	0	3	0	0	2	0	1	0	0	0	0	1	.00	0	.500	.625	.500
Moore, Lacarlo*	of	W Michigan	Det	A	24	43	164	49	4	1	0	55	27	17	16	1	26	1	1	0	8	3	.73	7	.299	.365	.335
		Lakeland	Det	A+	24	36	94	23	4	1	0	29	15	6	9	0	18	0	0	1	6	3	.67	3	.245	.308	.309
Moore, Ryan*	3b	Vermont	Mon	A-	23	26	103	27	4	1	2	39	16	12	13	1	21	2	0	1	1	3	.25	1	.262	.353	.379
		Jupiter	Mon	A+	23	5	10	2	0	0	1	5	2	1	1	0	5	0	0	0	0	0	.00	0	.200	.273	.500
Mora, Juan*	of	Lakeland	Det	A+	22	3	8	1	1	0	0	2	1	0	0	0	3	0	1	0	0	0	.00	0	.125	.125	.250
Moraga, Omar*	2b	Mahoning Vy	Cle	A-	23	67	248	57	21	2	4	94	35	37	21	0	69	1	2	4	3	2	.60	5	.230	.288	.379
Morales, Stephen#	c	Kane County	Fla	A	22	28	96	26	5	0	2	37	12	11	4	0	16	1	2	0	0	0	.00	2	.271	.307	.385
Morales, Victor#	1b	St.Cathrnes	Tor	A-	22	43	132	29	4	0	0	33	10	16	11	0	24	5	4	0	7	0	1.00	5	.220	.304	.250
Morban, Jose	ss	Rangers	Tex	R	20	54	205	58	10	5	4	90	45	18	31	2	70	2	4	3	19	14	.58	1	.283	.378	.439
Morency, Vernand	of	Rockies	Col	R	20	44	160	47	7	4	2	68	36	18	19	0	49	2	0	1	25	5	.83	3	.294	.374	.425
Moreno, Jorge	of	Mahoning Vy	Cle	A-	19	69	230	59	10	2	9	100	38	38	31	0	61	5	2	7	15	7	.68	4	.257	.348	.435
Moreno, Jose	dh	Wisconsin	Sea	A	22	3	4	0	0	0	0	0	0	0	0	0	0	0	0	0	0	1	.00	1	.000	.000	.000
		Lancaster	Sea	A+	22	23	68	11	2	0	0	13	9	4	7	0	12	1	1	0	4	1	.80	2	.162	.250	.191
Moreno, Juan	of	St. Lucie	NYM	A+	24	120	424	127	18	5	4	167	64	47	51	0	70	2	7	4	28	11	.72	10	.300	.374	.394
Moreno, Mikel	of	Lansing	ChC	A	23	5	19	3	0	1	1	8	1	2	0	0	2	0	0	0	1	0	1.00	0	.158	.158	.421
Moreno, Omar#	of	Yakima	LA	A-	20	44	133	26	1	0	0	27	30	8	33	0	28	2	6	1	11	8	.58	4	.195	.361	.203
Morillo, Luis*	of	Dunedin	Tor	A+	22	4	3	0	0	0	0	0	1	0	0	0	1	0	0	0	0	0	.00	0	.000	.000	.000
Morla, Gilberto	c	Burlington	Cle	R+	20	5	9	1	0	0	0	1	0	0	1	0	6	1	0	0	0	1	.00	0	.111	.273	.111
Morneau, Justin*	dh	Twins	Min	R	19	17	53	16	5	0	0	21	3	9	2	0	6	1	1	1	0	1	.00	2	.302	.333	.396
Morrison, Greg*	1b	Dunedin	Tor	A+	24	81	260	69	17	1	2	94	31	34	15	1	32	0	1	2	2	1	.67	6	.265	.303	.362
Morrissey, Adam	2b	Cubs	ChC	R	19	44	169	50	7	3	2	69	23	23	21	0	28	2	2	2	4	7	.36	6	.296	.376	.408
Morrow, Alvin	of	Beloit	Mil	A	22	82	296	69	11	0	3	89	29	41	47	0	121	1	0	3	0	0	.00	8	.233	.337	.301
Mota, Pedro*	of	San Jose	SF	A+	22	50	171	46	3	4	3	66	26	19	12	1	38	0	2	2	3	7	.30	2	.269	.314	.386
Motley, Brittan#	of	Idaho Falls	SD	R+	21	41	153	36	6	0	1	45	23	20	16	0	40	1	0	0	11	1	.92	6	.235	.312	.294
Mott, Bill*	dh	Lk Elsinore	Ana	A+	24	25	88	28	5	1	1	38	16	12	10	0	18	1	2	2	6	3	.67	1	.318	.386	.432
Mounts, J.R.	of	Burlington	CWS	A	21	95	326	69	14	1	6	103	40	32	25	0	129	6	1	2	11	7	.61	1	.212	.279	.316
Moye, Melvin	of	South Bend	Ari	A	21	72	244	62	13	1	3	86	33	30	19	0	75	5	1	2	4	2	.67	10	.254	.319	.352
Moyer, Kyle*	1b	Burlington	Cle	R+	19	38	132	35	5	0	1	43	15	10	21	2	40	0	0	1	0	0	.00	2	.265	.364	.326
Mulqueen, Dave#	1b-3b	Rockies	Col	R	19	53	169	42	9	3	1	60	32	17	42	0	63	3	0	2	6	3	.67	2	.249	.403	.355
Mulvehill, Chase	of	Capital Cty	NYM	A	22	116	427	122	23	6	9	184	65	58	29	0	97	12	5	5	29	13	.69	6	.286	.345	.431
Munoz, Billy*	1b	Kinston	Cle	A+	25	106	378	96	25	1	9	150	46	55	48	2	108	1	1	1	3	2	.60	9	.254	.339	.397
Munson, Eric*	1b-dh	Lakeland	Det	A+	22	2	6	2	0	0	0	2	0	1	1	0	1	0	0	0	0	0	.00	0	.333	.429	.333
		W Michigan	Det	A	22	67	252	67	16	1	14	127	42	44	37	3	47	9	0	1	3	1	.75	4	.266	.378	.504
Murch, Jeremy*	dh	Hudson Val	TB	A-	21	39	131	28	7	2	5	54	18	18	12	1	36	1	0	1	1	2	.33	2	.214	.283	.412
Muthig, Dean	1b-3b	Batavia	Phi	A-	22	31	107	28	7	2	1	42	16	18	4	0	28	0	0	3	1	0	1.00	1	.262	.281	.393
Myers, Corey	ss	Missoula	Ari	R+	20	66	272	75	13	2	5	107	43	44	22	0	65	2	0	1	6	3	.67	9	.276	.333	.393
Myers, Tootie	2b	Cape Fear	Mon	A	21	137	515	115	19	8	11	183	61	52	35	1	147	10	6	1	30	16	.65	9	.223	.285	.355
Na, Jim*	of	Cape Fear	Mon	A	24	67	221	48	10	4	1	69	24	18	17	0	45	6	2	0	7	5	.58	3	.217	.291	.312
Nanita, Manny	dh of	Elizabothtn	Min	R+	20	38	135	31	0	1	2	45	20	19	9	0	40	1	0	0	1	0	1.00	1	.230	.283	.333
Navarro, Ibrahim	ss	Lansing	ChC	A	20	55	156	31	7	1	1	43	19	18	15	0	39	2	0	3	2	0	1.00	7	.199	.273	.276
Ndungidi, Ntema*	of	Delmarva	Bal	A	21	64	217	42	8	2	0	54	33	24	49	2	54	3	1	1	18	2	.90	7	.194	.348	.249
		Frederick	Bal	A+	21	60	192	51	10	3	0	67	40	18	39	0	43	3	1	1	4	2	.67	6	.266	.396	.349
Neal, Steve*	1b	High Desert	Ari	A+	23	6	20	5	0	0	2	11	3	2	1	0	7	0	0	0	0	0	.00	2	.250	.286	.550
		South Bend	Ari	A	23	69	249	70	14	2	7	109	41	53	40	2	72	1	0	3	6	2	.75	3	.281	.379	.438

1999 Batting — Single-A and Rookie Leagues

BATTING																					BASERUNNING				PERCENTAGES		
Player	Pos	Team	Org	Lg	A	G	AB	H	2B	3B	HR	TB	R	RBI	TBB	IBB	SO	HBP	SH	SF	SB	CS	SB%	GDP	Avg	OBP	SLG
Nelson, Brian	dh	Wisconsin	Sea	A	24	58	171	35	10	0	3	54	17	21	22	0	54	2	0	0	2	1	.67	4	.205	.303	.316
Nelson, Eric#	2b	Spokane	KC	A-	23	69	284	79	18	4	8	129	51	52	33	0	65	1	1	2	12	2	.86	6	.278	.353	.454
Nelson, Reggie	2b	Lakeland	Det	A+	21	3	7	2	0	0	0	2	0	0	0	0	1	0	0	0	0	0	.00	0	.286	.286	.286
		Oneonta	Det	A-	21	67	249	59	11	3	1	79	44	20	36	0	42	3	4	1	32	8	.80	4	.237	.339	.317
Nelson, Tim	3b	Bluefield	Bal	R+	22	33	115	26	3	2	3	42	19	16	6	0	35	5	0	1	0	0	.00	0	.226	.291	.365
Nettles, Jeff	1b	Yankees	NYY	R	21	44	142	39	8	1	6	67	24	31	15	0	27	3	1	5	1	2	.33	4	.275	.345	.472
Neuberger, Scott	of	St. Pete	TB	A+	22	127	442	115	14	3	10	165	55	63	24	0	104	8	1	6	1	2	.33	12	.260	.306	.373
Newton, Kimani	of	San Berndno	LA	A+	21	40	143	35	3	4	0	46	19	16	13	0	39	2	0	0	9	3	.75	2	.245	.316	.322
		Vero Beach	LA	A+	21	62	211	56	7	2	0	67	29	18	29	0	67	1	0	1	7	5	.58	4	.265	.355	.318
Nicholson, Derek*	dh	Michigan	Hou	A	24	66	216	69	8	5	3	96	40	39	30	0	25	1	1	2	3	4	.43	6	.319	.402	.444
Nicolas, Jose	of	Williamsprt	Pit	A-	21	29	99	20	6	1	1	31	8	11	7	0	32	1	0	0	2	2	.50	4	.202	.262	.313
Nieckula, Aaron	c	Sou Oregon	Oak	A-	23	15	50	13	4	0	1	20	11	9	9	0	12	2	0	1	2	1	.67	2	.260	.387	.400
		Visalia	Oak	A+	23	25	65	18	4	0	0	22	13	10	8	0	17	4	2	2	2	0	1.00	0	.277	.380	.338
Niemet, Bob	1b	Salem-Keizr	SF	A-	23	18	56	12	1	0	0	13	8	4	6	0	5	1	0	0	1	2	.33	1	.214	.302	.232
		Bakersfield	SF	A+	23	27	57	15	4	0	0	19	7	7	13	0	9	4	0	1	3	1	.75	3	.263	.427	.333
Nieves, Juan	of	Hagerstown	Tor	A	23	47	130	19	3	1	1	27	14	14	12	0	28	2	3	2	7	1	.88	3	.146	.226	.208
Nieves, Wilbert	c	Rancho Cuca	SD	A+	22	120	427	140	26	2	7	191	58	61	40	1	54	5	1	4	2	7	.22	12	.328	.389	.447
Nina, Amaurys	of	Charlotte	Tex	A+	22	112	426	113	15	5	2	144	65	29	45	0	101	3	5	2	24	12	.67	9	.265	.338	.338
Noboa, Joel	3b	South Bend	Ari	A	20	11	39	7	2	0	0	9	2	3	0	0	17	0	0	0	0	0	.00	2	.179	.179	.231
		Diamondbcks	Ari	R	20	52	215	67	11	1	12	116	31	41	6	0	60	3	0	2	5	1	.83	3	.312	.336	.540
		Missoula	Ari	R+	20	5	18	2	0	0	0	2	1	2	1	0	9	0	0	0	1	0	1.00	0	.111	.158	.111
Nolasco, Regino	2b	Delmarva	Bal	A	20	23	59	7	0	0	0	7	10	6	5	0	16	1	2	1	1	1	.50	1	.119	.197	.119
		Bluefield	Bal	R+	20	58	198	40	5	3	1	54	35	26	19	0	49	2	2	0	5	0	1.00	6	.202	.279	.273
Norrell, Troy	c	Batavia	Phi	A-	23	28	100	25	7	2	6	54	16	21	8	1	45	1	0	0	1	0	1.00	1	.250	.312	.540
Novak, John	of	Savannah	Tex	A	23	66	215	54	13	1	8	93	38	36	28	0	65	5	0	2	3	2	.60	3	.251	.348	.433
Nowlin, Cody*	of	Savannah	Tex	A	20	56	204	37	6	1	4	57	25	26	19	0	58	2	0	3	1	2	.33	3	.181	.254	.279
		Pulaski	Tex	R+	20	58	227	63	10	1	8	99	45	49	21	1	34	3	1	3	5	0	1.00	4	.278	.343	.436
Nunez, Abraham#	of	High Desert	Ari	A+	20	130	488	133	29	6	22	240	106	93	86	2	122	2	1	8	40	13	.75	10	.273	.378	.492
Nunez, Edward*	of	Twins	Min	R	20	29	43	10	1	1	0	13	9	5	10	1	9	0	1	1	3	2	.60	0	.233	.370	.302
Nunez, Hector	3b	Tigers	Det	R	22	10	26	8	4	0	0	12	4	6	4	0	3	0	0	0	4	1	.80	0	.308	.400	.462
		Oneonta	Det	A-	22	33	102	29	9	2	0	42	6	15	6	0	13	2	0	0	0	0	.00	1	.284	.336	.412
Nunez, Jorge	2b	Hagerstown	Tor	A	22	133	564	151	28	11	14	243	116	61	40	1	103	2	1	2	51	8	.86	8	.268	.317	.431
Nunez, Jose	3b	New Jersey	StL	A-	21	45	157	48	11	1	1	64	29	13	20	1	18	2	3	0	6	3	.67	4	.306	.391	.408
Nye, Rodney	3b	Pittsfield	NYM	A-	23	70	255	78	30	2	7	133	45	48	32	1	36	5	0	4	10	4	.71	5	.306	.389	.522
Nykoluk, Kevin	c	Peoria	StL	A	25	55	177	46	13	1	2	67	24	19	14	0	25	2	0	1	0	1	.00	6	.260	.320	.379
Ochoa, Javier	c	Auburn	Hou	A-	21	15	47	13	2	1	0	17	5	11	3	0	7	0	0	2	0	1	.00	2	.277	.308	.362
O'Connor, Brian	c	Martinsvlle	Hou	R+	23	13	38	7	1	0	1	11	3	2	8	0	4	0	0	0	2	3	.40	1	.184	.326	.289
		Michigan	Hou	A	23	21	64	10	2	0	0	12	8	5	9	0	29	0	2	1	0	1	.00	2	.156	.257	.188
Oglesby, Travis	c	Diamondbcks	Ari	R	22	35	109	24	8	0	4	44	20	13	19	0	40	2	0	0	0	0	.00	3	.220	.346	.404
		Missoula	Ari	R+	22	3	5	0	0	0	0	0	0	0	0	0	2	0	0	0	0	0	.00	0	.000	.000	.000
O'Keefe, Mike*	of	Boise	Ana	A-	22	72	264	86	13	1	9	128	52	70	54	2	41	6	0	5	4	1	.80	7	.326	.444	.485
Olivares, Teuris	ss	Greensboro	NYY	A	21	110	451	126	18	6	11	189	78	52	26	0	78	6	3	4	14	7	.67	10	.279	.324	.419
Oliver, Bill	1b	Cedar Rapds	Ana	A	25	21	61	5	1	0	1	9	6	1	6	0	28	3	0	0	0	0	.00	1	.082	.200	.148
Oliver, Brian	ss	Cedar Rapds	Ana	A	23	66	252	69	16	1	6	105	43	29	26	0	30	6	4	4	12	1	.92	3	.274	.351	.417
Oliver, Johnny	of	Clinton	Cin	A	22	17	52	6	0	0	1	9	7	2	5	0	16	0	0	0	0	2	.00	3	.115	.193	.173
		Augusta	Bos	A	22	33	120	25	4	0	0	29	9	7	10	0	36	1	1	0	1	0	1.00	3	.208	.275	.242
Olivo, Miguel	c	Modesto	Oak	A+	21	73	243	74	13	6	9	126	46	42	21	1	60	2	1	1	4	5	.44	6	.305	.363	.519
Olmeda, Jose#	ss	Sarasota	Bos	A+	22	53	160	43	12	1	3	66	20	20	6	0	39	2	1	2	1	3	.25	3	.269	.300	.413
		Columbus	Cle	A	22	30	106	28	3	2	3	44	16	16	11	0	32	2	0	1	5	1	.83	3	.264	.342	.415
Olmedo, Ranier	2b-ss	Reds	Cin	R	19	54	195	46	12	1	1	63	30	19	12	0	28	1	1	2	13	7	.65	1	.236	.281	.323
O'Neill, Dan	of	Phillies	Phi	R	23	10	27	9	3	1	0	14	6	4	10	0	7	1	0	0	2	0	1.00	0	.333	.526	.519
		Batavia	Phi	A-	23	34	106	20	2	0	1	25	11	8	14	0	27	1	1	0	7	2	.78	2	.189	.289	.236
Orgill, Peter*	1b	Butte	Ana	R+	23	58	217	70	8	1	5	95	43	36	26	1	38	12	0	2	0	0	.00	6	.323	.420	.438
Oropeza, Asdrubal	3b	Jamestown	Atl	A-	19	74	266	78	12	1	14	134	56	46	32	0	60	6	0	6	10	2	.83	3	.293	.374	.504
Ortega, Jose	1b	New Jersey	StL	A-	22	30	100	19	1	0	0	20	12	8	1	0	32	5	1	1	4	0	1.00	1	.190	.234	.200
Ortega, Sixto	c	Rockies	Col	R	20	25	82	19	3	0	0	22	8	14	4	0	20	3	1	0	3	2	.60	0	.232	.292	.268
		Portland	Col	A-	20	1	4	1	0	0	0	1	1	0	0	0	0	0	0	0	1	0	1.00	0	.250	.250	.250
Ortiz, Daniel	1b-dh	Princeton	TB	R+	19	43	141	22	4	1	1	31	15	11	16	0	74	4	0	0	0	2	.00	4	.156	.261	.220
Ortiz, Jorge	3b-dh	Athletics	Oak	R	19	22	52	10	1	0	0	11	6	5	13	0	29	2	1	0	1	1	.50	0	.192	.373	.212
Ortiz, Juan	of	Cape Fear	Mon	A	21	16	44	7	1	0	0	8	7	2	7	0	21	1	3	0	1	1	.50	0	.159	.288	.182
		Vermont	Mon	A-	21	32	115	27	0	1	1	32	16	9	6	0	29	2	1	0	6	1	.86	2	.235	.285	.278
Ortiz, Miguel	dh	Butte	Ana	R+	21	31	124	48	8	3	6	80	24	29	2	0	19	0	1	0	3	3	.50	3	.387	.397	.645
Osborn, Jason	of	Mets	NYM	R	20	1	3	2	1	0	0	3	0	2	0	0	0	0	0	0	0	0	.00	0	.667	.667	1.000
Osborne, Mark*	dh	High Desert	Ari	A+	22	113	335	83	15	3	11	137	52	69	40	0	88	2	2	4	1	3	.25	9	.248	.328	.409
Osilka, Garret	2b	Stockton	Mil	A+	22	100	278	71	11	1	4	96	43	28	24	0	60	7	5	2	7	9	.44	2	.255	.328	.345
Osorio, Isrrael	1b	Princeton	TB	R+	19	60	205	57	15	2	12	112	36	50	37	1	79	3	0	2	8	4	.67	3	.278	.393	.546
O'Sullivan, Pat	dh	Kingsport	NYM	R+	23	51	161	43	8	0	4	63	22	23	10	1	42	1	4	1	4	2	.67	3	.267	.312	.391
Otero, William	2b	San Jose	SF	A+	23	96	402	134	28	3	10	198	81	56	37	0	67	2	1	1	20	4	.83	5	.333	.391	.493
Ottevaere, Derek	of	Savannah	Tex	A	24	97	337	92	11	5	7	134	45	43	27	0	70	8	0	3	3	1	.75	2	.273	.339	.398
Overbay, Lyle*	1b	Missoula	Ari	R+	23	75	306	105	25	7	12	180	66	101	40	2	53	2	0	4	10	3	.77	14	.343	.418	.588
Owens, Jeremy	of	Fort Wayne	SD	A	23	129	513	144	26	12	9	221	111	66	63	2	153	9	4	6	65	14	.82	5	.281	.365	.431
		Rancho Cuca	SD	A+	23	9	38	6	1	0	0	7	2	1	1	0	13	1	0	1	2	1	.67	1	.158	.195	.184
Ozarowski, Rich#	2b	Lakeland	Det	A+	25	52	173	47	8	6	2	73	24	23	14	0	23	3	4	2	4	1	.80	4	.272	.333	.422
Pacheco, Juan#	2b	Tigers	Det	R	20	43	147	32	6	0	0	38	23	12	17	0	29	7	3	1	12	7	.63	1	.218	.326	.259
Padgett, Matt*	of-dh	Kane County	Fla	A	22	45	159	53	9	0	5	77	34	23	20	0	40	1	0	1	1	0	1.00	4	.333	.409	.484
Padilla, Jorge	of	Piedmont	Phi	A	20	44	168	35	10	1	3	56	13	17	5	0	44	4	0	1	0	0	.00	5	.208	.247	.333
		Batavia	Phi	A-	20	65	238	60	10	1	3	81	28	30	22	1	79	7	1	2	2	1	.67	3	.252	.331	.340

1999 Batting — Single-A and Rookie Leagues

BATTING																					BASERUNNING				PERCENTAGES		
Player	Pos	Team	Org	Lg	A	G	AB	H	2B	3B	HR	TB	R	RBI	TBB	IBB	SO	HBP	SH	SF	SB	CS	SB%	GDP	Avg	OBP	SLG
Pagan, Andres	c	Padres	SD	R	19	27	91	17	3	0	1	23	15	6	9	0	25	1	0	0	3	0	1.00	1	.187	.267	.253
Pagan, Carlos	c	Wilmington	KC	A+	24	4	8	0	0	0	0	0	0	0	0	0	3	0	0	0	0	0	.00	0	.000	.000	.000
		Chstn-WV	KC	A	24	50	154	35	9	0	6	62	19	21	13	0	40	0	0	2	2	2	.50	1	.227	.284	.403
Pagan, Felix	3b	Fort Myers	Min	A+	25	7	24	2	0	0	0	2	2	1	4	0	10	0	0	0	1	0	1.00	0	.083	.214	.083
Palafox, Sergio	2b	Mexico	—	R	—	42	148	40	5	2	0	49	29	17	17	0	16	3	2	1	10	1	.91	6	.270	.355	.331
Palmieri, Jon	1b	Boise	Ana	A-	23	48	151	49	10	2	2	69	34	31	17	0	10	6	0	4	4	4	.50	3	.325	.404	.457
Palomares, Luis	of	Ogden	Mil	R+	21	66	223	55	4	1	9	88	40	34	18	0	59	1	5	2	10	5	.67	6	.247	.303	.395
Paredes, Reny	of	Cubs	ChC	R	20	35	122	34	10	0	2	50	16	17	2	0	32	1	1	0	2	3	.40	1	.279	.296	.410
Parker, Chris	c	Lakeland	Det	A+	20	3	8	1	1	0	0	2	1	0	0	0	3	0	0	0	0	0	.00	1	.125	.125	.250
		Oneonta	Det	A-	20	38	116	23	5	0	2	34	10	17	12	0	38	3	0	2	0	1	.00	3	.198	.286	.293
Parker, Clark*	2b	Burlington	CWS	A	24	32	77	12	1	1	0	15	13	4	16	0	24	2	1	0	6	2	.75	2	.156	.316	.195
Parnell, Sean	of	Everett	Sea	A-	22	36	131	32	8	0	0	40	25	18	12	0	24	1	1	2	5	3	.63	3	.244	.308	.305
Pascucci, Valentino	of	Vermont	Mon	A-	21	72	259	91	26	1	7	140	62	48	53	3	46	14	0	2	17	2	.89	5	.351	.482	.541
Pass, Patrick	of	Utica	Fla	A-	22	1	2	0	0	0	0	0	1	0	1	0	1	0	0	0	0	0	.00	0	.000	.333	.000
Paterson, Joe	of	Ogden	Mil	R+	21	35	94	23	4	0	2	33	11	20	9	0	26	0	1	1	0	2	.00	3	.245	.308	.351
Patten, Chris	2b	Beloit	Mil	A	21	124	478	136	16	7	7	187	69	65	30	1	100	8	8	4	6	5	.55	9	.285	.335	.391
Patterson, Corey*	of	Lansing	ChC	A	20	112	475	152	35	17	20	281	94	79	25	1	85	5	0	4	33	9	.79	5	.320	.358	.592
Patton, Cory	of	St. Lucie	NYM	A+	24	9	13	1	0	0	0	1	3	0	3	0	8	0	0	0	0	0	.00	0	.077	.250	.077
Paulino, David	2b	Marlins	Fla	R	20	46	141	28	0	0	0	28	21	4	18	1	24	1	1	0	22	7	.76	2	.199	.294	.199
Paulino, Robert	ss	Cubs	ChC	R	18	21	53	11	1	0	0	12	3	4	3	0	22	0	0	1	1	1	.50	3	.208	.246	.226
Paulino, Ronny	c	Pirates	Pit	R	19	29	83	21	2	4	1	34	6	13	8	0	19	1	1	2	1	2	.33	0	.253	.319	.410
Paxton, Chris*	dh-c	Frederick	Bal	A+	23	58	169	42	8	0	6	68	26	28	34	1	54	5	1	1	0	0	.00	5	.249	.388	.402
Pecci, Jay#	ss	Visalia	Oak	A+	23	119	377	95	14	2	1	116	60	43	42	0	56	10	7	1	12	7	.63	9	.252	.342	.308
Peeples, Mike	of-3b	Dunedin	Tor	A+	23	132	541	156	34	6	20	262	100	68	49	1	80	7	5	5	20	11	.65	7	.288	.352	.484
Pelfrey, Brice	2b	Pirates	Pit	R	20	31	108	26	1	0	0	27	19	7	8	0	15	5	2	3	6	3	.67	3	.241	.315	.250
		Williamsprt	Pit	A-	20	14	50	6	0	1	0	8	1	2	1	0	12	3	0	0	1	0	1.00	1	.120	.185	.160
Pellerano, Cristian	of	Athletics	Oak	R	21	48	178	49	11	1	3	71	34	29	11	0	45	5	0	2	1	1	.50	3	.275	.332	.399
Pena, Carlos*	1b	Charlotte	Tex	A+	22	136	501	128	31	8	18	229	85	103	74	2	135	16	0	6	2	5	.29	7	.255	.365	.457
Pena, Jose	of	Red Sox	Bos	R	20	12	32	12	1	0	1	16	9	7	2	0	7	6	0	0	2	1	.67	0	.375	.500	.500
		Augusta	Bos	A	20	49	168	38	8	1	5	63	23	24	10	0	50	2	0	3	1	2	.33	2	.226	.273	.375
Pena, Jose	of	Charlotte	Tex	A+	23	64	187	43	9	3	2	64	39	24	17	0	32	1	2	1	8	7	.53	1	.230	.296	.342
Pena, Pelagio	c	Mariners	Sea	R	20	21	77	28	5	1	0	35	11	14	4	0	13	1	0	1	3	1	.75	1	.364	.398	.455
Pena, Rodolfo	c	Augusta	Bos	A	21	99	320	76	15	1	3	102	35	37	16	0	79	7	4	1	1	1	.50	8	.238	.288	.319
Pena, Wilton	c	Athletics	Oak	R	21	41	129	31	14	1	5	62	18	21	14	0	39	9	0	1	0	0	.00	3	.240	.353	.481
Pena, Wily	of-dh	Yankees	NYY	R	18	45	166	41	10	1	7	74	21	26	12	0	54	7	0	1	3	2	.60	2	.247	.323	.446
Penberthy, Aaron	c-dh	New Jersey	StL	A-	23	15	48	12	4	1	0	18	6	6	3	0	17	3	0	0	0	0	.00	2	.250	.333	.375
		Johnson Cy	StL	R+	23	1	2	0	0	0	0	0	0	0	0	0	0	0	0	0	0	0	.00	1	.000	.000	.000
Pene, Ryan*	of	Salem-Keizr	SF	A-	23	40	125	24	5	0	2	35	18	21	19	1	40	1	0	0	1	0	1.00	0	.192	.303	.280
Peralta, Marco	c	Mexico	—	R	—	5	21	4	1	0	0	5	1	1	0	0	6	0	0	0	0	0	.00	0	.190	.190	.238
Perea, Carlos	ss	Royals	KC	R	20	4	8	0	0	0	0	0	1	0	1	0	1	0	0	0	0	0	.00	0	.000	.111	.000
Perez, Antonio	ss-2b	Rockford	Cin	A	18	119	385	111	20	3	7	158	69	41	43	0	80	13	8	3	35	24	.59	3	.288	.376	.410
Perez, Deivi	ss	Hickory	Pit	A	19	25	83	17	4	0	2	27	13	9	14	0	26	0	0	0	2	0	1.00	0	.205	.320	.325
		Williamsprt	Pit	A-	19	48	148	28	7	0	3	44	20	9	18	1	35	1	2	0	2	0	1.00	5	.189	.281	.297
Perez, Jay#	c-dh	Martinsvlle	Hou	R+	20	43	139	38	9	0	2	53	25	36	24	0	47	7	0	2	17	4	.81	2	.273	.401	.381
Perez, Jersen	ss	St. Lucie	NYM	A+	24	128	468	120	15	7	7	170	60	45	27	0	117	8	9	3	7	5	.58	10	.256	.306	.363
Perez, Josue#	of	Vero Beach	LA	A+	22	62	201	56	14	1	2	78	24	22	21	0	29	2	1	2	14	11	.56	5	.279	.350	.388
		Clearwater	Phi	A+	22	23	93	23	2	0	0	25	15	6	7	0	17	1	0	2	6	1	.86	3	.247	.301	.269
Perez, Juan	of	Johnson Cy	StL	R+	19	46	171	40	11	1	1	56	31	11	18	0	41	5	5	0	13	7	.65	1	.234	.325	.327
Perez, Nestor	ss	St. Pete	TB	A+	23	111	364	96	8	1	0	106	33	23	10	0	53	2	14	1	4	5	.44	8	.264	.286	.291
Perez, Rafael*	of	White Sox	CWS	R	21	51	179	37	7	5	3	63	26	22	20	0	64	2	3	2	11	5	.69	1	.207	.291	.352
Perich, Joshua	of	Mets	NYM	R	20	47	158	43	5	1	0	50	21	22	20	0	37	4	1	1	6	2	.75	6	.272	.366	.316
Perini, Mike*	dh	Staten Ilnd	NYY	A-	22	43	97	18	4	1	2	30	11	13	6	1	40	0	0	2	1	0	1.00	0	.186	.229	.309
Perkins, Kevin	3b-of	Utica	Fla	A-	22	60	202	58	11	4	2	83	35	23	19	0	41	8	3	5	2	3	.40	4	.287	.363	.411
Pernalete, Marco#	2b-ss	San Jose	SF	A+	21	99	370	88	19	0	3	116	50	32	30	1	105	5	5	2	10	3	.77	2	.238	.302	.314
Pernell, Brandon	of	Rancho Cuca	SD	A+	23	133	529	148	30	7	21	255	96	84	50	1	156	8	5	6	33	14	.70	14	.280	.347	.482
Peters, Samone	of-dh	Clinton	Cin	A	21	83	290	64	13	1	15	124	32	46	17	0	131	3	0	2	0	2	.00	5	.221	.269	.428
		Billings	Cin	R+	21	29	111	25	3	0	9	55	13	23	5	0	57	1	0	2	0	0	.00	0	.225	.261	.495
Peters, Tony	of	Dunedin	Tor	A+	25	116	316	77	12	2	14	135	58	50	44	1	97	6	4	3	15	4	.79	3	.244	.344	.427
Phelps, Josh	dh	Dunedin	Tor	A+	22	110	406	133	27	4	20	228	72	88	28	0	104	8	2	4	6	3	.67	13	.328	.379	.562
Phillips, Andy	3b	Staten Ilnd	NYY	A-	23	64	233	75	11	7	7	121	35	48	37	1	40	3	0	3	3	3	.50	4	.322	.417	.519
Phillips, Brandon	ss	Expos	Mon	R	19	47	169	49	11	3	1	69	23	21	15	0	35	3	0	0	12	3	.80	6	.290	.358	.408
Phillips, Dan	of	Portland	Col	A-	21	71	280	80	19	4	10	137	38	53	14	1	72	6	0	3	8	2	.80	9	.286	.330	.489
Pichardo, Gilberto	of	Butte	Ana	R+	21	41	137	32	6	2	4	54	32	16	9	0	39	3	2	1	2	0	1.00	4	.234	.293	.394
Pichardo, Henry	2b	Burlington	Cle	R+	21	62	233	61	12	3	4	91	44	32	14	0	30	2	2	3	8	5	.62	8	.262	.306	.391
		Mahoning Vy	Cle	A-	21	2	5	2	1	0	0	3	0	1	0	0	1	0	0	0	0	0	.00	0	.400	.400	.600
Pickering, Kelvin	dh	Orioles	Bal	R	20	23	72	14	2	0	1	19	8	3	4	0	25	1	0	0	0	0	.00	3	.194	.247	.264
Piedra, Jorge*	of	San Berndno	LA	A+	21	8	30	9	2	0	0	11	6	3	3	0	3	0	1	2	1	0	1.00	0	.300	.343	.367
		Vero Beach	LA	A+	21	15	59	17	3	1	1	25	13	6	7	1	9	0	0	1	2	2	.50	0	.288	.358	.424
Piercy, Brad*	of-c	Cape Fear	Mon	A	23	90	323	75	12	2	6	109	40	23	17	0	111	2	3	0	17	11	.61	5	.232	.275	.337
Piercy, Mike*	of	Hickory	Pit	A	24	8	18	3	0	0	0	3	7	0	3	0	2	1	1	0	1	1	.50	0	.167	.318	.167
		Pirates	Pit	R	24	10	35	11	1	0	0	12	6	3	7	0	7	0	0	0	3	1	.75	1	.314	.429	.343
		Williamsprt	Pit	A-	24	8	26	5	0	0	1	8	3	5	6	0	7	0	0	0	0	3	.00	0	.192	.344	.308
Pierre, Juan*	of	Asheville	Col	A	22	140	585	187	28	5	1	228	93	55	38	2	37	8	11	6	66	19	.78	12	.320	.366	.390
Pimentel, Baez	3b	Johnson Cy	StL	R+	21	3	10	3	1	0	0	4	0	2	0	0	0	0	0	0	0	0	.00	1	.300	.300	.400
Pimentel, Francisco	3b	Cubs	ChC	R	19	29	83	24	4	3	1	37	13	8	10	0	27	3	1	0	3	0	1.00	2	.289	.385	.446
Pimentel, Franklin#	2b	Visalia	Oak	A+	21	3	2	1	0	0	0	1	0	1	0	0	0	0	0	1	0	1	.00	0	.500	.333	.500
		Athletics	Oak	R	21	54	174	48	6	2	8	82	40	40	38	1	36	1	1	2	6	4	.60	3	.276	.405	.471

1999 Batting — Single-A and Rookie Leagues

BATTING																					BASERUNNING				PERCENTAGES		
Player	Pos	Team	Org	Lg	A	G	AB	H	2B	3B	HR	TB	R	RBI	TBB	IBB	SO	HBP	SH	SF	SB	CS	SB%	GDP	Avg	OBP	SLG
Pina, Emmanuel	c	Cubs	ChC	R	20	18	51	11	1	0	0	12	3	3	4	0	11	1	0	1	2	2	.50	1	.216	.281	.235
Pinero, Juan#	of	Eugene	ChC	A-	22	10	34	8	1	1	0	11	5	6	4	0	4	3	0	0	5	1	.83	1	.235	.366	.324
		Lansing	ChC	A	22	27	82	24	5	0	1	32	19	8	13	0	14	4	1	1	1	2	.33	0	.293	.410	.390
Pines, Greg	1b	Mariners	Sea	R	21	31	97	29	7	2	3	49	14	17	8	0	15	1	2	1	0	0	.00	1	.299	.355	.505
Pinto, Rene	c	Greensboro	NYY	A	22	19	58	15	1	1	2	24	9	6	5	0	13	1	0	0	0	1	.00	2	.259	.328	.414
		Tampa	NYY	A+	22	22	70	16	5	2	1	28	9	6	3	0	19	1	1	1	0	0	.00	3	.229	.267	.400
Pittman, Thomas	1b	Cape Fear	Mon	A	20	131	505	143	26	3	22	241	74	97	25	0	146	11	0	4	12	17	.41	9	.283	.328	.477
Poe, Adam	of	Pulaski	Tex	R+	22	49	171	51	12	0	2	69	26	31	16	0	30	4	3	3	11	3	.79	1	.298	.366	.404
Pointer, Corey	of	Lynchburg	Pit	A+	24	108	327	59	18	1	15	124	55	44	44	0	147	14	2	2	13	12	.52	3	.180	.302	.379
Polidor, Wil#	3b-2b	Clearwater	Phi	A+	26	52	151	36	9	0	0	45	18	14	11	2	18	2	0	1	1	0	1.00	4	.238	.297	.298
		Piedmont	Phi	A	26	26	95	21	3	1	0	26	7	7	2	0	15	0	1	0	0	1	.00	1	.221	.237	.274
Pond, Ryan	2b	Cedar Rapds	Ana	A	25	44	167	41	12	0	4	65	18	21	11	1	34	2	3	1	2	1	.67	2	.246	.298	.389
Pond, Simon*	dh-1b	Jupiter	Mon	A+	23	127	434	111	25	1	10	168	47	77	48	3	83	14	1	11	4	8	.33	10	.256	.341	.387
Porter, Colin*	of	Michigan	Hou	A	24	127	453	132	28	9	18	232	91	68	53	2	123	7	3	8	23	13	.64	4	.291	.369	.512
Porter, Jamie	of	Sou Oregon	Oak	A-	24	44	129	31	5	1	2	44	30	16	11	0	32	3	2	1	9	4	.69	1	.240	.313	.341
Postell, Matt*	3b	Utica	Fla	A-	23	45	148	39	8	2	0	51	15	21	18	0	50	2	1	3	4	2	.67	5	.264	.345	.345
Poulsen, Chris	c	Jamestown	Atl	A-	24	37	123	27	8	0	2	41	10	14	2	0	22	3	0	1	2	2	.50	4	.220	.248	.333
Powers, Jeff*	ss	Columbus	Cle	A	24	76	233	62	10	0	2	78	34	30	24	2	24	4	3	4	2	3	.40	0	.266	.340	.335
Pratt, Scott*	2b	Kinston	Cle	A+	23	133	486	120	27	6	9	186	86	54	77	3	95	6	1	3	47	11	.81	6	.247	.355	.383
Pregnalato, Bob	of	Ogden	Mil	R+	22	42	130	43	7	1	3	61	34	14	18	0	19	7	3	1	14	4	.78	2	.331	.436	.469
Presichi, Cristian	3b	Mexico	—	R	—	52	190	61	8	6	4	93	29	23	16	0	37	1	3	3	4	1	.80	4	.321	.371	.489
Pressley, Josh*	1b	Chston-SC	TB	A	20	118	437	106	22	0	9	155	50	64	49	5	80	5	0	4	1	4	.20	11	.243	.323	.355
Price, Corey#	2b	Rockford	Cin	A	23	6	9	0	0	0	0	0	0	1	0	0	2	0	0	0	0	0	.00	0	.000	.000	.000
		Delmarva	Bal	A	23	22	82	20	4	0	0	24	8	9	8	0	24	0	1	1	0	0	.00	2	.244	.308	.293
Price, Duane	of	Billings	Cin	R+	24	10	29	6	0	0	0	6	6	7	6	0	5	0	1	2	2	1	.67	1	.207	.324	.207
		Clinton	Cin	A	24	37	96	16	1	0	0	17	8	5	9	1	30	1	3	2	4	2	.67	3	.167	.241	.177
Prieto, Jonathan*	2b	Hickory	Pit	A	20	61	244	74	9	1	1	88	42	21	22	0	55	2	3	1	10	7	.59	4	.303	.364	.361
Proctor, Jerry	dh	Yakima	LA	A-	22	10	36	7	2	0	0	9	4	3	5	0	15	1	0	0	0	0	.00	0	.194	.310	.250
Puccinelli, John	3b	Padres	SD	R	19	50	177	47	12	0	1	62	34	20	22	0	35	3	1	0	3	2	.60	3	.266	.356	.350
Pugh, Josh	c	Myrtle Bch	Atl	A+	22	41	115	19	2	0	0	21	4	12	10	0	32	1	1	2	0	0	.00	2	.165	.234	.183
Pujols, Rafael#	c	Modesto	Oak	A+	22	71	233	55	16	0	3	80	28	32	24	0	34	1	0	2	5	6	.45	4	.236	.308	.343
Punto, Nick#	ss	Clearwater	Phi	A+	22	106	400	122	18	6	1	155	65	48	67	3	53	3	3	5	16	7	.70	13	.305	.404	.388
Purkiss, Matt*	1b	Delmarva	Bal	A	24	107	366	77	15	0	11	125	44	46	57	0	124	6	0	1	0	0	.00	8	.210	.326	.342
Pursell, Mike*	1b	Columbus	Cle	A	24	18	69	15	4	1	0	21	9	6	6	0	11	0	0	1	1	0	1.00	3	.217	.276	.304
Quaccia, Luke*	1b	Potomac	StL	A+	25	125	429	106	26	2	13	175	46	80	42	0	112	14	2	6	4	5	.44	7	.247	.330	.408
Quero, Pedro	of-1b	Jupiter	Mon	A+	22	114	419	100	16	2	4	132	36	52	16	1	83	2	1	7	13	12	.52	12	.239	.266	.315
Quezada, Juan	c	Mexico	—	R	—	20	55	11	2	0	0	13	8	3	9	1	19	4	2	0	0	0	.00	3	.200	.353	.236
Quickstad, Barry*	of	Twins	Min	R	19	32	96	23	4	2	1	34	20	9	21	1	29	1	0	0	11	0	1.00	3	.240	.381	.354
Quinlan, Robb	3b	Boise	Ana	A-	23	73	295	95	20	1	9	144	51	77	35	2	52	4	0	1	5	3	.63	5	.322	.400	.488
Quinones, Marcus#	ss	Charlotte	Tex	A+	24	7	23	6	1	0	0	7	2	3	1	0	5	1	0	0	0	1	.00	0	.261	.320	.304
		Savannah	Tex	A	24	37	123	25	9	0	0	34	17	9	14	0	28	1	4	1	2	1	.67	4	.203	.288	.276
Quintana, Wilfredo	of	Mariners	Sea	R	22	16	58	22	8	0	2	36	10	18	2	0	11	1	0	1	2	2	.50	2	.379	.403	.621
		Lancaster	Sea	A+	22	10	37	11	1	1	3	23	7	8	2	0	14	1	0	0	1	0	1.00	1	.297	.350	.622
		Everett	Sea	A-	22	19	62	10	3	0	1	16	6	5	0	0	21	0	0	2	0	1	.00	2	.161	.156	.258
Quintero, Humberto	c	Bristol	CWS	R+	20	48	155	43	5	2	0	52	30	15	9	0	19	6	3	0	11	1	.92	8	.277	.341	.335
Quiroz, Guillermo	c	Medcine Hat	Tor	R+	18	63	208	46	7	0	9	80	25	28	18	0	55	4	2	0	0	2	.00	4	.221	.296	.385
Radcliff, Vic	of	Wilmington	KC	A+	23	114	393	104	22	8	7	163	62	56	28	1	69	18	3	6	13	3	.81	5	.265	.337	.415
Raines, Tim	of	Delmarva	Bal	A	20	117	415	103	24	8	2	149	80	49	71	1	130	3	3	4	49	16	.75	1	.248	.359	.359
Ralph, Brian*	of	Hickory	Pit	A	24	16	48	8	3	0	0	11	7	2	6	0	8	1	1	0	3	2	.60	0	.167	.273	.229
Ramirez, Anthony*	dh-3b	Martinsvlle	Hou	R+	19	22	64	22	7	0	4	41	13	20	9	0	11	1	0	1	1	2	.33	0	.344	.427	.641
Ramirez, Charlie	of	Chstn-WV	KC	A	21	28	70	14	0	0	0	14	5	4	7	1	16	0	1	1	1	2	.33	3	.200	.269	.200
		Spokane	KC	A-	21	54	179	47	7	3	2	66	34	15	14	0	30	0	2	1	8	3	.73	6	.263	.314	.369
Ramirez, Edgar	of	Hudson Val	TB	A-	20	34	120	23	6	1	2	37	14	6	10	0	46	1	2	0	2	1	.67	1	.192	.260	.308
Ramirez, Frankelis*	1b	Great Falls	LA	R+	21	74	281	82	9	3	3	106	39	42	22	3	34	3	4	5	7	4	.64	5	.292	.344	.377
Ramirez, Joel	ss	Lancaster	Sea	A+	26	106	376	90	17	7	2	127	55	42	29	0	64	13	4	5	10	8	.56	3	.239	.312	.338
Ramirez, Oscar	3b	Mariners	Sea	R	21	47	159	52	15	2	1	74	44	26	28	0	28	3	0	3	9	4	.69	2	.327	.430	.465
		Everett	Sea	A-	21	6	13	4	3	0	0	7	4	5	4	0	3	0	0	0	0	0	.00	0	.308	.471	.538
Ramos, Eddy#	of	Rangers	Tex	R	21	55	180	36	0	2	0	40	20	16	21	1	54	1	4	2	12	1	.92	2	.200	.284	.222
Ramos, Kelly#	c	St. Lucie	NYM	A+	23	24	80	15	3	1	2	26	6	11	8	1	16	0	4	3	0	0	.00	4	.188	.253	.325
		Capital Cty	NYM	A	23	82	262	67	14	0	10	111	31	34	9	0	52	10	2	1	4	2	.67	5	.256	.305	.424
Ramsey, Brad	c-dh	Daytona	ChC	A+	23	105	330	70	15	0	9	112	47	44	40	1	67	16	2	6	1	3	.25	17	.212	.321	.339
Randolph, Jaisen	of	Daytona	ChC	A+	21	130	511	139	16	5	2	171	70	37	43	1	86	8	4	0	25	26	.49	4	.272	.338	.335
Ransom, Troy	of	Salem-Keizr	SF	A-	21	26	50	7	1	2	0	12	6	6	5	0	19	1	3	1	1	2	.33	2	.140	.228	.240
Rasmussen, Wes	ss	Braves	Atl	R	19	36	122	27	5	1	1	37	16	15	19	0	40	2	1	1	2	2	.50	1	.221	.333	.303
Rauls, Ian*	of	Phillies	Phi	R	22	51	175	53	8	0	0	61	31	17	34	0	32	6	4	0	27	8	.77	3	.303	.433	.349
Ravelo, Manny	of	Williamsprt	Pit	A-	18	55	201	43	2	1	1	50	27	10	17	1	43	0	2	2	23	7	.77	2	.214	.273	.249
Raymundo, Gregg	3b	Spokane	KC	A-	23	67	254	82	16	1	11	133	44	44	32	4	37	4	2	3	1	1	.50	9	.323	.403	.524
Reding, Josh	ss	Jupiter	Mon	A+	23	121	415	109	10	2	2	129	54	31	22	0	73	1	12	6	30	9	.77	6	.263	.297	.311
Redman, Prentice	of	Kingsport	NYM	R+	20	58	200	59	14	1	6	93	40	29	24	0	42	2	3	2	16	11	.59	0	.295	.373	.465
Reed, Brian	of	Brevard Cty	Fla	A+	22	19	56	12	2	0	0	14	3	1	3	0	20	1	0	0	2	1	.67	2	.214	.267	.250
Reed, Keith	of	Bluefield	Bal	R+	21	4	16	3	0	0	0	3	2	0	1	0	3	0	0	0	0	1	.00	0	.188	.235	.188
		Delmarva	Bal	A	21	61	240	62	14	3	4	94	36	25	22	0	53	3	2	2	3	2	.60	4	.258	.326	.392
Reed, Matthew	ss	Twins	Min	R	19	27	65	12	1	0	0	13	8	7	4	0	10	1	2	1	1	1	.50	0	.185	.239	.200
Repko, Jason	ss	Great Falls	LA	R+	19	49	207	63	9	9	8	114	51	32	21	0	43	3	1	1	12	5	.71	1	.304	.375	.551
Requena, Ruben#	of	Mahoning Vy	Cle	A-	19	61	214	50	6	3	0	62	44	18	36	0	64	6	4	1	44	12	.79	0	.234	.358	.290
Restovich, Michael	of	Quad City	Min	A	21	131	493	154	30	6	19	253	91	107	74	4	100	13	0	5	7	9	.44	9	.312	.412	.513
Rewers, Nathan#	2b	Billings	Cin	R+	23	3	15	1	1	0	0	2	3	2	1	0	2	0	0	0	1	0	1.00	1	.067	.125	.133

1999 Batting — Single-A and Rookie Leagues

Player	Pos	Team	Org	Lg	A	G	AB	H	2B	3B	HR	TB	R	RBI	TBB	IBB	SO	HBP	SH	SF	SB	CS	SB%	GDP	Avg	OBP	SLG
BATTING																					**BASERUNNING**				**PERCENTAGES**		
Reyes, Ambiorix	ss	Batavia	Phi	A-	21	25	77	18	1	0	0	19	4	5	3	0	7	0	1	0	6	2	.75	1	.234	.263	.247
		Piedmont	Phi	A	21	78	257	63	7	3	0	76	30	15	11	0	23	6	3	0	14	5	.74	5	.245	.292	.296
Reyes, Christian#	3b	Athletics	Oak	R	22	49	187	53	11	8	1	83	39	39	26	1	54	1	1	1	3	1	.75	4	.283	.372	.444
Reyes, Dadny#	3b	Utica	Fla	A-	21	30	78	20	3	2	0	27	9	3	6	0	17	1	0	1	2	1	.67	4	.256	.314	.346
Reyes, Deurys*	of	Oneonta	Det	A-	20	12	38	13	3	1	2	24	8	9	5	0	12	0	0	1	3	0	1.00	0	.342	.409	.632
		W Michigan	Det	A	20	46	134	33	11	3	5	65	23	27	16	3	53	2	2	0	8	1	.89	1	.246	.336	.485
Reyes, Eduardo	3b	Helena	Mil	R+	20	66	223	65	12	3	6	101	51	33	19	0	38	8	1	2	13	4	.76	3	.291	.365	.453
Reyes, Guillermo#	2b	White Sox	CWS	R	18	54	200	50	5	3	0	61	27	15	20	0	25	4	0	3	18	10	.64	1	.250	.326	.305
Reyes, Ivan	ss	Yankees	NYY	R	19	45	122	16	5	1	0	23	15	12	25	0	55	1	1	1	1	4	.20	2	.131	.282	.189
Reyes, Jose	c	Lynchburg	Pit	A+	27	30	65	10	4	0	1	17	7	4	11	0	28	1	0	0	1	0	1.00	1	.154	.286	.262
		Hickory	Pit	A	27	23	80	22	4	1	5	43	11	15	4	0	18	4	0	0	3	1	.75	3	.275	.341	.538
Reyes, Julio*	of	White Sox	CWS	R	20	33	127	39	8	3	2	59	23	20	7	0	16	3	0	0	1	2	.33	1	.307	.358	.465
Reyes, Manuel	c	Mets	NYM	R	20	11	22	4	0	0	0	4	3	3	1	0	5	0	0	0	0	0	.00	2	.182	.217	.182
Reyes, Rene#	dh-1b	Rockies	Col	R	22	22	97	35	4	4	1	50	21	20	4	0	14	2	0	0	6	1	.86	2	.361	.398	.515
		Asheville	Col	A	22	40	160	56	6	1	3	73	26	19	6	0	22	1	0	0	1	0	1.00	1	.350	.377	.456
Reynolds, Dusty#	c	Tigers	Det	R	23	19	54	13	2	1	0	17	5	5	10	0	6	0	1	1	1	2	.33	0	.241	.354	.315
Reynoso, Ismael	ss	San Jose	SF	A+	22	79	253	63	12	1	3	86	26	26	12	0	48	5	6	1	12	3	.80	7	.249	.295	.340
Rhodes, Dusty*	of	Staten Ilnd	NYY	A-	24	45	169	42	11	0	1	56	28	13	33	0	42	4	2	2	3	5	.38	2	.249	.380	.331
		Greensboro	NYY	A	24	67	234	69	10	3	4	97	43	44	43	2	57	5	2	5	7	5	.58	3	.295	.408	.415
Rhodes, Nick	c	St. Pete	TB	A+	21	1	2	1	0	0	1	4	2	1	1	0	0	0	0	0	0	0	.00	0	.500	.667	2.000
		Chston-SC	TB	A	21	19	46	11	0	2	0	15	6	0	5	0	11	1	0	0	0	0	.00	2	.239	.327	.326
Ribaudo, Mike	c	Capital Cty	NYM	A	25	58	199	49	12	0	7	82	22	33	4	0	53	0	3	1	0	1	.00	5	.246	.260	.412
Rich, Bill	of	W Michigan	Det	A	23	108	394	99	20	1	9	148	64	50	47	1	87	5	1	2	6	4	.60	8	.251	.337	.376
Richards, Rowan	of	Rangers	Tex	R	26	10	30	8	1	0	1	12	4	8	2	0	8	3	0	1	0	0	.00	0	.267	.361	.400
		Charlotte	Tex	A+	26	9	34	9	1	0	1	13	5	5	0	0	8	0	0	1	0	1	.00	0	.265	.257	.382
Richardson, Corey	of	Oneonta	Det	A-	23	41	125	33	2	1	0	37	25	9	25	1	34	4	1	1	19	4	.83	1	.264	.400	.296
Richardson, Juan	3b	Piedmont	Phi	A	19	4	12	2	1	0	0	3	0	2	1	0	5	0	1	0	0	0	.00	1	.167	.231	.250
		Phillies	Phi	R	19	46	164	37	14	0	5	66	27	23	11	1	46	5	1	3	7	5	.58	5	.226	.290	.402
		Batavia	Phi	A-	19	7	24	3	0	0	1	6	1	2	2	0	8	1	0	0	0	1	.00	0	.125	.222	.250
Richardson, Miguel	of	Mariners	Sea	R	19	37	128	35	3	4	7	67	26	26	13	0	49	4	0	0	1	1	.50	1	.273	.359	.523
Rickon, Jim	c	Burlington	Cle	R+	24	31	96	29	5	0	4	46	16	17	19	0	25	1	0	0	2	1	.67	2	.302	.422	.479
		Mahoning Vy	Cle	A-	24	8	25	5	0	0	1	8	3	4	2	0	7	0	1	0	0	0	.00	2	.200	.259	.320
Rico, Diego*	of	Daytona	ChC	A+	24	100	344	97	22	5	4	141	50	42	26	2	66	6	3	4	10	4	.71	6	.282	.339	.410
Riek, Clifford	1b-3b	Pirates	Pit	R	19	24	84	19	2	0	1	24	10	6	6	1	22	0	0	0	1	0	1.00	1	.226	.278	.286
Riepe, Andrew	c	Lowell	Bos	A-	23	31	100	31	12	0	1	46	16	15	6	0	14	2	3	2	0	0	.00	3	.310	.355	.460
Riggins, Auntwan#	1b	St.Cathrnes	Tor	A-	24	44	105	25	3	1	0	30	16	11	12	0	34	5	0	0	12	2	.86	0	.238	.344	.286
Riggs, Eric#	ss	San Berndno	LA	A+	23	130	523	144	18	10	16	230	105	69	70	2	92	6	7	5	27	11	.71	6	.275	.364	.440
Rigsby, Randy*	of	Brevard Cty	Fla	A+	23	106	362	95	16	6	2	129	41	37	34	2	76	6	3	3	6	3	.67	6	.262	.333	.356
Rincon, Carlos	of	Martinsvlle	Hou	R+	20	55	180	43	11	3	3	69	29	21	16	0	59	3	0	2	24	6	.80	2	.239	.308	.383
Rinne, James	of	High Desert	Ari	A+	23	104	268	75	10	0	11	118	45	39	27	0	66	1	3	3	5	5	.50	9	.280	.344	.440
Riordan, Matt	of-dh	Orioles	Bal	R	22	8	24	6	1	0	0	7	4	3	2	0	2	0	0	1	2	1	.67	0	.250	.296	.292
		Bluefield	Bal	R+	22	5	21	7	1	1	1	13	2	6	3	0	3	0	0	0	1	1	.50	0	.333	.417	.619
		Delmarva	Bal	A	22	54	204	59	12	4	3	88	22	38	24	2	46	5	1	3	6	5	.55	0	.289	.373	.431
Rios, Alexis	of	Medcine Hat	Tor	R+	19	67	234	63	7	3	0	76	35	13	17	0	31	1	0	0	8	4	.67	6	.269	.321	.325
Rios, Brian	3b	Lakeland	Det	A+	25	119	430	121	27	7	6	180	60	44	24	1	47	5	0	6	7	3	.70	13	.281	.323	.419
Rios, Fernando	of	Rockford	Cin	A	21	24	81	23	7	0	0	30	9	8	11	3	9	1	0	1	2	3	.40	2	.284	.372	.370
		Clinton	Cin	A	21	75	275	76	16	0	2	98	36	42	21	0	34	1	2	3	3	2	.60	2	.276	.327	.356
Risinger, Ben	3b	Hickory	Pit	A	22	124	449	112	20	3	4	150	56	44	39	0	80	12	9	3	2	4	.33	12	.249	.324	.334
Rivas, Justo	of	Danville	Atl	R+	20	60	215	67	11	6	2	96	35	42	21	0	44	4	1	2	10	5	.67	3	.312	.380	.447
Rivera, Carlos*	1b	Hickory	Pit	A	22	119	457	147	30	1	13	218	63	86	15	2	45	11	0	4	2	1	.67	13	.322	.355	.477
Rivera, Erick	of	Phillies	Phi	R	19	31	100	15	4	0	2	25	8	10	4	0	32	1	0	2	0	2	.00	3	.150	.187	.250
Rivera, Francisco*	c	Billings	Cin	R+	20	31	112	24	1	0	2	31	11	15	4	0	14	2	1	2	2	0	1.00	5	.214	.250	.277
		Clinton	Cin	A	20	15	50	16	6	1	0	24	7	6	4	0	10	0	0	0	0	0	.00	1	.320	.370	.480
Rivera, Juan	of	Yankees	NYY	R	21	5	18	6	0	0	1	9	7	4	4	0	1	0	0	0	0	0	.00	1	.333	.455	.500
		Tampa	NYY	A+	21	109	426	112	20	2	14	178	50	77	26	3	67	5	0	8	5	4	.56	13	.263	.308	.418
Rivera, Luis	c	Vermont	Mon	A-	22	31	97	22	6	1	1	33	14	12	14	1	28	1	0	1	0	2	.00	3	.227	.327	.340
Rizzo, Jeff*	3b	Idaho Falls	SD	R+	22	29	97	20	3	2	2	33	19	19	21	0	28	5	1	7	3	0	1.00	0	.206	.354	.340
Roach, Jason	3b	St. Lucie	NYM	A+	24	115	409	88	21	0	15	154	51	62	30	0	122	9	3	6	6	0	1.00	11	.215	.280	.377
Roberts, Brian#	ss	Delmarva	Bal	A	22	47	167	40	12	1	0	54	22	21	27	0	42	1	5	1	17	5	.77	0	.240	.347	.323
Robinson, Bo	3b	Wisconsin	Sea	A	24	138	499	164	50	3	13	259	101	102	108	4	75	4	0	8	4	1	.80	18	.329	.446	.519
Robinson, Coby	of	Cubs	ChC	R	21	30	80	15	1	2	2	26	12	9	11	0	25	6	0	0	0	1	.00	4	.188	.330	.325
Robles, Kevin	1b	Everett	Sea	A-	22	62	214	56	12	0	5	83	27	32	16	0	44	5	0	5	0	0	.00	5	.262	.321	.388
Rodeheaver, Roger	1b	Phillies	Phi	R	23	40	123	29	7	1	1	41	14	14	16	1	36	6	0	1	4	1	.80	1	.236	.349	.333
Rodgers, Mackeel#	ss	Royals	KC	R	19	31	105	21	3	0	1	27	10	14	4	0	30	2	2	0	3	2	.60	2	.200	.243	.257
Rodriguez, Carlos	of	Augusta	Bos	A	23	33	119	23	6	1	3	40	14	8	8	0	41	3	1	0	1	2	.33	4	.193	.262	.336
		Lowell	Bos	A-	23	60	228	57	13	5	12	116	37	46	13	0	66	2	0	0	17	3	.85	5	.250	.296	.509
Rodriguez, Erick	1b-c	Mexico	—	R	—	39	127	36	0	0	0	36	17	10	9	1	13	0	5	0	2	1	.67	3	.283	.331	.283
Rodriguez, Felix	c	Staten Ilnd	NYY	A-	22	1	2	0	0	0	0	0	0	0	0	0	1	0	0	0	0	0	.00	0	.000	.000	.000
Rodriguez, Guill.	c	Bakersfield	SF	A+	22	41	93	27	5	0	1	35	10	11	3	0	18	4	3	2	4	0	1.00	2	.290	.333	.376
		Salem-Keizr	SF	A-	22	33	114	29	5	0	6	52	16	34	9	1	28	3	0	0	1	3	.25	2	.254	.325	.456
Rodriguez, Jeff	c	Jamestown	Atl	A-	23	48	174	50	10	0	0	60	23	14	11	0	27	5	1	0	3	0	1.00	2	.287	.347	.345
		Myrtle Bch	Atl	A+	23	1	1	0	0	0	0	0	0	0	0	0	1	0	0	0	0	0	.00	0	.000	.000	.000
Rodriguez, John*	of	Yankees	NYY	R	22	3	7	2	0	1	0	4	1	1	3	0	0	0	0	0	0	0	.00	0	.286	.500	.571
		Tampa	NYY	A+	22	71	269	82	14	3	8	126	37	43	41	7	52	3	1	3	2	5	.29	5	.305	.399	.468
Rodriguez, Juan#	1b-of	Lk Elsinore	Ana	A+	25	86	315	95	12	6	6	137	54	50	32	0	70	2	4	1	7	5	.58	5	.302	.369	.435
Rodriguez, Junior	ss	Greensboro	NYY	A	22	69	191	36	3	3	5	60	28	25	37	0	75	4	4	1	1	2	.33	2	.188	.330	.314
Rodriguez, Luis#	2b	Quad City	Min	A	20	119	434	117	20	0	3	146	63	50	53	0	49	4	13	9	8	4	.67	10	.270	.348	.336

1999 Batting — Single-A and Rookie Leagues

BATTING																					BASERUNNING				PERCENTAGES		
Player	Pos	Team	Org	Lg	A	G	AB	H	2B	3B	HR	TB	R	RBI	TBB	IBB	SO	HBP	SH	SF	SB	CS	SB%	GDP	Avg	OBP	SLG
Rodriguez, Mike	3b	Dunedin	Tor	A+	25	80	260	73	17	1	4	104	36	30	17	0	40	2	3	0	3	2	.60	9	.281	.330	.400
Rodriguez, Ronny	2b-ss	Sarasota	Bos	A+	19	4	12	3	1	0	0	4	4	0	0	0	2	0	1	0	0	0	.00	1	.250	.250	.333
		Red Sox	Bos	R	19	54	170	42	5	1	1	52	19	13	14	0	32	3	1	1	7	2	.78	5	.247	.314	.306
Rodriguez, Serafin	of	Billings	Cin	R+	21	33	150	44	13	1	0	59	30	13	2	0	23	1	3	1	2	0	1.00	2	.293	.305	.393
		Clinton	Cin	A	21	28	115	29	4	2	1	40	10	6	4	0	17	1	1	2	6	0	1.00	3	.252	.279	.348
Rodriguez, Steve	1b	Tigers	Det	R	22	50	178	49	14	0	4	75	18	29	11	0	50	0	0	2	2	2	.50	6	.275	.314	.421
Roehler, Trent	c	White Sox	CWS	R	23	9	15	1	1	0	0	2	1	0	1	0	6	0	0	0	0	0	.00	0	.067	.125	.133
Rogers, Ed	ss	Orioles	Bal	R	18	53	177	51	5	1	1	61	34	19	23	0	22	4	4	2	20	3	.87	2	.288	.379	.345
Rogowski, Casey*	1b	White Sox	CWS	R	19	52	160	46	7	2	0	57	23	27	26	1	34	1	1	3	2	1	.67	2	.288	.384	.356
Rogue, Francisco	c	Stockton	Mil	A+	24	8	15	5	1	0	0	6	2	3	1	0	0	0	1	0	0	1	.00	0	.333	.375	.400
Rohena, Omar	1b	Cubs	ChC	R	19	20	60	15	2	0	1	20	11	5	4	0	21	1	0	0	0	0	.00	1	.250	.308	.333
Rojas, Alex	2b	Batavia	Phi	A-	22	45	176	50	6	3	0	62	38	16	15	0	37	3	2	0	39	7	.85	4	.284	.351	.352
Rojas, Clara	2b	Helena	Mil	R+	21	43	151	42	4	1	3	57	26	20	14	0	21	1	2	1	7	1	.88	4	.278	.341	.377
Rojas, Mo	of	Chstn-WV	KC	A	23	18	33	3	1	0	0	4	4	3	3	0	12	1	0	0	1	2	.33	1	.091	.189	.121
Rollins, Antwon	of	Savannah	Tex	A	20	8	33	8	0	0	0	8	7	1	4	0	14	0	1	0	3	0	1.00	0	.242	.324	.242
		Rangers	Tex	R	20	1	4	1	1	0	0	2	1	2	0	0	0	0	0	0	0	0	.00	0	.250	.250	.500
Rolls, Damian	3b	Vero Beach	LA	A+	22	127	474	141	20	2	9	198	68	54	38	2	66	14	4	5	24	13	.65	8	.297	.361	.418
Roman, Junior#	ss	Bristol	CWS	R+	19	44	131	34	8	0	0	42	21	12	16	0	22	1	2	0	15	2	.88	1	.260	.345	.321
Romano, Jason	2b	Charlotte	Tex	A+	21	120	459	143	27	14	13	237	84	71	39	2	72	13	4	7	34	16	.68	4	.312	.376	.516
Romano, Jimmie	c	Savannah	Tex	A	23	44	134	27	2	0	2	35	13	14	5	0	26	0	1	0	1	0	1.00	-2	.201	.230	.261
Rombley, Danny	of	Expos	Mon	R	20	45	134	33	4	1	0	39	20	15	12	0	29	1	0	2	8	4	.67	4	.246	.309	.291
Romero, Gabe	of	Braves	Atl	R	20	13	35	7	1	0	0	8	4	2	2	0	12	0	1	0	0	0	.00	0	.200	.243	.229
Romero, Nicholas	ss	Padres	SD	R	20	45	181	53	4	3	3	72	31	23	16	1	59	2	1	1	16	4	.80	2	.293	.355	.398
Roneberg, Brett*	of	Kane County	Fla	A	21	132	511	147	32	4	8	211	88	68	79	4	82	4	0	5	3	2	.60	11	.288	.384	.413
Rooi, Vince	3b	Expos	Mon	R	18	36	111	21	4	0	0	25	17	10	22	0	24	2	0	2	3	2	.60	4	.189	.328	.225
Roper, Doug	ss	Medcine Hat	Tor	R+	22	45	137	34	7	2	0	45	20	10	20	0	25	0	2	0	8	2	.80	0	.248	.344	.328
Rosa, Ivan*	of	Athletics	Oak	R	21	32	72	14	4	0	2	24	18	11	11	0	30	1	0	1	0	2	.00	0	.194	.306	.333
Rosado, Omar	1b-2b	Expos	Mon	R	19	41	140	33	7	0	0	40	12	22	9	0	10	3	0	3	4	1	.80	3	.236	.290	.286
Rosamond, Mike	of	Auburn	Hou	A-	22	61	230	61	9	4	6	96	34	24	23	0	63	3	0	1	22	6	.79	5	.265	.339	.417
		Michigan	Hou	A	22	4	10	1	0	0	0	1	0	2	2	0	3	0	0	1	0	1	.00	0	.100	.231	.100
Rosario, Carlos#	2b	Visalia	Oak	A+	20	37	123	29	5	1	0	36	27	16	21	0	29	2	5	1	11	6	.65	1	.236	.354	.293
		Sou Oregon	Oak	A-	20	63	260	59	9	5	2	84	51	27	44	0	56	2	4	3	31	13	.70	2	.227	.340	.323
Rosario, Melvin*	of	Portland	Col	A-	21	50	185	45	5	3	0	56	29	8	15	0	46	0	1	0	12	2	.86	3	.243	.300	.303
Rosario, Omar*	of	Modesto	Oak	A+	22	116	419	125	23	6	5	175	82	57	70	1	94	6	4	4	19	12	.61	4	.298	.403	.418
Rosario, Vicente	of	Mets	NYM	R	22	3	5	1	0	0	0	1	0	0	0	0	2	0	0	0	0	0	.00	0	.200	.200	.200
Ross, Cody	of	Tigers	Det	R	19	42	142	31	8	3	4	57	19	18	16	0	28	2	2	1	3	1	.75	3	.218	.304	.401
Ross, David	c	Vero Beach	LA	A+	23	114	375	85	19	1	7	127	47	39	46	1	111	7	1	6	5	10	.33	10	.227	.318	.339
Ross, Donovan*	3b	Royals	KC	R	22	31	91	23	10	0	0	33	12	19	25	0	34	1	2	3	1	1	.50	1	.253	.408	.363
		Chstn-WV	KC	A	22	6	17	3	1	0	0	4	1	0	4	0	6	1	1	0	0	0	.00	1	.176	.364	.235
Ross, Jason	of	Myrtle Bch	Atl	A+	26	133	482	129	23	13	12	214	80	64	43	2	136	8	1	2	31	5	.86	11	.268	.336	.444
Ross, Justin*	of	Cedar Rapds	Ana	A	23	51	184	53	14	0	3	76	43	23	53	2	30	1	0	0	10	3	.77	5	.288	.450	.413
		Lk Elsinore	Ana	A+	23	22	66	17	3	1	0	22	10	5	16	0	16	0	0	2	2	1	.67	2	.258	.393	.333
Rowan, Chris	ss	Stockton	Mil	A+	21	121	431	102	25	4	11	168	53	55	30	1	142	9	5	4	9	5	.64	6	.237	.297	.390
Rowand, Aaron	of	Winston-Sal	CWS	A+	22	133	512	143	37	3	24	258	96	88	33	2	94	13	2	5	15	10	.60	13	.279	.336	.504
Rowden, Monte	c	Cubs	ChC	R	23	15	37	7	0	1	1	12	4	7	2	0	8	3	0	0	0	0	.00	2	.189	.286	.324
Rozich, John	c	Yakima	LA	A-	23	40	134	31	5	2	2	46	20	16	23	0	41	0	2	0	1	3	.25	2	.231	.344	.343
Ruan, Wilken	of	Cape Fear	Mon	A	20	112	397	89	16	4	1	116	43	47	18	0	79	6	7	0	29	17	.63	5	.224	.268	.292
Ruiz, Ramon	3b	Yakima	LA	A-	24	46	167	49	10	1	8	85	34	32	24	3	33	2	1	0	6	2	.75	3	.293	.389	.509
Ruiz, Randy	dh-1b	Reds	Cin	R	22	33	102	29	8	0	3	46	12	9	12	0	33	4	0	1	5	2	.71	5	.284	.378	.451
		Clinton	Cin	A	22	2	8	5	2	0	0	7	3	2	1	0	0	0	0	1	0	0	.00	1	.625	.600	.875
Ruiz, Willy	2b	Spokane	KC	A-	21	6	11	3	1	0	0	4	3	0	1	0	3	0	0	0	2	1	.67	0	.273	.333	.364
		Chstn-WV	KC	A	21	57	191	58	6	1	0	66	31	19	34	0	44	0	4	0	24	14	.63	1	.304	.409	.346
Rumfield, Brock	3b	Delmarva	Bal	A	24	119	421	96	13	1	4	123	60	56	47	1	101	7	7	3	3	0	1.00	13	.228	.314	.292
Rummel, Jason	2b	Bristol	CWS	R+	23	56	191	51	10	1	8	87	39	36	48	1	32	5	1	3	11	2	.85	3	.267	.421	.455
Runnells, T.J.	2b	W Michigan	Det	A	22	88	288	66	10	1	0	78	35	32	29	0	42	1	5	6	5	4	.56	15	.229	.296	.271
Rupert, Bryan	c	Potomac	StL	A+	25	40	121	23	7	1	2	38	11	16	9	0	42	1	1	1	0	0	.00	3	.190	.250	.314
Ryan, Jeff	of	Eugene	ChC	A-	23	45	149	41	6	5	2	63	26	16	17	0	39	0	2	2	9	1	.90	4	.275	.345	.423
Ryan, Kelvin	of	Chston-SC	TB	A	21	128	478	113	20	3	12	175	63	66	30	0	107	7	4	5	12	4	.75	10	.236	.288	.366
Ryan, Mike*	2b	Fort Myers	Min	A+	22	131	507	139	26	5	8	199	85	71	63	2	60	5	4	6	3	4	.43	11	.274	.356	.393
Ryden, Karl	dh	Auburn	Hou	A-	23	31	117	39	8	0	3	56	24	15	19	0	19	4	0	2	10	4	.71	1	.333	.437	.479
Saba, Cesar#	ss	Lowell	Bos	A-	18	69	284	78	16	3	2	106	38	30	28	0	49	4	2	0	1	3	.25	9	.275	.348	.373
St. Pierre, Maxim	c	Oneonta	Det	A-	20	51	175	44	7	0	1	54	12	22	11	0	29	3	0	1	9	0	1.00	2	.251	.305	.309
Salargo, Steve	of	Bluefield	Bal	R+	23	50	170	52	12	1	5	81	46	45	37	0	28	1	0	4	8	2	.80	2	.306	.425	.476
		Frederick	Bal	A+	23	3	10	1	0	0	0	1	0	0	0	0	5	0	0	0	0	0	.00	1	.100	.100	.100
Salas, Jose#	c-dh	Braves	Atl	R	18	42	140	38	7	1	1	50	19	16	14	0	27	1	0	0	2	1	.67	1	.271	.342	.357
Salas, Juan	2b	Princeton	TB	R+	18	53	193	50	9	0	2	65	19	15	13	0	50	3	1	1	1	6	.14	1	.259	.314	.337
Salazar, Erick	of	Martinsvlle	Hou	R+	20	17	41	8	0	0	0	8	6	0	3	0	15	5	0	0	3	0	1.00	1	.195	.327	.195
Salazar, Jeremy	c	Piedmont	Phi	A	24	98	345	87	17	0	10	134	37	36	27	0	90	7	1	4	1	0	1.00	9	.252	.316	.388
		Clearwater	Phi	A+	24	2	10	3	1	0	0	4	1	1	0	0	2	0	0	0	0	0	.00	0	.300	.300	.400
Salazar, Oscar	dh	Modesto	Oak	A+	22	130	525	155	26	18	18	271	100	105	39	1	106	1	0	9	14	6	.70	10	.295	.340	.516
Salazar, Ruben	2b	Elizabethtn	Min	R+	22	64	262	105	24	2	14	175	66	65	18	2	13	5	1	2	11	4	.73	8	.401	[illegible]	.668
Salinas, Trey	dh	St. Pete	TB	A+	25	10	32	8	6	0	0	14	5	2	0	0	6	0	0	0	0	0	.00	1	.250	.250	.438
Sampson, Chris	ss	Auburn	Hou	A-	22	51	159	38	7	3	1	54	23	19	22	1	49	1	1	1	21	5	.81	2	.239	.333	.340
Sampson, Jacob	of	Great Falls	LA	R+	21	37	102	27	6	1	2	41	17	17	12	0	24	3	1	0	7	3	.70	1	.265	.359	.402
Samuel, Tomas	c	Salem	Col	A+	20	1	0	0	0	0	0	0	0	0	0	0	0	0	0	0	0	0	.00	0	.000	.000	.000
		Rockies	Col	R	20	42	170	49	18	1	2	75	30	35	11	0	48	8	0	3	6	1	.86	2	.288	.354	.441
Sanchez, Jose	ss	Mexico	—	R	—	39	136	33	2	0	0	35	20	9	12	0	27	0	4	3	6	2	.75	3	.243	.298	.257
Sanchez, Marcos#	c	Rockford	Cin	A	25	20	57	14	2	2	1	23	6	7	3	0	23	0	0	1	4	1	.80	1	.246	.279	.404

1999 Batting — Single-A and Rookie Leagues

						BATTING															BASERUNNING				PERCENTAGES		
Player	Pos	Team	Org	Lg	A	G	AB	H	2B	3B	HR	TB	R	RBI	TBB	IBB	SO	HBP	SH	SF	SB	CS	SB%	GDP	Avg	OBP	SLG
Sanchez, Tino#	c	Portland	Col	A-	21	31	101	17	3	1	1	25	10	9	9	0	11	1	2	1	0	0	.00	2	.168	.241	.248
Sanchez, Well.	ss	Beloit	Mil	A	23	71	261	68	14	3	0	88	35	23	25	0	58	4	4	0	9	3	.75	5	.261	.334	.337
Sandberg, Eric*	1b	Elizabethtn	Min	R+	20	67	255	78	16	2	15	143	60	62	45	2	51	2	1	4	3	2	.60	9	.306	.408	.561
Sandberg, Jared	3b	St. Pete	TB	A+	22	136	504	139	24	1	22	231	73	96	51	0	133	9	1	5	8	2	.80	12	.276	.350	.458
Sandoval, Danny#	ss	Burlington	CWS	A	21	76	255	58	5	1	3	74	34	37	17	0	39	0	6	2	8	5	.62	7	.227	.274	.290
Sandoval, Michael	3b	Twins	Min	R	18	55	194	62	13	3	0	81	30	34	15	3	21	2	0	3	5	7	.42	1	.320	.369	.418
Sandusky, Scott	c	Jupiter	Mon	A+	24	108	354	90	9	1	1	104	31	22	20	0	72	8	7	0	4	5	.44	6	.254	.309	.294
Santamarina, Juan*	3b	Burlington	CWS	A	20	29	95	17	2	0	1	22	12	10	14	0	15	0	0	0	5	0	1.00	0	.179	.284	.232
		Bristol	CWS	R+	20	60	213	54	10	1	5	81	36	22	16	1	41	0	1	1	5	5	.50	5	.254	.304	.380
Santana, Em.*	c	Royals	KC	R	19	26	83	13	3	0	0	16	8	14	19	0	18	0	0	1	1	1	.50	2	.157	.311	.193
Santana, Gamalier*	2b	Twins	Min	R	19	20	44	15	1	1	0	18	7	6	8	0	4	0	1	0	3	0	1.00	1	.341	.442	.409
Santana, Osmany*	of	Columbus	Cle	A	23	38	133	43	6	0	0	49	23	17	10	1	21	1	1	1	15	6	.71	0	.323	.372	.368
		Kinston	Cle	A+	23	43	145	35	8	0	3	52	16	20	8	0	26	1	1	0	7	0	1.00	2	.241	.286	.359
Santana, Pedro	of	Staten Ilnd	NYY	A-	21	67	237	76	18	1	9	123	35	41	9	2	57	0	1	0	5	4	.56	6	.321	.346	.519
Santiago, Daniel#	c	Reds	Cin	R	21	24	65	7	0	0	0	7	7	2	9	1	20	3	1	1	2	1	.67	1	.108	.244	.108
		Rockford	Cin	A	21	1	2	0	0	0	0	0	0	0	0	0	2	0	0	0	0	0	.00	0	.000	.000	.000
Santiago, Ramon#	ss	Tigers	Det	R	18	35	134	43	9	2	0	56	25	11	9	0	17	1	4	3	20	7	.74	3	.321	.361	.418
		Oneonta	Det	A-	18	12	50	17	1	2	1	25	9	8	2	0	12	1	1	0	5	0	1.00	0	.340	.377	.500
Santillan, Manuel	c	Martinsvlle	Hou	R+	20	21	72	13	3	1	2	24	13	9	4	0	21	0	1	0	2	2	.50	2	.181	.224	.333
Santini, Travis	of	Burlington	Cle	R+	19	44	169	48	6	2	4	70	17	29	10	1	45	1	1	1	0	1	.00	5	.284	.326	.414
Santonocito, Justin*	2b	Reds	Cin	R	23	3	10	1	0	0	0	1	1	0	0	0	1	0	0	0	0	0	.00	0	.100	.100	.100
		Clinton	Cin	A	23	26	61	11	2	0	1	16	5	5	5	0	12	0	1	0	0	0	.00	1	.180	.242	.262
Santora, Jack#	2b	Missoula	Ari	R+	23	51	195	51	9	1	1	65	46	31	34	0	33	2	6	2	36	7	.84	3	.262	.373	.333
Santoro, Patrick	2b	Red Sox	Bos	R	21	8	23	4	1	0	1	8	2	3	2	0	6	0	0	0	0	1	.00	0	.174	.240	.348
Santos, Angel#	2b	Augusta	Bos	A	20	130	466	126	30	2	15	205	83	55	62	4	88	5	2	3	25	10	.71	12	.270	.360	.440
Santos, Chad*	1b	Royals	KC	R	19	48	177	48	9	0	4	69	20	35	12	0	54	1	1	1	1	0	1.00	4	.271	.319	.390
Santos, Jose	3b	Kane County	Fla	A	22	128	459	124	30	5	19	221	93	105	83	2	130	17	0	5	18	4	.82	6	.270	.397	.481
Santos, Jose	3b	Boise	Ana	A-	23	1	1	0	0	0	0	0	0	0	0	0	0	0	0	0	0	0	.00	0	.000	.000	.000
Santos, Juan#	c	St.Cathrnes	Tor	A-	22	43	128	22	6	0	1	31	16	8	20	0	38	3	1	0	1	1	.50	1	.172	.298	.242
Santos, Luis	ss-2b	Missoula	Ari	R+	21	43	123	30	3	0	0	33	19	15	26	0	24	0	3	1	5	2	.71	4	.244	.373	.268
Sapp, Damian	1b	Sarasota	Bos	A+	24	86	289	57	11	1	13	109	38	48	44	0	102	12	0	2	0	0	.00	8	.197	.326	.377
Sarabia, Eliot	ss	Williamsprt	Pit	A-	24	34	100	20	1	1	0	23	12	10	14	0	12	4	1	0	7	1	.88	2	.200	.322	.230
Sassanella, Jer.#	1b	W Michigan	Det	A	21	14	41	3	1	0	0	4	2	6	1	0	18	0	0	0	0	0	.00	1	.073	.095	.098
		Oneonta	Det	A-	21	54	170	46	7	0	0	53	16	13	13	0	57	2	0	2	1	0	1.00	0	.271	.326	.312
Scales, Bobby#	2b	Idaho Falls	SD	R+	22	44	169	49	14	6	1	78	47	30	29	0	31	2	2	1	7	2	.78	6	.290	.398	.462
Scanlon, Mike*	3b	Elizabethtn	Min	R+	22	57	240	85	16	5	6	129	54	48	36	0	45	6	1	1	8	0	1.00	5	.354	.449	.538
		Quad City	Min	A	22	16	53	10	2	1	1	17	8	5	2	0	8	1	1	1	0	0	.00	1	.189	.228	.321
Scarborough, Steve	ss	Ogden	Mil	R+	22	16	39	9	3	1	0	14	7	6	4	0	10	1	0	0	3	2	.60	0	.231	.318	.359
		Helena	Mil	R+	22	32	113	37	11	0	5	63	29	18	19	2	16	2	0	1	6	2	.75	0	.327	.430	.558
Schader, Troy	3b	Idaho Falls	SD	R+	23	68	268	90	16	7	19	177	61	69	35	1	75	4	0	5	2	2	.50	0	.336	.413	.660
Schaeffer, Jon	c-1b	Quad City	Min	A	24	116	390	113	33	4	17	205	97	65	92	1	69	20	2	5	2	3	.40	12	.290	.444	.526
Schaffer, Jake	ss	Michigan	Hou	A	25	7	23	3	0	0	0	3	2	2	1	0	8	0	0	0	0	0	.00	0	.130	.167	.130
Scharrer, Jim	1b-dh	Myrtle Bch	Atl	A+	23	119	466	121	18	0	7	160	52	54	30	4	120	3	3	4	0	1	.00	7	.260	.306	.343
Schaub, Greg	of	Stockton	Mil	A+	23	119	422	106	18	5	5	149	51	43	21	2	71	5	3	8	4	7	.36	6	.251	.289	.353
Scheid, Jeremy*	1b	Sou Oregon	Oak	A-	24	60	213	54	9	1	3	74	28	35	32	2	60	1	0	2	0	0	.00	6	.254	.351	.347
Schell, Barry*	dh-of	Utica	Fla	A-	22	33	95	17	2	1	2	27	13	10	7	0	37	1	0	2	2	0	1.00	1	.179	.238	.284
Scheschuk, John*	1b	Fort Wayne	SD	A	23	66	242	61	14	0	3	84	35	36	43	4	34	2	1	6	3	1	.75	4	.252	.362	.347
Schill, Vaughn	ss	Wisconsin	Sea	A	22	25	79	28	4	0	0	32	13	7	13	0	16	1	1	2	7	1	.88	2	.354	.442	.405
Schilling, Chris	c	Ogden	Mil	R+	19	16	33	10	1	0	0	11	3	2	3	0	8	1	1	0	0	1	.00	1	.303	.378	.333
Schley, Joe	of	Batavia	Phi	A-	23	36	71	14	3	1	1	22	15	7	16	0	24	1	3	0	8	3	.73	1	.197	.352	.310
Schmidt, J.P.*	ss	Athletics	Oak	R	20	34	90	25	2	2	0	31	20	14	28	0	21	0	2	0	2	5	.29	0	.278	.449	.344
Schmitt, Brian*	1b	Martinsvlle	Hou	R+	21	51	180	48	11	1	4	73	27	26	29	1	48	0	0	1	4	4	.50	1	.267	.367	.406
Schnall, Kevin	c	Billings	Cin	R+	23	18	54	17	4	0	2	27	22	14	20	0	10	2	0	0	0	0	.00	2	.315	.513	.500
		Reds	Cin	R	23	1	1	1	0	0	0	1	0	0	0	0	0	0	0	0	0	0	.00	0	1.000	1.000	1.000
Schneider, Matt*	of-dh	Williamsprt	Pit	A-	22	24	76	15	4	1	2	27	10	11	9	0	27	0	0	2	1	0	1.00	1	.197	.276	.355
Schneidmiller, Gary	3b	Visalia	Oak	A+	20	85	239	66	8	2	0	78	56	22	49	0	57	0	6	2	4	2	.67	4	.276	.397	.326
Schrager, Tony	2b	Lansing	ChC	A	23	122	392	106	31	4	16	193	83	73	103	2	101	5	1	8	8	3	.73	8	.270	.421	.492
Schreimann, Eric	dh	Piedmont	Phi	A	25	78	257	62	10	5	12	118	35	37	16	0	77	19	1	3	1	1	.50	5	.241	.329	.459
Schuda, Justin*	c	Princeton	TB	R+	19	33	111	35	9	0	4	56	17	19	14	0	44	1	0	0	0	0	.00	0	.315	.397	.505
Schumacher, Sh.*	c	New Jersey	StL	A-	23	47	154	35	6	0	3	50	14	23	11	0	8	4	0	3	2	3	.40	9	.227	.291	.325
Schwartzbauer, Br.*	dh	Salem	Col	A+	23	58	179	46	3	1	2	57	21	19	26	0	44	6	5	1	1	3	.25	3	.257	.368	.318
Scioneaux, Damian*	of	Chston-SC	TB	A	25	5	18	2	0	0	0	2	1	0	2	0	3	0	0	0	2	0	1.00	2	.111	.200	.111
Seabol, Scott	3b	Greensboro	NYY	A	25	138	543	171	55	6	15	283	86	89	45	1	91	9	0	11	6	5	.55	9	.315	.370	.521
Seal, Scott*	of	Rancho Cuca	SD	A+	24	123	439	109	23	2	13	175	67	70	45	5	96	10	3	2	7	3	.70	13	.248	.331	.399
Seale, Marvin#	of	Kingsport	NYM	R+	21	63	210	49	7	3	2	68	46	20	24	0	75	0	2	1	22	4	.85	1	.233	.311	.324
Sears, Todd*	1b	Salem	Col	A+	24	109	385	108	21	0	14	171	58	59	58	1	99	4	0	1	11	2	.85	9	.281	.379	.444
Secoda, Joe	of	Peoria	StL	A	22	116	400	101	14	2	2	125	61	30	62	0	97	9	6	1	15	9	.63	2	.253	.364	.313
Seestedt, Michael	c	Orioles	Bal	R	22	6	15	3	1	0	0	4	0	4	0	0	1	0	0	0	0	0	.00	0	.200	.200	.267
		Delmarva	Bal	A	22	27	80	21	3	0	0	24	8	3	10	0	20	0	5	0	0	0	.00	1	.263	.344	.300
Seever, Brian	of	Boise	Ana	A-	23	36	103	33	5	1	0	40	32	7	21	0	27	1	1	1	14	3	.82	1	.320	.437	.388
Segura, Rolando	3b	Williamsprt	Pit	A-	21	29	108	36	10	0	4	58	20	24	12	1	26	2	0	0	1	1	.50	4	.333	.410	.537
		Hickory	Pit	A	21	40	142	43	8	0	6	69	23	21	12	0	30	2	0	0	0	3	.00	3	.303	.365	.486
Seiber, Antron	of	Red Sox	Bos	R	20	13	46	12	0	2	0	16	6	10	4	0	11	0	0	1	2	2	.50	1	.261	.314	.348
Sein, Javier*	1b	Yankees	NYY	R	21	37	114	24	4	0	2	34	9	15	15	1	39	1	0	2	0	1	.00	6	.211	.303	.298
Selander, Craig*	of	Quad City	Min	A	23	100	345	78	17	3	2	107	41	32	21	2	56	0	6	2	2	1	.67	6	.226	.269	.310
Senegal, Terence	of	Reds	Cin	R	21	50	148	30	2	0	0	32	17	9	11	0	36	2	3	0	8	1	.89	3	.203	.267	.216
Serrano, Hector#	c	Phillies	Phi	R	20	10	26	3	0	0	0	3	0	1	4	0	14	1	1	0	0	0	.00	1	.115	.258	.115

1999 Batting — Single-A and Rookie Leagues

BATTING																					BASERUNNING				PERCENTAGES		
Player	Pos	Team	Org	Lg	A	G	AB	H	2B	3B	HR	TB	R	RBI	TBB	IBB	SO	HBP	SH	SF	SB	CS	SB%	GDP	Avg	OBP	SLG
Serrano, Raymond	c	Braves	Atl	R	19	38	97	25	6	0	5	46	14	21	13	0	15	0	1	1	1	0	1.00	0	.258	.342	.474
Serrano, Sammy	c	Bakersfield	SF	A+	23	125	463	128	30	1	9	187	55	80	30	1	78	5	0	6	4	6	.40	16	.276	.323	.404
Serrano, Yalian	c	Princeton	TB	R+	19	7	10	0	0	0	0	0	0	0	0	0	8	0	0	0	0	0	.00	0	.000	.000	.000
Shackelford, Brian*	of	Chstn-WV	KC	A	23	73	260	52	14	2	10	100	25	30	26	0	80	1	1	1	1	1	.50	3	.200	.274	.385
Shaffer, Josh*	ss	Boise	Ana	A-	20	66	225	47	11	0	1	61	46	21	30	0	65	0	4	0	3	4	.43	6	.209	.302	.271
Shanks, James	of	Spokane	KC	A-	21	69	260	67	9	0	0	76	41	29	19	0	52	3	11	1	19	5	.79	6	.258	.314	.292
Sharp, Preston#	of-2b	Butte	Ana	R+	23	26	98	32	3	4	1	46	25	12	11	0	15	1	2	1	9	2	.82	0	.327	.396	.469
Shearin, Jarrett	of	Spokane	KC	A-	23	51	183	46	14	1	3	71	37	20	31	0	42	2	1	2	16	5	.76	3	.251	.362	.388
Sheffield, Jeff#	of	Yankees	NYY	R	21	3	4	0	0	0	0	0	0	0	0	0	1	0	0	0	0	0	.00	0	.000	.000	.000
Shelley, Jason	3b	Pirates	Pit	R	23	8	17	0	0	0	0	0	0	1	2	0	4	0	0	1	0	0	.00	0	.000	.100	.000
		Hickory	Pit	A	23	20	54	14	2	0	1	19	8	6	1	0	14	1	0	2	0	1	.00	0	.259	.276	.352
Sheppard, Greg	dh	Winston-Sal	CWS	A+	25	79	224	45	5	0	7	71	22	27	21	2	74	5	1	1	6	2	.75	5	.201	.283	.317
Sherlock, Brian	1b	Medcine Hat	Tor	R+	24	73	265	77	16	0	6	111	43	50	46	0	49	3	2	2	17	5	.77	3	.291	.399	.419
Sherrill, J.J.#	of	Burlington	Cle	R+	19	64	233	48	11	6	3	80	55	24	29	0	64	26	5	0	28	8	.78	0	.206	.358	.343
		Mahoning Vy	Cle	A-	19	3	8	3	0	0	0	3	1	1	1	0	4	0	0	0	0	0	.00	0	.375	.444	.375
Shier, Pete	ss	Orioles	Bal	R	19	9	26	9	1	0	0	10	6	1	3	0	4	0	1	0	3	4	.43	0	.346	.414	.385
Shipp, Brian	ss	Pittsfield	NYM	A-	21	65	240	57	10	4	1	78	25	19	18	0	56	2	2	2	8	6	.57	2	.238	.294	.325
Shipp, Charles	of	Eugene	ChC	A-	23	6	14	3	1	0	0	4	3	1	1	0	3	0	0	0	0	0	.00	2	.214	.267	.286
Shrum, Allen	c	Quad City	Min	A	24	68	191	45	12	0	1	60	14	22	16	0	52	3	1	2	0	0	.00	8	.236	.302	.314
Sickles, Jeremy	c	Williamsprt	Pit	A-	22	27	94	15	2	0	1	20	4	1	4	0	19	2	0	0	0	1	.00	1	.160	.210	.213
Siegfried, Jason	dh	Oneonta	Det	A-	23	24	61	10	3	0	0	13	6	3	6	0	28	0	1	0	0	0	.00	1	.164	.239	.213
Sienko, Ryan	c	Savannah	Tex	A	24	37	86	13	3	0	1	19	7	6	8	0	25	2	0	1	0	0	.00	2	.151	.237	.221
Silvestre, Juan	of	Wisconsin	Sea	A	22	137	534	154	34	4	21	259	89	107	47	1	124	6	0	8	5	4	.56	17	.288	.348	.485
Simmons, Jerry	of	Jamestown	Atl	A-	24	62	232	50	9	5	4	81	37	27	20	0	46	5	0	0	19	6	.76	2	.216	.292	.349
Sing, Brandon	3b	Cubs	ChC	R	19	17	68	18	4	1	2	30	4	12	5	0	16	0	0	1	1	1	.50	2	.265	.311	.441
Singletary, Dan*	of-dh	South Bend	Ari	A	24	95	306	72	8	6	5	107	47	43	54	2	53	1	0	5	15	9	.63	7	.235	.347	.350
Sitzman, Jay*	of	Batavia	Phi	A-	22	49	169	50	5	5	2	71	33	22	9	0	37	1	0	4	15	5	.75	2	.296	.328	.420
Skrehot, Shaun	ss	Hickory	Pit	A	24	115	461	108	17	5	1	138	53	37	16	0	72	5	7	4	12	8	.60	8	.234	.265	.299
Sledge, Terrmel*	of	Everett	Sea	A-	23	62	233	74	8	3	5	103	43	32	27	0	35	9	2	2	9	8	.53	2	.318	.406	.442
Smalls, Terrence*	3b	Kane County	Fla	A	24	8	22	5	0	1	0	7	2	2	1	0	2	0	1	1	1	0	1.00	1	.227	.250	.318
		Brevard Cty	Fla	A+	24	32	77	16	1	0	0	17	5	5	6	0	8	2	2	0	5	2	.71	1	.208	.282	.221
Smiley, Jermaine*	of	Royals	KC	R	20	5	15	1	0	0	0	1	0	1	0	0	6	0	0	1	0	0	.00	0	.067	.063	.067
Smith, Casey	c	Columbus	Cle	A	23	47	153	36	6	0	1	45	21	13	28	0	48	7	1	1	0	2	.00	1	.235	.376	.294
		Kinston	Cle	A+	23	39	129	21	6	0	2	33	15	15	14	0	48	3	0	0	0	1	.00	2	.163	.260	.256
Smith, Fred	of	St.Cathrnes	Tor	A-	22	40	130	29	3	1	1	37	10	12	22	0	50	4	2	2	13	3	.81	2	.223	.348	.285
Smith, Jason*	ss	Daytona	ChC	A+	22	39	142	37	5	2	5	61	22	26	12	3	29	3	0	1	9	3	.75	2	.261	.329	.430
Smith, Nestor#	of	Fort Myers	Min	A+	22	96	329	93	14	6	4	131	39	34	16	1	67	8	2	5	8	7	.53	3	.283	.327	.398
Smith, Ryan	c	Kingsport	NYM	R+	21	31	86	16	2	1	0	20	8	9	7	0	20	1	0	0	1	1	.50	1	.186	.255	.233
		Pittsfield	NYM	A-	21	12	35	5	0	0	1	8	1	5	0	0	5	1	0	0	0	0	.00	0	.143	.167	.229
		Capital Cty	NYM	A	21	1	3	0	0	0	0	0	0	0	0	0	1	0	0	0	0	0	.00	0	.000	.000	.000
Smith, Sam	1b	Asheville	Col	A	21	87	316	86	16	0	8	126	42	39	12	0	79	10	0	0	7	2	.78	4	.272	.320	.399
Smith, Toebius	of	Braves	Atl	R	20	29	94	18	3	0	0	21	11	7	10	0	24	1	0	0	6	0	1.00	1	.191	.276	.223
Smith, Tony*	dh	Reds	Cin	R	19	21	65	16	2	2	0	22	12	11	6	0	10	0	0	0	3	0	1.00	2	.246	.310	.338
Smothers, Stewart	of	Myrtle Bch	Atl	A+	24	56	185	28	8	3	1	45	19	14	15	1	71	0	0	5	2	2	.50	3	.151	.210	.243
		Macon	Atl	A	24	63	219	62	12	0	7	95	32	39	16	0	61	0	2	5	2	3	.40	2	.283	.325	.434
Snead, Esix#	of	Potomac	StL	A+	24	67	249	45	8	5	0	63	37	14	32	0	57	4	3	3	35	12	.74	2	.181	.281	.253
		Peoria	StL	A	24	59	181	35	7	1	2	50	35	18	35	0	42	2	7	1	29	9	.76	3	.193	.329	.276
Snelling, Chris*	of	Everett	Sea	A-	18	69	265	81	15	3	10	132	46	50	33	2	24	6	3	5	8	9	.47	4	.306	.388	.498
Snow, Chris	of	Great Falls	LA	R+	19	12	40	11	0	1	0	13	9	2	1	0	4	0	0	0	2	1	.67	1	.275	.293	.325
Snyder, Earl	1b	Capital Cty	NYM	A	24	136	486	130	25	4	28	247	73	97	55	0	117	2	0	9	2	2	.50	5	.267	.339	.508
Snyder, Michael*	3b	Medcine Hat	Tor	R+	19	62	196	41	7	0	3	57	30	19	31	1	47	1	0	0	3	4	.43	3	.209	.320	.291
Sobet, Renato	of	Padres	SD	R	20	39	129	29	4	1	2	41	11	13	13	1	28	1	0	0	3	1	.75	6	.225	.301	.318
Soler, Ramon#	ss	Chston-SC	TB	A	18	108	389	92	17	2	1	116	74	28	56	0	93	4	6	1	46	14	.77	5	.237	.338	.298
Solorzano, Lenin	3b	White Sox	CWS	R	20	51	180	48	6	5	1	67	21	30	13	0	45	1	2	0	5	5	.50	8	.267	.320	.372
Sorensen, Zach#	ss	Kinston	Cle	A+	23	130	508	121	16	7	7	172	79	59	62	1	126	2	8	2	24	12	.67	6	.238	.322	.339
Sosa, Jorge#	of	Portland	Col	A-	22	35	113	23	3	0	2	32	15	8	13	0	57	1	0	0	2	3	.40	0	.204	.291	.283
Sosa, Jovanny	of	Hickory	Pit	A	19	108	402	84	16	1	22	168	61	53	37	1	145	8	0	4	2	2	.50	9	.209	.286	.418
Sosa, Nick	1b	Visalia	Oak	A+	22	100	339	74	14	1	13	129	53	67	65	1	106	7	0	7	4	2	.67	7	.218	.349	.381
Soto, Jorge	1b-dh	Sou Oregon	Oak	A-	22	45	160	39	9	0	11	81	37	30	38	1	63	10	0	2	1	2	.33	0	.244	.414	.506
Soto, Jose#	of	Marlins	Fla	R	20	49	175	40	8	0	4	60	17	20	14	1	56	3	1	1	10	8	.56	0	.229	.295	.343
Soules, Ryan*	dh	Tampa	NYY	A+	24	22	71	18	5	1	2	31	12	12	14	0	22	1	0	3	0	0	.00	0	.254	.371	.437
Southall, Rick*	1b	Lancaster	Sea	A+	23	1	2	0	0	0	0	0	0	0	0	0	2	0	0	0	0	0	.00	0	.000	.000	.000
		Wisconsin	Sea	A	23	102	337	83	19	1	10	134	47	51	42	1	101	4	0	0	4	1	.80	5	.246	.337	.398
Southward, De.	of	Elizabethtn	Min	R+	22	50	173	43	10	2	1	60	34	25	28	0	30	2	1	2	16	4	.80	4	.249	.356	.347
Sowers, Doug*	3b	Orioles	Bal	R	22	4	14	4	0	0	0	4	0	1	0	0	1	0	0	0	1	1	.50	0	.286	.286	.286
		Bluefield	Bal	R+	22	53	181	45	14	1	8	85	32	35	33	1	54	2	0	3	2	1	.67	0	.249	.365	.470
Spencer, Jeff	of	Myrtle Bch	Atl	A+	23	111	397	98	28	4	11	167	59	42	34	1	126	2	0	4	2	6	.25	4	.247	.307	.421
Spoerl, Josh	dh	Billings	Cin	R+	21	66	258	74	15	1	8	115	43	45	24	0	64	6	0	1	1	0	1.00	9	.287	.360	.446
Spooner, Brent	c	Johnson Cy	StL	R+	22	42	126	27	9	0	1	39	17	10	16	0	24	3	0	0	0	3	.00	2	.214	.317	.310
Sprowl, Jon*	c	Cubs	ChC	R	19	31	97	38	9	2	0	51	19	14	18	1	14	1	0	2	1	1	.50	4	.392	.483	.526
Stanley, Derek	of	Bristol	CWS	R+	20	39	135	31	5	3	1	45	20	9	17	0	31	3	3	0	6	6	.50	3	.230	.329	.333
Stanton, Tom*	dh	St. Lucie	NYM	A+	24	37	82	14	6	1	2	28	10	5	12	0	38	3	1	0	1	1	.50	2	.171	.299	.341
Steele, Alex	dh	Lakeland	Det	A+	24	16	52	11	3	0	0	14	3	3	6	0	17	1	0	0	0	0	.00	0	.212	.305	.269
Steelmon, Wyley*	1b-dh	High Desert	Ari	A+	24	32	91	20	6	0	1	29	13	10	9	0	19	2	0	0	1	1	.50	1	.220	.304	.319
Stewart, Colin	of	Macon	Atl	A	23	29	72	15	4	0	0	19	8	3	5	0	16	1	0	0	3	1	.75	3	.208	.269	.264
Stockam, Travis	dh	Pittsfield	NYM	A-	24	41	128	28	4	1	4	46	19	19	8	1	32	11	1	0	1	3	.25	1	.219	.320	.359

1999 Batting — Single-A and Rookie Leagues

BATTING																					BASERUNNING				PERCENTAGES		
Player	Pos	Team	Org	Lg	A	G	AB	H	2B	3B	HR	TB	R	RBI	TBB	IBB	SO	HBP	SH	SF	SB	CS	SB%	GDP	Avg	OBP	SLG
Stodgel, Jeff#	of-2b	Vero Beach	LA	A+	24	44	123	26	1	2	0	31	14	8	10	0	24	1	1	0	3	4	.43	3	.211	.276	.252
Stone, John#	c	Idaho Falls	SD	R+	21	28	98	20	6	0	0	26	11	8	11	0	38	2	1	0	5	1	.83	1	.204	.297	.265
Storke, Jon	3b	Orioles	Bal	R	22	25	71	11	3	1	0	16	13	5	12	0	28	2	0	0	4	1	.80	1	.155	.294	.225
Story-Harden, Tho.	dh	Great Falls	LA	R+	20	13	45	9	2	0	2	17	7	6	5	0	17	3	0	0	2	0	1.00	0	.200	.321	.378
Stratton, Robert	of-dh	Capital Cty	NYM	A	22	95	318	87	17	3	21	173	58	60	48	4	112	5	0	3	7	1	.88	1	.274	.374	.544
Strickland, Greg*	of-dh	Macon	Atl	A	24	86	314	82	13	8	7	132	58	34	26	1	74	2	0	1	27	12	.69	1	.261	.321	.420
Stryhas, Paul	3b-dh	Helena	Mil	R+	23	37	123	35	8	0	2	49	18	14	13	0	24	1	0	2	1	1	.50	4	.285	.353	.398
Stuart, Rich	dh-of	Lk Elsinore	Ana	A+	23	11	43	8	1	1	0	11	3	3	1	0	11	1	0	0	1	2	.33	0	.186	.222	.256
		Cedar Rapds	Ana	A	23	67	250	72	16	2	15	137	46	55	30	1	53	2	0	0	8	4	.67	5	.288	.369	.548
Suarez, Luis	ss	Burlington	CWS	A	21	51	173	42	10	0	4	64	24	25	19	0	32	3	3	2	5	4	.56	1	.243	.325	.370
		Winston-Sal	CWS	A+	21	74	241	49	7	2	2	66	20	26	22	0	66	2	5	3	3	2	.60	4	.203	.272	.274
Suarez, Marc	c	Clinton	Cin	A	24	33	95	15	2	0	2	23	8	10	16	0	31	1	1	4	0	3	.00	3	.158	.276	.242
		Rockford	Cin	A	24	4	13	6	1	0	1	10	4	1	3	0	2	0	0	0	2	0	1.00	0	.462	.563	.769
Summers, John#	1b	Bakersfield	SF	A+	23	114	403	119	19	2	7	163	50	51	40	0	65	5	0	1	2	5	.29	4	.295	.365	.404
Suriel, Miguel	c	Hudson Val	TB	A-	23	33	121	28	8	0	0	36	15	7	8	0	15	1	2	0	1	1	.50	6	.231	.285	.298
		Chston-SC	TB	A	23	80	257	58	18	0	3	85	24	22	31	0	35	3	1	1	2	1	.67	9	.226	.315	.331
Sutter, Chad	c	Staten Ilnd	NYY	A-	22	36	77	10	1	0	2	17	8	7	11	0	18	0	2	2	1	0	1.00	1	.130	.233	.221
Sykes, Jamie	of	South Bend	Ari	A	25	127	479	137	34	10	15	236	75	83	53	1	111	4	1	4	17	8	.68	9	.286	.359	.493
Tamburrino, Brett#	1b	Twins	Min	R	18	14	43	9	0	0	0	9	9	5	7	0	10	0	1	0	1	0	1.00	2	.209	.320	.209
Tapia, Roman	3b	White Sox	CWS	R	20	21	50	15	4	0	0	19	7	6	7	0	12	0	3	0	0	3	.00	1	.300	.386	.380
Taveras, Jose	of	Chstn-WV	KC	A	23	91	335	82	14	2	4	112	41	29	19	0	78	5	2	0	38	10	.79	2	.245	.295	.334
Taveras, Luis	c	Charlotte	Tex	A+	22	95	308	81	18	4	6	125	36	46	30	0	69	3	3	4	10	4	.71	6	.263	.330	.406
Taylor, Adam	c	Kinston	Cle	A+	26	6	16	3	0	0	1	6	2	2	2	0	7	0	0	0	0	1	.00	0	.188	.278	.375
		Columbus	Cle	A	26	8	27	8	2	0	1	13	4	4	2	0	9	0	0	0	0	0	.00	0	.296	.345	.481
Taylor, Corey	of	Reds	Cin	R	25	1	3	2	0	0	0	2	2	1	2	0	0	0	0	0	0	0	.00	0	.667	.800	.667
Taylor, Josh	2b	Lancaster	Sea	A+	23	6	13	1	0	0	0	1	0	2	1	0	6	0	0	0	0	0	.00	0	.077	.143	.077
		Everett	Sea	A-	23	42	90	19	1	0	1	23	11	8	17	0	21	2	3	2	0	1	.00	2	.211	.342	.256
Taylor, Seth	ss	Staten Ilnd	NYY	A-	22	74	283	83	11	1	5	111	57	36	35	1	40	8	2	3	23	6	.79	8	.293	.383	.392
		Greensboro	NYY	A	22	4	10	3	1	0	0	4	1	1	1	0	0	1	1	0	1	0	1.00	0	.300	.417	.400
Teilon, Nilson	2b	Bristol	CWS	R+	19	68	240	71	12	2	9	114	43	51	29	0	68	8	1	3	6	4	.60	3	.296	.386	.475
Templeton, Garry	2b-of	Butte	Ana	R+	21	33	93	19	0	0	0	19	16	11	8	0	28	3	2	1	4	1	.80	0	.204	.286	.204
Terhune, Mike#	ss-3b	Myrtle Bch	Atl	A+	24	92	312	70	10	3	1	89	24	26	27	0	51	0	6	1	3	2	.60	11	.224	.285	.285
Terni, Chaz	3b	Augusta	Bos	A	21	36	123	22	3	4	1	36	10	10	9	0	36	2	0	0	1	1	.50	3	.179	.246	.293
		Lowell	Bos	A-	21	38	119	24	6	1	0	32	10	7	10	0	35	3	2	2	1	2	.33	1	.202	.276	.269
Terrell, Jeff*	2b	Clearwater	Phi	A+	25	109	385	109	18	4	2	141	63	45	42	2	44	5	3	5	13	8	.62	8	.283	.357	.366
Terrell, Jim*	3b	Winston-Sal	CWS	A+	22	119	436	118	31	5	3	168	74	47	52	0	79	7	7	4	16	6	.73	9	.271	.355	.385
Terrero, Luis	of	Missoula	Ari	R+	20	71	272	78	13	7	8	129	74	40	32	1	91	5	3	6	27	10	.73	2	.287	.365	.474
Terveen, Bryce*	c	Danville	Atl	R+	22	50	157	38	9	0	5	62	21	27	25	1	44	5	1	0	0	1	.00	2	.242	.364	.395
Testa, Chris*	of	Rockies	Col	R	19	47	168	49	10	1	1	64	22	22	24	0	27	4	0	1	11	6	.65	3	.292	.391	.381
Thames, Damon	ss	New Jersey	StL	A-	23	47	180	41	5	1	0	48	22	16	7	0	42	4	4	1	10	5	.67	1	.228	.271	.267
Theodorou, Nick#	of	San Berndno	LA	A+	25	104	355	110	11	4	0	129	57	44	72	3	62	7	5	1	14	14	.50	7	.310	.434	.363
Thomas, Charles	of	Great Falls	LA	R+	20	54	194	49	11	4	3	77	32	23	22	0	48	2	4	1	10	2	.83	1	.253	.333	.397
Thomas, Gary	of	Modesto	Oak	A+	20	99	344	111	14	4	7	154	69	38	33	1	45	9	8	4	23	6	.79	7	.323	.392	.448
Thomas, J.J.	1b-dh	Kissimmee	Hou	A+	24	88	287	66	15	0	16	129	36	44	20	0	109	2	1	4	0	0	.00	4	.230	.281	.449
Thomas, Mark*	1b	Vermont	Mon	A-	24	44	152	48	5	3	1	62	23	23	27	1	28	1	0	2	10	3	.77	3	.316	.418	.408
Thompson, Alva	c	Braves	Atl	R	23	27	76	17	3	0	3	29	11	11	13	0	22	2	0	0	1	1	.50	2	.224	.352	.382
		Danville	Atl	R+	23	11	36	13	3	1	2	24	7	10	6	0	10	0	0	1	0	0	.00	0	.361	.442	.667
Thompson, Andrew*	c	Capital Cty	NYM	A	26	61	185	42	11	0	0	53	14	17	22	0	45	6	0	0	0	0	.00	4	.227	.329	.286
Thompson, Eric*	of	Columbus	Cle	A	21	74	280	70	9	0	0	79	48	15	31	0	83	1	3	0	22	9	.71	3	.250	.327	.282
Thompson, Nick	dh	Clearwater	Phi	A+	25	9	27	3	1	0	0	4	4	1	4	0	12	2	0	0	0	1	.00	0	.111	.273	.148
Thompson, Tyler	of	Hagerstown	Tor	A	24	130	440	115	28	3	17	200	84	81	79	0	122	4	2	5	20	3	.87	7	.261	.375	.455
Thornton-Murray, J.	3b-2b	Cubs	ChC	R	19	34	112	23	2	1	0	27	12	4	9	0	24	4	2	0	0	3	.00	1	.205	.288	.241
Thorpe, A.D.#	ss	Clinton	Cin	A	23	6	12	4	2	0	0	6	2	1	0	0	2	1	1	0	1	2	.33	0	.333	.385	.500
		Rockford	Cin	A	23	7	8	2	0	0	0	2	3	0	1	0	0	0	0	0	1	1	.50	1	.250	.333	.250
Thurston, Joe*	ss	Yakima	LA	A-	20	71	277	79	10	3	0	95	48	32	27	1	34	21	6	3	27	17	.61	3	.285	.387	.343
		San Berndno	LA	A+	20	2	3	0	0	0	0	0	0	0	0	0	1	1	0	0	0	0	.00	0	.000	.250	.000
Ticehurst, Brad*	of	Staten Ilnd	NYY	A-	23	63	221	56	12	5	8	102	29	39	22	1	51	6	0	6	4	3	.57	2	.253	.329	.462
Ticen, Kevin	3b	Boise	Ana	A-	24	14	48	14	5	0	0	19	5	9	3	0	10	3	0	1	1	0	1.00	3	.292	.364	.396
		Cedar Rapds	Ana	A	24	27	88	25	4	0	1	32	8	10	8	0	24	3	1	0	0	1	.00	4	.284	.364	.364
Tindell, Matt	c	Helena	Mil	R+	20	29	100	28	6	0	2	40	20	11	7	0	24	2	0	0	4	1	.80	3	.280	.339	.400
Tolli, Barry	of	Tigers	Det	R	20	43	137	33	7	1	2	48	19	17	15	0	39	1	2	0	12	3	.80	1	.241	.320	.350
Tomaszewski, Dane	c	Great Falls	LA	R+	20	34	131	39	9	1	5	65	22	24	5	0	25	1	2	0	3	2	.60	2	.298	.328	.496
Tommasini, Kevin	of-dh	San Jose	SF	A+	25	108	382	97	17	2	6	136	52	34	48	1	86	5	3	1	3	3	.50	12	.254	.344	.356
Tomshack, Steven	c	Diamondbcks	Ari	R	23	44	144	48	9	1	3	68	21	22	19	2	24	3	0	3	0	0	.00	1	.333	.414	.472
Toomey, Chris	of	Clinton	Cin	A	22	100	307	80	19	1	6	119	51	41	41	0	87	15	2	4	5	3	.63	7	.261	.371	.388
Tope, Stephen	dh	Twins	Min	R	18	18	55	11	3	0	0	14	14	10	9	0	10	4	1	0	2	1	.67	0	.200	.353	.255
Topolski, Jon*	of	Auburn	Hou	A-	23	67	255	62	11	6	2	91	46	38	50	1	72	3	0	3	27	13	.68	2	.243	.370	.357
Torcato, Tony*	3b	Bakersfield	SF	A+	20	110	422	123	25	0	4	160	50	58	30	3	67	3	1	7	2	1	.67	6	.291	.338	.379
Torrealba, Steve	c	Myrtle Bch	Atl	A+	22	52	175	37	9	0	6	64	23	23	13	0	47	2	3	0	1	0	1.00	4	.211	.274	.366
Torres, Andres#	of	W Michigan	Det	A	22	117	407	96	20	5	2	132	72	34	92	1	116	10	9	5	39	18	.68	2	.236	.385	.324
Torres, Bernie	2b	Burlington	CWS	A	20	65	268	69	12	4	2	95	40	21	15	0	32	2	4	2	7	2	.78	4	.257	.300	.354
Torres, Digno*	of-1b	Twins	Min	R	20	53	166	46	7	1	1	58	20	26	26	1	36	4	1	2	10	2	.83	4	.277	.384	.349
Torres, Franklin	2b	Elizabethtn	Min	R+	20	52	187	47	7	3	7	81	44	30	32	0	60	4	0	0	12	3	.80	3	.251	.372	.433
Torres, Frederick	c	Pulaski	Tex	R+	20	60	240	73	19	0	8	116	35	45	7	0	53	3	4	0	1	0	1.00	9	.304	.332	.483
Torres, Gabby	c	Elizabethtn	Min	R+	22	7	24	6	1	0	1	10	5	3	4	0	1	1	1	0	1	1	.50	3	.250	.379	.417
		Fort Myers	Min	A+	22	22	68	15	3	0	1	21	7	6	3	0	8	2	1	1	0	0	.00	5	.221	.270	.309
Torres, Jaime	c	Yankees	NYY	R	29	11	30	10	2	0	1	15	5	3	2	1	1	2	0	0	0	1	.00	0	.333	.412	.500

1999 Batting — Single-A and Rookie Leagues

BATTING																					BASERUNNING				PERCENTAGES		
Player	Pos	Team	Org	Lg	A	G	AB	H	2B	3B	HR	TB	R	RBI	TBB	IBB	SO	HBP	SH	SF	SB	CS	SB%	GDP	Avg	OBP	SLG
		Tampa	NYY	A+	29	9	33	9	1	0	0	10	1	3	1	0	4	2	0	0	1	0	1.00	4	.273	.333	.303
Torres, Jason*	c	Savannah	Tex	A	21	43	126	21	3	2	0	28	6	8	10	0	31	0	0	1	2	1	.67	4	.167	.226	.222
		Pulaski	Tex	R+	21	25	65	18	4	1	4	36	18	8	12	0	16	1	0	0	0	0	.00	0	.277	.397	.554
Torres, Rafael	of	Wilmington	KC	A+	21	76	252	61	7	0	1	71	15	20	15	0	51	5	2	2	0	4	.00	3	.242	.296	.282
Torres, Reynaldo	1b	Johnson Cy	StL	R+	21	36	105	16	6	0	1	25	8	10	6	0	52	3	0	2	1	0	1.00	1	.152	.216	.238
Tosca, Dan*	c-dh	Phillies	Phi	R	19	50	157	37	8	0	4	57	19	22	22	1	38	2	0	3	3	1	.75	1	.236	.332	.363
Treanor, Matt	c	Kane County	Fla	A	24	86	308	88	21	1	10	141	56	53	36	0	65	15	2	2	4	1	.80	9	.286	.385	.458
Trout, Casey	3b	Ogden	Mil	R+	23	49	142	35	5	0	1	43	14	11	14	0	26	1	1	0	2	3	.40	1	.246	.318	.303
Truitt, Steve	of	Helena	Mil	R+	22	54	185	57	10	1	11	102	51	50	37	0	40	5	0	4	19	5	.79	6	.308	.429	.551
Trzesniak, Nick	dh-c	Padres	SD	R	19	29	108	26	3	1	0	31	17	16	14	0	39	3	1	0	7	1	.88	1	.241	.344	.287
Tsoukalas, John*	dh	San Jose	SF	A+	29	64	208	67	15	1	9	111	36	41	25	2	42	1	0	0	0	1	.00	3	.322	.397	.534
Tucent, Francisco#	3b	Beloit	Mil	A	23	38	102	19	4	0	1	26	9	10	0	0	26	1	1	1	0	1	.00	4	.186	.192	.255
Tucker, Mamon	of	Bluefield	Bal	R+	20	58	233	59	9	5	0	78	52	18	29	0	44	2	0	0	7	0	1.00	6	.253	.341	.335
Turco, Paul#	ss	Salem-Keizr	SF	A-	23	44	116	21	3	0	0	24	8	5	10	0	27	1	6	0	3	1	.75	2	.181	.252	.207
Turnquist, Tyler	3b	Michigan	Hou	A	24	118	456	141	25	7	11	213	89	67	62	1	69	5	1	7	5	4	.56	14	.309	.392	.467
Twombley, Dennis	c	Tampa	NYY	A+	25	15	37	9	1	0	0	10	3	3	6	0	11	0	0	0	0	0	.00	1	.243	.349	.270
		Greensboro	NYY	A	25	44	142	34	6	0	7	61	19	22	17	0	44	5	1	2	0	0	.00	4	.239	.337	.430
Tyson, Torre#	2b	Red Sox	Bos	R	24	10	19	2	0	0	0	2	4	3	4	0	2	0	0	1	1	1	.50	1	.105	.250	.105
Uccello, Jeff	c	Sarasota	Bos	A+	26	10	32	9	4	0	0	13	4	2	3	0	6	0	1	0	0	0	.00	0	.281	.343	.406
Ugueto, Luis#	ss	Brevard Cty	Fla	A+	21	12	30	4	0	0	0	4	1	3	7	0	5	0	1	0	1	0	1.00	3	.133	.297	.133
		Marlins	Fla	R	21	1	3	0	0	0	0	0	0	2	1	0	0	0	0	1	0	0	.00	0	.000	.200	.000
		Utica	Fla	A-	21	56	217	60	11	2	1	78	33	26	18	0	46	1	3	0	9	4	.69	4	.276	.335	.359
Ullery, Dave*	c	Wilmington	KC	A+	25	60	199	46	18	0	2	70	20	27	18	1	70	2	0	4	0	0	.00	3	.231	.296	.352
Umbria, Jose	c	Hagerstown	Tor	A	22	62	186	54	5	0	3	68	24	20	26	0	36	0	0	2	2	2	.50	4	.290	.374	.366
Uribe, Juan	ss	Asheville	Col	A	19	125	430	115	28	3	9	176	57	46	20	0	79	6	11	4	11	7	.61	12	.267	.307	.409
Urquhart, Derick*	of	Jupiter	Mon	A+	24	23	44	8	1	0	0	9	5	5	7	0	7	0	0	0	2	0	1.00	0	.182	.294	.205
		Cape Fear	Mon	A	24	54	169	52	4	4	3	73	31	18	26	1	19	1	2	0	6	8	.43	1	.308	.403	.432
Urquiola, Carlos*	2b	South Bend	Ari	A	20	93	384	139	13	3	0	158	66	35	22	0	32	5	1	3	20	14	.59	2	.362	.401	.411
Ust, Brant	3b	Oneonta	Det	A-	21	58	226	59	12	3	5	92	23	34	16	2	54	4	1	3	3	4	.43	3	.261	.317	.407
Valderrama, Carlos	of	San Jose	SF	A+	22	26	90	23	2	0	0	25	12	12	4	0	19	0	2	0	8	4	.67	1	.256	.287	.278
		Salem-Keizr	SF	A-	22	40	134	39	3	1	2	50	27	18	12	0	34	0	3	0	17	2	.89	0	.291	.349	.373
Valdez, Angel	of	Staten Ilnd	NYY	A-	22	34	71	15	3	0	1	21	11	13	5	0	16	1	2	0	3	2	.60	1	.211	.273	.296
		Greensboro	NYY	A	22	35	125	31	4	0	1	41	11	14	2	0	32	5	0	0	2	3	.40	2	.272	.311	.328
Valdez, Castulo	c	Hudson Val	TB	A-	22	12	26	6	0	0	0	6	4	0	5	0	4	1	1	0	0	0	.00	0	.231	.375	.231
Valdez, Darlin	dh-c	Expos	Mon	R	20	14	48	13	2	1	0	17	3	4	4	0	10	0	0	0	0	0	.00	1	.271	.327	.354
Valdez, Eladio	3b	Yakima	LA	A-	23	39	136	33	5	0	4	50	20	21	4	0	18	4	4	2	1	2	.33	3	.243	.281	.368
Valdez, Jerry	c-dh	Piedmont	Phi	A	26	39	126	28	5	0	2	39	11	13	11	1	26	1	1	2	0	0	.00	2	.222	.286	.310
Valdez, Toribio#	3b	Rangers	Tex	R	20	10	27	1	0	0	0	1	0	1	2	0	5	0	0	0	0	0	.00	0	.037	.103	.037
Valdez, Wilson	ss	Expos	Mon	R	20	22	82	24	2	0	0	26	12	7	5	0	7	0	2	1	10	0	1.00	1	.293	.330	.317
		Vermont	Mon	A-	20	36	130	32	7	0	1	42	19	10	7	0	21	0	0	1	4	3	.57	3	.246	.283	.323
Valent, Eric*	of	Clearwater	Phi	A+	23	134	520	150	31	9	20	259	91	106	58	5	110	5	1	10	5	3	.63	10	.288	.359	.498
Valenzuela, Mario	of	Burlington	CWS	A	23	122	477	154	31	6	10	227	89	70	44	0	77	6	3	3	13	6	.68	16	.323	.385	.476
Valera, Greg	ss	South Bend	Ari	A	21	53	186	29	4	2	0	37	18	10	9	0	46	1	1	0	1	2	.33	6	.156	.199	.199
		Diamondbcks	Ari	R	21	13	0	0	0	0	0	0	0	0	0	0	0	0	0	0	0	0	.00	0	.000	.000	.000
Valera, Ramon#	ss-2b	Lancaster	Sea	A+	24	17	54	10	1	0	0	11	10	1	10	0	10	1	1	0	4	4	.50	0	.185	.323	.204
		Wisconsin	Sea	A	24	99	382	103	14	4	2	131	72	33	75	1	92	1	4	1	42	19	.69	3	.270	.390	.343
Van Buizen, Rod.	2b	Great Falls	LA	R+	19	69	259	74	9	0	4	95	43	33	17	0	38	6	6	4	9	4	.69	4	.286	.339	.367
Vandemore, An.*	of	Padres	SD	R	23	50	185	51	7	3	3	73	32	39	23	1	51	1	0	2	2	6	.25	3	.276	.355	.395
		Fort Wayne	SD	A	23	5	18	5	2	0	0	7	0	0	1	0	5	0	0	0	0	0	.00	0	.278	.316	.389
Van Horn, Ryan	c	Cubs	ChC	R	22	18	40	6	2	0	0	8	4	4	0	0	8	2	0	1	1	0	1.00	1	.150	.186	.200
Van Iten, Bob*	1b	Clearwater	Phi	A+	22	98	345	91	16	1	5	124	48	51	31	1	63	4	4	7	3	4	.43	7	.264	.326	.359
Van Pareren, Tim#	2b	Vermont	Mon	A-	20	30	82	17	2	0	0	19	9	3	12	0	23	3	1	2	4	1	.80	1	.207	.323	.232
Van Vark, Wade#	of	Phillies	Phi	R	23	34	106	22	1	0	0	23	6	6	12	0	26	2	1	1	4	2	.67	1	.208	.298	.217
Vann, Eric#	of	Chstn-WV	KC	A	24	14	27	2	0	0	0	2	1	1	4	0	11	1	0	0	2	1	.67	1	.074	.219	.074
Vargas, Arias	c	Tigers	Det	R	22	5	10	4	0	0	1	7	2	2	1	0	1	0	0	0	0	0	.00	0	.400	.455	.700
		Lakeland	Det	A+	22	21	41	5	0	0	0	5	2	2	4	0	13	1	1	0	0	0	.00	0	.122	.217	.122
Vasquez, Alejandro*	of	Kissimmee	Hou	A+	22	79	275	65	6	4	4	91	31	29	14	0	40	1	0	1	3	5	.38	8	.236	.275	.331
Vasquez, Geraldo	ss	Johnson Cy	StL	R+	20	49	167	38	6	0	5	59	28	25	13	0	43	5	5	0	7	5	.58	4	.228	.303	.353
Vasquez, Sandy	of	Yakima	LA	A-	23	75	271	71	11	1	6	102	46	44	44	2	91	13	0	1	18	8	.69	3	.262	.389	.376
Vaughn, Clint	1b	Clinton	Cin	A	23	104	374	89	25	4	3	131	45	54	18	1	87	8	1	5	2	2	.50	8	.238	.284	.350
Vazquez, Carlos	dh	Hudson Val	TB	A-	21	29	91	18	1	0	0	19	3	7	7	0	18	0	0	2	0	0	.00	1	.198	.250	.209
Velazquez, Gil	ss	Kingsport	NYM	R+	20	62	225	59	8	0	1	70	24	19	19	0	43	3	2	4	4	0	1.00	5	.262	.323	.311
		Capital Cty	NYM	A	20	21	75	17	4	1	0	23	9	6	3	0	14	1	2	3	0	1	.00	2	.227	.256	.307
Velazquez, Jose*	1b	St. Pete	TB	A+	24	112	404	105	15	2	3	133	43	69	37	4	46	3	2	7	2	5	.29	5	.260	.322	.329
Venales, Luis	c	Marlins	Fla	R	20	28	67	6	2	0	0	8	6	5	18	0	27	0	0	0	1	2	.33	2	.090	.282	.119
Vento, Mike	of	Tampa	NYY	A+	22	70	255	66	10	1	7	99	37	28	17	1	69	3	0	2	2	3	.40	1	.259	.310	.388
		Greensboro	NYY	A	22	40	148	37	11	1	3	59	20	16	14	1	46	2	0	1	3	1	.75	1	.250	.321	.399
Ventura, Juan	2b	Rockies	Col	R	19	46	193	77	9	4	0	94	35	23	12	0	24	2	0	5	25	9	.74	2	.399	.429	.487
Vessel, Andrew	of	Lansing	ChC	A	25	13	52	16	4	2	0	24	7	11	2	0	3	1	0	1	1	0	1.00	3	.308	.339	.462
		Daytona	ChC	A+	25	20	77	16	4	0	2	26	7	8	2	0	15	1	0	0	1	0	1.00	1	.208	.238	.338
Victorino, Shane	of	Great Falls	LA	R+	19	55	225	63	7	6	2	88	53	25	20	0	31	0	6	3	20	5	.80	3	.280	.335	.391
Villar, Jose	of	Jamestown	Atl	A-	21	39	133	33	6	1	4	53	14	17	11	0	43	2	0	1	5	3	.63	5	.248	.313	.398
Villegas, Ernest	1b	Rangers	Tex	R	21	11	35	10	1	2	0	15	6	5	5	0	7	3	0	1	1	1	.50	0	.286	.409	.429
Vilorio, Miguel	2b	Portland	Col	A-	20	21	77	26	3	0	1	32	14	5	7	0	14	1	1	1	13	4	.76	2	.338	.395	.416
Vizcaino, Maximo	ss	Diamondbcks	Ari	R	19	12	46	13	0	1	0	15	7	4	4	0	3	2	0	1	1	0	1.00	4	.283	.358	.326
Volquez, Angel	ss	Princeton	TB	R+	18	58	202	55	8	1	1	68	23	20	13	0	57	3	1	0	9	4	.69	5	.272	.326	.337
Wade, Mike	1b	Orioles	Bal	R	24	2	4	0	0	0	0	0	0	0	0	0	2	0	0	0	0	0	.00	0	.000	.000	.000

1999 Batting — Single-A and Rookie Leagues

BATTING																					BASERUNNING				PERCENTAGES		
Player	Pos	Team	Org	Lg	A	G	AB	H	2B	3B	HR	TB	R	RBI	TBB	IBB	SO	HBP	SH	SF	SB	CS	SB%	GDP	Avg	OBP	SLG
Wagner, Jeff	dh	Butte	Ana	R+	23	8	34	13	4	0	2	23	7	10	0	0	5	0	0	0	0	0	.00	2	.382	.382	.676
Wagner, Mike	of	Padres	SD	R	22	34	128	40	9	4	5	72	27	27	21	1	37	3	0	4	13	4	.76	3	.313	.410	.563
		Fort Wayne	SD	A	22	13	46	12	1	0	2	19	10	8	8	0	15	1	0	1	0	0	.00	0	.261	.375	.413
Waldron, Jeff*	c-dh	Lowell	Bos	A-	23	39	125	22	3	1	1	30	17	13	14	1	22	6	0	0	0	1	.00	4	.176	.290	.240
Walker, Javon	of	Utica	Fla	A-	21	8	11	0	0	0	0	0	0	0	1	0	7	0	0	0	0	0	.00	0	.000	.083	.000
Walker, Keronn#	c	Royals	KC	R	21	18	37	12	1	0	1	16	4	4	9	0	9	2	1	0	0	0	.00	1	.324	.479	.432
Wallis, Jacob	c	Reds	Cin	R	20	15	47	6	1	0	0	7	3	2	7	0	8	1	0	0	0	3	.00	0	.128	.255	.149
		Billings	Cin	R+	20	26	94	22	6	0	0	28	10	12	8	0	31	1	0	1	0	0	.00	3	.234	.298	.298
Wandall, Chad	ss	Elizabethtn	Min	R+	23	65	271	67	12	1	2	87	56	27	46	0	71	1	1	2	6	4	.60	6	.247	.356	.321
Ward, Brian	2b	Idaho Falls	SD	R+	22	68	287	91	23	2	7	139	50	60	32	2	46	3	0	4	6	3	.67	7	.317	.387	.484
Ward, Corey	of	Billings	Cin	R+	21	49	167	45	7	4	3	69	24	19	12	0	49	1	3	1	8	4	.67	0	.269	.320	.413
Ware, Anthony	3b-dh	Tigers	Det	R	19	33	102	19	2	0	2	27	11	8	6	0	48	0	1	1	0	0	.00	2	.186	.229	.265
Ware, Ryan	2b	Charlotte	Tex	A+	24	67	181	33	3	0	1	39	16	15	22	1	40	1	5	3	6	3	.67	3	.182	.271	.215
Warren, Chris	3b	Rockies	Col	R	23	40	144	37	4	1	1	46	30	16	23	0	22	3	2	2	18	2	.90	3	.257	.366	.319
Warren, Chris	of	Augusta	Bos	A	23	42	153	26	4	0	5	45	16	16	11	0	53	2	3	1	4	0	1.00	4	.170	.234	.294
		Lowell	Bos	A-	23	56	215	48	13	3	5	82	29	25	12	0	69	2	2	3	3	2	.60	5	.223	.267	.381
Warren, Tom#	of	Ogden	Mil	R+	20	35	87	13	5	0	0	18	14	3	13	0	34	5	2	0	5	2	.71	1	.149	.295	.207
Warriax, Brandon	ss	Savannah	Tex	A	21	43	144	22	3	1	1	30	10	13	15	0	43	0	2	2	7	1	.88	1	.153	.230	.208
		Pulaski	Tex	R+	21	65	232	59	9	2	9	99	44	35	18	0	68	3	6	2	11	1	.92	3	.254	.314	.427
Washington, Dion	1b	Greensboro	NYY	A	23	84	284	62	14	2	7	101	46	34	30	0	107	6	0	1	15	6	.71	4	.218	.305	.356
Washington, Kelley	ss	Marlins	Fla	R	20	4	15	2	0	0	0	2	2	2	2	0	9	0	0	0	0	0	.00	0	.133	.235	.133
		Brevard Cty	Fla	A+	20	57	197	53	6	4	4	79	30	30	11	0	56	2	4	2	13	7	.65	4	.269	.311	.401
Washington, Mo	of	Williamsprt	Pit	A-	21	5	16	2	0	0	0	2	0	0	2	0	11	1	0	0	0	0	.00	0	.125	.263	.125
Washington, Rico*	c	Hickory	Pit	A	22	76	287	102	15	1	13	158	70	50	48	7	45	8	0	6	5	1	.83	4	.355	.453	.551
		Lynchburg	Pit	A+	22	57	205	58	7	0	7	86	31	32	30	0	45	4	1	2	4	1	.80	8	.283	.382	.420
Wathan, Derek#	ss	Kane County	Fla	A	23	125	469	119	18	4	1	148	71	49	53	2	54	5	10	3	33	12	.73	13	.254	.334	.316
Watkins, Tommy	2b	Twins	Min	R	20	49	152	40	10	0	1	53	30	12	28	1	21	2	7	1	4	4	.50	5	.263	.383	.349
Watson, Brandon*	of	Expos	Mon	R	18	33	119	36	2	0	0	38	15	12	11	2	11	1	2	2	4	2	.67	0	.303	.361	.319
Watson, Matt*	of	Vermont	Mon	A-	21	70	284	108	12	3	7	147	55	47	30	1	27	3	2	4	17	7	.71	6	.380	.439	.518
Weber, Jon*	of	Billings	Cin	R+	22	22	80	19	6	0	5	40	16	17	16	1	15	0	0	0	1	1	.50	2	.238	.365	.500
Weekly, Chris*	2b	Medcine Hat	Tor	R+	23	71	257	77	18	2	6	117	43	42	29	0	43	1	1	2	12	2	.86	6	.300	.370	.455
Weichard, Paul#	of	Hickory	Pit	A	20	89	316	71	7	3	5	99	44	37	28	0	92	0	4	0	23	7	.77	4	.225	.288	.313
Welch, Ed*	of	Butte	Ana	R+	20	31	122	42	4	2	0	50	29	19	18	0	30	0	0	0	24	6	.80	0	.344	.429	.410
Welsh, Eric*	1b	Rockford	Cin	A	23	101	368	103	23	0	16	174	52	64	23	3	57	1	0	2	3	2	.60	9	.280	.322	.473
Wenner, Mike	of	Athletics	Oak	R	21	49	207	80	12	7	2	112	56	28	17	0	31	5	4	2	36	12	.75	4	.386	.442	.541
Wesson, Barry	of	Kissimmee	Hou	A+	23	115	352	76	15	1	4	105	32	34	26	0	84	4	2	2	8	7	.53	3	.216	.276	.298
West, Kevin	of	Elizabethtn	Min	R+	20	63	229	72	12	6	12	132	43	55	22	2	68	16	0	2	4	2	.67	3	.314	.409	.576
Weston, Aron*	of	Pirates	Pit	R	19	33	119	26	2	1	0	30	26	5	20	0	36	1	0	0	14	5	.74	1	.218	.336	.252
Wheat, Trey	of	White Sox	CWS	R	24	16	58	17	1	0	0	18	7	4	5	0	9	0	0	0	7	0	1.00	0	.293	.349	.310
Whitby, Cory*	c	Augusta	Bos	A	24	35	70	15	4	0	1	22	12	5	18	0	20	3	0	0	2	1	.67	0	.214	.396	.314
		Sarasota	Bos	A+	24	3	5	1	0	0	0	1	0	0	2	0	1	0	0	0	0	0	.00	0	.200	.429	.200
White, Greg	1b	Butte	Ana	R+	24	55	205	67	15	2	9	113	37	47	26	1	50	4	0	3	1	2	.33	5	.327	.408	.551
Whitehead, Braxton	c	Clinton	Cin	A	24	82	272	81	19	0	3	109	41	38	30	1	42	5	0	1	0	0	.00	7	.298	.377	.401
Whitehurst, Tom	of	Asheville	Col	A	22	33	100	24	1	0	1	28	15	6	2	0	23	5	1	1	3	2	.60	1	.240	.287	.280
Whitlock, Brian	of	Kinston	Cle	A+	25	13	32	8	1	0	0	9	3	3	1	0	10	1	0	1	0	2	.00	0	.250	.286	.281
Wickersham, Jack	2b	Fort Wayne	SD	A	24	39	140	33	7	1	0	42	24	20	12	0	28	4	4	0	6	6	.50	4	.236	.314	.300
		Rancho Cuca	SD	A+	24	56	174	49	10	0	0	59	28	14	15	0	37	4	4	1	13	5	.72	6	.282	.351	.339
Wiese, Brian	of	Lowell	Bos	A-	23	21	79	25	4	1	5	46	16	18	9	0	25	2	0	0	2	2	.50	1	.316	.400	.582
		Augusta	Bos	A	23	23	68	8	2	0	0	10	7	2	10	0	18	4	1	1	1	0	1.00	2	.118	.265	.147
Wigand, Tom	2b	Phillies	Phi	R	22	15	27	4	0	0	0	4	8	2	10	1	11	2	0	1	2	3	.40	2	.148	.400	.148
Wigginton, Ty	2b	St. Lucie	NYM	A+	22	123	456	133	23	5	21	229	69	73	56	4	82	4	4	2	9	12	.43	5	.292	.373	.502
Wilder, Paul*	of	Chston-SC	TB	A	22	44	150	26	4	0	4	42	15	13	21	0	61	3	0	0	7	1	.88	3	.173	.287	.280
William, Jovany	c	Peoria	StL	A	23	67	240	49	8	0	8	81	30	27	14	0	59	8	3	3	2	3	.40	6	.204	.268	.338
Williams, Brady	3b-dh	Red Sox	Bos	R	20	39	121	31	4	2	5	54	19	25	29	0	45	2	0	3	3	3	.50	4	.256	.400	.446
Williams, Charles#	of	New Jersey	StL	A-	22	28	90	22	4	4	2	40	16	8	19	0	25	1	4	0	3	5	.38	2	.244	.382	.444
Williams, Clyde*	1b	Vermont	Mon	A-	20	63	256	60	14	2	2	84	23	37	16	1	85	1	1	2	1	4	.20	6	.234	.280	.328
Williams, Jewell	of	Mahoning Vy	Cle	A-	23	62	220	60	9	0	8	93	37	42	31	1	60	6	0	1	14	7	.67	7	.273	.376	.423
Williams, P.J.	of	Wisconsin	Sea	A	23	115	371	111	14	5	2	141	65	46	48	0	63	6	5	3	22	7	.76	5	.299	.386	.380
Williams, Peanut	1b	Wisconsin	Sea	A	22	9	32	8	1	0	2	15	6	7	4	0	12	1	0	0	0	0	.00	0	.250	.351	.469
		Lancaster	Sea	A+	22	68	272	88	12	0	26	178	60	59	35	1	89	4	0	1	0	0	.00	5	.324	.407	.654
Williamson, Bryan	of	Elizabethtn	Min	R+	23	24	67	17	3	1	0	22	6	6	7	0	11	1	1	0	0	1	.00	2	.254	.333	.328
Williamson, Casey*	of	Oneonta	Det	A-	23	48	139	34	8	0	1	45	19	15	14	0	38	7	1	0	5	1	.83	0	.245	.344	.324
Williford, Dan*	1b	South Bend	Ari	A	23	8	24	2	0	0	0	2	1	0	2	0	10	1	0	0	0	0	.00	0	.083	.185	.083
		Missoula	Ari	R+	23	16	50	7	4	0	1	14	6	6	4	0	19	2	0	0	0	0	.00	1	.140	.232	.280
Willis, Dave	1b	Wilmington	KC	A+	25	116	441	115	26	1	16	191	58	72	20	0	84	7	0	7	4	4	.50	10	.261	.299	.433
Wilson, Andy	of	Rancho Cuca	SD	A+	24	105	351	103	18	5	1	134	60	39	48	1	50	4	3	2	26	14	.65	8	.293	.383	.382
Wilson, Jack	ss	Peoria	StL	A	22	64	251	86	22	4	3	125	47	28	15	0	23	2	3	0	11	5	.69	2	.343	.384	.498
		Potomac	StL	A+	22	64	257	76	10	1	2	94	44	18	19	1	31	1	3	1	7	4	.64	2	.296	.345	.366
Wilson, Josh	ss	Marlins	Fla	R	19	53	203	54	9	4	0	71	29	27	24	0	36	5	1	4	14	2	.88	4	.266	.352	.350
Wilson, Travis	2b	Macon	Atl	A	22	90	363	112	20	4	11	173	65	63	9	1	66	15	0	3	14	8	.64	8	.309	.349	.477
Winchester, Jeff	c	Asheville	Col	A	20	86	310	72	18	1	18	146	45	48	27	0	92	9	0	1	0	1	.00	8	.232	.311	.471
Winrow, Gary*	of	Yankees	NYY	R	19	46	180	57	9	3	0	72	31	28	21	0	28	0	0	1	5	1	.83	2	.317	.386	.400
		Tampa	NYY	A+	19	3	7	3	0	0	0	3	1	0	0	0	0	0	0	0	0	0	.00	1	.429	.429	.429
Winter, Jon	2b-ss	Chston-SC	TB	A	23	13	32	8	2	0	0	10	3	3	7	0	10	2	0	0	0	1	.00	2	.250	.415	.313
Wise, DeWayne*	of	Rockford	Cin	A	22	131	502	127	20	13	11	206	70	81	42	2	81	7	5	14	35	13	.73	6	.253	.312	.410
Wong, Jerrod*	of	Myrtle Bch	Atl	A+	26	58	201	45	11	4	5	79	27	31	6	0	52	4	4	2	1	2	.33	7	.224	.258	.393
Woodward, Mattson	1b	Wisconsin	Sea	A	24	58	150	32	1	0	0	33	15	9	24	0	45	1	0	0	0	3	.00	5	.213	.326	.220

1999 Batting — Single-A and Rookie Leagues

Player	Pos	Team	Org	Lg	A	G	AB	H	2B	3B	HR	TB	R	RBI	TBB	IBB	SO	HBP	SH	SF	SB	CS	SB%	GDP	Avg	OBP	SLG
Woody, Dominic	c-dh	Utica	Fla	A-	21	48	181	50	11	0	4	73	26	22	16	1	34	13	0	2	0	2	.00	1	.276	.373	.403
Wren, Cliff	1b	Yakima	LA	A-	23	64	254	80	21	0	10	131	46	44	18	2	39	4	5	0	11	5	.69	5	.315	.370	.516
Wrenn, Michael	1b-c	Twins	Min	R	22	42	129	33	8	1	4	55	24	21	15	0	19	2	4	1	6	0	1.00	0	.256	.340	.426
Wright, Brad*	of	Pittsfield	NYM	A-	24	63	236	61	9	3	1	79	38	23	18	0	31	4	6	1	9	4	.69	4	.258	.320	.335
Wright, Corey*	of	Savannah	Tex	A	20	95	316	83	15	5	1	111	61	23	64	1	73	5	1	1	13	13	.50	2	.263	.394	.351
Wright, Gavin	of	Martinsvlle	Hou	R+	21	61	236	73	17	3	2	102	37	29	25	0	46	1	0	1	32	2	.94	0	.309	.376	.432
Wright, Michael	c	Salem-Keizr	SF	A-	24	24	63	17	4	0	1	24	14	7	17	0	12	2	0	1	0	0	.00	0	.270	.434	.381
Yakopich, Joe*	2b	Diamondbcks	Ari	R	19	47	154	47	5	3	0	58	37	22	30	0	31	1	0	0	6	2	.75	5	.305	.422	.377
Yancy, Mike	of	Kingsport	NYM	R+	21	65	215	61	6	3	2	79	36	29	15	0	50	13	2	2	24	7	.77	2	.284	.363	.367
Yates, Chris	of	Kissimmee	Hou	A+	24	16	36	9	1	0	0	10	2	4	4	0	8	1	0	0	3	4	.43	1	.250	.341	.278
Yingling, Joe	c	Tigers	Det	R	19	5	11	1	1	0	0	2	2	0	3	0	6	1	0	0	0	0	.00	0	.091	.333	.182
Young, Mike	2b-ss	Dunedin	Tor	A+	23	129	495	155	36	3	5	212	86	83	61	2	78	4	1	5	30	6	.83	10	.313	.389	.428
Young, Walter*	1b	Pirates	Pit	R	20	37	130	30	6	2	0	40	9	15	4	1	34	3	1	0	2	2	.50	4	.231	.270	.308
Zambrano, Alan#	2b	Wisconsin	Sea	A	21	90	282	57	14	0	5	86	33	30	29	1	79	6	3	3	6	7	.46	5	.202	.288	.305
Zapata, Alexis	of	Lakeland	Det	A+	23	115	404	99	15	5	5	139	52	45	33	0	116	2	3	2	7	5	.58	16	.245	.304	.344
Zapata, Juan	of	Auburn	Hou	A-	22	16	44	10	0	0	1	13	7	5	0	0	10	0	1	0	4	0	1.00	0	.227	.227	.295
Zapey, Winton	of	Marlins	Fla	R	20	29	74	16	6	0	1	25	8	10	7	0	17	4	0	0	1	0	1.00	1	.216	.318	.338
Zapp, A.J.*	1b	Macon	Atl	A	22	119	428	98	24	1	22	190	60	65	40	0	163	7	0	4	1	0	1.00	4	.229	.303	.444
Zaragoza, Anthony	2b	Kingsport	NYM	R+	27	36	84	13	2	1	0	17	8	3	15	0	27	4	1	1	4	2	.67	0	.155	.308	.202
Zardis, Alex	3b	Kingsport	NYM	R+	22	33	43	5	4	0	0	9	10	3	7	0	18	1	1	0	0	3	.00	0	.116	.255	.209
Zavala, Juan	of	Mexico	—	R	—	36	107	16	1	1	0	19	9	8	12	0	50	10	2	0	2	1	.67	3	.150	.295	.178
Zeber, Ryan	c	Clinton	Cin	A	22	2	2	0	0	0	0	0	0	0	0	0	0	0	0	0	0	0	.00	0	.000	.333	.000
		Reds	Cin	R	22	3	6	1	0	0	0	1	1	0	1	0	0	0	0	0	0	0	.00	0	.167	.286	.167
		Rockford	Cin	A	22	39	106	27	6	1	0	35	11	10	7	1	21	3	0	1	1	5	.17	3	.255	.316	.330
Zepeda, Jesse#	3b	Hagerstown	Tor	A	26	89	222	50	8	1	5	75	26	34	42	1	36	1	4	2	3	0	1.00	4	.225	.348	.338
Zoccolillo, Pete*	1b	Eugene	ChC	A-	23	64	183	43	7	1	1	55	20	15	22	1	26	2	0	2	3	2	.60	2	.235	.321	.301
Zumwalt, Sean	of	Braves	Atl	R	19	51	188	39	3	1	3	53	19	22	15	0	48	5	0	0	1	2	.33	6	.207	.284	.282
Zuniga, Tony	3b	San Jose	SF	A+	25	136	533	144	33	3	10	213	82	66	65	0	89	13	3	4	9	4	.69	8	.270	.361	.400

1999 Pitching — Single-A and Rookie Leagues

HOW MUCH HE PITCHED											WHAT HE GAVE UP												THE RESULTS					
Player	Team	Org	Lg	A	G	GS	CG	GF	IP	BFP	H	R	ER	HR	SH	SF	HB	TBB	IBB	SO	WP	Bk	W	L	Pct.	ShO	Sv	ERA
Abreu, Miguel	Utica	Fla	A-	21	15	0	0	6	22.1	102	23	16	16	7	0	1	1	17	0	12	3	0	1	0	1.000	0	0	6.45
Abreu, Winston	Macon	Atl	A	23	14	14	0	0	69.1	272	41	17	13	3	0	2	4	26	0	95	7	1	7	2	.778	0	0	1.69
	Myrtle Bch	Atl	A+	23	13	12	0	0	68.2	290	53	26	25	7	2	4	0	41	0	76	3	1	3	2	.600	0	0	3.28
Acevedo, Jose	Clinton	Cin	A	22	24	24	1	0	133.2	553	119	65	56	14	2	3	0	43	0	136	5	3	8	6	.571	1	0	3.77
Achilles, Matt	Frederick	Bal	A+	23	16	15	1	1	94	413	103	57	45	6	2	6	5	32	2	77	5	0	5	8	.385	0	0	4.31
Acosta, Jhon	Cubs	ChC	R	20	5	0	0	2	9	35	7	1	0	0	1	1	2	0	0	9	0	0	1	0	1.000	0	1	0.00
	Eugene	ChC	A-	20	13	3	0	0	35.1	156	39	29	26	7	0	1	1	14	1	43	0	0	1	0	1.000	0	0	6.62
Adair, Derek	Piedmont	Phi	A	24	8	6	1	2	38.1	166	44	28	20	4	0	1	0	6	0	15	2	2	2	4	.333	0	0	4.70
	Clearwater	Phi	A+	24	9	0	0	4	14	58	16	5	5	0	0	0	0	1	0	9	0	0	1	0	1.000	0	3	3.21
Adams, Chris	Eugene	ChC	A-	22	17	0	0	14	18.2	94	24	14	11	0	0	1	0	14	1	17	5	0	1	1	.500	0	4	5.30
Adkins, Jon	Modesto	Oak	A+	22	26	15	0	2	102	460	113	65	54	6	4	6	9	30	1	93	8	0	9	5	.643	0	1	4.76
Advincola, Jose*	Orioles	Bal	R	20	12	5	0	4	28	131	37	20	17	1	1	0	2	16	0	23	8	1	1	1	.500	0	0	5.46
Affeldt, Jeremy*	Chstn-WV	KC	A	21	27	24	2	1	143.1	637	140	78	61	4	9	4	8	80	0	111	14	4	7	7	.500	1	0	3.83
Ainsworth, Kurt	Salem-Keizr	SF	A-	21	10	10	1	0	44.2	187	34	18	8	1	3	2	3	18	0	64	3	0	3	3	.500	0	0	1.61
Akin, Aaron	Brevard Cty	Fla	A+	23	27	15	1	5	108.2	496	149	79	62	17	4	6	12	34	0	55	3	1	5	8	.385	0	0	5.13
Albertus, Roberto*	Braves	Atl	R	18	13	4	0	0	32.2	146	36	23	22	1	1	2	0	17	1	27	1	0	1	2	.333	0	0	6.06
Albin, Scott	Vermont	Mon	A-	24	26	0	0	16	55	226	50	22	16	3	0	1	1	11	1	57	3	0	4	2	.667	0	6	2.62
	Jupiter	Mon	A+	24	2	0	0	2	2	12	4	4	1	0	0	1	0	1	1	3	0	0	0	1	.000	0	1	4.50
Alcala, Jason	Pirates	Pit	R	19	10	0	0	9	14.2	59	12	7	2	0	1	1	0	0	0	9	1	1	0	1	.000	0	2	1.23
	Williamsprt	Pit	A-	19	6	0	0	4	12.1	56	11	7	6	1	0	0	2	6	0	11	0	0	0	0	.000	0	0	4.38
Alcantara, Over	Marlins	Fla	R	19	4	0	0	3	10	40	7	1	1	0	1	0	0	3	0	4	1	0	0	0	.000	0	0	0.90
Aldridge, Mike	Yankees	NYY	R	23	7	0	0	0	7.1	34	6	7	7	0	0	1	0	5	0	12	3	0	2	0	1.000	0	0	8.59
Almonte, Edwin	Burlington	CWS	A	23	37	5	2	16	115.2	480	107	48	39	5	2	1	2	28	4	85	6	1	9	12	.429	0	5	3.03
Alston, Travis	Batavia	Phi	A-	23	15	3	0	3	32	149	35	19	15	1	0	3	1	17	0	29	6	0	1	0	1.000	0	0	4.22
Altman, Gene	Reds	Cin	R	21	3	3	0	0	10	41	6	2	2	0	0	0	0	4	0	10	0	0	1	0	1.000	0	0	1.80
	Clinton	Cin	A	21	3	3	0	0	14	60	7	9	6	0	0	0	3	7	0	19	0	0	0	2	.000	0	0	3.86
	Rockford	Cin	A	21	11	11	0	0	53.1	254	63	41	36	4	1	3	3	34	0	51	6	0	2	6	.250	0	0	6.08
Alvarado, Carlos	Lynchburg	Pit	A+	22	20	18	0	0	90.2	400	89	52	46	4	0	1	2	46	0	75	8	4	4	6	.400	0	0	4.57
Alvarez, Larry	Cubs	ChC	R	20	8	0	0	1	17	74	17	7	6	0	0	0	1	8	0	10	0	0	2	0	1.000	0	0	3.18
Ammons, Cary*	Chstn-WV	KC	A	23	16	16	0	0	90.2	371	80	41	30	3	4	2	2	34	0	92	5	0	8	5	.615	0	0	2.98
Anderson, An.*	Marlins	Fla	R	21	13	0	0	6	28.2	123	28	13	11	1	1	1	1	9	0	26	1	0	2	1	.667	0	2	3.45
Anderson, Craig*	Everett	Sea	A-	19	15	15	2	0	90	360	81	42	32	7	3	2	3	13	1	82	5	1	10	2	.833	1	0	3.20
Andersen, Derek*	Hudson Val	TB	A-	22	20	5	0	5	55.1	220	46	19	16	0	2	1	2	14	0	56	2	2	2	3	.400	0	0	2.60
Anderson, Travis	Auburn	Hou	A-	22	9	8	0	0	39.2	175	42	31	23	2	0	2	3	17	0	29	5	0	1	5	.167	0	0	5.22
Anderson, Wes	Kane County	Fla	A	20	23	23	2	0	137.1	565	111	55	49	8	3	5	5	51	0	134	4	0	9	5	.643	1	0	3.21
Andra, Jeff*	San Jose	SF	A+	24	13	7	0	0	50	217	54	28	25	3	2	2	0	19	1	54	3	1	4	2	.667	0	0	4.50
Andrade, Jancy	Bluefield	Bal	R+	22	3	3	0	0	15.2	65	17	8	5	1	1	1	1	0	0	16	1	0	1	0	1.000	0	0	2.87
	Delmarva	Bal	A	22	26	8	0	3	75	339	73	61	46	8	1	2	4	44	0	63	8	2	2	5	.286	0	0	5.52
Andujar, Jesse	Vermont	Mon	A-	20	5	0	0	1	4.1	31	2	11	9	0	0	1	4	10	0	2	2	0	0	0	.000	0	0	18.69
Anez, Omar	Orioles	Bal	R	19	14	6	0	2	31.1	161	38	38	29	2	0	0	2	29	0	23	13	3	1	6	.143	0	0	8.33
Aponte, Carlos	Helena	Mil	R+	21	21	1	0	10	36	155	36	24	23	4	3	1	1	17	2	28	2	0	2	3	.400	0	1	5.75
Aracena, Juan	Columbus	Cle	A	23	32	0	0	30	35.2	138	32	13	13	7	1	0	1	3	0	30	1	0	2	0	1.000	0	18	3.28
	Kinston	Cle	A+	23	5	0	0	2	7	28	7	2	2	0	1	0	0	1	0	7	1	0	1	1	.500	0	0	2.57
	Frederick	Bal	A+	23	2	0	0	2	2	7	2	1	0	0	0	0	0	0	0	0	0	0	0	0	.000	0	0	0.00
Aragon, Angel	Rancho Cuca	SD	A+	26	53	0	0	36	68.2	291	55	33	27	3	4	3	6	28	3	76	6	1	2	7	.222	0	19	3.54
Aramboles, Ricardo	Yankees	NYY	R	20	9	7	0	2	34.2	149	35	18	15	1	3	4	1	14	0	42	6	0	2	3	.400	0	0	3.89
	Greensboro	NYY	A	20	6	6	1	0	34.2	136	25	9	9	1	1	1	0	12	0	34	5	0	1	2	.333	0	0	2.34
Arauz, Alexis	Diamondbcks	Ari	R	20	16	8	0	3	51	246	60	40	25	1	2	4	1	26	0	38	12	2	2	3	.400	0	1	4.41
Arellan, Felix*	Great Falls	LA	R+	19	15	3	0	6	31	156	32	31	29	1	0	2	2	32	0	38	11	1	1	2	.333	0	0	8.42
Arias, Pablo	Tigers	Det	R	21	12	12	1	0	65.2	282	57	31	22	2	1	2	8	22	1	60	2	0	3	2	.600	0	0	3.02
Arieta, Corey*	Helena	Mil	R+	23	15	15	1	0	88.2	386	83	51	38	5	2	2	6	27	0	60	7	1	6	3	.667	0	0	3.86
Armstrong, Charles*	Princeton	TB	R+	23	3	0	0	1	2.2	18	7	5	4	0	0	1	0	3	0	2	0	1	0	0	.000	0	0	13.50
Arthurs, Shane	Cape Fear	Mon	A	20	25	21	2	2	136.1	596	144	77	63	8	7	5	7	52	1	87	10	0	7	8	.467	0	0	4.16
Asencio, Domingo	White Sox	CWS	R	18	11	0	0	5	10.2	56	24	13	13	1	0	0	0	4	0	5	4	1	1	0	1.000	0	0	10.97
Atchison, Scott	Wisconsin	Sea	A	24	15	13	0	0	81.2	326	67	34	31	4	2	2	3	25	1	85	4	1	4	5	.444	0	0	3.42
Avery, Paul*	Vero Beach	LA	A+	23	32	7	0	10	78.1	369	82	51	42	5	5	9	4	46	2	57	9	3	2	7	.222	0	0	4.83
Babula, Shaun*	Bluefield	Bal	R+	23	4	0	0	0	8	33	4	2	1	0	0	0	0	5	0	10	0	0	1	0	1.000	0	0	1.13
	Delmarva	Bal	A	23	16	0	0	7	13.2	65	17	7	5	3	5	2	0	5	0	16	1	1	0	2	.000	0	2	3.29
Backsmeyer, Justin	Pulaski	Tex	R+	20	12	7	0	0	42.2	211	55	41	32	8	0	0	5	30	0	31	10	2	3	1	.750	0	0	6.75
Baek, Cha	Mariners	Sea	R	20	8	4	0	1	27	112	30	13	11	2	0	0	0	6	0	25	2	3	3	0	1.000	0	0	3.67
Baerlocher, Ryan	Spokane	KC	A-	22	15	15	0	0	74.2	326	78	43	39	7	2	0	6	32	0	68	0	0	7	2	.778	0	0	4.70
Baginski, Tom*	Tigers	Det	R	23	10	0	0	1	20	74	11	4	4	2	0	1	1	4	0	24	0	0	2	0	1.000	0	0	1.80
	Lakeland	Det	A+	23	6	0	0	2	7	37	10	5	5	1	0	1	0	7	0	5	0	0	0	0	.000	0	0	6.43
	Oneonta	Det	A-	23	3	0	0	2	6	29	8	4	3	0	1	1	0	4	0	6	0	0	1	1	.500	0	1	4.50
Bailey, Ben	Clinton	Cin	A	25	9	2	0	1	21.1	88	20	12	12	3	0	0	2	8	0	16	2	0	1	0	1.000	0	0	5.06
Bailey, David	Cubs	ChC	R	23	4	0	0	3	6.2	29	8	7	7	2	0	0	0	2	0	10	0	0	0	0	.000	0	1	9.45
Baisley, Brad	Piedmont	Phi	A	20	23	23	3	0	147.2	606	116	56	37	5	5	5	14	55	1	110	6	2	10	7	.588	2	0	2.26
Baker, Brad	Red Sox	Bos	R	19	4	3	0	0	11.1	48	10	3	1	0	1	0	1	2	0	10	0	1	1	0	1.000	0	0	0.79
Baker, Chris	Medcine Hat	Tor	R+	22	3	1	0	1	8.2	37	8	4	3	0	0	0	1	2	0	9	1	1	0	1	.000	0	0	3.12
	St.Cathrnes	Tor	A-	22	12	10	0	0	49.1	221	61	37	34	6	1	0	1	14	1	55	7	2	2	4	.333	0	0	6.20
Balbuena, Caleb	Wisconsin	Sea	A	23	9	8	0	0	44	201	48	33	26	6	2	1	1	16	0	37	4	2	1	3	.250	0	0	5.32
Baldassano, J.R.	Vermont	Mon	A-	20	6	0	0	4	8	45	9	7	6	0	0	0	2	9	0	11	4	1	0	1	.000	0	0	6.75
	Expos	Mon	R	20	12	0	0	7	19.2	101	27	22	20	1	1	3	0	13	0	20	6	0	1	2	.333	0	4	9.15
Balfour, Grant	Quad City	Min	A	22	19	14	0	2	91.2	368	66	39	36	7	1	1	6	37	0	95	1	0	8	5	.615	0	1	3.53
Baranowski, Bran.	Royals	KC	R	23	24	0	0	9	35	151	27	14	11	1	1	0	1	19	2	53	3	0	1	2	.333	0	1	2.83
Barbarossa, Josh*	Idaho Falls	SD	R+	20	3	3	0	0	9.1	39	8	4	3	1	0	0	0	4	0	7	0	0	1	0	1.000	0	0	2.89
Barker, Billy*	Expos	Mon	R	23	10	0	0	7	14.1	61	13	6	5	2	1	0	0	8	0	10	2	0	2	2	.500	0	3	3.14

1999 Pitching — Single-A and Rookie Leagues

HOW MUCH HE PITCHED											WHAT HE GAVE UP												THE RESULTS					
Player	Team	Org	Lg	A	G	GS	CG	GF	IP	BFP	H	R	ER	HR	SH	SF	HB	TBB	IBB	SO	WP	Bk	W	L	Pct.	ShO	Sv	ERA
Barnes, Pat*	Everett	Sea	A-	20	15	10	1	0	49.1	236	59	40	31	4	4	1	5	26	0	39	8	1	3	3	.500	1	0	5.66
Barnett, Aaron*	Oneonta	Det	A-	23	23	0	0	6	35.2	161	35	21	20	2	3	1	0	22	1	35	5	0	5	0	1.000	0	0	5.05
Barnsby, Scott	Vero Beach	LA	A+	24	4	0	0	0	7.2	39	12	10	7	1	0	0	0	2	0	7	2	0	0	0	.000	0	0	8.22
Barr, Adam*	Burlington	Cle	R+	19	9	7	0	0	18	105	21	22	15	0	1	0	4	28	0	21	2	0	0	4	.000	0	0	7.50
Barreto, Joel	Twins	Min	R	19	11	9	3	1	56.1	222	45	18	16	2	3	0	0	17	0	41	4	2	4	3	.571	1	0	2.56
Barrett, Jimmy	Martinsvlle	Hou	R+	19	6	3	0	1	18.1	82	15	9	9	0	1	1	4	10	0	12	2	1	0	1	.000	0	0	4.42
Barrett, Scott*	Auburn	Hou	A-	21	5	2	0	0	11.1	49	8	5	4	0	0	2	0	6	0	13	1	1	0	0	.000	0	0	3.18
Barry, Shawn*	St. Lucie	NYM	A+	25	46	0	0	11	37.1	199	35	33	29	4	4	2	6	46	3	40	12	0	3	4	.429	0	0	6.99
Barton, Chris	Stockton	Mil	A+	23	7	2	0	1	18.1	90	23	23	21	1	1	0	3	15	0	8	4	0	1	1	.500	0	0	10.31
	Beloit	Mil	A	23	16	0	0	3	28	143	31	27	17	5	0	0	7	16	0	18	9	1	0	1	.000	0	2	5.46
Bartosh, Cliff*	Fort Wayne	SD	A	20	35	20	1	1	129.2	567	136	76	64	14	0	4	10	49	0	100	7	2	5	12	.294	1	0	4.44
Bauder, Mike*	Lakeland	Det	A+	25	28	0	0	12	43	201	56	22	21	1	6	1	2	19	3	30	4	0	1	3	.250	0	1	4.40
Bauer, Rick	Frederick	Bal	A+	23	26	26	4	0	152	662	159	85	77	17	3	11	12	54	2	123	11	1	10	9	.526	0	0	4.56
Bauer, Ryan	Fort Wayne	SD	A	23	36	15	1	12	110.1	495	111	75	60	10	2	5	7	55	0	86	6	0	4	9	.308	0	5	4.89
Bausher, Andy*	Lynchburg	Pit	A+	23	25	24	1	0	143.1	648	165	98	77	12	4	4	6	52	1	89	7	2	6	15	.286	0	0	4.83
Bautista, Francisco	Chstn-WV	KC	A	24	7	0	0	4	10.1	54	11	7	5	1	0	0	1	12	1	5	2	0	0	1	.000	0	0	4.35
Bautista, Martin	Columbus	Cle	A	22	15	12	0	0	67.1	311	80	46	37	5	1	2	6	20	0	51	5	0	6	3	.667	0	0	4.95
	Kinston	Cle	A+	22	20	0	0	6	42.1	179	31	16	13	3	5	3	3	20	1	44	2	0	6	1	.857	0	2	2.76
Baxter, Gerik	Padres	SD	R	20	8	7	0	0	36	153	27	7	6	0	3	0	5	15	0	45	2	0	3	0	1.000	0	0	1.50
	Idaho Falls	SD	R+	20	5	5	0	0	24.1	110	21	15	13	3	1	0	2	17	0	29	1	0	2	0	1.000	0	0	4.81
Bazan, Juan	Williamsprt	Pit	A-	22	8	8	1	0	47.2	191	37	17	16	4	0	2	1	16	0	33	2	0	4	3	.571	0	0	3.02
Bazzell, Shane	Sou Oregon	Oak	A-	21	5	5	0	0	29	126	27	15	6	1	0	2	1	9	0	18	0	4	3	1	.750	0	0	1.86
	Visalia	Oak	A+	21	8	8	0	0	40.1	182	50	27	23	4	1	1	0	19	0	29	0	1	2	4	.333	0	0	5.13
Bechler, Steve	Delmarva	Bal	A	20	26	26	1	0	152.1	642	137	69	60	12	5	2	4	58	0	139	9	0	8	12	.400	1	0	3.54
Beckman, Jacob	Athletics	Oak	R	21	12	2	0	4	28.1	126	31	16	12	2	0	0	2	10	0	19	4	1	4	1	.800	0	1	3.81
Becks, Ryan*	Cape Fear	Mon	A	24	34	6	0	11	93.2	408	96	52	40	10	2	2	6	32	1	62	5	0	10	6	.625	0	1	3.84
Bedard, Erik*	Orioles	Bal	R	21	8	6	0	1	29	117	20	7	6	1	0	0	0	13	0	41	3	0	2	1	.667	0	0	1.86
Beech, Matt*	Clearwater	Phi	A+	28	2	2	0	0	4.2	24	7	5	4	0	0	1	0	2	0	3	0	0	0	0	.000	0	0	7.71
Behn, Brendan*	Pittsfield	NYM	A-	24	15	1	0	10	40	172	39	18	14	3	3	0	2	11	1	39	2	0	2	2	.500	0	1	3.15
	Capital Cty	NYM	A	24	1	0	0	1	1	8	4	4	4	0	0	0	0	1	0	1	2	0	0	0	.000	0	0	36.00
Beimel, Joe*	Hickory	Pit	A	23	29	22	0	3	130	570	146	81	64	12	4	5	12	43	0	102	10	2	5	11	.313	0	0	4.43
Beitey, Jason	Savannah	Tex	A	22	21	1	0	9	48.2	228	54	38	29	4	1	5	6	28	0	38	5	2	1	3	.250	0	2	5.36
Belcher, B.J.	Charlotte	Tex	A+	22	15	4	0	3	37	173	48	22	19	4	1	2	2	19	0	15	0	1	2	2	.500	0	0	4.62
Belisle, Matt	Danville	Atl	R+	20	14	14	0	0	71.1	329	86	50	38	3	0	2	8	23	0	60	6	2	2	5	.286	0	0	4.79
Bell, Casey	Fort Wayne	SD	A	21	2	0	0	0	6.2	28	8	5	5	1	0	0	0	1	0	3	1	0	0	0	.000	0	0	6.75
	Idaho Falls	SD	R+	21	15	13	0	1	78.1	362	85	57	41	3	4	2	1	39	1	37	11	0	3	6	.333	0	0	4.71
Bell, Heath	Capital Cty	NYM	A	22	55	0	0	48	62.1	251	47	23	18	3	2	0	0	17	0	68	3	1	1	7	.125	0	25	2.60
Bell, Scott	San Berndno	LA	A+	24	28	0	0	13	50.2	239	66	40	34	4	3	6	3	22	1	37	5	0	2	5	.286	0	3	6.04
Bell, Tom	Marlins	Fla	R	19	13	0	0	9	24.2	105	21	11	11	2	0	1	1	7	0	9	0	0	1	0	1.000	0	3	4.01
Bellhorn, Todd*	Capital Cty	NYM	A	23	38	0	0	10	58.2	265	55	38	28	3	2	2	3	32	0	46	6	0	5	4	.556	0	0	4.30
Bello, Emerson	Lancaster	Sea	A+	22	9	0	0	1	13.1	65	15	12	10	3	0	0	3	9	0	13	1	0	0	0	.000	0	0	6.75
Bello, Jilberto	Delmarva	Bal	A	23	38	0	0	21	65.2	292	68	36	29	4	5	1	2	29	0	46	5	1	6	4	.600	0	4	3.97
Beltran, Francis	Cubs	ChC	R	19	7	0	0	6	10.2	38	5	3	0	0	0	0	1	1	0	8	0	0	0	1	.000	0	2	0.00
	Eugene	ChC	A-	19	16	0	0	7	28	142	41	32	26	2	0	1	3	14	0	28	6	0	0	2	.000	0	0	8.36
Beltre, Sandy	White Sox	CWS	R	18	13	10	0	2	67.2	305	85	38	31	5	2	1	3	21	0	58	7	1	5	4	.556	0	0	4.12
Benitez, Angel	Cubs	ChC	R	19	16	0	0	6	26.2	132	37	24	23	2	2	2	3	11	0	15	0	1	0	3	.000	0	0	7.76
Bennett, Jeff	Pirates	Pit	R	20	8	8	0	0	44.2	191	53	27	21	1	2	1	0	9	0	28	2	3	3	4	.429	0	0	4.23
	Hickory	Pit	A	20	8	6	0	2	35	161	48	25	23	5	2	0	1	9	0	16	2	0	2	2	.500	0	0	5.91
Bennett, Tom	Visalia	Oak	A+	24	36	8	0	5	87.2	463	113	91	78	7	3	4	2	94	1	87	39	1	1	9	.100	0	0	8.01
Benoit, Joaquin	Charlotte	Tex	A+	21	22	22	0	0	105	483	117	67	62	5	1	7	11	50	0	83	3	2	7	4	.636	0	0	5.31
Berger, Craig	St. Lucie	NYM	A+	24	36	0	0	26	38.2	188	49	22	21	2	3	0	3	25	3	21	3	0	1	3	.250	0	9	4.89
Bergman, Dusty*	Boise	Ana	A-	22	15	15	0	0	74.1	340	102	58	54	12	1	1	1	18	2	46	6	0	5	5	.500	0	0	6.54
Bermudez, Manny	Bakersfield	SF	A+	23	32	22	1	1	145.2	687	183	121	97	8	7	5	18	66	1	65	7	1	5	14	.263	0	0	5.99
Bernero, Adam	W Michigan	Det	A	23	15	15	2	0	95.2	386	75	36	27	8	0	2	4	23	0	80	3	3	8	4	.667	1	0	2.54
Berroa, Oliver	Wisconsin	Sea	A	22	21	0	0	10	29.1	124	22	8	6	1	2	1	4	17	0	28	6	0	1	0	1.000	0	1	1.84
Berry, Jonathan	Yakima	LA	A-	22	16	10	0	1	58	299	81	68	56	3	1	4	3	46	0	31	15	0	1	6	.143	0	0	8.69
Berryman, Brian	Fort Wayne	SD	A	22	9	9	0	0	46.2	205	43	25	21	2	0	2	2	24	0	19	0	2	4	2	.667	0	0	4.05
Berryman, Chad	Boise	Ana	A-	23	24	0	0	11	46	181	34	16	12	4	0	1	2	13	1	42	8	2	1	1	.500	0	1	2.35
Berube, Martin	Orioles	Bal	R	18	11	0	0	8	17	69	8	5	1	0	0	1	2	10	1	11	0	0	0	0	.000	0	2	0.53
Bess, Stephen	Oneonta	Det	A-	23	7	1	0	2	17	67	9	2	2	1	1	0	0	7	2	23	1	0	0	0	.000	0	2	1.06
	W Michigan	Det	A	23	12	0	0	7	19.1	76	12	2	2	0	0	0	0	7	0	23	1	0	1	1	.500	0	3	0.93
Bevis, P.J.	Missoula	Ari	R+	19	15	15	0	0	85.2	357	83	51	44	11	1	0	7	30	0	69	6	2	6	2	.750	0	0	4.62
Biddlestone, Jason	Pirates	Pit	R	21	12	4	0	3	46.1	195	39	19	15	1	0	2	4	16	0	45	0	0	4	1	.800	0	0	2.91
	Williamsprt	Pit	A-	21	1	1	0	0	5	26	7	6	5	0	0	1	0	3	0	2	0	0	0	1	.000	0	0	9.00
Bido, Jose	High Desert	Ari	A+	21	11	0	0	5	13	74	23	19	18	3	0	1	3	9	0	14	0	0	0	0	.000	0	3	12.46
Bieniasz, Derek	Lancaster	Sea	A+	26	15	9	0	0	52.1	249	75	48	46	7	2	2	6	20	0	29	4	1	1	8	.111	0	0	7.91
Birdsong, Tim	Clinton	Cin	A	23	24	23	0	0	128.2	555	131	75	61	9	0	8	4	50	0	95	7	0	5	8	.385	0	0	4.27
Black, Brett	Clearwater	Phi	A+	25	34	0	0	19	45.1	194	55	30	26	5	2	4	2	6	4	27	0	1	3	3	.500	0	3	5.16
Blackmore, John	Michigan	Hou	A	22	37	0	0	25	49.1	241	64	44	41	9	4	3	2	29	2	43	10	4	3	4	.429	0	7	7.48
Blanco, Roger	Macon	Atl	A	23	19	6	0	5	38	199	63	46	41	8	0	1	5	16	0	28	3	3	1	3	.250	0	0	9.71
Blevins, Jeremy	Tampa	NYY	A+	22	1	0	0	0	1.2	11	4	0	0	0	0	0	1	1	0	0	0	0	0	0	.000	0	0	0.00
	Greensboro	NYY	A	22	19	19	0	0	106.2	449	105	56	48	7	1	3	3	30	0	81	8	0	10	5	.667	0	0	4.05
Blitstein, Jeff	Auburn	Hou	A-	24	17	5	0	6	54.1	234	58	33	26	4	2	2	4	9	0	29	2	2	4	5	.444	0	1	4.31
Bloomer, Chris	South Bend	Ari	A	25	43	0	0	39	49.2	210	44	28	22	3	2	1	2	16	0	54	8	1	1	2	.333	0	21	3.99
Bluma, Marc	St.Cathrnes	Tor	A-	23	24	0	0	23	24.1	106	22	16	16	3	1	0	1	7	1	32	2	0	3	4	.429	0	13	5.92
Blumenstock, Brad	Athletics	Oak	R	25	3	2	0	0	5	28	10	4	3	0	0	0	0	6	0	4	2	0	0	0	.000	0	0	5.40
Blythe, Billy	Macon	Atl	A	24	1	0	0	1	1	5	2	1	1	0	0	0	0	0	0	1	2	0	0	0	.000	0	0	9.00

1999 Pitching — Single-A and Rookie Leagues

HOW MUCH HE PITCHED											WHAT HE GAVE UP												THE RESULTS					
Player	Team	Org	Lg	A	G	GS	CG	GF	IP	BFP	H	R	ER	HR	SH	SF	HB	TBB	IBB	SO	WP	Bk	W	L	Pct.	ShO	Sv	ERA
Bond, Aaron	Charlotte	Tex	A+	23	8	7	0	1	37.2	183	54	34	27	1	2	2	3	23	0	18	3	0	2	4	.333	0	0	6.45
Bong, Jung*	Macon	Atl	A	19	26	20	0	2	108.2	484	111	61	48	8	5	1	11	50	0	100	9	4	6	5	.545	0	1	3.98
Bonner, Luke	Mahoning Vy	Cle	A-	23	19	1	0	5	38	170	46	20	20	4	2	1	4	8	0	37	2	1	4	3	.571	0	0	4.74
Book, Jeremy	Peoria	StL	A	22	27	16	0	1	103	458	110	70	61	9	2	3	11	32	0	67	6	6	6	5	.545	0	0	5.33
Booker, Chris	Daytona	ChC	A+	23	42	0	0	29	73	328	72	45	32	6	2	3	3	37	1	68	5	0	2	5	.286	0	6	3.95
Borges, Reece	Michigan	Hou	A	24	37	1	0	6	64.1	295	74	45	36	4	2	2	6	23	2	37	5	1	6	2	.750	0	2	5.04
Borne, Matt	Burlington	CWS	A	23	22	0	0	14	30.1	149	35	20	16	3	1	1	5	22	3	24	5	2	2	4	.333	0	2	4.75
	Winston-Sal	CWS	A+	23	10	1	0	3	16.2	83	21	14	13	0	1	2	2	12	3	8	1	0	1	2	.333	0	0	7.02
Bost, Ronald*	St.Cathrnes	Tor	A-	20	4	0	0	1	3.2	16	2	3	3	1	0	0	0	3	0	2	0	0	0	0	.000	0	0	7.36
Bottenfield, Jason	Lowell	Bos	A-	23	23	0	0	2	36.1	166	36	29	23	3	3	2	2	17	0	24	2	3	1	2	.333	0	0	5.70
Boublis, Dan	Savannah	Tex	A	23	30	9	2	14	84	399	116	66	59	10	0	5	4	35	0	59	9	1	7	3	.700	0	0	6.32
Bowe, Brandon	Brevard Cty	Fla	A+	24	9	0	0	3	20	86	18	7	7	4	0	0	0	10	0	21	3	1	2	0	1.000	0	1	3.15
	Utica	Fla	A-	24	6	0	0	1	12.1	54	14	6	4	0	0	0	0	2	0	24	1	0	2	0	1.000	0	0	2.92
Bowen, Patrick	Butte	Ana	R+	23	20	7	0	0	55.1	287	81	59	47	9	3	5	8	35	0	48	15	0	2	2	.500	0	0	7.64
Bowles, Brian	Hagerstown	Tor	A	23	48	1	0	22	79.1	355	73	41	35	4	3	4	12	39	3	80	9	0	6	2	.750	0	3	3.97
Bowyer, Travis	Twins	Min	R	18	1	0	0	0	1	3	0	0	0	0	0	0	0	0	0	1	0	0	1	0	1.000	0	0	0.00
Box, John*	St. Pete	TB	A+	25	42	0	0	16	57	259	71	34	32	6	3	4	4	15	0	39	9	0	2	2	.500	0	0	5.05
	Chston-SC	TB	A	25	2	0	0	1	2	6	2	0	0	0	0	0	0	0	0	1	0	0	1	0	1.000	0	0	0.00
Boyanich, Vincent	Twins	Min	R	23	15	0	0	10	33.1	159	45	33	28	1	3	1	3	11	1	38	6	2	2	5	.286	0	2	7.56
Brackeen, Colin*	Dunedin	Tor	A+	25	40	0	0	14	53.1	247	60	29	23	4	0	0	8	28	0	33	3	0	2	1	.667	0	3	3.88
Bradley, Bobby	Pirates	Pit	R	19	6	6	0	0	31	128	31	13	10	2	0	2	2	4	0	31	5	0	1	1	.500	0	0	2.90
Bradley, David	Billings	Cin	R+	22	17	9	0	0	64.2	292	69	43	35	3	2	3	5	24	0	51	4	1	5	4	.556	0	0	4.87
Brantley, Brian	Asheville	Col	A	24	34	3	0	13	90.1	406	89	65	59	6	7	2	11	44	0	100	13	1	6	6	.500	0	3	5.88
Bravo, Franklin	Hickory	Pit	A	21	34	8	0	6	95	415	82	47	34	11	6	3	9	42	2	81	3	2	7	1	.875	0	0	3.22
Brazoban, Melvin	Savannah	Tex	A	23	29	5	0	11	66	335	72	63	52	6	1	3	2	60	0	75	13	2	1	2	.333	0	2	7.09
Brea, Lesli	St. Lucie	NYM	A+	21	32	18	0	9	120.2	516	95	64	50	4	2	2	4	68	1	136	7	3	1	7	.125	0	3	3.73
Breitenstein, Keith*	Lynchburg	Pit	A+	28	33	8	0	4	85	362	85	37	25	4	5	4	5	25	0	62	5	0	1	2	.333	0	0	2.65
Brewer, Clint	Clinton	Cin	A	21	24	9	0	4	73.2	308	61	41	34	10	4	1	2	28	0	39	2	0	8	2	.800	0	0	4.15
	Rockford	Cin	A	21	10	0	0	5	17.2	82	19	15	12	2	1	0	0	9	1	16	3	1	1	0	1.000	0	0	6.11
Brewer, Dustin	Orioles	Bal	R	19	4	0	0	0	9.1	47	13	11	3	0	0	1	2	2	0	8	1	1	1	1	.500	0	0	2.89
	Bluefield	Bal	R+	19	1	0	0	0	1	6	2	1	0	0	0	0	0	1	0	0	0	0	0	0	.000	0	0	0.00
Brewington, Jamie	Kinston	Cle	A+	28	36	5	0	15	81.1	353	74	42	35	6	2	4	2	37	0	81	8	1	1	10	.091	0	4	3.87
Briceno, Pablo	Helena	Mil	R+	22	12	6	0	1	42.1	182	36	26	21	6	1	0	2	21	0	23	4	0	1	4	.200	0	0	4.46
Bridenbaugh, Chri.*	Great Falls	LA	R+	20	17	12	0	1	79	384	114	77	64	11	3	2	4	25	0	54	2	2	0	6	.000	0	0	7.29
Bridges, Donnie	Cape Fear	Mon	A	21	8	8	1	0	47.1	189	37	12	12	2	2	0	5	17	0	44	5	0	6	1	.857	1	0	2.28
	Jupiter	Mon	A+	21	18	18	1	0	99	429	116	53	45	5	3	8	2	36	0	63	7	0	4	6	.400	1	0	4.09
Bridges, Doug*	Cedar Rapds	Ana	A	23	22	22	3	0	150.1	628	136	67	60	12	7	4	7	45	0	128	7	2	15	5	.750	2	0	3.59
	Lk Elsinore	Ana	A+	23	5	5	2	0	35.1	156	42	19	17	4	2	0	0	11	0	34	3	0	3	2	.600	0	0	4.33
Brito, Eude*	Phillies	Phi	R	18	12	3	0	3	28.2	139	39	22	16	0	2	2	0	19	0	23	4	1	0	1	.000	0	0	5.02
Brookman, Ryan	Batavia	Phi	A-	23	14	0	0	5	19.2	83	17	5	1	0	0	2	0	7	2	13	3	1	1	0	1.000	0	1	0.46
Brooks, Frank*	Batavia	Phi	A-	21	16	12	1	2	77.1	312	64	26	25	2	0	1	2	33	0	58	2	6	7	3	.700	1	0	2.91
Brooks, Jacob	Lk Elsinore	Ana	A+	22	27	0	0	15	36.2	176	38	33	29	7	2	3	1	29	1	43	9	1	3	3	.500	0	4	7.12
Brown, Andrew	Braves	Atl	R	19	11	11	0	0	42.1	183	40	15	11	4	1	0	3	16	0	57	1	4	1	1	.500	0	0	2.34
Brown, Craig*	Mahoning Vy	Cle	A-	23	18	0	0	7	29.1	136	34	20	20	0	1	1	2	15	0	33	4	1	1	1	.500	0	1	6.14
Brown, Derek	Frederick	Bal	A+	23	43	0	0	37	51.1	232	49	31	23	6	4	1	4	20	1	36	4	1	6	5	.545	0	14	4.03
Brown, Graeme	Kingsport	NYM	R+	22	18	3	0	3	46.1	203	47	24	17	6	3	1	4	19	1	46	5	0	4	3	.571	0	1	3.30
Brown, Paul*	Reds	Cin	R	21	14	4	1	4	48	204	53	30	23	2	4	4	1	13	0	20	1	0	0	3	.000	0	1	4.31
Brown, Steve	Auburn	Hou	A-	24	18	7	0	4	52.2	243	57	40	31	4	0	3	4	21	1	43	5	0	3	2	.600	0	1	5.30
Brown, Tighe	Bristol	CWS	R+	23	7	0	0	4	9.2	52	18	12	11	1	1	1	0	5	1	11	0	0	1	2	.333	0	1	10.24
	Burlington	CWS	A	23	4	0	0	1	4.2	25	3	4	4	1	0	0	0	6	0	8	1	0	0	0	.000	0	0	7.71
Brown, Zay	Clinton	Cin	A	21	3	0	0	2	4.1	20	4	2	2	0	0	0	0	3	1	1	1	0	0	1	.000	0	0	4.15
	Billings	Cin	R+	21	18	7	1	4	56	253	60	30	23	6	4	2	5	21	0	36	2	0	3	3	.500	0	0	3.70
Bruback, Matt	Lansing	ChC	A	21	25	25	0	0	135	633	151	92	81	15	5	3	10	87	0	118	10	1	9	8	.529	0	0	5.40
Brueggemann, D.*	Salem	Col	A+	24	37	0	0	17	61	288	64	46	40	7	6	1	4	43	1	52	13	2	3	3	.500	0	2	5.90
Brummett, Sean*	Boise	Ana	A-	22	17	3	0	2	32.1	148	41	25	24	3	1	0	1	12	1	26	1	0	1	2	.333	0	0	6.68
Brunet, Michael	Butte	Ana	R+	23	9	0	0	6	10.2	43	8	2	2	1	0	0	0	4	0	12	1	0	1	0	1.000	0	3	1.69
Buchanan, Brian*	Greensboro	NYY	A	23	48	0	0	14	51	238	41	21	17	1	2	3	6	40	0	58	8	1	4	3	.571	0	1	3.00
Buehrle, Mark*	Burlington	CWS	A	21	20	14	1	4	98.2	412	105	49	45	8	2	2	5	16	1	91	3	6	7	4	.636	1	3	4.10
Buirley, Matt	Hickory	Pit	A	24	46	0	0	33	55	253	44	34	23	4	2	0	9	32	3	63	7	1	8	4	.667	0	11	3.76
Bukowski, Stan	Butte	Ana	R+	18	10	5	0	1	28	124	26	13	10	0	1	3	3	16	0	29	1	1	1	2	.333	0	0	3.21
Buller, Sean*	Lakeland	Det	A+	24	1	0	0	1	3	15	4	3	3	0	0	1	0	2	0	2	0	0	0	0	.000	0	0	9.00
	W Michigan	Det	A	24	31	17	2	2	120.1	528	133	78	66	11	3	6	5	55	1	72	9	0	10	10	.500	0	0	4.94
Bullinger, Jim	Vero Beach	LA	A+	34	6	6	0	0	19	90	23	17	16	5	1	1	0	10	0	18	1	0	0	2	.000	0	0	7.58
Bullock, Jeremiah*	Pulaski	Tex	R+	20	13	13	0	0	67.2	315	78	60	43	7	1	3	6	31	0	39	10	3	2	3	.400	0	0	5.72
Bumatay, Mike*	Pirates	Pit	R	20	11	3	0	6	40.1	154	35	16	13	4	0	0	1	8	0	39	2	0	2	1	.667	0	2	2.90
Burch, Matt	Royals	KC	R	23	5	4	0	0	14	67	17	10	7	0	0	0	3	10	0	9	1	0	0	2	.000	0	0	4.50
	Chstn-WV	KC	A	23	21	15	0	2	73.2	355	95	62	52	14	3	3	6	41	1	43	7	2	3	11	.214	0	1	6.35
Bureau, Stephen	Braves	Atl	R	19	11	0	0	5	11.2	66	13	17	13	0	0	1	6	14	0	8	6	0	0	0	.000	0	0	10.03
Burgos, Ricardo	Yakima	LA	A-	21	18	0	0	17	41.2	194	50	31	20	6	3	0	1	9	1	24	3	0	1	2	.333	0	4	4.32
Burke, Erick*	Oneonta	Det	A-	22	15	0	0	6	16.1	107	28	26	16	2	2	3	3	25	0	15	8	2	1	1	.500	0	0	8.82
Burkhart, B.J.*	Ogden	Mil	R+	23	10	0	0	5	21.2	102	27	21	12	9	0	3	1	5	0	13	0	1	1	0	1.000	0	0	4.98
	Helena	Mil	R+	23	8	0	0	4	8	32	13	4	3	1	0	0	0	1	0	4	1	0	1	1	.500	0	0	3.38
Burns, Casey	Idaho Falls	SD	R+	22	12	9	0	0	39.2	181	44	24	16	1	0	1	2	22	0	48	4	4	1	2	.333	0	0	3.63
Burnside, Adrian*	San Berndno	LA	A+	23	26	22	0	0	131.2	571	124	69	61	7	3	4	11	55	0	129	10	2	10	9	.526	0	0	4.17
Burruezo, Joe	Pirates	Pit	R	19	7	0	0	3	9.1	40	6	6	5	0	0	1	1	9	0	8	0	0	0	1	.000	0	0	4.82
Burton, Tim	Everett	Sea	A-	23	26	0	0	13	38.2	181	40	25	16	2	3	1	0	21	5	28	6	0	2	3	.400	0	1	3.72
Butler, Mark	New Jersey	StL	A-	23	18	0	0	5	19.2	111	22	18	16	1	0	0	9	22	0	8	3	0	2	0	1.000	0	0	7.32

1999 Pitching — Single-A and Rookie Leagues

HOW MUCH HE PITCHED											WHAT HE GAVE UP												THE RESULTS					
Player	Team	Org	Lg	A	G	GS	CG	GF	IP	BFP	H	R	ER	HR	SH	SF	HB	TBB	IBB	SO	WP	Bk	W	L	Pct.	ShO	Sv	ERA
Butler, Matt	Braves	Atl	R	20	11	10	0	0	38	168	36	20	17	4	1	2	0	22	0	38	0	0	2	4	.333	0	0	4.03
Button, Sammy*	Burlington	Cle	R+	22	13	12	0	0	50.1	236	55	38	29	3	1	2	5	26	0	44	8	0	1	5	.167	0	0	5.19
Bynum, Mike*	Idaho Falls	SD	R+	22	5	3	0	0	17	60	7	0	0	0	1	0	0	4	0	21	0	0	1	0	1.000	0	0	0.00
	Rancho Cuca	SD	A+	22	7	7	0	0	38.1	159	35	17	14	1	1	1	2	8	0	44	2	2	3	1	.750	0	0	3.29
Byrd, Mike	Mahoning Vy	Cle	A-	22	9	0	0	2	20	89	17	12	6	0	0	0	1	10	0	23	1	0	2	0	1.000	0	1	2.70
Byron, Terence	Utica	Fla	A-	21	6	6	1	0	29	110	17	7	4	0	0	0	3	7	0	31	2	2	3	0	1.000	1	0	1.24
Cabaj, Chris	Royals	KC	R	22	11	2	0	3	44	179	42	15	13	1	0	1	2	6	0	38	4	0	6	0	1.000	0	0	2.66
Cabrera, Yunior*	Mets	NYM	R	19	13	11	0	0	54.1	249	58	35	23	0	1	1	4	26	0	59	7	1	2	3	.400	0	0	3.81
Calandriello, Do.*	Modesto	Oak	A+	24	38	0	0	13	48	210	36	22	19	2	2	3	4	31	1	44	7	1	4	1	.800	0	1	3.56
Calvo, Jose	Auburn	Hou	A-	20	5	0	0	1	7	36	9	9	4	0	0	1	1	4	0	5	2	0	0	2	.000	0	1	5.14
Calzada, Javier	Athletics	Oak	R	21	10	8	0	1	46	177	32	19	13	4	0	2	1	11	0	30	3	1	5	1	.833	0	0	2.54
	Visalia	Oak	A+	21	8	0	0	4	19	85	24	17	14	4	1	4	1	4	1	15	2	1	2	0	1.000	0	0	6.63
Cameron, Ryan	Portland	Col	A-	22	4	0	0	3	5	18	1	0	0	0	1	0	0	1	1	4	0	0	1	0	1.000	0	1	0.00
	Asheville	Col	A	22	17	0	0	5	34.2	140	18	10	9	1	0	0	1	18	1	40	4	0	3	1	.750	0	2	2.34
Camp, Shawn	Rancho Cuca	SD	A+	24	53	0	0	28	66	285	68	37	29	4	4	4	1	25	3	78	7	1	1	5	.167	0	6	3.95
Campbell, Jarrett	Princeton	TB	R+	20	11	9	0	0	46.1	215	51	35	26	3	1	3	5	15	0	29	7	3	4	2	.667	0	0	5.05
Campos, David*	Marlins	Fla	R	22	8	0	0	4	10.1	84	20	9	9	1	1	0	2	6	0	20	3	0	3	1	.750	0	0	4.19
	Brevard Cty	Fla	A+	22	13	0	0	7	25.1	121	25	24	19	3	0	3	2	16	0	17	2	0	0	2	.000	0	0	6.75
Cannon, Jon*	Daytona	ChC	A+	25	33	11	1	12	95.2	424	83	55	47	8	7	5	10	66	3	77	6	2	3	5	.375	0	0	4.42
Caple, Chance	New Jersey	StL	A-	21	7	7	0	0	37	164	35	24	18	4	0	1	2	18	0	36	2	1	0	4	.000	0	0	4.38
Caraballo, Angel	Bristol	CWS	R+	20	13	13	1	0	81	352	88	40	36	11	2	0	4	27	0	88	10	5	8	2	.800	0	0	4.00
Caraccioli, Lance*	San Berndno	LA	A+	22	28	26	0	0	140	645	124	90	78	9	7	10	10	126	0	98	8	1	6	7	.462	0	0	5.01
Cardona, Steve	Winston-Sal	CWS	A+	26	17	0	0	10	26	126	29	20	18	1	0	2	1	17	0	24	4	1	1	0	1.000	0	1	6.23
	South Bend	Ari	A	26	14	0	0	10	21.2	103	31	18	15	3	2	1	1	5	0	26	4	0	1	2	.333	0	0	6.23
Cardwell, Brian	Medcine Hat	Tor	R+	19	10	4	0	2	29.2	137	34	22	17	5	1	1	4	8	0	26	3	1	2	1	.667	0	1	5.16
Carey, Ben*	Phillies	Phi	R	21	17	4	0	3	39.1	172	40	20	16	1	0	1	4	15	0	35	2	0	2	2	.500	0	0	3.66
Carlson, Jeff	Staten Ilnd	NYY	A-	24	6	0	0	3	6.2	29	2	2	2	0	0	0	2	3	0	6	2	0	0	0	.000	0	0	2.70
Carmody, Brian*	Lancaster	Sea	A+	24	16	2	0	3	39.1	179	43	22	16	2	1	0	1	18	1	45	5	1	3	3	.500	0	0	3.66
Carmona, Cesarin	Idaho Falls	SD	R+	23	25	0	0	7	53	237	58	33	29	1	2	1	1	24	0	47	7	1	4	1	.800	0	0	4.92
Carnes, Matt	Fort Myers	Min	A+	24	52	1	0	20	81	343	74	48	33	4	8	7	2	26	0	67	6	1	4	4	.500	0	4	3.67
Carpenter, Justin	Greensboro	NYY	A	23	40	0	0	17	57.2	258	57	39	26	6	0	3	3	29	0	45	9	0	3	2	.600	0	0	4.06
Carr, Tim	Capital Cty	NYM	A	22	45	0	0	18	68.1	280	58	18	12	4	3	0	7	20	2	64	4	0	6	4	.600	0	0	1.58
Carrasco, Danny	Williamsprt	Pit	A-	23	18	4	0	6	51.2	212	43	20	17	2	1	3	3	23	0	49	7	4	4	2	.667	0	0	2.96
	Lynchburg	Pit	A+	23	2	0	0	0	5.2	29	9	8	4	0	1	0	0	3	0	4	0	0	0	1	.000	0	0	6.35
Carreras, Marino*	Everett	Sea	A-	20	22	0	0	9	31.1	157	37	29	25	4	2	1	4	24	1	30	2	1	1	4	.200	0	2	7.18
Carter, Justin*	Asheville	Col	A	23	27	26	2	1	144	639	138	79	57	10	5	4	12	72	0	146	8	3	13	6	.684	1	0	3.56
Carter, Roger	Chston-SC	TB	A	21	12	1	0	4	12.1	65	11	15	12	2	0	0	2	17	0	14	1	0	0	3	.000	0	1	8.76
Casadiego, Gerardo	Expos	Mon	R	19	9	4	0	2	19.1	84	19	10	6	1	2	0	2	8	0	8	1	0	1	1	.500	0	0	2.79
Casey, Joe	Hagerstown	Tor	A	21	28	28	0	0	142	637	150	99	74	10	4	3	10	64	0	79	25	3	7	14	.333	0	0	4.69
Cassidy, Scott	Hagerstown	Tor	A	24	27	27	1	0	170.2	694	151	78	62	13	2	1	21	30	0	178	3	2	13	7	.650	0	0	3.27
Casteel, Ricky	Delmarva	Bal	A	22	29	21	2	6	134.2	591	152	92	75	13	4	8	4	53	0	100	4	1	3	14	.176	0	0	5.01
Castellano, Jon.	Mexico	—	R	—	16	12	1	2	76.2	336	86	45	39	2	0	3	5	30	0	71	9	3	5	3	.625	0	0	4.58
Castelli, Robert	Cape Fear	Mon	A	23	29	0	0	18	43.2	204	39	30	18	4	0	3	2	35	0	46	5	3	2	2	.500	0	3	3.71
Castillo, Jose	Lakeland	Det	A+	23	8	0	0	6	13.2	54	7	4	4	1	0	1	0	5	2	11	0	0	2	1	.667	0	0	2.63
Castillo, Marcos	San Berndno	LA	A+	21	27	27	1	0	167	720	182	90	76	14	2	4	8	48	1	130	6	2	14	9	.609	1	0	4.10
Castillo, Ramon	Marlins	Fla	R	21	11	10	0	0	52	222	56	21	20	3	1	1	4	12	1	34	2	0	1	2	.333	0	0	3.46
Castillo, Wilson	Yakima	LA	A-	21	8	0	0	2	20	110	26	25	18	3	2	1	4	22	0	11	6	1	1	0	1.000	0	0	8.10
	Great Falls	LA	R+	21	5	0	0	3	10	45	11	6	5	1	1	1	1	3	0	8	4	0	1	3	.250	0	0	4.50
Castro, Eleuterio	Red Sox	Bos	R	22	6	0	0	2	15	64	15	7	6	1	1	0	0	4	1	8	1	0	0	1	.000	0	0	3.60
	Sarasota	Bos	A+	22	3	1	0	2	13	55	13	6	6	2	0	1	0	6	1	8	0	0	1	0	1.000	0	0	4.15
Cavazos, Andy	Rangers	Tex	R	19	10	7	0	1	36.1	151	35	16	15	3	3	1	0	12	0	15	1	1	2	0	1.000	0	0	3.72
Cedeno, Jovanny	Charlotte	Tex	A+	20	1	1	0	0	5	24	7	3	3	1	0	0	1	1	0	5	0	0	1	0	1.000	0	0	5.40
	Rangers	Tex	R	20	6	6	1	0	27.1	101	13	3	1	0	0	0	2	4	0	32	1	0	3	0	1.000	1	0	0.33
Cenate, Josh*	Bluefield	Bal	R+	19	9	9	0	0	38.1	183	45	32	19	1	3	2	3	20	0	55	5	2	1	5	.167	0	0	4.46
Cento, Tony*	Elizabethtn	Min	R+	22	18	0	0	14	19.1	90	22	6	4	1	1	0	1	6	1	35	1	0	1	2	.333	0	5	1.86
	Quad City	Min	A	22	11	0	0	3	8.1	34	6	2	1	0	0	1	1	3	1	11	1	0	1	0	1.000	0	0	1.08
Cepeda, Victor	Lakeland	Det	A+	22	11	3	0	0	28	139	41	27	22	4	2	1	1	15	0	23	1	0	0	6	.000	0	0	7.07
Cepeda, Wellington	High Desert	Ari	A+	22	42	3	0	13	86.2	407	106	64	55	14	3	3	1	42	1	74	10	0	6	6	.500	0	2	5.71
Cercy, Rick	Portland	Col	A-	23	13	1	0	2	28.2	137	29	19	17	0	0	3	6	17	0	25	6	0	1	2	.333	0	0	5.34
Cerros, Juan	St. Lucie	NYM	A+	23	5	0	0	2	7.2	32	5	1	0	0	0	0	1	4	0	6	0	1	2	0	1.000	0	0	0.00
Cervantes, Chris*	South Bend	Ari	A	21	38	10	0	14	115	490	109	49	40	9	5	1	4	34	0	89	10	1	8	5	.615	0	3	3.13
	High Desert	Ari	A+	21	1	0	0	0	0.1	7	5	6	6	1	0	0	0	1	0	1	0	0	0	0	.000	0	0	162.00
Cervantes, Peter	San Berndno	LA	A+	25	40	1	0	12	79.2	345	92	38	37	4	2	3	1	21	1	89	5	0	4	3	.571	0	2	4.18
Cespedes, Rafael	Braves	Atl	R	19	14	0	0	5	28.2	124	19	16	11	2	1	4	4	11	1	24	1	0	1	5	.167	0	0	3.45
Cetani, Bryan*	Braves	Atl	R	18	13	9	0	0	41.1	185	48	27	21	1	1	2	4	15	0	17	3	1	1	3	.250	0	0	4.57
Chacin, Gustavo*	Medcine Hat	Tor	R+	20	15	9	0	2	64	280	68	33	22	6	4	4	7	23	0	50	4	3	4	3	.571	0	1	3.09
Chacon, Ernesto	Yankees	NYY	R	20	18	1	0	4	35	156	30	14	12	1	2	1	3	21	0	55	3	0	4	0	1.000	0	1	3.09
Chacon, Shawn	Salem	Col	A+	22	12	12	0	0	72	316	69	44	33	3	1	3	2	34	0	66	5	0	5	5	.500	0	0	4.13
Charles, Juan	Ogden	Mil	R+	22	6	0	0	5	8.1	45	18	11	11	2	0	0	0	4	0	8	0	0	0	1	.000	0	0	11.88
Charron, Eric	Expos	Mon	R	21	9	8	0	0	43	189	44	32	28	3	1	3	2	19	0	25	5	0	2	6	.250	0	0	5.86
Chavez, Chris	Danville	Atl	R+	24	11	0	0	10	12	50	9	5	5	0	0	0	1	5	0	15	1	1	1	1	.500	0	4	3.75
	Macon	Atl	A	24	13	0	0	10	15.1	64	14	9	6	1	1	1	0	6	2	18	1	0	1	2	.333	0	3	3.52
Chavez, Wilton	Cubs	ChC	R	19	14	13	1	0	67.1	328	89	57	44	5	2	1	6	31	0	68	4	2	5	5	.500	1	0	5.88
Cheek, Andrew*	Red Sox	Bos	R	22	18	0	0	9	29	125	27	16	11	2	1	1	1	17	1	20	2	0	2	1	.667	0	2	3.41
	Sarasota	Bos	A+	22	2	0	0	1	4	25	8	6	6	0	1	0	0	6	0	0	1	0	0	0	.000	0	0	13.50
Chenard, Ken	Kingsport	NYM	R+	21	14	13	1	0	76.1	317	64	32	26	6	1	4	3	25	1	80	8	2	6	3	.667	0	0	3.07
Chiasson, Scott	Sou Oregon	Oak	A-	22	15	13	0	1	69	318	80	52	40	6	3	2	5	39	0	51	3	0	2	2	.500	0	0	5.22

1999 Pitching — Single-A and Rookie Leagues

Player	Team	Org	Lg	A	G	GS	CG	GF	IP	BFP	H	R	ER	HR	SH	SF	HB	TBB	IBB	SO	WP	Bk	W	L	Pct.	ShO	Sv	ERA
Chiavacci, Ron	Cape Fear	Mon	A	22	20	8	0	6	62.2	295	60	39	25	5	3	3	6	34	0	67	1	0	5	3	.625	0	1	3.59
	Jupiter	Mon	A+	22	8	8	0	0	48.1	198	36	15	12	5	0	0	5	17	0	32	3	0	4	4	.500	0	0	2.23
Chighisola, Lou*	Billings	Cin	R+	24	16	0	0	6	21	105	25	23	12	2	3	0	4	12	0	19	4	0	0	2	.000	0	0	5.14
	Reds	Cin	R	24	7	0	0	5	9.1	38	9	4	4	0	4	0	0	4	1	11	1	0	1	2	.333	0	3	3.86
	Clinton	Cin	A	24	7	1	0	5	13	55	11	4	4	1	0	1	0	7	0	8	1	0	0	1	.000	0	0	2.77
Childers, Jason	Ogden	Mil	R+	25	3	3	0	0	13	50	10	4	2	1	0	0	1	3	0	14	1	0	0	0	.000	0	0	1.38
	Stockton	Mil	A+	25	12	12	1	0	73.1	314	78	39	29	12	2	2	3	11	0	73	3	1	2	8	.200	0	0	3.56
Childers, Matt	Beloit	Mil	A	21	20	19	0	0	100	448	129	72	66	9	1	5	5	30	1	52	0	2	3	10	.231	0	0	5.94
Chipperfield, Calvin	Oneonta	Det	A-	22	15	15	0	0	79.2	332	55	32	29	5	2	4	5	33	0	83	9	0	4	4	.500	0	0	3.28
Chisnall, Wes	Vermont	Mon	A-	19	9	9	0	0	41.2	214	57	57	40	10	3	2	10	20	0	26	5	1	2	5	.286	0	0	8.64
	Expos	Mon	R	19	4	4	0	0	14.2	72	20	13	12	1	1	0	0	6	0	8	2	0	0	2	.000	0	0	7.36
Chivers, Jason*	Kingsport	NYM	R+	21	20	1	0	10	25.1	137	29	18	12	0	2	2	3	29	3	30	2	1	3	1	.750	0	0	4.26
Choate, Randy*	Tampa	NYY	A+	24	47	0	0	17	50	224	51	25	25	4	4	0	2	24	5	62	4	0	2	2	.500	0	1	4.50
Christ, John	Burlington	Cle	A	22	23	0	0	19	35.1	158	35	19	16	3	3	1	1	18	3	36	2	0	3	4	.429	0	4	4.08
Christensen, Ben	Cubs	ChC	R	22	3	3	0	0	9	39	8	3	3	0	0	0	1	5	0	10	1	1	0	1	.000	0	0	3.00
	Eugene	ChC	A-	22	5	5	0	0	21.1	100	21	14	14	2	0	1	0	14	0	21	2	0	0	2	.000	0	0	5.91
	Daytona	ChC	A+	22	4	4	0	0	22.2	106	25	16	16	4	1	1	3	11	0	18	1	1	1	3	.250	0	0	6.35
Christensen, Deryck	Rockies	Col	R	19	18	0	0	5	25.1	125	33	14	10	1	3	0	1	18	0	20	2	1	2	1	.667	0	0	3.55
Christenson, Ryan	Peoria	StL	A	23	29	8	0	2	89.2	410	101	63	53	9	2	5	5	42	0	84	5	0	4	4	.500	0	0	5.32
Christman, Tim*	Salem	Col	A+	25	38	0	0	7	48.1	188	38	18	13	0	1	2	2	12	0	64	1	0	1	2	.333	0	2	2.42
Chrysler, Clint*	Wisconsin	Sea	A	24	51	0	0	28	56.2	243	47	22	13	4	4	4	3	22	3	59	5	1	5	7	.417	0	8	2.06
Chung, Rocky	San Berndno	LA	A+	26	9	0	0	2	21	78	13	5	4	2	0	1	1	3	0	23	1	1	1	0	1.000	0	1	1.71
Cisar, Mark	Augusta	Bos	A	25	52	0	0	47	68.1	288	57	22	17	0	3	2	4	22	3	64	4	0	3	6	.333	0	27	2.24
Clackum, Scott	Kane County	Bos	A	25	47	1	0	29	71	306	82	32	26	0	2	2	1	14	1	53	4	0	4	4	.500	0	10	3.30
Clark, Kevin	Mariners	Sea	R	22	16	0	0	3	28.1	138	34	22	18	1	3	1	2	20	1	22	4	1	2	0	1.000	0	0	5.72
Classen, Ender	Pirates	Pit	R	22	6	6	0	0	34.2	139	21	13	7	1	1	2	7	9	0	28	0	0	3	1	.750	0	0	1.82
	Williamsprt	Pit	A-	22	3	1	0	0	8.2	37	9	3	3	0	0	0	3	2	0	5	0	1	0	0	.000	0	0	3.12
Claussen, Brandon*	Yankees	NYY	R	21	2	2	0	0	11.1	42	7	4	4	2	0	0	0	2	0	16	0	0	1	0	1.000	0	0	3.18
	Staten Ilnd	NYY	A-	21	12	12	1	0	72	295	70	30	27	4	3	0	3	12	2	89	4	4	6	4	.600	0	0	3.38
	Greensboro	NYY	A	21	1	1	1	0	6	29	8	7	7	1	0	0	0	2	0	5	1	1	0	1	.000	0	0	10.50
Clifton, Derek	Danville	Atl	R+	20	13	13	0	0	60	273	81	52	44	3	1	1	2	16	0	46	4	3	4	4	.500	0	0	6.60
Coa, Jesus	Royals	KC	R	20	7	2	0	0	26.2	129	36	22	17	1	0	2	4	13	0	11	3	1	1	1	.500	0	0	5.74
Coco, Pasqual	Hagerstown	Tor	A	22	14	14	0	0	97.2	384	67	29	24	4	1	1	8	25	1	83	2	0	11	1	.917	0	0	2.21
	Dunedin	Tor	A+	22	13	13	2	0	75	338	81	50	47	7	3	3	6	36	0	59	7	2	4	6	.400	0	0	5.64
Coffey, Todd	Reds	Cin	R	19	5	2	0	0	16	78	9	12	6	1	0	1	1	10	0	14	2	2	1	1	.500	0	0	3.38
Cogan, Tony*	Spokane	KC	A-	23	27	0	0	11	39.2	160	26	10	6	0	6	1	2	14	2	37	3	1	1	3	.250	0	4	1.36
Cole, Joey	Mets	NYM	R	22	13	8	0	0	51	234	52	30	25	1	0	2	11	23	0	55	9	1	5	1	.833	0	0	4.41
Collins, Pat	Vermont	Mon	A-	22	12	11	0	0	54.1	243	57	35	21	3	0	3	6	21	0	39	5	1	2	4	.333	0	0	3.48
Colome, Jesus	Modesto	Oak	A+	20	31	22	0	2	128.2	564	125	63	48	6	1	6	9	60	2	127	13	2	8	4	.667	0	1	3.36
Colon, Jose	Burlington	Cle	R+	22	13	0	0	0	25	107	19	14	9	4	1	2	1	6	1	29	8	1	2	0	1.000	0	0	3.24
Colon, Roman	Jamestown	Atl	A-	20	15	15	1	0	77.1	329	77	48	39	4	1	3	2	25	0	61	7	2	7	5	.583	0	0	4.54
Colton, Kyle	Braves	Atl	R	19	13	10	0	0	50.1	207	35	11	10	1	0	0	3	27	0	30	2	3	2	1	.667	0	0	1.79
Colyer, Steve*	San Berndno	LA	A+	21	27	25	1	0	145.2	644	145	82	76	12	3	7	8	86	0	131	8	3	7	9	.438	0	0	4.70
Combs, Chris	Lynchburg	Pit	A+	25	32	13	0	8	89.2	415	112	73	65	18	3	5	5	40	0	69	4	1	5	3	.625	0	0	6.52
Comer, Scott*	Brevard Cty	Fla	A+	23	19	19	5	0	130	502	120	38	34	3	3	4	3	50	0	85	0	1	9	4	.692	1	0	2.35
Condrey, Clay	Fort Wayne	SD	A	24	42	0	0	39	47.2	202	40	24	20	5	0	2	0	19	4	47	4	1	2	3	.400	0	20	3.78
	Rancho Cuca	SD	A+	24	6	0	0	1	7.1	29	4	3	3	1	0	0	0	3	0	9	0	0	0	0	.000	0	0	3.68
Connolly, Keith	Bakersfield	SF	A+	25	54	0	0	22	83	364	61	41	40	8	4	3	8	47	1	95	6	0	7	8	.467	0	3	4.34
Conroy, Ken	Eugene	ChC	A-	21	11	11	0	0	59.2	274	75	37	29	5	1	3	2	23	0	48	4	0	5	3	.625	0	0	4.37
Coogan, Patrick	Potomac	StL	A+	24	19	19	2	0	101	457	112	73	65	14	4	5	7	43	0	67	5	0	4	7	.364	0	0	5.79
Cook, Aaron	Asheville	Col	A	21	25	25	2	0	121.2	561	157	99	87	17	2	1	9	42	0	73	15	0	4	12	.250	0	0	6.44
Cook, Andy	Capital Cty	NYM	A	27	26	0		1	149.2	628	150	66	47	16	4	4	3	42	0	124	10	1	12	7	.632	0	1	2.83
Cook, Brent	New Jersey	StL	A-	22	9	8	0	0	44.1	189	42	19	14	2	4	0	1	16	0	42	5	2	5	1	.833	0	0	2.84
Cooke, Andrew*	Elizabethtn	Min	R+	19	16	9	0	0	54.2	246	65	44	32	8	3	2	2	9	0	58	6	0	1	4	.200	0	0	5.27
Cooper, Eric	Rockford	Min	A	22	4	4	0	0	13.2	69	21	15	15	2	0	2	3	11	0	6	7	0	1	1	.500	0	0	9.88
	Reds	Cin	R	22	3	2	0	0	10.1	48	13	12	9	0	0	1	0	5	0	5	2	0	0	0	.000	0	0	7.84
	Billings	Cin	R+	22	2	2	0	0	8	37	11	8	8	2	0	0	0	3	0	6	1	0	1	1	.500	0	0	9.00
	Clinton	Cin	A	22	12	10	1	1	47.1	226	49	38	32	8	2	3	2	36	1	37	9	2	2	5	.286	0	0	6.08
Cordero, Frangil*	Cubs	ChC	R	19	14	13	0	1	69.1	317	68	48	31	6	1	2	6	31	0	78	6	4	2	6	.250	0	0	4.02
Cordero, Jesus	Great Falls	LA	R+	21	11	6	0	3	29.1	161	51	43	34	5	1	3	5	24	0	20	12	0	0	5	.000	0	0	10.43
Cordero, Victor	Helena	Mil	R+	20	22	0	0	7	40.1	193	45	39	31	6	2	4	6	22	1	41	7	4	5	3	.625	0	1	6.92
Cordova, Jorge	Marlins	Fla	R	22	7	0	0	5	14	51	8	3	2	0	0	0	0	2	0	18	2	0	1	0	1.000	0	1	1.29
	Brevard Cty	Fla	A+	22	6	0	0	1	12.1	52	9	6	6	1	0	2	0	6	0	11	1	0	1	0	1.000	0	0	4.38
	Kane County	Fla	A	22	12	0	0	3	19.1	73	6	2	1	0	0	0	2	10	0	17	1	0	1	0	1.000	0	0	0.47
Corey, Michael	Macon	Atl	A	25	11	0	0	17	33.2	126	18	4	2	2	1	0	1	7	0	39	6	0	1	1	.500	0	7	0.53
	Myrtle Bch	Atl	A+	25	22	0	0	16	32	139	32	19	17	4	3	0	0	11	0	31	1	0	2	1	.667	0	6	4.78
Cornejo, Jesse*	Chston-SC	TB	A	23	51	0	0	16	72	313	66	35	28	5	2	2	1	33	3	75	4	2	4	5	.444	0	2	3.50
Cornejo, Nate	W Michigan	Det	A	20	28	28	4	0	174.2	750	173	87	72	4	10	9	12	67	0	125	11	5	9	11	.450	1	0	3.71
Correa, Cristobal	New Jersey	StL	A-	20	9	9	0	0	52	217	41	20	17	5	0	2	1	26	0	59	3	1	3	3	.500	0	0	2.94
	Peoria	StL	A	20	5	5	0	0	20	99	26	24	23	4	0	2	0	14	0	15	2	1	0	2	.000	0	0	10.35
Correa, Elvis	San Berndno	LA	A+	21	40	0	0	14	68.2	307	87	42	38	7	2	6	5	17	2	40	8	0	2	2	.500	0	1	4.98
Cortez, Martin*	Mexico	—	R	20	2	0	0	2	27.1	122	32	13	11	0	1	0	3	10	0	22	0	3	1	3	.750	0	2	3.62
Coscia, Tony	Bakersfield	SF	A+	26	28	28	1	0	171.2	737	186	100	86	25	4	7	15	38	0	133	7	3	10	11	.476	0	0	4.51
Cosgrove, Mike	Fort Myers	Min	A+	24	7	0	0	4	10.2	52	12	8	4	2	1	1	1	6	0	9	0	0	1	0	1.000	0	1	3.38
	Quad City	Min	A	24	42	0	0	15	62.2	276	71	37	33	9	2	2	1	24	3	46	2	3	7	7	.500	0	4	4.74
Cotton, Joe	Clearwater	Phi	A+	25	38	3	0	5	69.1	263	41	17	15	5	1	3	1	15	2	43	1	0	5	3	.625	0	1	1.95

343

1999 Pitching — Single-A and Rookie Leagues

HOW MUCH HE PITCHED											WHAT HE GAVE UP												THE RESULTS					
Player	Team	Org	Lg	A	G	GS	CG	GF	IP	BFP	H	R	ER	HR	SH	SF	HB	TBB	IBB	SO	WP	Bk	W	L	Pct.	ShO	Sv	ERA
Cowie, Stephen	Mahoning Vy	Cle	A-	23	12	10	0	0	61.2	262	66	38	32	10	2	1	5	7	0	83	2	1	2	5	.286	0	0	4.67
Cowsill, Brendon	Lk Elsinore	Ana	A+	25	27	20	4	2	125.2	562	155	87	75	17	6	9	5	36	0	62	3	0	4	10	.286	1	1	5.37
Cox, Brian	Jamestown	Atl	A-	24	17	1	0	5	28	128	23	17	15	1	0	1	2	18	0	29	6	0	1	1	.500	0	1	4.82
Cox, Ryan	Salem-Keizr	SF	A-	23	8	8	0	0	34.1	139	39	13	12	1	2	1	1	10	0	20	0	2	2	1	.667	0	0	3.15
	Bakersfield	SF	A+	23	7	7	0	0	33.1	151	46	22	18	6	1	0	1	3	0	30	2	0	1	4	.200	0	0	4.86
Cozier, Vance	Salem-Keizr	SF	A-	22	15	10	0	1	61	260	61	34	31	4	3	1	2	24	1	46	1	0	5	4	.556	0	0	4.57
Crawford, Chris	Hudson Val	TB	A-	22	1	0	0	0	1	4	0	0	0	0	0	1	0	1	0	2	2	0	0	0	.000	0	0	0.00
Crawford, Danny	Hickory	Pit	A	25	16	9	0	3	59.2	260	66	35	27	7	1	1	1	21	1	38	1	1	6	4	.600	0	0	4.07
Crawford, Jeremy*	Sou Oregon	Oak	A-	21	19	0	0	14	38.2	174	40	20	17	2	1	1	3	14	1	24	2	0	2	1	.667	0	2	3.96
Crawford, Wes*	Boise	Ana	A-	23	11	9	2	0	61	251	52	23	15	3	0	1	1	17	0	54	6	0	5	1	.833	0	0	2.21
Cromer, Jason*	Princeton	TB	R+	19	11	8	0	1	41	204	69	45	34	6	2	0	3	14	0	26	9	0	1	5	.167	0	0	7.46
Cromer, Nathan*	Princeton	TB	R+	19	13	7	0	0	39.1	228	72	69	49	7	1	2	1	33	1	28	10	1	0	4	.000	0	0	11.21
Crowder, Chuck*	Portland	Col	A-	23	6	6	0	0	27	119	24	14	13	2	0	0	2	16	0	39	2	0	2	1	.667	0	0	4.33
Crowther, John	Expos	Mon	R	23	13	0	0	4	34.2	144	30	14	12	0	1	0	3	11	0	26	1	2	2	2	.500	0	1	3.12
Crudale, Mike	Johnson Cy	StL	R+	23	24	0	0	8	33	142	29	15	12	1	1	0	1	14	0	36	5	0	0	1	.000	0	1	3.27
Crumpton, Chuck	Vermont	Mon	A-	23	19	0	0	13	23.1	102	24	11	5	0	1	1	3	6	0	24	2	1	1	2	.333	0	5	1.93
	Cape Fear	Mon	A	23	13	0	0	13	19	74	15	3	1	0	0	0	1	3	0	15	0	0	2	1	.667	0	7	0.47
Cruz, Juan	Eugene	ChC	A-	19	15	15	0	0	80.1	374	97	59	50	11	1	4	0	33	0	65	4	0	5	6	.455	0	0	5.94
Cubillan, Darwin	Tampa	NYY	A+	25	55	0	0	28	75.1	311	57	27	21	6	4	1	3	32	6	76	2	0	7	4	.636	0	3	2.51
Cueto, Jose	Cubs	ChC	R	21	11	9	0	1	56.2	247	49	32	18	1	1	3	4	22	0	66	2	1	3	4	.429	0	0	2.86
	Eugene	ChC	A-	21	4	4	0	0	24	101	26	13	12	2	2	1	4	5	0	21	1	0	0	2	.000	0	0	4.50
Cullen, Ryan*	Pulaski	Tex	R+	20	19	0	0	12	40.2	169	33	20	16	1	1	0	1	17	0	47	7	0	1	2	.333	0	6	3.54
Cummings, Jeremy	New Jersey	StL	A-	23	14	14	1	0	85	341	88	42	34	5	3	0	5	7	0	62	4	4	6	6	.500	0	0	3.60
Cunningham, Jer.	Salem-Keizr	SF	A-	21	7	5	0	1	15.1	76	25	11	8	0	0	0	1	6	0	13	0	0	0	2	.000	0	1	4.70
Currens, Tim	Burlington	CWS	A	24	22	0	0	10	33.2	163	50	31	25	1	1	1	2	14	1	26	3	0	1	3	.250	0	0	6.68
	Winston-Sal	CWS	A+	24	14	0	0	8	21.2	98	21	8	6	1	2	0	1	13	2	17	5	0	1	1	.500	0	0	2.49
Curreri, Joe	Bristol	CWS	R+	23	16	0	0	12	24.2	103	17	10	8	2	0	1	3	9	0	24	0	0	1	0	1.000	0	5	2.92
Curtice, John*	Red Sox	Bos	R	20	8	6	0	0	14.2	80	16	22	12	1	1	0	6	12	0	19	3	0	0	5	.000	0	0	7.36
Curtis, Daniel	Jamestown	Atl	A-	20	15	15	1	0	74.2	323	74	41	38	10	1	1	6	24	0	61	7	1	5	6	.455	1	0	4.58
Curtis, Mark*	Medcine Hat	Tor	R+	22	10	5	0	1	31.1	152	47	29	24	7	1	1	0	15	0	36	10	1	1	3	.250	0	0	6.89
Curtis, Tom*	Danville	Atl	R+	23	18	0	0	10	32.1	143	35	25	16	1	2	0	1	9	0	48	6	0	2	2	.500	0	3	4.45
Cutchins, Todd*	St. Lucie	NYM	A+	24	25	25	1	0	129.2	579	127	68	57	10	4	4	5	82	0	106	4	1	6	7	.462	0	0	3.96
Cyr, Eric*	Padres	SD	R	21	11	5	0	1	38.2	159	34	19	14	2	2	1	1	15	0	39	0	0	2	1	.667	0	0	3.26
	Idaho Falls	SD	R+	21	1	1	0	0	5	19	5	1	1	0	0	0	0	1	0	3	1	0	1	0	1.000	0	0	1.80
Daboin, Jorge	Burlington	Cle	R+	20	15	0	0	7	31.1	130	29	16	13	2	1	2	1	9	0	26	3	1	1	1	.500	0	1	3.73
Dagley, Corey	Batavia	Phi	A-	23	15	12	0	1	65.1	287	77	35	31	1	0	4	6	19	0	44	5	1	5	5	.500	0	0	4.27
Dailey, Matt*	Princeton	TB	R+	22	4	0	0	1	7	30	5	1	1	0	0	0	2	3	0	6	0	1	0	0	.000	0	0	1.29
	Hudson Val	TB	A-	22	14	0	0	3	20.1	100	27	19	16	3	0	0	1	12	0	17	2	1	0	1	.000	0	0	7.08
Dansby, Justin	Macon	Atl	A	22	4	0	0	2	6	31	7	5	5	1	0	0	0	6	0	7	0	1	0	2	.000	0	0	7.50
	Jamestown	Atl	A-	22	24	0	0	13	38.1	187	45	29	28	3	0	2	4	24	0	43	5	1	1	4	.200	0	4	6.57
Dant, Larry	Lansing	ChC	A	23	43	0	0	31	54.1	244	54	35	30	5	2	4	7	19	2	52	2	0	3	1	.750	0	12	4.97
Darnell, Paul*	Billings	Cin	R+	24	9	9	0	0	48.1	226	55	37	28	5	1	4	3	22	0	39	4	0	3	3	.500	0	0	5.21
	Clinton	Cin	A	24	6	6	0	0	35.1	152	35	19	12	4	0	0	3	13	0	23	1	0	3	2	.600	0	0	3.06
Darr, Jay	Fort Wayne	SD	A	21	7	4	0	1	23	106	27	19	15	2	0	2	2	12	0	12	1	0	1	3	.250	0	0	5.87
	Idaho Falls	SD	R+	21	19	8	0	1	57	273	80	48	43	6	3	6	4	20	0	62	6	0	2	1	.667	0	0	6.79
Darrell, Tommy	Sarasota	Bos	A+	23	30	12	1	6	101	455	118	75	56	8	5	7	5	30	5	67	11	0	4	10	.286	0	3	4.99
Davies, Bob	Fort Myers	Min	A+	24	25	23	1	1	137.1	594	156	82	70	13	3	7	5	38	1	105	6	2	10	10	.500	1	0	4.59
Davis, Billy	Great Falls	LA	R+	23	5	0	0	0	2.1	25	4	12	12	0	0	1	1	14	0	0	9	0	0	0	.000	0	0	46.29
Davis, Clint	High Desert	Ari	A+	30	2	0	0	1	2	9	0	1	1	0	2	0	0	2	0	3	1	0	1	0	1.000	0	0	4.50
Davis, Lance*	Rockford	Cin	A	23	22	20	1	0	127.1	550	135	62	54	9	5	2	4	49	1	95	2	0	7	5	.583	0	0	3.82
Davis, Keith	Tampa	NYY	A+	27	11	0	0	1	16	75	17	9	4	0	0	1	1	5	0	15	2	0	2	1	.667	0	0	2.25
	Lakeland	Det	A+	27	25	0	0	1	34.1	144	36	15	13	2	1	1	5	10	0	24	8	0	3	0	1.000	0	0	3.41
Day, Zach	Yankees	NYY	R	22	5	4	0	0	16.2	74	20	10	7	1	0	0	1	4	0	17	0	0	1	1	.500	0	0	3.78
	Greensboro	NYY	A	22	2	2	0	0	8	42	14	11	2	0	0	1	1	1	0	4	0	0	0	1	.000	0	0	2.25
Dean, Aaron*	St.Cathrnes	Tor	A-	23	17	8	0	6	61.2	243	50	18	16	3	1	1	5	13	1	68	7	2	4	0	1.000	0	1	2.34
DeHart, Blair	Idaho Falls	SD	R+	22	10	10	0	0	56.1	237	50	28	20	4	3	3	2	17	0	43	2	2	3	1	.750	0	0	3.20
DeHart, Casey*	Reds	Cin	R	22	2	2	0	0	4.2	22	7	4	4	0	0	0	0	2	0	6	0	0	0	1	.000	0	0	7.71
	Clinton	Cin	A	22	24	0	0	4	21.1	97	16	10	8	1	1	0	0	16	0	17	7	0	2	0	1.000	0	0	3.38
de la Cruz, Andres	Staten Ilnd	NYY	A-	20	5	0	0	5	4	21	7	6	6	0	0	0	1	2	0	3	2	0	0	2	.000	0	2	13.50
	Greensboro	NYY	A	20	3	0	0	1	2.2	16	5	3	3	0	0	0	1	2	0	2	3	0	0	0	.000	0	0	10.13
de la Cruz, Luis	Yankees	NYY	R	19	3	0	0	1	3	13	2	0	0	0	0	0	0	2	0	2	0	0	0	0	.000	0	1	0.00
	Tampa	NYY	A+	19	5	0	0	0	8.2	40	9	2	2	0	0	0	0	5	0	1	1	1	2	0	1.000	0	0	2.08
Delaney, Donnie	Wilmington	KC	A+	26	23	0	0	14	25	125	25	17	15	2	2	2	2	28	2	26	2	0	0	3	.000	0	3	5.40
Delano, Mike*	Lansing	ChC	A	22	2	2	0	0	10.1	38	7	5	4	0	0	0	0	2	0	10	1	0	0	1	.000	0	0	3.48
de la Rosa, Cristian	Orioles	Bal	R	21	15	0	0	8	19.1	103	30	19	14	0	2	1	3	16	3	13	1	0	1	3	.250	0	0	6.52
de la Rosa, Jorge*	High Desert	Ari	A+	19	2	0	0	2	3	12	1	0	0	0	0	0	0	2	0	3	0	0	0	0	.000	0	0	0.00
	Diamondbcks	Ari	R	19	8	0	0	6	14	56	12	5	5	1	0	0	0	3	0	17	2	1	0	0	.000	0	2	3.21
	Missoula	Ari	R+	19	13	0	0	6	14.2	75	22	17	13	2	0	0	0	9	0	14	4	0	0	1	.000	0	2	7.98
Delatori, Keola	Lansing	ChC	A	21	15	4	0	4	30.2	144	34	28	26	1	0	1	2	20	0	27	1	1	3	5	.375	0	1	7.63
DeLeon, Jose	Potomac	StL	A+	23	59	0	0	31	70.2	316	68	48	43	4	4	4	0	42	2	47	11	0	5	6	.455	0	5	5.48
Delgado, Joseph	Wilmington	KC	A+	20	2	1	0	0	7.2	32	6	4	4	1	0	0	1	2	0	5	2	0	0	1	.000	0	0	4.70
	Royals	KC	R	20	1	1	0	0	[illegible]	[illegible]	0	0	0	0	0	0	0	1	0	4	0	0	1	0	1.000	0	0	0.00
	Chstn-WV	KC	A	20	11	11	0	0	45	208	53	29	23	1	0	3	4	21	0	31	3	3	3	4	.429	0	0	4.00
Demouy, Chris*	Cedar Rapds	Ana	A	24	46	0	0	28	48.2	212	39	18	13	3	7	3	0	28	2	51	8	0	2	1	.667	0	16	2.40
Denney, Kyle	Burlington	Cle	R+	22	12	3	0	4	34	143	26	17	13	7	4	1	2	15	0	37	2	3	3	4	.429	0	1	3.44
	Mahoning Vy	Cle	A-	22	1	1	0	0	5	16	5	1	1	1	0	0	0	0	0	5	0	0	1	0	1.000	0	0	1.80
Dent, Doug	Macon	Atl	A	23	17	17	0	0	89	375	78	42	34	8	1	3	2	30	0	64	5	1	4	5	.444	0	0	3.44

1999 Pitching — Single-A and Rookie Leagues

HOW MUCH HE PITCHED											WHAT HE GAVE UP												THE RESULTS					
Player	Team	Org	Lg	A	G	GS	CG	GF	IP	BFP	H	R	ER	HR	SH	SF	HB	TBB	IBB	SO	WP	Bk	W	L	Pct.	ShO	Sv	ERA
	Fort Wayne	SD	A	23	8	8	0	0	48.2	201	43	23	19	2	0	1	1	17	0	32	4	1	4	1	.800	0	0	3.51
DePaula, Julio	Portland	Col	A-	20	16	16	0	0	85.1	392	97	67	57	8	5	4	5	43	0	77	7	1	6	6	.500	0	0	6.01
DePaula, Miguel	Phillies	Phi	R	19	9	5	0	3	28.2	137	35	24	19	1	0	4	2	16	0	14	1	0	1	4	.200	0	0	5.97
Detwiler, Jim*	Medcine Hat	Tor	R+	24	3	2	0	0	11	48	10	6	6	2	0	2	0	6	0	14	0	0	0	0	.000	0	0	4.91
	St.Cathrnes	Tor	A-	24	14	6	0	3	44	199	45	23	16	3	0	0	1	25	0	45	2	4	2	4	.333	0	0	3.27
Deveraux, Dale	Diamondbcks	Ari	R	20	16	0	0	5	27.2	146	42	38	32	2	1	5	4	20	0	17	6	1	3	2	.600	0	0	10.41
Devey, Phil*	Yakima	LA	A-	23	13	13	1	0	78.1	330	70	43	34	6	2	0	9	27	0	56	6	1	5	4	.556	0	0	3.91
Devine, Travis	Idaho Falls	SD	R+	20	8	4	0	0	25.1	113	32	17	12	0	3	0	0	9	0	13	7	0	1	2	.333	0	0	4.26
Diaz, Alex	Athletics	Oak	R	20	22	0	0	17	42.1	184	54	21	15	2	0	1	2	10	1	26	1	0	2	1	.667	0	5	3.19
Diaz, Antonio	Rancho Cuca	SD	A+	21	9	0	0	5	12.1	52	7	7	7	3	0	1	0	7	0	7	0	0	0	0	.000	0	0	5.11
	Fort Wayne	SD	A	21	27	9	0	7	75.1	330	77	41	35	5	2	3	1	28	0	54	7	1	6	3	.667	0	0	4.18
Diaz, Eddy	Cubs	ChC	R	19	17	2	0	6	34.1	180	47	44	32	4	2	0	6	23	1	30	7	0	0	6	.000	0	2	8.39
Diaz, Luis	Tigers	Det	R	21	22	0	0	9	31.2	135	24	9	7	1	3	0	2	20	2	36	1	2	1	2	.333	0	2	1.99
Diaz, Zach*	Boise	Ana	A-	24	17	0	0	4	29.2	133	36	11	8	0	1	1	1	7	1	24	1	0	1	2	.333	0	2	2.43
Difelice, Mark	Salem	Col	A+	23	27	23	3	1	156.1	642	142	71	67	20	4	6	4	36	0	142	3	1	8	12	.400	0	0	3.86
Dinkel, Aaron	New Jersey	StL	A-	22	13	0	0	5	10.1	63	16	13	11	0	0	0	0	15	0	6	3	0	0	0	.000	0	0	9.58
Dittfurth, Ryan	Pulaski	Tex	R+	20	14	14	1	0	83	361	66	35	23	4	0	1	15	42	0	85	6	2	7	2	.778	1	0	2.49
Dittmer, Greg*	Princeton	TB	R+	21	28	0	0	7	44	202	48	28	16	2	0	2	5	16	0	32	0	1	1	3	.250	0	1	3.27
Dobis, Jason	Quad City	Min	A	24	23	4	0	4	57	249	67	36	32	5	1	1	1	17	2	36	5	0	5	1	.833	0	1	5.05
Dobson, Dwayne	Cedar Rapds	Ana	A	24	22	6	0	2	61.1	329	94	75	58	6	1	5	9	43	0	31	7	2	1	7	.125	0	0	8.51
Dobson, Mark	Fort Wayne	SD	A	24	41	0	0	13	80.1	376	92	65	58	10	0	1	0	48	1	83	2	0	2	0	1.000	0	0	6.50
Dorame, Randey*	Vero Beach	LA	A+	21	3	2	0	0	11	48	15	9	7	2	0	0	0	1	0	5	0	0	0	2	.000	0	0	5.73
	San Berndno	LA	A+	21	24	24	1	0	154.1	613	130	52	43	9	3	6	3	37	0	159	7	1	14	3	.824	1	0	2.51
Dorn, Grant	Vermont	Mon	A-	22	23	1	0	8	54.1	234	55	23	19	4	2	1	2	19	0	54	5	0	3	3	.500	0	3	3.15
Dotel, Melido	Vero Beach	LA	A+	23	31	6	0	14	72.2	344	56	45	36	6	1	1	5	73	0	57	8	1	6	5	.545	0	1	4.46
Douglass, Ryan	Spokane	KC	A-	21	4	4	0	0	20.1	87	24	13	10	0	0	0	1	6	0	14	3	0	0	1	.000	0	0	4.43
	Chstn-WV	KC	A	21	10	9	0	0	42	188	55	28	22	1	1	2	2	13	0	22	5	0	3	4	.429	0	0	4.71
Douglass, Sean	Frederick	Bal	A+	21	16	16	1	0	97.2	425	101	48	36	9	4	3	5	35	0	89	3	0	5	6	.455	0	0	3.32
Dowell, Brian	Padres	SD	R	22	2	0	0	0	1	14	2	8	5	0	0	0	1	6	0	0	1	0	0	0	.000	0	0	45.00
Drain, Brad	Mariners	Sea	R	20	13	11	0	0	65.1	273	63	38	31	3	1	1	7	13	0	71	9	0	6	5	.545	0	0	4.27
Dreier, Tom	Hagerstown	Tor	A	23	8	0	0	4	9.1	50	12	11	7	2	0	0	1	8	0	10	4	0	0	0	.000	0	0	6.75
	St.Cathrnes	Tor	A-	23	4	0	0	0	10.2	46	6	3	3	0	0	0	0	9	0	15	1	0	1	0	1.000	0	0	2.53
Drese, Ryan	Mahoning Vy	Cle	A-	24	5	5	0	0	17	66	8	6	5	1	0	2	1	7	0	26	0	1	0	2	.000	0	0	2.65
	Columbus	Cle	A	24	2	2	0	0	12	49	9	6	6	2	0	0	0	4	0	15	3	0	0	2	.000	0	0	4.50
	Kinston	Cle	A+	24	15	15	1	0	69.1	310	46	47	38	2	3	1	10	52	0	81	7	1	5	4	.556	0	0	4.93
Drew, Tim	Kinston	Cle	A+	21	28	28	2	0	169	713	154	79	70	12	5	3	10	60	0	125	7	0	13	5	.722	0	0	3.73
Duarte, Renney	Lk Elsinore	Ana	A+	21	3	3	0	0	14	71	22	13	10	2	0	0	1	8	1	6	0	1	0	1	.000	0	0	6.43
	Cedar Rapds	Ana	A	21	31	18	3	4	132.2	561	145	81	70	19	4	4	2	33	0	102	5	1	6	11	.353	2	1	4.75
Dubuc, Charles*	Expos	Mon	R	19	16	5	0	3	46.2	200	39	21	14	0	4	0	7	27	0	34	4	1	1	2	.333	0	2	2.70
Duchscherer, Justin	Augusta	Bos	A	22	6	6	0	0	41	150	21	1	1	0	0	0	0	8	0	39	1	0	4	0	1.000	0	0	0.22
	Sarasota	Bos	A+	22	20	18	0	0	112.1	475	101	62	56	14	2	5	12	30	0	105	5	0	7	7	.500	0	0	4.49
Duckworth, Bran.	Clearwater	Phi	A+	24	27	17	0	1	132	602	164	84	71	13	5	7	5	40	0	101	10	1	11	5	.688	0	1	4.84
Dukeman, Gregory	Danville	Atl	R+	21	17	0	0	6	24	113	30	16	9	2	0	0	2	6	1	21	3	1	0	1	.000	0	2	3.38
Duncan, Sean*	Charlotte	Tex	A+	27	45	0	0	25	80	360	71	38	28	4	4	6	2	52	3	65	9	2	7	6	.538	0	8	3.15
Dunn, Keith	Greensboro	NYY	A	22	35	18	1	14	135.1	561	134	61	47	7	5	4	12	16	1	109	14	0	9	9	.500	0	5	3.13
Dunn, Scott	Billings	Cin	R+	22	9	8	0	0	39.2	178	36	24	19	3	0	1	3	24	0	36	3	2	1	3	.250	0	0	4.31
Dunning, Justin	Wisconsin	Sea	A	23	25	8	0	12	69	329	79	50	43	8	2	1	8	36	0	76	17	0	4	4	.500	0	2	5.61
Dunphy, Micah*	Athletics	Oak	R	20	16	1	0	3	31	143	35	18	11	2	1	2	1	17	1	34	4	0	2	1	.667	0	1	3.19
Duprey, Pete*	Everett	Sea	A-	21	22	0	0	12	36	143	26	7	4	0	1	0	3	12	0	32	1	0	3	1	.750	0	3	1.00
Durkee, Jeremy*	Ogden	Mil	R+	19	16	1	0	5	31	140	31	19	14	0	1	1	5	13	0	32	3	1	2	3	.400	0	2	4.06
Durkovic, Peter*	Lakeland	Det	A+	26	17	0	0	8	21	88	19	12	11	4	1	1	2	5	0	11	1	1	1	1	.500	0	3	4.71
Eames, Todd	Missoula	Ari	R+	22	19	1	0	3	39.2	174	37	19	13	3	1	2	1	17	1	28	9	1	2	1	.667	0	1	2.95
Earl, Ryan*	Tigers	Det	R	19	7	7	0	0	37.1	160	34	20	19	4	1	2	1	18	0	20	7	2	3	2	.600	0	0	4.58
Earle, Scott	Mariners	Sea	R	23	7	0	0	1	12.1	54	14	4	2	0	0	1	0	2	0	13	0	0	1	1	.500	0	0	1.46
Easton, Eric	Butte	Ana	R+	21	16	0	0	5	18	107	29	37	24	3	0	1	0	20	0	18	4	0	0	1	.000	0	0	12.00
Eavenson, Clay	Staten Ilnd	NYY	A-	22	1	0	0	0	1.1	6	2	1	1	0	0	0	0	1	0	0	1	0	0	0	.000	0	0	6.75
	Greensboro	NYY	A	22	5	1	0	1	10.2	47	12	7	4	1	0	1	0	3	0	6	3	0	0	1	.000	0	0	3.38
Ebanks, Palmer	Boise	Ana	A-	23	27	0	0	13	48	209	44	23	21	4	0	2	3	22	2	53	2	0	6	3	.667	0	3	3.94
Echols, Justin	Rangers	Tex	R	19	14	4	0	3	34.2	144	27	14	10	1	1	0	1	21	1	32	0	3	2	2	.500	0	0	2.60
Ellison, Jason	Tampa	NYY	A+	24	49	0	0	42	54.1	226	42	15	13	0	4	2	4	19	1	56	0	0	0	2	.000	0	35	2.15
Emanuel, Brandon	Cedar Rapds	Ana	A	24	23	23	5	0	153	678	173	92	76	16	2	10	4	50	0	88	9	1	7	12	.368	0	0	4.47
	Lk Elsinore	Ana	A+	24	2	2	0	0	14	64	15	11	8	1	0	2	1	7	0	12	0	0	0	2	.000	0	0	5.14
Embry, Byron	Macon	Atl	A	23	25	0	0	4	45.1	194	35	17	12	3	2	2	0	25	0	42	5	1	5	2	.714	0	0	2.38
	Myrtle Bch	Atl	A+	23	2	0	0	1	6	19	1	0	0	0	0	0	1	0	0	5	0	0	0	0	.000	0	0	0.00
Emiliano, Jamie	Salem	Col	A+	25	45	0	0	23	53.2	240	50	26	21	4	3	2	5	29	1	47	8	0	5	1	.833	0	7	3.52
Encarnacion, Luis	Mariners	Sea	R	20	15	0	0	9	22.1	123	26	30	27	1	0	1	4	24	0	25	1	1	0	0	.000	0	1	10.88
Encarnacion, Or.	Pittsfield	NYM	A-	21	15	15	0	0	86	365	102	51	46	6	3	4	4	13	0	61	2	1	3	6	.333	0	0	4.81
Ennis, John	Danville	Atl	R+	20	13	13	0	0	65.2	296	71	46	37	7	3	2	9	21	0	60	3	2	4	3	.571	0	0	5.07
Eppeneder, James*	Eugene	ChC	A-	21	20	0	0	15	31.1	137	21	10	10	3	1	0	1	22	1	42	1	0	3	1	.750	0	1	2.87
Erazo, Rafael	Billings	Cin	R+	21	9	2	0	1	22	99	32	23	20	2	0	0	2	6	0	16	3	3	2	1	.667	0	1	8.18
Ericks, Dave	Cubs	ChC	R	20	16	1	0	6	29	156	35	31	27	3	0	1	3	29	0	22	7	1	1	3	.250	0	0	8.38
Escamilla, Paco	Billings	Cin	R+	23	5	5	0	0	28	113	18	11	11	0	1	0	2	9	0	33	2	0	3	0	1.000	0	0	3.54
	Clinton	Cin	A	23	12	9	0	1	55	244	56	36	32	4	2	2	6	20	0	52	4	0	1	6	.143	0	0	5.24
Espina, Rendy*	Batavia	Phi	A-	22	1	0	0	0	1	9	5	4	4	1	0	0	0	1	0	1	0	0	0	1	.000	0	0	36.00
	Phillies	Phi	R	22	2	0	0	2	1	4	1	0	0	0	0	0	0	0	0	1	0	0	1	0	1.000	0	1	0.00
	Piedmont	Phi	A	22	15	0	0	7	35	143	35	20	18	1	2	2	1	10	1	31	3	1	0	2	.000	0	3	4.63
Espinal, Jose	Twins	Min	R	20	10	4	0	3	30	140	35	29	23	3	2	3	2	13	0	23	4	2	4	3	.571	0	0	6.90

1999 Pitching — Single-A and Rookie Leagues

HOW MUCH HE PITCHED											WHAT HE GAVE UP												THE RESULTS					
Player	Team	Org	Lg	A	G	GS	CG	GF	IP	BFP	H	R	ER	HR	SH	SF	HB	TBB	IBB	SO	WP	Bk	W	L	Pct.	ShO	Sv	ERA
Espinal, Juan	Mariners	Sea	R	19	15	5	0	2	43	206	56	38	34	6	2	3	4	20	0	31	2	0	3	3	.500	0	0	7.12
Esslinger, Cam	Portland	Col	A-	23	14	14	0	0	80	351	76	37	34	1	4	2	10	35	1	68	3	2	6	3	.667	0	0	3.83
Estrella, Leo	Dunedin	Tor	A+	25	27	24	2	0	168	696	166	74	60	11	6	5	17	47	0	116	6	1	14	7	.667	2	0	3.21
Evans, Mike*	Asheville	Col	A	24	38	0	0	22	84	367	81	52	40	12	1	5	9	35	0	70	5	2	5	6	.455	0	7	4.29
Everett, Matt	Mahoning Vy	Cle	A-	24	3	0	0	1	4	15	4	2	2	0	1	0	0	1	0	5	0	0	0	0	.000	0	0	4.50
	Columbus	Cle	A	24	18	0	0	8	31.2	135	30	17	16	5	1	0	2	14	0	19	2	0	1	2	.333	0	1	4.55
Everly, Bill	San Berndno	LA	A+	25	60	0	0	57	63.1	272	66	26	24	6	4	0	3	21	3	51	3	0	7	4	.636	0	34	3.41
Evert, Brett	Braves	Atl	R	19	13	10	0	1	48.2	195	37	17	11	0	2	2	4	9	1	39	3	4	5	3	.625	0	0	2.03
Eyre, Willie	Elizabethtn	Min	R+	21	16	10	1	1	57.2	270	60	38	29	4	2	0	4	34	0	59	7	1	6	3	.667	0	0	4.53
	Quad City	Min	A	21	2	2	0	0	12.2	51	8	6	6	0	0	1	1	6	0	10	1	0	1	0	1.000	0	0	4.26
Fabricio, Benitez	Red Sox	Bos	R	19	13	8	0	2	57.2	241	55	34	21	0	3	1	0	14	0	40	4	2	4	4	.500	0	1	3.28
Fahrner, Evan	High Desert	Ari	A+	22	3	1	0	0	3	18	3	3	2	0	0	0	0	7	0	3	0	1	0	1	.000	0	0	6.00
	South Bend	Ari	A	22	20	1	0	9	37	172	39	27	25	3	0	0	1	21	0	45	5	2	3	1	.750	0	1	6.08
Fahs, Paul	New Jersey	StL	A-	22	30	0	0	15	34.2	149	25	17	13	1	0	3	4	19	1	21	6	0	1	2	.333	0	7	3.37
	Peoria	StL	A	22	2	0	0	1	2.1	10	3	0	0	0	0	0	0	0	0	2	0	0	1	0	1.000	0	0	0.00
Faigin, Jason	Staten Ilnd	NYY	A-	21	18	0	0	9	22.2	96	22	9	8	1	1	0	2	5	0	27	0	1	1	1	.500	0	1	3.18
Farizo, Brad	Kane County	Fla	A	21	34	12	0	9	112.2	500	143	81	66	10	5	3	4	37	0	80	7	2	4	7	.364	0	1	5.27
Farnsworth, Jeff	Lancaster	Sea	A+	24	26	9	0	6	72	351	91	61	52	7	1	10	15	43	1	43	10	0	3	6	.333	0	3	6.50
Farren, Dave	Orioles	Bal	R	19	10	2	0	4	19	81	17	6	2	1	0	0	2	7	0	12	1	1	1	1	.500	0	2	0.95
Fauske, Josh	Burlington	CWS	A	26	5	0	0	2	7	35	6	6	4	0	0	1	1	7	0	6	3	1	0	0	.000	0	0	5.14
Featherstone, Der.	Salem-Keizr	SF	A-	23	4	0	0	0	2.1	22	7	12	12	0	0	1	2	6	0	0	1	0	0	1	.000	0	0	46.29
	Bakersfield	SF	A+	23	6	0	0	4	10.2	65	13	17	9	0	0	1	1	17	0	13	4	0	0	0	.000	0	0	7.59
Felix, Miguel	Burlington	CWS	A	23	30	0	0	11	44.2	237	60	52	39	3	0	4	7	39	0	29	15	1	0	2	.000	0	0	7.86
	Winston-Sal	CWS	A+	23	9	0	0	4	14	62	11	8	3	1	0	1	5	7	0	7	2	0	1	0	1.000	0	1	1.93
Fenus, Justin	Piedmont	Phi	A	25	10	4	0	2	37	150	29	16	10	1	1	2	2	10	0	27	0	0	2	0	1.000	0	0	2.43
Fereira, Ramon	Auburn	Hou	A-	21	21	3	0	7	49	235	42	41	29	7	2	1	8	28	0	49	8	1	2	4	.333	0	1	5.33
Ferguson, Tony	Martinsvlle	Hou	R+	23	15	0	0	13	32.2	131	27	12	8	1	1	1	2	6	0	32	4	1	0	2	.000	0	3	2.20
	Michigan	Hou	A	23	5	0	0	1	4.2	28	8	4	4	1	0	0	0	6	0	2	1	0	0	2	.000	0	0	7.71
	Auburn	Hou	A-	23	3	0	0	2	7	26	3	1	1	0	0	0	1	1	0	8	1	0	0	0	.000	0	1	1.29
Fernandez, Osvaldo	San Jose	SF	A+	31	4	4	0	0	9	37	6	6	6	1	0	0	2	2	0	5	0	0	0	1	.000	0	0	6.00
Ferrand, Dario	White Sox	CWS	R	19	13	13	1	0	72.2	321	80	46	36	4	0	1	7	25	1	44	9	2	2	5	.286	0	0	4.46
Ferrand, Julian	Rockies	Col	R	20	13	0	0	5	20.2	99	25	22	19	2	0	1	1	15	0	14	7	1	0	1	.000	0	1	8.27
Ferrier, Shayne	Cedar Rapds	Ana	A	24	7	0	0	4	10.2	54	11	10	6	1	0	0	2	8	0	8	3	1	0	0	.000	0	0	5.06
	Boise	Ana	A-	24	4	0	0	3	3.1	24	9	10	10	2	0	0	1	4	0	2	1	0	0	0	.000	0	0	27.00
Fields, Brian*	Bakersfield	SF	A+	25	20	0	0	4	35.2	164	43	25	23	7	0	1	0	12	1	22	3	1	2	0	1.000	0	1	5.80
	Salem-Keizr	SF	A-	25	24	0	0	17	34.2	146	30	14	12	5	3	2	1	14	1	38	4	0	2	3	.400	0	8	3.12
Figueroa, Carlos*	Rangers	Tex	R	21	6	0	0	2	10.2	39	5	1	1	0	0	0	1	3	0	17	0	4	4	0	1.000	0	0	0.84
	Savannah	Tex	A	21	10	0	0	2	20	97	19	14	13	2	0	0	3	16	0	30	5	1	0	0	.000	0	1	5.85
Figueroa, Juan	Burlington	CWS	A	21	17	16	2	0	115.1	491	100	51	40	8	0	6	5	44	0	139	4	1	8	4	.667	0	0	3.12
	Winston-Sal	CWS	A+	21	10	10	1	0	56.1	252	67	47	33	2	3	2	2	19	0	50	3	0	2	5	.286	0	0	5.27
Fikac, Jeremy	Rancho Cuca	SD	A+	25	40	6	0	13	85	381	94	50	48	7	0	2	4	43	0	75	8	2	8	3	.727	0	0	5.08
File, Bob	Dunedin	Tor	A+	23	47	0	0	42	53	203	30	13	10	2	3	0	4	14	0	48	1	1	4	1	.800	0	26	1.70
Finnegan, Mike	Expos	Mon	R	23	1	0	0	0	2	11	5	0	0	0	0	0	0	0	0	1	0	0	1	0	1.000	0	0	0.00
	Vermont	Mon	A-	23	14	0	0	3	26.2	128	38	18	17	1	0	1	0	18	0	17	0	1	1	1	.500	0	0	5.74
Fiora, Chris	Johnson Cy	StL	R+	21	18	0	0	11	19.2	103	27	21	19	4	0	0	1	14	0	31	3	0	0	3	.000	0	2	8.69
Fischer, Eric*	Burlington	CWS	A	20	25	25	2	0	137	614	160	89	79	11	4	3	8	50	1	78	4	2	10	11	.476	1	0	5.19
Fischer, Mike	San Berndno	LA	A+	23	3	3	0	0	11	47	13	6	6	1	0	0	0	4	0	7	1	0	1	0	1.000	0	0	4.91
Fischer, Sean*	Frederick	Bal	A+	22	3	0	0	0	4.2	29	10	7	7	0	0	0	0	6	1	3	2	0	0	1	.000	0	0	13.50
	Bluefield	Bal	R+	22	17	1	0	5	32.2	164	38	37	24	3	3	2	1	24	0	32	10	0	1	2	.333	0	0	6.61
Fish, Steve	Lk Elsinore	Ana	A+	25	32	29	5	0	196.2	876	220	125	107	17	0	8	10	72	3	180	15	2	11	11	.500	2	0	4.90
Fisher, Louis	Daytona	ChC	A+	23	40	0	0	21	69.2	321	63	59	43	5	3	1	2	50	2	64	13	0	3	8	.273	0	9	5.56
Fisher, Pete	Fort Myers	Min	A+	22	25	24	0	0	146.2	639	171	74	61	10	3	6	9	38	0	91	14	3	5	10	.333	0	0	3.74
Fitts, Brian	Quad City	Min	A	23	37	12	0	5	100	448	109	73	62	15	4	4	10	32	0	71	11	0	6	4	.600	0	1	5.58
Fitzgerald, Ryan	Martinsvlle	Hou	R+	24	12	0	0	2	24.2	111	24	20	15	4	0	1	0	6	0	22	1	0	1	1	.500	0	0	5.47
Flading, Cameron	Butte	Ana	R+	21	20	0	0	4	27.1	140	39	26	22	0	0	3	7	17	0	19	6	0	1	0	1.000	0	0	7.24
Flanagan, Ryan	Twins	Min	R	21	8	4	0	3	20.2	91	10	11	9	0	3	0	4	16	0	14	3	3	1	2	.333	0	0	3.92
Fleck, Will	Myrtle Bch	Atl	A+	23	40	0	0	17	75	342	67	56	54	14	5	1	3	52	3	72	9	0	10	10	.500	0	0	6.48
Fleming, Emar	Charlotte	Tex	A+	23	24	22	1	1	142.1	608	138	81	68	19	4	6	10	62	0	100	4	3	9	9	.500	1	0	4.30
Fleming, Travis	Orioles	Bal	R	23	4	3	0	0	16	62	12	2	2	0	0	0	0	2	0	21	1	1	1	1	.500	0	0	1.13
	Delmarva	Bal	A	23	14	1	0	4	38.1	159	36	24	20	4	1	1	1	14	0	33	3	0	2	1	.667	0	1	4.70
Flock, Rick	Elizabethtn	Min	R+	22	22	0	0	9	27.2	122	30	19	16	4	0	1	1	7	1	37	2	0	2	3	.400	0	3	5.20
Flohr, Adam*	St. Pete	TB	A+	23	31	18	0	2	135	587	164	78	57	10	6	1	9	30	0	64	9	2	6	6	.500	0	0	3.80
Flores, Benito*	Bakersfield	SF	A+	24	34	6	0	7	81	357	81	42	33	3	1	2	2	34	2	63	6	0	2	1	.667	0	0	3.67
Flores, Pedro*	San Berndno	LA	A+	23	32	0	0	14	47.1	236	68	47	40	4	2	0	4	30	4	35	6	0	2	3	.400	0	1	7.61
Foote, Joe	Quad City	Min	A	20	44	18	1	7	135	582	131	72	59	6	4	4	5	44	2	111	9	1	7	5	.583	1	2	3.93
Foran, John	Rancho Cuca	SD	A+	26	25	20	0	0	105	482	113	70	56	12	0	6	10	53	0	89	13	1	9	5	.643	0	0	4.80
Forbes, Derek	Missoula	Ari	R+	21	13	12	0	0	59	273	77	45	37	4	2	2	3	20	0	63	6	0	3	1	.750	0	0	5.64
Forbes, Keith	Fort Wayne	SD	A	23	42	2	0	16	67	329	60	52	46	11	3	2	9	65	3	70	7	3	3	4	.429	0	3	6.18
Ford, Matt*	Medcine Hat	Tor	R+	19	13	7	0	0	48.1	193	31	11	11	0	0	0	0	23	0	68	1	0	4	0	1.000	0	0	2.05
Fossum, Casey*	Lowell	Bos	A-	22	5	5	0	0	14.1	56	6	2	2	1	0	0	2	5	0	16	0	4	0	1	.000	0	0	1.26
Foster, John*	Danville	Atl	R+	22	19	0	0	7	39	148	28	10	6	0	5	0	2	6	0	36	4	0	4	1	.800	0	1	1.38
Frachiseur, Zach	Macon	Atl	A	23	4	0	0	2	4	21	5	3	3	1	0	0	0	2	0	6	0	0	0	1	.000	0	0	6.75
	Myrtle Bch	Atl	A+	23	37	5	0	9	98	397	75	34	30	5	2	4	2	31	1	93	5	0	7	3	.700	0	2	2.76
Francisco, Franklin	Red Sox	Bos	R	20	12	7	0	1	53.1	252	58	39	27	3	1	1	4	35	0	48	7	3	2	4	.333	0	0	4.56
Franco, Edwin*	Royals	KC	R	23	2	0	0	0	3	9	1	0	0	0	0	0	0	0	0	4	0	0	0	0	.000	0	0	0.00
	Spokane	KC	A-	23	3	1	0	1	4.1	20	5	1	1	0	1	0	0	2	0	6	1	1	0	0	.000	0	0	2.08
Franco, Jose	Staten Ilnd	NYY	A-	18	30	0	0	18	41.1	171	29	14	13	1	3	1	1	14	1	58	3	1	3	3	.500	0	5	2.83

1999 Pitching — Single-A and Rookie Leagues

HOW MUCH HE PITCHED											WHAT HE GAVE UP												THE RESULTS					
Player	Team	Org	Lg	A	G	GS	CG	GF	IP	BFP	H	R	ER	HR	SH	SF	HB	TBB	IBB	SO	WP	Bk	W	L	Pct.	ShO	Sv	ERA
Franke, Aaron	Butte	Ana	R+	20	15	15	0	0	78.2	343	76	52	38	6	6	2	2	32	0	69	8	1	4	5	.444	0	0	4.35
Franks, Lance	Potomac	StL	A+	24	54	0	0	6	78.2	308	63	25	23	5	2	2	3	17	0	61	2	0	5	1	.833	0	0	2.63
Fraser, Joe	Vermont	Mon	A-	22	4	0	0	0	4	31	9	14	11	0	0	1	3	7	0	2	4	0	0	1	.000	0	0	24.75
	Expos	Mon	R	22	4	0	0	1	5.2	23	1	0	0	0	0	0	2	9	0	4	4	0	0	0	.000	0	0	0.00
Frasor, Jason	Oneonta	Det	A-	22	12	11	0	0	58.2	229	36	16	11	3	0	1	1	22	0	69	3	2	3	3	.500	0	0	1.69
	W Michigan	Det	A	22	4	4	1	0	24	97	17	10	7	2	0	0	2	9	0	33	0	3	2	1	.667	1	0	2.63
Frazier, Brad	Quad City	Min	A	23	33	0	0	6	48.1	243	52	37	29	1	3	3	9	39	5	26	9	2	1	3	.250	0	0	5.40
Frederick, Kevin	Twins	Min	R	23	2	0	0	0	2.1	14	6	5	4	0	0	1	0	1	0	3	0	0	0	0	.000	0	0	15.43
Freehill, Mike	Cedar Rapds	Ana	A	29	2	0	0	1	2.1	15	2	3	3	0	0	0	1	4	0	2	0	1	0	0	.000	0	0	11.57
	Charlotte	Tex	A+	29	17	0	0	16	17.2	79	15	11	7	1	1	0	2	9	0	18	5	0	2	2	.500	0	8	3.57
Freeman, Kai	Winston-Sal	CWS	A+	23	32	8	0	5	95.1	417	100	58	52	13	6	4	5	32	1	64	1	1	2	6	.250	0	1	4.91
Frendling, Neal	Princeton	TB	R+	20	4	3	0	0	18	76	16	8	5	1	0	0	2	5	0	18	2	0	2	1	.667	0	0	2.50
	Hudson Val	TB	A-	20	9	9	0	0	49.1	195	39	21	17	2	0	3	4	10	0	50	3	0	3	1	.750	0	0	3.10
Frey, Chris	Charlotte	Tex	A+	26	2	0	0	1	4	22	10	3	3	0	1	1	0	2	1	3	0	0	0	1	.000	0	0	6.75
	Savannah	Tex	A	26	31	0	0	12	59	247	53	27	16	1	1	0	2	15	0	55	7	0	2	0	1.000	0	5	2.44
Frias, Juan	Princeton	TB	R+	21	30	0	0	16	37	175	40	28	24	3	0	0	1	18	0	38	6	0	2	2	.500	0	2	5.84
Fry, Justin	Batavia	Phi	A-	23	25	0	0	20	33.1	127	18	5	5	1	0	0	2	10	2	59	6	1	4	0	1.000	0	6	1.35
Fuell, Jerrod	Tigers	Det	R	19	6	6	0	0	19	95	29	19	17	1	0	1	1	13	0	8	1	0	0	3	.000	0	0	8.05
Fuller, Jody	South Bend	Ari	A	23	36	11	0	10	116.1	524	133	68	58	6	1	7	4	43	0	83	7	0	7	4	.636	0	0	4.49
Gage, Matt	Sou Oregon	Oak	A-	22	18	5	0	7	65	292	78	49	41	11	4	3	4	16	3	39	4	1	8	7	.533	0	0	5.68
Gagliano, Steve	Brevard Cty	Fla	A+	22	15	7	0	5	48.2	227	59	38	25	6	0	4	4	14	0	29	3	0	2	5	.286	0	0	4.62
	Beloit	Mil	A	22	15	9	1	2	74.2	314	71	40	34	8	4	1	6	23	0	45	9	0	5	3	.625	1	1	4.10
Gallo, Mike*	Auburn	Hou	A-	23	3	3	0	0	14.2	63	13	4	2	0	0	0	0	7	0	11	0	0	1	0	1.000	0	0	1.23
	Michigan	Hou	A	23	12	12	0	0	60	268	76	47	39	6	1	2	1	23	0	32	1	0	2	3	.400	0	0	5.85
Galva, Claudio*	Athletics	Oak	R	20	14	11	0	0	68	275	64	23	18	0	3	2	2	16	0	59	4	1	6	2	.750	0	0	2.38
Gamble, Jerome	Lowell	Bos	A-	20	5	5	0	0	25.2	101	18	7	5	1	0	0	0	9	0	37	0	0	1	0	1.000	0	0	1.75
Gamboa, Javier	Royals	KC	R	26	3	3	0	0	5	22	6	2	2	1	0	0	0	2	0	4	0	0	0	0	.000	0	0	3.60
Gandy, Josh*	Fort Myers	Min	A+	24	47	1	0	24	73.2	324	75	33	30	2	4	3	0	36	0	64	3	0	4	3	.571	0	3	3.67
Gangemi, Joe*	Lk Elsinore	Ana	A+	24	21	15	1	2	81.2	388	118	81	65	10	1	2	5	41	1	55	7	0	3	11	.214	0	0	7.16
	Cedar Rapds	Ana	A	24	5	5	0	0	27.2	128	37	17	11	4	0	4	1	13	0	23	2	0	1	2	.333	0	0	3.58
Garcia, Abel*	Royals	KC	R	22	3	2	0	0	15	63	17	9	7	1	0	0	2	2	0	13	4	0	1	2	.333	0	0	4.20
Garcia, Gabe	Michigan	Hou	A	23	38	8	0	11	89.1	393	100	49	46	11	0	1	5	37	1	79	8	0	5	3	.625	0	3	4.63
	Kissimmee	Hou	A+	23	1	0	0	1	2	10	5	3	3	1	0	0	0	1	0	0	0	0	0	1	.000	0	0	13.50
Garcia, Joaquin	Mariners	Sea	R	22	12	7	0	2	52.2	235	64	33	27	1	1	5	6	13	0	51	1	0	4	3	.571	0	0	4.61
Garcia, Rafael	Royals	KC	R	22	9	5	0	0	41	184	44	24	21	2	1	4	5	13	0	44	2	0	4	2	.667	0	0	4.61
Garcia, Ramon	Red Sox	Bos	R	21	21	0	0	18	24.1	116	24	10	8	0	1	0	1	15	2	26	3	0	2	0	1.000	0	5	2.96
	Lowell	Bos	A-	21	5	0	0	5	5	22	5	2	2	0	0	2	0	2	0	5	1	1	0	0	.000	0	2	3.60
Garcia, Raul	Spokane	KC	A-	23	32	0	0	7	52.2	222	47	18	14	5	1	1	2	21	2	64	3	2	9	2	.818	0	1	2.39
Garcia, Reynaldo	Rangers	Tex	R	22	12	11	0	0	64	268	55	30	23	3	2	4	0	26	0	42	4	3	4	4	.500	0	0	3.23
Garcia, Rosman	Greensboro	NYY	A	21	9	9	0	0	42.1	204	60	33	30	4	0	1	2	20	0	31	12	3	2	3	.400	0	0	6.38
	Staten Ilnd	NYY	A-	21	18	10	0	1	69.2	310	86	40	33	3	3	3	4	14	2	40	4	1	2	6	.250	0	1	4.26
Garcia, Sonny	Delmarva	Bal	A	23	13	12	0	0	62	271	68	46	40	6	1	2	8	19	0	44	5	0	3	5	.375	0	0	5.81
Gardea, Mario	Yankees	NYY	R	20	14	0	0	2	19	84	11	10	6	1	0	0	3	13	0	34	6	0	1	3	.250	0	0	2.84
Gardner, Nathan	Rockford	Cin	A	25	34	0	0	15	46	219	51	31	26	1	1	3	3	31	3	27	8	0	3	2	.600	0	2	5.09
Gargano, Mike	New Jersey	StL	A-	21	21	7	0	0	49	233	57	34	31	3	1	2	8	27	0	20	6	0	1	4	.200	0	0	5.69
Garibaldi, Cecilio	St. Pete	TB	A+	22	21	15	0	1	99	429	109	56	48	7	3	4	12	28	2	52	6	1	6	6	.500	0	0	4.36
Garner, Brandon	Rockies	Col	R	20	14	13	1	0	79.1	327	74	37	32	1	4	3	6	5	0	67	6	3	4	5	.444	0	0	3.63
	Portland	Col	A-	20	1	0	0	0	1	6	2	1	1	0	0	0	0	1	0	1	0	0	0	0	.000	0	0	9.00
Garrett, Josh	Sarasota	Bos	A+	22	26	26	0	0	149	683	189	87	76	9	1	6	17	50	2	95	7	0	8	10	.444	0	0	4.59
Garris, Antonio	Expos	Mon	R	22	15	1	0	7	40.1	169	32	19	18	2	2	1	4	19	0	33	3	1	3	2	.600	0	1	4.02
Garvin, Robert	Brevard Cty	Fla	A+	21	1	0	0	0	2.2	12	2	0	0	0	0	0	0	2	0	3	0	0	0	0	.000	0	0	0.00
	Utica	Fla	A-	21	23	3	0	0	54.2	224	58	29	24	4	1	2	0	8	0	39	2	0	3	5	.375	0	0	3.95
Gaskill, Derek	Capital Cty	NYM	A	26	12	0	0	6	20.1	79	13	7	7	1	0	0	0	9	0	23	3	0	2	1	.667	0	0	3.10
	St. Lucie	NYM	A+	26	22	0	0	6	28	145	34	30	25	2	3	1	3	24	0	28	6	0	2	0	1.000	0	0	8.04
Gaud, Perfecto*	Medcine Hat	Tor	R+	21	14	2	0	4	20.2	103	23	22	19	3	0	1	4	16	1	26	4	0	0	1	.000	0	0	8.27
Gauger, Michael*	Mets	NYM	R	23	18	0	0	10	30	127	27	17	11	1	0	2	2	8	0	30	1	1	2	0	1.000	0	3	3.30
Gawer, Matt*	Jamestown	Atl	A-	22	21	0	0	13	30	128	24	12	11	1	0	2	2	18	0	44	4	0	2	1	.667	0	6	3.30
Geary, Geoff	Clearwater	Phi	A+	23	24	19	2	0	139	611	175	77	61	11	6	4	5	31	1	77	6	3	10	5	.667	0	0	3.95
Gehrke, Jay	Spokane	KC	A-	22	32	0	0	32	29	143	34	21	18	3	1	0	3	21	0	33	3	0	0	3	.000	0	13	5.59
Geitz, Scott	Beloit	Mil	A	24	52	0	0	17	69.1	315	75	44	40	5	3	1	7	31	0	56	4	0	1	3	.250	0	3	5.19
Gentile, Mark*	Missoula	Ari	R+	19	15	14	0	0	78	361	100	62	51	5	3	3	2	25	0	45	5	2	7	4	.636	0	0	5.88
George, Chris	Auburn	Hou	A-	22	21	0	0	15	30.1	129	28	9	5	1	0	1	3	9	0	41	3	0	2	1	.667	0	2	1.48
George, Chris*	Wilmington	KC	A+	20	27	27	0	0	145	618	142	65	58	8	3	4	5	53	0	142	5	1	9	7	.563	0	0	3.60
German, Franklyn	Sou Oregon	Oak	A-	20	15	15	0	0	73.2	344	89	52	49	10	0	4	4	45	1	58	4	0	3	5	.375	0	0	5.99
German, Yon*	Capital Cty	NYM	A	22	14	14	0	0	87.2	352	82	33	22	9	1	2	0	15	0	68	3	1	8	2	.800	0	0	2.26
	St. Lucie	NYM	A+	22	10	9	0	1	55	250	67	41	33	5	2	2	0	21	3	40	4	3	1	7	.125	0	0	5.40
Getz, Cody*	Hudson Val	TB	A-	21	11	11	0	0	60	247	56	22	19	4	2	0	7	17	0	69	3	0	5	1	.833	0	0	2.85
Giese, Daniel	Lowell	Bos	A-	23	18	0	0	8	34.1	131	17	8	7	2	1	1	2	10	1	27	2	0	3	0	1.000	0	2	1.83
	Augusta	Bos	A	23	9	0	0	1	17.1	71	15	4	4	1	1	0	3	5	0	11	1	0	1	0	1.000	0	0	2.08
Gilfillan, Jason	Chstn-WV	KC	A	23	8	0	0	1	11.2	66	22	21	19	2	0	0	1	6	0	9	1	0	0	1	.000	0	0	14.66
	Spokane	KC	A-	23	25	0	0	7	34.2	161	31	23	22	6	3	4	6	22	0	37	3	1	4	1	.800	0	1	5.71
Gilich, Denny	Cedar Rapds	Ana	A	24	51	0	0	19	64	290	62	36	30	5	4	1	11	31	0	79	4	2	3	7	.300	0	2	4.22
Ginter, Matt	White Sox	CWS	R	22	3	0	0	1	8.1	33	5	4	0	0	0	1	0	3	0	10	0	0	1	0	1.000	0	1	3.24
	Burlington	CWS	A	22	9	9	0	0	40	173	38	20	18	3	1	0	3	19	0	29	1	0	4	2	.667	0	0	4.05
Girdley, Josh*	Expos	Mon	R	19	12	11	0	1	43.1	182	41	19	16	2	0	1	3	16	0	49	3	0	0	2	.000	0	1	3.32
Giuliano, Joe	Rockford	Cin	A	24	43	1	0	11	73.2	348	79	51	33	6	3	5	8	39	7	54	8	1	3	4	.429	0	2	4.03
Glaser, Eric	Lowell	Bos	A-	22	14	14	0	0	78.2	324	65	37	30	7	2	1	2	26	0	82	1	0	4	5	.444	0	0	3.43

1999 Pitching — Single-A and Rookie Leagues

HOW MUCH HE PITCHED											WHAT HE GAVE UP												THE RESULTS					
Player	Team	Org	Lg	A	G	GS	CG	GF	IP	BFP	H	R	ER	HR	SH	SF	HB	TBB	IBB	SO	WP	Bk	W	L	Pct.	ShO	Sv	ERA
	Augusta	Bos	A	22	1	1	0	0	5	17	2	0	0	0	0	0	0	1	0	7	0	0	1	0	1.000	0	0	0.00
Glaser, Scott*	Williamsprt	Pit	A-	24	3	0	0	2	4	18	5	2	2	0	0	0	0	1	0	6	0	0	0	1	.000	0	0	4.50
	Hickory	Pit	A	24	17	0	0	7	20.1	90	23	12	10	3	0	1	1	3	0	10	0	0	1	1	.500	0	0	4.43
Glick, Dave*	Michigan	Hou	A	24	10	0	0	3	16.1	66	7	2	1	0	0	0	3	5	1	20	2	0	1	0	1.000	0	1	0.55
	Kissimmee	Hou	A+	24	32	0	0	10	44	206	47	29	23	1	2	2	4	22	2	41	3	0	0	3	.000	0	0	4.70
Glysch, Craig	Boise	Ana	A-	23	22	0	0	11	32.1	132	30	15	13	1	1	1	2	7	2	28	0	0	3	4	.429	0	2	3.62
Gobble, Jimmy*	Royals	KC	R	18	4	1	0	0	6.2	32	6	3	2	0	0	0	0	5	0	8	1	1	0	0	.000	0	0	2.70
Goetz, Geoff*	Kane County	Fla	A	21	16	12	0	0	50.2	223	52	28	24	4	0	4	6	24	0	43	7	0	5	3	.625	0	0	4.26
Gold, J.M.	Beloit	Mil	A	20	21	21	2	0	111.2	505	120	82	67	16	3	5	4	54	2	93	13	2	6	10	.375	0	0	5.40
Gomer, Jeramy*	Lansing	ChC	A	21	7	5	0	1	27.2	121	27	18	18	3	1	1	3	12	0	21	2	0	2	1	.667	0	0	5.86
	Eugene	ChC	A-	21	16	15	0	1	82.1	368	106	70	67	9	4	7	3	28	0	52	7	0	2	11	.154	0	0	7.32
Gomera, Rafael	Great Falls	LA	R+	22	19	2	0	7	36.2	200	64	54	45	1	0	4	6	24	0	23	10	2	2	5	.286	0	3	11.05
Gomes, Tony	Vero Beach	LA	A+	22	37	0	0	17	61.2	285	67	45	43	7	7	2	2	32	3	70	5	1	4	5	.444	0	2	6.28
Gomez, Diogenes	Portland	Col	A-	21	24	0	0	17	27.1	122	25	12	7	3	2	2	1	13	3	17	0	0	3	2	.600	0	7	2.30
Gomez, Odalis	Butte	Ana	R+	21	22	5	0	6	37	211	44	58	42	3	0	1	5	50	1	42	11	3	2	7	.222	0	0	10.22
Gomez, Rafael	Kingsport	NYM	R+	22	25	0	0	11	36.2	163	35	21	19	1	3	3	2	20	2	23	2	1	3	3	.500	0	4	4.66
Gonzales, Rick	Potomac	StL	A+	25	47	3	0	7	72	337	88	58	49	8	4	7	5	38	3	39	11	1	3	4	.429	0	0	6.13
Gonzalez, Edwin	Wilmington	KC	A+	22	5	0	0	0	11	52	14	12	8	3	1	0	0	4	0	8	0	0	1	1	.500	0	0	6.55
	Chstn-WV	KC	A	22	27	13	3	4	120.1	479	101	37	30	6	5	4	5	28	0	136	13	1	7	6	.538	2	2	2.24
Gonzalez, Miguel	Rockies	Col	R	20	10	1	0	4	16.1	90	24	18	12	1	0	0	3	12	0	15	6	1	0	1	.000	0	0	6.61
Gooch, Arnie	Reds	Cin	R	23	2	2	0	0	8	32	5	2	1	0	0	0	1	1	0	6	0	0	1	1	.500	0	0	1.13
	Clinton	Cin	A	23	2	2	0	0	8	36	8	5	4	1	0	0	0	3	0	5	0	0	1	1	.500	0	0	4.50
Good, Andrew	South Bend	Ari	A	20	27	27	0	0	153.2	662	160	80	70	9	3	9	9	42	0	146	7	0	11	10	.524	0	0	4.10
Good, Eric*	Vermont	Mon	A-	20	15	15	0	0	70	319	77	49	45	3	1	2	8	30	0	59	3	2	5	5	.500	0	0	5.79
Gooden, Derek	Peoria	StL	A	25	38	0	0	34	37.1	162	41	20	20	1	0	1	5	12	1	21	1	0	3	2	.600	0	12	4.82
Goodrich, Randy	San Jose	SF	A+	23	38	18	0	4	136.2	623	174	95	73	6	5	6	11	34	0	82	6	3	8	8	.500	0	1	4.81
Gordon, Justin*	Helena	Mil	R+	21	15	4	0	5	31.1	160	31	31	21	3	0	0	12	29	0	36	13	1	1	2	.333	0	0	6.03
Gordon, Kevin	Asheville	Col	A	23	2	1	0	0	7	31	7	4	2	1	0	1	0	3	0	8	0	0	0	1	.000	0	0	2.57
	Portland	Col	A-	23	8	0	0	0	9.2	55	14	18	10	2	1	0	0	7	0	11	1	0	0	1	.000	0	0	9.31
	Utica	Fla	A-	23	1	0	0	0	1.1	7	3	1	1	0	0	0	0	1	0	1	0	0	1	0	1.000	0	0	6.75
Gorman, Pat	Capital Cty	NYM	A	22	15	0	0	8	18.1	106	28	27	24	4	0	1	0	19	0	19	4	0	1	1	.500	0	0	11.78
	Pittsfield	NYM	A-	22	19	0	0	9	33.2	152	30	17	12	3	4	1	2	20	1	40	5	0	3	2	.600	0	1	3.21
Gourlay, Matt	Hagerstown	Tor	A	21	7	0	0	3	6.2	42	10	10	10	0	0	1	2	13	0	5	0	0	0	1	.000	0	0	13.50
	St.Cathrnes	Tor	A-	21	14	0	0	2	19	95	14	17	11	4	0	1	4	18	0	24	4	0	1	1	.500	0	0	5.21
Grabow, John*	Hickory	Pit	A	21	26	26	0	0	156.1	654	152	82	66	16	3	3	5	32	0	164	3	0	9	10	.474	0	0	3.80
Grace, Bryan	Staten Ilnd	NYY	A-	24	8	1	0	3	12.2	63	13	14	8	2	0	2	1	9	0	11	3	2	0	4	.000	0	0	5.68
	Tampa	NYY	A+	24	9	0	0	4	17.2	91	17	7	4	0	2	0	2	18	3	10	3	1	2	0	1.000	0	0	2.04
Gracesqui, Frank.*	St.Cathrnes	Tor	A-	20	15	10	0	1	46.1	220	44	30	26	4	0	2	3	41	0	45	6	2	2	3	.400	0	1	5.05
Graham, Frank	Kingsport	NYM	R+	21	14	14	0	0	80	348	69	42	33	4	1	1	7	33	0	79	7	1	3	3	.500	0	0	3.71
Graman, Alex*	Staten Ilnd	NYY	A-	22	14	14	0	0	81.1	324	74	30	27	7	3	1	1	16	0	85	1	1	6	3	.667	0	0	2.99
Granadillo, Adel	Columbus	Cle	A	21	2	0	0	0	3	14	3	5	5	1	1	1	0	3	0	1	1	0	0	1	.000	0	0	15.00
Granados, Bernie	Rockies	Col	R	21	16	0	0	7	27.1	140	38	28	17	2	5	1	3	12	1	25	1	5	1	1	.500	0	0	5.60
Grantham, Ryan	Expos	Mon	R	20	8	5	0	0	26.1	126	24	10	10	1	1	1	5	18	0	30	4	0	2	0	1.000	0	0	3.42
Grater, Kevin	Helena	Mil	R+	22	6	5	0	1	30.2	126	34	16	15	2	2	0	1	7	0	30	1	1	1	1	.500	0	0	4.40
	Beloit	Mil	A	22	9	8	1	1	60.1	240	47	17	16	3	1	0	6	17	0	65	2	3	5	3	.625	1	0	2.39
Graves, Donovan	Johnson Cy	StL	R+	19	19	5	0	5	43.2	187	40	24	18	3	2	2	1	17	0	51	2	0	3	1	.750	0	1	3.71
Gray, Michael*	Macon	Atl	A	23	46	1	0	22	81.1	349	88	45	33	6	3	2	7	12	1	57	2	1	5	4	.556	0	8	3.65
Greene, Ryan	Myrtle Bch	Atl	A+	25	44	0	0	29	82	339	65	32	31	7	5	1	2	29	1	85	11	0	3	5	.375	0	16	3.40
Greeny, Burdette	Ogden	Mil	R+	25	5	0	0	4	12	62	20	13	12	2	0	0	1	6	0	7	2	0	0	3	.000	0	0	9.00
	Beloit	Mil	A	25	19	0	0	12	28	126	38	20	18	2	0	0	3	7	0	22	2	1	0	0	.000	0	3	5.79
Grezlovski, Ben	Boise	Ana	A-	23	14	0	0	14	16.2	65	11	5	4	2	1	0	0	3	1	20	0	0	0	1	.000	0	7	2.16
Griffin, Kirk	Peoria	StL	A	25	57	0	0	37	65	258	42	28	26	4	5	3	1	22	2	53	3	1	3	4	.429	0	11	3.60
Griffiths, Jeremy	Kingsport	NYM	R+	22	14	14	1	0	76.1	321	68	40	28	6	1	3	1	36	1	74	5	1	3	5	.375	0	0	3.30
Grippo, Mike*	Johnson Cy	StL	R+	24	14	0	0	1	18.1	88	21	18	17	2	1	4	1	12	0	18	1	1	0	1	.000	0	1	8.35
Gross, Rafael	Kinston	Cle	A+	25	4	0	0	2	8.2	34	9	3	3	0	0	1	0	1	0	5	1	0	1	0	1.000	0	0	3.12
	Columbus	Cle	A	25	42	0	0	31	62.1	249	51	19	18	3	2	0	1	14	0	62	0	0	6	1	.857	0	7	2.60
Grunwald, Erik	Mariners	Sea	R	23	18	0	0	15	24	101	22	10	7	0	3	1	0	9	1	23	3	0	3	2	.600	0	3	2.63
	Everett	Sea	A-	23	4	0	0	3	4	22	5	1	1	0	0	0	0	4	0	4	1	0	0	0	.000	0	1	2.25
Guerrero, Junior	Chstn-WV	KC	A	20	19	19	0	0	104.1	441	90	39	32	6	4	5	3	45	0	113	10	2	7	3	.700	0	0	2.76
	Wilmington	KC	A+	20	9	9	0	0	51.1	206	30	10	8	2	1	1	0	26	0	68	4	0	4	2	.667	0	0	1.40
Guerrero, Neftali	Mets	NYM	R	20	15	0	0	14	21.2	87	16	6	4	1	2	0	0	5	0	17	2	0	1	2	.333	0	5	1.66
Guerrier, Matt	Bristol	CWS	R+	21	21	0	0	19	25.2	109	18	9	3	1	0	2	1	14	2	37	1	1	5	0	1.000	0	10	1.05
	Winston-Sal	CWS	A+	21	4	0	0	4	3.1	15	3	2	2	0	0	0	1	0	0	5	2	0	0	0	.000	0	2	5.40
Guillen, Elvin	Reds	Cin	R	19	7	0	0	4	8	42	9	9	8	0	0	0	1	11	0	7	3	2	0	0	.000	0	0	9.00
Guillory, Dan	Kinston	Cle	A+	24	25	0	0	15	31.2	152	36	20	18	2	3	1	2	16	4	32	6	1	1	3	.250	0	5	5.12
	Columbus	Cle	A	24	15	0	0	8	32.2	130	21	9	7	3	0	0	0	10	0	43	0	0	1	1	.500	0	0	1.93
Gulin, Lindsay*	Daytona	ChC	A+	23	3	1	0	0	13.2	53	7	0	0	0	1	0	0	7	0	19	0	0	2	0	1.000	0	0	0.00
Gunderson, Matt	Lansing	ChC	A	23	13	0	0	3	19.2	97	28	23	21	2	0	3	1	11	0	11	6	1	0	0	.000	0	0	9.61
	Eugene	ChC	A-	23	8	0	0	4	12.1	58	16	11	7	2	1	1	0	6	2	15	1	1	1	3	.250	0	1	5.11
Gutierrez, Lazaro*	W Michigan	Det	A	24	35	0	0	17	46.1	220	50	26	24	5	3	2	1	40	0	49	3	0	2	1	.667	0	1	4.66
Guttormson, Rick	Rancho Cuca	SD	A+	23	28	28	1	0	174.1	714	165	83	72	15	4	1	9	36	0	125	6	2	14	8	.636	0	0	3.72
Guy, Brad	Lynchburg	Pit	A+	21	40	0	0	37	73.1	308	77	35	33	2	5	2	1	17	2	60	7	1	6	6	.500	0	10	4.11
Guzman, Ambiorix	Savannah	Tex	A	22	29	1	0	18	71.2	301	71	37	35	10	6	4	5	16	0	73	2	2	3	7	.300	0	0	4.40
Guzman, Juan	Delmarva	Bal	A	22	29	18	0	8	124.1	531	124	51	49	10	2	2	7	44	0	134	6	4	9	5	.643	0	3	3.55
Guzman, Leiby	Rangers	Tex	R	23	1	1	0	0	3	11	2	0	0	0	0	0	0	0	0	1	0	0	0	0	.000	0	0	0.00
	Charlotte	Tex	A+	23	19	18	0	1	93.1	420	114	67	61	16	0	5	9	40	0	45	5	0	5	6	.455	0	0	5.88
Guzman, Wilson*	Lynchburg	Pit	A+	22	35	0	0	13	65.1	283	70	35	25	3	0	4	1	12	0	78	2	0	1	2	.333	0	2	3.44

1999 Pitching — Single-A and Rookie Leagues

HOW MUCH HE PITCHED											WHAT HE GAVE UP												THE RESULTS					
Player	Team	Org	Lg	A	G	GS	CG	GF	IP	BFP	H	R	ER	HR	SH	SF	HB	TBB	IBB	SO	WP	Bk	W	L	Pct.	ShO	Sv	ERA
Haase, Frank*	Portland	Col	A-	20	14	0	0	5	17.2	87	18	20	13	2	0	1	1	14	1	10	2	2	0	1	.000	0	0	6.62
Hadden, Randy	Yakima	LA	A-	22	16	11	0	3	86.2	371	94	51	46	7	0	4	3	25	1	53	6	1	6	5	.545	0	1	4.78
Haines, Talley	St. Pete	TB	A+	23	2	0	0	1	4.1	13	1	0	0	0	0	0	2	0	0	4	0	0	0	0	.000	0	0	0.00
	Chston-SC	TB	A	23	47	0	0	34	61	248	51	33	22	2	2	0	3	12	4	68	5	1	3	2	.600	0	18	3.25
Halisky, Scott	Orioles	Bal	R	22	3	0	0	2	5	23	7	4	4	1	0	0	0	3	1	3	2	0	0	0	.000	0	0	7.20
Halla, Ryan	Lynchburg	Pit	A+	26	46	0	0	29	54.1	246	60	34	31	5	5	4	2	20	1	56	7	0	2	7	.222	0	7	5.13
Halpin, Jeremy	Frederick	Bal	A+	25	45	1	0	22	83.1	359	95	44	33	7	2	4	3	18	2	53	4	0	5	3	.625	0	2	3.56
Halvorson, Greg	Mets	NYM	R	23	5	3	0	1	21	95	22	14	9	0	1	0	1	9	0	20	3	1	1	2	.333	0	0	3.86
Hamann, Robert	Medcine Hat	Tor	R+	23	15	13	0	1	75.2	337	95	54	33	9	3	4	2	17	0	45	7	0	2	8	.200	0	0	3.93
Hammons, Matt	Daytona	ChC	A+	23	15	11	0	3	59.2	262	54	36	33	6	4	3	4	32	0	53	6	0	2	4	.333	0	1	4.98
Hamulack, Tim*	Michigan	Hou	A	23	25	0	0	12	26.2	112	23	9	9	0	1	2	0	11	0	32	2	1	3	0	1.000	0	0	3.04
Hancock, Josh	Augusta	Bos	A	22	25	25	0	0	139.2	607	154	79	59	12	4	2	4	46	0	106	10	1	6	8	.429	0	0	3.80
Hancock, Rodney*	Williamsprt	Pit	A-	21	8	4	0	4	32	136	27	13	6	0	1	1	2	13	1	35	3	1	1	2	.333	0	0	1.69
Hand, Jon	Peoria	StL	A	24	58	0	0	17	81.2	352	90	43	33	4	1	5	5	22	2	55	3	3	3	3	.500	0	1	3.64
Hanson, David	Medcine Hat	Tor	R+	19	14	7	0	2	45.2	217	64	33	27	1	2	1	2	21	0	35	2	2	1	2	.333	0	0	5.32
Harang, Aaron	Pulaski	Tex	R+	22	16	10	1	6	78.1	309	64	22	20	5	2	3	4	17	1	87	2	1	9	2	.818	1	1	2.30
Harber, Ryan*	Kane County	Fla	A	23	24	14	0	4	98.1	438	110	50	39	10	6	7	3	33	0	77	5	2	3	5	.375	0	0	3.57
Harrell, Scott	Reds	Cin	R	25	2	0	0	0	4	20	6	4	3	1	0	0	1	1	0	2	0	0	0	0	.000	0	0	6.75
Harrell, Tim	San Berndno	LA	A+	24	44	0	0	14	74.2	324	78	40	40	10	4	4	0	36	2	78	13	0	5	2	.714	0	2	4.82
Harris, J.T.	Butte	Ana	R+	24	23	0	0	8	39.1	173	43	25	19	3	2	0	2	13	0	34	5	0	3	4	.429	0	0	4.35
Harris, Josh	Fort Wayne	SD	A	22	17	7	0	3	53.1	255	67	52	44	6	2	3	4	28	1	28	0	2	2	5	.286	0	0	7.43
Harris, Julian*	Butte	Ana	R+	22	17	16	0	0	81.2	409	132	95	76	7	1	4	2	36	0	67	15	0	2	9	.182	0	0	8.38
Harris, Silas*	Vermont	Mon	A-	23	23	1	0	7	30	158	32	24	24	3	1	2	5	30	3	32	6	0	0	5	.000	0	0	7.20
Harris, Toby	Missoula	Ari	R+	23	22	4	1	7	60.2	277	80	48	34	5	1	0	2	14	0	43	5	1	1	3	.250	0	1	5.04
Hart, Damien*	Clinton	Cin	A	25	26	0	0	8	34.2	160	34	25	21	3	3	4	2	18	3	20	5	0	2	5	.286	0	0	5.45
Harwas, Oliver	Cedar Rapds	Ana	A	24	37	0	0	16	51.1	240	50	40	32	3	4	1	9	29	1	37	12	0	3	4	.429	0	2	5.61
Hawkins, Barry	Pittsfield	NYM	A-	23	16	0	0	4	37.1	159	39	20	16	1	1	1	4	12	0	24	5	0	1	2	.333	0	0	3.86
Haworth, Brent	Boise	Ana	A-	23	15	0	0	4	20	106	30	26	15	2	0	1	1	14	0	14	4	1	0	0	.000	0	0	6.75
	Butte	Ana	R+	23	5	0	0	3	4.1	23	4	6	5	0	0	1	2	4	0	3	0	0	0	0	.000	0	1	10.38
Hayden, Terry*	Rockford	Cin	A	25	5	0	0	2	7	33	10	6	6	1	2	0	0	3	0	7	0	0	0	0	.000	0	0	7.71
	Clinton	Cin	A	25	33	14	1	4	109.2	470	98	51	29	9	8	3	6	39	0	72	6	0	8	6	.571	0	0	2.38
Haynes, Brad	Marlins	Fla	R	18	11	11	0	0	46.1	214	45	31	21	1	1	1	6	30	0	40	4	0	1	4	.200	0	0	4.08
Hearns, Shane	W Michigan	Det	A	24	51	0	0	30	69	294	41	26	18	1	3	4	1	39	2	101	15	1	5	4	.556	0	10	2.35
Heath, Woody	Dunedin	Tor	A+	23	22	14	0	1	102.2	462	109	67	57	11	1	5	3	47	1	89	3	1	6	4	.600	0	1	5.00
Heaverlo, Jeff	Everett	Sea	A-	22	3	0	0	1	8.2	35	5	5	2	1	1	0	1	2	0	9	1	0	1	0	1.000	0	0	2.08
	Wisconsin	Sea	A	22	3	3	1	0	17.2	75	15	6	5	1	1	0	1	7	0	24	0	1	1	0	1.000	1	0	2.55
Hebert, Cedric	San Berndno	LA	A+	22	16	5	0	4	44.1	203	57	34	29	3	0	1	3	19	0	37	3	1	2	2	.500	0	1	5.89
	Vero Beach	LA	A+	22	7	0	0	3	8.2	41	8	3	3	1	0	0	1	7	0	6	0	0	1	0	1.000	0	0	3.12
Hebson, Bryan	Cape Fear	Mon	A	24	6	6	0	0	33.2	142	22	13	10	2	1	1	3	17	0	34	2	0	0	1	.000	0	0	2.67
	Jupiter	Mon	A+	24	17	16	0	1	103.1	414	85	33	23	5	2	3	5	26	0	79	3	0	7	6	.538	0	0	2.00
Hecht, Brian	Michigan	Hou	A	22	27	0	0	13	34.1	152	42	13	12	0	1	1	2	10	2	26	2	0	4	1	.800	0	1	3.15
Hee, Aaron*	Kingsport	NYM	R+	21	12	12	0	0	48.2	250	64	48	41	4	1	0	8	37	0	38	10	0	0	4	.000	0	0	7.58
Heffernan, Greg	Capital Cty	NYM	A	25	5	0	0	3	7	31	7	8	4	2	0	0	0	5	0	5	0	0	0	0	.000	0	0	5.14
Held, Travis	Peoria	StL	A	23	2	2	0	0	10.2	47	14	3	3	1	1	0	0	4	0	7	1	1	1	0	1.000	0	0	2.53
	Potomac	StL	A+	23	24	21	0	1	111.2	500	140	76	67	11	6	4	10	25	0	85	6	1	2	10	.167	0	0	5.40
Hendricks, John*	Pittsfield	NYM	A-	22	15	14	0	0	80	340	78	38	27	4	4	2	3	19	0	64	2	1	5	4	.556	0	0	3.04
Henriquez, Hector*	Kane County	Fla	A	21	14	10	0	1	53.1	255	65	47	45	4	0	4	4	40	0	31	3	2	2	5	.286	0	0	7.59
	Utica	Fla	A-	21	12	1	0	1	16	74	16	12	11	2	0	1	1	13	0	12	2	1	1	1	.500	0	0	6.19
Hernandez, Carlos*	Martinsvlle	Hou	R+	20	13	9	0	0	55.1	227	36	21	9	2	1	1	6	23	0	82	6	0	5	1	.833	0	0	1.46
Herndon, Eric	Macon	Atl	A	23	27	2	0	5	72	314	72	42	32	9	1	1	1	27	0	75	2	2	5	4	.556	0	1	4.00
Herrera, Carlos	Phillies	Phi	R	19	12	5	0	0	45.1	209	46	30	22	4	3	1	6	25	0	40	2	0	0	3	.000	0	0	4.37
Herrera, Jose	Mariners	Sea	R	20	12	11	0	0	54	252	56	46	35	7	1	2	10	29	0	48	5	4	3	5	.375	0	0	5.83
Herrera, Pedro	Royals	KC	R	21	5	0	0	4	6	22	1	0	0	0	0	0	2	3	0	5	0	0	0	0	.000	0	3	0.00
	Spokane	KC	A-	21	16	0	0	3	20	100	27	18	14	1	0	0	3	14	0	14	5	0	1	0	1.000	0	0	6.30
Hertzel, Patrick	Chston-SC	TB	A	23	35	16	0	7	126.2	559	142	66	56	10	1	3	3	46	1	96	7	0	7	7	.500	0	0	3.98
Hickman, Ben	Utica	Fla	A-	23	24	0	0	19	38	149	36	12	9	1	4	0	1	4	0	38	0	1	3	2	.600	0	7	2.13
Hiles, Cary	Piedmont	Phi	A	24	44	0	0	40	61	255	52	20	15	3	6	0	3	12	0	84	9	0	3	2	.600	0	26	2.21
Hill, Jaime*	Rangers	Tex	R	23	21	1	0	12	46	181	32	12	12	0	2	0	1	20	0	38	0	2	2	0	1.000	0	2	2.35
Hill, Kendall	Fort Myers	Min	A+	25	39	4	0	12	80	378	99	68	57	8	3	1	4	42	0	55	11	3	2	5	.286	0	2	6.41
Hill, Ryan	Royals	KC	R	21	1	0	0	0	0.1	5	0	3	3	0	0	0	1	3	0	1	0	0	0	0	.000	0	0	81.00
Hill, Terrance*	Augusta	Bos	A	24	53	0	0	15	92.1	383	77	30	28	6	5	3	3	25	2	95	11	0	3	6	.333	0	1	2.73
Hills, Mark*	Salem-Keizr	SF	A-	21	16	7	0	1	52.1	253	70	49	39	3	3	3	1	27	0	41	4	1	0	2	.000	0	0	6.71
Hilton, Nate	Sou Oregon	Oak	A-	22	16	14	0	0	67.1	324	80	63	51	7	3	1	6	28	0	50	7	0	2	4	.333	0	0	6.82
Hines, Carlos	Reds	Cin	R	19	5	0	0	0	10	53	15	12	9	0	2	0	0	8	1	7	5	1	0	0	.000	0	0	8.10
Hlodan, George	Pirates	Pit	R	24	4	0	0	3	10	43	11	4	4	1	1	0	0	3	0	3	0	0	0	0	.000	0	1	3.60
Hoard, Brent*	Quad City	Min	A	23	28	28	1	0	149.2	643	143	68	57	9	4	3	2	64	1	139	7	1	12	7	.632	0	0	3.43
Hoerman, Jared	Mariners	Sea	R	23	11	1	0	5	32	126	24	6	5	0	0	0	1	6	0	46	1	0	1	0	1.000	0	2	1.41
	Lancaster	Sea	A+	23	4	0	0	1	7.2	36	8	6	6	2	0	1	0	7	0	6	1	0	0	0	.000	0	0	7.04
Hoff, Steve*	Cubs	ChC	R	22	3	3	0	0	6	29	6	4	3	1	0	0	0	5	0	9	0	0	0	1	.000	0	0	4.50
Hoffman, Matt	Portland	Col	A-	23	23	0	0	8	33	161	35	27	23	2	4	1	3	23	0	22	3	0	4	1	.800	0	1	6.27
Hollifield, Alec	White Sox	CWS	R	19	16	0	0	7	18.1	99	29	19	14	2	2	4	3	11	3	14	2	1	1	5	.167	0	0	6.87
Hollingsworth, Scott	Pulaski	Tex	R+	24	12	0	0	5	19.2	95	24	18	12	3	0	1	1	14	0	20	2	0	0	1	.000	0	0	5.49
Holmes, Mike	Modesto	Oak	A+	24	34	18	0	9	145.2	629	184	100	79	14	3	4	5	15	3	84	3	1	9	6	.600	0	6	4.88
Hopper, Josh*	Mets	NYM	R	22	16	2	0	4	44.1	190	42	13	8	0	1	0	1	19	0	50	4	2	3	1	.750	0	2	1.62
Horgan, Joe*	Bakersfield	SF	A+	23	25	19	1	1	117.1	520	129	76	68	18	2	2	10	43	0	101	5	2	6	10	.375	0	0	5.22
Horne, Travis*	Helena	Mil	R+	19	3	2	0	0	5.2	27	5	5	5	1	0	0	0	9	0	2	1	0	1	0	1.000	0	0	7.94
Horney, Michael	Billings	Cin	R+	22	8	0	0	5	16	67	15	6	5	0	0	0	4	4	0	11	2	1	4	1	.800	0	1	2.81

1999 Pitching — Single-A and Rookie Leagues

HOW MUCH HE PITCHED											WHAT HE GAVE UP												THE RESULTS					
Player	Team	Org	Lg	A	G	GS	CG	GF	IP	BFP	H	R	ER	HR	SH	SF	HB	TBB	IBB	SO	WP	Bk	W	L	Pct.	ShO	Sv	ERA
Hosford, Clinton	Great Falls	LA	R+	19	10	0	0	6	17.2	78	18	13	12	2	1	0	0	11	0	12	5	1	1	0	1.000	0	1	6.11
Hostetler, Jim	Lakeland	Det	A+	23	31	0	0	17	41.1	201	51	44	39	5	0	7	0	31	1	27	3	0	0	0	.000	0	0	8.49
Houle, Marc	Bluefield	Bal	R+	22	20	0	0	7	44	212	57	44	35	5	0	6	5	27	0	36	10	4	0	3	.000	0	0	7.16
House, Craig	Portland	Col	A-	22	26	0	0	19	34.2	154	28	14	8	0	1	0	5	14	0	58	4	2	2	1	.667	0	11	2.08
House, Jeff	Ogden	Mil	R+	23	17	0	0	8	33	169	47	41	30	3	3	2	3	19	4	31	7	0	1	3	.250	0	0	8.18
Houser, Kyle	Asheville	Col	A	25	4	3	0	1	11	51	14	12	10	5	0	1	0	3	0	19	2	1	0	1	.000	0	0	8.18
Houston, Ryan	Medcine Hat	Tor	R+	20	14	7	0	1	45.2	216	61	41	34	4	1	3	3	19	0	30	6	2	3	4	.429	0	1	6.70
Howard, Ben	Fort Wayne	SD	A	21	28	28	0	0	144.2	666	123	100	76	17	4	3	5	110	0	131	19	1	6	10	.375	0	0	4.73
Howard, Tom*	Quad City	Min	A	24	15	1	0	4	29.1	118	26	6	5	1	0	0	0	4	0	22	2	0	2	1	.667	0	0	1.53
	Fort Myers	Min	A+	24	22	0	0	14	42.2	194	43	28	24	3	1	3	2	25	0	22	4	0	1	2	.333	0	0	5.06
Hubbel, Travis	St.Cathrnes	Tor	A-	21	5	3	0	2	20	83	16	5	4	1	0	0	1	7	0	19	0	0	0	0	.000	0	1	1.80
Hudson, Luke	Asheville	Col	A	23	21	20	1	1	88	372	89	47	42	10	2	2	8	24	0	96	3	3	6	5	.545	0	0	4.30
Huffaker, Mike	Potomac	StL	A+	24	54	0	0	13	67.2	322	59	33	29	5	5	2	9	51	3	79	11	0	1	5	.167	0	0	3.86
Huggins, David	Dunedin	Tor	A+	24	42	3	0	12	70	325	72	29	24	3	2	0	1	52	4	57	3	1	2	3	.400	0	1	3.09
Hughes, Mike*	Columbus	Cle	A	24	6	2	0	3	18	71	15	11	9	2	0	1	0	3	0	22	1	1	0	0	.000	0	1	4.50
	Expos	Mon	R	24	2	2	0	0	8	28	4	1	0	0	0	0	0	0	0	9	0	0	0	0	.000	0	0	0.00
	Jupiter	Mon	A+	24	17	2	0	6	30.2	145	41	17	16	2	1	3	3	16	0	22	2	0	1	2	.333	0	0	4.70
Hughes, Rocky*	White Sox	CWS	R	21	13	6	0	2	46	202	53	23	17	2	3	1	0	20	2	47	2	0	3	3	.500	0	1	3.33
Hughes, Travis	Savannah	Tex	A	22	30	23	1	5	157	646	127	60	49	9	3	3	11	54	0	150	9	2	11	7	.611	0	2	2.81
Huller, Mike*	Salem-Keizr	SF	A-	22	3	0	0	2	3	21	6	5	4	0	0	1	2	3	0	4	1	1	0	0	.000	0	0	12.00
	Bakersfield	SF	A+	22	1	0	0	1	1	7	2	2	2	0	0	0	0	2	0	0	1	0	0	0	.000	0	0	18.00
Humrich, Chris	Vermont	Mon	A-	22	22	0	0	7	45.1	199	45	29	20	2	3	0	2	20	0	52	3	0	1	1	.500	0	0	3.97
Hundley, Jeff*	Cedar Rapds	Ana	A	23	25	25	6	0	158	698	163	99	71	17	5	8	8	62	0	140	10	2	9	9	.500	1	0	4.04
Hunter, John	Idaho Falls	SD	R+	25	29	0	0	14	49	240	55	41	30	5	1	0	4	34	0	54	10	0	3	4	.429	0	3	5.51
Huntsman, Brandon	Delmarva	Bal	A	24	7	2	0	3	22.1	96	20	12	11	3	1	1	0	9	0	25	0	0	1	1	.500	0	0	4.43
	Frederick	Bal	A+	24	11	10	0	0	44.2	207	58	37	34	8	0	0	4	19	0	29	4	0	4	4	.500	0	0	6.85
Hurtado, Ed	Boise	Ana	A-	23	4	0	0	0	4	25	8	9	8	2	0	0	0	3	0	3	2	0	0	0	.000	0	0	18.00
Hurtado, Victor	Brevard Cty	Fla	A+	23	4	4	0	0	21	99	28	22	22	2	0	2	1	7	1	6	2	0	0	2	.000	0	0	9.43
Husted, Brent	Vero Beach	LA	A+	24	47	0	0	44	54	222	42	30	25	9	2	3	1	17	0	41	2	0	2	4	.333	0	27	4.17
Hutchinson, Brian*	Jamestown	Atl	A-	23	14	0	0	4	22.2	103	24	19	16	3	1	1	5	12	0	22	5	0	1	2	.333	0	0	6.35
Igualada, Eric	Yankees	NYY	R	21	11	0	0	1	23.2	98	16	10	10	4	1	2	1	12	0	30	3	0	1	3	.250	0	0	3.80
Immel, Steve	High Desert	Ari	A+	23	19	0	0	5	40.2	192	61	36	25	7	1	3	5	12	0	35	0	1	4	1	.800	0	0	5.53
Incantalupo, Todd*	Beloit	Mil	A	24	40	7	0	8	95.1	443	115	71	64	7	3	5	7	40	1	62	4	0	4	4	.500	0	1	6.04
Infante, Asdrubal	Tigers	Det	R	18	14	2	1	9	32.2	134	17	5	4	0	1	0	1	20	0	51	2	0	3	0	1.000	0	2	1.10
	Lakeland	Det	A+	18	1	1	0	0	4	21	6	2	2	0	1	0	0	3	0	3	0	0	0	1	.000	0	0	4.50
Izquierdo, Hansel	Winston-Sal	CWS	A+	23	18	13	0	4	82.2	371	76	46	38	5	5	2	8	46	1	72	13	1	3	5	.375	0	0	4.14
Jackson, Brian	Mahoning Vy	Cle	A-	22	14	13	0	0	70.2	321	75	38	27	1	2	4	4	30	0	51	2	2	6	4	.600	0	0	3.44
Jackson, Jeremy*	Chstn-WV	KC	A	24	19	13	0	4	81.2	356	82	52	40	4	1	1	6	30	0	65	8	0	4	5	.444	0	0	4.41
	Capital Cty	NYM	A	24	5	4	0	0	28	105	22	5	5	1	1	0	0	3	0	26	1	0	1	0	1.000	0	0	1.61
Jackson, Jonathan	Spokane	KC	A-	22	19	0	0	3	35.1	166	49	27	22	6	2	1	5	18	1	32	0	0	0	2	.000	0	0	5.60
Jackson, Stosh*	Cubs	ChC	R	24	6	0	0	0	10.2	45	8	5	2	0	0	1	0	4	0	23	0	0	0	1	.000	0	0	1.69
	Eugene	ChC	A-	24	10	0	0	5	16.2	76	20	12	6	0	0	0	0	5	0	24	2	1	0	2	.000	0	1	3.24
Jacobs, Dwayne	Winston-Sal	CWS	A+	23	46	1	0	20	59	286	33	38	33	4	3	0	6	79	0	76	28	1	1	3	.250	0	4	5.03
Jacobs, Frankey	Athletics	Oak	R	22	12	0	0	2	21.1	90	20	14	13	0	0	4	0	11	0	15	3	0	1	2	.333	0	0	5.48
Jacobs, Greg*	Cedar Rapds	Ana	A	23	36	10	0	10	105.1	457	108	62	52	7	2	7	5	37	2	106	8	1	2	5	.286	0	1	4.44
Jacobs, Jake	Quad City	Min	A	22	48	0	0	21	71.1	347	63	52	38	7	3	4	15	55	4	70	6	0	0	3	.000	0	0	4.79
Jacobson, Andrew	Burlington	CWS	A	24	13	1	0	6	19.1	96	28	19	13	1	0	2	1	12	1	10	3	0	1	1	.500	0	0	6.05
James, Delvin	Chston-SC	TB	A	22	25	25	1	0	158.1	654	142	76	64	13	9	4	8	33	1	106	8	1	8	8	.500	0	0	3.64
	St. Pete	TB	A+	22	3	2	0	1	17	71	18	6	6	0	0	0	3	4	0	6	1	0	3	0	1.000	0	0	3.18
James, Nick	Kingsport	NYM	R+	22	2	0	0	1	1	5	1	0	0	0	0	0	0	1	0	2	1	0	0	0	.000	0	0	0.00
Jamison, Ryan	Auburn	Hou	A-	22	15	15	0	0	87.2	374	83	45	40	7	1	3	6	36	0	83	5	4	5	3	.625	0	0	4.11
Janke, Cheyenne	New Jersey	StL	A-	23	15	14	0	0	83.1	356	85	40	34	8	2	1	1	20	0	63	8	2	2	5	.286	0	0	3.67
Jelovcic, Rich	Yankees	NYY	R	22	14	0	0	2	17.1	78	12	6	6	0	0	0	2	15	0	10	0	0	1	1	.500	0	0	3.12
Jennings, Jason	Portland	Col	A-	21	2	2	0	0	9	33	5	1	1	0	0	0	0	2	0	11	0	0	1	0	1.000	0	0	1.00
	Asheville	Col	A	21	12	12	0	0	58.1	242	55	27	24	3	3	2	6	8	0	69	4	0	2	2	.500	0	0	3.70
Jensen, Jared	Visalia	Oak	A+	26	32	22	0	2	141.1	607	154	82	66	15	2	6	3	41	2	110	9	1	9	7	.563	0	0	4.20
Jerue, Tristan	Potomac	StL	A+	24	4	3	0	0	14.2	67	18	12	12	0	0	1	1	8	0	9	2	0	0	1	.000	0	0	7.36
Jimenez, Jason*	St. Pete	TB	A+	24	41	1	0	19	56.2	229	46	23	15	2	2	0	3	21	2	47	2	0	4	4	.500	0	5	2.38
Jimenez, Julio*	Mexico	—	R	—	13	10	0	1	61.1	277	75	40	32	3	1	0	4	28	0	38	5	0	3	5	.375	0	0	4.70
Jimenez, Reinaldo	Salem-Keizr	SF	A-	22	24	0	0	4	37.1	184	44	29	23	7	4	2	5	27	0	23	8	2	5	2	.714	0	0	5.54
Jimenez, Ronal	Phillies	Phi	R	19	20	0	0	13	33.1	144	29	13	13	2	0	3	1	16	0	30	1	0	6	2	.750	0	4	3.51
Jodie, Brett	Greensboro	NYY	A	23	25	20	2	3	120.1	497	125	59	51	10	0	1	1	18	0	106	9	0	9	6	.600	0	1	3.81
Johnson, Craig	Lakeland	Det	A+	24	26	25	0	1	144	638	176	93	82	20	6	7	6	31	0	98	2	0	11	11	.500	0	0	5.13
Johnson, D.J.	Salem	Col	A+	25	4	0	0	4	6	26	4	2	2	1	0	0	0	2	0	6	0	0	0	0	.000	0	0	3.00
Johnson, Derrick*	Martinsvlle	Hou	R+	21	21	0	0	11	47.1	198	32	23	22	6	2	0	6	32	0	46	2	2	2	2	.500	0	0	4.18
Johnson, Eric	Bakersfield	SF	A+	22	17	0	0	8	21.2	106	22	14	14	1	0	1	2	21	0	14	1	0	1	0	1.000	0	0	5.82
	Salem-Keizr	SF	A-	22	15	1	0	3	16.1	86	18	15	14	1	0	0	2	17	0	18	5	1	1	1	.500	0	0	7.71
Johnson, James*	Stockton	Mil	A+	23	29	23	1	1	129.1	568	146	83	68	13	6	5	2	47	1	135	23	1	5	6	.455	1	0	4.73
Johnson, Roney	Rockies	Col	R	19	9	8	0	0	33.1	163	48	34	32	4	0	1	1	18	0	22	2	4	2	3	.400	0	0	8.64
Johnson, Solomon*	Burlington	CWS	A	21	19	8	0	3	53	249	70	38	29	2	0	5	1	17	1	39	1	1	3	2	.600	0	0	4.92
	Winston-Sal	CWS	A+	21	17	0	0	4	24.1	114	25	11	9	1	4	1	2	15	1	22	1	0	1	2	.333	0	0	3.33
Johnston, Clint*	Hickory	Pit	A	22	34	10	0	4	90.1	[illegible]	[illegible]	[illegible]	[illegible]	[illegible]	[illegible]	1	6	49	0	94	7	0	5	6	.455	0	0	4.72
Johnston, Dave	Marlins	Fla	R	19	12	0	0	7	26	116	35	17	14	4	0	1	5	5	1	20	3	0	1	2	.333	0	0	4.85
Johnston, Michael*	Williamsprt	Pit	A-	21	14	2	0	3	42.1	193	46	26	20	5	0	0	3	18	0	30	3	1	3	2	.600	0	2	4.25
Johnston, Rikki*	Oneonta	Det	A-	19	12	12	1	0	60	256	57	33	27	2	1	4	2	30	0	36	7	0	1	6	.143	0	0	4.05
Johnston, Sean*	Daytona	ChC	A+	24	26	3	0	6	68.1	338	91	54	38	5	3	3	6	39	1	28	7	0	2	5	.286	0	0	5.00
Jones, Charlie	South Bend	Ari	A	24	7	6	0	0	30	130	27	13	9	4	0	0	0	19	1	25	3	0	2	3	.400	0	0	2.70

1999 Pitching — Single-A and Rookie Leagues

HOW MUCH HE PITCHED											WHAT HE GAVE UP												THE RESULTS					
Player	Team	Org	Lg	A	G	GS	CG	GF	IP	BFP	H	R	ER	HR	SH	SF	HB	TBB	IBB	SO	WP	Bk	W	L	Pct.	ShO	Sv	ERA
Jones, Chris*	San Jose	SF	A+	20	28	27	0	0	130.2	592	121	85	67	5	4	3	6	87	0	118	17	5	8	12	.400	0	0	4.61
Jones, Craig	Spokane	KC	A-	23	2	2	0	0	8.2	42	11	8	6	0	0	0	4	1	0	4	0	0	1	1	.500	0	0	6.23
Jones, Fontella	Beloit	Mil	A	25	36	5	0	19	76.2	347	84	44	37	10	0	1	2	35	0	76	11	1	4	3	.571	0	4	4.34
Jones, Geoff*	Padres	SD	R	20	14	0	0	7	39	176	38	25	18	5	0	5	3	18	0	32	1	0	4	2	.667	0	2	4.15
Jones, Greg	Cedar Rapds	Ana	A	23	34	0	0	29	40	165	37	18	17	5	2	0	0	13	2	41	5	0	2	4	.333	0	13	3.83
Jones, Sean	Bluefield	Bal	R+	22	13	11	0	0	60.1	302	82	54	41	3	0	0	5	33	0	52	3	0	1	3	.250	0	0	6.12
Jones, Travis*	Fort Wayne	SD	A	22	41	7	0	6	91.1	409	90	42	32	6	2	5	4	57	0	72	7	2	8	2	.800	0	0	3.15
Joseph, Glen	Reds	Cin	R	19	2	0	0	1	5	22	8	4	4	0	0	0	0	1	0	3	0	0	1	0	1.000	0	0	7.20
Joseph, Jake	Pittsfield	NYM	A-	22	11	6	0	1	43.1	189	35	19	14	1	0	1	0	27	0	26	7	1	3	2	.600	0	1	2.91
Josephson, Jared	Pirates	Pit	R	23	8	0	0	7	10	40	8	2	2	0	0	1	0	2	0	8	0	1	1	0	1.000	0	1	1.80
Julio, Jorge	Jupiter	Mon	A+	21	23	22	0	1	114.2	491	116	62	50	6	3	5	3	34	0	80	11	1	4	8	.333	0	0	3.92
Junge, Eric	Yakima	LA	A-	23	15	15	0	0	82	363	98	60	53	10	3	6	0	31	0	55	3	0	5	7	.417	0	0	5.82
Kalinowski, Josh*	Salem	Col	A+	23	27	27	1	0	162.1	659	119	47	38	3	4	2	6	71	0	176	11	1	11	6	.647	0	0	2.11
Kalita, Tim*	Oneonta	Det	A-	21	3	3	0	0	12.1	44	3	1	0	0	0	0	0	5	0	15	1	0	0	0	.000	0	0	0.00
	W Michigan	Det	A	21	9	9	0	0	47.1	213	46	26	22	2	1	1	5	27	0	35	4	1	4	1	.800	0	0	4.18
Kane, Kyle	Bristol	CWS	R+	24	5	5	0	0	28	112	19	8	8	2	2	0	2	11	0	23	3	0	2	0	1.000	0	0	2.57
	Burlington	CWS	A	24	12	0	0	5	18	100	28	29	27	3	0	2	3	12	0	17	5	1	1	0	1.000	0	1	13.50
Kann, Kris	Martinsvlle	Hou	R+	22	9	6	0	1	25.1	129	36	26	22	2	1	2	4	16	0	16	5	0	0	2	.000	0	0	7.82
Kanovich, Jason*	Cape Fear	Mon	A	23	36	0	0	16	62	267	52	28	22	3	1	3	3	28	1	46	9	2	4	2	.667	0	2	3.19
Kaye, Justin	Lancaster	Sea	A+	24	53	0	0	46	61	289	68	42	39	4	2	3	5	40	1	66	6	0	3	5	.375	0	14	5.75
Kearney, Ryan	Columbus	Cle	A	24	6	0	0	1	14.1	67	17	10	9	2	0	0	4	5	0	6	0	1	0	1	.000	0	0	5.65
	Mahoning Vy	Cle	A-	24	11	2	0	4	25	100	23	4	4	0	0	0	1	5	0	26	1	0	3	0	1.000	0	0	1.44
Keelin, Chris	Batavia	Phi	A-	23	14	0	0	5	21.1	103	19	18	12	2	0	2	5	16	0	27	3	1	1	0	1.000	0	0	5.06
	Piedmont	Phi	A	23	4	0	0	3	6	32	9	6	2	1	0	0	0	3	0	2	0	0	1	0	1.000	0	0	3.00
Kees, Justin	High Desert	Ari	A+	22	30	7	0	6	85.2	385	89	60	53	10	2	3	10	51	1	68	4	3	6	2	.750	0	1	5.57
Keller, Kris	W Michigan	Det	A	22	49	0	0	28	77	324	63	28	25	6	4	3	3	36	1	87	11	2	5	3	.625	0	8	2.92
Kelley, Chris	Mahoning Vy	Cle	A-	22	13	11	0	0	48	228	44	40	30	2	1	3	4	34	0	54	9	0	3	4	.429	0	0	5.63
Kelley, Jason	Ogden	Mil	R+	23	15	3	0	7	45	215	70	37	30	6	0	3	2	12	0	34	5	0	2	3	.400	0	1	6.00
Kendall, Phil	Stockton	Mil	A+	22	18	18	1	0	103	479	113	71	65	12	2	5	7	63	1	60	12	2	0	10	.000	0	0	5.68
Kennedy, Joe*	Hudson Val	TB	A-	21	16	16	1	0	95	376	78	33	28	2	1	1	4	26	0	101	7	1	6	5	.545	1	0	2.65
Kenny, Seth	Modesto	Oak	A+	23	18	0	0	11	23	110	26	13	9	0	0	0	2	13	2	18	1	0	0	3	.000	0	0	3.52
Kent, Steve*	Everett	Sea	A-	21	21	0	0	8	37	168	31	24	22	2	1	1	2	26	1	43	6	0	3	2	.600	0	4	5.35
Kessel, Kyle*	Mets	NYM	R	24	3	3	0	0	8	29	5	4	3	0	0	0	1	2	0	11	1	0	0	1	.000	0	0	3.38
	St. Lucie	NYM	A+	24	8	8	0	0	35	157	35	22	18	4	2	1	1	16	0	24	0	0	1	2	.333	0	0	4.63
Kesten, Mike*	Mariners	Sea	R	18	13	0	0	2	22	104	17	18	16	0	1	0	2	20	0	17	4	0	2	0	1.000	0	0	6.55
Key, Scott	Rockford	Cin	A	23	1	0	0	0	0.2	4	0	2	2	0	0	0	0	2	0	0	0	0	0	0	.000	0	0	27.00
Kibler, Ryan	Rockies	Col	R	19	14	14	2	0	81.1	337	77	35	23	3	2	0	10	14	1	55	2	0	6	2	.750	0	0	2.55
	Portland	Col	A-	19	1	1	0	0	3.1	21	8	8	8	1	0	0	0	4	0	4	0	0	0	0	.000	0	0	21.60
Kidd, Jake	Portland	Col	A-	22	11	0	0	6	17	67	10	6	5	1	1	1	2	5	0	17	2	0	2	1	.667	0	0	2.65
	Asheville	Col	A	22	9	1	0	4	24.1	94	16	7	4	2	2	0	3	3	0	21	0	0	2	1	.667	0	2	1.48
King, James*	Spokane	KC	A-	22	17	7	0	2	72	295	60	38	31	8	1	0	0	29	0	63	5	1	7	2	.778	0	0	3.88
Kingrey, Jarrod	Hagerstown	Tor	A	23	56	0	0	48	61	259	49	24	21	5	1	0	6	26	0	69	0	4	3	2	.600	0	27	3.10
Kirst, Mark	Stockton	Mil	A+	25	32	4	0	14	60	284	67	55	43	12	3	5	5	31	1	58	9	2	3	7	.300	0	2	6.45
Kirsten, Rick	Tigers	Det	R	21	11	4	0	4	25.2	112	18	15	15	2	3	2	2	17	0	27	1	0	1	1	.500	0	0	5.26
	Lakeland	Det	A+	21	2	2	1	0	16.2	60	7	1	1	0	0	0	0	6	0	8	1	0	2	0	1.000	1	0	0.54
Kiyono, Masashi	San Jose	SF	A+	25	32	3	0	13	56.2	290	87	62	47	5	2	2	3	29	0	31	10	0	2	1	.667	0	0	7.46
Klein, Cody*	Staten Ilnd	NYY	A-	21	16	0	0	4	22.2	89	17	9	9	2	0	1	0	6	0	23	5	0	0	0	.000	0	0	3.57
Klein, Matt	Visalia	Oak	A+	25	11	2	0	1	24.1	129	35	24	15	2	0	3	2	20	0	18	5	0	1	1	.500	0	0	5.55
Klepacki, Edward	Vermont	Mon	A-	22	14	14	1	0	78	347	92	54	41	1	0	4	5	18	1	40	10	2	5	4	.556	0	0	4.73
Klepaski, Jose	Lancaster	Sea	A+	22	1	0	0	1	2	7	0	0	0	0	0	0	0	1	0	0	0	0	0	0	.000	0	0	0.00
	Everett	Sea	A-	22	3	0	0	0	5.1	29	6	4	4	0	0	0	1	5	0	5	1	0	0	0	.000	0	0	6.75
Knapp, Ben	Bluefield	Bal	R+	20	14	14	0	0	61.1	320	88	77	62	12	2	1	13	40	0	50	10	1	4	6	.400	0	0	9.10
Knowles, Mike	Staten Ilnd	NYY	A-	20	3	2	0	0	6.1	37	15	12	10	0	0	1	0	4	0	5	2	1	0	0	.000	0	0	14.21
	Greensboro	NYY	A	20	11	2	0	5	27.1	137	45	27	25	1	0	0	2	10	0	27	5	1	1	1	.500	0	0	8.23
Koehler, Russ	Mariners	Sea	R	25	4	4	0	0	18.2	79	16	5	2	0	1	0	1	5	0	21	0	0	1	2	.333	0	0	0.96
	Lancaster	Sea	A+	25	7	7	0	0	24.2	125	33	28	22	5	1	0	2	18	0	19	5	0	0	3	.000	0	0	8.03
Koeth, Mark	Burlington	Cle	R+	22	20	2	0	4	47.1	222	55	40	28	8	3	2	3	19	0	51	12	0	3	4	.429	0	1	5.32
Kofler, Ed	Chston-SC	TB	A	22	27	27	2	0	157.1	661	153	85	70	10	4	7	11	37	0	136	10	4	9	11	.450	0	0	4.00
Kohl, Doug	High Desert	Ari	A+	20	30	11	0	3	89	421	114	79	73	13	1	5	6	40	2	74	7	0	9	5	.643	0	0	7.38
Kolb, Jason*	Princeton	TB	R+	22	2	0	0	0	2.2	14	4	3	3	2	0	0	0	1	0	1	0	0	0	0	.000	0	0	10.13
Koplove, Mike	South Bend	Ari	A	23	45	0	0	19	84	351	70	23	19	5	3	0	11	29	0	98	4	0	5	2	.714	0	7	2.04
Koronka, John*	Reds	Cin	R	19	7	7	0	0	37.1	148	25	11	7	1	1	1	3	14	0	27	1	1	3	3	.500	0	0	1.69
	Billings	Cin	R+	19	7	7	0	0	40.1	173	41	26	25	1	2	2	2	17	0	34	1	0	2	3	.400	0	0	5.58
Kosderka, Matt	Savannah	Tex	A	24	31	20	1	8	134.2	577	133	69	57	14	3	8	3	50	0	114	9	2	12	9	.571	1	4	3.81
Koutrouba, Tom*	W Michigan	Det	A	22	31	11	0	7	85	381	110	56	51	5	1	4	2	24	1	46	1	1	3	2	.600	0	0	5.40
Koziara, Matt	Reds	Cin	R	23	13	1	0	6	26.1	123	24	15	6	0	3	0	2	16	2	26	2	0	3	2	.600	0	0	2.05
	Rockford	Cin	A	23	8	3	0	0	28.2	131	39	19	13	1	1	0	1	13	1	15	2	0	1	2	.333	0	0	4.08
Kozlowski, Ben*	Braves	Atl	R	19	15	0	0	7	33.2	132	28	9	7	0	0	0	0	6	0	29	2	0	1	1	.500	0	3	1.87
Kramer, Aaron	Rancho Cuca	SD	A+	25	23	23	0	0	139	592	154	73	56	14	1	5	3	31	0	98	6	4	9	9	.500	0	0	3.63
Krawczyk, Jack	Beloit	Mil	A	24	6	0	0	6	6.1	24	5	0	0	0	0	0	0	1	0	11	0	0	0	0	.000	0	3	0.00
	Stockton	Mil	A+	24	41	1	0	13	77	331	87	48	40	8	5	3	1	19	2	74	3	0	5	4	.556	0	2	4.68
Kremer, John	Staten Ilnd	NYY	A-	23	23	0	0	4	38	162	31	14	12	5	1	0	0	17	1	59	5	0	3	0	1.000	0	0	2.84
Kringen, Jake*	Salem	Col	A+	24	8	0	0	4	17.2	93	30	14	13	0	1	0	0	9	0	17	0	0	0	1	.000	0	0	6.62
Krismer, Jeremy	Helena	Mil	R+	23	12	9	0	1	46.1	198	49	26	25	5	1	1	5	17	0	27	4	0	4	3	.571	0	0	4.86
Krug, Dustin	Lansing	ChC	A	23	46	0	0	23	59	278	75	34	22	1	4	5	4	25	0	32	9	0	3	7	.300	0	5	3.36
Kubes, Greg*	Piedmont	Phi	A	23	27	27	4	0	164.2	705	162	65	48	4	8	3	3	47	0	147	4	0	11	12	.478	0	0	2.62
Kurtz-Nicholl, Jes.*	Spokane	KC	A-	23	24	0	0	4	38	165	39	19	13	0	2	0	0	14	2	38	4	0	5	2	.714	0	0	3.08

1999 Pitching — Single-A and Rookie Leagues

HOW MUCH HE PITCHED											WHAT HE GAVE UP												THE RESULTS					
Player	Team	Org	Lg	A	G	GS	CG	GF	IP	BFP	H	R	ER	HR	SH	SF	HB	TBB	IBB	SO	WP	Bk	W	L	Pct.	ShO	Sv	ERA
Kusiewicz, Mike*	Rockies	Col	R	23	6	6	0	0	24.2	112	26	16	15	0	1	1	2	9	0	27	1	1	1	3	.250	0	0	5.47
Labitzke, Jesse*	Asheville	Col	A	22	14	1	0	8	32.1	159	40	29	29	2	1	3	2	25	0	35	3	0	0	2	.000	0	0	8.07
	Portland	Col	A-	22	18	0	0	5	27	121	24	15	11	0	1	0	1	17	0	30	2	0	1	1	.500	0	3	3.67
LaChapelle, Yan	Dunedin	Tor	A+	24	15	7	0	2	44.2	205	46	28	26	3	3	3	7	22	0	36	5	0	2	3	.400	0	1	5.24
Lackey, John	Boise	Ana	A-	21	15	15	1	0	81.1	372	81	59	45	7	5	2	8	50	1	77	14	1	6	2	.750	0	0	4.98
LaCorte, Vince	Boise	Ana	A-	21	11	9	0	1	50	224	64	38	30	5	1	1	3	15	2	32	5	1	2	6	.250	0	0	5.40
Lajara, Eddy*	Marlins	Fla	R	20	8	2	0	2	21.2	93	13	6	5	0	0	0	2	14	0	23	4	0	1	2	.333	0	0	2.08
LaMarsh, Robert*	Rangers	Tex	R	23	3	0	0	1	9	35	7	2	2	1	0	0	1	1	0	6	0	0	2	0	1.000	0	0	2.00
	Charlotte	Tex	A+	23	1	1	0	0	3.1	18	9	1	1	0	0	0	0	0	0	0	0	0	0	0	.000	0	0	2.70
LaMattina, Ryan*	Asheville	Col	A	24	38	0	0	25	79.2	334	68	36	31	10	2	2	6	29	1	78	5	0	3	4	.429	0	9	3.50
Lamber, Justin*	Wilmington	KC	A+	24	39	2	0	18	68.2	304	68	29	28	2	1	0	2	33	2	67	8	0	5	3	.625	0	6	3.67
Lambert, Jeremy	Peoria	StL	A	21	21	0	0	1	34.1	175	48	36	34	5	0	2	2	27	0	27	3	0	2	1	.667	0	0	8.91
Lambert, Kris*	Lynchburg	Pit	A+	24	13	5	0	3	45	183	43	16	13	1	0	0	1	12	0	37	2	0	1	3	.250	0	0	2.60
Lampley, Danny	Sarasota	Bos	A+	24	25	25	2	0	140.1	623	152	85	71	13	1	5	18	54	1	126	7	0	10	8	.556	1	0	4.55
Landkamer, Michael	Billings	Cin	R+	23	20	0	0	10	21.2	104	23	17	17	0	0	2	1	19	0	19	1	0	2	2	.500	0	1	7.06
Lanfranco, Otoniel	Potomac	StL	A+	23	21	21	0	0	115.1	475	105	59	55	13	4	3	9	35	0	83	4	1	8	6	.571	0	0	4.29
Langen, Brian*	New Jersey	StL	A-	22	26	0	0	6	29.1	138	26	20	15	2	2	0	3	21	2	24	4	0	1	3	.250	0	0	4.60
Langston, Mike	Staten Ilnd	NYY	A-	21	2	0	0	0	1.1	10	3	3	3	0	0	0	0	3	0	0	1	0	0	0	.000	0	0	20.25
Lankford, Frank	Yankees	NYY	R	29	1	1	0	0	2	8	2	1	1	0	0	0	0	1	0	2	1	0	0	0	.000	0	0	4.50
Lanzetta, Tobin	Vero Beach	LA	A+	24	4	0	0	3	5.1	23	3	2	2	0	1	0	1	3	1	2	1	0	0	1	.000	0	0	3.38
LaPlante, Reggie	Yankees	NYY	R	20	8	7	0	0	38	165	40	25	22	3	1	1	2	15	0	40	2	0	1	2	.333	0	0	5.21
Lara, Nelson	Kane County	Fla	A	21	46	0	0	34	52	257	50	38	35	5	3	3	7	47	1	45	8	0	3	2	.600	0	10	6.06
LaRoche, Jeff*	Kane County	Fla	A	22	17	0	0	6	31	144	32	18	16	3	3	1	3	20	0	15	1	0	1	4	.200	0	0	4.65
	Utica	Fla	A-	22	26	0	0	9	37	187	62	37	33	5	1	2	5	15	0	29	3	0	3	3	.500	0	1	8.03
LaRosa, Dancy	Twins	Min	R	21	11	11	2	0	59	258	66	30	24	2	2	3	0	20	1	42	4	1	5	2	.714	0	0	3.66
LaRosa, Tom	Hagerstown	Tor	A	25	12	0	0	4	11.1	60	9	8	6	0	0	1	2	16	0	18	8	0	0	0	.000	0	1	4.76
Latham, Jason	Martinsvlle	Hou	R+	23	15	6	0	3	45	208	51	35	26	7	1	1	3	19	0	45	3	1	3	3	.500	0	0	5.20
Lavery, Tim*	Eugene	ChC	A-	21	15	2	0	4	39.2	169	42	21	16	2	0	0	0	17	0	43	2	3	3	2	.600	0	3	3.63
Law, Keith	Oneonta	Det	A-	23	22	1	0	10	45	199	35	23	17	5	1	1	5	28	0	32	10	0	2	2	.500	0	2	3.40
Lawrence, Brian	Rancho Cuca	SD	A+	24	27	27	4	0	175.1	723	178	72	66	6	7	5	10	30	1	166	7	5	12	8	.600	3	0	3.39
Lawrence, Clint*	Dunedin	Tor	A+	23	15	3	0	7	23.2	115	29	23	20	5	1	0	0	20	0	16	3	0	1	2	.333	0	1	7.61
Lawson, Jarrod	Batavia	Phi	A-	21	4	4	0	0	17.1	90	27	19	16	2	2	2	1	12	0	11	9	0	0	4	.000	0	0	8.31
Layfield, Scotty	New Jersey	StL	A-	23	23	3	0	15	34.1	150	27	16	12	3	1	1	2	21	1	26	4	0	2	2	.500	0	8	3.15
Layne, Roger	Mahoning Vy	Cle	A-	23	4	0	0	1	6.2	35	8	4	4	1	0	1	0	7	0	9	0	0	0	0	.000	0	0	5.40
	Burlington	Cle	R+	23	11	0	0	2	30	142	36	23	15	4	1	2	1	8	1	22	6	0	1	2	.333	0	0	4.50
	Columbus	Cle	A	23	1	1	0	0	6	21	4	1	1	0	0	0	0	0	0	7	0	0	1	0	1.000	0	0	1.50
Leach, Bryan	Red Sox	Bos	R	22	1	0	0	1	2	9	2	1	0	0	0	0	0	1	0	1	1	0	0	0	.000	0	0	0.00
	Lowell	Bos	A-	22	13	4	0	1	45.1	194	41	23	18	4	0	1	0	18	0	52	2	0	5	2	.714	0	0	3.57
Leahy, Bart	Marlins	Fla	R	23	8	0	0	1	17	94	22	19	16	2	1	1	5	18	0	16	2	0	0	1	.000	0	1	8.47
Ledden, Ryan	Hudson Val	TB	A-	22	20	0	0	4	30.1	148	33	23	22	1	0	1	4	27	0	16	10	3	3	1	.750	0	0	6.53
Ledezma, Wilfredo*	Red Sox	Bos	R	19	13	6	0	2	57.1	242	51	28	21	2	1	1	1	20	0	52	3	1	5	1	.833	0	1	3.30
Lee, Andy*	Lowell	Bos	A-	25	26	1	0	6	48.2	216	52	22	19	7	1	3	3	16	0	58	6	3	2	1	.667	0	0	3.51
Lee, Fletcher	Salem-Keizr	SF	A-	24	26	0	0	16	37.2	166	33	15	13	3	1	1	2	20	1	34	5	6	2	1	.667	0	5	3.11
Lee, Garrett	Jamestown	Atl	A-	23	13	13	1	0	77.1	323	79	39	35	8	1	5	6	16	0	47	0	2	4	3	.571	0	0	4.07
	Myrtle Bch	Atl	A+	23	3	3	0	0	17.2	77	21	12	10	1	1	0	0	3	0	12	0	0	1	1	.500	0	0	5.09
Lee, Wayne	Chstn-WV	KC	A	23	48	0	0	22	88.2	366	82	45	39	11	3	3	3	26	4	77	4	2	7	2	.778	0	6	3.96
Leek, Randy*	Oneonta	Det	A-	23	21	3	1	4	63.1	249	58	16	11	0	1	1	2	9	1	66	2	0	6	3	.667	0	1	1.56
Legette, Richard	Phillies	Phi	R	19	12	6	0	1	31	144	34	26	25	2	0	2	0	23	0	23	2	1	2	1	.667	0	0	7.26
Lehr, Justin	Sou Oregon	Oak	A-	22	14	4	0	7	42.1	207	62	36	28	3	5	1	2	17	3	40	9	0	2	6	.250	0	0	5.95
Lelless, Alex	Danville	Atl	R+	20	18	0	0	4	28	137	34	26	22	1	0	2	2	18	0	20	5	1	1	0	1.000	0	1	7.07
Lesner, Ken	Twins	Min	R	23	13	0	0	4	23	109	32	16	12	0	1	2	1	9	1	13	1	0	0	2	.000	0	1	4.70
Levan, Matt*	Brevard Cty	Fla	A+	25	35	2	0	14	66.1	291	52	39	30	6	4	2	1	39	3	84	9	0	2	3	.400	0	2	4.07
Levesque, Ben	Pirates	Pit	R	20	11	11	1	0	43	210	38	44	36	1	2	6	6	40	0	20	6	0	2	7	.222	0	0	7.53
Levy, Tye*	Clinton	Cin	A	22	7	0	0	2	8.2	43	12	4	4	2	1	2	0	4	0	6	0	1	1	1	.500	0	1	4.15
	Billings	Cin	R+	22	9	0	0	8	9.1	41	11	8	6	2	0	1	0	3	0	10	1	0	0	0	.000	0	0	5.79
Lewis, Colby	Pulaski	Tex	R+	20	14	11	1	0	64.2	280	46	24	14	3	0	3	7	27	0	84	3	4	7	3	.700	1	0	1.95
Lewis, Craig	Tampa	NYY	A+	23	5	1	0	0	13.2	62	18	9	8	1	2	0	0	3	0	12	2	1	0	1	.000	0	0	5.27
	Greensboro	NYY	A	23	9	5	0	1	47.1	197	42	17	14	3	1	2	2	7	1	51	3	0	4	0	1.000	0	1	2.66
Lewis, Derrick	Myrtle Bch	Atl	A+	24	24	23	0	0	131	551	100	44	35	9	1	3	3	81	0	102	6	1	8	4	.667	0	0	2.40
Lewis, Jeremy*	Tigers	Det	R	19	10	10	0	0	40	181	34	16	12	1	2	1	2	28	0	31	2	0	4	5	.444	0	0	2.70
Lewis, Peyton	St.Cathrnes	Tor	A-	24	15	1	0	3	41.1	164	26	8	6	2	1	2	2	15	0	54	2	1	2	1	.667	0	2	1.31
	Hagerstown	Tor	A	24	2	0	0	2	2	8	0	0	0	0	0	0	0	1	0	5	2	0	0	0	.000	0	0	0.00
Lewis, Rickey	Beloit	Mil	A	23	16	14	0	1	64.1	315	70	59	43	9	0	7	2	55	0	42	10	2	5	6	.455	0	0	6.02
	Ogden	Mil	R+	23	11	11	0	0	59.2	284	75	53	48	4	2	1	5	44	0	35	4	0	1	7	.125	0	0	7.24
Lewter, John	Pirates	Pit	R	23	13	0	0	8	24	116	28	20	15	2	3	0	2	8	0	14	4	0	2	1	.667	0	1	5.63
Lidge, Brad	Kissimmee	Hou	A+	23	6	6	0	0	21.1	82	13	8	8	0	0	0	0	11	0	19	2	0	0	2	.000	0	0	3.38
Lima, Frank	Tigers	Det	R	21	20	3	0	3	48.1	206	48	28	23	1	2	1	0	14	0	53	1	2	1	2	.333	0	0	4.28
Linarelli, Tom	Red Sox	Bos	R	23	1	1	0	0	1.1	9	2	3	2	0	1	0	0	2	0	1	0	0	0	0	.000	0	0	13.50
Lira, James	St. Pete	TB	A+	23	36	0	0	13	44.1	191	45	18	15	1	2	2	2	17	1	25	4	0	4	1	.800	0	0	3.05
Little, Rodney	Portland	Col	A-	21	6	0	0	0	9	55	12	15	13	0	0	2	1	17	1	4	4	0	0	1	.000	0	0	13.00
Little, Roger	Portland	Col	A-	21	12	4	0	3	33.1	160	41	27	23	2	0	1	3	15	0	21	2	0	0	4	.000	0	0	6.21
Lockridge, Sherwin	Elizabethtn	Min	R+	23	16	0	0	4	17.2	91	10	17	12	0	0	0	5	16	0	21	3	0	0	1	.000	0	0	6.11
Lockwood, Luke*	Expos	Mon	R	18	11	7	0	4	41.1	184	46	21	21	3	0	2	2	13	0	32	0	0	1	2	.333	0	0	4.57
Lohrman, Dave	St. Lucie	NYM	A+	24	43	1	0	16	76	325	64	33	26	3	4	1	4	46	4	75	5	0	4	0	1.000	0	0	3.08
Longo, Neil	Wisconsin	Sea	A	22	5	5	3	0	37.2	140	24	9	4	0	1	1	0	8	0	18	1	1	2	2	.500	1	0	0.96
	Lancaster	Sea	A+	22	23	19	0	2	127.2	576	163	87	81	15	2	6	9	46	0	76	5	1	6	7	.462	0	0	5.71
Lontayo, Alex*	Augusta	Bos	A	24	40	0	0	14	58.2	255	55	31	28	7	1	2	4	26	0	80	3	1	2	0	1.000	0	0	4.30

1999 Pitching — Single-A and Rookie Leagues

HOW MUCH HE PITCHED											WHAT HE GAVE UP												THE RESULTS					
Player	Team	Org	Lg	A	G	GS	CG	GF	IP	BFP	H	R	ER	HR	SH	SF	HB	TBB	IBB	SO	WP	Bk	W	L	Pct.	ShO	Sv	ERA
Looper, Aaron	Wisconsin	Sea	A	23	38	7	0	10	90	391	89	47	41	8	1	3	6	26	0	73	6	1	9	6	.600	0	3	4.10
Lopez, Aquilino	Everett	Sea	A-	19	15	15	1	0	87.2	365	76	44	37	8	1	2	2	30	2	93	2	0	7	6	.538	0	0	3.80
Lopez, Gustavo	Utica	Fla	A-	21	13	13	0	0	63.2	261	59	28	25	5	0	1	1	17	0	46	5	0	4	2	.667	0	0	3.53
Lopez, Ignacio	Rangers	Tex	R	20	12	9	0	2	56.2	235	60	22	17	2	1	1	5	5	0	31	1	0	7	2	.778	0	1	2.70
Lopez, Javier*	South Bend	Ari	A	22	20	20	0	0	99	458	122	74	66	9	1	4	3	43	0	70	9	0	4	6	.400	0	0	6.00
Lopez, Jorge	Reds	Cin	R	18	10	0	0	2	25	112	31	19	17	2	1	2	2	9	0	17	2	1	1	1	.500	0	0	6.12
Lopez, Jose	Winston-Sal	CWS	A+	24	19	0	0	5	26.2	138	38	22	14	0	1	0	4	14	0	10	3	0	0	1	.000	0	1	4.72
Lopez, Jose	Mets	NYM	R	20	2	2	0	0	6.1	37	12	8	6	0	0	0	2	8	0	4	1	2	0	2	.000	0	0	8.53
Lopez, Juan*	White Sox	CWS	R	20	14	2	0	6	27	132	32	27	22	2	1	4	1	16	1	27	2	4	2	2	.500	0	2	7.33
Lopez, Rafael	Mets	NYM	R	19	12	8	0	1	58	245	43	20	14	1	0	3	3	29	0	42	4	1	7	1	.875	0	0	2.17
Lorenzo, Javier	Rockies	Col	R	21	20	1	0	14	33.2	159	36	23	16	3	0	0	1	19	0	41	2	0	6	4	.600	0	2	4.28
Loudon, Gary	Reds	Cin	R	24	15	5	0	5	36.1	176	34	27	26	3	3	4	2	33	0	45	3	1	1	2	.333	0	1	6.44
Loux, Shane	W Michigan	Det	A	20	8	8	0	0	47.1	215	55	39	33	5	1	2	8	16	1	43	4	0	1	3	.250	0	0	6.27
	Lakeland	Det	A+	20	17	17	0	0	91	412	92	48	41	8	2	5	10	47	0	52	7	1	6	5	.545	0	0	4.05
Love, Brandon	Reds	Cin	R	20	7	6	0	0	24.2	118	30	21	21	0	2	1	4	9	0	17	1	1	0	4	.000	0	0	7.66
Love, Jeff	Kissimmee	Hou	A+	26	15	0	0	7	25.2	120	34	24	19	2	1	1	1	9	2	20	1	0	2	3	.400	0	0	6.66
Lovingood, Ray*	Rockford	Cin	A	22	16	1	0	9	29.2	133	27	16	16	2	0	1	2	16	0	24	3	0	1	0	1.000	0	0	4.85
Lowe, Matt	Capital Cty	NYM	A	21	1	0	0	1	2	9	3	2	2	1	0	0	0	0	0	2	0	0	0	0	.000	0	0	9.00
	Pittsfield	NYM	A-	21	16	11	0	4	69	309	67	42	35	3	3	2	7	37	0	33	11	1	3	5	.375	0	2	4.57
Lowery, Phil*	Utica	Fla	A-	23	2	0	0	0	6	26	7	4	4	1	0	0	1	1	0	5	0	1	1	0	1.000	0	0	6.00
	Kane County	Fla	A	23	1	1	0	0	5	19	5	1	1	0	0	0	0	0	0	3	0	0	1	0	1.000	0	0	1.80
Lugo, Ruddy	Ogden	Mil	R+	20	6	6	0	0	24	117	35	23	21	2	1	0	1	12	0	26	1	0	1	2	.333	0	0	7.88
Lundberg, Dave	Charlotte	Tex	A+	23	30	21	4	1	156	656	162	63	49	4	2	6	9	44	1	81	4	4	14	7	.667	1	0	2.83
Luque, Roger*	Fort Wayne	SD	A	20	46	3	0	20	77.1	337	67	39	33	2	3	5	2	40	3	79	4	1	4	5	.444	0	2	3.84
	Rancho Cuca	SD	A+	20	3	0	0	0	1.2	11	3	2	2	1	0	0	1	2	0	2	1	0	0	0	.000	0	0	10.80
Lutz, Ken	Reds	Cin	R	18	12	9	0	0	44.1	210	58	40	32	1	3	3	3	20	0	37	0	0	0	4	.000	0	0	6.50
Lynch, Jim	Kissimmee	Hou	A+	24	28	21	3	2	129.2	588	131	82	71	14	4	5	10	61	2	99	12	0	3	14	.176	0	0	4.93
Lynch, Pat	Hagerstown	Tor	A	22	24	18	0	2	127.2	529	133	55	50	10	7	3	6	22	0	106	1	1	10	5	.667	0	1	3.52
	Asheville	Col	A	22	2	2	0	0	12	48	8	4	4	0	0	1	1	2	0	14	0	1	1	1	.500	0	0	3.00
Lyons, Curt	Yankees	NYY	R	25	1	0	0	0	2	9	1	0	0	0	1	0	0	2	0	3	0	0	0	0	.000	0	0	0.00
Lyons, Jonathan	Sarasota	Bos	A+	25	23	0	0	7	24.1	131	44	25	16	2	1	1	1	11	2	18	2	0	1	2	.333	0	0	5.92
	Augusta	Bos	A	25	19	0	0	10	29.1	123	26	9	7	1	1	2	1	9	0	32	0	0	1	1	.500	0	2	2.15
Maas, Steve	Chstn-WV	KC	A	26	21	0	0	13	27.2	118	28	17	16	1	0	1	0	12	0	33	0	0	0	4	.000	0	2	5.20
MacDougal, Mike	Spokane	KC	A-	23	11	11	0	0	46.1	196	43	25	23	3	1	1	6	17	0	57	8	1	2	2	.500	0	0	4.47
Macias, Jose	Burlington	Cle	R+	20	12	3	0	4	28.2	139	30	28	26	3	0	0	0	25	0	37	10	1	0	2	.000	0	1	8.16
	Mahoning Vy	Cle	A-	20	1	1	0	0	5	19	2	1	1	0	0	1	0	2	0	1	0	0	1	0	1.000	0	0	1.80
	Columbus	Cle	A	20	1	0	0	1	2	7	1	0	0	0	1	0	0	0	0	2	0	0	0	0	.000	0	0	0.00
Madero, Francisco	San Berndno	LA	A+	21	12	2	0	4	26.2	111	28	10	8	1	0	1	1	9	2	33	2	1	3	2	.600	0	0	2.70
	Vero Beach	LA	A+	21	12	10	1	2	69	302	75	43	39	9	4	1	3	25	1	45	3	1	2	6	.250	0	0	5.09
Madison, Scott*	Columbus	Cle	A	25	10	4	0	2	31.1	140	37	19	16	6	1	0	1	13	0	22	1	0	2	2	.500	0	0	4.60
Madson, Ryan	Batavia	Phi	A-	19	15	15	0	0	87.2	383	80	51	46	5	2	4	10	43	0	75	10	0	5	5	.500	0	0	4.72
Madson, Will	W Michigan	Det	A	24	8	0	0	3	8	44	15	10	9	3	0	1	0	6	1	7	0	0	1	2	.333	0	0	10.13
Majewski, Gary	Bristol	CWS	R+	20	13	13	1	0	76.2	325	67	34	26	4	4	1	7	37	0	91	1	0	7	1	.875	1	0	3.05
	Burlington	CWS	A	20	2	0	0	0	3.1	28	11	14	14	3	1	0	2	4	0	1	0	0	0	0	.000	0	0	37.80
Maldonado, Es.	Kissimmee	Hou	A+	24	8	1	0	3	10.2	50	6	6	4	1	0	0	2	12	0	4	6	0	0	0	.000	0	0	3.38
Malerich, Will*	San Jose	SF	A+	24	45	0	0	14	72.2	338	95	43	36	5	3	2	4	38	1	59	3	0	5	4	.556	0	1	4.46
Maleski, Eric	Mahoning Vy	Cle	A-	23	22	0	0	17	37.1	158	42	21	20	3	2	0	2	6	0	32	3	0	4	1	.800	0	8	4.82
Malko, Bryan	Fort Myers	Min	A+	23	30	18	2	4	110.1	492	120	60	55	8	2	3	9	48	0	102	5	0	7	9	.438	1	1	4.49
Mallette, Brian	Stockton	Mil	A+	25	28	0	0	14	36	162	38	16	6	1	0	1	3	16	1	34	0	0	2	0	1.000	0	4	1.50
Mallory, Andrew	Lansing	ChC	A	23	5	0	0	1	4.2	31	12	11	7	2	0	0	2	4	0	2	1	0	0	0	.000	0	0	13.50
Malone, Corwin*	White Sox	CWS	R	19	10	0	0	3	18	90	16	19	16	1	0	0	1	16	0	24	5	4	0	2	.000	0	0	8.00
Mancha, Tony	Chstn-WV	KC	A	21	40	3	0	24	82.2	370	89	50	48	6	1	3	9	38	4	76	2	2	4	3	.571	0	2	5.23
Maness, Nick	Capital Cty	NYM	A	21	23	22	0	0	107.1	469	92	74	59	8	3	5	6	57	0	99	20	2	5	6	.455	0	0	4.95
Mangum, Mark	Cape Fear	Mon	A	21	26	26	1	0	159.1	677	156	85	62	14	1	7	16	54	0	107	15	0	10	11	.476	0	0	3.50
Manning, Mike	Burlington	Cle	R+	22	4	0	0	2	8	39	9	6	3	0	2	1	0	4	2	9	2	0	0	2	.000	0	0	3.38
	Mahoning Vy	Cle	A-	22	20	0	0	14	33.2	138	25	11	10	0	0	1	1	12	0	34	7	0	2	1	.667	0	3	2.67
Manzueta, Roberto	High Desert	Ari	A+	21	40	0	0	19	66.2	294	63	29	26	4	1	2	8	31	2	59	8	0	2	2	.500	0	2	3.51
Marietta, Ron*	Columbus	Cle	A	22	11	11	0	0	48	244	71	48	44	9	1	0	8	19	0	40	7	0	3	6	.333	0	0	8.25
Marin, Willy	Hudson Val	TB	A-	21	23	1	0	11	56.2	237	43	23	21	2	2	1	9	13	1	47	1	0	2	3	.400	0	2	3.34
Marini, Anthony*	Mahoning Vy	Cle	A-	23	13	11	0	1	65	281	64	31	26	4	1	4	3	25	1	56	4	3	5	3	.625	0	0	3.60
Markwell, Di.*	St.Cathrnes	Tor	A-	19	14	13	0	0	59.1	295	72	55	50	8	1	1	4	38	0	54	6	0	3	4	.429	0	0	7.58
Marr, Jason	Potomac	StL	A+	24	50	0	0	45	53	237	57	36	31	5	2	3	1	21	3	40	6	0	1	6	.143	0	21	5.26
Marrero, Darwin	Jupiter	Mon	A+	19	2	0	0	0	1.1	7	1	2	2	0	0	0	0	2	0	4	1	0	0	0	.000	0	0	13.50
	Vermont	Mon	A-	19	14	14	0	0	76.2	343	86	53	45	7	4	3	5	27	0	74	5	2	3	3	.500	0	0	5.28
Marriott, Mike	Brevard Cty	Fla	A+	23	8	8	0	0	34	172	50	36	34	5	4	1	4	21	0	22	6	1	1	5	.167	0	0	9.00
Marshall, Lee	Fort Myers	Min	A+	23	28	0	0	18	36.2	144	32	10	6	1	4	3	0	5	0	25	1	0	2	2	.500	0	5	1.47
Marsonek, Sam	Charlotte	Tex	A+	21	15	15	2	0	91	420	111	69	56	8	4	4	14	27	0	61	4	1	3	9	.250	0	0	5.54
Martin, Jeff	Hickory	Pit	A	26	13	0	0	3	24	97	19	6	5	1	1	0	3	8	1	23	1	0	0	2	.000	0	0	1.88
	Lynchburg	Pit	A+	26	10	3	0	2	30.2	143	34	27	19	2	0	1	1	13	1	27	3	0	2	1	.667	0	0	5.58
Martin, Kelly	Billings	Cin	R+	21	5	3	0	0	19.1	81	16	13	10	4	0	0	0	8	0	25	1	0	2	0	1.000	0	0	4.66
Martin, Scott	Great Falls	LA	R+	22	16	15	2	0	102.2	435	115	55	44	11	3	4	3	23	0	69	1	1	4	4	.500	0	0	3.86
Martines, Jason	High Desert	Ari	A+	24	43	0	0	37	71.2	306	68	33	18	5	2	1	2	28	4	73	1	1	9	7	.563	0	9	2.26
Martinez, Anastacio	Augusta	Bos	A	19	10	10	0	0	40	188	44	37	28	7	0	0	2	18	0	36	1	3	2	4	.333	0	0	6.30
	Lowell	Bos	A-	19	11	11	0	0	51.1	234	61	36	21	4	0	1	4	18	0	43	9	2	0	3	.000	0	0	3.68
Martinez, Carlos*	Royals	KC	R	21	11	7	1	1	50.1	197	40	20	17	5	0	1	1	7	0	36	0	1	4	3	.571	1	0	3.04
Martinez, Daniel*	White Sox	CWS	R	21	13	0	0	6	15.1	75	18	6	4	0	2	1	1	10	1	20	3	1	2	0	1.000	0	1	2.35
Martinez, David*	Yankees	NYY	R	20	12	11	2	0	66.2	273	52	29	22	2	5	1	3	22	0	67	8	1	5	3	.625	1	0	2.97

1999 Pitching — Single-A and Rookie Leagues

HOW MUCH HE PITCHED											WHAT HE GAVE UP												THE RESULTS					
Player	Team	Org	Lg	A	G	GS	CG	GF	IP	BFP	H	R	ER	HR	SH	SF	HB	TBB	IBB	SO	WP	Bk	W	L	Pct.	ShO	Sv	ERA
Martinez, Erineido	Reds	Cin	R	19	17	0	0	9	26.2	124	27	14	11	0	5	2	3	16	2	17	2	0	3	3	.500	0	1	3.71
Martinez, Jesus*	Sarasota	Bos	A+	26	16	2	0	8	32.2	151	36	20	19	2	2	6	3	17	1	20	5	0	1	2	.333	0	0	5.23
Martinez, Juan	Mexico	—	R	21	15	13	3	2	85.1	346	76	36	31	3	2	2	1	27	0	86	2	2	5	5	.500	1	1	3.27
Martinez, Lionel	Braves	Atl	R	20	12	0	0	1	26.1	109	28	16	10	1	1	0	1	8	0	16	2	0	2	1	.667	0	0	3.42
	Myrtle Bch	Atl	A+	20	1	0	0	1	1	5	1	0	0	0	0	0	0	0	0	1	0	0	1	0	1.000	0	0	0.00
Martinez, Luis*	Ogden	Mil	R+	20	15	7	0	4	50.1	259	66	65	39	3	1	3	3	34	0	43	13	0	0	7	.000	0	1	6.97
Martinez, Obispo	Cape Fear	Mon	A	22	7	0	0	4	8	40	12	10	9	1	0	2	0	3	0	4	1	0	0	0	.000	0	0	10.13
Martinez, Oscar	Yankees	NYY	R	21	23	0	0	19	24.1	103	23	8	5	0	1	0	0	8	2	29	2	0	2	1	.667	0	9	1.85
Marx, Tom*	Tigers	Det	R	20	8	8	0	0	42	191	35	24	16	0	3	1	3	32	0	39	3	0	3	2	.600	0	0	3.43
	Oneonta	Det	A-	20	6	4	0	0	22.1	98	20	14	8	2	0	1	0	13	0	19	1	0	2	1	.667	0	0	3.22
Mastrolonardo, Da.	Orioles	Bal	R	25	3	0	0	0	4.1	16	2	1	1	0	0	0	0	2	0	9	0	0	2	0	1.000	0	0	2.08
	Bluefield	Bal	R+	25	1	0	0	0	1.2	5	0	0	0	0	0	0	0	0	0	2	1	0	0	0	.000	0	0	0.00
	Frederick	Bal	A+	25	8	0	0	1	8	37	6	7	7	0	0	0	2	6	0	5	1	0	0	0	.000	0	1	7.88
Matcuk, Steve	Salem	Col	A+	24	26	26	1	0	152.2	672	157	100	86	10	8	1	20	64	0	103	6	0	8	11	.421	0	0	5.07
Mateo, Julio	Wisconsin	Sea	A	20	20	0	0	10	29	131	31	18	14	2	2	1	1	8	2	27	2	0	1	3	.250	0	4	4.34
Matew, Francisco	New Jersey	StL	A-	21	19	0	0	1	32.2	135	34	17	13	0	0	2	1	8	0	28	1	0	1	1	.500	0	0	3.58
Mathews, Dan	Beloit	Mil	A	24	19	3	0	9	29	156	41	34	28	5	0	0	2	25	0	26	5	0	3	4	.429	0	3	8.69
Matias, Adalberto	Butte	Ana	R+	21	17	7	0	0	47	233	68	47	41	3	2	4	10	23	0	27	11	2	0	2	.000	0	0	7.85
Matos, Jesus	Rockies	Col	R	21	18	3	0	4	36	165	48	28	22	1	3	2	1	9	0	31	3	0	2	1	.667	0	0	5.50
Matos, Josue	Wisconsin	Sea	A	22	25	22	2	0	138	596	143	78	71	19	1	5	4	42	1	136	4	6	9	9	.500	1	0	4.63
Matsko, Rick	Columbus	Cle	A	23	42	0	0	8	85	374	70	49	43	8	2	6	11	43	1	93	13	0	7	5	.583	0	0	4.55
Mattson, John	Capital Cty	NYM	A	23	1	0	0	0	3	16	6	3	3	1	0	0	0	2	0	2	1	0	0	0	.000	0	0	9.00
	Pittsfield	NYM	A-	23	11	0	0	3	18	95	32	20	18	1	1	1	1	10	0	20	5	0	1	3	.250	0	0	9.00
Matz, Brian*	Jupiter	Mon	A+	25	41	1	0	17	91.1	375	77	30	24	3	7	0	6	31	1	46	4	1	5	2	.714	0	7	2.36
Matzenbacher, Bri.	Missoula	Ari	R+	23	24	0	0	22	26	113	22	13	9	0	1	0	1	13	2	28	1	1	3	3	.500	0	11	3.12
Maurer, Mike	Athletics	Oak	R	27	7	0	0	6	7.1	26	4	1	1	1	0	0	0	1	0	8	0	0	0	0	.000	0	2	1.23
	Modesto	Oak	A+	27	15	0	0	3	17	81	23	8	5	1	0	0	1	5	0	15	3	0	1	0	1.000	0	1	2.65
Mays, Jarrod	Kinston	Cle	A+	25	45	1	0	32	73.1	293	48	23	17	5	7	2	6	18	2	75	4	0	5	5	.500	0	19	2.09
Mazur, Bryan*	Sou Oregon	Oak	A-	22	23	0	0	20	40.1	172	36	20	15	5	2	3	1	17	2	29	3	0	5	2	.714	0	8	3.35
Mazur, Graham*	Bristol	CWS	R+	24	10	0	0	3	22	87	17	7	5	0	1	0	0	3	0	34	3	0	2	2	.500	0	0	2.05
McCall, Travis*	Modesto	Oak	A+	22	43	0	0	18	71.1	322	79	46	36	8	5	9	1	31	4	67	6	1	9	3	.750	0	3	4.54
McCarter, Jason	Pittsfield	NYM	A-	23	21	0	0	14	35	160	33	17	13	1	0	1	2	25	0	36	5	0	4	0	1.000	0	2	3.34
McClain, Jeremy	Lowell	Bos	A-	24	16	7	0	0	51.2	230	59	41	31	4	1	3	2	17	1	53	4	3	3	6	.333	0	0	5.40
McClain, Kevin	Butte	Ana	R+	22	18	11	0	1	58.1	297	85	67	58	13	2	2	10	28	1	51	9	0	4	5	.444	0	0	8.95
McClellan, Matt	Dunedin	Tor	A+	23	26	25	1	0	147.1	612	114	69	62	15	1	5	10	61	0	146	6	3	13	5	.722	0	0	3.79
McClendon, Matt	Jamestown	Atl	A-	22	7	7	0	0	23	94	18	11	10	2	0	0	1	11	0	24	2	0	1	1	.500	0	0	3.91
McCloud, Josh	Yankees	NYY	R	19	3	0	0	1	2.2	21	9	8	8	0	0	0	1	3	0	4	0	1	0	0	.000	0	0	27.00
McClung, Seth	Princeton	TB	R+	19	13	10	0	0	45.2	244	53	47	39	3	0	1	9	48	0	46	20	0	2	4	.333	0	0	7.69
McConnell, Gary	Ogden	Mil	R+	22	17	0	0	7	34.1	166	38	24	20	5	1	3	2	28	2	34	5	0	1	2	.333	0	0	5.24
McCormick, Terry*	Hudson Val	TB	A-	21	9	6	0	0	29.2	134	22	15	13	2	2	0	6	15	0	23	3	0	3	1	.750	0	0	3.94
McCullem, Ryan*	Medcine Hat	Tor	R+	19	9	5	0	0	23.2	114	34	17	16	1	2	0	0	11	0	19	3	1	2	1	.667	0	0	6.08
McCurtain, Paul	Brevard Cty	Fla	A+	24	40	0	0	32	57.2	261	59	32	22	1	0	1	2	25	0	49	2	1	3	2	.600	0	12	3.43
McDonald, Corey*	Oneonta	Det	A-	23	19	0	0	8	34.2	153	34	18	18	5	1	4	0	23	0	30	8	0	3	3	.500	0	0	4.67
McDonald, Jon*	St. Pete	TB	A+	23	10	0	0	2	15	70	19	12	10	1	0	1	0	6	0	10	1	0	1	0	1.000	0	0	6.00
	Chston-SC	TB	A	23	14	0	0	8	20.2	97	26	19	16	3	0	0	0	5	1	19	1	0	0	0	.000	0	0	6.97
McEvoy, Casey	Clinton	Cin	A	23	7	0	0	1	9.2	48	12	12	11	1	0	0	2	8	1	13	2	1	0	1	.000	0	0	10.24
	Billings	Cin	R+	23	5	5	0	0	33	133	28	10	8	1	0	0	2	7	0	35	2	1	4	0	1.000	0	0	2.18
	Rockford	Cin	A	23	6	5	1	0	24.1	118	32	26	21	1	0	0	3	10	0	21	2	1	1	2	.333	0	0	7.77
McGee, Chris	Ogden	Mil	R+	22	17	0	0	17	24	97	18	8	8	0	0	2	1	7	1	28	2	0	3	1	.750	0	7	3.00
McGill, Frankie	Savannah	Tex	A	20	26	26	0	0	141.1	641	163	92	82	13	4	2	9	56	0	128	13	0	8	14	.364	0	0	5.22
McGinnis, Johnny	Danville	Atl	R+	20	14	14	0	0	70	312	70	48	39	4	0	1	8	23	0	70	8	0	6	5	.545	0	0	5.01
McGinnis, Ronny	Phillies	Phi	R	23	4	0	0	2	4	30	9	10	10	0	0	0	0	8	0	2	0	0	0	0	.000	0	0	22.50
McGowan, Brian	W Michigan	Det	A	23	39	0	0	8	62.1	309	66	58	35	4	7	2	2	47	1	40	16	2	2	5	.286	0	0	5.05
McKey, Dustin	Princeton	TB	R+	22	26	0	0	9	44.1	221	62	49	43	10	1	1	5	18	1	31	8	2	1	1	.500	0	0	8.73
McKoin, Heath*	Hudson Val	TB	A-	20	15	14	0	0	57.1	272	67	52	40	4	0	3	6	33	0	51	6	0	2	7	.222	0	0	6.28
McLeary, Marty	Sarasota	Bos	A+	25	8	0	0	0	12.2	73	29	20	17	1	2	1	1	7	0	11	2	0	1	0	1.000	0	0	12.08
	Augusta	Bos	A	25	35	9	0	16	80.2	338	73	34	28	8	3	2	4	25	1	90	5	2	5	6	.455	0	3	3.12
McWhirter, Kris.	Bristol	CWS	R+	21	12	1	0	5	25.2	116	25	16	12	2	1	0	1	12	0	23	2	5	0	1	.000	0	2	4.21
Mead, David	Rangers	Tex	R	19	11	7	0	1	36	163	40	23	20	5	2	1	2	11	0	34	3	4	1	3	.250	0	0	5.00
Meagher, Brian*	Salem-Keizr	SF	A-	23	17	6	0	0	51.2	236	56	32	28	2	0	0	4	28	0	41	2	3	3	2	.600	0	0	4.88
Mears, Chris	Wisconsin	Sea	A	22	13	13	2	0	89	359	76	33	24	1	2	3	5	16	0	78	1	0	10	1	.909	1	0	2.43
	Lancaster	Sea	A+	22	10	10	0	0	54.2	250	71	44	43	12	1	1	3	18	0	45	3	2	3	6	.333	0	0	7.08
Medrano, Juan	Spokane	KC	A-	21	15	15	0	0	68.2	311	77	46	37	10	4	1	7	25	1	30	7	2	3	5	.375	0	0	4.85
Meeks, Eric	Sou Oregon	Oak	A-	21	6	3	0	0	19	91	21	22	19	2	0	1	3	11	0	10	0	1	0	0	.000	0	0	9.00
Mejia, Juan	Braves	Atl	R	20	16	0	0	9	29	143	40	23	19	3	2	0	3	8	1	24	4	1	0	3	.000	0	0	5.90
Melson, Nate	Elizabethtn	Min	R+	21	22	0	0	5	36.1	166	40	22	10	2	2	0	4	10	1	23	3	0	3	1	.750	0	2	2.48
Mendez, David*	Danville	Atl	R+	20	12	12	0	0	61	273	61	32	22	6	2	0	2	28	0	74	5	0	6	3	.667	0	0	3.25
Mendible, Franklin	Pirates	Pit	R	20	4	0	0	1	5.2	22	4	1	1	0	0	0	0	4	0	3	0	0	0	1	.000	0	0	1.59
Mendoza, Ger.	Burlington	CWS	A	22	28	28	0	0	157.1	713	186	96	81	10	3	3	8	60	5	119	7	0	9	8	.529	0	0	4.63
Mendoza, Hatuey	South Bend	Ari	A	20	13	11	0	2	57.2	283	64	57	53	5	0	1	8	45	0	36	20	2	3	9	.250	0	0	8.27
	Diamondbcks	Ari	R	20	13	13	0	0	71.2	338	83	64	45	3	1	6	5	31	0	69	14	3	2	7	.222	0	0	5.65
	Missoula	Ari	R+	20	1	0	0	1	[illegible]	15	0	0	0	0	0	0	0	[illegible]	0	[illegible]	[illegible]	0	0	0	.000	0	0	0.00
Mendoza, Mario	Boise	Ana	A-	21	15	15	0	0	78.2	355	93	58	48	5	4	2	7	29	1	47	9	2	8	2	.800	0	0	5.49
Mercedes, Carlos	Kissimmee	Hou	A+	24	41	1	0	10	75	340	82	51	41	5	2	6	2	31	3	39	8	2	2	4	.333	0	2	4.92
Merrill, Darren	Expos	Mon	R	23	6	0	0	3	11.2	49	13	4	4	0	2	0	0	2	0	5	0	3	2	0	1.000	0	0	3.09
Messenger, Randy	Marlins	Fla	R	18	13	2	0	6	26.1	122	28	25	22	1	0	1	3	19	0	23	1	0	0	3	.000	0	2	7.52
Messer, Brian	Pirates	Pit	R	23	3	2	0	1	6	25	7	3	3	0	0	0	0	1	0	5	0	0	0	1	.000	0	0	4.50

1999 Pitching — Single-A and Rookie Leagues

HOW MUCH HE PITCHED											WHAT HE GAVE UP												THE RESULTS					
Player	Team	Org	Lg	A	G	GS	CG	GF	IP	BFP	H	R	ER	HR	SH	SF	HB	TBB	IBB	SO	WP	Bk	W	L	Pct.	ShO	Sv	ERA
Messman, Joey	Kissimmee	Hou	A+	24	45	0	0	40	59.1	251	38	20	16	6	4	0	4	35	2	47	6	2	3	4	.429	0	15	2.43
	San Jose	SF	A+	24	2	0	0	2	1.2	13	6	5	5	0	0	0	0	3	0	0	3	0	0	0	.000	0	0	27.00
Meyer, John	Idaho Falls	SD	R+	21	2	1	0	0	5	35	13	13	8	1	0	1	2	3	0	1	7	0	0	1	.000	0	0	14.40
	Padres	SD	R	21	21	0	0	14	32.2	163	34	29	22	2	1	1	3	30	0	31	6	0	1	3	.250	0	6	6.06
Mikels, Jason	Danville	Atl	R+	20	16	3	0	5	37.1	168	32	20	11	4	0	2	4	16	0	42	4	4	1	2	.333	0	1	2.65
	Macon	Atl	A	20	5	0	0	2	12	48	9	7	4	2	1	1	0	4	0	6	0	0	0	1	.000	0	1	3.00
Mikkola, Shaun	Mets	NYM	R	20	5	4	0	0	24	111	28	14	11	0	0	0	0	15	0	9	2	2	1	0	1.000	0	0	4.13
	Kingsport	NYM	R+	20	8	0	0	5	11	62	17	13	13	1	0	0	1	12	0	10	4	0	0	0	.000	0	0	10.64
Miller, Aaron*	Quad City	Min	A	23	25	18	0	1	83.1	378	55	53	40	3	2	3	8	73	2	87	6	0	6	6	.500	0	1	4.32
Miller, Benji	San Jose	SF	A+	24	47	0	0	38	59.2	248	53	26	20	3	2	4	1	17	0	61	6	2	3	2	.600	0	20	3.02
Miller, Corey	Athletics	Oak	R	23	18	0	0	17	23	90	15	3	2	1	0	0	1	9	1	28	0	3	2	0	1.000	0	11	0.78
	Sou Oregon	Oak	A-	23	5	0	0	1	12	44	5	4	3	1	0	0	1	2	0	10	1	0	1	1	.500	0	0	2.25
Miller, Greg*	Augusta	Bos	A	20	25	25	1	0	136.2	558	109	54	47	8	1	0	5	56	0	146	4	3	10	6	.625	0	0	3.10
Miller, Jim	Beloit	Mil	A	24	6	1	0	2	14.1	59	13	6	6	4	0	0	0	5	0	9	2	0	0	1	.000	0	0	3.77
	Stockton	Mil	A+	24	28	17	1	7	124.1	557	137	91	61	13	3	4	13	44	1	101	8	4	8	9	.471	0	1	4.42
Miller, Justin	Salem	Col	A+	22	8	8	0	0	37	159	35	18	17	3	0	0	5	11	0	35	5	0	1	2	.333	0	0	4.14
Mills, Ryan*	Fort Myers	Min	A+	22	27	21	0	3	95.1	499	121	107	94	6	0	6	16	87	1	70	20	0	3	10	.231	0	0	8.87
Minaya, Edwin	Athletics	Oak	R	20	14	11	0	0	59.2	274	76	49	41	1	1	3	1	24	0	41	4	3	5	3	.625	0	0	6.18
Minaya, Pedro	Clinton	Cin	A	22	36	11	0	10	84	397	88	65	52	4	4	2	7	58	0	74	11	4	4	6	.400	0	0	5.57
Minaya, Richard	Reds	Cin	R	18	16	0	0	10	27.1	124	25	19	14	1	0	4	0	16	1	19	7	2	2	2	.500	0	0	4.61
Miniel, Rene	Red Sox	Bos	R	19	21	0	0	13	37.2	175	40	28	17	2	1	1	1	16	0	37	7	0	1	2	.333	0	1	4.06
Miniel, Roberto	Beloit	Mil	A	20	10	0	0	3	16.1	87	23	19	17	5	0	0	0	16	0	11	3	0	0	0	.000	0	0	9.37
	Ogden	Mil	R+	20	15	14	1	0	85.2	387	98	58	42	5	3	5	5	34	0	77	7	1	5	4	.556	0	0	4.41
Minix, Travis	Hudson Val	TB	A-	22	27	0	0	19	56.1	221	36	11	9	2	5	2	2	12	2	68	3	0	2	2	.500	0	7	1.44
Minter, Matt*	Lynchburg	Pit	A+	27	41	0	0	22	62.2	272	67	40	35	5	3	4	1	16	1	55	5	0	3	2	.600	0	3	5.03
Mlodik, Kevin	Savannah	Tex	A	25	14	0	0	14	20	81	12	5	2	1	1	0	0	8	0	32	2	1	2	2	.500	0	5	0.90
	Charlotte	Tex	A+	25	25	0	0	13	48.2	229	52	29	22	2	5	4	3	30	0	33	12	0	0	4	.000	0	0	4.07
Mobley, Kevin	Lakeland	Det	A+	25	46	5	0	12	96.2	414	107	48	41	11	5	8	3	26	1	73	5	0	7	4	.636	0	2	3.82
Montenegro, Chris	Mariners	Sea	R	23	19	0	0	11	27	114	19	11	9	1	1	0	2	15	1	35	4	3	0	1	.000	0	7	3.00
Montero, Francisco	Piedmont	Phi	A	24	25	9	0	7	85.2	365	84	48	29	13	2	0	2	20	0	70	2	0	4	3	.571	0	2	3.05
Montero, Oscar	Ogden	Mil	R+	22	13	8	0	1	61	285	67	47	36	8	0	1	2	42	0	63	6	1	2	7	.222	0	0	5.31
Montgomery, Steve	Vero Beach	LA	A+	26	9	6	0	1	37	145	28	12	10	5	0	0	4	10	0	33	4	0	0	4	.000	0	0	2.43
Montilla, Felix	Williamsprt	Pit	A-	20	23	0	0	21	29.1	126	29	14	13	3	0	1	1	11	0	29	0	2	1	2	.333	0	10	3.99
	Hickory	Pit	A	20	2	0	0	0	3.1	16	6	2	2	0	0	0	0	0	0	1	0	1	0	0	.000	0	0	5.40
Montoya, Saul	Diamondbcks	Ari	R	19	17	0	0	4	29	132	33	14	13	3	0	1	1	11	0	39	5	1	2	1	.667	0	1	4.03
Monzon, Yoel	Portland	Col	A-	23	17	7	0	3	57	272	65	43	30	3	3	6	7	29	0	37	2	4	3	4	.429	0	1	4.74
Moore, Brad	Modesto	Oak	A+	24	34	0	0	15	37	182	37	24	21	2	2	2	5	31	2	42	11	0	3	2	.600	0	0	5.11
Moore, Bryan	Utica	Fla	A-	23	26	0	0	23	35	146	29	13	6	1	0	0	4	5	1	36	2	0	2	1	.667	0	9	1.54
Moore, Chris	Brevard Cty	Fla	A+	21	13	0	0	1	28.1	125	20	20	17	5	2	1	2	20	0	16	1	2	0	0	.000	0	0	5.40
	Kane County	Fla	A	21	25	0	0	7	46	198	41	12	11	1	1	0	8	23	0	52	3	1	3	0	1.000	0	2	2.15
Moore, Darin	Sou Oregon	Oak	A-	23	5	2	0	0	12.2	55	9	4	2	0	1	0	2	6	1	14	1	0	1	0	1.000	0	0	1.42
	Modesto	Oak	A+	23	12	0	0	2	20.2	111	21	27	27	0	2	0	5	26	0	21	12	0	1	1	.500	0	0	11.76
Moore, Eric	Savannah	Tex	A	24	23	0	0	17	34.2	148	38	16	11	0	1	1	6	7	0	28	4	0	1	1	.500	0	1	2.86
Moore, Greg	Boise	Ana	A-	21	10	4	0	2	28.2	132	39	22	16	6	1	0	1	6	0	24	1	1	2	2	.500	0	0	5.02
Moore, Joel	Rockies	Col	R	27	4	3	0	0	10.1	60	25	19	15	1	0	0	2	1	0	9	1	0	0	1	.000	0	0	13.06
Morel, Francis	Diamondbcks	Ari	R	21	7	0	0	2	15.2	78	23	15	14	1	1	0	2	5	0	18	1	0	2	1	.667	0	1	8.04
Morel, Jesus	Twins	Min	R	19	14	0	0	6	31.2	156	34	26	16	2	0	4	5	15	0	31	2	6	0	1	.000	0	1	4.55
Morel, Ramon	Expos	Mon	R	25	2	2	0	0	2	17	7	8	6	0	0	0	0	4	0	1	1	0	0	1	.000	0	0	27.00
Moreno, Edgar	Mexico	—	R	—	18	0	0	18	20.2	93	23	13	6	0	0	2	2	5	0	22	0	2	4	2	.667	0	3	2.61
Moreno, Victor	Diamondbcks	Ari	R	20	7	0	0	4	10	53	17	13	11	0	1	0	0	6	0	7	1	0	1	2	.333	0	2	9.90
Mori, Kazuma	Jupiter	Mon	A+	24	3	0	0	3	3.2	19	3	4	3	0	0	1	1	2	0	2	1	0	0	1	.000	0	0	7.36
Morrison, Cody	Lk Elsinore	Ana	A+	25	45	0	0	27	67.2	332	65	57	40	2	3	1	11	50	7	64	7	1	4	8	.333	0	3	5.32
Morse, Bryan*	Utica	Fla	A-	22	14	14	0	0	78.1	324	73	41	30	5	2	1	3	19	0	74	6	1	3	5	.375	0	0	3.45
Moser, Todd*	Utica	Fla	A-	23	14	14	3	0	88	343	63	20	15	2	1	1	2	24	0	86	4	2	8	2	.800	1	0	1.53
Mosher, Andy	Helena	Mil	R+	24	24	0	0	21	25.2	118	25	17	16	3	3	0	0	15	2	30	4	0	1	1	.500	0	12	5.61
Moskau, Ryan*	Vero Beach	LA	A+	22	17	17	0	0	104	443	99	54	48	8	3	4	7	40	0	68	6	4	5	5	.500	0	0	4.15
	Brevard Cty	Fla	A+	22	9	9	2	0	63.2	261	50	22	19	4	4	0	1	21	0	40	0	0	4	3	.571	0	0	2.69
Mowday, Chris	Medcine Hat	Tor	R+	18	16	1	0	7	28.2	137	34	25	19	3	4	2	2	12	0	28	7	1	2	6	.250	0	1	5.97
Mowel, Mike	Augusta	Bos	A	20	21	21	0	0	101	459	131	68	55	9	1	2	4	40	1	76	9	0	5	13	.278	0	0	4.90
Mozingo, Dan*	Bristol	CWS	R+	20	13	13	1	0	67	323	79	59	45	3	0	1	7	32	0	68	14	1	4	7	.364	1	0	6.04
Mundy, Mike	Asheville	Col	A	24	37	0	0	22	58	286	65	43	38	6	0	4	4	42	0	59	10	2	3	3	.500	0	2	5.90
Munoz, Arnaldo*	White Sox	CWS	R	18	14	0	0	7	12	61	13	10	7	1	0	0	2	8	0	12	1	1	0	2	.000	0	1	5.25
Murphy, Brian	Frederick	Bal	A+	24	26	0	0	11	53.1	224	51	36	25	6	1	0	3	10	0	39	0	0	1	2	.333	0	3	4.22
Murphy, Matt*	Lansing	ChC	A	21	25	2	0	10	46.1	198	50	22	18	2	1	1	1	16	0	39	1	1	3	1	.750	0	2	3.50
Murray, Steve*	St.Cathrnes	Tor	A-	20	12	8	0	2	57	252	68	46	36	7	0	4	1	16	0	46	5	0	1	4	.200	0	1	5.68
Musser, Neal*	Mets	NYM	R	19	8	7	0	0	31.1	134	26	13	7	1	0	0	0	18	0	22	4	0	2	1	.667	0	0	2.01
Myers, Aaron	Stockton	Mil	A+	24	22	10	0	2	83	360	88	52	42	7	3	6	8	25	2	81	3	4	3	4	.429	0	1	4.55
Myers, Brett	Phillies	Phi	R	19	7	5	0	0	27	105	17	8	7	0	0	0	2	7	0	30	2	0	2	1	.667	0	0	2.33
Myers, Taylor	Royals	KC	R	22	3	3	0	0	4	24	10	8	8	1	0	0	2	2	0	3	0	0	0	2	.000	0	0	18.00
Myers, Todd	Missoula	Ari	R+	23	5	1	0	1	7	44	12	11	10	1	1	1	3	6	0	4	1	0	0	0	.000	0	0	12.86
	Diamondbcks	Ari	R	23	3	0	0	2	5.1	26	6	3	1	0	0	0	1	3	0	4	0	0	0	0	.000	0	0	1.69
Nakamura, Mike	Fort Myers	Min	A+	23	14	0	0	6	19.2	74	9	5	4	1	2	2	0	5	0	18	1	0	2	0	1.000	0	2	1.83
Nall, T.J.	Great Falls	LA	R+	19	15	14	2	1	92.2	401	115	60	51	13	6	3	5	13	0	70	2	0	3	8	.273	0	0	4.95
Nanninga, Matt	Billings	Cin	R+	23	14	0	0	1	27.2	132	40	30	24	2	2	2	5	10	0	19	2	1	1	3	.250	0	0	7.81
	Reds	Cin	R	23	6	2	0	0	15	73	17	19	16	1	2	1	2	10	0	4	3	3	1	1	.500	0	0	9.60
Nannini, Mike	Auburn	Hou	A-	19	11	11	2	0	75.2	295	55	19	16	2	3	3	4	17	0	86	1	0	5	3	.625	1	0	1.90

1999 Pitching — Single-A and Rookie Leagues

HOW MUCH HE PITCHED											WHAT HE GAVE UP												THE RESULTS					
Player	Team	Org	Lg	A	G	GS	CG	GF	IP	BFP	H	R	ER	HR	SH	SF	HB	TBB	IBB	SO	WP	Bk	W	L	Pct.	ShO	Sv	ERA
	Michigan	Hou	A	19	15	15	0	0	87.1	398	107	56	43	8	2	7	4	31	1	68	3	0	4	10	.286	0	0	4.43
Nantkes, Kurt	Athletics	Oak	R	20	15	11	0	0	70	287	55	25	17	3	0	1	5	18	0	64	6	3	5	4	.556	0	0	2.19
Nation, Joey*	Macon	Atl	A	21	6	6	0	0	27.1	118	27	10	9	1	0	1	1	9	0	31	2	1	1	1	.500	0	0	2.96
	Myrtle Bch	Atl	A+	21	19	17	0	0	96.1	401	88	51	47	7	2	4	2	37	0	87	4	0	5	4	.556	0	0	4.39
	Daytona	ChC	A+	21	2	2	0	0	13	47	8	2	2	0	0	0	0	2	0	11	0	0	2	0	1.000	0	0	1.38
Navarro, Hector	Mexico	—	R	—	11	1	0	2	25.2	123	35	24	22	2	1	1	2	12	1	15	2	4	3	1	.750	0	0	7.71
Navarro, Jason*	Potomac	StL	A+	24	39	14	0	3	111.1	508	134	82	75	12	3	6	5	49	0	66	7	1	5	13	.278	0	0	6.06
Navarro, Scott*	Kissimmee	Hou	A+	25	37	11	1	5	112.2	452	108	39	36	4	5	5	3	17	3	86	7	2	8	3	.727	1	0	2.88
Neal, Blaine	Kane County	Fla	A	22	26	0	0	18	31	117	21	8	8	2	2	0	0	10	0	31	1	0	4	2	.667	0	6	2.32
Neal, Brian*	Great Falls	LA	R+	20	15	4	0	7	32.2	156	32	23	21	1	2	1	2	29	0	23	7	1	0	2	.000	0	1	5.79
Nebel, Jeffrey	Butte	Ana	R+	23	29	0	0	23	31	139	34	15	14	2	0	0	4	12	0	26	7	0	3	2	.600	0	5	4.06
Needle, Chad	St.Cathrnes	Tor	A-	21	15	0	0	7	20	86	18	13	13	5	1	1	2	5	0	20	0	0	1	2	.333	0	0	5.85
Negron, Jose	Sou Oregon	Oak	A-	22	13	1	0	5	25.2	124	16	21	16	2	3	1	6	23	0	25	1	3	0	4	.000	0	1	5.61
Neu, Michael	Rockford	Cin	A	22	9	0	0	2	18	84	17	10	9	1	0	1	2	12	1	23	4	0	0	1	.000	0	1	4.50
Neugebauer, Nick	Beloit	Mil	A	19	18	18	0	0	80.2	372	50	41	35	4	2	3	6	80	0	125	10	2	7	5	.583	0	0	3.90
Newman, Tim	Medcine Hat	Tor	R+	21	23	0	0	7	26.2	121	26	21	14	5	1	2	0	10	1	20	5	0	1	0	1.000	0	2	4.72
Nichols, Brian	Mets	NYM	R	22	9	0	0	0	20	85	22	12	11	1	0	0	0	8	0	11	1	2	3	1	.750	0	0	4.95
Nicholson, John	Jupiter	Mon	A+	22	4	4	0	0	8.1	60	9	21	20	1	1	1	6	19	0	3	4	0	0	4	.000	0	0	21.60
	Expos	Mon	R	22	2	0	0	1	3	11	0	0	0	0	0	0	1	2	0	4	0	0	0	0	.000	0	0	0.00
Nickle, Doug	Clearwater	Phi	A+	25	60	0	0	50	70.2	299	60	25	18	1	1	1	4	23	3	70	6	0	2	4	.333	0	28	2.29
Nix, Wayne	Modesto	Oak	A+	23	34	18	0	4	119.1	532	109	76	56	10	3	5	9	69	2	105	8	3	9	6	.600	0	2	4.22
Noel, Todd	Tampa	NYY	A+	21	17	17	0	0	93.1	415	101	56	45	3	2	9	4	33	1	80	7	2	3	7	.300	0	0	4.34
Nogowski, Bran.*	Visalia	Oak	A+	24	33	2	0	11	65	290	71	40	29	4	2	3	2	19	1	60	5	0	5	4	.556	0	3	4.02
Noriega, Ray*	Visalia	Oak	A+	26	60	0	0	34	69.1	308	67	36	31	6	4	4	2	32	2	62	6	0	5	3	.625	0	11	4.02
Norris, Shon	Lowell	Bos	A-	23	27	0	0	25	41	179	41	25	23	2	2	2	2	13	0	29	7	0	4	4	.500	0	3	5.05
Norton, Jason	Augusta	Bos	A	24	30	17	2	5	136	544	106	50	35	11	1	2	4	28	1	150	7	0	9	6	.600	1	0	2.32
Novits, Carey*	Mahoning Vy	Cle	A-	24	12	3	0	3	34.2	166	46	30	21	5	2	2	1	19	0	33	4	0	2	4	.333	0	1	5.45
Nowakowski, Brian	Elizabethtn	Min	R+	20	16	0	0	5	20.2	99	17	12	7	3	0	2	4	11	0	26	3	0	1	0	1.000	0	0	3.05
Noyce, David*	Kane County	Fla	A	23	16	16	2	0	101	419	82	43	37	5	3	5	3	29	0	86	6	1	7	3	.700	2	0	3.30
Nunez, Franklin	Piedmont	Phi	A	23	13	13	1	0	77	326	69	39	29	4	4	1	6	25	0	88	2	1	4	8	.333	0	0	3.39
Nunez, Jose*	Kingsport	NYM	R+	21	13	13	0	0	69.2	296	75	36	29	6	0	2	4	15	0	63	4	0	3	4	.429	0	0	3.75
Nunley, Derrick	St.Cathrnes	Tor	A-	19	7	0	0	3	8.2	35	8	3	3	1	0	1	1	2	0	10	0	1	0	0	.000	0	0	3.12
Oase, Ryan	Hudson Val	TB	A-	22	1	0	0	0	1.1	8	3	1	1	0	0	0	0	1	0	1	0	0	0	0	.000	0	0	6.75
Obando, Omar	Yankees	NYY	R	23	2	0	0	0	4	20	5	4	0	1	3	0	0	3	0	3	0	0	1	0	1.000	0	0	0.00
Obermuelle, Wes	Royals	KC	R	23	11	7	0	2	38.1	159	33	16	11	2	0	1	1	12	1	39	2	1	2	1	.667	0	0	2.58
Ochoa, Pablo	Capital Cty	NYM	A	24	3	0	0	2	5.2	19	2	0	0	0	0	0	0	1	0	4	0	0	0	0	.000	0	1	0.00
Ochsner, Alan	Yankees	NYY	R	24	4	0	0	1	4.2	21	4	4	3	1	1	0	0	4	0	6	0	0	1	1	.500	0	0	5.79
Odom, Lance	Twins	Min	R	21	20	0	0	17	23.1	113	33	18	15	0	0	1	3	7	1	13	2	2	0	2	.000	0	5	5.79
Ohm, Joe	Eugene	ChC	A-	23	21	1	0	7	41.1	196	50	31	29	3	4	2	2	19	0	32	7	1	0	5	.000	0	0	6.31
Ohman, Will*	Daytona	ChC	A+	22	31	15	2	12	106.2	457	102	59	41	11	2	4	8	41	1	97	6	1	4	7	.364	2	5	3.46
Ojeda, Joseph	Salem-Keizr	SF	A-	23	16	0	0	3	33	155	39	27	24	3	0	2	5	17	1	20	6	1	2	3	.400	0	0	6.55
Olean, Chris	Ogden	Mil	R+	23	2	0	0	1	3	17	4	6	6	0	0	0	0	3	1	3	0	0	0	0	.000	0	0	18.00
	Helena	Mil	R+	23	14	8	2	4	58.2	243	56	30	18	3	5	4	0	12	1	27	2	0	6	1	.857	0	4	2.76
Oleksik, George	High Desert	Ari	A+	26	4	0	0	2	7	39	14	11	3	1	0	0	0	6	0	5	2	0	0	2	.000	0	0	3.86
	Rockford	Cin	A	26	21	0	0	9	28.1	133	32	22	20	4	1	0	5	12	2	24	5	0	0	1	.000	0	2	6.35
Oliver, Scott	Staten Ilnd	NYY	A-	23	2	2	0	0	6.1	33	9	9	7	1	0	0	0	4	0	4	2	1	0	1	.000	0	0	9.95
	Yankees	NYY	R	23	6	5	0	0	32.2	133	28	7	6	0	2	0	2	8	0	31	2	0	4	1	.800	0	0	1.65
	Greensboro	NYY	A	23	7	7	1	0	43.2	182	42	22	18	3	2	1	1	8	0	37	2	2	1	1	.500	0	0	3.71
Olivo, Carlos	Johnson Cy	StL	R+	20	6	6	0	0	32	144	35	19	15	2	0	0	4	13	1	31	4	1	2	1	.667	0	0	4.22
Olore, Kevin	Everett	Sea	A-	21	22	0	0	12	31.1	141	31	21	17	5	0	0	2	21	1	31	4	2	0	0	.000	0	2	4.88
Olsen, Kevin	Brevard Cty	Fla	A+	23	11	11	0	0	57	253	70	37	32	8	1	1	1	13	0	45	3	0	2	5	.286	0	0	5.05
	Kane County	Fla	A	23	10	9	0	0	61.1	257	65	25	23	3	0	3	2	16	0	52	2	0	5	2	.714	0	0	3.38
O'Reilly, John	High Desert	Ari	A+	25	21	4	0	6	46	230	53	46	37	5	4	2	2	36	0	47	4	2	1	4	.200	0	1	7.24
	South Bend	Ari	A	25	4	2	0	1	11.1	56	17	11	11	4	0	0	0	5	0	15	1	0	0	1	.000	0	0	8.74
Orloski, Joe	St.Cathrnes	Tor	A-	21	17	7	0	3	64.2	290	80	48	33	9	0	1	1	22	0	57	7	0	3	9	.250	0	1	4.59
Ormond, Rodney	Bluefield	Bal	R+	23	4	0	0	4	9.1	36	2	4	0	0	0	1	0	3	0	11	1	0	1	0	1.000	0	0	0.00
	Delmarva	Bal	A	23	17	1	0	7	37.1	156	29	16	12	1	0	0	4	19	0	38	5	2	1	2	.333	0	3	2.89
Ortega, Carlos*	Great Falls	LA	R+	21	17	6	0	8	54.2	232	45	25	14	0	0	2	2	23	0	52	5	0	3	3	.500	0	2	2.30
Ortega, Jose*	Royals	KC	R	21	17	0	0	7	37.1	166	41	17	15	3	0	0	3	18	0	32	3	0	2	1	.667	0	3	3.62
Ortega, Jose	Royals	KC	R	20	12	9	0	0	53.1	257	67	48	35	1	2	5	5	30	0	27	3	1	1	5	.167	0	0	5.91
Ortiz, J.C.*	Auburn	Hou	A-	24	23	0	0	8	36.2	168	39	25	19	1	2	1	4	22	0	28	1	0	1	2	.333	0	0	4.66
Ortiz, Javier	Yankees	NYY	R	20	12	10	1	0	50.2	246	63	40	32	4	1	1	4	35	0	46	2	0	3	2	.600	0	0	5.68
Ortiz, Jose	Hudson Val	TB	A-	22	29	0	0	27	46.2	183	31	14	9	0	2	0	3	14	0	35	1	1	4	3	.571	0	9	1.74
Ortiz, Omar	Idaho Falls	SD	R+	22	6	5	0	0	29	127	25	18	11	2	0	1	3	13	0	24	5	1	2	1	.667	0	0	3.41
	Fort Wayne	SD	A	22	4	4	0	0	18.2	91	17	16	14	0	0	0	2	20	0	9	1	0	1	2	.333	0	0	6.75
Osting, Jimmy*	Macon	Atl	A	23	27	22	0	5	147	581	130	52	47	13	2	1	5	30	0	131	2	0	14	4	.778	0	2	2.88
Oswalt, Roy	Michigan	Hou	A	22	22	22	2	0	151.1	643	144	78	75	8	2	5	7	54	0	143	8	4	13	4	.765	0	0	4.46
Outlaw, Mark*	Batavia	Phi	A-	23	23	0	0	10	33.1	134	26	10	6	1	2	3	0	9	2	45	5	0	1	1	.500	0	4	1.62
Ovalles, Juan	Diamondbcks	Ari	R	18	14	7	0	0	60	257	48	25	16	1	3	3	8	25	0	36	4	1	7	2	.778	0	0	2.40
Oyler, Scott	Sou Oregon	Oak	A-	24	4	0	0	0	7	[illegible]	11	14	[illegible]	0	0	1	[illegible]	6	1	4	[illegible]	[illegible]	0	0	.000	0	0	15.43
Ozias, Todd	Bakersfield	SF	A+	23	52	0	0	49	56.1	235	47	21	16	6	0	2	1	25	1	67	6	0	5	5	.500	0	26	2.56
Pacheco, Delvis	Myrtle Bch	Atl	A+	22	40	3	0	16	99.1	429	87	47	38	9	5	2	6	42	3	87	7	0	6	5	.545	0	2	3.44
Pacheco, En.	Asheville	Col	A	20	15	15	1	0	85	383	98	60	50	4	2	7	4	29	0	59	4	2	3	9	.250	0	0	5.29
	Portland	Col	A-	20	12	12	1	0	73	327	73	43	32	7	2	3	7	21	1	44	4	1	4	3	.571	0	0	3.95
Padilla, Charly	Boise	Ana	A-	21	10	0	0	4	18.2	92	21	16	15	4	0	1	0	13	0	14	0	1	1	0	1.000	0	0	7.23
Padilla, Roy*	Columbus	Cle	A	24	30	0	0	11	59.2	263	53	27	20	3	0	2	10	27	0	56	9	0	2	2	.500	0	3	3.02
	Kinston	Cle	A+	24	8	0	0	2	13	57	9	6	6	1	0	0	2	10	0	7	0	0	0	0	.000	0	1	4.15

1999 Pitching — Single-A and Rookie Leagues

HOW MUCH HE PITCHED											WHAT HE GAVE UP												THE RESULTS					
Player	Team	Org	Lg	A	G	GS	CG	GF	IP	BFP	H	R	ER	HR	SH	SF	HB	TBB	IBB	SO	WP	Bk	W	L	Pct.	ShO	Sv	ERA
Padua, Geraldo	Greensboro	NYY	A	23	21	21	1	0	139.2	569	120	53	44	12	0	1	2	35	0	155	13	1	9	4	.692	1	0	2.84
	Rancho Cuca	SD	A+	23	7	7	0	0	40.2	174	43	21	21	4	0	0	0	18	0	41	6	0	3	3	.500	0	0	4.65
Palki, Jeromy	Twins	Min	R	24	3	1	0	0	5	16	0	0	0	0	0	0	0	1	0	3	0	0	0	0	.000	0	0	0.00
Palma, Ricardo*	Lansing	ChC	A	20	22	22	2	0	134.2	571	134	61	44	6	1	4	3	44	0	79	8	4	7	7	.500	0	0	2.94
Pamus, Javier	Chstn-WV	KC	A	25	44	0	0	17	90.1	398	87	37	28	1	5	0	5	34	2	81	3	0	3	3	.500	0	4	2.79
Paradis, Mike	Delmarva	Bal	A	22	2	2	0	0	3	16	3	5	5	0	1	0	0	4	0	6	0	1	0	1	.000	0	0	15.00
Paredes, Carlos	Wilmington	KC	A+	24	36	0	0	12	55	253	47	31	25	3	0	2	2	48	2	49	9	0	6	0	1.000	0	3	4.09
Parker, Allan	Cedar Rapds	Ana	A	28	1	0	0	0	1	10	7	6	6	1	0	0	0	0	0	0	0	0	0	0	.000	0	0	54.00
Parker, Beau	Yakima	LA	A-	21	3	1	0	0	6.2	27	6	0	0	0	0	0	0	1	0	4	0	0	1	0	1.000	0	0	0.00
Parker, Brandon	Lancaster	Sea	A+	24	27	27	0	0	139.2	640	164	95	79	12	5	10	14	67	0	147	5	3	9	7	.563	0	0	5.09
Parker, Daniel	Martinsvlle	Hou	R+	20	14	13	1	0	73.2	324	73	47	32	5	1	1	6	30	0	71	19	0	6	4	.600	0	0	3.91
Parker, Matt	Johnson Cy	StL	R+	21	23	0	0	15	31.1	124	22	13	9	3	1	0	0	11	2	43	2	0	1	1	.500	0	2	2.59
Parkerson, Michael*	Pirates	Pit	R	21	14	0	0	5	33	141	25	14	12	1	3	1	2	21	0	31	3	5	0	1	.000	0	1	3.27
Parra, Christian	Jamestown	Atl	A-	22	9	9	0	0	49.1	207	46	21	17	2	0	0	1	19	0	62	1	1	1	2	.333	0	0	3.10
	Macon	Atl	A	22	6	6	0	0	32.2	139	33	15	12	3	0	1	3	12	0	37	1	1	1	1	.500	0	0	3.31
Parrish, Wade*	Yakima	LA	A-	22	17	8	0	5	60	261	57	30	27	4	0	2	1	24	0	48	2	0	4	3	.571	0	2	4.05
Partenheimer, Bri.*	Sarasota	Bos	A+	25	17	0	0	6	30	117	26	8	6	3	1	2	0	3	0	28	2	0	1	0	1.000	0	2	1.80
	Brevard Cty	Fla	A+	25	21	0	0	8	44	180	29	13	11	1	3	1	6	14	1	29	2	0	2	3	.400	0	2	2.25
Pasqualicchio, Mi.*	Stockton	Mil	A+	25	4	4	0	0	13.2	56	15	9	8	3	2	0	0	4	0	12	0	0	0	1	.000	0	0	5.27
Pate, Dustin	Cubs	ChC	R	19	12	11	0	0	48.2	233	70	53	52	2	0	3	5	21	0	42	8	1	1	5	.167	0	0	9.62
Patten, Michael	White Sox	CWS	R	19	15	5	0	3	38.2	174	27	22	18	0	0	2	11	30	1	27	11	0	0	4	.000	0	0	4.19
Pautz, Brad	Batavia	Phi	A-	23	13	13	2	0	77.2	326	77	37	35	4	2	1	1	30	1	58	4	1	8	4	.667	2	0	4.06
Pavlovich, Tony	Hickory	Pit	A	25	56	0	0	39	73.1	287	55	29	19	8	1	3	1	16	4	78	1	0	5	1	.833	0	20	2.33
Paz, Rolando	Orioles	Bal	R	21	13	0	0	3	25	124	23	28	24	1	1	2	2	25	1	23	6	1	1	1	.500	0	0	8.64
Pearce, Josh	New Jersey	StL	A-	22	14	14	1	0	77.2	336	78	45	43	8	2	6	5	20	0	78	14	1	3	7	.300	1	0	4.98
Pearson, Dale*	Great Falls	LA	R+	23	7	0	0	7	16	74	16	10	8	2	1	0	0	8	0	11	0	1	1	1	.500	0	1	4.50
Peavy, Jacob	Padres	SD	R	19	13	11	1	0	73.2	286	52	16	11	4	2	0	3	23	0	90	5	3	7	1	.875	0	0	1.34
	Idaho Falls	SD	R+	19	2	2	0	0	11	40	5	0	0	0	0	0	0	1	0	13	0	0	2	0	1.000	0	0	0.00
Peck, Brandon*	New Jersey	StL	A-	23	31	0	0	16	35.2	147	37	17	16	3	4	0	0	11	0	29	0	1	1	4	.200	0	0	4.04
Pederson, Justin	Wilmington	KC	A+	25	34	4	0	8	77.1	349	67	46	39	4	0	4	9	40	1	67	6	0	4	4	.500	0	2	4.54
Peeples, Jim*	Yankees	NYY	R	19	16	0	0	4	16.1	87	21	13	9	0	1	0	1	16	0	21	3	0	0	0	.000	0	0	4.96
Peguero, Darwin*	Michigan	Hou	A	21	24	20	0	2	114	483	115	58	52	7	2	2	5	35	1	88	6	3	7	7	.500	0	0	4.11
Peguero, Radhame	Hudson Val	TB	A-	22	4	4	0	0	26	96	13	8	7	0	0	0	3	11	0	24	2	0	2	1	.667	0	0	2.42
	Chston-SC	TB	A	22	11	11	0	0	56.1	249	61	31	26	2	3	2	3	25	0	29	3	0	0	4	.000	0	0	4.15
Pena, Juan*	Visalia	Oak	A+	21	33	18	0	4	131.1	609	168	106	84	10	3	3	0	61	2	107	9	3	9	5	.643	0	1	5.76
Penney, Mike	Beloit	Mil	A	23	27	27	4	0	170	740	171	94	80	16	2	3	7	70	2	109	11	2	9	12	.429	2	0	4.24
Pepen, Robert	Mets	NYM	R	21	19	0	0	16	30.2	119	20	7	5	0	2	0	0	7	0	34	2	0	3	1	.750	0	2	1.47
Percell, Brody*	Columbus	Cle	A	24	6	6	0	0	29.1	116	22	15	14	3	1	1	1	10	0	30	0	0	1	3	.250	0	0	4.30
	Kinston	Cle	A+	24	5	5	0	0	23	101	25	12	11	3	0	0	0	11	0	22	1	0	0	0	.000	0	0	4.30
Perez, Elvis	Danville	Atl	R+	20	21	0	0	4	29.1	157	37	42	32	6	0	3	6	22	0	28	5	1	2	1	.667	0	0	9.82
Perez, Franklin	Phillies	Phi	R	19	12	7	0	3	41.1	192	44	36	29	2	1	2	5	27	0	35	6	0	3	4	.429	0	0	6.31
Perez, George	Medcine Hat	Tor	R+	21	15	8	0	3	56	258	65	46	36	9	3	0	4	26	0	41	8	0	2	2	.500	0	1	5.79
Perez, Norberto	Delmarva	Bal	A	22	25	2	0	10	41	188	43	31	28	7	3	2	5	17	0	39	4	1	0	4	.000	0	1	6.15
Perez, Oliver*	Padres	SD	R	18	15	2	0	7	28.1	133	28	20	16	1	1	0	1	16	0	37	0	2	1	2	.333	0	3	5.08
Perez, Randy*	Delmarva	Bal	A	20	21	0	0	11	25.1	118	28	22	20	4	2	0	2	15	0	9	2	0	0	2	.000	0	2	7.11
	Bluefield	Bal	R+	20	14	5	1	4	50	211	51	26	15	4	0	1	2	12	0	39	4	0	4	3	.571	0	0	2.70
	Frederick	Bal	A+	20	2	1	0	1	7	35	14	8	7	0	1	0	0	1	0	4	1	0	0	1	.000	0	0	9.00
Perkins, Greg	Diamondbcks	Ari	R	19	4	3	0	0	12	58	13	11	9	0	1	0	1	8	0	11	1	0	0	0	.000	0	0	6.75
Perkins, Mike	Johnson Cy	StL	R+	21	15	11	0	1	61.2	270	71	34	28	2	0	2	2	19	0	50	1	2	6	1	.857	0	0	4.09
Perozo, Felix	Lk Elsinore	Ana	A+	26	32	0	0	23	36.1	172	44	26	23	3	2	1	2	18	1	23	5	0	0	5	.000	0	2	5.70
Perry, Tim	Fort Wayne	SD	A	22	10	10	0	0	51.1	241	50	39	29	4	1	4	3	34	0	46	5	0	2	5	.286	0	0	5.08
Pesqueira, Omar	Fort Wayne	SD	A	20	47	2	0	15	78	344	84	49	44	7	2	3	2	30	1	56	3	0	4	5	.444	0	2	5.08
Phelps, Travis	St. Pete	TB	A+	22	24	23	1	0	133.2	574	148	70	63	6	4	4	11	39	0	101	2	0	10	8	.556	1	0	4.24
Phillips, James	Orioles	Bal	R	19	15	0	0	6	27.2	123	25	16	12	1	0	1	3	17	1	16	6	0	1	1	.500	0	2	3.90
Phillips, Matt	Augusta	Bos	A	25	39	1	0	14	73.2	326	85	55	39	7	3	4	4	23	3	69	3	0	2	5	.286	0	1	4.76
Pichardo, Carlos	Spokane	KC	A-	22	4	4	0	0	14.1	70	14	15	6	0	1	0	1	10	0	10	0	0	1	2	.333	0	0	3.77
	Chstn-WV	KC	A	22	10	8	0	0	42	187	44	19	12	1	2	2	3	22	0	24	3	0	2	3	.400	0	0	2.57
Pidgeon, Chip*	Mets	NYM	R	21	4	0	0	0	4.1	27	5	6	5	0	0	1	3	6	0	4	3	0	0	0	.000	0	0	10.38
Pidgeon, Matt	Kane County	Fla	A	23	40	7	0	8	100	447	126	59	55	6	3	2	8	36	2	64	3	1	7	6	.538	0	0	4.95
Piedra, Alex	Great Falls	LA	R+	20	18	0	0	10	30.1	147	22	21	19	1	3	2	1	36	0	25	9	0	3	2	.600	0	0	5.64
Pierce, Tony	Jamestown	Atl	A-	24	17	0	0	14	26.2	107	14	9	8	0	0	1	2	12	0	44	1	0	0	1	.000	0	8	2.70
	Macon	Atl	A	24	8	0	0	3	15	63	11	3	3	1	0	1	0	7	0	23	4	0	0	0	.000	0	0	1.80
Pike, Tom	Billings	Cin	R+	23	26	0	0	24	27	127	31	18	9	1	1	0	1	12	0	28	6	0	2	2	.500	0	12	3.00
Pilato, Chris	Batavia	Phi	A-	22	11	0	0	5	14	69	15	8	7	0	3	0	3	9	1	18	7	1	0	0	.000	0	0	4.50
	Piedmont	Phi	A	22	4	4	0	0	22	92	20	12	11	0	0	1	0	8	0	15	2	0	1	2	.333	0	0	4.50
Pine, Chris	Beloit	Mil	A	23	7	0	0	4	14.1	65	13	7	5	1	0	2	1	10	0	17	2	0	0	1	.000	0	0	3.14
Pineda, Isauro	Sarasota	Bos	A+	21	11	8	0	2	51.2	230	56	32	30	3	1	3	3	24	0	32	0	0	2	1	.667	0	0	5.23
	Augusta	Bos	A	21	8	8	0	0	42.2	195	51	24	16	0	2	3	3	15	0	36	5	0	2	1	.667	0	0	3.38
Pineda, Jairo	Michigan	Hou	A	23	4	4	0	0	19.1	91	30	24	19	1	0	2	2	5	0	6	0	0	0	2	.000	0	0	8.84
	Auburn	Hou	A-	23	15	15	1	0	84.1	360	70	35	27	5	0	3	8	31	0	67	3	2	9	2	.818	0	0	2.88
Pineda, Luis	W Michigan	Det	A	22	24	3	0	19	40.1	175	30	18	16	2	2	5	1	26	2	55	5	0	0	2	.000	0	7	3.57
	Lakeland	Det	A+	22	8	0	0	8	8.2	39	6	2	1	0	0	0	0	7	0	8	0	0	0	1	.000	0	0	1.04
Pipes, Joey	Cedar Rapds	Ana	A	26	7	6	1	1	42.2	184	45	24	14	1	1	1	4	11	0	23	2	1	4	1	.800	0	0	2.95
	Lk Elsinore	Ana	A+	26	2	2	1	0	16	64	16	3	3	1	1	0	0	4	0	19	0	1	1	0	1.000	0	0	1.69
Pirkl, Greg	Kinston	Cle	A+	29	6	0	0	6	6.1	32	11	6	5	0	1	1	0	3	0	5	0	0	0	1	.000	0	2	7.11
Place, Eric*	Hagerstown	Tor	A	25	40	0	0	13	72	306	55	34	25	2	8	3	2	38	1	56	3	1	6	4	.600	0	0	3.13
Plank, Terry	Bluefield	Bal	R+	22	20	1	0	6	32.1	152	42	26	24	6	1	0	2	12	0	46	4	2	1	3	.250	0	0	6.68

1999 Pitching — Single-A and Rookie Leagues

HOW MUCH HE PITCHED											WHAT HE GAVE UP												THE RESULTS					
Player	Team	Org	Lg	A	G	GS	CG	GF	IP	BFP	H	R	ER	HR	SH	SF	HB	TBB	IBB	SO	WP	Bk	W	L	Pct.	ShO	Sv	ERA
Poe, Ryan	Beloit	Mil	A	22	49	5	0	28	96	398	94	46	38	9	1	2	3	16	3	108	5	1	6	10	.375	0	9	3.56
Poeck, Chad	Charlotte	Tex	A+	27	9	0	0	3	15	59	10	3	2	0	2	0	0	6	0	12	2	0	0	0	.000	0	1	1.20
Polanco, Elvis	Eugene	ChC	A-	22	10	0	0	6	15.1	77	22	16	14	0	1	1	3	9	0	13	0	0	0	0	.000	0	1	8.22
	Lansing	ChC	A	22	25	0	0	16	37.2	187	54	34	27	3	2	2	3	16	2	29	0	0	0	4	.000	0	4	6.45
Polk, Scott	Kingsport	NYM	R+	23	23	0	0	11	48	207	32	24	17	2	3	1	3	30	3	70	9	2	4	5	.444	0	4	3.19
Polo, Bienvenido	Johnson Cy	StL	R+	21	20	0	0	5	25	147	47	47	36	3	0	1	6	19	0	11	5	1	0	5	.000	0	0	12.96
Pomar, Jason	Sou Oregon	Oak	A-	23	16	1	0	6	49.2	232	55	31	21	2	0	1	2	25	1	42	5	0	2	0	1.000	0	0	3.81
Poplin, Paul	Elizabethtn	Min	R+	22	21	0	0	11	37	174	50	25	18	4	1	1	1	11	1	37	5	0	6	3	.667	0	3	4.38
Porter, Scott	Medcine Hat	Tor	R+	23	18	0	0	17	19.2	95	23	16	12	1	0	0	1	10	0	29	2	0	1	3	.250	0	8	5.49
Poturnicki, Adam	Helena	Mil	R+	23	16	2	0	4	35.2	167	37	27	19	2	2	1	3	16	0	32	5	1	3	0	1.000	0	0	4.79
Pourron, Joe	San Jose	SF	A+	23	14	0	0	7	23.1	118	17	18	16	0	2	2	2	32	0	23	8	0	2	0	1.000	0	0	6.17
	Salem-Keizr	SF	A-	23	8	0	0	5	7	40	13	10	9	1	0	2	0	6	0	6	2	0	0	0	.000	0	0	11.57
Prata, Danny*	Bakersfield	SF	A+	21	27	27	0	0	142.2	632	143	80	62	22	2	2	9	54	0	87	6	1	9	9	.500	0	0	3.91
Prater, Andy	Hickory	Pit	A	22	15	12	0	0	63.2	284	71	46	41	14	5	2	4	18	0	52	1	1	2	3	.400	0	0	5.80
	Williamsprt	Pit	A-	22	10	10	1	0	38.1	183	45	36	26	8	0	3	6	18	0	21	2	0	2	4	.333	0	0	6.10
Prather, Scott*	Peoria	StL	A	20	27	27	0	0	147.1	642	134	81	63	10	4	4	11	77	0	132	5	0	9	10	.474	0	0	3.85
Pratt, Andy*	Savannah	Tex	A	20	13	13	1	0	71.2	299	66	30	23	4	4	2	4	16	0	100	4	0	4	4	.500	1	0	2.89
Prempas, Lyle*	Lynchburg	Pit	A+	25	6	6	0	0	25.1	112	27	19	16	3	0	2	0	7	0	25	3	0	2	3	.400	0	0	5.68
Price, Kevin	Princeton	TB	R+	21	4	0	0	1	5	34	9	14	4	1	0	0	1	5	0	6	2	0	0	0	.000	0	0	7.20
Price, Ryan	Salem	Col	A+	22	28	27	1	0	171.2	762	198	102	94	13	6	5	8	57	0	143	22	0	10	12	.455	0	0	4.93
Pridie, Jon	Elizabethtn	Min	R+	20	14	14	0	0	76.1	347	93	44	38	4	1	5	5	33	0	64	10	1	5	6	.455	0	0	4.48
Prinz, Bret	South Bend	Ari	A	23	30	23	0	3	138.2	594	129	82	69	16	5	7	8	52	0	98	10	4	6	10	.375	0	0	4.48
Proctor, Scott	Yakima	LA	A-	23	16	6	0	5	50	235	57	45	40	4	1	4	5	26	0	41	7	1	4	2	.667	0	0	7.20
Prokop, Michael	Capital Cty	NYM	A	22	37	0	0	23	40	189	51	21	17	1	2	1	5	17	1	33	5	0	5	2	.714	0	4	3.83
Pruett, Jason*	Hudson Val	TB	A-	21	25	0	0	5	40.2	166	32	13	9	1	6	1	1	8	0	29	1	1	4	2	.667	0	1	1.99
Pruitt, Jason*	Bluefield	Bal	R+	19	17	8	0	5	54	245	56	41	36	9	1	1	1	31	0	57	8	0	2	4	.333	0	1	6.00
Puffer, Brandon	Clinton	Cin	A	24	59	0	0	55	63.1	277	53	20	14	2	2	2	11	24	3	60	4	1	1	2	.333	0	34	1.99
Puga, Sergio	Mexico	—	R	—	13	3	1	9	30	141	33	23	20	4	0	0	6	12	0	20	1	3	1	1	.500	0	0	6.00
Pugmire, Rob	Columbus	Cle	A	21	10	10	0	0	57.2	229	43	20	17	4	1	1	2	14	0	71	1	1	6	1	.857	0	0	2.65
	Kinston	Cle	A+	21	16	16	0	0	96	396	85	44	39	8	4	1	8	25	0	89	3	0	7	1	.875	0	0	3.66
Purvis, Rob	White Sox	CWS	R	22	4	0	0	3	9	48	12	10	4	0	0	0	0	6	0	7	1	4	0	1	.000	0	2	4.00
	Burlington	CWS	A	22	6	0	0	3	11.1	50	10	5	3	1	0	0	1	4	0	8	0	1	0	0	.000	0	1	2.38
Putz, J.J	Everett	Sea	A-	23	10	0	0	3	22.1	99	23	13	12	2	1	1	2	11	1	17	0	1	0	0	.000	0	2	4.84
Queen, Mike*	Pittsfield	NYM	A-	22	15	15	0	0	77.1	322	68	33	28	5	0	4	5	24	0	69	3	3	5	3	.625	0	0	3.26
Quintal, Craig	Lakeland	Det	A+	25	26	16	2	4	109.2	490	129	74	59	10	3	3	10	27	3	45	2	0	1	11	.083	0	2	4.84
Rahrer, Josh	Rangers	Tex	R	19	15	0	0	4	33	143	29	18	16	5	0	1	1	12	0	16	1	0	4	4	.500	0	0	4.36
Rajotte, Jason*	Bakersfield	SF	A+	27	47	0	0	22	53.1	248	63	35	31	4	4	4	1	26	1	43	3	0	1	1	.500	0	2	5.23
Rakers, Aaron	Bluefield	Bal	R+	23	3	0	0	1	7	28	5	2	2	1	0	0	0	3	0	12	0	0	0	0	.000	0	0	2.57
	Delmarva	Bal	A	23	18	0	0	16	25.1	97	9	6	4	0	0	1	0	13	0	38	1	1	4	1	.800	0	8	1.42
Ramirez, Enrique	Orioles	Bal	R	20	9	0	0	9	11	46	9	3	3	0	0	0	1	3	0	7	0	0	0	0	.000	0	5	2.45
	Bluefield	Bal	R+	20	13	0	0	11	14.2	74	18	9	5	0	0	1	4	9	0	14	1	0	0	1	.000	0	1	3.07
Ramirez, Erasmo*	San Jose	SF	A+	24	31	0	0	12	57.1	219	42	18	17	2	2	4	1	8	0	52	2	0	2	0	1.000	0	5	2.67
Ramirez, Horacio*	Macon	Atl	A	20	17	14	1	0	77.2	316	70	30	23	6	2	5	2	25	0	43	1	1	6	3	.667	1	0	2.67
Ramirez, Santiago	Martinsvlle	Hou	R+	19	25	0	0	25	31	127	26	9	5	1	1	0	0	14	1	35	7	1	2	1	.667	0	17	1.45
Ramos, Fernando	Piedmont	Phi	A	24	38	0	0	25	68.2	286	61	31	22	12	3	1	1	19	1	73	4	0	3	6	.333	0	4	2.88
Ramos, Juan	Lancaster	Sea	A+	24	42	0	0	29	61.2	309	82	58	43	9	2	1	8	36	0	41	13	1	1	4	.200	0	1	6.28
Rangel, Tuli	Tampa	NYY	A+	24	12	9	0	1	55.1	225	48	23	18	1	1	2	2	17	1	36	4	0	3	3	.500	0	1	2.93
Rasmussen, Brent	Royals	KC	R	23	17	0	0	7	32	130	28	8	8	3	1	1	2	11	0	16	0	0	2	1	.667	0	0	2.25
Rauch, Jon	Bristol	CWS	R+	21	14	9	0	3	56.2	264	65	44	28	4	1	2	3	16	1	66	6	2	4	4	.500	0	2	4.45
	Winston-Sal	CWS	A+	21	1	1	0	0	6	26	4	3	2	1	0	0	0	3	0	7	1	0	0	0	.000	0	0	3.00
Rayborn, Kris*	Johnson Cy	StL	R+	20	13	13	0	0	65.1	301	79	54	42	2	2	3	8	33	0	34	11	2	1	7	.125	0	0	5.79
Reames, Britt	Potomac	StL	A+	26	10	8	0	0	36.2	163	34	21	13	2	2	1	3	21	0	22	4	0	3	2	.600	0	0	3.19
Redding, Tim	Michigan	Hou	A	22	43	11	0	24	105	470	84	69	58	4	6	5	3	76	1	141	19	2	8	6	.571	0	14	4.97
Regalado, Maximo	Vero Beach	LA	A+	23	20	19	1	0	90	429	110	65	58	16	5	3	12	49	0	58	7	0	2	12	.143	0	0	5.80
Regilio, Nick	Pulaski	Tex	R+	21	11	8	1	0	49.2	194	30	12	9	2	0	1	3	16	0	58	4	1	4	2	.667	1	0	1.63
Reid, Justin	Williamsprt	Pit	A-	23	16	11	0	4	62.1	277	71	41	32	4	0	3	3	23	0	68	0	4	2	6	.250	0	1	4.62
Reimers, Cameron	Medcine Hat	Tor	R+	21	13	5	0	3	44.1	184	39	21	16	2	1	3	2	12	0	29	7	3	1	5	.167	0	2	3.25
Reinike, Chris	Columbus	Cle	A	23	11	11	0	0	48	222	55	28	23	3	0	1	4	21	0	41	1	1	3	4	.429	0	0	4.31
Reisinger, Justin	Yankees	NYY	R	20	8	0	0	1	7.1	42	11	12	9	1	0	1	3	6	0	7	5	1	1	0	1.000	0	0	11.05
Reith, Brian	Tampa	NYY	A+	22	26	23	0	0	139.2	616	174	87	73	12	7	4	4	35	1	101	4	0	9	9	.500	0	0	4.70
Reitsma, Chris	Sarasota	Bos	A+	22	19	19	0	0	96.1	440	116	71	60	11	1	4	10	31	1	79	7	3	4	10	.286	0	0	5.61
Renovato, Nestor	Mexico	—	R	—	9	9	0	0	47	217	62	39	36	3	1	1	4	14	0	41	6	2	3	3	.500	0	0	6.89
Renwick, Tyler	St.Cathrnes	Tor	A-	21	16	5	0	6	39	182	35	28	23	2	1	2	1	33	0	32	10	0	2	4	.333	0	0	5.31
Reyes, Junior*	Cubs	ChC	R	18	7	0	0	2	10.2	69	24	24	23	6	0	0	1	13	0	5	0	0	0	1	.000	0	0	19.41
Reynolds, Jacob	Burlington	Cle	R+	20	3	3	0	0	10	52	13	14	10	1	0	0	1	8	0	7	2	0	0	2	.000	0	0	9.00
Rhea, Thad	Pirates	Pit	R	23	2	0	0	1	2.2	13	2	1	1	0	0	0	1	3	0	1	0	0	0	1	.000	0	0	3.38
Riccobono, Rick	Lowell	Bos	A-	20	15	14	0	0	77.1	368	93	63	45	4	3	5	11	30	0	54	9	0	4	6	.400	0	0	5.24
Rice, Nathan*	Bakersfield	SF	A+	26	3	0	0	1	4.1	36	11	14	11	1	0	0	1	10	0	3	1	0	0	0	.000	0	0	22.85
Rice, Scott*	Orioles	Bal	R	18	9	6	0	0	17.1	101	26	34	20	2	1	0	3	20	1	14	3	1	1	4	.200	0	0	10.38
Richards, Mark	Brevard Cty	Fla	A+	26	26	24	2	2	133.2	624	171	107	91	14	7	5	13	51	0	54	5	2	6	14	.300	0	2	6.13
Richardson, Jason	Twins	Min	R	20	12	10	0	0	49.1	211	46	21	13	2	2	1	9	23	1	54	3	0	1	2	.333	0	0	2.37
Richardson, Kasey*	Frederick	Bal	A+	23	38	0	0	15	61	277	63	38	36	7	6	2	6	32	5	44	4	0	5	2	.714	0	2	5.31
Ridenour, Ryan*	Greensboro	NYY	A	23	17	1	0	6	31	163	33	35	33	3	2	1	7	31	0	32	20	1	0	2	.000	0	0	9.58
	Staten Ilnd	NYY	A-	23	2	0	0	1	2	8	2	1	1	0	0	0	0	0	0	4	1	0	0	0	.000	0	0	4.50
	Yankees	NYY	R	23	3	1	0	0	8.2	36	5	5	2	0	0	1	0	5	0	13	0	2	0	0	.000	0	0	2.08
Riggan, Jerrod	St. Lucie	NYM	A+	26	44	0	0	26	73	305	69	33	27	4	6	1	5	24	5	66	4	0	5	5	.500	0	12	3.33
Rijo, Fernando	Yakima	LA	A-	22	18	4	0	10	57.1	271	63	57	49	14	0	5	9	31	0	39	9	0	1	4	.200	0	2	7.69

1999 Pitching — Single-A and Rookie Leagues

HOW MUCH HE PITCHED											WHAT HE GAVE UP												THE RESULTS					
Player	Team	Org	Lg	A	G	GS	CG	GF	IP	BFP	H	R	ER	HR	SH	SF	HB	TBB	IBB	SO	WP	Bk	W	L	Pct.	ShO	Sv	ERA
Rijo, Hector*	Expos	Mon	R	19	15	0	0	9	26.1	116	25	11	10	1	2	2	2	12	0	16	0	3	1	1	.500	0	3	3.42
Rincon, Jose	Helena	Mil	R+	20	15	15	3	0	108	425	79	36	32	5	1	0	1	28	0	87	6	3	10	2	.833	1	0	2.67
Rincon, Juan	Quad City	Min	A	21	28	28	0	0	163.1	683	146	67	53	8	1	3	2	66	3	153	11	0	14	8	.636	0	0	2.92
Riveles, Mike	Johnson Cy	StL	R+	22	4	0	0	1	7.1	40	12	10	4	1	0	0	0	4	0	4	1	0	0	0	.000	0	0	4.91
Rivera, Homero*	Oneonta	Det	A-	21	23	0	0	8	49.2	218	44	19	15	3	6	4	4	22	3	47	5	1	5	2	.714	0	0	2.72
Rivera, Leyson	Burlington	Cle	R+	19	17	0	0	10	23.1	126	29	30	20	5	2	0	1	19	0	25	6	0	0	1	.000	0	0	7.71
Rivera, Luis	Myrtle Bch	Atl	A+	22	25	13	0	2	66.2	262	45	25	23	3	2	1	1	23	0	81	7	0	0	2	.000	0	0	3.11
Rivera, Samuel	Tigers	Det	R	20	7	1	0	1	15.1	66	9	6	4	1	0	0	1	11	0	19	4	0	1	0	1.000	0	1	2.35
Rivera, Saul	Quad City	Min	A	22	60	0	0	54	69.2	283	42	12	11	0	2	0	0	36	5	102	2	0	4	1	.800	0	23	1.42
Riviere, Rhett	Elizabethtn	Min	R+	20	7	0	0	2	8	37	7	3	2	0	0	1	0	4	0	6	0	0	1	0	1.000	0	0	2.25
Rizo, Miguel	Johnson Cy	StL	R+	20	20	0	0	4	31.1	133	26	12	11	2	0	0	1	14	1	22	5	0	2	3	.400	0	1	3.16
Roberts, Mike	Wilmington	KC	A+	24	9	0	0	6	10.1	42	10	2	2	1	1	0	0	1	0	6	0	0	0	0	.000	0	1	1.74
Roberts, Nick	Martinsvlle	Hou	R+	23	10	7	1	1	47.1	188	43	11	10	0	1	0	1	6	0	56	2	3	4	2	.667	0	1	1.90
Roberts, Phil	Mahoning Vy	Cle	A-	23	3	0	0	1	4.1	25	6	5	3	0	0	0	1	4	0	4	0	0	0	0	.000	0	0	6.23
Roberts, Rick*	W Michigan	Det	A	21	1	1	0	0	3	16	5	5	4	1	0	1	0	2	0	1	1	0	0	0	.000	0	0	12.00
	Vero Beach	LA	A+	21	11	10	0	1	44.2	208	54	35	30	7	3	2	2	25	0	29	6	0	1	4	.200	0	0	6.04
	Yakima	LA	A-	21	11	6	0	1	34.2	176	52	34	28	5	0	3	0	23	0	26	4	1	1	3	.250	0	0	7.27
Robertson, Nate*	Utica	Fla	A-	22	5	5	0	0	26	101	22	9	8	0	1	2	0	8	0	26	0	0	2	0	1.000	0	0	2.77
	Kane County	Fla	A	22	8	8	1	0	51	197	42	14	13	1	0	2	0	12	0	33	0	0	6	1	.857	1	0	2.29
Robinson, Dustin	Clinton	Cin	A	24	44	1	0	11	70	312	67	51	37	8	7	6	4	29	3	53	4	0	3	6	.333	0	0	4.76
Robinson, Jeff	Ogden	Mil	R+	23	9	8	2	1	54.2	223	45	25	18	3	1	0	4	16	0	51	5	0	5	2	.714	1	0	2.96
	Helena	Mil	R+	23	1	1	0	0	7	31	4	4	1	0	0	0	1	3	0	14	1	0	0	0	.000	0	0	1.29
Robinson, Jeremy*	Chston-SC	TB	A	22	29	16	0	3	116.1	499	144	59	57	9	5	2	6	29	2	67	2	1	5	8	.385	0	0	4.41
Rochez, Angel	Pulaski	Tex	R+	21	18	3	0	4	39.1	191	54	40	33	8	1	2	2	20	0	29	1	0	2	1	.667	0	3	7.55
Rodgers, Marcus	Burlington	CWS	A	23	4	0	0	2	2.2	22	10	10	10	2	0	1	1	3	0	5	1	0	0	0	.000	0	0	33.75
Rodney, Fernando	Tigers	Det	R	19	22	0	0	20	30	129	20	8	8	1	3	2	3	21	0	39	1	1	3	3	.500	0	9	2.40
	Lakeland	Det	A+	19	4	0	0	4	6.1	25	7	1	1	0	0	0	1	1	0	5	0	0	1	0	1.000	0	2	1.42
Rodriguez, Alej.	Phillies	Phi	R	19	5	5	0	0	24	101	24	9	7	2	1	0	1	8	0	22	3	2	1	1	.500	0	0	2.63
Rodriguez, Alfredo	Rangers	Tex	R	22	9	0	0	6	12.1	55	14	6	3	0	0	0	1	1	0	8	0	0	0	1	.000	0	3	2.19
	Pulaski	Tex	R+	22	6	0	0	2	8.1	44	13	10	9	2	0	1	2	5	0	5	0	2	0	1	.000	0	0	9.72
Rodriguez, Anthony	Staten Ilnd	NYY	A-	21	13	0	0	5	18.1	89	24	15	14	1	0	2	0	13	0	19	8	0	1	0	1.000	0	0	6.87
Rodriguez, Cris.	Cape Fear	Mon	A	21	26	25	0	1	121	525	100	68	56	12	2	4	7	65	0	128	12	3	5	8	.385	0	0	4.17
Rodriguez, Fran.	Butte	Ana	R+	18	12	9	1	0	51.2	211	33	21	19	1	3	0	3	21	1	69	10	3	1	1	.500	0	0	3.31
	Boise	Ana	A-	18	1	1	0	0	5	22	3	4	3	0	0	1	0	1	0	6	0	0	1	0	1.000	0	0	5.40
Rodriguez, Jose	Chston-SC	TB	A	22	7	0	0	4	12.1	67	20	15	9	1	2	1	0	7	0	11	3	0	0	1	.000	0	1	6.57
Rodriguez, Jose	Braves	Atl	R	18	16	6	0	5	42.1	180	33	22	17	2	0	0	0	21	0	38	3	2	1	2	.333	0	1	3.61
Rodriguez, Luis	Pulaski	Tex	R+	18	1	0	0	1	1	4	2	0	0	0	0	0	0	0	0	1	0	0	0	0	.000	0	0	0.00
	Rangers	Tex	R	18	17	5	1	3	49.1	217	46	24	19	2	1	2	6	18	0	26	7	1	4	2	.667	1	1	3.47
Rodriguez, Wil.*	Kissimmee	Hou	A+	21	25	24	0	1	153.1	624	108	55	49	8	2	5	13	62	0	148	5	1	15	7	.682	0	0	2.88
Rogers, Brad	Orioles	Bal	R	18	6	0	0	2	10.2	46	11	3	2	0	0	3	1	3	1	8	2	1	1	1	.500	0	0	1.69
Rogers, Brian	Tampa	NYY	A+	23	25	23	1	0	134	577	141	62	57	13	2	1	2	43	1	129	7	0	8	10	.444	1	0	3.83
Rogers, Devin	Burlington	Cle	R+	21	8	6	0	1	20.1	99	26	23	17	0	0	2	0	15	0	21	6	3	0	2	.000	0	0	7.52
Rogers, Lionel	Kingsport	NYM	R+	22	14	0	0	11	29.1	121	17	7	6	1	2	1	1	17	2	34	5	0	3	1	.750	0	2	1.84
Rohling, Stuart	Bristol	CWS	R+	22	16	1	0	5	32.2	147	34	19	16	3	1	0	2	17	0	44	5	0	0	2	.000	0	1	4.41
Rojas, Chris	Williamsprt	Pit	A-	23	15	15	1	0	81.1	374	72	57	44	4	1	3	11	43	0	85	10	1	5	7	.417	1	0	4.87
Roller, Adam	Sarasota	Bos	A+	22	1	0	0	0	2.2	14	5	5	5	1	0	0	0	2	0	2	0	0	0	0	.000	0	0	16.88
	Lowell	Bos	A-	22	23	0	0	23	39	186	30	16	11	1	3	2	9	29	2	41	7	1	4	5	.444	0	2	2.54
Roman, Orlando	Mets	NYM	R	21	12	11	1	1	61	254	41	20	16	0	0	4	5	21	0	64	3	0	6	0	1.000	1	0	2.36
Romero, Jordan	Delmarva	Bal	A	23	24	9	0	11	76	359	87	55	40	10	6	3	6	38	0	61	11	1	3	7	.300	0	2	4.74
	Frederick	Bal	A+	23	9	0	0	2	15.1	70	11	9	5	1	1	0	1	13	1	11	2	0	0	0	.000	0	0	2.93
	Kinston	Cle	A+	23	1	0	0	1	1	5	1	1	1	0	0	0	0	1	0	2	0	0	0	0	.000	0	0	9.00
Romero, Josmir	Twins	Min	R	19	11	11	3	0	67	267	61	33	24	5	1	4	1	7	1	40	0	5	5	3	.625	1	0	3.22
Romo, Eduardo	Mexico	—	R	—	12	3	0	1	29	152	46	35	26	0	0	1	3	17	0	17	1	0	0	5	.000	0	0	8.07
Roque, Darryl	Expos	Mon	R	23	1	0	0	0	0.2	4	1	0	0	0	0	0	1	0	0	0	0	0	1	0	1.000	0	0	0.00
	Vermont	Mon	A-	23	12	7	0	0	44.2	191	44	27	23	4	1	3	9	12	0	37	1	0	2	3	.400	0	0	4.63
Rosa, Cristy	Salem	Col	A+	22	8	2	0	3	21.2	99	27	13	7	0	0	1	1	7	0	12	3	0	1	1	.500	0	0	2.91
	Asheville	Col	A	22	7	4	0	2	22.1	105	26	21	16	5	1	1	4	9	0	11	3	0	0	2	.000	0	1	6.45
Rosado, Juan*	Beloit	Mil	A	25	8	0	0	3	10	54	11	12	11	1	0	0	1	14	0	4	2	0	0	0	.000	0	0	9.90
	Savannah	Tex	A	25	20	0	0	12	33.1	161	35	29	18	2	2	3	2	23	0	35	2	0	0	1	.000	0	4	4.86
Rosario, Hipolito	Idaho Falls	SD	R+	20	2	0	0	1	4	17	3	2	2	0	0	0	0	2	0	2	1	0	0	0	.000	0	0	4.50
	Padres	SD	R	20	16	0	0	9	25.2	137	47	34	28	4	0	0	4	13	0	16	1	4	0	1	.000	0	1	9.82
Rosario, Juan	St. Pete	TB	A+	24	15	15	0	0	94.1	391	80	34	28	2	5	3	11	25	0	37	2	1	5	3	.625	0	0	2.67
Rosario, Rodrigo	Martinsvlle	Hou	R+	20	14	14	0	0	78.2	345	78	46	41	9	7	3	11	32	0	86	7	0	5	5	.500	0	0	4.69
Rose, Brian	Sarasota	Bos	A+	27	5	0	0	2	7.1	36	10	5	5	0	0	0	0	5	0	9	2	0	1	0	1.000	0	1	6.14
	Clinton	Cin	A	27	24	1	0	4	32.2	129	27	2	2	1	3	0	1	11	1	24	0	0	7	0	1.000	0	0	0.55
	Rockford	Cin	A	27	24	0	0	22	34.2	154	38	22	20	6	0	1	2	12	2	40	3	0	4	2	.667	0	6	5.19
Rose, Johnathan*	Phillies	Phi	R	23	5	2	0	0	18	74	15	5	5	1	3	0	0	7	0	17	1	0	2	1	.667	0	0	2.50
	Piedmont	Phi	A	23	21	1	0	12	30	147	40	24	21	5	1	1	1	17	1	34	5	0	0	5	.000	0	1	6.30
	Clearwater	Phi	A+	23	8	0	0	0	9.1	44	12	7	7	3	0	0	0	6	0	7	1	0	0	1	.000	0	0	6.75
Rosengren, Phil	Mahoning Vy	Cle	A-	23	11	9	0	1	49.2	215	40	30	28	4	0	1	1	24	0	41	1	0	2	3	.400	0	0	5.07
Ross, Lew*	Missoula	Ari	R+	22	20	0	0	10	38.2	160	27	21	12	1	3	1	2	13	0	50	4	1	4	3	.571	0	4	2.79
Roundtree, Monte*	Reds	Cin	R	22	7	3	0	1	22.1	96	16	8	6	0	0	0	2	11	0	19	5	0	1	1	.500	0	0	2.42
Rowe, Casey	Oneonta	Det	A-	21	15	15	1	0	76	330	76	42	29	6	2	3	1	30	0	50	5	9	3	4	.429	1	0	3.43
Royer, Jason	South Bend	Ari	A	21	32	18	0	6	119	531	135	77	62	6	2	1	6	43	0	62	8	1	7	7	.500	0	1	4.69
Rubio, Miguel	Diamondbcks	Ari	R	20	2	2	0	0	3	15	6	2	2	0	0	0	0	3	0	3	0	0	0	1	.000	0	0	6.00
	High Desert	Ari	A+	20	27	11	0	7	77.2	368	96	61	53	8	4	5	8	33	0	53	5	0	2	5	.286	0	1	6.14
Ruhl, Nathan	Chston-SC	TB	A	23	36	0	0	13	55.1	234	31	20	18	3	2	3	1	34	1	82	9	1	4	4	.500	0	2	2.93
	St. Pete	TB	A+	23	4	0	0	4	7	32	9	2	2	0	0	0	1	3	0	5	0	0	2	0	1.000	0	0	2.57

1999 Pitching — Single-A and Rookie Leagues

HOW MUCH HE PITCHED											WHAT HE GAVE UP												THE RESULTS					
Player	Team	Org	Lg	A	G	GS	CG	GF	IP	BFP	H	R	ER	HR	SH	SF	HB	TBB	IBB	SO	WP	Bk	W	L	Pct.	ShO	Sv	ERA
Ruiz, Juan	Mexico	—	R	21	1	1	0	0	4	17	5	1	1	0	0	0	0	1	0	3	0	0	0	0	.000	0	0	2.25
Rundles, Richard*	Red Sox	Bos	R	19	5	1	0	0	12.2	53	13	3	3	1	0	1	0	1	0	11	2	0	1	0	1.000	0	0	2.13
Rupp, Mike	Lowell	Bos	A-	22	18	8	0	1	57.1	275	72	46	37	2	0	4	3	33	2	48	4	1	1	5	.167	0	0	5.81
Russo, Dennis	Reds	Cin	R	20	2	2	0	0	4	19	6	3	2	0	0	0	0	2	0	1	1	1	0	0	.000	0	0	4.50
Russo, Mike	Chstn-WV	KC	A	22	10	0	0	5	10.1	60	18	18	16	1	0	2	1	10	1	10	4	0	0	2	.000	0	0	13.94
	Spokane	KC	A-	22	21	1	0	4	41.2	190	39	19	16	4	0	3	6	23	1	29	2	0	1	2	.333	0	0	3.46
Ryba, Jason	Bluefield	Bal	R+	21	18	3	0	2	47	225	55	40	31	5	2	0	3	23	0	42	5	0	1	3	.250	0	0	5.94
Sabathia, C.C.*	Mahoning Vy	Cle	A-	19	6	6	0	0	19.2	77	9	5	4	0	0	2	0	12	0	27	0	0	0	0	.000	0	0	1.83
	Columbus	Cle	A	19	3	3	0	0	16.2	64	8	2	2	1	1	0	1	5	0	20	1	0	2	0	1.000	0	0	1.08
	Kinston	Cle	A+	19	7	7	0	0	32	143	30	22	19	3	3	3	1	19	0	29	6	0	3	3	.500	0	0	5.34
Sabens, Mike	Williamsprt	Pit	A-	23	5	0	0	1	6.2	39	8	8	8	1	1	2	2	9	1	6	1	1	1	1	.500	0	0	10.80
	Pirates	Pit	R	23	7	0	0	5	8	35	6	4	3	0	1	0	1	4	0	3	0	0	0	1	.000	0	0	3.38
Sabino, Miguel	Salem-Keizr	SF	A-	21	10	6	0	0	43.1	193	48	35	31	5	1	0	3	18	1	29	3	0	1	2	.333	0	0	6.44
Sadler, Carl*	Burlington	Cle	R+	23	5	5	0	0	23	93	18	10	8	0	1	0	0	10	0	22	5	0	1	0	1.000	0	0	3.13
	Mahoning Vy	Cle	A-	23	1	1	0	0	2	17	8	7	7	0	0	0	0	3	0	3	1	0	0	1	.000	0	0	31.50
Saenz, Jason*	Capital Cty	NYM	A	23	27	27	0	0	134	617	147	80	81	16	0	5	18	68	0	125	16	2	10	8	.556	0	0	5.44
St. Amand, Reuben	Medcine Hat	Tor	R+	20	15	0	0	4	28	133	31	23	19	5	0	2	1	17	0	24	4	1	0	1	.000	0	0	6.11
Saladin, Miguel	Auburn	Hou	A-	22	8	0	0	3	17.2	92	23	19	14	1	2	0	7	7	0	10	1	2	1	4	.200	0	0	7.13
	Martinsvlle	Hou	R+	22	11	0	0	4	16	79	24	12	9	1	0	0	4	4	0	19	0	1	1	0	1.000	0	1	5.06
Salazar, Luis	Marlins	Fla	R	21	14	0	0	7	32.1	148	26	14	12	0	3	1	1	23	1	27	6	1	5	3	.625	0	1	3.34
Salmon, Brad	Billings	Cin	R+	20	16	6	0	2	49.1	239	67	46	41	2	2	4	6	19	1	43	2	3	2	2	.500	0	1	7.48
Samadani, Ali	Jamestown	Atl	A-	24	22	0	0	5	40.1	178	41	28	24	6	0	3	0	17	0	37	6	1	3	1	.750	0	1	5.36
Samora, Santo	Johnson Cy	StL	R+	20	18	2	0	4	32.2	133	26	12	9	2	1	0	1	11	0	17	2	1	2	0	1.000	0	1	2.48
Sams, Aaron*	Lansing	ChC	A	24	17	17	0	0	96.1	428	99	57	50	6	1	4	3	52	0	83	12	0	6	4	.600	0	0	4.67
	Daytona	ChC	A+	24	10	10	1	0	55	239	53	31	29	4	0	1	4	26	0	41	5	1	2	5	.286	0	0	4.75
Sanches, Brian	Spokane	KC	A-	21	9	9	0	0	34	146	32	19	18	2	0	0	1	12	0	51	0	0	1	1	.500	0	0	4.76
Sanchez, Cade	Sou Oregon	Oak	A-	23	9	0	0	4	21.1	103	20	15	9	0	0	3	0	21	0	15	4	1	0	1	.000	0	0	3.80
Sanchez, Duaner	High Desert	Ari	A+	20	3	3	0	0	14.1	63	15	13	12	2	0	1	1	9	0	9	0	0	0	0	.000	0	0	7.53
	Missoula	Ari	R+	20	13	11	0	0	63.1	269	54	34	22	3	1	1	3	23	0	51	8	0	5	3	.625	0	0	3.13
Sanchez, Simon	High Desert	Ari	A+	22	40	1	0	26	71.2	330	79	45	42	8	3	3	8	31	3	53	4	0	3	5	.375	0	7	5.27
Sanchez, Sinuhe*	Butte	Ana	R+	22	27	0	0	5	36.1	171	52	36	24	5	3	5	3	11	1	33	5	0	3	3	.500	0	2	5.94
Sanchez, Willmen*	Burlington	Cle	R+	21	10	0	0	2	22.1	93	26	8	8	4	1	0	2	3	0	26	0	1	0	1	.000	0	1	3.22
	Columbus	Cle	A	21	13	0	0	5	22.1	108	29	23	16	4	0	2	1	10	0	10	5	0	1	1	.500	0	1	6.45
Sanders, David*	White Sox	CWS	R	20	7	1	0	2	16.1	66	12	3	2	0	1	0	1	6	3	26	1	0	1	0	1.000	0	1	1.10
Sandoval, Marcos	Hagerstown	Tor	A	19	27	10	0	5	83	368	89	47	42	6	2	1	15	32	0	53	8	1	4	3	.571	0	4	4.55
Sansom, Trevor	New Jersey	StL	A-	24	20	0	0	7	23.1	121	34	28	20	3	1	1	1	16	2	18	4	0	1	3	.250	0	0	7.71
Santana, Hum.*	Mets	NYM	R	23	2	0	0	1	3	9	0	0	0	0	0	0	0	0	0	2	0	0	1	0	1.000	0	0	0.00
	Pittsfield	NYM	A-	23	4	0	0	1	9.1	38	7	2	0	1	0	0	0	2	1	12	0	0	1	0	1.000	0	0	0.00
	Capital Cty	NYM	A	23	10	2	0	1	25	101	19	12	9	2	0	1	0	4	0	19	3	0	3	1	.750	0	1	3.24
Santana, Johan*	Michigan	Hou	A	21	27	26	1	0	160.1	688	162	94	83	14	1	6	10	55	0	150	10	1	8	8	.500	0	0	4.66
Santos, Josh*	San Jose	SF	A+	23	13	13	1	0	66.2	308	75	47	32	6	2	4	8	29	0	47	2	0	3	6	.333	0	0	4.32
Satterfield, Jeremy	Jamestown	Atl	A-	24	23	0	0	13	33.2	148	25	17	16	0	2	4	4	22	0	36	7	0	2	2	.500	0	1	4.28
Satterfield, Troy*	Williamsprt	Pit	A-	23	17	0	0	5	37	150	33	11	7	1	3	0	1	11	2	28	0	0	2	1	.667	0	0	1.70
Sauer, Marc	Marlins	Fla	R	20	13	13	1	0	69.2	284	75	28	21	2	2	0	0	7	1	57	0	0	5	4	.556	1	0	2.71
Sawyell, Matt*	Mets	NYM	R	23	8	0	0	1	10	49	14	7	7	1	0	0	0	4	0	13	1	0	0	0	.000	0	0	6.30
Schmidt, Donnie	Wisconsin	Sea	A	25	5	0	0	0	8	39	5	6	4	0	2	0	1	9	1	8	1	1	0	1	.000	0	0	4.50
	Lancaster	Sea	A+	25	21	0	0	8	36	178	46	20	14	1	0	4	3	25	0	21	4	1	1	2	.333	0	0	3.50
Schmidt, Pat*	Danville	Atl	R+	21	13	0	0	6	17	96	9	11	9	0	2	3	2	37	0	16	7	0	0	1	.000	0	0	4.76
Schoening, Brent	Quad City	Min	A	22	6	1	0	1	11	45	7	3	3	1	0	0	0	5	0	11	1	1	0	1	.000	0	1	2.45
Schreyer, Brett	Butte	Ana	R+	23	10	0	0	7	10.2	48	9	3	3	0	0	0	0	9	0	6	4	0	0	0	.000	0	0	2.53
	Boise	Ana	A-	23	9	0	0	4	8.1	40	6	5	1	0	0	0	1	7	0	8	0	0	0	0	.000	0	2	1.08
Schubmehl, Brian	Stockton	Mil	A+	25	43	1	0	18	77.1	360	81	52	35	4	7	2	3	47	3	71	5	1	6	6	.500	0	9	4.07
Schuldt, Matt	St. Pete	TB	A+	24	19	2	0	7	31.2	147	36	19	17	5	1	1	3	16	0	23	5	1	2	0	1.000	0	0	4.83
	Chston-SC	TB	A	24	26	1	0	15	33	149	31	24	18	2	2	3	1	20	0	26	3	0	1	4	.200	0	1	4.91
Schultz, Eric	Charlotte	Tex	A+	25	19	1	0	4	45.1	196	56	30	27	3	4	1	2	9	0	44	4	1	2	2	.500	0	1	5.36
Schultz, Jeff	Modesto	Oak	A+	24	23	11	0	4	82.2	388	90	58	50	5	5	2	5	49	0	63	7	0	2	9	.182	0	3	5.44
Schurman, Ryan	Clinton	Cin	A	23	44	3	0	15	86.1	380	74	41	34	8	6	2	7	50	6	83	7	2	3	3	.500	0	2	3.54
Schwager, Matthew	Delmarva	Bal	A	22	10	0	0	2	21.1	99	32	15	13	2	0	0	0	6	0	20	1	1	0	1	.000	0	0	5.48
	Bluefield	Bal	R+	22	22	0	0	21	30	127	31	19	12	2	0	1	1	5	0	29	2	0	3	1	.750	0	7	3.60
Sclafani, Anthony	Braves	Atl	R	18	17	0	0	15	28	111	21	9	8	1	1	0	1	9	0	22	0	0	3	2	.600	0	0	2.57
Scott, Brian	Winston-Sal	CWS	A+	24	25	25	1	0	147.2	637	135	75	56	7	7	3	5	60	3	132	17	0	8	8	.500	0	0	3.41
Scuglik, Mike*	Pulaski	Tex	R+	23	18	0	0	8	29	129	36	15	10	2	0	1	2	10	2	36	1	0	2	2	.500	0	3	3.10
Seabury, Jaron	Dunedin	Tor	A+	24	35	0	0	18	53.2	231	59	33	32	1	3	0	3	19	1	34	5	0	4	3	.571	0	3	5.37
Seale, Dustin*	St.Cathrnes	Tor	A-	22	3	0	0	2	3.1	16	2	1	1	0	2	0	0	2	1	4	1	0	0	1	.000	0	0	2.70
	Cape Fear	Mon	A	22	3	0	0	3	5	19	3	1	1	0	0	1	0	1	0	4	0	0	1	0	1.000	0	0	1.80
	Vermont	Mon	A-	22	14	0	0	7	20.1	85	13	1	1	0	0	0	0	13	2	16	5	3	2	1	.667	0	2	0.44
Seaman, John	Brevard Cty	Fla	A+	23	25	0	0	7	54.2	238	47	32	27	3	2	2	5	27	1	47	7	0	5	2	.714	0	0	4.45
	Kane County	Fla	A	23	13	0	0	6	21	95	27	15	13	1	1	1	2	4	0	12	4	1	1	2	.333	0	0	5.57
Searles, Jon	Pirates	Pit	R	19	8	0	0	1	13	65	14	10	6	1	0	2	1	9	0	9	3	0	1	0	1.000	0	0	4.15
Seaver, Mark	Modesto	Oak	A+	25	31	17	0	6	134	606	158	85	64	10	3	3	8	57	2	112	7	0	12	4	.750	0	2	4.30
Seberino, Ronni*	Chston-SC	TB	A	21	50	0	0	11	74.2	315	57	29	22	5	0	4	1	38	3	73	10	1	6	2	.750	0	0	2.65
Sedlacek, Shawn	Wilmington	KC	A+	23	17	17	1	0	92	411	111	61	54	7	6	3	6	26	0	69	4	0	4	6	.400	0	0	5.28
Sents, Marcus	Elizabethtn	Min	R+	19	13	13	0	0	63	295	56	48	43	8	1	1	7	48	0	60	15	1	5	1	.833	0	0	6.14
Seo, Jae	St. Lucie	NYM	A+	23	3	3	0	0	14.2	55	8	3	3	0	0	1	0	2	0	14	0	0	2	0	1.000	0	0	1.84
Seo, Jung	Red Sox	Bos	R	26	13	0	0	6	32	137	29	14	10	2	1	1	3	10	1	26	4	0	3	2	.600	0	1	2.81
Sequea, Jacobo	Reds	Cin	R	18	1	1	0	0	2	7	2	1	1	0	0	0	0	0	0	3	0	0	0	0	.000	0	0	4.50
	Rockford	Cin	A	18	16	16	2	0	89.2	393	88	52	49	6	2	5	7	44	0	67	9	6	4	6	.400	1	0	4.92
	Delmarva	Bal	A	18	6	6	0	0	30	134	35	19	13	4	1	0	2	16	0	25	3	3	0	2	.000	0	0	3.90

1999 Pitching — Single-A and Rookie Leagues

HOW MUCH HE PITCHED											WHAT HE GAVE UP												THE RESULTS					
Player	Team	Org	Lg	A	G	GS	CG	GF	IP	BFP	H	R	ER	HR	SH	SF	HB	TBB	IBB	SO	WP	Bk	W	L	Pct.	ShO	Sv	ERA
Sergent, Joe*	Utica	Fla	A-	21	10	0	0	1	19.1	74	9	4	3	2	0	0	0	7	1	23	0	0	0	0	.000	0	1	1.40
	Kane County	Fla	A	21	8	0	0	2	12.2	59	17	10	10	1	1	1	1	4	1	9	0	0	2	1	.667	0	0	7.11
Serrano, Alex	Rockies	Col	R	19	18	0	0	13	30	126	21	10	4	1	3	0	1	14	0	23	5	0	3	2	.600	0	5	1.20
Serrano, Elio	Batavia	Phi	A-	21	19	3	0	2	39.1	176	38	22	18	3	0	2	3	20	1	29	2	0	0	4	.000	0	1	4.12
Serrano, Jim	Jupiter	Mon	A+	24	44	1	0	24	93	365	59	25	22	4	2	5	7	27	4	118	8	0	8	5	.615	0	8	2.13
Serrano, Willy	Tigers	Det	R	19	6	5	0	0	25.1	113	30	19	18	4	0	0	0	13	0	14	2	0	0	3	.000	0	0	6.39
Sessions, Doug	Michigan	Hou	A	23	12	0	0	12	13	44	6	1	1	1	1	0	1	1	0	18	0	0	0	0	.000	0	5	0.69
	Kissimmee	Hou	A+	23	35	0	0	27	45.2	183	35	11	10	1	1	0	1	14	1	55	2	0	3	0	1.000	0	13	1.97
Shaffar, Ben	Eugene	ChC	A-	22	14	13	0	0	65.1	311	79	54	42	5	0	1	9	27	1	76	6	5	4	5	.444	0	0	5.79
Shearn, Tom	Kissimmee	Hou	A+	22	24	24	0	0	145.1	624	144	75	63	11	5	5	4	53	2	107	15	1	10	6	.625	0	0	3.90
Sheets, Ben	Ogden	Mil	R+	21	2	2	0	0	8	33	8	5	5	2	0	0	1	2	0	12	0	0	0	1	.000	0	0	5.63
	Stockton	Mil	A+	21	5	5	0	0	27.2	115	23	11	11	1	0	1	1	14	0	28	1	0	1	0	1.000	0	0	3.58
Sheets, Matt	Elizabethtn	Min	R+	22	12	12	0	0	62	276	69	40	33	4	2	1	7	20	0	55	7	0	3	3	.500	0	0	4.79
Sheldon, Kyle	Cape Fear	Mon	A	23	26	0	0	23	44	175	39	13	10	3	3	0	1	10	2	30	2	0	5	1	.833	0	9	2.05
	Jupiter	Mon	A+	23	20	0	0	12	29.2	133	37	13	11	2	0	2	3	7	1	22	0	0	1	1	.500	0	1	3.34
Shepherd, Alvie	Bluefield	Bal	R+	26	2	2	0	0	9	44	11	8	4	0	0	0	1	4	0	7	3	0	1	1	.500	0	0	4.00
	Frederick	Bal	A+	26	3	2	0	0	5.1	33	7	7	7	2	0	0	0	10	0	6	1	0	0	2	.000	0	0	11.81
	Lk Elsinore	Ana	A+	26	5	0	0	2	5.2	32	11	11	10	2	0	0	2	3	0	6	2	0	0	0	.000	0	0	15.88
	Cedar Rapds	Ana	A	26	6	0	0	3	7.2	36	4	5	4	0	0	2	0	8	0	5	0	0	0	0	.000	0	0	4.70
Sheredy, Kevin	Potomac	StL	A+	25	41	12	0	12	104	462	100	58	46	6	3	6	6	53	1	69	13	0	5	5	.500	0	0	3.98
Shibilo, Andy	Peoria	StL	A	23	27	24	2	0	135.2	621	157	105	77	10	3	8	14	41	0	96	6	2	4	13	.235	0	0	5.11
Shields, Drew	Kane County	Fla	A	21	14	0	0	2	23	110	30	14	14	3	0	0	3	9	0	20	2	0	1	0	1.000	0	0	5.48
	Utica	Fla	A-	21	13	2	0	3	24.1	126	30	28	23	2	3	0	6	17	1	33	5	0	2	3	.400	0	0	8.51
Shiell, Jason	Myrtle Bch	Atl	A+	23	26	17	0	1	114.2	485	118	51	48	5	4	2	3	36	0	90	9	0	6	7	.462	0	0	3.77
Shipp, Kevin	Clearwater	Phi	A+	25	32	7	0	2	83.1	374	108	56	51	5	4	1	3	22	1	54	3	2	7	4	.636	0	0	5.51
Shiyuk, Todd*	Idaho Falls	SD	R+	23	23	0	0	10	39.2	184	46	30	25	5	2	1	5	17	1	49	2	1	5	0	1.000	0	4	5.67
Siciliano, Jess	Hickory	Pit	A	23	6	0	0	3	5.2	35	11	8	6	0	0	0	2	6	0	4	2	0	0	2	.000	0	0	9.53
Sido, Wilson	Kinston	Cle	A+	24	9	7	0	0	36.1	163	33	26	24	4	1	1	5	22	1	22	6	0	1	2	.333	0	0	5.94
	Columbus	Cle	A	24	13	12	0	0	49	232	63	43	40	5	2	2	3	23	0	51	4	3	3	7	.300	0	0	7.35
Silva, Carlos	Piedmont	Phi	A	21	26	26	3	0	164.1	708	176	79	57	6	8	6	9	41	2	99	8	2	11	8	.579	1	0	3.12
Silva, Doug	Savannah	Tex	A	20	7	0	0	4	17.2	72	15	5	4	2	0	0	0	3	0	18	1	0	0	1	.000	0	1	2.04
	Charlotte	Tex	A+	20	24	12	0	6	94.2	404	103	58	41	8	2	2	1	25	1	55	5	1	4	4	.500	0	0	3.90
Silverio, Carlos	Phillies	Phi	R	21	5	1	0	2	9.2	46	12	6	6	1	0	0	0	5	0	8	1	0	1	0	1.000	0	0	5.59
Silverio, Marcelino	Idaho Falls	SD	R+	21	23	0	0	5	46.1	199	47	38	35	4	1	1	1	20	1	41	5	0	7	3	.700	0	0	6.80
Silverthorn, Will*	Princeton	TB	R+	21	7	0	0	4	9.2	52	16	10	2	0	0	0	1	7	0	9	5	0	0	0	.000	0	0	1.86
Simon, Ben	Vero Beach	LA	A+	25	38	5	0	12	88.2	382	79	44	34	5	4	2	10	29	2	89	7	1	7	4	.636	0	2	3.45
Simonson, Chris	Helena	Mil	R+	23	6	6	0	0	37	160	34	21	8	2	0	0	3	8	0	29	0	0	3	0	1.000	0	0	1.95
	Stockton	Mil	A+	23	15	1	0	6	31.1	136	31	13	11	0	2	1	1	12	2	31	0	1	2	1	.667	0	2	3.16
Simontacchi, Jason	Hickory	Pit	A	26	23	7	0	8	69.1	297	71	34	31	8	2	1	6	19	1	66	5	3	4	6	.400	0	1	4.02
Simpson, Allan	Wisconsin	Sea	A	22	24	13	1	3	90.1	402	83	56	44	4	4	8	3	48	0	88	4	1	2	9	.182	0	0	4.38
	Lancaster	Sea	A+	22	9	0	0	0	21.1	96	17	16	15	4	0	2	2	14	0	25	2	1	0	0	.000	0	0	6.33
Simpson, Andre	Bristol	CWS	R+	19	13	13	1	0	72	297	69	33	24	2	2	3	1	22	0	79	6	0	7	1	.875	0	0	3.00
Simpson, Cory	Macon	Atl	A	22	14	9	0	0	50.2	229	37	37	34	4	2	5	2	44	0	40	3	1	3	5	.375	0	0	6.04
Simpson, Joe	Rockies	Col	R	21	14	3	0	0	35.1	166	39	28	24	0	0	4	1	31	0	21	8	2	1	3	.250	0	0	6.11
Sims, Ken	Frederick	Bal	A+	24	35	1	0	11	69	312	83	38	32	7	3	1	4	19	3	41	1	0	4	4	.500	0	2	4.17
Sirianni, Jay*	Burlington	Cle	R+	24	11	10	1	0	56	245	62	36	28	6	2	1	3	12	0	66	3	0	1	5	.167	0	0	4.50
	Mahoning Vy	Cle	A-	24	3	2	1	0	13.1	56	15	6	4	1	1	0	0	4	0	16	0	0	2	0	1.000	1	0	2.70
Sismondo, Bobby*	W Michigan	Det	A	23	27	27	1	0	169.1	708	153	86	69	12	4	5	7	62	2	135	8	1	9	12	.429	1	0	3.67
Smith, Brandon	Michigan	Hou	A	24	18	0	0	10	24.1	117	25	19	18	2	0	1	1	20	1	19	5	0	1	2	.333	0	0	6.66
	Martinsvlle	Hou	R+	24	8	0	0	5	13.1	52	6	3	2	1	0	1	0	10	0	10	2	0	2	0	1.000	0	0	1.35
Smith, Chad	Phillies	Phi	R	22	22	2	0	20	34.1	143	29	19	11	2	2	1	1	9	1	31	1	0	3	5	.375	0	8	2.88
	Batavia	Phi	A-	22	3	0	0	0	5	28	9	8	6	1	0	0	0	1	0	8	3	0	0	0	.000	0	0	10.80
Smith, Clint	W Michigan	Det	A	23	20	14	0	1	87.1	397	88	60	41	6	2	3	8	48	0	73	13	4	4	7	.364	0	0	4.23
	Lakeland	Det	A+	23	7	7	0	0	37.1	170	42	29	21	3	1	2	0	18	0	32	5	1	3	2	.600	0	0	5.06
Smith, Jesse	Helena	Mil	R+	24	19	1	0	9	31	149	37	23	15	0	1	1	4	16	1	29	5	0	2	3	.400	0	3	4.35
Smith, Justin*	Everett	Sea	A-	23	2	0	0	0	5.2	21	3	3	2	1	0	0	0	1	0	8	0	0	1	0	1.000	0	0	3.18
	Wisconsin	Sea	A	23	7	7	0	0	37.1	163	41	22	20	6	2	1	3	10	0	29	0	1	1	1	.500	0	0	4.82
Smith, Matt	Kingsport	NYM	R+	21	18	0	0	4	24	132	33	35	29	2	0	3	5	20	1	28	8	2	1	1	.500	0	0	10.88
Smith, Robert*	Peoria	StL	A	20	9	9	0	0	54	219	53	20	17	4	1	3	2	16	0	59	2	1	4	1	.800	0	0	2.83
	Potomac	StL	A+	20	18	18	0	0	103.1	433	91	47	34	2	3	2	9	32	0	93	4	0	4	9	.308	0	0	2.96
Smith, Taylor	Hagerstown	Tor	A	21	28	28	1	0	171.1	724	158	87	72	11	3	4	12	51	0	119	5	0	7	10	.412	1	0	3.78
Smuin, Shane	Utica	Fla	A-	21	23	0	0	6	43	179	33	20	19	3	3	0	5	21	0	51	5	0	1	3	.250	0	1	3.98
Smyth, Steve*	Eugene	ChC	A-	22	5	5	0	0	24.2	110	29	17	12	2	1	3	0	7	0	14	2	1	1	1	.500	0	0	4.38
	Lansing	ChC	A	22	10	10	0	0	50.2	238	68	40	39	5	0	2	2	30	0	46	6	0	5	3	.625	0	0	6.93
Snyder, Kyle	Spokane	KC	A-	22	7	7	0	0	24	103	20	13	11	1	2	1	2	7	0	25	1	0	1	0	1.000	0	0	4.13
Sobchuk, Justin	Athletics	Oak	R	19	15	6	0	2	48.1	216	51	34	31	3	3	4	1	28	0	47	4	0	3	1	.750	0	1	5.77
Sobkowiak, Scott	Myrtle Bch	Atl	A+	22	27	26	0	1	139.1	572	100	50	44	10	3	2	2	63	1	161	12	1	9	4	.692	0	0	2.84
Solano, Alex	Augusta	Bos	A	20	9	5	0	1	28	126	32	25	15	5	0	2	2	7	0	18	3	1	1	2	.333	0	0	4.82
	Red Sox	Bos	R	20	5	5	0	0	26.1	118	30	12	7	1	1	0	2	7	0	15	1	1	1	3	.250	0	0	2.39
	Lowell	Bos	A-	20	6	6	0	0	33.2	150	40	23	21	6	1	3	1	7	1	26	2	3	1	2	.333	0	0	5.61
Solano, Francisco	Chstn-WV	KC	A	20	32	6	1	12	89.2	414	100	63	55	8	2	3	13	37	1	52	3	1	1	6	.143	0	4	5.52
Sollenberg, Matt*	Mets	NYM	R	23	18	0	0	7	27.2	118	30	16	11	1	3	0	1	6	1	27	3	0	1	5	.167	0	2	3.58
Song, Seung	Red Sox	Bos	R	20	13	9	0	2	54.2	233	47	29	14	2	0	2	4	20	0	61	2	4	5	5	.500	0	0	2.30
Sonnier, Shawn	Wilmington	KC	A+	23	44	0	0	38	59.1	237	46	20	19	1	2	0	1	19	2	73	2	0	1	2	.333	0	13	2.88
Sopkin, Josh	Royals	KC	R	20	16	1	0	2	30	145	37	22	19	0	0	1	1	23	0	19	4	0	3	1	.750	0	0	5.70
Soriano, Gabriel	Rockford	Cin	A	24	8	0	0	3	9.2	64	18	21	15	1	0	0	1	16	2	10	4	0	0	2	.000	0	0	13.97
Soriano, Rafael	Everett	Sea	A-	20	14	14	0	0	75.1	323	56	34	26	8	1	0	4	49	0	83	2	0	5	4	.556	0	0	3.11

1999 Pitching — Single-A and Rookie Leagues

Player	Team	Org	Lg	A	G	GS	CG	GF	IP	BFP	H	R	ER	HR	SH	SF	HB	TBB	IBB	SO	WP	Bk	W	L	Pct.	ShO	Sv	ERA
Soto, Darwin	Padres	SD	R	18	15	4	0	4	39	176	39	22	16	3	3	0	6	16	0	32	3	3	2	2	.500	0	1	3.69
Southard, Lee	St.Cathrnes	Tor	A-	22	5	0	0	3	4.1	29	2	5	5	0	0	0	0	14	0	6	4	0	0	0	.000	0	0	10.38
Sparks, Steve	Hickory	Pit	A	25	25	12	1	2	88.2	407	97	60	44	3	3	3	5	51	0	72	7	0	4	6	.400	1	0	4.47
	Lynchburg	Pit	A+	25	5	5	1	0	26	124	36	20	18	3	0	2	1	15	0	20	2	0	2	3	.400	0	0	6.23
Spear, Russell	Lakeland	Det	A+	22	8	2	0	1	12.2	77	15	17	13	1	0	1	4	24	0	8	5	0	0	0	.000	0	0	9.24
Spears, Ricky	Yankees	NYY	R	19	7	1	0	4	10.2	42	5	1	1	0	0	0	0	7	0	8	0	0	0	0	.000	0	0	0.84
Spencer, Corey*	Lowell	Bos	A-	23	19	0	0	3	29	127	33	12	8	0	0	0	0	7	0	38	1	0	1	0	1.000	0	1	2.48
	Augusta	Bos	A	23	7	1	0	2	11.2	49	13	6	6	1	0	0	0	5	0	13	0	0	1	0	1.000	0	1	4.63
Spenser, Kaipo	Kinston	Cle	A+	24	35	5	0	7	72	316	65	33	26	4	2	1	14	22	0	49	1	1	3	4	.429	0	1	3.25
Spiegel, Mike*	Columbus	Cle	A	24	7	7	0	0	35	145	27	13	11	4	1	0	1	14	0	38	2	2	2	0	1.000	0	0	2.83
	Kinston	Cle	A+	24	18	18	0	0	96	405	69	46	33	8	6	4	7	36	0	103	11	0	5	3	.625	0	0	3.09
Spille, Ryan*	St.Cathrnes	Tor	A-	23	1	1	0	0	5	17	2	0	0	0	0	0	1	0	0	5	0	1	1	0	1.000	0	0	0.00
	Hagerstown	Tor	A	23	14	11	0	0	69.2	263	49	20	17	3	3	1	4	15	0	49	1	1	7	1	.875	0	0	2.20
Spinelli, Mike*	Sarasota	Bos	A+	23	38	0	0	16	80.1	352	73	36	28	4	1	2	5	44	1	58	9	1	2	2	.500	0	2	3.14
Spooneybarger, Ti.	Danville	Atl	R+	20	12	0	0	2	24.1	103	15	11	7	0	0	0	0	14	0	36	5	0	3	0	1.000	0	0	2.59
	Macon	Atl	A	20	7	0	0	3	10	47	7	4	4	1	1	0	0	10	1	17	2	0	0	1	.000	0	0	3.60
Sprague, Kevin*	Johnson Cy	StL	R+	23	11	11	0	0	64	264	47	27	23	4	3	2	2	27	0	73	3	4	5	3	.625	0	0	3.23
Springston, Adam	Great Falls	LA	R+	22	4	0	0	3	8.2	32	4	4	2	1	0	0	0	3	0	12	0	0	1	1	.500	0	0	2.08
	Yakima	LA	A-	22	6	0	0	5	9	42	8	6	4	1	0	2	1	7	0	4	0	0	0	0	.000	0	0	4.00
Spurgeon, Jay	Frederick	Bal	A+	23	26	26	1	0	146	659	176	99	77	14	4	4	4	53	2	87	12	2	6	9	.400	0	0	4.75
Spurling, Chris	Greensboro	NYY	A	23	49	0	0	26	76.1	332	78	34	31	8	4	9	2	23	3	68	7	0	4	6	.400	0	4	3.66
Spykstra, Dave	Michigan	Hou	A	26	5	0	0	1	5.1	30	2	7	4	0	0	0	2	10	0	9	6	0	0	0	.000	0	0	6.75
Stabile, Paul*	Hickory	Pit	A	24	46	0	0	14	74.1	345	70	42	33	9	1	3	4	42	0	87	6	1	3	3	.500	0	1	4.00
Stafford, Mike*	Hagerstown	Tor	A	25	39	0	0	18	50	194	37	15	15	2	3	0	1	10	0	40	1	1	3	2	.600	0	5	2.70
Stamm, Steve*	Rangers	Tex	A	23	20	0	0	16	31	127	15	11	6	3	1	1	2	15	2	30	6	0	1	2	.333	0	8	1.74
Standridge, Jason	Chston-SC	TB	A	21	18	18	3	0	116	455	80	35	26	5	5	5	7	31	0	84	9	2	9	1	.900	2	0	2.02
	St. Pete	TB	A+	21	8	8	0	0	48.1	208	49	21	21	0	1	0	4	20	0	26	6	1	4	4	.500	0	0	3.91
Stanford, Derek	Martinsvlle	Hou	R+	21	11	9	0	1	59.2	250	39	28	19	2	3	1	11	25	0	75	8	0	4	4	.500	0	0	2.87
Stanley, Cody	Billings	Cin	R+	21	26	0	0	10	37	186	43	36	15	2	2	0	0	24	2	35	7	1	1	2	.333	0	2	3.65
Stanton, Tim*	Missoula	Ari	R+	21	21	0	0	7	32.1	146	35	19	14	5	0	0	3	9	0	35	1	0	3	3	.500	0	0	3.90
Staples, Dave*	Phillies	Phi	R	22	15	2	0	2	36.2	174	45	31	29	4	0	6	6	13	0	38	3	0	0	3	.000	0	0	7.12
Stark, Zac*	Lancaster	Sea	A+	25	49	0	0	15	79	345	75	44	35	9	2	0	4	29	2	72	4	0	1	2	.333	0	2	3.99
Stemle, Steve	Peoria	StL	A	23	28	28	0	0	148	688	177	104	90	11	3	5	6	67	0	113	12	0	7	10	.412	0	0	5.47
Stephens, Jason	Lk Elsinore	Ana	A+	24	15	11	1	0	68.2	310	84	39	32	6	3	1	2	24	2	66	2	0	3	3	.500	0	0	4.19
Stephens, John	Delmarva	Bal	A	20	28	27	4	0	170.1	702	148	75	61	10	5	4	10	36	0	217	4	0	10	8	.556	2	0	3.22
Stephenson, Brian	Cubs	ChC	R	26	1	0	0	0	2	6	1	0	0	0	0	0	0	0	0	2	0	0	0	0	.000	0	0	0.00
	Eugene	ChC	A-	26	2	2	0	0	4	22	4	5	2	0	0	0	1	4	0	4	0	0	1	0	1.000	0	0	4.50
Stevens, Josh	Medcine Hat	Tor	R+	21	23	0	0	17	29.1	121	27	14	8	2	2	1		5	0	34	2	0	5	1	.833	0	2	2.45
Stewart, Cory*	Billings	Cin	R+	21	10	10	0	0	48.2	217	50	25	17	2	0	3	3	21	0	37	1	0	2	0	1.000	0	0	3.14
Stewart, John*	Savannah	Tex	A	22	30	20	1	7	130.1	576	144	99	73	19	4	8	7	24	0	79	5	2	6	14	.300	0	1	5.04
Stewart, Josh*	Bristol	CWS	R+	21	5	0	0	2	18	71	13	5	3	0	1	0	2	5	0	25	0	0	1	0	1.000	0	0	1.50
	Burlington	CWS	A	21	16	0	0	3	29.2	138	32	25	24	6	0	2	2	21	0	35	1	0	2	0	1.000	0	0	7.28
Stewart, Paul	Stockton	Mil	A+	21	27	25	5	0	170.1	733	171	90	75	18	6	9	4	61	0	117	7	1	10	11	.476	1	0	3.96
Stewart, Steve*	Ogden	Mil	R+	21	13	10	0	1	70.2	310	73	47	31	6	1	2	3	27	0	50	6	0	2	3	.400	0	0	3.95
Stiles, Brad*	Royals	KC	R	19	4	0	0	2	5	20	3	1	1	0	1	0	1	3	0	5	0	0	1	0	1.000	0	0	1.80
Stine, Justin*	St.Cathrnes	Tor	A-	22	2	1	0	0	8.1	31	5	1	1	1	0	0	0	1	0	4	0	0	2	0	1.000	0	0	1.08
	Hagerstown	Tor	A	23	17	0	0	5	28	125	30	13	12	1	1	2	3	7	0	20	3	0	0	0	.000	0	0	3.86
Stokes, Brian	Princeton	TB	R+	20	33	0	0	27	37	163	33	20	16	2	2	1	1	21	0	39	8	1	2	3	.400	0	0	3.89
Story, Aaron*	Pirates	Pit	R	19	12	1	0	2	27.2	120	26	14	11	0	0	0	1	13	0	27	3	0	2	2	.500	0	0	3.58
Strange, Pat	Capital Cty	NYM	A	19	28	21	2	1	154	627	138	57	45	4	4	3	10	29	1	113	7	0	12	5	.706	1	0	2.63
Stumm, Jason	White Sox	CWS	R	19	3	2	0	0	11	47	13	4	4	2	0	1	1	3	0	9	1	0	0	0	.000	0	0	3.27
	Burlington	CWS	A	19	10	10	0	0	44	199	47	31	26	4	0	1	1	27	1	33	4	2	3	3	.500	0	0	5.32
Sturdy, Tim	Quad City	Min	A	21	13	13	0	0	60.1	282	85	48	42	4	3	0	5	16	0	39	2	1	2	7	.222	0	0	6.27
	Elizabethtn	Min	R+	21	12	12	0	0	73.1	311	71	33	27	2	1	1	0	17	0	64	9	1	6	1	.857	0	0	3.31
Suarez, Felipe	Boise	Ana	A-	24	5	5	0	0	29.2	135	32	26	20	2	1	1	2	11	0	33	2	0	1	2	.333	0	0	6.07
Suarez, Luis	Cedar Rapds	Ana	A		4	4	0	0	18	91	25	19	14	3	0	4	1	9	0	15	2	0	1	1	.500	0	0	7.00
Sullivan, Luke*	Boise	Ana	A-	23	2	0	0	0	1.1	7	2	2	1	0	0	0	2	0	1	0	0	0	0	.000	0	0	13.50
Sullivan, Shane	Lansing	ChC	A	22	13	0	0	3	17.2	95	28	20	16	1	0	1	1	13	0	9	3	1	2	0	1.000	0	0	8.15
	Daytona	ChC	A+	22	4	0	0	0	12	55	17	10	9	3	0	1	0	7	0	5	0	0	1	0	1.000	0	0	6.75
Sullivan, Ted*	Mahoning Vy	Cle	A-	23	13	0	0	9	12.1	57	14	9	9	2	0	1	3	7	0	13	0	0	1	1	.500	0	4	6.57
Sundbeck, Cody	High Desert	Ari	A+	22	14	14	0	0	67.1	311	81	59	53	7	1	3	7	35	0	68	12	2	4	5	.444	0	0	7.08
Sunderman, Nick*	Burlington	Cle	R+	21	16	0	0	2	30	135	30	17	12	1	1	1	3	15	0	42	3	3	0	0	.000	0	0	3.60
	Mahoning Vy	Cle	A-	23	4	0	0	1	4	18	2	2	2	0	0	0	2	2	0	4	0	0	0	0	.000	0	0	4.50
Surkont, Keith	Sou Oregon	Oak	A-	23	17	13	0	4	74.1	332	85	45	37	5	4	3	2	35	2	39	6	1	5	3	.625	0	1	4.48
Surridge, Lance	Augusta	Bos	A	23	37	10	0	5	106.1	459	102	52	36	3	3	1	3	38	1	88	4	0	9	5	.643	0	3	3.05
Suttles, Donnie	Columbus	Cle	A	23	16	16	1	0	77	349	86	55	39	6	1	1	11	29	0	66	11	1	4	6	.400	0	0	4.56
Sweeney, Mike	Mets	NYM	R	23	1	0	0	0	2	7	1	0	0	0	0	0	0	0	0	2	0	0	1	0	1.000	0	0	0.00
	Kingsport	NYM	R+	23	19	0	0	8	30.1	136	34	20	19	1	2	0	0	11	0	20	2	0	1	3	.250	0	1	5.64
Swiatkiewicz, Chris	Yankees	NYY	R	24	9	0	0	8	11	38	5	1	1	0	0	2	0	2	0	13	0	1	1	0	1.000	0	5	0.82
	Staten Isld	NYY	A-	21					9.2	42	13	8	6	2	0	0	0	3	0	6	0	0	0	0	.000	0	0	6.23
	Tampa	NYY	A+	24	2	0	0	2	2.1	9	1	0	0	0	0	0	0	0	0	1	0	0	0	0	.000	0	0	0.00
Sylvester, Billy	Macon	Atl	A	23					83.2	373	78	37	29	3	5	5	6	37	2	75	5	1	5	4	.556	0	2	3.12
Taczy, Craig*	Vero Beach	LA	A+	23	28	25	2	1	160.1	701	172	93	83	12	3	10	14	50	0	83	6	1	5	14	.263	0	0	4.66
Tankersley, Dennis	Red Sox	Bos	R	21	11	6	0	2	35.2	133	14	7	3	2	0	3	0	9	1	57	0	0	1	0	1.000	0	0	0.76
Tapia, Rafael	Delmarva	Bal	A	22	7	2	0	0	23	92	18	7	6	2	0	0	0	8	0	16	3	1	3	0	1.000	0	0	2.35
Targac, Matt*	Marlins	Fla	R	20	12	11	1	0	56	237	53	32	19	2	1	2	0	16	0	55	8	1	1	7	.125	0	0	3.05

1999 Pitching — Single-A and Rookie Leagues

HOW MUCH HE PITCHED											WHAT HE GAVE UP												THE RESULTS					
Player	Team	Org	Lg	A	G	GS	CG	GF	IP	BFP	H	R	ER	HR	SH	SF	HB	TBB	IBB	SO	WP	Bk	W	L	Pct.	ShO	Sv	ERA
Taschner, Jack*	Salem-Keizr	SF	A-	22	7	6	0	0	28.2	118	26	12	8	1	0	0	0	10	0	36	0	0	3	2	.600	0	0	2.51
Tate, Matt	Orioles	Bal	R	19	11	11	0	0	57.2	241	40	26	23	3	5	2	6	26	3	44	3	4	2	2	.500	0	0	3.59
Tauscher, Ryan*	Sou Oregon	Oak	A-	23	12	0	0	6	25	122	27	22	19	1	2	1	3	19	3	16	1	0	2	1	.667	0	0	6.84
Tavarez, David	Orioles	Bal	R	18	12	9	0	0	67.1	277	60	22	16	2	2	1	7	12	2	55	4	2	9	0	1.000	0	0	2.14
Taylor, Aaron	Macon	Atl	A	22	27	8	0	6	79.1	360	86	56	43	9	2	5	7	27	2	78	17	0	6	7	.462	0	1	4.88
Taylor, Jason	Tigers	Det	R	23	18	1	0	7	33.1	147	33	15	11	2	2	0	1	17	1	26	2	0	3	5	.375	0	0	2.97
Teekel, Josh	Johnson Cy	StL	R+	19	8	8	0	0	33.2	157	41	26	20	4	0	0	4	8	0	42	2	3	2	3	.400	0	0	5.35
Tejeda, Franklin	Johnson Cy	StL	R+	20	14	2	0	4	26.1	115	24	15	9	0	2	1	1	7	0	28	3	1	2	1	.667	0	1	3.08
Tejeda, Robinson	Phillies	Phi	R	18	12	9	0	2	46.1	206	47	27	22	5	3	1	2	27	0	39	1	1	1	3	.250	0	0	4.27
Terry, Mike*	Mets	NYM	R	24	2	0	0	2	2	6	1	0	0	0	0	0	0	0	0	0	0	0	0	0	.000	0	1	0.00
	Pittsfield	NYM	A-	24	18	0	0	11	32	142	33	19	19	1	3	2	4	14	0	24	0	0	2	1	.667	0	1	5.34
Tetz, Kris	Expos	Mon	R	21	1	0	0	0	4	15	1	1	1	0	0	0	1	1	0	4	0	0	0	0	.000	0	0	2.25
	Cape Fear	Mon	A	21	10	9	0	0	49.2	209	54	25	24	5	0	1	1	12	0	36	3	0	3	3	.500	0	0	4.35
Teut, Nate*	Daytona	ChC	A+	24	26	26	1	0	132.2	613	180	113	94	16	3	9	9	41	0	91	13	1	5	12	.294	0	0	6.38
Theodile, Simieon	Delmarva	Bal	A	23	33	1	0	17	54	259	68	44	35	4	4	3	1	27	1	45	4	0	1	2	.333	0	0	5.83
Thomas, Brad*	Fort Myers	Min	A+	22	27	27	1	0	152.2	666	182	99	81	11	4	3	6	46	0	108	8	1	8	11	.421	1	0	4.78
Thomas, Don*	Kissimmee	Hou	A+	24	18	18	0	0	90.2	413	129	77	70	8	4	3	2	28	2	44	11	1	8	6	.571	0	0	6.95
Thomas, Gaige	Utica	Fla	A-	21	13	11	0	1	40	193	41	34	24	4	1	2	8	30	0	32	16	0	0	5	.000	0	1	5.40
Thompson, Doug	Asheville	Col	A	23	25	0	0	12	56	250	56	29	27	9	1	2	6	18	0	72	5	3	3	3	.500	0	3	4.34
Thompson, Eric	Visalia	Oak	A+	22	31	20	0	5	126.2	595	150	91	79	9	2	6	11	56	2	110	10	1	9	6	.600	0	1	5.61
Thompson, John	Winston-Sal	CWS	A+	27	2	2	0	0	9	43	10	9	7	1	0	1	0	8	0	9	3	0	0	1	.000	0	0	7.00
	Wilmington	KC	A+	27	20	0	0	11	35	139	29	12	10	2	1	2	2	12	0	25	3	0	2	1	.667	0	4	2.57
Thompson, Matt	Red Sox	Bos	R	18	5	2	0	1	15	53	7	3	2	0	0	0	0	4	0	12	0	0	0	0	.000	0	0	1.20
Thompson, Mike	Padres	SD	R	19	13	13	0	0	65	300	78	52	44	8	2	3	4	27	0	62	3	4	1	7	.125	0	0	6.09
Thompson, Travis	Salem	Col	A+	25	56	0	0	52	62	267	54	19	12	1	7	1	2	24	4	53	5	0	3	3	.500	0	27	1.74
Thompson, Travis	Billings	Cin	R+	22	8	0	0	3	20.2	72	14	1	0	0	1	0	0	3	0	27	4	0	1	0	1.000	0	0	0.00
Thorn, Todd*	Wilmington	KC	A+	23	34	13	0	6	126.2	559	143	85	79	14	4	4	9	44	1	89	6	2	8	5	.615	0	2	5.61
Thornton, Matt*	Wisconsin	Sea	A	23	25	1	0	3	29.1	154	39	19	16	1	4	1	0	25	0	34	5	0	0	0	.000	0	1	4.91
Thrasher, Jesse	Phillies	Phi	R	19	5	1	0	0	8.1	57	15	16	14	1	0	2	2	15	0	6	0	0	0	1	.000	0	0	15.12
Thurman, Corey	Wilmington	KC	A+	21	27	27	0	0	149.1	667	160	89	81	11	4	5	9	64	0	131	11	1	8	11	.421	0	0	4.88
Tomaszewski, Eliot	Orioles	Bal	R	20	10	6	0	3	43.2	183	35	22	9	0	0	2	3	19	1	36	3	2	3	1	.750	0	2	1.85
	Bluefield	Bal	R+	20	1	1	0	0	5	23	8	5	4	0	0	0	1	1	0	1	0	0	0	0	.000	0	0	7.20
Tommassi, Carlos	Burlington	Cle	R+	20	12	0	0	5	25.1	119	29	22	10	0	1	2	1	9	0	24	6	0	1	1	.500	0	0	3.55
Toriz, Steve	Vermont	Mon	A-	23	21	4	0	9	39.1	180	34	25	20	4	3	1	1	31	2	31	4	1	2	2	.500	0	3	4.58
	Cape Fear	Mon	A	23	1	1	0	0	4	15	2	3	3	0	0	1	0	2	0	1	0	0	0	1	.000	0	0	6.75
Toropov, Alexandre	Great Falls	LA	R+	20	2	0	0	2	1.1	7	2	1	1	0	0	0	0	2	0	1	0	0	0	0	.000	0	0	6.75
Torres, Alex*	Tigers	Det	R	21	13	1	0	4	23.2	123	28	20	19	1	0	2	2	25	0	15	2	0	1	1	.500	0	0	7.23
Torres, Leo*	Lansing	ChC	A	24	51	0	0	20	62.1	259	51	22	19	2	2	1	3	28	1	47	1	1	2	0	1.000	0	3	2.74
Torres, Luis	Pirates	Pit	R	20	8	8	0	0	42.2	157	24	9	8	0	1	2	5	7	0	33	4	1	1	2	.333	0	0	1.69
	Hickory	Pit	A	20	7	7	0	0	38.2	168	40	17	14	3	2	2	4	20	1	26	6	0	3	2	.600	0	0	3.26
Torres, Luis	Expos	Mon	R	19	12	9	1	1	60	259	55	28	19	1	1	1	3	28	1	36	8	0	5	3	.625	1	0	2.85
Torres, Manny	Billings	Cin	R+	23	7	2	0	0	20.2	84	17	9	8	3	0	0	0	7	0	18	0	0	1	1	.500	0	0	3.48
	Rockford	Cin	A	23	8	7	1	0	38.2	177	48	33	26	2	0	1	2	11	0	29	1	1	1	6	.143	0	0	6.05
Torres, Melqui	Wisconsin	Sea	A	23	27	27	3	0	171.2	736	185	99	86	9	3	14	10	45	0	129	12	6	13	9	.591	2	0	4.51
Tovar, Angel	Yankees	NYY	R	22	8	0	0	4	7.2	42	12	8	7	0	0	0	1	5	0	7	2	0	0	1	.000	0	0	8.22
	Tampa	NYY	A+	22	3	0	0	3	1.2	10	5	2	2	0	0	0	0	1	0	1	0	0	1	1	.500	0	0	10.80
Trask, Cody	Rockies	Col	R	22	9	1	0	1	17.1	89	26	21	16	0	2	1	0	13	0	12	4	2	0	0	.000	0	0	8.31
Travis, Jesse	Bakersfield	SF	A+	25	14	9	0	0	45.1	218	71	47	44	8	0	2	1	20	0	27	3	0	2	5	.286	0	0	8.74
Trejo, Francisco*	High Desert	Ari	A+	20	3	0	0	2	6.2	32	5	6	5	1	0	0	1	7	0	6	3	0	0	0	.000	0	0	6.75
	Diamondbcks	Ari	R	20	17	0	0	6	28.1	131	28	18	10	0	2	0	1	19	0	30	10	1	0	2	.000	0	1	3.18
Trevino, Chris*	Braves	Atl	R	19	11	0	0	5	19.2	90	28	17	13	1	1	1	0	5	0	17	0	0	1	3	.250	0	1	5.95
Trinidad, Fernando	Orioles	Bal	R	20	15	0	0	7	35.1	155	40	23	20	1	1	0	3	9	2	19	1	0	0	4	.000	0	1	5.09
Truitt, Derrick	Jamestown	Atl	A-	22	18	0	0	3	35	149	28	20	18	3	3	1	4	18	0	30	4	0	2	3	.400	0	1	4.63
Tucker, Brad	Batavia	Phi	A-	23	17	1	0	9	26	112	24	15	11	4	0	1	3	11	0	15	0	1	0	1	.000	0	0	3.81
Turman, Jimmy	Lancaster	Sea	A+	24	31	12	1	9	97	436	116	66	56	12	1	2	6	35	1	78	14	0	4	10	.286	0	1	5.20
Turnbow, Derrick	Piedmont	Phi	A	22	26	26	4	0	161	651	130	67	60	10	1	2	7	53	0	149	8	0	12	8	.600	1	0	3.35
Turner, Jess	Twins	Min	R	21	17	2	0	6	35	148	38	18	16	2	3	2	0	13	1	39	2	0	6	0	1.000	0	0	4.11
Turner, Kyle*	Royals	KC	R	21	2	1	0	0	4	15	2	0	0	0	0	0	0	0	0	3	0	0	1	0	1.000	0	0	0.00
	Spokane	KC	A-	21	8	0	0	2	14.1	67	13	7	7	1	1	0	0	10	1	12	2	0	0	1	.000	0	0	4.40
Tynan, Chris	Savannah	Tex	A	21	21	21	0	0	112	512	140	96	87	19	0	5	7	38	0	97	7	1	4	10	.286	0	0	6.99
Ugas, Juan	Yakima	LA	A-	20	20	2	0	12	50.2	237	55	32	26	7	3	0	5	26	1	45	2	0	3	5	.375	0	3	4.62
Ulacia, Dennis*	White Sox	CWS	R	19	8	8	0	0	38	157	36	19	16	2	0	1	1	11	1	52	0	2	3	2	.600	0	0	3.79
Ulloa, Enmanuel	Wisconsin	Sea	A	21	35	10	0	17	88	384	90	50	45	9	1	0	1	36	2	98	8	6	7	3	.700	0	5	4.60
Underhill, Ray	Elizabethtn	Min	R+	21	17	0	0	6	25	128	36	24	20	2	0	2	1	15	0	18	5	1	0	1	.000	0	0	7.20
Urbina, Ulmer	Expos	Mon	R	20	14	0	0	9	25.1	123	22	19	18	1	1	1	3	24	0	20	1	1	3	2	.600	0	2	6.39
Urdaneta, Lino	Vero Beach	LA	A+	20	27	5	0	6	67	292	74	42	36	10	4	3	6	20	1	43	3	3	5	4	.556	0	0	4.84
Vael, Rob	Columbus	Cle	A	24	42	7	0	16	92.2	422	89	59	50	14	3	2	5	53	1	91	12	1	5	4	.556	0	0	4.86
Vail, Garet	Red Sox	Bos	R	23	7	0	0	1	14	63	15	10	5	2	0	1	0	6	0	5	0	2	1	1	.500	0	0	3.21
Valdez, Domingo	Pulaski	Tex	R+	20	3	3	0	0	16	74	20	14	12	2	0	1	2	7	0	14	2	0	0	0	.000	0	0	6.75
	Rangers	Tex	R	20	8	7	0	0	29.1	138	29	22	16	2	0	1	5	18	0	34	4	2	0	1	.000	0	0	4.91
Valdez, Jose	Reds	Cin	R	21	12	6	0	6	41.1	167	20	12	9	0	5	1	2	25	0	36	3	0	3	3	.500	0	2	1.96
	Clinton	Cin	A	21	3	1	0	0	5.2	35	16	10	10	0	0	0	0	4	0	3	0	0	0	1	.000	0	0	15.88
Valenti, Jon	Bakersfield	SF	A+	26	46	0	0	13	84.1	378	85	55	48	15	0	8	5	39	1	69	4	1	4	1	.800	0	1	5.12
Valentine, Jose	White Sox	CWS	R	20	3	0	0	1	4.1	14	2	0	0	0	0	0	0	1	0	2	0	0	0	0	.000	0	0	0.00
	Bristol	CWS	R+	20	11	0	0	7	16.2	90	27	17	13	2	0	3	3	9	0	14	1	1	0	0	.000	0	0	7.02
Valera, Nelson	Princeton	TB	R+	21	23	1	0	3	58.2	242	55	26	19	7	0	3	2	15	0	52	7	1	5	2	.714	0	1	2.91
	Hudson Val	TB	A-	21	2	1	0	0	2.2	16	4	5	5	1	0	1	1	2	0	3	0	0	0	1	.000	0	0	16.88

1999 Pitching — Single-A and Rookie Leagues

HOW MUCH HE PITCHED											WHAT HE GAVE UP												THE RESULTS					
Player	Team	Org	Lg	A	G	GS	CG	GF	IP	BFP	H	R	ER	HR	SH	SF	HB	TBB	IBB	SO	WP	Bk	W	L	Pct.	ShO	Sv	ERA
Valverde, Jose	Diamondbcks	Ari	R	20	20	0	0	17	28.2	138	34	21	13	1	0	0	4	10	0	47	1	1	1	2	.333	0	8	4.08
	South Bend	Ari	A	20	2	0	0	0	2.2	11	2	0	0	0	0	0	1	2	0	3	1	1	0	0	.000	0	0	0.00
Van Buren, Jer.	Asheville	Col	A	19	28	28	0	0	143	640	143	87	78	16	1	13	19	70	0	133	19	2	7	10	.412	0	0	4.91
Van De Weg, Ryan	Fort Wayne	SD	A	26	13	8	0	3	53.2	257	71	46	40	6	0	2	7	28	0	41	7	0	3	4	.429	0	1	6.71
Vandermeer, Scott	Princeton	TB	R+	19	14	11	0	0	58.1	269	58	54	43	10	2	4	2	36	0	32	13	2	2	8	.200	0	0	6.63
Van Gilder, Ryan	Cape Fear	Mon	A	24	1	0	0	0	0.2	6	2	4	4	0	0	0	0	2	0	0	0	0	0	1	.000	0	0	54.00
	Jupiter	Mon	A+	24	5	0	0	0	6	26	5	5	5	1	0	0	0	3	0	6	0	0	0	1	.000	0	0	7.50
VanHekken, An.*	Oneonta	Det	A-	20	11	10	0	0	50.1	210	44	17	12	3	0	0	3	16	0	50	1	0	4	2	.667	0	0	2.15
Vargas, Claudio	Kane County	Fla	A	21	19	19	1	0	99.2	426	97	47	43	8	2	3	0	41	0	88	2	2	5	5	.500	0	0	3.88
Vargas, Derrick*	Portland	Col	A-	23	18	0	0	3	31.2	158	26	17	14	0	0	1	7	32	0	33	5	4	1	0	1.000	0	0	3.98
Vargas, Jose	Columbus	Cle	A	23	34	6	0	5	85	374	88	47	44	10	1	2	5	29	0	103	1	1	2	5	.286	0	2	4.66
Vasquez, Luis*	Martinsvlle	Hou	R+	20	13	3	0	1	42	181	46	21	13	3	0	0	4	12	0	39	2	2	6	1	.857	0	1	2.79
Vega, Rene*	Capital Cty	NYM	A	23	29	22	1	2	146	593	101	57	51	8	3	2	12	50	1	148	6	4	11	7	.611	0	1	3.14
Velazquez, Elih*	Athletics	Oak	R	20	16	4	0	1	41.1	175	44	18	17	1	0	0	1	11	0	38	1	1	4	1	.800	0	0	3.70
Velazquez, Ernesto	Padres	SD	R	18	18	0	0	11	34	144	44	19	14	3	0	0	0	3	0	15	0	0	2	3	.400	0	2	3.71
Vent, Kevin	Salem-Keizr	SF	A-	23	17	6	0	10	39.1	174	44	25	22	4	2	2	1	18	0	31	2	1	2	3	.400	0	3	5.03
Veras, Enger	Princeton	TB	R+	19	14	14	0	0	60.2	299	74	57	48	5	1	4	7	50	1	48	10	1	3	5	.375	0	0	7.12
Verdugo, Oswaldo	Idaho Falls	SD	R+	19	33	0	0	32	38.1	155	34	13	10	2	0	3	2	9	0	54	4	1	5	1	.833	0	13	2.35
Veronie, Shanin	Danville	Atl	R+	23	18	0	0	15	25.1	91	12	4	2	2	0	0	1	4	0	41	0	0	2	2	.500	0	3	0.71
Viator, Dustin	Fort Wayne	SD	A	24	5	0	0	2	3.2	18	7	7	7	2	0	0	0	1	0	2	0	0	0	1	.000	0	0	17.18
Victery, Joe	Lancaster	Sea	A+	25	10	5	0	3	30.2	156	51	35	29	4	0	1	3	13	0	15	2	0	1	4	.200	0	0	8.51
Victoria, Lester*	Quad City	Min	A	24	41	0	0	8	51.1	235	41	30	23	2	1	1	3	42	2	58	10	0	1	1	.500	0	0	4.03
Vigeland, Ole	Charlotte	Tex	A+	23	5	0	0	2	8.2	41	14	7	7	0	0	1	0	4	0	9	0	0	0	0	.000	0	0	7.27
Viles, Jeff	Peoria	StL	A	24	58	0	0	15	70.2	307	59	47	42	15	3	1	4	34	0	79	3	0	3	5	.375	0	0	5.35
Villamil, William*	Rangers	Tex	R	19	14	0	0	6	23.2	108	24	14	13	0	1	1	0	12	0	17	2	4	0	1	.000	0	1	4.94
Villanueva, Bill	Marlins	Fla	R	21	11	11	1	0	58.1	251	58	29	25	0	0	1	4	21	0	42	1	0	2	5	.286	0	0	3.86
Villarreal, Oscar	Diamondbcks	Ari	R	18	14	11	0	1	64.1	286	64	39	27	1	2	3	10	25	0	51	6	4	1	5	.167	0	0	3.78
Vincentq, Matt*	Johnson Cy	StL	R+	23	24	0	0	8	28.1	127	24	14	12	3	2	1	1	18	1	36	1	1	1	2	.333	0	2	3.81
Vinton, Drew	Williamsprt	Pit	A-	24	17	7	1	5	62.2	283	58	43	29	1	1	8	7	33	0	49	11	4	1	4	.200	0	0	4.16
Viole, Paul	Pittsfield	NYM	A-	22	18	0	0	14	23	83	7	0	0	0	0	0	0	7	1	28	2	0	3	0	1.000	0	11	0.00
	Capital Cty	NYM	A	22	2	0	0	0	2	10	1	1	0	0	0	0	0	2	0	1	0	0	0	0	.000	0	0	0.00
Vitek, Josh	Padres	SD	R	20	12	10	0	0	47.1	212	43	22	21	3	0	4	8	24	0	48	2	0	6	2	.750	0	0	3.99
Vizcarra, Enrique	Mexico	—	R	—	11	0	0	5	15	60	9	3	3	0	0	1	2	7	2	15	2	0	0	1	.000	0	3	1.80
Vogt, Robert*	Pirates	Pit	R	21	3	0	0	3	3	16	5	4	4	0	0	1	0	2	0	3	1	0	0	0	.000	0	0	12.00
Vogtli, Robb	Greensboro	NYY	A	25	25	0	0	7	38.1	169	39	25	22	7	2	0	1	18	1	38	2	0	3	2	.600	0	1	5.17
Volkman, Keith*	Rancho Cuca	SD	A+	24	49	0	0	16	53.1	254	59	38	32	4	4	2	4	37	1	41	5	0	2	2	.500	0	2	5.40
Voyles, Brad	Macon	Atl	A	23	38	0	0	26	51.1	226	27	21	17	0	1	2	5	39	2	65	7	2	3	3	.500	0	14	2.98
	Myrtle Bch	Atl	A+	23	5	0	0	2	12	50	7	3	3	1	1	0	0	9	1	13	1	0	1	1	.500	0	0	2.25
Vracar, Paul	Eugene	ChC	A-	20	20	0	0	8	32	177	46	45	38	5	1	4	13	26	2	26	10	2	1	0	1.000	0	0	10.69
Wade, Matt	Burlington	Cle	R+	20	7	7	0	0	33	130	26	10	4	1	0	1	1	3	0	33	2	0	3	3	.500	0	0	1.09
Wade, Travis	Kissimmee	Hou	A+	24	1	0	0	1	1	4	1	0	0	0	0	0	0	0	0	2	0	0	0	0	.000	0	0	0.00
	Michigan	Hou	A	24	10	0	0	5	14	78	22	18	15	2	0	0	2	11	1	9	1	0	0	0	.000	0	2	9.64
	Auburn	Hou	A-	24	26	0	0	23	37.2	150	25	10	10	0	3	0	2	13	0	53	0	0	1	1	.500	0	11	2.39
Waechter, Doug	Princeton	TB	R+	19	11	7	0	0	35	189	46	45	38	2	0	5	4	35	0	38	21	1	0	5	.000	0	0	9.77
Wagner, Frank*	Helena	Mil	R+	22	11	0	0	1	11.1	70	18	19	16	0	1	0	2	16	0	6	5	1	0	1	.000	0	1	12.71
Wagner, Ken	Kinston	Cle	A+	25	14	0	0	6	26.2	122	31	25	20	4	0	0	0	12	0	21	1	0	1	1	.500	0	0	6.75
Waites, David	Visalia	Oak	A+	24	32	0	0	22	38.1	180	30	25	25	2	2	3	8	29	3	28	8	1	1	4	.200	0	7	5.87
Wakefield, Doug*	Butte	Ana	R+	23	3	0	0	3	4.1	18	5	2	2	2	0	0	0	1	0	3	0	0	0	0	.000	0	0	4.15
Waldron, Brad	Cape Fear	Mon	A	23	25	9	0	9	93.1	397	104	40	35	6	4	3	0	20	0	72	4	0	3	2	.600	0	5	3.38
Waldrum, Kevin	Eugene	ChC	A-	21	4	0	0	1	7.1	34	10	6	5	2	0	1	1	3	0	1	1	0	0	0	.000	0	0	6.14
Waligora, Tom	Lansing	ChC	A	23	50	1	0	20	82	365	78	44	39	8	5	5	4	38	1	56	8	0	2	6	.250	0	5	4.28
Walker, Adam*	Clearwater	Phi	A+	24	26	25	3	1	149	646	156	80	65	7	6	3	3	52	0	100	9	2	9	7	.563	2	0	3.93
Walker, Adrian*	Braves	Atl	R	20	13	0	0	3	23.2	104	22	11	11	2	0	3	0	15	0	30	3	0	0	2	.000	0	0	4.18
Walker, Josh	Helena	Mil	R+	24	3	0	0	0	6.2	30	10	4	4	0	1	0	0	0	0	3	1	0	0	0	.000	0	0	5.40
Walker, Kevin*	Rancho Cuca	SD	A+	23	27	1	0	9	39	169	35	19	15	2	1	2	3	19	3	35	1	0	1	1	.500	0	4	3.46
Wallace, Ben*	Ogden	Mil	R+	19	16	2	0	7	23	124	37	33	25	3	1	1	0	25	0	13	3	2	0	1	.000	0	0	9.78
Wallace, Chris	Tampa	NYY	A+	24	30	0	0	6	37.1	166	46	24	21	4	6	2	0	15	2	21	1	0	3	4	.429	0	0	5.06
	Staten Ilnd	NYY	A-	24	14	0	0	11	15.2	70	9	7	7	0	2	2	0	13	0	12	3	0	0	1	.000	0	8	4.02
Wallace, Jeff	Great Falls	LA	R+	23	4	0	0	3	4.2	24	5	2	2	0	0	1	0	5	0	5	0	1	0	0	.000	0	0	3.86
	Yakima	LA	A-	23	11	0	0	7	24.2	110	20	12	9	2	0	0	3	14	2	26	3	0	0	1	.000	0	2	3.28
Wallace, Justin*	Williamsprt	Pit	A-	23	19	0	0	8	31.2	143	35	22	19	2	0	4	2	16	1	23	1	2	0	0	.000	0	2	5.40
Wallace, Shane*	Burlington	Cle	R+	19	12	12	0	0	48	217	58	35	28	2	1	5	3	15	0	38	1	0	1	5	.167	0	0	5.25
Walling, Dave	Staten Ilnd	NYY	A-	21	14	14	0	0	80.1	331	76	31	28	3	1	2	2	18	1	82	1	3	8	2	.800	0	0	3.14
Walrond, Les*	Peoria	StL	A	23	21	20	0	0	109	489	115	77	69	12	2	5	3	59	0	78	6	0	7	10	.412	0	0	5.70
Walters, Jason	Yakima	LA	A-	22	8	0	0	7	7.2	39	9	10	7	2	0	2	2	7	0	13	2	0	0	1	.000	0	3	8.22
Walton, Sam*	Everett	Sea	A-	21	14	14	0	0	62	292	55	39	34	7	0	1	2	60	0	59	16	0	3	3	.500	0	0	4.94
Wamback, Trevor	Expos	Mon	R	23	2	2	0	0	12.1	48	12	5	4	1	0	0	0	1	0	12	0	0	1	0	1.000	0	0	2.92
	Cape Fear	Mon	A	23	24	14	1	2	104.2	414	98	39	33	10	2	2	3	14	0	77	3	1	6	3	.667	0	1	2.84
Ward, Matt*	Kane County	Fla	A	22	5	5	0	0	26.2	118	41	17	15	6	0	0	0	4	0	7	0	0	3	1	.750	0	0	5.06
	Utica	Fla	A	[illegible]	[illegible]	[illegible]	[illegible]	1	[illegible]	140	[illegible]	17	16	10	1	0	1	3	0	24	0	0	2	1	.667	0	0	4.00
Ward, Monty	Chstn-WV	KC	A	23	42	3	0	24	84.1	370	74	42	27	1	7	7	3	40	2	93	9	2	2	9	.182	0	7	2.88
Warren, Josh	Butte	Ana	R+	21	14	0	0	2	28	148	44	38	34	6	0	0	4	16	0	16	3	0	2	0	1.000	0	1	10.93
Washington, Porter	Reds	Cin	R	20	10	0	0	4	11.2	68	17	19	12	1	1	1	1	13	0	13	3	0	0	0	.000	0	0	9.26
Watkins, David	Braves	Atl	R	18	13	0	0	4	29.1	115	15	5	3	0	0	0	1	11	1	24	2	1	5	0	1.000	0	2	0.92
Watkins, Steve	Fort Wayne	SD	A	21	4	4	0	0	17	83	24	17	16	3	1	0	2	9	0	21	1	0	0	3	.000	0	0	8.47
	Idaho Falls	SD	R+	21	12	11	0	0	61.1	272	60	39	30	5	4	3	4	25	0	75	9	0	5	2	.714	0	0	4.40
Watson, Greg	Oneonta	Det	A-	23	31	0	0	27	33.2	150	23	18	12	2	2	0	9	17	2	33	4	0	1	2	.333	0	19	3.21

1999 Pitching — Single-A and Rookie Leagues

HOW MUCH HE PITCHED											WHAT HE GAVE UP												THE RESULTS					
Player	Team	Org	Lg	A	G	GS	CG	GF	IP	BFP	H	R	ER	HR	SH	SF	HB	TBB	IBB	SO	WP	Bk	W	L	Pct.	ShO	Sv	ERA
Wayne, Hawkeye	Everett	Sea	A-	22	15	7	0	0	33.2	186	47	39	31	1	2	1	5	32	0	34	13	0	0	2	.000	0	0	8.29
Weaver, Joseph	Pulaski	Tex	R+	22	18	0	0	8	21	107	30	17	15	1	0	0	1	15	0	17	1	0	6	0	1.000	0	0	6.43
Webb, John	Cubs	ChC	R	21	18	0	0	14	32.2	147	33	20	13	0	1	1	3	8	0	39	2	2	0	0	.000	0	3	3.58
	Eugene	ChC	A-	21	2	0	0	2	4	14	1	0	0	0	0	0	0	1	0	3	0	0	1	0	1.000	0	1	0.00
Weber, Brett	Greensboro	NYY	A	23	52	0	0	38	73	295	56	24	16	2	3	1	5	17	0	83	5	1	8	4	.667	0	23	1.97
Webster, Jeremy*	Idaho Falls	SD	R+	21	12	0	0	4	19	101	22	19	14	1	0	0	6	18	0	11	5	0	0	2	.000	0	0	6.63
	Padres	SD	R	21	7	0	0	1	12.2	67	13	11	6	2	0	0	2	13	0	16	2	0	1	0	1.000	0	0	4.26
Wedel, Jeremy	Piedmont	Phi	A	23	23	0	0	17	50	202	46	19	12	2	1	1	3	8	0	40	2	0	5	3	.625	0	3	2.16
	Clearwater	Phi	A+	23	4	0	0	1	5.1	21	4	1	1	0	0	0	0	1	0	3	1	0	0	0	.000	0	0	1.69
Weidert, Chris	Kinston	Cle	A+	26	27	2	0	13	52.1	223	49	15	15	2	5	2	1	22	5	42	3	0	4	3	.571	0	0	2.58
Weimer, Matt	Dunedin	Tor	A+	25	46	0	0	26	65.1	273	60	23	21	5	2	1	5	20	3	37	3	0	6	3	.667	0	6	2.89
Weinberg, Todd*	Athletics	Oak	R	28	6	0	0	2	4.1	18	5	5	2	1	0	0	0	0	0	3	1	0	0	0	.000	0	0	4.15
Weis, John*	Elizabethtn	Min	R+	22	26	0	0	12	33.1	147	24	15	8	2	0	1	1	17	0	39	3	0	0	1	.000	0	3	2.16
Wells, Matt	San Jose	SF	A+	25	57	0	0	24	90.2	400	73	41	37	4	4	8	1	65	0	100	6	0	8	5	.615	0	7	3.67
Wells, Roy	Everett	Sea	A-	21	2	0	0	0	2.1	15	5	5	5	0	0	1	0	4	0	3	0	1	0	2	.000	0	0	19.29
	Mariners	Sea	R	21	10	9	0	0	46.2	199	39	22	14	0	1	0	1	22	0	52	1	2	3	0	1.000	0	0	2.70
Wells, Zach	Bakersfield	SF	A+	23	4	0	0	3	6	27	6	4	2	2	0	0	2	1	0	3	0	0	0	0	.000	0	0	3.00
	Salem-Keizr	SF	A-	23	15	0	0	6	20.2	91	17	13	8	2	2	2	3	8	0	13	0	0	4	1	.800	0	1	3.48
Weslowski, Robert	Capital Cty	NYM	A	21	9	0	0	1	22.1	102	22	18	16	3	1	1	3	13	1	21	1	2	1	0	1.000	0	0	6.45
	Pittsfield	NYM	A-	21	14	14	0	0	83.2	344	79	35	31	2	1	2	5	22	1	62	1	0	4	4	.500	0	0	3.33
Wessel, Travis*	Pulaski	Tex	R+	24	21	0	0	19	29	128	28	15	13	1	1	4	2	11	0	36	1	0	5	1	.833	0	7	4.03
West, Brian	White Sox	CWS	R	19	2	0	0	1	4.2	25	10	7	7	0	1	2	0	2	0	3	0	0	0	1	.000	0	0	13.50
	Bristol	CWS	R+	19	8	1	0	2	18	98	26	25	21	4	1	0	1	14	2	17	5	0	1	2	.333	0	2	10.50
Westmoreland, Ken	Clearwater	Phi	A+	25	20	20	0	0	111.1	484	130	59	52	7	4	0	3	40	2	40	9	0	8	4	.667	0	0	4.20
Weymouth, Marty	Winston-Sal	CWS	A+	22	41	0	0	16	57.1	257	62	35	30	1	3	1	1	21	3	42	3	1	5	6	.455	0	2	4.71
Whatley, Brannon	Burlington	CWS	A	23	45	0	0	37	57	254	48	29	22	3	6	1	1	34	4	52	9	0	3	5	.375	0	20	3.47
Wheeler, David	Kingsport	NYM	R+	24	7	0	0	4	9	49	10	9	4	0	2	0	3	9	0	6	4	0	0	0	.000	0	0	4.00
White, James	Pirates	Pit	R	20	13	11	0	0	63	284	70	44	34	4	1	3	12	24	0	35	3	1	2	8	.200	0	0	4.86
White, Matt	St. Pete	TB	A+	21	21	20	2	0	113	498	125	75	65	6	2	6	8	33	0	92	10	1	9	7	.563	0	0	5.18
White, Matt*	Columbus	Cle	A	22	19	18	1	0	95.1	414	99	67	56	12	3	3	5	31	0	75	7	1	3	10	.231	0	0	5.29
White, Matt	High Desert	Ari	A+	22	31	17	0	4	91.2	418	101	70	59	15	2	3	3	49	1	78	5	0	2	8	.200	0	1	5.79
Whitecotton, Billy	Bluefield	Bal	R+	19	15	10	0	0	62.1	304	82	67	48	9	1	0	6	37	0	60	19	1	3	8	.273	0	0	6.93
Whiteley, Shad	Greensboro	NYY	A	25	15	8	0	1	55.1	276	67	52	47	7	1	0	6	42	0	62	5	4	1	9	.100	0	0	7.64
	Staten Ilnd	NYY	A-	25	12	12	0	0	61.2	279	69	39	34	1	1	3	2	26	0	71	9	0	3	4	.429	0	0	4.96
Whitesides, Johnny	Rockford	Cin	A	22	13	1	0	4	15.2	82	24	19	14	0	0	2	3	10	0	11	2	0	1	1	.500	0	0	8.04
	Auburn	Hou	A-	22	6	0	0	2	14.1	66	13	12	4	2	3	1	0	8	0	13	0	0	1	0	1.000	0	0	2.51
	Kissimmee	Hou	A+	22	14	0	0	9	25.1	119	34	20	12	1	2	3	1	6	1	11	3	0	1	1	.500	0	0	4.26
Whitney, Jacob*	Michigan	Hou	A	24	33	19	2	3	136.2	570	152	81	70	15	2	7	3	29	1	121	10	3	9	8	.529	0	1	4.61
Wiggins, Dan	Cubs	ChC	R	23	17	0	0	6	34.1	146	29	16	11	2	2	1	4	11	0	47	2	1	3	0	1.000	0	2	2.88
	Eugene	ChC	A-	23	3	0	0	1	6	25	4	5	4	1	1	0	0	3	0	8	2	0	1	0	1.000	0	0	6.00
Wiggins, Scott*	Greensboro	NYY	A	24	17	17	0	0	93.1	395	84	45	41	15	1	0	6	32	0	110	7	0	7	1	.875	0	0	3.95
Wilkerson, Byron	Auburn	Hou	A-	23	9	7	0	1	48	202	38	25	20	5	1	2	5	22	0	47	3	0	3	3	.500	0	0	3.75
Williams, Adam*	Great Falls	LA	R+	21	15	14	0	0	88.2	370	70	45	43	6	1	2	8	35	0	95	8	1	7	2	.778	0	0	4.36
Williams, David*	Williamsprt	Pit	A-	21	7	7	1	0	45.2	180	33	17	13	2	0	0	2	11	0	47	0	0	4	2	.667	1	0	2.56
	Hickory	Pit	A	21	9	9	1	0	59	228	42	22	21	5	0	2	6	11	0	46	2	0	3	1	.750	1	0	3.20
Williams, Jerome	Salem-Keizr	SF	A-	18	7	7	1	0	37	151	29	13	9	1	0	1	3	11	0	34	1	0	1	1	.500	1	0	2.19
Williams, Joel	Great Falls	LA	R+	20	13	0	0	4	22.2	114	30	26	21	3	1	0	1	16	0	15	2	0	2	3	.400	0	1	8.34
Williams, Larry	Lynchburg	Pit	A+	24	34	3	0	8	63.1	269	58	36	25	9	1	4	2	21	1	51	4	0	4	4	.500	0	0	3.55
Williams, Mike	Burlington	CWS	A	21	37	16	2	12	127.1	573	119	78	63	9	4	6	14	65	1	83	11	2	6	7	.462	0	2	4.45
Williams, Randy*	Daytona	ChC	A+	24	14	9	0	3	53	243	55	36	28	5	4	1	1	30	0	47	3	0	3	4	.429	0	1	4.75
Williamson, Brian	Pittsfield	NYM	A-	23	6	0	0	5	7.1	33	6	5	4	0	1	0	0	4	0	2	1	0	1	1	.500	0	1	4.91
Williamson, Charlie	Missoula	Ari	R+	22	25	0	0	13	35.2	160	33	16	10	1	3	0	5	12	1	34	5	0	2	2	.500	0	2	2.52
Willis, Craig	Wisconsin	Sea	A	23	39	1	0	17	61	293	81	47	40	6	3	3	4	26	2	49	5	1	2	2	.500	0	0	5.90
Willis, Jason	Yankees	NYY	R	21	4	4	0	0	16.1	64	13	4	4	0	0	1	0	6	0	17	2	0	1	1	.500	0	0	2.20
	Tampa	NYY	A+	21	3	3	0	0	13.1	55	9	3	3	0	1	0	0	7	0	10	0	0	2	0	1.000	0	0	2.03
	Staten Ilnd	NYY	A-	21	7	7	0	0	33	157	45	18	15	0	1	0	3	12	1	27	2	1	1	2	.333	0	0	4.09
Wilson, Jeff*	High Desert	Ari	A+	24	32	17	0	2	110.2	494	106	66	53	12	2	4	3	67	2	122	8	2	7	4	.636	0	1	4.31
Wilson, Mike	Batavia	Phi	A-	20	13	13	1	0	84	349	66	42	34	7	1	8	10	29	0	73	5	0	5	3	.625	0	0	3.64
Wimberly, Larry*	Hickory	Pit	A	24	17	5	0	3	47.2	182	32	8	8	2	2	1	1	11	3	57	3	0	3	1	.750	0	0	1.51
	Lynchburg	Pit	A+	24	11	10	0	0	55.1	257	77	40	31	5	2	0	5	13	0	41	2	1	5	3	.625	0	0	5.04
Winchester, Scott	Rockford	Cin	A	27	6	6	0	0	19.1	82	19	7	6	2	1	0	0	3	0	11	0	0	1	1	.500	0	0	2.79
Witte, Lou	Staten Ilnd	NYY	A-	23	25	0	0	4	41.1	174	42	21	14	2	0	0	1	12	1	39	1	0	5	2	.714	0	1	3.05
Wolfe, Brian	Twins	Min	R	19	9	5	2	0	38	153	33	14	12	2	1	1	1	9	0	40	2	0	4	0	1.000	0	0	2.84
Wollscheid, Jim	Missoula	Ari	R+	22	18	9	0	2	62.1	285	65	50	40	8	3	1	8	31	1	55	11	0	3	5	.375	0	0	5.78
Wood, Brandon	Missoula	Ari	R+	21	19	9	0	3	72	325	69	46	31	4	3	0	11	31	1	71	4	2	6	0	1.000	0	0	3.88
Wood, Stanton	Tampa	NYY	A+	23	50	0	0	19	81.2	355	89	43	34	2	3	2	2	23	3	66	4	0	4	1	.800	0	0	3.75
Woodards, Orlando	Hagerstown	Tor	A	22	44	3	0	12	80.1	352	66	45	37	5	6	1	7	43	3	79	7	1	7	4	.636	0	2	4.15
Wooten, Greg	Lancaster	Sea	A+	26	17	17	3	0	114.1	489	123	62	55	13	2	3	6	30	1	72	5	0	10	4	.714	0	0	4.33
Wooten, Shane*	Beloit	Mil	A	25	33	0	0	10	35	162	29	16	12	1	0	3	4	25	1	35	2	0	0	2	.000	0	1	3.09
Wright, Barrett	Chston-SC	TB	A	21	13	13	0	0	63.2	299	67	55	38	5	3	4	7	41	0	34	8	1	2	6	.250	0	0	5.37
	Hudson Val	TB	A-	21	10	9	0	1	58.1	250	55	29	24	1	3	1	7	24	0	40	5	1	4	2	.667	0	1	3.70
Wright, Chris	Chston-SC	TB	A	23	38	14	0	20	105.1	451	108	54	47	10	4	0	5	22	1	89	5	2	5	12	.294	0	8	4.02
Wright, Danny	Bristol	CWS	R+	22	10	0	0	3	18	79	14	8	2	1	0	0	1	9	1	18	3	0	2	0	1.000	0	1	1.00
	Burlington	CWS	A	22	2	0	0	0	6	26	5	4	4	1	0	0	1	3	0	3	0	0	0	0	.000	0	0	6.00
Wright, Shane	Williamsprt	Pit	A-	23	17	6	2	6	57.2	253	53	29	18	3	2	4	9	19	0	38	4	1	2	6	.250	0	1	2.81
Wrigley, Jase	Asheville	Col	A	24	28	0	0	18	58.1	259	63	32	20	2	2	2	2	16	0	58	6	2	3	2	.600	0	6	3.09
	Salem	Col	A+	24	8	0	0	5	9.1	36	9	1	1	0	0	0	0	0	0	6	1	0	2	0	1.000	0	0	0.96

1999 Pitching — Single-A and Rookie Leagues

Player	Team	Org	Lg	A	G	GS	CG	GF	IP	BFP	H	R	ER	HR	SH	SF	HB	TBB	IBB	SO	WP	Bk	W	L	Pct.	ShO	Sv	ERA
Wuertz, Mike	Lansing	ChC	A	21	28	28	1	0	161.1	716	191	104	86	11	2	10	1	44	0	127	11	0	11	12	.478	0	0	4.80
Wykoff, Jarred	Marlins	Fla	R	19	11	0	0	6	22.1	99	20	11	9	1	1	0	2	8	0	12	3	0	1	0	1.000	0	1	3.63
Wylie, Mitch	Burlington	CWS	A	23	6	6	0	0	32	134	28	11	7	0	0	3	2	11	0	27	0	0	1	0	1.000	0	0	1.97
Yacco, Anthony	Salem-Keizr	SF	A-	19	9	4	0	1	13	73	16	19	19	1	0	1	5	14	0	12	4	1	0	1	.000	0	1	13.15
Yates, Chad	New Jersey	StL	A-	23	12	0	0	4	17	69	9	7	7	3	1	1	0	10	0	20	1	0	1	1	.500	0	1	3.71
	Peoria	StL	A	23	22	0	0	9	24.1	103	16	8	7	2	1	2	0	14	0	26	4	2	1	2	.333	0	0	2.59
Yates, Tyler	Visalia	Oak	A+	22	47	1	0	19	82.1	382	98	64	50	12	3	2	4	35	3	74	12	0	2	5	.286	0	4	5.47
Yen, Buddy	Royals	KC	R	23	25	0	0	21	30	120	18	11	8	1	0	1	5	6	1	34	1	3	3	2	.600	0	10	2.40
	Wilmington	KC	A+	23	2	0	0	0	1	11	3	5	5	0	0	1	0	4	0	0	1	0	0	1	.000	0	0	45.00
Yepiz, Heriberto*	Mexico	—	R	—	15	0	0	4	29.1	112	24	10	9	2	0	0	0	6	0	28	0	1	0	0	.000	0	2	2.76
Young, Colin*	Portland	Col	A-	22	15	13	0	1	59	266	59	39	32	8	1	2	5	28	0	74	4	0	2	5	.286	0	0	4.88
Yount, Andy	W Michigan	Det	A	23	24	3	0	8	43.1	199	38	31	27	3	0	4		36	0	28	6	0	2	3	.400	0	1	5.61
Zallie, Chris*	Augusta	Bos	A	25	9	0	0	6	8.1	44	4	4	4	0	1	2	4	10	1	14	0	0	2	1	.667	0	0	4.32
Zamarripa, Tony	Lansing	ChC	A	23	11	0	0	1	15	68	21	13	12	1	0	0	0	5	0	7	0	0	2	0	1.000	0	0	7.20
Zambrano, Carlos	Lansing	ChC	A	19	27	24	2	2	153.1	663	150	87	71	9	5	4	10	62	1	98	10	2	13	7	.650	1	0	4.17
Zapata, Juan	Stockton	Mil	A+	24	30	0	0	12	54	267	65	52	40	7	1	2	4	30	2	35	0	0	1	4	.200	0	1	6.67
	Beloit	Mil	A	24	7	0	0	2	12.1	68	22	16	11	0	0	1	1	9	0	9	0	0	0	2	.000	0	0	8.03
Zazueta, Peter	Johnson Cy	StL	R+	20	11	11	1	0	56.2	261	62	43	36	7	1	0	4	26	0	56	7	0	3	6	.333	1	0	5.72
Zgoda, Derek	Yankees	NYY	R	27	2	0	0	1	5	22	5	2	2	0	1	0	0	0	0	5	0	0	0	0	.000	0	0	3.60
Zipser, Mike	Phillies	Phi	R	23	6	0	0	0	9	41	11	5	4	1	1	2	0	5	0	11	0	0	0	1	.000	0	0	4.00
	Batavia	Phi	A-	22	9	0	0	2	16.1	72	17	9	5	0	1	0	2	6	0	16	0	0	2	1	.667	0	0	2.76
Zirelli, Mike	Salem-Keizr	SF	A-	23	25	0	0	4	51	227	50	31	25	9	0	2	3	17	0	47	6	0	1	4	.200	0	2	4.41
Zorrilla, Reinaldo	White Sox	CWS	R	18	14	0	0	6	14	66	16	13	11	0	0	1	1	5	2	17	1	1	0	1	.000	0	1	7.07
Zyskowski, Garrett*	Michigan	Hou	A	24	14	0	0	5	16.1	78	21	14	14	3	1	1	3	12	1	12	3	0	2	0	1.000	0	1	7.71

1999 Team Statistics

How do the different leagues at a classification compare? This section answers that question, as team statistics for all 16 minor leagues follow. (A complete list of abbreviations can be found in the back of this book.)

For instance, a quick look at these numbers reveals that Triple-A hitters fare significantly better in the Pacific Coast League than in the International League. Or that the Eastern League is the most pitcher-friendly circuit in Double-A.

The team stats can help identify the most extreme parks in the minors. Check out the Texas League numbers, and you'll know why pitchers hate working in El Paso and Midland.

International League Batting - AAA

Team	Org	G	AB	H	2B	3B	HR	TB	R	RBI	TBB	IBB	SO	HBP	SH	SF	SB	CS	SB%	GDP	Avg	OBP	SLG
Durham	TB	143	4951	1460	336	39	186	2432	923	865	565	30	956	53	48	56	103	56	.65	110	.295	.369	.491
Columbus	NYY	141	4816	1391	305	34	171	2277	879	825	576	25	853	49	25	57	96	60	.62	114	.289	.367	.473
Charlotte	CWS	144	4843	1405	309	22	164	2250	836	777	506	20	850	70	52	48	95	37	.72	112	.290	.362	.465
Indianapolis	Cin	144	4977	1411	296	30	156	2235	788	748	479	23	878	51	28	51	83	41	.67	132	.284	.349	.449
Pawtucket	Bos	144	4897	1286	265	28	187	2168	776	726	593	20	1008	53	34	34	90	33	.73	91	.263	.346	.443
Buffalo	Cle	144	4829	1301	254	34	154	2085	748	697	542	20	947	46	39	46	143	46	.76	109	.269	.346	.432
Syracuse	Tor	144	4891	1311	257	32	154	2094	744	688	498	23	968	44	29	40	102	38	.73	121	.268	.339	.428
Louisville	Mil	144	4893	1299	265	36	166	2134	731	686	492	20	1003	47	40	43	168	47	.78	104	.265	.336	.436
Scranton-WB	Phi	144	4799	1220	290	29	132	1964	728	674	583	29	1035	53	31	47	90	36	.71	106	.254	.339	.409
Toledo	Det	144	4814	1241	250	32	176	2083	706	668	526	10	978	44	23	49	86	48	.64	103	.258	.333	.433
Norfolk	NYM	140	4688	1313	258	32	121	1998	675	631	468	23	782	52	50	45	115	73	.61	110	.280	.349	.426
Rochester	Bal	144	4931	1325	277	31	114	2006	668	615	414	18	858	50	48	46	91	58	.61	132	.269	.329	.407
Richmond	Atl	144	4774	1263	249	24	126	1938	661	617	455	17	956	44	42	48	132	66	.67	78	.265	.331	.406
Ottawa	Mon	144	4770	1216	246	32	120	1886	647	603	460	25	1057	82	40	58	146	78	.65	101	.255	.327	.395
Total		1003	67873	18442	3857	435	2127	29550	10510	9820	7157	303	13129	738	529	668	1540	716	.68	1523	.272	.345	.435

International League Pitching - AAA

Team	Org	G	GS	CG	GF	IP	BFP	H	R	ER	HR	SH	SF	HB	TBB	IBB	SO	WP	Bk	W	L	Pct.	ShO	Sv	ERA
Pawtucket	Bos	144	144	9	132	1266.2	5455	1283	682	565	161	42	41	54	393	16	900	51	14	76	68	.528	9	31	4.01
Richmond	Atl	142	142	4	138	1232	5316	1256	693	637	131	55	52	24	466	22	1040	74	8	64	78	.451	8	34	4.65
Buffalo	Cle	144	144	2	142	1246.2	5453	1278	706	601	137	43	53	47	491	34	818	64	13	72	72	.500	5	42	4.34
Norfolk	NYM	140	140	7	133	1219.2	5412	1283	712	620	156	45	28	47	532	50	984	66	13	77	63	.550	7	39	4.58
Scranton-WB	Phi	144	144	9	135	1253	5503	1363	715	641	115	35	50	33	494	31	912	65	9	78	66	.542	11	40	4.60
Columbus	NYY	141	141	9	132	1230	5355	1262	725	643	150	29	49	67	470	9	986	82	12	83	58	.589	5	34	4.70
Ottawa	Mon	144	144	2	142	1254.2	5542	1321	725	624	148	52	41	59	531	17	954	66	6	59	85	.410	6	36	4.48
Rochester	Bal	144	144	5	139	1274.1	5559	1290	740	662	174	28	47	54	511	14	1017	67	13	61	83	.424	8	30	4.68
Syracuse	Tor	144	144	4	140	1258	5596	1284	752	682	165	34	48	49	618	19	974	66	10	73	71	.507	4	41	4.88
Charlotte	CWS	144	144	12	132	1225	5397	1378	763	677	154	32	44	37	440	8	952	72	5	82	62	.569	4	42	4.97
Indianapolis	Cin	144	144	4	140	1264.2	5557	1386	773	696	137	41	61	63	496	27	853	66	8	75	69	.521	6	47	4.95
Durham	TB	143	143	2	141	1253	5574	1370	817	724	165	21	46	61	533	10	961	72	13	83	60	.580	2	39	5.20
Toledo	Det	144	144	11	133	1241	5559	1327	839	753	163	31	55	78	596	23	848	75	14	57	87	.396	2	22	5.46
Louisville	Mil	144	144	2	142	1271.2	5677	1361	868	765	171	41	53	65	586	23	929	70	5	63	81	.438	7	33	5.41
Total		1003	1003	84	919	17490.1	76985	18442	10510	9290	2127	529	668	738	7157	303	13129	956	136	1003	1003	.500	84	510	4.78

Pacific Coast League Batting - AAA

Team	Org	G	AB	H	2B	3B	HR	TB	R	RBI	TBB	IBB	SO	HBP	SH	SF	SB	CS	SB%	GDP	Avg	OBP	SLG
Fresno	SF	142	4857	1430	262	37	170	2276	849	784	483	23	883	42	58	56	145	61	.70	116	.294	.360	.469
Omaha	KC	141	4828	1395	277	20	231	2405	826	779	457	18	990	97	40	36	104	63	.62	112	.289	.360	.498
Salt Lake	Min	141	4736	1379	274	48	159	2226	814	766	521	14	951	62	34	40	84	48	.64	137	.291	.366	.466
Nashville	Pit	140	4757	1373	292	26	183	2266	806	759	440	19	855	57	39	54	93	50	.65	111	.289	.352	.476
Col. Springs	Col	139	4796	1422	303	28	194	2367	793	752	437	17	1012	57	46	47	100	53	.65	113	.297	.359	.494
Oklahoma	Tex	142	4819	1360	286	27	151	2153	787	738	469	29	970	55	29	46	84	45	.65	123	.282	.350	.447
Tucson	Ari	142	4885	1427	282	36	141	2204	766	705	449	18	941	53	46	49	86	46	.65	122	.292	.355	.451
Vancouver	Ana	142	4740	1339	272	37	124	2057	759	693	547	26	902	65	43	38	93	53	.64	149	.282	.362	.434
Memphis	StL	138	4666	1323	300	34	127	2072	743	683	472	19	1017	60	46	45	110	49	.69	95	.284	.354	.444
Albuquerque	LA	139	4703	1338	288	32	148	2134	742	694	472	16	979	47	61	38	119	83	.59	95	.284	.353	.454
Edmonton	Oak	139	4767	1338	272	31	137	2083	730	677	444	13	860	48	38	37	84	61	.58	108	.281	.346	.437
Calgary	Fla	139	4703	1327	315	34	159	2187	716	670	403	17	995	42	32	33	73	50	.59	121	.282	.342	.465
Iowa	ChC	141	4800	1261	287	29	156	2074	699	646	461	21	1093	60	45	34	116	62	.65	89	.263	.333	.432
Las Vegas	SD	142	4771	1261	297	31	135	2025	692	636	560	15	1106	51	36	29	105	41	.72	123	.264	.346	.424
Tacoma	Sea	139	4841	1359	272	35	102	2007	698	624	488	22	949	47	35	55	121	54	.69	108	.281	.349	.415
New Orleans	Hou	140	4711	1270	266	19	118	1928	674	618	454	15	914	38	41	32	75	62	.55	113	.270	.337	.409
Total		1123	76380	21602	4545	494	2435	34444	12085	11224	7557	302	15417	881	669	669	1592	881	.64	1835	.283	.351	.451

Pacific Coast League Pitching - AAA

Team	Org	G	GS	CG	GF	IP	BFP	H	R	ER	HR	SH	SF	HB	TBB	IBB	SO	WP	Bk	W	L	Pct.	ShO	Sv	ERA
Vancouver	Ana	142	142	6	136	1229	5291	1287	617	527	103	41	39	36	436	17	925	70	4	84	58	.592	11	43	3.86
Tacoma	Sea	139	139	8	131	1231.2	5346	1245	664	595	131	30	38	76	476	20	998	62	7	69	70	.496	6	34	4.35
Oklahoma	Tex	142	142	16	126	1233.2	5368	1349	696	638	131	26	38	43	456	9	900	62	3	83	59	.585	5	43	4.65
Nashville	Pit	140	140	4	136	1216	5384	1328	708	606	129	56	35	49	464	37	1042	62	3	80	60	.571	1	43	4.49
Iowa	ChC	141	141	6	135	1242.1	5444	1290	716	644	152	51	37	55	495	14	1014	63	7	65	76	.461	4	25	4.67
Memphis	StL	138	138	3	130	1195.1	5237	1250	730	602	165	47	35	48	408	16	918	67	6	71	91	.500	9	27	1.09
Omaha	KC	141	141	6	135	1226	5361	1313	744	650	177	33	36	62	438	15	957	64	8	81	60	.574	5	29	4.77
Edmonton	Oak	139	139	5	134	1213.1	5297	1365	746	666	157	24	43	41	421	12	936	57	6	65	74	.468	4	25	4.94
New Orleans	Hou	140	140	7	133	1209.2	5356	1332	750	676	137	52	42	56	416	27	851	66	10	55	85	.393	6	31	5.03
Las Vegas	SD	142	142	6	136	1230.2	5509	1437	791	695	164	41	55	57	451	13	1057	64	3	67	75	.472	6	30	5.08
Fresno	SF	142	142	5	137	1230	5482	1327	800	672	195	40	38	65	499	10	1107	97	12	73	69	.514	2	29	4.92
Albuquerque	LA	139	139	8	131	1206	5403	1363	805	713	175	41	47	67	514	21	1023	70	6	65	74	.468	5	34	5.32
Tucson	Ari	142	142	2	140	1222.1	5471	1400	807	700	144	55	36	57	523	38	1013	55	11	66	76	.465	6	32	5.15
Salt Lake	Min	141	141	4	137	1203.2	5441	1387	807	711	163	36	57	54	494	17	858	75	6	73	68	.518	2	35	5.32
Col. Springs	Col	139	139	10	134	1193.1	5409	1457	830	730	164	49	46	67	504	28	909	61	12	66	73	.475	2	34	5.51
Calgary	Fla	139	139	4	135	1171	5347	1424	866	760	148	47	43	53	511	11	882	73	6	57	82	.410	2	22	5.84
Total		1123	1123	100	1023	19454	86166	21602	12085	10645	2435	669	669	881	7557	302	15417	1058	109	1123	1123	.500	73	528	4.92

Eastern League Batting - AA

Team	Org	G	AB	H	2B	3B	HR	TB	R	RBI	TBB	IBB	SO	HBP	SH	SF	SB	CS	SB%	GDP	Avg	OBP	SLG
Trenton	Bos	142	4851	1352	251	23	150	2099	785	731	495	17	801	100	51	52	151	75	.67	119	.279	.342	.433
Norwich	NYY	142	4766	1259	232	39	129	1956	755	685	605	11	1129	94	30	40	168	84	.67	102	.264	.356	.410
Harrisburg	Mon	142	4723	1265	256	29	140	1999	714	666	543	25	910	38	51	41	119	72	.62	96	.268	.345	.423
Akron	Cle	140	4782	1266	248	40	132	1990	714	663	495	11	1066	56	27	31	84	41	.67	81	.265	.339	.416
Altoona	Pit	140	4723	1218	249	43	138	1967	695	664	519	10	964	85	58	50	105	76	.58	85	.258	.339	.416
Reading	Phi	142	4711	1237	236	43	116	1907	680	628	549	19	839	71	81	39	164	77	.68	119	.263	.346	.405
Bowie	Bal	141	4798	1245	229	27	118	1882	676	611	522	13	786	56	69	48	110	58	.65	92	.259	.336	.392
Erie	Ana	142	4686	1210	234	41	110	1856	671	612	581	18	1094	53	58	44	180	80	.69	96	.258	.344	.396
Portland	Fla	142	4774	1277	249	35	110	1926	646	587	521	11	990	49	54	38	133	55	.71	124	.267	.343	.403
Binghamton	NYM	142	4789	1218	224	33	113	1847	635	582	470	17	1130	55	52	35	168	73	.70	111	.254	.326	.386
New Britain	Min	141	4730	1232	237	26	106	1839	611	562	458	19	832	46	34	43	111	57	.66	114	.260	.329	.389
New Haven	Sea	142	4754	1219	222	25	97	1782	610	566	478	13	1000	62	31	30	110	67	.62	107	.256	.330	.375
Total		849	57087	14998	2867	404	1459	23050	8192	7557	6236	184	11541	765	596	491	1603	815	.66	1246	.263	.340	.404

Eastern League Pitching - AA

Team	Org	G	GS	CG	GF	IP	BFP	H	R	ER	HR	SH	SF	HB	TBB	IBB	SO	WP	Bk	W	L	Pct.	ShO	Sv	ERA
Trenton	Bos	142	142	7	135	1265.1	5347	1200	603	541	105	40	34	53	453	14	986	67	9	92	50	.648	17	42	3.85
Erie	Ana	142	142	19	123	1249.1	5345	1197	617	520	127	49	33	68	451	1	967	46	12	81	61	.570	7	37	3.75
New Haven	Sea	142	142	10	132	1244	5376	1215	625	532	104	41	36	66	549	13	1059	80	6	65	77	.458	7	36	3.85
Harrisburg	Mon	142	142	7	135	1232.2	5319	1200	649	560	137	62	35	79	496	9	812	58	8	76	66	.535	10	31	4.09
Bowie	Bal	141	141	9	132	1260.2	5496	1264	670	600	156	59	31	60	534	22	989	63	19	70	71	.496	7	33	4.28
Norwich	NYY	142	142	6	136	1242.1	5437	1209	680	545	82	40	52	40	550	30	981	73	10	78	64	.549	6	47	3.95
Altoona	Pit	140	140	4	136	1244.2	5497	1252	680	560	99	61	44	50	570	23	935	91	18	67	73	.479	5	32	4.05
Akron	Cle	140	140	2	138	1215.2	5373	1232	702	627	123	49	58	69	562	11	839	72	13	65	77	.493	6	41	4.64
Portland	Fla	140	140	2	140	1242	5484	1301	708	595	130	56	31	78	520	21	1068	73	11	65	77	.458	5	39	4.31
Reading	Phi	142	142	9	133	1249.2	5490	1295	732	645	145	45	48	70	494	21	984	48	11	73	69	.514	4	39	4.65
New Britain	Min	141	141	7	134	1224.1	5435	1336	759	653	126	45	51	50	500	10	982	53	7	59	82	.418	9	30	4.80
Binghamton	NYM	142	142	1	141	1255.2	5595	1297	767	639	125	49	38	82	557	9	939	48	10	54	88	.380	8	29	4.58
Total		849	849	83	766	14926.1	65194	14998	8192	7017	1459	596	491	765	6236	184	11541	772	134	849	849	.500	91	436	4.23

Southern League Batting - AA

Team	Org	G	AB	H	2B	3B	HR	TB	R	RBI	TBB	IBB	SO	HBP	SH	SF	SB	CS	SB%	GDP	Avg	OBP	SLG
Knoxville	Tor	140	4717	1312	274	29	151	2097	824	755	666	20	860	58	24	55	122	79	.61	119	.278	.370	.445
Jacksonville	Det	141	4952	1367	305	31	149	2181	792	743	561	9	1032	49	14	50	106	44	.71	99	.276	.352	.440
Chattanooga	Cin	140	4789	1327	270	35	147	2108	765	710	530	21	919	57	47	50	130	88	.60	117	.277	.353	.440
Mobile	SD	139	4686	1235	265	36	116	1920	711	664	570	24	1094	59	36	38	139	51	.73	103	.264	.348	.410
Birmingham	CWS	140	4671	1253	229	38	101	1861	699	636	491	19	883	56	46	40	160	76	.60	111	.268	.342	.398
Orlando	TB	138	4695	1319	254	26	118	1979	686	639	458	16	760	39	40	45	91	59	.61	125	.281	.347	.422
West Tenn	ChC	141	4648	1181	275	36	106	1846	646	595	482	30	1044	91	42	40	144	71	.67	86	.254	.333	.397
Huntsville	Mil	141	4698	1182	229	24	92	1735	646	582	542	24	915	79	42	44	178	72	.71	112	.252	.336	.369
Greenville	Atl	138	4558	1186	241	24	109	1802	640	594	432	16	884	66	46	42	108	88	.55	89	.260	.330	.395
Carolina	Col	140	4587	1169	260	34	110	1827	597	547	423	15	1017	59	47	41	103	58	.64	100	.255	.323	.398
Total		699	47001	12531	2602	313	1199	19356	7006	6465	5155	194	9408	613	384	445	1281	686	.65	1060	.267	.344	.412

Southern League Pitching - AA

Team	Org	G	GS	CG	GF	IP	BFP	H	R	ER	HR	SH	SF	HB	TBB	IBB	SO	WP	Bk	W	L	Pct.	ShO	Sv	ERA
West Tenn	ChC	141	141	8	133	1230.2	5323	1115	579	489	89	39	52	48	590	38	1133	83	7	84	57	.596	9	45	3.58
Birmingham	CWS	140	140	6	134	1207.1	5158	1108	592	511	103	27	37	69	475	4	876	76	9	73	67	.521	8	31	3.81
Chattanooga	Cin	140	140	3	137	1241.1	5426	1308	682	583	98	44	35	36	533	21	948	73	10	78	62	.557	8	35	4.23
Carolina	Col	140	140	8	132	1197	5376	1249	685	575	109	59	35	67	489	7	1020	78	14	60	80	.429	7	38	4.32
Jacksonville	Det	141	141	6	135	1252.1	5471	1280	710	595	126	30	42	66	466	9	877	41	10	75	66	.532	8	39	4.28
Huntsville	Mil	141	141	8	133	1240.2	5461	1299	724	619	146	44	42	81	503	23	833	79	12	64	77	.454	7	27	4.49
Orlando	TB	138	138	5	133	1200.1	5286	1259	742	638	130	25	54	77	469	16	953	64	19	70	68	.507	11	33	4.78
Knoxville	Tor	140	140	4	136	1222.1	5401	1300	757	646	114	35	48	54	549	8	974	68	13	71	69	.507	9	32	4.76
Greenville	Atl	138	138	4	134	1185.2	5384	1279	763	656	129	40	48	61	588	42	920	63	12	58	80	.420	6	30	4.98
Mobile	SD	139	139	7	132	1214.2	5398	1334	772	687	155	41	52	54	493	26	874	67	4	66	73	.475	6	30	5.09
Total		699	699	59	640	12192.1	53617	12531	7006	5999	1199	384	445	613	5155	194	9408	694	110	699	699	.500	79	340	4.43

Texas League Batting - AA

Team	Org	G	AB	H	2B	3B	HR	TB	R	RBI	TBB	IBB	SO	HBP	SH	SF	SB	CS	SB%	GDP	Avg	OBP	SLG
Midland	Oak	140	4786	1406	311	48	164	2305	884	818	586	29	916	64	32	54	138	77	.64	101	.294	.374	.482
Wichita	KC	140	4596	1286	257	28	122	1965	785	691	577	18	785	50	52	46	140	93	.60	104	.280	.363	.428
El Paso	Ari	140	4835	1375	303	46	107	2091	726	675	416	27	986	52	27	40	88	55	.62	95	.284	.345	.432
Tulsa	Tex	140	4798	1272	284	38	132	2028	720	657	491	19	910	47	23	37	130	46	.74	97	.265	.337	.423
San Antonio	LA	140	4733	1337	265	52	102	2012	710	658	516	17	915	30	53	41	171	90	.66	97	.282	.354	.425
Jackson	Hou	140	4670	1199	233	23	133	1877	628	576	402	13	918	65	50	41	127	77	.62	95	.257	.322	.402
Shreveport	SF	140	4581	1140	222	32	89	1693	613	573	484	18	944	57	41	32	103	62	.62	108	.249	.326	.370
Arkansas	StL	140	4405	1113	207	34	125	1763	527	489	328	7	950	67	44	38	79	56	.59	106	.253	.312	.400
Total		560	37404	10128	2082	301	974	15734	5593	5137	3800	148	7324	432	322	329	976	556	.64	803	.271	.342	.421

Texas League Pitching - AA

Team	Org	G	GS	CG	GF	IP	BFP	H	R	ER	HR	SH	SF	HB	TBB	IBB	SO	WP	Bk	W	L	Pct.	ShO	Sv	ERA
Shreveport	SF	140	140	4	136	1208.1	5125	1165	585	493	102	47	35	42	410	8	851	54	12	71	69	.507	13	39	3.67
Jackson	Hou	140	140	2	130	1219.2	5200	1183	632	510	129	40	29	71	465	16	988	70	11	68	72	.486	10	39	3.76
Wichita	KC	140	140	2	138	1196.2	5200	1339	643	568	118	33	37	46	377	36	772	59	8	83	57	.593	8	42	4.27
Tulsa	Tex	140	140	7	133	1228.1	5350	1218	666	563	132	37	42	56	487	13	984	82	6	74	66	.529	10	36	4.13
Arkansas	StL	140	140	5	135	1153	5075	1188	690	596	139	43	39	40	521	10	876	66	8	59	81	.421	7	36	4.65
San Antonio	LA	140	140	2	138	1212.1	5363	1235	733	583	103	51	49	64	518	19	951	65	6	67	73	.479	8	40	4.33
El Paso	Ari	140	140	8	132	1198.2	5352	1352	741	625	111	40	59	59	470	14	944	74	11	64	76	.457	7	31	4.69
Midland	Oak	140	140	3	137	1201	5553	1448	903	756	140	31	59	54	552	32	958	89	13	74	66	.529	2	35	5.67
Total		560	560	33	527	9618	42304	10128	5593	4694	974	322	329	432	3800	148	7324	559	75	560	560	.500	65	298	4.39

California League Batting - A+

Team	Org	G	AB	H	2B	3B	HR	TB	R	RBI	TBB	IBB	SO	HBP	SH	SF	SB	CS	SB%	GDP	Avg	OBP	SLG
High Desert	Ari	141	4941	1449	268	51	159	2296	903	827	583	13	1116	57	42	44	140	100	.58	97	.293	.371	.465
Modesto	Oak	140	4885	1410	300	63	120	2096	872	787	575	11	1075	73	28	67	193	88	.69	95	.289	.368	.450
Visalia	Oak	140	4791	1312	259	39	132	2045	871	783	701	19	1044	85	38	56	154	88	.64	108	.274	.372	.427
Lancaster	Sea	140	4892	1363	249	43	142	2124	812	726	500	17	1112	70	36	37	137	91	.60	87	.279	.352	.434
San Bernardino	LA	141	4936	1416	224	57	95	2039	764	685	517	27	918	68	51	44	145	78	.65	112	.287	.360	.413
Lake Elsinore	Ana	140	4831	1320	274	61	92	1992	753	669	496	11	1034	66	27	49	190	91	.68	91	.273	.346	.412
San Jose	SF	140	4780	1260	254	28	126	1948	722	649	529	15	1143	76	39	33	134	61	.69	97	.264	.344	.408
Rancho Cuca.	SD	140	4755	1300	237	33	100	1903	715	628	484	17	1016	78	35	36	136	78	.64	142	.273	.348	.400
Bakersfield	SF	140	4786	1281	224	43	66	1789	685	613	478	12	1116	77	23	43	187	99	.65	77	.268	.341	.374
Stockton	Mil	140	4787	1283	223	43	78	1826	654	596	406	19	991	75	38	58	126	95	.57	84	.268	.331	.381
Total		701	48384	13394	2512	461	1110	20158	7751	6963	5269	161	10565	725	357	467	1542	869	.64	990	.277	.354	.417

California League Pitching - A+

Team	Org	G	GS	CG	GF	IP	BFP	H	R	ER	HR	SH	SF	HB	TBB	IBB	SO	WP	Bk	W	L	Pct.	ShO	Sv	ERA
Rancho Cuca.	SD	140	140	6	134	1232.2	5242	1198	619	527	94	30	37	58	425	13	1110	84	23	76	64	.543	11	38	3.85
San Bernardino	LA	141	141	3	138	1266	5531	1321	697	611	96	36	55	62	546	16	1126	89	13	80	61	.567	8	46	4.34
San Jose	SF	140	140	2	138	1227	5409	1264	704	575	68	40	44	67	526	2	1068	97	21	75	65	.536	4	38	4.22
Modesto	Oak	140	140	0	140	1246	5572	1310	734	579	82	43	48	85	544	26	1099	103	11	88	52	.629	7	54	4.18
Lake Elsinore	Ana	140	140	21	119	1239	5531	1385	771	637	101	44	33	64	481	30	999	83	14	63	77	.450	9	19	4.63
Bakersfield	SF	140	140	3	137	1230.1	5509	1329	787	658	140	25	45	79	493	8	926	73	9	64	76	.457	2	33	4.81
Stockton	Mil	140	140	9	131	1228	5491	1316	802	627	129	51	51	67	523	22	1048	103	19	57	83	.407	8	34	4.60
Visalia	Oak	140	140	1	139	1235.1	5634	1376	832	680	108	33	53	55	577	21	1118	133	12	75	65	.536	3	38	4.95
High Desert	Ari	141	141	0	141	1231	5653	1391	890	744	144	32	49	89	621	16	1099	80	19	68	73	.482	0	28	5.44
Lancaster	Sea	140	140	4	136	1223	5644	1504	915	780	148	23	52	99	533	7	972	104	14	55	85	.393	4	21	5.74
Total		701	701	49	652	12358.1	55216	13394	7751	6418	1110	357	467	725	5269	161	10565	949	155	701	701	.500	56	349	4.67

Carolina League Batting - A+

Team	Org	G	AB	H	2B	3B	HR	TB	R	RBI	TBB	IBB	SO	HBP	SH	SF	SB	CS	SB%	GDP	Avg	OBP	SLG
Frederick	Bal	138	4667	1232	222	30	79	1751	699	623	589	10	952	56	43	53	171	72	.70	106	.264	.350	.375
Lynchburg	Pit	137	4568	1182	228	40	116	1838	680	614	582	14	1146	72	38	38	126	71	.64	106	.259	.349	.402
Wilmington	KC	138	4641	1208	209	33	85	1738	653	583	482	16	950	83	52	43	143	71	.67	97	.260	.338	.374
Kinston	Cle	137	4492	1132	241	36	92	1721	644	591	554	18	1088	53	42	29	142	59	.71	82	.252	.339	.383
Myrtle Beach	Atl	139	4763	1193	240	49	105	1846	637	578	427	21	1190	56	31	40	108	54	.67	93	.250	.317	.388
Winston-Salem	CWS	138	4623	1159	242	29	94	1741	635	571	458	14	1037	60	43	35	174	77	.69	80	.251	.324	.377
Potomac	StL	139	4610	1120	221	30	90	1671	619	573	475	8	1051	88	42	40	138	81	.63	99	.243	.323	.362
Salem	Col	138	4521	1116	206	37	61	1579	574	511	430	14	915	45	77	37	126	62	.67	85	.247	.316	.349
Total		552	36885	9342	1809	284	722	13885	5141	4644	3997	115	8329	513	368	315	1128	547	.67	748	.253	.332	.376

Carolina League Pitching - A+

Team	Org	G	GS	CG	GF	IP	BFP	H	R	ER	HR	SH	SF	HB	TBB	IBB	SO	WP	Bk	W	L	Pct.	ShO	Sv	ERA
Myrtle Beach	Atl	139	139	0	139	1248.2	5271	1056	552	486	95	48	35	31	559	17	1159	88	3	79	60	.568	10	41	3.50
Kinston	Cle	137	137	4	133	1184	5062	1031	569	478	83	51	35	86	492	13	1092	82	4	79	58	.577	11	47	3.63
Salem	Col	138	138	6	132	1205.1	5189	1152	600	513	73	46	30	67	468	6	1078	89	4	69	69	.500	8	38	3.83
Wilmington	KC	138	138	1	137	1221	5252	1165	607	541	78	39	33	60	503	11	1090	73	5	77	61	.558	9	40	3.99
Winston-Salem	CWS	138	138	7	131	1209.1	5348	1155	675	544	70	54	36	83	568	21	1065	123	5	63	75	.457	10	29	4.05
Lynchburg	Pit	137	137	6	131	1206	5265	1271	706	587	102	37	46	44	431	8	1008	81	10	64	73	.467	7	24	4.38
Frederick	Bal	138	138	8	130	1219	5381	1269	714	585	118	45	44	69	479	26	943	80	5	67	71	.486	8	26	4.32
Potomac	StL	139	139	3	136	1209	5323	1243	718	617	103	48	56	73	497	13	894	98	4	54	85	.388	8	26	4.59
Total		552	552	35	517	9702.1	42091	9342	5141	4351	722	368	315	513	3997	115	8329	714	41	552	552	.500	71	271	4.04

Florida State League Batting - A+

Team	Org	G	AB	H	2B	3B	HR	TB	R	RBI	TBB	IBB	SO	HBP	SH	SF	SB	CS	SB%	GDP	Avg	OBP	SLG
Dunedin	Tor	137	4659	1341	285	39	120	2064	760	695	414	12	835	70	51	45	159	74	.68	103	.288	.352	.443
Clearwater	Phi	136	4653	1307	232	48	87	1896	756	691	579	24	811	75	42	66	103	48	.68	110	.281	.365	.407
Charlotte	Tex	139	4583	1232	215	53	89	1820	702	636	521	18	914	71	39	40	180	101	.64	70	.269	.350	.397
Sarasota	Bos	139	4649	1250	238	31	106	1868	693	608	498	16	841	88	49	39	121	58	.68	94	.269	.348	.402
Fort Myers	Min	139	4635	1251	221	32	91	1809	686	626	507	16	801	61	32	48	95	54	.64	111	.270	.346	.390
Kissimmee	Hou	137	4554	1149	227	34	121	1807	652	589	486	14	1051	72	27	31	118	82	.59	80	.252	.332	.397
Lakeland	Det	138	4623	1221	231	41	64	1726	638	570	393	10	911	66	27	42	173	71	.71	111	.264	.328	.373
St. Lucie	NYM	138	4595	1199	203	39	98	1774	625	557	419	15	971	68	49	43	143	75	.66	98	.261	.329	.386
Tampa	NYY	136	4577	1208	219	55	90	1807	622	561	511	18	991	61	25	52	79	48	.62	99	.264	.342	.395
Brevard County	Fla	135	4541	1201	174	33	58	1615	591	537	396	12	842	62	39	47	140	68	.67	89	.264	.329	.356
Daytona	ChC	138	4452	1147	206	30	79	1650	589	526	378	18	795	81	35	40	128	76	.63	104	.258	.324	.371
St. Petersburg	TB	137	4491	1160	174	29	63	1581	579	519	367	10	851	62	45	36	93	58	.62	97	.258	.321	.352
Jupiter	Mon	138	4471	1126	184	28	57	1537	579	513	428	16	895	86	85	49	206	102	.67	87	.252	.326	.344
Vero Beach	LA	133	4262	1079	181	21	59	1479	531	451	428	13	884	71	48	39	125	110	.53	76	.253	.329	.347
Total		960	63745	16871	2990	513	1182	24433	9003	8079	6325	212	12393	994	593	611	1863	1025	.65	1329	.265	.337	.383

Florida State League Pitching - A+

Team	Org	G	GS	CG	GF	IP	BFP	H	R	ER	HR	SH	SF	HB	TBB	IBB	SO	WP	Bk	W	L	Pct.	ShO	Sv	ERA
Jupiter	Mon	138	138	6	132	1209.2	5041	1056	509	426	65	40	44	69	402	12	885	65	9	73	65	.529	13	32	3.17
Tampa	NYY	136	136	4	132	1194.2	5113	1154	561	455	60	46	33	42	415	26	1002	57	6	78	58	.574	9	42	3.43
St. Petersburg	TB	137	137	3	134	1177.1	5065	1227	585	483	57	41	37	102	362	9	805	75	7	74	63	.540	12	40	3.69
Dunedin	Tor	137	137	6	131	1195.2	5117	1131	592	515	87	36	33	78	475	11	967	60	10	86	51	.628	9	42	3.88
Kissimmee	Hou	137	137	9	128	1190.2	5093	1143	595	492	80	41	39	62	416	21	918	97	11	71	66	.518	8	31	3.72
St. Lucie	NYM	138	138	7	131	1201	5240	1177	637	511	71	52	32	56	533	29	957	67	13	68	70	.493	7	31	3.83
Charlotte	Tex	139	139	10	129	1189.2	5245	1275	669	550	83	39	58	75	481	7	816	70	16	69	70	.496	8	34	4.16
Vero Beach	LA	138	138	5	128	1219	4985	1145	679	584	122	47	51	79	482	11	819	77	16	48	85	.361	5	32	4.67
Lakeland	Det	138	138	7	131	1192.2	5230	1243	681	581	106	44	49	58	471	13	843	57	9	65	73	.471	3	28	4.38
Brevard County	Fla	135	135	13	122	1171.1	5153	1228	686	578	96	43	45	84	430	11	789	66	9	61	74	.452	7	27	4.44
Clearwater	Phi	136	136	5	131	1204.2	5302	1323	690	559	85	42	44	51	406	20	798	77	14	77	59	.566	11	44	4.18
Daytona	ChC	138	138	10	128	1164.2	5134	1151	694	550	103	41	42	73	540	12	981	91	7	63	75	.457	9	34	4.25
Sarasota	Bos	139	139	3	136	1189	5311	1311	709	586	88	37	50	102	443	24	929	93	6	67	72	.482	7	38	4.44
Fort Myers	Min	139	139	5	134	1187.2	5263	1307	716	601	79	44	54	63	469	6	884	89	11	60	79	.432	9	20	4.55
Total		960	960	93	867	16594.2	72292	16871	9003	7471	1182	593	611	994	6325	212	12393	1041	144	960	960	.500	117	475	4.05

Midwest League Batting - A

Team	Org	G	AB	H	2B	3B	HR	TB	R	RBI	TBB	IBB	SO	HBP	SH	SF	SB	CS	SB%	GDP	Avg	OBP	SLG
Lansing	ChC	140	4670	1278	288	60	147	2127	822	752	619	12	1031	70	10	54	133	61	.69	108	.274	.363	.455
Michigan	Hou	138	4747	1350	277	54	141	2158	810	741	401	13	873	61	31	55	105	67	.61	97	.284	.344	.455
Kane County	Fla	137	4681	1263	251	40	86	1852	777	674	554	14	1010	83	32	48	166	67	.71	88	.270	.354	.396
Quad City	Min	139	4655	1203	252	28	110	1841	743	658	658	21	893	80	51	52	96	58	.62	122	.258	.356	.395
Burlington	CWS	139	4604	1213	239	39	99	1827	734	661	610	13	1023	68	39	51	155	65	.70	87	.263	.355	.397
Wisconsin	Sea	138	4645	1243	247	26	90	1812	721	650	609	9	1027	52	28	37	122	72	.63	116	.268	.356	.390
Rockford	Cin	139	4587	1221	243	43	116	1898	700	621	451	22	975	84	28	52	227	123	.65	89	.266	.339	.414
West Michigan	Det	140	4688	1186	260	43	73	1751	696	627	521	10	1091	65	38	43	197	73	.73	91	.253	.333	.374
Beloit	Mil	139	4664	1227	231	34	94	1808	680	606	491	13	1056	49	46	40	94	39	.71	104	.263	.337	.388
Fort Wayne	SD	140	4668	1209	221	38	61	1689	672	593	571	20	1102	81	44	53	225	100	.69	96	.259	.346	.362
Cedar Rapids	Ana	138	4627	1178	235	35	90	1753	666	573	506	17	901	63	37	39	152	63	.71	90	.255	.334	.379
Clinton	Cin	137	4542	1159	234	38	75	1694	648	579	425	11	1045	57	28	43	157	76	.67	91	.255	.324	.373
South Bend	Ari	139	4712	1236	229	45	63	1744	642	578	447	11	986	47	9	43	108	73	.60	96	.262	.330	.370
Peoria	StL	139	4634	1178	228	41	69	1695	641	552	455	9	1049	74	45	29	125	79	.61	90	.254	.329	.366
Total		971	65124	17144	3435	564	1314	25649	9952	8865	7318	195	14062	934	466	639	2062	1016	.67	1365	.263	.343	.394

Midwest League Pitching - A

Team	Org	G	GS	CG	GF	IP	BFP	H	R	ER	HR	SH	SF	HB	TBB	IBB	SO	WP	Bk	W	L	Pct.	ShO	Sv	ERA
Kane County	Fla	137	137	6	131	1206	5241	1247	617	545	82	36	46	60	466	5	955	63	12	78	59	.569	11	29	4.07
Clinton	Cin	137	137	6	131	1180.2	5131	1093	643	513	96	48	40	72	516	19	964	92	14	68	69	.496	5	37	3.91
Quad City	Min	139	139	2	137	1220.2	5339	1194	649	534	78	31	32	69	569	32	1103	90	10	77	62	.554	10	31	3.94
Wisconsin	Sea	138	138	12	126	1197.2	5219	1194	653	544	90	40	50	60	434	12	1110	91	29	72	66	.522	10	29	4.09
West Michigan	Det	140	140	10	130	1219.2	5332	1170	682	548	80	41	50	65	570	12	1033	111	23	68	72	.486	9	30	4.04
Rockford	Cin	139	139	16	123	1204.1	5323	1232	690	567	72	37	36	67	524	33	1046	97	13	76	63	.547	18	32	4.24
South Bend	Ari	139	139	0	139	1214.1	5339	1222	702	591	92	30	40	65	482	1	1003	107	13	68	71	.489	6	36	4.38
Michigan	Hou	138	138	5	133	1192	5245	1264	732	639	96	26	47	62	483	15	1055	102	19	76	62	.551	5	37	4.82
Cedar Rapids	Ana	138	138	21	117	1195.2	5287	1242	741	596	117	43	64	70	459	7	976	102	16	61	77	.442	7	35	4.49
Peoria	StL	139	139	2	137	1201	5326	1240	748	634	104	35	51	70	511	6	978	64	18	63	76	.453	4	26	4.75
Lansing	ChC	140	140	5	135	1198.2	5374	1312	750	630	83	31	51	60	528	7	893	92	12	73	67	.521	4	32	4.73
Burlington	CWS	139	139	9	130	1194	5386	1291	763	635	89	26	46	77	519	23	953	87	21	71	68	.511	4	35	4.79
Beloit	Mil	139	139	8	131	1201.2	5419	1261	770	648	120	20	39	74	582	10	1002	106	17	59	80	.424	9	30	4.85
Fort Wayne	SD	140	140	2	138	1224.1	5540	1237	812	678	115	22	47	63	675	13	991	88	16	61	79	.436	5	33	4.98
Total		971	971	104	867	16850.2	74501	17144	9952	8302	1314	466	639	934	7318	195	14062	1290	233	971	971	.500	107	452	4.43

South Atlantic League Batting - A

Team	Org	G	AB	H	2B	3B	HR	TB	R	RBI	TBB	IBB	SO	HBP	SH	SF	SB	CS	SB%	GDP	Avg	OBP	SLG
Greensboro	NYY	141	4756	1245	251	46	122	1954	733	650	430	7	1232	7	26	44	106	62	.63	83	.262	.321	.411
Hagerstown	Tor	140	4826	1225	234	34	110	1857	731	646	562	9	1076	44	28	42	179	65	.73	86	.254	.334	.385
Hickory	Pit	140	4781	1222	226	25	134	1900	705	641	498	15	1119	79	39	35	96	62	.61	90	.256	.334	.397
Asheville	Col	141	4869	1352	263	20	106	1973	701	609	320	4	956	76	43	30	149	64	.70	92	.278	.330	.405
Columbus	Cle	141	4679	1231	222	40	110	1863	688	608	453	11	1005	70	33	43	179	88	.67	92	.263	.334	.398
Capital City	NYM	141	4682	1209	238	34	155	1980	688	626	406	6	1089	73	31	54	167	68	.71	72	.258	.324	.423
Macon	Atl	138	4633	1210	235	31	115	1852	661	584	415	8	1169	69	23	35	199	94	.68	96	.261	.329	.400
Charleston-SC	TB	142	4719	1118	207	29	88	1647	634	546	450	13	1117	69	48	39	132	64	.67	105	.237	.310	.349
Delmarva	Bal	138	4557	1092	203	41	47	1518	627	556	615	12	1175	73	46	39	163	80	.67	101	.240	.337	.333
Augusta	Bos	139	4657	1140	198	40	83	1667	626	532	427	5	1064	3	30	33	139	71	.66	116	.245	.307	.358
Cape Fear	Mon	140	4553	1161	222	38	81	1702	616	536	397	9	1109	71	37	27	173	155	.53	65	.255	.323	.374
Savannah	Tex	140	4621	1118	203	41	95	1688	607	556	424	7	1197	58	35	36	82	57	.59	81	.242	.311	.365
Charleston-WV	KC	141	4661	1135	227	35	65	1627	593	509	499	5	1138	75	50	27	270	105	.72	78	.244	.325	.349
Piedmont	Phi	140	4548	1111	214	38	64	1653	528	481	360	4	993	81	31	29	145	58	.71	90	.244	.309	.363
Total		981	65542	16569	3143	492	1395	24881	9138	8080	6256	115	15439	848	500	513	2179	1093	.67	1220	.253	.324	.380

South Atlantic League Pitching - A

Team	Org	G	GS	CG	GF	IP	BFP	H	R	ER	HR	SH	SF	HB	TBB	IBB	SO	WP	Bk	W	L	Pct.	ShO	Sv	ERA
Piedmont	Phi	140	140	16	124	1187.1	4995	1099	540	399	73	42	26	53	352	7	1041	58	8	69	71	.493	12	42	3.02
Macon	Atl	138	138	1	137	1193	5111	1083	585	476	101	31	40	67	466	10	1128	90	22	74	64	.536	5	40	3.59
Augusta	Bos	139	139	3	136	1216.2	5180	1157	585	453	86	30	29	54	407	13	1170	71	11	69	70	.496	14	35	3.35
Capital City	NYM	141	141	3	138	1220.2	5205	1115	611	494	94	30	30	76	448	6	1103	103	14	83	58	.589	11	37	3.64
Cape Fear	Mon	140	140	5	135	1216	5209	1172	613	483	96	33	43	71	441	7	952	83	9	75	65	.536	4	32	3.57
Hagerstown	Tor	140	110	0	100	1089	5250	1138	616	509	78	44	26	12	440	8	1049	82	15	84	56	.600	11	43	3.63
Greensboro	NYY	141	141	7	134	1223.1	5283	1204	646	541	100	25	33	64	406	6	1186	141	15	77	64	.546	6	36	3.98
Charleston-SC	TB	142	142	6	136	1243.1	5321	1192	651	529	87	44	40	59	430	17	1010	88	16	65	77	.458	9	33	3.83
Charleston-WV	KC	141	141	6	135	1245	5462	1252	689	556	72	47	45	75	532	16	1078	96	19	61	80	.433	10	28	4.02
Hickory	Pit	140	140	2	138	1247.1	5444	1243	702	553	129	39	33	88	470	18	1130	75	12	70	70	.500	9	33	3.99
Columbus	Cle	141	141	3	138	1220.1	5200	1207	703	594	132	25	32	88	443	3	1182	94	15	70	71	.496	7	34	4.38
Delmarva	Bal	138	138	7	131	1213	5289	1214	705	583	109	47	34	63	479	2	1134	82	20	58	80	.420	7	27	4.33
Asheville	Col	141	141	6	135	1211	5370	1231	743	627	121	32	53	7	492	2	1163	109	22	64	77	.454	4	35	4.66
Savannah	Tex	140	140	6	134	1206.2	5339	1262	749	608	117	31	49	71	450	0	1113	97	16	62	78	.443	12	34	4.53
Total		981	981	73	908	17105.2	73878	16569	9138	7405	1395	500	513	848	6256	115	15439	1269	214	981	981	.500	121	489	3.90

New York-Penn League Batting - A-

Team	Org	G	AB	H	2B	3B	HR	TB	R	RBI	TBB	IBB	SO	HBP	SH	SF	SB	CS	SB%	GDP	Avg	OBP	SLG
Mahoning Vlly	Cle	76	2429	607	119	19	49	911	406	350	305	2	623	45	13	32	115	49	.70	45	.250	.340	.375
Vermont	Mon	76	2680	732	126	24	45	1041	400	352	289	9	577	38	12	25	94	46	.67	53	.273	.349	.388
Auburn	Hou	76	2567	673	120	33	44	991	399	343	299	6	585	45	7	25	191	64	.75	43	.262	.346	.386
Lowell	Bos	76	2620	671	137	27	44	994	379	323	283	8	574	40	20	21	81	33	.71	56	.256	.335	.379
Batavia	Phi	76	2589	643	115	33	48	968	379	329	239	4	633	46	14	27	125	33	.79	34	.248	.320	.374
Staten Island	NYY	74	2457	626	126	23	51	951	372	332	278	9	597	40	16	27	67	34	.66	39	.255	.337	.387
Pittsfield	NYM	76	2536	631	137	21	41	933	368	317	270	5	591	46	29	15	125	49	.72	34	.249	.330	.368
Jamestown	Atl	76	2520	632	117	16	55	946	365	321	235	2	599	42	13	26	101	28	.78	45	.251	.322	.375
Utica	Fla	75	2530	655	136	29	36	957	357	310	279	6	570	53	22	27	69	44	.61	52	.259	.342	.378
Hudson Valley	TB	76	2620	647	132	22	53	982	340	292	233	6	644	36	18	23	74	36	.67	44	.247	.315	.375
St. Catharines	Tor	76	2455	604	115	16	42	877	332	292	286	4	655	56	23	35	96	46	.68	28	.246	.334	.357
Williamsport	Pit	76	2522	616	120	13	36	870	329	289	270	5	617	45	13	16	108	42	.72	51	.244	.326	.345
New Jersey	StL	76	2494	582	94	39	36	862	320	271	192	2	635	57	28	14	97	66	.60	45	.233	.301	.346
Oneonta	Det	75	2523	607	112	21	25	836	313	267	236	6	637	42	17	21	131	29	.82	30	.241	.314	.331
Total		530	35542	8926	1706	336	605	13119	5059	4388	3694	74	8537	631	245	334	1474	599	.71	599	.251	.330	.369

New York-Penn League Pitching - A-

Team	Org	G	GS	CG	GF	IP	BFP	H	R	ER	HR	SH	SF	HB	TBB	IBB	SO	WP	Bk	W	L	Pct.	ShO	Sv	ERA
Oneonta	Det	75	75	3	72	660.2	2832	565	302	230	41	23	28	35	306	9	609	70	14	41	34	.547	5	25	3.13
Hudson Valley	TB	76	76	1	75	687	2873	585	308	256	25	25	16	60	240	3	632	51	10	42	34	.553	8	20	3.35
Staten Island	NYY	74	74	1	73	647.1	2797	660	333	284	35	19	18	23	207	9	670	60	16	39	35	.527	3	20	3.95
Pittsfield	NYM	76	76	0	76	675	2903	655	336	277	32	24	21	39	247	5	540	51	7	41	35	.539	6	20	3.69
Utica	Fla	75	75	4	71	670.1	2828	631	338	275	54	18	13	42	219	3	622	56	8	42	33	.560	6	20	3.69
Batavia	Phi	76	76	4	72	668	2881	629	341	285	36	14	33	51	277	10	602	74	13	42	34	.553	6	15	3.84
Mahoning Vlly	Cle	76	76	1	75	648	2840	650	363	302	44	19	27	36	243	1	638	43	9	43	33	.566	2	19	4.19
Auburn	Hou	76	76	3	73	670	2905	607	364	276	41	19	25	60	258	1	616	41	12	39	37	.513	5	18	3.71
Williamsport	Pit	76	76	7	69	656.1	2877	622	372	284	41	10	35	58	276	5	565	44	22	32	44	.421	4	16	3.89
Jamestown	Atl	76	76	3	73	656.1	2851	630	377	327	50	11	25	41	263	1	638	64	8	38	38	.500	1	23	4.48
New Jersey	StL	76	76	2	74	665.1	2919	656	397	314	51	17	20	43	277	6	540	68	12	30	46	.395	2	16	4.25
St. Catharines	Tor	76	76	0	76	649.1	2888	637	393	324	62	10	16	33	317	5	653	69	16	34	42	.447	6	21	4.49
Lowell	Bos	76	76	0	76	674	2986	675	395	304	48	17	31	44	262	7	639	58	21	34	42	.447	0	10	4.06
Vermont	Mon	76	76	1	75	676	3076	724	460	362	45	19	26	66	302	9	573	67	15	33	43	.434	1	19	4.82
Total		530	530	30	500	9303.2	40456	8926	5059	4100	605	245	334	631	3694	74	8537	816	183	530	530	.500	58	262	3.97

Northwest League Batting - A-

Team	Org	G	AB	H	2B	3B	HR	TB	R	RBI	TBB	IBB	SO	HBP	SH	SF	SB	CS	SB%	GDP	Avg	OBP	SLG
Boise	Ana	76	2697	814	167	17	49	1162	556	495	381	11	515	44	13	31	77	32	.71	56	.302	.393	.431
South. Oregon	Oak	76	2631	708	136	26	73	1115	489	434	401	9	631	58	15	37	101	44	.70	39	.269	.373	.424
Spokane	KC	76	2648	749	138	16	62	1105	477	408	303	15	476	45	32	22	110	37	.75	61	.283	.363	.417
Salem-Keizer	SF	76	2582	677	117	13	48	964	426	373	312	12	544	47	30	14	128	54	.70	35	.262	.351	.373
Everett	Sea	76	2589	693	139	17	55	1031	423	369	310	9	563	40	18	33	83	46	.64	40	.268	.351	.398
Yakima	LA	76	2517	654	126	11	55	967	418	362	314	13	582	63	48	20	103	69	.60	43	.260	.354	.384
Portland	Col	76	2630	692	142	22	70	1088	416	369	279	10	684	32	15	24	71	34	.68	41	.263	.338	.414
Eugene	ChC	76	2576	684	123	14	57	1006	390	341	226	2	556	59	12	15	83	51	.62	56	.266	.337	.391
Total		304	20870	5671	1088	136	469	8438	3595	3151	2526	81	4551	388	183	196	756	367	.67	371	.272	.358	.404

Northwest League Pitching - A-

Team	Org	G	GS	CG	GF	IP	BFP	H	R	ER	HR	SH	SF	HB	TBB	IBB	SO	WP	Bk	W	L	Pct.	ShO	Sv	ERA
Spokane	KC	76	76	0	76	672.2	2970	669	383	313	57	28	13	55	298	10	624	50	9	44	32	.579	1	19	4.19
Everett	Sea	76	76	4	72	662.2	2954	626	395	316	55	27	19	36	355	13	640	70	7	41	35	.539	4	18	4.29
Salem-Keizer	SF	76	76	2	74	663.2	2998	705	432	359	54	24	26	49	319	5	570	58	19	37	39	.487	1	21	4.87
Portland	Col	76	76	1	75	668.2	3082	672	443	352	42	26	29	66	354	8	607	53	16	39	37	.513	1	24	4.74
Boise	Ana	76	76	3	73	669.1	2993	738	451	364	65	17	16	37	254	14	554	63	9	43	33	.566	2	17	4.89
South. Oregon	Oak	76	76	0	76	672.1	3101	742	486	386	59	28	28	47	333	18	484	53	13	38	38	.500	1	12	5.17
Eugene	ChC	76	76	0	76	672.1	3017	773	501	423	63	18	32	52	294	8	596	63	14	29	47	.382	4	12	5.85
Yakima	LA	76	76	1	75	667.1	3065	746	504	417	74	15	33	46	319	5	476	68	5	33	43	.434	1	17	5.62
Total		304	304	11	293	5327	24180	5671	3595	2930	469	183	196	388	2526	81	4551	478	92	304	304	.500	15	140	4.95

Appalachian League Batting - R+

Team	Org	G	AB	H	2B	3B	HR	TB	R	RBI	TBB	IBB	SO	HBP	SH	SF	SB	CS	SB%	GDP	Avg	OBP	SLG
Elizabethton	Min	70	2515	748	148	28	73	1171	505	449	346	8	589	52	8	17	74	31	.70	54	.297	.391	.466
Pulaski	Tex	69	2356	681	141	16	75	1079	475	410	269	5	545	40	24	28	86	19	.82	35	.289	.368	.458
Bluefield	Bal	68	2375	616	111	30	59	964	445	372	310	5	587	39	6	19	51	19	.73	30	.259	.352	.406
Danville	Atl	69	2343	631	121	28	30	898	408	340	304	3	594	49	15	18	85	45	.65	35	.269	.363	.383
Bristol	CWS	69	2308	635	108	14	46	909	392	329	275	6	478	40	20	21	131	47	.74	47	.275	.359	.394
Princeton	TB	70	2410	639	137	16	53	967	384	322	209	4	702	36	7	13	87	39	.69	36	.265	.331	.401
Kingsport	NYM	70	2373	646	110	18	40	912	378	313	237	5	566	61	35	17	130	55	.70	37	.272	.351	.384
Martinsville	Hou	70	2318	589	130	25	37	880	366	297	253	1	611	48	4	16	160	53	.75	25	.254	.338	.380
Johnson City	StL	69	2357	569	98	20	44	839	366	309	266	6	674	46	29	19	123	49	.72	38	.241	.328	.356
Burlington	Cle	70	2318	529	85	14	34	744	336	281	271	3	624	62	15	20	83	33	.72	44	.228	.323	.321
Total		347	23673	6283	1189	209	491	9363	4055	3422	2740	46	5970	473	163	188	1010	390	.72	381	.265	.351	.396

Appalachian League Pitching - R+

Team	Org	G	GS	CG	GF	IP	BFP	H	R	ER	HR	SH	SF	HB	TBB	IBB	SO	WP	Bk	W	L	Pct.	ShO	Sv	ERA
Martinsville	Hou	70	70	2	68	610.1	2632	556	323	242	44	20	13	62	245	1	646	70	12	41	29	.586	3	23	3.57
Pulaski	Tex	69	69	4	65	590	2611	579	343	261	49	0	21	50	262	3	589	50	15	48	21	.696	8	20	3.98
Bristol	CWS	69	69	4	65	592.1	2625	596	346	256	42	17	14	38	242	7	662	60	15	45	24	.652	4	25	3.89
Kingsport	NYM	70	70	2	68	612	2747	595	369	293	40	21	21	49	314	15	603	76	10	34	36	.486	2	12	4.31
Elizabethton	Min	70	70	1	69	612	2799	658	390	299	51	18	18	47	258	4	602	79	5	40	30	.571	3	16	4.40
Danville	Atl	69	69	0	69	596.2	2689	610	398	299	39	15	16	52	248	1	613	66	15	38	31	.551	2	15	4.51
Johnson City	StL	69	69	1	68	611.1	2744	637	408	324	46	16	16	38	268	5	584	58	17	30	39	.435	5	12	4.77
Burlington	Cle	70	70	1	69	602.1	2744	634	429	312	54	26	25	33	269	7	617	90	14	21	49	.300	1	9	4.66
Bluefield	Bal	68	68	1	67	584.2	2767	696	505	370	62	14	17	50	291	0	571	88	10	25	43	.368	0	9	5.70
Princeton	TB	70	70	0	70	594.1	2885	722	544	414	64	10	27	51	343	3	483	128	15	25	45	.357	0	13	6.27
Total		347	347	16	331	6006	27243	6283	4055	3070	491	163	188	473	2740	46	5970	765	128	347	347	.500	28	154	4.60

Pioneer League Batting - R+

Team	Org	G	AB	H	2B	3B	HR	TB	R	RBI	TBB	IBB	SO	HBP	SH	SF	SB	CS	SB%	GDP	Avg	OBP	SLG
Missoula	Ari	76	2668	759	142	33	59	1144	552	472	376	5	658	40	21	26	150	47	.76	60	.284	.370	.429
Idaho Falls	SD	75	2653	755	165	35	68	1194	546	467	334	5	646	52	9	28	153	39	.80	54	.285	.372	.450
Butte	Ana	75	2641	765	132	34	51	1118	529	446	284	6	585	54	22	26	109	43	.72	48	.290	.367	.423
Billings	Cin	75	2645	761	152	27	70	1177	489	433	292	4	613	43	26	23	50	27	.65	53	.288	.365	.445
Helena	Mil	75	2545	715	129	11	58	1040	468	381	283	4	490	54	19	21	143	45	.76	52	.281	.362	.409
Great Falls	LA	76	2637	708	106	31	40	996	438	353	224	3	498	42	39	26	108	49	.69	46	.268	.333	.378
Ogden	Mil	76	2631	737	137	19	55	1077	437	373	265	3	561	52	24	19	122	54	.69	54	.280	.355	.409
Medicine Hat	Tor	76	2536	647	123	18	45	941	389	323	310	2	530	31	18	19	86	36	.70	50	.255	.341	.371
Total		302	20956	5847	1086	208	446	8687	3848	3248	2368	32	4581	368	178	188	921	340	.73	417	.279	.359	.415

Pioneer League Pitching - R+

Team	Org	G	GS	CG	GF	IP	BFP	H	R	ER	HR	SH	SF	HB	TBB	IBB	SO	WP	Bk	W	L	Pct.	ShO	Sv	ERA
Helena	Mil	75	75	6	69	651.1	2856	633	404	312	49	25	12	47	264	7	509	69	12	47	28	.627	3	22	4.31
Idaho Falls	SD	75	75	0	75	668	3001	700	440	343	44	25	23	39	299	2	634	87	10	48	27	.640	1	20	4.62
Billings	Cin	75	75	1	74	658.1	2959	702	444	341	43	19	28	49	275	3	577	53	13	42	33	.560	2	18	4.66
Medicine Hat	Tor	76	76	0	76	648.2	2949	739	449	343	69	25	28	34	264	2	586	77	16	33	43	.434	2	21	4.76
Missoula	Ari	76	76	1	75	678	3034	719	457	338	53	23	11	51	255	6	593	73	10	45	31	.592	4	21	4.49
Great Falls	LA	76	76	4	72	663	3054	755	511	430	60	23	28	42	327	0	533	87	11	29	47	.382	1	9	5.84
Ogden	Mil	76	76	3	73	663.1	3090	787	541	410	64	15	27	41	336	8	577	70	6	26	50	.342	1	11	5.56
Butte	Ana	75	75	1	74	647.2	3125	812	602	479	64	23	31	65	348	4	572	115	10	32	43	.427	0	12	6.66
Total		302	302	16	286	5278.1	24068	5847	3848	2996	446	178	188	368	2368	32	4581	631	88	302	302	.500	14	134	5.11

Arizona League Batting - R

Team	Org	G	AB	H	2B	3B	HR	TB	R	RBI	TBB	IBB	SO	HBP	SH	SF	SB	CS	SB%	GDP	Avg	OBP	SLG
Athletics	Oak	56	1920	511	106	34	31	778	384	323	272	6	516	48	11	18	77	37	.68	30	.266	.368	.405
Rockies	Col	56	1929	559	97	29	15	759	346	290	210	3	450	51	4	24	157	45	.78	29	.290	.370	.393
Mariners	Sea	56	1940	553	118	24	27	800	342	275	182	1	414	30	20	14	78	43	.64	41	.285	.353	.412
Padres	SD	55	1861	488	70	28	25	689	323	273	225	5	482	33	7	21	123	38	.76	30	.262	.349	.370
Diamondbacks	Ari	56	1924	545	83	18	27	745	292	252	165	3	437	23	4	17	40	15	.73	47	.283	.344	.387
White Sox	CWS	56	1864	504	81	37	11	692	287	238	209	1	387	31	22	13	76	42	.64	40	.270	.351	.371
Mex. All-Stars	—	56	1845	480	58	31	25	675	263	204	189	6	455	27	28	13	41	21	.66	36	.260	.336	.366
Cubs	ChC	55	1887	493	88	25	31	724	249	214	164	2	442	40	8	13	44	36	.55	46	.261	.331	.384
Total		223	15170	4133	701	226	192	5862	2486	2069	1616	27	3583	283	104	133	636	277	.70	299	.272	.351	.386

Arizona League Pitching - R

Team	Org	G	GS	CG	GF	IP	BFP	H	R	ER	HR	SH	SF	HB	TBB	IBB	SO	WP	Bk	W	L	Pct.	ShO	Sv	ERA
Athletics	Oak	56	56	0	56	497	2112	497	250	196	21	8	19	17	172	3	416	37	13	39	17	.696	2	21	3.55
Mex. All-Stars	—	56	56	5	51	470.1	2073	522	289	243	20	5	12	30	177	3	397	28	20	28	28	.500	4	11	4.65
Padres	SD	55	55	1	54	482	2161	492	291	227	37	14	14	41	220	0	472	26	16	31	24	.564	3	15	4.24
White Sox	CWS	56	56	1	55	474.2	2142	519	301	233	22	13	20	34	204	15	461	53	24	23	33	.411	0	10	4.42
Mariners	Sea	56	56	0	56	492.2	2193	498	310	252	24	15	15	41	211	3	503	38	14	32	24	.571	2	16	4.60
Diamondbacks	Ari	56	56	1	55	474.1	2184	513	330	237	14	14	23	41	216	0	449	66	15	24	32	.429	3	16	4.50
Rockies	Col	56	56	3	53	480.1	2197	551	336	259	20	23	14	33	191	2	392	50	20	28	28	.500	2	8	4.85
Cubs	ChC	55	55	1	54	480.2	2250	541	379	295	34	12	16	46	225	1	493	39	14	18	37	.327	1	11	5.52
Total		223	223	12	211	3852	17312	4133	2486	1942	192	104	133	283	1616	27	3583	337	136	223	223	.500	17	108	4.54

Gulf Coast League Batting - R

Team	Org	G	AB	H	2B	3B	HR	TB	R	RBI	TBB	IBB	SO	HBP	SH	SF	SB	CS	SB%	GDP	Avg	OBP	SLG
Mets	NYM	60	1971	525	94	19	24	729	324	273	249	4	455	39	21	18	58	29	.67	49	.266	.357	.370
Royals	KC	60	1939	478	89	16	28	683	305	259	304	0	507	25	22	24	101	24	.81	37	.247	.352	.352
Orioles	Bal	60	1896	490	90	20	29	707	303	246	187	6	368	30	26	22	141	48	.75	30	.258	.331	.373
Rangers	Tex	60	1909	471	91	26	22	680	302	250	238	13	460	42	21	21	85	31	.73	35	.247	.340	.356
Twins	Min	60	1838	481	77	16	10	620	295	236	241	11	356	33	34	18	75	32	.70	33	.262	.354	.337
Yankees	NYY	60	1922	500	98	18	32	730	292	268	255	3	486	39	11	19	44	33	.57	37	.260	.355	.380
Red Sox	Bos	60	1915	461	72	19	23	640	279	232	226	3	401	36	10	20	65	45	.59	44	.241	.329	.334
Pirates	Pit	60	1990	497	84	16	22	679	274	231	177	3	431	32	12	21	82	27	.75	37	.250	.318	.341
Braves	Atl	60	2018	493	86	9	30	687	265	233	225	2	482	34	13	8	55	26	.68	29	.244	.329	.340
Phillies	Phi	60	1860	461	93	10	20	654	248	202	228	7	450	43	19	18	94	32	.75	40	.248	.341	.341
Tigers	Det	60	1851	470	98	15	19	655	240	209	190	2	463	27	17	16	96	41	.70	33	.254	.330	.354
Marlins	Fla	60	2015	486	95	20	11	654	239	196	218	3	456	40	10	15	100	44	.69	33	.241	.325	.325
Reds	Cin	60	1861	418	75	17	14	569	220	180	172	4	427	34	13	12	87	28	.76	36	.225	.300	.306
Expos	Mon	60	1898	451	66	10	8	561	215	186	180	2	348	28	11	15	73	24	.75	51	.238	.311	.296
Total		420	26883	6682	1208	231	292	9228	3801	3201	3090	63	6090	482	240	247	1156	464	.71	524	.249	.334	.343

Gulf Coast League Pitching - R

Team	Org	G	GS	CG	GF	IP	BFP	H	R	ER	HR	SH	SF	HB	TBB	IBB	SO	WP	Bk	W	L	Pct.	ShO	Sv	ERA
Rangers	Tex	60	60	2	58	510.1	2148	441	221	176	27	14	13	28	179	3	385	30	24	37	23	.617	4	16	3.10
Tigers	Det	60	60	2	58	490.1	2149	427	239	199	23	21	15	28	275	4	462	31	7	29	31	.483	3	14	3.65
Mets	NYM	60	60	1	59	522.2	2257	473	247	180	9	10	13	34	216	1	486	51	13	39	21	.650	2	15	3.10
Braves	Atl	60	60	0	60	525.2	2258	479	258	204	23	12	17	30	214	5	440	33	16	27	33	.450	4	7	3.49
Royals	KC	60	60	1	59	519	2242	498	263	212	24	7	18	41	197	4	441	33	8	33	27	.550	5	18	3.68
Expos	Mon	60	60	1	59	504.2	2216	481	264	224	20	20	15	41	241	1	387	45	11	29	31	.483	3	17	3.99
Yankees	NYY	60	60	3	57	502.2	2205	468	265	211	23	24	17	30	243	3	565	50	5	32	28	.533	5	16	3.78
Red Sox	Bos	60	60	0	60	511	2216	465	273	172	22	15	11	28	198	6	472	40	15	30	29	.508	3	12	3.03
Marlins	Fla	60	60	3	57	528.2	2303	522	274	222	21	13	11	36	201	4	428	42	2	25	35	.417	5	11	3.78
Pirates	Pit	60	60	0	54	514	2199	467	275	213	19	16	25	46	196	0	383	37	12	24	35	.407	1	8	3.73
Twins	Min	60	60	10	50	480.2	2084	490	276	215	21	21	23	29	165	7	403	33	23	33	26	.559	6	9	4.03
Orioles	Bal	60	60	0	60	504	2224	472	300	214	17	13	15	44	242	17	413	59	21	31	28	.525	2	14	3.82
Phillies	Phi	60	60	0	60	491.2	2235	516	318	265	29	17	27	35	262	1	438	38	5	26	34	.433	4	13	4.85
Reds	Cin	60	60	1	59	491	2218	483	328	258	14	37	27	32	261	7	387	49	15	23	37	.383	2	8	4.73
Total		420	420	25	395	7096.1	30954	6682	3801	2965	292	240	247	482	3090	63	6090	571	177	418	418	.500	49	178	3.76

1999 Leader Boards

It's hard to find leader boards like these. We offer plenty of categories and break them down five different ways. In addition to leader lists for Triple-A, Double-A, full-season Class-A and short-season leagues, you'll find a leader board for all full-season leagues regardless of classification.

Wondering who led the full-season minors in runs scored or stolen bases? Oakland prospect Adam Piatt crossed the plate more than any other minor leaguer, scoring 129 runs at Double-A Midland and Triple-A Vancouver. A gifted young shortstop in the Atlanta organization, Rafael Furcal, stole 96 bases between Class-A Macon and Myrtle Beach to lead all minor league players.

If a player appeared with more than one team in a given breakdown, we list him with his last team in that category. To qualify for leadership, full-season players had to have 383 plate appearances, 112 innings pitched, 18 starts (starting pitchers) or 40 games with fewer than 18 starts (relief pitchers). Short-season players required 150 plate appearances, 55 innings pitched, nine starts (starting pitchers) or 20 games with fewer than nine starts (relief pitchers).

League abbreviations are as follows:

INT—International League (AAA)
PCL—Pacific Coast League (AAA)
EL—Eastern League (AA)
SL—Southern League (AA)
TL—Texas League (AA)
CAL—California League (A+)
CAR—Carolina League (A+)
FSL—Florida State League (A+)
MWL—Midwest League (A)
SAL—South Atlantic League (A)
NYP—New York-Penn League (A-)
NWL—Northwest League (A-)
APP—Appalachian League (R+)
PIO—Pioneer League (R+)
AZL—Arizona League (R)
GCL—Gulf Coast League (R)

Full-Season Batting Leaders

Batting Average

Player, Team	Lg	Org	Avg
Erubiel Durazo, Tucson	**PCL**	**Ari**	**.404**
Sean Burroughs, Rancho Cuca.	CAL	SD	.363
Carlos Urquiola, South Bend	MWL	Ari	.362
Mark Quinn, Omaha	PCL	KC	.360
Jarrod Patterson, Tucson	PCL	Ari	.358
Nick Johnson, Norwich	EL	NYY	.345
Talmadge Nunnari, Harrisburg	EL	Mon	.344
Steve Cox, Durham	INT	TB	.341
Adam Piatt, Vancouver	PCL	Oak	.340
Jason Williams, Indianapolis	INT	Cin	.339

Catchers Batting Average

Player, Team	Lg	Org	Avg
Robert Hammock, High Desert	**CAL**	**Ari**	**.332**
Wilbert Nieves, Rancho Cuca.	CAL	SD	.328
Rod Barajas, El Paso	TL	Ari	.318
Ben Petrick, Colorado Springs	PCL	Col	.311
Javier Cardona, Jacksonville	SL	Det	.309
Javier Flores, Visalia	CAL	Oak	.296
Cody McKay, Midland	TL	Oak	.294
Jayson Werth, Bowie	EL	Bal	.294
Chris Heintz, Winston-Salem	CAR	CWS	.293
Robinson Cancel, Louisville	INT	Mil	.291

First Basemen Batting Average

Player, Team	Lg	Org	Avg
Erubiel Durazo, Tucson	**PCL**	**Ari**	**.404**
Nick Johnson, Norwich	EL	NYY	.345
Talmadge Nunnari, Harrisburg	EL	Mon	.344
Steve Cox, Durham	INT	TB	.341
Felipe Crespo, Fresno	PCL	SF	.332
Desi Wilson, Tucson	PCL	Ari	.323
Luis Lopez, Syracuse	INT	Tor	.322
Carlos Rivera, Hickory	SAL	Pit	.322
Pat Burrell, Scranton/Wilkes-Barre	INT	Phi	.320
Eduardo Perez, Memphis	PCL	StL	.320

Second Basemen Batting Average

Player, Team	Lg	Org	Avg
Carlos Urquiola, South Bend	**MWL**	**Ari**	**.362**
Jason Williams, Indianapolis	INT	Cin	.339
Josue Espada, Vancouver	PCL	Oak	.336
Belvani Martinez, High Desert	CAL	Ari	.333
William Otero, San Jose	CAL	SF	.333
Tony Medrano, Omaha	PCL	KC	.331
Jason Hardtke, Indianapolis	INT	Cin	.329
Adam Kennedy, Memphis	PCL	StL	.327
Brian Raabe, Columbus	INT	NYY	.327
Trace Coquillette, Ottawa	INT	Mon	.326

Third Basemen Batting Average

Player, Team	Lg	Org	Avg
Jarrod Patterson, Tucson	**PCL**	**Ari**	**.358**
Adam Piatt, Vancouver	PCL	Oak	.340
Bo Robinson, Wisconsin	MWL	Sea	.329
Aramis Ramirez, Nashville	PCL	Pit	.328
Rico Washington, Lynchburg	CAR	Pit	.325
Mike Lamb, Oklahoma	PCL	Tex	.324
Ken Woods, Fresno	PCL	SF	.324
Jimmy Gonzalez, San Bernardino	CAL	LA	.316
Scott Seabol, Greensboro	SAL	NYY	.315
Jim Tatum, Colorado Springs	PCL	Col	.313

Shortstops Batting Average

Player, Team	Lg	Org	Avg
D'Angelo Jimenez, Columbus	**INT**	**NYY**	**.327**
Rafael Furcal, Myrtle Beach	CAR	Atl	.322
Julio Lugo, Jackson	TL	Hou	.319
Jack Wilson, Potomac	CAR	StL	.319
Ismael Gallo, San Bernardino	CAL	LA	.314
Cesar Izturis, Dunedin	FSL	Tor	.308
John McDonald, Buffalo	INT	Cle	.307
Alex Cintron, High Desert	CAL	Ari	.307
Nick Punto, Clearwater	FSL	Phi	.305
Travis Dawkins, Chattanooga	SL	Cin	.300

Outfielders Batting Average

Player, Team	Lg	Org	Avg
Mark Quinn, Omaha	**PCL**	**KC**	**.360**
Roosevelt Brown, Iowa	PCL	ChC	.338
Jeff DaVanon, Edmonton	PCL	Ana	.338
Midre Cummings, Salt Lake	PCL	Min	.336
Raul Gonzalez, Trenton	EL	Bos	.335
Scott Sollmann, Huntsville	SL	Mil	.334
Jack Cust, High Desert	CAL	Ari	.334
Vernon Wells, Syracuse	INT	Tor	.334
Calvin Murray, Fresno	PCL	SF	.334
Dee Brown, Wichita	TL	KC	.331

Switch-Hitters Batting Average

Player, Team	Lg	Org	Avg
Jeff DaVanon, Edmonton	**PCL**	**Ana**	**.338**
Felipe Crespo, Fresno	PCL	SF	.332
Milton Bradley, Harrisburg	EL	Mon	.329
Jason Hardtke, Indianapolis	INT	Cin	.329
D'Angelo Jimenez, Columbus	INT	NYY	.327
Tony Mota, San Antonio	TL	LA	.325
Chris Latham, Salt Lake	PCL	Min	.322
Rafael Furcal, Myrtle Beach	CAR	Atl	.322
Aaron Miles, Michigan	MWL	Hou	.317
Nick Theodorou, San Bernardino	CAL	LA	.310

Full-Season Batting Leaders

Hits

Player, Team	Lg	Org	H
Jarrod Patterson, Tucson	**PCL**	**Ari**	**187**
Juan Pierre, Asheville	**SAL**	**Col**	**187**
Calvin Murray, Fresno	PCL	SF	183
Steve Cox, Durham	INT	TB	182
Mike Lamb, Oklahoma	PCL	Tex	177
Robb Gorr, San Bernardino	CAL	LA	174
D'Angelo Jimenez, Columbus	INT	NYY	172
Talmadge Nunnari, Harrisburg	EL	Mon	172
3 tied with			171

Extra-Base Hits

Player, Team	Lg	Org	XBH
Adam Piatt, Vancouver	**PCL**	**Oak**	**91**
Jacques Landry, Modesto	CAL	Oak	79
Steve Cox, Durham	INT	TB	78
Jack Cust, High Desert	CAL	Ari	77
Mike Lamb, Oklahoma	PCL	Tex	77
Jarrod Patterson, Tucson	PCL	Ari	77
Scott Seabol, Greensboro	SAL	NYY	76
Corey Patterson, Lansing	MWL	ChC	72
3 tied with			71

Doubles

Player, Team	Lg	Org	2B
Scott Seabol, Greensboro	**SAL**	**NYY**	**55**
Jarrod Patterson, Tucson	PCL	Ari	52
Mike Lamb, Oklahoma	PCL	Tex	51
Bo Robinson, Wisconsin	MWL	Sea	50
Steve Cox, Durham	INT	TB	49
Adam Piatt, Vancouver	PCL	Oak	49
Jason Hart, Modesto	CAL	Oak	48
Jacques Landry, Modesto	CAL	Oak	46
Jason Williams, Indianapolis	INT	Cin	45
2 tied with			44

Total Bases

Player, Team	Lg	Org	TB
Adam Piatt, Vancouver	**PCL**	**Oak**	**340**
Aaron McNeal, Michigan	MWL	Hou	315
Steve Cox, Durham	INT	TB	314
Jarrod Patterson, Tucson	PCL	Ari	308
D.T. Cromer, Indianapolis	INT	Cin	301
Mike Lamb, Oklahoma	PCL	Tex	301
Jacques Landry, Modesto	CAL	Oak	297
Calvin Murray, Fresno	PCL	SF	297
Chin-Feng Chen, San Bernardino	CAL	LA	296
Jack Cust, High Desert	CAL	Ari	296

Triples

Player, Team	Lg	Org	3B
Oscar Salazar, Modesto	**CAL**	**Oak**	**18**
Corey Patterson, Lansing	MWL	ChC	17
Jeff DaVanon, Edmonton	PCL	Ana	14
Jason Romano, Charlotte	FSL	Tex	14
Elpidio Guzman, Cedar Rapids	MWL	Ana	13
Jackson Melian, Tampa	FSL	NYY	13
Jason Ross, Myrtle Beach	CAR	Atl	13
DeWayne Wise, Rockford	MWL	Cin	13
7 tied with			12

Runs

Player, Team	Lg	Org	R
Adam Piatt, Vancouver	**PCL**	**Oak**	**129**
Jeff DaVanon, Edmonton	PCL	Ana	122
Calvin Murray, Fresno	PCL	SF	122
Jorge Nunez, Hagerstown	SAL	Tor	116
Nick Johnson, Norwich	EL	NYY	114
Jeremy Owens, Rancho Cuca.	CAL	SD	113
Jermaine Clark, Lancaster	CAL	Sea	112
Eric Byrnes, Midland	TL	Oak	111
David Eckstein, Trenton	EL	Bos	109
Jarrod Patterson, Tucson	PCL	Ari	109

Home Runs

Player, Team	Lg	Org	HR
J.R. Phillips, Colorado Springs	**PCL**	**Col**	**41**
Adam Piatt, Vancouver	PCL	Oak	39
Aaron McNeal, Michigan	MWL	Hou	38
Chris Norton, Portland	EL	Fla	38
Andy Tracy, Harrisburg	EL	Mon	37
Sean McNally, Wichita	TL	KC	36
Morgan Burkhart, Trenton	EL	Bos	35
Kit Pellow, Omaha	PCL	KC	35
Scott Morgan, Buffalo	INT	Cle	34
Luis Raven, Charlotte	INT	CWS	33

Runs Batted In

Player, Team	Lg	Org	RBI
Adam Piatt, Vancouver	**PCL**	**Oak**	**138**
Aaron McNeal, Michigan	MWL	Hou	131
Andy Tracy, Harrisburg	EL	Mon	128
Steve Cox, Durham	INT	TB	127
Luis Raven, Charlotte	INT	CWS	125
Chin-Feng Chen, San Bernardino	CAL	LA	123
Jason Hart, Modesto	CAL	Oak	123
Todd Mensik, Visalia	CAL	Oak	123
Tim Giles, Knoxville	SL	Tor	114
Jack Cust, High Desert	CAL	Ari	112

Full-Season Batting Leaders

Walks

Player, Team	Lg	Org	BB
Nick Johnson, Norwich	**EL**	**NYY**	**123**
Adam Melhuse, Syracuse	INT	Tor	118
Bo Robinson, Wisconsin	MWL	Sea	108
Tony Schrager, Lansing	MWL	ChC	103
Esteban German, Modesto	CAL	Oak	102
Albenis Machado, Cape Fear	SAL	Mon	102
Adam Piatt, Vancouver	PCL	Oak	99
Richard Paz, Bowie	EL	Bal	98
Jack Cust, High Desert	CAL	Ari	96
Eddy Furniss, Lynchburg	CAR	Pit	94

Stolen Bases

Player, Team	Lg	Org	SB
Rafael Furcal, Myrtle Beach	**CAR**	**Atl**	**96**
Mike Curry, Wilmington	CAR	KC	85
Jeremy Owens, Rancho Cuca.	CAL	SD	67
Richard Gomez, West Michigan	MWL	Det	66
Juan Pierre, Asheville	SAL	Col	66
Julio Ramirez, Portland	EL	Fla	64
Esix Snead, Peoria	MWL	StL	64
Ethan Faggett, Mobile	SL	SD	63
Rod Lindsey, Jacksonville	SL	Det	61
Trent Durrington, Erie	EL	Ana	59

Strikeouts

Player, Team	Lg	Org	K
Russ Branyan, Buffalo	**INT**	**Cle**	**187**
Bryon Gainey, Binghamton	EL	NYM	184
Tim Flaherty, San Jose	CAL	SF	168
Jeremy Owens, Rancho Cuca.	CAL	SD	166
A.J. Zapp, Macon	SAL	Atl	163
Troy Cameron, Macon	SAL	Atl	161
Jayson Bass, New Haven	EL	Sea	160
Darren Blakely, Lake Elsinore	CAL	Ana	159
Tom Quinlan, Iowa	PCL	ChC	159
Felipe Lopez, Hagerstown	SAL	Tor	157

On-Base Percentage

Player, Team	Lg	Org	OBP
Nick Johnson, Norwich	**EL**	**NYY**	**.525**
Erubiel Durazo, Tucson	PCL	Ari	.489
Sean Burroughs, Rancho Cuca.	CAL	SD	.467
Adam Piatt, Vancouver	PCL	Oak	.450
Jack Cust, High Desert	CAL	Ari	.450
Jarrod Patterson, Tucson	PCL	Ari	.448
Felipe Crespo, Fresno	PCL	SF	.447
Scott Sollmann, Huntsville	SL	Mil	.446
Bo Robinson, Wisconsin	MWL	Sea	.446
Jon Schaeffer, Quad City	MWL	Min	.444

Plate Appearances/Strikeout

Player, Team	Lg	Org	PA/K
Brian Raabe, Columbus	**INT**	**NYY**	**29.63**
Toby Hall, Orlando	SL	TB	22.00
Jesus Ametller, Memphis	PCL	StL	19.81
Jesus Azuaje, Huntsville	SL	Mil	18.46
Matt Howard, Nashville	PCL	Pit	18.21
Juan Pierre, Asheville	SAL	Col	17.51
Aaron Miles, Michigan	MWL	Hou	15.55
Jose Amado, Wichita	TL	KC	14.11
Brent Abernathy, Knoxville	SL	Tor	13.83
Jose Cepeda, Greenville	SL	Atl	13.80

Slugging Percentage

Player, Team	Lg	Org	SLG
Erubiel Durazo, Tucson	**PCL**	**Ari**	**.703**
Adam Piatt, Vancouver	PCL	Oak	.688
Jack Cust, High Desert	CAL	Ari	.651
Roosevelt Brown, Iowa	PCL	ChC	.634
Chris Norton, Portland	EL	Fla	.633
Felipe Crespo, Fresno	PCL	SF	.616
J.R. Phillips, Colorado Springs	PCL	Col	.614
Ben Petrick, Colorado Springs	PCL	Col	.603
Pat Burrell, Scranton/Wilkes-Barre	INT	Phi	.602
Israel Alcantara, Pawtucket	INT	Bos	.599

Hit By Pitch

Player, Team	Lg	Org	HBP
Nick Johnson, Norwich	**EL**	**NYY**	**37**
Corky Miller, Chattanooga	SL	Cin	31
Sal Fasano, Omaha	PCL	KC	26
David Eckstein, Trenton	EL	Bos	25
Trace Coquillette, Ottawa	INT	Mon	24
Darren Blakely, Lake Elsinore	CAL	Ana	20
Jon Schaeffer, Quad City	MWL	Min	20
Julio Zuleta, West Tenn	SL	ChC	20
5 tied with			19

Errors

Player, Team	Lg	Org	E
Luke Allen, San Antonio	**TL**	**LA**	**53**
Luis Suarez, Winston-Salem	CAR	CWS	52
Alex Fajardo, Piedmont	SAL	Phi	47
Chone Figgins, Salem	CAR	Col	45
Chris Rowan, Stockton	CAL	Mil	45
Wilmy Caceres, Clinton	MWL	Cin	42
Aramis Ramirez, Nashville	PCL	Pit	42
Juan Bautista, Tulsa	TL	Tex	41
Steve Lackey, Greenville	SL	Atl	41
3 tied with			40

Full-Season Pitching Leaders

Earned Run Average

Player, Team	Lg	Org	ERA
Mike Meyers, West Tenn	**SL**	**ChC**	**1.73**
Josh Kalinowski, Salem	CAR	Col	2.11
Bryan Hebson, Jupiter	FSL	Mon	2.17
Eric Ireland, Jackson	TL	Hou	2.24
Brad Baisley, Piedmont	SAL	Phi	2.26
Tomokazu Ohka, Pawtucket	INT	Bos	2.31
Junior Guerrero, Wilmington	CAR	KC	2.31
Jason Norton, Augusta	SAL	Bos	2.32
Scott Downs, West Tenn	SL	ChC	2.35
Rick Ankiel, Memphis	PCL	StL	2.35
Scott Comer, Brevard County	FSL	Fla	2.35
Derrick Lewis, Myrtle Beach	CAR	Atl	2.40
Winston Abreu, Myrtle Beach	CAR	Atl	2.48
Jason Standridge, St. Petersburg	FSL	TB	2.57
Edwin Gonzalez, Charleston (WV)	SAL	KC	2.60

Saves

Player, Team	Lg	Org	S
Jason Ellison, Tampa	**FSL**	**NYY**	**35**
Bill Everly, San Bernardino	CAL	LA	34
Brandon Puffer, Clinton	MWL	Cin	34
Joe Lisio, Norwich	EL	NYY	33
Jim Brink, Midland	TL	Oak	29
Doug Nickle, Clearwater	FSL	Phi	28
Jay Tessmer, Columbus	INT	NYY	28
Mark Cisar, Augusta	SAL	Bos	27
Francisco Cordero, Jacksonville	SL	Det	27
Brent Husted, Vero Beach	FSL	LA	27
Jarrod Kingrey, Hagerstown	SAL	Tor	27
Eddy Reyes, Orlando	SL	TB	27
Travis Thompson, Salem	CAR	Col	27
6 tied with			26

Wins

Player, Team	Lg	Org	W
Doug Bridges, Lake Elsinore	**CAL**	**Ana**	**18**
Bronson Arroyo, Nashville	PCL	Pit	15
Jason Beverlin, Norwich	EL	NYY	15
Matt Blank, Harrisburg	EL	Mon	15
Pasqual Coco, Dunedin	FSL	Tor	15
Jared Fernandez, Pawtucket	INT	Bos	15
Gary Knotts, Portland	EL	Fla	15
Tomokazu Ohka, Pawtucket	INT	Bos	15
Matt Perisho, Oklahoma	PCL	Tex	15
Jeromie Robertson, Jackson	TL	Hou	15
Wilfredo Rodriguez, Kissimmee	FSL	Hou	15
Mark Watson, Akron	EL	Cle	15
22 tied with			14

Games

Player, Team	Lg	Org	G
Pat Flury, Indianapolis	**INT**	**Cin**	**66**
Scott Brow, Edmonton	PCL	Ana	64
John Riedling, Indianapolis	INT	Cin	64
Mark Guerra, Norfolk	INT	NYM	63
Rick Greene, Indianapolis	INT	Cin	61
Bill Snyder, Jacksonville	SL	Det	61
Matt Dunbar, Nashville	PCL	Pit	60
Trevor Enders, Orlando	SL	TB	60
Dave Evans, Rochester	INT	Bal	60
Bill Everly, San Bernardino	CAL	LA	60
Gus Gandarillas, Salt Lake	PCL	Min	60
Doug Nickle, Clearwater	FSL	Phi	60
Ray Noriega, Visalia	CAL	Oak	60
Saul Rivera, Quad City	MWL	Min	60
6 tied with			59

Losses

Player, Team	Lg	Org	L
Nate Bump, Portland	**EL**	**Fla**	**16**
Derek Root, Jackson	**TL**	**Hou**	**16**
Andy Bausher, Lynchburg	CAR	Pit	15
Keith Evans, Ottawa	INT	Mon	15
Joel Pineiro, New Haven	EL	Sea	15
Jake Robbins, Norwich	EL	NYY	15
Bob Scanlan, New Orleans	PCL	Hou	15
10 tied with			14

Innings Pitched

Player, Team	Lg	Org	IP
Steve Fish, Lake Elsinore	**CAL**	**Ana**	**196.2**
Jeromie Robertson, Jackson	TL	Hou	191.0
Brian Cooper, Edmonton	PCL	Ana	189.0
Seth Etherton, Edmonton	PCL	Ana	189.0
Josh Towers, Bowie	EL	Bal	189.0
David Darwin, Jacksonville	SL	Det	187.1
Adam Pettyjohn, Jacksonville	SL	Det	186.1
Doug Bridges, Lake Elsinore	CAL	Ana	185.2
Ryan Cummings, Erie	EL	Ana	185.1
Eric Ireland, Jackson	TL	Hou	185.0
Jared Fernandez, Pawtucket	INT	Bos	182.0
Scot Shields, Erie	EL	Ana	182.0
Geraldo Padua, Rancho Cuca.	CAL	SD	180.1
Bryan Wolff, Las Vegas	PCL	SD	177.2
2 tied with			177.1

Full-Season Pitching Leaders

Walks

Player, Team	Lg	Org	BB
Lance Caraccioli, San Bernardino	**CAL**	**LA**	**126**
Ben Howard, Fort Wayne	MWL	SD	110
Robbie Beckett, Albuquerque	PCL	LA	106
Tom Bennett, Visalia	CAL	Oak	94
Jacob Shumate, Greenville	SL	Atl	94
Chad Hutchinson, Memphis	PCL	StL	93
Brian O'Connor, Altoona	EL	Pit	92
Matt Drews, Toledo	INT	Det	91
Paul Morse, Edmonton	PCL	Ana	88
Matt Bruback, Lansing	MWL	ChC	87
Chris Jones, San Jose	CAL	SF	87
Ryan Mills, Fort Myers	FSL	Min	87
Ryan Anderson, New Haven	EL	Sea	86
Steve Colyer, San Bernardino	CAL	LA	86
Jim Crowell, Chattanooga	SL	Cin	85

Strikeouts

Player, Team	Lg	Org	K
John Stephens, Delmarva	**SAL**	**Bal**	**217**
Geraldo Padua, Rancho Cuca.	CAL	SD	196
Rick Ankiel, Memphis	PCL	StL	194
Scot Shields, Erie	EL	Ana	194
Juan Figueroa, Winston-Salem	CAR	CWS	189
Matt Riley, Bowie	EL	Bal	189
Eric Gagne, San Antonio	TL	LA	185
Junior Guerrero, Wilmington	CAR	KC	181
Steve Fish, Lake Elsinore	CAL	Ana	180
Scott Cassidy, Hagerstown	SAL	Tor	178
Josh Kalinowski, Salem	CAR	Col	176
Brian Cooper, Edmonton	PCL	Ana	175
Scott Downs, West Tenn	SL	ChC	173
Mike Meyers, West Tenn	SL	ChC	173
Seth Etherton, Edmonton	PCL	Ana	172

Strikeouts/9 Innings—Starters

Player, Team	Lg	Org	K/9
Nick Neugebauer, Beloit	**MWL**	**Mil**	**13.95**
Rick Ankiel, Memphis	PCL	StL	12.68
John Stephens, Delmarva	SAL	Bal	11.47
Winston Abreu, Myrtle Beach	CAR	Atl	11.15
Robinson Checo, Albuquerque	PCL	LA	11.12
Mike Meyers, West Tenn	SL	ChC	11.10
Ryan Anderson, New Haven	EL	Sea	10.88
Junior Guerrero, Wilmington	CAR	KC	10.46
Scott Sobkowiak, Myrtle Beach	CAR	Atl	10.40
Lesli Brea, St. Lucie	FSL	NYM	10.14
John Patterson, Tucson	PCL	Ari	10.06
John Sneed, Knoxville	SL	Tor	10.02
Ryan Vogelsong, Shreveport	TL	SF	10.01
Cedrick Bowers, Orlando	SL	TB	9.94
Brad Penny, Portland	EL	Fla	9.93

Strikeouts/9 Innings—Relievers

Player, Team	Lg	Org	K/9
Eric Cammack, Norfolk	**INT**	**NYM**	**13.78**
Saul Rivera, Quad City	MWL	Min	13.18
Shane Heams, West Michigan	MWL	Det	13.17
Bo Donaldson, Chattanooga	SL	Cin	12.95
Matt Miller, Tulsa	TL	Tex	12.82
Bert Snow, Vancouver	PCL	Oak	12.78
Nathan Ruhl, St. Petersburg	FSL	TB	12.56
Cary Hiles, Piedmont	SAL	Phi	12.39
Erik Hiljus, Toledo	INT	Det	12.27
Alex Lontayo, Augusta	SAL	Bos	12.27
Jeff Sparks, Durham	INT	TB	12.27
Tim Redding, Michigan	MWL	Hou	12.09
Sean DePaula, Buffalo	INT	Cle	12.06
Juan Moreno, Tulsa	TL	Tex	11.92
Ivan Montane, New Haven	EL	Sea	11.76

Hits/9 Innings—Starters

Player, Team	Lg	Org	H/9
Nick Neugebauer, Beloit	**MWL**	**Mil**	**5.58**
Mike Meyers, West Tenn	SL	ChC	5.71
Aaron Miller, Quad City	MWL	Min	5.94
Winston Abreu, Myrtle Beach	CAR	Atl	6.13
Rene Vega, Capital City	SAL	NYM	6.23
Wilfredo Rodriguez, Kissimmee	FSL	Hou	6.34
Rick Ankiel, Memphis	PCL	StL	6.41
Scott Sobkowiak, Myrtle Beach	CAR	Atl	6.46
Eric Gagne, San Antonio	TL	LA	6.55
Mike Spiegel, Kinston	CAR	Cle	6.60
Josh Kalinowski, Salem	CAR	Col	6.60
Derrick Lewis, Myrtle Beach	CAR	Atl	6.87
Junior Guerrero, Wilmington	CAR	KC	6.94
Matt McClellan, Dunedin	FSL	Tor	6.96
Bryan Hebson, Jupiter	FSL	Mon	7.03

Hits/9 Innings—Relievers

Player, Team	Lg	Org	H/9
David Riske, Buffalo	**INT**	**Cle**	**3.33**
Juan Moreno, Tulsa	TL	Tex	4.74
Eric Cammack, Norfolk	INT	NYM	4.82
Brad Voyles, Myrtle Beach	CAR	Atl	4.83
Dwayne Jacobs, Winston-Salem	CAR	CWS	5.03
Bob File, Dunedin	FSL	Tor	5.09
Bo Donaldson, Chattanooga	SL	Cin	5.20
Shane Heams, West Michigan	MWL	Det	5.35
Saul Rivera, Quad City	MWL	Min	5.43
Wayne Franklin, Jackson	TL	Hou	5.56
Jim Serrano, Jupiter	FSL	Mon	5.71
Ivan Montane, New Haven	EL	Sea	5.75
Nathan Ruhl, St. Petersburg	FSL	TB	5.78
Kirk Griffin, Peoria	MWL	StL	5.82
Jarrod Mays, Kinston	CAR	Cle	5.89

Triple-A Batting Leaders

Batting Average

Player, Team	Lg	Org	Avg
Mark Quinn, Omaha	**PCL**	**KC**	**.360**
Steve Cox, Durham	INT	TB	.341
Calvin Murray, Fresno	PCL	SF	.334
Felipe Crespo, Fresno	PCL	SF	.332
Jason Hardtke, Indianapolis	INT	Cin	.329
Aramis Ramirez, Nashville	PCL	Pit	.328
Pedro Valdes, Oklahoma	PCL	Tex	.327
D'Angelo Jimenez, Columbus	INT	NYY	.327
Adam Kennedy, Memphis	PCL	StL	.327
Brian Raabe, Columbus	INT	NYY	.327

Third Basemen Batting Average

Player, Team	Lg	Org	Avg
Aramis Ramirez, Nashville	**PCL**	**Pit**	**.328**
Ken Woods, Fresno	PCL	SF	.324
Jim Tatum, Colorado Springs	PCL	Col	.313
Frank Menechino, Vancouver	PCL	Oak	.309
Jeff Ball, Vancouver	PCL	Oak	.309
Eddie Zosky, Louisville	INT	Mil	.294
Brad Seitzer, Tacoma	PCL	Sea	.287
Kit Pellow, Omaha	PCL	KC	.286
Gabe Alvarez, Toledo	INT	Det	.285
Howard Battle, Richmond	INT	Atl	.284

Catchers Batting Average

Player, Team	Lg	Org	Avg
George Williams, New Orleans	**PCL**	**Hou**	**.284**
Mike Hubbard, Oklahoma	PCL	Tex	.283
Toby Rumfield, Richmond	INT	Atl	.274
Tim Laker, Nashville	PCL	Pit	.269
Raul Chavez, Tacoma	PCL	Sea	.268
Tommy Davis, Rochester	INT	Bal	.257
Danny Ardoin, Vancouver	PCL	Oak	.253
Bobby Estalella, Scranton-WB	INT	Phi	.231
Francisco Morales, Ottawa	INT	Mon	.229

Shortstops Batting Average

Player, Team	Lg	Org	Avg
D'Angelo Jimenez, Columbus	**INT**	**NYY**	**.327**
Carlos Hernandez, New Orleans	PCL	Hou	.293
Luis Ordaz, Memphis	PCL	StL	.285
Jose Ortiz, Vancouver	PCL	Oak	.284
Benji Gil, Calgary	PCL	Fla	.279
Shane Halter, Norfolk	INT	NYM	.274
Juan Castro, Albuquerque	PCL	LA	.274
Chris Martin, Durham	INT	TB	.273
Mark DeRosa, Richmond	INT	Atl	.272
Jose Flores, Tacoma	PCL	Sea	.270

First Basemen Batting Average

Player, Team	Lg	Org	Avg
Steve Cox, Durham	**INT**	**TB**	**.341**
Felipe Crespo, Fresno	PCL	SF	.332
Desi Wilson, Tucson	PCL	Ari	.323
Luis Lopez, Syracuse	INT	Tor	.322
Eduardo Perez, Memphis	PCL	StL	.320
David Ortiz, Salt Lake	PCL	Min	.315
J.R. Phillips, Colorado Springs	PCL	Col	.311
Ryan Jackson, Tacoma	PCL	Sea	.308
Wes Chamberlain, Albuquerque	PCL	LA	.307
Andy Barkett, Oklahoma	PCL	Tex	.307

Outfielders Batting Average

Player, Team	Lg	Org	Avg
Mark Quinn, Omaha	**PCL**	**KC**	**.360**
Calvin Murray, Fresno	PCL	SF	.334
Darryl Brinkley, Nashville	PCL	Pit	.323
Chris Latham, Salt Lake	PCL	Min	.322
Chad Mottola, Charlotte	INT	CWS	.321
John Roskos, Calgary	PCL	Fla	.320
Kevin Grijak, Albuquerque	PCL	LA	.317
Lyle Mouton, Louisville	INT	Mil	.310
D.T. Cromer, Indianapolis	INT	Cin	.310
Ryan Thompson, New Orleans	PCL	Hou	.309

Second Basemen Batting Average

Player, Team	Lg	Org	Avg
Jason Hardtke, Indianapolis	**INT**	**Cin**	**.329**
Adam Kennedy, Memphis	PCL	StL	.327
Brian Raabe, Columbus	INT	NYY	.327
Trace Coquillette, Ottawa	INT	Mon	.326
Tilson Brito, Charlotte	INT	CWS	.318
Amaury Garcia, Calgary	PCL	Fla	.317
J.P. Roberge, Omaha	PCL	KC	.314
Tony Graffanino, Durham	INT	TB	.313
Scott Sheldon, Oklahoma	PCL	Tex	.311
Aaron Holbert, Durham	INT	TB	.311

Switch-Hitters Batting Average

Player, Team	Lg	Org	Avg
Felipe Crespo, Fresno	**PCL**	**SF**	**.332**
Jason Hardtke, Indianapolis	INT	Cin	.329
D'Angelo Jimenez, Columbus	INT	NYY	.327
Chris Latham, Salt Lake	PCL	Min	.322
Kimera Bartee, Toledo	INT	Det	.286
George Williams, New Orleans	PCL	Hou	.284
Torey Lovullo, Scranton-WB	INT	Phi	.279
Casey Candaele, New Orleans	PCL	Hou	.266
Greg Martinez, Louisville	INT	Mil	.265
Santiago Perez, Louisville	INT	Mil	.263

Triple-A Batting Leaders

Hits

Player, Team	Lg	Org	H
Calvin Murray, Fresno	**PCL**	**SF**	**183**
Steve Cox, Durham	INT	TB	182
D'Angelo Jimenez, Columbus	INT	NYY	172
Luis Lopez, Syracuse	INT	Tor	171
D.T. Cromer, Indianapolis	INT	Cin	166
Chad Mottola, Charlotte	INT	CWS	164
John Roskos, Calgary	PCL	Fla	162
Brian Raabe, Columbus	INT	NYY	161
Wendell Magee, Scranton-WB	INT	Phi	160
Dave Hajek, Colorado Springs	PCL	Col	157

Extra-Base Hits

Player, Team	Lg	Org	XBH
Steve Cox, Durham	**INT**	**TB**	**78**
D.T. Cromer, Indianapolis	INT	Cin	71
Kurt Bierek, Columbus	INT	NYY	69
Lyle Mouton, Louisville	INT	Mil	69
Luis Raven, Charlotte	INT	CWS	69
David Ortiz, Salt Lake	PCL	Min	68
John Roskos, Calgary	PCL	Fla	68
Kit Pellow, Omaha	PCL	KC	67
Scott Sheldon, Oklahoma	PCL	Tex	66
2 tied with			63

Doubles

Player, Team	Lg	Org	2B
Steve Cox, Durham	**INT**	**TB**	**49**
John Roskos, Calgary	PCL	Fla	44
Dave Hajek, Colorado Springs	PCL	Col	43
Lyle Mouton, Louisville	INT	Mil	43
Kurt Bierek, Columbus	INT	NYY	42
Billy McMillon, Scranton-WB	INT	Phi	38
D.T. Cromer, Indianapolis	INT	Cin	37
Amaury Garcia, Calgary	PCL	Fla	37
Jason Hardtke, Indianapolis	INT	Cin	37
3 tied with			36

Total Bases

Player, Team	Lg	Org	TB
Steve Cox, Durham	**INT**	**TB**	**314**
D.T. Cromer, Indianapolis	INT	Cin	301
Calvin Murray, Fresno	PCL	SF	297
J.R. Phillips, Colorado Springs	PCL	Col	294
Luis Raven, Charlotte	INT	CWS	289
David Ortiz, Salt Lake	PCL	Min	281
John Roskos, Calgary	PCL	Fla	278
Kit Pellow, Omaha	PCL	KC	277
Kurt Bierek, Columbus	INT	NYY	268
Scott Sheldon, Oklahoma	PCL	Tex	266

Triples

Player, Team	Lg	Org	3B
Kerry Robinson, Indianapolis	**INT**	**Cin**	**11**
David Roberts, Buffalo	INT	Cle	10
Amaury Garcia, Calgary	PCL	Fla	9
Frank Menechino, Vancouver	PCL	Oak	9
Kimera Bartee, Toledo	INT	Det	8
Jason Conti, Tucson	PCL	Ari	8
Chris Latham, Salt Lake	PCL	Min	8
Jose Macias, Toledo	INT	Det	8
Santiago Perez, Louisville	INT	Mil	8
9 tied with			7

Runs

Player, Team	Lg	Org	R
Calvin Murray, Fresno	**PCL**	**SF**	**122**
Steve Cox, Durham	INT	TB	107
Scott McClain, Durham	INT	TB	106
Frank Menechino, Vancouver	PCL	Oak	103
Jason Conti, Tucson	PCL	Ari	100
Felipe Crespo, Fresno	PCL	SF	98
5 tied with			97

Home Runs

Player, Team	Lg	Org	HR
J.R. Phillips, Colorado Springs	**PCL**	**Col**	**41**
Kit Pellow, Omaha	PCL	KC	35
Luis Raven, Charlotte	INT	CWS	33
Chad Hermansen, Nashville	PCL	Pit	32
Dave McCarty, Toledo	INT	Det	31
6 tied with			30

Runs Batted In

Player, Team	Lg	Org	RBI
Steve Cox, Durham	**INT**	**TB**	**127**
Luis Raven, Charlotte	INT	CWS	125
David Ortiz, Salt Lake	PCL	Min	110
D.T. Cromer, Indianapolis	INT	Cin	107
Torey Lovullo, Scranton-WB	INT	Phi	106
Scott McClain, Durham	INT	TB	104
J.R. Phillips, Colorado Springs	PCL	Col	100
Kit Pellow, Omaha	PCL	KC	99
Joe Vitiello, Omaha	PCL	KC	98
2 tied with			97

Triple-A Batting Leaders

Walks

Player, Team	Lg	Org	BB
Brad Seitzer, Tacoma	**PCL**	**Sea**	**89**
Jon Zuber, Scranton/Wilkes-Barre	INT	Phi	86
Jon Nunnally, Pawtucket	INT	Bos	85
Alonzo Powell, Columbus	INT	NYY	82
Dusty Allen, Las Vegas	PCL	SD	79
David Ortiz, Salt Lake	PCL	Min	79
Felipe Crespo, Fresno	PCL	SF	78
Torey Lovullo, Scranton-WB	INT	Phi	78
Keith Mitchell, Pawtucket	INT	Bos	78
Mario Valdez, Charlotte	INT	CWS	76

Strikeouts

Player, Team	Lg	Org	K
Russ Branyan, Buffalo	**INT**	**Cle**	**187**
Tom Quinlan, Iowa	PCL	ChC	159
Scott McClain, Durham	INT	TB	156
Chris Haas, Memphis	PCL	StL	155
Dusty Allen, Las Vegas	PCL	SD	143
J.R. Phillips, Colorado Springs	PCL	Col	143
Jose Fernandez, Ottawa	INT	Mon	136
Ernie Young, Tucson	PCL	Ari	129
Michael Coleman, Pawtucket	INT	Bos	128
2 tied with			127

Plate Appearances/Strikeout

Player, Team	Lg	Org	PA/K
Brian Raabe, Columbus	**INT**	**NYY**	**29.63**
Matt Howard, Nashville	PCL	Pit	18.21
Dave Hajek, Colorado Springs	PCL	Col	13.52
Todd Haney, Norfolk	INT	NYM	12.33
Ken Woods, Fresno	PCL	SF	11.51
Adam Kennedy, Memphis	PCL	StL	11.25
Jason Hardtke, Indianapolis	INT	Cin	10.65
Francisco Matos, Tacoma	PCL	Sea	10.32
Tony Tarasco, Columbus	INT	NYY	10.26
Luis Ordaz, Memphis	PCL	StL	10.05

Hit By Pitch

Player, Team	Lg	Org	HBP
Sal Fasano, Omaha	**PCL**	**KC**	**26**
Trace Coquillette, Ottawa	INT	Mon	24
Jerry Hairston Jr., Rochester	INT	Bal	19
Kit Pellow, Omaha	PCL	KC	18
Dave Hollins, Charlotte	INT	CWS	14
Brian Raabe, Columbus	INT	NYY	14
Jim Chamblee, Pawtucket	INT	Bos	13
Steve Gibralter, Omaha	PCL	KC	13
Scott Krause, Louisville	INT	Mil	13
Tom Quinlan, Iowa	PCL	ChC	13

Stolen Bases

Player, Team	Lg	Org	SB
Greg Martinez, Louisville	**INT**	**Mil**	**48**
Kerry Robinson, Indianapolis	INT	Cin	44
Calvin Murray, Fresno	PCL	SF	42
David Roberts, Buffalo	INT	Cle	39
Brandon Wilson, Iowa	PCL	ChC	31
Terry Jones, Ottawa	INT	Mon	30
Chris Stowers, Ottawa	INT	Mon	28
Scarborough Green, Oklahoma	PCL	Tex	26
D'Angelo Jimenez, Columbus	INT	NYY	26
Jon Nunnally, Pawtucket	INT	Bos	26

On-Base Percentage

Player, Team	Lg	Org	OBP
Felipe Crespo, Fresno	**PCL**	**SF**	**.447**
Trace Coquillette, Ottawa	INT	Mon	.434
Aramis Ramirez, Nashville	PCL	Pit	.425
Jon Zuber, Scranton/Wilkes-Barre	INT	Phi	.421
Bubba Carpenter, Columbus	INT	NYY	.419
Steve Cox, Durham	INT	TB	.415
Alonzo Powell, Columbus	INT	NYY	.414
David Ortiz, Salt Lake	PCL	Min	.412
Pedro Valdes, Oklahoma	PCL	Tex	.410
Mark Quinn, Omaha	PCL	KC	.409

Slugging Percentage

Player, Team	Lg	Org	SLG
Felipe Crespo, Fresno	**PCL**	**SF**	**.616**
J.R. Phillips, Colorado Springs	PCL	Col	.614
Mark Quinn, Omaha	PCL	KC	.598
David Ortiz, Salt Lake	PCL	Min	.590
Steve Cox, Durham	INT	TB	.588
Scott Sheldon, Oklahoma	PCL	Tex	.587
Kit Pellow, Omaha	PCL	KC	.583
Joe Vitiello, Omaha	PCL	KC	.579
Brooks Kieschnick, Edmonton	PCL	Ana	.569
Trace Coquillette, Ottawa	INT	Mon	.566

Errors

Player, Team	Lg	Org	E
Aramis Ramirez, Nashville	**PCL**	**Pit**	**42**
Dernell Stenson, Pawtucket	INT	Bos	34
Carlos Villalobos, New Orleans	PCL	Hou	34
Kit Pellow, Omaha	PCL	KC	33
Jose Fernandez, Ottawa	INT	Mon	31
Mike Moriarty, Salt Lake	PCL	Min	30
Santiago Perez, Louisville	INT	Mil	30
Benji Gil, Calgary	PCL	Fla	29
Jose Ortiz, Vancouver	PCL	Oak	28
2 tied with			27

Triple-A Pitching Leaders

Earned Run Average

Player, Team	Lg	Org	ERA
Mel Bunch, Tacoma	**PCL**	**Sea**	**3.10**
Brett Laxton, Vancouver	PCL	Oak	3.46
Ed Yarnall, Columbus	INT	NYY	3.47
Mike Fyhrie, Edmonton	PCL	Ana	3.47
Giovanni Carrara, Indianapolis	INT	Cin	3.47
Dave Borkowski, Toledo	INT	Det	3.50
Bob Wolcott, Pawtucket	INT	Bos	3.59
Doug Linton, Rochester	INT	Bal	3.65
Jose Mercedes, Norfolk	INT	NYM	3.70
Andrew Lorraine, Iowa	PCL	ChC	3.71
Doug Creek, Iowa	PCL	ChC	3.79
Paul Wagner, Buffalo	INT	Cle	3.82
Rod Bolton, Scranton-WB	INT	Phi	3.82
Jimmy Anderson, Nashville	PCL	Pit	3.84
Nelson Figueroa, Tucson	PCL	Ari	3.94

Wins

Player, Team	Lg	Org	W
Matt Perisho, Oklahoma	**PCL**	**Tex**	**15**
Denny Harriger, Indianapolis	INT	Cin	14
Bronswell Patrick, Fresno	PCL	SF	14
Brett Laxton, Vancouver	PCL	Oak	13
Larry Luebbers, Memphis	PCL	StL	13
Ed Yarnall, Columbus	INT	NYY	13
Giovanni Carrara, Indianapolis	INT	Cin	12
Jared Fernandez, Pawtucket	INT	Bos	12
Dan Murray, Norfolk	INT	NYM	12
Mike Romano, Syracuse	INT	Tor	12
Ramon Tatis, Durham	INT	TB	12
10 tied with			11

Losses

Player, Team	Lg	Org	L
Bob Scanlan, New Orleans	**PCL**	**Hou**	**15**
Matt Drews, Toledo	INT	Det	14
Keith Evans, Ottawa	INT	Mon	13
Dario Perez, Calgary	PCL	Fla	13
Bob Wolcott, Pawtucket	INT	Bos	13
Ryan Bradley, Columbus	INT	NYY	12
Mike Drumright, Calgary	PCL	Fla	12
Robert Ellis, New Orleans	PCL	Hou	12
Mike Johnson, Ottawa	INT	Mon	12
Jeff Juden, Columbus	INT	NYY	12
Jon Ratliff, Richmond	INT	Atl	12
Bryan Wolff, Las Vegas	PCL	SD	12
9 tied with			11

Saves

Player, Team	Lg	Org	S
Jay Tessmer, Columbus	**INT**	**NYY**	**28**
Eddie Gaillard, Durham	INT	TB	26
Todd Williams, Tacoma	PCL	Sea	25
Oscar Henriquez, Norfolk	INT	NYM	23
David Cortes, Richmond	INT	Atl	22
Dave Wainhouse, Col. Springs	PCL	Col	22
Rick Heiserman, Memphis	PCL	StL	20
Rich DeLucia, Buffalo	INT	Cle	19
Tony Fiore, Salt Lake	PCL	Min	19
Cory Bailey, Fresno	PCL	SF	18
Allen McDill, Oklahoma	PCL	Tex	18
Gabe Molina, Rochester	INT	Bal	18
Steve Sinclair, Tacoma	PCL	Sea	18
Luis Andujar, Charlotte	INT	CWS	16
Reggie Harris, Louisville	INT	Mil	16

Games

Player, Team	Lg	Org	G
Scott Brow, Edmonton	**PCL**	**Ana**	**64**
Mark Guerra, Norfolk	INT	NYM	63
Rick Greene, Indianapolis	INT	Cin	61
Dave Evans, Rochester	INT	Bal	60
Bryan Eversgerd, Memphis	PCL	StL	59
Eddie Gaillard, Durham	INT	TB	59
Joe Borowski, Louisville	INT	Mil	58
Steve Gajkowski, Iowa	PCL	ChC	58
Hector Ramirez, Louisville	INT	Mil	58
Darryl Scott, Scranton-WB	INT	Phi	57
Jeff Granger, Louisville	INT	Mil	56
Fred Rath, Salt Lake	PCL	Min	56
Richie Barker, Iowa	PCL	ChC	55
Jim Stoops, Colorado Springs	PCL	Col	55
2 tied with			54

Innings Pitched

Player, Team	Lg	Org	IP
Bryan Wolff, Las Vegas	**PCL**	**SD**	**177.2**
Jeff Juden, Columbus	INT	NYY	176.1
Mike Romano, Syracuse	INT	Tor	174.1
Reid Cornelius, Calgary	PCL	Fla	172.1
Denny Harriger, Indianapolis	INT	Cin	172.0
Calvin Maduro, Rochester	INT	Bal	169.0
Brady Raggio, Oklahoma	PCL	Tex	168.0
Ricky Stone, Albuquerque	PCL	LA	167.0
Bronswell Patrick, Fresno	PCL	SF	164.0
Bob Scanlan, New Orleans	PCL	Hou	163.2
Todd Van Poppel, Nashville	PCL	Pit	163.2
Jared Fernandez, Pawtucket	INT	Bos	163.1
Brandon Knight, Oklahoma	PCL	Tex	163.0
Nerio Rodriguez, Syracuse	INT	Tor	162.2
Wade Miller, New Orleans	PCL	Hou	162.1

Triple-A Pitching Leaders

Walks

Player, Team	Lg	Org	BB
Matt Drews, Toledo	**INT**	**Det**	**91**
Mike Romano, Syracuse	INT	Tor	84
Terrell Wade, Durham	INT	TB	80
Matt Perisho, Oklahoma	PCL	Tex	78
Jeff Juden, Columbus	INT	NYY	76
Ramon Tatis, Durham	INT	TB	74
Ryan Bradley, Columbus	INT	NYY	73
Everett Stull, Richmond	INT	Atl	73
Mike Drumright, Calgary	PCL	Fla	72
Ricky Stone, Albuquerque	PCL	LA	71
Dan Murray, Norfolk	INT	NYM	70
Reid Cornelius, Calgary	PCL	Fla	68
Ryan Jensen, Fresno	PCL	SF	68
Tom Fordham, Charlotte	INT	CWS	66
Horacio Estrada, Louisville	INT	Mil	65

Strikeouts

Player, Team	Lg	Org	K
Todd Van Poppel, Nashville	**PCL**	**Pit**	**157**
Aaron Fultz, Fresno	PCL	SF	151
Jeff Juden, Columbus	INT	NYY	151
Bryan Wolff, Las Vegas	PCL	SD	151
Ryan Jensen, Fresno	PCL	SF	150
Matt Perisho, Oklahoma	PCL	Tex	150
Calvin Maduro, Rochester	INT	Bal	149
Ruben Quevedo, Iowa	PCL	ChC	148
Ed Yarnall, Columbus	INT	NYY	146
Bronswell Patrick, Fresno	PCL	SF	142
Doug Creek, Iowa	PCL	ChC	140
Buddy Carlyle, Las Vegas	PCL	SD	138
Nerio Rodriguez, Syracuse	INT	Tor	137
Reid Cornelius, Calgary	PCL	Fla	135
Wade Miller, New Orleans	PCL	Hou	135

Strikeouts/9 Innings—Starters

Player, Team	Lg	Org	K/9
Mike Judd, Albuquerque	**PCL**	**LA**	**9.92**
Aaron Fultz, Fresno	PCL	SF	9.90
Doug Creek, Iowa	PCL	ChC	9.64
Blake Stein, Vancouver	PCL	Oak	9.11
Ed Yarnall, Columbus	INT	NYY	9.04
Dan Carlson, Tucson	PCL	Ari	9.03
Mike Fyhrie, Edmonton	PCL	Ana	8.92
Ruben Quevedo, Iowa	PCL	ChC	8.88
Joel Bennett, Scranton-WB	INT	Phi	8.86
Ryan Jensen, Fresno	PCL	SF	8.64
Matt Perisho, Oklahoma	PCL	Tex	8.64
Todd Van Poppel, Nashville	PCL	Pit	8.63
Mel Bunch, Tacoma	PCL	Sea	8.42
Everett Stull, Richmond	INT	Atl	8.16
Tom Fordham, Charlotte	INT	CWS	8.12

Strikeouts/9 Innings—Relievers

Player, Team	Lg	Org	K/9
Jeff Sparks, Durham	**INT**	**TB**	**12.27**
Johnny Ruffin, Albuquerque	PCL	LA	11.00
Oscar Henriquez, Norfolk	INT	NYM	10.83
Reggie Harris, Louisville	INT	Mil	10.13
Cory Bailey, Fresno	PCL	SF	10.10
Chris Clemons, Tucson	PCL	Ari	9.88
Jim Mann, Syracuse	INT	Tor	9.82
Eddie Gaillard, Durham	INT	TB	9.67
Sean Spencer, Tacoma	PCL	Sea	9.67
Eric Ludwick, Calgary	PCL	Fla	9.41
Anthony Chavez, Vancouver	PCL	Oak	9.39
David Holdridge, Tacoma	PCL	Sea	9.23
Brandon Kolb, Las Vegas	PCL	SD	9.19
Gabe Molina, Rochester	INT	Bal	9.10
Miguel Del Toro, Fresno	PCL	SF	8.96

Hits/9 Innings—Starters

Player, Team	Lg	Org	H/9
Mike Fyhrie, Edmonton	**PCL**	**Ana**	**7.11**
Kyle Peterson, Louisville	INT	Mil	7.43
Blake Stein, Vancouver	PCL	Oak	7.71
Doug Creek, Iowa	PCL	ChC	7.99
Everett Stull, Richmond	INT	Atl	8.03
Mel Bunch, Tacoma	PCL	Sea	8.06
Rob Ramsay, Tacoma	PCL	Sea	8.17
Giovanni Carrara, Indianapolis	INT	Cin	8.20
Mike Romano, Syracuse	INT	Tor	8.26
Jeff Juden, Columbus	INT	NYY	8.37
Ed Yarnall, Columbus	INT	NYY	8.42
Mark Thompson, Memphis	PCL	StL	8.46
Dave Borkowski, Toledo	INT	Det	8.50
Paul Wagner, Buffalo	INT	Cle	8.54
Wade Miller, New Orleans	PCL	Hou	8.65

Hits/9 Innings—Relievers

Player, Team	Lg	Org	H/9
Jeff Sparks, Durham	**INT**	**TB**	**6.50**
Alan Newman, Durham	INT	TB	6.61
Greg McCarthy, Columbus	INT	NYY	6.63
Johnny Ruffin, Albuquerque	PCL	LA	6.83
Gabe Molina, Rochester	INT	Bal	7.06
Mike McMullen, Fresno	PCL	SF	7.09
Jim Mann, Syracuse	INT	Tor	7.23
Rich DeLucia, Buffalo	INT	Cle	7.42
Sean Spencer, Tacoma	PCL	Sea	7.48
Radhames Dykhoff, Rochester	INT	Bal	7.54
Kevin Lovingier, Memphis	PCL	StL	7.62
Chad Bradford, Charlotte	INT	CWS	7.63
Bryan Eversgerd, Memphis	PCL	StL	7.64
Brendan Donnelly, Syracuse	INT	Tor	7.70
Jeff Kubenka, Albuquerque	PCL	LA	8.06

Double-A Batting Leaders

Batting Average

Player, Team	Lg	Org	Avg
Nick Johnson, Norwich	**EL**	**NYY**	**.345**
Adam Piatt, Midland	TL	Oak	.345
Jeff DaVanon, Midland	TL	Oak	.342
Josue Espada, Midland	TL	Oak	.338
Raul Gonzalez, Trenton	EL	Bos	.335
Pat Burrell, Reading	EL	Phi	.333
Milton Bradley, Harrisburg	EL	Mon	.329
Brady Clark, Chattanooga	SL	Cin	.326
Tony Mota, San Antonio	TL	LA	.325
Mike Lamb, Tulsa	TL	Tex	.324

Catchers Batting Average

Player, Team	Lg	Org	Avg
Rod Barajas, El Paso	**TL**	**Ari**	**.318**
Javier Cardona, Jacksonville	SL	Det	.309
Cody McKay, Midland	TL	Oak	.294
Geronimo Gil, San Antonio	TL	LA	.283
Brian Loyd, Knoxville	SL	Tor	.280
Paul Phillips, Wichita	TL	KC	.267
Heath Hayes, Akron	EL	Cle	.266
Brian Schneider, Harrisburg	EL	Mon	.264
Giu. Chiaramonte, Shreveport	TL	SF	.245
Victor Valencia, Norwich	EL	NYY	.222

First Basemen Batting Average

Player, Team	Lg	Org	Avg
Nick Johnson, Norwich	**EL**	**NYY**	**.345**
Pat Burrell, Reading	EL	Phi	.333
Tim Giles, Knoxville	SL	Tor	.311
David Gibralter, Trenton	EL	Bos	.299
Nate Rolison, Portland	EL	Fla	.299
Julio Zuleta, West Tenn	SL	ChC	.295
Chris Richard, Arkansas	TL	StL	.294
Rich Aude, Birmingham	SL	CWS	.290
Jose Amado, Wichita	TL	KC	.290
Larry Barnes, Erie	EL	Ana	.286

Second Basemen Batting Average

Player, Team	Lg	Org	Avg
Jason Williams, Chattanooga	**SL**	**Cin**	**.319**
David Eckstein, Trenton	EL	Bos	.313
Jesus Ametller, Arkansas	TL	StL	.307
Dustin Carr, Orlando	SL	TB	.302
Elvis Pena, Carolina	SL	Col	.301
Jamey Carroll, Harrisburg	EL	Mon	.292
Hiram Bocachica, San Antonio	TL	LA	.291
Brent Abernathy, Knoxville	SL	Tor	.291
Tom Sergio, Tulsa	TL	Tex	.291
Jackie Rexrode, El Paso	TL	Ari	.289

Third Basemen Batting Average

Player, Team	Lg	Org	Avg
Adam Piatt, Midland	**TL**	**Oak**	**.345**
Mike Lamb, Tulsa	TL	Tex	.324
Donny Leon, Norwich	EL	NYY	.302
Aubrey Huff, Orlando	SL	TB	.301
Steve Goodell, Greenville	SL	Atl	.299
Shawn Wooten, Erie	EL	Ana	.292
Chris Truby, Jackson	TL	Hou	.282
Rob Sasser, Jacksonville	SL	Det	.282
Sean McNally, Wichita	TL	KC	.282
Wilton Veras, Trenton	EL	Bos	.281

Shortstops Batting Average

Player, Team	Lg	Org	Avg
Josue Espada, Midland	**TL**	**Oak**	**.338**
Julio Lugo, Jackson	TL	Hou	.319
Alfonso Soriano, Norwich	EL	NYY	.305
Fausto Solano, Knoxville	SL	Tor	.305
Tom Nevers, Chattanooga	SL	Cin	.295
Alejandro Prieto, Wichita	TL	KC	.294
Mike Metcalfe, San Antonio	TL	LA	.293
Kevin Nicholson, Mobile	SL	SD	.288
Jesus Azuaje, Huntsville	SL	Mil	.281
Rudy Gomez, Knoxville	SL	Tor	.281

Outfielders Batting Average

Player, Team	Lg	Org	Avg
Jeff DaVanon, Midland	**TL**	**Oak**	**.342**
Raul Gonzalez, Trenton	EL	Bos	.335
Milton Bradley, Harrisburg	EL	Mon	.329
Brady Clark, Chattanooga	SL	Cin	.326
Tony Mota, San Antonio	TL	LA	.325
Adam Hyzdu, Altoona	EL	Pit	.316
Rick Short, Bowie	EL	Bal	.314
Jason Tyner, Binghamton	EL	NYN	.313
Mario Encarnacion, Midland	TL	Oak	.309
Eric Gillespie, Jacksonville	SL	Det	.306

Switch-Hitters Batting Average

Player, Team	Lg	Org	Avg
Jeff DaVanon, Midland	**TL**	**Oak**	**.342**
Milton Bradley, Harrisburg	EL	Mon	.329
Tony Mota, San Antonio	TL	LA	.325
Demond Smith, Greenville	SL	Atl	.305
Donny Leon, Norwich	EL	NYY	.302
Elvis Pena, Carolina	SL	Col	.301
Adam Melhuse, Knoxville	SL	Tor	.294
Mike Metcalfe, San Antonio	TL	LA	.293
Kevin Nicholson, Mobile	SL	SD	.288
Rick Prieto, Mobile	SL	SD	.287

Double-A Batting Leaders

Hits

Player, Team	Lg	Org	H
Mike Lamb, Tulsa	**TL**	**Tex**	**176**
Raul Gonzalez, Trenton	EL	Bos	169
Brent Abernathy, Knoxville	SL	Tor	168
Brady Clark, Chattanooga	SL	Cin	165
Jamey Carroll, Harrisburg	EL	Mon	164
Adam Piatt, Midland	TL	Oak	164
Rod Barajas, El Paso	TL	Ari	162
Jason Tyner, Binghamton	EL	NYM	162
Tim Giles, Knoxville	SL	Tor	157
2 tied with			151

Extra-Base Hits

Player, Team	Lg	Org	XBH
Adam Piatt, Midland	**TL**	**Oak**	**90**
Mike Lamb, Tulsa	TL	Tex	77
Aubrey Huff, Orlando	SL	TB	65
Andy Tracy, Harrisburg	EL	Mon	65
Cliff Brumbaugh, Tulsa	TL	Tex	63
Steve Hacker, New Britain	EL	Min	63
T.R. Marcinczyk, Midland	TL	Oak	63
Chris Norton, Portland	EL	Fla	63
3 tied with			62

Doubles

Player, Team	Lg	Org	2B
Mike Lamb, Tulsa	**TL**	**Tex**	**51**
Adam Piatt, Midland	TL	Oak	48
Scott Vieira, West Tenn	SL	ChC	44
Brent Abernathy, Knoxville	SL	Tor	42
Rod Barajas, El Paso	TL	Ari	41
Aubrey Huff, Orlando	SL	TB	40
Rob Sasser, Jacksonville	SL	Det	40
T.R. Marcinczyk, Midland	TL	Oak	39
Kevin Nicholson, Mobile	SL	SD	38
Tom Sergio, Tulsa	TL	Tex	38

Total Bases

Player, Team	Lg	Org	TB
Adam Piatt, Midland	**TL**	**Oak**	**335**
Mike Lamb, Tulsa	TL	Tex	300
Andy Tracy, Harrisburg	EL	Mon	276
Raul Gonzalez, Trenton	EL	Bos	264
Pat Burrell, Reading	EL	Phi	263
Brady Clark, Chattanooga	SL	Cin	261
Cliff Brumbaugh, Tulsa	TL	Tex	260
Aubrey Huff, Orlando	SL	TB	260
Sean McNally, Wichita	TL	KC	260
Chris Norton, Portland	EL	Fla	257

Triples

Player, Team	Lg	Org	3B
Luke Allen, San Antonio	**TL**	**LA**	**12**
Tike Redman, Altoona	**EL**	**Pit**	**12**
Jeff DaVanon, Midland	TL	Oak	11
Ethan Faggett, Mobile	SL	SD	11
Hiram Bocachica, San Antonio	TL	LA	10
Cleatus Davidson, New Britain	EL	Min	10
Tim Garland, Midland	TL	Oak	10
Donzell McDonald, Norwich	EL	NYY	10
Julio Ramirez, Portland	EL	Fla	10
Reggie Taylor, Reading	EL	Phi	10

Runs

Player, Team	Lg	Org	R
Adam Piatt, Midland	**TL**	**Oak**	**128**
Nick Johnson, Norwich	EL	NYY	114
David Eckstein, Trenton	EL	Bos	109
Brent Abernathy, Knoxville	SL	Tor	108
Brady Clark, Chattanooga	SL	Cin	103
Goefrey Tomlinson, Wichita	TL	KC	100
Mike Lamb, Tulsa	TL	Tex	98
Sean McNally, Wichita	TL	KC	97
Andy Tracy, Harrisburg	EL	Mon	96
2 tied with			95

Home Runs

Player, Team	Lg	Org	HR
Adam Piatt, Midland	**TL**	**Oak**	**39**
Chris Norton, Portland	EL	Fla	38
Andy Tracy, Harrisburg	EL	Mon	37
Sean McNally, Wichita	TL	KC	36
Chris Richard, Arkansas	TL	StL	29
Pat Burrell, Reading	EL	Phi	28
Chris Truby, Jackson	TL	Hou	28
Steve Hacker, New Britain	EL	Min	27
Javier Cardona, Jacksonville	SL	Det	26
Scott Morgan, Akron	EL	Cle	26

Runs Batted In

Player, Team	Lg	Org	RBI
Adam Piatt, Midland	**TL**	**Oak**	**135**
Andy Tracy, Harrisburg	EL	Mon	128
Tim Giles, Knoxville	SL	Tor	114
T.R. Marcinczyk, Midland	TL	Oak	111
Sean McNally, Wichita	TL	KC	109
Raul Gonzalez, Trenton	EL	Bos	103
Larry Barnes, Erie	EL	Ana	100
Mike Lamb, Tulsa	TL	Tex	100
Donny Leon, Norwich	EL	NYY	100
4 tied with			97

Double-A Batting Leaders

Walks

Player, Team	Lg	Org	BB
Nick Johnson, Norwich	**EL**	**NYY**	**123**
Adam Melhuse, Knoxville	SL	Tor	108
Sean McNally, Wichita	TL	KC	93
Adam Piatt, Midland	TL	Oak	93
Donzell McDonald, Norwich	EL	NYY	90
Kurt Airoso, Jacksonville	SL	Det	89
Brady Clark, Chattanooga	SL	Cin	89
David Eckstein, Trenton	EL	Bos	89
Brad Wilkerson, Harrisburg	EL	Mon	88
Vick Brown, Norwich	EL	NYY	83

Strikeouts

Player, Team	Lg	Org	K
Bryon Gainey, Binghamton	**EL**	**NYM**	**184**
Jayson Bass, New Haven	EL	Sea	160
Julio Ramirez, Portland	EL	Fla	150
Danny Peoples, Akron	EL	Cle	142
Victor Valencia, Norwich	EL	NYY	142
Jamie Gann, El Paso	TL	Ari	141
Andy Tracy, Harrisburg	EL	Mon	139
Chuck Abbott, Erie	EL	Ana	138
John Curl, Mobile	SL	SD	137
Yuri Sanchez, Binghamton	EL	NYM	135

Plate Appearances/Strikeout

Player, Team	Lg	Org	PA/K
Jesus Ametller, Arkansas	**TL**	**StL**	**19.62**
Jesus Azuaje, Huntsville	SL	Mil	18.46
Jose Amado, Wichita	TL	KC	14.11
Brent Abernathy, Knoxville	SL	Tor	13.83
Jason Tyner, Binghamton	EL	NYM	12.83
David Eckstein, Trenton	EL	Bos	12.81
John Barnes, New Britain	EL	Min	12.78
Jimmy Rollins, Reading	EL	Phi	12.72
Julius Matos, El Paso	TL	Ari	12.05
Brent Butler, Arkansas	TL	StL	12.02

Hit By Pitch

Player, Team	Lg	Org	HBP
Nick Johnson, Norwich	**EL**	**NYY**	**37**
David Eckstein, Trenton	EL	Bos	25
Julio Zuleta, West Tenn	SL	ChC	20
Kevin Haverbusch, Altoona	EL	Pit	19
Craig Wilson, Altoona	EL	Pit	19
Toby Kominek, Huntsville	SL	Mil	18
Rod Bair, Carolina	SL	Col	16
Gary Burnham, Reading	EL	Phi	15
4 tied with			13

Stolen Bases

Player, Team	Lg	Org	SB
Julio Ramirez, Portland	**EL**	**Fla**	**64**
Ethan Faggett, Mobile	SL	SD	63
Trent Durrington, Erie	EL	Ana	59
Mike Metcalfe, San Antonio	TL	LA	57
Donzell McDonald, Norwich	EL	NYY	54
Vick Brown, Norwich	EL	NYY	50
Jason Tyner, Binghamton	EL	NYM	49
Alex Sanchez, Orlando	SL	TB	48
Juan Tolentino, Erie	EL	Ana	47
Cleatus Davidson, New Britain	EL	Min	40

On-Base Percentage

Player, Team	Lg	Org	OBP
Nick Johnson, Norwich	**EL**	**NYY**	**.525**
Adam Melhuse, Knoxville	SL	Tor	.454
Adam Piatt, Midland	TL	Oak	.451
David Eckstein, Trenton	EL	Bos	.440
Pat Burrell, Reading	EL	Phi	.438
Brady Clark, Chattanooga	SL	Cin	.425
Jeff DaVanon, Midland	TL	Oak	.424
Josue Espada, Midland	TL	Oak	.420
Steve Goodell, Greenville	SL	Atl	.412
Sean McNally, Wichita	TL	KC	.411

Slugging Percentage

Player, Team	Lg	Org	SLG
Adam Piatt, Midland	**TL**	**Oak**	**.704**
Chris Norton, Portland	EL	Fla	.633
Pat Burrell, Reading	EL	Phi	.631
Adam Hyzdu, Altoona	EL	Pit	.612
Scott Morgan, Akron	EL	Cle	.596
Sean McNally, Wichita	TL	KC	.591
Javier Cardona, Jacksonville	SL	Det	.569
Jeff DaVanon, Midland	TL	Oak	.567
Chris Richard, Arkansas	TL	StL	.563
Andy Tracy, Harrisburg	EL	Mon	.560

Errors

Player, Team	Lg	Org	E
Luke Allen, San Antonio	**TL**	**LA**	**53**
Juan Bautista, Tulsa	TL	Tex	41
Eddy de los Santos, Orlando	SL	TB	39
Luis Rivas, New Britain	EL	Min	39
Josue Espada, Midland	TL	Oak	35
Donny Leon, Norwich	EL	NYY	35
Derek Mitchell, Jacksonville	SL	Det	35
Rob Sasser, Jacksonville	SL	Det	35
Tomas de la Rosa, Harrisburg	EL	Mon	34
Kevin Haverbusch, Altoona	EL	Pit	33

390

Double-A Pitching Leaders

Earned Run Average

Player, Team	Lg	Org	ERA
Pat Ahearne, New Haven	**EL**	**Sea**	**2.61**
Michael Tejera, Portland	EL	Fla	2.62
Eric Gagne, San Antonio	TL	LA	2.63
Tony McKnight, Jackson	TL	Hou	2.75
Tony Armas Jr., Harrisburg	EL	Mon	2.89
Jeromie Robertson, Jackson	TL	Hou	3.06
Jeff Yoder, West Tenn	SL	ChC	3.08
Brandon Villafuerte, Jacksonville	SL	Det	3.18
Matt Riley, Bowie	EL	Bal	3.22
Evan Thomas, Reading	EL	Phi	3.25
Seth Etherton, Erie	EL	Ana	3.27
Brian Cooper, Erie	EL	Ana	3.30
Jason Sekany, Trenton	EL	Bos	3.35
Mark Roberts, Birmingham	SL	CWS	3.40
Jason Secoda, Birmingham	SL	CWS	3.44

Saves

Player, Team	Lg	Org	S
Joe Lisio, Norwich	**EL**	**NYY**	**33**
Francisco Cordero, Jacksonville	SL	Det	27
Matt Montgomery, San Antonio	TL	LA	26
Steve Rain, West Tenn	SL	ChC	24
Hector Almonte, Portland	EL	Fla	23
Ryan Kohlmeier, Bowie	EL	Bal	23
Jason Davis, Shreveport	TL	SF	21
Wayne Franklin, Jackson	TL	Hou	20
Gene Stechschulte, Arkansas	TL	StL	19
Eric Cammack, Binghamton	EL	NYM	15
Pat Flury, Chattanooga	SL	Cin	15
Kevin Hite, Mobile	SL	SD	15
John Daniels, Orlando	SL	TB	14
Lariel Gonzalez, Carolina	SL	Col	14
4 tied with			13

Wins

Player, Team	Lg	Org	W
Bronson Arroyo, Altoona	**EL**	**Pit**	**15**
Jason Beverlin, Norwich	**EL**	**NYY**	**15**
Jeromie Robertson, Jackson	**TL**	**Hou**	**15**
David Darwin, Jacksonville	SL	Det	14
Jason Sekany, Trenton	EL	Bos	14
Jason Gooding, Wichita	TL	KC	13
Chandler Martin, Carolina	SL	Col	13
Michael Tejera, Portland	EL	Fla	13
Eric Gagne, San Antonio	TL	LA	12
Aaron Myette, Birmingham	SL	CWS	12
Victor Santos, Jacksonville	SL	Det	12
Josh Towers, Bowie	EL	Bal	12
Mike Bacsik, Akron	EL	Cle	11
Isabel Giron, Mobile	SL	SD	11
Jake Westbrook, Harrisburg	EL	Mon	11

Games

Player, Team	Lg	Org	G
Trevor Enders, Orlando	**SL**	**TB**	**60**
Joe Lisio, Norwich	EL	NYY	59
Benny Lowe, Knoxville	SL	Tor	58
Matt Montgomery, San Antonio	TL	LA	58
Eric Newman, West Tenn	SL	ChC	58
Jason Kershner, Reading	EL	Phi	57
Chad Ricketts, West Tenn	SL	ChC	57
Blake Mayo, El Paso	TL	Ari	56
Scott Rivette, Knoxville	SL	Tor	56
Danny Smith, West Tenn	SL	ChC	56
David Daniels, Altoona	EL	Pit	55
Craig Dingman, Norwich	EL	NYY	55
Ryan Kohlmeier, Bowie	EL	Bal	55
Joe Winkelsas, Greenville	SL	Atl	55
2 tied with			54

Losses

Player, Team	Lg	Org	L
Nate Bump, Portland	**EL**	**Fla**	**16**
Derek Root, Jackson	**TL**	**Hou**	**16**
Joel Pineiro, New Haven	EL	Sea	15
Ryan Anderson, New Haven	EL	Sea	13
Mark Corey, Binghamton	EL	NYM	13
Rich Dishman, Greenville	SL	Atl	13
Brett Herbison, Binghamton	EL	NYM	13
John Ambrose, Arkansas	TL	StL	12
A.J. Burnett, Portland	EL	Fla	12
David Darwin, Jacksonville	SL	Det	12
Jose Espinal, New Britain	EL	Min	12
Isabel Giron, Mobile	SL	SD	12
Ryan Jacobs, Carolina	SL	Col	12
Luke Prokopec, San Antonio	TL	LA	12
Jake Robbins, Norwich	EL	NYY	12

Innings Pitched

Player, Team	Lg	Org	IP
Jeromie Robertson, Jackson	**TL**	**Hou**	**191.0**
Josh Towers, Bowie	EL	Bal	189.0
David Darwin, Jacksonville	SL	Det	187.1
Jake Westbrook, Harrisburg	EL	Mon	174.2
Jason Beverlin, Norwich	EL	NYY	173.1
Victor Santos, Jacksonville	SL	Det	173.0
Bryan Braswell, Jackson	TL	Hou	171.1
Rodrigo Lopez, Mobile	SL	SD	169.1
Seth Etherton, Erie	EL	Ana	167.2
Eric Gagne, San Antonio	TL	LA	167.2
Joel Pineiro, New Haven	EL	Sea	166.0
Jason Brester, Reading	EL	Phi	164.2
Aaron Myette, Birmingham	SL	CWS	164.2
Andy Hazlett, Trenton	EL	Bos	164.1
Chandler Martin, Carolina	SL	Col	164.1

Double-A Pitching Leaders

Walks

Player, Team	Lg	Org	BB
Brian O'Connor, Altoona	**EL**	**Pit**	**92**
Ryan Anderson, New Haven	EL	Sea	86
Jim Crowell, Chattanooga	SL	Cin	85
Chad Hutchinson, Arkansas	TL	StL	85
Jason Beverlin, Norwich	EL	NYY	81
Brett Herbison, Binghamton	EL	NYM	81
Derek Root, Jackson	TL	Hou	79
Aaron Myette, Birmingham	SL	CWS	77
Cedrick Bowers, Orlando	SL	TB	76
Francisco de la Cruz, Norwich	EL	NYY	73
A.J. Burnett, Portland	EL	Fla	71
Ken Pumphrey, Binghamton	EL	NYM	71
Bobby Rodgers, Portland	EL	Fla	70
Jeff Yoder, West Tenn	SL	ChC	70
Clayton Andrews, Knoxville	SL	Tor	69

Strikeouts

Player, Team	Lg	Org	K
Eric Gagne, San Antonio	**TL**	**LA**	**185**
Ryan Anderson, New Haven	EL	Sea	162
Seth Etherton, Erie	EL	Ana	153
Michael Tejera, Portland	EL	Fla	152
Chad Hutchinson, Arkansas	TL	StL	150
Jason Beverlin, Norwich	EL	NYY	147
Victor Santos, Jacksonville	SL	Det	146
Brian Cooper, Erie	EL	Ana	143
Doug Walls, Carolina	SL	Col	140
Cedrick Bowers, Orlando	SL	TB	138
Rodrigo Lopez, Mobile	SL	SD	138
Jack Cressend, New Britain	EL	Min	136
Aaron Myette, Birmingham	SL	CWS	135
Brad Penny, Portland	EL	Fla	135
Jeromie Robertson, Jackson	TL	Hou	133

Strikeouts/9 Innings—Starters

Player, Team	Lg	Org	K/9
Ryan Anderson, New Haven	**EL**	**Sea**	**10.88**
John Patterson, El Paso	TL	Ari	10.53
Cedrick Bowers, Orlando	SL	TB	9.94
Brad Penny, Portland	EL	Fla	9.93
Eric Gagne, San Antonio	TL	LA	9.93
Chad Hutchinson, Arkansas	TL	StL	9.57
Matt Riley, Bowie	EL	Bal	9.38
A.J. Burnett, Portland	EL	Fla	9.02
Michael Tejera, Portland	EL	Fla	8.84
Corey Lee, Tulsa	TL	Tex	8.53
Rich Dishman, Greenville	SL	Atl	8.44
Doug Walls, Carolina	SL	Col	8.38
Seth Etherton, Erie	EL	Ana	8.21
Brian Cooper, Erie	EL	Ana	8.15
Bobby Rodgers, Portland	EL	Fla	8.00

Strikeouts/9 Innings—Relievers

Player, Team	Lg	Org	K/9
Eric Cammack, Binghamton	**EL**	**NYM**	**13.18**
Juan Moreno, Tulsa	TL	Tex	11.92
Pat Flury, Chattanooga	SL	Cin	11.64
Ivan Montane, New Haven	EL	Sea	11.52
Ryan Kohlmeier, Bowie	EL	Bal	11.20
Steve Rain, West Tenn	SL	ChC	10.92
Craig Dingman, Norwich	EL	NYY	10.90
Chad Ricketts, West Tenn	SL	ChC	10.75
Francisco Cordero, Jacksonville	SL	Det	9.97
Lance Carter, Wichita	TL	KC	9.95
Kevin Tolar, Chattanooga	SL	Cin	9.94
Jesus Pena, Birmingham	SL	CWS	9.66
Cam Smith, New Haven	EL	Sea	9.65
Eric Newman, West Tenn	SL	ChC	9.60
Danny Smith, West Tenn	SL	ChC	9.40

Hits/9 Innings—Starters

Player, Team	Lg	Org	H/9
Eric Gagne, San Antonio	**TL**	**LA**	**6.55**
Tony Armas Jr., Harrisburg	EL	Mon	7.40
Tony McKnight, Jackson	TL	Hou	7.52
Aaron Myette, Birmingham	SL	CWS	7.54
Jeff Yoder, West Tenn	SL	ChC	7.70
Carlos Chantres, Birmingham	SL	CWS	7.77
Victor Santos, Jacksonville	SL	Det	7.80
Jason Beverlin, Norwich	EL	NYY	7.94
Michael Tejera, Portland	EL	Fla	7.97
Jason Sekany, Trenton	EL	Bos	7.98
Matt Riley, Bowie	EL	Bal	8.09
Chad Hutchinson, Arkansas	TL	StL	8.11
Seth Etherton, Erie	EL	Ana	8.21
David Manning, West Tenn	SL	ChC	8.25
Brian Cooper, Erie	EL	Ana	8.32

Hits/9 Innings—Relievers

Player, Team	Lg	Org	H/9
Eric Cammack, Binghamton	**EL**	**NYM**	**4.45**
Juan Moreno, Tulsa	TL	Tex	4.74
Wayne Franklin, Jackson	TL	Hou	5.54
Jason Davis, Shreveport	TL	SF	5.91
Francisco Cordero, Jacksonville	SL	Det	6.02
Pat Flury, Chattanooga	SL	Cin	6.08
Jesus Pena, Birmingham	SL	CWS	6.11
Ivan Montane, New Haven	EL	Sea	6.26
J.D. Brammer, Akron	EL	Cle	6.30
Ryan Kohlmeier, Bowie	EL	Bal	6.32
Lance Carter, Wichita	TL	KC	6.33
Steve Rain, West Tenn	SL	ChC	6.35
Eric Newman, West Tenn	SL	ChC	6.51
Matt Dunbar, Altoona	EL	Pit	6.65
Hal Garrett, San Antonio	TL	LA	6.65

Class-A Batting Leaders

Batting Average

Player, Team	Lg	Org	Avg
Sean Burroughs, Rancho Cuca.	**CAL**	**SD**	**.363**
Carlos Urquiola, South Bend	MWL	Ari	.362
Eric Byrnes, Modesto	CAL	Oak	.337
Jack Cust, High Desert	CAL	Ari	.334
Belvani Martinez, High Desert	CAL	Ari	.333
William Otero, San Jose	CAL	SF	.333
Robert Hammock, High Desert	CAL	Ari	.332
Bo Robinson, Wisconsin	MWL	Sea	.329
Wilbert Nieves, Rancho Cuca.	CAL	SD	.328
Josh Phelps, Dunedin	FSL	Tor	.328

Third Basemen Batting Average

Player, Team	Lg	Org	Avg
Bo Robinson, Wisconsin	**MWL**	**Sea**	**.329**
Rico Washington, Lynchburg	CAR	Pit	.325
Jimmy Gonzalez, San Bernardino	CAL	LA	.316
Scott Seabol, Greensboro	SAL	NYY	.315
Jason Grabowski, Charlotte	FSL	Tex	.313
Jacques Landry, Modesto	CAL	Oak	.311
Tyler Turnquist, Michigan	MWL	Hou	.309
Juan Espinal, Sarasota	FSL	Bos	.299
Michael Cuddyer, Fort Myers	FSL	Min	.298
Damian Rolls, Vero Beach	FSL	LA	.297

Catchers Batting Average

Player, Team	Lg	Org	Avg
Robert Hammock, High Desert	**CAL**	**Ari**	**.332**
Wilbert Nieves, Rancho Cuca.	CAL	SD	.328
Javier Flores, Visalia	CAL	Oak	.296
Chris Heintz, Winston-Salem	CAR	CWS	.293
Jon Schaeffer, Quad City	MWL	Min	.290
Jason Hill, Cedar Rapids	MWL	Ana	.287
Mike Rivera, Lakeland	FSL	Det	.278
Humberto Cota, Hickory	SAL	Pit	.277
Sammy Serrano, Bakersfield	CAL	SF	.276
Paul Hoover, St. Petersburg	FSL	TB	.272

Shortstops Batting Average

Player, Team	Lg	Org	Avg
Rafael Furcal, Myrtle Beach	**CAR**	**Atl**	**.322**
Jack Wilson, Potomac	CAR	StL	.319
Ismael Gallo, San Bernardino	CAL	LA	.314
Cesar Izturis, Dunedin	FSL	Tor	.308
Alex Cintron, High Desert	CAL	Ari	.307
Nick Punto, Clearwater	FSL	Phi	.305
Eddie Lara, Visalia	CAL	Oak	.299
Eddy Martinez, Frederick	CAR	Bal	.291
Antonio Perez, Rockford	MWL	Cin	.288
Teuris Olivares, Greensboro	SAL	NYY	.279

First Basemen Batting Average

Player, Team	Lg	Org	Avg
Carlos Rivera, Hickory	**SAL**	**Pit**	**.322**
Robb Gorr, San Bernardino	CAL	LA	.319
Aaron McNeal, Michigan	MWL	Hou	.310
Jay Gibbons, Dunedin	FSL	Tor	.308
Jason Hart, Modesto	CAL	Oak	.305
Nick Caiazzo, Stockton	CAL	Mil	.300
Ross Gload, Brevard County	FSL	Fla	.298
Scott Kirby, Stockton	CAL	Mil	.296
John Summers, Bakersfield	CAL	SF	.295
Chris Walther, Lake Elsinore	CAL	Ana	.295

Outfielders Batting Average

Player, Team	Lg	Org	Avg
Eric Byrnes, Modesto	**CAL**	**Oak**	**.337**
Jack Cust, High Desert	CAL	Ari	.334
Doug Clark, Bakersfield	CAL	SF	.326
Mario Valenzuela, Burlington	MWL	CWS	.323
Gary Thomas, Modesto	CAL	Oak	.323
Al Benjamin, Cape Fear	SAL	Mon	.322
Corey Patterson, Lansing	MWL	ChC	.320
Juan Pierre, Asheville	SAL	Col	.320
Brian Cole, Capital City	SAL	NYM	.316
Chin-Feng Chen, San Bernardino	CAL	LA	.316

Second Basemen Batting Average

Player, Team	Lg	Org	Avg
Carlos Urquiola, South Bend	**MWL**	**Ari**	**.362**
Belvani Martinez, High Desert	CAL	Ari	.333
William Otero, San Jose	CAL	SF	.333
Marcus Giles, Myrtle Beach	CAR	Atl	.326
Aaron Miles, Michigan	MWL	Hou	.317
Jermaine Clark, Lancaster	CAL	Sea	.315
Mike Young, Dunedin	FSL	Tor	.313
Jason Romano, Charlotte	FSL	Tex	.312
Esteban German, Modesto	CAL	Oak	.311
Travis Wilson, Macon	SAL	Atl	.309

Switch-Hitters Batting Average

Player, Team	Lg	Org	Avg
Rafael Furcal, Myrtle Beach	**CAR**	**Atl**	**.322**
Aaron Miles, Michigan	MWL	Hou	.317
Nick Theodorou, San Bernardino	CAL	LA	.310
Cesar Izturis, Dunedin	FSL	Tor	.308
Alex Cintron, High Desert	CAL	Ari	.307
Nick Punto, Clearwater	FSL	Phi	.305
Geramel Castillo, Savannah	SAL	Tex	.301
Eddie Lara, Visalia	CAL	Oak	.299
John Summers, Bakersfield	CAL	SF	.295
Cesar Crespo, Brevard County	FSL	Fla	.286

Class-A Batting Leaders

Hits

Player, Team	Lg	Org	H
Juan Pierre, Asheville	**SAL**	**Col**	**187**
Robb Gorr, San Bernardino	CAL	LA	174
Scott Seabol, Greensboro	SAL	NYY	171
Jason Hart, Modesto	CAL	Oak	168
Quincy Foster, Brevard County	FSL	Fla	167
Rafael Furcal, Myrtle Beach	CAR	Atl	167
Aaron McNeal, Michigan	MWL	Hou	166
Cesar Izturis, Dunedin	FSL	Tor	165
Bo Robinson, Wisconsin	MWL	Sea	164
Sean Burroughs, Rancho Cuca.	CAL	SD	163

Extra-Base Hits

Player, Team	Lg	Org	XBH
Jacques Landry, Modesto	**CAL**	**Oak**	**79**
Jack Cust, High Desert	CAL	Ari	77
Scott Seabol, Greensboro	SAL	NYY	76
Corey Patterson, Lansing	MWL	ChC	72
Aaron McNeal, Michigan	MWL	Hou	70
Jason Hart, Modesto	CAL	Oak	69
Bo Robinson, Wisconsin	MWL	Sea	66
Aaron Rowand, Winston-Salem	CAR	CWS	64
Chin-Feng Chen, San Bernardino	CAL	LA	63
Brian Cole, Capital City	SAL	NYM	63

Doubles

Player, Team	Lg	Org	2B
Scott Seabol, Greensboro	**SAL**	**NYY**	**55**
Bo Robinson, Wisconsin	MWL	Sea	50
Jason Hart, Modesto	CAL	Oak	48
Jacques Landry, Modesto	CAL	Oak	46
Jack Cust, High Desert	CAL	Ari	42
Brian Cole, Capital City	SAL	NYM	41
Marcus Giles, Myrtle Beach	CAR	Atl	40
Al Benjamin, Cape Fear	SAL	Mon	38
Darren Blakely, Lake Elsinore	CAL	Ana	38
2 tied with			37

Total Bases

Player, Team	Lg	Org	TB
Aaron McNeal, Michigan	**MWL**	**Hou**	**315**
Jacques Landry, Modesto	CAL	Oak	297
Chin-Feng Chen, San Bernardino	CAL	LA	296
Jack Cust, High Desert	CAL	Ari	296
Scott Seabol, Greensboro	SAL	NYY	283
Corey Patterson, Lansing	MWL	ChC	281
Jason Hart, Modesto	CAL	Oak	277
Todd Mensik, Visalia	CAL	Oak	271
Oscar Salazar, Modesto	CAL	Oak	271
Jay Gibbons, Dunedin	FSL	Tor	268

Triples

Player, Team	Lg	Org	3B
Oscar Salazar, Modesto	**CAL**	**Oak**	**18**
Corey Patterson, Lansing	MWL	ChC	17
Jason Romano, Charlotte	FSL	Tex	14
Elpidio Guzman, Cedar Rapids	MWL	Ana	13
Jackson Melian, Tampa	FSL	NYY	13
Jason Ross, Myrtle Beach	CAR	Atl	13
DeWayne Wise, Rockford	MWL	Cin	13
5 tied with			12

Runs

Player, Team	Lg	Org	R
Jorge Nunez, Hagerstown	**SAL**	**Tor**	**116**
Jeremy Owens, Rancho Cuca.	CAL	SD	113
Jermaine Clark, Lancaster	CAL	Sea	112
Jack Cust, High Desert	CAL	Ari	107
Esteban German, Modesto	CAL	Oak	107
Abraham Nunez, High Desert	CAL	Ari	106
Rafael Furcal, Myrtle Beach	CAR	Atl	105
Eric Riggs, San Bernardino	CAL	LA	105
Billy Brown, Greensboro	SAL	NYY	102
3 tied with			101

Home Runs

Player, Team	Lg	Org	HR
Aaron McNeal, Michigan	**MWL**	**Hou**	**38**
Jack Cust, High Desert	CAL	Ari	32
Chin-Feng Chen, San Bernardino	CAL	LA	31
Todd Mensik, Visalia	CAL	Oak	29
Travis Hafner, Savannah	SAL	Tex	28
Earl Snyder, Capital City	SAL	NYM	28
Peanut Williams, Lancaster	CAL	Sea	28
Scott Kirby, Stockton	CAL	Mil	27
Jacques Landry, Modesto	CAL	Oak	27
3 tied with			25

Runs Batted In

Player, Team	Lg	Org	RBI
Aaron McNeal, Michigan	**MWL**	**Hou**	**131**
Chin-Feng Chen, San Bernardino	CAL	LA	123
Jason Hart, Modesto	CAL	Oak	123
Todd Mensik, Visalia	CAL	Oak	123
Jack Cust, High Desert	CAL	Ari	112
Travis Hafner, Savannah	SAL	Tex	111
Jacques Landry, Modesto	CAL	Oak	111
Jay Gibbons, Dunedin	FSL	Tor	108
Michael Restovich, Quad City	MWL	Min	107
Juan Silvestre, Wisconsin	MWL	Sea	107

Class-A Batting Leaders

Walks

Player, Team	Lg	Org	BB
Bo Robinson, Wisconsin	**MWL**	**Sea**	**108**
Tony Schrager, Lansing	MWL	ChC	103
Esteban German, Modesto	CAL	Oak	102
Albenis Machado, Cape Fear	SAL	Mon	102
Jack Cust, High Desert	CAL	Ari	96
Eddy Furniss, Lynchburg	CAR	Pit	94
Mike Edwards, Kinston	CAR	Cle	93
Jon Schaeffer, Quad City	MWL	Min	92
Andres Torres, West Michigan	MWL	Det	92
Ryan Hankins, Burlington	MWL	CWS	91

Stolen Bases

Player, Team	Lg	Org	SB
Rafael Furcal, Myrtle Beach	**CAR**	**Atl**	**96**
Mike Curry, Wilmington	CAR	KC	85
Jeremy Owens, Rancho Cuca.	CAL	SD	67
Richard Gomez, West Michigan	MWL	Det	66
Juan Pierre, Asheville	SAL	Col	66
Esix Snead, Peoria	MWL	StL	64
Rod Lindsey, Lakeland	FSL	Det	61
Quincy Foster, Brevard County	FSL	Fla	56
Nelson Castro, Lake Elsinore	CAL	Ana	53
2 tied with			52

Strikeouts

Player, Team	Lg	Org	K
Tim Flaherty, San Jose	**CAL**	**SF**	**168**
Jeremy Owens, Rancho Cuca.	CAL	SD	166
A.J. Zapp, Macon	SAL	Atl	163
Troy Cameron, Macon	SAL	Atl	161
Darren Blakely, Lake Elsinore	CAL	Ana	159
Felipe Lopez, Hagerstown	SAL	Tor	157
Brandon Pernell, Rancho Cuca.	CAL	SD	156
Junior Brignac, Myrtle Beach	CAR	Atl	152
Travis Hafner, Savannah	SAL	Tex	151
Jeff Deardorff, Stockton	CAL	Mil	150

On-Base Percentage

Player, Team	Lg	Org	OBP
Sean Burroughs, Rancho Cuca.	**CAL**	**SD**	**.467**
Jack Cust, High Desert	CAL	Ari	.450
Bo Robinson, Wisconsin	MWL	Sea	.446
Jon Schaeffer, Quad City	MWL	Min	.444
Skip Kiil, Clearwater	FSL	Phi	.436
Nick Theodorou, San Bernardino	CAL	LA	.434
Eric Byrnes, Modesto	CAL	Oak	.433
Esteban German, Modesto	CAL	Oak	.428
Rico Washington, Lynchburg	CAR	Pit	.424
Rusty Keith, Visalia	CAL	Oak	.423

Plate Appearances/Strikeout

Player, Team	Lg	Org	PA/K
Juan Pierre, Asheville	**SAL**	**Col**	**17.51**
Aaron Miles, Michigan	MWL	Hou	15.55
Ismael Gallo, San Bernardino	CAL	LA	13.37
Chris Walther, Lake Elsinore	CAL	Ana	13.35
Carlos Urquiola, South Bend	MWL	Ari	12.97
Javier Fuentes, Sarasota	FSL	Bos	12.77
Eric Byrnes, Modesto	CAL	Oak	11.86
Clay Snellgrove, Rancho Cuca.	CAL	SD	10.98
Brian Moon, Stockton	CAL	Mil	10.88
Carlos Rivera, Hickory	SAL	Pit	10.84

Slugging Percentage

Player, Team	Lg	Org	SLG
Jack Cust, High Desert	**CAL**	**Ari**	**.651**
Corey Patterson, Lansing	MWL	ChC	.592
Aaron McNeal, Michigan	MWL	Hou	.588
Jacques Landry, Modesto	CAL	Oak	.585
Chin-Feng Chen, San Bernardino	CAL	LA	.580
Josh Phelps, Dunedin	FSL	Tor	.562
Scott Kirby, Stockton	CAL	Mil	.559
Travis Hafner, Savannah	SAL	Tex	.546
Skip Kiil, Clearwater	FSL	Phi	.538
Todd Mensik, Visalia	CAL	Oak	.537

Hit By Pitch

Player, Team	Lg	Org	HBP
Darren Blakely, Lake Elsinore	**CAL**	**Ana**	**20**
Corky Miller, Rockford	**MWL**	**Cin**	**20**
Jon Schaeffer, Quad City	**MWL**	**Min**	**20**
Jess Graham, Sarasota	FSL	Bos	19
Eric Schreimann, Piedmont	SAL	Phi	19
Rod Lindsey, Lakeland	FSL	Det	18
Vic Radcliff, Wilmington	CAR	KC	18
5 tied with			17

Errors

Player, Team	Lg	Org	E
Luis Suarez, Winston-Salem	**CAR**	**CWS**	**52**
Alex Fajardo, Piedmont	SAL	Phi	47
Chone Figgins, Salem	CAR	Col	45
Chris Rowan, Stockton	CAL	Mil	45
Wilmy Caceres, Clinton	MWL	Cin	42
Caonabo Cosme, Modesto	CAL	Oak	40
Jose Santos, Kane County	MWL	Fla	40
Ramon Soler, Charleston (SC)	SAL	TB	40
3 tied with			39

Class-A Pitching Leaders

Earned Run Average

Player, Team	Lg	Org	ERA
Eric Ireland, Kissimmee	**FSL**	**Hou**	**2.06**
Josh Kalinowski, Salem	CAR	Col	2.11
Bryan Hebson, Jupiter	FSL	Mon	2.17
Brad Baisley, Piedmont	SAL	Phi	2.26
Junior Guerrero, Wilmington	CAR	KC	2.31
Jason Norton, Augusta	SAL	Bos	2.32
Scott Comer, Brevard County	FSL	Fla	2.35
Derrick Lewis, Myrtle Beach	CAR	Atl	2.40
Winston Abreu, Myrtle Beach	CAR	Atl	2.48
Jason Standridge, St. Petersburg	FSL	TB	2.57
Robert Averette, Rockford	MWL	Cin	2.58
Edwin Gonzalez, Charleston (WV)	SAL	KC	2.60
Greg Kubes, Piedmont	SAL	Phi	2.62
Pat Strange, Capital City	SAL	NYM	2.63
Terry Hayden, Clinton	MWL	Cin	2.70

Wins

Player, Team	Lg	Org	W
Doug Bridges, Lake Elsinore	**CAL**	**Ana**	**18**
Pasqual Coco, Dunedin	FSL	Tor	15
Wilfredo Rodriguez, Kissimmee	FSL	Hou	15
Marcos Castillo, San Bernardino	CAL	LA	14
Randey Dorame, San Bernardino	CAL	LA	14
Leo Estrella, Dunedin	FSL	Tor	14
Dicky Gonzalez, St. Lucie	FSL	NYM	14
Rick Guttormson, Rancho Cuca.	CAL	SD	14
Dave Lundberg, Charlotte	FSL	Tex	14
Jimmy Osting, Macon	SAL	Atl	14
Juan Rincon, Quad City	MWL	Min	14
11 tied with			13

Losses

Player, Team	Lg	Org	L
Andy Bausher, Lynchburg	**CAR**	**Pit**	**15**
Manny Bermudez, Bakersfield	CAL	SF	14
Joe Casey, Hagerstown	SAL	Tor	14
Ricky Casteel, Delmarva	SAL	Bal	14
Brandon Emanuel, Lake Elsinore	CAL	Ana	14
Jim Lynch, Kissimmee	FSL	Hou	14
Frankie McGill, Savannah	SAL	Tex	14
Mark Richards, Brevard County	FSL	Fla	14
John Stewart, Savannah	SAL	Tex	14
Craig Taczy, Vero Beach	FSL	LA	14
Joe Gangemi, Cedar Rapids	MWL	Ana	13
Mike Mowel, Augusta	SAL	Bos	13
Jason Navarro, Potomac	CAR	StL	13
Andy Shibilo, Peoria	MWL	StL	13
15 tied with			12

Saves

Player, Team	Lg	Org	S
Jason Ellison, Tampa	**FSL**	**NYY**	**35**
Bill Everly, San Bernardino	CAL	LA	34
Brandon Puffer, Clinton	MWL	Cin	34
Jim Brink, Modesto	CAL	Oak	29
Doug Nickle, Clearwater	FSL	Phi	28
Mark Cisar, Augusta	SAL	Bos	27
Brent Husted, Vero Beach	FSL	LA	27
Jarrod Kingrey, Hagerstown	SAL	Tor	27
Travis Thompson, Salem	CAR	Col	27
Bob File, Dunedin	FSL	Tor	26
Cary Hiles, Piedmont	SAL	Phi	26
Todd Ozias, Bakersfield	CAL	SF	26
Heath Bell, Capital City	SAL	NYM	25
Eddy Reyes, St. Petersburg	FSL	TB	25
2 tied with			23

Games

Player, Team	Lg	Org	G
Bill Everly, San Bernardino	**CAL**	**LA**	**60**
Doug Nickle, Clearwater	**FSL**	**Phi**	**60**
Ray Noriega, Visalia	**CAL**	**Oak**	**60**
Saul Rivera, Quad City	**MWL**	**Min**	**60**
Jose DeLeon, Potomac	CAR	StL	59
Brandon Puffer, Clinton	MWL	Cin	59
Jon Hand, Peoria	MWL	StL	58
Jeff Viles, Peoria	MWL	StL	58
Kirk Griffin, Peoria	MWL	StL	57
Matt Wells, San Jose	CAL	SF	57
Jarrod Kingrey, Hagerstown	SAL	Tor	56
Tony Pavlovich, Hickory	SAL	Pit	56
Travis Thompson, Salem	CAR	Col	56
Heath Bell, Capital City	SAL	NYM	55
Darwin Cubillan, Tampa	FSL	NYY	55

Innings Pitched

Player, Team	Lg	Org	IP
Steve Fish, Lake Elsinore	**CAL**	**Ana**	**196.2**
Doug Bridges, Lake Elsinore	CAL	Ana	185.2
Geraldo Padua, Rancho Cuca.	CAL	SD	180.1
Delvin James, St. Petersburg	FSL	TB	175.1
Brian Lawrence, Rancho Cuca.	CAL	SD	175.1
Nate Cornejo, West Michigan	MWL	Det	174.2
Rick Guttormson, Rancho Cuca.	CAL	SD	174.1
Pasqual Coco, Dunedin	FSL	Tor	172.2
Tony Coscia, Bakersfield	CAL	SF	171.2
Juan Figueroa, Winston-Salem	CAR	CWS	171.2
Ryan Price, Salem	CAR	Col	171.2
Melqui Torres, Wisconsin	MWL	Sea	171.2
Taylor Smith, Hagerstown	SAL	Tor	171.1
Scott Cassidy, Hagerstown	SAL	Tor	170.2
3 tied with			170.1

Class-A Pitching Leaders

Walks

Player, Team	Lg	Org	BB
Lance Caraccioli, San Bernardino	**CAL**	**LA**	**126**
Ben Howard, Fort Wayne	MWL	SD	110
Tom Bennett, Visalia	CAL	Oak	94
Matt Bruback, Lansing	MWL	ChC	87
Chris Jones, San Jose	CAL	SF	87
Ryan Mills, Fort Myers	FSL	Min	87
Steve Colyer, San Bernardino	CAL	LA	86
Todd Cutchins, St. Lucie	FSL	NYM	82
Derrick Lewis, Myrtle Beach	CAR	Atl	81
Jeremy Affeldt, Charleston (WV)	SAL	KC	80
Nick Neugebauer, Beloit	MWL	Mil	80
Dwayne Jacobs, Winston-Salem	CAR	CWS	79
Aaron Sams, Daytona	FSL	ChC	78
Scott Prather, Peoria	MWL	StL	77
Tim Redding, Michigan	MWL	Hou	76

Strikeouts

Player, Team	Lg	Org	K
John Stephens, Delmarva	**SAL**	**Bal**	**217**
Geraldo Padua, Rancho Cuca.	CAL	SD	196
Juan Figueroa, Winston-Salem	CAR	CWS	189
Junior Guerrero, Wilmington	CAR	KC	181
Steve Fish, Lake Elsinore	CAL	Ana	180
Scott Cassidy, Hagerstown	SAL	Tor	178
Josh Kalinowski, Salem	CAR	Col	176
Winston Abreu, Myrtle Beach	CAR	Atl	171
Brian Lawrence, Rancho Cuca.	CAL	SD	166
Randey Dorame, San Bernardino	CAL	LA	164
John Grabow, Hickory	SAL	Pit	164
Doug Bridges, Lake Elsinore	CAL	Ana	162
Scott Sobkowiak, Myrtle Beach	CAR	Atl	161
Rob Pugmire, Kinston	CAR	Cle	160
Juan Rincon, Quad City	MWL	Min	153

Strikeouts/9 Innings—Starters

Player, Team	Lg	Org	K/9
Nick Neugebauer, Beloit	**MWL**	**Mil**	**13.95**
John Stephens, Delmarva	SAL	Bal	11.47
Winston Abreu, Myrtle Beach	CAR	Atl	11.15
Junior Guerrero, Wilmington	CAR	KC	10.46
Scott Sobkowiak, Myrtle Beach	CAR	Atl	10.40
John Sneed, Dunedin	FSL	Tor	10.27
Lesli Brea, St. Lucie	FSL	NYM	10.14
Juan Figueroa, Winston-Salem	CAR	CWS	9.91
Luke Hudson, Asheville	SAL	Col	9.82
Geraldo Padua, Rancho Cuca.	CAL	SD	9.78
Josh Kalinowski, Salem	CAR	Col	9.76
Juan Guzman, Delmarva	SAL	Bal	9.70
Mike Spiegel, Kinston	CAR	Cle	9.69
Greg Miller, Augusta	SAL	Bos	9.61
Mike Gonzalez, Lynchburg	CAR	Pit	9.56

Strikeouts/9 Innings—Relievers

Player, Team	Lg	Org	K/9
Saul Rivera, Quad City	**MWL**	**Min**	**13.18**
Shane Heams, West Michigan	MWL	Det	13.17
Nathan Ruhl, St. Petersburg	FSL	TB	12.56
Cary Hiles, Piedmont	SAL	Phi	12.39
Alex Lontayo, Augusta	SAL	Bos	12.27
Tim Redding, Michigan	MWL	Hou	12.09
Dwayne Jacobs, Winston-Salem	CAR	CWS	11.59
Jim Serrano, Jupiter	FSL	Mon	11.42
Doug Sessions, Kissimmee	FSL	Hou	11.20
Randy Choate, Tampa	FSL	NYY	11.16
Denny Gilich, Cedar Rapids	MWL	Ana	11.11
Brad Voyles, Myrtle Beach	CAR	Atl	11.08
Shawn Sonnier, Wilmington	CAR	KC	11.07
Todd Ozias, Bakersfield	CAL	SF	10.70
Tim Corcoran, Capital City	SAL	NYM	10.68

Hits/9 Innings—Starters

Player, Team	Lg	Org	H/9
Nick Neugebauer, Beloit	**MWL**	**Mil**	**5.58**
Aaron Miller, Quad City	MWL	Min	5.94
Winston Abreu, Myrtle Beach	CAR	Atl	6.13
Rene Vega, Capital City	SAL	NYM	6.23
Randy Keisler, Tampa	FSL	NYY	6.31
Wilfredo Rodriguez, Kissimmee	FSL	Hou	6.34
Scott Sobkowiak, Myrtle Beach	CAR	Atl	6.46
Mike Spiegel, Kinston	CAR	Cle	6.60
Josh Kalinowski, Salem	CAR	Col	6.60
Derrick Lewis, Myrtle Beach	CAR	Atl	6.87
Junior Guerrero, Wilmington	CAR	KC	6.94
Matt McClellan, Dunedin	FSL	Tor	6.96
Bryan Hebson, Jupiter	FSL	Mon	7.03
Jason Standridge, St. Petersburg	FSL	TB	7.06
Brad Baisley, Piedmont	SAL	Phi	7.07

Hits/9 Innings—Relievers

Player, Team	Lg	Org	H/9
Brad Voyles, Myrtle Beach	**CAR**	**Atl**	**4.83**
Dwayne Jacobs, Winston-Salem	CAR	CWS	5.03
Bob File, Dunedin	FSL	Tor	5.09
Shane Heams, West Michigan	MWL	Det	5.35
Saul Rivera, Quad City	MWL	Min	5.43
Jim Serrano, Jupiter	FSL	Mon	5.71
Nathan Ruhl, St. Petersburg	FSL	TB	5.78
Kirk Griffin, Peoria	MWL	StL	5.82
Jarrod Mays, Kinston	CAR	Cle	5.89
Bill Snyder, Lakeland	FSL	Det	5.92
Doug Sessions, Kissimmee	FSL	Hou	6.29
Joey Messman, San Jose	CAL	SF	6.49
Keith Connolly, Bakersfield	CAL	SF	6.61
Tony Pavlovich, Hickory	SAL	Pit	6.75
Heath Bell, Capital City	SAL	NYM	6.79

Short-Season Batting Leaders

Batting Average

Player, Team	Lg	Org	Avg
Ben Broussard, Billings	**PIO**	**Cin**	**.407**
Ruben Salazar, Elizabethton	APP	Min	.401
Juan Ventura, Rockies	AZL	Col	.399
Kenneth Harvey, Spokane	NWL	KC	.397
Mike Wenner, Athletics	AZL	Oak	.386
Craig Brazell, Kingsport	APP	NYM	.385
Matt Watson, Vermont	NYP	Mon	.380
Pat Deschenes, Pittsfield	NYP	NYM	.374
Casey Bookout, Billings	PIO	Cin	.363
Kevin Mench, Pulaski	APP	Tex	.362

Catchers Batting Average

Player, Team	Lg	Org	Avg
Mike Jacobs, Mets	**GCL**	**NYM**	**.333**
Steven Tomshack, D'backs	**AZL**	**Ari**	**.333**
Eliezer Alfonzo, New Jersey	NYP	StL	.326
J.D. Closser, Missoula	PIO	Ari	.324
J.R. House, Williamsport	NYP	Pit	.315
Lee Jaramillo, Ogden	PIO	Mil	.308
Frederick Torres, Pulaski	APP	Tex	.304
Matt Ceriani, Helena	PIO	Mil	.302
Ryan Luther, Salem-Keizer	NWL	SF	.300
Thomas Gregorio, Boise	NWL	Ana	.296

First Basemen Batting Average

Player, Team	Lg	Org	Avg
Ken Harvey, Spokane	**NWL**	**KC**	**.397**
Craig Brazell, Kingsport	APP	NYM	.385
Casey Bookout, Billings	PIO	Cin	.363
Jason Jones, Pulaski	APP	Tex	.355
Ventura Cisneros, Mex. All-Stars	AZL	—	.349
Rick Elder, Bluefield	APP	Bal	.345
Lyle Overbay, Missoula	PIO	Ari	.343
Luis Medina, Eugene	NWL	ChC	.337
Sean McGowan, Salem-Keizer	NWL	SF	.335
Greg White, Butte	PIO	Ana	.327

Second Basemen Batting Average

Player, Team	Lg	Org	Avg
Ruben Salazar, Elizabethton	**APP**	**Min**	**.401**
Juan Ventura, Rockies	AZL	Col	.399
Mark Burnett, Billings	PIO	Cin	.326
Alfredo Amezaga, Boise	NWL	Ana	.318
Brian Ward, Idaho Falls	PIO	SD	.317
Joe Kerrigan, Lowell	NYP	Bos	.314
Victor Castillo, Yankees	GCL	NYY	.314
Joe Yakopich, Diamondbacks	AZL	Ari	.305
Frank Moore, Hudson Valley	NYP	TB	.304
Leandro Arias, Mets	GCL	NYM	.301

Third Basemen Batting Average

Player, Team	Lg	Org	Avg
Hank Blalock, Rangers	**GCL**	**Tex**	**.361**
Matt Scanlon, Elizabethton	APP	Min	.354
Cordell Lindsey, Butte	PIO	Ana	.341
Andrew Beinbrink, Hudson Valley	NYP	TB	.339
Jeff Brooks, Missoula	PIO	Ari	.339
Troy Schader, Idaho Falls	PIO	SD	.336
Curt Fiore, Danville	APP	Atl	.333
Oscar Ramirez, Everett	NWL	Sea	.326
Gregg Raymundo, Spokane	NWL	KC	.323
Robb Quinlan, Boise	NWL	Ana	.322

Shortstops Batting Average

Player, Team	Lg	Org	Avg
Ralph Flores, White Sox	**AZL**	**CWS**	**.337**
Brandon Jackson, St. Catharines	NYP	Tor	.332
Mark Ellis, Spokane	NWL	KC	.327
Ramon Santiago, Oneonta	NYP	Det	.326
Wilson Betemit, Danville	APP	Atl	.320
Guillermo Martinez, Mariners	AZL	Sea	.306
Enrique Cruz, Mets	GCL	NYM	.306
Jason Repko, Great Falls	PIO	LA	.304
Steve Scarborough, Helena	PIO	Mil	.303
B.J. Hawes, Reds	GCL	Cin	.302

Outfielders Batting Average

Player, Team	Lg	Org	Avg
Ben Broussard, Billings	**PIO**	**Cin**	**.407**
Michael Wenner, Athletics	AZL	Oak	.386
Matt Watson, Vermont	NYP	Mon	.380
Kevin Mench, Pulaski	APP	Tex	.362
Mike Lockwood, Southern Oregon	NWL	Oak	.361
Brett Cadiente, Pulaski	APP	Tex	.354
Valentino Pascucci, Vermont	NYP	Mon	.351
Ryan Knox, Helena	PIO	Mil	.349
Alex Gordon, Bluefield	APP	Bal	.348
Will Ford, Ogden	PIO	Mil	.341

Switch-Hitters Batting Average

Player, Team	Lg	Org	Avg
Jason Jones, Pulaski	**APP**	**Tex**	**.355**
Ramon Santiago, Oneonta	NYP	Det	.326
J.D. Closser, Missoula	PIO	Ari	.324
Wilson Betemit, Danville	APP	Atl	.320
Bill Curtis, Butte	PIO	Ana	.319
Shawn Garrett, Idaho Falls	PIO	SD	.307
Guillermo Martinez, Mariners	AZL	Sea	.306
Medardo Fernandez, Marlins	GCL	Fla	.306
Leandro Arias, Mets	GCL	NYM	.301
Kenichiro Kawabata, Red Sox	GCL	Bos	.297

Short-Season Batting Leaders

Hits

Player, Team	Lg	Org	H
Matt Watson, Vermont	**NYP**	**Mon**	**108**
Lyle Overbay, Missoula	PIO	Ari	105
Ruben Salazar, Elizabethton	APP	Min	105
Jeff Brooks, Missoula	PIO	Ari	100
Andrew Beinbrink, Hudson Valley	NYP	TB	99
Matt Cepicky, Vermont	NYP	Mon	99
Brett Cadiente, Pulaski	APP	Tex	97
Frank Moore, Hudson Valley	NYP	TB	97
Josh Hamilton, Hudson Valley	NYP	TB	96
Ryan Knox, Helena	PIO	Mil	96

Extra-Base Hits

Player, Team	Lg	Org	XBH
Lyle Overbay, Missoula	**PIO**	**Ari**	**44**
Troy Schader, Idaho Falls	PIO	SD	42
Cordell Lindsey, Butte	PIO	Ana	40
Ruben Salazar, Elizabethton	APP	Min	40
Kevin Mench, Pulaski	APP	Tex	39
Rodney Nye, Pittsfield	NYP	NYM	39
Andrew Beinbrink, Hudson Valley	NYP	TB	37
Josh Hamilton, Hudson Valley	NYP	TB	37
4 tied with			36

Doubles

Player, Team	Lg	Org	2B
Rodney Nye, Pittsfield	**NYP**	**NYM**	**30**
Valentino Pascucci, Vermont	NYP	Mon	26
Lyle Overbay, Missoula	PIO	Ari	25
Andrew Beinbrink, Hudson Valley	NYP	TB	24
Jason Jones, Pulaski	APP	Tex	24
Ruben Salazar, Elizabethton	APP	Min	24
Josh Hamilton, Hudson Valley	NYP	TB	23
Cordell Lindsey, Butte	PIO	Ana	23
Brian Ward, Idaho Falls	PIO	SD	23
4 tied with			22

Total Bases

Player, Team	Lg	Org	TB
Lyle Overbay, Missoula	**PIO**	**Ari**	**180**
Troy Schader, Idaho Falls	PIO	SD	177
Ruben Salazar, Elizabethton	APP	Min	175
Kevin Mench, Pulaski	APP	Tex	166
Jeff Brooks, Missoula	PIO	Ari	162
Andrew Beinbrink, Hudson Valley	NYP	TB	160
Matt Cepicky, Vermont	NYP	Mon	160
Josh Hamilton, Hudson Valley	NYP	TB	157
Alex Gordon, Bluefield	APP	Bal	156
2 tied with			154

Triples

Player, Team	Lg	Org	3B
Alex Gordon, Bluefield	**APP**	**Bal**	**10**
Chip Ambres, Utica	NYP	Fla	9
Jason Huth, Billings	PIO	Cin	9
Jason Repko, Great Falls	PIO	LA	9
Travis Bailey, New Jersey	NYP	StL	8
Ramon Carvajal, New Jersey	NYP	StL	8
Christian Reyes, Athletics	AZL	Oak	8
10 tied with			7

Runs

Player, Team	Lg	Org	R
Luis Terrero, Missoula	**PIO**	**Ari**	**74**
J.D. Closser, Missoula	PIO	Ari	73
Cordell Lindsey, Butte	PIO	Ana	72
Brett Cadiente, Pulaski	APP	Tex	69
Mark Ellis, Spokane	NWL	KC	67
Joe Jester, Salem-Keizer	NWL	SF	67
Chad Durham, Bristol	APP	CWS	66
Lyle Overbay, Missoula	PIO	Ari	66
Ruben Salazar, Elizabethton	APP	Min	66
Jason Jones, Pulaski	APP	Tex	65

Home Runs

Player, Team	Lg	Org	HR
Dan Grummitt, Hudson Valley	**NYP**	**TB**	**22**
Troy Schader, Idaho Falls	PIO	SD	19
Kirk Asche, Southern Oregon	NWL	Oak	17
Lamont Matthews, Yakima	NWL	LA	17
Hector Garcia, Helena	PIO	Mil	16
Kevin Mench, Pulaski	APP	Tex	16
Alex Gordon, Bluefield	APP	Bal	15
Sean McGowan, Salem-Keizer	NWL	SF	15
Eric Sandberg, Elizabethton	APP	Min	15
7 tied with			14

Runs Batted In

Player, Team	Lg	Org	RBI
Lyle Overbay, Missoula	**PIO**	**Ari**	**101**
Robb Quinlan, Boise	NWL	Ana	77
Mike O'Keefe, Boise	NWL	Ana	70
Troy Schader, Idaho Falls	PIO	SD	69
Kirk Asche, Southern Oregon	NWL	Oak	67
Alex Gordon, Bluefield	APP	Bal	66
Ruben Salazar, Elizabethton	APP	Min	65
Casey Bookout, Billings	PIO	Cin	63
3 tied with			62

Short-Season Batting Leaders

Walks

Player, Team	Lg	Org	BB
J.D. Closser, Missoula	**PIO**	**Ari**	**71**
Josh Holliday, St. Catharines	NYP	Tor	63
Ben Cordova, Spokane	NWL	KC	54
Mike O'Keefe, Boise	NWL	Ana	54
Michael Forbes, Danville	APP	Atl	53
Valentino Pascucci, Vermont	NYP	Mon	53
Kevin Burford, Portland	NWL	Col	52
Joe Jester, Salem-Keizer	NWL	SF	50
Jon Topolski, Auburn	NYP	Hou	50
Pedro Guerrero, Pulaski	APP	Tex	49

Strikeouts

Player, Team	Lg	Org	K
Brian Martin, Hudson Valley	**NYP**	**TB**	**107**
Justin Lincoln, Portland	NWL	Col	102
Curtis Gay, Mahoning Valley	NYP	Cle	98
Andy Brown, Staten Island	NYP	NYY	97
Luis Terrero, Missoula	PIO	Ari	91
Sandy Vasquez, Yakima	NWL	LA	91
Jesus Lebron, St. Catharines	NYP	Tor	90
Candido Martinez, Great Falls	PIO	LA	87
Lamont Matthews, Yakima	NWL	LA	87
Clyde Williams, Vermont	NYP	Mon	85

Plate Appearances/Strikeout

Player, Team	Lg	Org	PA/K
Shawn Schumacher, New Jersey	**NYP**	**StL**	**21.88**
Jon Palmieri, Boise	NWL	Ana	17.80
Omar Rosado, Expos	GCL	Mon	15.50
Emmanuel del Rosario, Orioles	GCL	Bal	15.20
Brian Hitchcox, Batavia	NYP	Phi	14.07
Chris Snelling, Everett	NWL	Sea	13.00
David Lutz, Expos	GCL	Mon	12.29
Matt Watson, Vermont	NYP	Mon	11.96
Jon Anderson, Lowell	NYP	Bos	11.77
Ryan Knox, Helena	PIO	Mil	11.52

Hit By Pitch

Player, Team	Lg	Org	HBP
J.J. Sherrill, Mahoning Valley	**NYP**	**Cle**	**26**
Joe Thurston, Yakima	NWL	LA	21
Antonio Alvarez, Williamsport	NYP	Pit	16
Kevin West, Elizabethton	APP	Min	16
Valentino Pascucci, Vermont	NYP	Mon	14
Sandy Vasquez, Yakima	NWL	LA	13
Dominic Woody, Utica	NYP	Fla	13
Mike Yancy, Kingsport	APP	NYM	13
Bo Hart, New Jersey	NYP	StL	12
Peter Orgill, Butte	PIO	Ana	12

Stolen Bases

Player, Team	Lg	Org	SB
Chad Durham, Bristol	**APP**	**CWS**	**57**
Ryan Knox, Helena	PIO	Mil	44
Ruben Requena, Mahoning Valley	NYP	Cle	44
Todd Donovan, Idaho Falls	PIO	SD	40
Alex Rojas, Batavia	NYP	Phi	39
Antonio Alvarez, Williamsport	NYP	Pit	38
Jack Santora, Missoula	PIO	Ari	36
Mike Wenner, Athletics	AZL	Oak	36
Modesto DeAza, Auburn	NYP	Hou	34
Chip Ambres, Utica	NYP	Fla	33

On-Base Percentage

Player, Team	Lg	Org	OBP
Ben Broussard, Billings	**PIO**	**Cin**	**.527**
Ruben Salazar, Elizabethton	APP	Min	.498
Valentino Pascucci, Vermont	NYP	Mon	.482
Kenneth Harvey, Spokane	NWL	KC	.477
Pat Deschenes, Pittsfield	NYP	NYM	.475
J.D. Closser, Missoula	PIO	Ari	.458
Rick Elder, Bluefield	APP	Bal	.451
Mike Lockwood, Southern Oregon	NWL	Oak	.451
Mike Scanlon, Elizabethton	APP	Min	.449
Kevin Burford, Portland	NWL	Col	.447

Slugging Percentage

Player, Team	Lg	Org	SLG
Ben Broussard, Billings	**PIO**	**Cin**	**.800**
Alex Gordon, Bluefield	APP	Bal	.678
Ruben Salazar, Elizabethton	APP	Min	.668
Rick Elder, Bluefield	APP	Bal	.667
Troy Schader, Idaho Falls	PIO	SD	.660
Luis Garcia, Mex. All-Stars	AZL	—	.649
Kevin Mench, Pulaski	APP	Tex	.638
Casey Bookout, Billings	PIO	Cin	.632
Cordell Lindsey, Butte	PIO	Ana	.604
Kenneth Harvey, Spokane	NWL	KC	.598

Errors

Player, Team	Lg	Org	E
Jeff Brooks, Missoula	**PIO**	**Ari**	**40**
Bill Hall, Ogden	PIO	Mil	38
Jason Repko, Great Falls	PIO	LA	38
Cesar Saba, Lowell	NYP	Bos	35
Chad Wandall, Elizabethton	APP	Min	35
Wilson Betemit, Danville	APP	Atl	33
Jason Moore, Idaho Falls	PIO	SD	33
Oscar Garcia, Burlington	APP	Cle	32
3 tied with			29

Short-Season Pitching Leaders

Earned Run Average

Player, Team	Lg	Org	ERA
Jacob Peavy, Idaho Falls	**PIO**	**SD**	**1.17**
Travis Minix, Hudson Valley	NYP	TB	1.44
Carlos Hernandez, Martinsville	APP	Hou	1.46
Todd Moser, Utica	NYP	Fla	1.53
Randy Leek, Oneonta	NYP	Det	1.56
Jason Frasor, Oneonta	NYP	Det	1.69
Mike Nannini, Auburn	NYP	Hou	1.90
Colby Lewis, Pulaski	APP	Tex	1.95
David Tavarez, Orioles	GCL	Bal	2.14
Rafael Lopez, Mets	GCL	NYM	2.17
Kurt Nantkes, Athletics	AZL	Oak	2.19
Wes Crawford, Boise	NWL	Ana	2.21
Aaron Harang, Pulaski	APP	Tex	2.30
Aaron Dean, St. Catharines	NYP	Tor	2.34
Orlando Roman, Mets	GCL	NYM	2.36

Saves

Player, Team	Lg	Org	S
Greg Watson, Oneonta	**NYP**	**Det**	**19**
Santiago Ramirez, Martinsville	APP	Hou	17
Marc Bluma, St. Catharines	NYP	Tor	13
Jay Gehrke, Spokane	NWL	KC	13
Oswaldo Verdugo, Idaho Falls	PIO	SD	13
Andy Mosher, Helena	PIO	Mil	12
Tom Pike, Billings	PIO	Cin	12
Craig House, Portland	NWL	Col	11
Brian Matzenbacher, Missoula	PIO	Ari	11
Corey Miller, Southern Oregon	NWL	Oak	11
Paul Viole, Pittsfield	NYP	NYM	11
Travis Wade, Auburn	NYP	Hou	11
Matt Guerrier, Bristol	APP	CWS	10
Felix Montilla, Williamsport	NYP	Pit	10
Buddy Yen, Royals	GCL	KC	10

Wins

Player, Team	Lg	Org	W
Craig Anderson, Everett	**NWL**	**Sea**	**10**
Jose Rincon, Helena	**PIO**	**Mil**	**10**
Raul Garcia, Spokane	NWL	KC	9
Aaron Harang, Pulaski	APP	Tex	9
Jacob Peavy, Idaho Falls	PIO	SD	9
Jairo Pineda, Auburn	NYP	Hou	9
David Tavarez, Orioles	GCL	Bal	9
Angel Caraballo, Bristol	APP	CWS	8
Matt Gage, Southern Oregon	NWL	Oak	8
Mario Mendoza, Boise	NWL	Ana	8
Todd Moser, Utica	NYP	Fla	8
Brad Pautz, Batavia	NYP	Phi	8
Dave Walling, Staten Island	NYP	NYY	8
15 tied with			7

Games

Player, Team	Lg	Org	G
Brian Stokes, Princeton	**APP**	**TB**	**33**
Oswaldo Verdugo, Idaho Falls	**PIO**	**SD**	**33**
Raul Garcia, Spokane	NWL	KC	32
Jay Gehrke, Spokane	NWL	KC	32
Brandon Peck, New Jersey	NYP	StL	31
Greg Watson, Oneonta	NYP	Det	31
Paul Fahs, New Jersey	NYP	StL	30
Jose Franco, Staten Island	NYP	NYY	30
Juan Frias, Princeton	APP	TB	30
John Hunter, Idaho Falls	PIO	SD	29
Jeffrey Nebel, Butte	PIO	Ana	29
Jose Ortiz, Hudson Valley	NYP	TB	29
Greg Dittmer, Princeton	APP	TB	28
5 tied with			27

Losses

Player, Team	Lg	Org	L
Jeramy Gomer, Eugene	**NWL**	**ChC**	**11**
Julian Harris, Butte	PIO	Ana	9
Joe Orloski, St. Catharines	NYP	Tor	9
Robert Hamann, Medicine Hat	PIO	Tor	8
T.J. Nall, Great Falls	PIO	LA	8
Scott Vandermeer, Princeton	APP	TB	8
James White, Pirates	GCL	Pit	8
Billy Whitecotton, Bluefield	APP	Bal	8
16 tied with			7

Innings Pitched

Player, Team	Lg	Org	IP
Jose Rincon, Helena	**PIO**	**Mil**	**108.0**
Scott Martin, Great Falls	PIO	LA	102.2
Joe Kennedy, Hudson Valley	NYP	TB	95.0
T.J. Nall, Great Falls	PIO	LA	92.2
Craig Anderson, Everett	NWL	Sea	90.0
Corey Arieta, Helena	PIO	Mil	88.2
Adam Williams, Great Falls	PIO	LA	88.2
Todd Moser, Utica	NYP	Fla	88.0
Ryan Jamison, Auburn	NYP	Hou	87.2
Aquilino Lopez, Everett	NWL	Sea	87.2
Ryan Madson, Batavia	NYP	Phi	87.2
Randy Hadden, Yakima	NWL	LA	86.2
Orlando Encarnacion, Pittsfield	NYP	NYM	86.0
P.J. Bevis, Missoula	PIO	Ari	85.2
Roberto Miniel, Ogden	PIO	Mil	85.2

Short-Season Pitching Leaders

Walks

Player, Team	Lg	Org	BB
Sam Walton, Everett	**NWL**	**Sea**	**60**
Odalis Gomez, Butte	PIO	Ana	50
John Lackey, Boise	NWL	Ana	50
Enger Veras, Princeton	APP	TB	50
Rafael Soriano, Everett	NWL	Sea	49
Seth McClung, Princeton	APP	TB	48
Marcus Sents, Elizabethton	APP	Min	48
Jonathan Berry, Yakima	NWL	LA	46
Franklyn German, South. Oregon	NWL	Oak	45
Tom Marx, Oneonta	NYP	Det	45
Rickey Lewis, Ogden	PIO	Mil	44
Julio DePaula, Portland	NWL	Col	43
Ryan Madson, Batavia	NYP	Phi	43
Chris Rojas, Williamsport	NYP	Pit	43
2 tied with			42

Strikeouts

Player, Team	Lg	Org	K
Brandon Claussen, Staten Island	**NYP**	**NYY**	**105**
Jacob Peavy, Idaho Falls	PIO	SD	103
Joe Kennedy, Hudson Valley	NYP	TB	101
Adam Williams, Great Falls	PIO	LA	95
Aquilino Lopez, Everett	NWL	Sea	93
Gary Majewski, Bristol	APP	CWS	91
Angel Caraballo, Bristol	APP	CWS	88
Jose Cueto, Eugene	NWL	ChC	87
Aaron Harang, Pulaski	APP	Tex	87
Jose Rincon, Helena	PIO	Mil	87
Juan Martinez, Mex. All-Stars	AZL	—	86
Todd Moser, Utica	NYP	Fla	86
Mike Nannini, Auburn	NYP	Hou	86
Rodrigo Rosario, Martinsville	APP	Hou	86
3 tied with			85

Strikeouts/9 Innings—Starters

Player, Team	Lg	Org	K/9
Brian Sanches, Spokane	**NWL**	**KC**	**13.50**
Carlos Hernandez, Martinsville	APP	Hou	13.34
Josh Cenate, Bluefield	APP	Bal	12.91
Kurt Ainsworth, Salem-Keizer	NWL	SF	12.90
Andrew Brown, Braves	GCL	Atl	12.12
Stephen Cowie, Mahoning Valley	NYP	Cle	12.11
Lorenzo Barcelo, White Sox	AZL	CWS	12.02
Francisco Rodriguez, Boise	NWL	Ana	11.91
Colby Lewis, Pulaski	APP	Tex	11.69
Brandon Claussen, Staten Island	NYP	NYY	11.34
Derek Stanford, Martinsville	APP	Hou	11.31
Christian Parra, Jamestown	NYP	Atl	11.31
Colin Young, Portland	NWL	Col	11.29
Mike MacDougal, Spokane	NWL	KC	11.07
Gerik Baxter, Idaho Falls	PIO	SD	11.04

Strikeouts/9 Innings—Relievers

Player, Team	Lg	Org	K/9
Justin Fry, Batavia	**NYP**	**Phi**	**15.93**
Craig House, Portland	NWL	Col	15.06
Jose Valverde, Diamondbacks	AZL	Ari	14.76
John Kremer, Staten Island	NYP	NYY	13.97
Brannon Baranowski, Royals	GCL	KC	13.63
Matt Gawer, Jamestown	NYP	Atl	13.20
Scott Polk, Kingsport	APP	NYM	13.13
Matt Guerrier, Bristol	APP	CWS	12.97
Terry Plank, Bluefield	APP	Bal	12.80
Oswaldo Verdugo, Idaho Falls	PIO	SD	12.68
Travis Wade, Auburn	NYP	Hou	12.66
Jose Franco, Staten Island	NYP	NYY	12.63
Matt Parker, Johnson City	APP	StL	12.35
Dan Wiggins, Eugene	NWL	ChC	12.27
Chris George, Auburn	NYP	Hou	12.16

Hits/9 Innings—Starters

Player, Team	Lg	Org	H/9
Jason Frasor, Oneonta	**NYP**	**Det**	**5.52**
Francisco Rodriguez, Boise	NWL	Ana	5.72
Carlos Hernandez, Martinsville	APP	Hou	5.86
Derek Stanford, Martinsville	APP	Hou	5.88
Orlando Roman, Mets	GCL	NYM	6.05
Jacob Peavy, Idaho Falls	PIO	SD	6.06
Calvin Chipperfield, Oneonta	NYP	Det	6.21
Matt Tate, Orioles	GCL	Bal	6.24
Kyle Colton, Braves	GCL	Atl	6.26
Colby Lewis, Pulaski	APP	Tex	6.40
Todd Moser, Utica	NYP	Fla	6.44
Mike Nannini, Auburn	NYP	Hou	6.54
Jose Rincon, Helena	PIO	Mil	6.58
Kevin Sprague, Johnson City	APP	StL	6.61
Rafael Soriano, Everett	NWL	Sea	6.69

Hits/9 Innings—Relievers

Player, Team	Lg	Org	H/9
Steve Stamm, Rangers	**GCL**	**Tex**	**4.35**
Justin Fry, Batavia	NYP	Phi	4.86
Corey Miller, Southern Oregon	NWL	Oak	5.14
Buddy Yen, Royals	GCL	KC	5.40
Travis Minix, Hudson Valley	NYP	TB	5.75
Tony Cogan, Spokane	NWL	KC	5.90
Travis Wade, Auburn	NYP	Hou	5.97
Jose Ortiz, Hudson Valley	NYP	TB	5.98
Scott Polk, Kingsport	APP	NYM	6.00
Fernando Rodney, Tigers	GCL	Det	6.00
James Eppeneder, Eugene	NWL	ChC	6.03
Derrick Johnson, Martinsville	APP	Hou	6.08
Greg Watson, Oneonta	NYP	Det	6.15
Jaime Hill, Rangers	GCL	Tex	6.26
Lew Ross, Missoula	PIO	Ari	6.28

1999 Triple-A and Double-A Splits

This section features lefty/righty and home/road splits for Triple-A and Double-A players. To be listed in this section, a hitter required 200 at-bats at a classification, while a pitcher needed either 200 at-bats against (lefty/righty) or 80 innings pitched (home/road).

These statistics will help you identify which hitters can handle all types of pitching, and vice versa. Other hitters might have to be platooned while certain pitchers may be best suited for specialized relief work. You'll also see which players had legitimate big seasons, and which were assisted by their ballparks.

Triple-A Batting vs. Lefthanded and Righthanded Pitchers

			vs Left					vs Right				
Player	Team	Org	AB	H	HR	RBI	Avg	AB	H	HR	RBI	Avg
Andy Abad	Pawtucket	Bos	56	15	1	6	.268	321	97	14	59	.302
Jeff Abbott	Charlotte	CWS	45	18	2	7	.400	232	70	7	30	.302
Dusty Allen	Las Vegas	SD	145	44	8	28	.303	309	80	10	61	.259
Jer. Allensworth	Norfolk	NYM	67	20	1	4	.299	206	52	4	16	.252
Gabe Alvarez	Toledo	Det	100	27	5	22	.270	310	90	16	45	.290
Alex Andreopoulos	Louisville	Mil	18	4	0	3	.222	183	49	5	28	.268
Danny Ardoin	Vancouver	Oak	105	28	1	15	.267	231	57	7	31	.247
Chris Ashby	Columbus	NYY	43	12	2	8	.279	163	43	7	24	.264
Carlos Baerga	Indianapolis	Cin	70	18	2	10	.257	151	46	1	17	.305
Kevin Baez	Norfolk	NYM	52	17	0	10	.327	163	41	1	23	.252
Jeff Ball	Vancouver	Oak	101	33	2	8	.327	247	75	6	43	.304
Kevin Barker	Louisville	Mil	68	10	2	12	.147	374	113	21	75	.302
Andy Barkett	Oklahoma	Tex	141	41	3	15	.291	345	108	7	61	.313
Kimera Bartee	Toledo	Det	113	36	1	11	.319	303	83	11	32	.274
Howard Battle	Richmond	Atl	103	27	5	16	.262	351	102	19	58	.291
Esteban Beltre	Rochester	Bal	86	31	1	10	.360	349	83	2	30	.238
Yamil Benitez	Louisville	Mil	68	15	2	6	.221	273	58	10	43	.212
Lance Berkman	New Orleans	Hou	97	29	3	19	.299	129	44	5	30	.341
Kurt Bierek	Columbus	NYY	116	30	5	18	.259	416	119	18	77	.286
Casey Blake	Syracuse	Tor	71	23	4	14	.324	316	72	18	61	.228
Geoff Blum	Ottawa	Mon	43	12	0	10	.279	225	59	10	27	.262
Jeff Branson	Indianapolis	Cin	98	23	1	14	.235	332	86	6	42	.259
Russell Branyan	Buffalo	Cle	110	22	10	26	.200	285	60	20	41	.211
Kary Bridges	Oklahoma	Tex	63	18	0	8	.286	201	67	7	31	.333
Darryl Brinkley	Nashville	Pit	110	41	7	30	.373	265	79	7	45	.298
Tilson Brito	Charlotte	CWS	89	32	2	12	.360	317	97	9	46	.306
Jerry Brooks	Norfolk	NYM	70	12	2	8	.171	171	45	7	19	.263
Emil Brown	Nashville	Pit	96	30	4	13	.313	337	102	14	47	.303
Kevin Brown	Syracuse	Tor	63	14	3	13	.222	232	62	10	38	.267
Roosevelt Brown	Iowa	ChC	70	24	3	19	.343	198	72	19	60	.364
Brian Buchanan	Salt Lake	Min	105	33	3	25	.314	286	83	7	35	.290
Darren Burton	Scranton-WB	Phi	108	31	6	23	.287	301	76	7	40	.252
Rich Butler	Durham	TB	62	12	0	8	.194	270	84	10	55	.311
Jimmie Byington	Omaha	KC	68	14	1	8	.206	160	33	1	15	.206
Jolbert Cabrera	Buffalo	Cle	59	13	0	5	.220	220	61	0	22	.277
Casey Candaele	New Orleans	Hou	159	48	1	14	.302	308	76	6	28	.247
Jay Canizaro	Fresno	SF	85	29	9	26	.341	279	73	17	52	.262
Bubba Carpenter	Columbus	NYY	76	13	3	13	.171	249	79	19	68	.317
Jeremy Carr	Omaha	KC	91	27	1	8	.297	184	45	3	17	.245
Jhonny Carvajal	Ottawa	Mon	75	13	0	8	.173	280	69	0	26	.246
Jovino Carvajal	Edmonton	Ana	98	17	1	7	.173	269	73	4	33	.271
Steve Carver	Scranton-WB	Phi	55	13	4	9	.236	233	55	7	29	.236
Juan Castro	Albuquerque	LA	153	45	4	19	.294	270	71	3	32	.263
Ramon Castro	Calgary	Fla	99	31	3	19	.313	250	59	12	42	.236
Andujar Cedeno	Columbus	NYY	50	15	0	6	.300	165	48	6	32	.291
Dan Cey	Salt Lake	Min	88	29	4	12	.330	315	90	7	44	.286
Wes Chamberlain	Albuquerque	LA	146	44	6	29	.301	229	71	12	49	.310
Jim Chamblee	Pawtucket	Bos	92	30	10	23	.326	372	97	14	65	.261
Frank Charles	Las Vegas	SD	91	23	1	8	.253	181	44	1	20	.243
Raul Chavez	Tacoma	Sea	90	25	1	8	.278	264	70	2	32	.265
Chris Clapinski	Calgary	Fla	71	25	2	10	.352	196	61	6	25	.311
Stubby Clapp	Memphis	StL	91	23	2	10	.253	302	79	12	52	.262
Howie Clark	Rochester	Bal	38	11	0	2	.289	241	71	6	26	.295
Edgard Clemente	Col. Springs	Col	88	30	4	22	.341	185	53	12	37	.286
Pat Cline	Iowa	ChC	109	26	2	19	.239	181	40	4	23	.221
Danny Clyburn	Durham	TB	62	16	3	7	.258	241	55	6	26	.228
Michael Coleman	Pawtucket	Bos	89	25	8	18	.281	378	100	22	56	.265
Jason Conti	Tucson	Ari	147	41	3	15	.279	373	110	6	42	.295
Brent Cookson	Albuquerque	LA	88	28	9	21	.318	189	61	19	49	.323
Mike Coolbaugh	Columbus	NYY	100	32	7	19	.320	291	76	8	47	.261
Scott Coolbaugh	Tucson	Ari	80	19	3	6	.237	132	35	4	25	.265
Trace Coquillette	Ottawa	Mon	82	20	5	12	.244	252	89	9	43	.353
Alex Cora	Albuquerque	LA	101	31	0	6	.307	201	62	4	31	.308
John Cotton	Col. Springs	Col	65	16	3	6	.246	170	58	12	42	.341
Steve Cox	Durham	TB	125	40	4	24	.320	409	142	21	103	.347
Rickey Cradle	Toledo	Det	101	22	3	12	.218	247	61	7	40	.247
Felipe Crespo	Fresno	SF	116	41	7	23	.353	269	87	17	61	.323
Brandon Cromer	Louisville	Mil	49	6	1	4	.122	281	65	23	57	.231
D.T. Cromer	Indianapolis	Cin	139	34	6	23	.245	396	132	24	84	.333
Ivan Cruz	Nashville	Pit	84	31	9	31	.369	189	58	16	50	.307
Jacob Cruz	Buffalo	Cle	67	20	1	14	.299	135	35	6	17	.259
Midre Cummings	Salt Lake	Min	65	18	0	11	.277	196	66	13	57	.337
Mike Darr	Las Vegas	SD	142	41	4	23	.289	241	73	6	39	.303
Ben Davis	Las Vegas	SD	73	23	4	21	.315	128	39	3	23	.305
Tommy Davis	Rochester	Bal	76	21	3	10	.276	337	85	8	46	.252
Steve Decker	Edmonton	Ana	63	17	3	12	.270	162	47	12	39	.290
Wilson Delgado	Fresno	SF	64	20	0	14	.313	149	44	1	19	.295
Joe DePastino	Pawtucket	Bos	45	6	2	5	.133	212	59	11	47	.278
Mark DeRosa	Richmond	Atl	80	19	1	14	.237	284	80	0	26	.282
Edwin Diaz	Tucson	Ari	121	40	6	23	.331	294	89	5	27	.303
Kelly Dransfeldt	Oklahoma	Tex	102	26	3	13	.255	257	59	7	31	.230
Todd Dunn	Rochester	Bal	39	10	1	6	.256	165	30	6	25	.182
Todd Dunwoody	Calgary	Fla	83	25	2	14	.301	163	42	7	22	.258
Bobby Estalella	Scranton-WB	Phi	96	25	1	13	.260	290	64	14	49	.221
Tom Evans	Oklahoma	Tex	135	31	3	18	.230	304	92	9	50	.303
Sal Fasano	Omaha	KC	81	23	6	13	.284	199	54	15	36	.271
Jeff Ferguson	Salt Lake	Min	83	28	1	12	.337	215	51	3	36	.237
Jose Fernandez	Ottawa	Mon	100	22	3	12	.220	365	104	11	56	.285
Jose Flores	Scranton-WB	Phi	52	11	0	2	.212	176	45	0	16	.256
Chad Fonville	Pawtucket	Bos	56	19	1	3	.339	201	46	0	11	.229
P.J. Forbes	Rochester	Bal	54	13	0	2	.241	295	79	0	17	.268
Mike Frank	Indianapolis	Cin	99	30	4	13	.303	334	98	5	49	.293
Lou Frazier	Scranton-WB	Phi	78	20	3	11	.256	230	56	3	21	.243
Ricky Freeman	Vancouver	Oak	82	28	4	17	.341	122	18	0	9	.148
Amaury Garcia	Calgary	Fla	136	48	4	15	.353	343	104	13	38	.303
Carlos Garcia	Las Vegas	SD	96	28	2	12	.292	178	49	1	16	.275

			vs Left					vs Right				
Player	Team	Org	AB	H	HR	RBI	Avg	AB	H	HR	RBI	Avg
Guillermo Garcia	Indianapolis	Cin	66	17	4	8	.258	167	50	6	20	.299
Jesse Garcia	Rochester	Bal	35	11	1	5	.314	185	45	1	18	.243
Luis Garcia	Toledo	Det	83	23	2	11	.277	225	59	1	23	.262
Steve Gibralter	Omaha	KC	116	33	8	26	.284	301	78	20	52	.259
Derrick Gibson	Col. Springs	Col	137	27	7	23	.197	248	79	10	44	.319
Benji Gil	Calgary	Fla	117	37	6	24	.316	295	78	11	40	.264
Shawn Gilbert	Albuquerque	LA	141	47	5	22	.333	280	81	5	30	.289
Tony Graffanino	Durham	TB	73	21	3	16	.288	272	87	6	42	.320
Scarborough Green	Oklahoma	Tex	105	26	1	14	.248	254	63	2	15	.248
Kevin Grijak	Albuquerque	LA	105	37	4	23	.352	296	90	14	57	.304
Aaron Guiel	Las Vegas	SD	90	20	4	10	.222	167	43	8	29	.257
Matt Guiliano	Scranton-WB	Phi	53	9	0	4	.170	163	32	2	20	.196
Mike Gulan	Calgary	Fla	83	26	3	18	.313	203	53	10	33	.261
Edwards Guzman	Fresno	SF	106	37	2	20	.349	252	61	5	28	.242
Chris Haas	Memphis	StL	117	24	4	16	.205	280	67	14	57	.239
Jerry Hairston Jr.	Rochester	Bal	79	26	3	10	.329	334	94	4	38	.281
Dave Hajek	Col. Springs	Col	176	57	5	21	.324	357	100	3	37	.280
Shane Halter	Norfolk	NYM	114	34	1	10	.298	360	96	5	25	.267
Todd Haney	Norfolk	NYM	116	34	1	11	.293	331	105	4	37	.317
Jason Hardtke	Indianapolis	Cin	113	39	1	13	.345	303	90	11	40	[illegible]
Chris Hatcher	Col. Springs	Col	129	44	10	24	.341	205	71	11	45	.346
Bret Hemphill	Edmonton	Ana	90	28	4	9	.311	156	49	3	22	.314
Chad Hermansen	Nashville	Pit	123	36	3	17	.293	376	98	29	80	.261
Carlos Hernandez	New Orleans	Hou	105	32	0	11	.305	250	72	0	32	.288
Ramon Hernandez	Vancouver	Oak	99	26	6	22	.263	192	50	7	33	.260
Phil Hiatt	Indianapolis	Cin	72	15	2	4	.208	239	59	16	50	.247
Aaron Holbert	Durham	TB	78	26	4	18	.333	269	82	8	38	.305
Damon Hollins	Indianapolis	Cin	110	33	3	11	.300	218	53	6	32	.243
Dave Hollins	Syracuse	Tor	39	12	2	9	.308	175	54	6	25	.309
Matt Howard	Nashville	Pit	110	35	0	8	.318	291	82	2	36	.282
Mike Hubbard	Oklahoma	Tex	125	34	6	17	.272	267	77	3	32	.288
Ken Huckaby	Tucson	Ari	106	33	0	14	.311	249	74	2	28	.297
David Hulse	Memphis	StL	47	12	2	7	.255	153	55	2	24	.359
Scott Hunter	Ottawa	Mon	96	21	2	11	.219	364	83	14	53	.228
Norm Hutchins	Edmonton	Ana	167	41	1	12	.246	354	89	6	39	.251
Garey Ingram	Pawtucket	Bos	81	13	1	6	.160	215	60	8	33	.279
Ryan Jackson	Tacoma	Sea	128	44	2	25	.344	281	82	6	37	.292
Robin Jennings	Iowa	ChC	81	24	1	16	.296	178	56	8	27	.315
Marcus Jensen	Memphis	StL	48	12	1	7	.250	189	57	7	37	.302
D'Angelo Jimenez	Columbus	NYY	102	31	1	13	.304	424	141	14	75	.333
Keith Johns	Edmonton	Ana	84	17	0	4	.202	152	32	3	22	.211
Keith Johnson	Tucson	Ari	102	31	4	16	.304	254	71	8	30	.280
Chris Jones	Syracuse	Tor	62	12	2	7	.194	217	54	6	33	.249
Terry Jones	Ottawa	Mon	88	30	0	8	.341	244	57	0	15	.234
Mike Kelly	Col. Springs	Col	131	38	2	14	.290	263	71	7	36	.270
Adam Kennedy	Memphis	StL	115	32	2	14	.278	252	88	8	49	.349
Brooks Kieschnick	Edmonton	TB	90	26	4	21	.289	206	67	19	52	.325
Mike Kinkade	Norfolk	NYM	79	19	3	12	.241	233	77	4	37	.330
Danny Klassen	Tucson	Ari	82	17	1	11	.207	163	49	5	22	.301
Randy Knorr	New Orleans	Hou	75	26	1	5	.347	195	69	10	36	.354
Scott Krause	Louisville	Mil	95	34	3	19	.358	404	104	12	70	.257
Tim Laker	Nashville	Pit	106	30	7	24	.283	301	80	5	41	.266
Jason LaRiviere	Memphis	StL	143	44	2	10	.308	354	98	7	37	.277
Jason LaRue	Indianapolis	Cin	66	12	4	8	.182	197	54	8	29	.274
Chris Latham	Salt Lake	Min	95	33	5	14	.347	287	90	10	37	.314
Jalal Leach	Fresno	SF	69	16	1	4	.232	302	93	14	71	.308
Derrek Lee	Calgary	Fla	100	27	5	20	.270	239	69	14	53	.289
Pat Lennon	Toledo	Det	100	30	6	17	.300	314	89	24	66	.283
Brian Lesher	Vancouver	Oak	112	37	6	19	.330	278	77	8	46	.277
Cole Liniak	Pawtucket	Bos	89	22	2	7	.247	259	70	10	35	.270
George Lombard	Richmond	Atl	56	9	0	3	.161	177	39	7	26	.220
Terrence Long	Norfolk	NYM	77	22	1	7	.286	227	77	6	40	.339
Luis Lopez	Syracuse	Tor	111	40	3	25	.360	420	131	1	44	.312
Mendy Lopez	Omaha	KC	56	17	5	14	.304	166	52	7	26	.313
Torey Lovullo	Scranton-WB	Phi	137	39	3	21	.285	382	106	18	85	.277
Terrell Lowery	Durham	TB	66	20	4	15	.303	209	72	11	42	.344
Lou Lucca	Scranton-WB	Phi	126	30	3	15	.238	407	113	9	55	.278
Keith Luuloa	Edmonton	Ana	111	41	2	12	.369	285	72	2	34	.253
Jose Macias	Toledo	Det	98	18	0	4	.184	340	89	2	32	.262
Wendell Magee	Scranton-WB	Phi	112	34	4	18	.304	454	126	16	61	.278
Marty Malloy	Richmond	Atl	64	17	0	5	.266	343	102	7	31	.297
Jeff Manto	Buffalo	Cle	68	21	7	18	.309	135	39	16	26	.289
Chris Martin	Durham	TB	71	23	2	9	.324	328	86	7	44	.262
Norberto Martin	Syracuse	Tor	55	13	1	4	.236	264	81	4	30	.307
Greg Martinez	Louisville	Mil	70	22	1	8	.314	349	89	3	21	.255
Eric Martins	Vancouver	Oak	91	18	0	6	.198	212	54	3	27	.255
Raul Marval	Fresno	SF	67	25	5	9	.373	213	59	2	37	.277
Damon Mashore	Fresno	SF	111	29	10	28	.261	236	62	10	41	.263
Ruben Mateo	Oklahoma	Tex	56	15	1	10	.268	197	70	17	52	.355
Francisco Matos	Tacoma	Sea	122	41	3	11	.336	271	81	0	22	.299
Pascual Matos	Richmond	Atl	46	12	2	5	.261	178	35	1	16	.197
Gary Matthews	Las Vegas	SD	150	33	4	19	.220	272	75	5	33	.276
Jason Maxwell	Toledo	Det	106	28	3	17	.264	313	71	12	45	.227
Derrick May	Rochester	Bal	56	19	1	11	.339	239	63	4	32	.264
Dave McCarty	Toledo	Det	116	38	9	22	.328	350	87	22	55	.249
Scott McClain	Durham	TB	115	30	8	23	.261	418	104	20	81	.249
John McDonald	Buffalo	Cle	51	12	0	4	.235	186	63	0	21	.339
Walt McKeel	Toledo	Det	75	23	6	21	.307	140	29	1	16	.207
Billy McMillon	Scranton-WB	Phi	106	32	4	24	.302	358	109	12	61	.304
Carlos Mendez	Omaha	KC	86	29	4	10	.337	207	53	6	27	.256
Carlos Mendoza	Durham	TB	58	17	0	6	.293	208	61	1	19	.293
Frank Menechino	Vancouver	Oak	159	53	5	31	.333	346	104	10	57	.301
Lou Merloni	Pawtucket	Bos	49	15	2	13	.306	180	49	5	23	.272
David Miller	Buffalo	Cle	74	14	1	8	.189	251	64	1	29	.255
Orlando Miller	Buffalo	Cle	75	21	2	8	.280	158	39	5	25	.247
Ryan Minor	Rochester	Bal	82	21	5	15	.256	301	77	16	52	.256

Triple-A Batting vs. Lefthanded and Righthanded Pitchers

Player	Team	Org	vs Left AB	H	HR	RBI	Avg	vs Right AB	H	HR	RBI	Avg
Doug Mirabelli	Fresno	SF	85	20	3	12	.235	235	80	11	39	.340
Keith Mitchell	Pawtucket	Bos	87	15	3	7	.172	344	96	9	45	.279
Ben Molina	Edmonton	Ana	78	20	3	16	.256	163	49	4	25	.301
Izzy Molina	Columbus	NYY	70	21	1	11	.300	268	62	3	40	.231
Jose Molina	Iowa	ChC	84	22	2	13	.262	156	41	2	13	.263
Shane Monahan	Tacoma	Sea	97	22	1	9	.227	302	80	6	23	.265
Ray Montgomery	Nashville	Pit	89	33	6	21	.371	186	58	11	32	.312
Brandon Moore	Charlotte	CWS	69	19	1	9	.275	230	66	0	32	.287
Melvin Mora	Norfolk	NYM	64	23	1	9	.359	240	69	7	27	.287
Francisco Morales	Ottawa	Mon	72	18	4	8	.250	273	61	6	36	.223
Mike Moriarty	Salt Lake	Min	86	16	3	13	.186	294	82	1	38	.279
Chad Mottola	Charlotte	CWS	106	32	5	25	.302	405	132	15	69	.326
Lyle Mouton	Rochester	Bal	99	30	4	28	.303	368	115	19	66	.313
Rob Mummau	Syracuse	Tor	97	26	2	12	.268	336	79	3	46	.235
Mike Murphy	Rochester	Bal	54	10	0	6	.185	163	39	1	15	.239
Calvin Murray	Fresno	SF	142	40	5	22	.282	406	143	18	51	.352
Mike Neal	New Orleans	Hou	91	23	3	15	.253	152	26	3	13	.171
Mike Neill	Vancouver	Oak	128	33	2	17	.258	241	75	8	44	.311
David Newhan	Las Vegas	SD	115	31	3	14	.270	259	76	11	35	.293
Warren Newson	Albuquerque	LA	72	14	4	12	.194	213	60	4	26	.282
Darrell Nicholas	Salt Lake	Min	86	23	1	11	.267	262	79	4	33	.302
Jose Nieves	Iowa	ChC	113	31	3	20	.274	279	74	8	39	.265
Les Norman	Omaha	KC	88	27	6	12	.307	245	64	7	28	.261
Jon Nunnally	Pawtucket	Bos	102	27	4	11	.265	392	105	19	65	.268
Joe Oliver	Durham	TB	42	15	3	14	.357	177	51	4	29	.288
Luis Ordaz	Memphis	StL	105	34	0	11	.324	257	69	1	34	.268
David Ortiz	Salt Lake	Min	128	38	7	34	.297	348	112	23	76	.322
Jose Ortiz	Vancouver	Oak	112	37	4	20	.330	265	70	5	25	.264
Luis Ortiz	Louisville	Mil	79	22	3	9	.278	225	58	8	24	.258
Craig Paquette	Norfolk	NYM	75	17	4	17	.227	208	60	11	37	.288
Jarrod Patterson	Tucson	Ari	86	26	1	8	.302	188	66	10	39	.351
Kit Pellow	Omaha	KC	137	35	13	24	.255	338	101	22	75	.299
Eduardo Perez	Memphis	StL	130	44	2	19	.338	286	89	16	63	.311
Santiago Perez	Louisville	Mil	72	16	0	9	.222	335	91	7	29	.272
Tomas Perez	Edmonton	Ana	83	20	2	12	.241	213	57	2	28	.268
Chan Perry	Buffalo	Cle	77	19	4	17	.247	196	58	6	42	.296
Chris Petersen	Col. Springs	Col	115	28	2	12	.243	255	68	4	22	.267
Ben Petrick	Col. Springs	Col	115	35	7	17	.319	188	58	12	47	.309
J.R. Phillips	Col. Springs	Col	162	44	7	31	.272	317	105	34	69	.331
Calvin Pickering	Rochester	Bal	75	14	4	19	.187	297	92	12	44	.310
A.J. Pierzynski	Salt Lake	Min	33	8	0	4	.242	195	51	1	21	.262
Kevin Polcovich	Nashville	Pit	54	11	1	7	.204	179	45	2	18	.251
Bo Porter	Iowa	ChC	134	46	11	27	.343	280	75	16	37	.268
Dave Post	Ottawa	Mon	72	27	3	12	.346	297	70	7	24	.236
Alonzo Powell	Columbus	NYY	90	30	4	19	.333	380	118	20	71	.311
Chris Prieto	Las Vegas	SD	115	35	3	10	.304	233	49	3	19	.210
Chris Pritchett	Edmonton	Ana	99	27	5	21	.273	249	70	7	24	.281
Tom Quinlan	Iowa	ChC	149	43	5	21	.289	323	75	12	37	.232
Mark Quinn	Omaha	KC	125	48	7	26	.384	303	106	18	58	.350
Brian Raabe	Columbus	NYY	95	23	0	7	.242	398	138	11	70	.347
Ryan Radmanovich	Tacoma	Sea	144	43	5	32	.299	276	77	12	48	.279
Alex Ramirez	Buffalo	Cle	86	29	3	17	.337	219	64	9	33	.292
Aramis Ramirez	Nashville	Pit	119	50	7	30	.420	341	101	14	44	.296
Omar Ramirez	New Orleans	Hou	121	27	2	14	.223	258	69	4	37	.267
Luis Raven	Charlotte	CWS	102	32	9	32	.314	430	118	24	93	.274
Glenn Reeves	Calgary	Fla	71	17	1	8	.239	165	34	1	13	.206
Brian Richardson	Salt Lake	Min	109	37	9	17	.339	342	88	9	56	.257
Adam Riggs	Albuquerque	LA	176	49	4	31	.278	337	101	9	50	.300
J.P. Roberge	Omaha	KC	127	53	3	24	.417	310	84	10	42	.271
David Roberts	Buffalo	Cle	81	17	0	10	.210	269	78	0	28	.290
Lonell Roberts	Richmond	Atl	119	27	0	7	.227	323	89	3	34	.276
Mike Robertson	Nashville	Pit	42	12	1	6	.279	177	56	6	25	.316
Kerry Robinson	Tacoma	Sea	105	41	0	15	.390	230	67	0	19	.291
Mandy Romero	Pawtucket	Bos	64	9	0	4	.141	176	47	4	27	.267
John Roskos	Calgary	Fla	145	46	8	29	.317	361	116	16	61	.321
Rico Rossy	Las Vegas	SD	80	19	3	9	.237	179	47	7	20	.263
Toby Rumfield	Richmond	Atl	106	36	5	16	.340	277	69	10	46	.249
Rob Ryan	Tucson	Ari	124	34	5	23	.274	290	86	14	65	.297
Marc Sagmoen	Oklahoma	Tex	81	23	3	12	.284	187	50	10	31	.267

Player	Team	Org	vs Left AB	H	HR	RBI	Avg	vs Right AB	H	HR	RBI	Avg
Anthony Sanders	Syracuse	Tor	82	21	5	16	.256	414	100	13	43	.242
Chance Sanford	Albuquerque	LA	51	5	1	6	.098	176	51	7	23	.290
Jamie Saylor	New Orleans	Hou	59	17	1	10	.288	271	57	3	26	.210
Gene Schall	Richmond	Atl	83	21	3	12	.253	272	83	9	41	.305
Marcos Scutaro	Buffalo	Cle	126	28	1	14	.222	336	98	7	37	.292
Scot Sealy	Tacoma	Sea	77	9	2	6	.117	124	28	4	18	.226
Fernando Seguignol	Ottawa	Mon	76	25	8	19	.329	236	64	15	55	.271
Brad Seitzer	Tacoma	Sea	137	32	0	21	.234	337	104	9	45	.309
Bill Selby	Buffalo	Cle	95	29	5	24	.305	352	103	15	61	.293
Chris Sheff	Vancouver	Oak	130	34	5	15	.262	291	87	10	55	.299
Scott Sheldon	Oklahoma	Tex	115	41	9	26	.357	338	100	19	71	.296
Joe Siddall	Toledo	Det	43	5	1	4	.116	201	42	7	29	.209
Dave Silvestri	Edmonton	Ana	91	31	0	13	.341	227	70	6	29	.308
Brian Simmons	Charlotte	CWS	74	17	3	12	.230	211	60	7	32	.284
Mitch Simons	Charlotte	CWS	92	27	0	10	.293	382	110	7	42	.289
Steve Sisco	Richmond	Atl	117	39	6	19	.333	378	115	12	57	.304
Bobby Smith	Durham	TB	43	14	2	4	.326	182	61	12	43	.335
Chris Snopek	Pawtucket	Bos	125	40	3	21	.320	337	87	9	53	.258
Scott Stahoviak	Iowa	ChC	82	12	0	4	.146	192	53	14	40	.276
Mike Stefanski	Memphis	StL	74	21	2	8	.284	127	39	2	14	.307
Dernell Stenson	Pawtucket	Bos	97	24	2	21	.247	343	95	16	61	.277
Darond Stovall	Calgary	Fla	92	21	1	9	.228	134	34	9	25	.195
Chris Stowers	Ottawa	Mon	96	24	2	10	.250	335	78	3	27	.233
Pedro Swann	Toledo	Det	35	9	0	1	.257	297	77	10	36	.259
Mark Sweeney	Indianapolis	Cin	80	18	1	7	.225	231	82	11	44	.355
Tony Tarasco	Columbus	NYY	84	29	4	16	.345	262	73	15	45	.279
Jim Tatum	Col. Springs	Col	130	42	4	23	.323	266	82	10	41	.308
Andy Thompson	Syracuse	Tor	46	15	1	4	.326	183	52	15	38	.284
Ryan Thompson	New Orleans	Hou	130	36	4	10	.277	274	89	12	48	.325
Jake Thrower	Las Vegas	SD	90	39	1	8	.322	177	48	1	14	.271
Ozzie Timmons	Tacoma	Sea	110	31	9	28	.282	187	50	12	38	.267
Andy Tomberlin	Norfolk	NYM	53	9	1	7	.170	250	85	15	54	.340
Dave Toth	Charlotte	CWS	51	17	1	5	.333	210	47	5	28	.224
Chris Turner	Buffalo	Cle	54	12	3	9	.222	111	24	4	14	.288
Brad Tyler	Richmond	Atl	82	25	3	16	.305	331	93	18	63	.281
Pedro Valdes	Oklahoma	Tex	115	38	7	22	.330	379	110	5	54	.326
Mario Valdez	Charlotte	CWS	84	25	3	13	.298	318	85	23	63	.267
Roberto Vaz	Vancouver	Oak	109	28	3	13	.257	161	69	4	25	.264
Carlos Villalobos	New Orleans	Hou	159	51	6	23	.321	340	90	3	27	.265
Julio Vinas	Rochester	Bal	86	27	5	14	.281	388	124	15	69	.320
Joe Vitiello	Omaha	KC	133	50	8	29	.376	314	92	20	69	.293
Daryle Ward	New Orleans	Hou	85	22	14	28	.338	316	83	14	37	.358
Ron Warner	Memphis	StL	105	31	6	20	.295	140	40	5	13	.286
Gabe Whatley	Richmond	Atl	60	15	1	5	.250	191	53	6	23	.277
Derrick White	Iowa	ChC	168	48	2	24	.286	335	84	11	53	.251
Darrell Whitmore	Indianapolis	Cin	45	2	1	1	.044	193	65	9	41	.337
Rick Wilkins	Albuquerque	LA	74	17	1	3	.230	226	59	7	30	.261
Eddie Williams	Salt Lake	Min	90	30	3	11	.333	255	79	14	46	.310
George Williams	Salt Lake	Min	102	32	2	14	.314	226	61	7	31	.270
Keith Williams	Fresno	SF	90	31	7	22	.344	204	52	4	28	.255
Brandon Wilson	Iowa	ChC	147	53	3	18	.361	325	78	9	31	.240
Desi Wilson	Tucson	Ari	134	35	0	17	.261	413	111	6	45	.349
Tom Wilson	Durham	TB	105	40	4	18	.400	165	40	12	36	.242
Randy Winn	Durham	TB	39	15	1	4	.385	168	58	2	26	.345
Kevin Witt	Syracuse	Tor	98	29	4	12	.296	323	88	20	59	.272
Ken Woods	Fresno	SF	120	42	1	19	.350	349	110	5	54	.315
Chris Woodward	Syracuse	Tor	49	21	1	4	.429	232	61	0	16	.263
Ernie Young	Tucson	Ari	137	44	10	26	.321	316	89	20	69	.282
Eddie Zosky	Louisville	Mil	94	27	2	13	.287	321	95	10	34	.296
Jon Zuber	Scranton-WB	Phi	100	31	1	14	.310	287	83	5	40	.289
Mike Zywica	Oklahoma	Tex	153	37	3	15	.242	342	94	6	64	.275

Triple-A Batting at Home and on the Road

			Home					Road				
Player	Team	Org	AB	H	HR	RBI	Avg	AB	H	HR	RBI	Avg
Andy Abad	Pawtucket	Bos	192	56	5	24	.292	185	56	10	41	.303
Jeff Abbott	Charlotte	CWS	139	37	4	15	.266	138	51	5	22	.370
Dusty Allen	Las Vegas	SD	227	69	8	41	.304	227	55	10	48	.242
Jer. Allensworth	Norfolk	NYM	132	31	1	11	.235	141	41	4	9	.291
Gabe Alvarez	Toledo	Det	202	61	9	34	.302	208	56	12	33	.269
Alex Andreopoulos	Louisville	Mil	111	33	3	16	.297	90	20	2	15	.222
Danny Ardoin	Vancouver	Oak	168	47	2	22	.280	168	38	6	24	.226
Chris Ashby	Columbus	NYY	112	31	4	16	.277	94	24	5	16	.255
Carlos Baerga	Indianapolis	Cin	102	28	2	14	.275	119	36	1	13	.303
Kevin Baez	Norfolk	NYM	106	24	0	14	.226	109	34	1	19	.312
Jeff Ball	Vancouver	Oak	144	49	1	21	.340	202	58	7	30	.287
Kevin Barker	Louisville	Mil	228	66	11	44	.289	214	57	12	43	.266
Andy Barkett	Oklahoma	Tex	227	75	6	51	.330	259	74	4	25	.286
Kimera Bartee	Toledo	Det	202	60	8	26	.297	214	59	4	17	.276
Howard Battle	Richmond	Atl	218	56	10	28	.257	236	73	14	46	.309
Esteban Beltre	Rochester	Bal	228	68	0	21	.298	207	46	3	19	.222
Yamil Benitez	Louisville	Mil	181	43	8	32	.238	160	30	4	17	.188
Lance Berkman	New Orleans	Hou	104	35	4	26	.337	122	38	4	23	.311
Kurt Bierek	Cólumbus	NYY	253	80	11	43	.316	279	69	12	52	.247
Casey Blake	Syracuse	Tor	185	47	11	31	.254	202	48	11	44	.238
Geoff Blum	Ottawa	Mon	140	38	5	19	.271	128	33	5	18	.258
Jeff Branson	Indianapolis	Cin	219	55	3	26	.251	211	54	4	30	.256
Russell Branyan	Buffalo	Cle	173	30	9	24	.173	222	52	21	43	.234
Kary Bridges	Oklahoma	Tex	120	38	2	15	.317	144	46	5	24	.319
Darryl Brinkley	Nashville	Pit	195	65	7	38	.333	177	55	7	37	.311
Tilson Brito	Charlotte	CWS	204	68	7	32	.333	202	61	4	26	.302
Jerry Brooks	Norfolk	NYM	123	28	3	15	.228	118	29	6	12	.246
Emil Brown	Nashville	Pit	202	63	7	28	.312	228	69	11	32	.303
Kevin Brown	Syracuse	Tor	158	46	9	35	.291	137	30	4	16	.219
Roosevelt Brown	Iowa	ChC	139	46	12	41	.331	129	50	10	37	.388
Brian Buchanan	Salt Lake	Min	161	47	10	36	.292	230	69	0	24	.300
Darren Burton	Scranton-WB	Phi	210	55	6	34	.262	199	52	7	29	.261
Rich Butler	Durham	TB	174	48	5	36	.276	158	48	5	27	.304
Jimmie Byington	Omaha	KC	131	25	1	13	.191	97	22	1	10	.227
Jolbert Cabrera	Buffalo	Cle	124	31	0	8	.250	155	43	0	19	.277
Casey Candaele	New Orleans	Hou	213	57	3	18	.268	254	67	4	24	.264
Jay Canizaro	Fresno	SF	175	52	15	45	.297	189	50	11	33	.265
Bubba Carpenter	Columbus	NYY	150	41	9	39	.273	175	51	13	42	.291
Jeremy Carr	Omaha	KC	139	39	3	14	.281	136	33	1	11	.243
Jhonny Carvajal	Ottawa	Mon	171	36	0	14	.211	184	46	0	20	.250
Jovino Carvajal	Edmonton	Ana	177	40	1	23	.226	190	50	4	17	.263
Steve Carver	Scranton-WB	Phi	146	35	6	16	.240	142	33	5	22	.232
Juan Castro	Albuquerque	LA	208	58	3	25	.279	215	58	4	26	.270
Ramon Castro	Calgary	Fla	139	44	5	20	.317	210	46	10	41	.219
Andujar Cedeno	Columbus	NYY	109	28	3	18	.257	106	35	3	20	.330
Dan Cey	Salt Lake	Min	214	72	6	31	.336	189	47	5	25	.249
Wes Chamberlain	Albuquerque	LA	190	64	11	41	.337	185	51	7	37	.276
Jim Chamblee	Pawtucket	Bos	232	56	10	49	.241	232	71	14	39	.306
Frank Charles	Las Vegas	SD	127	31	2	16	.244	145	36	0	12	.248
Raul Chavez	Tacoma	Sea	178	42	0	15	.236	176	53	3	25	.301
Chris Clapinski	Calgary	Fla	129	43	5	20	.333	138	43	3	15	.312
Stubby Clapp	Memphis	StL	182	46	4	26	.253	211	56	10	36	.265
Howie Clark	Rochester	Bal	134	34	1	11	.254	145	48	5	17	.331
Edgard Clemente	Col. Springs	Col	106	32	6	21	.302	167	51	10	38	.305
Pat Cline	Iowa	ChC	141	33	2	23	.234	149	33	4	19	.221
Danny Clyburn	Durham	TB	157	33	4	14	.210	146	38	5	19	.260
Michael Coleman	Pawtucket	Bos	253	71	17	44	.281	214	54	13	30	.252
Jason Conti	Tucson	Ari	252	79	5	38	.313	268	72	4	19	.269
Brent Cookson	Albuquerque	LA	155	51	18	45	.329	122	38	10	25	.311
Mike Coolbaugh	Columbus	NYY	178	47	7	33	.264	213	61	8	33	.286
Scott Coolbaugh	Tucson	Ari	114	32	2	19	.281	98	22	5	12	.224
Trace Coquillette	Ottawa	Mon	143	49	7	23	.343	191	60	7	32	.314
Alex Cora	Albuquerque	LA	132	36	0	14	.273	170	57	4	23	.335
John Cotton	Col. Springs	Col	129	42	9	25	.326	106	32	6	23	.302
Steve Cox	Durham	TB	270	100	17	70	.370	264	82	8	57	.311
Rickey Cradle	Toledo	Det	168	34	6	22	.202	180	49	4	30	.272
Felipe Crespo	Fresno	SF	207	65	12	42	.314	178	63	12	42	.354
Brandon Cromer	Louisville	Mil	164	40	14	36	.244	166	31	10	25	.187
D.T. Cromer	Indianapolis	Cin	253	71	9	43	.281	282	95	21	64	.337
Ivan Cruz	Nashville	Pit	148	49	14	50	.331	125	40	11	31	.320
Jacob Cruz	Buffalo	Cle	86	17	1	8	.198	116	38	6	23	.328
Midre Cummings	Salt Lake	Min	127	42	10	34	.331	134	42	3	34	.313
Mike Darr	Las Vegas	SD	192	59	6	36	.307	191	55	4	26	.288
Ben Davis	Las Vegas	SD	114	37	4	23	.325	87	25	3	21	.287
Tommy Davis	Rochester	Bal	209	56	5	28	.268	204	50	6	28	.245
Steve Decker	Edmonton	Ana	100	27	4	13	.270	125	37	11	38	.296
Wilson Delgado	Fresno	SF	104	31	1	17	.298	109	33	0	16	.303
Joe DePastino	Pawtucket	Bos	135	34	6	27	.252	122	31	7	25	.254
Mark DeRosa	Richmond	Atl	182	52	0	23	.286	182	47	1	17	.258
Edwin Diaz	Tucson	Ari	230	81	10	41	.352	185	48	1	9	.259
Kelly Dransfeldt	Oklahoma	Tex	180	48	3	27	.267	179	37	7	17	.207
Todd Dunn	Rochester	Bal	106	25	4	20	.236	98	15	3	11	.153
Todd Dunwoody	Calgary	Fla	110	34	4	17	.309	136	33	5	19	.243
Bobby Estalella	Scranton-WB	Phi	188	46	11	33	.245	198	43	4	29	.217
Tom Evans	Oklahoma	Tex	217	66	5	35	.304	222	57	7	33	.257
Sal Fasano	Omaha	KC	117	29	11	20	.248	163	48	10	29	.294
Jeff Ferguson	Salt Lake	Min	129	38	1	23	.295	169	41	3	25	.243
Jose Fernandez	Ottawa	Mon	215	53	6	30	.247	250	73	8	38	.292
Jose Flores	Scranton-WB	Phi	98	23	0	11	.235	130	33	0	7	.254
Chad Fonville	Pawtucket	Bos	138	34	0	5	.246	119	31	1	9	.261
P.J. Forbes	Rochester	Bal	171	48	0	10	.281	178	44	0	9	.247
Mike Frank	Indianapolis	Cin	189	59	2	25	.312	244	69	7	37	.283
Lou Frazier	Scranton-WB	Phi	142	38	4	13	.268	166	38	2	19	.229
Ricky Freeman	Vancouver	Oak	102	22	2	15	.216	100	23	2	9	.230
Amaury Garcia	Calgary	Fla	246	91	11	34	.370	233	61	6	19	.262
Carlos Garcia	Las Vegas	SD	124	32	0	11	.258	150	45	3	17	.300

			Home					Road				
Player	Team	Org	AB	H	HR	RBI	Avg	AB	H	HR	RBI	Avg
Guillermo Garcia	Indianapolis	Cin	98	31	3	10	.316	135	36	7	18	.267
Jesse Garcia	Rochester	Bal	82	19	0	7	.232	138	37	2	16	.268
Luis Garcia	Toledo	Det	145	35	1	14	.241	163	47	2	20	.288
Steve Gibralter	Omaha	KC	160	37	12	32	.231	257	74	16	46	.288
Derrick Gibson	Col. Springs	Col	166	50	7	29	.301	219	56	10	38	.256
Benji Gil	Calgary	Fla	204	57	11	37	.279	208	58	6	27	.279
Shawn Gilbert	Albuquerque	LA	226	72	4	28	.319	195	56	6	24	.287
Tony Graffanino	Durham	TB	160	52	6	34	.325	185	56	3	24	.303
Scarborough Green	Oklahoma	Tex	171	44	1	14	.257	188	45	2	15	.239
Kevin Grijak	Albuquerque	LA	209	66	11	44	.316	192	61	7	36	.318
Aaron Guiel	Las Vegas	SD	135	33	7	21	.244	122	30	5	18	.246
Matt Guiliano	Scranton-WB	Phi	99	20	1	11	.202	117	21	1	13	.179
Mike Gulan	Calgary	Fla	133	36	8	36	.271	153	43	5	15	.281
Edwards Guzman	Fresno	SF	186	49	6	23	.263	172	49	1	25	.285
Chris Haas	Memphis	StL	198	45	12	45	.227	199	46	6	28	.231
Jerry Hairston Jr.	Rochester	Bal	206	62	5	26	.301	207	58	2	22	.280
Dave Hajek	Col. Springs	Col	258	80	4	37	.310	275	77	4	21	.280
Shane Halter	Norfolk	NYM	233	74	3	19	.318	241	56	3	16	.232
Todd Haney	Norfolk	NYM	208	68	1	21	.327	239	71	4	27	.297
Jason Hardtke	Indianapolis	Cin	200	69	6	27	.345	216	68	6	34	.315
Chris Hatcher	Col. Springs	Col	135	50	12	37	.370	199	65	9	32	.327
Bret Hemphill	Edmonton	Ana	134	43	3	17	.321	112	34	4	14	.304
Chad Hermansen	Nashville	Pit	241	69	16	55	.286	255	65	16	42	.255
Carlos Hernandez	New Orleans	Hou	162	52	0	19	.321	193	52	0	24	.269
Ramon Hernandez	Vancouver	Oak	121	27	4	23	.223	170	49	9	32	.288
Phil Hiatt	Indianapolis	Cin	150	29	7	25	.193	161	45	11	29	.280
Aaron Holbert	Durham	TB	162	49	4	21	.302	185	59	8	35	.319
Damon Hollins	Indianapolis	Cin	157	44	6	24	.280	171	42	3	19	.246
Dave Hollins	Syracuse	Tor	85	25	2	12	.294	129	41	6	22	.318
Matt Howard	Nashville	Pit	186	54	1	16	.290	213	63	1	28	.296
Mike Hubbard	Oklahoma	Tex	208	53	3	26	.255	184	58	6	23	.315
Ken Huckaby	Tucson	Ari	188	61	1	28	.324	167	46	1	14	.275
David Hulse	Memphis	StL	119	39	4	23	.328	81	28	0	8	.346
Scott Hunter	Ottawa	Mon	217	48	8	27	.221	243	56	8	37	.230
Norm Hutchins	Edmonton	Ana	242	60	2	15	.248	279	70	5	36	.251
Garey Ingram	Pawtucket	Bos	159	43	6	20	.270	137	30	3	19	.219
Ryan Jackson	Tacoma	Sea	203	59	4	30	.291	206	67	4	32	.325
Robin Jennings	Iowa	ChC	139	43	5	25	.309	120	37	4	18	.308
Marcus Jensen	Memphis	StL	117	38	1	17	.325	120	31	7	27	.258
D'Angelo Jimenez	Columbus	NYY	264	91	10	47	.345	262	81	5	41	.309
Keith Johns	Edmonton	Ana	107	27	1	16	.252	129	22	2	10	.171
Keith Johnson	Tucson	Ari	179	52	4	25	.291	177	50	8	21	.282
Chris Jones	Syracuse	Tor	103	22	3	12	.214	176	44	5	28	.250
Terry Jones	Ottawa	Mon	163	40	0	10	.245	169	47	0	13	.278
Mike Kelly	Col. Springs	Col	192	53	4	28	.276	202	56	5	22	.277
Adam Kennedy	Memphis	StL	199	68	6	34	.342	168	52	4	29	.310
Brooks Kieschnick	Edmonton	TB	135	43	13	39	.319	161	50	10	34	.311
Mike Kinkade	Norfolk	NYM	164	51	4	24	.311	148	45	3	25	.304
Danny Klassen	Tucson	Ari	143	39	1	15	.273	102	27	5	18	.265
Randy Knorr	New Orleans	Hou	148	51	6	22	.345	122	44	5	19	.361
Scott Krause	Louisville	Mil	241	64	6	44	.266	258	74	9	45	.287
Tim Laker	Nashville	Pit	207	50	1	29	.242	198	59	11	36	.298
Jason LaRiviere	Memphis	StL	230	68	6	30	.296	267	74	3	17	.277
Jason LaRue	Indianapolis	Cin	142	33	3	20	.232	121	33	9	17	.273
Chris Latham	Salt Lake	Min	194	62	6	26	.320	188	61	9	25	.324
Jalal Leach	Fresno	SF	190	59	9	47	.311	182	50	6	28	.275
Derrek Lee	Calgary	Fla	175	57	13	44	.326	164	39	6	29	.238
Pat Lennon	Toledo	Det	200	52	14	37	.260	214	67	16	46	.313
Brian Lesher	Vancouver	Oak	161	43	2	21	.267	226	70	12	43	.310
Cole Liniak	Pawtucket	Bos	161	44	8	21	.273	187	48	4	21	.257
George Lombard	Richmond	Atl	96	13	1	9	.135	137	35	6	20	.255
Terrence Long	Norfolk	NYM	148	57	2	24	.385	156	42	5	23	.269
Luis Lopez	Syracuse	Tor	255	82	2	37	.322	276	89	2	32	.322
Mendy Lopez	Omaha	KC	130	44	8	24	.338	92	25	4	16	.272
Torey Lovullo	Scranton-WB	Phi	248	71	6	47	.286	271	74	15	59	.273
Terrell Lowery	Durham	TB	120	39	5	21	.325	155	53	10	36	.342
Lou Lucca	Scranton-WB	Phi	269	63	1	33	.234	264	80	11	37	.303
Keith Luuloa	Edmonton	Ana	204	69	2	24	.338	192	44	2	22	.229
Jose Macias	Toledo	Det	223	53	2	20	.238	215	54	0	16	.251
Wendell Magee	Scranton-WB	Phi	269	72	7	30	.268	297	88	13	49	.296
Marty Malloy	Richmond	Atl	201	58	3	22	.289	206	61	4	14	.296
Jeff Manto	Buffalo	Cle	115	35	15	27	.304	88	25	8	17	.284
Chris Martin	Durham	TB	220	63	3	22	.286	179	46	6	31	.257
Norberto Martin	Syracuse	Tor	150	50	3	15	.333	169	44	2	19	.260
Greg Martinez	Louisville	Mil	203	55	3	18	.271	216	56	1	11	.259
Eric Martins	Vancouver	Oak	155	34	1	11	.219	146	38	2	22	.260
Raul Marval	Fresno	SF	160	55	6	26	.344	120	29	1	20	.242
Damon Mashore	Fresno	SF	184	54	13	41	.293	163	37	7	28	.227
Ruben Mateo	Oklahoma	Tex	136	50	10	36	.368	117	35	8	26	.299
Francisco Matos	Tacoma	Sea	205	58	0	17	.283	188	64	3	16	.340
Pascual Matos	Richmond	Atl	104	23	0	8	.221	120	24	3	13	.200
Gary Matthews	Las Vegas	SD	203	56	4	29	.276	219	52	5	23	.237
Jason Maxwell	Toledo	Det	208	52	7	34	.250	211	47	8	28	.223
Derrick May	Rochester	Bal	152	42	3	25	.276	143	40	2	18	.280
Dave McCarty	Toledo	Det	208	57	15	43	.274	258	68	16	34	.264
Scott McClain	Durham	TB	264	63	14	45	.239	269	71	14	59	.264
John McDonald	Buffalo	Cle	112	41	0	15	.366	125	34	0	10	.272
Walt McKeel	Toledo	Det	106	29	5	23	.274	109	23	2	14	.211
Billy McMillon	Scranton-WB	Phi	212	75	10	54	.354	252	66	6	31	.262
Carlos Mendez	Omaha	KC	152	42	6	25	.276	141	40	4	12	.284
Carlos Mendoza	Durham	TB	120	36	1	9	.300	146	42	0	16	.288
Frank Menechino	Vancouver	Oak	230	70	4	38	.304	271	85	11	50	.314
Lou Merloni	Pawtucket	Bos	121	37	4	20	.306	108	27	3	16	.250
David Miller	Buffalo	Cle	175	44	0	23	.251	150	34	2	14	.227
Orlando Miller	Buffalo	Cle	93	21	0	11	.226	140	39	7	22	.279
Ryan Minor	Rochester	Bal	183	46	8	25	.251	200	52	13	42	.260

Triple-A Batting at Home and on the Road

Player	Team	Org	Home AB	H	HR	RBI	Avg	Road AB	H	HR	RBI	Avg
Doug Mirabelli	Fresno	SF	141	42	9	27	.298	179	58	5	24	.324
Keith Mitchell	Pawtucket	Bos	217	57	5	31	.263	214	54	7	21	.252
Ben Molina	Edmonton	Ana	108	25	3	16	.231	133	44	4	25	.331
Izzy Molina	Columbus	NYY	160	38	1	20	.237	178	45	3	31	.253
Jose Molina	Iowa	ChC	105	27	0	11	.257	135	36	4	15	.267
Shane Monahan	Tacoma	Sea	213	50	2	14	.235	186	52	5	18	.280
Ray Montgomery	Nashville	Pit	153	48	9	27	.314	119	42	7	25	.353
Brandon Moore	Charlotte	CWS	138	41	0	18	.297	161	44	1	23	.273
Melvin Mora	Norfolk	NYM	135	41	3	21	.304	169	51	5	15	.302
Francisco Morales	Ottawa	Mon	181	38	6	25	.210	164	41	4	19	.250
Mike Moriarty	Salt Lake	Min	189	50	3	25	.265	191	48	1	26	.251
Chad Mottola	Charlotte	CWS	256	75	12	51	.293	255	89	8	43	.349
Lyle Mouton	Rochester	Bal	216	56	8	43	.259	251	89	15	51	.355
Rob Mummau	Syracuse	Tor	206	51	3	30	.248	227	54	2	28	.238
Mike Murphy	Rochester	Bal	114	23	0	8	.202	103	26	1	13	.252
Calvin Murray	Fresno	SF	268	96	17	43	.358	280	87	6	30	.311
Mike Neal	New Orleans	Hou	118	22	0	7	.186	125	27	6	21	.216
Mike Neill	Vancouver	Oak	145	38	5	22	.262	220	70	5	39	.318
David Newhan	Las Vegas	SD	184	54	8	27	.293	190	53	6	22	.279
Warren Newson	Albuquerque	LA	127	36	3	14	.283	158	38	5	24	.241
Darrell Nicholas	Salt Lake	Min	167	63	2	30	.377	181	39	3	14	.215
Jose Nieves	Iowa	ChC	180	42	2	20	.233	212	63	9	39	.297
Les Norman	Omaha	KC	137	40	8	19	.292	196	51	5	21	.260
Jon Nunnally	Pawtucket	Bos	234	66	11	36	.282	260	66	12	40	.254
Joe Oliver	Durham	TB	95	29	2	11	.305	124	37	5	32	.298
Luis Ordaz	Memphis	StL	176	57	1	28	.324	186	46	0	17	.247
David Ortiz	Salt Lake	Min	231	75	15	66	.325	245	75	15	44	.306
Jose Ortiz	Vancouver	Oak	173	42	1	14	.243	204	65	8	31	.319
Luis Ortiz	Louisville	Mil	132	38	3	13	.288	172	42	8	20	.244
Craig Paquette	Norfolk	NYM	143	43	6	27	.301	140	34	9	27	.243
Jarrod Patterson	Tucson	Ari	121	47	4	19	.388	153	45	7	28	.294
Kit Pellow	Omaha	KC	223	57	18	48	.256	252	79	17	51	.313
Eduardo Perez	Memphis	StL	192	66	7	34	.344	224	67	11	48	.299
Santiago Perez	Louisville	Mil	211	59	5	24	.280	196	48	2	14	.245
Tomas Perez	Edmonton	Ana	131	37	4	20	.282	165	40	0	20	.242
Chan Perry	Buffalo	Cle	113	36	4	31	.319	160	41	6	28	.256
Chris Petersen	Col. Springs	Col	199	64	3	21	.322	171	32	3	13	.187
Ben Petrick	Col. Springs	Col	109	36	6	30	.330	173	53	13	34	.301
J.R. Phillips	Col. Springs	Col	247	82	21	56	.332	232	67	20	44	.289
Calvin Pickering	Rochester	Bal	179	52	11	34	.291	193	54	5	39	.280
A.J. Pierzynski	Salt Lake	Min	135	34	0	18	.252	93	25	1	7	.269
Kevin Polcovich	Nashville	Pit	111	26	1	11	.234	120	30	2	14	.248
Bo Porter	Iowa	ChC	212	63	13	27	.297	202	58	14	37	.287
Dave Post	Ottawa	Mon	199	53	9	25	.266	176	44	1	11	.250
Alonzo Powell	Columbus	NYY	236	82	12	45	.347	234	66	12	45	.282
Chris Prieto	Las Vegas	SD	162	40	1	9	.247	186	44	5	20	.237
Chris Pritchett	Edmonton	Ana	146	40	7	31	.274	202	57	5	14	.282
Tom Quinlan	Iowa	ChC	226	57	8	27	.252	246	61	9	31	.248
Mark Quinn	Omaha	KC	172	57	10	31	.331	256	97	15	53	.379
Brian Raabe	Columbus	NYY	251	93	7	49	.371	242	64	2	26	.281
Ryan Radmanovich	Tacoma	Sea	199	53	3	24	.266	221	67	14	56	.303
Alex Ramirez	Buffalo	Cle	131	32	4	15	.244	174	61	8	35	.351
Aramis Ramirez	Nashville	Pit	221	75	9	36	.339	239	76	12	38	.318
Omar Ramirez	New Orleans	Hou	173	46	1	26	.266	206	50	5	25	.243
Luis Raven	Charlotte	CWS	279	84	18	67	.301	253	66	15	58	.261
Glenn Reeves	Calgary	Fla	105	30	1	12	.286	131	21	1	9	.160
Brian Richardson	Salt Lake	Min	225	65	8	42	.289	226	60	10	30	.265
Adam Riggs	Albuquerque	LA	249	77	7	44	.309	264	73	6	37	.277
J.P. Roberge	Omaha	KC	215	76	8	45	.353	222	61	5	21	.275
David Roberts	Buffalo	Cle	166	42	0	21	.253	184	53	0	17	.288
Lonell Roberts	Richmond	Atl	221	56	2	21	.253	221	60	1	20	.271
Mike Robertson	Nashville	Pit	88	25	4	14	.284	132	43	5	17	.326
Kerry Robinson	Tacoma	Sea	158	50	0	12	.316	177	58	0	22	.328
Mandy Romero	Pawtucket	Bos	120	38	3	22	.317	120	18	1	9	.150
John Roskos	Calgary	Fla	252	77	14	51	.306	254	85	10	39	.335
Rico Rossy	Las Vegas	SD	125	38	5	13	.304	134	28	5	16	.209
Toby Rumfield	Richmond	Atl	194	51	8	36	.263	189	54	7	26	.286
Rob Ryan	Tucson	Ari	207	64	7	41	.309	207	56	12	47	.271
Marc Sagmoen	Oklahoma	Tex	136	39	8	23	.287	132	34	5	20	.258
Anthony Sanders	Syracuse	Tor	255	69	11	33	.271	241	52	7	26	.216
Chance Sanford	Albuquerque	LA	109	27	6	16	.248	118	29	2	13	.246
Jamie Saylor	New Orleans	Hou	166	34	1	20	.205	164	40	3	16	.244
Gene Schall	Richmond	Atl	158	46	6	25	.291	197	58	6	28	.294
Marcos Scutaro	Buffalo	Cle	218	59	4	29	.271	244	67	4	22	.275
Scot Sealy	Tacoma	Sea	88	13	3	12	.148	113	24	3	12	.212
Fernando Seguignol	Ottawa	Mon	173	52	12	43	.301	139	37	11	31	.266
Brad Seitzer	Tacoma	Sea	231	65	4	33	.281	243	71	5	33	.292
Bill Selby	Buffalo	Cle	214	62	11	37	.290	233	70	9	48	.300
Chris Sheff	Vancouver	Oak	180	50	3	35	.278	241	71	12	35	.295
Scott Sheldon	Oklahoma	Tex	241	70	12	47	.290	212	71	16	50	.335
Joe Siddall	Toledo	Det	118	21	4	10	.178	126	26	4	23	.206
Dave Silvestri	Edmonton	Ana	135	48	4	24	.356	183	53	2	18	.290
Brian Simmons	Charlotte	CWS	170	52	6	28	.306	115	25	4	16	.217
Mitch Simons	Charlotte	CWS	248	69	6	31	.278	226	68	1	21	.301
Steve Sisco	Richmond	Atl	243	76	8	33	.313	252	78	10	43	.310
Bobby Smith	Durham	TB	93	30	5	17	.323	132	45	9	30	.341
Chris Snopek	Pawtucket	Bos	212	66	4	35	.311	250	61	8	39	.244
Scott Stahoviak	Iowa	ChC	129	32	6	21	.248	145	33	8	23	.228
Mike Stefanski	Memphis	StL	93	29	3	12	.312	108	31	1	10	.287
Dernell Stenson	Pawtucket	Bos	217	55	5	28	.253	196	56	11	28	.286
Darond Stovall	Calgary	Fla	132	32	7	20	.242	134	23	3	14	.172
Chris Stowers	Ottawa	Mon	211	70	9	42	.332	185	54	5	22	.292
Pedro Swann	Toledo	Det	174	49	7	23	.282	158	37	3	14	.234
Mark Sweeney	Indianapolis	Cin	142	46	6	27	.324	169	54	6	24	.320
Tony Tarasco	Columbus	NYY	150	46	8	33	.307	196	56	11	28	.286
Jim Tatum	Col. Springs	Col	211	70	9	42	.332	185	54	5	22	.292
Andy Thompson	Syracuse	Tor	119	40	10	28	.336	110	27	6	14	.245
Ryan Thompson	New Orleans	Hou	196	49	6	23	.250	208	76	10	35	.365
Jake Thrower	Las Vegas	SD	119	31	1	10	.261	148	46	3	20	.311
Ozzie Timmons	Tacoma	Sea	122	32	5	23	.262	175	49	16	43	.280
Andy Tomberlin	Norfolk	NYM	156	53	9	33	.340	147	41	7	28	.279
Dave Toth	Charlotte	CWS	135	38	5	20	.281	126	21	1	13	.206
Chris Turner	Buffalo	Cle	107	29	4	21	.271	112	30	5	12	.274
Brad Tyler	Richmond	Atl	196	52	6	24	.265	217	66	15	55	.304
Pedro Valdes	Oklahoma	Tex	170	55	9	30	.324	224	74	12	42	.330
Mario Valdez	Charlotte	CWS	204	56	16	41	.275	198	54	10	35	.273
Roberto Vaz	Vancouver	Oak	166	41	2	14	.247	201	56	5	24	.279
Carlos Villalobos	New Orleans	Hou	256	73	3	24	.285	243	68	6	26	.280
Julio Vinas	Rochester	Bal	232	57	7	28	.246	252	79	13	55	.313
Joe Vitiello	Omaha	KC	208	70	20	57	.337	239	72	8	41	.301
Daryle Ward	New Orleans	Hou	162	47	9	22	.290	140	54	19	43	.386
Ron Warner	Memphis	StL	107	27	6	16	.252	138	44	5	17	.319
Gabe Whatley	Richmond	Atl	121	31	2	12	.240	122	37	6	22	.303
Derrick White	Iowa	ChC	227	62	9	35	.273	276	70	4	42	.254
Darrell Whitmore	Indianapolis	Cin	121	35	5	21	.289	131	28	5	21	.214
Rick Wilkins	Albuquerque	LA	146	40	5	19	.274	154	36	3	14	.234
Eddie Williams	Salt Lake	Min	135	67	9	36	.362	160	42	8	21	.262
George Williams	Salt Lake	Min	188	50	4	33	.266	140	43	5	22	.307
Keith Williams	Fresno	SF	143	43	7	25	.301	151	40	4	25	.265
Brandon Wilson	Iowa	ChC	251	71	9	27	.283	221	60	3	21	.271
Desi Wilson	Tucson	Ari	229	77	2	31	.336	223	69	4	31	.309
Tom Wilson	Durham	TB	127	36	8	24	.283	88	24	8	20	.273
Randy Winn	Durham	TB	117	46	3	24	.393	90	27	0	6	.300
Kevin Witt	Syracuse	Tor	200	60	13	37	.300	221	57	11	34	.258
Ken Woods	Fresno	SF	216	73	5	38	.338	253	79	1	35	.312
Chris Woodward	Syracuse	Tor	141	42	0	11	.298	140	40	1	9	.286
Ernie Young	Tucson	Ari	73	18	5	7	.247	260	62	10	38	.238
Eddie Zosky	Louisville	Mil	219	64	6	25	.292	196	58	6	22	.296
Jon Zuber	Scranton-WB	Phi	202	62	1	25	.307	185	52	5	29	.281
Mike Zywica	Oklahoma	Tex	224	55	2	35	.246	271	76	7	44	.280

Triple-A Pitching vs. Lefthanded and Righthanded Batters

			vs Left					vs Right				
Player	Team	Org	AB	H	HR	SO	Avg	AB	H	HR	SO	Avg
Willie Adams	Pawtucket	Bos	133	36	3	23	.271	139	46	4	14	.331
Paul Ah Yat	Nashville	Pit	72	22	3	14	.306	186	53	7	27	.285
Jose Alberro	Calgary	Fla	88	34	5	13	.386	159	45	4	30	.283
Jimmy Anderson	Nashville	Pit	104	27	2	16	.260	425	126	3	77	.296
Luis Andujar	Charlotte	CWS	82	19	2	22	.232	146	43	1	37	.295
Rick Ankiel	Memphis	StL	72	14	0	26	.194	256	59	7	93	.230
Brian Barber	Omaha	KC	195	51	9	33	.262	286	77	12	42	.269
Richie Barker	Iowa	ChC	80	23	3	16	.287	206	49	4	36	.238
Brian Barnes	Memphis	StL	58	15	1	17	.259	292	89	15	71	.305
Manuel Barrios	Indianapolis	Cin	133	38	1	20	.286	219	56	7	53	.256
Jose Bautista	Ottawa	Mon	189	49	7	28	.259	273	95	13	37	.348
Kevin Beirne	Charlotte	CWS	188	56	7	24	.298	264	78	7	39	.295
Jason Bell	Salt Lake	Min	141	40	4	31	.284	178	56	8	41	.315
Joel Bennett	Scranton-WB	Phi	177	41	3	37	.232	312	93	7	88	.298
Shayne Bennett	Ottawa	Mon	110	26	4	20	.236	236	70	8	50	.297
Brent Billingsley	Calgary	Fla	110	31	5	18	.282	351	102	10	61	.291
Kurt Bogott	Syracuse	Tor	96	20	2	33	.208	238	60	9	43	.252
Rod Bolton	Scranton-WB	Phi	208	47	3	29	.226	388	114	7	56	.294
Dave Borkowski	Toledo	Det	199	61	6	33	.307	275	58	10	61	.211
Joe Borowski	Louisville	Mil	110	30	2	21	.273	232	64	5	49	.276
Shawn Boskie	Albuquerque	LA	112	33	5	25	.295	241	78	9	37	.324
Heath Bost	Col. Springs	Col	117	37	3	26	.316	242	83	7	41	.343
Shane Bowers	Salt Lake	Min	189	61	11	27	.323	309	88	14	76	.285
Micah Bowie	Richmond	Atl	33	9	2	8	.273	237	56	2	74	.236
Jason Boyd	Tucson	Ari	105	31	1	12	.295	198	47	5	50	.237
Chad Bradford	Charlotte	CWS	87	26	1	10	.299	186	37	1	46	.199
Ryan Bradley	Columbus	NYY	252	85	15	44	.337	315	78	13	74	.248
Billy Brewer	Scranton-WB	Phi	65	11	1	19	.169	188	48	4	38	.255
Antone Brooks	Richmond	Atl	69	20	0	12	.290	141	37	2	27	.262
Scott Brow	Edmonton	Ana	101	31	5	18	.307	211	63	2	30	.299
Jim Brower	Buffalo	Cle	225	55	11	26	.244	383	109	12	50	.285
Mark Brownson	Col. Springs	Col	170	51	7	32	.300	237	69	17	49	.291
Mike Buddie	Columbus	NYY	99	27	1	24	.273	200	53	1	44	.265
Mel Bunch	Tacoma	Sea	165	35	4	49	.212	302	77	7	68	.255
Terry Burrows	Rochester	Bal	60	8	3	13	.133	268	66	6	62	.246
Mike Busby	Memphis	StL	121	40	3	19	.331	192	72	9	31	.375
Mickey Callaway	Durham	TB	119	34	1	21	.286	192	52	4	35	.271
Dan Carlson	Tucson	Ari	154	51	10	27	.331	311	79	9	91	.254
Buddy Carlyle	Las Vegas	SD	234	63	9	52	.269	395	117	16	86	.296
Giovanni Carrara	Indianapolis	Cin	221	63	9	36	.285	364	81	11	78	.223
Carlos Castillo	Charlotte	CWS	218	67	14	39	.307	325	83	14	66	.255
Frank Castillo	Nashville	Pit	161	35	3	43	.217	318	104	12	47	.327
Mike Cather	Richmond	Atl	102	30	2	27	.294	158	41	2	33	.259
Anthony Chavez	Vancouver	Oak	103	25	3	25	.243	161	42	5	47	.261
Robinson Checo	Albuquerque	LA	88	25	6	27	.284	209	43	9	71	.206
Bruce Chen	Richmond	Atl	40	5	0	21	.125	251	68	10	69	.271
Jin Ho Cho	Pawtucket	Bos	158	38	6	27	.241	251	61	6	53	.243
Bobby Chouinard	Tucson	Ari	96	31	1	24	.323	142	39	7	39	.275
Chris Clemons	Tucson	Ari	84	28	5	22	.333	187	49	6	53	.262
Steve Connelly	Fresno	SF	123	41	3	17	.333	174	52	5	30	.299
Jim Converse	Louisville	Mil	94	27	5	16	.287	157	49	3	24	.312
Bryan Corey	Toledo	Det	101	24	3	15	.238	161	39	3	21	.242
Reid Cornelius	Calgary	Fla	261	63	1	54	.241	402	121	8	81	.301
Doug Creek	Iowa	ChC	95	22	4	36	.232	387	94	16	104	.243
Nelson Cruz	Toledo	Det	104	21	2	18	.202	118	26	3	23	.220
Chris Cumberland	Pawtucket	Bos	57	13	1	14	.228	172	43	3	21	.250
Pat Daneker	Charlotte	CWS	79	27	4	14	.342	129	37	6	22	.287
Doug Davis	Oklahoma	Tex	71	20	2	18	.282	221	57	2	56	.258
Kane Davis	Nashville	Pit	68	24	3	5	.353	133	41	5	26	.308
Javier de la Hoya	Rochester	Bal	124	27	4	29	.218	195	61	10	29	.313
Luis de los Santos	Columbus	NYY	115	42	7	16	.365	155	39	4	29	.252
Miguel del Toro	Fresno	SF	106	38	6	22	.358	175	38	5	49	.217
Shane Dennis	Las Vegas	SD	97	33	3	21	.340	369	107	16	83	.290
John DeSilva	Ottawa	Mon	121	22	1	23	.182	202	51	3	52	.252
Kris Detmers	Memphis	StL	103	29	5	22	.282	385	106	12	68	.275
Mike Diorio	New Orleans	Hou	104	38	4	9	.365	187	47	6	23	.251
Brendan Donnelly	Durham	TB	81	21	2	18	.259	173	40	4	52	.231
Octavio Dotel	Norfolk	NYM	121	23	3	43	.190	134	29	6	47	.216
Jim Dougherty	Nashville	Pit	58	17	2	14	.293	182	52	7	41	.286
Matt Drews	Toledo	Det	220	74	6	33	.336	332	97	15	37	.292
Travis Driskill	Buffalo	Cle	173	43	6	30	.249	340	103	15	60	.303
Al Drumheller	Las Vegas	SD	68	16	1	16	.235	167	56	6	30	.335
Mike Drumright	Toledo	Det	180	46	6	33	.256	280	70	11	43	.250
Radhames Dykhoff	Rochester	Bal	80	19	1	15	.237	222	50	10	42	.225
Derrin Ebert	Richmond	Atl	116	41	2	8	.353	473	132	11	74	.279
Dave Eiland	Durham	TB	86	26	3	21	.302	142	34	4	25	.239
Robert Ellis	New Orleans	Hou	210	71	8	36	.338	413	105	12	69	.254
Todd Erdos	Columbus	NYY	109	33	4	22	.303	128	37	6	31	.289
Horacio Estrada	Louisville	Mil	82	26	5	7	.317	408	102	16	105	.250
Dave Evans	Rochester	Bal	99	25	1	31	.253	171	45	10	34	.263
Keith Evans	Ottawa	Mon	184	53	8	27	.288	304	90	9	47	.296
Bryan Eversgerd	Memphis	StL	69	17	3	16	.246	178	39	6	30	.219
Scott Eyre	Charlotte	CWS	78	21	[illegible]	10	[illegible]	[illegible]	[illegible]	1	11	[illegible]
Steve Falteisek	Louisville	Mil	103	38	5	14	.369	207	60	8	20	.290
Mike Farmer	Col. Springs	Col	95	31	4	17	.326	379	139	20	58	.367
Jared Fernandez	Pawtucket	Bos	230	53	7	39	.230	401	119	13	37	.297
Nelson Figueroa	Tucson	Ari	176	51	5	36	.290	315	77	11	70	.244
Huck Flener	Tacoma	Sea	45	16	1	11	.356	214	56	5	37	.262
Ben Ford	Columbus	NYY	105	42	3	13	.400	162	27	1	27	.167
Tom Fordham	Charlotte	CWS	107	30	7	25	.280	356	114	18	76	.320
Ryan Franklin	Tacoma	Sea	180	52	4	33	.289	346	90	13	61	.260
Aaron Fultz	Fresno	SF	142	34	9	38	.239	389	107	23	113	.275
Chris Fussell	Omaha	KC	119	31	5	38	.261	182	35	6	42	.192
Mike Fyhrie	Edmonton	Ana	133	26	5	40	.195	280	64	3	73	.229
Eddie Gaillard	Durham	TB	83	22	5	22	.265	169	45	1	45	.266
Steve Gajkowski	Iowa	ChC	90	24	4	19	.267	214	55	4	45	.257

			vs Left					vs Right				
Player	Team	Org	AB	H	HR	SO	Avg	AB	H	HR	SO	Avg
Gus Gandarillas	Salt Lake	Min	81	18	5	19	.222	176	55	3	28	.313
Keith Glauber	Indianapolis	Cin	125	39	5	13	.312	146	45	3	38	.308
Gary Glover	Syracuse	Tor	127	40	6	23	.315	181	53	4	34	.293
Ryan Glynn	Oklahoma	Tex	109	29	1	11	.266	230	52	6	44	.226
Jeff Granger	Louisville	Mil	87	24	1	22	.276	149	48	7	28	.322
Beiker Graterol	Toledo	Det	133	37	4	18	.278	172	52	6	29	.302
Tyler Green	Scranton-WB	Phi	71	25	2	13	.352	145	53	6	18	.366
Rick Greene	Indianapolis	Cin	109	24	0	21	.220	176	54	3	19	.307
Jason Grilli	Fresno	SF	227	70	10	42	.308	361	110	19	61	.305
Mark Guerra	Norfolk	NYM	123	34	2	20	.276	223	56	3	50	.251
Luther Hackman	Col. Springs	Col	174	47	4	40	.270	214	59	3	48	.276
Chris Haney	Buffalo	Cle	40	10	1	5	.250	175	40	3	32	.229
Erik Hanson	Calgary	Fla	166	52	7	37	.313	256	74	8	48	.289
Denny Harriger	Indianapolis	Cin	264	69	6	43	.261	406	114	9	67	.281
Derek Hasselhoff	Charlotte	CWS	95	39	3	17	.411	190	44	4	48	.232
Ryan Hawblitzel	Edmonton	Ana	104	29	3	14	.279	159	52	5	23	.327
Mike Heathcott	Charlotte	CWS	219	59	3	36	.269	335	118	11	41	.352
Rick Heiserman	Memphis	StL	80	25	4	16	.313	159	42	3	41	.264
Rod Henderson	Louisville	Mil	188	56	12	23	.298	281	63	8	52	.224
Oscar Henriquez	Norfolk	NYM	76	14	2	28	.184	130	40	6	37	.308
Matt Herges	Albuquerque	LA	130	39	4	23	.300	367	96	13	65	.262
Erik Hiljus	Toledo	Det	84	23	1	31	.274	130	26	4	42	.200
Brett Hinchliffe	Tacoma	Sea	170	48	3	32	.282	335	93	14	75	.278
Kevin Hodges	Tacoma	Sea	161	52	5	15	.323	268	70	4	43	.261
David Holdridge	Tacoma	Sea	81	26	0	20	.321	179	41	3	48	.229
Mark Holzemer	Col. Springs	Col	78	26	3	18	.333	156	51	7	31	.327
Kevin Jarvis	Vancouver	Oak	139	31	1	22	.223	268	79	13	42	.295
Ryan Jensen	Fresno	SF	236	70	8	51	.297	365	90	9	99	.247
Barry Johnson	Scranton-WB	Phi	204	68	5	31	.333	342	89	7	57	.260
Jonathan Johnson	Oklahoma	Tex	85	25	2	14	.294	193	66	7	24	.342
Mike Johnson	Ottawa	Mon	231	68	13	54	.294	363	106	11	66	.292
Mike Judd	Albuquerque	LA	147	41	9	45	.279	302	91	13	77	.301
Jeff Juden	Columbus	NYY	271	80	13	59	.295	391	84	11	92	.215
Jarod Juelsgaard	Iowa	ChC	124	43	3	20	.347	208	49	9	34	.236
Bill King	Vancouver	Oak	136	24	3	29	.176	245	81	8	31	.331
Scott Klingenbeck	Indianapolis	Cin	119	36	1	23	.303	171	53	7	30	.310
Brandon Knight	Oklahoma	Tex	242	59	5	36	.244	403	114	18	61	.283
Brandon Kolb	Las Vegas	SD	79	24	3	16	.304	166	48	0	47	.289
Dan Kolb	Oklahoma	Tex	[illegible]	[illegible]	2	9	[illegible]	139	40	2	12	.288
Rick Krivda	Omaha	KC	100	30	3	17	.300	390	124	14	53	.318
Jeff Kubenka	Albuquerque	LA	60	14	3	15	.233	192	46	3	48	.240
Tim Kubinski	Vancouver	Oak	64	20	0	16	.313	213	50	2	40	.235
Kerry Lacy	Iowa	ChC	107	24	2	22	.224	260	81	3	47	.312
Brett Laxton	Vancouver	Oak	247	72	5	48	.291	351	86	3	64	.245
Richie Lewis	Norfolk	NYM	202	60	7	38	.297	278	68	12	63	.245
Ted Lilly	Ottawa	Mon	55	16	4	20	.291	280	65	8	58	.232
Mike Lincoln	Salt Lake	Min	81	26	6	17	.321	164	56	6	22	.341
Doug Linton	Rochester	Bal	216	61	7	46	.282	249	59	6	51	.237
Felipe Lira	Toledo	Det	221	76	10	23	.344	260	87	15	47	.335
Kevin Lomon	Edmonton	Ana	183	70	11	37	.383	328	100	12	54	.305
Brian Looney	Toledo	Det	84	20	4	20	.238	183	50	6	44	.273
Johan Lopez	Norfolk	NYM	150	41	5	27	.273	236	57	8	57	.242
Andrew Lorraine	Iowa	ChC	118	21	2	29	.178	439	128	14	67	.292
Kevin Lovingier	Memphis	StL	71	16	2	14	.225	225	50	6	52	.222
Eric Ludwick	Calgary	Fla	92	26	3	22	.283	136	39	2	39	.287
Larry Luebbers	Memphis	StL	206	58	8	34	.282	293	76	7	50	.259
Mark Lukasiewicz	Syracuse	Tor	94	26	5	19	.277	294	83	15	58	.282
Calvin Maduro	Rochester	Bal	256	69	10	59	.270	405	110	13	90	.272
Ron Mahay	Vancouver	Oak	98	33	2	15	.337	317	83	10	58	.262
Jim Mann	Syracuse	Tor	90	22	4	22	.244	154	31	7	50	.201
Tim Manwiller	Vancouver	Oak	89	23	3	11	.258	134	49	6	19	.366
Damaso Marte	Tacoma	Sea	56	14	4	14	.250	235	65	9	45	.277
Jason McCommon	Rochester	Bal	189	52	6	28	.275	303	91	15	40	.300
Mike McMullen	Fresno	SF	88	24	2	15	.273	149	28	3	41	.188
Brian McNichol	Iowa	ChC	153	49	5	37	.320	496	145	16	83	.292
Paul Menhart	Edmonton	Ana	135	36	4	19	.267	198	70	6	32	.354
Jose Mercedes	Las Vegas	SD	163	51	8	19	.313	312	89	8	51	.285
Chris Michalak	Tucson	Ari	100	21	3	27	.210	247	71	6	39	.287
Bob Milacki	Nashville	Pit	164	41	2	31	.250	283	89	12	48	.314
Wade Miller	New Orleans	Hou	211	45	6	52	.213	417	111	10	83	.266
Blas Minor	Louisville	Mil	167	39	5	26	.234	260	79	8	51	.304
Scott Mitchell	Ottawa	Mon	84	29	6	11	.345	166	49	5	17	.295
Greg Mix	Pawtucket	Bos	126	45	6	18	.357	209	44	3	61	.211
Doug Mlicki	Memphis	StL	80	24	4	6	.300	189	54	12	20	.286
Gabe Molina	Rochester	Bal	82	16	2	18	.195	131	29	1	40	.221
Norm Montoya	Edmonton	Ana	90	33	2	11	.367	180	59	3	19	.328
Eric Moody	Oklahoma	Tex	83	28	2	9	.337	203	50	3	22	.246
Mark Mulder	Vancouver	Oak	97	26	0	20	.268	409	126	13	61	.308
Scott Mullen	Omaha	KC	139	44	8	34	.317	339	106	16	53	.313
Bobby Munoz	Durham	TB	88	17	2	20	.193	126	38	3	30	.302
Peter Munro	Syracuse	Tor	105	25	3	27	.238	167	45	3	41	.269
Dan Murray	Norfolk	NYM	250	68	11	36	.272	311	81	11	60	.260
Heath Murray	Las Vegas	SD	49	17	1	7	.347	279	82	4	58	.294
Joe Nathan	Fresno	SF	112	26	5	29	.232	167	42	6	53	.251
Alan Newman	Durham	TB	98	19	1	32	.194	191	40	1	44	.209
Chris Nichting	Columbus	NYY	193	54	10	50	.280	303	81	12	60	.267
Phillip Norton	Iowa	ChC	88	27	3	20	.307	233	71	17	41	.305
Mark Nussbeck	Memphis	StL	152	56	12	23	.368	278	89	11	59	.320
Ryan Nye	Scranton-WB	Phi	97	27	4	20	.278	161	42	4	43	.261
Tomokazu Ohka	Pawtucket	Bos	108	26	1	37	.241	153	34	4	26	.222
Kevin Ohme	Salt Lake	Min	88	24	2	19	.273	234	70	6	29	.299
Kirt Ojala	Calgary	Fla	58	22	2	8	.379	268	88	10	46	.328
Jason Olsen	Charlotte	CWS	104	39	5	14	.375	152	45	7	35	.296
Eddie Oropesa	Fresno	SF	78	17	4	16	.218	326	96	11	45	.294
Ramon Ortiz	Edmonton	Ana	76	16	4	22	.211	127	30	3	42	.236
Gavin Osteen	Albuquerque	LA	87	22	1	17	.253	335	105	9	48	.313

Triple-A Pitching vs. Lefthanded and Righthanded Batters

Player	Team	Org	vs Left					vs Right				
			AB	H	HR	SO	Avg	AB	H	HR	SO	Avg
Vicente Padilla	Tucson	Ari	142	47	1	17	.331	224	60	5	41	.268
Bronswell Patrick	Fresno	SF	251	70	13	58	.279	413	124	20	84	.300
Dave Pavlas	Columbus	NYY	95	22	1	18	.232	147	47	4	31	.320
Dario Perez	Calgary	Fla	224	72	14	36	.321	291	78	8	30	.268
Matt Perisho	Oklahoma	Tex	111	29	3	31	.261	482	131	11	119	.272
Kyle Peterson	Louisville	Mil	172	39	6	45	.227	240	51	7	50	.213
Ricky Pickett	Oklahoma	Tex	47	14	2	12	.298	184	63	10	43	.342
Rafael Pina	Rochester	Bal	161	45	5	29	.280	273	68	10	59	.249
Erik Plantenberg	Durham	TB	65	16	1	13	.246	263	84	19	59	.319
Lou Pote	Edmonton	Ana	235	63	8	58	.268	355	108	11	60	.304
Jeremy Powell	Ottawa	Mon	129	35	2	30	.271	206	50	3	42	.243
Eddie Priest	Indianapolis	Cin	52	13	1	10	.250	223	73	9	25	.327
Ruben Quevedo	Richmond	Atl	179	38	7	47	.212	226	74	19	51	.327
Rob Radlosky	Salt Lake	Min	149	41	6	24	.275	241	57	6	44	.237
Brady Raggio	Oklahoma	Tex	228	84	6	28	.368	437	109	10	86	.249
Jason Rakers	Buffalo	Cle	199	53	6	42	.266	334	98	11	43	.293
Hector Ramirez	Louisville	Mil	135	36	3	15	.267	222	55	10	40	.248
Roberto Ramirez	Col. Springs	Col	42	8	1	14	.190	195	56	5	41	.287
Robert Ramsay	Pawtucket	Bos	80	23	3	19	.287	365	91	18	60	.249
Fred Rath	Salt Lake	Min	98	38	3	10	.388	214	50	6	26	.234
Gary Rath	Salt Lake	Min	77	18	2	23	.234	335	111	10	44	.331
Jon Ratliff	Richmond	Atl	237	68	8	54	.287	367	86	16	75	.234
Mark Redman	Salt Lake	Min	104	26	1	27	.250	415	115	11	87	.277
Brandon Reed	Toledo	Det	151	41	1	26	.272	211	60	5	33	.284
Dan Reichert	Omaha	KC	187	49	6	50	.262	217	43	3	73	.198
Paul Rigdon	Buffalo	Cle	142	37	4	25	.261	275	77	7	35	.280
Dan Rios	Omaha	KC	128	39	2	11	.305	235	72	11	33	.306
Todd Rizzo	Charlotte	CWS	84	20	1	14	.238	180	48	4	32	.267
Willis Roberts	Toledo	Det	147	44	5	19	.299	218	68	5	33	.312
Nerio Rodriguez	Syracuse	Tor	263	65	4	65	.247	357	96	13	72	.269
Mike Romano	Syracuse	Tor	252	64	7	42	.254	404	96	14	62	.238
Glendon Rusch	Omaha	KC	111	37	2	22	.333	355	106	8	80	.299
Jason Ryan	Salt Lake	Min	79	18	5	15	.228	132	39	3	19	.295
Matt Ryan	Nashville	Pit	107	30	1	23	.280	206	57	6	29	.277
Erik Sabel	Tucson	Ari	86	22	0	15	.256	189	57	4	23	.302
A.J. Sager	Indianapolis	Cin	77	26	4	6	.338	143	53	1	12	.371
Matt Saier	Omaha	KC	97	33	5	15	.340	148	36	8	29	.243
Mike Saipe	Col. Springs	Col	72	21	4	12	.292	135	41	7	27	.304
Rich Sauveur	Nashville	Pit	98	17	0	34	.173	182	52	6	34	.286
Bob Scanlan	New Orleans	Hou	242	83	7	31	.343	422	125	5	47	.296
Aaron Scheffer	Tacoma	Sea	69	14	3	20	.203	149	33	3	42	.221
Darryl Scott	Scranton-WB	Phi	143	33	4	26	.231	258	67	7	65	.260
Chris Seelbach	Richmond	Atl	75	20	1	15	.267	142	31	3	33	.218
Stephen Shoemaker	Col. Springs	Col	134	39	5	23	.291	189	61	3	23	.323
Anthony Shumaker	Scranton-WB	Phi	78	22	0	14	.282	282	97	15	35	.344
Brian Sikorski	New Orleans	Hou	201	54	9	31	.269	422	115	16	91	.273
Joe Slusarski	New Orleans	Hou	89	20	1	20	.225	156	51	4	20	.327
Aaron Small	Durham	TB	212	75	11	16	.354	283	81	8	47	.286

Player	Team	Org	vs Left					vs Right				
			AB	H	HR	SO	Avg	AB	H	HR	SO	Avg
Mark Small	Ottawa	Mon	87	32	3	17	.368	185	53	6	26	.286
Chuck Smith	Oklahoma	Tex	95	23	2	26	.242	213	50	5	50	.235
Dan Smith	Ottawa	Mon	112	27	4	21	.241	149	34	3	38	.228
Pete Smith	Memphis	StL	166	40	4	27	.241	278	90	10	55	.324
Matt Snyder	Rochester	Bal	133	37	6	22	.278	206	58	8	37	.282
Steve Soderstrom	Fresno	SF	129	32	3	32	.248	175	58	13	26	.331
Clint Sodowsky	Memphis	StL	118	35	3	21	.297	191	50	11	31	.262
Stan Spencer	Las Vegas	SD	84	25	1	21	.298	140	44	5	29	.314
Kennie Steenstra	Tacoma	Sea	75	21	0	12	.280	130	39	5	12	.300
Blake Stein	Vancouver	Oak	154	35	4	46	.227	249	59	5	65	.237
Scott Stewart	Norfolk	NYM	104	30	3	26	.288	292	79	6	59	.271
Ricky Stone	Albuquerque	LA	251	80	6	51	.319	419	125	17	81	.298
Jim Stoops	Col. Springs	Col	111	36	5	18	.324	217	57	6	39	.263
Everett Stull	Richmond	Atl	194	45	6	54	.232	317	79	11	72	.249
Tanyon Sturtze	Charlotte	CWS	172	38	4	41	.221	216	45	3	66	.208
Brendan Sullivan	Las Vegas	SD	87	35	4	15	.402	187	53	2	35	.283
Ramon Tatis	Durham	TB	105	20	1	21	.190	503	158	18	76	.314
Dave Telgheder	Buffalo	Cle	161	41	1	29	.255	257	68	7	31	.265
Jay Tessmer	Columbus	NYY	80	21	0	13	.262	134	31	4	29	.231
Dave Tuttle	Tucson	Ari	116	33	4	20	.284	208	67	4	35	.322
Todd Van Poppel	Nashville	Pit	232	63	7	53	.272	406	110	16	104	.271
Ben VanRyn	Charlotte	CWS	87	22	4	20	.253	188	61	5	34	.324
Ismael Villegas	Richmond	Atl	135	39	1	16	.289	215	54	6	45	.251
Terrell Wade	Durham	TB	88	36	5	13	.409	322	104	16	48	.323
Paul Wagner	Buffalo	Cle	179	50	5	36	.279	316	73	6	59	.231
Pete Walker	Col. Springs	Col	73	22	3	16	.301	166	42	6	41	.253
Derek Wallace	Norfolk	NYM	70	18	2	16	.257	135	35	4	22	.259
Kent Wallace	New Orleans	Hou	93	28	5	9	.301	138	33	4	34	.239
Scott Watkins	Iowa	ChC	77	20	2	21	.260	169	51	9	33	.302
Ben Weber	Fresno	SF	114	26	4	17	.228	205	52	2	50	.254
Mike Welch	Scranton-WB	Phi	110	36	5	13	.327	154	42	3	15	.273
Dan Wheeler	Durham	TB	140	55	8	20	.393	196	48	8	38	.245
Matt Whiteside	Las Vegas	SD	121	35	7	31	.289	240	64	6	45	.251
Jeff Williams	Albuquerque	LA	100	34	4	24	.340	390	117	10	62	.300
Shad Williams	Edmonton	Ana	91	26	3	9	.286	210	54	6	30	.257
Bob Wolcott	Pawtucket	Bos	198	50	7	33	.253	293	81	10	36	.276
Randy Wolf	Scranton-WB	Phi	73	16	3	21	.219	223	57	5	51	.256
Bryan Wolff	Las Vegas	SD	249	72	7	52	.289	440	127	15	99	.289
Brad Woodall	Iowa	ChC	34	8	0	12	.235	182	59	9	29	.324
Jamey Wright	Col. Springs	Col	182	50	4	30	.275	228	83	9	45	.364
Ed Yarnall	Columbus	NYY	127	28	2	51	.220	413	108	3	95	.262
Jay Yennaco	Syracuse	Tor	141	52	5	14	.369	185	55	6	31	.297
Dave Zancanaro	Columbus	NYY	59	12	0	13	.203	248	73	11	32	.294

Triple-A Pitching at Home and on the Road

			Home					Road				
Player	Team	Org	G	IP	W	L	ERA	G	IP	W	L	ERA
Jimmy Anderson	Nashville	Pit	12	78.0	6	2	3.46	9	55.2	5	0	4.37
Rick Ankiel	Memphis	StL	8	46.0	4	1	2.74	8	42.0	3	2	3.64
Brian Barber	Omaha	KC	9	59.0	4	1	3.97	10	61.0	5	4	5.16
Brian Barnes	Memphis	StL	19	46.0	3	1	5.09	17	43.2	1	2	5.98
Manuel Barrios	Indianapolis	Cin	25	53.0	1	5	6.28	24	37.0	1	2	3.89
Jose Bautista	Ottawa	Mon	17	54.2	4	2	5.76	19	56.1	3	3	5.11
Kevin Beirne	Charlotte	CWS	10	58.2	3	0	4.45	10	54.0	2	5	6.50
Joel Bennett	Scranton-WB	Phi	8	44.2	3	3	5.84	12	82.0	7	1	3.95
Shayne Bennett	Ottawa	Mon	19	46.0	1	5	5.48	19	43.0	2	4	4.60
Brent Billingsley	Calgary	Fla	10	55.0	0	6	7.36	11	61.0	2	3	3.98
Kurt Bogott	Syracuse	Tor	23	46.2	6	1	4.05	23	39.0	2	5	5.31
Rod Bolton	Scranton-WB	Phi	13	81.1	8	3	4.32	11	71.0	3	7	3.30
Dave Borkowski	Toledo	Det	8	52.0	2	2	3.63	11	74.0	4	6	3.41
Joe Borowski	Louisville	Mil	30	46.2	4	1	4.44	28	42.0	2	1	6.64
Shawn Boskie	Albuquerque	LA	9	53.0	2	5	4.92	6	33.0	2	3	7.36
Heath Bost	Col. Springs	Col	17	50.0	3	3	6.48	21	36.0	2	1	4.25
Shane Bowers	Salt Lake	Min	15	59.2	3	2	6.64	16	62.0	4	2	4.79
Jason Boyd	Tucson	Ari	27	49.0	5	0	2.57	22	31.0	1	5	6.97
Ryan Bradley	Columbus	NYY	14	69.1	3	8	6.10	15	75.0	2	4	6.36
Jim Brower	Buffalo	Cle	14	84.0	5	7	4.71	13	75.1	6	4	4.78
Mark Brownson	Col. Springs	Col	8	46.2	3	2	7.52	9	56.0	3	4	5.14
Mel Bunch	Tacoma	Sea	11	63.2	4	2	4.24	10	61.0	6	0	1.92
Terry Burrows	Rochester	Bal	11	65.0	1	4	2.49	6	27.2	0	2	7.48
Mickey Callaway	Durham	TB	8	45.0	3	0	4.40	7	36.0	4	1	4.00
Dan Carlson	Tucson	Ari	16	60.2	2	5	4.90	16	57.0	2	4	6.00
Buddy Carlyle	Las Vegas	SD	11	68.0	3	5	5.03	14	92.0	8	3	4.79
Giovanni Carrara	Indianapolis	Cin	20	73.1	4	4	3.56	19	84.0	8	3	3.43
Carlos Castillo	Charlotte	CWS	13	84.0	5	4	5.79	7	52.0	4	2	4.15
Frank Castillo	Nashville	Pit	7	47.0	5	1	3.45	12	72.0	2	4	5.50
Jin Ho Cho	Pawtucket	Bos	7	49.0	4	1	2.02	10	60.2	5	2	4.60
Reid Cornelius	Calgary	Fla	12	77.0	2	3	5.14	15	95.1	8	3	3.97
Doug Creek	Iowa	ChC	12	56.2	4	0	3.81	13	74.0	3	3	3.77
Javier de la Hoya	Rochester	Bal	7	39.2	0	2	6.13	7	41.2	4	1	4.10
Shane Dennis	Las Vegas	SD	18	62.2	1	5	5.46	16	53.0	2	5	5.77
John DeSilva	Ottawa	Mon	11	43.2	1	1	3.09	11	46.2	3	0	2.70
Kris Detmers	Memphis	StL	8	48.0	3	2	4.13	15	77.0	3	6	5.73
Matt Drews	Toledo	Det	15	80.1	2	7	6.50	13	55.0	0	7	10.96
Travis Driskill	Buffalo	Cle	14	58.0	3	5	4.81	17	74.0	6	3	4.86
Mike Drumright	Toledo	Det	9	52.2	2	0	3.93	12	68.0	4	7	7.54
Radhames Dykhoff	Rochester	Bal	21	39.2	1	0	4.31	26	42.2	1	0	3.59
Derrin Ebert	Richmond	Atl	13	79.0	4	3	3.99	12	71.0	4	4	4.69
Robert Ellis	New Orleans	Hou	14	83.0	3	1	5.53	13	72.0	4	2	5.38
Horacio Estrada	Louisville	Mil	13	68.0	4	2	5.82	12	63.0	2	4	5.57
Keith Evans	Ottawa	Mon	12	58.2	1	6	4.45	12	63.0	1	7	5.14
Mike Farmer	Col. Springs	Col	13	55.0	4	4	9.16	12	58.0	4	6	6.67
Jared Fernandez	Pawtucket	Bos	13	79.0	7	5	5.47	14	84.0	5	4	3.11
Nelson Figueroa	Tucson	Ari	12	63.2	5	3	4.38	12	64.0	6	3	3.52
Tom Fordham	Charlotte	CWS	15	56.0	1	2	6.75	14	56.0	3	5	7.88
Ryan Franklin	Tacoma	Sea	16	73.0	3	4	3.33	13	62.0	3	5	6.39
Aaron Fultz	Fresno	SF	16	57.2	4	2	5.62	21	79.1	5	6	4.54
Chris Fussell	Omaha	KC	7	44.0	5	2	1.43	7	37.0	5	1	6.08
Mike Fyhrie	Edmonton	Ana	10	66.0	6	2	2.32	9	48.0	3	3	5.06
Ryan Glynn	Oklahoma	Tex	8	46.0	3	1	3.72	8	44.0	3	1	3.07
Jason Grilli	Fresno	SF	16	84.0	4	4	6.21	11	57.0	4	6	6.16
Mark Guerra	Norfolk	NYM	26	35.2	1	2	4.29	37	53.0	7	1	2.04
Luther Hackman	Col. Springs	Col	6	39.0	4	2	3.92	9	61.2	3	4	3.65
Erik Hanson	Calgary	Fla	15	62.2	3	5	6.61	9	45.2	2	4	4.93
Denny Harriger	Indianapolis	Cin	16	107.1	9	2	3.02	11	64.1	5	4	5.88
Mike Heathcott	Charlotte	CWS	15	60.0	5	2	4.35	17	79.0	5	6	5.81
Rod Henderson	Louisville	Mil	14	57.2	4	4	5.46	14	63.0	3	7	7.14
Matt Herges	Albuquerque	LA	9	57.0	3	2	4.58	12	74.0	5	1	4.86
Brett Hinchliffe	Tacoma	Sea	11	65.1	4	5	5.79	10	65.0	5	2	4.57
Kevin Hodges	Tacoma	Sea	11	65.2	2	4	3.56	8	44.1	2	2	5.28
Kevin Jarvis	Vancouver	Oak	8	42.0	4	0	3.00	9	61.0	6	2	3.98
Ryan Jensen	Fresno	SF	11	69.1	7	4	4.93	16	86.1	4	6	5.32
Barry Johnson	Scranton-WB	Phi	12	61.0	2	3	4.72	19	75.0	4	7	5.28
Mike Johnson	Ottawa	Mon	14	65.0	1	6	7.06	14	82.0	5	6	4.06
Mike Judd	Albuquerque	LA	11	55.0	4	3	7.04	10	55.2	4	4	6.31
Jeff Juden	Columbus	NYY	11	74.1	6	4	4.72	16	101.1	5	8	6.22
Jarod Juelsgaard	Iowa	ChC	10	36.0	2	3	5.50	13	47.0	2	4	5.74
Bill King	Vancouver	Oak	18	45.0	6	2	2.40	27	53.0	3	4	4.42
Brandon Knight	Oklahoma	Tex	13	75.1	6	1	5.02	14	87.1	3	7	4.84
Rick Krivda	Omaha	KC	9	54.0	2	3	4.33	12	61.0	4	5	6.93
Kerry Lacy	Iowa	ChC	23	40.0	1	6	6.98	26	52.0	2	2	4.33
Brett Laxton	Vancouver	Oak	15	108.0	11	2	1.50	10	53.0	2	6	7.47
Richie Lewis	Norfolk	NYM	10	60.2	4	4	6.08	10	62.0	3	4	4.06
Ted Lilly	Ottawa	Mon	8	45.0	4	1	3.60	8	44.0	4	4	4.09
Doug Linton	Rochester	Bal	9	59.2	4	2	2.87	9	58.2	3	3	4.45
Felipe Lira	Toledo	Det	15	50.0	1	5	7.02	15	64.0	1	6	6.47
Kevin Lomon	Edmonton	Ana	9	52.0	4	3	6.23	14	71.1	3	5	5.43
Johan Lopez	Norfolk	NYM	18	53.0	2	3	3.91	15	49.0	1	2	4.41
Andrew Lorraine	Iowa	ChC	10	69.0	6	2	3.00	12	74.0	3	6	4.38
[illegible]	Memphis	StL	10	70.0	7	0	[illegible]	6	33.2	0	1	3.02
Mark Lukasiewicz	Syracuse	Tor	20	53.2	1	1	4.70	17	44.0	3	3	6.14
Calvin Maduro	Rochester	Bal	13	82.0	6	5	4.06	16	86.1	5	6	3.96
Ron Mahay	Vancouver	Oak	16	53.0	1	0	3.40	16	53.2	6	2	5.20
Jason McCommon	Rochester	Bal	16	72.0	3	8	5.88	13	52.0	4	2	3.81
Brian McNichol	Iowa	ChC	14	94.0	4	5	3.64	14	67.0	6	6	8.33
Paul Menhart	Edmonton	Ana	9	44.2	3	4	7.46	8	36.1	2	1	3.96
Jose Mercedes	Las Vegas	SD	8	45.0	0	6	5.60	7	43.0	2	0	2.93
Chris Michalak	Tucson	Ari	22	45.1	2	0	3.97	23	47.0	4	0	4.60
Bob Milacki	Nashville	Pit	10	54.0	3	5	4.83	12	57.0	3	3	4.89
Wade Miller	New Orleans	Hou	12	75.0	5	4	4.08	14	87.1	6	5	4.64
Blas Minor	Louisville	Mil	10	52.0	3	2	4.85	11	56.0	1	2	4.34
Greg Mix	Pawtucket	Bos	23	38.2	1	1	3.96	23	46.2	3	3	3.47
Mark Mulder	Vancouver	Oak	12	72.0	4	5	3.63	10	56.0	2	2	4.66
Scott Mullen	Omaha	KC	11	63.2	4	4	7.35	9	55.2	2	3	5.01
Dan Murray	Norfolk	NYM	13	78.0	8	3	3.00	16	67.0	4	7	7.25
Heath Murray	Las Vegas	SD	7	38.2	2	1	3.49	8	43.2	3	3	4.95
Alan Newman	Durham	TB	31	50.2	6	0	1.60	19	29.2	4	0	3.34
Chris Nichting	Columbus	NYY	11	64.0	4	3	5.20	14	63.2	4	2	5.37
Mark Nussbeck	Memphis	StL	13	44.2	3	4	7.66	23	57.0	3	6	8.68
Kevin Ohme	Salt Lake	Min	30	46.0	1	1	4.30	21	36.0	4	2	3.25
Eddie Oropesa	Fresno	SF	9	48.0	3	0	3.94	12	54.0	3	5	5.67
Gavin Osteen	Albuquerque	LA	20	65.0	3	5	5.40	14	38.0	3	3	4.74
Vicente Padilla	Tucson	Ari	8	43.0	2	3	4.40	10	50.2	5	1	3.20
Bronswell Patrick	Fresno	SF	16	95.1	7	7	5.10	12	68.1	7	4	4.61
Dario Perez	Calgary	Fla	15	74.0	5	6	5.72	13	58.0	2	7	5.74
Matt Perisho	Oklahoma	Tex	15	86.1	8	4	4.38	12	69.1	7	3	4.93
Kyle Peterson	Louisville	Mil	8	45.2	3	2	3.35	10	63.0	4	4	3.71
Rafael Pina	Rochester	Bal	26	65.1	4	7	4.41	22	45.2	4	3	4.34
Erik Plantenberg	Durham	TB	20	38.0	3	2	6.16	20	42.2	4	3	5.70
Lou Pote	Edmonton	Ana	13	85.0	4	6	3.81	11	64.1	3	3	5.46
Jeremy Powell	Ottawa	Mon	8	48.0	1	3	2.63	8	43.0	2	2	3.35
Ruben Quevedo	Richmond	Atl	10	50.2	3	2	5.15	11	55.0	3	3	5.56
Rob Radlosky	Salt Lake	Min	8	38.0	3	2	3.55	14	63.0	5	2	4.14
Brady Raggio	Oklahoma	Tex	15	101.1	6	3	3.29	15	66.0	0	8	8.05
Jason Rakers	Buffalo	Cle	9	58.2	3	2	3.38	14	73.0	4	6	6.16
Hector Ramirez	Louisville	Mil	33	58.0	3	2	3.10	25	36.2	0	1	4.91
Robert Ramsay	Pawtucket	Bos	10	63.2	3	4	4.38	10	50.2	3	2	6.57
Fred Rath	Salt Lake	Min	32	46.2	4	3	4.24	24	36.0	3	2	3.50
Gary Rath	Salt Lake	Min	9	42.0	2	3	7.50	11	57.0	1	5	4.26
Jon Ratliff	Richmond	Atl	16	95.0	2	5	4.26	11	62.2	3	7	4.74
Mark Redman	Salt Lake	Min	15	84.1	7	6	3.74	9	49.0	2	3	7.35
Brandon Reed	Toledo	Det	27	55.2	5	3	3.72	17	35.2	3	2	4.79
Dan Reichert	Omaha	KC	8	57.0	4	0	3.47	9	54.0	5	2	4.00
Paul Rigdon	Buffalo	Cle	11	62.2	4	3	4.02	8	40.2	3	1	5.31
Dan Rios	Omaha	KC	27	47.2	8	0	4.34	20	41.0	2	4	8.12
Willis Roberts	Toledo	Det	16	42.2	1	5	8.23	15	49.0	4	3	4.59
Nerio Rodriguez	Syracuse	Tor	14	74.0	5	5	5.23	13	88.1	5	3	3.97
Mike Romano	Syracuse	Tor	14	78.0	6	3	4.85	15	96.1	6	5	3.55
Glendon Rusch	Omaha	KC	10	55.2	1	4	4.69	10	58.0	3	3	4.19
Bob Scanlan	New Orleans	Hou	13	83.0	5	5	3.47	15	80.0	3	1	7.88
Darryl Scott	Scranton-WB	Phi	32	63.0	6	3	2.29	25	42.0	1	3	6.86
Stephen Shoemaker	Col. Springs	Col	9	46.0	3	3	7.04	7	35.0	1	3	4.63
Anthony Shumaker	Scranton-WB	Phi	5	32.0	0	2	5.34	9	57.0	3	3	6.00
Brian Sikorski	New Orleans	Hou	14	77.0	3	5	5.03	14	81.0	4	5	4.89
Aaron Small	Durham	TB	16	59.2	2	5	7.39	16	60.1	3	2	6.41
Chuck Smith	Oklahoma	Tex	18	50.0	5	0	1.98	14	35.0	0	4	4.37
Pete Smith	Memphis	StL	11	50.1	4	3	5.72	10	59.0	2	5	3.97
Matt Snyder	Rochester	Bal	21	35.0	1	2	5.14	27	49.0	5	4	5.33
Clint Sodowsky	Memphis	StL	11	48.0	3	2	3.75	8	32.0	1	3	6.47
Blake Stein	Vancouver	Oak	7	42.2	0	1	3.59	12	67.0	4	1	4.43
Scott Stewart	Norfolk	NYM	15	67.0	3	3	4.16	20	32.0	3	1	5.06
Ricky Stone	Albuquerque	LA	16	102.1	2	7	5.28	11	64.0	4	3	5.91
Jim Stoops	Col. Springs	Col	28	45.0	3	2	4.40	27	43.2	0	5	5.98
Everett Stull	Richmond	Atl	16	76.0	4	5	4.86	14	62.2	4	3	4.02
Tanyon Sturtze	Charlotte	CWS	17	46.0	5	3	4.11	16	58.0	4	1	4.03
Ramon Tatis	Durham	TB	14	75.1	6	4	6.09	14	79.1	6	4	4.99
Dave Telgheder	Buffalo	Cle	14	54.0	1	6	4.33	15	53.0	7	2	3.57
Dave Tuttle	Tucson	Ari	21	49.2	1	3	6.34	14	34.2	1	2	6.75
Todd Van Poppel	Nashville	Pit	15	89.0	5	4	5.76	12	74.1	5	2	4.00
Ismael Villegas	Richmond	Atl	25	54.0	4	1	3.67	19	38.0	2	6	5.45
Terrell Wade	Durham	TB	16	52.0	0	2	7.44	18	46.0	1	5	11.93
Paul Wagner	Buffalo	Cle	10	53.0	3	2	3.23	13	76.1	5	2	4.24
Ben Weber	Fresno	SF	25	43.0	1	3	3.56	26	43.0	1	1	3.14
Dan Wheeler	Durham	TB	6	39.0	3	3	4.62	8	43.0	4	2	5.23
Matt Whiteside	Las Vegas	SD	28	48.2	5	1	4.44	19	41.0	4	4	5.93
Jeff Williams	Albuquerque	LA	21	54.0	4	4	5.33	21	71.1	5	3	4.79
Bob Wolcott	Pawtucket	Bos	14	67.1	3	6	2.94	12	57.2	3	7	4.37
Bryan Wolff	Las Vegas	SD	14	90.0	5	6	4.60	14	87.1	3	6	4.74
Jamey Wright	Col. Springs	Col	8	48.2	2	5	5.55	9	51.2	3	2	7.32
Ed Yarnall	Columbus	NYY	13	89.0	8	3	2.63	10	56.0	5	1	4.82
Jay Yennaco	Syracuse	Tor	8	45.0	1	2	5.40	7	35.0	1	4	8.74

Double-A Batting vs. Lefthanded and Righthanded Pitchers

			vs Left					vs Right				
Player	Team	Org	AB	H	HR	RBI	Avg	AB	H	HR	RBI	Avg
Chuck Abbott	Erie	Ana	144	38	3	15	.264	300	68	3	31	.227
Brent Abernathy	Knoxville	Tor	180	53	3	20	.294	397	115	10	42	.290
Carlos Adolfo	Harrisburg	Mon	75	24	5	17	.320	146	36	5	24	.247
Kurt Airoso	Jacksonville	Det	157	40	3	18	.255	379	106	7	54	.280
Israel Alcantara	Trenton	Bos	70	21	5	13	.300	223	65	15	47	.291
Chad Alexander	Jackson	Hou	98	28	4	12	.286	219	70	5	32	.320
Jeff Alfano	Huntsville	Mil	75	18	0	6	.240	172	43	5	25	.250
Luke Allen	San Antonio	LA	202	49	1	23	.243	331	101	13	59	.305
Wady Almonte	Bowie	Bal	121	32	4	17	.264	361	109	13	66	.302
Jose Amado	Wichita	KC	179	59	7	35	.330	280	74	6	58	.264
Jesus Ametller	Arkansas	StL	128	43	2	17	.336	269	79	8	36	.294
Rich Aude	Birmingham	CWS	141	40	2	30	.284	345	101	10	55	.293
Jesus Azuaje	Huntsville	Mil	110	36	4	18	.327	281	74	6	42	.263
Ed Bady	Akron	Cle	69	20	0	5	.290	161	36	2	28	.224
Rod Bair	Carolina	Col	148	51	6	27	.345	324	92	7	54	.284
Ryan Balfe	Mobile	SD	130	44	8	30	.338	270	68	3	40	.252
Rod Barajas	El Paso	Ari	156	57	4	32	.365	354	105	10	63	.297
John Barnes	New Britain	Min	106	28	2	14	.264	346	91	11	44	.263
Larry Barnes	Erie	Ana	177	49	9	48	.277	320	93	11	52	.291
Blake Barthol	Carolina	Col	102	30	5	12	.294	220	60	3	15	.273
Jayson Bass	New Haven	Sea	110	27	4	18	.245	321	87	17	49	.271
Fletcher Bates	Portland	Fla	153	37	0	12	.242	384	99	9	43	.258
Juan Bautista	Tulsa	Tex	141	26	1	10	.184	330	90	7	35	.273
Trey Beamon	Binghamton	NYM	73	17	0	6	.233	173	42	2	14	.243
Brian Becker	Orlando	TB	162	40	7	28	.247	318	81	11	46	.255
Mike Berry	Carolina	Col	107	33	5	24	.308	199	41	4	14	.206
Junior Betances	Akron	Cle	85	20	0	8	.235	221	70	2	20	.317
Todd Betts	Akron	Cle	89	20	3	13	.225	286	85	16	54	.297
Hiram Bocachica	San Antonio	LA	156	48	4	17	.308	321	91	7	43	.283
Justin Bowles	Midland	Oak	159	39	6	21	.245	330	101	14	52	.306
Milton Bradley	Harrisburg	Mon	90	35	4	17	.389	256	79	8	33	.309
Danny Bravo	Birmingham	CWS	102	30	1	19	.294	168	46	1	19	.274
Tarrik Brock	West Tenn	ChC	116	26	1	7	.224	291	69	7	25	.237
Dee Brown	Wichita	KC	86	24	4	14	.279	149	59	8	42	.396
Richard Brown	Norwich	NYY	115	33	1	14	.287	268	67	5	40	.250
Vick Brown	Norwich	NYY	147	40	4	17	.272	335	81	1	31	.242
Mo Bruce	Binghamton	NYM	158	38	4	25	.241	342	97	5	51	.284
Cliff Brumbaugh	Tulsa	Tex	157	48	10	32	.306	356	96	15	57	.270
Mark Budzinski	Akron	Cle	71	18	1	9	.254	226	66	5	37	.292
Morgan Burkhart	Trenton	Bos	56	13	2	6	.232	183	42	10	35	.230
Gary Burnham	Reading	Phi	69	14	2	8	.203	285	74	10	41	.260
Kevin Burns	Jackson	Hou	90	22	1	8	.244	262	77	11	50	.294
Pat Burrell	Reading	Phi	108	41	10	30	.380	309	98	18	60	.317
Andy Burress	Chattanooga	Cin	90	20	0	5	.222	167	50	7	23	.299
Brent Butler	Arkansas	StL	199	51	3	24	.256	329	91	10	30	.277
Rob Butler	Knoxville	Tor	79	22	0	10	.278	179	65	2	26	.363
Michael Byas	Shreveport	SF	196	51	0	20	.260	291	81	0	21	.278
Robinson Cancel	Huntsville	Mil	57	15	0	6	.263	166	41	5	26	.247
Ben Candelaria	Jacksonville	Det	127	25	5	19	.197	337	100	13	58	.297
Javier Cardona	Jacksonville	Det	124	43	9	33	.347	294	86	17	59	.293
Dustin Carr	Orlando	TB	143	43	4	19	.301	318	96	2	44	.302
Jamey Carroll	Harrisburg	Mon	174	58	2	22	.333	387	106	3	41	.274
Carlos Casimiro	Bowie	Bal	136	32	4	15	.235	390	84	14	49	.215
Jose Castro	Midland	Oak	134	36	3	17	.269	234	60	4	25	.256
Virgil Chevalier	Trenton	Bos	115	36	7	22	.313	394	113	6	54	.287
Giu. Chiaramonte	Shreveport	SF	154	35	6	21	.227	246	63	13	53	.256
McKay Christensen	Birmingham	CWS	115	30	1	9	.261	178	55	2	19	.309
Eddie Christian	Erie	Ana	59	16	2	12	.271	146	42	1	15	.288
Brady Clark	Chattanooga	Cin	151	49	6	22	.325	355	116	11	53	.327
Kevin Clark	El Paso	Ari	128	37	5	29	.289	245	74	3	35	.302
Roberto Colina	Orlando	TB	71	16	0	10	.225	244	70	6	43	.287
Joe Crede	Birmingham	CWS	90	26	1	15	.289	201	47	3	27	.234
John Curl	Mobile	SD	167	46	5	25	.275	307	89	17	51	.290
Brian Dallimore	Jackson	Hou	74	16	0	6	.216	177	51	5	13	.288
Jeff DaVanon	Midland	Oak	136	36	1	16	.265	238	92	10	44	.387
Cleatus Davidson	New Britain	Min	109	28	1	10	.257	382	92	1	30	.241
Glenn Davis	San Antonio	LA	170	47	3	19	.276	322	81	7	44	.252
Tim DeCinces	Bowie	Bal	49	12	2	5	.245	209	55	10	31	.263
Tomas de la Rosa	Harrisburg	Mon	146	43	2	14	.295	321	79	4	29	.246
Jason Dellaero	Birmingham	CWS	86	23	4	16	.267	186	50	6	28	.269
Eddy de los Santos	Orlando	TB	148	40	1	14	.270	300	83	2	35	.277
Darrell Dent	Bowie	Bal	48	8	0	1	.167	202	45	0	16	.223
Cesar Devarez	Bowie	Bal	54	11	0	2	.204	146	42	4	27	.288
Alejandro Diaz	Chattanooga	Cin	78	22	4	20	.282	142	36	3	15	.254
Juan Diaz	San Antonio	LA	89	27	2	15	.303	165	50	7	37	.303
Juan Dilone	Shreveport	SF	133	33	2	13	.248	207	53	3	31	.256
Jeremy Dodson	Wichita	KC	152	33	3	14	.217	300	83	18	44	.277
Erubiel Durazo	El Paso	Ari	70	29	0	15	.414	156	62	14	40	.397
Trent Durrington	Erie	Ana	133	44	0	9	.331	263	70	3	25	.266
David Eckstein	Trenton	Bos	111	37	3	15	.333	372	114	3	37	.306
Dave Elliott	Huntsville	Mil	128	30	4	19	.234	276	64	8	36	.232
Mario Encarnacion	Midland	Oak	113	41	3	17	.363	240	68	15	54	.283
Matt Erickson	Portland	Fla	76	18	0	5	.237	285	79	0	30	.277
Roman Escamilla	Wichita	KC	101	24	0	13	.238	100	25	1	15	.250
Emiliano Escandon	Wichita	KC	103	23	4	19	.223	237	65	3	38	.274
Josue Espada	Midland	Oak	161	66	1	13	.410	274	81	5	38	.296
Adam Everett	Trenton	Bos	87	20	2	7	.230	251	69	8	37	.275
Ethan Faggett	Mobile	SD	157	46	1	18	.293	370	82	5	25	.222
Cordell Farley	Arkansas	StL	155	46	4	16	.297	266	63	4	25	.237
Pedro Feliz	Shreveport	SF	177	43	6	27	.243	314	81	7	50	.258
Dave Feuerstein	Carolina	Col	112	25	0	8	.223	175	38	1	10	.217
Luis Figueroa	Altoona	Pit	100	24	0	11	.240	318	86	3	39	.270
David Francia	Reading	Phi	75	25	2	11	.333	264	67	2	32	.254
Dan Fraraccio	Orlando	TB	110	33	2	10	.300	144	40	5	18	.278
Alejandro Freire	Jacksonville	Det	89	29	5	21	.326	154	43	5	22	.279
Joe Funaro	Portland	Fla	61	28	1	16	.459	207	70	2	24	.338

			vs Left					vs Right				
Player	Team	Org	AB	H	HR	RBI	Avg	AB	H	HR	RBI	Avg
Bryon Gainey	Binghamton	NYM	136	34	7	26	.250	366	85	18	52	.232
Shawn Gallagher	Tulsa	Tex	147	34	8	26	.231	305	94	10	52	.308
Jamie Gann	El Paso	Ari	137	42	1	14	.307	306	74	8	42	.242
Tim Garland	Midland	Oak	160	51	2	13	.319	303	83	4	42	.274
David Gibralter	Trenton	Bos	109	32	9	29	.294	339	102	15	68	.301
Geronimo Gil	San Antonio	LA	121	31	6	20	.256	222	66	9	39	.297
Tim Giles	Knoxville	Tor	175	36	3	28	.206	330	121	15	86	.367
Eric Gillespie	Jacksonville	Det	135	37	2	14	.274	339	108	17	74	.319
Chip Glass	Norwich	NYY	67	14	0	10	.209	172	46	6	24	.267
Mike Glavine	Greenville	Atl	72	16	2	4	.222	233	66	15	48	.283
Ramon Gomez	Birmingham	CWS	103	29	0	12	.282	171	49	0	14	.287
Rudy Gomez	Knoxville	Tor	141	44	9	34	.312	286	76	8	58	.266
Raul Gonzalez	Trenton	Bos	110	34	5	28	.309	395	135	13	75	.342
Wiki Gonzalez	Mobile	SD	83	35	8	23	.422	142	41	2	26	.289
Steve Goodell	Greenville	Atl	127	49	4	25	.386	211	52	11	33	.246
Chad Green	Huntsville	Mil	128	29	0	6	.227	294	75	10	40	.255
Steve Hacker	New Britain	Min	110	36	11	37	.327	351	103	16	60	.293
Tom Hage	Bowie	Bal	74	21	0	7	.284	352	97	8	58	.276
Pat Hallmark	Wichita	KC	98	36	4	9	.367	144	33	1	15	.229
Brian Harris	Reading	Phi	119	35	4	19	.294	261	49	1	22	.188
Adonis Harrison	New Haven	Sea	101	29	1	15	.287	348	93	1	30	.267
Kevin Haverbusch	Altoona	Pit	93	26	5	21	.280	239	69	9	40	.289
Kraig Hawkins	Orlando	TB	90	20	0	6	.222	206	69	0	21	.335
Heath Hayes	Akron	Cle	107	30	5	23	.280	311	81	11	45	.260
Alex Hernandez	Altoona	Pit	115	26	2	16	.226	360	96	13	47	.267
Shea Hillenbrand	Trenton	Bos	74	20	1	7	.270	208	53	6	29	.255
Rich Hills	New Haven	Sea	58	8	1	1	.138	224	66	3	28	.295
Todd Hogan	Arkansas	StL	104	25	3	12	.240	176	31	1	9	.176
Tyrone Horne	Reading	Phi	55	13	2	12	.236	207	57	3	25	.275
Jim Horner	New Haven	Sea	75	18	0	6	.240	203	57	6	44	.281
Aubrey Huff	Orlando	TB	168	50	5	23	.298	323	98	17	55	.303
B.J. Huff	Binghamton	NYM	57	12	1	7	.211	148	39	6	25	.264
Larry Huff	Reading	Phi	108	29	0	11	.269	319	82	3	43	.257
Adam Hyzdu	Altoona	Pit	75	22	3	19	.293	270	87	21	59	.322
Jesse Ibarra	Tulsa	Tex	85	18	2	10	.212	240	54	9	39	.225
Jeff Inglin	Birmingham	CWS	134	47	8	31	.351	298	79	7	32	.265
Darron Ingram	Chattanooga	Cin	73	21	3	14	.288	194	38	8	26	.196
Adam Johnson	Greenville	Atl	140	42	5	37	.300	254	72	9	35	.283
J.J. Johnson	Jackson	Hou	136	41	3	20	.301	301	69	15	49	.229
Nick Johnson	Norwich	NYY	133	50	7	34	.376	287	95	7	53	.331
Ric Johnson	Jackson	Hou	102	20	0	5	.196	221	59	1	22	.267
Jaime Jones	Portland	Fla	67	17	2	5	.254	177	45	5	26	.254
Ryan Jones	Jacksonville	Det	150	39	5	21	.260	337	84	14	52	.249
Randy Jorgensen	Mobile	SD	78	22	2	17	.282	174	59	5	37	.339
Robbie Kent	Mobile	SD	126	41	3	19	.325	210	50	5	37	.238
Brad King	West Tenn	ChC	79	15	0	5	.190	140	36	0	19	.257
Cesar King	Tulsa	Tex	102	21	1	9	.206	219	52	10	36	.237
Brendan Kingman	New Haven	Sea	119	35	1	10	.294	390	107	9	46	.274
Eugene Kingsale	Bowie	Bal	91	25	2	9	.275	177	38	1	14	.215
Chris Kirgan	Carolina	Col	163	36	2	28	.221	311	69	11	56	.222
Stacy Kleiner	Arkansas	StL	105	26	2	10	.248	130	26	0	6	.200
Larry Kleinz	Portland	Fla	84	23	2	10	.274	192	49	3	33	.255
Josh Klimek	Huntsville	Mil	113	26	2	14	.230	318	77	12	57	.242
Toby Kominek	Huntsville	Mil	125	32	6	20	.256	331	74	6	39	.224
Hector Kuilan	Portland	Fla	78	23	2	10	.295	167	41	0	22	.246
Steve Lackey	Greenville	Atl	114	41	0	13	.360	201	51	4	25	.254
Mike Lamb	Tulsa	Tex	198	57	6	35	.288	346	119	15	65	.344
Ryan Lane	Tulsa	Tex	94	30	5	18	.319	170	42	4	30	.247
Stephen Larkin	Chattanooga	Cin	101	36	0	11	.356	163	43	4	31	.264
Joe Lawrence	Knoxville	Tor	69	19	2	9	.275	181	47	5	15	.260
Chris Lemonis	Jacksonville	Det	59	18	2	7	.305	206	57	3	31	.277
Donny Leon	Norwich	NYY	144	43	4	25	.299	313	95	17	75	.304
Jose Leon	Arkansas	StL	107	22	5	18	.206	228	56	13	36	.246
Marc Lewis	New Britain	Min	104	28	3	19	.269	280	72	6	33	.257
Tal Light	Carolina	Col	90	15	0	8	.167	169	33	9	22	.195
David Lindstrom	Jacksonville	Det	76	21	4	13	.276	138	37	3	22	.268
Garrett Long	Altoona	Pit	73	16	7	13	.219	282	71	11	43	.252
Mickey Lopez	Huntsville	Mil	90	26	5	18	.289	225	68	0	22	.302
Pedro Lopez	Jackson	Hou	80	11	2	5	.138	175	36	4	23	.206
Brian Loyd	Knoxville	Tor	106	29	2	21	.274	258	73	9	44	.283
Julio Lugo	Jackson	Hou	126	39	4	12	.310	319	103	6	30	.323
Fernando Lunar	Greenville	Atl	120	31	2	17	.258	223	46	1	18	.206
Ryan Luzinski	Mobile	SD	80	25	2	13	.313	153	40	0	17	.261
Scott Lydy	Birmingham	CWS	109	37	8	23	.339	291	69	12	42	.237
Jon Macalutas	Huntsville	Mil	84	20	2	14	.238	222	61	3	31	.275
Garry Maddox	El Paso	Ari	151	43	5	24	.285	341	102	10	51	.299
Ricky Magdaleno	New Haven	Sea	66	17	0	10	.258	192	53	1	14	.276
Chris Magruder	Shreveport	SF	192	49	5	31	.255	284	73	1	29	.257
T.R. Marcinczyk	Midland	Oak	163	43	10	46	.264	314	90	13	65	.287
Felix Martinez	Wichita	KC	122	30	1	9	.246	205	58	3	28	.283
Pablo Martinez	Greenville	Atl	86	24	1	8	.279	142	30	0	11	.211
Jared Mathis	Huntsville	Mil	59	15	1	6	.254	159	34	1	18	.214
Joe Mathis	New Haven	Sea	70	15	1	5	.214	170	50	1	25	.294
Julius Matos	El Paso	Ari	140	39	3	19	.279	285	80	2	22	.281
Luis Matos	Bowie	Bal	68	16	2	8	.235	215	51	7	28	.237
Donzell McDonald	Norwich	NYY	158	46	2	15	.291	375	99	2	18	.264
John McDonald	Akron	Cle	53	18	0	7	.340	173	49	1	19	.283
Cody McKay	Midland	Oak	108	24	2	5	.222	225	74	4	38	.329
Dan McKinley	Akron	Cle	102	31	0	9	.304	361	88	3	28	.244
Sean McNally	Wichita	KC	162	51	12	42	.315	278	73	24	67	.263
Tony Medrano	Wichita	KC	89	29	2	16	.326	168	58	3	16	.345
Adam Melhuse	Knoxville	Tor	132	42	7	25	.318	242	68	12	44	.281
Carlos Mendoza	Shreveport	SF	118	26	2	12	.220	214	41	1	22	.192
Mike Metcalfe	San Antonio	LA	160	49	1	18	.306	301	86	2	39	.286
Chad Meyers	West Tenn	ChC	84	26	1	9	.310	154	43	2	20	.279
Damon Minor	Shreveport	SF	189	46	3	22	.243	284	83	17	60	.292

Double-A Batting vs. Lefthanded and Righthanded Pitchers

Player	Team	Org	vs Left					vs Right				
			AB	H	HR	RBI	Avg	AB	H	HR	RBI	Avg
Derek Mitchell	Jacksonville	Det	126	30	1	12	.238	296	72	6	37	.243
Chad Moeller	New Britain	Min	89	22	3	9	.247	161	40	1	15	.248
Wonderful Monds	Chattanooga	Cin	66	17	4	8	.258	245	64	7	24	.261
Kenderick Moore	Wichita	KC	111	30	0	11	.270	132	31	0	16	.235
Willie Morales	Midland	Oak	120	32	5	20	.287	223	64	11	51	.287
Ramon Moreta	San Antonio	LA	139	42	1	17	.302	258	79	1	25	.306
Scott Morgan	Akron	Cle	94	29	5	15	.309	250	68	21	55	.272
Jeremy Morris	Norwich	NYY	119	27	1	11	.227	273	70	8	41	.256
Julio Mosquera	Orlando	TB	106	37	1	11	.349	153	42	3	26	.275
Rick Moss	New Britain	Min	34	8	0	1	.235	218	60	4	28	.275
Tony Mota	San Antonio	LA	123	39	5	25	.317	222	73	10	50	.329
Kelcey Mucker	New Britain	Min	62	15	0	2	.242	306	85	1	23	.278
Nate Murphy	Erie	Ana	122	26	5	17	.213	237	70	9	39	.295
Adrian Myers	Tulsa	Tex	120	25	1	6	.208	237	59	0	22	.249
Bry Nelson	West Tenn	ChC	141	42	2	21	.298	330	84	14	57	.255
Garrett Neubart	Binghamton	NYM	79	24	1	6	.304	181	51	2	15	.282
Tom Nevers	Chattanooga	Cin	139	37	7	22	.266	241	75	10	43	.311
Doug Newstrom	Birmingham	CWS	55	15	1	9	.273	198	57	2	14	.288
Kevin Nicholson	Mobile	SD	169	49	5	31	.290	320	92	8	50	.287
Dax Norris	Greenville	Atl	163	44	5	27	.270	240	68	10	39	.283
Chris Norton	Portland	Fla	119	31	11	31	.261	287	87	27	66	.303
Talmadge Nunnari	Harrisburg	Mon	86	22	2	12	.256	153	57	4	17	.373
Augie Ojeda	Bowie	Bal	113	23	3	14	.204	347	100	7	46	.288
Pablo Ozuna	Portland	Fla	146	44	2	15	.301	356	97	5	31	.272
Pete Paciorek	Mobile	SD	59	9	2	5	.153	167	41	2	12	.246
Jarrod Patterson	El Paso	Ari	76	37	3	18	.487	169	57	5	32	.337
Josh Paul	Birmingham	CWS	94	27	2	15	.287	225	62	2	27	.276
Richard Paz	Bowie	Bal	68	15	0	4	.221	205	63	2	16	.307
Rudy Pemberton	Birmingham	CWS	92	28	5	13	.304	215	57	13	47	.265
Elvis Pena	Carolina	Col	125	38	2	12	.304	231	69	0	19	.299
Tyrone Pendergrass	Greenville	Atl	109	29	3	16	.266	235	61	3	15	.260
Danny Peoples	Akron	Cle	113	28	4	18	.248	381	96	17	60	.252
Jhony Perez	Jackson	Hou	93	28	2	8	.301	183	41	2	17	.224
Tommy Peterman	New Britain	Min	138	35	2	15	.254	400	106	18	69	.265
Paul Phillips	Wichita	KC	150	38	0	22	.253	243	67	3	34	.276
Adam Piatt	Midland	Oak	154	46	10	35	.299	322	118	29	100	.366
Kirk Pierce	Reading	Phi	71	21	3	12	.296	184	45	6	28	.245
Jose Pimentel	Greenville	Atl	137	35	5	24	.263	227	42	3	21	.185
Juan Piniella	Tulsa	Tex	158	43	1	16	.272	300	78	0	31	.260
Enohel Polanco	West Tenn	ChC	104	22	2	8	.212	250	63	1	22	.252
Nick Presto	Chattanooga	Cin	56	12	0	4	.214	168	48	2	24	.286
Alejandro Prieto	Wichita	KC	133	37	2	12	.278	227	69	4	29	.304
Rick Prieto	Mobile	SD	144	47	4	24	.326	215	56	2	19	.260
Julio Ramirez	Portland	Fla	147	27	2	11	.184	421	121	11	53	.287
Tike Redman	Altoona	Pit	128	35	0	10	.273	404	108	3	50	.267
Jackie Rexrode	Birmingham	Ari	63	19	0	9	.302	150	38	0	16	.253
Chris Richard	Arkansas	StL	167	42	9	29	.251	275	88	20	65	.320
Luis Rivas	New Britain	Min	127	34	2	10	.268	400	100	5	39	.250
Adam Robinson	Akron	Cle	40	7	0	7	.175	198	59	5	23	.298
Liu Rodriguez	Birmingham	CWS	80	26	2	18	.325	164	45	1	19	.274
Sammy Rodriguez	Binghamton	NYM	80	15	2	14	.188	123	31	1	10	.252
Nate Rolison	Portland	Fla	120	34	2	15	.283	321	92	12	50	.287
Jimmy Rollins	Reading	Phi	146	37	4	20	.253	386	108	7	36	.280
Aaron Royster	Reading	Phi	147	29	5	31	.283	190	56	4	31	.295
Chad Rupp	Knoxville	Tor	83	21	5	11	.253	158	41	11	33	.259
Rich Saitta	San Antonio	LA	106	35	2	22	.330	148	39	0	12	.264
Jerry Salzano	Chattanooga	Cin	67	20	1	11	.299	196	66	3	27	.337
Alex Sanchez	Orlando	TB	155	41	0	12	.265	345	86	2	17	.249
Victor Sanchez	Jackson	Hou	152	40	6	25	.263	255	62	11	43	.243
Yuri Sanchez	Binghamton	NYM	111	28	2	10	.252	270	60	3	20	.222

Player	Team	Org	vs Left					vs Right				
			AB	H	HR	RBI	Avg	AB	H	HR	RBI	Avg
Pedro Santana	Jacksonville	Det	152	36	1	14	.237	360	107	4	35	.297
Rob Sasser	Jacksonville	Det	132	39	4	18	.295	292	81	3	43	.277
Luis Saturria	Arkansas	StL	176	45	7	23	.256	308	73	9	38	.237
Chris Saunders	Chattanooga	Cin	55	13	2	9	.236	161	55	5	26	.342
Brian Schneider	Harrisburg	Mon	131	39	2	19	.298	290	72	15	47	.248
Chip Sell	El Paso	Ari	107	24	2	12	.224	222	77	6	23	.347
Tom Sergio	Tulsa	Tex	196	55	4	30	.281	316	94	6	42	.297
Rick Short	Bowie	Bal	95	32	4	13	.337	297	91	12	49	.306
Demond Smith	Greenville	Atl	154	40	2	17	.260	262	87	7	42	.332
Jeff Smith	New Britain	Min	40	7	1	2	.175	225	60	5	29	.267
Fausto Solano	Knoxville	Tor	108	32	6	16	.296	240	74	8	45	.308
Alfonso Soriano	Norwich	NYY	106	27	7	14	.255	255	83	8	54	.325
Juan Sosa	Carolina	Col	146	40	2	13	.274	344	95	5	29	.276
Dorian Speed	West Tenn	ChC	126	36	3	16	.286	289	75	11	41	.260
Ryan Stromsborg	Knoxville	Tor	122	28	2	11	.230	255	66	7	34	.259
John Tamargo	Binghamton	NYM	98	23	1	11	.235	265	55	3	26	.208
Reggie Taylor	Reading	Phi	123	30	2	10	.244	403	110	13	51	.273
Nate Tebbs	Trenton	Bos	80	20	1	10	.250	285	79	3	25	.277
Fausto Tejero	Erie	Ana	72	16	0	1	.222	109	29	0	17	.209
Juan Thomas	New Haven	Sea	70	14	3	8	.200	197	51	13	43	.259
Andy Thompson	Knoxville	Tor	79	19	8	20	.241	175	43	7	33	.246
Jorge Toca	Binghamton	NYM	76	21	4	13	.276	203	65	16	54	.320
Juan Tolentino	Erie	Ana	164	40	6	16	.244	325	83	15	45	.255
Goefrey Tomlinson	Wichita	KC	171	49	2	20	.287	308	85	2	26	.276
Yorvit Torrealba	Shreveport	SF	79	23	2	10	.291	138	30	2	9	.217
Andy Tracy	Harrisburg	Mon	177	46	8	38	.260	316	89	29	90	.282
Chris Truby	Jackson	Hou	144	43	7	25	.299	321	88	21	62	.274
Pete Tucci	Mobile	SD	112	29	6	15	.259	200	49	5	20	.245
Jon Tucker	Harrisburg	Mon	119	30	3	18	.252	243	63	10	37	.259
Josh Tyler	Shreveport	SF	123	29	2	18	.236	208	58	1	21	.279
Jason Tyner	Binghamton	NYM	162	40	0	9	.247	356	122	0	24	.343
Victor Valencia	Norwich	NYY	108	24	7	25	.222	288	64	15	47	.222
Yohanny Valera	Binghamton	NYM	52	13	2	5	.250	152	46	7	34	.303
Ramon Vazquez	New Haven	Sea	98	21	1	5	.214	340	92	4	40	.271
Wilton Veras	Trenton	Bos	109	36	2	16	.330	365	97	9	59	.266
Scott Vieira	West Tenn	ChC	147	46	2	20	.313	308	87	8	38	.282
Chris Wakeland	Jacksonville	Det	57	16	3	6	.281	155	52	10	30	.335
Ron Walker	West Tenn	ChC	80	17	1	12	.213	222	49	8	30	.221
Jeremy Ware	Harrisburg	Mon	116	31	4	22	.267	265	69	5	34	.260
Dusty Wathan	New Haven	Sea	72	23	0	8	.319	261	70	4	29	.268
Pat Watkins	Carolina	Col	92	36	0	13	.391	220	57	3	27	.259
Jake Weber	New Haven	Sea	129	39	3	10	.261	378	96	8	49	.254
Luke Wilcox	Orlando	TB	103	19	4	16	.184	230	71	16	48	.309
Brad Wilkerson	Harrisburg	Mon	133	32	2	13	.256	230	62	8	36	.225
Glenn Williams	Greenville	Atl	75	20	2	7	.267	129	26	2	8	.202
Jason Williams	Chattanooga	Cin	91	33	0	16	.363	241	73	7	29	.303
Craig Wilson	Altoona	Pit	89	30	6	18	.337	273	67	14	51	.245
Mike Wolff	Erie	Ana	112	29	1	15	.259	195	47	9	25	.241
Jason Woolf	Arkansas	StL	104	30	2	7	.288	216	57	6	8	.264
Shawn Wooten	Erie	Ana	179	52	7	27	.291	339	99	12	61	.292
Travis Young	Shreveport	SF	162	45	3	15	.278	254	65	2	23	.256
Junior Zamora	Binghamton	NYM	82	22	5	15	.268	173	39	5	18	.225
Julio Zuleta	West Tenn	ChC	151	43	3	25	.285	331	99	18	72	.299

Double-A Batting at Home and on the Road

			Home					Road				
Player	Team	Org	AB	H	HR	RBI	Avg	AB	H	HR	RBI	Avg
Chuck Abbott	Erie	Ana	205	57	1	22	.278	239	49	5	24	.205
Brent Abernathy	Knoxville	Tor	286	90	10	33	.315	291	78	3	29	.268
Carlos Adolfo	Harrisburg	Mon	96	33	7	26	.344	125	27	3	15	.216
Kurt Airoso	Jacksonville	Det	261	66	5	28	.253	275	80	5	44	.291
Israel Alcantara	Trenton	Bos	152	42	8	27	.276	141	44	12	33	.312
Chad Alexander	Jackson	Hou	170	52	5	20	.306	147	46	4	24	.313
Jeff Alfano	Huntsville	Mil	138	34	4	20	.246	109	27	1	11	.248
Luke Allen	San Antonio	LA	252	63	2	22	.250	281	87	12	60	.310
Wady Almonte	Bowie	Bal	238	74	10	46	.311	244	67	7	37	.275
Jose Amado	Wichita	KC	210	59	7	48	.281	249	74	6	45	.297
Jesus Ametller	Arkansas	StL	183	59	8	28	.322	214	63	2	25	.294
Rich Aude	Birmingham	CWS	238	76	8	52	.319	248	65	4	33	.262
Jesus Azuaje	Huntsville	Mil	175	48	4	20	.274	216	62	6	40	.287
Ed Bady	Akron	Cle	120	32	2	21	.267	110	24	0	12	.218
Rod Bair	Carolina	Col	237	74	8	42	.312	235	69	5	39	.294
Ryan Balfe	Mobile	SD	184	56	7	35	.304	216	56	4	35	.259
Rod Barajas	El Paso	Ari	244	92	9	60	.377	266	70	5	35	.263
John Barnes	New Britain	Min	221	54	11	31	.244	231	65	2	27	.281
Larry Barnes	Erie	Ana	238	70	7	46	.294	259	72	13	54	.278
Blake Barthol	Carolina	Col	156	44	7	15	.282	166	46	1	12	.277
Jayson Bass	New Haven	Sea	225	62	13	33	.276	206	52	8	34	.252
Fletcher Bates	Portland	Fla	260	60	3	25	.231	277	76	6	30	.274
Juan Bautista	Tulsa	Tex	200	48	3	18	.240	271	68	5	27	.251
Trey Beamon	Binghamton	NYM	116	26	1	11	.224	130	33	1	9	.254
Brian Becker	Orlando	TB	224	52	11	36	.232	256	69	7	38	.270
Mike Berry	Carolina	Col	174	44	5	24	.253	132	30	4	14	.227
Junior Betances	Akron	Cle	149	44	1	11	.295	157	46	1	17	.293
Todd Betts	Akron	Cle	188	55	8	29	.293	187	50	11	38	.267
Hiram Bocachica	San Antonio	LA	216	55	3	21	.255	261	84	8	39	.322
Justin Bowles	Midland	Oak	250	74	11	44	.296	239	66	9	29	.276
Milton Bradley	Harrisburg	Mon	163	54	7	30	.331	183	60	5	20	.328
Danny Bravo	Birmingham	CWS	140	35	0	20	.250	130	41	2	18	.315
Tarrik Brock	West Tenn	ChC	210	55	0	13	.262	197	40	8	19	.203
Dee Brown	Wichita	KC	110	38	5	22	.345	125	45	7	34	.360
Richard Brown	Norwich	NYY	177	43	2	31	.243	206	57	4	23	.277
Vick Brown	Norwich	NYY	235	59	2	22	.251	247	62	3	26	.251
Mo Bruce	Binghamton	NYM	252	72	2	41	.286	248	63	7	35	.254
Cliff Brumbaugh	Tulsa	Tex	259	73	13	45	.282	254	71	12	44	.280
Mark Budzinski	Akron	Cle	141	40	2	17	.284	156	44	4	29	.282
Morgan Burkhart	Trenton	Bos	121	28	4	16	.231	118	27	8	25	.229
Gary Burnham	Reading	Phi	182	39	7	27	.214	172	49	5	22	.285
Kevin Burns	Jackson	Hou	155	34	5	21	.219	197	65	7	37	.330
Pat Burrell	Reading	Phi	211	74	13	45	.351	206	65	15	45	.316
Andy Burress	Chattanooga	Cin	122	35	5	17	.287	135	35	2	11	.259
Brent Butler	Arkansas	StL	250	65	3	23	.260	277	77	10	31	.278
Rob Butler	Knoxville	Tor	131	45	1	22	.344	127	42	1	14	.331
Michael Byas	Shreveport	SF	231	67	0	24	.290	256	65	0	17	.254
Robinson Cancel	Huntsville	Mil	100	27	2	17	.270	123	29	3	15	.236
Ben Candelaria	Jacksonville	Det	220	66	12	40	.300	244	59	6	37	.242
Javier Cardona	Jacksonville	Det	200	55	10	36	.275	218	74	16	56	.339
Dustin Carr	Orlando	TB	218	74	3	36	.339	243	65	3	27	.267
Jamey Carroll	Harrisburg	Mon	277	85	3	38	.307	284	79	2	25	.278
Carlos Casimiro	Bowie	Bal	251	61	8	32	.243	275	55	10	32	.200
Jose Castro	Midland	Oak	175	54	4	28	.309	193	42	3	14	.218
Virgil Chevalier	Trenton	Bos	244	71	5	34	.291	265	78	8	42	.294
Giu. Chiaramonte	Shreveport	SF	197	49	8	38	.249	202	49	11	36	.243
McKay Christensen	Birmingham	CWS	149	45	2	16	.302	144	40	1	12	.278
Eddie Christian	Erie	Ana	98	29	2	16	.296	107	29	1	11	.271
Brady Clark	Chattanooga	Cin	260	95	8	41	.365	246	70	9	34	.285
Kevin Clark	El Paso	Ari	193	61	3	32	.316	180	50	5	32	.278
Roberto Colina	Orlando	TB	132	36	2	17	.273	183	50	4	36	.273
Joe Crede	Birmingham	CWS	131	43	1	22	.328	160	30	3	20	.188
John Curl	Mobile	SD	243	73	13	45	.300	231	62	9	31	.268
Brian Dallimore	Jackson	Hou	134	34	2	7	.254	117	33	3	12	.282
Jeff DaVanon	Midland	Oak	191	74	6	33	.387	183	54	5	27	.295
Cleatus Davidson	New Britain	Min	249	62	1	20	.249	242	58	1	20	.240
Glenn Davis	San Antonio	LA	235	59	5	30	.251	257	69	5	33	.268
Tim DeCinces	Bowie	Bal	119	31	4	17	.261	139	36	8	19	.259
Tomas de la Rosa	Harrisburg	Mon	221	60	3	19	.271	246	62	3	24	.252
Jason Dellaero	Birmingham	CWS	130	33	2	16	.254	142	40	8	28	.282
Eddy de los Santos	Orlando	TB	201	53	0	21	.264	247	70	3	28	.283
Darrell Dent	Bowie	Bal	113	25	0	5	.221	137	28	0	12	.204
Cesar Devarez	Bowie	Bal	107	31	2	22	.290	93	22	2	7	.237
Alejandro Diaz	Chattanooga	Cin	101	24	3	16	.238	119	34	4	19	.286
Juan Diaz	San Antonio	LA	112	33	7	29	.295	142	44	2	23	.310
Juan Dilone	Shreveport	SF	162	41	3	23	.253	178	45	2	21	.253
Jeremy Dodson	Wichita	KC	229	60	11	31	.262	223	56	10	27	.251
Erubiel Durazo	El Paso	Ari	118	42	8	34	.356	108	49	6	21	.454
Trent Durrington	Erie	Ana	195	49	2	19	.251	201	65	1	15	.323
David Eckstein	Trenton	Bos	248	81	2	24	.327	235	70	4	28	.298
Dave Elliott	Huntsville	Mil	189	39	4	20	.206	215	55	8	35	.256
Mario Encarnacion	Midland	Oak	202	67	10	45	.332	151	42	8	26	.278
Matt Erickson	Portland	Fla	178	57	0	25	.320	183	40	0	10	.219
Roman Escamilla	Wichita	KC	96	21	1	9	.219	105	28	0	19	.267
Emiliano Escandon	Wichita	KC	175	45	3	31	.257	165	43	4	26	.261
Josue Espada	Midland	Oak	234	81	6	37	.346	201	66	0	14	.328
Adam Everett	Trenton	Bos	167	44	4	20	.263	171	45	6	24	.263
Ethan Faggett	Mobile	SD	252	55	3	17	.218	275	73	3	26	.265
Cordell Farley	Arkansas	StL	202	59	7	30	.292	219	50	1	11	.228
Pedro Feliz	Shreveport	SF	248	63	6	35	.254	243	61	7	42	.251
Dave Feuerstein	Carolina	Col	149	31	1	10	.208	138	32	0	8	.232
Luis Figueroa	Altoona	Pit	209	54	1	24	.258	209	56	2	26	.268
David Francia	Reading	Phi	163	48	4	27	.294	176	44	0	16	.250
Dan Fraraccio	Orlando	TB	137	37	5	17	.270	117	36	2	11	.308
Alejandro Freire	Jacksonville	Det	104	29	2	17	.279	139	43	8	26	.309
Joe Funaro	Portland	Fla	138	59	2	29	.428	130	39	1	11	.300

			Home					Road				
Player	Team	Org	AB	H	HR	RBI	Avg	AB	H	HR	RBI	Avg
Bryon Gainey	Binghamton	NYM	240	56	11	32	.233	262	63	14	46	.240
Shawn Gallagher	Tulsa	Tex	225	64	9	41	.284	227	64	9	37	.282
Jamie Gann	El Paso	Ari	215	64	4	34	.298	228	52	5	22	.228
Tim Garland	Midland	Oak	236	74	3	33	.314	227	60	3	22	.264
David Gibralter	Trenton	Bos	235	76	17	58	.323	213	58	7	39	.272
Geronimo Gil	San Antonio	LA	160	49	7	30	.306	183	48	8	29	.262
Tim Giles	Knoxville	Tor	249	84	12	67	.337	256	73	6	47	.285
Eric Gillespie	Jacksonville	Det	239	62	8	37	.259	235	83	11	51	.353
Chip Glass	Norwich	NYY	96	28	2	13	.292	143	32	4	21	.224
Mike Glavine	Greenville	Atl	159	48	13	39	.302	146	34	4	13	.233
Ramon Gomez	Birmingham	CWS	129	35	0	9	.271	145	43	0	17	.297
Rudy Gomez	Knoxville	Tor	201	53	11	41	.264	226	67	6	51	.296
Raul Gonzalez	Trenton	Bos	265	92	7	52	.347	240	77	11	51	.321
Wiki Gonzalez	Mobile	SD	110	34	6	20	.309	115	42	4	29	.365
Steve Goodell	Greenville	Atl	179	61	10	35	.341	159	40	5	23	.252
Chad Green	Huntsville	Mil	228	50	6	26	.219	194	54	4	20	.278
Steve Hacker	New Britain	Min	222	72	14	44	.324	239	67	13	53	.280
Tom Hage	Bowie	Bal	197	50	4	33	.254	229	68	4	32	.297
Pat Hallmark	Wichita	KC	122	37	3	13	.303	120	32	2	11	.267
Brian Harris	Reading	Phi	183	42	2	17	.230	197	42	3	24	.213
Adonis Harrison	New Haven	Sea	218	59	2	30	.271	231	63	0	15	.273
Kevin Haverbusch	Altoona	Pit	178	52	7	30	.292	154	43	7	31	.279
Kraig Hawkins	Orlando	TB	141	46	0	14	.326	155	43	0	13	.277
Heath Hayes	Akron	Cle	193	48	7	32	.249	225	63	9	36	.280
Alex Hernandez	Altoona	Pit	219	51	7	35	.233	256	71	8	28	.277
Shea Hillenbrand	Trenton	Bos	154	39	3	18	.253	128	34	4	18	.266
Rich Hills	New Haven	Sea	95	36	2	15	.379	187	38	2	14	.203
Todd Hogan	Arkansas	StL	137	31	3	12	.226	143	25	1	9	.175
Tyrone Horne	Reading	Phi	116	32	5	20	.276	146	38	0	17	.260
Jim Horner	New Haven	Sea	140	40	2	21	.286	138	35	4	29	.254
Aubrey Huff	Orlando	TB	230	63	13	36	.274	261	85	9	42	.326
B.J. Huff	Binghamton	NYM	112	23	2	17	.205	93	28	5	15	.301
Larry Huff	Reading	Phi	208	57	1	25	.274	219	54	2	29	.247
Adam Hyzdu	Altoona	Pit	157	51	8	38	.325	188	58	16	40	.309
Jesse Ibarra	Tulsa	Tex	162	40	7	29	.247	163	32	4	20	.196
Jeff Inglin	Birmingham	CWS	205	60	6	29	.293	227	66	9	34	.291
Darron Ingram	Chattanooga	Cin	131	32	5	19	.244	136	27	6	21	.199
Adam Johnson	Greenville	Atl	208	65	10	50	.313	186	49	4	22	.263
J.J. Johnson	Jackson	Hou	218	52	8	29	.239	218	58	10	40	.266
Nick Johnson	Norwich	NYY	199	74	5	46	.372	221	71	9	41	.321
Ric Johnson	Jackson	Hou	157	38	0	11	.242	167	41	1	16	.246
Jaime Jones	Portland	Fla	118	23	3	13	.195	126	39	4	18	.310
Ryan Jones	Jacksonville	Det	228	60	13	35	.263	259	63	6	38	.243
Randy Jorgensen	Mobile	SD	109	29	5	22	.266	143	52	2	32	.364
Robbie Kent	Mobile	SD	142	38	2	22	.268	194	53	6	34	.273
Brad King	West Tenn	ChC	105	22	0	10	.210	127	31	0	15	.244
Cesar King	Tulsa	Tex	134	31	6	21	.231	187	42	5	24	.225
Brendan Kingman	New Haven	Sea	235	52	5	21	.221	274	90	5	35	.328
Eugene Kingsale	Bowie	Bal	134	34	2	12	.254	134	29	1	11	.216
Chris Kirgan	Carolina	Col	234	52	6	46	.222	240	53	7	38	.221
Stacy Kleiner	Arkansas	StL	108	19	1	4	.176	127	33	1	12	.260
Larry Kleinz	Portland	Fla	142	31	4	17	.218	134	41	1	26	.306
Josh Klimek	Huntsville	Mil	218	50	9	35	.229	213	53	5	36	.249
Toby Kominek	Huntsville	Mil	236	54	7	34	.229	220	52	5	25	.236
Hector Kuilan	Portland	Fla	123	35	2	21	.285	122	29	0	11	.238
Steve Lackey	Greenville	Atl	161	56	1	27	.348	154	36	3	11	.234
Mike Lamb	Tulsa	Tex	260	88	12	49	.338	284	88	9	51	.310
Ryan Lane	Tulsa	Tex	117	34	7	26	.291	147	38	2	22	.259
Stephen Larkin	Chattanooga	Cin	137	43	3	20	.314	127	36	1	22	.283
Joe Lawrence	Knoxville	Tor	118	30	2	8	.254	132	36	5	16	.273
Chris Lemonis	Jacksonville	Det	122	31	3	18	.254	143	44	2	20	.308
Donny Leon	Norwich	NYY	209	60	7	46	.287	248	78	14	54	.315
Jose Leon	Arkansas	StL	161	41	8	29	.255	174	37	10	25	.213
Marc Lewis	New Britain	Min	198	55	5	32	.278	186	45	4	20	.242
Tal Light	Carolina	Col	117	23	6	15	.197	142	25	3	15	.176
David Lindstrom	Jacksonville	Det	101	27	5	18	.267	113	31	2	17	.274
Garrett Long	Altoona	Pit	182	45	8	29	.247	173	42	10	27	.243
Mickey Lopez	Huntsville	Mil	158	48	3	18	.304	157	46	2	22	.293
Pedro Lopez	Jackson	Hou	128	27	3	16	.211	127	20	3	12	.157
Brian Loyd	Knoxville	Tor	179	42	4	33	.235	185	60	7	32	.324
Julio Lugo	Jackson	Hou	217	61	6	22	.281	228	81	4	20	.355
Fernando Lunar	Greenville	Atl	161	41	1	17	.255	182	36	2	18	.198
Ryan Luzinski	Mobile	SD	116	29	2	20	.250	117	36	0	10	.308
Scott Lydy	Birmingham	CWS	205	58	11	34	.283	195	48	9	31	.246
Jon Macalutas	Huntsville	Mil	158	46	2	24	.291	148	35	3	21	.236
Garry Maddox	El Paso	Ari	241	79	4	34	.328	251	66	11	41	.263
Ricky Magdaleno	New Haven	Sea	145	44	1	18	.303	113	26	0	6	.230
Chris Magruder	Shreveport	SF	242	57	3	38	.236	234	65	3	22	.278
T.R. Marcinczyk	Midland	Oak	248	79	16	68	.319	229	54	7	43	.236
Felix Martinez	Wichita	KC	146	36	2	10	.247	181	52	2	27	.287
Pablo Martinez	Greenville	Atl	121	29	0	11	.240	107	25	1	8	.234
Jared Mathis	Huntsville	Mil	109	29	0	11	.266	109	20	2	13	.183
Joe Mathis	New Haven	Sea	131	36	2	22	.275	109	29	0	8	.266
Julius Matos	El Paso	Ari	216	63	1	23	.292	209	56	4	18	.268
Luis Matos	Bowie	Bal	128	33	4	22	.258	155	34	5	14	.219
Donzell McDonald	Norwich	NYY	247	73	2	10	.296	286	72	2	23	.252
John McDonald	Akron	Cle	99	34	1	18	.343	127	33	0	8	.260
Cody McKay	Midland	Oak	163	47	1	18	.288	170	51	5	25	.300
Dan McKinley	Akron	Cle	234	61	0	13	.261	229	58	3	24	.253
Sean McNally	Wichita	KC	207	53	16	46	.256	233	71	20	63	.305
Tony Medrano	Wichita	KC	117	45	4	25	.385	140	42	1	7	.300
Adam Melhuse	Knoxville	Tor	176	54	7	28	.307	198	56	12	41	.283
Carlos Mendoza	Shreveport	SF	157	28	1	18	.178	175	39	2	16	.223
Mike Metcalfe	San Antonio	LA	217	59	2	29	.272	244	76	1	28	.311
Chad Meyers	West Tenn	ChC	109	36	2	16	.330	129	33	1	13	.256
Damon Minor	Shreveport	SF	229	62	8	41	.271	244	67	12	41	.275

Double-A Batting at Home and on the Road

Player	Team	Org	Home					Road				
			AB	H	HR	RBI	Avg	AB	H	HR	RBI	Avg
Derek Mitchell	Jacksonville	Det	197	41	3	20	.208	225	61	4	29	.271
Chad Moeller	New Britain	Min	119	37	1	14	.311	131	25	3	10	.191
Wonderful Monds	Chattanooga	Cin	160	45	4	18	.281	151	36	7	14	.238
Kenderick Moore	Wichita	KC	127	34	0	15	.268	116	27	0	12	.233
Willie Morales	Midland	Oak	177	54	8	37	.305	166	42	8	34	.253
Ramon Moreta	San Antonio	LA	168	42	1	15	.250	229	79	1	27	.345
Scott Morgan	Akron	Cle	158	44	10	32	.278	186	53	16	38	.285
Jeremy Morris	Norwich	NYY	205	49	5	25	.239	187	48	4	27	.257
Julio Mosquera	Orlando	TB	104	35	2	17	.337	155	44	2	20	.284
Rick Moss	New Britain	Min	119	38	3	18	.319	133	30	1	11	.226
Tony Mota	San Antonio	LA	171	51	4	28	.298	174	61	11	47	.351
Kelcey Mucker	New Britain	Min	175	51	0	11	.291	193	49	1	14	.254
Nate Murphy	Erie	Ana	170	42	8	32	.247	189	54	6	24	.286
Adrian Myers	Tulsa	Tex	147	32	0	15	.218	210	52	1	13	.248
Bry Nelson	West Tenn	ChC	220	55	6	34	.250	251	71	10	44	.283
Garrett Neubart	Binghamton	NYM	116	38	2	13	.328	144	37	1	8	.257
Tom Nevers	Chattanooga	Cin	158	42	6	21	.266	222	70	11	44	.315
Doug Newstrom	Birmingham	CWS	134	37	1	9	.276	119	35	2	14	.294
Kevin Nicholson	Mobile	SD	253	72	8	39	.285	236	69	7	42	.292
Dax Norris	Greenville	Atl	207	60	6	41	.290	196	52	9	25	.265
Chris Norton	Portland	Fla	154	44	20	55	.288	184	54	18	42	.293
Talmadge Nunnari	Harrisburg	Mon	120	45	2	16	.375	119	34	4	13	.286
Augie Ojeda	Bowie	Bal	225	64	5	25	.284	235	59	5	36	.251
Pablo Ozuna	Portland	Fla	254	74	5	25	.291	248	67	2	21	.270
Pete Paciorek	Mobile	SD	123	27	3	11	.220	103	23	1	6	.223
Jarrod Patterson	El Paso	Ari	144	59	4	35	.410	105	36	4	16	.343
Josh Paul	Birmingham	CWS	144	39	2	23	.271	175	50	2	19	.286
Richard Paz	Bowie	Bal	125	39	1	8	.312	148	39	1	12	.264
Rudy Pemberton	Birmingham	CWS	152	41	7	31	.270	155	44	11	29	.284
Elvis Pena	Carolina	Col	179	52	1	17	.291	177	51	1	14	.311
Tyrone Pendergrass	Greenville	Atl	176	49	4	20	.278	168	41	2	11	.244
Danny Peoples	Akron	Cle	222	61	13	40	.275	272	63	8	38	.232
Jhonny Perez	Jackson	Hou	149	40	4	15	.268	127	29	0	10	.228
Tommy Peterman	New Britain	Min	274	71	10	43	.259	264	70	10	41	.265
Paul Phillips	Wichita	KC	189	52	2	33	.275	204	53	1	23	.260
Adam Piatt	Midland	Oak	176	62	11	54	.343	228	79	17	57	.346
Kirk Pierce	Reading	Phi	118	32	3	21	.271	137	34	6	19	.248
Jose Pimentel	Greenville	Atl	189	39	2	22	.206	184	43	2	23	.223
Juan Piniella	Tulsa	Tex	245	70	5	27	.206	213	51	4	10	.230
Enohel Polanco	West Tenn	ChC	176	42	1	19	.239	178	43	2	16	.242
Nick Presto	Chattanooga	Cin	137	33	1	18	.241	87	27	1	10	.310
Alejandro Prieto	Wichita	KC	175	52	3	17	.295	184	54	3	24	.293
Rick Prieto	Mobile	SD	175	53	3	18	.303	184	50	3	25	.272
Julio Ramirez	Portland	Fla	278	82	8	38	.295	290	66	5	26	.228
Tike Redman	Altoona	Pit	251	59	1	20	.235	281	84	2	40	.299
Jackie Rexrode	Birmingham	Ari	97	27	0	13	.278	116	30	0	12	.259
Chris Richard	Arkansas	StL	214	60	12	44	.280	228	70	17	50	.307
Luis Rivas	New Britain	Min	283	81	5	28	.286	244	53	2	21	.217
Adam Robinson	Akron	Cle	133	39	1	13	.293	105	27	4	17	.257
Liu Rodriguez	Birmingham	CWS	137	35	0	15	.255	107	36	3	22	.336
Sammy Rodriguez	Binghamton	NYM	104	23	2	14	.221	99	23	1	10	.232
Nate Rolison	Portland	Fla	216	58	6	30	.269	222	73	11	35	.329
Jimmy Rollins	Reading	Phi	264	78	9	33	.295	268	67	2	23	.250
Aaron Royster	Reading	Phi	140	42	6	25	.300	197	48	2	23	.282
Chad Rupp	Knoxville	Tor	125	38	10	30	.304	116	24	6	14	.207
Rich Saitta	San Antonio	LA	116	26	1	13	.224	138	48	1	21	.348
Jerry Salzano	Chattanooga	Cin	147	50	2	24	.340	116	36	2	14	.310
Alex Sanchez	Orlando	TB	249	66	2	14	.265	251	61	0	15	.243
Victor Sanchez	Jackson	Hou	203	50	12	32	.246	204	52	5	36	.255
Yuri Sanchez	Binghamton	NYM	169	36	2	11	.213	212	52	3	19	.245

Player	Team	Org	Home					Road				
			AB	H	HR	RBI	Avg	AB	H	HR	RBI	Avg
Pedro Santana	Jacksonville	Det	261	64	2	13	.245	252	79	3	36	.313
Rob Sasser	Jacksonville	Det	206	57	4	26	.277	218	63	3	35	.289
Luis Saturria	Arkansas	StL	230	60	9	30	.261	254	58	7	31	.228
Chris Saunders	Chattanooga	Cin	99	38	3	19	.384	117	30	4	16	.256
Brian Schneider	Harrisburg	Mon	207	58	10	36	.280	214	53	7	30	.248
Chip Sell	El Paso	Ari	172	63	3	21	.366	157	38	5	14	.242
Tom Sergio	Tulsa	Tex	243	66	2	30	.272	269	83	8	42	.309
Rick Short	Bowie	Bal	205	68	8	37	.332	187	55	8	25	.294
Demond Smith	Greenville	Atl	207	71	9	42	.343	209	56	0	17	.268
Jeff Smith	New Britain	Min	124	35	3	14	.282	141	32	3	17	.227
Fausto Solano	Knoxville	Tor	165	48	6	30	.291	183	58	8	31	.317
Alfonso Soriano	Norwich	NYY	175	55	7	34	.314	186	55	8	34	.296
Juan Sosa	Carolina	Col	236	75	2	25	.318	254	60	5	17	.236
Dorian Speed	West Tenn	ChC	183	52	7	32	.284	232	59	7	25	.254
Ryan Stromsborg	Knoxville	Tor	189	43	4	21	.228	188	51	5	24	.271
John Tamargo	Binghamton	NYM	170	40	2	19	.235	193	38	2	18	.197
Reggie Taylor	Reading	Phi	271	78	6	26	.288	255	62	9	35	.243
Nate Tebbs	Trenton	Bos	156	44	1	15	.282	209	55	3	20	.263
Fausto Tejero	Erie	Ana	89	21	1	7	.236	122	24	2	11	.197
Juan Thomas	New Haven	Sea	150	40	10	30	.267	117	25	6	21	.214
Andy Thompson	Knoxville	Tor	120	31	5	27	.258	134	31	10	26	.231
Jorge Toca	Binghamton	NYM	143	45	14	39	.315	136	41	6	28	.301
Juan Tolentino	Erie	Ana	222	53	6	29	.239	267	70	3	32	.262
Goefrey Tomlinson	Wichita	KC	236	65	4	29	.275	243	69	0	17	.284
Yorvit Torrealba	Shreveport	SF	109	26	3	8	.239	108	27	1	11	.250
Andy Tracy	Harrisburg	Mon	227	67	20	65	.295	266	68	17	63	.256
Chris Truby	Jackson	Hou	219	76	21	54	.347	245	55	7	33	.224
Pete Tucci	Mobile	SD	167	47	9	23	.281	145	31	2	12	.214
Jon Tucker	Harrisburg	Mon	181	51	9	34	.282	181	42	4	21	.232
Josh Tyler	Shreveport	SF	161	40	2	20	.248	170	47	1	19	.276
Jason Tyner	Binghamton	NYM	262	84	0	18	.321	256	78	0	15	.305
Victor Valencia	Norwich	NYY	193	38	6	27	.197	203	50	16	45	.246
Yohanny Valera	Binghamton	NYM	109	33	6	25	.303	95	26	3	14	.274
Ramon Vazquez	New Haven	Sea	214	58	5	27	.271	224	55	0	18	.246
Wilton Veras	Trenton	Bos	234	69	8	45	.295	240	64	3	30	.267
Scott Vieira	West Tenn	ChC	219	59	3	24	.269	236	74	7	34	.314
Chris Wakeland	Jacksonville	Det	109	36	7	19	.330	103	32	6	17	.311
Ron Walker	West Tenn	ChC	135	33	3	16	.244	167	33	6	24	.198
Joromy Waro	Harrisburg	Mon	185	56	7	37	.303	196	44	2	19	.224
Dusty Wathan	New Haven	Sea	166	48	1	19	.289	167	45	3	18	.269
Pat Watkins	Carolina	Col	165	49	2	22	.297	147	44	1	18	.299
Jake Weber	New Haven	Sea	230	50	2	21	.217	233	59	9	38	.290
Luke Wilcox	Orlando	TB	161	39	12	41	.242	172	51	8	23	.297
Brad Wilkerson	Harrisburg	Mon	199	51	4	24	.256	223	48	4	25	.215
Glenn Williams	Greenville	Atl	108	27	3	12	.250	96	19	1	3	.198
Jason Williams	Chattanooga	Cin	169	56	4	29	.331	163	50	3	16	.307
Craig Wilson	Altoona	Pit	181	47	8	28	.260	181	50	12	41	.276
Mike Wolff	Erie	Ana	158	43	8	26	.272	149	33	2	14	.221
Jason Woolf	Arkansas	StL	107	34	2	7	.318	213	53	6	8	.249
Shawn Wooten	Erie	Ana	249	65	7	34	.261	269	86	12	54	.320
Travis Young	Shreveport	SF	195	53	2	17	.272	221	57	3	21	.258
Junior Zamora	Binghamton	NYM	139	33	4	16	.237	116	28	6	17	.241
Julio Zuleta	West Tenn	ChC	226	71	11	48	.314	256	71	10	49	.277

Double-A Pitching vs. Lefthanded and Righthanded Batters

			vs Left					vs Right				
Player	Team	Org	AB	H	HR	SO	Avg	AB	H	HR	SO	Avg
Stevenson Agosto	Mobile	SD	75	14	2	22	.187	227	67	11	37	.295
Paul Ah Yat	Altoona	Pit	96	22	1	25	.229	261	64	5	65	.245
Pat Ahearne	New Haven	Sea	205	50	3	34	.244	254	64	3	46	.252
Jay Akin	Huntsville	Mil	85	28	5	16	.329	248	65	4	46	.262
Victor Alvarez	San Antonio	LA	73	26	2	9	.356	145	32	3	34	.221
John Ambrose	Arkansas	StL	153	54	6	26	.353	244	54	5	52	.221
Jason Anderson	Midland	Oak	109	34	2	19	.312	352	114	13	55	.324
Ryan Anderson	New Haven	Sea	98	30	4	32	.306	407	101	5	130	.248
Clayton Andrews	Knoxville	Tor	94	23	4	23	.245	415	120	9	70	.289
Jeff Andrews	El Paso	Ari	120	35	0	15	.292	168	52	6	25	.310
Tony Armas Jr.	Harrisburg	Mon	237	52	5	32	.219	307	71	5	74	.231
Bronson Arroyo	Altoona	Pit	309	99	9	45	.320	286	68	6	55	.238
Justin Atchley	Chattanooga	Cin	71	18	0	15	.254	315	96	9	55	.305
Ross Atkins	Akron	Cle	146	33	1	22	.226	194	57	9	21	.294
Mike Bacsik	Akron	Cle	151	37	5	29	.245	431	127	19	55	.295
Benito Baez	Midland	Oak	68	18	1	19	.265	150	50	4	32	.333
John Bale	Knoxville	Tor	47	13	3	17	.277	201	51	4	74	.254
Marty Barnett	Reading	Phi	82	16	0	12	.195	118	27	2	21	.229
Jim Baron	Altoona	Pit	134	34	4	18	.254	422	107	9	57	.254
Chuck Beale	Trenton	Bos	103	30	3	24	.291	130	41	3	17	.315
Ray Beasley	Greenville	Atl	74	19	3	18	.257	240	65	5	53	.271
Matt Beaumont	Erie	Ana	124	26	1	27	.210	275	71	12	49	.258
Greg Beck	Huntsville	Mil	203	57	14	28	.281	377	100	10	65	.265
Robbie Beckett	San Antonio	LA	100	15	2	32	.150	259	67	5	60	.259
Todd Belitz	Orlando	TB	95	21	1	19	.221	532	148	22	99	.278
Mike Bell	Bowie	Bal	157	33	7	31	.210	350	101	6	48	.289
Rob Bell	Chattanooga	Cin	110	31	4	30	.282	162	44	3	38	.272
Rafael Betancourt	Trenton	Bos	81	21	3	27	.259	121	29	4	30	.240
Bobby Bevel	Carolina	Col	52	10	1	17	.192	208	60	6	41	.288
Jason Beverlin	Norwich	NYY	303	71	9	67	.234	340	82	7	80	.241
Nick Bierbrodt	El Paso	Ari	67	16	0	14	.239	226	62	3	41	.274
Alberto Blanco	Jacksonville	Det	56	11	1	10	.196	206	47	9	52	.228
Matt Blank	Harrisburg	Mon	77	20	1	10	.260	253	74	13	32	.292
David Bleazard	Knoxville	Tor	124	32	0	15	.258	191	49	4	34	.257
Cedrick Bowers	Orlando	TB	79	21	2	24	.266	400	104	16	114	.260
Josh Bradford	Knoxville	Tor	136	40	2	26	.294	266	69	7	57	.259
J.D. Brammer	Akron	Cle	128	24	2	31	.188	145	29	4	38	.200
Bryan Braswell	Jackson	Hou	141	37	7	32	.262	531	143	20	99	.269
Jason Brester	Reading	Phi	107	31	2	27	.290	291	74	6	60	.254
	Carolina	Col	44	9	0	6	.205	194	62	8	38	.320
Ryan Brewer	Wichita	KC	101	29	2	9	.287	161	56	7	25	.348
Corey Brittan	Binghamton	NYM	157	33	2	28	.210	188	51	4	32	.271
Jamie Brown	Akron	Cle	227	70	5	39	.308	290	70	6	59	.241
Bucky Buckles	Tulsa	Tex	100	28	6	14	.280	171	43	4	25	.251
Nate Bump	Shreveport	SF	122	35	5	23	.287	229	50	4	36	.218
A.J. Burnett	Portland	Fla	204	54	4	49	.265	265	78	11	72	.294
Kiko Calero	Wichita	KC	208	64	6	41	.308	304	79	8	51	.260
Aaron Cames	Portland	Fla	149	47	9	30	.315	227	63	8	36	.278
Ken Carlyle	Greenville	Atl	99	25	5	9	.253	199	64	6	24	.322
Lance Carter	Wichita	KC	89	24	0	13	.270	162	25	1	64	.154
Silvio Censale	Reading	Phi	65	23	2	12	.354	155	51	13	24	.329
Carlos Chantres	Birmingham	CWS	197	43	4	42	.218	323	79	9	63	.245
Jake Chapman	Wichita	KC	91	29	0	25	.319	188	58	3	28	.309
Trevor Cobb	Tulsa	Tex	80	14	0	21	.175	223	65	13	23	.291
Derrick Cook	Tulsa	Tex	193	66	4	30	.342	273	71	8	41	.260
Brian Cooper	Erie	Ana	276	68	6	57	.246	318	78	11	86	.245
Mark Corey	Binghamton	NYM	315	80	8	59	.254	305	95	10	52	.311
Edwin Corps	Shreveport	SF	129	41	2	11	.318	208	57	7	23	.274
Robbie Crabtree	Shreveport	SF	75	13	0	15	.173	157	37	2	50	.236
Paxton Crawford	Trenton	Bos	297	67	6	67	.226	319	84	6	44	.263
Jack Cressend	Trenton	Bos	289	78	4	68	.270	340	93	9	68	.274
Jason Crews	El Paso	Ari	87	24	4	13	.276	145	49	3	17	.338
Jim Crowell	Chattanooga	Cin	105	30	1	15	.286	485	143	11	65	.295
Derek Dace	El Paso	Ari	60	14	2	14	.233	142	44	2	20	.310
Pat Daneker	Birmingham	CWS	134	36	3	27	.269	280	70	3	44	.250
David Daniels	Altoona	Pit	96	26	0	18	.271	155	29	6	45	.187
David Darwin	Jacksonville	Det	138	32	1	33	.232	598	162	18	67	.271
Allen Davis	San Antonio	LA	121	27	3	23	.223	394	113	10	64	.287
Doug Davis	Tulsa	Tex	43	10	1	10	.233	234	55	8	69	.235
Jason Davis	Shreveport	SF	50	10	0	5	.200	173	32	1	49	.185
Kane Davis	Altoona	Pit	186	50	0	23	.269	185	47	5	30	.254
Joey Dawley	Greenville	Atl	130	33	4	32	.254	210	43	1	57	.205
Fran. de la Cruz	Norwich	NYY	242	68	5	51	.281	279	73	5	40	.262
Javier de la Hoya	Bowie	Bal	133	33	4	32	.248	155	31	8	36	.200
Pete Della Ratta	Binghamton	NYM	140	38	2	26	.271	168	37	2	42	.220
Marc Deschenes	Akron	Cle	102	29	2	21	.284	135	28	3	43	.207
Matt DeWitt	Arkansas	StL	226	70	9	27	.310	351	83	12	80	.236
Scott DeWitt	Carolina	Col	75	14	1	17	.187	203	70	1	48	.345
R.A. Dickey	Tulsa	Tex	156	41	5	29	.263	215	64	8	30	.298
Craig Dingman	Norwich	NYY	105	23	1	29	.219	166	33	1	61	.199
Rich Dishman	Greenville	Atl	184	50	6	48	.272	354	96	13	83	.271
Robert Dodd	Reading	Phi	93	29	1	28	.312	212	49	7	51	.231
Brian Doughty	Mobile	SD	174	50	5	17	.287	374	111	15	52	.297
Scott Downs	West Tenn	ChC	55	6	0	24	.109	234	50	2	77	.214
AJ Drumheller	Mobile	SD	48	12	1	13	.250	218	66	6	42	.303
Eric DuBose	Midland	Oak	75	17	2	22	.227	227	72	8	46	.317
Geoff Duncan	Portland	Fla	86	22	2	16	.256	161	37	6	43	.230
Chad Durbin	Wichita	KC	241	62	7	49	.257	357	92	13	73	.258
Adam Eaton	Reading	Phi	146	33	3	35	.226	135	27	6	32	.200
Trevor Enders	Orlando	TB	79	14	0	9	.177	272	72	4	54	.265
Jose Espinal	New Britain	Min	233	71	3	32	.305	300	89	7	58	.297
Jake Esteves	Shreveport	SF	127	31	1	16	.244	212	45	6	37	.212
Luis Estrella	Shreveport	SF	110	28	0	17	.255	227	49	2	58	.216
Seth Etherton	Erie	Ana	282	63	5	80	.223	353	90	9	73	.255
Brian Falkenborg	Bowie	Bal	145	31	2	33	.214	173	46	9	44	.266
Brian Fitzgerald	New Haven	Sea	55	17	0	12	.309	150	41	2	25	.273

			vs Left					vs Right				
Player	Team	Org	AB	H	HR	SO	Avg	AB	H	HR	SO	Avg
Josh Fogg	Birmingham	CWS	92	27	3	15	.293	131	39	5	25	.298
Rick Forney	Greenville	Atl	95	21	1	25	.221	170	46	4	45	.271
Aaron France	Altoona	Pit	167	29	3	48	.174	186	50	5	22	.269
Brian Fuentes	New Haven	Sea	53	16	0	11	.302	155	37	5	55	.239
Eric Gagne	San Antonio	LA	232	40	4	78	.172	374	82	13	107	.219
Apostol Garcia	San Antonio	LA	144	40	3	17	.278	250	70	2	33	.280
Hal Garrett	San Antonio	LA	136	28	2	24	.206	203	42	6	52	.207
John Geis	Arkansas	StL	45	12	3	6	.267	172	53	6	23	.308
Isabel Giron	Mobile	SD	216	59	6	53	.273	405	109	23	73	.269
Chris Gissell	West Tenn	ChC	158	48	2	17	.304	230	73	8	40	.317
Gary Glover	Knoxville	Tor	104	28	2	18	.269	208	42	3	59	.202
Gary Goldsmith	Jacksonville	Det	94	32	1	11	.340	206	52	7	19	.252
Jason Gooding	Wichita	KC	102	31	4	19	.304	451	145	12	44	.322
Chris Gorrell	Midland	Oak	96	42	5	11	.438	160	50	2	30	.313
Kevin Gregg	Midland	Oak	152	29	3	29	.191	188	46	4	37	.245
Kevin Gryboski	New Haven	Sea	90	26	2	17	.289	147	41	3	24	.279
Domingo Guzman	Mobile	SD	64	20	1	16	.313	140	40	1	22	.286
Luther Hackman	Carolina	Col	96	21	0	21	.219	140	32	4	29	.229
Phil Haigler	New Britain	Min	108	35	3	6	.324	114	39	3	12	.342
Travis Harper	Orlando	TB	82	21	4	29	.256	196	52	6	39	.265
D.J. Harris	Knoxville	Tor	85	20	2	9	.235	162	53	7	27	.327
Tommy Harrison	Greenville	Atl	98	33	3	18	.337	158	42	8	24	.266
Al Hawkins	Huntsville	Mil	130	39	2	18	.300	269	87	8	38	.323
Andy Hazlett	Trenton	Bos	187	46	4	42	.246	431	109	11	81	.253
Andy Heckman	Shreveport	SF	103	23	3	19	.223	413	119	8	51	.288
Scott Henderson	Portland	Fla	132	32	1	39	.242	170	35	3	44	.206
Mark Hendrickson	Knoxville	Tor	34	12	0	5	.353	195	61	4	34	.313
Russ Herbert	Reading	Phi	156	47	5	27	.301	164	43	2	28	.262
Brett Herbison	Binghamton	NYM	256	66	8	31	.258	324	95	12	29	.293
Maximo Heredia	Bowie	Bal	114	34	7	18	.298	187	46	5	38	.246
Elvin Hernandez	West Tenn	ChC	212	52	7	30	.245	393	122	9	68	.310
Santos Hernandez	Orlando	TB	73	18	2	15	.247	134	25	3	32	.187
Junior Herndon	Mobile	SD	199	63	14	27	.317	437	109	10	60	.249
Kevin Hite	Mobile	SD	66	27	2	5	.409	165	44	4	47	.267
David Hooten	New Britain	Min	159	33	2	32	.208	232	61	8	57	.263
Scott Huntsman	Huntsville	Mil	94	29	4	6	.309	174	43	4	25	.247
Chad Hutchinson	Arkansas	StL	218	47	4	63	.216	304	80	8	87	.263
Ryan Jacobs	Carolina	Col	102	28	0	20	.275	347	92	10	69	.265
Tom Jacquez	Reading	Phi	134	32	3	27	.239	373	117	17	41	.314
Marty Janzen	Chattanooga	Cin	70	26	3	9	.371	135	28	3	32	.207
Mark Johnson	Norwich	NYY	143	30	3	22	.210	201	58	4	30	.289
Doug Johnston	Huntsville	Mil	167	46	4	24	.275	289	82	13	56	.284
Jason Karnuth	Arkansas	StL	238	65	8	30	.273	380	110	8	41	.289
Ryan Karp	Tulsa	Tex	50	8	0	10	.160	179	42	5	39	.235
Brad Kaufman	Norwich	NYY	143	34	2	39	.238	173	42	4	42	.243
Greg Keagle	Jacksonville	Det	93	28	2	16	.301	121	30	2	12	.248
Al Kermode	El Paso	Ari	115	30	2	23	.261	156	38	5	33	.244
Jason Kershner	Reading	Phi	117	23	1	36	.197	241	76	13	55	.315
Tim Kester	Jackson	Hou	100	29	3	14	.290	203	62	6	37	.305
Sun Kim	Trenton	Bos	269	85	9	57	.316	312	75	7	73	.240
Andy Kimball	Midland	Oak	133	39	8	23	.293	231	73	6	64	.316
Matt Kinney	New Britain	Min	91	27	2	22	.297	148	42	6	28	.284
Brian Knoll	Shreveport	SF	155	39	7	37	.252	321	78	8	54	.243
Eric Knott	El Paso	Ari	139	39	1	23	.281	515	159	10	60	.309
Gary Knotts	Portland	Fla	145	36	4	31	.248	165	43	8	32	.261
Ryan Kohlmeier	Bowie	Bal	98	23	5	31	.235	122	21	5	47	.172
Eric LeBlanc	Chattanooga	Cin	101	32	4	18	.317	144	31	3	19	.215
Corey Lee	Tulsa	Tex	81	27	0	15	.333	418	105	11	106	.251
Derek Lee	Huntsville	Mil	75	17	1	12	.227	462	126	15	65	.273
Brandon Leese	Portland	Fla	148	52	4	19	.351	193	58	4	33	.301
Allen Levrault	Huntsville	Mil	121	20	5	29	.165	240	57	6	53	.237
Julian Leyva	Midland	Oak	119	41	5	14	.345	142	45	5	25	.317
Joe Lisio	Norwich	NYY	97	24	2	23	.247	117	34	2	26	.291
Kyle Lohse	New Britain	Min	131	44	3	16	.336	145	43	6	25	.297
Rodrigo Lopez	Mobile	SD	183	64	5	39	.350	470	123	9	99	.262
Benny Lowe	Knoxville	Tor	74	12	0	26	.162	182	56	8	44	.308
Mike Lyons	Binghamton	NYM	138	34	3	32	.246	163	42	3	38	.258
Scott MacRae	Chattanooga	Cin	183	45	9	33	.246	313	94	9	48	.300
Kats Maeda	Norwich	NYY	150	42	2	19	.280	147	40	5	29	.272
Alan Mahaffey	New Britain	Min	111	36	8	23	.324	276	73	7	66	.264
Oswaldo Mairena	Norwich	NYY	100	24	2	23	.240	116	24	1	24	.207
Randi Mallard	Chattanooga	Cin	108	45	4	13	.417	183	47	3	32	.257
David Manning	West Tenn	ChC	154	51	4	19	.331	301	62	3	59	.206
Julio Manon	Orlando	TB	112	35	3	19	.313	165	45	6	34	.273
Tim Manwiller	Midland	Oak	155	47	3	24	.303	177	48	3	34	.271
Adrian Manzano	Greenville	Atl	90	24	0	17	.267	147	37	6	34	.252
Jason Marquis	Greenville	Atl	75	18	4	12	.240	141	34	3	23	.241
Chandler Martin	Carolina	Col	258	62	7	56	.240	362	91	7	74	.251
Jose Martinez	Tulsa	Tex	150	44	4	25	.293	245	68	12	45	.278
Romulo Martinez	Jacksonville	Det	85	27	0	11	.318	208	58	5	35	.279
Willie Martinez	Akron	Cle	276	73	2	39	.264	308	90	18	52	.292
Troy Mattes	Harrisburg	Mon	166	47	3	33	.283	210	67	9	25	.319
Dave Maurer	Mobile	SD	61	10	0	15	.164	206	49	7	44	.238
Blake Mayo	San Antonio	LA	108	38	2	18	.352	208	66	3	31	.317
Sam McConnell	Altoona	Pit	67	17	3	14	.254	186	65	4	26	.349
Scott McCrary	Binghamton	NYM	112	30	2	15	.268	105	42	6	14	.400
Mike McDougal	Bowie	Bal	100	36	6	20	.360	143	34	4	27	.238
Tony McKnight	Jackson	Hou	260	73	7	48	.281	344	61	8	70	.177
Gil Meche	New Haven	Sea	77	14	0	20	.182	144	37	3	36	.257
Carlos Medina	Bowie	Bal	79	21	1	20	.266	223	65	5	50	.291
Jason Middlebrook	Mobile	SD	79	27	4	7	.342	179	51	5	31	.285
Chad Miles	Jacksonville	Det	51	8	2	18	.157	199	70	7	32	.352
Matt Montgomery	San Antonio	LA	100	31	0	17	.310	129	34	1	22	.264
Juan Moreno	Tulsa	Tex	61	8	0	29	.131	154	25	5	54	.162
Paul Morse	Erie	Ana	155	34	3	23	.219	199	49	6	29	.246
Tony Mounce	Jackson	Hou	70	18	1	11	.257	196	46	5	69	.235

Double-A Pitching vs. Lefthanded and Righthanded Batters

Player	Team	Org	vs Left AB	H	HR	SO	Avg	vs Right AB	H	HR	SO	Avg
Aaron Myette	Birmingham	CWS	228	52	9	48	.228	386	86	10	87	.223
Eric Newman	West Tenn	ChC	99	20	1	34	.202	199	41	4	56	.206
Geronimo Newton	New Haven	Sea	55	17	0	8	.309	171	43	8	40	.251
Randy Niles	Midland	Oak	155	46	2	24	.297	225	80	5	22	.356
Ben Norris	El Paso	Ari	87	29	2	17	.333	380	103	11	70	.271
Phillip Norton	West Tenn	ChC	68	14	1	16	.206	245	58	4	65	.237
Brian O'Connor	Altoona	Pit	134	44	5	29	.328	452	108	5	77	.239
Tomokazu Ohka	Trenton	Bos	126	31	3	26	.246	144	32	6	27	.222
Paul O'Malley	Jackson	Hou	97	20	3	25	.206	173	55	7	40	.318
Pablo Ortega	Orlando	TB	187	44	7	27	.235	313	103	7	47	.329
Ramon Ortiz	Erie	Ana	194	50	4	38	.258	178	38	8	48	.213
Mick Pageler	Portland	Fla	98	35	2	14	.357	120	35	2	30	.292
Roberto Paredes	Huntsville	Mil	57	16	1	9	.281	144	32	3	26	.222
Christian Parker	Harrisburg	Mon	142	39	6	16	.275	187	47	5	29	.251
John Patterson	El Paso	Ari	171	46	5	45	.269	212	52	11	72	.245
Brad Penny	El Paso	Ari	147	43	3	34	.293	212	66	6	66	.311
Adam Pettyjohn	Jacksonville	Det	90	20	0	20	.222	407	114	13	72	.280
Tommy Phelps	Harrisburg	Mon	56	17	3	7	.304	208	59	10	29	.284
Joel Pineiro	New Haven	Sea	314	80	6	66	.255	342	110	12	50	.322
Trey Poland	Tulsa	Tex	109	34	4	19	.312	370	105	7	61	.284
Cliff Politte	Reading	Phi	169	41	1	39	.243	246	71	11	58	.289
Eddie Priest	Chattanooga	Cin	56	18	2	9	.321	260	81	4	51	.312
Steve Prihoda	Wichita	KC	91	23	4	13	.253	227	68	4	38	.300
Luke Prokopec	San Antonio	LA	235	66	6	55	.281	382	106	12	73	.277
Denis Pujals	Orlando	TB	92	32	2	7	.348	191	50	4	32	.262
Ken Pumphrey	Binghamton	NYM	230	55	2	41	.239	293	91	8	43	.311
David Pyc	Reading	Phi	92	26	1	14	.283	234	69	8	37	.295
Scott Randall	Carolina	Col	144	41	2	39	.285	238	60	4	63	.252
Kevin Rawitzer	Carolina	Col	53	17	1	14	.321	216	56	4	40	.259
Steve Reed	Arkansas	StL	126	33	9	19	.262	191	54	6	26	.283
Ray Ricken	Mobile	SD	168	55	6	15	.327	269	67	9	52	.249
Chad Ricketts	West Tenn	ChC	74	25	5	23	.338	174	30	3	57	.172
Matt Riley	Bowie	Bal	109	31	2	29	.284	359	82	11	102	.228
Michael Riley	Shreveport	SF	84	21	1	24	.250	314	59	5	83	.188
Scott Rivette	Knoxville	Tor	100	32	0	23	.320	203	53	2	51	.261
Jake Robbins	Norwich	NYY	227	58	3	31	.256	205	60	4	32	.293
Chris Roberts	Carolina	Col	70	19	0	14	.271	241	57	10	38	.237
Grant Roberts	Binghamton	NYM	235	66	4	35	.281	271	69	5	59	.255
Mark Roberts	Birmingham	CWS	166	38	5	29	.229	304	70	6	55	.230
Jeromie Robertson	Jackson	Hou	141	42	7	26	.298	586	142	15	107	.242
Bobby Rodgers	Portland	Fla	225	70	6	40	.311	268	77	7	69	.287
J.C. Romero	New Britain	Min	10	1	1	10	.100	153	41	5	43	.268
Derek Root	Jackson	Hou	130	39	5	24	.300	483	128	12	105	.265
Matt Saier	Wichita	KC	84	21	1	24	.250	256	72	6	37	.281
Cody Salter	Erie	Ana	95	34	1	4	.358	122	31	1	12	.254
Martin Sanchez	El Paso	Ari	163	44	6	25	.270	216	51	4	48	.236
Frankie Sanders	Akron	Cle	211	69	7	38	.327	265	70	5	34	.264
Victor Santos	Jacksonville	Det	223	52	4	48	.233	427	98	12	98	.230
Ryan Saylor	Harrisburg	Mon	104	22	2	37	.212	114	28	5	18	.246
Trevor Schaffer	Knoxville	Tor	62	18	3	6	.290	157	51	7	17	.325
Brian Schmack	Birmingham	CWS	77	21	0	17	.273	164	39	3	39	.238
Scott Schroeffel	El Paso	Ari	84	20	4	23	.238	176	55	5	29	.313
Carl Schutz	West Tenn	ChC	53	14	1	20	.264	147	40	3	26	.272
Jason Secoda	Birmingham	CWS	166	43	3	38	.259	258	57	4	56	.221

Player	Team	Org	vs Left AB	H	HR	SO	Avg	vs Right AB	H	HR	SO	Avg
Jason Sekany	Trenton	Bos	273	62	3	55	.227	323	81	5	61	.251
Scot Shields	Erie	Ana	110	27	2	35	.245	154	30	8	46	.195
Anthony Shumaker	Reading	Phi	49	6	0	17	.122	176	42	3	43	.239
Jacob Shumate	Greenville	Atl	78	15	2	20	.192	122	28	4	28	.230
Ted Silva	Tulsa	Tex	94	23	4	15	.245	180	41	6	33	.228
Steve Smetana	Trenton	Bos	110	32	2	15	.291	215	58	6	46	.270
Dan Smith	West Tenn	ChC	78	17	3	24	.218	203	53	6	54	.261
Toby Smith	Wichita	KC	125	35	3	13	.280	188	51	3	27	.271
Gabe Sollecito	Tulsa	Tex	107	29	5	20	.271	250	56	1	60	.224
Cam Spence	Norwich	NYY	180	59	4	31	.328	192	59	3	31	.307
Dennis Stark	New Haven	Sea	243	75	5	36	.309	320	76	9	67	.237
Jason Stevenson	Knoxville	Tor	148	41	4	30	.277	215	58	4	43	.270
Brian Sweeney	New Haven	Sea	182	45	7	42	.247	257	80	11	41	.311
Michael Tejera	Portland	Fla	143	36	6	43	.252	433	101	7	109	.233
Robert Theodile	Huntsville	Mil	121	40	3	21	.331	252	78	6	39	.310
Evan Thomas	Reading	Phi	197	48	3	54	.244	283	75	4	73	.265
Kevin Tolar	Chattanooga	Cin	49	11	0	19	.224	164	50	2	41	.305
Josh Towers	Bowie	Bal	368	96	14	51	.261	371	108	12	55	.291
Keith Troutman	Erie	Ana	106	32	5	21	.302	125	34	3	28	.272
T.J. Tucker	Harrisburg	Mon	188	43	7	20	.229	254	07	5	59	.204
Brad Tweedlie	Trenton	Bos	99	28	0	16	.283	125	31	3	15	.248
Jeff Urban	Shreveport	SF	51	15	2	10	.294	243	85	6	44	.350
Mike Vavrek	Carolina	Col	54	17	4	10	.315	152	54	7	31	.355
Jason Verdugo	Shreveport	SF	74	15	3	14	.203	166	43	4	32	.259
Brandon Villafuerte	Portland	Fla	140	33	4	29	.236	231	64	7	56	.277
Luis Vizcaino	Midland	Oak	185	63	10	26	.341	233	57	8	62	.245
Tyler Walker	Binghamton	NYM	103	28	6	29	.272	164	50	5	30	.305
Doug Walls	Carolina	Col	224	69	7	50	.308	356	90	7	90	.253
Mark Watson	Akron	Cle	104	34	0	15	.327	339	109	9	42	.322
Alan Webb	Jacksonville	Det	69	22	2	10	.319	460	118	15	78	.257
Neil Weber	San Antonio	LA	56	23	0	4	.411	162	39	3	27	.241
Clint Weibl	Arkansas	StL	174	48	3	44	.276	254	73	8	31	.287
Kip Wells	Birmingham	CWS	107	19	0	20	.178	141	30	5	24	.213
Jake Westbrook	Harrisburg	Mon	289	77	8	29	.266	367	103	6	61	.281
Dan Wheeler	Orlando	TB	82	25	3	17	.305	140	31	4	36	.221
Curtis Whitley	Birmingham	CWS	56	22	1	8	.393	145	36	3	16	.248
Kris Wilson	Wichita	KC	129	48	7	15	.372	173	43	4	30	.249
Joe Winkelsas	Greenville	Atl	80	20	1	9	.250	161	54	4	29	.309
Matt Wise	Erie	Ana	184	43	2	35	.234	195	59	8	37	.303
Widd Workman	San Antonio	LA	80	26	2	12	.325	128	47	7	15	.367
L.J. Yankosky	Greenville	Atl	150	39	1	15	.260	287	83	4	47	.289
Nate Yeskie	New Britain	Min	247	72	8	48	.291	271	85	7	54	.314
Jeff Yoder	West Tenn	ChC	178	41	1	47	.230	313	74	9	62	.236
Danny Young	West Tenn	ChC	42	10	1	12	.238	175	38	1	55	.217
Victor Zambrano	Orlando	TB	104	34	2	21	.327	225	58	3	60	.258
Pete Zamora	San Antonio	LA	68	17	0	11	.250	182	62	5	30	.341
Dave Zancanaro	Norwich	NYY	63	17	1	12	.270	224	47	3	49	.210

Double-A Pitching at Home and on the Road

			Home					Road				
Player	Team	Org	G	IP	W	L	ERA	G	IP	W	L	ERA
Stevenson Agosto	Mobile	SD	21	46.0	0	3	5.09	19	35.0	3	0	6.94
Paul Ah Yat	Altoona	Pit	7	46.0	4	2	2.35	9	49.0	4	2	3.67
Pat Ahearne	New Haven	Sea	10	72.0	4	2	2.25	7	52.0	4	1	3.12
Jay Akin	Huntsville	Mil	27	49.0	1	3	3.86	19	34.2	1	2	4.67
John Ambrose	Arkansas	StL	17	47.2	2	6	5.66	17	59.0	2	6	3.97
Jason Anderson	Midland	Oak	10	48.0	2	3	6.19	13	63.0	2	6	7.43
Ryan Anderson	New Haven	Sea	13	75.1	5	7	3.82	11	58.0	4	6	5.43
Clayton Andrews	Knoxville	Tor	13	73.0	6	2	2.71	12	59.2	4	6	5.43
Tony Armas Jr.	Harrisburg	Mon	13	79.1	6	3	2.38	11	70.0	3	4	3.47
Bronson Arroyo	Altoona	Pit	17	109.1	10	4	2.80	8	43.2	5	0	5.77
Justin Atchley	Chattanooga	Cin	6	32.2	0	3	6.06	11	64.1	4	6	2.10
Ross Atkins	Akron	Cle	15	35.0	4	5	7.20	18	52.0	2	3	4.85
Mike Bacsik	Akron	Cle	15	84.0	5	8	4.82	11	65.0	6	3	4.43
Jim Baron	Altoona	Pit	14	70.0	6	1	2.19	15	75.0	3	8	5.64
Ray Beasley	Greenville	Atl	26	47.0	5	0	2.68	24	34.0	2	4	7.41
Matt Beaumont	Erie	Ana	17	60.0	2	5	4.50	15	46.0	3	1	5.09
Greg Beck	Huntsville	Mil	14	76.0	6	4	4.62	12	75.0	4	5	4.32
Robbie Beckett	San Antonio	LA	8	47.0	5	3	2.87	10	50.0	2	4	7.38
Todd Belitz	Orlando	TB	17	100.0	8	6	5.67	11	60.2	1	3	5.93
Mike Bell	Bowie	Bal	22	75.1	2	3	3.94	19	55.2	5	4	5.50
Jason Beverlin	Norwich	NYY	12	80.1	5	5	2.91	16	92.1	10	4	4.39
Matt Blank	Harrisburg	Mon	5	35.0	3	1	3.09	10	50.0	3	2	4.50
David Bleazard	Knoxville	Tor	6	39.2	3	0	1.13	9	47.0	2	3	4.98
Cedrick Bowers	Orlando	TB	12	58.2	4	5	6.44	15	66.0	2	4	5.59
Josh Bradford	Knoxville	Tor	16	50.2	3	2	4.97	18	54.0	2	2	5.67
Bryan Braswell	Jackson	Hou	14	87.1	4	3	4.02	14	83.1	5	7	5.08
Jason Brester	Reading	Phi	9	59.0	5	2	2.90	7	46.0	2	3	4.89
Corey Brittan	Binghamton	NYM	28	47.2	0	3	2.83	26	43.0	2	1	2.72
Jamie Brown	Akron	Cle	11	67.0	2	5	4.84	12	71.0	3	4	4.31
Nate Bump	Shreveport	SF	8	48.0	3	4	1.69	9	44.0	1	6	5.11
A.J. Burnett	Portland	Fla	13	61.0	5	4	5.31	13	59.2	1	8	5.73
Kiko Calero	Wichita	KC	13	66.0	6	1	4.77	13	63.0	3	2	3.43
Aaron Cames	Portland	Fla	10	42.0	1	2	6.21	13	53.2	2	4	5.03
Carlos Chantres	Birmingham	CWS	18	90.1	4	3	2.99	10	50.2	2	5	4.44
Derrick Cook	Tulsa	Tex	11	54.0	2	3	5.83	10	60.0	5	3	5.55
Brian Cooper	Erie	Ana	9	62.0	2	2	3.48	13	96.0	8	3	3.19
Mark Corey	Binghamton	NYM	17	85.0	4	7	5.93	13	70.0	3	6	4.76
Edwin Corps	Shreveport	SF	11	40.2	2	2	4.43	13	43.2	3	2	4.74
Paxton Crawford	Trenton	Bos	15	82.1	3	5	5.47	13	80.1	4	3	2.69
Jack Cressend	Trenton	Bos	15	92.0	5	7	4.79	13	68.0	3	3	4.37
Jim Crowell	Chattanooga	Cin	14	78.0	6	2	5.08	13	70.0	4	3	5.14
Pat Daneker	Birmingham	CWS	7	48.0	3	3	3.19	9	60.2	3	5	3.26
David Darwin	Jacksonville	Det	14	89.1	4	8	4.43	14	97.1	10	4	2.77
Allen Davis	San Antonio	LA	13	66.0	5	3	2.32	16	64.0	2	7	6.19
Kane Davis	Altoona	Pit	9	58.0	2	3	2.64	7	37.0	2	3	5.59
Joey Dawley	Greenville	Atl	13	45.0	3	3	5.20	13	46.0	2	0	2.93
Fran. de la Cruz	Norwich	NYY	12	55.2	4	1	5.01	17	77.1	2	4	4.31
Pete Della Ratta	Binghamton	NYM	22	41.0	0	3	2.41	19	41.0	1	1	1.98
Matt DeWitt	Arkansas	StL	13	73.0	6	5	4.56	13	75.0	3	3	4.32
R.A. Dickey	Tulsa	Tex	18	54.0	4	3	4.17	17	41.0	2	4	5.05
Rich Dishman	Greenville	Atl	17	88.1	4	6	3.67	13	51.0	2	7	5.12
Robert Dodd	Reading	Phi	24	48.0	7	2	3.75	18	32.0	3	0	3.94
Brian Doughty	Mobile	SD	19	68.0	4	5	5.56	17	69.0	4	5	4.04
Scott Downs	West Tenn	ChC	9	53.0	6	0	1.02	4	27.0	2	1	2.00
Chad Durbin	Wichita	KC	14	82.1	5	3	3.61	14	74.0	3	7	5.84
Trevor Enders	Orlando	TB	26	40.2	2	1	3.54	34	54.2	6	1	3.13
Jose Espinal	New Britain	Min	15	78.0	3	6	4.15	14	53.2	0	6	7.55
Jake Esteves	Shreveport	SF	7	42.0	4	0	3.86	8	49.2	4	2	3.44
Luis Estrella	Shreveport	SF	20	43.0	4	1	2.30	20	49.0	2	3	3.67
Seth Etherton	Erie	Ana	11	76.1	5	3	2.95	13	91.0	5	7	3.56
Brian Falkenborg	Bowie	Bal	8	38.0	2	3	3.08	8	45.0	1	3	4.40
Aaron France	Altoona	Pit	17	41.2	1	1	3.24	16	54.0	3	4	4.00
Eric Gagne	San Antonio	LA	13	83.0	8	2	2.17	13	84.1	4	2	3.09
Apostol Garcia	San Antonio	LA	15	51.0	3	3	2.29	17	50.0	4	2	4.50
Hal Garrett	San Antonio	LA	21	51.2	3	4	2.26	21	43.0	2	5	5.23
Isabel Giron	Mobile	SD	15	89.0	7	7	5.66	13	69.1	4	5	5.19
Chris Gissell	West Tenn	ChC	8	39.2	1	4	5.45	12	58.0	2	4	6.36
Gary Glover	Knoxville	Tor	7	47.0	4	1	3.83	6	39.0	4	1	3.23
Jason Gooding	Wichita	KC	12	68.1	7	4	5.53	11	70.0	6	3	3.99
Kevin Gregg	Midland	Oak	8	40.0	1	5	5.63	8	51.0	3	2	2.29
Al Hawkins	Huntsville	Mil	9	47.2	3	6	4.91	10	52.0	5	3	5.71
Andy Hazlett	Trenton	Bos	15	96.1	7	4	3.18	12	67.1	2	5	5.61
Andy Heckman	Shreveport	SF	12	74.0	6	1	2.80	11	58.0	4	5	5.74
Scott Henderson	Portland	Fla	27	52.0	3	0	2.60	19	33.0	3	3	3.55
Russ Herbert	Reading	Phi	15	46.2	2	1	5.40	11	36.2	1	4	3.93
Brett Herbison	Binghamton	NYM	15	78.0	3	9	7.62	12	71.0	2	4	3.93
Elvin Hernandez	West Tenn	ChC	12	57.2	2	4	3.43	17	93.1	7	5	5.88
Junior Herndon	Mobile	SD	13	81.1	5	6	4.87	13	81.0	5	3	4.56
David Hooten	New Britain	Min	24	55.2	4	3	2.59	28	48.0	2	3	4.69
Chad Hutchinson	Arkansas	StL	13	79.1	4	6	3.74	12	61.0	3	5	6.05
Ryan Jacobs	Carolina	Col	14	60.0	2	7	5.40	14	54.0	4	5	5.17
Tom Jacquez	Reading	Phi	20	63.0	4	1	4.00	18	59.2	2	4	6.64
Mark Johnson	Norwich	NYY	9	51.2	5	2	3.48	7	36.0	4	1	4.00
Doug Johnston	Huntsville	Mil	12	67.0	4	7	5.37	9	51.0	3	4	4.59
Jason Karnuth	Arkansas	StL	13	81.0	4	4	5.33	13	79.0	3	7	5.13
Brad Kaufman	Norwich	NYY	18	39.0	1	1	4.15	22	44.0	2	1	4.09
Jason Kershner	Reading	Phi	31	48.0	1	2	4.88	26	44.2	3	2	6.65
Sun Kim	Trenton	Bos	14	81.1	5	2	3.10	12	67.0	4	6	7.12
Andy Kimball	Midland	Oak	26	50.0	6	2	4.50	21	39.0	3	3	6.69
Brian Knoll	Shreveport	SF	16	66.1	5	2	2.17	17	61.2	4	5	4.96
Eric Knott	El Paso	Ari	12	65.0	3	3	5.54	15	96.1	4	8	3.92
Gary Knotts	Portland	Fla	5	35.2	3	0	2.27	7	46.0	3	3	4.89
Corey Lee	Tulsa	Tex	11	63.0	4	2	3.86	11	64.0	4	3	5.06
Derek Lee	Huntsville	Mil	12	71.0	4	4	4.18	14	69.0	4	4	3.52
Brandon Leese	Portland	Fla	8	27.2	0	2	6.18	12	54.0	4	2	5.50
Allen Levrault	Huntsville	Mil	5	28.0	2	1	4.50	11	71.1	7	1	3.03
Rodrigo Lopez	Mobile	SD	14	84.0	5	4	4.18	14	85.0	5	4	4.66
Scott MacRae	Chattanooga	Cin	20	69.1	2	5	4.93	19	58.2	6	2	3.84
Alan Mahaffey	New Britain	Min	15	53.0	4	4	4.58	18	45.0	4	2	3.60
David Manning	West Tenn	ChC	11	62.0	3	3	3.19	12	61.0	5	4	4.72
Tim Manwiller	Midland	Oak	9	49.0	5	0	3.31	8	35.0	1	2	3.86
Chandler Martin	Carolina	Col	12	83.0	8	1	1.84	15	81.0	5	7	5.78
Jose Martinez	Tulsa	Tex	18	58.0	3	3	5.28	15	40.0	1	1	5.63
Willie Martinez	Akron	Cle	13	80.0	5	5	4.84	11	67.0	4	3	3.22
Troy Mattes	Harrisburg	Mon	10	48.0	3	3	4.50	10	49.0	2	5	6.24
Tony McKnight	Jackson	Hou	13	85.0	5	5	3.18	11	75.0	4	4	2.28
Paul Morse	Erie	Ana	7	45.0	4	2	4.00	8	52.0	4	4	2.77
Aaron Myette	Birmingham	CWS	16	97.1	8	3	2.87	12	67.0	4	4	4.84
Eric Newman	West Tenn	ChC	29	40.0	1	2	3.15	29	44.0	4	1	3.27
Randy Niles	Midland	Oak	12	44.0	3	3	6.55	11	44.0	1	3	4.91
Ben Norris	El Paso	Ari	11	69.0	6	2	3.26	9	49.2	4	4	5.44
Phillip Norton	West Tenn	ChC	9	62.2	7	1	1.44	5	24.0	0	3	4.88
Brian O'Connor	Altoona	Pit	11	60.2	2	5	2.97	17	92.1	5	6	5.56
Pablo Ortega	Orlando	TB	7	44.0	5	0	3.27	15	86.1	3	1	4.17
Ramon Ortiz	Erie	Ana	6	40.0	4	1	2.70	9	62.0	5	3	2.90
Christian Parker	Harrisburg	Mon	15	41.0	5	2	3.29	21	47.2	3	3	3.97
John Patterson	El Paso	Ari	10	52.0	4	3	4.67	8	48.0	4	3	4.88
Brad Penny	El Paso	Ari	10	52.0	1	3	5.19	7	37.2	1	4	4.30
Adam Pettyjohn	Jacksonville	Det	10	67.0	5	4	4.03	10	59.2	4	1	5.43
Joel Pineiro	New Haven	Sea	14	83.0	7	7	4.66	14	83.0	3	8	4.77
Trey Poland	Tulsa	Tex	10	55.0	3	4	5.40	11	63.0	2	4	4.57
Cliff Politte	Reading	Phi	19	51.2	6	3	2.79	18	57.0	3	5	4.42
Luke Prokopec	San Antonio	LA	13	79.1	4	4	3.74	14	78.0	4	8	7.15
Ken Pumphrey	Binghamton	NYM	12	66.1	4	3	4.34	13	64.1	2	6	5.32
David Pyc	Reading	Phi	10	47.0	3	1	4.40	7	34.0	2	1	4.24
Scott Randall	Carolina	Col	10	65.1	4	3	2.48	6	34.0	1	5	5.29
Steve Reed	Arkansas	StL	16	42.0	4	4	6.86	20	39.0	0	4	3.92
Ray Ricken	Mobile	SD	11	70.0	5	3	3.99	9	40.2	2	4	7.75
Matt Riley	Bowie	Bal	10	60.0	5	3	4.65	10	65.1	5	3	1.93
Michael Riley	Shreveport	SF	15	55.0	5	1	1.31	15	56.0	3	2	2.89
Jake Robbins	Norwich	NYY	13	74.0	2	8	6.08	7	37.0	1	4	4.14
Chris Roberts	Carolina	Col	22	35.0	2	4	3.86	21	45.2	3	0	3.74
Grant Roberts	Binghamton	NYM	12	68.0	4	4	4.10	11	63.0	3	4	5.71
Mark Roberts	Birmingham	CWS	17	63.0	3	3	2.71	16	61.0	2	5	4.13
Jeromie Robertson	Jackson	Hou	15	108.1	11	3	2.74	13	82.0	4	4	3.51
Bobby Rodgers	Portland	Fla	14	68.0	2	6	6.09	12	54.0	3	4	4.67
Derek Root	Jackson	Hou	14	85.0	2	1	4.87	14	71.0	5	6	4.44
Matt Saier	Wichita	KC	8	49.0	5	3	4.78	11	60.0	4	4	5.25
Martin Sanchez	El Paso	Ari	22	52.2	2	3	3.25	20	44.0	2	2	4.70
Frankie Sanders	Akron	Cle	17	62.0	4	1	3.19	16	58.2	2	5	6.60
Victor Santos	Jacksonville	Det	13	75.0	4	4	3.48	15	97.1	8	2	3.51
Jason Secoda	Birmingham	CWS	11	56.2	3	2	2.70	11	58.0	5	5	4.19
Jason Sekany	Trenton	Bos	11	59.0	3	0	2.29	16	102.1	11	4	3.96
Steve Smetana	Trenton	Bos	22	53.0	2	3	3.74	17	32.2	3	1	4.41
Gabe Sollecito	Tulsa	Tex	28	49.0	2	1	3.49	25	47.0	3	3	1.34
Cam Spence	Norwich	NYY	8	32.2	2	2	7.16	11	59.0	3	3	5.03
Dennis Stark	New Haven	Sea	11	65.1	5	3	3.99	15	81.1	4	8	4.76
Jason Stevenson	Knoxville	Tor	11	46.0	1	6	7.43	10	46.0	3	1	5.09
Brian Sweeney	New Haven	Sea	12	63.0	1	5	4.29	11	48.0	3	1	5.25
Michael Tejera	Portland	Fla	12	76.1	7	2	2.48	13	78.0	6	2	2.77
Robert Theodile	Huntsville	Mil	29	62.0	2	2	4.94	18	30.1	1	5	7.42
Evan Thomas	Reading	Phi	22	71.0	5	1	3.04	14	56.0	4	4	3.54
Josh Towers	Bowie	Bal	14	89.1	5	4	3.73	15	99.1	7	3	3.81
T.J. Tucker	Harrisburg	Mon	12	73.1	5	2	4.30	7	42.2	3	3	3.80
Brandon Villafuerte	Portland	Fla	10	53.0	3	5	3.57	12	47.0	3	3	3.45
Luis Vizcaino	Midland	Oak	13	53.2	5	2	4.53	12	51.0	3	5	7.24
Doug Walls	Carolina	Col	13	77.1	4	6	4.19	13	72.1	6	3	3.11
Mark Watson	Akron	Cle	11	68.0	5	5	2.91	8	42.0	4	3	6.64
Alan Webb	Jacksonville	Det	12	66.0	3	4	3.82	14	73.1	6	5	6.01
Clint Weibl	Arkansas	StL	12	49.0	2	2	3.86	16	60.2	2	7	5.34
Jake Westbrook	Harrisburg	Mon	14	95.1	6	1	3.68	13	79.0	5	4	4.22
Matt Wise	Erie	Ana	8	51.0	5	3	4.24	8	46.2	3	2	3.28
L.J. Yankosky	Greenville	Atl	9	48.2	2	2	4.44	11	59.2	3	6	4.07
Nate Yeskie	New Britain	Min	14	69.0	5	3	4.57	11	60.2	0	8	6.08
Jeff Yoder	West Tenn	ChC	16	73.0	8	4	1.97	13	61.0	2	1	4.43
Victor Zambrano	Orlando	TB	16	33.2	3	1	5.08	24	48.2	4	1	4.25

1999 Major League Equivalencies

When Bill James first devised Major League Equivalencies 14 years ago, he said it was easily the most important research he ever had done. That's quite a statement, considering how much he has contributed to the study of baseball.

An MLE translates a Double-A or Triple-A hitter's statistics into big league numbers. It does this by making a series of adjustments for a player's minor league home ballpark, his minor league and his future major league home park. If he plays in a pitcher's league, his MLE will get a boost. If he's a Rockies prospect, then his numbers will be inflated, just like they are for all hitters at Coors Field. The MLE also recognizes that it's significantly tougher to hit in the majors than in the upper minors, and makes a further adjustment.

The end result is an estimation of what the hitter would have done had he gotten similar playing time in the major leagues with his parent club in 1999. Please understand that an MLE is not a projection for the future. If a player's MLE gives him 30 homers, that doesn't mean he'll hit 30 homers in the majors if given a chance to play in 2000. Treat an MLE as a single season in the major league career of a player. It's quite possible that a player with a banner MLE had the misfortune of spending his career year in Triple-A or Double-A.

The MLE can't tell you if a player is going to get a chance to play in the majors. But it can show you, with a high degree of accuracy, what he would have done with that opportunity in 1999. Ages are as of June 30, 1999.

Major League Equivalencies for 1999 AAA/AA Batters

ANAHEIM ANGELS		Age	Avg	G	AB	R	H	2B	3B	HR	RBI	BB	SO	SB	CS	OBP	SLG
Abbott,Chuck	SS	24	.218	125	432	59	94	11	0	5	39	34	147	6	10	.275	.278
Barnes,Larry	1B	24	.263	130	482	62	127	22	7	17	85	35	106	10	3	.313	.444
Carvajal,Jovino	OF	30	.213	108	352	28	75	12	2	3	30	15	66	12	13	.245	.284
Christian,Eddie	OF	27	.235	97	340	42	80	13	0	5	34	23	68	12	6	.284	.318
Colangelo,Mike	OF	22	.312	54	202	29	63	13	2	0	17	19	41	3	4	.371	.396
DaVanon,Jeff	OF	25	.293	134	474	86	139	29	9	11	55	44	98	18	14	.353	.462
Decker,Steve	3B	33	.248	64	214	38	53	15	1	11	38	33	39	0	0	.348	.481
Durrington,Trent	2B	23	.262	107	382	71	100	23	0	2	29	37	70	42	16	.327	.338
Foster,Jim	C	27	.220	74	236	18	52	10	0	1	24	17	35	2	2	.273	.275
Hemphill,Bret	C	24	.275	74	233	21	64	12	0	5	23	23	60	0	0	.340	.391
Hutchins,Norm	OF	23	.216	126	499	60	108	21	5	5	38	30	133	17	6	.261	.309
Johno,Koith	SS	27	.176	81	227	24	40	7	1	2	19	10	39	1	0	.240	.242
Luuloa,Keith	2B	24	.247	115	376	40	93	19	0	3	34	33	55	4	7	.308	.322
Molina,Ben	C	24	.249	65	229	21	57	13	0	5	30	11	17	0	2	.283	.371
Murphy,Nate	OF	24	.246	104	349	41	86	15	6	12	47	39	91	4	5	.322	.427
Perez,Tomas	SS	25	.226	83	283	23	64	13	0	3	30	14	45	1	2	.263	.304
Pritchett,Chris	1B	29	.244	96	332	45	81	12	0	9	33	35	73	0	1	.316	.361
t'Hoen,E.J.	2B-3B	23	.171	65	210	16	36	10	0	1	17	10	62	4	2	.209	.233
Tejero,Fausto	C	30	.195	67	221	18	43	7	0	2	16	11	43	0	2	.233	.253
Tolentino,Juan	OF	23	.229	136	475	52	109	16	4	7	52	34	124	34	13	.281	.324
Wolff,Mike	DH	28	.225	91	298	36	67	18	2	8	34	45	91	2	6	.327	.379
Wooten,Shawn	3B	26	.267	137	501	59	134	23	0	16	75	36	109	2	1	.317	.409

ARIZ. DIAMONDBACKS		Age	Avg	G	AB	R	H	2B	3B	HR	RBI	BB	SO	SB	CS	OBP	SLG
Barajas,Rod	C	23	.278	127	482	55	134	34	1	10	68	14	78	1	0	.298	.415
Clark,Kevin	DH	26	.260	106	354	31	92	20	2	5	46	12	80	0	2	.284	.370
Conti,Jason	OF	24	.258	133	497	75	128	20	5	6	43	41	93	15	6	.314	.354
Coolbaugh,Scott	3B	33	.229	92	262	29	60	14	0	7	35	31	60	0	1	.311	.363
Diaz,Edwin	2B-SS	24	.278	107	396	54	110	20	0	8	37	12	80	4	7	.299	.389
Durazo,Erubiel	1B	25	.361	94	321	58	116	21	2	17	60	36	57	1	1	.426	.598
Gann,Jamie	OF	24	.227	109	423	49	96	20	4	6	40	19	151	4	11	.260	.336
Herrick,Jason	OF	25	.214	99	309	27	66	21	0	5	24	13	105	1	7	.245	.330
Huckaby,Ken	C	28	.268	107	339	33	91	17	0	1	31	9	34	0	0	.287	.327
Johnson,Keith	2B	28	.256	124	407	58	104	24	0	11	44	24	92	1	5	.297	.396
Klassen,Danny	SS	23	.238	64	235	28	56	13	2	4	25	15	53	3	3	.284	.362
Maddox,Garry	OF	24	.257	127	467	57	120	29	6	10	53	18	113	14	5	.285	.409
Matos,Julius	SS	24	.243	120	404	38	98	14	3	3	29	7	39	3	2	.255	.314
Patterson,Jarrod	3B	25	.317	142	492	79	156	43	4	13	71	58	86	3	3	.389	.500
Rexrode,Jackie	2B	20	.257	107	342	49	88	11	4	1	27	36	49	13	7	.328	.322
Ryan,Rob	OF	26	.258	117	396	54	102	26	3	14	66	42	73	2	3	.329	.444
Sell,Chip	OF	28	.277	122	390	44	108	17	1	5	38	14	84	14	9	.302	.364
Wilson,Desi	1B	30	.288	130	430	49	124	23	5	4	47	25	79	1	3	.327	.393
Young,Ernie	OF	29	.261	126	433	59	113	21	0	22	72	43	135	2	1	.328	.462

ATLANTA BRAVES		Age	Avg	G	AB	R	H	2B	3B	HR	RBI	BB	SO	SB	CS	OBP	SLG
Battle,Howard	3B	27	.255	121	436	63	111	25	0	18	58	26	69	1	3	.297	.436
DeRosa,Mark	SS	24	.245	105	351	32	86	14	1	0	31	16	51	5	6	.278	.291
Glavine,Mike	1B	26	.231	107	290	33	67	20	0	11	37	30	69	0	3	.303	.414
Goodell,Steve	3B	24	.259	102	320	49	83	21	1	10	41	33	65	5	6	.329	.425
Johnson,Adam	OF	23	.256	118	414	41	106	23	1	9	55	20	84	0	7	.290	.382
Lackey,Steve	SS	24	.254	80	299	36	76	15	2	2	27	12	58	6	8	.283	.338
Lombard,George	OF	23	.181	74	226	19	41	9	2	5	22	27	102	15	5	.269	.305

Major League Equivalencies for 1999 AAA/AA Batters

ATLANTA BRAVES		Age	Avg	G	AB	R	H	2B	3B	HR	RBI	BB	SO	SB	CS	OBP	SLG
Lunar,Fernando	C	22	.191	105	329	23	63	12	0	2	25	7	68	0	1	.208	.246
Malloy,Marty	2B	26	.263	114	391	45	103	20	0	5	28	41	54	13	15	.333	.353
Martinez,Pablo	SS	30	.188	120	399	34	75	13	4	0	27	31	87	13	11	.247	.241
Matos,Pascual	C	24	.184	66	217	13	40	6	0	2	16	4	49	2	1	.199	.240
Norris,Dax	1B	26	.240	120	383	42	92	22	0	10	47	25	63	1	1	.287	.376
Pendergrass,Ty.	OF	22	.226	100	328	43	74	10	2	4	22	22	65	12	14	.274	.305
Pimentel,Jose	OF-3B	24	.183	106	350	39	64	15	0	5	32	14	85	13	5	.214	.269
Roberts,Lonell	OF	28	.237	119	427	52	101	16	4	2	32	26	99	12	9	.280	.307
Rumfield,Toby	C-1B	26	.245	111	368	45	90	20	0	11	49	24	59	0	2	.291	.389
Schall,Gene	1B	29	.264	100	341	38	90	22	0	9	41	27	88	0	1	.318	.408
Sisco,Steve	2B	29	.281	128	474	63	133	31	1	13	60	30	77	9	7	.323	.432
Smith,Demond	OF	26	.266	132	394	50	105	16	5	6	42	33	77	20	8	.323	.378
Tyler,Brad	OF	30	.257	122	397	57	102	17	1	15	62	54	103	13	3	.346	.418
Whatley,Gabe	OF	27	.241	82	241	27	58	12	1	6	26	30	68	5	4	.325	.373
BALTIMORE ORIOLES		Age	Avg	G	AB	R	H	2B	3B	HR	RBI	BB	SO	SB	CS	OBP	SLG
Almonte,Wady	OF	24	.268	124	466	58	125	23	2	15	70	22	77	7	10	.301	.423
Casimiro,Carlos	2B	22	.201	139	513	62	103	19	0	16	54	27	109	5	12	.241	.331
Clark,Howie	OF	25	.267	118	390	42	104	21	2	6	33	35	37	1	2	.327	.377
Davis,Tommy	C	26	.234	110	401	41	94	15	0	9	47	20	68	0	4	.271	.339
DeCinces,Tim	C	25	.236	100	301	37	71	17	0	11	36	38	68	0	2	.322	.402
Dent,Darrell	OF	22	.180	117	272	37	49	7	1	1	18	28	70	18	6	.257	.224
Forbes,P.J.	2B-3B	31	.215	110	404	44	87	13	0	0	17	25	54	3	0	.261	.248
Garcia,Jesse	SS	25	.230	62	213	21	49	8	1	1	19	9	22	6	6	.261	.291
Hage,Tom	1B	24	.252	128	412	45	104	18	2	6	55	35	64	0	1	.311	.350
Hairston Jr.,Jerry	2B	23	.266	107	399	55	106	20	3	6	40	25	53	14	10	.309	.376
Isom,Johnny	OF	25	.257	72	237	32	61	15	0	2	21	16	56	0	2	.304	.346
Kingsale,Gene	OF	22	.241	115	444	62	107	16	2	3	36	33	74	16	19	.294	.306
Matos,Luis	OF	20	.215	66	275	34	59	9	0	8	30	10	42	10	4	.242	.335
May,Derrick	OF	30	.253	71	285	33	72	16	2	4	36	18	29	3	2	.297	.365
Minor,Ryan	3B	25	.234	101	372	47	87	20	0	18	57	30	126	2	1	.291	.433
Ojeda,Augie	SS	24	.244	135	447	62	109	15	2	8	51	39	51	4	2	.305	.340
Paz,Richard	3B	21	.261	79	264	33	69	10	1	1	17	36	37	7	3	.350	.318
Pickering,Calvin	1B	22	.259	103	359	53	93	17	0	13	53	50	104	0	3	.350	.415
Short,Rick	OF	26	.290	112	379	51	110	16	0	14	52	30	51	4	0	.342	.443
Vinas,Julio	DH	26	.287	126	467	57	134	27	1	17	70	20	77	3	3	.316	.458
BOSTON RED SOX		Age	Avg	G	AB	R	H	2B	3B	HR	RBI	BB	SO	SB	CS	OBP	SLG
Abad,Andy	OF	26	.274	102	365	47	100	20	3	10	50	39	52	4	1	.344	.427
Alcantara,Israel	OF	26	.269	101	364	49	98	27	0	22	66	25	113	2	1	.316	.525
Burkhart,Morgan	1B-DH	27	.214	66	234	33	50	14	0	9	33	21	46	1	0	.278	.389
Chamblee,Jim	2B	24	.251	127	450	65	113	20	2	18	68	33	132	3	2	.302	.424
Chevalier,Virgil	OF	25	.276	131	497	66	137	28	3	10	62	35	78	5	8	.323	.404
Coleman,Michael	OF	23	.245	115	453	74	111	28	1	23	57	39	134	9	5	.305	.464
DePastino,Joe	C	25	.225	83	271	31	61	12	0	10	44	23	45	0	0	.286	.380
Eckstein,David	2B	24	.294	131	470	90	138	21	3	4	42	62	51	20	8	.376	.377
Everett,Adam	SS	22	.245	98	330	46	81	10	0	8	36	28	68	13	5	.304	.348
Fonville,Chad	2B	28	.229	74	249	24	57	3	1	0	10	15	32	3	3	.273	.249
Gibralter,David	1B	24	.280	124	436	62	122	21	0	19	80	22	72	3	4	.314	.459
Gonzalez,Raul	OF	25	.316	127	491	66	155	32	3	14	85	35	76	7	2	.361	.479
Hillenbrand,Shea	C	23	.243	69	276	33	67	14	0	5	29	9	28	4	4	.267	.348
Ingram,Garey	OF	28	.226	85	288	38	65	14	2	6	30	13	54	7	1	.259	.351

Major League Equivalencies for 1999 AAA/AA Batters

BOSTON RED SOX		Age	Avg	G	AB	R	H	2B	3B	HR	RBI	BB	SO	SB	CS	OBP	SLG
Jackson,Gavin	SS	25	.160	76	206	22	33	2	0	0	7	31	45	2	0	.270	.170
McKeel,Walt	C	27	.213	67	207	16	44	7	0	6	29	20	33	1	2	.282	.333
Merloni,Lou	SS-3B	28	.257	66	222	35	57	13	0	5	28	23	39	0	0	.327	.383
Mitchell,Keith	OF-DH	29	.238	117	420	55	100	31	3	9	40	61	72	5	0	.335	.390
Nunnally,Jon	OF	27	.244	133	479	70	117	23	2	16	59	66	108	16	7	.336	.401
Stenson,Dernell	1B	21	.248	121	427	50	106	27	1	13	64	43	124	1	0	.317	.407
Tebbs,Nate	OF	26	.258	111	361	40	93	15	0	3	28	21	72	13	5	.298	.324
Veras,Wilton	3B	21	.263	116	463	53	122	22	1	8	61	16	58	4	5	.288	.367
CHICAGO CUBS		Age	Avg	G	AB	R	H	2B	3B	HR	RBI	BB	SO	SB	CS	OBP	SLG
Almanzar,Richard	2B	23	.249	75	237	34	59	7	2	1	17	17	27	13	8	.299	.308
Brock,Tarrik	OF	25	.230	120	405	61	93	19	4	7	28	55	130	11	8	.322	.348
Brown,Roosevelt	OF	23	.310	108	377	40	117	32	1	10	72	24	87	6	4	.352	.552
Cedeno,Andujar	3B	29	.259	62	205	20	53	11	1	4	28	8	32	0	1	.286	.380
Cline,Pat	C	24	.203	98	281	21	57	17	0	5	32	20	76	0	2	.256	.317
Encarnacion,Ang.	C	26	.219	64	224	16	49	11	0	0	26	7	32	1	1	.242	.268
Gazarek,Marty	OF	26	.283	75	247	24	70	18	0	9	36	6	40	1	6	.300	.466
Jennings,Robin	OF	27	.281	80	299	45	84	19	3	11	48	22	42	4	4	.330	.475
King,Brad	C	24	.211	92	227	25	48	9	0	0	22	28	36	1	1	.298	.251
King,Brett	SS	26	.190	86	248	36	47	10	0	5	18	42	80	8	7	.307	.290
Liniak,Cole	3B	22	.243	95	338	43	82	24	0	9	32	31	59	0	4	.306	.393
Meyers,Chad	2B	23	.291	108	398	70	116	28	2	2	37	41	63	28	13	.358	.387
Molina,Jose	C	24	.223	88	265	19	59	11	0	3	24	16	70	0	1	.267	.298
Nelson,Bry	3B	25	.253	129	462	58	117	21	3	15	69	31	55	7	7	.300	.409
Nieves,Jose	SS	24	.241	104	378	43	91	21	2	9	46	18	68	7	8	.275	.378
Polanco,Enohel	SS	23	.225	116	347	39	78	19	3	2	26	15	95	9	8	.257	.314
Porter,Bo	OF	26	.266	111	399	67	106	20	1	23	50	51	127	10	17	.349	.494
Quinlan,Tom	3B	31	.225	133	457	48	103	22	0	14	45	32	166	0	1	.276	.365
Rennhack,Mike	OF	24	.221	115	326	31	72	15	0	5	26	40	91	3	1	.306	.313
Speed,Dorian	OF	25	.253	121	407	62	103	19	6	13	50	20	113	16	6	.288	.425
Stahoviak,Scott	1B	29	.211	83	265	40	56	13	0	10	34	34	92	2	1	.301	.374
Vieira,Scott	OF	25	.276	126	445	56	123	40	3	9	51	40	134	7	6	.336	.440
Walker,Ron	3B	23	.205	105	297	37	61	18	0	8	37	29	92	1	0	.276	.347
White,Derrick	OF-1B	29	.237	132	486	58	115	26	0	11	60	36	98	7	8	.289	.358
Wilson,Brandon	2B	30	.251	123	455	64	114	24	4	10	38	26	79	22	8	.291	.387
Zuleta,Julio	1B	24	.280	133	472	66	132	34	3	20	86	26	130	3	3	.317	.492
CHICAGO WHITE SOX		Age	Avg	G	AB	R	H	2B	3B	HR	RBI	BB	SO	SB	CS	OBP	SLG
Abbott,Jeff	OF	26	.287	67	265	33	76	20	0	7	29	12	28	1	3	.318	.442
Aude,Rich	1B	27	.269	129	472	54	127	29	1	10	73	25	95	11	3	.306	.398
Beltre,Esteban	SS	31	.236	130	420	59	99	22	2	1	32	24	83	5	3	.277	.305
Bravo,Danny	3B-2B	22	.246	88	289	42	71	10	0	1	33	30	47	4	5	.317	.291
Brito,Tilson	2B	27	.286	111	388	47	111	25	3	8	46	27	68	4	4	.333	.428
Christensen,McK.	OF	23	.265	76	287	45	76	7	4	2	24	22	48	13	6	.317	.338
Crede,Joe	3B	21	.232	74	284	32	66	12	0	3	36	16	49	1	6	.273	.306
Dellaero,Jason	SS	22	.246	81	264	34	65	11	2	7	38	10	80	4	8	.274	.383
Eddie,Steve	3B	28	.207	95	290	25	60	11	0	1	20	13	51	0	3	.241	.255
Gomez,Ramon	OF	23	.263	99	266	40	70	9	4	0	22	22	85	19	7	.319	.327
Hollins,Dave	3B	33	.275	67	204	40	56	15	0	5	28	28	43	3	1	.357	.422
Inglin,Jeff	OF	23	.263	131	457	60	120	23	3	14	60	45	74	14	6	.329	.418
Lydy,Scott	OF	30	.236	130	453	72	107	23	0	17	66	55	79	12	3	.319	.400
Moore,Brandon	SS	26	.231	126	403	44	93	20	2	0	43	28	63	4	4	.281	.290

Major League Equivalencies for 1999 AAA/AA Batters

CHICAGO WHITE SOX		Age	Avg	G	AB	R	H	2B	3B	HR	RBI	BB	SO	SB	CS	OBP	SLG
Mottola,Chad	OF	27	.290	140	489	75	142	27	3	15	74	47	86	13	6	.353	.450
Newstrom,Doug	C	27	.261	82	245	25	64	9	0	2	19	21	44	2	4	.320	.322
Paul,Josh	C	24	.258	93	310	40	80	17	2	3	36	21	72	4	6	.305	.355
Pemberton,Rudy	DH	29	.252	110	369	52	93	18	2	16	60	24	71	5	3	.298	.442
Raven,Luis	DH	30	.252	139	511	77	129	27	3	25	99	39	132	3	0	.305	.464
Rodriguez,Liu	2B-SS	22	.270	64	237	36	64	9	0	2	32	16	36	3	3	.316	.333
Simmons,Brian	OF	25	.241	78	274	42	66	11	0	7	35	29	61	5	2	.314	.358
Simons,Mitch	2B-3B	30	.259	119	455	67	118	27	0	5	41	35	69	15	6	.312	.352
Toth,Dave	C	29	.218	79	252	28	55	12	0	4	26	19	39	0	2	.273	.313
CINCINNATI REDS		Age	Avg	G	AB	R	H	2B	3B	HR	RBI	BB	SO	SB	CS	OBP	SLG
Branson,Jeff	SS	32	.221	124	412	41	91	15	1	5	40	34	90	1	1	.280	.299
Burress,Andy	OF	21	.240	63	246	31	59	10	0	5	21	12	43	7	3	.275	.341
Clark,Brady	OF	26	.293	138	482	78	141	33	2	12	56	59	62	17	6	.370	.444
Cromer,D.T.	OF-1B	28	.275	136	509	60	140	32	2	23	78	33	102	2	1	.319	.481
Diaz,Alejandro	OF	20	.232	55	211	20	49	8	5	5	26	5	33	4	1	.250	.389
Frank,Mike	OF	24	.260	121	412	53	107	31	4	6	45	27	57	7	5	.305	.398
Garcia,Guillermo	C	27	.253	75	261	29	66	9	2	7	25	17	52	0	0	.299	.383
Hardtke,Jason	2B-3B	27	.292	101	394	54	115	33	1	9	44	27	45	5	3	.337	.449
Hiatt,Phil	1B	30	.205	78	298	33	61	9	0	13	39	22	108	0	0	.259	.366
Hollins,Damon	OF	25	.229	106	314	42	72	16	0	6	31	23	46	7	1	.282	.338
Ingram,Darron	OF	23	.194	85	258	31	50	9	2	8	30	18	101	3	6	.246	.337
Larkin,Stephen	1B	25	.266	104	252	25	67	14	1	3	31	20	47	4	2	.320	.365
LaRue,Jason	C	25	.218	70	252	30	55	10	1	8	27	11	54	0	2	.251	.361
Melo,Juan	SS	22	.192	89	308	30	59	10	1	3	21	12	70	6	5	.222	.260
Nevers,Tom	SS	27	.262	111	363	46	95	20	1	12	49	10	79	2	4	.282	.421
Presto,Nick	SS	24	.237	73	215	25	51	7	0	1	21	25	36	3	6	.317	.284
Robinson,Kerry	OF	25	.278	113	446	64	124	16	7	0	40	15	58	33	12	.302	.345
Salzano,Jerry	3B	24	.281	79	260	33	73	17	0	3	29	26	46	9	9	.346	.381
Saunders,Chris	1B	28	.282	58	206	23	58	11	0	5	26	22	44	0	0	.351	.408
Snopek,Chris	SS	28	.242	127	442	55	107	27	2	8	53	34	68	13	5	.296	.367
Sweeney,Mark	OF	29	.285	86	295	48	84	15	0	9	37	44	42	2	1	.378	.427
Whitmore,Darrell	OF	30	.247	83	227	28	56	15	0	7	30	18	67	1	0	.302	.405
Williams,Jason	2B	25	.303	127	466	70	141	39	2	6	47	40	68	4	3	.358	.433
CLEVELAND INDIANS		Age	Avg	G	AB	R	H	2B	3B	HR	RBI	BB	SO	SB	CS	OBP	SLG
Bady,Ed	OF	26	.230	69	226	37	52	12	2	1	29	24	72	14	5	.304	.314
Baerga,Carlos	3B	30	.247	73	295	33	73	14	0	3	25	12	23	1	0	.277	.325
Betances,Junior	2B	26	.280	89	300	36	84	13	3	1	24	23	56	6	6	.331	.353
Betts,Todd	3B	26	.266	104	368	53	98	23	0	16	59	45	69	1	1	.346	.459
Branyan,Russ	3B	23	.191	109	387	42	74	10	0	25	56	43	196	6	3	.272	.411
Budzinski,Mark	OF	25	.267	133	420	71	112	22	6	6	54	54	104	9	6	.350	.390
Cabrera,Jolbert	OF	26	.246	71	272	36	67	12	3	0	22	21	45	15	5	.300	.313
Dishington,Nate	OF	24	.197	89	249	38	49	11	0	10	38	24	131	0	4	.267	.361
Hayes,Heath	C	27	.251	119	410	45	103	14	1	13	60	30	118	1	1	.302	.385
McDonald,John	SS	24	.288	121	451	52	130	22	0	0	43	23	51	9	6	.323	.337
McKinley,Dan	OF	23	.244	111	455	61	111	19	4	2	32	18	93	2	5	.273	.316
Miller,David	OF	25	.223	101	318	31	71	19	2	1	31	27	59	9	5	.284	.305
Miller,Orlando	SS	30	.238	68	227	22	54	15	0	5	27	10	54	3	0	.270	.370
Morgan,Scott	OF	25	.256	136	503	89	129	32	1	28	87	43	141	5	4	.315	.491
Peoples,Danny	1B	24	.237	127	485	66	115	22	2	18	69	41	152	1	1	.297	.402
Perry,Chan	1B	26	.264	116	417	57	110	28	0	14	75	23	63	3	1	.302	.432

Major League Equivalencies for 1999 AAA/AA Batters

CLEVELAND INDIANS		Age	Avg	G	AB	R	H	2B	3B	HR	RBI	BB	SO	SB	CS	OBP	SLG
Ramirez,Alex	OF	24	.284	75	296	41	84	18	1	9	41	14	54	3	5	.316	.443
Roberts,David	OF	27	.252	89	341	54	86	15	7	0	31	36	54	29	11	.324	.337
Robinson,Adam	2B-SS	24	.262	66	233	32	61	11	3	4	26	15	52	3	1	.306	.386
Scutaro,Marcos	2B	23	.255	129	451	63	115	22	1	6	42	51	72	15	6	.331	.348
Selby,Bill	DH	29	.276	122	435	62	120	29	3	16	71	47	66	3	3	.346	.467
Turner,Chris	C	30	.253	69	225	30	57	8	0	7	27	28	47	1	2	.336	.382
COLORADO ROCKIES		Age	Avg	G	AB	R	H	2B	3B	HR	RBI	BB	SO	SB	CS	OBP	SLG
Bair,Rod	OF	24	.317	125	482	63	153	35	6	15	73	21	77	10	12	.346	.508
Barthol,Blake	C	26	.293	96	328	37	96	18	3	9	24	24	61	0	1	.341	.448
Berry,Mike	3B	28	.254	90	311	32	79	15	2	10	34	20	60	0	2	.299	.412
Clemente,Edgard	OF	23	.302	75	275	35	83	22	0	17	46	15	53	3	5	.338	.567
Cotton,John	3B	28	.296	112	395	62	117	26	0	23	66	17	100	2	3	.325	.537
Feuerstein,Dave	OF	25	.230	101	291	24	67	9	3	1	16	13	42	4	2	.263	.292
Gibson,Derrick	OF	24	.273	110	384	52	105	18	5	17	51	23	80	8	6	.314	.479
Hajek,Dave	2B	31	.289	127	529	64	153	41	2	8	44	19	41	9	8	.314	.420
Hatcher,Chris	OF	30	.342	98	333	48	114	22	1	21	53	17	86	8	4	.374	.604
Kelly,Mike	OF	29	.273	114	392	53	107	25	2	9	38	44	90	6	7	.346	.416
Kirgan,Chris	1B	26	.233	133	481	50	112	28	2	15	76	46	114	0	0	.300	.393
Monds,Wonderful	OF	26	.231	75	299	36	69	12	1	8	24	11	52	10	7	.258	.358
Pena,Elvis	2B	22	.293	123	403	54	118	27	7	2	28	39	66	17	7	.355	.409
Petersen,Chris	SS	28	.255	107	368	43	94	20	0	6	26	22	83	2	0	.297	.359
Petrick,Ben	C	22	.313	104	351	59	110	20	5	23	69	40	70	8	7	.384	.595
Phillips,J.R.	1B	29	.301	124	472	67	142	21	0	36	77	41	139	2	3	.357	.574
Sosa,Juan	SS	23	.293	131	526	65	154	22	5	9	41	24	64	28	11	.324	.405
Tatum,Jimmy	3B	31	.310	109	394	44	122	22	0	14	49	25	83	0	2	.351	.472
Watkins,Pat	OF	26	.309	100	346	37	107	28	1	3	37	19	53	4	5	.345	.422
DETROIT TIGERS		Age	Avg	G	AB	R	H	2B	3B	HR	RBI	BB	SO	SB	CS	OBP	SLG
Airoso,Kurt	OF	24	.235	134	510	69	120	22	4	8	52	55	121	6	3	.310	.341
Alvarez,Gabe	3B	25	.256	110	394	55	101	20	0	18	52	45	84	0	3	.333	.444
Bartee,Kimera	OF	26	.256	104	399	50	102	10	6	11	34	30	79	15	5	.308	.393
Candelaria,Ben	OF	24	.233	120	442	47	103	25	2	14	56	21	99	4	7	.268	.394
Cardona,Javier	C	23	.270	108	396	61	107	25	0	21	67	28	73	2	2	.318	.492
Cradle,Rickey	OF	26	.211	110	336	45	71	22	1	8	41	33	86	7	6	.282	.354
Freire,Alejandro	1B-DH	24	.257	66	230	32	59	16	0	8	31	14	47	1	0	.299	.430
Garcia,Luis	SS	24	.234	89	295	23	69	16	0	2	26	3	43	2	3	.242	.308
Gillespie,Eric	OF	24	.267	118	449	58	120	22	4	15	64	32	95	7	2	.316	.434
Jones,Ryan	1B	24	.219	125	466	48	102	17	2	15	53	31	123	0	1	.268	.361
Lemonis,Chris	2B	25	.243	75	251	25	61	13	0	4	27	11	48	0	2	.275	.343
Lennon,Patrick	OF-DH	31	.264	111	401	61	106	17	0	25	68	45	111	2	5	.339	.494
Lindstrom,David	C	24	.232	66	203	21	47	13	0	5	16	14	37	0	3	.281	.369
Macias,Jose	2B	25	.216	112	422	34	91	14	6	1	28	28	62	7	5	.264	.284
Maxwell,Jason	SS	27	.210	119	405	47	85	14	1	13	49	41	91	4	3	.283	.346
McCarty,Dave	1B	29	.242	132	450	67	109	20	2	27	60	55	115	4	6	.325	.476
Mitchell,Derek	SS	24	.208	124	404	40	84	13	0	5	35	32	125	2	2	.266	.277
Santana,Pedro	2B	22	.241	120	486	65	117	28	4	4	35	21	104	23	8	.272	.340
Sasser,Rob	3B	24	.243	122	420	45	102	31	0	5	44	35	110	5	5	.301	.352
Siddall,Joe	O	31	.109	84	237	22	40	12	0	0	20	20	77	2	1	.251	.295
Swann,Pedro	OF	28	.231	103	320	40	74	11	1	8	29	28	70	2	1	.293	.347
Wakeland,Chris	OF	25	.280	55	200	30	56	13	2	10	26	21	56	3	5	.348	.515

Major League Equivalencies for 1999 AAA/AA Batters

FLORIDA MARLINS		Age	Avg	G	AB	R	H	2B	3B	HR	RBI	BB	SO	SB	CS	OBP	SLG
Bates,Fletcher	OF	25	.229	139	520	59	119	24	8	6	45	27	116	13	6	.267	.340
Castro,Ramon	C	23	.218	97	331	30	72	17	0	10	43	17	67	0	0	.256	.360
Clapinski,Chris	3B	27	.276	81	250	36	69	16	5	5	24	21	55	3	1	.332	.440
Dunwoody,Todd	OF	24	.232	65	233	24	54	13	5	5	25	7	58	4	8	.254	.395
Erickson,Matt	2B	23	.241	107	348	31	84	17	1	0	28	36	69	1	3	.313	.296
Funaro,Joe	3B	26	.333	74	255	34	85	16	0	2	33	22	23	4	6	.386	.420
Garcia,Amaury	2B	24	.273	119	450	66	123	30	7	11	37	31	82	11	11	.320	.444
Gil,Benji	SS	26	.237	116	389	52	92	23	0	11	45	19	106	11	5	.272	.380
Gulan,Mike	3B	28	.233	84	270	29	63	18	1	8	36	7	86	1	1	.253	.396
Hastings,Lionel	C	26	.210	95	262	26	55	7	0	2	13	25	61	2	2	.279	.260
Jones,Jaime	OF	22	.219	114	366	40	80	18	0	5	29	40	117	1	3	.296	.309
Kleinz,Larry	3B	25	.233	94	266	24	62	18	0	3	35	27	53	1	3	.304	.335
Kuilan,Hector	C	23	.233	76	236	18	55	9	0	1	26	7	44	0	0	.255	.284
Lee,Derrek	1B	23	.241	89	320	42	77	16	0	12	51	21	94	2	4	.287	.403
Lobaton,Jose	SS	25	.209	94	239	24	50	10	0	1	15	13	75	2	2	.250	.264
Norton,Chris	DH	28	.262	120	390	61	102	22	0	30	80	50	132	0	2	.345	.549
Ozuna,Pablo	SS	20	.254	117	484	51	123	22	5	5	38	9	53	23	9	.268	.351
Ramirez,Julio	OF	21	.235	138	549	71	129	26	8	10	52	27	160	46	18	.271	.366
Reeves,Glenn	OF	25	.174	97	235	23	41	6	0	1	14	26	50	2	6	.257	.213
Robertson,Ryan	C	26	.239	103	284	23	68	13	0	1	21	33	48	0	2	.319	.296
Rolison,Nate	1B	22	.269	124	420	58	113	17	0	12	57	48	119	0	1	.344	.395
Roskos,John	OF	24	.274	134	474	60	130	35	0	16	63	37	117	1	1	.327	.449
HOUSTON ASTROS		Age	Avg	G	AB	R	H	2B	3B	HR	RBI	BB	SO	SB	CS	OBP	SLG
Alexander,Chad	OF	25	.261	112	395	37	103	28	2	7	39	26	89	6	6	.306	.395
Berkman,Lance	OF	23	.282	64	213	30	60	18	0	4	35	27	53	4	1	.363	.423
Betzsold,Jim	OF	26	.193	101	311	44	60	18	0	8	32	24	109	4	5	.251	.328
Burns,Kevin	1B	23	.249	113	337	43	84	19	1	8	45	27	83	4	3	.305	.383
Candaele,Casey	2B	38	.231	126	446	40	103	30	2	4	30	33	61	2	9	.284	.334
Dallimore,Brian	2B	25	.237	70	241	29	57	11	0	3	14	10	49	9	3	.267	.320
Hernandez,Carlos	SS	23	.255	94	337	40	86	12	0	0	31	19	71	15	6	.295	.291
Johnson,J.J.	OF	25	.221	131	420	44	93	25	1	12	54	30	133	7	11	.273	.371
Johnson,Ric	OF	25	.218	99	312	21	68	17	0	0	21	8	49	3	5	.238	.272
Knorr,Randy	C	30	.308	77	253	24	78	19	0	7	29	14	45	0	1	.345	.466
Lopez,Pedro	C	30	.174	100	305	23	53	13	0	5	29	12	66	0	1	.205	.266
Lugo,Julio	SS	23	.285	116	424	60	121	22	3	7	32	28	59	17	7	.330	.401
Miller,Ryan	2B	26	.202	91	238	16	48	7	0	0	21	4	43	3	2	.215	.231
Neal,Mike	OF	27	.171	94	234	24	40	8	0	3	20	19	67	2	0	.233	.244
Perez,Jhonny	2B	22	.222	76	266	28	59	14	3	2	19	12	49	4	8	.255	.320
Ramirez,Omar	OF	28	.218	110	362	40	79	13	1	3	37	21	54	5	3	.261	.285
Sanchez,Victor	1B	27	.220	125	391	47	86	16	0	11	53	26	104	7	9	.269	.345
Saylor,Jamie	OF	24	.192	113	317	27	61	12	3	2	26	24	91	5	10	.249	.268
Thompson,Ryan	OF	31	.268	112	381	43	102	20	1	10	42	26	85	2	9	.314	.404
Truby,Chris	3B	25	.248	124	444	61	110	19	2	19	68	23	98	14	5	.285	.428
Villalobos,Carlos	3B	25	.245	133	474	59	116	29	0	5	36	38	110	7	3	.301	.338
Ward,Daryle	1B	24	.304	61	224	40	68	13	0	18	47	16	47	0	1	.350	.603
Williams,George	C	30	.244	103	311	39	76	18	0	5	31	39	76	0	4	.329	.350
KANSAS CITY ROYALS		Age	Avg	G	AB	R	H	2B	3B	HR	RBI	BB	SO	SB	CS	OBP	SLG
Amado,Jose	1B	24	.259	121	440	53	114	24	1	9	70	34	37	3	2	.312	.380
Brown,Dee	OF	21	.318	65	223	44	71	11	2	9	42	22	41	6	7	.380	.507
Byington,Jimmie	OF	25	.185	89	222	22	41	8	0	1	18	15	45	2	6	.236	.234

Major League Equivalencies for 1999 AAA/AA Batters

KANSAS CITY ROYALS		Age	Avg	G	AB	R	H	2B	3B	HR	RBI	BB	SO	SB	CS	OBP	SLG
Carr,Jeremy	OF	28	.237	73	266	37	63	10	0	3	19	32	57	10	7	.319	.308
Dodson,Jeremy	OF	22	.228	133	435	47	99	16	0	15	44	32	96	5	4	.281	.368
Escandon,Emil.	DH-2B	24	.232	120	328	44	76	15	4	5	43	46	46	3	6	.326	.348
Fasano,Sal	C	27	.245	88	269	49	66	12	0	16	38	32	68	2	1	.326	.468
Gibralter,Steve	OF	26	.239	110	402	60	96	18	0	22	61	21	96	4	2	.277	.448
Hallmark,Pat	OF	25	.254	75	232	26	59	5	1	3	18	13	63	9	6	.294	.323
Lopez,Mendy	SS	24	.282	61	213	32	60	6	0	9	31	14	40	1	1	.326	.437
Martinez,Felix	SS	25	.239	95	335	44	80	22	2	3	29	24	47	12	11	.290	.343
McNally,Sean	3B	26	.251	129	422	73	106	20	1	27	82	59	134	4	2	.343	.495
Medrano,Tony	2B	24	.296	106	351	45	104	17	0	4	42	20	37	2	1	.334	.379
Mendez,Carlos	1B	25	.252	84	282	29	71	21	0	7	29	4	31	2	2	.262	.401
Moore,Kenderlck	OF	26	.222	80	234	27	52	9	0	0	20	12	55	12	9	.260	.261
Norman,Les	OF	30	.246	89	321	41	79	17	1	10	31	10	44	4	2	.269	.399
Pellow,Kit	3B	25	.260	131	458	69	119	24	3	27	78	15	116	4	4	.283	.502
Phillips,Paul	C	22	.238	108	378	44	90	16	1	2	42	16	38	5	8	.269	.302
Prieto,Alejandro	SS-2B	23	.264	114	345	42	91	19	3	4	31	22	47	7	5	.308	.371
Quinn,Mark	OF	25	.328	107	408	52	134	23	0	19	66	21	68	4	8	.361	.525
Roberge,J.P.	2B	26	.284	116	419	60	119	26	2	10	52	20	58	11	4	.317	.427
Tomlinson,Goefrey	OF	22	.250	128	460	75	115	26	3	3	34	45	83	15	6	.317	.339
Vitiello,Joe	DH-1B	29	.287	122	428	55	123	28	0	22	77	51	83	2	3	.363	.507
LA DODGERS		Age	Avg	G	AB	R	H	2B	3B	HR	RBI	BB	SO	SB	CS	OBP	SLG
Allen,Luke	3B	20	.236	137	501	65	118	12	6	9	59	26	108	9	8	.273	.337
Bocachica,Hiram	2B	23	.244	123	447	60	109	17	5	7	43	36	75	19	7	.300	.351
Castro,Juan	SS-3B	27	.225	116	396	35	89	19	2	4	35	22	72	1	3	.266	.313
Chamberlain,Wes	1B	33	.255	111	349	36	89	14	1	12	53	16	68	2	7	.288	.404
Cookson,Brent	OF	29	.268	85	257	39	69	13	0	18	48	25	58	4	1	.333	.529
Cora,Alex	SS	23	.254	80	280	35	71	8	3	2	25	8	38	6	5	.274	.325
Davis,Glenn	OF-1B	23	.217	134	465	52	101	24	1	7	45	41	136	3	7	.281	.318
Diaz,Juan	1B	23	.256	66	238	30	61	16	0	6	37	15	81	0	0	.300	.399
Gil,Geronimo	C	23	.238	106	323	34	77	20	0	10	42	29	61	1	0	.301	.393
Gilbert,Shawn	OF	34	.253	114	392	60	99	26	1	6	35	41	87	16	6	.323	.370
Grijak,Kevin	OF	28	.263	119	372	39	98	21	0	12	55	12	51	1	6	.286	.417
Metcalfe,Mike	SS	26	.247	123	433	56	107	18	1	2	41	38	49	36	14	.308	.307
Moreta,Ramon	OF	23	.258	117	372	40	96	10	1	1	30	10	69	17	6	.277	.298
Mota,Tony	OF	21	.276	98	322	47	89	22	0	10	54	24	58	8	5	.327	.438
Newson,Warren	OF	34	.213	95	268	28	57	16	0	5	26	29	72	1	4	.290	.328
Ortiz,Hector	C	29	.231	95	268	21	62	9	0	4	22	10	46	1	4	.259	.310
Ortiz,Nicky	SS	25	.230	91	278	28	64	17	1	1	12	15	59	0	2	.270	.309
Riggs,Adam	2B	26	.242	133	479	59	116	22	3	8	55	36	118	16	6	.295	.351
Saitta,Rich	SS	23	.244	91	238	18	58	8	2	1	24	4	45	4	4	.256	.307
Sanford,Chance	3B	27	.201	77	214	25	43	10	0	5	19	20	57	3	3	.269	.318
Stovall,Darond	OF	26	.191	95	299	33	57	12	2	7	30	25	123	5	5	.253	.314
Wilkins,Rick	C	32	.208	92	283	26	59	6	0	5	22	19	90	0	0	.258	.283
MILWAUKEE BREWERS		Age	Avg	G	AB	R	H	2B	3B	HR	RBI	BB	SO	SB	CS	OBP	SLG
Alfano,Jeff	C	22	.218	83	238	15	52	13	0	3	23	22	68	2	0	.285	.311
Azuaje,Jesus	SS	26	.251	119	375	47	94	18	0	7	45	45	27	22	8	.331	.355
Barker,Kevin	1B	23	.246	121	423	67	104	23	3	16	66	45	96	1	1	.318	.428
Benitez,Yamil	OF	26	.188	99	330	35	62	20	1	8	37	22	105	9	3	.239	.327
Cancel,Robinson	C	23	.261	105	326	42	85	14	0	6	45	24	67	9	5	.311	.359
Cromer,Brandon	2B	25	.188	115	319	35	60	10	0	17	46	30	105	4	0	.258	.379

Major League Equivalencies for 1999 AAA/AA Batters

MILWAUKEE BREWERS		Age	Avg	G	AB	R	H	2B	3B	HR	RBI	BB	SO	SB	CS	OBP	SLG
Elliott,Dave	OF	25	.205	123	390	51	80	19	0	8	41	38	116	7	5	.276	.315
Green,Chad	OF	24	.219	116	407	42	89	19	2	6	34	29	112	19	7	.271	.319
Iapoce,Anthony	OF	25	.201	76	209	16	42	7	0	0	3	12	55	5	3	.244	.234
Klimek,Josh	3B	25	.210	123	415	34	87	24	0	10	53	21	81	2	1	.248	.340
Kominek,Toby	OF-1B	26	.205	128	440	42	90	17	2	8	44	33	123	4	9	.260	.307
Krause,Scott	OF	25	.246	133	479	43	118	22	5	10	67	25	107	7	5	.284	.376
Light,Tal	OF	25	.195	80	262	23	51	18	0	10	27	12	120	0	3	.230	.378
Lopez,Mickey	2B	25	.273	132	473	75	129	27	4	6	53	57	72	28	13	.351	.385
Macalutas,Jon	1B	25	.235	93	294	37	69	17	0	3	33	24	33	2	2	.292	.323
Martinez,Greg	OF	27	.237	132	497	73	118	13	3	2	26	48	63	39	13	.305	.288
Mathis,Jared	SS	23	.199	74	211	17	42	4	0	1	18	5	33	1	2	.218	.232
Mouton,Lyle	OF	30	.278	127	446	69	124	36	1	16	72	30	100	15	1	.324	.471
Ortiz,Luis	DH	29	.235	96	293	27	69	9	0	8	25	17	42	0	1	.277	.348
Perez,Santiago	SS	23	.235	108	392	43	92	20	5	4	28	23	95	15	5	.277	.342
Williamson,Antone	DH	25	.225	80	213	18	48	8	0	3	19	27	35	2	0	.313	.305
Zosky,Eddie	3B	31	.264	116	398	45	105	19	2	8	35	17	69	3	0	.294	.382

MINNESOTA TWINS		Age	Avg	G	AB	R	H	2B	3B	HR	RBI	BB	SO	SB	CS	OBP	SLG
Barnes,John	OF	23	.241	129	439	51	106	19	0	10	48	34	43	7	2	.296	.353
Buchanan,Brian	OF	25	.259	107	371	47	96	20	0	6	42	19	91	7	2	.295	.361
Cey,Dan	2B	23	.257	117	382	44	98	15	2	7	39	22	70	6	2	.297	.361
Cummings,Midre	OF	27	.301	93	336	58	101	22	3	10	60	28	61	4	5	.354	.473
Davidson,Cleatus	2B	22	.225	127	479	72	108	15	8	1	33	37	121	29	11	.281	.296
Ferguson,Jeff	3B-2B	26	.229	95	284	31	65	13	1	2	33	19	41	4	5	.277	.303
Hacker,Steve	DH	24	.271	126	465	59	126	34	0	22	82	30	119	0	3	.315	.486
Latham,Chris	OF	26	.283	94	361	65	102	21	6	10	36	38	103	12	13	.351	.457
Lewis,Marc	OF	24	.241	101	374	31	90	25	0	7	43	27	86	4	4	.292	.364
Moeller,Chad	C	24	.226	89	243	24	55	10	2	3	19	14	48	0	0	.268	.321
Moriarty,Mike	SS	25	.223	128	363	44	81	18	5	2	36	39	66	4	4	.299	.317
Moss,Rick	3B	23	.249	90	245	23	61	12	0	3	24	17	40	0	5	.298	.335
Mucker,Kelcey	OF	24	.249	109	357	21	89	15	0	0	20	22	62	0	3	.293	.291
Nicholas,Darrell	OF	27	.255	106	330	38	84	16	1	3	31	23	81	9	7	.303	.336
Ortiz,David	1B	23	.277	130	451	60	125	30	2	22	77	56	112	1	2	.357	.499
Peterman,Tommy	1B	24	.242	140	524	56	127	26	0	17	69	43	91	0	2	.300	.389
Pierzynski,A.J.	C	22	.221	67	217	20	48	8	0	0	17	11	31	0	0	.259	.258
Richardson,Brian	3B	23	.240	130	429	54	103	20	3	12	51	38	111	0	0	.302	.385
Rivas,Luis	SS	19	.234	132	513	64	120	28	5	5	40	29	100	22	8	.275	.337
Smith,Jeff	C	25	.237	84	274	23	65	14	0	5	27	16	44	0	0	.279	.343
Valdez,Mario	1B	24	.242	121	385	62	93	14	1	19	60	60	94	0	0	.344	.431
Williams,Eddie	DH	34	.276	97	326	39	90	20	0	11	40	24	72	0	1	.326	.439

MONTREAL EXPOS		Age	Avg	G	AB	R	H	2B	3B	HR	RBI	BB	SO	SB	CS	OBP	SLG
Adolfo,Carlos	OF	23	.227	92	264	33	60	15	0	8	40	19	65	2	1	.279	.375
Bergeron,Peter	OF	21	.294	100	343	52	101	24	3	5	30	34	73	16	13	.358	.426
Blum,Geoff	SS	26	.242	77	260	35	63	13	0	7	30	30	40	4	0	.321	.373
Bradley,Milton	OF	21	.301	87	332	50	100	21	4	8	40	22	65	10	9	.345	.461
Camilli,Jason	2B	23	.210	98	248	30	52	11	0	3	18	24	52	2	1	.279	.290
Carroll,Jamey	2B	24	.266	141	541	63	144	31	4	3	50	32	62	15	5	.307	.355
Carvajal,Jhonny	SS	24	.211	106	346	22	73	18	3	0	27	17	70	5	2	.248	.280
Coquillette,Trace	2B	25	.299	98	321	45	96	30	2	10	45	36	71	7	3	.370	.498
de la Rosa,Tomas	SS	21	.237	135	452	56	107	20	2	4	34	28	68	19	7	.281	.316
Fernandez,Jose	3B	24	.247	124	450	59	111	28	1	10	55	25	142	10	6	.286	.380

Major League Equivalencies for 1999 AAA/AA Batters

MONTREAL EXPOS		Age	Avg	G	AB	R	H	2B	3B	HR	RBI	BB	SO	SB	CS	OBP	SLG
Hunter,Scott	OF	23	.200	128	445	33	89	15	0	11	50	23	111	5	10	.239	.308
Jones,Terry	OF	28	.239	88	322	40	77	16	1	0	18	19	69	22	8	.282	.295
Morales,Francisco	C	26	.206	99	335	35	69	10	0	7	36	25	97	0	0	.261	.299
Nunnari,Talmadge	1B	24	.304	63	230	36	70	15	0	4	23	26	49	4	1	.375	.422
Post,Dave	2B	25	.238	113	382	44	91	16	1	7	31	27	60	8	7	.289	.340
Schneider,Brian	C	22	.240	121	408	38	98	17	0	12	53	21	59	1	1	.277	.370
Seguignol,Fern.	1B	24	.259	87	301	44	78	16	2	16	60	32	100	2	7	.330	.485
Stowers,Chris	OF	24	.217	118	420	49	91	16	3	3	30	32	96	20	7	.272	.290
Tracy,Andy	3B	25	.248	134	476	77	118	24	1	27	103	48	148	4	0	.317	.473
Tucker,Jon	1B	22	.234	112	351	42	82	19	1	9	44	34	91	2	3	.301	.370
Ware,Jeremy	OF	23	.238	111	369	46	88	21	1	6	45	28	84	8	4	.292	.350
Wilkerson,Brad	OF	22	.214	138	411	50	88	19	2	6	39	60	107	2	4	.314	.314
NEW YORK METS		**Age**	**Avg**	**G**	**AB**	**R**	**H**	**2B**	**3B**	**HR**	**RBI**	**BB**	**SO**	**SB**	**CS**	**OBP**	**SLG**
Allensworth,Jer.	OF	27	.227	81	260	33	59	16	3	3	15	27	40	6	5	.300	.346
Baez,Kevin	2B-SS	32	.234	80	205	13	48	6	0	0	24	20	26	1	0	.302	.263
Beamon,Trey	OF	25	.212	89	288	33	61	15	0	1	19	21	53	10	10	.265	.274
Brooks,Jerry	1B	32	.203	79	231	24	47	10	0	6	20	25	52	0	2	.281	.325
Bruce,Mo	2B	24	.238	133	479	63	114	21	3	6	59	40	143	21	9	.297	.332
Buccheri,Jim	OF	30	.239	87	264	20	63	8	0	0	15	13	44	6	4	.274	.269
Gainey,Bryon	1B	23	.210	137	485	53	102	23	4	19	61	26	197	0	2	.250	.392
Halter,Shane	SS	29	.239	127	452	58	108	18	2	4	26	45	94	12	18	.308	.314
Haney,Todd	2B	33	.274	122	424	62	116	20	4	3	36	55	45	4	9	.357	.361
Kinkade,Mike	3B	26	.268	84	295	40	79	16	1	4	37	15	32	4	1	.303	.369
Livingstone,Scott	1B	33	.242	78	223	18	54	8	0	0	22	16	25	2	1	.293	.278
Mora,Melvin	SS-OF	27	.264	82	288	41	76	14	1	5	27	30	56	12	8	.333	.372
Neubart,Garrett	OF	25	.239	96	285	32	68	11	3	2	17	18	49	14	6	.284	.319
Rodriguez,Sammy	C	23	.192	74	203	12	39	8	0	3	21	15	54	1	2	.248	.276
Romero,Mandy	C	31	.203	74	231	11	47	11	0	2	23	16	45	0	0	.255	.277
Sanchez,Yuri	SS	25	.206	116	369	33	76	8	0	3	23	24	144	3	5	.254	.252
Tamargo,John	3B	24	.188	112	351	21	66	10	2	2	29	26	58	4	5	.244	.245
Toca,George	1B-OF	24	.281	124	431	66	121	22	0	17	74	25	70	3	8	.320	.450
Tomberlin,Andy	OF	32	.274	97	288	45	79	17	0	11	46	30	77	1	1	.343	.448
Tyner,Jason	OF	22	.278	132	504	71	140	16	3	0	26	41	54	32	13	.332	.321
Valera,Yohanny	C	22	.222	80	257	28	57	12	2	6	34	14	77	1	1	.262	.354
Zamora,Junior	3B	23	.208	67	245	22	51	14	0	7	26	7	66	1	1	.230	.351
NEW YORK YANKEES		**Age**	**Avg**	**G**	**AB**	**R**	**H**	**2B**	**3B**	**HR**	**RBI**	**BB**	**SO**	**SB**	**CS**	**OBP**	**SLG**
Ashby,Chris	OF	24	.229	99	301	43	69	15	0	8	37	22	61	6	7	.282	.359
Bierek,Kurt	1B	26	.246	135	508	63	125	35	2	17	71	35	102	3	3	.295	.423
Brown,Richard	OF	22	.237	104	371	38	88	16	5	5	45	23	85	3	8	.282	.348
Brown,Vick	2B	26	.229	132	468	71	107	17	0	4	40	58	107	34	13	.314	.291
Carpenter,Bubba	OF	30	.248	101	310	58	77	17	1	16	61	56	70	4	3	.363	.465
Coolbaugh,Mike	3B-OF	27	.241	114	373	49	90	26	1	10	49	28	116	3	7	.294	.397
Glass,Chip	OF	28	.234	118	384	54	90	13	3	6	50	37	84	6	9	.302	.331
Jimenez,D'Angelo	SS	21	.291	126	499	73	145	26	3	11	66	43	77	18	7	.347	.421
Johnson,Nick	1B	20	.319	132	404	95	129	29	3	11	72	86	93	5	6	.439	.488
Leon,Donny	3B	23	.277	118	441	57	122	30	1	17	83	23	107	0	0	.313	.465
McDonald,Donzell	OF	24	.248	137	516	79	128	16	6	3	27	62	115	37	14	.329	.320
Molina,Izzy	C	28	.215	97	325	33	70	13	0	2	38	13	48	2	2	.246	.274
Morris,Jeremy	DH	24	.226	111	381	41	86	14	0	7	43	21	96	5	2	.266	.318
Powell,Alonzo	DH	34	.280	130	447	73	125	19	0	17	68	61	114	0	3	.366	.436

Major League Equivalencies for 1999 AAA/AA Batters

NEW YORK YANKEES		Age	Avg	G	AB	R	H	2B	3B	HR	RBI	BB	SO	SB	CS	OBP	SLG
Raabe,Brian	2B	31	.289	130	467	70	135	29	3	8	58	35	19	3	7	.339	.415
Soriano,Alfonso	SS	21	.255	109	427	53	109	21	2	13	64	25	89	17	7	.296	.405
Tarasco,Tony	OF	28	.261	95	330	54	86	19	0	14	46	36	40	6	5	.333	.445
Valencia,Victor	C	22	.202	119	386	47	78	16	0	17	60	31	150	0	0	.261	.376
OAKLAND ATHLETICS		Age	Avg	G	AB	R	H	2B	3B	HR	RBI	BB	SO	SB	CS	OBP	SLG
Ardoin,Danny	C	24	.242	109	331	49	80	12	1	7	43	45	80	2	3	.332	.347
Ball,Jeff	3B	30	.295	96	339	46	100	21	1	7	47	33	58	5	2	.358	.425
Bowles,Justin	OF	25	.245	131	462	50	113	22	5	13	50	25	128	6	7	.283	.398
Castro,Jose	2B-SS	24	.221	119	349	47	77	13	1	4	29	21	93	13	5	.265	.298
Encarnacion,Mario	OF	21	.252	133	473	63	119	21	2	13	64	31	135	9	13	.298	.387
Espada,Josue	SS	23	.292	119	432	59	126	12	1	3	35	37	57	14	7	.348	.345
Garland,Tim	OF	30	.247	119	437	58	108	18	6	3	38	16	61	18	7	.274	.336
Hernandez,Ramon	C	23	.248	77	286	35	71	10	2	11	51	20	38	0	2	.297	.413
Lesher,Brian	1B-OF	28	.279	103	380	61	106	27	1	12	59	37	73	6	2	.343	.450
Long,Terrence	OF	23	.269	118	439	45	118	21	3	6	54	26	72	14	10	.310	.371
Marcinczyk,T.R.	1B	25	.237	127	451	60	107	32	0	15	76	35	114	1	0	.292	.408
Martins,Eric	2B	26	.226	97	296	36	67	14	3	2	30	28	48	1	1	.293	.314
McKay,Cody	C	25	.252	94	314	40	79	17	0	4	29	21	41	0	2	.299	.344
Menechino,Frank	3B	28	.295	130	491	96	145	29	7	13	82	66	99	3	5	.379	.462
Morales,Willie	C	26	.231	107	337	30	78	22	0	10	50	13	60	1	0	.260	.386
Neill,Mike	OF	29	.282	96	358	57	101	22	1	9	57	51	99	8	5	.372	.425
Ortiz,Jose	SS	22	.270	107	370	61	100	27	1	8	42	26	51	10	4	.318	.414
Piatt,Adam	3B	23	.291	135	460	88	134	39	2	25	95	58	108	4	3	.371	.548
Sheff,Chris	OF	28	.274	118	413	58	113	22	0	13	65	40	89	7	6	.338	.421
Vaz,Roberto	OF-DH	24	.259	119	390	52	101	19	3	6	43	50	79	5	6	.343	.369
PHIL. PHILLIES		Age	Avg	G	AB	R	H	2B	3B	HR	RBI	BB	SO	SB	CS	OBP	SLG
Burnham,Gary	1B	24	.231	116	346	39	80	19	0	10	41	29	53	7	3	.291	.373
Burrell,Pat	1B	22	.298	127	436	73	130	27	4	23	78	60	120	2	2	.383	.537
Burton,Darren	OF	26	.239	118	397	48	95	29	2	10	49	35	104	5	2	.301	.398
Carver,Steve	1B	26	.214	98	280	26	60	17	0	8	30	27	108	1	0	.283	.361
Estalella,Bobby	C	24	.210	110	376	45	79	21	1	11	44	44	107	2	1	.293	.359
Finn,John	SS	31	.193	82	233	26	45	7	0	3	14	26	29	5	1	.274	.262
Francia,David	OF	24	.254	107	331	34	84	21	4	3	35	15	62	9	4	.286	.369
Frazier,Lou	OF	34	.224	89	299	42	67	15	5	4	25	35	85	15	5	.305	.348
Guiliano,Matt	SS	26	.171	71	211	15	36	14	0	1	18	13	65	2	2	.219	.251
Harris,Brian	2B	24	.204	119	372	35	76	13	2	4	34	33	64	6	5	.269	.282
Horne,Tyrone	OF	28	.247	80	255	30	63	12	1	4	30	31	69	9	8	.329	.349
Huff,Larry	3B	27	.240	130	433	63	104	28	2	2	45	47	77	19	7	.315	.328
Lovullo,Torey	2B	33	.255	139	502	71	128	35	2	17	83	63	96	2	4	.338	.434
Lucca,Lou	3B	28	.244	136	516	48	126	31	1	9	55	17	100	2	6	.268	.360
Magee,Wendell	OF	26	.258	142	547	75	141	32	1	15	62	44	132	7	8	.313	.402
McMillon,Billy	OF	27	.279	132	448	76	125	36	3	12	67	52	84	7	2	.354	.453
Pierce,Kirk	C	26	.238	83	248	30	59	9	0	7	33	30	61	2	3	.320	.359
Rollins,Jimmy	SS	20	.247	137	530	67	131	21	6	9	46	37	53	17	6	.296	.360
Royster,Aaron	OF	26	.269	91	301	44	81	16	1	6	40	34	98	7	5	.343	.389
Taylor,Reggie	OF	22	.248	127	513	62	127	16	8	12	51	13	86	28	11	.266	.380
Zuber,Jon	1B	29	.268	111	373	54	100	22	1	4	42	69	51	5	1	.382	.365
PITTSBURGH PIRATES		Age	Avg	G	AB	R	H	2B	3B	HR	RBI	BB	SO	SB	CS	OBP	SLG
Brinkley,Darryl	OF	30	.284	111	352	47	100	31	1	9	52	21	60	3	4	.324	.455
Brown,Emil	OF	24	.268	110	407	68	109	17	3	12	42	24	84	10	4	.309	.413

Major League Equivalencies for 1999 AAA/AA Batters

PITTSBURGH PIRATES		Age	Avg	G	AB	R	H	2B	3B	HR	RBI	BB	SO	SB	CS	OBP	SLG
Cruz,Ivan	1B	31	.278	78	270	40	75	17	0	17	59	14	66	0	1	.313	.530
Dunn,Todd	OF	28	.167	78	227	16	38	5	0	4	25	17	79	1	2	.225	.242
Figueroa,Luis	SS	25	.234	131	402	45	94	14	3	2	37	33	47	6	8	.292	.299
Haverbusch,Kevin	3B	23	.255	93	318	42	81	20	1	10	45	7	64	4	2	.271	.418
Hermansen,Chad	OF	21	.235	125	473	62	111	24	2	22	68	24	124	13	9	.272	.433
Hernandez,Alex	OF	22	.228	126	457	56	104	23	2	11	47	34	117	7	7	.281	.359
Howard,Matt	2B	31	.256	114	379	28	97	15	1	1	30	17	25	8	9	.288	.309
Hyzdu,Adam	OF	27	.269	117	405	54	109	23	1	20	71	30	90	5	3	.320	.479
Laker,Tim	C	29	.235	112	387	33	91	25	2	8	45	20	71	2	0	.273	.372
Long,Garrett	OF-1B	22	.216	109	342	45	74	10	3	13	41	39	107	3	5	.297	.377
Montgomery,Ray	OF	28	.292	90	257	40	75	20	1	11	36	16	51	3	2	.333	.506
Oliver,Joe	C	33	.267	67	206	18	53	15	0	4	20	4	52	0	0	.271	.000
Patzke,Jeff	2B	25	.228	112	355	37	81	15	0	2	27	42	78	3	3	.310	.287
Polcovich,Kevin	SS	29	.206	80	223	26	46	8	0	2	17	14	54	4	3	.253	.269
Ramirez,Aramis	3B	21	.288	131	434	64	125	31	0	14	52	51	58	3	2	.363	.456
Redman,Tike	OF	22	.239	136	511	62	122	18	9	2	44	33	55	19	7	.285	.321
Robertson,Mike	1B	28	.261	120	376	46	98	24	0	12	41	22	60	1	2	.302	.420
Wilson,Craig	DH	22	.239	111	348	42	83	19	2	14	51	25	111	0	2	.290	.425
ST. LOUIS CARDINALS		Age	Avg	G	AB	R	H	2B	3B	HR	RBI	BB	SO	SB	CS	OBP	SLG
Ametller,Jesus	2B	24	.282	118	387	44	109	23	1	8	44	3	22	1	1	.287	.408
Bieser,Steve	OF	31	.237	104	329	39	78	15	2	5	32	27	69	7	3	.295	.340
Butler,Brent	SS	21	.248	139	513	57	127	19	0	10	45	18	49	0	4	.273	.343
Clapp,Stubby	2B-OF	26	.238	110	382	60	91	23	1	12	51	44	99	5	7	.317	.398
Farley,Cordell	OF	26	.237	122	409	36	97	14	5	6	34	13	102	17	6	.261	.340
Haas,Chris	3B	22	.209	114	387	52	81	17	1	15	61	55	161	2	4	.308	.375
Hogan,Todd	OF	23	.179	91	273	30	49	6	4	3	17	14	72	5	7	.220	.264
Jensen,Marcus	C	26	.266	72	229	31	61	17	2	6	36	25	60	0	0	.339	.437
Kennedy,Adam	2B	23	.302	91	354	57	107	20	2	8	52	24	37	15	5	.347	.438
Kleiner,Stacy	C	24	.201	85	229	19	46	7	1	1	13	17	63	1	1	.256	.253
LaRiviere,Jason	OF	25	.263	133	482	75	127	32	2	7	39	39	66	13	4	.319	.382
Leon,Jose	3B	22	.214	112	327	31	70	15	0	15	45	17	120	2	3	.253	.398
McDonald,Keith	C	26	.278	88	266	33	74	15	0	5	33	26	62	0	0	.342	.391
Ordaz,Luis	SS	23	.262	107	351	25	92	22	2	0	37	20	41	2	4	.302	.336
Paquette,Craig	3B	30	.234	70	269	30	63	16	2	10	41	7	49	2	0	.254	.420
Perez,Eduardo	1B	29	.296	119	402	56	119	28	0	15	68	37	95	5	8	.355	.478
Richard,Chris	1B	25	.276	137	445	67	123	24	2	25	81	30	81	5	7	.322	.508
Saturria,Luis	OF	22	.223	139	471	55	105	27	2	13	51	24	142	11	8	.261	.372
Warner,Ron	OF	30	.266	90	237	29	63	12	0	9	27	26	72	5	2	.338	.430
Woolf,Jason	SS	22	.248	86	310	38	77	16	2	6	12	19	90	7	3	.292	.371
SAN DIEGO PADRES		Age	Avg	G	AB	R	H	2B	3B	HR	RBI	BB	SO	SB	CS	OBP	SLG
Allen,Dusty	1B-OF	26	.231	128	429	46	99	23	1	12	60	52	151	1	5	.314	.373
Balfe,Ryan	3B	23	.236	111	377	47	89	22	1	7	48	28	103	0	1	.289	.355
Charles,Frank	C	30	.205	80	258	17	53	14	1	1	19	6	64	1	0	.223	.279
Curl,John	OF	26	.240	133	446	54	107	23	1	14	52	44	148	5	5	.308	.390
Darr,Mike	OF	23	.249	100	358	38	89	26	0	6	42	33	109	6	3	.312	.372
Faggett,Ethan	OF	24	.202	128	500	56	101	13	6	4	29	30	136	39	15	.247	.276
Garcia,Carlos	1B	31	.230	78	258	24	61	14	0	2	19	11	64	3	0	.268	.314
Gonzalez,Wiki	C	25	.273	85	297	34	81	16	1	11	41	19	40	0	0	.316	.444
Guiel,Aaron	OF	26	.198	84	242	31	48	19	1	7	26	29	91	3	4	.284	.372
Johnson,A.J.	OF	26	.207	107	309	24	64	11	0	4	24	8	79	2	5	.227	.282

430

Major League Equivalencies for 1999 AAA/AA Batters

SAN DIEGO PADRES		Age	Avg	G	AB	R	H	2B	3B	HR	RBI	BB	SO	SB	CS	OBP	SLG
Jorgensen,Randy	1B	27	.272	72	235	28	64	11	0	4	37	20	49	1	2	.329	.370
Kent,Robbie	2B	25	.230	109	318	33	73	13	1	5	38	25	76	1	0	.286	.324
Luzinski,Ryan	C	25	.240	77	221	19	53	16	0	1	21	23	62	0	1	.311	.326
Matthews Jr.,Gary	OF	24	.213	121	399	38	85	16	1	6	35	38	111	10	6	.281	.303
Newhan,David	2B	25	.239	98	351	33	84	19	0	9	33	20	89	14	5	.280	.370
Nicholson,Kevin	SS	23	.243	127	460	58	112	28	1	9	56	26	100	10	5	.284	.367
Paciorek,Pete	1B	23	.181	83	215	26	39	6	1	2	11	21	64	1	3	.254	.247
Prieto,Chris	OF	26	.200	108	330	45	66	10	3	3	19	30	54	13	5	.267	.276
Prieto,Rick	OF	26	.243	118	338	42	82	10	2	4	29	32	59	17	6	.308	.320
Rossy,Rico	SS	35	.215	93	246	28	53	9	0	7	19	27	28	2	1	.293	.337
Thrower,Jake	2B	23	.227	112	392	37	89	18	3	4	38	28	87	3	7	.279	.319
Tucci,Pete	OF	23	.212	83	297	31	63	11	0	8	24	15	89	7	6	.250	.330
SF GIANTS		Age	Avg	G	AB	R	H	2B	3B	HR	RBI	BB	SO	SB	CS	OBP	SLG
Byas,Michael	OF	23	.256	134	496	73	127	9	0	0	39	58	91	25	10	.334	.274
Canizaro,Jay	2B	25	.241	105	345	56	83	16	1	19	58	37	84	11	5	.314	.458
Chiaramonte,Giu.	C	23	.230	114	392	50	90	18	1	17	69	32	96	3	2	.288	.411
Crespo,Felipe	1B	26	.290	112	362	73	105	21	3	18	62	59	79	11	8	.390	.514
Delgado,Wilson	SS	23	.259	57	201	20	52	8	1	0	24	13	37	2	2	.304	.308
Dilone,Juan	OF	26	.237	112	333	48	79	17	4	4	41	37	96	8	7	.314	.348
Feliz,Pedro	3B	22	.235	131	480	48	113	22	4	11	72	15	98	3	2	.259	.367
Guzman,Edwards	3B	22	.238	90	341	35	81	10	0	5	35	12	53	4	5	.263	.311
Leach,Jalal	OF	30	.256	116	352	43	90	15	3	11	56	20	71	5	7	.296	.409
Magruder,Chris	OF	22	.240	133	466	73	112	19	2	5	56	56	94	13	12	.322	.322
Marval,Raul	SS	23	.255	99	267	31	68	12	0	5	34	12	52	1	4	.287	.356
Mashore,Damon	OF	29	.224	110	330	46	74	16	0	14	51	28	104	4	3	.285	.400
Mendoza,Carlos	SS	19	.187	111	326	32	61	14	2	2	31	29	71	0	4	.254	.261
Minor,Damon	1B	25	.259	136	464	71	120	30	3	19	77	64	125	0	0	.348	.459
Mirabelli,Doug	C	28	.272	86	302	47	82	19	0	10	38	36	59	5	2	.349	.434
Murray,Calvin	OF	27	.291	130	515	91	150	25	4	16	54	37	94	29	11	.339	.449
Torrealba,Yorvit	C	20	.224	82	272	29	61	10	0	4	24	10	48	0	3	.252	.305
Tyler,Josh	OF	25	.247	105	324	38	80	15	0	2	36	24	57	10	5	.299	.312
Williams,Keith	OF	27	.244	89	279	34	68	19	2	8	37	25	53	2	2	.306	.412
Woods,Ken	3B	28	.281	124	441	57	124	19	2	4	54	24	48	13	4	.318	.361
Young,Travis	2B	24	.241	134	494	74	119	26	1	5	43	32	105	14	13	.287	.328
SEATTLE MARINERS		Age	Avg	G	AB	R	H	2B	3B	HR	RBI	BB	SO	SB	CS	OBP	SLG
Bass,Jayson	OF	25	.254	123	425	78	108	21	4	21	66	60	171	26	10	.346	.471
Brown,Randy	2B	29	.241	90	316	42	76	12	4	10	45	24	89	3	6	.294	.399
Chavez,Raul	C	25	.247	102	344	34	85	17	0	2	35	25	66	0	3	.298	.314
Flores,Jose	SS	26	.245	106	359	56	88	10	1	2	27	62	70	12	6	.356	.295
Harrison,Adonis	2B	22	.259	120	441	53	114	15	0	2	44	32	80	17	6	.309	.306
Hills,Rich	3B	25	.248	84	282	29	70	14	0	3	28	33	50	0	3	.327	.330
Horner,Jim	C	25	.259	76	274	28	71	16	0	5	49	14	54	0	1	.295	.372
Jackson,Ryan	1B	27	.284	105	395	51	112	22	1	7	55	32	67	9	3	.337	.397
Kingman,Brendan	1B	26	.269	130	502	57	135	18	0	9	55	21	76	0	0	.298	.359
Magdaleno,Ricky	SS	24	.247	95	332	34	82	16	0	0	28	22	68	0	4	.294	.295
Mathis,Joe	OF	24	.247	93	324	35	80	16	4	2	35	17	74	9	5	.284	.340
Matos,Francisco	2B	29	.289	100	381	38	110	21	2	2	29	16	43	3	6	.317	.370
Monahan,Shane	OF	24	.235	108	388	45	91	18	1	6	28	17	85	7	3	.267	.332
Murphy,Mike	OF	27	.229	108	336	48	77	11	4	1	36	39	103	12	7	.309	.295
Radmanovich,Ry.	OF	27	.263	109	407	61	107	21	2	15	71	47	87	7	4	.339	.435

Major League Equivalencies for 1999 AAA/AA Batters

SEATTLE MARINERS		Age	Avg	G	AB	R	H	2B	3B	HR	RBI	BB	SO	SB	CS	OBP	SLG
Seitzer,Brad	3B	29	.265	130	460	71	122	30	0	8	59	79	90	0	2	.373	.383
Thomas,Juan	DH-1B	27	.235	71	264	46	62	12	0	15	50	11	98	0	0	.265	.451
Timmons,Ozzie	OF	28	.253	82	289	50	73	19	0	18	59	47	85	0	2	.357	.505
Vazquez,Ramon	SS	22	.246	127	431	57	106	25	2	5	44	52	82	6	1	.327	.348
Wathan,Dusty	C	25	.268	96	328	36	88	15	1	3	36	20	64	3	1	.310	.348
Weber,Jake	OF	23	.243	136	481	63	117	20	1	11	58	55	78	3	7	.321	.358
TAMPA BAY DEVIL RAYS		Age	Avg	G	AB	R	H	2B	3B	HR	RBI	BB	SO	SB	CS	OBP	SLG
Becker,Brian	1B	24	.220	129	460	49	101	20	0	13	54	25	95	0	0	.260	.348
Butler,Rich	OF	26	.248	90	314	35	78	23	1	7	43	27	73	1	4	.308	.395
Carr,Dustin	2B	24	.265	125	438	55	116	19	2	4	46	43	66	4	1	.331	.345
Clyburn,Danny	OF	25	.197	82	289	26	57	9	0	6	22	12	77	1	0	.229	.291
Colina,Roberto	DH	28	.239	99	301	32	72	17	0	4	38	22	50	0	0	.291	.336
Cox,Steve	1B	24	.297	134	501	73	149	41	2	18	87	45	77	1	2	.355	.495
de los Santos,Ed.	SS	21	.241	128	428	38	103	20	2	2	35	17	73	2	1	.270	.311
Fraraccio,Dan	OF	28	.248	97	270	38	67	18	2	5	22	17	50	1	3	.293	.385
Graffanino,Tony	2B	27	.269	87	324	45	87	21	4	6	39	25	48	10	8	.321	.414
Hawkins,Kraig	OF	27	.263	94	281	30	74	8	0	0	19	23	48	12	9	.319	.292
Holbert,Aaron	2B	26	.267	100	326	52	87	15	2	8	38	16	58	9	4	.301	.399
Huff,Aubrey	3B	22	.267	133	468	62	125	34	2	17	57	39	82	1	2	.323	.457
Kieschnick,Brooks	DH	27	.257	100	354	44	91	21	2	18	57	16	76	0	0	.289	.480
Lowery,Terrell	OF	28	.288	71	257	47	74	16	3	10	39	29	65	6	4	.360	.490
Martin,Chris	SS	31	.233	120	378	43	88	16	0	6	36	32	64	9	1	.293	.323
McClain,Scott	3B	27	.215	137	508	72	109	27	0	19	71	49	163	2	1	.284	.380
Mendoza,Carlos	OF	24	.251	75	251	39	63	6	2	0	17	21	39	5	7	.309	.291
Mosquera,Julio	C	27	.268	80	246	26	66	11	0	2	27	9	42	0	0	.294	.337
Sanchez,Alex	OF	22	.219	124	488	50	107	10	2	1	21	16	94	32	12	.244	.254
Silvestri,Dave	2B	31	.276	80	304	41	84	15	0	4	31	16	45	2	3	.313	.365
Smith,Bobby	3B	25	.289	57	211	35	61	12	2	9	32	18	64	8	3	.345	.493
Wilcox,Luke	OF	25	.252	129	445	64	112	30	3	21	69	35	75	1	3	.306	.474
Wilson,Tom	C	28	.244	97	303	36	74	17	0	15	46	44	97	0	1	.340	.449
TEXAS RANGERS		Age	Avg	G	AB	R	H	2B	3B	HR	RBI	BB	SO	SB	CS	OBP	SLG
Barkett,Andy	1B	24	.292	132	476	61	139	29	4	9	66	38	73	5	6	.344	.426
Bautista,Juan	SS	24	.237	127	465	54	110	13	2	7	40	19	120	13	8	.267	.318
Bridges,Kary	2B	26	.304	85	257	33	78	12	0	6	34	18	19	4	2	.349	.420
Brumbaugh,Cliff	OF	25	.266	139	515	85	137	32	2	22	80	54	95	13	3	.336	.464
Dransfeldt,Kelly	SS	24	.224	102	353	48	79	19	1	8	38	21	112	4	2	.267	.351
Evans,Tom	3B	24	.265	128	430	73	114	32	2	10	59	58	103	3	3	.352	.419
Gallagher,Shawn	1B	22	.270	112	444	55	120	28	2	15	70	20	89	0	0	.302	.444
Green,Scar.	OF	25	.235	104	353	59	83	14	6	2	25	29	88	19	7	.293	.326
Hubbard,Mike	C	28	.268	110	384	42	103	17	0	7	43	21	72	3	0	.306	.367
Ibarra,Jesse	DH	26	.198	108	389	35	77	9	1	10	48	37	113	0	0	.268	.303
King,Cesar	C	21	.215	95	316	37	68	17	1	9	40	24	74	1	0	.271	.361
Lamb,Mike	3B	23	.312	139	536	88	167	48	4	20	90	40	68	2	2	.359	.528
Lane,Ryan	DH	24	.261	94	307	38	80	21	4	9	47	24	59	4	3	.314	.443
Mateo,Ruben	OF	21	.317	63	246	46	78	11	0	15	54	12	37	4	2	.349	.545
Myers,Adrian	OF	24	.227	99	353	54	80	11	3	0	25	33	66	23	9	.293	.275
Piniella,Juan	OF	21	.253	124	451	62	114	21	1	7	41	47	127	10	5	.323	.350
Rosario,Mel	C	26	.197	61	203	19	40	10	0	7	27	5	53	0	0	.216	.350
Sagmoen,Marc	OF	28	.261	83	264	36	69	10	2	12	37	21	60	2	1	.316	.451
Sergio,Tom	2B	24	.281	128	505	79	142	35	5	9	65	44	62	13	4	.339	.424

Major League Equivalencies for 1999 AAA/AA Batters

TEXAS RANGERS		Age	Avg	G	AB	R	H	2B	3B	HR	RBI	BB	SO	SB	CS	OBP	SLG
Sheldon,Scott	2B	30	.294	122	442	82	130	32	2	24	85	49	116	8	1	.365	.538
Valdes,Pedro	DH	26	.315	121	419	65	132	28	0	19	66	51	68	0	1	.389	.518
Zywica,Mike	OF	24	.251	135	486	70	122	28	2	7	69	29	123	3	0	.293	.360
TORONTO BLUE JAYS		Age	Avg	G	AB	R	H	2B	3B	HR	RBI	BB	SO	SB	CS	OBP	SLG
Abernathy,Brent	2B	21	.256	136	550	79	141	37	0	9	45	34	50	23	8	.300	.373
Blake,Casey	3B	25	.230	110	379	61	87	15	1	19	66	54	86	7	5	.326	.425
Brown,Kevin L.	C	26	.242	88	289	34	70	17	1	11	45	18	82	0	1	.287	.422
Butler,Rob	OF	29	.296	64	243	35	72	11	4	1	26	11	22	2	5	.327	.387
Giles,Tim	1B	23	.272	133	478	56	130	21	1	12	84	35	99	0	2	.322	.395
Gomez,Rudy	SS-3B	24	.246	122	407	54	100	23	2	12	67	47	67	6	4	.324	.400
Jones,Chris	DH	33	.220	81	273	39	60	11	2	6	35	16	77	8	3	.263	.341
Lawrence,Joe	3B	22	.230	70	239	38	55	14	1	5	17	35	51	4	6	.328	.360
Lopez,Luis	1B	25	.304	136	517	67	157	33	1	3	61	35	60	0	0	.348	.389
Loyd,Brian	C	25	.245	104	347	39	85	15	0	7	47	28	61	6	2	.301	.349
Martin,Norberto	SS-2B	32	.277	81	311	39	86	10	1	4	30	10	34	11	1	.299	.354
Melhuse,Adam	OF	27	.259	128	425	71	110	26	0	14	64	75	102	3	7	.370	.419
Mummau,Rob	2B	27	.228	123	425	46	97	28	2	4	51	24	64	1	1	.269	.332
Rupp,Chad	OF	27	.203	104	345	48	70	18	1	15	44	39	129	6	2	.284	.391
Sanders,Anthony	OF	25	.228	124	486	62	111	21	4	15	52	40	116	14	10	.287	.381
Solano,Fausto	SS	25	.261	113	357	48	93	15	0	10	47	35	59	7	16	.327	.387
Stromsborg,Ryan	OF	24	.216	99	361	39	78	15	2	6	33	17	97	3	4	.251	.319
Thompson,Andy	OF	23	.242	129	467	78	113	30	3	23	76	39	105	8	3	.300	.467
Wells,Vernon	OF	20	.293	59	225	30	66	12	1	5	30	15	39	8	3	.338	.422
Witt,Kevin	1B-OF	23	.259	114	410	63	106	23	2	20	62	56	114	0	0	.348	.471
Woodward,Chris	SS	23	.274	75	274	40	75	19	2	0	17	33	51	3	1	.352	.358

Appendix

Minor League Team	Organization	League	Level
Akron Aeros	Indians	EL	AA
Albuquerque Dukes	Dodgers	PCL	AAA
Altoona Curve	Pirates	EL	AA
Arkansas Travelers	Cardinals	TL	AA
Asheville Tourists	Rockies	SAL	A
Athletics (Phoenix)	Athletics	AZL	R
Auburn Doubledays	Astros	NYP	A-
Augusta GreenJackets	Red Sox	SAL	A
Bakersfield Blaze	Giants	CAL	A+
Batavia Muckdogs	Phillies	NYP	A-
Beloit Snappers	Brewers	MWL	A
Billings Mustangs	Reds	PIO	R+
Binghamton Mets	Mets	EL	AA
Birmingham Barons	White Sox	SL	AA
Bluefield Orioles	Orioles	APP	R+
Boise Hawks	Angels	NWL	A-
Bowie Baysox	Orioles	EL	AA
Braves (Orlando)	Braves	GCL	R
Brevard County Manatees	Marlins	FSL	A+
Bristol Sox	White Sox	APP	R+
Buffalo Bisons	Indians	IL	AAA
Burlington Bees	White Sox	MWL	A
Burlington Indians	Indians	APP	R+
Butte Copper Kings	Angels	PIO	R+
Calgary Cannons	Marlins	PCL	AAA
Cape Fear Crocs	Expos	SAL	A
Capital City Bombers	Mets	SAL	A
Carolina Mudcats	Rockies	SL	AA
Cedar Rapids Kernels	Angels	MWL	A
Charleston (S.C.) RiverDogs	Devil Rays	SAL	A
Charleston (W.Va.) Alley Cats	Royals	SAL	A
Charlotte Knights	White Sox	IL	AAA
Charlotte Rangers	Rangers	FSL	A+
Chattanooga Lookouts	Reds	SL	AA
Clearwater Phillies	Phillies	FSL	A+
Clinton LumberKings	Reds	MWL	A
Colorado Springs Sky Sox	Rockies	PCL	AAA
Columbus Clippers	Yankees	IL	AAA
Columbus RedStixx	Indians	SAL	A
Cubs (Mesa)	Cubs	AZL	R
Danville Braves	Braves	APP	R+
Daytona Cubs	Cubs	FSL	A+
Delmarva Shorebirds	Orioles	SAL	A
Diamondbacks (Tucson)	Diamondbacks	AZL	R
Dunedin Blue Jays	Blue Jays	FSL	A+
Durham Bulls	Devil Rays	IL	AAA
Edmonton Trappers	Angels	PCL	AAA
El Paso Diablos	Diamondbacks	TL	AA
Elizabethton Twins	Twins	APP	R+
Erie SeaWolves	Angels	EL	AA
Eugene Emeralds	Cubs	NWL	A-

Minor League Team	Organization	League	Level
Everett AquaSox	Mariners	NWL	A-
Expos (Jupiter)	Expos	GCL	R
Frederick Keys	Orioles	CAR	A+
Fresno Grizzlies	Giants	PCL	AAA
Fort Myers Miracle	Twins	FSL	A+
Fort Wayne Wizards	Padres	MWL	A
Great Falls Dodgers	Dodgers	PIO	R+
Greensboro Bats	Yankees	SAL	A
Greenville Braves	Braves	SL	AA
Hagerstown Suns	Blue Jays	SAL	A
Harrisburg Senators	Expos	EL	AA
Helena Brewers	Brewers	PIO	R+
Hickory Crawdads	Pirates	SAL	A
High Desert Mavericks	Diamondbacks	CAL	A+
Hudson Valley Renegades	Devil Rays	NYP	A-
Huntsville Stars	Brewers	SL	AA
Idaho Falls Braves	Padres	PIO	R+
Indianapolis Indians	Reds	IL	AAA
Iowa Cubs	Cubs	PCL	AAA
Jackson Generals	Astros	TL	AA
Jacksonville Suns	Tigers	SL	AA
Jamestown Jammers	Braves	NYP	A-
Johnson City Cardinals	Cardinals	APP	R+
Jupiter Hammerheads	Expos	FSL	A+
Kane County Cougars	Marlins	MWL	A
Kingsport Mets	Mets	APP	R+
Kinston Indians	Indians	CAR	A+
Kissimmee Cobras	Astros	FSL	A+
Knoxville Smokies	Blue Jays	SL	AA
Lake Elsinore Storm	Angels	CAL	A+
Lakeland Tigers	Tigers	FSL	A+
Lancaster JetHawks	Mariners	CAL	A+
Lansing Lugnuts	Cubs	MWL	A
Las Vegas Stars	Padres	PCL	AAA
Louisville RiverBats	Brewers	IL	AAA
Lowell Spinners	Red Sox	NYP	A-
Lynchburg Hillcats	Pirates	CAR	A+
Macon Braves	Braves	SAL	A
Mahoning Valley Scrappers	Indians	NYP	A-
Mariners (Peoria)	Mariners	AZL	R
Marlins (Melbourne)	Marlins	GCL	R
Martinsville Astros	Astros	APP	R+
Medicine Hat Blue Jays	Blue Jays	PIO	R+
Memphis Redbirds	Cardinals	PCL	AAA
Mets (Port St. Lucie)	Mets	GCL	R
Mexican All-Stars (Tucson)	—	AZL	R
Michigan Battle Cats	Astros	MWL	A
Midland RockHounds	Athletics	TL	AA
Missoula Osprey	Diamondbacks	PIO	R+
Mobile BayBears	Padres	SL	AA
Modesto A's	Athletics	CAL	A+

Minor League Team	Organization	League	Level	Minor League Team	Organization	League	Level
Myrtle Beach Pelicans	Braves	CAR	A+	St. Petersburg Devil Rays	Devil Rays	FSL	A+
Nashville Sounds	Pirates	PCL	AAA	Salem Avalanche	Rockies	CAR	A+
New Britain Rock Cats	Twins	EL	AA	Salem-Keizer Volcanoes	Giants	NWL	A-
New Haven Ravens	Mariners	EL	AA	Salt Lake Buzz	Twins	PCL	AAA
New Jersey Cardinals	Cardinals	NYP	A-	San Antonio Missions	Ddogers	TL	AA
New Orleans Zephyrs	Astros	PCL	AAA	San Bernardino Stampede	Dodgers	CAL	A+
Norfolk Tides	Mets	IL	AAA	San Jose Giants	Giants	CAL	A+
Norwich Navigators	Yankees	EL	AA	Sarasota Red Sox	Red Sox	FSL	A+
Ogden Raptors	Brewers	PIO	R+	Savannah Sand Gnats	Rangers	SAL	A
Oklahoma Redhawks	Rangers	PCL	AAA	Scranton/Wilkes-Barre Red Barons	Phillies	IL	AAA
Omaha Golden Spikes	Royals	PCL	AAA	Shreveport Captains	Giants	TL	AA
Oneonta Tigers	Tigers	NYP	A-	South Bend Silver Hawks	Diamondbacks	MWL	A
Orioles (Sarasota)	Orioles	GCL	R	Southern Oregon Timberjacks	Athletics	NWL	A-
Orlando Rays	Devil Rays	SL	AA	Spokane Indians	Royals	NWL	A-
Ottawa Lynx	Expos	IL	AAA	Staten Island Yankees	Yankees	NYP	A-
Padres (Peoria)	Padres	AZL	R	Stockton Ports	Brewers	CAL	A+
Pawtucket Red Sox	Red Sox	IL	AAA	Syracuse SkyChiefs	Blue Jays	IL	AAA
Peoria Chiefs	Cardinals	MWL	A	Tacoma Rainiers	Mariners	PCL	AAA
Phillies (Clearwater)	Phillies	GCL	R	Tampa Yankees	Yankees	FSL	A+
Piedmont Boll Weevils	Phillies	SAL	A	Tigers (Lakeland)	Tigers	GCL	R
Pirates (Bradenton)	Pirates	GCL	R	Toledo Mud Hens	Tigers	IL	AAA
Pittsfield Mets	Mets	NYP	A-	Tucson Sidewinders	Diamondbacks	PCL	AAA
Portland Sea Dogs	Marlins	EL	AA	Trenton Thunder	Red Sox	EL	AA
Portland Rockies	Rockies	NWL	A-	Tulsa Drillers	Rangers	TL	AA
Potomac Cannons	Cardinals	CAR	A+	Twins (Fort Myers)	Twins	GCL	R
Princeton Devil Rays	Devil Rays	APP	R+	Utica Blue Sox	Marlins	NYP	A-
Pulaski Rangers	Rangers	APP	R+	Vancouver Canadians	Athletics	PCL	AAA
Quad City River Bandits	Twins	MWL	A	Vermont Expos	Expos	NYP	A-
Rancho Cucamonga Quakes	Padres	CAL	A+	Vero Beach Dodgers	Dodgers	FSL	A+
Rangers (Port Charlotte)	Rangers	GCL	R	Visalia Oaks	Athletics	CAL	A+
Reading Phillies	Phillies	EL	AA	West Michigan Whitecaps	Tigers	MWL	A
Red Sox (Fort Myers)	Red Sox	GCL	R	West Tenn Diamond Jaxx	Cubs	SL	AA
Reds (Sarasota)	Reds	GCL	R	White Sox (Tucson)	White Sox	AZL	R
Richmond Braves	Braves	IL	AAA	Wichita Wranglers	Royals	TL	AA
Rochester Red Wings	Orioles	IL	AAA	Williamsport Crosscutters	Pirates	NYP	A-
Rockford Reds	Reds	MWL	A	Wilmington Blue Rocks	Royals	CAR	A+
Rockies (Tucson)	Rockies	AZL	R	Winston-Salem Warthogs	White Sox	CAR	A+
Royals (Baseball City)	Royals	GCL	R	Wisconsin Timber Rattlers	Mariners	MWL	A
St. Catharines Stompers	Blue Jays	NYP	A-	Yakima Bears	Ddogers	NWL	A-
St. Lucie Mets	Mets	FSL	A+	Yankees (Tampa)	Yankees	GCL	R

435

About STATS, Inc.

STATS, Inc. is the nation's leading independent sports information and statistical analysis company, providing detailed sports services for a wide array of commercial clients.

As one of the fastest growing companies in sports, STATS provides the most up-to-the-minute sports information to professional teams, print and broadcast media, software developers and interactive service providers around the country. STATS was recently recognized as "One of Chicago's 100 most influential technology players" by *Crain's Chicago Business* and a two-time finalist for KPMG/Peat Marwick's Illinois High Tech Award. Some of our major clients are ESPN, the Associated Press, America Online, *The Sporting News*, Fox Sports, Yahoo!, CNNSI, Electronic Arts, MSNBC, SONY and Topps. Much of the information we provide is available to the public via our site on AOL (keyword: STATS) and our web site: www.stats.com. With a computer and a modem, you can follow action in the four major professional sports, as well as NCAA football and basketball and other professional and college sports. . . as it happens!

STATS Publishing, a division of STATS, Inc., produces 12 annual books, including the *Major League Handbook*, *The Scouting Notebook*, the *Pro Football Handbook*, the *Pro Basketball Handbook* and the *Hockey Handbook*. In 1998, we introduced two baseball encyclopedias, *The All-Time Major League Handbook* and *The All-Time Baseball Sourcebook*. Together they combine for more than 5,000 pages of baseball history. We also published *Ballpark Sourcebook: Diamond Diagrams*, an authoritative look at major and minor league ballparks of today and yesterday. Also available is *From Abba Dabba to Zorro: The World of Baseball Nicknames*, a wacky look at monikers and their origins. A new football title was launched in 1999, the *Pro Football Scoreboard*. These publications deliver STATS' expertise to fans, scouts, general managers and media around the country.

In addition, STATS offers the most innovative—and fun—fantasy sports games around, from Bill James Fantasy Baseball and Bill James Classic Baseball to STATS Fantasy Football and our newest game, Diamond Legends Internet Baseball. Check out our immensely popular Fantasy Portfolios and our great new web-based product, STATS Fantasy Advantage.

Information technology has grown by leaps and bounds in the last decade, and STATS will continue to be at the forefront as a provider of the most up-to-date, in-depth sports information available.

For more information on our products, or on joining our reporter network, contact us on:

America Online — (Keyword: STATS)

Internet — www.stats.com

Toll Free in the USA at 1-800-63-STATS (1-800-637-8287)

Outside the USA at 1-847-470-8798

Or write to:

STATS, Inc.
8130 Lehigh Ave.
Morton Grove, IL 60053

About Howe Sportsdata

Howe Sportsdata has been compiling statistics on professional baseball since 1910. Currently, Howe is the official statistician for all 17 U.S.-based National Association professional baseball leagues. Howe also compiles statistics for the Arizona Fall League, the Hawaiian Winter League and winter leagues located in Mexico, Puerto Rico, the Dominican Republic, Venezuela and Australia. In addition, Howe keeps the official statistics of the Continental Basketball Association, all professional minor hockey leagues and the National Professional Soccer League.

Originally based in Chicago, Howe Sportsdata is now located in Boston, MA and is under the ownership of SportsTicker Enterprises, L.P., the instant sports news and information service of ESPN, Inc. All told, Howe is responsible for maintaining statistics for more than 300 teams who collectively play more than 14,000 games per year.

Howe also provides statistical information to all 30 major league teams and to major media outlets such as *USA Today*, *The Sporting News*, *Baseball America*, the Associated Press and *Sports Illustrated*. Howe also counts as its customers many leading newspapers, of which the following are a small representative sample: the *Los Angeles Times*, the *Detroit Free Press*, the *Miami Herald* and both the *Chicago Sun-Times* and *Chicago Tribune*. For more information about Howe, write to:

Howe Sportsdata
Boston Fish Pier, West Building #1, Suite 302
Boston, Massachusetts 02110

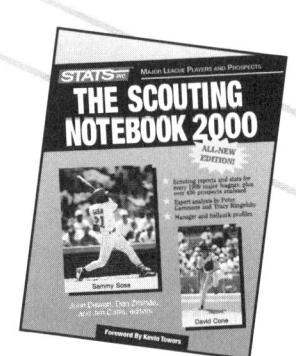

STATS' Power Hitters

STATS Major League Handbook 2000

- Career stats for every 1999 major leaguer
- Bill James' & STATS' exclusive player projections for the 2000 season
- Complete fielding stats for every player at every position
- Expanded and exclusive leader boards
- Managerial performances and tendencies

"STATS consistently provides a thorough and innovative analysis of the game of baseball."
Ron Schueler, GM, Chicago White Sox

Item #HB00, $19.95, Available Now!
Comb-bound #HC00, $24.95, Available Now!

STATS Player Profiles 2000

Extensive season and five-year breakdowns including:

- Lefty-righty splits for hitters and pitchers
- Breakdowns for clutch situations
- Home vs. road, day vs. night, grass vs. turf
- Batting in different lineup spots for hitters
- Pitching after various days of rest

"*Player Profiles* is my companion on all road trips."
Rod Beaton, *USA Today*

Item #PP00, $19.95, Available Now!
Comb-bound #PC00, $24.95, Available Now!

One of a Kind STATS!

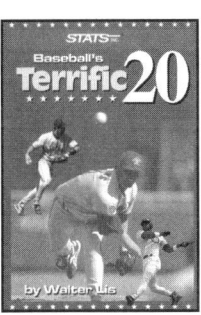

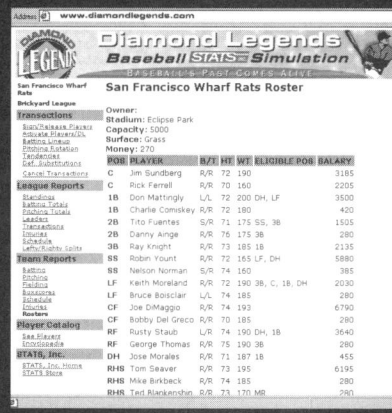

Mail:
STATS, Inc.
8130 Lehigh Avenue
Morton Grove, IL 60053

Phone:
1-800-63-STATS
(847) 677-3322

Fax:
(847) 470-9140

Bill To:
Company_____
Name_____
Address_____
City_____State_____Zip_____
Phone (   )_____Ext.____Fax (   )_____
E-mail Address_____

Ship To: *(Fill in this section if shipping address differs from billing address)*
Company_____
Name_____
Address_____
City_____State_____Zip_____
Phone (   )_____Ext.____Fax (   )_____
E-mail Address_____

Method of payment:
All prices stated
in U.S. Dollars

❏ Charge to my *(circle one)*
   Visa
   MasterCard
   American Express
   Discover

❏ Check or Money Order
   (U.S. funds only)

Please include credit card number
and expiration date with charge orders!

Exp. Date [____/____]
   Month Year

X_____
   Signature *(as shown on credit card)*

Totals for STATS Products:

Books	[____]
Books Under $10 *	[____]
Prior Book Editions *	[____]
order 2 or more books/subtract: $1.00/book *(Does not include prior editions)*	[____]
Illinois residents add 8.5% sales tax	[____]
Sub Total	[____]

Shipping Costs

Canada	Add $3.50/book	[____]
* All books under $10	Add $2.00/book	[____]
Fantasy Games		[____]
	Grand Total	[____]

(No other discounts apply)

(Orders subject to availability)

Free First-Class Shipping for Books Over $10

Books (Free first-class shipping for books over $10)

Qty	Product Name	Item Number	Price	Total
	STATS Major League Handbook 2000	HB00	$19.95	
	STATS Major League Handbook 2000 (Comb-bound)	HC00	$24.95	
	The Scouting Notebook 2000	SN00	$19.95	
	The Scouting Notebook 2000 (Comb-bound)	SC00	$24.95	
	STATS Minor League Handbook 2000	MH00	$19.95	
	STATS Minor League Handbook 2000 (Comb-bound)	MC00	$24.95	
	STATS Player Profiles 2000	PP00	$19.95	
	STATS Player Profiles 2000 (Comb-bound)	PC00	$24.95	
	STATS Minor League Scouting Notebook 2000	MN00	$19.95	
	STATS Batter Vs. Pitcher Match-Ups! 2000	BP00	$24.95	
	STATS Ballpark Sourcebook: Diamond Diagrams	BSDD	$24.95	
	STATS Baseball Scoreboard 2000	SB00	$19.95	
	STATS Diamond Chronicles 2000	CH00	$19.95	
	STATS Pro Football Handbook 1999	FH99	$19.95	
	STATS Pro Football Handbook 1999 (Comb-bound)	FC99	$24.95	
	STATS Pro Football Scoreboard 1999	SF99	$19.95	
	STATS Hockey Handbook 1999-2000	HH00	$19.95	
	STATS Pro Basketball Handbook 1999-2000	BH00	$19.95	
	STATS All-Time Major League Handbook, 2nd Edition	ATHB	$79.95	
			Total	

Books Under $10 (Please include $2.00 S&H for each book)

	From Abba-Dabba to Zorro: The World of Baseball Nicknames	ABBA	$ 9.95	
	STATS Baseball's Terrific 20	KID1	$ 9.95	
	STATS Player Projections Update 2000	PJUP	$ 9.95	
			Total	

Previous Editions (Please circle appropriate years and include $2.00 S&H for each book)

	Product Name	Years	Price	Total
	STATS Major League Handbook	'91 '92 '93 '94 '95 '96 '97 '98 '99	$ 9.95	
	The Scouting Notebook/Report	'94 '95 '96 '97 '98 '99	$ 9.95	
	STATS Player Profiles	'93 '94 '95 '96 '97 '98 '99	$ 9.95	
	STATS Minor League Handbook	'92 '93 '94 '95 '96 '97 '98 '99	$ 9.95	
	STATS Minor League Scouting Notebook	'95 '96 '97 '98 '99	$ 9.95	
	STATS Batter Vs. Pitcher Match-Ups!	'94 '95 '96 '97 '98 '99	$ 9.95	
	STATS Diamond Chronicles	'97 '98 '99	$ 9.95	
	STATS Baseball Scoreboard	'92 '93 '94 '95 '96 '97 '98 '99	$ 9.95	
	Pro Football Revealed: The100-Yard War	'94 '95 '96 '97 '98	$ 9.95	
	STATS Pro Football Handbook	'95 '96 '97 '98	$ 9.95	
	STATS Hockey Handbook	'96-97 '97-98 '98-99	$ 9.95	
	STATS Pro Basketball Handbook	'93-94 '94-95 '95-96 '96-97 '97-98 '98-99	$ 9.95	
			Total	

Fantasy Games

	Bill James Classic Baseball	BJCB	$129.95	
	Bill James Fantasy Baseball	PJUP	$ 89.95	
	STATS Fantasy Football	SFF	$ 49.95	
			Total	

1st Fantasy Team Name (ex. Colt 45's):_____
   Which Fantasy Game is the team for?_____

2nd Fantasy Team Name (ex. Colt 45's):_____
   Which Fantasy Game is the team for?_____

Note: $1.00/player is charged for all roster moves and transactions.